RESTORATION SCRIPTURES

TRUE NAME EDITION©

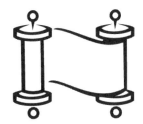

כיתבי הקודש של עם ישראל המתקן

Scriptural Supervision and Doctrinal Oversight
by
Rabbi Moshe Yoseph Koniuchowsky

Your Arms To Yisrael Publishing
NORTH MIAMI BEACH, FLORIDA - 2004

Restoration Scriptures True Name Edition

Copyright ©2004 by
Your Arms To Yisrael Publishing

Permission to reproduce in any form
must be secured from the publisher.

www.yourarmstoisrael.org
info@yourarmstoisrael.org

To order additional copies contact us online or write:
YATI Publishing
7378 W. Atlantic Blvd. #112
Margate, FL. 33063
1-305-868-8787

Library of Congress Control Number 2004102592
ISBN 0-9752514-0-6

Printed for the Publisher by
Gateway Press, Inc.
1001 N. Calvert Street
Baltimore, MD 21202-3897

www.Gatewaypress.com

Printed in the United States of America

Yirmiyahu/Jeremiah 31:31-34

In The Masoretic Text The Verses Are Numbered As Seen Below In the Hebrew

³⁰הִנֵּה יָמִים בָּאִים נְאֻם יהוה וְכָרַתִּי אֶת בֵּית יִשְׂרָאֵל וְאֶת בֵּית יְהוּדָה בְּרִית חֲדָשָׁה׃ ³¹ לֹא כַבְּרִית אֲשֶׁר כָּרַתִּי אֶת אֲבוֹתָם בְּיוֹם הֶחֱזִיקִי בְיָדָם לְהוֹצִיאָם מֵאֶרֶץ מִצְרַיִם אֲשֶׁר הֵמָּה הֵפֵרוּ אֶת בְּרִיתִי וְאָנֹכִי בָּעַלְתִּי בָם נְאֻם יהוה׃ ³² כִּי זֹאת הַבְּרִית אֲשֶׁר אֶכְרֹת אֶת בֵּית יִשְׂרָאֵל אַחֲרֵי הַיָּמִים הָהֵם נְאֻם יהוה נָתַתִּי אֶת תּוֹרָתִי בְּקִרְבָּם וְעַל לִבָּם אֶכְתֲּבֶנָּה וְהָיִיתִי לָהֶם לֵאלֹהִים וְהֵמָּה יִהְיוּ לִי לְעָם׃ ³³ וְלֹא יְלַמְּדוּ עוֹד אִישׁ אֶת רֵעֵהוּ וְאִישׁ אֶת אָחִיו לֵאמֹר דְּעוּ אֶת יהוה כִּי כוּלָּם יֵדְעוּ אוֹתִי לְמִקְּטַנָּם וְעַד גְּדוֹלָם נְאֻם יהוה כִּי אֶסְלַח לַעֲוֹנָם וּלְחַטָּאתָם לֹא אֶזְכָּר עוֹד׃

31 Behold, the days come, says יהוה that I will make a Renewed Covenant with Beit Yisrael and Beit Yahudah: 32 Not according to the covenant that I made with their fathers, in the day that I took them by the hand to bring them out of the land of Egypt; which My covenant they broke, although I was a Husband to them says יהוה. 33 But this shall be the covenant I will make with Beit Yisrael; after those days, says יהוה, I will put My Torah in their inward parts, and write it on their hearts; and I will be their Elohim and they shall be My people. 34 And they shall not teach any more every man his neighbor, and every man his brother, saying, Know יהוה: for they shall all know me, from the least of them unto the greatest of them, says יהוה: for I will forgive their iniquity, and I will remember their sin no more.

Scrolls Of The Restoration Scriptures

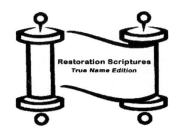

Table Of Scrolls

Hebrew is read from right to left.

Torah-Instructions

To Our Forefathers Yisrael

Niviim-Prophets

To Our Forefathers Yisrael

Ketuvim-Writings

To Our Forefathers Yisrael

Brit Chadasha-Renewed Covenant

To All Nations

To The Believing Remnant Of Yisrael

To The Shepherds of Yisrael

To Yisrael's Final Generation

YATI Publishing extends a heartfelt todah rabah (thank you) to all who gave of their time effort and talents, to make this very special end-time tool a reality. May YHWH give them special favor in life and in eternal habitations.

YATI Publishing invites all of our friends and students of YHWH's Word to write us regarding any typos, grammar or spelling errors found. We will then make the corrections for future editions. Write us at info@yourarmstoisrael.org or 7378 W. Atlantic Blvd. #112 Margate, FL 33063

Key

Restoration Scriptures
True Name Edition

יהוה-The Name of The Father in bold preserved as it appears in the First Covenant Text and inserted into the Renewed Covenant Text based on scholarship, consistency, and the Torah command of Exodus 3:15

יהושע-The True Name of YHWH's Only Begotten Son in bold, recovered as it initially appeared prior to His days on earth, meaning YHWH who does the saving. The use of "Yahshua/Yahoshua" rather than "Y'shua" or "Yeshua" as the name of Moshiach, greatly depends on the historical context. For the *Restoration Scriptures True Name Edition*, we have opted for "Yahshua/Yahoshua" because (as found in our research) this was the form of the Name prior to the Babylonian captivity, and also because of its clear linkage in the prophetic Scriptures, such as in Zechariah 6:11-12. Add to that the fact that Yahshua came in His Father's name, which most obviously contains the letter **hey** as in "**Yah**oshua." However, in terms of what Moshiach was actually called at the time of His first advent, both the *Aramaic Peshitta* and *Old Syriac* texts refer to him as **yud-shen-vav-ayin** rather than **yud hey vav shen ayin**. We have opted for the full name including the letter **hey** as revealed prior to corruption.

Normal Text-Indicates Scriptures pertaining to Yisrael's history, physical growth, division, and ultimate prophetic two-house restoration. This includes any references to Yisraelite events, including casual Yisraelite contact with other nations, places and events. Normal text is used to reference both believers in Yahshua and those who are not believers in Moshiach. Normal text also will indicate non-Yisraelite peoples, places and events, with the context being the determining factor.

Italics-Words of YHWH The Father and Yahshua the Son in the first person in both covenants.

Bakersville Font-Indicates the week's Torah; Haftarah; and Brit Chadasha portions to be read in the congregation or in private devotion to Abba YHWH. These subheadings can be found throughout the Torah or the first five scrolls of the Restoration Scriptures. Following the Torah portion will assure that the entire Torah can be covered on an annual cycle.

About The Restoration Scriptures True Name Edition

Why Now?

The Restoration Scriptures True Name Edition has been in the heart of Father YHWH from the very dawn of His covenant with Jacob/Yaakov. YHWH being in control of all things knew Yisrael's entire future – including our exile, dispersion and regathering through the Moshiach. The Moshiach has come, and we are the result of His faithful mission, the return of all the believing exiles of all 12 tribes, both physically and spiritually.

Meeting The Need

In order to meet the needs of this growing remnant community, The Father ordained the vision for this edition around the year 2000 CE. We did not act upon the vision at that time for many reasons. One being that the task was so monumental and daunting for us, due to the fact that we would have to self-publish any such "two-house Scriptures." However, after the strong and increasing frequency of the prompting by the Set-Apart Ruach HaKodesh, we decided that we could no longer postpone YHWH's will. He desired a translation that would edify and confirm the renewed Yisraelite heritage and identity of many believers in the Moshiach Yahshua, who desired to live out their lifestyle as part of the true Commonwealth of Yisrael. Once we decided to obey our Abba's orders, the world's first two-house True Name Bible has now become a wonderful living reality.

Underlying Text

To publish the unique *Restoration Scriptures True Name Edition*, we used the Masoretic Text as our foundational text for the First Covenant Tanach. We then proceeded to correct obvious anti-Yahshua redactions, shamefully tampered with by the Masoretics. Moreover, we reinserted the true Name back into this foundational source.

For the Renewed Covenant, we have used the greatly appreciated and widely accepted Textus Receptus, or Received Text in the Greek. After prayerful consideration and scholarship, we have heartily used other key sources such as the Aramaic Peshitta, Matthew Shem Tov, Dead Sea Scrolls, and the Septuagint, along with consulting many other legitimate sources. Most often those sources were Semitic, since we believe the Renewed Covenant was inspired in the Semitic languages of Aramaic and Hebrew.

So then the resulting *Restoration Scriptures True Name Edition* is a blend of the Masoretic Text and the Textus Receptus and their reliability, combined with valid Hebraic understandings gained from other reliable Semitic sources.

Our Purpose

Our purpose in publishing *The Restoration Scriptures True Name Edition* is to give all Yisraelite believers a translation that first and foremost uplifts and proclaims the true Names of YHWH and Yahshua, as it originally appeared in the First Covenant almost 7,000 times, as well as restoring it in the Renewed Covenant directly from the Aramaic Peshitta, and other reliable Semitic historical sources. Additional insertions were based on the consistency and immutability of the Heavenly Father, whose Name did not change (Shemot 3:14-15) just because His Son came into the world, and was greatly misunderstood.

A "Thought For Thought" Translation

The Restoration Scriptures True Name Edition is not a "word for word" translation. It is not designed to be. First of all, all translations in a real honest sense are all paraphrases. Simply put, there is no such thing as a literal "word for word" translation. It is just that some publishers and editors are pretty crafty at covering up that fact. They don't want you to know that they were forced by linguistic constraints and limitations to paraphrase, or add words, or even often reverse word orders. Some may find that shocking, but it remains nonetheless true. Therefore the *Restoration Scriptures True Name Edition* has had to employ all of the above traditional translation methods. And we desire to be up front and honest about it.

Paraphrase

Paraphrase means "an intentional re-wording to make a point" (Webster's New World Dictionary, Second Edition, p. 1031). This we have done. The rewording and Hebraic insertions have been made in order to bring clarity to YHWH's covenant faithfulness in all its unchanging beauty (Malaki 3:6, Ivrim 13:8).

For example, in Hebrew there are over 10 legitimate words for the English word "praise." In English, however, translators have taken all 10 different Hebrew words for "praise" and have translated it simply as "praise" in English. That is not a literal translation; for if it were, all 10 words for praise would have to appear differently-translated in English. But since there are not 10 words for praise in English due to English language constraints, all 10 Hebrew words are lumped into a single English word.

The same problem can be found in the Greek, for example, with the word "love." There are at least three common words for love, and yet all three words are translated as the single English word "love." Were the Greek-based Renewed Covenant translated literally rather than reworded, all three forms would have to appear as three different English words. These are just two common examples of the problems facing all translators. So rather than deal with such unsolvable issues, we have decided to publish the best "thought for thought" paraphrased translation, as it pertains to our vision. We have therefore reworded verses in order to capture, proclaim, and declare the thoughts of YHWH, as perhaps never before seen, due to the biases of ancient and modern translators – both Jewish and Christian. If we have recaptured YHWH's true intentions, then we have recaptured the true message of the kingdom, and its restoration through YHWH's Son.

No other translations we know of have set out to focus on the true, central and primary meaning of the message of the kingdom. Rather, they have presented the Tov News (Evangel) as a message for the whole world, without any true understanding or discernment of YHWH's intense compassionate heart for his nation Yisrael and their scattered sheep. *The Restoration Scriptures True Name Edition* has corrected what we believe to be the wrong emphasis of other translations that discount Yisrael. More specifically, they have altogether discounted the ten tribes returning through the Tov News. That unbalance is corrected in the *The Restoration Scriptures True Name Edition*, displaying that Yahshua's primary mission was first to reunite Yisrael (Judah and Ephraim) and only then to reach out to those from the nations – not the other way around.

Mah-Nishtana? - What's The Difference?

Our vision as given to us by Abba-YHWH was to publish the world's first and only known two-house restoration Bible. As such, our overriding aim was to show the following clearly and without disputation:

That YHWH has one elect people called Yisrael, and that all His words and actions are eternally centered on that special chosen nation in both covenants. *The Restoration Scriptures True Name Edition* therefore has taken extra special care to preserve the same message of YHWH towards Yisrael in both the First and Renewed Covenants. In order to do that, there are times when we have added a word or a phrase in order to capture the consistency and eternal commitment of YHWH's message to Yisrael. By adding a word or phrase in this paraphrased translation, we manage to show that Rav Shaul (Paul) was writing to Yisraelite assemblies in exile, even as Yahshua Himself attended to the regathering of all Yisrael, thereby capturing the Father's consistency and immutability, along with His covenant faithfulness.

One such example is found in Qorintyah Alef-First Corinthians 1:2:

"To the Yisraelite congregation of יהוה which is at Qorintyah, to them that are set-apart in ha Moshiach יהושע, called to be kidushim, with all that in every place call upon the Name of יהושע ha Moshiach our Master, both theirs and ours."

Changing YHWH's Words

Some may rightly ask about the prohibition and dire warnings against adding or subtracting words from the Scriptures. To that we wholeheartedly agree and would never think of rewording, altering or changing the original manuscripts also known as the autographs. In order to violate these prohibitions as found in such places as Proverbs 30:6, Deuteronomy 12:32, and Revelation 22:18-19, one would by definition have to have access to the autographs (originals) and proceed to tamper with them. This we have not done; for the fear of YHWH and His awesome Word is both the beginning and fullness of all wisdom. Simply put, we have paraphrased and reversed some word orders to properly fit the original Semitic languages into understandable English. Nevertheless we have managed to remain true to the text, without major changes.

In this, we have not departed from other translations and their practices, be they advertised as "word for word" "literal," or as "paraphrased" editions. As stated earlier, once a translation is made from the original autographs, it in essence becomes a paraphrase, as any honest and knowledgeable linguist will attest to.

"Dispensationalist Traps" Have Been Removed

The Restoration Scriptures True Name Edition is a translation of YHWH's Word, that is "dispensationalist protected." That means that by studying *The Restoration Scriptures True Name Edition*, one cannot be trapped or deceived by such manmade and unscriptural issues as law versus grace, Old versus New Testament, Church versus Synagogue, Replacement or Separate Entity Theology, or the "Torah has been nailed to the cross" theology, that are all kissing cousins of dispensationalist falsehoods. The core of dispensationalism is that Yisrael was YHWH's people at one time, but are now no longer His chosen, and that born-again Yisraelites are no longer part of Yisrael, but part of a "new economy" called "church grace," or the "dispensation of grace." Following and studying *The Restoration Scriptures True Name Edition* should help to clear up that abominable falsehood, to those seeking true and lasting spiritual healing and truth, for their own hidden man of the heart.

Two-House Message Reclaimed

Another main purpose of *The Restoration Scriptures True Name Edition* is to fully capture and reclaim the centrality of the two-house message as vital to even a basic understanding of the word of YHWH. The alarming absence of any known translation that emphasizes the return of all 12 tribes of Yisrael by Moshiach Yahshua is alarming. By studying most modern day Bibles, one is left with the feeling that the 10 tribes of Yisrael are lost and are never going to return. Moreover, that YHWH somehow doesn't care to find or restore them. Since the entire message of the Bible is YHWH's covenant promises and covenant-keeping ability, any translation that does not declare the manner in which YHWH has kept covenant with Yisrael by His Son, is a flawed translation, regardless of how literal or "word for word" it may claim to be.

Knowing this, we have decided to capture YHWH's heart and His mind as seen in His covenant faithfulness to a single people called Yisrael, and to all who by their own volition choose to join that single redeemed people. For the purposes of the latter-day move of the Ruach HaKodesh, a translation was needed that truly lays hold on YHWH's plans towards us, the redeemed of YHWH, as He places us back into the nation birthed at Sinai. *The Restoration Scriptures True Name Edition* has at long last captured and laid hold on His heart and His mind for His nation. For that reason, this "thought for thought" translation will serve His people best; simply because no translation in existence has purposed to override the ongoing scourge of Separate Entity and Replacement Theology, as has *The Restoration Scriptures True Name Edition*. By capturing YHWH's mind, we can bypass the bias in many other translations that subtly fuel – rather than eliminate – these problems.

A Running Yisraelite Commentary

To provide the open-hearted and searching believer with the true Tov News of the kingdom, *The Restoration Scriptures True Name Edition* provides literally thousands of notes in a running commentary format, in order to assist the student and seeker of truth in their hunger for righteousness. The running commentary footnotes, when used properly, will weave a wonderful scarlet cord in all of YHWH's doings and dealings with His chosen nation. The running commentary is presented so as to bring about the full richness of the two-house, and True Name message, to all who desire to join Yisrael's commonwealth.

Restoring The True Names

The Restoration Scriptures True Name Edition has been compiled to give full honor to the True Names of the Father and His Son, by placing them in the Hebrew font, thereby bypassing any controversy over the exact pronunciation of the Names. We did not want that kind of a discussion diluting the message and heart of the Father for both houses of scattered Yisrael, presented in this edition.

We also have highlighted the Father's and Yahshua's words in italics in both covenants for easy identification purposes. This is done in contrast to most translations where the words of YHWH and Yahshua are not highlighted, or worse yet, where Yahshua's words are, but the Father's are not (in either covenant). *The Restoration Scriptures True Name Edition* has corrected that undesirable reality by italicizing all the words of both the Father and His Son in both covenants.

Order of the Scrolls

The order of the scrolls as listed in *The Restoration Scriptures True Name Edition* is such that it highlights YHWH and His eternal covenants with all Yisrael, from the days of the marriage on Sinai, the united nation under David and Solomon, through the exiles, and all the way to the Tov News brought by Yahshua to both houses. The Tov News was declared to the nation's leaders, then the renewed assembly, and ultimately to the final generation of Yisraelites in the Scroll of Revelation. The order of the scrolls as presented also helps to dispel any myths of dispensationalist understanding.

Use of Hebrew Words

In this "thought for thought" translation, *The Restoration Scriptures True Name Edition* desires to preserve key Hebrew words and phrases to add to the Hebraic flavor of the translation. These key Hebrew words give added insight into the full restoration message. Towards that end, we have inserted key Hebrew words from the ancient texts. However, we have chosen not to preserve variations of words in their past and future forms. To do so would create huge problems in exact wording and an overabundance of Hebrew words, thus obscuring the basic English text with some Hebraic flavoring. We maintained the Hebrew root of a given word, in the simple present tense. In this manner, the reader can easily process the Hebrew with his or her own comprehension of both the text and the Hebraic thoughts of YHWH towards His people Yisrael.

Variations In Spelling

Some Hebrew words transliterated from Hebrew to English have different spellings. As seen in the glossary, a word like "fathers" may alternately read as **ahvot** or **avot**. "Firstborn" may read as **bachor** or **bechor**. "Set-apart" may read as **kodesh** or **kadosh**. These are just a few of many examples. Since these words are being transliterated into English, there is no standard or commonly accepted spelling, since transliteration is not an exact science. Transliteration is done by matching sounds as closely as possible. There is no standard transliteration tool such as a dictionary or a thesaurus, for consultation, clarity or uniformity. Moreover different editors transliterated many parts of *The Restoration Scriptures True Name Edition* at different times. As such, some variations occurred in the transliteration process. The Glossary however has listed all the variant spellings for ease in comprehension. We do not believe this has diminished in any way from the substance of the text.

Glossary

All non-English words other than proper names appearing in the actual body of the text have been listed in the Glossary, to promote quick and easy comprehension.

Parshas

The Restoration Scriptures True Name Edition has the weekly readings of the Torah, Haftarah (prophets), and the Brit Chadasha (Renewed Covenant) neatly interwoven into the text. This will greatly assist the reader who desires to follow the Jewish weekly portions designed to cover the full Torah in a full year. This added blessing will greatly enhance all those desiring a true commitment to their new life in Yisrael, as they no longer have to check calendars to seek out the weekly portions.

Agenda

Unlike many crafty translators and their translations that do not admit to an underlying agenda in their publications, *The Restoration Scriptures True Name Edition* has an overriding and clear agenda in publishing this project. We admit that! It is our most sincere desire and heartfelt prayer, that this translation will help end the exile of our people, by bringing believers from all backgrounds into their Hebraic heritage. We desire that *The Restoration Scriptures True Name Edition* will lead to a repentance and return to YHWH for many, so as to experience life in His sight as a practicing Torah-keeping born-again Yisraelite. We can see the days when many will study His Word as preserved in *The Restoration Scriptures True Name Edition*, and will come to have the same love for the restoration of our people that the eleven disciples had in their final question to our Master when they asked "Master; will You at this time restore the kingdom to Yisrael?" It is our earnest expectation that not only will the reader adopt this same burden, but will also become aware of their own special place in that promised restoration.

Rabbi Moshe Yoseph Koniuchowsky
General Editor/Publisher
North Miami Beach, Florida
February 2004

בראשית

Beresheeth - Genesis
To Our Forefathers Yisrael

Torah Parsha 1
Beresheeth 1:1-6:8
Haftara Yeshayahu 42:5-43:10
Brit Chadasha Yochanan 1:1-18

1 Beresheeth bara Elohim Aleph-Taf[1] ha shamayim v-et ha-aretz. 2 And the earth was without form, and void; and darkness was upon the face of the deep. And the Ruach of Elohim moved upon the face of the mayim. 3 And Elohim said, *Let there be Light:* and Light was. 4 And Elohim saw the Light, that it was tov: and Elohim divided the light from the darkness. 5 And Elohim called the light Day, and the darkness He called Night. And the evening and the morning were Yom Rishon. 6 And Elohim said, *Let there be a firmament in the midst of the mayim, and let it divide the mayim from the mayim.* 7 And Elohim made the firmament, and divided the mayim that were under the firmament from the mayim that were above the firmament: and it was so. 8 And Elohim called the firmament Shamayim. And the evening and the morning were Yom Shanee. 9 And Elohim said, *Let the mayim under the shamayim be gathered together to one place, and let the dry land appear*: and it was so. 10 And Elohim called the dry land Earth; and the gathering together of the mayim He called Seas: and Elohim saw that it was tov. 11 And Elohim said, *Let the earth bring out grass, the herb yielding zera, and the fruit eytz yielding fruit after its kind, whose zera is in itself, upon the earth:* and it was so. 12 And the earth brought out grass, and herb yielding zera after its kind, and the eytz yielding fruit, whose zera was in itself, after its kind: and Elohim saw that it was tov.

13 And the evening and the morning were Yom Shlishi. 14 And Elohim said, *Let there be lights in the firmament of the shamayim to divide the day from the night; and let them be for signs, and for moadim, and for days, and years:* 15 And let them be for lights in the firmament of the shamayim to give light upon the earth: and it was so. 16 And Elohim made two great lights; the greater light to rule the day, and the lesser light to rule the night: He made the chochavim also. 17 And Elohim set them in the firmament of the shamayim to give light upon the earth, 18 And to rule over the day and over the night, and to divide the light from the darkness: and Elohim saw that it was tov. 19 And the evening and the morning were Yom Revee. 20 And Elohim said, *Let the mayim bring out abundantly the moving creature that has chayim, and fowl that may fly above the earth in the open firmament of the shamayim.* 21 And Elohim created great whales, and every living creature that moves, which the mayim brought out abundantly, after their kind, and every winged fowl after its kind: and Elohim saw that it was tov. 22 And Elohim blessed them, saying, *Be fruitful, and multiply, and fill the mayim in the seas, and let fowls multiply in the earth.* 23 And the evening and the morning were Yom Chameeshe. 24 And Elohim said, *Let the earth bring out the living creature after its kind, cattle, and creeping thing, and beast of the earth after its kind:* and it was so. 25 And Elohim made the beast of the earth after its kind, and cattle after their kind, and every thing that creeps upon the earth after its kind: and Elohim saw that it was tov. 26 And Elohim said, *Let Us make man in Our image, after Our likeness:* [2] and let

---

[1] The Hebrew word here is **et** spelled **Aleph Taf**, which are the first and last letters of the Hebrew alphabet and are used to describe YHWH's Son in the Renewed Covenant. Colossians 1:16 and Proverbs 30:4 confirm that the Son is the true Creator and the Abba is the Master designer.

[2] "Our image and our likeness," speaks of the plurality of the one YHWH.

them have dominion over the fish of the sea, and over the fowl of the air, and over the cattle, and over all the earth, and over every creeping thing that creeps upon the earth. 27 So the Word of Elohim[1] created man in His own image, in the image of Elohim He created him; male and female He created them. 28 And Elohim blessed them, and Elohim said to them, *Be fruitful, and multiply, and replenish the earth,* [2] *and subdue it: and have dominion over the fish of the sea, and over the fowl of the air, and over every living thing that moves upon the earth.* 29 And Elohim said, *See, I have given you every herb bearing zera, which is upon the face of all the earth, and every eytz, which is the fruit of a eytz yielding zera; to you it shall be for food.* 30 *And to every beast of the earth, and to every fowl of the air, and to every thing that creeps upon the earth, in which there is chayim, I have given every green herb for food: and it was so.* 31 And Elohim saw every thing that He had made; and see; it was very tov. And the evening and the morning were Yom Sheshi.

2 So the shamayim and the earth were finished, and all their hosts. 2 And on the seventh day Elohim ended His work that He had made; and He rested on the seventh day from all His work that He had made. 3 And Elohim blessed the seventh day, and set it apart it: because in it He had rested from all His work that Elohim created and made. 4 These are the generations of the shamayim and of the earth when they were created, in the day that יהוה Elohim made the earth and the shamayim, 5 And every plant of the field before it was in the earth, and every herb of the field before it grew: for יהוה Elohim had not caused it to rain upon the earth, and there was not a man to till the ground. 6 But there went up a mist from the earth, and watered the whole face of the ground. 7 And יהוה Elohim formed man from the dust of the ground, and

breathed into his nostrils the breath of chayim; and man became a living being. 8 And יהוה Elohim planted a garden eastward in Aden; and there He put the man whom He had formed. 9 And out of the ground made יהוה Elohim to grow every eytz that is pleasant to the sight, and tov for food; the eytz chayim also in the midst of the garden, and the eytz of the da'at of tov and evil. 10 And a river went out of Aden to mayim the garden; and from there it parted, and became four riverheads. 11 The name of the first is Pishon: that is the one surrounding the whole land of Havilah, where there is gold; 12 And the gold of that land is tov: Bdellium is there and the onyx stone. 13 And the name of the second river is Gihon: the same one that surrounds the whole land of Ethiopia. 14 And the name of the third river is Hiddekel: that is the one that goes toward the east of Ashshur. And the fourth river is Euphrates. 15 And יהוה Elohim took the man, and put him into Gan-Aden to work it and to guard it. 16 And יהוה Elohim commanded the man, saying, *Of every eytz of the Gan-Adan you may freely eat:* 17 *But of the eytz of the da'at of tov and evil, you shall not eat of it: for in the day that you eat from it you shall surely die.* 18 And יהוה Elohim said, *It is not tov that the man should be alone; I will make for him a helper as his counterpart.*[3] 19 And out of the ground יהוה Elohim formed every beast of the field, and every fowl of the air; and brought them to Adam to see what he would call them: and whatever Adam called every living creature; that was the name of it. 20 And Adam gave names to all the cattle, and to the fowls of the air, and to every beast of the field; but for Adam there was not found a helper. 21 And יהוה Elohim caused a deep sleep to fall upon Adam and he slept: and He took one of his ribs, and closed up the flesh in its place; 22 And with the rib that יהוה Elohim had taken from man, He made a woman, and brought her to the man. 23 And Adam said,

---

[1] Aramaic Targum; Jonathan.
[2] To create a single family or assembly of set apart chosen people to fill the earth.

[3] To bring forth a people after His heart and image.

This is now bone of my bones, and flesh of my flesh: she shall be called Isha, because she was taken out of Ish. 24 Therefore shall a man leave his abba and his ima, and shall cleave to his wife: and they shall be basar echad. 25 And they were both naked, the ish and his isha, and were not ashamed.

3 Now the serpent was craftier than any beast of the field that יהוה Elohim had made. And he said to the woman, Is it emet? Has Elohim said, You shall not eat of every eytz of the garden? 2 And the woman said to the serpent, We may eat of the fruit of the eytzim of the garden: 3 But of the fruit of the eytz which is in the midst of the garden, Elohim has said, You shall not eat of it, neither shall you touch it, lest you die. 4 And the serpent said to the woman, You shall not surely die: 5 For Elohim does know that in the day you eat of it, then your eyes shall be opened, and you shall be like Elohim, knowing tov and evil. 6 And when the woman saw that the eytz was tov for food, and that it was pleasant to the eyes, and an eytz to be desired to make one wise, she took of the fruit of it, and did eat, and gave it also to her husband with her; and he did eat. 7 And the eyes of both of them were opened, and they knew that they were naked; and they sewed fig leaves together, and made themselves aprons. 8 And they heard the voice of יהוה Elohim walking in the garden in the cool of the day: and Adam and his wife hid themselves from the presence of יהוה Elohim among the eytzim of the garden. 9 And יהוה Elohim called to Adam, and said to him, *Where are you?* 10 And he said, I heard Your voice in the garden, and I was afraid, because I was naked; and I hid myself. 11 And He said, *Who told you that you were naked? Have you eaten of the eytz that I commanded you that you should not eat?* 12 And the man said, The woman whom You gave to be with me, she gave me of the eytz, and I did eat. 13 And יהוה Elohim said to the woman, *What is this that you have done?*

And the woman said, The serpent deceived me, and I did eat. 14 And יהוה Elohim said to the serpent, *Because you have done this, you are cursed above all cattle, and above every beast of the field; upon your belly shall you go, and dust shall you eat all the days of your chayim:* 15 *And I will put enmity between you and the woman, and between your zera and her Zera; He shall crush your head, and you shall bruise His heel.*[1] 16 Unto the woman He said, *I will greatly multiply your sorrow and your conception; in sorrow you shall bring out children; and your desire shall be to your husband, and he shall rule over you.* 17 And to Adam He said, *Because you have listened to the voice of your wife, and have eaten of the eytz, of which I commanded you, saying, You shall not eat of it: cursed is the ground for your sake; in sorrow shall you eat from it all the days of your chayim;* 18 *Thorns also and thistles shall it bring out for you; and you shall eat the herb of the field;* 19 *By the sweat of your face shall you eat lechem, until you return to the ground; for out of it were you taken: for dust you are, and to dust shall you return.* 20 And Adam called his wife's name Chavah; because she was the ima of all living. 21 Unto Adam also and to his wife did יהוה Elohim make coats of skins, and clothed them. 22 And יהוה Elohim said, *See, the man has become as one of Us, to know tov and evil: and now, lest he put out his hand, and take also of the eytz chayim, and eat, and live le-olam-va-ed:* 23 Therefore יהוה Elohim sent him out from the Gan-Aden, to work the ground from where he was taken. 24 So He drove out the man; and He placed at the east of the Gan-Aden cheruvim, and a flaming sword that turned in every direction, to guard the way back to the eytz chayim.

4 And Adam knew Chavah his wife; and she conceived, and bore Qayin, and

---

[1] The **proto-evangelium**, or the first proclamation of the **besarot**. While the Seed here is Moshiach Yahshua, it also speaks of the nation of Yisrael overcoming the serpent's people.

said, I have gotten a man from **יהוה**.[1]
2 And she again bore his brother Hevel. And Hevel was a guardian of sheep, but Qayin was a tiller of the ground. 3 And in process of time[2] it came to pass, that Qayin brought from the fruit of the ground an offering to **יהוה**. 4 And Hevel, also brought of the bechorot of his flock and of its fat. And **יהוה** had respect for Hevel and to his offering: 5 But to Qayin and to his offering He had not respect. And Qayin was very angry, and his face displayed hate. 6 And **יהוה** said to Qayin, *Why are you angered and annoyed? And why is your face displaying hate? 7 If you do well, shall you not be accepted? And if you do not do well, sin lies at your door. And its desire is for you, but you should rule over it.* 8 And Qayin talked with Hevel his brother: Let us go out into the plain.[3] And it came to pass, when they were in the field, that Qayin rose up against Hevel his brother, and killed him. 9 And **יהוה** said to Qayin, *Where is Hevel your brother? And he said, I don't know: Am I my brother's guardian?* 10 And He said, *What have you done? The voice of your brother's dom cries to Me from the ground. 11 And now are you cursed from the earth, that has opened its mouth to receive your brother's dom from your hand; 12 When you till the ground, it shall not from now on yield to you its strength; a fugitive and a vagabond shall you be in the earth.* 13 And Qayin said to **יהוה**, My punishment is greater than I can bear. 14 See, You have driven me out this day from the face of the earth; and from Your face shall I be hidden; and I shall be a fugitive and a vagabond in the earth; and it shall come to pass, that every one that finds me shall try and kill me. 15 And **יהוה** said to him, *Therefore whoever kills Qayin, vengeance shall be taken on him sevenfold.* And **יהוה** set a mark upon Qayin, lest any

finding him should kill him.[4] 16 And Qayin went out from the presence of **יהוה**, and dwelt in the land of Nod, at the east of Aden. 17 And Qayin knew his wife;[5] and she conceived, and bore Enoch: and he built a city, and called the name of the city, after the name of his son, Enoch. 18 And to Enoch was born Irad: and Irad begat Mehuya-El: and Mehuya-El begat Methusa-El: and Methusa-El begat Lamech. 19 And Lamech took to him two wives: the name of the one was Adah, and the name of the other Zillah. 20 And Adah bore Yaval: he was the abba of such as dwell in tents, and of such as have cattle. 21 And his brother's name was Yuval: he was the abba of all such as handle the harp and organ. 22 And Zillah, she also bore Tuval-Cain, an instructor in every kind of brass and iron tool: and the sister of Tuval-Cain was Naamah. 23 And Lamech said to his wives, Adah and Zillah, Listen to my voice; you wives of Lamech, listen to my speech: for I have slain a man to my own wounding, and a young man to my hurt. 24 If Qayin shall be avenged sevenfold, truly Lamech seventy-sevenfold.[6] 25 And Adam knew his wife again; and she bore a son, and called his name Sheth: For Elohim, she said, has appointed me another zera instead of Hevel, whom Qayin killed. 26 And to Sheth, also there was born a son; and he called his name Enosh: then men began to call upon the Name of **יהוה**.[7]

5 This is the scroll of the generations of Adam. In the day that Elohim created man, in the likeness of Elohim He made him; 2 Male and female He created them; and blessed them, and called their name Adam, in the day when they were created. 3 And Adam lived a hundred thirty years, and begat a son in his own likeness, after his own image; and called his name Sheth:[8] 4 And the days of Adam after he had

[4] Eternal **rachamim**/unmerited favor.
[5] His sister, which was allowed before Torah was fully revealed in greater detail.
[6] Just wishful thinking.
[7] A long time before Moshe in Shemot 3:15.
[8] Not in YHWH's image since this is after the fall.

[1] The first false moshiach. Chavah hoped that Qayin was the promised seed of Genesis 3:15.
[2] Probably YHWH had already revealed the moadim.
[3] Found in LXX.

begotten Sheth were eight hundred years: and he begat sons and daughters: 5 And all the days that Adam lived were nine hundred thirty years: and he died. 6 And Sheth lived a hundred five years, and begat Enosh: 7 And Sheth lived after he begat Enosh eight hundred seven years, and begat sons and daughters: 8 And all the days of Sheth were nine hundred twelve years: and he died. 9 And Enosh lived ninety years, and begat Caiynan: 10 And Enosh lived after he begat Caiynan eight hundred fifteen years, and begat sons and daughters: 11 And all the days of Enosh were nine hundred five years: and he died. 12 And Caiynan lived seventy years, and begat Mahalal-El: 13 And Caiynan lived after he begat Mahalal-El eight hundred forty years, and begat sons and daughters: 14 And all the days of Caiynan were nine hundred ten years: and he died. 15 And Mahalal-El lived sixty-five years, and begat Yared: 16 And Mahalal-El lived after he begat Yared eight hundred thirty years, and begat sons and daughters: 17 And all the days of Mahalal-El were eight hundred ninety five years: and he died. 18 And Yared lived a hundred sixty-two years, and he begat Enoch: 19 And Yared lived after he begat Enoch eight hundred years, and begat sons and daughters: 20 And all the days of Yared were nine hundred sixty two years: and he died. 21 And Enoch lived sixty-five years, and begat Metushelach: 22 And Enoch had his halacha with Elohim after he begat Metushelach three hundred years, and begat sons and daughters: 23 And all the days of Enoch were three hundred sixty five years: 24 And Enoch had his halacha with Elohim: and he was not; for Elohim took him. 25 And Metushelach lived a hundred eighty seven years, and begat Lamech: 26 And Metushelach lived after he begat Lamech seven hundred eighty two years, and begat sons and daughters: 27 And all the days of Metushelach[1] were nine hundred sixty nine years: and he died. 28 And Lamech lived a hundred eighty two years, and begat a son: 29 And he called his name Noach, saying, This one shall comfort us concerning our work and toil of our hands, because of the ground that יהוה has cursed. 30 And Lamech lived after he begat Noach five hundred ninety five years, and begat sons and daughters: 31 And all the days of Lamech were seven hundred seventy seven years: and he died. 32 And Noach was five hundred years old: and Noach begat Shem, Ham, and Yahpheth.

6 And it came to pass, when men began to multiply on the face of the earth, and daughters were born to them,[2] 2 That the sons of Elohim[3] saw the daughters of men that they were beautiful; and they took for themselves wives of all which they chose. 3 And יהוה said, *My Ruach shall not always strive with man, for that he also is flesh: yet his days shall be one hundred twenty years.* 4 There were Nephilim in the earth in those days; and also after that, when the sons of Elohim came in to the daughters of men, and they bore children to them, the same became mighty men who were of old, men of fame.[4] 5 And Elohim saw that the wickedness of man was great in the earth, and that every imagination of the thoughts of his lev was only evil continually. 6 And it bothered יהוה that He had made man on the earth, and it grieved Him at His lev. 7 And יהוה said, *I will destroy man whom I have created from the face of the earth; both man, and beast, and the creeping thing, and the fowls of the air; for it bothers Me that I have made them.* 8 But Noach found favor[5] in the eyes of יהוה.

---

[1] Meaning "when he dies it shall be sent," speaking of the flood.

[2] As per YHWH's plan to fill the earth with His people.

[3] Fallen **melachim**/angels.

[4] To stop YHWH's eternal plan to fill the earth with one pure people.

[5] Eternal unmerited favor/**rachamim**.

Torah Parsha 2
Noach 6:9-11:32
Haftarah Yeshayahu 54:1-55:5
Brit Chadasha Mattityahu 24:36-44

9 These are the generations of Noach: Noach was a tzadik man and perfect in his generations, and Noach had his halacha with Elohim. 10 And Noach begat three sons, Shem, Ham, and Yahpheth. 11 The earth also was corrupt before Elohim, and the earth was filled with violence. 12 And Elohim looked upon the earth, and, see, it was corrupt; for all flesh had corrupted its way upon the earth. 13 And Elohim said to Noach, *The end of all flesh has come before Me; for the earth is filled with violence through them; and, see, I will destroy them with the earth. 14 Make a tavah of gopher wood; rooms you shall make in the tavah, and shall cover it inside and outside with tar. 15 And this is the design that you shall make it: The length of the tavah shall be three hundred cubits, the width of it fifty cubits, and the height of it thirty cubits. 16 A window shall you make to the tavah, and in a cubit shall you finish it above; and the door of the tavah shall you set in the side of it; with lower, second, and third stories shall you make it. 17 And, see, I, even I, do bring a flood of mayim upon the earth, to destroy all flesh, in which is the breath of chayim, from under the shamayim; and everything that is in the earth shall die. 18 But with you I will establish My covenant; and you shall come into the tavah, you, and your sons, and your wife, and your sons' wives with you. 19 And of every living thing of all flesh, two of every sort shall you bring into the tavah, to keep them alive with you; they shall be male and female. 20 Of fowls after their kind, and of cattle after their kind, of every creeping thing of the earth after its kind, two of every sort shall come to you, to keep them alive. 21 And take for you all food that is eaten, and you shall gather it to you; and it shall be for food for you, and for them. 22 So* Noach did according to all that Elohim commanded him; so he did.[1]

7 And יהוה said to Noach, *Come you and all your bayit into the tavah; for you have I seen tzadik before Me in this generation. 2 Of every clean beast you shall take by sevens,[2] the male and the female: and of beasts that are not clean by two, the male and the female. 3 Of fowls also of the air by sevens, the male and the female; to keep all zera alive upon the face of all the earth. 4 For in seven days, and I will cause it to rain upon the earth forty days and forty nights; and every living substance that I have made I will destroy from off the face of the earth.* 5 And Noach did according to all that יהוה commanded him.[3] 6 And Noach was six hundred years old when the flood of mayim was upon the earth. 7 And Noach went in, and his sons, and his wife, and his sons' wives with him, into the tavah, because of the mayim of the flood. 8 Of clean beasts, and of beasts that are not clean, and of fowls, and of every thing that creeps upon the earth, 9 They went in two by two to Noach into the tavah, the male and the female, as Elohim had commanded Noach. 10 And it came to pass after seven days, that the mayim of the flood was upon the earth. 11 In the six hundredth year of Noach's chayim, in the second month, the seventeenth day of the month, the same day were all the fountains of the great deep broken up, and the windows of the shamayim were opened. 12 And the rain was upon the earth forty days and forty nights. 13 In the same day entered Noach, and Shem, and Ham, and Yahpheth, the sons of Noach, and Noach's wife, and the three wives of his sons with them, into the tavah; 14 They, and every beast after its kind, and all the cattle after their kind, and every creeping thing that creeps upon the earth after its kind, and every fowl after its kind, every bird of every sort. 15 And they

---

[1] Followed Torah as it was progressively revealed.
[2] Noach had a revelation of **kashrut** or kosher animals.
[3] Kept Torah.

went in to Noach into the tavah, two by two of all flesh, in which is the breath of chayim. 16 And they that went in, went in male and female of all flesh, as Elohim had commanded him: and **יהוה** shut him in.[1] 17 And the flood was forty days upon the earth; and the mayim increased, and lifted up the tavah, and it was lifted up above the earth. 18 And the mayim prevailed, and were increased greatly upon the earth; and the tavah went upon the face of the mayim. 19 And the mayim prevailed exceedingly upon the earth; and all the high hills that were under the entire shamayim were covered. 20 Fifteen cubits upward did the mayim prevail; and the mountains were covered. 21 And all flesh died that moved upon the earth, both of fowl, and of cattle, and of beast, and of every creeping thing that creeps upon the earth, and every man: 22 All in whose nostrils was the breath of chayim, of all that was in the dry land, died. 23 And every living substance was destroyed that was upon the face of the ground, both man, and cattle, and the creeping things, and the fowls of the shamayim; and they were destroyed from the earth: and Noach only remained alive, and they that were with him in the tavah. 24 And the mayim prevailed upon the earth a hundred fifty days.

8 And Elohim remembered Noach, and every living thing, and all the cattle that were with him in the tavah: and Elohim made a wind to pass over the earth, and the mayim subsided; 2 The fountains also of the deep and the windows of shamayim were stopped, and the rain from the shamayim was restrained; 3 And the mayim returned from off the earth continually: and after the end of the hundred fifty days the mayim were abated. 4 And the tavah rested in the seventh month, on the seventeenth day of the month, upon the mountains of Ararat.[2]

5 And the mayim decreased continually until the tenth month: in the tenth month, on the first day of the month, were the tops of the mountains seen. 6 And it came to pass at the end of forty days, that Noach opened the window of the tavah that he had made: 7 And he sent out a raven, which went out back and forth, until the mayim were dried up from off the earth. 8 Also he sent out a yonah from him, to see if the mayim were abated from off the face of the ground; 9 But the yonah found no rest for the sole of her foot, and she returned to him into the tavah, for the mayim were on the face of the whole earth: then he put out his hand, and took her, and pulled her in to him into the tavah. 10 And he stayed yet seven more days; and again he sent out the yonah out of the tavah; 11 And the yonah came in to him in the evening; and, see, in her mouth was an olive leaf plucked off: so Noach knew that the mayim were abated from off the earth. 12 And he stayed yet seven more days; and sent out the yonah; which returned not again to him any more. 13 And it came to pass in the six hundred first year, in the first month, on the first day of the month,[3] the mayim were dried up from off the earth: and Noach removed the covering of the tavah, and looked, and, see, the face of the ground was dry. 14 And in the second month, on the twenty-seventh day of the month, the earth was dried. 15 And Elohim spoke to Noach, saying, 16 *Go out from the tavah, you, and your wife, and your sons, and your sons' wives with you. 17 Bring out with you every living thing that is with you, of all flesh, both of fowl, and of cattle, and of every creeping thing that creeps upon the earth; that they may breed abundantly in the earth, and be fruitful, and multiply upon the earth.*[4] 18 And Noach went out, and his sons, and his wife, and his son's wives with him: 19 Every beast, every creeping thing, and every fowl, and whatever creeps upon the earth, after their kinds, went out of the

---

[1] More rachamim.
[2] During Sukkot an appropriate time indeed for a sukkah in the form of an ark for the fathers of the future redeemed people of Yisrael.
[3] A New Year for a renewed family and earth.
[4] YHWH refills the earth with Noach's seed.

tavah. 20 And Noach built an altar to **יהוה**; and took of every clean beast, and of every clean fowl, and offered burnt offerings on the altar. 21 And **יהוה** smelled a sweet fragrance; and **יהוה** said in His lev, *I will not again curse the ground any more for man's sake; for the imagination of man's lev is evil from his youth; neither will I again smite any more every living thing, as I have done.* 22 *While the earth remains, seedtime and harvest, and cold and heat, and summer and winter, and day and night shall not cease.*

9 And Elohim blessed Noach and his sons, and said to them, *Be fruitful, and multiply, and replenish the earth.[1] 2 And the fear of you and the dread of you shall be upon every beast of the earth, and upon every fowl of the air, upon all that moves upon the earth, and upon all the fishes of the sea; into your hand are they delivered. 3 Every moving thing that lives shall be food for you; even as the green herb have I given you all things. 4 But flesh with the chayim in it, which is its dom, shall you not eat.[2] 5 And surely the dom of your lives I will require; at the hand of every beast will I require it, and at the hand of man; at the hand of every man's brother will I require the chayim of man. 6 Whosoever sheds man's dom, by man, shall his dom be shed: for in the image of Elohim He made man.[3] 7 And you, be fruitful, and multiply; bring out abundantly in the earth, and multiply in it.[4] 8 And Elohim spoke to Noach, and to his sons with him, saying, 9 And I, even I,[5] will establish My covenant with you, and with your zera after you; 10 And with every living creature that is with you, the fowl, the cattle, and every beast of the earth with you; from all that go out of the tavah, to every beast of the earth. 11 And I will establish*

My covenant with you; neither shall all flesh be cut off any more by the mayim of a flood; neither shall there any more be a flood to destroy the earth.[6] 12 And Elohim said, This is the token of the covenant that I make between Me and you and every living creature that is with you, for perpetual generations: 13 I do set My bow in the cloud, and it shall be for a token of a covenant between the earth and Me. 14 And it shall come to pass, when I bring a cloud over the earth, that the bow shall be seen in the cloud: 15 And I will remember My covenant, which is between Me and you and every living creature of all flesh; and the mayim shall no more become a flood to destroy all flesh. 16 And the bow shall be in the cloud; and I will look upon it, that I may remember the everlasting covenant between Elohim and every living creature of all flesh that is upon the earth.[7] 17 And Elohim said to Noach, This is the token of the covenant, which I have established between My word and all flesh that is upon the earth. 18 And the sons of Noach that went out from the tavah were Shem, and Ham, and Yahpheth: and Ham is the abba of Kanaan. 19 These are the three sons of Noach: and from them was the whole earth filled.[8] 20 And Noach began to be a man of the soil, and he planted a vineyard: 21 And he drank of the wine, and became drunk; and he was uncovered within his tent. 22 And Ham, the abba of Kanaan, saw the nakedness of his abba, and told his two brothers outside. 23 And Shem and Yahpheth took a garment, and laid it upon both their shoulders, and went in backwards, and covered the nakedness of their abba; and their faces were backward, and they saw not their abba's nakedness. 24 And Noach awoke from his wine, and

---

[1] See note on chapter 8 verse 17.
[2] Noach obeys Torah.
[3] YHWH installs the right ruling of capital punishment as an act of mercy to deter evil.
[4] The plan is unchanged. Yisrael the elect of YHWH will be birthed.
[5] Duality in **echad**.

[6] The physical multiplicity provision of the Edenic Covenant renewed in Noach.
[7] Forgiven and redeemed Yisrael will eventually inherit this same evelasting covenant in Yirmeyah 31:31.
[8] The Hebrew word is **maaleh** the same root used in Genesis 48:19 for "fullness-melo." YHWH made every human after the flood from Noach, a single person. We see that again when He populates all the earth's nations through a single person - Yaakov/Yaakov.

knew what his younger son had done to him. 25 And he said, Cursed be Kanaan; an eved of avadim shall he be to his brothers.[1] 26 And he said, Barchu-et-יהוה Elohim of Shem; and Kanaan shall be his eved. 27 Elohim shall enlarge Yahpheth, and he shall dwell in the tents of Shem; and Kanaan shall be his eved.[2] 28 And Noach lived after the flood three hundred fifty years. 29 And all the days of Noach were nine hundred fifty years: and he died.

10 Now these are the generations of the sons of Noach, Shem, Ham, and Yahpheth: and to them were sons born after the flood. 2 The sons of Yahpheth; Gomer, and Magog, and Madai, and Yavan, and Tuval, and Meshech, and Tiras. 3 And the sons of Gomer; Ashkenaz, and Riphath, and Togarmah. 4 And the sons of Yavan; Elishah, and Tarshish, Kittim, and Dodanim. 5 By these were the isles of the gentiles divided in their lands, every one after his tongue, after their mishpachot, in their nations.[3] 6 And the sons of Ham; Cush, and Mitzrayim, and Phut, and Kanaan. 7 And the sons of Cush; Seba, and Havilah, and Savtah, and Raamah, and Savtecha: and the sons of Raamah; Sheba, and Dedan. 8 And Cush begat Nimrod: he began to be a mighty one in the earth. 9 He was a mighty hunter before יהוה: That is why it is said, Even as Nimrod the mighty hunter before יהוה.[4] 10 And the beginning of his malchut was Bavel, and Erech, and Accad, and Calneh, in the land of Shinar. 11 Out of that land went out Ashshur, who built Nineveh, and the city Rehovoth, and Calah,[5] 12 And Resen between Nineveh and Calah: the same is a great city. 13 And Mitzrayim begat Ludim, and Anamim, and Lehavim, and Naphtuhim, 14 And Pathrusim, and Casluhim, out of whom came Philistim, and Caphtorim. 15 And Kanaan begat Tzidon his bachor, and Cheth, 16 And the Yevusite, and the Amorite, and the Girgashite, 17 And the Hivite, and the Arkite, and the Sinite, 18 And the Arvadite, and the Zemarite, and the Hamathite: and afterward were the mishpachot of the Kanaanites spread abroad. 19 And the border of the Kanaanites was from Sidon, as you come to Gerar, to Gaza, as you go, to Sedom, and Amorah, and Admah, and Zevoim, even to Lasha. 20 These are the sons of Ham, after their mishpachot, after their tongues, in their countries, and in their nations. 21 Unto Shem also, the abba of all the children of Ever, the brother of Yahpheth the zachen, even to him were children born. 22 The children of Shem; Eylam, and Ashshur, and Arphaxad, and Lud, and Aram.[6] 23 And the children of Aram; Uz, and Hul, and Gether, and Mash. 24 And Arphaxad begat Caynan and Caynan[7] begat Salah; and Salah begat Ever. 25 And to Ever were born two sons: the name of one was Peleg; for in his days was the earth divided; and his brother's name was Yoktan. 26 And Yoktan begat Almodad, and Sheleph, and Hazar-Maveth, and Yourah, 27 And Hadoram, and Uzal, and Diklah, 28 And Oval, and Avima-El, and Sheva, 29 And Ophir, and Havilah, and Yovab: all these were the sons of Yoktan. 30 And their dwelling was from Mesha, as you are going to Sephar a mountain of the east. 31 These are the sons of Shem, after their mishpachot, after their tongues, in their lands, after their nations.[8] 32 These are the mishpachot of the sons of Noach, after their generations, in their nations. By these

---

[1] This is not a perpetual curse on blacks or any race. Rather it's a curse on one individual Cannan, who would be in servitude.
[2] A clear-cut prophecy (not question) that all humanity will one day be gathered as Shemites or in the House of Righteous Shem, later to become the single renewed Yisraelite body of Moshiach. That's exactly what Moshiach has done, gathering all believers in Shem's tent as Yisrael!
[3] These are the same gentile nations that would one day be filled with Shem's seed.
[4] Nimrod was worshipped and hunted men's souls away from YHWH.
[5] Where Ephraim Yisrael would be taken.
[6] The father of the Arameans, who were Semites and of the same race as the Hebrews.
[7] From LXX that provides the missing link between Arphaxad and Salah.
[8] Shem's seed already spread out in many nations.

mishpachot were the nations divided in the earth after the flood.

11 And the whole earth was of one language, and of one speech. 2 And it came to pass, as they journeyed from the east, that they found a plain in the land of Shinar; and they dwelt there. 3 And they said one to another, Come, let us make brick, and burn them thoroughly. And they had brick for stone, and slime had they for mortar. 4 And they said, Come, let us build us a city and a tower, whose top may reach to the shamayim; and let us make us a name, lest we be scattered abroad upon the face of the whole earth. 5 And **יהוה** came down to see the city and the tower that the children of men built. 6 And **יהוה** said, *See, the people are echad, and they all have one language; and this they begin to do: and now nothing will be restrained from them, which they have imagined to do. 7 Come, let Us* [1] *go down, and there confound their language, that they may not understand one another's speech.* 8 So **יהוה** scattered them abroad from there upon the face of all the earth: and they ceased to build the city. [2] 9 Therefore its name is called Bavel; because **יהוה** did there confuse the language of all the earth: and from there did **יהוה** scatter them abroad upon the face of all the earth. 10 These are the generations of Shem: Shem was an hundred years old, and begat Arphaxad two years after the flood: 11 And Shem lived after he begat Arphaxad five hundred years, and begat sons and daughters. 12 And Arphaxad lived thirty-five years, and begat Salah: 13 And Arphaxad lived after he begat Salah four hundred three years, and begat sons and daughters. 14 And Salah lived thirty years, and begat Ever: 15 And Salah lived after he begat Ever four hundred three years, and begat sons and daughters. 16 And Ever lived thirty-four years, and begat Peleg: 17 And Ever lived after he begat Peleg four hundred thirty years, and begat sons and daughters. 18 And Peleg lived thirty years, and begat Reu: 19 And Peleg lived after he begat Reu two hundred and nine years, and begat sons and daughters. 20 And Reu lived thirty-two years, and begat Serug: 21 And Reu lived after he begat Serug two hundred seven years, and begat sons and daughters. 22 And Serug lived thirty years, and begat Nachor: 23 And Serug lived after he begat Nachor two hundred years, and begat sons and daughters. 24 And Nachor lived twenty-nine years, and begat Terah: 25 And Nachor lived after he begat Terah one hundred nineteen years, and begat sons and daughters. 26 And Terah lived seventy years, and begat Avram, Nachor, and Charan. 27 Now these are the generations of Terah: Terah begat Avram, Nachor, and Charan; and Charan begat Lot. 28 And Charan died before his abba Terah in the land of his nativity, in Ur of the Chaldees. 29 And Avram and Nachor took wives: the name of Avram's wife was Sarai; and the name of Nachor's wife, Milcah, the daughter of Charan, the abba of Milcah, and the abba of Iscah. 30 But Sarai was barren; she had no child. 31 And Terah took Avram his son, and Lot the son of Charan his son's son, and Sarai his daughter in law, his son Avram's wife; and they went out with them from Ur of the Chaldees, to go into the land of Kanaan; and they came to Charan, and dwelt there. 32 And the days of Terah were two hundred five years: and Terah died in Charan.

Torah Parsha 3
Lech Lecha 12:1-17:27
Haftara Yeshayahu 40:27-41:16
Brit Chadasha Romiyah 3:19-5:6

12 Now **יהוה** had said to Avram, *Get out of your country, and from your mishpocha, and from your abba's bayit, to a land that I will show you: 2 And I will make of you a great nation,* [3] *and I will bless you, and make your name great; and you shall*

---
[1] Plurality of YHWH.
[2] The plan to spread Shem's seed from the east into the entire globe.

[3] Yisrael.The blessed nation.

be a bracha: 3 *And I will bless them that bless you, and curse him that curses you: and in you shall all mishpachot of the earth be blessed - mixed.*[1] 4 So Avram departed, as **יהוה** had spoken to him; and Lot went with him: and Avram was seventy-five years old when he departed out of Charan. 5 And Avram took Sarai his wife, and Lot his brother's son, and all their substance that they had gathered, and the beings that they had gotten in Charan; and they went out to go into the land of Kanaan; and into the land of Kanaan they came. 6 And Avram passed through the land to the place of Shechem, to the plain of Moreh. And the Canaanite was then in the land. 7 And **יהוה** appeared to Avram, and said, *To your zera will I give this land:* and there he built an altar to **יהוה**, who appeared to him. 8 And he moved from there to a mountain on the east of Beth-El, and pitched his tent, having Beth-El on the west, and Ai on the east: and there he built an altar to **יהוה**, and called upon the Name of **יהוה**.[2] 9 And Avram journeyed, going on still toward the south. 10 And there was a famine in the land: and Avram went down into Mitzrayim to sojourn there; for the famine was severe in the land. 11 And it came to pass, when he was come near to enter into Mitzrayim, that he said to Sarai his wife, See now, I know that you are a beautiful woman to look upon: 12 Therefore it shall come to pass, when the Mitzrites shall see you, that they shall say, This is his wife: and they will kill me, but they will save you alive. 13 Say, Please, you are my sister: that it may be well with me for your sake; and my being shall live because of you. 14 And it came to pass, that, when Avram came into Mitzrayim, the Mitzrites beheld the woman that she was very beautiful. 15 The princes

also of Pharaoh saw her, and commended her before Pharaoh: and the woman was taken into Pharaoh's bayit.[3] 16 And he treated Avram well for her sake: and he had sheep, and oxen, and male donkeys, and male avadim, and female avadim, and female donkeys, and camels. 17 And **יהוה** plagued Pharaoh and his bayit with great plagues because of Sarai Avram's wife. 18 And Pharaoh called Avram, and said, What is this that you have done to me? Why did you not tell me that she was your wife? 19 Why did you say, She is my sister? So I might have mistakenly taken her to me as my wife: now therefore see your wife, take her, and go your way. 20 And Pharaoh commanded his men concerning him: and they sent him away, and his wife, and all that he had.

13 And Avram went up out of Mitzrayim, he, and his wife, and all that he had, and Lot with him, into the south. 2 And Avram was very rich in cattle, in silver, and in gold. 3 And he went on his journeys from the south even to Beth-El, to the place where his tent had been at the beginning, between Beth-El and Ai; 4 To the place of the altar, which he had made there at the first: and there Avram called on the Name of **יהוה**. 5 And Lot also, who went with Avram, had flocks, and herds, and tents. 6 And the land was not able to bear them so that they might dwell together: for their substance was great, so that they could not dwell together. 7 And there was strife between the herdsmen of Avram's cattle and the herdsmen of Lot's cattle: and the Canaanite and the Perizzite dwelt then in the land. 8 And Avram said to Lot, Let there be no strife, please, between you, and me and between my herdsmen and your herdsmen, for we are brothers. 9 Is not the whole land before you? Separate yourself, please, from me: if you will take the left hand, then I will go to the right; or if you depart to the right hand, then I will go to the

---

[1] Hebrew for blessed here is **nivrechu** and not only means "blessed" but also "mixed." All nations will have Avraham's seed mixed into their populations. For more details on **nivrechu** see: **The Truth About All Israel** under the section on **nivrechu** at:
http://yourarmstoisrael.org/The_Truth/THE_TRUTH_ABOUT_ALL_ISRAEL_by_Rabbi_Moshe_Koniuchowsky.pdf
[2] Avraham knew the true Name.

[3] As Yisrael would one day be.

left. 10 And Lot lifted up his eyes, and beheld all the plain of Yarden, that it was well watered everywhere, before יהוה destroyed Sedom and Amorah, even as the Gan-Adan of יהוה , like the land of Mitzrayim, as you come to Tzoar. 11 Then Lot chose for himself all the plain of the Yarden; and Lot journeyed east: and they separated themselves from one another. 12 Avram dwelt in the land of Kanaan, and Lot dwelt in the cities of the plain, and pitched his tent toward Sedom. 13 But the men of Sedom were wicked and sinners before יהוה exceedingly. 14 And יהוה said to Avram, after Lot was separated from him, *Lift up now yours eyes, and look from the place where you are northward, and southward, and eastward, and westward: 15 For all the land which you see, to you will I give it, and to your zera le-olam-va-ed.[1] 16 And I will make your zera as the dust of the earth: so that if a man can number the dust of the earth, then your zera also can be numbered.[2] 17 Arise, walk through the land in the length and in the width, for I will give it to you.* 18 Then Avram removed his tent, and came and dwelt in the plain of Mamre, which is in Hevron, and built there an altar to יהוה.

14 And it came to pass in the days of Amraphel melech of Shinar, Arioch melech of Ellasar, Chedarlaomer melech of Eylam, and Tidal melech of nations, 2 That these made war with Bera melech of Sedom, and with Birsha melech of Amorah, Shinav melech of Admah, and Shemever melech of Zevoiim, and the melech of Bela, which is Tzoar. 3 All these were joined together in the vale of Siddim, which is the Salt Sea. 4 Twelve years they served Chedarlaomer, and in the thirteenth year they rebelled. 5 And in the fourteenth year came Chedarlaomer, and the melechim that were with him, and smote the Rephalim in Ashteroth Karnayim, and the Zuzims in

Ham, and the Emims in Shaveh Kiryat-Aim, 6 And the Horites in their Mount Seir, to El-Paran, which is by the wilderness. 7 And they returned, and came to En-Mishpat, which is Kadesh, and smote all the country of the Amalekites, and also the Amorites that dwelt in Hazezon-Tamar. 8 And there went out the melech of Sedom, and the melech of Amorah, and the melech of Admah, and the melech of Zevoiim, and the melech of Bela (the same is Tzoar), and they joined battle with them in the vale of Siddim; 9 With Chedarlaomer the melech of Eylam, and with Tidal melech of nations, and Amraphel melech of Shinar, and Arioch melech of Ellasar; four melechim against five. 10 And the vale of Siddim was full of tar pits; and the melechim of Sedom and Amorah fled, and fell there; and they that remained fled to the mountain. 11 And they took all the items of Sedom and Amorah, and all their food, and went their way. 12 And they took Lot, Avram's brother's son, who dwelt in Sedom, and his items, and departed. 13 And there came one that had escaped, and told Avram the Ivri;[3] for he dwelt in the plain of Mamre the Amorite, brother of Eschol, and brother of Aner: and these were in confederate with Avram. 14 And when Avram heard that his brother was taken captive, he armed his trained avadim, born in his own bayit, three hundred and eighteen, and pursued them to Dan. 15 And he divided himself against them, he and his avadim, by night, and smote them, and pursued them to Hovah, which is on the left hand of Dameshek. 16 And he brought back all the items, and also brought again his brother Lot, and his items, and the women also, and the people. 17 And the melech of Sedom went out to meet him after his return from the slaughter of Chedarlaomer, and of the melechim that were with him, at the Valley of Shaveh, which is the melech's valley. 18 And Malki-Tzedek melech of Salem brought out lechem and wine: and He was the Kohen of

---

[1] Yisrael's eternal home.
[2] A literal promise to a literal **zera**/seed.
[3] Avraham was not a Jew.

El-Elyon.[1] 19 And He blessed him, and said, *Blessed be Avram of El-Elyon, Possessor of the shamayim and earth:* 20 *And blessed be El-Elyon, who has delivered your enemies into your hand.* And he paid Him ma'aser of all.[2] 21 And the melech of Sedom said to Avram, Give me the persons, and take the items to yourself. 22 And Avram said to the melech of Sedom, I have lifted up my hand to יהוה, El-Elyon, the Possessor of the shamayim and earth, 23 That I will not take from you a thread or even a shoe latchet, and that I will not take anything that is yours, lest you should say, I have made Avram rich: 24 Except what the young men have eaten, and the portion of the men who went with me. Aner, Eshcol, and Mamre. Let them take their portion.

15 After these things the word of יהוה came to Avram in a vision, saying, *Fear not, Avram: I am your shield, and your exceeding great reward.* 2 And Avram said, Sovereign יהוה, what will You give me, seeing I go childless, and the steward of my bayit is this Eliezer of Dameshek? 3 And Avram said, See, to me You have given no zera: and, see, one born in my bayit is my heir. 4 And, see, the word of יהוה came to him, saying, *This shall not be your heir; but he that shall come out out of your own bowels shall be your heir.*[3] 5 And He brought him out abroad, and said, *Look now toward the shamayim, and count the chochavim, if you are able to number them:* and He said to him, *So shall your zera be.*[4] 6 And he believed in the Word of יהוה;[5] and He counted it to him as tzedakah.[6] 7 And He said to him, *I am יהוה that brought you out of Ur of the Chaldees, to give you this land to inherit it.* 8 And he said, Melech-יהוה, how shall I know that I

shall inherit it? 9 And He said to him, *Take a heifer three years old, and a female goat three years old, and a ram three years old, and a turtledove, and a young pigeon.* 10 And he took for Him all these, and divided them in the midst, and laid each piece one against another: but the birds he divided not. 11 And when the fowls came down upon the carcasses, Avram drove them away. 12 And when the sun was going down, a deep sleep fell upon Avram; and, see, a horror of great darkness fell upon him. 13 And He said to Avram, *Know of a certainty that your zera shall be gerim in a land that is not theirs, and shall serve them; and they shall afflict them four hundred years;*[7] 14 *And also that nation, whom they shall serve, will I shophet: and afterward shall they come out with great substance.* 15 *And you shall go to your ahvot in shalom; you shall be buried in a tov old age.* 16 *But in the fourth generation they shall come here again: for the iniquity of the Amorites is not yet full.* 17 And it came to pass, that, when the sun went down, and it was dark, see a smoking furnace, and a burning lamp that passed between those pieces.[8] 18 In the same day יהוה made a covenant with Avram, saying, *To your zera have I given this land, from the River of Mitzrayim to the Great River, the River Euphrates:* 19 *The land of the Kenites, and the Kenizzites, and the Kadmonites,* 20 *And the Hittites, and the Perizzites, and the Rephaim,* 21 *And the Amorites, and the Kanaanites, and the Girgashites, and the Yevusites.*

16 Now Sarai Avram's wife bore him no children: and she had a handmaid, a Mitzrite, whose name was Hagar. 2 And Sarai said to Avram, See now, יהוה has restrained me from bearing: Please, go in to my maid; it may be that I may obtain children by her; And Avram listened to the voice of Sarai. 3 And Sarai

---

[1] Obvious reference to Yahshua YHWH's Son.
[2] Tithing predates the Mt. Sinai marriage to Yisrael.
[3] YHWH rebukes Avraham's request for gentile offspring.
[4] Not metaphorical - the literal plan to fill the earth with Abraham, Isaac and Jacob's zera.
[5] Aramaic Targum Onkelos.
[6] How did Avraham get saved? By trusting the promise of physical multiplicity. If you are Abraham's seed, you must believe what Abraham believed.

[7] General approximation of Yisrael's time of slavery in Egypt.
[8] The Divine **Shechinah**.

Avram's wife took Hagar her maid the Mitzrite, after Avram had dwelt ten years in the land of Kanaan, and gave her to her husband Avram to be his wife. 4 And he went in to Hagar, and she conceived: and when she saw that she had conceived, her mistress was despised in her eyes. 5 And Sarai said to Avram, My wrong is upon you: I have given my maid into your bosom; and when she saw that she had conceived, I was despised in her eyes: **יהוה** shophet between me and you. 6 But Avram said to Sarai, See, your maid is in your hand; do to her as it pleases you. And when Sarai dealt harshly with her, she fled from her face. 7 And the Malach- **יהוה** found her by a fountain of mayim in the wilderness, by the fountain on the way to Shur. 8 And He said, *Hagar, Sarai's maid, where did you come from? And where will you go?* And she said, I flee from the face of my mistress Sarai. 9 And the Malach- **יהוה** said to her, *Return to your mistress, and submit yourself under her hands.* 10 And the Malach- **יהוה** said to her, *I will multiply your zera exceedingly, that it shall not be numbered for multitude.* 11 And the Malach- **יהוה** said to her, *See, you are with child, and shall bear a son, and shall call his name Yishma-El; because* **יהוה** *has heard your affliction. 12 And he will be a wild man; his hand will be against every man, and every man's hand against him; and he shall dwell in the presence of all his brothers.* 13 And she called on the Name of **יהוה** that spoke to her, You are El-Roi: for she said, Have I even here looked upon Him that sees me? 14 Therefore the well was called Beer-Lahai-Roi; and it is between Kadesh and Bered. 15 And Hagar bore Avram a son: and Avram called his son's name, which Hagar bore, Yishma-El. 16 And Avram was eight-six years old, when Hagar bore Yishma-El to Avram.

17 And when Avram was ninety-nine years old, **יהוה** appeared to Avram, and said to him, *I am El-Shaddai; have your halacha before Me, and be perfect. 2 And I will make My covenant between Me and you, and will multiply you exceedingly.* 3 And Avram fell on his face: and Elohim talked with him, saying, 4 *As for Me, see, My covenant is with you, and you shall be the abba of many nations.[1] 5 Neither shall your name any more be called Avram, but your name shall be Avraham;[2] for the abba of many nations I have made you.[3] 6 And I will make you exceeding fruitful, and I will make nations from you, and melechim shall come from you. 7 And I will establish My covenant between My word[4] and you and your zera after you in their generations as an everlasting covenant, to be an Elohim to you, and to your zera after you. 8 And I will give to you, and to your zera after you, the land in which you are a Ger, all the land of Kanaan, for an everlasting possession; and I will be their Elohim.* 9 And Elohim said to Avraham, *You shall keep My covenant therefore, you, and your zera after you in their generations. 10 This is My covenant that you shall keep, between Me and you and your zera after you; every male child among you shall enter brit-milah. 11 And you shall brit-milah the flesh of your foreskin; and it shall be a token of the covenant between you and Me. 12 And he that is eight days old shall be circumcised among you, every male child in your generations, he that is born in the bayit, or bought with the money of any Ger, which is not of your zera. 13 He that is born in your bayit, and he that is bought with your money, must enter brit-milah: and My covenant shall be in your flesh for an everlasting covenant.[5] 14 And the uncircumcised male-child whose flesh of his foreskin is not circumcised, that being shall*

---

[1] These many nations would come to pass through Isaac and Yaakov as we are later told, not Ishmael the abba of one large nation.
[2] By adding the Hebrew letter **"hey"** or the breath of YHWH to give life to Abraham's seed. Moreover, **"hey"** is the second letter of the **Tetragrammaton**; thus by changing the name to Avra**ham** he carried YHWH's Name and breath, signifying new birth and new life as a Hebrew.
[3] See note at Genesis 17:4. The promise repeated.
[4] **Memra** in Aramaic Targum.
[5] Therefore the Renewed Covenant cannot possibly teach against an eternal ordinance.

be cut off from his people; he has broken My covenant. [1] 15 And Elohim said to Avraham, *As for Sarai your wife, you shall not call her name Sarai, but Sarah shall be her name. 16 And I will bless her, and give you a son also by her: And I will bless her, and she shall be an ima of nations;* [2] *melechim of peoples shall be from her.* 17 Then Avraham fell upon his face, and laughed, and said in his lev, Shall a child be born to him that is a hundred years old? And shall Sarah, that is ninety years old, bear? 18 And Avraham said to Elohim, O that Yishma-El might live before You! 19 And Elohim said, *Sarah your wife shall bear you a son indeed; and you shall call his name Yitzchak: and I will establish My covenant with him for an everlasting covenant, and with his zera after him.* [3] *20 And as for Yishma-El, I have heard you: See, I have blessed him, and will make him fruitful, and will multiply him exceedingly; twelve princes shall he beget, and I will make him a great nation.* [4] *21 But My covenant will I establish with Yitzchak, whom Sarah shall bear to you at this set time in the next year.* [5] 22 And He stopped talking with him, and Elohim went up from Avraham. 23 And Avraham took Yishma-El his son, and all that were born in his bayit, and all that were bought with his money, every male among the men of Avraham's bayit; and circumcised the flesh of their foreskin in the very same day, that Elohim had spoken to him. 24 And Avraham was ninety-nine years old, when he was circumcised in the flesh of his foreskin. 25 And Yishma-El his son was thirteen years old, when he was circumcised in the flesh of his foreskin. 26 In the very same day was Avraham circumcised, and Yishma-El his son. 27 And all the men of his bayit, born in the bayit, and bought with money of the Ger, [6] were circumcised with him.

Torah Parsha 4
Vayera 18:1-22:24
Haftarah Melechim Bet 4:1-37
Brit Chadasha Yaakov 2:14-24

18 And יהוה appeared to him in the plains of Mamre: and Avraham sat in the tent door in the heat of the day. 2 And Avraham lifted up his eyes and looked, and, see, three men stood by him: and when he saw them, he ran to meet them at the tent door, and bowed himself toward the ground, 3 And Avraham said, יהוה; if now I have found favor in Your sight, please do not leave Your eved: 4 Please let a little mayim, be took, and wash Your feet, and rest yourselves under the eytz: 5 And I will get a morsel of lechem, and so comfort Your levim; after that You shall go Your way: for this is why You have come to Your eved. And they said, Go do, as you have said. 6 And Avraham ran into the tent to Sarah, and said, Make ready quickly three measures of fine flour, knead it, and make cakes. 7 And Avraham ran to the herd, and took a tov tender calf, and gave it to a young man; and he hurried to prepare it. 8 And he took butter, and milk, and the calf that he had prepared, and set it before them; and he stood by them under the eytz, and they did eat. [7] 9 And they said to him, Where is Sarah your wife? And he said, See; in the tent. 10 And He said, *I will certainly return to you according to the time of chayim; and, see; Sarah your wife shall have a son.* And Sarah heard it in the tent door that was behind Him. [8] 11 Now Avraham and Sarah were old and well stricken in age; and it ceased to be with Sarah after the manner of women. 12 Therefore Sarah laughed within herself, saying, After I am grown old shall I have pleasure, my master being old also? 13 And יהוה said to Avraham, *Why did*

---

[1] That has not changed for all Yisraelites.
[2] Mother of nations is **vehaytah legoyim;** she will become nations - a promise not given to Hagar, who would mother just one nation.
[3] The promised seed of physical multiplicity goes through Yitzchak not through Ishmael.
[4] Notice one nation not many nations.
[5] A covenant is more detailed and extensive than the mere blessing that Ishmael experienced.

[6] All who joined his faith including strangers.
[7] We see meat and dairy mixing fully legal according to Torah, with Avraham, and YHWH Himself in his tent.
[8] The promised seed.

Sarah laugh, saying, Shall I of a certainty bear a child, seeing I am old? 14 *Is any thing too hard for* יהוה *? At the time appointed I will return to you, according to the time of chayim, and Sarah shall have a son.* 15 Then Sarah denied, saying, I laughed not; for she was afraid. And He said, *No; but you did laugh.* 16 And the men rose up from there, and looked toward Sedom: and Avraham went with them to bring them on the way. 17 And יהוה said, *Shall I hide from Avraham that thing which I must do;* 18 *Seeing that Avraham shall surely become a great and mighty nation, and all the nations of the earth shall be blessed in him?* 19 *For I know him, that he will command his children and his household after him, and they shall keep the halacha of* יהוה*, to do justice and mishpat; that* יהוה *may bring upon Avraham that which He has spoken about him.*[1] 20 And יהוה said, *Because the cry of Sedom and Amorah is great, and because their sin is very severe;* 21 *I will go down now, and see whether they have done altogether according to the cry of it, which is come to Me; and if not, I will know.* 22 And the men turned their faces from there, and went toward Sedom: but Avraham still stood before יהוה. 23 And Avraham drew near, and said, Will You also destroy the tzadikim with the wicked? 24 Suppose there are fifty tzadikim within the city: will You also destroy and not spare the place for the fifty tzadikim that are in it? 25 That be far from You to do after this manner, to kill the tzadikim with the wicked: and that the tzadikim should be as the wicked, that be far from You: Shall not the Shophet of all the earth do right? 26 And יהוה said, *If I find in Sedom fifty tzadikim within the city, then I will spare the entire place for their sakes.* 27 And Avraham answered and said, See now, I have taken upon me to speak to יהוה, which am but dust and ashes: 28 Suppose there shall lack five from the fifty tzadikim: will You destroy the whole city for lack of

five? And He said, *If I find forty-five, I will not destroy it.* 29 And he spoke to Him yet again, and said, Suppose there shall be forty found there. And He said, *I will not do it for forty's sake.* 30 And he said to Him, Oh let not יהוה be angry, and I will speak: Suppose there shall thirty be found there. And He said, *I will not do it, if I find thirty there.* 31 And he said, See now, I have taken it upon me to speak to יהוה: Suppose there shall be twenty found there. And He said, *I will not destroy it for twenty's sake.* 32 And he said, Oh let not יהוה be angry, and I will speak yet but this once more: Suppose ten shall be found there. And He said, *I will not destroy it for ten's sake.*[2] 33 And יהוה went His way, as soon as He had left communing with Avraham: and Avraham returned to his place.

19 And there came two heavenly messengers to Scdom at evening; and Lot sat in the gate of Sedom: and Lot seeing them rose up to meet them; and he bowed himself with his face toward the ground; 2 And he said, See now, my masters, turn in and stay here, Please, into your eved's bayit, and stay all night, and wash your feet, and You shall rise up early, and go on your ways. And they said, No; but we will stay in the street all night. 3 And he pressured them greatly; and they turned in to stay with him, and entered into his bayit; and he made them a feast, and did bake matzah, and they did eat.[3] 4 But before they lay down, the men of the city of Sedom, surrounded the bayit all round, both old and young, all the people from every quarter: 5 And they called to Lot, and said to him, Where are the men who came in to you this night? Bring them out to us, that we may know them. 6 And Lot went out of the door to them, and shut the door behind him, 7 And said, Please, brothers, do not do this wickedness. 8 See now, I have two daughters who have not known a man; let

---
[1] A Torah keeper.

[2] YHWH fulfilled this promise in a sense when He spared the 10 tribes of non-Jewish Yisrael.
[3] Possibly at Pesach.

me, please, bring them out to you, and do to them as you desire: only to these men do nothing; because they came they under the shadow of my roof. 9 And they said, Stand back; And they said again, This one fellow came in here to sojourn, and he desires to be a shophet: now will we deal worse with you, than with them. And they leaned heavily upon Lot, and came close to breaking down the door. 10 But the men put out their hand, and pulled Lot into the bayit to them, and shut the door. 11 And they smote the men that were at the door of the bayit with blindness, both small and great: so that they struggled to find the door. 12 And the men said to Lot, Do you have anyone else here? A son-in-law, and your sons, and your daughters, and whomever else you have in the city, bring them out of this place: 13 For we will destroy this place, because their sinful cry has grown great before the face of יהוה; and יהוה has sent us to destroy it. 14 And Lot went out, and spoke to his sons in law, who married his daughters, and said, Get up, get out of this place; for יהוה will destroy this city. But he seemed as one that mocked to his sons in law. 15 And when the morning dawned, then the heavenly messengers hurried Lot, saying, Arise, take your wife, and your two daughters, who are here; lest you be consumed in the punishment of the city. 16 And while he lingered, the men laid hold upon his hand, and upon the hand of his wife, and upon the hand of his two daughters; יהוה being full of rachamim to him: and they brought him out, and placed him outside the city. [1] 17 And it came to pass, when they had brought them out, that he said, Escape for your chayim; look not behind you, and do not stay in any part of the plain; escape to the mountain, lest you be consumed. 18 And Lot said to them, Please don't, my master: 19 See now, your eved has found favor in your sight, and you have magnified your rachamim, which you have shown to me in saving my chayim; and I cannot escape to the mountain, lest some evil take me, and I die: 20 See now, this city is near to flee to, and it is a little one: Oh, let me escape there - is it not a small matter - and my being shall be rescued. 21 And he said to him, See, I have accepted you concerning this thing also, that I will not overthrow the city, about which you have spoken. 22 Hurry and escape there; for I cannot do anything until you get there. Therefore the name of the city was called Tzoar. 23 The sun had risen upon the earth when Lot entered into Tzoar. 24 Then the Word[2] of יהוה [3] rained upon Sedom and upon Amorah brimstone and fire from יהוה out of the shamayim;[4] 25 And He overthrew those cities, and all the plain, and all the inhabitants of the cities, and that which grew up from the ground. 26 But his wife looked back from behind him, and she became a pillar of salt. 27 And Avraham got up early in the morning to the place where he stood before יהוה: 28 And he looked toward Sedom and Amorah, and toward all the land of the plain, and beheld, and, see, the smoke of the country went up as the smoke of a furnace. 29 And it came to pass, when Elohim destroyed the cities of the plain, that Elohim remembered Avraham, and sent Lot out of the midst of the overthrow, when He overthrew the cities where Lot dwelt. 30 And Lot went up out of Tzoar, and dwelt in the mountain, and his two daughters with him; for he feared to dwell in Tzoar: and he dwelt in a cave, he and his two daughters. 31 And the bachor said to the younger, Our abba is old, and there is not a man in the earth to come in to us after the manner of all the earth: 32 Come, let us make our abba drink wine, and we will lie with him, that we may preserve zera for our abba. 33 And they made their abba drink wine that night: and the bachor went in, and lay with her abba; and he did not perceive when she lay down,

---

[1] YHWH's mercy did not start at Golgotha.

[2] Aramaic **Memra** or Word.
[3] Aramaic Targum considered authoritative and used in the ancient synagogues.
[4] The Greater and Lesser YHWH; the Sender and the Sent.

or when she arose. 34 And it came to pass the next day, that the bachor said to the younger, See, I lay last night with my abba: let us make him drink wine this night also; and go you in, and lie with him, that we may preserve zera for our abba. 35 And they made their abba drink wine that night also: and the younger arose, and lay with him; and he perceived not when she lay down, nor when she arose. 36 So both the daughters of Lot were with a child by their abba. 37 And the bachor bore a son, and called his name Moav: the same is the abba of the Moavites to this day. 38 And the younger, she also bore a son, and called his name Ben-Ammi: the same is the abba of the children of Ammon to this day.

20 And Avraham journeyed from there toward the south country, and dwelt between Kadesh and Shur, and sojourned in Gerar. 2 And Avraham said of Sarah his wife, She is my sister: and Avimelech melech of Gerar sent, and took Sarah. 3 But Elohim came to Avimelech in a dream by night, and said to him, *See, you are but a dead man, because of the woman whom you have taken; for she is a man's wife.* 4 But Avimelech had not come near her: and he said, **יהוה**, will You kill also a tzadik nation? 5 Didn't he say to me, She is my sister? And she, even said herself, He is my brother. In the integrity of my lev and innocence of my hands have I done this. 6 And Elohim said to him in a dream, *Yes, I know that you did this in the integrity of your lev; for I also withheld you from sinning against Me: therefore I allowed you not to touch her. 7 Now therefore restore the man to his wife; for he is a navi, and he shall make tefillah for you, and you shall live: and if you restore her not, know that you shall surely die, you, and all that belongs to you.* 8 Therefore Avimelech rose early in the morning, and called all his avadim, and told all these things to them: and the men were very afraid. 9 Then Avimelech called Avraham, and said to

him, What have you done to us? And how have I offended you that you have brought on me and on my malchut a great sin? You have done deeds to me that ought not to be done. 10 And Avimelech said to Avraham, What were you thinking seeing that you have done this thing? 11 And Avraham said, Because I thought, Surely the fear of Elohim is not in this place; and they will kill me for my wife's sake. 12 And yet indeed she is my sister; she is the daughter of my abba, but not the daughter of my ima; and she became my wife. 13 And it came to pass, when Elohim caused me to wander from my abba's bayit, that I said to her, This is your chesed which you shall show to me; in every place where we shall come, say about me, He is my brother. 14 And Avimelech took sheep, and oxen, and male avadim, and female avadim, and gave them to Avraham, and restored him to Sarah his wife. 15 And Avimelech said, See, my land is before you: dwell where it pleases you. 16 And to Sarah he said, See, I have given your brother a thousand pieces of silver: see, he is to you a covering of the eyes, to all that are with you, and with all others: by this she was reproved. 17 So Avraham prayed to Elohim: and Elohim healed Avimelech, and his wife, and his female avadim; and they bore children. 18 For **יהוה** had closed up all the wombs of the bayit of Avimelech, because of Sarah Avraham's wife.

21 And **יהוה** visited Sarah as He had said, and **יהוה** did to Sarah as He had spoken. 2 For Sarah conceived, and bore Avraham a son in his old age, at the set time of which Elohim had spoken to him. 3 And Avraham called the name of his son that was born to him, whom Sarah bore to him, Yitzchak. 4 And Avraham circumcised his son Yitzchak being eight days old, as Elohim had commanded him. 5 And Avraham was a hundred years old, when his son Yitzchak was born to him. 6 And Sarah said, Elohim has made me to laugh, so that

all that hear will laugh with me. 7 And she said, Who would have said to Avraham, that Sarah should nurse children? For I have born him a son in his old age. 8 And the child grew, and was weaned: and Avraham made a great feast the same day that Yitzchak was weaned. 9 And Sarah saw the son of Hagar the Mitzrite, whom she had birthed for Avraham, mocking. 10 So she said to Avraham, Cast out this bondwoman and her son: for the son of this bondwoman shall not be heir with my son, Yitzchak. 11 And the thing was very severe in Avraham's sight because of his son. 12 And Elohim said to Avraham, *Let it not be severe in your sight because of the lad, and because of your bondwoman; in all that Sarah has said to you, listen to her voice; for in Yitzchak shall your zera be called.* 13 And also of the son of the slave woman will I make a nation,[1] because he is your zera. 14 And Avraham rose up early in the morning, and took lechem, and a bottle of mayim, and gave it to Hagar, putting it on her shoulder, and the child, and sent her away: and she left, and wandered in the wilderness of Beer-Sheva. 15 And the mayim was used up in the bottle, and she cast the child under one of the shrubs. 16 And she went, and sat down opposite him a tov ways off, about the distance of a bowshot: for she said, Let me not see the death of the child. And she sat opposite him, and lifted up her voice, and wept. 17 And Elohim heard the voice of the lad; and the heavenly messenger of Elohim called to Hagar out of the shamayim, and said to her, What is the matter with you, Hagar? Fear not, for Elohim has heard the voice of the lad where he is. 18 Arise, lift up the lad, and hold him in your hand; for I will make him a great nation. 19 And Elohim opened her eyes, and she saw a well of mayim; and she went, and filled the bottle with mayim, and gave the lad drink. 20 And Elohim was with the lad; and he grew, and dwelt in the wilderness, and became an archer. 21 And

he dwelt in the wilderness of Paran: and his ima took him a wife for him out of the land of Mitzrayim. 22 And it came to pass at that time, that Avimelech and Phichol the chief captain of his army spoke to Avraham, saying, Elohim is with you in all that you do: 23 Now therefore swear to me here by Elohim that you will not deal falsely with me, nor with my son, nor with my son's son: but according to the chesed that I have done to you, you shall do to me, and to the land in which you have sojourned. 24 And Avraham said, I will swear. 25 And Avraham reproved Avimelech because of a well of mayim, which Avimelech's avadim had violently taken away. 26 And Avimelech said, I don't know who has done this thing: neither did you tell me, neither did I hear of it, until today. 27 And Avraham took sheep and oxen, and gave them to Avimelech; and both of them made a covenant. 28 And Avraham set seven ewe lambs of the flock by themselves. 29 And Avimelech said to Avraham, What do these seven ewe lambs mean that you have set by themselves? 30 And he said, For these seven ewe lambs shall you take of my hand, that they may be a witness to me, that I have dug this well. 31 So he called that place Beer-Sheva; because there both of them swore. 32 So they made a covenant at Beer-Sheva: then Avimelech rose up, and Phichol the chief captain of his army, and they returned into the land of the Philistines. 33 And Avraham planted a grove in Beer-Sheva, and called there on the Name of יהוה, El-Olam. 34 And Avraham sojourned in the Philistines land many days.

22 And it came to pass after these things, that Elohim did test Avraham, and said to him, Avraham: and he said, See, Hinayni. 2 And He said, *Take now your son, your only son Yitzchak,[2] whom you love, and get into the land of Moriyah; and offer him there for a burnt*

---

[1] Nation, not nations.

offering upon one of the mountains[1] which I will tell you of. 3 And Avraham rose up early in the morning, and saddled his donkey, and took two of his young men with him, and Yitzchak his son, and cut the wood for the burnt offering, and rose up, and went to the place that Elohim had told him. 4 Then on the third day Avraham lifted up his eyes, and saw the place far off. 5 And Avraham said to his young men, Stay here with the donkey; and I and the lad will go over there and worship, and come again to you,[2] 6 And Avraham took the wood of the burnt offering, and laid it upon Yitzchak his son; and he took the fire in his hand, and a knife; and they went both of them together. 7 And Yitzchak spoke to Avraham his abba, and said, My abba: and he said, Hinayni, my son. And he said, See the fire and the wood: but where is the lamb for a burnt offering? 8 And Avraham said, My son, Elohim will provide Himself a Lamb for the burnt offering: [3] so they went both of them together. 9 And they came to the place that Elohim had told him about; and Avraham built an altar there, and laid the wood in order, and bound Yitzchak his son, and laid him on the altar upon the wood. 10 And Avraham stretched out his hand, and took the knife to kill his son. 11 And the Malach-יהוה called to him out of the shamayim, and said, *Avraham, Avraham*: and he said, Hinayni. 12 And He said, *Lay not your hand upon the lad, neither do anything to him: for now I know that you fear Elohim, seeing you have not withheld your son, your only son from Me.* 13 And Avraham lifted up his eyes, and looked, and see behind him a ram caught in a thicket by its horns: and Avraham went and took the ram, and offered it up for a burnt offering instead of his son. 14 And Avraham called the name of that place יהוה-Yireh: as it is said to this day, On the mountain[4] יהוה is seen. 15 And the Malach-יהוה called to Avraham out of

the shamayim the second time, 16 And said, *By Myself have I sworn, says* יהוה, *because you have done this thing, and have not withheld your son, your only son:* 17 *That in bracha I will bless you, and in multiplying I will multiply your zera as the chochavim of the shamayim, and as the sand that is upon the seashore; and your zera shall possess the gate of its enemies;*[5] 18 *And in your zera shall all the nations of the earth be blessed; because you have obeyed My voice.*[6] 19 So Avraham returned to his young men, and they rose up and went together to Beer-Sheva; and Avraham dwelt at Beer-Sheva. 20 And it came to be after these things, that it was told Avraham, saying, See, Milcah, she has also born children to your brother Nachor; 21 Huz his bachor, and Buz his brother, and Kemu-El the abba of Aram, 22 And Chesed, and Hazo, and Pildash, and Yidlaph, and Bethu-El. 23 And Bethu-El begat Rivkah: these eight Milcah did bear to Nachor, Avraham's brother. 24 And his concubine, whose name was Reumah, she bore also Tevah, and Gaham, and Thahash, and Maachah.

Torah Parsha 5
Chayai Sarah 23:1-25:18
Haftarah Melechim Alef 1:1-31
Brit Chadasha Mattityahu 8:19-22
Luke 9:57-62

23 And Sarah was one hundred twenty-seven years old: these were the years of the chayim of Sarah. 2 And Sarah died in Kiryath-Arba; the same is Hevron in the land of Kanaan: and Avraham came to mourn for Sarah, and to weep for her. 3 And Avraham stood up from before his dead, and spoke to the sons of Cheth, saying, 4 I am a Ger and a sojourner with you: give me a possession for a burial-place with you, that I may bury my dead out of my sight. 5 And the children of Cheth

---

[1] Mt. of Olives.
[2] Faith in Yitzchak's resurrection.
[3] YHWH Himself will become the Lamb.
[4] Olivet.

[5] The Yisraelite nations would be among the world's stronger end-time nations.
[6] The repetition of this same promise seems redundant, but YHWH knew most wouldn't grasp its full implication. Therefore, it needed to be repeated.

answered Avraham, saying to him, 6 Hear us, my master: you are a mighty sar among us: in the choice of our sepulchers bury your dead; none of us shall withhold from you his sepulcher, so that you may bury your dead. 7 And Avraham stood up, and bowed himself to the people of the land, even to the children of Cheth. 8 And he communed with them, saying, If it be your mind that I should bury my dead out of my sight; listen to me, and inquire for me to Ephron the son of Tzohar, 9 That he may give me the cave of Machpelah, which he has, which is at the end of his field; for as much money as it is worth he shall give it me for a possession for a burial-place among you. 10 And Ephron dwelt among the children of Cheth: and Ephron the Hittite answered Avraham in the audience of the children of Cheth, even all those that went in at the gate of his city, saying, 11 No, my master, hear me: the field I give you, and the cave that is in it, I give it to you; in the presence of the sons of my people I give it to you: bury your dead. 12 And Avraham bowed down himself before the people of the land. 13 And he spoke to Ephron in the audience of the people of the land, saying, But if you will give it to me, Please, hear me: I will give you money for the field; take it from me, and I will bury my dead there. 14 And Ephron answered Avraham, saying to him, 15 My master, listen to me: the land is worth four hundred shekels of silver; what is that between you and me? Bury therefore your dead. 16 And Avraham listened to Ephron; and Avraham weighed to Ephron the silver, which he had named in the presence of the sons of Cheth, four hundred shekels of silver, current money with the merchant. 17 And the field of Ephron, which was in Machpelah, which was before Mamre, the field, and the cave that were in it, and all the eytzim that were in the field, that were in all the borders all around, were made sure. 18 Unto Avraham for a possession in the presence of the children of Cheth, before all that went in at the gate of

his city. 19 And after this, Avraham buried Sarah his wife in the cave of the field of Machpelah before Mamre: the same is Hevron in the land of Kanaan. 20 And the field, and the cave that is in it, were deeded to Avraham for a possession of a burial-place by the sons of Cheth.

24 And Avraham was old, and well stricken in age: and **יהוה** had blessed Avraham in all things. 2 And Avraham said to his eldest eved of his bayit, that ruled over all that he had, Please put your hand under my thigh: 3 And I will make you swear by **יהוה**, the Elohim of the shamayim, and the Elohim of the earth, that you shall not take a wife for my son of the daughters of the Kanaanites, among whom I dwell: 4 But you shall go to my country, and to my mishpocha, and take a wife for my son Yitzchak.[1] 5 And the eved said to him, Suppose the woman will not be willing to follow me to this land: do I need to bring your son again to the land from where you came? 6 And Avraham said to him, Beware that you bring not my son there again.[2] 7 **יהוה** Elohim of the shamayim, who took me from my abba's bayit, and from the land of my mishpocha, and who spoke to me, and that swore to me, saying, Unto your zera will I give this land; He shall send His Malach before you, and you shall take a wife for my son from there. 8 And if the woman will not be willing to follow you, then you shall be clear from this oath: only bring not my son there again. 9 And the eved put his hand under the thigh of Avraham his master, and swore to him concerning that matter. 10 And the eved took ten camels from the camels of his master, and departed; for all the items of his master were in his hand: and he arose, and went to Mesopotamia, to the city of Nachor. 11 And he made his camels to kneel down outside the city by a well of mayim at the time of the evening, even the time that

---

[1] A Hebrew.
[2] Separation unto YHWH.

women go out to draw mayim. 12 And he said, O **יהוה** , Elohim of my master Avraham, Please, send me with bracha this day, and show chesed to my master Avraham. 13 See, I stand here by the well of mayim; and the daughters of the men of the city come out to draw mayim: 14 And let it come to pass, that the young girl to whom I shall say, Please let down your pitcher, that I may drink; and she shall say, Drink, and I will give your camels drink also: let the same be she that you have appointed for your eved Yitzchak; and thereby shall I know that you have shown chesed to my master. 15 And it came to pass, before he had done speaking, that, see, Rivkah came out, who was born to Bethu-El, son of Milcah, the wife of Nachor, Avraham's brother, with her pitcher upon her shoulder. 16 And the young girl was very beautiful to look at, a virgin, neither had any man known her: and she went down to the well, and filled her pitcher, and came up. 17 And the eved ran to meet her, and said, Please let me drink a little mayim from your pitcher. 18 And she said, Drink, my master: and she hurried and let down her pitcher upon her hand, and gave him drink. 19 And when she had done giving him drink, she said, I will draw mayim for your camels also, until they have done drinking. 20 And she hurried, and emptied her pitcher into the trough, and ran again to the well to draw mayim, and drew for all his camels. [1] 21 And the man wondering about her held his silence, to see whether **יהוה** had made his journey prosperous or not. 22 And it came to pass, as the camels had done drinking, that the man took a golden earring of half a shekel weight, and two bracelets for her hands of ten shekels weight of gold; 23 And said, whose daughter are you? Please tell me: is there room in your abba's bayit for us to lodge in? 24 And she said to him, I am the daughter of Bethu-El the son of Milcah that she bore to Nachor. 25 She said moreover to

him, We have both straw and fodder enough, and room to lodge in. 26 And the man bowed down his head, and worshipped **יהוה** . 27 And he said, Barchu-et- **יהוה** Elohim of my master Avraham, who has not left destitute my master of His rachamim and His emet: I was traveling in the way, and now **יהוה** has led me to the bayit of my master's brothers. 28 And the young girl ran, and told them of her ima's bayit these things. 29 And Rivkah had a brother, and his name was Lavan: and Lavan ran out to the man, to the well. 30 And it came to pass, when he saw the earring and bracelets upon his sister's hands, and when he heard the words of Rivkah his sister, saying, This is what the man spoke to me; then Lavan came to the man; as he stood by the camels at the well. 31 And he said, Come in, you blessed of **יהוה**; Why do you stand outside? For I have prepared the bayit, and room for the camels. 32 And the man came into the bayit: and he undressed his camels, and gave straw and fodder for the camels, and mayim to wash his feet, and the men's feet that were with him. 33 And there was set food before him to eat: but he said, I will not eat, until I have told of my errand. And he said, Speak on. 34 And he said, I am Avraham's eved. 35 And **יהוה** has blessed my master greatly; and he is become great: and He has given him flocks, and herds, and silver, and gold, and male avadim, and female avadim, and camels, and donkeys. 36 And Sarah my master's wife bore a son to my master when she was old: and to him has he given all that he has. 37 And my master made me swear, saying, You shall not take a wife for my son of the daughters of the Kanaanites, in whose land I dwell: 38 But you shall go to my abba's bayit, and to my mishpocha, and take a wife for my son. 39 And I said to my master, Suppose the woman will not follow me? 40 And he said to me, **יהוה**, before whom I have my halacha, will send His Malach with you, and prosper your derech; and you shall take a wife for my son of my mishpocha, and of my abba's bayit: 41 Then

---

[1] Ten camels drinking in the land from a mother of Yisrael, shows beautiful typology of Ephraim's return in physical abundance and in the Spirit.

shall you be clear from this my oath, when you come to my mishpocha; if they give you no one, you shall be clear from my oath. 42 And I came this day to the well, and said, O יהוה, Elohim of my master Avraham, if now You do prosper my derech in which I go; 43 See, I stand by the well of mayim; and it shall come to pass, that when the virgin comes out to draw mayim, and I say to her, Please give me a little mayim from your pitcher to drink; 44 And she says to me, Drink and I will also draw for your camels too. Let therefore the same one be the woman whom יהוה has appointed for my master's son. 45 And before I had done speaking in my lev, see, Rivkah came out with her pitcher on her shoulder; and she went down to the well, and drew mayim: and I said to her, Please let me drink. 46 And she hurried, and let down her pitcher from her shoulder, and said, Drink, and I will give your camels drink also: so I drank, and she gave the camels drink also. 47 And I asked her, and said, Whose daughter are you? And she said, The daughter of Bethu-El, Nachor's son, whom Milcah bore to him: and I put the earring upon her face, and the bracelets upon her hands. 48 And I bowed down my head, and worshipped יהוה, and blessed יהוה Elohim of my master Avraham, who had led me in the right derech to take my master's brother's daughter to his son. 49 And now if you will deal kindly and truly with my master, tell me: and if not, tell me; that I may turn to the right hand, or to the left. 50 Then Lavan and Bethu-El answered and said, This thing proceeds from יהוה: we cannot speak to you bad or tov. 51 See, Rivkah is before you, take her, and go, and let her be your master's son's wife, as יהוה has spoken. 52 And it came to pass, that, when Avraham's eved heard their words, he worshipped יהוה, bowing himself to the earth. 53 And the eved brought out jewels of silver, and jewels of gold, and clothing, and gave them to Rivkah: he gave also to her brother and to her ima precious things.

54 And they did eat and drink, he and the men that were with him, and stayed all night; and they rose up in the morning, and he said, Send me away to my master. 55 And her brother and her ima said, Let the young girl stay with us a few days, at least ten; after that she shall go. 56 And he said to them, Do not hinder me, seeing יהוה has prospered my way; send me away that I may go to my master. 57 And they said, We will call the young girl, and ask her. 58 And they called Rivkah, and said to her, Will you go with this man? And she said, I will go. 59 And they sent away Rivkah their sister, and her nurse, and Avraham's eved, and his men. 60 And they blessed Rivkah, and said to her, You are our sister, now become the ima of thousands of millions,[1] and let your zera possess the gate of those who hate them. 61 And Rivkah arose, and her young girls, and they rode upon the camels, and followed the man: and the eved took Rivkah, and went his way. 62 And Yitzchak came from the way of the well Lachai-Roee, for he dwelt in the south country. 63 And Yitzchak went out to meditate in the field in the evening: and he lifted up his eyes, and saw, and, see, the camels were coming. 64 And Rivkah lifted up her eyes, and when she saw Yitzchak, she was lifted from off the camel. 65 For she had said to the eved, What man is this that walks in the field to meet us? And the eved had said, It is my master: therefore she took a veil,[2] and covered herself. 66 And the eved told Yitzchak all things that he had done. 67 And Yitzchak brought her into his ima Sarah's tent, and took Rivkah, and she became his wife; and he loved her: and Yitzchak was comforted after his ima's death.

25 Then again Avraham took a wife, and her name was Keturah. 2 And she bore him Zimran, and Yokshan, and

---

[1] Billions – Rivkah was said to have billions of biological offspring. These are those who would spring forth through Jacob/Yisrael and become biological Yisraelites.
[2] Sign of authority and submission.

Medan, and Midyan, and Ishvak, and Shuah. 3 And Yokshan begat Sheva, and Dedan. And the sons of Dedan were Ashurim, and Letushim, and Leummim. 4 And the sons of Midyan; Ephah, and Epher, and Hanoch, and Avida, and Eldah. All these were the children of Keturah. 5 And Avraham gave all that he had to Yitzchak. [1] 6 But to the sons of the concubines, whom Avraham had, Avraham gave gifts, and sent them away from Yitzchak his son, eastward, to the east country. 7 And these are the days of the years of Avraham's chayim that he lived, a hundred seventy five years. 8 Then Avraham gave up the ruach, and died in a tov old age, an old man, and full of years; and was gathered to his people. 9 And his sons Yitzchak and Yishma-El buried him in the cave of Machpelah, in the field of Ephron the son of Tzoar the Hittite, which is before Mamre, 10 The field that Avraham purchased from the sons of Cheth: there was Avraham buried, and Sarah his wife. 11 And it came to pass after the death of Avraham, that Elohim blessed his son Yitzchak; and Yitzchak dwelt by the well Lachai-Roee. 12 Now these are the generations of Yishma-El, Avraham's son, whom Hagar the Mitzrite, Sarah's handmaid, bore to Avraham: 13 And these are the names of the sons of Yishma-El, by their names, according to their generations: the bachor of Yishma-El, Nevayoth; and Kedar, and Adveel, and Mivsam, 14 And Mishma, and Dumah, and Massa, 15 Hadar, and Tema, Yetur, Naphish, and Kedemah: 16 These are the sons of Yishma-El, and these are their names, by their towns, and by their settlements, twelve princes according to their tribes. [2] 17 And these are the years of the chayim of Yishma-El, one hundred thirty seven years: and he gave up the ruach and died; and was gathered to his people. 18 And they dwelt from Havilah to Shur that is before Mitzrayim, as you go towards

Ashshur: and he died in the presence of all his brothers.

Torah Parsha 6
Toldot 25:19-28:9
Haftarah Malachi 1:1-2:7
Brit Chadasha Romiyah 9:6-16

19 And these are the generations of Yitzchak, Avraham's son: Avraham begat Yitzchak: 20 And Yitzchak was forty years old when he took Rivkah to be his wife, the daughter of Bethu-El the Aramean of Padan-Aram, the sister of Lavan the Aramean. [3] 21 And Yitzchak sought יהוה for his wife, because she was barren: and יהוה was found by him, and Rivkah his wife conceived. 22 And the children struggled together within her; and she said, If it is so, why am I like this? And she went to inquire of יהוה. 23 And יהוה said to her, *Two nations are in your womb, and two kinds of peoples shall be separated from your bowels; and the one people shall be stronger than the other people; and the elder shall serve the younger.* [4] 24 And when her days to be delivered were fulfilled, see, there were twins in her womb. 25 And the first came out red, all over like a hairy garment; and they called his name Esav. 26 And after that came out his brother, and his hand took hold on Esav's heel; and his name was called Yaakov: and Yitzchak was sixty years old when she bore them. 27 And the boys grew: and Esav was a skilled hunter, a man of the field; and Yaakov was a plain man, dwelling in tents. 28 And Yitzchak loved Esav, because he did eat of his venison: but Rivkah loved Yaakov. 29 And Yaakov cooked pottage: and Esav came from the field, and he was faint: 30 And Esav said to Yaakov, Please feed me with that same red pottage; for I am faint: therefore was his name called Edom. 31 And Yaakov said, Sell me this day your bachor. 32 And Esav said, See, I am at the point of death: and what profit shall this

---

[1] Due to covenant.
[2] Tribes, not nations.
[3] Notice Rivkah was not Jewish, but an Aramean who crossed over to be a Hebrew.
[4] Yisraelite people and Edomite people.

bachor be to me? 33 And Yaakov said, Swear to me this day; and he swore to him: and he sold his bachor to Yaakov. 34 Then Yaakov gave Esav lechem and a pottage of lentiles; and he did eat and drink, and rose up, and went his way: so Esav despised his bachor.[1]

26 And there was a famine in the land, beside the first famine that was in the days of Avraham. And Yitzchak went to Avimelech melech of the Philistines to Gerar. 2 And יהוה appeared to him, and said, *Go not down into Mitzrayim; dwell in the land that I shall tell you about: 3 Sojourn in this land, and I will be with you, and will bless you; for to you, and to your zera, I will give all these countries, and I will perform the oath which I swore to Avraham your abba;[4] 4 And I will make your zera to multiply as the chochavim of shamayim, and will give to your zera all these countries; and in your zera shall all the nations of the earth be blessed;[3] 5 Because Avraham obeyed My voice, and kept My charge, My mitzvot, My chukim, and My Torot.[4]* 6 And Yitzchak dwelt in Gerar: 7 And the men of the place asked him about his wife; and he said, She is my sister: for he feared to say, She is my wife; lest, said he, the men of the place should kill me for Rivkah; because she was beautiful to look at. 8 And it came to pass; when he had been there a long time that Avimelech melech of the Philistines looked out at a window, and saw Yitzchak playing with Rivkah his wife. 9 And Avimelech called Yitzchak, and said, See, of a certainty she is your wife. So why did you say you, She is my sister? And Yitzchak said to him, Because, I said otherwise I will die because of her. 10 And Avimelech said, What is this you have done to us? One of our people might have unknowingly lain with your wife, and you would have brought guilt upon us. 11 And Avimelech charged all his people, saying, He that touches this man or his wife shall surely be put to death. 12 Then Yitzchak sowed in that land, and received in that same year a hundredfold return: and יהוה blessed him. 13 And the man grew great, and went forward, and grew until he became very great:[5] 14 For he had possession of flocks, and possessions of herds, and a great supply of avadim: and the Philistines envied him. 15 For all the wells that his abba's avadim had dug in the days of Avraham his abba, the Philistines had stopped them, and filled them with earth. 16 And Avimelech said to Yitzchak, Go from us; for you are much mightier than us. 17 And Yitzchak departed from there, and pitched his tent in the Valley of Gerar, and dwelt there. 18 And Yitzchak dug again the wells of mayim, which they had dug in the days of Avraham his abba; for the Philistines had stopped them after the death of Avraham: and he called their names by the names that his abba had called them. 19 And Yitzchak's avadim dug in the valley, and found there a well of springing mayim. 20 And the herdsmen of Gerar did strive with Yitzchak's herdsmen, saying, The mayim is ours: and he called the name of the well Esek; because they strove with him. 21 And they dug another well, and strove over that one also: and he called the name of it Sitnah. 22 And he moved from there, and dug another well; and for that they strove not: and he called the name of it Rehovoth; and he said, For now יהוה has made room for us, and we shall be fruitful in the land. 23 And he went up from there to Beer-Sheva. 24 And יהוה appeared to him the same night, and said, *I am the Elohim of Avraham your abba: fear not, for I am with you, and will bless you, and multiply your zera for My eved Avraham's sake.* 25 And he built an altar there, and called upon the

---

[1] In the natural, the twins vied for being the chosen seed of promise. But in the spirit all things were already decided. Yisrael was to be the chosen seed, YHWH's Son, His firstborn.
[2] Greater Yisrael is a massive land including many countries of Yisraelite seed, not merely one country, as many believe.
[3] The promise of physical multiplicity renewed in Yitzchak.
[4] Chosen because of his obedience to Torah, as revealed to him in stages.

[5] As promised.

Name of **יהוה**[1] and pitched his tent there, and Yitzchak's avadim dug a well. 26 Then Avimelech went to him from Gerar, and Ahuzzath one of his friends, and Phichol the chief captain of his army. 27 And Yitzchak said to them, Why do you come to me, seeing you hate me, and have sent me away from you? 28 And they said, We saw certainly that **יהוה** was with you: and we said, Let there be now an oath between us, even between us and you, and let us make a covenant with you; 29 That you will do us no hurt, as we have not touched you, and as we have done to you nothing but tov, and have sent you away in shalom: you are now the blessed of **יהוה**. 30 And he made for them a feast, and they did eat and drink. 31 And they rose up early in the morning, and swore one to another: and Yitzchak sent them away, and they departed from him in shalom. 32 And it came to pass the same day that Yitzchak's avadim came, and told him concerning the well that they had dug, and said to him, We have found mayim. 33 And he called it Shevah: therefore the name of the city is Beer-Sheva to this day. 34 And Esav was forty years old when he took his wife Yahudite the daughter of Beeri the Hittite, and Bashemath the daughter of Elon the Hittite: 35 Which caused grief of mind to Yitzchak and to Rivkah.

27 And it came to pass, that when Yitzchak was old, and his eyes were dim, so that he could not see, he called Esav his eldest son, and said to him, My son: and he said to him, See, here am I. 2 And he said, See now, I am old; I know not the day of my death: 3 Now please take your weapons, your quiver and your bow, and go out to the field, and find me some venison;[2] 4 And make me tasty meat, such as I love, and bring it to me, that I may eat it; that my being may bless you before I die. 5 And Rivkah heard when Yitzchak spoke to Esav his son. And Esav went to the field to hunt

for venison, and to bring it. 6 And Rivkah spoke to Yaakov her son, saying, See, I heard your abba speak to Esav your brother, saying, 7 Bring me venison, and make me tasty meat, that I may eat, and bless you before **יהוה** before my death. 8 Now therefore, my son, obey my voice according to that which I command you. 9 Go now to the flock, and get me from there two tov kids of the goats; and I will make from them tasty meat for your abba, such as he loves: 10 And you shall bring it to your abba, that he may eat, and that he may bless you before his death. 11 And Yaakov said to Rivkah his ima, See, Esav my brother is a hairy man, and I am a smooth man: 12 My abba will feel me, and I shall seem to him as a deceiver; and I shall bring a curse upon me, and not a bracha. 13 And his ima said to him, Upon me be your curse, my son: only obey my voice, and go get them for me. 14 And he went, and took, and brought them to his ima: and his ima made tasty meat, such as his abba loved. 15 And Rivkah took nice clothing from her eldest son Esav, which were with her in the bayit, and put them upon Yaakov her younger son: 16 And she put the skins of the kids of the goats upon his hands, and upon the smooth parts of his neck: 17 And she gave the tasty meat and the lechem, which she had prepared, into the hand of her son Yaakov. 18 And he came to his abba, and said, My abba: and he said, Hinayni; who are you, my son? 19 And Yaakov said to his abba, I am Esav your bachor; I have done accordingly as you told me: Please arise sit up and eat of my venison, that your being may bless me. 20 And Yitzchak said to his son, How is it that you have found it so quickly, my son? And he said, Because **יהוה** your Elohim brought it to me. 21 And Yitzchak said to Yaakov, Please come near so that I may feel you, my son, whether you are really my son Esav or not. 22 And Yaakov went near to Yitzchak his abba; and he felt him, and said, The voice is Yaakov's voice, but the hands are the hands of Esav.

---

[1] Isaac knew YHWH's Name.
[2] Deer skin eaten as food.

23 And he discerned him not, because his hands were hairy, as his brother Esav's hands: so he blessed him. 24 And he said, Are you really my son Esav? And he said, I am. 25 And he said, Bring it near to me, and I will eat of my son's venison, that my being may bless you. And he brought it near to him, and he did eat: and he brought him wine, and he drank. 26 And his abba Yitzchak said to him, Come near now, and kiss me, my son. 27 And he came near, and kissed him: and he smelled the smell of his clothing, and blessed him, and said, See, the smell of my son is as the smell of a field that יהוה has blessed: 28 Therefore Elohim give you from the dew of the shamayim, and the fatness of the earth, and plenty of corn and wine: 29 Let people serve you, and nations bow down to you: be master over your brothers, and let your ima's sons bow down to you: cursed be every one that curses you, and blessed be he that blesses you. 30 And it came to pass, as soon as Yitzchak had made an end of bracha Yaakov, and Yaakov had hardly gone out from the presence of Yitzchak his abba, that Esav his brother came in from his hunting. 31 And he also had made tasty meat, and brought it to his abba, and said to his abba, Let my abba arise, and eat of his son's venison, that your being may bless me. 32 And Yitzchak his abba said to him, Who are you? And he said, I am your son, your bachor Esav. 33 And Yitzchak trembled very exceedingly, and said, Who? Where is he that has taken venison, and brought it me, and I have eaten of all before you came, and have blessed him? Yes, and he shall be blessed. 34 And when Esav heard the words of his abba, he cried with a great and exceedingly bitter cry, and said to his abba, Bless me also, O my abba. 35 And he said, Your brother came with subtilty, and has taken away your bracha. 36 And he said, Is not he rightly named Yaakov? For he has supplanted me these two times: he took away my bachor; and, see, now he has taken away my bracha![1] And Esav said, Have you not reserved a bracha for me? 37 And Yitzchak answered and said to Esav, See, I have made him your master, and all his brothers have I given to him for avadim; and with corn and wine have I sustained him: and what shall I do now for you, my son? 38 And Esav said to his abba, Have you not just one bracha, my abba? Bless me, even me also, O my abba. And Esav lifted up his voice, and wept. 39 And Yitzchak his abba answered and said to him, See, your dwelling shall be the fatness of the earth, and of the dew of the shamayim from above; 40 And by your sword shall you live, and shall serve your brother; and it shall come to pass when you shall have the dominion, that you shall break his yoke from off your neck.[2] 41 And Esav hated Yaakov because of the bracha with which his abba blessed him: and Esav said in his lev, The days of mourning for my abba are at hand; then will I kill my brother Yaakov. 42 And these words of Esav her zachen son were told to Rivkah: and she sent and called Yaakov her younger son, and said to him, See, your brother Esav, concerning you, does comfort himself by purposing to kill you. 43 Now therefore, my son, obey my voice; and arise, flee to Lavan my brother to Charan; 44 And stay with him a few days, until your brother's anger turns away; 45 Until your brother's anger turns away from you, and he forgets what you have done to him: then I will send, and get you from there: why should I be deprived of both of you in one day? 46 And Rivkah said to Yitzchak, I am weary of my chayim because of the daughters of Cheth: if Yaakov takes a wife from the daughters of Cheth, such as these who are of the daughters of the land, what tov shall my chayim be to me?

---

[1] They go together as part of the **bachor** and both were foreordained. Both "my birthright" **bachorati** and "my blessing" **berchati** sound the same in Hebrew.
[2] From about 600 CE with the rise of Islam to present 1967.

28 And Yitzchak called Yaakov, and blessed him, and charged him, and said to him, You shall not take a wife of the daughters of Kanaan. 2 Arise, go to Padan-Aram, to the bayit of Bethu-El your ima's abba; and take a wife from there from the daughters of Lavan your ima's brother. 3 And El-Shaddai bless you, and make you fruitful, and multiply you and you shall become a congregation of nations;[1] 4 And El-Shaddai give you the bracha of Avraham, to you, and to your zera with you; that you may inherit the land in which you are a Ger, which Elohim gave to Avraham. 5 And Yitzchak sent Yaakov away: and he went to Padan-Aram to Lavan, son of Bethu-El the Aramean, the brother of Rivkah, Yaakov's and Esav's ima. 6 When Esav saw that Yitzchak had blessed Yaakov, and sent him away to Padan-Aram, to take him a wife from there; and that as he blessed him he gave him a charge, saying, You shall not take a wife from the daughters of Kanaan; 7 And that Yaakov obeyed his abba and his ima, and had gone to Padan-Aram. 8 And Esav seeing that the daughters of Kanaan pleased not Yitzchak his abba; 9 Then went Esav to Yishma-El, and took besides the wives that he already had Mahalath the daughter of Yishma-El Avraham's son, the sister of Nevayoth, to be his wife.

Torah Parsha 7
Vayetze 28:10-32:3
Haftarah Hoshea 12:13-14:10
Brit Chadasha Yochanan 1:43-51

10 And Yaakov went out from Beer-Sheva, and went toward Charan. 11 And he came upon a certain place, and stayed there all night, because the sun was set; and he took of the stones of that place, and used them for his pillows, and lay down in that place to sleep. 12 And he dreamed, and see a ladder set up on the earth, and the top of it reached to the shamayim: and see the heavenly messengers of Elohim ascending and descending on it. 13 And, see, **יהוה** stood above it, and said, *I am* **יהוה** *Elohim of Avraham your abba, and the Elohim of Yitzchak: the land where you lie, to you will I give it, and to your zera; 14 And your zera shall be as the dust of the earth, and you shall break out[2] abroad to the west, and to the east, and to the north, and to the south: and in you and in your zera shall all the mishpachot of the earth be blessed. 15 And, see, I am with you, and will keep you in all the places where you are going, and will bring you again into this land; for I will not leave you, until I have done that which I have spoken to you.* 16 And Yaakov awoke out of his sleep, and he said, Surely **יהוה** is in this place; and I knew it not. 17 And he was afraid, and said, How awesome is this place! This is no other place but Beit Elohim, and this is the gate of the shamayim. 18 And Yaakov rose up early in the morning, and took the stone that he had put for his pillow, and set it up for a pillar, and poured oil upon the top of it. 19 And he called the name of that place Beth-El: but the name of that city was called Luz at the first. 20 And Yaakov vowed a vow, saying, If the word of Elohim will be with me, and will keep me in this way that I go, and will give me lechem to eat, and clothing to put on, 21 So that I come again to my abba's bayit in shalom; then shall the word of **יהוה** be my Elohim: 22 And this stone, which I have set for a pillar, shall be Elohim's Bayit: and of all that You shall give me I will surely give the ma'aser to You.

29 Then Yaakov went on his journey, and came into the land of the people of the east. 2 And he looked, and see a well in the field, and, see, there were three flocks of sheep lying by it; for out of that well they watered the flocks: and a great stone was upon the well's mouth. 3 And there were all the flocks gathered: and they rolled the stone from the well's mouth, and watered

---

[1] **Kahal Goyim** - an obvious reference to Moshiach's congregation, which is the physical and spiritual offspring of the redeemed remnant, from all the Yisraelite nations. Notice not a congregation of Jews only.

[2] **Uparatztah** – Break forth.

the sheep, and put the stone again upon the well's mouth in its place. 4 And Yaakov said to them, My brothers, where are you from? And they said, From Charan are we. 5 And he said to them, Do you know Lavan the son of Nachor? And they said, We know him, 6 And he said to them, Is he well? And they said, He is well, and see, Rachel his daughter comes with the sheep. 7 And he said, See, it is still bright, neither is it time that the cattle should be gathered together: mayim the sheep, and go and feed them. 8 And they said, We cannot, until all the flocks are gathered together, and until they roll the stone from the well's mouth; then we mayim the sheep. 9 And while he yet spoke with them, Rachel came with her abba's sheep: for she kept them. 10 And it came to pass, when Yaakov saw Rachel the daughter of Lavan his ima's brother, and the sheep of Lavan his ima's brother, that Yaakov went near, and rolled the stone from the well's mouth, and watered the flock of Lavan his ima's brother. 11 And Yaakov kissed Rachel, and lifted up his voice, and wept. 12 And Yaakov told Rachel that he was her abba's relative, and that he was Rivkah's son: and she ran and told her abba. 13 And it came to pass, when Lavan heard the tidings of Yaakov his sister's son, that he ran to meet him, and embraced him, and kissed him, and brought him to his bayit. And he told Lavan all these things. 14 And Lavan said to him, Surely you are my bone and my flesh. And he abode with him the space of a month. 15 And Lavan said to Yaakov, Because you are my relative, should you therefore serve me for nothing? Tell me, what shall your wages be? 16 And Lavan had two daughters: the name of the zachen was Leah, and the name of the younger was Rachel. 17 Leah's eyes were tender; but Rachel was beautiful and well favored. 18 And Yaakov loved Rachel; and said, I will serve you seven years for Rachel your younger daughter. 19 And Lavan said, It is better that I give her to you, than that I should give her to another man: stay with me. 20 And Yaakov served seven years for Rachel; and they seemed to him but a few days, for the love he had for her. 21 And Yaakov said to Lavan, Give me my wife, for my days are fulfilled, that I may go in to her. 22 And Lavan gathered together all the men of the place, and made a feast. 23 And it came to pass in the evening, that he took Leah his daughter, and brought her to him; and he went in to her. 24 And Lavan gave to his daughter Leah, Zilpah his maid for a handmaid. 25 And it came to pass, that in the morning, see, it was Leah: and he said to Lavan, What is this you have done to me? Did I not serve with you for Rachel? Why then have you deceived me? 26 And Lavan said, It must not be so done in our country, to give the younger before the bachor. 27 Fulfill her seven years, and we will give you Rachel also for the service that you shall serve with me yet seven more years. 28 And Yaakov did so, and fulfilled her seven years: and he gave him Rachel his daughter for a wife also. 29 And Lavan gave to Rachel his daughter Bilhah his handmaid to be her maid. 30 And he went in also to Rachel, and he loved also Rachel more than Leah, and served with him yet seven more years. 31 And when יהוה saw that Leah was hated, He opened her womb: [1] but Rachel was barren. 32 And Leah conceived, and bore a son, and she called his name Reuven: for she said, Surely יהוה has looked upon my affliction; now therefore my husband will love me. 33 And she conceived again, and bore a son; and said, Because יהוה has heard that I was hated, he has therefore given me this son also: and she called his name Shimeon. 34 And she conceived again, and bore a son; and said, Now this time will my husband be joined to me, because I have born him three sons: therefore was his name called Levi. 35 And she conceived again, and bore a son: and she said, Now will I hallel יהוה: therefore she called his name Yahudah; and ceased bearing.

_____
[1] Chesed.

30 And when Rachel saw that she bore Yaakov no children, Rachel envied her sister; and said to Yaakov, Give me children, or else I will die. 2 And Yaakov's anger was kindled against Rachel: and he said, Am I in Elohim's place; who has withheld from you the fruit of the womb? 3 And she said, See my maid Bilhah, go in to her; and she shall bear upon my knees that I may also have children by her. 4 And she gave him Bilhah her handmaid to be his wife: and Yaakov went in to her. 5 And Bilhah conceived, and bore Yaakov a son. 6 And Rachel said, Elohim has judged me, and has also heard my voice, and has given me a son: therefore she called his name Dan. 7 And Bilhah Rachel's maid conceived again, and bore Yaakov a second son. 8 And Rachel said, With great wrestlings have I wrestled with my sister, and I have prevailed: and she called his name Naphtali. 9 When Leah saw that she had left bearing, she took Zilpah her maid, and gave her to Yaakov to be his wife. 10 And Zilpah Leah's maid bore Yaakov a son. 11 And Leah said, A troop comes: and she called his name Gad. 12 And Zilpah Leah's maid bore Yaakov a second son. 13 And Leah said, Happy am I, for the daughters will call me blessed: and she called his name Asher. 14 And Reuven went in the days of wheat harvest, and found love apples in the field, and brought them to his ima Leah. Then Rachel said to Leah, Please give me some of your son's love apples.[1] 15 And Leah said to her, Is it a small matter that you have taken my husband? And would you take away my son's love apples also? And Rachel said, Therefore let him lie with you tonight for your son's love apples. 16 And Yaakov came out of the field in the evening, and Leah went out to meet him, and said, You must come in to me; for surely I have hired you with my son's love apples. And he lay with her that night. 17 And Elohim listened to Leah, and she

conceived, and bore Yaakov the fifth son. 18 And Leah said, Elohim has given me my hire, because I have given my maiden to my husband: and she called his name Yissacher. 19 And Leah conceived again, and bore Yaakov the sixth son. 20 And Leah said, Elohim has endued me with a tov dowry; now will my husband dwell with me, because I have born him six sons: and she called his name Zevulon. 21 And afterwards she bore a daughter, and called her name Dinah. 22 And Elohim remembered Rachel, and Elohim listened to her, and opened her womb. 23 And she conceived, and bore a son; and said, Elohim has taken away my reproach: 24 And she called his name Yoseph; and said, יהוה shall add to me another son. 25 And it came to pass, when Rachel had born Yoseph, that Yaakov said to Lavan, Send me away, that I may go to my own place, and to my country. 26 Give me my wives and my children, for whom I have served you, and let me go: for you know my service that I have done you. 27 And Lavan said to him, Please, if I have found favor in yours eyes, stay: for I have learned by experience that יהוה has blessed me for your sake. 28 And he said, Appoint me your wages, and I will give it. 29 And he said to him, You know how I have served you, and how your cattle were with me. 30 For it was little which you had before I came, and it is now increased to a multitude; and יהוה has blessed you since my coming: and now when shall I provide for my own bayit also? 31 And he said, What shall I give you? And Yaakov said, You shall not give me anything: if you will do this thing for me, I will again feed and keep your flock: 32 I will pass through all your flock today, removing from there all the speckled and spotted cattle, and all the brown cattle among the sheep, and the spotted and speckled among the goats: and those shall be my hire. 33 So shall my tzedakah answer for me in time to come, when it shall come for my hire before your face: every one that is not speckled and spotted among the goats,

[1] A plant and fruit used as a love or fertility stimulant, sought by Rachel to overcome her barren womb.

and brown among the sheep, that shall be counted as stolen with me. 34 And Lavan said, See, I would it might be according to your word. 35 And he removed that day the male goats that were ring streaked and spotted, and all the female goats that were speckled and spotted, and every one that had some white in it, and all the brown among the sheep, and gave them into the hand of his sons. 36 And he set three days' journey between himself and Yaakov: and Yaakov fed the rest of Lavan's flocks. 37 And Yaakov took rods of green poplar, and of the hazel and chesnut eytz; and rounded white streaks in them, and made the white appear that was in the rods. 38 And he set the rods that he had rounded before the flocks in the gutters in the watering troughs when the flocks came to drink, that they should conceive when they came to drink. 39 And the flocks conceived before the rods, and brought out cattle ring streaked, speckled, and spotted. 40 And Yaakov did separate the lambs, and set the faces of the flocks toward the ring streaked, and all the brown in the flock of Lavan; and he put his own flocks by themselves, and did not put them in Lavan's cattle. 41 And it came to pass, whenever the stronger cattle did conceive, that Yaakov laid the rods before the eyes of the cattle in the gutters, that they might conceive among the rods. 42 But when the cattle were feeble, he put them not in: so the feebler were Lavan's, and the stronger Yaakov's. 43 And the man increased exceedingly, and had much cattle, and female avadim, and male avadim, and camels, and donkeys.

31 And he heard the words of Lavan's sons, saying, Yaakov has taken away all that was our abba's; and of that which was our abba's has he gotten all this tifereth. 2 And Yaakov beheld the face of Lavan, and, see, it was not towards him as before. 3 And יהוה said to Yaakov, *Return to the land of your ahvot, and to your mishpocha; and I will be with you.* 4 And

Yaakov sent and called Rachel and Leah to the field to his flock, 5 And said to them, I see your abba's face that it is not toward me as before; but the Elohim of my abba has been with me. 6 And you know that with all my power I have served your abba. 7 And your abba has deceived me, and changed my wages ten times; but Elohim did not allow him to hurt me. 8 When he said, The speckled cattle shall be your wages; then all the cattle bore speckled: and when he said so, The ring streaked shall be your hire; then all the cattle bore ring streaked. 9 So Elohim has taken away the cattle of your abba, and given them to me. 10 And it came to pass at the time that the cattle conceived, that I lifted up my eyes, and saw in a dream, and, see, the rams that leaped upon the cattle were ring streaked, speckled, and grisled. 11 And the Malach-Elohim spoke to me in a dream, saying, *Yaakov:* And I said, Hinayni. 12 And he said, *Lift up now yours eyes, and see, all the rams which leap upon the cattle are ring streaked, speckled, and grisled: for I have seen all that Lavan does to you.* 13 I am the El of Beth-El, where you anointed the pillar, and where you vowed a vow to Me: now arise, get out from this land, and return to the land of your mishpocha. 14 And Rachel and Leah answered and said to him, Is there yet any portion or inheritance for us in our abba's bayit? 15 Are we not counted as gerim by him? For he has sold us, and has fully devoured our money also. 16 For all the riches that Elohim has taken from our abba, that is ours, and our children's: now then, whatever Elohim has said to you, do. 17 Then Yaakov rose up, and set his sons and his wives upon camels. 18 And he carried away all his cattle, and all his items that he had gotten, the cattle of his getting, which he had gotten in Padan-Aram, to go to Yitzchak his abba in the land of Kanaan. 19 And Lavan went to shear his sheep: and Rachel had stolen the images that were her abba's. 20 And Yaakov went away without telling Lavan the Aramean, in that he told him not that he fled. 21 So he fled with all that he had; and he rose up, and passed over the river, and set his face toward Mount Gilead. 22 And it was told to Lavan on the third day that Yaakov had fled. 23 And he took his brothers with him, and pursued after him a seven days' journey; and they overtook him in the Mount Gilead. 24 And Elohim came to Lavan the Aramean in a dream by night, and said to him, *Take heed that you speak not to Yaakov either tov or bad.* 25 Then Lavan overtook Yaakov. Now Yaakov had pitched his tent in the Mount: and Lavan with his brothers pitched in the Mount of Gilead. 26 And Lavan said to Yaakov, What have you done, that you have gone away without telling me, and carried away my daughters, as captives taken with a sword? 27 Why did you flee away secretly, and deceive me; and did not tell me, so that I could have sent you away with simcha, and with shirim, with tabret, and with harp? 28 And you have not allowed me to kiss my sons and my daughters? You have now done foolishly in so doing. 29 It is in the power of my hand to do you harm: but the El of your abba's bayit spoke to me last night, saying, *Take heed that you speak not to Yaakov either tov or bad.* 30 And now, you have gone, because you greatly long for your abba's bayit, but why have you stolen my elohim? 31 And Yaakov answered and said to Lavan, Because I was afraid: for I said, Suppose you would take by force your daughters from me. 32 With whomever you find your elohim, let him not live: before our brothers discern what is and isn't mine, and take it with you. For Yaakov knew not that Rachel had stolen them. 33 And Lavan went into Yaakov's tent, and into Leah's tent, and into the two female avadim's tents; but he found them not. Then went he out of Leah's tent, and entered into Rachel's tent. 34 Now Rachel had taken the images, and put them in the camel's furniture, and sat upon them. And Lavan searched the entire tent, but found them not. 35 And she said to her abba, Let it not displease my master that I cannot rise up before you; for the custom of women is upon me. And he searched, but found not the images. 36 And Yaakov was angry, and contended with Lavan: and Yaakov answered and said to Lavan, What is my trespass? What is my sin; that you have so hotly pursued after me? 37 Why you have searched all my items, what have you found from all your household items? Set it here before my brothers and your brothers, that they may shophet between us both. 38 These twenty years have I been with you; your ewes and your female goats have not cast their young, and the rams of your flock have I not eaten. 39 That which was torn of beasts I brought not to you; I bore the loss of it; of my hand did you require it, whether stolen by day, or stolen by night. 40 So I was; in the day the drought consumed me, and the frost by night; and my sleep departed from my eyes. 41 Therefore have I been twenty years in your bayit; I served you fourteen years for your two daughters, and six years for your cattle: and you have changed my wages ten times. 42 Except the Elohim of my abba, the Elohim of Avraham, and the Fear of Yitzchak, had been with me, surely you would have sent me away now empty. Elohim has seen my affliction and the labor of my hands, and rebuked you last night. 43 And Lavan answered and said to Yaakov, These daughters are my daughters, and these children are my children, and these cattle are my cattle, and all that you see is mine: and what can I do this day to these my daughters, or to their children which they have born? 44 Now therefore come, let us make a covenant, you and I; and let it be for a witness between you and me. 45 And Yaakov took a stone, and set it up for a pillar. 46 And Yaakov said to his brothers, Gather stones; and they took stones, and made a heap: and they did eat there upon the heap. 47 And Lavan called it Yegar-Sahadutha: but Yaakov called it Gal-Ed. 48 And Lavan said, This heap is a witness between you and me this day. Therefore was the name of it called Gal-Ed. 49 And Mitzpah; for he said, **יהוה** watch between you and me, when we are absent one from another. 50 If you shall afflict my daughters, or if you shall take other wives beside my daughters, no man is with us; see, Elohim is witness between you and me. 51 And Lavan said to Yaakov, See this heap, and see this pillar, which I have set between you; and me 52 This heap be witness, and this pillar be witness, that I will not pass over this heap to you, and that you shall not pass over this heap and this pillar to me, for harm. 53 The Elohim of Avraham, and the Elohim of Nachor, the Elohim of their abba, shophet between us. And Yaakov swore by the Fear of his abba Yitzchak. 54 Then Yaakov offered sacrifice upon the Mount, and called his brothers to eat lechem: and they did eat lechem, and stayed all night in the Mount. 55 And early in the morning Lavan rose up, and kissed his sons and his daughters, and blessed them: and Lavan departed, and returned to his place.

32 And Yaakov went on his way, and the heavenly messengers of Elohim met him. 2 And when Yaakov saw them, he said, This is Elohim's army: and he called the name of that place Machanayim.

Torah Parsha 8
Vayishlach 32:4-36:43
Haftarah Hoshea 11:7-12:12
Brit Chadasha Qorintiyah Alef 5:1-13

3 And Yaakov sent messengers before him to Esav his brother to the land of Seir, the country of Edom. 4 And he commanded them, saying, So shall you speak to my master Esav; Your eved Yaakov says this, I have sojourned with Lavan, and stayed there until now: 5 And I have oxen, and donkeys, flocks, and male avadim, and female avadim: and I have sent to tell my master, that I may find favor in your sight. 6 And the messengers returned to Yaakov, saying,

We came to your brother Esav, and also he comes to meet you, and four hundred men with him. 7 Then Yaakov was greatly afraid and distressed: and he divided the people that were with him, and the flocks, and herds, and the camels, into two camps - groups;[1] 8 And said, If Esav comes to the one company, and smites it, then the other company that is left shall escape. 9 And Yaakov said, O Elohim of my abba Avraham, and Elohim of my abba Yitzchak, **יהוה** who said to me, *Return to your country, and to your mishpocha, and I will deal well with you:* 10 I am not worthy of the least of all the rachamim, and of all the emet, which You have shown to Your eved; for with just my staff I passed over this Yarden; and now I have become two camps of peoples. 11 Please deliver me from the hand of my brother, from the hand of Esav: for I fear him, lest he will come and smite me, and the ima with the children.[2] 12 And You did say, *I will surely do you tov, and make your zera as the sand of the sea, which cannot be numbered for multitude.* 13 And he lodged there that same night; and took of that which came to his hand a present for Esav his brother; 14 Two hundred female goats, and twenty male goats, two hundred ewes, and twenty rams, 15 Thirty milk camels with their colts, forty cows, and ten bulls, twenty female donkeys, and ten foals. 16 And he delivered them into the hand of his avadim, every drove by themselves; and said to his avadim, Go ahead of me, and put a space between drove and drove. 17 And he commanded the foremost, saying, When Esav my brother meets you, and asks you, saying, Whose are you? And where are you going? And whose are these before you? 18 Then you shall say, They be your eved Yaakov's; it is a present sent to my master Esav: and, see, also

---

[1] **Shnai Machanot** - two camps. This has always been one of the main reasons for Yisrael being divided into two houses. For preservation from attack and annihilation. Yaakov here operates in the full mind of YHWH.
[2] Trials from Edomites always bring two-house understanding. These events will be played out again in the last days according to the prophet Obadiah.

Yaakov is behind us. 19 And so in like manner he commanded the second, and the third, and all that followed the droves, saying, In this manner shall you speak to Esav, when you find him. 20 And say also, See, your eved Yaakov is behind us. For he said, I will appease him with the present that goes before me, and after that I will see his face; I suppose he will then accept me. 21 So the present went before him: and he himself lodged that night in the company. 22 And he rose up that night, and took his two wives, and his two female avadim, and his eleven sons, and passed over the ford Yavvok. 23 And he took them, and sent them over the brook, and sent over what he had. 24 And Yaakov was left alone; and there wrestled a Man with Yaakov until the breaking of the day.[1] 25 And when the Man saw that He prevailed not against him, the Man touched the hollow of Yaakov's thigh; and the hollow of Yaakov's thigh was out of joint, as the Man wrestled with Yaakov. 26 And the Man said, *Let Me go, for the day breaks*. And Yaakov said, I will not let You go, except You bless me. 27 And the Man said to Yaakov, *What is your name?* And he answered, Yaakov. 28 And the Man said, *your name shall no longer be called Yaakov, but Yisrael:[2] for as a sar you have power with Elohim and with men, and have prevailed.* 29 And Yaakov asked Him, and said, Please tell me Your Name. And He said, *Why is it that you do ask about My Name?[3]* And He blessed him there. 30 And Yaakov called the name of the place Peni-El: for I have seen Elohim panayim-el-panayim, and still - my chayim has been

preserved.[4] 31 And as he passed over Penu-El the sun rose upon him, and he limped on his hip. [5] ,32 Therefore the children of Yisrael eat not of the sinew which shrank, that is upon the socket of the thigh, to this day: because He touched the socket of Yaakov's thigh in the sinew of the hip.

33 And Yaakov lifted up his eyes, and looked, and, see, Esav came, and with him four hundred men. And he divided the children to Leah, and to Rachel, and to the two handmaids. 2 And he put the handmaids and their children in the front, and Leah and her children after them, and Rachel and Yoseph in the back. 3 And he passed over before them, and bowed himself to the ground seven times, until he came near to his brother. 4 And Esav ran to meet him, and embraced him, and fell on his neck, and kissed him: and they wept. 5 And Esav lifted up his eyes, and saw the women and the children; and said, Who are those with you? And Yaakov said, The children that Elohim has by His unmerited favor given to your eved. 6 Then the handmaidens came near, they and their children, and they bowed themselves. 7 And Leah also with her children came near, and bowed themselves: and after came Yoseph near with Rachel, and they bowed themselves. 8 And he said, What do you mean by all this company that I met? And Yaakov said, These are to find favor in the sight of my master. 9 And Esav said, I have enough, my brother; keep what you have for yourself. 10 And Yaakov said, No, Please, if now I have found favor in your sight, then receive my present from my hand: because I see your face towards me, as though I had seen the face of Elohim, and you were pleased with me. 11 Please take my bracha that is brought to you; because Elohim has dealt with me through unmerited favor, and

---

[1] A Man: Recognized later as Elohim Himself by Yaakov, a clear reference to Yahshua, since no mortal man can see the Father and live. Here Jacob sees the same one Abraham saw on His way to destroy Sedom and Amorah.
[2] "Overcoming believers" who wrestle with Moshiach and are established by Him and are often sealed with a name change as a result of that regeneration experience. Returning Yisraelites from both houses should strongly consider a name change to a legal Hebrew name, as an outward seal of an inner reality and understanding concerning what Yahshua has truly come to do.
[3] In other words - I'm here to change your name and heart, you are not here to ask questions about my Name. That answer would be provided later in Yahshua's first advent.

[4] The visible part of YHWH that was later to be sent as His Son.
[5] Physical marking is often a sign of one's painful calling by YHWH to surrender all in order to fully serve Him. YHWH often gives Yisraelites a thorn in the flesh to keep them humble and submissive, marked as regenerated Yisrael.

because I have enough. And he urged him, and Esav took it. 12 And he said, Let us take our journey, and let us go, and I will go before you. 13 And he said to him, My master knows that the children are tender, and the flocks and herds with young are with me: and if men should overdrive them one day, all the flock will die. 14 Please let my master pass over before his eved. And I will lead on gently, according to the pace of the cattle that goes before me, and the pace that the children are able to endure, until I come to my master to Seir. 15 And Esav said, Let me now leave with you some of the folks that are with me. And Yaakov said, What nccd do I have for them? Let me find favor in the sight of my master. 16 So Esav returned that day on his derech to Seir. 17 And Yaakov journeyed to Sukkoth, and built himself a bayit, and made booths for his cattle: therefore the name of the place is called Sukkoth. 18 And Yaakov came to Shalem, a city of Shechem, which is in the land of Kanaan, when he came from Padan-Aram; and pitched his tent before the city. 19 And he bought a parcel of a field, where he had spread his tent, at the hand of the children of Chamor, Shechem's abba, for an hundred pieces of money. 20 And he erected there an altar, and called it El-Elohe-Yisrael.

34 And Dinah the daughter of Leah, who she bore to Yaakov, went out to see the daughters of the land. 2 And when Shechem the son of Chamor the Hivite, sar of the country, saw her, he took her, and lay with her, and defiled her. 3 And his being cut to Dinah the daughter of Yaakov, and he loved the young girl, and spoke kindly to the young girl. 4 And Shechem spoke to his abba Chamor, saying, Get me this young girl to be my wife. 5 And Yaakov heard that he had defiled Dinah his daughter: now his sons were with his cattle in the field: and Yaakov held his silence until they had come. 6 And Chamor the abba of Shechem went out to Yaakov to commune with him.

7 And the sons of Yaakov came out of the field when they heard it: and the men were grieved, and they were very angry, because he had wrought folly in Yisrael in lying with Yaakov's daughter; which thing should not to be done. 8 And Chamor communed with them, saying, The being of my son Shechem longs for your daughter: Please give her to him to be his wife. 9 And make many marriages with us, and give your daughters to us, and take our daughters to you. 10 And you shall dwell with us: and the land shall be before you; dwell and trade you in it, and get possessions in it. 11 And Shechem said to her abba and to her brothers, Let me find favor in your eyes, and what you shall say to me I will give. 12 Ask me much dowry and gift, and I will give it according as you shall tell me: but give me the young girl to bc my wife. 13 And the sons of Yaakov answered Shechem and Chamor his abba deceitfully, because he had defiled Dinah their sister: 14 And they said to them, We cannot do this thing, to give our sister to one that is uncircumcised; for that would be a reproach to us: 15 But in this request we will we consent to you: If you will be as we are, that every male of yours become circumcised; 16 Then will we give our daughters to you, and we will take your daughters to us, and we will dwell with you, and we will become one people. 17 But if you will not listen to us, to be circumcised; then will we take our daughter, and we will be gone. 18 And their words pleased Chamor, and Shechem Chamor's son. 19 And the young man did not hesitate to become circumcised, because he delighted in Yaakov's daughter: and he was more honorable than all in the bayit of his abba. 20 And Chamor and Shechem his son came to the gate of their city, and communed with the men of their city, saying, 21 These men are in shalom with us; therefore let them dwell in the land, and trade in it; for look at the land; it is large enough for them also; let us take their daughters to us for our wives, and let us

give them our daughters. 22 Only in this manner will the men consent to dwell with us, to be one people, if every male among us becomes circumcised, as they are circumcised. 23 Shall not their cattle and their substance and every beast of theirs become ours? Only let us consent to them, and they will dwell with us. 24 And to Chamor and to Shechem his son heard all that went out of the gate of his city; and every male was circumcised including all that went out of the gate of his city. 25 And it came to pass on the third day, when the men were still sore, that two of the sons of Yaakov, Shimeon and Levi, Dinah's brothers, took each man his sword, and came upon the city boldly, and killed all the males. 26 And they killed Chamor and Shechem his son with the edge of the sword, and took Dinah out of Shechem's bayit, and went out. 27 The sons of Yaakov came upon the slain, and plundered the city, because they had defiled their sister. 28 They took their sheep, and their oxen, and their donkeys, and that which was in the city, and that which was in the field, 29 And all their wealth, and all their little ones, and their wives they took captive, and plundered even all that was in the bayit. 30 And Yaakov said to Shimeon and Levi, You have troubled me to make me to stink among the inhabitants of the land, among the Kanaanites and the Perizzites: and I being few in number, they shall gather themselves together against me, and kill me; and I shall be destroyed, I and also kol Beit Yisrael. 31 And they said to Yaakov, Should he deal with our sister as with a harlot?

35 And Elohim said to Yaakov, *Arise, go up to Beth-El, and dwell there: and make there an altar to El, that appeared to you when you fled from the face of Esav your brother.* 2 Then Yaakov said to his household, and to all that were with him, Put away the strange elohim that are among you, and be clean, and change your garments:[1] 3 And let us arise, and go up to Beth-El; and I will make there an altar to El, who answered me in the day of my distress, and was with me in the way which I went. 4 And they gave to Yaakov all the strange elohim that were in their hand, and all their earrings that were in their ears; and Yaakov hid them under the oak which was by Shechem.[2] 5 And they journeyed: and the terror of Elohim was upon the cities that were around them, so that they did not pursue after the sons of Yaakov. 6 So Yaakov came to Luz, which is in the land of Kanaan, that is, Beth-El, he and all the people that were with him. 7 And he built there an altar, and called the place El-Beth-El: because there Elohim appeared to him, when he fled from the face of his brother. 8 But Devorah Rivkah's nurse died, and she was buried beneath Beth-El under an oak: and the name of it was called Allon-Bachuth. 9 And Elohim appeared to Yaakov again, when he came out of Padan-Aram, and blessed him. 10 And Elohim said to him, *Your name is Yaakov: your name shall not be called any more Yaakov, but Yisrael shall be your name: and He called his name Yisrael.*[3] 11 And Elohim said to him, I am El-Shaddai: be fruitful and multiply; a nation-goy; and a congregation of nations-kahal-goyim; shall come from you, and melechim[4] shall come out of your loins;[5][6] 12 *And the land that I gave Avraham and Yitzchak, to you I will give it, and to your*

---

[1] This calling is ongoing to all Yisraelites in all generations, especially in the end-times, for without repentance Yisrael will remain divided and in exile.
[2] Notice Yisrael always struggled with idolatry just like the nations and instead of destroying idols they hid them.
[3] An overcomer with man and with YHWH.
[4] Many of the royal houses of both the east and west came from Jacob and had Yisraelite dom. This issue has been well documented by scholars. A perfect example is the Ethiopian royalty, as well as the royalty of Western Europe.
[5] A nation, the Jews (**goy**), and a company of nations, or a congregation of nations (**kahal goyim**), a clear prophesy that from Yaakov's body would come two physical houses; one Jewish and one "gentile."
[6] Also notice that Yisrael is called a "**goy**", just like today non-Yisraelites are called goyim. So when one is called a goy, that does not by any means eliminate Yisraelite DNA; for if that were true, the Jews of today also would not be Yisraelites, as often they are referred to as **goy** or the **goyim** of YHWH in Scripture.

zera after you will I give the land. [1] 13 And Elohim went up from him in the place where He talked with him. 14 And Yaakov set up a pillar in the place where He talked with him, even a pillar of stone: and he poured a drink offering on it, and he poured oil on it. 15 And Yaakov called the name of the place where Elohim spoke with him, Beth-El. 16 And they journeyed from Beth-El; and there was just a little way to go to Ephrath: and Rachel travailed, and she had hard labor. 17 And it came to pass, when she was in hard labor, that the midwife said to her, Fear not; you shall have this son also. 18 And it came to pass, as her chayim was leaving, - for she died - that she called his name Ben-Oni: but his abba called him Benyamin. 19 And Rachel died, and was buried on the way to Ephrath, which is Beth-Lechem. 20 And Yaakov set a pillar upon her grave: that is the pillar of Rachel's grave to this day. 21 And Yisrael journeyed, and spread his tent beyond the tower of Edar. 22 And it came to pass, when Yisrael dwelt in that land, that Reuven went and lay with Bilhah his abba's concubine: and Yisrael heard it. Now the sons of Yaakov were twelve: 23 The sons of Leah; Reuven, Yaakov's bachor, and Shimeon, and Levi, and Yahudah, and Yissacher, and Zevulon: 24 The sons of Rachel; Yoseph, and Benyamin: 25 And the sons of Bilhah, Rachel's handmaid; Dan, and Naphtali: 26 And the sons of Zilpah, Leah's handmaid; Gad, and Asher: these are the sons of Yaakov, who were born to him in Padan-Aram. 27 And Yaakov came to Yitzchak his abba to Mamre, to the city of Arbah, which is Hevron, where Avraham and Yitzchak sojourned. 28 And the days of Yitzchak were ond hundred eighty years. 29 And Yitzchak gave up the ruach, and died, and was gathered to his people, being old and full of days: and his sons Esav and Yaakov buried him.

36 Now these are the generations of Esav, who is Edom. 2 Esav took his wives of the daughters of Kanaan; Adah the daughter of Elon the Hittite, and Aholivamah the daughter of Anah the daughter of Ziveon the Hivite. 3 And Bashemath Yishma-El's daughter, sister of Nevayoth. 4 And Adah bore to Esav Eliphaz; and Bashemath bore Reuel; 5 And Aholivamah bore Yeush, and Yaalam, and Korah: these are the sons of Esav, which were born to him in the land of Kanaan. 6 And Esav took his wives, and his sons, and his daughters, and all the persons of his bayit, and his cattle, and all his beasts, and all his substance, that he had gotten in the land of Kanaan; and went into the country away from the face of his brother Yaakov. 7 For their riches were more than what would allow them to dwell together; and the land in which they were gerim[2] could not bear them both because of their cattle. 8 So Esav dwelt in Mount Seir: Esav is Edom.[3] 9 And these are the generations of Esav the abba of the Edomites in Mount Seir: 10 These are the names of Esav's sons; Eliphaz the son of Adah the wife of Esav, Reu-El the son of Bashemath the wife of Esav. 11 And the sons of Eliphaz were Teman, Omar, Zepho, and Gatam, and Kenaz. 12 And Timna was concubine to Eliphaz Esav's son; and she bore to Eliphaz Amalek: these were the sons of Adah Esav's wife. 13 And these are the sons of Reuel; Nahath, and Zerah, Shammah, and Mizzah: these were the sons of Bashemath Esav's wife. 14 And these were the sons of Aholivamah, the daughter of Anah the daughter of Ziveon, Esav's wife: and she bore to Esav Yeush, and Yaalam, and Korah. 15 These were chiefs of the sons of Esav: the sons of Eliphaz the bachor son of Esav; chief Teman, chief Omar, chief Zepho, chief Kenaz, 16 Chief Korah, chief Gatam, and chief Amalek: these are the

---

[1] Yisrael's homeland.

[2] Interesting text; Yisrael himself is called a **Ger**. So **gerim** who settled amongst the nations were always considered Yisrael in Scripture's view.
[3] Not In Yisrael.

chiefs that came of Eliphaz in the land of Edom; these were the sons of Adah. 17 And these are the sons of Reuel Esav's son; chief Nahath, chief Zerah, chief Shammah, chief Mizzah: these are the chiefs that came from Reuel in the land of Edom; these are the sons of Bashemath Esav's wife. 18 And these are the sons of Aholivamah Esav's wife; chief Yeush, chief Yaalam, chief Korah: these were the chiefs that came from Aholivamah the daughter of Anah, Esav's wife. 19 These are the sons of Esav, who is Edom, and these are their chiefs. 20 These are the sons of Seir the Horite, who inhabited the land; Lotan, and Shoval, and Ziveon, and Anah, 21 And Dishon, and Ezer, and Dishan: these are the chiefs of the Horites, the children of Seir in the land of Edom. 22 And the children of Lotan were Hori and Hemam; and Lotan's sister was Timna. 23 And the children of Shoval were these; Alvan, and Manahath, and Eval, Shepho, and Onam. 24 And these are the children of Ziveon; both Ayah, and Anah: this was that Anah that found the mules in the wilderness, as he fed the donkeys of Ziveon his abba. 25 And the children of Anah were these; Dishon, and Aholivamah the daughter of Anah. 26 And these are the children of Dishon; Hemdan, and Eshvan, and Ithran, and Cheran. 27 The children of Ezer are these; Bilhan, and Zaavan, and Akan. 28 The children of Dishan are these: Uz, and Aran. 29 These are the chiefs that came from the Horites; chief Lotan, chief Shoval, chief Ziveon, chief Anah, 30 Chief Dishon, chief Ezer, and chief Dishan: these are the chiefs that came from Hori, among their chiefs in the land of Seir. 31 And these are the melechim that reigned in the land of Edom, before there reigned any melech over the children of Yisrael. 32 And Bela the son of Beor reigned in Edom: and the name of his city was Dinhavah. 33 And Bela died, and Yovav the son of Zerah of Bozrah reigned in his place. 34 And Yovav died, and Husham of the land of Temani reigned in his place. 35 And Husham died, and Hadad the son of Bedad, who smote Midyan in the field of Moav, reigned in his place: and the name of his city was Avith. 36 And Hadad died, and Samlah of Masrekah reigned in his place. 37 And Samlah died, and Shaul of Rehovoth by the river reigned in his place. 38 And Shaul died, and Baal-Hanan the son of Achvor reigned in his place. 39 And Baal-Hanan the son of Achvor died, and Hadar reigned in his place: and the name of his city was Pau; and his wife's name was Mehetavel, the daughter of Matred, the daughter of Mezahav. 40 And these are the names of the chiefs that came from Esav, according to their mishpachot, after their places, by their names; chief Timnah, chief Alvah, chief Yetheth, 41 Chief Aholivamah, chief Elah, chief Pinon, 42 Chief Kenaz, chief Teman, chief Mivzar, 43 Chief Magdiel, chief Iram: these are the chiefs of Edom, according to their dwellings in the land of their possession: he is Esav the abba of the Edomites.[1]

Torah Parsha 9
Vayeshev 37:1-40:23
Haftarah Amoz 2:6-3:8
Brit Chadasha MaAseh Shlichim 7:9-16

37 And Yaakov dwelt in the land in which his abba was a Ger, in the land of Kanaan. 2 These are the generations of Yaakov. Yoseph, being seventeen years old, was feeding the flock with his brothers; and the lad was with the sons of Bilhah, and with the sons of Zilpah, his abba's wives: and Yoseph brought to his abba their evil report. 3 Now Yisrael loved Yoseph more than all his children, because he was the son of his old age: and he made him a coat of many colors. 4 And when his brothers saw

---

[1] Edom's genealogy is included in a book about Yisrael in order to document that Arabs are not considered native Yisraelites. Many still erroneously teach that Edomites are part of the chosen seed emanating from Abraham. However as these genealogies show they cannot be the chosen seed, since they do not proceed from Abraham, Isaac and Jacob, but merely through Abraham. Nevertheless, individuals from these Edomite tribes can and do become Yisrael as repentant individuals, when they place faith in Yahshua the Moshiach and His Torah.

that their abba loved him more than all his brothers, they hated him, and could not speak nicely to him. 5 And Yoseph dreamed a dream, and he told it his brothers: and they hated him even more. 6 And he said to them, Please listen to this dream that I have dreamed: 7 For, see, we were binding sheaves in the field, and, see, my sheaf arose, and also stood upright; and, see, your sheaves stood all around, and bowed to my sheaf. 8 And his brothers said to him, Shall you indeed reign over us? Or shall you indeed have dominion over us? And they hated him even more for his dreams, and for his words. 9 And he dreamed another dream, and told it his brothers, and said, See, I have dreamed another dream more; and, see, the sun and the moon and the eleven chochavim bowed down to me. 10 And he told it to his abba, and to his brothers: and his abba rebuked him, and said to him, What is this dream that you have dreamed? Shall your ima and I and your brothers indeed come to bow down to you to the earth? 11 And his brothers envied him; but his abba observed the saying. [1] 12 And his brothers went to feed their abba's flock in Shechem. 13 And Yisrael said to Yoseph, Do not your brothers feed the flock in Shechem? Come, and I will send you to them. And he said to him, Heynani. 14 And he said to him, Please go and see whether things are well with your brothers, and well with the flocks; and bring me word again. So he sent him out of the Valley of Hevron, and he came to Shechem. 15 And a certain man found Yoseph, as he was wandering in the field: and the man asked him, saying, What are you looking for? 16 And he said, I seek my brothers: Please tell me where they feed their flocks. 17 And the man said, They have departed from here; for I heard them say, Let us go to Dothan. And Yoseph went after his brothers, and found them in Dothan. 18 And when they saw him far off, even before he came near to them, they conspired against him to kill him. [2] 19 And they said one to another, See, the dreamer is coming. 20 Come now, and let us kill him, and cast him into some pit, and we will say, Some evil beast has devoured him: and we shall see what will become of his dreams. 21 And Reuven heard it, and he delivered him out of their hands; and said, Let us not kill him. 22 And Reuven said to them, Shed no dom, but cast him into this pit that is in the wilderness, and lay no hand upon him; that he might remove him out of their hands, to deliver him to his abba again. 23 And it came to pass, when Yoseph came to his brothers, that they stripped Yoseph of his coat of many colors that was on him. 24 And they took him, and cast him into a pit: and the pit was empty, there was no mayim in it. 25 And they sat down to eat lechem: and they lifted up their eyes and looked, and, see, a company of Yishmaelites came from Gilead with their camels bearing spices and balm and myrrh, going to carry it down to Mitzrayim. 26 And Yahudah said to his brothers, What profit is it if we kill our brother, and conceal his dom? 27 Come, and let us sell him to the Yishmaelites, and let not our hand be upon him; for he is our brother and our flesh. And his brothers were content. [3] 28 Then there passed by Midyanite traders; and they drew and lifted up Yoseph out of the pit, and sold Yoseph to the Ishmaelites for twenty pieces of silver: and they brought Yoseph into Mitzrayim. 29 And Reuven returned to the pit; and, see, Yoseph was not in the pit; and he tore his clothes. 30 And he returned to his brothers, and said, The child is not here; and I, where shall I go? 31 And they took Yoseph's coat, and killed a kid of the goats, and dipped the coat in the dom. [4] 32 And

---

[1] Because Yaakov knew the promise to Yisrael and took the dreams in stride in a "wait and see" attitude.

[2] Joseph and his seed have always been misunderstood and separated from the rest of Yisrael.
[3] Historically Yahudah has desired separation from Joseph, not necessarily his total demise. This continues today.
[4] Today Joseph's gentile children become Yisrael again, regardless of their skin color, by the dom of salvation. The muti colored coat represents all nations and racial colors dipped in Yahshua's dom.

they sent the coat of many colors, and they brought it to their abba; and said, This have we found: and we don't know whether it be your son's coat or not. 33 And he knew it, and said, It is my son's coat; an evil beast has devoured him; Yoseph is without a doubt torn in pieces. 34 And Yaakov tore his clothes, and put sackcloth upon his loins, and mourned for his son many days. 35 And all his sons and all his daughters rose up to comfort him; but he refused to be comforted; and he said, For I will go down to the grave mourning my son. So his abba wept for him. 36 And the Midyanites sold him into Mitzrayim to Potiphar, an officer of Pharaoh's, and captain of the guard.

38 And it came to pass at that time that Yahudah went down from his brothers, and turned in to a certain Adullamite, whose name was Hirah. 2 And Yahudah saw there a daughter of a certain Canaanite, whose name was Shuah; and he took her, and went in to her. 3 And she conceived, and bore a son; and he called his name Er. 4 And she conceived again, and bore a son; and she called his name Onan. 5 And she yet again conceived, and bore a son; and called his name Shelah: and he was at Chezib, when she bore him. 6 And Yahudah took a wife for Er his bachor, whose name was Tamar. 7 And Er, Yahudah's bachor, was wicked in the sight of **יהוה** ; and **יהוה** killed him. 8 And Yahudah said to Onan, Go in to your brother's wife, and marry her, and raise up zera for your brother. 9 And Onan knew that the zera should not be his; and it came to pass, when he went in to his brother's wife, that he spilled it on the ground, lest he should give zera to his brother. 10 And the thing that he did displeased **יהוה**: So He killed him also.[1] 11 Then said Yahudah to Tamar his daughter in law, Remain a widow at your abba's bayit, until Shelah my son be

grown: for he said, Lest suppose he die also, as his brothers did. And Tamar went and dwelt in her abba's bayit. 12 And in process of time the daughter of Shuah Yahudah's wife died; and Yahudah was comforted, and went up to his sheepshearers to Timnath, he and his friend Hirah the Adullamite. 13 And it was told Tamar, saying, See your abba-in-law goes up to Timnath to shear his sheep. 14 And she put her widow's garments off from her, and covered herself with a veil, and wrapped herself, and sat in an open entrance, which is by the way to Timnath; for she saw that Shelah was grown, and she was not given to him to be his wife. 15 When Yahudah saw her, he thought she was a harlot because she had covered her face. 16 And he turned to her by the way, and said, Please go get ready and let me come in to you; - for he knew not that she was his daughter in law. - She said, What will you give me that you may come in to me? 17 And he said, I will send you a kid from the flock. And she said, Will you give me a pledge, until you send it? 18 And he said, What pledge shall I give you? And she said, Your signet, and your bracelets, and your staff that is in your hand. And he gave it her, and came in to her, and she conceived by him. 19 And she arose, and went away, and removed her veil from her, and put on the garments of her widowhood. 20 And Yahudah sent the kid by the hand of his friend the Adullamite, to receive his pledge from the woman's hand: but he found her not. 21 Then he asked the men of that place, saying, Where is the harlot, that was openly by the way side? And they said, There was no harlot in this place. 22 And he returned to Yahudah, and said, I cannot find her; and also the men of the place said, that there was no harlot in this place. 23 And Yahudah said, Let her take it to her, lest we be shamed: see, I sent this kid, and you have not found her. 24 And it came to pass about three months after, that it was told Yahudah, saying, Tamar your daughter in law has played the harlot; and also, see, she is with

---

[1] Not a reference to masturbation but to Onan sinning against YHWH's plan to multiply Yisrael among the nations, and also for breaking the Torah requirement of refusing to raise up seed for a dead brother and thus build his brother's house.

child by whoredom. And Yahudah said, Bring her out, and let her be burnt. 25 When she was brought out, she sent to her abba in law, saying, By the man, whose these are, am I with child: and she said, Please discern, whose are these, the signet, and bracelets, and staff. 26 And Yahudah acknowledged them, and said, She has been more tzadik than I; because that I gave her not to Shelah my son. And he knew her again no more. 27 And it came to pass in the time of her travail, that twins were in her womb. 28 And it came to pass, when she travailed, that the one put out his hand: and the midwife took it and bound upon his hand a scarlet thread, saying, This one came out first, 29 And it came to pass, he drew back his hand, so that his brother came out first: and she said, How have you broken out? This breach is upon you: therefore his name was called Pharez. 30 And afterward came out his brother, who had the scarlet thread upon his hand: and his name was called Zarah.

39 And Yoseph was brought down to Mitzrayim; and Potiphar, an officer of Pharaoh, captain of the guard, a Mitzrite, bought him of the hands of the Yishmaelites, who had brought him down there. 2 And יהוה was with Yoseph, and he was a prosperous man; and he was in the bayit of his master the Mitzrite. 3 And his master saw that יהוה was with him, and that יהוה made all that he did to prosper in his hand. 4 And Yoseph found favor in his sight, and he served him: and he made him overseer over his bayit, and all that he had he put into Yoseph's hand. 5 And it came to pass from the time that he had made him overseer in his bayit, and over all that he had, that יהוה blessed the Mitzrite's bayit for Yoseph's sake; and the bracha of יהוה was upon all that he had in the bayit, and in the field. 6 And he left all that he had in Yoseph's hand; and he knew not what he had, except the lechem that he did eat. And Yoseph was handsome in form and

appearance. 7 And it came to pass after these things, that his master's wife cast her eyes upon Yoseph; and she said, Lie with me. 8 But he refused, and said to his master's wife, See, my master does not know what is with me in the bayit, and he has committed all that he has to my hand; 9 There is none greater in this bayit than I; neither has he kept back anything from me but you, because you are his wife: how then can I do this great wickedness, and sin against Elohim? 10 And it came to pass, as she spoke to Yoseph day by day, that he listened not to her, to lie with her, or to be with her. 11 And it came to pass about this time, that Yoseph went into the bayit to do his business; and none of the men of the bayit were there with him. 12 And she caught him by his garment, saying, Lie with me: and he left his garment in her hand, and fled outside. 13 And it came to pass, when she saw that he had left his garment in her hand, and had fled, 14 That she called to the men of her bayit, and spoke to them, saying, See, he has brought in an Ivri to us to mock us; he came in to me to lie with me, and I cried with a loud voice: 15 And it came to pass, when he heard that I lifted up my voice and cried, that he left his garment with me, and fled, and went outside. 16 And she placed his garment by her, until his master came home. 17 And she spoke to him according to these words, saying, The Ivri eved, who you have brought to us, came in to me to mock me: 18 And it came to pass, as I lifted up my voice and cried, that he left his garment with me, and fled out. 19 And it came to pass, when his master heard the words of his wife, which she spoke to him, saying, After this manner did your eved to me; that his anger was kindled. 20 And Yoseph's master took him, and put him into the prison, a place where the melech's prisoners were bound: and he was there in the prison. 21 But יהוה was with Yoseph, and showed him rachamim, and gave him favor in the sight of the guard of the prison. 22 And the guardian of the prison committed to Yoseph's hand all the prisoners that were in the prison; and whatever they did there, he was the doer of it. 23 The guardian of the prison looked not at anything that was under his authority; because יהוה was with him, and that which he did, יהוה made it to prosper.

40 And it came to pass after these things, that the butler of the melech of Mitzrayim and his baker had offended their master the melech of Mitzrayim. 2 And Pharaoh was angry against two of his officers, against the chief of the butlers, and against the chief of the bakers. 3 And he put them in prison in the bayit of the captain of the guard, into the prison, the place where Yoseph was bound. 4 And the captain of the guard charged Yoseph with them, and he served them: and they continued a season in prison. 5 And they dreamed a dream both of them, each man his dream in one night, each man according to the interpretation of his dream, the butler and the baker of the melech of Mitzrayim, who were bound in the prison. 6 And Yoseph came in to them in the morning, to check on them, and, see, they were sad. 7 And he asked Pharaoh's officers that were with him in the prison of his master's bayit, saying, Why do you look so sad today? 8 And they said to him, We have dreamed a dream, and there is no interpreter of it. And Yoseph said to them, Do not interpretations belong to Elohim? Please tell them to me. 9 And the chief butler told his dream to Yoseph, and said to him, In my dream, see, a vine was before me; 10 And in the vine were three branches: and it was as though it budded, and her blossoms shot out; and the clusters of it brought out ripe grapes: 11 And Pharaoh's cup was in my hand: and I took the grapes, and pressed them into Pharaoh's cup, and I gave the cup into Pharaoh's hand. 12 And Yoseph said to him, This is the interpretation of it: The three branches are three days: 13 Within three days shall Pharaoh lift up your head, and restore you to your place: and you shall deliver

Pharaoh's cup into his hand, like in the past when you were his butler. 14 But remember me when it shall be well with you, and show chesed, to me, and please make mention of me to Pharaoh, and bring me out of this bayit: 15 For indeed I was stolen away out of the land of the Ivrim: and here also have I done nothing that they should put me into the dungeon. 16 When the chief baker saw that the interpretation was tov, he said to Yoseph, I also was in my dream, and I had three white baskets on my head: 17 And in the uppermost basket there was of all manner of baked foods for Pharaoh; and the birds did eat them out of the basket upon my head. 18 And Yoseph answered and said, This is the interpretation of it: The three baskets are three days: 19 Yet within three days shall Pharaoh lift up your head from off of you, and shall hang you on an eytz; and the birds shall eat your flesh from off of you. 20 And it came to pass the third day, which was Pharaoh's birthday, that he made a feast to all his avadim: and he lifted up the head of the chief butler and of the chief baker among his avadim.[1] 21 And he restored the chief butler to his butlership again; and he gave the cup into Pharaoh's hand: 22 But he hanged the chief baker: as Yoseph had interpreted to them. 23 Yet the chief butler did not remember Yoseph, but forgot him.

Torah Parsha 10
Mikketz 41:1-44:17
Haftarah Melechim Alef 3:15-4:1
Brit Chadasha MaAseh Shlichim 7:9-16

41 And it came to pass at the end of two full years, that Pharaoh dreamed: and, see, he stood by the river. 2 And, see, there came up out of the river seven well-favored cows; and they fed in a meadow. 3 And, see, seven other cows came up after them out of the river, ill-favored and lean; and stood by the other

---

[1] Birthdays in Scripture are never portrayed in a positive light. They are not part of Hebrew culture. Hebrews or Yisraelites honor the blessed memory and the day of one's passing. This was clearly displayed in Yahshua's Memorial Supper.

cows upon the edge of the river. 4 And the ugly and lean cows did eat up the seven well-favored and fat cows. So Pharaoh awoke. 5 And he slept and dreamed the second time: and, see, seven ears of corn came up upon one stalk, abundant and tov. 6 And, see, seven thin ears and blasted with the east wind sprung up after them. 7 And the seven thin ears devoured the seven abundant and full ears. And Pharaoh awoke, and, see, it was a dream. 8 And it came to pass in the morning that his ruach was troubled; and he sent and called for all the magicians of Mitzrayim, and all the wise men: and Pharaoh told them his dream; but there was none that could interpret them to Pharaoh. 9 Then spoke the chief butler to Pharaoh, saying, I do remember my faults this day: 10 Pharaoh was angry with his avadim, and put me in prison in the captain of the guard's bayit, both me and the chief baker: 11 And we dreamed a dream in one night, both he and I; we dreamed each man according to the interpretation of his dream. 12 And there was there with us a young man, an Ivri,[1] an eved to the captain of the guard; and we told him, and he interpreted to us our dreams; to each man according to his dream he did interpret. 13 And it came to pass, as he interpreted to us, so it was; me he restored to my office, and him he hanged. 14 Then Pharaoh sent and called Yoseph, and they brought him quickly out of the dungeon: and he shaved himself, and changed his clothing, and came in to Pharaoh. 15 And Pharaoh said to Yoseph, I have dreamed a dream, and there is none that can interpret it: and I have heard it said of you, that you can understand a dream to interpret it. 16 And Yoseph answered Pharaoh, saying, It is not in me: Elohim shall give Pharaoh an answer with shalom. 17 And Pharaoh said to Yoseph, In my dream, see, I stood upon the bank of the river: 18 And, see, there came up out of the river seven cows, fat-fleshed and well-favored; and they fed in a meadow: 19 And,

see, seven other cows came up after them, poor and very ugly and lean, such as I never saw in all the land of Mitzrayim for ugliness: 20 And the lean and the ill-favored cows did eat up the first seven fat cows: 21 And when they had eaten them up, it could not be known that they had eaten them; but they were ugly, as at the beginning. So I awoke. 22 And I saw in my dream, and, see; seven ears came up in one stalk, full and tov: 23 And, see, seven ears, withered, thin, and blasted with the east wind, sprung up after them: 24 And the thin ears devoured the seven tov ears: and I told this to the magicians; but there was none that could declare it to me. 25 And Yoseph said to Pharaoh, The dreams of Pharaoh are echad: Elohim has shown Pharaoh what He is about to do. 26 The seven tov cows are seven years; and the seven tov ears are seven years: the dream is echad. 27 And the seven thin and ugly cows that came up after them are seven years; and the seven empty ears blasted with the east wind shall be seven years of famine. 28 This is the thing that I have spoken to Pharaoh: What Elohim is about to do he shows to Pharaoh. 29 See, there comes seven years of great plenty throughout all the land of Mitzrayim: 30 And there shall arise after them seven years of famine; and all the plenty shall be forgotten in the land of Mitzrayim; and the famine shall consume the land; 31 And the plenty shall not be known in the land by reason of the famine following, for it shall be very severe. 32 And for that the dream was doubled to Pharaoh twice; it is because the thing is established by Elohim, and Elohim will shortly bring it to pass. 33 Now therefore let Pharaoh seek for a man discreet and wise, and set him over the land of Mitzrayim. 34 Let Pharaoh do this, and let him appoint officers over the land, and take up the fifth part of the land of Mitzrayim in the seven plentiful years. 35 And let them gather all the food of those tov years that come, and lay up corn under the hand of Pharaoh, and let them keep food in the

---

[1] Yoseph was a Hebrew not a Jew.

cities. 36 And that food shall be for storage to the land against the seven years of famine, which shall be in the land of Mitzrayim; so that the land perishes not through the famine. 37 And the thing was tov in the eyes of Pharaoh, and in the eyes of all his avadim. 38 And Pharaoh said to his avadim, Can we find such a one as this is, a man in whom is the Ruach of Elohim? 39 And Pharaoh said to Yoseph, Seeing that Elohim has shown you all this, there is none so discreet and wise as you are: 40 You shall be over all my bayit, and according to your word shall all my people be ruled: only in the throne will I be greater than you. 41 And Pharaoh said to Yoseph, See, I have set you over all the land of Mitzrayim. 42 And Pharaoh took off his ring from his hand, and put it upon Yoseph's hand, and prepared him in garments of fine linen, and put a gold chain around his neck; 43 And he made him to ride in the second chariot that he had; and they cried before him, Bow the knee: and he made him ruler over all the land of Mitzrayim. 44 And Pharaoh said to Yoseph, I am Pharaoh, and without you shall no man lift up his hand or foot in all the land of Mitzrayim. 45 And Pharaoh called Yoseph's name Zaphnath-Paaneah;[1] and he gave him as his wife Asenath the daughter of Poti-Pherah kohen of On. And Yoseph went out over all the land of Mitzrayim. 46 And Yoseph was thirty years old when he stood before Pharaoh melech of Mitzrayim. And Yoseph went out from the presence of Pharaoh, and went throughout all the land of Mitzrayim. 47 And in the seven plentiful years the earth brought out by handfuls. 48 And he gathered up all the food for the seven years, which was in the land of Mitzrayim, and laid up the food in the cities: the food of the field, which was all around every city, he laid up the same. 49 And Yoseph gathered much corn as the sand of the sea, until he stopped numbering; for it was without number. 50 And to Yoseph were born two sons before the years of famine came, which Asenath the daughter of Poti-Pherah kohen of On bore to him. 51 And Yoseph called the name of the bachor Menashsheh: For he said Elohim, has made me forget all my toil, and all my past in my abba's bayit. 52 And the name of the second son he called Ephraim: For Elohim has caused me to be fruitful in the land of my affliction.[2] 53 And the seven years of plenty that was in the land of Mitzrayim, had ended. 54 And the seven years of scarcity began to come, according to what Yoseph had said: and the scarcity was in all lands; but in all the land of Mitzrayim there was lechem. 55 And when all the land of Mitzrayim was famished, the people cried to Pharaoh for lechem: and Pharaoh said to all the Mitzrites, Go to Yoseph; what he says to you, do. 56 And the famine was over all the face of the earth: and Yoseph opened all the storehouses, and sold to the Mitzrites; and the famine grew very severe in the land of Mitzrayim. 57 And all countries came into Mitzrayim to Yoseph to buy corn because the famine was so severe in all the lands.

42 Now when Yaakov saw that there was corn in Mitzrayim, Yaakov said to his sons, Why do you look at each other? 2 And he said, See, I have heard that there is corn in Mitzrayim: go down there, and buy from there; that we may live, and not die. 3 And Yoseph's ten brothers went down to buy corn in Mitzrayim.[3] 4 But Benyamin, Yoseph's brother, Yaakov did not send with his brothers; for he said, Perhaps mischief may befall him. 5 And the sons of Yisrael came to buy corn among those that came: for the famine was in the land of Kanaan. 6 And Yoseph was the governor over the land, and it was he that

---

[1] A Hebrew heir with a gentile name and gentile clothes, married to a heathen priestess, yet still a biological Hebrew man later restored to Yisrael; Just as his offspring would one day be, as they would experience the same pattern of restoration.

[2] Despite being Hebrews by birth, Menashshe and Ephraim were assimilated into pagan society, as would be their offspring, the ten tribes of Ephraim-Yisrael.

[3] A picture of the ten tribes in starvation in their exile.

sold to all the people of the land: and Yoseph's brothers came, and bowed down themselves before him with their faces to the earth. 7 And Yoseph saw his brothers, and he knew them, but made himself strange to them, and spoke roughly to them; and he said to them, Where do you come from? And they said, From the land of Kanaan to buy food. 8 And Yoseph knew his brothers, but they knew him not.[1] 9 And Yoseph remembered the dreams that he dreamed about them, and said to them, You are spies; You have come only to see the secrets and operations of the land. 10 And they said to him, No, my master, but to buy food have your avadim come. 11 We are all one man's sons; we are emet men, your avadim are not spies. 12 And he said to them, No, but to see the operations of the land you have come. 13 And they said, Your avadim are twelve brothers, the sons of one man in the land of Kanaan; and, see, the youngest is this day with our abba, and one is not. 14 And Yoseph said to them, That is it what I spoke to you, saying, You are spies: 15 Hereby you shall be proven: By the chayim of Pharaoh you shall not go out from here, except your youngest brother come here. 16 Send one of you, and let him get your brother, and you shall be kept in prison, that your words may be proven, whether there be any emet in you: or else by the chayim of Pharaoh surely you are spies. 17 And he put them all into the prison for three days. 18 And Yoseph said to them the third day, This do, and live; for I fear Elohim: 19 If you are emet men, let one of your brothers be bound in the bayit of your prison: but go, carry corn for the famine of your bayits: 20 But bring your youngest brother to me; so shall your words be verified, and you shall not die. And they did so. 21 And they said one to another, We are truly guilty concerning our brother, in that

we saw the anguish of his being, when he begged us, and we would not listen; therefore is this distress come upon us.[2] 22 And Reuven answered them, saying, Did not I warn you not to sin against the child; and you would not listen? Therefore, see, now his dom is required. 23 And they knew not that Yoseph understood them, for he spoke to them by an interpreter. 24 And he turned himself around from them, and wept; and returned to them again, and communed with them, and took from them Shimeon, and bound him before their eyes. 25 Then Yoseph commanded to fill their sacks with corn, and to restore every man's money into his sack, and to give them provision for the way: and this he did for them. 26 And they loaded their donkeys with the corn, and departed there. 27 And as one of them opened his sack to give his donkey fodder in the inn, he saw his money; for, see, it was in his sack's mouth. 28 And he said to his brothers, My money is restored; and, see, it is even in my sack: and their levim failed them, and they were afraid, saying one to another, What is this that Elohim has done to us? 29 And they came to Yaakov their abba to the land of Kanaan, and told him all that happened to them; saying, 30 The man, who is master of the land, spoke roughly to us, and saw us as spies of his country. 31 And we said to him, We are emet men; we are not spies: 32 We are twelve brothers, sons of our abba; one is not, and the youngest is this day with our abba in the land of Kanaan. 33 And the man, the master of the country, said to us, Hereby shall I know that you are emet men; leave one of your brothers here with me, and take food for the famine of your households, and go: 34 And bring your youngest brother to me: then shall I know that you are not spies, but that you are emet men: so I will deliver your brother to you, and you shall move around freely in the land. 35 And it came to pass as they emptied their sacks, that, see, every man's bundle of money was in his sack: and

---

[1] The same exact situation exists today. Ephraimites or Yospehites can easily recognize Judah and their Jewish brothers. However his Jewish brothers often cannot recognize Joseph, because of their strange gentile names, clothing, foods, holidays and lifestyles.

[2] The inevitable cry of latter-day repentance among Yisrael.

when both they and their abba saw the bundles of money, they were afraid. 36 And Yaakov their abba said to them, All of you have bereaved me of my children: Yoseph is not, and Shimeon is not, and now you will take Benyamin away: all these things are done against me. 37 And Reuven spoke to his abba, saying, Slay my two sons, if I bring him not back to you: deliver him into my hand, and I will bring him to you again. 38 And he said, My son shall not go down with you; for his brother is dead, and he is left alone: if mischief befalls him by the way in which you go, then shall you bring down my old age with sorrow to the grave.

43 And the famine was severe in the land. 2 And it came to pass, when they had eaten up the corn which they had brought out of Mitzrayim, their abba said to them, Go again, buy us a little more food. 3 And Yahudah spoke to him, saying, The man did solemnly warn us, saying, You shall not see my face, except your brother is with you. 4 If you will send our brother with us, we will go down and buy you food: 5 But if you will not send him, we will not go down: for the man said to us, You shall not see my face, except your brother is with you. 6 And Yisrael said, Why did you deal so badly with me, so as to tell the man whether you had another brother? 7 And they said, The man asked us persistently of our state, and of our mishpocha, saying, Is your abba yet alive? Have you another brother? And we answered him according to these words: could we certainly have known that he would say, Bring your brother down? 8 And Yahudah said to Yisrael his abba, Send the lad with me, and we will arise and go; that we may live, and not die, both we, and you, and also our little ones. 9 I will be surety for him; of my hand shall you require him: if I bring him not to you, and set him again before you, then let me bear the blame le-olam-va-ed: 10 For if we had not lingered, surely by now we would have returned this second time. 11 And their abba Yisrael said to them, If it must be so now, do this; take of the best fruits in the land in your vessels, and carry down a present to the man, a little balm, and a little honey, spices, and myrrh, nuts, and almonds: 12 And take double money in your hand; and the money that was brought again in the mouth of your sacks, carry it again in your hand; It could have been a mistake. 13 Take also your brother, and arise, go again to the man: 14 And El-Shaddai give you rachamim before the man, that he may send away your other brother, and Benyamin. If I will be bereaved of my children, I am bereaved. 15 And the men took that present, and they took double money in their hand, and Benyamin; and rose up, and went down to Mitzrayim, and stood before Yoseph. 16 And when Yoseph saw Benyamin with them, he said to the ruler of his bayit, Bring these men home, and make a slaughtering, and make ready; for these men shall dine with me at noon. 17 And the man did as Yoseph asked; and the man brought the men into Yoseph's bayit. 18 And the men were afraid, because they were brought into Yoseph's bayit; and they said, Because of the money that was returned in our sacks at the first time are we brought in; that he may seek occasion against us, and fall upon us, and take us for avadim, and our donkeys. 19 And they came near to the steward of Yoseph's bayit, and they communed with him at the door of the bayit, 20 And said, O sir, we indeed came down the first time to buy food: 21 And it came to pass, when we came to the inn, that we opened our sacks, and, see, every man's money was in the mouth of his sack, our money in full weight: and we have brought it again in our hand. 22 And other money have we brought down in our hands to buy food: we cannot tell who put our money in our sacks. 23 And he said, Shalom be to you, fear not: your Elohim, and the Elohim of your abba, has given you treasure in your sacks: I had your money. And he brought Shimeon out to them. 24 And the man

brought the men into Yoseph's bayit, and gave them mayim, and they washed their feet; and he gave their donkeys fodder. 25 And they made ready the present for Yoseph's coming at noon: for they heard that they should eat lechem there. 26 And when Yoseph came home, they brought him the present that was in their hand into the bayit, and bowed themselves to him to the earth. 27 And he asked them of their welfare, and said, Is your abba well, the old man of whom you spoke? Is he yet alive? 28 And they answered, Your eved our abba is in tov health, he is yet alive. And they bowed down their heads, and made obeisance. 29 And he lifted up his eyes, and saw his brother Benyamin, his ima's son, and said, Is this your younger brother, about whom you spoke to me? And he said, Elohim give you unmerited favor, my son. 30 And Yoseph hurried; for his emotions did yearn for his brother: and he sought somewhere to weep; and he entered into his room, and wept there. 31 And he washed his face, and went out to refrain himself, and said, Serve the food. 32 And they set the table for him by himself, and for them by themselves, and for the Mitzrites by themselves, because the Mitzrites do not eat lechem with the Ivrim, for that is an abomination to the Mitzrites.[1] 33 And they sat before him, the bachor according to his birthright, and the youngest according to his youth: and the men marveled at one another. 34 And he took and sent portions to them from before him: but Benyamin's portion was five times as much as any of theirs. And they drank, and had simcha with him.

44 And he commanded the steward of his bayit, saying, Fill the men's sacks with food, as much as they can carry, and put every man's money in his sack's mouth. 2 And put my cup, the silver cup, in the sack's mouth of the youngest, and his

corn money. And he did according to the word that Yoseph had spoken. 3 As soon as the morning was light, the men were sent away, they and their donkeys. 4 And when they were gone out of the city, and not that far off, Yoseph said to his steward, Rise up, follow the men; and when you do overtake them, say to them, Why have you rewarded evil for tov? 5 Is not this cup the one from which my master drinks, and by which he divines? You have done evil in so doing. 6 And he overtook them, and he spoke to them these same words. 7 And they said to him, Why says my master these words? Elohim forbid that your avadim should do according to this thing: 8 See, the money, which we found in our sacks' mouths, we brought again to you out of the land of Kanaan: why then should we steal out of your master's bayit his silver or gold? 9 With whomever of your avadim it is found, let him die, and we also will be my master's avadim. 10 And he said, Now also let it be according to your words; he with whom it is found shall be my eved; and you shall be blameless. 11 Then they speedily took down every man his sack to the ground, and opened every man his sack. 12 And he searched, and began at the eldest, and stopped at the youngest: and the cup was found in Benyamin's sack. 13 Then they tore their clothes, and loaded every man his donkey and returned to the city. 14 And Yahudah and his brothers came to Yoseph's bayit; for he was still there: and they fell before him to the ground. 15 And Yoseph said to them, What deed is this that you have done? Did you not know that such a man as I can certainly divine? 16 And Yahudah said, What shall we say to my master? What shall we speak? Or how shall we clear ourselves? Elohim has found out the iniquity of your avadim: see, we are my master's avadim, both we, and he also with whom the cup is found. 17 And he said, Elohim forbid that I should do so: but the man in whose hand the cup is found, he

---

[1] Actually it is the other way around. Yisraelites ought not to share unclean food with heathen at heathen tables of fellowship. If worldly people in Egypt understand this why don't Yisraelites?

shall be my eved; and as for the rest of you, go in shalom to your abba.

Torah Parsha 11
Vayigash 41:18-47:27
Haftarah Yehchezkel 37:15-28
Brit Chadasha Yochanan 10:11-19

18 Then Yahudah came near to him, and said, Oh my master; please let your eved speak a word in my master's ears, and let not your anger burn against your eved: for you are even as Pharaoh. 19 My master asked his avadim, saying, Have you an abba, or a brother? 20 And we said to my master, We have an abba, an old man, and a child of his old age, a little one; and his brother is dead, and he alone is left of his ima, and his abba loves him. 21 And you did you say to your avadim, Bring him down to me, that I may set my eyes upon him. 22 And we said to my master, The lad cannot leave his abba: for if he should leave his abba, his abba would die. 23 And you did you say to your avadim, Except your youngest brother come down with you, you shall see my face no more. 24 And it came to pass when we came up to your eved my abba, we told him the words of my master. 25 And our abba said, Go again, and buy us a little food. 26 And we said, We cannot go down: if our youngest brother be with us, then will we go down: for we may not see the man's face, except our youngest brother be with us. 27 And your eved my abba said to us, You know that my wife bore me two sons: 28 And the one went out from me, and I said, Surely he is torn in pieces; and I saw him not since: 29 And if you take this one also from me, and mischief befall him, you shall bring down my old age with sorrow to the grave. 30 Now therefore when I come to your eved my abba, and the lad is not with us; seeing that his chayim is bound up in the lad's chayim; 31 It shall come to pass, when he sees that the lad is not with us, that he will die: and your avadim shall bring down the old age of your eved our abba with sorrow to the grave. 32 For your eved

became surety for the lad to my abba, saying, If I bring him not again to you, then I shall bear the blame to my abba le-olam-va-ed. 33 Now therefore, please, let your eved stay instead of the lad an eved to my master; and let the lad go up with his brothers.[1] 34 For how shall I go up to my abba, and the lad be not with me? For then I will see the evil that would come on my abba.

45 Then Yoseph could not refrain himself before all them that stood by him; and he cried, Make every man to go out from me. And there stood no man with him, while Yoseph made himself known to his brothers.[2] 2 And he wept aloud: and the Mitzrites and the bayit of Pharaoh heard. 3 And Yoseph said to his brothers, I am Yoseph;[3] does my abba still live? And his brothers could not answer him; for they were trembling at his presence. 4 And Yoseph said to his brothers, Come near to me please. And they came near. And he said, I am Yoseph your brother, whom you sold into Mitzrayim. 5 Now therefore be not grieved, nor angry with yourselves that you sold me here: for Elohim did send me before you to preserve chayim.[4] 6 For these two years have the famine been in the land: and yet there are still five more years, in which there shall be neither ploughing nor harvest. 7 And Elohim sent me before you to preserve for you a remnant[5] in the earth, and to save your lives by a great deliverance. 8 So now it was not you that sent me here, but Elohim: and He has made me an abba to Pharaoh, and master of all his bayit, and a ruler throughout all the land of Mitzrayim. 9 Hurry, and go up to my abba,

---

[1] Yahudah seeks leadership in the family as guardian
[2] Declaring yourself to your Jewish brethren as Joseph returning and revealed is a painful and trying experience for many.
[3] The cry of restoration.
[4] Like their father Joseph, YHWH sent Ephraim to preserve life into the **olam** as dispersed Yisrael in order to preserve and proclaim eternal life through the Tov News of Moshiach's Kingdom.
[5] Only a remnant from both houses of physical Yisrael will be saved.

and say to him, This says your son Yoseph, Elohim has made me master of all Mitzrayim: come down to me, do not delay: 10 And you shall dwell in the land of Goshen, and you shall be near to me, you, and your children, and your children's children, and your flocks, and your herds, and all that you have: 11 And there will I nourish you; for there are still five years of famine; lest you, and your household, and all that you have, come to poverty. 12 And, see, your eyes see, and the eyes of my brother Benyamin, that it is my mouth that speaks to you. 13 And you shall tell my abba of all my tifereth in Mitzrayim, and of all that you have seen; and you shall hurry and bring down my abba here. 14 And he fell upon his brother Benyamin's neck, and wept; and Benyamin wept upon his neck. 15 Moreover he kissed all his brothers, and wept upon them: and after that his brothers talked with him.[1] 16 And the report was heard in Pharaoh's bayit, saying, Yoseph's brothers have come: and it pleased Pharaoh well, and his avadim. 17 And Pharaoh said to Yoseph, Say to your brothers, This do; load your beasts, and go, into the land of Kanaan; 18 And take your abba and your households, and come to me: and I will give you the tov of the land of Mitzrayim, and you shall eat the fat of the land. 19 Now you are commanded, this do; take wagons out of the land of Mitzrayim for your little ones, and for your wives, and bring your abba, and come. 20 Also do not worry about your items; for the tov of all the land of Mitzrayim is now yours. 21 And the children of Yisrael did so: and Yoseph gave them wagons, according to the commandment of Pharaoh, and gave them provision for the way. 22 To all of them he gave each man changes of clothing; but to Benyamin he gave three hundred pieces of silver, and five changes of clothing. 23 And to his abba he sent the following; ten donkeys loaded with the tov things of Mitzrayim, and ten female donkeys loaded with corn and lechem and food for his abba by the way. 24 So he sent his brothers away, and they departed: and he said to them, See that you don't quarrel on the way. 25 And they went up out of Mitzrayim, and came into the land of Kanaan to Yaakov their abba, 26 And told him, saying, Yoseph is still alive, and he is governor over all the land of Mitzrayim. And Yaakov's lev fainted, for he believed them not. 27 And they told him all the words of Yoseph that he had said to them: and when he saw the wagons that Yoseph had sent to carry him, the ruach of Yaakov their abba revived:[2] 28 And Yisrael said, It is enough; Yoseph my son is still alive: I will go and see him before I die.

46 And Yisrael took his journey with all that he had, and came to Beer-Sheva, and offered sacrifices to the Elohim of his abba Yitzchak. 2 And Elohim spoke to Yisrael in the visions of the night, and said, *Yaakov, Yaakov.* And he said, Hinayni. 3 And He said, *I am El, the El of your abba: fear not to go down into Mitzrayim; for I will there make of you a great nation – a goy[3] gadol:[4] 4 I will go down with you into Mitzrayim; and I will also surely bring you up again: and Yoseph shall put his hand upon your eyes.* 5 And Yaakov rose up from Beer-Sheva: and the sons of Yisrael carried Yaakov their abba, and their little ones, and their wives, in the wagons that Pharaoh had sent to carry him. 6 And they took their cattle, and their items, which they had gotten in the land of Kanaan, and came into Mitzrayim, Yaakov, and all his zera with him: 7 His sons, and his sons' sons with him, his daughters, and his sons' daughters, and all his zera he brought with him into Mitzrayim. 8 And these are the names of the children of Yisrael, who came into Mitzrayim, Yaakov and his sons: Reuven,

---

[1] Dialogue as equal heirs along with repentance will lead to reconciliation and restoration.

[2] Yospeh's revelation of himself will bring revival to Yisrael.
[3] Yisrael called YHWH's **goy**.
[4] There (in spite of famine) physical multiplication will begin in earnest.

Yaakov's bachor. 9 And the sons of Reuven; Hanoch, and Phallu, and Hetzron, and Carmi. 10 And the sons of Shimeon; Yemu-El, and Yamin, and Ohad, and Yachin, and Tzoar, and Shaul the son of a Canaanitish woman. 11 And the sons of Levi; Gershon, Kohath, and Merari. 12 And the sons of Yahudah; Er, and Onan, and Shelah, and Pharez, and Zerah: but Er and Onan died in the land of Kanaan.[1] And the sons of Pharez were Hetzron and Hamul. 13 And the sons of Yissacher; Tola, and Phuvah, and Iyov, and Shimron. 14 And the sons of Zevulon; Sered, and Elon, and Yahle-El. 15 These are the sons of Leah, which she bore to Yaakov in Padan-Aram, with his daughter Dinah: all the beings of his sons and his daughters were thirty-three. 16 And the sons of Gad; Ziphion, and Haggi, Shuni, and Ezvon, Eri, and Arodi, and Areli. 17 And the sons of Asher; Yimnah, and Ishuah, and Isui, and Beriyah, and Serah their sister: and the sons of Beriyah; Hever, and Malchi-El. 18 These are the sons of Zilpah, whom Lavan gave to Leah his daughter, and these she bore to Yaakov, even sixteen beings. 19 The sons of Rachel Yaakov's wife; Yoseph, and Benyamin. 20 And to Yoseph in the land of Mitzrayim were born Menashsheh and Ephraim, who Asenath the daughter of Poti-Pherah kohen of On bore to him. 21 And the sons of Benyamin were Belah, and Becher, and Ashvel, Gera, and Naaman, Ehi, and Rosh, Muppim, and Huppim, and Ard. 22 These are the sons of Rachel, who were born to Yaakov: all the beings were fourteen. 23 And the sons of Dan; Hushim. 24 And the sons of Naphtali; Yahze-El, and Guni, and Yezer, and Shillem. 25 These are the sons of Bilhah, who Lavan gave to Rachel his daughter, and she bore these to Yaakov: all the beings were seven. 26 All the beings that came with Yaakov into Mitzrayim, who came out of his loins, besides Yaakov's sons' wives, all the beings were sixty-six. 27 And the sons of Yoseph, who were born to him in Mitzrayim, were two beings: all the beings of Beit Yaakov, who came into Mitzrayim, were seventy-five.[2] 28 And he sent Yahudah before him to Yoseph, to direct his face to Goshen; and they came into the land of Goshen.[3] 29 And Yoseph made ready his chariot, and went up to meet Yisrael his abba, in Goshen, and presented himself before him; and he fell on his neck, and wept on his neck a long while. 30 And Yisrael said to Yoseph, Now let me die, since I have seen your face, because you are still alive. 31 And Yoseph said to his brothers, and to his abba's bayit, I will go up, and show Pharaoh, and say to him, My brothers, and my abba's bayit, who were in the land of Kanaan, have come to me; 32 And the men are shepherds, for their trade has been to feed cattle; and they have brought their flocks, and their herds, and all that they have. 33 And it shall come to pass, when Pharaoh shall call you, and shall say, What is your occupation? 34 That you shall say, Your avadim's trade has been with cattle from our youth even until now, both we, and also our ahvot: that you may dwell in the land of Goshen; le-olam-va-ed shepherd is an abomination to the Mitzrites.[4]

47 Then Yoseph came and told Pharaoh, and said, My abba and my brothers, and their flocks, and their herds, and all that they have, came out of the land of Kanaan; and, see, they are in the land of Goshen. 2 And he took some of his brothers, even five men, and presented them to Pharaoh. 3 And Pharaoh said to his brothers, What is your occupation? And they said to Pharaoh, Your avadim are shepherds, both we, and also our ahvot. 4 They said moreover to Pharaoh, To sojourn in the land we have come; for your avadim have no pasture for their flocks; for the famine is severe in the land of Kanaan:

---

[1] For violating the Torah principle of physical multiplicity.

[2] According to the LXX, Dead Sea Scrolls and the Brit Chadasha.
[3] Yahudah will lead the way in the restoration, when they behold two-house truth and Yahshua in all its fullness.
[4] Restored Yisrael is to be a nation of shepherds of truth and love in the midst of a pagan culture.

therefore we ask you, let your avadim dwell in the land of Goshen. 5 And Pharaoh spoke to Yoseph, saying, Your abba and your brothers have come to you: 6 The land of Mitzrayim is before you; in the best of the land make your abba and brothers to dwell; in the land of Goshen let them dwell: and if you know any able men among them, then make them rulers over my cattle. 7 And Yoseph brought in Yaakov his abba, and set him before Pharaoh: and Yaakov blessed Pharaoh. 8 And Pharaoh said to Yaakov, How old are you? 9 And Yaakov said to Pharaoh, The days of the years of my pilgrimage[1] are a hundred thirty years: few and evil have the days ot the years ot my chayim been, and I have not attained to the days of the years of the chayim of my ahvot in the days of their pilgrimage. 10 And Yaakov blessed Pharaoh, and went out from before Pharaoh. 11 And Yoseph placed his abba and his brothers, and gave them a possession in the land of Mitzrayim, in the best of the land, in the land of Rameses, as Pharaoh had commanded. 12 And Yoseph nourished his abba, and his brothers, and his abba's entire household, with lechem, according to their mishpachot. 13 And there was no lechem in all the land; for the famine was very sore, so that the land of Mitzrayim and all the land of Kanaan grew weak because of thc famine. 14 And Yoseph gathered up all the money that was found in the land of Mitzrayim, and in the land of Kanaan, for the corn which they bought: and Yoseph brought the money into Pharaoh's bayit. 15 And when money failed in the land of Mitzrayim, and in the land of Kanaan, all the Mitzrites came to Yoseph, and said, Give us lechem: for why should we die in your presence? For the money is gone. 16 And Yoseph said, Give me your cattle; and I will give you food for your cattle, if the money is gone. 17 And they brought their cattle to Yoseph: and Yoseph gave them lechem in exchange for horses, and for the flocks, and for the cattle of the herds, and for the donkeys: and he fed them with lechem for all their cattle for that year. 18 When that year ended, they came to him the second year, and said to him, We will not hide it from my master, how that our money is spent; my master also has our herds of cattle; there is nothing left in the sight of my master, but our bodies, and our lands: 19 Why shall we die before your eyes, both our land and us? Buy us and our land for lechem, and we will be avadim to Pharaoh: and give us zera, that we may live, and not die, that the land be not desolate. 20 And Yoseph bought all the land of Mitzrayim for Pharaoh; for the Mitzrites sold every man his field, because the famine prevailed over them: so the land became Pharaoh's. 21 And as for the people, he removed them to cities from one end of the borders of Mitzrayim even to the other end of it. 22 Only the land of the kohanim bought he not; for the kohanim had a portion assigned to them by Pharaoh, and did eat their portion which Pharaoh gave them: That is why they did not sell their lands. 23 Then Yoseph said to the people, See, I have bought you this day and your land for Pharaoh: look, here is zera for you, and you shall sow the land. 24 And it shall come to pass in the increase, that you shall give the fifth part to Pharaoh, and four parts shall be your own, for zera of the field, and for your food, and for those of your households, and for food for your little ones. 25 And they said, You have saved our lives: let us find favor in the sight of my master, and we will be Pharaoh's avadim. 26 And Yoseph made it a law over the land of Mitzrayim to this day, that Pharaoh should have the fifth part; except the land of the kohanim, which did not become Pharaoh's. 27 And Yisrael dwelt in the land of Mitzrayim, in the country of Goshen; and they had possessions in it, and grew, and multiplied exceedingly.

[1] Note the correct attitude of a born again Yisraelite. The earth is not our home in this age, but in the age to come –olam habah - when the heavens and earth will become one, even as the two houses are becoming one.

Torah Parsha 12
Vayechi 47:28-50:26
Haftarah Melechim Alef 2:1-12
Brit Chadasha Ivrim 11:21-22
Kepha Alef 2:11-17

28 And Yaakov lived in the land of Mitzrayim seventeen years: so the whole age of Yaakov was a hundred forty-seven years. 29 And the time drew near that Yisrael must die: and he called his son Yoseph, and said to him, If now I have found favor in your sight, Please put your hand under my thigh for the oath, and deal in chesed and emet with me. Please do not bury me in Mitzrayim: 30 But I will lie with my ahvot, and you shall carry me out of Mitzrayim, and bury me in their burial-place. And he said, I will do as you have said. 31 And he said, Swear to me. And he swore to him. And Yisrael bowed himself upon the bed's head.

48 And it came to pass after these things, that one told Yoseph, See, your abba is sick: and he took with him his two sons, Menashsheh and Ephraim. 2 And one told Yaakov, and said, See, your son Yoseph comes to you: and Yisrael strengthened himself, and sat upon the bed. 3 And Yaakov said to Yoseph, El-Shaddai appeared to me at Luz in the land of Kanaan, and blessed me, 4 And said to me, *See, I will make you fruitful, and multiply you, and I will make you into a congregation of nations – kahal amim;[1] and will give this land to your zera after you for an everlasting possession.* 5 And now your two sons, Ephraim and Menashsheh, who were born to you in the land of Mitzrayim before I came to you in Mitzrayim, are mine; as Reuven and Shimeon, they shall be mine.[2] 6 And your issue, which you beget

after them, shall be yours, and shall be called after the name of their brothers in their inheritance.[3] 7 And as for me, when I came from Padan, Rachel died next to me in the land of Kanaan on the way, when yet there was but a little way to come to Ephrath: and I buried her there in the way of Ephrath; the same is Beth-Lechem. 8 And Yisrael beheld Yoseph's sons, and said, Who are these?[4] 9 And Yoseph said to his abba, They are my sons, whom Elohim has given me in this place. And he said, Please bring them to me, and I will bless them. 10 Now the eyes of Yisrael were dim for age, so that he could not see. And he brought them near to him; and he kissed them, and embraced them. 11 And Yisrael said to Yoseph, I had not thought to see your face ever again: and, see, Elohim has shown me also your zera. 12 And Yoseph brought them out from between his knees, and he bowed himself with his face to the earth. 13 And Yoseph took them both, Ephraim in his right hand toward Yisrael's left hand, and Menashsheh in his left hand toward Yisrael's right hand, and brought them near to him.[5] 14 And Yisrael stretched out his right hand, and laid it upon Ephraim's head, who was the younger, and his left hand upon Menashsheh's head, guiding his hands wittingly; for Menashsheh was the bachor.[6] 15 And he blessed Yoseph, and said, Elohim, before whom my ahvot Avraham and Yitzchak did have their halacha, the Elohim who fed me all my chayim long to this day, 16 The Malach who redeemed me from all evil,[7] bless the lads; and let my name-Yisrael be named on

---

[1] Le kahal amim or congregation of nations as fulfilled by Moshiach the Restorer of our nation, who has assembled a congregation from out of all the scattered Yisraelite nations.
[2] A profound event and declaration. They are Yaakov's physical grandchildren, and as such they are already physical Yisrael. But here he equates them to a status of his sons, not merely his grandsons, and officially places them into the tribal equation.

[3] Yisrael demands that Ephraim and Menashsheh be considered and verbally called Yisrael/Yisraelites along with all their children for all future generations.
[4] Perhaps Yisrael is testing Yoseph to see if he grasped the prior declarations. Of course his sight is diminishing as well.
[5] The right hand is the one of imparted favor and blessing. Reserved for the firstborn.
[6] This is no mistake. Notice the term "wittingly." YHWH was taking the next step to bring about Yisrael's growth, division and end-time regathering.
[7] The Malach of His Presence, or Yahshua, called the guardian or Metatron who alone can redeem from sin's wages.

them,[1] and the name of my ahvot Avraham and Yitzchak; and let them grow into a multitude like fish –Vayi-dag-oo lerov[2] in the midst of the earth. 17 And when Yoseph saw that his abba laid his right hand upon the head of Ephraim, it displeased him: and he held up his abba's hand, to remove it from Ephraim's head to Menashsheh's head. 18 And Yoseph said to his abba, Not so, my abba: for this is the bachor; put your right hand upon his head.[3] 19 And his abba refused, and said, I know it, my son, I know it:[4] he also shall become a people,[5] and he also shall be great: but truly his younger brother shall be greater than him, and his zera shall become the fullness of the nations – melo ha-goyim.[6] 20 And he blessed them that day,[7] saying, In you shall Yisrael bless, saying, Elohim make you as Ephraim and as Menashsheh:[8] and he set Ephraim before Menashsheh. [9] 21 And Yisrael said to Yoseph, See, I die: but Elohim shall be with you, and bring you again to the land of your ahvot.[10] 22 Moreover I have given to you one portion above your brothers that I took out of the hand of the Amorite with my sword and with my bow.[11]

49 And Yaakov called to his sons, and said, Gather yourselves together,[12] that I may tell you that which shall befall you in the last days.[13] [14] 2 Gather yourselves together, and listen, you sons of Yaakov, and listen to Yisrael your abba. 3 Reuven, you are my bachor, my might, and the beginning of my strength, the excellency of dignity, and the excellency of power: 4 Unstable as mayim, you shall not excel; because you went up to your abba's bed; then you defiled it: he went up to my couch.[15] 5 Shimeon and Levi are brothers; instruments of cruelty are in their dwellings. 6 O my being, come not into their secret; let not my honor, be united to their congregation:[16] for in their anger they killed a man, and in their displeasure and self-will they they hamstrung an ox in pleasure. 7 Cursed be their anger, for it was fierce; and their anger, for it was cruel: I will divide them in Yaakov, and scatter them in Yisrael. 8 Yahudah, you are he whom your brothers shall hallel: your hand shall be on the neck of your enemies; your abba's children shall bow down before you. 9 Yahudah is a lion's whelp: from the prey, my son, you have gone up: he stooped down; he couched as a lion, and as an old lion; who shall rouse him up? 10 The scepter shall not depart from Yahudah nor a lawgiver from between His feet, until Shiloh comes; To Him shall the gathering of the

[1] His name was Yisrael, and he declares again that Ephraim's and Menashsheh's descendants are physical Yisrael carrying that very literal name.
[2] **Vayidagoo lerov**, may they grow into a multitude of fish in the midst of the olam or earth. This is an amazing prophecy, whereby YHWH through the dying man Yisrael, pinpoints that the offspring of the people of Ephraim and Menashsheh, known later on as the 10 tribes (not two), would literally fill the globe with Yisraelites. We see the ingathering officially begin later in Mattityahu/Matthew 4:19, where the disciples are sent to fish for the men of Yisrael and are called to be Yahshua's fishermen sent to catch the wandering and floating fish of Yisrael in the midst of all the earth.
[3] Man's ways are not YHWH's ways.
[4] Yaakov knew what he was doing in the Spirit. Do you?
[5] Could this be a specific nation?
[6] **Melo ha-goyim** or the "fullness of the gentiles." Ephraim's seed later collected in the ten tribes of the northern kingdom would produce the "fullness of the gentiles." This is a marvelous revelation that most so-called gentiles are in fact Yisrael's physical children. Of course, they still need dom-atonement-salvation to become true redeemed remnant Yisrael. Paul confirms this clear understanding in Romans 11:25-26, when he speaks of the "fullness of the gentiles" as those who will come in as believing Yisrael in the last of the last days.
[7] He sealed the revelation through prayer and the laying on of hands, a Yisraelite custom.
[8] This sealing of Yisrael's non-Jewish peoples is still found in the Jewish Daily Prayer book - the siddur.
[9] For Yahshua's assembly is greater than any individual physical nation. Yahshua's nation is both physical and spiritual Yisrael, as opposed to a mere physical nation.
[10] Yoseph is once again declaring this truth. Ephraim, or the ten tribes are even now returning to the land of Yisrael.

[11] The wealth of the gentile heathen Amorites are laid up for redeemed Yisrael. Yisrael is the head and never the tail. Do not let anyone steal your birthright as the firstborn.
[12] All twelve tribes will be gathered in the last days. That is why this message is in the forefront of YHWH's agenda at this point in man's history.
[13] This bedside meeting is a plain foreshadow of Yisrael's sons gathered to hear YHWH's word in the latter days.
[14] An in-depth study on these tribal fulfillments is at http://yourarmstoisrael.org/Articles_new/articles/?page=tribes&type=6.
[15] Firstborn status transferred to Ephraim.
[16] A type of any assembly or religious institution that destroys those who teach Renewed Covenant circumcision as did these sons in the incident in Shechem (chapter 34), destroying newly circumcised covenant men desiring to join Yisrael. Let Yisrael heed Jacob's warning not to be joined to such foolishness.

nations be.[1] [2] 11 Binding his foal to the vine, and his donkey's colt to the choice vine; he washed his garments in wine, and his clothes in the dom of grapes:[3] 12 His eyes shall be red with wine, and his teeth white with milk. 13 Zevulon shall dwell at the haven of the sea; and he shall be for a haven of ships; and his border shall be to Tzidon. 14 Yissacher is a strong donkey couching down between two burdens:[4] 15 And he saw that rest was tov, and the land that it was pleasant; and bowed his shoulder to bear, and became an eved to tribute. 16 Dan shall shophet his people, as one of the tribes of Yisrael. 17 Dan shall be a serpent in the Way,[5] an adder in the path that bites the horse's heels, so that its rider shall fall backward.[6] 18 I have waited for Your Yahshua, O יהוה. 19 Gad, a troop shall overcome him: but he shall overcome at the end. 20 Out of Asher his lechem shall be fat, and he shall yield royal dainties. 21 Naphtali is a deer let loose: he gives beautiful words. 22 Yoseph is a fruitful bough, even a fruitful bough by a well; whose branches run over the wall: 23 The archers have severely grieved him, and shot at him, and hated him: 24 But his bow abode in strength, and the arms of his hands were made strong by the hands of the Mighty Elohim of Yaakov; (from there comes the Shepherd, the Stone of Yisrael) 25 Even by the El of your abba, who shall help you; and by the Almighty, who shall bless you with brachot of the shamayim above, brachot of the deep that lies beneath, brachot of the breasts, and of the womb:

26 The brachot of your abba have prevailed above the brachot of my ancestors to the utmost border of the everlasting hills: they shall be on the head of Yoseph, and on the keter of the head of him that was separate from his brothers.[7] 27 Benyamin shall tear as a wolf: in the morning he shall devour the prey, and at night he shall divide the plunder. 28 All these are the twelve tribes of Yisrael: and this is what their abba spoke to them, and blessed them; every one according to his bracha he blessed them. 29 And he charged them, and said to them, I am to be gathered to my people: bury me with my ahvot in the cave that is in the field of Ephron the Hittite, 30 In the cave that is in the field of Machpelah, which is before Mamre, in the land of Kanaan, that Avraham bought along with the field of Ephron the Hittite for a possession for a burial-place. 31 There they buried Avraham and Sarah his wife; there they buried Yitzchak and Rivkah his wife; and there I buried Leah. 32 The purchase of the field and of the cave that is there was from the children of Cheth. 33 And when Yaakov had made an end of commanding his sons, he gathered up his feet into the bed, and yielded up the ruach, and was gathered to his people.

50 And Yoseph fell upon his abba's face, and wept upon him, and kissed him. 2 And Yoseph commanded his avadim the physicians to embalm his abba: and the physicians embalmed Yisrael. 3 And forty days were fulfilled for him; for so are fulfilled the days of those who are embalmed: and the Mitzrites mourned for him seventy days. 4 And when the days of his mourning were past, Yoseph spoke to the bayit of Pharaoh, saying, If now I have found favor in your eyes, please speak to Pharaoh, saying, 5 My abba made me swear, saying, See, I desire to die in my grave that I have dug for myself in the land of Kanaan, there shall you bury me. Now

---

[1] The end-time Yisraelite nations gathered into one, along with all other non-biological Yisraelite believing peoples, who have joined as friends through Moshiach's dom. See notes on Ezekiel, chapter 37:16-28.
[2] Covered in detail at:
http://yourarmstoisrael.org/Articles_new/restoration/?page=21 &type=12.
[3] His (Moshiach's) dom likened unto grapes of red.
[4] Many who love and long for Yisrael's two-house restoration can be found carrying burdens and love for both houses, and are from Zevulon.
[5] Early Torah keeping believers were called the "Way."
[6] The latter-day anti-Moshiach will come from Dan, biting Yahshua on the white horse (Rev. 19:11), causing Yaakov to cry out for YHWH's deliverance during "Yaakov's Trouble," as they experience the hate of Dan's anti-Moshiach, as seen in the very next verse.

[7] Remains true today.

therefore let me go up, please, and bury my abba, and I will return again. 6 And Pharaoh said, Go up, and bury your abba, even as he made you swear. 7 And Yoseph went up to bury his abba: and with him went up all the avadim of Pharaoh, the shamashim of his bayit, and all the shamashim of the land of Mitzrayim, 8 And all of Beit Yoseph, and his brothers, and his abba's bayit: only their little ones, and their flocks, and their herds, they left in the land of Goshen. 9 And there went up with him both mirkavot and horsemen: and it was a very great company. 10 And they came to the threshing floor of Atad, which is beyond the Yarden River, and there they mourned with a great and very severe lamentation: and he mourned for his abba sheva yamim.[1] 11 And when the inhabitants of the land, the Kanaanites, saw the mourning in the floor of Atad, they said, This is a severe mourning to the Mitzrites: Therefore the name of it was called Hevel-Mitzraim, which is beyond the Yarden. 12 And his sons did to him according to all he commanded them: 13 For his sons carried him into the land of Kanaan, and buried him in the cave of the field of Machpelah, that Avraham bought along with the field as a possession for a burial-place from Ephron the Hittite, before Mamre. 14 And Yoseph returned into Mitzrayim, he, and his brothers, and all that went up with him to bury his abba, after he had buried his abba. 15 And when Yoseph's brothers saw that their abba was dead, they said, Yoseph maybe will hate us, and will certainly repay us all the evil that we did to him. 16 And they sent a messenger to Yoseph, saying, Your abba did command before he died, saying,

17 So shall you say to Yoseph, Please forgive the trespass of your brothers, for their sin; for they did to you evil: and now, we beg you, forgive the trespass of the avadim of the Elohim of your abba. And Yoseph wept when they spoke to him. 18 And his brothers also went and fell down before his face; and they said, See, we will be your avadim. 19 And Yoseph said to them, Fear not: for am I in the place of Elohim? 20 But as for you, you thought evil against me; but Elohim meant it for tov, to bring to pass, as it is this day, to save many people alive. 21 Now therefore fear not: I will nourish you, and your little ones. And he comforted them, and spoke kindly to them. 22 And Yoseph dwelt in Mitzrayim, he, and his abba's bayit: and Yoseph lived a hundred ten years. 23 And Yoseph saw Ephraim's children until the third generation: the children also of Machir, the son Menashsheh, were brought up upon Yoseph's knees. 24 And Yoseph said to his brothers, I will soon die: and Elohim will surely visit you, and bring you out of this land to the land which he swore to Avraham, to Yitzchak, and to Yaakov. 25 And Yoseph took an oath from the children of Yisrael, saying, Elohim will surely visit you, and you shall carry up my bones from here. 26 So Yoseph died, being a hundred ten years old: and they embalmed him, and he was put in a coffin in Mitzrayim.

Chazak Chazak VeNitchazak
Be Strong Be Strong!
And May We Be Strengthened!

---

[1] This is the origin of the Yisraelite custom of sitting **shiva**, or sitting for seven days of mourning for the dead.

שמות

Shemoth - Exodus
To Our Forefathers Yisrael

Torah Parsha 13
Shemot 1:1-6:1
Haftarah Yeshayahu 27:6-28:13
Brit Chadasha Yochanan 17:1-26

1 Now these are the shemot of the children of Yisrael, which came into Mitzrayim; every man and his household came with Yaakov. 2 Reuven, Shimeon, Levi, and Yahudah, 3 Yissacher, Zevulun, and Benyamin, 4 Dan, and Naphtali, Gad, and Asher. 5 And all the beings that came.out of the waists of Yaakov were seventy-five [1] beings: for Yoseph was in Mitzrayim already. 6 And Yoseph died, and all his brothers, and all that generation. 7 And the children of Yisrael were fruitful, and increased abundantly, and multiplied, and became exceeding mighty; and the land was filled with them.[2] 8 Now there arose up a new melech over Mitzrayim, who knew not Yoseph. 9 And he said to his people, See, the people of the children of Yisrael are more and mightier than us:[3] 10 Come, let us ephah wisely with them; lest they multiply, and it come to pass, that, when there comes upon us any war, they join with our enemies, and fight against us, and then leave the land. 11 Therefore they did set over them eved-masters to afflict them with their burdens. And they built for Pharaoh the treasure cities, of Pithom and Raamses. 12 But the more they afflicted them, the more they multiplied and grew.[4] And they were grieved because of the children of Yisrael. 13 And the Mitzrites made the children of Yisrael to serve with harshness:

14 And they made their lives bitter with hard bondage, with mortar, and with brick, and with all manner of service in the field: all their service, which they made them serve, was with harshness. 15 And the melech of Mitzrayim spoke to the Ivree midwives, of which the name of the one was Shiphrah, and the name of the other Puah: 16 And he said, When you perform the office of a midwife to the Ivree women, and see them upon the stools; if it be a son, then you shall kill him: but if it be a daughter, then she shall live.[5] 17 But the midwives feared Elohim, and did not obey what the melech of Mitzrayim commanded them, but saved the male children alive. 18 And the melech of Mitzrayim called for the midwives, and said to them, Why have you done this thing, and have saved the male children alive? 19 And the midwives said to Pharaoh, Because the Ivree women are not as the Mitzrite women; for they are lively, and are delivered before the midwives come in to help them. 20 Therefore Elohim dealt well with the midwives: and the people multiplied, and became very mighty. [6] 21 And it came to pass, because the midwives feared Elohim, that He made them batiym. 22 And Pharaoh charged all his people, saying, Every son that is born to you, him shall you cast into the river, but every daughter you shall save alive.

2 And there went a man from the bayit of Levi, and took as a wife a daughter of Levi. 2 And the woman conceived, and bore a son: and when she saw him that he was a beautiful child, she hid him three months. 3 And when she could not longer hide him, she took for him an ark of wicker,

---

[1] LXX, Dead Sea Scrolls, and Brit Chadasha say 75.
[2] The promise of physical multiplicity was already quite active, leading to the entire episode on just how Pharaoh would deal with his problem and their promise. He decided to use murder to stop Yisrael's calling to fill the nations with the zera of Jacob.
[3] See note on verse 7.
[4] A principle that would be eternal. They would fill every nation where they were dispersed in spite of persecution and often because of persecution.
[5] The world's "final solution" to Yisrael's blessing and favor is genocide. A pattern seen throughout the centuries.
[6] As promised.

and coated it with slime and with pitch, and put the child inside; and she laid it in the reeds by the river's bank. 4 And his sister stood far off, to know what would happen to him. 5 And the daughter of Pharaoh came down to wash herself at the river; and her female servants walked along by the river's side; and when she saw the ark among the reeds, she sent her eved to get it. 6 And when she had opened it, she saw the child: and, see, the baby wept. And she had compassion on him, and said, This is one of the Ivree's children. 7 Then said his sister to Pharaoh's daughter, Shall I go and call for you a nurse from the Ivree women, that she may nurse the child for you? 8 And Pharaoh's daughter said to her, Go. And the eved went and called the child's ima. 9 And Pharaoh's daughter said to her, Take this child away, and nurse it for me, and I will give you your wages. And the woman took the child, and nursed it. 10 And the child grew, and she brought him to Pharaoh's daughter, and he became her son. And she called his name Moshe: [1] and she said, Because I drew him out of the mayim. 11 And it came to pass in those days, when Moshe was grown, that he went out to his brothers, and looked on their burdens: and he saw a Mitzrite smiting a Ivree, one of his brothers. 12 And he looked all around, and when he saw that there was no man, he killed the Mitzrite, and hid him in the sand. 13 And when he went out the second day, see, two men of the Ivrim argued together: and he said to him that did the wrong, Why did you smite your neighbor? 14 And he said, Who made you a prince and a shophet over us? Do you intend to kill me, as you killed the Mitzrite? And Moshe feared, and said, Surely this thing is known. 15 Now when Pharaoh heard this thing, he sought to slay Moshe. But Moshe fled from the face of Pharaoh, and dwelt in the land of Midyan: and he sat down by a well. 16 Now the kohen of Midyan had seven daughters: and they came and drew mayim, and filled the bowls to mayim their abba's flock. 17 And the shepherds came and drove them away: but Moshe stood up and helped them, and watered their flock. 18 And when they came to Reu-El their abba, he said, How is it that you came back so soon today? 19 And they said, A Mitzrite delivered us out of the hand of the shepherds, and also drew enough mayim for us, and watered the flock. 20 And he said to his daughters, And where is he? Why is it that you have left the man? Call him, that he may eat a meal. 21 And Moshe was content to dwell with the man: and he gave Moshe Tzipporah his daughter. 22 And she bore him a son, and he called his name Gershom: for he said, I have been a Ger in a strange land. 23 And it came to pass in due time that the melech of Mitzrayim died: and the children of Yisrael sighed because of the bondage, and they cried, and their cry came up to Elohim because of the bondage. 24 And Elohim heard their groaning, and Elohim remembered His covenant with Avraham, with Yitzchak, and with Yaakov.[2] 25 And Elohim looked upon the children of Yisrael, and Elohim knew them.[3]

3 Now Moshe kept the flock of Yithro his abba-in-law, the kohen of Midyan: and he led the flock to the backside of the desert, and came to the mountain of Elohim, even to Horev. 2 And the Malach- יהוה [4] appeared to him in a flame of fire out of the midst of a bush: and he looked, and, see, the bush burned with fire, and the bush was not consumed. 3 And Moshe said, I will now turn aside, and see this great sight, why the bush is not burnt. 4 And when יהוה saw that he turned aside to see, Elohim called to him out of the midst of the bush, and said, *Moshe, Moshe.* And he said, Hinani. 5 And He said, *Draw not near here: put off your sandals from off your feet, for the place on*

---

[1] Drawn out, as he would help do to Yisrael from Egypt.

[2] To bring them out after 400 or so years to the Promised Land.
[3] Or knew the hour of their redemption was at hand.
[4] Called Elohim in verse 4.

which you stand is kadosh [1] ground. 6 Moreover He said, *I am the Elohim of your abba, the Elohim of Avraham, the Elohim of Yitzchak, and the Elohim of Yaakov.* And Moshe hid his face; for he was afraid to look upon Elohim. 7 And יהוה said, *I have surely seen the affliction of My people which are in Mitzrayim, and have heard their cry because of their eved-masters; for I know their sorrows; 8 And I have come down to deliver them out of the hand of the Mitzrites, and to bring them up out of that land to a lovely and large land, to a land flowing with milk and honey; to the place of the Kanaanites, and the Hittites, and the Amorites and the Perizzites, and the Hivites, and the Yevusites. 9 Now therefore, see, the cry of the children of Yisrael has come to Me: and I have also seen the oppression with which the Mitzrites oppress them. 10 Come now therefore, and I will send you to Pharaoh, that you may bring forth My people the children of Yisrael out of Mitzrayim.* 11 And Moshe said to Elohim, Who am I, that I should go to Pharaoh, and that I should bring forth the children of Yisrael out of Mitzrayim? 12 And He said, *Certainly I will be with you; and this shall be a sign to you, that I have sent you: When you have brought forth the people out of Mitzrayim, you shall serve Elohim upon this mountain.* 13 And Moshe said to Elohim, See, when I come to the children of Yisrael, and shall say to them, The Elohim of your ahvot has sent me to you; and they shall say to me, What is His Name? What shall I say to them? 14 And the Word of Elohim said to Moshe, *eyeh asher eyeh:* and He said, *This shall you say to the children of Yisrael, EYEH has sent me to you.* 15 And Elohim said moreover to Moshe, *This shall you say to the children of Yisrael, יהוה Elohim of your ahvot, the Elohim of Avraham, the Elohim of Yitzchak, and the Elohim of Yaakov, has sent me to you: this is My Name le-olam-va-ed, and*

this is My memorial to all generations. [2] 16 Go, and gather the zachanim of Yisrael together, and say to them, יהוה Elohim of your ahvot, the Elohim of Avraham, of Yitzchak, and of Yaakov, appeared to me, saying, I have surely visited you, and have seen that which is done to you in Mitzrayim: [3] 17 And I have said, I will bring you up out of the affliction of Mitzrayim to the land of the Kanaanites, and the Hittites, and the Amorites, and the Perizzites, and the Hivites, and the Yevusites, to a land flowing with milk and honey. 18 And they shall listen to your voice: and you shall come, you and the zachanim of Yisrael, to the melech of Mitzrayim, and you shall say to him, יהוה Elohim of the Ivrim has met with us: and now please let us go, on a three days' journey into the wilderness, that we may sacrifice to יהוה our Elohim. 19 And I am sure that the melech of Mitzrayim will not let you go, no, not even by a mighty hand. 20 And I will stretch out My hand, and smite Mitzrayim with all My wonders that I will do in the midst of it: and after that he will let you go. 21 And I will give this people favor in the sight of the Mitzrites: and it shall come to pass, that, when you go, you shall not go empty: 22 But every woman shall take from her neighbor, and from her that sojourns in her bayit, jewels of silver, and jewels of gold, and garments: and you shall put them upon your sons, and upon your daughters; and you shall plunder the Mitzrites.

4 And Moshe answered and said, But, see, they will not believe me, nor listen to my voice: for they will say, יהוה has not appeared to you. 2 And יהוה said to him,

---

[2] Regardless of any other man-made substitute names and regardless of translators hiding His Name almost 7,000 times in most English translations, YHWH assures all Yisrael that YHWH is His true everlasting Name, regardless of which language man speaks or writes.
[3] Yisrael obviously knew the Name already, which is why YHWH told Moshe to make sure to use it as a point of validation for his role as their deliverer. Also, in order to be reborn and renewed Yisrael, the Name is a mark or a identification of YHWH's true people as later seen in Revelation 14:1.

What is that in your hand? And he said, A rod. 3 And He said, *Cast it on the ground.* And he cast it on the ground, and it became a serpent; and Moshe fled from before it. 4 And יהוה said to Moshe, *Put forth your hand, and take it by the tail.* And he put forth his hand, and caught it, and it became a rod in his hand: 5 *So that they may believe that* יהוה *Elohim of their ahvot, the Elohim of Avraham, the Elohim of Yitzchak, and the Elohim of Yaakov, has appeared to you.* 6 And יהוה said furthermore to him, *Put now your hand into your bosom.* And he put his hand into his bosom: and when he took it out, see, and his hand was leprous as snow. 7 And He said, *Put your hand back into your bosom again.* And he put his hand back into his bosom again; and plucked it out of his bosom, and, see, it had turned again as his other flesh. 8 *And it shall come to pass, if they will not believe you, neither listen to the voice of the first sign, that they will believe the voice of the latter sign.* 9 *And it shall come to pass, if they will not believe also these two signs, neither listen to your voice, that you shall take from the mayim of the river, and pour it upon the dry land: and the mayim which you take out of the river shall become dom upon the dry land.* 10 And Moshe said to יהוה, O יהוה, I am not eloquent, neither before, nor since have You spoken to Your eved: but I am slow of speech, and of a slow tongue. 11 And יהוה said to him, *Who has made man's mouth? Or who makes the dumb, or deaf, or the seeing, or the blind? Have not I* יהוה*?* 12 *Now therefore go, and I will be with your mouth, and teach you what you shall say.* 13 And he said, O יהוה, I beg You; by the hand of someone else please send deliverance. 14 And the anger of יהוה burned against Moshe, and He said, *Is not Aharon Ha Levi your brother? I know that he can speak well. And also, see, he comes forth to meet you: and when he sees you, he will have simcha in his lev.* 15 *And you shall speak to him, and put words in his mouth: and I will be with your mouth, and with his*

mouth, and will teach you what you shall do. 16 *And he shall be your spokesman to the people: and he shall be to you like a mouth, and you shall be to him like an Elohim.* 17 *And you shall take this rod in your hand, with which you shall do the signs.* 18 And Moshe went and returned to Yithro[1] his abba-in-law, and said to him, Let me go, please, and return to my brothers who are in Mitzrayim, and see whether they still are alive. And Yithro said to Moshe, Go in shalom. 19 And יהוה said to Moshe in Midyan, *Go, return into Mitzrayim: for all the men are dead who sought your chayim.* 20 And Moshe took his wife and his sons, and put them upon a donkey, and he returned to the land of Mitzrayim: and Moshe took the rod of Elohim in his hand. 21 And יהוה said to Moshe, *When you go to return to Mitzrayim, see that you do all those wonders before Pharaoh, which I have put in your hand: but I will harden his lev, that he shall not let the people go.* 22 *And you shall say to Pharaoh, This said* יהוה, *Yisrael is My son, even My bachor:*[2] 23 *And I say to you, Let My son go, that he may serve Me: and if you refuse to let him go, see, I will slay your son, even your bachor.* 24 And it came to pass by the way in the lodging place that יהוה met Moshe, and sought to kill him. 25 Then Tzipporah took a sharp stone, and cut off the foreskin of her son,[3] and cast it at his feet, and said, Surely a bloody husband are you to me. 26 So יהוה let Moshe go: then she said, A bloody husband you are, because of the circumcision.[4] 27 And יהוה said to Aharon, *Go into the wilderness to meet Moshe.* And he went, and met him on the Mount of Elohim, and kissed him. 28 And Moshe told Aharon all the words of יהוה who had sent him, and all the signs, which He had

---

[1] Jethro.
[2] Proof that Yahshua is YHWH's Son for the natural realm is patterned after the reality of the unseen spirit realm. Yisrael as a nation is called "the son" of YHWH's own choosing.
[3] Did Moshe's job for him.
[4] Moshe in his complaining and attempts to avoid his calling, forgot to do brit milah/circumcision on Gershom; YHWH took this as another sign of Moshe's unwillingness to trust, as well as his covenant-breaking attitude.

commanded him. 29 And Moshe and Aharon went and gathered together all the zachanim of the children of Yisrael: 30 And Aharon spoke all the words that יהוה had spoken to Moshe, and did the signs in the sight of the people. 31 And the people believed: and when they heard that יהוה had visited the children of Yisrael, and that He had looked upon their affliction, then they bowed their heads and worshipped.

5 And afterward Moshe and Aharon went in, and told Pharaoh, This says יהוה Elohim of Yisrael, *Let My people go, that they may hold a moed to Me in the wilderness.*[1] 2 And Pharaoh said, Who is this יהוה that I should obey His voice to let Yisrael go? I know not יהוה, neither will I let Yisrael go. 3 And they said, The Elohim of the Ivrim has met with us: let us go, for a three day journey into the desert, and sacrifice to יהוה our Elohim; lest He fall upon us with pestilence, or with the sword. 4 And the melech of Mitzrayim said to them, Why do you, Moshe and Aharon, take the people away from their work? Get back to your burdens. 5 And Pharaoh said, See, the people of the land now are many,[2] and you make them rest from their burdens. 6 And Pharaoh commanded the same day the eved-masters of the people, and their officers, saying, 7 You shall no more give the people straw to make bricks, as before: let them go and gather straw for themselves. 8 And the same amount of bricks, which they did make before, you shall require it of them; you shall not diminish any of it: for they are idle; therefore they cry, saying, Let us go and sacrifice to our Elohim. 9 Let even more work be laid upon the men, that they may labor inside; and let them not regard vain words. 10 And the eved-masters of the people went out, and their officers, and they spoke to the people, saying, This said Pharaoh, I will not give you straw. 11 Go get your straw wherever you can find

it: yet none of your work shall be diminished. 12 So the people were scattered abroad throughout all the land of Mitzrayim to gather stubble instead of straw. 13 And the eved-masters hurried them, saying, fulfill your work, your daily tasks just like when there was straw. 14 And the foremen of the children of Yisrael, which Pharaoh's eved-masters had set over them, were beaten, and asked, Why have you not fulfilled your task in making bricks both yesterday and today, as before? 15 Then the foremen of the children of Yisrael came and cried to Pharaoh, saying, Why do you treat your avadim this way? 16 There is no straw given to your avadim, and they say to us, Make bricks: and, see, your avadim are beaten; but the fault is with your own people. 17 But he said, You are idle; therefore you say, Let us go and do sacrifice to יהוה. 18 Go therefore now, and work; for there shall no straw be given to you, yet shall you deliver the same amount of bricks. 19 And the officers of the children of Yisrael did see that they were in trouble, after it was said, You shall not diminish any from the bricks of your daily task. 20 And they met Moshe and Aharon, who stood in the way, as they came forth from Pharaoh: 21 And they said to them, יהוה look upon you, and shophet; because you have made us to be abhorred in the eyes of Pharaoh, and in the eyes of his avadim, to put a sword in their hand to slay us. 22 And Moshe returned to יהוה, and said, יהוה, why have You done this evil to this people? Why is it that You have sent me? 23 For since I came to Pharaoh to speak in Your Name,[3] he has done evil to this people; neither have You delivered Your people at all.

6 Then יהוה said to Moshe, *Now shall you see what I will do to Pharaoh: for*

---

[1] To receive Torah
[2] Multiplying according to promise.

[3] Sometimes it seems that using the true Name is harmful to the evangel or to one's calling; but that lie is merely a mirage, as it is the actual key to deliverance and life in and as Yisrael. Time always will bear that out.

with a strong hand shall he let them go, and with a strong hand shall he drive them out of his land.

Torah Parsha 14
Vayera 6:2-9:35
Haftarah Yechezkel 28:25-29:21
Brit Chadasha Romiyah 9:14-17,
Qorintiyah Bet 6:14-7:1

2 And Elohim spoke to Moshe, and said to him, *I am* יהוה : 3 *And I appeared to Avraham, to Yitzchak, and to Yaakov, as El-Shaddai, but by My Name* יהוה *was I not known to them?* [1] 4 *And I have also established My covenant with them, to give them the land of Kanaan, the land of their pilgrimage, where they were strangers.* 5 *And I have also heard the groaning of the children of Yisrael, whom the Mitzrites shomer in bondage; and I have remembered My covenant.* 6 *Therefore say to the children of Yisrael, I am* יהוה*, and I will bring you out from under the burdens of the Mitzrites, and I will deliver you out of their bondage, and I will redeem you with a stretched out arm, and with great mishpatim: 7 And I will take you to Me for a people, and I will be Your Elohim: and you shall know that I am* יהוה *Your Elohim, who brings you out from under the burdens of the Mitzrites. 8 And I will bring you in to the land, concerning which I did swear to give it to Avraham, to Yitzchak, and to Yaakov; and I will give it you for an heritage: I am* יהוה. 9 And Moshe spoke so to the children of Yisrael: but they listened not to Moshe because of their anguish of ruach, and cruel bondage. 10 And יהוה spoke to Moshe, saying, 11 *Go in, speak to Pharaoh melech of Mitzrayim, so that he lets the children of Yisrael go out of his land.* 12 And Moshe spoke before יהוה, saying, See, the children of Yisrael have not listened to me; how then shall Pharaoh listen to me, I who am of uncircumcised lips? 13 And יהוה spoke to Moshe and to Aharon, and gave them a command for the children of Yisrael, and to Pharaoh melech of Mitzrayim, to bring the children of Yisrael out from the land of Mitzrayim. 14 These are the heads of their ahvot's batiym: The sons of Reuven the bachor of Yisrael; Hanoch, and Pallu, Hetzron, and Carmi: these are the families of Reuven. 15 And the sons of Shimeon, Yemu-El, and Yamin, and Ohad, and Yachin, and Zohar, and Shaul the son of a Kanaanite woman:[2] these are the families of Shimeon. 16 And these are the names of the sons of Levi according to their generations; Gershon, and Kohath, and Merari: and the years of the chayim of Levi were one hundred thirty seven years. 17 The sons of Gershon; Libni, and Shimi, according to their families. 18 And the sons of Kohath; Amram, and Izhar, and Hevron, and Uzziel: and the years of the chayim of Kohath were one hundred thirty three years. 19 And the sons of Merari; Mahali and Mushi: these are the families of Levi according to their generations. 20 And Amram took him Yochebed his abba's sister as a wife; and she bore him Aharon and Moshe: and the years of the chayim of Amram were a hundred thirty seven years. 21 And the sons of Izhar; Korah, and Nepheg, and Zichri. 22 And the sons of Uzzi-El; Misha-El, and Elzaphan, and Zithri. 23 And Aharon took him Elisheva, daughter of Amminadav, sister of Naashon, as a wife; and she bore him Nadav, and Avihu, El-Azar, and Ithamar. 24 And the sons of Korah; Assir, and Elchanah, and Aviasaph: these are the families of the Korhites. 25 And El-Azar Aharon's son took him one of the daughters of Putiel to wife; and she bore him Phinehas: these are the heads of the ahvot of the Leviim according to their families.

---

[1] Not an introduction of the Name, but a question showing that in fact it was an established Name among the children of Yisrael. The actual Hebrew is in the form of a rhetorical question. Anyone reading Genesis realizes that the patriarchs all knew, used and treasured YHWH's Name, and it was not introduced to Moshe as a new revelation.

[2] A perfect example of the tribe of Shimeon being filled with non-Yisraelite dom that later mixed with Yisrael. Yisrael has always been a mixed and diverse people.

26 These are Aharon and Moshe, to whom יהוה said, *Bring out the children of Yisrael from the land of Mitzrayim according to their divisions.* 27 These are they which spoke to Pharaoh melech of Mitzrayim, to bring out the children of Yisrael from Mitzrayim: this is that Moshe and Aharon. 28 And it came to pass on the day when יהוה spoke to Moshe in the land of Mitzrayim, 29 That יהוה spoke to Moshe, saying, *I am* יהוה *: speak to Pharaoh melech of Mitzrayim all that I say to you.* 30 And Moshe said before יהוה, See, I am of uncircumcised lips, and why should Pharaoh listen to me?

7 And יהוה said to Moshe, *See, I have made you like elohim to Pharaoh: and Aharon your brother shall be your navi.* 2 *You shall speak all that I command you: and Aharon your brother shall speak to Pharaoh, that he send the children of Yisrael out of his land. 3 And I will harden Pharaoh's lev, and multiply My signs and My wonders in the land of Mitzrayim. 4 But Pharaoh shall not listen to you, that I may lay My hand upon Mitzrayim, and bring forth My divisions, and My people the children of Yisrael, out of the land of Mitzrayim by great mishpatim. 5 And the Mitzrites shall know that I am* יהוה*, when I stretch forth My hand upon Mitzrayim, and bring out the children of Yisrael from among them.* 6 And Moshe and Aharon did as יהוה commanded them, so did they. 7 And Moshe was eighty years old, and Aharon eighty-three years old, when they spoke to Pharaoh. 8 And יהוה spoke to Moshe and to Aharon, saying, 9 *When Pharaoh shall speak to you, saying, Show a miracle for yourselves: then you shall say to Aharon, Take your rod, and cast it before Pharaoh, and it shall become a serpent.* 10 And Moshe and Aharon went in to Pharaoh, and they did so as יהוה had commanded, and Aharon cast down his rod before Pharaoh, and before his avadim, and it became a serpent. 11 Then Pharaoh also called the wise men and the sorcerers: and the magicians of Mitzrayim, they also did in like manner with their enchantments. 12 For they cast down every man his rod, and they became serpents: but Aharon's rod swallowed up their rods. 13 And He hardened Pharaoh's lev, so that he listened not to them; as יהוה had said. 14 And יהוה said to Moshe, *Pharaoh's lev is hardened; he refuses to let the people go.* 15 *Go to Pharaoh in the morning; see, he goes out to the mayim; and you shall stand by the river's bank to meet him; and the rod which was turned to a serpent shall you take in your hand.* 16 *And you shall say to him,* יהוה *Elohim of the Ivrim has sent me to you, saying, Let My people go, that they may serve Me in the wilderness: and, see, before you would not listen.* 17 This says יהוה*, In this you shall know that I am* יהוה *: see, I will smite with the rod that is in my hand upon the mayim, which are in the river, and they shall be turned to dom.* 18 *And the fish that is in the river shall die, and the river shall stink; and the Mitzrites shall find it impossible to drink of the mayim of the river.* 19 And יהוה spoke to Moshe, *Say to Aharon, Take your rod, and stretch out your hand upon the mayim of Mitzrayim, upon their streams, upon their rivers, and upon their ponds, and upon all their pools of mayim, that they may become dom; and that there may be dom throughout all the land of Mitzrayim, both in vessels of wood, and in vessels of stone.* 20 And Moshe and Aharon did so, as יהוה commanded; and he lifted up the rod, and smote the mayim that were in the river, in the sight of Pharaoh, and in the sight of his avadim; and all the mayim that were in the river were turned to dom. 21 And the fish that were in the river died; and the river smelled, and the Mitzrites could not drink of the mayim of the river; and there was dom throughout all the land of Mitzrayim. 22 And the magicians of Mitzrayim did so with their enchantments: and Pharaoh's lev

was hardened, neither did he listen to them; as **יהוה** had said. 23 And Pharaoh turned and went into his bayit neither did he set his lev to this also. 24 And all the Mitzrites dug all around the river for mayim to drink; for they could not drink of the mayim of the river. 25 And seven days were fulfilled, after **יהוה** had smitten the river.

8 And **יהוה** spoke to Moshe, *Go to Pharaoh, and say to him, This says* **יהוה**, *Let My people go, that they may serve Me.* 2 *And if you refuse to let them go, see, I will smite all your borders with frogs: 3 And the river shall bring forth frogs abundantly, which shall go up and come into your bayit, and into your bedroom, and upon your bed, and into the bayit of your avadim, and upon your people, and into your ovens, and into your kneading bowls: 4 And the frogs shall come up both on you, and upon your people, and upon all your avadim.* 5 And **יהוה** spoke to Moshe, *Say to Aharon, Stretch forth your hand with your rod over the streams, over the rivers, and over the ponds, and cause frogs to come up upon the land of Mitzrayim.* 6 And Aharon stretched out his hand over the mayim of Mitzrayim; and the frogs came up, and covered the land of Mitzrayim. 7 And the magicians did so with their enchantments, and brought up frogs upon the land of Mitzrayim. 8 Then Pharaoh called for Moshe and Aharon, and said, Make tefillah to **יהוה**, that he may take away the frogs from me, and from my people; and I will let the people go, that they may do sacrifice to **יהוה**. 9 And Moshe said to Pharaoh, Explain yourself to me: when shall I make tefillah for you, and for your avadim, and for your people, to destroy the frogs from you and your batiym, that they may remain in the river only? 10 And he said, Tomorrow. And Moshe said, Be it according to your word: that you may know that there is none like **יהוה** our Elohim. 11 And the frogs shall depart from you, and from your batiym, and from your avadim, and from your people; they shall

remain in the river only. 12 And Moshe and Aharon went out from Pharaoh: and Moshe cried to **יהוה** because of the frogs that He had brought against Pharaoh. 13 And **יהוה** did according to the word of Moshe; and the frogs died out of the batiym, out of the villages, and out of the fields. 14 And they gathered them together upon heaps: and the land smelled. 15 But when Pharaoh saw that there was relief, he hardened his lev, and listened not to them; as **יהוה** had said. 16 And **יהוה** said to Moshe, *Say to Aharon, Stretch out your rod, and smite the dust of the land, that it may become lice throughout all the land of Mitzrayim.* 17 And they did so; for Aharon stretched out his hand with his rod, and smote the dust of the earth, and it became lice in man, and in beast; all the dust of the land became lice throughout all the land of Mitzrayim. 18 And the magicians did so with their enchantments to bring forth lice, but they could not: so there were lice upon man, and upon beast. 19 Then the magicians said to Pharaoh, This is the finger of Elohim: and Pharaoh's lev was hardened, and he listened not to them; as **יהוה** had said. 20 And **יהוה** said to Moshe, *Rise up early in the morning, and stand before Pharaoh; see, he comes forth to the mayim; and say to him, This says* **יהוה**, *Let My people go, that they may serve Me.* 21 *Or else, if you will not let My people go, see, I will send swarms of flies upon you, and upon your avadim, and upon your people, and into your batiym: and the batiym of the Mitzrites shall be full of swarms of flies, and also the ground where they are.* 22 *And I will separate in that day the land of Goshen, in which My people dwell, that no swarms of flies shall be there; to the end that you may know that I am* **יהוה** *in the midst of the earth.* 23 *And I will put a division between My people and your people: tomorrow shall this sign be.* 24 And **יהוה** did so; and there came a grievous swarm of flies into the bayit of Pharaoh, and into his avadim's batiym, and into all the land of Mitzrayim: the land was ruined by reason of the swarm of flies. 25 And Pharaoh called for Moshe and for Aharon, and said, Go you, sacrifice to Your Elohim in the land. 26 And Moshe said, It is not right to do so; for we would be sacrificing the abomination of the Mitzrites to יהוה our Elohim: see, shall we sacrifice the abomination of the Mitzrites before their eyes, and will they not stone us? 27 We will go three days' journey into the wilderness, and sacrifice to יהוה our Elohim, as He shall command us. 28 And Pharaoh said, I will let you go, that you may sacrifice to יהוה Your Elohim in the wilderness; only you shall not go very far away: make tefillah for me. 29 And Moshe said, See, I go out from you, and I will make tefillah to יהוה that the swarms of flies may depart from Pharaoh, from his avadim, and from his people, tomorrow: but let not Pharaoh ephah deceitfully any more in not letting the people go to sacrifice to יהוה. 30 And Moshe went out from Pharaoh, and prayed to יהוה. 31 And יהוה did according to the word of Moshe; and He removed the swarms of flies from Pharaoh, from his avadim, and from his people; there remained not one. 32 And Pharaoh hardened his lev at this time also, neither would he let the people go.

9 Then יהוה said to Moshe, *Go in to Pharaoh, and tell him, This says יהוה Elohim of the Ivrim, Let My people go, that they may serve Me. 2 For if you refuse to let them go, and will hold them still, 3 See, the hand of יהוה is upon your cattle that is in the field, upon the horses, upon the donkeys, upon the camels, upon the oxen, and upon the sheep: there shall be a very grievous pestilence. 4 And יהוה shall separate between the cattle of Yisrael and the cattle of Mitzrayim: and there shall nothing die of all that is the children of Yisrael's. 5 And יהוה appointed a set time, saying, Tomorrow יהוה shall do this thing in the land. 6 And יהוה* did that thing on the next day, and all the cattle of Mitzrayim died: but of the cattle of the children of Yisrael not one died. 7 And Pharaoh sent, and, see, there was not one of the cattle of the Yisraelites dead. And the lev of Pharaoh was hardened, and he did not let the people go. 8 And יהוה said to Moshe and to Aharon, *Take handfuls of ashes of a furnace, and let Moshe sprinkle it toward the shamayim in the sight of Pharaoh. 9 And it shall become small dust in all the land of Mitzrayim, and shall be for boils breaking forth with sores upon man, and upon beast, throughout all the land of Mitzrayim.* 10 And they took ashes of the furnace, and stood before Pharaoh; and Moshe sprinkled it up toward the shamayim; and it became a boil breaking forth with sores upon man, and upon beast. 11 And the magicians could not stand before Moshe because of the boils; for the boils were upon the magicians, and upon all the Mitzrites. 12 And יהוה hardened the lev of Pharaoh, and he listened not to them; as יהוה had spoken to Moshe. 13 And יהוה said to Moshe, *Rise up early in the morning, and stand before Pharaoh, and say to him, This says יהוה Elohim of the Ivrim, Let My people go, that they may serve Me. 14 For I will at this time send all My plagues upon your lev, and upon your avadim, and upon your people; that you may know that there is none like Me in all the earth. 15 For now I will stretch out My hand, that I may smite you and your people with pestilence; and you shall be cut off from the earth. 16 And indeed for this cause have I raised you up, for to show in you My power; and that My Name[1] may be declared throughout all the earth. 17 You still yet exalt you yourself against My people, that you will not let them go? 18 See, tomorrow about this time I will cause it to rain a very grievous hail, such as has not been in Mitzrayim since the foundation of it even until now. 19 Therefore now, send for and gather your cattle, and all that you have in the field; for upon every man and beast*

---

[1] Pharaoh's lev was hardened so that YHWH's Name may be known and honored among men.

which shall be found in the field, and shall not be brought home, the hail shall come down upon them, and they shall die. 20 He that feared the word of **יהוה** among the avadim of Pharaoh made his avadim and his cattle flee into their batiym: 21 But those that regarded not the word of **יהוה** left their avadim and their cattle in the field. 22 And **יהוה** said to Moshe, *Stretch forth your hand toward the shamayim, that there may be hail in all the land of Mitzrayim, upon man, and upon beast, and upon every herb of the field, throughout the land of Mitzrayim.* 23 And Moshe stretched forth his rod toward the shamayim: and **יהוה** sent thunder and hail, and the fire ran along upon the ground; and **יהוה** rained hail upon the land of Mitzrayim. 24 So there was hail, and fire mingled with the hail, very grievous, such as there was none like it in all the land of Mitzrayim since it became a nation. 25 And the hail smote throughout all the land of Mitzrayim all that was in the field, both man and beast; and the hail smote every herb of the field, and broke every eytz of the field. 26 Only in the land of Goshen, where the children of Yisrael were, was there no hail. 27 And Pharaoh sent, and called for Moshe and Aharon, and said to them, I have sinned this time: **יהוה** is Tzadik, and my people and I are wicked. 28 Make tefillah to **יהוה** - for it is enough Let there be no more mighty thunderings and hail; and I will let you go, and you shall stay no longer. 29 And Moshe said to Him, As soon as I am gone out of the city, I will spread abroad my hands to **יהוה**; and the thunder shall cease, neither shall there be any more hail; that you may know how that the earth is **יהוה**'s. 30 But as for you and your avadim, I know that you will not yet fear **יהוה** Elohim. 31 And the flax and the barley was smitten: for the barley was in the ear, and the flax was in bud. 32 But the wheat and the spelt were not smitten: for they were late crops. 33 And Moshe went out of the city from Pharaoh, and spread abroad his hands to **יהוה**: and the thunders

and hail ceased, and the rain was not poured upon the earth. 34 And when Pharaoh saw that the rain and the hail and the thunders were ceased, he sinned yet more, and hardened his lev, he and his avadim. 35 And the lev of Pharaoh was hardened, neither would he let the children of Yisrael go; as **יהוה** had spoken by Moshe.

Torah Parsha 15
Bo 10:1-13:16
Haftarah Yirmeyahu 46:13-28
Brit Chadasha Gilyahna 19:1-16

10 And **יהוה** said to Moshe, *Go in to Pharaoh: for I have hardened his lev, and the lev of his avadim, that I might show these My signs before him: 2 And that you may tell it in the ears of your son, and of your son's son, what things I have done in Mitzrayim, and My signs which I have done among them; that you may know that I am* **יהוה**. 3 And Moshe and Aharon came in to Pharaoh, and said to him, This says **יהוה** Elohim of the Ivrim, *How long will you refuse to humble yourself before Me? Let My people go, that they may serve Me. 4 Or else, if you refuse to let My people go, see, tomorrow will I bring the locusts into your coast: 5 And they shall cover the face of the earth, that one cannot be able to see the earth: and they shall eat the residue of that which is escaped, which remains to you from the hail, and shall eat every eytz which grows for you out of the field: 6 And they shall fill your batiym, and the batiym of all your avadim, and the batiym of all the Mitzrites; which neither your ahvot, nor your ahvot' ahvot have seen, since the day that they were upon the earth to this day. And he turned, and went out from Pharaoh.* 7 And Pharaoh's avadim said to him, How long shall this man be a snare to us? Let the men go, that they may serve **יהוה** their Elohim: Do you not yet know that Mitzrayim is destroyed? 8 And Moshe and Aharon were brought again to Pharaoh: and he said to them, Go, serve **יהוה** Your Elohim: but who are they that shall go?

9 And Moshe said, We will go with our young and with our old, with our sons and with our daughters, with our flocks and with our herds will we go; for we must hold a moed to יהוה. 10 And he said to them, Let יהוה be so with you, as I will let you go, and your little ones: but be warned that evil is before you. 11 Not so: go now you that are men, and serve יהוה; for that is what you did desire. And they were driven out from Pharaoh's presence. 12 And יהוה said to Moshe, *Stretch out your hand over the land of Mitzrayim for the locusts, that they may come up upon the land of Mitzrayim, and eat every herb of the land, even all that the hail has left.* 13 And Moshe stretched forth his rod over the land of Mitzrayim, and יהוה brought an east wind upon the land all that day, and all that night; and when it was morning, the east wind brought the locusts. 14 And the locusts went up over all the land of Mitzrayim, and rested in all the coasts of Mitzrayim: very grievous were they; before then there were no such locusts as those, neither after them shall be such. 15 For they covered the face of the whole earth, so that the land was darkened; and they did eat every herb of the land, and all the fruit of the eytzim which the hail had left: and there remained not any green thing on the eytzim, or in the herbs of the field, throughout all the land of Mitzrayim. 16 Then Pharaoh called for Moshe and Aharon in haste; and he said, I have sinned against יהוה Your Elohim, and against you. 17 Now therefore forgive, my sin only this once, and make tefillah to יהוה Your Elohim, that He may take away from me this death. 18 And he went out from Pharaoh, and prayed to יהוה. 19 And יהוה turned a mighty strong west wind, which took away the locusts, and cast them into the Sea of Reeds; there remained not one locust in all the coasts of Mitzrayim. 20 But יהוה hardened Pharaoh's lev, so that he would not let the children of Yisrael go. 21 And יהוה said to Moshe, *Stretch out your hand toward the shamayim, that there may be darkness over the land of Mitzrayim, even darkness that may be felt.* 22 And Moshe stretched forth his hand toward the shamayim; and there was a thick darkness in all the land of Mitzrayim for three days: 23 They saw not one another, neither rose any from his place for three days: but all the children of Yisrael had light in their dwellings. [1] 24 And Pharaoh called to Moshe, and said, Go, serve יהוה; only let your flocks and your herds stay: let your little ones also go with you. 25 And Moshe said, You must give us also sacrifices and burnt offerings, that we may sacrifice to יהוה our Elohim. 26 Our cattle also shall go with us; there shall not be a hoof left behind; for we must take them to serve יהוה our Elohim; for we know not with what we must serve יהוה, until we come there. 27 But יהוה hardened Pharaoh's lev, and he would not let them go. 28 And Pharaoh said to him, Get away from me, watch yourself, and never see my face again! For in that day that you see my face you shall die. 29 And Moshe said, You have spoken well, I will see your face again no more!

11 And יהוה said to Moshe, *Yet will I bring one more plague upon Pharaoh, and upon Mitzrayim; afterwards he will let you go from here: when he shall let you go, he shall surely drive you out from here altogether. 2 Speak now in the ears of the people, and let every man ask from his neighbor, and every woman from her neighbor, jewels of silver, and jewels of gold. 3 And* יהוה gave the people favor in the sight of the Mitzrites. Moreover the man Moshe was very great in the land of Mitzrayim, in the sight of Pharaoh's avadim, and in the sight of the people. 4 And Moshe said, *This says* יהוה, *About midnight will I go out into the midst of Mitzrayim: 5 And all the bachor in the land of Mitzrayim shall die, from the bachor of Pharaoh that sits*

---

[1] Yisrael is called to walk in light as a people, even while the world walks in darkness.

upon his throne, even to the bachor of the female eved that is behind the mill; and all the bachor of beasts. 6 And there shall be a great cry throughout all the land of Mitzrayim, such as there was none like it, nor shall be like it anymore. 7 But against any of the children of Yisrael shall no dog move his tongue, against man or beast: that you may know that יהוה does put a difference between the Mitzrites and Yisrael.[1] 8 And all these your avadim shall come down to me, and bow down themselves to me, saying, Get out, and all the people that follow you: and after that I will go out. And he went out from Pharaoh in a great anger. 9 And יהוה said to Moshe, Pharaoh shall not listen to you; that My wonders may be multiplied in the land of Mitzrayim. 10 And Moshe and Aharon did all these wonders before Pharaoh: and יהוה hardened Pharaoh's lev, so that he would not let the children of Yisrael go out of his land.

12 And יהוה spoke to Moshe and Aharon in the land of Mitzrayim, saying, 2 This month shall be for you the beginning of months: it shall be the first month of the year for you.[2] 3 Speak you to all the congregation of Yisrael, saying, In the tenth day of this month they shall take for themselves every man a lamb, according to the bayit of their ahvot, a lamb for a bayit: 4 And if the household is too little for the lamb, let him and his neighbor next to his bayit take it according to the number of their beings; every man according to his needs you shall make your count for the lamb. 5 Your lamb shall be without blemish, a male of the first year: you shall take it out from the sheep, or from the goats: 6 And you shall shomer it up until the fourteenth day of the same month: and the whole assembly of the congregation of Yisrael shall kill it in between the evenings. 7 And they shall take of the dom, and strike it on

the two side posts and on the upper doorpost of their batiym, in which they shall eat it. 8 And they shall eat the flesh in that night, roasted with fire, and matzah; and with bitter herbs they shall eat it. 9 Eat none of it raw, nor boiled at all with mayim, but roasted with fire; its head with its legs, with the inside parts. 10 And you shall let nothing of it remain until the morning; and that which remains until the morning you shall burn with fire. 11 And this is how you shall eat it; with your waists dressed, your shoes on your feet, and your staff in your hand; and you shall eat it in a great hurry: it is יהוה's Pesach.[3] 12 For I will pass through the land of Mitzrayim this night, and will smite all the bachor in the land of Mitzrayim, both man and beast; and against all the elohim of Mitzrayim I will execute mishpat: I am יהוה. 13 And the dom shall be to you for a sign upon the batiym where you are: and when I see the dom, I will pass over you,[4] and the plague shall not be upon you to destroy you, when I smite the land of Mitzrayim. 14 And this day shall be to you for a memorial; and you shall shomer it a moed to יהוה throughout your generations; you shall shomer it a moed by a mishpat le-olam-va-ed.[5] 15 Seven days shall you eat matzah; even the first day you shall put away chametz out of your batiym: for whoever eateth chametz-lechem from the first day until the seventh day, that being shall be cut off from Yisrael. 16 And in the first day there shall be a miqra kodesh,[6] and on the seventh day there shall be a miqra kodesh to you; no manner of work shall be done in them, except that which every man must eat, that only may be done of you. 17 And you shall observe Chag Matzoth; for on this very day have I brought your divisions out of the land of Mitzrayim: therefore shall you observe this day in your

---

[1] That is why YHWH Himself considers all believers in Yisrael's Moshiach Hebrews, or Yisraelites.
[2] Aviv.
[3] Notice that it is not exclusively the Jewish Passover, but YHWH's Passover for all His children.
[4] True salvation and deliverance has always been by the dom of the Pesach/Paschal Lamb.
[5] No dispensations. Passover is for all times and forever, for all believers.
[6] Hebrew: **miqra kodesh**-set-apart gathering.

generations by a mishpat le-olam-va-ed. 18 In the first month, on the fourteenth day of the month between the evenings, you shall eat matzah, until the twenty-first day of the month at evening. 19 Seven days shall there be no chametz found in your batiym: for whoever eats that which is chametz, even that being shall be cut off from the congregation of Yisrael, whether he be a Ger, or born in the land. 20 You shall eat nothing with chametz; in all your dwellings shall you eat matzah. 21 Then Moshe called for all the zachanim of Yisrael, and said to them, Choose and take a lamb according to your families, and kill the Pesach. 22 And you shall take a bunch of hyssop, and dip it in the dom that is in the bason, and strike the lintel and the two side posts with the dom that is in the bason; and none of you shall go out the door of his bayit until the morning. 23 For יהוה will pass through to smite the Mitzrites; and when He sees the dom upon the lintel, and on the two side posts, יהוה will pass over the door, and will not allow the destroyer to come in to your batiym to smite you. 24 And you shall observe this word as a mishpat for you, and for your sons' le-olam-va-ed. 25 And it shall come to pass, when you have come to the land that יהוה will give you, according as He has promised, that you shall shomer this service. 26 And it shall come to pass, when your children shall say to you, What do you mean by this service? 27 That you shall say, It is the sacrifice of יהוה 's Pesach, who passed over the batiym of the children of Yisrael in Mitzrayim, when He smote the Mitzrites, and delivered · our batiym. And the people bowed their heads and worshipped. 28 And the children of Yisrael went away, and did as יהוה had commanded Moshe and Aharon, so they did. 29 And it came to pass, that at midnight יהוה smote all the bachor in the land of Mitzrayim, from the bachor of Pharoah that sat on his throne to the bachor of the captive that was in the dungeon; and all the bachor of cattle. 30 And Pharaoh rose up in the night, he, and all his avadim, and all the Mitzrites; and there was a great cry in Mitzrayim, for there was not a bayit where there was not one dead. 31 And he called for Moshe and Aharon by night, and said, Rise and get out from among my people, both you and the children of Yisrael; and go, serve יהוה, as you have said. 32 Also take your flocks and your herds, as you have said, and be gone; and bless me also. 33 And the Mitzrites greatly urged the people, that they might send them out of the land in a great hurry; for they said, We will all be dead men. 34 And the people took their dough before it was chametz, their kneading bowls being bound up in their clothes upon their shoulders. 35 And the children of Yisrael did according to the word of Moshe; and they asked of the Mitzrites jewels of silver, and jewels of gold, and garments: 36 And יהוה gave the people favor in the sight of the Mitzrites, so that they gave to them such things as they required. And they plundered the Mitzrites. 37 And the children of Yisrael journeyed from Rameses to Succoth, about six hundred thousand on foot that were men, beside children.[1] 38 And a mixed multitude[2] went up also with them; and flocks, and herds, even very much cattle. 39 And they baked unleavened cakes of the dough which they brought forth out of Mitzrayim, for it was not chametz; because they were driven out of Mitzrayim, and could not delay, neither had they prepared for themselves any food. 40 Now the sojourning of the children of Yisrael, who dwelt in Mitzrayim, was four hundred thirty years. 41 And it came to pass at the end of the four hundred and thirty years, even on the very same day of their entry it came to pass, that all the divisions of יהוה went out from the land of Mitzrayim. 42 It is a night to be much observed to יהוה for bringing them

---

[1] This an important figure to note. These were just the men. If we include all others, we would estimate the exodus to be about 3-4 million strong. This number will come into play later in Devarim 1:10-11.
[2] Those who were not biological Yisraelites but became Yisrael.

out from the land of Mitzrayim: this is a night unto יהוה to be observed by all the children of Yisrael in all their generations. 43 And יהוה said to Moshe and Aharon, *This is the mishpat of the Pesach: There shall no Ger eat of it: 44 But every man's eved that is bought for money, when you have circumcised him, then shall he eat of it. 45 A foreigner and an hired eved shall not eat of it. 46 In one bayit shall it be eaten;[1] you shall not carry forth any of the flesh outside of the bayit, neither shall you break a bone of it.[2] 47 All the congregation of Yisrael shall shomer it. 48 And when a Ger shall sojourn with you, and will shomer the Pesach to יהוה; all his males must be circumcised, and then let him come near and shomer it; and he shall be as one that is born in the land: for no uncircumcised person shall eat of it.[3] 49 One Torah shall be for him that is native, and for the Ger that sojourns among you.[4] 50 This did all* the children of Yisrael; as יהוה commanded Moshe and Aharon, so did they. 51 And it came to pass the very same day that יהוה did bring the children of Yisrael out of the land of Mitzrayim by their divisions.

13 And יהוה spoke to Moshe, saying, *2. Set-Apart to Me all the bachor, whatever opens the womb among the children of Yisrael, both of man and of beast: it is Mine.* 3 And Moshe said to the people, Remember this day,[5] in which you came out from Mitzrayim, out of the bayit of bondage; for by the strength of His hand יהוה brought you out from this place: there shall no chametz-lechem be eaten. 4 This day came you out in the month of Aviv. 5 And it shall be when יהוה shall bring you into the land of the Kanaanites, and the

Hittites, and the Amorites, and the Hivites, and the Yevusites, which He swore to your ahvot to give you, a land flowing with milk and honey, that you shall shomer this service in this month. 6 Seven days you shall eat matzah, and in the seventh day shall be a moed to יהוה. 7 Matzah shall be eaten seven days; and there shall no chametz-lechem be seen with you, neither shall there be chametz seen with you in all your borders. 8 And you shall inform your son in that day, saying, This is done because of what יהוה did for me when I came forth out of Mitzrayim. 9 And it shall be for a sign to you upon your hand, and for a memorial between your eyes, that the Torah of יהוה may be in your mouth: for with a strong hand has יהוה brought you out of Mitzrayim. 10 You shall therefore shomer this mishpat in its appointed time from year to year. 11 And it shall be when יהוה shall bring you into the land of the Kanaanites, as He swore to you and to your ahvot, and shall give it you, 12 That you shall set-apart to יהוה all that pehters the womb, and every bachor that comes from a beast which you have; all the males belong to יהוה. 13 And every bachor of a donkey you shall redeem with a lamb; and if you will not redeem it, then you shall break its neck: and all the bachor males among your children shall you redeem. 14 And it shall be when your son asks you in times to come, saying, What is this? That you shall say to him, By the strength of His hand יהוה brought us out from Mitzrayim, from the bayit of bondage: 15 And it came to pass, when Pharaoh would hardly let us go, that יהוה killed all the bachor in the land of Mitzrayim, both the bachor of man, and the bachor of beast: therefore I sacrifice to יהוה all that opens the womb, being males; but all the bachor of my children I redeem. 16 And it shall be for a sign upon your hand, and for frontlets between your eyes: for by strength of hand יהוה brought us forth out of Mitzrayim.

---

[1] Pesach is designed to bring both houses (all Yisrael) to the same table of fellowship, all in the one reunited house, by the dom of the Lamb as seen in verse 47 as well.
[2] Yahshua's bones as the Lamb of Yah were never broken.
[3] Very plain - no one can eat the Passover without circumcision and without dwelling by choice with the nation of Yisrael.
[4] This truth is what makes being Yisrael so special. All believers receive the same blessings of doing the same Torah.
[5] Aviv 15.

Torah Parsha 16
B'shallach 13:17-17:16
Haftarah Shophtim 4:4-5:31
Brit Chadasha Gilyahna 15:1-8

17 And it came to pass, when Pharaoh had let the people go, that Elohim led them not through the way of the land of the Philistines, although that was near; for Elohim said, Lest the people regret when they see war, and they return to Mitzrayim: 18 But Elohim led the people around, through the way of the wilderness of the Sea of Reeds: and the children of Yisrael went up armed [1] out of the land of Mitzrayim. 19 And Moshe took the bones of Yoseph with him: for he had certainly made the children of Yisrael swear, saying, Elohim will surely visit you; and you shall carry up my bones away from here with you. 20 And they took their journey from Succoth, and encamped in Etham, in the edge of the wilderness. 21 And יהוה went before them by day in a pillar of a cloud, to lead them in the way; and by night in a pillar of fire, to give them light; to go with them by day and night: 22 He took not away the pillar of the cloud by day, nor the pillar of fire by night, from before the people. 4

14 And יהוה spoke to Moshe, saying, *2 Speak to the children of Yisrael that they turn and encamp before Pi-Hahiroth, between Migdol and the sea, opposite Baal-Zephon: before it shall you encamp by the sea. 3 For Pharaoh will say of the children of Yisrael, They are entangled in the land; the wilderness has shut them in. 4 And I will harden Pharaoh's lev, that he shall follow after them; and I will be honored through Pharaoh, and over all his army; that the Mitzrites may know that I am יהוה*. And they did so. 5 And it was told the melech of Mitzrayim that the people fled: and the lev of Pharaoh and of his avadim was turned against the people, and they said, Why have we done this, that

we have let Yisrael go from serving us? 6 And he made ready his mirkavah, and took his people with him: 7 And he took six hundred chosen mirkavot, and all the mirkavot of Mitzrayim, and captains over every one of them. 8 And יהוה hardened the lev of Pharaoh melech of Mitzrayim, and he pursued after the children of Yisrael: and the children of Yisrael went out with a high hand. 9 But the Mitzrites pursued after them, all the horses and mirkavot of Pharaoh, and his horsemen, and his army, and overtook them camping by the sea, beside Pi-Hahiroth, before Baal-Zephon. 10 And when Pharaoh drew near, the children of Yisrael lifted up their eyes, and, see, the Mitzrites marched after them; and they were much afraid: and the children of Yisrael cried out to יהי. 11 And they said to Moshe, Because there were no graves in Mitzrayim, have you now taken us away to die in the wilderness? Why have you dealt with us in this manner, to carry us forth out of Mitzrayim? 12 Is not this the word that we did tell you in Mitzrayim, saying, Leave us alone, that we may serve the Mitzrites? For it had been better for us to serve the Mitzrites, than that we should die in the wilderness. 13 And Moshe said to the people, Fear not, stand still, and see the salvation of יהי, which He will show to you today: for the Mitzrites whom you have seen today, you shall see them again no more le-olam-va-ed. 14 יהוה shall fight for you, and you shall stay still. 15 And יהוה said to Moshe, *Why do you cry to Me? Speak to the children of Yisrael that they may go forward: 16 But lift up your rod, and stretch out your hand over the sea, and divide it: and the children of Yisrael shall go on dry ground through the middle of the sea. 17 And I, see, I will harden the levim of the Mitzrites, and they shall follow them: and I will get for Myself honor through Pharaoh, and upon all his armies, upon his mirkavot, and upon his horsemen. 18 And the Mitzrites shall know that I am יהוה, when I have gotten honor for Myself*

---

[1] With victory.

through Pharaoh, his mirkavot, and his horsemen. 19 And the Malach-Elohim, who went before the camp of Yisrael, moved and went behind them; and the pillar of the cloud went from before their face, and stood behind them:[1] 20 And it came between the camp of the Mitzrites and the camp of Yisrael; and it was a cloud and darkness to them, but it gave light by night to these: so that the one came not near the other all the night. 21 And Moshe stretched out his hand over the sea; and יהוה caused the sea to go back by a strong east wind all that night, and made the sea dry land, and the mayim were divided. 22 And the children of Yisrael went into the midst of the sea upon the dry ground: and the mayim were a wall to them on their right hand, and on their left. 23 And the Mitzrites pursued, and went in after them to the midst of the sea, even all Pharaoh's horses, his mirkavot, and his horsemen. 24 And it came to pass, that in the morning watch יהוה looked to the armies of the Mitzrites through the pillar of fire and of the cloud, and troubled the army of the Mitzrites, 25 And took off their mirkavah wheels, that they drove them with difficulty: so that the Mitzrites said, Let us flee from the face of Yisrael; for יהוה fights for them against the Mitzrites. 26 And יהוה said to Moshe, *Stretch out your hand over the sea, that the mayim may come again upon the Mitzrites, upon their mirkavot, and upon their horsemen.* 27 And Moshe stretched forth his hand over the sea, and the sea returned to its usual flow when the morning appeared; and the Mitzrites fled right into it; and יהוה overthrew the Mitzrites in the midst of the sea. 28 And the mayim returned, and covered the mirkavot, and the horsemen, and all the army of Pharaoh that came into the sea after them; there remained not even one of them alive. 29 But the children of Yisrael walked upon dry land in the midst of the sea; and the mayim were a wall to them on their right hand, and on their left. 30 So יהוה saved

Yisrael that day out of the hand of the Mitzrites; and Yisrael saw the Mitzrites dead upon the seashore. 31 And Yisrael saw that great work which יהוה did upon the Mitzrites: and the people feared יהוה, and believed יהוה, and His eved Moshe.

15 Then sang Moshe and the children of Yisrael this shir to יהוה, and spoke, saying, I will sing to יהוה, for He has triumphed gloriously: the horse and his rider has He thrown into the sea. 2 **YAH** is my strength and shir, and He has become my Yahshua:[2] He is my El, and I will hallel Him; my abba's Elohim, and I will exalt Him. 3 יהוה is a Man of war: יהוה is His Name. 4 Pharaoh's mirkavot and his army has He cast into the sea: his chosen captains also are drowned in the Sea of Reeds. 5 The depths have covered them: they sank into the bottom as a stone. 6 Your Right Hand,[3] O יהוה, has become tiferet in power: Your Right Hand, O יהוה, has dashed in pieces the enemy. 7 And in the greatness of Your Excellency You have overthrown them that rose up against You: You sent forth Your anger, which consumed them as stubble. 8 And with the blast of Your nostrils the mayim were gathered together, the floods stood upright as a heap, and the depths became stiff in the lev of the sea. 9 The enemy said, I will pursue, I will overtake, I will divide the plunder; my desire shall be satisfied upon them; I will draw my sword, my hand shall destroy them. 10 You did blow with Your wind, the sea covered them: they sank as lead in the mighty mayim. 11 Me-chamocha, O יהוה, among the mighty ones? Who is like You, beautiful in set-apartness, awesome in tehilot, doing wonders?[4] 12 You stretched out Your Right Hand,[5] the earth swallowed them. 13 You in Your rachamim have led forth the people whom You have redeemed: You have

---

[1] Yahshua and the **Shechinah** or Divine Presence.

[2] A **remez** or hint of the ultimate deliverance from Egypt or the world, found in YHWH's Son, when YHWH became Yahshua for mankind's sins.
[3] Yahshua.
[4] The famous Hebrew liturgy **Me-camocha.**
[5] Idiomatic expression for Moshiach.

guided them in Your strength to Your kadosh dwelling. 14 The people shall hear, and be afraid: sorrow shall take hold on the inhabitants of Philistia. 15 Then the rulers of Edom shall be amazed; the mighty men of Moav, trembling shall take hold upon them; all the inhabitants of Kanaan shall melt away. 16 Fear and dread shall fall upon them; by the greatness of Your Arm they shall be as still as a stone; until Your people pass over, O יהוה, until the people pass over, whom You have purchased. 17 You shall bring them in, and plant them in the mountain of Your inheritance, in the place, O יהוה, which You have made for Yourself to dwell in, in the Set-Apart-Place, O יהוה, that Your hands have established. 18 יהוה shall reign le-olam-va-ed. 19 For the horse of Pharaoh went in with his mirkavot and with his horsemen into the sea, and יהוה brought again the mayim of the sea upon them; but the children of Yisrael went on dry land in the midst of the sea. 20 And Miryam the neviyah, the sister of Aharon, took a timbrel in her hand; and all the women went out after her with timbrels and with dances.[1] 21 And Miryam answered them, Sing to יהוה, for He has triumphed gloriously; the horse and his rider has He thrown into the sea. 22 So Moshe brought Yisrael from the Sea of Reeds, and they went out into the wilderness of Shur; and they went three days in the wilderness, and found no mayim. 23 And when they came to Marah, they could not drink of the mayim of Marah, for they were bitter: therefore the name of it was called Marah. 24 And the people murmured against Moshe, saying, What shall we drink? 25 And he cried to יהוה; and יהוה showed him an eytz, which when he had cast into the mayim, the mayim were made sweet: there He made for them a chuk and a mishpat, and there He tested them,[2] 26 And said, If you will diligently listen to the voice of יהוה Your

Elohim, and will do that which is right in His sight, and will give ear to His mitzvot, and shomer all His chukim, I will put none of these diseases upon you, which I have brought upon the Mitzrites: for I am יהוה-Rophechah.[3] 27 And they came to Eylim, where were twelve wells of mayim, and seventy palm eytzim: and they encamped there by the mayim.[4]

16 And they took their journey from Eylim, and all the congregation of the children of Yisrael came to the wilderness of Sin, which is between Eylim and Sinai, on the fifteenth day of the second month after their departing out of the land of Mitzrayim. 2 And the whole congregation of the children of Yisrael murmured against Moshe and Aharon in the wilderness: 3 And the children of Yisrael said to them, Would to Elohim we had died by the hand of יהוה in the land of Mitzrayim, when we sat by the pots of meat, and when we did eat lechem until we were full; for you have brought us forth into this wilderness, to kill this whole congregation with hunger. 4 Then said יהוה to Moshe, See, I will rain lechem from the shamayim for you; and the people shall go out and gather a certain amount every day, that I may test them, whether they will have their halacha in My Torah, or not. 5 And it shall come to pass, that on the sixth day they shall prepare that which they bring in; and it shall be twice as much as they gather daily. 6 And Moshe and Aharon said to all the children of Yisrael, At evening, then you shall know that יהוה has brought you out from the land of Mitzrayim: 7 And in the morning, then you shall see the tifereth of יהוה ; for He shemas your murmurings against יהוה : and what are we that you murmur against us? 8 And Moshe said, This shall be, when יהוה shall give you in the evening meat to eat, and in the morning

---

[1] In Yisrael women are fully equal and able to serve YHWH in their assigned roles.
[2] A true foreshadow of Yahshua's healing tree of sacrifice, making life sweet when placed in life's bitter waters.
[3] Your-Healer.
[4] Twelve wells represent YHWH's living water for all 12 tribes. The 70 palm trees represent the 70 ruling elders of Yisrael and later the 70 rulers of the great assembly or Sanhedrin.

lechem to the satisfaction; for יהוה shemas your murmurings that you murmur against Him: and what are we? Your murmurings are not against us, but against יהוה. 9 And Moshe spoke to Aharon, Say to all the congregation of the children of Yisrael, Come near before יהוה: for He has heard your murmurings. 10 And it came to pass, as Aharon spoke to the whole congregation of the children of Yisrael, that they looked toward the wilderness, and, see, the tifereth of יהוה appeared in the cloud. 11 And יהוה spoke to Moshe, saying, 12 I have heard the murmurings of the children of Yisrael: speak to them, saying, At evening you shall eat meat, and in the morning you shall be filled with lechem; and you shall know that I am יהוה Your Elohim. 13 And it came to pass, that at evening the quails came up, and covered the camp: and in the morning the dew lay all around the camp. 14 And when the dew that lay was gone up, see, upon the face of the wilderness there lay a small round thing, as small as the frost on the ground. 15 And when the children of Yisrael saw it, they said one to another, It is manna: for they did not know what it was. And Moshe said to them, This is the lechem that יהוה has given you to eat. 16 This is the thing which יהוה has commanded, Gather of it every man according to eating, an omer for every man, according to the number of your persons; take some for every man who is in his tent. 17 And the children of Yisrael did so, and gathered, some more, some less. 18 And when they did measure it with an omer, he that gathered much had nothing over, and he that gathered little had no lack; they gathered every man according to his need. 19 And Moshe said, Let no man leave any of it until the morning. 20 Nevertheless they listened not to Moshe; but some of them left of it until the morning, and it bred worms, and smelled: and Moshe was angry with them. 21 And they gathered it every morning, every man according to his need: and when the sun became hot, it melted. 22 And it came to pass, that on the sixth day they gathered twice as much lechem, two omers for one man: and all the rulers of the congregation came and told Moshe. 23 And He said to them, This is that which יהוה has said, Tomorrow is the rest of the kadosh Shabbat to יהוה: bake that which you will bake today, and cook what you will cook; and that which remains leftover, store up for yourselves until the morning. 24 And they stored up until the morning, as Moshe commanded: and it did not stink, neither was there any worm inside. 25 And Moshe said, Eat that today; for today is a Shabbat to יהוה: today you shall not find it in the field. 26 Six days you shall gather it; but on the seventh day, which is the Shabbat, in it there shall be none. 27 And it came to pass, that there went out some of the people on the seventh day to gather, and they found none. 28 And יהוה said to Moshe, How long do you refuse to shomer My mitzvot and My Torot? 29 See, for that יהוה has given you the Shabbat, therefore He gives you on the sixth day the lechem for two days; abide every man in his place, let no man go out of his place on the seventh day. 30 So the people rested on the seventh day. 31 And the bayit of Yisrael called the name of it Manna: and it was like coriander zera, white; and the taste of it was like wafers made with honey. 32 And Moshe said, This is the thing which יהוה commands, Fill an omer of it to be kept for your generations; that they may see the lechem with which I have fed you in the wilderness, when I brought you forth from the land of Mitzrayim. 33 And Moshe said to Aharon, Take a pot, and put an omer full of manna inside, and store it up before יהוה, to be kept for your generations. 34 As יהוה commanded Moshe, so Aharon stored it before the Testimony, to be kept. 35 And the children of Yisrael did eat manna forty years, until they came to a land inhabited; they did eat manna, until they came to the borders of the land of Kanaan. 36 Now an omer is the tenth part of an ephah. 17 And all the congregation of the children of Yisrael journeyed from the wilderness of Tzin, after their journeys, according to the mitzvah of יהוה, and pitched in Rephidim: and there was no mayim for the people to drink. 2 Wherefore the people did strive with Moshe, and said, Give us mayim that we may drink. And Moshe said to them, Why do you strive you with me? Why do you test יהוה? 3 And the people thirsted there for mayim; and the people murmured against Moshe, and said, Why is this that you have brought us up out of Mitzrayim, to kill us and our children and our cattle with thirst? 4 And Moshe cried to יהוה, saying, What shall I do with this people? They are almost ready to stone me. 5 And יהוה said to Moshe, *Go on before the people, and take with you of the zachanim of Yisrael; and your rod, with which you smote the river, take it in your hand, and go. 6 See, I will stand before you there upon the Rock in Horev; and you shall smite the Rock, and there shall come mayim out of it, so that the people may drink.* And Moshe did so in the sight of the zachanim of Yisrael. 7 And he called the name of the place Massah, and Merivah, because of the striving of the children of Yisrael, and because they tested יהוה, saying, Is יהוה among us, or not? 8 Then came Amalek, and fought with Yisrael in Rephidim. 9 And Moshe said to Yahoshua, Choose us out men, and go out, fight with Amalek: tomorrow I will stand on the top of the hill with the rod of Elohim in my hand. 10 So Yahoshua did as Moshe had said to him, and fought with Amalek: and Moshe, Aharon, and Hur went up to the top of the hill. 11 And it came to pass, when Moshe held up his hand, that Yisrael prevailed: and when he let down his hand, Amalek prevailed. 12 But Moshe's hands were heavy; and they took a stone, and put it under him, and he sat down; and Aharon and Hur held up his hands, the one on the one side, and the other on the other side; and his hands were steady until the going down of the sun. 13 And Yahoshua defeated

Amalek and their people with the edge of the sword. 14 And יהוה said to Moshe, *Write this for a memorial in a scroll, and rehearse it in the ears of Yahoshua: for I will utterly put out the remembrance of Amalek from under the shamayim.* 15 And Moshe built an altar, and called the Name of it יהוה-Nissi:[1] 16 For he said, Because His hand is on the throne of Yah; יהוה will have a war with Amalek from generation to generation.

Torah Parsha 17
Yitro 18:1-20:23
Haftarah Yeshayahu 6:1-7:14
Brit Chadasha Timtheous Alef 3:1-14

18 When Yithro, the kohen of Midyan, Moshe's abba-in-law, heard of all that Elohim had done for Moshe, and for Yisrael His people, and that יהוה had brought Yisrael out of Mitzrayim; 2 Then Yithro, Moshe's abba-in-law, took Tzipporah, Moshe's wife, after he had sent her back, 3 And her two sons; of which the name of the one was Gershom; for he said, I have been a Ger in a strange land: 4 And the name of the other was Eliezer; for the Elohim of my abba, said he, was mine help, and delivered me from the sword of Pharaoh: 5 And Yithro, Moshe's abba-in-law, came with his sons and his wife to Moshe into the wilderness, where he camped at the Mount of Elohim: 6 And he said to Moshe, I your abba-in-law Yithro have come to you, and your wife, and her two sons with her. 7 And Moshe went out to meet his abba-in-law, and bowed down,[2] and kissed him; and they asked each other of their welfare; and they came into the tent. 8 And Moshe told his abba-in-law all that יהוה had done to Pharaoh and to the Mitzrites for Yisrael's sake, and all the travail that had come upon them by the way, and how יהוה delivered them. 9 And Yithro rejoiced for all the tov that יהוה had done to Yisrael, whom he had delivered out of the

---

[1] YHWH my Banner.
[2] Not worship but a custom.

hand of the Mitzrites. 10 And Yithro said, Blessed be **יהוה**, who has delivered you out of the hand of the Mitzrites, and out of the hand of Pharaoh, who has delivered the people from under the hand of the Mitzrites. 11 Now I know that **יהוה** is greater than all elohim: for in the thing in which they dealt proudly He was above them. 12 And Yithro, Moshe's abba-in-law, took a burnt offering and sacrifices for Elohim: and Aharon came, and all the zachanim of Yisrael, to eat lechem with Moshe's abba-in-law before Elohim. 13 And it came to pass the next day, that Moshe sat to shophet the people: and the people stood by Moshe from the morning to the evening. 14 And when Moshe's abba-in-law saw all that he did for the people, he said, What is this thing that you do for all the people? Why do you sit alone, and all the people stand before you from morning to even? 15 And Moshe said to his abba-in-law, Because the people come to me to inquire of Elohim: 16 When they have a matter, they come to me; and I shophet between one and another, and I do make them know the chukim of Elohim, and His Torot. 17 And Moshe's abba-in-law said to him, The thing that you do is not tov. 18 You will surely wear away, both you, and this people that is with you: for this thing is too heavy for you; you are not able to perform it yourself all alone.[1] 19 Listen now to my voice, I will give you counsel, and Elohim shall be with you: Stand before Elohim for the people, that you may bring the matters to Elohim: 20 And you shall teach them the ordinances and Torot, and shall show them the derech in which they must have their halacha,[2] and the work that they must do. 21 Moreover you shall provide out of all the people able men, such as fear Elohim, men of emet, hating covetousness; and place such over them, to be rulers of thousands, and rulers of hundreds, rulers of fifties, and rulers of

tens:[3] 22 And let them shophet the people at all seasons: and it shall be, that every great matter they shall bring to you, but every small matter they shall shophet: so shall it be easier for yourself, and they shall bear the burden with you. 23 If you shall do this thing, and Elohim command you so, then you shall be able to endure, and the entire people shall also go to their place in shalom. 24 So Moshe listened to the voice of his abba-in-law, and did all that he had said. 25 And Moshe chose able men out of all Yisrael, and made them heads over the people, rulers of thousands, rulers of hundreds, rulers of fifties, and rulers of tens. 26 And they judged the people at all seasons: the hard matters they brought to Moshe, but every small matter they judged themselves. 27 And Moshe let his abba-in-law depart; and he went his way into his own land.

19 In the third month, when the children of Yisrael had gone forth out of the land of Mitzrayim, the same day they came into the wilderness of Sinai. 2 For they were departed from Rephidim, and were come to the desert of Sinai, and had pitched in the wilderness; and there Yisrael camped before the Mount. 3 And Moshe went up to Elohim, and **יהוה** called to him out of the mountain, saying, *This shall you say to the bayit of Yaakov, and tell the children of Yisrael; 4 You have seen what I did to the Mitzrites, and how I bore you on eagles' wings, and brought you to Myself. 5 Now therefore, if you will obey My voice indeed, and shomer My covenant, then you shall be a peculiar treasure to Me above all peoples: for all the earth is Mine: 6 And you shall be to Me a malchut of kohanim,[4] and a kadosh nation. These are the words that you shall speak to the children of Yisrael.* 7 And Moshe came and

---

[1] True ministry for YHWH can never be done alone; it must be done in tandem with a chosen and called out team.
[2] Hebrew: **halacha**, meaning way or way to walk or conduct one's life.
[3] Notice Yisrael and its Kingdom is not a democracy and no elections are held. Service is by divine appointment and submission.
[4] That's what Yahshua came to do in His people. First Peter 2:9.

called for the zachanim of the people, and laid before their faces all these words that יהוה commanded him. 8 And all the people answered together, and said, All that יהוה has spoken we will do. And Moshe returned the words of the people to יהוה. 9 And יהוה said to Moshe, *See, I come to you in a thick cloud, that the people may hear when I speak with you, and believe you le-olam-va-ed.* And Moshe told the words of the people to יהוה. 10 And יהוה said to Moshe, *Go to the people, and set them apart today and tomorrow, and let them wash their clothes, 11 And be ready by the third day: for on the third day יהוה will come down in the sight of all the people upon Mount Sinai. 12 And you shall set borders for the people all around, saying, Be careful, that you go not up into the Mount, or touch the border of it: whoever touches the Mount shall be surely put to death: 13 There shall not a hand touch it, but he shall surely be stoned, or shot through; whether it be beast or man, it shall not live: when the shofar sounds long, they shall come near the mountain.* 14 And Moshe went down from the Mount to the people, and set-apart the people; and they washed their clothes. 15 And he said to the people, Be ready for the third day: come not at your wives in intimacy. 16 And it came to pass on the third day in the morning, that there were thunders and lightnings, and a thick cloud upon the Mount, and the voice of the shofar exceedingly loud; so that all the people that were in the camp trembled. 17 And Moshe brought forth the people out of the camp to meet with Elohim; and they stood at the foot of the mountain. 18 And Mount Sinai was altogether in smoke, because יהוה descended upon it in fire: and the smoke of it ascended as the smoke of a furnace, and the whole Mount shook greatly. 19 And when the voice of the shofar sounded long, and became louder and louder, Moshe spoke, and Elohim answered him by a voice. 20 And יהוה came down upon Mount Sinai, on the top of the Mount: and יהוה called Moshe up to the top of the

Mount; and Moshe went up. 21 And יהוה said to Moshe, *Go down, and warn the people,[1] lest they break through to יהוה to see, and many of them perish. 22 And let the kohanim also, who come near to יהוה, set themselves apart, lest יהוה break forth upon them.* 23 And Moshe said to יהוה, The people cannot come up to Mount Sinai: for you warned us, saying, Set borders around the mountain, and set it apart. 24 And יהוה said to him, *Away, get you down, and you shall come up, you, and Aharon with you: but let not the kohanim and the people break through to come up to יהוה, lest He break forth upon them.* 25 So Moshe went down to the people, and spoke to them.

20 And the word of Elohim spoke all these words, saying, 2 *I am יהוה Your Elohim, who has brought you out of the land of Mitzrayim, out of the bayit of bondage. 3 You shall have no other elohim before My face. 4 You shall not make to you any graven image, or any likeness of any thing that is in the shamayim above, or that is in the earth beneath, or that is in the mayim under the earth: 5 You shall not bow down yourself to them, nor serve them: for I יהוה Your Elohim am a jealous Elohim, visiting the iniquity of the ahvot upon the children to the third and fourth generation of those that hate Me; 6 And showing rachamim to thousands of them that love Me, and shomer My mitzvot. 7 You shall not bring the Name of יהוה Your Elohim to vain emptiness; for יהוה will not hold him guiltless that brings His Name to vain emptiness.[2] 8 Remember Yom Shabbat, to shomer it as kadosh. 9 Six days shall you labor, and do all your work: 10 But the seventh day is the Shabbat of יהוה Your Elohim: in it you shall not do any work, you, nor your son, nor your daughter, your male*

---

[1] **Chesed.**
[2] Most religions blatantly violate this command. The Hebrew for vain is **shavah** meaning "to bring to nothing or erasing from man's usage." It does not mean as erroneously taught that using it in vain is actually saying it. The truth is just the opposite.

eved, nor your female eved, nor your cattle, nor your Ger that is within your gates: 11 *For in six days* יהוה *made the shamayim and earth, the sea, and all that is in them, and rested on the seventh day: therefore* יהוה *blessed the Shabbat day, and set it apart. 12 Honor your abba and your ima: that your days may be long upon the land that* יהוה *Your Elohim gives you.* [1] *13 You shall not kill. 14 You shall not commit adultery. 15 You shall not steal. 16 You shall not bear false witness against your neighbor. 17 You shall not covet your neighbor's bayit; you shall not covet your neighbor's wife, or his male eved, or his female eved, or his ox, or his donkey, or anything that is your neighbor's. 18 And all* the people saw the thunderings, and the lightnings, and the noise of the shofar, and the mountain smoking: and when the people saw it, they moved back, and stood at a distance. 19 And they said to Moshe, You speak with us, and we will listen: but let not Elohim speak with us, lest we die. 20 And Moshe said to the people, Fear not: for Elohim is come to test you, and that His fear may be before your faces, that you sin not. 21 And the people stood far off, and Moshe drew near to the thick darkness where Elohim was. 22 And יהוה said to Moshe, *This you shall say to the children of Yisrael, You have seen that I have talked with you from the shamayim. 23 You shall not make besides Me elohim of silver; neither shall you make for yourselves elohim of gold. 24 An altar of earth you shall make for Me, and shall sacrifice there your burnt offerings, and your shalom offerings, your sheep, and your oxen: in all places where I record My Name I will come to you, and I will bless you. 25 And if you will make Me an altar of stone, you shall not build it of cut stone: for if you lift up your tool upon it, you have polluted it. 26 Neither shall you go up by steps to My altar, that your nakedness be not discovered on it.*

---

[1] Rav Shaul/Paul quotes this command to the Ephesian (6:1-2) Yisraelites, proving their Yisraelite heritage.

Parsha 18
Mishpatim 21:1-24:18
Haftarah Yirmeyahu 34:8-22, 31:31-34
Brit Chadasha Ivrim 9:15-22

21 *Now these are the mishpatim that you shall set before them. 2 If you buy an Ivree eved, six years he shall serve: and in the seventh he shall go out free for nothing. 3 If he came in by himself, he shall go out by himself: if he was married, then his wife shall go out with him. 4 If his master has given him a wife, and she has born him sons or daughters; the wife and her children shall be her master's, and he shall go out by himself. 5 And if the eved shall plainly say, I love my master, my wife, and my children; I will not go out free: 6 Then his master shall bring him to the shophtim; he shall also bring him to the door, or to the door post; and his master shall pierce his ear through with an awl; and he shall serve him le-olam-va-ed. 7 And if a man sells his daughter to be a female eved, she shall not go out as the menservants do. 8 If she please not her master, who has betrothed her to himself, then shall he let her be redeemed: to sell her to a strange nation he shall have no power, seeing he has dealt deceitfully with her. 9 And if he has betrothed her to his son, he shall ephah with her after the manner of daughters. 10 If he takes himself another wife; her food, her garment, and her duty of marriage, shall he not diminish. 11 And if he does not these three to her, then shall she go out free without money. 12 He that smites a man, so that he dies, shall be surely put to death. 13 And if a man lies not in wait, but Elohim delivers him into his hand; then I will appoint you a place where he shall flee. 14 But if a man come presumptuously upon his neighbor, to kill him with guile; you shall take him from My altar that he may die. 15 And he that hits his abba, or his ima, shall be surely put to death. 16 And he that kidnaps a man, and sells him, or if he be found in his hand, he shall surely be put to death. 17 And he that*

curses his abba, or his ima, shall surely be put to death. 18 And if men strive together, and one smites another with a stone, or with his fist, and he does not die, but is confined to his bed: 19 If he rise again, and walks outside with his staff, then shall he that smote him be innocent: only he shall pay for the loss of his time, and shall see to it that he is thoroughly healed. 20 And if a man smites his eved, or his eved, with a rod, and he die under his hand; he shall be surely punished. 21 But if he remains alive a day or two, he shall not be punished: for he is his property. 22 If men fight, and hurt a woman with child, so that her child departs from her, and yet no mischief follows: he shall be surely punished, according to what the woman's husband will determine; and he shall pay as the shophtim determine. 23 And if there is any injury, then you shall give chayim for chayim, 24 Eye for eye, tooth for tooth, hand for hand, foot for foot,[1] 25 Burning for burning, wound for wound, stripe for stripe. 26 And if a man smites the eye of his eved, or the eye of his female eved, that it perish; he shall let him go free for his eye's sake. 27 And if he smites out his male eved's tooth, or his female eved's tooth, he shall let them go free for the tooth's sake. 28 If an ox gores a man or a woman that they die: then the ox shall be surely stoned, and his flesh shall not be eaten; but the owner of the ox shall be innocent. 29 But if the ox was in the habit of goring in times past, and it had been told to the owner, and he had not kept it in, but that it had killed a man or a woman; the ox shall be stoned, and its owner also shall be put to death. 30 If there be laid on him a sin covering penalty, then he shall give for the ransom of his chayim whatever is laid upon him. 31 Whether it has gored a son, or has gored a daughter, according to this mishpat shall it be done to him. 32 If the ox shall gore a male eved or a female eved, he shall

give to their master thirty shekels of silver, and the ox shall be stoned. 33 And if a man shall open a pit, or if a man shall dig a pit, and not cover it, and an ox or an donkey fall inside; 34 The owner of the pit shall repay, and give money to the owner of them; and the dead beast shall be his. 35 And if one man's ox hurts another's, so that he dies; then they shall sell the live ox, and divide the money of it; and the dead ox also they shall divide. 36 Or if it is known that the ox has gored in times past, and his owner has not kept him in; he shall surely repay ox for ox; and the dead ox shall be his own.

22 If a man shall steal an ox, or a sheep, and kill it, or sell it; he shall restore five oxen for an ox, and four sheep for a sheep. 2 If a thief be found breaking in, and be smitten so that he dies, there shall no dom be shed for him. 3 If the sun is risen upon him, there shall be domshed for him; for he should make full restitution; if he has nothing, then he shall be sold for his theft. 4 If the theft is certainly found in his hand alive, whether it is an ox, or donkey, or sheep; he shall restore double. 5 If a man shall cause a field or vineyard to be eaten, and shall put in his beast, and shall feed in another man's field; he repays from the best of his own field, and from the best of his own vineyard, shall he make restitution. 6 If a fire breaks out, and spreads to thorn bushes, so that the stacked corn, or the standing grain, or the field, is consumed; he that kindled the fire shall surely make restitution. 7 If a man shall deliver to his neighbor money or goods to shomer, and it be stolen out of the man's bayit; if the thief is found, let him repay double. 8 If the thief is not found, then the master of the bayit shall be brought to the shophtim, to see whether he has put his hand into his neighbor's goods. 9 For all manner of trespass, whether it be for ox, for donkey, for sheep, for garment, or for any manner of lost thing, which another challenges to be his, the cause of both parties shall come

---

[1] Idiomatic expressions used for equity and justice to be sought. This is not to be understood as divinely sanctioned mutilation.

before the shophtim; and whomever the shophtim shall declare wrong, he shall repay double to his neighbor. 10 If a man deliver to his neighbor a donkey, or an ox, or a sheep, or any beast, to shomer; and it dies, or is hurt, or driven away, no man seeing it: 11 Then shall an oath of יהוה be between them both, that he has not put his hand to his neighbor's goods; and the owner of it shall accept it, and he shall not repay. 12 And if it is stolen from him, he shall make restitution to the owner of it. 13 If it is torn in pieces, then let him bring it for witness, and he shall not repay that which was torn. 14 And if a man borrow anything from his neighbor, and it is hurt, or dies, the owner of it not being with it, he shall surely repay. 15 But if the owner of it is with it, he shall not repay: if it is a hired thing, it came for his hire. 16 And if a man entices a virgin that is not engaged, and lies with her, he shall surely endow her to be his wife. 17 If her abba utterly refuses to give her to him, he shall pay money according to the dowry of virgins. 18 You shall not allow a witch to live. 19 Whoever lies with a beast shall surely be put to death. 20 He that sacrifices to any elohim, except to יהוה only, he shall be utterly destroyed. 21 You shall neither vex a Ger, nor oppress him: for you were strangers in the land of Mitzrayim. 22 You shall not afflict any widow, or fatherless child. 23 If you afflict them in any way, and they cry out to Me, I will surely hear their cry; 24 And My anger shall wax hot, and I will kill you with the sword; and your wives shall be widows, and your children fatherless. 25 If you lend money to any of My people that is poor among you, you shall not be to him as one who lends on interest to him, neither shall you lay upon him interest. 26 If you take your neighbor's garment as a pledge, you shall deliver it to him before the sun goes down: 27 For that is his covering only, it is his garment for his skin: with what shall he sleep? And it shall come to pass, when he calls out to Me, that I will listen; for I am gracious.[1] 28 You shall not revile Elohim, nor curse a ruler of your people.[2] 29 You shall not delay to offer the first of your ripe fruits, and of your liquors: the bachor of your sons shall you give to Me. 30 Likewise shall you do with your oxen, and with your sheep: seven days it shall be with his ima; on the eighth day you shall give it Me. 31 And you shall be kadosh men to Me: neither shall you eat any flesh that is torn of the beasts in the field; you shall cast it to the dogs.

23 You shall not raise a false report: put not your hand with the wicked to be an unrighteous witness. 2 You shall not follow a crowd to do evil; neither shall you speak in a cause to turn aside after many to turn aside what is right: 3 Neither shall you favor a poor man in his cause. 4 If you meet your enemy's ox or his donkey going astray, you shall surely bring it back to him again. 5 If you see the donkey of him that hates you lying under his burden, you shall refrain from leaving it to him, you shall surely help with him. 6 You shall not turn aside the right ruling of your poor in his cause. 7 Keep far from a false matter; and the innocent and tzadik kill not: for I will not justify the wicked. 8 And you shall take no bribe: for the bribe blinds the wise, and twists the words of the tzadik. 9 Also you shall not oppress a Ger: for you know the lev of a Ger, seeing you were strangers in the land of Mitzrayim.[3] 10 And six years you shall sow your land, and shall gather in the fruits of it: 11 But the seventh year you shall let it rest[4] and lie still; that the poor of your people may eat: and what they leave the beasts of the field shall eat. In like manner you shall ephah with your vineyard, and with your oliveyard. 12 Six days you shall do your work, and on the seventh day

---

[1] Eternally full of rachamim.
[2] Sadly, many in Yisrael continue to live under a divine curse, not realizing that they cannot come against a leader of Yisrael even when he or she may be wrong.
[3] An important word in season for Judah, in their treatment of returning brother Ephraim.
[4] Land Shabbat or **shemetah**.

you shall rest: that your ox and your donkey may rest, and the son of your handmaid, and the Ger, may be refreshed. 13 And in all things that I have said to you take heed: and make no mention of the name of other elohim, neither let it be heard out of you mouth.[1] 14 Three regalim you shall shomer as chagim to Me in the year.[2] 15 You shall shomer Chag Matzah: - you shall eat matzah seven days, as I commanded you, in the time appointed in the month Aviv; for in it you came out from Mitzrayim: and none shall appear before Me empty - 16 And Chag Shavuot - the harvest - the firstfruits of your labors,[3] which you have sown in the field: and the Chag of Ingathering – Sukkot - [4] that is toward the end of the year, [5] when you have gathered in your labors out of the field. 17 Three times in the year all your males shall appear before יהוה Elohim.[6] 18 You shall not offer the dom of My sacrifice with chametz-lechem; neither shall the fat of My sacrifice remain until the morning. 19 The first of the firstfruits of your land you shall bring into the Bayit of יהוה Your Elohim. You shall not cook a kid in its ima's milk.[7] 20 See, I send a Malach before you,[8] to guide you in the derech, and to bring you into the place that I have prepared. 21 Beware of Him, and obey His voice, provoke Him not; for otherwise He will not pardon your transgressions: for My Name is in Him.[9] 22 But if you shall indeed obey His voice, and do all that I speak; then I will be an enemy to your enemies, and an adversary to your adversaries. [10] 23 For My Malach shall go before you, and bring you into the land of the Amorites, and the Hittites, and the Perizzites, and the Kanaanites, and the Hivites, and the Yevusites: and I will cut them off. 24 You shall not bow down to their elohim, nor serve them, nor do after their works: but you shall utterly overthrow them, and without fail break down their images. 25 And you shall serve יהוה Your Elohim, and He shall bless your lechem, and your mayim; and I will take sickness away from the midst of you. 26 There shall nothing miscarry, nor be barren, in your land: the number of your days I will fill. 27 I will send My fear before you, and will destroy all the people to whom you shall come, and I will make all your enemies turn their backs to you. 28 And I will send hornets before you, which shall drive out the Hivite, the Kanaanite, and the Hittite, from before you. 29 I will not drive them out from before you in one year; lest the land become desolate, and the beast of the field multiply against you. 30 Little by little I will drive them out from before you, until you be increased, and inherit the land. 31 And I will set your borders from the Sea of Reeds even to the Sea of the Philistines, and from the desert to the river: for I will deliver the inhabitants of the land into your hand; and you shall drive them out from before you. 32 You shall make no covenant with them, or with their elohim.[11] 33 They shall not dwell in your land, lest they make you sin against Me: for if you serve their elohim, it will surely be a snare to you.

24 And the word יהוה said to Moshe, Come up to יהוה, you, and Aharon, Nadav, and Avihu, and seventy of the zachanim of Yisrael; and worship far off. 2 And Moshe alone shall come near יהוה: but they shall not come near; neither shall the people go up with him. 3 And Moshe

---

[1] Which is why knowing and using YHWH's true Name is so important. It protects you from judgment.
[2] Three ascension feasts (or the **shalosh regalim**) out of 7 annual feasts.
[3] Shavuot.
[4] Sukkot.
[5] Towards the end of the harvest cycle, or yearly harvest cycle.
[6] And by definition all under the male's covering or authority; and thereby not limited to males.
[7] Forbidding torture of a mother by cooking the offspring, as did the heathen. This is not a prohibition of mixing meat and dairy.
[8] Widely acknowledged as the Guardian of Yisrael, or the young Man **Metatron**/Yahshua.
[9] The young man Metatron has YHWH's Name and can pardon Yisrael's sin. This Man has to be His pre-incarnate Son.

[10] Widely acknowledged as the Guardian of Yisrael or the young Man **Metatron**/Yahshua.
[11] All peace accords with others on the land are forbidden.

came and told the people all the words of יהוה, and all the mishpatim: and all the people answered with kol echad, and said, All the words that יהוה has said we will do. 4 And Moshe wrote all the words of יהוה, and rose up early in the morning, and built an altar under the hill, and twelve pillars, according to the twelve tribes of Yisrael. 5 And he sent young men of the children of Yisrael, which offered burnt offerings, and sacrificed shalom offerings of oxen to יהוה. 6 And Moshe took half of the dom, and put it in basons; and half of the dom he sprinkled on the altar. 7 And he took the scroll of the covenant, and read it in the audience of the people: and they said, All that יהוה has said will we do, and be obedient. 8 And Moshe took the dom, and sprinkled it on the people, and said, See the dom of the covenant,[1] that יהוה has made with you concerning all these words. 9 Then went up Moshe, and Aharon, Nadav, and Avihu, and seventy of the zachanim of Yisrael: 10 And they saw the Elohim of Yisrael: and there was under His feet as it were a paved work of a sapphire stone, and as it were the body of the shamayim in His clearness.[2] 11 And upon the nobles of the children of Yisrael He laid not His hand: also they saw Elohim, and did eat and drink.[3] 12 And יהוה said to Moshe, *Come up to Me into the Mount, and be there: and I will give you tablets of stone, and a Torah, and mitzvot that I have written; that you may teach them.* 13 And Moshe rose up, and his assistant Yahoshua: and Moshe went up into the Mount of Elohim. 14 And he said to the zachanim, Wait here for us, until we come again to you: and, see, Aharon and Hur are with you: if any man has any matters to do, let him come to them. 15 And

Moshe went up into the Mount, and a cloud covered the Mount. 16 And the tifereth of יהוה abode upon Mount Sinai, and the cloud covered it six days: and on the seventh day He called to Moshe out of the midst of the cloud. 17 And the sight of the tifereth of יהוה was like a consuming fire on the top of the Mount in the eyes of the children of Yisrael. 18 And Moshe went into the midst of the cloud, and went up to the Mount: and Moshe was in the Mount forty days and forty nights.

Torah Parsha 19
Terumah 25:1-27:19
Haftarah Melechim Alef 5:26-6:13
Brit Chadasha Ivrim 8:1-13

25 And יהוה spoke to Moshe, saying, 2 *Speak to the children of Yisrael, that they bring Me an offering: of every man that gives it willingly with his lev you shall take My offering. 3 And this is the offering that you shall take from them; gold, and silver, and brass, 4 And blue, and purple, and scarlet, and fine linen, and goats' hair, 5 And rams' skins dyed red, and badgers' skins, and shittim wood, 6 Oil for the light, spices for anointing oil, and for sweet incense, 7 Onyx stones, and stones to be set in the shoulder garment, and in the breastplate. 8 And let them make Me a Set-Apart-Place; that I may dwell among them. 9 According to all that I show you, after the pattern of the Tabernacle, and the pattern of all the instruments of it, even so shall you make it. 10 And they shall make an ark of shittim wood: two cubits and a half shall be the length of it, and a cubit and a half the width of it, and a cubit and a half the height of it. 11 And you shall cover it with pure gold, within and without shall you cover it, and shall make upon it a keter of gold all around. 12 And you shall cast four rings of gold for it, and put them in the four corners of it; and two rings shall be in the one side of it, and two rings in the other side of it. 13 And you shall make poles of shittim wood, and cover them with gold. 14 And*

---

[1] The dom of the lamb sealed the Torah, just as the dom of the Lamb also seals the Renewed Covenant. YHWH truly never changes either the means of atonement, or the nation who are the recipients of His atonement.
[2] They saw Elohim and did not die. The Elohim they saw is called the body or bone of the heavens or **ke-etzem hashamayim**. So we see that they see a part of YHWH corporally. No doubt they did not see Abba-YHWH, but His Son.
[3] See note on Exodus 24 verse 10.

you shall put the poles into the rings by the sides of the ark, that the ark may be carried with them. 15 *The poles shall be in the rings of the ark: they shall not be taken from it.* 16 *And you shall put into the ark the testimony that I shall give you.* 17 *And you shall make a lid of atonement of pure gold: two cubits and a half shall be the length of it, and a cubit and a half the width of it.* 18 *And you shall make two cheruvim of gold; of beaten work shall you make them, on the two ends of the lid of atonement.* 19 *And make one cheruv on the one end, and the other cheruv on the other end: even of the lid of atonement shall you make the cheruvim on the two ends of it.*[1] 20 *And the cheruvim shall stretch forth their wings on high, covering the lid of atonement with their wings, and their faces shall look one to another; toward the lid of atonement shall the faces of the cheruvim be.*[2] 21 *And you shall put the lid of atonement above upon the ark; and in the ark you shall put the testimony that I shall give you.* 22 *And there I will meet with you, and I will commune with you from above the lid of atonement, from between the two cheruvim that are upon the Ark of the Covenant, of all things which I will give you in mitzvoth to the children of Yisrael.* 23 *You shall also make a table of shittim wood: two cubits shall be the length of it, and a cubit the width of it, and a cubit and a half the height of it.* 24 *And you shall cover it with pure gold, and make a keter molding of gold all around.* 25 *And you shall make to it a border of a hand width all around it, and you shall make a golden keter to the border of it all around.* 26 *And you shall make for it four rings of gold, and put the rings in the four corners that are on the four feet of it.* 27 *Over against the border shall the rings be for places for the poles to bear the table.* 28 *And you shall make the poles of shittim*

wood, and cover them with gold, that the table may be borne with them. 29 *And you shall make the dishes of it, and spoons of it, and the covers of it, and bowls of it, to cover all over: of pure gold shall you make them.* 30 *And you shall put the Lechem of the Panayim on the table before Me always.* 31 *And you shall make a menorah of pure gold: of beaten work shall the menorah be made: its shaft, and its branches, its bowls, its knobs, and its blossoms, shall be of the same.* 32 *And six branches shall come out of the sides of it; three branches of the menorah out of the one side, and three branches of the menorah out of the other side:*[3] 33 *Three cups made like almonds, with a knob and a blossom in one branch; and three cups made like almonds in the other branch, with a knob and a blossom: for the six branches that come out of the menorah.* 34 *And on the menorah itself shall be four cups made like almonds, with their knobs and their blossom.* 35 *And there shall be a knob under two branches of the same, and a knob under two branches of the same, and a knob under two branches of the same, according to the six branches that proceed out of the menorah.* 36 *Their knobs and their branches shall be the same: all it shall be one beaten work of pure gold.*[4] 37 *And you shall make the seven lamps of it: and they shall light the lamps of it, that they may give light opposite it.*[5] 38 *And the snuffers of it, and the trays of it, shall be of pure gold.* 39 *Of a talent of pure gold shall he make it, with all these vessels.* 40 *See to it that you make them after their pattern, which was shown you in the Mount.*

26 Moreover *you shall make the Tabernacle with ten curtains of fine twined linen, and blue, and purple, and scarlet: with cheruvim of skilled work shall you make them.* 2 *The length of one curtain*

---

[1] Two cherubim represent both houses of Yisrael; with the dom atonement in the middle on the lid of atonement indicating dom redemption for what would eventually become the two houses of lost Yisrael.
[2] Both houses are to seek out or look for each other.

[3] A type and shadow of YHWH's Light, shining on both sides of Yisrael's future divided family.
[4] From both houses comes one beaten yet united nation, fully pure and holy; symbolized by the gold of the menorah.
[5] A perfect light to a reunited house.

shall be eight and twenty cubits, and the width of one curtain four cubits: and every one of the curtains shall have one measure. 3 The five curtains shall be coupled together one to another; and other five curtains shall be coupled one to another. 4 And you shall make loops of blue upon the edge of the end curtain on one set; and likewise shall you make in the uttermost edge of the end curtain, in the coupling of the second. 5 Fifty loops shall you make in the one curtain, and fifty loops shall you make in the edge of the curtain that is in the coupling of the second; that the loops may take hold one of another. [1] 6 And you shall make fifty hooks of gold, and couple the curtains together with the hooks: and it shall be one Tabernacle. [2] 7 And you shall make curtains of goats' hair to be a covering upon the Tabernacle: eleven curtains shall you make. 8 The length of one curtain shall be thirty cubits, and the width of one curtain four cubits: and the eleven curtains shall be all of one measure. 9 And you shall couple five curtains by themselves, and six curtains by themselves, and shall double the sixth curtain in the forefront of the Tabernacle. 10 And you shall make fifty loops on the edge of the one curtain that is outmost in the coupling, and fifty loops in the edge of the curtain and second set. 11 And you shall make fifty hooks of brass, and put the hooks into the loops, and couple the tent together, that it may be one. 12 And the remnant that remains of the curtains of the tent, the half curtain that remains, shall hang over the backside of the Tabernacle. 13 And a cubit on the one side, and a cubit on the other side of that which remains in the length of the curtains of the tent, it shall hang over the sides of the Tabernacle on this side and on that side, to cover it. 14 And you shall make a covering for the tent of rams' skins dyed red, and a covering above of badgers'

skins. 15 And you shall make boards for the Tabernacle of shittim wood standing up. 16 Ten cubits shall be the length of a board, and a cubit and a half shall be the width of one board. 17 Two tenons shall there be in one board, set in order one against another: this shall you make for all the boards of the Tabernacle. 18 And you shall make the boards for the Tabernacle, twenty boards on the south side southward. 19 And you shall make forty sockets of silver under the twenty boards; two sockets under one board for his two tenons, and two sockets under another board for his two tenons. 20 And for the second side of the Tabernacle on the north side there shall be twenty boards: 21 And their forty sockets of silver; two sockets under one board, and two sockets under another board. 22 And for the sides of the Tabernacle westward you shall make six boards. 23 And two boards shall you make for the corners of the Tabernacle in the two sides. 24 And they shall be coupled together beneath, and they shall be coupled together above the head of it to one ring: this shall it be for them both; they shall be for the two corners. 25 And they shall be eight boards, and their sockets of silver, sixteen sockets; two sockets under one board, and two sockets under another board. 26 And you shall make bars of shittim wood; five for the boards of the one side of the Tabernacle, 27 And five bars for the boards of the other side of the Tabernacle, and five bars for the boards of the side of the Tabernacle, for the two sides westward. 28 And the middle bar in the midst of the boards shall reach from end to end. 29 And you shall cover the boards with gold, and make their rings of gold for places for the bars: and you shall cover the bars with gold. 30 And you shall raise up the Tabernacle according to the fashion of it that was shown you on the Mount. 31 And you shall make a veil of blue, and purple, and scarlet, and fine twined linen of skilled work: with cheruvim shall it be made: 32 And you shall hang it upon four pillars of shittim wood covered

---

[1] Two curtains symbolize both eventual houses meeting in set-apartness, symbolized by the gold hooks holding the two curtains together, forming one dwelling place for YHWH. When Moshiach restores both houses fully, His Set-Apart-Place will once again be in our midst.
[2] See note on Lev. 26 verse 5.

with gold: their hooks shall be of gold, upon the four sockets of silver. 33 And you shall hang up the veil from the hooks, that you may bring it in inside within the veil the Ark of the Covenant: and the veil shall divide between the kadosh place and the Most-Kadosh-Place. 34 And you shall put the lid of atonement upon the Ark of the Covenant in the Most-Kadosh-Place. 35 And you shall set the table outside the veil, and the menorah opposite the table on the side of the Tabernacle toward the south: and you shall put the table on the north side. 36 And you shall make a hanging for the door of the tent, of blue, and purple, and scarlet, and fine twined linen, made with needlework. 37 And you shall make for the hanging five pillars of shittim wood, and cover them with gold, and their hooks shall be of gold: and you shall cast five sockets of brass for them.

27 And you shall make an altar of shittim wood, five cubits long, and five cubits broad; the altar shall be foursquare: and the height of it shall be three cubits. 2 And you shall make the horns of it upon the four corners of it: its horns shall be the same: and you shall cover it with brass. 3 And you shall make its pans to receive its ashes, and its shovels, and its basons, and its flesh hooks, and its firepans: all the vessels of it you shall make of brass. 4 And you shall make for it a grate of network of brass; and upon the net shall you make four brass rings in the four corners of it. 5 And you shall put it under the compass of the altar beneath that the net may be even to the midst of the altar. 6 And you shall make poles for the altar, poles of shittim wood, and cover them with brass. 7 And the poles shall be put into the rings, and the poles shall be upon the two sides of the altar, to bear it. 8 Hollow with boards shall you make it: as it was shown you in the Mount, so shall they make it. 9 And you shall make the court of the Tabernacle: for the south side southward there shall be hangings for the court of fine twined linen

of an hundred cubits long for one side: 10 And the twenty pillars of it and their twenty sockets shall be of brass; the hooks of the pillars and their bands shall be of silver. 11 And likewise for the north side in length there shall be hangings of an hundred cubits long, with its twenty pillars and their twenty sockets of brass; the hooks of the pillars and their bands of silver. 12 And for the width of the court on the west side shall be hangings of fifty cubits: their pillars ten, and their sockets ten. 13 And the width of the court on the east side eastward shall be fifty cubits. 14 The hangings of one side of the gate shall be fifteen cubits: their pillars three, and their sockets three. 15 And on the other side shall be hangings fifteen cubits: their pillars three, and their sockets three. 16 And for the gate of the court shall be an hanging of twenty cubits, of blue, and purple, and scarlet, and fine twined linen, made with needlework: and their pillars shall be four, and their sockets four. 17 All the pillars all around the court shall be banded with silver; their hooks shall be of silver, and their sockets of brass. 18 The length of the court shall be a hundred cubits, and the width fifty everywhere, and the height five cubits of fine twined linen, and their sockets of brass. 19 All the vessels of the Tabernacle in all the service of it, and all the pegs of it, and all the pegs of the court, shall be of brass.

Torah Parsha 20
Tetzaveh 27:20-30:10
Haftarah Yechezkel 43:10-27
Brit Chadasha Phylypseyah 4:10-20

20 And you shall command the children of Yisrael that they bring you pure oil olive beaten for the light, to cause the lamp to burn always. 21 In the Tabernacle of the congregation outside the veil, which is before the testimony, Aharon and his sons shall tend it from evening to morning before יהרה: it shall be a chuk le-olam-va-ed to their generations on behalf of the children of Yisrael.

28 *And bring near Aharon your brother, and his sons with him, from among the children of Yisrael, that he may serve Me in the kohen's office, even Aharon, Nadav and Avihu, El-Azar and Ithamar, Aharon's sons. 2 And you shall make kadosh garments for Aharon your brother for tifereth and for beauty. 3 And you shall speak to all that are wise hearted, who I have filled with the Ruach of cochma, that they may make Aharon's garments to consecrate him, that he may attend to Me in the kohen's office. 4 And these are the garments which they shall make; a breastplate, and an shoulder garment, and a robe, and a broidered coat, a turban, and a girdle: and they shall make kadosh garments for Aharon your brother, and his sons, that he may attend to Me in the kohen's office. 5 And they shall take gold, and blue, and purple, and scarlet, and fine linen. 6 And they shall make the shoulder garment of gold, of blue, and of purple, of scarlet, and fine twined linen, with skilled work. 7 It shall have the two shoulder pieces joined at the two edges of it; and so it shall be joined together.[1] 8 And the embroidered band of the shoulder garment, which is upon it, shall be of the same, according to the work of it; even of gold, of blue, and purple, and scarlet, and fine twined linen. 9 And you shall take two onyx stones,[2] and inscribe on them the names of the children of Yisrael: 10 Six of their names on one stone, and the other six names of the rest on the other stone, according to their birth. 11 With the work of an engraver in stone, like the engravings of a signet, shall you engrave the two stones with the names of the children of Yisrael: you shall make them to be set in settings of gold.[3] 12 And you shall put the two stones upon the shoulders of the shoulder garment for stones of memorial to the children of Yisrael: and*

Aharon shall bear their names before יהוה upon his two shoulders for a memorial.[4] 13 And you shall make settings of gold; 14 And two chains of pure gold at the ends; of braided cords shall you make them, and fasten the braided cords to the settings. 15 And you shall make the breastplate of mishpat with skilled work; like the work of the shoulder garment you shall make it; of gold, of blue, and of purple, and of scarlet, and of fine twined linen, shall you make it. 16 Foursquare it shall be being doubled; a span shall be the length of it, and a span shall be the width of it. 17 And you shall set in it settings of stones, even four rows of stones: the first row shall be a sardius, a topaz, and a carbuncle: this shall be the first row. 18 And the second row shall be an emerald, a sapphire, and a diamond. 19 And the third row a ligure, an agate, and an amethyst. 20 And the fourth row a beryl, and an onyx, and a jasper: they shall be set in gold in their settings. 21 And the stones shall be with the names of the children of Yisrael, twelve, according to their names, like the engravings of a signet; every one with its name shall they be according to the twelve tribes.[5] 22 And you shall make upon the breastplate chains at the ends of corded work of pure gold. 23 And you shall make upon the breastplate two rings of gold, and shall put the two rings on the two ends of the breastplate.[6] 24 And you shall put the two-corded chains of gold in the two rings that are on the ends of the breastplate. 25 And the other two ends of the two-corded chains you shall fasten in the two settings, and put them on the shoulder pieces of the shoulder garment before it. 26 And you shall make two rings of gold, and you shall put them upon the two ends of the breastplate in the border of it, which is in

---

[1] The job of Yisrael's **Kohen HaGadol** is to carry the burdens of both baytim to Abba YHWH.
[2] One for each future divided house of Yisrael.
[3] Two stones each with six tribes on the High Priest's shoulder, a prophetic foreshadowing of Yisrael's two-house re-gathering and restoration.

[4] Both houses are the golden vessels of YHWH for all ages.
[5] The **Kohen HaGadol** carried all 12 tribes on his lev, which is the heart for unity of the Father. However the reality of a divided house full of burdens was always on the Priest's shoulders, even as it was on Yahshua's shoulders when He came looking for Yisrael's lost sheep, manifesting the heart of His Father.
[6] More two-house prophetic typology.

the side of the shoulder garment inward. 27 And two other rings of gold you shall make, and shall put them on the two sides of the shoulder garment underneath, on the front of it, opposite the other coupling of it, above the embroidered band of the shoulder garment. 28 And they shall bind the breastplate by the rings of it to the rings of the shoulder garment with a lace of blue, that it may be above the embroidered band of the shoulder garment, and that the breastplate is not loosed from the shoulder garment. 29 And Aharon shall bear the names of the children of Yisrael on the breastplate of mishpat upon his lev, when he goes in to the kadosh place, for a memorial before יהוה continually.[1] 30 And you shall put on the breastplate of mishpat the Urim and the Thummim; and they shall be upon Aharon's lev, when he goes in before יהוה: and Aharon shall bear the mishpat of the children of Yisrael upon his lev before יהוה continually. 31 And you shall make the robe of the shoulder garment all of blue. 32 And there shall be an hole in the top of it, in the midst of it: it shall have a binding of woven work all around the hole of it, as it were the hole of strong armor that it be not torn. 33 And beneath upon the hem of it you shall make pomegranates of blue, and of purple, and of scarlet, all around the hem of it; and bells of gold between them all around: 34 A golden bell and a pomegranate, a golden bell and a pomegranate, upon the hem of the robe round all around. 35 And it shall be upon Aharon to attend: and its sound shall be heard when he goes in to the kadosh place before יהוה, and when he comes out, that he die not. 36 And you shall make a plate of pure gold, and grave upon it, like the engravings of a signet, Kadosh-Le-יהוה. 37 And you shall put it on a blue lace that it may be upon the turban; upon the forefront of the turban it shall be. 38 And it shall be upon Aharon's forehead, that Aharon may bear the iniquity of the

kadosh things, which the children of Yisrael shall set-apart in all their kadosh gifts; and it shall be always upon his forehead, that they may be accepted before יהוה.[2] 39 And you shall embroider the coat of fine linen, and you shall make the turban of fine linen, and you shall make the girdle of needlework. 40 And for Aharon's sons you shall make coats, and you shall make for them girdles, and turbins shall you make for them, for tifereth and for beauty. 41 And you shall put them upon Aharon your brother, and his sons with him; and shall anoint them, and consecrate them, and set-apart them, that they may attend to Me in the kohen's office. 42 And you shall make them linen breeches to cover their nakedness; from the waists even to the thighs they shall reach: 43 And they shall be upon Aharon, and upon his sons, when they come in to the Tabernacle of the congregation, or when they come near to the altar to attend in the kadosh place; that they bear not iniquity, and die: it shall be a chuk le-olam-va-ed to him and his zera after him.[3]

29

And this is the thing that you shall do to them to set apart them, to attend to Me in the kohen's office: Take one young bullock, and two rams without blemish. 2 And matzah, and cakes unleavened tempered with oil, and wafers unleavened anointed with oil: of wheat flour shall you make them. 3 And you shall put them into one basket, and bring them in the basket, with the bullock and the two rams. 4 And Aharon and his sons you shall bring to the door of the Tabernacle of the congregation, and shall wash them with mayim. 5 And you shall take the garments, and put upon Aharon the coat, and the robe of the shoulder garment, and the shoulder garment, and the breastplate, and gird him with the embroidered band of the shoulder

---

[1] Moshiach Yahshua does the same today as well, in the heavenly Set-Apart Place, the place of the original design.

[2] Without YHWH's set-apart Name all of men's gifts will not be accepted.
[3] Take careful note. Yisraelites of both sexes must not allow their undergarments to be exposed forever.

garment: 6 *And you shall put the turban upon his head, and put the kadosh keter upon the turban.*[1] *7 Then shall you take the anointing oil, and pour it upon his head, and anoint him. 8 And you shall bring his sons, and put long shirts upon them. 9 And you shall gird them with girdles, Aharon and his sons, and put the turbans on them: and the kohen's office shall be theirs for a perpetual chuk: and you shall consecrate Aharon and his sons. 10 And you shall cause a bullock to be brought before the Tabernacle of the congregation: and Aharon and his sons shall put their hands upon the head of the bullock. 11 And you shall kill the bullock before* יהוה*, by the door of the Tabernacle of the congregation.*[2] *12 And you shall take of the dom of the bullock, and put it upon the horns of the altar with your finger, and pour all the dom beside the bottom of the altar. 13 And you shall take all the fat that covers the inwards, and the appendage that is above the liver, and the two kidneys, and the fat that is upon them, and burn them upon the altar. 14 But the flesh of the bullock, and his skin, and his dung, shall you burn with fire outside the camp: it is a sin offering. 15 You shall also take one ram; and Aharon and his sons shall put their hands upon the head of the ram. 16 And you shall slay the ram, and you shall take its dom, and sprinkle it all around upon the altar. 17 And you shall cut the ram in pieces, and wash the inwards of it, and its legs, and put them upon its pieces, and on its head. 18 And you shall burn the whole ram upon the altar: it is a burnt offering to* יהוה*: it is a sweet savor, an offering made by fire to* יהוה*. 19 And you shall take the other ram; and Aharon and his sons shall put their hands upon the head of the ram. 20 Then shall you kill the ram, and take of its dom, and put it upon the tip of the right ear of Aharon, and upon the tip of the right ear of his sons, and upon the thumb of their*

right hand, and upon the great toe of their right foot, and sprinkle the dom upon the altar all around. 21 And you shall take of the dom that is upon the altar, and of the anointing oil, and sprinkle it upon Aharon, and upon his garments, and upon his sons, and upon the garments of his sons with him: and he shall be set-apart, and his garments, and his sons, and his sons' garments with him. 22 Also you shall take of the ram the fat and the rump, and the fat that covers the inwards, and the appendage above the liver, and the two kidneys, and the fat that is upon them, and the right shoulder; for it is a ram of consecration: 23 And one loaf of lechem, and one cake of oiled lechem, and one wafer out of the basket of the matzah that is before* יהוה*: 24 And you shall put all in the hands of Aharon, and in the hands of his sons; and shall wave them for a wave offering before* יהוה*. 25 And you shall receive them of their hands, and burn them upon the altar for a burnt offering, for a sweet savor before* יהוה*: it is an offering made by fire to* יהוה*. 26 And you shall take the breast of the ram of Aharon's consecration, and wave it for a wave offering before* יהוה*: and it shall be your portion. 27 And you shall set-apart the breast of the wave offering, and the shoulder of the contribution offering, which is waved, and which is heaved up, of the ram of the consecration, even of that which is for Aharon, and of that which is for his sons: 28 And it shall be Aharon's and his sons' by a chuk le-olam-va-ed from the children of Yisrael: for it is a contribution offering: and it shall be a contribution offering from the children of Yisrael of the sacrifice of their shalom offerings, even their contribution offering to* יהוה*. 29 And the kadosh garments of Aharon shall be his sons' after him, to be anointed in them, and to be consecrated in them. 30 And that son that is kohen in his place shall put them on seven days, when he comes into the Tabernacle of the congregation to attend in the kadosh place. 31 And you shall take the ram of the consecration, and cook its flesh*

---

[1] Yisraelite priests wear head coverings in both covenants.
[2] In the east, where Yahshua died "before YHWH," on the Mt.Olivet.

in the kadosh place. 32 And Aharon and his sons shall eat the flesh of the ram, and the lechem that is in the basket, by the door of the Tabernacle of the congregation. 33 And they shall eat those things with which the atonement was made, to consecrate and to set-apart them: but a Ger shall not eat of it, because they are kadosh. 34 And if any of the flesh of the consecrations, or of the lechem, remain to the morning, then you shall burn the remainder with fire: it shall not be eaten, because it is kadosh. 35 And this shall you do to Aharon, and to his sons, according to all things that I have commanded you: seven days shall you consecrate them. 36 And you shall offer every day a bullock for a sin offering for atonement: and you shall cleanse the altar, when you have made an atonement for it, and you shall anoint it, to set it apart. 37 Seven days you shall make atonement for the altar, and set-apart it; and it shall be an altar most kadosh: whatever touches the altar shall be kadosh. 38 Now this is that which you shall offer upon the altar; two lambs of the first year day by day continually. [1] 39 The one lamb you shall offer in the morning; and the other lamb you shall offer at even: [2] 40 And with the one lamb a tenth ephah of flour mingled with the fourth part of an hin of beaten oil; and the fourth part of an hin of wine for a drink offering. 41 And the other lamb you shall offer at evening, and shall do like according to the meat offering of the morning, and according to the drink offering of it, for a sweet savor, an offering made by fire to יהוה. 42 This shall be a continual burnt offering throughout your generations at the door of the Tabernacle of the congregation before יהוה: where I will meet you, to speak there to you. 43 And there I will meet with the children of Yisrael, and the Tabernacle shall be set-apart by My tifereth. 44 And I will set-apart the Tabernacle of the congregation, and the altar: I will set-apart also both Aharon and his sons, to attend to Me in the kohen's office. 45 And I will dwell among the children of Yisrael, and will be their Elohim. 46 And they shall know that I am יהוה their Elohim, that brought them forth out of the land of Mitzrayim, that I may dwell among them: I am יהוה their Elohim.

30 And you shall make an altar to burn incense upon: of shittim wood shall you make it. 2 A cubit shall be the length of it, and a cubit the width of it; foursquare shall it be: and two cubits shall be the height of it: the horns of it shall be of the same. 3 And you shall cover it with pure gold, the top of it, and the sides of it all around, and the horns of it; and you shall make for it a keter of gold all around. 4 And two golden rings shall you make for it under the keter of it, by the two corners of it, upon the two sides of it shall you make it; and they shall be for places for the poles to bear it with. 5 And you shall make the poles of shittim wood, and cover them with gold. 6 And you shall put it before the veil that is by the Ark of the Covenant, before the lid of atonement that is over the testimony, where I will meet with you. 7 And Aharon shall burn on it sweet incense every morning: when he prepares the lamps, he shall burn incense upon it. 8 And when Aharon lights the lamps at evening, he shall burn incense upon it, perpetual incense before יהוה throughout your generations. [3] 9 You shall offer no strange incense on it, or burnt sacrifice, or meat offering; neither shall you pour a drink offering on it. 10 And Aharon shall make an atonement upon the horns of it once in a year with the dom of the sin offering of atonement: once in the year shall he make atonement upon it throughout your generations: it is most kadosh to יהוה.

---

[1] Daily lamb sacrifices for both houses symbolized by the two lambs.
[2] Biblical **shacrit** and **maariv**.

[3] Daily part of shacrit and maariv.

Torah Parsha 21
Ki Tissa 30:11-34:35
Haftarah Melechim Alef 18:1-39
Brit Chadasha Qorintyah Bet 3:1-8

11 And יהוה spoke to Moshe, saying, 12 When you take the census of the children of Yisrael after their number, then shall they give every man a ransom for his being to יהוה, when you number them; that there be no plague among them, when you number them. 13 This they shall give, every one that passes among them that are numbered, half a shekel after the shekel of the Set-Apart-Place: (a shekel is twenty gerahs:) an half shekel shall be the offering of יהוה. 14 Every one that passes among them that is numbered, from twenty years old and above, shall give an offering to יהוה. 15 The rich shall not give more, and the poor shall not give less than half a shekel, when they give an offering to יהוה, to make an atonement for your beings. 16 And you shall take the atonement money of the children of Yisrael, and shall appoint it for the service of the Tabernacle of the congregation; that it may be a memorial to the children of Yisrael before יהוה, to make an atonement for your beings. [1] 17 And יהוה spoke to Moshe, saying, 18 You shall also make a basin of brass, and its foot also of brass, to wash with: and you shall put it between the Tabernacle of the congregation and the altar, and you shall put mayim inside. 19 For Aharon and his sons shall wash their hands and their feet there: 20 When they go into the Tabernacle of the congregation, they shall wash with mayim, that they die not; or when they come near to the altar to attend, to burn offering made by fire to יהוה: 21 So they shall wash their hands and their feet, so that they die not: and it shall be a chuk le-olam-va-ed to them, even to him and to his zera throughout their generations. 22 Moreover יהוה spoke to Moshe, saying, 23 Take for you principal spices, of pure myrrh five hundred shekels, and of sweet cinnamon half so much, even two hundred and fifty shekels, and of sweet calamus two hundred and fifty shekels, 24 And of cassia five hundred shekels, after the shekel of the Set-Apart-Place, and of olive oil a hin: 25 And you shall make it into an oil of kadosh ointment, an ointment compound after the work of the perfumer: it shall be a kadosh anointing oil. 26 And you shall anoint the Tabernacle of the congregation with it, and the Ark of the Covenant, 27 And the table and all its vessels, and the menorah and its vessels, and the altar of incense, 28 And the altar of burnt offering with all its vessels, and the basin and its stand. 29 And you shall set them apart, that they may be most kadosh: so that whatever touches them shall be kadosh. 30 And you shall anoint Aharon and his sons, and consecrate them, that they may attend to Me in the kohen's office. 31 And you shall speak to the children of Yisrael, saying, This shall be a kadosh anointing oil to Me throughout your generations. 32 Upon man's flesh shall it not be poured, neither shall you make any other like it, after the composition of it: it is kadosh, and it shall be kadosh to you. 33 Whoever produces any like it, or whoever puts any of it upon a Ger, shall even be cut off from his people. 34 And יהוה said to Moshe, Take to you sweet spices, stacte, and onycha, and galbanum; these sweet spices with pure frankincense: of each shall there be a like weight: 35 And you shall make it a perfume, a confection after the work of a perfumer, salted, pure and kadosh: 36 And you shall beat some of it very small, and put of it before the testimony in the Tabernacle of the congregation, where I will meet with you: it shall be to you most kadosh. 37 And as for the incense that you shall make, you shall not make to yourselves according to the composition of it: it shall be to you kadosh for יהוה. 38 Whoever shall make anything like it, to smell it, shall even be cut off from his people.

---

[1] Not atonement for sin, but for paganism and the idolatry that so easily seeps in.

31 And יהוה spoke to Moshe, saying, 2 *See, I have called by name Betzale-El the son of Uri, the son of Hur, of the tribe of Yahudah: 3 And I have filled him with the Ruach of Elohim, in cochma, and in understanding, and in knowledge, and in all manner of workmanship, 4 To devise skilled works, to work in gold, and in silver, and in brass, 5 And in cutting of stones, to set them, and in carving of timber, to work in all manner of workmanship.* 6 *And I, see, I have given with him Aholiav, the son of Ahisamach, of the tribe of Dan: and in the levim of all that are wise hearted I have put cochma, that they may make all that I have commanded you; 7 The Tabernacle of the congregation, and the Ark of the Covenant, and the lid of atonement that is on it, and all the furniture of the Tabernacle, 8 And the table and its furniture, and the pure menorah with all its furniture, and the altar of incense, 9 And the altar of burnt offering with all its furniture, and the basin and its stand. 10 And the cloths of service, and the kadosh garments for Aharon the kohen, and the garments of his sons, to attend in the kohen's office, 11 And the anointing oil, and sweet incense for the kadosh place: according to all that I have commanded you shall they do.* 12 And יהוה spoke to Moshe, saying, 13 *Speak also to the children of Yisrael, saying, Truly My Shabbats you shall shomer: for it is a sign between Me and you throughout your generations; that you may know that I am* יהוה *that does set you apart.*[1] 14 *You shall shomer the Shabbat therefore; for it is kadosh for you: every one that defiles it shall surely be put to death: for whoever does any work on it, that being shall be cut off from among his people. 15 Six days may work be done; but on the seventh is the Shabbat of rest, kadosh to* יהוה*: whomever does any work on the Shabbat day; he shall surely be put to death. 16 Therefore the children of Yisrael shall shomer the Shabbat, to observe the Shabbat throughout their generations, for an everlasting covenant. 17 It is a sign between Me and the children of Yisrael le-olam-va-ed: for in six days* יהוה *made the shamayim and the earth, and on the seventh day He rested, and was refreshed. 18 And He gave to Moshe, when He had made an end of communing with him upon Mount Sinai, two tables of testimony, tables of stone, written with the finger of Elohim.*

32 And when the people saw that Moshe delayed to come down out of the Mount, the people gathered themselves together to Aharon, and said to him, Get up, make us elohim, that shall go before us; for as for this Moshe, the man that brought us up out of the land of Mitzrayim, we do not know what has become of him. 2 And Aharon said to them, Break off the golden earrings, which are in the ears of your wives, of your sons, and of your daughters, and bring them to me. 3 And all the people broke off the golden earrings that were in their ears, and brought them to Aharon. 4 And he received them at their hand, and fashioned it with a graving tool, after he had made it a golden calf: and they said, These be your elohim, O Yisrael, which brought you up out of the land of Mitzrayim. 5 And when Aharon saw it, he built an altar before it; and Aharon made a proclamation, and said, Tomorrow is a moed to יהוה. 6 And they rose up early in the morning, and offered burnt offerings, and brought shalom offerings; and the people sat down to eat and to drink, and rose up to play. 7 And יהוה said to Moshe, *Go, get yourself down; for your people, which you brought out of the land of Mitzrayim, have corrupted themselves: 8 They have turned aside quickly out of the halacha which I commanded them: they have made themselves a molded calf, and have worshiped it, and have sacrificed to it, and said, These be your elohim, O Yisrael, which have brought you up out of the land of Mitzrayim.* 9 And יהוה said to

---
[1] Forever even after Moshiach comes.

Moshe, *I have seen this people, and see; it is a stiff-necked people:* 10 *Now therefore leave Me alone, that My anger may wax hot against them, and that I may consume them: and I will make of you a great nation.* [1] 11 And Moshe besought יהוה his Elohim, and said, יהוה, why does Your anger wax hot against Your people, which You have brought forth out of the land of Mitzrayim with great power, and with a mighty hand? 12 Why should the Mitzrites speak, and say, For mischief did He bring them out, to slay them in the mountains, and to consume them from the face of the earth? Turn from Your fierce anger, and relent of this evil against Your people. 13 Remember Avraham, Yitzchak, and Yisrael, Your avadim, to whom You swore by Your own self, and said to them, I will multiply Your zera as the chochavim of the shamayim, and all this land that I have spoken of will I give to Your zera, and they shall inherit it le-olam-va-ed. 14 And יהוה relented of the evil which He thought to do to His people. 15 And Moshe turned, and went down from the Mount, and the two tables of the testimony were in his hand: the tables were written on both their sides; on the one side and on the other were they written. 16 And the tables were the work of Elohim, and the writing was the writing of Elohim, inscribed upon the tables. 17 And when Yahoshua heard the noise of the people as they shouted, he said to Moshe, There is a noise of war in the camp. 18 And Moshe said, It is not the voice of them that shout for strength, neither is it the voice of them that cry in weakness: but the noise of them that sing do I hear. 19 And it came to pass, as soon as he came near to the camp, that he saw the calf, and the dancing: and Moshe's anger became hot, and he cast the tables out of his hands, and broke them beneath the Mount. [2] 20 And he took the calf that they had made, and burnt it in the fire, and ground it to powder, and scattered it upon the mayim, and made the children of Yisrael drink of it. 21 And Moshe said to Aharon, What did this people do to you, that you have brought so great a sin upon them? 22 And Aharon said, Let not the anger of my master burn: you know the people that they are set on evil. 23 For they said to me, Make us elohim, which shall go before us: for as for this Moshe, the man that brought us up out of the land of Mitzrayim, we do not know what is become of him. 24 And I said to them, Whoever has any gold, let them break it off. So they gave it me: then I cast it into the fire, and there came out this calf. 25 And when Moshe saw that the people were naked; for Aharon had made them naked to their shame among their enemies: 26 Then Moshe stood in the gate of the camp, and said, Who is on יהוה's side? Let him come to me. And all the sons of Levi gathered themselves together to him. 27 And he said to them, This said יהוה Elohim of Yisrael, *Put every man his sword by his side, and go in and out from tent to tent throughout the camp, and slay every man his brother, and every man his companion, and every man his neighbor.* 28 And the children of Levi did according to the word of Moshe: and there died of the people that day about three thousand men. 29 For Moshe had said, Ordain yourselves today for service to יהוה, since every man was against his son, and upon his brother; that he may bestow upon you a bracha this day. 30 And it came to pass on the next day, that Moshe said to the people, You have sinned a great sin: and now I will go up to יהוה; perhaps I shall make an atonement for your sin. 31 And Moshe returned to יהוה, and said, Oh, this people have sinned a great sin, and have made for themselves elohim of gold. 32 Yet now, if You will forgive their sin, but if not, please blot me, I ask You, out of Your scroll that You have written. 33 And יהוה said to Moshe, *Whoever has sinned against Me, him will I blot out of My scroll.* 34 *Therefore now go*

---

[1] YHWH still would have been faithful to the promise of physical multiplicity, had He decided to take this route at this particular time.
[2] Even the giver broke the Torah literally and spiritually, which is why Yahshua is greater than Moshe **Rabainu**.

lead the people to the place of which I have spoken to you: see, My Malach[1] shall go before you: nevertheless in the day when I visit I will visit their sin upon them. 35 And יהוה plagued the people, because they made the calf, which Aharon made.

33 And יהוה said to Moshe, *Depart, and go up from here, you and the people who you have brought up out of the land of Mitzrayim, to the land which I swore to Avraham, to Yitzchak, and to Yaakov, saying, Unto your zera will I give it:* 2 *And I will send a Malach before you;[2] and I will drive out the Kanaanite, the Amorite, and the Hittite, and the Perizzite, the Hivite, and the Yevusite.* 3 *Unto a land flowing with milk and honey: for I will not go up in the midst of you; for you are a stiff-necked people: lest I consume you in the way.* 4 And when the people heard these evil tidings, they mourned: and no man did put on him his ornaments. 5 For יהוה had said to Moshe, *Say to the children of Yisrael, You are a stiff-necked people: I will come up into the midst of you in a moment, and consume you: therefore now put off your ornaments from you, that I may know what to do to you.* 6 And the children of Yisrael stripped themselves of their ornaments by the Mount Horev. 7 And Moshe took the Tabernacle, and pitched it outside the camp, far off from the camp, and called it the Tabernacle of the congregation. And it came to pass, that every one who sought יהוה went out to the Tabernacle of the congregation, which was outside the camp. 8 And it came to pass, when Moshe went out to the Tabernacle that all the people rose up, and stood every man at his tent door, and looked at Moshe, until he was gone into the Tabernacle. 9 And it came to pass, as Moshe entered into the Tabernacle, the cloudy pillar descended, and stood at the door of the Tabernacle, and יהוה talked with Moshe. 10 And all the people saw the cloudy pillar stand at the Tabernacle door: and all the people rose up and worshipped, every man in his tent door. 11 And יהוה spoke to Moshe panayim-el-panayim, as a man speaks to his friend.[3] And he returned again into the camp: but his eved Yahoshua, the son of Nun, a young man, departed not out of the Tabernacle. 12 And Moshe said to יהוה, See, You said to me, Bring up this people: and You have not let me know whom You will send with me.[4] *Yet You have said, I know You by Name, and You have also found favor in My sight.* 13 Now therefore, I ask You, if I have found favor in Your sight, show me now Your Way,[5] that I may know You, that I may find favor in Your sight: and consider that this nation is Your people.[6] 14 And He said, *My Presence shall go with you, and I will give you rest.* 15 And he said to Him, If Your Presence go not with me, carry us not up there. 16 For how shall it be known here that I, and Your people have found favor in Your sight? Is it not in that You go with us? So shall we be separated, I, and Your people, from all the nations that are upon the face of the earth. 17 And יהוה said to Moshe, *I will do this thing also that you have spoken: for you have found favor in My sight, and I know you by name.* 18 And Moshe said, I beg You, show me Your tifereth. 19 And He said, *I will make all My tov to pass before you, and I will proclaim the Name of* יהוה *before you; And will show unmerited favor to whom I will, and will show rachamim to whom I will.*[7] 20 And He said, *You cannot see My face: for there shall no man see Me, and live.*[8] 21 And יהוה said, *See, there is a place by Me, and you shall stand upon a rock:* 22 *And it shall come to pass, while My*

---

[1] Metatron.
[2] Malach-YHWH.

[3] Obviously the face of the Son or the young Man **Metatron**.
[4] Moshe desired to know the Name of the Malach-YHWH, as did Yisrael before him. Today we know His Name since the fullness of time has come.
[5] Yochanan 14:6.
[6] This "nation is Your **goy**" in the Hebrew. Yisrael was YHWH's goy. So today we should not find it strange that non-Jewish Yisraelites are still called goyim.
[7] The manifest part of YHWH, who proclaims the Name of YHWH, is Yahshua, as He did on earth in Yochanan chapter 17.
[8] Abba's face.

tifereth passes by, that I will put you in a cleft of the rock, and will cover you with My hand while I pass by: 23 And I will take away My hand, and you shall see My back parts:[1] But My face shall not be seen.

34 And יהוה said to Moshe, *Cut two tables of stone like to the first: and I will write upon these tables the words that were on the first tables, which you broke.[2] 2 And be ready in the morning, and come up in the morning to Mount Sinai, and present yourself there to Me on the top of the Mount.* 3 *And no man shall come up with you, neither let any man be seen throughout the entire Mount; neither let the flocks nor herds feed before the Mount.* 4 And he cut two tables of stone like the first; and Moshe rose up early in the morning, and went up to Mount Sinai, as יהוה had commanded him, and took in his hand the two tables of stone. 5 And יהוה descended in the cloud, and stood with him there, and proclaimed the Name of יהוה.[3] 6 And יהוה passed by before him, and proclaimed, יהוה, יהוה. *An El, full of rachamim and favor, longsuffering, and abundant in tov, chesed, and emet,* 7 *Keeping rachamim for thousands, forgiving iniquity and transgression and sin, and will by no means clear the guilty; visiting the iniquity of the ahvot upon the children, and upon the children's children, to the third and to the fourth generation.* 8 And Moshe hurried, and bowed his head toward the earth, and worshipped. 9 And he said, If now I have found favor in Your sight, O יהוה, let יהוה, I beg You, go among us; for it is a stiff-necked people; and pardon our iniquity and our sin, and take us for Your inheritance. 10 And He said, *See, I make a covenant: before all your people I will do marvels,* such as have not been done in all the earth, nor in any nation: and all the people among whom you are, shall see the work of יהוה: for it is an awesome thing that I will do with you. 11 *Observe that which I command you this day: see, I drive out from before you the Amorite, and the Kanaanite, and the Hittite, and the Perizzite, and the Hivite, and the Yevusite.* 12 *Guard yourself, lest you make a covenant with the inhabitants of the land where you go, lest it be for a snare in the midst of you:* 13 *But you shall destroy their altars, break their images, and cut down their groves:* 14 *For you shall worship no other El: for* יהוה, *whose Name is Jealous, is a jealous El:* 15 *Lest you make a covenant with the inhabitants of the land, and they go a whoring after their elohim, and do sacrifice to their elohim, and one calls to you, and you eat of his sacrifice;* 16 *And you take of their daughters for your sons, and their daughters go whoring after their elohim, and make your sons go whoring after their elohim.* 17 *You shall make you no molded elohim.* 18 *Chag Matzoth shall you shomer. Seven days you shall eat matzah, as I commanded you, at the time of the month Aviv: for in the month Aviv you came out from Mitzrayim.* 19 *All that opens the womb is Mine; and every bachor among your cattle, whether ox or sheep, that is male.* 20 *But the bachor of a donkey you shall redeem with a lamb: and if you redeem him not, then shall you break his neck. All the bachor of your sons you shall redeem. And none shall appear before Me empty.* 21 *Six days you shall work, but on the seventh day you shall rest: in ploughing time and in harvest time you shall rest.* 22 *And you shall observe Chag Shavout, of the firstfruits of wheat harvest, and the chag of the ingathering-Sukkot at the year's end.* 23 *Three times in the year shall all your male children appear before* יהוה *Elohim, the Elohim of Yisrael.* 24 *For I will cast out the nations before you, and enlarge your borders:[4] neither shall any man desire your*

---

[1] Anthropomorphic expression meaning His manifest Presence; but not the Abba's face. This is exactly what Yahshua came to do. Reveal the Father, but continue to hide His face.
[2] Renewal of the covenant, not a new covenant like the Brit Chadasha.
[3] The plurality of divinity. One YHWH declares the Name of the other.

[4] To the four winds later in time.

land, when you shall go up to appear before יהוה *Your Elohim three times in the year.* 25 *You shall not offer the dom of My sacrifice with chametz; neither shall the sacrifice of the moed of the Pesach be left to the morning.* 26 *The first of the firstfruits of your land you shall bring to the Bayit of* יהוה *Your Elohim. You shall not cook a kid in its ima's milk.* 27 And יהוה said to Moshe, *Write you these words: for according to the mouth of these words I have made a covenant with you and with Yisrael.* 28 And Moshe was there with יהוה forty days and forty nights; he did neither eat lechem, nor drink mayim. And he wrote upon the tables the words of the covenant, the ten mitzvot. 29 And it came to pass, when Moshe came down from Mount Sinai with the two tables of testimony in Moshe's hand, when he came down from the Mount, that Moshe did not know that the skin of his face shone while he talked with Him. 30 And when Aharon and all the children of Yisrael saw Moshe, see, the skin of his face shone; and they were afraid to come near him. 31 And Moshe called to them; and Aharon and all the rulers of the congregation returned to him: and Moshe talked with them. 32 And afterward all the children of Yisrael came near: and he gave them in commands all that יהוה had spoken with him on Mount Sinai. 33 And until Moshe had done speaking with them, he put a veil on his face. 34 But when Moshe went in before יהוה to speak with Him, he took the veil off, until he came out. And he came out, and spoke to the children of Yisrael that which he was commanded. 35 And the children of Yisrael saw the face of Moshe that the skin of Moshe's face shone: and Moshe put the veil upon his face again, until he went in to speak with him.

Torah Parsha 22
Vayachel 35:1-38:20
In regular 12-month years,
read with Parsha 23.
In years with 13 months, read separately
Haftarah Melechim Alef 7:40-50
Brit Chadasha Ivrim 9:1-14

35 And Moshe gathered all the congregation of the children of Yisrael together, and said to them, These are the words that יהוה has commanded, that you should do them. 2 *Six days shall work be done, but on the seventh day there shall be to you a kadosh day, a Shabbat of rest to* יהוה*: whoever does work on it shall be put to death.* 3 *You shall kindle no fire throughout your dwellings upon the Shabbat day.* 4 And Moshe spoke to all the congregation of the children of Yisrael, saying, This is the thing that יהוה commanded, saying, 5 *Take from among you an offering to* יהוה*: whoever is of a willing lev, let him bring it, an offering of* יהוה*; gold, and silver, and brass,* 6 *And blue, and purple, and scarlet, and fine linen, and goats' hair,* 7 *And rams' skins dyed red, and badgers' skins, and shittim wood,* 8 *And oil for the light, and spices for anointing oil, and for the sweet incense,* 9 *And onyx stones, and stones to be set for the shoulder garment, and for the breastplate.* 10 *And every wise hearted among you shall come, and make all that* יהוה *has commanded;* 11 *The Tabernacle, its tent, and its covering, its hooks, and its boards, its bars, its pillars, and its sockets,* 12 *The ark, and the poles of it, with the lid of atonement, and the veil of the covering,* 13 *The table, and its poles, and all its vessels, and the Lechem of the Panayim,* 14 *The menorah also for the light, and its furniture, and its lamps, with the oil for the light,* 15 *And the incense altar, and its poles, and the anointing oil, and the sweet incense, and the hanging for the door at the entrance of the Tabernacle,* 16 *The altar of burnt offering, with its bronze grating, its poles, and all its vessels, the basin and its stand,* 17 *The hangings of*

the court, its pillars, and their sockets, and the hanging for the door of the court, 18 *The pegs of the Tabernacle, and the pegs of the court, and their cords,* 19 *The cloths of service, to do service in the kadosh place, the kadosh garments for Aharon the kohen, and the garments of his sons, to attend in the kohen's office.* 20 And all the congregation of the children of Yisrael departed from the presence of Moshe. 21 And they came, every one whose lev was stirred up, and every one whose ruach was willing, and they brought יהוה's offering to the work of the Tabernacle of the congregation, and for all its service, and for the kadosh garments. 22 And they came, both men and women, as many as were willing hearted, and brought bracelets, and earrings, and rings, and tablets, all jewels of gold: and every man that offered a wave offering of gold to יהוה. 23 And every man, with whom was found blue, and purple, and scarlet, and fine linen, and goats' hair, and red skins of rams, and badgers' skins, brought them. 24 Every one that did offer an offering of silver and brass brought an offering to יהוה: and every man, with whom was found shittim wood for any work of the service, brought it. 25 And all the women that were wise hearted did spin with their hands, and brought that which they had spun, both of blue, and of purple, and of scarlet, and of fine linen. 26 And all the women whose lev stirred them up in cochma spun goats' hair. 27 And the rulers brought onyx stones, and stones to be set, for the shoulder garment, and for the breastplate; 28 And spices, and oil for the light, and for the anointing oil, and for the sweet incense. 29 The children of Yisrael brought a willing offering to יהוה, every man and woman, whose lev made them willing to bring something for all manner of work, which יהוה had commanded to be made by the hand of Moshe. 30 And Moshe said to the children of Yisrael, See, יהוה has called by name Betzal-El the son of Uri, the son of Hur, of the tribe of Yahudah;

31 And he has filled him with the Ruach of Elohim, in cochma, in understanding, and in knowledge, and in all manner of workmanship; 32 And to design, to work in gold, and in silver, and in brass, 33 And in the cutting of stones, to set them, and in carving of wood, to make all manner of skilled work. 34 And He has put this in his lev that he may teach, both he, and Aholiav, the son of Ahisamach, of the tribe of Dan. 35 Them has He filled with cochma of lev, to work all manner of work, of the engraver, and of the skilled workman, and of the embroiderer, in blue, and in purple, in scarlet, and in fine linen, and of the weaver, even of them that do any work, and of those that design skilled work.

36 Then made Betzal-El and Aholiav, and every wise hearted man, in whom יהוה put cochma and understanding to know how to work all manner of work for the service of the Set-Apart-Place, according to all that יהוה had commanded. 2 And Moshe called Betzal-El and Aholiav, and every wise hearted man, in whose lev יהוה had put cochma, even every one whose lev was stirred up to come to the work to do it: 3 And they received from Moshe all the offerings, which the children of Yisrael had brought for the work of the service of the Set-Apart-Place, to make it complete. And they brought to him free will offerings every morning. 4 And all the wise men, that were doing all the work of the Set-Apart-Place, came every man from his work that they made; 5 And they spoke to Moshe, saying, The people bring much more than enough for the service of the work, which יהוה commanded to make. 6 And Moshe gave mitzvah, and they caused it to be proclaimed throughout the camp, saying, Let neither man nor woman make any more work for the offering of the Set-Apart-Place. So the people were restrained from bringing. 7 For that which they had was sufficient for all the work to be made; and it was too much. 8 And every

wise hearted man among them that made the work of the Tabernacle made ten curtains of fine twined linen, and blue, and purple, and scarlet: with cheruvim of skilled work he made them. 9 The length of one curtain was twenty and eight cubits, and the width of one curtain four cubits: the curtains were all of one size. 10 And he coupled the five curtains one to another: and the other five curtains he coupled one to another. 11 And he made loops of blue on the edge of one curtain from one set in the coupling: likewise he made them in the end curtain, in the coupling of the second. 12 Fifty loops made he in one curtain, and fifty loops made he in the edge of the curtain that was in the coupling of the second: the loops held one curtain to another. 13 And he made fifty hooks of gold, and coupled the curtains one to another with the hooks: so it became one Tabernacle. 14 And he made curtains of goats' hair for the tent over the Tabernacle: eleven curtains he made them. 15 The length of one curtain was thirty cubits, and four cubits was the width of one curtain: the eleven curtains were of one size. 16 And he coupled five curtains by themselves, and six curtains by themselves. 17 And he made fifty loops upon the uttermost edge of the curtain in the coupling, and fifty loops he made upon the edge of the curtain that couples the second. 18 And he made fifty hooks of brass to couple the tent together, that it might be one. 19 And he made a covering for the tent of rams' skins dyed red, and a covering of badgers' skins above that. 20 And he made boards for the Tabernacle of shittim wood, standing up. 21 The length of a board was ten cubits, and the width of a board one cubit and a half. 22 One board had two tenons, equally distant one from another: so did he make for all the boards of the Tabernacle. 23 And he made boards for the Tabernacle; twenty boards for the south side southward: 24 And forty sockets of silver he made under the twenty boards; two sockets under one board for his two tenons, and two sockets under another board for his

two tenons. 25 And for the other side of the Tabernacle, which is toward the north corner, he made twenty boards, 26 And their forty sockets of silver; two sockets under one board, and two sockets under another board. 27 And for the sides of the Tabernacle westward he made six boards. 28 And two boards made he for the corners of the Tabernacle in the two sides. 29 And they were coupled beneath, and coupled together at the head of it, to one ring: this he did to both of them in both the corners. 30 And there were eight boards; and their sockets were sixteen sockets of silver, under every board two sockets. 31 And he made bars of shittim wood; five for the boards of the one side of the Tabernacle, 32 And five bars for the boards of the other side of the Tabernacle, and five bars for the boards of the Tabernacle for the sides westward. 33 And he made the middle bar to shoot through the boards from the one end to the other. 34 And he covered the boards with gold, and made their rings of gold to be places for the bars, and covered the bars with gold. 35 And he made a veil of blue, and purple, and scarlet, and fine twined linen: with cheruvim he made it of skilled work. 36 And he made four pillars of shittim wood, and covered them with gold: their hooks were of gold; and he cast for them four sockets of silver. 37 And he made a covering for the Tabernacle door of blue, and purple, and scarlet, and fine twined linen, of needlework; 38 And the five pillars of it with their hooks: and he covered their tops and their rings with gold: but their five sockets were of brass.

37 And Betzal-El made the ark of shittim wood: two cubits and a half was the length of it, and a cubit and a half the width of it, and a cubit and a half the height of it: 2 And he covered it with pure gold inside and outside and made a keter of gold for it all around. 3 And he cast for it four rings of gold, to be set by the four corners of it; even two rings upon the one

side of it, and two rings upon the other side of it. 4 And he made poles of shittim wood, and covered them with gold. 5 And he put the poles into the rings by the sides of the ark, to bear the ark. 6 And he made the lid of atonement of pure gold: two cubits and a half was the length of it, and one cubit and a half the width of it. 7 And he made two cheruvim of gold, beaten out of one piece he made them, on the two ends of the lid of atonement; 8 One cheruv on the end on this side, and another cheruv on the other end on that side: out of the lid of atonement he made the cheruvim on the two ends of it. 9 And the cheruvim spread out their wings on high, and covered with their wings over the lid of atonement, with their faces one to another; even towards the lid of atonement were turned the faces of the cheruvim.[1] 10 And he made the table of shittim wood: two cubits was the length of it, and a cubit the width of it, and a cubit and a half the height of it: 11 And he covered it with pure gold, and made on it a keter of gold all around. 12 Also he made on it a border of a handbreadth all around; and made a keter of gold for the border of it all around. 13 And he cast for it four rings of gold, and put the rings upon the four corners that were in the four legs of it. 14 Opposite the border were the rings, the places for the poles to bear the table. 15 And he made the poles of shittim wood, and covered them with gold, to bear the table. 16 And he made the vessels which were upon the table, his dishes, and his spoons, and his bowls, and his covers to cover with, of pure gold. 17 And he made the menorah of pure gold: of beaten work he made the menorah; its shaft, and its branch, its cups, its knobs, and its blossoms, were the same: 18 And six branches going out of the sides of it; three branches of the menorah out of the one side of it, and three branches of the menorah out of the other side of it: 19 Three cups made after the fashion of almonds in one branch, a knob

and a blossom; and three cups made like almonds in another branch, a knob and a blossom: so was done throughout the six branches going out of the menorah. 20 And in the menorah were four cups made like almonds, its knobs, and its blossoms: 21 And a knob under two branches of the same, and a knob under two branches of the same, and a knob under two branches of the same, according to the six branches going out of it. 22 Their knobs and their branches were the same: all of it was one beaten work of pure gold. 23 And he made its seven lamps, and its snuffers, and its trays, of pure gold. 24 Of a talent of pure gold he made it, and all the vessels of it. 25 And he made the incense altar of shittim wood: the length of it was a cubit, and the width of it a cubit; it was foursquare; and two cubits was the height of it; the horns of it were of the same. 26 And he covered it with pure gold, both the top of it, and the sides of it all around, and the horns of it: also he made to it a keter of gold all around. 27 And he made two rings of gold for it under the keter of it, by the two corners of it, upon the two sides of it, to be places for the poles to lift it. 28 And he made the poles of shittim wood, and covered them with gold. 29 And he made the kadosh anointing oil, and the pure incense of sweet spices, according to the work of the perfumer.

38 And he made the altar of burnt offering of shittim wood: five cubits was the length of it, and five cubits the width of it; it was foursquare; and three cubits the height of it. 2 And he made the horns of it on the four corners of it; the horns of it were of the same: and he covered it with brass. 3 And he made all the vessels of the altar, the pots, and the shovels, and the basons, and the flesh hooks, and the firepans: all the vessels of it he made of brass. 4 And he made for the altar a brass-grated network, under its rim, midway from the bottom. 5 And he cast four rings for the four ends of the grate of brass, to be places

---

[1] Type of two-houses touching each other by the rachamim of Moshiach's dom.

for the poles. 6 And he made the poles of shittim wood, and covered them with brass. 7 And he put the poles into the rings on the sides of the altar, to lift it; he made the altar hollow with boards. 8 And he made the basin of brass, and the stand from brass, from the bronze mirrors of the women assembling, who did service at the door of the Tabernacle of the congregation. 9 And he made the court: on the south side southward the hangings of the court were of fine twined linen, a hundred cubits: 10 Their pillars were twenty, and their brasen sockets twenty; the hooks of the pillars and their bands were of silver. 11 And for the north side the hangings were a hundred cubits, their pillars were twenty, and their sockets of brass twenty; the hooks of the pillars and their bands of silver. 12 And for the west side were hangings of fifty cubits, their pillars ten, and their sockets ten; the hooks of the pillars and their bands of silver. 13 And for the east side eastward fifty cubits. 14 The hangings of the one side of the gate were fifteen cubits; their pillars three, and their sockets three. 15 And for the other side of the court gate, on this hand and that hand, were hangings of fifteen cubits; their pillars three, and their sockets three. 16 All the hangings of the court all around were of fine twined linen. 17 And the sockets for the pillars were of brass; the hooks of the pillars and their bands of silver; and the covering of their tops of silver; and all the pillars of the court were banded with silver. 18 And the hanging for the gate of the court was needlework, of blue, and purple, and scarlet, and fine twined linen: and twenty cubits was the length, and the height in the width was five cubits, corresponding to the screens of the court. 19 And their pillars were four, and their sockets of brass four; their hooks of silver, and the covering of their tops and their bands of silver. 20 And all the pegs of the Tabernacle, and of the court all around, were of brass.

Torah Parsha 23
Pekudei 38:21-40:38
In 12-month years, read with Parsha 22.
In years with 13 months read separately.
Haftarah Melechim Alef 7:51-8:21
Brit Chadasha MaAseh Shlichim 1:1-11

21 This is the census of the Tabernacle, even of the Tabernacle of testimony, as it was counted, according to the mitzvah of Moshe, for the service of the Leviim, by the hand of Ithamar, son to Aharon the kohen. 22 And Betzal-El the son of Uri, the son of Hur, of the tribe of Yahudah, made all that יהוה commanded Moshe. 23 And with him was Aholiav, son of Ahisamach, of the tribe of Dan, an engraver, and a skilled workman, and an embroiderer in blue, and in purple, and in scarlet, and fine linen. 24 All the gold that was used for the work in all the work of the kadosh place, even the gold of the offering, was twenty-nine talents, and seven hundred thirty shekels, according to the shekel of the Set-Apart-Place. 25 And the silver from them that were numbered of the congregation was a hundred talents, and one thousand seven hundred seventy five shekels, after the shekel of the Set-Apart-Place: 26 A bekah for every man, that is, half a shekel, after the shekel of the Set-Apart-Place, for every one that went to be numbered, from twenty years old and upward, for six hundred thousand three thousand five hundred fifty men. 27 And from the hundred talents of silver were cast the sockets of the Set-Apart-Place, and the sockets of the veil; a hundred sockets from the hundred talents, a talent for a socket. 28 And from the one thousand seven hundred seventy five shekels he made hooks for the pillars, and covered their tops, and made bands for them. 29 And the brass from the offering was seventy talents, and two thousand four hundred shekels. 30 And with it he made the sockets to the door of the Tabernacle of the congregation, and the brasen altar, and the brasen grate for it, and all the vessels of the altar, 31 And the sockets of the court all around, and the

sockets of the court gate, and all the pegs of the Tabernacle, and all the pegs of the court all around.

39 And of the blue, and purple, and scarlet, they made cloths of service, to do service in the kadosh place, and made the kadosh garments for Aharon; as יהוה commanded Moshe. 2 And he made the shoulder garment of gold, blue, and purple, and scarlet, and fine twined linen. 3 And they did beat the gold into thin plates, and cut it into wires, to work it in the blue, and in the purple, and in the scarlet, and in the fine linen, with skilled work. 4 They made shoulder pieces for it, to couple it together: by the two edges was it coupled together. 5 And the embroidered band of his shoulder garment, that was upon it, was of the same, according to the work of it; of gold, blue, and purple, and scarlet, and fine twined linen; as יהוה commanded Moshe. 6 And they made onyx stones enclosed in settings of gold, graven, as signets are graven, with the names of the children of Yisrael. 7 And he put them on the shoulders of the shoulder garment, that they should be stones for a memorial to the children of Yisrael; as יהוה commanded Moshe. 8 And he made the breastplate of skilled work, like the work of the shoulder garment; of gold, blue, and purple, and scarlet, and fine twined linen. 9 It was foursquare; they made the breastplate double: a span was the length of it, and a span the width of it, being doubled. 10 And they set in it four rows of stones: the first row was a sardius, a topaz, and a carbuncle: this was the first row. 11 And the second row, an emerald, a sapphire, and a diamond. 12 And the third row, a ligure, an agate, and an amethyst. 13 And the fourth row, a beryl, an onyx, and a jasper: they were enclosed in settings of gold. 14 And the stones were according to the names of the children of Yisrael, twelve, according to their names, like the engravings of a signet, every one with his name, according to the twelve tribes. 15 And they made upon the breastplate chains at the ends, of wreathen work of pure gold. 16 And they made two settings of gold, and two gold rings; and put the two rings in the two ends of the breastplate. 17 And they put the two cords of gold in the two rings on the ends of the breastplate. 18 And the two ends of the two cords they fastened in the two settings, and put them on the shoulder pieces of the shoulder garment, before it. 19 And they made two rings of gold, and put them on the two ends of the breastplate, upon the border of it, which was on the side of the shoulder garment inward. 20 And they made two other golden rings, and put them on the two sides of the shoulder garment underneath, toward the front of it, opposite the other coupling of it, above the embroidered band of the shoulder garment. 21 And they did bind the breastplate by its rings to the rings of the shoulder garment with a lace of blue, that it might be above the embroidered band of the shoulder garment, and that the breastplate might not be loosed from the shoulder garment; as יהוה commanded Moshe. 22 And he made the robe of the shoulder garment of woven work, all of blue. 23 And there was a hole in the midst of the robe, as the hole of a strong armor, with a band all around the hole that it should not tear. 24 And they made upon the hems of the robe pomegranates of blue, and purple, and scarlet, and twined linen. 25 And they made bells of pure gold, and put the bells between the pomegranates upon the hem of the robe, all around between the pomegranates; 26 A bell and a pomegranate, a bell and a pomegranate, all around the hem of the robe to attend in; as יהוה commanded Moshe. 27 And they made coats of fine linen of woven work for Aharon, and for his sons, 28 And a turban of fine linen, and beautiful turban ornaments of fine linen, and linen breeches of fine twined linen, 29 And a girdle of fine twined linen, and blue, and purple, and scarlet, of needlework; as יהוה commanded Moshe. 30 And they made the plate of the kadosh keter of pure gold, and wrote upon it a writing, like the engravings of a signet, Kadosh-Le-**יהוה**. 31 And they tied to it a lace of blue, to fasten it high upon the turban; as **יהוה** commanded Moshe. 32 So all the work of the Tabernacle of the tent of the congregation was finished: and the children of Yisrael did according to all that **יהוה** commanded Moshe, so they did. 33 And they brought the Tabernacle to Moshe, the tent, and all its furniture, its hooks, its boards, its bars, and its pillars, and its sockets, 34 And the covering of rams' skins dyed red, and the covering of badgers' skins, and the veil of the covering, 35 The Ark of the Covenant, and its poles, and the lid of atonement, 36 The table, and all the vessels of it, and the Lechem of the Panayim, 37 The pure menorah, with the lamps of it, even with the lamps to be set in order, and all the vessels of it, and the oil for light, 38 And the golden altar, and the anointing oil, and the sweet incense, and the hanging for the Tabernacle door, 39 The brasen altar, and its grate of brass, its poles, and all its vessels, the basin and its stand, 40 The hangings of the court, its pillars, and its sockets, and the hanging for the court gate, its cords, and its pegs, and all the vessels of the service of the Tabernacle, for the tent of the congregation, 41 The cloths of service to do service in the kadosh place, and the kadosh garments for Aharon the kohen, and his sons' garments, to attend in the kohen's office. 42 According to all that **יהוה** commanded Moshe, so the children of Yisrael made all the work. 43 And Moshe did look upon all the work, and, see, they had done it as **יהוה** had commanded, even so had they done it: and Moshe blessed them.

40 And **יהוה** spoke to Moshe, saying, 2 *On the first day of the first month shall you set up the Tabernacle of the tent of the congregation,* [1] 3 *And you shall put inside the Ark of the Covenant, and cover the ark with the veil. 4 And you shall bring in the table, and set in order the things that are to be set in order upon it; and you shall bring in the menorah, and light the lamps of it. 5 And you shall set the altar of gold for the incense before the Ark of the Covenant, and put the hanging of the door to the Tabernacle. 6 And you shall set the altar of the burnt offering before the door of the Tabernacle of the tent of the congregation. 7 And you shall set the basin between the tent of the congregation and the altar, and shall put mayim inside. 8 And you shall set up the court all around, and hang up the hanging at the court gate. 9 And you shall take the anointing oil, and anoint the Tabernacle, and all that is inside, and shall set it apart, and all the vessels of it: and it shall be kadosh. 10 And you shall anoint the altar of the burnt offering, and all its vessels, and set-apart the altar: and it shall be an altar most kadosh. 11 And you shall anoint the basin and its stand, and set-apart it. 12 And you shall bring Aharon and his sons to the door of the Tabernacle of the congregation, and wash them with mayim. 13 And you shall put upon Aharon the kadosh garments, and anoint him, and set-apart him; that he may attend to Me in the kohen's office. 14 And you shall bring his sons, and clothe them with long robes: 15 And you shall anoint them, as you did anoint their abba that they may attend to Me in the kohen's office: for their anointing shall surely be an everlasting priesthood throughout their generations.* 16 So Moshe did: according to all that **יהוה** commanded him, so did he. 17 And it came to pass in the first month in the second year, on the first day of the month; that the Tabernacle was raised up. 18 And Moshe raised up the Tabernacle, and fastened its sockets, and set up the boards of it, and put in the bars of it, and raised up its pillars. 19 And he spread abroad the tent over the Tabernacle, and put the covering of the tent above it; as **יהוה** commanded Moshe. 20 And he took and put the testimony into the ark, and set the poles

---

[1] True New Year.

on the ark, and put the lid of atonement above the ark: 21 And he brought the ark into the Tabernacle, and set up the veil of the covering, and covered the Ark of the Covenant; as יהוה commanded Moshe. 22 And he put the table in the tent of the congregation, upon the side of the Tabernacle northward, outside the veil. 23 And he set the lechem in order upon it before יהוה ; as יהוה had commanded Moshe. 24 And he put the menorah in the tent of the congregation, opposite the table, on the side of the Tabernacle southward. 25 And he lighted the lamps before יהוה; as יהוה commanded Moshe. 26 And he put the golden altar in the tent of the congregation before the veil: 27 And he burnt sweet incense on it; as יהוה commanded Moshe. 28 And he set up the hanging at the door of the Tabernacle. 29 And he put the altar of burnt offering by the door of the Tabernacle of the tent of the congregation, and offered upon it the burnt offering and the grain offering; as יהוה commanded Moshe. 30 And he set the basin between the tent of the congregation and the altar, and put mayim there, to wash there.

31 And Moshe and Aharon and his sons washed their hands and their feet there: 32 When they went into the tent of the congregation, and when they came near to the altar, they washed; as יהוה commanded Moshe. 33 And he raised up the court all around the Tabernacle and the altar, and set up the hanging of the court gate. So Moshe finished the work. 34 Then a cloud covered the tent of the congregation, and the tifereth of יהוה filled the Tabernacle. 35 And Moshe was not able to enter into the tent of the congregation, because the cloud dwelt on it, and the tifereth of יהוה filled the Tabernacle. 36 And when the cloud was taken up from over the Tabernacle, the children of Yisrael went onward in all their journeys: 37 But if the cloud was not taken up, then they journeyed not until the day that it was taken up. 38 For the cloud of יהוה was upon the Tabernacle by day, and fire was on it by night, in the sight of all the bayit of Yisrael, throughout all their journeys.

Chazak Chazak VeNitchazak
Be Strong Be Strong!
And May We Be Strengthened!

ויקרא

Vayiqra – Leviticus

To Our Forefathers Yisrael

Torah Parsha 24
Vayiqra 1:1-6:7
Haftarah Yeshayahu 43:21-44:23
Brit Chadasha Romiyah 8:1-13

1 And **יהוה** called to Moshe, and spoke to him out of the Tabernacle of the congregation, saying, 2 Speak to the children of Yisrael, and say to them, *If any man of you bring an offering to* **יהוה***, you shall bring your offering of the cattle, even of the herd, and of the flock. 3 If his offering be a burnt sacrifice of the herd, let him offer a male without blemish: he shall offer it of his own voluntary will at the door of the Tabernacle of the congregation before* **יהוה** *. 4 And he shall put his hand upon the head of the burnt offering; and it shall be accepted for him to make atonement for him. 5 And he shall kill the bull before* **יהוה** *: and the kohanim, Aharon's sons, shall bring the dom, and sprinkle the dom all around upon the altar that is by the door of the Tabernacle of the congregation. 6 And he shall skin the burnt offering, and cut it into pieces. 7 And the sons of Aharon the kohen shall put fire upon the altar, and lay the wood in order upon the fire: 8 And the kohanim, Aharon's sons, shall lay the splits, the head, and the fat, in order upon the wood that is on the fire that is upon the altar: 9 But his inwards and his legs shall he wash in mayim: and the kohen shall burn all on the altar, to be a burnt sacrifice, an offering made by fire, of a sweet fragrance to* **יהוה** *. 10 And if his offering is of the flocks, namely, of the sheep, or of the goats, for a burnt sacrifice; he shall bring it a male without blemish. 11 And he shall kill it on the north side of the altar before* **יהוה***:[1] and the kohanim, Aharon's sons, shall*

sprinkle his dom all around upon the altar. 12 And he shall cut it into its pieces, with its head and its fat: and the kohen shall lay them in order on the wood that is on the fire that is upon the altar: 13 But he shall wash the inwards and the legs with mayim: and the kohen shall bring it all, and burn it upon the altar: it is a burnt sacrifice, an offering made by fire, a sweet fragrance to **יהוה**. 14 And if the burnt sacrifice for his offering to **יהוה** be of fowls, then he shall bring his offering of turtledoves, or of young pigeons. 15 And the kohen shall bring it to the altar, and wring off its head, and burn it on the altar; and the dom of it shall be drained out at the side of the altar: 16 And he shall pluck away his crop with his feathers, and cast it beside the altar on the east part, by the place of the ashes: 17 And he shall cleave it at its wings, but shall not divide it asunder: and the kohen shall burn it upon the altar, upon the wood that is upon the fire: it is a burnt sacrifice, an offering made by fire, a sweet fragrance to **יהוה**.

2 And when any will offer a grain offering to **יהוה**, his offering shall be of fine flour; and he shall pour oil upon it, and put frankincense on it: 2 And he shall bring it to Aharon's sons the kohanim: and he shall take from it his handful of the flour of it, and of the oil of it, with all the frankincense of it; and the kohen shall burn the remembrance portion of it upon the altar, to be an offering made by fire, of a sweet fragrance to **יהוה**: 3 And the remnant of the grain offering shall be Aharon's and his sons: it is a thing most set-apart of the offerings of **יהוה** made by fire. 4 And if you bring an offering of a grain offering baked in the oven, it shall be unleavened cakes of fine flour mixed with oil, or unleavened

---

[1] "Before YHWH" in the east, always facing westward toward the Set-Apart Place, the way back into His presence. This term appears throughout scripture reminding Yisrael that the way back to Eden is heading west.

wafers anointed with oil. 5 And if your offering is a grain offering baked in a pan, it shall be of fine flour unleavened, mixed with oil. 6 You shall part it in pieces, and pour oil on it: it is a grain offering. 7 And if your offering is a grain offering baked in the frying pan, it shall be made of fine flour with oil. 8 And you shall bring the grain offering that is made of these things to יהוה *: And when it is presented to the kohen, he shall bring it to the altar. 9 And the kohen shall take from the grain offering a remembrance portion, and shall burn it upon the altar: it is an offering made by fire, of a sweet fragrance to* יהוה*. 10 And that which is left of the grain offering shall be Aharon's and his sons: it is a thing most set-apart of the offerings of* יהוה *made by fire. 11 No grain offering, which you shall bring to* יהוה*, shall be made with chametz: for you shall burn no chametz, nor any honey, in any offering of* יהוה *made by fire.[1] 12 Regarding the offering of firstfruits, you shall offer them to* יהוה*: but they shall not be burnt on the altar for a sweet fragrance. 13 And every offering of your grain offering shall you season with salt; neither shall you suffer the salt of the covenant of Your Elohim to be lacking from your grain offering: with all your offerings you shall offer salt.[2] 14 And if you offer a grain offering of your firstfruits to* יהוה*, you shall offer for the grain offering of your firstfruits green ears of corn dried by the fire, even corn crushed out of full ears. 15 And you shall put oil upon it, and lay frankincense on it: it is a grain offering. 16 And the kohen shall burn the remembrance portion of it, part of the crushed corn of it, and part of the oil of it, with all the frankincense of it: it is an offering made by fire to* יהוה*.*

3 *And if his offering is a sacrifice of a shalom offering, if he offer it of the herd; whether it be a male or female, he shall offer it without blemish before* יהוה*. 2 And he shall lay his hand upon the head of his offering, and kill it at the door of the Tabernacle of the congregation: and Aharon's sons the kohanim shall sprinkle the dom upon the altar all around. 3 And he shall offer of the sacrifice of the shalom offering an offering made by fire to* יהוה*; the fat that covers the inwards, and all the fat that is upon the inwards, 4 And the two kidneys, and the fat that is on them, which is by the flanks, and the appendage above the liver, with the kidneys, it shall he take away. 5 And Aharon's sons shall burn it on the altar upon the burnt sacrifice, which is upon the wood that is on the fire: it is an offering made by fire, a sweet fragrance to* יהוה*. 6 And if his offering for a sacrifice of shalom offering to* יהוה *be of the flock; male or female, he shall offer it without blemish. 7 If he offer a lamb for his offering, then shall he offer it before* יהוה*. 8 And he shall lay his hand upon the head of his offering, and kill it before the Tabernacle of the congregation: and Aharon's sons shall sprinkle the dom of it upon the altar all around. 9 And he shall offer of the sacrifice of the shalom offering an offering made by fire to* יהוה*; the fat of it, and the whole tail, it shall he take off hard by the backbone; and the fat that covers the inwards, and all the fat that is upon the inwards, 10 And the two kidneys, and the fat that is upon them, which is by the flanks, and the appendage above the liver, with the kidneys, it shall he take away. 11 And the kohen shall burn it upon the altar: it is the food of the offering made by fire to* יהוה*. 12 And if his offering is a goat, then he shall offer it before* יהוה*. 13 And he shall lay his hand upon the head of it, and kill it before the Tabernacle of the congregation: and the sons of Aharon shall sprinkle the dom of it upon the altar all around. 14 And he shall offer of it his offering, even an offering made by fire to*

---

[1] Leaven (a type of sin) and honey (a type of bribery) are foods used by pagans to obtain favor from false elohim. They are to be kept off YHWH's altar.
[2] For a full treatment see:
http://yourarmstoisrael.org/Articles_new/restoration/?page=27&type=12

יהוה; the fat that covers the inwards, and all the fat that is upon the inwards, 15 And the two kidneys, and the fat that is upon them, which is by the flanks, and the appendage above the liver, with the kidneys, it shall he take away. 16 And the kohen shall burn them upon the altar: it is the food of the offering made by fire for a sweet fragrance: all the fat is יהוה's. 17 It shall be a chuk le-olam-va-ed for your generations throughout all your dwellings, that you eat neither fat nor dom.[1]

4 And יהוה spoke to Moshe, saying, 2 Speak to the children of Yisrael, saying, If a being shall sin through ignorance against any of the mitzvot of יהוה concerning things which ought not be done, and shall do against any of them: 3 If the anointed kohen commits sin, like the sin of the people; then let him bring for his sin, which he has sinned, a young bull without blemish to יהוה for a sin offering. 4 And he shall bring the bull to the door of the Tabernacle of the congregation before יהוה ; and shall lay his hand upon the bull's head, and kill the bull before יהוה. 5 And the kohen that is anointed shall take of the bull's dom, and bring it to the Tabernacle of the congregation: 6 And the kohen shall dip his finger in the dom, and sprinkle the dom seven times before יהוה, before the vail of the Set-Apart-Place. 7 And the kohen shall put some of the dom upon the horns of the altar of sweet incense before יהוה, which is in the Tabernacle of the congregation: and shall pour all the dom of the bull at the bottom of the altar of the burnt offering, which is at the door of the Tabernacle of the congregation. 8 And he shall take off from it all the fat of the bull for the sin offering; the fat that covers the inwards, and all the fat that is upon the inwards, 9 And the two kidneys, and the fat that is upon them, which is by the flanks, and the appendage above the liver, with the kidneys, it shall he take away, 10 As it was taken off from the bull of

the sacrifice of shalom offerings: and the kohen shall burn them upon the altar of the burnt offering. 11 And the skin of the bull, and all its flesh, with its head, and with its legs, and its inwards, and its dung, 12 Even the whole bull shall he carry forth outside the camp to a clean place, where the ashes are poured out, and burn it on the wood with fire: where the ashes are poured out shall he be burnt. 13 And if the whole congregation of Yisrael sin through ignorance, and the thing be hidden from the eyes of the congregation, and they have done something against any of the mitzvot of יהוה concerning things which should not be done, and are guilty; 14 When the sin, which they have sinned against it, is known, then the congregation shall offer a young bull for the sin, and bring him before the Tabernacle of the congregation. 15 And the zachanim of the congregation shall lay their hands upon the head of the bull before יהוה : and the bull shall be killed before יהוה. 16 And the kohen that is anointed shall bring of the bull's dom to the Tabernacle of the congregation: 17 And the kohen shall dip his finger in some of the dom, and sprinkle it seven times before יהוה, even in front of the vail. 18 And he shall put some of the dom upon the horns of the altar which is before יהוה, that is in the Tabernacle of the congregation, and shall pour out all the dom at the bottom of the altar of the burnt offering, which is at the door of the Tabernacle of the congregation. 19 And he shall take all its fat from it, and burn it upon the altar. 20 And he shall do with the bull as he did with the bull for a sin offering, so shall he do with this: and the kohen shall make atonement for them, and it shall be forgiven them. 21 And he shall carry forth the bull outside the camp, and burn it as he burned the first bull: it is a sin offering for the congregation. 22 When a ruler has sinned, and done something through ignorance against any of the mitzvot of יהוה his Elohim concerning things that should not be done, and is guilty; 23 Or if

---

[1] YHWH knew how to protect Yisrael. True health insurance.

- 105 -

VAYIQRA – LEVITICUS 4

his sin, that he has sinned, comes to his knowledge; he shall bring his offering, a kid of the goats, a male without blemish: 24 And he shall lay his hand upon the head of the goat, and kill it in the place where they kill the burnt offering before יהוה: it is a sin offering. 25 And the kohen shall take of the dom of the sin offering with his finger, and put it upon the horns of the altar of burnt offering, and shall pour out its dom at the bottom of the altar of burnt offering. 26 And he shall burn all its fat upon the altar, as the fat of the sacrifice of the shalom offerings: and the kohen shall make atonement for him as concerning his sin, and it shall be forgiven him. 27 And if any one of the common people sin through ignorance, while he does something against any of the mitzvot of יהוה concerning things which ought not to be done, and is guilty; 28 Or if his sin, which he has sinned, comes to his knowledge: then he shall bring his offering, a kid of the goats, a female without blemish, for his sin which he has sinned. 29 And he shall lay his hand upon the head of the sin offering, and slay the sin offering in the place of the burnt offering. 30 And the kohen shall take of the dom of it with his finger, and put it upon the horns of the altar of burnt offering, and shall pour out all the dom of it at the bottom of the altar. 31 And he shall take away all the fat of it, as the fat is taken away from off the sacrifice of shalom offerings; and the kohen shall burn it upon the altar for a sweet fragrance to יהוה; and the kohen shall make atonement for him, and it shall be forgiven him. 32 And if he brings a lamb for a sin offering, he shall bring it a female without blemish. 33 And he shall lay his hand upon the head of the sin offering, and slay it for a sin offering in the place where they kill the burnt offering. 34 And the kohen shall take of the dom of the sin offering with his finger, and put it upon the horns of the altar of burnt offering, and shall pour out all the dom of it at the bottom of the altar: 35 And he shall take away all

the fat of it, as the fat of the lamb is taken away from the sacrifice of the shalom offerings; and the kohen shall burn them upon the altar, according to the offerings made by fire to יהוה: and the kohen shall make atonement for his sin that he has committed, and it shall be forgiven him.

5 And if a being sins, and hears the voice of swearing, and is a witness, whether he has seen or known of it; if he does not reveal it, then he shall bear his iniquity. 2 Or if a being touches any unclean thing, whether it be a carcass of an unclean beast, or a carcass of unclean cattle, or the carcass of unclean creeping things, and if it is hidden from him; he also shall be unclean, and guilty. 3 Or if he touchs the uncleanness of man, whatever uncleanness it is that a man shall be defiled, and it be hidden from him; when he knows of it, then he shall be guilty. 4 Or if a being swears, speaking with his lips to do evil, or to do tov, whatever it be that a man shall pronounce with an oath, and it be hidden from him; when he knows of it, then he shall be guilty in one of these. 5 And it shall be, when he shall be guilty in one of these things, that he shall confess that he has sinned in that thing: 6 And he shall bring his guilt offering to יהוה for his sin that he has sinned, a female from the flock, a lamb or a kid of the goats, for a sin offering; and the kohen shall make atonement for him concerning his sin. 7 And if he be not able to bring a lamb, then he shall bring for his guilt, which he has committed, two turtledoves, or two young pigeons, to יהוה; one for a sin offering, and the other for a burnt offering.[1] 8 And he shall bring them to the kohen, who shall offer that which is for the sin offering first, and wring off its head from its neck, but shall not divide it asunder: 9 And he shall sprinkle of the dom of the sin offering upon the side of the altar; and the rest of the dom shall be drained out

---

[1] **Chesed**/grace to the poor. Chesed did not start with the coming of Moshiach.

- 106 -

at the bottom of the altar: it is a sin offering. 10 And he shall offer the second for a burnt offering, according to the manner: and the kohen shall make atonement for him for his sin that he has sinned, and it shall be forgiven him. 11 But if he be not able to bring two turtledoves, or two young pigeons, then he that sinned shall bring for his offering the tenth part of an ephah of fine flour for a sin offering; he shall put no oil upon it, neither shall he put any frankincense on it: for it is a sin offering.[1] 12 Then shall he bring it to the kohen, and the kohen shall take his handful of it, even a remembrance portion of it, and burn it on the altar, according to the offerings made by fire to יהוה: it is a sin offering. 13 And the kohen shall make atonement for him as touching his sin that he has sinned in one of these, and it shall be forgiven him: and the remnant shall be the kohen's, as a grain offering. 14 And יהוה spoke to Moshe, saying, 15 If a being commit a guilt, and sin through ignorance, in the set-apart things of יהוה; then he shall bring for his guilt to יהוה a ram without blemish out of the flocks, with your estimation by shekels of silver, after the shekel of the Set-Apart-Place, for a guilt offering: 16 And he shall make amends for the harm that he has done in the set-apart thing, and shall add a fifth part to it, and give it to the kohen: and the kohen shall make atonement for him with the ram of the guilt offering, and it shall be forgiven him. 17 And if a being sin, and commit any of these things which are forbidden to be done by the mitzvot of יהוה; though he knew it not, yet is he guilty, and shall bear his iniquity. 18 And he shall bring a ram without blemish out of the flock, with your estimation, for a guilt offering, to the kohen: and the kohen shall make atonement for him concerning his ignorance where he made a mistake and did not know it, and it shall be forgiven him. 19 It is a guilt offering: he has certainly trespassed against יהוה.

6 And יהוה spoke to Moshe, saying, 2 If a being sins, and commits a guilt against יהוה, and lies to his neighbor in that which was delivered to him to keep, or in pledge, or in a thing taken away by violence, or has deceived his neighbor; 3 Or have found that which was lost, and lies about it, and swears falsely; in any of all these that a man does by sinning: 4 Then it shall be, because he has sinned, and is guilty, that he shall restore that which he took violently away, or the thing which he has deceitfully gotten, or that which was delivered to him to keep, or the lost thing which he found, 5 Or all that about which he has sworn falsely; he shall even restore its principal, and shall add the fifth part more to it, and give it to him to whom it belongs, in the day of his guilt offering.[2] 6 And he shall bring his guilt offering to יהוה, a ram without blemish out of the flock, with your estimation, for a guilt offering, to the kohen: 7 And the kohen shall make atonement for him before יהוה: and it shall be forgiven him for anything of all that he has done in trespassing in it.

Torah Parsha 25
Tzav 6:8-8:36
Haftarah Yirmeyahu 7:21-8:3
Brit Chadasha Romiyah 12:1-8

8 And יהוה spoke to Moshe, saying, 9 Command Aharon and his sons, saying, This is the Torah of the burnt offering: It is the burnt offering, because of the burning upon the altar all night to the morning, and the fire of the altar shall be burning in it. 10 And the kohen shall put on his linen garment, and his linen breeches shall he put upon his flesh, and take up the ashes which the fire has consumed with the burnt offering on the altar, and he shall put them beside the altar. 11 And he shall put off his garments, and put on other garments, and carry forth the ashes outside the camp to a clean place. 12 And the fire upon the altar

---

[1] See note on verse 7.

[2] Yisrael was not only to repent and atone for sin; but also make real restitution for damages done.

shall be burning in it; it shall not be put out: and the kohen shall burn wood on it every morning, and lay the burnt offering in order upon it; and he shall burn on it the fat of the shalom offerings. 13 The fire shall always be burning upon the altar; it shall never go out.[1] 14 And this is the Torah of the grain offering: the sons of Aharon shall offer it before יהוה, before the altar. 15 And he shall take of it his handful, of the flour of the grain offering, and of the oil of it, and all the frankincense which is upon the grain offering, and shall burn it upon the altar for a sweet fragrance, even the remembrance portion of it, to יהוה. 16 And the remainder of it shall Aharon and his sons eat: with unleavened lechem shall it be eaten in the Set-Apart-Place; in the court of the Tabernacle of the congregation they shall eat it. 17 It shall not be baked with chametz. I have given it to them for their portion of My offerings made by fire; it is most set-apart, as is the sin offering, and as the guilt offering. 18 All the males among the children of Aharon shall eat of it. It shall be a chuk le-olam-va-ed in your generations concerning the offerings of יהוה made by fire: every one that touches them shall be set-apart. 19 And יהוה spoke to Moshe, saying, 20 This is the offering of Aharon and of his sons, which they shall offer to יהוה in the day when he is anointed; the tenth part of an ephah of fine flour for a grain offering perpetual, half of it in the morning, and half of it at night. 21 In a pan it shall be made with oil; and when it is baked, you shall bring it in: and the baked pieces of the grain offering shall you offer for a sweet fragrance to יהוה. 22 And the kohen from his sons that is anointed in his place shall offer it: it is a chuk le-olam-va-ed to יהוה, it shall be wholly burnt. 23 For every grain offering for the kohen shall be wholly burnt: it shall not be eaten. 24 And יהוה spoke to Moshe, saying, 25 Speak to Aharon and to his sons, saying, This is the Torah of the sin offering: In the place where the burnt offering is killed shall the sin offering be killed before יהוה: it is most set-apart. 26 The kohen that offers it for sin shall eat it: in the Set-Apart-Place shall it be eaten, in the court of the Tabernacle of the congregation. 27 Whatever shall touch the flesh of it shall be set-apart: and when there is sprinkled of the dom of it upon any garment, you shall wash that on which it was sprinkled in the Set-Apart-Place. 28 But the earthen vessel in which it is cooked shall be broken: and if it be cooked in a brasen pot, it shall be both scoured, and rinsed in mayim. 29 All the males among the kohanim shall eat of it: it is most set-apart. 30 And no sin offering, from which any of the dom is brought into the Tabernacle of the congregation to make atonement in the Set-Apart-Place, shall be eaten: it shall be burnt in the fire.

7 Likewise this is the Torah of the guilt offering: it is most set-apart. 2 In the place where they kill the burnt offering shall they kill the guilt offering: and the dom of it shall he sprinkle all around upon the altar. 3 And he shall offer of it all the fat of it; the tail, and the fat that covers the inwards, 4 And the two kidneys, and the fat that is on them, which is by the flanks, and the appendage that is above the liver, with the kidneys, it shall he take away: 5 And the kohen shall burn them upon the altar for an offering made by fire to יהוה: it is a guilt offering. 6 Every male among the kohanim shall eat of it: it shall be eaten in the Set-Apart-Place: it is most set-apart. 7 As the sin offering is, so is the guilt offering: there is one Torah for them: the kohen that makes atonement with it shall have it. 8 And the kohen that offers any man's burnt offering, even the kohen shall have to himself the skin of the burnt offering that he has offered. 9 And the entire grain offering that is baked in the oven, and all that is dressed in the frying pan, and in the pan, shall be the

---

[1] YHWH's presence is always among His people. Today this is substituted in the form of a **neir tamid**, or the electric lamp in front of the ark of the Torah in most synagogues, that is never turned off.

kohen's that offers it. 10 *And every grain offering, mixed with oil, and dry, shall all the sons of Aharon have, one as much as another.* 11 *And this is the Torah of the sacrifice of shalom offerings, which he shall offer to* יהוה. 12 *If he offers it for a hodu, then he shall offer with the sacrifice of hodu unleavened cakes mixed with oil, and unleavened wafers anointed with oil, and cakes mixed with oil, of fine flour, fried.* 13 *Besides the cakes, he shall offer for his offering leavened lechem with the sacrifice of hodu of his shalom offerings.* 14 *And of it he shall offer one out of the whole offering for a contribution to* יהוה, *and it shall be the kohen's that sprinkles the dom of the shalom offerings.* 15 *And the flesh of the sacrifice of his shalom offerings for hodu shall be eaten the same day that it is offered; he shall not leave any of it until the morning.* 16 *But if the sacrifice of his offering be a vow, or a voluntary offering, it shall be eaten the same day that he offers his sacrifice: and on the next day also the remainder of it shall be eaten:* 17 *But the remainder of the flesh of the sacrifice on the third day shall be burnt with fire.* 18 *And if any of the flesh of the sacrifice of his shalom offerings be eaten at all on the third day, it shall not be accepted, neither shall it be imputed to him that offers it: it shall be an abomination, and the being that eats of it shall bear his iniquity.* 19 *And the flesh that touches any unclean thing shall not be eaten; it shall be burnt with fire: and as for the flesh, all that is clean shall eat of it.* 20 *But the being that eats of the flesh of the sacrifice of shalom offerings, that pertains to* יהוה, *having his uncleanness upon him, even that being shall be cut off from his people.* 21 *Moreover the being that shall touch any unclean thing, as the uncleanness of man, or any unclean beast, or any abominable unclean thing, and eats of the flesh of the sacrifice of shalom offerings, which pertains to* יהוה, *even that being shall be cut off from his people.* 22 And יהוה spoke to Moshe, saying, 23 *Speak to the children of Yisrael, saying, You shall eat no manner of fat, of ox, or of sheep, or of goat.* 24 *And the fat of the beast that dies by itself, and the fat of that which is torn by living creatures, may be used in any other use: but you shall in no wise eat of it.* 25 *For whoever eats the fat of the beast, of which men offer an offering made by fire to* יהוה, *even that being that eats it shall be cut off from his people.* 26 *Moreover you shall eat no manner of dom, whether it be of fowl or of beast, in any of your dwellings.* 27 *Whatever being it be that eats any manner of dom, even that being shall be cut off from his people.* 28 And יהוה spoke to Moshe, saying, 29 *Speak to the children of Yisrael, saying, He that offers the sacrifice of his shalom offerings to* יהוה *shall bring his offering to* יהוה *of the sacrifice of his shalom offerings.* 30 *His own hands shall bring the offerings of* יהוה *made by fire, the fat with the breast, it shall he bring, that the breast may be waved for a wave offering before* יהוה. 31 *And the kohen shall burn the fat upon the altar: but the breast shall be Aharon's and his sons'.* 32 *And the right shoulder shall you give to the kohen for a contribution offering of the sacrifices of your shalom offerings.* 33 *He among the sons of Aharon, that offers the dom of the shalom offerings, and the fat, shall have the right shoulder for his part.* 34 *For the wave breast and the heave shoulder have I taken of the children of Yisrael from off the sacrifices of their shalom offerings, and have given them to Aharon the kohen and to his sons by a chuk le-olam-va-ed from among the children of Yisrael.* 35 This is the portion of the anointing of Aharon, and of the anointing of his sons, out of the offerings of יהוה made by fire, in the day when he presented them to attend to יהוה in the kohen's office; 36 Which יהוה commanded to be given to them by the children of Yisrael, in the day that He anointed them, by a chuk le-olam-va-ed throughout their generations. 37 This is the Torah of the burnt offering, of the grain offering, and of the sin offering, and of the guilt offering, and of the ordinations, and of the sacrifice of the shalom offerings; 38 Which יהוה commanded Moshe on Mount Sinai, in the day that He commanded the children of Yisrael to offer their offerings to יהוה , in the wilderness of Sinai.

8 And יהוה spoke to Moshe, saying, 2 *Take Aharon and his sons with him, and the garments, and the anointing oil, and a bull for the sin offering, and two rams, and a basket of unleavened lechem; 3 And gather the entire congregation together to the door of the Tabernacle of the congregation. 4 And Moshe did as* יהוה *commanded him; and the congregation was gathered together to the door of the Tabernacle of the congregation.* 5 And Moshe said to the congregation, This is the thing that יהוה commanded to be done. 6 And Moshe brought Aharon and his sons, and washed them with mayim. 7 And he put upon him the coat, and dressed him with the girdle, and clothed him with the robe, and put the ephod upon him, and he dressed him with the long shirt of the ephod, and bound it to him with it. 8 And he put the breastplate upon him; also he put in the breastplate the Urim and the Thummim. 9 And he put the turban upon his head; also upon the turban, [1] even upon its forefront, did he put the golden plate, the set-apart keter, as יהוה commanded Moshe. 10 And Moshe took the anointing oil, and anointed the Tabernacle and all that was in it, and set them apart. 11 And he sprinkled it upon the altar seven times, and anointed the altar and all its vessels, both the basin and its stand, to set them apart. 12 And he poured of the anointing oil upon Aharon's head, and anointed him, to set him apart. 13 And Moshe brought Aharon's sons, and put robes upon them, and dressed them with girdles,

and put turbins upon them; [2] as יהוה commanded Moshe. 14 And he brought the bull for the sin offering: and Aharon and his sons laid their hands upon the head of the bull for the sin offering. 15 And he killed it; and Moshe took the dom, and put it upon the horns of the altar all around with his finger, and purified the altar, and poured the dom at the bottom of the altar, and set it apart, to make atonement upon it. 16 And he took all the fat that was upon the inwards, and the appendage above the liver, and the two kidneys, and their fat, and Moshe burnt it upon the altar. 17 But the bull, and its hide, its flesh, and its dung, he burnt with fire outside the camp; as יהוה commanded Moshe. 18 And he brought the ram for the burnt offering: and Aharon and his sons laid their hands upon the head of the ram. 19 And he killed it; and Moshe sprinkled the dom upon the altar all around. 20 And he cut the ram into pieces; and Moshe burnt the head, and the pieces, and the fat. 21 And he washed the inwards and the legs in mayim; and Moshe burnt the whole ram upon the altar: it was a burnt sacrifice for a sweet fragrance, and an offering made by fire to יהוה; as יהוה commanded Moshe. 22 And he brought the other ram, the ram of consecration, and Aharon and his sons laid their hands upon the head of the ram. 23 And he killed it; and Moshe took of the dom of it, and put it upon the tip of Aharon's right ear, and upon the thumb of his right hand, and upon the great toe of his right foot. 24 And he brought Aharon's sons, and Moshe put some of the dom upon the tip of their right ear, and upon the thumbs of their right hands, and upon the great toes of their right feet: and Moshe sprinkled the dom upon the altar all around.[3] 25 And he took the fat, and the tail, and all the fat that was upon the inwards, and the appendage above the liver, and the two kidneys, and their fat, and the right

---

[1] Men were to always have their heads covered especially as a nation of kohanim. The same holds true today. The Scriptures do not command the modern skullcap or **yarmulke,** but do call for a head covering or turban.

[2] See note on verse 9.
[3] This ceremony was done to symbolize what Moshiach Yahshua did who is now at the right side of the Father, serving as Kohen HaGadol over Renewed Covenant Yisrael.

shoulder: 26 And out of the basket of unleavened lechem, that was before **יהוה**, he took one unleavened cake, and a cake of oiled lechem, and one wafer, and put them on the fat, and upon the right shoulder: 27 And he put all upon Aharon's hands, and upon his sons' hands, and waved them for a wave offering before **יהוה**. 28 And Moshe took them from off their hands, and burnt them on the altar upon the burnt offering: they were for consecrations for a sweet fragrance: it is an offering made by fire to **יהוה**. 29 And Moshe took the breast, and waved it for a wave offering before **יהוה**: Taken from the ram of consecration it was Moshe's part as **יהוה** commanded Moshe. 30 And Moshe took of the anointing oil, and of the dom which was upon the altar, and sprinkled it upon Aharon, and upon his garments, and upon his sons, and upon his sons' garments with him; and set Aharon apart, and his garments, and his sons, and his sons' garments with him. 31 And Moshe said to Aharon and to his sons, Boil the flesh at the door of the Tabernacle of the congregation: and there eat it with the lechem that is in the Basket of Consecration, as I commanded, saying, Aharon and his sons shall eat it. 32 And that which remains of the flesh and of the lechem shall you burn with fire. 33 And you shall not go out of the door of the Tabernacle of the congregation for seven days, until the days of your consecration are at an end: for seven days shall he be consecrated. 34 As he has done this day, so **יהוה** has commanded to do, to make atonement for you. 35 Therefore shall you abide at the door of the Tabernacle of the congregation day and night seven days, and guard the charge of **יהוה**, that you do not die: for so I am commanded. 36 So Aharon and his sons did all things that **יהוה** commanded by the hand of Moshe.

Torah Parsha 26
Shmini 9:1-11:47
Haftarah Schmuel Bet 6:1-7:17
Brit Chadasha Moshe-Markus 7:1-23

9 And it came to pass on the eighth day, that Moshe called Aharon and his sons, and the zachanim of Yisrael. 2 And he said to Aharon, Take a young calf for a sin offering, and a ram for a burnt offering, without blemish, and offer them before **יהוה**. 3 And to the children of Yisrael you shall speak, saying, Take a kid of the goats for a sin offering; and a calf and a lamb, both of the first year, without blemish, for a burnt offering; 4 Also a bull and a ram for shalom offerings, to sacrifice before **יהוה**; and a grain offering mixed with oil: for today **יהוה** will appear to you. 5 And they brought that which Moshe commanded before the Tabernacle of the congregation: and all the congregation drew near and stood before **יהוה**. 6 And Moshe said, This is the thing that **יהוה** commanded that you should do: and the tiferet of **יהוה** shall appear to you. 7 And Moshe said to Aharon, Go to the altar, and offer your sin offering, and your burnt offering, and make atonement for yourself, and for the people: and offer the offering of the people, and make atonement for them; as **יהוה** commanded. 8 Aharon therefore went to the altar, and killed the calf of the sin offering, which was for himself. 9 And the sons of Aharon brought the dom to him: and he dipped his finger in the dom, and put it upon the horns of the altar, and poured out the dom at the bottom of the altar: 10 But the fat, and the kidneys, and the appendage above the liver of the sin offering, he burnt upon the altar; as **יהוה** commanded Moshe. 11 And the flesh and the hide he burnt with fire outside the camp. 12 And he killed the burnt offering; and Aharon's sons presented to him the dom, which he sprinkled all around upon the altar. 13 And they presented the burnt offering to him, with the pieces of it, and the head: and he burnt them upon the altar. 14 And he did wash the

inwards and the legs, and burnt them upon the burnt offering on the altar. 15 And he brought the people's offering, and took the goat, which was the sin offering for the people, and killed it, and offered it for sin, as the first. 16 And he brought the burnt offering, and offered it according to the prescribed manner. 17 And he brought the grain offering, and took a handful of it, and burnt it upon the altar, beside the burnt sacrifice of the morning. 18 He killed also the bull and the ram for a sacrifice of shalom offerings, which was for the people: and Aharon's sons presented to him the dom, which he sprinkled upon the altar all around, 19 And the fat of the bull and of the ram, the tail, and that, which covers the inwards, and the kidneys, and the appendage above the liver: 20 And they put the fat upon the breasts, and he burnt the fat upon the altar: 21 And the breasts and the right shoulder Aharon waved for a wave offering before יהוה ; as Moshe commanded. 22 And Aharon lifted up his hand toward the people, and blessed them, and came down from offering the sin offering, and the burnt offering, and shalom offerings. 23 And Moshe and Aharon went into the Tabernacle of the congregation, and came out, and blessed the people: and the tiferet of יהוה appeared to all the people. 24 And there came a fire out from before יהוה , and consumed upon the altar the burnt offering and the fat: which when all the people saw, they shouted, and fell on their faces.

10 And Nadav and Avihu, the sons of Aharon, took either of them his censer, and put fire in it, and put incense on it, and offered strange fire before יהוה , which He commanded them not. 2 And there went out fire from יהוה, and devoured them, and they died before יהוה.[1] 3 Then Moshe said to Aharon, This is it that יהוה spoke, saying, I will be set-apart in them that come near Me, and before all the people I will be esteemed. And Aharon held his silence. 4 And Moshe called Misha-el and El-Tzaphan, the sons of Uzziel the uncle of Aharon, and said to them, Come near, carry your brothers from before the Set-Apart-Place out of the camp. 5 So they went near, and carried them in their coats out of the camp; as Moshe had said. 6 And Moshe said to Aharon, and to El-Azar and to Ithamar, his sons, Uncover not your heads,[2] neither tear your clothes; lest you die, and lest wrath come upon all the people: but let your brothers, kol Beit Yisrael, mourn the burning which יהוה has kindled. 7 And you shall not go out from the door of the Tabernacle of the congregation, lest you die: for the anointing oil of יהוה is upon you. And they did according to the word of Moshe. 8 And יהוה spoke to Aharon, saying, 9 *Do not drink wine nor strong drink, you, nor your sons with you, when you go into the Tabernacle of the congregation, lest you die: it shall be a chuk le-olam-va-ed throughout your generations:* [3] 10 *And that you may put a difference between that which is set-apart and defiled, and between unclean and clean;* 11 *And that you may teach the children of Yisrael all the chukim, which יהוה has spoken to them by the hand of Moshe.* 12 And Moshe spoke to Aharon, and to El-Azar and to Ithamar, his sons that were left, Take the grain offering that remains of the offerings of יהוה made by fire, and eat it without chametz beside the altar: for it is most set-apart: 13 And you shall eat it in the Set-Apart-Place, because it is your due, and your sons' due, of the sacrifices of יהוה made by fire: for so I am commanded. 14 And the wave breast and contribution thigh shall you eat in a clean place; you, and your sons, and your daughters with you: for they are your dues, and your sons' dues, which are given out of

---

[1] Apparently the incense was offered incorrectly and YHWH considered that worthy of death. Perhaps their heads were uncovered or they were drunk, or even partially naked by having torn cloths as we read a few verses later.

[2] The possible strange fire seen earlier, where YHWH in mercy is explaining to Aharon's other sons how to avoid further disaster.
[3] See note on verse 2.

the sacrifices of the shalom offerings of the children of Yisrael. 15 The contribution thigh and the wave breast shall they bring with the offerings made by fire of the fat, to wave it for a wave offering before יהוה; and it shall be yours, and your sons' with you, by a chuk le-olam-va-ed; as יהוה has commanded. 16 And Moshe diligently sought the goat of the sin offering, and, see, it was burnt: and he was angry at El-Azar and Ithamar, the sons of Aharon which were left alive, saying, 17 Why have you not eaten the sin offering in the Set-Apart-Place, seeing it is most set-apart, and Elohim has given it you to bear the iniquity of the congregation, to make atonement for them before יהוה? 18 See, the dom of it was not brought in within the Set-Apart-Place: you should indeed have eaten it in the Set-Apart-Place, as I commanded. 19 And Aharon said to Moshe, See, this day have they offered their sin offering and their burnt offering before יהוה; and such things have befallen me: and if I had eaten the sin offering today, would it have been right in the sight of יהוה? 20 And when Moshe heard that, he was content.

11 And יהוה spoke to Moshe and to Aharon, saying to them, 2 *Speak to the children of Yisrael, saying, These are the living creatures that you shall eat* [1] *among all the living creatures that are on the earth. 3 Whatever splits the hoof, and is cloven-footed, and chews the cud, among the living creatures, that shall you eat. 4 Nevertheless these shall you not eat of those that chew the cud, or of those that divide the hoof: the camel, because he chews the cud, but divides not the hoof; he is unclean to you. 5 And the rabbit, because he chews the cud, but divides not the hoof; he is unclean to you. 6 And the hare, because he chews the cud, but divides not the hoof; he is unclean to you. 7 And the pig, though he divides the hoof, and be cloven-footed, yet he chews not the cud; he is unclean to you. 8 Of their flesh shall you not eat, and their carcass shall you not touch; they are unclean to you. 9 These shall you eat of all that are in the mayim: whatever has fins and scales in the mayim, in the seas, and in the rivers, them shall you eat. 10 And all that have not fins and scales in the seas, and in the rivers, of all that move in the mayim, and of any living thing that is in the mayim, they shall be an abomination to you: 11 They shall be even an abomination to you; you shall not eat of their flesh, but you shall hold their carcasses in abomination. 12 Whatever has no fins or scales in the mayim; that shall be an abomination to you. 13 And these are they that you shall hold in abomination among the fowls; they shall not be eaten, they are an abomination: the eagle, and the vulture, and the black vulture, 14 And the hawk, and the falcon after its kind; 15 Every raven after its kind; 16 And the ostrich, and the nighthawk, and the seagull, and the hawk after its kind, 17 And the little owl, and the fisher owl, and the great owl, 18 And the swan, and the pelican, and the bat, 19 And the stork, the heron after its kind, and the wild hen, and the bat. 20 All flying insects, creeping upon all fours, shall be an abomination to you. 21 Yet these may you eat of every flying creeping thing that goes upon all fours, which have legs above their feet, to leap with upon the earth; 22 Even these of them you may eat; the locust after its kind, and the bald locust after its kind, and the beetle after its kind, and the grasshopper after its kind. 23 But all other flying creeping things, which have four feet, shall be an abomination to you. 24 And for these you shall be unclean: whoever touches the carcass of them shall be unclean until the evening. 25 And whoever picks up any part of the carcass of them shall wash his clothes, and be unclean until the evening. 26 The carcasses of every beast that divides the hoof, and is not cloven-footed, nor chews the cud, are*

---

[1] All believers in YHWH and His Son as outlined in Acts 15; Yisrael must not break these eternal requirements.

unclean to you: every one that touches them shall be unclean. 27 And whatever goes upon his paws, among all manner of living creatures that go on all four, those are unclean to you: anyone who touches their carcass shall be unclean until the evening. 28 And he that picks up the carcass of them shall wash his clothes, and be unclean until the evening: they are unclean to you. 29 These also shall be unclean to you among the creeping things that creep upon the earth; the weasel, and the mouse, and the frog after its kind, 30 And the porcupine, and the land lizard, and the lizard, and the snail, and the mole.[1] 31 These are unclean to you among all that creep: whoever touches them, when they are dead, shall be unclean until the evening. 32 And upon whatever any of them, when they are dead, falls, it shall be unclean; whether it be any vessel of wood, or clothing, or skin, or sack, whatever vessel it is, in which any work is done, it must be put into mayim, and it shall be unclean until the evening; so it shall be cleansed. 33 And every earthen vessel, on which any of them falls, whatever is in it shall be unclean; and you shall break it. 34 Of all grain that may be eaten, that on which such mayim comes shall be unclean: and all drink that may be drunk in every such vessel shall be unclean. 35 And every thing whereupon any part of their carcass falls shall be unclean; whether it be oven, or stoves for cooking pots, they shall be broken down: for they are unclean, and shall be unclean to you. 36 Nevertheless a fountain or pit, in which there is plenty of mayim, shall be clean: but that which touches their carcass shall be unclean. 37 And if any part of their carcass falls upon any planting seed that is to be sown, it shall be clean. 38 But if any mayim is put upon the seed, and any part of their carcass falls on it, it shall be unclean to you. 39 And if any beast, of which you may eat, dies; he that touches the carcass of it shall be unclean until the evening. 40 And he that eats of the carcass

of it shall wash his clothes, and be unclean until the evening: he also that picks up the carcass of it shall wash his clothes, and be unclean until the evening. 41 And every creeping thing that creeps upon the earth shall be an abomination; it shall not be eaten. 42 Whatever goes upon the belly, and whatever goes upon all fours, or whatever has more feet among all creeping things that creep upon the earth, them you shall not eat; for they are an abomination. 43 You shall not make yourselves abominable with any creeping thing that creeps; neither shall you make yourselves unclean with them, that you should be defiled thereby. 44 For I am יהוה Your Elohim: you shall therefore set Him apart yourselves, and you shall be set-apart; for I am set-apart: neither shall you defile yourselves with any manner of creeping thing that creeps upon the earth. 45 For I am יהוה that brings you up out of the land of Mitzrayim, to be Your Elohim: you shall therefore be set-apart, for I am set-apart. 46 This is the Torah of the living creatures, and of the fowls, and of every living creature that moves in the mayim, and of every creature that creeps upon the earth: 47 To make a difference between the unclean and the clean, and between the beast that may be eaten and the beast that may not be eaten.[2]

Torah Parsha 27
Tazria 12:1-13:59
In regular 12-month years,
read with Parsha 28.
In years with 13 months, read separately. Haftarah
Melechim Bet 4:42-5:19
Brit Chadasha Mattityahu 8:1-4,
Luka 17:11-19

12 And יהוה spoke to Moshe, saying, 2 Speak to the children of Yisrael, saying, If a woman has conceived, and has born a male child: then she shall be unclean seven days; as in the days of the monthly

---

[1] Stone Edition Tanach p. 269

[2] Herein lies the whole purpose of Vayiqra and other Scriptures that are designed to separate Yisrael. To make a difference between YHWH and other Elohim, and Yisrael and the nations.

separation for her infirmity shall she be unclean. 3 And in the eighth day the flesh of his foreskin shall be circumcised. 4 And she shall then continue in the dom of her purifying thirty-three days; she shall touch no set-apart thing, nor come into the Set-Apart-Place, until the days of her purifying be fulfilled. 5 But if she bear a female child, then she shall be unclean two weeks, as in her monthly separation: and she shall continue in the dom of her purifying sixty-six days. 6 And when the days of her purifying are fulfilled, for a son, or for a daughter, she shall bring a lamb of the first year for a burnt offering, and a young pigeon, or a turtledove, for a sin offering, to the door of the Tabernacle of the congregation, to the kohen: 7 Who shall offer it before יהוה, and make atonement for her; and she shall be cleansed from the discharge of her dom. This is the Torah for her that has born a male or a female. 8 And if she is not able to bring a lamb, then she shall bring two turtles, or two young pigeons; the one for the burnt offering, and the other for a sin offering: and the kohen shall make atonement for her, and she shall be clean.[1]

13 And יהוה spoke to Moshe and Aharon, saying, 2 When a man shall have in the skin of his flesh a swelling, a scab, or a bright spot, and it be in the skin of his flesh like the plague of leprosy; then he shall be brought to Aharon the kohen, or to one of his sons the kohanim: 3 And the kohen shall look on the plague in the skin of the flesh: and if the hair in the plague is turned white, and the plague in sight is deeper than the skin of his flesh, it is a plague of leprosy: and the kohen shall look on him, and pronounce him unclean. 4 If the bright spot is white in the skin of his flesh, and in sight be not deeper than the skin, and the hair of it be not turned white; then the kohen shall shut him up that has the plague

seven days: 5 And the kohen shall look on him the seventh day: and, see, if the plague in his sight is as it was, and the plague did not spread in the skin; then the kohen shall shut him up seven days more: 6 And the kohen shall look on him again the seventh day: and, see, if the plague be something dark, and the plague spread not in the skin, the kohen shall pronounce him clean: it is but a scab: and he shall wash his clothes, and be clean. 7 But if the scab spread much further in the skin, after he has been seen by the kohen for his cleansing, he shall be seen of the kohen again: 8 And if the kohen sees that, the scab spreads in the skin, then the kohen shall pronounce him unclean: it is a leprosy. 9 When the plague of leprosy is in a man, then he shall be brought to the kohen. 10 And the kohen shall see him: and, see, if the rising is white in the skin, and it has turned the hair white, and there be quick raw flesh in the rising; 11 It is an old leprosy in the skin of his flesh, and the kohen shall pronounce him unclean, and shall not shut him up: for he is unclean. 12 And if a leprosy breaks out further in the skin, and the leprosy covers all the skin of the one that has the plague from his head even to his foot, wherever the kohen looks; 13 Then the kohen shall consider: and, see, if the leprosy has covered all his flesh, he shall pronounce him clean that has the plague: it is all turned white: he is clean. 14 But when raw flesh appears in him, he shall be unclean. 15 And the kohen shall see the raw flesh, and pronounce him to be unclean: for the raw flesh is unclean: it is a leprosy. 16 Or if the raw flesh changes again, and be changed to white, he shall come to the kohen; 17 And the kohen shall see him: and, see, if the plague has turned into white; then the kohen shall pronounce him clean that has the plague: he is clean. 18 The flesh also, in which, even in the skin of it, was a boil, and is healed, 19 And in the place of the boil there be a white rising, or a bright spot, white, and something reddish, and it be shown to the kohen;

---

[1] Performed by Miryam, Yahshua's mother, and given for those poor in Yisrael.

20 *And if, when the kohen sees it, see, it be in sight lower than the skin, and the hair of it is turned white; the kohen shall pronounce him unclean: it is a plague of leprosy broken out of the boil.* 21 *But if the kohen look on it, and, see, there are no white hairs on it, and if it is not lower than the skin, but is something dark; then the kohen shall shut him up seven days:* 22 *And if it spread much further in the skin, then the kohen shall pronounce him unclean: it is a plague.* 23 *But if the bright spot stays in its place, and spread not, it is a burning boil; and the kohen shall pronounce him clean.* 24 *Or if there be any flesh, in the skin in which there is a hot burning, and the quick flesh that burns has a white bright spot, something reddish, or white;* 25 *Then the kohen shall look upon it: and, see, if the hair in the bright spot be turned white, and it be in sight deeper than the skin; it is a leprosy broken out of the burning: therefore the kohen shall pronounce him unclean: it is the plague of leprosy.* 26 *But if the kohen look at it, and, see, there is no white hair in the bright spot, and it be no lower than the other skin, but be something dark; then the kohen shall shut him up seven days:* 27 *And the kohen shall look upon him the seventh day: and if it is spread much further in the skin, then the kohen shall pronounce him unclean: it is the plague of leprosy.* 28 *And if the bright spot stay in its place, and spreads not in the skin, but it is something dark; it is a rising of the burning, and the kohen shall pronounce him clean: for it is an inflammation of the burning.* 29 *If a man or woman have a plague upon the head or the beard;* 30 *Then the kohen shall see the plague: and, see, if it be in sight deeper than the skin; and there be in it a yellow thin hair; then the kohen shall pronounce him unclean: it is a leprosy upon the head or beard.* 31 *And if the kohen looks at the infection and, see, it is not in sight deeper than the skin, and that there is no black hair in it; then the kohen shall shut him up that has the infection seven days:* 32 *And in the seventh day the kohen shall look on the plague: and, see, if the infection did not spread, and there be in it no yellow hair, and the infection is not in sight deeper than the skin;* 33 *He shall be shaven, but the infection shall he not shave; and the kohen shall shut him up that has the infection seven more days:* 34 *And in the seventh day the kohen shall look on the infection: and, see, if the infection is not spread further in the skin, nor is in sight deeper than the skin; then the kohen shall pronounce him clean: and he shall wash his clothes, and be clean.* 35 *But if the infection spread much into the skin after his cleansing;* 36 *Then the kohen shall look at him: and, see, if the infection is spread in the skin, the kohen shall not seek for yellow hair; he is unclean.* 37 *But if the infection is in his sight not spread, and that there is black hair grown up on it; the infection is healed, he is clean: and the kohen shall pronounce him clean.* 38 *If a man also or a woman has in the skin of their flesh bright spots, even white bright spots;* 39 *Then the kohen shall look: and, see, if the bright spots in the skin of their flesh be darkish white; it is a freckled spot that grows in the skin; he is clean.* 40 *And the man whose hair is fallen off his head, he is bald; yet is he clean.* 41 *And he that has his hair fallen off from the part of his head toward his face, he is forehead bald: yet is he clean.* 42 *And if there be in the bald head, or bald forehead, a white reddish sore; it is a leprosy sprung up in his bald head, or his bald forehead.* 43 *Then the kohen shall look upon it: and, see, if the rising of the sore be white reddish in his bald head, or in his bald forehead, as the leprosy appears in the skin of the flesh;* 44 *He is a leprous man, he is unclean: the kohen shall pronounce him utterly unclean; his plague is in his head.* 45 *And the leper in whom the plague is, his clothes shall be torn, and his head bare, and he shall put a covering upon his upper lip, and shall cry, Unclean, unclean.* 46 *All the days in which the plague shall be in him he shall be*

defiled; he is unclean: he shall dwell alone; outside the camp shall his dwelling be. 47 The garment also that the plague of leprosy is in, whether it be a woollen garment, or a linen garment; 48 Whether it be in the warp, or woof; of linen, or of wool; whether in a skin, or in any thing made of skin; 49 And if the plague be greenish or reddish in the garment, or in the skin, either in the warp, or in the woof, or in any thing of skin; it is a plague of leprosy, and shall be shown to the kohen: 50 And the kohen shall look upon the plague, and shut him up that has the plague seven days: 51 And he shall look on the plague on the seventh day: if the plague is spread in the garment, either in the warp, or in the woof, or in a skin, or in any work that is made of skin; the plague is an active leprosy; it is unclean. 52 He shall therefore burn that garment, whether warp or woof, in wool or in linen, or any thing of skin, in which the plague is: for it is a active leprosy; it shall be burnt in the fire. 53 And if the kohen shall look, and, sees, that the plague is not spread in the garment, either in the warp, or in the woof, or in any thing of skin; 54 Then the kohen shall command that they wash the thing in which the plague is, and he shall shut it up seven days more: 55 And the kohen shall look on the plague, after that it is washed: and, see, if the plague has not changed its color, and the plague is not spread; it is unclean; you shall burn it in the fire; it is eaten inward, whether it be bare within or outside. 56 And if the kohen look, and, see, the plague be something dark after the washing of it; then he shall tear it out of the garment, or out of the skin, or out of the warp, or out of the woof: 57 And if it appears still in the garment, either in the warp, or in the woof, or in any thing of skin; it is a spreading plague: you shall burn that in which the plague is with fire. 58 And the garment, either warp, or woof, or whatever thing of skin it be, which you shall wash, if the plague is departed from them, then it shall be washed the second time, and shall

be clean. 59 This is the Torah of the plague of leprosy in a garment of wool or linen, either in the warp, or woof, or any thing of skin, to pronounce it clean, or to pronounce it unclean.

Torah Parsha 28
Mtzora 14:1-15:33
In regular 12-month years,
read with Parsha 27.
In years with 13 months, read separately. Haftarah
Melechim Bet 7:3-20
Brit Chadasha Moshe-Markus 5:24b-34

14 And יהוה spoke to Moshe, saying, 2 This shall be the Torah of the leper in the day of his cleansing: He shall be brought to the kohen: 3 And the kohen shall go forth out of the camp; and the kohen shall look, and, see, if the plague of leprosy is healed in the leper; 4 Then shall the kohen command to take for him that is to be cleansed two birds alive and clean, and cedar wood, and scarlet, and hyssop: 5 And the kohen shall command that one of the birds be killed in an earthen vessel over running mayim: 6 As for the living bird, he shall take it, and the cedar wood, and the scarlet, and the hyssop, and shall dip them and the living bird in the dom of the bird that was killed over the running mayim: 7 And he shall sprinkle upon him that is to be cleansed from the leprosy seven times, and shall pronounce him clean, and shall let the living bird loose into the open field. 8 And he that is to be cleansed shall wash his clothes, and shave off all his hair, and wash himself in mayim, that he may be clean: and after that he shall come into the camp, and shall stay out of his tent seven days. 9 But it shall be on the seventh day, that he shall shave all his hair off his head and his beard and his eyebrows, even all his hair he shall shave off: and he shall wash his clothes, also he shall wash his flesh in mayim, and he shall be clean. 10 And on the eighth day he shall take two male lambs without blemish, and one ewe lamb of the first year without blemish, and three tenth of an

ephah of fine flour for a grain offering, mixed with oil, and one log of oil. 11 And the kohen that makes him clean shall present the man that is to be made clean, and those things, before יהוה, at the door of the Tabernacle of the congregation: 12 And the kohen shall take one male lamb, and offer him for a guilt offering, and the log of oil, and wave them for a wave offering before יהוה: 13 And he shall slay the lamb in the place where he shall kill the sin offering and the burnt offering, in the Set-Apart-Place: for as the sin offering is the kohen's, so is the guilt offering: it is most set-apart: 14 And the kohen shall take some of the dom of the guilt offering, and the kohen shall put it upon the tip of the right ear of him that is to be cleansed, and upon the thumb of his right hand, and upon the great toe of his right foot:[1] 15 And the kohen shall take some of the log of oil, and pour it into the palm of his own left hand: 16 And the kohen shall dip his right finger in the oil that is in his left hand, and shall sprinkle of the oil with his finger seven times before יהוה: 17 And of the rest of the oil that is in his hand shall the kohen put upon the tip of the right ear of him that is to be cleansed, and upon the thumb of his right hand, and upon the great toe of his right foot, upon the dom of the guilt offering:[2] 18 And the remnant of the oil that is in the kohen's hand he shall pour upon the head of him that is to be cleansed: and the kohen shall make atonement for him before יהוה. 19 And the kohen shall offer the sin offering, and make atonement for him that is to be cleansed from his uncleanness; and afterward he shall kill the burnt offering: 20 And the kohen shall offer the burnt offering and the grain offering upon the altar: and the kohen shall make atonement for him, and he shall be clean. 21 And if he is poor, and cannot get so much; then he shall take one lamb for a guilt offering to be waved, to make atonement for him, and one

tenth deal of fine flour mixed with oil for a grain offering, and a log of oil; 22 And two turtledoves, or two young pigeons, such as he is able to get; and the one shall be a sin offering, and the other a burnt offering. 23 And he shall bring them on the eighth day for his cleansing to the kohen, to the door of the Tabernacle of the congregation, before יהוה. 24 And the kohen shall take the lamb of the guilt offering, and the log of oil, and the kohen shall wave them for a wave offering before יהוה: 25 And he shall kill the lamb of the guilt offering, and the kohen shall take some of the dom of the guilt offering, and put it upon the tip of the right ear of him that is to be cleansed, and upon the thumb of his right hand, and upon the great toe of his right foot:[3] 26 And the kohen shall pour of the oil into the palm of his own left hand: 27 And the kohen shall sprinkle with his right finger some of the oil that is in his left hand seven times before יהוה: 28 And the kohen shall put of the oil that is in his hand upon the tip of the right ear of him that is to be cleansed, and upon the thumb of his right hand, and upon the great toe of his right foot, upon the place of the dom of the guilt offering:[4] 29 And the rest of the oil that is in the kohen's hand he shall put upon the head of him that is to be cleansed, to make atonement for him before יהוה 30 And he shall offer the one of the turtledoves, or of the young pigeons, such as he can get; 31 Even such as he is able to get, the one for a sin offering, and the other for a burnt offering, with the grain offering: and the kohen shall make atonement for him that is to be cleansed before יהוה. 32 This is the Torah for the one who has the plague of leprosy, whose hand is not able to get that which pertains to his cleansing. 33 And יהוה spoke to Moshe and to Aharon, saying, 34 When you be come into the land of Kanaan, which I give to you for a possession, and I put the plague of leprosy in a bayit of the land of your possession;

---

[1] See note on Leviticus 8:24.
[2] See note on Leviticus 8:24.
[3] See note on Leviticus 8:24.
[4] See note on Leviticus 8:24.

35 *And he that owns the bayit shall come and tell the kohen, saying, It seems to me there is as it were a plague in the bayit:* 36 *Then the kohen shall command that they empty the bayit, before the kohen go into it to see the plague, that all that is in the bayit be not made unclean: and afterward the kohen shall go in to see the bayit:* 37 *And he shall look on the plague, and, see, if the plague be in the walls of the bayit with sunken places, greenish or reddish, which in sight are deep into the wall;* 38 *Then the kohen shall go out of the bayit to the door of the bayit, and shut up the bayit for seven days:* 39 *And the kohen shall come again the seventh day, and shall look: and, see, if the plague is spread in the walls of the bayit;* 40 *Then the kohen shall command that they take away the stones in which the plague is, and they shall cast them into an unclean place outside the city:* 41 *And he shall cause the bayit to be scraped inside all around, and they shall pour out the dust that they scrape off outside the city into an unclean place:* 42 *And they shall take other stones, and put them in the place of those stones; and he shall take other morter, and shall plaster the bayit.* 43 *And if the plague come again, and break out in the bayit, after that he has taken away the stones, and after he has scraped the bayit, and after it is plastered;* 44 *Then the kohen shall come and look, and, see, if the plague is spread in the bayit, it is an active leprosy in the bayit: it is unclean.* 45 *And he shall break down the bayit, the stones of it, and the timber of it, and all the morter of the bayit; and he shall carry them forth out of the city into an unclean place.* 46 *Moreover he that goes into the bayit all the while that it is shut up shall be unclean until the evening.* 47 *And he that lies in the bayit shall wash his clothes; and he that eats in the bayit shall wash his clothes.* 48 *And if the kohen shall come in, and look upon it, and, see, the plague has not spread in the bayit, after the bayit was plastered: then the kohen shall pronounce the bayit clean, because the* plague is healed. 49 *And he shall take to cleanse the bayit two birds, and cedar wood, and scarlet, and hyssop:* 50 *And he shall kill the one of the birds in an earthen vessel over running mayim:* 51 *And he shall take the cedar wood, and the hyssop, and the scarlet, and the living bird, and dip them in the dom of the slain bird, and in the running mayim, and sprinkle the bayit seven times:* 52 *And he shall cleanse the bayit with the dom of the bird, and with the running mayim, and with the living bird, and with the cedar wood, and with the hyssop, and with the scarlet:* 53 *But he shall let the living bird go out of the city into the open fields, and make atonement for the bayit: and it shall be clean.* 54 *This is the Torah for all manner of plague of leprosy, and eruption,* 55 *And for the leprosy of a garment, and of a bayit,* 56 *And for a rising, and for a scab, and for a bright spot:* 57 *To teach when it is unclean, and when it is clean: this is the Torah of leprosy.*

15 And יהוה spoke to Moshe and to Aharon, saying, 2 *Speak to the children of Yisrael, and say to them, When any man has a running discharge out of his flesh, because of his discharge he is unclean.* 3 *And this shall be his uncleanness in his discharge: whether his flesh run with his discharge, or his flesh be stopped from his discharge, it is his uncleanness.* 4 *Every bed, on which he lies that has the discharge, is unclean: and every object, on which he sits, shall be unclean.* 5 *And whoever touches his bed shall wash his clothes, and bathe himself in mayim, and be unclean until the evening.* 6 *And he that sits on any thing on which he sat that has the discharge shall wash his clothes, and bathe himself in mayim, and be unclean until the evening.* 7 *And he that touches the flesh of him that has the discharge shall wash his clothes, and bathe himself in mayim, and be unclean until the evening.* 8 *And if he that has the discharge spit upon him that is clean; then he shall wash his clothes, and bathe himself* in mayim, and be unclean until the evening. 9 And whatever saddle he rides upon that has the discharge shall be unclean. 10 And whoever touches any object that was under him shall be unclean until the evening: and he that picks up any of those things shall wash his clothes, and bathe himself in mayim, and be unclean until the evening. 11 And whoever touches the one that has the discharge, and has not rinsed his hands in mayim, he shall wash his clothes, and bathe himself in mayim, and be unclean until the evening. 12 And the vessel of earth, that he touches which has the discharge, shall be broken: and every vessel of wood shall be rinsed in mayim. 13 And when he that has a discharge is cleansed of his discharge; then he shall count for himself seven days for his cleansing, and wash his clothes, and bathe his flesh in running mayim, and shall be clean. 14 And on the eighth day he shall take with him two turtledoves, or two young pigeons, and come before יהוה to the door of the Tabernacle of the congregation, and give them to the kohen: 15 And the kohen shall offer them, the one for a sin offering, and the other for a burnt offering; and the kohen shall make atonement for him before יהוה for his discharge. 16 And if any man's semen of emission goes out from him, then he shall wash all his flesh in mayim, and be unclean until the evening 17 And every garment, and every skin, on which is the semen of emission, shall be washed with mayim, and be unclean until the evening. 18 The woman also who lies with a man having semen of emission, they shall both bathe themselves in mayim, and be unclean until the evening. 19 And if a woman has a discharge, and in her discharge of her flesh shall be found dom, she shall be separated seven days: and whoever touches her shall be unclean until the evening. 20 And every thing that she lies upon in her separation shall be unclean: every thing also that she sits upon shall be unclean. 21 And whoever touches her bed shall wash his clothes, and bathe himself in mayim, and be unclean until the evening. 22 And whoever touches any thing that she sat upon shall wash his clothes, and bathe himself in mayim, and be unclean until the evening. 23 And if it be on her bed, or on any thing on which she sits, when he touches it, he shall be unclean until the evening. 24 And if any man lie with her at all, and her discharge be upon him, he shall be unclean seven days; and all the bed on which he lies shall be unclean. 25 And if a woman has a discharge of her dom many days out of the time of her separation, or if it run beyond the time of her separation; all the days of the discharge of her uncleanness shall be as the days of her separation: she shall be unclean. 26 Every bed on which she lies all the days of her discharge shall be to her as the bed of her separation: and whatever she sits upon shall be unclean, as the uncleanness of her separation. 27 And whoever touches those things shall be unclean, and shall wash his clothes, and bathe himself in mayim, and be unclean until the evening. 28 But if she is cleansed of her discharge, then she shall count to herself seven days, and after that she shall be clean. 29 And on the eighth day she shall take with her two turtles, or two young pigeons, and bring them to the kohen, to the door of the Tabernacle of the congregation. 30 And the kohen shall offer the one for a sin offering, and the other for a burnt offering; and the kohen shall make atonement for her before יהוה for the discharge of her uncleanness. 31 And so shall you separate the children of Yisrael from their uncleanness; that they die not in their uncleanness, when they defile My Tabernacle that is among them. 32 This is the Torah of him that has a discharge, and of him whose semen goes from him, and is defiled by it; 33 And of her that is sick in her monthly separation, and of him that has a discharge, of the man, and of the woman, and of him that lies with her that is unclean.

Torah Parsha 29
Acharei Mot 16:1-18:30
In regular 12-month years,
read with Parsha 30.
In years with 13 months, read separately. Haftarah
Yeshayahu 53:1-12
Brit Chadasha Ivrim 7:23-10:25

16 And יהוה spoke to Moshe after the death of the two sons of Aharon, when they offered before יהוה, and died; 2 And יהוה said to Moshe, *Speak to Aharon your brother, that he come not at all times into the most Set-Apart-Place within the vail before the rachamim seat, which is upon the ark; that he die not: for I will appear in the cloud upon the rachamim seat. 3 Thus shall Aharon come into the Set-Apart-Place: with a young bull for a sin offering, and a ram for a burnt offering. 4 He shall put on the set-apart linen coat, and he shall have the linen breeches upon his flesh, and shall be dressed with a linen girdle, and with the linen turban shall he be attired: these are set-apart garments; therefore shall he wash his flesh in mayim, and so put them on. 5 And he shall take from the congregation of the children of Yisrael two kids of the goats for a sin offering, and one ram for a burnt offering. 6 And Aharon shall offer his bull of the sin offering, which is for himself, and make atonement for himself, and for his bayit. 7 And he shall take the two goats, and present them before* יהוה *at the door of the Tabernacle of the congregation. 8 And Aharon shall cast lots upon the two goats; one lot for* יהוה*, and the other lot for the scapegoat. 9 And Aharon shall bring the goat upon which* יהוה*'s lot fell, and offer it for a sin offering. 10 But the goat, on which the lot fell to be the scapegoat, shall be presented alive before* יהוה *, to make atonement with him, and to let it go for a scapegoat into the wilderness. 11 And Aharon shall bring the bull of the sin offering, which is for himself, and shall make atonement for himself, and for his bayit, and shall kill the bull of the sin offering which is for himself: 12 And he* shall take a censer full of burning coals of fire from off the altar before יהוה, and his hands full of sweet incense crushed small, and bring it within the vail: 13 And he shall put the incense upon the fire before יהוה, that the cloud of the incense may cover the rachamim seat that is upon the testimony, that he die not: 14 And he shall take of the dom of the bull, and sprinkle it with his finger upon the rachamim seat that is eastward; and before the rachamim seat shall he sprinkle of the dom with his finger seven times. 15 Then shall he kill the goat of the sin offering, that is for the people, and bring its dom within the vail, and do with that dom as he did with the dom of the bull, and sprinkle it upon the rachamim seat, and before the rachamim seat: 16 And he shall make atonement for the Set-Apart-Place, because of the uncleanness of the children of Yisrael, and because of their transgressions in all their sins: and so shall he do for the Tabernacle of the congregation, that remains among them in the midst of their uncleanness. 17 And there shall be no man in the Tabernacle of the congregation when he goes in to make atonement in the Set-Apart-Place, until he comes out, and has made atonement for himself, and for his household, and for all the congregation of Yisrael.* [1] *18 And he shall go out to the altar that is before* יהוה*, and make atonement for it; and shall take of the dom of the bull, and of the dom of the goat, and put it upon the horns of the altar all around. 19 And he shall sprinkle of the dom upon it with his finger seven times, and cleanse it, and set it apart from the uncleanness of the children of Yisrael. 20 And when he has made an end of reconciling the Set-Apart-Place, and the Tabernacle of the congregation, and the altar, he shall bring the live goat: 21 And Aharon shall lay both his hands upon the*

---

[1] **Yom HaKippurim** (literally, the Day of Atonements) for all Yisrael. All Yisrael was cleansed of both willful and unintentional sin by this annual atonement. The same "one for all ordinance" is found in Moshiach's one-time offering of Himself.

head of the live goat, and confess over it all the iniquities of the children of Yisrael, and all their transgressions in all their sins, putting them upon the head of the goat, and shall send it away by the hand of a fit man[1] into the wilderness: 22 And the goat shall bear upon him all their iniquities to a land not inhabited: and he shall let go the goat in the wilderness. 23 And Aharon shall come into the Tabernacle of the congregation, and shall put off the linen garments, which he put on when he went into the Set-Apart-Place, and shall leave them there: 24 And he shall wash his flesh with mayim in the Set-Apart-Place, and put on his garments, and come forth, and offer his burnt offering, and the burnt offering of the people, and make atonement for himself, and for the people. 25 And the fat of the sin offering shall he burn upon the altar. 26 And he that let go the goat to Azazel[2] shall wash his clothes, and bathe his flesh in mayim, and afterward come into the camp. 27 And the bull for the sin offering, and the goat for the sin offering, whose dom was brought in to make atonement in the Set-Apart-Place, shall one carry forth outside the camp; and they shall burn in the fire their skins, and their flesh, and their dung. 28 And he that burns them shall wash his clothes, and bathe his flesh in mayim, and afterward he shall come into the camp. 29 And this shall be a chuk le-olam-va-ed to you: that in the seventh month, on the tenth day of the month, you shall afflict your beings,[3] and do no work at all, whether it be one of your own country, or a Ger that sojourns among you: 30 For on that day shall the kohen make atonement for you, to cleanse you, that you may be clean from all your sins

before יהוה. 31 It shall be a Shabbat-Shabbaton[4] of rest to you, and you shall afflict your beings, by a chuk le-olam-va-ed.[5] 32 And the kohen, whom he shall anoint, and whom he shall consecrate to attend in the kohen's office in his abba's place, shall make the atonement, and shall put on the linen clothes, even the set-apart garments: 33 And he shall make atonement for the most set-apart Set-Apart-Place, and he shall make atonement for the Tabernacle of the congregation, and for the altar, and he shall make atonement for the kohanim, and for all the people of the congregation. 34 And this shall be an everlasting chuk to you, to make atonement for the children of Yisrael for all their sins once a year. And Aharon did as יהוה commanded Moshe.[6]

17 And יהוה spoke to Moshe, saying, 2 Speak to Aharon, and to his sons, and to all the children of Yisrael, and say to them; This is the thing that יהוה has commanded, saying, 3 Anyone of Beit Yisrael, that kills an ox, or lamb, or goat, in the camp, or that kills it out of the camp, 4 And does not bring it to the door of the Tabernacle of the congregation, to offer an offering to יהוה before the Tabernacle of יהוה; dom shall be imputed to that man; he has shed dom; and that man shall be cut off from among his people:[7] 5 To the end that the children of Yisrael may bring their sacrifices, which they offer in the open field, even that they may bring them to יהוה, to the door of the Tabernacle of the

---

[1] In Yisrael's history, only Yahshua was a fit man forever by reason of His immortality.
[2] **Azazel** is considered in Hebraic literature the wasteland of spiritual destruction, or even Gehenna. The symbolism is that YHWH loves Yisrael so much, that He annually sent their sins far away to a place called Azazel, far outside the camp, never to return. This was done yearly to portray YHWH's forgiveness for all Yisrael as well as the future redemption through the "fit man" chosen for Yisrael by YHWH Himself (First Tim 2:5, Isaiah 59:16).
[3] Could mean fasting but fasting is not clearly specified.

[4] **Shabbat-Shabbaton** - The same term used for Moshiach's resurrection in Matthew 28:1, Mark 16:2, Luke 24:1, and John 20:1, since there is no Greek word for Shabbat. He rose on **Shabbat-Shabbaton.**
[5] Continued in and by Moshiach Yahshua, in the true tabernacle - not pitched with men's hands - in the shamayim.
[6] A rejection of Moshiach's dom leaves a person with no atonement, hence no forgiveness. Thankfully YHWH's love for Yisrael has never changed, and this is seen in the provision of YHWH Himself as the Lamb.
[7] Meaning if a Yisraelite just likes killing and is not killing the animal for use in the direct worship of YHWH. Misusing the offerings by not offering them to YHWH was considered an act of demonic allegiance worthy of death. How many offerings in modern religion are truly offered to YHWH? Those people are at the very least removed or cut off from Renewed Covenant Yisrael and live as saved individuals separate or cut off from community.

congregation, to the kohen, and offer them for shalom offerings to **יהוה**. 6 And the kohen shall sprinkle the dom upon the altar of **יהוה** at the door of the Tabernacle of the congregation, and burn the fat for a sweet fragrance to **יהוה**. 7 And they shall no more offer their sacrifices to demons,[1] after whom they have gone whoring. This shall be a chuk le-olam-va-ed to them throughout their generations.[2] 8 And you shall say to them, Whatever man there be of the bayit of Yisrael, or of the Gerim that sojourn among you, that offers a burnt offering of sacrifice, 9 And brings it not to the door of the Tabernacle of the congregation, to offer it to **יהוה**; even that man shall be cut off from among his people. 10 And whatever man there be of the bayit of Yisrael, or of the Gerim that sojourn among you, that eats any manner of dom; I will even set My face against that being that eats dom, and will cut him off from among his people. 11 For the life of the flesh is in the dom: and I have given it to you upon the altar to make atonement for your beings: for it is the dom that makes atonement for the being.[3] 12 Therefore I said to the children of Yisrael, No being shall eat dom; neither shall any Ger that sojourns among you eat dom. 13 And whatever man there be of the children of Yisrael, or of the Gerim that sojourn among you, which hunts and catches any beast or fowl that may be eaten; he shall even pour out the dom of it, and cover it with dust. 14 For it is the life of all flesh; the dom of it is for the life of it: therefore I said to the children of Yisrael, You shall eat the dom of no manner of flesh: for the life of all flesh is the dom of it: whoever eats it shall be cut off. 15 And every being that eats that which died by itself, or that which was torn with living creatures, whether it be one of your own

country, or a Ger, he shall both wash his clothes, and bathe himself in mayim, and be unclean until the evening: then shall he be clean. 16 But if he wash them not, nor bathe his flesh; then he shall bear his iniquity.

18 And **יהוה** spoke to Moshe, saying, 2 Speak to the children of Yisrael, and say to them, I am **יהוה** Your Elohim. 3 After the doings of the land of Mitzrayim, in which you dwelt, shall you not do: and after the doings of the land of Kanaan, where I bring you, shall you not do: neither shall you have your halacha in their ordinances. 4 You shall do My mishpatim, and shomer My ordinances, to have your halacha in it: I am **יהוה** Your Elohim. 5 You shall therefore guard My chukim, and My mishpatim: which if a man does, he shall live in them: I am **יהוה**.[4] 6 None of you shall approach to any that is close mishpacha, to uncover their nakedness: I am **יהוה**. 7 The nakedness of your abba, or the nakedness of your ima, shall you not uncover: she is your ima; you shall not uncover her nakedness. 8 The nakedness of your abba's wife shall you not uncover: it is your abba's nakedness. 9 The nakedness of your sister, the daughter of your abba, or daughter of your ima, whether she be born at home, or born abroad, even their nakedness you shall not uncover. 10 The nakedness of your son's daughter, or of your daughter's daughter, even their nakedness you shall not uncover: for theirs is your own nakedness. 11 The nakedness of your abba's wife's daughter, begotten of your abba, she is your sister, you shall not uncover her nakedness. 12 You shall not uncover the nakedness of your abba's sister: she is your abba's flesh. 13 You shall not uncover the nakedness of your ima's sister: for she is your ima's near flesh. 14 You shall not uncover the nakedness of your abba's brother, you shall not approach to his wife:

---

[1] Demons and s.a.tan are not Christian inventions but are recorded in **Torah** and **Tanach**.
[2] Meaning for all time Yisrael must forsake all forms of worship that does not honor YHWH and His Son in a Torah foundation, including anti-nomian pagan systems.
[3] Let all those who pursue Judaism in any form without YHWH's Son and His dom take careful note.

[4] This does not mean that Torah keeping brings eternal life as some teach. Rather, those who do them shall live their lifestyles in a full commitment to them.

she is your aunt. 15 You shall not uncover the nakedness of your daughter-in-law: she is your son's wife; you shall not uncover her nakedness. 16 You shall not uncover the nakedness of your brother's wife: it is your brother's nakedness. 17 You shall not uncover the nakedness of a woman and her daughter, neither shall you take her son's daughter, or her daughter's daughter, to uncover her nakedness; for they are her near relatives: it is wickedness. 18 Neither shall you take a woman, as a rival to her sister, to uncover her nakedness while the sister is alive. 19 Also you shall not approach to a woman to uncover her nakedness, as long as she is put apart for her monthly uncleanness. 20 Moreover you shall not lie carnally with your neighbor's wife, to defile yourself with her. 21 And you shall not let any of your offspring pass through the fire to Molech, neither shall you defile the Name of Your Elohim: I am יהוה. 22 You shall not lie with mankind, as with womankind: it is abomination.[1] 23 Neither shall you lie with any beast to defile yourself with it: neither shall any woman stand before a beast to lie down to it: it is perversion. 24 Defile not yourselves in any of these things: for in all these the nations are defiled which I cast out before you: 25 And the land is defiled: therefore I do visit the iniquity of it upon it, and the land itself vomits out her inhabitants. 26 You shall therefore guard My chukim and My mishpatim, and shall not commit any of these abominations; neither any of your own nation, nor any Ger that sojourns among you: 27 For all these abominations have the men of the land done, which were before you, and the land is defiled; 28 That the land spit you not out also, when you defile it, as it spit out the nations who were before you. 29 For whoever shall commit any of these abominations, even the beings that commit them shall be cut off from among their people. 30 Therefore shall you guard My ordinance, that you commit not

any one of these abominable customs, which were committed before you, and that you defile not yourselves by them: I am יהוה Your Elohim.

Torah Parsha 30
Kedoshim 19:1-20:27
In regular 12-month years,
read with Parsha 29.
In years with 13 months, read separately. Haftarah
Amos 9:7-15
Brit Chadasha MaAseh Shlichim 15:1-21

19 And יהוה spoke to Moshe, saying, 2 Speak to all the congregation of the children of Yisrael, and say to them, You shall be kidushim: for I יהוה Your Elohim am set-apart. 3 You shall fear every man his ima, and his abba, and guard My Shabbats: I am יהוה Your Elohim.[2] 4 Turn not to idols, nor make yourselves molded elohim: I am יהוה Your Elohim. 5 And if you offer a sacrifice of shalom offerings to יהוה, you shall offer it from your own freewill.[3] 6 It shall be eaten the same day you offer it, and on the next day: and if anything remains until the third day, it shall be burnt in the fire. 7 And if it be eaten at all on the third day, it is abominable; it shall not be accepted. 8 Therefore every one that eats it shall bear his iniquity, because he has profaned the set-apart thing of יהוה: and that being shall be cut off from among his people. 9 And when you reap the harvest of your land, you shall not wholly reap the corners of your field, neither shall you gather the gleanings of your harvest. 10 And you shall not glean your vineyard, neither shall you gather every grape of your vineyard; you shall leave them for the poor and Ger:[4] I am יהוה Your Elohim. 11 You shall not steal, neither deal falsely, neither lie one to another. 12 And you shall not swear by My Name falsely, neither shall you

---

[1] Homosexual behavior is called an abomination.

[2] By implication honor and fear their Shabbats as Yisraelites.
[3] All service to YHWH must be by choice and not compulsion.
[4] An example of YHWH's mercy/**rachamim** that is eternal and did not start with the coming of Moshiach as so many teach.

defile the Name of Your Elohim: I am **יהוה**.[1]
13 You shall not defraud your neighbor, neither rob him: the wages of him that is hired shall not abide with you all night until the morning.[2] 14 You shall not curse the deaf, nor put a stumblingblock before the blind, but shall fear Your Elohim: I am **יהוה**. 15 You shall do no unrighteousness in mishpat: you shall not respect the person of the poor, nor honor the person of the mighty: but in tzedakah shall you mishpat your neighbor. 16 You shall not go up and down as a slanderer among your people: neither shall you stand against the dom of your neighbor: I am **יהוה**.[3] 17 You shall not hate your brother in your lev: you may rebuke your neighbor, and not suffer sin because of him. 18 You shall not take vengeance, nor bear any grudge against the children of your people, but you shall love your neighbor as yourself: I am **יהוה**.[4] 19 You shall guard My chukim.[5] You shall not let your cattle mate with a diverse kind: you shall not sow your field with mixed zera:[6] neither shall a garment mixed of linen and wool come upon you.[7] 20 And whoever lies carnally with a woman, that is a female slave, engaged to a husband, and not at all redeemed, nor set free; there shall be an inquiry; they shall not be put to death, because she was not free. 21 And he shall bring his guilt offering to **יהוה**, to the door of the Tabernacle of the congregation, even a ram for a guilt offering. 22 And the kohen shall make atonement for him with the ram of the guilt offering before **יהוה** for his sin that he has done: and the sin, which he has done, shall be forgiven him. 23 And when you shall come into the land, and shall have planted all manner of eytzim for food, then you shall count the fruit of it as unharvested: three years shall it be as unharvested for you: it shall not be eaten.[8] 24 But in the fourth year all the fruit of it shall be set-apart to hallel **יהוה** with. 25 And in the fifth year shall you eat of the fruit of it, that it may yield to you the increase of it: I am **יהוה** Your Elohim. 26 You shall not eat any thing with the dom: neither shall you use enchantment, nor observe times.[9] 27 You shall not round the corners of your heads; neither shall you destroy the peot of your beard.[10] 28 You shall not make any cuttings in your flesh for the dead, nor print any tattoo marks upon you: I am **יהוה**. 29 Do not prostitute your daughter, to cause her to be a whore; lest the land fall to whoredom, and the land become full of wickedness. 30 You shall guard My Shabbats, and reverence My Set-Apart-Place: I am **יהוה**. 31 Regard not them that are mediums, neither seek after spiritists, to be defiled by them: I am **יהוה** Your Elohim. 32 You shall rise up before the grey head, and honor the face of the old man, and fear Your Elohim: I am **יהוה**. 33 And if a Ger sojourn with you in your land, you shall not vex him.[11] 34 But the Ger that dwells with you shall be to you as one born among you, and you shall love him as yourself; for you were Gerim in the land of Mitzrayim: I am **יהוה** Your Elohim. 35 You shall do no unrighteousness in mishpat, in measurement of length, in weight, or in measuring liquids. 36 Just

---

[1] This is not any kind of a prohibition against using YHWH's Name. Rather it is a prohibition about using it to lie or perpetuate falsehood.
[2] It seems that daily pay is the Torah way not monthly or weekly pay.
[3] Spilling dom with the tongue. All forms of **lashon hara** are forbidden.
[4] Yahshua renewed that Torah in our hearts.
[5] Nothing to pray about.
[6] This is a positive proof that all believers in the Moshiach are part of the olive tree of Yisrael, for if the non-Jews truly were gentile pagans they would not be considered part of the Olive Tree, since that would be a violation of the Torah of mixing seed or **kilayim**. For more details see: **Kilayim** at: http://yourarmstoisrael.org/Articles_new/guest/?page=the_torah_of_kilayim_and_the_olive_tree&type=13
[7] **Shatnez**: A prohibition of wearing two specific fabrics, linen and wool, in one garment. Not a general prohibition against mixing other fabrics, since others are not specifically mentioned.

[8] Applies only in the land of Yisrael.
[9] Pagan calendars and reckoning of time.
[10] Notice that Yisraelite men were expected and commanded to wear beards. Also this does not specifically prohibit the trimming of side locks or **peot**. Rather the command is to not destroy them or be fully clean-shaven.
[11] Yahudah must learn how to end his pre-disposition to vex Ephraim through the love of Moshiach according to Isaiah 11:13

balances, just weights, a just ephah, and a just hin, shall you have: I am יהוה Your Elohim, who brought you out of the land of Mitzrayim.¹ 37 Therefore shall you observe all My chukim, and all My mishpatim, and do them: I am יהוה.

20 And יהוה spoke to Moshe, saying, 2 Again, you shall say to the children of Yisrael, Whoever he be of the children of Yisrael, or of the Gerim that sojourn in Yisrael, that gives any of his offspring to Molech; he shall surely be put to death: the people of the land shall stone him with stones. 3 And I will set My face against that man, and will cut him off from among his people; because he has given of his offspring to Molech, to defile My Set-Apart-Place, and to defile My set-apart Name. 4 And if the people of the land do any way hide their eyes from the man, when he gives his offspring to Molech, and kill him not: 5 Then I will set My face against that man, and against his mishpacha, and will cut him off, and all that go a whoring after him, to commit whoredom with Molech, from among their people.² 6 And the being that turns after such as have spiritists, and after mediums, to go whoring after them, I will even set My face against that being, and will cut him off from among his people. 7 Set yourselves apart therefore, and be you kidushim: for I am יהוה Your Elohim. 8 And you shall guard My chukim, and do them: I am יהוה who sets you apart. 9 For every one that curses his abba or his ima shall be surely put to death: he has cursed his abba or his ima; his dom shall be upon him. 10 And the man that commits adultery with another man's wife, even he that commits adultery with his neighbor's wife,

the adulterer and the adulteress shall surely be put to death. 11 And the man that lies with his abba's wife has uncovered his abba's nakedness: both of them shall surely be put to death; their dom shall be upon them. 12 And if a man lie with his daughter-in-law, both of them shall surely be put to death: they have made confusion; their dom shall be upon them. 13 If a man also lie with mankind, as he lies with a woman, both of them have committed an abomination: they shall surely be put to death; their dom shall be upon them. 14 And if a man take a wife with her ima, it is wickedness: they shall be burnt with fire, both he and they; that there be no wickedness among you. 15 And if a man lies with a beast, he shall surely be put to death: and you shall slay the beast. 16 And if a woman approaches any beast, and lies down with it, you shall kill the woman, and the beast: they shall surely be put to death; their dom shall be upon them. 17 And if a man shall take his sister, his abba's daughter, or his ima's daughter, and see her nakedness, and she see his nakedness; it is a wicked thing; and they shall be cut off in the sight of their people: he has uncovered his sister's nakedness; he shall bear his iniquity. 18 And if a man shall lie with a woman during her sickness, and shall uncover her nakedness; he has discovered her flow, and she has uncovered the fountain of her dom: and both of them shall be cut off from among their people. 19 And you shall not uncover the nakedness of your ima's sister, nor of your abba's sister: for he uncovers his near kin: they shall bear their iniquity. 20 And if a man shall lie with his uncle's wife, he has uncovered his uncle's nakedness: they shall bear their sin; they shall die childless. 21 And if a man shall take his brother's wife, it is an unclean thing: he has uncovered his brother's nakedness; they shall be childless. 22 You shall therefore guard all My chukim, and all My mishpatim, and do them: that the land, where I bring you to dwell in, spit you not out. 23 And you

---

¹ When dealing with what would become the two houses of Yisrael, we must always apply equal weights and measures by treating both houses with equity, not treating one as better than the other, and by recognizing both as legitimate equal heirs in Yisrael.
² True Yisraelites confront paganism that has crept into the faith, and failure to do so is forsaking our calling as Yisrael. To confront and rebuke paganism is a loving act and are matters of obedience to YHWH.

shall not have your halacha in the manners of the nations, which I cast out before you: for they committed all these things, and therefore I abhorred them. 24 But I have said to you, You shall inherit their land, and I will give it to you to possess it, a land that flows with milk and honey: I am יהוה Your Elohim, who has separated you from other peoples. 25 You shall therefore put difference between clean living creatures and unclean, and between unclean fowls and clean: and you shall not make your beings abominable by beast, or by fowl, or by any manner of living thing that creeps on the ground, which I have separated from you as unclean. 26 And you shall be kidushim to Me: for I יהוה am set-apart, and have separated you from other peoples, that you should be Mine. 27 A man or woman who is a spiritist, or that is a medium, shall surely be put to death: they shall stone them with stones: their dom shall be upon them.

Torah Parsha 31
Emor 21:1-24:23
Haftarah Yechezkel 44:15-31
Brit Chadasha Qolesayah 2:11-23

21 And יהוה said to Moshe, Speak to the kohanim the sons of Aharon, and say to them, There shall none be defiled for the dead among his people: 2 Except for his relatives, that are near to him, that is, for his ima, and for his abba, and for his son, and for his daughter, and for his brother, 3 And for his sister a virgin that is near to him, which has had no husband; for her may he be defiled. 4 But he shall not defile himself, being a ruler among his people, to defile himself. 5 They shall not make baldness upon their head, neither shall they fully shave off the corner of their beard, nor make any cuttings in their flesh. 6 They shall be kidushim to their Elohim, and not defile the Name of their Elohim: for the offerings of יהוה made by fire, and the lechem of their Elohim, they do offer: therefore they shall be set-apart. 7 They

shall not take a wife that is a whore, or a defiled woman; neither shall they take a woman put away from her husband: for he is set-apart to his Elohim. 8 You shall set him apart therefore; for he offers the lechem of Your Elohim: he shall be set-apart to you: for I יהוה, who am setting him apart, am Set-Apart. 9 And the daughter of any kohen, if she defiled herself by playing the whore, she profanes her abba: she shall be burnt with fire. 10 And he that is the Kohen HaGadol among his brothers, upon whose head the anointing oil was poured, and that is consecrated to put on the garments, shall not uncover his head,[1] nor tear his clothes. 11 Neither shall he go in to any dead body, nor defile himself for his abba, or for his ima; 12 Neither shall he go out of the Set-Apart-Place, nor defile the Set-Apart-Place of his Elohim; for the keter of the anointing oil of his Elohim is upon him: I am יהוה. 13 And he shall take a wife in her virginity.[2] 14 A widow, or a divorced woman, or defiled, or a harlot, these shall he not take: but he shall take a virgin of his own people as a wife.[3] 15 Neither shall he defile his offspring among his people: for I יהוה do set him apart him. 16 And יהוה spoke to Moshe, saying, 17 Speak to Aharon, saying, Whoever he be of your offspring in their generations that has any blemish, let him not approach to offer the lechem of his Elohim.[4] 18 For whatever man he be that has a blemish, he shall not approach: a blind man, or a lame, or he that is disfigured, or deformed, 19 Or a man that is broken footed, or broken handed, 20 Or hunchback, or a dwarf, or he that has a defect in his eye, or has skin inflammation,

---

[1] Yisraelite men are eternally called to wear head coverings, if they claim to be a royal priesthood of the chosen nation of Renewed Covenant Yisrael.
[2] As opposed to pagan religions, Yisraelite priests in Yisrael are encouraged and even commanded to marry.
[3] Netsarim are priests of the Renewed Covenant, and as such, should be careful to marry only those in Yisrael with a Torah lifestyle and a commitment to the eternal Torah of YHWH. A Shabbat-keeper yoked with a Sunday-keeper, or a Je- -s and Yahshua believer, by being unequally yoked in marriage, are defiling the people, as well as themselves.
[4] The disqualifications of Aharon's sons for priesthood.

or is scabbed, or a eunuch; 21 No man that has a blemish of the offspring of Aharon the kohen shall come near to offer the offerings of יהוה made by fire: he has a blemish; he shall not come near to offer the lechem of his Elohim. 22 He shall eat the lechem of his Elohim, both of the most set-apart, and of the set-apart. 23 Only he shall not go into the vail, nor come near to the altar, because he has a blemish; that he defile not My Set-Apart-Places: for I יהוה do set them apart them. 24 And Moshe told it to Aharon, and to his sons, and to all the children of Yisrael.

22 And יהוה spoke to Moshe, saying, 2 Speak to Aharon and to his sons, that they separate themselves from the set-apart offerings of the children of Yisrael, and that they defile not My set-apart Name in those things which they set-apart to Me: I am יהוה. 3 Say to them, Whoever he be of all your offspring among your generations, that draws near to the set-apart things, which the children of Yisrael set-apart to יהוה, having his uncleanness upon him, that being shall be cut off from My presence: I am יהוה. 4 If anyone of the zera of Aharon is a leper, or has a running discharge; he shall not eat of the set-apart things, until he be clean. And whoever touches any thing that is unclean by the dead, or a man whose semen goes from him; 5 Or whoever touches any creeping thing, whereby he may be made unclean, or a man of whom he may take uncleanness, whatever uncleanness he has; 6 The being that has touched any such shall be unclean until evening, and shall not eat of the set-apart things, unless he washes his flesh with mayim. 7 And when the sun is down, he shall be clean, and shall afterward eat of the set-apart things, because it is his food.[1] 8 That which dies by itself, or is torn with living creatures, he shall not eat to defile himself with it: I am יהוה. 9 They shall therefore guard My ordinance, lest they

bear sin for it, and die therefore, if they defile it: I יהוה do set them apart. 10 There shall no Ger eat of the set-apart thing: a sojourner of the kohen, or a hired eved, shall not eat of the set-apart thing. 11 But if the kohen buy any being with his money, he shall eat of it, and he that is born in his bayit: they shall eat of his grain. 12 If the kohen's daughter also is married to a Ger, she may not eat of an offering of the set-apart things. 13 But if the kohen's daughter be a widow, or divorced, and have no child, and returns to her abba's bayit, as in her youth, she shall eat of her abba's grain:[2] but there shall no Ger eat of it. 14 And if a man eats of the set-apart thing by mistake, then he shall add the fifth part of it to it, and shall give it to the kohen with the set-apart thing. 15 And they shall not defile the set-apart things of the children of Yisrael, which they offer to יהוה; 16 Or allow them to bear the iniquity of guilt, when they eat their set-apart things: for I יהוה do set them apart. 17 And יהוה spoke to Moshe, saying, 18 Speak to Aharon, and to his sons, and to all the children of Yisrael, and say to them, Anyone from Beit Yisrael, or from the Gerim in Yisrael, that will offer his offering for all his vows, and for all his freewill offerings which they will offer to יהוה for a burnt offering; 19 You shall offer at your own will a male without blemish, of the cattle, of the sheep, or of the goats. 20 But whatever has a blemish that shall you not offer: for it shall not be acceptable for you. 21 And whoever offers a sacrifice of shalom offerings to יהוה to accomplish his vow, or a freewill offering in cattle or sheep, it shall be perfect to be accepted; there shall be no blemish in it. 22 Blind, or broken, or maimed, or having a cut, or scurvy, or scabbed, you shall not offer these to יהוה, nor make an offering by fire of them upon the altar to יהוה. 23 Either a bull or a lamb that has anything deformed or dwarfed, that may you offer for a freewill offering; but for a vow it shall not be accepted. 24 You shall

---

[1] Rachamim.

[2] Rachamim.

not offer to **יהוה** that which is bruised, or crushed, or broken, or cut; neither shall you make any offering of it in your land. 25 Neither from a Ger's hand shall you offer the lechem of Your Elohim of any of these; because their corruption is in them, and blemishes are in them: they shall not be accepted for you. 26 And **יהוה** spoke to Moshe, saying, 27 When a bull, or a sheep, or a goat, is brought forth, then it shall be seven days with its ima; and from the eighth day and thereafter it shall be accepted for an offering made by fire to **יהוה**. 28 And whether it is cow or sheep, you shall not kill it and her young both in one day.[1] 29 And when you will offer a sacrifice of hodu to **יהוה**, offer it at your own will for your acceptance. 30 On the same day it shall be eaten up; you shall leave none of it until the next day: I am **יהוה**. 31 Therefore shall you guard My mitzvot, and do them: I am **יהוה**. 32 Neither shall you defile My Set-Apart Name; but I will be set-apart among the children of Yisrael: I am **יהוה** who sets you apart, 33 That brought you out of the land of Mitzrayim, to be Your Elohim: I am **יהוה**.

23 And **יהוה** spoke to Moshe, saying, 2 Speak to the children of Yisrael, and say to them, The moadim of **יהוה**, which you shall proclaim to be miqra qedoshim, even these are My moadim.[2] 3 Six days shall work be done: but the seventh day is a Shabbat-Shabbaton of rest, a miqra qodesh. You shall do no work in it: it is the Shabbat of **יהוה** in all your dwellings.[3] 4 These are the moadim of **יהוה**, even miqra qedoshim, which you shall proclaim in their appointed times.[4] 5 On the fourteenth day of the first month between the evenings[5] is **יהוה**'s Pesach. 6 And on the fifteenth day of the same month is Chag

HaMatzoth to **יהוה**: seven days you must eat matzah. 7 In the first day you shall have a miqra qodesh: you shall do no laborious work on it. 8 But you shall offer an offering made by fire to **יהוה** for seven days: on the seventh day is a miqra qodesh: you shall do no laborious work on it. 9 And **יהוה** spoke to Moshe, saying, 10 Speak to the children of Yisrael, and say to them, When you have come into the land which I give to you, and shall reap the harvest of it, then you shall bring a sheaf of the bikkurm of your harvest to the kohen: 11 And he shall wave the sheaf before **יהוה**, to be accepted for you: on the next day after the first day[6] the kohen shall wave it. 12 And you shall offer that day when you wave the sheaf a he lamb without blemish of the first year for a burnt offering to **יהוה**. 13 And the grain offering of it shall be two tenths of an ephah of fine flour mixed with oil, an offering made by fire to **יהוה** for a sweet fragrance: and the drink offering of it shall be of wine, the fourth part of a hin. 14 And you shall eat neither lechem, nor parched corn, nor green ears, until the same day that you have brought an offering to Your Elohim:[7] it shall be a chuk le-olam-va-ed throughout your generations in all your dwellings. 15 And you[8] shall count from the next day after the Shabbat,[9] from the day that you brought the sheaf of the wave offering; seven full weeks:[10] 16 Until the next day after the last week shall you number fifty days, and you shall offer a new grain offering to **יהוה**.[11] 17 You shall bring out of your dwellings two wave loaves of two-tenths of an ephah: they shall be of fine flour; they shall be baked with

---

[1] YHWH's proper compassion on all life.
[2] Notice the fixed times are not exclusively Jewish, but belong to all Yisrael who desire to serve YHWH.
[3] The weekly Shabbat is the first of YHWH's listed moadim, in all Yisraelite lands.
[4] It is up to us to re-establish them among believers, as YHWH calls us to proclaim His appointed times.
[5] **Ben HaArbayim.**

[6] LXX .The day after Unleavened Bread or Aviv 16. For more deails go to: http://yourarmstoisrael.org/Articles_new/articles/?page=Bringin g_Yisrael_Back&type=26
[7] Aviv 16; **MeMacharat HaShabbat**
[8] You meaning every Yisraelite.
[9] Aviv 16; **MeMacharat HaShabbat**
[10] LXX.
[11] LXX.

chametz; they are the bikkurim to יהוה.[1]
18 And you shall offer with the lechem
seven lambs without blemish of the first
year, and one young bull, and two rams:
they shall be for a burnt offering to יהוה,
with their grain offering, and their drink
offerings, even an offering made by fire, of
sweet fragrance to יהוה. 19 Then you shall
sacrifice one kid of the goats for a sin
offering, and two male lambs of the first
year for a sacrifice of shalom offerings.
20 And the kohen shall wave them with the
lechem of the firstfruits for a wave offering
before יהוה, with the two lambs.[2] They
shall be set-apart to יהוה for the kohen.
21 And you shall proclaim on the same day,
that it may be a miqra qodesh to you: you
shall do no laborious work on it: it shall be
a chuk le-olam-va-ed in all your dwellings
throughout your generations.[3] 22 And when
you reap the harvest of your land, you shall
not harvest the corners of your field when
you reap, neither shall you gather any
gleaning of your harvest: you shall leave
them to the poor, and to the Ger: I am יהוה
Your Elohim.[4] 23 And יהוה spoke to
Moshe, saying, 24 Speak to the children of
Yisrael, saying, In the seventh month, on the
first day of the month, you shall have a
Shabbaton, a remembrance of blowing of
shofar blasts, a miqra qodesh. 25 You shall
do no laborious work on it: but you shall
offer an offering made by fire to יהוה.
26 And יהוה spoke to Moshe, saying,
27 Also on the tenth day of this seventh
month there shall be a Yom HaKippurim: it
shall be a miqra qodesh to you; and you
shall afflict your beings, and offer an
offering made by fire to יהוה. 28 And you

shall do no work in that same day: for it is
the Yom HaKippur, to make atonement for
you before יהוה Your Elohim. 29 For any
being that shall not be afflicted in that same
day, he shall be cut off from among his
people. 30 And whatever being it is that
does any work in that same day, the same
being will I destroy from among his people.[5]
31 You shall do no manner of work: it shall
be a chuk le-olam-va-ed throughout your
generations in all your dwellings. 32 It shall
be to you a Shabbat-Shabbaton, and you
shall afflict your beings: on the ninth day of
the month at evening, from evening to
evening,[6] shall you celebrate your Shabbat.
33 And יהוה spoke to Moshe, saying,
34 Speak to the children of Yisrael, saying,
The fifteenth day of this seventh month shall
be the Chag HaSukkot for seven days to
יהוה. 35 On the first day shall be a miqra
qodesh: you shall do no laborious work in
it. 36 Seven days you shall offer an offering
made by fire to יהוה: on the eighth day
shall be a miqra qodesh to you; and you
shall offer an offering made by fire to יהוה:
it is a solemn gathering; and you shall do
no laborious work on it. 37 These are the
moadim of יהוה, which you shall proclaim
to be miqra qedoshim, to offer an offering
made by fire to יהוה, a burnt offering, and
a grain offering, a sacrifice, and drink
offerings, as commanded every day:
38 Beside the Shabbats of יהוה, and beside
your gifts, and beside all your vows, and
beside all your freewill offerings, which you
give to יהוה. 39 Also on the fifteenth day of
the seventh month, when you have gathered
in the fruit of the land, you shall celebrate a
chag to יהוה seven days: on the first day
shall be a Shabbaton, and on the eighth day
shall be a Shabbaton. 40 And you shall take
on the first day the boughs of tov eytzim,
branches of palm eytzim, and the boughs of

---

[1] On Shavuot the Torah and Ruach HaKodesh were given to
Yisrael. The events of Acts 2 circa 33CE is symbolically
proclaimed annually by the High Priest's waving of two
leavened loaves before YHWH, as the first fruits of Shavuot
symbolizing the restoration and regathering of Yisrael's two
houses, by the hands and work of the High Priest.
[2] This took place on Shavuot, one lamb for each future house
of Yisrael, fulfilling the principle of one lamb per house. Notice
how the two-houses are set-apart for and by the High Priest, a
perfect picture of Moshiach Yahshua.
[3] YHWH's laws are eternal, as are His one true people.
[4] Unmerited favor is the basis of Torah, and Yahshua did not
introduce it as some teach.

[5] The threat here is sharper than working on other feasts
where the penalty is a cutting off, whereas here (for working
on Yom HaKippurim), the penalty is the utter destruction of
the individual.
[6] So much for the flawed and growing theory that biblical days
start at sunrise.

thick eytzim, and willows of the brook; and you shall have simcha before יהוה Your Elohim seven days. 41 And you shall celebrate it a chag to יהוה seven days in the year. It shall be a chuk le-olam-va-ed in your generations: you shall celebrate it in the seventh month. 42 You shall dwell in sukkot seven days; all that are native Yisraelites shall dwell in sukkot:[1] 43 That your generations may know that I made the children of Yisrael to dwell in sukkot, when I brought them out of the land of Mitzrayim: I am יהוה Your Elohim. 44 And Moshe spoke to the children of Yisrael about the moadim of יהוה.

24 And יהוה spoke to Moshe, saying, 2 Command the children of Yisrael that they bring to you pure olive oil for the light, to cause the lamps of the menorah to burn continually. 3 Outside the vail of the testimony, in the Tabernacle of the congregation, shall Aharon arrange it from the evening to the morning before יהוה continually: it shall be a chuk le-olam-va-ed in your generations.[2] 4 He shall arrange the lamps upon the menorah before יהוה continually. 5 And you shall take fine flour, and bake twelve cakes: two tenths of an ephah shall be in one cake.[3] 6 And you shall set them in two rows,[4] six on a row, upon the clean table before יהוה.[5] 7 And you shall put pure frankincense upon each row so that it may be on the lechem for a remembrance portion, even an offering made by fire to יהוה. 8 Every Shabbat he shall set it in order before יהוה continually, being taken from the children of Yisrael by

an everlasting covenant.[6] 9 And it shall be Aharon's and his sons'; and they shall eat it in the Set-Apart-Place: for it is most set-apart to him of the offerings of יהוה made by fire by an eternal chuk.[7] 10 And the son of a Yisraelite woman, whose abba was a Mitzrite, went out among the children of Yisrael: and this son of the Yisraelite woman and a man of Yisrael strove together in the camp; 11 And the Yisraelite woman's son blasphemed the Name of יהוה,[8] and cursed. And they brought him to Moshe: and his ima's name was Shelomith, the daughter of Divri, of the tribe of Dan.[9] 12 And they put him in under guard, that the mind of יהוה might be shown them. 13 And יהוה spoke to Moshe, saying, 14 Bring forth him that has cursed outside the camp; and let all that heard him lay their hands upon his head, and let the entire congregation stone him. 15 And you shall speak to the children of Yisrael, saying, Whoever curses his Elohim shall bear his sin.[10] 16 And he that blasphemes the Name of יהוה, he shall surely be put to death, and all the congregation shall certainly stone him: as well the Ger, as he that is born in the land, when he blasphemes the Name of יהוה, shall be put to death.[11] 17 And he that kills any man shall surely be put to death. 18 And he that kills a beast shall make it tov; beast for beast. 19 And if a man causes a blemish in his neighbor; as he has done, so shall it be done to him; 20 Fracture for

---

[1] Since there's only one Torah for the native and the stranger, the same command applies to all Yisrael.
[2] Continues today in Yahshua as the Light that never goes out.
[3] The Bread of His Presence was divided into 12 cakes set in two rows, a beautiful view of how that nation of 12 tribes would become a divided house of two separated peoples, who would both one day receive the Light of the menorah that never went out. That eternal Light is Moshiach who by His light will cause both houses to make teshuvah and re-enter the Light that never goes out.
[4] Twelve tribes in two rows or houses.
[5] See note on verse 5.
[6] The two houses of Yisrael are so fresh and uppermost in YHWH's heart that He made sure the people understood that they would be continually renewed through the years. The changing of the Bread of His Presence, displayed that all Yisrael stays fresh in His presence, as they enter into His Shabbat rest. Therefore the Shabbat was appointed as the day of refreshing, as there remains therefore rest to Yisrael according to Hebrews/Ivrim 4:9.
[7] The Bread of His Presence was the most set-apart food for the priests.
[8] The blasphemy is using YHWH's Name as a curse, or in dishonesty, or bringing it to nothing, not in merely pronouncing it as rabbinical Judaism falsely teaches.
[9] The end-time anti-Moshiach will come from Dan, and will continue in the traditions of his tribe by cursing and blaspheming YHWH's set-apart Name in a global manner.
[10] Here it cannot be clearer just what entails blasphemy. It is cursing His Name not using it to bless Him and others.
[11] For more details see: http://yourarmstoisrael.org/Articles_new/?page=home&type=1

fracture, eye for eye, tooth for tooth: as he has caused a blemish in a man, so shall it be done to him again.[1] 21 And he that kills a beast, he shall restore it: and he that kills a man, he shall be put to death. 22 You shall have one mishpat of Torah, for the Ger, and for the native: for I am יהוה Your Elohim. 23 And Moshe spoke to the children of Yisrael that they should bring forth him that had cursed out of the camp, and stone him with stones. And the children of Yisrael did as יהוה commanded Moshe.

Torah Parsha 32
BaHar 25:1-26:2
In regular 12-month years,
read with Parsha 33,
in years with 13 months read separately.
Haftarah Yirmeyahu 32:6-27
Brit Chadasha Luka 4:16-21,
Galutyah 5:1-13

25 And יהוה spoke to Moshe on Mount Sinai, saying, 2 *Speak to the children of Yisrael, and say to them, When you come into the land that I give you, then shall the land keep a Shabbat to יהוה. 3 Six years you shall sow your field, and six years you shall prune your vineyard, and gather in the fruit of it; 4 But in the seventh year shall be a Shabbat Shabbaton to the land, a Shabbat for יהוה:[2] you shall neither sow your field, nor prune your vineyard. 5 That which grows of its own accord of your harvest you shall not reap, neither gather the grapes of your vine undressed: for it is a year of Shabbaton to the land. 6 And the Shabbat of the land shall be grain for you; for you, and for your eved, and for your female eved, and for your hired eved, and for your Ger that sojourns with you, 7 And for your cattle, and for the beast that are in your land, shall all the increase of it be grain. 8 And you shall number seven Shabbats of years, seven times seven years; and the space of the seven Shabbats of years*

shall be to you forty-nine years. 9 Then shall you cause the shofar of the Yovel[3] to sound on the tenth day of the seventh month, on the Yom HaKippur shall you make the shofar sound throughout all your land. 10 And you shall set-apart the fiftieth year, and proclaim liberty throughout all the land to all the inhabitants of it: it shall be a Yovel to you; and you shall return every man to his possession, and you shall return every man to his mishpacha. 11 A Yovel shall that fiftieth year be to you: you shall not sow; neither reap that which grows by itself in it, nor gather the grapes in it of your vine undressed. 12 For it is the Yovel; it shall be set-apart to you: you shall eat the increase of it out of the field. 13 In the year of this Yovel you shall return every man to his possession. 14 And if you sell some item to your neighbor, or buy from your neighbor's hand, you shall not oppress one another: 15 According to the number of years after the Yovel you shall buy from your neighbor, and according to the number of years of the fruits he shall sell to you: 16 According to the multitude of years you shall increase the price of it, and according to the fewness of years you shall diminish the price of it: for according to the number of the years of the fruits does he sell to you. 17 You shall not therefore oppress one another; but you shall fear Your Elohim: for I am יהוה Your Elohim. 18 Wherefore you shall do My chukim, and guard My mishpatim, and do them; and you shall dwell in the land in safety. 19 And the land shall yield her fruit, and you shall eat your fill, and dwell there in safety. 20 And if you shall say, What shall we eat the seventh year? See, we shall not sow, nor gather in our increase: 21 Then I will command My blessing upon you in the sixth year, and it shall bring forth fruit for three years. 22 And you shall sow the eighth year, and eat yet of old fruit until the ninth year; until her fruits come in you shall eat of the old

[1] Metaphorically speaking of equitable restitution not literally maiming one another.
[2] **Shmitta** or the land Shabbat is for YHWH, not man. The weekly Shabbat and moadim are for man.

[3] Jubilee.

store. 23 *The land shall not be sold le-olam-va-ed: for the land is Mine; for you are settlers and sojourners with Me.[1] 24 And in all the land you possess you shall grant a redemption for the land. 25 If your brother becomes poor, and has sold away some of his possession, and if any of his relatives come to redeem it, then shall he redeem that which his brother sold. 26 And if the man has no one to redeem it, but he himself becomes able to redeem it; 27 Then let him count the years since the sale, and restore the remainder to the man to whom he sold it; that he may return to his possession. 28 But if he be not able to restore it to him, then that which is sold shall remain in the hand of him that has bought it until the year of Yovel: and in the Yovel it shall be released, and he shall return to his possession. 29 And if a man sells a dwelling bayit in a walled city, then he may redeem it within a whole year after it is sold; within a full year may he redeem it. 30 And if it be not redeemed within the space of a full year, then the bayit that is in the walled city shall be established le-olam-va-ed to him that bought it throughout his generations: it shall not go out in the Yovel. 31 But the houses of the villages, which have no wall around them, shall be counted as the fields of the country: they may be redeemed, and they shall go out in the Yovel. 32 As for the cities of the Levites, and the houses of the cities of their possession, the Levites can redeem them at any time. 33 And if a man purchase from the Levites, then the bayit that was sold, and the city of his possession, shall go out in the year of Yovel: for the houses of the cities of the Levites are their possession among the children of Yisrael. 34 But the field of the suburbs of their cities may not be sold; for it is their perpetual possession. 35 And if your brother become poor, and he falters in your area; then you shall strengthen him; that he may live with you, like a Ger or soujourner. 36 Take no*

interest from him, or increase: but fear Your Elohim; that your brother may live with you. 37 You shall not give him your money with interest, nor lend him your supplies for your profit. 38 I am יהוה *Your Elohim, which brought you forth out of the land of Mitzrayim, to give you the land of Kanaan, and to be Your Elohim. 39 And if your brother that dwells in your area becomes poor, and sells himself to you; you shall not force him to serve as a slave: 40 But as an hired eved, and as a resident, he shall be with you, and shall serve you to the year of Yovel: 41 And then shall he depart from you, both he and his children with him, and shall return to his own mishpacha, and to the possession of his ahvot shall he return. 42 For they are My avadim, which I brought forth out of the land of Mitzrayim: they shall not be sold as avadim. 43 You shall not rule over him with harshness; but shall fear Your Elohim. 44 Both your male and female avadim, which you shall have, shall be from the heathen that are all around you; of them shall you buy male and female avadim. 45 Moreover from the children of the Gerim that do sojourn among you, from them shall you buy, and of their mishpachot that are with you, which they shall bring forth in your land: and they shall be your possession. 46 And you shall take them as an inheritance for your children after you, to inherit them for a possession; they shall be your avadim le-olam-va-ed: but over your brothers the children of Yisrael, you shall not rule one over another with harshness. 47 And if a resident or Ger grows rich with you, and your brother that dwell by him grow poor, and sells himself to the resident or sojourner with you, or to a member of the Ger's mishpacha: 48 After that he is sold he may be redeemed again; one of his brothers may redeem him: 49 Either his uncle, or his uncle's son, may redeem him, or any that are close relatives to him of his mishpacha may redeem him; or if he is able, he may redeem himself. 50 And he shall reckon with him that bought*

---

[1] The land of Yisrael belongs to YHWH and no one else. He is the landlord and gives it to whom He will.

him from the year that he was sold until the year of Yovel: and the price of his purchase shall be divided according to the number of years, according to the time of a paid eved. 51 If there be yet many years behind, according to them he shall give again the price of his redemption out of the money that he was bought for. 52 And if there remain just a few years to the year of Yovel, then he shall count with him, and according to his years shall he give him again the price of his redemption. 53 And as a yearly hired eved shall he be with him: and the other shall not rule with harshness over him in your sight. 54 And if he be not redeemed in these years, then he shall go out in the year of Yovel, both he, and his children with him. 55 Because the children of Yisrael are My avadim; they are My avadim whom I brought forth out of the land of Mitzrayim: I am יהוה Your Elohim.[1]

26 You shall make you no idols nor graven image, neither rear you up a standing image, neither shall you set up any

image of stone in your land, to bow down to it: for I am יהוה Your Elohim. 2 You shall guard My Shabbats, and reverence My Set-Apart-Place: I am יהוה.

Torah Parsha 33
BeChukkotai 26:3-27:34
In regular 12-month years
read with Parsha 32,
in years with 13 months, read separately.
Haftarah Yirmeyahu 16:19-17:14
Brit Chadasha Ephsiya 2: 11-19

3 If you have your halacha in My chukim, and guard My mitzvot, and do them; 4 Then I will give you rain in due season, and the land shall yield her increase, and the eytzim of the field shall yield their fruit. 5 And your threshing shall reach to the vintage, and the vintage shall reach to the sowing time: and you shall eat your lechem to the full, and dwell in your land safely. 6 And I will give shalom in the land, and you shall lie down, and none shall make you afraid: and I will rid evil living beasts out of the land, neither shall the sword go through your land. 7 And you shall chase your enemies, and they shall fall before you by the sword. 8 And five of you shall chase a hundred, and a hundred of you shall put ten thousand to flight: and your enemies shall fall before you by the sword. 9 For I will have respect to you, and make you fruitful, and multiply you, and establish My covenant with you.[2] 10 And you shall eat old supply, and clear the old because of the new. 11 And I will set My Tabernacle among you: and My being shall not reject you. 12 And I will walk among you, and will be Your Elohim, and you shall be My people. 13 I am יהוה Your Elohim, which brought you forth out of the land of Mitzrayim, that you should not be their avadim; and I have broken the bands of your yoke, and made you go upright. 14 But if you will not listen to Me, and will not do all these mitzvot; 15 And if you shall despise My chukim, or if your being despises My

---

[1] The overriding theme that reoccurs during these verses on the Jubilee or Yovel is that of freedom, release, and a nation that owns nothing permanent except YHWH. As Yisrael owns YHWH so YHWH owns Yisrael. Yisrael is never again to be slaves to anyone after Egypt, and YHWH makes sure that generational slavery does not reoccur by proclaiming release every 50 years. The idea of either Yahudah being enslaved by Ephraim or of Ephraim being enslaved by Yahudah should be as abominable to us as it is to YHWH. With **yovel**, Yahudah and Ephraim could never claim any kind of long-term domination or ownership over each other like the gentiles. Both houses are owned by YHWH and not by each other, making both houses equal before Abba YHWH. The command for the release of debts, relationships, pledges cancelled, and all other forms of slavery (individual, personal or financial), is YHWH's way of making sure that Yisrael as a nation maintains no worldly long-term possessions or entanglements. The very principle of **yovel** continues to be the hallmark of theocracy and a society that walks in forgiveness of debts, along with the liberty to proclaim release, restoration, and freedom. What we can glean from this overriding joy of liberty and release, is that Yisraelite brothers are called to love by forgiving all debts real and imagined. And as such, the **yovel** is a call to two battling brothers Yahudah and Ephraim to return and release each other in **yovel**, proclaiming liberty throughout both the land and nation of Yisrael, which is why Moshiach came according to Isaiah 61:1. To proclaim release to both houses of Yisrael (Isaiah 8:14) in the Jubilee generation or 2,000 years (2,000 divided by 40 years per generation), after the birth of the Hebrew nation; with the choosing and calling of Abraham. Also if you count the 2,000 years from Moshiach until now, then this generation is the 50th generation from Moshiach, and the first one since 1996 to experience a true re-awakening in both houses unto yovel.

[2] Physical multiplicity restated.

mishpatim, so that you will not do all My mitzvot, but that you break My covenant: 16 I also will do this to you; I will even appoint over you terror, consumption, and inflammation, that shall destroy the eyes, and cause sorrow of lev: and you shall sow your zera in vain, for your enemies shall eat it. 17 And I will set My face against you, and you shall be slain before your enemies: they that hate you shall reign over you; and you shall flee when none pursues you. 18 And if you will not yet for all this listen to Me, then I will punish you seven times more for your sins. 19 And I will break the pride of your power; and I will make your heavens as iron, and your earth as brass: 20 And your strength shall be spent in vain: for your land shall not yield her increase, neither shall all the eytzim of the land yield their fruits. 21 And if you walk contrary to Me, and will not listen to Me; I will bring seven times more plagues upon you according to your sins. 22 I will also send wild living creatures among you, which shall rob you of your children, and destroy your cattle, and make you few in number; and your highways shall be desolate. 23 And if you will not be reformed by Me by these things, but will walk contrary to Me; 24 Then will I also walk contrary to you, and will punish you yet seven times for your sins. 25 And I will bring a sword upon you, that shall avenge the vengeance of My covenant: and when you are gathered together within your cities, I will send the pestilence among you; and you shall be delivered into the hand of the enemy. 26 And when I have broken the supply of your lechem, ten women shall bake your lechem in one oven, and they shall deliver you your lechem again by weight: and you shall eat, and not be satisfied. 27 And if you will not for all this listen to Me, but walk contrary to Me; 28 Then I will walk contrary to you also in fury; and I, even I, will chastise you seven times for your sins. 29 And you shall eat the flesh of your sons, and the flesh of your daughters shall you eat. 30 And I will destroy your high places, and cut down your sun-pillars, and cast your carcasses upon the carcasses of your idols, and My being shall abhor you. 31 And I will make your cities waste, and bring your sanctuaries to desolation, and I will not smell the fragrance of your sweet odors. 32 And I will bring the land into desolation: and your enemies which dwell there shall be astonished at it. 33 And I will scatter you among the heathen, and will draw out a sword after you: and your land shall be desolate, and your cities waste. 34 Then shall all the land enjoy her Shabbats, as long as it lies desolate, while you are in your enemies' land; even then shall all the land rest, and enjoy her Shabbats. 35 As long as it lies desolate it shall rest; because it did not rest in your Shabbats, when you dwelt upon it. 36 And upon them that are left alive of you I will send a faintness into their levim in the lands of their enemies; and the sound of a shaken leaf shall chase them; and they shall flee, as fleeing from a sword; and they shall fall when none pursues. 37 And they shall fall one upon another, as it were before a sword, when none pursues: and you shall have no power to stand before your enemies. 38 And you shall perish among the heathen, and the land of your enemies shall eat you up. 39 And they that are left of you shall pine away in their iniquity in your enemies' lands; and also in the iniquities of their ahvot shall they pine away with them. 40 If they shall confess their iniquity, and the iniquity of their ahvot, with their guilt, which they trespassed against Me, and that also, they have walked contrary to Me; 41 And that I also have walked contrary to them, and have brought them into the land of their enemies; if then their uncircumcised levim be humbled, and they then accept the punishment of their iniquity: 42 Then will I remember My covenant with Yaakov, and also My covenant with Yitzchak, and also My covenant with Avraham will I remember; and I will remember the land.

43 *The land also shall be left of them, and shall enjoy her Shabbats, while she lies desolate without them: and they shall accept the punishment of their iniquity: because they despised My mishpatim, and because their being abhorred My chukim.* 44 *And yet for all that, when they be in the land of their enemies, I will not cast them away, neither will I abhor them, to destroy them utterly, and to break My covenant with them: for I am* יהוה *their Elohim.* 45 *But I will for their sakes remember the covenant of their ancestors, whom I brought forth out of the land of Mitzrayim in the sight of the heathen, that I might be their Elohim: I am* יהוה . 46 *These are the chukim and mishpatim and Torot, which* יהוה *made between Him and the children of Yisrael on Mount Sinai by the hand of Moshe.*[1]

27 And יהוה spoke to Moshe, saying, 2 *Speak to the children of Yisrael, and say to them, If a man shall make a singular vow, regarding evaluation of lives unto* יהוה. 3 *And your estimation shall be of the male from twenty years old even to sixty years old; even your estimation shall be fifty shekels of silver, after the shekel of the Set-Apart-Place.* 4 *And if it is a female, then your estimation shall be thirty shekels.* 5 *And if it is from five years old even to twenty years old, then your estimation shall be of the male twenty shekels, and for the female ten shekels.* 6 *And if it is from a month old even to five years old, then your estimation shall be of the male five shekels of silver, and for the female your estimation shall be three shekels of silver.* 7 *And if it be*

from sixty years old and above; if it be a male, then your estimation shall be fifteen shekels, and for the female ten shekels. 8 *But if he is too poor to pay your estimation, then he shall present himself before the kohen, and the kohen shall set a value for him; according to his ability that vowed shall the kohen value him.*[2] 9 *And if it is a beast, of which men bring an offering to* יהוה, *all that any man gives of such to* יהוה *shall be set-apart.* 10 *He shall not alter it, nor change it, a tov for a bad, or a bad for a tov: and if he shall at all change beast for beast, then it and the exchange of it shall be set-apart.* 11 *And if it be any unclean beast, of which they do not offer a sacrifice to* יהוה, *then he shall present the beast before the kohen:* 12 *And the kohen shall value it, whether it be tov or bad: as you value it, O kohen, so shall it be.* 13 *But if he will at all redeem it, then he shall add a fifth part of it to your estimation.* 14 *And when a man shall set apart his bayit to* יהוה, *then the kohen shall estimate it, whether it be tov or bad: as the kohen shall estimate it, so shall it stand.* 15 *And if he that set it apart it will redeem his bayit, then he shall add the fifth part of the money of your estimation to it, and it shall be his.* 16 *And if a man shall set apart to* יהוה *some part of a field of his possession, then your estimation shall be according to the zera of it: a homer of barley zera shall be valued at fifty shekels of silver.* 17 *If he set apart his field from the year of Yovel, according to your estimation it shall stand.* 18 *But if he set apart his field after the Yovel, then the kohen shall reckon to him the money according to the years that*

---

[1] The seven-fold prophesied vengeance by YHWH against Yisrael for idolatry and waywardness, takes form in multiples of 7, as seen in many verses here in Leviticus such as verses 24 and 28. Based on these declared multiples of seven, and doing a little math from Ezekiel 4, we have discovered that Ephraim, who was perishing among the heathen as heathen, had their total years in exile prophesied beforehand. Their punishment was in fact multiplied sevenfold due to hardness of heart, and as promised in Lev. 26, they had their punishment at long last come to an end in 1996 CE. Historically that was the year when the two-house restoration moved into high gear, with hearts of understanding and revelation opening in great numbers. For details on this exact calculation, see: http://yourarmstoisrael.org/misc/charts/?page=ephraim_and_ju dahs_punishment

[2] A voluntary vow called **"Arech"** in Hebrew. To some this may seem like male chauvinism, or some unfair way of assigning a monetary value to human life, as opposed to all Yisraeltes being equal. That is not what is happening here. This vow was done voluntarily, not under compulsion. Thus YHWH did not assign monetary values to different kinds of people. The key word in these verses is "if." If certain individuals took vows, they had to have an assigned monetary value to successfully pay off that vow faithfully. It was only on this basis that monetary assigned value became acceptable. Were YHWH to assign value and make an act mandatory we can be sure that all beings would hold the same value monetarily, or otherwise, regardless of gender or age.

VAYIQRA – LEVITICUS 27

remain, even to the year of the Yovel, and it shall be deducted from your estimation. 19 And if he that set-apart the field will in any way redeem it, then he shall add the fifth part of the money of your evaluation to it, and it shall be assured to him. 20 And if he will not redeem the field, or if he has sold the field to another man, it shall not be redeemed any more. 21 But the field, when it is released in the Yovel, shall be set-apart to יהוה, as a field devoted; the possession of it shall be the kohen's. 22 And if a man set apart to יהוה a field that he has bought, which is not of the field of his possession; 23 Then the kohen shall reckon to him the worth of your estimation, even to the year of the Yovel: and he shall give your estimation in that day, as a set-apart thing to יהוה. 24 In the year of the Yovel, the field shall return to him from whom it was bought, even to him to whom the possession of the land did belong. 25 And all your estimations shall be according to the shekel of the Set-Apart-Place: twenty gerahs shall be the shekel. 26 Only the firstling of the living creatures, which should be יהוה's firstling, no man shall set it apart; whether it be ox, or sheep: it is יהוה's. 27 And if it be of an unclean beast, then he shall redeem it according to your estimation, and shall add a fifth part of it to it: or if it be not redeemed, then it shall be sold according to your estimation.

28 Notwithstanding no devoted thing, that a man shall devote to יהוה of all that he has, both of man and beast, and of the field of his possession, shall be sold or redeemed: every devoted thing is most set-apart to יהוה. 29 No one under the ban of men shall be redeemed; but shall surely be put to death. 30 And all the ma'aser of the land, whether of the zera of the land, or of the fruit of the eytz, is יהוה's: it is set-apart to יהוה. 31 And if a man indeed redeems any of his ma'aser, he shall add to it the fifth part of it. 32 And concerning the ma'aser of the herd, or of the flock, even whatever passes under the rod, the tenth shall be set-apart to יהוה. 33 He shall not search whether it be tov or bad, neither shall he change it: and if he change it at all, then both it and the change of it shall be set apart; it shall not be redeemed. 34 These are the mitzvot, which יהוה commanded Moshe for the children of Yisrael on Mount Sinai.[1]

Chazak Chazak VeNitchazak
Be Strong Be Strong! And May We Be Strengthened!

---

[1] As always, YHWH's love for the community of Yisrael leads Him to open (Lev.1: 2) and close His scrolls and thoughts with Yisrael His people foremost on His mind.

במדבר

Bamidbar - Numbers
To Our Forefathers Yisrael

Torah Parsha 34
BaMidbar 1:1-4:20
Haftarah Hoshea 2:1-22
Brit Chadasha Gilyahna 7:1-17

1 And **יהוה** spoke to Moshe in the wilderness of Sinai, in the Tabernacle of the congregation, on the first day of the second month, in the second year after they had come out of the land of Mitzrayim, saying, 2 *Take a census of all the congregation of the children of Yisrael, after their mishpachot, by the bayit of their ahvot, with the number of their names, every male head by head,*[1] *3 From twenty years old and upward, all that are able to go out to war in Yisrael: you and Aharon shall number them by their divisions.*[2] *4 And with you there shall be a man of every tribe; every one head of the bayit of his ahvot. 5 And these are the names of the men that shall stand with you:*[3] *From the tribe of Reuven; Elitzur the son of Shedeyur. 6 Of Shimeon; Shelumi-El the son of Tzurishaddai. 7 Of Yahudah; Nahcshon the son of Amminadav. 8 Of Yissachar; Nethane-El the son of Tzuar. 9 Of Zevulun; Eliav the son of Helon. 10 Of the children of Yoseph: of Ephraim; Elyshama the son of Ammihud: of Menashsheh; Gamaliel the son of Pedahtzur. 11 Of Benyamin; Avidan the son of Gidoni. 12 Of Dan; Ahizer the son of Ammishaddai. 13 Of Asher; Pagi-El the son of Okran. 14 Of Gad; Elyasaph the son of Deu-El. 15 Of Naphtali; Ahira the son of Enan.* 16 These were the leaders of the congregation, leaders of the tribes of their ahvot, heads of thousands in Yisrael.

17 And Moshe and Aharon took these men who were are expressed by their names: 18 And they assembled the entire congregation together on the first day of the second month, and they declared their ancestry after their mishpachot, by the bayit of their ahvot, according to the number of the names, from twenty years old and upward, head by head 19 As **יהוה** commanded Moshe, so he numbered them in the wilderness of Sinai. 20 And the children of Reuven, Yisrael's eldest son, by their generations, after their mishpachot, by the bayit of their ahvot, according to the number of the names, head by head, every male from twenty years old and upward, all that were able to go to war; 21 Those that were numbered of them, even of the tribe of Reuven, were forty six thousand five hundred. 22 Of the children of Shimeon, by their generations, after their mishpachot, by the bayit of their ahvot, those that were numbered of them, according to the number of the names, head by head, every male from twenty years old and upward, all that were able to go out to war; 23 Those that were numbered of them, even of the tribe of Shimeon, were fifty nine thousand three hundred. 24 Of the children of Gad, by their generations, after their mishpachot, by the bayit of their ahvot, according to the number of the names, from twenty years old and upward, all that were able to go out to war; 25 Those that were numbered of them, even of the tribe of Gad, were forty five thousand six hundred fifty. 26 Of the children of Yahudah, by their generations, after their mishpachot, by the bayit of their ahvot, according to the number of the names, from twenty years old and upward, all that were able to go out to war; 27 Those that were numbered of them, even of the tribe of Yahudah, were seventy four thousand six hundred. 28 Of the children of Yissakar, by their generations,

---

[1] **Le goolgelotam** meaning each head, a derivation of the Hebrew **Golgotha**, where every Yisraelite head is counted to see if that individual is for Him or against Him.
[2] In Yisrael, YHWH counts only the warriors not the others. He can count only on the warriors in the Ruach.
[3] YHWH chooses Yisrael's leaders, not the nation. This is an eternal principle, which was violated in Matthew 23 by the Prushim.

after their mishpachot, by the bayit of their ahvot, according to the number of the names, from twenty years old and upward, all that were able to go out to war; 29 Those that were numbered of them, even of the tribe of Yissakar, were fifty four thousand four hundred. 30 Of the children of Zevulon, by their generations, after their mishpachot, by the bayit of their ahvot, according to the number of the names, from twenty years old and upward, all that were able to go out to war; 31 Those that were numbered of them, even of the tribe of Zevulon, were fifty seven thousand four hundred. 32 Of the children of Yoseph, namely, of the children of Ephraim, by their generations, after their mishpachot, by the bayit of their ahvot, according to the number of the names, from twenty years old and upward, all that were able to go out to war; 33 Those that were numbered of them, even of the tribe of Ephraim, were forty thousand five hundred.[1] 34 Of the children of Menashsheh, by their generations, after their mishpachot, by the bayit of their ahvot, according to the number of the names, from twenty years old and upward, all that were able to go out to war; 35 Those that were numbered of them, even of the tribe of Menashsheh, were thirty two thousand two hundred. 36 Of the children of Benyamin, by their generations, after their mishpachot, by the bayit of their ahvot, according to the number of the names, from twenty years old and upward, all that were able to go out to war; 37 Those that were numbered of them, even of the tribe of Benyamin, were thirty five thousand four hundred. 38 Of the children of Dan, by their generations, after their mishpachot, by the bayit of their ahvot, according to the number of the names, from twenty years old and upward, all that were able to go out to war; 39 Those that were numbered of them, even of the tribe of Dan, were sixty two thousand seven hundred.

---

[1] Proof that the multitudes of Ephraim come from all ten tribes, known after the division of the House of David as Ephraim, or non-Jewish Yisrael. Ephraim by itself as a single tribe never brought forth the multitudes.

40 Of the children of Asher, by their generations, after their mishpachot, by the bayit of their ahvot, according to the number of the names, from twenty years old and upward, all that were able to go out to war; 41 Those that were numbered of them, even of the tribe of Asher, were forty one thousand five hundred. 42 Of the children of Naphtali, throughout their generations, after their mishpachot, by the bayit of their ahvot, according to the number of the names, from twenty years old and upward, all that were able to go out to war; 43 Those that were numbered of them, even of the tribe of Naphtali, were fifty three thousand four hundred. 44 These are those that were numbered, which Moshe and Aharon numbered, and the leaders of Yisrael, being twelve men: each one was for the bayit of his ahvot. 45 So were all those that were numbered of the children of Yisrael, by the bayit of their ahvot, from twenty years old and upward, all that were able to go out to war in Yisrael; 46 Even all they that were numbered were six hundred three thousand five hundred fifty. 47 But the Leviim after the tribe of their ahvot were not numbered among them. 48 For יהוה had spoken to Moshe, saying, 49 *Only you shall not number the tribe of Levi, neither take their census among the children of Yisrael: 50 But you shall appoint the Leviim over the Tabernacle of testimony, and over all the vessels of it, and over all things that belong to it: they shall bear the Tabernacle, and all the vessels of it; and they shall serve in it, and shall camp all around the Tabernacle. 51 And when the Tabernacle moves forward, the Leviim shall take it down: and when the Tabernacle is to be pitched, the Leviim shall set it up: and the Ger that comes near shall be put to death. 52 And the children of Yisrael shall pitch their tents, every man by his own camp, and every man by his own banner, throughout their divisions. 53 But the Leviim shall pitch all around the Tabernacle of testimony, that there is no wrath upon the congregation of*

the children of Yisrael: and the Leviim shall keep the duty of the Tabernacle of the testimony. 54 And the children of Yisrael did according to all that יהוה commanded Moshe, so they did.

2 And יהוה spoke to Moshe and to Aharon, saying, 2 *Every man of the children of Yisrael shall pitch by his own banner, with the sign of their abba's bayit: at a long distance around the Tabernacle of the congregation shall they pitch.* 3 *And on the east side toward the rising of the sun shall those of the banner of the camp of Yahudah pitch throughout their divisions: and Nachshon the son of Amminadav shall be leader of the children of Yahudah.* 4 And his host, and those that were numbered of them, were seventy four thousand six hundred. 5 *And those that do pitch next to him shall be the tribe of Yissakar: and Nethan-El the son of Tzuar shall be leader of the children of Yissakar.* 6 And his host, and those that were numbered of it, were fifty four thousand four hundred. 7 *Then the tribe of Zevulon: and Eliav the son of Helon shall be leader of the children of Zevulon.* 8 And his host, and those that were numbered of it, were fifty seven thousand four hundred. 9 All that were numbered in the camp of Yahudah were one hundred eighty six thousand four hundred, throughout their divisions. *These shall set out first.*[1] 10 *On the south side shall be the banner of the camp of Reuven according to their divisions: and the leader of the children of Reuven shall be Elitzur the son of Shedey-Ur.* 11 And his host, and those that were numbered of it, were forty six thousand five hundred. 12 *And those who camp next to him shall be the tribe of Shimeon: and the leader of the children of Shimeon shall be Shelumi-El the son of Tzuri-Shaddai.* 13 And his host, and those that were numbered of them, were fifty nine

thousand three hundred. 14 *Then the tribe of Gad: and the leader of the sons of Gad shall be Elyasaph the son of Reu-El.* 15 And his host, and those that were numbered of them, were forty five thousand six hundred fifty. 16 *All that were numbered in the camp of Reuven were one hundred fifty one thousand four hundred fifty, throughout their divisions.* And they shall set out as second to depart. 17 *Then the Tabernacle of the congregation shall move forward with the camp of the Leviim in the midst of the camp: as they camp, so shall they move forward, every man in his place by their banners.* 18 *On the west side shall be the banner of the camp of Ephraim according to their divisions: and the leader of the sons of Ephraim shall be Eli-Shama the son of Ammichud.* 19 And his host, and those that were numbered of them, were forty thousand five hundred. 20 *And next to him shall be the tribe of Menashsheh: and the leader of the children of Menashsheh shall be Gamali-El the son of Pedahtzur.* 21 And his host, and those that were numbered of them, were thirty two thousand two hundred. 22 *Then the tribe of Benyamin: and the leader of the sons of Benyamin shall be Avidan the son of Gideoni.* 23 And his host, and those that were numbered of them, were thirty five thousand four hundred. 24 All that were numbered of the camp of Ephraim were one hundred eight thousand one hundred, throughout their divisions. *And they shall go forward as the third to depart.* 25 *The banner of the camp of Dan shall be on the north side by their divisions: and the leader of the children of Dan shall be Achiezer the son of Ammi-Shaddai.* 26 And his host, and those that were numbered of them, were sixty two thousand seven hundred. 27 *And those that camp next to him shall be the tribe of Asher: and the leader of the children of Asher shall be Pagi-El the son of Ocran.* 28 And his host, and those that were numbered of them, were forty one thousand five hundred. 29 *Then the tribe of Naphtali: and the leader of the*

---

[1] Yahudah is usually first; as in hearing about Moshiach, marching to battle, breaking camp, and the first to return to the land in the end-time two house restoration as seen in Zacharyah 12:7.

children of Naphtali shall be Ahira the son of Enan. 30 And his host, and those that were numbered of them, were fifty three thousand four hundred. 31 All they that were numbered in the camp of Dan were one hundred fifty seven thousand six hundred. *They shall go last with their banners.* 32 These are those who were numbered of the children of Yisrael by the bayit of their ahvot: all those that were numbered of the camps throughout their divisions were six hundred three thousand five hundred fifty. 33 But the Leviim were not numbered among the children of Yisrael; as יהוה commanded Moshe. 34 And the children of Yisrael did according to all that יהוה commanded Moshe: so they pitched by their banners, and so they moved forward, every one after their mishpachot, according to the bayit of their ahvot.

3 These also are the generations of Aharon and Moshe in the day that יהוה spoke with Moshe in Mount Sinai. 2 And these are the names of the sons of Aharon; Nadav the bachor, and Avihu, El-Azar, and Ithamar. 3 These are the names of the sons of Aharon, the kohanim who were anointed, whom he consecrated to serve in the kohen's office. 4 And Nadav and Avihu died before יהוה, when they offered strange fire before יהוה, in the wilderness of Sinai,[1] and they had no children: and El-Azar and Ithamar ministered in the kohen's office in the sight of Aharon their abba. 5 And יהוה spoke to Moshe, saying, 6 *Bring the tribe of Levi near, and present them before Aharon the kohen, that they may serve him. 7 And they shall keep his duty, and the duty of the whole congregation before the Tabernacle of the congregation, to do the service of the Tabernacle. 8 And they shall keep all the instruments of the Tabernacle of the congregation, and the duty of the children of Yisrael, to do the service of the Tabernacle. 9 And you shall give the Leviim*

to Aharon and to his sons: they are wholly given to him out of the children of Yisrael. 10 And you shall appoint Aharon and his sons, and they shall guard their kohen's office: and the Ger that comes near shall be put to death.* 11 And יהוה spoke to Moshe, saying, 12 *See, I have taken the Leviim from among the children of Yisrael instead of all the bachor that pehter[2] the womb among the children of Yisrael: therefore the Leviim shall be Mine; 13 Because all the bachor are Mine; for on the day that I smote all the bachor in the land of Mitzrayim I made all the bachor in Yisrael kodesh to Me, both man and beast: they shall be Mine: I am* יהוה. 14 And יהוה spoke to Moshe in the wilderness of Sinai, saying, 15 *Number the children of Levi after the bayit of their ahvot, by their mishpachot: every male from a month old and upward shall you number them.* 16 And Moshe numbered them according to the word of יהוה, as he was commanded. 17 And these were the sons of Levi by their names; Gershon, and Qehath, and Merari. 18 And these are the names of the sons of Gershon by their mishpachot; Livni, and Shimei. 19 And the sons of Kohath by their mishpachot; Amram, and Yitzhar, Hevron, and Uzzi-El. 20 And the sons of Merari by their mishpachot; Mahli, and Mushi. These are the mishpachot of the Leviim according to the bayit of their ahvot. 21 Of Gershon was the mishpacha of the Livnites, and the mishpacha of the Shimites: these are the mishpachot of the Gershonites. 22 Those that were numbered of them, according to the number of all the males, from a month old and upward, even those that were numbered of them were seven thousand five hundred. 23 *The mishpachot of the Gershonites shall pitch behind the Tabernacle westward. 24 And the leader of the bayit of the abba of the Gershonites shall be Eliyasaph the son of Le-El. 25 And*

[1] See note on Leviticus 10:2.

[2] **Pehter**: or open, as in open the womb. It is of special interest to note that Peter, Yahshua's disciple, opened the womb of Renewed Covenant Yisrael, on the Day of Pentecost in the Temple (YHWH's House not an upper room) allowing Yisrael's promised renewal to begin. In Greek **peter** is rock; but in Hebrew it means, "to open."

the duty of the sons of Gershon in the Tabernacle of the congregation shall be the Tabernacle, and the tent, the covering of it, and the covering for the door of the Tabernacle of the congregation, 26 And the hangings of the court, and the curtain for the door of the court, which is by the Tabernacle, and by the altar all around, and the cords of it for all its service. 27 And of Kohath was the mishpacha of the Amramites, and the mishpacha of the Yisharites, and the mishpacha of the Hevronites, and the mishpacha of the Uzzielites: these are the mishpachot of the Kohathites. 28 The number of all the males, from a month old and upward were eight thousand six hundred, keeping the duty of the Set-Apart-Place. 29 *The mishpachot of the sons of Kohath shall pitch on the side of the Tabernacle southward.* 30 *And the leader of the bayit of the abba of the mishpachot of the Kohathites shall be Elizaphan the son of Uzzi-El:* 31 *And their duty shall be the Ark, and the table, and the Menorah, and the altars, and the vessels of the Set-Apart-Place with which they serve, and the covering, and all its service.* 32 And El-Azar the son of Aharon the kohen shall be leader over the leader of the Leviim, and has the oversight of them that keep the duty of the Set-Apart-Place. 33 Of Merari was the mishpacha of the Mahlites, and the mishpacha of the Mushites: these are the mishpachot of Merari. 34 And those that were numbered of them, according to the number of all the males, from a month old and upward, were six thousand two hundred. 35 *And the leader of the bayit of the abba of the mishpachot of Merari was Zuri-El the son of Avihail: these shall pitch on the side of the Tabernacle northward.* 36 *And under the custody and duty of the sons of Merari shall be the boards of the Tabernacle, and the bars of it, and the columns of it, and the sockets of it, and all the vessels of it, and all its service,* 37 *And the columns of the court all around, and*

their sockets, and their pins, and their cords. 38 *But those that camp before the Tabernacle toward the east, even before the Tabernacle of the congregation eastward, shall be Moshe, and Aharon and his sons, keeping the duty of the Set-Apart-Place for the duty of the children of Yisrael; and the Ger that comes near shall be put to death.* 39 All that were numbered of the Leviim, which Moshe and Aharon numbered at the command of יהוה, by their mishpachot, all the males from a month old and upward, were twenty two thousand. 40 And יהוה said to Moshe, *Number all the bachor of the males of the children of Yisrael from a month old and upward, and take the number of their names.* 41 *And you shall take the Leviim for Me - I am*יהוה *- instead of all the bachor among the children of Yisrael, and the cattle of the Leviim instead of all the bachor among the cattle of the children of Yisrael.* 42 And Moshe numbered, as יהוה commanded him, all the bachor among the children of Yisrael. 43 And all the bachor males by the number of names, from a month old and upward, of those that were numbered, were twenty two thousand two hundred senety three. 44 And יהוה spoke to Moshe, saying, 45 *Take the Leviim instead of all the bachor among the children of Yisrael, and the cattle of the Leviim instead of their cattle; and the Leviim shall be Mine: I am* יהוה. 46 *And for those that are to be redeemed of the two hundred and seventy threee of the bachor of the children of Yisrael, which are more than the Leviim;* 47 *You shall even take five shekels apiece by the poll, after the shekel of the Set-Apart-Place shall you take them, the shekel of twenty gerahs.* 48 *And you shall give the money, by which the odd number of them is to be redeemed, to Aharon and to his sons.* 49 And Moshe took the redemption money of them that were over and above those that were redeemed by the Leviim: 50 Of the bachor of the children of Yisrael he took the money; one thousand three hundred sixty five shekels, after the shekel of the Set-Apart-Place: [1] 51 And Moshe gave the money of those that were redeemed to Aharon and to his sons, according to the word of **יהוה**, as **יהוה** commanded Moshe.

4 And **יהוה** spoke to Moshe and to Aharon, saying, 2 *Take the census of the sons of Kohath from among the sons of Levi, after their mishpachot, by the bayit of their ahvot, 3 From thirty years old[2] and upward even until fifty years old, all who enter into the service, to do the work in the Tabernacle of the congregation. 4 This shall be the service of the sons of Kohath in the Tabernacle of the congregation, about the most set-apart things: 5 And when the camp moves forward, Aharon shall come, and his sons, and they shall take down the covering vail, and cover the Ark of the testimony with it: 6 And shall put on it the covering of fine leather, and shall spread over it an all blue cloth, and shall put in the poles of it. 7 And upon the Table of the Faces they shall spread a cloth of blue, and put on it the dishes, and the spoons, and the bowls, and covers to cover it fully: and the eternal lechem shall be on it: 8 And they shall spread upon them a cloth of scarlet, and cover the same with a covering of fine leather, and shall put in the poles of it. 9 And they shall take a cloth of blue, and cover the Menorah of the light, and its lamps, and its snuffers, and its trays, and all the oil vessels of it, by which they serve it: 10 And they shall put it and all the vessels of it inside a covering of leather skin, and shall put it upon a bar. 11 And upon the golden altar they shall spread a cloth of blue, and cover it with a covering of leather skin, and shall put in the poles of it: 12 And they shall take all the instruments of ministry, by which they serve in the Set-Apart-Place, and put them in a cloth of* blue, and cover them with a covering of leather skin, and shall put them on a bar: 13 And they shall take away the ashes from the altar, and spread a purple cloth over it: 14 And they shall put upon it all the vessels of it, by which they serve about it, even the censers, the meathooks, and the shovels, and the basins, all the vessels of the altar; and they shall spread over it a covering of leather skin, and put in the poles of it. 15 And when Aharon and his sons have made an end of covering the Set-Apart-Place, and all the vessels of the Set-Apart-Place, as the camp moves forward; after that, the sons of Kohath shall come to bear it: but they shall not touch any set-apart thing, lest they die. These things are the burden of the sons of Kohath in the Tabernacle of the congregation.[3] 16 And to the oversight of El-Azar the son of Aharon the kohen, pertains the oil for the light, and the sweet incense, and the daily grain offering, and the anointing oil, and the oversight of all the Tabernacle, and of all that is in it, in the Set-Apart-Place, and in the vessels of it.* 17 And **יהוה** spoke to Moshe and to Aharon, saying, 18 *Do not cut off the tribe of the mishpachot of the Kohathites from among the Leviim: 19 But this do to them, that they may live, and not die, when they approach to the most set-apart things: Aharon and his sons shall go in, and appoint everyone to his service and to his burden: 20 But they shall not go in to see when the set-apart things are covered, lest they die.*

Torah Parsha 35
Naso 4:21-7:89
Haftarah Shophtim 13:2-25
Brit Chadasha MaAseh Shlichim 21:17-32

21 And **יהוה** spoke to Moshe, saying, 22 *Take also the census of the sons of Gershon, throughout the houses of their*

---

[1] There were 273 more firstborn than Levites. The 273 were then redeemed for five shekels a piece, and the money given to the High Priest.
[2] Yahshua began His ministry among the congregation of Yisrael at 30 as well.

[3] The items of the Tabernacle were all portable, which is most significant to understand, as it expresses YHWH's will to be with and in the midst of His people, wherever they go, a scene that was fully realized when His Son Yahshua came and lived in our midst on the earth.

ahvot, by their mishpachot; 23 *From thirty years old and upward until fifty years old shall you number them; all that enter in to perform the service, to do the work in the Tabernacle of the congregation.* 24 *This is the service of the mishpachot of the Gershonites, to serve, and for their burdens:* 25 *And they shall bear the curtains of the Tabernacle, and the Tabernacle of the congregation, its covering, and the covering of the leather skin that is on it, and the covering for the door of the Tabernacle of the congregation,* 26 *And the hangings of the court, and the covering for the door of the gate of the court, which is by the Tabernacle and by the altar all around, and their cords, and all the instruments of their service, and all that is made for them: so shall they serve.* 27 *At the appointment of Aharon and his sons shall be all the service of the sons of the Gershonites, in all their burdens, and in all their service: and you shall appoint to them their duty all their burdens.* [1] 28 *This is the service of the mishpachot of the sons of Gershon in the Tabernacle of the congregation: and their duty shall be under the hand of Ithamar the son of Aharon the kohen.* 29 *As for the sons of Merari, you shall number them after their mishpachot, by the bayit of their ahvot;* 30 *From thirty years old and upward even to fifty years old shall you number them, every one that enters into the service, to do the work of the Tabernacle of the congregation.* 31 *And this is the duty of their burden, according to all their service in the Tabernacle of the congregation; the boards of the Tabernacle, and the bars of it, and the columns of it, and sockets of it,* 32 *And the columns of the court all around, and their sockets, and their pins, and their cords, with all their instruments, and all their service: and by their name you shall assign the instruments of the duty of their burden.* 33 *This is the service of the mishpachot of the sons of Merari, according*

to all their service, in the Tabernacle of the congregation, under the hand of Ithamar the son of Aharon the kohen. 34 And Moshe and Aharon and the leader of the congregation numbered the sons of the Kohathites after their mishpachot, and after the bayit of their ahvot, 35 From thirty years old and upward even to fifty years old, every one that enters into the service, for the work in the Tabernacle of the congregation: 36 And those that were numbered of them by their mishpachot were two thousand seven hundred fifty. 37 These were they that were numbered of the mishpachot of the Kohathites, all that might do service in the Tabernacle of the congregation, which Moshe and Aharon did number according to the command of יהוה by the hand of Moshe. 38 And those who were numbered of the sons of Gershon, throughout their mishpachot, and by the bayit of their ahvot, 39 From thirty years old and upward even to fifty years old, every one that enters into the service, for the work in the Tabernacle of the congregation, 40 Even those that were numbered of them, throughout their mishpachot, by the bayit of their ahvot, were two thousand six hundred thirty. 41 These are they that were numbered of the mishpachot of the sons of Gershon, of all that might do service in the Tabernacle of the congregation, whom Moshe and Aharon did number according to the command of יהוה. 42 And those who were numbered of the mishpachot of the sons of Merari, throughout their mishpachot, by the bayit of their ahvot, 43 From thirty years old and upward even to fifty years old, every one that enters into the service, for the work in the Tabernacle of the congregation, 44 Even those that were numbered of them after their mishpachot, were three thousand two hundred. 45 These are those that were numbered of the mishpachot of the sons of Merari, whom Moshe and Aharon numbered according to the word of יהוה by the hand of Moshe. 46 All those that were numbered of the Leviim, whom Moshe and

---

[1] In Yisrael, every position of responsibility and leadership is by divine appointment, not election or democratic vote.

Aharon and the leader of Yisrael numbered, after their mishpachot, and after the bayit of their ahvot, 47 From thirty years old and upward even to fifty years old, everyone that came to do the service of the ministry, and the service of the burden in the Tabernacle of the congregation, 48 Even those that were numbered of them, were eight thousand five hundred eighty. 49 According to the command of יהוה they were numbered by the hand of Moshe, every one according to his service, and according to his burden: thus were they numbered by him, as יהוה commanded Moshe.

5 And יהוה spoke to Moshe, saying, 2 Command the children of Yisrael, that they put out of the camp every leper, and everyone that has an issue, and whoever is defiled by the dead: 3 Both male and female shall you put out, outside the camp shall you put them; that they defile not their camps, in the midst of which I dwell. 4 And the children of Yisrael did so, and put them out outside the camp: as יהוה spoke to Moshe, so did the children of Yisrael. 5 And יהוה spoke to Moshe, saying, 6 Speak to the children of Yisrael, When a man or woman shall commit any sin that men commit, to do a trespass against יהוה, and that person be guilty; 7 Then they shall confess their sin that they have done: and he shall repay his trespass with its principal, and then add to it the one-fifth, and give it to him against whom he has trespassed.[1] 8 But if the man has no relative to repay the trespass to, let the trespass be paid to יהוה, for the kohen; in addition to the ram of the atonement, with which an atonement shall be made for him. 9 And every offering of all the set-apart things of the children of Yisrael, which they bring to the kohen, shall be his. 10 And every man's set-apart gifts shall be his: whatever any man gives the kohen, it shall be his. 11 And יהוה spoke to Moshe, saying, 12 Speak to the children of Yisrael, and say to them, If any man's wife goes aside, and commit a trespass against him, 13 And a man lies with her carnally, and it be hidden from the eyes of her husband, and be kept secret, and she be defiled, and there be no witness against her, nor was she caught; 14 And the ruach of jealousy come upon him, and he becomes jealous of his wife, and she be defiled: or if the ruach of jealousy come upon him, and he be jealous of his wife, and she is not defiled: 15 Then shall the man bring his wife to the kohen, and he shall bring the offering for her, the tenth part of an ephah of barley meal; he shall pour no oil upon it, nor put frankincense on it; for it is an offering of jealousy, an offering of memorial, bringing iniquity to remembrance. 16 And the kohen shall bring her near, and set her before יהוה: 17 And the kohen shall take set-apart mayim in an earthen vessel; of the dust that is on the floor of the Tabernacle the kohen shall take some, and put it into the mayim: 18 And the kohen shall set the woman before יהוה, and uncover the woman's head,[2] and put the offering of memorial in her hands, which is the jealousy offering: and the kohen shall have in his hand the bitter mayim that causes the curse: 19 And the kohen shall put her under an oath, and say to the woman, If no man has lain with you, and if you have not gone aside to uncleanness with another instead of your husband, be free from this bitter mayim that causes the curse: 20 But if you have gone aside to another instead of your husband, and if you are defiled, and some man has lain with you beside your husband: 21 Then the kohen shall charge the woman with an oath of cursing, and the kohen shall say to the woman, יהוה make you a curse and an oath among your people, when יהוה makes your thigh to rot, and your belly to swell; 22 And this mayim that causes the curse shall go into your bowels, to make your belly to swell, and your thigh

[1] Restitution.

[2] Yisraelite women did and are still required to continue to wear head coverings as seen here.

to rot: And the woman shall say, Amein, amein. 23 And the kohen shall write these curses in a scroll, and he shall blot them out with the bitter mayim: [1] 24 And he shall cause the woman to drink the bitter mayim that causes the curse: and the mayim that causes the curse shall enter into her, and become bitter. 25 Then the kohen shall take the jealousy offering out of the woman's hand, and shall wave the offering before יהוה, and offer it upon the altar: 26 And the kohen shall take a handful of the offering, as a memorial offering, and burn it upon the altar, and afterward shall cause the woman to drink the mayim. 27 And when he has made her to drink the mayim, then it shall come to pass, that, if she be defiled, and has done trespass against her husband, that the mayim that causes the curse shall enter into her, and become bitter, and her belly shall swell, and her thigh shall rot: and the woman shall be a curse among her people. 28 And if the woman is not defiled, but is clean; then she shall be free, and shall conceive zera. 29 This is the Torah of jealousy, when a wife turns aside to another instead of her husband, and is defiled; 30 Or when the ruach of jealousy comes upon him, and he be jealous over his wife, and shall set the woman before יהוה, and the kohen shall do to her all this Torah. 31 Then shall the man be guiltless from iniquity, but the woman shall bear her iniquity.

6 And יהוה spoke to Moshe, saying, 2 Speak to the children of Yisrael, and say to them, When either man or woman shall separate themselves to vow a vow of a Nazirite, to separate themselves to יהוה: 3 He shall separate himself from wine and strong drink, and shall drink no vinegar of wine, or vinegar of strong drink, neither

shall he drink any liquor of grapes, nor eat moist grapes, or dried. 4 All the days of his separation shall he eat nothing that is made of the vine eytz, from the zera even to the skin. 5 All the days of the vow of his separation there shall no razor come upon his head: until the days be fulfilled, in which he separates himself to יהוה, he shall be set-apart, and shall let the locks of the hair of his head grow. 6 All the days that he separates himself to יהוה he shall not come near a dead body. 7 He shall not make himself unclean for his abba, or for his mother, for his brother, or for his sister, when they die: because the separation of his Elohim is upon his head. 8 All the days of his separation he is set-apart to יהוה. 9 And if any man die suddenly near him, and he has defiled the head of his separation; then he shall shave his head in the day of his cleansing, on the seventh day shall he shave it. 10 And on the eighth day he shall bring two turtledoves, or two young pigeons, to the kohen, to the door of the Tabernacle of the congregation: 11 And the kohen shall offer one for a sin offering, and the other for a burnt offering, and make an atonement for him, for that he sinned by reason of the dead body, and shall set-apart his head that same day. 12 And he shall consecrate to יהוה the days of his separation, and shall bring a lamb of the first year for a trespass offering: but the days that were before shall be lost, because his separation was defiled. 13 And this is the Torah of the Nazirite, when the days of his separation are fulfilled: he shall be brought to the door of the Tabernacle of the congregation: 14 And he shall offer his offering to יהוה, one male lamb of the first year without blemish for a burnt offering, and one ewe lamb of the first year without blemish for a sin offering, and one ram without blemish for shalom offerings, 15 And a basket of unleavened lechem, cakes of fine flour mingled with oil, and wafers of unleavened lechem anointed with oil, and their grain offering, and their drink

---

[1] Yahshua nailed the curse of Yisrael's unfaithfulness to His execution stake, as Yisrael corporately had violated the Torah of a jealous husband; In so doing, Yahshua took the book with all Yisrael's violations and canceled the curses that resulted from Yisrael's unfaithfulness that were recorded in the book by the Kohen HaGadol. That is referenced clearly in Colossians 2:14.

offerings. 16 *And the kohen shall bring them before* יהוה, *and shall offer his sin offering, and his burnt offering:* 17 *And he shall offer the ram for a sacrifice of shalom offerings to* יהוה, *with the basket of unleavened lechem: the kohen shall offer also his grain offering, and his drink offering.* 18 *And the Nazirite shall shave the head of his separation at the door of the Tabernacle of the congregation, and shall take the hair of the head of his separation, and put it in the fire which is under the sacrifice of the shalom offerings.* 19 *And the kohen shall take the boiled shoulder of the ram, and one unleavened cake out of the basket, and one unleavened wafer, and shall put them upon the hands of the Nazirite, after the hair of his separation is shaven:* 20 *And the kohen shall wave them for a wave offering before* יהוה: *this is set-apart for the kohen, with the wave breast offering and the thigh of the contribution: and after that the Nazirite may drink wine.* 21 *This is the Torah of the Nazirite who has vowed, and of his offering to* יהוה *for his separation, and besides whatever else his hands are able to get: according to the vow which he vowed, so he must do after the Torah of his separation.* 22 And יהוה spoke to Moshe, saying, 23 *Speak to Aharon and to his sons, saying, This is the way you shall bless the children of Yisrael, saying to them,* 24 יהוה *bless you, and keep you:* 25 יהוה *make His face shine upon you, and be gracious to you:* 26 יהוה *lift up His countenance upon you, and give you shalom.* 27 *And they shall put My Name upon the children of Yisrael; and I will bless them.*[1]

7 And it came to pass on the day that Moshe had fully set up the Tabernacle, and had anointed it, and set it apart, and all the instruments of it, both the altar and all its vessels, and had anointed them, and set them apart; 2 That the leaders of Yisrael, heads of the bayit of their ahvot, who were the leaders of the tribes, and were over them that were numbered, drew near: 3 And they brought their offering before יהוה, six covered wagons, and twelve cattle; a wagon le-olam-va-ed two of the leaders, and for each one a bull: and they brought them before the Tabernacle. 4 And יהוה spoke to Moshe, saying, 5 *Accept these from them, that they may be for the service of the Tabernacle of the congregation; and you shall give them to the Leviim, to every man according to his service.* 6 And Moshe took the wagons and the cattle, and gave them to the Leviim. 7 Two wagons and four cattle he gave to the sons of Gershon, according to their service: 8 And four wagons and eight cattle he gave to the sons of Merari, according to their service, under the hand of Ithamar the son of Aharon the kohen. 9 But to the sons of Kohath he gave none: because the service of the Set-Apart-Place belonging to them they should carry it upon their shoulders. 10 And the leaders offered for dedicating of the altar in the day that it was anointed, even the leaders offered their offering before the altar. 11 And יהוה said to Moshe, *They shall offer their offering, each leader on his day, for the dedicating of the altar.* 12 And he that offered his offering the first day was Nachshon the son of Amminadav, of the tribe of Yahudah: 13 And his offering was one silver charger, the weight of it was a hundred and thirty shekels, one silver bowl of seventy shekels, after the shekel of the Set-Apart-Place; both of them were full of fine flour mingled with oil for a grain offering: 14 One spoon of ten shekels of gold, full of incense: 15 One young bullock, one ram, one lamb of the first year, for a burnt offering: 16 One kid of the male goats for a sin offering: 17 And for a sacrifice of shalom offerings, two cattle, five rams, five male goats, and five lambs of the first year: this was the offering of

---

[1] The official means by which all Yisraelites carry the true Name. The true Name is so crucial to Abba-YHWH, that He deemed it necessary that all professing Yisraelites carry it all the days of their lives. As such, any Yisraelite from Yahudah or Ephraim who does not carry it in their heart and on their tongue at all times simply cannot meet the biblical criteria of a true ordained Yisraelite, who is in position for YHWH's blessing.

Nachshon the son of Amminadav. 18 On the second day Nethane-El the son of Tzuar, leader of Yissakar, brought it near: 19 He offered for his offering one silver charger, the weight of which was an hundred and thirty shekels, one silver bowl of seventy shekels, after the shekel of the Set-Apart-Place; both of them full of fine flour mingled with oil for a grain offering: 20 One spoon of gold of ten shekels, full of incense: 21 One young bullock, one ram, one lamb of the first year, for a burnt offering: 22 One kid of the male goats for a sin offering: 23 And for a sacrifice of shalom offerings, two cattle, five rams, five male goats, and five lambs of the first year: this was the offering of Nethane-El the son of Tzuar. 24 On the third day Eliav the son of Helon, leader of the children of Zevulon, drew near: 25 His offering was one silver charger, the weight of which was an hundred and thirty shekels, one silver bowl of seventy shekels, after the shekel of the Set-Apart-Place; both of them full of fine flour mingled with oil for a grain offering: 26 One golden spoon of ten shekels, full of incense: 27 One young bullock, one ram, one lamb of the first year, for a burnt offering: 28 One kid of the male goats for a sin offering: 29 And for a sacrifice of shalom offerings, two oxen, five rams, five male goats, and five lambs of the first year: this was the offering of Eliav the son of Helon. 30 On the fourth day Elizur the son of Shedey-Ur, leader of the children of Reuven, did offer: 31 His offering was one silver charger of the weight of an hundred and thirty shekels, one silver bowl of seventy shekels, after the shekel of the Set-Apart-Place; both of them full of fine flour mingled with oil for a grain offering: 32 One golden spoon of ten shekels, full of incense: 33 One young bullock, one ram, one lamb of the first year, for a burnt offering: 34 One kid of the male goats for a sin offering: 35 And for a sacrifice of shalom offerings, two oxen, five rams, five male goats, and five lambs of the first year:

this was the offering of Elizur the son of Shedey-Ur. 36 On the fifth day Shelumi-El the son of Zurishaddai, leader of the children of Shimeon, did draw near: 37 His offering was one silver charger, the weight of which was an hundred and thirty shekels, one silver bowl of seventy shekels, after the shekel of the Set-Apart-Place; both of them full of fine flour mingled with oil for a grain offering: 38 One golden spoon of ten shekels, full of incense: 39 One young bullock, one ram, one lamb of the first year, for a burnt offering: 40 One kid of the male goats for a sin offering: 41 And for a sacrifice of shalom offerings, two oxen, five rams, five male goats, and five lambs of the first year: this was the offering of Shelumi-El the son of Zurishaddai. 42 On the sixth day Elyasaph the son of Deu-El, leader of the children of Gad, offered: 43 His offering was one silver charger of the weight of a hundred and thirty shekels, a silver bowl of seventy shekels, after the shekel of the Set-Apart-Place; both of them full of fine flour mingled with oil for a grain offering: 44 One golden spoon of ten shekels, full of incense: 45 One young bullock, one ram, one lamb of the first year, for a burnt offering: 46 One kid of the male goats for a sin offering: 47 And for a sacrifice of shalom offerings, two oxen, five rams, five male goats, and five lambs of the first year: this was the offering of Elyasaph the son of Deu-El. 48 On the seventh day Elyshama the son of Ammihud, leader of the children of Ephraim, offered: 49 His offering was one silver charger, the weight of which was a hundred and thirty shekels, one silver bowl of seventy shekels, after the shekel of the Set-Apart-Place; both of them full of fine flour mingled with oil for a grain offering: 50 One golden spoon of ten shekels, full of incense: 51 One young bullock, one ram, one lamb of the first year, for a burnt offering: 52 One kid of the male goats for a sin offering: 53 And for a sacrifice of shalom offerings, two oxen, five rams, five male goats, and five lambs of the first year: this was the offering of Elyshama the son of Ammihud. 54 On the eighth day offered Gamaliel the son of Pedahtzur, leader of the children of Menashsheh: 55 His offering was one silver charger of the weight of a hundred thirty shekels, one silver bowl of seventy shekels, after the shekel of the Set-Apart-Place; both of them full of fine flour mingled with oil for a grain offering: 56 One golden spoon of ten shekels, full of incense: 57 One young bullock, one ram, one lamb of the first year, for a burnt offering: 58 One kid of the male goats for a sin offering: 59 And for a sacrifice of shalom offerings, two oxen, five rams, five male goats, and five lambs of the first year: this was the offering of Gamaliel the son of Pedahtzur. 60 On the ninth day Avidan the son of Gidoni, leader of the children of Benyamin, offered: 61 His offering was one silver charger, the weight of which was a hundred and thirty shekels, one silver bowl of seventy shekels, after the shekel of the Set-Apart-Place; both of them full of fine flour mingled with oil for a grain offering: 62 One golden spoon of ten shekels, full of incense: 63 One young bullock, one ram, one lamb of the first year, for a burnt offering: 64 One kid of the male goats for a sin offering: 65 And for a sacrifice of shalom offerings, two oxen, five rams, five male goats, and five lambs of the first year: this was the offering of Avidan the son of Gidoni. 66 On the tenth day Ahiezer the son of Ammishaddai, leader of the children of Dan, offered: 67 His offering was one silver charger, the weight of which was a hundred and thirty shekels, one silver bowl of seventy shekels, after the shekel of the Set-Apart-Place; both of them full of fine flour mingled with oil for a grain offering: 68 One golden spoon of ten shekels, full of incense: 69 One young bullock, one ram, one lamb of the first year, for a burnt offering: 70 One kid of the male goats for a sin offering: 71 And for a sacrifice of shalom offerings, two oxen, five rams, five male goats, five lambs of the first

year: this was the offering of Ahiezer the son of Ammishaddai. 72 On the eleventh day Pagi-El the son of Ocran, leader of the children of Asher, offered: 73 His offering was one silver charger, the weight of which was a hundred and thirty shekels, one silver bowl of seventy shekels, after the shekel of the Set-Apart-Place; both of them full of fine flour mingled with oil for a grain offering: 74 One golden spoon of ten shekels, full of incense: 75 One young bullock, one ram, one lamb of the first year, for a burnt offering: 76 One kid of the male goats for a sin offering: 77 And for a sacrifice of shalom offerings, two oxen, five rams, five male goats, and five lambs of the first year: this was the offering of Pagi-El the son of Ocran. 78 On the twelfth day Ahira the son of Enan, leader of the children of Naphtali, offered: 79 His offering was one silver charger, the weight of which was a hundred and thirty shekels, one silver bowl of seventy shekels, after the shekel of the Set-Apart-Place; both of them full of fine flour mingled with oil for a grain offering: 80 One golden spoon of ten shekels, full of incense: 81 One young bullock, one ram, one lamb of the first year, for a burnt offering: 82 One kid of the male goats for a sin offering: 83 And for a sacrifice of shalom offerings, two oxen, five rams, five male goats, and five lambs of the first year: this was the offering of Ahira the son of Enan. 84 This was the dedication of the altar, when it was anointed by the leaders of Yisrael, with twelve chargers of silver, twelve silver bowls, and twelve spoons of gold:[1] 85 Each charger of silver weighing a hundred thirty shekels, each bowl seventy: all the silver vessels weighed two thousand four hundred shekels, after the shekel of the Set-Apart-Place: 86 The golden spoons were twelve, full of incense, weighing ten shekels apiece, after the shekel

---

[1] This anointing of the altar is very likely the pattern that YHWH will use to anoint the 144,000 Yisraelites from all 12 tribes sealed with YHWH's Name on their heads in Revelation 7, as one tribe is sealed every day for 12 days. This also may be the pattern for the Millennial Temple in Jerusalem, at the altar dedication.

of the Set-Apart-Place: all the gold of the spoons was a hundred twenty shekels. 87 All the cattle for the burnt offering were twelve bullocks, the rams twelve, the lambs of the first year twelve, with their grain offering: and the kids of the male goats for sin offering twelve. 88 And all the oxen for the sacrifice of the shalom offerings were twenty- four bullocks, the rams sixty, the male goats sixty, the lambs of the first year sixty. This was the dedication of the altar, after it was anointed. 89 And when Moshe went into the Tabernacle of the congregation to speak with Him, then he heard the voice of One speaking to him from above the rachamim seat that was upon the Ark of testimony, from between the two cheruvim:[1] and He spoke to him.

Torah Parsha 36
B'Haalotcha 8:1-12:16
Haftarah Zecharyah 2:14-4:7
Brit Chadasha Ivrim 4:1-16

8 And יהוה spoke to Moshe, saying, 2 *Speak to Aharon, and say to him, When you light the lamps, the seven lamps shall give light in front of the menorah.* 3 And Aharon did so; he lit the lamps in front of the Menorah, as יהוה commanded Moshe. 4 And this work of the menorah was of beaten gold, to the shaft of it, to its blossoms it was beaten work: according to the pattern that יהוה had shown Moshe, so he made the menorah. 5 And יהוה spoke to Moshe, saying, 6 *Take the Leviim from among the children of Yisrael, and cleanse them. 7 And this shall you do to them, to cleanse them: Sprinkle mayim of purifying upon them, and let them shave all their body, and let them wash their clothes, and so make themselves clean. 8 Then let them take a young bullock with its grain offering, even fine flour mingled with oil, and* another young bullock shall you take for a sin offering. 9 And you shall bring the Leviim before the Tabernacle of the congregation: and you shall gather the whole congregation of the children of Yisrael together: 10 And you shall bring the Leviim before יהוה : and the children of Yisrael shall lay their hands upon the Leviim: 11 And Aharon shall offer the Leviim before יהוה for an offering from the children of Yisrael so that they may perform the service of יהוה. 12 And the Leviim shall lay their hands upon the heads of the bullocks: and you shall offer one for a sin offering, and the other for a burnt offering, to יהוה , to make an atonement for the Leviim. 13 And you shall set the Leviim before Aharon, and before his sons, and offer them for an offering to יהוה. 14 So shall you separate the Leviim from among the children of Yisrael: and the Leviim shall be Mine. 15 And after that shall the Leviim go in to do the service of the Tabernacle of the congregation: and you shall cleanse them, and offer them for an offering. 16 For they are wholly given to Me from among the children of Yisrael, instead of such as open every womb, even instead of the bachor of all the children of Yisrael, have I taken them to Me. 17 For all the bachor of the children of Yisrael are Mine, both man and beast: on the day that I smote every bachor in the land of Mitzrayim I set them apart for Myself. 18 And I have taken the Leviim instead of all the bachor of the children of Yisrael. 19 And I have given the Leviim as a gift to Aharon and to his sons from among the children of Yisrael, to do the service for the children of Yisrael in the Tabernacle of the congregation, and to make an atonement for the children of Yisrael: that there be no plague among the children of Yisrael, when the children of Yisrael come near to the Set-Apart-Place. 20 And Moshe, and Aharon, and all the congregation of the children of Yisrael, did to the Leviim according to all that יהוה commanded Moshe concerning the Leviim, so did the children of Yisrael to

---

[1] The two cherubims are symbolic of both houses of Yisrael, receiving **rachamim** by the dom of atonement and being in unity, so that together they can hear the voice of YHWH. The cherubim touched and were of equal size, displaying that in YHWH's sight both houses are equal and strong when touching each other in unity.

them. 21 And the Leviim were purified, and they washed their clothes; and Aharon offered them as an offering before יהוה; and Aharon made atonement for them to cleanse them. 22 And after that went the Leviim in to do their service in the Tabernacle of the congregation before Aharon, and before his sons: as יהוה had commanded Moshe concerning the Leviim, so they did to them. 23 And יהוה spoke to Moshe, saying, 24 *This applies to the Leviim: from twenty-five years old and upward they shall go in to wait upon the service of the Tabernacle of the congregation:* 25 *And from the age of fifty years they shall cease waiting upon the service of it, and shall serve no more:* 26 *But shall serve with their brothers in the Tabernacle of the congregation, to shomer the duty, but shall do no service. This shall you do to the Leviim regarding their duties.*

9 And יהוה spoke to Moshe in the wilderness of Sinai, in the first month of the second year after they were come out of the land of Mitzrayim, saying, 2 Let the children of Yisrael also keep the Pesach at its appointed time. 3 In the fourteenth day of this month, in the evening, you shall keep it in its appointed time: according to all the rites of it, and according to all the ceremonies of it, shall you keep it. 4 And Moshe spoke to the children of Yisrael, that they should keep the Pesach. 5 And they kept the Pesach on the fourteenth day of the first month in the evening in the wilderness of Sinai: according to all that יהוה commanded Moshe, so did the children of Yisrael. 6 And there were certain men, who were defiled by the dead body of a man, that they could not keep the Pesach on that day: and they came before Moshe and before Aharon on that day: 7 And those men said to him, We are defiled by the dead body of a man: Why are we kept back, that we may not offer an offering to יהוה in His appointed time among the children of Yisrael? 8 And Moshe said to them, Stand

still, and I will hear what יהוה will command concerning you. 9 And יהוה spoke to Moshe, saying, 10 Speak to the children of Yisrael, saying, If any man of you or of your offspring shall be unclean by reason of a dead body, or is on a far off journey, he shall still keep the Pesach to יהוה.[1] 11 The fourteenth day of the second month at evening they shall keep it, and eat it with unleavened lechem and bitter herbs. 12 They shall leave none of it until the morning, nor break any bone of it: according to all the ordinances of the Pesach they shall keep it. 13 But the man that is clean, or is not on a journey, and fails to keep the Pesach, even the same being shall be cut off from among his people: because he brought not the offering of יהוה at its appointed time, that man shall bear his sin. 14 And if a Ger shall sojourn among you, and will keep the Pesach to יהוה; according to the ordinance of the Pesach, and according to the manner of it, so shall he do: you shall have one ordinance, both for the Ger, and for him that was born in the land.[2] 15 And on the day that the Tabernacle was raised up the cloud covered the Tabernacle, the tent of the testimony: and at evening there was upon the Tabernacle as it were the appearance of fire, until the morning. 16 So it was always: the cloud covered it by day, and the appearance of fire by night. 17 And when the cloud was taken up from the Tabernacle, then the children of Yisrael journeyed: and in the place where the cloud stopped, there the children of Yisrael pitched their tents. 18 At the command of יהוה the children of Yisrael journeyed, and at the command of יהוה they pitched: as long as the cloud stayed upon the Tabernacle they rested in their tents. 19 And when the cloud tarried for a long time upon the Tabernacle many days, the children of Yisrael kept the duty of יהוה, and did not journey. 20 And so it was, when the cloud was a few days upon the Tabernacle;

[1] Known as **"Pesach shanei,"** or the "second Passover."
[2] One Torah for all Yisraelites, not one for Jews and one for believing "gentiles."

according to the command of **יהוה** they stayed in their tents, and according to the command of **יהוה** they journeyed. 21 And so it was, when the cloud stayed from evening to the morning, and that the cloud was taken up in the morning, then they journeyed: whether it was by day or by night when the cloud was taken up, they journeyed. 22 Or whether it was two days, or a month, or a year, that the cloud tarried upon the Tabernacle, remaining on it, the children of Yisrael stayed in their tents, and did not journey: but when it was taken up, they journeyed. 23 At the command of **יהוה** they rested in the tents, and at the command of **יהוה** they journeyed: they kept the duty of **יהוה**, at the command of **יהוה** by the hand of Moshe.

10 And **יהוה** spoke to Moshe, saying, 2 *Make two trumpets of silver; of a whole piece shall you make them: that you may use them for the calling of the congregation, and for the journeying of the camp. 3 And when they shall blow with them, the entire congregation shall assemble themselves to you at the door of the Tabernacle of the congregation. 4 And if they blow but with one trumpet, then the leaders, who are heads of the thousands of Yisrael, shall gather themselves to you. 5 When you blow an alarm, then the camps that lie on the east parts shall go forward. 6 When you blow an alarm the second time, then the camps that lie on the south side shall take their journey: they shall blow an alarm for their journeys. 7 But when the congregation is to be gathered together, you shall blow, but you shall not sound an alarm. 8 And the sons of Aharon, the kohanim, shall blow with the trumpets; and they shall be to you for an ordinance le-olam-va-ed throughout your generations.[1] 9 And if you go to war in your land against the enemy that oppresses you, then you shall blow an alarm with the trumpets; and you*

shall be remembered before **יהוה** *Your Elohim, and you shall be saved from your enemies.* 10 *Also in the day of your simcha, and in your moadim,[2] and in the beginnings of your Chodashim,[3] you shall blow with the trumpets over your burnt offerings, and over the sacrifices of your shalom offerings; that they may be to you for a memorial before Your Elohim: I am* **יהוה** *Your Elohim.* 11 And it came to pass on the twentieth day of the second month, in the second year, that the cloud was taken up from off the Tabernacle of the testimony. 12 And the children of Yisrael took their journeys out of the wilderness of Sinai; and the cloud rested in the wilderness of Paran. 13 And they first took their journey according to the command of **יהוה** by the hand of Moshe. 14 In the first place went the banner of the camp of the children of Yahudah according to their divisions: and over his host was Nachshon the son of Amminadav. 15 And over the host of the tribe of the children of Yissakar was Nethane-El the son of Tzuar. 16 And over the host of the tribe of the children of Zevulon was Eliav the son of Helon. 17 And the Tabernacle was taken down; and the sons of Gershon and the sons of Merari moved forward, bearing the Tabernacle. 18 And the banner of the camp of Reuven moved forward according to their divisions: and over his host was Elitzur the son of Shedey-Ur. 19 And over the host of the tribe of the children of Shimeon was Shelumi-El the son of Tzurishaddai. 20 And over the host of the tribe of the children of Gad was Elyasaph the son of Deu-El. 21 And the Kohathites moved forward, bearing the Set-Apart-Place objects: and the others did set up the Tabernacle before they came. 22 And the banner of the camp of the children of Ephraim set forward according to their divisions: and over his host was Ely-Shama the son of Ammihud. 23 And over the host of the tribe of the children of Menashsheh was Gamli-El the son of

---

[1] Today in order to call both houses home from exile in the Ruach, the twin **chatsrot** should be sounded in faith so that in YHWH's timing the whole congregation will respond as **echad**.

[2] Feasts.
[3] **Rosh Chodesh**.

Pedahtzur. 24 And over the host of the tribe of the children of Benyamin was Avidan the son of Gidoni. 25 And the banner of the camp of the children of Dan moved forward, which was the rear guard of all the camps throughout their divisions: and over their division was Ahiezer the son of Ammishaddai. 26 And over the host of the tribe of the children of Asher was Pagi-El the son of Ocran. 27 And over the host of the tribe of the children of Naphtali was Ahira the son of Enan. 28 Such were the journeyings of the children of Yisrael according to their divisions, when they moved forward. 29 And Moshe said to Hovav, the son of Reu-El the Midyanite, Moshe's abba-in-law, We are journeying to the place of which יהוה said, I will give it you: come with us, and we will do you tov: for יהוה has spoken tov concerning Yisrael. 30 And he said to Moshe, I will not go; but I will depart to my own land, and to my kindred. 31 And Moshe said, Leave us not, I ask you; because you know how we are to camp in the wilderness, and you may be to us as eyes. 32 And it shall be, if you go with us, yes, it shall be, that what tov יהוה shall do to us, the same will we do to you. 33 And they departed from the Mount of יהוה three days' journey: and the Ark of the Covenant of יהוה went before them in the three days' journey, to search out a resting place for them. 34 And the cloud of יהוה was upon them by day, when they went out of the camp. 35 And it came to pass, when the Ark moved forward, that Moshe said, Rise up, יהוה, and let Your enemies be scattered; and let them that hate you flee before you.[1] 36 And when it rested, he said, Shuvee, O יהוה, to the countless myriad thousands of Yisrael.[2]

___
[1] The source of the universal liturgical **Vayehee Beensoah HaAron;** said in the Torah processional in synagogues of all denominations.
[2] The countless thousands here indicates Moshe was resting in the promise of YHWH to make Yisrael the largest nation on earth, even though this was ultimately played out in the latter-days and not in his time.

11 And when the people complained, it displeased יהוה: and יהוה heard it; and His anger was kindled; and the fire of יהוה burnt among them, and consumed them that were at the outskirts of the camp. 2 And the people cried to Moshe; and when Moshe made tefillah to יהוה, the fire was quenched. 3 And he called the name of the place Taverah: because the fire of יהוה burnt among them. 4 And the mixed multitude that was among them lusted greatly: and the children of Yisrael also wept again, and said, Who shall give us meat to eat? 5 We remember the fish, which we did eat in Mitzrayim freely; the cucumbers, and the melons, and the leeks, and the onions, and the garlic: 6 But our throat is dried up: there is nothing at all, beside this manna, before our eyes. 7 And the manna was as coriander zera, and the color of it as the color of bdellium. 8 And the people went about, and gathered it, and ground it on millstones, or beat it in the mortar, and baked it in pans, and made cakes from it: and the taste of it was as the taste of fresh oil. 9 And when the dew fell upon the camp in the night, the manna fell upon it. 10 Then Moshe heard the people weep throughout their mishpachot, every man in the door of his tent: and the anger of יהוה was kindled greatly; Moshe also was displeased. 11 And Moshe said to יהוה, Why have You afflicted Your servant? And why have I not found favor in Your sight, in that You lay the burden of this entire people upon me? 12 Have I conceived all of this people; Have I begotten them, that You should say to me, Carry them in Your bosom, as a nursing abba bears the nursing child, to the land that You swore to their ahvot? 13 Where should I find meat to give to this entire people? For they weep to me, saying, Give us meat that we may eat. 14 I am not able to bear this entire people alone, because it is too heavy for me. 15 And if You do this to me, kill me altogether, if I have found favor in Your sight; and let me not see my evil. 16 And יהוה said to

Moshe, *Gather to Me seventy men of the zachanim of Yisrael, whom you know to be the zachanim of the people, and officers over them; and bring them to the Tabernacle of the congregation, that they may stand there with you. 17 And I will come down and talk with you there: and I will take of the Ruach which is upon you, and will put it upon them;[1] and they shall bear the burden of the people with you, that you bear it not yourself alone. 18 And say to the people, Set yourselves apart for tomorrow, and you shall eat meat: for you have wept in the ears of יהוה, saying, Who shall give us meat to eat? For it was well with us in Mitzrayim: therefore יהוה will give you meat, and you shall eat. 19 You shall not eat one day, nor two days, nor five days, neither ten days, nor twenty days; 20 But even a whole month, until it comes out of your nostrils, and it becomes loathsome to you: because you have despised יהוה who is among you, and have wept before Him, saying, Why did we come out of Mitzrayim?* 21 And Moshe said, The people, among whom I am, are six hundred thousand footmen; and you have said, I will give them meat, that they may eat a whole month. 22 Shall the flocks and the herds be slain for them, to suffice them? Or shall all the fish of the sea be gathered together just for them, to suffice them? 23 And יהוה said to Moshe, *Is יהוה's Arm too short? You shall see now whether My Word meets you or not.[2]* 24 And Moshe went out, and told the people the words of יהוה, and gathered the seventy men of the zachanim of the people, and set them all around the Tabernacle. 25 And יהוה came down in a cloud, and spoke to him, and took of the Ruach that was upon him, and gave it to the seventy zachanim: and it came to pass, that, when the Ruach rested upon them, they prophesied, and did not cease. 26 But there

remained two of the men in the camp, the name of the one was Eldad, and the name of the other Medad: and the Ruach rested upon them; and they were among those listed, but went not out to the Tabernacle: and they prophesied in the camp. 27 And there ran a young man, and told Moshe, and said, Eldad and Medad do prophesy in the camp. 28 And Yahoshua the son of Nun, the assistant of Moshe, one of his young men, answered and said, My master Moshe, forbid them. 29 And Moshe said to him, Are you jealous for my sake? O that all יהוה's people were neviim, and that יהוה would put His Ruach upon them! 30 And Moshe returned into the camp, he and the zachanim of Yisrael. 31 And there went out a wind from יהוה, and brought quails from the sea, and let them fall by the camp, as it were a day's journey on this side, and as it were a day's journey on each side, all around the camp, and as it were two cubits high upon the surface of the earth. 32 And the people stayed up all that day, and all that night, and all the next day, and they gathered the quails: he that gathered least gathered ten homers: and they spread them out for themselves all around the camp. 33 And while the meat was yet between their teeth, before it was chewed, the wrath of יהוה was kindled against the people, and יהוה smote the people with a very great plague. 34 And he called the name of that place Kibroth-Hattaavah: because there they buried the people that lusted. 35 And the people journeyed from Kivroth-Hattaavah to Hatzeroth; and stayed at Hatzeroth.

12 And Miryam and Aharon spoke against Moshe because of the Ethiopian woman whom he had married: for

---

[1] The **Ruach HaKodesh** has always existed, and was not introduced in the Renewed Covenant for the first time.
[2] The "Arm of YHWH" is a metaphor for Yahshua, and the "Word of YHWH," is also a reference to Yahshua, who will provide for Yisrael the meat they desire.

he had married an Ethiopian woman.[1] 2 And they said, Has **יהוה** indeed spoken only by Moshe? Has He not spoken also by us? And **יהוה** heard it. 3 Now the man Moshe was very meek, above all the men that were upon the face of the earth. 4 And **יהוה** spoke suddenly to Moshe, and to Aharon, and to Miryam, *Come out you three to the Tabernacle of the congregation.* And those three came out. 5 And **יהוה** came down in the pillar of the cloud, and stood in the door of the Tabernacle, and called Aharon and Miryam: and they both came out. 6 *And He said, Hear now My words: If there be a navi among you, I* **יהוה** *will make Myself known to him in a vision, and will speak to him in a dream.* 7 *My servant Moshe is not so, who is faithful in all My bayit.* 8 *With him will I speak mouth to mouth, even apparently, and not in dark speeches; and the form of* **יהוה** *shall he see: why then were you not afraid to speak against My servant Moshe?*[2] 9 And the anger of **יהוה** was kindled against them; and He departed. 10 And the cloud departed from off the Tabernacle; and, see, Miryam became leprous, white as snow: and Aharon looked upon Miryam, and, see, she was leprous. 11 And Aharon said to Moshe, Oh, my master, I beg you, lay not the sin upon us, in which we have done foolishly, and in which we have sinned. 12 Let her not be as one dead, of whom the flesh is half consumed when it comes out of its mother's womb. 13 And Moshe cried to **יהוה**,

saying, Heal her now, O El, I beg You. 14 And **יהוה** said to Moshe, *If her abba had but spit in her face, should she not be ashamed seven days? Let her be shut out from the camp seven days, and after that let her be received in again.*[3] 15 And Miryam was shut out from the camp seven days: and the people journeyed not till Miryam was brought in again. 16 And afterward the people left from Hatzeroth, and pitched in the wilderness of Paran.

Torah Parsha 37
Shlach Lecha 13:1-15:41
Haftarah Yahoshua 2:1-24
Brit Chadasha Ivrim 3:7-19

13 And **יהוה** spoke to Moshe, saying, 2 *Send men that they may search the land of Kanaan, which I give to the children of Yisrael: from every tribe of their ahvot shall you send a man, every one a leader among them.* 3 And Moshe by the command of **יהוה** sent them from the wilderness of Paran: all those men were heads of the children of Yisrael. 4 And these were their names: of the tribe of Reuven, Shammua the son of Zakur. 5 Of the tribe of Shimeon, Shaphat the son of Hori. 6 Of the tribe of Yahudah, Calev the son of Yephunneh.[4] 7 Of the tribe of Yissakar, Igal the son of Yoseph. 8 Of the tribe of Ephraim, Hoshea the son of Nun.[5][6] 9 Of the tribe of Benyamin, Palti the son of Raphu. 10 Of the tribe of Zevulon, Gaddi-El the son of Sodi. 11 Of the tribe of Yoseph, namely, of the tribe of Menashsheh, Gaddi the son of Susi. 12 Of the tribe of Dan, Ammi-El the son of Gemalli. 13 Of the tribe of Asher, Shethur the son of Mikael. 14 Of

---

[1] Racial prejudice in Yisrael is deadly and can lead to further lusting for power and position over others. Racism is a manifestation of a corrupted lev. In Yisrael, as it was in days of old, we are made up of all colors and pigmentations, especially as we recall that Ephraim and Menashsheh carried Hamite dom and brown skin, having been born in Mitzrayim and having an Egyptian mother. Also, Moshe's children were dark-skinned, due to Tzippora being an Ethiopian. So in the restoration of all things, we realize full well that many multitudes of modern day black people are the biological offspring of the true people of Yisrael. While the world may be shocked by the reality of black Jews, we should know our nation's true history better and not find our multicolored nation to be of any great shock or surprise.
[2] First note how YHWH defends His true leaders. If you speak evil of any truly called (not perfect) leader, you are doomed. Also note that the reason Moshe's relationship was above that of the other Yisraelite leaders was due to the fact that he saw YHWH's form. Since the Father has no form, we know of a certainty that he saw Yahshua the Son of YHWH, who was and remains the manifest form of YHWH.

[3] **Kal VaChomer**. If she sins against her earthly father for 7 days of banishment, how much more should her sins against the Heavenly Father be dealt with by some kind of reprimand?
[4] Caleb was not a Jew. His father was not even a biological Yisraelite, yet settled in the tribe of Yahudah.
[5] Yahoshua was an Ephraimite, not a Jew.
[6] These two spies were the true witnesses from the 12, to establish the matter of YHWH's tov report in the earth. The same holds true today. Ephraim proclaims the son of YHWH, and Yahudah proclaims the Torah of YHWH, thereby confirming YHWH's truth in the earth. Even before the breakup of the House of David in 921 BCE, Yahudah and Ephraim were always the two faithful witnesses for YHWH's purposes. Joshua was from Ephraim and Caleb from Judah.

the tribe of Naphtali, Nahvi the son of Vophsi. 15 Of the tribe of Gad, Geu-El the son of Machi. 16 These are the names of the men that Moshe sent to spy out the land. And Moshe called Hoshea the son of Nun Yahoshua.[1] 17 And Moshe sent them to spy out the land of Kanaan, and said to them, Go up this way southward, and go up into the mountain: 18 And see the land, what it is; and the people that dwell there, whether they be strong or weak, few or many; 19 And what the land is that they dwell in, whether it be tov or bad; and what cities there are that they dwell in, whether in tents, or in strongholds; 20 And what the land is, whether it be fat or lean, whether there be wood there, or not. And be of tov courage, and bring of the fruit of the land. Now the time was the time of the first ripe grapes. 21 So they went up, and searched the land from the wilderness of Tzin to Rehov, as men come to Hamath. 22 And they ascended by the south, and came to Hevron; where Ahiman, Sheshai, and Talmai, the children of Anak, were. Now Hevron was built seven years before Zoan in Mitzrayim. 23 And they came to the brook of Eshcol, and cut down from there a branch with one cluster of grapes, and they bore it between the two of them on a pole; and they brought of the pomegranates, and of the figs. 24 The place was called the Brook Eshcol, because of the cluster of grapes that the children of Yisrael cut down from there. 25 And they returned from searching the land after forty days. 26 And they went and came to Moshe, and to Aharon, and to all the congregation of the children of Yisrael, to the wilderness of Paran, to Kadesh; and brought back word to them, and to all the congregation, and shown them the fruit of the land. 27 And they told him, and said, We came to the land where you sent us, and surely it flows with milk and honey; and this is the fruit of it. 28 Nevertheless the people are strong that dwell in the land, and the cities are walled,

and very great: and moreover we saw the children of Anak there. 29 The Amalekites dwell in the land of the south: and the Hittites, and the Yevusites, and the Amorites, dwell in the mountains: and the Kanaanites dwell by the sea, and by the coast of Yarden. 30 And Calev quieted the people before Moshe, and said, Let us go up at once, and possess it; for we are well able to overcome it. 31 But the men that went up with him said, We are not able to go up against the people; for they are stronger than we are. 32 And they brought up an evil report of the land which they had searched to the children of Yisrael, saying, The land, through which we have gone to search, is a land that eats up its inhabitants; and all the people that we saw in it are men of great size. 33 And there we saw the Nephilim, the sons of Anak, who came from the Nephilim: and we were in our own sight as grasshoppers, and so we were in their sight.[2]

14 And the entire congregation lifted up their voice, and cried; and the people wept that night. 2 And all the children of Yisrael murmured against Moshe and against Aharon: and the whole congregation said to them, Would to Elohim that we had died in the land of Mitzrayim! or would to Elohim we had died in this wilderness! 3 And why has יהוה brought us to this land, to kill us by the sword, that our wives and our children should be a prey? Is it not better for us to return to Mitzrayim? 4 And they said one to another, Let us make a leader, and let us return to Mitzrayim. 5 Then Moshe and Aharon fell on their faces before all the congregation of the children of Yisrael. 6 And Yahoshua the son of Nun, and Calev the son of Yephunneh, who were of them that searched the land, tore their clothes: 7 And they spoke to all the company of the children of Yisrael, saying, The land, which we passed through

---

[1] By adding the **yud** and the **vav**, both inserts of the Tetragrammaton letters of YHWH.

[2] It is possible that these **Nephilim** were unclean spirits in the spirit realm after the flood, and then later came back into the daughters of men. Or, Nephiliim may simply be a term for giants, not connected with the events of Genesis 6.

to search it, is an exceedingly tov land. 8 If יהוה delights in us, then He will bring us into this land, and give it to us; a land that flows with milk and honey. 9 Only rebel not against יהוה, neither fear the people of the land; for they are lechem for us: their defence is departed from them, and יהוה is with us: fear them not. 10 But the entire congregation wanted to stone them with stones. And the tifereth of יהוה appeared in the Tabernacle of the congregation before all the children of Yisrael. 11 And יהוה said to Moshe, *How long will this people provoke Me? And how long will it be until they believe us,[1] for all the signs that I have shown among them? 12 I will smite them with the pestilence, and disinherit them, and will make of you a greater goy[2] and mightier than them.* 13 And Moshe said to יהוה, *Then the Mitzrites shall hear it, for You brought up this people in Your might from among them; 14 And they will tell it to the inhabitants of this land: for they have heard that You* יהוה *are among this people, that You* יהוה *are seen face to face, and that Your cloud stands over them, and that You go before them, by day in a pillar of a cloud, and in a pillar of fire by night. 15 Now if You shall kill this entire people as one man, then the nations who have heard of Your fame will speak, saying, 16 Because* יהוה *was not able to bring this people into the land which He swore to them, therefore He has slain them in the wilderness. 17 And now, I beg You, let the power of* יהוה *be great, according as You have spoken, saying, 18* יהוה *is longsuffering, and of great rachamim, forgiving iniquity and transgression, and by no means clearing the guilty, visiting the iniquity of the ahvot upon the children to the third and fourth generation. 19 Pardon, I beg You, the iniquity of this people according to the greatness of Your rachamim, and as You have forgiven this people, from Mitzrayim even until now.*

20 And יהוה said, *I have pardoned according to your word:[3] 21 But as truly as I live, all the earth shall be filled with the tifereth of* יהוה. *22 Because all those men who have seen My tifereth, and My nisim, which I did in Mitzrayim and in the wilderness, and have tempted Me now these ten times, and have not listened to My voice; 23 Surely they shall not see the land that I swore to their ahvot, neither shall any of them that provoked Me see it: 24 But My servant Calev, because he had another Ruach in him, and has followed Me fully, him will I bring into the land where he went; and his zera shall possess it. 25 (Now the Amalekites and the Kanaanites dwelt in the valley) Tomorrow turn, and set out into the wilderness by the derech of the Sea Of Reeds.* 26 And יהוה spoke to Moshe and to Aharon, saying, 27 *How long shall I bear with this evil congregation, who murmur against Me? I have heard the murmurings of the children of Yisrael that they murmur against Me. 28 Say to them, As truly as I live, says* יהוה, *as you have spoken in My ears, so will I do to you: 29 Your carcases shall fall in this wilderness; and all that were numbered among you, according to your whole number, from twenty years old and upward, who have murmured against Me, 30 Doubtless you shall not come into the land, concerning which I swore to make you dwell there, except Calev the son of Yephunneh, and Yahoshua the son of Nun. 31 But your little ones, who you said should be a prey, them will I bring in, and they shall know the land that you have despised.[4] 32 But as for you, your carcasses, they shall fall in this wilderness. 33 And your children shall wander in the wilderness forty years, and bear your whorings, until your carcasses be wasted in the wilderness. 34 After the number of the days in which you searched the land, even forty days, each day for a year, shall you bear your iniquities, even forty years, and you shall know the*

---

[1] **HaAminu** Believe Us - Plurality of YHWH.
[2] Yisrael often called a **goy**, so why should it surprise some that **goyim** or Ephraimites can also be Yisraelites?

[3] Mercy or **rachamim**.
[4] **Rachamim**.

result of straying from Me. 35 *I* יהוה *have said, I will surely do it to this entire evil congregation that are gathered together against Me: in this wilderness they shall be consumed, and there they shall die.* 36 And the men, who Moshe sent to search the land, who returned, and made all the congregation to murmur against Him, by bringing up slander about the land, 37 Even those men that did bring up the evil report from the land, died by the plague before יהוה . 38 But Yahoshua the son of Nun, and Calev the son of Yephunneh, who were of the men that went to search the land, still lived. 39 And Moshe told these sayings to all the children of Yisrael: and the people mourned greatly. 40 And they rose up early in the morning, and got up into the top of the mountain, saying, See, we are here, and will go up to the place which יהוה has promised: for we have sinned. 41 And Moshe said, Why do you now still transgress the command of יהוה ? But it shall not prosper. 42 Go not up, for יהוה is not among you; that you be not smitten by your enemies. 43 For the Amalekites and the Kanaanites are there before you, and you shall fall by the sword: because you are turned away from יהוה, therefore יהוה will not be with you. 44 But they presumed to go up to the hill top: nevertheless the Ark of the Covenant of יהוה, and Moshe, departed not out of the camp. 45 Then the Amalekites came down, and the Kanaanites who dwelt in that hill, and smote them, and beat them down, even to Hormah.

15 And יהוה spoke to Moshe, saying, 2 *Speak to the children of Yisrael, and say to them, When you come into the land of your dwellings, which I give to you, 3 And will make an offering by fire to* יהוה, *a burnt offering, or a sacrifice in performing a vow, or in a freewill offering, or in your moadim, to make a sweet fragrance to* יהוה, *of the herd, or of the flock: 4 Then shall he that offers his offering to* יהוה *bring a grain offering of a tenth deal of flour mingled with the fourth part of a hin of oil. 5 And the fourth part of a hin of wine for a drink offering shall you prepare with the burnt offering or sacrifice, for one lamb. 6 Or for a ram, you shall prepare for a grain offering two tenth deals of flour mingled with the third part of a hin of oil. 7 And for a drink offering you shall offer the third part of a hin of wine, for a sweet fragrance to* יהוה. *8 And when you prepare a bullock for a burnt offering, or for a sacrifice in performing a vow, or shalom offerings to* יהוה: *9 Then shall he bring with a bullock a grain offering of three tenth deals of flour mingled with half a hin of oil. 10 And you shall bring for a drink offering half a hin of wine, for an offering made by fire, of a sweet fragrance to* יהוה. *11 This shall be done for one bullock, or for one ram, or for a lamb, or for a kid. 12 According to the number that you shall prepare, so shall you do to every one according to their number. 13 All that are natives of the country shall do these things after this manner, in offering an offering made by fire, of a sweet fragrance to* יהוה. *14 And if a Ger sojourn with you, or whoever is among you in your generations, and will offer an offering made by fire, of a sweet fragrance to* יהוה; *as you do, so he shall do. 15 One ordinance shall be both for you of the congregation, and also for the Ger that sojourns with you, an ordinance le-olam-va-ed in your generations: as you are, so shall the Ger be before* יהוה. *16 One Torah and one manner shall be for you, and for the Ger that sojourns with you.[1] 17 And* יהוה *spoke to Moshe, saying, 18 Speak to the children of Yisrael, and say to them, When you come into the land where I bring you, 19 Then it shall be, that, when you eat of the lechem of the land, you shall offer up a terumah offering to* יהוה. *20 You shall offer up a cake of the first of your dough for a terumah offering: as you do the terumah offering of the threshing floor, so shall you present it. 21 Of the first of your dough you*

---

[1] The only unifying truth for believers in both covenants.

shall give to יהוה *a terumah offering in your generations. 22 And if you have erred, and not observed all these mitzvot, which* יהוה *has spoken to Moshe, 23 Even all that* יהוה *has commanded you by the hand of Moshe, from the day that* יהוה *commanded Moshe, and onward throughout all your generations; 24 Then it shall be, if anything be committed by ignorance without the knowledge of the congregation, that all the congregation shall offer one young bullock for a burnt offering, for a sweet fragrance to* יהוה, *with its grain offering, and its drink offering, according to the manner, and one kid of the male goats for a sin offering. 25 And the kohen shall make an atonement for all the congregation of the children of Yisrael, and it shall be forgiven them; for it is ignorance: and they shall bring their offering, a sacrifice made by fire to* יהוה, *and their sin offering before* יהוה, *for their ignorance: 26 And it shall be forgiven all the congregation of the children of Yisrael, and the Ger that sojourns among them; seeing all the people were in ignorance. 27 And if any being sin through ignorance, then he shall bring a female goat of the first year for a sin offering. 28 And the kohen shall make an atonement for the being that sins ignorantly, when he sins by ignorance before* יהוה, *to make an atonement for him; and it shall be forgiven him. 29 You shall have one Torah for him that sins through ignorance, both for him that is born among the children of Yisrael, and for the Ger that sojourns among them. 30 But the being that does something defiantly, whether he be born in the land, or a Ger, the same reproaches* יהוה; *and that being shall be cut off from among his people. 31 Because he has despised the word of* יהוה, *and has broken His command, that being shall be utterly be cut off; his iniquity shall be upon him.* 32 And while the children of Yisrael were in the wilderness, they found a man that gathered sticks on the Shabbat day. 33 And they that found him gathering sticks brought him to Moshe and Aharon, and to

the entire congregation. 34 And they put him under guard, because it was not declared what should be done to him. 35 And יהוה said to Moshe, *The man shall be surely put to death: the entire congregation shall stone him with stones outside the camp.* 36 And all the congregation brought him outside the camp, and stoned him with stones, and he died; as יהוה commanded Moshe. 37 And יהוה spoke to Moshe, saying, 38 *Speak to the children of Yisrael, and tell them that they make them tzitziyot in the wings of their garments throughout their generations, and that they put upon the tzitzit of the wings a cord of techelet: 39 And it shall be to you for a tzitzit, that you may look upon it, and remember all the mitzvot of* יהוה, *and do them; and that you seek not after your own lev and your own eyes, after that you used to go whoring: 40 That you may remember, and do all My mitzvot, and be set-apart to Your Elohim. 41 I am* יהוה *Your Elohim, who brought you out of the land of Mitzrayim, to be Your Elohim: I am* יהוה *Your Elohim.*

Torah Parsha Korach 16:1-18:32
Haftarah Schmuel Alef 11:14-12:22
Brit Chadasha Yahudah 1-25

16 Now Korach, the son of Izhar, the son of Kohath, the son of Levi, and Dathan and Aviram, the sons of Eliav, and On, the son of Peleth, sons of Reuven, took men: 2 And they rose up before Moshe, with certain of the children of Yisrael, two hundred fifty leaders of the congregation, famous in the congregation, men of name recognition: 3 And they gathered themselves together against Moshe and against Aharon, and said to them, You take too much upon you, seeing all the congregation is set-apart, every one of them, and יהוה is among them: why then do you lift up yourselves above the congregation of יהוה? 4 And when Moshe heard it, he fell upon his face: 5 And he spoke to Korach and to all his company, saying, Even tomorrow יהוה will show who are His, and who is set-apart; and will cause him to come near to Him: even him whom He has chosen will He cause to come near to Him. 6 Do this; Take censers, Korach, and all your company; 7 And put fire in it, and put incense in them before יהוה tomorrow: and it shall be that the man whom יהוה does choose, he shall be set-apart: you take too much upon you, you sons of Levi. 8 And Moshe said to Korach, Hear, I ask you, you sons of Levi: 9 Is it but a small thing to you, that the Elohim of Yisrael has separated you from the congregation of Yisrael, to bring you near to Himself to do the service of the Tabernacle of יהוה, and to stand before the congregation to serve them? 10 And He has brought you near to Him, and all your brothers the sons of Levi with you: and now you seek the priesthood also? 11 For which cause both you and all your company are gathered together against יהוה: and what is Aharon that you murmur against him? 12 And Moshe sent to call Dathan and Aviram, the sons of Eliav: who said, We will not come up: 13 Is it a small thing that you have brought us up out of a land that flows with milk and honey, to kill us in the wilderness, except perhaps to make yourself a leader over us? 14 Moreover you have not brought us into a land that flows with milk and honey, or given us inheritance of fields and vineyards: will you now put out the eyes of these men? We will not come up. 15 And Moshe was very angry, and said to יהוה, Respect not their offering: I have not taken one donkey from them, neither have I hurt one of them. 16 And Moshe said to Korach, You and all your company come before יהוה with Aharon tomorrow: 17 And take every man his censer, and put incense in them, and bring it before יהוה every man his censer, two hundred fifty censers; you also, and Aharon, each of you his censer. 18 And they took every man his censer, and put fire in them, and laid incense on it, and stood in the door of the Tabernacle of the congregation with Moshe

and Aharon. 19 And Korach gathered the entire congregation against them to the door of the Tabernacle of the congregation: and the tifereth of יהוה appeared to all the congregation. 20 And יהוה spoke to Moshe and to Aharon, saying, 21 *Separate yourselves from among this congregation, that I may consume them in a moment.* 22 And they fell upon their faces, and said, O Elohim, the El of the ruachim of all flesh, shall one man sin, and will you be angry with all the congregation? 23 And יהוה spoke to Moshe, saying, 24 *Speak to the congregation, saying, Move away from around the tents of Korach, Dathan, and Aviram.* 25 And Moshe rose up and went to Dathan and Aviram; and the zachanim of Yisrael followed him. 26 And he spoke to the congregation, saying, Depart, I ask you, from the tents of these wicked men, and touch nothing of theirs, lest you be consumed in all their sins. 27 So they got away from the tents of Korach, Dathan, and Aviram, on every side: and Dathan and Aviram came out, and stood in the door of their tents, and their wives, and their sons, and their little children. 28 And Moshe said, Hereby you shall know that יהוה has sent me to do all these works; for I have not done them from my own lev. 29 If these men die the common death of all men, or if they are visited after the visitation of all men; then יהוה has not sent me. 30 But if יהוה makes a new thing, and the earth opens her mouth, and swallows them up, with all that pertains to them, and they go down quick into the grave; then you shall understand that these men have provoked יהוה. 31 And it came to pass, as he had made an end of speaking all these words, that the ground split open that was under them: 32 And the earth opened its mouth, and swallowed them up, and their houses, and all the men with Korach, and all their goods. 33 They, and all that pertained to them, went down alive into the grave, and the earth closed upon them: and they perished from among the congregation.

34 And all Yisrael that were around them fled at their cry: for they said, Lest the earth swallow us up also. 35 And there came out a fire from יהוה, and consumed the two hundred and fifty men that offered incense. 36 And יהוה spoke to Moshe, saying, 37 *Speak to El-Azar the son of Aharon the kohen, that he take up the censers out of the blaze, and scatter the fire away; for they are set-apart. 38 The censers of these sinners against their own beings, let them make from them broad plates as a covering for the altar: for they offered them before יהוה, therefore they are set-apart: and they shall be a sign to the children of Yisrael.* 39 And El-Azar the kohen took the brazen censers, by which they that were burnt had offered; and they were made broad plates for a covering of the altar: 40 To be a memorial to the children of Yisrael, that no stranger, who is not of the zera of Aharon, come near to offer incense before יהוה; that he be not as Korach, and as his company: as יהוה said to him by the hand of Moshe. 41 But on the next day all the congregation of the children of Yisrael murmured against Moshe and against Aharon, saying, You have killed the people of יהוה. 42 And it came to pass, when the congregation was gathered against Moshe and against Aharon, that they looked toward the Tabernacle of the congregation: and, see, the cloud covered it, and the tifereth of יהוה appeared. 43 And Moshe and Aharon came before the Tabernacle of the congregation. 44 And יהוה spoke to Moshe, saying, 45 *Get you up from among this congregation, that I may consume them in a moment. And they fell upon their faces.* 46 And Moshe said to Aharon, Take a censer, and put fire on it from off the altar, and put on incense, and go quickly to the congregation, and make an atonement for them: for there is anger gone out from יהוה; the plague has begun. 47 And Aharon took as Moshe commanded, and ran into the midst of the congregation; and, see, the plague was begun among the people: and he put on incense, and made atonement for the people. 48 And he stood between the dead and the living; and the plague was stopped. 49 Now they that died in the plague were fourteen thousand seven hundred, besides them that died after the matter of Korach. 50 And Aharon returned to Moshe to the door of the Tabernacle of the congregation: and the plague was stopped.

17 And יהוה spoke to Moshe, saying, 2 *Speak to the children of Yisrael, and take of every one of them a rod according to the bayit of their ahvot, of all their leaders according to the bayit of their ahvot twelve rods: write every man's name upon his rod. 3 And you shall write Aharon's name upon the rod of Levi: for one rod shall be for the head of the bayit of their ahvot. 4 And you shall lay them in the Tabernacle of the congregation before the testimony, where I will meet with you. 5 And it shall come to pass, that the man's rod, whom I shall choose, shall blossom: and I will make to cease from before Me the murmurings of the children of Yisrael, whereby they murmur against you.* 6 And Moshe spoke to the children of Yisrael, and every one of their leaders gave him a rod apiece, for each leader one, according to their ahvot's houses, even twelve rods: and the rod of Aharon was among their rods. 7 And Moshe laid up the rods before יהוה in the Tabernacle of witness. 8 And it came to pass, that on the next day Moshe went into the Tabernacle of witness; and, see, the rod of Aharon for the bayit of Levi had budded, and brought out buds, and bloomed blossoms, and yielded almonds. 9 And Moshe brought out all the rods from before יהוה to all the children of Yisrael: and they looked, and took every man his rod. 10 And יהוה said to Moshe, *Bring Aharon's rod again before the testimony, to be kept for a token against the rebels; and you shall put away their murmurings from Me, that they do not die.* 11 And Moshe did so: as יהוה commanded him, so did he. 12 And the

children of Yisrael spoke to Moshe, saying, See, we die, we perish, we all perish. 13 Whoever comes anywhere near to the Tabernacle of **יהוה** shall die: shall we be consumed with dying?

18

And **יהוה** said to Aharon, *You and your sons and your abba's bayit with you shall bear the iniquity of the Set-Apart-Place: and you and your sons with you shall bear the iniquity of your priesthood. 2 And your brothers also of the tribe of Levi, the tribe of your abba, bring with you, that they may be joined to you, and serve to you: but you and your sons with you shall serve before the Tabernacle of witness. 3 And they shall keep your duty, and the duty of the entire Tabernacle: only they shall not come near the vessels of the Set-Apart-Place and the altar that neither they, nor you also, die. 4 And they shall be joined to you, and keep the duty of the Tabernacle of the congregation, for all the service of the Tabernacle: and a Ger shall not come near to you. 5 And you shall keep the duty of the Set-Apart-Place, and the duty of the altar: that there be no wrath any more upon the children of Yisrael. 6 And I, see, I have taken your brothers the Leviim from among the children of Yisrael: to you they are given as a gift from* **יהוה**, *to do the service of the Tabernacle of the congregation. 7 Therefore you and your sons with you shall shomer your kohen's office for all things pertaining to the altar, and inside the vail; and you shall serve: I have given your kohen's office to you as a gift for service: and the stranger that comes near shall be put to death.* 8 And **יהוה** spoke to Aharon, *See, I also have given you the duty of My terumah offerings of all the set-apart things of the children of Yisrael; to you have I given them by reason of the anointing, and to your sons, by an ordinance le-olam-va-ed. 9 This shall be yours of the most set-apart things, reserved from the fire: every oblation of theirs, every grain offering of theirs, and every sin offering of theirs, and every trespass offering of theirs, which they shall render to Me, shall be most set-apart for you and for your sons. 10 In the most Set-Apart-Place shall you eat it; every male shall eat it: it shall be set-apart to you. 11 And this is yours; the terumah offering of their gift, with all the wave offerings of the children of Yisrael: I have given them to you, and to your sons and to your daughters with you, by a chuk le-olam-va-ed: every one that is clean in your bayit shall eat of it. 12 All the best of the oil, and all the best of the wine, and of the wheat, the firstfruits of them which they shall offer to* **יהוה**, *them have I given you. 13 And whatever is first ripe in the land, which they shall bring to* **יהוה**, *shall be yours; every one that is clean in your bayit shall eat of it. 14 Everything devoted in Yisrael shall be yours. 15 Everything that opens the womb in all flesh, which they bring to* **יהוה**, *whether it be of men or beasts, shall be yours: nevertheless the bachor of man shall you surely redeem, and the firstling of unclean beasts shall you redeem. 16 And those that are to be redeemed from a month old shall you redeem, according to your estimation, for the money of five shekels, after the shekel of the Set-Apart-Place, which is twenty gerahs. 17 But the firstling of a cow, or the firstling of a sheep, or the firstling of a goat, you shall not redeem; they are set-apart: you shall sprinkle their dom upon the altar, and shall burn their fat for an offering made by fire, for a sweet fragrance to* **יהוה**. *18 And the meat of them shall be yours, as the wave breast and as the right thigh are yours. 19 All the terumah offerings of the set-apart things, which the children of Yisrael offer to* **יהוה**, *have I given you, and your sons and your daughters with you, by a chuk le-olam-va-ed: it is a covenant of salt le-olam-va-ed before* **יהוה** *to you and to your zera with you. 20 And* **יהוה** *spoke to Aharon, You shall have no inheritance in their land, neither shall you have any part among them: I am your part and your* inheritance among the children of Yisrael. 21 And, see, I have given the children of Levi all the tenth in Yisrael for an inheritance, for their service in which they serve, even the service of the Tabernacle of the congregation. 22 Neither must the children of Yisrael from now on come near the Tabernacle of the congregation, lest they bear sin, and die. 23 But the Leviim shall do the service of the Tabernacle of the congregation, and they shall bear their iniquity: it shall be a chuk le-olam-va-ed throughout your generations, that among the children of Yisrael they have no inheritance. 24 But the ma'aser of the children of Yisrael, which they offer as a terumah offering to יהוה, I have given to the Leviim to inherit: therefore I have said to them, Among the children of Yisrael they shall have no inheritance. 25 And יהוה spoke to Moshe, saying, 26 Speak to the Leviim, and say to them, When you take from the children of Yisrael the ma'aser which I have given you from them for your inheritance, then you shall offer up a terumah offering of it for יהוה, even a tenth part of the tithe. 27 And your terumah offering shall be reckoned to you, as though it were the corn of the threshing floor, and as the fullness of the winepress. 28 So you also shall offer a terumah offering to יהוה of all your ma'aser, that you receive from the children of Yisrael; and you shall give of it יהוה's terumah offering to Aharon the kohen. 29 Out of all your gifts you shall offer every terumah offering to יהוה, of all the best of it, even the set-apart part of it out of it. 30 Therefore you shall say to them, When you have heaved the best of it from it, then it shall be counted to the Leviim as the increase of the threshing floor, and as the increase of the winepress. 31 And you shall eat it in every place, you and your households: for it is your reward for your service in the Tabernacle of the congregation. 32 And you shall bear no sin by reason of it, when you have heaved the best of it: neither shall you pollute the set-

apart things of the children of Yisrael, lest you die.

Torah Parsha 39
Chukkat 19:1-22:1
In regular years, read with Pasrsha 40.
In 13 month-years read separately.
Haftarah Shophtim 11:1-33
Brit Chadasha Yochanan 3:9-21

19 And יהוה spoke to Moshe and to Aharon, saying, 2 This is the ordinance of the Torah which יהוה has commanded, saying, Speak to the children of Yisrael, that they bring you a red heifer without spot, in which is no blemish, and upon which never came a yoke: 3 And you shall give her to El-Azar the kohen, that he may bring it out outside the camp, and one shall slay it before him: 4 And El-Azar the kohen shall take of its dom with his finger, and sprinkle of its dom directly before the Tabernacle of the congregation seven times: 5 And one shall burn the heifer in his sight; its skin, and its flesh, and its dom, with its dung, shall he burn: 6 And the kohen shall take cedarwood, and hyssop, and scarlet, and cast it into the midst of the burning of the heifer. 7 Then the kohen shall wash his clothes, and he shall bath his body in mayim, and afterward he shall come into the camp, and the kohen shall be unclean until the evening. 8 And he that burns it shall wash his clothes in mayim, and bathe his body in mayim, and shall be unclean until the evening. 9 And a man that is clean shall gather up the ashes of the heifer, and lay them up outside the camp in a clean place, and it shall be kept for the congregation of the children of Yisrael for a mayim of separation: it is for purification for sin. 10 And he that gathers the ashes of the heifer shall wash his clothes, and be unclean until the evening: and it shall be to the children of Yisrael, and to the Ger that sojourns among them, for a law le-olam-va-ed. 11 He that touches the dead body of any man shall be unclean seven days. 12 He shall purify himself with it on the third day, *and on the seventh day he shall be clean: but if he does not purify not himself the third day, then the seventh day he shall not be clean. 13 Whosoever touches the dead body of any man that is dead, and purifies not himself, defiles the Tabernacle of* יהוה*; and that being shall be cut off from Yisrael: because the mayim of separation was not sprinkled upon him, he shall be unclean; his uncleanness is yet upon him. 14 This is the Torah, of when a man dies in a tent: all that come into the tent, and all that is in the tent, shall be unclean seven days. 15 And every open vessel, which has no covering fastened upon it, is unclean. 16 And whoever touches one that is slain with a sword in the open fields, or a dead body, or a bone of a man, or a grave, shall be unclean seven days. 17 And for an unclean person they shall take of the ashes of the burnt heifer of purification for sin, and running mayim shall be put into a vessel: 18 And a clean person shall take hyssop, and dip it in the mayim, and sprinkle it upon the tent, and upon all the vessels, and upon the persons that were there, and upon him that touched a bone, or one slain, or one dead, or a grave: 19 And the clean person shall sprinkle upon the unclean on the third day, and on the seventh day: and on the seventh day he shall purify himself, and wash his clothes, and bathe himself in mayim, and shall be clean at evening. 20 But the man that shall be unclean, and shall not purify himself, that being shall be cut off from among the congregation, because he has defiled the Set-Apart-Place of* יהוה *: the mayim of separation has not been sprinkled upon him; he is unclean. 21 And it shall be a perpetual chuk to them, that he that sprinkles the mayim of separation shall wash his clothes; and he that touches the mayim of separation shall be unclean until evening. 22 And whatever the unclean person touches shall be unclean; and the being that touches it shall be unclean until evening.*

20 Then came the children of Yisrael, even the whole congregation, into the desert of Tzin in the first month: and the people stayed in Kadesh; and Miryam died there, and was buried there. 2 And there was no mayim for the congregation: and they gathered themselves together against Moshe and against Aharon. 3 And the people contended with Moshe, and spoke, saying, Would to Elohim that we had died when our brothers died before יהוה! 4 And why have you brought up the congregation of יהוה into this wilderness, that we and our cattle should die there? 5 And why have you made us to come up out of Mitzrayim, to bring us into this evil place? It is not a place of seed, or of figs, or of vines, or of pomegranates; neither is there any mayim to drink. 6 And Moshe and Aharon went from the presence of the congregation to the door of the Tabernacle of the congregation, and they fell upon their faces: and the tifereth of יהוה appeared to them. 7 And יהוה spoke to Moshe, saying, 8 *Take the rod, and gather the congregation together, you, and Aharon your brother, and speak to the Rock before their eyes; and it shall give out its mayim, and you shall bring them mayim out of the Rock: so you shall give the congregation and their beasts drink.*[1] 9 And Moshe took the rod from before יהוה, as He commanded him. 10 And Moshe and Aharon gathered the congregation together before the Rock, and he said to them, Hear now, you rebels; must we fetch you mayim out of this Rock? 11 And Moshe lifted up his hand, and with his rod he smote the Rock twice:[2] and the mayim came out abundantly, and the congregation drank, and their beasts also. 12 And יהוה spoke to Moshe and Aharon, *Because you believed Me not, to set Me apart in the eyes of the*

---

[1] Father's care for Yisrael.
[2] That Rock was Moshiach (First Corinthians 10:4) and as such we speak to Him, and He provides living water for us. Moshe not only did not speak to the Rock, but also hit it twice, when Moshiach would only be smitten once, thereby misrepresenting YHWH, a grievous sin that YHWH calls a failure to set Him apart by revealing His plan as something different than it would actually one day be.

children of Yisrael, therefore you shall not bring this congregation into the land which I have given them. 13 This is the mayim of Merivah; because the children of Yisrael strove with **יהוה**, and He was set-apart in them. 14 And Moshe sent messengers from Kadesh to the melech of Edom, This says your brother Yisrael, You know all the travail that has befallen us: 15 How our ahvot went down into Mitzrayim, and we had dwelt in Mitzrayim a long time; and the Mitzrites did evil to us, and our ahvot: 16 And when we cried to **יהוה**, He heard our voice, and sent a Malach, and has brought us out out of Mitzrayim: and, see, we are in Kadesh, a city on the edge of your border: 17 Let us pass, I ask you, through your country: we will not pass through the fields, or through the vineyards, neither will we drink of the mayim of the wells: we will go by the melech's highway, we will not turn to the right hand nor to the left, until we have passed your borders. 18 And Edom said to him, You shall not pass by me, lest I come out against you with the sword. 19 And the children of Yisrael said to him, We will go by the highway: and if my cattle and I drink of your mayim, then I will pay for it: Let me only pass through on foot without a word. 20 And he said, You shall not go through. And Edom came out against him with much people, and with a strong hand. 21 Thus Edom refused to give Yisrael passage through his border: therefore Yisrael turned away from him. 22 And the children of Yisrael, even the whole congregation, journeyed from Kadesh, and came to Mount Hor. 23 And **יהוה** spoke to Moshe and Aharon in Mount Hor, by the coast of the land of Edom, saying, 24 *Aharon shall be gathered to his people: for he shall not enter into the land that I have given to the children of Yisrael, because you rebelled against My word at the mayim of Merivah. 25 Take Aharon and El-Azar his son, and bring them up to Mount Hor: 26 And strip Aharon of his garments, and put them upon El-Azar his*

son: and Aharon shall be gathered to his people, and shall die there. 27 And Moshe did as **יהוה** commanded: and they went up into Mount Hor in the sight of the entire congregation. 28 And Moshe stripped Aharon of his garments, and put them upon El-Azar his son; and Aharon died there at the top of the Mount: and Moshe and El-Azar came down from the Mount. 29 And when the entire congregation saw that Aharon was dead, they mourned for Aharon thirty days, even all Beit Yisrael.

21 And when melech Arad the Kanaanite, who dwelt in the south, heard tell that Yisrael came by the way of the spies; then he fought against Yisrael, and took some of them prisoners. 2 And Yisrael vowed a vow to **יהוה**, and said, If You will indeed deliver this people into my hand, and then I will utterly destroy their cities. 3 And **יהוה** listened to the voice of Yisrael, and delivered up the Kanaanites; and they utterly destroyed them and their cities: and he called the name of the place Hormah. 4 And they journeyed from Mount Hor by the way of the Sea Of Reeds, to go around the land of Edom: and the beings of the people were very discouraged because of this route. 5 And the people spoke against Elohim, and against Moshe, Why have you brought us up out of Mitzrayim to die in the wilderness? For there is no lechem, and neither is there any mayim, and our being hates this light lechem. 6 And **יהוה** sent fiery serpents among the people, and they bit the people; and many of the people of Yisrael died. 7 Therefore the people came to Moshe, and said, We have sinned, for we have spoken against **יהוה**, and against you; ask **יהוה** , that He may take away the serpents from us. And Moshe made tefillah for the people. 8 And **יהוה** said to Moshe, *Make you a fiery serpent, and set it upon a pole: and it shall come to pass, that everyone that is bitten, when he looks upon it, shall live.* 9 And Moshe made a serpent of brass, and put it upon a pole, and it came

to pass, that if a serpent had bitten any man, when he looked at the serpent of brass, he lived. 10 And the children of Yisrael set forward, and pitched in Ovoth. 11 And they journeyed from Ovoth, and pitched at Iye Ha-Avarim, in the wilderness that is before Moav, toward the sunrising. 12 From there they moved, and pitched in the valley of Zered. 13 From there they moved, and pitched on the other side of Arnon, which is in the wilderness that comes out of the coasts of the Amorites: for Arnon is the border of Moav, between Moav and the Amorites. 14 Therefore it is said in the Scroll of the Wars of **יהוה**,[1] what He did in the Sea Of Reeds, and in the brooks of Arnon, 15 And at the stream of the brooks that goes down to the dwelling of Ar, and lies upon the border of Moav. 16 And from there they went to Beer: that is the well of which **יהוה** had spoken to Moshe, *Gather the people together, and I will give them mayim.* 17 Then Yisrael sang this shir, Spring up O well; sing to it: 18 The leaders digged the well, the nobles of the people digged it, by the direction of the Torah-Giver, with their shovels. And from the wilderness they went to Mattanah: 19 And from Mattanah to Nahali-El: and from Nahali-El to Bamoth: 20 And from Bamoth in the valley, that is in the country of Moav, to the top of Pisgah, which looks toward Yeshimon. 21 And Yisrael sent messengers to Sihon melech of the Amorites, saying, 22 Let me pass through your land: we will not turn into the fields, or into the vineyards; we will not drink of the mayim of the well: but we will go along by the melech's highway, until we are past your borders. 23 And Sihon would not allow Yisrael to pass through his border: but Sihon gathered all his people together, and went out against Yisrael into the wilderness: and he came to Yahatz, and fought against Yisrael. 24 And Yisrael smote him with the edge of the sword, and possessed his land from Arnon to Yavvok, even to the children

of Ammon: for the border of the children of Ammon was strong. 25 And Yisrael took all these cities: and Yisrael dwelt in all the cities of the Amorites, in Cheshbon, and in all the villages of it. 26 For Cheshbon was the city of Sihon the melech of the Amorites, who had fought against the former melech of Moav, and taken all his land out of his hand, even to Arnon. 27 Wherefore they that speak in proverbs say, Come into Cheshbon, let the city of Sihon be built and prepared: 28 For there is a fire gone out of Cheshbon, a flame from the city of Sihon: it has consumed Ar of Moav, and the masters of the high places of Arnon. 29 Woe to you, Moav! you are undone, O people of Chemosh: he has given his sons that escaped, and his daughters, into captivity to Sihon melech of the Amorites. 30 We have shot at them; Cheshbon is perished even to Divon, and we have laid them waste even to Nophah, which reaches to Medeva. 31 So Yisrael dwelt in the land of the Amorites. 32 And Moshe sent to spy out Yaatzer, and they took the villages of it, and drove out the Amorites that were there. 33 And they turned and went up by the way of Bashan: and Og the melech of Bashan went out against them, he, and all his people, to the battle at Edrei. 34 And **יהוה** said to Moshe, *Fear him not: for I have delivered him into your hand, and all his people, and his land; and you shall do to him as you did to Sihon melech of the Amorites, who dwelt at Cheshbon.* 35 So they smote him, and his sons, and all his people, until there was none left him alive: and they possessed his land.

22 And the children of Yisrael set forward, and pitched in the plains of Moav on this side of the Yarden by Yericho.

---

[1] Now extinct.

Torah Parsha 40
Balak 22:2-25:9
In regular 12-month years,
read with Pasrsha 39.
In 13-month years read separately.
Haftarah Mikah 5:6-6:8
Brit Chadasha Kefa Bet 2:1-22

2 And Balak the son of Tzippor saw all that Yisrael had done to the Amorites. 3 And Moav was very afraid of the people, because they were many: [1] and Moav was distressed because of the children of Yisrael. 4 And Moav said to the zachanim of Midyan, Now shall this company lick up all that are around us, as the ox licks up the grass of the field. And Balak the son of Tzippor was melech of the Moavites at that time. 5 He sent messengers therefore to Bilam the son of Beor to Pethor, which is by the river of the land of the children of his people, to call him, saying, See, there is a people come out from Mitzrayim: see, they cover the face of the earth, and they abide opposite me: [2] 6 Come now therefore, I ask you, curse for me this people; for they are too mighty for me: perhaps I shall prevail, that we may smite them, and then I may drive them out of the land: for I know that he whom you bless is blessed, and he whom you curse is cursed. 7 And the zachanim of Moav and the zachanim of Midyan departed with the rewards of divination in their hand; and they came to Bilam, and spoke to him the words of Balak. 8 And he said to them, Stay here this night, and I will bring you word again, as יהוה shall speak to me: and the leaders of Moav stayed with Bilam. 9 And Elohim came to Bilam, and said, *What men are these with you?* 10 And Bilam said to Elohim, Balak the son of Tzippor, melech of Moav, has sent to me, saying, 11 See, there is a people come out of Mitzrayim, who cover the face of the earth: [3] come now, curse them; perhaps I then shall

be able to overcome them, and drive them out. 12 And Elohim said to Bilam, *You shall not go with them; you shall not curse the people: for they are blessed.* 13 And Bilam rose up in the morning, and said to the leaders of Balak, Get into your land: for יהוה refuses to give me leave to go with you. 14 And the leaders of Moav rose up, and they went to Balak, and said, Bilam refuses to come with us. 15 And Balak sent again more leaders, and more honorable than them. 16 And they came to Bilam, and said to him, This says Balak the son of Tzippor, Let nothing, I ask you, hinder you from coming to me: 17 For I will promote you to very great honor, and I will do whatever you say to me: come therefore, I ask you, curse for me this people. 18 And Bilam answered and said to the avadim of Balak, If Balak would give me his bayit full of silver and gold, I cannot go beyond the word of יהוה my Elohim, to do less or more. 19 Now therefore, I ask you, stay here also tonight, that I may know what more יהוה will say to me. 20 And Elohim came to Bilam at night, and said to him, *If the men come to call you, rise up, and go with them; but only the word that I shall say to you, that shall you do.* 21 And Bilam rose up in the morning, and saddled his donkey, and went with the leaders of Moav. 22 And Elohim's anger was kindled because he went: and the Malach-יהוה [4] stood in the way as an adversary against him. Now he was riding upon his donkey, and his two avadim were with him. 23 And the donkey saw the Malach of יהוה standing in the way, and His sword drawn in His hand: and the donkey turned aside out of the way, and went into the field: and Bilam smote the donkey, to turn her back on the way. 24 But the Malach of יהוה stood in a path of the vineyards, a wall being on this side, and a wall on that side. 25 And when the donkey saw the Malach of יהוה, she thrust herself to the wall, and crushed Bilam's foot against

---

[1] Large multitudes.
[2] Funny how pagans can see Yisrael's blessing of filling the earth, even in those days.
[3] Probably the largest nation numerically speaking in the ancient world. All their enemies from Egypt to Edom and here to Moab recognized this fact.

---

[4] Yahshua or **Metatron**, "the Guardian" of Yisrael.

the wall: and he smote her again. 26 And the Malach of יהוה went further, and stood in a narrow place, where was no way to turn either to the right hand or to the left. 27 And when the donkey saw the Malach of יהוה, she fell down under Bilam: and Bilam's anger was kindled, and he smote the donkey with his staff. 28 And יהוה opened the mouth of the donkey, and she said to Bilam, What have I done to you, that you have smitten me these three times? 29 And Bilam said to the donkey, Because you have mocked me: I wish there were a sword in my hand, for now would I kill you. 30 And the donkey said to Bilam, Am not I your donkey, upon which you have ridden ever since I was yours to this day? Was I ever inclined to do this to you? And he said, No. 31 Then יהוה opened the eyes of Bilam, and he saw the Malach of יהוה standing in the way, and His sword drawn in His hand: and he bowed down his head, and fell flat on his face.[1] 32 And the Malach of יהוה said to him, *Why have you smitten your donkey these three times? See, I went out to stand against you, because your way is perverted before Me: 33 And the donkey saw Me, and turned from Me these three times: unless she had turned from Me, surely now also I had slain you, and saved her alive.* 34 And Bilam said to the Malach of יהוה, I have sinned; for I knew not that You stood in the derech against me: now therefore, if it displeases You, I will go back again. 35 And the Malach of יהוה said to Bilam, *Go with the men: but only the word that I shall speak to you, that you shall speak.*[2] So Bilam went with the leaders of Balak. 36 And when Balak heard that Bilam was come, he went out to meet him at a city of Moav, which is in the border of Arnon, which is in the border coast. 37 And Balak said to Bilam, Did I not urgently send for you to call you? Why did you delay in coming to me? Am I not able indeed to promote you to honor? 38 And Bilam said to Balak, See, I have come to you: do I now have any power at all to say something? The word that Elohim puts in my mouth, that shall I speak.[3] 39 And Bilam went with Balak, and they came to Kiryath-Huzoth. 40 And Balak offered cattle and sheep, and sent to Bilam, and to the leaders that were with him. 41 And it came to pass on the next day, that Balak took Bilam, and brought him up into the high places of Baal, that there he might see the outside part of the people.

23 And Bilam said to Balak, Build me here seven altars, and prepare for me here seven bulls and seven rams. 2 And Balak did as Bilam had spoken; and Balak and Bilam offered on every altar a bullock and a ram. 3 And Bilam said to Balak, Stand by your burnt offering, and I will go: perhaps יהוה will come to meet me: and whatever He shows me I will tell you. And he went to a high place. 4 And Elohim met Bilam: and he said to Him, I have prepared seven altars, and I have offered upon every altar a bullock and a ram. 5 And יהוה put a word in Bilam's mouth, and said, *Return to Balak, and so you shall speak.* 6 And he returned to him, and, see, he stood by his burnt sacrifice, he, and all the leaders of Moav. 7 And he took up his mishle, and said, Balak the melech of Moav has brought me from Aram, out of the mountains of the east, saying, Come, curse for me Yaakov, and come, rage at Yisrael. 8 How shall I curse, whom El has not cursed? Or how shall I rage, at he whom יהוה has not raged? 9 For from the top of the rocks I see Him, and from the hills I see Him: look, a people dwelling alone, and shall not be

---

[1] Further proof that this is Metatron, the Guardian of Yisrael, or the Son of Yah. Here He receives worship.
[2] Here this Malach speaks YHWH's word with authority, as if He's delivering it in the first person.

[3] The same Elohim that was the Malach that met Him, and guarded Yisrael from a curse.

reckoned among the nations.[1] 10 Who can count the dust of Yaakov, and the number of the fourth part of Yisrael?[2] Let me die the death of the tzadik, and let my last end be like his! 11 And Balak said to Bilam, What have you done to me? I took you to curse my enemies, and, see, you have kept on blessing. 12 And he answered and said, Must I not take heed to speak that, which יהוה has put in my mouth? 13 And Balak said to him, Come, I ask you, with me to another place, from where you may see them: you shall see only the extremity, and shall not see them all: and curse them for me from there. 14 And he brought him into the field of Tzophim, to the top of Pisgah, and built seven altars, and offered a bullock and a ram on every altar. 15 And he said to Balak, Stand here by your burnt offering, while I meet יהוה there. 16 And יהוה met Bilam, and put a word in his mouth, and said, *Go again to Balak, and say this.* 17 And when he came to him, see, he stood by his burnt offering, and the leaders of Moav with him. And Balak said to him, What has יהוה spoken? 18 And he took up his mishle, and said, Rise up, Balak, and hear; listen to me, you son of Tzippor: 19 El is not a man, that He should lie, neither a ben-adam, that He should repent: has He said, and shall He not do it? Or has He spoken, and shall He not make it tov? 20 See, I have received an order to bless: and He has blessed; and I cannot reverse it. 21 He has not beheld iniquity in Yaakov, neither has He seen perverseness in Yisrael: יהוה His Elohim is with him, and the shout of a Melech is among them.[3] 22 El brought

them out of Mitzrayim; He has as it were the strength of a wild ox.[4] 23 Surely there is no enchantment against Yaakov, neither is there any divination against Yisrael: according to this time it shall be said of Yaakov and of Yisrael, What El has done![5] 24 See, the people shall rise up as a great lion, and lift up himself as a young lion: he shall not lie down until he eats of the prey, and drinks the dom of the slain.[6] 25 And Balak said to Bilam, Neither curse them at all, nor bless them at all. 26 But Bilam answered and said to Balak, Did I not tell you, saying, All that יהוה speaks, that I must do? 27 And Balak said to Bilam, Come, I ask you, I will bring you to another place; perhaps it will please Elohim that you may curse them for me from there.[7] 28 And Balak brought Bilam to the top of Peor looking toward Yeshimon. 29 And Bilam said to Balak, Build me here seven altars, and prepare me here seven bullocks and seven rams. 30 And Balak did as Bilam had said, and offered a bullock and a ram on every altar.

24 And when Bilam saw that it pleased יהוה to bless Yisrael, he went not, as at other times, to seek for enchantments, but he set his face toward the wilderness. 2 And Bilam lifted up his eyes, and he saw Yisrael abiding in his tents according to their tribes; and the Ruach of Elohim came upon him. 3 And he took up his mishle, and said, Bilam the son of Beor has said, and the man whose eyes are open has said: 4 He has said, who heard the words of El, who saw the vision of the Almighty, falling into a trance, but having his eyes open: 5 How tov are your tents, O

---

[1] Despite the prophet's madness and greed, YHWH used him to deliver some startling end-time prophecies and insights. Here he declares that Yisrael will be a nation set apart from all nations, so that in heaven's view, Yisrael is not reckoned among the nations, meaning all citizens from both redeemed houses of Yisrael are not to be counted or reckoned as pagans or gentiles from among the nations, but rather as the Commonwealth of Yisrael.
[2] Here YHWH's Ruach declares that 25% of Yisrael's population is so large that it cannot be counted. This may seem like a metaphor, but remember, this was the day of no computers or calculators.
[3] A messianic prophecy that one day YHWH will see Yisrael as a pure spotless bride, when the King Elohim Moshiach arrives

to shouts of Halleluyah, as He is coming to remove all iniquity from Yisrael.
[4] A wild ox, with strength in two horns, to push the people of Yaakov to the ends of the earth.
[5] Divination cannot work against Yisrael, since Yisrael's Torah forbids divination, and the people are guarded from it.
[6] A prophecy of Yisrael's powerful and overwhelming entry into the Promised Land.
[7] Pagan practice of associating access to their Elohim with shifting places of worship as we find in John chapter 4.

Yaakov, and your tabernacles, O Yisrael![1]
6 As the valleys are they spread out, as gardens by the river's side, as the eytzim of aloes that **יהוה** has planted, and as cedar eytzim beside the mayim. 7 He shall pour the mayim out of his buckets, and his zera shall be in many mayim, and his melech shall be higher than Agag, and his malchut shall be exalted.[2] 8 El brought him out out of Mitzrayim; He has as it were the strength of a wild ox: He shall eat up the nations His enemies, and shall break their bones, and pierce them through with His arrows.[3] 9 He couched, He lay down as a Lion, and as a great Lion: who shall stir Him up?[4] Blessed is he that blesses you, and cursed is he that curses you.[5] 10 And Balak's anger was kindled against Bilam, and he smote his hands together: and Balak said to Bilam, I called you to curse my enemies, and, see, you have continued to bless them these three times. 11 Therefore now flee to your place: I sought to promote you to great honor; but see, **יהוה** has kept you back from honor. 12 And Bilam said to Balak, Did not I speak also to your messengers whom you sent to me, saying, 13 If Balak would give me his bayit full of silver and gold, I cannot go beyond the command of **יהוה**, to do either tov or bad of my own mind; but what **יהוה** says, that will I speak? 14 And now, see, I go to my people: come therefore, and I will advise you what this people Yisrael shall do to your people in the latter-days. 15 And he took up his mishle, and said, Bilam the son of Beor has said, and the man whose eyes are open has said: 16 He has said, who heard the words of Elohim, and knew the knowledge of the most High, who saw the vision of the

Almighty, falling into a trance, but having his eyes open: 17 *I shall see Him, but not now: I shall see Him, but not near: there shall come a Chochav out of Yaakov, and a Sceptre shall rise out of Yisrael, and shall smite the corners of Moav, and destroy all the children of Sheth.[6] 18 And Edom shall be a possession, Seir also shall be a possession for his enemies; and Yisrael shall do valiantly.[7] 19 Out of Yaakov shall He come that shall have dominion, and shall destroy the remains of the city.[8]*
20 And when he looked on Amalek, he took up his mishle, and said, Amalek was the first of the nations; but his latter-end shall be that he perishes le-olam-va-ed.[9] 21 And he looked on the Qeynites, and took up his mishle, and said, Strong is your dwelling place, and you put your nest in a rock. 22 Nevertheless the Qeynite shall be wasted, until Asshur shall take you captive.[10] 23 And he took up his mishle, and said, Oh, who shall live when El does this! 24 And ships shall come from the coast of Chittim,[11] and shall afflict Ashshur; and shall afflict the Ivrim; they also shall perish le-olam-va-ed.[12] 25 And Bilam rose up, and went and returned to his place: and Balak also went his way.

25 And Yisrael stayed in Shittim, and the people began to whore with the daughters of Moav. 2 And they called the people to the sacrifices of their elohim: and

---

[1] **Mah tovu ohalecha Yaakov mishkenotecha Yisrael.** The famous liturgy is taken from here.
[2] A prophecy of Yisrael's seed being in many waters, or in many nations of the earth, and not limited to the Promised Land. The exalted king is David, and the kingdom is his, and ultimately his Son's the Moshiach, whose kingdom is an everlasting kingdom.
[3] Military strength of many later-day Yisraelite nations.
[4] A reference to the King Moshiach Yahshua, coming forth from Yahudah.
[5] A renewal of the promise to the patriarchs.

[6] As stated in verse 14, this is a latter-day prophecy of the reign of Yisrael in the kingdom of heaven over all the earth and of all the enemies of our people being subdued. The star is **kochav** in Hebrew and is a reference to the King Moshiach, who will set up his end-time kingdom and subdue all YHWH's enemies. The star may have been a reference to the **kochav** of Bethlehem announcing Yahshua's birth to mankind, as His star rose in the east and then rose over Yisrael as a sign of Moshiach's birth. The scepter or **shevet** is the rule that will come over the earth through Yisrael's end-time King. The enemies that are specified to be conquered are Esau's sons and the illegitimate sons of Lot, the Moabites and Ammonites.
[7] See note on verse 17.
[8] See note on verse 17.
[9] Yisrael's enemies wind up with the curses.
[10] A prophecy of Ephraim Yisrael's exile into Assyria and control over Canaan until then.
[11] Lands of the east including China.
[12] Aramaic Peshitta. A possible reference to the Babylonians from the east who conquered the Medo-Persians, who conquered the Assyrians, and who also afflicted the Hebrews.

the people did eat, and bowed down to their elohim. 3 And Yisrael joined himself to Baal-Peor: and the anger of יהוה was kindled against Yisrael. 4 And יהוה said to Moshe, *Take all the heads of the people, and hang them up before יהוה before the sun, that the fierce anger of יהוה may be turned away from Yisrael.* 5 And Moshe said to the shophtim of Yisrael, Slay everyone his men that were joined to Baal-Peor. 6 And, see, one of the children of Yisrael came and brought to his brothers a Midyanite woman in the sight of Moshe, and in the sight of all the congregation of the children of Yisrael, who were weeping before the door of the Tabernacle of the congregation. 7 And when Pinchus, the son of El-Azar, the son of Aharon the kohen, saw it, he rose up from among the congregation, and took a javelin in his hand; 8 And he went after the man of Yisrael into the tent, and thrust both of them through, the man of Yisrael, and the woman through her belly. So the plague was stopped from the children of Yisrael. 9 And those that died in the plague were twenty-four thousand.

Pinchus 25:10-29:40
Haftarah Melechim Alef 18:46-19:21
Brit Chadasha MaAseh Shlichim 2:1-21

10 And יהוה spoke to Moshe, saying, 11 *Pinchus, the son of El-Azar, the son of Aharon the kohen, has turned My wrath back from the children of Yisrael, while he was zealous for My sake among them, that I consumed not the children of Yisrael in My jealousy. 12 Therefore say, See, I give to him My covenant of shalom: 13 And he shall have it, and his zera after him, even the covenant of an everlasting priesthood; because he was zealous for His Elohim, and made atonement for the children of Yisrael.[1]* 14 Now the name of the Yisraelite that was

slain, with the Midyanite woman, was Zimri, the son of Salu, a leader of an abba's bayit among the Shimeonites. 15 And the name of the Midyanite woman that was slain was Kozbi, the daughter of Tzur; he was head over a people, and of an abba's bayit in Midyan. 16 And יהוה spoke to Moshe, saying, 17 *Distress the Midyanites, and smite them: 18 For they distressed you with their tricks, by which they have beguiled you in the matter of Peor, and in the matter of Kozbi, the daughter of a leader of Midyan, their sister, who was slain in the day of the plague because of the matter of Peor.*

26 And it came to pass after the plague that יהוה spoke to Moshe and to El-Azar the son of Aharon the kohen, saying, 2 *Take a census of all the congregation of the children of Yisrael, from twenty years old and upward, throughout their abba's bayit, all that are able to go to war in Yisrael.* 3 And Moshe and El-Azar the kohen spoke with them in the plains of Moav by Yarden near Yericho, saying, 4 Take the census of the people, from twenty years old and upward; as יהוה commanded Moshe and the children of Yisrael, who went out out of the land of Mitzrayim. 5 Reuven, the eldest son of Yisrael: the children of Reuven; Hanoch, of whom comes the mishpacha of the Hanochites: of Pallu, the mishpacha of the Palluites: 6 Of Hetzron, the mishpacha of the Hetzronites: of Carmi, the mishpacha of the Carmites. 7 These are the mishpachot of the Reuvenites: and they that were numbered from them were forty three thousand seven hundred thirty. 8 And the sons of Pallu; Eliav. 9 And the sons of Eliav; Nemu-El, and Dathan, and Aviram. This is that Dathan and Aviram, who were famous in the congregation, who strove against Moshe and against Aharon in the company of Korach, when they strove against יהי: 10 And the earth opened her mouth, and swallowed them up together

---

[1] A case where the death or sacrifice of two people, through the act of one righteous man, resulted in an act of atonement for the entire nation of Yisrael, just as Moshiach's death as Moshiach ben Yoseph would atone for the nation as well.

with Korach, when that company died, the time the fire devoured two hundred fifty men: and they became a sign. 11 But the children of Korach died not. 12 The sons of Shimeon after their mishpachot: of Nemu-El, the mishpacha of the Nemuelites: of Yamin, the mishpacha of the Yaminites: of Yachin, the mishpacha of the Yachinites: 13 Of Zerah, the mishpacha of the Zarhites: of Shaul, the mishpacha of the Shaulites. 14 These are the mishpachot of the Shimeonites, twenty two thousand two hundred. 15 The children of Gad after their mishpachot: of Zephon, the mishpacha of the Zephonites: of Haggi, the mishpacha of the Haggites: of Shuni, the mishpacha of the Shunites: 16 Of Ozni, the mishpacha of the Oznites: of Eri, the mishpacha of the Erites: 17 Of Arod, the mishpacha of the Arodites: of Areli, the mishpacha of the Arelites. 18 These are the mishpachot of the children of Gad according to those that were numbered of them, forty thousand five hundred. 19 The sons of Yahudah were Er and Onan: and Er and Onan died in the land of Kanaan. 20 And the sons of Yahudah after their mishpachot were; of Shelah, the mishpacha of the Shelanites: of Pharez, the mishpacha of the Pharezites: of Zerah, the mishpacha of the Zarhites. 21 And the sons of Pharez were; of Hetzron, the mishpacha of the Hetzronites: of Hamul, the mishpacha of the Hamulites. 22 These are the mishpachot of Yahudah according to those that were numbered of them, seventy six thousand five hundred. 23 Of the sons of Yissakar after their mishpachot: of Tola, the mishpacha of the Tolaites: of Pua, the mishpacha of the Punites: 24 Of Yashuv, the mishpacha of the Yashuvites: of Shimron, the mishpacha of the Shimronites. 25 These are the mishpachot of Yissakar according to those that were numbered of them, sixty four thousand three hundred. 26 Of the sons of Zevulon after their mishpachot: of Sered, the mishpacha of the Sardites: of Elon, the mishpacha of the Elonites: of Yahle-El, the mishpacha of the Yahleelites. 27 These are the mishpachot of the Zevulunites according to those that were numbered of them, sixty thousand five hundred. 28 The sons of Yoseph after their mishpachot were Menashsheh and Ephraim. 29 Of the sons of Menashsheh: of Machir, the mishpacha of the Machirites: and Machir begat Gilead: from Gilead come the mishpacha of the Gileadites. 30 These are the sons of Gilead: of Yeezer, the mishpacha of the Yeezerites: of Helek, the mishpacha of the Helekites: 31 And of Asri-El, the mishpacha of the Asrielites: and of Shechem, the mishpacha of the Shechemites: 32 And of Shemida, the mishpacha of the Shemidaites: and of Hepher, the mishpacha of the Hepherites. 33 And Zelophehad the son of Hepher had no sons, but daughters: and the names of the daughters of Zelophehad were Mahlah, and Noah, Hoglah, Milcah, and Tirzah. 34 These are the mishpachot of Menashsheh, and those that were numbered of them, fifty two thousand seven hundred. 35 These are the sons of Ephraim after their mishpachot: of Shuthelah, the mishpacha of the Shuthalhites: of Becher, the mishpacha of the Bachrites: of Tahan, the mishpacha of the Tahanites. 36 And these are the sons of Shuthelah: of Eran, the mishpacha of the Eranites. 37 These are the mishpachot of the sons of Ephraim according to those that were numbered of them, thirty two thousand five hundred. These are the sons of Yoseph after their mishpachot. 38 The sons of Benyamin after their mishpachot: of Bela, the mishpacha of the Belaites: of Ashvel, the mishpacha of the Ashvelites: of Ahiram, the mishpacha of the Ahiramites: 39 Of Shupham, the mishpacha of the Shuphamites: of Hupham, the mishpacha of the Huphamites. 40 And the sons of Bela were Ard and Naaman: of Ard, the mishpacha of the Ardites: and of Naaman, the mishpacha of the Naamites. 41 These are the sons of Benyamin after their mishpachot: and they that were numbered of them were forty five thousand six hundred.

42 These are the sons of Dan after their mishpachot: of Shuham, the mishpacha of the Shuhamites. These are the mishpachot of Dan after their mishpachot. 43 All the mishpachot of the Shuhamites, according to those that were numbered of them, were sixty four thousand four hundred. 44 Of the children of Asher after their mishpachot: of Yimna, the mishpacha of the Yimnahites: of Yishwi, the mishpacha of the Yishwites: of Beriah, the mishpacha of the Beriites. 45 Of the sons of Beriyah: of Hever, the mishpacha of the Heverites: of Malchi-El, the mishpacha of the Malchielites. 46 And the name of the daughter of Asher was Sarah. 47 These are the mishpachot of the sons of Asher according to those that were numbered of them; who were fifty three thousand four hundred. 48 Of the sons of Naphtali after their mishpachot: of Yahze-El, the mishpacha of the Yahzeelites: of Guni, the mishpacha of the Gunites: 49 Of Yezer, the mishpacha of the Yezerites: of Shillem, the mishpacha of the Shillemites. 50 These are the mishpachot of Naphtali according to their mishpachot: and they that were numbered of them were forty five thousand four hundred. 51 These were the numbered of the children of Yisrael, six hundred one thousand seven hundred thirty. 52 And יהוה spoke to Moshe, saying, 53 *Unto these the land shall be divided for an inheritance according to the number of names. 54 To many you shall give the greater inheritance, and to few you shall give the smaller inheritance: to each one shall their inheritance be given according to those that were numbered of them. 55 But the land shall be divided by lot according to the names of the tribes of their ahvot they shall inherit it. 56 According to the lot shall the possession of it be divided between many and few.* 57 And these are they that were numbered of the Leviim after their mishpachot: of Gershon, the mishpacha of the Gershonites: of Kohath, the mishpacha of the Kohathites: of Merari, the mishpacha of the Merarites. 58 These are the

mishpachot of the Leviim: the mishpacha of the Livnites, the mishpacha of the Hevronites, the mishpacha of the Mahlites, the mishpacha of the Mushites, the mishpacha of the Korathites: And Kohath begat Amram. 59 And the name of Amram's wife was Yocheved, the daughter of Levi, whom her mother bare to Levi in Mitzrayim: and she bore to Amram Aharon and Moshe, and Miryam their sister. 60 And to Aharon was born Nadav, and Avihu, El-Azar, and Ithamar. 61 And Nadav and Avihu died, when they offered strange fire before יהוה . 62 And those that were numbered of them were twenty three thousand, all males from a month old and upward: for they were not numbered among the children of Yisrael, because there was no inheritance given them among the children of Yisrael. 63 These are those that were numbered by Moshe and El-Azar the kohen, who numbered the children of Yisrael in the plains of Moav by Yarden near Yericho. 64 But among these there was not a man of them whom Moshe and Aharon the kohen numbered, when they numbered the children of Yisrael in the wilderness of Sinai. 65 For יהוה had said of them, They shall surely die in the wilderness. And there was not left a man of them, save Calev the son of Yephunneh, and Yahoshua the son of Nun.

27 Then came the daughters of Zelophehad, the son of Hepher, the son of Gilead, the son of Machir, the son of Menashsheh, of the mishpachot of Menashsheh the son of Yoseph: and these are the names of his daughters; Mahlah, Noah, and Hoglah, and Milcah, and Tirzah. 2 And they stood before Moshe, and before El-Azar the kohen, and before the leaders and the entire congregation, by the door of the Tabernacle of the congregation, saying, 3 Our abba died in the wilderness, and he was not in the company of them that gathered themselves together against יהוה in the company of Korach; but died in his

own sin, and had no sons. 4 Why should the name of our abba be done away from among his mishpacha, because he has no son? Give to us therefore a possession among the brothers of our abba. 5 And Moshe brought their cause before **יהוה**.

6 And **יהוה** spoke to Moshe, saying, 7 *The daughters of Zelophehad speak right: you shall surely give them a possession of an inheritance among their abba's brothers; and you shall cause the inheritance of their abba to pass to them. 8 And you shall speak to the children of Yisrael, saying, If a man dies, and has no son, then you shall cause his inheritance to pass to his daughter.* [1]

9 *And if he has no daughter, then you shall give his inheritance to his brothers. 10 And if he has no brothers, then you shall give his inheritance to his abba's brothers. 11 And if his abba has no brothers, then you shall give his inheritance to his relative that is next to him of his mishpacha, and he shall possess it: and it shall be to the children of Yisrael a chuk of mishpat, as* **יהוה** *commanded Moshe.* 12 And **יהוה** said to Moshe, *Get you up into this Mount Avarim, and see the land that I have given to the children of Yisrael. 13 And when you have seen it, you also shall be gathered to your people, as Aharon your brother was gathered. 14 For you rebelled against My command in the desert of Tzin, in the strife of the congregation, to set Me apart at the mayim before their eyes: that is the mayim of Merivah in Kadesh in the wilderness of Tzin.* 15 And Moshe spoke to **יהוה**, saying, 16 *Let* **יהוה**, *the Elohim of the ruachim of all flesh, set a man over the congregation, 17 Who may go out before them, and who may go in before them, and who may lead them out, and who may bring them in; that the congregation of* **יהוה** *be not as sheep who have no shepherd.* 18 And **יהוה** said to Moshe, *Take Yahoshua the son of Nun, a man in whom is the Ruach, and lay yours*

hand upon him; 19 *And set him before El-Azar the kohen, and before the entire congregation; and give him a charge in their sight. 20 And you shall put some of your honor upon him, that all the congregation of the children of Yisrael may be obedient. 21 And he shall stand before El-Azar the kohen, who shall ask counsel for him after the mishpat of Urim before* **יהוה**: *at His word shall they go out, and at His word they shall come in, both he, and all the children of Yisrael with him, even all the congregation.* 22 And Moshe did as **יהוה** commanded him: and he took Yahoshua, and set him before El-Azar the kohen, and before the entire congregation: 23 And he laid his hands upon him, and gave him a charge, as **יהוה** commanded by the hand of Moshe.

28 And **יהוה** spoke to Moshe, saying, 2 *Command the children of Yisrael, and say to them, My offering, and My lechem for My sacrifices made by fire, for a sweet fragrance to Me, shall you observe to offer to Me in their due time. 3 And you shall say to them, This is the offering made by fire which you shall offer to* **יהוה**; *two lambs of the first year without spot day by day, for a continual burnt offering. 4 The one lamb shall you offer in the shacrit, and the other lamb shall you offer at ma'ariv; 5 And a tenth part of an ephah of flour for a grain offering, mingled with the fourth part of an hin of beaten oil. 6 It is a continual burnt offering, which was ordained in Mount Sinai for a sweet fragrance, a sacrifice made by fire to* **יהוה**. *7 And the drink offering of it shall be the fourth part of an hin for the one lamb: in the Set-Apart-Place shall you cause the strong wine to be poured to* **יהוה** *for a drink offering. 8 And the other lamb shall you offer at ma'ariv: as the grain offering of the morning, and as the drink offering of it, you shall offer it, a sacrifice made by fire, of a sweet fragrance to* **יהוה**. *9 And on the Shabbat day two lambs of the first year without spot, and two*

---

[1] The inheritance of property and royalty can pass through the daughter according to Torah. Therefore Yahshua as King could and did inherit David's throne through Miryam his mother; this is an eternal ordinance in Yisrael.

tenth deals of flour for a grain offering, mingled with oil, and the drink offering of it: 10 This is the burnt offering of every Shabbat, beside the continual burnt offering, and its drink offering. 11 And in the beginnings of your months you shall offer a burnt offering to **יהוה**; two young bullocks, and one ram, seven lambs of the first year without spot; 12 And three tenths of an ephah of flour for a grain offering, mingled with oil, for one bullock; and two tenth deals of flour for a grain offering, mingled with oil, for one ram; 13 And a tenth of an ephah of flour mingled with oil for a grain offering to one lamb; for a burnt offering of a sweet fragrance, a sacrifice made by fire to **יהוה**. 14 And their drink offerings shall be half an hin of wine to a bullock, and the third part of an hin to a ram, and a fourth part of an hin to a lamb: this is the burnt offering of every month throughout the months of the year. 15 And one kid of the male goats for a sin offering to **יהוה** shall be offered, beside the continual burnt offering, and its drink offering. 16 And in the fourteenth day of the first month is the Pesach of **יהוה**. 17 And in the fifteenth day of this month is the moed: seven days shall matzah be eaten. 18 In the first day shall be a miqra-qodesh; you shall do no manner of laborious work.[1] 19 But you shall offer a sacrifice made by fire for a burnt offering to **יהוה**; two young bullocks, and one ram, and seven lambs of the first year: they shall be to you without blemish: 20 And their grain offering shall be of flour mingled with oil: three tenths of an ephah shall you offer for a bullock, and two tenth deals for a ram; 21 One tenth of an ephah shall you offer le-olam-va-ed lamb, for each of the seven lambs: 22 And one goat for a sin offering, to make atonement for you. 23 You shall offer these beside the burnt offering in the morning, which is for a continual burnt offering. 24 After this manner you shall offer daily, throughout the seven days, the food of the sacrifice made by fire, of a sweet fragrance to **יהוה**: it shall be offered beside the continual burnt offering, and its drink offering. 25 And on the seventh day you shall have a set-apart convocation; you shall do no laborious work. 26 Also on the day of bikkurim, when you bring a new grain offering to **יהוה**, at your moed of Shavout, you shall have a miqra-qodesh; you shall do no laborious work: 27 But you shall offer the burnt offering for a sweet fragrance to **יהוה**; two young bullocks, one ram, seven lambs of the first year; 28 And their grain offering of flour mingled with oil, three tenths of an ephah for one bullock, two tenths of an ephah to one ram, 29 One tenth of an ephah to one lamb, for each of the seven lambs; 30 And one kid of the male goats, to make atonement for you. 31 You shall offer them beside the continual burnt offering, and the grain offering, they shall be to you without blemish and their drink offerings.

29 And in the seventh month, on the first day of the month, you shall have a miqra-qodesh; you shall do no laborious work: it is a day of blowing the trumpets for you. 2 And you shall offer a burnt offering for a sweet fragrance to **יהוה**; one young bullock, one ram, and seven lambs of the first year without blemish: 3 And their grain offering shall be of flour mingled with oil, three tenths of an ephah for a bullock, and two tenths of an ephah for a ram, 4 And one tenth of an ephah for one lamb, for all the seven lambs: 5 And one kid of the male goats for a sin offering, to make atonement for you: 6 Beside the burnt offering of the month, and the grain offering, and the daily burnt offering, and the grain offering, and their drink offerings, according to their manner, for a sweet fragrance, a sacrifice made by fire to **יהוה**. 7 And you shall have on the tenth day of this seventh month a miqra-qodesh; and you shall afflict your beings: you shall not do any work on it: 8 But you shall offer a burnt offering to **יהוה** for a sweet fragrance; one

---

[1] Labor, normal labor and labor for pay.

young bullock, one ram, and seven lambs of the first year; they shall be to you without blemish: 9 And their grain offering shall be of flour mingled with oil, three tenths of an ephah to a bullock, and two tenths of an ephah to one ram, 10 One tenth of an ephah for one lamb, for each of the seven lambs: 11 One kid of the male goats for a sin offering; beside the sin offering of atonement, and the continual burnt offering, and the grain offering of it, and their drink offerings. 12 And on the fifteenth day of the seventh month you shall have a miqra-qodesh; you shall do no laborious work, and you shall keep a moed to יהוה seven days: 13 And you shall offer a burnt offering, a sacrifice made by fire, of a sweet fragrance to יהוה; thirteen young bullocks, two rams, and fourteen lambs of the first year; they shall be without blemish: 14 And their grain offering shall be of flour mingled with oil, three tenths of an ephah to every bullock of the thirteen bullocks, two tenths of an ephah to each ram of the two rams, 15 And a tenth of an ephah to each lamb of the fourteen lambs: 16 And one kid of the male goats for a sin offering; beside the continual burnt offering, its grain offering, and its drink offering. 17 And on the second day you shall offer twelve young bullocks, two rams, and fourteen lambs of the first year without spot: 18 And their grain offering and their drink offerings for the bullocks, for the rams, and for the lambs, shall be according to their number, after the manner: 19 And one kid of the male goats for a sin offering; beside the continual burnt offering, and the grain offering of it, and their drink offerings. 20 And on the third day eleven bullocks, two rams, fourteen lambs of the first year without blemish; 21 And their grain offering and their drink offerings for the bullocks, for the rams, and for the lambs, shall be according to their number, after the manner: 22 And one goat for a sin offering; beside the continual burnt offering, and its grain offering, and its drink offering. 23 And on the fourth day ten bullocks, two rams, and fourteen lambs of the first year without blemish: 24 Their grain offering and their drink offerings for the bullocks, for the rams, and for the lambs, shall be according to their number, after the manner: 25 And one kid of the male goats for a sin offering; beside the continual burnt offering, its grain offering, and its drink offering. 26 And on the fifth day nine bullocks, two rams, and fourteen lambs of the first year without spot: 27 And their grain offering and their drink offering for the bullocks, for the rams, and for the lambs, shall be according to their number, after the manner: 28 And one goat for a sin offering; beside the continual burnt offering, and its grain offering, and its drink offering. 29 And on the sixth day eight bullocks, two rams, and fourteen lambs of the first year without blemish: 30 And their grain offering and their drink offerings for the bullocks, for the rams, and for the lambs, shall be according to their number, after their manner: 31 And one goat for a sin offering; beside the continual burnt offering, its grain offering, and its drink offering. 32 And on the seventh day seven bullocks, two rams, and fourteen lambs of the first year without blemish: 33 And their grain offering and their drink offerings for the bullocks, for the rams, and for the lambs, shall be according to their number, after the manner: 34 And one goat for a sin offering; beside the continual burnt offering, its grain offering, and its drink offering. 35 On the eighth day you shall have a miqra-qodesh: you shall do no laborious work on it: 36 But you shall offer a burnt offering, a sacrifice made by fire, of a sweet fragrance to יהוה: one bullock, one ram, and seven lambs of the first year without blemish: 37 Their grain offering and their drink offerings for the bullock, for the ram, and for the lambs, shall be according to their number, after the manner: 38 And one goat for a sin offering; beside the continual burnt offering, and its grain offering, and its drink offering.

39 *These things you shall do to* יהוה *in your moadim, beside your vows, and your terumah offerings, for your burnt offerings, and for your grain offerings, and for your drink offerings, and for your shalom offerings.* 40 And Moshe told the children of Yisrael according to all that יהוה commanded Moshe.

Torah Parsha 42
Mattot 30:1-32:42
In regular 12-month years,
read with Pasrsha 43,
in 13 month years read separately.
Haftarah Yirmeyahu 1:1-2:3
Brit Chadasha Mattityahu 5:33-37

30 And Moshe spoke to the heads of the tribes concerning the children of Yisrael, saying, This is the thing that יהוה has commanded. 2 If a man vows a vow to יהוה, or swears an oath to bind his being with some agreement; he shall not break his word, he shall do according to all that proceeds out of his mouth. 3 If a woman also vows a vow to יהוה, and binds herself by an agreement, being in her abba's bayit in her youth; 4 And her abba hears her vow, and her agreement by which she has bound her being, and her abba shall hold his shalom at her: then all her vows shall stand, and every agreement by which she has bound her being shall stand. 5 But if her abba disallows it in the day that he hears it; not any of her vows, or of her agreements by which she has bound her being, shall stand: and יהוה shall forgive her, because her abba disallowed it for her. 6 And if she has a husband, when she vowed, or uttered ought out of her lips, by which she bound her being; 7 And her husband heard it, and held his shalom at her in the day that he heard it: then her vows shall stand, and her agreements by which she bound her being shall stand. 8 But if her husband disallowed it on the day that he heard it; then he has nullified her vow which she vowed, and that which she uttered with her lips, by which she bound her being, shall be of none effect:

and יהוה shall forgive her. 9 But every vow of a widow, and of her that is divorced, by which they have bound their beings, shall stand against her. 10 And if she vowed in her husband's bayit, or bound herself by an agreement with an oath; 11 And her husband heard it, and held his shalom at her, and disallowed it not: then all her vows shall stand, and every agreement by which she bound her being shall stand. 12 But if her husband has utterly made them void on the day he heard them; then what ever proceeded out of her lips concerning her vows, or concerning the agreement of her being, shall not stand: her husband has made them void; and יהוה shall forgive her. 13 Every vow, and every binding oath to afflict the being, her husband may establish it, or her husband may make it void.[1] 14 But if her husband altogether hold his shalom at her from day to day; then he established all her vows, or all her agreements, which are upon her: he confirms thcm, bccause he held his shalom at her in the day that he heard them. 15 But if he shall in any way make them void after he has heard them; then he shall bear her iniquity. 16 These are the chukim, which יהוה commanded Moshe, between a man and his wife, between the abba and his daughter, being yet in her youth in her abba's bayit.

31 And יהוה spoke to Moshe, saying, 2 *Avenge the children of Yisrael against the Midyanites: afterward shall you be gathered to your people.* 3 And Moshe spoke to the people, saying, Some of you arm for war; and let them go against the Midyanites, and avenge יהוה on Midyan. 4 Of every tribe a thousand, throughout all the tribes of Yisrael, shall you send to the war: 5 So there were delivered out of the thousands of Yisrael, a thousand of every tribe, twelve thousand armed for war. 6 And Moshe sent them to the war, a thousand of

---

[1] This is the true Yisraelite concept of binding and loosing spoken of by Yahshua; to bind means to disallow; to loose means to allow.

- 178 -

every tribe, them and Pinchus the son of El-Azar the kohen, to the war, with the set-apart instruments, and the trumpets to blow in his hand. 7 And they warred against the Midyanites, as יהוה commanded Moshe; and they killed all the males. 8 And they killed the melechim of Midyan, beside the rest of them that were slain; namely, Evi, and Rekem, and Zur, and Hur, and Reva, five melechim of Midyan: Bilam also the son of Beor they slew with the sword. 9 And the children of Yisrael took all the women of Midyan captives, and their little ones, and took the spoil of all their cattle, and all their flocks, and all their goods. 10 And they burnt all their cities in which they dwelt, and all their encampments, with fire. 11 And they took all the spoil, and all the prey, both of men and of beasts. 12 And they brought the captives, and the prey, and the spoil, to Moshe, and El-Azar the kohen, and to the congregation of the children of Yisrael, to the camp at the plains of Moav, which is by Yarden near Yericho. 13 And Moshe, and El-Azar the kohen, and all the leaders of the congregation, went out to meet them outside the camp. 14 And Moshe was angry with the officers of the army, with the captains over thousands, and captains over hundreds, who came from the battle. 15 And Moshe said to them, Have you saved all the women alive? 16 See, these caused the children of Yisrael, through the counsel of Bilam, to commit trespass against יהוה in the matter of Peor, and there was a plague among the congregation of יהוה. 17 Now therefore kill every male among the little ones, and kill every woman that has known a man by lying with him. 18 But all the female children, that have not known a man by lying with him, keep alive for yourselves. 19 And abide outside the camp seven days: whoever has killed any person, and whoever has touched any slain, purify both yourselves and your captives on the third day, and on the seventh day. 20 And purify all your raiment, and all that is made of skins, and all work of goats' hair,

and all things made of wood. 21 And El-Azar the kohen said to the men of war who went out to the battle, This is the ordinance of the Torah that יהוה commanded Moshe; 22 Only the gold, and the silver, the brass, the iron, the tin, and the lead, 23 Everything that may abide in the fire, you shall make it go through the fire, and it shall be clean: nevertheless it shall be purified with the mayim of separation: and all that passes not through the fire you shall make go through the mayim. 24 And you shall wash your clothes on the seventh day, and you shall be clean, and afterward you shall come into the camp. 25 And יהוה spoke to Moshe, saying, 26 *Take the census of the prey that was taken, both of man and of beast, you, and El-Azar the kohen, and the heads of the ahvot of the congregation: 27 And divide the prey into two parts; between them that took the war upon them, who went out to battle, and between the entire congregation: 28 And levy a tribute to יהוה of the men of war who went out to battle: one being of five hundred, both of the persons, and of the cattle, and of the donkeys, and of the sheep: 29 Take it from their half, and give it to El-Azar the kohen, for a terumah offering for יהוה. 30 And of the children of Yisrael's half, you shall take one portion of fifty, of the persons, of the cattle, of the donkeys, and of the flocks, of all manner of beasts, and give them to the Leviim, who keep the duty of the Tabernacle of יהוה. 31 And* Moshe and El-Azar the kohen did as יהוה commanded Moshe. 32 And the spoils, being the rest of the prey which the men of war had caught, was six hundred seventy five thousand sheep, 33 And seventy-two thousand cattle, 34 And sixty-one thousand donkeys, 35 And thirty-two thousand persons in all, of woman that had not known a man by lying with him. 36 And the half, which was the portion of those that went out to war, was in number three hundred thirty seven thousand five hundred sheep: 37 And יהוה's tribute of the sheep was six hundred seventy five. 38 And the cattle were thirty six thousand; of which יהוה's tribute was seventy-two. 39 And the donkeys were thirty thousand five hundred; of which יהוה's tribute was sixty-one. 40 And the persons were sixteen thousand; of which יהוה's tribute was thirty-two persons. 41 And Moshe gave the tribute, which was יהוה's terumah offering, to El-Azar the kohen, as יהוה commanded Moshe. 42 And of the children of Yisrael's half, which Moshe divided from the men that were at war, 43 Now the half that pertained to the congregation was three hundred thirty seven thousand five hundred sheep, 44 And thirty six thousand cattle, 45 And thirty thousand five hundred donkeys, 46 And sixteen thousand persons; 47 Even of the children of Yisrael's half, Moshe took one portion of fifty, both of man and of beast, and gave them to the Leviim, who kept the duty of the Tabernacle of יהוה ; as יהוה commanded Moshe. 48 And the officers, who were over thousands of the army, the captains of thousands, and captains of hundreds, came near to Moshe: 49 And they said to Moshe, Your avadim have taken the census of the men of war who are under our duty, and there lacks not one man among us. 50 We have therefore brought an offering for יהוה, what every man has gotten, of jewels of gold, chains, and bracelets, rings, earrings, and tablets, to make an atonement for our beings before יהוה. 51 And Moshe and El-Azar the kohen took the gold from them, even all the fashioned jewels. 52 And all the gold of the offering that they offered up to יהוה, of the captains of thousands, and of the captains of hundreds, was sixteen thousand seven hundred fifty shekels. 53 For the men of war had taken spoil, every man for himself. 54 And Moshe and El-Azar the kohen took the gold of the captains of thousands and of hundreds, and brought it into the Tabernacle of the congregation for a memorial for the children of Yisrael before יהוה.

32 Now the children of Reuven and the children of Gad had a very great multitude of cattle: and when they saw the land of Yazer, and the land of Gilead, that the place was a tov place for cattle; 2 The children of Gad and the children of Reuven came and spoke to Moshe, and to El-Azar the kohen, and to the leaders of the congregation, saying, 3 Ataroth, and Divon, and Yazer, and Nimrah, and Cheshbon, and Elealeh, and Shevam, and Nevo, and Beon, 4 Even the country which יהוה smote before the congregation of Yisrael, is a land for cattle, and your avadim have cattle: 5 Therefore, they said, If we have found favor in your sight, let this land be given to your avadim for a possession, and bring us not over the Yarden. 6 And Moshe said to the children of Gad and to the children of Reuven, Shall your brothers go to war, while you shall sit here? 7 And why do you discourage the lev of the children of Yisrael from going over into the land that יהוה has given them? 8 This did your ahvot, when I sent them from Kadesh-Barnea to see the land. 9 For when they went up to the Valley of Eshcol, and saw the land, they discouraged the lev of the children of Yisrael, that they should not go into the land that יהוה had given them. 10 And יהוה's anger was kindled at the same time, and He swore, saying, 11 *Surely none of the men that came up out of Mitzrayim, from twenty years old and upward, shall see the land which I swore to Avraham, to Yitzchak, and to Yaakov; because they had not fully followed Me:* 12 *Except Calev the son of Yephunneh the Kenezite,[1] and Yahoshua the son of Nun: for they have wholly followed* יהוה. 13 And יהוה's anger was kindled against Yisrael, and He made them wander in the wilderness forty years, until all the generation, that had done evil in the sight of יהוה, was consumed. 14 And, see, now you have risen up in your abba's stead, an

---

[1] Calev was considered a Yahudite, despite his father being a non-Yisraelite. All who join Yisrael are Yisrael, without any conversion process necessary. Beware of any manmade conversion process.

increase of sinful men, to add more to the fierce anger of יהוה towards Yisrael. 15 For if you turn away from after Him, He will yet again leave them in the wilderness; and you shall destroy this entire people. 16 And they came near to him, and said, We will build sheepfolds here for our cattle, and cities for our little ones: 17 But we ourselves will go ready armed before the children of Yisrael, until we have brought them to their place: and our little ones shall dwell in the fenced cities because of the inhabitants of the land. 18 We will not return to our houses, until the children of Yisrael have inherited every man his inheritance.[1] 19 For we will not inherit with them on other side Yarden, or beyond; because our inheritance is fallen to us on this side of the Yarden eastward. 20 And Moshe said to them, If you will do this thing, if you will go armed before יהוה to war, 21 And will go all of you armed over Yarden before יהוה, until He has driven out His enemies from before Him, 22 And the land be subdued before יהוה : then afterward you shall return, and be guiltless before יהוה, and before Yisrael; and this land shall be your possession before יהוה. 23 But if you will not do so, see, you will have sinned against יהוה: and be sure your sin will find you out.[2] 24 Build cities for your little ones, and folds for your sheep; and do that which has proceeded out of your mouth. 25 And the children of Gad and the children of Reuven spoke to Moshe, saying, Your avadim will do as my master commands. 26 Our little ones, our wives, our flocks, and all our cattle, shall be there in the cities of Gilead: 27 But your avadim will pass over, every man armed for war, before יהוה to battle, as my master says. 28 So concerning them Moshe commanded El-Azar the kohen, and Yahoshua the son of Nun, and the leaders, ahvot of the tribes of the children of Yisrael: 29 And Moshe said to them, If the children of Gad and the children of Reuven will pass with you over Yarden, every man armed to battle, before יהוה, and the land shall be subdued before you; then you shall give them the land of Gilead for a possession: 30 But if they will not pass over with you armed, they shall have possessions among you in the land of Kanaan. 31 And the children of Gad and the children of Reuven answered, saying, As יהוה has said to your avadim, so will we do. 32 We will pass over armed before יהוה into the land of Kanaan, that the possession of our inheritance on this side of the Yarden may be ours. 33 And Moshe gave to them, even to the children of Gad, and to the children of Reuven, and to half the tribe of Menashsheh the son of Yoseph, the malchut of Sihon melech of the Amorites, and the malchut of Og melech of Bashan, the land, with the cities of it in the coasts, even the cities of the country all around. 34 And the children of Gad built Dibon, and Ataroth, and Aroer, 35 And Atroth, Shophan, and Yaazer, and Yogvehah, 36 And Beth-nimrah, and Beth-haran, fenced cities: and folds for sheep. 37 And the children of Reuven built Cheshbon, and Elealeh, and Kirjathaim, 38 And Nevo, and Baal-Meon - their names being changed - and Shivmah: and gave other names to the cities that they built. 39 And the children of Machir the son of Menashsheh went to Gilead, and took it, and dispossessed the Amorite that was in it. 40 And Moshe gave Gilead to Machir the son of Menashsheh; and he dwelt there. 41 And Yair the son of Menashsheh went and took the small towns of it, and called them Havoth-Yair. 42 And Novah went and took Kenath, and the villages of it, and called it Novah, after his own name, for a memorial for the children of Yisrael before יהוה.

---

[1] The correct attitude of all those called into Yisrael's restoration. We will not return to our homes and agendas until all Yisrael has received their inheritance and place in Yisrael's commonwealth.

[2] A tov warning to all who do not allow and do not fight for full equality and inheritance for both houses of Yisrael. Failure to do so is sin, and YHWH will expose that sin for what it is.

Parsha 43
Masaei 33:1-36:13
In regular years with 12-months,
read with Pasrsha 42.
In years with 13-months, ead separately. Haftarah
Yirmeyahu 2:4-28
Brit Chadasha Yaakov 4:1-12

33 These are the journeys of the children of Yisrael, who went out of the land of Mitzrayim with their divisions under the hand of Moshe and Aharon. 2 And Moshe wrote their goings out according to their journeys by the command of יהוה : and these are their journeys according to their starting points. 3 And they departed from Rameses in the first month, on the fifteenth day of the first month; on the day after the Pesach the children of Yisrael went out with a high hand in the sight of all the Mitzrites. 4 For the Mitzrites buried all their bachor, which יהוה had smitten among them: upon their elohim also יהוה executed mishpatim. 5 And the children of Yisrael moved from Rameses, and pitched in Succoth. 6 And they departed from Succoth, and pitched in Etham, which is in the edge of the wilderness. 7 And they moved from Etham, and turned again to Pi-Hahiroth, which is before Baal-Zephon: and they pitched before Migdol. 8 And they departed from Pi-Hahiroth, and passed through the midst of the sea into the wilderness, and went three days' journey in the wilderness of Etham, and pitched in Marah. 9 And they moved from Marah, and came to Elim: and in Elim were twelve fountains of mayim, and seventy palm eytzim; and they pitched there. 10 And they moved from Eylim, and encamped by the Sea Of Reeds. 11 And they removed from the Sea Of Reeds, and encamped in the wilderness of Tzin. 12 And they took their journey out of the wilderness of Tzin, and encamped in Dophkah. 13 And they departed from Dophkah, and encamped in Alush. 14 And they moved from Alush, and encamped at Rephidim, where was no mayim for the people to drink. 15 And they departed from Rephidim, and pitched in the wilderness of Sinai. 16 And they moved from the desert of Sinai, and pitched at Kivroth-Hattaavah. 17 And they departed from Kivroth-Hattaavah, and encamped at Hazeroth. 18 And they departed from Hazeroth, and pitched in Rithmah. 19 And they departed from Rithmah, and pitched at Rimmon-Parez. 20 And they departed from Rimmon-Parez, and pitched in Livnah. 21 And they moved from Livnah, and pitched at Rissah. 22 And they journeyed from Rissah, and pitched in Kehelathah. 23 And they went from Kehelathah, and pitched in Mount Shapher. 24 And they moved from Mount Shapher, and encamped in Haradah. 25 And they moved from Haradah, and pitched in Makheloth. 26 And they moved from Makheloth, and encamped at Tahath. 27 And they departed from Tahath, and pitched at Tarah. 28 And they moved from Tarah, and pitched in Mithcah. 29 And they went from Mithcah, and pitched in Hashmonah. 30 And they departed from Hashmonah, and encamped at Moseroth. 31 And they departed from Moseroth, and pitched in Bene-Yaakan. 32 And they moved from Bene-Yaakan, and encamped at Hor-hagidgad. 33 And they went from Hor-Hagidgad, and pitched in Yotvathah. 34 And they moved from Yotvathah, and encamped at Evronah. 35 And they departed from Evronah, and encamped at Ezion-Gaver. 36 And they removed from Ezion-Gaver, and pitched in the wilderness of Tzin, which is Kadesh. 37 And they removed from Kadesh, and pitched in Mount Hor, in the edge of the land of Edom. 38 And Aharon the kohen went up into Mount Hor at the command of יהוה, and died there, in the fortieth year after the children of Yisrael were come out of the land of Mitzrayim, in the first day of the fifth month. 39 And Aharon was a hundred twenty three years old when he died in Mount Hor. 40 And melech Arad the Kanaanite, which dwelt in the south in the land of Kanaan, heard of the coming of the children of Yisrael. 41 And they departed from Mount Hor, and pitched in Zalmonah. 42 And they departed from Zalmonah, and pitched in Punon. 43 And they departed from Punon, and pitched in Ovoth. 44 And they departed from Ovoth, and pitched in Iye-Ha-Avarim, at the border of Moav. 45 And they departed from Iyim, and pitched in Divon-Gad. 46 And they removed from Divon-Gad, and encamped in Almon-Divlathayim. 47 And they removed from Almon-Divlathayim, and pitched in the mountains of Avarim, before Nevo. 48 And they departed from the mountains of Avarim, and pitched in the plains of Moav by Yarden near Yericho. 49 And they pitched by Yarden, from Beth-Yesimoth even to Avel-Shittim in the plains of Moav. 50 And יהוה spoke to Moshe in the plains of Moav by Yarden near Yericho, saying, 51 *Speak to the children of Yisrael, and say to them, When you pass over Yarden into the land of Kanaan; 52 Then you shall drive out all the inhabitants of the land from before you, and destroy all their stone images, and destroy all their molded images, and demolish all their high places: 53 And you shall dispossess the inhabitants of the land, and dwell there: for I have given you the land to possess it. 54 And you shall divide the land by lot for an inheritance among your mishpachot: and to the larger you shall give the greater inheritance, and to the fewer you shall give the smaller inheritance: every man's inheritance shall be in the place where his lot falls; according to the tribes of your ahvot you shall inherit. 55 But if you will not drive out the inhabitants of the land from before you; then it shall come to pass, that those which you let remain of them shall be pricks in your eyes, and thorns in your sides, and shall distress you in the land in which you dwell. 56 Moreover it shall come to pass, that I shall do to you, as I thought to do to them.*

34 And יהוה spoke to Moshe, saying, 2 *Command the children of Yisrael,*

and say to them, When you come into the land of Kanaan; this is the land that shall fall to you for an inheritance, even the land of Kanaan with the coasts of it: 3 Then your south quarter shall be from the wilderness of Tzin along by the coast of Edom, and your southern border shall be the outmost coast of the Salt Sea eastward: 4 And your border shall turn from the south to the ascent of Akravvim, and pass on to Tzin: and the going out of it shall be from the south to Kadesh-Barnea, and shall go on to Hazar-Addar, and pass on to Azmon: 5 And the border shall turn around from Azmon to the river of Mitzrayim, and the goings out of it shall be at the sea. 6 And as for the western border, you shall even have the Great Sea for a border: this shall be your western border. 7 And this shall be your north border: from the Great Sea you shall mark out Mount Hor: 8 From Mount Hor you shall mark out your border to the entrance of Hamath; and the goings out of the border shall be to Zedad: 9 And the border shall go on to Ziphron, and the goings out of it shall be at Hazar-Enan: this shall be your north border. 10 And you shall mark out your east border from Hazar-Enan to Shepham: 11 And the coast shall go down from Shepham to Rivlah, on the east side of Ain; and the border shall descend, and shall reach to the side of the sea of Chinnereth eastward: 12 And the border shall go down to Yarden, and the goings out of it shall be at the Salt Sea: this shall be your land with the coasts of it all around.* 13 And Moshe commanded the children of Yisrael, saying, This is the land that you shall inherit by lot, which יהוה commanded to give to the nine tribes, and the half tribe: 14 For the tribe of the children of Reuven according to the bayit of their ahvot, and the tribe of the children of Gad according to the bayit of their ahvot, have received their inheritance; and half the tribe of Menashsheh has received their inheritance: 15 The two tribes and the half tribe have received their inheritance on this side of the Yarden near

Yericho eastward, toward the sunrising. 16 And יהוה spoke to Moshe, saying, 17 *These are the names of the men who shall divide the land to you: El-Azar the kohen, and Yahoshua the son of Nun. 18 And you shall take one leader of every tribe, to divide the land among you by inheritance. 19 And the names of the men are these: Of the tribe of Yahudah, Calev the son of Yephunneh. 20 And of the tribe of the children of Shimeon, Shemu-El the son of Ammihud. 21 Of the tribe of Benyamin, Elidad the son of Chislon. 22 And the leader of the tribe of the children of Dan, Bukki the son of Yogli. 23 The leader of the children of Yoseph, for the tribe of the children of Menashsheh, Hanni-El the son of Ephod. 24 And the leader of the tribe of the children of Ephraim, Kemu-El the son of Shiphtan. 25 And the leader of the tribe of the children of Zevulon, Elyzaphan the son of Parnach. 26 And the leader of the tribe of the children of Yissakar, Palti-El the son of Azzan. 27 And the leader of the tribe of the children of Asher, Ahihud the son of Shelomi. 28 And the leader of the tribe of the children of Naphtali, Pedah-El the son of Ammihud.* 29 These are they whom יהוה commanded to divide the inheritance to the children of Yisrael in the land of Kanaan.[1]

35 And יהוה spoke to Moshe in the plains of Moav by Yarden near Yericho, saying, 2 *Command the children of Yisrael that they give to the Leviim of the inheritance of their possession cities to dwell in; and you shall give also to the Leviim suburbs for the cities all around them. 3 And the cities shall they have to dwell in; and the suburbs shall be for their cattle, and for their goods, and for all their beasts. 4 And the suburbs of the cities, which you shall give to the Leviim, shall reach from the wall of the city and outward a thousand cubits all around. 5 And you shall measure from outside the city on the* east side two thousand cubits, and on the south side two thousand cubits, and on the west side two thousand cubits, and on the north side two thousand cubits and the city shall be in the midst: this shall be to them the suburbs of the cities. 6 And among the cities which you shall give to the Leviim there shall be six cities for refuge, which you shall appoint for the manslayer, that he may flee there: and to these you shall add forty-two cities. 7 So all the cities that you shall give to the Leviim shall be forty and eight cities: them shall you give with their suburbs. 8 And the cities which you shall give shall be from the possession of the children of Yisrael: from them that have many you shall give many; but from them that have few you shall give few: every one shall give of his cities to the Leviim according to his inheritance which he inherits.* 9 And יהוה spoke to Moshe, saying, 10 *Speak to the children of Yisrael, and say to them, When you are come over Yarden into the land of Kanaan; 11 Then you shall appoint cities to be cities of refuge for you; that the killer may flee there, who kills any person accidentally. 12 And they shall be for you cities for refuge from the avenger; that the killer dies not, until he stands before the congregation in mishpat. 13 And of these cities which you shall give six cities shall you have for refuge. 14 You shall give three cities on this side of Yarden, and three cities shall you give in the land of Kanaan, which shall be cities of refuge. 15 These six cities shall be a refuge, both for the children of Yisrael, and for the Ger, and for the sojourner among them: that anyone that kills any person by accident may flee there.[2] 16 And if he smites him by an instrument of iron, so that he dies, he is a murderer: the murderer shall surely be put to death. 17 And if he smites him by throwing a stone, by which he may die, and he dies, he is a murderer: the murderer shall surely be put to death. 18 Or if he smites him with a hand weapon of wood, by*

---

[1] In a theocracy, YHWH chooses, calls, and names the leadership Himself.

[2] Unmerited favor/**rachamim**.

which he may die, and he dies, he is a murderer: the murderer shall surely be put to death. 19 *The revenger of dom himself shall slay the murderer: when he meets him, he shall slay him.* 20 *But if he threw him because of hatred, or hurled something at him while laying in wait, that he dies;* 21 *Or in enmity smite him with his hand so that he dies: he that smote him shall surely be put to death; for he is a murderer: the revenger of dom shall slay the murderer, when he meets him.* 22 *But if he threw him suddenly without enmity, or has thrown at him anything without laying in wait,* 23 *Or with any stone, by which a man may die, seeing him not, and cast it at him, that he dies, and was not his enemy, neither sought his harm:* 24 *Then the congregation shall shophet between the slayer and the revenger of dom according to these mishpatim:* 25 *And the congregation shall deliver the slayer out of the hand of the revenger of dom, and the congregation shall restore him to the city of his refuge, where he had fled: and he shall abide in it until the death of the Kohen HaGadol, who was anointed with the set-apart oil.* 26 *But if the slayer shall at any time come outside the border of the city of his refuge, where he fled;* 27 *And the revenger of dom finds him outside the borders of the city of his refuge, and the revenger of dom kill the slayer; he shall not be guilty of dom:* 28 *Because he should have remained in the city of his refuge until the death of the Kohen HaGadol: but after the death of the Kohen HaGadol the slayer shall return into the land of his possession.* 29 *So these things shall be for a chuk of mishpat to you throughout your generations in all your dwellings.* 30 *Whoever kills any person, the murderer shall be put to death by the mouth of witnesses: but one witness shall not testify against any person to cause him to die.* 31 *Moreover you shall take no ransom for the chayim of a murderer, who is guilty of death: but he shall be surely put to death.* 32 *And you shall take no ransom for him that is fled to the city of his refuge,* that he should come again to dwell in the land, until the death of the kohen. 33 *So you shall not pollute the land in which you are: for dom defiles the land: and the land cannot be cleansed of the dom that is shed on it, except by the dom of him that shed it.* 34 *Defile not the land that you shall inhabit, in which I dwell: for I* יהוה *dwell among the children of Yisrael.*

36 And the leaders of the ahvot of the mishpachot of the children of Gilead, the son of Machir, the son of Menashsheh, of the mishpachot of the sons of Yoseph, came near, and spoke before Moshe, and before the leaders, the main ahvot of the children of Yisrael: 2 And they said, יהוה commanded my master to give the land for an inheritance by lot to the children of Yisrael: and my master was commanded by יהוה to give the inheritance of Zelophehad our brother to his daughters. 3 And if they are married to any of the sons of the other tribes of the children of Yisrael, then shall their inheritance be taken from the inheritance of our ahvot, and shall be put to the inheritance of the tribe into which they are received: so shall it be taken from the lot of our inheritance. 4 And when the Yovel of the children of Yisrael shall be, then shall their inheritance be put to the inheritance of the tribe into which they are received: so shall their inheritance be taken away from the inheritance of the tribe of our ahvot. 5 And Moshe commanded the children of Yisrael according to the word of יהוה , saying, The tribe of the sons of Yoseph have spoken well. 6 This is the thing which יהוה does command concerning the daughters of Zelophehad, saying, Let them marry whom they think best; but only to the mishpacha of the tribe of their abba shall they marry. 7 So shall the inheritance of the children of Yisrael not be moved from tribe to tribe: each one of the children of Yisrael shall keep himself in the inheritance of the tribe of his ahvot. 8 And every daughter, that possesses an inheritance in any tribe of the children of Yisrael, shall be wife to one of the mishpacha of the tribe of her abba, that the children of Yisrael may enjoy every man the inheritance of his ahvot. 9 Neither shall the inheritance move from one tribe to another tribe; but every one of the tribes of the children of Yisrael shall keep himself in his own inheritance. [1] 10 Even as יהוה commanded Moshe, so did the daughters of Zelophehad: 11 For Mahlal, Tirzah, and Hoglah, and Milcah, and Noah, the daughters of Zelophehad, were married to their abba's brothers' sons: 12 And they were married into the mishpachot of the sons of Menashsheh the son of Yoseph, and

their inheritance remained in the tribe of the mishpacha of their abba. 13 These are the mitzvot and the mishpatim, which יהוה commanded by the hand of Moshe to the children of Yisrael in the plains of Moav by Yarden near Yericho.

Chazak Chazak VeNitchazak
Be Strong Be Strong!
And May We Be Strengthened!

---

[1] This principle is still vital to the restoration today. Now that the two sticks of Ezekiel 37 are being made one, Yahudah must not seek to consume Ephraim by converting them to a different house, by becoming Jews. And, neither should Ephraim take Jews and demand that they join with Ephraim and any of their unbiblical manners in a Sunday church system. Rather, each house has a special and unique role to play, and that role in order to be preserved remains separate; and yet both houses are well on their way to becoming one reconstituted people in Torah and in Moshiach.

דברים

Devarim - Deuteronomy
To Our Forefathers Yisrael

Torah Parsha 44
Devarim 1:1-3:22
Haftarah Yeshayahu 1:1-27
Brit Chadasha Yochanan 15:1-11

1 These are the words that Moshe spoke to all Yisrael[1] beyond the Yarden in the wilderness, in the plain over opposite the Sea of Reeds, between Paran, and Tophel, and Lavan, and Hatzeroth, and Dizahav. 2 (There are eleven days' journey from Horev by the way of Mount Seir to Kadesh-Barnea.) 3 And it came to pass in the fortieth year, in the eleventh month, on the first day of the month, that Moshe spoke to the children of Yisrael, according to all that יהוה had given him in mitzvah to them; 4 After he had slain Sihon the melech of the Amorites, who dwelt in Cheshbon, and Og the melech of Bashan, who dwelt at Astaroth in Edrei: 5 Beyond Yarden, in the land of Moav, Moshe began to declare this Torah, saying, 6 יהוה our Elohim spoke to us in Horev, saying, *You have dwelt long enough in this Mount:* 7 *Turn, and take your journey, and go to the Mount of the Amorites, and to all the places near there, in the plain, in the hills, and in the low country, and in the south, and by the sea side, to the land of the Kanaanites, and to Levanon, to the great river, the River Euphrates.* 8 See, I have set the land before you: go in and possess the land which יהוה swore to your ahvot, Avraham, Yitzchak, and Yaakov, to give to them and to their zera after them. 9 And I spoke to you at that time, saying, I am not able to bear you alone by myself: 10 יהוה Your Elohim has multiplied you, and, see, you are this day as the chochavim of the shamayim for multitude. 11 יהוה Elohim of Your ahvot will make you a thousand times more than you are now, and bless you, as He has promised you![2] 12 How can I by myself all alone bear your pressure, and your burden, and your strife? 13 Take wise and understanding men, known among your tribes, and I will make them heads over you. 14 And you answered me, and said, The thing, which you have spoken, is tov for us to do. 15 So I took the heads of your tribes, wise men, and well known, and made them heads over you, captains over thousands, and captains over hundreds, and captains over fifties, and captains over tens, and officers among your tribes. 16 And I charged your shophtim at that time, saying, hear the causes between your brothers, and shophet in tzedakah between every man and his brother, and the Ger that is with him. 17 You shall not respect persons in mishpat; but you shall hear the small as well as the great; you shall not be afraid of the face of man; for the mishpat belongs to Elohim: and the cause that is too hard for you, bring it to me, and I will hear it. 18 And I commanded you at that time all the things that you should do. 19 And when we departed from Horev, we went through that entire huge and awesome wilderness, which you saw by the way of the mountain of the Amorites, as יהוה our Elohim commanded us; and we came to Kadesh-Barnea. 20 And I said to you, You are come to the mountain of the Amorites, which יהוה our Elohim does give to us. 21 See, יהוה Your Elohim has set the land before you: go up and possess it, as יהוה Elohim of your ahvot has said to you; fear not, neither be discouraged. 22 And you came near to me every one of you, and said, We will send men before us,

---

[1] An intense recital of many of the key benchmarks in our nation's history.

[2] Four million Yisraelites including men, women, and children left Egypt. Yet Moshe said that this number in order to fulfill the covenant of physical multiplicity would be multiplied by one thousand. That brings us to a latter-day total of approximately 4 billion or four out of every six humans, whether they know who they really are or not.

and they shall search out the land, and bring us word again by which way we must go up, and into what cities we shall come. 23 And the saying pleased me: and I took twelve men from you, one per tribe: 24 And they turned and went up into the mountain, and came to the valley of Eshcol, and searched it out. 25 And they took of the fruit of the land in their hands, and brought it down to us, and brought us word again, and said, It is a tov land that יהוה our Elohim gives us. 26 Nevertheless you would not go up, but rebelled against the mitzvah of יהוה Your Elohim: 27 And you grumbled in your tents, and said, Because יהוה hated us, He has brought us forth out of the land of Mitzrayim, to deliver us into the hand of the Amorites, to destroy us. 28 Where shall we go up? Our brothers have discouraged our levim, saying, The people are greater and taller than us; the cities are great and walled up to the shamayim; and we have seen the sons of the Anakims there. 29 Then I said to you, Dread not, neither be afraid of them. 30 יהוה Your Elohim who goes before you, He shall fight for you, according to all that He did for you in Mitzrayim before your eyes; 31 And in the wilderness, where you have seen how יהוה Your Elohim carried you, as a man carries his son, in all the way that you went, until you came into this place. 32 Yet in this matter you did not believe יהוה Your Elohim, 33 Who went in the way before you, to search out a place to pitch your tents in, in fire by night, to show you which way you should go, and in a cloud by day. 34 And יהוה heard the voice of your words, and was angry, and swore, saying, 35 *Surely there shall not one of these men of this evil generation see that tov land, which I swore to give to your ahvot. 36 Except Kalev the son of Yephunneh,[1] he shall see it, and to him will I give the land that he has walked upon, and to his children, because he has fully followed* יהוה. 37 Also יהוה was angry with me for

your sakes, saying, You also shall not go in there. 38 But Yahoshua the son of Nun, who stands before you, he shall go in there: encourage him: for he shall cause Yisrael to inherit it. 39 And your little ones, which you said should be a prey, and your children, which in that day had no knowledge between tov and evil, they shall go in there, and to them will I give it, and they shall possess it. 40 But as for you, turn, and take your journey into the wilderness by the way of the Sea of Reeds. 41 Then you answered and said to me, We have sinned against יהוה, we will go up and fight, according to all that יהוה our Elohim commanded us. And when you had girded on every man his weapons of war, you were ready to go up into the hill. 42 And יהוה said to me, *Say to them. Go not up, neither fight; for I am not among you; lest you be smitten before your enemies.* 43 So I spoke to you; and you would not listen, but rebelled against the mitzvah of יהוה, and went presumptuously up into the mountain. 44 And the Amorites, who dwelt in that mountain, came out against you, and chased you, as bees do, and destroyed you in Seir, even to Hormah. 45 And you returned and wept before יהוה; but יהוה would not listen to your voice, nor give ear to you. 46 So you dwelt in Kadesh many days, according to the days that you dwelt there.

2 Then we turned, and took our journey into the wilderness by the way of the Sea of Reeds, as יהוה spoke to me: and we circled Mount Seir many days. 2 And יהוה spoke to me, saying, 3 *You have circled this mountain long enough: turn northward. 4 And command the people, saying, You are to pass through the coast of your brothers the children of Esav, who dwell in Seir; and they shall be afraid of you: take you tov heed to yourselves therefore: 5 Strive not with them; for I will not give you of their land, no, not so much as a footstep; because I have given Mount Seir to Esav for a*

---

[1] Considered a Yahudite even though his abba was not a native.

possession.[1] 6 *You shall buy food from them for money, that you may eat; and you shall also buy water from them for money, that you may drink.* 7 For יהוה Your Elohim has blessed you in all the works of your hand: He knows your wandering through this great wilderness: these forty years יהוה Your Elohim has been with you; you have lacked nothing. 8 And when we passed by from our brothers the children of Esav, who dwelt in Seir, through the way of the plain from Elath, and from Etzion-Gever, we turned and passed by the way of the wilderness of Moav. 9 And יהוה said to me, *Distress not the Moavites, neither contend with them in battle: for I will not give you their land as a possession; because I have given Ar to the children of Lot as a possession.* 10 The Emitess dwelt there in times past, a people great, and many, and tall, as the Anakims; 11 Which also were reckoned as giants, like the Anakims; but the Moavites called them Emites. 12 The Horites also dwelt in Seir before; but the children of Esav succeeded them, when they had destroyed them, and dwelt in their place; as Yisrael did to the land of their possession, which יהוה gave to them. 13 Now rise up, I said, and go over the brook Zered. And we went over the brook Zered. 14 And the time from which we came from Kadesh-Barnea, until we came over the brook Zered, was thirty-eight years; until all the generation of the men of war were consumed from among the camp, as יהוה swore to them. 15 For indeed the hand of יהוה was against them, to destroy them from among the camp, until they were consumed. 16 So it came to pass, when all the men of war had perished from among the people, 17 That יהוה spoke to me, saying, 18 *You are to pass over through Ar, the coast of Moav, this day:* 19 *And when you come near opposite the children of Ammon, distress them not, nor strive with*

them: *for I will not give you the land of the children of Ammon as a possession; because I have given it to the children of Lot for a possession.* 20 (That also was accounted a land of giants: giants dwelt there in old times; and the Ammonites call them Zamzummims; 21 A people great, and many, and as tall, as the Anakim; but יהוה destroyed them before them; and they succeeded them, and dwelt in their place: 22 As He did to the children of Esav, who dwelt in Seir, when He destroyed the Horites from before them; and they succeeded them, and dwelt in their place even to this day: 23 And the Avims who dwelt in Hazerim, even to Azzah, the Kaphtorim, who came forth out of Kaphtor, destroyed them, and dwelt in their place). 24 *Rise up, take your journey, and pass over the river Arnon: see, I have given into your hand Sihon the Amorite, melech of Cheshbon, and his land: begin to possess it, and contend with him in battle.* 25 *This day will I begin to put the dread of you and the fear of you upon the nations that are under the whole shamayim, who shall hear reports of you, and shall tremble, and be in anguish because of you.*[2] 26 And I sent messengers out of the wilderness of Kedemoth to Sihon melech of Cheshbon with words of shalom, saying, 27 Let me pass through your land: I will go along by the high way; I will neither turn to the right hand nor to the left. 28 You shall sell me meat for money that I may eat; and give me water for money, that I may drink: only I will pass through on my feet; 29 As the children of Esav who dwell in Seir, and the Moavites who dwell in Ar, did to me; until I shall pass over Yarden into the land that יהוה our Elohim gives us. 30 But Sihon melech of Cheshbon would not let us pass by him: for יהוה Your Elohim hardened his ruach, and made his lev obstinate, that He might deliver him into your hand, as can be seen this day. 31 And יהוה said to me, *See, I have begun to give*

---

[1] Esau is not homeless. He has Mt. Seir but doesn't like his home, and due to anger and jealousy has come to the land of Yisrael to destroy Jews in his unresolved anger over selling his birthright.

[2] The whole world fears Yisrael's power, influence and might, now and le-olam-va-edmore.

Sihon and his land before you: begin to possess, that you may inherit his land. 32 Then Sihon came out against us, he and all his people, to fight at Yahaz. 33 And יהוה our Elohim delivered him before us; and we smote him, and his sons, and all his people. 34 And we took all his cities at that time, and utterly destroyed the men, and the women, and the little ones, of every city, we left none to remain: 35 Only the cattle we took for a prey to ourselves, and the spoil of the cities that we took. 36 From Aroer, which is by the brink of the river of Arnon, and from the city that is by the river, even to Gilead, there was not one city too strong for us: יהוה our Elohim delivered all of them to us: 37 Only to the land of the children of Ammon you did not come, nor to any place of the river Yavvok, nor to the cities in the mountains, nor to whatever יהוה our Elohim has forbidden us.

3 Then we turned, and went up the way to Bashan: and Og the melech of Bashan came out against us, he and all his people, to battle at Edrei. 2 And יהוה said to me, *Fear him not: for I will deliver him, and all his people, and his land, into your hand; and you shall do to him as you did to Sihon melech of the Amorites, who dwelt at Cheshbon.* 3 So יהוה our Elohim delivered Og into our hands also, the melech of Bashan, and all his people: and we smote him until none of them was left to him. 4 And we took all his cities at that time; there was not a city that we didn't take from them, sixty cities, all the region of Argov, and the malchut of Og in Bashan. 5 All these cities were fenced with high walls, gates, and bars; and many unwalled towns. 6 And we utterly destroyed them, as we did to Sihon melech of Cheshbon, utterly destroying the men, women, and children, of every city. 7 But all the cattle, and the spoil of the cities, we took for a prey for ourselves. 8 And we took at that time out of the hand of the two melechim of the Amorites the land that was beyond Yarden,

from the river of Arnon to Mount Hermon; 9 (Hermon is the place that the Tzidonians call Sirion; and the Amorites call it Shenir) 10 All the cities of the plain, and all Gilead, and all Bashan, to Salchah and Edrei, cities of the malchut of Og in Bashan. 11 For only Og melech of Bashan remained of the remnant of giants; see his bedstead was a bedstead of iron; is it not in Ravvath of the children of Ammon? Nine cubits was the length of it, and four cubits the width of it, after the cubit of a man. 12 And this land, which we possessed at that time, from Aroer, which is by the river Arnon, and half of Mount Gilead, and the cities of it, I gave to the Reuvenites and to the Gadites. 13 And the rest of Gilead, and all Bashan, being the malchut of Og, I gave to the half tribe of Menashsheh; all the region of Argov, with all Bashan, which was called the land of giants. 14 Yair the son of Menashsheh took all the country of Argov to the coasts of Geshuri and Maachathi; and called them after his own name, Bashan-Havoth-Yair, to this day. 15 And I gave Gilead to Machir. 16 And to the Reuvenites and to the Gadites I gave from Gilead even to the river Arnon half the valley, and the border even to the river Yavvok, which is the border of the children of Ammon; 17 The plain also, and Yarden, and the coast off it, from Kinnereth even to the sea of the plain, even the Salt Sea, under the slopes of Pisgah eastward. 18 And I commanded you at that time, saying, יהוה Your Elohim has given you this land to possess it: you shall pass over armed before your brothers the children of Yisrael, all that are fit for the war. 19 But your wives, and your little ones, and your cattle, for I know that you have much cattle; shall abide in your cities that I have given you; 20 Until יהוה has given rest to your brothers, as well as to you, and until they also possess the land which יהוה Your Elohim has given them beyond Yarden: and then shall you return every man to his possession, which I have given you. 21 And I commanded Yahoshua at that time, saying, Your eyes have seen all that יהוה Your Elohim has done to these two melechim: so shall יהוה do to all the malchutim where you are going. 22 You shall not fear them: for יהוה Your Elohim He shall fight for you.

Torah Parsha 45
VaEtchanan 3:23-7:11
Haftarah Yeshayahu 40:1-26
Brit Chadasha Moshe-Markus 12:28-34
Mattiyahu 4:1-11

23 And I pleaded with יהוה at that time, saying, 24 O Sovereign יהוה, You have begun to show Your eved Your greatness, and Your mighty hand: for what El is there in the shamayim or in the earth, that can do according to Your works, and according to Your might? 25 I asked You, let me go over, and see the tov land that is beyond Yarden, that beautiful mountain, and Levanon. 26 But יהוה was angry with me for your sakes, and would not listen me: and יהוה said to me, *Enough of that already! Speak no more to Me about this matter. 27 Get up into the top of Pisgah, and lift up your eyes westward, and northward, and southward, and eastward, and see it with your eyes: for you shall not go over this Yarden. 28 But charge Yahoshua, and encourage him, and strengthen him: for he shall go over before this people, and he shall cause them to inherit the land that you shall see.* 29 So we dwelt in the valley opposite Beth-Peor.

4 Now therefore shema, O Yisrael, to the chukim and to the mishpatim, which I teach you, for to do them, that you may live, and go in and possess the land which יהוה Elohim of your ahvot gives you. 2 You shall not add to the word, which I command you, neither shall, you take away anything from it, that you may shomer the mitzvot of יהוה Your Elohim that I command you. 3 Your eyes have seen what יהוה did because of Baal-Peor: for all the men that followed Baal-Peor, יהוה Your

Elohim has destroyed them from among you. 4 But you who cling to יהוה Your Elohim are alive every one of you this day. 5 See, I have taught you chukim and mishpatim, even as יהוה My Elohim commanded me, that you should do so in the land where you go to possess it. 6 Keep therefore and do them; for this is your chochma and your understanding in the sight of the nations, who shall hear all these chukim, and say, Surely this great nation is a wise and understanding people.[1] 7 For what nation is there so great, who has Elohim so near to them, as יהוה our Elohim is in all things that we call upon Him for? 8 And what nation is there so great, that has chukim and mishpatim so tzadik as all this Torah, which I set before you this day? 9 Only take heed to yourself, and shomer your being diligently, lest you forget the things which your eyes have seen, and lest they depart from your lev all the days of your chayim: but teach them to your sons, and your son's sons; 10 The day that you stood before יהוה Your Elohim in Horev, when יהוה said to me, *Gather the people to Me together, and I will make them hear My words, that they may learn to fear Me all the days that they shall live upon the earth, and that they may teach their children.* 11 And you came near and stood under the mountain; and the mountain burned with fire to the midst of the shamayim, with darkness, clouds, and thick darkness. 12 And יהוה spoke to you out of the midst of the fire: you heard the voice of the words but saw no likeness,[2] only you heard a voice. 13 And He declared to you His covenant, which He commanded you to perform, even the Ten Commandments, and He wrote them upon two tables of stone.[3] 14 And יהוה commanded me at that time to teach you chukim and mishpatim, that you might do them in the land where you are going to possess it. 15 Take therefore tov

---

[1] Torah will separate us above all nations.
[2] The nation didn't see Yahshua, as did Moshe.
[3] Symbolizing His Torah for the eventuality of both houses of Yisrael.

heed to yourselves, for you saw no manner of form on the day that **יהוה** spoke to you in Horev out of the midst of the fire: 16 Lest you corrupt yourselves, and make a graven image, the form of any figure, the likeness of male or female, 17 The likeness of any beast that is on the earth, the likeness of any winged fowl that flies in the air, 18 The likeness of any thing that creeps on the ground, the likeness of any fish that is in the mayim beneath the earth: 19 And lest you lift up your eyes to the shamayim, and when you see the sun, and the moon, and the chochavim, even all the host of the shamayim, should be drawn to worship them, and serve them, which **יהוה** Your Elohim has divided to all nations under the whole shamayim. 20 But **יהוה** has taken you, and brought you forth out of the iron furnace, even out of Mitzrayim, to be to Him a people of inheritance, as you are this day. 21 And **יהוה** was angry with me for your sakes, and swore that I should not go over the Yarden, and that I should not go in to that tov land, which **יהוה** Your Elohim gives you for an inheritance: 22 But I must die in this land, I must not go over the Yarden: but you shall go over, and possess that tov land. 23 Take heed to yourselves, lest you forget the covenant of **יהוה** Your Elohim, which He made with you, and make you a graven image, or the likeness of any thing, that **יהוה** Your Elohim has forbidden you. 24 For **יהוה** Your Elohim is a consuming fire, even a jealous El.[1] 25 When you shall beget children, and children's children, and you shall have remained a long time in the land, and shall corrupt yourselves, and make a graven image, or the likeness of any thing, and shall do evil in the sight of **יהוה** Your Elohim, to provoke Him to anger: 26 I call the shamayim and earth to witness against you this day that you shall soon utterly perish from off the land where you are going over Yarden to possess it; you shall not prolong your days upon it, but shall utterly be destroyed.

27 And **יהוה** shall scatter you among the nations, and you shall be left few in number among the heathen,[2] where **יהוה** shall lead you. 28 And there you shall serve elohim, the work of men's hands, wood and stone, which neither see, nor hear, nor eat, nor smell. 29 But if from there you shall seek **יהוה** Your Elohim, you shall find Him, if you seek Him with all your lev and with all your being. [3] 30 When you are in tribulation,[4] and all these things have come upon you, even in the latter-days, then you shall make teshuvah to **יהוה** Your Elohim, and shall be obedient to His voice. 31 For **יהוה** Your Elohim is an El of rachamim, He will not forsake you, neither destroy you,[5] nor forget the covenant of your ahvot, which He swore to them. 32 For ask now for the days that are past, which were before you, since the day that Elohim created man upon the earth, and ask from the one side of the shamayim to the other, whether there has been any Word as great as this, or anything that has been heard like it? 33 Did any other people hear the voice of Elohim speaking out of the midst of the fire, as you have heard, and live? 34 Or has Elohim tried to go and take for Him a nation from the midst of another nation, by trials, by signs, and by wonders, and by war, and by a mighty hand, and by a stretched-out Arm,[6] and by great deeds, according to all that **יהוה** Your Elohim did for you in Mitzrayim before your eyes? 35 To you it was shown, that you might know that **יהוה** He is Elohim; there is none else beside Him. 36 Out of the shamayim He made you to hear His voice, that He might instruct you: and upon earth He showed you His great fire; and you heard His words out of the midst of the fire. 37 And because He loved

---

[1] This warning later repeated to Renewed Covenant Yisrael.

[2] Few in recognizable numbers not actual numbers since they will look and behave like gentiles.
[3] Always the answer.
[4] Generally any kind of tribulation, specifically the time of Yakkov's Trouble or the Great Tribulation.
[5] Ephraim has to exist and they cannot possibly disappear or be lost. The same applies to Yahudah, since YHWH promised to never fully destroy any part of Yisrael.
[6] A metaphoric expression referring to Yahshua as the right arm of YHWH the Abba.

your ahvot, therefore He chose their zera after them, and brought you out in His sight with His mighty power out of Mitzrayim; 38 To drive out nations from before you greater and mightier than you are, to bring you in, to give you their land for an inheritance, as it is this day. 39 Know therefore this day, and consider it in your lev, that יהוה He is Elohim in the shamayim above, and upon the earth beneath: there is none else. 40 You shall therefore shomer His chukim, and His mitzvot, which I command you this day, that it may go well with you, and with your children after you, and that you may prolong your days upon the earth, which יהוה Your Elohim gives you, le-olam-va-ed. 41 Then Moshe separated three cities on this side of the Yarden toward the rising sun; 42 That the killer might flee there, who might kill his neighbor unintentionally, without hating him in times past; and that fleeing to one of these cities he might live:[1] 43 Namely, Bezer in the wilderness, in the plain country, of the Reuvenites; and Ramoth in Gilead, of the Gadites; and Golan in Bashan, of the Menashshites. 44 And this is the Torah that Moshe set before the children of Yisrael:[2] 45 These are the testimonies, and the chukim, and the mishpatim, which Moshe spoke to the children of Yisrael, after they came forth out of Mitzrayim. 46 On this side of Yarden, in the valley opposite Beth-Peor, in the land of Sihon melech of the Amorites, who dwelt at Cheshbon, whom Moshe and the children of Yisrael smote, after they were come forth out of Mitzrayim: 47 And they possessed his land, and the land of Og melech of Bashan, two melechim of the Amorites, who were on this side of Yarden toward the sunrising; 48 From Aroer, which is by the bank of the river Arnon, even to Mount Sion, which is Hermon, 49 And all the plain on this side of the Yarden eastward, even to the sea of the plain, under the slopes of Pisgah.

5 And Moshe called all Yisrael, and said to them, Shema, O Yisrael, the chukim and mishpatim which I speak in your hearing this day, that you may learn them, and shomer, and do them. 2 יהוה our Elohim made a covenant with us in Horev. 3 יהוה made not this covenant with our ahvot, but with us, who are all of us here alive this day. 4 יהוה talked with you face to face in the Mount out of the midst of the fire, 5 (I stood between יהוה and you at that time, to show you the word of יהוה:[3] For you were afraid because of the fire, and went not up into the Mount) saying, 6 *I am יהוה Your Elohim, who brought you out of the land of Mitzrayim, from the bayit of slavery. 7 You shall have no other elohim before My face. 8 You shall not make any graven image, or any likeness of any thing that is in the shamayim above, or that is on the earth beneath, or that is in the mayim beneath the earth: 9 You shall not bow down to them, nor serve them: for I* יהוה *Your Elohim am a jealous El, visiting the iniquity of the ahvot upon the children to the third and fourth generation of them that hate Me, 10 And showing rachamim to thousands of them that love Me and shomer My mitzvot. 11 You shall not bring the Name of* יהוה *Your Elohim to vain emptiness:* [4] *for* יהוה *will not hold him guiltless that brings His Name to vain emptiness. 12 Keep the Shabbat day to set it apart it, as* יהוה *Your Elohim has commanded you. 13 Six days you shall labor, and do all your work: 14 But the seventh day is the Shabbat of* יהוה *Your Elohim: in it you shall not do any work, you, nor your son, nor your daughter, nor your male eved, nor your female eved, nor your ox, nor your donkey, nor any of your cattle, nor your Ger that is within your gates; that your male eved and your female eved may*

---

[1] **Chesed**/unmerited favor
[2] **Vezot HaTorah asher saam Moshe** used in the synagogue Torah liturgy.
[3] Yahshua.
[4] Bring it to nothing.

rest as well as you.[1] 15 *And remember that you were a eved in the land of Mitzrayim, and that* יהוה *Your Elohim brought you out from there through a mighty hand and by a stretched-out arm: therefore* יהוה *Your Elohim commanded you to shomer the Shabbat day.* 16 *Honor your abba and your ima, as* יהוה *Your Elohim has commanded you; that your days may be prolonged, and that it may go well with you, in the land that* יהוה *Your Elohim gives you.* 17 *You shall not kill.* 18 *Neither shall you commit adultery.* 19 *Neither shall you steal.* 20 *Neither shall you bear false witness against your neighbor.* 21 *Neither shall you desire your neighbor's wife, neither shall you covet your neighbor's bayit, his field, nor his male eved, nor his female eved, his ox, or his donkey, or any thing that is your neighbor's.* 22 These words יהוה spoke to all your congregation in the Mount out of the midst of the fire, of the cloud, and of the thick darkness, with a great voice: and He added no more. And He wrote them in two tables of stone, and delivered them to me. 23 And it came to pass, when you heard the voice out of the midst of the darkness, for the mountain did burn with fire, that you came near to me, even all the heads of your tribes, and your zachanim; 24 And you said, See, יהוה our Elohim has shown us His tifereth and His greatness, and we have heard His voice out of the midst of the fire: we have seen this day that Elohim does talk with man, and man still lives. 25 Now therefore why should we die? For this great fire will consume us: if we hear the voice of יהוה our Elohim any more, then we shall die. 26 For who is there of all flesh, that has heard the voice of the living Elohim speaking out of the midst of the fire, as we have, and lived? 27 You go near, and hear all that יהוה our Elohim shall say: and speak to us all that יהוה our Elohim shall speak to you; and we will listen to it, and do it.[2] 28 And יהוה heard the voice of your

words, when you spoke to me; and יהוה said to me, *I have heard the voice of the words of this people, which they have spoken to you: they have well said all that they have spoken.* 29 *O that there were such a lev in them, that they would fear Me, and shomer all My mitzvot always, that it might be well with them, and with their children le-olam-va-ed!* 30 Go say to them, Get into your tents again. 31 But as for you, stand here by Me, and I will speak to you all the mitzvot, and the chukim, and the mishpatim, which you shall teach them, that they may do them in the land that I give them to possess it. 32 You shall shomer to do therefore as יהוה Your Elohim has commanded you: you shall not turn aside to the right hand or to the left. 33 You shall have your halacha in all the halachot that יהוה Your Elohim has commanded you, that you may live, and that it may be well with you, and that you may prolong your days in the land that you shall possess.

6 Now these are the mitzvot, the chukim, and the mishpatim, which יהוה Your Elohim commanded to teach you, that you might do them in the land where you go to possess it: 2 That you might fear יהוה Your Elohim, to shomer all His chukim and His mitzvot, which I command you, you, and your son, and your son's son, all the days of your chayim; and that your days may be prolonged. 3 Shema, O Yisrael, and shomer to do it; that it may be well with you, and that you may increase mightily,[3] as יהוה Elohim of your ahvot has promised you, in the land that flows with milk and honey. 4 Shema, O Yisrael: יהוה is our Elohim, יהוה is Echad:[4] 5 And you shall love יהוה Your Elohim with all your lev, and with all your being, and with all your might. 6 And these words, which I command you this day, shall be in your lev:

---

[1] All Yisrael benefits from Torah.
[2] Yisrael always needed an intercessor, as they were unable or unwilling to hear directly from YHWH. The same holds true today for both houses, for without Yahshua, neither house will hear clearly and without fear.
[3] Physical multiplicity.
[4] The **Shema**. YHWH is **echad** not **yachid**, meaning He is, and always will be, a plurality in divinity.

7 And you shall teach them diligently to your children, and shall talk of them when you sit in your bayit, and when you walk by the way, and when you lie down, and when you rise up. 8 And you shall bind them for a sign upon your hand, and they shall be as frontlets[1] between your eyes. 9 And you shall write them upon the posts of your bayit, and on your gates.[2] 10 And it shall be, when יהוה Your Elohim shall have brought you into the land which He swore to your ahvot, to Avraham, to Yitzchak, and to Yaakov, to give you great and tov cities, which you did not build, 11 And houses full of all tov things, which you filled not, and wells dug, which you did not dig, vineyards and olive eytzim, which you planted not; when you shall have eaten and are full; 12 Then beware lest you forget יהוה, who brought you forth out of the land of Mitzrayim, from the bayit of slavery. 13 You shall fear יהוה Your Elohim, and serve Him, and shall swear by His Name.[3] 14 You shall not go after other elohim, the elohim of the peoples who are all around you; 15 (For יהוה Your Elohim is a jealous El among you) lest the anger of יהוה Your Elohim be lit against you, and destroy you from off the face of the earth. 16 You shall not try יהוה Your Elohim, as you tried Him in Massah. 17 You shall diligently shomer the mitzvot of יהוה Your Elohim, and His testimonies, and His chukim, which He has commanded you. 18 And you shall do that which is right and tov in the sight of יהוה: that it may be well with you, and that you may go in and possess the tov land that יהוה swore to your ahvot. 19 To cast out all your enemies from before you, as יהוה has spoken. 20 And when your son asks you in times to come, saying, What means these testimonies, and the chukim, and the mishpatim, which יהוה our Elohim has commanded you? 21 Then you shall say to your son, We were Pharaoh's avadim in Mitzrayim; and יהוה brought us out of

Mitzrayim with a mighty hand: 22 And יהוה shown signs and wonders, great and grievous, upon Mitzrayim, upon Pharaoh, and upon his entire household, before our eyes: 23 And He brought us out from there, that He might bring us in, to give us the land that He swore to our ahvot. 24 And יהוה commanded us to do all these chukim, to fear יהוה our Elohim, for our tov always, that He might preserve us alive, as it is at this day. 25 And it shall be our tzedakah, if we shomer to do all these mitzvot before יהוה our Elohim, as He has commanded us.[4]

7 When יהוה Your Elohim shall bring you into the land where you are going to possess it, and has cast out many nations before you, the Hittites, and the Girgashites, and the Amorites, and the Kanaanites, and the Perizzites, and the Hivites, and the Yevusites, seven nations greater and mightier than you; 2 And when יהוה Your Elohim shall deliver them before you; you shall smite them, and utterly destroy them; you shall make no covenant with them, nor show rachamim to them:[5] 3 Neither shall you make marriages with them; your daughter you shall not give to his son, nor his daughter shall you take to your son. 4 For they will turn away your son from following Me, that they may serve other elohim: so will the anger of יהוה be lit against you, and destroy you suddenly.[6] 5 But this is how you shall deal with them; you shall destroy their altars, and break down their images, and cut down their groves, and burn their graven images with fire. 6 For you are a kadosh people to יהוה Your Elohim: יהוה Your Elohim has chosen you to be a special people to Himself, above all people that are upon the

---

[1] Known today as **Tefillin.**
[2] **Mezuzot.**
[3] For oaths.

[4] This does not mean that Torah justifies. It means that our tzedakah in Moshiach's atonement will be guarded and kept secure by obedience, which protects us from falling away.
[5] To guarantee set-apartness and victory.
[6] Redeemed Yisraelites must not intermarry with those who still do not obey Torah, even if they profess a mental assent to salvation. Ephraimites and Yahudites are free to marry each other as long as both love Moshiach and Torah.

face of the earth. 7 **יהוה** did not set His love upon you, nor choose you, because you were more in number than any people; for you were the fewest of all people:[1] 8 But because **יהוה** loved you, and because He would shomer the oath which He had sworn to your ahvot, has **יהוה** brought you out with a mighty hand, and redeemed you out of the bayit of avadim, from the hand of Pharaoh melech of Mitzrayim. 9 Know that **יהוה** Your Elohim, He is Elohim, the faithful El, who keeps covenant and rachamim with them that love Him and shomer His mitzvot to a thousand generations;[2] 10 And repays them that hate Him to their face, to destroy them: He will not be slack to anyone that hates Him; He will repay him to his face. 11 You shall therefore shomer the mitzvot, and the chukim, and the mishpatim, which I command you this day, to do them.

Torah Parsha 46
Ekev 7:12-11:25
Haftarah Yeshayahu 49:14-51:3, 52:1-15
Brit Chadasha Luka 4:1-13

12 Therefore it shall come to pass, if you listen to these mishpatim, and shomer, and do them, that **יהוה** Your Elohim shall shomer with you the covenant and the rachamim which He swore to your ahvot: 13 And He will love you, and bless you, and multiply you: He will also bless the fruit of your womb, and the fruit of your land, your corn, and your wine, and your oil, the increase of your cattle, and the flocks of your sheep, in the land which He swore to your ahvot to give you. 14 You shall be blessed above all peoples: there shall not be male or female barren among you, or among your cattle. 15 And **יהוה** will take away from you all sickness, and will put none of the evil diseases of Mitzrayim, which you

know about, upon you; but will lay them upon all them that hate you. 16 And you shall consume all the peoples that **יהוה** Your Elohim shall deliver you; your eye shall have no pity upon them: neither shall you serve their elohim; for that will be a snare to you. 17 If you shall say in your lev, These nations are more than I; how can I dispossess them? 18 You shall not be afraid of them: but shall well remember what **יהוה** Your Elohim did to Pharaoh, and to all Mitzrayim; 19 The great temptations which your eyes saw, and the signs, and the wonders, and the mighty hand, and the stretched-out arm, whereby **יהוה** Your Elohim brought you out: so shall **יהוה** Your Elohim do to all the peoples of whom you fear. 20 Moreover **יהוה** Your Elohim will send the hornet among them, until they that are left, who hide themselves from you, will be destroyed. 21 You shall not be afraid of them: for **יהוה** Your Elohim is among you, a Mighty-El and awesome. 22 And **יהוה** Your Elohim will put out those nations before you little by little: you may not consume them at once, lest the beasts of the field increase upon you. 23 But **יהוה** Your Elohim shall deliver them to you, and shall destroy them with a mighty destruction, until they are destroyed. 24 And He shall deliver their melechim into your hand, and you shall destroy their name from under the shamayim: there shall no man be able to stand before you, until you have destroyed them. 25 The graven images of their elohim shall you burn with fire: you shall not desire the silver or gold that is on them, nor take it for you, lest you be snared with it: for it is an abomination to **יהוה** Your Elohim. 26 Neither shall you bring an abomination into your bayit, lest you be a cursed thing like it: but you shall utterly detest it, and you shall utterly abhor it; for it is a cursed thing.

8 All the mitzvot, which I command you this day, shall you shomer to do, that you may live, and multiply, and go in and

---

[1] At first prior to divine election.
[2] If a generation is 50 years, and YHWH promises love to 1,000 generations of Yisrael, that means His love for Yisrael is for a minimum of 50,000 years. That means that there is no church apart from Yisrael, the single elect community of faith for all believers and **kidushim**.

possess the land that יהוה swore to your ahvot. 2 And you shall remember all the ways that יהוה Your Elohim led you these forty years in the wilderness, to humble you, and to prove you, to know what was in your lev, whether you would shomer His mitzvot, or not. 3 And He humbled you, and allowed you to hunger, and fed you with manna, which you knew not, neither did your ahvot know; that He might make you know that man does not live by lechem only, but by every word that proceeds out of the mouth of יהוה does man live. 4 Your garment did not wear out on you; neither did your foot swell, these forty years. 5 You shall also consider in your lev, that, as a man disciplines his son, so יהוה Your Elohim disciplines you. 6 Therefore you shall shomer the mitzvot of יהוה Your Elohim, to have your halacha in His halachot, and to fear Him. 7 For יהוה Your Elohim brings you into a tov land, a land of brooks of water, of fountains and depths that spring out of valleys and hills; 8 A land of wheat, and barley, and vines, and fig eytzim, and pomegranates; a land of olive oil, and honey; 9 A land where you shall eat lechem without scarceness, you shall not lack any thing in it; a land whose stones are iron, and out of whose hills you may dig brass. 10 When you have eaten and are full, then you shall bless יהוה Your Elohim for the tov land that He has given you.[1] 11 Beware that you forget not יהוה Your Elohim, in not keeping His mitzvot, and His mishpatim, and His chukim, which I command you this day: 12 Lest when you have eaten and are full, and have built nice houses, and dwelt in them; 13 And when your herds and your flocks multiply, and your silver and your gold is multiplied, and all that you have is multiplied;[2] 14 That your lev be lifted up, and you forget יהוה Your Elohim, who brought you forth out of

the land of Mitzrayim, from the bayit of slavery; 15 Who led you through that great and awesome wilderness, where there were fiery serpents, and scorpions, and drought, where there was no water; who brought forth water out of the rock of flint; 16 Who fed you in the wilderness with manna, which your ahvot knew not, that He might humble you, and that He might prove you, to do you tov at your latter-end, 17 And you say in your lev, My power and the might of my hand has gotten me this wealth. 18 But you shall remember יהוה Your Elohim: for it is He that gives you power to get wealth, that He may establish His covenant which He swore to your ahvot, as it is this day.[3] 19 And it shall be, if you do in any manner forget יהוה Your Elohim, and walk after other elohim, and serve them, and worship them, I testify against you this day that you shall surely perish. 20 And like the nations that יהוה destroyed before your face, so shall you also perish; because you would not be obedient to the voice of יהוה Your Elohim.

9 Shema, O Yisrael: You are to pass over Yarden this day, to go in to possess nations greater and mightier than yourself, cities great and fenced up to the shamayim, 2 A people great and tall, the children of the Anakim, whom you know, and of whom you have heard say, Who can stand before the children of Anak! 3 Understand therefore this day, that יהוה Your Elohim is He who goes over before you; as a consuming fire He shall destroy them, and He shall bring them down before your face: so shall you drive them out, and destroy them quickly, as יהוה has said to you. 4 Do not say in your lev, after יהוה Your Elohim has cast them out from before you, saying, For my tzedakah יהוה has brought me in to possess this land: rather for the wickedness of those nations יהוה does drive them out from before you. 5 Not for

---

[1] Proper "grace after meals." Hebrews say "grace" after meals, when they have fully experienced YHWH's tov provision. "Grace" before meals is not scriptural, though it is permitted to say a brief blessing.
[2] According to promise.

[3] Wealth for Yisrael is a sign of the covenant of being Yisrael, not a guarantee of eternal life in Moshiach.

your tzedakah, or for the uprightness of your lev, do you go to possess their land: but for the wickedness of these nations יהוה Your Elohim does drive them out from before you, and that He may perform the word which יהוה swore to your ahvot, Avraham, Yitzchak, and Yaakov. *6 Understand therefore, that יהוה Your Elohim does not give you this tov land to possess it for your tzedakah; for you are a stiff-necked people. 7 Remember, and don't forget, how you provoked יהוה Your Elohim to wrath in the wilderness: from the day that you did depart out of the land of Mitzrayim, until you came to this place, you have been rebellious against יהוה . 8 Also in Horev you provoked יהוה to wrath, so that יהוה was angry with you and wanted to destroy you. 9 When I had gone up into the Mount to receive the tables of stone, even the tables of the covenant that יהוה made with you, then I dwelt in the Mount forty days and forty nights, I neither did eat lechem nor drink water: 10 And יהוה delivered to me two tables of stone written with the finger of Elohim; and on them was written according to all the words, which יהוה spoke with you in the Mount out of the midst of the fire in the day of the congregation. 11 And it came to pass at the end of forty days and forty nights, that יהוה gave me the two tables of stone, even the tables of the covenant. 12 And יהוה said to me, Arise, get down quickly from here; for your people who you have brought forth out of Mitzrayim have corrupted themselves; they have quickly turned aside out of the derech which I commanded them; they have made for themselves a molded image. 13 And יהוה spoke to me, saying, I have seen this people, and, see, it is a stiff-necked people: 14 Leave Me alone, that I may destroy them, and blot out their name from under the shamayim: and I will make from you a nation mightier and greater than they are. 15 So I turned and came down from the Mount, and the Mount burned with*

fire: and the two tables of the covenant were in my two hands. 16 And I looked, and, saw that, you had sinned against יהוה Your Elohim, and had made a molded calf: you had turned aside quickly out of the derech that יהוה had commanded you. 17 And I took the two tables, and cast them out of my two hands, and broke them before your eyes. 18 And I fell down before יהוה, as at first, forty days and forty nights: I did neither eat lechem, nor drink water, because of all your sins which you sinned, in doing wickedly in the sight of יהוה, to provoke Him to anger. 19 For I was afraid of the anger and hot displeasure, with which יהוה was angry against you to destroy you. But יהוה heard to me at that time also. 20 And יהוה was very angry with Aharon to have destroyed him: and I made tefillah for Aharon also at the same time. 21 And I took your sin, the calf which you had made, and burnt it with fire, and stamped it, and ground it very small, even until it was as small as dust: and I cast the dust into the brook that descended out of the Mount. 22 And at Taverah, and at Massah, and at Kivroth-Hattaavah, you provoked יהוה to wrath. 23 And when יהוה sent you from Kadesh-Barnea, saying, Go up and possess the land that I have given you; then you rebelled against the mitzvah of יהוה Your Elohim, and you believed Him not, nor heard to His voice. 24 You have been rebellious against יהוה from the day that I knew you. 25 So I fell down before יהוה forty days and forty nights, as I fell down at the first; because יהוה had said He would destroy you. 26 I made tefillah therefore to יהוה, and said, O Sovereign יהוה, destroy not your people and your inheritance, whom you have redeemed through your greatness, whom you have brought out of Mitzrayim with a mighty hand. 27 Remember your avadim, Avraham, Yitzchak, and Yaakov; look not to the stubbornness of this people, nor to their wickedness, nor to their sin: 28 Lest the land from where you brought us out say, Because יהוה was not able to bring them into the land which He promised them, and because He hated them, He has brought them out to slay them in the wilderness. 29 Yet they are Your people and Your inheritance, which You brought out by Your mighty power and by Your stretched-out Arm. 10 At that time יהוה said to me, Cut two tables of stone like the first, and come up to Me into the Mount, and make an Ark of wood. 2 And I will write on the tables the words that were in the first tables that you broke, and you shall put them in the Ark. 3 And I made an Ark of shittim wood, and cut two tables of stone like the first, and went up into the Mount, having the two tables in my hand. 4 And He wrote on the tables, according to the first writing, the ten mitzvot, which יהוה spoke to you in the Mount out of the midst of the fire in the day of the congregation: and יהוה gave them to me. 5 And I turned and came down from the Mount, and put the tables in the Ark that I had made; and there they are, as יהוה commanded me. 6 And the children of Yisrael took their journey from Beeroth of the children of Yaakan to Mosera: there Aharon died, and there he was buried; and El-Azar his son served in the kohen's office in his place. 7 From there they journeyed to Gudgodah; and from Gudgodah to Yotbath, a land of rivers of mayim. 8 At that time יהוה separated the tribe of Levi, to bear the Ark of the Covenant of יהוה, to stand before יהוה to attend to Him, and to bless in His Name, to this day.[1] 9 Therefore Levi has no part or inheritance with his brothers; יהוה is his inheritance, as יהוה Your Elohim promised him. 10 And I stayed in the Mount, according to the first time, forty days and forty nights; and יהוה heard to me at that time also, and יהוה chose not destroy you. 11 And יהוה said to me, Arise, take your journey before the people, that they may go in and possess the land, which I

swore to their ahvot to give to them. 12 And now, Yisrael, what does יהוה Your Elohim require of you, but to fear יהוה Your Elohim, to have your halacha in all His ways, and to love Him, and to serve יהוה Your Elohim with all your lev and with all your being, 13 To shomer the mitzvot of יהוה, and His chukim, which I command you this day for your tov. 14 See, the shamayim and the shamayim of shamayim is יהוה's Your Elohim, the earth also, with all that is in it. 15 Only יהוה had a delight in your ahvot to love them, and He chose their zera after them, even you above all peoples, as it is this day. 16 Brit-milah therefore the foreskin of your lev,[2] and be no more stiff-necked. 17 For יהוה Your Elohim is the Elohim of all mighty ones, and Sovereign of all sovereigns, a great El, Mighty, and Awesome, who shows no partiality, nor takes bribes: 18 He does execute the mishpat of the fatherless and widow, and loves the Ger, in giving him food and garment. 19 Ahav therefore the Ger: for you were Gerim in the land of Mitzrayim.[3] 20 You shall fear יהוה Your Elohim; Him shall you serve, and to Him shall you cleave, and swear by His Name. 21 He is your tehilla, and He is Your Elohim, that has done for you these great and awesome things, which your eyes have seen. 22 Your ahvot went down into Mitzrayim with seventy-five persons;[4] and now יהוה Your Elohim has made you as the chochavim of the shamayim for multitude.[5]

11 Therefore you shall love יהוה Your Elohim, and shomer His charge, and His chukim, and His mishpatim, and His mitzvot, always.[6] 2 And know you

---

[1] How far we have fallen?

[2] Be born again o Yisrael! Known in Hebrew as **Brit HaLev**.
[3] A word in due season for the House of Yahudah, as they welcome back returning Ephraim Yisrael.
[4] Following the Torah of two or more witnesses here, from the LXX Shemot 1:5 and Acts 7:14.
[5] A nation of four million one of the largest of the ancient world, about to become 4 billion in the end of days.
[6] Even after Moshiach comes.

this day. for I speak not with your children who have not known, and who have not seen the chastisement of יהוה Your Elohim, His greatness, His mighty hand, and His stretched-out Arm, 3 And His nisim, and His acts, which He did in the midst of Mitzrayim to Pharaoh the melech of Mitzrayim, and to all his land; 4 And what He did to the army of Mitzrayim, to their horses, and to their chariots; how He made the water of the Sea of Reeds to overflow them as they pursued after you, and how יהוה has destroyed them to this day; 5 And what He did for you in the wilderness, until you came into this place; 6 And what He did to Dathan and Aviram, the sons of Eliav, the son of Reuven: how the earth opened its mouth, and swallowed them up, and their households, and their tents, and all the substance that was in their possession, in the midst of all Yisrael: 7 But your eyes have seen all the great acts of יהוה which He did. 8 Therefore shall you shomer all the mitzvot which I command you this day, that you may be strong, and go in and possess the land, where you are going to possess it; 9 And to prolong your days in the land, which יהוה swore to your ahvot to give to them and to their zera, a land that flows with milk and honey. 10 For the land, where you go in to possess it, is not as the land of Mitzrayim, from where you came out, where you sowed your zera, and watered it by foot, as a garden of herbs: 11 But the land, where you are going to possess it, is a land of hills and valleys, and drinking water from the rain of the shamayim: 12 A land that יהוה Your Elohim cares for: the eyes of יהוה Your Elohim are always upon it, from the beginning of the year even to the end of the year. 13 *And it shall come to pass, if you shall listen diligently to My mitzvot which I command you this day, to love יהוה Your Elohim, and to serve Him with all your lev and with all your being, 14 That I will give you the rain of your land in its due season, the first rain and the latter rain, that you may gather in your corn, and your wine, and your oil. 15 And I will send grass in your fields for your cattle, that you may eat and be full. 16 Take heed to yourselves, that your lev be not deceived, and you turn aside, and serve other elohim, and worship them;* 17 And then יהוה 's wrath be lit against you, and He will shut up the shamayim, that there be no rain, and that the land yield not its fruit; and lest you perish quickly from off the tov land which יהוה gives you. 18 *Therefore shall you lay up My words in your lev and in your being, and bind them for a sign upon your hand, that they may be as frontlets between your eyes. 19 And you shall teach them to your children, speaking of them when you sit in your bayit, and when you walk by the way, when you lie down, and when you rise up. 20 And you shall write them upon the doorposts of your bayit, and upon your gates:* 21 That your days may be multiplied, and the days of your children, in the land which יהוה swore to your ahvot to give them, as the days of the shamayim upon the earth. 22 For if you shall diligently shomer all these mitzvot that I command you, to do them, to love יהוה Your Elohim, to have your halacha in all His halachot, and to cleave to Him; 23 Then will יהוה drive out all these nations from before you, and you shall possess greater nations and mightier ones than yourselves. 24 Every place the soles of your feet shall tread shall be yours: from the wilderness and Levanon, from the River Euphrates, even to the Western Sea shall your coast be. 25 There shall no man be able to stand before you: for יהוה Your Elohim shall lay the fear of you and the dread of you upon all the land that you shall tread upon, as He has said to you.

Torah Parsha 47
Re'eh 11:26-16:17
Haftarah Yeshayahu 44:11-45:5
Brit Chadasha Yochanan Alef 4:1-6, 2:18-25

26 See, I set before you this day a blessing and a curse; 27 A blessing, if you obey the

mitzvot of יהוה Your Elohim, which I command you this day: 28 And a curse, if you will not obey the mitzvot of יהוה Your Elohim, but turn aside out of the derech which I command you this day, to go after other elohim, which you have not known. 29 And it shall come to pass, when יהוה Your Elohim has brought you into the land where you go to possess it, that you shall put the blessing upon Mount Gerizim, and the curse upon Mount Eval. 30 Are they not on the other side of the Yarden, by the way where the sun goes down, in the land of the Kanaanites, who dwell in the desert plain opposite Gilgal, beside the plains of Moreh? 31 For you shall pass over the Yarden to go in to possess the land that יהוה Your Elohim gives you, and you shall possess it, and dwell therein. 32 And you shall shomer to do all the chukim and mishpatim that I set before you this day.

12 These are the chukim and mishpatim, which you shall shomer to do in the land, which יהוה Elohim of your ahvot gives you to possess it, all the days that you live upon the earth. 2 You shall utterly destroy all the places, in which the nations, which you shall possess, served their elohim, upon the high mountains, and upon the hills, and under every green eytz: 3 And you shall overthrow their altars, and break their pillars, and burn their Asherim with fire; and you shall cut down the graven images of their elohim, and destroy the names[1] of them out of that place. 4 You shall not do so to יהוה Your Elohim. 5 But to the place that יהוה Your Elohim shall choose out of all your tribes to put His Name there, even to His dwelling shall you seek, and there you shall come:[2] 6 And there you shall bring your burnt offerings, and your sacrifices, and your tithes, and heave offerings of your hand, and your vows, and your terumah offerings, and the bechorot of

your herds and of your flocks: 7 And there you shall eat before יהוה Your Elohim, and you shall gilah in all that you put your hand to, you and your households, in which יהוה Your Elohim has blessed you. 8 You shall not do after all the things that we do here this day; every man whatever is right in his own eyes. 9 For you have not as yet come to the rest and to the inheritance, which יהוה Your Elohim gives you. 10 But when you go over the Yarden, and dwell in the land which יהוה Your Elohim gives you to inherit, and when He gives you rest from all your enemies all around, so that you dwell in safety; 11 Then there shall be a place which יהוה Your Elohim shall choose to cause His Name to dwell there; there shall you bring all that I command you; your burnt offerings, and your sacrifices, your tithes, and the heave offering of your hand, and all your choice vows which you vow to יהוה: 12 And you shall gilah before יהוה Your Elohim, you, and your sons, and your daughters, and your male avadim, and your female avadim, and the Ha Levi that is within your gates; because he has no part or inheritance with you. 13 Take heed to yourself that you offer not your burnt offerings in every place that you see: 14 But in the place which יהוה shall choose in one of your tribes, there you shall offer your burnt offerings, and there you shall do all that I command you. 15 Whatever you desire you may kill and eat in all your gates, according to the blessing of יהוה Your Elohim which He has given you: the unclean and the clean may eat of it, as of the gazelle, and deer alike.[3] 16 Only you shall not eat the dom; you shall pour it upon the earth as water. 17 You may not eat within your gates the tithe of your corn, or of your wine, or of your oil, or the bechorot of your herds or of your flock, nor any of your vows which you vowed, nor your terumah offerings, or heave offering of your hand: 18 But you must eat them before יהוה Your

---

[1] Yirseal must destroy the name of false deities, even though they may be familiar and comfortable. Only YHWH's set-apart Name should be in our midst.
[2] **Yahrushalayim**

[3] Any animal whether clean or unclean can eat any other animal used for offering, but the dom must be poured out. This is not an allowance for Yisrael to eat unclean food.

Elohim in the place which יהוה Your Elohim shall choose, you, and your son, and your daughter, and your male eved, and your female eved, and the Ha Levi that is within your gates: and you shall gilah before יהוה Your Elohim in all that you put your hands to. 19 Guard yourself that you forsake not the Ha Levi as long as you live upon the earth.[1] 20 When יהוה Your Elohim shall enlarge your border, as He has promised you, and you shall say, I will eat meat, because your being longs to eat flesh; you may eat flesh, whatever your being desires after. 21 If the place where יהוה Your Elohim has chosen to put His Name is too far from you, then you shall kill of your herd and of your flock, which יהוה has given you, as I have commanded you, and you shall eat in your gates whatever your being desires. 22 Even as the gazelle and the deer are eaten, so you shall eat them: the unclean and the clean shall eat of them alike. 23 Only be sure that you eat not the dom: for the dom is the chayim; and you may not eat the chayim with the meat. 24 You shall not eat it; you shall pour it upon the earth as water. 25 You shall not eat it; that it may go well with you, and with your children after you, when you shall do that which is right in the sight of יהוה.[2] 26 Only your kadosh things which you have, and your vows, you shall take, and go to the place which יהוה shall choose: 27 And you shall offer your burnt offerings, the meat and the dom, upon the altar of יהוה Your Elohim: and the dom of your sacrifices shall be poured out upon the altar of יהוה Your Elohim, and you shall eat the meat. 28 Shomer and hear all these words which I command you, that it may go well with you, and with your children after you le-olam-va-ed, when you do that which is tov and right in the sight of יהוה Your Elohim. 29 When יהוה Your Elohim shall cut off the nations from before you, where

you are going to possess them, and you dispossess them, and dwell in their land; 30 Guard yourself that you are not ensnared by following them, after they are destroyed from before you; and that you inquire not after their elohim, saying, How did these nations serve their elohim? Even so will I do too. 31 You shall not do so to יהוה Your Elohim: for every abomination to יהוה, that He hates, have they done to their elohim; for even their sons and their daughters they have burnt in the fire to their elohim. 32 Whatever I am commanding you, shomer to do it: you shall not add to it, nor take away from it.

13 If there arise among you a navi, or a dreamer of dreams, and gives you a sign or a wonder, 2 And the sign or the wonders come to pass,[3] which he spoke to you, saying, Let us go after other elohim, which you have not known, and let us serve them; 3 You shall not listen to the words of that navi, or that dreamer of dreams: for יהוה Your Elohim tests you, to know whether you love יהוה Your Elohim with all your lev and with all your being. 4 You shall have your halacha after יהוה Your Elohim, and fear Him, and shomer His mitzvot, and obey His voice, and you shall serve Him, and cleave to Him. 5 And that navi, or that dreamer of dreams, shall be put to death; because he has spoken to turn you away from יהוה Your Elohim, who brought you out of the land of Mitzrayim, and redeemed you out of the bayit of slavery, to draw you out of the halacha that יהוה Your Elohim commanded you to have your halachia in. So shall you put the evil away from the midst of you. 6 If your brother, the son of your ima, or your son, or your daughter, or the wife of your bosom, or your friend, which is as your own being, entice you secretly, saying, Let us go and serve other elohim, whom you have not known,

---

[1] Yisrael is eternally responsible for providing for their leaders in both covenants.
[2] Drinking and eating dom is characteristic of pagan worship and diet.

[3] Signs coming to pass are not in itself a validating mark of a person's ministry. The greater question is do they point people to YHWH or away from YHWH, and do they follow a Torah-obedient life?

you, nor your ahvot; 7 Namely, of the elohim of the people who are all around you, near to you, or far off from you, from one end of the earth even to the other end of the earth; 8 You shall not agree with him, or listen to him; neither shall your eye pity him, neither shall you spare, neither shall you conceal him: 9 But you shall surely kill him; your hand shall be first upon him to put him to death, and afterwards the hand of all the people. 10 And you shall stone him with stones, that he die; because he has sought to tear you away from **יהוה** Your Elohim, which brought you out of the land of Mitzrayim, from the bayit of slavery.[1] 11 And all Yisrael shall hear, and fear, and shall do no more any such wickedness as this among you. 12 If you shall hear something from one of your cities, that **יהוה** Your Elohim has given you to dwell there, saying, 13 Certain men, the children of Belial, have gone out from among you, and have withdrawn the inhabitants of their city, saying, Let us go and serve other elohim, whom you have not known; 14 Then shall you inquire, and search, and ask diligently; and, see, if it be emet, and if the thing is certain, that such abomination is done among you; 15 You shall surely smite the inhabitants of that city with the edge of the sword, destroying it utterly, and all that is in it, and the cattle of it, with the edge of the sword. 16 And you shall gather all the spoil of it into the midst of the street of it, and shall burn with fire the city, and all the spoil of it, for **יהוה** Your Elohim: and it shall be a heap le-olam-va-ed; it shall not be built again. 17 And there shall cleave none of the cursed thing to your hand: that **יהוה** may turn from the fierceness of His anger, and show you rachamim, and have compassion upon you, and multiply you, as He has sworn to your ahvot;[2] 18 When you shall listen to the voice of **יהוה** Your

Elohim, to shomer all His mitzvot that I command you this day, to do that which is tzadik in the eyes of **יהוה** Your Elohim.

14 You are the children of **יהוה** Your Elohim: you shall not cut yourselves, nor shave between your eyes for the dead. 2 For you are a kadosh people to **יהוה** Your Elohim, and **יהוה** has chosen you to be a treasured possession, a people for Himself, above all the nations that are upon the earth. 3 You shall not eat any abominable thing. 4 These are the beasts that you shall eat: the ox, the sheep, and the goat, 5 The deer, and the gazelle, and the fallow deer, and the wild goat, and the mountain goat, and the wild ox, and the mountain goat. 6 And every beast that parts the hoof, and splits the hoof in two, and chews the cud among the beasts that you shall eat. 7 Nevertheless these you shall not eat of them that chew the cud, or of them that split the hoof; like the camel, and the hare, and the rabbit: for they chew the cud, but split not the hoof; therefore they are unclean to you. 8 And the swine, because it parts the hoof, yet chews not the cud, it is unclean to you: you shall not eat of their flesh, nor touch their dead body. 9 These you shall eat of all that are in the mayim: all that have fins and scales shall you eat: 10 And whatever has not fins and scales you may not eat; it is unclean to you. 11 Of all clean birds you shall eat. 12 But these are they of which you shall not eat: the eagle, and the vulture, and the black vulture, 13 And the red kite, and the falcon and the buzzard after their kinds, 14 And every raven after its kind. 15 And the ostrich, and the nighthawk, and the seagull, and the hawk after its kind, 16 The little owl, and the great owl, and the white owl, 17 And the pelican, and the carrion vulture, and the fisher owl, 18 And the stork, and the heron after its kind, and the lapwing, and the bat. 19 And every creeping thing that flies is unclean to you: they shall not be eaten. 20 But of all clean birds you may eat.

---

[1] This is what Yahudah's leaders wrongly believed Yahshua was doing, namely, pulling people to other Elohim, when in fact as He said He was not drawing men after Himself, but restoring them to His Abba.
[2] Paganism destroys Yisrael from within.

21 You shall not eat of anything that dies by itself: you shall give it to the Ger that is in your gates, that he may eat it; or you may sell it to an alien: for you are a kadosh people to יהוה Your Elohim. You shall not cook a kid in its ima's milk. 22 You shall truly tithe all the increase of your zera that the field brings forth year by year. 23 And you shall eat before יהוה Your Elohim, in the place that He shall choose to place His Name there, the tithe of your corn, of your wine, and of your oil, and the bechorot of your herds and of your flocks; that you may learn to fear יהוה Your Elohim always. 24 And if the way is too long for you, so that you are not able to carry it; or if the place is too far from you, that יהוה Your Elohim shall choose to set His Name there, when יהוה Your Elohim has blessed you: 25 Then shall you turn it into money, and bind up the money in your hand, and shall go to the place which יהוה Your Elohim shall choose:[1] 26 And you shall bestow that money for whatever your being desires after, for oxen, or for sheep, or for wine, or for strong drink, or for whatever your being desires: and you shall eat there before יהוה Your Elohim, and you shall gilah, you, and your household, 27 And the Ha Levi that is within your gates; you shall not forsake him; for he has no part or inheritance with you. 28 At the end of three years you shall bring forth all the tithe of your increase the same year, and shall lay it up within your gates: 29 And the Ha Levi, (because he has no part nor inheritance with you,) and the Ger, and the fatherless, and the widow, which are within your gates, shall come, and shall eat and be satisfied; that יהוה Your Elohim may bless you in all the work of your hands which you do.[2]

15 At the end of every seven years you shall make a release. 2 And this is the manner of the release: Every creditor that lends anything to his neighbor shall release it; he shall not require it from his neighbor, or from his brother; because it is called יהוה's release. 3 Of a foreigner you may exact it again: but that which is yours with your brother your hand shall release; 4 There shall be no poor among you; for יהוה shall greatly bless you in the land which יהוה Your Elohim gives you for an inheritance to possess it: 5 Only if you carefully listen to the voice of יהוה Your Elohim, to shomer and to do all these mitzvot which I command you this day. 6 For יהוה Your Elohim will bless you, as He promised you: and you shall lend to many nations, but you shall not borrow; and you shall reign over many nations, but they shall not reign over you. 7 If there be among you a poor man of one of your brothers within any of your gates in your land which יהוה Your Elohim gives you, you shall not harden your lev, nor shut your hand from your poor brother: 8 But you shall open your hand wide to him, and shall surely lend him sufficient for his need, in that which he needs.[3] 9 Beware that there be not a thought of Beliy-al[4] in your lev, saying, The seventh year, the year of release, is at hand; and your eye be evil against your poor brother, and you give him no release; and he cry to יהוה against you, and it become sin for you. 10 You shall surely give him the release, and your lev shall not be grieved when you give it to him: because for this thing יהוה Your Elohim shall bless you in all your works, and in all that you put your hand to. 11 For the poor shall never cease out of the land: therefore I command you, saying, You shall open your hand wide to your brother, to your poor, and to your needy, in your land.[5] 12 And if your brother, an Ivri man, or an Ivri woman, be sold to you, and serve you six years; then in the seventh year you shall let him go free from

---

[1] Moneychangers in the Temple were fine according to Torah. The problem the moneychangers later developed when they engaged in dishonest business and sold blemished animals for sacrifice.
[2] A different tithe for the needy and Ha Levi. Normal tithes paid annually belonged to YHWH.

[3] Giving is fine. But not to someone merely taking advantage of you.
[4] s.a.tan.
[5] Yisraelites are their brother's keepers.

you. 13 And when you send him out free from you, you shall not let him go away empty: 14 You shall furnish him liberally out of your flock, and out of your floor, and out of your winepress: of that which יהוה Your Elohim has blessed you, you shall give to him. 15 And you shall remember that you were a eved in the land of Mitzrayim, and יהוה Your Elohim redeemed you: therefore I command you this thing today. 16 And it shall be, if he says to you, I will not go away from you; because he loves you and your bayit, because he is well with you; 17 Then you shall take an awl, and thrust it through his ear to the door, and he shall be your eved le-olam-va-ed. And also to your female eved you shall do likewise. 18 It shall not seem hard to you, when you send him away free from you; for he has been worth a double hired eved to you, in serving you six years: and יהוה Your Elohim shall bless you in all that you do. 19 All the bachor males that come from your herd and from your flock you shall set it apart to יהוה Your Elohim: you shall do no work with the bachor of your herd, nor shear the bachor of your sheep. 20 You shall eat it before יהוה Your Elohim year by year in the place that יהוה shall choose, you and your household. [1] 21 And if there be any blemish in it, such as if it is lame, or blind, or have any ill blemish, you shall not sacrifice it to יהוה Your Elohim. 22 You shall eat it within your gates: the unclean and the clean person shall eat it alike, as the gazelle, and as the deer. 23 Only you shall not eat the dom of it; you shall pour it upon the ground as water.

16

Shomer the month of Aviv, and shomer the Pesach to יהוה Your Elohim: for in the month of Aviv יהוה Your Elohim brought you forth out of Mitzrayim by night. 2 You shall therefore sacrifice the Pesach to יהוה Your Elohim, from the flock and the herd, in the place that יהוה shall choose to place His Name there. 3 You shall eat no leavened lechem with it; seven days shall you eat matzah with it, even the lechem of affliction; for you came forth out of the land of Mitzrayim in haste: that you may remember the day when you came forth out of the land of Mitzrayim all the days of your chayim. 4 And there shall be no leavened lechem seen with you in all your borders seven days; neither shall any of the meat, which you sacrificed the first day at evening, remain all night until the morning. 5 You may not sacrifice the Pesach within any of your gates, which יהוה Your Elohim gives you: 6 But at the place that יהוה Your Elohim shall choose to place His Name in, there you shall sacrifice the Pesach at evening, at the going down of the sun, at the season that you came forth out of Mitzrayim.[2] 7 And you shall roast and eat it in the place that יהוה Your Elohim shall choose: and you shall return in the morning, and go to your tents. 8 Six days you shall eat matzah: and on the seventh day shall be a miqra-kodesh to יהוה Your Elohim: you shall do no work in it. 9 Seven weeks shall you number: begin to number the seven weeks from such time as you begin to put the sickle to the corn.[3] 10 And you shall shomer the Chag Shavout to יהוה Your Elohim with a tribute of a terumah offering from your hand, which you shall give to יהוה Your Elohim, according to how יהוה Your Elohim has blessed you: 11 And you shall gilah before יהוה Your Elohim, you, and your son, and your daughter, and your male eved, and your female eved, and the Ha Levi that is within your gates, and the Ger, and the fatherless, and the widow, that are among you, in the place which יהוה Your Elohim has chosen to place His Name there. 12 And you shall remember that you were a eved in Mitzrayim: and you shall shomer and do these chukim. 13 You shall shomer Chag Sukkot seven days, after you have gathered

---

[1] Yahrushalayim.

[2] After Temple was built.
[3] Not from the wave offering as is commonly taught.

in your corn and your wine: 14 And you shall gilah in your chag, you, and your son, and your daughter, and your male eved, and your female eved, and the Ha Levi, the Ger, and the fatherless, and the widow, that are within your gates. 15 Seven days shall you shomer a solemn chag to **יהוה** Your Elohim in the place which **יהוה** shall choose: because **יהוה** Your Elohim shall bless you in all your increase, and in all the works of your hands, therefore you shall surely gilah. 16 Three times in a year shall all your males appear before **יהוה** Your Elohim in the place which He shall choose; at Chag Matzot, and at Chag Shavout, and at Chag Sukkot: and they shall not appear before **יהוה** empty:[1] 17 Every man shall give, as he is able; according to the bracha of **יהוה** Your Elohim; that He has given you.

Torah Parsha 48
Shoftim 16:18-21:9
Haftarah Yeshayahu 9:1-6
Yeshayahu 49:1-6
Brit Chadasha MaAseh Shlichim 7:35-60

18 Shophtim and officers shall you make you in all your gates, which **יהוה** Your Elohim gives you, throughout your tribes: and they shall shophet the people with just mishpat. 19 You shall not distort mishpat; you shall not respect persons, neither take a bribe: for a bribe does blind the eyes of the wise, and pervert the words of the tzadik. 20 That which is fully tzedakah shall you follow, that you may live, and inherit the land that **יהוה** Your Elohim gives you. 21 You shall not plant a grove of any eytzim near the altar of **יהוה** Your Elohim, which you shall make. 22 Neither shall you set up any pillar;[2] which **יהוה** Your Elohim hates.

17 You shall not sacrifice to **יהוה** Your Elohim any bull, or sheep, in which there is blemish, or any evil matter: for that is an abomination to **יהוה** Your Elohim. 2 If there be found among you,

within any of your gates which **יהוה** Your Elohim gives you, man or woman, that has done wickedness in the sight of **יהוה** Your Elohim, in transgressing His covenant, 3 And has gone and served other elohim, and worshipped them, either the sun, or moon, or any of the host of the shamayim, which I have not commanded; 4 And it be told you, and you have heard of it, and inquired diligently, and, see, it is emet, and the thing certain, that such abomination is done in Yisrael. 5 Then shall you bring forth that man or that woman, that has committed that wicked thing, to your gates, even that man or that woman, and shall stone them with stones, until they die. 6 At the mouth of two witnesses, or three witnesses, shall he that is worthy of death be put to death; but at the mouth of one witness he shall not be put to death. 7 The hands of the witnesses shall be first upon him to put him to death, and afterward the hands of all the people. So you shall put the evil away from among you. 8 If there arise a matter too hard for you in mishpat, between dom and dom, between plea and plea, and between stroke and stroke, being matters of controversy within your gates: then shall you arise, and get up into the place which **יהוה** Your Elohim shall choose; 9 And you shall come to the kohanim the leviim, and to the shophet that shall be in those days, and inquire; and they shall show you the sentence of mishpat: 10 And you shall do according to the sentence, which they of that place which **יהוה** shall choose shall show you; and you shall shomer to do according to all that they inform you: 11 According to the sentence of the Torah that they shall teach you, and according to the mishpat that they shall tell you, you shall do: you shall not decline from the ruling which they shall show you, to the right hand, nor to the left.[3] 12 And the man

---

[1] Ascension feasts or **shalosh regallim**.
[2] That would include pillars with symbols like steeples.

[3] This verse is used by traditional Judaism to prove that the unsaved rabbis lead Yisrael, and that somehow their rulings are binding on the Jewish people. But these verses speak of priests and judges, in temple times, and the Sanhedrin or the judges have not sat over Yisrael for some 1700 years.

that will do arrogantly, and will not listen to the kohen that stands to attend there before יהוה Your Elohim, or to the shophet, even that man shall die: and you shall put away the evil from Yisrael. 13 And all the people shall hear, and fear, and not do arrogantly. 14 When you are come to the land that יהוה Your Elohim gives you, and shall possess it, and shall dwell in it, and shall say, I will set a melech over me, like all the nations that are around me; 15 You shall certainly set a melech over you, whom יהוה Your Elohim shall choose: one from among your brothers shall you set as melech over you: you may not set a Ger over you, which is not your brother. 16 But he shall not multiply horses to himself, nor cause the people to return to Mitzrayim, so that he can multiply horses: because as יהוה has said to you, You shall not return any more that way. 17 Neither shall he multiply wives to himself, so that his lev turns not away: neither shall he greatly multiply for himself silver and gold. 18 And it shall be, when he sits upon the throne of his malchut, that he shall write himself a copy of this Torah in a scroll out of that which is before the kohanim the leviim: 19 And it shall be with him, and he shall read it all the days of his chayim: that he may learn to fear יהוה His Elohim, to shomer all the words of this Torah and these chukim, to do them: [1] 20 That his lev be not lifted up above his brothers, and that he turn not aside from the mitzvah, to the right hand, or to the left: to the end that he may prolong his days in his malchut, he, and his children, in the midst of Yisrael.

18 The kohanim the leviim, and all the tribe of Levi, shall have no part or inheritance with Yisrael: they shall eat the offerings of יהוה made by fire, and his inheritance. 2 They shall have no inheritance among their brothers: יהוה is their inheritance, as He has said to them. 3 And this shall be the kohen's due from the people, from them that offer a sacrifice, whether it be ox or sheep; and they shall give to the kohen the shoulder, and the two cheeks, and the stomach. 4 The firstfruit also of your corn, of your wine, and of your oil, and the first of the fleece of your sheep, shall you give him. 5 For יהוה Your Elohim has chosen him out of all your tribes, to stand to attend in the Name of יהוה, [2] him and his sons le-olam-va-ed. 6 And if a Ha Levi comes from any of your gates out of all Yisrael, where he sojourned, and comes with all the desire of his mind to the place that יהוה shall choose; 7 Then he shall attend in the Name of יהוה His Elohim, as all his brothers the leviim do, who stand there before יהוה. 8 They shall have like portions to eat, beside that which comes from the sale of his patrimony. 9 When you have come into the land that יהוה Your Elohim gives you, you shall not learn to do after the abominations of those nations. 10 There shall not be found among you anyone that makes his son or his daughter to pass through the fire, or that uses divination, or an observer of times, or an enchanter, or a witch. 11 Or a spell caster, or a consulter with familiar spirits, or a wizard, or one who calls up the dead. 12 For all that do these things are an abomination to יהוה: and because of these abominations יהוה Your Elohim does drive them out from before you. 13 You shall be perfect with יהוה Your Elohim. 14 For these nations, which you shall possess, heard to observers of times, and to diviners: but as for you, יהוה Your Elohim has not allowed you to do so. 15 יהוה Your Elohim will raise up to you a Navi from the midst of you, of your brothers, like me; to Him you shall listen; 16 According to all that you desired of יהוה Your Elohim in Horev in the day of the congregation, saying, Let me not hear again the voice of יהוה My Elohim, neither let me see this great fire any more, that I die not. 17 And יהוה said to

---

[1] Every believer today should do the same.

[2] Don't tithe to any man who does not stand to minister in YHWH's true Name, a requirement for even receiving tithes.

me, *They have well spoken that which they have spoken. 18 I will raise them up a Navi from among their brothers, like you, and will put My words in His mouth; and He shall speak to them all that I shall command Him. 19 And it shall come to pass, that whoever will not* listen *to My words that He shall speak in My Name, I will require it of him.[1] 20 But the navi, who shall presume to speak a word in My Name, which I have not commanded him to speak, or that shall speak in the Name of other elohim, even that navi shall die. 21 And if you say in your lev, How shall we know the word that* יהוה *has not spoken? 22 When a navi speaks in the Name of* יהוה*, if the thing follows not, nor comes to pass, that is the thing which* יהוה *has not spoken, but the navi has spoken it presumptuously: you shall not be afraid of him.*

19

When יהוה Your Elohim has cut off the nations, whose land יהוה Your Elohim gives you, and you dispossess them, and dwell in their cities, and in their houses; 2 You shall separate three cities for you in the midst of your land, which יהוה Your Elohim gives you to possess it. 3 You shall prepare a derech, and divide the coasts of your land, which יהוה Your Elohim gives you to inherit, into three parts, that every killer may flee there. 4 And this is the case of the killer, who shall flee there, that he may live: Whoever kills his neighbor ignorantly, whom he hated not in times past; 5 As when a man goes into the wood with his neighbor to cut wood, and his hand swings with the axe to cut down the eytz, and the head slips from the handle, and strikes his neighbor, so that he dies; he shall flee to one of those cities, and live:[2] 6 Lest the revenger of the dom pursue the killer,

while his lev is hot, and overtake him, because the way is long, and slays him; whereas he was not worthy of death, because he hated him not in times past. 7 Therefore I commanded you, saying, You shall separate three cities for you. 8 And if יהוה Your Elohim enlarges your coast, as He has sworn to your ahvot, and gives you all the land that He promised to give to your ahvot;[3] 9 If you shall shomer all these mitzvot to do them, which I command you this day, to love יהוה Your Elohim, and to have your halacha always in His halachot; then shall you add three cities more for you, beside these three:[4] 10 That innocent dom be not shed in your land, which יהוה Your Elohim gives you for an inheritance, and so dom be upon you. 11 But if any man hates his neighbor, and lies in wait for him, and rises up against him, and smites him so that he dies, and flees into one of these cities: 12 Then the zachanim of his city shall send and fetch him there, and deliver him into the hand of the revenger of dom that he may die. 13 Your eye shall not pity him, but you shall put away the guilt of innocent dom from Yisrael, that it may go well with you. 14 You shall not remove your neighbor's landmark, which those of past times have set in your inheritance, which you shall inherit in the land that יהוה Your Elohim gives you to possess it. 15 One witness shall not rise up against a man for any iniquity, or for any sin, in any sin that he sins: at the mouth of two witnesses, or at the mouth of three witnesses, shall the matter be established. 16 If a false witness rises up against any man to testify against him, that which is wrong; 17 Then both the men, between whom the controversy is, shall stand before יהוה, before the kohanim and the shophtim, which shall be in those days; 18 And the shophtim shall make diligent inquiry: and, see, if the witness be a false witness, and has testified falsely against his brother; 19 Then shall you do to him, as he

---

[1] According to Renewed Covenant Yisrael, and the Brit Chadasha, this promise is of the Moshiach, who (like Moshe) would be a final and glorious Deliverer of Yisrael, by bringing the Paschal dom and the words of Abba's Torah. Islam claims this to be fulfilled in Mohammad. The problem with that understanding is that the promise is that Moshiach will come from among Moshe's brethren or the children of Yisrael, not Esau.
[2] **Chesed.**

[3] The promise of prosperity.
[4] More rachamim.

had thought to have done to his brother: so shall you put the evil away from among you. 20 And those who remain shall hear, and fear, and shall commit no more any such evil among you. 21 And your eye shall not pity; but chayim shall go for chayim, eye for eye, tooth for tooth, hand for hand, foot for foot.[1]

20 When you go out to battle against your enemies, and see horses, and chariots, and a people more than you, be not afraid of them: for **יהוה** Your Elohim is with you, who brought you up out of the land of Mitzrayim. 2 And it shall be, when you are come near to the battle, that the kohen shall approach and speak to the people, 3 And shall say to them, Shema, O Yisrael, you approach this day to battle against your enemies: let not your levim faint, fear not, and do not tremble, neither be terrified because of them; 4 For **יהוה** Your Elohim is He that goes with you, to fight for you against your enemies, to save you. 5 And the officers shall speak to the people saying, What man is there that has built a new bayit, and has not dedicated it? Let him go and return to his bayit, lest he die in the battle, and another man dedicate it. 6 And what man is he that has planted a vineyard, and has not yet eaten of it? Let him also go and return to his bayit, lest he dies in the battle, and another man eat of it. 7 And what man is there that has engaged a wife, and has not taken her? Let him go and return to his bayit, lest he die in the battle, and another man take her. 8 And the officers shall speak further to the people, and they shall say, What man is there that is fearful and fainthearted? Let him go and return to his bayit, lest his brother's lev faint as well as his lev.[2] 9 And it shall be, when the officers have made an end of speaking to the people that they shall make captains of the armies to lead the people. 10 When you

come near to a city to fight against it, then proclaim shalom to it. 11 And it shall be, if it gives you an answer of shalom, and opens to you, then it shall be, that all the people that are found in it shall be compulsory labor to you, and they shall serve you. 12 And if it will make no shalom with you, but will make war against you, then you shall besiege it: 13 And when **יהוה** Your Elohim has delivered it into your hands, you shall smite every male in it with the edge of the sword: 14 But the women, and the little ones, and the cattle, and all that is in the city, even all the spoil in it, shall you take for yourself; and you shall eat the spoil of your enemies, which **יהוה** Your Elohim has given you.[3] 15 This shall you do to all the cities which are very far off from you, which are not of the cities of these nations. 16 But of the cities of these people, which **יהוה** Your Elohim does give you for an inheritance, you shall save alive nothing that breathes: 17 But you shall utterly destroy them; namely, the Hittites, and the Amorites, the Kanaanites, and the Perizzites, the Hivites, and the Yevusites; as **יהוה** Your Elohim has commanded you: 18 That they teach you not to do after all their abominations, which they have done to their elohim; so do not sin against **יהוה** Your Elohim. 19 When you shall besiege a city a long time, in making war against it to take it, you shall not destroy the eytzim in it by weilding an axe against them: for you may eat of them, and you shall not cut them down - for the eytz of the field is man's chayim - to use them in the siege: 20 Only the eytzim that you know that they are not eytzim for food, you shall destroy and cut them down; and you shall build bulwarks against the city that makes war with you, until it falls.

21 If one be found slain in the land which **יהוה** Your Elohim gives you to possess it, lying in the field, and it be not

---

[1] Judicial justice not mutilation.
[2] Only willing spiritual soldiers can be Yisraelites. All else are sent home. Large numbers don't help Yisrael because YHWH is our Man of War.

[3] The only exception to this rule of sparing women and children is when there is paganism involved, so that they do not influence Yisrael.

known who has slain him: 2 Then your zachanim and your shophtim shall come forth, and they shall measure the distance to the cities, which are around him, that is slain: 3 And it shall be, that the city that is next to the slain man, even the zachanim of that city shall take a heifer, which has not been worked with, and which has not drawn in the yoke; 4 And the zachanim of that city shall bring down the heifer to a rough valley, which is neither plowed nor sown, and shall cut off the heifer's neck there in the valley: 5 And the kohanim the sons of Levi shall come near; for them יהוה Your Elohim has chosen to attend to Him, and to bless in the Name of יהוה; and by their word shall every controversy and every stroke be tried: 6 And all the zachanim of that city, that are next to the slain man, shall wash their hands over the heifer that is beheaded in the valley: 7 And they shall answer and say, Our hands have not shed this dom, neither have our eyes seen it. 8 Be full of chesed, O יהוה, to Your people Yisrael, whom You have redeemed, and lay not innocent dom to Your people Yisrael's charge. And the dom shall be forgiven them. 9 So shall you put away the guilt of innocent dom from among you, when you shall do that which is right in the sight of יהוה.

Torah Parsha 49
Ki Teze 21:10-25:19
Haftarah Yeshayahu 40:1-11
Brit Chadasha Moshe Markus 1:1-14

10 When you go forth to war against your enemies, and יהוה Your Elohim has delivered them into your hands, and you have taken them captive, 11 And see among the captives a beautiful woman, and have a desire for her, that you would have her to be your wife; 12 Then you shall bring her home to your bayit, and she shall shave her head, and trim her nails; 13 And she shall put the garment of her captivity from off her, and shall remain in your bayit, and bewail her abba and her ima a full month: and after that you shall go in to her, and be

her husband, and she shall be your wife. 14 And it shall be, if you have no delight in her, then you shall let her go where she will; but you shall not sell her at all for money, you shall not make merchandise of her, because you have humbled her. 15 If a man have two wives, one beloved, and another hated, and they have born him children, both the beloved and the hated; and if the bachor son be hers that was hated: 16 Then it shall be, when he makes his sons to inherit that which he has, that he may not make the son of the beloved bachor before the son of the hated, which is indeed the bachor: 17 But he shall acknowledge the son of the hated for the bachor, by giving him a double portion of all that he has: for he is the beginning of his strength; the right of the bachor is his. 18 If a man have a stubborn and rebellious son, who will not obey the voice of his abba, or the voice of his ima, and that, when they have disciplined him, will not listen to them: 19 Then shall his abba and his ima lay hold on him, and bring him out to the zachanim of his city, and to the gate of his place; 20 And they shall say to the zachanim of his city, This our son is stubborn and rebellious, he will not obey our voice; he is a glutton, and a drunkard. 21 And all the men of his city shall stone him with stones, that he dies: so shall you put evil away from among you; and all Yisrael shall hear, and fear. 22 And if a man has committed a sin worthy of death, then he shall be put to death, and you hang him on a eytz: 23 His body shall not remain all night upon the eytz, but you shall bury him that day; (for he that is hanged is cursed by Elohim;) that your land be not defiled, which יהוה Your Elohim gives you for an inheritance.[1]

22 You shall not see your brother's ox or his sheep go astray, and hide yourself from them: you shall without fail bring them again to your brother. 2 And if

---

[1] Which is why Yahshua's body had to be down before nightfall, for He became a curse for the people and the land in order to cleanse them.

your brother be not near to you, or if you know him not, then you shall bring it to your own bayit, and it shall be with you until your brother seeks after it, and you shall restore it to him again. 3 In like manner shall you do with his donkey; and so shall you do with his garment; and with all lost things of your brother's, which he has lost, and you have found, shall you do likewise: you may not hide yourself. 4 You shall not see your brother's donkey or his ox fall down by the way, and hide yourself from them: you shall surely help him to lift them up again.[1] 5 The woman shall not wear that which pertains to a man, neither shall a man put on a woman's garment: for all that do so are an abomination to יהוה Your Elohim.[2] 6 If a bird's nest by chance is before you in the way in any eytz, or on the ground, whether they are young ones, or eggs, and the ima sitting upon the young, or upon the eggs, you shall not take the ima with the young: 7 But you shall in any case let the ima go, and take the young to you; that it may be well with you, and that you may prolong your days. 8 When you build a new bayit, then you shall make a guard rail for your roof, that you bring not dom upon your bayit, if any man falls from there. 9 You shall not sow your vineyard with different zera: lest the fruit of your zera that you have sown, and the fruit of your vineyard, be defiled.[3] 10 You shall not plow with an ox and a donkey together.[4] 11 You shall not wear a garment of different sorts, as of wool and linen together.[5] [6] 12 You shall make for yourself fringes upon the four corners of your garment, with which you cover yourself. 13 If any man takes a wife, and goes in to her, and hates her, 14 And makes abusive charges against her, and brings up an evil name upon her, and says, I took this woman, and when I came to her, I found her not a virgin: 15 Then shall the abba of the damsel, and her ima, take and bring forth the tokens of the damsel's virginity to the zachanim of the city in the gate: 16 And the damsel's abba shall say to the zachanim, I gave my daughter to this man to wife, and he hates her; 17 And, see, he has made accusation against her, saying, I found not your daughter a virgin; and yet these are the tokens of my daughter's virginity. And they shall spread the cloth before the zachanim of the city. 18 And the zachanim of that city shall take that man and discipline him; 19 And they shall fine him a hundred shekels of silver, and give them to the abba of the damsel, because he has brought up an evil name upon a virgin of Yisrael: and she shall be his wife; he may not put her away all his days. 20 But if this thing is emet, and the tokens of virginity are not found for the damsel: 21 Then they shall bring out the damsel to the door of her abba's bayit, and the men of her city shall stone her with stones so that she dies: because she has done folly in Yisrael, to play the whore in her abba's bayit: so shall you put evil away from among you. 22 If a man be found lying with a woman married to an husband, then they shall both of them die, both the man that lay with the woman, and the woman: so shall you put away evil from Yisrael. 23 If a damsel that is a virgin be engaged to a husband, and a man finds her in the city, and lie with her; 24 Then you shall bring them both out to the gate of that city, and you shall stone them with stones that they die; the damsel, because she cried not, being in the city; and the man, because he has humbled his neighbor's wife: so you shall put away evil from among you. 25 But if a man finds an engaged damsel in the field, and the man forces her, and lies with her: then the man only that lay with her shall die. 26 But to the damsel you shall do

---

[1] Brotherhood in Yisrael. This speaks of physical and spiritual brotherhood.
[2] This is the problem Rav Shaul dealt with in the Yisraelite congregation in Corinth. As seen in First Corinthians 11, where men are not allowed to veil their face with hair.
[3] Torah of **Kilayim** proving that all believers are Yisrael, for the olive tree cannot contain differing branches or differing seed. All branches are Yisrael.
[4] YHWH's kingdom cannot be plowed with a "Jew and gentile" theology, but only with men of the same breed, which is why YHWH sees all believers as the seed of Yisrael.
[5] See note for verse #9.
[6] Only these two fabrics cannot be mixed. No mention is made of mixing other fabrics.

nothing; there is in the damsel no sin worthy of death: for as when a man rises against his neighbor, and slays him, even so is this matter: 27 For he found her in the field, and the engaged damsel cried, and there was none to save her. 28 If a man find a damsel that is a virgin, who is not engaged, and lays hold on her, and lies with her, and they be found; 29 Then the man that lay with her shall give to the damsel's abba fifty shekels of silver, and she shall be his wife; because he has humbled her, he may not put her away all his days. 30 A man shall not take his abba's wife, nor discover his abba's skirt.

23 He that is wounded in the stones, or has his private member cut off, shall not enter into the congregation of יהוה. 2 A bastard shall not enter into the congregation of יהוה; even to his tenth generation shall he not enter into the congregation of יהוה. 3 An Ammonite or Moavite shall not enter into the congregation of יהוה; even to their tenth generation shall they not enter into the congregation of יהוה le-olam-va-ed: 4 Because they met you not with lechem and with water in the way, when you came forth out of Mitzrayim; and because they hired Balaam the son of Beor of Pethor of Mesopotamia against you, to curse you. 5 Nevertheless יהוה Your Elohim would not listen to Balaam; but יהוה Your Elohim turned the curse into a blessing for you, because יהוה Your Elohim loved you. 6 You shall not seek their shalom nor their prosperity all your days le-olam-va-ed. 7 You shall not abhor an Edomite; for he is your brother: you shall not abhor a Mitzrite; because you were a Ger in his land. 8 The children that are begotten of them shall enter into the congregation of יהוה in their third generation. 9 When your army goes forth against your enemies, then guard yourself from every wicked thing. 10 If there be among you any man, that is not clean by reason of emission at night, then shall he go abroad out of the camp, he shall not come within the camp: 11 But it shall be, when evening comes, he shall wash himself with water: and when the sun is down, he shall come into the camp again. 12 You shall have a place also outside the camp, where you shall go forth abroad: 13 And you shall have a paddle upon your weapon; and it shall be, when you will ease yourself outside, you shall dig there, and shall turn and cover your excrement: 14 For יהוה Your Elohim walks in the midst of your camp, to deliver you, and to give up your enemies before you; therefore shall your camp be kadosh: that He sees no unclean thing in you, and turns away from you. 15 You shall not deliver back to his master the eved who has escaped from his master to you: 16 He shall dwell with you, even among you, in that place which he shall choose in one of your gates, where it suits him best: you shall not oppress him. 17 There shall be no whore of the daughters of Yisrael, nor a sodomite of the sons of Yisrael. 18 You shall not bring the hire of a whore, or the price of a dog, into the Bayit of יהוה Your Elohim for any vow: for even both these are abomination to יהוה Your Elohim. 19 You shall not lend upon interest to your brother; interest of money, interest of food, interest of any thing that is lent upon interest: 20 Unto a Ger you may lend upon interest; but to your brother you shall not lend upon interest: that יהוה Your Elohim may bless you in all that you set your hand to in the land where you go to possess it. 21 When you shall vow a vow to יהוה Your Elohim, you shall not be slack to pay it: for יהוה Your Elohim will surely require it of you; and it would be sin to you. 22 But if you shall abstain to vow, it shall be no sin in you. 23 That which is gone out of your lips you shall shomer and perform; even a terumah offering, according as you have vowed to יהוה Your Elohim, which you have promised with your mouth. 24 When you come into your neighbor's vineyard, then you may eat grapes to your fill at your own pleasure; but you shall not put any in your vessel. 25 When you come into the standing corn of your neighbor, then you may pluck the ears with your hand; but you shall not use a sickle for your neighbor's standing corn.1 24 When a man has taken a wife, and married her, and it come to pass that she find no favor in his eyes, because he has found some uncleanness in her: then let him write her a Get, and put it in her hand, and send her out of his bayit. 2 And when she is departed out of his bayit, she may go and be another man's wife. 3 And if the latter husband hate her, and write her a Get, and puts it in her hand, and sends her out of his bayit; or if the latter husband dies, who took her to be his wife; 4 Her former husband, who sent her away, may not take her again to be his wife, after that she is defiled; for that is abomination before יהוה: and you shall not cause the land to sin, which יהוה Your Elohim gives you for an inheritance. 2 5 When a man has taken a new wife, he shall not go out to war, neither shall he be charged with any business: but he shall be free at home one year, and shall cheer up his wife which he has taken.3 6 No man shall take the mill or the upper millstone as a pledge: for he takes a man's chayim as a pledge.4 7 If a man be found kidnapping any of his brothers of the children of Yisrael, and makes merchandise of him, or sells him; then that thief shall die; and you shall put evil away from among you. 8 Take heed in the plague of leprosy, that you shomer diligently, and do according to all that the kohanim the leviim shall teach you: as I commanded them, so you shall shomer to do. 9 Remember what יהוה Your Elohim did to Miryam by the derech, after you had come forth out of Mitzrayim. 10 When you lend your brother anything, you shall not go into his bayit to get his pledge.5 11 You

shall stand outside, and the man to whom you do lend shall bring out the pledge outside to you. 12 And if the man is poor, you shall not sleep with his pledge: 13 In any case you shall deliver to him the pledge again when the sun goes down, that he may sleep in his own garment, and bless you: and it shall be tzedakah to you before יהוה Your Elohim. 14 You shall not oppress a hired eved that is poor and needy, whether he be of your brothers, or of your Gerim that are in your land within your gates: 15 Daily you shall give him his wages, neither shall the sun go down upon it; for he is poor, and sets his lev upon it: lest he cries against you to יהוה, and it is sin to you.6 |16 The ahvot shall not be put to death for the children, neither shall the children be put to death for the ahvot: every man shall be put to death for his own sin. 17 You shall not pervert the mishpat of the Ger, nor of the fatherless; nor take a widow's garment: 18 But you shall remember that you were an eved in Mitzrayim, and יהוה Your Elohim redeemed you there: therefore I command you to do this thing. 19 When you cut down your harvest in your field, and have forgotten a sheaf in the field, you shall not go again to get it: it shall be for the Ger, for the fatherless, and for the widow: that יהוה Your Elohim may bless you in all the work of your hands. 20 When you beat your olive eytz, you shall not examine the branch behind you: it shall be for the Ger, for the fatherless, and for the widow.7 21 When you gather the grapes of your vineyard, you shall not glean it afterward: it shall be for the Ger, for the fatherless, and for the widow.8 22 And you shall remember that you were a eved in the land of Mitzrayim: therefore I command you to do this thing.

25 If there be a controversy between men, and they come to mishpat, that the shophtim may shophet them; then they

---

1 A **chesed** provision for the poor in Yisrael.
2 Only with the death of the husband can she remarry, which is why Yahshua died to release the bride back to the Abba.
3 **Chesd**/Unmerited favor. Biblical honeymoon is one year.
4 Torah forbids a creditor taking anything from a debtor that he needs to make a living to survive. Unmerited favor/rachamim.
5 Respecting a man's private property.

6 Biblical pay is daily, not weekly.
7 **Chesed**.
8 **Chesed**.

shall justify the tzadik, and condemn the wicked. 2 And it shall be, if the wicked man is worthy to be beaten, that the shophet shall cause him to lie down, and to be beaten before his face, according to his fault, by a certain number. 3 Forty stripes he may give him, and not more: lest, if he should continue to beat him above these with many stripes, then your brother should be degraded before you. 4 You shall not muzzle the ox when he treads out the corn.[1] 5 If brothers dwell together, and one of them die, and have no child, the wife of the dead shall not marry a Ger: her husband's brother shall go in to her, and take her to him as a wife, and perform the duty of an husband's brother to her. 6 And it shall be, that the bachor whom she bears shall succeed in the name of his brother that is dead, that his name be not put out of Yisrael. 7 And if the man does not like to take his brother's wife, then let his brother's wife go up to the gate to the zachanim, and say, My husband's brother refuses to raise up to his brother a name in Yisrael, he will not perform the duty of my husband's brother. 8 Then the zachanim of his city shall call him, and speak to him: and if he stands to it, and says, I desire not to take her; 9 Then shall his brother's wife come to him in the presence of the zachanim, and loose his shoe from off his foot, and spit in his face, and shall answer and say, So shall it be done to that man that will not build up his brother's bayit.[2] 10 And his name shall be called in Yisrael, The bayit of him that has his shoe loosed. 11 When men strive together one with another, and the wife of the one draws near for to deliver her husband out of the hand of the one that smites him, and puts forth her hand, and takes him by the private parts: 12 Then you shall cut off her hand, your eye shall not pity her. 13 You shall not have in your bag

different weights, a great and a small.[3] 14 You shall not have in your bayit different measures, a great and a small.[4] 15 But you shall have a perfect and just weight, a perfect and just measure shall you have: that your days may be lengthened in the land that יהוה Your Elohim gives you.[5] 16 For all that do such things, and all that do unrighteously, are an abomination to יהוה Your Elohim.[6] 17 Remember what Amalek did to you by the way, when you came out of Mitzrayim; 18 How he met you by the way, and attacked your rear, even all that were feeble behind you, when you were faint and weary; and he feared not Elohim. 19 Therefore it shall be, when יהוה Your Elohim has given you rest from all your enemies all around, in the land which יהוה Your Elohim gives you for an inheritance to possess it, that you shall blot out the remembrance of Amalek from under the shamayim; you shall not forget to do it.

Torah Parsha 50
Ki Tavo 26:1-29:8
Haftarah Yeshayahu 60:1-22
Brit Chadasha Mattityahu 13:1-23

26 And it shall be, when you are come in to the land that יהוה Your Elohim gives you for an inheritance, and possess it, and dwell in it; 2 That you shall take of the first of all the fruit of the earth, which you shall bring of your land that יהוה Your Elohim gives you, and shall put it in a basket, and shall go to the place which יהוה Your Elohim shall choose to place His Name there. 3 And you shall go to the kohen that shall be in those days, and say to him, I profess this day to יהוה Your Elohim, that I am come to the country

---

[1] Meaning that he should not be deprived of food and nourishment while laboring. Same applies to avadim of YHWH.
[2] A warning to those who refuse to work with Moshiach to gather and restore all the brethren from both houses of Yisrael and refuse to build their brother's house.

[3] Another warning to those who treat Yahudah and Ephraim differently; favoring one over the other, such as forcing Ephraimites to prove something that cannot be proven such as their ancient genealogy, while not requiring Jews to prove their own genealogy by factual temple records that no longer exist. All Yisrael must learn to walk with equity towards both houses.
[4] In the house of Yisrael as well.
[5] Long life is a benefit of treating Yahudah and Ephraim equally with love and respect.
[6] Yisraelite brethren mistreat each other by using unequal weights and measures.

which יהוה swore to our ahvot to give us. 4 And the kohen shall take the basket out of your hand, and set it down before the altar of יהוה Your Elohim. 5 And you shall speak and say before יהוה Your Elohim, an Aramean[1] ready to perish was my abba, and he went down into Mitzrayim, and sojourned there with a few, and became there a nation, great, mighty, and populous:[2] 6 And the Mitzrites treated us wickedly, and afflicted us, and laid upon us hard slavery: 7 And when we cried to יהוה Elohim of our ahvot, יהוה heard our voice, and looked on our affliction, and our labor, and our oppression: 8 And יהוה brought us forth out of Mitzrayim with a mighty hand, and with an outstretched arm, and with great fear, and with signs, and with wonders: 9 And He has brought us into this place, and has given us this land, even a land that flows with milk and honey. 10 And now, see, I have brought the bikkurim of the land, which you, O יהוה, have given me. And you shall set it before יהוה Your Elohim, and worship before יהוה Your Elohim: 11 And you shall gilah in every tov thing that יהוה Your Elohim has given to you, and to your bayit, you, and the Ha Levi, and the Ger that is among you. 12 When you have made an end of tithing all the tithes of your increase the third year, which is the year of tithing, and have given it to the Ha Levi, the Ger, the fatherless, and the widow, that they may eat within your gates, and be filled; 13 Then you shall say before יהוה Your Elohim, I have brought away the kadosh things out of my bayit, and also have given them to the Ha Levi, and to the Ger, to the fatherless, and to the widow, according to all your mitzvot which you have commanded me: I have not transgressed your mitzvot, neither have I forgotten them. 14 I have not eaten any of it in my mourning, neither have I taken away

any of it for any unclean use, nor given any of it for the dead: but I have heard to the voice of יהוה My Elohim, and have done according to all that you have commanded me. 15 Look down from your kadosh dwelling, from the shamayim, and bless your people Yisrael, and the land that you have given us, as You swore to our ahvot, a land that flows with milk and honey. 16 This day יהוה Your Elohim has commanded you to do these chukim and mishpatim: you shall therefore shomer and do them with all your lev, and with all your being. 17 You have caused יהוה this day to be Your Elohim, and to have your halacha in His ways, and to shomer His chukim, and His mitzvot, and His mishpatim, and to listen to His voice: 18 And יהוה has caused you this day to be His treasured people, as He has promised you, and that you should shomer all His mitzvot; 19 And to make you high above all nations that He has made, in tehilla, and in name, and in honor; and that you may be a kadosh people to יהוה Your Elohim, as He has spoken.

27 And Moshe with the zachanim of Yisrael commanded the people, saying, Shomer all the mitzvot that I command you this day. 2 And it shall be on the day when you shall pass over the Yarden to the land which יהוה Your Elohim gives you, that you shall set up great stones, and plaster them with plaster: 3 And you shall write upon them all the words of this Torah, when you have passed over, that you may go in to the land that יהוה Your Elohim gives you, a land that flows with milk and honey, as יהוה Elohim of your ahvot has promised you. 4 Therefore it shall be when you have gone over Yarden, that you shall set up these stones, which I command you this day, in Mount Eval, and you shall plaster them with plaster. 5 And there shall you build an altar to יהוה Your Elohim, an altar of stones: you shall not lift up any iron tool upon them. 6 You shall build the altar of יהוה Your Elohim of

---

[1] Note that the original patriarchs and their wives were not Jewish or native Hebrews and that non-natives are the fathers of the nation of Yisrael. Therefore all non-natives who join Yisrael by choice through Moshiach Yahshua, are considered Yisraelites like the patriarchs themselves.
[2] Physical multiplicity.

whole stones: and you shall offer burnt offerings on it to יהוה Your Elohim: 7 And you shall offer shalom offerings, and shall eat there, and gilah before יהוה Your Elohim. 8 And you shall write upon the stones all the words of this Torah very plainly. 9 And Moshe and the kohanim the leviim spoke to all Yisrael, saying, Take heed, and listen, O Yisrael; this day you have become the people of יהוה Your Elohim. 10 You shall therefore obey the voice of יהוה Your Elohim, and do His mitzvot and His chukim, which I command you this day. 11 And Moshe charged the people the same day, saying, 12 These tribes shall stand upon Mount Gerizim to bless the people, when you go over Yarden; Shimeon, and Levi, and Yahudah, and Yissacher, and Yoseph, and Benyamin: 13 And these tribes shall stand upon Mount Eval to curse; Reuven, Gad, and Asher, and Zevulon, Dan, and Naphtali. 14 And the leviim shall speak, and say to all the men of Yisrael with a loud voice, 15 Cursed be the man that makes any graven or molded image, an abomination to יהוה, the work of the hands of the craftsman, and puts it in a secret place. And all the people shall answer and say, Amein. 16 Cursed be he that makes light of his abba or his ima. And all the people shall say, Amein. 17 Cursed be he that removes his neighbor's landmark. And all the people shall say, Amein. 18 Cursed be he that makes the blind to wander out of the way. And all the people shall say, Amein. 19 Cursed be he that perverts the mishpat of the Ger, fatherless, and widow. And all the people shall say, Amein. 20 Cursed be he that lies with his abba's wife; because he uncovers his abba's skirt. And all the people shall say, Amein. 21 Cursed be he that lies with any manner of beast. And all the people shall say, Amein. 22 Cursed be he that lies with his sister, the daughter of his abba, or the daughter of his ima. And all the people shall say, Amein. 23 Cursed be he that lies with his ima-in-law. And all the people shall say,

Amein. 24 Cursed be he that smites his neighbor secretly. And all the people shall say, Amein. 25 Cursed be he that takes a reward to slay an innocent person. And all the people shall say, Amein. 26 Cursed be he that confirms not all the words of this Torah to do them. And all the people shall say, Amein.[1]

28 And it shall come to pass, if you shall listen diligently to the voice of יהוה Your Elohim, to shomer and to do all His mitzvot which I command you this day, that יהוה Your Elohim will set you on high above all nations of the earth: 2 And all these blessings shall come on you, and overtake you, if you shall listen to the voice of יהוה Your Elohim. 3 Blessed shall you be in the city, and blessed shall you be in the field. 4 Blessed shall be the fruit of your body, and the fruit of your ground, and the fruit of your cattle, the increase of your cattle, and the flocks of your sheep. 5 Blessed shall be your basket and your bowl. 6 Blessed shall you be when you come in, and blessed shall you be when you go out. 7 יהוה shall cause your enemies that rise up against you to be smitten before your face: they shall come against you one way, and flee before you seven ways. 8 יהוה shall command the blessing upon you in your storehouses, and in all that you set your hand to; and He shall bless you in the land that יהוה Your Elohim gives you. 9 יהוה shall establish you as a kadosh people to Himself, as He has sworn to you, if you shall shomer the mitzvot of יהוה Your Elohim, and have your halacha in His halachot. 10 And all people of the earth shall see that you are called by the Name of יהוה ;[2] and they shall be afraid of you. 11 And יהוה shall make you have plenty in goods, in the fruit of your body, and in the fruit of your cattle, and in the fruit of your ground, in the land which יהוה swore to your ahvot to give you. 12 יהוה shall open

---

[1] Ephraim's cursed past was due to violating this truth.
[2] Are you called by that Name?

to you His tov treasure, the shamayim to give the rain to your land in its season, and to bless all the work of your hand: and you shall lend to many nations, and you shall not borrow. 13 And **יהוה** shall make you the head, and not the tail; and you shall be above only, and you shall not be beneath; if you listen to the mitzvot of **יהוה** Your Elohim, which I command you this day, to shomer and to do them: 14 And you shall not go aside from any of the words that I command you this day, to the right hand, or to the left, to go after other elohim to serve them. 15 But it shall come to pass, if you will not listen to the voice of **יהוה** Your Elohim, to shomer to do all His mitzvot and His chukim that I command you this day; that all these curses shall come upon you, and overtake you: 16 Cursed shall you be in the city, and cursed shall you be in the field. 17 Cursed shall be your basket and your bowl. 18 Cursed shall be the fruit of your body, and the fruit of your land, the increase of your cattle, and the flocks of your sheep. 19 Cursed shall you be when you come in, and cursed shall you be when you go out. 20 **יהוה** shall send upon you cursing, vexation, and rebuke, in all that you set your hand to do, until you are destroyed, and until you perish quickly; because of the wickedness of your doings, whereby you have forsaken Me. 21 **יהוה** shall make the pestilence cleave to you, until it has consumed you from off the land, where you are going to possess it. 22 **יהוה** shall smite you with confusion, and with a fever, and with an inflammation, and with an extreme burning, and with the sword, and with blight, and with mildew; and they shall pursue you until you perish. 23 And your shamayim that is over your head shall be brass, and the earth that is under you shall be iron. 24 **יהוה** shall make the rain of your land powder and dust: from the shamayim shall it come down upon you, until you be destroyed. 25 **יהוה** shall cause you to be smitten before your enemies: you shall go out one way against them, and flee seven

ways before them: and shall be removed into all the malchutim of the earth.[1] 26 And your body shall be food to all fowls of the air, and to the beasts of the earth, and no man shall frighten them away. 27 **יהוה** will smite you with the boils of Mitzrayim, and with the tumors, and with the scab, and with the itch, of which you cannot be healed. 28 **יהוה** shall smite you with madness, and blindness, and astonishment of lev: 29 And you shall grope at noonday, as the blind gropes in darkness, and you shall not prosper in your ways: and you shall be only oppressed and spoiled all your days, and no man shall save you. 30 You shall engage a wife, and another man shall lie with her: you shall build a bayit, and you shall not dwell in it: you shall plant a vineyard, and shall not gather the grapes of it. 31 Your ox shall be slain before your eyes, and you shall not eat of it: your donkey shall be violently taken away from before your face, and shall not be restored to you: your sheep shall be given to your enemies, and you shall have none to rescue them. 32 Your sons and your daughters shall be given to another people, and your eyes shall look, and fail with longing for them all the day long; and there shall be no might in your hand. 33 The fruit of your land, and all your labors, shall a nation that you know not eat up; and you shall be only oppressed and crushed always: 34 So that you shall be mad for the sight of your eyes and what you shall see. 35 **יהוה** shall smite you in the knees, and in the legs, with a sore boil that cannot be healed, from the sole of your foot to the top of your head. 36 **יהוה** shall bring you, and your melech which you shall set over you, to a nation which neither you nor your ahvot have known; and there shall you serve other elohim, wood and stone. 37 And you shall become an astonishment, a proverb, and a mockery, among all nations[2] where

---

[1] A prophecy of Yisrael's dispersions into all nations for their disobedience to Torah and also to fulfill covenant to make Yisrael the fullness of all nations.
[2] Not just Anglo-Saxon nations as some erroneously teach.

יהוה shall lead you.[1] 38 You shall carry much zera out into the field, and shall gather little in; for the locust shall consume it. 39 You shall plant vineyards, and dress them, but shall neither drink of the wine, nor gather the grapes; for worms shall eat them. 40 You shall have olive eytzim throughout all your coasts, but you shall not anoint yourself with the oil; for your olive shall cast its fruit. 41 You shall beget sons and daughters, but you shall not enjoy them; for they shall go into captivity. 42 All your eytzim and fruit of your land shall the locust consume. 43 The Ger that is within you shall come up above you very high; and you shall come down very low. 44 He shall lend to you, and you shall not lend to him: he shall be the head, and you shall be the tail. 45 Moreover all these curses shall come upon you, and shall pursue you, and overtake you, until you are destroyed; because you heard not to the voice of יהוה Your Elohim, to shomer His mitzvot and His chukim which He commanded you: 46 And they shall be upon you for a sign and for a wonder, and upon your zera le-olam-va-ed. 47 Because you did not serve יהוה Your Elohim with simcha, and with gladness of lev, for the abundance of all things; 48 Therefore shall you serve your enemies that יהוה shall send against you, in hunger, and in thirst, and in nakedness, and in want of all things: and He shall put a yoke of iron upon your neck, until He has destroyed you.[2] 49 יהוה shall bring a nation against you from far, from the end of the earth, as swift as the eagle flies; a nation whose tongue you shall not understand; 50 A nation of fierce countenance that shall not regard the person of the old, nor show favor to the young:[3] 51 And they shall eat the fruit of your cattle, and the fruit of your land, until you are destroyed: who also shall not leave you either corn, wine, or oil, or the increase of your cattle, or flocks of your sheep, until they have destroyed you. 52 And they shall besiege you in all your gates, until your high and fenced walls come down, in which you trusted, throughout all your land: and they shall besiege you in all your gates throughout all your land, which יהוה Your Elohim has given you. 53 And you shall eat the fruit of your own body, the flesh of your sons and of your daughters, which יהוה Your Elohim has given you, in the siege, and in the tribulation, in which your enemies shall distress you:[4] 54 So that the man that is tender among you, and very delicate, his eye shall be evil toward his brother, and toward the wife of his bosom, and toward the remnant of his children that he shall leave: 55 So that he will not give to any of them of the flesh of his children whom he shall eat: because he has nothing left him in the siege, and in the tribulation, in which your enemies shall distress you in all your gates. 56 The tender and delicate woman among you; who would not adventure to set the sole of her foot upon the ground for delicateness and tenderness, her eye shall be evil toward the husband of her bosom, and toward her son, and toward her daughter, 57 And toward her young one that comes out from between her feet, and toward her children which she shall bear: for she shall eat them for want of all things secretly in the siege and tribulation, in which your enemy shall distress you in your gates. 58 If you will not shomer to do all the words of this Torah that are written in this scroll, that you may fear this glorious and fearful Name, יהוה Your Elohim; 59 Then יהוה will make your plagues extraordinary, and the plagues of your zera, even great plagues of long duration, and sore sicknesses of long duration. 60 Moreover He will bring upon you all the diseases of Mitzrayim, which you were afraid of; and they shall cleave to you. 61 Also every sickness, and every

---

[1] Exile foretold.
[2] Not totally, but until He has destroyed their pride and self-sufficiency.
[3] Most likely Rome with the symbol of the eagle. Rome caused the dispersion of Jewish Yisrael.

[4] Possible dual application, with the same thing occurring in the time of Yaakov's Trouble, as in the days of the Roman exile of the Jews.

plague, which is not written in the scroll of this Torah, them will יהוה bring upon you, until you are destroyed. 62 And you shall be left few in number, whereas you were as the chochavim of the shamayim for multitude; because you would not obey the voice of יהוה Your Elohim.[1] 63 And it shall come to pass, that as יהוה rejoiced over you to do you tov, and to multiply you; so יהוה will gilah over you to destroy you, and to bring you to nothing; and you shall be plucked from off the land where you are going to possess it. 64 And יהוה shall scatter you among all peoples and nations, from the one end of the earth even to the other; and there you shall serve other elohim, which neither you nor your ahvot have known, even wood and stone. 65 And among these nations shall you find no ease, neither shall the sole of your foot have rest: but יהוה shall give you there a trembling lev, and failing of eyes, and sorrow of mind:[2] 66 And your chayim shall hang in doubt before you; and you shall fear day and night, and shall have no assurance of your chayim: 67 In the morning you shall say, Would to Elohim it were evening! and at evening you shall say, Would to Elohim it were morning! for the fear of your lev with which you shall fear, and for the sight of your eyes which you shall see. 68 And יהוה shall bring you into Mitzrayim again with ships,[3] the way of which I said to you, You shall see it no more again: and there you shall be sold to your enemies for avadim and female avadim, and no man shall buy you.

29 These are the words of the covenant, which יהוה commanded Moshe to make with the children of Yisrael in the land of Moav, besides the covenant that He made with them in Horev.[4] 2 And Moshe called to all Yisrael, and said to them, You have seen all that יהוה did before your eyes in the land of Mitzrayim to Pharaoh, and to all his avadim, and to all his land; 3 The great trials which your eyes have seen, the signs, and those great nisim: 4 Yet יהוה has not given you a lev to perceive, and eyes to see, and ears to hear, to this day. 5 And I have led you forty years in the wilderness: your clothes are not worn old upon you, and your shoe is not worn old upon your foot. 6 You have not eaten lechem, neither have you drunk wine or strong drink: that you might know that I am יהוה Your Elohim. 7 And when you came to this place, Sihon the melech of Cheshbon, and Og the melech of Bashan, came out against us to battle, and we smote them: 8 And we took their land, and gave it for an inheritance to the Reuvenites, and to the Gadites, and to the half tribe of Menashsheh.

Torah Parsha 51
Nitzavim 29:9-30:20
In regular years, read with Parsha 52.
In years with 13 months, read separately. Haftarah
Yeshayahu 61:1-63:9
Brit Chadasha Romiyah 9:30-10:13

9 Keep therefore the words of this covenant, and do them, that you may prosper in all that you do. 10 You stand this day all of you before יהוה Your Elohim; your captains of your tribes, your zachanim, and your officers, with all the men of Yisrael, 11 Your little ones, your wives, and your Gerim that are in your camp, from the cutter of your wood to the drawer of your water: 12 That you should enter into covenant with יהוה Your Elohim, and into His oath, which יהוה Your Elohim makes with you this day: 13 That He may establish you today for a people to Himself, and that He

---

[1] Few in recognizable or identifiable number, not in actual number, since most Yisraelites live and act like gentiles thus are not distinguishable from them, unless a reawakening and regeneration occurs by emunah in Moshiach.
[2] The exile of the whole nation to all nations.
[3] This could be a spiritual Egypt or at various points in later history, Yisraeltes fled to Egypt for protection only to be discovered and captured. These isolated incidents where not national bondage, so there may be a spiritual/**sod** meaning here as well.

[4] The same covenant renewed on the east bank of the Yarden. We see no new covenant, but a recital and renewal. The Brit Chadasha of Moshiach should be viewed as the renewal and internalization of the Torah, as opposed to a totally new covenant with totally foreign concepts.

may be to you an Elohim, as He has said to you, and as He has sworn to your ahvot, to Avraham, to Yitzchak, and to Yaakov. 14 Neither with you only do I make this covenant and this oath; 15 But with him that stands here with us this day before יהוה our Elohim, and also with him that is not here with us this day:[1] 16 For you know how we have dwelt in the land of Mitzrayim; and how we came through the nations that you passed by; 17 And you have seen their abominations, and their idols, wood and stone, silver and gold, which were among them: 18 Lest there should be among you man, or woman, or family, or tribe, whose lev turns away this day from יהוה our Elohim, to go and serve the elohim of these nations; lest there should be among you a root that bears bitterness and wormwood; 19 And it come to pass, when he hears the words of this curse, that he blesses himself in his lev, saying, I shall have shalom, though I have my halacha in the imagination of my lev, to add drunkenness to thirst: 20 יהוה will not spare him, but then the anger of יהוה and His jealousy shall smoke against that man, and all the curses that are written in this scroll shall lie upon him, and יהוה shall blot out his name from under the shamayim. 21 And יהוה shall separate him to evil out of all the tribes of Yisrael, according to all the curses of the covenant that are written in this scroll of the Torah: 22 So that the generation to come of your children that shall rise up after you, and the Ger that shall come from a far land, shall say, when they see the plagues of that land, and the sicknesses which יהוה has laid upon it; 23 And that the whole land is like that which is brimstone, and salt, and burning, that it is not sown, nor bears, nor any grass grows in it, like the overthrow of Sedom, and Amorah, Admah, and Zevoim, which יהוה overthrew in His anger, and in His wrath: 24 Even all nations shall say, Why has יהוה done this to this land? What means the heat of this great anger? 25 Then

men shall say, Because they have forsaken the covenant of יהוה Elohim of their ahvot, which He made with them when He brought them forth out of the land of Mitzrayim: 26 For they went and served other elohim, and worshipped them, elohim whom they knew not, and whom He had not given to them: 27 And the anger of יהוה was lit against this land, to bring upon it all the curses that are written in this scroll: 28 And יהוה rooted them out of their land in anger, and in wrath, and in great indignation, and cast them into another land,[2] as it is this day. 29 The secret things belong to יהוה our Elohim: but those things that are revealed belong to us and to our children le-olam-va-ed, that we may do all the words of this Torah.[3]

30 And it shall come to pass, when all these things are come upon you, the blessing and the curse, which I have set before you, and you shall call them to mind among all the nations,[4] where יהוה Your Elohim has driven you, 2 And shall teshuvah to יהוה Your Elohim, and shall obey His voice according to all that I command you this day, you and your children, with all your lev, and with all your being; 3 That then יהוה Your Elohim will turn your captivity, and have compassion upon you, and will return and gather you from all the nations, where יהוה Your Elohim has scattered you.[5] 4 If any of you be driven out to the farthest parts of the shamayim, from there will יהוה Your

---

[2] **Eretz Acheret**-An interesting phrase, since all other Scriptures of exile, speak of all nations. Taken with those, here is a singe nation of exile, singled out from other nations of exile. This could definitely be a clear reference to the United States of America, which houses literally hundreds of millions of both Jews and Ephraimites, in varying forms of Christian expression. The **Mishna** (Sanhedrin 10) opines that this verse in Deuteronomy refers to the lost ten tribes who are ordained to remain in "**Eretz Acheret**" until close to the end of this age. The American hemisphere when first revealed in our era to European eyes was known as "The New World," another translation of the term "**eretz acheret**." For more details see: http://yourarmstoisrael.org/Articles_new/guest/?page=eretz_ac herit
[3] In context, the secret things are the whereabouts of all of Yisrael's exiles.
[4] All nations.
[5] Through and by the mission of Moshiach Yahshua.

Elohim gather you, and from there will He fetch you: 5 And יהוה Your Elohim will bring you into the land that your ahvot possessed, and you shall possess it; and He will do you tov, and multiply you above your ahvot.[1] 6 And יהוה Your Elohim will brit-milah your lev, and the lev of your zera, to love יהוה Your Elohim with all your lev, and with all your being, that you may live. 7 And יהוה Your Elohim will put all these curses upon your enemies, and on them that hate you, who persecute you. 8 And you shall make teshuvah and obey the voice of יהוה , and do all His mitzvot which I command you this day. 9 And יהוה Your Elohim will make you have excess in every work of your hand, in the fruit of your body, and in the fruit of your cattle, and in the fruit of your land, for tov: for יהוה will again gilah over you for tov, as He rejoiced over your ahvot: 10 If you shall listen to the voice of יהוה Your Elohim, to shomer His mitzvot and His chukim which are written in this scroll of the Torah, and if you turn to יהוה Your Elohim with all your lev, and with all your being. 11 For this mitzvah, which I command you, this day, it is not hidden from you, neither is it far off. 12 It is not in the shamayim, that you should say, Who shall go up for us to the shamayim, and bring it to us, that we may hear, and do it? 13 Neither is it beyond the sea that you should say, Who shall go over the sea for us, and bring it to us, that we may hear, and do it? 14 But the Word is very near to you, in your mouth, and in your lev,[2] that you may do it.[3] 15 See, I have set before you this day chayim and tov, and death and evil; 16 In that I command you this day to love יהוה Your Elohim, to have your halacha in His ways, and to shomer His mitzvot and His chukim and His mishpatim, that you may live and multiply:[4] and יהוה Your

Elohim shall bless you in the land where you are going to possess it. 17 But if your lev turn away, so that you will not hear, but shall be drawn away, and worship other elohim, and serve them; 18 I declare to you this day, that you shall surely perish, and that you shall not prolong your days upon the land, where you pass over the Yarden to go to possess it. 19 I call the shamayim and earth to record this day against you, that I have set before you chayim and death, blessing and cursing: therefore choose chayim, that both you and your zera may live: 20 That you may love יהוה Your Elohim, and that you may obey His voice, and that you may cleave to Him: for He is your chayim, and the length of your days: that you may dwell in the land which יהוה swore to your ahvot, to Avraham, to Yitzchak, and to Yaakov, to give them.

Torah Parsha 52
Vayelech 31:1-30
In regular years, read with Parsha 51.
In years with 13 months, read separately.
Haftarah Hoshea 14:2-10
Brit Chadasha Ivrim 13:5-8
Mattityahu 28:16-20

31 And Moshe went and spoke these words to all Yisrael. 2 And he said to them, I am a hundred twenty years old this day; I can no more go out and come in: also יהוה has said to me, You shall not go over this Yarden. 3 יהוה Your Elohim, He will go over before you, and He will destroy these nations from before you, and you shall possess them: and Yahoshua, he shall go over before you, as יהוה has said. 4 And יהוה shall do to them as He did to Sihon and to Og, melechim of the Amorites, and to their land which He destroyed. 5 And יהוה shall give them up before your face, that you may do to them according to all the mitzvot which I have commanded you. 6 Be strong and of a tov courage, fear not, nor be afraid of them: for יהוה Your Elohim, He it is that does go with you; He will not fail you, nor forsake you. 7 And Moshe called

---

[1] Physical multiplication.
[2] Yahshua; Romans 10:8-10.
[3] According to the Brit Chadasha, the Torah itself is the word of faith renewed through the **besarot** and proclaimed by the **shlichiim**, as opposed to a dispensationalist mindset of Torah versus faith.
[4] Physical multiplicity.

to Yahoshua, and said to him in the sight of all Yisrael, Be strong and of a tov courage: for you must go with this people to the land which **יהוה** has sworn to their ahvot to give them; and you shall cause them to inherit it. 8 And **יהוה**, He it is that does go before you; He will be with you, He will not fail you, neither forsake you: fear not, neither be dismayed. 9 And Moshe wrote this Torah, and delivered it to the kohanim the sons of Levi, who bore the Ark of the Covenant of **יהוה**, and to all the zachanim of Yisrael. 10 And Moshe commanded them, saying, At the end of every seven years, in the solemnity of the year of release, at Chag Sukkot, 11 When all Yisrael comes to appear before **יהוה** Your Elohim in the place that He shall choose, you shall read this Torah before all Yisrael in their hearing. 12 Gather the people together, men and women, and children,[1] and your Ger that is within your gates, that they may hear, and that they may learn, and fear **יהוה** Your Elohim, and shomer to do all the words of this Torah: 13 And that their children, who have not known anything, may hear, and learn to fear **יהוה** Your Elohim, as long as you live in the land where you go over the Yarden to possess it. 14 And **יהוה** said to Moshe, *See, your days approach that you must die: call Yahoshua, and present yourselves in the tabernacle of the congregation, that I may give him a command.* And Moshe and Yahoshua went, and presented themselves in the tabernacle of the congregation. 15 And **יהוה** appeared in the tabernacle in a pillar of a cloud: and the pillar of the cloud stood over the door of the tabernacle. 16 And **יהוה** said to Moshe, *See, you shall sleep with your ahvot; and this people will rise up, and whore after the elohim of the Gerim of the land, where they are going to be among them, and will forsake Me, and break My covenant that I have made with them. 17 Then My anger shall be lit against them in that day, and I*

will forsake them, and I will hide My face from them, and they shall be devoured, and many evils and troubles shall befall them; so that they will say in that day, Are not these evils come upon us, because our Elohim is not among us? 18 And I will surely hide My face in that day for all the evils that they shall do, in that they will have turned to other elohim. 19 Now therefore write this song for you, and teach it the children of Yisrael: put it in their mouths, that this song may be a witness for Me against the children of Yisrael. 20 For when I shall have brought them into the land which I swore to their ahvot, that flows with milk and honey; and they shall have eaten and filled themselves, and grown fat; then will they turn to other elohim, and serve them, and provoke Me, and break My covenant. 21 And it shall come to pass, when many evils and troubles are befallen them, that this song shall testify against them as a witness; for it shall not be forgotten out of the mouths of their zera: for I know their imaginations that they entertain, even now, before I have brought them into the land which I swore to them.

22 Moshe therefore wrote this shir the same day, and taught it to the children of Yisrael. 23 And he gave Yahoshua the son of Nun a command, and said, Be strong and of a tov courage: for you shall bring the children of Yisrael into the land which I swore to them: and I will be with you. 24 And it came to pass, when Moshe had made an end of writing the words of this Torah in a scroll, until they were finished, 25 That Moshe commanded the leviim, who bore the Ark of the Covenant of **יהוה**, saying, 26 Take this scroll of the Torah, and put it inside of the Ark of the Covenant of **יהוה** Your Elohim, that it may be there for a witness against you. 27 For I know your rebellion, and your stiff neck: see, while I am yet alive with you this day, you have been rebellious against **יהוה**; and how much more after my death? 28 Gather to Me all the zachanim of your tribes, and your officers, that I may speak

---

[1] Notice; the children did not go to separate children's programs; but were required to hear all of Torah with the adults.

these words in their ears, and call the shamayim and earth to record it against them. 29 For I know that after my death you will fully corrupt yourselves, and turn aside from the derech which I have commanded you; and evil will befall you in the latter-days;[1] because you will do evil in the sight of יהוה, to provoke Him to anger through the work of your hands. 30 And Moshe spoke in the ears of all the congregation of Yisrael the words of this song, until they were ended.

Torah Parsha 53
HaAzinu 32:1-52
Haftarah Schmuel Bet 22:1-51
Brit Chadasha Romiyah 10:14-21

32 Give ear, O you shamayim, and I will speak; and listen, O earth, the words of my mouth. 2 My doctrine shall drop as the rain; my speech shall drop down as the dew, as the small rain upon the tender herb, and as the showers upon the grass: 3 Because I will publish the Name of יהוה:[2] ascribe greatness to our Elohim. 4 He is the Rock, His work is perfect: for all His halachot are mishpat: An El of emet and without iniquity, Tzadik and right is He. 5 They have corrupted themselves, they are blemished and are not His children: they are a perverse and crooked generation. 6 Are these the things you return to יהוה,[3] O foolish and unwise people? Is not He your Abba that has bought you? Has He not made you, and established you? 7 Remember the days of old, consider the years of many generations: ask your Abba,[4] and He will show you; your zachanim, and they will tell you. 8 When the Most High divided to the nations their inheritance, when He separated the sons of Adam, He set the boundaries of the nations according to the number of the heavenly messengers

of Elohim.[5] [6] 9 For יהוה's portion is His people; Yaakov His allotted inheritance.[7] 10 He found him in a desert land, and in the waste howling wilderness; He led him about, He instructed him, He kept him as the apple of His eye. 11 As an eagle stirs up her nest, flutters over her young, spreads abroad her wings, takes them, and bears them on her wings: 12 So יהוה alone did lead him, and there was no strange El with him. 13 He made him ride on the high places of the earth, that he might eat the increase of the fields; and He made him to suck honey out of the rock, and oil out of the flinty rock; 14 Butter of cattle, and milk of sheep, with fat of lambs, and rams of the breed of Bashan, and goats, with the fat of kidneys of wheat; and you did drink the pure dom of the grape, the tov wine. 15 But Yeshurun[8] grew fat, and kicked: you are waxed fat, you are grown thick, you are covered with fatness; then he forsook Eloah who made him, and lightly esteemed the Rock of his salvation. 16 They provoked Him to jealousy with strange elohim, with abominations they provoked Him to anger. 17 They sacrificed to shadim, not to Eloah; to elohim whom they knew not, to new ones that popped up; whom your ahvot feared not. 18 Of the Rock that begat you, you are not mindful, and have forgotten the El that formed you. 19 And when יהוה saw it, He abhorred them, because of their provoking of His sons, and of His daughters. 20 And He said, *I will hide My face from them, I will see what their end shall be: for they are a very perverse generation, children in whom is no emunah. 21 They have moved Me to jealousy with that which is not El;*

---

[1] Starting in circa 33CE.
[2] A defining characteristic of true Yisrael. Those who refuse to proclaim the true Name of Abba cannot be considered Yisrael, as both heaven and earth record and testify the same along with Moshe's Song.
[3] Idolatry and forsaking His Name.
[4] The concept of YHWH as Abba is not a Christian invention.

[5] Speaking of YHWH's command for key messengers/heavenly messengers to guard specific nations (LXX and DSS).
[6] Alternate translation according to the Peshitta and Masoretic texts reads: "According to the number of the sons of Yisrael." If one accepts this rendering, then the nations were divided geographically based on the criteria of how many of Yisrael's exiles that nation could hold. Based on that sole criteria YHWH would allot a certain amount of land. This rendering further displays the vastness of the billions of Yisraelites in the latter-days.
[7] Yaakov's inheritance will eventually fill all nations.
[8] Pet name for Yisrael.

they have provoked Me to anger with their vanities: and I will move them to jealousy with those who are Lo-Ami; I will provoke them to anger with a foolish nation.[1] 22 For a fire is lit in My anger, and shall burn to the lowest Sheol, and shall consume the land with its increase, and set on fire the foundations of the mountains. 23 I will gather evils upon them; I will send My arrows upon them. 24 They shall be wasted with hunger, and devoured with burning heat, and with bitter destruction: I will also send the teeth of beasts upon them, with the poison of serpents of the dust. 25 The sword without, and fear within, shall destroy both the young man and the virgin, the nursing child also with the man of gray hairs. 26 I said, I would scatter them into the four corners, I would make the remembrance of them to cease from among men:[2] 27 Were it not that I feared the wrath of the enemy, lest their adversaries should behave themselves strangely, and lest they should say, Our hand is high, and יהוה has not done all this. 28 For they are a nation void of counsel, neither is there any understanding in them. 29 O that they were wise, that they understood this, that they would consider their latter end! 30 How should one chase a thousand, and two put ten thousand to flight, except their Rock had sold them, and יהוה had given them up? 31 For their rock is not as our Rock, even our enemies themselves are shophtim. 32 For their vine is of the vine of Sedom, and of the fields of Amorah: their grapes are grapes of gall, their clusters are bitter: 33 Their wine is the poison of dragons, and the cruel venom of asps. 34 Is not this laid up in store with Me, and sealed up among My treasures? 35 To Me belongs vengeance and repayment; their foot shall slide in due time: for the day of their

calamity is at hand, and the things that shall come upon them make haste. 36 For יהוה shall shophet His people, and have rachamim for His avadim, when He sees that their power is gone, and there is none remaining shut up, or at large. 37 And He shall say, Where are their elohim, their rock in whom they trusted, 38 Who did eat the fat of their sacrifices, and drank the wine of their drink offerings? Let them rise up and help you, and be your protection. 39 See now that I, even I, am He, and there is no elohim with Me: I kill, and I make alive; I wound, and I heal: neither is there any that can deliver out of My hand. 40 For I lift up My hand to the shamayim, and say, I live le-olam-va-ed. 41 If I sharpen My flashing sword, and My hand takes hold on mishpat; I will render vengence to My enemies, and will reward them that hate Me. 42 I will make My arrows drunk with dom, and My sword shall devour flesh; and that with the dom of the slain and of the captives, from the keter of the head of the enemy. 43 Rejoice, O shamayim, with Him, and let all the heavenly messengers worship Him:[3] O gilah you nations with His people,[4] and let all the sons of Elohim strengthen themselves in Him; for He will avenge the dom of His sons, and will render mishpat to His adversaries, and will reward them that hate Him, and יהוה will make an atonement for the land and for His people. 44 And Moshe came and spoke all the words of this song in the ears of the people, he, and Yahoshua the son of Nun. 45 And Moshe made an end of speaking all these words to all Yisrael: 46 And he said to them, Set your levim to all the words that I testify among you this day, which you shall command your children to shomer and to do, all the words of this Torah. 47 For it is not a vain thing for you; because it is your chayim: and through this thing you shall prolong

---

[1] This reference refers to Yisrael being stunned and angered by a people that resemble non-Yisraelites in culture and lifestyle, claiming to be the "Yisrael of YHWH" in the latter-days. From Scriptures in Hosea1: 9, First Peter 2:10, and Romans 9:25-27, the Lo-Ami foolish or goy nation, was and is returning Ephraim Yisrael.
[2] Ephraim Yisrael, all but forgotten by mankind until the last days, and the coming of Moshiach Yahshua.
[3] Speaking of Moshiach Yahshua as quoted in Ivrim/Hebrews 1:6 and from the LXX.
[4] From the LXX and quoted in Romans 15:10 validating this usage encouraging all nations to be Yisrael and join in with Yisrael, not Yisrael with other religions, or nations.

your days in the land, where you go over the Yarden to possess it. 48 And **יהוה** spoke to Moshe that same day, saying, 49 *Get up into this mountain Avarim, to Mount Nevo, which is in the land of Moav that is opposite Yericho; and see the land of Kanaan, which I give to the children of Yisrael for a possession: 50 And die on the Mount where you go up, and be gathered to your people; as Aharon your brother died on Mount Hor, and was gathered to his people: 51 Because you trespassed against Me among the children of Yisrael at the mayim of Merivah-Kadesh, in the wilderness of Tzin; because you did not set Me apart in the midst of the children of Yisrael. 52 Yet you shall see the land before you; but you shall not go there to the land that I give the children of Yisrael.*

Torah Parsha 54
VeZot HaBrachah 33:1-34:12
Haftarah Yahoshua 1:1-18
Brit Chadasha Mattityahu 17:1-9
Yahudah 8-9

33 And this is the blessing, with which Moshe the man of Elohim blessed the children of Yisrael before his death. 2 And he said, **יהוה** came from Sinai, and rose up from Seir to them; He shined forth from Mount Paran, and He came with ten thousands of kidushim: from His Right Hand[1] went a fiery Torah for them. 3 Yes, He loved the people; all His kidushim are in your hand: and they sat down at your feet; every one shall receive of your words. 4 Moshe commanded us a Torah, even the inheritance of the congregation of Yaakov. 5 And He was melech in Yeshurun, when the heads of the people and the tribes of Yisrael were gathered together.[2] 6 Let Reuven live, and not die; and let not his men be few. 7 And this is the blessing of Yahudah: and he said, Shema, **יהוה**, to the voice of Yahudah, and bring him to his people: let his hands be

sufficient for him; and be a help to him from his enemies. 8 And of Levi he said, Let your Thummim and your Urim be with your Kadosh-One, whom you did test at Massah, and with whom you did contend at the mayim of Merivah; 9 Who said to his abba and to his ima, I have not seen him; neither did he acknowledge his brothers, or know his own children: for they have observed Your word, and kept Your covenant. 10 They shall teach Yaakov Your mishpatim, and Yisrael Your Torah: they shall put incense before You, and whole burnt sacrifices upon Your altar. 11 **יהוה** Bless, His substance, and accept the work of his hands; smite through the loins of them that rise against him, and of them that hate him, that they rise not again. 12 And of Benyamin he said, The beloved of **יהוה** shall dwell in safety by Him; and **יהוה** shall cover him all the day long, and he shall dwell between His shoulders. 13 And of Yoseph he said, Blessed of **יהוה** be his land, for the precious things of the shamayim, for the dew, and for the deep that lies beneath, 14 And for the precious fruits brought forth by the sun, and for the precious things put forth by the moon, 15 And for the best things of the ancient mountains, and for the precious things of the lasting hills, 16 And for the precious things of the earth and fullness off it, and for the tov will of him that dwelt in the bush: let the blessing come upon the head of Yoseph, and upon the top of the head of him that was separated from his brothers. 17 His splendor is like a first-born bull, and his horns are like the horns of the wild ox: with them he shall push the peoples together to the ends of the earth: and they are the myriads of Ephraim, and they are the thousands of Menashsheh.[3]

---

[1] Reference to Moshiach

[2] YHWH is truly King when He receives honor for gathering all Yisrael back in spite of their exile and hard levim.

[3] Just as a goring ox thrusts things forward and outward, so will the multitudes of Yisrael be found in Ephraim Yisrael, or the collective term for the later 10 tribes of the northern kingdom. This dominant tribe of the north will be responsible for pushing the peoples of Yisrael into all the nations, as outlined in many other references.

- 225 -

18 And of Zevulon he said, Rejoice, Zevulon, in your going out; and, Yissacher, in your tents. 19 They shall call the people to the mountain; there they shall offer sacrifices of tzedakah: for they shall suck of the abundance of the seas, and of treasures hidden in the sand. 20 And of Gad he said, Blessed be he that enlarges Gad:[1] he dwells as a lion, and tears the arm with the keter of the head. 21 And he provided the first part for himself, because there, the portion of the Torah giver, was hidden; and he came with the heads of the people, he did the tzedakah of יהוה, and his mishpatim with Yisrael.[2] 22 And of Dan he said, Dan is a lion's whelp: he shall leap from Bashan. 23 And of Naphtali he said, O Naphtali, satisfied with favor, and full with the blessing of יהוה : possess the west and the south. 24 And of Asher he said, Let Asher be blessed with children; let him be acceptable to his brothers, and let him dip his foot in oil. 25 Your shoes shall be iron and brass; and as your days, so shall your strength be. 26 There is none like the El of Yeshurun, who rides upon the shamayim for your help, and in His excellency rides the skies. 27 The Elohim of old is your refuge, and underneath are the everlasting arms: and He shall thrust out the enemy from before you; and shall say, Destroy them. 28 Yisrael then shall dwell in safety alone: the fountain of Yaakov shall be upon a land of corn and wine; also His shamayim shall drop down dew. 29 Favored are you, O Yisrael: who is like you, O people saved by יהוה , the Shield of your help, who is the Sword of Your Excellency! And your enemies shall be found to be liars to you; and you shall tread down their high places.

34 And Moshe went up from the plains of Moav to the mountain of Nevo, to the top of Pisgah that is opposite Yericho.

And יהוה showed him all the land of Gilead, as far as Dan, 2 And all of Naphtali, and the land of Ephraim, and Menashsheh, and all the land of Yahudah, to the Western Sea, 3 And the south, and the plain of the Valley of Yericho, the city of palm eytzim, to Tzoar. 4 And יהוה said to him, *This is the land which I swore to Avraham, to Yitzchak, and to Yaakov, saying, I will give it to your zera: I have caused you to see it with your eyes, but you shall not go over there.* 5 So Moshe the eved of יהוה died there in the land of Moav, according to the Word of יהוה.[3] 6 And He buried him in a valley in the land of Moav, opposite Beth-Peor: but no man knows of his burial place to this day. 7 And Moshe was one hundred twenty years old when he died: his eye was not dim, nor his natural force gone. 8 And the children of Yisrael wept for Moshe in the plains of Moav thirty days: so the days of weeping and mourning for Moshe were ended. 9 And Yahoshua the son of Nun was full of the Ruach of chochma; for Moshe had laid his hands upon him: and the children of Yisrael heard to him, and did as יהוה commanded Moshe. 10 And there arose not a navi since in Yisrael like Moshe, whom יהוה knew panayim-el-panayim, [4] 11 In all the signs and the wonders, which יהוה sent him to do in the land of Mitzrayim to Pharaoh, and to all his avadim, and to all his land, 12 And in all that his mighty hand did, and in all the great fearsome deeds that Moshe showed forth in the sight of kol Yisrael.

Chazak Chazak VeNitchazak
Be Strong Be Strong! And May We Be Strengthened!

---

[1] To house the scepter.
[2] For more details See The **Mystery Of The Hidden Scepter** at:
http://yourarmstoisrael.org/Articles_new/restoration/?page=21&type=12

[3] Joshua probably penned this verse to the chapter's end.
[4] Until the coming of YHWH's Son

יהושע

Yahoshua - Joshua
To Our Forefathers Yisrael

1 Now after the death of Moshe the eved of יהוה, it came to pass, that יהוה spoke to Yahoshua [1] the son of Nun, Moshe's assistant, saying, 2 *Moshe My eved is dead; now therefore arise, go over this the Yarden River, you, and this entire people, to the land that I do give to them, even to the children of Yisrael. 3 Every place that the sole of your foot shall tread upon, that have I given to you, as I said to Moshe. 4 From the wilderness of Levanon even to the great river, the River Euphrates, all the land of the Hittites, and to the great sea toward the going down of the sun, shall be your border. 5 There shall not be any man able to resist you all the days of your chayim: as I was with Moshe, so I will be with you.[2] I will not fail you, nor forsake you. 6 Be strong and courageous: for to this people shall you divide for an inheritance the land, which I swore to their ahvot to give them. 7 Only be strong and very courageous, that you may shomer to do according to all the Torah, which Moshe My eved commanded you: turn not from it to the right hand or to the left, that you may prosper wherever you go. 8 This scroll of the Torah shall not depart out of your mouth; but you shall meditate on it day and night, that you may shomer to do according to all that is written in it: for then you shall make your derech prosperous, and then you shall have tov success. 9 Have not I commanded you? Be strong and courageous; be not afraid, neither be dismayed: for* יהוה *Your Elohim is with you wherever you go.* 10 Then Yahoshua commanded the officers of the people, saying, 11 Pass through the camp, and command the people, saying, Prepare for yourselves provisions; for within three days you shall pass over this the Yarden River, to go in to possess the land, which יהוה Your Elohim gives you to possess it. 12 And to the Reuvenites, and to the Gadites, and to half the tribe of Menashsheh, spoke Yahoshua, saying, 13 Remember the word that Moshe the eved of יהוה commanded you, saying, יהוה Your Elohim has given you rest, and has given you this land. 14 Your wives, your little ones, and your cattle, shall remain in the land which Moshe gave you on this side of the Yarden River; nevertheless you shall pass with your brothers armed, all the mighty men of valor, and help them; 15 Until יהוה has given your brothers rest, as He has given you, and they also have possessed the land which יהוה Your Elohim gives them: then you shall return to the land of your possession, and enjoy it, which Moshe יהוה's eved gave you on this side of the Yarden River toward the sunrising. 16 And they answered Yahoshua, saying, All that you command us we will do, and wherever you send us, we will go. 17 As we listened to Moshe in all things, so will we shema to you: only יהוה Your Elohim be with you, as He was with Moshe. 18 Whoever he is that does rebel against your commandment, and will not shema to your words in all that you command him, he shall be put to death: only be strong and courageous.

2 And Yahoshua the son of Nun sent out of Shittim two men to spy secretly, saying, Go view the land, even Yericho. And they went, and came to a harlot's bayit, named Rachav, and lodged there. 2 And it was told the melech of Yericho, saying, See, there came men in here tonight from the children of Yisrael to search out the land. 3 And the melech of Yericho sent to

---

[1] The full Name of our Moshiach is shortened to Yahshua. The spelling of Yahoshua preserves the Yah O syllables in the true Name.
[2] A promise to all Yisrael for all times.

Rachav, saying, Bring forth the men that have come to you, which have entered into your bayit: for they have come to search out all the land. 4 And the woman took the two men, and hid them, and said, There came men to me, but I didn't know where they were from: 5 And it came to pass about the time of the shutting of the gate, when it was dark, that men from the melech went out: She said to them, Where those men went, I don't know: Pursue after them quickly; for you shall overtake them. 6 But she had brought them up to the roof of the bayit, and hid them with the stalks of flax, which she had piled up on the roof. 7 And the men pursued after them the derech to the Yarden River to the fords: and as soon as those who pursued after them had gone out after the spies, they shut the gate. 8 And before they were laid down for the night, she came up to them up on the roof; 9 And she said to the men, I know that יהוה has given you the land, and that your fear is fallen upon us, and that all the inhabitants of the land faint because of you. 10 For we have heard how יהוה dried up the mayim of the Sea of Reeds for you, when you came out of Mitzrayim; and what you did to the two melechim of the Amorites, that were on the other side of the Yarden River, Sihon and Og, whom you utterly destroyed. 11 And as soon as we had heard these things, our levim did melt, neither did there remain any more courage in us, because of you: for יהוה Your Elohim, He is Elohim in the shamayim above, and in earth beneath. 12 Now therefore, please, swear to me by יהוה, since I have shown you chesed; that you will also show chesed to my abba's bayit, and give me an emet sign of that chesed: 13 And that you will keep alive my abba, and my ima, and my brothers, and my sisters, and all that they have, and deliver our chayim from death. 14 And the men answered her, Our chayim for yours, if you utter nothing about this business. And it shall be, when יהוה has given us the land that we will deal in chesed and in emet with

you. 15 Then she let them down by a rope through the window: for her bayit was upon the town wall, and she dwelt upon the wall. 16 And she said to them, Get to the mountain, lest the pursuers meet you; and hide yourselves there three days, until the pursuers return: and afterward you can go your way. 17 And the men said to her, We will be blameless of this your oath which you have made us swear. 18 Unless you do this; when we come into the land, you shall bind this cord of scarlet thread in the window from which you did let us down by: and you shall bring your abba, and your ima, and your brothers, and all your abba's household to stay with you. 19 And it shall be, that whosoever shall go out of the doors of your bayit into the street, his spilled dom shall be his own fault, and we will be guiltless: and whoever shall be with you in the bayit, if they are hurt, his dom shall become our fault, if any harm be upon him. 20 And if you mention this business to anyone, then we will be free of your oath that you have made us to swear. 21 And she said, According to your words, so be it. And she sent them away, and they departed: and she bound the scarlet line in the window. 22 And they went, and came to the mountain, and stayed there three days, until the pursuers had returned: and the pursuers sought them throughout all the derech, but found them not. 23 So the two men returned, and descended from the mountain, and passed over, and came to Yahoshua the son of Nun, and told him all things that had happened to them: 24 And they said to Yahoshua, Truly יהוה has delivered into our hands all the land; for even all the inhabitants of the land do faint because of us.

3 And Yahoshua rose early in the morning; and they set out from Shittim, and came to the Yarden River, he and all the children of Yisrael, and lodged there before they passed over. 2 And it came to pass after three days that the officers went

through the camp; 3 And they commanded the people, saying, When you see the Ark of the Covenant of יהוה Your Elohim, and the kohanim, the Leviim, bearing it; then you shall set out from your place, and follow it. 4 Only, there shall be a space between you and it, about two thousand cubits by measure: come not near to it, that you may know the derech by which you must go: for you have not passed this derech before. 5 And Yahoshua said to the people, Set yourselves apart: for tomorrow יהוה will do wonders among you. 6 And Yahoshua spoke to the kohanim, saying, Take up the Ark of the Covenant, and pass over before the people. And they took up the Ark of the Covenant, and went before the people. 7 And יהוה said to Yahoshua, *This day will I begin to magnify you in the sight of all Yisrael; that they may know that, as I was with Moshe, so I will be with you. 8 And you shall command the kohanim that bear the Ark of the Covenant, saying, When you have come to the brink of the mayim of the Yarden River, you shall stand still in the middle of the Yarden River.* 9 And Yahoshua said to the children of Yisrael, Come here, and shema the words of יהוה Your Elohim. 10 And Yahoshua said, By this you shall know that the living Elohim is among you, and that He will without fail drive out from before you the Kanaanites, and the Hittites, and the Hivites, and the Perizzites, and the Girgashites, and the Amorites, and the Yevusites. 11 See; the Ark of the Covenant of יהוה of all the earth passes over before you into the Yarden River. 12 Now therefore take twelve men out of the tribes of Yisrael, out of every tribe a man. 13 And it shall come to pass, as soon as the soles of the feet of the kohanim that bear the Ark of יהוה, Master of all the earth, shall rest in the mayim of the Yarden River, that the mayim of the Yarden River shall be cut off from the mayim that come down from upstream; and they shall stand still like a pile. 14 And it came to pass, when the people removed from their tents,

to pass over the Yarden River, and the kohanim bearing the Ark of the Covenant before the people; 15 And as they that bore the Ark were come to the Yarden River, and the feet of the kohanim that bore the Ark were dipped at the edge of the mayim - for the Yarden River overflows all its banks all the time at harvest - 16 That the mayim which came down from the north stopped and rose up into a pile very far away at Aram, that is beside Tzaretan: and the mayim that came down toward the sea of the plain, even the salt sea, failed, and were cut off: and the people passed over just opposite Yericho. 17 And the kohanim that bore the Ark of the Covenant of יהוה stood firm on dry ground in the midst of the Yarden River, and all the Yisraelites passed over on dry ground, until all the people had passed completely over the Yarden River.

4 And it came to pass, when all the people had completely passed over the Yarden River, that יהוה spoke to Yahoshua, saying, 2 *Take twelve men out of the people, out of every tribe a man, 3 And command them, saying, Take out of the midst of the Yarden River, out of the place where the kohanim's feet stood firm, twelve stones, and you shall carry them over with you, and leave them in the lodging place, where you shall lodge this night.* 4 Then Yahoshua called the twelve men, whom he had prepared from the children of Yisrael, out of every tribe a man: 5 And Yahoshua said to them, Pass over before the Ark of יהוה Your Elohim into the midst of the Yarden River, and take up every man a stone upon his shoulder, according to the number of the tribes of the children of Yisrael: 6 That this may be a sign among you, that when your children ask their ahvot in times to come, saying, What is the meaning of these stones? 7 Then you shall answer them, That the mayim of the Yarden River was cut off before the Ark of the Covenant of יהוה; when it passed over the Yarden River, the mayim of the Yarden

River was cut off: and these stones shall be for a memorial to the children of Yisrael le-olam-va-ed. 8 And the children of Yisrael did so as Yahoshua commanded, and took up twelve stones out of the midst of the Yarden River, as יהוה spoke to Yahoshua, according to the number of the tribes of the children of Yisrael, and carried them over with them to the place where they lodged, and laid them down there. 9 And Yahoshua set up twelve stones in the midst of the Yarden River, in the place where the feet of the kohanim who bore the Ark of the Covenant stood: and they are there to this day. 10 For the kohanim who bore the Ark stood in the midst of the Yarden River, until everything was finished that יהוה commanded Yahoshua to speak to the people, according to all that Moshe commanded Yahoshua: and the people hurried and passed over. 11 And it came to pass, when all the people had completely passed over, that the Ark of יהוה passed over, and the kohanim, in the presence of the people. 12 And the children of Reuven, and the children of Gad, and half the tribe of Menashsheh, passed over armed before the children of Yisrael, as Moshe spoke to them: 13 About forty thousand prepared for war passed over before יהוה to battle, to the plains of Yericho. 14 On that day יהוה magnified Yahoshua in the sight of all Yisrael; and they feared him, just as they feared Moshe, all the days of his chayim. 15 And יהוה spoke to Yahoshua, saying, 16 *Command the kohanim that bear the Ark of the testimony that they come up out of the Yarden River.* 17 Yahoshua therefore commanded the kohanim, saying, Come up out of the Yarden River. 18 And it came to pass, when the kohanim that bore the Ark of the Covenant of יהוה came up out of the midst of the Yarden River, and the soles of the kohanim's feet were lifted up to the dry land, that the mayim of the Yarden River returned to its place and flowed over all its banks, as they did before. 19 And the people

came up out of the Yarden River on the tenth day of the first month, and camped in Gilgal, on the east border of Yericho. 20 And those twelve stones, which they took out of the Yarden River, did Yahoshua set up in Gilgal. 21 And he spoke to the children of Yisrael, saying, When your children shall ask their ahvot in times to come, saying, What is the meaning of these stones? 22 Then you shall let your children know, saying, Yisrael came over this Yarden River on dry land. 23 For יהוה Your Elohim dried up the mayim of the Yarden River from before you, until you had passed over, just as יהוה Your Elohim did to the Sea of Reeds, which He dried up before us, until we had gone over: 24 That all the people of the earth might know the Hand of יהוה, that it is mighty: that you might fear יהוה Your Elohim le-olam-va-ed.

5 And it came to pass, when all the melechim of the Amorites, who were on the side of the Yarden River westward, and all the melechim of the Kanaanites, which were by the sea, heard that יהוה had dried up the mayim of the Yarden River from before the children of Yisrael, until we were passed over, that their lev melted, neither was there ruach in them any more, because of the children of Yisrael. 2 At that time יהוה said to Yahoshua, Make yourselves sharp knives and brit-milah again the children of Yisrael a second time. 3 And Yahoshua made a sharp knife, and circumcised the children of Yisrael at the hill of the foreskins. 4 And this is the reason why Yahoshua did brit-milah the people: All the people that came out of Mitzrayim, that were males, even all the men of war, died in the wilderness, on the derech after they came out of Mitzrayim. 5 Now all the people that came out were circumcised: but all the people that were born in the wilderness by the derech as they came out of Mitzrayim, they had not been

circumcised.[1] 6 For the children of Yisrael walked forty years in the wilderness, until all the people that were men of war, who came out of Mitzrayim, were consumed, because they obeyed not the voice of יהוה: to whom יהוה swore that He would not show them the land, which יהוה swore to their ahvot that He would give us, a land that flows with milk and honey. 7 And their children, whom He raised up in their place, them Yahoshua circumcised: for they were uncircumcised, because they had not circumcised them in the derech. 8 And it came to pass, when they had done circumcising all the people, that they abode in their places in the camp, until they were healed. 9 And יהוה said to Yahoshua, *This day have I rolled away the reproach of Mitzrayim from off you.* Therefore the name of the place is called Gilgal to this day. 10 And the children of Yisrael encamped in Gilgal, and kept the Pesach on the fourteenth day of the month in the evening in the plains of Yericho. 11 And they did eat of the old corn of the land on the day after the Pesach, unleavened cakes, and parched corn on the same day.[2] 12 And the manna ceased on the next day after they had eaten of the old corn of the land; neither had the children of Yisrael manna any more; but they did eat of the fruit of the land of Kanaan that year. 13 And it came to pass, when Yahoshua was by Yericho, that he lifted up his eyes and looked, and, see, there stood a Man over against him with His sword drawn in His hand: and Yahoshua went to Him, and said to Him, Are You for us, or for our enemies? 14 And He said, No; but as Captain of the armies[3] of יהוה am I now come. And Yahoshua fell on his face to the earth, and did worship, and said to Him, What says My Master to His eved? 15 And the captain of יהוה's camp said to Yahoshua, Loose your sandals from off your feet; for the place where you stand is kadosh ground. And Yahoshua did so.[4]

6 Now Yericho was tightly shut up because of the children of Yisrael: none went out, and none came in. 2 And יהוה said to Yahoshua, *See, I have given into your hand Yericho, and the melech of it, and the mighty men of valor. 3 And you shall go around the city, all the men of war, shall go around the city once. This shall you do for six days. 4 And seven kohanim shall carry before the Ark seven trumpets of shofars: and on the seventh day you shall go around the city seven times, and the kohanim shall blow with the shofars.* 5 And it shall come to pass, that when they make a tekiyah gedollah with the shofars and when you shema the sound of the shofars, that all the people shall shout with a great shout; and the wall of the city shall fall down flat, and the people shall ascend up every man directly before him. 6 And Yahoshua the son of Nun called the kohanim, and said to them, Take up the Ark of the Covenant, and let seven kohanim bear the seven trumpets of shofars before the Ark of יהוה. 7 And he said to the people, Pass over, and surround the city, and let him that is armed go before the Ark of יהוה. 8 And it came to pass, when Yahoshua had spoken to the people, that the seven kohanim bearing the seven shofars passed on before יהוה, and blew with the shofars: and the Ark of the Covenant of יהוה followed them. 9 And the armed men went before the kohanim that

---

[1] Here we see that faith in YHWH comes before circumcision. The Galatian heresy was that Ephraimites had started performing circumcisions to please the Yahudim, having not yet entered into the fullness of faith or of Torah. As with Avraham, circumcision came much later, after faith. Yaakov-James in Acts 15 later affirmed this, so that the pattern is clear and the Galatians had broken the pattern.
[2] Concrete proof that Bikkurim (the Firstfruit wave offering), had to be the day after the annual Shabbat of Aviv 15, not the day after the weekly Shabbat, since eating grain is forbidden until the first fruit wave offering. If the wave offering was done on a Sunday annually and Passover fell on a weekday as it often did, then Joshua caused all Yisrael to violate Torah. That cannot be. For full details see: **Bringing Yisrael Back from Omer Error** at:
http://yourarmstoisrael.org/Articles_new/articles/?page=Bringing_Yisrael_Back&type=26

[3] An appearance of Yahshua, or **Metatron**, the Guardian of Yisrael known to Moshe as the Messenger of YHWH, but here as the Captain of YHWH's armies, and in Hebrews as the Captain of our salvation.
[4] YHWH appeared to Moshe in the burning bush in like manner as He does here, further confirming that this was none other than YHWH the sent one.

blew with the shofars, and the rear guard came after the Ark, and behind the kohanim blowing with shofars. 10 And Yahoshua had commanded the people, saying, You shall not shout, nor make any noise with your voice, neither shall any word proceed out of your mouth, until the day I tell you to shout; then shall you shout. 11 So the Ark of יהוה circled the city, going around it once: and they came into the camp, and lodged in the camp. 12 And Yahoshua rose early in the morning, and the kohanim took up the Ark of יהוה. 13 And seven kohanim bearing seven shofars before the Ark of יהוה went on continually, and blew with the shofars: and the armed men went before them; but the rear guard came after the Ark of יהוה, and after the kohanim blowing with the shofars. 14 And the second day they circled the city once, and returned into the camp: so they did the same six days. 15 And it came to pass on the seventh day, that they rose early about the dawning of the day, and circled the city after the same manner seven times: only on that day they circled the city seven times. 16 And it came to pass at the seventh time, when the kohanim blew with the trumpets, Yahoshua said to the people, Shout; for יהוה has given you the city. 17 And the city shall be cursed, and all that is in it belongs to יהוה: Only Rachav the harlot shall live, she and all that are with her in her bayit, because she hid the messengers that we sent. 18 And, under all circumstances you shall guard yourselves from the cursed things, lest you make yourselves cursed, when you take of the cursed things, and make the camp of Yisrael a curse, and trouble it. 19 But all the silver, and gold, and vessels of brass and iron, are set-apart to יהוה: they shall come into the treasury of יהוה. 20 So the people shouted when the kohanim blew with the shofars: and it came to pass, when the people heard the sound of the shofars, that the people shouted with a great shout, that the walls fell down flat, so that the people went up into the city every man directly before him,

and they took the city. 21 And they utterly destroyed all that was in the city, man and woman, young and old, and ox, and sheep, and donkey, with the edge of the sword. 22 But Yahoshua had said to the two men that had spied out the land, Go into the harlot's bayit, and bring out from there the woman, and all that she has, as you swore to her.[1] 23 And the young men that were spies went in, and brought Rachav, and her abba, and her ima, and her brothers, and all that she had; and they brought out all her relatives, and left them outside the camp of Yisrael.[2] 24 And they burnt the city with fire, and all that was in it: only the silver, and the gold, and the vessels of brass and of iron, they put into the treasury of the Bayit of יהוה. 25 And Yahoshua saved Rachav the harlot alive, and her abba's household, and all that she had; and she dwells in Yisrael even to this day;[3] because she hid the messengers, which Yahoshua had sent to spy out Yericho. 26 And Yahoshua warned them at that time, saying, Cursed be the man before יהוה, that rises up and rebuilds this city Yericho: he shall lay the foundation of it with the death of his firstborn, and with the death of his youngest son shall he set up the gates of it. 27 So יהוה was with Yahoshua, and his fame was reported throughout all the land.

7 But the children of Yisrael committed a trespass in the cursed thing: for Achan, the son of Karmi, the son of Zavdi, the son of Zerah, of the tribe of Yahudah, took of the cursed thing: and the anger of

---

[1] The two men are a type of the two houses of Yisrael, which will eventually take back the land of Yisrael.
[2] A type of both houses, defiled by harlotry, being kept outside the camp until cleansed by Yahshua. After contact with her, even the two messengers (Ephraim and Yahudah) were brought outside the camp. How much more were the actual two houses that became an adulterous bride, brought outside the camp until Yahshua arrived to lead them back in?
[3] Hear this really well. Even a gentile whore can become Yisrael when obeying Yisrael's King Moshiach and Torah, and chooses to dwell with the people in culture and lifestyle. Rahab is rewarded officially as a mother of Yisrael by being placed in the genealogy of Yahshua. Based on modern Judaism and Messianic Judaism, she probably would not have been allowed to be a Yisraelite unless she converted and became a certain type of a Jewish woman, like an orthodox Jewish convert.

יהוה burned against the children of Yisrael. 2 And Yahoshua sent men from Yericho to Ai, which is beside Beth-Aven, on the east side of Beth-El, and spoke to them, saying, Go up and view the land. And the men went up and viewed Ai. 3 And they returned to Yahoshua, and said to him, Let not all the people go up; but let about two or three thousand men go up and smite Ai; and make not all the people to labor there; for they are just a few. 4 So there went up from the people about three thousand men: and they fled before the men of Ai. 5 And the men of Ai smote about thirty-six men: for they chased them from before the gate even to Shevarim, and smote them in the descent: therefore the levim of the people melted, and became as mayim. 6 And Yahoshua tore his clothes, and fell to the earth upon his face before the Ark of יהוה until the evening, he and the zachanim of Yisrael, and put dust upon their heads. 7 And Yahoshua said, O Master יהוה, why have You even brought this people over the Yarden River, to deliver us into the hand of the Amorites, to destroy us? Would to Elohim we had been content, and stayed on the other side of the Yarden River! 8 O יהוה, what shall I say, when Yisrael turns their backs before their enemies! 9 For the Kanaanites and all the inhabitants of the land shall shema of it, and shall surround us, and cut off our name from the earth: and what will You do for Your great Name?[1] 10 And יהוה said to Yahoshua, *Get up; why do you lie down this way upon your face? 11 Yisrael has sinned, and they have also transgressed My covenant, which I commanded them: for they have even taken of the cursed things, and have also stolen, and deceived also, and they have put it even among their own belongings. 12 Therefore the children of Yisrael could not stand before their enemies, but turned their backs before their enemies, because they were cursed: neither will I be with you any more,*

except you destroy the cursed things from among you. 13 Rise up, set the people apart, and say, Set yourselves apart for tomorrow: for this says יהוה *Elohim of Yisrael, There is a cursed thing in the midst of you, O Yisrael: you cannot stand before your enemies, until you take away the cursed thing from among you. 14 In the morning therefore you shall be brought near according to your tribes: and it shall be, that the tribe which* יהוה *calls for shall come according to their mishpachot; and the mishpocha which* יהוה *shall call for will come by household; and the household which* יהוה *shall call for shall come forth man by man. 15 And it shall be, that he that is found with the cursed thing shall be burnt with fire, he and all that he has: because he has transgressed the covenant of* יהוה, *and because he has worked wickedness in Yisrael.* 16 So Yahoshua rose up early in the morning, and brought Yisrael by their tribes; and the tribe of Yahudah was selected: 17 And he brought the mishpocha of Yahudah; and he took the mishpocha of the Zarhites: and he brought the mishpocha of the Zarhites man by man; and Zavdi was taken: 18 And he brought his household man by man; and Achan, the son of Karmi, the son of Zavdi, the son of Zerah, of the tribe of Yahudah, was selected. 19 And Yahoshua said to Achan, My son, I beg you, give tifereth to יהוה Elohim of Yisrael, and make confession to Him; and tell me now what you have done; hide it not from me. 20 And Achan answered Yahoshua, and said, Indeed I have sinned against יהוה Elohim of Yisrael, and this is what I did: 21 When I saw among the spoils a lovely garment from Shinar, and two hundred shekels of silver, and a bar of gold of fifty shekels weight, then I coveted them, and took them; and, see, they are hidden in the earth under the middle of my tent, and the silver is under it. 22 So Yahoshua sent messengers, and they ran to the tent; and, see, it was hidden in his tent, and the silver under it. 23 And they took them out of the

---

[1] s.a.tan's grand design is to obliterate both the Name of YHWH and Yisrael.

midst of the tent, and brought them to Yahoshua, and to all the children of Yisrael, and laid the items out before יהוה. 24 And Yahoshua, and all Yisrael with him, took Achan the son of Zerah, and the silver, and the garment, and the bar of gold, and his sons, and his daughters, and his oxen, and his donkeys, and his sheep, and his tent, and all that he had: and they brought them to the Valley of Achor.[1] 25 And Yahoshua said, Why have you troubled us? יהוה shall trouble you this day. And all Yisrael stoned him with stones, and burned them with fire, after they had stoned them with stones. 26 And they raised over him a great heap of stones to this day. So יהוה turned from the fierceness of His anger. Therefore the name of that place was called, The Valley of Achor, to this day.[2]

8 And יהוה said to Yahoshua, *Fear not, neither be dismayed: take all the people of war with you, and arise, go up to Ai: see, now I have given into your hand the melech of Ai, and his people, and his city, and his land: 2 And you shall do to Ai and her melech as you did to Yericho and her melech: only the spoil, and the cattle, shall you take for a prey to yourselves: now go lay an ambush for the city behind it.* 3 So Yahoshua arose, and all the people of war, to go up against Ai: and Yahoshua chose thirty thousand mighty men of valor, and sent them away by night. 4 And he commanded them, saying, See, you shall lie in wait against the city, even behind the city: go not very far from the city, but you all be ready: 5 And I, and all the people that are with me, will approach the city: and it shall come to pass, when they come out against us, as the last time, that we will turn and run before them, 6 For they will come out after us. When we have drawn them from the city; they will say, They flee from before us, as last time: then we will flee before them. 7 Then you shall rise up from the ambush, and seize the city: for יהוה Your Elohim will deliver it into your hand. 8 And it shall be, when you have taken the city, that you shall set the city on fire: according to the commandment of יהוה shall you do. See, I have commanded you. 9 Yahoshua therefore sent them forth: and they went to lie in ambush, and stay between Beth-El and Ai, on the west side of Ai: but Yahoshua lodged that night among the people. 10 And Yahoshua rose up early in the morning, and numbered the people, and went up, he and the zachanim of Yisrael, ahead of the people to Ai. 11 And all the people, even the people of war that were with him, went up, and drew near, and came before the city, and pitched on the north side of Ai: now there was a valley between them and Ai. 12 And he took about five thousand men, and set them to lie in ambush between Beth-El and Ai, on the west side of the city. 13 And when they had set the people in position, even all the army, positioned to the north of the city, and those who lie in wait positioned to the west of the city, that Yahoshua went that night into the midst of the valley. 14 And it came to pass, when the melech of Ai saw it, that they quickly rose up early, and the men of the city went out against Yisrael to battle, he and all his people, at a time appointed, before the plain; but he did not know that there was an ambush against him behind the city. 15 And Yahoshua and all Yisrael pretended as if they were beaten before them, and fled by the way of the wilderness. 16 And all the people that were in Ai were called together to pursue after them: and they pursued after Yahoshua, and were drawn away from the city. 17 And there was not a man left in Ai or Beth-El, that went not out chasing after Yisrael: and they left the city wide open, and pursued after

---

[1] Valley of Tribulation.
[2] The name of the place means Valley of Tribulation or the time and place of tribulation as it relates to Yisrael's full future return during the end-time tribulation. It is written in Hosea 2:15, that a door of hope and deliverance will be opened in that valley, and Yisrael will sing and be delivered as in the day of the historical Egyptian redemption. Even this valley of Achan's burial, and Yisrael's curse, will be turned into a valley of restoration and singing in the day Yisrael is restored from her exile and tribulation.

Yisrael. 18 And **יהוה** said to Yahoshua, *Stretch out the spear that is in your hand toward Ai; for I will give it into your hand.* And Yahoshua stretched out the spear that he had in his hand toward the city. 19 And the ambush arose quickly out of their places, and they ran as soon as he had stretched out his hand: and they entered into the city, and took it, and immediately set the city on fire. 20 And when the men of Ai looked behind them, they saw, and, see, the smoke of the city ascended up to the shamayim, and they had no power to flee in any direction: and the people that fled to the wilderness turned back towards the pursuers. 21 And when Yahoshua and all Yisrael saw that the ambush had taken the city, and that the smoke of the city ascended, then they turned again, and killed the men of Ai. 22 And the others also ran out of the city; so they were in the midst of Yisrael, some on this side, and some on that side: and they smote them, so that they let none of them remain or escape. 23 And the melech of Ai they took alive, and brought him to Yahoshua. 24 And it came to pass, when Yisrael had made an end of killing all the inhabitants of Ai in the field, and in the wilderness where they chased them, and when they had all fallen by the edge of the sword, until they were consumed, that all the Yisraelites returned to Ai, and smote it with the edge of the sword. 25 And so it was, that all that fell that day, both of men and women, were twelve thousand, even all the men of Ai. 26 For Yahoshua drew not his hand back, with which he stretched out the spear, until he had utterly destroyed all the inhabitants of Ai. 27 Only the cattle and the spoil of that city Yisrael took for a prey to themselves, according to the word of **יהוה** which He commanded Yahoshua. 28 And Yahoshua burnt Ai, and made it a heap le-olam-va-ed, even a desolation to this day. 29 And the melech of Ai he hanged on a tree until evening: and as soon as the sun was down, Yahoshua commanded that they should take his body down from

the tree, and cast it at the entrance of the gate of the city, and raised on it a great pile of stones, that remains to this day. 30 Then Yahoshua built an altar to **יהוה** Elohim of Yisrael in Mount Eval, 31 As Moshe the eved of **יהוה** commanded the children of Yisrael, as it is written in the scroll of the Torah of Moshe, an altar of whole stones, over which no man has lifted up any cutting tool: and they offered on it burnt offerings to **יהוה**, and sacrificed shalom offerings. 32 And he wrote there on top of the stones a copy of the Torah of Moshe, which he wrote in the presence of the children of Yisrael. 33 And all Yisrael, and their zachanim, and officers, and their shophtim, stood on both sides of the Ark of the Covenant before the kohanim the Leviim, who bore the Ark of the Covenant of **יהוה**, as well the Ger, as he that was born among them;[1] half of them over against Mount Gerizim, and half of them over against Mount Eval; as Moshe the eved of **יהוה** had commanded before, that they should bless the people of Yisrael. 34 And afterwards he read all the words of the Torah, the brachot and kelalot, according to all that is written in the scroll of the Torah. 35 There was not a single word of all that Moshe commanded, which Yahoshua did not read before all the congregation of Yisrael,[2] with the women, and the little ones,[3] and the gerim that were accompanying them.

9 And it came to pass, when all the melechim which were on this side of the Yarden River, in the hills, and in the valleys, and in all the borders of the Great Sea toward Levanon, the Hittite, and the Amorite, the Kanaanite, the Perizzite, the

---

[1] We see again, that no one who dwells with Yisrael and worships with Yisrael as Yisrael, is to be considered a non-Yisraelite.
[2] The entire Torah was given to Moshe in written and not verbal format. In order for Joshua to have read all the words with no words missing, there could not by definition be any other words delivered verbally that were not written and subsequently read. Therefore the so-called oral Torah is mere opinion, though oftentimes is insightful.
[3] Notice that in Yisrael, little children are to hear the Torah along with the adults and not separate from them into children's classrooms.

Hivite, and the Yevusite, heard of it; 2 That they gathered themselves together, to fight with Yahoshua and with Yisrael, with one accord. 3 And when the inhabitants of Giveon heard what Yahoshua had done to Yericho and to Ai, 4 They did work slyly, and went and pretended to be ambassadors, and took old sacks upon their donkeys, and wine bottles, old, and torn, and bound up; 5 And old shoes or bound their feet with sandals, and old garments upon them, and all the lechem of their provision was dry and moldy. 6 And they went to Yahoshua to the camp at Gilgal, and said to him, and to the men of Yisrael, We come from a far land: now therefore make a covenant with us. 7 And the men of Yisrael said to the Hivites, It is possible that you dwell among us; and how shall we make a covenant with you? 8 And they said to Yahoshua, We are your avadim. And Yahoshua said to them, Who are you? And from where do you come? 9 And they said to him, From a very far land your avadim have come because of the Name of יהוה Your Elohim: for we have heard the fame of Him, and all that He did in Mitzrayim, 10 And all that He did to the two melechim of the Amorites, that were beyond the Yarden River, to Sihon melech of Cheshbon, and to Og melech of Bashan, which was at Ashtaroth. 11 Why our zachanim and all the inhabitants of our land spoke to us, saying, Take food with you for the journey, and go to meet them, and say to them, We are your avadim: therefore now make a covenant with us. 12 This our lechem we took fresh for our provision out of our bayits on the day we left to go to you; but now, see, it is dry, and it is moldy: 13 And these skins of wine, which we filled, were new; and, see, they are torn: and these garments and our shoes have become old because of the very long journey. 14 And the men took of their food, and asked not counsel at the mouth of יהוה. 15 And Yahoshua made shalom with them, and made a covenant with them, to let them live: and the leaders of the congregation

swore to them. 16 And it came to pass at the end of three days after they had made a covenant with them, that they heard that they were their neighbors, and that they dwelt among them. 17 And the children of Yisrael journeyed, and came to their cities on the third day. Now their cities were Giveon, and Khephirah, and Beeroth, and Kiryath-Yearim. 18 And the children of Yisrael smote them not, because the leaders of the congregation had sworn to them by יהוה Elohim of Yisrael. And the entire congregation murmured against the leaders. 19 But all the leaders said to the entire congregation, We have sworn to them by יהוה Elohim of Yisrael: now therefore we may not touch them. 20 This we will do to them; we will even let them live, lest wrath be upon us, because of the oath that we swore to them. 21 And the leaders said to them, Let them live; but let them be avadim as cutters of wood and drawers of mayim for all the congregation; as the leaders had promised them. 22 And Yahoshua called for them, and he spoke to them, saying, Why have you tricked us, saying, We are very far from you, when you dwell among us? 23 Now therefore you are cursed, and there shall none of you be freed from being avadim, and cutters of wood and drawers of mayim for the Bayit of My Elohim. 24 And they answered Yahoshua, and said, Because it was certainly told your avadim, how that יהוה Your Elohim commanded His eved Moshe to give you all the land, and to destroy all the inhabitants of the land from before you, therefore we were very afraid of our chayim because of you, and have done this thing. 25 And now, see, we are in your hand: as it seems tov and right to you to do to us, do. 26 And so he did to them, and delivered them out of the hand of the children of Yisrael, that they killed them not. 27 And Yahoshua made them that day cutters of wood and drawers of mayim for the congregation, and for the altar of יהוה, even to this day, in the place that he would choose.

10 Now it came to pass, when Adoni-Tzedek, melech of Yahrushalayim had heard how Yahoshua had taken Ai, and had utterly destroyed it; as he had done to Yericho and her melech, and as he had done to Ai and her melech; and how the inhabitants of Giveon had made shalom with Yisrael, and were among them; 2 That they feared greatly, because Giveon was a great city, as one of the royal cities, and because it was greater than Ai, and all the men there were mighty. 3 Why Adoni-Tzedek melech of Yahrushalayim sent to Hoham melech of Hevron, and to Piram melech of Yarmuth, and to Yaphia, melech of Lachish, and to Devir melech of Eglon, saying, 4 Come up to me, and help me, that we may smite Giveon: for they have made shalom with Yahoshua and with the children of Yisrael. 5 Therefore the five melechim of the Amorites, the melech of Yahrushalayim, the melech of Hevron, the melech of Yarmuth, the melech of Lachish, the melech of Eglon, gathered themselves together, and went up, with all their armies, and camped before Giveon, and made war against them. 6 And the men of Giveon sent to Yahoshua to the camp to Gilgal, saying, Hold not back your hand from your avadim; come up to us quickly, and accept us, and help us: for all the melechim of the Amorites that dwell in the mountains are gathered together against us. 7 So Yahoshua ascended from Gilgal, he, and all the people of war with him, and all the mighty men of valor. 8 And יהוה said to Yahoshua, *Fear them not: for I have delivered them into your hand; there shall not a man of them stand before you.* 9 Yahoshua therefore came to them suddenly, and went up from Gilgal all night. 10 And יהוה confused them before Yisrael, and killed them with a great slaughter at Giveon, and chased them along the derech that goes up to Beth-Horon, and smote them to Azekah, and to Makkedah. 11 And it came to pass, as they fled from before Yisrael, and were going down to Beth-Horon, that יהוה cast down great stones from the shamayim upon them to Azekah, and they died: there were more who died with hailstones than those whom the children of Yisrael killed with the sword. 12 Then spoke Yahoshua to יהוה in the day when יהוה delivered up the Amorites before the children of Yisrael, and he said in the sight of Yisrael, Sun, stand still over Giveon; and, Moon, in the Valley of Ayalon. 13 And the sun stood still, and the moon stopped, until the people had avenged themselves upon their enemies. Is not this written in the Scroll of Yasher?[1] So the sun stood still in the midst of the shamayim, and did not set for about a whole day. 14 And there was no day like that before it or after it, that יהוה listened to the voice of a man: for יהוה fought for Yisrael. 15 And Yahoshua returned, and all Yisrael with him, to the camp to Gilgal. 16 But these five melechim fled, and hid themselves in a cave at Makkedah. 17 And it was told Yahoshua, saying, The five melechim have been found hiding in a cave at Makkedah. 18 And Yahoshua said, Roll great stones upon the opening of the cave, and set men by it to guard them: 19 And don't stay, but pursue after your enemies, and smite in their rear guard; Do not allow them to enter into their cities: for יהוה Your Elohim has delivered them into your hand. 20 And it came to pass, when Yahoshua and the children of Yisrael had made an end of killing them with a very great slaughter, until they were consumed, that the rest which remained of them entered into fenced cities. 21 And all the people returned to the camp to Yahoshua at Makkedah in shalom: none murmured against any of the children of Yisrael. 22 Then said Yahoshua, Open the mouth of the cave, and bring out those five melechim to me. 23 And they did so, and brought forth those five melechim to him, the melech of Yahrushalayim, the melech of Hevron, the melech of Yarmuth, the melech of Lachish, and the melech of Eglon. 24 And it came to pass, when they brought out those melechim

---

[1] The Scroll of **Yasher** has been preserved.

to Yahoshua, that Yahoshua called for all the men of Yisrael, and said to the captains of the men of war who went with him, Come near, put your feet upon the necks of these melechim. And they came near, and put their feet upon their necks.[1] 25 And Yahoshua said to them, Fear not, nor be dismayed, be strong and courageous: for this is what יהוה will do to all your enemies against whom you fight. 26 And afterward Yahoshua smote them, and killed them, and hanged them on five trees: and they were hanging upon the trees until the evening. 27 And it came to pass at the time of the going down of the sun, that Yahoshua commanded, and they took them down off the trees, and cast them into the cave where they had been hidden, and laid great stones in the cave's mouth, which remain until this very day. 28 And that day Yahoshua took Makkedah, and smote it with the edge of the sword, and the melech he utterly destroyed, and all the beings that were in it; he let none remain: and he did to the melech of Makkedah as he had done to the melech of Yericho. 29 Then Yahoshua passed from Makkedah, and all Yisrael with him, to Livnah, and fought against Livnah: 30 And יהוה delivered it also, and the melech of it, into the hand of Yisrael; and he smote it with the edge of the sword, and all the beings that were in it; he let none remain in it; but did to that melech as he had done to the melech of Yericho. 31 And Yahoshua passed from Livnah, and all Yisrael with him, to Lachish, and camped against it, and fought against it: 32 And יהוה delivered Lachish into the hand of Yisrael, taking it on the second day, and smote it with the edge of the sword, and all the beings that were in it, according to all that he had done to Livnah. 33 Then Horam melech of Gezer came up to help Lachish; and Yahoshua smote him and his people, until he had left him none remaining. 34 And from Lachish Yahoshua passed to Eglon, and all Yisrael

with him; and they camped against it, and fought against it: 35 And they took it on that day, and smote it with the edge of the sword, and all the beings that were in it he utterly destroyed that day, according to all that he had done to Lachish. 36 And Yahoshua went up from Eglon, and all Yisrael with him, to Hevron; and they fought against it: 37 And they took it, and smote it with the edge of the sword, and the melech of it, and all the cities of it, and all the beings that were in it; he left none remaining, according to all that he had done to Eglon; but destroyed it utterly, and all the beings that were in it. 38 And Yahoshua returned, and all Yisrael with him, to Devir; and fought against it: 39 And he took it, and the melech of it, and all the cities of it; and they smote them with the edge of the sword, and utterly destroyed all the beings that were in it; he left none remaining: as he had done to Hevron, so he did to Devir, and to the melech of it; as he had done also to Livnah, and to her melech. 40 So Yahoshua smote all the land of the hills, and of the south, and of the low country, and of the springs, and all their melechim: he left none remaining, but utterly destroyed all that breathed, as יהוה Elohim of Yisrael commanded. 41 And Yahoshua smote them from Kadesh-Barnea even to Gaza, and all the land of Goshen, even to Giveon. 42 And all these melechim and their land did Yahoshua take at one time, because יהוה Elohim of Yisrael fought for Yisrael. 43 And Yahoshua returned, and all Yisrael with him, to the camp to Gilgal.

11 And it came to pass, when Yavin melech of Chatzor had heard those things, that he sent to Yovav melech of Madon, and to the melech of Shimron, and to the melech of Achshaph, 2 And to the melechim that were on the north of the mountains, and of the plains south of Kinneroth, and in the valley, and in the borders of Dor on the west, 3 And to the

---

[1] This is our eternal position and calling in all the circumstances in our lives, as overcomers through YHWH.

Kanaanite on the east and on the west, and to the Amorite, and the Hittite, and the Perizzite, and the Yevusite in the mountains, and to the Hivite under Hermon in the land of Mitzpeh. 4 And they went out, they and all their armies with them, much people, even as the sand that is upon the seashore in multitude, with horses and mirkavot very many. 5 And when all these melechim met together, they came and pitched together at the mayim of Merom, to fight against Yisrael. 6 And יהוה said to Yahoshua, *Be not afraid because of them: for tomorrow about this time will I deliver them up all slain before Yisrael: you shall destroy their horses, and burn their mirkavot with fire.* 7 So Yahoshua came, and all the people of war with him, against them by the mayim of Merom suddenly; and they fell upon them. 8 And יהוה delivered them into the hand of Yisrael, who smote them, and chased them to great Tzidon, and to Misrephoth-Mayim, and to the Valley of Mitzpeh eastward; and they smote them, until they left them none remaining. 9 And Yahoshua did to them as יהוה told him: he destroyed their horses, and burnt their mirkavot with fire. 10 And Yahoshua at that time turned back, and took Chatzor, and smote the melech of it with the sword: for Chatzor previously was the head of all those malchutim. 11 And they smote all the beings that were in it with the edge of the sword, utterly destroying them: there was not any left to breath: and he burnt Chatzor with fire. 12 And all the cities of those melechim, and all the melechim of them, did Yahoshua take, and smote them with the edge of the sword, and he utterly destroyed them, as Moshe the eved of יהוה commanded. 13 But as for the cities that stood still in their strength, Yisrael burned none of them, except Chatzor only; that did Yahoshua burn. 14 And all the spoil of these cities, and the cattle, the children of Yisrael took for a prey to themselves; but every man they smote with the edge of the sword, until they had destroyed them, neither were

any left. 15 As יהוה commanded Moshe His eved, so did Moshe command Yahoshua, and so did Yahoshua; he left nothing undone of all that יהוה commanded Moshe. 16 So Yahoshua took all that land, the hills, and all the southland, and all the land of Goshen, and the valley, and the plain, and the mountain of Yisrael, and the valley of the same; 17 Even from the Mount Halak, that goes up to Seir, even to Baal-Gad in the Valley of Levanon under Mount Hermon: and all their melechim he took, and smote them, and killed them. 18 Yahoshua made war a long time with all those melechim. 19 There was not a city that made shalom with the children of Yisrael, except the Hivites, the inhabitants of Giveon: all the others they took in battle. 20 For it was from יהוה to harden their levim, that they should come against Yisrael in battle, that He might destroy them utterly, and that they might have no favor, but that He might destroy them, as יהוה commanded Moshe. 21 And at that time came Yahoshua, and cut off the giants from the mountains, from Hevron, from Devir, from Anav, and from all the mountains of Yahudah, and from all the mountains of Yisrael: Yahoshua destroyed them utterly with their cities. 22 There was none of the giants left in the land of the children of Yisrael: only in Gaza, in Gath, and in Ashdod, some remained. 23 So Yahoshua took the whole land, according to all that יהוה said to Moshe; and Yahoshua gave it for an inheritance to Yisrael according to their divisions by their tribes. And the land rested from war.

12 Now these are the melechim of the land, that the children of Yisrael smote, and possessed their land on the other side the Yarden River toward the rising of the sun, from the river Arnon to Mount Hermon, and all the plain on the east: 2 Sihon melech of the Amorites, who dwelt in Cheshbon, and ruled from Aroer, which is upon the bank of the river Arnon, and

from the middle of the river, and from half of Gilead, even to the river Yabbok, which is the border of the children of Ammon; 3 And from the plain to the sea of Kinneroth on the east, and to the sea of the plain, even the Salt Sea on the east, the way to Beth-Yeshimoth; and from the south, under Ashdoth-Pisgah: 4 And the border of Og, melech of Bashan, which was of the remnant of the giants, that dwelt at Ashtaroth and at Edrei, 5 And reigned in Mount Hermon, and in Salcah, and in all Bashan, to the border of the Geshurites and the Maachathites, and half of Gilead, the border of Sihon, melech of Cheshbon. 6 Them did Moshe the eved of יהוה and the children of Yisrael smite: and Moshe the eved of יהוה gave it for a possession to the Reuvenites, and the Gadites, and the half tribe of Menashsheh. 7 And these are the melechim of the land which Yahoshua and the children of Yisrael smote on this side of the Yarden River on the west, from Baal-Gad in the Valley of Levanon even to Mount Halak, that goes up to Seir; which Yahoshua gave to the tribes of Yisrael for a possession according to their divisions; 8 In the mountains, and in the valleys, and in the plains, and in the springs, and in the wilderness, and in the southland; the Hittites, the Amorites, and the Kanaanites, the Perizzites, the Hivites, and the Yevusites: 9 The melech of Yericho, one; the melech of Ai, which is beside Beth-El, one; 10 The melech of Yahrushalayim, one; the melech of Hevron, one; 11 The melech of Yarmuth, one; the melech of Lachish, one; 12 The melech of Eglon, one; the melech of Gezer, one; 13 The melech of Devir, one; the melech of Geder, one; 14 The melech of Hormah, one; the melech of Arad, one; 15 The melech of Livnah, one; the melech of Adullam, one; 16 The melech of Makkedah, one; the melech of Beth-El, one; 17 The melech of Tappuah, one; the melech of Hepher, one; 18 The melech of Aphek, one; the melech of Lasharon, one; 19 The melech of Madon, one; the melech

of Chatzor, one; 20 The melech of Shimron-Meron, one; the melech of Achshaph, one; 21 The melech of Taanach, one; the melech of Megiddo, one; 22 The melech of Kedesh, one; the melech of Yokneam of Carmel, one; 23 The melech of Dor in the border of Dor, one; the melech of the nations of Gilgal, one; 24 The melech of Tirzah, one: all the melechim thirty-one.

13 Now Yahoshua was old and advanced in years; and יהוה said to him, *You are old and advanced in years, and there remains yet very much land to be possessed. 2 This is the land that yet remains: all the borders of the Philistines, and all Geshuri, 3 From Sihor, which is before Mitzrayim, even to the borders of Ekron northward, which is counted to the Kanaanite: five masters of the Philistines; the Gazathites, and the Ashdothites, the Eshkalonites, the Gittites, and the Ekronites; also the Avites: 4 From the south, all the land of the Kanaanites, and Mearah that is beside the Tsidonians, to Aphek, to the borders of the Amorites: 5 And the land of the Giblites, and all Levanon, toward the sunrising, from Baal-Gad under Mount Hermon to the enterance into Hamath. 6 All the inhabitants of the hill land from Levanon to Misrephoth-Mayim, and all the Tsidonians, them will I drive out from before the children of Yisrael: Now divide it by lot to the Yisraelites for an inheritance, as I have commanded you. 7 Now therefore divide this land for an inheritance to the nine tribes, and the half a tribe of Menashsheh, 8 With whom the Reuvenites and the Gadites have received their inheritance, which Moshe gave them, beyond the Yarden River eastward, even as Moshe the eved of יהוה gave them;* 9 From Aroer, that is upon the bank of the river Arnon, and the city that is in the midst of the river, and all the plain of Medeva to Divon, 10 And all the cities of Sihon, melech of the Amorites, who reigned in Cheshbon, to the border of the children of

Ammon; 11 And Gilead, and the border of the Geshurites and Maachathites, and all of Mount Hermon, and all Bashan to Salcah; 12 All the malchut of Og in Bashan, who reigned in Ashtaroth and in Edrei, who remained of the remnant of the giants: for these did Moshe smite, and cast them out. 13 Nevertheless the children of Yisrael expelled not the Geshurites, nor the Maachathites: but the Geshurites and the Maachathites dwell among the Yisraelites until this day. 14 Only to the tribe of Levi he gave no inheritance; the sacrifices of יהוה Elohim of Yisrael made by fire are their inheritance, as he said to them. 15 And Moshe gave to the tribe of the children of Reuven inheritance according to their mishpachot. 16 And their border was from Aroer, which is on the bank of the river Arnon, and the city that is in the midst of the river, and all the plain by Medeva; 17 Cheshbon, and all her cities that are in the plain; Divon, and Bamoth-Baal, and Beth-Baal-Meon, 18 And Yahazah, and Kedemoth, and Mephaath, 19 And Kiryathaim, and Sibmah, and Zareth-Shahar in the Mount of the valley, 20 And Beth-Peor, and Ashdoth-Pisgah, and Beth-Yeshimoth, 21 And all the cities of the plain, and all the malchut of Sihon, melech of the Amorites, who reigned in Cheshbon, whom Moshe smote with the leaders of Midian, Evi, and Rekem, and Zur, and Hur, and Reva, which were princes of Sihon, dwelling in the land. 22 Bilam also the son of Beor, the soothsayer, did the children of Yisrael slay with the sword among those that were slain by them. 23 And the border of the children of Reuven was the Yarden River, and the border of it. This was the inheritance of the children of Reuven after their mishpachot, the cities and the villages of it. 24 And Moshe gave inheritance to the tribe of Gad, even to the children of Gad according to their mishpachot. 25 And their border was Yazer, and all the cities of Gilead, and half the land of the children of Ammon, to Aroer that is before Ravah;

26 And from Cheshbon to Ramath-Mitzpeh, and Betonim; and from Mahanaim to the border of Devir; 27 And in the valley, Beth-Aram, and Beth-Nimrah, and Succoth, and Zaphon, the rest of the malchut of Sihon, melech of Cheshbon, the Yarden River and its border, even to the edge of the sea of Kinnereth on the other side of the Yarden River eastward. 28 This is the inheritance of the children of Gad after their mishpachot, the cities, and their villages. 29 And Moshe gave inheritance to the half tribe of Menashsheh: and this was the possession of the half tribe of the children of Menashsheh by their mishpachot. 30 And their border was from Mahanayim, all Bashan, all the malchut of Og melech of Bashan, and all the towns of Yair, which are in Bashan, sixty cities: 31 And half Gilead, and Ashtaroth, and Edrei, cities of the malchut of Og in Bashan, were pertaining to the children of Machir the son of Menashsheh, even to one half of the children of Machir by their mishpachot. 32 These are the countries that Moshe did distribute for inheritance in the plains of Moav, on the other side of the Yarden River, by Yericho, eastward. 33 But to the tribe of Levi Moshe gave not any inheritance: יהוה Elohim of Yisrael was their inheritance, as He said to them.

14 And these are the countries that the children of Yisrael inherited in the land of Kanaan, which El-Azar the kohen, and Yahoshua the son of Nun, and the heads of the ahvot of the tribes of the children of Yisrael, distributed for an inheritance to them. 2 By lot was their inheritance, as יהוה commanded by the hand of Moshe, for the nine tribes, and for the half tribe. 3 For Moshe had given the inheritance of two tribes and a half tribe on the other side the Yarden River: but to the Leviim he gave no inheritance among them. 4 For the children of Yoseph were two tribes, Menashsheh and Ephraim: therefore they gave no part to the Leviim in the land, except cities to dwell in, with their suburbs

for their cattle and for their substance. 5 As יהוה commanded Moshe, so the children of Yisrael did, and they divided the land. 6 Then the children of Yahudah came to Yahoshua in Gilgal: and Kalev the son of Yephunneh the Kenezite said to him, You know the thing that יהוה said to Moshe the man of Elohim concerning me and you in Kadesh-Barnea. 7 I was forty years old when Moshe the eved of יהוה sent me from Kadesh-Barnea to spy out the land; and I brought him word again as it was in my lev. 8 Nevertheless my brothers that went up with me made the lev of the people melt: but I fully followed יהוה My Elohim. 9 And Moshe swore on that day, saying, Surely the land upon which your feet have trodden shall be your inheritance, and your children's le-olam-va-ed, because you have fully followed יהוה My Elohim. 10 And now, see, יהוה has kept me alive, as He said, these forty-five years, ever since יהוה spoke this word to Moshe, while the children of Yisrael wandered in the wilderness: and now, I am this day eighty-five years old. 11 Yet I am as strong this day as I was in the day that Moshe sent me: as my strength was then, even so is my strength now, for war, both to go out, and to come in. 12 Now therefore give me this mountain, of which יהוה spoke in that day; for you heard in that day how the giants were there, and that the cities were great and fenced: if so be יהוה will be with me, then I shall be able to drive them out, as יהוה said. 13 And Yahoshua blessed him, and gave to Kalev the son of Yephunneh, Hevron for an inheritance. [1] 14 Hevron therefore became the inheritance of Kalev the son of Yephunneh the Kenezite to this day, because that he fully followed יהוה Elohim of Yisrael. 15 And the name of Hevron before was Kiryath-Arba; because

Arba was the greatest man among the giants. And the land had rest from war.

15 This then was the lot of the tribe of the children of Yahudah by their mishpachot; even to the border of Edom the wilderness of Tzin southward was the uttermost part of the south border. 2 And their south border was from the shore of the Salt Sea, from the bay that looks southward: 3 And it went out to the south side to Maaleh-Acravvim, and passed along to Tzin, and ascended up on the south side to Kadesh-Barnea, and passed along to Chetzron, and went up to Adar, and went around to Karkaa: 4 And it passed toward Azmon, and went out to the river of Mitzrayim; and the goings out of that border was at the sea: this shall be your south border. 5 And the east border was the Salt Sea, even to the end of the Yarden River. And the border in the north side began from the bay of the sea at the uttermost part of the Yarden River: 6 And the border went up to Beth-Hogla, and passed along by the north of Beth-Aravah; and the border went up to the stone of Bohan the son of Reuven: 7 And the border went up toward Devir from the Valley of Achor, and so northward, looking toward Gilgal, that is before the going up to Adummim, which is on the south side of the river: and the border passed toward the mayim of Enshemesh, and ended at Enrogel: 8 And the border went up by the Valley of the son of Hinnom to the south side of the Yevusite; the same is Yahrushalayim: and the border went up to the top of the mountain that lies before the Valley of Hinnom westward, which is at the end of the valley of the giants northward: 9 And the border was drawn from the top of the hill to the fountain of the mayim of Nephtoah, and went out to the cities of Mount Ephron; and the border went around to Ba-Alah, which is Kiryath-Yearim: 10 And the border turned around from Ba-Alah westward to Mount Seir, and passed along to the side of Mount Yearim, which is

---

[1] It is interesting that a united Yisrael's future capital city, would be the inheritance of a non-biological Yisraelite, who was actually considered more of a faithful Yisraelite, than many others who were biological, but had evil in their hearts and expressed a lack of trust with their lips.

Kesalon, on the north side, and went down to Beth-Shemesh, and passed on to Timnah: 11 And the border went out to the side of Ekron northward: and the border went around to Shicron, and passed along to Mount Ba-Alah, and went out to Yavneel; and the border ended at the sea. 12 And the west border was to the Great Sea, and the border of it. This is the border of the children of Yahudah all round according to their mishpachot. 13 And to Kalev the son of Yephunneh he gave a part among the children of Yahudah, according to the commandment of יהוה to Yahoshua, even the city of Arba the abba of Anak, that city is Hevron. 14 And Kalev drove out the three sons of Anak, Sheshai, and Ahiman, and Talmai, the children of Anak. 15 And he went up from there to the inhabitants of Devir: and the name of Devir before was Kiryath-Sepher. 16 And Kalev said, He that smites Kiryath-Sepher, and takes it, to him will I give Achsah my daughter as a wife. 17 And Othni-El the son of Kenaz, the brother of Kalev, took it: and he gave him Achsah his daughter as a wife. 18 And it came to pass, as she came to him, that she moved him to ask from her abba a field: and she got off her donkey; and Kalev said to her, What is the matter my daughter? 19 She answered, Give me a bracha; for you have given me a southland; give me also springs of mayim. And he gave her the upper springs, and the lower springs. 20 This is the inheritance of the tribe of the children of Yahudah according to their mishpachot. 21 And the furthest cities of the tribe of the children of Yahudah toward the border of Edom southward were Kavzeel, and Eder, and Yagur, 22 And Kinah, and Dimonah, and Adadah, 23 And Kedesh, and Chatzor, and Ithnan, 24 Ziph, and Telem, and Bealoth, 25 And Chatzor, Hadattah, and Kerioth, and Chetzron, which is Chatzor, 26 Amam, and Shema, and Moladah, 27 And Hazargaddah, and Heshmon, and Beth-Palet, 28 And Hazarshual, and Beer-Sheva, and Bizyothyah, 29 Baalah, and

Yim, and Azem, 30 And Eltolad, and Chesil, and Hormah, 31 And Ziklag, and Madmannah, and Sansannah, 32 And Levaoth, and Shilhim, and Ain, and Rimmon: all the cities were twenty-nine, with their villages: 33 And in the valley, Eshtaol, and Zoreah, and Ashnah, 34 And Zanoah, and Engannim, Tappuah, and Enam, 35 Yarmuth, and Adullam, Socoh, and Azekah, 36 And Sharaim, and Adithaim, and Gederah, and Gederothaim; fourteen cities with their villages: 37 Zenan, and Hadashah, and Migdalgad, 38 And Dilean, and Mitzpeh, and Yoktheel, 39 Lachish, and Bozkath, and Eglon, 40 And Cavon, and Lahmam, and Kithlish, 41 And Gederoth, Beth-Dagon, and Naamah, and Makkedah; sixteen cities with their villages: 42 Livnah, and Ether, and Ashan, 43 And Yiphtah, and Ashnah, and Neziv, 44 And Keilah, and Achziv, and Mareshah; nine cities with their villages: 45 Ekron, with her towns and her villages: 46 From Ekron even to the sea, all that was near Ashdod, with their villages: 47 Ashdod with her towns and her villages, Gaza with her towns and her villages, to the river of Mitzrayim, and the Great Sea, and the border of it: 48 And in the mountains, Shamir, and Yattir, and Socoh, 49 And Dannah, and Kiryath-Sannah, which is Devir, 50 And Anav, and Eshtemoh, and Anim, 51 And Goshen, and Holon, and Giloh; eleven cities with their villages: 52 Arav, and Dumah, and Eshean, 53 And Yanum, and Beth-Tappuah, and Aphekah, 54 And Humtah, and Kiryath-arva, which is Hevron, and Tzior; nine cities with their villages: 55 Maon, Carmel, and Ziph, and Yuttah, 56 And Yezreel, and Yokdeam, and Zanoah, 57 Cain, Gibeah, and Timnah; ten cities with their villages: 58 Halhul, Bethzur, and Gedor, 59 And Maarath, and Beth-Anoth, and Eltekon; six cities with their villages: 60 Kiryath-Baal, which is Kiryath-Yearim, and Ravh; two cities with their villages: 61 In the wilderness, Beth-Arabah, Middin, and Secacah, 62 And

Nivshan, and the City of Salt, and Engedi; six cities with their villages. 63 As for the Yevusites, the inhabitants of Yahrushalayim, the children of Yahudah could not drive them out: but the Yevusites dwell with the children of Yahudah at Yahrushalayim to this day.

16 And the lot of the children of Yoseph fell from the Yarden River by Yericho, to the mayim of Yericho on the east, to the wilderness that goes up from Yericho throughout Mount Beth-El, 2 And goes out from Beth-El to Luz, and passes along to the borders of Archi to Ataroth, 3 And goes down westward to the border of Yaphleti, to the border of Beth-Horon the lower, and to Gezer: and the goings out of it is at the sea. 4 So the children of Yoseph, Menashsheh and Ephraim, took their inheritance. 5 And the border of the children of Ephraim according to their mishpachot was this: even the border of their inheritance on the east side was Atarothaddar, to Beth-Horon the upper; 6 And the border went out toward the sea to Michmethah on the north side; and the border went about eastward to Taanath-Shiloh, and passed by it on the east to Yanohah; 7 And it went down from Yanohah to Ataroth, and to Naarath, and came to Yericho, and went out at the Yarden River. 8 The border went out from Tappuah westward to the river Kanah; and the goings out of it were at the sea. This is the inheritance of the tribe of the children of Ephraim by their mishpachot. 9 And the separate cities for the children of Ephraim were among the inheritance of the children of Menashsheh, all the cities with their villages. 10 And they did not drive out the Kanaanites that dwelt in Gezer: but the Kanaanites dwell among the Ephraimites to this day, and serve under slave labor.[1]

---

[1] This is a prophetic declaration when taken on the **remez** level, that one of the plagues of the future northern kingdom of Ephraim, was the full infiltration of the ways and paganism of the Canaanites, who dwell within Ephraim (later to become the ten tribes), until this present hour. Of course, the ways of the Canaanites were adopted in large part by such empires as Assyria, Greece, Babylon and Rome.

17 There was also a lot for the tribe of Menashsheh; for he was the firstborn of Yoseph; for Machir the firstborn of Menashsheh, the abba of Gilead: because he was a man of war, therefore he had Gilead and Bashan. 2 And for the rest of the children of Menashsheh by their mishpachot; for the children of Aviezer, and for the children of Helek, and for the children of Asriel, and for the children of Shechem, and for the children of Hepher, and for the children of Shemida: these were the male children of Menashsheh the son of Yoseph by their mishpachot. 3 But Zelophehad, the son of Hepher, the son of Gilead, the son of Machir, the son of Menashsheh, had no sons, but daughters: and these are the names of his daughters, Mahlah, and Noah, Hoglah, Milcah, and Tirzah. 4 And they came near before El-Azar the kohen, and before Yahoshua the son of Nun, and before the leaders, saying, יהוה commanded Moshe to give us an inheritance among our brothers. Therefore according to the commandment of יהוה he gave them an inheritance among the brothers of their abba. 5 And there fell ten portions to Menashsheh, beside the land of Gilead and Bashan, which were on the other side the Yarden River; 6 Because the daughters of Menashsheh had an inheritance among his sons: and the rest of Menashsheh's sons had the land of Gilead. 7 And the border of Menashsheh was from Asher to Michmethah that lies before Shechem; and the border went along on the right hand to the inhabitants of Entappuah. 8 Menashsheh had the land of Tappuah: but Tappuah on the border of Menashsheh belonged to the children of Ephraim; 9 And the border descended to the river Kanah, southward of the river: these cities of Ephraim are among the cities of Menashsheh: the border of Menashsheh also was on the north side of the river, and the outgoings of it were at the sea: 10 Southward it was Ephraim's, and northward it was Menashsheh's, and the sea

is his border; and they met together in Asher in the north, and in Yissaker in the east. 11 And Menashsheh had in Yissaker and in Asher Beth-Shean and her towns, and Ivleam and her towns, and the inhabitants of Dor and her towns, and the inhabitants of Endor and her towns, and the inhabitants of Ta-Anach and her towns, and the inhabitants of Megiddo and her towns, three districts. 12 Yet the children of Menashsheh could not drive out the inhabitants of those cities; but the Kanaanites would dwell in that land. 13 Yet it came to pass, when the children of Yisrael were growing strong, that they put the Kanaanites to slave labor; but did not utterly drive them out.[1] 14 And the children of Yoseph spoke to Yahoshua, saying, Why have you given us just one lot and one portion to inherit,[2] seeing we are a great people, whom **יהוה** has blessed until now?[3] 15 And Yahoshua answered them, If you are a great people, then get up to the forests, and clear out a place for yourself there in the land of the Perizzites and of the Rephaites, since the hills of Ephraim are too narrow for you. 16 And the children of Yoseph said, The hills of Ephraim are not enough for us: and besides, all the Kanaanites that dwell in the land of the valley have mirkavot of iron, both those who are of Beth-Shean and its towns, and those who are in the Valley of Yezreel. 17 And Yahoshua spoke to the Beit Yoseph, even to Ephraim and to Menashsheh, saying, You are a great people,[4] and have great power: you shall not have only one lot:[5] 18 But the mountain shall be yours; for though it is a forest, you shall cut it down: and its farthest limits shall be yours: for you

shall drive out the Kanaanites, though they have iron mirkavot, and though they are strong.

18 And the whole congregation of the children of Yisrael assembled together at Shiloh, and set up the tabernacle of the congregation there. And the land was subdued before them. 2 And there remained among the children of Yisrael seven tribes, which had not yet received their inheritance. 3 And Yahoshua said to the children of Yisrael, How long are you slack to go to possess the land, which **יהוה** Elohim of your ahvot has given you? 4 Appoint three men from each tribe: and I will send them, and they shall rise, and go through the land, and describe it according to their inheritance; and they shall come back to me. 5 And they shall divide it into seven parts: Yahudah shall abide in their border on the south, and Beit Yoseph shall abide in their borders on the north. 6 You shall therefore describe the land in seven parts, and bring the description here to me, that I may cast lots for you here before **יהוה** our Elohim. 7 But the Leviim have no part among you; for the priesthood of **יהוה** is their inheritance: and Gad, and Reuven, and half the tribe of Menashsheh, have received their inheritance beyond the Yarden River on the east, which Moshe the eved of **יהוה** gave them. 8 And the men arose, and went away: and Yahoshua charged them that went to describe the land, saying, Go and walk through the land, and describe it, and come again to me, that I may cast lots here for you before **יהוה** in Shiloh. 9 And the men went and passed through the land, and described it by cities into seven parts in a scroll, and came back to Yahoshua to the camp at Shiloh. 10 And Yahoshua cast lots for them in Shiloh before **יהוה** : and Yahoshua divided the land to the children of Yisrael according to their divisions. 11 And the lot of the tribe of the children of Benyamin came up according to their mishpachot: and the border of their lot came forth between

---

[1] The same mixing with paganism that befell Ephraim. Both main northern tribes were always willing to live with and compromise with paganism.
[2] **Yoseph**; Strong's Hebrew #3130. **Yoseph** means YHWH has added or enlarged.
[3] Standing on the covenant of physical multiplicity, Yoseph planned for the future in order to accommodate the children of that promise. This request had both an immediate as well as end-time application.
[4] Hebrew: **Am rav atah**, or "a great nation," thus indicating a nation within a nation.
[5] Then like today, Yoseph or the ten tribes, have to ask and fight for their rights and the right to return home to their land, even if it means living where others do not want to settle.

the children of Yahudah and the children of Yoseph.[1] 12 And their border on the north side was from the Yarden River; and the border went up to the side of Yericho on the north side, and went up through the mountains westward; and the endings of it were at the wilderness of Beth-Aven. 13 And the border went over from there toward Luz, to the side of Luz, which is Beth-El, southward; and the border descended to Atarothadar, near the hill that lies on the south side of the nether Beth-Horon. 14 And the border was drawn there, and went around the corner of the sea southward, from the hill that lies before Beth-Horon southward; and it ended at Kiryath-Baal, which is Kiryath-Yearim, a city of the children of Yahudah: this was the west side. 15 And the south side was from the end of Kiryath-Yearim, and the border went out on the west, and went out to the well of mayim of Nephtoah: 16 And the border came down to the end of the mountain that lies before the Valley of the son of Hinnom, which is in the valley of the giants on the north, and descended to the Valley of Hinnom, to the side of Yevusi on the south, and descended to Enrogel, 17 And was drawn from the north, and went forth to En-Shemesh, and went forth toward Geliloth, which is opposite the going up of Adummim, and went down to the stone of Bohan the son of Reuven, 18 And passed along toward the side opposite Aravah northward, and went down to Aravah: 19 And the border passed along to the side of Beth-Hoglah northward: and the end of the border was at the north bay of the Salt Sea at the south end of the Yarden River: this was the south border. 20 And the Yarden River was the border of it on the east side. This was the inheritance of the children of Benyamin, by the boundaries of it all around, according to their mishpachot. 21 Now the cities of the tribe of the children of Benyamin according to their mishpachot

were Yericho, and Beth-Hoglah, and the Valley of Keziz, 22 And Beth-Aravah, and Zemaraim, and Beth-El, 23 And Avim, and Parah, and Ophrah, 24 And Khephar-Haammonai, and Ophni, and Gava; twelve cities with their villages: 25 Giveon, and Ramah, and Beeroth, 26 And Mitzpeh, and Chephirah, and Motzah, 27 And Rekem, and Irpeel, and Taralah, 28 And Zelah, Eleph, and Yevusi, which is Yahrushalayim, Giveath, and Kiryath; fourteen cities with their villages. This is the inheritance of the children of Benyamin according to their mishpachot.

19 And the second lot came forth to Shimeon, for the tribe of the children of Shimeon according to their mishpachot: and their inheritance was within the inheritance of the children of Yahudah. 2 And they had in their inheritance Beer-Sheva, or Sheva, and Moladah, 3 And Hazarshual, and Balah, and Azem, 4 And Eltolad, and Bethul, and Hormah, 5 And Ziklag, and Beth-Marcavoth, and Chatzarsusah, 6 And Beth-LeVaoth, and Sharuhen; thirteen cities and their villages: 7 Ain, Remmon, and Ether, and Ashan; four cities and their villages: 8 And all the villages that were around these cities to Baalathveer, Ramath of the south. This is the inheritance of the tribe of the children of Shimeon according to their mishpachot. 9 Out of the portion of the children of Yahudah was the inheritance of the children of Shimeon: for the part of the children of Yahudah was too much for them:[2] [3] therefore the children of Shimeon had their inheritance within their inheritance. 10 And the third lot came up for the children of Zevulon according to their mishpachot: and the border of their inheritance was to Sarid: 11 And their border went up toward the sea, and Maralah,

---

[1] This geographic location was symbolic of the tribe of Benjamin being torn in their later historical allegiance between the House of Joseph and the House of Judah.

[2] Yahudah has always been only a small part of greater Yisrael. Nothing has changed in any way. The Yahudites today, continue to represent only a small part of the exiled nation.
[3] The House of Judah still has many Simeonites within it ranks. These two tribes always have been intermingled.

and reached to Davasheth, and reached to the river that is before Yokneam; 12 And turned from Sarid eastward toward the sunrising to the border of Chisloth-Tavor, and then goes out to Daverath, and goes up to Yaphia, 13 And from there passes on along on the east to Gath-Hepher, to Et-Katsin, and goes out to Rimmon to Neah; 14 And the border went around it on the north side to Hannathon: and ended in the Valley of Yiphthah-El: 15 And Kattath, and Nahallal, and Shimron, and Idalah, and Beth-Lehem: twelve cities with their villages. 16 This is the inheritance of the children of Zevulon according to their mishpachot, these cities with their villages. 17 The fourth lot came out to Yissaker, for the children of Yissaker according to their mishpachot. 18 And their border was toward Yezreel, and Chesulloth, and Shunem, 19 And Hapharaim, and Shion, and Anaharath, 20 And Ravith, and Kishion, and Avez, 21 And Remeth, and En-Gannim, and En-Haddah, and Beth-Pazzez; 22 And the border reachs to Tavor, and Shahazimah, and Beth-Shemesh; and the outgoings of their border was at the Yarden River: sixteen cities with their villages. 23 This is the inheritance of the tribe of the children of Yissaker according to their mishpachot, the cities and their villages. 24 And the fifth lot came out for the tribe of the children of Asher according to their mishpachot. 25 And their border was Helkath, and Hali, and Beten, and Achshaph, 26 And Alammelech, and Amad, and Misheal; and reaches to Carmel westward, and to Shihor-Livnath; 27 And turns toward the sunrising to Beth-Dagon, and reachs to Zevulon, and to the valley of Yiphthah-El toward the north side of Beth-Emek, and Neiel, and goes out to Cavul on the left hand, 28 And Hevron, and Rehovb, and Hammon, and Kanah, even to great Tzidon; 29 And then the border turns to Ramah, and to the strong city Tsor; and the border turns to Hosah; and the outgoings of it are at the sea from the border to Achziv: 30 Ummah also, and

Aphek, and Rehov: twenty-two cities with their villages. 31 This is the inheritance of the tribe of the children of Asher according to their mishpachot, these cities with their villages. 32 The sixth lot came out to the children of Naphtali, even for the children of Naphtali according to their mishpachot. 33 And their border was from Heleph, from Allon to Zaanannim, and Adami, Nekev, and Yavne-El, to Lakum; and the outgoings of it were at the Yarden River: 34 And then the border turns westward to Aznothtavor, and goes out from there to Hukkok, and reaches to Zevulon on the south side, and reaches to Asher on the west side, and to Yahudah upon the Yarden River toward the sunrising. 35 And the fenced cities are Ziddim, Zer, and Hammath, Rakkath, and Chinnereth, 36 And Adamah, and Ramah, and Chatzor, 37 And Kedesh, and Edrei, and Enhazor, 38 And Yiron, and Migdalel, Horem, and Beth-Anath, and Beth-Shemesh; nineteen cities with their villages. 39 This is the inheritance of the tribe of the children of Naphtali according to their mishpachot, the cities and their villages. 40 And the seventh lot came out for the tribe of the children of Dan according to their mishpachot. 41 And the border of their inheritance was Zorah, and Eshtaol, and Yir-Shemesh, 42 And Shaalavin, and Ayalon, and Yethlah, 43 And Elon, and Thimnathah, and Ekron, 44 And Eltekeh, and Givethon, and Baalath, 45 And Yehud, and Beneberak, and Gath-Rimmon, 46 And Meyarkon, and Rakkon, with the border before Yapho. 47 And the border of the children of Dan was too little for them: therefore the children of Dan went up to fight against Leshem, and took it, and smote it with the edge of the sword, and possessed it, and dwelt in it, and called it Leshem-Dan, after the name of Dan their abba.[1] 48 This is the inheritance of the tribe of the children of Dan according to their mishpachot, these

---

[1] This custom would follow them in their westward migrations and throughout Europe, at the Danube River and other such places, as they continued to name towns and rivers after Dan their father.

cities with their villages. 49 When they had made an end of dividing the land for inheritance by their borders, the children of Yisrael gave an inheritance to Yahoshua the son of Nun among them: 50 According to the word of **יהוה** they gave him the city that he asked for, even Timnath-Serah in Mount Ephraim: and he built the city, and dwelt in it.[1] 51 These are the inheritances, which El-Azar the kohen, and Yahoshua the son of Nun, and the heads of the ahvot of the tribes of the children of Yisrael, divided for an inheritance by lot in Shiloh before **יהוה**, at the door of the tabernacle of the congregation. So they made an end of dividing the land.

20 And **יהוה** also spoke to Yahoshua, saying, 2 *Speak to the children of Yisrael, saying, Appoint for yourselves cities of refuge, which I spoke to you about through Moshe: 3 That the slayer that kills anyone accidently, or unintentionally may flee there: and these cities shall be your refuge from the revenger of dom. 4 And when he that does flee to one of those cities shall stand at the entrance of the gate of the city, and shall declare his cause in the ears of the zachanim of that city, they shall take him into the city, and give him a place, that he may dwell among them. 5 And if the revenger of dom pursues after him, then they shall not deliver the slayer up into his hand; because he smote his neighbor unwittingly, and did not hate him previously.* 6 And he shall dwell in that city, until he stands before the congregation for mishpat, and until the death of the Kohen HaGadol that shall be in those days: then shall the slayer return, and come to his own city, and to his own bayit, to the city from where he fled.[2] 7 And they appointed Kedesh in Galilee in Mount Naphtali, and Shechem in Mount Ephraim, and Kiryath-Arba, which is Hevron, in the mountain of Yahudah. 8 And on the other side of the

Yarden River by Yericho eastward, they assigned Bezer in the wilderness upon the plain out of the tribe of Reuven, and Ramoth in Gilead out of the tribe of Gad, and Golan in Bashan out of the tribe of Menashsheh. 9 These were the cities appointed for all the children of Yisrael, and for the Ger that sojourns among them that whoever kills any person unintentionally might flee there, and not die by the hand of the revenger of dom, until he stood before the congregation.

21 Then came near the heads of the ahvot of the Leviim to El-Azar the kohen, and to Yahoshua the son of Nun, and to the heads of the ahvot of the tribes of the children of Yisrael; 2 And they spoke to them at Shiloh in the land of Kanaan, saying, **יהוה** commanded through Moshe to give us cities to dwell in, with the suburbs of it for our cattle. 3 And the children of Yisrael gave to the Leviim out of their inheritance, at the commandment of **יהוה**, these cities and their suburbs. 4 And the lot came out for the mishpachot of the Kohathites: and the children of Aharon the kohen, who were of the Leviim, had by lot out of the tribe of Yahudah, and out of the tribe of Shimeon, and out of the tribe of Benyamin, thirteen cities. 5 And the rest of the children of Kohath had by lot out of the mishpachot of the tribe of Ephraim, and out of the tribe of Dan, and out of the half tribe of Menashsheh, ten cities. 6 And the children of Gershon had by lot out of the mishpachot of the tribe of Yissaker, and out of the tribe of Asher, and out of the tribe of Naphtali, and out of the half tribe of Menashsheh in Bashan, thirteen cities. 7 The children of Merari by their mishpachot had out of the tribe of Reuven, and out of the tribe of Gad, and out of the tribe of Zevulon, twelve cities. 8 And the children of Yisrael gave by lot to the Leviim these cities with their suburbs, as **יהוה** commanded through Moshe. 9 And they gave out of the tribe of the children of

---

[1] Note that Yahoshua was an Ephraimite (not a Jew) whose heart was for his people.
[2] Chesed for Yisrael.

Yahudah, and out of the tribe of the children of Shimeon, these cities that are here mentioned by name, 10 Which the children of Aharon, being of the mishpachot of the Kohathites, who were of the children of Levi, had: for theirs was the first lot. 11 And they gave them the city of Arba the abba of Anak, which city is Hevron, in the hill land of Yahudah, with the suburbs of it around it. 12 But the fields of the city, and the villages of it, they gave to Kalev the son of Yephunneh for his possession. 13 So they gave to the children of Aharon the kohen Hevron with its suburbs, to be a city of refuge for the slayer; and Livnah with its suburbs, 14 And Yattir with its suburbs, and Eshtemoa with its suburbs, 15 And Holon with its suburbs, and Devir with its suburbs, 16 And Ain with its suburbs, and Yuttah with its suburbs, and Beth-Shemesh with its suburbs; nine cities out of those two tribes. 17 And out of the tribe of Benyamin, Giveon with its suburbs, Geva with its suburbs, 18 Anathoth with its suburbs, and Almon with its suburbs; four cities. 19 All the cities of the children of Aharon, the kohanim, were thirteen cities with their suburbs. 20 And the mishpachot of the children of Kohath, the Leviim that remained of the children of Kohath, even they had the cities of their lot out of the tribe of Ephraim. 21 For they gave them Shechem with its suburbs in Mount Ephraim, to be a city of refuge for the slayer; and Gezer with its suburbs, 22 And Kivzaim with its suburbs, and Beth-Horon with its suburbs; four cities. 23 And out of the tribe of Dan, Eltekeh with its suburbs, Givethon with its suburbs, 24 Aiyalon with its suburbs, Gath-Rimmon with its suburbs; four cities. 25 And out of the half tribe of Menashsheh, Tan-Tch with its suburbs, and Gath-Rimmon with its suburbs; two cities. 26 All the cities were ten with their suburbs for the mishpachot of the children of Kohath that remained. 27 And to the children of Gershon, of the mishpachot of the Leviim, out of the other half tribe of Menashsheh

they gave Golan in Bashan with its suburbs, to be a city of refuge for the slayer; and Beeshterah with its suburbs; two cities. 28 And out of the tribe of Yissaker, Kishon with its suburbs, Davareh with its suburbs, 29 Yarmuth with its suburbs, En-Gannim with its suburbs; four cities. 30 And out of the tribe of Asher, Mishal with its suburbs, Avdon with its suburbs, 31 Helkath with its suburbs, and Rehov with its suburbs; four cities. 32 And out of the tribe of Naphtali, Kedesh in Galilee with its suburbs, to be a city of refuge for the slayer; and Hammothdor with its suburbs, and Kartan with its suburbs; three cities. 33 All the cities of the Gershonites according to their mishpachot were thirteen cities with their suburbs. 34 And to the mishpachot of the children of Merari, the rest of the Leviim, out of the tribe of Zevulon, Yokneam with its suburbs, and Kartah with its suburbs, 35 Dimnah with its suburbs, Nahalal with its suburbs; four cities. 36 And out of the tribe of Reuven, Bezer with its suburbs, and Yahazah with its suburbs, 37 Kedemoth with its suburbs, and Mephaath with its suburbs; four cities. 38 And out of the tribe of Gad, Ramoth in Gilead with its suburbs, to be a city of refuge for the slayer; and Mahanayim with its suburbs, 39 Cheshbon with its suburbs, Yazer with its suburbs; four cities in all. 40 So all the cities for the children of Merari by their mishpachot, that were remaining of the mishpachot of the Leviim, were by their lot twelve cities. 41 All the cities of the Leviim within the possession of the children of Yisrael were forty-eight cities with their suburbs. 42 These cities each had suburbs around them: as it was with all these cities. 43 And יהוה gave to Yisrael all the land which He swore to give to their ahvot; and they possessed it, and dwelt in it. 44 And יהוה gave them rest all around, according to all that He swore to their ahvot: and there stood not a man of all their enemies before them; יהוה delivered all their enemies into their hand. 45 There failed nothing of any tov word that יהוה had spoken to Beit Yisrael; all came to pass.

22 Then Yahoshua called the Reuvenites, and the Gadites, and the half tribe of Menashsheh, 2 And said to them, You have kept all that Moshe the eved of יהוה commanded you, and have obeyed my voice in all that I commanded you: 3 You have not left your brothers these many days to this day, but have kept the charge of the commandment of יהוה Your Elohim. 4 And now יהוה Your Elohim has given rest to your brothers, as He promised them: therefore now return, and go to your tents, and to the land of your possession, which Moshe the eved of יהוה gave you on the other side of the Yarden River. 5 But take diligent heed to do the commandment and the Torah, which Moshe the eved of יהוה charged you, to love יהוה Your Elohim, and to have your halacha in all His halachot, and to keep His commandments, and to cleave to Him, and to serve Him with all your lev and with all your being. 6 So Yahoshua blessed them, and sent them away: and they went to their tents. 7 Now to the one half of the tribe of Menashsheh Moshe had given possession in Bashan: but to the other half of it gave Yahoshua among their brothers on this side of the Yarden River westward. And when Yahoshua sent them away also to their tents, then he blessed them, 8 And he spoke to them, saying, Return with much riches to your tents, and with much cattle, with silver, and with gold, and with brass, and with iron, and with much clothing: divide the spoil of your enemies with your brothers. 9 And the children of Reuven and the children of Gad and the half tribe of Menashsheh returned, and departed from the children of Yisrael out of Shiloh, which is in the land of Kanaan, to go to the land of Gilead, to the land of their possession, which they possessed, according to the word of יהוה through Moshe. 10 And when they came to the borders of the Yarden River, that are in the land of Kanaan, the children of Reuven and the children of Gad and the half tribe of Menashsheh built there an altar by the Yarden River, a great altar for all to see. 11 And the children of Yisrael who heard it said, See, the children of Reuven and the children of Gad and the half tribe of Menashsheh have built an altar opposite the land of Kanaan, in the borders of the Yarden, at the passage of the children of Yisrael. 12 And when the children of Yisrael heard it, the whole congregation of the children of Yisrael gathered themselves together at Shiloh, to go up to war against them. 13 And the children of Yisrael sent to the children of Reuven, and to the children of Gad, and to the half tribe of Menashsheh, into the land of Gilead, Pinchus the son of El-Azar the kohen, 14 And with him ten leaders, one from each bayit a leader throughout all the tribes of Yisrael; and each one was a head of the bayit of their ahvot among the thousands of Yisrael. 15 And they came to the children of Reuven, and to the children of Gad, and to the half tribe of Menashsheh, to the land of Gilead, and they spoke with them, saying, 16 This says the whole congregation of יהוה, What trespass is this that you have committed against the Elohim of Yisrael, to turn away this day from following יהוה, in that you have built an altar, that you might rebel this day against יהוה? 17 Is the iniquity of Peor too little for us, from which we are not cleansed until this day, although there was a plague in the congregation of יהוה; 18 That you must turn away this day from following יהוה? And it will be, if you rebel today against יהוה, that tomorrow He will be angry with the whole congregation of Yisrael. 19 And, if the land of your possession is unclean, then pass over to the land of the possession of יהוה, where יהוה's tabernacle dwells, and take possession among us: but rebel not against יהוה, nor rebel against us, in building an altar besides

the altar of **יהוה** our Elohim in Shiloh.[1]
20 Did not Achan the son of Zerah commit a trespass in the cursed thing, and wrath fell on all the congregation of Yisrael? And that man did not perish alone in his iniquity. 21 Then the children of Reuven and the children of Gad and the half tribe of Menahsheh answered, and said to the heads of the thousands of Yisrael, 22 **יהוה** El of Elohim, **יהוה** El of Elohim, He knows our reasons, and let Yisrael also know our reasons; if it was built in rebellion, or in transgression against **יהוה**, then let Him not save us this day, 23 If we have built an altar to turn away from following **יהוה**, or to offer on it burnt offerings or meat offerings, or if to offer shalom offerings on it, let **יהוה** Himself enact retribution; 24 But truly because of fear we built it, saying, perhaps in times to come your children might speak to our children, saying, What have you to do with **יהוה** Elohim of Yisrael? 25 For **יהוה** has made the Yarden River a border between us and you, you children of Reuven and children of Gad; you have no part with **יהוה** : so shall your children make our children cease from fearing **יהוה** . 26 Therefore we said, Let us now prepare to build us an altar, not for burnt offering, or for sacrifice: 27 But that it may serve as a witness between us, and you, and our generations after us, that we might do the service of **יהוה** before Him with our burnt offerings, and with our sacrifices, and with our shalom offerings; that your children may not say to our children in time to come, You have no part with **יהוה**. 28 Therefore we said, that it shall be, if they should say this to us or to our generations in times to come, that we may say again, See the pattern of the altar of **יהוה**, which our ahvot made, not for burnt offerings, nor for sacrifices; but it is a witness between us and you. 29 Far be it from us to rebel against

יהוה, and turn this day from following **יהוה**, to build an altar for burnt offerings, for meat offerings, or for sacrifices, beside the altar of **יהוה** our Elohim that is before His tabernacle. 30 And when Pinchus the kohen, and the leaders of the congregation and heads of the thousands of Yisrael which were with him, heard the words that the children of Reuven and the children of Gad and the children of Menahsheh spoke, it pleased them. 31 And Pinchus the son of El-Azar the kohen said to the children of Reuven, and to the children of Gad, and to the children of Menahsheh, This day we perceive that **יהוה** is among us, because you have not committed this trespass against **יהוה**: now you have delivered the children of Yisrael out of the hand of **יהוה**. 32 And Pinchus the son of El-Azar the kohen, and the leaders, returned from the children of Reuven, and from the children of Gad, out of the land of Gilead, to the land of Kanaan, to the children of Yisrael, and brought them word again. 33 And the thing pleased the children of Yisrael; and the children of Yisrael blessed Elohim, and no longer intended to go up against them in battle, to destroy the land where the children of Reuven and Gad dwelt. 34 And the children of Reuven and the children of Gad called the altar "Ed," for it shall serve as a witness between us that **יהוה** is both of our Elohim.

23 And it came to pass a long time after that **יהוה** had given rest to Yisrael from all their enemies all around, that Yahoshua grew old and advanced in age. 2 And Yahoshua called for all Yisrael, and for their zachanim, and for their heads, and for their shoptim, and for their officers, and said to them, I am old and advanced in age: 3 And you have seen all that **יהוה** Your Elohim has done to all these nations because of you; for **יהוה** Your Elohim is He that has fought for you. 4 See; I have divided to you by lot these nations that remain, to be an inheritance for your tribes,

---

[1] As has occurred throughout the ten tribe's history, they would have a tendency to change YHWH's altars and feasts, in violation of the Torah. Here we see two and a half tribes of what would later be a part of the ten tribes of Ephraim building another altar beside the true one at Shiloh. This time, however, it was for tov motives.

from the Yarden River, with all the nations that I have cut off, even to the Great Sea westward. 5 And **יהוה** Your Elohim, He shall expel them from before you, and drive them out of your sight; and you shall possess their land, as **יהוה** Your Elohim has promised to you. 6 Be you therefore very courageous to keep and to do all that is written in the scroll of the Torah of Moshe, that you turn not aside from it either to the right hand or to the left; 7 That you come not among these nations, these that remain among you; neither make mention of the name of their elohim, nor swear by them, neither serve them, nor bow yourselves to them:[1] 8 But cleave to **יהוה** Your Elohim, as you have done until this day. 9 For **יהוה** has driven out from before you great nations and strong: but as for you, no man has been able to stand before you until this day. 10 One man of yours shall chase a thousand: for **יהוה** Your Elohim, He it is that fights for you, as He has promised you. 11 And you shall carefully guard yourselves, that you fully love **יהוה** Your Elohim. 12 But if you do in any way go back, and cleave to the remnant of these nations, even these that remain among you, and shall make marriages with them, and go in to them, and they to you: 13 Know for a certainty that **יהוה** Your Elohim will no longer drive out any of these nations from before you; but they shall be snares and traps to you, and whips in your sides, and thorns in your eyes, until you perish from off this tov land that **יהוה** Your Elohim has given you. 14 And, see, this day I am going the way of all the earth: and you know in all your levim and in all your beings, that not one thing has failed of all the tov things which **יהוה** Your Elohim spoke concerning you; all has come to pass for you, and not one word has failed. 15 Therefore it shall come to pass, that as all the tov things have come upon you, which **יהוה** Your Elohim promised you; so shall **יהוה** bring upon you

all evil things, until He has destroyed you from off this tov land which **יהוה** Your Elohim has given you. 16 When you have transgressed the covenant of **יהוה** Your Elohim, which He commanded you, and have gone and served other elohim, and bowed yourselves to them; then shall the anger of **יהוה** be kindled against you, and you shall perish quickly from off the tov land which He has given to you.

24 And Yahoshua gathered all the tribes of Yisrael to Shechem, and called for the zachanim of Yisrael, and for their heads, and for their shoptim, and for their officers; and they presented themselves before Elohim. 2 And Yahoshua said to all the people, This says **יהוה** Elohim of Yisrael, *Your ahvot dwelt on the other side of the River Euphrates in old times, even Terah, the abba of Avraham, and the abba of Nachor: and they served other elohim. 3 And I took your abba Avraham from the other side of the River Euphrates,[2] and led him throughout all the land of Kanaan, and multiplied his seed,[3] and gave him Yitzchak. 4 And I gave to Yitzchak, Yaakov and Esav: and I gave to Esav Mount Seir, to possess it; but Yaakov and his children went down into Mitzrayim. 5 I sent Moshe also and Aharon, and I plagued Mitzrayim, according to that which I did among them: and afterward I brought you out. 6 And I brought your ahvot out of Mitzrayim: and you came to the sea; and the Mitzrites pursued after your ahvot with mirkavot and horsemen to the Sea of Reeds. 7 And when they cried to **יהוה**, He put darkness between you and the Mitzrites, and brought the sea upon them, and covered them; and your eyes have seen what I have done in Mitzrayim: and you dwelt in the wilderness for a long season. 8 And I brought you into the land of the Amorites, who dwelt on the other side of the Yarden River; and they fought with you: and I gave them into your hand, that you might possess*

---

[1] Yisraelites must unlearn all names but that of Yahweh. They must be removed from out hearts, lips, vocabulary and speech. That is His charge to us.

[2] Like our father Avraham, we must hear and respond to the call to leave Babylon.

[3] As has happened throughout the centuries.

their land; and I destroyed them from before you. 9 Then Balak the son of Tzippor, melech of Moav, arose and warred against Yisrael, and sent and called Bilam the son of Beor to curse you: 10 But I would not shema to Bilam; therefore he blessed you still: so I delivered you out of his hand. 11 And you went over the Yarden River, and came to Yericho: and the men of Yericho fought against you, the Amorites, and the Perizzites, and the Kanaanites, and the Hittites, and the Girgashites, the Hivites, and the Yevusites; and I delivered them into your hand. 12 And I sent the hornet before you, that drove them out from before you, even the two melechim of the Amorites; but not with your sword, nor with your bow. 13 And I have given you a land for which you did not labor, and cities that you built not, and now you dwell in them; and eat of the vineyards and olive trees, which you did not plant. 14 Now therefore fear יהוה, and serve Him in sincerity and in emet: and put away the elohim which your ahvot served on the other side of the River Euphrates, and in Mitzrayim; and serve יהוה. 15 And if it seems evil to you to serve יהוה, choose you this day whom you will serve; whether the elohim which your ahvot served that were on the other side of the River Euphrates, or the elohim of the Amorites, in whose land you dwell: but as for me and my bayit, we will serve יהוה. [1] 16 And the people answered and said, far be it from us that we should forsake יהוה, to serve other elohim; 17 For יהוה our Elohim, He it is that brought us up and our ahvot out of the land of Mitzrayim, from the bayit of bondage, and which did those great signs in our sight, and preserved us in all the derech where we went, and among all the peoples through whom we passed: 18 And יהוה drove out from before us all the peoples, even the Amorites who dwelt in the land: therefore will we also serve יהוה, for He is our Elohim. 19 And Yahoshua said to the

people, You cannot serve יהוה: for He is a kodesh Elohim; He is also a jealous Elohim; He will not forgive your transgressions or your sins. 20 If you forsake יהוה, and serve strange elohim, then He will turn and do you hurt, and consume you, even after He has done you tov. 21 And the people said to Yahoshua, No; but we will serve יהוה. 22 And Yahoshua said to the people, You are witnesses against yourselves that you have chosen יהוה, to serve Him. And they said, We are witnesses. 23 Now therefore put away, the strange elohim that are among you, and incline your lev to יהוה Elohim of Yisrael. 24 And the people said to Yahoshua, יהוה our Elohim will we serve, and His voice will we obey. 25 So Yahoshua made a covenant with the people that day, and established for them a statute and an ordinance in Shechem. 26 And Yahoshua wrote these words in the scroll of the Torah of Elohim, and took a great stone, and set it up there under an oak, that was by the Dwelling Place of יהוה. 27 And Yahoshua said to all the people, See, this stone shall be a witness to us; for it has heard all the words of יהוה that He spoke to us: it shall be therefore a witness to you, lest you deny Your Elohim. 28 So Yahoshua let the people depart, every man to his inheritance. 29 And it came to pass after these things, that Yahoshua the son of Nun, the eved of יהוה, died, being a hundred ten years old. 30 And they buried him in the border of his inheritance in Timnath-Serah, which is in Mount Ephraim, on the north side of the hill of Gaash. 31 And Yisrael served יהוה all the days of Yahoshua, and all the days of the zachanim that outlived Yahoshua, who had known all the works of יהוה, that He had done for Yisrael. 32 And the bones of Yoseph, which the children of Yisrael brought up out of Mitzrayim, were buried in Shechem, in a parcel of ground which Yaakov bought from the sons of Hamor the abba of Shechem for one hundred pieces of silver: and it became the inheritance of the children

---

[1] A declaration that should soon come to pass for all the house of Yisrael.

of Yoseph. 33 And El-Azar the son of
Aharon died; and they buried him in a hill
that belonged to Pinchus his son, which was
given him in Mount Ephraim.

שופטים

Shophtim - Judges
To Our Forefathers Yisrael

1 Now after the death of Yahoshua it came to pass, that the children of Yisrael asked **יהוה**, saying, Who shall go up for us against the Kanaanites first, to fight against them? 2 And **יהוה** said, *Yahudah shall go up: see, I have delivered the land into his hand.* 3 And Yahudah said to Shimeon his brother, Come up with me into my lot, that we may fight against the Kanaanites; and I likewise will go with you into your lot. So Shimeon went with him. 4 And Yahudah went up; and **יהוה** delivered the Kanaanites and the Perizzites into their hand: and they killed in Bezek ten thousand men. 5 And they found Adoni-Bezek in Bezek: and they fought against him, and they killed the Kanaanites and the Perizzites. 6 But Adoni-Bezek fled; and they pursued after him, and caught him, and cut off his thumbs and his great toes. 7 And Adoni-Bezek said, Seventy melechim, having their thumbs and their great toes cut off, gathered their food under my table: as I have done, so Elohim has repaid me. And they brought him to Yahrushalayim, and there he died. 8 Now the children of Yahudah had fought against Yahrushalayim, and had taken it, and smote it with the edge of the sword, and set the city on fire. 9 And afterward the children of Yahudah went down to fight against the Kanaanites, who dwelt in the mountain, and in the south, and in the valley. 10 And Yahudah went against the Kanaanites that dwelt in Hevron - now the name of Hevron before was Kiryath-Arba - and they killed Sheshai, and Ahiman, and Talmai. 11 And from there he went against the inhabitants of Devir: and the name of Devir before was Kiryath-Sepher: 12 And Calev said, He that smites Kiryath-Sepher, and takes it, to him will I give Achsah my daughter as a wife. 13 And Othni-El the son of Kenaz, Calev's

younger brother, took it: and he gave him Achsah his daughter as a wife. 14 And it came to pass, when she came to him, that she moved him to ask of her abba a field: and she dismounted from off her donkey; and Calev said to her, What do you want? 15 And she said to him, Give me a bracha: for you have given me a south land; give me also the springs of mayim. And Calev gave her the upper springs and the lower springs. 16 And the children of the Kenite, Moshe's abba-in-law, went up out of the city of palm eytzim with the children of Yahudah into the wilderness of Yahudah, which lies south of Arad; and they went and dwelt among the people. 17 And Yahudah went with Shimeon his brother, and they killed the Kanaanites that inhabited Zephath, and utterly destroyed it. And the name of the city was called Hormah. 18 Also Yahudah took Gaza with its border, and Ashkelon with its border, and Ekron with its border. 19 And **יהוה** was with Yahudah; and He drove out the inhabitants of the mountain; but Yisrael could not drive out the inhabitants of the valley, because the had mirkavot of iron. 20 And they gave Hevron to Calev, as Moshe said: and he expelled from there the three sons of Anak. 21 And the children of Benyamin did not drive out the Yevusites that inhabited Yahrushalayim; but the Yevusites dwell with the children of Benyamin in Yahrushalayim to this day. 22 And Beit Yoseph also went up against Beth-El: and **יהוה** was with them. 23 And Beit Yoseph sent some to spy in Beth-El - now the name of the city before was formerly Luz. 24 And the spies saw a man come forth out of the city, and they said to him, Show us, we ask you, the entrance into the city, and we will show you rachamim. 25 And when he showed them the entrance into the city, they smote the city with the edge of the sword; but they let the man go along with all his mishpocha. 26 And the man went into the land of the Hittites, and built a city, and called the name of it Luz: which is the name of it to this day. 27 Neither did Menashsheh drive out the inhabitants of Beth-Shean and its villages, nor Taanach and its villages, nor the inhabitants of Dor and its villages, nor the inhabitants of Ivleam and its villages, nor the inhabitants of Megiddo and its villages: but the Kanaanites would dwell in that land. 28 And it came to pass, when Yisrael was strong, that they put the Kanaanites to slave labor, and did not utterly drive them out. [1] 29 Neither did Ephraim drive out the Kanaanites that dwelt in Gezer; but the Kanaanites dwelt in Gezer among them. 30 Neither did Zevulun drive out the inhabitants of Kitron, nor the inhabitants of Nachalol; but the Kanaanites dwelt among them, and became slave laborers. 31 Neither did Asher drive out the inhabitants of Accho, nor the inhabitants of Tzidon, nor of Achlab, nor of Achzib, nor of Helvah, nor of Aphik, nor of Rehov: 32 But the Asherites dwelt among the Kanaanites, the inhabitants of the land: for they did not drive them out. 33 Neither did Naphtali drive out the inhabitants of Beth-Shemesh, nor the inhabitants of Beth-Anath; but they dwelt among the Kanaanites, the inhabitants of the land: Nevertheless the inhabitants of Beth-Shemesh and of Beth-Anath became slave laborers to them. 34 And the Amorites forced the children of Dan into the mountain: for they would not allow them to come down to the valley: 35 But the Amorites would dwell in Mount Heres in Aiyalon, and in Shaalvim: yet the hand of Beit Yoseph prevailed, so that they became slave laborers. 36 And the border of the Amorites was from the going up to Akravim, from Sela, and upward.

2 And the Malach-**יהוה**[2] came up from Gilgal to Bochim, and said, *I made you to go up out of Mitzrayim, and have brought you to the land that I swore to your ahvot; and I said, I will never break My covenant with you. 2 And you shall make no covenant with the inhabitants of this land; you shall throw down their altars: but you have not obeyed My voice: why have you done this? 3 Therefore I also said, I will not drive them out from before you; but they shall be as thorns in your sides, and their elohim shall be a trap to you.* 4 And it came to pass, when the Malach-**יהוה** spoke these words to all the children of Yisrael, that the people lifted up their voice, and wept. 5 And they called the name of that place Bochim: and they sacrificed there to **יהוה**. 6 And when Yahoshua had let the people go, the children of Yisrael went every man to his inheritance to possess the land. 7 And the people served **יהוה** all the days of Yahoshua, and all the days of the zachanim that outlived Yahoshua, who had seen all the great nisim of **יהוה**, that He did for Yisrael. 8 And Yahoshua the son of Nun, the eved of **יהוה**, died, being one hundred ten years old. 9 And they buried him in the border of his inheritance in Timnath-Cheres, in the Mount of Ephraim, on the north side of the hill Gaash. 10 And also all that generation was gathered to their ahvot: and there arose another generation after them, who knew not **יהוה**, nor the nisim that He had done for Yisrael. 11 And the children of Yisrael did evil in the sight of **יהוה**, and served many of the Baalim: [3] 12 And they forsook **יהוה** Elohim of their ahvot, who brought them out of the land of Mitzrayim, and followed other elohim, even the elohim of the peoples that were all around them, and bowed themselves to them, and provoked **יהוה** to anger. 13 And they forsook **יהוה**, and served Baal and Ashtaroth.[4] 14 And the anger of **יהוה** was

---

[1] Disobedience to YHWH.

[2] The same Guardian-**Metatron** that has YHWH's Name speaking in the first person is no doubt Yahshua.
[3] lords in Hebrew.
[4] lords in Hebrew.

hot against Yisrael, and He delivered them into the hands of spoilers that plundered them, and He sold them into the hands of their enemies all around, so that they could not any longer stand before their enemies. 15 Wherever they went out, the hand of יהוה was against them for evil, as יהוה had said, and as יהוה had sworn to them: and they were greatly distressed. 16 Nevertheless יהוה raised up shophtim, who delivered them out of the hand of those that plundered them. 17 And yet they would not shema to their shophtim, but they went whoring after other elohim, and bowed themselves to them: they turned quickly out of the halacha which their ahvot walked in, who obeyed the mitzvoth of יהוה; but they did not do so. 18 And when יהוה raised up their shophtim, then יהוה was with the shophet, and delivered them out of the hand of their enemies all the days of the shophet's chayim: for יהוה had rachamim because of their groanings because of those that oppressed them and crushed them. 19 And it came to pass, when the shophet was dead, that they returned, and corrupted themselves more than their ahvot, in following other elohim to serve them, and to bow down to them; they ceased not from their own doings, nor from their stubborn halachot. 20 And the anger of יהוה was hot against Yisrael; and He said, *Because this people has transgressed My covenant which I commanded their ahvot, and have not listened to My voice; 21 I will also no longer drive out from before them any of the nations that Yahoshua left when he died: 22 That through them I may test Yisrael, whether they will keep the halacha of יהוה to have their halacha in it, as their ahvot did keep it, or not.* 23 Therefore יהוה left those nations, without driving them out quickly; neither did He deliver them into the hand of Yahoshua.

3 Now these are the nations that יהוה left, to test Yisrael, even many in Yisrael who had not known all the wars of Kanaan; 2 Only so that the generations of the children of Yisrael might know, to teach them war, at the least such as before knew nothing about war; 3 Namely, five masters of the Philistines, and all the Kanaanites, and the Tsidonians, and the Hivites that dwelt in Mount Levanon, from Mount Baal-Hermon to the entering in of Hamath. 4 And they were to test Yisrael by them, to know whether they would shema to the mitzvoth of יהוה, which He commanded their ahvot through Moshe. 5 And the children of Yisrael dwelt among the Kanaanites, Hittites, and Amorites, and Perizzites, and Hivites, and Yevusites: 6 And they took their daughters to be their wives, and gave their daughters to their sons, and served their elohim.[1] 7 And the children of Yisrael did evil in the sight of יהוה, and forgot יהוה their Elohim, and served the Baalim and the Asherahot. 8 Therefore the anger of יהוה was hot against Yisrael, and He sold them into the hand of Chushan-Rishathayim melech of Mesopotamia: and the children of Yisrael served Chushan-Rishathayim eight years. 9 And when the children of Yisrael cried to יהוה, יהוה raised up a deliverer for the children of Yisrael, who delivered them, even Othni-El the son of Kenaz, Calev's younger brother. 10 And the Ruach of יהוה[2] came upon Othni-El, and He gave mishpat to Yisrael, and went out to war: and יהוה delivered Chushan-Rishathayim melech of Mesopotamia into his hand; and his hand prevailed against Chushan-Rishathayim. 11 And the land had rest for forty years. And Othni-El the son of Kenaz died. 12 And the children of Yisrael did evil again in the sight of יהוה : and יהוה strengthened Eglon the melech of Moav against Yisrael, because they had done evil

---

[1] Intermarriages are the death note for Yisraelites. This would include all those believers in Yahshua, who are not committed to a Torah-guarding lifestyle.
[2] The Ruach of YHWH was and is His Power not a third person. This Ruach would come and go throughout the period of the Judges. As can be seen religions did not invent this concept of the Set-Apart Spirit. It was always an exclusive possession of those faithful within Yisrael.

in the sight of **יהוה**. 13 And Eglon gathered to him the children of Ammon and Amalek, and went and smote Yisrael, and possessed the city of palm eytzim.[1] 14 So the children of Yisrael served Eglon the melech of Moav eighteen years. 15 But when the children of Yisrael cried to **יהוה**, **יהוה** raised them up a deliverer, Ehud the son of Gera, a Benyamite, a man impeded in his right hand:[2] and by him the children of Yisrael sent a present to Eglon the melech of Moav. 16 But Ehud made him a dagger that had two edges, of a cubit length; and he did gird it under his robe upon his right thigh. 17 And he brought the present to Eglon melech of Moav: and Eglon was a very fat man. 18 And when he had made an end of offering the present, he sent away the people that brought the present. 19 But he himself turned again from the stone images that were by Gilgal, and said, I have a secret message to you, O melech: who then said, Keep silent. And all that stood by him went out from him. 20 And Ehud came to him; and he was sitting in a cool room, which he had for himself alone. And Ehud said, I have a message from Elohim to you. And he arose out of his seat. 21 And Ehud put forth his left hand, and took the dagger from his right thigh, and thrust it into his belly: 22 And the handle also went in after the blade; and the body fat closed over the blade, so that he could not draw the dagger out of his belly; and it came out behind him. 23 Then Ehud went forth through the porch, and shut the doors of the cool room upon him, and locked them. 24 When he had gone out, his avadim came; and when they saw that, see, the doors of the cool room were locked, they said, Surely he covers his feet in his summer bedroom. 25 And they tarried until they were ashamed: and, see, he did not open the doors of the cool room; therefore they took a key, and opened them: and, see, their master was fallen down dead on the earth. 26 And Ehud escaped while

they tarried, and passed beyond the stone images, and escaped to Seirath. 27 And it came to pass, when he was come, that he blew a shofar in the mountain of Ephraim, and the children of Yisrael went down with him from the Mount, and he went before them. 28 And he said to them, Follow after me: for **יהוה** has delivered your enemies the Moavites into your hand. And they went down after him, and took the fords of the Yarden River toward Moav, and allowed not any man to pass over. 29 And they killed from Moav at that time about ten thousand men, all were robust, and all men of valor; and there escaped not a single man. 30 So Moav was subdued that day under the hand of Yisrael. And the land had rest eighty years. 31 And after him was Shamgar the son of Anath, who killed of the Philistines six hundred men with an ox goad: and he also delivered Yisrael.

4 And the children of Yisrael again did evil in the sight of **יהוה**, when Ehud was dead. 2 And **יהוה** sold them into the hand of Yavin melech of Kanaan, that reigned in Hatzor; the captain of the army was Sisera, who dwelt in Harosheth Ha-Goyim. 3 And the children of Yisrael cried to **יהוה** : for Sisera had nine hundred mirkavot of iron, and for twenty years he harshly oppressed the children of Yisrael. 4 And Devorah, a neviyah, the wife of Lapidoth, gave mishpat to Yisrael at that time. 5 And she dwelt under the palm eytz of Devorah between Ramah and Beth-El in Mount Ephraim: and the children of Yisrael came up to her for mishpat.[3] 6 And she sent and called Barak the son of Avinoam out of Kedesh-Naphtali, and said to him, Has not **יהוה** Elohim of Yisrael commanded us saying, *Go and draw towards Mount Tavor, and take with you ten thousand men of the children of Naphtali and of the children of Zevulun? 7 And I will draw to you Sisera, the captain of Yavin's army, with his mirkavot and his multitude; and I will*

---

[1] Jericho.
[2] Most faithful men of YHWH have handicaps that YHWH uses to show Himself strong.

[3] Women have always had key leadership roles in Yisrael.

deliver him into your hand. 8 And Barak said to her, If you will go with me, then I will go: but if you will not go with me, then I will not go.[1] 9 And she said, I will surely go with you: nevertheless the journey that you take shall not be for your honor; for יהוה shall sell Sisera into the hand of a woman. And Devorah arose, and went with Barak to Kedesh. 10 And Barak called Zevulun and Naphtali to Kedesh; and he went up with ten thousand men at his feet: and Devorah went up with him. 11 Now Chever the Kenite, who was of the children of Chovav the abba-in-law of Moshe, had separated himself from the Kenites, and pitched his tent to the plain of Zaanayim, which is by Kedesh. 12 And they showed Sisera that Barak the son of Avinoam had gone up to Mount Tavor. 13 And Sisera gathered together all his mirkavot, even nine hundred mirkavot of iron, and all the people that were with him, from Harosheth Ha-Goyim to the river of Kishon. 14 And Devorah said to Barak, Go up; for this is the day in which יהוה has delivered Sisera into your hand: has not יהוה gone out before you? So Barak went down from Mount Tavor, and ten thousand men after him. 15 And יהוה destroyed Sisera, and all his mirkavot, and all his army, with the edge of the sword before Barak; so that Sisera went down off his mirkavah, and fled away on his feet. 16 But Barak pursued after the mirkavot, and after the army, to Charosheth Ha-Goyim: and all the army of Sisera fell by the edge of the sword; and there was not a man left. 17 However Sisera fled away on his feet to the tent of Yah-El the wife of Chever the Kenite: for there was shalom between Yavin the melech of Chazor and the bayit of Chever the Kenite. 18 And Yah-El went out to meet Sisera, and said to him, Turn in, my master, turn in to me; fear not. And when he had turned in to her into the tent, she covered him with a mantle. 19 And he said to her, Give me, I beg you, a little mayim to drink, for I am thirsty. And she opened a bottle of milk, and gave him to drink, and covered him. 20 Again he said to her, Stand in the door of the tent, and it shall be, when any man does come and ask you, Is there any man here? You shall say, No. 21 Then Yah-El Cheber's wife took a nail of the tent, and took a hammer in her hand, and went quietly to him, and smote the nail into his temples, and nailed it into the ground: for he was fast asleep and weary. So he died. 22 And, see, as Barak pursued Sisera, Yah-El came out to meet him, and said to him, Come, and I will show you the man whom you seek. And when he came into her tent, see, Sisera lay dead, and the nail was in his temple. 23 So Elohim subdued on that day Yavin the melech of Kanaan before the children of Yisrael. 24 And the hand of the children of Yisrael prospered, and prevailed against Yavin the melech of Kanaan, until they had destroyed Yavin melech of Kanaan.

5 Then sang Devorah and Barak the son of Avinoam on that day, saying, 2 Hallelu-et- יהוה for the avenging of Yisrael, when the people willingly offered themselves. 3 Shema, O you melechim; give ear, O you princes; I, will shir to יהוה; I will shir tehilot to יהוה Elohim of Yisrael. 4 יהוה, when You went out of Seir, when You marched out of the field of Edom, the earth trembled, and the shamayim dropped, the clouds also dropped mayim. 5 The mountains melted from before יהוה, even Sinai from before יהוה Elohim of Yisrael. 6 In the days of Shamgar the son of Anath, in the days of Yah-El, the highways were unoccupied, and the travelers walked through byways. 7 They began to live behind walled towns until it ceased, it ceased in Yisrael, until I Devorah - an ima in Yisrael, arose. 8 They chose new elohim; then there was war in the gates. Was there a shield or spear seen among forty thousand in Yisrael? 9 My lev is for the Torah leaders of Yisrael, who offered themselves willingly among the people. Barchu-et

---

[1] Ministry team. Women function best in these situations.

יהוה. 10 Speak up, you that ride on white donkeys, you that sit in mishpat, and walk along the derech. 11 They that are delivered from the noise of archers in the places of drawing mayim, there shall they rehearse the tzadik acts of יהוה, even the tzadik acts toward the inhabitants of his villages in Yisrael: then shall the people of יהוה go down to the gates. 12 Awake, awake, Devorah: awake, awake, and utter a song: arise, Barak, and lead your captivity captive, you son of Avinoam. 13 Then He made him that remains to have dominion over the nobles among the people: יהוה made me have dominion over the mighty. 14 Out of Ephraim was there a root of them against Amalek; after you, Benyamin, among your people; out of Machir came Torah instructors, and out of Zevulun they that handle the pen of the Torah sopher. 15 And the princes of Yissacher were with Devorah; even Yissacher, and also Barak: he was sent on foot into the valley. For the divisions of Reuven there was great searching of lev. 16 Why did you remain among the sheepfolds, to shema the bleatings of the flocks? For the divisions of Reuven there was great searching of lev. 17 Gilead stayed beyond the Yarden River: and why did Dan remain in ships? Asher continued on the seashore, and stayed in his ports. 18 Zevulun and Naphtali were a people that jeopardized their lives to the death in the high places of the field. 19 The melechim came and fought, then fought the melechim of Kanaan in Taanach by the waters of Megiddo; they took no spoils of silver. 20 They fought from the shamayim; the cochavim in their courses fought against Sisera. 21 The River Kishon swept them away, that ancient river, the River Kishon. O my being, you have trampled in strength. 22 Then were the horse hoofs of the enemy broken by the means of the prancing, of their mighty ones. 23 Curse Meroz, said the heavenly messenger of יהוה, curse bitterly the inhabitants of it; because they came not to the help of יהוה, to the help of יהוה

against the mighty. 24 Blessed above women shall Yah-El the wife of Chever the Kenite be, blessed shall she be above women in the tents. 25 He asked mayim, and she gave him milk; she brought forth butter in a noble dish. 26 She put her hand to the nail, and her right hand to the workmen's hammer; and with the hammer she smote Sisera, she smashed his head, when she had pierced and struck through his temples. 27 Between her feet he bowed, he fell, he lay down: between her feet he bowed, he fell: where he bowed, there he fell down dead. 28 The ima of Sisera looked out at a window, and cried through the lattice, Why is his mirkavah so long in coming home? Why are the wheels of his mirkavot delayed? 29 Her wise ladies answered her; yes, she indeed answered herself, 30 Have they not divided the spoil? Have they not divided the spoil; to every man a woman or two; to Sisera a spoil of divers colors, a spoil of divers colors of needlework, of divers colors of needlework on both sides, made for the necks of them that took the spoil? 31 So let all Your enemies perish, O יהוה: but let them that love Him be as the sun when it goes forth in its might. And the land had rest forty years.

6 And the children of Yisrael did evil in the sight of יהוה: and יהוה delivered them into the hand of Midyan seven years. 2 And the hand of Midyan prevailed against Yisrael: and because of the Midyanites the children of Yisrael made dens that are in the mountains, and caves, and strongholds. 3 And so it was, when Yisrael had sown zera, that the Midyanites came up, and the Amalekites, and the children of the east, they all came up against them. 4 And they encamped against them, and destroyed the increase of the earth, all the way to Gaza, and left no food for Yisrael, neither sheep, nor ox, nor donkey. 5 For they came up with their cattle and their tents, and they came as grasshoppers for multitude; for both they and their camels were without

number: and they entered into the land to destroy it. 6 And Yisrael was greatly impoverished because of the Midyanites; and the children of Yisrael cried to **יהוה**. 7 And it came to pass, when the children of Yisrael cried to **יהוה** because of the Midyanites, 8 That **יהוה** sent a navi to the children of Yisrael, who said to them, This says **יהוה** Elohim of Yisrael, *I brought you up from Mitzrayim, and brought you forth out of the bayit of bondage; 9 And I delivered you out of the hand of the Mitzrites, and out of the hand of all that oppressed you, and drove them out from before you, and gave you their land; 10 And I said to you, I am* **יהוה** *Your Elohim; fear not the elohim of the Amorites, in whose land you dwell: but you have not obeyed My voice.* 11 And there came the Malach-**יהוה**, who sat under an oak that was in Ophrah that belonged to Yoash the Avi-Ezrite: and his son Gidyon threshed wheat by the winepress, to hide it from the Midyanites. 12 And the Malach-**יהוה** appeared to him, and said to him, **יהוה** *is with you, you mighty man of valor.* 13 And Gidyon said to him, Oh My Master, if **יהוה** is with us, why then is all this happened to us? And where are all His nisim which our ahvot told us about, saying, Did not **יהוה** bring us up from Mitzrayim? But now **יהוה** has forsaken us, and delivered us into the hands of the Midyanites. 14 And **יהוה** looked upon him,[1] and said, *Go in this your might, and you shall save Yisrael from the hand of the Midyanites: have not I sent you?* 15 And he said to Him, Oh My Master, with what shall I save Yisrael? See, my mishpocha is poor in Menashsheh, and I am the least in my abba's bayit. 16 And **יהוה** said to him, *Surely I will be with you, and you shall smite the Midyanites as one man.* 17 And he said to Him, If now I have found favor in Your sight, then show me a sign that it is You who is talking with me. 18 Depart not from here, I ask You, until I come to You, to bring forth my present, and set it before

You. And He said, I will stay until you come again. 19 And Gidyon went in, and made ready a young goat, and unleavened cakes of an ephah of flour: the meat he put in a basket, and he put the broth in a pot, and brought it out to him under the oak, and presented it. 20 And the Malach-**יהוה** said to him, *Take the flesh and the unleavened cakes, and lay them upon this rock, and pour out the broth.* And he did so. 21 Then the Malach-**יהוה** put forth the end of the staff that was in His hand, and touched the meat and the unleavened cakes; and there rose up fire out of the rock, and consumed the meat and the unleavened cakes. Then the Malach-**יהוה** departed out of his sight. 22 And when Gidyon perceived that He was the Malach-**יהוה**, Gidyon said, Oy, Oy **יהוה**-Elohim! I have seen the Malach-**יהוה** panayim-el-panayim. 23 And **יהוה** said to him, *Shalom be to you; fear not: you shall not die.*[2] 24 Then Gidyon built an altar there to **יהוה**, and called it **יהוה**-Shalom: to this day it is yet in Ophrah of the Avi-Ezrites. 25 And it came to pass the same night, that **יהוה** said to him, *Take your abba's young bull, even the second bull of seven years old, and throw down the altar of Baal that your abba has, and cut down the Asherah that is by it: 26 And build an altar to* **יהוה** *Your Elohim on the top of this rock, in the ordered place, and take the second bull, and offer a burnt sacrifice with the wood of the Asherah that you shall cut down.* 27 Then Gidyon took ten men of his avadim,[3] and did as **יהוה** had said to him: and so it was, because he feared his abba's household, and the men of the city, that he could not do it by day, so he did it by night. 28 And when the men of the city arose early in the morning, and see, the altar of Baal was cast down, and the Asherah was cut down that was by it, and the second bull was offered upon the altar that was built. 29 And they said one to another, Who has done this thing? And when they inquired

---

[1] Note that the **Malach**-YHWH is YHWH here in this verse.

[2] Because he only saw the sent YHWH, and not Abba YHWH.
[3] A type or picture of the ten tribes of Ephraim, forsaking the pagan elohim of their fathers, and returning to YHWH.

and asked, they said, Gidyon the son of Yoash has done this thing. 30 Then the men of the city said to Yoash, Bring out your son, that he may die: because he has cast down the altar of Baal,[1] and because he has cut down the Asherah that was by it. 31 And Yoash said to all that stood against him, Will you plead for Baal? Will you save him? He that will plead for him, let him be put to death while it is yet morning: if he be a real elohim, let him plead for himself, because someone has cast down his altar. 32 Therefore on that day Yoash called Gidyon; Yahrubaal, saying, Let Baal plead against him, because his altar is thrown down. 33 Then all the Midyanites and the Amalekites and the children of the east were gathered together, and went over, and pitched in the Valley of Yezreel. 34 But the Ruach of יהוה came upon Gidyon, and he blew a shofar; and Avi-Ezer was gathered to him. 35 And he sent messengers throughout all Menashsheh; who also were gathered to him: and he sent messengers to Asher, and to Zevulun, and to Naphtali; and they came up to meet them. 36 And Gidyon said to Elohim, If You will save Yisrael by my hand, as You have said, 37 See, I will put a fleece of wool on the floor; and if the dew is on the fleece only, and it is dry upon all the earth next to it, then shall I know that You will save Yisrael by my hand, as You have said. 38 And it was so: for he rose up early in the morning, and squeezed the fleece together, and wrung the dew out of the fleece, filling a bowl full of mayim. 39 And Gidyon said to Elohim, Let not Your anger be hot against me, and I will speak only once more: let me test once more with the fleece; let it now be dry only upon the fleece, and upon all the ground next to it let there be dew. 40 And Elohim did so that night: for it was dry upon the fleece only, and there was dew on all the ground.

7 Then Yahrubaal, who is Gidyon, and all the people that were with him, rose up early, and pitched beside the well of Harod: so that the army of the Midyanites were on the north side of them, by the hill of Moreh, in the valley. 2 And יהוה said to Gidyon, *The people that are with you are too many for Me to give the Midyanites into their hands, lest Yisrael boast themselves against Me, saying, my own hand has saved me.*[2] 3 *Now therefore go to, proclaim in the ears of the people, saying, Anyone who is fearful and afraid, let him return and depart early from Mount Gilead.* And there returned from the people twenty-two thousand; and there remained ten thousand. 4 And יהוה said to Gidyon, *The people are yet too many; bring them down to the mayim, and I will test them for you there: and it shall be, that of whom I say to you, This one shall go with you, the same shall go with you; and of whomever I say to you, This one shall not go with you, the same one shall not go.* 5 So he brought down the people to the mayim: and יהוה said to Gidyon, *Everyone that laps of the mayim with his tongue, as a dog laps, him shall you set by himself; likewise every one that bows down upon his knees to drink.* 6 And the number of those that lapped; putting their hands to their mouth were three hundred men: but all the rest of the people bowed down upon their knees to drink mayim. 7 And יהוה said to Gidyon, *By the three hundred men that lapped will I save you, and deliver the Midyanites into your hand: and let all the other people go every man to his place.*[3] 8 So the people took food in their hands, and their shofars: and he sent all the rest of Yisrael every man to his tent, and retained those three hundred men: and the army of Midyan was beneath them in

---

[1] The lord.

[2] People want to know why more believers don't understand and receive the two-house message. Here is our answer. YHWH always and only, deals with a remnant of Yisrael taken from the large numbers.

[3] If one is not ready to deal with the enemies of Yisrael's restoration and victory, it's better for that individual to go home, lest he bring fear, doubt and unemunah, to those who have heard YHWH's call in this final hour.

the valley. 9 And it came to pass the same night, that יהוה said to him, *Arise, get down to the army, for I have delivered it into your hand.* 10 *But if you fear to go down, go with Phurah your eved down to the army:* 11 *And you shall shema what they say; and afterward shall your hands be strengthened to go down to the army.* Then he went down with Phurah his eved to the edge of the armed men that were in the camp. 12 And the Midyanites and the Amalekites and all the children of the east lay along in the valley like grasshoppers for multitude; and their camels were without number, as the sand by the seaside for multitude. 13 And when Gidyon had come, see, there was a man that told a dream to his chaver, and said, See, I dreamed a dream, and, a cake of barley lechem tumbled into the army of Midyan, and came to a tent, and smote it so that it fell, and overturned it, that the tent lay flat. 14 And his companion answered and said, This is nothing other than the sword of Gidyon the son of Yoash, a man of Yisrael: for into his hand has Elohim delivered Midyan, and all the army. 15 And it was so, when Gidyon heard the telling of the dream, and the interpretation of it, that he worshipped, and returned to the army of Yisrael, and said, Arise; for יהוה has delivered into your hand the army of Midyan. 16 And he divided the three hundred men into three companies, and he put a shofar in every man's hand, with empty jars, and torches in the jars. 17 And he said to them, Look at me, and do likewise: and, see, when I come to the outside of the camp, it shall be that, as I do, so shall you do. 18 When I blow with the shofar, I and all that are with me, then blow your shofars also on every side of the camp, and say, The sword of יהוה, and of Gidyon. 19 So Gidyon, and the hundred men that were with him, came to the outside of the camp at the start of the middle watch; and they had just set their watch: and they blew the shofars, and broke the jars that were in their hands. 20 And the three companies

blew the shofars, and broke the jars, and held the torches in their left hands, and the shofars in their right hands to blow with: and they cried, The sword of יהוה, and of Gidyon. 21 And they stood every man in his place around the camp: and all the army ran, and cried, and fled. 22 And the three hundred blew the shofars, and יהוה set every man's sword against his fellow, even throughout all the army: and the army fled to Beth-Shittah in Tzererath, and to the border of Avel-Meholah, to Tavvath. 23 And the men of Yisrael gathered themselves together out of Naphtali, and out of Asher, and out of all Menashsheh, and pursued after the Midyanites. 24 And Gidyon sent messengers throughout all Mount Ephraim, saying, Come down against the Midyanites, and take from them the watering places to Beth-Barah and of the Yarden River. Then all the men of Ephraim gathered themselves together, and took the watering places in Beth-Barah and also of the Yarden River. 25 And they took two princes of the Midyanites, Orev and Zeev; and they killed Orev upon the rock Orev, and Zeev they killed at the winepress of Zeev, and pursued Midyan, and brought the heads of Orev and Zeev to Gidyon on the other side of the Yarden River.

8 And the men of Ephraim said to him, Why have you treated us like this, that you did not call us, when you went to fight with the Midyanites? And they did argue with him sharply.[1] 2 And he said to them, What have I done now in comparison to you? Is not the gleaning of the grapes of Ephraim better than the vintage of Avi-Ezer? 3 Elohim has delivered into your hands the princes of Midyan, Orev and Zeev: and what was I able to do in comparison to you? Then their anger was abated toward him, when he had said that. 4 And Gidyon came to the Yarden River, and passed over, he, and the three hundred

---

[1] Ephraim always has and continues to have, a rejection and inferiority complex, feeling left out in the things that belong to Yisrael's inheritance.

men that were with him, weary, yet pursuing them. 5 And he said to the men of Succoth, Give, I ask you, loaves of lechem to the people that follow me; for they are weary, and I am pursuing after Tzevah and Tzalmunna, melechim of Midyan. 6 And the princes of Succoth said, Are the hands of Tzevah and Tzalmunna now in your hand, that we should give lechem to your army? 7 And Gidyon said, Therefore when יהוה has delivered Tzevah and Tzalmunna into my hand, and then I will tear your flesh with the thorns of the wilderness and with briers. 8 And he went up to Penu-El, and spoke to them likewise: and the men of Penu-El answered him just as the men of Succoth had answered him. 9 And he spoke also to the men of Penu-El, saying, When I come again in shalom, I will break down this tower. 10 Now Tzevah and Tzalmunna were in Karkor, and their armies with them, about fifteen thousand men, all that were left of all the armies of the children of the east: for there fell a hundred twenty thousand men that drew the sword. 11 And Gidyon went up by the derech of those that dwelt in tents on the east of Novah and Yogvehah, and smote the army: for the army was secure. 12 And when Tzevah and Tzalmunna fled, he pursued after them, and took the two melechim of Midyan, Tzevah and Tzalmunna, and destroyed all the army. 13 And Gidyon the son of Yoash returned from battle before the sun was up, 14 And caught a young man of the men of Succoth, and inquired of him: and he described to him the princes of Succoth, and their zachanim, even seventy-seven men. 15 And he came to the men of Succoth, and said, See Tzevah and Tzalmunna, about whom you taunted me, saying, Are the hands of Tzevah and Tzalmunna now in your hand, that we should give lechem to your men that are weary? 16 And he took the zachanim of the city, and thorns of the wilderness and briers, and with them he taught the men of Succoth a lesson. 17 And he beat down the tower of Penu-El, and killed the men of the

city. 18 Then said he to Tzevah and Tzalmunna, What manner of men were they whom you killed at Tavor? And they answered, As you are, so were they: Each one resembled the children of a Melech.[1] 19 And he said, They were my brothers, even the sons of my ima: as יהוה lives, if you had saved them alive, I would not kill you now. 20 And he said to Yether his firstborn, Rise up, and kill them. But the youth drew not his sword: for he feared, because he was still a youth. 21 Then Tzevah and Tzalmunna said, Rise and fall upon us: for as the man is, so is his strength. And Gidyon arose, and killed Tzevah and Tzalmunna, and took away the ornaments that were on their camels' necks. 22 Then the men of Yisrael said to Gidyon, Rule over us, both you, and your son, and your son's son also: for you have delivered us from the hand of Midyan. 23 And Gidyon said to them, I will not rule over you, neither shall my son rule over you: יהוה shall rule over you. 24 And Gidyon said to them, I would desire a request from you, that you would give me every man the earrings of his spoil - For they had golden earrings because they were Ishmaelites.[2] 25 And they answered, We will willingly give them. And they spread a garment, and did cast in it every man the earrings of his spoil. 26 And the weight of the golden earrings that he requested was a thousand seven hundred shekels of gold; besides ornaments, and collars, and purple raiment that was on the melechim of Midyan, and besides the chains that were around their camels' necks. 27 And Gidyon made it into an ephod shoulder garment, like the one worn by the Kohen Ha-Gadol, and put it in his city, even in Ophrah: and all Yisrael went there whoring after it: it then became a

---

[1] Yisraelites are to appear to the heathen as children of the true eternal King.
[2] Note that men wearing earrings, is part of the culture of Ishmael and not of Yisrael.

trap to Gidyon, and to his bayit.[1] 28 So Midyan was subdued before the children of Yisrael, so that they lifted up their heads no more. And the country was in shalom forty years in the days of Gidyon. 29 And Yahrubaal the son of Yoash went and dwelt in his own bayit. 30 And Gidyon had seventy sons from his own body: for he had many wives. 31 And his concubine that was in Shechem, she also bore him a son, whose name he called Avimelech. 32 And Gidyon the son of Yoash died in a tov old age, and was buried in the tomb of Yoash his abba, in Ophrah of the Avi-Ezrites. 33 And it came to pass, as soon as Gidyon was dead, that the children of Yisrael turned again, and went whoring after the Baalim, and made Baal-Berith[2] their elohim. 34 And the children of Yisrael remembered not יהוה their Elohim, who had delivered them out of the hands of all their enemies on every side: 35 Neither showed they chesed to the bayit of Yahrubaal, named, Gidyon, according to all the tov that he had showed to Yisrael.

9 And Avimelech the son of Yahrubaal went to Shechem to his ima's brothers, and communed with them, and with all the mishpocha of the bayit of his ima's abba, saying, 2 Speak, I ask you, in the ears of all the men of Shechem, What is better for you, should all the sons of Yahrubaal, which are seventy persons, reign over you, or just one reign over you? Remember also that I am your bone and your flesh. 3 And his ima's brothers spoke of him in the ears of all the men of Shechem all these words: and their levim inclined to follow Avimelech; for they said, He is our brother. 4 And they gave him seventy pieces of silver out of the bayit of Baal-Berith, with which Avimelech hired the am-ha-aretz, who followed him. 5 And he went to his abba's bayit at Ophrah,

and killed his brothers the sons of Yahrubaal, being seventy persons, upon one stone: not counting Yotham the youngest son of Yahrubaal was left; for he hid himself. 6 And all the men of Shechem gathered together, and all the bayit of Millo, and went, and made Avimelech melech, by the oak of Matzpiyah near the pillar that was in Shechem. 7 And when they told it to Yotham, he went and stood on the top of Mount Gerizim, and lifted up his voice, and cried, and said to them, Shema to me, you men of Shechem, that Elohim may shema to you. 8 The eytzim went forth once upon a time to anoint a melech over them; and they said to the olive eytz, Reign over us. 9 But the olive eytz said to them, Should I leave my fatness, with which by me they honor Elohim and man, and go to be promoted over the other eytzim? 10 And the other eytzim said to the fig eytz, Come, and reign over us. 11 But the fig eytz said to them, Should I forsake my sweetness, and my tov fruit, and go to be promoted over the other eytzim? 12 Then said the other eytzim to the vine, Come, and reign over us. 13 And the vine said to them, Should I leave my wine, which cheers Elohim and man, and go to be promoted over the other eytzim? 14 Then said all the other eytzim to the bramble, Come, and reign over us. 15 And the bramble said to the eytzim, If in emet you will anoint me melech over you, then come and put your trust in my shadow: and if not, let fire come out of the bramble, and devour the cedars of Levanon.[3] 16 Now therefore, if you have done truly and sincerely, in that you have made Avimelech melech, and if you have dealt well with Yahrubaal and his bayit, and have done to him according to the deserving of his hands; 17 For my abba fought for you, and risked his chayim, and delivered you out of the hand of Midyan: 18 And you have risen up against my abba's bayit this day, and have

---

[1] In pride he sought to wear that which pertains only to the **Kohen HaGadol** and thus drew attention to the object causing idolatry, all the while being puffed up with pride over the military prowess given to him by YHWH. As Yahshua taught all Yisrael, it is not how you start, but how you finish in your walk with YHWH.
[2] lord of the covenant.

[3] A parable or **drash** given by Gideon's son, to show how self-promotion in Yisrael never works, and that just like Yahshua taught us, the road to greatness in Yisrael is in service to others.

slain his sons, seventy persons, upon one stone, and have made Avimelech, the son of his female eved, melech over the men of Shechem, because he is your brother; 19 If you then have dealt truly and sincerely with Yahrubaal and with his bayit this day, then gilah in your choice of Avimelech, and let him also gilah in you: 20 But if not, let fire come out from Avimelech, and devour the men of Shechem, and the bayit of Millo; and let fire come out from the men of Shechem, and from the bayit of Millo, and devour Avimelech.[1] 21 And Yotham ran away, and fled, and went to Beer, and dwelt there, for fear of Avimelech his brother. 22 And Avimelech had reigned three years over Yisrael, 23 Then Elohim sent an evil ruach between Avimelech and the men of Shechem; and the men of Shechem dealt treacherously against Avimelech: 24 That the cruelty done to the seventy sons of Yahrubaal might come, and their dom be laid upon Avimelech their brother, who killed them; and upon the men of Shechem, who aided him in the killing of his brothers. 25 And the men of Shechem set an ambush for him in the top of the mountains, and they robbed all that came along that way: and it was told Avimelech. 26 And Gaal the son of Eved came with his brothers, and went over to Shechem: and the men of Shechem put their confidence in him. 27 And they went out into the fields, and gathered their vineyards, and trode the grapes, and made glad, and went into the bayit of their elohim, and did eat and drink, and cursed Avimelech. 28 And Gaal the son of Eved said, Who is Avimelech, and who is Shechem, that we should serve him? Is not he the son of Yahrubaal? And is not Tzevul his officer? Serve the men of Chamor the abba of Shechem! But why should we serve him? 29 And would to Elohim this people were under my hand! Then would I remove Avimelech. And he said to Avimelech, Increase your army, and come out. 30 And when Tzevul the ruler of the city

heard the words of Gaal the son of Eved, his anger was kindled. 31 And he sent messengers to Avimelech privately, saying, See, Gaal the son of Eved and his brothers have come to Shechem; and, see, they fortify the city against you. 32 Now therefore go up by night, you and the people that are with you, and lie in wait in the field: 33 And it shall be, that in the morning, as soon as the sun is up, you shall rise early, and set upon the city: and, see, when he and the people that are with him come out against you, then may you do to them as you shall find occasion. 34 And Avimelech rose up, and all the people that were with him, by night, and they laid wait against Shechem in four companies. 35 And Gaal the son of Eved went out, and stood in the entrance of the gate of the city: and Avimelech rose up, and the people that were with him, from lying in wait. 36 And when Gaal saw the people, he said to Tzevul, See, there come people down from the top of the mountains. And Tzevul said to him, You see the shadow of the mountains as if they were men. 37 And Gaal spoke again and said, See; there comes people down by the middle of the land, and another company comes along by the plain of Meonenim. 38 Then said Tzevul to him, Where is now your mouth, with what you said, Who is Avimelech, that we should serve him? Is not this the people that you have despised? Go out now, I tell you, and fight with them. 39 And Gaal went out before the men of Shechem, and fought with Avimelech. 40 And Avimelech chased him, and he fled before him, and many were overthrown and wounded, even to the entrance of the gate. 41 And Avimelech dwelt at Arumah: and Tzevul thrust out Gaal and his brothers, so that they should not dwell in Shechem. 42 And it came to pass in the morning that the people went out into the field; and they told Avimelech. 43 And he took the people, and divided them into three companies, and laid wait in the field, and looked, and the people had come forth out of the city; and he rose up

---

[1] The fruit of rebellion is corruption, death, and the devouring one of another.

against them, and smote them. 44 And Avimelech, and the company that was with him, rushed forward, and stood in the entrance of the gate of the city: and the two other companies ran upon all the people that were in the fields, and killed them. 45 And Avimelech fought against the city all that day; and he took the city, and killed the people that were in it, and beat down the city, and sowed it with salt. 46 And when all the men of the tower of Shechem heard that, they entered into a stronghold of the bayit of the El-Berith. 47 And it was told Avimelech, that all the men of the tower of Shechem were gathered together. 48 And Avimelech went up to Mount Tzalmon, he and all the people that were with him; and Avimelech took an axe in his hand, and cut down a branch from the eytzim, and took it, and laid it on his shoulder, and said to the people that were with him, What you have seen me do, hurry up, and do as I have done. 49 And all the people likewise cut down every man his branch, and followed Avimelech, and put them to the stronghold, and set the stronghold on fire above them, so that all the men of the tower of Shechem died also, about a thousand men and women. 50 Then went Avimelech to Thevez, and encamped against Thevez, and took it. 51 But there was a strong tower within the city, and there fled all the men and women, and all those of the city, and shut it to them, and they got up to the top of the tower. 52 And Avimelech came to the tower, and fought against it, and approached the door of the tower to burn it with fire. 53 And a certain woman dropped a piece of millstone upon Avimelech's head, and crushed his skull. 54 Then he called quickly to the young man his armor bearer, and said to him, Draw your sword, and kill me, that men say not of me that, A woman killed him. And his young man thrust him through, and he died. 55 And when the men of Yisrael saw that Avimelech was dead, they departed every man to his place. 56 So Elohim repaid the wickedness to Avimelech, which he did to his abba, in killing his seventy brothers: 57 And all the evil of the men of Shechem did Elohim repay upon their heads: and upon them came the curse of Yotham the son of Yahrubaal.

10 And after Avimelech there arose to defend Yisrael Tola the son of Puah, the son of Dodo, a man of Yissacher; and he dwelt in Shamir in Mount Ephraim. 2 And he gave mishpat to Yisrael twenty-three years, and died, and was buried in Shamir. 3 And after him arose Yair, a Gileadite, and gave mishpat to Yisrael twenty-two years. 4 And he had thirty sons that rode on thirty donkey colts, and they had thirty cities, which are called Chavoth-Yair to this day, which are in the land of Gilead. 5 And Yair died, and was buried in Camon. 6 And the children of Yisrael did evil again in the sight of יהוה, and served the Baalim, and Ashtaroth, and the elohim of Aram, and the elohim of Tzidon, and the elohim of Moav, and the elohim of the children of Ammon, and the elohim of the Philistines, and forsook יהוה, and did not serve Him. 7 And the anger of יהוה was hot against Yisrael, and He sold them into the hands of the Philistines, and into the hands of the children of Ammon. 8 And that year they crushed and oppressed the children of Yisrael: eighteen years, all the children of Yisrael that were on the other side of the Yarden River in the land of the Amorites, which is in Gilead. 9 Moreover the children of Ammon passed over the Yarden River to fight also against Yahudah, and against Benyamin, and against the bayit of Ephraim; so that Yisrael was very distressed. 10 And the children of Yisrael cried to יהוה, saying, We have sinned against you, both because we have forsaken our Elohim, and also served the Baalim. 11 And יהוה said to the children of Yisrael, *Did not I deliver you from the Mitzrites, and from the Amorites, from the children of Ammon, and from the Philistines? 12 The*

Tzidonians also, and the Amalekites, and the Maonites, did oppress you; and you cried to Me, and I delivered you out of their hand. 13 Yet you have forsaken Me, and served other elohim: therefore I will deliver you no more. 14 Go and cry to the elohim whom you have chosen; let them deliver you in the time of your tribulation.¹ 15 And the children of Yisrael said to יהוה, We have sinned: do to us whatever seems tov to You; deliver us only today, we ask You. 16 And they put away the strange elohim from among them, and served יהוה: and His being was grieved for the misery of Yisrael. 17 Then the children of Ammon were gathered together, and camped in Gilead. And the children of Yisrael assembled themselves together, and camped in Mitzpeh. 18 And the people and princes of Gilead said one to another, What man is he that will begin the fight against the children of Ammon? Let him be the head over all the inhabitants of Gilead.

11 Now Yiphtah the Gileadite was a mighty man of valor, and he was the son of a harlot: and Gilead begat Yiphtah. 2 And Gilead's wife bore him sons; and his wife's sons grew up, and they threw out Yiphtah, and said to him, You shall not inherit in our abba's bayit; for you are the son of a strange woman. 3 Then Yiphtah fled from his brothers, and dwelt in the land of Tov: and there were gathered the am-ha-aretz to Yiphtah, who went out with him. 4 And it came to pass in the process of time, that the children of Ammon made war against Yisrael. 5 And it was so, that when the children of Ammon made war against Yisrael, the zachanim of Gilead went to fetch Yiphtah out of the land of Tov: 6 And they said to Yiphtah, Come, and be our captain, that we may fight with the children of Ammon. 7 And Yiphtah said to the zachanim of Gilead, Did you not hate me, and expel me out of my abba's bayit? And

why have you come to me now when you are in distress? 8 And the zachanim of Gilead said to Yiphtah, Therefore we turn again to you now, that you may go with us, and fight against the children of Ammon, and be our head over all the inhabitants of Gilead. 9 And Yiphtah said to the zachanim of Gilead, If you bring me home again to fight against the children of Ammon, and יהוה deliver them before me, shall I be your head? 10 And the zachanim of Gilead said to Yiphtah, יהוה be witness between us, if we do not obey you according to your words. 11 Then Yiphtah went with the zachanim of Gilead, and the people made him head and captain over them: and Yiphtah uttered all his words before יהוה in Mitzpeh. 12 And Yiphtah sent messengers to the melech of the children of Ammon, saying, What have you to do with me, that you have come against me to fight in my land? 13 And the melech of the children of Ammon answered to the messengers of Yiphtah, Because Yisrael took away my land, when they came up out of Mitzrayim, from Arnon even to Yavvok, and to the Yarden River: now therefore restore those lands again in shalom. 14 And Yiphtah sent messengers again to the melech of the children of Ammon: 15 And said to him, This says Yiphtah, Yisrael took not away the land of Moav, nor the land of the children of Ammon: 16 But when Yisrael came up from Mitzrayim, and walked through the wilderness to the Sea of Reeds, and came to Kadesh; 17 Then Yisrael sent messengers to the melech of Edom, saying, Let me, I ask you, pass through your land: but the melech of Edom would not shema. And in like manner they sent to the melech of Moav: but he would not consent: and Yisrael stayed in Kadesh. 18 Then they went along through the wilderness, and around the land of Edom, and the land of Moav, and came by the east side of the land of Moav, and pitched on the other side of Arnon, but did not go within the border of Moav: for Arnon was the

¹ Dual application in both the historic setting and also to both houses, as they enter the Great Tribulation.

border of Moav. 19 And Yisrael sent messengers to Sihon melech of the Amorites, the melech of Cheshbon; and Yisrael said to him, Let us pass, we ask you, through your land into my place. 20 But Sihon trusted not Yisrael to pass through his border: but Sihon gathered all his people together, and pitched in Yahaz, and fought against Yisrael. 21 And יהוה Elohim of Yisrael delivered Sihon and all his people into the hand of Yisrael, and they smote them: so Yisrael possessed all the land of the Amorites, the inhabitants of that country. 22 And they possessed all the borders of the Amorites, from Arnon even to Javvok, and from the wilderness even to the Yarden River. 23 So now יהוה Elohim of Yisrael has dispossessed the Amorites from before His people Yisrael, and should you possess it? 24 Will not you possess that which Chemosh your elohim gives you to possess? So anyone יהוה our Elohim shall drive out from before us, them will we possess. 25 And now are you any better or different than Balaq the son of Tzippor, melech of Moav? Did he ever strive against Yisrael, or did he ever fight against them, 26 While Yisrael dwelt in Cheshbon and her towns, and in Aroer and her towns, and in all the cities that are along the borders of Arnon, three hundred years? Why therefore did you not recover them within that time? 27 So I have not sinned against you, but you do me wrong to war against me: יהוה the Shophet is Shophet this day between the children of Yisrael and the children of Ammon. 28 However the melech of the children of Ammon listened not to the words of Yiphtah who he sent him. 29 Then the Ruach of יהוה came upon Yiphtah, and he passed over Gilead, and Menashsheh, and passed over Mitzpeh of Gilead, and from Mitzpeh of Gilead he passed over to the children of Ammon. 30 And Yiphtah made a vow to יהוה, and said, If You shall without fail deliver the children of Ammon into my hands, 31 Then it shall be, that whatever comes forth from the doors of my bayit to meet me, when I return in shalom from the children of Ammon, shall surely belong to יהוה, and I will offer it up for a burnt offering. 32 So Yiphtah passed over to the children of Ammon to fight against them; and יהוה delivered them into his hands. 33 And he smote them from Aroer, even until Minnith, even twenty cities, and also the plain of the vineyards, with a very great slaughter. So the children of Ammon were subdued before the children of Yisrael. 34 And Yiphtah came to Mitzpeh to his bayit, and, see, his daughter came out to meet him with timbrels and with dancing: and she was his only child; beside her he had neither son nor daughter. 35 And it came to pass, when he saw her, that he tore his clothes, and said, Oy oy, my daughter! You have brought me into depression, and you are one of them that cause me trouble: for I have opened my mouth to יהוה, and I cannot go back on my word. 36 And she said to him, My abba, if you have opened your mouth to יהוה, do to me according to that which has proceeded out of your mouth; because יהוה has taken vengeance for you of your enemies, even the children of Ammon. 37 And she said to her abba, Let this thing be done for me: leave me alone for two months, that I may wander upon the mountains, and bewail my virginity, my friends and I. 38 And he said, Go. And he sent her away for two months: and she went with her chaverim, and bewailed her virginity upon the mountains. 39 And it came to pass at the end of two months, that she returned to her abba, who did with her according to his vow which he had made:[1] and she knew no man. And it was a custom in Yisrael, 40 That the daughters of Yisrael went yearly to mourn

---

[1] This is not about human sacrifice. This is about keeping vows to YHWH. The point being that YHWH can deliver your enemies without you putting your foot in your mouth. Once the vow was made, eternal binding Torah principles kicked in which were irreversible. Moreover, nowhere does the text state that YHWH required the daughter as a human sacrifice. Rather that YHWH accepted the vow to receive the daughter in some fashion, not necessarily in the fashion or manner in which Jephtah offered her to YHWH.

the daughter of Yiphtah the Gileadite four days every year.

12 And the men of Ephraim gathered themselves together, and went northward, and said to Yiphtah, Why then did you pass over to fight against the children of Ammon, and did not call us to go with you? We will burn your bayit upon you with fire.[1] 2 And Yiphtah said to them, my people and I were all in great strife with the children of Ammon, and when I called you, you delivered me not out of their hands. 3 And when I saw that you delivered me not, I put my chayim in my hands, and passed over against the children of Ammon, and **יהוה** delivered them into my hand: why then have you come up to me this day, to fight against me? 4 Then Yiphtah gathered together all the men of Gilead, and fought with Ephraim: and the men of Gilead smote Ephraim, because they said, You Gileadites are fugitives of Ephraim, as Ephraimites, living among the people of Menashsheh.[2] 5 And the Gileadites took the passages of of the Yarden River before the Ephraimites: and it was so, that when those Ephraimites who had escaped said, Let me go over; that the men of Gilead said to him, Are you an Ephraimite? If he said, No; 6 Then they said to him, Say now the word Shivoleth: and he said Sivoleth: for if he could not pronounce it right;[3] they took him, and killed him at the passages of the Yarden River: and there fell at that time of the Ephraimites forty-two thousand. 7 And Yiphtah gave mishpat to Yisrael six years. Then Yiphtah the Gileadite died, and was buried in one of the cities of Gilead. 8 And after him Ivzan of Beth-Lechem gave

mishpat to Yisrael. 9 And he had thirty sons, and thirty daughters, whom he sent abroad, and took in thirty daughters from abroad for his sons. And he gave mishpat to Yisrael seven years. 10 Then died Ivzan, and was buried at Beth-Lechem. 11 And after him Elon, a Zevulonite, gave mishpat to Yisrael; and he gave mishpat to Yisrael ten years. 12 And Elon the Zevulonite died, and was buried in Aiyalon in the country of Zevulun. 13 And after him Avdon the son of Hillel, a Pirathonite, gave mishpat to Yisrael. 14 And he had forty sons and thirty nephews who rode on seventy donkey colts: and he gave mishpat to Yisrael eight years. 15 And Avdon the son of Hillel the Pirathonite died, and was buried in Pirathon in the land of Ephraim, in the Mount of the Amalekites.

13 And the children of Yisrael did evil again in the sight of **יהוה**; and **יהוה** delivered them into the hand of the Philistines for forty years. 2 And there was a certain man of Tzorah, of the mishpocha of the Danites, whose name was Manoah; and his wife was barren, and bore not. 3 And the Malach- **יהוה** appeared to the woman, and said to her, *See now, you are barren, and bear not: but you shall conceive, and bear a son. 4 Now therefore beware, I tell you, and drink no wine or strong drink, and eat not any unkosher-unclean thing: 5 For, look, you shall conceive, and bear a son; and no razor shall come on his head: for the child shall be a Nazarite to Elohim from the womb: and he shall begin to deliver Yisrael out of the hand of the Philistines.* 6 Then the woman came and told her husband, saying, A Man of Elohim came to me, and His countenance was like the countenance of a heavenly messenger of Elohim, very awesome: but I asked him not from where He was, neither did He tell me His Name: 7 But He said to me, See, you shall conceive, and bear a son; and now drink no wine or strong drink, neither eat any

---

[1] This trait as stated earlier, is a battle within Ephraim that manifests against others including Yahudah when he feels neglected and left out, or when his inferiority complex kicks in. This trait is still found in Ephraimites today. It is designed to be removed only by Moshiach Yahshua, as ordained by Abba-YHWH.
[2] Ephraim enters civil strife with other tribes in Yisrael. We see this unrest in an embryonic stage, even before the actual division of the nation some 400 years later.
[3] Apparently different dialects had set in, even amongst the different tribes.

unkosher-unclean thing: for the child shall be a Nazarite to Elohim from the womb to the day of his death. 8 Then Manoah intreated יהוה, and said, O My Master, let the Man of Elohim that You did send come again to us, and teach us what we shall do for the child that shall be born. 9 And Elohim listened to the voice of Manoah; and the Malach-Elohim came again to the woman as she sat in the field: but Manoah her husband was not with her. 10 And the woman hurried, and ran, and showed her husband, and said to him, See, the Man has appeared to me again, that came to me the other day. 11 And Manoah arose, and went after his wife, and came to the Man, and said to him, Are You the Man that spoke to the woman? And He said, I AM. 12 And Manoah said, Now let Your words come to pass. How shall we bring up the child, and how shall we prepare him? 13 And the Malach-יהוה said to Manoah, *Of all that I said to the woman let her shomer. 14 She may not eat anything that comes from the vine, neither let her drink wine or strong drink, nor eat any unkosher-unclean thing: all that I commanded her let her shomer.* 15 And Manoah said to the Malach-יהוה, I ask You, let us detain You, until we shall have made ready a young goat for You. 16 And the Malach-יהוה said to Manoah, *Though you detain Me, I will not eat of your lechem: and if you will offer a burnt offering, you must offer it to יהוה.* [1] For Manoah knew not that He was the Malach-יהוה. 17 And Manoah said to the Malach-יהוה, What is Your Name, that when Your sayings come to pass we may do You honor? 18 And the Malach-יהוה said to him, *Why do you ask My Name, seeing it is secret-sod?* [2] 19 So Manoah took a young goat with a meat offering, and offered it upon a rock to יהוה: and the Malach -יהוה gave hallel to יהוה; and Manoah and his

wife looked on. [3] 20 For it came to pass, when the flame went up toward the shamayim from off the altar that the Malach-יהוה ascended in the flame of the altar. And Manoah and his wife looked on it, and fell on their faces to the ground. 21 But the Malach- יהוה did not appear again to Manoah and to his wife. Then Manoah knew that He was the Malach-יהוה. 22 And Manoah said to his wife, We shall surely die, because we have seen Elohim. [4] 23 But his wife said to him, If יהוה had desired to kill us, He would not have received a burnt offering and a meat offering at our hands, neither would He have showed us all these things, nor would He at this time have told us such things as these. [5] 24 And the woman bore a son, and called his name Shimshon: and the child grew, and יהוה blessed him. 25 And the Ruach of יהוה began to move him at times in the camp of Dan between Tzorah and Eshtaol.

14

And Shimshon went down to Timnath, and saw a woman in Timnath of the daughters of the Philistines. 2 And he came up, and told his abba and his ima, and said, I have seen a woman in Timnath of the daughters of the Philistines: now therefore get her for me as my wife. [6] 3 Then his abba and his ima said to him, Is there not a woman among the daughters of your brothers, or among all my people, that you go to take a wife of the uncircumcised Philistines? And Shimshon said to his abba, Get her for me; for she pleases me well. 4 But his abba and his ima knew not that it was from יהוה, that He sought an occasion against the Philistines: for at that time the Philistines had dominion over Yisrael. 5 Then Shimshon went down, and his abba and his ima, to Timnath, and came to the

---

[3] The Son worshiping His Father.
[4] They knew this was no ordinary messenger.
[5] Women in Yisrael are often more spiritually discerned and sensitive than the men who trust YHWH.
[6] A head-start to trouble. Torah is clear. Nazarene Yisraelites must not marry outside of the faith, or even outside of those who dwell with Yisrael in their daily lifestyle.

---

[1] Yahshua directing all worship to His Father; His Elohim, even as He did in the Renewed Covenant.
[2] A temporary secret to be revealed only in the fullness of times.

vineyards of Timnath: and, see, a young lion roared against him. 6 And the Ruach of יהוה came mightily upon him, and he tore him as he would have torn a young goat, and he had nothing in his hand: but he told not his abba or his ima what he had done. 7 And he went down, and talked with the woman; and she pleased Shimshon well. 8 And after a time he returned to take her, and he turned aside to see the carcase of the lion: and, see, there was a swarm of bees and honey in the carcase of the lion. 9 And he took some of it in his hands, and went on eating, and came to his abba and ima, and he gave them, and they did eat: but he told them not that he had taken the honey out of the carcase of the lion. 10 So his abba went down to the woman: and Shimshon made there a feast; for this is what the young men used to do. 11 And it came to pass, when they saw him that they brought thirty chaverim to be with him. 12 And Shimshon said to them, I will now put forth a riddle to you: if you can certainly declare it to me within the seven days of the feast, and find out the answer, then I will give you thirty sheets and thirty changes of garments: 13 But if you cannot declare it me, then shall you give me thirty sheets and thirty changes of garments. And they said to him, Put forth your riddle, that we may shema it. 14 And he said to them, Out of the eater came forth meat, and out of the strong came forth sweetness. And they could not in three days expound the riddle. 15 And it came to pass on the seventh day, that they said to Shimshon's wife, Entice your husband, that he may declare to us the riddle, lest we burn you and your abba's bayit with fire: have you called us to take that we have? Is it not so? 16 And Shimshon's wife wept before him, and said, You hate me, and love me not: you have put forth a riddle to the children of my people, and have not told it me. And he said to her, See, I have not told it my abba nor to my ima, and shall I tell it you? 17 And she wept before him the seven days, while their feast lasted: and it came to

pass on the seventh day, that he told her, because she pressed him: and she told the riddle to the children of her people. 18 And the men of the city said to him on the seventh day before the sun went down, What is sweeter than honey? And what is stronger than a lion? And he said to them, If you had not plowed with my heifer, you would have not found out my riddle. 19 And the Ruach of יהוה came upon him, and he went down to Ashkelon, and killed thirty men there, and took their spoil, and gave changes of garments to those who expounded the riddle. And his anger was kindled, and he went up to his abba's bayit. 20 But Shimshon's wife was given to his companion, who used to be his chaver.

15 But it came to pass after some time, in the time of Shavout, that Shimshon visited his wife with a young goat; and he said, I will go into my wife in the bedroom. But her abba would not allow him to go in. 2 And her abba said, I truly thought that you had utterly hated her; therefore I gave her to your chaver: is not her younger sister prettier than her? Take her, I ask you, instead of her. 3 And Shimshon said concerning them, Now this time I will be blameless regarding the Philistines, if I do them evil. 4 And Shimshon went and caught three hundred foxes, and took torches, and turned tail to tail, and put a firebrand in the midst between two tails. 5 And when he had set the torches on fire, he let them go into the standing corn of the Philistines, and burnt up both the shocks, and also the standing corn, with the vineyards and olives. 6 Then the Philistines said, Who has done this? And they answered, Shimshon, the son-in-law of the Timnite, because he had taken his wife, and given her to his chaver. And the Philistines came up, and burnt her and her abba with fire. 7 And Shimshon said to them, Though you have done this, yet will I be avenged of you, and after that I will

cease. 8 And he smote them hip and thigh[1] with a great slaughter: and he went down and dwelt in the cleft of the rock Eytam. 9 Then the Philistines went up, and pitched in Yahudah, and spread out in Lehi. 10 And the men of Yahudah said, Why have you come up against us? And they answered, To bind Shimshon have we come up, to do to him as he has done to us. 11 Then three thousand men of Yahudah went to the top of the rock Eytam, and said to Shimshon, You know not that the Philistines are rulers over us? What is this that you have done to us? And he said to them, As they did to me, so have I done to them. 12 And they said to him, We have come down to bind you so that we may deliver you into the hand of the Philistines. And Shimshon said to them, Swear to me, that you will not fall upon me yourselves. 13 And they spoke to him, saying, No; but we will bind you hard, and deliver you into their hand: but surely we will not kill you. And they bound him with two new cords, and brought him up from the rock. 14 And when he came to Lehi, the Philistines shouted against him: and the Ruach of יהוה came mightily upon him, and the cords that were upon his arms became as linen that was burnt with fire, and his bands were loosed from off his hands. 15 And he found a new jawbone of a donkey, and put forth his hand, and took it, and killed a thousand men with it. 16 And Shimshon said, With the jawbone of a donkey, one heap, two heaps; with the jaw of a donkey have I slain a thousand men. 17 And it came to pass, when he had made an end of speaking, that he cast away the jawbone out of his hand, and called that place Ramath-Lehi. 18 And he was very thirsty, he called on יהוה, and said, You have given this great deliverance into the hand of Your eved: and now shall I die for thirst, and fall into the hands of the uncircumcised? 19 But Elohim split a hollow place that was in the Lehi, and there came mayim out; and when he had drunk, his ruach came again, and he revived: therefore he called the name of it En-Chakkore, which is in Lehi to this day. 20 And he gave mishpat to Yisrael in the days of the Philistines twenty years.

16 Then went Shimshon to Gaza, and saw there a harlot, and went into her. 2 And it was told the Gazites, saying, Shimshon is come here. And they surrounded him in, and lay in wait for him all night in the gate of the city, and were quiet all the night, saying, In the morning, when it is day, we shall kill him. 3 And Shimshon lay until midnight, and arose at midnight, and took the doors of the gate of the city, and the two posts, and went away with them, bar and all, and put them upon his shoulders, and carried them up to the top of a hill that is before Hevron. 4 And it came to pass afterward, that he loved a woman in the Valley of Sorek, whose name was Delilah. 5 And the rulers of the Philistines came up to her, and said to her, Entice him, and see where his great strength lies, and by what means we may prevail against him, that we may bind him to afflict him: and we will give you every one of us eleven hundred pieces of silver. 6 And Delilah said to Shimshon, Tell me, I ask you, where does your great strength lie, and with what and how might you be bound in order to afflict you. 7 And Shimshon said to her, If they bind me with seven fresh cords that were never dried, then shall I be weak, and be like any another man. 8 Then rulers of the Philistines brought up to her seven fresh cords that had not been dried, and she bound him with them. 9 Now there were men lying in wait, abiding with her in the bedroom. And she said to him, The Philistines be upon you, Shimshon. And he broke the cords, as a strand of yarn is broken when it touches the fire. So his strength was not known. 10 And Delilah said to Shimshon, See, you have mocked me, and told me lies: now tell me, I ask you,

---

[1] A Hebraic idiomatic expression meaning: completely, or fully.

with what might you be bound. 11 And he said to her, If they bind me tightly with new ropes that never were used, then shall I be weak, and be as another man. 12 Delilah therefore took new ropes, and bound him, and said to him, The Philistines be upon you, Shimshon. And there were those lying in wait abiding in the bedroom. And he broke them from off his arms like a thread. 13 And Delilah said to Shimshon, Until now you have mocked me, and told me lies: tell me with what you might be bound. And he said to her, If you weave the seven locks of my head with the web. 14 And she tightened it with the pin, and said to him, The Philistines be upon you, Shimshon. And he awoke out of his sleep, and went away with the pin of the loom, and with the web. 15 And she said to him, How can you say, I love you, when your lev is not with me? You have mocked me these three times, and have not told me where your great strength lies. 16 And it came to pass, when she pressed him daily with her words, and urged him, so that his being was wearied to death; 17 That he told her all his lev, and said to her. There has not come a razor upon my head; for I have been a Nazarite to Elohim from my ima's womb: if I am shaved, then my strength will go from me, and I shall become weak, and be like any other man. 18 And when Delilah saw that he had told her all his lev, she sent and called for the rulers of the Philistines, saying, Come up at once, for he has shown me all his lev. Then the rulers of the Philistines came up to her, and brought money in their hands. 19 And she made him sleep upon her knees; and she called for a man, and she caused him to shave off the seven locks of his head; and she began to afflict him, and his strength went from him. 20 And she said, The Philistines be upon you, Shimshon. And he awoke out of his sleep, and said, I will go about things as at other times before, and simply shake myself. But he did not know that יהוה had departed from him. 21 But the Philistines

took him, and put out his eyes, and brought him down to Gaza, and bound him with bronze shackles; and he became a grinder in the prison bayit. 22 However the hair of his head began to grow again after he had been shaven. 23 Then rulers of the Philistines gathered together to offer a great sacrifice to Dagon their elohim, and to make gilah: for they said, Our elohim has delivered Shimshon our enemy into our hands. 24 And when the people saw him, they praised their elohim: for they said, Our elohim has delivered into our hands our enemy, and the destroyer of our country, who killed many of us. 25 And it came to pass, when their levim were glad, that they said, Call for Shimshon, that he may entertain us. And they called for Shimshon out of the prison bayit; and he entertained them: and they set him between the pillars. 26 And Shimshon said to the lad that held him by the hand, Allow me that I may feel the pillars upon which the bayit stands, that I may lean upon them. 27 Now the bayit was full of men and women; and all the rulers of the Philistines were there; and there were upon the roof about three thousand men and women, who beheld while Shimshon entertained them. 28 And Shimshon called to יהוה, and said, O יהוה Elohim, remember me, I ask You, and strengthen me, I ask You, only this once, O Elohim, that I may be avenged of the Philistines for my two eyes. 29 And Shimshon took hold of the two middle pillars upon which the bayit stood, and on which it was supported, one with his right hand, and the other with his left.[1] 30 And Shimshon said, Let me die with the Philistines. And he bowed himself with all his might; and the bayit fell upon the rulers, and upon all the people that were in it. So those who he killed at his death were more

---

[1] A beautiful type of Yisrael, called to be separate from their birth at Sinai, just like Samson the Nazarite, that had gone whoring after other elohim in spiritual adultery and becoming fully blind to the things of YHWH, forcing YHWH to remove His favor and His Ruach HaKodesh, causing both houses symbolized by both pillars to bring the entire house of Yisrael to ruin.

than those that he killed in his chayim. 31 Then his brothers and all the bayit of his abba came down, and took him, and brought him up, and buried him between Tzorah and Eshtaol in the burying place of Manoah his abba. And he gave mishpat to Yisrael twenty years.

17 And there was a man of Mount Ephraim, whose name was Michayahu. 2 And he said to his ima, The eleven hundred shekels of silver that were taken from you, about which you cursed, and spoke of also in my ears, see, the silver is with me; I took it. And his ima said, Blessed are you of יהוה, my son. 3 And when he had restored the eleven hundred shekels of silver to his ima, his ima said, I had wholly dedicated the silver to יהוה from my hand for my son, to make a graven image and a molded image: now therefore I will restore it to you. 4 Yet he restored the money to his ima; and his ima took two hundred shekels of silver, and gave them to the silversmith, who made it into a graven image and a molded image: and they were in the bayit of Michayahu. 5 And the man Michayahu had a bayit of elohim, and made an ephod, and teraphim, and consecrated one of his sons, who became his kohen.[1] 6 In those days there was no melech in Yisrael, but every man did that which was right in his own eyes. 7 And there was a young man out of Beth-Lechem Yahudah of the mishpocha of Yahudah, who was a Levite, and he sojourned there. 8 And the man departed out of the city from Beth-Lechem Yahudah to sojourn where he could find a place: and he came to Mount Ephraim to the bayit of Michayahu, as he journeyed. 9 And Michayahu said to him, From where do you come? And he said to him, I am a Levite of Beth-Lechem Yahudah, and I went to sojourn where I may find a place. 10 And Michayahu said to him, Dwell with me, and be to me an abba

and a kohen, and I will give you ten shekels of silver for the year, and a suit of apparel, and your food. So ha Levi went in.[2] 11 And ha Levi was content to dwell with the man; and the young man was to him as one of his sons. 12 And Michayahu consecrated ha Levi; and the young man became his kohen, and was in the bayit of Michayahu. 13 Then said Michayahu, Now I know that יהוה will do me tov, seeing I have a Levite as my kohen.

18 In those days there was no melech in Yisrael: and in those days the tribe of the Danites sought an inheritance to dwell in; for until that day all their inheritance had not yet fallen to them among the tribes of Yisrael. 2 And the children of Dan sent of their mishpocha five men from their borders, men of valor, from Tzorah, and from Eshtaol, to spy out the land, and to search it; and they said to them, Go, search the land: who when they came to Mount Ephraim, to the bayit of Michayahu, they lodged there. 3 When they were by the bayit of Michayahu, they knew the voice of the young man ha Levi: and they turned in there, and said to him, Who brought you here? And what are you making in this place? And what have you here? 4 And he said to them, Michayahu did such and such with me, and has hired me, and I am his kohen. 5 And they said to him, Ask counsel, we ask you, of Elohim, that we may know whether our way which we go shall be prosperous. 6 And the kohen said to them, Go in shalom: before יהוה, is your journey in which you go. 7 Then the five men departed, and came to Layish, and saw the people that were in it, how they dwelt careless, after the manner of the Tzidonians, quiet and secure; and there was no civil authority in the land, that might put them to shame in any wrong thing and they were far from the Tzidonians, and had kept to

---

[1] A nice Ephraimite religion, void of YHWH's counsel and mind.

[2] We'll see this again later. Part of Ephraim's appeal to Yahudah was to come north and be priests for Jeroboam's new calendar and holidays, as Ephraim Yisrael wandered further and further away from YHWH.

themselves. 8 And they came to their brothers to Tzorah and Eshtaol: and their brothers said to them, What say you? 9 And they said, Arise, that we may go up against them: for we have seen the land, and, see, it is very tov: and are you standing still? Be not lazy to go, and enter to possess the land. 10 When you go, you shall come to a people secure, and to a large land: for Elohim has given it into your hands; a place where there is no want of anything that is in the earth. 11 And there went from there from the mishpocha of the Danites, out of Tzorah and out of Eshtaol, six hundred men appointed with weapons of war. 12 And they went up, and pitched in Kiryath-Yearim, in Yahudah: wherefore they called that place Machaneh-Dan to this day: see, it is behind Kiryath-Yearim. 13 And they passed there to Mount Ephraim, and came to the bayit of Michayahu. 14 Then answered the five men that went to spy out the country of Layish, and said to their brothers, Do you know that there is among these houses an ephod, and teraphim, and a graven image, and a molded image? Now therefore consider what you have to do. 15 And they turned aside, and came to the bayit of the young man ha Levi, even to the bayit of Michayahu, and saluted him. 16 And the six hundred men appointed with their weapons of war, which were of the children of Dan, stood by the entrance of the gate. 17 And the five men that went to spy out the land went up, and came in there, and took the graven image, and the ephod, and the teraphim, and the molded image: and the kohen stood in the entrance of the gate with the six hundred men that were appointed with weapons of war. 18 And these went into Michayahu's bayit, and fetched the carved image, the ephod, and the teraphim, and the molded image. Then said the kohen to them, What are you doing? 19 And they said to him, Hold your silence, lay your hand upon your mouth, and go with us, and be to us an abba and a kohen: is it better for you to be a kohen to

the bayit of one man, or that you be a kohen to a whole tribe and a mishpocha in Yisrael?[1] 20 And the kohen's lev was in simcha, and he took the ephod, and the teraphim, and the graven image, and went out in the midst of the people. 21 So they turned and departed, and put the little ones and the cattle and the carriage before them. 22 And when they were a certain distance from the bayit of Michayahu, the men that were in the houses near to Michayahu's bayit were gathered together, and overtook the children of Dan. 23 And they cried to the children of Dan. And they turned their faces, and said to Michayahu, What's wrong with you, that you come with such a company? 24 And he said, You have taken away my elohim that I made, and the kohen, and you are gone away: and what have I left? And now you say to me, What bothers you? 25 And the children of Dan said to him, Let not your voice be heard among us, lest angry fellows come upon you, and you lose your chayim, with the chayim of your household.[2] 26 And the children of Dan went their way: and when Michayahu saw that they were too strong for him, he turned and went back to his bayit. 27 And they took the things that Michayahu had made, and the kohen that he had, and came to Layish, to a people that were in shalom and secure: and they smote those people with the edge of the sword, and burnt the city with fire. 28 And there was no deliverer, because it was far from Tzidon, and they had no business with any man; and it was in the valley that lies near Beth-Rechov. And they built a city, and dwelt in it. 29 And they called the name of the city Dan, after

---

[1] Dan, seeing Ephraim's little "in-house setup," was impressed, and demanded that the false priest relocate, offering him a bigger ministry with a better salary, even though it would be false worship. Today not much has changed, as many of Dan and Ephraim's sons seek crowds and vain reputation, rather than truth and heavenly treasures.
[2] A sad and yet somewhat humorous fight between Ephraim and Dan, over who gets to control the idolatry and rebellion against YHWH. We see this again later after the split of the two houses, when Ephraim demanded to control the false worship, and wound up putting one of two golden calves in Dan to please Dan's desire to lead in the north's abominations before YHWH.

the name of Dan their abba, who was born to Yisrael: but the name of the city was Layish first.[1] 30 And the children of Dan set up the graven image: and Yahonathan, the son of Gershom, the son of Menashsheh, he and his sons were kohanim to the tribe of Dan until the day of the captivity of the land. 31 And they set them up Michayahu's graven image, which he made, all the time that the Bayit of Elohim was in Shiloh.

19 And it came to pass in those days, when there was no melech in Yisrael, that there was a certain Levite sojourning on the side of Mount Ephraim, who took to him a concubine out of Beth-Lechem Yahudah. 2 And his concubine played the whore against him, and went away from him to her abba's bayit to Beth-Lechem Yahudah, and was there four whole months. 3 And her husband arose, and went after her, to speak friendly to her, and to bring her again, having his eved with him, and a couple of donkeys: and she brought him into her abba's bayit: and when the abba of the woman saw him, he gilahed to meet him. 4 And his abba-in-law, the woman's abba, retained him; and he stayed with him three days: so they did eat and drink, and lodged there. 5 And it came to pass on the fourth day, when they arose early in the morning, that he rose up to depart: and the woman's abba said to his son-in-law, Comfort your lev with a morsel of lechem, and afterward go your way. 6 And they sat down, and did eat and drink both of them together: for the woman's abba had said to the man, Be content, I ask you, and stay all night, and let your lev be glad. 7 And when the man rose up to depart, his abba-in-law urged him to stay: therefore he lodged there again. 8 And he arose early in the morning on the fifth day to depart: and the woman's abba said, Comfort your lev, I ask you. And they tarried until afternoon, and they did eat both of them. 9 And when

the man rose up to depart, he, and his concubine, and his eved, his abba-in-law, the woman's abba, said to him, See, now the day draws toward evening, I ask you stay all night: see, the day grows to an end, lodge here, that your lev may be glad; and in the morning go early on your way, that you may go home. 10 But the man would not stay that night, but he rose up and departed, and came over against Yevus, which is Yahrushalayim; and there were with him two donkeys saddled, his concubine also was with him. 11 And when they were by Yevus, the day was almost over; and the eved said to his master, Come, I ask you, and let us turn in into this city of the Yevusites, and lodge in it. 12 And his master said to him, We will not turn aside here into the city of a Ger that is not of the children of Yisrael; we will pass over to Giveah. 13 And he said to his eved, Come, and let us draw near to one of these places to lodge all night, in Giveah, or in Ramah. 14 And they passed on and went their way; and the sun went down upon them when they were by Giveah, which belongs to Benyamin. 15 And they turned aside there, to go in and to lodge in Giveah: and when he went in, he sat down in a street of the city: for there was no man that took them into his bayit for lodging. 16 And, see, there came an old man from his work out of the field at evening, which was also of Mount Ephraim; and he sojourned in Giveah: but the men of the place were Benyamites. 17 And when he had lifted up his eyes, he saw a wayfaring man in the street of the city: and the old man said, Where are you going? And from where do you come? 18 And he said to him, We are passing from Beth-Lechem Yahudah toward the side of Mount Ephraim; from there am I: and I went to Beth-Lechem Yahudah, but I am now going to the Bayit of יהוה; and there is no man that receives me into his bayit. 19 Yet there is both straw and fodder for our donkeys; and there is lechem and wine also for me, and for your female eved, and

---

[1] This pattern continued, especially as Dan later worked their way west into Europe, where many peoples and places are named after Dan, like the Dan-ish or Dan from Layish.

for the young man who is with your avadim: there is no want of any thing. 20 And the old man said, Shalom be with you; however, let all your wants lie upon me; only lodge not in the street. 21 So he brought him into his bayit, and gave fodder to the donkeys: and they washed their feet, and did eat and drink. 22 Now as they were making their levim glad, see, the men of the city, certain sons of Beliyaal, circled the bayit all around, and beat on the door, and spoke to the master of the bayit, the old man, saying, Bring forth the man that came into your bayit, that we may know him. 23 And the man, the master of the bayit, went out to them, No, my brothers, no, I ask you, do not so wickedly; seeing that this man is come into my bayit, do not this folly. 24 See, here is my daughter a young woman, and this man's concubine; them I will bring out now, and humble them, and do with them what seems tov to you: but to this man do not so vile a thing. 25 But the men would not shema to him: so the man took his concubine, and brought her forth to them; and they knew her, and abused her all the night until the morning: and when the day began to spring, they let her go. 26 Then came the woman in the dawning of the day, and fell down at the door of the man's bayit where her master was, until it was light. 27 And her master rose up in the morning, and opened the doors of the bayit, and went out to go his way: and, see, the woman his concubine was fallen down at the door of the bayit, and her hands were upon the threshold. 28 And he said to her, Up, and let us be going. But none answered. Then the man took her up upon a donkey, and the man rose up, and returned to his place. 29 And when he had come into his bayit, he took a knife, and laid hold on his concubine, and divided her, together with her bones, into twelve pieces, and sent her into all the borders of Yisrael. 30 And it was so, that all that saw it said, There was no such deed done nor seen from the day that the children of Yisrael came up out of

the land of Mitzrayim to this day: consider it, take advice, and speak up.

20 Then all the children of Yisrael went out, and the congregation was gathered together as one man, from Dan even to Beer-Sheva, with the land of Gilead, to יהוה in Mitzpeh. 2 And the leaders of all the people, even of all the tribes of Yisrael, presented themselves in the congregation of the people of Elohim, four hundred thousand footmen that drew the sword. 3 Now the children of Benyamin heard that the children of Yisrael had gone up to Mitzpeh. Then said the children of Yisrael, Tell us, how was this wickedness done? 4 And ha Levi, the husband of the woman that was slain, answered and said, I came into Giveah that belongs to Benyamin, I and my concubine to lodge. 5 And the men of Giveah rose up against me, and circled the bayit all around and came upon me by night, and thought to have slain me: and my concubine have they sexually forced, so that she is dead. 6 And I took my concubine, and cut her in pieces, and sent her throughout all the country of the inheritance of Yisrael: for they have committed lewdness and folly in Yisrael. 7 See, you are all children of Yisrael; give here your advice and counsel. 8 And all the people arose as one man, saying, We will not any of us go to his tent, neither will any of us return to his bayit. 9 But now this shall be the thing that we will do to Giveah; we will go up by lot against it; 10 And we will take ten men out of a hundred throughout all the tribes of Yisrael, and a hundred out of a thousand, and a thousand out of ten thousand, to fetch food for the people, to prepare them, when they come to Giveah of Benyamin, according to all the folly that they have wrought in Yisrael. 11 So all the men of Yisrael were gathered against the city, knit together as one man. 12 And the tribes of Yisrael sent men through all the tribe of Benyamin, saying, What wickedness is this that is done among

you? 13 Now therefore deliver to us these men, the children of Beliyaal, who are in Giveah, that we may put them to death, and put away the evil from Yisrael. But the children of Benyamin would not shema to the voice of their brothers the children of Yisrael: 14 But the children of Benyamin gathered themselves together out of the cities to Giveah, to go out to battle against the children of Yisrael. 15 And the children of Benyamin were numbered at that time out of the cities twenty six thousand men that drew the sword, besides the inhabitants of Giveah, who were numbered seven hundred chosen men. 16 Among all the people there were seven hundred chosen men left-handed; every one could sling stones at a hair's width, and not miss. 17 And the men of Yisrael, against Benyamin, were numbered four hundred thousand men that drew the sword: all these were men of war. 18 And the children of Yisrael arose, and went up to the Bayit of Elohim, and asked counsel from Elohim, and said, Which of us shall go up first to the battle against the children of Benyamin? And יהוה said, *Yahudah shall go up first.* 19 And the children of Yisrael rose up in the morning, and encamped against Giveah. 20 And the men of Yisrael went out to battle against Benyamin; and the men of Yisrael put themselves in array to fight against them at Giveah. 21 And the children of Benyamin came forth out of Giveah, and cut down to the ground of the Yisraelites that day twenty-two thousand men. 22 And the people the men of Yisrael encouraged themselves, and set their battle again in array in the place where they put themselves in array the first day. 23 And the children of Yisrael went up and wept before יהוה until evening, and asked counsel of יהוה, saying, Shall I go up again to battle against the children of Benyamin my brother? And יהוה said, *Go up against him.* 24 And the children of Yisrael came near to the children of Benyamin the second day. 25 And Benyamin went forth against them

out of Giveah the second day, and cut down to the ground of the children of Yisrael again eighteen thousand men; all these drew the sword. 26 Then all the children of Yisrael, and all the people, went up, and came to the Bayit of Elohim, and wept, and sat there before יהוה, and fasted that day until evening, and offered burnt offerings and shalom offerings before יהוה. 27 And the children of Yisrael inquired of יהוה, for the Ark of the Covenant of Elohim was there in those days, 28 And Pinchus, the son of Eleazar, the son of Aharon, stood before it in those days, saying, Shall I yet again go out to battle against the children of Benyamin my brother, or shall I cease? And יהוה said, *Go up; for tomorrow morning I will deliver them into your hand.* 29 And Yisrael set an ambush in wait around Giveah. 30 And the children of Yisrael went up against the children of Benyamin on the third day, and put themselves in array against Giveah, as at other times. 31 And the children of Benyamin went out against the people, and were drawn away from the city; and they began to smite the people, and kill, as at other times, in the highways, one of which goes up to the Bayit of Elohim, and the other to Giveah in the field, about thirty men of Yisrael. 32 And the children of Benyamin said, They are smitten before us, as the first time. But the children of Yisrael said, Let us flee, and draw them from the city to the highways. 33 And all the men of Yisrael rose up out of their place, and put themselves in array at Baal-Tamar: and the ambushers of Yisrael came forth out of their places, even out of the meadows of Giveah. 34 And there came against Giveah ten thousand chosen men out of kol Yisrael, and the battle was fierce: but they knew not that evil was near them. 35 And יהוה smote Benyamin before Yisrael: and the children of Yisrael destroyed from the Benyamites that day twenty-five thousand one hundred men: all these drew the sword. 36 So the children of Benyamin saw that they were smitten: for the men of Yisrael gave ground to the Benyamites, because they trusted the ambushers that they had set next to Giveah. 37 And the ambushers hurried, and rushed upon Giveah; and the ambushers in wait drew themselves along, and smote the entire city with the edge of the sword. 38 Now there was an appointed sign between the men of Yisrael and the ambushers in wait that they should make a great flame with smoke rising up out of the city. 39 And when the men of Yisrael turned in the battle, Benyamin began to smite and kill of the men of Yisrael about thirty persons: for they said, Surely they are smitten down before us, as in the first battle. 40 But when the flame began to rise up out of the city with a pillar of smoke, the Benyamites looked behind them, and, see, the flame of the city ascended up to the shamayim. 41 And when the men of Yisrael turned again, the men of Benyamin were amazed: for they saw that evil had come upon them. 42 Therefore they turned their backs before the men of Yisrael to the way of the wilderness; but the battle overtook them; and those who came out of the cities they destroyed in the midst of them. 43 They surrounded the Benyamites all around, and chased them, and trampled them down with ease over against Giveah toward the east. 44 And there fell of Benyamin eighteen thousand men; all these were men of valor. 45 And they turned and fled toward the wilderness to the Rock of Rimmon: and they cut down in the highways five thousand men; and pursued hard after them to Gidom, and killed two thousand of them. 46 So that all that fell that day of Benyamin were twenty five thousand men that drew the sword; all these were men of valor. 47 But six hundred men turned and fled to the wilderness to the Rock Rimmon, and stayed in the Rock Rimmon for four months. 48 And the men of Yisrael turned again upon the children of Benyamin, and smote them with the edge of the sword, men and beasts of every city, and all that were

found: also they set fire to all the cities that they came to.[1]

21 Now the men of Yisrael had sworn in Mitzpeh, saying, There shall not any of us give his daughter to Benyamin as a wife. 2 And the people came to the Bayit of Elohim, and stayed there until evening before Elohim, and lifted up their voices, and wept sore; 3 And said, O יהוה Elohim of Yisrael, why is this come to pass in Yisrael, that there should be today one tribe missing in Yisrael? 4 And it came to pass in the morning, that the people rose early, and built there an altar, and offered burnt offerings and shalom offerings. 5 And the children of Yisrael said, Who is there among all the tribes of Yisrael that came not up with the congregation to יהוה? For they had made a great oath concerning him that would not come up to יהוה to Mitzpeh, saying, He shall surely be put to death. 6 And the children of Yisrael repented for what had occurred to Benyamin their brother, and said, There is one tribe cut off from Yisrael this day.[2] 7 What shall we do to give them wives for those that remain, seeing we have sworn by יהוה that we will not give them our daughters as wives? 8 And they said, Which one of the tribes of Yisrael did not come up to Mitzpeh to יהוה? And, see, there came none from Yavesh-Gilead to the congregation.[3] 9 For the people were numbered, and, see, there were none of the inhabitants of Yavesh-Gilead there. 10 And the congregation sent there twelve thousand of the bravest men, and commanded them, saying, Go and smite the inhabitants of Yavesh-Gilead with the edge of the sword, with the women and the children. 11 And this is the thing that you

---

[1] A perfect example of tribal infighting way before the official split.
[2] This ought to be Yahudah's heartfelt cry for any Ephraimites still not present in the congregation of YHWH. Rather than rejoice, they ought to be heartbroken, crying and even looking for the tribes that cut themselves off like Benyamin due to Torah violation.
[3] Yabesh Gilead was east of the Jordan River, and as such housed the tribes of Reuben, Gad and half of Menashshe. Apparently these tribes were missing from the congregation.

shall do, You shall utterly destroy every male, and every woman that has lain with a man. 12 And they found among the inhabitants of Yavesh-Gilead four hundred young virgins, that had known no man by lying with any male: and they brought them to the camp at Shiloh, which is in the land of Kanaan. 13 And the whole congregation sent delegates to speak to the children of Benyamin that were in the Rock Rimmon, and to call to them offering shalom. 14 And Benyamin returned at that time; and the congregation gave them wives that they had saved alive from the women of Yavesh-Gilead: and yet there were more men than women. 15 And the people were sorry for Benyamin, because that יהוה had made a breach in the tribes of Yisrael. 16 Then the zachanim of the congregation said, What shall we do for wives for them that remain, seeing the women are destroyed out of Benyamin? 17 And they said, There must be an inheritance for them that are escaped of Benyamin, that a tribe be not destroyed out of Yisrael. 18 However we may not give them wives of our daughters: for the children of Yisrael have sworn, saying, Cursed be he that gives a wife to Benyamin. 19 Then they said, See, there is a moed of יהוה in Shiloh yearly in a place which is on the north side of Beth-El, on the east side of the highway that goes up from Beth-El to Shechem, and on the south of Levonah.

20 Therefore they commanded the children of Benyamin, saying, Go and lie in wait in the vineyards; 21 And see, if the daughters of Shiloh come out to dance in dances, then come out of the vineyards, and catch every man his wife from the daughters of Shiloh, and go to the land of Benyamin. 22 And it shall be, when their ahvot or their brothers come to us to complain, that we will say to them, Be favorable to them for our sakes: because we reserved not to each man his wife in the war: for you did not give them wives at this time, that you should be guilty.[1] 23 And the children of Benyamin did so, and took wives, according to their number, of those that danced, whom they caught: and they went and returned to their inheritance, and repaired the cities, and dwelt in them. 24 And the children of Yisrael departed from there at that time, every man to his tribe and to his mishpocha, and they went out from there every man to his inheritance. 25 In those days there was no melech in Yisrael: every man did that which was right in his own eyes.

---

[1] The elders found a way around this vow to YHWH, in order to preserve Yisrael. Technically, through this plan, not only was Benjamin preserved in Yisrael, the other tribes did not break their vow by giving the Benjamite men their wives from the other tribes who had not made the vow and who were not in a vow of marriage. The men of Benjamin "took" the wives from Shiloh, so they technically were not given but taken. This great wisdom preserved a tribe on the verge of extinction due to sodomite behavior. Therefore Benjamites today are full of the dom from many other tribes, as is all of Judah, since Benjamin settled in Judah after the split of the kingdom in 921 BCE.

שמואל א

Schmuel Alef - First Samuel
To Our Forefathers Yisrael

1 Now there was a certain male of Ramathayim-Zophim, of Mount Ephraim, and his name was Elchanah, the son of Yeroham, the son of Elihu, the son of Tohu, the son of Zuph, an Ephratite:[1] 2 And he had two wives; the name of the one was Channah, and the name of the other Peninnah: and Peninnah had children, but Channah had no children. 3 And this male went up out of his city yearly to worship and to sacrifice to יהוה of hosts in Shiloh. And the two sons of Eli, Hophni and Phinehas, the kohanim of יהוה, were there. 4 And when the time was that Elchanah made an offering, he gave to Peninnah his wife, and to all her sons and her daughters, portions: 5 But to Channah he gave a double portion; for he loved Channah: but יהוה had shut up her womb. 6 And her adversary also provoked and aggravated her, to make her anxious, because יהוה had shut up her womb. 7 And as he did so year by year, when she went up to the Bayit of יהוה, so she provoked her; therefore she wept, and did not eat.[2] 8 Then said Elchanah her husband to her, Channah, why do you weep? And why do you eat nothing? Also why is your lev grieved? Am I not better to you than ten sons? 9 So Channah rose up after they had eaten in Shiloh, and after they had drunk. Now Eli the kohen sat upon a seat by a post of the Tent of יהוה. 10 And she was in bitterness of chayim, and made tefillah to יהוה, and wept greatly. 11 And she vowed a vow, and said, O יהוה of hosts, if You will indeed look on the affliction of Your female eved, and remember me, and not forget Your female eved, but will give to Your female eved a male child, then I will give him to יהוה all the days of his chayim, and there shall no razor come upon his head.[3] 12 And it came to pass, as she continued making tefillah before יהוה, that Eli watched her mouth. 13 Now Channah, she spoke in her lev; only her lips moved, but her voice was not heard: therefore Eli thought she was drunk. 14 And Eli said to her, How long will you be drunk? Put away your wine from you. 15 And Channah answered and said, No, my master, I am a woman of a heavy ruach: I have drunk neither wine nor strong drink, but have poured out my chayim before יהוה. 16 Count not your female eved as a daughter of Beliyaal:[4] for out of the abundance of my complaints and grief have I spoken until now. 17 Then Eli answered and said, Go in shalom: and the Elohim of Yisrael grant you your request that you have asked of Him. 18 And she said, Let your female eved find favor in your sight. So the woman went her way, and did eat, and her appearance was no longer sad. 19 And they rose up in the morning early, and worshipped shachrit before יהוה, and returned, and came to their bayit in Ramah: and Elchanah knew Channah his wife; and יהוה remembered her request. 20 Therefore it came to pass, when the time was come about after Channah had conceived, that she bore a son, and called his name Schmuel, saying, Because I have asked him from יהוה. 21 And the man Elchanah, and all his bayit, went up to offer to יהוה the yearly sacrifice, and his vow.[5] 22 But Channah did not go up; for she said to her husband, I will

---

[1] "Every prince or great man that arose in Yisrael was given the name Ephrati. "Ephrati" is defined as one who is an aristocrat or noble man. The Talmud believed that descendents of the House of Ephraim became noble aristocrats wherever they were scattered. In the Babylonian Talmud Yalkut Shimeoni A77, commenting on 1 Samuel 1:1, Rabbi Raddak states "Ephrati is taken to mean someone from the tribe of Ephraim and of noble birth."
[2] Provoked by the other wife, which is why polygamy was allowed but caused many problems and did not remain in YHWH's perfect will.

[3] Will be a lifelong Nazarite.
[4] "lord" or s.a.tan disguised as a lord.
[5] Yom Kippur.

not go up while the child is weaned, after that I will bring him, that he may appear before יהוה, and there stay le-olam-va-ed. 23 And Elchanah her husband said to her, Do what seems tov to you; stay here until you have nursed him; only יהוה establish His word. So the woman stayed, and gave her son nursing until she weaned him. 24 And when she had weaned him, she took him up with her, with three bullocks, and one ephah of flour, and a bottle of wine, and brought him to the Bayit of יהוה in Shiloh: and the child was young. 25 And they killed a bull, and brought the child to Eli. 26 And she said, Oh my master, as your chayim lives, my master, I am the woman that stood by you here, making tefillah to יהוה . 27 For this child I made tefillah; and יהוה has given me my request which I have asked of Him: 28 Therefore also I have promised him to יהוה; as long as he lives he shall be given to יהוה . And she worshipped יהוה there.

2 And Channah made tefillah, and said, My lev has gilah in יהוה, my lev is exalted in יהוה: my mouth is enlarged over my enemies; because I gilah in Your deliverance. 2 There is none Set-Apart as יהוה: for there is none beside You: neither is there any Rock like our Elohim. 3 Talk no more so exceeding proudly; let not arrogance come out of your mouth: for יהוה is an El of da'at, and by Him your actions are weighed. 4 The bows of the mighty men are broken, and they that stumbled are girded with strength. 5 They that were full have sought work for lechem; and they that were hungry have ceased: Also the barren has born seven; and she that has many children has become feeble. 6 יהוה kills, and makes alive: He brings down to the grave, and brings up. 7 יהוה makes poor, and makes rich: He brings low, and lifts up. 8 He raises up the poor out of the dust, and lifts up the beggar from the dunghill, to set them with rulers, and to make them inherit the throne of tifereth: for

the pillars of the earth are יהוה's, and He has set the olam hazeh upon them. 9 He will guard the feet of His kidushim, and the wicked shall be silent in darkness; for by his own strength shall no man prevail. 10 The adversaries of יהוה shall be broken to pieces; out of the shamayim shall He thunder upon them: יהוה shall shophet the ends of the earth; and He shall give strength to His melech, and exalt the position of His anointed. 11 And Elchanah went to Ramah to his bayit. And the child did serve before יהוה in the presence of Eli the kohen. 12 Now the sons of Eli were sons of Beliyaal; they knew not יהוה. 13 And the kohen's custom with the people was, that, when any man offered sacrifice, the kohen's eved came, while the meat was cooking, with a three-pronged hook in his hand, 14 And he struck it into the pan, or kettle, or caldron, or pot; so that all that the flesh-hook brought up the kohen took for himself. So this they did in Shiloh to all the Yisraelites that came there. 15 Also before they burnt the fat, the kohen's eved came, and said to the man that sacrificed, Give the meat for the kohen to roast; for he will not have cooked meat from you, but raw. 16 And if any man said to him, Let the fat burn first, and then take as much as your being desires; then he would answer him, No; but you shall give it to me now: and if not, I will take it by force. 17 Therefore the sin of the young men was very great before יהוה : for men despised the offering of יהוה. 18 But Schmuel served before יהוה, being a child, dressed with a linen shoulder garment. 19 Moreover his ima made him a little coat, and brought it to him from year to year, when she came up with her husband to offer the yearly sacrifice. 20 And Eli blessed Elchanah and his wife, and said, יהוה give you zera of this woman for the promise that is given to יהוה. And they went to their own home. 21 And יהוה visited Channah, so that she conceived, and bore three sons and two daughters. And the child Schmuel grew before יהוה. 22 Now

Eli was very old, and heard all that his sons did to kol Yisrael; and how they had relations with the women that assembled at the door of the tabernacle of the congregation. 23 And he said to them, Why do you do such things? For I shema of your evil dealings from all the people. 24 No, my sons; for it is not a tov report that I shema: for you make יהוה's people to transgress. 25 If one man sins against another, the shophet shall render mishpat for him: but if a man sins against יהוה, who shall help him? Nevertheless they listened not to the voice of their abba, because יהוה would kill them. 26 And the child Schmuel grew up, and was in favor both with יהוה, and also with men. 27 And there came a man of Elohim to Eli, and said to him, This said יהוה, *Did I not plainly appear to the bayit of your abba, when they were in Mitzrayim in Pharaoh's bayit? 28 And didn't I choose him out of all the tribes of Yisrael to be My kohen, to offer upon My altar, to burn incense, to wear a shoulder ephod before Me? And didn't I give to the bayit of your ahvot all the offerings made by fire by the children of Yisrael? 29 Why do you deal wrongly with My sacrifice and keep My offering, which I have commanded in My dwelling; and honor your sons above Me, to make yourselves fat with the best of all the offerings of Yisrael My people?* 30 Therefore יהוה Elohim of Yisrael says, *I said indeed that your bayit, and the bayit of your ahvot, should have their halacha before Me le-olam-va-ed: but now* יהוה said, *Be it far from Me; for them that honor Me I will honor, and they that despise Me shall be lightly esteemed. 31 See, the days come, that I will cut off your arm, and the arm of your abba's bayit, that there shall not be an old man in your bayit. 32 And you shall see an enemy in My Dwelling Place, despite all the wealth which Elohim shall give Yisrael: and there shall not be an old man in your bayit le-olam-va-ed. 33 And any of the men of your bayit, whom I shall not cut off from My altar, shall still*

consume your eyes, and grieve your lev: and all the increase of your bayit shall die in their youth. 34 And this shall be a sign to you, that what now comes upon your two sons, on Hophni and Phinehas; in one day they shall die both of them. 35 And I will raise Me up a faithful Kohen, that shall do according to that which is in My lev and in My mind: and I will build Him a sure Bayit; and He shall have His halacha before My anointing le-olam-va-ed.[1] *36 And it shall come to pass, that every one that is left in your bayit shall come and crouch before him for a piece of silver and a piece of lechem, and shall say, Put me, I ask you, into one of the kohanim's offices, that I may eat even a piece of lechem.*[2]

3 And the child Schmuel served before יהוה and in front of Eli. And the word of יהוה was rare in those days; there was no open vision. 2 And it came to pass at that time, when Eli had laid down in his bed, and his eyes began to grow dim, that he could not see; 3 And the neir tamid of Elohim went out in the Tent of יהוה, where the Ark of Elohim was, and Schmuel was laying down ready to sleep; 4 That יהוה called *Schmuel*: and he answered, Hinayni. 5 And he ran to Eli, and said, Hinayni; for you called me. And he said, I did not call you; go lie down again. And he went and lay down. 6 And יהוה called yet again, *Schmuel.* And Schmuel arose and went to Eli, and said, Hinayni; for you did call me. And he answered, I did not call you, my son; go lie down again. 7 Now Schmuel did not yet know יהוה neither was the word of יהוה yet revealed to him. 8 And יהוה called Schmuel again the third time. And he arose and went to Eli, and said, Hinayni; for you did call me. And Eli then perceived that יהוה had called the child. 9 Therefore Eli said to Schmuel, Go, lie down: and it shall

---

[1] Moshiach; the promised Kohen HaGadol – High Priest – that would be given to all Yisrael as a faithful Mediator for all Yisrael.
[2] Entry in to the Renewed Covenant priesthood will depend fully on Yahshua choosing and supplying the needs for His priests.

be, if He calls you, that you shall say, Speak, יהוה ; for Your eved hears. So Schmuel went and lay down in his place. 10 And יהוה came, and stood, and called as at the other times, *Schmuel, Schmuel.* Then Schmuel answered, Speak; for Your eved hears. 11 And יהוה said to Schmuel, *See, I will do a thing in Yisrael, at which both ears of every one that hears shall tingle. 12 In that day I will perform against Eli all things that I have spoken concerning his bayit: when I begin, I will also make an end. 13 For I have told him that I will shophet his bayit le-olam-va-ed for the iniquity which he knows about; because his sons made themselves vile and reviled the people, and he restrained them not. 14 And therefore I have sworn to the bayit of Eli, that the iniquity of Eli's bayit shall not be purged with sacrifice nor offering le-olam-va-ed.* 15 And Schmuel lay until the morning, and opened the doors of the Bayit of יהוה. And Schmuel feared to show Eli the vision. 16 Then Eli called Schmuel, and said, Schmuel, my son. And he answered, Hinayni. 17 And he said, What is the thing that יהוה has said to you? I ask you hide it not from me: Elohim do all He has shown you, and even more also, if you hide anything from me of all the things that He said to you. 18 And Schmuel told him every thing, and hid nothing from him. And he said, It is from יהוה : let Him do what seems tov to Him. 19 And Schmuel grew, and יהוה was with him, and he did not ignore even one of His words. 20 And all Yisrael from Dan even to Beer-Sheva knew that Schmuel was established to be a navi of יהוה .[1] 21 And יהוה appeared again in Shiloh: for יהוה revealed Himself to Schmuel in Shiloh by the word of יהוה.[2]

4 And the word of Schmuel came to kol Yisrael.[3] Now Yisrael went out against the Philistines to battle, and pitched beside Even-Ezer: and the Philistines pitched in Aphek. 2 And the Philistines put themselves in battle against Yisrael: and when they joined battle, Yisrael was smitten before the Philistines: and they killed of the army in the field about four thousand men. 3 And when the people had come into the camp, the zachanim of Yisrael said, Why has יהוה smitten us to day before the Philistines? Let us get the Ark of the Covenant of יהוה out of Shiloh to us, so that when it comes among us, it may save us out of the hand of our enemies. 4 So the people sent to Shiloh, that they might bring from there the Ark of the Covenant of יהוה of hosts, who dwells between the cheruvim: and the two sons of Eli, Hophni and Phinehas, were there with the Ark of the Covenant of Elohim. 5 And when the Ark of the Covenant of יהוה came into the camp, all Yisrael shouted with a great shout, so that the earth shook. 6 And when the Philistines heard the noise of the shout, they said, What means the noise of this great shout in the camp of the Ivrim?[4] And they understood that the Ark of יהוה had come into the camp. 7 And the Philistines were afraid, for they said, Elohim has come into the camp. And they said, Woe to us! For there has not been such a thing before. 8 Woe to us! Who shall deliver us out of the hand of these mighty Elohim? These are the Elohim that smote the Mitzrites with all the plagues in the wilderness. 9 Be strong, and behave yourselves like men, O you Philistines, that you be not avadim to the Ivrim, as they have been to you: behave yourselves like men, and fight. 10 And the Philistines fought, and Yisrael was smitten, and they fled every man into his tent: and there was a very great slaughter; for there fell in Yisrael thirty thousand foot soldiers. 11 And the Ark of Elohim was taken; and the two sons of Eli, Hophni and Phinehas, were killed. 12 And there ran a man of Benyamin out of the army, and came to Shiloh the same day with his clothes torn,

---

[1] All Yisrael recognized his authority.
[2] Duality of YHWH.
[3] United nation.

[4] Note there were no Jews in those unified days. Yisrael was known as the "Hebrews."

and with dust upon his head. 13 And when he came, see, Eli sat upon a seat by the wayside watching: for his lev trembled over the Ark of Elohim. And when the man came into the city, and told it to them, the entire city shouted out. 14 And when Eli heard the noise of the crying, he said, What means the noise of this tumult? And the man came in hastily, and told Eli. 15 Now Eli was ninety-eight years old; and his eyes were dim, so that he could not see. 16 And the man said to Eli, I am he that came out of the army, and I fled here today out of the battle. And he said, What is going on there, my son? 17 And the messenger answered and said, Yisrael has fled before the Philistines, and there has been also a great slaughter among the people, and your two sons also, Hophni and Phinehas, are dead, and the Ark of Elohim has been taken. 18 And it came to pass, when he made mention of the Ark of Elohim, that he fell from off the seat backward by the side of the gate, and his neck brake, and he died: for he was an old man, and very heavy. And he had been shophet in Yisrael for forty years. 19 And his daughter-in-law, Pinchus's wife, was with child, near to be delivered: and when she heard the news that the Ark of Elohim was taken, and that her abba-in-law and her husband were dead, she bowed herself and gave birth; for her labor pains came upon her. 20 And about the time of her death the women that stood by her said to her, Fear not; for you have born a son. But she answered nothing and neither did she care. 21 And she named the child Ichavod, saying, The tifereth has departed from Yisrael: because the Ark of Elohim was taken, and because of her abba-in-law and her husband. 22 And she said, The tifereth is departed from Yisrael: for the Ark of Elohim is taken.

5 And the Philistines took the Ark of Elohim, and brought it from Even-Ezer to Ashdod. 2 When the Philistines took the Ark of Elohim, they brought it into the bayit of Dagon, and set it by Dagon. 3 And when those of Ashdod arose early in the morning, see, Dagon was thrown down upon his face to the earth before the Ark of יהוה. And they took Dagon, and set him back in his place again. 4 And when they arose early on the next morning, see, Dagon was thrown down upon his face to the ground before the Ark of יהוה; and the head of Dagon and both the palms of his hands were cut off upon the threshold; only the stump of Dagon was left to him. 5 Therefore neither the priests of Dagon, nor any that come into Dagon's bayit, step on the threshold of Dagon in Ashdod to this day. 6 But the hand of יהוה was heavy upon them of Ashdod, and He destroyed them, and smote them with tumors, even Ashdod and the borders of it. 7 And when the men of Ashdod saw that it was so, they said, The Ark of the Elohim of Yisrael shall not stay with us: for His hand is heavy upon us, and upon Dagon our elohim. 8 They sent therefore and gathered all the rulers of the Philistines to them, and said, What shall we do with the Ark of the Elohim of Yisrael? And they answered, Let the Ark of the Elohim of Yisrael be moved to Gath. And they carried the Ark of the Elohim of Yisrael there. 9 And it was so, that, after they had removed it, the hand of יהוה was against the city with a very great destruction: and He smote the men of the city, both small and great, and they had tumors in their private parts. 10 Therefore they sent the Ark of Elohim to Ekron. And it came to pass, as the Ark of Elohim came to Ekron, that the Ekronites shouted out, saying, They have brought here the Ark of the Elohim of Yisrael to us, to kill us and our people. 11 So they sent and gathered together all the rulers of the Philistines, and said, Send away the Ark of the Elohim of Yisrael, and let it go again to its own place, that it kill us not, and kill not our people: for there was a deadly destruction throughout all the city; the hand of Elohim was very heavy there. 12 And the men that

did not die were smitten with the tumors: and the cry of the city went up to the shamayim.

6 And the Ark of יהוה was in the country of the Philistines seven months. 2 And the Philistines called for their priests and the diviners, saying, What shall we do to the Ark of יהוה? Tell us by what means shall we send it to its place. 3 And they said, If you send away the Ark of the Elohim of Yisrael, send it not away empty; you shall surely bring Him a trespass offering: then you shall be healed, and it shall be known to you why His hand is not turned aside from you. 4 Then said they, What shall be the trespass offering that we shall return to Him? They answered, Five golden tumors, and five golden mice, according to the number of masters of the Philistines: for one plague was on all of you, and on your masters. 5 And you shall make images of your tumors, and images of your mice that ruin the land; and you shall give tifereth to the Elohim of Yisrael: perhaps then He will lighten His hand from off of you, and from off of your elohim, and from off of your land. 6 Why then do you harden your levim, as the Mitzrites and Pharoah hardened their levim? When He had done wonderfully among them, did they not let the people go, and they departed? 7 Now therefore make a new cart, and take two milking cows, which have never been yoked, and tie the cows to the cart, and bring their calves home away from them: 8 And take the Ark of יהוה, and lay it upon the cart; and put the jewels of gold, which you return to Him for a trespass offering, in a chest by the side of it; and send it away, that it may go. 9 And see, if it goes up to its own border to Beth-Shemesh, then He has done us this great evil: but if not, then we shall know that it was not His hand that smote us; it was an accident that happened to us. 10 And the men did so; and took two milking cows, and tied them to the cart, and shut up their calves at home: 11 And they laid the Ark of יהוה upon the cart, and the chest with the mice of gold and the images of their tumors. 12 And the cows went immediately to the way of Beth-Shemesh, and went along the highway, bellowing as they went, and turned not aside to the right hand or to the left; and the rulers of the Philistines went after them to the border of Beth-Shemesh. 13 And those of Beth-Shemesh were reaping their wheat harvest in the valley: and they lifted up their eyes, and saw the Ark, and rejoiced to see it. 14 And the cart came into the field of Yahoshua, a Beth-Shemite, and stood there, where there was a great stone: and they split the wood of the cart, and offered the cows as a burnt offering to יהוה. 15 And the Levites took down the Ark of יהוה, and the chest that was with it, in which the jewels of gold were, and put them on the great stone: and the men of Beth-Shemesh offered burnt offerings and sacrificed sacrifices the same day to יהוה. 16 And when the five masters of the Philistines had seen it, they returned to Ekron the same day. 17 And these are the golden tumors which the Philistines returned for a trespass offering to יהוה; for Ashdod one, for Gaza one, for Ashkelon one, for Gath one, for Ekron one; 18 And the golden mice, according to the number of all the cities of the Philistines belonging to the five masters, both of fenced cities, and of the country villages, even to the great stone of Avel, where they set down the Ark of יהוה: which stone remains to this day in the field of Yahoshua, the Beth-Shemite. 19 And He smote the men of Beth-Shemesh, because they had looked into the Ark of יהוה, even He smote of the people five thousand seventy men: and the people lamented, because יהוה had smitten many of the people with a great slaughter. 20 And the men of Beth-Shemesh said, Who is able to stand before this set-apart יהוה Elohim? And who shall carry up from us the Ark? 21 And they sent messengers to the inhabitants of Kiryath-Yearim, saying, The

Philistines have brought again the Ark of יהוה; come down, and take it to you.

7 And the men of Kiryath-Yearim came, and got the Ark of יהוה, and brought it into the bayit of Aviniadav on the hill, and set apart El-Azar his son to keep the Ark of יהוה. 2 And it came to pass, while the Ark stayed in Kiryath-Yearim, that the time was long; for it was twenty years: and all Beit Yisrael yearned after יהוה. 3 And Schmuel spoke to all Beit Yisrael, saying, If you do teshuvah to יהוה with all your levim, then put away the strange elohim and Ashtaroth from among you, and prepare your levim for יהוה, and serve Him only: then He will deliver you out of the hand of the Philistines. 4 Then the children of Yisrael did put away the Baalim and Ashtaroth, and served יהוה only. 5 And Schmuel said, Gather kol Yisrael[1] to Mitzpeh, and I will make tefillah for you to יהוה. 6 And they gathered together to Mitzpeh, and drew mayim, and poured it out before יהוה, and fasted on that day, and said there, We have sinned against יהוה. And Schmuel was shophet over the children of Yisrael in Mitzpeh. 7 And when the Philistines heard that the children of Yisrael were gathered together to Mitzpeh, the rulers of the Philistines went up against Yisrael. And when the children of Yisrael heard it, they were afraid of the Philistines. 8 And the children of Yisrael said to Schmuel, Don't stop crying to יהוה our Elohim for us, that He will save us out of the hand of the Philistines. 9 And Schmuel took a sucking lamb, and offered it for a burnt offering wholly to יהוה: and Schmuel shouted to יהוה for Yisrael; and יהוה heard him. 10 And as Schmuel was offering up the burnt offering, the Philistines drew near to battle against Yisrael: but יהוה thundered with a great thunder on that day upon the Philistines, and troubled them; and they were smitten before Yisrael. 11 And the men of Yisrael went out of Mitzpeh, and

pursued the Philistines, and smote them, until they came under Beth-Kar. 12 Then Schmuel took a stone, and set it between Mitzpeh and Shen, and called the name of it Even-Ezer, saying, So far has יהוה helped us. 13 So the Philistines were subdued, and they came no more into the borders of Yisrael: and the hand of יהוה was against the Philistines all the days of Schmuel. 14 And the cities which the Philistines had taken from Yisrael were restored to Yisrael, from Ekron even to Gath; and all its borders did Yisrael deliver out of the hands of the Philistines. And there was shalom between Yisrael and the Amorites. 15 And Schmuel was shophet in Yisrael all the days of his chayim. 16 And he went from year to year and made rounds to Bethel, and Gilgal, and Mitzpeh, and was shophet in Yisrael in all those places. 17 And he returned to Ramah; for there was his bayit; and there he was also the shophet in Yisrael; and there he built an altar to יהוה.

8 And it came to pass, when Schmuel was old, that he made his sons the shophtim over Yisrael. 2 Now the name of his firstborn was Yoel; and the name of his second, Aviyah: and they were shophtim in Beer-Sheva. 3 And his sons walked not in his halacha, but turned aside after gain, and took bribes, and perverted mishpat. 4 Then all the zachanim of Yisrael gathered themselves together, and came to Schmuel to Ramah, 5 And said to him, See, you are old, and your sons walk not in your ways: now make us a melech to shophet us like all the pagan nations. 6 But the thing displeased Schmuel, when they said, Give us a melech to shophet us. And Schmuel made tefillah to יהוה. 7 And יהוה said to Schmuel, *Shema to the voice of the people in all that they say to you: for they have not rejected you, but they have rejected Me, that I should not reign over them. 8 According to all the works that they have done since the day that I brought them up out of Mitzrayim even to this day, forsaking*

---
[1] Still united.

Me, and serving other elohim, so do they also to you. 9 *Now therefore shema to their voice: but sternly warn them, and show them the kind of melech that shall reign over them.* 10 And Schmuel told all the words of יהוה to the people that asked for this melech from him. 11 And he said, This will be the manner of the melech that shall reign over you: He will take your sons, and appoint them for himself, for his mirkavot, and to be his horsemen; and some shall run before his mirkavot. 12 And he will appoint him captains over thousands, and captains over fifties; and will set them to plough his ground, and to reap his harvest, and to make his instruments of war, and instruments for his mirkavot. 13 And he will take your daughters to be perfume makers, and to be cooks, and to be bakers. 14 And he will take your fields, and your vineyards, and your oliveyards, even the best of them, and give them to his avadim. 15 And he will take the ma'aser of your zera, and of your vineyards, and give it to his officers, and to his avadim. 16 And he will take your male avadim, and your female avadim, and your best young men, and your donkeys, and put them to his own work. 17 He will take the ma'aser of your sheep: and you shall be his avadim. 18 And you shall cry out in that day because of your melech that you have chosen; and יהוה will not shema you in that day. 19 Nevertheless the people refused to obey the voice of Schmuel; and they said, No; but we still will have a melech over us; 20 That we also may be like all the nations,[1] and that our melech may shophet us, and go out before us, and fight our battles. 21 And Schmuel heard all the words of the people, and he repeated them in the ears of יהוה. 22 And יהוה said to Schmuel, *Shema to their voice, and make them a melech.* And Schmuel said to the men of Yisrael, Go home every man to his city.

9 Now there was a man of Benyamin, whose name was Kish, the son of Aviel, the son of Zeror, the son of Bechorath, the son of Aphiyah, a Benyamite, a mighty man of power. 2 And he had a son, whose name was Shaul, a choice young male, and handsome: and there was not among the children of Yisrael a better-looking person than him: from his shoulders and upward he was taller than any of the people. 3 And the donkeys of Kish Shaul's abba were lost. And Kish said to Shaul his son, Take now one of the avadim with you, and arise, go seek the donkeys. 4 And he passed through Mount Ephraim, and passed through the land of Shalishah, but they found them not: then they passed through the land of Shalim, and they were not there: and he passed through the land of the Benyamites, but they found them not. 5 And when they had come to the land of Zuph, Shaul said to his eved that was with him, Come, and let us return; lest my abba stop caring for the donkeys, and get worried about us. 6 And he said to him, See now, there is in this city a man of Elohim, and he is an honorable man; all that he says comes surely to pass: now let us go there; perhaps he can show us the way that we should go. 7 Then said Shaul to his eved, But, see, if we go, what shall we bring the man? For the lechem is gone in our vessels, and there is not a present to bring to the man of Elohim: what do we have? 8 And the eved answered Shaul again, and said, See, I have here at hand the fourth part of a shekel of silver: that will I give to the man of Elohim, to tell us our way. 9 In the past in Yisrael, when a man went to inquire of Elohim, he spoke like this, Come, and let us go to the seer: for he that is now called a Navi used to be called a Seer. 10 Then said Shaul to his eved, Well said; come, let us go. So they went to the city where the man of Elohim was. 11 And as they went up the hill to the city, they found young maidens going out to draw mayim, and said to them, Is the seer here? 12 And they answered them, and said, He is; see, he is in front of you: hurry now, for he came today to the city; for there is a

---

[1] Pagan nations.

sacrifice of the people today in the high place: 13 As soon as you are come into the city, you shall find him immediately, before he goes up to the high place to eat: for the people will not eat until he comes, because he does bless the sacrifice; and afterwards they eat that are invited. Now therefore go; for about this time you shall find him. 14 And they went up into the city: and when they were come into the city, see, Schmuel came out toward them, going up to the high place. 15 Now יהוה had told Schmuel in his ear a day before Shaul came, saying, 16 *Tomorrow about this time I will send you a man out of the land of Benyamin, and you shall anoint him to be leader over My people Yisrael, that he may save My people out of the hand of the Philistines: for I have looked upon My people, because their cry is come to Me.* 17 And when Schmuel saw Shaul, יהוה said to him, *See the man whom I spoke to you of! He shall reign over My people.* 18 Then Shaul drew near to Schmuel in the gate, and said, Tell me, please, where the seer's bayit is. 19 And Schmuel answered Shaul, and said, I am the seer: go up before me to the high place; for you shall eat with me today, and tomorrow I will let you go, and will tell you all that is in your lev. 20 And as for your donkeys that were lost three days ago, set not your mind on them; for they are found. And for who is all the desire of Yisrael? Is it not on you, and all your abba's bayit? 21 And Shaul answered and said, Am not a Benyamite, of the smallest of the tribes of Yisrael? And my family is the least of all the families of the tribe of Binyamin? Why then do you speak like this to me? 22 And Schmuel took Shaul and his eved, and brought them into the hall, and made them sit in the best place among them that were invited, which were about thirty persons. 23 And Schmuel said to the cook, Bring the portion that I gave you, of which I said to you, Set it aside. 24 And the cook took up the shoulder, and that which was upon it, and set it before

Shaul. And Schmuel said, See that which is left! Set it before you, and eat: for this time has it been kept for you since I said, I have invited the people. So Shaul did eat with Schmuel that day. 25 And when they were come down from the high place into the city, Schmuel communed with Shaul upon the top of the bayit. 26 And they rose early: and it came to pass about the dawning of the day, that Schmuel called Shaul to the top of the bayit, saying, Come up, that I may send you on your way. And Shaul arose, and they went out both of them, he and Schmuel, outside. 27 And as they were going down to the end of the city, Schmuel said to Shaul, Ask your eved to go on ahead of us, and he went on, but stay here for a while, that I may show you the word of Elohim.

10 Then Schmuel took a flask of oil, and poured it upon his head, and kissed him, and said, Is it not because יהוה has anointed you to be leader over his inheritance? 2 When you are departed from me today, then you shall find two men by Rachel's tomb at the border of Benyamin at Zelzah; and they will say to you, The donkeys which you went to seek are found: and, see, your abba has stopped caring about the donkeys, and worries about you, saying, What shall I do about my son? 3 Then shall you go on forward from there, and you shall come to the plain of Tabor, and there shall meet you three men going up to Elohim to Beth-El, one carrying three young goats, and another carrying three loaves of lechem, and another carrying a skin of wine: 4 And they will greet you, and give you two loaves of lechem; which you shall receive from their hands. 5 After that you shall come to the hill of Elohim, where is the watch-post of the Philistines: and it shall come to pass, when you are come there to the city, that you shall meet a group of niviim coming down from the high place with a stringed instrument, and a flute, and a pipe, and a harp, before them; and they

shall prophesy: 6 And the Ruach of יהוה will come upon you, and you shall prophesy with them, and shall be turned into another man.[1] 7 And let it be, when these signs are come to you, that you do whatever your hand finds to do; for Elohim is with you. 8 And you shall go down before me to Gilgal; and, see, I will come down to you, to offer burnt offerings, and to sacrifice the sacrifices of the shalom offerings: seven days shall you stay, until I come to you, and show you what you shall do. 9 And it was so, that when he had left Schmuel, Elohim gave him another lev:[2] and all those signs came to pass that day. 10 And when they came there to the hill, see, a group of niviim met him; and the Ruach of Elohim came upon him, and he prophesied among them. 11 And it came to pass, when all that knew him from before saw that, see, he prophesied among the niviim, then the people said one to another, What is this that has happened to the son of Kish? Is Shaul also among the niviim? 12 And a man of the same place answered and said, But who is their abba? Therefore it became a mishle, Is Shaul also among the niviim? 13 And when he had made an end of prophesying, he came to the high place. 14 And Shaul's uncle said to him and to his eved, Where did you go? And he said, To seek the donkeys: and when we saw that they were nowhere, we came to Schmuel. 15 And Shaul's uncle said, Tell me, what did Schmuel say to you? 16 And Shaul said to his uncle, He told us plainly that the donkeys were found. But of the matter of the malchut, about which Schmuel spoke, he told him not. 17 And Schmuel called the people together to יהוה at Mitzpeh; 18 And said to the children of Yisrael, This said יהוה Elohim of Yisrael, *I brought up Yisrael out of Mitzrayim, and delivered you out of the hand of the Mitzrites, and out of the hand of all the malchutim, and from them that oppressed you:* 19 *And you have*

this day rejected Your Elohim, who Himself saved you out of all your adversities and your tribulations; and you have said to him, No, but set a melech over us. Now therefore present yourselves before יהוה by your tribes, and by your thousands. 20 And when Schmuel had caused all the tribes of Yisrael to come near, the tribe of Benyamin was taken. 21 When he had caused the tribe of Benyamin to come near by their families, the family of Matri was taken, and Shaul the son of Kish was taken: and when they sought him, he could not be found. 22 Therefore they inquired of יהוה further, if the man should yet come there. And יהוה answered, *See, he has hidden himself among the baggage.* 23 And they ran and got him there: and when he stood among the people, he was taller than any of the people from his shoulders and upward. 24 And Schmuel said to all the people, See the man whom יהוה has chosen, that there is none like him among all the people? And all the people shouted, Long live the melech![3] 25 Then Schmuel told the people the manner of the malchut, and wrote it in a scroll, and laid it up before יהוה. And Schmuel sent all the people away, every man to his bayit. 26 And Shaul also went home to Giveah; and there went with him a band of men, whose levim Elohim had touched. 27 But the children of Beliyaal said, How shall this man save us? And they despised him, and brought him no presents. But he held his silence.

11 Then Nachash [4] the Ammonite came up, and camped against Yavesh-Gilead: and all the men of Yavesh said to Nachash, Make a covenant with us, and we will serve you. 2 And Nachash the Ammonite answered them, On this condition will I make a covenant with you, that I may thrust out all your right eyes, and lay it for a reproach upon all Yisrael. 3 And the zachanim of Yavesh said to him, Give

---

[1] Yisraelites were always the recipient of the Spirit, and it always turned people into new persons.
[2] Born-again.

[3] The United Kingdom has their first of only three kings.
[4] Means: "the snake."

us seven days to rest, that we may send messengers to all the borders of Yisrael: and then, if there is no man to save us, we will come out to you. 4 Then came the messengers to Giveah of Shaul, and told the news in the ears of the people: and all the people lifted up their voices, and wept. 5 And, see, Shaul came behind the herd out of the field; and Shaul said, What is wrong with the people that they weep? And they told him the news of the men of Yavesh. 6 And the Ruach of Elohim came upon Shaul when he heard the news, and his anger was kindled greatly. 7 And he took a yoke of cattle, and cut them in pieces, and sent them throughout all the borders of Yisrael by the hands of messengers, saying, Whoever comes not forth with Shaul and Schmuel to battle, so shall it be done to him like unto his cattle. And the fear of יהוה fell on the people, and they came out in one accord. 8 And when he numbered them in Bezek, the children of Yisrael were three hundred thousand, and the men of Yahudah thirty thousand.[1] 9 And they said to the messengers that came, This shall you say to the men of Yavesh-Gilead, Tomorrow, by the time the sun is hot, you shall have help. And the messengers came and showed it to the men of Yavesh; and they were glad. 10 Therefore the men of Yavesh said, Tomorrow we will come out to meet you, and you shall do with us all that seems tov to you. 11 And it was so on the next day, that Shaul put the people in three companies; and they came into the midst of the camp in the morning watch, and killed the Ammonites until the heat of the day: and it came to pass, that they who remained were scattered, so that not even two of them were left together. 12 And the people said to Schmuel, Who is he that said, Shall Shaul reign over us? Bring the men, that we may put them to death. 13 And Shaul said, There shall not a man be put to death this day: for today יהוה has brought deliverance in Yisrael. 14 Then said Schmuel to the people, Come, and let us go to Gilgal, and renew the malchut there.[2] 15 And all the people went to Gilgal; and there they made Shaul melech before יהוה in Gilgal; and there they sacrificed the sacrifices of shalom offerings before יהוה; and there Shaul and all the men of Yisrael gilahed greatly.

12 And Schmuel said to all Yisrael, See, I have listened to your voice in all that you said to me, and have made a melech over you. 2 And now, see, the melech walks before you: and I am old and gray-headed; and, see, my sons are with you: and I have had my halacha before you from my childhood to this day. 3 See, here I am: witness against me before יהוה, and before His anointed: whose cattle have I taken? Or whose donkey have I taken? Or whom have I defrauded? Whom have I oppressed? Or from whose hand have I received any bribe to blind my eyes with it? If so I will restore it you. 4 And they said, You have not defrauded us, nor oppressed us, neither have you taken anything from any man's hand. 5 And he said to them, יהוה is witness against you, and His anointed is witness this day, that you have not found anything in my hand. And they answered, He is a witness. 6 And Schmuel said to the people, It is יהוה that advanced Moshe and Aharon, and that brought your ahvot up out of the land of Mitzrayim. 7 Now therefore stand still, that I may rehearse with you before יהוה all the tzadik acts of יהוה, which He did to you and to your ahvot. 8 When Yaakov had come into Mitzrayim, and your ahvot cried out to יהוה, then יהוה sent Moshe and Aharon, who brought forth your ahvot out of Mitzrayim, and made them dwell in this place. 9 And when they forgot יהוה their Elohim, He sold them into the hand of Sisera, leader of the host of Hatzor, and into

---

[1] A clear mention of two separate counts for both houses, even before the actual split.

[2] A type of the call of Yahshua in His first advent, calling all Yisrael to renew the kingdom, as seen in Acts 1:6.

the hand of the Philistines, and into the hand of the melech of Moav, and they fought against them. 10 And they cried out to יהוה, and said, We have sinned, because we have forsaken יהוה, and have served Baalim and Ashtaroth: but now deliver us out of the hand of our enemies, and we will serve you. 11 And יהוה sent Yeruvaal, and Bedan, and Yephthah, and Schmuel, and delivered you out of the hand of your enemies on every side, and you dwelt safely. 12 And when you saw that Nachash the melech of the children of Ammon came against you, you said to me, No; but a melech shall reign over us: when יהוה Your Elohim was Your melech. 13 Now therefore see the melech whom you have chosen, and whom you have desired! And, see, יהוה has set a melech over you. 14 If you will fear יהוה, and serve Him, and obey His voice, and not rebel against the commandments of יהוה, then shall both you and also the melech that reigns over you continue following יהוה Your Elohim: 15 But if you will not obey the voice of יהוה, but rebel against the commandment of יהוה, then shall the hand of יהוה be against you, as it was against your ahvot. 16 Now therefore stand and see this great thing, which יהוה will do before your eyes. 17 Is it not wheat harvest today? I will call to יהוה, and He shall send thunder and rain; that you may perceive and see that your wickedness is great, which you have done in the sight of יהוה, in asking for a melech. 18 So Schmuel called to יהוה; and יהוה sent thunder and rain that day: and all the people greatly feared יהוה and Schmuel. 19 And all the people said to Schmuel, Make tefillah for your avadim to יהוה Your Elohim, that we die not: for we have added to all our sins this evil, to ask for a melech. 20 And Schmuel said to the people, Fear not: you have done all this wickedness: yet turn not aside from following יהוה, but serve יהוה with all your lev; 21 And turn not aside: for then should you go after worthless things, which

cannot profit nor deliver; for they are worthless. 22 For יהוה will not forsake His people for His great Name's sake: because it has pleased יהוה to make you His people. 23 Moreover as for me, Elohim forbid that I should sin against יהוה in ceasing to make tefillah for you: but I will teach you the tov and the correct halacha: 24 Only fear יהוה, and serve Him in emet with all your lev: for consider how great things He has done for you. 25 But if you shall still do wickedly, you shall be consumed, both you and your melech.

13 Shaul reigned one year; and when he had reigned two years over Yisrael, 2 Shaul chose three thousand men of Yisrael; of which two thousand were with Shaul in Michmash and in Mount Bethel, and a thousand were with Yonathan in Giveah of Benyamin: and the rest of the people he sent every man to his tent. 3 And Yonathan smote the watch-post of the Philistines that was in Geva, and the Philistines heard of it. And Shaul blew the shofar throughout all the land, saying, Let the Ivrim shema. 4 And all Yisrael heard that Shaul had smitten a watch-post of the Philistines, and that Yisrael also was held in contempt by the Philistines. And the people were called together by Shaul to Gilgal. 5 And the Philistines gathered themselves together to fight with Yisrael, thirty thousand mirkavot, and six thousand horsemen, and people as the sand which is on the sea shore in multitude: and they came up, and pitched in Michmash, eastward from Beth-Aven. 6 When the men of Yisrael saw that they were in trouble, for the people were distressed, then the people did hide themselves in caves, and in thickets, and in rocks, and in high places, and in pits. 7 And some of the Ivrim went over the Yarden River to the land of Gad and Gilead. As for Shaul, he was yet in Gilgal, and all the people followed him trembling. 8 And he tarried seven days, according to the set time that Schmuel had

appointed: but Schmuel came not to Gilgal; and the people were scattered from him. 9 And Shaul said, Bring here a burnt offering to me, and shalom offerings. And he offered the burnt offering. 10 And it came to pass, that as soon as he had made an end of offering the burnt offering, see, Schmuel came; and Shaul went out to meet him, that he might greet him. 11 And Schmuel said, What have you done? And Shaul said, Because I saw that the people were scattered from me, and that you came not within the days appointed, and that the Philistines gathered themselves together at Michmash; 12 Therefore said I, The Philistines will come down now upon me to Gilgal, and I have not made supplication to יהוה: I forced myself therefore, and offered a burnt offering. 13 And Schmuel said to Shaul, You have done foolishly: you have not kept the commandment of יהוה Your Elohim, which He commanded you: for now would יהוה have established your malchut upon Yisrael le-olam-va-ed. [1] 14 But now your malchut shall not continue: יהוה has sought Him a man after His own lev, and יהוה has commanded him to be the leader over His people, because you have not kept that which יהוה commanded you. 15 And Schmuel arose, and got up from Gilgal to Giveah of Benyamin. And Shaul numbered the people that were present with him, about six hundred men. 16 And Shaul, and Yonathan his son, and the people that were present with them, stayed in Giveah of Benyamin: but the Philistines camped in Michmash. 17 And the spoilers came out of the camp of the Philistines in three troops: one troop turned to the way that leads to Ophrah, to the land of Shual: 18 And another troop turned the way to Beth-Horon: and another troop turned to the way of the border that looks to the Valley of Zevoim toward the wilderness. 19 Now there was no blacksmith found throughout all the land of Yisrael: for the Philistines said, Lest the

Ivrim make them swords or spears: 20 But all the Yisraelites went down to the Philistines, to sharpen every man his sickle, and his forks, and his axe, and his mattock. 21 Yet they had a broad file for the mattocks, and for the coulters, and for the forks, and for the axes, and to sharpen the goads. 22 So it came to pass in the day of battle, that there was neither sword nor spear found in the hand of any of the people that were with Shaul and Yonathan: but with Shaul and with Yonathan his son they were found. 23 And the watch-post of the Philistines went out to the passage of Michmash.

14 Now it came to pass upon a day, that Yonathan the son of Shaul said to the young man that bore his armor, Come, and let us go over to the Philistines' watch-post, that is on the other side. But he told not his abba. 2 And Shaul stayed in the outskirts of Giveah under a pomegranate eytz, which is in Migron: and the people that were with him were about six hundred men; 3 And Ahiyah, the son of Ahituv, Ichabod's brother, the son of Phinehas, the son of Eli, יהוה's kohen in Shiloh, was girded with a ephod shoulder garment. And the people knew not that Yonathan was gone. 4 And between the passages, by which Yonathan sought to go over to the Philistines' watch-post, there was a sharp rock on the one side and a sharp rock on the other side: and the name of the one was Bozez, and the name of the other Seneh. 5 One edge was on the north over against Michmash, and the other south over against Giveah. 6 And Yonathan said to the young man that bore his armor, Come, and let us go over to the watch-post of these uncircumcised: it may be that יהוה does work for us: for there is no limit for יהוה to save by many or by just a few. 7 And his armor-bearer said to him, Do all that is in your lev: turn and see, that I am with you according to your lev. 8 Then said Yonathan, See, we will pass over to these

---

[1] Only sons of Aaron can offer sacrifices.

men, and we will reveal ourselves to them. 9 If they say this to us, Stay until we come to you; then we will stand still in our place, and will not go up to them. 10 But if they say this, Come up to us; then we will go up: for יהוה has delivered them into our hand: and this shall be a sign to us. 11 And both of them revealed themselves to the watch-post of the Philistines: and the Philistines said, See, the Ivrim come forth out of the holes where they had hidden themselves. 12 And the men of the watch-post answered Yonathan and his armor-bearer, and said, Come up to us, and we will show you a thing. And Yonathan said to his armor-bearer, Come up after me: for יהוה has delivered them into the hand of Yisrael. 13 And Yonathan climbed up upon his hands and upon his feet, and his armor-bearer after him: and they fell before Yonathan, and his armor-bearer and were killed. 14 And that first slaughter, which Yonathan and his armor-bearer made, was about twenty men, within about a half acre of land, which a yoke of cattle usually plows. 15 And there was trembling in the camp, in the field, and among all the people: the watch-post, and the invaders, they also trembled, so that the earth quaked: so it was a very great trembling. 16 And the watchmen of Shaul in Giveah of Benyamin looked; and, see, the multitude melted away, and they went away very confused. 17 Then said Shaul to the people that were with him, Count and see who is gone from us. And when they had numbered, see, Yonathan and his armor-bearer were not there. 18 And Shaul said to Ahiyah, Bring here the Ark of Elohim. For the Ark of Elohim was at that time with the children of Yisrael. 19 And it came to pass, while Shaul talked to the kohen, that the noise that was in the camp of the Philistines went on and increased: and Shaul said to the kohen, Withdraw your hand. 20 And Shaul and all the people that were with him assembled themselves, and they came to the battle: and, see, every man's sword was against his

fellow, and there was a very great confusion. 21 Moreover the Ivrim that were with the Philistines before that time, who went up with them into the camp from the country all around, even they also turned to be with the Yisraelites who were with Shaul and Yonathan. 22 Likewise all the men of Yisrael which had hidden themselves in Mount Ephraim, when they heard that the Philistines fled, even they also followed hard after them in the battle. 23 So יהוה saved Yisrael that day: and the battle moved to Beth-Aven. 24 And the men of Yisrael were distressed that day: for Shaul had adjured the people, saying, Cursed be the man that eats any food until evening, that I may be avenged on my enemies. So none of the people tasted any food.[1] 25 And all they of the land came to a wood; and there was honey upon the ground. 26 And when the people were come into the wood, see, the honey dropped; but no man put his hand to his mouth: for the people feared the oath. 27 But Yonathan heard not that his abba charged the people with the oath: wherefore he put forth the end of the rod that was in his hand, and dipped it in a honeycomb, and put his hand to his mouth; and his eyes were enlightened. 28 Then answered one of the people, and said, Your abba strictly charged the people with an oath, saying, Cursed be the man that eats any food this day. And the people were weak. 29 Then said Yonathan, My abba has troubled the land: see, I ask you, how my eyes have been enlightened, because I tasted a little of this honey. 30 How much better, if the people had eaten freely today of the spoil of their enemies that they found? For would there not have been a much greater slaughter among the Philistines? 31 And they smote the Philistines that day from Michmash to Ayalon: and the people were very weak. 32 And the people flew upon the spoil, and took sheep, and cattle, and calves, and killed them on the ground: and the people

---

[1] Another sin by making Yisrael too weak to fight.

did eat them with the dom.[1] 33 Then they told Shaul, saying, See, the people sin against יהוה, in that they eat with the dom. And he said, You have transgressed: roll a great stone to me this day. 34 And Shaul said, Disperse yourselves among the people, and say to them, Bring me here every man his cattle, and every man his sheep, and kill them here, and eat; and sin not against יהוה in eating with the dom. And all the people brought every man his cattle with him that night, and killed them there. 35 And Shaul built an altar to יהוה: this was the first altar that he built to יהוה. 36 And Shaul said, Let us go down after the Philistines by night, and spoil them until the morning light, and let us not leave a man of them alive. And they said, Do whatever seems tov to you. Then said the kohen, Let us draw near here to Elohim. 37 And Shaul asked counsel of Elohim, Shall I go down after the Philistines? Will you deliver them into the hand of Yisrael? But he answered him not that day. 38 And Shaul said, Draw near here, all the heads of the people: and know and see what this sin has been this day. 39 For, as יהוה lives, who saves Yisrael, though it be in Yonathan my son, he shall surely die. But there was not a man among all the people that answered him. 40 Then said he to kol Yisrael, Be on one side, and I and Yonathan my son will be on the other side. And the people said to Shaul, Do what seems tov to you. 41 Therefore Shaul said to יהוה Elohim of Yisrael, Give me a perfect lot. And Shaul and Yonathan were taken: but the people escaped. 42 And Shaul said, Cast lots between me and Yonathan my son. And Yonathan was taken. 43 Then Shaul said to Yonathan, Tell me what you have done. And Yonathan told him, and said, I did but taste a little honey with the end of the rod that was in my hand, and, see, I must die. 44 And Shaul answered, Elohim do so and more also: for you shall surely die, Yonathan. 45 And the people said to Shaul, Shall Yonathan die,

who has brought this great deliverance in Yisrael? Elohim forbid: as יהוה lives, there shall not one hair of his head fall to the ground; for he has wrought with Elohim this day. So the people rescued Yonathan, so that he did not die. 46 Then Shaul stopped from following the Philistines: and the Philistines went to their own place. 47 So Shaul took the malchut over Yisrael, and fought against all his enemies on every side, against Moav, and against the children of Ammon, and against Edom, and against the melechim of Zovah, and against the Philistines: and wherever he turned, he troubled them. 48 And he gathered an army, and smote the Amalekites, and delivered Yisrael out of the hands of those that plundered them. 49 Now the sons of Shaul were Yonathan, and Ishui, and Melchi-Shua: and the names of his two daughters were these; the name of the firstborn Merav, and the name of the younger Michal: 50 And the name of Shaul's wife was Achinoam, the daughter of Ahimaaz: and the name of the leader of his army was Avner, the son of Ner, Shaul's uncle. 51 And Kish was the abba of Shaul; and Ner the abba of Avner was the son of Aviel. 52 And there was heavy war against the Philistines all the days of Shaul: and when Shaul saw any strong man, or any brave man, he took him for himself.

15 Schmuel also said to Shaul, יהוה sent me to anoint you to be melech over His people, over Yisrael: now therefore shema to the voice of the words of יהוה . 2 This said יהוה of hosts, *I remember that which Amalek did to Yisrael, how he laid wait for him in the derech, when he came up from Mitzrayim. 3 Now go and smite Amalek, and utterly destroy all that they have, and spare them not; but kill both man and woman, infant and the nursing, cattle and sheep, camel and donkey.* 4 And Shaul gathered the people together, and numbered them in Telaim, two hundred thousand footmen, and ten

---

[1] Another of Saul's sins. People ate dom due to hunger.

thousand men of Yahudah. 5 And Shaul came to a city of Amalek, and laid wait in the valley. 6 And Shaul said to the Kenites, Go, depart, get away from among the Amalekites, lest I destroy you with them: for you showed chesed to all the children of Yisrael, when they came up out of Mitzrayim. So the Kenites departed from among the Amalekites. 7 And Shaul smote the Amalekites from Havilah until you come to Shur, that is over against Mitzrayim. 8 And he took Agag the melech of the Amalekites alive, and utterly destroyed all the people with the edge of the sword. 9 But Shaul and the people spared Agag, along with the best of the sheep, and of the cattle, and of the fatlings, and the lambs, and all that was tov, and would not utterly destroy them: but everything that was vile and useless, that they destroyed utterly. 10 Then came the word of יהוה[1] to Schmuel, saying, 11 *It repents Me that I have set up Shaul to be melech: for he is turned back from following Me, and has not performed My orders.* And it grieved Schmuel; and he shouted to יהוה all night. 12 And when Schmuel rose early to meet Shaul in the morning, it was told Schmuel, saying, Shaul came to Carmel, and, see, he set up a place, and has gone out, and moved on, and gone down to Gilgal. 13 And Schmuel came to Shaul: and Shaul said to him, Yev-er-ech-echah יהוה : I have performed the order of יהוה . 14 And Schmuel said, What means then this bleating of the sheep in my ears, and the bellowing of the cattle which I shema? 15 And Shaul said, They have brought them from the Amalekites: for the people spared the best of the sheep and of the cattle, to sacrifice to יהוה Your Elohim; and the rest we have utterly destroyed. 16 Then Schmuel said to Shaul, Stay, and I will tell you what יהוה has said to me this night. And he said to him, Go ahead speak. 17 And Schmuel said, When you were little

in your own sight, were you not made the head of the tribes of Yisrael, and יהוה anointed you melech over kol Yisrael? 18 And יהוה sent you on a journey, and said, *Go and utterly destroy the sinners, the Amalekites, and fight against them until they are consumed.* 19 Why then did you not obey the voice of יהוה, but did jump upon the spoil, and did evil in the sight of יהוה? 20 And Shaul said to Schmuel, But yes, I have obeyed the voice of יהוה, and have gone on the derech that יהוה sent me, and have brought Agag the melech of Amalek, and have utterly destroyed the Amalekites. 21 But the people took of the spoil, sheep and cattle, the best of the things that should have been utterly destroyed, to sacrifice to יהוה Your Elohim in Gilgal. 22 And Schmuel said, Has יהוה as great a delight in burnt offerings and sacrifices, as in obeying the voice of יהוה? See, to obey is better than sacrifice, and to shema than the fat of rams. 23 For rebellion is as the sin of witchcraft, and stubbornness is as iniquity and idolatry. Because you have rejected the word of יהוה, He has also rejected you from being melech. 24 And Shaul said to Schmuel, I have sinned: for I have transgressed the order of יהוה, and your words: because I feared the people, and obeyed their voice. 25 Now therefore, I beg you, pardon my sin, help me make teshuvah again, that I may worship יהוה. 26 And Schmuel said to Shaul, I will not make teshuvah with you: for you have rejected the word of יהוה, and יהוה has rejected you from being melech over kol Yisrael. 27 And as Schmuel turned about to go away, he laid hold upon the robe of his mantle, and it tore. 28 And Schmuel said to him, יהוה has torn the malchut of Yisrael from you this day, and has given it to a neighbor of yours, that is better than you. 29 And also the Strength of Yisrael will not lie nor repent: for He is not a man that He should repent. 30 Then he said, I have sinned: yet honor me now, I beg you, before the zachanim of my people, and before

---

[1] The eternal Word is always a reference to Yahshua in both covenants.

Yisrael, and make teshuvah with me, that I may worship יהוה Your Elohim. 31 So Schmuel made teshuvah with Shaul; and then Shaul worshipped יהוה. 32 Then said Schmuel, Bring here to me Agag the melech of the Amalekites. And Agag came to him with delight. And Agag said, Surely the bitterness of death is past. 33 And Schmuel said, As your sword has made women childless, so shall your ima be childless among women. And Schmuel cut Agag in pieces before יהוה in Gilgal. 34 Then Schmuel went to Ramah; and Shaul went up to his bayit to Giveah of Shaul. 35 And Schmuel came no more to see Shaul until the day of his death: nevertheless Schmuel mourned for Shaul: and יהוה regretted that He had made Shaul melech over all Yisrael.

16 And יהוה said to Schmuel, *How long will you mourn for Shaul, seeing I have rejected him from reigning over all Yisrael? Fill your horn with oil, and go, I will send you to Yishai the Beth-Lechemite: for I have provided for Me a melech from among his sons.* 2 And Schmuel said, How can I go? If Shaul will shema it, he will kill me. And יהוה said, *Take a heifer with you, and say, I have come to sacrifice to יהוה.* 3 And call Yishai to the sacrifice, and I will show you what you shall do: and you shall anoint for Me the very one whom I name to you. 4 And Schmuel did that which יהוה spoke, and came to Beth-Lechem. And the zachanim of the town trembled at his coming, and said, Are you coming in shalom? 5 And he said, With shalom: I have come to sacrifice to יהוה: set yourselves apart, and come with me to the sacrifice. And he set apart Yishai and his sons, and called them to the sacrifice. 6 And it came to pass, when they were come, that he looked on Eliav, and said, Surely יהוה's anointed is before Him. 7 But יהוה said to Schmuel, *Look not on his appearance, or on his height; because I have refused him: for יהוה sees not as mankind sees; for mankind looks on the*

outward appearance, but יהוה looks on the lev. 8 Then Yishai called Aviniadav, and made him pass before Schmuel. And he said, Neither has יהוה chosen this one. 9 Then Yishai made Shammah to pass by. And he said, Neither has יהוה chosen this one. 10 Again, Yishai made seven of his sons to pass before Schmuel. And Schmuel said to Yishai, יהוה has not chosen any of these. 11 And Schmuel said to Yishai, Are all your children here? And he said, There remains yet the youngest, and, see, he keeps the sheep. And Schmuel said to Yishai, Send and get him: for we will not sit down until he comes here. 12 And he sent, and brought him in. Now he was dark-skinned and reddish, with a beautiful appearance, and tov-looking. And יהוה said, *Arise, and anoint him: for this is the one.* 13 Then Schmuel took the horn of oil, and anointed him in the midst of his brothers: and the Ruach of יהוה came upon David from that day forward. So Schmuel rose up, and went to Ramah. 14 But the Ruach of יהוה departed from Shaul, and an evil ruach from יהוה troubled him. 15 And Shaul's avadim said to him, See now, an evil ruach from Elohim troubles you. 16 Let our master now command your avadim, which are before you, to seek out a man, who is a skilled player on a harp: and it shall come to pass, when the evil ruach from Elohim is upon you, that he shall play with his hand, and you shall be well. 17 And Shaul said to his avadim, Provide me now a man that can play well, and bring him to me. 18 Then answered one of the avadim, and said, See, I have seen a son of Yishai the Beth-Lechemite, that is skilled in playing, and a mighty brave man, and a man of war, and prudent in all matters, and a handsome person, and יהוה is with him. 19 So Shaul sent messengers to Yishai, and said, Send me David your son, which is with the sheep. 20 And Yishai took a donkey loaded with lechem, and a bottle of wine, and a goat, and sent them by David his son to Shaul. 21 And David came to Shaul, and stood before him: and he loved him greatly; and he became his armor-bearer. 22 And Shaul sent to Yishai, saying, Let David, stand before me; for he has found favor in my sight. 23 And it came to pass, when the evil ruach from Elohim was upon Shaul, that David took a harp, and played with his hand: so Shaul was refreshed, and was well, and the evil ruach departed from him.

17 Now the Philistines gathered together their armies to battle, and were gathered together at Shochoh, which belongs to Yahudah, and pitched between Shochoh and Azekah, in Ephes-Dammim. 2 And Shaul and the men of Yisrael were gathered together, and pitched by the Valley of Elah, and began the battle in battle against the Philistines. 3 And the Philistines stood on a mountain on the one side, and Yisrael stood on a mountain on the other side: and there was a valley between them. 4 And there went out a champion out of the camp of the Philistines, named Golyath, of Gath, whose height was six cubits and a span. 5 And he had a helmet of bronze upon his head, and he was armed with a coat of scaled armor; and the weight of the coat was five thousand shekels of bronze. 6 And he had shin guards of bronze upon his legs, and a spear of bronze between his shoulders. 7 And the wood of his spear was like a weaver's beam; and his spear's head weighed six hundred shekels of iron: and his shield-bearer went before him. 8 And he stood and shouted to the armies of Yisrael, and said to them, Why are you come out to set yourselves in battle? Am not I a Philistine, and you avadim to Shaul? Choose a man from among you, and let him come down to me. 9 If he is able to fight with me, and to kill me, then will we be your avadim: but if I prevail against him, and kill him, then shall you be our avadim, and serve us. 10 And the Philistine said, I defy the armies of Yisrael this day; give me a man that we may fight together. 11 When Shaul and all Yisrael heard the words of the

Philistine, they were dismayed, and greatly afraid. 12 Now David was the son of the Ephrathite of Beth-Lechem Yahudah, whose name was Yishai; and he had eight sons: and in the days of Shaul, the man Yishai was old and advanced in years. 13 And the three eldest sons of Yishai went and followed Shaul to the battle: and the names of his three sons that went to the battle were Eliav the firstborn, and next to him Aviniadav, and the third Shammah. 14 And David was the youngest: and the three eldest followed Shaul. 15 But David went and returned from Shaul to feed his abba's sheep at Beth-Lechem. 16 And the Philistine drew near morning and evening, and presented himself for forty days. 17 And Yishai said to David his son, Take now for your brothers an ephah of this parched corn, and these ten loaves, and run to the camp to your brothers; 18 And carry these ten cheeses to the leader of their thousand, and look and see how your brothers are doing, and bring back news. 19 Now Shaul, and they, and all the men of Yisrael, were in the Valley of Elah, fighting with the Philistines. 20 And David rose up early in the morning, and left the sheep with a guardian, and took the items, and went, as Yishai had commanded him; and he came to the trench, as the host was going forth to the fight, and shouted for the battle. 21 For Yisrael and the Philistines were dressed for battle, army against army. 22 And David left his supplies in the hand of the guardian of the supplies, and ran into the army, and came and greeted his brothers. 23 And as he talked with them, see, there came up the champion, the Philistine of Gath, Golyath by name, out of the armies of the Philistines, and spoke the same threatening words: and David heard them. 24 And all the men of Yisrael, when they saw the man, fled from him, and were heavy with fear. 25 And the men of Yisrael said, Have you seen this man that has come up? Surely to defy Yisrael he is come up: and it shall be, that the man who kills him, the melech will enrich him with great riches, and will give him his daughter, and make his abba's bayit receive exemptions in Yisrael. 26 And David spoke to the men that stood by him, saying, What shall be done to the man that kills this Philistine, and takes away the reproach from Yisrael? For who is this uncircumcised Philistine, that he should defy the armies of the living Elohim? 27 And the people answered him after this manner, saying, So shall it be done to the man that kills him. 28 And Eliav his eldest brother heard when he spoke to the men; and Eliav's anger was kindled against David, and he said, Why did you come down here? And with whom have you left those few sheep in the wilderness? I know your pride, and the evil of your lev; for you are come down that you might watch the battle. 29 And David said, What have I now done? I was just talking. 30 And he turned from him toward another, and spoke after the same manner: and the people answered him again after the former manner. 31 And when the words were heard that David spoke, they repeated them before Shaul: and he sent for him. 32 And David said to Shaul, Let no man's lev fail because of him; your eved will go and fight with this Philistine. 33 And Shaul said to David, You are not able to go against this Philistine to fight with him: for you are but a youth, and he is a man of war from his youth. 34 And David said to Shaul, Your eved kept his abba's sheep, and there came a lion, and a bear, and took a lamb out of the flock: 35 And I went out after him, and smote him, and delivered it out of his mouth: and when he arose against me, I caught him by his beard, and smote him, and killed him. 36 Your eved killed both the lion and the bear: and this uncircumcised Philistine shall be as one of them, seeing he has defied the armies of the living Elohim. 37 David said moreover, יהוה that delivered me out of the paw of the lion, and out of the paw of the bear, He will deliver me out of the hand of this Philistine. And Shaul said to David, Go,

and יהוה be with you. 38 And Shaul armed David with his armor, and he put a helmet of bronze upon his head; also he armed him with a coat of armor. 39 And David girded his sword upon his armor, and he began to go; but stopped for he had not tried them. And David said to Shaul, I cannot go with these; for I have not tried them. And David took them off. 40 And he took his staff in his hand, and chose him five smooth stones out of the brook, and put them in a shepherd's bag which he had, even in a pouch; and his sling was in his hand: and he drew near to the Philistine. 41 And the Philistine came on and drew near to David; and the man that bore the shield went before him. 42 And when the Philistine looked around, and saw David, he despised him: for he was but a youth, and dark-skinned and ruddy, and of a handsome appearance. 43 And the Philistine said to David, Am I a dog; that you come to me with sticks? And the Philistine cursed David by his pagan elohim. 44 And the Philistine said to David, Come to me, and I will give your flesh to the fowls of the air, and to the beasts of the field. 45 Then said David to the Philistine, You come to me with a sword, and with a spear, and with a shield: but I come to you in the Name of יהוה of hosts, the Elohim of the armies of Yisrael, whom you have defied.[1] 46 This day will יהוה deliver you into mine hand; and I will smite you, and take your head from you; and I will give the dead bodies of the armies of the Philistines this day to the fowls of the air, and to the wild beasts of the earth; that all the earth may know that Yisrael has Elohim. 47 And all this congregation[2] shall know that יהוה saves not with sword and spear: for the battle is יהוה's, and He will give you into our hands. 48 And it came to pass, when the Philistine arose, and came and drew near to meet David, that David hurried, and ran toward the army to meet the Philistine. 49 And David put his hand in his bag, and

---

[1] What name do you come in?
[2] **Kahal** – same word for congregation translated as **ekklesia** in the Brit Chadashah and LXX.

took a stone, and slang it, and smote the Philistine in his forehead, that the stone sunk into his forehead; and he fell upon his face to the earth. 50 So David prevailed over the Philistine with a sling and with a stone, and smote the Philistine, and killed him; but there was no sword in the hand of David. 51 Therefore David ran, and stood upon the Philistine, and took his sword, and drew it out of the sheath, and killed him, and cut off his head with it. And when the Philistines saw that their champion was dead, they fled. 52 And the men of Yisrael and of Yahudah arose,[1] and shouted, and pursued the Philistines, until you come to the valley, and to the gates of Ekron. And the wounded of the Philistines fell down by the way to Shaaraim, even to Gath, and to Ekron. 53 And the children of Yisrael returned from chasing after the Philistines, and they plundered their tents. 54 And David took the head of the Philistine, and brought it to Yahrushalayim; but he put his armor in his tent. 55 And when Shaul saw David go forth against the Philistine, he said to Avner, the leader of the army, Avner, whose son is this youth? And Avner said, As your chayim lives, O melech, I cannot tell. 56 And the melech said, Find out whose son the young man is. 57 And as David returned from the slaughter of the Philistine, Avner took him, and brought him before Shaul with the head of the Philistine in his hand. 58 And Shaul said to him, Whose son are you, you young man? And David answered, I am the son of your eved Yishai the Beth-Lechemite.

18 And it came to pass, when he had made an end of speaking to Shaul, that the chayim of Yonathan was knit with the chayim of David, and Yonathan loved him as his own chayim. 2 And Shaul took him that day, and would not let him go home to his abba's bayit. 3 Then Yonathan and David made a covenant, because he loved him as his own chayim. 4 And Yonathan stripped himself of the robe that was upon him, and gave it to David, and his garments, even to his sword, and to his bow, and to his girdle. 5 And David went out wherever Shaul sent him, and behaved himself wisely: and Shaul set him over the men of war, and he was accepted in the sight of all the people, and also in the sight of Shaul's avadim. 6 And it came to pass as they came, when David had returned from the slaughter of the Philistine, that the women came out of all cities of Yisrael, singing and dancing, to meet melech Shaul, with tambourines, with simcha, and with instruments of music. 7 And the women sang as they played, and said, Shaul has killed his thousands, and David his ten of thousands. 8 And Shaul was very angry, and the saying displeased him; and he said, They have ascribed to David ten thousands, and to me they have ascribed only thousands: and what can he have more but the malchut itself? 9 And Shaul eyed David carefully from that day and forward. 10 And it came to pass on the next day, that the evil ruach from Elohim came upon Shaul, and he prophesied evil in the midst of the bayit: and David played the harp with his hand, as at other times: and there was a javelin in Shaul's hand. 11 And Shaul cast the javelin; for he said, I will smite David even to the wall with it. And David withdrew from his presence twice. 12 And Shaul was afraid of David, because יהוה was with him, and had departed from Shaul. 13 Therefore Shaul removed David from his presence, and made him his leader over a thousand; and he went out and came in before the people. 14 And David behaved himself wisely in all his halachot; and יהוה was with him. 15 So when Shaul saw that David behaved himself very wisely, he was afraid of him. 16 But all Yisrael and Yahudah loved David,[2] because he went out and came in before them. 17 And Shaul said to David, See my

---

[1] Another interesting two-house reference, especially in light of the fact that the split had not yet occurred officially.

[2] Another interesting pre-split reference; apparently there were seething problems below the surface that started around the time of Yisrael's call for a king.

eldest daughter Merav, I will give her to you as a wife: only be brave for me, and fight יהוה's battles. For Shaul said, Let not my hand kill him, but let the hand of the Philistines kill him. 18 And David said to Shaul, Who am I? And what is my chayim, or my abba's family in Yisrael, that I should be son-in-law to the melech? 19 But it came to pass at the time when Merav Shaul's daughter should have been given to David, that she was given to Adriel the Meholathite as his wife. 20 And Michal Shaul's daughter loved David: and they told Shaul, and the thing pleased him. 21 And Shaul said, I will give him to her, that she may be a snare to him, and that the hand of the Philistines may be against him. So Shaul said to David a second time, You shall this day be my son-in-law. 22 And Shaul commanded his avadim, saying, Commune with David secretly, and say, See, the melech delights in you, and all his avadim love you: now therefore be the melech's son-in-law. 23 And Shaul's avadim spoke those words in the ears of David. And David said, Does it seem to you a small thing to be a melech's son-in-law, seeing that I am a poor man, and lightly esteemed? 24 And the avadim of Shaul told him, saying, In this manner did David react. 25 And Shaul said, This shall you say to David, The melech desires no dowry, but only a hundred foreskins of the Philistines, to be avenged of the melech's enemies. But Shaul thought to kill David by the hands of the Philistines. 26 And when his avadim told David these words, it pleased David well to be the melech's son-in-law: and the days were not expired. 27 So David arose and went, he and his men, and killed of the Philistines two hundred men; and David brought their foreskins, and they gave them all to the melech, that he might be the melech's son-in-law. And Shaul gave him Michal his daughter as a wife. 28 And Shaul saw and knew that יהוה was with David, and that Michal Shaul's daughter loved him. 29 And Shaul was yet even more afraid of David;

and Shaul became David's enemy continually. 30 Then the rulers of the Philistines went forth: and it came to pass, after they went forth, that David behaved himself more wisely than all the avadim of Shaul; so that his name came to be very precious.

19 And Shaul spoke to Yonathan his son, and to all his avadim, that they should kill David. 2 But Yonathan Shaul's son delighted much in David: and Yonathan told David, saying, Shaul my abba seeks to kill you: now therefore, I beg you, take heed until the morning, and stay in a secret place, and hide yourself: 3 And I will go out and stand beside my abba in the field where you are, and I will commune with my abba about you, and what I see, that I will tell you. 4 And Yonathan spoke tov of David to Shaul his abba, and said to him, Let not the melech sin against his eved, against David, because he has not sinned against you, and because his works towards you have been very tov: 5 For he did take his chayim into his hands, and killed the Philistine, and יהוה brought a great deliverance for all Yisrael: you saw it, and did gilah: why then will you sin against innocent dom, to kill David without a cause? 6 And Shaul listened to the voice of Yonathan: and Shaul swore, As יהוה lives, he shall not be killed. 7 And Yonathan called David, and Yonathan showed him all those things. And Yonathan brought David to Shaul, and he was in his presence, as in times past. 8 And there was war again: and David went out, and fought with the Philistines, and killed them with a great slaughter; and they fled from him. 9 And the evil ruach from יהוה was upon Shaul again, as he sat in his bayit with his javelin in his hand: and David played the harp with his hand. 10 And Shaul sought to smite David even to the wall with the javelin; but he slipped away out of Shaul's presence, and he smote the javelin into the wall: and David fled, and escaped that night. 11 Shaul also sent

messengers to David's bayit, to watch him, and to kill him in the morning: and Michal David's wife told him, saying, If you save not your chayim tonight, tomorrow you shall be killed. 12 So Michal let David down through a window: and he went, and fled, and escaped. 13 And Michal took a bayit idol, and laid it in the bed, and put a pillow of goats' hair in place of his head, and covered it with a cloth. 14 And when Shaul sent messengers to take David, she said, He is sick. 15 And Shaul sent the messengers again to see David, saying, Bring him up to me in the bed, that I may kill him. 16 And when the messengers had come in, see, there was an image in the bed, with a pillow of goats' hair in place of his head. 17 And Shaul said to Michal, Why have you deceived me so, and sent away my enemy, that he is escaped? And Michal answered Shaul, He said to me, Let me go; why should I kill you? 18 So David fled, and escaped, and came to Schmuel in Ramah, and told him all that Shaul had done to him. And he and Schmuel went and dwelt in Naioth. 19 And it was told Shaul, saying, See, David is at Naioth in Ramah. 20 And Shaul sent messengers to take David: and when they saw the group of the niviim prophesying, and Schmuel standing as appointed over them, the Ruach of Elohim was upon the messengers of Shaul, and they also prophesied. 21 And when it was told Shaul, he sent other messengers, and they prophesied likewise. And Shaul sent messengers again the third time, and they prophesied also. 22 Then went he also to Ramah, and came to a great well that is in Sechu: and he asked and said, Where are Schmuel and David? And one said, See, they are at Naioth in Ramah. 23 And he went there to Naioth in Ramah: and the Ruach of Elohim was upon him also, and he went on, and prophesied, until he came to Naioth in Ramah. 24 And he stripped off his clothes also, and prophesied before Schmuel in like manner, and lay down naked all that day and all that night. Which is why they say, Is Shaul also among the niviim?

20 And David fled from Naioth in Ramah, and came and said before Yonathan, What have I done? What is my iniquity? And what is my sin before your abba, that he seeks my chayim? 2 And he said to him, Elohim forbid; you shall not die: see, my abba will do nothing either great or small, but that he will show it me: and why should my abba hide this thing from me? It is not so. 3 And David swore moreover, and said, Your abba certainly knows that I have found favor in your eyes; and he said, Let not Yonathan know this, lest he be grieved: but truly as יהוה lives, and as your chayim lives, there is but a step between me and death. 4 Then said Yonathan to David, Whatever your chayim desires, I will even do it for you. 5 And David said to Yonathan, See, tomorrow is the Rosh Chodesh, and I should be sitting with the melech to eat: but let me go, that I may hide myself in the field until the third day at evening. 6 If your abba misses me at all, then say, David earnestly asked leave of me that he might run to Beth-Lechem his city: for there is a yearly sacrifice there for all the family. 7 If he says this, It is well; your eved shall have shalom: but if he be very angry, then be sure that evil is determined by him. 8 Therefore you shall deal kindly with your eved; for you have brought your eved into a covenant of יהוה with you: nevertheless, if there be in me iniquity, kill me yourself; for why should you bring me to your abba? 9 And Yonathan said, Far be it from you: for if I knew certainly that evil were determined by my abba to come upon you, then would I not tell it to you? 10 Then said David to Yonathan, Who shall tell me? Or what if your abba answers you sharply? 11 And Yonathan said to David, Come, and let us go out into the field. And they went out both of them into the field. 12 And Yonathan said to David, O יהוה Elohim of

Yisrael be my witness, when I have sought for my abba sometime tomorrow, or the third day, and, see, if there be tov toward David, and I then send not to you, and show it to you; 13 Then יהוה do so and much more to Yonathan: but if it please my abba to do you evil, then I will show it you, and send you away, that you may go in shalom: and יהוה be with you, as He has been with my abba. 14 And you shall while yet I live show me the chesed of יהוה; that I die not: 15 And also you shall not cut off your chesed to my bayit le-olam-va-ed: when יהוה has cut off all the enemies of David from the face of the earth. 16 So Yonathan made a covenant, so his bayit would flourish with Beit David, saying, Let יהוה take vengeance against David's enemies. 17 And Yonathan caused David to swear again, because he loved him: for he loved him as he loved his own chayim. 18 Then Yonathan said to David, Tomorrow is Rosh Chodesh: and you shall be missed, because your seat will be empty. 19 And when you have stayed three days, then you shall go down quickly, and come to the place where you hid yourself, and shall remain by the stone Ezel. 20 And I will shoot three arrows on the side of the stone, as though I shot at a mark. 21 And, see, I will send a lad, saying, Go, find out the arrows. If I expressly say to the lad, See, the arrows are on this side of you, take them; then come out: for there is shalom to you, and no hurt; as יהוה lives. 22 But if I say this to the young man, See, the arrows are beyond you; then go your way: for יהוה has sent you away. 23 And as touching the matter which you and I have spoken of, see, יהוה be witness between you and me le-olam-va-ed. 24 So David hid himself in the field: and when the Rosh Chodesh had come, the melech sat down to eat. 25 And the melech sat upon his seat, as at other times, even upon a seat by the wall: and Yonathan arose, and Avner sat by Shaul's side, and David's place was empty. 26 Nevertheless Shaul spoke not anything that day: for he thought, Something has

happened to him, he is not clean; surely he is not clean. 27 And it came to pass on the next day, which was the second day of the month, that David's place was empty: and Shaul said to Yonathan his son, Why did not the son of Yishai come to eat, neither yesterday, nor today? 28 And Yonathan answered Shaul, David earnestly asked my permission to go to Beth-Lechem: 29 And he said, Let me go, I ask you; for our family has a sacrifice in the city; and my brother, he has commanded me to be there: and now, if I have found favor in your eyes, let me go, I ask you, and see my brothers. Therefore he came not to the melech's table. 30 Then Shaul's anger was kindled against Yonathan, and he said to him, You son of the perverse rebellious woman, do not I know that you have chosen the son of Yishai to your own shame, and to the shame of your ima's nakedness? 31 For as long as the son of Yishai lives upon the earth, you shall not be established, in your malchut. And now send and get him for me, for he shall surely die. 32 And Yonathan answered Shaul his abba, and said to him, Why shall he be killed? What has he done? 33 And Shaul cast a javelin at him to smite him: whereby Yonathan knew that it was determined by his abba to kill David. 34 So Yonathan arose from the table in fierce anger, and did eat no food the second day of the month: for he was grieved for David, because his abba had done him shame. 35 And it came to pass in the morning, that Yonathan went out into the field at the time appointed with David, and a little lad with him. 36 And he said to his lad, Run and find out where the arrows that I shoot will land. And as the lad ran, he shot an arrow beyond him. 37 And when the lad was come to the place of the arrow which Yonathan had shot, Yonathan shouted after the lad, and said, Is not the arrow beyond you? 38 And Yonathan shouted after the lad, Hurry, hurry, stay not. And Yonathan's lad gathered up the arrows, and came to his master. 39 But the lad knew not any thing:

only Yonathan and David knew the matter. 40 And Yonathan gave his artillery to his lad, and said to him, Go, carry them to the city. 41 And as soon as the lad was gone, David arose out of a place toward the south, and fell on his face to the ground, and bowed himself three times: and they kissed one another, and wept one with another, but David wept more. 42 And Yonathan said to David, Go in shalom, since we have sworn both of us in the Name of **יהוה**, saying, **יהוה** be witness between me and you, and between my zera and your zera le-olam-va-ed. And he arose and departed: and Yonathan went into the city.

21 Then came David to Nob to Achimelech the kohen: and Achimelech was afraid at the meeting of David, and said to him, Why are you alone, and no man with you? 2 And David said to Achimelech the kohen, The melech has commanded me a word, and has said to me, Let no man know any thing of the business about which I send you, and what I have commanded you: and I have appointed my avadim to such and such a place. 3 Now therefore what is under your hand? Give me five loaves of lechem in my hand, or what there is present. 4 And the kohen answered David, and said, There is no common lechem on hand, but there is set-apart lechem; if the young men have kept themselves at least from women. 5 And David answered the kohen, and said to him, Of an emet women have been kept from us around three days, since I came out, and the vessels of the young men are set-apart, but the lechem is practically common, even though it was set-apart this day in the vessel. 6 So the kohen gave him set-apart lechem: for there was no lechem there but the Lechem of the Faces, that was taken from before **יהוה**, to put hot lechem in the day when it was taken away. 7 Now a certain man of the avadim of Shaul was there that day, detained before **יהוה**; and his name was Doeg, an Edomite, the head

of the herdsmen that belonged to Shaul. 8 And David said to Achimelech, And is there not here under your hand spear or sword? For I have neither brought my sword nor my weapons with me, because the melech's business was urgent. 9 And the kohen said, The sword of Golyath the Philistine, whom you killed in the Valley of Elah, see, it is here wrapped in a cloth behind the shoulder garment: if you want to take that, take it: for there is no other one except that here. And David said, There is none like that; give it me. 10 And David arose, and fled that day for fear of Shaul, and went to Achish the melech of Gath. 11 And the avadim of Achish said to him, Is not this David the melech of the land? Did they not sing one to another of him in dances, saying, Shaul has killed his thousands, and David his ten thousands? 12 And David laid up these words in his lev, and was very afraid of Achish the melech of Gath. 13 And he changed his behavior before them, and pretended to be crazy in their hands, and scratched on the doors of the gate, and let his saliva fall down upon his beard. 14 Then said Achish to his avadim, Look, you see the man is crazy: why then have you brought him to me? 15 Have I need of crazy men, that you have brought this fellow to play the crazy man in my presence? Shall this fellow even come into my bayit?

22 David therefore departed from there, and escaped to the cave Adullam: and when his brothers and all his abba's bayit heard it, they went down there to him. 2 And every one that was in distress, and every one that was in debt, and every one that was discontented, gathered themselves to him; and he became a leader over them: and there were with him about four hundred men. 3 And David went there to Mitzpeh of Moav: and he said to the melech of Moav, Let my abba and my ima, I ask you, come forth, and be with you, until I know what Elohim will do for me. 4 And

he brought them before the melech of Moav: and they dwelt with him all the while that David was in the stronghold. 5 And the navi Gad said to David, Do not stay in the stronghold; depart, and get you into the land of Yahudah. Then David departed, and came into the forest of Hareth. 6 When Shaul heard that David was discovered, and the men that were with him, now Shaul stayed in Giveah under an eytz in Ramah, having his spear in his hand, and all his avadim were standing around him; 7 Then Shaul said to his avadim that stood arout him, Shema now, you Benyamites; will the son of Yishai give every one of you fields and vineyards, and make you all captains of thousands, and captains of hundreds; 8 Seeing that all of you have conspired against me, and there is none that has shown me that my son has made a pact with the son of Yishai, and there is none of you that is sorry for me, or shown to me that my son has stirred up my eved against me, to lie in wait, as at this day? 9 Then answered Doeg the Edomite, which was set over the avadim of Shaul, and said, I saw the son of Yishai coming to Nob, to Achimelech the son of Ahituv. 10 And he inquired of יהוה for him, and gave him food, and gave him the sword of Golyath the Philistine. 11 Then the melech sent to call Achimelech the kohen, the son of Ahituv, and all his abba's bayit, the kohanim that were in Nob: and they came all of them to the melech. 12 And Shaul said, Shema now, you son of Ahituv. And he answered, Here I am, my master. 13 And Shaul said to him, Why have you conspired against me, you and the son of Yishai, in that you have given him lechem, and a sword, and have inquired of Elohim for him, that he should rise against me, to lie in wait, as at this day? 14 Then Achimelech answered the melech, and said, And who is so faithful among all your avadim as David, which is the melech's son-in-law, and goes at your bidding, and is honorable in your bayit? 15 Did I then begin to inquire of Elohim for him? Be it

far from me: let not the melech impute anything unto his eved, nor to all the bayit of my abba: for your eved knew nothing of all this, not a little, not a lot. 16 And the melech said, You shall surely die, Achimelech, you, and all your abba's bayit. 17 And the melech said to the footmen that stood about him, Turn, and ki!l the kohanim of יהוה; because their hand also is with David, and because they knew when he fled, and did not show it to me. But the avadim of the melech would not put forth their hand to fall upon the kohanim of יהוה. 18 And the melech said to Doeg, Turn you, and fall upon the kohanim. And Doeg the Edomite turned, and he fell upon the kohanim, and killed on that day eighty-five persons that did wear a linen shoulder garment. 19 And Nob, the city of the kohanim, Doeg smote with the edge of the sword, both men and women, children and those nursing, and cattle, and donkeys, and sheep, with the edge of the sword. 20 And one of the sons of Achimelech the son of Ahituv, named Aviathar, escaped, and fled after David. 21 And Aviathar showed David that Shaul had killed יהוה 's kohanim. 22 And David said to Aviathar, I knew it that day, when Doeg the Edomite was there, that he would surely tell Shaul: I have caused the death of all the persons of your abba's bayit. 23 Stay with me, fear not: for he that seeks my chayim seeks your chayim: but with me you shall be safe.

23 Then they told David, saying, See, the Philistines fight against Keilah, and they rob the threshing floors. 2 Therefore David inquired of יהוה, saying, Shall I go and smite these Philistines? And יהוה said to David, Go, and smite the Philistines, and save Keilah. 3 And David's men said to him, See, we are afraid here in Yahudah: how much more then if we come to Keilah against the armies of the Philistines? 4 Then David inquired of יהוה yet again. And יהוה answered him and said, Arise, go down to

Keilah, for I will deliver the Philistines into your hand. 5 So David and his men went to Keilah, and fought with the Philistines, and brought away their cattle, and smote them with a great slaughter. So David saved the inhabitants of Keilah. 6 And it came to pass, when Aviathar the son of Achimelech fled to David to Keilah, that he came down with a shoulder garment in his hand. 7 And it was told Shaul that David was come to Keilah. And Shaul said, Elohim has delivered him into my hand; for he is shut in, by entering into a town that has gates and bars. 8 And Shaul called all the people together to war, to go down to Keilah, to besiege David and his men. 9 And David knew that Shaul secretly plotted mischief against him; and he said to Aviathar the kohen, Bring here the shoulder garment. 10 Then said David, O יהוה Elohim of Yisrael, Your eved has certainly heard that Shaul seeks to come to Keilah, to destroy the city for my sake. 11 Will the men of Keilah deliver me up into his hand? Will Shaul come down, as Your eved has heard? O יהוה Elohim of Yisrael, I beseech You, tell Your eved. And יהוה said, He will come down. 12 Then said David, Will the men of Keilah deliver me and my men into the hand of Shaul? And יהוה said, They will deliver you up. 13 Then David and his men, who were about six hundred, arose and departed out of Keilah, and went wherever they could go. And it was told Shaul that David was escaped from Keilah; and he ceased to go forth. 14 And David stayed in the wilderness in strongholds, and remained in a mountain in the wilderness of Ziph. And Shaul sought him every day, but Elohim delivered him not into his hand. 15 And David saw that Shaul was come out to seek his chayim: and David was in the wilderness of Ziph at Choresh. 16 And Yonathan Shaul's son arose, and went to David at Choresh, and strengthened his hand in Elohim. 17 And he said to him, Fear not: for the hand of Shaul my abba

shall not find you; and you shall be melech over Yisrael, and I shall be next to you; and that also Shaul my abba knows. 18 And the two of them made a covenant before יהוה: and David stayed in the Choresh, and Yonathan went to his bayit. 19 Then came up the Ziphites to Shaul to Giveah, saying, Does not David hide himself with us in strongholds in the forest, in the hill of Hachilah, which is on the south of Yeshimon? 20 Now therefore, O melech, come down according to all the desire of your chayim to come down; and our part shall be to deliver him into the melech's hand. 21 And Shaul said, Blessed are you of יהוה ; for you have rachamim on me. 22 Go, I ask you, prepare yet further, and know and see his place where his hide-out is, and who has seen him there: for it is told to me that he deals very subtly. 23 See therefore, and take da'at of all the hiding places where he hides himself, and come again to me with the certainty of his place, and I will go with you: and it shall come to pass, if he is in the land, that I will search him out throughout all the thousands of Yahudah. 24 And they arose, and went to Ziph before Shaul: but David and his men were in the wilderness of Maon, in the plain on the south of Yeshimon. 25 Shaul also and his men went to seek him. And they told David: therefore he came down into a rock, and stayed in the wilderness of Maon. And when Shaul heard that, he pursued after David in the wilderness of Maon. 26 And Shaul went on this side of the mountain, and David and his men on the other side of the mountain: and David made a rapid getaway to get away for fear of Shaul; for Shaul and his men surrounded David and his men to take them. 27 But there came a messenger to Shaul, saying, Hurry and get back, and come, for the Philistines have invaded the land. 28 So Shaul returned from pursuing after David, and went against the Philistines: therefore they called that place Sela-Hamm-Ahlek-Oth. 29 And David went up from there, and dwelt in strongholds at En-Gedi.

24 And it came to pass, when Shaul had returned from following the Philistines, that it was told him, saying, See, David is in the wilderness of En-Gedi. 2 Then Shaul took three thousand chosen men out of all Yisrael, and went to seek David and his men upon the rocks of the wild goats. 3 And he came to the sheepfolds and on the way, where was a cave; and Shaul went in to relieve himself: and David and his men remained in the sides of the cave. 4 And the men of David said to him, See the day of which יהוה said to you, See, I will deliver your enemy into your hand, that you may do to him as it shall seem tov to you. Then David arose, and cut off the corner of Shaul's robe privately. 5 And it came to pass afterward, that David's lev smote him, because he had cut off Shaul's robe. 6 And he said to his men, יהוה forbid that I should do this thing to my master, יהוה's anointed, to stretch forth my hand against him, seeing he is the anointed of יהוה. 7 So David stopped his avadim with these words, and allowed them not to rise against Shaul. But Shaul rose up out of the cave, and went on his way. 8 David also arose afterward, and went out of the cave, and shouted after Shaul, saying, My master the melech. And when Shaul looked behind him, David stooped with his face to the earth, and bowed himself. 9 And David said to Shaul, Why do you shema to men's words, saying, See, David seeks your hurt? 10 See, this day your eyes have seen how that יהוה had delivered you today into my hand in the cave: and some urged me to kill you: but my eye spared you; and I said, I will not put forth my hand against my master; for he is יהוה 's anointed. 11 Moreover, my abba, see the corner of your robe in my hand: for in that I cut off the corner of your robe and killed you not, now you know and see that there is neither

evil nor transgression in my hand, and I have not sinned against you; yet you hunt my chayim to take it. 12 יהוה shophet between us, and יהוה avenge me from you: but my own hand shall not be upon you. 13 As said the mishle of the ancients, Wickedness proceeds from the wicked: but my hand shall not be upon you. 14 After whom is the melech of Yisrael come out? After whom do you pursue? After a dead dog, or after a flea? 15 יהוה therefore is Shophet, and He will shophet between me and you, and see, and I will plead my cause, to be delivered out of your hand. 16 And it came to pass, when David had made an end of speaking these words to Shaul, that Shaul said, Is this your voice, my son David? And Shaul lifted up his voice, and wept. 17 And he said to David, You are more tzadik than I: for you have rewarded me tov, whereas I have rewarded you evil. 18 And you have showed me this day how that you have dealt well with me: seeing that when יהוה had delivered me into your hand, you killed me not. 19 For if a man finds his enemy, will he let him go away whole? Therefore יהוה reward you tov for what you have done to me this day. 20 And now, see, I know well that you shall surely be melech, and that the malchut of Yisrael shall be established in your hand. 21 Swear now therefore to me by יהוה, that you will not cut off my zera after me, and that you will not destroy my name out of my abba's bayit. 22 And David swore to Shaul. And Shaul went home; but David and his men went up to the stronghold.

25 And Schmuel died; and all the Yisraelites were gathered together, and lamented him, and buried him in his bayit at Ramah. And David arose, and went down to the wilderness of Paran. 2 And there was a man in Maon, whose possessions were in Carmel; and the man was very great, and he had three thousand sheep, and a thousand goats: and he was shearing his sheep in Carmel. 3 Now the

name of the man was Naval; and the name of his wife Avigail: and she was a woman of tov understanding, and of a beautiful appearance: but the man was hardened and evil in his doings; and he was of the bayit of Calev. 4 And David heard in the wilderness that Naval did shear his sheep. 5 And David sent out ten young men, and David said to the young men, Get up to Carmel, and go to Naval, and greet him in my name: 6 And say to him that lives in prosperity, Shalom be both to you, and shalom be to your bayit, and shalom be to all that you have. 7 And now I have heard that you have shearers: now your shepherds that were with us, we hurt them not, neither was there anything missing to them, all the while they were in Carmel. 8 Ask your young men, and they will tell you. So let the young men find favor in your eyes: for we come in a tov day: give, I ask you, whatever comes to your hand to your avadim, and to your son David. 9 And when David's young men came, they spoke to Naval according to all those words in the name of David, and waited. 10 And Naval answered David's avadim, and said, Who is David? And who is the son of Yishai? There are many avadim nowadays that break away every man from his master. 11 Shall I then take my lechem, and my mayim, and my food that I have killed for my shearers, and give it to men, whom I know not from where they are? 12 So David's young men turned their way, and went again, and came and told him all those sayings. 13 And David said to his men, Put on every man his sword. And they put on every man his sword; and David also put on his sword: and there went up after David about four hundred men; and two hundred stayed by the baggage. 14 But one of the young men told Avigail, Naval's wife, saying, See, David sent messengers out of the wilderness to greet our master; and he railed on them. 15 But the men were very tov to us, and we were not hurt, neither did we miss anything, as long as we were accompanying them,

when we were in the fields: 16 They were like a wall to us both by night and day, all the time we were with them keeping the sheep. 17 Now therefore know and consider what you will do; for evil is determined against our master, and against all his household: for he is such a son of Beliyaal, that a man cannot even speak to him. 18 Then Avigail hurried, and took two hundred loaves, and two bottles of wine, and five sheep made ready, and five measures of parched corn, and a hundred clusters of raisins, and two hundred cakes of figs, and laid them on donkeys. 19 And she said to her avadim, Go before me, and I will come after you. But she told it not her husband Naval. 20 And it was so, as she rode on the donkey, that she came down under the cover of the hill, and, see, David and his men came down toward her; and she met them. 21 Now David had said, Surely for nothing have I kept all that this fellow has in the wilderness, so that nothing was missed of all that pertained to him: and he has repaid me evil for tov. 22 Let Elohim do this and even more to the enemies of David, if I leave even one adult man to him by the morning light. 23 And when Avigail saw David, she hurried, and got off the donkey, and fell before David on her face, and bowed herself to the ground, 24 And fell at his feet, and said, Upon me, my master, upon me let this iniquity be: and let your female eved, I beg you, speak in your hearing, and shema the words of your female eved. 25 Let not my master, I beg you, regard this man of Beliyaal, even Naval: for as his name is, so is he; Naval is his name, and folly is with him: but I your female eved did not see the young men of my master, whom you did send. 26 Now therefore, my master, as יהוה lives, and as your being lives, seeing יהוה has withheld you from coming to shed dom, and from avenging yourself with your own hand, now let your enemies, and they that seek evil to my master, be as Naval. 27 And now this blessing that your female eved has brought to my master, let it even be given to the young men that follow my master. 28 I beg you, forgive the trespass of your female eved: for **יהוה** will certainly make my master a sure and secure bayit; because my master fights the battles of **יהוה**, and evil has not been found in you all your days. 29 Yet a man has risen to pursue you, and to seek your chayim: but the chayim of my master shall be bound in the bundle of chayim with **יהוה** Your Elohim; and the beings of your enemies, them shall he sling out, as out of the middle of a sling. 30 And it shall come to pass, when **יהוה** shall have done to my master according to all the tov that He has spoken concerning you, and shall have appointed you ruler over Yisrael; 31 That this shall bring no grief to you, no offence of lev to my master, either that you have shed dom without cause, or that my master has avenged himself: but when **יהוה** shall have dealt well with my master, then remember your female eved. 32 And David said to Avigail, Blessed be **יהוה** Elohim of Yisrael, who sent you this day to meet me: 33 And blessed is your advice, and blessed are you, who have kept me this day from coming to shed dom, and from avenging myself with my own hand. 34 For in very deed, as **יהוה** Elohim of Yisrael lives, which has kept me back from hurting you, except you had hurried and come to meet me, surely there had not been left to Naval by the morning light any man. 35 So David received from her hand that which she had brought him, and said to her, Go up in shalom to your bayit. See, I have listened to your voice, and have accepted your whole person. 36 And Avigail came to Naval; and, see, he held a feast in his bayit, like the feast of a melech; and Naval's lev was cheerful within him, for he was very drunk: wherefore she told him nothing, at all, until the morning light. 37 But it came to pass in the morning, when Naval was sober, and his wife had told him these things that his lev died within him; and he became as a stone lev. 38 And it came to pass about ten days

after that **יהוה** smote Naval, so that he died. 39 And when David heard that Naval was dead, he said, Barchu et **יהוה**, that has pleaded the cause of my reproach from the hand of Naval, and has kept his eved from doing evil: for **יהוה** has returned the wickedness of Naval upon his own head, And David sent and communicated with Avigail, to take her to him as a wife. 40 And when the avadim of David were come to Avigail to Carmel, they spoke to her, saying, David sent us to you to take you to him as his wife. 41 And she arose, and bowed herself on her face to the earth, and said, See, let your female eved be an eved to wash the feet of the avadim of my master. 42 And Avigail hurried, and arose, and rode upon a donkey, with five young women of hers that went after her; and she went after the messengers of David, and became his wife. 43 David also took Achinoam of Yezreel; and they were also both of them his wives. 44 But Shaul had given Michal his daughter, David's wife, to Phalti the son of Layish, which was of Gallim.

26 And the Ziphites came to Shaul to Giveah, saying, Does not David hide himself in the hill of Hachilah, which is before Yeshimon? 2 Then Shaul arose, and went down to the wilderness of Ziph, having three thousand chosen men of Yisrael with him, to seek David in the wilderness of Ziph. 3 And Shaul pitched in the hill of Hachilah, which is before Yeshimon, along the way. But David stayed in the wilderness, and he saw that Shaul came after him into the wilderness. 4 David therefore sent out spies, and understood that Shaul had come indeed. 5 And David arose, and came to the place where Shaul had pitched: and David beheld the place where Shaul lay, and Avner the son of Ner, the leader of his army: and Shaul lay in the trench, and the people pitched round about him. 6 Then answered David and said to Achimelech the Hittite, and to Avishai the

son of Zeruiah, brother to Yoav, saying, Who will go down with me to Shaul to the camp? And Avishai said, I will go down with you. 7 So David and Avishai came to the people by night: and, see, Shaul lay sleeping within the camp, and his spear stuck in the ground at his bolster: but Avner and the people lay around him. 8 Then said Avishai to David, Elohim has delivered your enemy into your hand this day: now therefore let me smite him, I ask you, with the spear even to the earth at once, and I will not smite him the second time. 9 And David said to Avishai, Destroy him not: for who can stretch forth his hand against יהוה 's anointed, and be guiltless?[1] 10 David said furthermore, As יהוה lives, יהוה shall smite him; or his day shall come to die; or he shall descend into battle, and perish. 11 But יהוה forbid that I should stretch forth my hand against יהוה's anointed: but, I ask you, take now the spear that is at his bolster, and the jug of mayim, and let us go. 12 So David took the spear and the jug of mayim from Shaul's bolster; and they got away, and no man saw it, nor knew it, neither was awakened: for they were all asleep; because a deep sleep from יהוה had fallen upon them. 13 Then David went over to the other side, and stood on the top of a hill far off; a great space being between them: 14 And David shouted to the people, and to Avner the son of Ner, saying, Don't you answer, Avner? Then Avner answered and said, Who are you that shouts at the melech? 15 And David said to Avner, Are not you a brave man? And who is like you in Yisrael? Why then have you not guarded your master the melech? For there came one of the people in to destroy the melech your master. 16 This thing is not tov that you have done. As יהוה lives, you are worthy to die, because you have not guarded your master, יהוה 's anointed. And now see where the melech's spear is, and the jug of mayim that was at his bolster. 17 And Shaul

knew David's voice, and said, Is this your voice, my son David? And David said, It is my voice, my master, O melech. 18 And he said, Why does my master still pursue after his eved? For what have I done? Or what evil is in my hand? 19 Now therefore, I beg you, let my master the melech shema the words of his eved. If יהוה has stirred you up against me, let Him accept an offering: but if they are the children of men, cursed are they before יהוה; for they have driven me out this day from abiding in the inheritance of יהוה, saying, Go, serve other elohim. 20 Now therefore, let not my dom fall to the earth before the face of יהוה: for the melech of Yisrael is come out to seek a flea, as when one does hunt a partridge in the mountains. 21 Then said Shaul, I have sinned: return, my son David: for I will no more do you harm, because my chayim was precious in your eyes this day: see, I have played the fool, and have greatly strayed. 22 And David answered and said, See the melech's spear! Let one of the young men come over and get it. 23 יהוה render to every man his tzedakah and his faithfulness: for יהוה delivered you into my hand today, but I would not stretch forth my hand against יהוה's anointed. 24 And, see, as your chayim was much valued this day in my eyes, so let my chayim be much valued in the eyes of יהוה, and let Him deliver me out of all tribulation. 25 Then Shaul said to David, Blessed be you, my son David: you shall both do great things, and also shall prevail. So David went on his way, and Shaul returned to his place.

27 And David said in his lev, I shall now perish one day by the hand of Shaul: there is nothing better for me than that I should speedily escape into the land of the Philistines; so that Shaul shall give up searching for me, to seek me any more in any of the borders of Yisrael: so shall I escape out of his hand. 2 And David arose, and he passed over with the six hundred men that were with him to Achish, the son

---

[1] A lesson Renewed Covenant Yisraelites need to grasp before wrath comes.

of Maoch, melech of Gath. 3 And David dwelt with Achish at Gath, he and his men, every man with his household, even David with his two wives, Achinoam the Yezreelitess, and Avigail the Carmelitess, Naval's wife. 4 And it was told Shaul that David had fled to Gath: and he sought no more again for him. 5 And David said to Achish, If I have now found favor in your eyes, let them give me a place in some town in the country, that I may dwell there: for why should your eved dwell in the royal city with you? 6 Then Achish gave him Ziklag that day: wherefore Ziklag belongs to the melechim of Yahudah to this day. 7 And the time that David dwelt in the country of the Philistines was a full year and four months. 8 And David and his men went up, and invaded the Geshurites, and the Gezrites, and the Amalekites: for those pagan nations were of old the inhabitants of the land, as you head to Shur, even to the land of Mitzrayim. 9 And David smote the land, and left neither man nor woman alive, and took away the sheep, and the cattle, and the donkeys, and the camels, and the apparel, and returned, and came to Achish. 10 And Achish said, Where have you made a raid today? And David said, Against the south of Yahudah, and against the south of the Yerahmeelites, and against the south of the Kenites. 11 And David saved neither man nor woman alive, to bring news to Gath, saying, Lest they should tell on us, saying, So did David, and so will be his manner all the while he dwells in the country of the Philistines. 12 And Achish believed David, saying, He has made his people Yisrael utterly to hate him; therefore he shall be my eved le-olam-va-ed.

28 And it came to pass in those days, that the Philistines gathered their armies together for warfare, to fight with Yisrael. And Achish said to David, You know of course, that you shall go out with me to battle, you and your men. 2 And David said to Achish, Surely you shall know what your eved can do. And Achish said to David, Therefore will I make you guardian of my head le-olam-va-ed. 3 Now Schmuel was dead, and all Yisrael had lamented him, and buried him in Ramah, even in his own city. And Shaul had put away those that had familiar spirits, and the wizards, out of the land. 4 And the Philistines gathered themselves together, and came and pitched in Shunem: and Shaul gathered all Yisrael together, and they pitched in Gilvoa. 5 And when Shaul saw the host of the Philistines, he was afraid, and his lev greatly trembled. 6 And when Shaul inquired of יהוה, יהוה answered him not, neither by dreams nor by Urim, nor by niviim. 7 Then said Shaul to his avadim, Seek for me a woman who is a medium, that I may go to her, and inquire of her. And his avadim said to him, See, there is a woman that is a medium at Endor. 8 And Shaul disguised himself, and put on other clothes, and he went, and two men with him, and they came to the woman by night: and he said, I ask you, divine for me by a familiar ruach, and bring me up, the one I shall name to you. 9 And the woman said to him, See, you know what Shaul has done, how he has cut off the mediums, and the wizards, out of the land: why then do you lay a snare for my chayim, to cause me to die? 10 And Shaul swore to her by יהוה, saying, As יהוה lives, there shall no punishment happen to you for this thing. 11 Then said the woman, Whom shall I bring up to you? And he said, Bring me up Schmuel. 12 And when the woman saw Schmuel, she shouted with a loud voice: and the woman spoke to Shaul, saying, Why have you deceived me? For you are Shaul. 13 And the melech said to her, Be not afraid: what did you see? And the woman said to Shaul, I saw a ruach ascending out of the earth. 14 And he said to her, What does he look like? And she said, An old man comes up; and he is covered with a mantle. And Shaul perceived that it was Schmuel, and he stooped with

his face to the ground, and bowed himself. 15 And Schmuel said to Shaul, Why have you disturbed my rest, to bring me up?[1] And Shaul answered, I am heavy distressed; for the Philistines make war against me, and Elohim has departed from me, and answers me no longer, neither by niviim, nor by dreams: therefore I have called you, that you may make known to me what I shall do. 16 Then said Schmuel, Why then do you ask of me, seeing יהוה has departed from you, and has become your enemy? 17 And יהוה has done to you, as He spoke by me: for יהוה has torn the malchut out of your hand, and given it to your neighbor, even to David: 18 Because you obeyed not the voice of יהוה , nor executed His fierce wrath upon Amalek, therefore has יהוה done this thing to you this day. 19 Moreover יהוה will also deliver Yisrael with you into the hand of the Philistines: and tomorrow you and your sons will be with me: [2] יהוה also shall deliver the armies of Yisrael into the hand of the Philistines. 20 Then Shaul fell immediately on the earth, and was very afraid, because of the words of Schmuel: and there was no strength in him, for he had eaten no lechem all the day, and all the night. 21 And the woman came to Shaul, and saw that he was heavily troubled, and said to him, See, your female eved has obeyed your voice, and I have put my chayim in my hands, and have listened to your words which you spoke to me. 22 Now therefore, I beg you, Shema also to the voice of your female eved, and let me set a piece of lechem before you; and eat, that you may have strength, when you go on your derech. 23 But he refused and said, I will not eat. But his avadim, together with the woman, compelled him; and he listened to their voice. So he arose from the earth, and sat upon the bed. 24 And the woman had a fat calf in the bayit; and she hurried, and killed it, and took flour, and kneaded it, and did bake matzah from it: 25 And she brought it before Shaul, and before his avadim; and they did eat. Then they rose up, and went away that night.

29 Now the Philistines gathered together all their armies to Aphek: and the Yisraelites pitched by a fountain that is in Yezreel. 2 And the rulers of the Philistines passed on by hundreds, and by thousands: but David and his men passed on in the rear guard with Achish. 3 Then said the rulers of the Philistines, What are these Ivrim doing here? And Achish said to the rulers of the Philistines, Is not this David, the eved of Shaul the melech of Yisrael, which has been with me these days, and these years, and I have found no fault in him since he came to me until this day? 4 And the rulers of the Philistines were angry with him; and the rulers of the Philistines said to him, Make this fellow return, that he may go again to his place which you have appointed him, and let him not go down with us to battle, lest in the battle he be an adversary to us: for how can he reconcile himself to his master? Except with the heads of these our men? 5 Is not this David, of whom they sang one to another in dances, saying, Shaul killed his thousands, and David his ten thousands? 6 Then Achish called David, and said to him, Surely, as יהוה lives, you have been a tzadik, and your going out and your coming in with me in the army is tov in my sight: for I have not found evil in you since the day of your coming to me to this day: nevertheless the other rulers' opinion is not favorable of you. 7 So now return, and go in shalom, that you displease not the rulers of the Philistines. 8 And David said to Achish, But what have I done? And what have you found in your eved so long as I have been with you to this day, that I may not go fight against the enemies of my master the

---

[1] Notice that like all other righteous men in YHWH in the Tanach, Samuel is in Abraham's Bosom in the earth waiting for the revelation of Moshiach to release him to eternal life in the heavens. He is certainly not sleeping in the ruach but is most conscious.
[2] In Sheol or the other compartment in the earth, where the unrighteous went before Moshiach, never to be released but held for the Great White Throne Judgment of Revelation 20.

melech? 9 And Achish answered and said to David, I know that you are as tov in my sight, as a messenger of Elohim: nevertheless the rulers of the Philistines have said, He shall not go up with us to the battle. 10 So now rise up early in the morning with your master's avadim that have come with you: and as soon as you are up early in the morning, and have light, depart. 11 So David and his men rose up early to depart in the morning, to return into the land of the Philistines. And the Philistines went up to Yezreel.

30 And it came to pass, when David and his men were come to Ziklag on the third day, that the Amalekites had invaded the south, and Ziklag, and smitten Ziklag, and burned it with fire; 2 And had taken the women captives, that were there: they killed not any, either great or small, but carried them away, and went on their way. 3 So David and his men came to the city, and, see, it was burned with fire; and their wives, and their sons, and their daughters, were taken captives. 4 Then David and the people that were with him lifted up their voice and wept, until they had no more power to weep. 5 And David's two wives were taken captives, Achinoam the Yezreelitess, and Avigail the wife of Naval the Carmelite. 6 And David was greatly distressed; for the people spoke of stoning him, because the chayim of all the people was grieved, every man for his sons and for his daughters: but David encouraged himself in יהוה His Elohim. 7 And David said to Aviathar the kohen, Achimelech's son, I ask you, bring me here the shoulder garment. And Aviathar brought there the shoulder garment to David. 8 And David inquired of יהוה, saying, Shall I pursue after this troop? Shall I overtake them? And He answered him, *Pursue, for you shall surely overtake them, and without fail recover all.* 9 So David went, he and the six hundred men who were with him, and came to the brook Besor, where those that were

left behind stayed. 10 But David pursued, he and four hundred men: for two hundred stayed behind, who were so weak that they could not go over the brook Besor. 11 And they found a Mitzrite in the field, and brought him to David, and gave him lechem, and he did eat; and they made him drink mayim; 12 And they gave him a piece of a cake of figs, and two clusters of raisins: and when he had eaten, his ruach came again to him: for he had not eaten lechem, nor drunk any mayim, three days and three nights. 13 And David said to him, To whom do you belong? Where are you from? And he said, I am a young man of Mitzrayim, an eved to an Amalekite; and my master left me, because three days ago I fell sick. 14 We made an invasion upon the south of the Cherethites, and upon the border that belongs to Yahudah, and upon the south of Calev; and we burned Ziklag with fire. 15 And David said to him, Can you bring me down to this troop? And he said, Swear to me by Elohim, that you will neither kill me, nor deliver me into the hands of my master, and I will bring you down to this troop. 16 And when he had brought him down, see, they were spread abroad upon all the land, eating and drinking, and dancing, because of all the great spoil that they had taken out of the land of the Philistines, and out of the land of Yahudah. 17 And David smote them from the twilight, even to the evening of the next day: and there escaped not a man of them, except four hundred young men, who rode upon camels, and fled. 18 And David recovered all that the Amalekites had carried away: and David rescued his two wives. 19 And there was nothing lacking to them, neither small nor great, neither sons nor daughters, neither spoil, nor anything that they had taken from them: David recovered all. 20 And David took all the flocks and the herds, which they drove before those other cattle, and said, This is David's spoil. 21 And David came to the two hundred men, which were so weak that they could not follow David, whom they had made to stay at the brook Besor: and they went forth to meet David, and to meet the people that were with him: and when David came near to the people, he greeted them. 22 Then answered all the wicked men and the men of Beliyaal, of those that went with David, and said, Because they went not with us, we will not give them anything of the spoil that we have recovered, except to every man his wife and his children, that they may go away, and depart. 23 Then said David, You shall not do so, my brothers, with that which יהוה has given us, who has preserved us, and delivered the troop that came against us into our hand. 24 For who will shema to you in this matter? But as the part is for those that went down to the battle, so shall the part be for those that stayed by the baggage: they shall also share the spoil. 25 And it was so from that day forward, that he made it a statute and an ordinance for Yisrael to this day. 26 And when David came to Ziklag, he sent some things from the spoil to the zachanim of Yahudah, even to his friends, saying, See a present for you from the spoil of the enemies of יהוה; 27 To them which were in Beth-El, and to them which were in south Ramoth, and to them which were in Yattir, 28 And to them which were in Aroer, and to them that were in Siphmoth, and to them that were in Eshtemoa, 29 And to them which were in Rachal, and to them that were in the cities of the Yerahmeelites, and to them that were in the cities of the Kenites, 30 And to them that were in Hormah, and to them that were in Chor-Ashan, and to them that were in Athach, 31 And to them that were in Hevron, and to all the places where David himself and his men had been traveling.

31 Now the Philistines fought against Yisrael: and the men of Yisrael fled from before the Philistines, and fell down killed in Mount Gilboa. 2 And the Philistines overtook Shaul and his sons; and the Philistines killed Yonathan, and Aviniadav, and Malchi-Shua, Shaul's sons. 3 And the battle was strong against Shaul, and the archers hit him; so he was heavily wounded by the archers. 4 Then said Shaul to his armor-bearer, Draw your sword, and thrust me through with it, lest these uncircumcised come and thrust me through, and abuse me. But his armor-bearer would not, for he was very afraid. Therefore Shaul took a sword, and fell upon it himself. 5 And when his armor-bearer saw that Shaul was dead, he fell likewise upon his sword, and died with him. 6 So Shaul died, and his three sons, and his armor-bearer, and all his men, that same day together. 7 And when the men of Yisrael that were on the other side of the valley, and they that were on the other side of the Yarden River, saw that the men of Yisrael fled, and that Shaul and his sons were dead, they forsook their cities, and fled; and the Philistines came and dwelt in them. 8 And it came to pass on the next day, when the Philistines came to strip the killed, that they found Shaul and his three sons fallen in Mount Gilboa. 9 And they cut off his head, and stripped off his armor, and sent word into the land of the Philistines around, to publish it in the bayit of their idols, and among the people. 10 And they put his armor in the bayit of Ashtaroth: and they fastened his body to the wall of Beth-Shan. 11 And when the inhabitants of Yavesh-Gilead heard of that which the Philistines had done to Shaul; 12 All the brave men arose, and went all night, and took the body of Shaul and the bodies of his sons from the wall of Beth-Shan, and came to Yavesh, and burnt them there. 13 And they took their bones, and buried them under an eytz at Yavesh, and fasted shiva seven days.[1]

---

[1] Notice they fasted but did not mourn over the unrighteous King Saul.

שמואל ב

Schmuel Bet - Second Samuel
To Our Forefathers Yisrael

1 Now it came to pass after the death of Shaul, when David was returned from the slaughter of the Amalekites, and David had stayed two days in Ziklag; 2 It came even to pass on the third day, that, see, a man came out of the camp from Shaul with his clothes torn, with earth upon his head: and so it was, when he came to David, that he fell to the earth, and did reverence. 3 And David said to him, Where do you come from? And he said to him, Out of the camp of Yisrael I have escaped. 4 And David said to him, How went the matter? I ask you, tell me. And he answered, The people are fleeing from the battle, and many of the people also are fallen and are dead; and Shaul and Yonathan his son are dead also. 5 And David said to the young man that told him, How do you know you that Shaul and Yonathan his son are dead? 6 And the young man that told him said, By chance I was on Mount Gilboa, and I saw, Shaul leaned upon his spear; and, see, the mirkavot and horsemen overtook him. 7 And when he looked behind him, he saw me, and called to me. And I answered, Here am I. 8 And he said to me, Who are you? And I answered him; I am an Amalekite. 9 And he said to me again, Stand, I beg you, over me, and slay me: for anguish has come upon me, but my chayim is still in me. 10 So I stood upon him, and killed him, because I was sure that he could not live after that he was fallen: and I took the keter that was upon his head, and the bracelet that was on his arm, and have brought them here to my master. 11 Then David took hold of his own clothes, and tore them, and likewise all the men that were with him: 12 And they mourned, and wept, and fasted until evening, for Shaul, and for Yonathan his son, and for the people of יהוה, and for kol Beit Yisrael; because they were fallen by the sword. 13 And David said to the young man that told him, Where are you from? And he answered, I am the son of a stranger, an Amalekite. 14 And David said to him, How were you not afraid to stretch forth your hand to destroy יהוה's anointed? 15 And David called one of the young men, and said, Go near, and fall upon him. And he smote him so that he died. 16 And David said to him, Your dom be upon your head; for your mouth has testified against yourself, saying, I have slain יהוה 's anointed. 17 And David lamented with this lamentation over Shaul and over Yonathan his son: 18 Also he ordered The Bow to be taught to the children of Yahudah: see, it is written in the Scroll of Yashar.[1] 19 The beauty of Yisrael is slain upon your high places: how are the mighty fallen! 20 Tell it not in Gath, publish it not in the streets of Ashkelon; lest the daughters of the Philistines have gilah, lest the daughters of the uncircumcised triumph. 21 You mountains of Gilboa, let there be no dew, neither let there be rain, upon you, nor fields of offerings: for there the shield of the mighty lays rejected, the shield of Shaul, without the anointing oil. 22 From the dom of the slain, from the fat of the mighty, the bow of Yonathan did not return, and the sword of Shaul did not return empty of dom. 23 Shaul and Yonathan were lovely and pleasant in their lives, and in their death they were not divided: they were swifter than eagles; they were stronger than lions. 24 You daughters of Yisrael, weep over Shaul, who clothed you in scarlet, along

---

[1] According to the Book of Jasher, chapter 55:35B: "Ephraim and Manasseh, remained constantly in the house of Jacob [in Goshen-Egypt], together with the children of the sons of Jacob their brethren, to learn the ways of the Lord and His Law." We see then that the people, who would later fill the nations through the 10 tribes, began life in Jacob's house in Egypt learning Torah. That alone makes Ephraimites bona fide Yisraelites!

with other delights, who put on ornaments of gold upon your clothes. 25 How are the mighty fallen in the midst of the battle! O Yonathan, you were slain in your high places. 26 I am distressed for you, my brother Yonathan: very pleasant have you been to me: your ahava to me was wonderful, surpassing the ahava of women.[1] 27 How are the mighty fallen, and the weapons of war perished!

2 And it came to pass after this, that David inquired of יהוה, saying, Shall I go up into any of the cities of Yahudah? And יהוה said to him, *Go up;* And David said, Where shall I go up? And He said, *Unto Hevron.* 2 So David went up there, and his two wives also, Ahinoam the Yizreelitess, and Avigail the widow of Naval the Carmelite. 3 And his men that were with him did David bring up, every man with his household: and they dwelt in the cities of Hevron. 4 And the men of Yahudah came, and there they anointed David melech over Beit Yahudah.[2] And they told David, saying, That the men of Yavesh-Gilead were those that buried Shaul. 5 And David sent messengers to the men of Yavesh-Gilead, and said to them, Blessed are you of יהוה that you have showed this chesed to your master, even to Shaul, and have buried him. 6 And now יהוה show chesed and emet to you: and I also will repay you this chesed, because you have done this thing. 7 Therefore now let your hands be strengthened, and be brave: for your master Shaul is dead, and also Beit Yahudah has anointed me melech over them. 8 But Avner the son of Ner, captain of Shaul's army, took Ish-Bosheth the son of Shaul, and brought him over to Machanayim; 9 And made him melech over Gilead, and over the Ashurites,[3] and over Yezreel, and over Ephraim, and over Benyamin, and over all Yisrael. 4 10 Ish-Bosheth Shaul's son was forty years old when he began to reign over Yisrael, and reigned two years. But Beit Yahudah followed David. 11 And the time that David was melech in Hevron over Beit Yahudah was seven years and six months. 12 And Avner the son of Ner, and the avadim of Ish-Bosheth the son of Shaul, went out from Machanayim to Giveon. 13 And Yoav the son of Tzeruiah, and the avadim of David, went out, and met together by the pool of Giveon: and they sat down, the one on the one side of the pool, and the other on the other side of the pool. 14 And Avner said to Yoav, Let the young men now arise, and compete before us. And Yoav said, Let them arise. 15 Then there arose and went over by number twelve of Benyamin, which pertained to Ish-Bosheth the son of Shaul, and twelve of the avadim of David. 16 And each one grasped his opponent by the head, and thrust his sword in his opponent's side; so they fell down together: wherefore that place was called Helkath-Hazzurim, which is in Giveon. 17 And there was a very fierce battle that day; and Avner was beaten, and the men of Yisrael, before the avadim of David. 18 And there were three sons of Tzeruiah there, Yoav, and Avishai, and Asahel: and Asahel was as fast as a desert gazelle. 19 And Asahel pursued after Avner; and in going he turned not to the right hand, nor to the left from following Avner. 20 Then Avner looked behind him, and said, Are you Asahel? And he answered, I am. 21 And Avner said to him, Turn aside to your right hand or to your left, and lay hold on one of the young men, and take his armor. But Asahel would not turn aside from following after him.

---

[1] This is not a reference to any alleged homosexual relationship as some perversely declare. It is a mere figure of speech in a song.

[2] But not yet over the House of Ephraim Yisrael. Even before unification under David, there was some subtle division between the North and South, though we cannot say for certain that the numbers of ten tribes versus two tribes + Levi was the same as in the eventual Jeroboam-Rehoboam split.

[3] Also note that the Assyrians were not biological Yisraelites at this time but still were considered Yisrael, by joining the House of Yisrael along with other tribes.

[4] We see the two houses at an embryonic point, although the alignment shifted when the big split occurred in 921 BCE; when Benyamin was in the south with Yahudah and no longer with Ephraim.

22 And Avner said again to Asahel, Turn you aside from following me: why should I smite you to the ground? How then could I face Yoav your brother? 23 However he refused to turn aside: so Avner with the blunt end of the spear smote him him under the stomach, so that the spear came out through his back; and he fell down there, and died in the same place: and it came to pass, that as many as came to the place where Asahel fell down and died stood still. 24 Yoav also and Avishai pursued after Avner: and the sun went down when they were come to the hill of Ammah, that lies before Giah by the way of the wilderness of Giveon. 25 And the children of Benyamin gathered themselves together behind Avner, and became one troop, and took their stand on the top of a hill. 26 Then Avner called to Yoav, and said, Shall the sword devour le-olam-va-ed? Don't you know that it will be bitter in the latter end? How long shall it be then, And when are you going to tell the people to return from following their brothers? 27 And Yoav said, As Elohim lives, unless you had spoken up, surely not until morning would the people have quit from following their brothers. 28 So Yoav blew a shofar, and all the people stood still, and pursued after Yisrael no more, neither fought they any more.[1] 29 And Avner and his men walked all that night through the plain, and passed over the Yarden River, and went through all Bithron, and they came to Machanayim. 30 And Yoav returned from following Avner: and when he had gathered all the people together, there lacked of David's avadim nineteen men and Asahel. 31 But the avadim of David had killed from Benyamin, and of Avner's men, so that three hundred sixty men died. 32 And they took up Asahel, and buried him in the tomb of his abba, which was in Beth-Lechem. And Yoav and his men went all night, and they came to Hevron at daybreak.

3 Now there was long war between Beit Shaul and Beit David: but David grew stronger and stronger, and Beit Shaul grew weaker and weaker.[2] 2 And to David were sons born in Hevron: and his firstborn was Amnon, of Ahinoam the Yizreelitess; 3 And his second, Chileav, of Avigail the widow of Naval the Carmelite; and the third, Avshalom the son of Maacah the daughter of Talmai melech of Geshur;[3] 4 And the fourth, Adoniyah the son of Haggith; and the fifth, Shephatyah the son of Avital; 5 And the sixth, Yithream, by Eglah David's wife. These were born to David in Hevron. 6 And it came to pass, while there was war between Beit Shaul and Beit David, that Avner made himself strong for Beit Shaul. 7 And Shaul had a concubine, whose name was Ritzpah, the daughter of Ayah: and Ish-Bosheth said to Avner, Why have you gone in to my abba's concubine? 8 Then was Avner very angry at the words of Ish-Bosheth, and said, Am I a dog's head, that belongs to Yahudah, to show chesed this day to Beit Shaul your abba, to his brothers, and to his friends, and have not allowed you to fall into the hand of David, that you now charge me today with a sin concerning this woman? 9 So do Elohim to Avner, and more also, if I do not perform all that יהוה has sworn to David, in his service, 10 To transfer the malchut from Beit Shaul, and to set up kesay David over Yisrael and over Yahudah, from Dan even to Beer-Sheva.[4] 11 And he could not answer Avner a word again, because he feared him. 12 And Avner sent messengers to David on his behalf, saying, Whose is this land? Saying also, Make your covenant with me, and, see, my hand shall be with you, to bring kol

---

[1] A two-house military encounter, ended by words of shalom and sanity. May there be more people today sounding forth this message of shalom between the two houses of Yisrael.

[2] Two houses before they were unified.
[3] Avshalom had non-Yisraelite dom from his mother.
[4] Avner swears to now switch to David's side and help unite both houses under David, in revenge against Ishbosheth's false accusation.

Yisrael to you.[1] 13 And he said, Very well; I will make a covenant with you: but one thing I require of you, and that is, that you shall not see my face, until you first bring Michal Shaul's daughter, when you come to see my face. 14 And David sent messengers to Ish-Bosheth Shaul's son, saying, Deliver to me my wife Michal, whom I engaged in exchange for a hundred foreskins of the Philistines. 15 And Ish-Bosheth sent, and took her from her husband, even from Paltiel the son of Layish. 16 And her husband went with her along weeping behind her to Bahurim. Then said Avner to him, Go, return. And he returned. 17 And Avner had communication with the zachanim of Yisrael, saying, You sought for David in times past to be melech over you: 18 Now then do it: for יהוה has spoken of David, saying, By the hand of My eved David I will save My people Yisrael out of the hand of the Philistines, and out of the hand of all their enemies. 19 And Avner also spoke in the ears of Benyamin: and Avner went also to speak in the ears of David in Hevron all that seemed tov to Yisrael, and that seemed tov to the whole bayit of Benyamin.[2] [3] 20 So Avner came to David to Hevron, and twenty men with him. And David made Avner and the men that were with him a feast. 21 And Avner said to David, I will arise and go, and will gather all Yisrael to my master the melech, that they may make a covenant with you, and that you may reign over all that your lev desires. And David sent Avner away; and he went in shalom. [4] 22 And, See, the avadim of David and Yoav came from a raid, and brought in a great spoil with them: but Avner was not with David in Hevron; for he had sent him away, and he was gone

in shalom. 23 When Yoav and all the army that was with him had come, they told Yoav, saying, Avner the son of Ner came to the melech, and he has sent him away, and he is gone in shalom. 24 Then Yoav came to the melech, and said, What have you done? See, Avner came to you; why is it that you have sent him away, and he is gone in shalom? 25 Don't you know Avner the son of Ner; that he came to deceive you, and to know your going out and your coming in, and to know all that you do. 26 And when Yoav was come out from David, he sent messengers after Avner, who brought him again from the well of Sirah: but David did not know it. 27 And when Avner returned to Hevron, Yoav took him aside in the gate to speak with him quietly, and smote him there under the stomach, that he died, for the dom of Asahel his brother.[5] 28 And afterward when David heard of it, he said, my malchut and I are guiltless before יהוה le-olam-va-ed from the dom of Avner the son of Ner: 29 Let it rest on the head of Yoav, and on all his abba's bayit; and let there not fail from the bayit of Yoav one that has an issue, or that is a leper, or that leans on a staff, or that falls on the sword, or that lacks lechem.[6] 30 So Yoav and Avishai his brother killed Avner, because he had slain their brother Asahel at Giveon in the battle. 31 And David said to Yoav, and to all the people that were with him, Tear your clothes, and gird yourselves with sackcloth, and mourn over Avner. And melech David himself followed the coffin. 32 And they buried Avner in Hevron: and the melech lifted up his voice, and wept at the grave of Avner; and all the people wept.[7] 33 And the melech lamented over Avner, and said, Should Avner have died as a fool dies? 34 Your hands were not bound,

---

[1] May all believers enter a similar covenant with YHWH, to bring all believers back to the House of David and out of the nations and their false elohim.
[2] Avner becomes a key figure in uniting both houses under David.
[3] In those days the house of Benjamin was synonymous with the house of Ephraim and the house of Yisrael.
[4] Avner was performing YHWH's will as it remains to this day. Only through David's son the King Moshiach can Yisrael be one again.

[5] All two-house messengers seeking unity like Avner, are targets for death inflicted by the enemies of Yisraelite unity.
[6] David pronounces a curse on anyone in Yoav's future lineage. A curse from YHWH also remains on anyone who tries to stop two-house unity and restoration either in ignorance or with malice and purpose. Remember: The curse on those who fight YHWH's perfect will, will be like the one placed on Yoav.
[7] Weeping for the unity that could have come sooner.

nor your feet put into fetters: as a man falls before wicked men, so fell you. And all the people wept again over him. 35 And when all the people came to cause David to eat food while it was yet day, David swore, saying, So do Elohim to me, and more also, if I taste lechem, or anything else, until the sun is down. 36 And all the people took notice of it, and it pleased them: and whatever the melech did pleased all the people. [1] 37 For all the people and all Yisrael understood that day that it was not the desire of the melech to slay Avner the son of Ner. 38 And the melech said to his avadim, Don't you know that there is a prince and a great man fallen this day in Yisrael? 39 And I am weak today, though I am anointed melech; and these men the sons of Tzeruiah are too harsh for me: יהוה shall reward the doer of evil according to his wickedness.

4 And when Shaul's son heard that Avner was dead in Hevron, his hands were feeble, and all the Yisraelites were troubled. 2 And Shaul's son had two men that were officers of bands: the name of the one was Baanah, and the name of the other Rechav, the sons of Rimmon a Beerothite, of the children of Benyamin: for Beeroth also was counted with Benyamin:[2] 3 And the Beerothites fled to Gittayim, and are sojourners there until this day. 4 And Yonathan, Shaul's son, had a son that was lame of his feet. He was five years old when the news came of Shaul and Yonathan out of Yezreel, and his nurse took him, and fled: and it came to pass, as she hurried to flee, that he fell, and became lame. And his name was Mephibosheth. 5 And the sons of Rimmon the Beerothite, Rechav and Baanah, went, and came about the mid-day to the bayit of Ish-Bosheth, who lay on a bed at noon. 6 And they came there into the

midst of the bayit, pretending as though they would have gotten wheat; and they smote him under the stomach: and Rechav and Baanah his brother escaped. 7 For when they came into the bayit, he lay on his bed in his bedchamber, and they smote him, and killed him, and beheaded him, and took his head, and got away through the plain all night. 8 And they brought the head of Ish-Bosheth to David in Hevron, and said to the melech, See the head of Ish-Bosheth the son of Shaul your enemy, which sought your chayim; and יהוה has avenged my master the melech this day of Shaul, and of his zera.[3] 9 And David answered Rechav and Baanah his brother, the sons of Rimmon the Beerothite, and said to them, As יהוה lives, who has redeemed my chayim out of all adversity, 10 When one told me, saying, See, Shaul is dead, thinking to have brought tov news, I took hold of him, and killed him in Ziklag, who thought that I would have given him a reward for his news: 11 How much more, when wicked men have slain a tzadik person in his own bayit upon his bed? Shall I not therefore now require his dom at your hand, and take you away from the earth? 12 And David commanded his young men, and they killed them, and cut off their hands and their feet, and hanged them up over the pool in Hevron. But they took the head of Ish-Bosheth, and buried it in the tomb of Avner in Hevron.

5 Then came all the tribes of Yisrael[4] to David to Hevron, and spoke, saying, See, we are your bone and your flesh. 2 Also in times past, when Shaul was melech over us, you were he that led out and brought in Yisrael: and יהוה said to you, you shall feed My people Yisrael, and you shall be a ruler over Yisrael. 3 So all the zachanim of Yisrael came to the melech to Hevron; and melech David made a covenant with them in Hevron before יהוה: and they anointed David melech over kol

---

[1] The House of Shaul or Yisrael was so impressed with David's love for both houses, that even former enemies made shalom.
[2] Non-Yisraelies mixed with Benjamin; and today Benjamin is mixed primarily with Judah. So even Jewish-Yisrael is full of dom from the nations.

[3] We see the Benjamites in part begin to change allegiance from the House of Yisrael/Shaul to the House of David.
[4] All 12 tribes seek unity.

Yisrael.[1] 4 David was thirty years old when he began to reign,[2] and he reigned forty years. 5 In Hevron he reigned over Yahudah seven years and six months: and in Yahrushalayim he reigned thirty-three years over kol Yisrael and kol Yahudah.[3] 6 And the melech and his men went to Yahrushalayim to the Yevusites, the inhabitants of the land: who spoke to David, saying, Except you take away the blind and the lame,[4] you shall not come in here: and they said, David cannot come in here. 7 Nevertheless David took the stronghold of Tzion: the same is the city of David. 8 And David said on that day, Whoever goes up to the mayim-shaft, and smites the Yevusites, and the lame and the blind, that hate David's chayim, he shall become chief and captain. Therefore they said, The blind and the lame shall not come into the bayit. 9 So David dwelt in the fort, and called it the city of David. And David built around it from Millo on inward. 10 And David went on, and grew great, and יהוה Elohim of hosts was with him. 11 And Hiram melech of Tzor[5] sent messengers to David, cedar eytzim, and carpenters, and masons: and they built David a bayit. 12 And David perceived that יהוה had established him as melech over all Yisrael, and that he had exalted his malchut for his people Yisrael's sake. 13 And David took more concubines and wives out of Yahrushalayim, after he was come from Hevron: and there were yet more sons and daughters born to David. 14 And these are the names of those that were born to him in Yahrushalayim; Shammua, and Shovab, and Nathan, and Shlomo, 15 Ivhar also, and Elishua, and Nepheg, and Yaphia, 16 And Elishama, and Eliada, and Eliphalet. 17 But when the Philistines heard that they had anointed David melech over Yisrael, all the Philistines came up to seek David; and

David heard of it, and went down to the fort. 18 The Philistines also came and spread out in the Valley of Rephaim. 19 And David inquired of יהוה, saying, Shall I go up to the Philistines? Will You deliver them into my hand? And יהוה said to David, *Go up: for I will no doubt deliver the Philistines into your hand.* 20 And David came to Baal-Peratzim, and David smote them there, and said, יהוה has broken forth upon my enemies before me, as the breach of mayim. Therefore he called the name of that place Baal-Peratzim. 21 And there they left their idols, and David and his men burned them.[6] 22 And the Philistines came up yet again, and spread out in the Valley of Rephaim. 23 And when David inquired of יהוה, He said, *You shall not go up; but turn around behind them, and come upon them in front of the mulberry eytzim. 24 And let it be, when you shema the sound of a movement in the tops of the mulberry eytzim, that then you shall become strong: for then shall* יהוה *go out before you, to smite the army of the Philistines.* 25 And David did so, as יהוה had commanded him; and smote the Philistines from Geva until you come to Gazer.

6 Again, David gathered together all the chosen men of Yisrael, thirty thousand. 2 And David arose, and went with all the people that were with him from Ba-Ale of Yahudah, to bring up from there the Ark of Elohim, whose name is called by the Name of יהוה of hosts that dwells between the cheruvim. 3 And they set the Ark of Elohim upon a new cart, and brought it out of the bayit of Avinadav that was in Giveah: and Uzzah and Ahyo, the sons of Avinadav, drove the new cart. 4 And they brought it out of the bayit of Avinadav that was at Giveah, accompanying the Ark of Elohim: and Ahyo went before the Ark. 5 And David and all Beit Yisrael played and danced before יהוה on all kinds of

---

[1] Over all 12 tribes.
[2] Same as Yahshua who began public ministry at 30.
[3] Both houses.
[4] Idiomatic expression meaning we will fight to the last man.
[5] A land that was colonized under Solomon.

[6] A pattern for all Yisrael regarding pagan religions.

instruments made of fir wood, even on harps, and on psalteries, and on timbrels, and on cornets, and on cymbals. 6 And when they came to Nachon's threshing floor, Uzzah put forth his hand to the Ark of Elohim, and took hold of it, for the ox had broken loose from the harness. 7 And the anger of יהוה was kindled against Uzzah; and Elohim smote him there for his error; and there he died by the Ark of Elohim. 8 And David was displeased, because יהוה had made a breach upon Uzzah: and he called the name of the place Peretz-Uzzah to this day. 9 And David was afraid of יהוה that day, and said, How shall the Ark of יהוה come to me? 10 So David would not remove the Ark of יהוה to him into the city of David: but David carried it into the bayit of Oved-Edom the Gittite. 11 And the Ark of יהוה continued in the bayit of Oved-Edom the Gittite[1] three months: and יהוה blessed Oved-Edom, and his entire household. 12 And it was told melech David, saying, יהוה has blessed the bayit of Oved-Edom, and all that pertains to him, because of the Ark of Elohim. So David went and brought up the Ark of Elohim from the bayit of Oved-Edom into the city of David with simcha. 13 And it was so, that when they that bore the Ark of יהוה had gone six paces, he sacrificed oxen and fatlings. 14 And David danced before יהוה with all his might; and David was girded with a linen shoulder garment. 15 So David and kol Beit Yisrael brought up the Ark of יהוה with shouting, and with the sound of the shofar. 16 And as the Ark of יהוה came into the city of David, Michal Shaul's daughter looked through a window, and saw melech David leaping and dancing before יהוה; and she despised him in her lev. 17 And they brought in the Ark of יהוה, and set it in its place, in the midst of the tent that David had pitched for it: and David offered burnt offerings and shalom

offerings before יהוה. 18 And as soon as David had made an end of offering burnt offerings and shalom offerings, he blessed the people in the Name of יהוה of hosts.[2] 19 And he dealt among all the people, even among the whole multitude of Yisrael; to each one, both women and men, he gave a container of wine,[3] a tov piece of meat, and a fine loaf of lechem. So all the people departed every one to his bayit. 20 Then David returned to bless his household. And Michal the daughter of Shaul came out to meet David, and said, How beautiful was the melech of Yisrael today, who uncovered himself today in the eyes of the female avadim, as one of the am ha-aretz shamelessly uncovers himself! 21 And David said to Michal, It was before יהוה, who chose me before your abba, and before all his bayit, to appoint me ruler over the people of יהוה, over Yisrael: therefore will I play before יהוה. 22 And I will yet be more abased than this, and will be base in my own sight: and of the female avadim that you have spoken of, from them shall I have honor. 23 Therefore Michal the daughter of Shaul had no child to the day of her death.

7 And it came to pass, when the melech sat in his bayit, and יהוה had given him shalom all around from all his enemies; 2 That the melech said to Nathan the navi, See now, I dwell in a bayit of cedar, but the Ark of Elohim dwells within curtains. 3 And Nathan said to the melech, Go, do all that is in your lev; for יהוה is with you. 4 And it came to pass that night, that the word of יהוה came to Nathan, saying, 5 *Go and tell My eved David, This said יהוה, Shall you build Me a Bayit for Me to dwell in? 6 For I have not dwelt in any bayit since*

---

[1] The Ark of the Covenant dwelt in the house of a non-biological Yisraelite, but one who joined them by choice. The pattern for becoming Yisrael remains the same and has never been altered.

[2] The only way to seal YHWH's favor.
[3] Yisraelites always use wine to live before YHWH, as did the Matser Yahshua Himself. They always partake, but are never to enter into excess. The custom that believers don't or should not even taste wine is a pagan tradition perpetrated by the so-called churches of Romanism and Protestantism. The only kind of Yisraelite that cannot drink wine is one under a Nazarite vow.

the time that I brought up the children of Yisrael out of Mitzrayim, even to this day, but have moved about in tents. 7 In all the places where I have moved with all the children of Yisrael did I ever speak a word to any of the tribes of Yisrael, whom I commanded to feed My people Yisrael, saying, Why did you not build Me a bayit of cedar? 8 Now therefore so shall you say to My eved David, This says יהוה of hosts, I took you from the sheepfold, from following the sheep, to be ruler over My people, over Yisrael: 9 And I was with you wherever you went, and have cut off all your enemies out of your sight, and have made you a great name, like the name of the great men that are in the earth. 10 Moreover I will appoint a place for My people Yisrael, and will plant them, that they may dwell in a place of their own, and move no more; neither shall the children of wickedness afflict them any more, as before;[1] 11 Even from the time that I commanded shophtim to rule over My people Yisrael, and have now caused you to rest from all your enemies. Also יהוה declared to you that He will make you a bayit. 12 And when your days are fulfilled, and you shall rest with your ahvot, I will set up your zera after you, which shall proceed out of your loins, and I will establish his malchut. 13 He shall build a Bayit for My Name, and I will establish the kesay of his malchut le-olam-va-ed. 14 I will be his Father, and he shall be My son. If he commits Torah violations, I will chasten him with the rod of men, and with the stripes of the children of men:[2] 15 But My rachamim shall not depart away from him, as I took it from Shaul, whom I put away before you. 16 And your bayit and your malchut shall be established le-olam-va-ed before you: your throne shall be established le-olam-va-ed.[3] 17 According to all these words, and according to all this vision, so did Nathan speak to David. 18 Then went melech David in, and sat before יהוה, and he said, Who am I, O Master יהוה? And what is my bayit, that You have brought me this far? 19 And this was yet a small thing in Your sight, O Master יהוה; but You have spoken also of Your eved's bayit for a great while to come. And is this the manner of man, O Master יהוה? 20 And what can David say more to You? For You, Master יהוה, know Your eved. 21 For Your word's sake, and according to Your own lev, have You done all these great things, to make Your eved know them. 22 Therefore You are great, O יהוה Elohim: for there is none like You, neither is there any Elohim beside You, according to all that we have heard with our ears. 23 And what one nation on the earth is like Your people, like Yisrael, whom Elohim went to redeem as a people to Himself, and to make for Himself a Name,[4] and to do for you great and awesome things, for Your land, before Your people, whom You redeemed to You from Mitzrayim, from the nations and their elohim? 24 For You have confirmed for Yourself Your people Yisrael to be a people to You le-olam-va-ed: and You, יהוה, have become their Elohim. 25 And now, O יהוה Elohim, the word that You have spoken concerning Your eved, and concerning his bayit, to establish it le-olam-va-ed, and now

---

[1] This is an amazing prophecy that Yisrael will one day be preserved for a time at least in another place until they return. This is a clear reference to the USA where most of the 250 million people are composed of Yahudites and Ephraimites in exile. Yahweh spoke to David and the entire nation in the future tense. He "will appoint" (Hebrew: vesamti), "will plant", (Hebrew: oontativ), and "they shall dwell in a place of their own." Consider this apparent contradiction. Scripture teaches that Israel in the Holy Land of Canaan promised to our patriarchs, is our appointed and prepared place, where we are to find dwelling and peace from all the sons of wickedness (traditional enemies such as Ishmaelites and Edomites). While the nation was strong and fortified and at rest from all her enemies, Yahweh declared that there would yet be a future place of planting and appointment, where the traditional enemies of Israel (children of wickedness) will no longer oppress and harass the nation. He called this future land a place of their own, despite the fact that when this prophesy was given they were in a land of their own. For more details, see:
http://yourarmstoisrael.org/Articles_new/restoration/?page=6&type=12

[2] This cannot be a messianic reference to Moshiach as some teach due to the fact that Moshiach did not and could not violate Torah. This speaks of Solomon.
[3] Through Moshiach Yahshua.
[4] Yisrael was ultimately formed to proclaim and represent YHWH's Name.

do as You have said. 26 And let Your Name be magnified le-olam-va-ed, saying, יהוה of hosts is the Elohim over Yisrael: and let the bayit of Your eved David be established before You. 27 For You, O יהוה of hosts, Elohim of Yisrael, have revealed to Your eved, saying, I will build You a Bayit: therefore has Your eved found it in his lev to make this tefillah to You. 28 And now, O Master יהוה, You are Elohim, and Your words are emet, and You have promised this chesed to Your eved: 29 Therefore now let it please You to bless the bayit of Your eved, that it may continue le-olam-va-ed before You: for You, O Master יהוה, have spoken it: and with Your bracha let the bayit of Your eved be blessed le-olam-va-ed.

8 And after this it came to pass, that David smote the Philistines, and subdued them: and David took Metheg-Ammah out of the hand of the Philistines. 2 And he smote Moav, and measured them with a line, causing them to lie down on the ground; with two lines he measured those to be put to death, and with one complete line to keep alive. And so the Moavites became David's avadim, and brought gifts. 3 David smote also Hadadezer, the son of Rehov, melech of Zovah, as he went to recover his border at the River Euphrates. 4 And David took from him a thousand mirkavot, and seven hundred horsemen, and twenty thousand footmen: and David destroyed all the mirkavah horses, but reserved from them one hundred mirkavot. 5 And when the Arameans of Dameshek came to help Hadadezer melech of Zovah, David killed twenty-two thousand Aramean men. 6 Then David put governors in Aram of Dameshek: and the Arameans became avadim to David, and brought gifts. And יהוה preserved David wherever he went. 7 And David took the shields of gold that were on the avadim of Hadadezer, and brought them to Yahrushalayim. 8 And from Betah, and from Berothai, cities of Hadadezer, melech

David took much bronze. 9 When Toi melech of Hamath heard that David had killed the entire army of Hadadezer, 10 Then Toi sent Yoram his son to melech David, to greet him, and to bless him, because he had fought against Hadadezer, and killed him: for Hadadezer had wars with Toi. And Yoram brought with him vessels of silver, and vessels of gold, and vessels of brass: 11 That melech David did dedicate to יהוה, with the silver and gold that he had dedicated from all nations that he subdued; 12 Of Aram, and of Moav, and of the children of Ammon, and of the Philistines, and of Amalek, and of the spoil of Hadadezer, son of Rehov, melech of Zovah.[1] 13 And David made a name for himself when he returned from smiting the Arameans in the Valley of Salt, being eighteen thousand men. 14 And he put governors in Edom; throughout all Edom he put governors, and all those of Edom became David's avadim. And יהוה preserved David wherever he went. 15 And David reigned over kol Yisrael; and David executed mishpat and justice to all his people. 16 And Yoav the son of Tzeruiah was over the army; and Yehoshaphat the son of Ahilud was recorder; 17 And Tzadok the son of Ahituv, and Ahimelech the son of Aviathar, were the kohanim; and Serayah was the sopher; 18 And Benayah the son of Yehoiada was over both the Cherethites and the Pelethites; and David's sons were princes.

9 And David said, Is there yet any that is left of Beit Shaul, that I may show him chesed for Yonathan's sake? 2 And there was of Beit Shaul an eved whose name was Ziva. And when they had called him to David, the melech said to him, Are you Ziva? And he said, your eved is he. 3 And the melech said, Is there not yet any left of Beit Shaul, that I may show the chesed of Elohim to him? And Ziva said to

---

[1] All became Yisraelite colonies, and in a sense Yisraelite nations with a certain amount of intermingling of seed, even prior to the exiles of both houses.

the melech, Yonathan has yet a son, who is lame on his feet. 4 And the melech said to him, Where is he? And Ziva said to the melech, See, he is in the bayit of Machir, the son of Ammiel, in Lo-Devar. 5 Then melech David sent, and fetched him out of the bayit of Machir, the son of Ammiel, from Lo-Devar. 6 Now when Mephibosheth, the son of Yonathan, the son of Shaul, had come to David, he fell on his face, and did reverence. And David said, Mephibosheth. And he answered, See your eved! 7 And David said to him, Fear not: for I will surely show you chesed for Yonathan your abba's sake, and will restore to you all the land of Shaul your abba; and you shall eat lechem at my table continually. 8 And he bowed himself, and said, What is your eved, that you should look upon such a dead dog as I am? 9 Then the melech called to Ziva, Shaul's eved, and said to him, I have given to your master's son all that pertains to Shaul and to all his bayit. 10 You therefore, and your sons, and your avadim, shall work the land for him, and you shall bring in the fruits, that your master's son may have food to eat: but Mephibosheth your master's son shall eat lechem always at my table. Now Ziva had fifteen sons and twenty avadim. 11 Then said Ziva to the melech, According to all that my master the melech has commanded his eved, so shall your eved do. As for Mephibosheth, said the melech, he shall eat at my table, as one of the melech's sons. 12 And Mephibosheth had a young son, whose name was Micha. And all that dwelt in the bayit of Ziva were avadim to Mephibosheth. 13 So Mephibosheth dwelt in Yahrushalayim: for he did eat continually at the melech's table; and was lame on both his feet.[1]

10 And it came to pass after this, that the melech of the children of Ammon died, and Hanun his son reigned in his stead. 2 Then said David, I will show chesed to Hanun the son of Nahash, as his abba showed chesed to me. And David sent to comfort him by the hand of his avadim concerning his abba. And David's avadim came into the land of the children of Ammon. 3 And the princes of the children of Ammon said to Hanun their master, Do you think that David does honor your abba, in that he has sent comforters to you? Has not David rather sent his avadim to you, to search the city, and to spy it out, to overthrow it? 4 Wherefore Hanun took David's avadim, and shaved off the one half of their beards, and cut off their garments in the middle, even to their buttocks, and sent them away. 5 When they told it to David, he sent to meet them, because the men were greatly ashamed: and the melech said, Stay at Yericho until your beards be grown, and then return.[2] 6 And when the children of Ammon saw that they had become a stench before David, the children of Ammon sent and hired the Arameans of Beth-Rehov, and the Arameans of Zova, twenty thousand footmen, and of melech Maacah a thousand men, and of Ish-Tov twelve thousand men. 7 And when David heard of it, he sent Yoav, and all the army of the mighty men. 8 And the children of Ammon came out, and put themselves in battle in array at the entering in of the gate: and the Arameans of Zova, and of Rehov, and Ish-Tov, and Maacah, were by themselves in the field. 9 When Yoav saw that the battle was against him in front and behind, he chose of all the choice men of Yisrael, and put them in array against the Arameans: 10 And the rest of the people he delivered into the hand of Avishai his brother, that he might put

---

[1] A beautiful typology of sinners, lame in every way, being forgiven and restored to Yisrael by covenant despite the fact that many were cut off and, were dead non-Yisraelite dogs. Now however, they eat bread always at Yahshua the King's table.

[2] Beards are not a choice for Yisraelites. They must be worn. Being clean-shaven is a sign of rebellion as Torah also commands by stating that men in Yisrael must not fully shave their facial corners. Leviticus 19:27: Ye shall not round the corners of your heads; neither shall you mar the corners of your beard.

them in array against the children of Ammon. 11 And he said, If the Arameans be too strong for me, then you shall help me: but if the children of Ammon be too strong for you, then I will come and help you. 12 Be of great courage, and let us show strength for our people, and for the cities of our Elohim: and יהוה do that which seems tov to Him. 13 And Yoav drew near, and the people that were with him, to the battle against the Arameans: and they fled before him. 14 And when the children of Ammon saw that the Arameans were fled, then they fled also before Avishai, and entered into the city. So Yoav returned from the children of Ammon, and came to Yahrushalayim. 15 And when the Arameans saw that they were killed before Yisrael, they gathered themselves together. 16 And Hadarezer sent, and brought out the Arameans that were beyond the river: and they came to Helam; and Shovach the captain of the army of Hadarezer went before them. 17 And when it was told David, he gathered all Yisrael together, and passed over the Yarden River, and came to Helam. And the Arameans set themselves in array against David, and fought with him. 18 And the Arameans fled before Yisrael; and David killed the men of the seven hundred mirkavot of the Arameans, and forty thousand horsemen, and smote Shovach the captain of their army, who died there. 19 And when all the melechim that were avadim to Hadarezer saw that they were killed before Yisrael, they made shalom with Yisrael, and served them. So the Arameans feared to help the children of Ammon any more.

11 And it came to pass, after the year was expired, at the time when melechim go forth to battle, that David sent Yoav, and his avadim with him, and all Yisrael; and they destroyed the children of Ammon, and besieged Ravah. But David stayed still at Yahrushalayim. 2 And it came to pass one evening time, that David arose from his bed, and walked upon the roof of the melech's bayit: and from the roof he saw a woman washing herself; and the woman was very beautiful to look upon. 3 And David sent and asked about the woman. And one said, Is not this Bath-Sheva, the daughter of Eliam, the wife of Uriyah the Hittite? 4 And David sent messengers, and took her; and she came in to him, and he lay with her; for she was purified from her uncleanness: and she returned to her bayit. 5 And the woman conceived, and sent and told David, and said, I am with child. 6 And David sent to Yoav, saying, Send me Uriyah the Hittite. And Yoav sent Uriyah to David. 7 And when Uriyah came to him, David demanded of him how Yoav did, and how the people did, and how the war was going. 8 And David said to Uriyah, Go down to your bayit, and wash your feet. And Uriyah departed out of the melech's bayit, and there followed him a gift of food from the melech. 9 But Uriyah slept at the door of the melech's bayit with all the avadim of his master, and went not down to his bayit. 10 And when they had told David, saying, Uriyah went not down to his bayit, David said to Uriyah, Didn't you come from your journey? Why then did you not go down to your bayit? 11 And Uriyah said to David, The Ark, and Yisrael, and Yahudah,[1] still stay in tents; and my master Yoav, and the avadim of my master, are encamped in the open fields; shall I then go into my bayit, to eat and to drink, and to lie with my wife? As you live, and as your chayim lives, I will not do this thing. 12 And David said to Uriyah, Stay here today also, and tomorrow I will let you depart. So Uriyah stayed in Yahrushalayim that day, and the next. 13 And when David had called him, he did eat and drink before him; and he made him drunk: and at evening he went out to lie on his bed with the avadim of his master, but did not go down to his bayit. 14 And it came to pass in the morning, that David wrote a letter to

---

[1] Both houses.

Yoav, and sent it by the hand of Uriyah. 15 And he wrote in the letter, saying, Put Uriyah in the front of the hottest battle, and then abandon him, that he may be killed, and die. 16 And it came to pass, when Yoav observed the city that he assigned Uriyah to a place where he knew that brave men were. 17 And the men of the city went out, and fought with Yoav: and there fell some of the people of the avadim of David; and Uriyah the Hittite died also. 18 Then Yoav sent and told David all the things concerning the war; 19 And commanded the messenger, saying, When you have made an end of telling the matters of the war to the melech, 20 And if it so be that the melech's anger arise, and he say to you, Why did you approach so near to the city when you fought? Did you not know they would shoot from the wall? 21 The same people who smote Avimelech the son of Yeruvesheth? Did not a woman cast a piece of a millstone upon him from the wall that he died in Thebez? Why did you go near the wall? Then you shall say, Your eved Uriyah the Hittite is dead also. 22 So the messenger went, and came and showed David all that Yoav had sent him for. 23 And the messenger said to David, Surely the men prevailed against us, and came out to us into the field, and we were upon them even to the entering of the gate. 24 And the shooters shot from off the wall upon your avadim; and some of the melech's avadim are dead, and your eved Uriyah the Hittite is dead also. 25 Then David said to the messenger, This shall you say to Yoav, Let not this thing displease you, for the sword devours one as well as another: make your battle more strong against the city, and overthrow it: and encourage him. 26 And when the wife of Uriyah heard that Uriyah her husband was dead, she mourned for her husband. 27 And when the mourning was past, David sent and fetched her to his bayit, and she became his wife, and bore him a son. But the thing that David had done displeased יהוה.

12 And יהוה sent Nathan to David. And he came to him, and said to him, There were two men in one city; the one rich, and the other poor. 2 The rich man had exceedingly many flocks and herds: 3 But the poor man had nothing, save one little ewe lamb, which he had bought and nourished up: and it grew up together with him, and with his children; it did eat of his own food, and drank of his own cup, and lay in his bosom, and was to him as a daughter. 4 And there came a traveler to the rich man, and he spared to take of his own flock and of his own herd, to dress for the traveling man that was come to him; but took the poor man's lamb, and prepared it for the man that was come to him. 5 And David's anger was greatly kindled against the man; and he said to Nathan, As יהוה lives, the man that has done this thing shall surely die: 6 And he shall restore the lamb fourfold, because he did this thing, and because he had no rachamim. 7 And Nathan said to David, You are the man. This says יהוה Elohim of Yisrael, *I anointed you melech over Yisrael, and I delivered you out of the hand of Shaul; 8 And I gave you your master's bayit, and your master's wives into your bosom, and gave you Beit Yisrael and Beit Yahudah;[1] and if that had been too little, I would moreover have given to you much more. 9 Why have you despised the commandment of יהוה, to do evil in His sight? You have killed Uriyah the Hittite with the sword, and have taken his wife to be your wife, and have slain him with the sword of the children of Ammon. 10 Now therefore the sword shall never depart from your bayit; because you have despised Me, and have taken the wife of Uriyah the Hittite to be your wife. 11 This says יהוה, See, I will raise up evil against you out of your own bayit, and I will take your wives before your eyes, and give them to your neighbor, and he shall lie with your wives publicly in the sight of the sun. 12 For you did it secretly: but I will do this thing before*

---

[1] Both houses.

all Yisrael, and before the sun. 13 And David said to Nathan, I have sinned against **יהוה**. And Nathan said to David, **יהוה** has put away your sin; you shall not die. 14 However, because by this deed you have given great occasion to the enemies of **יהוה** to blaspheme, the child also that is born to you shall surely die. 15 And Nathan departed to his bayit. And **יהוה** struck the child that Uriyah's wife bore to David, and it was very sick. 16 David therefore besought Elohim for the child; and David fasted, and went in, and lay all night upon the earth. 17 And the zachanim of his bayit arose, and went to him, to raise him up from the earth: but he would not, neither did he eat lechem with them. 18 And it came to pass on the seventh day, that the child died. And the avadim of David feared to tell him that the child was dead: for they said, See, while the child was yet alive, we spoke to him, and he would not shema to our voice: how will he then react, if we tell him that the child is dead? 19 But when David saw that his avadim whispered, David perceived that the child was dead: therefore David said to his avadim, Is the child dead? And they said, He is dead. 20 Then David arose from the earth, and washed, and anointed himself, and changed his clothes, and came into the Bayit of **יהוה**, and worshipped: then he came to his own bayit; and when he asked, they set food before him, and he did eat. 21 Then said his avadim to him, What thing is this that you have done? You did fast and weep for the child, while he was alive; but when the child was dead, you did rise and eat food. 22 And he said, While the child was yet alive, I fasted and wept: for I said, Who can tell whether Elohim will grant me unmerited favor that the child may live? 23 But now he is dead, why should I fast? Can I bring him back again? I shall go to him, but he shall not return to me.¹ 24 And David comforted Bath-Sheva his wife, and went in to her, and lay with her:

and she bore a son, and he called his name Shlomo: and **יהוה** loved him. 25 And he sent by the hand of Nathan the navi; and he called his name Yedidyah, because of **יהוה**. 26 And Yoav fought against Ravah of the children of Ammon, and took the royal city. 27 And Yoav sent messengers to David, and said, I have fought against Ravah, and have taken the city of mayim. 28 Now therefore gather the rest of the people together, and encamp against the city, and take it: lest I take the city, and it be called after my name. 29 And David gathered all the people together, and went to Ravah, and fought against it, and took it. 30 And he took their melech's keter from off his head, the weight of it was a talent of gold with the precious stones: and it was set on David's head. And he brought forth the spoil of the city in great abundance. 31 And he brought forth the people that were there, and put them under saws, and under instruments of iron, and under axes of iron, and made them pass through the brickworks: and so he did to all the cities of the children of Ammon. So David and all the people returned to Yahrushalayim.

13 And it came to pass after this, that Avshalom the son of David had a beautiful sister, whose name was Tamar; and Amnon the son of David loved her. 2 And Amnon was so troubled, that he became sick for his sister Tamar; for she was a virgin; and Amnon thought it hard for him to do any thing to her. 3 But Amnon had a friend, whose name was Yonadah, the son of Shimeah David's brother: and Yonadah was a very wise man. 4 And he said to him, Why are you, being the melech's son, becoming thinner from day to day? Will you not tell me? And Amnon said to him, I love Tamar, my brother Avshalom's sister. 5 And Yonadah said to him, Lay down on your bed, and make yourself sick: and when your abba comes to see you, say to him, I ask you, let my sister Tamar come, and give me food, and prepare

---

¹ A clear reference that babies' spirits and those too young to know right from wrong do go to heaven.

the food in my sight, that I may see it, and eat it from her hand. 6 So Amnon lay down, and made himself sick: and when the melech had come to see him, Amnon said to the melech, I ask you, let Tamar my sister come, and make me a couple of cakes in my sight, that I may eat at her hand. 7 Then David sent home to Tamar, saying, Go now to your brother Amnon's bayit, and make him food. 8 So Tamar went to her brother Amnon's bayit; and he was lying down. And she took flour, and kneaded it, and made cakes in his sight, and did bake the cakes. 9 And she took a pan, and poured them out before him; but he refused to eat. And Amnon said, Have all men leave me. And every man went out from him. 10 And Amnon said to Tamar, Bring the food into the bedroom, that I might eat from your hand. And Tamar took the cakes that she had made, and brought them into the bedroom to Amnon her brother. 11 And when she had brought them to him to eat, he grabbed her, and said to her, Come lie with me, my sister. 12 And she answered him, No, my brother, do not force me, for no such thing is to be done in Yisrael: do not do this wickedness. 13 And I, how then shall I ever cause my shame to depart? And as for you, you shall be as one of the fools in Yisrael. Now therefore, I beg you, speak to the melech; for he will not withhold me from you. 14 But he would not shema to her voice: but, being stronger than her, forced her, and lay with her. 15 Then Amnon hated her exceedingly; so that the hatred with which he hated her was even greater than the ahava with which he had loved her. And Amnon said to her, Arise, and get out of here. 16 And she said to him, There is no cause: this evil in sending me away is greater than the other evil that you did to me. But he would not shema to her. 17 Then he called his eved that served him, and said, Put now this woman out of my room, and bolt the door after her. 18 And she had a garment of divers colors upon her: for with such robes were the melech's

daughters that were virgins dressed. Then his eved brought her out, and bolted the door after her. 19 And Tamar put ashes on her head, and tore her garment of divers colors that was on her, and laid her hand on her head, and went away crying. 20 And Avshalom her brother said to her, Has Amnon your brother been with you? But hold now your silence, my sister: he is your brother; regard not this thing. So Tamar remained desolate and horrified in her brother Avshalom's bayit. 21 But when melech David heard of all these things, he was very angry. 22 And Avshalom spoke to his brother Amnon neither tov nor bad: for Avshalom hated Amnon, because he had forced his sister Tamar to lie with him. 23 And it came to pass after two full years, that Avshalom had sheepshearers in Baal-Hazor, which is next to Ephraim: and Avshalom invited all the melech's sons. 24 And Avshalom came to the melech, and said, See now, your eved has sheepshearers; let the melech, I ask you, and his avadim go with your eved. 25 And the melech said to Avshalom, No, my son, let us not all now go, lest we be a burden to you. And he pressured him: however he would not go, but blessed him. 26 Then said Avshalom, If not, I beg you, let my brother Amnon go with us. And the melech said to him, Why should he go with you? 27 But Avshalom pressured him so that he let Amnon and all the melech's sons go with him. 28 Now Avshalom had commanded his avadim, saying, Take note now when you see Amnon's lev drunk with wine, and when I say to you, Smite Amnon; then kill him, fear not: have not I commanded you? Be courageous and be brave. 29 And the avadim of Avshalom did to Amnon as Avshalom had commanded. Then all the melech's sons arose, and every man got up upon his mule, and fled. 30 And it came to pass, while they were on the way, that news came to David, saying, Avshalom has slain all the melech's sons, and there is not one of them left. 31 Then the melech arose, and tore his garments, and lay on the earth; and all his avadim stood by with their clothes torn. 32 And Yonadav, the son of Shimeah David's brother, answered and said, Let not my master suppose that they have slain all the young men the melech's sons; for Amnon only is dead: for by the order of Avshalom this has been determined from the day that he forced his sister Tamar. 33 Now therefore let not my master the melech take the thing to his lev, to think that all the melech's sons are dead: for Amnon only is dead. 34 But Avshalom fled. And the young man that kept the guard lifted up his eyes, and looked, and, see, there came many people by the way of the hillside behind him. 35 And Yonadav said to the melech, See, the melech's sons come: as your eved said, so it is. 36 And it came to pass, as soon as he had made an end of speaking, that, see, the melech's sons came, and lifted up their voice and wept: and the melech also and all his avadim wept very hard. 37 But Avshalom fled, and went to Talmai, the son of Ammihud, melech of Geshur. And David mourned for his son every day. 38 So Avshalom fled, and went to Geshur, and was there three years. 39 And the chayim of melech David longed to go forth to Avshalom: for he was comforted concerning Amnon, because he was dead.

14 Now Yoav the son of Tzeruiah perceived that the melech's lev was longing for Avshalom. 2 And Yoav sent to Tekoah, and fetched there a wise woman, and said to her, I ask you, feign yourself to be a mourner, and put on now mourning clothes, and anoint not yourself with oil, but be as a woman that had a long time mourned for the dead: 3 And come to the melech, and speak in this manner to him. So Yoav put the words in her mouth. 4 And when the woman of Tekoah spoke to the melech, she fell on her face to the ground, and did reverance, and said, Help, O melech. 5 And the melech said to her, What

bothers you? And she answered, I am indeed a widow woman, and my husband is dead. 6 And your female eved had two sons, and they two strove together in the field, and there was none to part them, but the one smote the other, and killed him. 7 And, see, the whole family is risen against your female eved, and they said, Deliver him that smote his brother, that we may kill him, for the chayim of his brother whom he killed; and we will destroy the heir also: and so they shall quench my spark of chayim which is left, and shall not leave to my husband neither name nor remnant upon the earth. 8 And the melech said to the woman, Go to your bayit, and I will give orders concerning you. 9 And the woman of Tekoah said to the melech, My master, O melech, the Torah violations be on me, and on my abba's bayit: and the melech and his throne be guiltless. 10 And the melech said, Whoever said anything to you, bring him to me, and he shall not touch you any more. 11 Then said she, I beg you, let the melech remember יהוה Your Elohim, that you would not allow the revengers of dom to destroy any more, lest they destroy my son. And he said, As יהוה lives, there shall not one hair of your son fall to the earth. 12 Then the woman said, Let your female eved, I ask you, speak one more word to my master the melech. And he said, Go ahead. 13 And the woman said, Why then have you thought such a thing against the people of Elohim? For the melech does speak this thing as one who is at fault, in that the melech does not bring home again his banished. 14 For we must needs die, and are as mayim spilt on the ground, which cannot be gathered up again; neither does Elohim respect any person: yet he devises means, that his banished be not cast out from Him. 15 Now therefore that I am come to speak of this thing to my master the melech, it is because the people have made me afraid: and your female eved said, I will now speak to the melech; it may be that the melech will perform the request of his female eved.

16 For the melech will shema, to deliver his female eved out of the hand of the man that would destroy me and my son together out of the inheritance of Elohim. 17 Then your female eved said, The word of my master the melech shall now be comfortable: for as a heavenly messenger of Elohim, so is my master the melech to discern tov and bad: therefore יהוה Your Elohim will be with you. 18 Then the melech answered and said to the woman, Hide it not from me, I ask you, the thing that I shall ask you. And the woman said, Let my master the melech now speak. 19 And the melech said, Is not the hand of Yoav with you in all this? And the woman answered and said, As your chayim lives, my master the melech, none can turn to the right hand or to the left from anything that my master the melech has spoken: for your eved Yoav, he ordered me, and he put all these words in the mouth of your female eved: 20 To change the appearance of the matter has your eved Yoav done this thing: and my master is wise, according to the chochma of a heavenly messenger of Elohim, to know all things that are in the earth. 21 And the melech said to Yoav, See now, I have done this thing: go therefore and bring the young man Avshalom again. 22 And Yoav fell to the ground on his face, and bowed himself, and thanked the melech: and Yoav said, Today your eved knows that I have found favor in your sight, my master, O melech, in that the melech has fulfilled the request of his eved. 23 So Yoav arose and went to Geshur, and brought Avshalom back to Yahrushalayim. 24 And the melech said, Let him turn to his own bayit, and let him not see my face. So Avshalom returned to his own bayit, and saw not the melech's face. 25 But in all Yisrael there was none to be so much esteemed as Avshalom for his beauty: from the sole of his foot even to the keter of his head there was no blemish in him. 26 And when he cut his hair, for it was at every year's end that he cut it: because the hair was long on him, therefore he cut it: he

weighed the hair of his head at two hundred shekels after the melech's weight. 27 And to Avshalom there were born three sons, and one daughter, whose name was Tamar: she was a woman of a beautiful countenance. 28 So Avshalom dwelt two full years in Yahrushalayim, and saw not the melech's face. 29 Therefore Avshalom sent for Yoav, to have sent him to the melech; but he would not come to him: and when he sent again the second time, he would not come. 30 Therefore he said to his avadim, See, Yoav's field is near me, and he has barley there; go and set it on fire. And Avshalom's avadim set the field on fire. 31 Then Yoav arose, and came to Avshalom to his bayit, and said to him, Why have your avadim set my field on fire? 32 And Avshalom answered Yoav, See, I sent to you, saying, Come here, that I may send you to the melech, to say, Why am I come from Geshur? It would have been tov for me to be there still: now therefore let me see the melech's face; and if there be any Torah violations in me, let him kill me. 33 So Yoav came to the melech, and told him: and when he had called for Avshalom, he came to the melech, and bowed himself on his face to the ground before the melech: and the melech kissed Avshalom.

15 And it came to pass after this, that Avshalom prepared mirkavot and horses, and fifty men to run before him. 2 And Avshalom rose up early, and stood beside the way of the gate: and it was so, that when any man that had a controversy and came to the melech for mishpat, then Avshalom called to him, and said, Of what city are you? And he said, Your eved is of one of the tribes of Yisrael. 3 And Avshalom said to him, See, your matters are tov and right; but there is no man authorized of the melech to shema you. 4 Avshalom said moreover, If I were made shophet in the land, every man who had any suit or cause might come to me, and I would bring him justice! 5 And it was so, that when any

man came near to him to do him reverence, he put forth his hand, and took him, and kissed him. 6 And in this manner did Avshalom to all Yisrael that came to the melech for mishpat: so Avshalom stole the levim of the men of Yisrael. 7 And it came to pass after forty years, that Avshalom said to the melech, I ask you, let me go and pay my vow, which I have vowed to **יהוה**, in Hevron. 8 For your eved vowed a vow while I stayed at Geshur in Aram, saying, If **יהוה** shall bring me again indeed to Yahrushalayim, then I will serve **יהוה**. 9 And the melech said to him, Go in shalom. So he arose, and went to Hevron. 10 But Avshalom sent spies throughout all the tribes of Yisrael, saying, As soon as you shema the sound of the shofar, then you shall say, Avshalom reigns in Hevron. [1] 11 And with Avshalom went two hundred men out of Yahrushalayim, that were called; and they went unsuspecting, and they knew not any thing. 12 And Avshalom sent for Ahithophel the Gilonite, David's counselor, from his city, even from Giloh, while he offered sacrifices. And the conspiracy was strong; for the people increased continually who were with Avshalom. 13 And there came a messenger to David, saying, The levim of the men of Yisrael are with Avshalom. 14 And David said to all his avadim that were with him at Yahrushalayim, Arise, and let us flee; for otherwise we shall not escape from Avshalom: let's hurry to depart, lest he overtake us suddenly, and bring evil upon us, and destroy the city with the edge of the sword. 15 And the melech's avadim said to the melech, See; your avadim are ready to do whatever my master the melech shall appoint. 16 And the melech went forth, and his entire household after him. And the melech left ten women, who were concubines, to keep the bayit. 17 And the melech went forth, and all the people after him, and stayed in a place that was far off. 18 And all his avadim passed on with him;

and all the Cherethites, and all the Pelethites, and all the Gittites, six hundred men that came after him from Gath, passed on before the melech. 19 Then said the melech to Ittai the Gittite, Why do you also go with us? Return to your place, and stay with the melech: for you are a stranger, and also an exile from your own place. 20 Whereas you came just yesterday, should I this day make you go up and down with us? Seeing I go where I have to, return, and go back with your brothers: rachamim and emet be with you. 21 And Ittai answered the melech, and said, As **יהוה** lives, and as my master the melech lives, surely in whatever place my master the melech shall be, whether in death or chayim, even there also will your eved be. 22 And David said to Ittai, Go and pass over. And Ittai the Gittite passed over, and all his men, and all the little ones that were with him. 23 And all the country wept with a loud voice, and all the people passed over: the melech also himself passed over the brook Kidron, and all the people passed over, toward the way of the wilderness. 24 And see Tzadok also, and all the Leviim were with him, bearing the Ark of the Covenant of Elohim: and they put down the Ark of Elohim; and Aviathar went up, until all the people had done passing out of the city. 25 And the melech said to Tzadok, Carry back the Ark of Elohim into the city: if I shall find favor in the eyes of **יהוה**, He will bring me again, and show me both it, and His dwelling: 26 But if He says, I have no delight in you; see, hinayni, let Him do to me as seems tov to Him. 27 The melech said also to Tzadok the kohen, Are not you a seer? Return into the city in shalom with your two sons with you; Ahimaaz your son, and Yonathan the son of Aviathar. 28 See, I will stay in the plain of the wilderness, until there comes word from you to inform me. 29 Tzadok therefore and Aviathar carried the Ark of Elohim again to Yahrushalayim: and they stayed there. 30 And David went up by the ascent of Mount of Olives, and

---

[1] Internal uprising.

wept as he went up, and had his head covered,[1] and he went barefoot: and all the people that were with him covered every man his head,[2] and they went up, weeping as they went up. 31 And one told David, saying, Ahithophel is among the conspirators with Avshalom. And David said, O יהוה, I make tefillah to You; turn the counsel of Ahithophel into foolishness. 32 And it came to pass, that when David was come to the top of the Mount, where he worshipped Elohim, see, Hushai the Archite came to meet him with his coat torn, and earth upon his head: 33 To whom David said, If you pass on with me, then you shall be a burden to me: 34 But if you return to the city, and say to Avshalom, I will be your eved, O melech; as I have been your abba's eved now will I be your eved: then I may defeat the counsel of Ahithophel. 35 And have you not there with you Tzadok and Aviathar the kohanim? Therefore it shall be, that whatever thing you shall shema out of Avshalom's bayit, you shall tell it to Tzadok and Aviathar the kohanim. 36 See, they have there with them their two sons, Ahimaaz Tzadok's son, and Yonathan Aviathar's son; and by them you shall send to me everything that you can shema. 37 So Hushai David's friend came into the city, and Avshalom came into Yahrushalayim.

16 And when David was a little past the top of the hill, see, Ziva the eved of Mephibosheth met him, with a couple of donkeys saddled, and upon them two hundred loaves of lechem, and one hundred bunches of raisins, and an hundred summer fruits and a bottle of wine. 2 And the melech said to Ziva, What is the purpose for all these? And Ziva said, The donkeys are for the melech's household to ride on; and the lechem and summer fruit for the young men to eat; and the wine that such as be faint in the wilderness may drink. 3 And the melech said, And where is your master's son? And Ziva said to the melech, See, he stays at Yahrushalayim: for he said, Today shall Beit Yisrael restore to me the malchut of my abba.[3] 4 Then said the melech to Ziva, See; all that pertains to Mephibosheth is now yours. And Ziva said, I humbly beseech you that I may find favor in your sight, my master, O melech. 5 And when melech David came to Bahurim, see, there came out a man of the family of Beit Shaul, whose name was Shimei, the son of Gera: he came forth, and cursed still as he came. 6 And he cast stones at David, and at all the avadim of melech David: and all the people and all the mighty men were on his right hand and on his left. 7 And Shimei said when he cursed, Come out, come out, you bloody man; you man of Beliyaal: 8 יהוה has returned upon you all the dom of Beit Shaul, in whose place you have reigned; and יהוה has delivered the malchut into the hand of Avshalom your son: and, see, you are taken in your mischief, because you are a bloody man. 9 Then said Avishai the son of Tzeruiah to the melech, Why should this dead dog curse my master the melech? Let me go over, I beg you, and take off his head. 10 And the melech said, What have I to do with you, you sons of Tzeruiah? So let him curse, because יהוה has said to him, Curse David. Who shall then say, why did this happen? 11 And David said to Avishai, and to all his avadim, See, my son, who came out of my loins, seeks my chayim: so how much more then that can this Benyamite do? Leave him alone, and let him curse; for יהוה has ordered him. 12 It may be that יהוה will look on my affliction, and that יהוה will repay me tov for his cursing this day. 13 And as David and his men went by the way, Shimei went along on the hill's side opposite him, and

---

[1] Men wore head coverings in Yisrael as an eternal custom.
[2] All Yisraelites are seen here in head coverings not only the priests or kings. Since YHWH does not change, all believers must continue in the practice; at the very least in public worship and assembly.

[3] Many from the former House of Shaul or Ephraim Yisrael joined with Avimelech. Here even Mephiboshet, who had joined the House of Yahudah by eating continually from David's table, speaks of the House of Shaul returning to power as the House of Yisrael under Avimelech.

cursed as he went, and threw stones at him, and cast dust. 14 And the melech, and all the people that were with him, became weary, and refreshed themselves there. 15 And Avshalom, and all the people the men of Yisrael, came to Yahrushalayim, and Ahithophel with him. 16 And it came to pass, when Hushai the Archite, David's friend, was come to Avshalom that Hushai said to Avshalom, Lechayim to the melech, Lechayim to the melech. 17 And Avshalom said to Hushai, Is this your chesed to your friend? Why didn't you go with your friend? 18 And Hushai said to Avshalom, No; but whom יהוה, and this people, and all the men of Yisrael, choose, his will I be, and with him will I stay. 19 And again, whom should I serve? Should I not serve in the presence of his son? As I have served in your abba's presence, so will I be in your presence. 20 Then said Avshalom to Ahithophel, Give counsel among you what we shall do. 21 And Ahithophel said to Avshalom, Go in to your abba's concubines, which he has left to keep the bayit; and all Yisrael shall shema that you are abhorred by your abba: then shall the hands of all that are with you be strong. 22 So they spread Avshalom a tent upon the top of the bayit; and Avshalom went in to his abba's concubines in the sight of all Yisrael. 23 And the counsel of Ahithophel, which he advised in those days, was as if a man had inquired of the words of Elohim: so was all the advice of Ahithophel both with David and with Avshalom.

17 Moreover Ahithophel said to Avshalom, Let me now choose out twelve thousand men, and I will arise and pursue after David this night: 2 And I will come upon him while he is weary and weak-handed, and will make him afraid: and all the people that are with him shall flee; and I will smite the melech only: 3 And I will bring back all the people to you: when all the people return except the man whom you seek; then all the people

shall be in shalom. 4 And the saying pleased Avshalom well, and all the zachanim of Yisrael. 5 Then said Avshalom, Call now Hushai the Archite also, and let us shema likewise what he said. 6 And when Hushai was come to Avshalom, Avshalom spoke to him, saying, Ahithophel has spoken after this manner: shall we do what he advises? If not, tell me. 7 And Hushai said to Avshalom, The counsel that Ahithophel has given is not tov at this time. 8 For, said Hushai, you know your abba and his men, that they are mighty men, and they are bitter, as a bear robbed of her cubs in the field: and your abba is a man of war, and will not be staying with the people. 9 See, he is hidden now in some pit, or in some other place: and it will come to pass, when some of them are overthrown at the start, that whoever hears it will say, There is a slaughter among the people that follow Avshalom. 10 And he also that is brave, whose lev is as the lev of a lion, shall utterly melt: for all Yisrael knows that your abba is a mighty man, and those who are with him are brave men. 11 Therefore I advise that all Yisrael be gathered to you, from Dan even to Beer-Sheva, as the sand that is by the sea for multitude; and that you go to battle yourself in their midst. 12 So shall we come upon him in some place where he shall be found, and we will fall upon him as the dew falls on the ground: and of him and of all the men that are with him there shall not be left even one. 13 Moreover, if he has gone into a city, then shall all Yisrael bring ropes to that city, and we will draw it into the river, until there is not one small stone found there. 14 And Avshalom and all the men of Yisrael said, The counsel of Hushai the Archite is better than the counsel of Ahithophel. For יהוה had appointed to defeat the tov counsel of Ahithophel, to the intent that יהוה might bring evil upon Avshalom. 15 Then said Hushai to Tzadok and to Aviathar the kohanim, This and this did Ahithophel counsel Avshalom and the zachanim of

Yisrael; and this and this have I advised. 16 Now therefore send quickly, and tell David, saying, Stay not this night in the plains of the wilderness, but quickly pass over; lest the melech be swallowed up, and all the people that are with him. 17 Now Yonathan and Ahimaaz stayed by En-Rogel; for they might not be seen to come into the city: and a female eved went and told them; and they went and told melech David. 18 Nevertheless a youth saw them, and told Avshalom: but they went both of them away quickly, and came to a man's bayit in Bahurim, which had a well in his court; where they went down into it. 19 And the woman took and spread a covering over the well's mouth, and spread ground corn on it; and the thing was not known. 20 And when Avshalom's avadim came to the woman to the bayit, they said, Where is Ahimaaz and Yonathan? And the woman said to them, They have gone over the brook of mayim. And when they had sought and could not find them, they returned to Yahrushalayim. 21 And it came to pass, after they were departed, that they came up out of the well, and went and told melech David, and said to David, Arise, and pass quickly over the mayim: for this is what Ahithophel advised against you. 22 Then David arose, and all the people that were with him, and they passed over the Yarden River: by the morning light not even one of them had not gone over the Yarden River. 23 And when Ahithophel saw that his counsel was not followed, he saddled his donkey, and arose, and came home to his bayit, to his city, and put his household in order, and hanged himself, and died, and was buried in the tomb of his abba. 24 Then David came to Machanayim. And Avshalom passed over the Yarden River, he and all the men of Yisrael with him. 25 And Avshalom made Amasa captain of the army instead of Yoav: which Amasa was a man's son, whose name was Ithra an Israelite, that went in to Avigail the daughter of Nahash, sister to Tzeruiah Yoav's ima. 26 So Yisrael and Avshalom pitched in the land of Gilead. 27 And it came to pass, when David was come to Machanayim, that Shovi the son of Nahash of Ravah of the children of Ammon, and Machir the son of Ammiel of Lo-Devar, and Barzillai the Gileadite of Rogelim, 28 Brought beds, and basons, and earthen vessels, and wheat, and barley, and flour, and parched corn, and beans, and lentils, and parched pulse, 29 And honey, and butter, and sheep, and cheese of cows, for David, and for the people that were with him, to eat: for they said, The people are hungry, and weary, and thirsty, in the wilderness.

18

And David numbered the people that were with him, and set officers of thousands and officers of hundreds over them. 2 And David sent out a third part of the people under the hand of Yoav, and a third part under the hand of Avishai the son of Tzeruiah, Yoav's brother, and a third part under the hand of Ittai the Gittite. And the melech said to the people, I will surely go forth with you myself also. 3 But the people answered, You shall not go forth: for if we flee away, they will not care about us; neither if half of us die, will they care about us: but now you are worth ten thousand of us: therefore now it is better that you support us out of the city. 4 And the melech said to them, What seems to you best I will do. And the melech stood beside the gate, and all the people came out by hundreds and by thousands. 5 And the melech commanded Yoav and Avishai and Ittai, saying, Deal gently for my sake with the young man, even with Avshalom. So all the people heard when the melech gave all the officers orders concerning Avshalom. 6 So the people went out into the field against Yisrael: and the battle was in the woods of Ephraim;[1] 7 There the people of Yisrael were slain before the avadim of David, and there was there a great slaughter that day of

---

[1] A typical two-house war, which is just one of many over the course of 3,000 years. We have yet to see an end to this battle.

twenty thousand men. 8 For the battle was there scattered over the face of all the country: and the woods devoured more people that day than the sword devoured. 9 And Avshalom met the avadim of David. And Avshalom rode upon a mule, and the mule went under the thick branches of a great oak, and his head caught hold of the oak, and he was hung up between the shamayim and the earth; and the mule that was under him went away. 10 And a certain man saw it, and told Yoav, and said, See, I saw Avshalom hung in an oak. 11 And Yoav said to the man that told him, And, you saw him, why then did you not smite him there to the ground? And I would have given you ten shekels of silver, and a belt. 12 And the man said to Yoav, Though I should receive a thousand shekels of silver in my hand, yet would I not put forth my hand against the melech's son: for in our hearing the melech charged you and Avishai and Ittai, saying, Beware that none touch the young man Avshalom. 13 Otherwise I would have brought falsehood into my own chayim: for there is no matter hidden from the melech, and you yourself would have set yourself against me. 14 Then said Yoav, I won't waste time here with you. And he took three spears in his hand, and thrust them through the lev of Avshalom, while he was still alive in the midst of the oak. 15 And ten young men that bore Yoav's armor also surrounded about and smote Avshalom, and killed him. 16 And Yoav blew the shofar, and the people returned from pursuing after Yisrael: for Yoav held back the people. 17 And they took Avshalom, and cast him into a great pit in the wood, and laid a very great heap of stones upon him: and all Yisrael fled every one to his tent. 18 Now Avshalom in his lifetime had taken and built up for himself a pillar, which is in the melech's valley: for he said, I have no son to keep my name in remembrance: and he called the pillar after his own name: and it is called to this day, Avshalom's Monument. 19 Then said

Ahimaaz the son of Tzadok, Let me now run, and bear the melech news, how that יהוה has avenged him of his enemies. 20 And Yoav said to him, You shall not bear news this day, but you shall bear news another day: but this day you shall bear no news, because the melech's son is dead. 21 Then said Yoav to the Cushite, Go tell the melech what you have seen. And Cushite bowed himself to Yoav, and ran. 22 Then said Ahimaaz the son of Tzadok yet again to Yoav, But however, let me, I ask you, also run after Cushi. And Yoav said, Why will you run, my son, seeing that you have no news to bring you reward? 23 But, said he, what is the difference, let me run. And he said to him, Run. Then Ahimaaz ran by the way of the plain, and overtook Cushi. 24 And David sat between the two gates: and the watchmen went up to the roof over the gate to the wall; and lifted up his eyes, and looked, and see a man running alone. 25 And the watchman cried, and told the melech. And the melech said, If he is alone, there is news in his mouth. And he came closer and drew near. 26 And the watchman saw another man running: and the watchman called to the gatekeeper, and said, See another man is running alone. And the melech said, He also brings news. 27 And the watchman said, I think the running of the first is like the running of Ahimaaz the son of Tzadok. And the melech said, He is a tov man, and comes with tov news. 28 And Ahimaaz called, and said to the melech, All is well. And he fell down to the earth upon his face before the melech, and said, Blessed be יהוה Your Elohim, who has delivered up the men that lifted up their hand against my master the melech. 29 And the melech said, Is the young man Avshalom safe? And Ahimaaz answered, When Yoav sent the melech's eved, and me your eved, I saw a great tumult, but I knew not what it was. 30 And the melech said to him, Turn aside, and stand here. And he turned aside, and stood still. 31 And, see, the Cushite came; and the

Cushite said, There is news, my master the melech: for **יהוה** has avenged you this day of all them that rose up against you. 32 And the melech said to the Cushite, Is the young man Avshalom safe? And the Cushite answered, The enemies of my master the melech, and all that rise against you to do you hurt, be as that young man is. 33 And the melech was much moved, and went up to the bedroom over the gate, and wept: and as he went, this he said, Oy my son Avshalom, my son, my son Avshalom! Would to Elohim I had died for you, O Avshalom, my son, my son!

19 And it was told Yoav, See, the melech weeps and mourns for Avshalom. 2 And the victory that day was turned into mourning for all the people: for the people heard that day how the melech was grieved for his son. 3 And the people concealed themselves that day as they returned back into the city, as people who are ashamed flee in battle. 4 But the melech covered his face, and the melech cried with a loud voice, Oy my son Avshalom, Oy Avshalom, my son, my son! 5 And Yoav came into the bayit to the melech, and said, You have put to shame this day all your avadim, who have saved your chayim, and the lives of your sons and of your daughters, and the lives of your wives, and the lives of your concubines; 6 In that you loved your enemies, and hated your friends. For you have declared this day, that you regard neither your princes or avadim: for this day I perceive, that if Avshalom had lived, and all of us had died this day, then it would have pleased you well. 7 Now therefore arise, go forth, and speak comfortably to your avadim: for I swear by **יהוה**, if you go not forth, there will not stay one minute with you this night: and that will be worse to you than all the evil that befell you from your youth until now. 8 Then the melech arose, and sat in the gate. And they told to all the people, saying, See, the melech does sit in the gate. And all the

people came before the melech: for Yisrael had fled every man to his tent. 9 And all the people were at strife throughout all the tribes of Yisrael, saying, The melech saved us out of the hand of our enemies, and he delivered us out of the hand of the Philistines; but now he is fled out of the land for Avshalom. 10 And Avshalom, whom we anointed over us, is dead in battle. Now therefore why are you silent about bringing the melech back? 11 And melech David sent to Tzadok and to Aviathar the kohanim, saying, Speak to the zachanim of Yahudah, saying, Why are you the last to bring the melech back to his bayit? Seeing the speech of all Yisrael is come to the melech, even to his bayit. 12 You are my brothers, you are my bones and my flesh: why then are you the last to bring back the melech? 13 And say to Amasa, Are you not of my bone, and of my flesh? Elohim do so to me, and more also, if you be not captain of the army before me continually in place of Yoav. 14 And he bowed the lev of all the men of Yahudah, even as the lev of one man; so that they sent this word to the melech, Return, and all your avadim. 15 So the melech returned, and came to the Yarden River. And Yahudah came to Gilgal, to go to meet the melech, to accompany the melech over the Yarden River. 16 And Shimei the son of Gera, a Benyamite, which was of Bahurim, hurried and came down with the men of Yahudah to meet melech David. 17 And there were a thousand men of Benyamin with him, and Ziva the eved of the bayit of Shaul, and his fifteen sons and his twenty avadim with him; and they went over the Yarden River before the melech. 18 And they built rafts to bring over the melech's household, and to do what he thought tov. And Shimei the son of Gera fell down before the melech, as he was come over the Yarden River; 19 And said to the melech, Let not my master impute Torah violations to me, neither remember that which your eved did perversely the day that my master the melech went out of Yahrushalayim, that the melech should take it to his lev. 20 For your eved does know that I have sinned: therefore, see, I have come today as the first of all Beit Yoseph to go down to meet my master the melech.[1] 21 But Avishai the son of Tzeruiah answered and said, Shall not Shimei be put to death for this, because he cursed יהוה's anointed? 22 And David said, What have I to do with you, you sons of Tzeruiah, that you should this day be adversaries to me? Shall there any man be put to death this day in Yisrael? For do not I know that I am this day melech over Yisrael? 23 Therefore the melech said to Shimei, You shall not die. And the melech swore to him. 24 And Mephibosheth the son of Shaul came down to meet the melech, and had neither dressed his feet, nor trimmed his beard, nor washed his clothes, from the day the melech departed until the day he came again in shalom. 25 And it came to pass, when he was come to Yahrushalayim to meet the melech, that the melech said to him, Why did you not go with me, Mephibosheth? 26 And he answered, My master, O melech, my eved deceived me: for your eved said, I will saddle me a donkey, that I may ride on it, and go to the melech; because your eved is lame. 27 And he has slandered your eved to my master the melech; but my master the melech is as a heavenly messenger of Elohim: do therefore what is tov in your eyes. 28 For all of my abba's bayit were but dead men before my master the melech: yet did you set your eved among them that did eat at your own table. What right therefore have I yet to cry any more to the melech? 29 And the melech said to him, Why speak you any more of your matters? I have said, You and Ziva divide the land. 30 And Mephibosheth said to the melech, Yes, let him take all, forasmuch as my master the melech is come again in shalom to his own bayit. 31 And Barzillai the Gileadite came down from Rogelim, and went over the Yarden River with the melech, to accompany him over the Yarden River. 32 Now Barzillai was a very aged man, even eighty years old: and he had provided the melech provisions while he lay at Machanayim, for he was a very rich man. 33 And the melech said to Barzillai, Come over with me, and I will feed you with me in Yahrushalayim. 34 And Barzillai said to the melech, How long have I to live, that I should go up with the melech to Yahrushalayim? 35 I am this day eighty years old: and can I discern between tov and evil? Can your eved taste what I eat or what I drink? Can I shema any more the voice of singing men and singing women? Why then should your eved be still a burden to my master the melech? 36 Your eved can hardly cross over the Yarden River with the melech: and why should the melech repay me with such a reward? 37 Let your eved, I beg you, turn back again, that I may die in my own city, and be buried by the grave of my abba and of my ima. But see your eved Chimham; let him go over with my master the melech; and do to him what shall seem tov to you. 38 And the melech answered, Chimham shall go over with me, and I will do to him that which shall seem tov to you: and whatever you shall require of me, that will I do for you. 39 And all the people went over the Yarden River. And when the melech was come over, the melech kissed Barzillai, and blessed him; and he returned to his own place. 40 Then the melech went on to Gilgal, and Chimham went on with him: and all the people of Yahudah accompanied the melech, and also half the people of Yisrael.[2] 41 And, see, all the men of Yisrael came to the melech, and said to the melech, Why have our brothers the men of Yahudah stolen you away, and have brought the melech, and his household, and all David's men with him, over the Yarden

---

[1] Another reminder that Benjamin was once part of the House of Yisrael and that most followers of Avshalom were from the House of Joseph, who had already rebelled against the House of David.

[2] Yahudah came to bring him back to Yahrushalayim.

River?¹ 42 And all the men of Yahudah answered the men of Yisrael, Because the melech is a near relative to us! Why then are you angry about this matter? Have we eaten at all at the melech's expense? Or has he given us any special gift?² 43 And the men of Yisrael answered the men of Yahudah, and said, We have ten parts in the melech, and we have also more right in David than you: why then did you despise us, was it not our advice first to bring back our melech?³ And the words of the men of Yahudah were fiercer than the words of the men of Yisrael.⁴

20 And there happened to be there a man of Beliyaal,⁵ whose name was Sheva, the son of Bichri, a Benyamite:⁶ and he blew a shofar, and said, We have no part in David, neither have we any inheritance in the son of Yishai: every man back to his tents, O Yisrael.⁷ 2 So every man of Yisrael

---

¹ Ephraim is jealous of Judah as usual and complains. The fact that they weren't invited nor welcome to bring David back, was because they has just finished conspiring against David by aiding and abetting Avshalom, in his rebellion against the House of David. But that didn't seem to stop their jealousy.

² Judah's answer is not bringing up the rebellion of Ephraim, but one of pride and arrogance. They claim that Ephraim should not be involved in David's return to the capital, because the king is a Yahudite and as such is naturally or biologically predisposed to being closer to Yahudah than to Ephraim. Today like yesterday, Judah desires to leave Ephraim out of kingdom restoration, just because the Ephraimites are merely Yisraelites, and not Jewish Yisraelites like the King Moshiach.

³ Ephraim's argument is that while they may not be Jewish, they are still the larger part of biological Yisrael, with ten tribes, rather than just two, and were also far more numerous than Yahudah. Not only that, it was their idea first to bring David back to the capital. In these exchanges we see both houses vying for supremacy over the other, a condition that is terminal, unless YHWH reveals to us the error of our ways.

⁴ This short but succinct comment is YHWH's commentary on the argument. Judah was more harsh and unkind than Ephraim. Why? Because Judah taunted Ephraim with a situation they could not possibly change (that of being non-Jews), whereas the king was a Jew. We find the same trends in certain denominations today, where Ephraimites are always reminded that though they are accepted, they can never be considered Jews who will benefit from a life of full obedience to Torah. This taunting led YHWH to make this startling comment. It serves all Yisrael well to remember YHWH's own words and commentary, about the harshness used by Judah against returning Ephraim.

⁵ Someone who is opposed to two-house truth is called here a son of s.a.tan or Beliyaal.

⁶ Benjamin was once considered part of Ephraim Yisrael.

⁷ This is the result of rejection and vexation. A feeling of not really being Yisrael, even though biologically they certainly were. The same applies to returning Ephraim of today. "To

---

went up from following after David, and followed Sheva the son of Bichri: but the men of Yahudah clave to their melech, from the Yarden River even to Yahrushalayim.⁸ 3 And David came to his bayit at Yahrushalayim; and the melech took the ten women his concubines, whom he had left to look after the bayit, and put them in a protected bayit, and fed them, but went not in to them. So they were shut up to the day of their death, living in widowhood. 4 Then said the melech to Amasa, Assemble me the men of Yahudah within three days, and be you here present. 5 So Amasa went to assemble the men of Yahudah: but he stayed longer than the set time that he had appointed him. 6 And David said to Avishai, Now shall Sheva the son of Bichri do us more harm than did Avshalom: take you your master's avadim, and pursue after him, lest he get for himself fenced cities, and escapes us. 7 And there went out after him Yoav's men, and the Cherethites, and the Pelethites, and all the mighty men: and they went out of Yahrushalayim, to pursue after Sheva the son of Bichri. 8 When they were at the great stone that is in Giveon, Amasa went before them. And Yoav's garment that he had put on was girded to him, and upon it a girdle with a sword attached to his waist in the sheath; and as he went forward it fell out. 9 And Yoav said to Amasa, Shalom, my brother? And Yoav took Amasa by the beard with the right hand to kiss him. 10 But Amasa took no heed to the sword that was in Yoav's hand: so he smote him with it in the stomach, and shed out his insides to the ground, and struck him not again; and he died. So Yoav and Avishai his brother pursued after Sheva the son of Bichri. 11 And one of Yoav's men stood by him, and said, He that favors Yoav, and is also for David, let him follow Yoav. 12 And Amasa wallowed in dom in the midst of the highway. And when the man saw that all the people stood still, he

---

your tents" often can mean back to false religion, after feeling rejected by Judah.

⁸ Sharp division.

removed Amasa out of the highway into the field, and cast a cloth upon him, when he saw that every one that came by him stood still. 13 When he was removed out of the highway, all the people went on after Yoav, to pursue after Sheva the son of Bichri. 14 And he went through all the tribes of Yisrael to Avel, and to Beth-Maachah, and all the Berites: and they were gathered together, and went also after him. 15 And they came and besieged him in Avel of Beth-Maachah, and they cast up a siege mound against the city, and it stood in the trench: and all the people that were with Yoav battered the wall, to throw it down. 16 Then cried a wise woman out of the city, Shema, shema; Please say to Yoav, Come near here, so that I may speak with you. 17 And when he was come near to her, the woman said, Are you Yoav? And he answered, I am he. Then she said to him, Shema the words of your female eved. And he answered, I do shema. 18 Then she spoke, saying, In former times, they said, They shall surely ask counsel at Avel: and so as to end all matters. 19 I am one of those that are peaceful and faithful in Yisrael: you seek to destroy a city and an ima in Yisrael: why will you swallow up the inheritance of יהוה ? 20 And Yoav answered and said, Far be it, far be it from me, that I should swallow up or destroy you or your city. 21 That's not the issue: but a man of Mount Ephraim, Sheva the son of Bichri by name, has lifted up his hand against the melech, even against David: deliver him only, and I will depart from the city. And the woman said to Yoav, See, his head shall be thrown to you over the wall. 22 Then the woman went to all the people in her chochma. And they cut off the head of Sheva the son of Bichri, and cast it out to Yoav. And he blew a shofar, and they retired from the city, every man to his tent. And Yoav returned to Yahrushalayim to the melech.[1] 23 Now Yoav was over all the

army of Yisrael: and Benayah the son of Yehoiada was over the Cherethites and over the Pelethites: 24 And Adoram was over the tribute: and Yehoshaphat the son of Ahilud was recorder: 25 And Shewa was sopher: and Tzadok and Aviathar were the kohanim: 26 And Aza also the Yairite was a kohen to David.

21 Then there was a famine in the days of David three years, year after year; and David inquired of יהוה. And יהוה answered, *It is for Shaul, and for his bloody bayit, because he killed the Giveonites.* 2 And the melech called the Giveonites, and said to them - now the Giveonites were not of the children of Yisrael, but of the remnant of the Amorites; and the children of Yisrael had sworn to them: and Shaul sought to slay them in his zeal to the children of Yisrael and Yahudah - 3 Therefore David said to the Giveonites, What shall I do for you? And how shall I make the atonement that you may bless the inheritance of יהוה? 4 And the Giveonites said to him, We will have no silver or gold from Shaul, nor from his bayit; neither for us shall you kill any man in Yisrael. And he said, What you shall say, that will I do for you. 5 And they answered the melech, The man that consumed us, and that devised against us that we should be destroyed from remaining in any of the coasts of Yisrael, 6 Let seven men of his sons be delivered to us, and we will hang them up to יהוה in Giveah of Shaul, whom יהוה did choose. And the melech said, I will give them. 7 But the melech spared Mephibosheth, the son of Yonathan the son of Shaul, because of יהוה's oath that was between them, between David and Yonathan the son of Shaul. 8 But the melech took the two sons of Ritzpah the daughter of Ayah, whom she bore to Shaul, Armoni and Mephibosheth; and the five sons of Michal the daughter of Shaul, whom she brought up for Adriel the son of Barzillai the Meholathite: 9 And he

[1] This is the ultimate result to all who ruthlessly sow division between the two houses rather than unite them through Moshiach and Torah.

delivered them into the hands of the Giveonites, and they hanged them in the hill before יהוה : and they fell all seven together, and were put to death in the days of harvest, in the first days, in the beginning of the barley harvest. 10 And Ritzpah the daughter of Ayah took sackcloth, and spread it for her upon the rock, from the beginning of harvest until mayim dropped upon them out of the shamayim, and suffered neither the birds of the air to rest on them by day, nor the beasts of the field by night. 11 And it was told David what Ritzpah the daughter of Ayah, the concubine of Shaul, had done. 12 And David went and took the bones of Shaul and the bones of Yonathan his son from the men of Yavesh-Gilead, who had stolen them from the street of Beth-Shan, where the Philistines had hanged them, when the Philistines had slain Shaul in Gilboa: 13 And he brought up from there the bones of Shaul and the bones of Yonathan his son; and they gathered the bones of them that were hanged. 14 And the bones of Shaul and Yonathan his son they buried in the country of Benyamin in Zelah, in the tomb of Kish his abba: and they performed all that the melech commanded. And after that Elohim heard the tefillah for the land. 15 Moreover the Philistines had war again with Yisrael; and David went down, and his avadim with him, and fought against the Philistines: and David grew weary. 16 And Yishbo-Benov, who was of the sons of the giant, the weight of whose spear weighed three hundred shekels of bronze in weight, he being girded with a new sword, thought he had slain David. 17 But Avishai the son of Tzeruiah helped him, and smote the Philistine, and killed him. Then the men of David swore to him, saying, You shall go no more out with us to battle, that you quench not the light of Yisrael. 18 And it came to pass after this, that there was again a battle with the Philistines at Gov: then Sivechai the Hushathite killed Saph, who was of the sons of the giant. 19 And there

was again a battle in Gov with the Philistines, where Elchanan the son of Yaare-Oregim, a Beth-Lechemite, killed the brother of Golyath the Gittite, the staff of whose spear was like a weaver's beam. 20 And there was a battle in Gath again, where was a man of great stature, that had on every hand six fingers, and on every foot six toes, twenty-four in total; and he also was born to the giant. 21 And when he defied Yisrael, Yonathan the son of Shimea the brother of David killed him. 22 These four were born to the giant in Gath, and fell by the hand of David, and by the hand of his avadim.

22 And David spoke to יהוה the words of this song in the day that יהוה had delivered him out of the hand of all his enemies, and out of the hand of Shaul: 2 And he said, יהוה is My Rock, and My Fortress, and My Deliverer; 3 The Elohim of My Rock; in Him will I trust: He is my shield, and the horn of My Yahshua, My High Tower, and My Refuge, My Savior; you save me from violence. 4 I will call on יהוה, who is worthy to be praised: so shall I be saved from my enemies. 5 When the waves of death surrounded me, the floods of wicked men made me afraid; 6 The sorrows of the grave surrounded me; the snares of death were before me; 7 In my distress I called upon יהוה, and cried to My Elohim: and He did shema my voice out of His Hekal, and my cry did enter into His ears. 8 Then the earth shook and trembled; the foundations of the shamayim moved and shook, because He was angry. 9 There went up a smoke out of His nostrils, and devouring fire out of His mouth: coals were kindled by it. 10 He bowed the shamayim also, and came down; and darkness was under His feet. 11 And He rode upon a cheruv, and did fly: and He was seen upon the wings of the wind. 12 And He made darkness pavilions round about Him, dark mayim, and thick clouds of the skies. 13 Through the brightness before Him were

coals of fire kindled. 14 **יהוה** thundered from the shamayim, and the most High uttered His voice. 15 And He sent out arrows, and scattered them; lightning, and discomfited them. 16 And the channels of the sea appeared; the foundations of the olam were discovered, at the rebuking of **יהוה**, at the blast of the breath of His nostrils. 17 He sent from above, He took me; He drew me out of many mayim; 18 He delivered me from my strong enemy, and from them that hated me: for they were too strong for me. 19 They confronted me in the day of my calamity: but **יהוה** was My support. 20 He brought me forth also into a large place: He delivered me, because He delighted in me. 21 **יהוה** rewarded me according to my tzedakah: according to the cleanness of my hands has He repaid me. 22 For I have kept the halacha of **יהוה**, and have not wickedly departed from My Elohim. 23 For all His mishpatim were before me: and as for His chukim, I did not depart from them. 24 I was also upright before Him, and have kept myself from Torah violations. 25 Therefore **יהוה** has repaid me according to my tzedakah; according to my cleanness in His eyes. 26 With those showing rachamim You will show Yourself with rachamim, and with the tzadik man You will show Yourself tzadik. 27 With the pure You will show Yourself pure; and with the perverse You will show Yourself twisted. 28 And the afflicted people you will save: but Your eyes are upon the proud, that You may bring them down. 29 For You are My Lamp, O **יהוה**: and **יהוה** will lighten my darkness. 30 For by You I have run through a troop: by My Elohim have I leaped over a wall. 31 As for El, His way is perfect; the word of **יהוה** is tried: He is a shield to all those that trust in Him. 32 For who is El, except **יהוה**? And who is a Rock, except our Elohim? 33 El is my strength and power: and He makes my way perfect. 34 He makes my feet like the feet of deer: and sets me upon my high places. 35 He teachs my hands to make war;

so that a bow of steel is broken by my arms. 36 You have also given me the shield of Your Yahshua: and Your gentleness has made me great. 37 You have enlarged my steps under me; so that my feet did not slip. 38 I have pursued my enemies, and destroyed them; and returned not again until I had consumed them. 39 And I have consumed them, and wounded them, so that they could not rise: yes, they are fallen under my feet. 40 For You have girded me with strength to battle: them that rose up against me have You subdued under me. 41 You have also given me the necks of my enemies, that I might destroy them that hate me. 42 They looked, but there was none to save; even to **יהוה**, but He answered them not. 43 Then did I beat them as small as the dust of the earth, I did stamp them as the dirt of the street, and did spread them abroad. 44 You also have delivered me from the strivings of my people, You have kept me to be head of the heathen nations: a people whom I knew not shall serve me. 45 Strangers shall submit themselves to me: as soon as they shema, they shall be obedient to me. 46 Strangers shall fade away, and they shall be restrained from their ways. 47 **יהוה** lives; and blessed be My Rock; and exalted is the Elohim of the Rock of My Yahshua. 48 El who avenges me, and that brings down the peoples under me, 49 And that brings me forth from my enemies: You also have lifted me up on high above them that rose up against me: You have delivered me from the violent man. 50 Therefore I will give hodu to You, O **יהוה**, among the heathen, and I will sing tehillot to Your Name. 51 He is the tower of salvation for His melech: and shows rachamim to His anointed, to David, and to his zera le-olam-va-ed.

23 Now these are the last words of David. David the son of Yishai said, and the man who was raised up on high, the anointed of the Elohim of Yaakov, and the sweet psalmist of Yisrael, said,

2 The Ruach of יהוה spoke by me, and His word was in my tongue. 3 The Elohim of Yisrael said, the Rock of Yisrael spoke to me, He that rules over men must be just, ruling in the fear of Elohim. 4 And he shall be as the light of the morning, when the sun rises, even a morning without clouds, as the tender grass springing out of the earth by clear shining after rain. 5 Although my bayit be not so with El; yet He has made with me an everlasting covenant, ordered me in all sure things: for this is all for my salvation, and all for my desire; He will not allow others to grow. 6 The sons of Beliyaal shall be all of them as thorns thrust away, because they cannot be taken with hands: 7 But the man that shall touch them must be fenced with iron and the staff of a spear; and they shall be utterly burned with fire in the same place. 8 These are the names of the mighty men whom David had: The Tachmonite that sat in the seat, chief among the officers; the same was Adino the Eznite: he lifted up his spear against eight hundred, whom he killed at one time. 9 And after him was El-Azar the son of Dodo the Ahohite, one of the three mighty men with David, when they defied the Philistines that were there gathered together to battle, when the men of Yisrael had gone up: 10 He arose, and smote the Philistines until his hand was weary, and his hand clung to the sword: and יהוה brought a great victory that day; and the people returned after him only to spoil. 11 And after him was Shammah the son of Agee the Hararite. And the Philistines were gathered together into a company, where was a piece of ground full of lentils: and the people fled from the Philistines. 12 But he stood in the midst of the ground, and defended it, and killed the Philistines: and יהוה brought a great victory. 13 And three of the valiant men went down, and came to David in the harvest time to the cave of Adullam: and the troop of the Philistines pitched in the Valley of Rephaim. 14 And David was then in a stronghold, and the watch-post of the Philistines was then in Beth-Lechem. 15 And David longed, and said, Oh that one would give me drink from the mayim of the well of Beth-Lechem, which is by the gate! 16 And the three mighty men broke through the army of the Philistines, and drew mayim out of the well of Beth-Lechem, that was by the gate, and took it, and brought it to David: nevertheless he would not drink it, but poured it out to יהוה. 17 And he said, Be it far from me, O יהוה, that I should do this: is not this the dom of the men that went in jeopardy of their lives? Therefore he would not drink it. These things did these three mighty men. 18 And Avishai, the brother of Yoav, the son of Tzeruiah, was first among three. And he lifted up his spear against three hundred, and killed them, and had a name among three. 19 Was he not most honorable of the three? Therefore he was their captain: but he did not come to the first three. 20 And Benanyahu the son of Yehoyada, the son of a brave man, of Kavzeel, who had done many acts, he killed two lionlike men of Moav: he went down also and killed a lion in the midst of a pit in the time of snow: 21 And he killed an Mitzrite, an impressive man: and the Mitzrite had a spear in his hand; but he went down to him with a staff, and plucked the spear out of the Mitzrite's hand, and killed him with his own spear. 22 These things did Benanyahu of Yehoyada, and had the name among three mighty men. 23 He was more honorable than the thirty, but he attained not to the first three. And David set him over his guard. 24 Asah-El the brother of Yoav was one of the thirty; Elchanan the son of Dodo of Beth-Lechem, 25 Shammah the Harodite, Elika the Harodite, 26 Helez the Paltite, Ira the son of Ikkesh the Tekoite, 27 Avi-Ezer the Anethothite, Mevunnai the Hushathite, 28 Tzalmon the Ahohite, Maharai the Netophathite, 29 Helev the son of Baanah, a Netophathite, Ittai the son of Rivai out of Giveah of the children of Benyamin, 30 Benayahu the Pirathonite,

Hiddai of the brooks of Gaash, 31 Avi-Alvon the Arvathite, Azmaveth the Barhumite, 32 Elyahva the Shaalvonite, of the sons of Yashen, Yonathan, 33 Shammah the Hararite, Ahyam the son of Sharar the Hararite, 34 Eliphelet the son of Ahasvai, the son of the Maachathite, Eliyam the son of Ahithophel the Gilonite, 35 Hetzrai the Carmelite, Paarai the Arvite, 36 Yigal the son of Nathan of Tzovah, Bani the Gadite, 37 Tzelek the Ammonite, Naharai the Beerothite, armor-bearer to Yoav the son of Tzeruiah, 38 Ira the Yithrite, Garev a Yithrite, 39 And Uriyah the Hittite: thirty-seven in all.

24 And again the anger of יהוה was kindled against Yisrael, and He moved David against them to say, Go, number Yisrael and Yahudah.[1] 2 For the melech said to Yoav the captain of the army, who was with him, Go now through all the tribes of Yisrael, from Dan even to Beer-Sheva, and number the people, that I may know the number of the people. 3 And Yoav said to the melech, Now even if יהוה Your Elohim adds to the people, a hundredfold more than there are, so that the eyes of my master the melech may see it: but why does my master the melech delight in this thing? 4 Nevertheless the melech's word prevailed against Yoav, and against the officers of the army. And Yoav and the officers of the army went out from the presence of the melech, to number the people of Yisrael. 5 And they passed over the Yarden River, and pitched in Aroer, on the right side of the city that lies in the midst of the river of Gad, and toward Yazer: 6 Then they came to Gilead, and to the land of Tahtim-Hodshi; and they came to Dan-Yaan, and around to Tzidon, 7 And came to the stronghold of Tzor, and to all the cities of the Hivites, and of the Kanaanites: and they went out to the south

of Yahudah, even to Beer-Sheva. 8 So when they had gone through all the land, they came to Yahrushalayim at the end of nine months and twenty days. 9 And Yoav gave up the sum of the number of the people to the melech: and there were in Yisrael eight hundred thousand brave men that drew the sword; and the men of Yahudah were five hundred thousand men. 10 And David's lev convicted him after he had numbered the people. And David said to יהוה, I have sinned greatly in what I have done: and now, I beseech you, O יהוה, take away the Torah violations of Your eved; for I have done very foolishly. 11 For when David was up in the morning, the word of יהוה came to the navi Gad, David's seer, saying, 12 Go and say to David, This said יהוה, *I offer you three things; choose one of them, that I may do it to you.* 13 So Gad came to David, and told him, and said to him, Shall seven years of famine come to you in your land? Or will you flee three months before your enemies, while they pursue you? Or will you that there be three days' pestilence in your land? Now advise me, and see what answer I shall return to Him that sent me. 14 And David said to Gad, I am in a great trouble now: let us fall now into the hand of יהוה, for His cheseds are great: and let me not fall into the hand of man. 15 So יהוה sent a pestilence upon Yisrael from the morning even to the time appointed: and there died of the people from Dan even to Beer-Sheva seventy thousand men. 16 And when the Malach stretched out His hand upon Yahrushalayim to destroy it, יהוה relented of the evil, and said to the Malach that destroyed the people, It is enough: now stop Your hand. And the Malach יהוה was by the threshing place of Araunah the Yevusite. 17 And David spoke to יהוה when he saw the heavenly messenger that smote the people, and said, See, I have sinned, and I have done wickedly: but these sheep, what have they done? Let Your hand, I beg you, be against me, and against my abba's bayit. 18 And Gad came that day

---

[1] Two-house reference. Another Scripture in First Chronicles 21:1 says s.a.tan moved David. There is no contradiction here, since YHWH caused s.a.tan to move David to achieve His purpose.

to David, and said to him, Go up, raise an altar to יהוה on the threshing floor of Araunah the Yevusite. 19 And David, according to the saying of Gad, went up as יהוה commanded. 20 And Araunah looked, and saw the melech and his avadim coming toward him: and Araunah went out, and bowed himself before the melech with his face upon the ground. 21 And Araunah said, Why is my master the melech come to his eved? And David said, To buy the threshing floor from you, to build an altar to יהוה, that the plague may be stopped from among the people. 22 And Araunah said to David, Let my master the melech take and offer up what seems tov to him: see, here are cattle for burnt sacrifice, and threshing instruments and other instruments of the cattle for wood. 23 All these things O Melech, Araunah gives to the melech. And Araunah said to the melech, May יהוה Your Elohim accept you.

24 And the melech said to Araunah, No; but I will surely buy it from you at a price: neither will I offer burnt offerings to יהוה My Elohim of that which costs me nothing. So David bought the threshing floor and the cattle for fifty shekels of silver. 25 And David built there an altar to יהוה, and offered burnt offerings and shalom offerings. So יהוה answered the tefillot for the land, and the plague was stopped from Yisrael.[1]

---

[1] There is a corresponding account in First Chronicles 21:15-29, and many confuse these two accounts as the purchase of the same field. But David actually bought two fields, from two different persons, for two different amounts of money. The first one was on the Mt. of Olives, which would become the altar of purifying from the red heifer with the ashes placed into the waters of purification as per Numbers 19. The other altar was to be built on Mt. Moriyah for the sacrifices in the Temple (First Chronicles 21:15-29) when it would be built. Both purchases were done in relation to the plague being lifted from Yisrael for David's sin of numbering the people. For more details, see: **An Altar Of Authority** available at: http://store.yourarmstoisrael.org/Qstore/Qstore.cgi?CMD=011&PROD=1065766783

מלכים א

Melechim Aleph - First Kings
To Our Forefathers Yisrael

1 Now melech David was old and advanced in years; and they covered him with clothes, but he could not get warm. 2 Therefore his avadim said to him, Let there be sought for my master the melech a young virgin: and let her stand before the melech, and let her cherish him, and let her lie in your bosom, that my master the melech may be warm. 3 So they sought for a lovely young woman throughout all the borders of Yisrael, and found Avishag a Shunammite, and brought her to the melech. 4 And the young woman was very lovely, and cherished the melech, and was a chaver to him: but the melech knew her not. 5 Then Adoniyah the son of Haggith exalted himself, saying, I will be melech: and he prepared mirkavot and horsemen, and fifty men to run before him. 6 And his abba had not rebuked him at any time in saying, Why have you done this? And he also was a very handsome man; and his ima bare him after Avshalom. 7 And he conferred with Yoav the son of Zeruyah, and with Aviathar the kohen: and they supported Adoniyah and helped him. 8 But Tzadok the kohen, and Benayahu the son of Yehoiada, and Nathan ha navi, and Shimei, and Rei, and the mighty men who belonged to David, were not with Adoniyah. 9 And Adoniyah offered sheep and oxen and fat cattle by the stone of Zoheleth, which is by En-Rogel, and called all his brothers the melech's sons, and all the men of Yahudah the melech's avadim: 10 But Nathan ha navi, and Benayahu, and the mighty men, and Shlomo his brother, he did not call. 11 Nathan then spoke to Bath-Sheva the ima of Shlomo, saying, Have you not heard that Adoniyah the son of Haggith has become melech, and David our master does not know it? 12 Now therefore come, let me, I ask you, give you advice, that you

may save your own chayim, and the chayim of your son Shlomo. 13 Go to the melech David, and say to him, Did you not, my master, O melech, swear to your female eved, saying, Certainly Shlomo your son shall reign after me, and he shall sit upon my throne? Why then does Adoniyah reign? 14 See, while you yet talk there with the melech, I also will come in after you, and confirm your words. 15 And Bath-Sheva went in to the melech into the bedroom: and the melech was very old; and Avishag the Shunammite was serving the melech. 16 And Bath-Sheva bowed, and did obeisance to the melech. And the melech said, What do you want? 17 And she said to him, My master, you swore by יהוה Your Elohim to your female eved, saying, Certainly Shlomo your son shall reign after me, and he shall sit upon my throne. 18 And now, see, Adoniyah reigns; and now, my master the melech, you don't even know it. 19 And he has sacrificed oxen and fat cattle and sheep in abundance, and has called all the sons of the melech, and Aviathar the kohen, and Yoav the captain of the army: but Shlomo your eved has he not called. 20 And you, my master, O melech, the eyes of all Yisrael are upon you, that you should tell them who shall sit on the throne of my master the melech after him. 21 Otherwise it shall come to pass, when my master the melech shall die with his ahvot, that I and my son Shlomo shall be considered as sinners. 22 And, see, while she yet talked with the melech, Nathan ha navi also came in. 23 And they told the melech, saying, See Nathan ha navi is here. And when he had come in before the melech, he bowed himself before the melech with his face to the ground. 24 And Nathan said, My master, O melech, Did you say, Adoniyah shall reign after me, and he shall sit upon my throne? 25 For he is gone down this day, and has sacrificed oxen and fat cattle and sheep in abundance, and has called all the melech's sons, and the captains of the army, and Aviathar the kohen; and, see, they eat and drink before him, and say, Le-Chayim melech Adoniyah. 26 But me, even me your eved, and Tzadok the kohen, and Benayahu the son of Yehoiada, and your eved Shlomo, all of us has he not called. 27 Is this thing done by my master the melech, and you have not shown it to him, who should sit on the throne of my master the melech after him? 28 Then melech David answered and said, Call Bath-Sheva. And she came into the melech's presence, and stood before the melech. 29 And the melech swore, and said, As יהוה lives, that has redeemed my being out of all distress, 30 Even as I swore to you by יהוה Elohim of Yisrael, saying, Certainly Shlomo your son shall reign after me, and he shall sit upon my throne in my place; even so will I certainly do again this day. 31 Then Bath-Sheva bowed with her face to the earth, and did reverence to the melech, and said, Let my master melech David live le-olam-va-ed. 32 And melech David said, Call me Tzadok the kohen, and Nathan ha navi, and Benayahu the son of Yehoiada. And they came before the melech. 33 The melech also said to them, Take with you the avadim of your master, and have Shlomo my son to ride upon my own mule, and bring him down to Gihon: 34 And let Tzadok the kohen and Nathan ha navi anoint him there melech over Yisrael: and blow with the shofar, and say, Let melech Shlomo live. 35 Then you shall come up after him, that he may come and sit upon my throne; for he shall be melech in my place: and I have appointed him to be ruler over Yisrael and over Yahudah.[1] 36 And Benayahu the son of Yehoiada answered the melech, and said, Amein: יהוה Elohim of my master the melech says so too. 37 As יהוה has been with my master the melech, even so let Him

be with Shlomo, and make his throne greater than the throne of my master melech David. 38 So Tzadok the kohen, and Nathan ha navi, and Benayahu the son of Yehoiada, and the Cherethites, and the Pelethites, went down, and had Shlomo to ride upon melech David's mule, and brought him to Gihon. 39 And Tzadok the kohen took a horn of oil out of the Tabernacle, and anointed Shlomo. And they blew the shofar; and all the people said, Let melech Shlomo live. 40 And all the people came up after him, and the people played the flutes, and had gilah with great simcha, so that the earth was split with their noise. 41 And Adoniyah and all the guests that were with him heard it as they had finished eating. And when Yoav heard the sound of the shofar, he said, Why is this noise of the city in an uproar? 42 And while he yet spoke, see, Yonathan the son of Aviathar the kohen came: and Adoniyah said to him, Come in; for you are a brave man, and bring tov news. 43 And Yonathan answered and said to Adoniyah, Truly our master melech David has made Shlomo melech. 44 And the melech has sent with him Tzadok the kohen, and Nathan ha navi, and Benayahu the son of Yehoiada, and the Cherethites, and the Pelethites, and they have caused him to ride upon the melech's mule: 45 And Tzadok the kohen and Nathan ha navi have anointed him melech in Gihon: and they are come up from there having gilah, so that the city rang again. This is the noise that you have heard. 46 And now Shlomo sits on the throne of the malchut. 47 And moreover the melech's avadim came to bless our master melech David, saying, Elohim make the name of Shlomo better than your name, and make his throne greater than your throne. And the melech bowed himself upon the bed. 48 And also the melech said, Blessed be יהוה Elohim of Yisrael, who has given one to sit on my throne this day, my eyes even seeing it. 49 And all the guests that were with Adoniyah were afraid, and rose up, and went every man his way. 50 And Adoniyah

---

[1] To continue the uneasy unity that existed.

feared because of Shlomo, and arose, and went, and took hold of the horns of the altar. 51 And it was told Shlomo, saying, See, Adoniyah fears melech Shlomo: for, see, he has caught hold on the horns of the altar, saying, Let melech Shlomo swear to me today that he will not kill his eved with the sword. 52 And Shlomo said, If he will show himself a worthy man, there shall not a hair of his fall to the earth: but if wickedness shall be found in him, he shall die. 53 So melech Shlomo sent, and they brought him down from the altar. And he came and bowed himself to melech Shlomo: and Shlomo said to him, Go to your bayit.

2 Now the days of David's death drew near; and he commanded Shlomo his son, saying, 2 I go the way of all the earth: be strong therefore, and show yourself a man; 3 And shomer the command of יהוה Your Elohim, to have your halacha in His halachot, to keep His chukim, and His mishpatim, and His testimonies, as it is written in the Torah of Moshe, that you may prosper in all that you do, and wherever you go: 4 That יהוה may continue His word which He spoke concerning me, saying, If your children take heed to their halacha, to have their halacha before Me in emet with all their lev and with all their being saying, there shall not cease from you a man to sit on the throne of Yisrael. 5 Moreover you know also what Yoav the son of Zeruyah did to me, and also what he did to the two captains of the hosts of Yisrael, to Avner the son of Ner, and to Amasa the son of Yether, whom he killed, and shed the dom of war in a time of shalom, and put the dom of war upon his belt that was around his waist, and on his sandals that were on his feet. 6 Do therefore according to your chochma, and let not his gray hair go down to the grave in shalom. 7 But show chesed to the sons of Barzillai the Gilyadite, and let them be of those that eat at your table: for so they came to me when I fled because of Avshalom your brother. 8 And, see, you

have with you Shimei the son of Gera, a Benyamite of Bahurim, who cursed me with a hard curse in the day when I went to Machanayim: but he came down to meet me at the River Yarden, and I swore to him by יהוה, saying, I will not put you to death with the sword. 9 So now do not hold him guiltless: for you are a wise man, and know what you ought to do to him; but his gray head bring down to the grave with dom. 10 So David slept with his ahvot, and was buried in the city of David. 11 And the days that David reigned over Yisrael were forty years: seven years he reigned in Hevron, and thirty-three years he reigned in Yahrushalayim. 12 Then Shlomo sat upon the throne of David his abba; and his malchut was established greatly. 13 And Adoniyah the son of Haggith came to Bath-Sheva the ima of Shlomo. And she said, Do you come in shalom? And he said, In Shalom. 14 He said moreover, I have something to say to you. And she said, Go ahead. 15 And he said, You know that the malchut was mine, and that kol Yisrael looked to me, that I should reign. But the malchut has turned around, and has become my brother's: for it was his from יהוה. 16 And now I ask one request of you, do not deny me. And she said to him, Say it. 17 And he said, Speak, I ask, to Shlomo the melech, for he will not say no to you, that he give me Avishag the Shunammite as my wife. 18 And Bath-Sheva said, Well; I will speak for you to the melech. 19 Bath-Sheva therefore went to melech Shlomo, to speak to him for Adoniyah. And the melech rose up to meet her, and bowed himself to her, and sat down on his throne, and had a throne set for the melech's ima; and she sat on his right hand. 20 Then she said, I desire one small request from you; I'll ask you, and do not tell me no. And the melech said to her, Ask on, my ima: for I will not say no to you. 21 And she said, Let Avishag the Shunammite be given to Adoniyah your brother to be his wife. 22 And melech Shlomo answered and said to his ima, And why do you ask Avishag the Shunammite for Adoniyah? Ask for him the malchut also; for he is my elder brother; and why don't you ask for the malchut for Aviathar the kohen also, and for Yoav the son of Zeruyah. 23 Then melech Shlomo swore by יהוה, saying, Elohim do so to me, and more also, if Adoniyah has not spoken this request against his own chayim. 24 Now therefore, as יהוה lives, who has established me, and set me on the throne of David my abba, and who has made me a bayit, as He promised, Adoniyah shall be put to death this day. 25 And melech Shlomo sent Benayahu the son of Yehoiada; and he killed him that he died. 26 And to Aviathar the kohen said the melech, Go to Anathoth, to your own fields; for you are worthy of death: but I will not at this time put you to death, because you bore the Ark of the Master יהוה before David my abba, and because you have been afflicted in all that my abba was afflicted. 27 So Shlomo expelled Aviathar from being kohen to יהוה; that he might fulfill the word of יהוה, which He spoke concerning the bayit of Eli in Shiloh. 28 Then news came to Yoav: for Yoav had followed after Adoniyah, though he did not follow after Avshalom. And Yoav fled to the Tabernacle of יהוה, and took hold of the horns of the altar. 29 And it was told melech Shlomo that Yoav was fled to the Tabernacle of יהוה; and, see, he is by the altar. Then Shlomo sent Benayahu the son of Yehoiada, saying, Go, and kill him. 30 And Benayahu came to the Tabernacle of יהוה, and said to him, This says the melech, Come out. And he said, No; but I will die here. And Benayahu brought the melech word again, saying, This said Yoav, and so he answered me. 31 And the melech said to him, Do as he has said, and fall upon him, and bury him; that you may take away the innocent dom, which Yoav shed, from me, and from the bayit of my abba. 32 And יהוה shall return his dom upon his own head, who fell upon two men more tzadik and better than he,

and killed them with the sword, my abba David not knowing about it, Avner the son of Ner, captain of the army of Yisrael, and Amasa the son of Yether, captain of the army of Yahudah. [1] 33 Their dom shall therefore return upon the head of Yoav, and upon the head of his zera le-olam-va-ed: but upon David, and upon his zera, and upon his bayit, and upon his throne, shall there be shalom le-olam-va-ed from יהוה. 34 So Benayahu the son of Yehoiada went up, and fell upon him, and killed him: and he was buried in his own bayit in the wilderness. 35 And the melech put Benayahu the son of Yehoiada in his place over the army: and Tzadok the kohen did the melech put in the place of Aviathar. 36 And the melech sent and called for Shimei, and said to him, Build a bayit in Yahrushalayim, and dwell there, and go not out from there anywhere. 37 For it shall be, that on the day you go out, and pass over the brook Kidron, you shall know for certain that you shall surely die: your dom shall be upon your own head. 38 And Shimei said to the melech, The saying is tov: as my master the melech has said, so will your eved do. And Shimei dwelt in Yahrushalayim many days. 39 And it came to pass at the end of three years, that two of the avadim of Shimei ran away to Achish son of Maachah melech of Gath. And they told Shimei, saying, See, your avadim are in Gath. 40 And Shimei arose, and saddled his donkey, and went to Gath to Achish to seek his avadim: and Shimei went out, and brought his avadim from Gath. 41 And it was told Shlomo that Shimei had gone from Yahrushalayim to Gath, and had come back. 42 And the melech sent and called for Shimei, and said to him, Did I not make you to swear by יהוה, and warned you, saying, Know for certain, on the day you go out, and walk abroad anywhere, that you shall surely die? And you said to me, The word that I have heard is tov. 43 Why then have you not kept the oath to יהוה, and the commandment that I have

---

[1] Two-house reference.

commanded you? 44 The melech said moreover to Shimei, You know all the wickedness that your lev is aware of, that you did to David my abba: therefore יהוה shall return your wickedness upon your own head; 45 And melech Shlomo shall be blessed, and the throne of David shall be established before יהוה le-olam-va-ed. 46 So the melech commanded Benayahu the son of Yehoiada; who went out, and fell upon him, so that he died. And the malchut was established in the hand of Shlomo.

3 And Shlomo became son in law to Pharaoh melech of Mitzrayim, and took Pharaoh's daughter, and brought her into the city of David, until he had made an end of building his own bayit, and the Bayit of יהוה, and the wall of Yahrushalayim all around. 2 Only the people sacrificed in the high places, because there was no bayit built for the Name of יהוה, before those days. 3 And Shlomo loved יהוה, walking in the chukim of David his abba: only he sacrificed and burnt incense in the high places. 4 And the melech went to Giveon to sacrifice there; for that was the great high place: a thousand burnt offerings did Shlomo offer upon that altar. 5 In Giveon יהוה appeared to Shlomo in a dream by night: and Elohim said, *Ask what I shall give you.* 6 And Shlomo said, You have shown to Your eved David my abba great chesed, as he had his halacha before You in emet, and in tzedakah, and in uprightness of lev; and You have kept for him this great chesed, that You have given him a son to sit on his throne, as it is this day. 7 And now, O יהוה My Elohim, You have made Your eved melech instead of David my abba: and I am like a little child: I know not how to go out or come in. 8 And Your eved is in the midst of Your people that You have chosen, a great people that cannot be numbered nor counted for multitude.[1] 9 So give Your eved a lev of binah to shophet Your people, that I

may discern between tov and bad: for who is able to shophet this Your great people? 10 And the words pleased יהוה , that Shlomo had asked this thing. 11 And Elohim said to him, *Because you have asked this thing, and have not asked for yourself long chayim; neither have asked riches for yourself, nor have asked for the chayim of your enemies; but have asked for yourself binah to discern mishpat; 12 See, I have done according to your words: see, I have given you a wise lev of binah; so that there was none like you before you, neither after you shall any arise like you. 13 And I have also given you that which you have not asked, both riches, and honor: so that there shall not be any among the melechim like you all your days. 14 And if you will have your halacah in My halachot, to keep My chukim and My mitzvoth, as your abba David did, then I will lengthen your days.* 15 And Shlomo awoke; and see; it was a dream. And he came to Yahrushalayim, and stood before the Ark of the Covenant of יהוה, and offered up burnt offerings, and offered shalom offerings, and made a feast for all his avadim. 16 Then came two women, that were harlots, to the melech, and stood before him. 17 And the one woman said, O my master, this woman and I dwell in one bayit; and I was delivered of a child with her in the bayit. 18 And it came to pass the third day after that I gave birth, that this woman gave birth also: and while we were together; there was no stranger with us in the bayit, except the two of us in the bayit. 19 And this woman's child died in the night; because she lay on it. 20 And she arose at midnight, and took my son from beside me, while your female eved slept, and laid it in her bosom, and laid her dead child in my bosom. 21 And when I rose in the morning to nurse my child, see, it was dead: but when I had considered it in the morning, see, it was not my son, which I did bear. 22 And the other woman said, No; but the living is my son, and the dead is your son. And this said, No; but the dead is your

---

[1] The on-going increase according to the promise of physical multiplicity.

son, and the living is my son. This they spoke before the melech. 23 Then said the melech, The one says, This is my son that lives, and your son is the dead one: and the other says, No; but your son is the dead son, and my son is the living. 24 And the melech said, Bring me a sword. And they brought a sword before the melech. 25 And the melech said, Divide and cut the living child in two, and give half to the one ima, and half to the other ima. 26 Then spoke the woman of the living child to the melech, for her rachamim within her for her son, and she said, O my master, I'll give her the living child, and in no way kill it. But the other said, Let it be neither mine, or yours, but kill it and divide it. 27 Then the melech answered and said, Give her the living child, and in no way kill it: she is its ima. 28 And all Yisrael heard of the mishpat that the melech had issued; and they feared melech: for they saw that the chochma of Elohim was in him, to do mishpat.

4 So melech Shlomo was melech over kol Yisrael. [1] 2 And these were the rulers which he had; Azaryahu the son of Tzadok the kohen, 3 Elihoreph and Ahiyah, the sons of Shisha, scribes; Yehoshaphat the son of Ahilud, the recorder. 4 And Benayahu the son of Yehoiada was over the army: and Tzadok and Aviathar were the kohanim: 5 And Azaryahu the son of Nathan was over the officers: and Zavud the son of Nathan was principal officer, and the melech's friend: 6 And Ahishar was over the household: and Adoniram the son of Avda was over the compulsory labor. 7 And Shlomo had twelve officers over all Yisrael, which provided food for the melech and his household: each man made provision for one month a year. 8 And these are their names: The son of Hur, in Mount Ephraim: 9 The son of Dekar, in Makaz, and in Shaalvim, and Beth-Shemesh, and Elon-Beth-Hanan: 10 The son of Chesed, in Aruvoth; to him pertained Sochoh, and all

the land of Chepher: 11 The son of Avinadav, in all the region of Dor; which had Taphath the daughter of Shlomo as wife: 12 Baana the son of Ahilud; to him pertained Taanach and Megiddo, and all Beth-Shean, which is by Zartanah beneath Yezreel, from Beth-Shean to Avel-Meholah, even to the place that is beyond Yokneam: 13 The son of Geber, in Ramoth-Gilead; to him pertained the towns of Yair the son of Menashsheh, which are in Gilead; to him also pertained the region of Argov, which is in Bashan, sixty great cities with walls and bronze bars: 14 Ahinadav the son of Iddo had Machanayim: 15 Ahimaaz was in Naphtali; he also took Basmath the daughter of Shlomo to wife: 16 Baanah the son of Hushai was in Asher and in Aloth: 17 Yehoshaphat the son of Paruah, in Yissachar: 18 Shimei the son of Elah, in Benyamin: 19 Gever the son of Uri was in the country of Gilead, in the country of Sihon melech of the Amorites, and of Og melech of Bashan; and he was the only officer who was in the land. 20 Yahudah and Yisrael were many, as the sand that is by the sea in multitude, eating and drinking, and making simcha. [2] 21 And Shlomo reigned over all malchutim from the river to the land of the Philistines, and to the border of Mitzrayim: they brought presents, and

---

[2] History tells us that the united Tabernacle of David that King Solomon inherited was in fact the beginning of global Yisraelite expansion. Yisraelite colonies were established throughout the known world and colonialist Yisraelites began to intermingle with those of other nations producing a Yisraelite empire of global proportions. It was during the time of King David that Israel's **zera** or seed started its global proliferation. This colonialism is confirmed in 1 Kings 4:20-26, which clearly states that the start of this accelerated phase of the dust of the earth promise, began when the concept of the two-houses began to emerge. The text states, "Yahudah and Yisrael were as many as the sand of the sea." Not Judah alone. Even though both kingdoms acknowledged Solomon's reign, we see YHWH's promise to the patriarchs begin to accelerate through unadulterated and unchecked Yisraelite colonialism. What YHWH began via colonialism; He continued later via dispersion and scattering. Second Chronicles 8:2 shows how Hiram deeded Phoenician cities to Solomon, and how Solomon settled Yisraelites there. There were Yisraelites in every nation and city of the earth, since according to 1 Chronicles 9:23-24, all the subjected kings and their subjected empires appeared before Solomon annually to present gifts. The full documentation of Yisraelite global colonialism under the reign of King Solomon is well chronicled and documented by many.

---

[1] Both houses.

served Shlomo all the days of his chayim. 22 And Shlomo's provision for one day was thirty measures of fine flour, and sixty measures of meal, 23 Ten fatted cattle, and twenty cattle out of the pastures, and an hundred sheep, besides deer, and gazelles, and roebucks, and fatted fowl. 24 For he had dominion over the entire region on this side of the river, from Tiphsah even to Azzah, over all the melechim on this side of the river: and he had shalom on all sides all round him. 25 And Yahudah and Yisrael dwelt safely,[1] every man under his vine and under his fig eytz,[2] from Dan even to Beer-Sheva, all the days of Shlomo. 26 And Shlomo had forty thousand stalls of horses for his mirkavot, and twelve thousand horsemen. 27 And those officers provided food for melech Shlomo, and for all that came to melech Shlomo's table, every man in his month: they lacked nothing. 28 Barley also and straw for the horses and steeds they brought to the place where the officers were, every man according to his command. 29 And Elohim gave Shlomo chochma and binah in great abundance, and largeness of lev, even as the sand that is on the seashore. 30 And Shlomo's chochma excelled the chochma of all the children of the east country, and all the chochma of Mitzrayim. 31 For he was wiser than all men; than Ethan the Ezrahite, and Heman, and Chalcol, and Darda, the sons of Mahol: and his fame was in all nations all around. 32 And he spoke three thousand mishle: and his shirim were one thousand five. 33 And he spoke with da'at about eytzim, from the cedar eytz that is in Levanon even to the hyssop that springs out of the wall: he spoke also of beasts, and of fowls, and of creeping things, and of fishes with great chochma. 34 And there came from all nations to shema the chochma of Shlomo, from all the melechim of the olam,[3] who had heard of his chochma.

5 And Hiram melech of Tzor sent his avadim to Shlomo; for he had heard that they had anointed him melech in the place of his abba: for Hiram always had an ahava for David. 2 And Shlomo sent to Hiram, saying, 3 You know how that David my abba could not build a Bayit to the Name of יהוה His Elohim for the wars which were around him on every side, until יהוה put them under the soles of his feet. 4 But now יהוה My Elohim has given me rest on every side, so that there is neither adversary nor evil incident. 5 And, see, I purpose to build a Bayit to the Name of יהוה my Elohim, as יהוה spoke to David my abba, saying, Your son, whom I will set upon your throne in your place, he shall build a Bayit to My Name. 6 So now command that they cut me cedar eytzim out of Levanon; and my avadim shall be with your avadim, and to you will I will pay wages for your avadim according to all that you shall appoint. For you know that there is not among us any that has the skill to cut timber like the Tzidonians. 7 And it came to pass, when Hiram heard the words of Shlomo, that he had great gilah, and said, Blessed be יהוה this day, who has given to David a wise son over this great people. 8 And Hiram sent to Shlomo, saying, I have considered the things that you sent to me for: and I will do all your desire concerning timber of cedar, and concerning the cypress logs. 9 My avadim shall bring them down from Levanon to the sea: and I will convey them by sea in floats to the place that you shall appoint me, and will cause them to be unloaded there, and you shall receive them: and you shall accomplish my desire, by giving food for my household. 10 So Hiram gave Shlomo cedar eytzim and cypress logs according to all his desire. 11 And Shlomo gave Hiram twenty thousand measures of wheat for food to his household, and twenty measures of pure oil: this Shlomo gave to Hiram every year. 12 And יהוה gave Shlomo chochma, as He promised him: and there was shalom between Hiram and

---

[1] Unity and shalom to both houses under Solomon.
[2] The Vine is a symbol of YHWH and the fig tree symbol is national Yisrael.
[3] Worldwide Yisraelite empire.

Shlomo, and the two made a covenant together. 13 And melech Shlomo raised compulsory labor out of all Yisrael; and the compulsory labor was thirty thousand men. 14 And he sent them to Levanon ten thousand a month in turns: a month they were in Levanon, and two months at home: and Adoniram was over the compulsory labor. 15 And Shlomo had seventy thousand that bore burdens, and eighty thousand stonecutters in the mountains: 16 Beside the chief of Shlomo's officers who were over the work, three thousand three hundred, who ruled over the people that labored in the work. 17 And the melech commanded, and they brought great stones, costly stones, and cut stones, to lay the foundation of the Bayit. 18 And Shlomo's builders and Hiram's builders did cut them, and the stonemasons: so they prepared timber and stones to build the Bayit.

6 And it came to pass in the four hundred eightieth year after the children of Yisrael were come out of the land of Mitzrayim, in the fourth year of Shlomo's reign over Yisrael, in the month Zif, which is the second month, that he began to build the Bayit of יהוה. 2 And the Bayit which melech Shlomo built for יהוה, the length was sixty cubits, and the width twenty cubits, and the height thirty cubits. 3 And the porch before the Beit HaMikdash of the Bayit, twenty cubits was the length, according to the width of the Bayit; and ten cubits was the width in front of the Bayit. 4 And for the Bayit he made windows with narrow frames. 5 And against the wall of the Bayit he built rooms all around, against the walls of the Bayit all around, both of the Beit HaMikdash and of the Speaking Place: and he made rooms all around: 6 The lowest room was five cubits wide, and the middle was six cubits wide, and the third was seven cubits wide: for outside in the wall of the Bayit he made narrow ledges all around, so that the beams should not be fastened in the walls of the Bayit. 7 And the Bayit, when it

was being built, was built of finished stone made ready before it was brought there: so that there was neither hammer nor axe nor any tool of iron heard in the Bayit, while it was being built. 8 The door for the middle room was on the right side of the Bayit: and they went up with winding stairs into the middle side rooms, and out of the middle into the third. 9 So he built the Bayit, and finished it; and panelled the Bayit with beams and boards of cedar. 10 And then he built side rooms against all the Bayit, five cubits high: and they rested on the Bayit with cedar beams. 11 And the word of יהוה came to Shlomo, saying, 12 *Concerning this Bayit which you are building, if you will have your halacha in My chukim, and execute My mishpatim, and keep all My mitzvoth to have your halacha in them, then will I perform My word with you, which I spoke to David your abba: 13 And I will dwell among the children of Yisrael, and will not forsake My people Yisrael.* 14 So Shlomo built the Bayit, and finished it. 15 And he built the walls of the Bayit within with boards of cedar, both the floor of the Bayit, and the walls to the ceiling: and he paneled them on the inside with wood, and he paneled the floor of the Bayit with planks of cypress. 16 And he built twenty cubits at the rear of the Bayit, from the floor to the walls with boards of cedar: he even built it inside the partition to be the Most Set-Apart Place. 17 And the Bayit, that is, the Hekel before it, was forty cubits long. 18 And the cedar of the Bayit within was carved with ornaments and open flowers: all was cedar; there was no stone seen. 19 And the Speaking Place he prepared in the Bayit within, to put there the Ark of the Covenant of יהוה. 20 And the Speaking Place in the front was twenty cubits in length, and twenty cubits in width, and twenty cubits in the height: and he overlaid it with pure gold; and so covered the altar which was of cedar. 21 So Shlomo overlaid the Bayit within with pure gold: and he made a partition by the chains of gold before the Speaking Place; and he overlaid it with gold. 22 And the whole Bayit he overlaid with gold, until he had finished all the Bayit: also the whole altar that was by the Speaking Place he overlaid with gold. 23 And within the Speaking Place he made two cheruvim[1] from olive eytz,[2] each ten cubits high. 24 And five cubits was the one wing of the cheruv, and five cubits the other wing of the cheruv: from the uttermost part of the one wing to the uttermost part of the other were ten cubits. 25 And the other cheruv was ten cubits: both the cheruvim were of one measure and one size.[3] 26 The height of the one cheruv was ten cubits, as was the other cheruv. 27 And he set the cheruvim inside the inner Bayit: and they stretched out the wings of the cheruvim, so that the wing of the one touched one wall, and the wing of the other cheruv touched the other wall; and their wings touched one another in the midst in the middle of the room.[4] 28 And he overlaid the cheruvim with gold.[5] 29 And he carved all the walls of the Bayit all around with carved figures of cheruvim and palm eytzim and open flowers, inside and outside. 30 And the floor of the Bayit he overlaid with gold, inside and outside. 31 And for the entrance of the Speaking Place he made doors of olive eytz:[6] the lintel and side posts were a fifth part of the wall. 32 The two doors also were of olive eytz; and he carved upon them carvings of cheruvim and palm eytzim and open flowers, and overlaid them with gold,[7] and spread gold upon the cheruvim, and upon the palm eytzim. 33 So also he made for the door of the Beit HaMikdash posts of olive eytz,[8] a fourth part of the wall. 34 And the two doors were of cypress eytz: the two leaves of the one door folded, and the two leaves of the other door were folded.[9] 35 And he carved on them cheruvim and palm eytzim and open flowers: and covered them with gold laid upon the carved work. 36 And he built the inner court with three rows of cut stone, and a row of cedar beams. 37 In the fourth year was the foundation of the Bayit of יהוה laid, in the month Zif: 38 And in the eleventh year, in the month Bul, which is the eighth month, was the Bayit finished in all its details, and according to all its plans. So he took seven years to build it.[10]

7 And Shlomo was building his own bayit for thirteen years, and he finished his bayit. 2 He built also the bayit of the forest of Levanon; the length was a hundred cubits, and the width fifty cubits, and the height thirty cubits, with four rows of cedar pillars, with cedar beams on the pillars. 3 And it was paneled with cedar above the beams that were on forty-five pillars, fifteen in a row. 4 And there were windows in three rows, and window was opposite window in three tiers. 5 And all the doors

---

[1] Each cherub representing one house of Yisrael, each in the Speaking Place symbolizing YHWH's desire to speak and meet with both houses of Yisrael. The design of each cherub was identical, thus indicating YHWH's desire for equality to, for and between both houses of Yisrael. The annual **Yom Kippur** ceremony took place before YHWH, and Yisrael's Kohen HaGadol, the type and forerunner of Yahshua. The Holy of Holies itself is a detailed plan for Yisrael's redemption and unity. For more details see: **A Testimony of Yahshua** http://store.yourarmstoisrael.org/Qstore/Qstore.cgi?CMD=011 &PROD=000065.
[2] According to Jeremiah 11 and Romans 11 the olive tree represents both houses of Yisrael. As such, each cherub representing one house of Yisrael was made from olive wood or olive tree and served as a confirmation of the two trees of Ezekiel 37, becoming one in YHWH's hands.
[3] Equal weights and measures must be used - and were - for both houses of Yisrael.
[4] When both houses treat each other with equal weights and measures, centering on the mercy seat and the dom of Yahshua's atonement, then true unity will occur along with a manifestation of His **shekinah** (the divine presence). The presence of YHWH filled the Holy of Holies and will fill the restored Tabernacle of David, if we truly put aside all past misunderstandings about Yisrael and adopt Scripture's admonitions for all Yisrael. Let the two wings touch in your life, as you become a restorer of that bond of unity.
[5] Symbolic of the King Moshiach covering both sticks for both houses of Yisrael, as they reach out and touch each other, with His purity and Kingly authority.

[6] The two doors of olive wood represent both houses, and their entrance back to YHWH. All believers are to see themselves as part of the olive tree and thus that truth lies as the very entrance back into the presence of His mercy and forgiveness.
[7] Both doors covered with Moshiach's purity.
[8] Two olive posts. A two-house symbolic reference.
[9] Symbolic of both houses being flexible and led by YHWH's Ruach or wind.
[10] A type of the 7-year time of Jacob's Trouble, during which Yisrael's restoration will be fully completed by King Yahshua.

and doorposts had square frames, and window was opposite window three times. 6 And he made the porch of pillars; the length was fifty cubits, and the width thirty cubits: and the porch was in front of them: and the other pillars and the roof was in front of them. 7 Then he made a hall for the throne where he might shophet, even the hall of mishpat: and it was paneled with cedar from one side of the floor to the other. 8 And his bayit where he lived had another courtyard within the hall, which was of like work. Shlomo also made a bayit for Pharaoh's daughter, whom he had taken as his wife, just like his. 9 All these were of costly stones, according to the measures of cut stones, cut with saws, inside and outside, even from the foundation to the coping, and so on the outside towards the great courtyard. 10 And the foundation was of costly stones, large stones of ten cubits, and stones of eight cubits. 11 And above were costly stones, cut stones to size, and cedars. 12 And the great courtyard all around was with three rows of cut stones, and a row of cedar beams, both for the inner court of the Bayit of יהוה, and for the porch of the Bayit. 13 And melech Shlomo sent and fetched Hiram out of Tzor. 14 He was a widow's son of the tribe of Naphtali, and his abba was a man of Tzor, a worker in brass: and he was filled with chochma, and binah, and skilled to work all works in brass. And he came to melech Shlomo, and did all his work. 15 For he cast two pillars of brass, of eighteen cubits high apiece: and a line of twelve cubits measured the circumference of each one. 16 And he made two capitals of cast brass, to set upon the tops of the pillars: the height of the one capital was five cubits, and the height of the other capital was five cubits: 17 And a network of carved ornaments and wreaths of chain work, for the capitals that were on the top of the pillars; seven for the one capital, and seven for the other capital. 18 And he made the pillars, and two rows all around above the one network, to cover

the capitals that were at the top, with pomegranates: and he did also the same for the other capital. 19 And the capitals that were upon the top of the pillars were of bulging work shaped like lilies in the hall, four cubits. 20 And the capitals upon the two pillars had pomegranates also above, by the bulge next to the network: and the pomegranates were two hundred in rows all around on each of the capitals. 21 And he set up the pillars in the porch of the Hekel: and he set up the right pillar, and called the name of it Yahchin: and he set up the left pillar, and he called the name of it Boaz.[1] 22 And upon the top of the pillars was lily work: so the work of the pillars was finished. 23 And he made a cast basin, ten cubits from the one brim to the other: it was round all around, and the height was five cubits: and a line of thirty cubits measured around it. 24 And under the brim of it all around there were ornaments compassing it, ten in a cubit, all around the basin all around: the ornaments were cast in two rows,[2] when it was cast. 25 It stood upon twelve oxen,[3] three looking toward the north, and three looking toward the west, and three looking toward the south, and three looking toward the east: and the basin was set above upon them, and all their back parts were inward.[4] 26 And it was a handbreath thick, and its brim was made like the brim of a cup, with flowers of lilies: it contained two thousand gallons of mayim.[5] 27 And he made ten stands of brass; four cubits was the length of one base, and four cubits the width, and three cubits the height of it. 28 And the work of the stands was like this: they had side panels, and the side panels were between

---

[1] Two-house reference. Boaz means "fleetness," Yachin means "He will establish," so combined it means "with swiftness He will establish." The two pillars indicate just what He will establish. Unity between the two houses of Yisrael to become His renewed Temple, for all those who seek Him.
[2] The ceremonial washing of both houses of Yisrael symbolized by the two rows on the basin of ceremonial mayim cleansing.
[3] Symbolizing the cleansing for all 12 tribes of Yisrael.
[4] Symbolizing the future exile of all 12 tribes of Yisrael
[5] One thousand gallons of mayim, for the cleansing of each house of Yisrael.

the frames: 29 And on the side panels that were between the frames were lions, oxen, and cheruvim: and upon the frames there was a pedestal above: and beneath the lions and oxen were certain additions made of thin work. 30 And every base had four bronze wheels, and plates of brass: and the four feet had support; under the laver were cast supports, at the side of every addition. 31 And the opening of it within the capital above was a cubit: but the opening was round after the work of the base, a cubit and a half: and also on the opening of it were engravings with their panels, foursquare, not round. 32 And under the side panels were four wheels; and the axle pins of the wheels were joined to the base: and the height of a wheel was a cubit and a half a cubit. 33 And the work of the wheels was like the work of a mirkavah wheel: their axle pins, and their rims, and their hubs, and their spokes, were all cast. 34 And there were four supports to the four corners of one base: and the supports were of the very base itself. 35 And at the top of the base was there a round compass of half a cubit high: and on the top of the base the ledges and the side panels were the same. 36 For on the plates of the ledges, and on the side panels, he engraved cheruvim, lions, and palm eytzim, according to the proportion of every one, and additions all around. 37 After this manner he made the ten stands: all of them had one casting, one measure, and one size. 38 Then he made ten basins of brass: one laver contained forty gallons: and every laver was four cubits: and upon every one of the ten stands one laver. 39 And he put five stands on the right side of the bayit, and five on the left side of the bayit: and he set the basin on the right side of the bayit eastward facing south. 40 And Hiram made the basins, and the shovels, and the bowls. So Hiram made an end of doing all the work that he made for melech Shlomo for the Bayit of יהוה : 41 The two pillars, and the two bowls of the capitals that were on the top of the two

pillars; and the two networks, to cover the two bowls of the capitals which were upon the top of the pillars; 42 And four hundred pomegranates for the two networks, two rows of pomegranates for each network, to cover the two bowls of the capitals that were on top of the pillars; 43 And the ten stands, and ten basins on the stands; 44 And one basin, and twelve oxen under the basin; 45 And the pots, and the shovels, and the bowels: and all these vessels, which Hiram made for melech Shlomo for the Bayit of יהוה, were of polished brass. 46 In the plain of the Yarden did the melech cast them, in the clay ground between Succoth and Tzarthan. 47 And Shlomo left all the vessels unweighed, because they were too many: neither was the weight of the brass sought for. 48 And Shlomo made all the vessels that pertained to the Bayit of יהי: the altar of gold, and the table of gold, on which the Bread of the Faces was, 49 And the menorot of pure gold, five on the right side, and five on the left, before the Speaking Place,[1] with the flowers, and the lamps, and the tongs of gold, 50 And the bowls, and the saucers, and the basons, and the spoons, and the censers of pure gold; and the hinges of gold, both for the doors of the inner Bayit, the Most Set-Apart Place, and for the doors of the Bayit of the Hekel. 51 So was finished all the work that melech Shlomo made for the Bayit of יהוה. And Shlomo brought in the things which David his abba had dedicated; even the silver, and the gold, and the vessels, did he put in the treasury of the Bayit of יהי.

8 Then Shlomo assembled the zachanim of Yisrael, and all the heads of the tribes, the chief of the ahvot of the children of Yisrael, to melech Shlomo in Yahrushalayim, that they might bring up the Ark of the Covenant of יהוה out of the city of David, which is Tzion. 2 And all the men of Yisrael assembled themselves to melech

---

[1] The ten tribes of Yisrael, proclaiming the Light of Moshiach after His first coming.

Shlomo at the feast in the month Eythanim, which is the seventh month. 3 And all the zachanim of Yisrael came, and the kohanim took up the Ark. 4 And they brought up the Ark of יהוה, and the tent of meeting, and all the set-apart vessels that were in the tent, even those did the kohanim and the Leviim bring up. 5 And melech Shlomo, and all the congregation of Yisrael, that were assembled to him, who were with him before the Ark, sacrificed sheep and oxen, that could not be counted or numbered for multitude. 6 And the kohanim brought in the Ark of the Covenant of יהוה to its place, into the Speaking Place of the Bayit, to the Most Set-Apart Place, even under the wings of the cheruvim. 7 For the cheruvim spread out their two wings over the place of the Ark, and the cheruvim covered the Ark and the poles of it above.[1] 8 And the poles extended so that the ends of the poles were seen sticking out into the Set-Apart Place in front of the Speaking Place, but they were not seen from outside: and they are there to this day. 9 There was nothing in the Ark except the two tables of stone, which Moshe put there at Horev, when יהוה made a covenant with the children of Yisrael, when they came out of the land of Mitzrayim. 10 And it came to pass, when the kohanim were come out of the Set-Apart Place, that the shechinah filled the Bayit of יהוה, 11 So that the kohanim could not stand to serve because of the shechinah: for the tifereth of יהוה had filled the Bayit of יהוה. 12 Then spoke Shlomo, יהוה said that He would dwell in the thick dark shechinah. 13 I have surely built You a Bayit to dwell in, a settled place for You to stay in le-olam-va-ed. 14 And the melech turned his face around, and blessed all the congregation of Yisrael: while all the congregation of Yisrael stood; 15 And he said, Blessed be יהוה Elohim of Yisrael, who spoke with His mouth to David my abba, and has with His hand fulfilled it,

saying, 16 *Since the day that I brought out My people Yisrael out of Mitzrayim, I chose no city out of all the tribes of Yisrael to build a Bayit, that My Name might be there; but I chose David to be over My people Yisrael.* 17 And it was in the lev of David my abba to build a Bayit for the Name of יהוה Elohim of Yisrael. 18 And יהוה said to David my abba, *Because it was in your lev to build a Bayit to My Name, you did do well that it was in your lev.* 19 *Nevertheless you shall not build the Bayit; but your son that shall come out of your waist, he shall build the Bayit to My Name.* 20 And יהוה has performed His word that He spoke, and I am risen up in the place of David my abba, and sit on the throne of Yisrael, as יהוה promised, and have built a Bayit for the Name of יהוה Elohim of Yisrael. 21 And I have set there a place for the Ark, in which is the covenant of יהוה, that He made with our ahvot, when He brought them out of the land of Mitzrayim. 22 And Shlomo stood before the altar of יהוה in the presence of all the congregation of Yisrael, and spread out his hands toward the shamayim: 23 And he said, יהוה Elohim of Yisrael, there is no Elohim like You, in the shamayim above, or on earth beneath, who keeps covenant and chesed with Your avadim that have their halacha before You with all their lev: 24 Who has kept with your eved David my abba what You promised him: You spoke also with Your mouth, and have fulfilled it with Your hand, as it is this day. 25 Therefore now, יהוה Elohim of Yisrael, keep with Your eved David my abba what You promised him, saying, *There shall not fail for you to have a man in My sight to sit on the throne of Yisrael; so that your children take heed to their halachot, that they have their halacha before Me as you have had your halacha before Me.* 26 And now, O Elohim of Yisrael let Your word, I ask You, be verified, which You spoke to Your eved David my abba. 27 But will Elohim indeed dwell on the earth? See, the shamayim and

---

[1] The four cherubim all symbolized Yisreal being scattered and dwelling in the four corners of the earth.

the shamayim of shamayim cannot contain You; how much less this Bayit that I have built? 28 Yet have respect to the tefillah of Your eved, and to his supplication, O יהוה My Elohim, to shema to the cry and to the tefillah, which Your eved prays before You today: 29 That Your eyes may be open toward this Bayit night and day, even toward the place of which You have said, My Name shall be there: that You may shema to the tefillah which Your eved shall make toward this place. 30 And shema to the supplication of Your eved, and of Your people Yisrael, when they shall make tefillah toward this place: and shema in the shamayim Your dwelling place: and when You shema, forgive. 31 If any man trespass against his neighbor, and an oath be laid upon him to cause him to swear, and the oath come before Your altar in this Bayit: 32 Then shema in the shamayim, and act, and shophet Your avadim, condemning the wicked, to bring his way upon his head; and justifying the tzadik, to give him according to his tzedakah. 33 When Your people Yisrael be smitten down before an enemy, because they have sinned against You, and shall turn again to You, and confess Your Name, and make tefillah, and make supplication to You in this Bayit:[1] 34 Then shema in the shamayim, and forgive the sin of Your people Yisrael, and bring them again to the land which You gave to their ahvot. 35 When the shamayim are shut up, and there is no rain, because they have sinned against You; if they make tefillah toward this place, and confess Your Name,[2] and turn from their sin, when You afflict them: 36 Then shema in the shamayim, and forgive the sin of Your avadim, and of Your people Yisrael, so that You teach them the tov halacha in which they should have their halacha, and give rain upon Your land, which You have given to Your people for

an inheritance. 37 If there be famine in the land, if there be pestilence, mildew, blight, locust, or if there be grasshoppers; when their enemy besieges them in the land of their cities; with any plague, or any sickness; 38 If any tefillah or supplication be made by any man, or by all Your people Yisrael, with every man knowing the plague of his own lev, and shall spread out his hands toward this Bayit:[3] 39 Then shema in the shamayim Your dwelling place, and forgive, and act, and give to every man according to his ways, whose lev You know; for You, even You alone, know the levim of all the children of men; 40 That they may fear You all the days that they live in the land that You gave to our ahvot. 41 Moreover concerning a Ger, that is not of Your people Yisrael, but comes out of a far country for Your Name's sake;[4] 42 For they shall shema of Your great Name,[5] and of Your strong hand, and of Your stretched out Arm; when he shall come and make tefillah toward this Bayit; 43 Shema in the shamayim Your dwelling place, and do according to all that the Ger calls to You for: so all people of the earth may know Your Name, to fear You, as do Your people Yisrael; and that they may know that this Bayit, which I have built, is called by Your Name. 44 If Your people go out to battle against their enemy, wherever You shall send them, and shall make tefillah to יהוה towards the city which You have chosen, and toward the Bayit that I have built for Your Name: 45 Then shema in the shamayim their tefillah and their supplication, and maintain their cause. 46 If they sin against You - for there is no man that sins not - and You are angry with them, and deliver them to the enemy, so that they carry them away captive to the land of the enemy, far and near; 47 Yet if they shall turn back in their lev in the land where they were carried captives, and repent, and make

---

[1] Not merely making teshuvah but confessing the name of YHWH (not "hashem"). The Diaspora will not come to a complete end, until both houses learn and walk in his true name.
[2] Confess his true Name.

[3] Praying and worshipping with lifted hands is a Yisraelite custom, not one started by Ch- - -tians.
[4] Non-Yisraelites or else the latter-day returning Ephraimites.
[5] YHWH's name draws men into becoming Yisrael.

supplication to You in the land of those that carried them captives, saying, We have sinned, and have done perversely, we have committed wickedness, 48 And so return to You with all their lev, and with all their being, in the land of their enemies, that led them away captive, and make tefillah to You toward their land, which You gave to their ahvot, the city which You have chosen, and the Bayit which I have built for Your Name; 49 Then shema their tefillah and their supplication in the shamayim Your dwelling place, and maintain their cause, 50 And forgive Your people that have sinned against You and all their transgressions in which they have transgressed against You, and give them rachamim before those who carried them captive, that they may have rachamim on them: 51 For they are Your people, and Your inheritance, which You brought out of Mitzrayim, from the midst of the furnace of iron: 52 That Your eyes may be open to the supplication of Your eved, and to the supplication of Your people Yisrael, to shema to them in all that they call for to You. 53 For You did separate them from among all the peoples of the earth, to be Your inheritance, as You spoke by the hand of Moshe Your eved, when You brought our ahvot out of Mitzrayim, O Melech יהוה. 54 And it was so, that when Shlomo had made an end of praying all of this tefillah and supplication to יהוה, he arose from before the altar of יהוה, from kneeling on his knees with his hands spread up to the shamayim. 55 And he stood, and blessed all the congregation of Yisrael with a loud voice, saying, 56 Barchu-et יהוה, that has given rest to His people Yisrael, according to all that He promised: there has not failed one word of all His tov promise, which He promised by the hand of Moshe His eved. 57 יהוה Our Elohim be with us, as He was with our ahvot: let Him not leave us, nor forsake us: 58 That He may incline our levim to Him, to have our halacha in all His halachot, and to keep His mitzvoth, and His

chukim, and His mishpatim, which He commanded our ahvot. 59 And let these my words, with which I have made supplication before יהוה, be near to יהוה Our Elohim day and night, that He maintain the cause of His eved, and the cause of His people Yisrael at all times, as the matters of the future shall require: 60 That all the people of the earth may know that יהוה is Elohim, and that there is none else. 61 Let your lev therefore be perfect with יהוה our Elohim, to have your halacha in His chukim, and to keep His mitzvoth, as at this day. 62 And the melech, and all Yisrael with him, offered sacrifices before יהוה. 63 And Shlomo offered a sacrifice of shalom offerings, which he offered to יהוה, twenty-two thousand oxen, and a hundred twenty thousand sheep. So the melech and all the children of Yisrael dedicated the Bayit of יהוה. 64 The same day did the melech hallow the middle of the court that was in front of the Bayit of יהוה: for there he offered burnt offerings, and meat offerings, and the fat of the shalom offerings: because the bronze altar that was before יהוה was too little to receive the burnt offerings, and meat offerings, and the fat of the shalom offerings. 65 And at that time Shlomo held a feast, and all Yisrael with him, a great congregation, from the entrance of Hamath to the River of Mitzrayim, before יהוה our Elohim, for fourteen days. 66 On the eighth day he sent the people away: and they blessed the melech, and went to their tents with simcha and gilah of lev for all the tov that יהוה had done for David His eved, and for Yisrael His people.

9 And it came to pass, when Shlomo had finished the building of the Bayit of יהוה, and the melech's bayit, and all Shlomo's desire which he was pleased to do, 2 That יהוה appeared to Shlomo the second time, as He had appeared to him at Giveon. 3 And יהוה said to him, *I have heard your tefillah and your supplication,*

that you have made before Me: I have set-apart this Bayit, which you have built, to put My Name there le-olam-va-ed; and My eyes and My lev shall be there perpetually. 4 And if you will have your halacha before Me, as David your abba had his halacha, in integrity of lev, and in uprightness, to do according to all that I have commanded you, and will keep My chukim and My mishpatim: 5 Then I will establish the throne of your malchut over Yisrael le-olam-va-ed, as I promised to David your abba, saying, There shall not cease for you a man to sit upon the throne of Yisrael. 6 But if you shall turn away from following Me, you or your children, and will not keep My mitzvoth and My chukim which I have set before you, but go and serve other elohim, and worship them: 7 Then will I cut off Yisrael out of the land which I have given them; and this Bayit, which I have set-apart for My Name, will I cast out of My sight; and Yisrael shall be a mishle and a mockery among all peoples:[1] 8 And at this Bayit, which is exalted, every one that passes by it shall be astonished, and shall hiss; and they shall say, Why has יהוה done this to this land, and to this Bayit? 9 And they shall answer, Because they forsook יהוה their Elohim, who brought out their ahvot out of the land of Mitzrayim, and have taken hold of other elohim, and have worshipped them, and served them: therefore has יהוה brought upon them all this evil. 10 And it came to pass at the end of twenty years, when Shlomo had built the two houses,[2] the Bayit of יהוה, and the melech's bayit, 11 Hiram the melech of Tzor had furnished Shlomo with cedar eytzim and cypress eytzim, and with gold, according to all his desire, that melech Shlomo gave Hiram twenty cities in the land of Galilee. 12 And Hiram came out from Tzor to see the cities that Shlomo had given him; and they pleased him not. 13 And he said, What cities are these that

you have given me, my brother? And he called them the land of Cavul to this day. 14 And Hiram sent to the melech one hundred twenty talents of gold. 15 And this is the reason of the compulsory labor which melech Shlomo raised; to build the Bayit of יהוה, and his own bayit, and Millo, and the wall of Yahrushalayim, and Hazor, and Megiddo, and Gezer. 16 For Pharaoh melech of Mitzrayim had gone up, and taken Gezer, and burnt it with fire, and slain the Kanaanites that dwelt in the city, and given it for a present to his daughter, Shlomo's wife. 17 And Shlomo built Gezer, and lower Beth-Horon. 18 And Baalath, and Tadmor in the wilderness, in the land, 19 And all the cities of storage that Shlomo had, and cities for his mirkavot, and cities for his horsemen, and that which Shlomo desired to build in Yahrushalayim, and in Levanon, and in all the land of his dominion. 20 And all the people that were left of the Amorites, Hittites, Perizzites, Hivites, and Yevusites, which were not of the children of Yisrael, 21 Their children that were left after them in the land, whom the children of Yisrael were not able utterly to destroy; upon those did Shlomo place in compulsory labor until this day. 22 But of the children of Yisrael did Shlomo make no avadim: but they were men of war, and his avadim, and his rulers, and his captains, and rulers of his mirkavot, and his horsemen. 23 These were the chief of the officers that were over Shlomo's work, five hundred fifty, who had rule over the people that labored in the work. 24 But Pharaoh's daughter came up out of the city of David to her bayit which Shlomo had built for her: then did he build Millo. 25 And three times in a year did Shlomo offer burnt offerings and shalom offerings upon the altar which he built to יהוה, and he burnt incense upon the altar that was before יהוה. So he finished the Bayit. 26 And melech Shlomo made a navy of ships in Ezion-Gever, which is beside Elath, on the shore of the Sea of Reeds, in the land of Edom. 27 And Hiram

---

[1] Exile foretold.
[2] A **remez** or hint at both houses built strong under Solomon.

sent in the navy his avadim, shipmen that had da'at of the sea, with the avadim of Shlomo.[1] 28 And they came to Ophir, and fetched from there gold, four hundred twenty talents, and brought it to melech Shlomo.

10 And when the malqa of Sheba heard of the fame of Shlomo concerning the Name of יהוה,[2] she came to test him with hard questions. 2 And she came to Yahrushalayim with a very great company, with camels that bare spices, and very much gold, and precious stones: and when she had come to Shlomo, she communed with him of all that was in her lev. 3 And Shlomo answered all her questions: there was not anything hidden from the melech, which he told her not. 4 And when the malqa of Sheba had seen all Shlomo's chochma, and the Bayit that he had built, 5 And the meat at his table, and the sitting of his avadim, and the service of his waiters, and their attire, and his cupbearers, and his burnt offerings which he offered in the Bayit of יהוה; there was no more ruach in her. 6 And she said to the melech, It was an emet report that I heard in my own land of your acts and of your chochma. 7 But I believed not the words, until I came, and my eyes have seen it: and, see, not even the half of your greatness was told to me: your chochma and prosperity exceeds the fame which I heard. 8 Favored are your men, favored are these, your avadim, who stand continually before you, and that shema your chochma. 9 Barchu-et יהוה Your Elohim, who delighted in you, to set you on the throne of Yisrael: because יהוה loved Yisrael le-olam-va-ed, therefore He made you melech, to do mishpat and justice. 10 And she gave the melech one hundred twenty talents of gold, and of spices very many, and precious stones: there came no more such an abundance of

spices as those which the malqa of Sheba gave to melech Shlomo. 11 And the navy also of Hiram, that brought gold from Ophir, brought in from Ophir a great amount of sandalwood, and precious stones. 12 And the melech made of the sandalwood pillars for the Bayit of יהוה, and for the melech's bayit, harps also and lyres for singers: there came no such sandalwood before, nor were any seen to this day. 13 And melech Shlomo gave to the malqa of Sheba all her desire, whatever she asked, besides that which Shlomo gave her of his royal bounty. So she turned and went to her own country, she and her avadim.[3] 14 Now the weight of gold that came to Shlomo in one year was six hundred sixty six talents of gold. 15 Beside that he had much from the merchantmen, and from the profit from traders, and from all the melechim of Arabia, and of the governors of the country. 16 And melech Shlomo made two hundred large shields of beaten gold: six hundred shekels of gold went into one shield. 17 And he made three hundred shields of beaten gold; three pounds of gold went into one shield: and the melech put them in the bayit of the forest of Levanon. 18 Moreover the melech made a great throne of ivory, and overlaid it with the best gold. 19 The throne had six steps, and the top of the throne was round in the back: and there were armrests on either side on the place of the seat, and two lions stood beside the

---

[1] A three-part alliance, between Hiram of Tyre or later Phoenicia, Egypt and Yisrael. A real commonwealth.
[2] YHWH's Name draws people to truth. Withholding it keeps them in error and religion.

[3] "To illustrate a point about Yisraelite ethnicity (or the lack thereof), we look here at 1 Kings 10:1-13. Here, we are told the queen of Sheba, having heard about the fame of Solomon, came to Jerusalem to visit him. And; according to Ethiopian tradition, Sheba (called Makeda) married Solomon, and their son, Menelik I, founded the royal dynasty of Ethiopia. Let us for a moment assume that Sheba did number among the 'hundreds' who were Solomon's 'wives' (1 Kings 11:3), and that a son was born of their union, and that when he was born, he looked just like his dark-skinned Ethiopian mother. "Now let us realize that this son, regardless of looks, was, like his abba, of the tribe of Judah. Taking this concept a step further, let us assume this son grew up and married an Ethiopian lady and that they had sons, all of whom grew up to marry Ethiopian ladies and to have sons. On and on the process goes. And while we are asleep at night, He who has in the past both "opened" and "closed" wombs (Gen 20:18; 30:22), could have been turning all of Ethiopia into the tribe of Judah. Descendants of the twelve tribes could be anywhere, everywhere. And we would never know." *Wootten, Who Is Israel? pp. 73-74.*

armrests. 20 And twelve lions stood one on each side of the six steps: there was not any like it made in any malchut.[1] 21 And all melech Shlomo's drinking vessels were of gold, and all the vessels of the Bayit of the forest of Levanon were of pure gold; none were of silver: for silver was counted as nothing in the days of Shlomo. 22 For the melech had at sea a navy of Tharshish with the navy of Hiram: once every three years came the navy of Tharshish,[2] bringing gold, and silver, ivory, and apes, and peacocks. 23 So melech Shlomo exceeded all the melechim of the earth for riches and for chochma.[3] 24 And all the earth came to Shlomo, to shema his chochma, which Elohim had put in his lev.[4] 25 And they brought every man his present, vessels of silver, and vessels of gold, and garments, and armor, and spices, horses, and mules year by year. 26 And Shlomo gathered together mirkavot and horsemen: and he had a thousand four hundred mirkavot, and twelve thousand horsemen, whom he stationed in the cities for mirkavot, and with the melech at Yahrushalayim. 27 And the melech made silver as common in Yahrushalayim as stones, and cedars to be as plenty as the sycamore eytzim that are on the plain. 28 And Shlomo had horses brought out of Mitzrayim, and the melech's merchants received a commission on the items they bought. 29 And a mirkavah came up and went out of Mitzrayim for six hundred shekels of silver, and an horse for a hundred fifty: and so for all the melechim of the Hittites, and for the melechim of Aram, did they bring them out by their own trading.

11 But melech Shlomo loved many strange[5] women, together with the daughter of Pharaoh, women of the Moavites, Ammonites, Edomites,

Tzidonians, and Hittites; 2 Of the nations concerning which יהוה said to the children of Yisrael, You shall not go in to them, neither shall they come in to you: for surely they will turn away your lev after their elohim: Shlomo clung to these in ahava. 3 And he had seven hundred wives, princesses, and three hundred concubines: and his wives turned away his lev. 4 For it came to pass, when Shlomo was old, that his wives turned away his lev after other elohim: and his lev was not perfect with יהוה His Elohim, as was the lev of David his abba. 5 For Shlomo went after Ashtoreth the mighty one of the Tzidonians, and after Milcom the abomination of the Ammonites. 6 And Shlomo did evil in the sight of יהוה, and did not follow after יהוה fully, as did David his abba. 7 Then Shlomo built a high place for Chemosh, the abomination of Moav, in the hill that is before Yahrushalayim, and for Molech, the abomination of the children of Ammon. 8 And likewise he did for all his strange wives, who burnt incense and sacrificed to their elohim. 9 And יהוה was angry with Shlomo, because his lev was turned from יהוה Elohim of Yisrael, who had appeared to him twice, 10 And had commanded him concerning this thing; that he should not go after other elohim: but he kept not that which יהוה commanded. 11 And יהוה said to Shlomo, *Seeing that this is done by you, and you have not kept My covenant and My chukim, which I have commanded you, I will surely tear the malchut from you, and will give it to your eved.[6] 12 Nevertheless, in your days I will not do it for David your abba's sake: but I will tear it out of the hand of your son.[7] 13 However I will not tear away all the malchut; but will give one tribe to your son for David My eved's sake, and for Yahrushalayim's sake which I have chosen.[8]* 14 And יהוה stirred up an

---

[1] Twelve lions; for the twelve tribes, on two sides of the steps symbolizing the future division of the House of David.
[2] Spain; Europe.
[3] Global empire.
[4] Global empire.
[5] Strangers to Torah.

[6] As punishment for Solomon's mixed worship the House of David or the 12 tribes, would be divided into two houses with ten tribes going to his servant.
[7] The kingdom will be divided after Solomon's death.
[8] Tribe of Yahudah, including Benjamin and Levi incorporated within Yahudah.

adversary to Shlomo, Hadad the Edomite: he was of the melech's zera in Edom. [1] 15 For it came to pass, when David was in Edom, and Yoav the captain of the army had gone up to bury the dead, after he had smitten every male in Edom that, 16 For six months Yoav remained there with all Yisrael, until he had cut off every male in Edom: 17 That Hadad fled, he and certain Edomites of his abba's avadim with him, to go into Mitzrayim; Hadad being yet a little child. 18 And they arose out of Midyan, and came to Paran: and they took men with them out of Paran, and they came to Mitzrayim, to Pharaoh melech of Mitzrayim; who gave him a bayit, and appointed him food, and gave him land. 19 And Hadad found great favor in the sight of Pharaoh, so that he gave him as a wife the sister of his own wife, the sister of Tahpenes the malqa. 20 And the sister of Tahpenes bore him Genuvath his son, whom Tahpenes nursed in Pharaoh's bayit: and Genuvath was in Pharaoh's household among the sons of Pharaoh. 21 And when Hadad heard in Mitzrayim that David slept with his ahvot, and that Yoav the captain of the army was dead, Hadad said to Pharaoh, Let me depart, that I may go to my own country. 22 Then Pharaoh said to him, But what have you lacked with me, that, see, you seek to go to your own country? And he answered, Nothing: but let me go anyway. 23 And Elohim stirred up another adversary, Rezon the son of El-Yadah, who fled from his master Hadadezer melech of Zovah: 24 And he gathered men to him, and became captain over a band, when David killed them of Zovah: and they went to Dameshek, and dwelt there, and reigned in Dameshek. 25 And he was an adversary to Yisrael all the days of Shlomo, beside the mischief that Hadad did: and he abhorred Yisrael, and reigned over Aram. 26 And

Yehravoam[2] the son of Nevat, an Ephrathite from Ephraim of Tzereda, Shlomo's eved, whose ima's name was Tzeruah, a widow woman, even he lifted up his hand against the melech. 27 And this was the reason that he lifted up his hand against the melech: Shlomo built Millo, and repaired the breaches of the city of David his abba. 28 And the man Yehravoam was a mighty man of valor: and Shlomo seeing the young man that he was industrious, made him ruler over all the compulsory labor of Beit Yoseph.[3] 29 And it came to pass at that time when Yehravoam went out of Yahrushalayim, that the navi Ahiyah the Shilonite met him on the way; and he had prepared himself with a new garment; and the two were alone in the field: 30 And Ahiyah grabbed the new garment that was on him, and tore it into twelve pieces:[4] 31 And he said to Yehravoam, Take for yourself ten pieces: for this says יהוה, the Elohim of Yisrael, *See, I will tear the malchut out of the hand of Shlomo, and will give ten tribes to you:*[5] 32 *But he shall have one tribe for My eved David's sake, and for Yahrushalayim's sake, the city which I have chosen out of all the tribes of Yisrael:*[6] 33 *Because they have forsaken Me, and have worshipped Ashtoreth the false elohim of the Tzidonians, Chemosh the elohim of the Moavites, and Milcom the elohim of the children of Ammon, and have not kept their halacha in My halachot, to do that which is right in My eyes, and to keep My chukim and My mishpatim, as did David his abba.* 34 *But I will not take the whole malchut out of his hand: but I will make him prince all the days of his chayim for David My eved's*

[2] Yehravoam, Means "Yah increases the nation." How true that through the ten tribes to be placed under Yehravoam, all nations would become full of Yisraelite seed.
[3] Solomon in error divided the Ephraimites from the rest of Yisrael and made them servants in violation of Torah, which forbids Yisraelites from being enslaved to other Yisraelites. This was the seed of discord.
[4] Symbolizing all 12 tribes.
[5] YHWH created the impenetrable boundaries between both houses according to His will. As YHWH, He also chose not to fully heal that animosity and division, until after the coming of His beloved Son Yahshua, the Greater and latter-day David.
[6] Tribe of Yahudah, including Benjamin and Levi incorporated within Yahudah.

[1] A clear reference proving that Yisrael's seed is even well mixed in with Edom, along with all the world's nations.

sake, whom I chose, because he kept My mitzvoth and My chukim: 35 But I will take the malchut out of his son's hand, and will give it to you, even ten tribes.[1] 36 And to his son[2] will I give one tribe, that David My eved may have a light always before Me in Yahrushalayim, the city which I have chosen for Me to put My Name there. 37 And I will take you, and you shall reign according to all that your being desires, and you shall be melech over Yisrael. 38 And it shall be, if you will shema to all that I command you, and will have your halacha in My halachot, and do what is right in My sight, to keep My chukim and My mitzvoth, as David My eved did; that I will be with you, and build you a sure bayit, as I built for David, and will give Yisrael to you.[3] 39 And I will for this afflict the zera of David, but not le-olam-va-ed.[4] 40 Shlomo sought therefore to kill Yehravoam. And Yehravoam arose, and fled into Mitzrayim, to Shishak melech of Mitzrayim, and was in Mitzrayim until the death of Shlomo. 41 And the rest of the acts of Shlomo, and all that he did, and his chochma, are they not written in the Scroll of the Acts of Shlomo?[5] 42 And the time that Shlomo reigned in Yahrushalayim over all Yisrael[6] was forty years[7]. 43 And Shlomo slept with his ahvot, and was buried in the city of David his abba: and Rehavoam his son reigned in his place.

---

[1] The ten tribes would now officially become the House of Yisrael/Ephraim/Joseph, also known in times past even under the monarchy of David as the former House of Saul or sometimes even as the former House of Benjamin, since Saul son of Kish was a Benjamite who in those days affiliated with the embryonic House of Yisrael. In this verse the split becomes officially pronounced and ordained by YHWH, although it seethed below the surface in earlier times.
[2] Rehoboam.
[3] If he would prove faithful, YHWH would reconstitute all Yisrael under him. But of course this was not to be, neither was it His will.
[4] Even though He will split Yisrael into two houses it will not be forever, as they will reunite in the days of the King Moshiach Yahshua.
[5] Missing Scroll.
[6] Both houses.
[7] Forty signifying the doomed House of David, as 40 is the symbolic number of divine judgment.

12 And Rehavoam went to Shechem: for all Yisrael had come to Shechem to make him melech. 2 And it came to pass, when Yehravoam the son of Nevat, who was yet in Mitzrayim, heard of it, because he had fled from the presence of melech Shlomo, and Yehravoam dwelt in Mitzrayim, 3 That they sent and called him. And Yehravoam and all the congregation of Yisrael came, and spoke to Rehavoam, saying, 4 Your abba made our yoke hard: now therefore make the compulsory labor of your abba, and his heavy yoke that he put upon us, lighter, and we will serve you. 5 And he said to them, Depart for three days, then come back to me. And the people departed. 6 And melech Rehavoam consulted with the zachanim that stood before Shlomo his abba while he still lived, and said, How do you advise that I may answer this people? 7 And they spoke to him, saying, If you will be an eved to this people this day, and will serve them, and answer them, and speak tov words to them, then they will be your avadim le-olam-va-ed. 8 But he forsook the counsel of the zachanim, which they had given him, and consulted with the young men with whom he had grown up with, and who stood before him: 9 And he said to them, What counsel do you give that we may answer this people, who have spoken to me, saying, Make the yoke which your abba did put upon us lighter? 10 And the young men that were grown up with him spoke to him, saying, This shall you say to this people that spoke to you, saying, Your abba made our yoke heavy, but you make it lighter on us; this shall you say to them, My little finger shall be thicker than my abba's waist. 11 And now my abba did lay on you a heavy yoke, yet I will add to your yoke: my abba has chastised you with whips, but I will chastise you with scorpions.[8] 12 So Yehravoam and all the people came to Rehavoam the third day, as the melech had

---

[8] A promise to continue their compulsory labor, in even worse conditions.

appointed, saying, Come back to me again on the third day, 13 And the melech answered the people roughly, and forsook the zachanim's counsel that they gave him; 14 And spoke to them after the counsel of the young men, saying, My abba made your yoke heavy, and I will add to your yoke: my abba also chastised you with whips, but I will chastise you with scorpions. 15 So the melech did not shema to the people, for the cause was from יהוה , that He might perform His saying, which יהוה spoke by Ahiyah the Shilonite to Yehravoam the son of Nevat.[1] 16 So when all Yisrael saw that the melech listened not to them, the people answered the melech, saying, What portion have we in Beit David? Neither have we an inheritance in the son of Yishai: to your tents, O Yisrael: now see to your own bayit, David. So Yisrael departed to their tents.[2] 17 But as for the children of Yisrael who dwelt in the cities of Yahudah, Rehavoam reigned over them.[3] 18 Then melech Rehavoam sent Adoram, who was over the compulsory labor; and all Yisrael stoned him with stones, that he died.[4] Therefore melech Rehavoam huried to get into his mirkavah, to flee to Yahrushalayim. 19 So Yisrael rebelled against Beit David to this day.[5] 20 And it came to pass, when all Yisrael heard that Yehravoam had returned, that they sent and called him to the congregation, and made him melech over all Yisrael: there was none that followed Beit David, except the tribe of Yahudah only. 21 And when Rehavoam was come to Yahrushalayim, he assembled all of Beit Yahudah, with the tribe of Benyamin, one hundred eighty thousand chosen men, who were warriors, to fight against Beit Yisrael, to return the malchut again to Rehavoam the son of Shlomo.[6] 22 But the word of Elohim came to Shemayah the man of Elohim, saying, 23 *Speak to Rehavoam, the son of Shlomo, melech of Yahudah, and to all of Beit Yahudah and Benyamin, and to the rest of the people, saying, 24 This says* יהוה, *You shall not go up, nor fight against your brothers the children of Yisrael: return every man to his bayit; for this thing[7] is from Me.[8]* They heard and obeyed the word of יהוה, and returned, according to the word of יהוה. 25 Then Yehravoam rebuilt Shechem in Mount Ephraim, and dwelt there; and went out from there, and rebuilt Penu-El. 26 And Yehravoam said in his lev, Now shall the malchut return to Beit David: 27 If this people goes up to do sacrifice in the Bayit of יהוה at Yahrushalayim, then shall the lev of this people return again to their master, even to Rehavoam melech of Yahudah, and they shall kill me, and go again to Rehavoam melech of Yahudah. 28 So the melech took counsel, and made two calves of gold, and said to them, It is too hard for you to go up to Yahrushalayim: see your elohim, O Yisrael, that brought you up out of the land of Mitzrayim. 29 And he set one in Beth-El, and the other

---

[1] This was one reason for YHWH allowing the split, but there was a far greater divine purpose as seen in the footnote on verse 24 later in this key chapter.
[2] The official split. They saw no future of being part of the House of David, and saw rather a people that were committed to withholding their freedom, and their rights as free citizens of Yisrael. They left the House of David and the breech has been with us to this day. For more insight and understanding see: http://yourarmstoisrael.org/Articles_new/restoration/?page=home&type=2.
[3] As seen here there was some crossover between the two houses and both houses literally have the dom of all 12 tribes, though Judah has more Jewish dom and Ephraim has more non-Jewish dom, but no one can deny limited crossover periods or patterns.
[4] Anger against injustice.
[5] This sad commentary by YHWH still holds true. Ephraim often knowing the errors of Christianity refuses to forsake the comfortable and familiar ways of their ahvot, instead clinging to traditions that are abominable in YHWH's sight. Fortunately Yahshua has started to change that.

---

[6] This is the first of many attempts to reunite the two houses in the flesh. This periodically takes place today by many on both sides of the fence. Oftentimes through the centuries, it has resulted in domshed between Ephraimites and Jews in many forms including Jewish and Christian hatred towards each other, such as in the crusades and early first century. All attempts to bring unity are destined to fail without Yahshua opening the hearts of both houses to walk in concern, unity, and forgiveness.
[7] This division.
[8] Prophetically, after becoming the single tribe of Ephraim, ten of the twelve tribes became known collectively as Ephraim, the ten were being removed from the House of David and given over to Jeroboam, son of Nebat. The primary purpose of this removal was to fill the globe with Yisraelites by gradually dispersing them into and among the nations. Scripture is clear that YHWH Himself allowed this division within the people of Israel, to fulfill the covenant promise of global physical multiplicity.

he put in Dan. 30 And this thing became a sin: for the people went to worship before one or the other, even in Dan. 31 And he made a bayit of idols, and made kohanim from the am-ha-aretz, who were not from the sons of Levi. 32 And Yehravoam ordained a feast in the eighth month, on the fifteenth day of the month, like the moed that is in Yahudah,[1] and he offered upon the altar. He did the same in Beth-El, sacrificing to the calves that he had made: and he placed and appointed in Beth-El the kohanim of the idol temples, which he had made. 33 So he offered upon the altar which he had made in Beth-El the fifteenth day of the eighth month, even in the month which he had devised from his own lev; and ordained a feast to the children of Yisrael: and he offered upon the altar, and burnt incense.

13 And, see, there came a man of Elohim out of Yahudah by the word of **יהוה** to Beth-El: and Yehravoam stood by the altar to burn incense. 2 And he cried against the altar by the word of **יהוה**, and said, O altar, altar, this says **יהוה**; *See, a child shall be born to Beit David, Yoshiyahu by name; and upon you O altar shall he offer the kohanim of the high places that burn incense upon you, and men's bones shall be burnt upon you.* 3 And he gave a sign the same day, saying, This is the sign that **יהוה** has spoken; *See, the altar shall be torn, and the ashes that are upon it shall be poured out.* 4 And it came to pass, when melech Yehravoam heard the saying of the man of Elohim, who had cried against the altar in Beth-El, that he put out his hand from the altar, saying, Lay hold on him. And his hand, which he put out against him, dried up, so that he could not pull it in again to him. 5 The altar also was torn, and the

ashes poured out from the altar, according to the sign that the man of Elohim had given by the word of **יהוה**. 6 And the melech answered and said to the man of Elohim, Seek for me before the face of **יהוה** Your Elohim, and make tefillah for me, that my hand may be restored to me again. And the man of Elohim besought **יהוה**, and the melech's hand was restored to him again, and became as it was before. 7 And the melech said to the man of Elohim, Come home with me, and refresh yourself, and I will give you a reward. 8 And the man of Elohim said to the melech, If you will give me half your bayit, I will not go in with you, neither will I eat lechem nor drink mayim in this place: 9 For so was it commanded me by the word of **יהוה**, saying, *Eat no lechem, nor drink mayim nor return by the same way that you came.* 10 So he went another way, and returned not by the way that he came to Beth-El. 11 Now there dwelt an old navi in Beth-El; and his sons came and told him all the works that the man of Elohim had done that day in Beth-El: the words which he had spoken to the melech, which they told also to their abba. 12 And their abba said to them, Which way did he go? For his sons had seen what way the man of Elohim went, who came from Yahudah. 13 And he said to his sons, Saddle me the donkey. So they saddled him the donkey: and he rode on it, 14 And went after the man of Elohim, and found him sitting under an oak: and he said to him, Are you the man of Elohim that came from Yahudah? And he said, I am. 15 Then he said to him, Come home with me, and eat lechem. 16 And he said, I may not return with you, nor go in with you: neither will I eat lechem nor drink mayim with you in this place: 17 For it was said to me by the word of **יהוה**, *You shall eat no lechem nor drink mayim there or turn again to go by the derech that you came.* 18 He said to him, I am a navi also as you are; and a heavenly messenger spoke to me by the word of **יהוה**, saying, Bring him back with

---

[1] A false feast to replace **Sukkoth** (Tabernacles), moving it from the 7th month to the 8th month. A favorite practice of Ephraimites to this day is to change YHWH's calendar to suit their own pagan twisting of set-apart days, such as the celebration of Easter for Passover and Christmas for Sukkoth. Then perhaps the worst of all sins is presenting those days to believers as the true times and seasons of YHWH.

you into your bayit, that he may eat lechem and drink mayim. But he lied to him. 19 So he went back with him, and did eat lechem in his bayit, and drank mayim. 20 And it came to pass, as they sat at the table, that the word of יהוה truly came to the navi that brought him back: 21 And he cried to the man of Elohim that came from Yahudah, saying, This says יהוה, *Forasmuch as you have disobeyed the mouth of יהוה, and have not kept the commandment which יהוה Your Elohim commanded you, 22 But came back, and have eaten lechem and drunk mayim in the place, of which יהוה did say to you, Eat no lechem, and drink no mayim; your body shall not come to the tomb of your ahvot.* 23 And it came to pass, after he had eaten lechem, and after he had drunk, that he saddled the donkey, for the navi whom he had brought back. 24 And when he was gone, a lion met him by the way, and killed him: and his body was cast in the way, and the donkey stood by it, the lion also stood by the body. 25 And, see, men passed by, and saw the body cast in the way, and the lion standing by the body: and they came and told it in the city where the old navi dwelt. 26 And when the navi that brought him back from the way heard about it, he said, It is the man of Elohim, who was disobedient to the word of יהוה. Therefore יהוה has delivered him to the lion, which has torn him, and slain him, according to the word of יהוה, which He spoke to him. 27 And he spoke to his sons saying; Saddle for me the donkey. And they saddled him. 28 And he went and found his body cast in the way, and the donkey and the lion standing by the body: the lion had not eaten the body, nor torn the donkey. 29 And the navi took up the body of the man of Elohim, and laid it upon the donkey, and brought it back: and the old navi came to the city, to mourn and to bury him. 30 And he laid his body in his own grave; and they mourned over him, saying, Oy Oy, my brother! 31 And it came to pass, after he had buried him, that he spoke to his sons, saying,

When I am dead, then bury me in the tomb in which the man of Elohim is buried; lay my bones beside his bones: 32 For the saying that he cried by the word of יהוה against the altar in Beth-El, and against all the houses and the temples of idols which are in the cities of Shomron, shall surely come to pass. 33 After this thing Yehravoam returned not from his evil halacha, but made again from the am-ha-aretz, kohanim for the high places: whoever wished to be one, he ordained him, and they became one of the kohanim of the temple of idols. 34 And this thing became sin to Beit Yehravoam, [1] even to cut it off, and to destroy it from off the face of the earth.

14 At that time Aviyah the son of Yehravoam fell sick. 2 And Yehravoam said to his wife, Arise, I beg you, and disguise yourself, that you be not known to be the wife of Yehravoam; and go to Shiloh: see, there is Ahiyah the navi, who told me that I should be melech over this people. 3 And take with you ten loaves, and cakes, and a jar of honey, and go to him: he shall tell you what shall become of the child. 4 And Yehravoam's wife did so, and arose, and went to Shiloh, and came to the bayit of Ahiyah. But Ahiyah could not see; for his eyes were failing by reason of his age. 5 And יהוה said to Ahiyah, *See, the wife of Yehravoam comes to ask a thing from you for her son; for he is sick: this and this shall you say to her: for it shall be, when she comes in, that she shall pretend to be another woman.* 6 And it was so, when Ahiyah heard the sound of her feet as she came in at the door, that he said, Come in, wife of Yehravoam; why do you pretend to be someone else? For I am sent to you with some heavy news. 7 Go, tell Yehravoam, This says יהוה Elohim of Yisrael, *Since I exalted you from among the people and made you ruler over My people Yisrael, 8 And tore the malchut away from Beit David, and gave it you: and yet you have*

---

[1] House of Yisrael/Ephraim.

not been as My eved David, who kept My mitzvoth, and who followed Me with all his lev, to do that only which was right in My eyes; 9 But have done evil above all that were before you: for you have gone and made other elohim, and molded images, to provoke Me to anger, and have cast Me behind your back: 10 Therefore, see, I will bring evil upon Beit Yehravoam, and will cut off from Yehravoam every male, and him that possesses authority in Yisrael, and will take away the remnant of Beit Yehravoam, as a man takes away dung, until it be all gone. 11 Him that dies of Yehravoam's bayit in the city shall the dogs eat; and him that dies in the field shall the fowls of the air eat: for יהוה has spoken it. 12 Arise therefore, go to your own bayit: and when your feet enter into the city, the child shall die. 13 And all Yisrael shall mourn for him, and bury him: for only him from Yehravoam's bayit shall come to the grave, because in him there is found some tov thing toward יהוה Elohim of Yisrael in the bayit of Yehravoam. 14 Moreover יהוה shall raise up a melech over Yisrael, who shall cut off Beit Yehravoam this day, even now. 15 For יהוה shall smite Yisrael, as a reed is shaken in the mayim, and He shall root up Yisrael out of this tov land, which He gave to their ahvot, and shall scatter them beyond the river,[1] because they have made their groves, provoking יהוה to anger.[2] 16 And he shall give Yisrael up because of the sins of Yehravoam,[3] who did sin, and who made kol Yisrael to sin. 17 And Yehravoam's wife arose, and departed, and came to Tirtzah: and when she came to the threshold of the door, the child died: 18 And they buried him; and all Yisrael mourned for him, according to the word of יהוה, which He spoke by the hand of His eved Ahiyah the navi. 19 And the rest of the acts of Yehravoam, how he warred, and how he reigned, see, they are written in the Scroll of Divre HaYamim

about the melechim of Yisrael. 20 And the days that Yehravoam reigned were twenty-two years: and he slept with this ahvot, and Nadav his son reigned in his place. 21 And Rehavoam the son of Shlomo reigned in Yahudah. Rehavoam was forty-one years old when he began to reign, and he reigned seventeen years in Yahrushalayim, the city that יהוה did choose out of all the tribes of Yisrael, to put His Name there. And his ima's name was Naamah an Ammonitess.[4] 22 And Yahudah did evil in the sight of יהוה, and they provoked Him to jealousy with their sins which they had committed, above all that their ahvot had done.[5] 23 For they also built themselves temples for idols, and pillars, and Asherim, on every high hill, and under every green eytz. 24 And there were also sodomites in the land: and they did according to all the abominations of the nations that יהוה cast out before the children of Yisrael. 25 And it came to pass in the fifth year of melech Rehavoam, that Shishak melech of Mitzrayim came up against Yahrushalayim: 26 And he took away the treasures of the Bayit of יהוה, and the treasures of the melech's bayit; he even took away all: and he took away all the shields of gold which Shlomo had made. 27 And melech Rehavoam made in their place bronze shields, and committed them to the hands of the chief of the guard, who guarded the door of the melech's bayit. 28 And it was so, when the melech went into the Bayit of יהוה, that the guard brought them, and brought them back into the guards' bedroom. 29 Now the rest of the acts of Rehavoam, and all that he did, are they not written in the Scroll of Divre HaYamim about the melechim of Yahudah? 30 And there was war between Rehavoam

---

[1] Euphrates.
[2] Their exile in 721 BCE is prophesied to Jeroboam's wife.
[3] To become **Lo-Ami** and **Lo-Ruchamah**.

[4] Even the first official king of the kingdom of Judah was not really Jewish because his mother was an Ammonite; according to traditional Judaism ancestry is traced from the mother. Of course biblically, if we follow the truth of the Commonwealth of Yisrael, we know that ancestry comes through the father. Anyone becomes Yisrael if they want to be by adopting YHWH's standards, which are trust in Moshiach Yahshua and Torah.
[5] Yahudah also was evil and wicked and often was even worse than Ephraim.

and Yehravoam all their days.[1] 31 And Rehavoam slept with his ahvot, and was buried with his ahvot in the city of David. And his ima's name was Naamah an Ammonitess. And Aviyam his son reigned in his place.

15 Now in the eighteenth year of melech Yehravoam the son of Nevat reigned Aviyam over Yahudah. 2 Three years he reigned in Yahrushalayim. And his ima's name was Maachah, the daughter of Avishalom. 3 And he had his halacha in all the sins of his abba, which he had done before him: and his lev was not perfect with יהוה His Elohim, as the lev of David his abba. 4 Nevertheless for David's sake did יהוה His Elohim give him a lamp in Yahrushalayim, to set up his son after him, and to establish Yahrushalayim: 5 Because David did that which was right in the eyes of יהוה, and turned not aside from anything that He commanded him all the days of his chayim, except only in the matter of Uriyah the Hittite. 6 And there was war between Rehavoam and Yehravoam all the days of his chayim. 7 Now the rest of the acts of Aviyam, and all that he did, are they not written in the Scroll of Divre HaYamim about the melechim of Yahudah? And there was war between Aviyam and Yehravoam.[2] 8 And Aviyam slept with his ahvot; and they buried him in the city of David: and Asa his son reigned in his place. 9 And in the twentieth year of Yehravoam melech of Yisrael Asa reigned over Yahudah. 10 And forty-one years he reigned in Yahrushalayim. And his ima's name was Maachah, the daughter of Avishalom. 11 And Asa did that which was right in the eyes of יהוה , as did David his abba. 12 And he took away the sodomites out of the land, and removed all the idols that his ahvot had made. 13 And also Maachah his ima, even her he removed from being malqa, because she had made an idol in a grove; and Asa destroyed her idol, and burnt it by the brook Kidron. 14 But the high places were not removed: nevertheless Asa's lev was perfect with יהוה all his days. 15 And he brought in the things that his abba had dedicated, and the things which he himself had dedicated, into the Bayit of יהוה, silver, and gold, and vessels. 16 And there was war between Asa and Ba-Asha melech of Yisrael all their days.[3] 17 And Ba-Asha melech of Yisrael went up against Yahudah, and rebuilt Ramah, that he might not allow any to go out or come in to Asa melech of Yahudah. 18 Then Asa took all the silver and the gold that were left in the treasures of the Bayit of יהוה, and the treasures of the melech's bayit, and delivered them into the hand of his avadim: and melech Asa sent them to Ben-Hadad, the son of Tavrimon, the son of Hetzion, melech of Aram, that dwelt at Dameshek, saying, 19 There is a covenant between me and you, and between my abba and your abba: see, I have sent to you a present of silver and gold; come and break your covenant with Ba-Asha melech of Yisrael, that he may depart from me. 20 So Ben-Hadad listened to melech Asa, and sent the captains of the armies which he had against the cities of Yisrael, and smote Iyon, and Dan, and Avel-Beth-Maachah, and all Cinneroth, with all the land of Naphtali. 21 And it came to pass, when Ba-Asha heard of it, that he stopped the rebuilding of Ramah, and dwelt in Tirtzah. 22 Then melech Asa made a proclamation throughout all Yahudah; none was exempted: and they took away the stones of Ramah, and the timber, with which Ba-Asha had build; and melech Asa rebuilt with them Geva of Benyamin, and Mizpah. 23 The rest of all the acts of Asa, and all his might, and all that he did, and the cities which he built, are they not written in the Scroll of Divre HaYamim about the melechim of Yahudah? Nevertheless in the

---

[1] And continues in various political and religious forms until this day.
[2] Another two-house civil war battle.

[3] Another two-house civil war.

time of his old age he was diseased in his feet. 24 And Asa slept with his ahvot, and was buried with his ahvot in the city of David his abba, and Yehoshaphat his son reigned in his place. 25 And Nadav the son of Yehravoam began to reign over Yisrael in the second year of Asa melech of Yahudah, and reigned over Yisrael two years. 26 And he did evil in the sight of יהוה, and had his halacha in the derech of his abba, and in his sin that he made Yisrael to sin. 27 And Ba-Asha the son of Ahiyah, of the bayit of Yissachar, conspired against him; and Ba-Asha smote him at Givethon, which belonged to the Philistines; for Nadav and all Yisrael laid siege to Givethon. 28 Even in the third year of Asa melech of Yahudah did Ba-Asha kill him, and reigned in his place. 29 And it came to pass, when he reigned, that he smote all of Beit Yehravoam; he left not to Yehravoam any offspring that breathed, until he had destroyed him, according to the saying of יהוה, which He spoke by His eved Ahiyah the Shilonite: 30 Because of the sins of Yehravoam which he sinned, and which he made Yisrael sin, by his provocation by which he provoked יהוה Elohim of Yisrael to anger. 31 Now the rest of the acts of Nadav, and all that he did, are they not written in the Scroll of the Divre HaYamim about the melechim of Yisrael? 32 And there was war between Asa and Ba-Asha melech of Yisrael all their days.[1] 33 In the third year of Asa melech of Yahudah began Ba-Asha the son of Ahiyah to reign over all Yisrael in Tirtzah, twenty-four years. 34 And he did evil in the sight of יהוה, and had his halacha in the derech of Yehravoam, and in his sin by which he made Yisrael to sin.

16 Then the word of יהוה came to Yehu the son of Hanani against Ba-Asha, saying, 2 *Forasmuch as I exalted you out of the dust, and made you prince over My people Yisrael; and you have had your halacha in the way of Yehravoam, and have made My people Yisrael to sin, to provoke Me to anger with their sins; 3 See, I will take away the posterity of Ba-Asha, and the posterity of his bayit; and will make your bayit like the bayit of Yehravoam the son of Nevat. 4 Him that dies of Ba-Asha in the city shall the dogs eat; and him that dies of Ba-Asha in the fields shall the fowls of the air eat.* 5 Now the rest of the acts of Ba-Asha, and what he did, and his might, are they not written in the Scroll of the Divre HaYamim about the melechim of Yisrael? 6 So Ba-Asha slept with his ahvot, and was buried in Tirtzah: and Elah his son reigned in his place. 7 And also by the hand of the navi Yehu the son of Hanani came the word of יהוה against Ba-Asha, and against his bayit, even for all the evil that he did in the sight of יהוה, in provoking Him to anger with the work of his hands, in being like Beit Yehravoam; and because he killed him. 8 In the twenty-sixth year of Asa melech of Yahudah began Elah the son of Ba-Asha to reign over Yisrael in Tirtzah, two years. 9 And his eved Zimri, captain of half his mirkavot, conspired against him, as he was in Tirtzah, drinking himself drunk in the bayit of Arza steward of his bayit in Tirtzah. 10 And Zimri went in and smote him, and killed him, in the twenty-seventh year of Asa melech of Yahudah, and reigned in his place. 11 And it came to pass, when he began to reign, as soon as he sat on his throne, that he killed all the bayit of Ba-Asha: he left him not one male, neither any of his relatives, nor of his friends. 12 So Zimri destroyed all the bayit of Ba-Asha, according to the word of יהוה, which he spoke against Ba-Asha by Yehu the navi, 13 For all the sins of Ba-Asha, and the sins of Elah his son, by which they sinned, and by which they made Yisrael to sin, in provoking יהוה Elohim of Yisrael to anger with their worthless deeds. 14 Now the rest of the acts of Elah, and all that he did, are they not written in the Scroll of the Divre HaYamim about the melechim of Yisrael?

---

[1] Another two-house civil war.

15 In the twenty-seventh year of Asa melech of Yahudah did Zimri reign seven days in Tirtzah. And the people were encamped against Givethon, which belonged to the Philistines. 16 And the people that were encamped heard it said, Zimri has conspired, and has also slain the melech: therefore all Yisrael made Omri, the captain of the army, melech over Yisrael that day in the camp. 17 And Omri went up from Givethon, and all Yisrael with him, and they besieged Tirtzah. 18 And it came to pass, when Zimri saw that the city was taken, that he went into the palace of the melech's bayit, and burnt the melech's bayit over him with fire, and died, 19 For his sins which he sinned in doing evil in the sight of יהוה , in walking in the derech of Yehravoam, and in his sin which he did, to make Yisrael to sin. 20 Now the rest of the acts of Zimri, and his treason that he made, are they not written in the Scroll of the Divre HaYamim of the melechim of Yisrael? 21 Then were the people of Yisrael divided into two parts: half of the people followed Tivni the son of Ginath, to make him melech; and half followed Omri. 22 But the people that followed Omri prevailed against the people that followed Tivni the son of Ginath: so Tivni died, and Omri reigned. 23 In the thirty-first year of Asa melech of Yahudah began Omri to reign over Yisrael, twelve years: six years he reigned in Tirtzah. 24 And he bought the hill Shomron from Shemer for two talents of silver, and built on the hill, and called the name of the city that he built, after the name of Shemer, owner of the hill, Shomron. 25 But Omri did evil in the eyes of יהוה, and did worse than all that were before him. 26 For he had his halacha in all the halacha of Yehravoam the son of Nevat, and in his sin by which he made Yisrael to sin, to provoke יהוה Elohim of Yisrael to anger with their worthless deeds. 27 Now the rest of the acts of Omri that he did, and his might that he showed, are they not written in the Scroll of the Divre HaYamim about

the melechim of Yisrael? 28 So Omri slept with his ahvot, and was buried in Shomron: and Ahav his son reigned in his place. 29 And in the thirty-eighth year of Asa melech of Yahudah began Ahav the son of Omri to reign over Yisrael: and Ahav the son of Omri reigned over Yisrael in Shomron twenty-two years. 30 And Ahav the son of Omri did evil in the sight of יהוה , above all that were before him. 31 And it came to pass, as if it had been a small thing for him to have his halacha in the sins of Yehravoam the son of Nevat, that he took as his wife Isavel the daughter of Ethbaal melech of the Tzidonians, and went and served Baal,[1] and worshipped him. 32 And he reared up an altar for Baal in the bayit of Baal, which he had built in Shomron. 33 And Ahav made a grove; and Ahav did more to provoke יהוה Elohim of Yisrael to anger than all the melechim of Yisrael that were before him. 34 In his days did Hiel[2] the Bethelite rebuilt Yericho: he laid the foundation of it in Aviram his firstborn, and set up the gates of it with his youngest son Seguv, according to the word of יהוה, which He spoke by Yahoshua the son of Nun.

17 And Eliyahu the Tishbite, who was of the inhabitants of Gilead,[3] said to Ahav, As יהוה Elohim of Yisrael lives, before whom I stand, there shall not be dew nor rain these years, without my word. 2 And the word of יהוה came to him, saying, 3 *Get away from here, and turn eastward, and hide yourself by the brook Cherith, that flows into the River Yarden. 4 And it shall be, that you shall drink of the brook; and I have commanded the ravens to feed you there.* 5 So he went and did according to the word of יהוה: for he went and dwelt by the brook Cherith, that flows into the River Yarden. 6 And the ravens brought him lechem and meat in the morning, and lechem and meat in the

---

[1] "The lord."
[2] One of s.a.tan's titles.
[3] An Ephraimite from the ten tribes.

evening; and he drank from the brook. 7 And it came to pass after a while, that the brook dried up, because there had been no rain in the land. 8 And the word of **יהוה** came to him, saying, 9 *Arise, go to Tzaraphath, which belongs to Tzidon, and dwell there: see, I have commanded a widow woman there to sustain you.* 10 So he arose and went to Tzaraphath. [1] And when he came to the gate of the city, see, the widow woman was there gathering sticks,[2] and he called to her, and said, Get me, I ask you, a little mayim in a vessel, that I may drink. 11 And as she was going to get it, he called to her, and said, Bring me please, a morsel of lechem in your hand. 12 And she said, As **יהוה** Your Elohim lives, I have not lechem, except a handful of flour in a bin, and a little oil in a jar, and I am gathering two sticks,[3] that I may go in and prepare it[4] for my son and me, so that we may eat it, and then die. 13 And Eliyahu said to her, Fear not; go and do as you have said: but make me a little lechem first, and bring it to me, and after that make some for you and for your son. 14 For this says **יהוה** Elohim of Yisrael, *The bin of flour shall not waste away, neither shall the jar of oil run dry, until the day that* **יהוה** *sends rain upon the earth.* 15 And she went and did according to the saying of Eliyahu: and she, and he, and her bayit, did eat many days.[5] 16 And the bin of meal wasted not, neither did the jar of oil fail, according to the word of **יהוה** , which he spoke by Eliyahu.

17 And it came to pass after these things, that the son of the woman, who owned the bayit, fell sick; and his sickness was so severe, that there was no breath left in him. 18 And she said to Eliyahu, What have I to do with you, O man of Elohim? Have you come to me to call my sin to remembrance, and to kill my son? 19 And he said to her, Give me your son. And he took him out of her bosom, and carried him up into an upper room, where he was staying, and laid him on his own bed. 20 And he cried to **יהוה**, and said, O **יהוה** My Elohim; have You also brought evil upon the widow with whom I sojourn, by killing her son? 21 And he stretched himself upon the child three times, and cried to **יהוה**, and said, O **יהוה** My Elohim, I make tefillah, let this child's chayim come into him again. 22 And **יהוה** heard the voice of Eliyahu, and the chayim of the child came into him again, and he revived. 23 And Eliyahu took the child, and brought him down out of the upper room into the bayit, and delivered him to his ima: and Eliyahu said, See, your son lives. 24 And the woman said to Eliyahu, Now; by this, I know that you are a man of Elohim, and that the word of **יהוה** in your mouth is emet.

18 And it came to pass after many days, that the word of **יהוה** came to Eliyahu in the third year,[6] saying, Go, show yourself to Ahav; and I will send rain upon the earth. 2 And Eliyahu went to show himself to Ahav. And there was a severe famine in Shomron. 3 And Ahav called Ovadyah, who was the governor of his bayit. Now Ovadyah feared **יהוה** greatly: 4 For it was, when Isavel cut down the neviim of **יהוה** , that Ovadyah took a hundred neviim, and hid them by fifty in a cave, and fed them with lechem and mayim. 5 And Ahav said to Ovadyah, Go into the land, to all fountains of mayim, and to all

---

[1] Luke 4:25-26, 28.
[2] A Yisraelite surviving among the nations, or a true non-Yisraelite; who has joined Yisrael by choice through faith.
[3] The gathering of two sticks or two houses among the nations in Zaraphath, is highly symbolic of the latter-day move of YHWH working through his quickened bride, the woman, out among the nations. The Hebrew for two sticks here is **shenayim eytzim,** or literally two **eytzim**/sticks, the exact same wording we find in Ezekiel 37:16-17.
[4] The woman symbolic of Renewed Covenant Yisrael uses the two sticks to start the flames or fires of revival, as she awaits the revelation of the ministry of Elijah. She uses the two sticks symbolizing the two houses in the nations. Elijah furthers the work by turning the hearts of the fathers or Judah back to the children, or Ephraim. Elijah then will give way to the second coming of Moshiach who finishes the task Himself.
[5] The fire of two-house revival is not a passing fad, but survives many days until Moshiach returns to complete the task.

[6] After 2,000 years in the 3rd year, or start of the third millennium since Yahshua, YHWH sends the rains of restoration, after the two sticks are gathered and used to start revival flames for the whole nation of Yisrael.

brooks: perhaps we may find grass to save the horses and mules alive, that we lose not all the livestock. 6 So they divided the land between them to pass throughout it: Ahav went one way by himself, and Ovadyah went another way by himself. 7 And as Ovadyah was on his way, see, Eliyahu met him: and he knew him, and fell on his face, and said, Is that you my master Eliyahu? 8 And he answered him, I am: go, tell your master, See, Eliyahu is here. 9 And he said, What have I sinned, that you would deliver your eved into the hand of Ahav, to kill me? 10 As יהוה Your Elohim lives, there is no nation or malchut, where my master has not sent to seek you: and when they said, He is not there; he made the malchut and nation take an oath, that they did not find you. 11 And now you say, Go, tell your master; See, Eliyahu is here. 12 And it shall come to pass, as soon as I am gone from you, that the Ruach of יהוה shall take you somewhere I know not; and so when I come and tell Ahav, and he cannot find you, he shall kill me: but I your eved have feared יהוה from my youth. 13 Was it not told my master what I did when Isavel killed the neviim of יהוה, how I hid a hundred men of יהוה's neviim by fifty in a cave, and fed them with lechem and mayim? 14 And now you say, Go, tell your master; See, Eliyahu is here: and he shall kill me. 15 And Eliyahu said, As יהוה of hosts lives, before whom I stand, I will surely show myself to him today. 16 So Ovadyah went to meet Ahav, and told him: and Ahav went to meet Eliyahu. 17 And it came to pass, when Ahav saw Eliyahu, that Ahav said to him, Are you he that troubles and disturbs Yisrael?[1] 18 And he answered, I have not troubled Yisrael; but you, and your abba's bayit, in that you have forsaken the mitzvoth- Torah of יהוה , and you have followed Baalim.[2][3] 19 Now therefore send,

and gather to me all Yisrael to Mount Carmel, and the neviim of Baal [4] four hundred fifty, and the neviim of the Asherah four hundred, who eat at Isavel's table. 20 So Ahav sent to all the children of Yisrael, and gathered the neviim together to Mount Carmel. 21 And Eliyahu came to all the people, and said, How long do you keep hopping between two opinions? If יהוה is Elohim, follow Him: but if Baal, [5] then follow him. And the people answered him not a word. 22 Then said Eliyahu to the people, I alone, remain a navi of יהוה; but Baal's neviim are four hundred fifty men. 23 Let them therefore give us two bullocks; and let them choose one bullock for themselves, and cut it in pieces, and lay it on wood, and put no fire under: and I will prepare the other bullock, and lay it on wood, and put no fire under: 24 And call you on the Name of your elohim, and I will call on the Name of יהוה: and the Elohim that answers by fire; let him be Elohim. And all the people answered and said, It is well spoken.[6] 25 And Eliyahu said to the neviim of Baal, Choose one bullock for yourselves, and prepare it first; for you are many; and call on the name of your elohim, but put no fire under it. 26 And they took the bullock which was given them, and they prepared it, and called on the name of Baal from morning even until noon, saying, O lord-Baal, shema to us. But there was no voice, nor any that answered.[7] And they leaped upon the altar that was made. 27 And it came to pass at noon, that Eliyahu mocked them, and said, Cry louder: for he is an elohim; either he is talking, or he is busy, or he is on a journey, or perhaps he sleeps, and must be awakened. 28 And they cried louder, and cut themselves after their rules with knives and spears, until the dom gushed out upon them. 29 And it came to

---

[1] Any man or woman who works in the ministry of restoration, to call and bring the north or Ephraim to repentance and back to Yisraelite status, faces or will face the same accusation. "Are you the one causing trouble in Yisrael?" Spirit-filled prophets trouble the unrighteous.
[2] Our true and firm response to Ephraim and their paganism.

[3] Baalim-lords.
[4] the lord.
[5] the lord.
[6] The name of YHWH and its usage is a key test to the legitimacy of any prophet.
[7] "lord" is not a name for YHWH; but for many things including demons and humans.

pass, when midday was past, and they prophesied until the time of the offering of the ma'ariv sacrifice, that there was neither voice, nor any to answer, nor any that paid attention. 30 And Eliyahu said to all the people, Come near to me. And all the people came near to him. And he repaired the altar of יהוה that was broken down.[1] 31 And Eliyahu took twelve stones, according to the number of the tribes of the sons of Yaakov, to whom the word of יהוה came, saying, Yisrael shall be your name:[2] 32 And with the stones he built an altar in the Name of יהוה:[3] and he made a trench around the altar, as large as would contain two seahs of zera.[4] 33 And he put the wood in order, and cut the bullock in pieces, and laid them down on the wood, and said, Fill four barrels[5] with mayim, and pour it on the burnt sacrifice, and on the wood. 34 And he said, Do it the second time. And they did it the second time. And he said, Do it the third time. And they did it the third time. 35 And the mayim ran all around the altar; and he filled the trench also with mayim.[6] 36 And it came to pass at the time of the offering of

the ma'ariv sacrifice, that Eliyahu the navi came near, and said, יהוה Elohim of Avraham, Yitzchak, and of Yisrael, let it be known this day that You are Elohim in Yisrael, and that I am Your eved, and that I have done all these things at Your word. 37 Answer me,[7] O יהוה, answer me,[8] that this people may know that You are יהוה[9] Elohim, and that You have restored their lev back again.[10] 38 Then the fire of יהוה fell, and consumed the burnt sacrifice, and the wood, and the stones, and the dust, and licked up the mayim that was in the trench.[11] 39 And when all the people saw it, they fell on their faces: and they said, יהוה, He is the Elohim;[12] יהוה, He is the Elohim.[13][14] 40 And Eliyahu said to them, Take the neviim of Baal; let not one of them escape. And they took them: and Eliyahu brought them down to the brook Kishon, and killed them there.[15] 41 And Eliyahu said to Ahav, Get up, eat and drink, for there is a sound of abundance of rain. 42 So Ahav went up to eat and to drink. And Eliyahu went up to the top of Carmel; and he cast himself down upon the earth, and put his face between his knees, 43 And said to his eved, Go up now, look toward the sea. And he went up, and looked, and said, There is not a speck of rain. And seven times he said, Go again. 44 And it came to pass the seventh time, that he said, See, there arises a little cloud out of the sea, like a man's hand. And he said, Go up, and say to Ahav, Prepare your mirkavah, and go

---

[1] An "Elijah calling" will focus on repairing the people and altar of YHWH to restore true worship for both houses.
[2] True worship after a renunciation of all pagan ways, is the restoration of that worship among all 12 tribes and every altar rebuilt and restored must include all 12 tribes or both houses of Yisrael, or it cannot be considered a true altar of pure worship. The rebuilding of David's Tabernacle and all the worship in it must be with all 12 foundation stones.
[3] When Yisrael is restored with all 12 tribes being repaired, the worship and homage will be done only and exclusively to and in the Name of YHWH. Any other form of worship or service does not meet the standard of Yisrael restored and rebuilt.
[4] The two seahs or measures of seed are symbolic of the word of YHWH and the word of restoration going to both houses involved with restoring the worship of YHWH to all 12 stones or tribes. Notice that both houses need the seed or the word of restoration, since both are partially blind and both are in a muddy ditch.
[5] Symbolic of the four winds, or corners of the earth from where Yisrael would be restored in their return and the altar (12 tribes) rebuilt in revival flames, through fearless restoration prophets and a return to the true Name of YHWH, as men forsake their generic "lords."
[6] The little revival flame that started with one woman rubbing the two sticks, now leads to the mayim of revival flowing for all the tribes, symbolized by the trench or pit where all 12 tribes have been blind and stuck, being filed and overflowing with the full flow of the Ruach HaKodesh and the mayim of revival and restoration. The mayim watered the two measures or **seahs**, touching both houses of Yisrael. By Biblical definition, when one house gets quickened the other house does as well. The renewal and rebuilding of both-houses or seahs of seed, is a simultaneous event.

[7] The declaration of Yahudah.
[8] The declaration of Ephraim.
[9] Know your true Name and character.
[10] That you have sent me to kindle the fire of Yisrael's restoration in both houses.
[11] YHWH's fire fell on both houses of Yisrael, causing national repentance and acknowledgment of idolatry, along with a renunciation of all false lords.
[12] Yahudah's proclamation.
[13] Ephraim's proclamation.
[14] All Yisrael accepts truth and the rebuilding of the nation, along with the leaders of that restoration.
[15] The unpleasant part of restoration is the destruction of the pagan prophets as well as their altars. In this area, most believers lose heart and become emotionally disturbed when they see true prophets verbally destroying false religious systems. These true restoration warriors often are accused of being mean-spirited. One wonders what today's naysayers would say about the deeds of Elijah, chasing and then killing the false prophets in cold dom.

down, before the rain stops you. 45 And meanwhile it came to pass, that the shamayim were black with clouds and wind, and there was a great rain. And Ahav rode, and went to Yezreel. 46 And the hand of יהוה was on Eliyahu; and he girded up his waist, and ran before Ahav to the entrance of Yezreel.

19 And Ahav told Isavel all that Eliyahu had done, and also how he had slain all the neviim with the sword. 2 Then Isavel sent a messenger to Eliyahu, saying, So let elohim do to me, and more also, if I make not your chayim as the chayim of one of them by tomorrow about this time. 3 And when he saw that, he arose, and ran for his chayim, and came to Beer-Sheva, which belongs to Yahudah, and left his eved there. 4 But he himself went a day's journey into the wilderness, and came and sat down under a juniper eytz: and he requested for himself that he might die; and said, I have had enough; now, O יהוה, take away my chayim; for I am not better than my ahvot. 5 And as he lay and slept under a juniper eytz, see, a heavenly messenger touched him, and said to him, Arise and eat. 6 And he looked, and, see, there was a cake of lechem baked on the coals, and a jar of mayim at his head. And he did eat and drink, and lay down again. 7 And the heavenly messenger of יהוה came again the second time, and touched him, and said, Arise and eat, because the journey is too great for you. 8 And he arose, and did eat and drink, and went in the strength of that food forty days and forty nights to Horev - Sinai the Mount of Elohim. 9 And he came there to a cave, and stayed there; and, see, the word of יהוה[1] came to him, and He said to him, *What are you doing here, Eliyahu?* 10 And he said, I have been very jealous for יהוה Elohim of hosts, but the children of Yisrael have forsaken Your covenant, thrown down Your altars, and slain Your neviim with the sword. Now I

alone am left; and they seek my chayim, to take it away. 11 And He said, *Go out, and stand upon the Mount before יהוה.* And, see, יהוה passed by, and a great and strong wind tore at the mountains, and broke in pieces the rocks before יהוה; but יהוה was not in the wind: and after the wind an earthquake; but יהוה was not in the earthquake: 12 And after the earthquake a fire, but יהוה was not in the fire: and after the fire a still small voice. 13 And it was so, when Eliyahu heard it, that he wrapped his face in his mantle, and went out, and stood at the entrance of the cave. And, see, there came a voice to him, and said, *What are you doing here, Eliyahu?* 14 And he said, I have been very jealous for יהוה Elohim of hosts: because the children of Yisrael have forsaken Your covenant, thrown down Your altars, and slain Your neviim with the sword; and I alone am left; and they seek my chayim, to take it away. 15 And יהוה said to him, *Go, return on your way to the wilderness of Dameshek: and when you come, anoint Haza-El to be melech over Aram: 16 And Yehu the son of Nimshi shall you anoint to be melech over Yisrael: and Elisha the son of Shaphat of Avel-Meholah shall you anoint to be navi in your place. 17 And it shall come to pass, that him that escapes the sword of Haza-El shall Yehu kill: and him that escapes from the sword of Yehu shall Elisha kill. 18 Yet I have left for Myself seven thousand in Yisrael,[2] all the knees that have not bowed to Baal-the lord, and every mouth that has not kissed him[3].* 19 So he departed from there, and found Elisha the son of Shaphat, who was plowing with twelve yoke of oxen before him,[4] and he along with the twelfth: and Eliyahu passed by him, and cast his mantle upon

---

[1] Yahshua.

[2] Representing all Yisraelites of this age or 7,000 years since creation, who have not kissed "the lord," but serve YHWH and His Son who will all surely enter into the resurrection of the just.
[3] True Yisraelites refuse to substitute a generic "lord" for YHWH.
[4] Elisha's calling like that of Elijah, was to be burdened and work with all 12 tribes, symbolized by the 12 yoke of oxen in their return to truth and repentance.

him.[1] 20 And he left the oxen, and ran after Eliyahu, and said, Let me, I beg you, kiss my abba and my ima, and then I will follow you. And he said to him, Go and turn back again: for what have I done to you? 21 And he returned back to him, and took a yoke of oxen, and killed them, and boiled their flesh with the instruments of the oxen, and gave to the people, and they did eat. Then he arose, and went after Eliyahu, and became his eved.

20 And Ben-Hadad the melech of Aram gathered all his army together: and there were thirty-two other melechim with him, and horses, and mirkavot: and he went up and besieged Shomron, and warred against it. 2 And he sent messengers to Ahav melech of Yisrael into the city, and said to him, This says Ben-Hadad, 3 Your silver and your gold is mine; your wives also and your children, even the best of all, are mine. 4 And the melech of Yisrael answered and said, My master, O melech, according to your saying, I am yours, and all that I have. 5 And the messengers came again, and said, This speaks Ben-Hadad, saying, Although I have sent to you, saying, You shall deliver to me your silver, and your gold, and your wives, and your children; 6 Yet I will send my avadim to you tomorrow about this time, and they shall search your bayit, and the houses of your avadim; and it shall be, that whatever is valued in your eyes, they shall put it in their hand, and take it away. 7 Then the melech of Yisrael called all the zachanim of the land, and said, Please know, and see how this man seeks mischief: for he sent to me for my wives, and for my children, and for my silver, and for my gold; and I did not refuse. 8 And all the zachanim and all the people said to him, Shema not to him, nor consent. 9 So he said to the messengers of Ben-Hadad, Tell my master the melech, All that you did send for

to your eved the first time I will do: but this thing I may not do. And the messengers departed, and brought him word again. 10 And Ben-Hadad sent to him, and said, The elohim do so to me, and more also, if the dust of Shomron shall be enough as handfuls for all the people that follow me. 11 And the melech of Yisrael answered and said, Tell him, Let not him that puts on his armor boast like one that puts it off. 12 And it came to pass, when Ben-Hadad heard this message, as he was drinking, along with the melechim in booths, that he said to his avadim, Set yourselves in array. And they set themselves in array against the city. 13 And, see, there came a navi to Ahav melech of Yisrael, saying, This says יהוה, *Have you seen all this great multitude? See, I will deliver it in to your hand this day; and you shall know that I am* יהוה. 14 And Ahav said, By whom? And he said, This says יהוה, *Even by the young men of the rulers of the provinces.* Then he said, Who shall order the battle? And he answered, *You.* 15 Then he numbered the young men of the rulers of the provinces, and they were two hundred thirty two: and after them he numbered all the people, even all the children of Yisrael, being seven thousand. 16 And they went out at noon. But Ben-Hadad was drinking himself drunk in the booths, he and the melechim, the thirty-two melechim that helped him. 17 And the young men of the rulers of the provinces went out first; and Ben-Hadad sent out, and they told him, saying, There are men coming out of Shomron. 18 And he said, If they come out for shalom, take them alive; or if they are come out for war, take them alive. 19 So these young men of the rulers of the provinces came out of the city, and the army that followed them. 20 And they killed every one his man: and the Arameans fled; and Yisrael pursued them: and Ben-Hadad the melech of Aram escaped on a horse with the horsemen. 21 And the melech of Yisrael went out, and smote the horses and mirkavot, and killed the

---

[1] Only after seeing Elisha's willingness to work with all 12 tribes, as seen in this symbolism.

Arameans with a great slaughter. 22 And the navi came to the melech of Yisrael, and said to him, Go, strengthen yourself, and know, and see what you do: for at the turn of the year the melech of Aram will come up against you again. 23 And the avadim of the melech of Aram said to him, Their elohim are elohim of the hills; therefore they were stronger than us; but let us fight against them in the plain, and surely we shall be stronger than they. 24 And do this thing, Take the melechim away, every man out of his place, and put officers in their places: 25 And number an army, like the army that you have lost, horse for horse, and mirkavah for mirkavah: and we will fight against them in the plain, and surely we shall be stronger than them. And he listened to their voice, and did so. 26 And it came to pass at the turn of the year, that Ben-Hadad numbered the Arameans, and went up to Aphek, to fight against Yisrael. 27 And the children of Yisrael were numbered, and were all present, and went against them: and the children of Yisrael pitched before them like two little flocks of goats; but the Arameans filled the country. 28 And there came a man of Elohim, and spoke to the melech of Yisrael, and said, This says יהוה , *Because the Arameans have said,* יהוה *is Elohim of the hills, but He is not Elohim of the valleys, therefore will I deliver all this great multitude into your hand, and you shall know that I am* יהוה. 29 And they camped opposite each other seven days. And so it was, that in the seventh day the battle was started: and the children of Yisrael killed of the Arameans a hundred thousand footmen in one day. 30 But the rest fled to Aphek, into the city, and there a wall fell upon twenty seven thousand of the men that were left. And Ben-Hadad fled, and came into the city, into an inner bedroom. 31 And his avadim said to him, See now, we have heard that the melechim of Beit Yisrael are merciful melechim: let us, I beg you, put sackcloth on our waist, and ropes upon our heads, and

go out to the melech of Yisrael: perhaps he will save your chayim. 32 So they girded sackcloth on their waist, and put ropes around their heads, and came to the melech of Yisrael, and said, Your eved Ben-Hadad says, I beg you, let me live. And he said, Is he yet alive? He is my brother.[1] 33 Now the men did diligently observe whether anything would come from him, and quickly grasped it: and they said, Your brother Ben-Hadad. Then he said, Go, bring him. Then Ben-Hadad came out to him; and caused him to come up into the mirkavah. 34 And Ben-Hadad said to him, The cities, which my abba took from your abba, I will restore; and you shall build streets for yourself in Dameshek, as my abba made in Shomron. Then said Ahav, I will send you away with this covenant. So he made a covenant with him, and sent him away. 35 And a certain man of the sons of the neviim said to his neighbor by the word of יהוה , Smite me, please. And the man refused to smite him. 36 Then said he to him, Because you have not obeyed the voice of יהוה , see, as soon as you are departed from me, a lion shall kill you. And as soon as he was departed from him, a lion found him, and killed him. 37 Then he found another man, and said, Smite me, please. And the man smote him, so that in smiting he wounded him. 38 So the navi departed, and waited for the melech on a road, and disguised himself with ashes upon his face. 39 And as the melech passed by, he cried to the melech: and he said, Your eved went out into the midst of the battle; and, see, a man came over, and brought a man to me, and said, Guard this man: if by any means he is missing, then shall your chayim be for his chayim, or else you shall pay a talent of silver. 40 And as your eved

---

[1] Here is a beautiful crystal-clear reference to the well-known fact in those days, that Arameans and Yisraelites were the very same people. Most of the congregations Rav Shaul planted in Asia Minor were in the land of Aram due north of Yisrael. Rachel and Leah were Arameans. Here Ahab calls Ben-Hadad his physical brother. They certainly couldn't be "spiritual brothers," since neither he nor Ben-Hadad were true faithful believers in YHWH.

was busy here and there, he left. And the melech of Yisrael said to him, Your mishpat is right; you yourself have decided it. 41 And he quickly removed the ashes away from his face; and the melech of Yisrael discerned that he was one of the neviim. 42 And he said to him, This says יהוה, *Because you have let go out of your hand a man whom I appointed to utter destruction, therefore your chayim shall go for his chayim, and your people for his people.* 43 And the melech of Yisrael went to his bayit bitter and displeased, and came to Shomron.

21 And it came to pass after these things, that Navoth the Yezreelite had a vineyard, which was in Yezreel, near by the palace of Ahav melech of Shomron. 2 And Ahav spoke to Navoth, saying, Give me your vineyard, that I may have it for a gan of herbs, because it is near to my bayit: and I will give you for it a better vineyard; or if it seems tov to you, I will give you its worth in silver. 3 And Navoth said to Ahav, יהוה forbid, that I should give the inheritance of my ahvot to you. 4 And Ahav came into his bayit bitter and displeased because of the word which Navoth the Yezreelite had spoken to him: for he had said, I will not give you the inheritance of my ahvot. And he lay down upon his bed, and turned his face, and would eat no food. 5 But Isavel his wife came to him, and said to him, Why is your ruach so sad, that you eat no lechem? 6 And he said to her, Because I spoke to Navoth the Yezreelite, and said to him, Give me your vineyard for money; or else, if it pleases you, I will give you another vineyard for it: and he answered, I will not give you my vineyard. 7 And Isavel his wife said to him, Do you now govern the malchut of Yisrael? Arise, and eat lechem, and let your lev be in simcha: I will give you the vineyard of Navoth the Yezreelite. 8 So she wrote letters in Ahav's name, and sealed them with his seal, and sent the letters to the

zachanim and to the nobles that were in the city, dwelling with Navoth. 9 And she wrote in the letters, saying, Proclaim a fast, and set Navoth at the head of the people: 10 And set two men, sons of Beliyaal, before him, to bear witness against him, saying, You did blaspheme Elohim and the melech. And then carry him out, and stone him, that he may die. 11 And the men of his city, even the zachanim and the nobles who were the inhabitants in his city, did as Isavel had sent to them, and as it was written in the letters that she had sent to them. 12 They proclaimed a fast, and set Navoth at the head of the people. 13 And there came in two men, children of Beliyaal,[1] and sat before him: and the men of Beliyaal witnessed against him, even against Navoth, in the presence of the people, saying, Navoth did blaspheme Elohim and the melech. Then they carried him out out of the city, and stoned him with stones, that he died. 14 Then they sent to Isavel, saying, Navoth is stoned, and is dead. 15 And it came to pass, when Isavel heard that Navoth was stoned, and was dead, that Isavel said to Ahav, Arise, take possession of the vineyard of Navoth the Yezreelite, which he refused to give you for money: for Navoth is not alive, but dead. 16 And it came to pass, when Ahav heard that Navoth was dead, that Ahav rose up to go down to the vineyard of Navoth the Yezreelite, to take possession of it. 17 And the word of יהוה came to Eliyahu the Tishbite, saying, 18 *Arise, go down to meet Ahav melech of Yisrael, who is in Shomron: see, he is in the vineyard of Navoth, where he has gone down to possess it.* 19 *And you shall speak to him, saying,* This says יהוה, *Have you killed, and also taken possession? And you shall speak to him, saying,* This says יהוה, *In the place where dogs licked the dom of Navoth shall dogs lick your dom, even your" " " ."*[2] 20 And Ahav said to Eliyahu, Have you found me, O my enemy? And he

---

[1] s.a.tan
[2] Missing words probably indicate distasteful descriptions of body parts that apparently YHWH wanted left out.

answered, I have found you: because you have sold yourself to work evil in the sight of יהוה. 21 *See, I will bring evil upon you, and will consume your descendants, and will cut off from Ahav every male, both him that is shut up and him that is left in Yisrael, 22 And will make your bayit like Beit Yehravoam the son of Nevat, and like the bayit of Ba-Asha the son of Ahiyah, for the provocation by which you have provoked Me to anger, and made Yisrael to sin.* 23 And of Isavel also spoke יהוה, saying, *The dogs shall eat Isavel by the wall of Yezreel.* 24 *Him that dies of Ahav in the city the dogs shall eat; and him that dies in the field shall the fowls of the air eat.* 25 But there was none like Ahav, who did sell himself to work wickedness in the sight of יהוה, whom Isavel his wife stirred up. 26 And he did very abominably in following idols, according to all things as did the Amorites, whom יהוה cast out before the children of Yisrael. 27 And it came to pass, when Ahav heard those words, that he tore his clothes, and put sackcloth upon his flesh, and fasted, and lay in sackcloth, and went softly. 28 And the word of יהוה came to Eliyahu the Tishbite, saying, 29 *Do you see how Ahav humbled himself before Me? Because he humbled himself before Me, I will not bring the evil in his days: but in his son's days will I bring the evil upon his bayit.*

22 And they continued three years without war between Aram and Yisrael. 2 And it came to pass in the third year, that Yehoshaphat the melech of Yahudah came down to the melech of Yisrael. 3 And the melech of Yisrael said to his avadim, You know that Ramoth in Gilead is ours, and we are silent, and yet we do not take it away from the hand of the melech of Aram? 4 And he said to Yehoshaphat, Will you go with me to battle to Ramoth-Gilead? And Yehoshaphat said to the melech of Yisrael, I am as you are, my people as your people, my horses as

your horses.[1] [2] 5 And Yehoshaphat said to the melech of Yisrael, Enquire, for the word of יהוה today. 6 Then the melech of Yisrael gathered the neviim together, about four hundred men, and said to them, Shall I go against Ramoth-Gilead to battle, or shall I refrain? And they said, Go up; for יהוה shall deliver it into the hand of the melech. 7 And Yehoshaphat said, Is there not here a navi of יהוה besides these that we might enquire of him also? 8 And the melech of Yisrael said to Yehoshaphat, There is yet one man, Michayah the son of Yimlah, by whom we may enquire from יהוה: but I hate him; for he does not prophesy tov concerning me, but only evil. And Yehoshaphat said, Let not the melech say so. 9 Then the melech of Yisrael called an officer, and said, Hurry and bring here Micahyah the son of Yimlah. 10 And the melech of Yisrael and Yehoshaphat the melech of Yahudah sat each on his throne, having put on their robes, in a threshing floor at the entrance of the Gate of Shomron; and all the neviim prophesied before them. 11 And Tzedkayahu the son of Chenaanah made horns of iron: and he said, This says יהוה, With these shall you push the Arameans, until you have consumed them. 12 And all the neviim prophesied the same, saying, Go up to Ramoth-Gilead, and prosper: for יהוה shall deliver it into the melech's hand. 13 And the messenger that was gone to call Micahyah spoke to him, saying, See now, the words of the neviim declare tov to the melech with one accord: let your word, I ask you, be like the words of one of them, and speak that which is tov. 14 And Micayah said, As יהוה lives, what יהוה says to me, that will I speak. 15 So he

---

[1] A temporary truce between the two houses; to unite against other Aramean-Yisraelites.

[2] "Scripture does speak of some intermingling and intermarriage between the two kingdoms but, while men were free to move from their tribal land to that of another, they could not take their land inheritance with them. Land could be sold on a lease basis, but not permanently (Lev 25:13, 29-31). Surely this restriction tended to limit intermingling. But most important, if one did move to a different tribal territory, that move would not, could not change one's tribal lineage. *Who Is Israel? Wootten.*

came to the melech. And the melech said to him, Michayah, shall we go against Ramoth-Gilead to battle, or shall we refrain? And he answered him, Go, and prosper: for יהוה shall deliver it into the hand of the melech. 16 And the melech said to him, How many times shall I make you swear that you tell me nothing but that which is emet in the Name of יהוה? 17 And he said, I saw all Yisrael scattered upon the hills, as sheep that have not a shepherd: and יהוה said, *These have no master: let them return every man to his bayit in shalom.* 18 And the melech of Yisrael said to Yehoshaphat, Did I not tell you that he would prophesy evil concerning me? 19 And he said, Shema therefore the word of יהוה: *I saw יהוה sitting on His throne, and all the armies of the shamayim standing by Him on His right hand and on His left.* 20 And יהוה said, *Who shall persuade Ahav, that he may go up and fall at Ramoth-Gilead?* And one said one thing, and another said another thing. 21 And there came forward a ruach, and stood before יהוה, and said, I will entice him. 22 And יהוה said to him, *In what way?* And he said, I will go out, and I will be a lying ruach in the mouth of all his neviim. And He said, *You shall persuade him, and prevail also: go out, and do so.* 23 Now therefore, see, יהוה has put a lying ruach in the mouth of all these your neviim, but יהוה has spoken evil concerning you. 24 But Tzedkayahu the son of Chenaanah went near, and smote Michayah on the cheek, and said, Which way did the Ruach of יהוה go from me to speak to you? 25 And Michayah said, See, you shall see in that day, when you shall go into an inner room to hide yourself. 26 And the melech of Yisrael said, Take Michayah, and carry him back to Amon the governor of the city, and to Yoash the melech's son, 27 And say, This says the melech, Put this fellow in the prison, and feed him with the lechem of affliction and with the mayim of affliction, until I come in shalom. 28 And Michayah

said, If you return at all in shalom, יהוה has not spoken by me. And he said, Shema, O people, every one of you. 29 So the melech of Yisrael and Yehoshaphat the melech of Yahudah went up to Ramoth-Gilead. 30 And the melech of Yisrael said to Yehoshaphat, I will disguise myself, and enter into the battle; but you put on your robes. And the melech of Yisrael disguised himself, and went into the battle. 31 But the melech of Aram commanded his thirty-two captains that had rule over his mirkavot, saying, Fight neither with small nor great, save only with the melech of Yisrael. 32 And it came to pass, when the captains of the mirkavot saw Yehoshaphat, that they said, Surely it is the melech of Yisrael. And they turned aside to fight against him: and Yehoshaphat cried out. 33 And it came to pass, when the captains of the mirkavot perceived that it was not the melech of Yisrael that they turned back from pursuing him. 34 And a certain man drew a bow aimlessly, and smote the melech of Yisrael between the joints of his armor: therefore he said to the driver of his mirkavah, Turn around, and carry me out of the battle; for I am wounded. 35 And the battle increased that day: and the melech was propped up in his mirkavah against the Arameans, and died at evening: and the dom ran out of the wound into the midst of the mirkavah. 36 And there went a proclamation throughout the army at sundown, saying, Every man to his city, and every man to his own country. 37 So the melech died, and was brought to Shomron; and they buried the melech in Shomron. 38 And one washed his mirkavah in the pool of Shomron; and the dogs licked up his dom; and the whores washed in it; according to the word of יהוה which he spoke. 39 Now the rest of the acts of Ahav, and all that he did, and the ivory Bayit which he made, and all the cities that he built, are they not written in the Scroll of the Divre HaYamim about the melechim of Yisrael? 40 So Ahav slept with his ahvot; and Ahazyahu his son reigned in his place.

41 And Yehoshaphat the son of Asa began to reign over Yahudah in the fourth year of Ahav melech of Yisrael. 42 Yehoshaphat was thirty-five years old when he began to reign; and he reigned twenty-five years in Yahrushalayim. And his ima's name was Azuvah the daughter of Shilhi. 43 And he had his halacha in all the ways of Asa his abba; he turned not aside from it, doing that which was right in the eyes of יהוה : nevertheless the temples of idols were not taken away; for the people still offered and burnt incense in the temples of idols. 44 And Yehoshaphat made shalom with the melech of Yisrael. 45 Now the rest of the acts of Yehoshaphat, and his might that he showed, and how he waged war, are they not written in the Scroll of the Divre HaYamim about the melechim of Yahudah? 46 And the remnant of the cult prostitutes, which remained in the days of his abba Asa, he took out of the land. 47 There was then no melech in Edom: a deputy was melech. 48 Yehoshaphat made ships of Tharshish to go to Ophir for gold: but they went not, for the ships were broken at Ezion-Gever.

49 Then said Ahazyahu the son of Ahav to Yehoshaphat, Let my avadim go with your avadim in the ships. But Yehoshaphat would not. 50 So Yehoshaphat slept with his ahvot, and was buried with his ahvot in the city of David his abba: and Yehoram his son reigned in his place. 51 Ahazyahu the son of Ahav began to reign over Yisrael in Shomron the seventeenth year of Yehoshaphat melech of Yahudah, and reigned two years over Yisrael. 52 And he did evil in the sight of יהי, and had his halacha in the derech of his abba, and in the derech of his ima, and in the derech of Yehravoam the son of Nevat, who made Yisrael to sin: 53 For he served Baal, and worshipped him, and provoked to anger יהוה Elohim of Yisrael, according to all that his abba had done.

מלכים ב

Melechim Bet - Second Kings
To Our Forefathers Yisrael

1 Then Moav rebelled against Yisrael after the death of Ahav. 2 And Ahazyahu fell down through a lattice in his upper room that was in Shomron, and was sick: and he sent messengers, and said to them, Go, inquire of Baal-Zevuv the elohim of Ekron whether I shall be healed of this disease. 3 But a heavenly messenger of יהוה said to Eliyahu the Tishbite, Arise, go up to meet the messengers of the melech of Shomron, and say to them, Is it because there is no Elohim in Yisrael, that you go to inquire of Baal-Zevuv the elohim of Ekron? 4 Now therefore this says יהוה, *You shall not come down from that bed on which you have gone up, but shall surely die.* And Eliyahu departed. 5 And when the messengers turned back to him, he said to them, Why have you now come back? 6 And they said to him, There came a man up to meet us, and said to us, Go, turn back to the melech that sent you, and say to him, This says יהוה, *Is it because there is no Elohim in Yisrael, that you sent to inquire of Baal-Zevuv the elohim of Ekron? Therefore you shall not come down from that bed on which you have gone up, but shall surely die.* 7 And he said to them, What kind of man was he who came up to meet you, and told you these words? 8 And they answered him, He was a hairy man, and dressed with a girdle of leather around his waste. And he said, It is Eliyahu the Tishbite. 9 Then the melech sent to him a captain of fifty with his fifty. And he went up to him: and, see, he sat on the top of a hill. And he spoke to him, You man of Elohim, the melech has said, Come down. 10 And Eliyahu answered and said to the captain of fifty, If I be a man of Elohim, then let fire come down from the shamayim, and consume you and your fifty. And fire came down fire from the shamayim, and

consumed him and his fifty. 11 Again also he sent to him another captain of fifty with his fifty. And he answered and said to him, O man of Elohim, this has the melech said, Come down quickly. 12 And Eliyahu answered and said to them, If I be a man of Elohim, let fire come down from the shamayim, and consume you and your fifty. And the fire of Elohim came down from the shamayim, and consumed him and his fifty. 13 And he sent again a captain of the third fifty with his fifty. And the third captain of fifty went up, and came and fell on his knees before Eliyahu, and pleaded with him, and said to him, O man of Elohim, I beg you, let my chayim, and the chayim of these fifty of your avadim, be precious in your sight. 14 See, there came fire down from the shamayim, and burnt up the two captains of the former fifties with their fifties: therefore let my chayim now be precious in your sight. 15 And the Malach-יהוה said to Eliyahu, *Go down with him: be not afraid of him.* And he arose, and went down with him to the melech. 16 And he said to him, This says יהוה, *Since you have sent messengers to inquire of Baal-Zevuv the elohim of Ekron, is it because there is no Elohim in Yisrael to inquire of His word? Therefore you shall not come down off that bed on which you have gone up, but shall surely die.* 17 So he died according to the word of יהוה which Eliyahu had spoken. And Yehoram reigned in his place in the second year of Yehoram the son of Yehoshaphat melech of Yahudah; because he had no son. 18 Now the rest of the acts of Ahazyahu that he did, are they not written in the scroll of the Divre HaYamim about the melechim of Yisrael?

2 And it came to pass, when יהוה would take up Eliyahu into the

shamayim by a whirlwind, that Eliyahu went with Elisha from Gilgal. 2 And Eliyahu said to Elisha, Stay here, I ask you; for יהוה has sent me to Beth-El. And Elisha said to him, As יהוה lives, and as your being lives, I will not leave you. So they went down to Beth-El. 3 And the sons of the neviim that were at Beth-El came forth to Elisha, and said to him, Do you know that יהוה will take away your master from being over you today? And he said, Ken, I know it; hold you your silence. 4 And Eliyahu said to him, Elisha, stay here, I ask you; for יהוה has sent me to Yericho. And he said, As יהוה lives, and as your being lives, I will not leave you. So they came to Yericho. 5 And the sons of the neviim that were at Yericho came to Elisha, and said to him, Do you know that יהוה will take away your master from being over you today? And he answered, Ken; I know it; be silent! 6 And Eliyahu said to him, Stay here, I ask you, for יהוה has sent me to Yarden. And he said, As יהוה lives, and as your being lives, I will not leave you. And the two went on. 7 And fifty men of the sons of ha neviim went, and stood far off to view: and the two of them stood by Yarden. 8 And Eliyahu took his mantle, and wrapped it together, and struck the mayim, and they were divided this derech and that derech, so that the two of them went over on dry ground. 9 And it came to pass, when they had gone over, that Eliyahu said to Elisha, Ask me what I shall do for you, before I be taken away from you. And Elisha said, I ask you, let a double portion of your Ruach be upon me. 10 And he said, You have asked a hard thing: nevertheless, if you see me when I am taken from you, it shall be so to you; but if not, it shall not be so. 11 And it came to pass, as they still went on, and talked, that, see, there appeared a mirkavah of fire, and horses of fire, and separated them; and Eliyahu went up by a whirlwind into the shamayim. 12 And Elisha saw it, and he cried, My abba, my abba, the Mirkavah of Yisrael, and their

horsemen. And he saw him no more: and he took hold of his own clothes, and tore them in two pieces. 13 He took up also the mantle of Eliyahu that fell from him, and went back, and stood by the bank of the Yarden; 14 And he took the mantle of Eliyahu that fell from him, and struck the mayim, and said, Where is יהוה Elohim of Eliyahu? And when he also had struck the mayim, they parted this derech and that derech: and Elisha went over. 15 And when the sons of ha neviim who were at Yericho saw him, they said, The Ruach of Eliyahu does rest on Elisha. And they came to meet him, and bowed themselves to the ground before him. 16 And they said to him, See now, there be with your avadim fifty strong men; let them go, we ask you, and seek your master: if perhaps the Ruach of יהוה has taken him up, and cast him upon some mountain, or into some valley. And he said, You shall not send anyone. 17 And when they urged him until he was ashamed, he relented and said, Send. They sent therefore fifty men; and they sought him for three days, but found him not. 18 And when they came again to him, for he tarried at Yericho, he said to them, Did I not say to you, Go not? 19 And the men of the city said to Elisha, See, We ask you, the situation of this city is pleasant, as my master sees: but the mayim is spoiled, and the ground barren. 20 And he said, Bring me a new bowl, and put salt in it. And they brought it to him. 21 And he went forth to the spring of the mayim, and cast the salt in there, and said, This says יהוה, *I have healed these mayim; there shall not be from them any more death or barren land.* 22 So the mayim were healed to this day, according to the saying of Elisha which he spoke. 23 And he went up from there to Beth-El: and as he was going up by the derech, there came forth little children out of the city, and mocked him, and said to him, Go up, you bald head; go up, you bald head.[1] 24 And he

---

[1] Yisraelites ought to take careful note to never speak evil against or ridicule the designated and anointed leadership in our nation, regardless of outward appearance.

turned back, and looked on them, and cursed them in the Name of **יהוה**. And there came forth two female bears out of the woods, and tore up forty-two of the children. 25 And he went from there to Mount Carmel, and from there he returned to Shomron.

3 And Yehoram son of Ahav began to reign over Yisrael at Shomron in the eighteenth year of Yehoshaphat melech of Yahudah, and reigned twelve years. 2 And he worked evil in the sight of **יהוה**; but not like his abba, and like his ima: for he put away the image of Baal that his abba had made. 3 Nevertheless he cleaved to the sins of Yeravoam the son of Nevat, who made Yisrael to sin; he departed not from them. 4 And Mesha melech of Moav was a sheep-breeder, and rendered to the melech of Yisrael a hundred thousand lambs, and a hundred thousand rams, with the wool. 5 But it came to pass, when Ahav was dead, that the melech of Moav rebelled against the melech of Yisrael. 6 And melech Yehoram went out of Shomron the same time, and numbered all Yisrael. 7 And he went and sent to Yehoshaphat the melech of Yahudah, saying, The melech of Moav has rebelled against me: will you go with me against Moav to battle? And he said, I will go up: I am as you are, my people as your people, and my horses as your horses.[1] 8 And he said, Which derech shall we go up? And he answered, The derech that goes through the wilderness of Edom. 9 So the melech of Yisrael went, and the melech of Yahudah, and the melech of Edom: and they went a journey of seven days: and there was no mayim for the armies, and for the cattle that followed them. 10 And the melech of Yisrael said, Oy Vey! Has **יהוה** has called these three melechim together, to deliver them into the hand of Moav! 11 But Yehoshaphat said, Is there not here a navi of **יהוה** that we may inquire of **יהוה** through him? And one of the melech of

Yisrael's avadim answered and said, Here is Elisha the son of Shaphat, who poured mayim on the hands of Eliyahu. 12 And Yehoshaphat said, The word of **יהוה** is with him. So the melech of Yisrael and Yehoshaphat and the melech of Edom went down to him. 13 And Elisha said to the melech of Yisrael, What have I to do with you? Go to ha neviim of your abba, and to ha neviim of your ima. And the melech of Yisrael said to him, No: for **יהוה** has called these three melechim together, to deliver them into the hand of Moav. 14 And Elisha said, As **יהוה** of hosts lives, before whom I stand, surely, were it not that I regard and respect the presence of Yehoshaphat the melech of Yahudah, I would not even look at you, nor see you. 15 But now bring me a harpist. And it came to pass, when the harpist played, that the Hand of **יהוה** came upon him. 16 And he said, This says **יהוה**, *Make this valley full of ditches.* 17 For this says **יהוה**, *You shall not see wind, neither shall you see rain; yet that valley shall be filled with mayim, that you may drink, both you, and your cattle, and your beasts.* 18 And this is but a minor thing in the sight of **יהוה**: He will also deliver the Moavites into your hand. 19 And you shall kill every fenced city, and every choice city, and shall cut down every tov eytz, and stop all wells of mayim, and ruin every tov piece of land with stones. 20 And it came to pass in the morning, when the grain offering was offered, that, see, there came mayim by the derech of Edom, and the country was filled with mayim. 21 And when all the Moavites heard that the melechim were come up to fight against them, they gathered all that were able to put on armor, and the older ones also, and stood in the border. 22 And they rose up early in the morning, and the sun shone upon the mayim, and the Moavites saw the mayim on the other side as red as dom: 23 And they said, This is dom: the melechim are surely killed, and they have killed one another: now therefore, Moav, go to the spoil. 24 And when they

---

[1] Another brief taste of unity against a common enemy.

came to the camp of Yisrael, the Yisraelites rose up and killed the Moavites, so that they fled before them: but they went forward smiting the Moavites, even into their country. 25 And they beat down the cities, and on every tov piece of land cast every man his stone, and filled it; and they stopped all the wells of mayim, and cut all the tov eytzim: only in Kir-Haraseth they left the stones; but the stone slingers went around it, and killed it. 26 And when the melech of Moav saw that the battle was too heavy for him, he took with him seven hundred men that drew swords, to break through even to the melech of Edom: but they could not. 27 Then he took his eldest son that should have reigned in his place, and offered him as a burnt offering upon the wall. And there was great indignation against Yisrael: and they departed from him, and returned to their own land.

4 Now there cried a certain woman of the wives of the sons of ha neviim to Elisha, saying, Your eved my husband is dead; and you know that your eved did fear יהוה: and the creditor is come to take my two sons to be avadim. 2 And Elisha said to her, What should I do for you? Tell me, what have you in the bayit? And she said, Your female eved has nothing in the bayit, except a pot of oil. 3 Then he said, Go, and borrow vessels everywhere from all your neighbors, even empty vessels; do not get just a few. 4 And when you have returned, you shall shut the door behind you and behind your sons, and shall pour out into all those vessels, and you shall set aside those that are full. 5 So she went from him, and shut the door behind her and behind her sons, who brought the vessels to her; and she poured them out. 6 And it came to pass, when the vessels were full, that she said to her son, Bring me another vessel. And he said to her, There are no more vessels. And the oil ceased. 7 Then she came and told the man of Elohim. And he said, Go, sell the oil, and pay your debt, and live off of the rest with your children. 8 And it came to be on a day, that Elisha passed to Shunem, where there was a wealthy prominent woman; and she constrained him to eat lechem. And so it was, that as often as he passed by, he turned in there to eat lechem. 9 And she said to her husband, See now, I perceive that this is a set-apart man of Elohim, who passes by us continually. 10 Let us make a little room, I ask you, on the wall; and let us put for him there a bed, and a table, and a stool, and a candlestick: and it shall be, when he comes to us, that he shall stay there. 11 And it came to be one day, that he came there, and he went into the room, and lay there. 12 And he said to Gechazi his eved, Call this Shunammite. And when he had called her, she stood before him. 13 And he said to his eved, Say now to her, See, you have troubled yourself for us with all this care; what is to be done for you? Would you like to be mentioned to the melech, or to the captain of the armies? And she answered; I dwell among my own people. 14 And he said, What then is to be done for her? And Gechazi answered, Truly she has no child and her husband is old. 15 And he said, Call her. And when he had called her, she stood in the door. 16 And he said, About this season, according to the times of chayim, you shall embrace a son. And she said, No, my master, man of Elohim, please do not lie to your female eved. 17 And the woman conceived, and bore a son at that season that Elisha had said to her, according to the times of chayim. 18 And when the child was grown, it came to pass, that he went out to his abba who was with the reapers. 19 And he said to his abba, My head, my head. And he said to a lad, Carry him to his ima. 20 And when he had taken him, and brought him to his ima, he sat on her knees until noon, and then died. 21 And she went up, and laid him on the bed of the man of Elohim, and shut the door behind him, and went out. 22 And she called to her husband, and said, Send me, I ask you, one of the young men, and one of

the donkeys, that I may run to the man of Elohim, and come again. 23 And he said, Why will you go to him today? It is neither Rosh Chodesh, nor Shabbat. And she said, All shall be well. 24 Then she saddled a donkey, and said to her eved, Drive, and go forward; and do not slow down, unless I tell you to. 25 So she went and came to the man of Elohim to Mount Carmel. And it came to pass, when the man of Elohim saw her far off, that he said to Gechazi his eved, See, over there is that Shunammite: 26 Run now, I tell you, to meet her, and say to her, Is it well with you? Is it well with your husband? Is it well with the child? And she answered, All is well. 27 And when she came to the man of Elohim on the hill, she caught him by the feet: but Gechazi came near to push her away. And the man of Elohim said, Leave her alone; for her being is troubled within her, and יהוה has hidden it from me, and has not told me. 28 Then she said, Did I desire a son from my master? Did I not say, Do not deceive me? 29 Then he said to Gechazi, Gird up your waste, and take my staff in your hand, and go your derech: if you meet any man, greet him not; and if any man greet you, do not answer him. Go and lay my staff upon the face of the child. 30 And the ima of the child said, As יהוה lives, and as your being lives I will not leave you. And he arose, and followed her. 31 And Gechazi passed on before them, and laid the staff upon the face of the child; but there was neither voice, nor hearing. Therefore he went again to meet him, and told him, saying, The child is not awake. 32 And when Elisha had come into the bayit, see, the child was dead, and laid upon his bed. 33 He went in therefore, and shut the door behind the two of them, and made tefillah to יהוה. 34 And he went up, and lay on top of the child, and put his mouth upon his mouth, and his eyes upon his eyes, and his hands upon his hands: and he stretched himself upon the child; and the flesh of the child grew warm. 35 Then he returned, and walked in the bayit back and forth; and went up again, and stretched himself upon him: and the child sneezed seven times, and the child opened his eyes. 36 And he called Gechazi, and said, Call this Shunammite. So he called her. And when she had come in to him, he said, Pick up your son. 37 Then she went in, and fell at his feet, and bowed herself to the ground, and picked up her son, and went out. 38 And Elisha came again to Gilgal: and there was a famine in the land; and the sons of ha neviim were sitting before him: and he said to his eved, Put on the large pot, and cook pottage for the sons of ha neviim. 39 And one went out into the field to gather herbs, and found a wild vine, and gathered from there wild cucumbers that filled his lap, and came and shredded them into the pot of pottage: for they did not know what they were. 40 So they poured out for the men to eat. And it came to pass, as they were eating of the pottage, that they cried out, and said, O man of Elohim, there is death in the pot. And they could not eat it. 41 But he said, Then bring flour. And he cast it into the pot; and he said, Pour it out for the people, that they may eat. And there was no harm in the pot. 42 And there came a man from Baal-Shalisha, and brought the man of Elohim lechem of the bikkurim, twenty loaves of barley, and full ears of corn in his knapsack. And he said; Give to the people that they may eat. 43 And his servant said, What, should I set this before a hundred men? He said again, Give the people that they may eat: for this says יהוה, *They shall eat, and shall leave leftovers.* 44 So he set it before them, and they did eat, and had leftovers, according to the word of יהוה.

5 Now Naaman, captain of the armies of the melech of Aram,[1] was a great man with his master, and honorable, because through him יהוה had given deliverance to Aram: he was also a mighty man and brave, but he was a leper. 2 And the Aramaens had gone out on raids, and had taken away captive from the land of Yisrael a little maid; and she waited on Naaman's wife. 3 And she said to her mistress, I wish before Elohim that my master was with ha navi that is in Shomron! For he would heal him of his leprosy. 4 And one went in, and told his master, saying, This is what the maid said that is of the land of Yisrael. 5 And the melech of Aram said, Go enter, and I will send a letter to the melech of Yisrael. And he departed, and took with him ten talents of silver, and six thousand pieces of gold, and ten changes of raiment. 6 And he brought the letter to the melech of Yisrael, saying, Now when this letter is come to you, see, I have sent Naaman my eved to you, that you may heal him of his leprosy. 7 And it came to pass, when the melech of Yisrael had read the letter, that he tore his clothes, and said, Am I Elohim, to kill and to make alive, that this man does send to me to heal a man of his leprosy? Therefore consider, I ask you, and see how he seeks to start a quarrel against me. 8 And it was so, when Elisha the man of Elohim had heard that the melech of Yisrael had torn his clothes that he sent to the melech, saying, Why have you torn your clothes? Let him come now to me, and he shall know that there is a navi in Yisrael. 9 So Naaman came with his horses and with his mirkavah, and stood at the door of the bayit of Elisha. 10 And Elisha sent a messenger to him, saying, Go and wash in the Yarden River

seven times, and your flesh shall be restored, and you shall be clean. 11 But Naaman was angry, and went away, and said, See, I thought, He will surely come out to me, and stand, and call on the Name of יהוה His Elohim, and wave his hand over the place, and heal the leprosy. 12 Are not Avana and Pharpar, rivers of Dameshek, better than all the mayim of Yisrael? May I not wash in them, and be clean? So he turned and went away in a rage. 13 And his avadim came near, and spoke to him, and said, My abba, if ha navi had told you do some great matter, should you not have done it? How much rather then, when he says to you, Wash, and be clean? 14 Then he went down, and dipped himself seven times in the Yarden River, according to the saying of the man of Elohim: and his flesh was restored like the flesh of a little child, and he was clean. 15 And he returned to the man of Elohim, with all his company, and came, and stood before him: and he said, See, now I know that there is no Elohim in all the earth, but in Yisrael:[2] now therefore, I beg you, take a blessing from your eved. 16 But he said, As יהוה lives, before whom I stand, I will receive nothing. And he urged him to take it; but he refused. 17 And Naaman said, Shall there not then, I beg you, be given to your eved two mule loads of earth? For your eved will from now on offer neither burnt offering nor sacrifice to any other elohim, but to יהוה. 18 In this thing יהוה pardon Your eved, that when my master the melech goes into the bayit of Rimmon to worship there, and he leans on my hand, and I bow myself in the bayit of Rimmon: when I bow down myself in the bayit of Rimmon, let יהוה pardon Your eved in this thing. 19 And he said to him, Go in shalom. So he departed from him a little distance. 20 But Gechazi, the eved of Elisha the man of Elohim, said, See, my master has spared Naaman this Aramean, in not receiving from his hands that which he

---

[1] The matriarchs of Yisrael (Rivkah, Leah and Rachel) were Arameans and the dom of the Arameans is highly prevalent throughout all 12 tribes. Even though they often lived separate from Yisraelites, they are one people with Yisrael. Most of Paul's congregations established in Asia Minor due north of Yisrael, were in modern Turkey or the former Aramean lands. The Aramaic Peshitta uses Arameans througout the Renewed Covenant, as opposed to the word references for "Greek," meaning that non-Jewish Ephraimites had much Aramean dom.

[2] A confession made by returning Arameans in the Renewed Covenant as they rejoin the Commonwealth of Yisrael.

brought: but, as **יהוה** lives, I will run after him, and take something from him. 21 So Gechazi pursued after Naaman. And when Naaman saw him running after him, he got down from the mirkavah to meet him, and said, Is all well? 22 And he said, All is well. My master has sent me, saying, See, even now there have come to me from Mount Ephraim two young men of the sons of ha neviim: give them, I ask you, a talent of silver, and two changes of garments. 23 And Naaman said, Be content, take two talents. And he urged him, and bound two talents of silver in two bags, with two changes of garments, and laid them upon two of his avadim; and they bore them before him. 24 And when he came to a secret place, he took them from their hand, and stored them in the bayit: and he let the men go, and they departed. 25 But he went in, and stood before his master. And Elisha said to him, Where are you coming from Gechazi? And he said, Your eved went nowhere. 26 And he said to him, Did not my lev go with you, when the man turned again from his mirkavah to meet you? Is it a time to receive silver, and to receive garments, and oliveyards, and vineyards, and sheep, and oxen, and men avadim, and female avadim? 27 The leprosy therefore of Naaman shall cleave to you, and to your zera le-olam-va-ed. And he went out from his presence a leper as white as snow.

6 And the sons of ha neviim said to Elisha, See now, the place where we dwell with you is too small for us. 2 Let us go, we ask you, to the Yarden, and take there every man a beam, and let us make us a place there, where we may dwell. And he answered, Go! 3 And one said, Be content, I ask you, and go with your avadim. And he answered, I will go. 4 So he went with them. And when they came to the Yarden, they cut down wood. 5 But as one was cutting a beam, the axe head fell into the mayim: and he cried, and said, Oy Vey! Master! For it was borrowed. 6 And the

man of Elohim said, Where did it fall? And he showed him the place. And he cut down a stick, and cast it in there; and the iron did swim. 7 Therefore said he, Pick it up. And he put out his hand, and took it. 8 Then the melech of Aram warred against Yisrael, and took counsel with his avadim, saying, In such and such a place shall be my camp. 9 And the man of Elohim sent to the melech of Yisrael, saying, Beware that you pass not at this place; for there the Aramaens have come down. 10 And the melech of Yisrael sent to the place where the man of Elohim told him and warned him of, and saved himself there, more than once or twice. 11 Therefore the lev of the melech of Aram was heavy troubled for this thing; and he called his avadim, and said to them, Will you not show me which of us is a traitor for the melech of Yisrael? 12 And one of his avadim said, None, my master, O melech: but Elisha, ha navi that is in Yisrael, tells the melech of Yisrael the words that you speak in your bedroom. 13 And he said, Go and spy where he is, that I may send and get him. And it was told him, saying, See, he is in Dothan. 14 Therefore, he sent there horses, and mirkavot, and great armies: and they came by night, and surrounded the city. 15 And when the eved of the man of Elohim had risen early, and gone forth, see, armies surrounded the city both with horses and mirkavot. And his eved said to him, Oy Vey! My master! What shall we do? 16 And he answered, Fear not: for they that are with us are more than they that be with them.[1] 17 And Elisha made tefillah, and said, **יהוה**; I ask open his eyes, that he may see. And **יהוה** opened the eyes of the young man; and he saw: and, see, the mountain was full of horses and mirkavot of fire all around Elisha. 18 And when they came down to him, Elisha made tefillah to **יהוה**, and said, Destroy this people, I ask you, with blindness. And he destroyed them with blindness according to the word of Elisha.

---

[1] Yirsael is surrounded with legions of YHWH's warring hosts of heaven.

19 And Elisha said to them, This is not the derech, neither is this the city: follow me, and I will bring you to the man whom you seek. But he led them to Shomron. 20 And it came to pass, when they were come into Shomron, that Elisha said, יהוה, open the eyes of these men, that they may see. And יהוה opened their eyes, and they saw; and, see, they were in the midst of Shomron. 21 And the melech of Yisrael said to Elisha, when he saw them, My abba, shall I kill them? Shall I kill them? 22 And he answered, You shall not kill them: would you kill those who you have taken captive with your sword and with your bow? Set lechem and mayim before them, that they may eat and drink, and go to their master. 23 And he prepared great provision for them: and when they had eaten and drank, he sent them away, and they went to their master. So the bands of Aramean raiders came no more into the land of Yisrael. 24 And it came to pass after this, that Ben-Hadad melech of Aram gathered all his armies, and went up, and besieged Shomron. 25 And there was a great famine in Shomron: and, see, they besieged it, until a donkey's head was sold for eighty pieces of silver, and the fourth part of a pint of dove's dropping for five pieces of silver. 26 And as the melech of Yisrael was passing by upon the wall, there cried a woman to him, saying, Help, my master, O melech. 27 And he said, If יהוה does not help you, how shall I help you? From the threshing floor, or from the winepress? 28 And the melech said to her, What bothers you? And she answered, This woman said to me, Give me your son, that we may eat him today, and we will eat my son tomorrow. 29 So we boiled my son, and did eat him: and I said to her on the next day, Give your son, that we may eat him: and she has hidden her son. 30 And it came to pass, when the melech heard the words of the woman, that he tore his clothes; and he passed by upon the wall, and the people looked, and, see, he had sackcloth on his body underneath. 31 Then he said, Elohim do so and more also to me, if the head of Elisha the son of Shaphat shall stay on him this day. 32 But Elisha sat in his bayit, and the zachanim sat with him; and the melech sent a man ahead of him: but before the messenger came to him, he said to the zachanim, See how this son of a murderer has been sent to take away my head? Look, when the messenger comes, shut the door, and hold him back at the door: is not the sound of his master's feet behind him? 33 And while he yet talked with them, see, the messenger came down to him: and he said, See, this evil is from יהוה ; why should I wait for יהוה any longer?

7 Then Elisha said, Shema you the word of יהוה ; This says יהוה, *Tomorrow about this time shall a measure of fine flour be sold for a shekel, and two measures of barley for a shekel, in the gate of Shomron.* 2 Then a master on whose hand the melech leaned answered the man of Elohim, and said, See, if יהוה would make windows in the shamayim, would this thing be? And he said, See, you shall see it with your eyes, but shall not eat of it. 3 And there were four leprous men at the entrance of the gate: and they said one to another, Why do we sit here until we die? 4 If we say, We will enter into the city, then the famine is in the city, and we shall die there: and if we sit still here, we die also. Now therefore come, and let us fall to the armies of the Aramaens: if they save us alive, we shall live; and if they kill us, we shall but die. 5 And they rose up in the twilight, to go to the camp of the Aramaens: and when they were come to the outskirts of the camp of Aram, see, there was no man there. 6 For יהוה had made the armies of the Aramaens to shema a noise of mirkavot, and a noise of horses, even the noise of great armies: and they said one to another, Look, the melech of Yisrael has hired against us the melechim of the Hittites, and the melechim of the Mitzrites, to come upon us. 7 Therefore they arose

and fled in the twilight, and left their tents, and their horses, and their donkeys, even the camp as it was, and fled for their chayim. 8 And when these lepers came to the outskirts of the camp, they went into one tent, and did eat and drink, and carried there silver, and gold, and raiment, and went and hid it; and came again, and entered into another tent, and carried there also, and went and hid it. 9 Then they said one to another, We do not well: this day is a day of tov tidings, and we hold our silence: if we stay until the morning light, some mischief will come upon us: now therefore come, that we may go and tell the melech's household. 10 So they came and called to the porter of the city: and they told them, saying, We came to the camp of the Aramaens, and, see, there was no man there, neither voice of man, but horses tied, and donkeys tied, and the tents as they were. 11 And he called the porters; and they told it to the melech's bayit within. 12 And the melech arose in the night, and said to his avadim, I will now show you what the Aramaens have done to us. They know that we are hungry; therefore they have gone out of the camp to hide themselves in the field, saying, When they come out of the city, we shall catch them alive, and get into the city. 13 And one of his avadim answered and said, Let some take, I ask you, five of the horses that remain, which are left in the city, see, they are as all the multitude of Yisrael that are left in it: see, I say, they are even as all the multitude of the Yisraelites that are consumed: and let us send and see. 14 They took therefore two mirkavah horses; and the melech sent them in the direction of the Aramaens, saying, Go and see. 15 And they went after them to the Yarden: and, see, all the derech was full of garments and vessels, which the Aramaens had cast away in their haste. And the messengers returned, and told the melech. 16 And the people went out, and spoiled the tents of the Aramaens. So a measure of fine flour was sold for a shekel, and two

measures of barley for a shekel, according to the word of יהוה. 17 And the melech appointed the officer on whose hand he leaned to have the charge of the gate: and the people trampled him in the gate, and he died, as the man of Elohim had said, who spoke when the melech came down to him. 18 And it came to pass as the man of Elohim had spoken to the melech, saying, Two measures of barley for a shekel, and a measure of fine flour for a shekel, shall be tomorrow about this time in the gate of Shomron: 19 And that master answered the man of Elohim, and said, Now, see, if יהוה should make windows in the shamayim, should such a thing be? And he said, See, you shall see it with your eyes, but shall not eat of it. 20 And so it came to be for him: for the people trampled him in the gate, and he died.

8 Then spoke Elisha to the woman, whose son he had restored to chayim, saying, Arise, and go with your household, and sojourn wherever you can sojourn: for יהוה has called for a famine; and it shall also come upon the land for seven years. 2 And the woman arose, and obeyed the saying of the man of Elohim: and she went with her household, and sojourned in the land of the Philistines seven years. 3 And it came to pass at the seven years' end, that the woman returned out of the land of the Philistines: and she went forth to cry to the melech for her bayit and for her land. 4 And the melech talked with Gechazi the eved of the man of Elohim, saying, Tell me, I ask you, all the great things that Elisha has done. 5 And it came to pass, as he was telling the melech how he had restored a dead body to chayim, that, see, the woman, whose son he had restored to chayim, cried to the melech for her bayit and for her land. And Gechazi said, My master, O melech, this is the woman, and this is her son, whom Elisha restored to chayim. 6 And when the melech asked the woman, she told him. So the melech appointed to her a certain

officer, saying, Restore all that was hers, and all the fruits of the field since the day that she left the land, even until now. 7 And Elisha came to Dameshek; and Ben-Hadad the melech of Aram was sick; and it was told to him, saying, The man of Elohim has come here. 8 And the melech said to Haza-El, Take a present in your hand, and go, meet the man of Elohim, and inquire of יהוה by him, saying, Shall I be healed from this disease? 9 So Haza-El went to meet him, and took a present with him, even of every tov thing of Dameshek, forty camels' loads, and came and stood before him, and said, Your son Ben-Hadad melech of Aram has sent me to you, saying, Shall I be healed from this disease? 10 And Elisha said to him, Go, say to him, You will certainly be healed: but יהוה has showed me that he shall surely die. 11 And he stared at him, until he was ashamed: and the man of Elohim wept. 12 And Haza-El said, Why does my master weep? And he answered, Because I know the evil that you will do to the children of Yisrael: their strongholds will you set on fire, and their young men will you slay with the sword, and will dash their children, and rip up their women with child. 13 And Haza-El said, But what, is your eved a dog, that he should do this great thing to Yisrael? And Elisha answered, יהוה has showed me that you shall be melech over Aram. 14 So he departed from Elisha, and came to his master; who said to him, What did Elisha say to you? And he answered; He told me that you should surely be healed. 15 And it came to pass the next day, that he took a thick cloth, and dipped it in mayim, and spread it on his face, so that he died: and Haza-El reigned in his place. 16 And in the fifth year of Yehoram the son of Ahav melech of Yisrael, Yehoshaphat being then melech of Yahudah, Yehoram the son of Yehoshaphat melech of Yahudah began to reign. 17 Thirty-two years old was he when he began to reign; and he reigned eight years in Yahrushalayim. 18 And he had his halacha in the derech of the melechim of Yisrael, as did Beit Ahav: for the daughter of Ahav was his wife:[1] and he did evil in the sight of יהוה. 19 Yet יהוה would not destroy Yahudah for David His eved's sake, as He promised him to give him always a light, and his children le-olam-va-ed. 20 In his days Edom revolted from under the hand of Yahudah, and made a melech over themselves. 21 So Yehoram went over to Zair, and all the mirkavot with him: and he rose by night, and killed the Edomites who surrounded him, and the captains of the mirkavot: and the people fled into their tents. 22 Yet Edom revolted from under the hand of Yahudah to this day. Then Livnah revolted at the same time.[2] 23 And the rest of the acts of Yehoram, and all that he did, are they not written in the scroll of the Divre HaYamim about the melechim of Yahudah? 24 And Yehoram slept with his ahvot, and was buried with his ahvot in the city of David: and Ahazyahu his son reigned in his place. 25 In the twelfth year of Yehoram the son of Ahav melech of Yisrael did Ahazyahu the son of Yehoram melech of Yahudah begin to reign. 26 Ahazyahu was twenty-two years of age when he began to reign; and he reigned one year in Yahrushalayim. And his ima's name was Athalyah, the daughter of Omri melech of Yisrael. 27 And he had his halacha in the derech of Beit Ahav, and did evil in the sight of יהוה, as did Beit Ahav: for he was the son-in-law of Beit Ahav. 28 And he went with Yehoram the son of Ahav to the war against Haza-El melech of Aram in Ramoth-Gilead; and the Aramaens wounded Yehoram. 29 And melech Yehoram went back to be healed in Yezreel from the wounds that the Aramaens had given him at Ramah, when he fought against Haza-El melech of Aram. And Ahazyahu the son of Yehoram melech of

---

[1] There was some very limited intermingling between the two-houses after the split.
[2] As seen here even Jewish-Yisrael is full of Edomite and Aramean dom. How much more is Ephraim's dom mixed among the nations?

Yahudah went down to see Yehoram the son of Ahav in Yezreel, because he was sick.

9 And Elisha ha navi called one of the sons of ha neviim, and said to him, Gird up your waste, and take this flask of oil in your hand, and go to Ramoth-Gilead: 2 And when you come there, look for Yehu the son of Yehoshaphat the son of Nimshi, and go in, and make him rise up from among his brothers, and carry him to an inner room; 3 Then take the flask of oil, and pour it on his head, and say, This says יהוה, *I have anointed you melech over Yisrael.* Then open the door, and flee, and stay not. 4 So the young man, even the young man ha navi, went to Ramoth-Gilead. 5 And when he came, see, the captains of the armies were sitting; and he said, I have a message for you, O commander. And Yehu said, For which one of us? And he said, For you, O commander. 6 And he arose, and went into the bayit; and he poured the oil on his head, and said to him, This says יהוה Elohim of Yisrael; *I have anointed you melech over the people of יהוה, even over Yisrael. 7 And you shall kill Beit Ahav your master, that I may avenge the dom of My avadim ha neviim, and the dom of all the avadim of יהוה, at the hands of Isavel. 8 For the whole of Beit Ahav shall perish: and I will cut off from Ahav every male, and him that is shut up and left in Yisrael: 9 And I will make Beit Ahav like Beit Yeravoam the son of Nevat, and like the Beit Baasha the son of Ahiyah: 10 And the dogs shall eat Isavel in the portion of Yezreel, and there shall be none to bury her.* And he opened the door, and fled. 11 Then Yehu came forth to the avadim of his master: and one said to him, Is all well? Why did this crazy man come to you? And he said to them, You know the man, and his communication. 12 And they said, That's a lie! Tell us now. And he said, This and this he spoke to me, saying, This says יהוה, *I have anointed you melech over Yisrael.* 13 Then they hurried and took

every man his garment, and put it under him on the top of the stairs, and blew with shofars, saying, Yehu is melech. 14 So Yehu the son of Yehoshaphat the son of Nimshi conspired against Yehoram. Now Yehoram had kept Ramoth-Gilead, he and all Yisrael, because of Haza-El melech of Aram. 15 But melech Yehoram had returned to be healed in Yezreel from the wounds that the Aramaens had given him, when he fought with Haza-El melech of Aram. And Yehu said, If this is your desire, then let none go forth nor escape out of the city to go to tell it in Yezreel. 16 So Yehu rode in a mirkavah, and went to Yezreel; for Yehoram lay there. And Ahazyahu melech of Yahudah had come down to see Yehoram. 17 And there stood a watchman on the tower in Yezreel, and he saw the company of Yehu as he came, and said, I see a company. And Yehoram said, Take a horseman, and go meet them, and let him say, Is it in shalom? 18 So there went one on horseback to meet him, and said, This says the melech, Is it in shalom? And Yehu said, What have you to do with shalom? Get behind me and follow me. And the watchman told, saying, The messenger came to them, but he did not come back. 19 Then he sent out a second on horseback, who came to them, and said, This says the melech, Is it in shalom? And Yehu answered, What have you to do with shalom? Get behind me and follow me 20 And the watchman told, saying, He came even to them, and does not return: and the driving is like the driving of Yehu the son of Nimshi; for he drives furiously. 21 And Yehoram said, Make ready. And his mirkavah was made ready. And Yehoram melech of Yisrael and Ahazyahu melech of Yahudah went out, each in his mirkavah, and they went out against Yehu, and met him in the field of Navoth the Yezreelite. 22 And it came to pass, when Yehoram saw Yehu, that he said, Is it in shalom, Yehu? And he answered, What shalom, as long as the whoredoms of your ima Isavel and her witchcrafts are so many? 23 And Yehoram turned his hands, and fled, and said to Ahazyahu, There is treachery, O Ahazyahu. 24 And Yehu drew a bow with his full strength, and killed Yehoram between his arms, and the arrow went out at his lev, and he sunk down in his mirkavah. 25 Then said Yehu to Bidkar his captain, Take up, and cast him in the portion of the field of Navoth the Yezreelite: for remember how that, when I and you rode together after Ahav his abba, יהוה laid this burden upon him; 26 *Surely I have seen yesterday the dom of Navoth, and the dom of his sons,* says יהוה; *and I will repay you in this field,* says יהוה. Now therefore take and cast him into the flat of ground, according to the word of יהוה. 27 But when Ahazyahu the melech of Yahudah saw this, he fled by the derech of the Gan-Bayit. And Yehu followed after him, and said, kill him also in the mirkavah. And they did so at the going up to Gur, which is by Yivleam. And he fled to Megiddo, and died there. 28 And his avadim carried him in a mirkavah to Yahrushalayim, and buried him in his tomb with his ahvot in the city of David. 29 And in the eleventh year of Yehoram the son of Ahav began Ahazyahu to reign over Yahudah. 30 And when Yehu was come to Yezreel, Isavel heard of it; and she painted her face, and adorned her head, and looked out a window. 31 And as Yehu entered in at the gate, she said, Has Zimri shalom, who killed his master? 32 And he lifted up his face to the window, and said, Who is on my side? Who? And there looked down at him two or three eunuchs. 33 And he said, Throw her down. So they threw her down: and some of her dom was sprinkled on the wall, and on the horses: and he trampled her under foot. 34 And when he was come in, he did eat and drink, and said, Go, see now this cursed woman, and bury her: for she is a melech's daughter. 35 And they went to bury her: but they found no more than her skull, and the feet, and the palms of her hands. 36 Therefore they came again, and told him. And he said, This is the word of יהוה, which He spoke by His eved Eliyahu the Tishbite, saying, *In the portion of Yezreel shall dogs eat the flesh of Isavel*: 37 And the carcass of Isavel shall be as dung upon the face of the field in the portion of Yezreel; so that they shall not even be able to say, This is Isavel.

10 And Ahav had seventy sons in Shomron. And Yehu wrote letters, and sent to Shomron, to the rulers of Yezreel, to the zachanim, and to them that brought up Ahav's children, saying, 2 Now as soon as this letter comes to you, seeing your master's sons are with you, and there are with you mirkavot and horses, a fenced city also, and armor; 3 Choose the best and most upright of your master's sons, and set him on his abba's throne, and fight for your master's bayit. 4 But they were exceedingly afraid, and said, See, two melechim stood not before him: how then shall we stand? 5 And he that was over the bayit, and he that was over the city, the zachanim also, and the guardians of the children, sent to Yehu, saying, We are your avadim, and will do all that you shall tell us; we will not crown any melech; do what is tov in your eyes. 6 Then he wrote a letter the second time to them, saying, If you are for me, and if you will shema to My voice, take the heads of the men your master's sons, and come to me to Yezreel tomorrow at this time. Now the melech's sons, being seventy persons, were with the great men of the city, who brought them up. 7 And it came to pass, when the letter came to them, that they took the melech's sons, and killed seventy persons, and put their heads in baskets, and sent them to Yezreel. 8 And there came a messenger, and told him, saying, They have brought the heads of the melech's sons. And he said, Lay them in two heaps at the entrance of the gate until the morning. 9 And it came to pass in the morning, that he went out, and stood, and said to all the people, You are tzadik: see, I conspired

against my master, and killed him: but who killed all these? 10 Know now that there shall fall to the earth nothing of the word of יהוה, which יהוה spoke concerning Beit Ahav: for יהוה has done that which He spoke by His eved Eliyahu. 11 So Yehu killed all that remained of Beit Ahav in Yezreel, and all his great men, and his relatives, and his kohanim, until he left him none remaining. 12 And he arose and departed, and came to Shomron. And on the derech he destroyed the bayit of idols. 13 Yehu met with the brothers of Ahazyahu melech of Yahudah, and said, Who are you? And they answered, We are the brothers of Ahazyahu; and we go down to greet the children of the melech and the children of the queen. 14 And he said, Take them alive. And they took them alive, and killed them at the pit of the shearing bayit, even forty-two men; neither did he leave any of them. 15 And when he was departed, he met Yehonadav the son of Rechav coming to meet him: and he saluted him, and said to him, Is your lev right, as my lev is with your lev? And Yehonadav answered, It is. If it is, give me your hand. And he gave him his hand; and he took him up to him into the mirkavah. 16 And he said, Come with me, and see my zeal for יהוה. So they made him ride in his mirkavah. 17 And when he came to Shomron, he killed all that remained to Ahav in Shomron, until he had destroyed him, according to the saying of יהוה, which He spoke by Eliyahu. 18 And Yehu gathered all the people together, and said to them, Ahav served Baal a little; but Yehu shall serve him much. 19 Now therefore call to me all ha neviim of Baal, all his avadim, and all his kohanim; let none be missing: for I have a great sacrifice to do to Baal; whoever shall be missing, he shall not live. But Yehu did it deceptively, to the intent that he might destroy the worshippers of Baal. 20 And Yehu said, Proclaim a solemn meeting for Baal. And they proclaimed it. 21 And Yehu sent through all Yisrael: and all the worshippers of Baal came, so that there was not a man left that did not come. And they came into the bayit of Baal; and the bayit of Baal was full from one end to another.[1] 22 And he said to him that was over the wardrobe, Bring forth garments for all the worshippers of Baal. And he brought them forth garments. 23 And Yehu and Yehonadav the son of Rechav, went into the bayit of Baal, and said to the worshippers of Baal, Search, and look that there be here with you none of the avadim of יהוה, but the worshippers of Baal only.[2] 24 And when they went in to offer sacrifices and burnt offerings, Yehu appointed eighty men outside, and said, If any of the men whom I have brought into your hands escapes, he that lets him go, his chayim shall be in place of the chayim of him that escaped. 25 And it came to pass, as soon as he had made an end of offering the burnt offering, that Yehu said to the guard and to the officers, Go in, and slay them; let none come forth. And they killed them with the edge of the sword; and the guard and the officers cast them out, and went to the city of the bayit of Baal. 26 And they brought forth the images out of the bayit of Baal, and burned them. 27 And they broke down the image of Baal, and broke down the bayit of Baal, and made it a latrine to this day. 28 In this manner Yehu destroyed Baal out of Yisrael. 29 However from the sins of Yeravoam the son of Nevat, who made Yisrael to sin, Yehu departed not from after them, from the golden calves that were in Beth-El, and that were in Dan. 30 And יהוה said to Yehu, *Because you have done well in executing that which is tzadik in My eyes, and have done to Beit Ahav according to all that was in My lev, your children until the fourth generation shall sit on the throne of Yisrael.* 31 But Yehu took no heed to have his halacha in the Torah of יהוה Elohim of Yisrael with all his lev: for he departed not from the sins of Yeravoam,

---

[1] The "lord's" followers always get large crowds. YHWH's people on the other hand are a small remnant.
[2] YHWH's people are spared from the fate of all "lord" worshippers.

who made Yisrael to sin. 32 In those days יהוה began to cut Yisrael short: and Haza-El killed them in all the borders of Yisrael; 33 From Yarden eastward, all the land of Gilead, the Gadites, and the Reuvenites, and the Menashshehites, from Aroer, which is by the river Arnon, even Gilead and Bashan. 34 Now the rest of the acts of Yehu, and all that he did, and all his might, are they not written in the scroll of the Divre HaYamim about the melechim of Yisrael? 35 And Yehu slept with his ahvot: and they buried him in Shomron. And Yehoahaz his son reigned in his place. 36 And the time that Yehu reigned over Yisrael in Shomron was twenty-eight years.

11 And when Athalyah the ima of Ahazyahu saw that her son was dead, she arose and destroyed all the royal offspring. 2 But Yehosheva, the daughter of melech Yehoram, sister of Ahazyahu, took Yehoash the son of Ahazyahu and stole him from among the melech's sons that were killed; and they hid him, even him and his nurse, in the bedroom from Athalyah, so that he was not killed. 3 And he was with her hidden in the Bayit of יהוה six years. And Athalyah did reign over the land. 4 And the seventh year Yehoyada sent and got the rulers over hundreds, with the captains and the guard, and brought them to him into the Bayit of יהוה, and made a covenant with them, and took an oath from them in the Bayit of יהוה, and showed them the melech's son. 5 And he commanded them, saying, This is the thing that you shall do; A third part of you that enter in on the Shabbat shall even be guards of the melech's bayit; 6 And a third part shall be at the Gate of Sur; and a third part at the gate behind the guard: so shall you keep the watch of the bayit; that it is not broken down. 7 And two parts of all that go forth on the Shabbat, even they shall keep the watch of the Bayit of יהוה for the melech. 8 And you shall surround the melech all around, every man with his weapons in his hand: and he that comes inside the ranks, let him be killed: and be you with the melech as he goes out and as he comes in. 9 And the captains over the hundreds did according to all things that Yehoyada the kohen commanded: and they took every man his men that were to come in on the Shabbat, with them that should go out on the Shabbat, and came to Yehoyada the kohen. 10 And to the captains over hundreds did the kohen give melech David's spears and shields, that were in the Beit HaMikdash of יהוה. 11 And the guard stood, every man with his weapons in his hand, all around the melech, from the right corner of the Beit HaMikdash to the left corner of the Beit HaMikdash, along by the altar of the Beit HaMikdash. 12 And he brought forth the melech's son, and put the keter upon him, and gave him the testimony; and they made him melech, and anointed him; and they clapped their hands, and said, Le-Chayim to the melech. 13 And when Athalyah heard the noise of the guards and of the people, she came to the people into the Beit HaMikdash of יהוה. 14 And when she looked, see, the melech stood by a pillar, as the manner was, and the princes and the trumpeters by the melech, and all the people of the land rejoiced, and blew with shofars: and Athalyah tore her clothes, and cried, Treason! Treason! 15 But Yehoyada the kohen commanded the captains of the hundreds, the officers of the armies, and said to them, Taker her away outside the ranks: and whoever follows her kill with the sword. For the kohen had said, Let her not be killed in the Bayit of יהוה. 16 And they laid hands on her; and she went by the derech that the horses came into the melech's bayit: and there was she killed. 17 And Yehoyada made a covenant between יהוה and the melech and the people that they should be יהוה's people; between the melech also and the people. 18 And all the people of the land went into the bayit of Baal, and broke it down; his altars and his images they broke in pieces

fully, and killed Mattan the pagan priest of Baal before the altars. And the kohen appointed officers over the Bayit of יהוה. 19 And he took the rulers over hundreds, and the captains, and the guard, and all the people of the land; and they brought down the melech from the Bayit of יהוה, and came by the derech of the gate of the guard to the melech's bayit. And he sat on the throne of the melechim. 20 And all the people of the land rejoiced, and the city was in shalom: and they killed Athalyah with the sword next to the melech's bayit. 21 Seven years old was Yehoash when he began to reign.

12 In the seventh year of Yehu, Yehoash began to reign; and forty years he reigned in Yahrushalayim. And his ima's name was Ziviah of Beer-Sheva. 2 And Yehoash did that which was right in the sight of יהוה all his days in which Yehoyada the kohen instructed him. 3 But the temples of idols were not taken away: the people still sacrificed and burnt incense in the temples of idols. 4 And Yehoash said to the kohanim, All the silver of the dedicated things that is brought into the Bayit of יהוה, even the silver of every one's assessment - the silver that every man has is assessed - and all the silver that comes into any man's lev to freely bring into the Bayit of יהוה, 5 Let the kohanim take for themselves, every man from his friend: and let them repair the damages of the bayit, wherever any damage shall be found. 6 But it was so, that in the twenty-third year of melech Yehoash the kohanim had not repaired the damages of the Bayit. 7 Then melech Yehoash called for Yehoyada the kohen, and the other kohanim, and said to them, Why did you not repair the damages of the Bayit? Now therefore receive no more silver from your friends, but deliver it for the repairing of the Bayit. 8 And the kohanim consented to receive no more silver from the people, neither to repair the damages of the Bayit.

9 But Yehoyada the kohen took a chest, and bore a hole in the lid of it, and set it beside the altar, on the right side as one comes into the Bayit of יהוה: and the kohanim that kept the door put in it all the silver that was brought into the Bayit of יהוה. 10 And it was so, when they saw that there was much silver in the chest, that the melech's sopher and the Kohen HaGadol came up, and they put up in bags, and took the silver that was found in the Bayit of יהוה. 11 And they gave the silver, being weighed, into the hands of them that did the work; who had the oversight of the Bayit of יהוה: and they laid it out to the carpenters and builders, who worked upon the Bayit of יהוה, 12 And to masons, and cutters of stone, and to buy timber and hewed stone to repair the damages of the Bayit of יהוה, and for all that was laid out for the Bayit to repair it. 13 However there were not made for the Bayit of יהוה bowls of silver, snuffers, basons, shofars, any vessels of gold, or vessels of silver, from the silver that was brought into the Bayit of יהוה: 14 But they gave that to the workmen, and repaired with it the Bayit of יהוה. 15 Moreover they did not ask for an accounting from the men, into whose hand they delivered the silver to be paid to the workmen: for they dealt faithfully. 16 The silver for the trespass offerings and the silver for the sin offerings were not brought into the Bayit of יהוה: it belonged to the kohanim. 17 Then Haza-El melech of Aram went up, and fought against Gath, and took it: and Haza-El set his face to go up to Yahrushalayim. 18 And Yehoash melech of Yahudah took all the set-apart things that Yehoshaphat, and Yehoram, and Ahazyahu, his ahvot, melechim of Yahudah, had dedicated, and his own set-apart things, and all the gold that was found in the treasures of the Bayit of יהוה and in the melech's bayit, and sent it to Haza-El melech of Aram: and he went away from Yahrushalayim. 19 And the rest of the acts of Yehoash, and all that he did, are they not written in the scroll of the

Divre HaYamim of the melechim of Yahudah? 20 And his avadim arose, and made a conspiracy, and killed Yehoash in the bayit of Millo that goes down to Silla. 21 For Yozachar the son of Shimath, and Yehozavad the son of Shomer, his avadim, killed him, and he died; and they buried him with his ahvot in the city of David: and Amatsyah his son reigned in his place.

13 In the twenty-third year of Yehoash the son of Ahazyahu melech of Yahudah Yehoahaz the son of Yehu began to reign over Yisrael in Shomron, and reigned seventeen years. 2 And he did that which was evil in the sight of יהוה, and followed the sins of Yeravoam the son of Nevat, who made Yisrael to sin; he departed not from them. 3 And the anger of יהוה was kindled against Yisrael, and He delivered them into the hand of Haza-El melech of Aram, and into the hand of Ben-Hadad the son of Haza-El, all their days. 4 And Yehoahaz besought יהוה, and יהוה listened to him: for He saw the oppression of Yisrael, because the melech of Aram oppressed them. 5 And יהוה gave Yisrael a savior, so that they went out from under the hand of the Aramaens: and the children of Yisrael dwelt in their tents, as before. 6 Nevertheless they departed not from the sins of Beit Yeravoam, who made Yisrael sin, but walked in it: and there remained the Asherah also in Shomron. 7 For He left of Yehoahaz's army only fifty horsemen, and ten mirkavot, and ten thousand footmen; for the melech of Aram had destroyed them, and had made them like the dust at threshing. 8 Now the rest of the acts of Yehoahaz, and all that he did, and his might, are they not written in the scroll of the Divre HaYamim about the melechim of Yisrael? 9 And Yehoahaz slept with his ahvot; and they buried him in Shomron: and Yehoash his son reigned in his place. 10 In the thirty-seventh year of Yehoash melech of Yahudah began Yehoash the son of Yehoahaz to reign over Yisrael in Shomron, and reigned sixteen years. 11 And he did that which was evil in the sight of יהוה; he departed not from all the sins of Yeravoam the son of Nevat, who made Yisrael, sin: but he had his halacha in it. 12 And the rest of the acts of Yehoash, and all that he did, and his might with which he fought against Amatsyah melech of Yahudah, are they not written in the scroll of the Divre HaYamim about the melechim of Yisrael? 13 And Yehoash slept with his ahvot; and Yeravoam sat upon his throne: and Yehoash was buried in Shomron with the melechim of Yisrael. 14 Now Elisha had fallen sick and died of his sickness. And Yehoash the melech of Yisrael came down to him, and wept over his face, and said, O My abba, My abba, the Mirkavah of Yisrael, and their horsemen. 15 And Elisha said to him, Take bow and arrows. And he took to him bow and arrows. 16 And he said to the melech of Yisrael, Put your hand upon the bow. And he put his hand upon it: and Elisha put his hands upon the melech's hands. 17 And he said, Open the window eastward. And he opened it. Then Elisha said, Shoot. And he shot. And he said, The arrow of יהוה's deliverance, and the arrow of deliverance from Aram: for you shall kill the Aramaens in Aphek, until you have consumed them. 18 And he said, Take the arrows. And he took them. And he said to the melech of Yisrael, strike the ground. And he struck it three times, and stopped. 19 And the man of Elohim was angry with him, and said, You should have struck it five or six times; then you would have smitten Aram until you had consumed it: whereas now you shall smite Aram only three times. 20 And Elisha died, and they buried him. And the bands of the Moavites invaded the land at the spring of the year. 21 And it came to pass, as they were burying a man, that, see, they saw a band of raiding men; and they cast the man into the tomb of Elisha: and when the man was let down, and touched the bones of Elisha, he revived, and stood up on his feet.

22 But Haza-El melech of Aram oppressed Yisrael all the days of Yehoahaz. 23 And יהוה was full of unmerited favor to them, and had compassion on them, and had respect to them, because of His covenant with Avraham, Yitzchak, and Yaakov, and would not destroy them, neither cast them from His presence as yet. 24 So Haza-El melech of Aram died; and Ben-Hadad his son reigned in his place. 25 And Yehoash the son of Yehoahaz took again out of the hand of Ben-Hadad the son of Haza-El the cities, which he had taken out of the hand of Yehoahaz his abba by war. Three times did Yehoash beat him, and recovered the cities of Yisrael.

14 In the second year of Yehoash son of Yehoahaz melech of Yisrael reigned Amatsyah the son of Yehoash melech of Yahudah. 2 He was twenty-five years old when he began to reign, and reigned twenty-nine years in Yahrushalayim. And his ima's name was Yehoaddan of Yahrushalayim. 3 And he did that which was right in the sight of יהוה, yet not like David his abba: he did according to all things as Yehoash his abba did. 4 However the temples of idols were not taken away: as yet the people did sacrifice and burnt incense in the temples of idols. 5 And it came to pass, as soon as the malchut was confirmed in his hand, that he killed his avadim that had killed the melech his abba. 6 But the children of the murderers he killed not: according to that which is written in the scroll of the Torah of Moshe, in which יהוה commanded, saying, The ahvot shall not be put to death for the children, nor the children be put to death for the ahvot; but every man shall be put to death for his own sin. 7 He killed of Edom in the Valley of Salt ten thousand, and took Selah by war, and called the name of it Yoktheel to this day. 8 Then Amatsyah sent messengers to Yehoash, the son of Yehoahaz son of Yehu, melech of Yisrael, saying, Come, let us look one another in the face. 9 And Yehoash the melech of Yisrael sent to Amatsyah melech of Yahudah, saying, The thistle that was in Levanon sent to the cedar that was in Levanon, saying, Give your daughter to my son as a wife: and there passed by a wild beast that was in Levanon, and trampled down the thistle. 10 You have indeed killed Edom, and your lev has lifted you up: be esteemed by this, and stay at home: for why should you meddle to your hurt, that you should fall - you and Yahudah with you? 11 But Amatsyah would not shema. Therefore Yehoash melech of Yisrael went up; and he and Amatsyah melech of Yahudah looked one another in the face at Beth-Shemesh, which belongs to Yahudah. 12 And Yahudah was smitten before Yisrael; and they fled every man to their tents. 13 And Yehoash melech of Yisrael took Amatsyah melech of Yahudah, the son of Yehoash the son of Ahazyahu, at Beth-Shemesh, and came to Yahrushalayim, and broke down the wall of Yahrushalayim from the Gate of Ephraim to the Corner Gate, four hundred cubits. 14 And he took all the gold and silver, and all the vessels that were found in the Bayit of יהוה, and in the treasures of the melech's bayit, and he took hostages, and returned to Shomron. 15 Now the rest of the acts of Yehoash which he did, and his might, and how he fought with Amatsyah melech of Yahudah, are they not written in the scroll of the Divre HaYamim about the melechim of Yisrael? 16 And Yehoash slept with his ahvot, and was buried in Shomron with the melechim of Yisrael; and Yeravoam his son reigned in his place. 17 And Amatsyah the son of Yehoash melech of Yahudah lived after the death of Yehoash son of Yehoahaz melech of Yisrael fifteen years. 18 And the rest of the acts of Amatsyah, are they not written in the scroll of the Divre HaYamim about the melechim of Yahudah? 19 Now they made a conspiracy against him in Yahrushalayim: and he fled to Lachish; but they sent after him to Lachish, and killed him there.

20 And they brought him on horses: and he was buried at Yahrushalayim with his ahvot in the city of David. 21 And all the people of Yahudah took Azaryah, who was sixteen years old, and made him melech instead of his abba Amatsyah. 22 He built Elath, and restored it to Yahudah, after that the melech slept with his ahvot. 23 In the fifteenth year of Amatsyah the son of Yehoash melech of Yahudah Yeravoam the son of Yehoash melech of Yisrael began to reign in Shomron, and reigned forty-one years. 24 And he did that which was evil in the sight of יהוה: he departed not from all the sins of Yeravoam the son of Nevat, who made Yisrael to sin. 25 He restored the coast of Yisrael from the entering of Hamath to the sea of the plain, according to the word of יהוה Elohim of Yisrael, which he spoke by the hand of his eved Yonah, the son of Amittai, ha navi, who was of Gath-Hepher. 26 For יהוה saw the affliction of Yisrael, that it was very bitter: for there was not any shut up, nor any left, nor any helper for Yisrael. 27 And יהוה said not that he would blot out the name of Yisrael from under the shamayim: but he saved them by the hand of Yeravoam the son of Yehoash. 28 Now the rest of the acts of Yeravoam, and all that he did, and his might, how he fought, and how he recovered Dameshek, and Hamath, which belonged to Yahudah, for Yisrael, are they not written in the scroll of the Divre HaYamim about the melechim of Yisrael? 29 And Yeravoam slept with his ahvot, even with the melechim of Yisrael; and Zecharyah his son reigned in his place.

15 In the twenty-seventh year of Yeravoam melech of Yisrael began Azaryah son of Amatsyah melech of Yahudah to reign. 2 Sixteen years old was he when he began to reign, and he reigned fifty-two years in Yahrushalayim. And his ima's name was Yecholyah of Yahrushalayim. 3 And he did that which was right in the sight of יהוה, according to all that his abba Amatsyah had done; 4 But the temple of idols was not removed: the people sacrificed and burnt incense still in the temple of idols. 5 And יהוה killed the melech, so that he was a leper to the day of his death, and dwelt in a separate bayit. And Yotham the melech's son was over the bayit, bringing mishpat to the people of the land. 6 And the rest of the acts of Azaryah, and all that he did, are they not written in the scroll of the Divre HaYamim about the melechim of Yahudah? 7 So Azaryah slept with his ahvot; and they buried him with his ahvot in the city of David: and Yotham his son reigned in his place. 8 In the thirty-eighth year of Azaryah melech of Yahudah did Zecharyah the son of Yeravoam reign over Yisrael in Shomron six months. 9 And he did that which was evil in the sight of יהוה, as his ahvot had done: he departed not from the sins of Yeravoam the son of Nevat, who made Yisrael to sin. 10 And Shallum the son of Yavesh conspired against him, and killed him before the people, and reigned in his place. 11 And the rest of the acts of Zecharyah, see, they are written in the scroll of the Divre HaYamim of the melechim about Yisrael. 12 This was the word of יהוה which he spoke to Yehu, saying, Your sons shall sit on the throne of Yisrael to the fourth generation. And so it came to pass. 13 Shallum the son of Yavesh began to reign in the thirty-ninth year of Uzziyah melech of Yahudah; and he reigned a full month in Shomron. 14 For Menachem the son of Gadi went up from Tirtzah, and came to Shomron, and killed Shallum the son of Yavesh in Shomron, and reigned in his place. 15 And the rest of the acts of Shallum, and his conspiracy which he made, see, they are written in the scroll of the Divre HaYamim about the melechim of Yisrael. 16 Then Menachem killed Tiphsah, and all that were in it, and the borders from Tirzah: because they did not open it to him, therefore he killed it; and all the women in it that were with child he ripped open. 17 In the thirty-ninth year of Azaryah melech of Yahudah began

Menachem the son of Gadi to reign over Yisrael, and reigned ten years in Shomron. 18 And he did that which was evil in the sight of **יהוה**: he departed not all his days from the sins of Yeravoam the son of Nevat, who made Yisrael to sin. 19 And Pul the melech of Ashshur came against the land: and Menachem gave Pul a thousand talents of silver, that his hand might be with him to confirm the malchut in his hand. 20 And Menachem exacted the silver of Yisrael, even of all the mighty men of wealth, of each man fifty shekels of silver, to give to the melech of Ashshur. So the melech of Ashshur turned back, and stayed not there in the land. 21 And the rest of the acts of Menachem, and all that he did, are they not written in the scroll of the Divre HaYamim about the melechim of Yisrael? 22 And Menachem slept with his ahvot; and Pekahyah his son reigned in his place. 23 In the fiftieth year of Azaryah melech of Yahudah, Pekahyah the son of Menachem began to reign over Yisrael in Shomron, and reigned two years. 24 And he did that which was evil in the sight of **יהוה**: he departed not from the sins of Yeravoam the son of Nevat, who made Yisrael to sin. 25 But Pekah the son of Remalyah, a captain of his, conspired against him, and killed him in Shomron, in the palace of the melech's bayit, with Argov and Arieh, and with him fifty men of the Gileadites: and he killed him, and reigned in his room. 26 And the rest of the acts of Pekahyah, and all that he did, see, they are written in the scroll of the Divre HaYamim of the melechim of Yisrael. 27 In the fifty-second year of Azaryah melech of Yahudah Pekah the son of Remalyah began to reign over Yisrael in Shomron, and reigned twenty years. 28 And he did that which was evil in the sight of **יהוה** : he departed not from the sins of Yeravoam the son of Nevat, who made Yisrael to sin. 29 In the days of Pekah melech of Yisrael came Tiglath-Pileser melech of Ashshur, and took Iyon, and Avel-Beth-Maachah, and Yonoah, and

Kedesh, and Hatzor, and Gilead, and Galilee, all the land of Naphtali, and carried them captive to Ashshur.[1] 30 And Hoshea the son of Elah made a conspiracy against Pekah the son of Remalyah, and killed him, and killed him, and reigned in his place, in the twentieth year of Yotham the son of Uzziyah. 31 And the rest of the acts of Pekah, and all that he did, see, they are written in the scroll of the Divre HaYamim about the melechim of Yisrael. 32 In the second year of Pekah the son of Remalyah melech of Yisrael began Yotham the son of Uzziyah melech of Yahudah to reign. 33 Twenty-five years old was he when he began to reign, and he reigned sixteen years in Yahrushalayim. And his ima's name was Yerusha, the daughter of Tzadok. 34 And he did that which was right in the sight of **יהוה**: he did according to all that his abba Uzziyah had done. 35 But the temple of idols, were not removed: the people sacrificed and burned incense still in the temple of idols. He built the Higher Gate of the Bayit of **יהוה**. 36 Now the rest of the acts of Yotham, and all that he did, are they not written in the scroll of the Divre HaYamim about the melechim of Yahudah? 37 In those days **יהוה** began to send against Yahudah Rezin the melech of Aram, and Pekah the son of Remalyah. 38 And Yotham slept with his ahvot, and was buried with his ahvot in the city of David his abba: and Ahaz his son reigned in his place.

16 In the seventeenth year of Pekah the son of Remalyah Ahaz the son of Yotham melech of Yahudah began to reign. 2 Twenty years old was Ahaz when he began to reign, and reigned sixteen years in Yahrushalayim, and did not that which was right in the sight of **יהוה** His Elohim, like David his abba. 3 But he had his halacha in the derech of the melechim of

---

[1] The north fell in stages of Assyrian captivity. This first invasion probably was around 735 BCE under Tiglath Pilser the third, with Samaria the capital falling finally in 721 BCE under the attack of Sargon the second.

Yisrael, and made his son to pass through the fire, according to the abominations of the heathen, whom יהוה cast out from before the children of Yisrael. 4 And he sacrificed and burnt incense in the temple of idols, and on the hills, and under every green eytz. 5 Then Rezin melech of Aram and Pekah son of Remalyah melech of Yisrael came up to Yahrushalayim to war: and they besieged Ahaz, but could not overcome him. 6 At that time Rezin melech of Aram recovered Elath for Aram, and drove the men of Yahudah from Elath: and the Aramaens came to Elath, and dwelt there to this day. [1] 7 So Ahaz sent messengers to Tiglath-Pileser melech of Ashshur, saying, I am your eved and your son: come up, and save me out of the hand of the melech of Aram, and out of the hand of the melech of Yisrael, who rise up against me. 8 And Ahaz took the silver and gold that was found in the Bayit of יהוה, and in the treasures of the melech's bayit, and sent it for a present to the melech of Ashshur. 9 And the melech of Ashshur listened to him: for the melech of Ashshur went up against Dameshek, and took it, and carried the people of it captive to Kir, and killed Rezin. 10 And melech Ahaz went to Dameshek to meet Tiglath-Pileser melech of Ashshur, and saw an altar that was at Dameshek: and melech Ahaz sent to Uriyah the kohen a sketch of the altar, and its pattern, according to all its workmanship. 11 And Uriyah the kohen built an altar according to all that melech Ahaz had sent from Dameshek: so Uriyah the kohen made it before melech Ahaz came from Dameshek. 12 And when the melech had come from Dameshek, the melech saw the altar: and the melech approached the altar, and offered on it. 13 And he burnt his burnt offering and his grain offering, and poured his drink offering, and sprinkled the dom of his shalom offerings, upon the altar. 14 And

he brought also the bronze altar, which was before יהוה, from the forefront of the Bayit, from between the altar and the Bayit of יהוה, and put it on the north side of the altar. 15 And melech Ahaz commanded Uriyah the kohen, saying, Upon the great altar burn the shachrit burnt offering, and the ma'ariv grain offering, and the melech's burnt sacrifice, and his grain offering, with the burnt offering of all the people of the land and their grain offering, and their drink offerings; and sprinkle upon it all the dom of the burnt offering, and all the dom of the sacrifice: and the bronze altar shall be for me to inquire by. 16 This did Uriyah the kohen, according to all that melech Ahaz commanded. 17 And melech Ahaz cut off the borders of the bases, and removed the laver from off them; and took down the sea from off the bronze oxen that were under it, and put it upon a pavement of stones. 18 And the shelter for the Shabbat that they had built in the bayit, and the melech's entry outside, he took from the Bayit of יהוה for the melech of Ashshur. 19 Now the rest of the acts of Ahaz which he did, are they not written in the scroll of the Divre HaYamim about the melechim of Yahudah? 20 And Ahaz slept with his ahvot, and was buried with his ahvot in the city of David: and Hizqiyahu his son reigned in his place.

17 In the twelfth year of Ahaz melech of Yahudah began Hoshea the son of Elah to reign in Shomron over Yisrael nine years. 2 And he did that which was evil in the sight of יהוה, but not as the melechim of Yisrael that were before him. 3 Against him came up Shalmaneser melech of Ashshur; and Hoshea became his eved, and gave him presents.[2] 4 And the melech of Ashshur found Hoshea in a conspiracy: for he had sent messengers to Sho melech of Mitzrayim, and brought no present to the melech of Ashshur, as he had done year by year: therefore the melech of Ashshur arrested him, and bound him in prison.

---

[1] The Arameans lived in Yisrael proper on and off throughout Yisrael's history and often mixed with Yisrael, becoming Yisrael, as in the case of the Aramean matriarchs of our forefathers.

[2] The final fall of Ephraim Yisrael under Shalmaneser.

5 Then the melech of Ashshur came up throughout all the land, and went up to Shomron, and besieged it three years.[1] 6 In the ninth year of Hoshea the melech of Ashshur took Shomron, and carried Yisrael away into Ashshur, and placed them in Chalah and in Havor by the River Gozan, and in the cities of the Medes.[2][3][4] 7 For so it was, that the children of Yisrael[5] had sinned against יהוה their Elohim, who had brought them up out of the land of Mitzrayim, from under the hand of Pharoah melech of Mitzrayim, and had feared other elohim, 8 And walked in the chukim of the heathen, whom יהוה cast out from before the children of Yisrael, and of the melechim of Yisrael, which they had made. 9 And the children of Yisrael did secretly those things that were not right against יהוה their Elohim, and they built themselves temples of idols in all their cities, from the watchtower to the walled city. 10 And they set up images and Asherim in every high hill, and under every green eytz: 11 And there they burnt incense in all the temples of idols, as did the heathen whom יהוה carried away before them; and worked wicked things to provoke יהוה to anger: 12 For they served idols, of which יהוה had said to them, You shall not do this thing. 13 Yet יהוה testified against Yisrael, and against Yahudah, by all ha neviim, and by all the seers, saying, Make teshuvah from your evil halachot, and keep My mitzvot and My chukim, according to all the Torah which I commanded your ahvot, and which I sent to you by My avadim ha neviim.

14 But they would not shema, but hardened their necks, like the necks of their ahvot, that did not believe in יהוה their Elohim. 15 And they rejected His chukim, and His covenant that He made with their ahvot, and His testimonies which He testified against them; and they followed vanity, and became vain, and went after the heathen that were all around them, concerning whom יהוה had ordered them, that they should not do like them. 16 And they left all the mitzvot of יהוה their Elohim, and made molten images, even two calves, and made an Asherah, and worshipped all the hosts of the shamayim, and served Baal. 17 And they caused their sons and their daughters to pass through the fire, and used divination and enchantments, and sold themselves to do evil in the sight of יהוה, to provoke Him to anger. 18 Therefore יהוה was very angry with Yisrael, and removed them out of His sight: there was none left but the tribe of Yahudah only.[6] 19 Also Yahudah did not guard the mitzvot of יהוה their Elohim, but had their halacha in the chukim of Yisrael that they made.[7] 20 And יהוה rejected all the zera of Yisrael,[8] and afflicted them, and delivered them into the hand of spoilers, until He had cast them out of His sight. 21 For He tore Yisrael away from Beit David; and they made Yeravoam the son of Nevat melech: and Yeravoam drove Yisrael away from following יהוה, and made them sin a great sin. 22 For the children of Yisrael had their halacha in all the sins of Yeravoam that he did; they departed not from them; 23 Until יהוה removed Yisrael out of His sight, as He had said by all His avadim ha neviim. So Yisrael was carried away out of their own land to Ashshur until this day.[9] 24 And the melech of Ashshur

---

[1] Final assault.
[2] Fall of the capital.
[3] These areas were later key cities of the Medo-Persian Empire. This exile is 200 years before Yahudah was driven to Babylon. The Ephraimite exile was beyond the river Euphrates in a northeast direction, whereas as the Yahudim went to the area of the River Cheber due east into Babylon. There were two-houses, in two different dispersions, at two different times. They were not the same people at that time.
[4] Halah, Habor and Gozan were in the Mesopotamian region of the Assyrian empire, but the cities of the Medes were located southeast of the Caspian Sea in modern Iran. It is likely that the Assyrians settled the Israelites in many different areas of their empire (not just Nineveh), in order to prevent them from consolidating their strength; "The Lost Ten Tribes Of Israel Found," Steven M. Collins, p. 119.
[5] House of Yisrael in context.

[6] Today as then, the tribes of Ephraim are not existing anymore as a independent sovereign nation, but are in fact being called out and rescued from the nations on an individual basis, one by one, by the Tov News of Moshiach Yahshua.
[7] Both houses became abominable in His sight.
[8] Ephraim.
[9] The exile remains in effect and has never ended, until the Tov News is proclaimed and received by truth seeking individuals.

brought men from Bavel, and from Cuthah, and from Ava, and from Hamath, and from Sepharvayim, and placed them in the cities of Shomron instead of the children of Yisrael: and they possessed Shomron, and dwelt in the cities thereof.[1] 25 And so it was at the beginning of their dwelling there, that they feared not יהוה: therefore יהוה sent lions among them, that killed some of them. 26 Therefore they spoke to the melech of Ashshur, saying, The nations whom you have removed, and placed in the cities of Shomron, know not the manner of the Elohim of the land: therefore he has sent lions among them, and, see, they are being killed, because they know not the manner of the Elohim of the land. 27 Then the melech of Ashshur commanded, saying, Carry there one of the kohanim whom you brought from there; and let them go and dwell there, and let him teach them the manner of the Elohim of the land. 28 Then one of the kohanim whom they had carried away from Shomron came and dwelt in Beth-El, and taught them how they should fear יהוה. 29 Yet every nation made elohim of their own, and put them in the bayits of the idol temples that the Shomronim had made, every nation in their cities in which they dwelt. 30 And the men of Bavel made Succoth-Benoth, and the men of Cuth made Nergal, and the men of Hamath made Ashima, 31 And the Avites made Nivhaz and Tartak, and the Sepharvites burnt their children in fire to Adram-Melech and Anam-Melech, the elohim of Sepharvaim. 32 So they feared יהוה, but also made for themselves from the lowest of them priests for the idol temples, who sacrificed for them in the bayits of the idol temples. 33 They feared יהוה, but they also served their own elohim, after the manner of the nations whom they carried away from

there.[2] 34 To this day they do after their former manners and behaviors: they fear not יהוה, neither do they follow His chukim, or ordinances, or Torah or mitzvot that יהוה commanded the children of Yaakov, whom he named Yisrael;[3] 35 With whom יהוה had made a covenant, and charged them saying, You shall not fear other elohim, nor bow yourselves to them, nor serve them, nor sacrifice to them: 36 But יהוה, who brought you up out of the land of Mitzrayim with great power and an stretched-out Arm, Him shall you fear, and Him shall you worship, and to Him shall you do sacrifice. 37 And the chukim, and the mishpatim, and the Torah, and the mitzvot, which He wrote for you, you shall observe to do le-olam-va-ed; and you shall not fear other elohim. 38 And the covenant that I have made with you you shall not forget; neither shall you fear other elohim. 39 But יהוה Your Elohim you shall fear; and He shall deliver you out of the hand of all your enemies. 40 But they did not shema, but they did after their former manners and behaviors. 41 So these nations feared יהוה, and also served their graven images, both their children, and their children's children: as did their ahvot, so do they to this day.[4]

18 Now it came to pass in the third year of Hoshea son of Elah melech of Yisrael, that Hizqiyahu the son of Ahaz melech of Yahudah began to reign. 2 Twenty-five years old was he when he began to reign; and he reigned twenty-nine years in Yahrushalayim. His ima's name also was Avi, the daughter of Zecharyah. 3 And he did that which was right in the sight of יהוה, according to all that David

---

[1] Their descendants were the much-despised Samaritans of the Renewed Covenant. They were hybrids between the Ephraimites and Assyrians settlers; who were settled in the former lands of victory. So as the Ephraimites came to Assyria; so did the Assyrians come to Ephraim in the north of Yisrael.

[2] The problem with Yisraelites in exile today and the words religions as well, is the deadly mixture of truth and error, where the truth is obscured by the error, and the error chokes the seeker of truth. This deadly combination is far more dangerous and nefarious than benign paganism itself.
[3] Until this very day most of the earth's 3-4 billion dom Yisraelites do not follow his Torah. Yahudah does not follow the living Torah Yahshua and Ephraim does not follow the written Torah. So both houses continue in partial darkness.
[4] An ongoing problem in Yisrael. Mixed worship of truth and error, or the tree of the knowledge of tov and evil that brings death.

his abba did. 4 He removed the idol temples, and broke the images, and cut down the Asherim, and broke in pieces the bronze serpent that Moshe had made: for in those days the children of Yisrael did burn incense to it: and called it Nehushtan. 5 He trusted in יהוה Elohim of Yisrael; so that after him was none like him among all the melechim of Yahudah, nor any that were before him. 6 For he clave to יהוה, and departed not from following Him, but kept His mitzvot, which יהוה commanded Moshe. 7 And יהוה was with him; and prospered him wherever he went: and he rebelled against the melech of Ashshur, and did not serve him. 8 He killed the Philistines, even to Gaza, and the borders of it, from the Tower of the Watchmen to the fenced city. 9 And it came to pass in the fourth year of melech Hizqiyahu, which was the seventh year of Hoshea son of Elah melech of Yisrael, that Shalmaneser melech of Ashshur came up against Shomron, and besieged it. 10 And at the end of three years they took it:[1] even in the sixth year of Hizqiyahu, that is the ninth year of Hoshea melech of Yisrael, Shomron was taken. 11 And the melech of Ashshur did carry away Yisrael to Ashshur, and put them in Chalah and in Chavor by the River Gozan, and in the cities of the Medes: 12 Because they obeyed not the voice of יהוה their Elohim, but transgressed His covenant, and all that Moshe the eved of יהוה commanded, and would not shema to them, nor do them. 13 Now in the fourteenth year of melech Hizqiyahu did Sanheriv melech of Ashshur come up against all the fenced cities of Yahudah, and took them. 14 And Hizqiyahu melech of Yahudah sent to the melech of Ashshur to Lachish, saying, I have done wrong; return from me: that which you put on me will I bear. And the melech of Ashshur appointed to Hizqiyahu melech of Yahudah three hundred talents of silver and thirty talents of gold. 15 And

Hizqiyahu gave him all the silver that was found in the Bayit of יהוה, and in the treasures of the melech's bayit. 16 At that time did Hizqiyahu cut off the gold from the doors of the Beit HaMikdash of יהוה, and from the pillars which Hizqiyahu melech of Yahudah had overlaid, and gave it to the melech of Ashshur. 17 And the melech of Ashshur sent Tartan and Ravsaris and Rav-Shakeh from Lachish to melech Hizqiyahu with great armies against Yahrushalayim. And they went up and came to Yahrushalayim. And when they had come up, they came and stood by the conduit of the upper pool, which is in the highway of the Launderer's Field. 18 And when they had called to the melech, there came out to them Elyaquim the son of Hilkiyahu, who was over the household, and Shevna the sopher, and Yoah the son of Asaph the recorder. 19 And Rav-Shakeh said to them, Speak now to Hizqiyahu, This says the great melech, the melech of Ashshur, What confidence is this in which you trust? 20 You say, but they are but vain words, I have counsel and strength for the war. Now on whom do you trust, that you rebel against me? 21 Now, see, you trust upon the staff of this bruised reed, even upon Mitzrayim, on which if a man lean, it will go into his hand, and pierce it: so is Pharoah melech of Mitzrayim to all that trust in him. 22 But if you say to me, We trust in יהוה Our Elohim: is not that He, whose idol temples and whose altars Hizqiyahu has taken away, and has said to Yahudah and Yahrushalayim, You shall worship before this altar in Yahrushalayim? 23 Now therefore, I ask you, give pledges to my master the melech of Ashshur, and I will deliver you two thousand horses, if you are able to put riders on them. 24 How then will you turn away the face of one captain of the least of my master's avadim, and put your trust in Mitzrayim for mirkavot and for horsemen? 25 Have I now come up without יהוה against this place to destroy it? יהוה said to me, Go up against this land, and

---

[1] Ephraim fell in stages and the deportations also took place in stages.

destroy it. 26 Then said Elyaquim the son of Hilkiyah, and Shevna, and Yoah, to Rav-Shakeh, Speak, I ask you, to your avadim in the Aramean language; for we understand it: but do not talk with us in the Yahudite language in the ears of the people that are on the wall.[1] 27 But Rav-Shakeh said to them, Has my master sent me to your master, and to you, to speak these words? Has he not sent me to the men who sit on the wall, that they may eat their own dung, and drink their own urine with you. 28 Then Rav-Shakeh stood and cried with a loud voice in the Yahudite's language, and spoke, saying, Shema the word of the great melech, the melech of Ashshur: 29 This says the melech, Let not Hizqiyahu deceive you: for he shall not be able to deliver you out of his hand: 30 Neither let Hizqiyahu make you trust in יהוה, saying, יהוה will surely deliver us, and this city shall not be delivered into the hand of the melech of Ashshur. 31 Listen not to Hizqiyahu: for this says the melech of Ashshur, Make an agreement with me by a present, and come out to me, and then eat every man of his own vine, and every man of his own fig eytz, and drink every man the mayim of his own cistern: 32 Until I come; and take you away to a land like your own land, a land of corn and wine, a land of lechem and vineyards, a land of olive eytzim and of honey, that you may live, and not die: and shema not to Hizqiyahu, when he misleads you, saying, יהוה will deliver us. 33 Have any of the elohim of the nations delivered at all its land out of the hand of the melech of Ashshur? 34 Where are the elohim of Hamath, and of Arpad? Where are the elohim of Sepharvaim, Hena, and Ivah? Have they delivered Shomron out of my hand? 35 Who are they among all the elohim of the countries that have delivered their country out of my hand; that יהוה should deliver Yahrushalayim out of my hand? 36 But the people held their silence,

and answered him not a word: for the melech's commandment said, Answer him not. 37 Then came Elyaquim the son of Hilkiyah, who was over the household, and Shevna the sopher, and Yoah the son of Asaph the recorder, to Hizqiyahu with their clothes torn, and told him all the words of Rav-Shakeh.

19 And it came to pass, when melech Hizqiyahu heard it, that he tore his clothes, and covered himself with sackcloth, and went into the Bayit of יהוה. 2 And he sent Elyaquim, who was over the household, and Shevna the sopher, and the zachanim of the kohanim, covered with sackcloth, to Yeshayahu ha navi the son of Amotz. 3 And they said to him, This says Hizqiyahu, This day is a day of trouble, and of rebuke, and blasphemy: for the children are come to the birth, and there is not strength to bring forth. 4 It may be יהוה Your Elohim will shema all the words of Rav-Shakeh, whom the melech of Ashshur his master has sent to reproach the living Elohim; and will reprove the words which יהוה Your Elohim has heard. Therefore lift up your tefillah for the remnant that are left. 5 So the avadim of melech Hizqiyahu came to Yeshayahu. 6 And Yeshayahu said to them, This shall you say to your master, This says יהוה, *Be not afraid of the words which you have heard, with which the avadim of the melech of Ashshur have blasphemed Me. 7 See, I will send a blast upon him, and he shall shema a rumor, and shall return to his own land; and I will cause him to fall by the sword in his own land.* 8 So Rav-Shakeh returned, and found the melech of Ashshur warring against Livnah: for he had heard that he was departed from Lachish. 9 And when the melech heard concerning Tirhakah melech of Ethiopia, See, he is come out to fight against you: he sent messengers again to Hizqiyahu, saying, 10 This shall you speak to Hizqiyahu melech of Yahudah, saying, Let not Your Elohim in whom you trust

---

[1] A clear-cut statement that the people of Yisrael knew and spoke Aramaic; and therefore were later able to pen the Renewed Covenant in Aramaic as well.

deceive you, saying, Yahrushalayim shall not be delivered into the hand of the melech of Ashshur. 11 See, you have heard what the melechim of Ashshur have done to all the lands, by destroying them utterly: and shall you be delivered? 12 Have the elohim of the nations delivered them whom my ahvot have destroyed; as Gozan, and Haran, and Rezeph, and the children of Aden that were in Thelasar? 13 Where is the melech of Hamath, and the melech of Arpad, and the melech of the city of Sepharvaim, of Hena, and Ivah? 14 And Hizqiyahu received the letter from the hand of the messengers, and read it: and Hizqiyahu went up into the Bayit of יהוה, and spread it before יהוה. 15 And Hizqiyahu made tefillah before יהוה, and said, O יהוה Elohim of Yisrael, who dwells between the cheruvim, You are the Elohim, even You alone, of all the malchutim of the earth: You have made the shamayim and earth. 16 יהוה, incline Your ear, and shema: open, יהוה, Your eyes, and see: and shema the words of Sanheriv, which he has sent to reproach the living Elohim. 17 Of an emet, יהוה, the melechim of Ashshur have destroyed the nations and their lands, 18 And have cast their elohim into the fire: for they were no elohim, but the work of men's hands, wood and stone: therefore they have destroyed them. 19 Now therefore, O יהוה our Elohim, I beg You, save us out of his hand, that all the malchutim of the earth may know that You are יהוה Elohim, even You alone. 20 Then Yeshayahu the son of Amotz sent to Hizqiyahu, saying, This says יהוה Elohim of Yisrael, *That which you have made tefillah to Me against Sanheriv melech of Ashshur I have heard.* 21 This is the word that יהוה has spoken concerning him; *The virgin the daughter of Tzion has despised you, and laughed you to scorn; the daughter of Yahrushalayim has shaken her head at you. 22 Whom have you reproached and blasphemed? And against whom have you exalted your voice, and lifted up your eyes on high? Even against the Set-Apart*

One of Yisrael. 23 By the messengers you have reproached יהוה, *and have said, With the multitude of my mirkavot I am come up to the height of the mountains, to the sides of Levanon, and will cut down the tall cedar eytzim, and the choice cypress eytzim: and I will enter into the lodgings of his borders, and into the forest of Carmel. 24 I have digged and drunk strange mayim, and with the sole of My feet have I dried up all the rivers of defence. 25 Have you not heard long ago how I have done it, and of ancient times that I have formed it? Now have I brought it to pass, that you should lay waste fenced cities into ruinous heaps. 26 Therefore their inhabitants were of small power, they were dismayed and confounded; they were as the grass of the field, and as the green herb, as the grass on the housetops, and as grass blasted before it is grown up. 27 But I know your sitting down, and your going out, and your coming in, and your rage against Me. 28 Because your rage against Me and your tumult is come up into My ears, therefore I will put My hook in your nose, and My bridle in your lips, and I will turn you back by the derech by which you came. 29 And this shall be a sign to you, You shall eat this year such things as grow of themselves, and in the second year that which springs of the same; and in the third year sow, and reap, and plant vineyards, and eat the fruits of it. 30 And the remnant that is escaped from Beit Yahudah shall yet again take root downward, and bear fruit upward. 31 For out of Yahrushalayim shall go forth a remnant, and they that escape out of Har Tzion: the zeal of* יהוה *of hosts shall do this.* 32 Therefore this says יהוה *concerning the melech of Ashshur, He shall not come into this city, nor shoot an arrow there, nor come before it with shield, nor cast a bank against it. 33 By the derech that he came, by the same derech shall he return, and shall not come into this city,* says יהוה. 34 *For I will defend this city, to save it, for My own sake, and for My eved*

David's sake. 35 And it came to pass that night; that the heavenly messenger of **יהוה** went out, and killed in the camp of the Ashurim one hundred eighty five thousand men: and when they arose early in the morning, see, they were all dead corpses. 36 So Sanheriv melech of Ashshur departed, and went and returned, and dwelt at Nineveh. 37 And it came to pass, as he was worshipping in the bayit of Nisroch his elohim, that Adram-Melech and Sharezer his sons killed him with the sword: and they escaped into the land of Armenia. And Esar-Haddon his son reigned in his place.

20 In those days was Hizqiyahu sick and near death. And ha navi Yeshayahu the son of Amotz came to him, and said to him, This says **יהוה**, Set your bayit in order; for you shall die, and not live. 2 Then he turned his face to the wall, and made tefillah to **יהוה**, saying, 3 I beg You, O **יהוה**, remember now how I have had my halacha before You in emet and with a perfect lev, and have done that which is tov in Your sight. And Hizqiyahu wept heavily. 4 And it came to pass, before Yeshayahu had gone out into the middle court, that the word of **יהוה** came to him, saying, Return, and tell Hizqiyahu the leader of My people, This says **יהוה**, the Elohim of David your abba, I have heard your tefillah, I have seen your tears: see, I will heal you:1 on the third day you shall go up to the Bayit of **יהוה**. 6 And I will add to your days fifteen years; and I will deliver you and this city out of the hand of the melech of Ashshur; and I will defend this city for My own sake, and for My eved David's sake. 7 And Yeshayahu said, Take a lump of figs. And they took and laid it on the boil, and he recovered. 8 And Hizqiyahu said to Yeshayahu, What shall be the sign that **יהוה** will heal me, and that I shall go up into the Bayit of **יהוה** the third day? 9 And Yeshayahu said, This sign shall you

have of **יהוה**, that **יהוה** will do the thing that He has spoken: shall the shadow go forth ten degrees, or go back ten degrees? 10 And Hizqiyahu answered, It would be easy for the shadow to go down ten degrees: no, but let the shadow return backward ten degrees. 11 And Yeshayahu ha navi cried to **יהוה** : and He brought the shadow ten degrees backward, by which it had gone down in the dial of Ahaz. 12 At that time Berodach-Baladan, the son of Baladan, melech of Bavel, sent letters and a present to Hizqiyahu: for he had heard that Hizqiyahu had been sick. 13 And Hizqiyahu listened to them, and showed them all the bayit of his precious things, the silver, and the gold, and the spices, and the precious ointment, and all the bayit of his armor, and all that was found in his treasures: there was nothing in his bayit, nor in all his dominion, that Hizqiyahu showed them not. 14 Then came Yeshayahu ha navi to melech Hizqiyahu, and said to him, What did these men say? And from where did they come to you? And Hizqiyahu said, They are come from a far country, even from Bavel. 15 And he said, What have they seen in your bayit? And Hizqiyahu answered, All the things that are in my bayit have they seen: there is nothing among my treasures that I have not showed them. 16 And Yeshayahu said to Hizqiyahu, Shema the word of **יהוה**. 17 See, the days come, that all that is in your bayit, and that which your ahvot have laid up in store until this day, shall be carried into Bavel: nothing shall be left, says **יהוה**. 18 And of your sons that shall issue from you, that you shall beget, shall they take away; and they shall be eunuchs in the palace of the melech of Bavel. 19 Then said Hizqiyahu to Yeshayahu, Tov is the word of **יהוה** which you have spoken. And he said, Is it not tov, if shalom and emet be in my days? 20 And the rest of the acts of Hizqiyahu, and all his might, and how he made a pool, and a conduit, and brought mayim into the city, are they not written in the scroll of the

---

[1] Miraculous healing did not start with Yahshua but was and remains the inheritance of righteous Yisrael.

Divre HaYamim about the melechim of Yahudah? 21 And Hizqiyahu slept with his ahvot: and Menashsheh his son reigned in his place.

21 Menashsheh was twelve years old when he began to reign, and reigned fifty-five years in Yahrushalayim. And his ima's name was Hephtzi-Bah. 2 And he did that which was evil in the sight of יהוה , after the abominations of the heathen, whom יהוה cast out before the children of Yisrael. 3 For he built up again the idol temples that Hizqiyahu his abba had destroyed; and he reared up altars for Baal, and made an Asherah, as did Ahav melech of Yisrael; and worshipped all the hosts of the shamayim, and served them. 4 And he built altars in the Bayit of יהוה, of which יהוה said, In Yahrushalayim will I put My Name. 5 And he built altars for all the hosts of the shamayim in the two courts of the Bayit of יהוה. 6 And he made his son pass through the fire, and observed times, and used enchantments, and dealt with familiar ruachim and mediums: he worked much wickedness in the sight of יהוה, to provoke Him to anger. 7 And he set a graven image of the Asherah that he had made in the bayit, of which יהוה said to David, and to Shlomo his son, *In this bayit, and in Yahrushalayim, which I have chosen out of all tribes of Yisrael, will I put My Name le-olam-va-ed*: 8 *Neither will I make the feet of Yisrael move any more out of the land which I gave their ahvot; only if they will observe to do according to all that I have commanded them, and according to all the Torah that My eved Moshe commanded them.* 9 But they listened not: and Menashsheh seduced them to do more evil than did the nations whom יהוה destroyed before the children of Yisrael. 10 And יהוה spoke by His avadim ha neviim, saying, 11 *Because Menashsheh melech of Yahudah has done these abominations, and has done wickedly above all that the Amorites did, who were before*

him, and has made Yahudah also to sin with his idols: 12 Therefore this says יהוה Elohim of Yisrael, *See, I am bringing such evil upon Yahrushalayim and Yahudah that whoever hears of it, both his ears shall tingle.* 13 *And I will stretch over Yahrushalayim the line of Shomron, and the plummet of Beit Ahav: and I will wipe Yahrushalayim as a man wipes a dish, wiping it, and turning it upside down.* 14 *And I will forsake the remnant of My inheritance, and deliver them into the hand of their enemies; and they shall become a prey and a spoil to all their enemies;* 15 *Because they have done that which was evil in My sight, and have provoked Me to anger, since the day their ahvot came forth out of Mitzrayim, even to this day.* 16 Moreover Menashsheh shed much innocent dom, until he had filled Yahrushalayim from one end to another; beside his sin by with he made Yahudah to sin, in doing that which was evil in the sight of יהוה. 17 Now the rest of the acts of Menashsheh, and all that he did, and his sin that he sinned, are they not written in the scroll of the Divre HaYamim about the melechim of Yahudah? 18 And Menashsheh slept with his ahvot, and was buried in the gan of his own bayit, in the Gan of Uzza: and Amon his son reigned in his place. 19 Amon was twenty-two years old when he began to reign, and he reigned two years in Yahrushalayim. And his ima's name was Meshullemeth, the daughter of Harutz of Yotevah. 20 And he did that which was evil in the sight of יהוה, as his abba Menashsheh did. 21 And he had his halacha in all the halachot that his abba walked in, and served the idols that his abba served, and worshipped them: 22 And he forsook יהוה Elohim of his ahvot, and did not have his halacha in the derech of יהוה. 23 And the avadim of Amon conspired against him, and killed the melech in his own bayit. 24 And the people of the land killed all them that had conspired against melech Amon; and the people of the land made Yoshiyahu his son melech in his place. 25 Now the rest of the acts of Amon that he did, are they not written in the scroll of the Divre HaYamim about the melechim of Yahudah? 26 And he was buried in his tomb in the Gan of Uzza: and Yoshiyahu his son reigned in his place.

22 Yoshiyahu was eight years old when he began to reign, and he reigned thirty-one years in Yahrushalayim. And his ima's name was Yedidah, the daughter of Adayah of Botscath. 2 And he did that which was right in the sight of יהוה, and had his halacha in all the derech of David his abba, and turned not aside to the right hand or to the left. 3 And it came to pass in the eighteenth year of melech Yoshiyahu, that the melech sent Shaphan the son of Azalyah, the son of Meshullam, the sopher, to the Bayit of יהוה, saying, 4 Go up to Hilkiyah the Kohen HaGadol, that he may weigh the silver that is brought into the Bayit of יהוה, which the doorkeepers have gathered from the people: 5 And let them deliver it into the hand of the doers of the work; that have the oversight of the Bayit of יהוה: and let them give it to the doers of the work which is in the Bayit of יהוה, to repair the damages of the bayit, 6 Unto the carpenters, and builders, and masons, and to buy timber and cut stone to repair the bayit. 7 However there was no accounting made with them of the silver that was delivered into their hand, because they acted faithfully. 8 And Hilkiyah the Kohen HaGadol said to Shaphan the sopher, I have found the scroll of the Torah in the Bayit of יהוה. And Hilkiyah gave the scroll to Shaphan, and he read it. 9 And Shaphan the sopher came to the melech, and brought the melech word again, and said, Your avadim have gathered the silver that was found in the bayit, and have delivered it into the hand of those that do the work, that have the oversight of the Bayit of יהוה. 10 And Shaphan the sopher

showed the melech, saying, Hilkiyah the kohen has delivered to me a scroll. And Shaphan read it before the melech. 11 And it came to pass, when the melech had heard the words of the scroll of the Torah, that he tore his clothes. 12 And the melech commanded Hilkiyah the kohen, and Ahikam the son of Shaphan, and Achvor the son of Michayah, and Shaphan the sopher, and Asayah an eved of the melech, saying, 13 Go, inquire of יהוה for me, and for the people, and for all Yahudah, concerning the words of this scroll that is found: for great is the wrath of יהוה that is kindled against us, because our ahvot have not listened to the words of this scroll, to do according to all that which is written concerning us. 14 So Hilkiyah the kohen, and Ahikam, and Achvor, and Shaphan, and Asayah, went to Huldah ha naviyah, the wife of Shallum the son of Tikvah, the son of Harhas, keeper of the wardrobe; now she dwelt in Yahrushalayim in the yeshiva studying Torah; and they communed with her. 15 And she said to them, This says יהוה Elohim of Yisrael, *Tell the man that sent you to Me,* 16 This says יהוה, *See, I will bring evil upon this place, and upon the inhabitants of it, even all the words of the scroll that the melech of Yahudah has read:* 17 *Because they have forsaken Me, and have burned incense to other elohim, that they might provoke Me to anger with all the works of their hands; therefore My wrath shall be kindled against this place, and shall not be quenched.* 18 But to the melech of Yahudah who sent you to inquire of יהוה, this shall you say to him, This says יהוה Elohim of Yisrael, about the words which you have heard; 19 *Because your lev was tender, and you have humbled yourself before יהוה, when you heared what I spoke against this place, and against the inhabitants of it, that they should become a desolation and a curse, and have torn your clothes, and wept before Me; I also have heard you, says יהוה. 20 See therefore, I will gather you to your ahvot, and you shall be gathered into your grave in shalom; and your eyes shall not see all the evil that I will bring upon this place.* And they brought the melech word again.

23 And the melech sent, and they gathered to him all the zachanim of Yahudah and of Yahrushalayim. 2 And the melech went up into the Bayit of יהוה, and all the men of Yahudah and all the inhabitants of Yahrushalayim with him, and the kohanim, and ha neviim, and all the people, both small and great: and he read in their ears all the words of the scroll of the covenant which was found in the Bayit of יהוה. 3 And the melech stood by a pillar, and made a covenant before יהוה, to have his halacha in the halachot of יהוה, and to keep His mitzvot and His mishpatim and His chukim with all His lev and all His being, to perform the words of this covenant that were written in this scroll. And all the people agreed to the covenant. 4 And the melech commanded Hilkiyah the Kohen HaGadol, and the kohanim of the second order, and the keepers of the door, to bring forth out of the Beit HaMikdash of יהוה all the vessels that were made for Baal, and for the Asherah, and for all the hosts of the shamayim: and he burned them outside of Yahrushalayim in the fields of Kidron, and carried the ashes of them to Beth-El. 5 And he put down the idolatrous kohanim, whom the melechim of Yahudah had ordained to burn incense in the idol temples in the cities of Yahudah, and in the places around Yahrushalayim; those also that burned incense to Baal, to the sun, and to the moon and to the planets, and to all the hosts of the shamayim. 6 And he brought out the Asherah from the Bayit of יהוה, outside Yahrushalayim, to the brook Kidron, and burned it at the brook Kidron, and grinded it to small powder, and cast the powder upon the graves of the children of the people. 7 And he broke down the bayits of the sodomites that was in the Bayit of יהוה, where the women wove hangings for the Asherah. 8 And he brought all the kohanim out of the cities of Yahudah, and destroyed the idol temples where the kohanim had burned incense, from Geva to Beer-Sheva, and broke down the idol temples of the gates that were in the entrance of the gate of Yahoshua the governor of the city, which were on a man's left hand at the gate of the city. 9 Nevertheless the priests of the idol temples came not up to the altar of יהוה in Yahrushalayim, but they did eat of the matzah among their brothers. 10 And he destroyed Topheth, which is in the Valley of the Children of Hinnom, that no man might make his son or his daughter to pass through the fire to Molech. 11 And he took away the horses that the melechim of Yahudah had given to the sun, at the entering in of the Bayit of יהוה, by the room of Natan-Melech the eunuch that was in the court, and burned the mirkavot of the sun with fire. 12 And the altars that were on the top of the upper room of Ahaz, which the melechim of Yahudah had made, and the altars which Menashsheh had made in the two courts of the Bayit of יהוה, did the melech beat down, and broke them down from there, and cast the dust of them into the brook Kidron. 13 And the idol temples that were before Yahrushalayim, which were on the right hand of the Mount of corruption, which Shlomo the melech of Yisrael had built for Ashtoreth the abomination of the Tzidonians, and for Chemosh the abomination of the Moavites, and for Milcom the abomination of the children of Ammon, did the melech destroy. 14 And he broke in pieces the images, and cut down the Asherim, and filled their places with the bones of men. 15 Moreover the altar that was at Beth-El, and the high place which Yeravoam the son of Nevat, who made Yisrael to sin, had made, both that altar and the idol temple he broke down, and burned the idol temple, and grinded it to small powder, and burned the Asherah. 16 And as Yoshiyahu turned, he saw the tombs that were there in the Mount

and sent and took the bones out of the tombs, and burned them upon the altar, and polluted it, according to the word of יהוה which the man of Elohim proclaimed, who proclaimed these words. 17 Then he said, What tombstone do I see? And the men of the city told him, It is the tomb of the man of Elohim, who came from Yahudah, and proclaimed these things that you have done against the altar of Beth-El. 18 And he said, Leave him alone; let no man move his bones. So they left his bones alone, with the bones of ha navi that came out of Shomron. 19 And all the bayits also of the idol temples that were in the cities of Shomron, which the melechim of Yisrael had made to provoke יהוה to anger, Yoshiyahu took away, and did to them according to all the things that he had done in Beth-El. 20 And he killed all the priests of the idol temples that were there upon the altars, and burned men's bones upon them, and returned to Yahrushalayim. 21 And the melech commanded all the people, saying, Keep the Pesach to יהוה Your Elohim, as it is written in the scroll of this covenant. 22 Surely there was no such Pesach prepared from the days of the shophtim that gave mishpat to Yisrael, nor in all the days of the melechim of Yisrael, nor of the melechim of Yahudah; 23 But in the eighteenth year of melech Yoshiyahu, this Pesach was held to יהוה in Yahrushalayim. 24 Moreover the workers with familiar ruachim, and the mediums, and the images, and the idols, and all the abominations that were seen in the land of Yahudah and in Yahrushalayim, did Yoshiyahu put away, that he might perform the words of the Torah that were written in the scroll that Hilkiyah the kohen found in the Bayit of יהוה. 25 And before him there was no melech like him, that made teshuvah to יהוה with all his lev, and with all his being, and with all his might, according to all the Torah of Moshe; and neither after him arose there any like him. [1] 26 However יהוה

turned not from the fierceness of His great wrath, with which His anger was kindled against Yahudah, because of all the provocations that Menashsheh had provoked him with. 27 And יהוה said, *I will remove Yahudah also out of My sight, as I have removed Yisrael, and will cast off this city Yahrushalayim which I have chosen, and the Bayit of which I said, My Name shall be there.* 28 Now the rest of the acts of Yoshiyahu, and all that he did, are they not written in the scroll of the Divre HaYamim about the melechim of Yahudah? 29 In his days Pharaoh-Nechoh melech of Mitzrayim went up against the melech of Ashshur to the River Euphrates: and melech Yoshiyahu went against him to fight against him and Pharaoh said to him, I have not come against you, go away from me. But Yoshiyahu did not shema to him. So Pharaoh killed him at Megiddo when he saw him there. 30 And his avadim carried him in a mirkavah dead from Megiddo, and brought him to Yahrushalayim, and buried him in his own tomb. And the people of the land took Yehoahaz the son of Yoshiyahu, and anointed him, and made him melech in his abba's place. 31 Yehoahaz was twenty-three years old when he began to reign; and he reigned three months in Yahrushalayim. And his ima's name was Hamutal, the daughter of Yirmeyahu of Livnah. 32 And he did that which was evil in the sight of יהוה, according to all that his ahvot had done. 33 And Pharaoh-Nechoh put him in chains at Rivlah in the land of Hamath, that he might not reign in Yahrushalayim; and put the land to a tribute of an hundred talents of silver, and a talent of gold. 34 And Pharaoh-Nechoh made Elyaquim the son of Yoshiyahu melech in the place of Yoshiyahu his abba, and changed his name to Yehoyakim, and took Yehoahaz away: and he came to Mitzrayim, and died there. 35 And Yehoyakim gave the silver and the gold to Pharaoh; but he taxed the land to give the silver according to the

---

[1] Perhaps with an even better record of service than David himself.

commandment of Pharaoh: he exacted the silver and the gold from the people of the land, of everyone according to his taxation, to give it to Pharaoh-Nechoh. 36 Yehoyakim was twenty-five years old when he began to reign; and he reigned eleven years in Yahrushalayim. And his ima's name was Zevidah, the daughter of Pedayah of Rumah. 37 And he did that which was evil in the sight of יהוה , according to all that his ahvot had done.

24 In his days Nebuchadnetzar melech of Bavel came up, and Yehoyakim became his eved three years: then he turned and rebelled against him. 2 And יהוה sent against him raiding bands of the Chaldeans, and raiding bands of the Aramaens, and raiding bands of the Moavites, and raiding bands of the children of Ammon, and sent them against Yahudah to destroy it, according to the word of יהוה, which He spoke by His avadim ha neviim. 3 Surely at the commandment of יהוה came this upon Yahudah, to remove them out of His sight, for the sins of Menashsheh, according to all that he did; 4 And also for the innocent dom that he shed: for he filled Yahrushalayim with innocent dom; which יהוה would not pardon.[1] 5 Now the rest of the acts of Yehoyakim, and all that he did, are they not written in the scroll of the Divre HaYamim about the melechim of Yahudah? 6 So Yehoyakim slept with his ahvot: and Yehoyakin his son reigned in his place. 7 And the melech of Mitzrayim came not again any more out of his land: for the melech of Bavel had taken all that belonged to the melech of Mitzrayim, from the River of Mitzrayim to the River Euphrates. 8 Yehoyakin was eighteen years old when he began to reign, and he reigned in Yahrushalayim three months. And his ima's name was Nehushta, the daughter of El-Natan of Yahrushalayim. 9 And he did that which was evil in the sight of יהוה , according to all that his abba had done.

10 At that time the avadim of Nebuchadnetzar melech of Bavel came up against Yahrushalayim, and the city was besieged. 11 And Nebuchadnetzar melech of Bavel came against the city, and his avadim did besiege it. 12 And Yehoyakin the melech of Yahudah went out to the melech of Bavel, he, and his ima, and his avadim, and his princes, and his officers: and the melech of Bavel took him in the eighth year of his reign. 13 And he carried out from there all the treasures of the Bayit of יהוה, and the treasures of the melech's bayit, and cut in pieces all the vessels of gold which Shlomo melech of Yisrael had made in the Beit HaMikdash of יהוה, as יהוה had said. 14 And he carried away all Yahrushalayim, and all the princes, and all the mighty men of valor, even ten thousand captives, and all the craftsmen and smiths: none remained, except the poorest people of the land. 15 And he carried away Yehoyakin to Bavel, and the melech's ima, and the melech's wives, and his officers, and the mighty of the land, those he carried into captivity from Yahrushalayim to Bavel. 16 And all the men of might, even seven thousand, and craftsmen and smiths a thousand, all that were strong and fit for war, even them the melech of Bavel brought captive to Bavel. 17 And the melech of Bavel made Mattanyah his abba's brother melech in his place, and changed his name to Tsidqiyahu. 18 Tsidqiyahu was twenty-one years old when he began to reign, and he reigned eleven years in Yahrushalayim. And his ima's name was Hamutal, the daughter of Yirmeyahu of Livnah. 19 And he did that which was evil in the sight of יהוה, according to all that Yehoyakim had done. 20 For through the anger of יהוה all this came to pass in Yahrushalayim and Yahudah, until He had cast them out from His presence, that Tsidqiyahu rebelled against the melech of Bavel.

25 And it came to pass in the ninth year of his reign, in the tenth

---

[1] Yahudah being expelled and exiled for 70 years.

month, in the tenth day of the month, that Nebuchadnetzar melech of Bavel came, he, and all his armies, against Yahrushalayim, and pitched against it; and they built forts against it all around. 2 And the city was besieged to the eleventh year of melech Tsidqiyahu. 3 And on the ninth day of the fourth month the famine prevailed in the city, and there was no lechem for the people of the land. 4 And the city was broken up, and all the men of war fled by night by the derech of the gate between two walls, which is by the melech's gan: now the Chaldeans were against the city all around it: and the melech went the derech toward the plain. 5 And the army of the Chaldeans pursued after the melech, and overtook him in the plains of Yericho: and all his army was scattered from him. 6 So they took the melech, and brought him up to the melech of Bavel to Rivlah; and they gave mishpat upon him. 7 And they killed the sons of Tsidqiyahu before his eyes, and put out the eyes of Tsidqiyahu, and bound him with fetters of bronze, and carried him to Bavel. 8 And in the fifth month, on the seventh day of the month, which is the nineteenth year of melech Nebuchadnetzar melech of Bavel, came Nebuzar-Adan, captain of the guard, an eved of the melech of Bavel, to Yahrushalayim: 9 And he burnt the Bayit of יהוה, and the melech's bayit, and all the bayits of Yahrushalayim, and every great man's bayit he burnt with fire. 10 And all the army of the Chaldeans, that were with the captain of the guard, broke down the walls of Yahrushalayim all around. 11 Now the rest of the people that were left in the city, and the fugitives that fell away to the melech of Bavel, with the remnant of the multitude, did Nebuzar-Adan the captain of the guard carry away. 12 But the captain of the guard left the poor of the land to be vinedressers and farmers. 13 And the pillars of bronze that were in the Bayit of יהוה, and the bases, and the bronze sea that was in the Bayit of יהוה, did the Chaldeans break in pieces, and carried their bronze to

Bavel. 14 And the pots, and the shovels, and the snuffers, and the spoons, and all the vessels of bronze with which they ministered, were taken away. 15 And the firepans, and the bowls, and such things as were of gold, or in gold, and of silver, or in silver, the captain of the guard took away. 16 The two pillars, one sea, and the bases which Shlomo had made for the Bayit of יהוה; the bronze of all these vessels was without weight. 17 The height of the one pillar was eighteen cubits, and the capital upon it was bronze: and the height of the capital three cubits; and the network, and pomegranates upon the capital all around, all of bronze: and like these had also the second pillar with a network. 18 And the captain of the guard took Seraiah the chief kohen, and Zephanyah the second kohen, and the three doorkeepers: 19 And out of the city he took an officer that was set over the men of war, and five of them that were in the melech's presence, which were found in the city, and the chief sopher of the armies, who mustered the people of the land, and sixty men of the people of the land that were found in the city: 20 And Nebuzar-Adan captain of the guard took these, and brought them to the melech of Bavel to Rivlah: 21 And the melech of bn governor, there came to Gedalyah to Mitzpah, even Ishmael the son of Nethanyah, and Yochanan the son of Careah, and Serayah the son of Tanhumeth the Netophathite, and Yaazanyah the son of a Maachathite, they and their men. 24 And Gedalyah swore to them, and to their men, and said to them, Fear not to be the avadim of the Chaldeans: dwell in the land, and serve the melech of Bavel; and it shall be well with you. 25 But it came to pass in the seventh month, that Ishmael the son of Nethanyah, the son of Elishama, of the royal offspring, came, and ten men with him, and killed Gedalyah, that he died, and the Yahudim and the Chaldeans that were with him at Mitzpah. 26 And all the people, both small and great, and the captains of the armies, arose, and came to Mitzrayim: for they were afraid of the Chaldeans. 27 And it came to pass in the thirty-seventh year of the captivity of Yehoyakin melech of Yahudah, in the twelfth month, on the twenty-seventh day of the month, that Evil-Merodach melech of Bavel in the year that he began to reign released Yehoyakin melech of Yahudah out of prison; 28 And he spoke kindly to him, and set his throne above the thrones of the melechim that were with him in Bavel; 29 And changed his prison garments: and he did eat lechem continually before him all the days of his chayim. 30 And his allowance was a continual allowance given to him by the melech, a daily rate every day, all the days of his chayim.

ישעיהו

Yeshayahu - Isaiah

To Our Forefathers Yisrael

1 The vision of Yeshayahu the son of Amotz, which he saw concerning Yahudah and Yahrushalayim in the days of Uzziyah, Yotham, Ahaz, and Hizqiyahu, melechim of Yahudah. 2 Shema, O shamayim, and shema, O earth: for יהוה has spoken, *I have nourished and brought up children, and they have rebelled against Me.* 3 *The ox knows his owner, and the donkey his master's crib: but Yisrael does not know Me, My people have not understood Me.* [1] 4 *Ah sinful nation, a people loaded with iniquity, a zera of evildoers, children that are corrupt: they have forsaken* יהוה, *they have provoked the Set-Apart One of Yisrael to anger, and they have gone backwards. 5 Why should you be beaten any more? Yet you will continue in apostasy: the whole head is sick, and the whole lev faint. 6 From the sole of the foot even to the head there is no soundness; but wounds, and bruises, and open sores: they have not been closed, neither bound up, neither soothed with ointment. 7 Your country is desolate, your cities are burned with fire: your land, foreigners devour it in Your presence, and it is desolate, foreigners overthrow it. 8 And the daughter of Tzion is left as a cottage in a vineyard,[2] as a hut in a garden of cucumbers, as a besieged city.* 9 *Except* יהוה *of hosts had left to us a very small remnant,[3] we would have become just like Sedom, and we would have been just like Amorah.[4] 10 Shema the word of* יהוה, *you rulers of Sedom; give ear to the Torah of Our Elohim, you people of Amorah.[5] 11 To what purpose is the multitude of your sacrifices to Me? Says* יהוה: *I am full of the burnt offerings of rams, and the fat of fed beasts; and I delight not in the dom of bulls, or of lambs, or of goats.[6] 12 When you come to appear before Me, who has required this at your hand, to trample My courts? 13 Bring no more vain offerings; incense is an abomination to Me; the Rosh Chodashim and the Shabbats, the calling of miqra kodashim,[7] I cannot put up with; it is iniquity, even the set-apart meetings.[8] 14 Your Rosh Chodashim and your moadim My being hates:[9] they are a trouble to Me; I am weary of bearing them.[10] 15 And when you spread forth your hands, I will hide My eyes from you: even though you make many tefillot, I will not shema: your hands are full of dom. 16 Wash yourself and make yourself clean; put away the evil of your doings from before My eyes; cease to do evil; 17 Learn to do tov; seek mishpat, relieve the oppressed, defend the fatherless, and plead for the widow. 18 Come now, and let us reason together, says* יהוה: *though your sins are as scarlet, they shall be as white as snow; though they are red like crimson, they shall be as wool.[11] 19 If you are willing and obedient, you shall eat*

---

[1] The problem with our nation has been in not knowing YHWH personally through His Son, and not having complete understanding of His truth.
[2] A vineyard is often used as a symbol of all 12 tribes of the nation.
[3] From both houses only a redeemed remnant will inherit the promises of Scripture. As stated in Romans 9:6-7-8, not all of physical Yisrael will be the final regathered Yisrael ("not all Yisrael is Yisrael"), as seen in the restored kingdom.
[4] If Moshiach had not been sent to redeem all the lost sheep of both houses, we would no doubt have become like the cities of the plains in their total and permanent destruction.

[5] Speaking to Judah's leaders in Jerusalem.
[6] With a wrong heart YHWH does not care about the dom sacrifices. With a right humble heart, they become potent.
[7] Set-apart meetings.
[8] Since Yisrael's leadership in Judah is corrupt in heart and full of evil, all the Torah rituals not only become futile and unfruitful religious exercises, they are an abomination to YHWH, whose patience has run out and who takes no delight in their performance, since the worshipper is not loving Him by obeying Him, but seeking Him by mere rote.
[9] When Yisrael's heart is not right, YHWH sees these feasts as a flesh trip, turning "His times" into their "own times" of self indulgence.
[10] See note on verse 13.
[11] This promise is to all those who reason with YHWH, through the ordained mediator the Moshiach Yahshua.

the tov of the land:[1] 20 *But if you refuse and rebel, you shall be devoured with the sword: for the mouth of* יהוה *has spoken it.* 21 *How is it that the faithful city[2] became a harlot! It was full of mishpat; tzedakah lodged in it; but now murderers.* 22 *Your silver has become dross, your wine mixed with mayim:* 23 *Your rulers are rebellious, and are companions of thieves: everyone loves bribes, and follows after rewards: they do not defend the fatherless, neither does the cause of the widow concern them.* 24 Therefore says the Master, יהוה of hosts, the Mighty One of Yisrael, *Ah; I will be eased from My adversaries, and avenged of My enemies:* 25 *And I will turn My hand against you, and purge away the dross of your rebellious men, and take away all your sin:[3]* 26 *And I will restore your shophtim as at the first, and your counselors as at the beginning: afterward you shall be called, The city of tzedakah, the faithful city.*[4] 27 *Tzion shall be redeemed[5] with mishpat, and her restored ones[6] with tzedakah.*[7] 28 *And the destruction of the transgressors and of the sinners shall be together, and also they that forsake* יהוה *shall be consumed.* 29 *For they shall be ashamed about the oak eytzim which they have desired,[8] and you shall be embarrassed because of the gardens that you have chosen.* 30 *For you shall be as an oak whose leaf fades, and as a garden that has no mayim.* 31 *And the strong shall be for cotton, and his work as a spark, and they shall both burn together, and there shall be none to extinguish it.*

2 The word that Yeshayahu the son of Amotz saw concerning Yahudah and Yahrushalayim. 2 *And it shall come to pass in the yamim acharonim, that the mountain of* יהוה's *Bayit shall be established on the top of the mountains, and shall be exalted above the hills; and all nations shall flow to it.[9]* 3 *And many nations shall go and say, Come, and let us make aliyah [10] to the mountain of* יהוה *, to the Bayit of the Elohim of Yaakov; and He will teach us His halachot, and we will have our halacha in His paths: for out of Tzion shall go forth the Torah, and the word of* יהוה *from Yahrushalayim.[11]* 4 *And He shall be a shofet between the nations, [12] and shall rebuke many peoples:[13] and they shall beat their swords into plowshares, and their spears into pruning hooks:[14] nation shall not lift up sword against nation, neither shall they learn war any more.[15]* 5 *O Beit Yaakov, [16] come, and let us have our halacha in the Light of* יהוה*.[17]* 6 *Therefore You have forsaken Your people Beit Yaakov, [18] because they are self-satisfied like the old days, and practice magic like the Philistines, and they please themselves with the children of foreigners.[19]* 7 *Their land also is full of silver and gold, neither is there any end of their treasures; their land is also full of horses, neither is there any end of their mirkavot:* 8 *Their land also is full of idols; they worship the work of their own hands, that which their own fingers have made:* 9 *And the humble bows down, and the great man humbles himself: You do not forgive them.* 10 *Enter into the Rock, and hide in the dust, for the fear of* יהוה*, and for the tiferet of His excellence.* 11 *The*

---

[1] Obedience allows Yisrael to eat the fruits of the land of Yisrael, whereas disobedience removes Yisrael from the fruit of the land, as well as from the fruit of the Ruach.

[2] Jerusalem.

[3] Through judgment and later through the coming of Moshiach.

[4] In the millennial kingdom.

[5] Brought back to YHWH.

[6] The restored ones of Judah and Ephraim.

[7] The imparted righteousness of Moshiach Yahshua.

[8] A popular place for heathen worship.

[9] All nations will be gathered to Jerusalem to worship YHWH or be subjected by YHWH.

[10] The gathering spoken of in the Renewed Covenant.

[11] Many nations will seek a return to Torah. Specifically, the exiles of both houses in the nations, coming from those nations, will seek YHWH and His Torah, as Jerusalem is restored as the world's chief city. Of course the ultimate fulfillment of this is found in the **atid lavoh**.

[12] Moshiach shall settle disputes between nations.

[13] Rebuke with Torah and right-ruling.

[14] Global shalom in the kingdom on earth.

[15] Those who learned war will now learn Torah.

[16] All 12 tribes.

[17] The light of YHWH is called Yahshua in John 8:12.

[18] All 12 tribes.

[19] Heathen.

proud looks of man shall be humbled, and the pride of men shall be brought down, and **יהוה** alone shall be exalted in that day.[1] 12 For the Yom **יהוה** of hosts shall be upon everyone that is proud and lofty, and upon everyone that is lifted up; and he shall be brought low: 13 And upon all the cedars of Levanon,[2] that are high and lifted up, and upon all the oaks of Bashan,[3] 14 And upon all the high mountains, and upon all the hills that are lifted up, 15 And upon every high tower, and upon every fenced wall, 16 And upon all the ships of Tarshish, and upon all desirable sights. 17 And the loftiness of man shall be bowed down, and the pride of men shall be brought low: and **יהוה** alone shall be exalted in that day.[4] 18 And the idols He shall utterly abolish. 19 And they shall go into the holes of the rocks, and into the caves of the earth, for the fear of **יהוה**, and for the tiferet of His excellence, when He arises to shake the earth mightily. 20 In that day a man shall cast his idols of silver, and his idols of gold, which they made each one for himself to worship, to the moles and to the bats; 21 To go into the clefts of the rocks, and into the tops of the ragged rocks, for the fear of **יהוה**, and for the tiferet of His excellence, when He arises to shake the earth mightily. 22 Cease from man, whose breath is in his nostrils: for he doesn't count for much, does he?

3 For, see, the Master, **יהוה** of hosts, He takes away from Yahrushalayim and from Yahudah the stock and the store, the whole supply of lechem, and the whole supply of mayim, 2 The mighty man, and the man of war, the shofet, and ha navi, and the diviner, and the zachen, 3 The captain of fifty, and the honorable man, and the counselor, and the skilled craftsman, and the expert enchanter. 4 And I will give children to be their rulers, and babies shall

rule over them. 5 And the people shall be oppressed, each one by another, and each one by his neighbor: the child shall behave himself proudly against the zachan, and the am ha-aretz against the honorable men. 6 When a man shall take hold of his brother of the bayit of his abba, saying, You have clothing, be our ruler, and let this ruin be your responsibility: 7 In that day shall he swear, saying, I am not a healer; for in My bayit is neither lechem nor clothing: do not make me a ruler of the people. 8 For Yahrushalayim is ruined, and Yahudah has fallen: because their tongue and their doings are against **יהוה**, to provoke the eyes of His tiferet. 9 The look of their faces does witness against them; and they display their sin as Sedom, they do not hide it. Woe to their being! For they have brought evil on themselves. 10 Say you to the tzadik that it shall be well with him: for they shall eat the fruit of their doings. 11 Woe to the wicked! There shall be evil with him: for the bribe of his hands shall be given to him. 12 As for My people, children are their oppressors, and women rule over them. O My people, those who lead you cause you to go astray, and destroy the halacha of your paths.[5] 13 **יהוה** stands up to plead, and stands to shofet the people. 14 **יהוה** will enter into mishpat with the zachanim of His people, and its rulers: for you have eaten up the vineyard;[6] the plunder of the poor is in your bayits. 15 What do you mean when you beat My people to pieces, and shame the faces of the poor? Says the Master **יהוה** of hosts. 16 Moreover **יהוה** says, Because the daughters of Tzion are haughty, and have their halacha with stretched forth necks and seductive eyes, walking and mincing as they go, and making a jingling with their anklets: 17 Therefore **יהוה** will smite the daughters of Tzion with a scab on the keter of their heads, and **יהוה** will

---

[1] The **atid lavoh.**
[2] Temple buildings.
[3] Idol temples.
[4] **Atid lavoh.**

[5] To this very day the leaders of Jewish Yisrael cause the fold to go astray from the King Moshiach Yahshua. Do not follow or chase after their approval or counsel.
[6] A metaphor for Yisrael.

expose their nakedness. 18 In that day[1] יהוה will take away the finery of their jingling ornaments around their feet, and their headbands, and their moon-shaped ornaments, 19 The chains, and the bracelets, and the veils, 20 The head coverings, and the ornaments of the legs, and the headbands, and the string of beads, and the perfume bottles and the earrings, 21 The rings, and nose jewels, 22 The expensive robes, and the mantles, and the shawls, and the purses, 23 The mirrors, and the fine linen, and the turbans, and the large veils. 24 And it shall come to pass, that instead of a sweet smell there shall be a stink; and instead of a belt a rope; and instead of well set hair baldness; and instead of a nice robe a sackcloth skirt; and burning instead of tiferet. 25 Your men shall fall by the sword, and your mighty in the war. 26 And her gates shall lament and mourn; and she being ruined shall sit upon the ground.

4 And in that day[2] seven women shall take hold of one man,[3] saying, We will eat our own lechem, and wear our own apparel: only let us be called by your name, to take away our reproach.[4] 2 In that day shall the Branch of יהוה be beautiful and full of tiferet, and the fruit of the land shall be excellent and comely for those that are escaped of Yisrael.[5] 3 And it shall come to pass, that he that is left in Tzion,[6] and he that remains in Yahrushalayim, shall be called set-apart, even everyone that is written among the living [7] in Yahrushalayim: 4 When יהוה shall have washed away the filth of the daughters of Tzion, and shall have purged the bloodguilt

of Yahrushalayim from the midst of it by the Ruach of mishpat, and by the Ruach of burning.[8] 5 And יהוה will create upon every dwelling place of Har Tzion, and upon her gatherings, a cloud and smoke by day, and the shining of a flaming of fire by night: for upon all the tiferet shall be an eternal shechinah covering.[9] 6 And there shall be a sukkah for a shadow in the daytime from the heat, and for a place of refuge, and for a cover from storm and from rain.[10]

5 Now will I shir to my Beloved a shir of my Beloved touching His vineyard.[11] My well Beloved has a vineyard in a very fruitful hill:[12] 2 And He fenced it in, and removed the stones, and planted it with the choicest vine, and built a tower in the midst of it, and also made a winepress in it: and He looked that it should bring forth grapes, but instead it brought forth wild grapes. 3 And now, O inhabitants of Yahrushalayim, and men of Yahudah, please shofet, between Me and My vineyard. 4 What could have been done more for My vineyard that I have not done in it? Why when I looked for grapes, it brought forth only wild grapes? 5 And now; I will tell you what I will do to My vineyard: I will take away the hedge of it, and it shall be eaten up; and break down its walls, and it shall be trampled down:[13] 6 And I will lay it waste: it shall not be pruned, nor dug; but there shall come up weeds and thorn bushes: I will also command the clouds that they do not rain upon it. 7 For the vineyard of יהוה of hosts is Beit Yisrael, and the men of Yahudah[14] His pleasant plant: and He looked for mishpat, but found oppression;

---

[1] Day of judgment.
[2] **Atid lavoh.**
[3] Yahshua.
[4] This verse does not support polygamy as some try to teach. It speaks of the daughter of Tzion in her kingdom perfection grabbing hold of the Man Yahshua, the branch of Jesse as seen in the next verse.
[5] The messianic redemption always speaks of only the surviving two-house remnant, but never the whole nation as Dual Covenant theology wrongly teaches.
[6] Redeemed remnant, after the Day of YHWH.
[7] Lamb's Book of Life.

[8] Cleansing through the fire of judgment.
[9] The everlasting cloud and fire of kingdom esteem covering all those who are part of the congregation of the redeemed.
[10] The tabernacle, symbolic of YHWH's covering over His remnant people in Mt. Zion forever.
[11] Matthew 21:33-46.
[12] Abba YHWH speaks to His Son about the Son's beloved vineyard Yisrael.
[13] In both the Babylonian siege, and later the Roman siege in 70CE.
[14] Both houses are seen as the vineyard.

for tzedakah, but found weeping. 8 *Woe to them that join bayit to bayit, that add field to field, until there is no room, that they may be placed alone in the midst of the land!*[1] 9 *In My hearing* **יהוה** *of hosts said, Of an emet many bayits shall be desolate, even the great and fine ones, without inhabitant.* 10 *Yes, ten acres of vineyard shall yield one bath, and a homer of zera shall yield an ephah.*[2] 11 *Woe to them that rise up early in the morning, that they may pursue strong drink; that continue until night, until their wine inflames them!* 12 *And the harp, and the lyre, the tambourine, and flute, and wine, are in their feasts: but they regard not the work of* **יהוה**, *neither consider the operation of His hands.* 13 *Therefore My people are gone into exile, because they have no da'at: and their honorable men are starved, and their multitude dried up with thirst.* 14 *Therefore Sheol has enlarged itself, and opened its mouth without measure: and their tiferet, and their multitude, and their pride, and he that has unjust simcha, shall descend into it.* 15 *And the mean-spirited man shall be brought down, and the mighty man shall be humbled, and the eyes of the proud shall be humbled:* 16 *But* **יהוה** *of hosts shall be exalted in mishpat, and El that is set-apart shall be set-apart in tzedakah.* 17 *Then shall the lambs feed after their pasture, and the waste places of the fat ones shall foreigners*[3] *eat.* 18 *Woe to them that draw iniquity with cords of falsehood, and sin as it were with wagon ropes:* 19 *That say, Let Him hurry, and hasten His work, that we may see it: and let the counsel of the Set-Apart One of Yisrael draw near and come, that we may know it!* 20 *Woe to them that call evil tov, and tov evil; that put darkness for light, and light for darkness; that put bitter for sweet, and sweet for bitter!* 21 *Woe to them that are wise in their own eyes, and clever in their own sight!* 22 *Woe to them that are mighty to drink wine, and men of strength who mix strong drink:* 23 *Who justify the wicked for a bribe, and take away the tzedakah of the tzadik from him!* 24 *Therefore as the fire devours the stubble, and the flame consumes the chaff, so their root shall be as rottenness, and their blossom shall go up as dust: because they have cast away the Torah of* **יהוה** *of hosts, and despised the word of the Set-Apart One of Yisrael.* 25 *Therefore is the anger of* **יהוה** *kindled against His people, and He has stretched forth His hand against them, and has smitten them: and the hills did tremble, and their corpses were torn in the midst of the streets. For all this His anger has not turned away, but His hand is stretched out still.* 26 *And He will lift up a banner to the nations from far, and will whistle to them from the ends of the earth: and, see, they shall come with speed swiftly:* 27 *None shall be weary nor stumble among them; none shall slumber nor sleep; neither shall the belt of their waist be loosed, nor the latchet of their sandals be broken:* 28 *Whose arrows are sharp, and all their bows bent, their horses' hoofs shall seem like flint, and their wheels like a whirlwind:* 29 *Their roaring shall be like a lion, they shall roar like young lions; they shall roar, and lay hold of the prey, and shall carry it away safely, and none shall rescue it.* 30 *And in that day they shall roar against them like the roaring of the sea: and if one looks to the land, see darkness and sorrow, and the light is darkened by the clouds over it.*[4]

6 In the year that melech Uzziyah died I also saw **יהוה** sitting upon a throne, high and lifted up, and the hem of His robe[5] filled the Beit HaMikdash. 2 Above it stood seraphim: each one had six wings; with two he covered his face, and with two he covered his feet, and with two he flew. 3 And one cried to another, and said, Kadosh,

---

[1] Greed and covetousness found in both houses.
[2] Great lack will come to the vineyard. Ephraim lacking Torah, and Judah lacking Moshiach.
[3] Heathen.

[4] Judgment upon the vineyard.
[5] Yahshua, since no man has or can see the Father, either in person or in vision.

kadosh, kadosh, is **יהוה** of hosts: the whole earth is full of His tiferet. 4 And the posts of the door shook at the voice of him that cried, and the Bayit[1] was filled with smoke. 5 Then I said, Woe is me! For I am undone, because I am a man of unclean lips, and I live in the midst of a people of unclean lips: for my eyes have seen the Melech,[2] **יהוה** of hosts. 6 Then flew one of the seraphim to me, having a live coal in his hand, which he had taken with the tongs from the altar: 7 And he laid it upon my mouth, and said, See, this has touched your lips; and now your iniquity is taken away from you, and your sin is purged. 8 Also I heard the voice of **יהוה**, saying, Whom shall I send, and who will go for Us?[3] Then I said, Hinani; send me. 9 And He said, *Go, and tell this people, You shema indeed, but understand nothing; and you see indeed, but perceive nothing. 10 Make the lev of this people fat, and make their ears heavy, and shut their eyes; lest they see with their eyes, and shema with their ears, and understand with their lev, and shall make teshuvah, and be healed.*[4] 11 Then said I, **יהוה**, how long? And He answered, *Until the cities be wasted without inhabitants, and the bayits without a man, and the land be utterly desolate,*[5] 12 And **יהוה** has removed men far away,[6] and there be a great forsaking in the midst of the land. 13 But yet in it[7] shall be a tenth,[8] and they shall return, and shall be eaten: as a pistachio eytz, and as an oak eytz, whose stump remains, after they cast their leaves: so the set-apart zera shall be the stump.[9]

7 And it came to pass in the days of Ahaz the son of Yotham, the son of Uzziyah, melech of Yahudah, that Rezin the melech of Aram, and Pekah the son of Remalyah, melech of Yisrael, went up toward Yahrushalayim to war against it, but could not prevail against it. 2 And it was told to Beit David,[10] saying, Aram is in alliance with Ephraim.[11] And His lev was moved, and the lev of His people, as the eytzim of the woods is moved with the strong wind. 3 Then said **יהוה** to Yeshayahu, *Go forth now to meet Ahaz, and take Shear-Yahsuv[12] your son, at the end of the channel of the upper pool in the highway of the Launderers Field, 4 And say to him, Take heed, and be quiet; fear not, neither be troubled by these two stubs of smoking firebrands,[13] [14] for the fierce anger of Rezin melech of Aram, and by the son of Remalyah. 5 Because Aram, Ephraim, and the son of Remalyah, have taken evil counsel against you, saying, 6 Let us go up against Yahudah, and trouble it, and let us break them open for ourselves, and set our own melech the son of Taveal in their midst,* 7 This says the Master **יהוה**, *It shall not stand, and neither shall it come to pass. 8 For the head of Aram is Dameshek, and the head of Dameshek is Rezin; and within sixty-five years shall Ephraim be broken, that it be Lo-Ami, not a people.*[15] 9 And the head of Ephraim is Shomron, and the head of Shomron is Remalyah's son. If you will not believe Me, surely you shall not be established.[16] 10 Moreover **יהוה** spoke again to Ahaz, saying, 11 *Ask a sign[17] from **יהוה** Your Elohim; ask it in depth, or make*

---

[1] The same "house" where the Ruach fell in Acts 2; and not in the upper room.
[2] Moshiach.
[3] A reference to the duality of powers in heaven; YHWH and His Word-the Son.
[4] When Yisrael refuses understanding and perception, their heart, like that of Pharaoh, just grows hard like wax.
[5] The dullness will last until the exile is over.
[6] The men of Ephraim Yisrael.
[7] The exile.
[8] People are curious as to how many will actually constitute the returning remnant. This verse indicates a tenth of 4 billion, or perhaps 400 million.
[9] The restored remnant seed of Jacob is called the stump.

[10] Judah.
[11] The 10 tribes of the north.
[12] Isaiah is instructed to take his son **Shear-Yahshuv**, meaning; "a remnant will return."
[13] Aram and Ephraim in league against Judah.
[14] "Weakening troublemakers" according to Aramaic Peshitta.
[15] This was written in 786BCE, as this foretells of Ephraim's exile completed in 721 BCE. The point is for the King of Judah not to worry, since Ephraim won't be around as a nation for much longer.
[16] In Judah's throne.
[17] Hebrew word is **OT**.

the request highly difficult.[1] 12 But Ahaz said, I will not ask, neither will I test ·.[2] 13 And Yeshayahu said, Shema now, O Beit David;[3] Is it a small thing for you[4] to weary men,[5] but will you weary My Elohim also? 14 Therefore יהוה Himself shall give you a sign; See, the[6] virgin[7] shall conceive, and bear a Son, and call [8] His Name Immanu-El.[9] [10] [11] 15 Butter and honey[12]

shall He eat, that He may know to refuse the evil, and choose the tov.[13] 16 For before the child shall know to refuse the evil, and choose the tov, the land that you abhor shall be forsaken of both her melechim.[14] 17 יהוה shall bring upon you, and upon your people, and upon your abba's bayit, days that have not come, from the day that Ephraim departed from Yahudah;[15] even the melech of Ashshur.[16] 18 And it shall come to pass in that day, that יהוה shall whistle for the fly that is in the uttermost part of the rivers of Mitzrayim, and for the bee that is in the land of Ashshur. 19 And they shall come, and shall rest all of them in the desolate valleys, and in the holes of the rocks, and upon all thorns, and upon all the bushes. 20 In the same day shall יהוה humiliate those beyond the river,[17] [18]by the melech of Ashshur, the head, and the hair of the feet: and they shall also shave off the

---

[1] To fully demonstrate this deliverance of Judah and of her king by YHWH, YHWH has mercy upon King Ahaz's anxiety disorder and asks him to ask for a sign or OT (supernatural demonstration) in Hebrew, to verify that YHWH will soon deliver him from this wicked alliance. YHWH tells him to ask big and deep, meaning as specific as Ahaz needs, because YHWH is planning on revealing something far greater than just a limited Word for just Ahaz and Judah at that historical hour.

[2] False humility since he was not a YHWH-seeker to begin with.

[3] King Ahaz in false humility, feigning to be righteous, said to YHWH, I will not ask for a sign, for I am too small to do such a thing. Therefore in verse 13 of Isaiah 7, YHWH bypasses King Ahaz and his false humility, and speaks directly to the whole House of David, or all 12 tribes. He states that they will not weary Him, as He was wearied by King Ahaz, and will speak even if Ahaz does not ask, and even if the whole House of David does not ask, because YHWH is bursting with the revelation of His virgin-born Moshiach.

[4] The words for "you," - appearing three times in verses 13 and 14 - are **mechem, lachem and lachem,** are all in the plural form in the actual Hebrew. That means that the words are no longer addressed to one individual, King Ahaz, but to the entire House of David. What is the sign for all of them, in all the House of David? The **almah** meaning "the virgin" or "the young maiden," (same thing in the time before Yahshua) will conceive and bear a Son and shall call His Name "Immanu-El," a metaphor for Moshiach, when Elohim dwells with us!

[5] Other Yisraelites.

[6] **Ha almah:** the definite article **ha** in Hebrew meaning not "a" but "**the.**"

[7] The Masoretic text uses **almah** in Isaiah 7:14 which means virgin, but then denies the virgin birth in spite of this word almah, claiming that **betulah** ought to have been used as if they have right to instruct YHWH. But the LXX (Septuagint) translates this as **parthenos,** which mean untouched virgin woman. The Aramaic Peshitta confirms the LXX with **betulah,** another synonymous, clear, Aramaic/Hebrew word for "virgin."

[8] The virgin will call his name **Emanu-El** or "El with us." Us in context, is the nation of Yisrael.

[9] The unsaved rabbis insist that this prophecy was about King Hezekiah. But this prophecy cannot be talking about Hezekiah, for one overriding reason. If Hezekiah was the promised Moshiach "Immanuel," then why did all ha neviim write of the still-future coming of the Moshiach long after Hezekiah, (for the span of 386 years after) who was a contemporary of Isaiah, had died? Malachi, Zechariah, Zephaniah, Jeremiah, and others all wrote well after Hezekiah had come. If Hezekiah were Immanuel, no further future prophesies would have been necessary! More than that, Mrs. Ahaz had already given birth to Hezekiah and Hezekiah was nine years old at this time! The prophecy is about a future birth, through a future maiden or virgin. At the time this prophecy was given, Mrs. Ahaz was not a virgin and Hezekiah was already born. Rabbi Hillel of Beth Hillel of the first-century school of learning, held to the "Hezekiah is Immanuel" theory and his entire life's work was held in dispute and in much disgrace by his contemporaries, who saw Rabbi Hillel's view

as an embarrassment to the truth. Then of course when the Hezekiah route does not work, the anti-Moshiach demons try the "Isaiah's son" routine, stating that **Shaar Yahshuuv** is Immanuel, and Mrs. Isaiah is the almah. The problem with that is that she couldn't have been an almah, since she already had a son (Shaar-Yahshuv); and if it speaks of a future son, that also wouldn't matter because she would no longer be a virgin/maiden.

[10] Keep in mind that the virgin (**betulah**) versus young woman (**almah**) controversy, began only after Yahshua of Nazareth. Before that there was no dissension at all, since all acknowledged that the terms were interchangeable.

[11] In the Hebrew; verse 14 reads **"lachen yetain adonai who la chem ot, henay ha almah harah veyoledet ben vekarat shemoh Immanuel."**

[12] Torah.

[13] The child in verse 15 is the Moshiach, who will always choose good over evil, making this child sinless due to His virgin birth.

[14] Verse 16 reverts back to **Shaar-Yeshuuv,** who is standing there hearing the prophecy, and YHWH says that before Isaiah's son grows up, and knows right from wrong, the land of Judah will be free from the attacks of the evil alliance between Ephraim-Yisrael and Syria-Aram. In essence, the son of Isaiah becomes proof of the veracity and surety of the almah/virgin birth prophecy. The virgin birth prophecy is so numbing and so astounding, that YHWH decided to bring little **Shaaer-Yahshuv** as a sign that in essence will say to all the House of David that "when you see both enemies of Judah defeated in Ahaz's days, before Isaiah's son grows up, then know of a certainty that the almah will conceive, and bring Yisrael their Savior, "Immanu-El" or "Elohim with us" in human form. YHWH is in essence challenging all Yisrael by declaring that only if Isaiah's son grows up and only if Judah's enemies are not yet defeated at that time; can this Messianic promise of redemption fail.

[15] From the days of the split in the Davidic monarchy.

[16] Judah need not worry as YHWH promises to send Ephraim (Judah's enemy) into exile by Assyria, and by their king.

[17] Jordan.

[18] Ephraimite territory.

beards. 21 *And it shall come to pass in that day, that a man shall nourish a young cow, and two sheep; 22 And it shall come to pass, for the abundance of milk that they shall give, he shall eat butter: for everyone left in the land shall eat curds. 23 And it shall come to pass in that day, that every place where there were a thousand vines worth a thousand shekels of silver, it shall even be for weeds and thorns.[1] 24 With arrows and with bows shall men come there; because all the land shall become weeds and thorns. 25 And on all hills that shall be dug with the hoe, there shall not come there the fear of weeds and thorns: but it shall be for the sending forth of oxen, and a place for sheep to roam.*

8 Moreover יהוה said to me, *Take a large scroll, and write in it with a man's pen concerning Maher-Shalal-Hash-Baz-the plunder hurries, the prey speeds along-[2] 2 And I took with me reliable witnesses to record, Uriyah the kohen, and Zacharyah the son of Berechiyah. 3 And I went in to the neviyah;*[3]*and she conceived, and bore a son.* Then said יהוה to me, *Call his name Maher-shalal-hash-baz. 4 For before the child shall have da'at to cry, My abba, and My ima, the riches of Dameshek and the plunder of Shomron shall be taken away before the melech of Ashshur. 5* יהוה spoke also to me again, saying, *6 Forasmuch as this people refuses the mayim of Shiloah[4] that flow softly, and instead have their simcha in Rezin and Remalyah's son;[5] 7 Now therefore, see,* יהוה *brings up upon them the mayim of the river, strong and mighty, even the melech of Ashshur, and all his tiferet: and He shall come up over all his channels, and go over all his banks:[6] 8 And He shall pass through*

Yahudah;[7] *He shall overflow and pass over, He shall reach even to the neck; and by the stretching out of His wings He shall fill the width of Your land, O Immanu-El.[8] 9 Be shattered O you people,[9] and you shall be broken in pieces; and shema, all of the far countries: prepare yourselves, and you shall be broken in pieces; put on yourselves, and you shall be broken in pieces. [10]*
10 *Take counsel together, and it shall come to nothing; speak the word, and it shall not stand: for El is with us.* 11 For יהוה spoke this to me with a strong hand, and instructed me that I should not follow in the halacha of this people, saying, 12 *Do not regard as an alliance what this nation calls an alliance; neither fear what they neither fear; nor be troubled by their alliance.[11]* 13 Set-Apart יהוה *of hosts Himself; Him shall you fear; and let Him be Your awe.[12] 14 And He shall be for a Place of Refuge[13]; but for a Stone of stumbling and for a Rock of offence[14] to both the bayits of Yisrael,[15] as a trap and a snare to the inhabitants of Yahrushalayim. 15 And many amongst both bayits shall stumble,[16] and fall, and be broken, and be snared, and be taken. [17]*
16 *Seal up the testimony; seal the Torah*

---

[1] When Ephraim is taken into exile.
[2] Ephraim's demise and exile.
[3] Isaiah's wife.
[4] "Shiloh" or "Shiloah," a title of the Moshiach. The "mayim of Shiloah" refers to the Ruach HaKodesh given to those resting and trusting in Moshiach Yahshua.
[5] Judah trusted in those who ultimately would do them no tov thing.
[6] Ephraim's impending doom.

---

[7] Threaten but not capture Judah.
[8] Here the land of Yisrael is called Emanu-El, a title, further proving that this is not the actual name of the Moshiach Yahshua.
[9] By Assyria.
[10] Repeated twice for the eventual exile of both houses.
[11] Ephraim's alliance will fail, for he does not align himself with YHWH of Hosts.
[12] YHWH should be Ephraim's Rock.
[13] For those who desire Him to be so.
[14] Moshiach-YHWH was that Stumbling Stone according to Acts 4:11, Ephesians 2:20, 1 Peter 2:4-8.
[15] Both houses have stumbled over the coming of Moshiach Yahshua, as prophesied here. Judah rejected the living Torah, YHWH's Son, and is blind. Ephraim or non-Jewish Yisrael has rejected their identity as the other house of Yisrael, along with their responsibilities to live in the eternal ways of the written Torah, and are therefore blind as well. In order for Ephraim or non-Jewish Yisrael to stumble at Moshiach Yahshua's arrival, by definition they had to be in existence to the supernatural eye of YHWH, even though the natural eye had lost track of them some 721 years before the Stumbling Stone arrived.
[16] Many amongst both houses shall stumble.
[17] Taken away to judgment. In Hebraic understanding "taken away" does not mean raptured to heaven, but left behind to be removed to wrath.

among My talmidim.[1] 17 And I will wait upon **יהוה**, that hides His face from Beit Yaakov,[2] and I will look for Him.[3] [4] 18 See, I and the children that **יהוה** has given me[5] are for signs and for wonders[6] in Yisrael from **יהוה** of hosts, who dwells on Har Tzion. 19 And when they shall say to you, Seek to them that have familiar ruachim, and to sorcerers that whisper and mutter[7]: should not a people seek for their Elohim? Who asks the dead about the living?[8] 20 To the Torah and to the testimony:[9] if they speak not according to this word,[10] it is because there is no Light in them.[11] 21 And they shall pass through it, hard pressed and hungry: and it shall come to pass, that when they shall be hungry, they shall be angered,[12] and they will curse their Melech and their Elohim, while looking upward.[13] 22 And they shall look to the earth; and see tribulation and darkness, gloom in anguish; and they shall be driven to darkness.[14]

9 Nevertheless the dimness[15] shall not be such as was in her distress,[16] when at first He lightly afflicted the land of Zevulon and the land of Naphtali, and afterward did more heavily afflict her by the way of the sea, beyond the Yarden,[17] in Galil of the gentiles.[18] [19] 2 The people that walked in darkness[20] have seen a great Light: they that live in the land of the shadow of death, upon them has the Light shined.[21] 3 You[22] have multiplied the nation,[23] and increased the simcha:[24] they simcha before You[25] like the simcha in harvest,[26] as men simcha when they divide the plunder. 4 For You have broken the yoke of his burden, and the staff of his shoulder, the rod of his oppressor, as in the day of Midyan.[27] 5 For every voice, which

---

[1] In contrast to those of both houses taken away, those left behind and protected by Moshiach Yahshua will have the testimony of His atonement and bodily resurrection plus the witness of Torah sealed in their levim and on their lips.
[2] He hides from both houses until they find Him and His truth in the manifested face of Yahshua (2nd Cor. 4:6) who then seals His testimony upon us.
[3] Both houses can remove their blindness by seeking Yahshua.
[4] Yahshua speaking in the Spirit of waiting for the right time to be revealed to Yisrael; as that time will be chosen by His Father alone.
[5] Yahshua the eternal brought-forth Son of YHWH speaks in the first person, as Abba YHWH gave all His children/disciples to Him, along with all other things such as Yahshua's power and His authority.
[6] Yahshua's talmidim are ordained to "perform miracles" in Yisrael amongst both houses, as seen in Mark 16:15-18 and Luke 10:16 to reveal to the world that they are Yahshua's Yisraelite children.
[7] Both houses have long been involved with various forms of witchcraft.
[8] Only the blind.
[9] True Yisraelites run to both the testimony of His resurrection, along with a life grounded in Torah-obedience.
[10] Moshiach Yahshua and Torah.
[11] The blindness of both houses does not allow light to enter, when one of the two key parts of true emunah are missing.
[12] In Assyrian exile.
[13] As both houses have often done through the years.
[14] Into exile and prolonged blindness and wandering.
[15] Blindness.
[16] Ephraim's punishment into exile.

[17] The Ephraimite exile took place in stages.
[18] The last stage was all of Galilee and Shomron the capital of the north.
[19] In Luke 1:79 Zechariah promises that Moshiach Yahshua will rescue those "who live in the shadow of death," a clear reference to Isaiah 9:1-3, where Moshiach Himself is prophesied to regather Zebulon, Naphtali and other former Yisraelites, in the "dark" Galilee area. His Light will shine brightest in the former Yisraelite areas of the north, now occupied by gentiles who are the direct descendants of those tribes. This is the main reason that Yahshua made His home in Capernaum, on the border of Zebulon and Naphtali. Yahshua was also a Nazarene or a consecrated one to YHWH by virtue of His chosen dwelling location. He settled in Galilee for the same reason, because He was a Nazarene or a separated Holy One to His Father, and desired to live separate from the religious order in Jerusalem, that had no care and concern for the welfare of their Ephraimite brothers.
[20] Ephraim Yisrael.
[21] Moshiach Himself is prophesied to regather Zebulon, Naphtali and other former Yisraelites, in the "dark" Galilee area. His Light will shine brightest in the former Yisraelite areas of the north, now occupied by goyim who are the direct descendants of those tribes.
[22] Yahshua.
[23] Yahshua increased Yisrael by bringing the northern tribes back into the fold and thereby did fulfill the promise to increase the nation from merely being that of Jewish-Yisrael, to the start of the restoration of both houses. He thus increased the nation numerically, along with the accompanying joy of a nation rebuilt.
[24] By bringing forgiveness and salvation, and the beginning of the promised end of the exile.
[25] The redeemed remnant of both houses.
[26] Like **Sukkot**, or Tabernacles and the final harvest.
[27] Only verse 4 of Isaiah 9 remains to be fulfilled in the **pashat** or literal sense and awaits His return to earth. Using **remez** or hint, the deliverance from Midianite captivity by a valiant spirit is done by Moshiach; in both the Spirit realm (heavenly tabernacle) and the physical realm (Ephraim's earthly restoration), whereas the historical deliverance from Midian has already taken place in the physical realm by Gideon. Moshiach Yahshua states in John 8:32-36 that He came to deliver the captive, and those who had been taken captive, who were in bondage under the yoke of sin, from which they could not free themselves. As such, there existed a spiritual yoke over Yisrael, worse than that of Midian or Rome. In Isaiah 9:1-4, we have both the literal fulfillment of Yahshua's restoration of the north, as well as His spiritual destruction of the yoke of sin, in the second level of Hebraic understanding.

is heard, brings fear, and garments rolled in dom; but this shall be with burning and fuel of fire.[1] 6 For to us a Child is born, to us a Son is given: and the government shall be upon His shoulder: and His Name shall be called Wonderful, Counselor, The Mighty-El, The Everlasting Abba, The Prince of Shalom. [2] 7 Of the increase [3] of His government and shalom there shall be no end, upon kesay David, and upon His malchut, to order it, and to establish it with mishpat and with justice from now on even le-olam-va-ed. The zeal of יהוה of hosts will perform this.[4] 8 יהוה sent a Word[5] into Yaakov, and it has Lighted [6] upon Yisrael.[7] 9 And all the people shall know, even Ephraim and the inhabitants of Shomron, that say in their pride and haughtiness of lev, 10 The bricks may have fallen down, but we will rebuild with cut stones: the sycamores are cut down, but we will change them into cedars. 11 Therefore יהוה shall set up the adversaries of Rezin against him, and join his enemies together; 12 The Arameans before, and the Philistines behind; and they shall devour Yisrael with open mouth. For all this His anger has not been turned away, but His hand is stretched out still. 13 For the people do not turn to Him that smites them, neither do they seek יהוה of hosts. 14 Therefore יהוה will cut off from Yisrael[8] head and tail, branch and reed, in one day. 15 The zachanim and the honorable, he is the head; and ha navi that teaches lies, he is the tail. 16 For the leaders of this people cause them to go astray; and they that are led by them are destroyed.[9] 17 Therefore יהוה shall have no simcha in their young men, neither shall He have rachamim on their fatherless and widows: for everyone is a hypocrite and an evildoer, and every mouth speaks folly. For all this His anger has not turned away, but His hand is stretched out against us still. 18 For wickedness burns as the fire: it shall devour the weeds and thorns, and shall kindle the thickets of the forest, and they shall be rolled up like the lifting up of

---

[1] Yahshua's victory over Yisrael's physical Midianite and Edomite enemies, in the Day of YHWH.
[2] In the Hebrew:" **Ki yelled yulad lanu ben netan lanu va te-he hamisrah al shichmoh va yiqra shemo pele yoetz, el gibor, avai ad, sar shalom."** In Hebrew grammar there exist two types of verbs. One is for a completed action and is known as a "perfect verb." The other verb is for an action not yet concluded, which by implication means a future or an ongoing action, and is known as an "imperfect verb." These references to "va te-he" and "va yiqra" both are imperfect verbs indicating future fulfillment, at the time of the prophecy in 768 BCE. The verbs **"yelled nolad"** and **"ben netan"** are in fact past tense perfect verbs. However there is yet a third category called the "prophetic perfect," meaning a writing style where the event is yet future, but is written in a past tense, or as a perfect completed action. Many prophecies in Tanach that are clearly future events use "perfect verbs" to describe still-future prophetic events, since YHWH knows the end from the beginning, and is prophetically declaring "a finished action," even though it hasn't yet actually taken place. One such example is found in Isaiah 5:13, where both houses of Yisrael are declared to be in exile, even though neither house of Yisrael had been sent out into exile at the time of the prophecy. Yet it is still written using a past perfect verb in a "prophetic perfect" future declaration. Another such example of the "prophetic perfect" is the Suffering Servant chapter of Isaiah 53, where the Servant is seen as having completed the work of atonement, yet its literal fulfillment is yet some 740 years in the future. Isaiah 9:6 contains the "prophetic perfect" in the words **"yelled nolad"** ("a child has been born"), **ben natan** ("a Son has been given"). Then later in verse 6 of Isaiah 9, Isaiah takes these "prophetic perfects" and combines them with the imperfect future verbs **"va te-he"** and **"va yiqra,"** and the government "will be," and He "shall be called." The literal reading is as follows. "Child born to us, Son given to us and the government will be (future tense at the time of prophecy in 786 BCE), and He will be called Wonderful Counselor, Mighty-El, Eternal Father, Prince of Peace." As you'll carefully note, the references to a future fulfillment in future terms is used four times in Isaiah 9:6, twice as imperfect future verbs (actions not completed) and twice as "prophetic perfect" references, thereby disqualifying any possible past fulfillment, as well as any possible immediate fulfillment in King Hezekiah, the son of King Ahaz. If in fact Hezekiah the righteous king of Judah was the "Eternal Father," it appears He died prematurely. Not a very "eternal" thing to do.
[3] The Messianic prophecy found in Yeshayahu 9:7 is a final evidence found in the original Hebrew words of the virgin birth of Isaiah 7:14. The closed **mem** is always used at the end of a Hebrew word. The only exception is where it is found in this prophecy in verse 7. Here, the closed **mem** is found in the middle of the word, which indicates (according to the modern rabbis) an increase in the Moshiach's government. That word is **le-marbe** meaning, "to increase." Normally (as any beginning Hebrew student would have learned), in the middle of the word the reader would find an open mem. The Zohar says, "The closed **mem** refers to the fact that the Moshiach would be born from a 'closed womb'." Richard Wurmbrand, the Messianic Jew who survived the Holocaust, (commenting on this portion of The Zohar, as he shared this with a Jewish rabbi) said, "Isaiah put a closed **mem** in the middle of the word to show the reader who was destined to understand it; that the Divine Child of whom this prophecy speaks, would be born of the closed womb of a virgin."
[4] Yahshua will rule forever by divine decree of Abba YHWH on David's throne, as the eternal King Moshiach.
[5] Yahshua.
[6] The Light to remove blindness and death.
[7] All 12 tribes.
[8] Ephraim.
[9] Yisraelites must never follow any leader denying either Yahshua or Torah, along with the restoration message, including the True Names of YHWH and Yahshua.

smoke. 19 Through the wrath of יהוה of hosts is the land darkened, and the people shall be as fuel for the fire: no man shall spare his brother. 20 And he shall snatch food on the right hand, and still be hungry; and he shall eat with the left hand, and shall not be satisfied: they shall eat every man the flesh of his own arm: 21 Menashsheh, Ephraim; and Ephraim, Menashsheh: and they together shall be against Yahudah.[1] For all this His anger is not turned away, but His hand is stretched out still.

10 *Woe to them that decree unrighteous decrees, and that write unjust decrees which they have prescribed; 2 To turn aside the needy from My mishpatim, and to take away the rights from the poor of My people, so that widows may be their prey, and so that they may rob the fatherless! 3 And what will you do in the day of Your visitation of punishment, and in the ruin that shall come from far? To whom will you run for help? And where will you leave your wealth? 4 Without Me they shall bow among the prisoners, and they shall fall among the slain. For all this His anger is not turned away, but His hand is stretched out still. 5 O Ashshur, the rod of My anger, and the staff in whose hand is My displeasure. 6 I will send him against a hypocritical nation,[2] and against the people of My wrath will I give him a command, to take the plunder, and to take the prey, and to trample them down like the mud of the streets. 7 But he does not intend to do this only, neither does his lev think that; but it is in his lev to destroy and cut off many nations. 8 For he says, Are not my rulers all melechim? 9 Is not Calno as Carchemish? Is not Hamath as Arphad? Is not Shomron as Dameshek? 10 Just as my hand has found the malchutim of the idols, whose graven images did exceed those of Yahrushalayim and of Shomron; 11 Shall I not, as I have done to Shomron and her idols, do also to Yahrushalayim and her idols? 12 Therefore it shall come to pass, that when יהוה has performed His whole work upon Har Tzion and on Yahrushalayim, I will punish the fruit of the proud lev of the melech of Ashshur, and the boasting of his proud looks. 13 For he says, By the strength of my hand I have done it, and by my chochma; for I am clever: and I have removed the boundaries of the nations, and have robbed their treasures, and I have put down the inhabitants like a brave man: 14 And my hand has found as a nest the riches of the people: and as one gathers eggs that are left, have I gathered all the earth; and there was none that moved the wing, or opened their mouth, with even a peep. 15 Shall the axe boast itself against him that cuts with it? Or shall the saw magnify itself against him that saws with it? As if the rod could wave those that lift it up, or as if the staff could lift that which is not wood. 16 Therefore shall the Master, יהוה of hosts, send among his rich ones leanness; and instead of His tiferet He shall kindle a burning like the burning of a fire. 17 And the Light of Yisrael[3] shall be for a fire, and His Set-Apart One as a flame: and it shall burn and devour his thorns and his weeds in one day;[4] 18 And shall consume the tiferet of his forest, and of his fruitful field, both being and body: and they shall be as when an invalid wastes away. 19 And the rest of the eytzim of his forest shall be few, so that a child may count them. 20 And it shall come to pass in that day,[5] that the restored remnant of Yisrael,[6] and such as have escaped belonging to Beit Yaakov, shall no more again trust him that smote them;[7] but shall trust and lean upon יהוה, the Set-Apart One of Yisrael, in emet.[8] 21 The*

---

[1] There is nothing new about this. The civil war is 2,900 years old and counting. In the alliance against Judah, Ephraim was united in purpose.
[2] Ephraim.
[3] Yahshua.
[4] Ephraim.
[5] End of the age.
[6] Dom atoned for minority from both houses.
[7] Assyria or any other heathen nation.
[8] When David's throne is established as chief of all the nations.

remnant shall return,[1] even the remnant of Yaakov,[2] to the Mighty-El. 22 For though Your people Yisrael be as the sand of the sea,[3] yet a remnant of them shall return:[4] their number decreased yet overflowing with tzedakah.[5] 23 For the Master יהוה of hosts shall make a full end of all that He has determined, in the midst of all the earth. 24 Therefore this says the Master יהוה of hosts, O My people that live in Tzion, be not afraid of Ashshur: he shall smite you with a rod, and shall lift up his staff against you, after the manner of Mitzrayim.[6] 25 For yet a very little while, and the displeasure shall cease, and My anger will be to their destruction.[7] 26 And יהוה of hosts shall stir up a beating for him like the slaughter of Midyan at the rock of Orev: and as His rod was upon the sea, so shall He lift it up after the manner of Mitzrayim. 27 And it shall come to pass in that day, that his burden shall be removed from your shoulder, and his yoke from off your neck, and the yoke shall be destroyed because of the anointing. 28 He is come to Ayath; he is passed to Migron; at Michmash he has laid up his supplies: 29 They are gone over the passage: they have taken up their lodging at Geva; Ramah is afraid; Giveah of Shaul has fled. 30 Lift up your voice, O daughter of Galliym: cause it to be heard to Laysh, O poor Anathoth. 31 Madmenah is removed; the inhabitants of Gevim gather themselves to flee. 32 As yet shall he remain at Nob that day: he shall shake his hand against the Mount of the daughter of Tzion, the hill of Yahrushalayim. 33 See, the Master, יהוה of hosts, shall loop off a branch with fear: and the tall ones are cut down, and the haughty shall be humbled. 34 And He shall cut down the thickets of the forest with iron, and Levanon shall fall as a mighty one.

11 And there shall come forth a rod out of the stem of Yishai, and a Netzer-Branch[8] shall grow out of His roots:[9] 2 And the Ruach HaKodesh of יהוה shall rest upon Him, the Ruach of chochma and binah, the Ruach of counsel and might, the Ruach of da'at and of the fear of יהוה;[10] 3 And shall make Him of quick binah in the fear of יהוה: and He shall not shofet after the sight of His eyes, neither reprove after the hearing of His ears:[11] 4 But with tzedakah shall He shofet the poor, and decide with equity for the meek of the earth: and He shall smite the earth with the rod of His mouth,[12] and with the breath of His lips[13] shall He slay the wicked. 5 And tzedakah shall be the belt of His loins, and faithfulness the belt of His waist. 6 The wolf also shall live with the lamb, and the leopard shall lie down with the young goat, and the calf and the young lion and the fattened lamb together, and a little child shall lead them.[14] 7 And the cow and the bear shall feed; their young ones shall lie down together, and the lion shall eat straw like an ox. 8 And the nursing child shall play on the hole of the cobra, and the weaned child shall put his hand on the viper's nest. 9 They shall not do evil nor destroy in My entire set-apart mountain: for the earth shall be full of the da'at of יהוה, as the mayim covers the sea.[15] 10 And in

---

[1] In context both houses, including Ephraim who used to trust in Assyria.
[2] From all 12 tribes.
[3] The metaphor referring to the promise of physical multiplicity.
[4] This is a clear word that from between 3-4 billion physical Yisraelites, only a remnant, or as seen earlier in Isaiah about 10 percent, or 400 million will return. Their accommodations will be in the "Greater Yisrael," promised to the patriarchs.
[5] The very imputed righteousness of Moshiach Yahshua Himself.
[6] Speaking to Judah, who will be protected for another 150 years or so.
[7] Egypt will battle them, and later Babylon will consume them.

[8] This was the prophecy where Yahshua the coming Moshiach was called **Netzer**, and His followers naturally **Netzarim** or Nazarenes. Matthew 2:23 speaks of this prophecy.
[9] The rabbis like Rashi teach that the **Netzer**, or the Nazarene is, Moshiach Ben Yoseph, called this because He will specifically be sent to find, locate and restore the ten tribes of Ephraim Yisrael.
[10] All these attributes are called sefirot of YHWH's Ruach and Moshiach.
[11] He will issue kingdom justice only by what is recorded in Torah.
[12] His words and rulings in Torah.
[13] Ruach HaKodesh without measure.
[14] In the **atid lavoh.**
[15] In the restored kingdom.

that day[1] there shall be a root of Yishai, which shall stand as a miraculous banner[2][3] to the people;[4] to it shall the gentile nations seek,[5] and His rest shall be with tiferet.[6] 11 And it shall come to pass in that day,[7] that יהוה shall set His hand[8] again a second time[9] to recover and restore[10] the remnant[11] of His people,[12] who shall be left,[13] from Ashshur,[14] and from Mitzrayim, and from Pathros, and from Cush, and from Eylam, and from Shinar,[15] and from Hamath, and from the coastlands of the sea.[16][17] 12 And He[18] shall set up a miraculous Banner[19] for the nations and He [20] shall gather the outcasts of Yisrael,[21][22] and gather together the dispersed of Yahudah[23] from the four corners of the earth.[24][25] 13 The envy also of Ephraim shall depart, [26] [27] and the adversaries of Yahudah shall be cut off.[28] Ephraim shall not envy Yahudah, [29] and Yahudah shall not trouble Ephraim. [30] 14 But they[31] shall fly upon the shoulders of the Philistines [32] toward the west; [33] they shall plunder them of the east together[34] they shall lay their hands upon Edom and Moav; and the children of Ammon shall be

---

[1] End of this age.
[2] Hebrew word is **Nes**, which can mean either banner, or miracle, or even miraculous banner.
[3] Moshiach Yahshua.
[4] The people of Yisrael.
[5] In a latter-day context, this refers to the seed of Ephraim Yisrael the "fullness of the nations" spoken of in Genesis 48:19 and Romans 11:26.
[6] Established on David's Throne.
[7] Kingdom.
[8] Yahshua.
[9] The first being in 520 BCE when Judah returned. The second time began in 1948, and will conclude with the return of the remnant of both houses.
[10] Or restore.
[11] Not all Yisrael, but a redeemed returning remnant.
[12] The Moshiach's banner being stretched out over the nations in order to perform a dual rescue of two parts of a scattered nation, in two unique stages.
[13] Remnant.
[14] Ephraim.
[15] Judah.
[16] Both houses.
[17] The Moshiach, or "The Banner," does the regathering back to the land. Not man or man's attempts to change immigration laws.
[18] Abba YHWH.
[19] Moshiach Yahshua.
[20] Yahshua; not immigration departments nor deals with the unredeemed orthodox.
[21] According to Jeremiah 3:8 and elsewhere, Ephraim was divorced and outcast from the covenant of Torah and the people of Yisrael. This term only can apply to them.
[22] Ephraim mixed with the nations (Hosea 8:9) and became as one with them. Presently they cannot be recognized nor differentiated from the true gentiles. That is why Yahshua's banner in Isaiah 11:12 is unfurled before all the nations, since verse 12 tells us that both outcast Yisrael and scattered Judah are in the nations. If you were Moshiach looking for Yisraelites, you would not unfurl your banner of love, revelation and restoration anywhere else. The natural understanding of the syntax in question is that Yisrael and Judah are the targets of this love.
[23] Judah on the other hand, was never fully or totally outcast, but were merely dispersed into all nations, but did manage in many instances to maintain their historical, spiritual, and cultural connections to the people and the land of Yisrael.

[24] The dom-washed remnant from both houses return from all four corners of the earth.
[25] If the Jews are all Yisrael, then why, when identifying the returnees in this same passage, does YHWH separate Judah and Yisrael into two categories of the "returning scattered" and the "returning outcasts"? If the covenant community concept applies only to modern Jewry, why was the Renewed Covenant promised to the community of all Yisrael, which includes two groupings of Yisraelites at the dawn of the messianic age?
[26] The result of Moshiach's work; Ephraim's desire to be Yisrael will be met, and their jealousy towards Judah will cease, as they return as equal heirs in the Commonwealth of Yisrael.
[27] This grievous envy is best-seen and illustrated in Yahshua's declaration of the parable of the prodigal son in Luke 15.
[28] Historical enemies such as Edom, Ammon, and Moab. With the help of returning Ephraim, the people of Yisrael will be numerically and militarily stronger, in defence of their national interests.
[29] Ephraim's desire has always been to be part of the House of David, and they have been envious of Judah's strong sense of national identity and family. Through Yahshua, Ephraim can reclaim their role in the House of David, and receive their full citizenship in Yisrael. As such their envy is no longer seen, as it is truly healed.
[30] Historically Judah has troubled or vexed Ephraim, by relegating them to different roles and tasks, all designed to send the same message of second-class or second-tier standing in Yisrael. This is seen historically when Ephraimites were identified as traitors from the House of Shaul, as well as when they were under compulsory slave labor to Judah in the days before Jeroboam was raised up as king, and down through the centuries where their image as pagan gentiles was reinforced by Judah, as Judah refused to accept them back into the fold, viewing Ephraim as the eternal apostates or the black sheep of the family. This denial or vexation even resulted in made-up doctrines of men, whereby Ephraim was said to be lost or the "lost ten tribes," thereby affording Judah the luxury of not having to extend recognition to Ephraim, since they were allegedly missing in action. This vexing continues to this day as most "messianic" organizations do not recognize Ephraim, and have not reckoned them as returning Yisrael, but as being merely "messianic gentiles," or gentiles with a "Jewish heart." But when Moshiach returns, both houses will be in shalom with each other, and Judah will no longer be allowed to vex his brother.
[31] Both houses.
[32] Palestinians in Gaza, the same home of the ancient Philistines. Even without a physical connection to the Philistines, they both live in the same land, and both are led by the same hatred of Zion.
[33] Fly them westward.
[34] Together both houses will fight the eastern front as well as the west.

subjected and obey them.[1] [2] 15 And **יהוה** shall utterly destroy the tongue of the Mitzrayim Sea; [3] and with His Mighty Rucah shall He shake His hand over the river,[4] and shall break it into seven streams, and shall cause Yisrael to trample it in their sandals.[5] 16 And there shall be a highway for the remnant of His people,[6] who shall be left, from Ashshur;[7] like as it was for all Yisrael in the day that they came up out of the land of Mitzrayim.[8]

12 And in that day[9] you shall say, O **יהוה**, I will hallel You: though You were angry with me, Your anger is turned away, and You have comforted me. 2 See, El is My Yahshua; I will trust, and will not be afraid: for Yah- **יהוה** is My Strength and My Shir; He also has become My Yahshua.[10] 3 Therefore with simcha shall you draw mayim out of the wells of Yahshua.[11] 4 And in that day shall you say, Baruch Hashem **יהוה**, call upon His Name, declare His doings among the nations,[12] make mention that His Name is exalted.[13] 5 Sing to **יהוה**, for He has done excellent things: this is known in all the earth. 6 Cry out and shout, you inhabitant of Tzion: for great is the Set-Apart One of Yisrael in the midst of you.[14]

13 The burden of Bavel, which Yeshayahu the son of Amotz did see. 2 *Lift up a banner upon the high mountain, exalt the voice to them, wave the hand that they may go into the gates of the nobles. 3 I have commanded My set-apart ones, I have also called My mighty ones for My anger, even them that simcha in My greatness. 4 The noise of a multitude in the mountains, like a great people; a tumultuous noise of the malchutim of the nations gathered together:* **יהוה** *of hosts gathers the army for the battle. 5 They come from a far country, from the end of the shamayim, even* **יהוה**, *and the weapons of His displeasure, to destroy the whole land.*

---

[1] These verses 14-15, and Obadiah 1:18-19 teach in the simplest possible terms, that the Jewish people will never ever conquer the Palestinians, Arabs, Edomites or the sons of Esau, until they are reunited to Ephraim with one heart, one Spirit and one accord, into one massive army, through the reconciliation of Jewish-Yisrael with non-Jewish-Yisrael. We (believers) will continue to struggle and fight ourselves, over the question of "who is the real Yisrael," instead of both camps recognizing the other house as also being legitimate heirs in Yisrael. Only a reunited Yisrael in these final last days of humanity will be able to overthrow the nefarious forces of Islam. This can become a reality in our lifetime. Islam cannot stand against a united Yisrael, for greater is He that is in us, than He that is in the world. We must look upon Ephraim in our midst, with great favor and grant them the recognition they deserve, so that they can take their rightful place in national Yisrael as physical, Spirit-filled, co-heirs, who are willing to join in military and spiritual warfare operations against Yisrael's historic enemies. We will receive the consolation of Jacob, only when we preserve the revelation of Jacob, found in Genesis 30:25.
[2] With a reunified Yisrael, the Middle East problem will end according to Scripture, when the west, along with all Yisrael, puts the Palestinians on airplanes and sends them away. Isaiah 11:14 in its most literal translation reads "they shall fly the Philistines away westward." Those, who in ignorance fight the two-house restoration, are actually postponing the inevitable Yisraelite victory over our enemies. Instead of worrying exclusively about learning Hebrew and keeping kosher, we should be concerned with victory. Biblical victory can be achieved only by a reunified two-house, two-front (spiritual and military) solution to the Arab-Israeli conflict (Obadiah 1:18). The spiritual part is our task as we abide in Him who is Yisrael's Prince. The military part is His work not ours. This truth by no means suggests that militarism is the answer, or militia-type theology, which is anti-Netsarim and wrought with doctrines of hate and superiority. When both houses are back in the Promised Land however, we will be at full force and in our most effective position to finally overcome our enemies.
[3] When both houses come together, another enemy that will be subdued are the strange languages that came forth from the Tower of Babel, as Hebrew is restored to the globe, so that the knowledge of YHWH can fill the earth in the language of revelation.
[4] Euphrates.
[5] YHWH finalizes the restoration with a perfect (7 streams) way of escape for all the seed of Yisrael stuck in countries influenced by the Egyptian tongue, and the pagan manners of that culture.
[6] YHWH always deals with only the remnant, while the world and the church systems attempt to deal in large numbers.
[7] Ephraim.
[8] Ephraim has great hope, as they look back on YHWH's faithfulness in the historic Egyptian redemption.

[9] When a highway of return is made for all Yisrael.
[10] There are those who falsely claim that Yahshua's Name as Savior, or as Yisrael's salvation, is found nowhere in Tanach/First Covenant Scripture. Yet here in the actual Hebrew it reads, "YHWH My strength, and My song, has become My Yahshua." That's what the besarot is all about: YHWH clothing Himself and manifesting as flesh, or YHWH becoming Yahshua.
[11] The fulfillment is found in John 7:38, and Isaiah 44:3, where Yisrael's seed receives the mayim of YHWH's Spirit.
[12] Where Yisrael is scattered.
[13] When both houses are restored as one, in the day of salvation/Yahshua, the Name will be declared along with the Besarot. The restoration itself will proclaim the Name.
[14] Salvation is the recognition of the fact that the Set-Apart One Himself, came to pitch His tabernacle among us, in the flesh of mankind.

6 *Howl, for Yom* יהוה *is at hand.¹ It shall come as a destruction from the Almighty. 7 Therefore shall all hands be faint, and every man's lev shall melt: 8 And they shall be afraid: pains and sorrows shall take hold of them; they shall be in pain as a woman that labors: they shall be amazed at one another; their faces shall be aflame. 9 See, Yom* יהוה *comes, cruel both with wrath and fierce anger, to lay the earth desolate: and He shall destroy the sinners out of it. 10 For the cochavim of the shamayim and its constellations shall not give their light: the sun shall be darkened in its going forth, and the moon shall not send her light to shine.² 11 And I will punish the olam for their evil, and the wicked for their iniquity; and I will cause the arrogance of the proud to cease, and will lay low the pride of the ruthless. 12 I will make a mortal man scarcer than fine gold; even mankind scarcer than the gold of Ophir. 13 Therefore I will shake the shamayim, and the earth shall move out of its place, in the wrath of* יהוה *of hosts, and in the day of His fierce anger. 14 And man shall be as the hunted gazelle, and as a sheep that no man takes up: every man shall turn to his own people, and flee into his own land. 15 Each one that is found shall be thrust through; and everyone that is joined to them shall fall by the sword. 16 Their children also shall be dashed to pieces before their eyes; their bayits shall be plundered, and their wives raped. 17 See, I will stir up the Medes against them, who shall not regard silver; and as for gold, they shall not delight in it.³ 18 Their bows also shall dash the young men to pieces; and they shall have no pity on the fruit of the womb; their eye shall not spare children. 19 And Bavel, the tiferet of all malchutim,* the tiferet of the Chaldean's pride shall become as when Elohim overthrew Sedom and Amorah. 20 It shall never be inhabited, neither shall it be dwelt in from generation to generation: neither shall the Arabian tar his tent; neither shall the shepherds rest their folds there. 21 But wild beasts of the desert shall lie there; and their bayits shall be full of owls; ostriches shall live there, and wild goats shall dance there. 22 And owls shall cry in their palaces, and jackals in their beautiful temples: and her time is near to come, and her days shall not be prolonged.*

14 *For* יהוה *will have rachamim on Yaakov, and will yet choose Yisrael,⁴ and set them in their own land:⁵ and the foreigners shall be joined with them, ⁶ and they shall cleave to Beit Yaakov.⁷ 2 And the nations shall take them, and bring them to their place:⁸ and Beit Yisrael shall possess them in the land of* יהוה⁹ *as avadim and female avadim:¹⁰ and they shall take them as captives, whose captives they once were; and they shall rule over their oppressors. 3 And it shall come to pass in the day that* יהוה *shall give you rest from your sorrow, and from your fear, and from the hard bondage in which you were made to serve others, 4 That you shall take up this mishle against the melech of Bavel, and say, How has the oppressor ceased! The golden city ceased! 5* יהוה *has broken the staff of the wicked, and the sceptre of their rulers. 6 He who smote the people¹¹ in wrath with continual blows, he that ruled the nations in anger, is persecuted, and none can hinder it. 7 The*

---

¹ Generally understood as the last seven years of this age, a time of judgment on the nations or the Babylonian system, and freedom for Yisrael's exiles.
² This grand and unprecedented cosmic disturbance during the Day of YHWH, is the actual sign of His soon second coming (Matthew 24:29-30).
³ As is often the case with an end-time text, there is also a prior historical fulfillment.

⁴ In the two-house regathering.
⁵ Aliyah back to the land led by Yahshua and not man.
⁶ All nations will join the 12 tribes, in the single Olive Tree, which is the community of Yisraelite faith.
⁷ The ten men from all nations will cling to the fringes of saved Yahudah as found in Zechariah 8:23.
⁸ Nations will return the Yisraelites they house, when Yahshua returns.
⁹ In Yisrael.
¹⁰ In the kingdom of YHWH, Yisrael will rule over all unregenerate heathen nations and individuals. Yisrael will be the rulers and not the captured.
¹¹ Yisrael.

whole earth is at rest, and is quiet: they break forth into singing. 8 Yes, the cypress eytzim simcha at you, and the cedars of Levanon, saying, Since you were cut down, no woodcutter has come up against us. 9 Sheol from beneath is moved to meet you at your upcoming death: it stirs up the dead for you, even all the ruling ones of the earth; it has raised up from their thrones all the melechim of the nations. 10 All they shall speak and say to you, Are you also become weak like us? Are you become like us?[1] 11 Your pride is brought down to the grave, and the noise of your stringed instruments: the worm is spread under you, and the worms cover you. 12 How are you fallen from the shamayim, O Heilel,[2] son of the morning![3] How are you cut down to the ground,[4] you who did weaken the nations![5] 13 For you have said in your lev, I will ascend into the shamayim, I will exalt my throne above the cochavim[6] of El: I will sit also upon the Mount of the Congregation,[7] on the sides of the north:[8] 14 I will ascend above the heights of the clouds; I[9] will be like El-Elyon. 15 Yet you shall be brought down to Sheol, to the sides of the pit.[10] 16 They that see you shall ponder and stare at you, saying, Is this the man that made the earth to tremble, that shook malchutim; 17 That made the olam as a wilderness, and destroyed its cities; that did not open the bayit of his prisoners? 18 All the melechim of the nations, even all of them, lie in tiferet, every one in his own grave. 19 But you are cast out of your grave like an abominable branch, and as the garment of those that are slain, who have been thrust through with a sword, that go down to the stones of the pit; like a trampled corpse. 20 You shall not be joined with them in burial, because you have destroyed your land, and slain your people: the zera of evildoers shall never be mentioned. 21 Prepare slaughter for his children for the iniquity of their ahvot; that they do not rise, nor possess the land, nor fill the face of the olam with cities. 22 For I will rise up against them, says יהוה of hosts, and cut off from Bavel the name, and the remnant, and the son, and the nephew, says יהוה. 23 I will also make it a possession for the owls, and pools of mayim, and I will sweep it with the broom of destruction, says יהוה of hosts. 24 יהוה of hosts has sworn, saying, Surely as I have thought, so shall it come to pass; and as I have purposed, so shall it stand: 25 That I will break Ashshur in My land, and upon My mountains trample him under foot: then shall his yoke depart from off them, and his burden depart from off their shoulders.[11] 26 This is the purpose that is purposed upon the whole earth: and this is the hand that is stretched out upon all the nations.[12] 27 For יהוה of hosts has purposed this, and who shall annul it? And His hand is stretched out, and who shall turn it back? 28 In the year that melech Ahaz died this following burden was received. 29 Rejoice not, all Philistia, because the rod of him that smote you is broken: for out of the serpent's root shall come forth a viper, and his fruit shall be a fiery flying serpent. 30 And the firstborn of the poor shall feed, and the needy shall lie down in safety: and I will kill your root with famine, and shall slay your remnant. 31 Howl, O gate; cry, O city! All of Philistia, shall melt: for there shall come from the north a smoke, and none shall be left at their pagan feasts. 32 What shall one

---

[1] The nations shall say to Babylon and her former greatness.
[2] s.a.tan. "Heilel" means "the shining one."
[3] Idiomatic expression for "an angel."
[4] Thrown out from heaven in eternity past.
[5] The evil of the Babylonian Empire is personified in s.a.tan. The text therefore goes from one topic in the pashat to the second level in the remez or hint level, meaning that the first level is spiritually tied into the second level, just as s.a.tan himself is the evil behind the Babylonian Empire, and is tied into that state as its head. More details can be found at: **Yahweh's Fallen Bride**
http://store.yourarmstoisrael.org/Qstore/Qstore.cgi?CMD=011&PROD=000071.
[6] Heavenly messengers.
[7] In the heavenly assembly.
[8] Third heaven.
[9] Notice all the usage of "I." s.a.tan can be seen as having great pride in himself and therefore has "I problems."
[10] YHWH's response to s.a.tan's "I problems," as well as Babylon's power and pride.

[11] Assyria along with Babylon will also be punished for their role in oppressing Yisrael.
[12] His hand and purpose.

then answer the messengers of the nation? That יהוה has founded Tzion, and the poor of His people shall trust in it.

15 The burden1 of Moav. Because in the night, Ar of Moav is laid waste, and brought to silence; because in the night, Kir of Moav is laid waste, and brought to silence; 2 He is gone up to the Bayit, and to Divon, the high places, to weep: Moav shall wail over Nevo, and over Medeva: on all their heads shall be baldness, and every beard cut shall be cut off. 3 In their streets they shall put on themselves sackcloth: on the tops of their bayits, and in their streets, every one shall wail, weeping abundantly. 4 And Cheshbon shall cry, and in Elealeh: their voice shall be heard even to Yahatz: therefore the armed soldiers of Moav shall cry out; their chayim shall tremble within them. 5 My lev shall cry out for Moav; her fugitives shall flee to Tzoar, like a heifer of three years old: for with weeping shall they go up by the ascending road of Luhith; for in the derech of Horonayim they shall raise up a cry of destruction. 6 For the mayim of Nimrim shall be desolate: for the hay will wither away, the grass fails, there is no green thing. 7 Therefore the abundance they have gotten, and that which they have laid up, shall they carry away to the brook of the willows. 8 For the cry has gone all around the borders of Moav; its howling to Eglayim, and its howling to Beer-Eylim. 9 For the mayim of Dimon shall be full of dom: for I will bring more upon Dimon, lions upon him that escapes from Moav, and upon the remnant of the land.

16 *Send a lamb to the ruler of the land from Sela to the wilderness, to the mountain of the daughter of Tzion. 2 For it shall be, that, as a wandering bird cast out of its nest, so the daughters of Moav shall be at the fords of Arnon. 3 Take counsel, execute mishpat; make your shadow as the night in the middle of the* day; hide the outcasts; betray not him that wanders.[2] 4 Let My outcasts live with you,[3] Moav; be a shelter to them from the face of the plunderer: for the extortioner is at an end, the plunderer ceases, the oppressors are consumed out of the land. 5 And in rachamim shall the throne be established: and He shall sit upon it in emet in the Sukkah of David, judging, and seeking mishpat, and bringing tzedakah speedily.[4] 6 We have heard of the pride of Moav; he is very proud: even proud of his pride, and his arrogance: but his lies shall not be so. 7 Therefore shall Moav wail for Moav, everyone shall wail: for the foundations of Kir-Hareseth shall you mourn; surely they are beaten. 8 For the fields of Cheshbon lose lev, and the vine of Sivmah: the mighty men of the heathen have broken down the choice plants, they are come even to Yazer, they wandered through the wilderness: her branches are stretched out, they are gone over the sea. 9 Therefore I will bewail with the weeping of Yazer for the vine of Sivmah: I will water you with my tears, O Cheshbon, and Elealeh: for an oppressor has come against your summer fruits and your harvest is fallen. 10 And simcha is taken away, and simcha out of the plentiful field; and in the vineyards there shall be no singing, neither shall there be shouting: the treaders shall trample out no wine in their presses; I have made their vine treaders to cease. 11 Therefore my inward parts shall sound like a harp for Moav, and my inward parts for Kir-Haresh. 12 And it shall come to pass, when it is seen that Moav is weary on the high place, that she shall come to her set-apart place to make tefillah; but she shall accomplish nothing.* 13 This is the word that יהוה has spoken concerning Moav since that time. 14 But now יהוה has spoken, saying, *Within three years, as the years of a hired man, and the tiferet of*

---

¹ Message or word.

² Be a shelter to the wandering Ephraim Yisraelites in your midst.
³ According to Jeremiah 3:8 and elsewhere, Ephraim was divorced and outcast from the covenant of Torah and the people of Yisrael. This term only can apply to them.
⁴ By Hezekiah and later Yahshua.

Moav shall be despised, with all that great multitude; and the remnant shall be very small and feeble.

17

The burden of Dameshek. *See, Dameshek is taken away from being a city, and it shall be a ruinous heap. 2 The cities of Aroer are forsaken: they shall be for flocks, which shall lie down, and none shall make them afraid. 3 Their stronghold also shall cease from Ephraim, and the malchut from Dameshek, and the remnant of Aram: they shall be as the tiferet of the children of Yisrael,* says יהוה *of hosts.[1] 4 And in that day it shall come to pass, that the tiferet of Yaakov shall be made thin, and the fatness of his flesh shall be lean. 5 And it shall be as when the harvester gathers the grain, and reaps the ears with his arm; and it shall be as he that gathers ears in the Valley of Rephayim.[2] 6 Yet gleaning grapes shall be left in it, as the shaking of an olive eytz, two or three olives in the top of the uppermost branch,[3] four or five in the outmost fruitful branches of it,* says יהוה *Elohim of Yisrael.[4] 7 At that day shall a man[5] look to his Maker, and his eyes shall have respect for the Set-Apart One of Yisrael. 8 And he shall not look to the altars, the work of his hands, neither shall he respect that which his fingers have made, neither the Asherim, nor the images. 9 In that day shall his strong cities be as a forsaken forest, and like a sheikdom, which was left destitute because of the children of Yisrael:[6] and there shall be ruin. 10 Because you have forgotten the Elohim of Your Yahshua, and have not been mindful of the Rock of Your strength, therefore shall you plant pleasant plants, and shall turn out foreign branches:[7] 11 In the day shall you make your plant to grow, and in the morning shall you make your zera to flourish: but the harvest shall be as a heap in the day of grief and desperate pain. 12 Woe to the army of many nations, who make a noise like the noise of the seas; and to the rushing of nations, that make a rushing like the rushing of mighty mayim! 13 The nations shall roar like the rushing of many mayim: but Elohim shall rebuke them, and they shall flee far away, and shall be chased as the chaff of the mountains before the wind, and like whirling objects in the whirlwind. 14 And see at sundown fear; and before the morning it is gone. This is the portion of them that plunder us, and the lot of them that rob us.[8]*

18

Woe to the land shadowing with wings, which is beyond the rivers of Ethiopia: 2 That sends ambassadors by the sea, even in vessels of reeds upon the mayim, saying, Go, swift messengers, to a nation scattered and peeled, to a people feared from their beginning forward; a nation mighty but trampled down, whose land the rivers have divided![9] 3 All you inhabitants of the olam, and dwellers on the earth, see, when He lifts up a banner on the mountains; and when He blows a shofar, shema.[10] 4 For this is what יהוה *said to me, I will take My rest, and I will look from My dwelling place like a clear heat upon the river, and like a cloud of dew in the day of harvest. 5 For before the harvest, when the bud is perfect, and the sour grape is ripening in the flower, He shall both cut off the twigs with pruning hooks, and take away and cut down the spreading branches.[11] 6 They shall be left together to the fowls of the mountains, and to the beasts*

---

[1] Since the Arameans played a large biological part in Yisrael's beginnings, YHWH will bring them into the covenant in the kingdom.
[2] Apparently many Arameans who have many Yisraelite dom lines, will be in the kingdom in large numbers, as through metaphor we see them enjoying the same kingdom benefits as Yisrael, meaning that they are part of Yisrael.
[3] When the Olive Tree is shaken, Aramean berries will be discovered in it.
[4] A remnant will be safe in the Olive Tree.
[5] An Aramean man.
[6] Because they went their own pagan ways, and refused to abide with the sons of Yaakov.

[7] Non-Yisraelite branches. Most Arameans with Yisraelite beginnings became Ishmaelites and/or Edomites, by assimilation and intermarriage.
[8] Even though Arameans have some Yisraelite fruit, most will be punished for their treatment of Judah, and for their league with Ephraim against Judah.
[9] Rivers of two-house division and exile.
[10] The banner is Yahshua, and the shofar is the trumpet of the final regathering.
[11] YHWH will prune His people to determine the remnant.

of the earth: and the fowls shall prey upon them, and all the beasts of the earth shall devour them. 7 In that time shall the present be brought to **יהוה** of hosts of a people scattered, tall and darkened, and from a people feared from their beginning forward; a nation dishonored and trampled under foot, whose land the rivers have divided,[1] to the place of the Name of **יהוה** of hosts, to Har Tzion.[2]

19

The burden of Mitzrayim.[3] See, **יהוה** rides upon a swift cloud, and He shall come into Mitzrayim: and the idols of Mitzrayim shall tremble at His presence, and the lev of Mitzrayim shall melt in the midst of it. 2 And I will set the Mitzrites against the Mitzrites: and they shall fight every one against his brother, and every one against his neighbor; city against city, and malchut against malchut. 3 And the ruach of Mitzrayim shall fail in the midst of it; and I will destroy the counsel of it: and they shall seek their idols, and their charmers, and those that have familiar ruachim, and their sorcerers. 4 And the Mitzrites will I give over into the hand of a cruel master; and a fierce melech shall rule over them, says the Master, **יהוה** of hosts. 5 And the mayim shall fail from the sea, and the river[4] shall be wasted and dried up. 6 And they shall turn the rivers far away; and the streams of defence shall be emptied and dried up: the reeds and rushes shall wither. 7 The rushes by the river, by the mouth of the river, and everything sown by the river, shall wither, be driven away, and be no more. 8 The fishermen also shall mourn, and all they that cast their angle into the river shall lament, and they that spread nets upon the mayim shall lose lev. 9 Moreover they that work in fine cotton, and they that weave fine fabric, shall be embarrassed. 10 And its foundations shall be broken; all that work for wages shall be grieved. 11 Surely the rulers of Tzoan are fools, the counsels of the wise counselors of Pharaoh are become brutish: how then do you say to Pharaoh, I am the son of the wise, the son of ancient melechim? 12 Where are they? Where are your wise men? And let them show you now, and let them know what **יהוה** of hosts has planed for Mitzrayim. 13 The rulers of Tzoan have become fools; the rulers of Noph are deceived; they have also seduced Mitzrayim, even they that are the cornerstone of her tribes. 14 **יהוה** has mixed a perverse ruach in the midst of it: and they have caused Mitzrayim to go astray in all her works, as a drunk man staggers in his vomit. 15 Neither shall there be any work to do in Mitzrayim, which the head or tail, palm branch or reed, may do. 16 In that day shall Mitzrayim become like women: and it shall be afraid and fear because of the shaking of the hand of **יהוה** of hosts, which He shakes over it. 17 And the land of Yahudah shall be a fear to Mitzrayim, everyone that makes mention of it shall be afraid within himself, because of the counsel of **יהוה** of hosts, which He has determined against it. 18 In that day shall five cities in the land of Mitzrayim speak the language of Kanaan,[5] and swear to **יהוה** of hosts;[6] and one shall be called, The City of Tzedakah.[7] 19 In that day shall there be an altar to **יהוה** in the midst of the land of Mitzrayim,[8] and a standing column[9] at its border to **יהוה**. 20 And it shall be for a sign and for a witness to **יהוה** of hosts in the land of Mitzrayim: for they shall cry to **יהוה** because of the oppressors, and He

---

[1] Yisrael.
[2] The final ingathering of Yisraelites from Africa, and lands beyond the rivers of Ethiopia like Zimbabwe.
[3] A full treatment of this grafting in of Edom and Ham into the Olive Tree in the latter days is found at http://yourarmstoisrael.org/Articles_new/restoration/?page=24 &type=12.
[4] Nile.

[5] Language of Tzion; Hebrew.
[6] Trust in YHWH.
[7] Many believe this to be a prophecy of the composition of the LXX (Septuagint) translated in Alexandria Egypt circa 150 BCE, the basis of the Brit Chadasha.
[8] Many from Egypt will also turn to YHWH in the day when the restoration of all things comes.
[9] Dolman or stone pillars built by the people of Yisrael wherever they wandered as a sign of their presence there.

shall send them a Savior, [1] and a Great One, [2] and He shall deliver them. [3] 21 And יהוה shall be known to Mitzrayim, [4] and the Mitzrites shall know יהוה in that day, [5] and shall do sacrifice and oblation; they shall vow a vow to יהוה, and perform it. [6] [7] 22 And יהוה shall smite Mitzrayim: He shall smite and heal it: and they shall return even to יהוה, [8] and He shall be sought by them, and He shall heal them. [9] 23 In that day [10] shall there be a highway out of Mitzrayim to Ashshur, and the Ashshurite shall come into Mitzrayim, and the Mitzrite into Ashshur, and the Mitzrites shall serve with the Ashshurim. [11] [12] 24 In that day shall Yisrael be the third with Mitzrayim and with Ashshur, even a bracha in the midst of the earth: [13] 25 Whom יהוה of hosts shall bless,

---

[1] The Savior of Egypt is the same one for Jacob. Yahshua of Nazareth. During their oppression or Great Tribulation distress, Egypt will seek YHWH for help.
[2] The Mighty El.
[3] Yahshua.
[4] By many of them accepting the besarot or tov news.
[5] **Atid lavoh.**
[6] In the **atid lavoh**, many of scattered Hamites and Ishmaelites will cry out to Yahweh, and He will send them Yahshua the Savior to bring them peace, life and national Yisraelite citizenship. These same redeemed Semites and Hamites will be allowed into the rebuilt millennial temple to make slaughter offerings, and to perform vows to the Prince and His Father, since they will be considered part of millennial Yisrael.
[7] After these individuals from Ham and Ishmael accept Yahshua, they will follow Torah as seen by their vows.
[8] After being smitten in the Great Tribulation.
[9] The full healing and acceptance of remnant Egypt into Yisrael.
[10] **Atid lavoh**/millennial kingdom.
[11] Both Assyria and Egypt will have remnants that join Yisrael by trust in Moshiach.
[12] Yisrael's historic enemies now join with them.
[13] In verses 23-25 we see some of the greatest glimpses into the peace plan amongst Arab nations hostile to Jewish Yisrael. In the days of Ishmael's ingathering to the rest of Yisrael, there shall be a Torah highway from Egypt to Syria. Assyria and those from Assyria/Syria will go to Egypt, and those from Egypt will go to Assyria. It will be the highway or path of return and teshuvah. Ishmaelites from both these nations are prophesied to come together in order to serve YHWH the Elohim of Yisrael. This renewed tripartite Yisraelite alliance in verse 24 that will enter the millennium under Moshiach, is said to be composed of Ephraim/Yisrael, Jewish/Yisrael, and Ishmael/Yisrael. All three parts are Yisrael. And why not? In Solomon's day before the Kingdom of Yisrael split, Ishmaelites in Lebanon and Syria, were already large parts of national Yisrael, as were the Arab lands and governors (Second Chronicles / Divre HaYamim 8:6, 9:14). In that Great Day of final ingathering, symbolized by the 7th day of the Feast of Sukkoth/Tabernacles, Jewish/Yisrael will be one of three main branches of Yisrael (Isaiah 17:6). Yahweh wants to take all the descendants of Noach's three sons, Shem, Ham, and Japheth, and bring them all under the Captain of their salvation, the only brought-forth Son of

by saying, Blessed be Mitzrayim My people, and Ashshur the work of My hands, and Yisrael My inheritance. [14]

20 In the year that Tartan came to Ashdod, when Sargon the melech of Ashshur sent him, and fought against Ashdod, and took it; 2 At the same time spoke יהוה by Yeshayahu the son of Amotz, saying, Go and loose the sackcloth from off your waist, and put off your sandals from your foot. And he did so, walking naked and barefoot. 3 And יהוה said, Like My eved Yeshayahu has walked naked and barefoot three years for a sign and wonder against Mitzrayim and upon Ethiopia; 4 So shall the melech of Ashshur lead away the Mitzrite prisoners, and the Ethiopians captives, young and old, naked and barefoot, even with their buttocks uncovered, to the shame of Mitzrayim. 5 And they shall be afraid and ashamed of Ethiopia their expectation, and of Mitzrayim their pride. 6 And the inhabitant of this coastland shall say in that day, See, such is our expectation, wherever we flee for help to be delivered from the melech of Ashshur: and so how then shall we escape?

21 The burden of the desert of the sea. As whirlwinds in the south pass through; so it comes from the desert, from an awesome land. 2 A grievous vision is declared to me; the treacherous dealer deals treacherously, and the plunderer spoils. Go up, O Eylam: besiege it, O Media, all the sighing of it I will make cease. 3 Therefore is my waist filled with pain: pains have taken hold upon me, as the pains of a

---

Righteousness for all of mankind, seated eternally on David's Throne in heaven, and one day soon in Yahrushalayim.
[14] In the days of the great Semitic/Ishmaelite awakening, many of Ishmael's sons scattered in and among the nations, along with a small remnant of Edom/Muslims who willingly denounce falsehood, will be joined together by Moshiach's dom, and will move Abba Yahweh to pronounce a new **bracha**/blessing, patterned after the Aaronic Benediction of (Numbers 6:23-27). May Yahweh bless Egypt My people/Ami, May Yahweh bless Assyria, the work of My hands, May Yahweh bless Yisrael/My inheritance (Isaiah 19:25). And in so doing, all three parts of Yisrael, Judah, Ephraim, and Ishmael, will carry the Name of Yahweh and "I Myself shall bless them, for I have returned them," says Yahweh (Numbers 6:27,10:36).

woman in labor: I was bowed down at the hearing of it; I was dismayed at the seeing of it. 4 My lev panted, fear overwhelmed me: the night of my pleasure has He turned into fear for me. 5 Prepare the table, watch in the watchtower, eat, and drink: arise, you rulers, and anoint the shield. 6 For this has יהוה said to me, *Go, set a watchman, and let him declare what he sees.* 7 And he saw a mirkavah with a couple of horsemen, a mirkavah of donkeys, and a mirkavah of camels; and he listened attentively, very carefully: 8 And he cried, A lion: My master, I stand continually upon the watchtower in the daytime, and I am set in my post every night: 9 And, see, here comes a mirkavah of men, with a couple of horsemen. And he answered and said, Bavel is fallen, it is fallen; and all the graven images of her elohim He has broken to the ground. 10 O my threshing, and the grain of my floor: that which I have heard from יהוה of hosts, the Elohim of Yisrael, have I declared to you. 11 The burden[1] of Dumah. He calls to me out of Seir, *Watchman, how much of the night? Watchman, how much of the night?* 12 The watchman said, morning came and also the night: if you will inquire, inquire and come again. 13 The burden upon Arabia. In the forest in Arabia shall you lodge, O you traveling companies of Dedanites. 14 The inhabitants of the land of Tema brought mayim to him that was thirsty, they met the fugitive with lechem. 15 For they fled from the swords, from the drawn sword, and from the bent bow, and from the stress of war. 16 For this has יהוה said to me, *Within a year, according to the year of a hired worker, all the men of Kedar shall come to an end:* 17 *And the residue of the number of archers, the mighty men of the children of Kedar, shall be diminished*: for יהוה Elohim of Yisrael has spoken it.

22 The burden of the Valley of Vision. What troubles you now that you all have gone up to the housetops?

2 You that are full of turmoil, a tumultuous city, and a noisy city: your slain men are not slain with the sword, nor are dead in battle. 3 All your rulers are fled together, the archers bind them: all that are found in you are bound together, who have fled from far. 4 Therefore said I, Look away from me; I will weep bitterly, don't bother to comfort me, because of the spoiling of the daughter of my people. 5 For it is a day of trouble, and of trampling down, and of perplexity by the Master יהוה of hosts in the Valley of Vision, breaking down the walls, and of crying to the mountains. 6 And Eylam bore the quiver with mirkavot of men and horsemen, and Kir carried the shield. 7 And it shall come to pass, that your best valleys shall be full of mirkavot, and the horsemen shall set themselves in battle array at the gate. 8 And He removed the covering of Yahudah, and you did look in that day to the armor of the bayit of the forest. 9 You have seen also the breaches of the city of David, that they are many: and you gathered together the mayim of the lower pool. 10 And you have numbered the bayits of Yahrushalayim, and the bayits have you broken down to fortify the wall. 11 You made also a ditch between the two walls for the mayim of the old pool: but you have not sought its Maker, neither seen Him that made it long ago. 12 And in that day the Master יהוה of hosts called for weeping, and for mourning, and for baldness, and for girding with sackcloth: 13 And see simcha upon simcha, slaying oxen, and killing sheep, eating meat, and drinking wine: let us eat and drink; for tomorrow we shall die. 14 And it was revealed in my ears by יהוה of hosts, *Surely this iniquity shall not be purged from you until you die,* says the Master יהוה of hosts. 15 This says the Master יהוה of hosts, *Go, get to this treasurer, even to Shevna,[2] who is over the bayit, and say,* 16 *What have you here? And who have you here that you have cut out a tomb here, as he that cuts out a tomb*

---

[1] Message.

[2] A deputy of King Hezekiah.

on high, and that carves a home for himself in a rock? 17 *See, O man,* יהוה *will throw you out, and will surely grab you.* 18 *He will surely violently turn and toss you like a ball into a large country: there shall you die, and there the mirkavot of your tiferet shall be the shame of your master's bayit.* 19 *And I will drive you from your office, and from your position He shall pull you down.* 20 *And it shall come to pass in that day, that I will call My eved Elyakim the son of Hilkiyah:* 21 *And I will clothe him with your robe, and strengthen him with your belt, and I will give your government into his hand: and he shall be an abba to the inhabitants of Yahrushalayim, and to Beit Yahudah.* [1] 22 *And the key of Beit David will I lay upon His shoulder; so He shall open, and none shall shut; and He shall shut, and none shall open.* [2] [3] 23 *And I will fasten Him as a nail in a sure place; and He shall become a Throne of tiferet to His Abba's Bayit.* 24 *And they shall hang upon Him all the tiferet of His Abba's Bayit, the honorable and the noble men, and all the vessels of small quantity, from the cups, even to the jars.* 25 *In that day, says* יהוה *of hosts, shall the Nail that is fastened in the secure place be removed, and be cut down, and fall; and the burden that was upon it shall be cut off: for* יהוה *has spoken it.* [4]

23 The burden of Tsor. *Howl, you ships of Tarshish; for it is laid waste, so that there is no bayit, no entering in: from the land of Chittim[5] it is revealed to us.* 2 *Be still, you inhabitants of the coastland; you whom the merchants of Tzidon, that pass over the sea, have replenished.* 3 *And on great mayim the grain of Sihor, the harvest of the river, is her revenue; and she was a market place of*

the nations. 4 *Be ashamed, O Tzidon: for the sea has spoken, even the strength of the sea, saying, I have not labored, nor brought forth children, neither do I nourish up young men, nor bring up virgins.* 5 *Like the report concerning Mitzrayim, so shall they be sorely pained at the report of Tsor.* 6 *Pass over to Tarshish; wail, you inhabitants of the coastland.* 7 *Is this your joyous city, whose antiquity is from days of old? Whose feet shall carry her far off to sojourn.* 8 *Who has taken this counsel against Tsor, the crowning city, whose merchants are rulers, whose traders are the honorable men of the earth?* 9 יהוה *of hosts has purposed it, to stain the pride of all its tiferet, and to bring into contempt all the honorable of the earth.* 10 *Pass through your land as a river, O daughter of Tarshish: there is no more strength.* 11 *He stretched out His hand over the sea, He shook the malchutim:* יהוה *has given a commandment against Kanaan, to destroy its strongholds.* 12 *And He said, You shall no more have your simcha, O oppressed virgin, daughter of Tzidon: arise, pass over to Chittim; there also shall you have no rest.* 13 *See the land of the Chaldeans; this people did not exist, Ashshur founded it for those wild beasts that live in the wilderness: they set up the towers of it, they raised up the palaces of it; so that it has been made a ruin.* 14 *Howl, you ships of Tarshish: for your stronghold is laid waste.* 15 *And it shall come to pass in that day, that Tsor shall be forgotten seventy years, according to the days of one melech: after the end of seventy years shall Tsor shir as a harlot.* 16 *Take a harp, go around the city, you harlot that has been forgotten; make sweet melodies, shir many shirim, that you may be remembered.* 17 *And it shall come to pass after the end of seventy years, that* יהוה *will visit Tsor, and she shall turn to her hire, and shall commit fornication with all the malchutim of the olam upon the face of the earth.* 18 *And her merchandise and her hire shall be set-apart to* יהוה*: it shall not*

---

[1] Eliakim will be clothed with Isaiah's authority.
[2] Eliakim is a clear type of Yahshua HaMoshiach.
[3] A dual prophecy showing that Moshiach in the person of Eliakim will oversee all 12 tribes in the restored House of David.
[4] Moshiach like the House of David before Him, was cut off or destroyed.
[5] China; Aramaic Peshitta.

be treasured nor laid up; for her merchandise shall be for them that live before יהוה, to eat sufficiently, and for durable clothing.[1]

24 See, יהוה makes the earth empty, and makes it a ruin, and turns it upside down, and scatters abroad its inhabitants.[2] 2 And it shall be, as with the people, so with the kohen; as with the eved, so with his master; as with the female eved, so with her mistress; as with the buyer, so with the seller; as with the lender, so with the borrower; as with the taker of interest so with the giver of interest to him. 3 The earth shall be utterly emptied, and utterly plundered: for יהוה has spoken this word. 4 The earth mourns and fades away,[3] the olam languishes and fades away, and the proud people of the earth lose lev. 5 The earth also is defiled under its inhabitants, because they have transgressed the Torot, changed the chukim, and broken the everlasting covenant.[4] 6 Therefore has the curse devoured the earth, and they that live in it are ruined: therefore the inhabitants of the earth are burned, and few men left.[5] 7 The new wine mourns, the vine languishes, all the glad at lev do sigh. 8 The simcha of tambourines ceases, the noise of them that simcha ends, the simcha of the harp ceases. 9 They shall not drink wine with a shir; strong drink shall be bitter to them that drink it. 10 The city is broken down: every bayit is shut, so that no man may enter. 11 There is a crying for wine in the streets; all simcha is darkened, the simcha of the earth shall be gone. 12 In the city is left ruin, and the gate is smitten with destruction. 13 When this shall be in the midst of the earth among the nations, there shall be like the shaking of an olive eytz, and as the gleaning grapes when the grape harvest is done.[6] 14 They shall lift up their voice, they shall shir for the excellency of יהוה, they shall cry aloud from the sea.[7] 15 Therefore lift up יהוה in the east,[8] even the Name of יהוה[9] Elohim of Yisrael in the coastlands of the sea. 16 From the furthest parts of the earth[10] we have heard shirim, even tiferet To The Tzadik One.[11] But I said, I am wasting away, woe to me! The treacherous have dealt treacherously; yes, the treacherous dealers have dealt very treacherously. 17 Fear, and the pit, and the trap, are upon you, O inhabitants of the earth. 18 And it shall come to pass, that he who flees from the noise of the fear shall fall into the pit; and he that comes up out of the midst of the pit shall be taken in the trap: for the windows from on high are open, and the foundations of the earth do shake. 19 The earth is utterly broken down, the earth is utterly removed, and the earth is moved exceedingly. 20 The earth shall reel to and fro like a drunkard, and shall be removed like a little hut; and the transgression of it shall be heavy upon it; and it shall fall, and not rise again. [12] 21 And it shall come to pass in that day, that יהוה shall punish the army of the high ones that are on high,[13] and the melechim of the earth upon the earth. 22 And they shall be gathered together, as prisoners are gathered in the pit, and shall be shut up in the prison, and after many days shall they be visited with mishpat. [14] 23 Then the

---

[1] Even Tyre and Zidon will be renewed in the millennial kingdom, as YHWH will appoint them, as food and supply centers for the Kingdom of Moshiach.
[2] During the awesome Day of YHWH. A day of dreads and fear for all those who remain unclaimed by the dom of Moshiach. Yisrael will be protected through preservation or through martyrdom.
[3] The current earth.
[4] The **chukim** and everlasting covenant that's was broken, in light of chronology, is the seventh-day Shabbat, since the everlasting covenant of Moshiach was still 700 years future.
[5] The current earth has an appointment with the cleansing fire of YHWH, as the first one had with water for 40 days and nights. A few will remain, as did 8 in Noach's days.

[6] While the world burns, the olive tree of Yisrael is merely shaken.
[7] While the world mourns, the remnant of Yisrael sings the songs of deliverance.
[8] Since Yahshua returns to the Eastern Gate to deliver Yisrael.
[9] We must all learn to adore not only YHWH; but also His very Name.
[10] Ephraim's dwellings.
[11] Ephraim's music to Yahshua in the midst of the "Day of YHWH" judgments.
[12] The old world will not rise, but will be renewed.
[13] Fallen heavenly messengers.
[14] Both fallen messengers and fallen kings, will be put in the pit or the Lake of Fire, with the messengers being in eternal torment, and the wicked kings being put to the second death.

moon shall blush, and the sun shall be ashamed, when **יהוה** of hosts shall reign in Har Tzion, and in Yahrushalayim, before His esteemed zachanim.[1]

25 O **יהוה**, You are My Elohim; I will exalt You, I will hallel Your Name; for You have done wonderful things; Your eternal counsels are faithfulness and emet.[2] 2 For You have made of a city a heap; a defended city a ruin: a palace of foreigners to be a city no more; it shall never be built. 3 Therefore the strong people[3] will give You tiferet; the cities of the ruthless nations shall fear You. 4 For You have been a strength to the poor, a strength to the needy in his distress, a refuge from the storm, a shadow from the heat, when the ruach of the ruthless is as a storm against the wall. 5 You shall bring down the noise of foreigners, as the heat in a dry place; even the heat with the shadow of a cloud: the heirs of the ruthless shall be brought low. 6 And in this mountain[4] shall **יהוה** of hosts make for all people a feast of choice pieces, a feast of old wines, of choice things full of marrow, of old wines, well refined. 7 And He will destroy in this mountain[5] the face of the covering cast over all nations, and the vail that is spread over all nations.[6] 8 *He will swallow up death in victory; and the Master* **יהוה** *will wipe away tears from off all faces; and the reproach of His people shall He take away from off all the earth:* for **יהוה** has spoken it.[7] 9 And it shall be said in that day,[8] See, this is our Elohim; we have waited for Him, and He will save us: this is **יהוה**; we have

waited for Him, we will be in gilah and simcha in His Yahshua. 10 For in this mountain[9] shall the hand of **יהוה** rest, and Moav shall be trampled down under Him, even as straw is trampled down for the dunghill. 11 And He shall spread forth His hands in their midst, as He that swims spreads forth His hands to swim: and He shall bring down their pride together with the spoils of their hands. 12 And the high stronghold of your walls shall He bring down, laid low, levelled to the ground, even to the dust.

26 In that day shall this shir be sung in the land of Yahudah; We have a strong city; Yahshua will Elohim appoint as our walls and ramparts.[10] 2 Open the gates, that the tzadik nation who shomers the emet may enter in.[11] 3 You will keep him in perfect shalom, whose mind is fixed on You: because he trusts in You. 4 Trust in **יהוה** le-olam-va-ed: for in Yah- **יה**, is everlasting strength: 5 For He brings down them that live on high; the proud city, He lays it low; He lays it low, even to the ground; He brings it even to the dust. 6 The foot shall trample it down, even the feet of the poor, and the steps of the needy. 7 The halacha of the just is uprightness: You, Most Tzadik, do weigh the derech of the just. 8 Yes, in the halacha of Your mishpatim, O **יהוה**, have we waited for You; the desire of our being is for Your Name,[12] and for the very remembrance of You. 9 With my being have I desired You in the night; yes, with all my ruach within me will I seek You early: for when Your mishpatim are in the earth, the inhabitants of this olam will learn tzedakah. 10 If favor be shown to the wicked, yet he still will not learn tzedakah: in the land of the tzadikim he will deal unjustly, and will not see the excellency of **יהוה**. 11 **יהוה**, when Your

---

[1] In the millennium His elders or saints will be immortal, which is what the Hebrew indicates here.
[2] All these verses are a description of the kingdom restored to Yisrael.
[3] Yisrael.
[4] Tzion.
[5] With the things of Tzion.
[6] Only with the things of Tzion such as Yahshua, the restoration of the two houses, Torah etc., will YHWH remove the veil of stupor and blindness that spiritually covers all the nations.
[7] The entire purpose of being Yisrael and loving Yahshua. Our death will be swallowed up in victory and overcoming, or in Yisrael.
[8] **Atid lavoh.**

[9] Mt. Tzion.
[10] More descriptions of the restored kingdom.
[11] Into the age to come; Yisrael is that nation.
[12] All born-again children must develop a love for the Name, not merely the character that the Name represents, but the very Name itself.

hand is lifted up, they will not see: but they shall see, and be ashamed for the zeal of Your people; yes, let the fire of the oven devour Your enemies. 12 **יהוה**, You will ordain shalom for us: for You also have done all our works in us.[1] 13 O **יהוה** Our Elohim, other masters besides You have had rule over us: but only in You will we make mention of Your Name.[2] 14 They are dead, they shall not live; they are deceased, they shall not rise: therefore have You visited and destroyed them, and made all their memory to perish.[3] 15 You shall increase the nation, O **יהוה**, You shall increase the nation:[4] You are lifted up: You had removed the nation far to all the ends of the earth.[5] 16 **יהוה**, in trouble have they visited You, they poured out a tefillah when Your chastening was upon them.[6] 17 Like a woman with child, that draws near the time of her delivery, is in pain, and cries out in her pains; so have we been in Your sight, O **יהוה**. 18 We have been with child, we have been in pain, we have as it were brought forth wind; we have not worked out any deliverance in the earth; neither have the inhabitants of the olam fallen. 19 Your dead men shall live; together with my dead body shall they arise.[7] Awake and shir, You that dwell in the dust: for Your dew is as the dew of first light, and the earth shall give birth to the departed healed [8] ruachim. [9] 20 Come, my people, [10] enter into your rooms, [11] and shut your doors all around you: hide yourself for just a little while, [12]

until the displeasure is past.[13] 21 For, see, **יהוה** comes out of His place to punish the inhabitants of the earth for their iniquity: the earth also shall disclose her bloodguilt, and shall no longer cover her slain.

27 In that day **יהוה** with His severe and great and strong sword shall punish Leviathan [14] the piercing serpent, even Leviathan that crooked serpent; and He shall slay the dragon that is in the sea. 2 In that day shir to her, A vineyard of red wine.[15] 3 *I* **יהוה** *do keep it; I will water it every moment: lest any hurt it, I will keep it night and day.[16] 4 Wrath is not in Me: who would set the weeds and thorns against Me in battle? I will trample it down and burn it up at once. 5 Unless it takes hold of My strength, in order to make shalom with Me; and he shall make shalom with Me. 6 He shall cause them that come of Yaakov to take root:[17] Yisrael shall blossom and bud, and fill the face of the olam with fruit.[18] 7 He shall not strike Yisrael, as He smote others that smote Yisrael; or is Yisrael slain according to the slaughter of them that are slain by Him? 8 In measure, by sending you away into exile: He will hold back His rough wind in the day of the east wind.[19] 9 By this therefore shall the iniquity of Yaakov be purged; and this is all the fruit of taking away his sin; when he makes all the stones of the altar as chalkstones that are beaten to dust, the Asherim and sun pillars shall rise no more. 10 Yet the defenced city shall be desolate, and the home forsaken, and left like a wilderness: there shall the calf feed, and there shall he lie down, and*

[1] Philippians 2:13.
[2] Only when YHWH does His full ruling over you, will you make frequent mention of His Name.
[3] The names of all false rulers and elohim will perish.
[4] Mentioned two times, one for the increase of each house.
[5] YHWH is not only regathering Yisrael from all four corners through His Son, He is also adding and increasing the nation through the two houses and all those joining the nation.
[6] Fully to come to pass in the Great Tribulation, when both houses will call on Him anew.
[7] Righteous Yisrael will all be raised from the dead at the end of the Great Tribulation, along with Isaiah the prophet.
[8] **Rephaim** from the root "**repha**."
[9] The long-awaited resurrection of the dead, by He who is the Resurrection according to John 11.
[10] Yisrael.
[11] Hiding places.
[12] A few years.

[13] Until the Great Tribulation is over; and Moshiach returns for our bodily resurrection.
[14] In the literal **pashat** this could be a sea dragon. In the **sod** this refers to heathen world powers that have sought to extinguish the people of Yisrael from off the face of the earth. YHWH in return will see to it that His vineyard is preserved, and that all heathen powers will be destroyed.
[15] Yisrael is seen as washed in the dom of redemption, as they sing after the heathen are subdued in the Great Tribulation.
[16] YHWH's watchful eye over Yisrael.
[17] Remnant Yisrael will overcome all gentile powers through their King Moshiach.
[18] Spiritual and physical fruit in the age to come.
[19] He will exile Yisrael, but not destroy them like He will do with Leviathan, and the Leviathan nations.

consume its branches. 11 *When its twigs are withered, they shall be broken off: the women come, and set them on fire: for it is a people of no binah: therefore He that made them will not have rachamim on them, and He that formed them will show them no favor.[1] 12 And it shall come to pass in that day, that* יהוה *shall stir up the people from the channel of the River Euphrates to the River of Mitzrayim, and you shall be gathered one by one, O b'nai Yisrael.[2] 13 And it shall come to pass in that day,[3] that the great shofar shall be blown, and they shall come who were ready to perish in the land of Ashshur,[4] and the outcasts in the land of Mitzrayim, and shall worship* יהוה *in the set-apart mountain at Yahrushalayim.*

28 *Woe to the keter of pride, to the drunkards of Ephraim, whose tiferet is a fading flower, which is on the head of the fertile valleys, of those that are overcome with wine! 2 See,* יהוה *has a mighty and strong one,[5] which as a storm of hail and a destroying storm, as a flood of mighty mayim overflowing, shall cast down to the earth with the hand. 3 The keter of pride, the drunkards of Ephraim, shall be trampled under feet: 4 And the tiferet, which is on the head of the fertile valley, shall be a fading flower, and as the first-fruit before the summer; which when he sees it, he eats it up while still in his hand. 5 In that day shall* יהוה *of hosts be for a keter of tiferet, and for a diadem of tiferet, to the remnant of His people,[6] 6 And for a Ruach of mishpat to him that desires mishpat,[7] and for strength to them that turn away the battle to the gate. 7 But they also have gone astray through wine, and through strong drink are away from the emet halacha; the kohen and ha navi have* gone astray through strong drink, they are swallowed up by wine, they are away from the emet halacha through strong drink; they go astray in vision, they stumble in mishpatim.[8] 8 *For all their tables are full of vomit and filthiness, so that there is no clean place. 9 To whom shall He teach da'at? And to whom shall He make to understand doctrine? Those that are weaned from the milk, and drawn away from the breasts.[9] 10 For precept must be laid upon precept, precept upon precept; line upon line, line upon line; here a little, and there a little: 11 For with stammering lips and another tongue will He speak to this people of Ephraim.[10] [11] 12 To whom He said, This is the rest by which you may cause the weary to rest;[12] and this is the refreshing:[13] yet they would not shema.[14] 13 But the word of* יהוה *was given to them precept upon precept, precept upon precept; line upon line, line upon line; here a little, and there a little; that they might go, and fall backward, and be broken, andsnared, and taken.[15]* 14 Therefore shema the word of יהוה, *you scornful men, that rule this people who are in Yahrushalayim. 15 Because you have said, We have made a*

---

[8] Ephraim has become like most of Yisrael. Drunk with wine and stupidity.
[9] To Yisraelites willing to grow up, away from believer's boredom as outlined in Hebrews 6:1-3.
[10] As per verse one of this chapter, specifically the drunkards of Ephraim. He will give them new wine in the form of tongues, and remove them from the old wine of death and stupidity.
[11] This is one of the least understood and yet most significant prophecies given to remnant, restored, and returning Ephraim. The gift of tongues placed upon the crown of Ephraim, or non-Jewish Yisrael is a sign to the world and to all with ears to hear, that these "tongue talkers" are the very same ten tribes of the exile. Paul addresses this clearly in First Corinthians 14:21, where he quotes this verse in Isaiah, identifying the Corinthian believers as the same people to whom YHWH said He would speak in tongues as a sign of lost Yisraelite heritage. More information is available at: **The Promise To Ephraim**
http://www.yourarmstoisrael.net/audio/promise_to_ephraim.ram.
[12] Weary and wandering Ephraim.
[13] Fresh wine revealed in new languages to get their doctrinal attention.
[14] Still Ephraim will reject the Torah despite the supernatural; and will separate the gift from the Torah, and are thus relegating the gift to abusive manifestations.
[15] YHWH fed them like the spiritual babies they are, so that when they refused to listen and they hardened their heart, they would fall away into error, as they refused to grasp even the most basic of truths and became for all intents and purposes just like their heathen captors.

---

[1] Branches from both houses will be cut off but never destroyed.
[2] "One by one" a redeemed remnant will return.
[3] **Atid lavoh.**
[4] Ephraim.
[5] Assyria.
[6] YHWH will bring remnant Ephraim home, with a crown of beauty.
[7] YHWH will teach Ephraim Torah, and how to conduct their lives in right-ruling.

covenant with death, and with Sheol are we in agreement; so that when the overflowing beatings shall pass through, it shall not come to us: for we have made lies our refuge, and under falsehood have we hidden ourselves. [1] 16 Therefore this says the Master יהוה, *See, I lay in Tzion for a foundation a Stone, a tried Stone, a precious Corner Stone, a Sure Foundation: he that believes[2] shall not hasten to do those things.[3] 17 Mishpat also will I lay to the line, and tzedakah to the plummet: and the hail shall sweep away the refuge of lies, and the mayim shall overflow the hiding place.[4] 18 And your covenant with death shall be annulled, and your agreement with Sheol shall not stand;[5] when the overflowing beating shall pass through, then you shall be trampled down by it.[6] 19 From the time that it goes forth it shall take hold of you: for morning by morning and, by day and by night: it shall cause only distress to even understand the report.[7] 20 For the bed[8] is shorter than that a man can stretch himself on it: and the covers too narrow to wrap himself in it.[9] 21 For* יהוה *shall rise up as in Mount Peratzim, He shall be angry as in the Valley of Giveon, that He may do His work, His strange work; and bring to pass His acts, His strange desires.[10]* 22 Now therefore be not mockers, lest your chains be made stronger: for I have heard from the Master יהוי of hosts a consumption

determined upon the whole earth.[11] 23 Give me your ear, and shema to my voice; and shema to my speech. 24 Does the plowman plow all day to sow? Does he keep turning his soil and breaking the clods? 25 When he has leveled the surface, does he not scatter the dill and sow the cummin? Does he not put wheat in rows and the barley where it belongs and plant the buckwheat around the edges? 26 For His Elohim does instruct him to use discretion, and does teach him. 27 For the dill is not threshed with a threshing instrument, neither is a cartwheel turned on top of the cummin; but the dills are beaten out with a staff, and the cummin with a rod. 28 Bread grain is crushed; so one does not thresh it le-olam-va-ed, nor break it with the wheel of his cart, nor crush it with his horsemen. 29 Even this comes from יהוה of hosts, who is wonderful in His counsel, and excellent in His chochma.[12]

29

Woe to Ariel, to Ariel, the city where David dwelt! Year to year; let moadim come around. 2 Yet I will distress Ariel, and there shall be heaviness and sorrow: and it shall be to Me as it is to Ariel. 3 And I will camp against you all around, and will lay siege against you with siege-mounds, and I will raise forts against you. 4 And you shall be brought down, and shall speak out of the ground, and your speech shall be low from the dust, and your voice shall be, like a medium's, out of the ground, and your speech shall whisper out of the dust. 5 Moreover the multitude of your foreigners shall be like small dust, and the multitude of the ruthless ones shall be as chaff that passes away: it shall be in an instant suddenly. 6 You shall be visited by יהוה *of hosts with thunder, and with earthquake, and great noise, with wind and storm, and the flame of devouring fire. 7 And the multitude of all the nations that*

---

[1] Judah's attitude in making deals with their neighbors that violate different parts of Torah, always lead to her death, or at the very least her demise before the nations. This can be seen in the current manmade move for Mideast peace.
[2] In Yahshua the Chief Corner Stone.
[3] Those who truly follow Moshiach's peace plan which is His second coming, will not make haste or hurry to make man-made covenants of death.
[4] YHWH's covenants on behalf of Yisrael alone will stand the test of time.
[5] YHWH alone decides Yisrael's future, both in and out of their land.
[6] The temporary results of making deals with the devil.
[7] Even the reports of carnal peace accords send fear and do damage.
[8] Bed of compromise.
[9] Man's future plans for Yisrael, just won't cover him in peace, or security, or salvation, or aliyah.
[10] They seem strange to man who knows nothing, as he ought to know. To the blind, two-house restoration seems like a strange or foreign/gentile work that's not from YHWH.

[11] What profit will man-made treaties be then?
[12] The point of verses 23-29 is that some things in Yisrael's dealings with the world cannot be harvested, but must be beaten and crushed for her own benefit.

fight against Ariel, even all that fight against her and her stronghold, and all that distress her, shall be as a dream of a night vision. 8 It shall even be as when a hungry man dreams, and, see, he eats; but he awakes, and his being is empty: or as when a thirsty man dreams, and, see, he drinks; but he awakes, and, see, he is faint, and his being has hunger: so shall the multitude of all the nations be, that fight against Har Tzion.[1] 9 Pause, and wonder; they cry out for trouble: they are drunk, but not with wine; they stagger, but not because of strong drink. 10 For יהוה has poured out upon you the ruach of deep sleep, and has closed your eyes:[2] ha neviim and your rulers, the seers also has He blinded. 11 And the vision of all[3] has become to you as the words of a scroll that is sealed, which men deliver to one that is learned, saying, Read this, please: and he says, I cannot; for it is sealed:[4] 12 And the scroll is delivered to him that is not learned, saying, Read this, please: and he says, I am not learned. 13 Therefore יהוה said, *Because this people draws near to Me with their mouths, and with their lips they do honor Me, but have removed their levim far from Me, and their fear of Me is taught by the commands of men:*[5] 14 *Therefore, see, I will proceed to do a marvelous work among this people, even a marvelous work and a wonder: for the chochma of their wise men shall perish, and the binah of their clever men shall be hidden.*[6] 15 Woe to them that seek deep places to hide their counsel far from יהוה, and their works are in the dark, and they say, Who sees us? And who knows us? 16 That is perverted! Should the Potter be counted as the clay? Should the created say

to the Creator, He made me not! Or shall the thing formed say of Him that formed it; He has no binah?[7] 17 Is it not yet a very little while, and Levanon shall be turned into a fruitful field, and the fruitful field shall be esteemed as a forest? 18 And in that day[8] shall the deaf shema the words of the scroll, and the eyes of the blind shall see out of gloom,[9] and out of darkness[10] [11] 19 The meek also shall increase their simcha in יהוה, and the poor[12] among men shall simcha in the Set-Apart One of Yisrael. 20 For the ruthless one is brought to nothing, and the scorner is consumed, and all that desire iniquity are cut off: 21 That make men to sin by their words, and lay a trap for him that rebukes evil in the gate, and turns aside the tzadik with empty reasoning. 22 Therefore this says יהוה, who redeemed Avraham,[13] concerning Beit Yaakov,[14] *Yaakov shall no longer be ashamed, and neither shall his face now grow pale. 23 But when he sees his children, the work of My hands, in the midst of him, they shall set-apart My Name, and set-apart the Set-Apart One of Yaakov, and shall fear the Elohim of Yisrael.*[15] 24 *They also that had gone astray in Ruach, shall come to binah, and they that grumbled shall learn Torah.*[16]

30 *Woe to the rebellious children,* says יהוה, *that take counsel, but not from Me; and that devise plans, but not from My Ruach, that they may add sin to sin: 2 That set to go down into Mitzrayim, and have not asked at My mouth; to*

---

[1] Left empty.
[2] Both houses remain blind in most cases.
[3] Yisrael.
[4] Yisrael has no answers apart from Yahshua.
[5] Yisrael's problem is and has always been one of the heart and false doctrines, denying either Yahshua, or His Torah, or both. Yahshua attributes this to Yisrael in Matthew 15:8-9 and Mark 7:6-7.
[6] The besarot of Moshiach will go forth from Tzion, regardless of the dullness of its leaders, through wonders and miracles, in order to get the common people's attention.

[7] Yisrael's pride is addressed.
[8] End of the age.
[9] Exile.
[10] The visionary remnant of both houses of Yisrael.
[11] This exciting time is the one in which we live in, where Ephraim sees himself for who he truly is, and Judah sees that YHWH has a Son, and that they have always been the marred clay in the Potter's Hand, as the Potter rebuilds the same lump called Yisrael into another Renewed Covenant people.
[12] In spirit.
[13] Note that the first Hebrew Avraham, also was not accepted by tov works, but received redemption from YHWH alone.
[14] All 12 tribes.
[15] His children will fear His Name, with a right heart attitude.
[16] In the restoration of the nation, YHWH will take grumblers and complainers, and those dull of understanding, and turn them into men and women of Torah and doctrine.

strengthen themselves in the strength of Pharaoh, and to trust in the shadow of Mitzrayim! 3 Therefore shall the strength of Pharaoh be your shame, and the trust in the shadow of Mitzrayim your confusion. 4 For his rulers were at Tzoan, and his ambassadors came to Hanes. 5 They go to a people that could not profit them, nor be a help nor a profit to them, but rather a shame, and also a reproach. 6 The burden of the beasts of the south: into the land of trouble and anguish, from where comes the young and old lion, the viper and fiery flying serpent, they will carry their riches upon the shoulders of young donkeys, and their treasures upon the humps of camels, to a people that shall not profit them. 7 For the Mitzrites shall help in vain, and to no avail: therefore have I called her, Rahav-Hem-Sheveth - Arrogance Doing Nothing. 8 Now go, write it before them on a tablet, and note it in a scroll, that it may be for the time to come le-olam-va-ed: 9 That this is a rebellious people, lying children that will not shema to the Torah of יהוה: 10 Who say to the seers, See not; and to ha neviim, Prophesy not to us right things, speak to us smooth nice things, prophesy deceits: [1] 11 Get out of His halacha, turn aside out of the derech, and cause the Set-Apart One of Yisrael to leave us alone. 12 Therefore this says the Set-Apart One of Yisrael, Because you despise this word, and trust in oppression and perverseness, and stay in that:[2] 13 Therefore this iniquity shall be to you as a breach ready to fall, growing in a high wall, whose breaking comes suddenly at an instant. 14 And He shall break it as the breaking of the potter's vessel that is broken in pieces; He shall not spare: so that there shall not be found any among the fragments to use to take fire from the fireplace, or to take mayim out of the cistern. 15 For this says the Master יהוה,

the Set-Apart One of Yisrael; In returning[3] and rest[4] shall you be saved;[5] in quietness and in trust shall be your strength: but you would not. 16 But you said, No; for we will flee upon horses; therefore shall you flee: and, We will ride upon the swift; therefore they that shall pursue you are swift. 17 One thousand shall flee at the rebuke of one; at the rebuke of five shall you flee: until you are left as a beacon upon the top of a mountain, and as a banner on a hill.[6] 18 And therefore will יהוה wait, that He may extend rachamim to you, and therefore will He be exalted, so that He may have rachamim upon you: for יהוה is a Elohim of mishpat: blessed are all they that wait for Him. 19 For the people shall live in Tzion at Yahrushalayim: [7] you shall weep no more: He will have great rachamim towards you at the voice of your cry; when He shall shema, He will answer you. 20 And though יהוה gave you the lechem of adversity, and the mayim of affliction, yet your teachers shall not be removed into a corner anymore, but your eyes shall see your teachers:[8] 21 And your ears shall shema a word behind you, saying, This is the halacha, have your halacha in this Way,[9] when you turn to the right hand, and when you turn to the left. 22 You shall defile also the covering of your graven images of silver, and the ornament of your molded images of gold: you shall cast them away as a menstruous cloth; you shall say to it, Get out![10] 23 Then shall He give the rain for your zera,[11] that you shall sow the ground; and lechem as the increase of the earth, and it shall be fat and filling: in that

---

[1] The same things are said to today's Yisraelite neviim. Whenever a prophetic word is perceived as too hard or harsh, the accusation of "unloving" always rears its head.
[2] Trusting in Egypt rather than YHWH.
[3] Returning to your Yisraelite heritage.
[4] Shabbat-keeping and all other forms of prescribed Yisraelite rest.
[5] Salvation leads to Yisraelite heritage.
[6] Yisrael will flee until they return to the comforts of Zion, when they will become the light of the world that they have been called to be.
[7] Both houses.
[8] Renewed Covenant Yisraelites with a public ministry.
[9] The voice of Moshiach Yahshua.
[10] The voice of the Way of Yahshua and Yisrael will cause you to defile all pagan practices as opposed to defiling YHWH in the name of g-d and other house idols.
[11] When Yisrael cleanses herself of false religion and idolatry, they reap immediate and long-term blessings.

day shall your cattle feed in large pastures. 24 The oxen and the young donkeys that work the ground, shall eat clean tasty mixtures, that has been winnowed with the shovel and with the fan. 25 And there shall be upon every high mountain, and upon every high hill, rivers and streams of mayim in the day of the great slaughter, when the towers fall.[1] 26 Moreover the light of the moon shall be as the light of the sun, and the light of the sun shall be magnified sevenfold, as the light of seven days, in the day that יהוה *binds up the breach of His people, and heals their wounds from His blows.[2] 27 See, the Name of* יהוה *comes from far,[3] burning with His anger, and the burden of it is heavy: His lips are full of displeasure, and His tongue as a devouring fire: 28 And His breath, as an overflowing river, shall reach to the midst of the neck, to sift the nations with the sieve of falsehood: and there shall be a bridle in the jaws of the nations, causing them to go astray.[4] 29 You[5] shall have a shir, in the night as when a set-apart moed is kept; and simcha of lev, as when one goes with a flute to come up to the mountain of* יהוה, *to the Mighty One of Yisrael. 30 And* יהוה *shall cause His voice of tiferet to be heard, and shall show the coming down of His Arm,[6] with the displeasure of His anger, and with the flame of a devouring fire, with scattering, and storm, and hailstones.[7] 31 By the voice of* יהוה *shall Ashshur be beaten down, who smote Yisrael with a rod. 32 And in every place where the ordained staff shall pass, which* יהוה *shall lay upon him, it shall be with tambourines and harps: in fierce battle will He fight against them. 33 For Tophet is ordained of old; yes, for the melech it is prepared; He made it deep and large: its fire pit with much wood; the breath of* יהוה, *like a river of brimstone, will burn it.*

31

Woe to them that go down to Mitzrayim for help; and rely on horses, and trust in mirkavot, because they are many; and in horsemen, because they are very strong; but they look not to the Set-Apart One of Yisrael, neither do they seek יהוה! 2 Yet He also is wise, and will bring evil, and will not take back His words: but will arise against the bayit of the evildoers, and against the helpers of those that work iniquity. 3 Now the Mitzrites are men, and not Eloah; and their horses are flesh, and not the Ruach HaKodesh. When יהוה shall stretch out His hand, both he that helps shall fall, and he that is being helped shall fall down, and they fall together. 4 For this has יהוה spoken to me, *Like as the lion and the young lion roaring on its prey, when a multitude of shepherds is called forth against him, he will not be afraid of their voice, nor humble himself for the noise of them:* so shall יהוה of hosts come down to fight for Har Tzion, and for its hill.[8] 5 As birds flying, so will יהוה of hosts defend Yahrushalayim; defending and delivering it; and passing over and preserving it. 6 Now make teshuvah to Him, from whom B'nai Yisrael has deeply fallen away. 7 For in that day every man shall cast away his idols of silver, and his idols of gold, which your own hands have made for yourselves to sin.[9] 8 Then shall Ashshur fall with the sword, not of a mighty man; and the sword, not from mankind, but he shall flee from the sword,[10] and his young men shall be put to

---

[1] Some say this was a prochecy of the Twin Towers of NYC falling on 9/11/01.
[2] All things will be brighter through renewal, including the healed people of Yisrael in the restoration of the nation in the millennial kingdom.
[3] "From far" denotes from the renewed circumcised lips of returning Ephraim Yisrael. Also YHWH uses His name to bring judgment on those in Yisrael who refuse to repent from idolatry.
[4] Even while Yisrael is being renewed, the nations go further astray. We see this happening more and more in the end times. The more "returning to Tzion" there is, the more those not willing to return recommit to their comfortable yet idolatrous ways.
[5] Redeemed Yisrael, on the other hand.
[6] Return of Yahshua.
[7] Yahshua comes down to judge the earth, and restore Yisrael simultaneously.

[8] He will come quietly in strength, not secretly or loudly to those who look for Him.
[9] In the day that the two trees of Ezekiel 37 come together.
[10] Of YHWH.

forced labor. 9 And he shall pass over to his stronghold for fear, and his rulers shall be afraid of the Banner, says **יהוה**, whose fire is in Tzion, and whose furnace in Yahrushalayim.[1]

32 See, a Melech shall reign in tzedakah,[2] and rulers shall rule in mishpat.[3] 2 And each man shall be as a hiding place from the wind, and a shelter from the storm; as rivers of mayim in a dry place, as the shadow of a great rock in a weary land. 3 And the eyes of them that see shall not be dim, and the ears of them that will shema shall shema. 4 The lev also of the quick to talk shall understand da'at, and the tongue of the stutterers shall be ready to speak plainly. 5 The fool shall be no more called noble, nor the scoundrel said to be respectable. 6 For the foolish person will speak folly, and his lev will work iniquity, to practice hypocrisy, and to utter error against **יהוה**, to make empty the being of the hungry, and to cause the drink of the thirsty to fail. 7 The instruments also of the scoundrel are evil: he plans wicked plans to destroy the poor with lying words, even when the needy asks for mishpat. 8 But the generous plans generous things; and by generous things shall he stand. 9 Rise up, you women that are at ease; shema to My voice, you carefree daughters; shema to My speech. 10 Many days and years shall you be troubled, you carefree women: for the grape harvest shall fail, the gathering shall not come.[4] 11 Tremble, you women that are at ease; be troubled, you carefree ones: strip yourself, and make yourselves bare, and put on sackcloth upon your waist.[5] 12 They shall lament for the breasts, for the pleasant fields, for the fruitful vine. 13 Upon the land of My people shall come up thorns and weeds; yes, upon all the bayits of simcha in the joyous city: 14 Because the palaces shall be forsaken; the crowded city deserted; the hills and watchtowers shall serve as caves le-olam-va-ed, a simcha of wild donkeys, a pasture of flocks will remain; 15 Until the Ruach is poured upon us from on high, and the wilderness is a fruitful field, and the fruitful field is counted as a forest.[6] 16 Then mishpat shall live in the wilderness, and tzedakah remain in the fruitful field. 17 And the work of tzedakah shall be shalom; and the effect of tzedakah rest and trust le-olam-va-ed. 18 And My people shall live in a homeland of shalom, and in secure dwellings, and in quiet resting places; 19 Even when it shall hail, coming down on the forest; and the city shall be laid low in humiliation. 20 Blessed are you that sow beside all kinds of mayim that send forth the feet of the ox and the donkey.[7]

33 Woe to you that plunders, and you were not plundered; and deals treacherously, and they dealt not treacherously with you! When you shall cease to plunder, you shall be plundered; and when you shall make an end to dealing treacherously, they shall deal treacherously with you. 2 O **יהוה**, show us favor; we have waited for You: be their Arm every morning, our Yahshua also in the time of trouble. 3 At the noise of rumbling the people fled; when You lift Yourself up the nations were scattered. 4 And Your plunder shall be gathered like the gathering of the caterpiller: as the running around of locusts shall He run upon them. 5 **יהוה** is exalted; for He dwells on high: He has filled Tzion with mishpat and tzedakah. 6 And chochma and da'at shall be the stability of your times, and strength of Yahshua: the fear of

---

[1] The source of His supernatural power resides among the people and land of Tzion.
[2] Moshiach Yahshua.
[3] His kidushim or saints.
[4] Those who do not take Yisrael's return and restoration seriously and are carefree towards it will see no spiritual harvest in their own lives, or in the lives of others, not to mention many days of anxiety. Restoration truth must be at the core position of any doctrine.
[5] Repentance is called for by those who harbor carefree attitudes towards YHWH's work in Zion between both houses in the latter-days.

[6] Without the outpouring of the Ruach, Yisrael and Jerusalem will remain desolate.
[7] Yisraelites must be ready to sow and reap in season and out of season, until the day of kingdom esteem.

יהוה - that is His treasure. 7 See, their brave ones shall cry outside: the ambassadors of shalom shall weep bitterly. 8 The highways lie deserted, the wayfaring man ceases: He has broken the covenant, he has despised the cities, he regards no man. 9 The earth mourns and languishes: Levanon is ashamed and cut down: Sharon is like a wilderness; and Bashan and Carmel shake off their fruits. 10 *Now will I rise, says* יהוה; *now will I be exalted; now will I lift up Myself.* 11 *You shall conceive chaff, you shall bring forth stubble: your breath, as fire, shall devour you.* 12 *And the people shall be as the burnings of lime: as thorns cut up shall they be burned in the fire.* 13 *Shema, you that are far off,[1] what I have done; and, you that are near,[2] acknowledge My might.* 14 The sinners in Tzion are afraid; trembling has seized the heathen. Who among us shall live with the devouring fire? Who among us shall live with everlasting burnings? 15 He that has their halacha righteously, and speaks uprightly; he that despises the gain of oppression, that holds back his hands from holding bribes, that stops his ears from hearing domshed, and shuts his eyes from seeing evil; 16 He shall live on high: his place of defence shall be the strongholds of rocks: lechem shall be given him; his mayim shall be sure. 17 Your eyes shall see the Melech in His tiferet: they shall see the land that is very far off. 18 Your lev shall ponder fear. Where is the sopher? Where is the weigher? Where is he that counts the towers? 19 You shall not see a fierce people, a people of an obscure language that you cannot perceive; with a stammering tongue that you cannot understand. 20 Look upon Tzion, the city of our moadim: Your eyes shall see Yahrushalayim a quiet home, a sukkah that shall not be taken down; not one of its pegs shall ever be removed, neither shall any of its cords be broken.[3] 21 But there Majestic יהוה will be to us a place of broad rivers and streams; in which shall go no boat with oars, neither shall large ships pass by. 22 For יהוה is Our Shofet, יהוה is Our Lawgiver, יהוה is Our Melech; He will save us.[4] 23 Your ropes are loosed; they could not well strengthen their mast, they could not spread the sail: then is the prey of a great plunder divided; the lame take the prey. 24 And the inhabitant shall not say, I am sick: the people that live in it shall be forgiven their iniquity.[5]

34

Come near, you nations, to shema; and shema, you people: let the earth shema, and all that is in it; the olam, and all things that come forth from it. 2 For the displeasure of יהוה *is upon all nations, and His fury upon all their armies: He shall utterly destroy them, He shall deliver them to the slaughter. 3 Their slain also shall be cast out, and their stink shall come up out of their corpses, and the mountains shall be melted with their dom. 4 And all the host of the shamayim shall be dissolved, and the shamayim shall be rolled together as a scroll: and all their host shall fall down, as the leaf falls off from the vine, and as a falling fig from the fig eytz. 5 For My sword shall be sharpened in the shamayim: see, it shall come down upon the Edomites, and upon the people of My curse, condemned in mishpat.[6] 6 The sword of* יהוה *is filled with dom, it shall overflow with fatness, and with the dom of lambs and goats, with the fat of the kidneys of rams: for* יהוה *has a sacrifice in Botzrah, and a great slaughter in the land of Edom. 7 And the wild ox shall come down with them, and the young bulls with the bulls; and their land shall be soaked with dom, and their*

---

[1] Ephraim Yisrael.
[2] Jewish Yisrael.

[3] Yahrushalayim is the permanent home of all the saved in Yisrael and it shall never be removed but shall be renewed for us to dwell there.
[4] Three wonderful manifestations of YHWH, and an indication of his echad nature.
[5] In the renewed Yahrushalayim.
[6] Verse 5 until the end of the chapter is the specific judgment of Edom.

dust made fat with fatness. 8 For it is the Yom of **יהוה**'s vengeance, and the year of paybacks for the controversy of Tzion. [1] 9 And its streams shall be turned into tar, and its dust into brimstone, and its land shall become burning tar. 10 It shall not be quenched night nor day; the smoke of it shall go up le-olam-va-ed: from generation to generation it shall lie in ruin; none shall pass through it le-olam-va-ed. [2] 11 But the pelican and the porcupine shall possess it; the owl also and the raven shall live in it: and He shall stretch out upon it the measuring line of confusion, and the stones of emptiness. 12 They shall call its nobles to the malchut, but none shall be there, and all her rulers shall become nothing. 13 And thorns shall come up in her palaces, nettles and brambles in its strongholds: and it shall be a home of jackals, and a courtyard for ostriches. 14 The wild beasts of the desert shall also meet in it with the wild beasts of the island, and the billy-goats shall call to each other; the night creature also shall rest there, and find for herself a place of rest. 15 There shall the hoot owl make her nest, and lay, and hatch, and gather under her shadow: there shall the vultures also be gathered, every one with its mate. 16 Seek for the scroll of **יהוה**, and read it: not one of these shall fail, none shall be without a mate: for my mouth He has commanded, and His Ruach shall gather them. 17 And He has cast the lot for them, and His hand has divided it to them by measuring line: they shall possess it le-olam-va-ed, from generation to generation shall they live in it. [3]

35 The wilderness and the solitary place shall be glad for them; and

the desert shall simcha, and blossom as the rose. [4] 2 It shall blossom abundantly, and simcha even with simcha and singing: the tiferet of Levanon shall be given to it, [5] the excellency of Carmel and Sharon, they shall see the tiferet of **יהוה**, and the excellency of Our Elohim. 3 Strengthen the weak hands, and make firm the feeble knees. 4 Say to them that are of a fearful lev, Be strong, and fear not: see, Your Elohim will come with vengeance, even Elohim with a recompense; He will come and save you. [6] 5 Then the eyes of the blind shall be opened, and the ears of the deaf shall be opened. [7] 6 Then shall the lame man leap as a hart, and the tongue of the dumb shir: for in the wilderness shall mayim break out, and streams in the desert. [8] 7 And the parched ground shall become a pool, and the thirsty land springs of mayim: in the home of jackals, where each one lay, there shall be grass with reeds and rushes. 8 And a highway shall be there, and A Way, and it shall be called The Way [9] of set-apartness; the unclean shall not pass over it; but it shall be for those who walk The Way: wayward fools shall not go astray in it. 9 No lion shall be there, nor any ravenous beast shall go up on it, they shall not be found there; but the redeemed shall have their halacha there: [10] 10 And the ransomed of **יהוה** shall return, and come to Tzion [11] with shirim and everlasting simcha upon their heads: they shall obtain simcha upon

---

[1] The Day of YHWH when He takes direct vengeance on Edom for the hate and violence towards Yisrael by trying to regain the birthright sold to Jacob through hate and death. YHWH Himself will settle the controversy of Zion's right to YHWH's birthright in the Day of YHWH or the Great Tribulation.
[2] The true and final end of all Yisrael's enemies.
[3] As opposed to Zion that will be inhabited by the redeemed remnant of Yisrael forever; vultures and creatures of the night along with their mates will inhabit Edom forever.

[4] While Edom is being judged, Israel will be fully restored.
[5] To "Greater Yisrael" in the millennium.
[6] YHWH will come to earth to repay Edom and rescue and deliver Yaakov.
[7] The signs of the Moshiach or Elohim with us. When these signs come to pass, we can know Moshiach Yahshua has come. These signs were surely performed as a sign of our salvation and Yisrael's renewal.
[8] Signs of the King Moshiach all performed in the person of Yahshua of Nazareth (Matthew 15:30, Matthew 11:5).
[9] A clear reference to the first Nazarene Yisraelites, also known as "followers of the Way" (in Acts 19:23, and 24:22), with Yahshua Himself called "The Way" in John 14:6.
[10] "The Way," is for redeemed Yisrael, not for fools, heathen, or unconverted Edomites.
[11] In YHWH's time by YHWH's Moshiach Yahshua, the redeemed will be restored and returned. The Way of set-apartness will restore us spiritually and physically back to our nation, and our YHWH.

simcha, and sorrow and sighing shall flee away.[1]

36 Now it came to pass in the fourteenth year of melech Hizqiyahu, that Sanheriv melech of Ashshur came up against all the defended cities of Yahudah, and took them. 2 And the melech of Ashshur sent Ravshakeh from Lachish to Yahrushalayim to melech Hizqiyahu with a great army. And he stood by the channel of the upper pool in the highway of the Launderers Field. 3 Then came forth to him Elyaqim, Hilqiyah's son, who was steward of the household, and Shevna the sopher, and Yoah, Asaph's son, the recorder. 4 And Ravshakeh said to them, Say now to Hizqiyahu, This says the great melech, the melech of Ashshur, What trust is this in which you trust? 5 I say, you speak of having counsel and strength for war, but they are but vain words: now upon whom do you trust, that you have rebelled against me? 6 See, you trust in the staff of this broken reed, on Mitzrayim; which if a man lean on, it will go into his hand, and pierce it: so is Pharaoh melech of Mitzrayim to all that trust in him. 7 But if you say to me, We trust in יהוה our Elohim: is it not He, whose high places and whose altars Hizqiyahu has taken away, and said to Yahudah and to Yahrushalayim, You shall worship before this altar? 8 Now therefore give a pledge, I ask you, to my master the melech of Ashshur, and I will give you two thousand horses, if you are able on your part to set riders upon them. 9 How then can you refuse one officer of the least of my master's avadim, and put your trust in Mitzrayim for mirkavot and for horsemen? 10 And am I now come up without יהוה against this land to destroy it? יהוה said to me, Go up against this land, and destroy it. 11 Then said Elyaqim and Shevna and Yoah to Ravshakeh, Please speak, to your avadim in the Aramaic language; for we

understand it: and speak not to us in the language of Yahudah,[2] in the ears of the people that are on the wall. 12 But Ravshakeh said, Has my master sent me to your master and to you to speak these words? Has he not sent me to the men that sit upon the wall, that they may eat their own dung, and drink their own urine with you? 13 Then Ravshakeh stood, and cried with a loud voice in Ivrit; language of Yahudah, and said, Shema to the words of the great melech, the melech of Ashshur. 14 This says the melech, Let not Hizqiyahu deceive you: for he shall not be able to deliver you. 15 Neither let Hizqiyahu make you trust in יהוה, saying, יהוה will surely deliver us: so that this city shall not be delivered into the hand of the melech of Ashshur. 16 Shema not to Hizqiyahu: for this says the melech of Ashshur, Make an agreement with me by a present, and come out to me: and eat every one of his vine, and every one of his fig eytz, and drink every one the mayim of his own cistern; 17 Until I come and take you away to a land like your own land, a land of grain and wine, a land of lechem and vineyards. 18 Beware lest Hizqiyahu persuade you, saying, יהוה will deliver us. Has any of the elohim of the nations delivered his land out of the hand of the melech of Ashshur? 19 Where are the elohim of Hamath and Arphad? Where are the elohim of Sepharvaim? Have they delivered Shomron out of my hand?[3] 20 Who are they among all the elohim of these lands, that have delivered their land out of my hand, that יהוה should deliver Yahrushalayim out of my hand? 21 But they held their shalom, and did not answer him even one word: for the melech's commandment said, Do not answer him. 22 Then came Elyaqim, the son of Hilqiyah, that was over the household, and Shevna the sopher, and Yoah, the son of Asaph, the

---

[1] The ultimate inheritance of every redeemed Yisraelite from either house.

[2] A crystal-clear reference to the fact that Hebrew was the original language of Yisrael, but also that many spoke and understood both Hebrew and Aramaic. Moreover we see that the Arameans were semites; and that these Assyrians very likely had clear dom ties to many in Yisrael.

[3] Shomron had already fallen frightening Judah even more.

recorder, to Hizqiyahu with their clothes torn, and told him all the words of Ravshakeh.

37 And it came to pass, when melech Hizqiyahu heard it, that he tore his clothes, and covered himself with sackcloth, and went into the Bayit of יהוה. 2 And he sent Elyaqim, who was over the household, and Shevna the sopher, and the zachanim of the kohanim covered with sackcloth, to Yeshayahu ha navi the son of Amotz. 3 And they said to him, This says Hizqiyahu, This day is a day of trouble, and of rebuke, and of scorn: for the children have come to the birth, and there is no strength to bring forth. 4 It may be יהוה Your Elohim will shema the words of Ravshakeh, whom the melech of Ashshur his master has sent to reproach the living Elohim, and will reprove the words which יהוה Your Elohim has heard: therefore lift up your tefillah for the remnant that is left. 5 So the avadim of melech Hizqiyahu came to Yeshayahu. 6 And Yeshayahu said to them, This shall you say to your master, This says יהוה, *Be not afraid of the words that you have heard, by which the avadim of the melech of Ashshur have blasphemed Me. 7 See, I will send a blast upon him, and he shall shema a rumor, and return to his own land; and I will cause him to fall by the sword in his own land.* 8 So Ravshakeh returned, and found the melech of Ashshur fighting against Livnah: for he had heard that he was departed from Lachish. 9 And he heard it said concerning Tirhachah melech of Ethiopia, He is come forth to make war with you. And when he heard it, he sent messengers to Hizqiyahu, saying, 10 This shall you say to Hizqiyahu melech of Yahudah, saying, Let not Your Elohim, in whom you trust, deceive you, saying, Yahrushalayim shall not be given into the hand of the melech of Ashshur. 11 See, you have heard what the melechim of Ashshur have done to all lands by destroying them utterly; and shall you be delivered?

12 Have the elohim of the nations delivered them that my ahvot have destroyed, like Gozan, and Haran, and Rezeph, and the children of Eden who were in Telassar? 13 Where is the melech of Hamath, and the melech of Arphad, and the melech of the city of Sepharvaim, Hena, and Ivah? 14 Hizqiyahu received the letter from the hands of the messengers, and read it: and Hizqiyahu went up to the Bayit of יהוה, and spread it before יהוה. 15 And Hizqiyahu made tefillah to יהוה, saying, 16 O יהוה of hosts, Elohim of Yisrael, You who live between the cheruvim,[1] You are the Elohim, even You alone, of all the malchutim of the earth: You alone have made the shamayim and the earth. 17 Incline Your ear, O יהוה, and shema; open Your eyes, O יהוה, and see: and shema to all the words of Sanheriv, which has been sent to reproach the living Elohim. 18 Of an emet, יהוה, the melechim of Ashshur have laid waste all the nations, and their countries, 19 And have cast their elohim into the fire: for they were not elohim, but the work of men's hands, wood and stone: therefore they have destroyed them. 20 Now therefore, O יהוה Our Elohim, save us from his hand, that all the malchutim of the earth may know that You are יהוה, even You alone. 21 Then Yeshayahu the son of Amotz sent to Hizqiyahu, saying, This says יהוה Elohim of Yisrael, *Because you have made tefillah to Me against Sanheriv melech of Ashshur:* 22 *This is the word that יהוה has spoken concerning him; The virgin, the daughter of Tzion, has despised you, and laughed you to scorn; the daughter of Yahrushalayim has shaken her head at you.* 23 *Whom have you reproached and blasphemed? And against whom have you exalted your voice, and lifted up your eyes on high? Even against the Set-Apart One of Yisrael.* 24 *By your avadim have you reproached יהוה, and have said, By the multitude of my mirkavot*

---

[1] Two cheruvim: symbolic of living between and amongst the two houses of Yisrael.

am I come up to the height of the mountains, to the sides of Levanon; and I will cut down the tall cedars of it, and the choice cypress eytzim of it: and I will enter into the height of its border, and the forest of its Carmel. 25 I have dug, and drunk mayim; and with the sole of my feet have I dried up all the rivers of the besieged places. 26 Have you not heard long ago, how I have done it; and of ancient times, that I have formed it? Now have I brought it to pass, that you should be allowed to lay waste defended cities into ruinous heaps. 27 Therefore their inhabitants were of small power, they were dismayed and embarrassed: they were as the grass of the field, and as the green herb, as the grass on the housetops, and as grain blasted before it is grown up. 28 But I know your sitting down, and your going out, and your coming in, and your rage against Me. 29 Because your rage against Me, and your pride, has come up into My ears, therefore will I put My hook in your nose, and My bridle in your lips, and I will turn you back by the same road by which you came. 30 And this shall be a sign to you, You shall eat this year such as grows by itself; and the second year that which springs of the same: and in the third year sow, and reap, and plant vineyards, and eat the fruit of it. 31 And the remnant that is escaped of Beit Yahudah shall again take root downward, and bear fruit upward: 32 For out of Yahrushalayim shall go forth a remnant, and they that escape out of Har Tzion: the zeal of יהוה of hosts shall do this.[1] 33 Therefore this says יהוה concerning the melech of Ashshur, He shall not come into this city, nor shoot an arrow there nor come before it with shields, nor build a siege mound against it. 34 By the road that he came, by the same road shall he return, and shall not come into this city, says יהוה. 35 For I will defend this city to save it for My own sake, and for My eved David's sake. 36 Then the heavenly messenger of יהוה went forth, and smote

the camp of the Ashurim one hundred eighty-five thousand: and when they arose early in the morning, see, they were all dead corpses. 37 So Sanheriv melech of Ashshur departed, and went and returned, and dwelt at Nineveh. 38 And it came to pass, as he was worshipping in the bayit of Nisroch his elohim, that Adram-Melech and Sharetzer his sons smote him with the sword; and they escaped into the land of Armenia: and Esar-Haddon his son reigned in his place.

38 In those days Hizqiyahu was sick and near death. And Yeshayahu ha navi the son of Amotz came to him, and said to him, This says יהוה, Set your bayit in order: for you shall die, and not live. 2 Then Hizqiyahu turned his face toward the wall, and made tefillah to יהוה, 3 And said, Remember now, O יהוה, I beg You, how I have had my halacha before You in emet and with a perfect lev, and have done that which is tov in Your sight. And Hizqiyahu wept heavily. 4 Then came the word of יהוה to Yeshayahu, saying, 5 Go, and tell Hizqiyahu, This says יהוה, the Elohim of David your abba, I have heard your tefillah, I have seen your tears: see, I will add to your days fifteen years. 6 And I will deliver you and this city out of the hand of the melech of Ashshur: and I will defend this city. 7 And this shall be a sign to you from יהוה, that יהוה will do this thing that He has spoken; 8 See, I will bring again the shadow of the degrees, which is gone down on the sundial of Ahaz, ten degrees backward. So the sun returned ten degrees on the dial, by the same degrees that it had gone down. 9 This then is the writing of Hizqiyahu melech of Yahudah, when he had been sick, and had later recovered from his sickness: 10 I said in the cutting off of my days, I shall go to the gates of the grave: I am deprived of the residue of my years. 11 I said, I shall not see Yah, Yah, in the land of the living: I shall see man no more with the inhabitants of the olam. 12 My chayim is departed, and is removed from

---

[1] A remnant shall escape in the end times.

me as a shepherd's tent: My chayim was shrunk like a weaver's web: He will cut me off with sickness: from one day to the next night You make an end of me. 13 I soothed myself until morning, but as a lion, so will He break all my bones: from one day to the next night will You make an end of me. 14 Like a swallow, so did I chatter: I did mourn as a yonah: my eyes became weary with looking upward: O יהוה , I am oppressed; take hold of this for me! 15 What shall I say? He has both spoken to me, and Himself has done it: I shall go humbly all my years in the bitterness of my being. 16 O יהוה, by these things men live, and in all these things is the chayim of my ruach: so restore me, and make me live. 17 See, for shalom I had great bitterness: but You have in Your ahava for my being delivered it from the pit of corruption: for You have cast all my sins behind Your back. 18 For the grave cannot hallel You, death cannot celebrate You: they that go down into the pit cannot tikvah for Your emet. 19 The living, yes, the living, shall hallel You, even as I do this day: the abba to their children shall make known Your emet. 20 יהוה came to save me: therefore we will shir my shirim with the stringed instruments all the days of our chayim in the Bayit of יהוה. 21 For Yeshayahu had said, Let them take a fig-plaster, and apply it upon the boil, and he shall recover: 22 Because Hizqiyahu asked, What is the sign that I shall be able to go up to the Bayit of יהוה?

39 At that time Merodach-Baladan, the son of Baladan, melech of Bavel, sent letters and a present to Hizqiyahu: for he had heard that he had been sick, and had recovered. 2 And Hizqiyahu was glad because of them, and in turn he showed them the bayit of his precious things, the silver, and the gold, and the spices, and the precious ointment, and all the bayit of his armor, and all that was found in his treasures: there was nothing in

his bayit, nor in all his dominion, that Hizqiyahu did not show them. 3 Then came Yeshayahu ha navi to melech Hizqiyahu, and said to him, What did those men say? And from where did they come? And Hizqiyahu said, They have come from a far country to me, even from Bavel. 4 Then he said, What have they seen in your bayit? And Hizqiyahu answered, All that is in my bayit have they seen: there is nothing among my treasures that I have not shown them. 5 Then said Yeshayahu to Hizqiyahu, Shema the word of יהוה of hosts: 6 *See, the days come, that all that is in your bayit, and that which your ahvot have laid up in store until this day, shall be carried to Bavel: nothing shall be left*, says יהוה. 7 *And of your sons that shall come from you, whom you shall bring forth, shall they take away; and they shall be eunuchs in the palace of the melech of Bavel.* 8 Then said Hizqiyahu to Yeshayahu, Tov is the word of יהוה which you have spoken. He said moreover, For there shall be shalom and emet in my days.

40 *Comfort you, comfort you My people,* [1] *says Your Elohim. 2 Speak comfortably to Yahrushalayim, and declare to her, that her warfare is finished,* [2] *that her iniquity is pardoned:* [3] *for she has received from* יהוה*'s hand double for all her sins.* [4] *3 The voice of him that cries in the wilderness, Prepare the Way of* יהוה*,* [5] [6] *make straight in the desert a highway for Our Elohim.* [7] *4 Every valley shall be exalted, and every mountain and hill shall be made low: and the crooked places shall be made straight, and the rough places*

---

[1] Two declarations of comfort for two houses of Yisrael.
[2] Her war between YHWH and man, and between the two houses of Yisrael, in their ongoing hatred for each other. That will come to an end.
[3] Sins forgiven and two-house restoration are the hallmarks of Moshiach and the restored kingdom.
[4] Yisrael has reaped what it has sown. Double punishment means two punishments for two houses.
[5] A prophecy about **Yochanan HaMatbeel**/John the Baptist.
[6] Notice the coming Elohim is called YHWH. The Moshiach is YHWH clothed in the flesh.
[7] Elohim is coming to earth to pardon Yisrael and speak gently to her with the **besarot** of the kingdom.

plain:[1] 5 *And the tiferet of* יהוה *shall be revealed, and all flesh shall see it together:*[2] *for the mouth of* יהוה *has spoken it.* 6 *The voice said, Cry. And he said, What shall I cry? All flesh is grass, and all the tov from it is as the flower of the field:* 7 *The grass whithers, the flower fades: when the Ruach HaKodesh of* יהוה *blows upon it: surely the people* [3] *are like grass.* 8 *The grass whithers, the flower fades: but the Word of Our Elohim shall abide and stand le-olam-va-ed.*[4] 9 *O Tzion, that brings tov tidings, get up into the high mountain; O Yahrushalayim, that brings tov tidings, lift up your voice with strength; lift it up, be not afraid; say to the cities of Yahudah, See Your Elohim!*[5] 10 *See, the Master* יהוה *will come with a strong Hand,*[6] *and His Arm shall rule for Him:*[7] *see, His reward is with Him,*[8] *and His work before Him.*[9] 11 *He shall feed His flock like a Shepherd: He shall gather the lambs with His Arm,*[10] *and carry them in His bosom, and shall gently lead those that are with young.* 12 *Who has measured the mayim in the hollow of His hand, and meted out the shamayim with the span, and gathered the dust of the earth in a measure, and weighed the mountains on scales, and the hills in a balance?* 13 *Who has directed the Ruach of* יהוה,[11] *or being His counselor has taught Him?* 14 *With whom did He take counsel, and who instructed Him, and taught Him in the derech of mishpat, and taught Him da'at, and showed Him the halacha of binah?* 15 *See, the nations are as a drop in a bucket, and are counted as the small dust on the balance: see, He lifts up the coastlands as fine dust.* 16 *And Levanon is not sufficient to burn, nor the beasts of it sufficient for a burnt offering.* 17 *All nations before Him are as nothing; and they are counted by Him as less than nothing, and emptiness.* 18 *To whom then will you liken Eloah? Or what likeness will you compare Him to?* 19 *The workman melts a graven image, and the goldsmith covers it with gold, and casts silver chains.* 20 *He that is so poor that he has no gold idol chooses an eytz that will not rot; he seeks for himself a skilled workman to prepare a graven image that shall not move.* 21 *Have you not known? Have you not heard? Has it not been told to you from the beginning? Have you not understood from the foundations of the earth?* 22 *It is He that sits upon the circle of the earth,*[12] *and the inhabitants of it are as a grasshopper; that stretches out the shamayim as a curtain, and spreads them out as a tent to live in:* 23 *That brings rulers to nothing; and makes the shophtim of the earth as vanity.* 24 *Yes, they shall not be planted; yes, they shall not be sown: yes, their stock shall not take root in the earth: and He shall also blow upon them, and they shall wither, and the whirlwind shall take them away as stubble.* 25 *To whom then will you liken Me, or to whom shall I be equal?* Says the Set-Apart One.[13] 26 *Lift up your eyes on high, and see who has created these things, that brings out their host by number: He calls them all by names*[14] *by the greatness of His might, for He is strong in power; and not one fails.* 27 *Why do you say, O Yaakov, and speak, O Yisrael, My halacha is hidden from* יהוה, *and mishpat is not issued from My Elohim?* 28 *Have you not known? Have you not heard, that the Everlasting Elohim,*

---

[1] Moshiach Yahshua will remove all obstacles to man's pardon and Yisrael's two-house reunion.
[2] The only way for flesh to see YHWH is for YHWH to become flesh, since no flesh can live in heaven in His abode.
[3] Of Yisrael.
[4] Yahshua abides forever.
[5] Yahshua would come to Judah since Ephraim was already in exile, and thus it would be their responsibility to proclaim Moshiach to their Ephraimite brethren, as Yahshua came to the cities of Judah.
[6] The coming Moshiach is the Strong Hand of YHWH, or YHWH Himself, not a mere impotent human.
[7] A metaphor for Yahshua.
[8] Salvation and eternal life is with Him.
[9] The work of redemption and restoration.
[10] The lambs of Yisrael that have been found; these words are addressed to Tzion in proper context.
[11] The Ruach is not a new concept.
[12] YHWH told Yisrael that the earth was a round circle long before modern science even existed.
[13] The Father has no equal. But He also does admit to having a Son according to Proverbs 30:4, Psalm 2:12, and Daniel 3:25.
[14] He not only knows the numbers of stars, but also has given each one a name.

יהוה, the Creator of the ends of the earth, faints not, neither is tired? There is no searching of His binah. 29 He gives power to the weary; and to them that have no might He increases strength. 30 Even the youths shall faint and be weary, and the young men shall stumble and fall: 31 But they that wait upon יהוה shall renew their strength;[1] they shall mount up with wings as eagles; they shall run, and not be weary; and they shall walk, and not faint.

41 Keep silent before Me, You coastlands; and let the people[2] renew their strength:[3] let them come near;[4] then let them speak: let us come together for mishpat.[5] 2 Who raised up the tzadik man from the east,[6] called him to His foot, gave the nations before Him, and made Him rule over melechim? He gave them as the dust for His sword, and as driven stubble for His bow. 3 He pursued them, and passed safely; even by the derech that He had not gone with His feet. 4 Who has wrought and done it, calling the generations[7] from the beginning? I יהוה, the first, and the last; I am He. 5 The coastlands saw it, and feared; the ends of the earth were afraid, they drew near, and came. 6 Each one helped his neighbor; and each one said to his brother, Be of tov courage. 7 So the craftsman encourages the goldsmith, and he that smooths with the hammer inspires him that strikes the anvil, saying, It is ready to be joined: and he fastens it with nails, that it should not be moved. 8 But you, Yisrael, are My eved, Yaakov whom I have chosen, the zera of Avraham My chaver. 9 You whom I have taken from the ends of the earth, and called you from the farthest parts of it, and said to you, You are My eved; I have chosen you, and not cast you away.[8] 10 Fear not; for I am with you: be not dismayed; for I am Your Elohim: I will strengthen you; yes, I will help you; yes, I will uphold you with the Right Hand[9] of My Tzedakah. 11 See, all they that were enraged against you shall be ashamed and embarrassed: they shall be as nothing; and they that strive with you shall perish. 12 You shall seek them, and shall not find them, even them that contended with you: they that war against you shall be as nothing, and as a thing of nothing.[10] 13 For I יהוה Your Elohim will hold your right hand, saying to you, Al-Tereh; I will help you. 14 Fear not, you worm Yaakov, and you men of Yisrael; I will help you, says יהוה, and Your Redeemer, the Set-Apart One of Yisrael.[11] 15 See, I will make you a new sharp threshing instrument having teeth: you shall thresh the mountains, and beat them small, and shall make the hills as chaff. 16 You shall fan them, and the wind shall carry them away, and the whirlwind shall scatter them: and you shall simcha in יהוה, and shall tiferet in the Set-Apart One of Yisrael.[12] 17 When the poor and needy seek mayim, and there is none, and their tongue fails for thirst, I יהוה will shema to them, I the Elohim of Yisrael will not forsake them. 18 I will open rivers in high places, and fountains in the midst of the valleys: I will make the wilderness a pool of mayim, and the dry land springs of mayim.[13] 19 I will plant in the wilderness the cedar, the acacia eytz, and the myrtle, and the oil eytz; I will set in the desert the cypress eytz,

---

[1] Yisraelites will be renewed through the Tov News.
[2] Of Yisrael.
[3] The exiles in all the coastlands.
[4] To YHWH and Zion.
[5] Both houses will come together to be free in YHWH's right rulings and justice.
[6] Avraham, and in an end-time setting the Moshiach.
[7] Of Yisrael.

[8] A prophecy of all 12 tribes returning from the ends of the earth, using the "prophetic perfect," meaning written in a way that makes the events seem past and fulfilled, when they are yet future or end-time events. Much of chapters 41-61 are written using this technique, since YHWH shows that He knows the end from the beginning.
[9] Fear not Yisrael, Moshiach will come and bring salvation and restoration.
[10] The ultimate end of Yisrael's struggles with her enemies. This will come to pass fully in the kingdom restored.
[11] Here there is Abba YHWH the Helper, and His Designated Redeemer. A duality of roles and powers; The Hebrew is VeGoalecha with the Ve prefix, meaning "and your Redeemer."
[12] In the kingdom Yisrael will be regathered, and the disobedient nations will in turn be scattered by judgment.
[13] The renewal of the land of Yisrael.

and the pine, and the box eytz together: 20 *That they may see, and know, and consider, and understand together, that the Hand of* יהוה *has done this, and the Set-Apart One of Yisrael has created it from nothing.* 21 *Produce your cause, says* יהוה; *bring forth your strong reasons, says the Melech of Yaakov.* 22 *Let them bring them forth, and show Us¹ what shall happen: let them show the former things, what they were, that we may consider them, and know the latter end of them; or declare to us things yet to come.* 23 *Show the things that are to come from now on, that We may know that you are elohim: yes, do tov, or do evil, that We may be amazed, and see it together.* 24 *See, you are nothing, and your work is nothing: an abomination is anyone that chooses you.* 25 *I have raised up one from the north, and he shall come: from the rising of the sun shall he call upon My Name:² and He shall come upon rulers as though morter, and as the potter tramples clay.* 26 *Who has declared from the beginning, that We may know? And ahead of time, that We may say, He is Tzadik? Yes, there is none that declares the future, yes, there is none that proclaims it, yes, yet there is none that hears Your words.* 27 *First He shall say to Tzion,³ here, see, now see then: I will give to Yahrushalayim One that brings tov tidings.* 28 *For I beheld, and there was no man;⁴ even among them, and there was no counselor, that, when I asked of them, could bring forth a word.⁵* 29 *See, they are all vanity; their works are nothing:*

their molded images are wind and confusion.⁶

42 *See My Eved, whom I uphold; My elect, in whom My being delights; I have put My Ruach upon Him:⁷ He shall bring forth mishpat to the nations.⁸* 2 *He shall not cry, nor lift up His voice, nor cause His voice to be heard in the street.* 3 *A bruised reed shall He not break, and the smoking cotton shall He not quench: He shall bring forth mishpat in accordance with emet.⁹* 4 *He shall not fail nor be discouraged,¹⁰ until He has set mishpat in the earth: and the coastlands shall wait for*

---

¹ Father And Son.
² A dual prophecy speaking of Cyrus the loving king who allowed Jewish-Yisrael to return from the northeast to rebuild the walls and city of Jerusalem, and moreover the Moshiach who will gather the ten tribes of Ephraim, and therefore is said to be coming from the northeast (the very initial lands of their exiles). Moreover, He will come declaring the true and only Name of Abba, which is "Yahweh."
³ The Tov News is first and primarily to Yisrael or Tzion, and then to the nations who become Tzion anyway, so that in Yahshua all Yisrael is gathered as Yisrael.
⁴ No mediator.
⁵ Abba YHWH is giving the Anointed One, because no true pure sinless High Priest or mediator was ever found amongst the sons of Yisrael.

⁶ Not qualified to mediate.
⁷ Moshiach.
⁸ The scattered seed of Yisrael.
⁹ Moshiach will bring justice through gentleness. This cannot be talking of the nation of Yisrael, since they were severely lacking in justice, tzedakah and gentleness, and did not have it themselves, much less were they able to impart it to the nations.
¹⁰ Moshiach Yahshua. This cannot be Yisrael since Yisrael did not keep the Torah properly, and they failed and often became discouraged in doing just that. Moreover, it must be brought to the nations according to justice and right ruling. How can they deliver right ruling, when they themselves did not abide in it at all, at any time, for any length of time? The "He" here is clearly YHWH's Son.

His Torah.[1] 5 This says the El-**יהוה**, *He that created the shamayim, and stretches them out; He that spreads forth the earth, and that which comes out of it; He that gives breath to the people upon it, and ruach to them that walk in it:* 6 *I* **יהוה** *have called You in tzedakah, and will hold Your hand, and will keep You, and give You for a covenant of the people,*[2] *for a Light to the nations;*[3] 7 *To open the blind eyes, to bring out the prisoners from the prison, and them that sit in darkness out of the prison bayit.*[4] 8 *I am* **יהוה***: that is My Name:*[5] *and My tiferet will I not give to another, neither My hallel to graven images.* 9 *See, the former things have come to pass, and new things do I declare: before they spring forth I tell you of them.*[6] 10 *Sing to* **יהוה** *a new shir,*[7]

and His hallel from the ends of the earth, you that go down to the sea, and all that is in it; the coastlands, and the inhabitants of it. 11 *Let the wilderness and the cities of it lift up their voice, the villages that Kedar does inhabit: let the inhabitants of the steep rocks shir; let them shout from the top of the mountains.* 12 *Let them give tiferet to* **יהוה** *, and declare His hallel in the coastlands.* 13 **יהוה** *shall go forth as a Mighty Man, He shall stir up jealousy like a Man of War: He shall cry, yes, roar; He shall prevail against His enemies.* 14 *I have held My shalom for a long while; I have been still, and refrained Myself: now will I cry like a travailing woman; I will destroy and devour at once.* 15 *I will make waste mountains and hills, and dry up all their herbs; and I will make the rivers coastlands, and I will dry up the pools.* 16 *And I will bring the blind by a halacha that they knew not; I will lead them in paths that they have not known: I will make darkness Light before them, and crooked things straight. These things will I do to them, and not forsake them.*[8] 17 *They shall make teshuvah, and then they shall be greatly ashamed, that have trusted in graven images, that say to the molded images, You are our elohim.* 18 *Shema, you who are deaf, and look, you who are blind, that you may see.*[9] 19 *Who is blind, but My eved? Or deaf, as My messenger that I sent? Who is as blind as he that is whole, and blind as* **יהוה***'s eved?*[10] 20 *Seeing many things, but you observe not; opening the ears, but He hears not.* 21 **יהוה** *is well pleased for the sake of His tzedakah, He will magnify the Torah,*[11] *and make it honorable.* 22 *But this is a people robbed and plundered; they are all of them snared in holes, and they are hidden in prison bayits: they are for a prey, and no one*

---

[1] In Matthew 12, in verses 15-20, Matthew quotes Isaiah 42 verses 1-4. There is no problem here. As is often the case in the Renewed Covenant a quote may be changed as the writer takes liberty to omit or omit a word or two, in order to enhance a point that YHWH desires to make. While these verses are not an exact quote, they do maintain the integrity of the text. As Hebraic authors using **Pardes** - the 4 levels of Hebraic understanding - Matthew receives revelation concerning this fulfillment, as do other authors. Therefore Matthew 12:16 has been changed to "trust in His Name" rather than "His Torah." Why was this done? Because both the Name of Yahshua (Acts 4:12), and the Torah of Yahshua are necessary for salvation: Since Isaiah presented the Torah of Moshiach, Matthew balanced that, and presented the Name of Moshiach, seeing that both are essentials for salvation according to Joel 2:32, and Romans 10:13. By no means does this mean that Moshiach Yahshua did not bring Torah to the nations, or in any way has failed in His mission to do so. Every born-again believer has the Torah in their Bible, and most of the world has the Torah in their native language through translation, and this is fully and solely due to the life, and work of the Moshiach. Through Yahshua and Him alone, one can find Torah in Africa, Australia, and every other nation and continent of the earth. Now it is a given that not all live or follow it, but all have had Torah made known and declared through proclamation of the Tov News, where Yahshua stated "if you love Me, you'll guard My commandments" (John 14:21). Contrary to anti-missionary pabulum, the Master Yahshua did proclaim the Torah to the nations, more so than any other leader or Jewish authority in the history of man. The "Great Commission" itself following the resurrection gives Yahshua's last instructions in Matthew 28:18-20, where He is found telling His true followers to "teach all things and guard all things, I have commanded you," an obvious reference to Torah. Furthermore Matthew quotes from the Greek LXX (Septuagint) and as such is quoting verbatim in Matthew 12:21, since in the LXX the phrase reads the same as in this gospel, calling on all nations to trust in His Name.

[2] Of Yisrael, specifically Judah, the nation from which Yahshua came.

[3] Ephraim; since in a latter-day context the nations are Ephraim.

[4] All 12 tribes.

[5] Not one of many names.

[6] The new thing in context is Yisrael's renewal through His servant the Moshiach.

[7] The new song of redemption and restoration.

[8] The role of the Moshiach to is take blind Yisrael in paths of renewal, light and tzedakah.

[9] A plea to both blind houses.

[10] YHWH's servant here is Yisrael since they, and not Moshiach are blind.

[11] Through the Renewed Covenant of Moshiach.

delivers them; for a plunder, and no one says, Restore![1] 23 Who among you will give ear to this? Who will shema and shema for the time to come?[2] 24 Who gave Yaakov for a plunder, and Yisrael to the robbers? Did not יהוה, He against whom we have sinned? For they would not have their halacha in His halachot, neither were they obedient to His Torah.[3] 25 Therefore He has poured upon Yaakov the fury of His anger, and the strength of battle: and has set him on fire all around, yet he did not understand why; and it burned him, yet he did not take it to lev.[4]

43 But now this says יהוה that created you, O Yaakov, and He that formed you, O Yisrael, *Fear not: for I have redeemed you, I have called you by Your name; you are Mine.*[5] 2 *When you pass through the mayim, I will be with you; and through the rivers, they shall not overflow you: when you walk through the fire, you shall not be burned; neither shall the flame kindle upon you.* 3 *For I am יהוה Your Elohim, the Set-Apart One of Yisrael, Your Savior: I gave Mitzrayim for your ransom, Ethiopia and Seva for you.*[6] 4 *Since you were precious in My sight, you have been honorable, and I have loved you: therefore will I give men for you, and people for Your chayim.*[7] 5 *Fear not: for I am with you: I will bring Your zera from the east, and gather you from the west;* 6 *I will say to the north, Give them up; and to the south, Keep them not back: bring My sons from far, and*

My daughters from the ends of the earth;[8] 7 *Even each one that is called by My Name:*[9] *for I have created him for My tiferet, I have formed him; yes, I have made him.* 8 *Bring forth the blind people that have eyes, and the deaf that have ears.* 9 *Let all the nations be gathered together,*[10] *and let the people be assembled;*[11] *who among them can declare this, and show us former things? Let them bring forth their witnesses, that they may be justified: or let them shema, and say, It is emet.*[12] 10 *You are My witnesses, says* יהוה,[13] *and My Eved*[14] *whom I have chosen: that you may know and believe Me, and understand that I am He: before Me there was no El formed, neither shall there be after Me.*[15] 11 *I, even I, am* יהוה; *and beside Me there is no Savior.*[16] 12 *I have declared, and have saved, and I have shown, when there was no*

---

[1] There is the problem with most of Yisrael's blind leaders in the church and synagogue; they shout and scream and speak in many tongues, but hardly any of them call out "Restore, Restore, Restore," when that's all mankind needs.

[2] The cry of the hour remains "Restore, Restore." Yet, who will heed this call for two-house truth?

[3] Both houses; which is why Ephraim must run to Yahshua, and not to apostate Judah in the land of Yisrael for their instruction in Torah.

[4] Despite the trials and fires of exile, the nation still has not come to its senses, and taken restoration to heart.

[5] All Yisrael.

[6] All nations are for redeemed Yisrael's pleasure and kingdom dominion.

[7] Others will inherit your nation, culture, life and your Elohim, through YHWH's Son.

[8] The end of the exile will be from all four corners and the returning Yisraelites will be called His sons and daughters, indicating their regeneration prior to their physical return.

[9] Yisraelites bear His Name, or they are not true Jews or Ephraimites regardless of pedigree.

[10] Into YHWH's Son, who came to re-establish the Commonwealth of Yisrael.

[11] In Yahshua.

[12] Let all mankind admit the truth of the "One Yisrael" that Yahshua has come to rebuild.

[13] Yisrael the nation reborn.

[14] The second witness is Yahshua the Suffering Servant Moshiach ben Yosef. These are the two witnesses for YHWH.

[15] Isaiah 43:10 makes it abundantly clear that there was no El or deity brought forth before or after Abba YHWH. Period. The creating of "a Yahshua" would contradict this simple declaration. If that is true (and it is), that must mean that Yahshua always was "in" Abba-YHWH, since He could not be created after YHWH. The Hebrew here as always sheds great light. "**Atem adai neum YHWH Ve Avdi asher bacaharti.**" In Hebrew this means there are actually two witnesses who testify that YHWH is One, and that He has not formed a different El before or after Him, thus ending the myth that Yahshua the Moshiach is some sort of a created being like Michael the angel, which would mean YHWH formed Yahshua after YHWH already was, which would be a violation of this text. What YHWH is simply saying in this verse is the exciting reality that there are two witnesses to His "echad compound unity" status. They are His eternal bride the people of Yisrael, and His chosen Suffering Servant Lamb, the Moshiach Yahshua. Both testify to the fact that He is and always will be **echad** (Mark 12:29).

[16] In many places such as here in the Tanach and Torah, the double repetitive first person "I, I," or "I even I," or in Hebrew "**Ani, Ani**" appears as here in Isaiah 43:11; proving once again that Yahshua is not an afterthought. And neither was He formed after YHWH, but is one of the two eternal "I"-s spoken of in this verse, as Yisrael's Savior. "I and I," or "I even I," or "I and also I," is/are the Savior. Both the Father and His Son are both called Moshiach/Savior not Saviors. If only Abba YHWH is Savior, then the term should read "**Ani**" not "**Ani, Ani.**" He is and always will be **echad**, a true compound unity (Mark 12:29).

stranger among you:[1] therefore you are My witnesses, [2] says יהוה , that I am El. 13 Yes, before the day was I am He; and there is none that can deliver out of My hand: I will work,[3] and who shall let it? 14 This says יהוה, Your Redeemer, the Set-Apart One of Yisrael; For Your sake I have sent to Bavel, and have brought down all their nobles, and the Chaldeans, whose cry is in their ships. 15 I am יהוה, Your Set-Apart One, the Creator of Yisrael, Your Melech. 16 This says יהוה, who makes a derech in the sea, and a derech in the mighty mayim, 17 Who brings forth the mirkavah and horse, the army and the power; they shall lie down together, they shall not rise: they are extinct; they are quenched like the wicked. 18 Remember not the former things, neither consider the things of old. 19 See, I will do a new thing; now it shall spring forth; shall you not know it? I will even make a derech in the wilderness, and rivers in the desert.[4] 20 The beast of the field shall honor Me, the jackals and the owls: because I give mayim in the wilderness, and rivers in the desert, to give drink to My people,[5] My chosen. 21 This people have I formed for Myself; they shall show forth My hallel. 22 But you have not called upon Me, O Yaakov; but you have been weary of Me, O Yisrael. 23 You have not brought Me the small cattle of your burnt offerings; neither have you honored Me with your sacrifices. I have not caused you to serve with an offering, nor wearied you with incense. 24 You have bought Me no sweet cane with money, neither have you filled Me with the fat of your sacrifices: but you have served Me with your sins, you have wearied Me with your iniquities. 25 I, even I,[6] am He that

blots out your transgressions for My own sake, and will not remember your sins. 26 Remember Me: let us reason together about mishpat: plead with Me, that you may be justified. 27 Your first abba has sinned,[7] and your advocates[8] have transgressed against Me. 28 Therefore I have profaned the rulers of the Set-Apart Place, and have given Yaakov to the curse, and Yisrael to scorn.

44 Yet now shema, O Yaakov My eved; and Yisrael, whom I have chosen:[9] 2 This says יהוה that made you, and formed you from the womb, who will help you; Fear not, O Yaakov, My eved; and you, Yeshurun,[10] whom I have chosen. 3 For I will pour mayim upon him that is thirsty, and floods upon the dry ground: I will pour My Ruach upon your zera, and My bracha upon your offspring:[11] 4 And they shall spring up as among the grass, as willows by the mayim streams. 5 One shall say, I am יהוה's; and another shall call himself by the name of Yaakov; and another shall write with his hand, Unto יהוה, and name himself by the name of Yisrael.[12] 6 This says יהוה the Melech of Yisrael,[13] and His Redeemer יהוה Tzevaot;[14] I am the first, and I am the last; and beside Me there is no Elohim.[15] 7 And who is like Me, let him call and declare it, and lay it before Me, since I appointed the ancient people? And the things that are coming, and shall come, let them show

[1] YHWH sees all His children as Yisrael, and reveals things as if there were no stranger among them.
[2] Yisrael and Yahshua are both witness that the Savior is echad not yachid.
[3] He alone will fully work the plan for Yisrael's redemption and restoration.
[4] A bright future is promised for all Yisraelites in the Renewed Covenant with YHWH through Yahshua.
[5] Renewed Covenant Yisrael.
[6] In Hebrew "Anochi, Anochi," dual first person reference.
[7] Adam and Abraham. If Adam is referred to here, it shows us how YHWH views Yisrael as the continual line from Adam; thus showing the utter foolishness of any form of dispensationalism, or a perceived "church age."
[8] Rulers and dishonest judges.
[9] YHWH's only eternal elect.
[10] Meaning: "straight and upright one."
[11] Through Moshiach.
[12] When Moshiach comes to rebuild Yisrael, all His children will be known by the name of Yisrael, and no longer by other titles such as "Jew" or "gentile."
[13] Abba YHWH.
[14] In Hebrew Ve goaloh YHWH Tzevaot, and His Redeemer YHWH of Hosts; meaning the tool by which He Himself will save us, is also YHWH. This is another reference to the Savior, emanating from Father-YHWH, without being the Father.
[15] So that the definition of Elohim is Abba-YHWH + His-Redeemer-YHWH=YHWH-Echad. Leaving out either Power leaves one with error rather than truth.

these things to them. 8 Fear not, neither be afraid: have not I told you from that time, and have declared it? You are even My witnesses. Is there an Eloah beside Me? Yes, there is no Rock beside Me; I know not of anyone. 9 They that make a graven image, all of them are vanity; and their delights shall not profit; and they are their own witnesses; they see not, neither know anything; that they may be ashamed. 10 Who has formed an El, or cast a graven image that is profitable for nothing? 11 See, all his fellows shall be ashamed: and the workmen, they are but men: let them all be gathered together, let them stand up; yet they shall fear, and they shall be ashamed together. 12 The craftsman with the tongs both works in the coals, and fashions it with hammers, and works it with the strength of his arms: yes, he is hungry, and his strength fails: he drinks no mayim, and is weak. 13 The carpenter stretches out his rule; he marks it out with a line; he fits it with planes, and he marks it out with the compass, and makes it after the figure of a man, according to the tiferet of a man; that it may remain in the bayit. 14 He cuts down cedars, and takes the cypress and the oak, which he raised for himself among the eytzim of the forest: he plants a pine, and the rain does nourish it. 15 Then shall it be for a man to burn: for he will take of it, and warm himself; yes, he kindles it, and bakes lechem; yes, he makes an El, and worships it; he makes it a graven image, and falls down before it. 16 He burns part of it in the fire; with part of it he eats flesh; he roasts roast, and is satisfied: yes, he warms himself, and says, Aha, I am warm, I have seen the fire: 17 And the residue of it he makes an El, even his graven image: he falls down to it, and worships it, and makes tefillah to it, and says; Deliver me, for you are my El. 18 They have not known nor understood: for He has shut their eyes, that they cannot see; and their levim, that they cannot understand. 19 And none considers in his lev, neither is there da'at nor binah to

say, I have burned part of it in the fire; yes, also I have baked lechem upon the coals of it; I have roasted flesh, and eaten it: and shall I make the residue of it into an abomination? Shall I fall down to the log of an eytz? 20 He feeds on ashes: a deceived lev has turned him aside, that he cannot deliver his being, nor say, Is there not a lie in my right hand? 21 Remember these, O Yaakov and Yisrael; for you are My eved: I have formed you; you are My eved: O Yisrael, you shall not be forgotten by Me.[1] 22 I have blotted out, as a thick cloud, your transgressions, and, as a cloud, your sins: make teshuvah to Me; for I have redeemed you.[2] 23 Sing, O shamayim; for יהוה has done it: shout, you depths of the earth: break forth into singing, you mountains, O forest, and every eytz in it: for יהוה has redeemed Yaakov, and lifted Himself up in Yisrael. [3] 24 This says יהוה , Your Redeemer, and He that formed you from the womb, I am יהוה that makes all things; that stretches forth the shamayim alone; that spreads abroad the earth by Myself; 25 That frustrates the signs of the liars, and makes diviners crazy; that turns wise men backward, and makes their da'at foolish; 26 That confirms the word of His eved, and performs the counsel of His messengers; that says to Yahrushalayim, You shall be inhabited; 4 and to the cities of Yahudah, You shall be rebuilt,[5] and I will raise up the ruined places of it: 27 That says to the deep, Be dry, and I will dry up your rivers:

---

[1] The ten tribes of Ephraim Yisrael cannot be lost or forgotten even in the nations.
[2] Through Moshiach.
[3] Redemption and His glory of salvation, is found only in all who are redeemed Yisrael.
[4] Restored.
[5] Restored.

28 *That says of Koresh, He is My shepherd, and shall perform all My pleasure: even saying to Yahrushalayim, You shall be rebuilt; and to the Beit HaMikdash, Your foundation shall be laid.*[1]

45 This says יהוה *to His anointed, to Koresh, whose right hand I have grasped, to subdue nations before him; and I will loose the waist of melechim, to open before him the double doors; so that the gates shall not be shut;* 2 *I will go before you, and make the crooked places straight: I will break in pieces the gates of brass, and cut down the bars of iron:* 3 *And I will give you the treasures of darkness, and the hidden riches of secret places, that you may know that I,* יהוה, *who call you by your name, am the Elohim of Yisrael.*[2] 4 *For Yaakov My eved's sake, and Yisrael My elect, I have even called you by your name: I have surnamed you, though you have not known Me.* 5 *I am* יהוה, *and there is none else, there is no Elohim beside Me: I dressed you, though you have not known Me:*[3] 6 *That they may know from the rising of the sun, and from the west, that there is none beside Me. I am* יהוה, *and there is none else.* 7 *I form the light, and create darkness: I make shalom, and create evil: I* יהוה *do all these things.* 8 *Drop down, you shamayim, from above, and let the skies pour down Tzedakah: let the earth open, and let them bring forth Yahshua, and let Tzedakah spring up together; I* יהוה *have created it.* 9 *Woe to him that strives with His Maker! An earthen vessel that strives with Him who made it! Shall the clay say to Him that fashioned it, Why did you make it like this? Or the handiwork saying to the Maker of it, He has*

no hands? 10 *Woe to him that says to his abba, Why did you beget me? Or to the ima, Why have you conceived me?* 11 *This says* יהוה, *the Set-Apart One of Yisrael, and His Maker,* [4] *Ask Me of things to come concerning My sons, and concerning the work of My hands command Me.*[5] 12 *I have made the earth, and created man upon it: I, even My hands, have stretched out the shamayim, and their entire host, have I commanded.* 13 *I have raised Him up in tzedakah, and I will direct all His halachot: He shall rebuild My city, and He shall let My exiles go,*[6] *not for a price or a bribe, says* יהוה *of hosts.*[7] 14 *This says* יהוה, *The labor of Mitzrayim, and merchandise of Ethiopia and of the Saveans, men of tall stature, shall come over to You, and they shall be Yours: they shall come after You; in chains they shall come over, and they shall fall down to You, they shall make supplication to You, saying, Surely El is in You; and there is none else, there is no other Elohim.*[8] 15 *Truly You are an El that hides Yourself, O Elohim of Yisrael, the Savior.* 16 *They shall be ashamed, and also be embarrassed, all of them: they shall go to confusion together that are makers of idols.* 17 *But Yisrael shall be saved in* יהוה *with an everlasting Yahshua: you shall not be ashamed nor embarrassed olam without end.*[9] 18 *For this says* יהוה *that created the shamayim; Elohim Himself that formed the earth and made it; He has established it, He created it not in vain, He formed it to be*

---

[1] YHWH raised up Cyrus/Koresh of Medo-Persia to restore Yahrushalayim. The reason that Cyrus was so benevolent towards Judah many say, was because he read his name here in this prophecy some 150 years before he was born, and came to trust in YHWH. The restoration allowed by Cyrus is but a small foretaste of the restoration coming to both houses of Yisrael, through the eternal, Redeemer and King Yahshua.
[2] See note on Chapter 44 verse 28.
[3] YHWH introduced Himself to Koresh through the Scriptures.

[4] Abba-YHWH; and His designated Maker for humanity the Moshiach Yahshua (Colossians 1:16, John 1:3). In Hebrew: **VeYitzro** "and His Maker." The plurality of **echad** is seen.
[5] This does not mean believers can command YHWH around. It means in essence - let the nations ask Me and command Me to tell them what tov things I have in store for My people Yisrael. We cannot order Him around as some subtly teach.
[6] Jewish-Yisrael in the time of Cyrus; and both houses by Yahshua in the end times.
[7] But as YHWH's servant, Yahshua will do the same in the **remez** as Koresh does in the **pashat**.
[8] Many Yisraelite exiles from Ephraim not in Medo-Persia will also come to Cyrus requesting clemency and freedom. In the end times the exiles of both houses will come to Yahshua, who fulfills these prophecies in a unique end-time context. Former black Yisraelites are seen here in their return to the nation through Yahshua.
[9] Yisrael will be redeemed and restored. Each of us must choose individually if we desire to plug into that covenant and that promise.

inhabited: I am יהוה; and there is none else. 19 I have not spoken in secret, in a dark place of the earth: I did not say to the zera of Yaakov, You seek Me in vain: I יהוה speak tzedakah; I declare things that are right. 20 Assemble yourselves and come; draw near together,[1] you that have escaped from the nations:[2] they have no da'at that set up the wood of their graven image, and make tefillah to an El that cannot save. 21 Declare, and bring them near, let them take counsel together: who has declared this from ancient time?[3] Who has told it from that time? Have not I יהוה? And there is no Elohim else beside Me; a just El and a Savior;[4] there is none besides Me.[5] 22 Look to Me, and be you saved, all the ends of the earth: for I am El, and there is none else. 23 I have sworn by Myself, the Word is gone out of My mouth[6] in tzedakah,[7] and shall not return, That to Me every knee shall bow, and every tongue shall swear.[8] 24 Surely, shall one say, in

יהוה I have tzedakah and strength: even to Him shall men come; and all that are incensed against Him shall be ashamed. 25 In יהוה shall all the zera of Yisrael be justified, and shall tiferet.[9]

46 Bel bows down, Nevo is stooping, their idols were upon the beasts, and upon the cattle: your carriages were burdened; they are a burden to the weary beast. 2 They stoop, they bow down together; they could not deliver the burden, but themselves have gone into exile.[10] 3 Shema to Me, O Beit Yaakov, and all the remnant of Beit Yisrael,[11] who are borne by Me from the belly, who are carried by Me from the womb: 4 And even to your old age I am He; and even to your gray hairs will I carry you: I have made you, and I will bear you; I will carry you, and will deliver you. 5 To whom will you liken Me, and make Me equal, and compare Me, that we may be alike? 6 They lavish gold out of the bag, and weigh silver in the balance, and hire a goldsmith; and he makes it into an El: they fall down, yes, they worship. 7 They bear him upon the shoulder, they carry him, and set him in his place, and he stands; from his place shall he not move: yes, one shall cry to him, yet he cannot answer, nor save him out of his trouble. 8 Remember this, and show yourselves to be men: bring it again to mind, O you transgressors. 9 Remember the former things of old: for I am El, and there is none else; I am Elohim, and there is none like Me, 10 Declaring the end from the beginning, and from ancient times the things that are not yet done, saying, My counsel shall stand, and I will

[1] A call to two-house unity.
[2] Both houses that have escaped from the pagan ways of the nations are to assemble as one under Yahshua and draw near to Him.
[3] Told of Yisrael's future.
[4] Literally; El-Tzadik, u moshiach "a just El and a Moshiach." Another example that the Savior equals Abba + Moshiach; not one at the expense of the other.
[5] If YHWH is the only Savior, why do we need another Savior named Yahshua? All these verses do is prove that YHWH is the source and architect of salvation. However as He manifested His salvation through Moses in the First Covenant, He manifests Himself as Savior through the promised "Prophet like Unto Moses" (Deuteronomy 18:18) in the Renewed Covenant. In the cases of Yahshua and Moses, both received their saving power through the Source, who was Abba-Father YHWH, and both merely manifested that saving power. Abba saves through His Son as confirmed in Psalm 2:12. Moreover, the very fact that Yahshua is called Savior by His disciples without any rebuke proves two things. First that Savior as a title is a direct link to YHWH, since all Yisrael knew that only YHWH carries that eternal title. By allowing that title to be used in reference to His mission on earth, He was ipso facto accepting the clear declaration that He was YHWH come in the flesh, as the direct and full manifestation of Abba-YHWH. Second that the Hebrew word "Savior" is the same root as "Moshiach," and so He allowed them to refer to Himself as both "The Savior" and "Moshiach," whom they had long expected.
[6] Yahshua.
[7] He was sinless.
[8] In Isaiah 45:23 it is clear that YHWH is the One to whom every knee shall bow, since only in YHWH is tzedakah, strength, and salvation. So some say in that case "Who needs Yahshua?" Philippians 2:9-11 quotes this verse as applicable to Yahshua. Once again we are left with the plain understanding that if every knee will bow to Yahshua, and every knee will bow to the Father, then both the Father and

the Moshiach are YHWH-Echad. Both receive worship and homage, though the Son redirects it to the Father. The Strength and Righteousness of Yisrael was manifested through His Son, as revealed in Isaiah 9:6, Heb.1:1-3 and Titus 3:13. As mentioned earlier, verses such as Isaiah 43:10 do not read "Elohim-Savior" but rather "Elohim and Savior," further substantiating that Yahshua the Moshiach and His Heavenly Father, His Elohim, are echad.
[9] Not all born Yisrael as seen in Romans 9:6-8, but all who willingly decide they need Yahshua to be declared righteous. All of those will be called and become righteous Yisrael.
[10] Babylonian elohim and the very carts that carry them are defeated and carried away into exile, along with their people.
[11] Only the redeemed remnant will hear.

do all My pleasure: 11 *Calling a ravenous bird from the east, the man[1] that executes My counsel from a far country: yes, I have spoken it, I will also bring it to pass; I have purposed it, I will also do it.* 12 *Shema to Me, you stubborn-hearted, that are far from tzedakah:* 13 *I bring near My Tzedakah; it shall not be far off, and My Yahshua shall not tarry: and I will place Yahshua in Tzion for Yisrael My tiferet.[2]*

47 *Come down, and sit in the dust, O virgin daughter of Bavel, sit on the ground: there is no more throne, O daughter of the Chaldeans: for you shall no more be called tender and delicate.* 2 *Take the millstones, and grind flour: uncover your veil, make bare the leg, lift up your skirt, pass through the rivers.* 3 *Your nakedness shall be uncovered, yes, your shame shall be seen: I will take vengeance, and I will not meet you as a man.[3]* 4 *As for Our Redeemer,* יהוה *of hosts is His Name, the Set-Apart One of Yisrael.* 5 *Sit in silence, and get into darkness, O daughter of the Chaldeans: for you shall no more be called, The lady of all malchutim.* 6 *I was angry with My people, I have polluted My inheritance, and given them into your hand: you did show them no rachamim; upon the elderly you have laid a heavy hand and yoke.* 7 *And you said, I shall be a lady le-olam-va-ed: so that you did not lay these things to your lev, neither did remember the latter end of them.* 8 *Therefore shema now to this, you that are given to pleasures, that live carelessly, that say in your lev, I am, and there is none else beside Me; I shall not sit as a widow, neither shall I know the loss of children:* 9 *But these two things shall come to you in a moment in one day, the loss of children, and widowhood: they shall come upon you in their fullness for the multitude of your sorceries, and for the great abundance of your evil spells.* 10 *For*

you have trusted in your wickedness: you have said, No one sees me. Your worldly chochma and your da'at, have perverted you; and you have said in your lev, I am, and there is none else beside me. 11 *Therefore shall evil come upon you; you shall not know from where it rises: and trouble shall befall you; you shall not be able to put it off of you: and ruin shall come upon you suddenly, which you shall not know.* 12 *Stand now with your enchantments, and with the multitude of your sorceries, in which you have labored from your youth; if so be that you shall be able to profit, if so be that you may prevail.* 13 *You are worn out by the multitude of your counsels. Let now the astrologers, the stargazers, the monthly prognosticators, stand up, and save you from these things that shall come upon you.* 14 *See, they shall be as stubble; the fire shall burn them; they shall not deliver themselves from the power of the flame: there shall not be a coal to be warmed by, nor fire to sit before it.* 15 *This shall they be to you and with those you have labored, even your merchants, from your youth: they shall wander every one to his own way; no one shall save you.[4]*

48 *Shema to this, O Beit Yaakov, who are called by the name of Yisrael, and are come forth out of the mayim of Yahudah, who swear by the Name of* יהוה, *and make mention of the Elohim of Yisrael, but not in emet, nor in tzedakah.* 2 *For they call themselves after the set-apart city, and lean upon the Elohim of Yisrael;* יהוה *of hosts is His Name.* 3 *I have declared the former things from the beginning; and they went forth out of My mouth, and I showed them; I did them suddenly, and they came to pass.* 4 *Because I knew that you are stubborn, and your neck is an iron sinew, and your forehead brass;* 5 *I have even from the beginning declared it to you; before it came to pass I showed it to you:*

---

[1] Cyrus.
[2] YHWH will place salvation into the world through Yisrael His beloved. Yahshua confirms this in John 4:22.
[3] YHWH will bring judgment on Babylon through Medo-Persia.

[4] The sharp contrast here is between Yisrael with her Redeemer, and Babylon void in redemption and salvation.

lest you should say, My idol has done them, and my graven image, and my molded image, has commanded them. 6 You have heard, and seen all this; and will you not declare it? I have shown you new things from this time, even hidden things, and you did not know them. 7 They are created now, and not from the beginning; even before this day you have not heard them; lest you should say, See, I knew them. 8 Yes, you heard not; yes, you knew not; yes, from that time that your ear was not opened: for I knew that you would deal very treacherously, and were called a transgressor from the womb. 9 For My Name's sake will I defer My anger, and for My hallel will I refrain from you, so that I cut you not off. 10 See, I have refined you, but not with silver; I have chosen you in the furnace of affliction.[1] 11 For My own sake, even for My own sake, will I do it: for how should My Name be polluted? And I will not give My tiferet to another. 12 Shema to Me, O Yaakov and Yisrael, My called; I am He; I am the first, I also am the last. 13 My Hand also has laid the foundation of the earth, and My Right Hand has spanned the shamayim: when I call to them, they stand up together. 14 All of you; assemble yourselves, and shema. Who among them has declared these things? יהוה Has loved him: he will do His pleasure on Bavel, and His Arm shall be on the Chaldeans. 15 I, even I,[2] have spoken; yes, I have called Him: I have brought Him, and he shall make His halacha prosperous. 16 Come near to Me, shema to this; I have not spoken in secret from the beginning; from the time that it was,[3] I was there: and now the Master יהוה, and His Ruach, has sent Me.[4] 17 This says יהוה, Your Redeemer, the Set-Apart One of Yisrael; I am יהוה Your Elohim who teaches you to profit, who leads

you by the halacha that you should go. 18 O that you had listened to My commandments! Then your shalom would have been there as a river, and your tzedakah as the waves of the sea: 19 Your zera also would have been as the sand, and the offspring of your inward parts like the gravel of it; his name should not have been cut off nor destroyed from before Me. 20 Go forth from Bavel, flee from the Chaldeans, with a voice of singing declare, tell this, utter it even to the ends of the earth; say, יהוה has redeemed His eved Yaakov.[5] 21 And they thirsted not when He led them through the deserts: He caused the mayim to flow out of the Rock for them: He split the Rock also, and the mayim gushed out. 22 There is no shalom, says יהוה, to the wicked.

49

Listen, O coastlands, to Me; and shema, you nations, from far;[6] יהוה has called Me from the womb;[7] from the inward parts of My ima has He made mention of My Name.[8] 2 And He has made My mouth like a sharp arrow;[9] in the shadow of His hand has He hidden me,[10] and made Me a polished shaft; in His quiver has He hidden Me; 3 And said to Me, You are My Eved, O Yisrael,[11] through whom I will be lifted up. 4 Then I said, I have labored in vain, I have spent My strength for nothing, and in vain: yet surely My mishpat is from יהוה, and My work from My Elohim.[12] 5 And now, says יהוה that formed Me[13] from the womb to be His

---

[1] Yisrael will go through the ultimate affliction of the Great Tribulation.
[2] Hebrew: **"Ani, Ani,"** a reference to the plurality of **echad.**
[3] This world.
[4] Yahshua speaking in the first person is being sent to rescue Yisrael along with the Power of YHWH, the Ruach HaKodesh. A clear view of the plurality of echad.

[5] That's the ongoing Tov News. YHWH has redeemed Yisrael physically many times in history as well as spiritually at the end of the age.
[6] Latter-day Ephraimite nations.
[7] The pre-existent Yahshua speaking in the first person.
[8] Yahshua was the Name given to Him before His birth according to Luke 2:21.
[9] He is the Word of YHWH, sharper than a two-edged sword.
[10] Yahshua was hidden in the Father in eternity past, before He was brought forth.
[11] The Servant here in the primary literal application is Yahshua, as the text will reveal, and not Yisrael the nation.
[12] This portrays a concern on behalf of Yisrael (the title in this context for the Moshiach, since He is the personification of all that is called Yisrael) that He might fail in His assignment given to Him by the Father.
[13] Not created but re-formed as the Word sent to Yaakov.

Eved,[1] to bring Yaakov again[2] to Him,[3] though Yisrael be not gathered,[4] yet I am esteemed with tiferet in the eyes of יהוה,[5] and My Elohim shall be My strength.[6] 6 And He said, It is a light, easy and small thing[7] that You should be My Eved to raise up the tribes of Yaakov,[8] [9] and to restore the preserved ones of Yisrael:[10] I will also give

---

[1] The willing Suffering Servant Moshiach Ben Yosef, formed from within YHWH in eternity past, who was ordained to suffer to bring the ten tribes home, and reunite them with believing Judah.
[2] To restore Yaakov; the Hebrew is **lashuv** or to return Yaakov.
[3] This has to be Moshiach, for Jacob cannot return Jacob from exile, any more than Yisrael can die for the sins of Yisrael, in a Torah-based system of substitutionary vicarious dom atonement.
[4] Without Moshiach Yisrael cannot be gathered.
[5] For a willingness to come to earth and be obedient.
[6] Abba-YHWH will give Him the mission, and the strength to perform that mission.
[7] Since Yahshua is in the full authority of Almighty YHWH, it is a small task for Him to regather the 12 tribes of both divided houses, back into one united Yisrael. What is impossible with man is possible and easy with YHWH.
[8] All 12 tribes.
[9] If Yahshua is the Moshiach, by Scriptural definition, He must be raising up all of physical Yisrael wherever they are. If He is not, and is just restoring Jews and gentiles (non-Israelites) alone to David's Tabernacle, then He is a false Moshiach. That is the issue at stake. The real Moshiach must arrive and gather all the exiles of Yisrael in both houses and all their non-Yisraelite companions (Ezekiel 37:15-17). If Yahshua is Moshiach, then rest assured that most of those being rescued from the nations are Joseph's House, and his non-Yisraelite companions.
[10] The term "preserved ones" is **ve-notsire (vav, nun, tzamech, yud, resh, yud)** or "**the notsire Yisrael.**" Those returning from the 12 tribes are called by this name. Yahshua's job is to restore and return all 12 tribes back into one family as His disciples, or the "preserved ones" of Yisrael, into one Olive Tree. Preserved believers from both houses, or all 12 tribes, are no longer referred to only as Ephraim-Yisrael, or Jewish-Yisrael, but as Nazarenes of Yisrael. Here the Hebrew word is **Notsire Yisrael** or the Nazarenes of Yisrael. Of course, the misguided traditional rabbis don't want anyone to accept that fact that the Nazarenes are really biological Yisraelites and not pagans. Therefore in many Jewish bibles such as the *Stone English Edition Tanach*, they have purposely left out the vowel pointing, to make it appear as a different word, and then added a different but similar word with vowel pointing in brackets, changing the **yud** to a **vav**, to purposely make the reader unable to pronounce the word **notsire** as it actually appears, and changing it to "**netsuri**" or "ruins." The two-house movement does not teach that the ten northern tribes were annihilated. Rather, we teach that preservation did take place, not as a nation or kingdom, but as individuals called the "preserved ones of Jacob" in Isaiah 49:6. The early believers in Jerusalem, Judea (Judah), and Shomron (Ephraim's former capital), were all called **Notzrim, Notsraei** or **Netsarim** Yisrael. They were the "preserved ones" from both houses from both from the 721 BCE and 586 BCE exiles. Believers are the preserved little branches, or notzrim of the main Vine, our Moshiach Yahshua. The Hebrew word for branches is **netsarim** the same term used here for "preserved ones." So we are the "preserved branches" of Yisrael. In John 15, Yahshua calls all believers regardless of race, Nazarenes, or branches/**netsarim**. Jeremiah 31:6 also makes reference to the watchmen or **Notsirim** returning to the

You for a Light to the heathen,[11] [12] that You may be My Yahshua to the ends of the earth.[13] 7 This says יהוה, the Redeemer of Yisrael, their Set-Apart One,[14] to Him whom man despises, to Him whom the nation abhors,[15] to be the Eved over rulers, Melechim shall see and arise, rulers also shall worship, because of יהוה that is faithful, and the Set-Apart One of Yisrael, and He shall choose You.[16] 8 This says יהוה, In an acceptable time have I heard You, and in the day of Yahshua have I helped You:[17] and I will preserve You, and give You for a covenant of the people, to restore the land, to cause You to inherit the desolate heritages;[18] 9 That You[19] may say to the prisoners, Go out; to them that are in darkness,[20] Show yourselves.[21] They shall feed on the ways, and their pastures shall be in all the bare hills. 10 They shall not hunger nor thirst; neither shall the heat nor

---

hills of Ephraim, or the **Notsirim** returning to the hills of the north, as YHWH becomes a Father to all the tribes or clans of Yisrael (Jeremiah 31:1) again.
[11] In addition to the primary role of regathering all 12 tribes from both houses, Yahshua will also be a Light to the heathen, who desire to join the Commonwealth of Yisrael. Notice that His primary mission is not to build a "gentile church" and invite Yisraelites to join. Religion has fully and totally reversed the primary order and main focus of His mission.
[12] Just so Yahshua does not get bored with His easy mission to both houses of Yisrael, YHWH will give him some true heathens to seek for as well.
[13] All who desire salvation must appoint Yahshua as Savior, and desire YHWH's salvation, and desire to live in accordance with Yisrael's eternal constitution called the Torah.
[14] The Set -Apart One for all 12 tribes; the Moshiach Yahshua.
[15] Many men among Yisrael and Judah's rulers hated this Yahshua, despite the fact that He came to search for them, find them, and forgive them. He came to be the ultimate Server and laid down his life as a ransom for many.
[16] Abba-YHWH has chosen Yahshua to bring Himself worshippers, from the ends of the earth, including kings, rulers, and presidents.
[17] Quoted by Rav Shaul in Second Corinthians 6:2, that these promises to physical Yisrael applied to the congregation at Corinth. This is further evidence that they were Ephraimites in Greek exile.
[18] Those calling on Moshiach will be the preserved of Yisrael, designated as a "**brit am**" or "covenant people" to restore the land, and cause other redeemed remnant covenant people, to inherit all the pagan or ruined inheritances and cultures; even those many of us once belonged to.
[19] Redeemed Yisraelites.
[20] Isaiah 9:1-3.
[21] The two-house message of restoration, is one that set the captives of both houses free from bondage and error, as well as guarantees their physical return to the land. Moreover, it cries out to the hidden, yet preserved of our people to stand up, declare themselves and show the world just who they are in Moshiach and the Commonwealth of Yisrael. The restoration message allows former pagan prisoners to show and declare themselves openly, as Yisrael.

sun smite them: for He that has rachamim on them shall also lead them, even by the springs of mayim shall He guide them.[1] [2] 11 And I will make all My mountains a path, and My highways shall be exalted.[3] 12 See, these shall come from far:[4] and, see, these from the north and from the west; and these from the land of Sinim.[5] 13 Sing, O shamayim; and be full of simcha, O earth; and break forth into singing, O mountains: for **יהוה** has comforted His people, and will have rachamim upon His afflicted.[6] 14 But Tzion said, **יהוה** has forsaken me, and My Master has forgotten me. 15 Can a woman forget her nursing child, that she should not have rachamim on the son of her womb? Yes perhaps, they may forget, yet will I not forget you.[7] 16 See, I have graven you upon the palms of My hands;[8] [9] your walls[10] are continually before Me. 17 Your children shall hurry back to Me; your destroyers and they that made you a ruin shall depart from you. 18 Lift up your eyes all around, and see: all these who have gathered themselves together, and have come to You.[11] As I live, says **יהוה**, you

shall surely clothe Yourself with them all, as with an ornament, and bind them on You, as does a bride.[12] 19 For your waste and your desolate places, and the land of your destruction, shall even now be too narrow by reason of the inhabitants, and they that swallowed you up shall be far away.[13] 20 The children which you shall have, after you have lost the others, shall say again in your ears, The place is too narrow for me: give place to me that I may live.[14] 21 Then shall you say in your lev, Who has begotten me these, seeing I have lost My children, and am barren, an exile, wandering back and forth? Who has brought these up in the aliyah? See, I was left alone; and now all these, where have they been?[15] 22 This says the Master **יהוה**, See, I will lift up My hand to the nations, and set up My Standard to the peoples:[16] and they shall bring Your sons in their arms, and Your daughters shall be carried upon their shoulders. [17] 23 And melechim shall be Your nursing ahvot, and their queens Your nursing mothers: [18] they shall bow down to You with their faces toward the earth, and lick up the dust of Your feet; and you shall know that I am **יהוה**: for they

---

[1] The return will be with great and wonderful guidance back to His Torah. He will not leave us comfortless in our return to Tzion, but will accompany us.
[2] This also speaks of the fact that the ten tribes of Ephraim-Yisrael will return and settle in an area not lacking in food and mayim.
[3] YHWH will open many roads of return to the 12 tribes.
[4] Ephraim Yisrael coming from the farthest points from Jerusalem on the earth.
[5] **Sinim**, according to Rashi and the Aramaic translation of verse 12, is the land of the south. The land farthest away and furthest south from Yisrael is Australia. In the Latin Vulgate translation of the Bible by Jerome, the word in verse 12 for "**Sinim**" is "**Australi**," or (in English) "Australia." Rashi attributes the lost tribe of Simeon to Australia, the "Great Southland." The name **Sinim** contains the root word for Sinai, both the mountain and the entire Sinai Peninsula. The Sinai Peninsula hosted a large population from the tribe of Simeon. In many respects Australia is similar to the Sinai Peninsula.
[6] In the restoration, return and regathering of all Yisrael, both the heavens and the earth will join as **echad** in great gladness.
[7] YHWH's eternal love for Yisrael is greater than any human love, reason, or emotion.
[8] Through Yahshua's impalement, He took the nails because of His love for you, and all Yisrael.
[9] This passage has to be referring to the House of Yisrael (Ephraim), since neither of the two major Jewish Diasporas (586 BCE and 70 CE) had yet occurred, when Isaiah was written in 720 BCE.
[10] Your earthly tabernacle.
[11] In the restoration of all Yisrael, He will gather both houses as one, and we will respond to Moshiach's mission by coming to Him and responding to His drawing power.

[12] In verse 18 of Isaiah 49, YHWH tells His Son Yahshua to put on regathered Ephraim as an ornament of YHWH's remarriage to His people.
[13] In verses 19-21 of Isaiah 49, we see a divinely mandated, major role reversal. In Moshiach's days, we see Ephraim's oppressors and captors being tormented with global dispersion, never to be regathered, while Ephraim-Yisrael has been regathered to the land of their former destruction. Those who did the swallowing will take Ephraim's place in the exile, as the swallowed. This is exactly what happened to the now-defunct Assyrian, Babylonian, Medo-Persian and Roman gentile empires.
[14] Verse 20 shows that returning Ephraim will be so numerous, that the land of Yisrael as it appears today, will not have enough space to contain Joseph's seed, let alone Judah's.
[15] In verse 21, the amazed peoples of Ephraim are flabbergasted at the fact that their brethren (other lost Yisraelites), are not only still extant, but, in fact, numerically multiplied and prosperous.
[16] Yahshua.
[17] Brethren carrying brethren. Jews and Ephraimites beginning to carry each other back to the land, when Moshiach is revealed. This is not talking about renting airplanes, and cutting deals with the orthodox Jews in Yisrael, promising them not to share the Tov News, or denying Yahshua, just to get in. Those of the nations are Yisraelites, encouraging other Yisraelites, to begin to return in the days of Moshiach, who will oversee the final ingathering. All the finer details are left up to King Moshiach.
[18] All nations will serve remnant Yisrael in the kingdom.

shall not be ashamed that wait for Me.[1] 24 Shall the prey be taken from the mighty, or the victors' exiles delivered? 25 But this says יהוה, Even the captives of the mighty shall be taken away, and the prey of the ruthless shall be delivered: for I will contend with him that contends with You, and I will save Your children.[2] 26 And I will feed them that oppress you with their own flesh; and they shall be drunk with their own dom, as with sweet wine: and all flesh shall know that I יהוה am Your Savior and Your Redeemer, the Mighty One of Yaakov.[3]

50 This says יהוה, Where is the bill of your ima's divorcement, whom I have put away? Or which of My creditors is it to whom I have sold you? See, for your iniquities you have sold yourselves, and for your transgressions was your ima put away.[4] 2 Why, when I came looking, was there no man?[5] When I called, was there none to answer? Is My Hand shortened so that it cannot redeem?[6] Or have I no power to deliver? See, at My rebuke I dry up the sea, I make the rivers into a wilderness: their fish stink, because there is no mayim, and they die for thirst. 3 I clothe the shamayim with blackness, and I make sackcloth their covering. 4 The Master יהוה has given Me the tongue of the learned, that I should know how to speak a word in season to him that is weary: he awakes morning by morning, He wakes up my ear to shema as the learned.[7] 5 The Master יהוה has opened My ear, and I was not rebellious,[8] neither did I turn away My back.[9] [10] 6 I gave My back to the smiters, and My cheeks to them that plucked off the hair: I hid not My face from shame and spitting.[11] 7 For the Master יהוה will help Me; therefore shall I not be embarrassed: therefore have I set My face like a flint, and I know that I shall not be ashamed.[12] 8 He is near that justifies Me;[13] who will contend with Me? Let us stand together:[14] Who is My adversary? Let him come near to Me.[15] 9 See, the Master יהוה will help Me; who is he that shall condemn Me? See, they all shall grow old as a garment; the moth shall eat them up.[16] 10 Who is among you that fears יהוה, that obeys the voice of His Eved,[17] that walks in darkness, and has no Light?[18] Let him trust in the Name of יהוה,[19] and lean upon His Elohim. 11 See, all you that kindle a fire, that surround yourselves with sparks: and follow in the light of your own fire, and in the sparks that you have kindled. This shall you have from My Hand; you shall lie down in sorrow.[20]

---

[1] In the return to YHWH spiritually speaking, all the kings and queens of the earth will bow down to us, as we subject them in right-ruling in the **atid lavoh**. However in the physical return to the land, we must wait for YHWH to speak to us and truly open a door in this age, or wait until the age to come. If we are forced to wait, we will not be ashamed, since our fallen inclinations and desires may lead us to deceive and mislead others in order to return to the land, in our own timing.
[2] Both houses can rest in that promise of salvation and restoration, through His deliverance.
[3] Yisrael will rule over every enemy she has ever had, as YHWH brings to pass His Torah promises in the Messianic Age, when Yisrael will be the head and no longer the tail.
[4] YHWH did not divorce Ephraim as a nation; she chose to divorce YHWH.
[5] No qualified intermediary to bring Yisrael back.
[6] Buy back Yisrael.
[7] Since YHWH found no mediator, He raised up Yahshua to reconnect Himself with Yisrael, and specifically Ephraim Yisrael the divorced house.
[8] He was the fully obedient Suffering Servant, unlike the nation He was being sent to.
[9] Moshiach has received all authority from Abba-YHWH to instruct Yisrael on the road back to restoration.
[10] As opposed to Yisrael.
[11] Yisrael's Restorer came to be impaled to buy back His bride, by the death of the Husband.
[12] Despite the apparent shame.
[13] Yahshua has come near to us.
[14] Judah and Ephraim.
[15] Yisrael restored is united and ready to stand against all her adversaries.
[16] All Moshiach's enemies will be vanquished through the Father (Hebrews 1:11).
[17] Yahshua.
[18] Yisrael.
[19] The only kind of acceptable faith there is includes loving His true Name.
[20] In contrast to those who trust YHWH for restoration, some who pervert the message by lighting their own flames for Yisrael's two-house return, will surely lie down in sorrow.

51

Shema to Me, you that follow after tzedakah, you that seek יהוה: look to the Rock from which you are cut, and to the hole of the pit from where you are dug.[1] 2 Look to Avraham your abba, and to Sarah that bore you:[2] for I called him alone,[3] and blessed him, and increased him. [4] [5] 3 For יהוה shall comfort Tzion: He will comfort all her waste places; and He will make her wilderness like Gan-Aden, and her desert like the Gan of יהוה;[6] simcha and gilah shall be found in it, hodu, and the voice of melody.[7] 4 Shema to Me, My people; and give ear to Me, O My nation:[8] for a Torah shall proceed from Me,[9] and My mishpat I will set as a light of the nations. 5 My Tzedakah is near;[10] My Yahshua[11] shall go forth, and My arms[12] shall shofet the nations; the coastlands shall wait upon Me, and on My Arm[13] shall they trust. 6 Lift up your eyes to the shamayim, and look upon the earth beneath: for the shamayim shall vanish away like smoke, and the earth shall grow old like a garment, and they that live in it shall die in like manner: but My Yahshua[14] shall be le-olam-va-ed and My Tzedakah shall never be abolished.[15] 7 Shema to Me, you that know tzedakah, the people in whose lev is My Torah; fear not the reproach of men, neither be afraid of their insults.[16] 8 For the moth shall eat them up like a garment, and the worm shall eat them like wool: but My Tzedakah shall be le-olam-va-ed,[17] and My Yahshua [18] from generation to generation. 9 Awake, awake, put on strength, O Arm of יהוה,[19] awake, as in the ancient days, in the generations of old. Wasn't it You that has decreed a severe sentence, and wounded the dragon? [20] 10 Are You not He who has dried the sea, the mayim of the great deep; that has made the depths of the sea a derech for the ransomed to pass over? 11 Therefore the redeemed of יהוה shall return,[21] and come with singing to Tzion; [22] and everlasting simcha shall be upon their head: they shall obtain simcha and joy; and sorrow and mourning shall flee away.[23] 12 I, even I, am He that comforts you: who are you, that you should be afraid of a man that shall die, and of the ben adam who shall be made as grass;[24] 13 And in turn forget יהוה Your Maker, that has stretched forth the shamayim, and laid the foundations of the earth; and you have feared continually every day because of the fury of the oppressor, as if he were ready to destroy? And where is the fury of the oppressor?[25] 14 The captive exile is in a hurry that he may be loosed, and that he should not die in the pit, nor that his lechem

---

[1] Any walk, path or lifestyle, that does not bring you all the way back to your Hebraic heritage, will find you looking in the wrong direction away from Yahshua and not back to Yahshua, who came to live the Torah, as He desires us to do.
[2] The first recorded man and woman to cross over or become Ivrim/Hebrews. We must leave all paganism and false notions behind in Babylon just like they did, in order to receive the same promises that they did.
[3] When starting out in your new return to the nation of your ancestors you can expect to walk as one, with no help from any humans other than YHWH. Eventually fellow Yisraelites will come along to encourage you.
[4] With the blessing of physical multiplicity and personal salvation, both contained in that single promise, as it is with us when we become Yisrael. We are both physically and spiritually blessed and increased.
[5] See Rebuilding Our Nation; For more details: http://store.yourarmstoisrael.org/Qstore/Qstore.cgi?CMD=011 &PROD=000088.
[6] In the atid lavoh.
[7] Millennial bliss.
[8] Moshiach came primarily for Yisrael and whosoever else wills.
[9] The Torah of the coming Moshiach. Yahshua came to reinforce and internalize Abba's Torah.
[10] Yahshua.
[11] Yishi in Hebrew.
[12] Yahshua and Torah. His dual "arms" to Yisrael.
[13] Yahshua.
[14] Yehshuati in Hebrew.

[15] This applies to the written Torah and the living Torah Yahshua.
[16] Your return to Yisrael must be with full devotion and conviction, or you will lose your inheritance in Tzion.
[17] All those Yisraelites clothed in Yahshua's tzedakah, will live forever, just like their Savior King.
[18] Hebrew: veyeshuati.
[19] Yahshua.
[20] Symbolizing Egypt and Pharaoh.
[21] In the two house restoration, limited to the ransomed and redeemed, not to biological apostate Jewish or Ephrayim-Yisrael.
[22] To the land and all the customs and culture as well.
[23] In the atid lavoh.
[24] Your love for personal Yisraelite restoration will help you overcome your fear of the opinions of others.
[25] Returning Yisraelites must be preoccupied with their return and not with the foes that threaten them.

should fail.[1] 15 But I am יהוה Your Elohim that divided the Sea of Reeds, whose waves roared: יהוה of hosts is His Name. 16 And I have put My words in Your mouth, and I have covered You in the shadow of My hand, that I may plant the shamayim,[2] and lay the foundations of the earth, and say to Tzion, You are My Ami-My People. [3] 17 Awake, awake, stand up, O Yahrushalayim, you who have drunk at the hand of יהוה and the cup of His fury; you have drunken the dregs of the cup of trembling, and drained them out. 18 There is none to guide her among all the sons whom she has brought forth; neither is there any that takes her by the hand of all the sons that she has brought up. [4] 19 These two things are coming upon you; who shall be sorry for you? Ruin, and destruction, the famine, and the sword: by whom shall I comfort you?[5] 20 Your sons have fainted, they lie at the head of all the streets, as a wild bull in a net: they are full of the fury of יהוה, the rebuke of Your Elohim. 21 Therefore shema to this right now, you who are afflicted, and drunk, but not with wine: 22 This says Your Master, יהוה, and Your Elohim[6] that pleads the cause of His people, See, I have taken out of your hand the cup of trembling, even the dregs of the cup of My fury; you shall no more drink it again:[7] 23 But I will put it into the hand of those that afflict you; who have said to your being, Bow down, that we may walk over you: and you have laid your body down like the ground, and like the street, to those that walked over you.[8]

52 Awake, awake; put on your strength, O Tzion; put on your beautiful garments, O Yahrushalayim, the set-apart city: from now on there shall no more come into you the uncircumcised and the unclean.[9] 2 Shake yourself from the dust; arise, and sit down, O Yahrushalayim: loose yourself from the bands of your neck, O captive daughter of Tzion.[10] 3 For this says יהוה, You have sold yourselves for nothing; and you shall be redeemed without money.[11] 4 For this says the Master יהוה, My people went down before into Mitzrayim to sojourn there; and Ashshur oppressed them without cause. 5 Now therefore, what have I here, says יהוה, that My people are taken away for nothing? Those that rule over them make them to wail, says יהוה; and My Name continually every day is despised and mocked.[12] 6 Therefore My People-Ami shall know My Name:[13] therefore they shall know in that day[14] that I am He that does speak: see, it is I. 7 How beautiful upon the mountains are the feet of Him that brings Tov News, that publishes shalom; that brings Tov News of tov things, that publishes Yahshua; that says to Tzion, Your Elohim reigns![15] 8 Your watchmen shall lift up the voice; with the voice together[16] shall they shir: for they shall see eye-to-eye, when יהוה shall return to Tzion. 9 Break forth into simcha, shir

---

[9] In the kingdom no uncircumcised people can enter the renewed Jerusalem, providing further evidence that Abba-YHWH sees all believers as Yisraelites.
[10] Don't just listen to the truth, act on it and loose yourself when you listen to the truth.
[11] Eternal life is free, and without cost, but discipleship brings about a great cost from our own lives.
[12] When YHWH's Name and His character are at stake, He moves very rapidly.
[13] Heed this well. You cannot be part of Yisrael without knowing, loving, using and proclaiming His Name. This Scripture is etched in simplicity and cannot be twisted or reasoned away.
[14] At the dawn of the age to come.
[15] The One coming with the Tov News is Yahshua and part of His proclamation is making sure that Tzion knows His Name and removes themselves from the manmade ban of the apostate rabbis. For more details see: **The Ban** at: http://store.yourarmstoisrael.org/Qstore/Qstore.cgi?CMD=011 &PROD=000082.
[16] Watchman from both houses join together in song, as they see eye-to-eye as **echad**, as both of them set their eyes on YHWH's return to Zion. This is a reference to the restored Kingdom and the second coming.

---

[1] Natural anxiety will accompany the return.
[2] The renewed heavens will follow the blueprint of the earthly renewal of Yisrael.
[3] Relax. YHWH has declared you to be His chosen nation. Enjoy the return, and don't let your enemies steal that joy.
[4] Therefore the need for Moshiach to lead us home in the true Way.
[5] Another reason for the need of Moshiach.
[6] Father and Son; "Your Elohim," who is said to plead for Yisrael; a clear reference to the Son's mediation role for Yisrael.
[7] Forgiveness is coming soon; by His Son.
[8] All the heathen empires throughout history, specifically Assyria, Babylon, Medo-Persia and Rome.

together, you waste places of Yahrushalayim: for **יהוה** has comforted His people, He has redeemed Yahrushalayim.[1] 10 **יהוה** has made bare His Set-Apart Arm in the eyes of all the nations; and all the ends of the olam shall see the Yahshua of Our Elohim.[2] 11 Depart, depart, go out from there, touch no unclean thing;[3] go out of the midst of her; be clean, that bear the vessels of **יהוה**.[4] 12 For you shall not come out with haste,[5] nor go by flight:[6] for **יהוה** will go before you;[7] and the Elohim of Yisrael will be your reward.[8] 13 See, My Eved shall work a wise work,[9] He shall be exalted and extolled, and be very high.[10] 14 Many were astonished at Him; His appearance was so marred more than any man,[11] and His form marred more than the sons of men:[12] 15 So shall He sprinkle many nations;[13] the melechim shall shut their mouths at Him: for that which had not been told to them shall they see; and that which they had not heard shall they consider.[14]

53 [15] [16] [17] Who has believed our report?[18] And to whom is the Arm of **יהוה**[19] revealed?[20] 2 For He shall grow up before Him[21] as a tender plant, and as a root out of a dry ground:[22] He has neither form nor beauty; and when we shall see Him, there is no tiferet that we should desire Him.[23] 3 He is despised and rejected of men;[24] a Man of sorrows, and acquainted with grief: and we hid as it were our faces from Him;[25] He was despised, and we esteemed Him not. 4 Surely He has borne our griefs, and carried our sorrows:[26] yet we did reckon Him beaten, smitten of Elohim, and afflicted.[27] 5 But He was wounded for our transgressions,

---

[1] Redemption songs will be sung in harmony by the love and joy for Yahshua and each other when Yisrael's capital and its dwellers receive the gift of pardon and redemption, by recognizing YHWH's Son, according to Zechariah 12:10.
[2] All nations drink of the tov of our YHWH.
[3] Touch nothing forbidden in Torah.
[4] Quoted by Rav Shaul in Second Corinthians 6:17-18, giving further evidence that he considered them Yisarel. To overcome in our restoration walk, we must come out of all religious systems that are founded in error, lest we be overcome, while being called to be overcomers.
[5] We will not come out of the exile in haste, but rather in slow progressive stages.
[6] Man-made plans will not bring the full restoration and kingdom. Only when YHWH goes before us, are we to make aliyah and not a nanosecond sooner.
[7] He alone will lead and plan this restoration and return.
[8] The end of the exile is not a Jewish experience without Yahshua as King.
[9] Salvation as a finished work, for both houses.
[10] Second only in the throne of the cosmos to His Elohim Abba-YHWH.
[11] The beaten and smitten Moshiach.
[12] He became unrecognizable as a human being.
[13] With the dom of atonement.
[14] Even though many kings and nobles will not be eyewitnesses, but will only hear of this Man's suffering for sin, yet the wonders of YHWH's love will cause them to hold their silence, and just allow themselves to be sprinkled with His dom. They will come to understand the events not by their actual attendance, but by a revelation of the Ruach.

[15] Isaiah 53, a chapter clearly speaking of the Suffering Servant Moshiach, containing Yahshua's Name by counting every 20th letter back from left to right beginning with the second yud in "ya'arik" in verse 10 is revealed as **"Yahshua-shem'i,"** or "Yahshua is My Name." Je--s is His Name" by Yacov Rambsel (Frontier Research Pub.) The Isaiah chapters pages 25-65, Page 28, Page 40.
[16] Many prophecies in Tanach that are clearly future events use "prophetic perfect verbs" to describe still future prophetic events, since YHWH knows the end from the beginning, and is prophetically declaring "a finished action," even though it hasn't actually taken place. The Suffering Servant chapter of Isaiah 53 is one such example, where the Servant is seen as having completed the work of atonement, yet its literal fulfillment is some 740 years in the future. Even the anti-missionaries see Isaiah 53 as national Yisrael (not Yahshua) suffering for mankind in the future, despite the actual language being written in a past tense, or "prophetic perfect" verb usage.
[17] Isaiah 53 is banned in the Shabbat **Haftarah** (prophetic portions read in synagogues during Shabbat services) portions. If this chapter does not speak clearly about Yahshua what are they running from? .
[18] The report about Yisrael's Suffering Servant Moshiach from Yisraelites to Yisarelites; is not a gentile message.
[19] Metaphor for His deliverance or redemption.
[20] Despite the telling and proclamation of the Besarot, many in Yisrael from both houses will stumble over the report as prophesied in Isaiah 8:14, and turn the tov report into one for stumbling and unemunah. This verse prophesies that the report of Moshiach's death, would meet with much rejection.
[21] "Before Abba YHWH," where all sacrifices had to be presented according to Torah.
For more details see **An Altar Of Authority** at:
http://store.yourarmstoisrael.org/Qstore/Qstore.cgi?CMD=011&PROD=1065766783.
[22] Normal roots grow in fertile ground. This is a **remez** or hint of the virgin birth.
[23] Moshiach looked just like us and was not dressed in king's clothing.
[24] "Men" is a synonym for the men of YHWH's flock, or Yisrael. Both houses rejected His message. Ephraim rejected His Torah and Judah His dom atonement.
[25] Both houses still run from the true message, either rejecting it outright, or else changing it into a gentile western anti-nomian perversion.
[26] The "our" is a reference to both houses of Yisrael.
[27] Both houses thought His suffering was for His own sins and not ours.

He was crushed for our iniquities: the chastisement for our shalom was upon Him; and with His stripes we are healed.[1] [2] 6 All we like sheep have gone astray;[3] we have turned each one to his own halacha; and יהוה has laid on Him the iniquity of us all.[4] 7 He was oppressed, and He was afflicted, yet He opened not His mouth: He is brought as a Lamb to the slaughter,[5] and as a sheep before its shearers is dumb, so He opens not His mouth.[6] 8 He was taken from prison and from mishpat:[7] and who shall declare His generation? For He was cut off[8] out of the land of the living: for the transgression of My People-Ami[9] was He beaten. 9 And He made His grave with the wicked, and with the rich in His death; because He had done no violence, neither was any deceit in His mouth.[10] [11] 10 Yet it pleased יהוה to crush Him; He has put Him to grief: when You shall make His being an asham[12] for sin, He shall see His zera, [13] He shall prolong His days,[14] [15] and the pleasure of

יהוה shall prosper in His hand.[16] 11 He shall see the Light[17] the result of the travail of His being, and shall be satisfied:[18] by His da'at shall My Tzadik Eved[19] justify many,[20] for He shall bear their iniquities. [21] 12 Therefore will I[22] divide Him a portion with the great, and He shall divide the plunder with the strong; because He has poured out His being to death:[23] and He was counted with the transgressors;[24] and He bore the sin of many, [25] and made intercession for the transgressors.[26]

54 Sing, O barren,[27] you that did not bear; break forth [28] into singing, and cry aloud,[29] you that did not travail with child:[30] for more are the children of

[15] Yahshua did have His human days prolonged on the earth by 40 days. This term **yaarich yamim** refers only to those 40 days after death between His resurrection and His ascension. This term does not refer to His past life in heaven, in YHWH's bosom, or now at YHWH's right hand as YHWH, since Isaiah speaks of His earthly days being prolonged. Isaiah properly uses the term, **yaarich yamim** to refer to those 40 days. Were Isaiah referring to Yahshua's eternality, He would have no doubt used a different term such as: **le-olam**, or **le-olam va-ed**, or **le-chayai-olam**.
[16] In His hand mankind and Yisrael will be restored.
[17] The missing word "light" is found in the LXX (Septuagint), and in the Dead Sea Scrolls. Therefore we see the Moshiach dying, and after death, seeing light again by His days being prolonged. By removing the word "light" after death, as in "light," or "life after death," the counter-missionaries have tried unsuccessfully to remove a clear reference to Moshiach's resurrection, after His death.
[18] YHWH's wrath at Yisrael's sin was fully brought forth upon Yahshua, and His righteous judgment upon that sin has been fully satisfied, which is why Yahshua cried out "It is finished."
[19] Unlike the nation of Yisrael, Isaiah 53:11 calls the Sufferer "righteous," and YHWH called Yisrael (as a nation) many things, but never called them blameless or righteous as Isaiah 53, calls the Suffering Servant.
[20] "Justify" means they will become reborn, just as if they've never sinned.
[21] He (Yahshua) has carried away all of Yisrael's sins, never to be brought back again.
[22] Abba-YHWH.
[23] Isaiah 53:12 must be taken in conjunction with Daniel 9:25, where it speaks of the "cutting off," or death of the Moshiach (in Hebrew **Ye Karet Moshiach).**
[24] Reckoned to be a mere common criminal with other common criminals, to His right and left.
[25] By a single act of love.
[26] When He prayed on the stake "Father forgive them. They know not what they do."
[27] Because of the events of the death, burial and resurrection of the Moshiach in Isaiah 53, the two-houses can begin to sing for joy, including the former barren house of Ephraim Yisrael, who would now begin to produce children because of the Moshiach bringing them back into the fold, and quickening their barren wombs to once again carry children for YHWH.
[28] Across the globe.
[29] Publish the **besarot.**
[30] Ephraim Yisrael.

---

[1] He brought shalom and healing between YHWH and man, and between both warring houses of Yisrael, if the individual allows His work to be internalized.
[2] Physical and spiritual healing are both part of the benefits of the atonement.
[3] Matthew 15:24 reminds us, that He suffered for the lost sheep of Yisrael from both houses.
[4] All Yisrael's sins fell on Him, since we were the former lost sheep of His fold.
[5] The Lamb of YHWH; Yisrael as a nation was never silent in the face of suffering.
[6] As seen by His refusal to defend Himself.
[7] Killed in violation of Torah and even Jewish halacha. Right-ruling was not enacted in His so-called trial. Yahshua arrived at trial straight from prison.
[8] Hebrew: **Nigzar.**
[9] **Pesha ami** or the transgression of my nation. Yisrael as a nation cannot die for Yisrael, since in order to be a valid Torah sacrifice, the sacrifice must be a substitution and vicarious in nature. He died for both houses of His nation.
[10] As seen in His burial in the tomb of Joseph of Ramatayim (a rich man); and His death between two wicked thieves.
[11] The Lamb here is declared by Abba-YHWH as spotless and without sin.
[12] Literally a special substituted type of sacrifice. This word **asham**, Strong's # 817, is used very rarely and is specifically related to an offering for guilt. Here Yahshua dies for Yisrael's collective guilt.
[13] In the very first book of Scripture, as in many other places "**zera**" can be used for seed other than human sperm as seen in Genesis 1:11, where fruit is seen to contain seed/**zera**. The Hebrew word here and in other places is **zera**. Of course, it is metaphoric, and through the centuries Yahshua has had billions of faithful children, who look to Him for full adoption into YHWH's eternal family. Both houses need that adoption.
[14] His life is prolonged after He is said to be dead; a reference to physical resurrection.

the desolate [1] than the children of the married wife,[2] says **יהוה**. 2 *Enlarge the place of your tent, and let them stretch forth the curtains of your dwellings: spare not, lengthen your cords, and strengthen your stakes;[3] 3 For you shall break forth on the right hand and on the left; and Your zera shall inherit the nations[4], and make the desolate cities to be inhabited.[5] 4 Fear not; for you shall not be ashamed: neither will you be embarrassed; for you shall not be put to shame: for you shall forget the shame of your youth, and shall not remember the reproach of your widowhood any more.[6] 5 For Your Maker is Your husbands;[7]* **יהוה** *of hosts is His Name; and Your Redeemer the Set-Apart One of Yisrael; The Elohim of the whole earth shall He be called.[8] 6 For* **יהוה** *has called you back as a woman forsaken and grieved in ruach, like a wife of youth, when you were refused,* says Your Elohim.[9] 7 *For a small moment have I forsaken you; but with great rachamim will I gather you.[10] 8 In an overflow of My wrath I hid My face from you for a moment;[11] but with everlasting chesed will I have rachamim on you,* says **יהוה** Your Redeemer. 9 *For this is as the mayim of Noach to Me: for as I have sworn that the mayim of Noach should no more go over the earth; so have I sworn that I would not be angry with you, nor rebuke you again.[12] 10 For the mountains shall depart, and the hills shall be removed; but My chesed shall not depart from you again, neither shall the covenant of My shalom be removed,[13]* says **יהוה** *that has rachamim on you. 11 O you afflicted, tossed with storms, and Lo-Ruchamah-Not Comforted, see, I will lay your stones with fair colors, and lay your foundations with sapphires.[14] 12 And I will make your windows of rubies, and your gates of crystal, and all your walls of precious stones. 13 And all your children shall be taught by* **יהוה***;[15] and great shall be the shalom of your children. 14 In tzedakah shall you be established:[16] you shall be far from oppression; for you shall not fear: and you shall be far from fear; for it shall not come near you. 15 See, they shall surely gather together, but not by Me:[17] whosoever shall gather against you shall fall for your sake.[18] 16 See, I have created the blacksmith that blows the coals in the fire, and that brings forth an instrument for his work; and I have also created the mayim that destroy. 17 No weapon that is formed against you shall prosper; and every tongue that shall rise up against you to shophet you, you shall*

---

[1] Ephraim's offspring is far more than the 16 or so million of Yahudah.

[2] The former barren one is Ephraim Yisrael, who had no husband due to her divorce. Subsequently and consequentially, she had no children. Now in and through the **besarot**, she who was divorced and barren is remarried, renewed and conceiving multitudes of Yisraelite children for YHWH; since she now operates in full obedience and compliance to Moshiach and His Torah. The former divorced woman (Ephraim or non-Jewish Yisrael) is still more fruitful than Yahudah, still bound in large part by the spirit of Ishmael working in the earthly city of Jerusalem among its residents.

[3] As Ephraim returns, Yisrael's tents will surely be enlarged as per covenant promise.

[4] Melo HaGoyim.

[5] The promise of Genesis 28:14 that through the Moshiach the seed of Yisrael would be regathered after breaking out **tefrotzyi**, from the root word **parats**, across the globe.

[6] Speaking to the former barren wombs of Ephraim Yisrael, who through the Suffering Servant have left widowhood.

[7] Hebrew: **ki baalecha asechah**, or "because your Husbands are your Maker." We see the plurality of **echad** again in the term "husbands." Also the Maker is YHWH, and His Redeemer, which in the Hebrew is **ve goalecha** or literally "your Redeemers." We see the Father and Son in this verse as **echad** in both cases.

[8] YHWH through Yahshua has taken Ephraim back to be with Judah.

[9] Ephraim was called back to YHWH through Yahshua, after being rejected in the past.

[10] In the restoration and regathering of both houses. It is YHWH through Yahshua, who does the regathering, not the elaborate fleshly plans of men.

[11] 721 years.

[12] A promise to redeemed Ephraim.

[13] Ephraim will never again experience separation and rejection by YHWH, due to the cutting of the everlasting Renewed Covenant, by the Suffering Servant our Yahshua.

[14] YHWH in essence is saying: I will reveal myself to you, by many stones, or **"sefirot-safiryim,"** or many manifestations of My love and no longer will I hide from you.

[15] John 6:45 is a clear indication that Yahshua who is teaching Yisrael, is the very YHWH spoken of in this verse, teaching Torah and **halacha** to the lost sheep of Epharim

[16] The tzedakah imparted by the Suffering Servant Yahshua.

[17] This is a nice little warning thrown in here. All attempts to gather Ephraim are destined to fail without Yahshua being King over both houses as outlined in Ezekiel 37. So do not trust every work or movement using or referring to the term "gathering," or "ingathering," or House of Joseph, if they deny Yahshua, or if they are not allowed to share Yahshua with all Yisrael.

[18] Gathering in any manner not prescribed in Scripture shall not stand; and actually does not hold Ephraim's best interests at heart.

condemn. This is the heritage of the avadim of **יהוה**,[1] and their tzedakah is from Me,[2] says **יהוה**.[3]

55 Hello, every one that thirsts, come to the mayim; and he that has no money; come, buy, and eat; yes, come, buy wine and milk without money and without price.[4] 2 Why do you spend money for that which is not lechem? And your labor for that which does not satisfies? Shema diligently to Me, and eat that which is tov, and let your being delight itself in fatness.[5] 3 Incline your ear, and come to Me: shema, and your being shall live; and I will make an Everlasting Covenant with you, even the sure rachamim of David.[6] 4 See, I have given Him[7] as a witness to the people, a Leader and Commander to the people.[8] 5 See, you shall call a nation that You knew not,[9] and nations that knew You not shall run to You[10] because of **יהוה** Your Elohim,[11] and for the Set-Apart One of Yisrael; for He has lifted You up. 6 Seek **יהוה** while He may be found, call upon Him while He is near:[12] 7 Let the wicked forsake his halacha, and the unrighteous man his thoughts: and let him make teshuvah to **יהוה**, for He will have rachamim upon him; and to Our Elohim, for He will abundantly pardon.[13] 8 For My thoughts are not your thoughts, neither are your halachot My halachot, says **יהוה**. 9 For as the shamayim are higher than the earth, so are My halachot higher than your own halachot, and My thoughts than your thoughts. 10 For as the rain comes down, and the snow from the shamayim, and returns not there, but waters the earth, and makes it bring forth and bud, that it may give zera to the sower, and lechem to the eater: 11 So shall My Word be that goes forth out of My mouth: it shall not return to Me void, but it shall accomplish that which I please, and it shall prosper in the thing where I sent it.[14] 12 For you shall go out with simcha, and be led forth with shalom:[15] the mountains and the hills shall break forth before you into singing,[16] and all the eytzim of the field shall clap their hands. [17] 13 Instead of the thorn shall come up the cypress eytz, and instead of the brier shall come up the myrtle eytz:[18] and it shall be to **יהוה** for a Name, for an everlasting sign that shall not be cut off.[19]

56 This says **יהוה**, Guard mishpat, and do justice: for My Yahshua[20] is near to come, and My Tzedakah to be revealed.[21] 2 Blessed is the man that does this, and the ben adam that lays hold on it, that shomers the Shabbat from polluting it, and shomers his hand from doing any evil.[22] 3 Neither let the son of the Ger, that has joined himself to **יהוה**, speak in this manner, saying, **יהוה** has utterly separated me from His people: neither let the eunuch

---

[1] Hebraic heritage.
[2] Dom atonement provided by Yahshua.
[3] Many Christians quote this verse-promise, but do not actually comprehend the depths of what they claim. Of course this is a verse of divine protection and guardianship, but moreover, it declares to them that they are Yisraelites, since this promise in context is given eternally to Yisrael, specifically to Ephraim-Yisrael.
[4] The proclamation of the **besorat** and salvation itself is free.
[5] Yisrael is called to receive living bread and milk from the lips of YHWH, along with His unmerited favor.
[6] The eternal covenant with all 12 tribes of Yisrael, brought in by Yahshua, the greater end-time, or eschatological David.
[7] Abba-YHWH gave Him.
[8] Yahshua is the Witness, Leader and Commander of all of Renewed Covenant Yisrael. He is called the "Faithful Witness" of Abba YHWH in the Book of Revelation (1:5).
[9] The individual lost sheep will become a reconstituted nation in Yahshua.
[10] Yisraelite nations that had lost their identity as Hebrews. Yahshua knew them, but they did not know Him, but ran to Him when hearing the Tov News of the kingdom.
[11] Moshiach has an Elohim over Him.
[12] A call and a plea to both houses of Yisrael.
[13] YHWH stands ready to pardon all Yisrael.

[14] The Word has in fact accomplished His will and purpose, in bringing atonement to both houses of Yisrael, since Yahshua is, was and will yet be YHWH's living Word, having now returned to the Father in great victory.
[15] Led forth from exile.
[16] The land will welcome Yisrael home.
[17] Kingdom joy. The trees as seen in Mark 8:22-25, are references to individual Yisraelites clapping their hands in celebration of the restoration of their nation.
[18] The curse on the land and on the earth is lifted.
[19] The regeneration of the land in the millennium will be for YHWH's esteem, and for a place where His Name can dwell, without it being defiled any more by His people.
[20] Hebrew: **yeshuati.**
[21] Through His Son.
[22] Those who are heirs of salvation must guard the Shabbat and the other eternal ordinances in Torah.

say, See, I am a dry eytz.[1] 4 For this says יהוה to the eunuchs that keep My Shabbats, and choose the things that please Me, and take hold[2] of My covenant; 5 Even to them will I give in My Bayit and within My walls[3] a place and a name better than that of sons and of daughters: I will give them an everlasting name, that shall not be cut off.[4] 6 Also the sons of the Ger, that join themselves to יהוה, to serve Him, and to love the Name of יהוה,[5] to be His avadim, every person that shomers the Shabbat from polluting it, and takes hold of My covenant;[6] 7 Even them will I bring to My set-apart mountain,[7] and make them full of simcha in My Beit-Tefillah: their burnt offerings and their sacrifices shall be accepted upon My altar; for My Bayit[8] shall be called a Beit-Tefillah for all the nations.[9] 8 The Master יהוה [10] who gathers the outcasts of Yisrael[11] says, Yet I will gather others to Him, [12] besides those that are being gathered to him.[13] 9 All you beasts of the field, come to devour, yes, all you beasts in the forest. [14] 10 His watchmen [15] are blind: they are all ignorant, they are all dumb dogs,[16] they cannot bark;[17] sleeping, lying down, loving to slumber. 11 Yes, they are greedy dogs who can never have enough, and they are shepherds that cannot understand: [18] they all look to their own halacha,[19] each one for his own gain, from his own view. 12 Come, they say, I will fetch wine, and we will fill ourselves with strong drink;[20] and tomorrow shall be as today, and much more abundant.[21]

57 The tzadik man perishes, and no man lays it to lev: and merciful and kind men are taken away, none considers that the tzadik is taken away from the evil to come.[22] 2 He shall enter into shalom: they shall rest in their beds, each one walking in his tzedakah.[23] 3 But come here, you sons of the sorceress, the zera of the adulterer and the whore.[24] 4 Against whom do you play games? Against whom do you open your mouth wide, and stick out your tongue? Are you not children of transgression, the zera of falsehood? 5 Comforting yourselves with idols under every green eytz, slaying the children in the

---

[1] Anyone joining Yisrael through Yahshua must never ever utter these forbidden words. No one in the Commonwealth of Yisrael, is a stranger, a sojourner, a visitor, a gentile, a eunuch or any kind of a dry eytz. The believer in Yahshua is declared to be righteous and part of the green Olive Tree of Yisrael. All separations, both physically and spiritually, are forbidden in confession and in practice.
[2] A Yisraelite must enter by the dom of Yahshua, but still must decide to "take hold" of Yisraelite culture and halacha on a daily basis.
[3] Within the walls of the Renewed Jerusalem.
[4] This falls in line with Matthew 5:19-21 where those not obeying Torah are least in the kingdom, yet by mercy remain sons and daughters, but have nothing to show for it. The ones here that are Torah-compliant and receive names and positions better than sons or daughters, are the great ones in the kingdom, with great fruit in this age and the age to come. They will be known as remnant Yisrael, the everlasting name that will never be cut off.
[5] Loving the true and only eternal Name of YHWH, is a prerequisite for being, or becoming, or staying, Yisrael. The word is simple, and we ought to take heed to it. Learning to love the Name "YHWH" is part of the "taking hold" process, for the redeemed from both houses of Yisrael.
[6] Even non-biological Yisraelites become Yisrael when they receive salvation; guard His Shabbats and take hold of Torah and Yahshua. They will also be considered full and equal heirs in Yisrael.
[7] Mt. Zion.
[8] Yisrael restored.
[9] All nations are called to worship as one now and also in the millennial rebuilt Beit HaMikdash, when the Prince Moshiach Yahshua, leads us in the true worship of His Father Abba-YHWH, using the true Name among all the people. The true faith must be one where all nations, colors, nationalities and races become Yisrael in accord with the "take hold" principle of His Torah.
[10] Abba.
[11] Ephraim.
[12] His **chaverim** or companions, according to Ezekiel 37.

[13] Abba brings all to Yahshua and gathers all Yisrael by Yahshua.
[14] While all this restoration is going on, the beasts or gentiles (heathens), will not be happy with the change in you, and will come to dissuade you in your personal return to Tzion. Expect them to pop out of the forests of misunderstanding.
[15] Pagan watchmen, or religionists, or even non-believers in the YHWH of restoration. Or even worse there are Jewish-Yisraelites, who stay in the one-house deception and are classified as watchmen asleep at the wheel, in full ignorance of YHWH's faithful working amongst Ephraim-Yisrael in these last days.
[16] Metaphor for gentiles.
[17] Those ignorant of two-house restoration cannot bark out the sounds of the times.
[18] The true and most fabulous latter-day move of YHWH in the world.
[19] Historically accepted yet misguided definitions of essential biblical terms such as "Jew" and "gentile" and "Ephraim."
[20] Temporal charismatic experiences.
[21] These false shepherds watch and yet are oblivious to Yisrael's bright future, as the two sticks/trees become one.
[22] Sometimes early departures from this age are to escape the evil ahead and prepare the saved for the **olam habah.**
[23] Eternal life.
[24] The topic now changes to the sons of Yisrael who refuse to repent and be restored.

valleys under the clefts of the rocks? 6 Among the smooth stones of the river is your portion; they are your lot: even to them have you poured a drink offering, you have offered a grain offering. Should I receive comfort in these works? 7 Upon a proud and high mountain have you set your bed: even there you went up to offer sacrifices. 8 Behind the doors also and the posts have you set up your remembrance: for you have gone up and uncovered yourself to another other than Me; you have enlarged your bed, and made a covenant with them also; you loved their bed where you saw their hand.[1] 9 And you went to the melech with ointment, and did increase your perfumes, and did send your messengers far off,[2] and did lower yourself even to Sheol. 10 You have wearied yourself in your many wanderings; yet you never said I give up and will stop. You have wasted your chayim with the guilt of your hands; therefore you were not grieved. 11 And of whom have you been afraid or feared, that you have lied, and have not remembered Me, nor taken it to your lev? Have not I held My shalom in the past, and you have not feared Me? 12 I will declare your tzedakah, and your works; for they shall not profit you. 13 When you cry for help, let your collection of idols deliver you; but the wind[3] shall carry them all away; vanity shall take them: but he that puts his trust in Me shall possess the land, and shall inherit My set-apart mountain;[4] 14 And shall say, Clear up, clear up, prepare the Way back, take away the stumblingblock out of the derech of My people.[5] 15 For this says the High and Exalted One that inhabits eternity, whose Name is Set-Apart; I live in the high and Set-Apart Place, with him that is of a contrite and humble ruach, to revive

the ruach of the humble, and to revive the lev of the contrite ones. 16 For I will not strive le-olam-va-ed, neither will I always be angry: for then their ruach would not survive before Me, even the beings that I have made. 17 For the iniquity of his covetousness was I angry, and smote him: I hid Myself, and was angry, and he went on backsliding in the halacha of his lev. 18 I have seen his halachot, and will heal him: I will lead him also, and restore comforts to him and to his mourners.[6] 19 I create the fruit of the lips;[7] Shalom, shalom to him that is far off,[8] and to him that is near,[9] says יהוה; and I will heal him.[10] 20 But the wicked are like the troubled sea, when it cannot rest, whose mayim casts up mud and dirt.[11] 21 There is no shalom, says My Elohim, to the wicked.[12]

58 Cry aloud, spare not, lift up your voice like a shofar, and show My people their transgression, and Beit Yaakov[13] their sins. 2 Yet they seek Me daily, and delight to know My halachot, as a nation that did tzedakah, and forsook not the ordinances of their Elohim: they ask from Me the ordinances of justice; they take delight in approaching their Elohim. 3 Why have we fasted, they say, and yet You do not see? Why have we afflicted our being, and You take no notice? See, in the day of your fast you do your own pleasure, while keeping your laborers working hard. 4 See, your fasts lead to strife and contention, and to hitting with violent blows: fasting on a day like today, will not make your voice to be heard on high. 5 Is this the kind of fast that I have chosen? A day for a man to mortify himself? Is the object to hang your

---

[1] Those in Yisrael who refused to be saved and restored.
[2] Sent away the prophets and swore allegiance to human kings.
[3] Of judgment.
[4] A sharp contrast between Nazarene Yisrael and deceived Yisrael.
[5] Restored Yisrael returns to Zion, while outcast adulterous Yisrael is leaving Zion.
[6] Only to those who desire restoration, since YHWH does not force Himself on anyone.
[7] Also known as praise.
[8] Ephraim-Yisrael.
[9] Jewish-Yisrael.
[10] YHWH's desire is to heal those backsliders from both houses, and bring them into His plan of full restoration, which is the healing of our nation.
[11] The wicked of Yisrael will remain wicked.
[12] There is shalom for both houses, but not for those Yisraelites who do not desire repentance.
[13] All 12 tribes.

YESHAYAHU - ISAIAH 58

head down like a reed, and to spread sackcloth and ashes under yourself? Will you call this a fast, an acceptable day to **יהוה**? 6 Rather is not this the fast that I have chosen? To loose the chains of wickedness, to untie the heavy burdens, and to let the oppressed go free, and to break off every yoke? 7 Is it not to distribute your lechem to the hungry, and to bring the poor that are cast out to your bayit? And when you see the naked, that you cover him; and that you fulfill your duties to your family?[1] 8 Then shall your light break forth as the morning, and your health shall spring forth speedily: and your tzedakah shall go before you; and the tiferet of **יהוה** shall be your reward. 9 Then shall you call, and **יהוה** shall answer; you shall cry, and He shall say, Hinayni. If you take away from your midst the yoke, the finger pointing, and the speaking of unrighteousness; 10 And if you extend your lev to the hungry, and satisfy the afflicted being; then shall your light rise in the darkness, and your darkness shall become as the noonday: 11 And **יהוה** shall guide you continually, and satisfy your being in drought, and make fat your bones: and you shall be like a watered garden, and like a spring of mayim, whose mayim fails not. 12 And they that shall be from among you shall build the old ruined places: you shall restore the foundations of many generations; and you shall be called, Gadar-Peretz,[2] The restorer of paths to live in.[3] 13 If you turn away your own foot from

the Shabbat, from doing your own pleasure on My set-apart day; and call the Shabbat a delight, the set-apart day of **יהוה**, honorable; and shall honor Him, not doing your own halachot, nor finding your own pleasure, nor speaking your own words:[4] 14 Then shall you delight yourself in **יהוה**;[5] and I will cause you to ride upon the high places of the earth, and feed you with the heritage of Yaakov your abba:[6] for the mouth of **יהוה**[7] has spoken it.

59 See, **יהוה**'s Hand is not shortened, that it cannot save;[8] neither His ear heavy, that it cannot shema: 2 But your iniquities have brought separation between you and Your Elohim, and your sins have hid His face from you, that He will not shema.[9] 3 For your hands are defiled with dom, and your fingers with iniquity; your lips have spoken lies, your tongue has muttered perverseness. 4 None calls for mishpat, nor any pleads for emet: they trust in vanity, and speak lies; they conceive mischief, and bring forth iniquity. 5 They hatch snakes' eggs, and weave the spider's web: He that eats of their eggs shall die, and when one is crushed a viper breaks out. 6 Their webs shall not become garments, neither shall they cover themselves with their works: their works are works of iniquity, and acts of violence are in their hands. 7 Their feet run to do evil, and they make haste to shed innocent dom: their thoughts are thoughts of iniquity; ruin and

---

[1] Fasting is not a day to improve ones self, or focus inward or lose weight. As Yisrael, fasting is a day to seek YHWH's love and concern towards others. In Yisrael it is a day to build up others less fortunate in the family of faith.
[2] Restorer of the Breach.
[3] If as a returning Yisraelite you learn the real purposes of the fast, and the true heart of the fast, and you are willing to lay aside the mere rote of habit, then YHWH will do the following: He will raise up others around you (even though you started out alone) to restore all the ruined things that have become desolate in our national heritage. He will provide you with a team of faithful co-laborers. He will give you the privilege of restoring the foundations of many lost generations, as you bring both houses to truth. He will make your name known and honored amongst Yisrael, as one who is a **Gadar Peretz**. He will make you a magnet that waters the lives of the hungry and the bound Yisraelites, still wandering the pagan cultures of the nations, by letting many find you as a restorer of paths to live in.

[4] Similar to the attitude a Renewed Covenant Yisraelite is called to have towards the fast days. The Shabbat is a time for YHWH alone, and for His people to serve them and not yourself. It is a day to focus, concentrate and meditate only on His Words and not on ours.
[5] You will show forth your true motive.
[6] All Yisraelites become Yisrael by Yahshua's dom, but still need to be fed "Jacob's Food" and "Hebraic heritage." That is reciprocal, meaning the hungrier you and I are for obedience and using the fast and Shabbat days for Him, the more kosher spiritual food we will be fed.
[7] Or Yahshua Himself.
[8] His "Hand" is a metaphor for Yahshua.
[9] What follows is a detailed list of the sins of both houses. As YHWH says here, it is not a matter of His inability or lack of desire to redeem Yisrael, but their long list of sins from which they desire no deliverance. This despite the fact that both Yisrael and YHWH know the sins backwards and forwards. The list follows in the upcoming verses.

destruction are in their paths. 8 The halacha of shalom they know not; and there is no mishpat in their goings: they have made for themselves crooked paths: whoever goes in it shall not know shalom. 9 Therefore is mishpat far from us, neither does justice overtake us: we wait for light, but see darkness; for brightness, but we walk in darkness. 10 We grope for the wall like a blind man, and we grope as if we had no eyes: we stumble at noonday as if it were the night; we are in desolate places as dead men. 11 We roar like bears, and mourn heavy like doves: we look for mishpat, but there is none; for Yahshua,[1] but it is far off from us. 12 For our transgressions are multiplied before You, and our sins testify against us: for our transgressions are with us; and as for our iniquities, we know them; 13 In transgressing and lying against יהוה, and departing away from our Elohim, speaking oppression and revolt, conceiving and uttering from the lev words of falsehood. 14 And mishpat is turned away, and justice stands far off: for emet is fallen in the street, and equity cannot enter. 15 Yes, emet fails; and he that departs from evil makes himself a prey: and יהוה saw it, and it displeased Him that there was no mishpat. 16 And He saw[2] that there was no Man, and wondered that there was no intercessor: therefore His Arm[3] brought Yahshua[4] to Him;[5] and His Tzedakah, it upheld Him.[6] 17 For He put on tzedakah as a breastplate, and a helmet of salvation upon His head, and He put on the garments of vengeance for clothing, and was clad with zeal as a cloke.[7] 18 According to their

deeds, accordingly He will repay,[8] wrath to His adversaries, recompense to His enemies; to the coastlands He will repay recompense. 19 So shall they fear the Name of יהוה from the west, and His tiferet from the rising of the sun.[9] When the enemy[10] shall come in like a river, the Ruach HaKodesh of יהוה shall lift up a standard against him to humble him.[11] 20 And the Redeemer shall come to Tzion, and to them that make teshuvah from transgression in Yaakov, says יהוה.[12] [13] 21 As for Me, this is My covenant with them, says יהוה; My Ruach that is upon You, and My words which I have put in Your mouth, shall not depart out of Your mouth, nor out of the mouth of Your zera, nor out of the mouth of Your zera's zera, says יה, from now on and le-olam-va-ed.[14] [15]

60 Arise, shine; for Your Light has come, and the tiferet of יהוה has risen upon you.[16] 2 For, see, the darkness shall cover the earth, and gross darkness the nations:[17] but יהוה shall arise upon you, and His tiferet shall be seen upon you.

---

[1] Hebrew: **Leyeshua.**
[2] Abba-YHWH.
[3] The deliverance and redeeming character of YHWH.
[4] Hebrew: **Vetosha.**
[5] An amazing prophecy; Abba YHWH looked for a righteous spotless and blameless Kohen Hagadol - High Priest in Yisrael, and found none, so He begat Yahshua into the world, even as in eternity past He brought forth His Son as the Word of YHWH.
[6] Upheld or justified His search.
[7] Yahshua's garments and dress as our High Priest, not a Roman soldier, for Isaiah never knew what a Roman solider looked like, since he lived some 600 years before Rome even existed. Moreover, Rav Shaul quotes this in Ephesians 6:13-17, and tells Yisraelites in Ephesus to dress just like their

Savior Yahshua. The Roman soldier analogy is a myth, produced by wayward sheep, darkened in their understanding.
[8] Yahshua, Yisrael's Guardian-**Metatron,** will repay all her enemies, both within and without the nation.
[9] Because of the work of Yahshua, YHWH's Name will be honored around the globe, as He said He would do in John 17.
[10] s.a.tan is the enemy of YHWH's Name being restored.
[11] YHWH's Spirit or power will clear the way for the restoration of all things, including the two houses, the Name of the Father, and Moshiach Yahshua's dom atonement.
[12] Moshiach Yahshua comes to all Yisrael, but specifically to those willing to turn from sin in Yisrael. This test ought to be enough for people to see that being Jacob is not the key to salvation, but turning from sin through the Redeemer to become redeemed, remnant Yisrael, is the key.
[13] Quoted in Romans 11 as applying to both houses of the Olive Tree, both to the cultivated and non-cultivated olive branches or Notsrim.
[14] Abba YHWH promises that part of this Renewed Covenant with those who turn from sin in Yisrael, will be to put His Ruach or Spirit upon them, even as He has done upon Yahshua without measure. Here Yahshua is said to have many spiritual children, all born again through the Spirit, associated with the Renewed Covenant, and not the will of man.
[15] Moshiah and His Yisraelite brethren are to carry YHWH's eternal words forever.
[16] Moshiach Yahshua our High Priest is the tiferet or beauty of YHWH.
[17] Ephraim.

3 *And the nations shall come to Your Light,[1] and melechim to the brightness of Your rising.[2] 4 Lift up your eyes all around, and see: all they gather themselves together,[3] they come to You: Your sons shall come from far,[4] and Your daughters shall be nursed at Your side. 5 Then You shall see, and flow together, and Your lev shall throb, and be enlarged; because the abundance of the sea[5] shall be turned to You, the wealth of the nations shall come to You. 6 The multitude of camels shall cover Your land, the dromedaries of Midyan and Ephah; all those from Sheva shall come: they shall bring gold and incense; and they shall proclaim the tehilot of* יהוה. *7 All the flocks of Kedar shall be gathered together to You, the rams of Nevayoth shall serve You: they shall come up with acceptance upon My altar, and I will bring splendor to the Bayit of My tiferet.[6] 8 Who are these that fly as a cloud, and as the yonahs[7] to their windows?[8] 9 Because the coastlands[9] shall wait for Me, and the ships of Tarshish[10] first, to bring Your sons from far, their silver and their gold with them, to the Name of* יהוה *Your Elohim, and to the Set-Apart One of Yisrael, because He has lifted you up.[11] 10 And the sons of foreigners shall build up Your walls, and their melechim shall serve You: for in My wrath I smote You,[12] but in My favor have I had rachamim on You.[13]*

11 *Therefore your gates shall be open continually; they shall not be shut day or night[14] that men may bring to you the wealth of the nations, and that their melechim may be brought. 12 For the nation and malchut that will not serve You shall perish; yes, those nations shall be utterly wasted. 13 The tiferet of Levanon shall come to you, the cypress eytz, the pine eytz, and the box together, to beautify the place of My Set-Apart Place; and I will remake the place of My feet with tiferet.[15] 14 The sons also of them that afflicted You shall come bowing to You; and all they that despised You shall bow themselves down at the soles of Your feet; and they shall call You, The city of* יהוה, *The Tzion of the Set-Apart One of Yisrael.[16] 15 Whereas You have been forsaken and hated, so that no man went through You, I will make you an Eternal Excellency,[17] a simcha of many generations.[18] 16 You shall also suck the milk of the nations, and shall suck the breasts of melechim: and you shall know that I* יהוה *am Your Savior and Your Redeemer, the Mighty One of Yaakov.[19] 17 For brass I will bring gold, and for iron I will bring silver, and for wood brass, and for stones iron: I will also make your officers shalom, and your leaders tzedakah. 18 Hamas[20] shall no more be heard in your land,[21] nor ruin and destruction within your borders; but you shall call your walls Yahshua, and your gates Tehilla. 19 The sun shall be no more your light by day;*

---

[1] Ephraim.
[2] Your advent.
[3] Yisrael will be gathered.
[4] Ephraim.
[5] A metaphor found in Genesis and elsewhere, referring to the "sand of the sea," or the physical multitudes of scattered and exiled Yisrael.
[6] Millennial Temple.
[7] The biblical and even modern symbol (doves) of wayward Ephraim, running to Yahshua to receive open windows of vision.
[8] Windows are symbolic of vision and understanding.
[9] All the earth.
[10] Spain/Europe.
[11] The returning exiles will come to Moshiach, because Abba has lifted Him up; and they will come to the true Name of YHWH that the Moshiach proclaims.
[12] At Golgotha.
[13] All nations and kings will serve Yahshua and the Ephraimites and other biological foreigners will rebuild the nation and the walls of the nation, in their return to join redeemed Judah.

[14] Now through the lifted up Suffering Servant we have access to Abba-YHWH day and night in any place Yisrael finds themselves.
[15] The Millennial Beit HaMikdash will have all the former Beit HaMikdash's beauty restored. Jerusalem will also be renewed as the place of His footstool.
[16] In the atid lavoh all the enemies of Yisrael and of Moshiach Yahshua, will come to be fully subjected with a rod of iron. Yahshua Himself will be known as the safe and secure city of YHWH's refuge, along with the city of Jerusalem.
[17] Yahshua.
[18] Now to go to YHWH, all men have to go through Yahshua according to John 14:6. This Scripture can also apply to Yisrael, as without being part of Yisrael, or going through her and her King, one remains outside the covenant.
[19] Through Moshiach, all 12 tribes will know that YHWH has visited them with salvation and redemption.
[20] The Hebrew word for violence.
[21] No more Palestinian squatters.

neither for brightness shall the moon give light to you: but יהוה shall be to you an everlasting Light, and Your Elohim Your tiferet. [1] 20 Your sun shall no more go down; neither shall your moon withdraw itself: for יהוה shall be Your everlasting Light, and the days of your mourning shall be ended. [2] 21 Your people also shall be all tzadik: they shall inherit the land le-olam-va-ed, the Branch-Netzer [3] of My planting, the work of My hands, that I may be lifted up. [4] 22 A little one shall become a thousand, and a small one a strong nation: I יהוה will quicken them in their time. [5]

61 The Ruach of the Master יהוה is upon Me; because יהוה has anointed Me to preach the besorah [6] to the meek; He has sent Me to bind up the brokenhearted, to proclaim liberty to the exiles, [7] recovery of sight to the blind [8] and the opening of the prison to them that are bound; [9] 2 To proclaim the acceptable year of יהוה, and the day of vengeance of Our Elohim; to comfort all that mourn; [10] 3 To appoint to them that mourn in Tzion, to give to them tiferet for ashes, the oil of simcha for mourning, the garment of hallel for the ruach of heaviness; that they might be called eytzim of tzedakah, [11] the planting of יהוה, that He might be lifted up. 4 And they shall rebuild the old ruins, they shall raise up the former desolations, and they shall repair the ruined cities, the desolations of many generations. [12] 5 And foreigners shall stand and feed your flocks, [13] and the sons of the alien shall be your plowmen and your vinedressers. [14] 6 But you shall be named the kohanim of יהוה: [15] men shall call you the avadim of our Elohim: you shall overcome the strength of the nations, [16] and in their tiferet [17] shall you boast yourselves. 7 For your shame you shall have a double portion of inheritance; [18] and you shall simcha in their portion: therefore in their land they shall possess the double portion: and everlasting simcha shall be theirs. [19] 8 For I יהוה love mishpat, I hate robbery for burnt offerings; and I will direct their work in emet, and I will make an Everlasting Covenant with them. [20] 9 And their zera shall be known among the nations, and their offspring among the peoples: all that see them shall acknowledge them, that they are the zera that יהוה has blessed. [21] 10 I will greatly simcha in יהוה, my being shall be full of simcha in My Elohim; for He has clothed me with the garments of Yahshua, [22] He has covered me with the robe of Tzedakah, as a bridegroom decks himself with ornaments, and as a bride adorns herself with her jewels. [23] 11 For as the earth brings forth her bud, and as the garden causes the things that are sown in it to spring forth; so the Master יהוה will

---

[1] The New Jerusalem enters eternity.
[2] The mourning of exile will be over in the restoration of the nation.
[3] Branch. The Hebrew word **Netzer**, from where comes the term **Netsarim** or Nazarenes, the first century name of the redeemed followers of Moshiach. In this verse Yahshua is the Hand of YHWH, or the Arm of redemption, planting branches or **Netsarim**, who are said to be the work of His hand.
[4] A true millennial covenant promise.
[5] The promise of physical multiplicity will be realized, understood, and brought to pass in the last days of the age. When the exile is over, even just the remnant of Yaakov will still be the largest nation on the planet.
[6] Gospel.
[7] Of Yisrael.
[8] In Isaiah 61:1 the Masoretic does not contain the phrase "recovery of sight to the blind." Yet Luke 4:18 does, as does the LXX. Obviously Yahshua is being quoted in Luke 4:18, as He quotes from the LXX's Isaiah scroll.
[9] Prisoners of exile from both houses.
[10] Over sin and exile.
[11] Yisraelites as per Mark 8.

[12] Those who receive Moshiach Yahshua, enter His ministry of the restoration of all things.
[13] Yisrael will also have teachers or rabbis to feed the sheep who are not Jewish but are Yisrael.
[14] All those not born Yisrael will all feed at and in the same pen.
[15] This came to pass as all redeemed Yisraelites became priests as found in Revelation 1:6.
[16] Ephraim.
[17] Their esteem is Yahshua; and so will Judah's be as well.
[18] "Ephraim" means "double fruit," or "double portion." Strong's H # 669. Ephraim shall have a double portion.
[19] Ephraim will finally live out the meaning of his namesake, as he reenters the land at the end of the age, to inherit a double portion of land and other kingdom benefits.
[20] With the remnant of Tzion.
[21] The blessed seed of redeemed Yaakov.
[22] Hebrew: **Yesha.**
[23] Clothed with Yahshua.

cause tzedakah and hallel to spring forth before all the nations.[1]

62 For Tzion's sake will I not hold My shalom, and for Yahrushalayim's sake I will not rest, until the tzedakah of it goes forth as brightness, and the Yahshua of it as a lamp that burns.[2] 2 And the nations[3] shall see Your tzedakah,[4] and all melechim Your tiferet:[5] and you shall be called by a new name, which the mouth of יהוה shall name. 3 You shall also be a keter of tiferet in the hand of יהוה, and a royal diadem in the hand of Your Elohim.[6] 4 You shall no more be termed: Uzuvah; Forsaken; neither shall your land any more be termed Desolate: but you shall be called: Hephzi-Vah-Delight In Her, and your land Beulah-Married: for יהוה delights in you, and your land shall be married.[7] 5 For as a young man marries a virgin, so shall Your sons marry you:[8] and as the bridegroom has simcha over the bride, so shall Your Elohim simcha over you.[9] 6 I have set watchmen[10] upon Your walls, O Yahrushalayim, which shall never hold their shalom day or night: you that make mention of יהוה, keep not silent, 7 And give Him no rest, until He establishes, and makes Yahrushalayim a hallel in the earth. [11]

8 יהוה has sworn by His Right Hand, and by the Arm of His strength,[12] Surely I will no more give your grain to be food for your enemies; and the sons of the Ger shall not drink your wine, that for which you have labored:[13] 9 But they that have gathered it shall eat it, and hallel יהוה; and they that

have brought it together shall drink it in the places of My set-apart courts.[14] 10 Go through, go through the gates; prepare the derech of the people;[15] build up, build up the highway;[16] get rid of the stones;[17] lift up a banner for the nations.[18] 11 See, יהוה has proclaimed to the ends of the olam,[19] Say to the daughter of Tzion, See, Your Yahshua[20] comes; see, His reward is with Him, and His work before Him.[21] 12 And they shall call them, The set-apart people,[22] The redeemed of יהוה: and you shall be called, Sought Out, A city not forsaken.[23]

63 Who is this that comes from Edom, with dyed garments from Bozrah? This that is with tiferet in His apparel, traveling in the greatness of His strength? It is I that speak in tzedakah, mighty to save.[24] 2 Why are you red in Your apparel, and Your garments like him that tramples in the winepress? 3 I have trampled the winepress alone; and from the nations there was none with Me: for I will trample them in My anger, and trample them in My fury; and their dom shall be sprinkled upon My garments, and I will stain all My garments.[25] 4 For the day of vengeance is in My lev,[26] and the year of My redeemed has come.[27] 5 And I looked, and there was none to help; and I wondered that there was

---

[1] From redeemed remnant Yisrael to all nations.
[2] YHWH's plan and pledge.
[3] Ephraim in a latter-day context.
[4] Yahshua our YHWH-Tzidkaynu.
[5] Moshiach.
[6] All 12 tribes.
[7] Married to Yisrael. The land will be restored to its tenants and its Owner, Yahshua and His bride Yisrael.
[8] In the **atid lavoh,** the sons of Yisrael will be remarried or restored to all their land, that YHWH gave the patriarchs.
[9] The joy and intimacy of restoration.
[10] Hebrew: **Shomerim,** from where comes Shomron capital of Ephraim. These watchmen are latter-day restored Ephraimites who watch over both houses for tov.
[11] Keep asking for the kingdom until it actually comes.
[12] Moshiach Yahshua.
[13] In the kingdom Yisrael will have no lack.

[14] Yisrael will be fully provided for and protected.
[15] Jewish-Yisrael.
[16] Restore the road back to YHWH, through the gates of Tzion.
[17] In context "heathen obstacles."
[18] Ephraim Yisrael.
[19] Calling both houses home.
[20] Hebrew: **Yeshecha.**
[21] Yahshua has come. His work was done. His reward is still with Him alone and available to any who desire to join the commonwealth by His dom. Notice how the action of saving is actually realized in the personification of that loving action in Yahshua of Nazareth.
[22] Yisrael.
[23] Jerusalem.
[24] YHWH speaks to an anonymous Edomite spectator. YHWH is the Warrior coming against Edom, holding a conversation with this person.
[25] YHWH will destroy Edom and Iraq just before the millennium. He challenges the Edomite in comparing the innocent Yisraelite dom shed on their garment, to the guilt-laden Edomite dom on YHWH's garment.
[26] Against Edom.
[27] For Yisrael. That is why the Day of YHWH (or Yom YHWH) is both great and terrible. Terrible for YHWH's enemies, and great for YHWH's redeemed.

none to uphold: therefore My own Arm brought Yahshua to Me;[1] and in My fury, it upheld Me.[2] 6 *And I will trample down the nations in My anger, and make them drunk in My fury, and I will bring down their strength to the earth.* 7 I will mention the loving chesed of **יהוה**, and the tehilot of **יהוה** , according to all that **יהוה** has bestowed on us, and the great tov toward Beit Yisrael,[3] which He has bestowed on them according to His many rachamim, and according to the multitude of His loving chesed. 8 For He said, *Surely they are Ami-My People, children that will not lie: so He became their Savior.*[4] 9 In all their affliction He was afflicted,[5] and the Malach of His Presence saved them: in His ahava and in His pity He redeemed them;[6] and He lifted them, and carried them all the days of old.[7] 10 But they rebelled, and grieved His Set-Apart Ruach: therefore He became their enemy, and He fought against them. 11 Then He remembered the days of old, Moshe, and His people, saying, Where is He that brought them up out of the sea with the shepherd of His flock? Where is He that put His Set-Apart Ruach within him? 12 That led them by the right hand of Moshe with His tiferet arm,[8] dividing the mayim before them, to make Himself an everlasting Name?[9] 13 That led them through the deep, and as a horse in the wilderness, that they should not stumble? 14 As a beast goes down into the valley, and the Ruach of **יהוה** causes him to rest: so did You lead Your people, to make for Yourself a wonderful Name. 15 Look down from the shamayim, and see from the home of Your Set-Apart Dwelling of tiferet:

where is Your zeal and Your strength, the sounding of Your inward parts and of Your cheseds toward me? Are they being withheld?[10] 16 Doubtless You are our Abba, though Avraham be ignorant of us, and Yisrael acknowledge us not: you, O **יהוה**, are Our Abba, Our Redeemer; Your Name is from everlasting. 17 O **יהוה**, why have You made us go astray from Your halachot, and hardened our lev from Your fear?[11] Return for Your avadim's sake, the tribes of Your inheritance.[12] [13] 18 Your set-apart nation has possessed the land but only for a little while: our adversaries have trampled down Your Set-Apart Place. 19 We are Yours: You never ruled over them; they were not called by Your Name.[14]

64 Oh that You would tear open the shamayim, that You would come down, that the mountains would shake at Your presence, 2 As when the melting fire burns, the fire causes the mayim to boil, to make Your Name known to Your adversaries, that the nations may tremble at Your presence! 3 When You did awesome things that we did not look for, You came down, and the mountains flowed down at Your presence. 4 For since the beginning of the olam hazeh men have not heard, nor perceived by the ear, neither has the eye seen, O Elohim, beside You,[15] what He has prepared[16] for him that waits for Him.[17] [18] 5 You shall meet with him that has simcha and works tzedakah, who remembers You and Your halachot: see, You were angry; when we sinned in those things for a long

---

[1] Hebrew: **Vetosha.**
[2] See notes on Isaiah 59:16.
[3] All 12 tribes.
[4] Hebrew: **Le Moshiyah.**
[5] Throughout Yisrael's history, YHWH felt the ongoing pain of His nation.
[6] The only Messenger that can redeem or bring Yisrael back to YHWH is Yahshua, who was surely the Malach-YHWH in the wilderness wanderings, and in many other places in Scripture as well.
[7] He does not change and neither does His people. He redeems today, in the same way He did back then.
[8] Yahshua is the right Arm of YHWH.
[9] His Name will be forever proclaimed by a remnant nation.

[10] Yisrael wandered during their 40 years in the wilderness.
[11] Blaming YHWH and His leaders, is a favorite Yisraelite pastime.
[12] Yisrael trying to lay guilt trip on the Father, as if their backslidings were His fault.
[13] Yahshua/YHWH's return will be to gather the tribes as **echad.**
[14] The lament of Yisrael in distress.
[15] Besides Elohim Yahshua.
[16] Abba-YHWH prepared the work, and only Yahshua knew the plan of redemption ahead of time.
[17] That wait for His return to Zion.
[18] First Corinthians 2:9 identifies the reason for the wait, which is to have His love revealed to us as remnant Yisrael.

time, and now, should we be saved?[1] 6 But we are all as an unclean thing, and all our tzedakah are as filthy rags;[2] and we all do fade as a leaf; and our iniquities, like the wind, have taken us away.[3] 7 And there is none that calls upon Your Name,[4] who stirs himself to take hold of You: for You have hidden Your face from us, and have consumed us, because of our iniquities. 8 But now, O יהוה, You are our Abba; we are the clay, and You our Potter; and we all are the work of Your hand. 9 Be not very angry, O יהוה, neither remember iniquity le-olam-va-ed: see, look, we beg You, we are all Your nation. 10 Your set-apart cities are a wilderness; Tzion is a wilderness, Yahrushalayim a ruin. 11 Our set-apart and beautiful Bayit, where our ahvot gave You hallel, is burned up with fire: and all our pleasant things are laid in ruin. 12 Will You restrain Yourself in light of all these things, O יהוה ? Will You hold Your response from us, and afflict us very heavily?

65 I am sought by them that asked not for Me;[5] I am found by those that did not seek Me:[6] I said, Hinayni, Hinayni, to a nation that was not called by My Name.[7] [8] 2 I have spread out My hands all the day to a rebellious people,[9] who walk in a halacha that was not tov, after their own thoughts; 3 A people that provokes Me to anger continually to My face; that sacrifices in gardens, and burns incense upon altars of brick; [10] 4 Who remain among the graves, and lodge in the monuments, which eat swine's flesh, and the broth of unclean meat is in their vessels; 5 Who say, Stand by yourself, come not near me; for I am more tzadik than you. These people are a smoke in My nose, a fire that burns all the day. 6 See, it is written before Me: I will not keep silent, but will repay, even recompense into their bosom, 7 Your iniquities, and the iniquities of your ahvot together, says יהוה , who have burned incense upon the mountains, and blasphemed Me upon the hills: therefore will I measure their former work and send it back into their bosom. 8 This says יהוה, As the new wine is found in the cluster, and one says, Destroy it not; for a bracha is in it: so will I do for My avadim's sakes, that I may not destroy them all.[11] 9 And I will bring forth a zera out of Yaakov, and out of Yahudah an heir of My mountains: and My chosen ones shall inherit it, and My avadim shall live there.[12] 10 And Sharon shall be for a fold of flocks, and the Valley of Achor a place for the herds to lie down in, for My people that have sought Me.[13] 11 But you are they that forsake יהוה,[14] that forget My set-apart mountain,[15] that prepare a table for G-d,[16] [17] and that furnish the drink

---

[1] Yisrael has a hard time grasping the reality of such a great salvation and allowing it to penetrate their eyes and ears, especially after such a darkened past.
[2] All Yisrael and all of mankind are sinful before YHWH. No one is without sin and thus no one can be cleansed by Torah alone, but is in need of an actual acceptable dom atonement.
[3] Away from YHWH's presence and His eternal home for us.
[4] Part of sinful man's behavior manifests in rebellion by refusing to call Him Abba-YHWH, whether by choice or mere ignorance.
[5] Ephraim.
[6] Ephraim.
[7] Ephraim was not called by His Name, as was Yahudah, with the poetic short form Yah-udah.
[8] This is quoted in Romans 10:20-21, as a reference to non-Jewish-Yisrael, contrasting verse 20 with verse 21, which refers to identifiable Jewish-Yisrael, who wanted no part of teshuvah, though they did want YHWH without teshuvah.
[9] Jewish-Yisrael.

---

[10] Even the altars were not according to the pattern of Torah.
[11] Many were and are being destroyed for their lack of desire to seek and know YHWH. But unlike the nations, not all Yisrael will be destroyed.
[12] A redeemed remnant from Judah will enter the kingdom as well.
[13] From both houses.
[14] The majority of both houses.
[15] Things of Zion.
[16] G-d's Table, or the "lord's table," from the Hebrew letters gimel, daled.
[17] Name of a pagan deity of strength or "troop strength." Yisraelites would forsake YHWH to worship what they thought was real carnal power. The Hebrew is spelled gimel, daled, with masoretic vowel pointing making it sound like God, not Gad, in Hebrew. This is close enough of a condemnation of using Gd or G-d in place of YHWH to be too close for comfort, and as such it is best and safer to stay away from worshiping a generic Gd, especially in light of clarion calls that demand that as Yisrael, we call on YHWH and His true Name alone. For more details see: **No G-d For Yisraelites** at: http://yourarmstoisrael.org/Editorials/?page=NO_GOD_FOR_ISRAELITES.

offering to Mani. [1] 12 *Therefore will I number you to the sword, and you shall all bow down to the slaughter: because when I called, you did not answer; when I spoke, you did not shema; but did evil before My eyes, and chose that in which I did not delight.* 13 Therefore this says the Master **יהוה**, *See, My avadim shall eat, but you shall be hungry: see, My avadim shall drink, but you shall be thirsty: see, My avadim shall simcha, but you shall be ashamed:* [2] 14 *See, My avadim shall shir for simcha of lev, but you shall cry for sorrow of lev, and shall wail for breaking of ruach.* 15 *And you shall leave your name for a curse to My chosen: for the Master* **יהוה** *shall slay you, and call His avadim by another name:* [3] 16 *That he who blesses himself in the earth shall bless himself in the Elohim of emet; and he that swears in the earth shall swear by the Elohim of emet; because the former troubles are forgotten, and because they are hidden from My eyes.* 17 *For, see, I create a renewed shamayim and a renewed earth: and the former shall not be remembered, nor come into mind.* [4] 18 *But gilah and simcha le-olam-va-ed in that which I recreate: for, see, I recreate Yahrushalayim for rejoicing, and her people for simcha.* [5] 19 *And I will simcha in Yahrushalayim, and simcha in Ami-My People: and the voice of weeping shall be no more be heard in her, nor the voice of crying.* [6] 20 *There shall be no more there an infant of just a few days, nor an old man that has not filled his days: for the child shall die a hundred years old; but the sinner*

being a hundred years old shall be cursed.[7] 21 *And they shall build bayits, and inhabit them; and they shall plant vineyards, and eat the fruit of them.* 22 *They shall not build, and another inhabit; they shall not plant, and another eat: for as the days of an eytz so are the days of My people, and My chosen people shall outlive the work of their hands.* 23 *They shall not labor in vain, nor conceive children for trouble; for they are the zera of the blessed of* **יהוה**, *and their offspring remains with them.* 24 *And it shall come to pass, that before they call, I will answer; and while they are yet speaking, I will shema.*[8] 25 *The wolf and the lamb shall feed together, and the lion shall eat straw like the ox: and dust shall be the serpent's food. They shall not hurt nor destroy in My entire set-apart mountain, says* **יהוה**.[9]

66 This says **יהוה**, *The shamayim are My throne, and the earth is My footstool: where is the Bayit that you will build for Me? And where is the place of My rest?* 2 *For all those things have My hands made, and all those things that have been, says* **יהוה**: *but to this man will I look, even to him that is poor and of a contrite ruach, and who trembles at My word.* 3 *He that kills an ox is as if he slew a man; he that sacrifices a lamb, as if he cut off a dog's neck; he that offers a grain offering, as if he offered pig's dom; he that burns incense, as if he blessed an idol. Yes, they have chosen their own halachot, and their beings delight in their own abominations.*[10] 4 *I also will choose their delusions, and will bring their fears upon them; because when I called, no one did answer; when I spoke, they did not shema: but they did evil before My eyes, and chose that in which I did not delight.*

---

[1] Luck. A deity of good fortune or luck, which has no place in the life of a believer. The Hebrew is **mem, nun, yud.** Many Yisraelites used to worship or trust in "luck," instead of YHWH, and still do today.
[2] Worshippers of G-d or Luck with pagan baggage cannot be Yisraelites, if they refuse to let go of those things that are clearly wrong as outlined in Scripture. Of course, YHWH gives us room to and time to grow into this truth. But Gd worshippers will suffer lack, while Yahwists will walk and move in abundance. That cannot be clearer in this verse.
[3] Branches or **Netsarim**; Redeemed Yisrael became **Netsarim**, or remnant Yisrael.
[4] As vividly detailed in Revelation 21 and 22.
[5] That is the plan. To renew Yisrael and the land; not to build new pagan Sunday institutions.
[6] Death will be conquered in victory in the **atid lavoh** and the **olam habah**.
[7] Meaning the subjected heathen.
[8] For Renewed Covenant Yisrael, petitions will be answered even before they are uttered.
[9] The Garden restored. Animals dwell in safety, unafraid of predators, as s.a.tan is permanently subdued.
[10] Meaning whatever they do at the point that the **atid lavoh** starts, it will not matter even if they have a sudden rush and urge to do right. It will be too late.

5 *Shema the word of* יהוה *, you that tremble at His word; your brothers that hated you, that cast you out for My Name's sake, said, Let* יהוה *be lifted up: but He shall appear to your simcha, and they shall be ashamed.*[1] 6 *A voice of noise from the city, a voice from the Beit HaMikdash,*[2] *the voice of* יהוה *that repays His enemies.* 7 *Before she travailed, she brought forth; before her pain came, she was delivered of a Male-Child.* 8 *Who has heard such a thing? Who has seen such things? Shall the earth be made to bring forth in one day? Or shall a nation be born at once?*[3] *For as soon as Tzion travailed,*[4] *she brought forth her children.*[5] 9 *Shall I bring to the birth, and not cause to bring forth? Says* יהוה*: shall I cause to bring forth, and shut the womb? Says Your Elohim.*[6] 10 *Rejoice with Yahrushalayim, and have gilah with her, all you that love her: simcha greatly with her, all you that mourn for her:*[7] 11 *That you may suck, and be satisfied with the breasts of her comforts; that you may drink deeply, and be delighted with the abundance of her tiferet.*[8] 12 *For this says* יהוה*, See, I will extend shalom to her like a river, and the tiferet of the nations like a flowing river: then shall you feed, you shall be carried upon her sides, and be bounced upon her knees.*[9] 13 *As one whom his ima comforts, so will I comfort you; and you shall be comforted in Yahrushalayim.*[10] 14 *And when you see this, your lev shall simcha, and your bones shall flourish like tender grass: and the Hand of* יהוה[11] *shall be known towards His avadim, but His displeasure toward His enemies.* 15 *For, see,* יהוה *will come with fire, and with His mirkavot like a whirlwind, to render His anger with fury, and His rebuke with flames of fire.*[12] 16 *For by fire and by His sword will* יהוה *plead with all flesh: and the slain of* יהוה *shall be many.* 17 *They that set themselves apart, and purify themselves in the gardens one behind another with an eytz in the midst, eating pigs' flesh, and the abomination, and the mouse, shall be taken away together, says* יהוה *.* 18 *For I knowing their works and their thoughts: shall come, and I will gather all nations and tongues; and they shall come, and see My tiferet.*[13] 19 *And I will put a sign on them, and I will send some of them as survivors to the nations,*[14] *to Tarshish, Pul, and Lud, that draw the bow, to Tuval, and Yavan, to the coastlands far off, that have not heard of My fame, neither have seen My tiferet; and they shall declare My tiferet among the nations.* 20 *And they shall bring all your brothers for an offering to* יהוה *out of all nations upon horses, and on mirkavot, and on litters, and upon wagons, and upon swift beasts, to My set-apart mountain Yahrushalayim, says* יהוה*, as the children of Yisrael bring an offering in a clean vessel into the Bayit of* יהוה*.*[15] [16] 21 *And I will also take from among them kohanim and Leviim, says* יהוה*.*[17] 22 *For as the renewed shamayim and the renewed earth, which I*

---

[1] Those from Yisrael who mock the remnant faithful Torah-keepers in Yahshua, will be ashamed and destroyed in the day when all YHWH's right-rulings kick in.

[2] Restored millennial Temple.

[3] The day Moshiach returns, and in a limited sense May 1948, when Judah returned in part and in unemunah.

[4] Entered the Great Tribulation.

[5] Both houses will manifest their remnant children throughout the Great Tribulation, and also the 144,000 will be sealed from all 12 tribes, and as such as soon as the travail begins, Zion will bring forth.

[6] YHWH intends to finish the restoration He started in these last days, far more fully during the Day of YHWH, or the Great Tribulation.

[7] If you mourned for her in times past, you are now to rejoice with her, for both her houses are returning in righteousness.

[8] Her kingdom esteem will feed and fill the nations.

[9] All the redeemed shall dance with her and be playful in her joy.

[10] Both houses will be comforted in Jerusalem.

[11] Yahshua.

[12] On the unredeemed.

[13] The great regathering of all of remnant Yisrael called in Hebrew the **kevutz galyut**, or "regathering of the exiles," is a term used throughout the teachings of Yahshua, to signify the gathering of Yisrael at the end of the age, as opposed to the pagan doctrine of the rapture.

[14] To declare a final chance at kingdom honor and life.

[15] This could be reference to a special group of **shlichim** (messengers), or even a direct reference to the 144,000, who will call all Yisrael home during the final ingathering during the Great Tribulation.

[16] Their mission is to cleanse Yisrael through the Tov News and return them safely to Jerusalem for the millennial kingdom, as they are presented to YHWH, as cleansed vessels for His millennial service.

[17] From the 144,000 marked and the others returning with them, as YHWH knows who are the **kohanim**, to be restored for Temple service.

will make, shall remain before Me, says **יהוה**, so shall Your zera and Your name remain.[1] 23 And it shall come to pass, that from one rosh chodesh to another, and from one Shabbat to another, all flesh[2] shall come to worship before Me,[3] says **יהוה**.[4]

24 And they shall go forth, and look upon the corpses of the men that have transgressed against Me:[5] for their worm shall not die,[6] neither shall their fire be quenched;[7] and they shall be repulsive to all flesh.

---

[1] Remnant Yisrael will live forever, just like Moshiach promised.
[2] All of humanity.
[3] Facing west.
[4] All humanity will keep the feasts, the Shabbat, and the new moons in the age to come. So the question that begs to be answered is this; If YHWH never changes, and Yahshua is the same yesterday, today, and forever, then how can mankind dispensationalize these ordinances away in this present time frame that we now live in, between comings? The answer is mankind can only do so at the peril of severe and swift judgment and loss of reward in the **olam habah**.

[5] Broken His Torah.
[6] "Their worm" is a Hebrew expression meaning "their evil memory."
[7] The fire in the Lake of Fire that consumes them will never be quenched, but the wicked being (him or her self), will be fully destroyed or annihilated. Just the opposite of all that saved Yisrael will inherit.

ירמיהו

Yirmeyahu - Jeremiah
To Our Forefathers Yisrael

1 The words of Yirmeyahu the son of Hilkiyah, of the kohanim that were in Anathoth in the land of Benyamin: 2 To whom the word of **יהוה** came in the days of Yoshiyahu the son of Amon melech of Yahudah, in the thirteenth year of his malchut. 3 It came also in the days of Yehoyaqim the son of Yoshiyahu melech of Yahudah, until the end of the eleventh year of Tzidkiyahu the son of Yoshiyahu melech of Yahudah, until the carrying away of Yahrushalayim into exile in the fifth month. 4 Then the word of **יהוה** [1]came to me, saying, 5 *Before I formed you in the belly I knew you;*[2] *and before you came forth out of the womb I set you apart, and I ordained you as a navi to the nations.*[3] 6 Then I said, Oy Vey, Master **יהוה**! See, I cannot speak: for I am only a child. 7 But **יהוה** said to me, *Do not say, I am a child: for you shall go to all that I shall send you, and whatever I command you, you shall speak. 8 Be not afraid of their faces: for I am with you to deliver you,* says **יהוה**.[4] 9 Then **יהוה** put forth His hand, and touched my mouth. And **יהוה** said to me, *See, I have put My words in your mouth. 10 See, I have this day set you over the nations and over the malchutim, to root out, and to pull down, and to destroy, and to throw down, to build, and to plant.*[5] 11 Moreover the word of **יהוה** came to me, saying, *Yirmeyahu, what do you see?* And I said, Master I see a branch of an almond eytz. 12 Then said

יהוה to me, *You have seen well: for I will hasten My word to perform it.* 13 And the word of **יהוה** came to me the second time, saying, *What do you see now?* And I said, I see a boiling pot; and it faces towards the north. 14 Then **יהוה** said to me, *Out of the north an evil shall break forth upon all the inhabitants of the land.*[6] 15 *For, see, I will call all the families of the malchutim of the north,* says **יהוה**; *and they shall come, and each one shall set his throne at the entrance of the gates of Yahrushalayim, and against all its walls all around, and against all the cities of Yahudah. 16 And I will utter My mishpatim against them regarding all their wickedness, who have forsaken Me, and have burned incense to other elohim, and worshipped the works of their own hands. 17 You therefore dress up your waist, and arise, and speak to them all that I command you: be not broken at their faces, lest I break you before them. 18 For, see, I have made you this day like a walled city, and an iron pillar, and bronze walls against the whole land, against the melechim of Yahudah, against its leaders, against its kohanim, and against the people of the land. 19 And they shall fight against you; but they shall not prevail against you; for I am with you,* says **יהוה**, *to deliver you.*

2 Moreover the word of **יהוה** came to me, saying, 2 *Go and cry in the hearing of Yahrushalayim, saying, This says* **יהוה**; *I remember you, and the kindness of your youth, the ahava of your bridehood, when you went after Me in the wilderness, in a land that was not sown. 3 Yisrael was set-apart to* **יהוה**, *and the bikkurim of his increase: all that devoured him became guilty; evil came upon them,* says **יהוה**. 4 Shema the word of **יהוה**, O Beit Yaakov,

---

[1] Yahshua.
[2] YHWH knows us before birth and as such abortion is murder and an attack on YHWH's revealed will to see us born.
[3] All true ordinations must originate from YHWH.
[4] A true prophet cannot care what people say either in words or by facial rejection.
[5] This is the outline for the only true calling to rebuild the Tabernacle of David. We are called to root out and destroy pagan roots and culture in the faith, all the while saving, preserving, and building up the remnant people of both houses. A true restorer of the nation must be prepared to do both, the pleasant work and the unpleasant task, of exposing error in Renewed Covenant Yisrael.

[6] Babylonian exile.

and all the families of Beit Yisrael: 5 This says יהוה, *What iniquity have your ahvot found in Me, that they are gone far from Me, and have had halacha after vanity, and have become worthless? 6 Neither did they say, Where is* יהוה *that brought us up out of the land of Mitzrayim, that led us through the wilderness, through a land of deserts and of pits, through a land of drought, and of the shadow of death, through a land that no man passed through, and where no man dwelt? 7 And I brought you into a plentiful country, to eat its fruit and the tov of it; but when you entered it, you defiled My land, and made My heritage an abomination. 8 The kohanim said not, Where is* יהוה*? And they that handle the Torah did not know Me:[1] the shepherds also transgressed against Me, and the neviim prophesied by Baal[2], and had their halacha after things that do not profit. 9 Therefore I will yet plead with you, says* יהוה*, and with your children's children will I also plead. 10 For pass over to the coastlands of Chittim[3], and see, and send to Qedar, and consider diligently, and see if there has ever been such a thing as this. 11 Have the gentiles changed their elohim, which are not the emet elohim? But My people have changed their tiferet for that which does not profit. 12 Be appalled, O shamayim, at this, and be amazed, says* יהוה*. 13 For My people have committed two evils; they have forsaken Me the fountain of living mayim, and hewed out cisterns for themselves, broken cisterns, that can hold no mayim.[4] 14 Is Yisrael an eved? Was he born as a bayit-eved? Why is he plundered? 15 The young lions roared upon him, and yelled, and they made his land wasted: his cities are burned without inhabitant. 16 Also the children of Noph and Tahpanes have shaved the keter of your head. 17 Have you not done this to yourself,*

in that you have forsaken יהוה *Your Elohim, when He led you in the right halacha? 18 And now what have you to do with the halacha of Mitzrayim, to drink the mayim of Sihor? Or what have you to do with the halacha of Ashshur, to drink the mayim of the river? 19 Your own wickedness shall correct you, and your backslidings shall reprove you: know therefore and see that it is an evil and bitter thing, in that you have forsaken* יהוה *Your Elohim, and that My fear is not in you, says the Master* יהוה *of hosts 20 For from old times I have broken your yoke, and cut your cords; and you said, I will not transgress; when upon every high hill and under every green eytz you wandered off, playing the harlot. 21 Yet I had planted you as a noble vine, a fully right zera[5]: how then are you turned into the foreign[6] plant of a strange vine before Me?[7] 22 For though you wash you with lye, and you use much soap, yet your iniquity is ingrained before Me, says the Master* יהוה*. 23 How can you say, I am not defiled, I have not gone after the Baalim? See your derech is in the valley, know what you have done: you are a swift dromedary breaking loose in her halacha; 24 A wild donkey used to the wilderness that sniffs up the wind at her desire; in her time of mating who can turn her away? All that seek her will weary themselves; only with her footprints can they find her. 25 Keep your foot from being bare, and your throat from thirst: but you said, It is useless, for I have loved strangers, and after them will I go. 26 As the thief is ashamed when he is caught, so is Beit Yisrael[8] ashamed; their melechim, their leaders, and their kohanim, and their neviim, 27 Saying to an eytz, You are my abba; and to a stone, You have given me birth: for they have turned their back on Me, and not their face: but in the time of*

---

[1] Same in Jewish Yisrael until this day, when they don't have Yahshua.
[2] Generic term for "lord." Today many prophecies are given in the name of baal/lord, but not YHWH. They normally can be dismissed as false.
[3] China.
[4] Leaving YHWH for other means of redemption.

[5] Of Yisrael.
[6] Hebrew word is **nokri**. Yisreal had started to act like the pagans since they sought to worship with them also.
[7] Despite being planted as Yisrael, they started producing gentile or strange fruit.
[8] All 12 tribes.

their trouble they will say, Arise, and save us.[1] 28 But where are your elohim that you have made? Let them arise, if they can save you in the time of your trouble: for according to the number of your cities so are your many elohim, O Yahudah. 29 Therefore will you complain to Me? You all have transgressed against Me, says יהוה. 30 In vain have I smitten your children; they received no correction: your own sword has devoured your neviim, like a destroying lion. 31 O wicked generation: See the word of יהוה.[2] Have I been like a wilderness to Yisrael? Like a land of darkness? Why then do My people say, We roam from You; we will not shuv to You? 32 Can a maiden forget her ornaments, or a bride her attire? Yet My people have forgotten Me for days without number. 33 Why do you adorn yourselves to seek ahava? Therefore you have also taught the wicked ones your halacha. 34 Also in your skirts is found the dom of the beings that are poor and innocent: I have not found it by a secret search, but upon all your skirts. 35 Yet you say, Because I am innocent, surely His anger shall turn from me. See, I will bring mishpat on you, because you say, I have not sinned. 36 Why are you so busy trying to change your halacha? You also shall be ashamed of Mitzrayim, as you were ashamed of Ashshur. 37 Yes, you shall go forth from there, with your hands upon your head: for יהוה has rejected those you trust, and you shall not prosper by them.

3 If a man puts away his wife, and she goes from him, and becomes another man's, shall he shuv to her again? Shall not that land be greatly defiled? But you have played the harlot with many lovers; yet returned again to Me, says יהוה. 2 Lift up your eyes to the high places, and see where you have not lain with men. In the roads have you sat for them, like an Arabian in the wilderness; and you have defiled the land with your whorings and with your wickedness. 3 Therefore the showers have been withheld, and there has been no malchut rain[3]; and you have a whore's forehead, you refuse to be ashamed. 4 Will you cry to Me from now on, My Abba, you are the guide of My youth? 5 Will He reserve His anger le-olam-va-ed? Will he keep it to the end of the age? See, you have spoken and done all the evil things that you could. 6 יהוה said also to me in the days of Yoshiyahu the melech, Have you seen that which backsliding Yisrael[4] has done? She is gone up to every high mountain and under every green eytz, and there has played the harlot. 7 And I said after she had done all these things, Teshuvah to Me. But she made no teshuvah. And her perverted sister Yahudah saw it. 8 And I saw, that for all the reasons which backsliding Yisrael committed adultery I had put her away, and given her a Get[5] of divorce; yet her perverted sister Yahudah feared not, but went and played the harlot also.[6] 9 And it came to pass through her excessive whoring, that she defiled the land, and committed adultery with stones and with eytzim. 10 And yet for all this her perverted sister Yahudah has not made teshuvah with her whole lev, but with falsehood, says יהוה. 11 And יהוה said to me, Backsliding Yisrael has justified herself more than perverted Yahudah.[7] 12 Go and proclaim these words toward the north, and say, Shuv, backsliding Yisrael, says יהוה[8]; and I will not cause My anger to fall upon you: for I am full of rachamim, says יהוה, and I will not keep My anger le-olam-va-ed. 13 Only acknowledge your iniquity, that

---

[1] During Yaakov's Trouble or the **Shivlay HaMoshiach**.
[2] Judah needs to see Yahshua.
[3] Latter rain in Hebrew is **malkosh;** which can mean kingdom rain.
[4] Ephraim.
[5] Certificate of divorce.
[6] Both houses have left YHWH. Returning Ephraimites must therefore be wise and not learn Torah from those who don't keep it, but from redeemed brother Judah, who loves Torah and YHWH's Son, the Moshiach.
[7] Both houses have no righteousness or answers apart from those given by Moshiach Yahshua.
[8] Obviously Jeremiah knew where to find the ten tribes or else YHWH wouldn't have told him to go and speak to them. The ten tribes were never lost, only swallowed up among the nations.

you have transgressed against יהוה Your Elohim, and have scattered your halacha to the strangers[1] under every green eytz, and you have not obeyed My voice, says יהוה. 14 Make teshuvah, O backsliding children, says יהוה. For I am married to you: and I will take you one from a city, and two from a mishpocha, and I will bring you to Tzion:[2] 15 And I will give you shepherds according to My lev, which shall feed you with da'at and binah.[3] 16 And it shall come to pass, when you are multiplied and increased in the land, in those days, says יהוה, they shall say no more, The ark of the covenant of יהוה : neither shall it come to mind: neither shall they remember it; neither shall they visit it; neither shall that ritual be done any more.[4][5] 17 At that time they shall call Yahrushalayim the Throne of יהוה ;[6] and all the nations shall be gathered to it,[7] to the Name of יהוה [8] to Yahrushalayim: neither shall they have their halacha any more after the imaginations of their evil lev.[9] 18 In those days[10] Beit Yahudah shall walk with Beit Yisrael, and they shall come together out of the land of the north to the land that I have given for an inheritance to your ahvot.[11] 19 I shall put you among the children of Yisrael [12], and give you a pleasant land, a tov heritage from the hosts of nations? And I said, You shall call Me, My Abba; and do not turn away from Me.[13] 20 Surely as a wife unfaithfully departs from her husband, so have you betrayed Me, O Beit Yisrael[14], says יהוה. 21 A voice was heard upon the high places, the weeping and supplications of the children of Yisrael: for they have perverted their halacha, and they have forgotten יהוה their Elohim. 22 Make teshuvah, you backsliding children, and I will heal your backslidings. See, we have come to you; for you are יהוה our Elohim. 23 Truly in vain is salvation hoped for from the high hills, and from the multitude of mountains: for truly in יהוה our Elohim is the salvation of Yisrael. 24 For shame has devoured the labor of our ahvot from our youth; their flocks and their herds, their sons and their daughters. 25 We lie down in our shame, and our confusion covers us: for we have sinned against יהוה our Elohim, we and our ahvot, from our youth even to this day, and have not obeyed the voice of יהוה our Elohim.

4 If you will make teshuvah, O Yisrael,[15] says יהוה, then make teshuvah to Me: and if you will put away your abominations out of My sight, then shall you cease to stray. 2 And you shall swear, יהוה lives, in emet, in mishpat, and in tzedakah; and the nations shall bless themselves in Him, and in Him shall they tiferet. 3 For this says

---

[1] Pagans.
[2] The end-time return to Zion will include only a remnant. Not all Yisrael will obey the call to return through Moshiach Yahshua. Many will choose a way of their own choosing, and will die in the spiritual and physical exile of our people. If most of your family doesn't "get it," that is ok. You need to see yourself as part of the "one from a city," and "two from a family" remnant.
[3] These are the leaders of Nazarene believers who love Yahshua, both covenants, and all things that pertain to the restoration of our nation.
[4] In the restored kingdom, the splendor will be so strong and the two-house reunion so central, that all searches and discussions over the ark of the covenant will not even come to mind, as Yisrael is multiplying and filling all of the original land given to the patriarchs. If there are ongoing discussions about the ark of the covenant and its location, that means that both houses have not been restored, and that the promised reunion has not taken place as many falsely teach.
[5] In the temple service that is restored in Ezekiel chapters 40-48, we see sacrifices restored but no Yom Kippur sacrifice is expressly mentioned, thus obviating the need to find and restore the Ark of the Covenant.
[6] In the millennium.
[7] The kingdom will be restored.
[8] Note that in the kingdom all nations will be gathered to the true Name of YHWH, not the names of false deities and false names for the true deity. The regathering is not only to the land, but also to the Name. So those who are truly the lost sheep of Yisrael, will find themselves being drawn back to the Name of YHWH.
[9] Remnant Yisrael will not invent and imagine names for YHWH from their own levim anymore.
[10] The days when the ark and its location no longer come to mind.

[11] This verse alone proves that Torah-keeping Ephraim is not called to learn Torah from the orthodox Jews in Yisrael. This and other key verses makes it clear that when YHWH opens the door of aliyah/immigration, both houses go together - rather than Ephraim running to apostate Jews now living in the land. Any aliyah without both houses having the same open door is a flesh trip of man's flesh and shall not stand.
[12] Aramaic Peshitta.
[13] In the days when the two houses walk together back to the land, He will place all Torah-keepers in among the children of Yisrael and in their inheritance. These are the companions or friends of Ezekiel 37.
[14] All 12 tribes.
[15] Both houses.

יהוה to the men of Yahudah and Yahrushalayim, *Break up your fallow ground, and sow not among thorns.* 4 *Brit milah yourselves to* יהוה, *and take away the foreskins of your lev,* [1] *you men of Yahudah and inhabitants of Yahrushalayim: lest My wrath come forth like fire, and burn so that none can quench it, because of the evil of your doings.* 5 *Declare in Yahudah, and publish in Yahrushalayim; and say, Blow the shofar in the land: cry, gather together, and say, Assemble yourselves, and let us go into the walled cities.* 6 *Lift up the banner toward Tzion: be strong and do not stand still: for I will bring evil from the north, and a great destruction.* 7 *The lion is come up from his thicket, and the destroyer of the nations is on his derech to you; he is gone forth from his place to make your land desolate; and your cities shall be laid waste, without any inhabitants.* 8 For this dress yourself with sackcloth, lament and wail: for the fierce anger of יהוה is not turned back from us. 9 *And it shall come to pass in that day,* says יהוה, *that the lev of the melech shall melt, and the lev of the leaders; and the kohanim shall be amazed, and the neviim shall wonder.* 10 Then said I, Oy Vey, Master יהוה! Surely You have greatly deceived this people and Yahrushalayim, saying, You shall have shalom; whereas the sword reaches to the being. 11 *At that time shall it shall be said to this people and to Yahrushalayim, A dry wind from the bare heights in the wilderness blows toward the daughter of My people, not to cool them, nor to cleanse them,* 12 *Even a full wind from those places shall come from Me: now also I will give mishpatim against them.* 13 *See, he shall come up as clouds, and his mirkavot shall be as a whirlwind: His horses are swifter than eagles. Woe to us! For we are plundered.* 14 *O Yahrushalayim, wash your lev from wickedness, that you may be saved. How long shall your worthless thoughts stay in you?* 15 *For a voice declares from*

Dan, and publishes affliction from Mount Ephraim. 16 *Announce to the nations; see, publish against Yahrushalayim, that captors will come from a far country, and raise their voice against the cities of Yahudah.* 17 *As keepers of a field, are they against her all around; because she has been rebellious against Me,* says יהוה. 18 *Your halacha and your doings have brought these things on you; this is your wickedness, because it is bitter, because it reaches to your lev.* 19 My inward parts, my inward parts! I am pained in my very lev; my lev makes a noise in me; I cannot hold my silence, because you have heard, O my being, the sound of the shofar, the alarm of a war. 20 Destruction upon destruction is being cried; for the whole land is plundered: suddenly are my tents plundered, and my curtains in a moment. 21 How long shall I see the banner of war, and shema the sound of the shofar? 22 *For My people are foolish, they have not known Me; they are stupid children, and they have no binah: they are wise to do evil, but to do tov they have no da'at.* 23 *I saw the earth, and, see, it was without form, and void; and the shamayim, and they had no light.* 24 *I saw the mountains, and, see, they trembled, and all the hills swayed.* 25 *I saw, and, see, there was no man, and all the birds of the shamayim had fled.* 26 *I saw, and, see, the fruitful place was a wilderness, and all the cities of it were broken down at the presence of* יהוה, *and by His fierce anger.* 27 For this has יהוה said, *The whole land shall be desolate; yet will I not make a full end of it.* 28 *For this shall the earth mourn, and the shamayim above shall be black: because I have spoken it, I have purposed it, and will not relent, neither will I turn back from it.* 29 *The whole city shall flee for the noise of the horsemen and bowmen; they shall go into bushes, and climb up upon the rocks: every city shall be forsaken, and not a man shall dwell in them.* 30 *And when you are plundered, what will you do? Though you clothe yourself with crimson, though*

---

[1] Become born-again.

you dress with ornaments of gold, though you enlarge your face with makeup, in vain shall you make yourself pretty; your lovers will despise you, they will seek your chayim. 31 For I have heard a voice as of a woman in labor, and the anguish as of her that brings forth her first child, the voice of the daughter of Tzion, that bewails herself, that spreads out her hands, saying, Woe is me now! For my being faints because of the murderers.

5 Run back and forth through the streets of Yahrushalayim, and see now, and know, and look in the open places, if you can find a man, if there be any that performs mishpat, that seeks the emet; and I will pardon it. 2 And though they say, יהוה lives; surely they swear falsely. 3 O יהוה, are not Your eyes upon the emet? You have stricken them, but they have not grieved; You have consumed them, but they have refused to receive correction: they have made their faces harder than a rock; they have refused to make teshuvah. 4 Therefore I said, Surely these are poor; they are foolish: for they know not the halacha of יהוה, nor the mishpatim of their Elohim. 5 I will find the great men, and will speak to them; for they have known the halacha of יהוה, and the mishpat of their Elohim: but these have altogether broken the yoke, and torn the bonds. 6 Therefore a lion out of the forest shall kill them, and a wolf of the evening shall plunder them, a leopard shall watch over their cities: every one that goes out there shall be torn in pieces: because their transgressions are many, and their backslidings have now increased. 7 How shall I pardon you for this? Your children have forsaken Me, and sworn by those that are not elohim at all: when I had fed them to the fullest, they then committed adultery, and assembled themselves in groups in the harlots' houses. 8 They were as fed horses in the morning: every one neighed after his neighbor's wife. 9 Shall I not visit mishpat for these things? Says יהוה: and shall not

My being be avenged on such a nation as this? 10 Go up upon her walls, and destroy them; but make not a full end of her: take away her branches;[1] for they are not יהוה's. 11 For Beit Yisrael and Beit Yahudah have dealt very treacherously against Me, says יהוה.[2] 12 They have been untrue to יהוה, and said, It is not He; neither shall evil come upon us; neither shall we see any sword nor famine: 13 And the neviim shall become wind, and My word is not in them: so shall it be done to them. 14 Therefore this says יהוה Elohim of hosts, Because you speak this word, see, I will make My words in your mouth fire, and this people wood, and it shall devour them. 15 I will bring a nation upon you from far, O Beit Yisrael,[3] says יהוה: it is a mighty nation, it is an ancient nation, a nation whose language you know not, neither understand what they say.[4] 16 Their quiver is as an open sepulcher; they are all mighty men. 17 And they shall eat up your harvest, and your lechem, which your sons and your daughters should eat: they shall eat up your flocks and your herds: they shall eat up your vines and your fig eytzim: they shall impoverish your fenced cities, in which you trusted, with the sword. 18 Nevertheless in those days, says יהוה, I will not make a full end of you. 19 And it shall come to pass, when you shall say, Why does יהוה our Elohim do all these things to us? Then shall you answer them, Just like you have forsaken Me, and served strange elohim in your land, so shall you serve strangers in a land that is not yours. 20 Declare this in Beit Yaakov[5], and publish it in Yahudah, saying, 21 Shema now to this, O foolish people, without binah; which have eyes, and see not; which have hearing, and shema not: 22 Don't you fear Me? says יהוה: Will you not tremble at My presence, that has placed the sand as a boundary of the sea by

---

[1] Judah and Ephraim are both the natural branches of the olive eytz, as seen in Romans 11 and Jeremiah 11:16-17.
[2] Both houses rebelled thus calling for two separate exiles.
[3] All 12 tribes.
[4] Babylon.
[5] Both houses.

an eternal decree, that it cannot pass it: and though the waves toss themselves, yet they cannot prevail against it; though they roar, yet they cannot pass over it? 23 But this people have a revolting and a rebellious lev; they have revolted and left Me. 24 Neither do say they in their lev, Let us now fear יהוה our Elohim, that gives both the teaching and the malchut rain, in due season: He guards for us the appointed Shavout of the harvest.[1] 25 Your iniquities have turned away these blessings, and your sins have withheld tov things from you. 26 For among My people are found wicked men: they lay in wait, as he that sets snares; they set a trap, to catch men.[2] 27 As a cage is full of birds, so are their houses full of deceit: therefore they are become great, and grown rich. 28 They are grown fat, they shine: yes, they overlook the deeds of the wicked: they shophet not the real causes, the cause of the fatherless, and the rights of those who are needy do they not shophet, and yet they prosper. 29 Shall I not visit punishment for these things? says יהוה: Shall not My being be avenged on such a nation as this? 30 An astounding and horrible matter is committed in the land; 31 The neviim prophesy falsely, and the kohanim bear rule by their own means; and My people love to have it like that: and what will you do in the end of it?

6 O you children of Benyamin, gather yourselves to flee out of the midst of Yahrushalayim, and blow the shofar in Tekoa, and set up a sign of fire in Beth-Hakerem: for evil appears out of the north, with great destruction. 2 I have likened the daughter of Tzion to a lovely and delicate woman. 3 The shepherds with their flocks shall come to her; they shall pitch their tents against her all around; they shall feed everyone in his own place. 4 Prepare war against her; arise, and let us go up at noon. Woe to us! For the day goes away, for the shadows of the evening are lengthened. 5 Arise, and let us go by night, and let us destroy her palaces. 6 For this יהוה of hosts said, Cut down eytzim, and cast a siege mound against Yahrushalayim: this is the city to be visited with correction; there is only oppression in her midst. 7 As a fountain casts out her mayim, so she casts out her wickedness: violence and plunder is heard in her; before Me continually is her grief and her wounds. 8 Be instructed, O Yahrushalayim, lest My being depart from you; lest I make you desolate, a land no longer inhabited. 9 This says יהוה of hosts, They shall completely glean the remnant of Yisrael[3] as a vine: pass your hand again over the branches as a grape gatherer. 10 To whom shall I speak, and give warning, that they may shema? See, their ear is uncircumcised, and they cannot shema: see, the word of יהוה is to them a reproach; they have no delight in it. 11 Therefore I am full of the wrath of יהוה; I am weary of holding it in: I will pour it out upon the children abroad, and upon the congregation of young men together: for even the husband with the wife shall be taken, the aged with him that is old. 12 And their houses shall be given to others, with their fields and wives together: for I will stretch out My hand upon the inhabitants of the land, says יהוה. 13 For from the least of them even to the greatest of them everyone is given to greed; and from ha navi even to the kohen every one deals falsely. 14 They have healed also the harm of the daughter of My people slightly, saying, Shalom, shalom; when there is no shalom. 15 Were they ashamed when they had committed abominations? No! They were not at all ashamed, neither could they blush: therefore they shall fall among them that fall: at the time that I visit them with punishment they shall be cast down, says יהוה. 16 This says יהוה, Stand in the halacha, and see, and ask for the old paths, where is the tov halacha, and walk in it, and

---

[1] The counting of the omer and the **Shavout** harvest.
[2] The men of the flock of Yisrael.

[3] Both houses.

you shall find rest for your beings. But they said, We will not walk in it.[1] 17 Also I set watchmen over you, saying, Shema to the sound of the shofar. But they said, We will not shema.[2] 18 Therefore shema, all nations,[3] and know, O congregation,[4] what is now upon them. 19 Shema, O earth: see, I will bring evil upon this people, even the fruit of their thoughts, because they have not listened to My words, nor to My Torah, but rejected it. 20 To what purpose comes to Me the incense from Sheba, and the sweet cane from a far country? Your burnt offerings are not acceptable, nor are your sacrifices sweet to Me. 21 Therefore this says יהוה, See, I will lay stumbling blocks before this people, and the ahvot and the sons together shall fall upon them; the neighbor and his friend shall perish.

22 This says יהוה, See, a people comes from the north country, and a great nation shall be raised from the furthest parts of the earth. 23 They shall lay hold on bow and spear; they are cruel, and have no rachamim; their voice roars like the sea; and they ride upon horses, set in battle gear as men for war against you, O daughter of Tzion. 24 We have heard the fame of them: our hands grow weak: anguish has taken hold of us, and pain, as of a woman in labor. 25 Go not forth into the field, nor walk by the derech; for the sword of the enemy and fear is on every side. 26 O daughter of My people, dress in sackcloth, and cover yourself in ashes: make mourning, as for an only son, most bitter lamentation: for the plunderer shall suddenly come upon us. 27 I have set you for a tester and a stronghold among My people, that you may know and try their halacha. 28 They are all serious rebels, walking as slanders: they are bronze and iron; they are all corrupters. 29 The bellows are burned, the fire consumes the lead; the refiner melts in vanity: for the wicked are not plucked away. 30 Rejected silver shall men call them, because יהוה has rejected them.

7 The word that came to Yirmeyahu from יהוה, saying, 2 Stand in the gate of יהוה's Bayit, and proclaim there this word, and say, Shema the word of יהוה, all you of Yahudah, that enter in at these gates to worship יהוה. 3 This says יהוה of hosts, the Elohim of Yisrael, Change your halacha and your doings, and I will cause you to dwell in this place. 4 Trust not in lying words, saying, The Beit HaMikdash of יהוה, The Beit HaMikdash of יהוה, The Beit HaMikdash of יהוה. 5 For if you completely change your halacha and your doings; if you completely execute mishpat between a man and his neighbor; 6 If you oppress not the stranger, the fatherless, and the widow, and shed not innocent dom in this place, neither follow after other elohim to your own harm: 7 Then will I cause you to dwell in this place, in the land that I gave to your ahvot, le-olam va-ed. 8 See, that you do not trust in a lying word that cannot profit. 9 Will you steal, murder, and commit adultery, and swear falsely, and burn incense to Baal, and walk after other elohim whom you know not; 10 And come and stand before Me in this Bayit, which is called by My Name, and say, We have been delivered to do all these abominations? 11 Is this Bayit, which is called by My Mame, become a den of robbers in your eyes? See, even I have seen it, says יהוה. 12 But go now to My place that was in Shiloh, where I put My Name at first, and see what I did to it for the wickedness of My people Yisrael. 13 And now, because you have done all these works, says יהוה, and I spoke to you, rising up early and speaking, but you did not shema; and I called to you,

---

[1] The healing for Yisrael is found in a return to the paths of Torah and the marriage covenant of Sinai. In that return there will be purpose, understanding, and rest for our souls. Yisrael must seek things that are renewed - not new things. For a full treatment of this subject, see:
http://store.yourarmstoisrael.org/Qstore/Qstore.cgi?CMD=011 &PROD=000211.
[2] Typical of Ephraim's reaction to the ancient Torah over the last 2,000 years.
[3] Ephraim.
[4] Judah.

but you answered not; 14 Therefore will I do to this Bayit, which is called by My Name, in which you trust, and to the place which I gave to you and to your ahvot, as I have done to Shiloh. 15 And I will cast you out of My sight, as I have cast out all your brothers, even the whole zera of Ephraim.[1] 16 Therefore do not make tefillah for this people, neither lift up a cry or a tefillah for them, neither make intercession to Me: for I will not shema you.[2] 17 Don't you see what they do in the cities of Yahudah and in the streets of Yahrushalayim? 18 The children gather wood, and the ahvot kindle the fire, and the women knead their dough, to make cakes to the malka of the shamayim,[3] and to pour out drink offerings to other elohim, that they may provoke Me to anger. 19 Do they provoke Me to anger? says יהוה: Do they not provoke themselves to the shame and confusion of their own faces? 20 Therefore this says the Master יהוה; See, My anger and My wrath shall be poured out upon this place, upon man, and upon beast, and upon the eytzim of the field, and upon the fruit of the ground; and it shall burn, and shall not be quenched. 21 This says יהוה of hosts, the Elohim of Yisrael; Put your burnt offerings to your sacrifices, and eat food. 22 For I spoke not to your ahvot, nor commanded them in the day that I brought them out of the land of Mitzrayim, concerning burnt offerings or sacrifices: 23 But this thing I commanded them, saying, Obey My voice, and I will be Your Elohim, and you shall be My people: and walk in all the halacha that I have commanded you, that it may be well you. 24 But they heard not, nor inclined their ear, but had their halacha in the counsels and in the imaginations of their evil lev, and went backwards, and not forwards. 25 Since the day that your ahvot came forth out of the land of Mitzrayim to this day I have

even sent to you all My avadim the neviim, daily rising up early and sending them: 26 Yet they listened not to Me, nor inclined their ear, but hardened their neck: they did worse than their ahvot. 27 Therefore you shall speak all these words to them; but they will not shema to you: you shall also call to them; but they will not answer you. 28 But you shall say to them, This is a nation that obeys not the voice of יהוה their Elohim, nor receives correction: emet has perished, and is cut off from their mouth. 29 Cut off your hair, O Yahrushalayim, and cast it away, and take up a lamentation on the bare heights; for יהוה has rejected and forsaken the generation of His wrath. 30 For the children of Yahudah have done evil in My sight, says יהוה: they have set their abominations in the Bayit that is called by My Name, to defile it. 31 And they have built the high places of Tophet, which is in the Valley of the Son of Hinnom, to burn their sons and their daughters in the fire; which I commanded them not, neither came it into My lev. 32 Therefore, see, the days come, says יהוה, that it shall no more be called Tophet, nor the Valley of the Son of Hinnom, but the Valley of Slaughter: for they shall bury in Tophet, until there is no more room. 33 And the corpses of this people shall be food for the fowls of the shamayim, and for the beasts of the earth; and none shall frighten them away. 34 Then will I cause to cease from the cities of Yahudah, and from the streets of Yahrushalayim, the voice of gilah, and the voice of simcha, the voice of the bridegroom, and the voice of the bride: for the land shall be desolate.

8 At that time, says יהוה, they shall bring out the bones of the melechim of Yahudah, and the bones of its leaders, and the bones of the kohanim, and the bones of the neviim, and the bones of the inhabitants of Yahrushalayim, out of their graves: 2 And they shall spread them before the sun, and the moon, and all the host of the

---

[1] Both houses need Moshiach's truth. One house is not to depend on the other in the return, since each house has its own unique evil to deal with.
[2] Judah's fate has been sealed.
[3] Today known as sinless Mother Mary the mother of G-d, but in the past known by many other names.

shamayim, whom they have loved, and whom they have served, and after whom they have had their halacha, and whom they have sought, and whom they have worshipped: they shall not be gathered, nor be buried; they shall be for dung upon the face of the earth. 3 And death shall be chosen rather than chayim by all the residue of them that remain of this evil mishpocha, which remains in all the places where I have driven them, says יהוה of hosts. 4 Moreover you shall say to them, This says יהוה; Shall they fall, and not arise? Shall they turn away, and not shuv? 5 Why then are this people in Yahrushalayim turned away by an everlasting backsliding? They hold fast to deceit, they refuse to make teshuvah. 6 I listened and gave ear to them, but they spoke not right: no man repented of his wickedness, saying, What have I done? Everyone turned to his course, like a horse rushes into the battle. 7 Yes, the stork in the shamayim knows her appointed times; and the turtledove and the crane and the swallow observe the time of their coming; but My people do not know the mishpatim of יהוה. 8 How do you say, We are wise, and the Torah of יהוה is with us? See, certainly the lying pen of the scribes has made it falsehood.[1] 9 The wise men are ashamed, they are broken and taken: see, they have rejected the word of יהוה ; so what chochma do they retain? 10 Therefore will I give their wives to others, and their fields to them that shall inherit them: for everyone from the least even to the greatest is given to greed, from ha navi even to the kohen every one deals falsely. 11 For they have healed the harm of the daughter of my people slightly, saying, Shalom, shalom;

when there is no shalom. 12 Were they ashamed when they had committed abominations? No, they were not at all ashamed, neither could they blush: therefore shall they fall among them that fall: in the time of their visitation of punishment they shall be cast down, says יהוה. 13 I will surely consume them, says יהוה: there shall be no grapes on the vine, nor figs on the fig eytz, and the leaf shall fade; and the things that I have given them shall pass away from them. 14 Why do we sit still? Assemble yourselves, and let us enter into the walled cities, and let us be silent there: for יהוה our Elohim has put us to silence, and given us mayim of poison to drink, because we have sinned against יהוה. 15 We looked for shalom, but no tov came; and for a time of health, and see trouble! 16 The snorting of His horses was heard from Dan: the whole land trembled at the sound of the neighing of His strong ones; for they have come, and have devoured the land, and all that is in it; the city, and those that dwell in it. 17 For, see, I will send serpents, adders, among you, which will not be charmed, and they shall bite you, says יהוה. 18 When I would comfort myself because of sorrow, my lev is sick in me. 19 See the voice of the cry of the daughter of my people because of them that dwell in a far country: Is not יהוה in Tzion? Is not her melech in her? Why have they provoked Me to anger with their carved images, and with strange vanities? 20 The harvest is past, the summer is ended, and we are not saved.[2] 21 For the harm of the daughter of My people am I harmed; I am black;[3] astonishment has taken hold of me. 22 Is there no balm in Gilead; is there no physician there? Why then is not the health of the daughter of My people recovered?[4]

---

[1] How can men know that the Torah is with us? One of the reasons Yisrael was judged was the changing of the Torah by lying scribes. These were the men who deliberately changed the Hebrew and Aramaic texts, so that translators cannot know for sure what YHWH wrote, in the original autographs. This is not a rebuke of translators and editors of later translations who vary on word meanings, but a rebuke on those who actually shema-ed the word, recorded it and then later changed the original scrolls. To them the warnings of Deuteronomy 12 and Revelation 22 apply.

[2] Judah's lament and ongoing condition. The end of the age is at hand, and it's almost too late.
[3] In context, this means "I am sick at lev over the judgment coming upon my people." It does not mean that YHWH is literally black or white or pink, as some racist Bible thumpers have tried to maintain.
[4] Yahshua is that prescribed balm, and without Him no healing of Judah can ever take place.

9 *Oh that my head were mayim, and my eyes a fountain of tears, that I might weep day and night for the slain of the daughter of My people! 2 Oh that I had in the wilderness a lodging place of travelers; that I might leave My people, and go from them! For they are all adulterers, a congregation of perverted men. 3 And they bend their tongues like their bow for lies: but they are not brave for the emet upon the earth; for they proceed from evil to evil, and they do not know Me,* says יהוה*. 4 Take heed every one of his neighbor and trust not in any brother: for every brother will utterly supplant, and every neighbor will walk with the slanderers.[1] 5 And they will deceive every one his neighbor, and will not speak the emet: they have taught their tongue to speak lies, and weary themselves to commit iniquity. 6 Your dwelling is in the midst of deceit; through deceit they refuse to know Me,* says יהוה*.

7 Therefore this says* יהוה *of hosts, See, I will melt them, and try them; for what shall I do because of the daughter of My people? 8 Their tongue is as an arrow shot out; it speaks deceit: one speaks with shalom to his neighbor with his mouth, but in lev he sets an ambush. 9 Shall I not visit them with punishment for these things? Says* יהוה*: Shall not My being be avenged on such a nation as this? 10 For the mountains will I take up a weeping and wailing, and for the dwellings of the wilderness a lamentation, because they are burned up, so that none can pass through them; neither can men shema the voice of the cattle; both the fowls of the shamayim and the beasts are fled; they are gone. 11 And I will make Yahrushalayim into heaps, and a den of jackals; and I will make the cities of Yahudah desolate, without an inhabitant. 12 Who is the wise man, that may understand this? And who is he to whom the mouth of* יהוה *has spoken, that he may declare it? For the land perishes and is* burned up like a wilderness, so that none passes through. 13 And* יהוה *says, Because they have forsaken My Torah which I set before them, and have not obeyed My voice, neither had their halacha in it; 14 But have had their halacha after the imagination of their own lev, and after Baalim, which their ahvot have taught them: 15 Therefore this says* יהוה *of hosts, the Elohim of Yisrael; See, I will feed them, even this people, with wormwood,[2] and give them mayim of poison to drink.[3] 16 I will scatter them also among the gentiles, whom neither they nor their ahvot have known: and I will send a sword after them, until I have consumed them.

17 This says* יהוה *of hosts, Use discernment, and call for the mourning women, that they may come; and send for wise women, that they may come: 18 And let them hurry, and take up a wailing for us, that our eyes may run down with tears, and our eyelids gush out with mayim. 19 For a voice of wailing is heard out of Tzion, How are we plundered! We are greatly ashamed, because we have forsaken the land, because our dwellings have cast us out. 20 Yet* shema the word of* יהוה*, O you women, and let your ear receive the word of His mouth, and teach your daughters wailing, and everyone her neighbor a lamentation. 21 For death is come up into our windows, and is entered into our palaces, to cut off the children from going outside, and the young men from the streets. 22 Speak, this says* יהוה*, Even the corpses of men shall fall as dung upon the open field, and as that which is cut by the reapers, and none shall gather them. 23 This says* יהוה*, Let not the wise man tiferet in his chochma, neither let the mighty man tiferet in his might, let not the rich man tiferet in his riches: 24 But let him that boasts boast in this, that he understands and knows Me,[4] that I am* יהוה *who exercises loving-kindness, mishpat, and*

---

[1] The two houses must rely on YHWH and His Son alone for instruction in their return, since both houses remain full of doctrinal error and each house has their share of liars.

[2] False doctrines of redemption.
[3] Theological and social confusion and upheaval.
[4] Quoted by Rav Shaul in First Corinthians 1:31; further evidence that they were an Ephraimite congregation in exile, since only Yisrael knew YHWH in the first place, and he takes that Scripture given to Yisrael and applies it to the Corinthians.

tzedakah, in the earth: for in these things I delight, says **יהוה**. 25 See, the days come, says **יהוה**, that I will punish all those who are circumcised[1] with the uncircumcised;[2] 26 Mitzrayim, and Yahudah, and Edom, and the children of Ammon, and Moav, and all that are in the furthest corners; that dwell in the wilderness: for all these nations are uncircumcised, and all of Beit Yisrael among them[3] are uncircumcised in the lev.

10 Shema the word that **יהוה** speaks to you, O Beit Yisrael:[4] 2 This says **יהוה**, Learn not the halacha of the heathen, and be not broken at the signs of the shamayim; for the heathen are broken with them. 3 For the customs of the nations are worthless: for one cuts an eytz out of the forest, the work of the hands of the workman, with the axe. 4 They deck it with silver and with gold; they fasten it with nails and with hammers, so that it does not move around.[5] 5 They are upright as the palm eytz, but speak not: they must be carried, because they cannot walk. Be not afraid of them; for they cannot do evil, neither can they do tov. 6 Forasmuch as there is none like You, O **יהוה**; You are great, and Your Name is great in might.[6] [7] 7 Who would not fear You, O Melech of nations? For to you does it apply: because among all the wise men of the nations, and in all their malchutim, there is none like You. 8 But they are altogether brutish and foolish: the eytz is a doctrine of vanities.[8] 9 Silver spread into plates is brought from Tarshish, and gold from Uphaz, the work of the smith, and of the hands of the refiner: blue and purple is their clothing: they are all the work of skilled workers. 10 But **יהוה** is the emet Elohim, He is the living Elohim, and an everlasting melech: at His wrath the earth shall tremble, and the nations shall not be able to stay His displeasure. 11 This shall you say to them, The elohim that have not made the shamayim and the earth, shall perish from the earth, and from under these shamayim. 12 He has made the earth by His power, He has established the olam by His chochma, and has stretched out the shamayim by His binah. 13 When He utters His voice, there is a multitude of mayim in the shamayim, and He causes the vapors to ascend from the ends of the earth; He makes lightnings for rain, and brings forth the wind out of His treasures. 14 Every man is brutish in his own da'at: every refiner is ashamed by the carved image: for his molded image is falsehood, and there is no ruach in them. 15 They are vanity, and the works of errors: in the time of their visitation of punishment they shall perish. 16 The Portion of Yaakov is not like them: for He is the maker of all things; and Yisrael is the mishpocha of His inheritance:[9] **יהוה** of hosts is His Name. 17 Gather up your items out of the land, O inhabitants of the strongholds. 18 For this says **יהוה**, See, I will sling out the inhabitants of the land all at once, and will distress them, so that they may feel it. 19 Woe is me for my harm! My wound is grievous: but I said, Truly this is a grief, and I must bear it. 20 My tabernacle is plundered, and all my cords are broken: my children are gone forth from me, and they are not: there is none to pitch my tent any more, and to set up my curtains. 21 For the shepherds have misbehaved, and have not sought **יהוה** : therefore they shall not prosper nor understand, and all their flocks shall be scattered.[10] 22 See, the noise of the report has come, and a great commotion

---

[1] Judah.
[2] Ephraim.
[3] Ephraim.
[4] Both houses.
[5] Do you have a Christmas tree? If you do, YHWH says that this is a pagan practice, and He desires for you and all Yisrael to end it immediately and learn the ways of Torah instead.
[6] This verse is most likely inauthentic, as it simply doesn't fit into the literal context of a warning to Yisrael about evil and pagan ways. It should be viewed accordingly. Both the LXX and the Dead Sea Scrolls omit this verse.
[7] Power in the true Name and the dom.
[8] The Christmas tree is a doctrine of vanity.
[9] If you are a part of His heirs, then you must be Yisrael.
[10] The ongoing problem with scattered Yisrael is the wayward shepherds who do not understand nor seek YHWH in truth. YHWH has promised to restore true shepherds to Yisrael in the days when He comes to earth as the Tov Shepherd, to teach His under-shepherds how to act for the tov of the sheep.

from the north country, to make the cities of Yahudah desolate, and a dwelling of jackals. 23 O יהוה, I know that the halacha of man is not found in himself: it is not for man to direct his own steps. 24 O יהוה, correct me, with mishpat; not in Your anger, lest You bring me to nothing. 25 Pour out Your wrath upon the heathen that know You not, and upon the families that call not on Your Name:[1] for they have eaten up Yaakov, and devoured him, and consumed him, and have made his home a ruin.

11 The word that came to Yirmeyahu from יהוה, saying, 2 *Shema the words of this covenant, and speak to the men of Yahudah, and to the inhabitants of Yahrushalayim;* 3 *And say you to them, This says* יהוה *Elohim of Yisrael; Cursed be the man that obeys not the words of this covenant,* 4 *Which I commanded your ahvot in the day that I brought them forth out of the land of Mitzrayim, from the iron furnace, saying, Obey My voice, and do them, according to all which I command you: so shall you be My people, and I will be Your Elohim:* 5 *That I may perform the oath which I have sworn to your ahvot, to give them a land flowing with milk and honey, as it is this day.* Then answered I, and said, Amein, יהוה. 6 Then יהוה said to me, *Proclaim all these words in the cities of Yahudah, and in the streets of Yahrushalayim, saying, Shema to the words of this covenant, and do them.* 7 *For I earnestly warned your ahvot in the day that I brought them up out of the land of Mitzrayim, even to this day, rising early and warning, saying, Obey My voice.* 8 *Yet they obeyed not, nor inclined their ear, but had their halacha each one in the imagination of their evil lev: therefore I will bring upon them all the words of this covenant, which I commanded them to do; but they did them not.* 9 And יהוה said to me, *A conspiracy is found among the men of Yahudah, and among the inhabitants of Yahrushalayim.* 10 *They are turned back to the iniquities of their forefathers, which refused to shema My words; and they went after other elohim to serve them: Beit Yisrael and Beit Yahudah have broken My covenant which I made with their ahvot.*[2] 11 Therefore this says יהוה, *See, I will bring evil upon them, which they shall not be able to escape; and though they shall cry to Me, I will not shema to them.* 12 *Then shall the cities of Yahudah and inhabitants of Yahrushalayim go, and cry to the elohim to whom they offer incense: but they shall not save them at all in the time of their trouble.* 13 *For according to the number of your cities were your elohim, O Yahudah; and according to the number of the streets of Yahrushalayim have you set up altars to do shameful things, to burn incense to Baal.* 14 *Therefore do not make tefillah for this people, neither lift up a cry or tefillah for them: for I will not shema to them in the time that they cry to Me for their trouble.* 15 *What has My beloved to do in My Bayit, seeing she has worked lewdness with many, and does your set-apart flesh remove you from doing evil? When you do evil, then you gilah.* 16 יהוה *called your name, A green olive tree, fair, and of tov fruit: but with the noise of a great tumult He has set fire upon it, and its branches arebroken.*[3] 17 For

---

[2] Both houses have broken covenant. Yet there are those that say Judah has been fully faithful so that they should lead in Yisrael's restoration. Yet YHWH says that only Moshiach can lead, as the state of both houses is not in tov condition.

[3] In Jeremiah 11 verse 16, YHWH teaches us that He has named the olive tree of His planting. The olive tree of His planting would be fair, green, and produce tov fruit. YHWH designed this tree of His planting to be a single, unified voice, sounding out the message of the Elohim of Yisrael. Apparently, the two olive trees evolved from the one tree, that the Father had initially ordained to represent him in purity and in holiness. It was His perfect, expressed desire, that this single olive tree would bear Him excellent polished fruit and produce for him Spirit-filled, Torah-obedient, pagan-rejecting disciples. Everything about this tree was perfect from the day that it was designed by the Master Architect. Yet something went astray from its original design. Instead of the olive tree being united and sounding out a single affirming plan and purpose of the Elohim of Yisrael for His people Yisrael, division and evil set in. The tov, green, once undefiled fruit of the original tree, turned against YHWH and against one another.

יהוה *of hosts, that planted you, has pronounced evil against you, for the evil of Beit Yisrael and Beit Yahudah, which they have done against themselves to provoke Me to anger in offering incense to Baal-the lord.*[1][2][3] 18 And יהוה *has given me da'at of it,*[4] *and I know it: then you showed me their doings.* 19 *But I was like a lamb or an ox that is brought to the slaughter; and I knew not that they had devised devices against me, saying, Let us destroy the eytz with the fruit of it, and let us cut him off from the land of the living, that his name may be no more remembered.*[5] 20 *But, O* יהוה *of hosts, that shophets righteously, that tries the kidneys and the lev, let me see Your vengeance on them: for to You have I revealed my cause.* 21 *Therefore this says* יהוה *of the men of Anathoth, that seek your chayim, saying, Prophesy not in the Name of* יהוה*; that you die not by our*

hand:*[6] 22 *Therefore this says* יהוה *of hosts, See, I will punish them: the young men shall die by the sword; their sons and their daughters shall die by famine:* 23 *And there shall be no remnant of them: for I will bring evil upon the men of Anathoth, even the year of their visitation of punishment.*

12 *Tzadik are You, O* יהוה*, when I plead with You: yet let me talk with You of Your mishpatim: Why does the halacha of the wicked prosper? Why are they all in simcha that deal very wickedly?* 2 *You have planted them, yes, they have taken root: they grow, yes, they bring forth fruit: You are near in their mouth, but far from their kidneys.* 3 *But You, O* יהוה*, know me: You have seen me, and tried my lev toward You: pull them out like sheep for the slaughter, and prepare them for the day of slaughter.* 4 *How long shall the land mourn, and the herbs of every field wither, for the wickedness of those that dwell in it? The beasts are consumed, and the birds; because they said, He shall not see our latter end.* 5 *If you have run with the footmen, and they have wearied you, then how can you contend with horses? And if in the land of shalom, in which you trust, they wearied you, then how will you manage to cross the raging Yarden River?*[7] 6 *For even your brothers, and the bayit of your abba, even they have dealt treacherously with you; yes, they have called a multitude after you: believe them not, though they speak flattering words to you.*[8] 7 *I have forsaken My Bayit, I have left My heritage; I have given the dearly beloved of My being into the hand of her enemies.* 8 *My heritage is to me as a lion in the forest; it roars against Me: therefore have I hated it.* 9 *My heritage is to Me as a speckled bird of prey, and the*

---

[1] Here we find two olive trees committing great evil. The tree no longer resembled love, brotherhood, unity, peace, singularity of mind and purpose. It no longer accurately portrayed the purity and holiness of its designer, a lost world full of pagan beggarly elements. For that evil and for that misrepresentation of the perfection of YHWH's planted olive eytz, He determined to bring evil upon it. The entire tree that had been planted in perfection became totally leavened. YHWH tells all with ears to shema that the tree has divided and its branches will be cut off because of the sin and evil found in the two olive trees, called or known as the House of Yisrael (ten tribes) and the House of Judah (two tribes plus Levi). The single nation typified by the image of the olive tree was tragically split into two olive trees or two separate houses. Even after their division into two houses, YHWH would further the discipline by cutting off all the individual branches of both trees via fire. Fire is symbolic of His wrath and indignation. YHWH planted one Yisrael that became two nations through division. Eventually, both nations were laid bare before all the other nations and are described as natural and unnatural or cultivated and uncultivated branches – yet both were cut off for unemunah.
[2] The olive tree therefore, consists of all Yisraelites (Ephraim and Judah). The non-Yisraelites are **gerim** (strangers) dwelling in Yisrael through Moshiach Yahshua and they are the ones who have received a reprieve and a new life in the olive tree of Yisrael, because branches from both houses were cut off to make room for them. YHWH discovered evil in both houses and determined to cut off branches from both houses, with great tumult and fire.
[3] YHWH is greatly angered by generic "lord" or "baal" worship. If we know Him, He expects all Yisrael to call on His Name.
[4] YHWH is the one who gives all knowledge relating to the mystery of the olive tree. For more information see: **The Mystery of the Olive Tree** at: http://yourarmstoisrael.org/Articles_new/restoration/?page=5&type=12.
[5] Yisrael's enemies and the enemies of the latter-day neviim of restoration desire to cut off the restored branches of the olive tree, as well as cut off YHWH's Name from those branches.

[6] When a Yisraelite prophesies truth in YHWH's Name, expect the world and the religious community who love false anti-Torah prophecies, to hate them, as they did with Jeremiah.
[7] Restoration advocates and soldiers like Jeremiah and Ezekiel, get easily wearied and discouraged, and must answer YHWH's piercing question.
[8] Restoration soldiers can expect many from their own house of faith to come against them.

birds all around are against her; come and assemble all the beasts of the field, come to devour. 10 *Many shepherds have destroyed My vineyard, they have trodden My portion[1] under foot, and they have made My pleasant portion into a desolate wilderness. 11 They have made it desolate, and being desolate it hurts Me; the whole land is made desolate, because no man takes this to lev. 12 The plunderers are come upon all the bare heights throughout the wilderness: for the sword of* יהוה *shall devour it from the one end of the land even to the other end of the land: no flesh shall have shalom. 13 They have sown wheat, but shall reap thorns: they have put themselves to hard work, but shall not profit: and they shall be ashamed of your harvest because of the fierce anger of* יהוה. 14 This says יהוה *against all My evil neighbors, that touch the inheritance that I have caused My people Yisrael[2] to inherit; See, I will pluck them out of their land, and pluck out Beit Yahudah from among them.[3]* 15 *And it shall come to pass, after that I have plucked them out I will shuv, and have rachamim on them, and will bring them again, every man to his heritage, and every man to his land. 16 And it shall come to pass, if they will diligently learn the halacha of My people, to swear by My Name,* יהוה *lives; as they taught My people to swear by Baal-the lord; then shall they be rebuilt in the midst of My people. 17 But if they will not obey, I will utterly pluck up and destroy that nation,[4] says* יהוה.

13 This says יהוה *to me, Go and get a linen girdle, and put it on your waist, and do not put it in mayim. 2 So I got a girdle according to the word of* יהוה, *and put it on my waist. 3 And the word of* יהוה *came to me the second time, saying, 4 Take the girdle that you have got, which is upon your waist, and arise, go to the Euphrates River, and hide it there in a hole of the rock.*

5 *So I went, and hid it by Euphrates, as* יהוה *commanded me. 6 And it came to pass after many days, that* יהוה *said to me, Arise, go to Euphrates, and take the girdle from there, which I commanded you to hide there. 7 Then I went to Euphrates, and dug, and took the girdle from the place where I had hid it: and, see, the girdle was marred, it was profitable for nothing. 8 Then the word of* יהוה *came to me, saying, 9 This says* יהוה, *After this manner will I mar the pride of Yahudah, and the great pride of Yahrushalayim. 10 This evil people, who refuse to shema to My words, who walk in the imagination of their lev, and walk after other elohim, to serve them, and to worship them, shall even be as this girdle, which is tov for nothing. 11 For as the girdle cleaves to the waist of a man, so have I caused to cleave to Me the whole Beit Yisrael and the whole Beit Yahudah,[5] says* יהוה; *that they might be to Me for a people, and for a name, and for a hallel, and for a tiferet: but they would not shema. 12 Therefore you shall speak to them this word; This says* יהוה *Elohim of Yisrael, Every jug shall be filled with wine: and they shall say to you, Do we not certainly know that every jug shall be filled with wine? 13 Then shall you say to them, This says* יהוה, *See, I will fill all the inhabitants of this land, even the melechim that sit upon David's throne, and the kohanim, and the neviim, and all the inhabitants of Yahrushalayim, with drunkenness[6]. 14 And I will dash them one against another, even the ahvot and the sons together, says* יהוה: *I will not pity, nor spare, nor have rachamim, but destroy them. 15 Shema, and give ear; be not proud: for* יהוה *has spoken. 16 Give tiferet to* יהוה *Your Elohim, before He cause darkness, and before your feet stumble upon the dark mountains, and, while you look for light, He turns it into the shadow of death, and makes it gross darkness. 17 But if you*

---

[1] Jerusalem.
[2] Judah.
[3] Babylon after the Jewish exile.
[4] Judah.

---

[5] Both houses.
[6] Confusion and paganism.

will not shema, my being shall weep in secret places for your pride; and my eye shall weep much, and run down with tears, because יהוה's flock is carried away to exile. 18 Say to the melech and to the rulers, Humble yourselves, sit down: for your rule shall come down, even the keter of your tiferet. 19 The cities of the south shall be shut, and none shall open them: Yahudah shall be carried away into exile all of it; it shall be fully carried away exile. 20 Lift up your eyes, and see them that come from the north: where is the flock that was given to you, your beautiful flock? 21 What will you say when He shall punish you? For you have taught them to be captains, and as chiefs over you: shall they not have sorrow, as a woman in labor? 22 *And if you say in your lev, Why do these things come upon me? For the greatness of your iniquity are your skirts uncovered, and your heels made bare. 23 Can the Ethiopian change his skin color, or the leopard its spots? Only then will you do tov; who are accustomed to do evil. 24 Therefore will I scatter them as the stubble that passes away by the wind of the wilderness. 25 This is your lot, the portion of your measures from Me,* says יהוה; *because you have forgotten Me, and trusted in falsehood. 26 Therefore will I uncover your skirts upon your face; that your shame may appear. 27 I have seen your adulteries, and your neighings, the lewdness of your whoring, and your abominations on the hills and in the fields. Woe to you, O Yahrushalayim! Will you not be made clean? How long shall it be before you are made clean?*[1]

14 The word of יהוה that came to Yirmeyahu concerning the drought. 2 *Yahudah mourns, and its gates languish; they are fallen to the ground; and the cry of Yahrushalayim is gone up. 3 And their nobles have sent their little ones for mayim: they came to the cisterns, and found no mayim; they returned with their vessels empty; they were ashamed and blushed, and covered their heads. 4 Because the ground became cracked, for there was no rain in the earth, the plowmen were put to shame; they covered their heads. 5 Yes, the deer also gave birth in the field, but left it, because there was no grass. 6 And the wild donkeys did stand in the high places, they snuffed up the wind like jackals; their eyes have failed, because there was no grass.* 7 O יהוה, *though our iniquities testify against us, You do it for Your Name's sake: for our backslidings are many; we have sinned against You. 8 O Expectation of Yisrael, the Savoir of it in time of trouble, why should You be as a stranger in the land, and as a traveler that turns in to stay for a night? 9 Why should You be as a man stunned, as a mighty man that cannot save? Yet You, O* יהוה, *are in the midst of us, and we are called by Your Name; do not leave us.* 10 This says יהוה to this people, *This have they loved to wander, they have not refrained their feet, therefore* יהוה *does not accept them; He will now remember their iniquity, and visit punishment for their sins.* 11 Then said יהוה to me, *Make no tefillah for this people for their tov. 12 When they fast, I will not shema to their cry; and when they offer burnt offering and an oblation, I will not accept them: but I will consume them by the sword, and by the famine, and by the pestilence.* 13 Then said I, Oy Vey, Master יהוה! See, the neviim say to them, You shall not see the sword, neither shall you have famine; but I will give you emet shalom in this place. 14 Then יהוה said to me, *The neviim prophesy lies in My Name: I sent them not, neither have I commanded them, neither have I spoken to them: they prophesy to you a false vision and divination, and a thing of vanity, and the deceit of their own lev. 15 Therefore this says* יהוה *concerning the neviim that prophesy in My Name, and I sent them not, yet they say, Sword and famine shall not be in this land; By sword and famine shall those neviim be consumed. 16 And the*

---

[1] Or how long until the Cleaner, the Moshiach shows up?

people to whom they prophesy shall be cast out in the streets of Yahrushalayim because of the famine and the sword; and they shall have no one to bury them, them, their wives, nor their sons, nor their daughters: for I will pour their wickedness upon them. 17 Therefore you shall say this word to them; Let my eyes run down with tears night and day, and let them not cease: for the virgin daughter of My people is broken with a great breach, with a very grievous blow. 18 If I go forth into the field, then see the slain with the sword! And if I enter into the city, then see them that are sick with famine! Yes, both the navi and the kohen go out into a land that they know not. 19 Have You utterly rejected Yahudah? Has Your being loathed Tzion? Why have You smitten us, and there is no healing for us? We looked for shalom, and there is no tov; and for the time of healing, and see trouble! 20 We acknowledge, O יהוה , our wickedness, and the iniquity of our ahvot: for we have sinned against You. 21 Do not despise us, for Your Name's sake, do not dishonor the throne of Your tiferet: remember; break not Your covenant with us. 22 Are there any among the worthless elohim of the gentiles that can cause rain? Or can the shamayim give showers? Are not You He, O יהוה our Elohim? Therefore we will wait upon You: for You have made all these things.

15 Then said יהוה to me, Though Moshe and Schmuel stood before Me, [1] yet My mind could not be changed toward this people: cast them out of My sight, and let them go forth. 2 And it shall come to pass, if they say to you, Where shall we go forth? Then you shall tell them, This says יהוה; Such as are for death, to death; and such as are for the sword, to the sword; and such as are for the famine, to the famine; and such as are for the exile, to the exile. 3 And I will appoint over them four kinds of punishment, says יהוה: the sword

to kill, and the dogs to tear, and the fowls of the shamayim, and the beasts of the earth, to devour and destroy. 4 And I will cause them to be removed into all the malchutim of the earth, [2] because of Menasheh the son of Hizqiyahu melech of Yahudah; for all that he did in Yahrushalayim. 5 For who shall have pity upon you, O Yahrushalayim? Or who shall mourn for you? Or who shall turn aside to ask how you are doing? 6 You have forsaken Me, says יהוה , you have gone backward: therefore will I stretch out My hand against you, and destroy you; I am weary of relenting. 7 And I will winnow them with a winnowing fan in the gates of the land; I will bereave them of children, I will destroy My people, since they shuv not from their own halacha. 8 Their widows are increased before Me more than the sand of the seas: I have brought upon them, against the ima of the young men, a plunderer at noon: I shall cause agitation and sudden alarm to fall on the city. 9 She that she that has borne seven languishes: she shall breathe her last; her sun is gone down while it was yet day: she has been ashamed and humiliated: and the rest of them will I deliver to the sword before their enemies, says יהוה. 10 Woe is me, my Ema, that you have borne me a man of strife and a man of contention to the whole earth! [3] I have neither lent on interest, nor men have lent to me on interest; yet every one of them does curse me. 11 יהוה said, Did I not direct you for your tov? Did I not intercede for you in a time of evil? And in a time of affliction against the enemy? 12 Shall iron break the northern iron and the steel? 13 Your substance and your treasures will I give to the plunderer without price, for all your sins, even in all your borders. 14 And I will make you to pass with your enemies into a land that you do not know: for a fire is kindled in My

---

[1] As mediators.

[2] If Judah is in all the nations, how much more Ephraim who was numerically greater and in exile longer.
[3] When you are called to teach the truth of YHWH's displeasure with man's ways, you will be labeled as a man of contention and division, as was Yahshua.

- 503 -

anger, which shall burn upon you. 15 O
יהוה, You know: remember me, and visit
me, and revenge me of my persecutors; take
me not away in Your patience: know that
for Your sake I have suffered rebuke.
16 Your words were found, and I did eat
them; and Your word was to me the simcha
and gilah of my lev: for I am called by Your
Name, O יהוה Elohim of hosts. 17 I sat not
in the congregation of the mockers, nor
rejoiced; I sat alone because of Your hand
upon my chayim: for You have filled me
with displeasure. 18 Why is my pain
everlasting, and my wound incurable, which
refuses to be healed? Will You be to me as
a mirage, which cannot be believed?
19 Therefore this says יהוה, If you make
teshuvah, then will I bring you again, and
you shall stand before Me: and if you take
out the precious from the vile, you shall be
as My mouth: let them shuv to you; but shuv
not to them. 20 And I will make you to this
people a fenced bronze wall: and they shall
fight against you, but they shall not prevail
against you: for I am with you to save you
and to deliver you, says יהוה. 21 And I will
deliver you out of the hand of the wicked,
and I will redeem you out of the hand of the
ruthless.

16 The word of יהוה came also to
me, saying, 2 You shall not take a
wife; neither shall you have sons or
daughters in this place. 3 For this says
יהוה concerning the sons and concerning
the daughters that are born in this place, and
concerning their imas that bare them, and
concerning their ahvot that begat them in
this land; 4 They shall die of grievous
deaths; they shall not be lamented; neither
shall they be buried; but they shall be as
dung upon the face of the earth: and they
shall be consumed by the sword, and by
famine; and their corpses shall be food for
the fowls of the shamayim, and for the
beasts of the earth. 5 For this says יהוה,
Enter not into the Bayit of mourning,
neither go to lament for them: for I have

taken away My shalom from this people,
says יהוה, even loving-kindness and
rachamim. 6 Both the great and the small
shall die in this land: they shall not be
buried, neither shall men lament for them,
nor cut themselves, nor make themselves
bald for them: 7 Neither shall men tear
themselves for them in mourning, to comfort
them for the dead; neither shall men give
them the cup of consolation to drink for
their abba or for their ima. 8 You shall not
also go into the Bayit of feasting, to sit with
them to eat and to drink.[1] 9 For this says
יהוה of hosts, the Elohim of Yisrael; See, I
will cause to cease out of this place in your
eyes, and in your days, the voice of gilah,
and the voice of simcha, the voice of the
bridegroom, and the voice of the bride.
10 And it shall come to pass, when you shall
show this people all these words, and they
shall say to you, Why has יהוה pronounced
all this great evil against us? Or what is our
iniquity? Or what is our sin that we have
committed against יהוה our Elohim?
11 Then shall you say to them, Because
your ahvot have forsaken Me, says יהוה,
and have had their halacha after other
elohim, and have served them, and have
worshipped them, and have forsaken Me,
and have not kept My Torah; 12 And you
have done worse than your ahvot; for, see,
you walk every one after the imagination of
his evil lev, that they may not shema to Me:
13 Therefore will I cast you out of this land
into a land that you know not, neither you
nor your ahvot; and there shall you serve
other elohim day and night; where I will not
show you favor. 14 Therefore, see, the days
come, says יהוה, that it shall no more be
said, יהוה lives, that brought up the
children of Yisrael out of the land of
Mitzrayim;[2] 15 But, יהוה lives, that
brought up the children of Yisrael from the
land of the north,[3] and from all the lands

---

[1] We must not celebrate the feasts with those not fully walking
in obedience to Torah.
[2] A greater exodus is coming that will make the first historical
one pale in comparison.
[3] Assyria.

where He had driven them:[1] and I will bring them again into their land that I gave to their ahvot.[2] 16 See, I will send for many fishers, says יהוה , and they shall fish them;[3] and after that will I send for many hunters, and they shall hunt them from every mountain, and from every hill, and out of the holes of the rocks[4]. 17 For My eyes are upon all their halacha: they are not hidden from My face, neither is their iniquity hidden from My eyes. 18 And first I will repay their iniquity and their sin double,[5] because they have defiled My land; they have filled My inheritance with the corpses of their detestable and abominable things. 19 O יהוה, My strength, and My stronghold, and My refuge in the Day of Tribulation,[6] the gentiles shall come to You from the ends of the earth,[7] and shall say,

Surely our ahvot have inherited only lies, only vanity, and things in which there is no profit.[8] 20 *Shall a man make elohim to himself that are not elohim? 21 Therefore, see, I will this time[9] cause them to know, I will cause them to know My Hand[10] and My Might,[11] and they shall know that My Name is יהוה.[12]*

17 *The sin of Yahudah is written with a pen of iron, and with the point of a diamond: it is carved upon the table of their lev, and upon the horns of your altars; 2 While their children remember their altars and their groves by the green eytzim on the high hills. 3 My mountain in the field, I will give your substance and all your treasures to be plundered, and your high places for sin, throughout all your borders. 4 And you, even yourself, shall discontinue from your heritage that I gave you; and I will cause you to serve your enemies in the land that you do not know: for you have kindled a fire in My anger, which shall burn le-olam-va-ed. 5 This says יהוה; Cursed be the man that trusts in man, and makes flesh his arm, and whose lev departs from יהוה. 6 For he shall be like the shrub in the desert, and shall not see when tov comes; but shall inhabit the parched places in the wilderness, a salt land that is not inhabited. 7 Blessed is the man that trusts in יהוה, and whose trust is in יהוה. 8 For he shall be as an eytz planted by the mayim, that spreads out its roots by the river, and shall not see when heat comes, but his leaf shall be green; and shall not be anxious in the year of drought, neither shall he cease from yielding fruit. 9 The lev is deceitful above all things, and desperately wicked: who can know it? 10 I יהוה search the lev; I try the kidneys, even to give every man according*

---

[1] All nations.
[2] YHWH speaks about the future messianic redemption when He will bring all the redeemed of Zion back to the land of Yisrael, not only from Egypt, but from all the nations, making this exodus far greater and more powerful than the first historic redemption. Also the fact that the final ingathering of the exiles will include upwards of 3 billion people as opposed to the 3-4 million of the historical exodus, makes this event a defining moment in YHWH's dealing with mankind. That's what the two houses are all about: the end of our long national nightmare of spiritual and physical exile from YHWH.
[3] The Torah-keeping disciples of Yahshua and those they led over the past 2,000 years by proclamation of the Tov News is what is referred to as the fishing stage or method by which the exiles from both houses are ordained to return. Yahshua in the Great Commission of Matthew 28:18-20; sent His disciples to all nations, since Yisrael was scattered into all nations. Yahshua said through the Tov News we would fish or search for men. As shown elsewhere "men" is a Hebraic idiomatic expression for Yisraelites, as opposed to the derogatory Hebraic terms for non-Yisraelites and pagan gentiles who are called dogs or pigs. The restoration and regathering of both houses takes place in two stages, with the first being the fishing stage, which by definition is the non-violent stage.
[4] Otherwise known as the time of Yaakov's Trouble, from which most of Yaakov will be saved according to Jeremiah 30:7. The hunters in every nation show the wandering Yisraelites that their life is in danger in the nations, and that the land of Yisrael is actually a much safer place under YHWH's protective care. The hunters are seen as anti-Semites, who hate Jews and Yahshua, as well as Ephraimite Torah-keepers, who are hounded and threatened by them without mercy. Anti-Semitism and fear will be the main weapon of the hunters.
[5] See notes on Ezekiel chapter 4.
[6] Great Tribulation.
[7] During Jacob's Trouble not only will both houses heed the call to return home, but even the non-Yisraelites will return to YHWH and seek Torah through His Son; they will confess that all their religion and western culture has not mounted up to a hill of beans, and that they are contrite and broken over their abominable sun worship offered by their ancestors which was not according to YHWH, His Son, and His Torah. Surely this confession will come to pass by millions of people, as they realize that Hebraic worship and comprehension of YHWH

remain His will, and is the only way that is not based on vain pagan philosophy, handed down through the generations.
[8] In non-Hebraic lifestyles.
[9] Great Tribulation.
[10] Yahshua.
[11] Ruach HaKodesh.
[12] All nations – either through the fishermen, or the hunting men – will know all things Hebraic, including the His Name, which is YHWH.

to his halacha the, fruit of his doings. 11 As the partridge sits on eggs, and hatches them not; so is he that gets riches, but not by doing right, it shall leave him in the midst of his days, and in the end he is a fool. 12 An exalted high throne from the beginning is the place of our Set-Apart Place. 13 O יהוה, the mikvah of Yisrael, all that forsake You shall be ashamed; *and they that depart from Me shall be written in the earth,[1] because they have forsaken* יהוה, *the Fountain of living mayim.*[2] 14 Heal me, O יהוה, and I shall be healed; save me, and I shall be saved: for You are my tehilla. 15 See, they say to me, Where is the word of יהוה? Let it come now! 16 As for me, I have not run away from being a shepherd who follows You: neither have I desired the dreadful day; You know that which has come out of my lips was tzadik before You. 17 Be not a ruin to me: You are my tikvah in the day of evil. 18 Let them be ashamed that persecute me, but let not I be ashamed: let them be broken, but let not I be broken: bring upon them the day of evil, and destroy them with double destruction. 19 This said יהוה to me; *Go and stand in the gate of the children of the people, where the melechim of Yahudah come in, and where they go out, and in all the gates of Yahrushalayim; 20 And say to them, Shema the word of* יהוה, *you melechim of Yahudah, and all Yahudah, and all the inhabitants of Yahrushalayim, that enter in by these gates: 21 This says* יהוה; *Guard yourselves, and bear no burden on the Shabbat, nor bring it in by the gates of Yahrushalayim; 22 Neither carry forth a burden out of your houses on the Shabbat, neither do any work, but set-apart the Shabbat, as I commanded your ahvot. 23 But they obeyed not, neither inclined their ear, but made their neck stiff, that they might not shema, and not receive instruction. 24 And it shall come to pass, if* you diligently shema to Me, says יהוה, *to bring in no burden through the gates of this city on the Shabbat, but set-apart the Shabbat, to do no work in it; 25 Then shall there enter into the gates of this city melechim and leaders sitting upon the throne of David, riding in mirkavot and on horses, they, and their leaders, the men of Yahudah, and the inhabitants of Yahrushalayim: and this city shall remain le-olam-va-ed. 26 And they shall come from the cities of Yahudah, and from the places around Yahrushalayim, and from the land of Benyamin, and from the plain, and from the mountains, and from the south, bringing burnt offerings, and sacrifices, and food offerings, and incense, and bringing sacrifices of hallel, to the Bayit of* יהוה. *27 But if you will not shema to Me to set-apart the Shabbat, and not to bear a burden, when entering the gates of Yahrushalayim on the Shabbat day; then will I kindle a fire in its gates, and it shall devour the palaces of Yahrushalayim, and it shall not be quenched.*

18 The word that came to Yirmeyahu from יהוה, saying, 2 *Arise, and go down to the potter's bayit, and there I will cause you to shema My words.* 3 Then I went down to the potter's bayit, and, see; he worked a work on the wheels. 4 And the vessel that he made of clay was marred[3] in the hand of the potter[4]: so he made it again another vessel,[5] as seemed tov to the potter to make it.[6] 5 Then the word of יהוה came to me, saying, 6 *O Beit Yisrael, cannot I do with you as this potter? says* יהוה. *See, as the clay is in the potter's hand, so are you in My hand, O Beit Yisrael.*[7][8] *7 The moment I shall speak concerning a nation, and*

---

[1] Literally fulfilled by Yahshua in John 8, when the names of all those forsaking Him were written in the earth.
[2] After rejecting Yahshua's call to drink from the wells of salvation in John 7, their names were recorded in the earth in John 8, and this prophecy was fulfilled.

[3] The marred vessel is the people of Yisrael. All 12 tribes.
[4] The potter is Father YHWH.
[5] The Renewed Covenant and the promise of ongoing renewal.
[6] According to His will.
[7] Both houses.
[8] For a full treatment on the Potter's house see: **One Lump Potter** at :
http://store.yourarmstoisrael.org/Qstore/Qstore.cgi?CMD=011&PROD=000142.

concerning a malchut, to pluck up, and to pull down, and to destroy it; 8 If that nation, against whom I have pronounced, turn from their evil, I will relent of the evil that I thought to do to them. 9 And the moment I shall speak concerning a nation, and concerning a malchut, to build and to plant it; 10 If it does evil in My sight, that it obeys not My voice, then I will relent of the tov that I said I would do for them. 11 Now therefore go to, speak to the men of Yahudah, and to the inhabitants of Yahrushalayim, saying, This says **יהוה** ; See, I allow evil against you, and devise a plan against you: shuv every one from his evil halacha, and make your halacha and your doings tov. 12 And they said, There is no tikvah: but we will have our halacha after our own plans, and we will all follow the imagination and stubbornness of our evil lev. 13 Therefore this says **יהוה**; Ask now among the nations, who has heard such things: the virgin of Yisrael has done a very horrible thing. 14 Will a man leave the snow of Levanon that comes from the rock of the field? Or shall the cool flowing mayim that comes from another place dry up? 15 Because My people have forgotten Me, they have burned incense to vanity, and they have caused them to stumble in their halacha away from the ancient paths, to walk in false paths, in a halacha not made by Me; 16 To make their land desolate, and an everlasting hissing; everyone that passes by shall be appalled, and shake his head. 17 I will scatter them as with an east wind[1] before the enemy; I will show them My back, and not My face, in the day of their calamity. 18 Then they said, Come, and let us devise plans against Yirmeyahu; for the Torah shall not perish from the kohen, nor counsel from the wise, nor the word from ha navi. Come, and let us smite him with the tongue, and let us not shema to any of his words. 19 Shema to me, O **יהוה**; and shema to the voice of those that contend with me. 20 Shall evil be repaid for tov? For

they have dug a pit for my being. Remember that I stood before You to speak tov for them, and to turn away Your wrath from them. 21 Therefore deliver up their children to the famine, and pour out their dom by the force of the sword; and let their wives be bereaved of their children, to be widows; and let their men be put to death; let their young men be slain by the sword in battle. 22 Let a cry be heard from their houses, when You shall bring a raiding unit suddenly upon them: for they have dug a pit to take me, and hidden snares for my feet. 23 Yet, **יהוה**, You know all their counsel against me to kill me: forgive not their iniquity, neither blot out their sin from Your sight, but let them be overthrown before You; deal with them in the time of Your anger.

19 This says **יהוה**, Go and get a potter's earthen jug, and take of the zechanim of the people, and of the zechanim of the kohanim; 2 And go forth to the Valley of the Son of Hinnom, which is by the entrance of the eastern gate, and proclaim there the words that I shall tell you, 3 And say, Shema the word of **יהוה**, O melechim of Yahudah, and inhabitants of Yahrushalayim; This says **יהוה** of hosts, the Elohim of Yisrael; See, I will bring evil upon this place that makes the ears of all who shema tingle. 4 Because they have forsaken Me, and have profaned this place, and have burned incense in it to other elohim, whom neither they nor their ahvot have known, nor the melechim of Yahudah have known, and have filled this place with the dom of innocents; 5 They have built also the high places of Baal, to burn their sons with fire for burnt offerings to Baal, which I commanded not, nor spoke it, neither did it come into My mind: 6 Therefore, see, the days come, says **יהוה**, that this place shall no more be called Tophet, nor the Valley of the Son of Hinnom, but the Valley of Slaughter. 7 And I will make void the counsel of Yahudah and Yahrushalayim in

---

[1] Wind of judgment.

this place; and I will cause them to fall by the sword before their enemies, and by the hands of those that seek their lives: and their corpses will I give for food for the fowls of the the shamayim, and for the beasts of the earth. 8 And I will make this city desolate, and a hissing; everyone that passes by shall be appalled and hiss because of all its plagues. 9 And I will cause them to eat the flesh of their sons and the flesh of their daughters, and they shall eat every one the flesh of his friend in the siege and in the distress, with which their enemies, and they that seek their lives, shall distress them 10 Then shall you break the jug in the sight of the men that go with you, 11 And shall say to them, This says יהוה of hosts; Even so will I break this people and this city, as one breaks a potter's vessel, that cannot be made whole again: and they shall bury them in Tophet, until there is no place left for burial. 12 This will I do to this place, says יהוה, and to the inhabitants of it, and I even will make this city as Tophet: 13 And the houses of Yahrushalayim, and the houses of the melechim of Yahudah, shall be defiled as the place of Tophet, because of all the houses upon whose roofs they have burned incense to all the hosts of the shamayim, and have poured out drink offerings to other elohim. 14 Then Yirmeyahu came from Tophet, where יהוה had sent him to prophesy; and he stood in the court of יהוה's Bayit; and said to all the people, 15 This says יהוה of hosts, the Elohim of Yisrael; See, I will bring upon this city and upon all her towns all the evil that I have pronounced against it, because they have hardened their necks, that they might not shema My words.

20 Now Pashur the son of Immer the kohen, who was also chief overseer in the Bayit of יהוה, heard that Yirmeyahu prophesied these things. 2 Then Pashur smote Yirmeyahu ha navi, and put him in the stocks that were in the High Gate of Benyamin, which was by the Bayit of יהוה.

3 And it came to pass on the next day, that Pashur brought forth Yirmeyahu out of the stocks. Then said Yirmeyahu to him, יהוה has not called your name Pashur, but Magor-Missaviv. 4 For this says יהוה, See, I will make you a fear to yourself, and to all your chaverim: and they shall fall by the sword of their enemies, and your eyes shall see it: and I will give all Yahudah into the hand of the melech of Bavel, and he shall carry them into exile into Bavel, and shall kill them with the sword. 5 Moreover I will deliver all the strength of this city, and all the labors of it, and all the precious things of it, and all the treasures of the melechim of Yahudah will I give into the hand of their enemies, that shall plunder them, and take them, and carry them to Bavel. 6 And you, Pashur, and all that dwell in your bayit shall go into exile: and you shall come to Bavel, and there you shall die, and shall be buried there, you, and all your chaverim, to whom you have prophesied lies. 7 O יהוה, You have enticed me, and I was deceived: You are stronger than I, and have prevailed: I have been ridiculed daily, everyone mocks me. 8 For when I speak, I cried out, declaring violence and plunder; because the word of יהוה was made a reproach to me, and a derision, daily. 9 Then I said, I will not make mention of Him, nor speak any more in His Name. But His word was in my lev as a burning fire shut up in my bones, and I was weary with holding back, and I could not stop. 10 For I heard many mockings, fear on every side. Expose, they say, and we will expose him. All my chaverim watched for my stumbling, saying, He will be lured away, and we shall prevail against him, and we shall take our revenge on him. 11 But יהוה is with me as a mighty awesome One: therefore my persecutors shall stumble, and they shall not prevail: they shall be greatly ashamed; for they shall not prosper: their everlasting confusion shall never be forgotten. 12 But, O יהוה of hosts, who tests the tzadik, and sees the kidneys and the lev, let me see

Your vengeance on them: for to You have I opened my cause. 13 Sing to יהוה, hallel יהוה: for He has delivered the being of the poor from the hand of evildoers. 14 Cursed be the day in which I was born: let not the day in which my ima bore me be blessed. 15 Cursed be the man who brought tidings to my abba, saying, A male child is born to you; giving him very much simcha. 16 And let that man be as the cities that יהוה overthrew, and repented not: and let him shema the cry in the morning, and the shouting at noon; 17 Because he killed me not from the womb, so that my ima might have been my grave, and her womb great le-olam-va-ed. 18 Why did I come forth from the womb to see labor and sorrow, that my days should be spent in shame?

21 The word which came to Yirmeyahu from יהוה, when melech Tzidkiyahu sent to him Pashur the son of Melchiyah, and Tzephanyah the son of Maaseyah the kohen, saying, 2 Inquire to יהוה for us; for Nebuchadnetzar melech of Bavel makes war against us; if so be that יהוה will deal with us according to all His wondrous works, so that the enemy withdraws from us. 3 Then said Yirmeyahu to them, This shall you say to Tzidkiyahu: 4 This says יהוה Elohim of Yisrael; *See, I will turn back the weapons of war that are in your hands, with which you fight against the melech of Bavel, and against the Chaldeans, which besiege you outside the walls, and I will gather them into the midst of this city. 5 And I Myself will fight against you with an outstretched hand and with a strong arm, even in rage, and in displeasure, and in great wrath. 6 And I will smite the inhabitants of this city, both man and beast: they shall die of a great pestilence. 7 And afterward,* says יהוה, *I will deliver Tzidkiyahu melech of Yahudah, and his avadim, and the people, and such as are left in this city from the pestilence, from the sword, and from the famine, into the hand of Nebuchadnetzar melech of Bavel,*

and into the hand of their enemies, and into the hand of those that seek their chayim: and He shall smite them with the edge of the sword; He shall not spare them, neither have pity, nor have rachamim. 8 And to this people you shall say, This says יהוה; See, I set before you the halacha of chayim, and the halacha of death. 9 He that stays in this city shall die by the sword, and by the famine, and by the pestilence: but he that goes out, and falls to the Chaldeans that besiege you, he shall live, and his chayim shall be to him for a prize. 10 For I have set My face against this city for evil, and not for tov, says יהוה: it shall be given into the hand of the melech of Bavel, and he shall burn it with fire. 11 And touching the bayit of the melech of Yahudah, say, Shema the word of יהוה; 12 O Beit David, this says יהוה; Execute mishpat in the morning, and deliver him that is plundered out of the hand of the oppressor, lest My wrath goes out like fire, and burns so that none can quench it, because of the evil of your doings. 13 See, I am against you, O inhabitant of the valley, and rock of the plain, says יהוה; who says, Who shall come down against us? Or who shall enter into our dwellings? 14 But I will punish you according to the fruit of your doings,* says יהוה: *and I will kindle a fire in its forest, and it shall devour all things all around.*

22 This says יהוה; *Go down to the bayit of the melech of Yahudah, and speak there this word, 2 And say, Shema the word of* יהוה, *O melech of Yahudah, that sits upon the throne of David, you, and your avadim, and your people that enter in by these gates: 3 This says* יהוה; *Execute mishpat and tzedakah, and deliver the plundered out of the hand of the oppressor: and do no wrong, do no violence to the stranger, the fatherless, nor the widow, neither shed innocent dom in this place. 4 For if you do this thing indeed, then shall there enter in by the gates of this bayit melechim sitting upon the throne of*

David, riding in mirkavot and on horses, he, and his avadim, and his people. 5 But if you will not shema these words, I swear by Myself, says יהוה, that this bayit shall become a ruin. 6 For this says יהוה to the melech's bayit of Yahudah; *You are Gilead to Me, and the head of Levanon: yet surely I will make you a wilderness, and cities that are not inhabited. 7 And I will prepare destroyers against you, every one with his weapons: and they shall cut down your choice cedars, and cast them into the fire. 8 And many nations shall pass by this city, and they shall say every man to his neighbor, Why has יהוה done this to this great city? 9 Then they shall answer, Because they have forsaken the covenant of יהוה their Elohim, and worshipped other elohim, and served them. 10 Weep not for the dead, neither mourn him: but weep bitterly for him that goes away: for he shall shuv no more, nor see his native country.* 11 For this says יהוה regarding Shallum the son of Yoshiyahu melech of Yahudah, who reigned in the place of Yoshiyahu his abba, who went forth out of this place; *He shall not shuv here any more: 12 But he shall die in the place where they have led him into exile, and shall see this land no more. 13 Woe to him that builds his bayit by unrighteousness, and his rooms by wrong; that uses his neighbor's service without wages, and gives him nothing for his work; 14 That says, I will build a wide bayit with large rooms, and cuts out windows; and it is paneled with cedar, and painted in red. 15 Shall you reign, just because you enclose yourself in cedar? Did not your abba eat and drink, and do mishpat and justice, and then it went well with him? 16 He defended the cause of the poor and needy; then it was well with him: was not this to know Me?* says יהוה. 17 *But your eyes and your lev are for nothing but your greed, and to shed innocent dom, and oppression, and the doing of violence.* 18 Therefore this says יהוה concerning Yehoyaqim the son of Yoshiyahu melech of Yahudah; *They shall not lament for him, saying, Oy Vey my brother! Or, Oy Vey my sister! They shall not lament for him, saying, Oy Vey master! Or, Oy Vey your excellency! 19 He shall be buried with the burial of a donkey, drawn out and cast out outside the gates of Yahrushalayim. 20 Go up to Levanon, and cry; and lift up your voice in Bashan, and cry from Avariym: for all your lovers are destroyed. 21 I spoke to you in your prosperity; but you said, I will not shema. This has been your manner from your youth, that you obeyed not My voice. 22 The wind of mishpat shall eat up all your shepherds, and your lovers shall go into exile: surely then shall you be ashamed and ashamed for all your wickedness. 23 O inhabitant of Levanon, that make your nest in the cedars, how you shall groan when birth pains come upon you, like the pain of a woman in labor!* 24 As I live, says יהוה, *though Coniyah the son of Yehoyaqim melech of Yahudah were the signet upon My right hand, yet would I pluck you off from there; 25 And I will give you into the hand of those that seek your chayim, and into the hand of those whose face you fear, even into the hand of Nebuchadnetzar melech of Bavel, and into the hand of the Chaldeans. 26 And I will cast you out, and your ima that bare you, into another country, where you were not born; and there shall you die. 27 But to the land where they desire to shuv, there shall they not shuv. 28 Is this man Coniyah a despised broken pot? Is he a vessel in which there is no pleasure? Why are they cast out, he and his zera, into a land which they do not know? 29 O land, land, land, shema the word of יהוה.*

30 This says יהוה, *Write this man childless, as a strong man that shall not prosper in his days: moreover no man of his zera shall prosper le-olam-va-ed, sitting upon the throne of David, and ruling any more in Yahudah.*[1]

23 *Woe be to the shepherds that destroy and scatter the sheep of My pasture!* says יהוה.[2] 2 Therefore this says יהוה Elohim of Yisrael against the shepherds that feed My people; *You have scattered My flock,*[3] *and driven them away, and have not visited them: see, I will visit upon you the evil of your doings,* says יהוה. 3 *And I will gather the remnant of My flock*[4] *out of all countries where I have driven*

them,[5] *and will bring them again to their folds; and they shall be fruitful and increase.* 4 *And I will set up shepherds*[6] *over them that shall feed them: and they shall fear no more, nor be broken,*[7] *neither shall they be lacking,* says יהוה. 5 *See, the days come,* says יהוה, *that I will raise to David a Tzadik Branch, and a Melech*[8] *shall rule and prosper, and shall execute mishpat and justice in the earth.*[9] 6 *In His days Yahudah shall be saved,*[10] *and Yisrael shall dwell safely:*[11] *and this is His Name by which He shall be called,* יהוה *- Tzidqaynu.*[12] 7 *Therefore, see, the days come,* says יהוה, *that they shall no more say,* יהוה *lives, who brought up the children of Yisrael out of the land of Mitzrayim;* 8 *But,* יהוה *lives, who brought up and which led the zera of Beit Yisrael out of the north country, and from all countries*[13] *where I had driven them; and they shall dwell in their own land.*[14] 9 My lev within me is broken because of the neviim; all my bones shake; I am like a drunken man, and like a man overcome by wine, because of יהוה, and because of His set-apart words. 10 *For the land is full of adulterers; for because of a curse the land mourns; the pleasant places of the wilderness are dried up, and their course is evil, and their force is not right.* 11 *For both navi and kohen are profane; yes, in My Bayit have I found their wickedness,* says

---

[1] The curse does not apply to Moshiach Yahshua, and furthermore substantiates that no one other than Yahshua of Nazareth could have been Moshiach. First of all YHWH signified, demonstrated and sealed the eternal curse on Coniah/Jeconiah's seed by removing the king's signet ring on his finger as found in verse 24. Knowing this, why would Matthew still list Coniah/Jeconiah, when he could have skipped him in his genealogy? Of course Matthew had no authority to remove any curse, even had he chosen not to list Coniah. In Haggai 2:23 the curse is definitely reversed. From this verse we see several things. First, Zerubabel was a chosen vessel to restore the Solomon line of descent, as YHWH who had removed the signet ring of kingship from Coniah/Jeconiah, now places it again on Zerubabel His chosen servant to restore and renew the Davidic lineage through Solomon. The Coniah/Jeconiah curse lasted only one generation due to YHWH's grace, and was reversed in his grandson Zerubabel, who became everything Coniah/Jeconiah was not. Also Jeconiah had children, even when YHWH told Jeremiah to record that the king would be childless. Matthew, knowing through the Spirit of Moshiach that this curse had been removed, felt free to include Coniah/Jeconiah in his genealogy. Let's assume that the curse had never been lifted in Zerubabel and is still on Solomon's lineage. That leaves us with an interesting scenario. Now, no Moshiach can come through Solomon, unless YHWH finds a way for the real Moshiach not to have any human father descending from Solomon. If YHWH Himself were to Father the Moshiach, then the curse would not need to be removed, but would be bypassed. He thus ordained the virgin birth, and the quickening of Miriam's womb by the Spirit Himself. Yahshua had no earthly father and therefore is the only man who can qualify now or then to be descended from Solomon's cursed line; again that is if one chooses to believe that the curse was never removed in Zerubabel, which it clearly was.
[2] All those who do not love the sheep, and those who deny them equal rights as Yisrael by dividing the body into Jew and gentile; as opposed to building and regathering all in the one fold of Renewed Yisrael as Yahshua has done and desires us to do.
[3] By divisive teachings; such as separate entity theology and replacement theology.
[4] Please note that the redeemed dom-washed remnant will be gathered. Not all Yisraelites will return, but only those under the banner of King Yahshua will occupy the land in the millennial kingdom.
[5] Both houses have been scattered to all nations; not just a select few to Europe.
[6] Renewed Covenant shepherds who understand the true plan of YHWH and the restoration of both houses. Shepherds who understand YHWH's plan will feed the flock in YHWH's desired and revealed manner.
[7] The people will no more fear separation from YHWH, nor of being outside His favor and favored nation.
[8] King Moshiach.
[9] Moshiach Yahshua will rule only by the precepts of Torah.
[10] In the atid lavoh, Judah will be redeemed by the dom of atonement, and Ephraim Yisrael will dwell safely back in the land having been redeemed and brought back safely by YHWH to the land.
[11] Both houses having their blindness removed.
[12] The King here is called YHWH; as it is YHWH and not a mere man who will restore both houses in salvation and aliyah. Any man-made attempts to restore both houses apart from Yahshua as King over both houses, is doomed not only to failure, but to His eternal unchanging wrath.
[13] The house of Yisrael is in all countries.
[14] The end of the exile of Judah and Ephraim will be so grand that it will make the historic Egyptian exile pale in comparison.

יהוה. 12 *Therefore their halacha shall be to them as a slippery derech in the darkness: they shall be driven on, and fall in it: for I will bring evil upon them, even the year of their visitation by punishment,* says יהוה. 13 *And I have seen folly in the neviim of Shomron; they prophesied in Baal,[1] and caused My people Yisrael to go astray. 14 I have seen also in the neviim of Yahrushalayim a horrible thing: they commit adultery, and walk in lies: they strengthen also the hands of the evildoers, that none does shuv from his wickedness: they are all of them before Me as Sedom, and the inhabitants of it as Amorah.* 15 Therefore this says יהוה of hosts *concerning the neviim; See, I will feed them with wormwood,[2] and make them drink the mayim of poison: for from the neviim of Yahrushalayim has defilement gone forth into all the land.* 16 This says יהוה of hosts, *Shema not to the words of the neviim that prophesy to you: they make you go astray: they speak a vision of their own lev, and not out of the mouth of* יהוה. 17 *They say still to them that despise Me,* יהוה *has said, You shall have shalom; and they say to everyone that walks after the imagination of his own lev, No evil shall come upon you.* 18 *For who has stood in the counsel of* יהוה, *and has perceived and heard His word? Who has marked His word, and heard it? 19 See, a whirlwind of* יהוה *has gone forth in wrath, even a whirlwind storm: it shall fall severely upon the head of the wicked. 20 The anger of* יהוה *shall not shuv, until He has done, and until He has established the thoughts of His lev: in the latter-days you shall consider it perfectly.[3] 21 I have not sent these neviim, yet they ran: I have not spoken to them, yet they prophesied. 22 But if they had stood in My counsel, and had caused My people to shema to My words, then they would have turned them from their evil halacha, and*

from the evil of their doings. 23 Am I an Elohim at hand,[4] says יהוה, *and not an Elohim far off?[5] 24 Can anyone hide himself in secret places where I shall not see him? Says* יהוה. *Do I not fill the shamayim and earth? Says* יהוה. *25 I have heard what the neviim said, that prophesy lies in My Name, saying, I have dreamed, I have dreamed. 26 How long shall this be in the lev of the neviim that prophesy lies? Yes, they are neviim of the deceit of their own lev; 27 Who attempt to cause My people to forget My Name by their dreams[6] that they tell every man to his neighbor, as their ahvot have forgotten My Name for Baal.[7][8] 28 The navi that has a dream, let him tell the dream; and he that has My word, let him speak My word faithfully. What is the chaff to the wheat? Says* יהוה. *29 Is not My word like a fire? Says* יהוה; *and like a hammer that breaks the rock in pieces? 30 Therefore, see, I am against the neviim,* says יהוה, *that steal My words every one from his neighbor. 31 See, I am against the neviim,* says יהוה, *that use their tongues, and say, He says. 32 See, I am against them that prophesy false dreams,* says יהוה, *and do tell them, and cause My people to go astray by their lies, and by their reckless boasting; yet I sent them not, nor commanded them: therefore they shall not profit this people at all,* says יהוה. *33 And when this people, or ha navi, or a kohen, shall ask you, saying, What is the burden of* יהוה*? You shall then say to them,*

---

[1] Literally:"The lord."
[2] False doctrines and spiritual confusion.
[3] In the latter-days both houses will reconsider their ways as they look for the truth of YHWH and His Son.

[4] Fo Judah.
[5] For Ephraim.
[6] Dreams, visions and other prophetic utterances cannot be deemed reliable without them using the true Name of the Father, i.e., the actual source from which these words are allegedly being given. Of course; even when these utterances are given in the Name of YHWH, they still must be individually tested.
[7] Literally:"the lord."
[8] A major part of the full restoration of Yisrael is the Father restoring His Name among our nation, overcoming the centuries of substituting titles like "hashem" and "lord" for "YHWH." YHWH states that those who do not actively teach and instruct in His true Name, are actually lying to the people and causing them to let go and forget the true Name, as did the false neviim to their ancestors. Either a returning Yisraelite will use, proclaim and return in the true Name, or YHWH will see to it that their fruits will be similar to the false prophets of yesteryear. As a leader in the two-house movement, are you causing people to remember or to forget His set-apart Name?

What burden? I will even forsake you, says יהוה. 34 And as for ha navi, and the kohen, and the people, that shall say, The burden of יהוה, I will even punish that man and his bayit. 35 This shall you say each person to his neighbor, and each person to his brother, What has יהוה answered? And, What has יהוה spoken? 36 And the burden of יהוה shall you mention no more: for every man's word shall be his own burden; for you have perverted the words of the living Elohim, יהוה of hosts our Elohim. 37 This shall you say to ha navi, What has יהוה answered you? And, What has יהוה spoken to you? 38 But since you say, The burden of יהוה;[1] therefore this says יהוה; Because you say this word, The burden of יהוה, and I have sent to you, saying, You shall not say, The burden of יהוה ; 39 Therefore, see, I, even I, will utterly forget you, and I will forsake you, and the city that I gave you and your ahvot, and cast you out of My presence: 40 And I will bring an everlasting reproach upon you, and an everlasting shame, that shall not be forgotten.

24 יהוה showed me, and, see, two baskets of figs were set before the Beit HaMikdash of יהוה , after that Nebuchadnetzar melech of Bavel had carried away into exile Yekonyahu the son of Yehoyaqim melech of Yahudah, and the leaders of Yahudah, with the craftsmen and smiths, from Yahrushalayim, and had brought them to Bavel. 2 One basket had very tov figs, even like the figs that are first ripe: and the other basket had very spoiled figs, which could not be eaten, they were so bad. 3 Then said יהוה to me, What do you see, Yirmeyahu? And I said, Figs; the tov figs, very tov; and the evil, very evil, so that they cannot be eaten, they are so evil. 4 Again the word of יהוה came to me, saying, 5 This says יהוה, the Elohim of Yisrael; Like these tov figs, so will I acknowledge them that are carried away from the exiles of Yahudah, whom I have sent out of this place into the land of the Chaldeans for their tov. 6 For I will set My eyes upon them for tov, and I will bring them again to this land: and I will build them, and not pull them down; and I will plant them, and not pluck them up. 7 And I will give them a lev to know Me, that I am יהוה: and they shall be My people, and I will be their Elohim: for they shall make teshuvah to Me with their whole lev. 8 And as for the evil figs, which cannot be eaten, they are so evil; surely this says יהוה, So will I give Tzidkiyahu the melech of Yahudah, and his leaders, and the residue of Yahrushalayim, that remain in this land, and them that dwell in the land of Mitzrayim: 9 And I will deliver them to be removed into all the malchutim of the earth for their harm, to be a reproach and a byword, a taunt and a curse word, in all the places where I shall drive them. 10 And I will send the sword, the famine, and the pestilence, among them, until they are consumed from off the land that I gave to them and to their ahvot.

25 The word that came to Yirmeyahu concerning all the people of Yahudah in the fourth year of Yehoyaqim the son of Yoshiyahu melech of Yahudah, that was the first year of Nebuchadnetzar melech of Bavel; 2 The which Yirmeyahu ha navi spoke to all the people of Yahudah, and to all the inhabitants of Yahrushalayim, saying, 3 From the thirteenth year of Yoshiyahu the son of Amon melech of Yahudah, even to this day, that is the twenty-third year, the word of יהוה had come to me, and I have spoken to you, rising early and speaking; but you have not heard. 4 And יהוה has sent to you all His avadim the neviim, rising early and sending them; but you have not heard, nor inclined your ear to shema. 5 They said, Teshuvah again now everyone from his evil halacha, and from the evil of your doings, and dwell in the land that יהוה has given to you and to your ahvot le-olam-va-ed: 6 And go not

---

[1] Meaning: "the weight of delivering YHWH's words is upon me," a claim that the false neviim always made.

after other elohim to serve them, and to worship them, and provoke Me not to anger with the works of your hands; and I will do you no harm. 7 Yet you have not listened to Me, says יהוה; that you might provoke Me to anger with the works of your hands to your own harm. 8 Therefore this says יהוה of hosts; Because you have not heard My words, 9 See, I will send and take all the families of the north, says יהוה , and Nebuchadnetzar the melech of Bavel, My eved, and will bring them against this land, and against the inhabitants of it, and against all these nations all around and will utterly destroy them, and make them an astonishment, and a hissing, and everlasting ruins. 10 Moreover I will take from them the voice of gilah, and the voice of simcha, the voice of the bridegroom, and the voice of the bride, the sound of the millstones, and the light of the candle. 11 And this whole land shall be a desolation, and a waste; and these nations shall serve the melech of Bavel seventy years. 12 And it shall come to pass, when seventy years are accomplished, that I will punish the melech of Bavel, and that nation, says יהוה, for their iniquity, and the land of the Chaldeans, and will make it everlasting ruins. 13 And I will bring upon that land all My words, which I have pronounced against it, even all that is written in this scroll, which Yirmeyahu has prophesied against all the nations. 14 For many nations and great melechim shall enslave them also: and I will repay them according to their deeds, and according to the works of their own hands. 15 For this says יהוה Elohim of Yisrael to me; Take the wine cup of this wrath at My hand, and cause all the nations, to whom I send you, to drink it. 16 And they shall drink, and shake, and be mad, because of the sword that I will send among them. 17 Then took I the cup at יהוה's hand, and made all the nations to drink it, to whom יהוה had sent me: 18 Namely, Yahrushalayim, and the cities of Yahudah, and the melechim of it, and the

leaders of it, to make them a desolation, an astonishment, a hissing, and a curse; as it is this day; 19 Pharaoh melech of Mitzrayim, and his avadim, and his leaders, and all his people; 20 And all the mixed multitude, and all the melechim of the land of Uz, and all the melechim of the land of the Philistines, and Ashkelon, and Azzah, and Ekron, and the remnant of Ashdod, 21 Edom, and Moav, and the children of Ammon, 22 And all the melechim of Tsor, and all the melechim of Tzidon, and the melechim of the coastlands which are beyond the sea, 23 Dedan, and Tema, and Buz, and all that are in the furthest corners, 24 And all the melechim of Arabia, and all the melechim of the mixed multitude who dwell in the desert, 25 And all the melechim of Zimri, and all the melechim of Eylam, and all the melechim of the Medes, 26 And all the melechim of the north, far and near, one with another, and all the malchutim of the olam, which are upon the face of the earth: and the melech of Sheshach shall drink with them. 27 Therefore you shall say to them, This says יהוה of hosts, the Elohim of Yisrael; Drink, and be drunk, and vomit, and fall, and rise no more, because of the sword which I will send among you. 28 And it shall be, if they refuse to take the cup at your hand to drink it, then shall you say to them, This says יהוה of hosts; You shall certainly drink it. 29 For, see, I begin to bring evil on the city that is called by My Name, and should you be utterly unpunished? You shall not be unpunished: for I will call for a sword upon all the inhabitants of the earth, says יהוה of hosts. 30 Therefore prophesy against them all these words, and say to them, יהוה shall roar from on high, and utter His voice from His set-apart dwelling; He shall mightily roar from His dwelling place; He shall give a shout, as they that tread the grapes, against all the inhabitants of the earth. [1]

---

[1] The following verses have a dual application, with the immediate context being the time of Judah's exile, but the eschatological context is when all nations will be in the Great Tribulation.

31 *A noise shall come even to the ends of the earth; for* יהוה *has a controversy with the nations, He will plead with all flesh; He will give them that are wicked to the sword, says* יהוה. 32 This says יהוה *of hosts, See, evil shall go forth from nation to nation, and a great whirlwind shall be raised up from the coasts of the earth.* 33 *And the slain of* יהוה *shall be at that day from one end of the earth even to the other end of the earth: they shall not be lamented, neither gathered, nor buried; they shall be dung upon the ground.* 34 *Howl, you shepherds, and cry; and cover yourselves in the ashes, you leaders of the flock: for the days of your slaughter and of your exiles are accomplished; and you shall fall like a choice vessel.* 35 *And the shepherds shall have no derech to flee, nor the leaders of the flock to escape.* 36 *A voice of the cry of the shepherds, and the howling of the leaders of the flock, shall be heard: for* יהוה *has plundered their pasture.* 37 *And their quiet dwellings are cut down because of the fierce anger of* יהוה. 38 *He has forsaken His hiding place, as the lion: for their land is desolate because of the fierceness of the oppressor, and because of His fierce anger.*

26 In the beginning of the malchut of Yehoyaqim the son of Yoshiyahu melech of Yahudah came this word from יהוה, saying, 2 This says יהוה; *Stand in the court of* יהוה*'s Bayit, and speak to all the cities of Yahudah, which come to worship in* יהוה*'s Bayit, all the words that I command you to speak to them; do not remove a word:* 3 *If perhaps they will shema, and make teshuvah every man from his evil halacha, that I may relent of the evil, which I purpose to do to them because of the evil of their doings.* 4 *And you shall say to them, This says* יהוה; *If you will not shema to Me, to have your halacha in My Torah, which I have set before you,* 5 *To shema to the words of My avadim the neviim, whom I send to you, both rising up*

early, and sending them, but you have not heard; 6 *Then will I make this bayit like Shiloh, and will make this city a curse to all the nations of the earth.* 7 So the kohanim and the neviim and all the people heard Yirmeyahu speaking these words in the Bayit of יהוה. 8 Now it came to pass, when Yirmeyahu had made an end of speaking all that יהוה had commanded him to speak to all the people, that the kohanim and the neviim and all the people took him, saying, You shall surely die.[1] 9 Why have you prophesied in the Name of יהוה, saying, This bayit shall be like Shiloh, and this city shall be desolate without an inhabitant? And all the people were gathered against Yirmeyahu in the Bayit of יהוה. 10 When the leaders of Yahudah heard these things, then they came up from the melech's bayit to the Bayit of יהוה, and sat down in the entrance of the New Gate of יהוה's Bayit. 11 Then spoke the kohanim and the neviim to the leaders and to all the people, saying, This man is worthy to die; for he has prophesied against this city, as you have heard with your own hearing. 12 Then spoke Yirmeyahu to all the leaders and to all the people, saying, יהוה sent me to prophesy against this bayit and against this city with all the words that you have heard. 13 Therefore now change your halacha and your doings, and obey the voice of יהוה Your Elohim; and יהוה will relent of the evil that He has pronounced against you. 14 As for me, see, I am in your hand: do with me as seems tov and right to you. 15 But know you for certain, that if you put me to death, you shall surely bring innocent dom upon yourselves, and upon this city, and upon the inhabitants of it: for of an emet יהוה has sent me to you to speak all these words in your hearing. 16 Then said the leaders and all the people to the kohanim and to the neviim; This man is not worthy to die: for he has spoken to us in the Name of יהוה our Elohim. 17 Then rose up

---

[1] A true navi will either be killed or be threatened with death; and of course be accused of being harsh and odious.

certain of the zachanim of the land, and spoke to all the congregation of the people, saying, 18 Micah the Morasthite prophesied in the days of Hizqiyahu melech of Yahudah, and spoke to all the people of Yahudah, saying, This says יהוה of hosts; *Tzion shall be plowed like a field, and Yahrushalayim shall become heaps, and the mountain of the bayit as the high places of a forest.* 19 Did Hizqiyahu melech of Yahudah and all Yahudah put him to death? Did he not fear יהוה, and sought יהוה, and יהוה relented of the evil that he had pronounced against them? We are doing great evil against ourselves. 20 And there was also a man that prophesied in the Name of יהוה, Uriyah the son of Shemayah of Kiryath-Yearyim, who prophesied against this city and against this land according to all the words of Yirmeyahu: 21 And when Yehoyaqim the melech, with all his mighty men, and all the leaders, heard his words, the melech sought to put him to death: but when Uriyah heard it, he was afraid, and fled, and went into Mitzrayim; 22 And Yehoyaqim the melech sent men into Mitzrayim, namely, El-Nathan the son of Achvor, and certain men with him into Mitzrayim. 23 And they brought Uriyah out of Mitzrayim, and brought him to Yehoyaqim the melech; who killed him with the sword, and cast his dead body into the graves of the am-ha-aretz. 24 Nevertheless the hand of Ahicham the son of Shaphan was with Yirmeyahu, that they should not give him into the hand of the people to put him to death.

27 In the beginning of the malchut of Yehoyaqim the son of Yoshiyahu melech of Yahudah came this word to Yirmeyahu from יהוה, saying, 2 This says יהוה to me; *Make for yourself bands and yokes, and put them upon your neck,* 3 *And send them to the melech of Edom, and to the melech of Moav, and to the melech of the Ammonites, and to the melech of Tsor, and to the melech of Tzidon, by the hand of the messengers that come to Yahrushalayim to Tzidkiyahu melech of Yahudah;* 4 *And command them to say to their masters, This says יהוה of hosts, the Elohim of Yisrael; This shall you say to your masters;* 5 *I have made the earth, the man and the beast that are upon the ground, by My great power and by My outstretched arm, and have given it to whom it seemed right to Me.* 6 *And now have I given all these lands to the hand of Nebuchadnetzar the melech of Bavel, My eved; and the beasts of the field have I given to him also to serve him.* 7 *And all nations shall serve him, and his son, and his son's son, to the very time of his land come: and then many nations and great melechim shall make him serve them.* 8 *And it shall come to pass, that the nation and malchut which will not serve the same Nebuchadnetzar the melech of Bavel, and that will not put their neck under the yoke of the melech of Bavel, that nation will I punish, says יהוה, with the sword, and with the famine, and with the pestilence, until I have consumed them by his hand.* 9 *Therefore shema not you to your neviim, nor to your diviners, nor to your dreamers, nor to your enchanters, nor to your sorcerers, who speak to you, saying, You shall not serve the melech of Bavel:* 10 *For they prophesy a lie to you, to remove you far from your land, and that I should drive you out, and that you should perish.* 11 *But the nations that bring their neck under the yoke of the melech of Bavel, and serve him, those will I let remain in their own land, says יהוה; and they shall till it, and dwell in it.* 12 I spoke also to Tzidkiyahu melech of Yahudah according to all these words, saying, *Bring your necks under the yoke of the melech of Bavel, and serve him and his people, and live.* 13 *Why will you die, you and your people, by the sword, by the famine, and by the pestilence, as יהוה has spoken against the nation that will not serve the melech of Bavel?* 14 *Therefore shema not to the words of the neviim that speak to you, saying, You shall not serve the melech*

of Bavel: for they prophesy a lie to you. 15 For I have not sent them, says יהוה, yet they prophesy a lie in My Name; that I might drive you out, and that you might perish, you, and the neviim who prophesy to you. 16 Also I spoke to the kohanim and to all the people, saying, This says יהוה; Shema not to the words of your neviim that prophesy to you, saying, See, the vessels of יהוה's Bayit shall now shortly be brought again from Bavel: for they prophesy a lie to you. 17 Shema not to them; serve the melech of Bavel, and live: why should this city be laid waste? 18 But if they are neviim, and if the word of יהוה is with them, let them now make intercession to יהוה of hosts, so that the vessels that are left in the Bayit of יהוה, and in the bayit of the melech of Yahudah, and at Yahrushalayim, do not go to Bavel. 19 For this says יהוה of hosts concerning the columns, and concerning the sea, and concerning the bases, and concerning the residue of the vessels that remain in this city, 20 Which Nebuchadnetzar melech of Bavel took not, when he carried away Yekonyahu the son of Yehoyaqim melech of Yahudah into exile from Yahrushalayim to Bavel, along with all the nobles of Yahudah and Yahrushalayim; 21 Yes, this says יהוה of hosts, the Elohim of Yisrael, concerning the vessels that remain in the Bayit of יהוה, and in the bayit of the melech of Yahudah and of Yahrushalayim; 22 They shall be carried to Bavel, and there shall they be to the day that I visit them with deliverance, says יהוה; then will I bring them up, and restore them to this place.

28 And it came to pass the same year, in the beginning of the malchut of Tzidkiyahu melech of Yahudah, in the fourth year, and in the fifth month, that Hananyah the son of Azur ha navi, who was of Giveon, spoke to me in the Bayit of יהוה, in the presence of the kohanim and of all the people, saying, 2 This speaks יהוה of hosts, the Elohim of Yisrael, saying, I have

broken the yoke of the melech of Bavel. 3 Within two full years will I bring again into this place all the vessels of יהוה's Bayit, that Nebuchadnetzar melech of Bavel took away from this place, and carried to Bavel: 4 And I will bring again to this place Yekonyahu the son of Yehoyaqim melech of Yahudah, with all the captives of Yahudah, that went into Bavel, says יהוה: for I will break the yoke of the melech of Bavel. 5 Then ha navi Yirmeyahu said to ha navi Hananyah in the presence of the kohanim, and in the presence of all the people that stood in the Bayit of יהוה, 6 Even ha navi Yirmeyahu said, Amein: יהוה do so: יהוה perform Your words which you have prophesied, to bring again the vessels of יהוה's Bayit, and all that is carried away into exile, from Bavel into this place. 7 Nevertheless shema now to this word that I speak in your hearing, and in the hearing of all the people; 8 The neviim that have been before me and before you from old prophesied both against many countries, and against great malchutim, of war, and of evil, and of pestilence. 9 The navi who prophesies of shalom, when the word of that navi shall come to pass, then shall ha navi be known, that יהוה has truly sent him. 10 Then Hananyah ha navi took the yoke from off ha navi Yirmeyahu's neck, and broke it. 11 And Hananyah spoke in the presence of all the people, saying, This says יהוה; Even so will I break the yoke of Nebuchadnetzar melech of Bavel from the neck of all nations within the space of two full years. And ha navi Yirmeyahu went his way. 12 Then the word of יהוה came to Yirmeyahu ha navi, after that Hananyah ha navi had broken the yoke from off the neck of ha navi Yirmeyahu, saying, 13 Go and tell Hananyah, saying, This says יהוה; You have broken the yokes of wood; but you shall make for them yokes of iron. 14 For this says יהוה of hosts, the Elohim of Yisrael; I have put a yoke of iron upon the neck of all these nations, that they may serve Nebuchadnetzar melech of Bavel; and *they shall serve him: and I have given him the beasts of the field also.* 15 Then said ha navi Yirmeyahu to Hananyah ha navi, Shema now, Hananyah; יהוה has not sent you; but you make this people trust in a lie. *16* Therefore this says יהוה; *See, I will cast you from off the face of the earth: this year you shall die, because you have taught rebellion against* יהוה. 17 So Hananyah ha navi died the same year in the seventh month.

29 Now these are the words of the letter that Yirmeyahu ha navi sent from Yahrushalayim to the rest of the zachanim who were carried away captive, and to the kohanim, and to the neviim, and to all the people whom Nebuchadnetzar had carried away in exile from Yahrushalayim to Bavel; 2 (After that Yekonyahu the melech, and the malka, and the eunuchs, the leaders of Yahudah and Yahrushalayim, and the carpenters, and the smiths, had departed from Yahrushalayim;) 3 By the hand of Elasah the son of Shaphan, and Gemaryah the son of Hilkiyah, (whom Tzidkiyahu melech of Yahudah sent to Bavel to Nebuchadnetzar melech of Bavel) saying, 4 This says יהוה of hosts, the Elohim of Yisrael, to all that are carried away captives, whom I have caused to be carried away from Yahrushalayim to Bavel; 5 *Build houses, and dwell in them; and plant gardens, and eat the fruit of them; 6 Take you wives, and beget sons and daughters; and take wives for your sons, and give your daughters to husbands, that they may bear sons and daughters; that you may be increased there,[1] and not diminished. 7 And seek the shalom of the city where I have caused you to be exiled, and make tefillah to* יהוה *for it: for in the shalom of it shall you have shalom.* 8 For this says יהוה of hosts, the Elohim of Yisrael; *Let not your neviim and your diviners, that are in the midst of you, deceive you, neither shema to your dreams which you are dreaming. 9 For they prophesy falsely to you in My Name: I have not sent them,* says יהוה. *10 For this* says יהוה , *After seventy years are accomplished at Bavel I will visit you, and perform My tov word toward you, in causing you to shuv to this place. 11 For I know the thoughts that I think toward you,* says יהוה, *thoughts of shalom, and not of evil, to give you tov tikvah in the end.[2] 12 Then shall you call upon Me, and you shall go and make tefillah to Me, and I will shema to you. 13 And you shall seek Me, and find Me, when you shall search for Me with all your lev. 14 And I will be found by you,* says יהוה: *and I will turn away your exile, and I will gather you from all the nations, and from all the places where I have driven you,* says יהוה; *and I will bring you back again into the place from where I caused you to go into exile. 15 Because you have said,* יהוה *has raised up neviim for us in Bavel; 16 Know this* says יהוה *of the melech that sits upon the throne of David, and of all the people that dwell in this city, and of your brothers that have not gone out with you into exile; 17 This says* יהוה *of hosts; See, I will send upon them the sword, the famine, and the pestilence, and will make them like vile figs, that cannot be eaten, they are so evil. 18 And I will persecute them with the sword, with the famine, and with the pestilence, and will deliver them to be removed to all the malchutim of the earth, to be a curse, and astonishment, and a hissing, and a reproach, among all the gentiles where I have driven them: 19 Because they have not listened to My words,* says יהוה, *which I sent to them by My avadim the neviim, rising up early and sending them; but you would not shema,* says יהוה. *20 Shema therefore the word of* יהוה, *all you of the exile, whom I have sent from Yahrushalayim to Bavel: 21 This says* יהוה *of hosts, the Elohim of Yisrael, about Ahav the son of Kolayah,*

---

[1] Regardless of where they go, the children of Yisrael always multiply physically, as per the patriarchal promise of covenant.

[2] In the end are the plan and the word of Judah's restoration to the land.

and Tzidkiyahu the son of Maaseyah, who prophesy a lie to you in My Name; *See, I will deliver them into the hand of Nebuchadnetzar melech of Bavel; and he shall kill them before your eyes; 22 And because of them all the exiles of Yahudah who are in Bavel shall use them as a curse, saying,* יהוה *make you like Tzidkiyahu and like Ahav, whom the melech of Bavel roasted in the fire; 23 Because they have committed evil in Yisrael, and have committed adultery with their neighbors' wives, and have spoken lying words in My Name, which I have not commanded them; even as I know, and am a witness, says* יהוה*. 24 This shall you also speak to Shemayah the Nehelamite, saying, 25 This speaks* יהוה *of hosts, the Elohim of Yisrael, saying, Because you have sent letters in your name to all the people that are at Yahrushalayim, and to Tzephanyah the son of Maaseyah the kohen, and to all the kohanim, saying, 26* יהוה *has made you kohen in place of Yehoyada the kohen, that you should be officers in the Bayit of* יהוה*, and for every man that is mad, and makes himself a navi, that you should put him in prison, and in the stocks. 27 Now therefore why have you not reproved Yirmeyahu of Anathoth, who makes himself a navi to you? 28 For therefore he sent to us in Bavel, saying, This exile is long: build houses, and dwell in them; and plant gardens, and eat the fruit of them.* 29 And Tzephanyah the kohen read this letter in the hearing of Yirmeyahu ha navi. 30 Then came the word of יהוה to Yirmeyahu, saying, 31 *Send to all them of the exile, saying, This says* יהוה *concerning Shemiyah the Nehelamite; Because Shemiyah has prophesied to you, and I sent him not, and he caused you to trust in a lie:* 32 Therefore this says יהוה*; See, I will punish Shemiyah the Nehelamite, and his zera: he shall not have a man to dwell among this people; neither shall he see the tov that I will do for My people, says* יהוה*; because he has taught rebellion against* יהוה*.*

30

The word that came to Yirmeyahu from יהוה, saying, 2 *This says* יהוה *Elohim of Yisrael, saying,* Write all the words that I have spoken to you in a scroll. 3 *For, see, the days come,* says יהוה, *that I will turn back the exile of My people Yisrael and Yahudah,* [1] says יהוה*; and I will cause them to shuv to the land that I gave to their ahvot, and they shall possess it.* [2] 4 And these are the words that יהוה spoke concerning Yisrael [3] and concerning Yahudah. [4] 5 For this says יהוה*; We have heard a voice of trembling, of fear, and not of shalom. 6 Ask now and see, whether a man does labor with child? Why do I see every man with his hands on his waist, as a woman in labor, and all faces are turned pale? 7 Oy! For that day is great, so that none is like it: it is even the time of Yaakov's Trouble; but he shall be saved out of it.* [5] 8 *For it shall come to pass in that day,* says יהוה *of hosts, that I will break his yoke from off your neck, and will burst your bonds, and strangers shall no more serve themselves of him:* [6] 9 *But they shall serve* יהוה *their Elohim, and David their Melech, whom I will raise up for them.* [7] 10 *Therefore fear not, O My eved Yaakov,* [8] says יהוה*; neither be discouraged, O Yisrael: for, see, I will save you from far,* [9] *and your zera from the land of their exile;* [10] *and Yaakov shall shuv,* [11] *and shall be in rest, and be in shalom, and no one shall*

---

[1] Both houses have been promised a return to the land and to redemption, not just Judah.
[2] Fully accomplished by YHWH alone through His Son, without help from any man or schemes of men.
[3] Ephraim.
[4] Applies to both houses.
[5] Jacob's Trouble is for both houses. But unlike the world, Yaakov will be spared from it through divine protection, or martyrdom.
[6] The end of the Great Tribulation will finally see the breaking of gentile or foreign dominion over Yisrael's two houses.
[7] At the end of Yaakov's Trouble we will also be serving only Yahshua our King, and be back in the land. It is great day for all Yisrael, but a dreadful day for the unrighteous.
[8] All 12 tribes.
[9] Ephraim in all nations.
[10] Judah in Babylon.
[11] Both houses.

make him afraid.[1] 11 *For I am with you,*
says **יהוה**, *to save you:[2] though I make a
full end of all nations where I have
scattered you, yet will I not make a full end
of you: but I will correct you in measure,
and will not leave you altogether
unpunished.[3]* 12 For this says **יהוה**, *Your
affliction is severe, and your wound is
grievous.* 13 *There is none to plead your
cause that you may be bound up: you have
no healing medicines.[4]* 14 *All your lovers
have forgotten you; they seek you not; for I
have wounded you with the wound of an
enemy, with the chastisement of a cruel one,
for the multitude of your iniquity; because
your sins were increased.* 15 *Why do you
cry about your affliction? Your sorrow is
incurable for the multitude of your iniquity:
because your sins were increased, I have
done these things to you.* 16 *Therefore all
they that devour you shall be devoured; and
all your adversaries, every one of them,
shall go into exile; and they that plunder
you shall be a plunder, and all that prey
upon you will I give for a prey.[5]* 17 *For I
will restore health to you,[6] and I will heal
you of your wounds,* says **יהוה**; *because
they called you an outcast, saying, This is
Tzion, whom no man seeks after.* 18 *This*
says **יהוה**; *See, I will turn back the exile of
Yaakov's tents, and have rachamim on his
dwelling places; and the city shall be
rebuilt upon its own heap, and the palace
shall remain in its right place.* 19 *And out of
them shall proceed hodu: and the voice of
them that make simcha: and I will multiply
them, and they shall not be few; I will also
grant them tiferet, and they shall not be*

small.[7] 20 *Their children also shall be as
before, and their congregation shall be
established before Me, and I will punish all
that oppress them.* 21 *And their Melech
shall be One of their own, and their
Governor shall proceed from their midst;
and I will cause Him to draw near, and He
shall approach Me: for who is this that
engaged His lev to approach to Me?* Says
יהוה.[8] 22 *And you shall be My people-Ami,
and I will be Your Elohim.[9]* 23 *See, the
whirlwind of* **יהוה** *goes forth with wrath, a
continuing whirlwind: it shall fall with pain
upon the head of the wicked.* 24 *The fierce
anger of* **יהוה** *shall not shuv, until He has
done it, and until He has performed the
intents of His lev: in the latter-days you
shall consider it.[10]*

31 *At the same time,[11] says* **יהוה**, *will
I be the Elohim of all the families of
Yisrael,[12] and they shall be My people-Ami.
2 This says* **יהוה**, *The people who were left
of the sword found favor in the wilderness;[13]
even Yisrael, when I went to cause him to
rest.* 3 **יהוה** *has appeared of old to me,
saying, Yes, I have loved you with an
everlasting ahava: therefore with loving-
kindness have I drawn you.[14]
4 Again I will rebuild you,[15] and you shall
be rebuilt, O virgin of Yisrael:[16] you shall
again take up your tambourines, and shall*

---

[1] This obviously cannot be speaking of 1948 as all of Jewish
Yisrael lives in fear for their life and Ephraim Yisrael has not
yet returned. This speaks of a true re-gathering at the end of
the Great Tribulation and not before.
[2] Both houses.
[3] In the end of the age, Yisrael will be corrected, whereas the
other nations will be eliminated as the kingdom is restored to
Yisrael; Yisrael will rule and reign over the earth with all
former nations now fully subjected to Yahshua from His throne
in Jerusalem.
[4] Until the coming of Yahshua the Moshiach.
[5] Only YHWH reserves the right to discipline Yisrael. No one
else can do so and escape His wrath.
[6] Spiritual healing by forgiveness and renewed creation status.

[7] Despite long and painful exiles, both houses will continue to
fill the nations with the seed of Jacob as per the covenant
promise of physical multiplicity, in this age and the age to
come.
[8] According to First Timothy 2:5, only Yahshua the Mediator
can make that approach.
[9] A reversal of the curse of Lo-Ami in Hosea chapter 1.
[10] Only in the latter-days, will the true meaning of this
marvelous two-house restoration be fully considered by
Yisrael.
[11] Atid lavoh.
[12] Jeremiah 31:1 is a definitive proclamation from YHWH, that
at the time of Jacob's (twelve tribes) return from all the lands
of their dispersion, YHWH will once again be the Master of all
the tribes of Yisrael.
[13] Salvation, regeneration and unmerited favor, all are found in
the wilderness of the nations for both houses, prior to their
physical return.
[14] YHWH speaking to His beloved Yisrael.
[15] YHWH – not man – does the building.
[16] All Yisrael -- i.e., both houses – will be rebuilt and return
together. Notice Ephraim does not meet Judah in the land, but
returns together with them from the nations, in the rebuilding
by YHWH through His Son.

go forth in the dances[1] of them that make simcha. 5 You shall yet plant vines upon the mountains of Shomron:[2] the planters shall plant, and shall treat them as normal. 6 For there shall be a day,[3] that the called out Netsarim-Notsrim[4] the ones who watch on the Mount Ephraim shall cry, Arise, and let us go up to Tzion to יהוה our Elohim.[5] 7 For this says יהוה; Sing with simcha for Yaakov, and shout among the chief of the nations:[6] publish, hallel saying, O יהוה, save Your people, the remnant of Yisrael.[7] 8 See, I will bring them from the north country, and gather them from the ends of the earth, and with them the blind and the lame,[8] the woman with child and her that labors with child

together: a great congregation-kahal gadol[9] shall shuv here.[10] 9 They shall come with weeping, and with tefillot I will lead them:[11] I will cause them to walk by the rivers of mayim in a straight halacha,[12] in which they shall not stumble: for I am an Abba to Yisrael, and Ephraim is My firstborn-bachor.[13] 10 Shema the word of יהוה, O you nations, and declare it in the coastlands far off, and say, He that scattered Yisrael will gather him, and keep him, as a Shepherd[14] does His flock.[15] 11 For יהוה has redeemed Yaakov, and ransomed him from the hand of him that was stronger than he.[16] 12 Therefore they shall come and shir in the heights of Tzion, and shall flow together[17] to the tov of יהוה,[18] for wheat, and for wine, and for oil, and for the young of the flock and of the herd: and their being shall be as a watered garden; and they shall not sorrow any more at all.[19] 13 Then shall the virgin gilah in the dance,[20] both young men and old together: for I will turn their mourning into simcha, and will comfort them, and make them gilah from their sorrow. 14 And I will fill the beings of the

---

[1] Hebraic dancing, and a growth in its interest, is also a sign that the daughter of Zion is being rebuilt.
[2] Capital of Ephraim showing YHWH's full intention to bring Ephraim home.
[3] Seventh-Day; or seven-thousandth year since Adam.
[4] In the course of time, the former northern territory of the land of Yisrael became known as Shomron, and the occupants of that land as Samaritans. These were a mixed breed of Ephraimite, food-growing landowners, and Assyrian colonists. Many Scriptures prophetically speak of a future day in the days around the time of the end of the exile, during which Notzrim will inhabit these same mountains of Shomron. These prophetic Scriptures reveal the glorious plan of the Father to turn these idolatrous territories into one of the future home bases of the Notzrim of Yisrael. The word Notzrim speaks of watchmen (guards) appointed by YHWH and assigned to the task of watching over the restoration of all Yisrael. Scripture refers to the Mountains of Ephraim (Shomron), which will produce the watchmen (guards) of the last days. The late Rabbi Isidor Zwirn, of blessed memory, a Messianic Jew, confirmed this in his extensive research on the term Notzrei-Yisrael, which he defined as Christian believers. He states: "Isaiah 11:1 clinched my acceptance of Yeshua HaNotzrei as the preserver of the twelve tribes of Yisrael, and the founding Father of the Notzrim." Another traditional Jew, Ben Cohen, states: "the way watchmen has been translated in our Bibles, it's a wonder we can see it right. The word is notzrim, and the root is natzar. The real explanation of the word in Hebrew is to 'safe keep,' 'to keep until a later time,' 'to hide it in a way that will be revealed later.' But, now take into consideration that the book of Jeremiah, of course, was written before there was Christianity. You look for a clue as to how it came about that Jeremiah used a word that was not used in his day at all, and it is the word used in Hebrew for Christians today. And it is translated 'preserved ones of Yisrael' (Isaiah 49:6, Isaac Lesser Edition) in English. Elsewhere it is translated as 'watchmen'. The word netzer is used only three times in the Bible, and everywhere it is mentioned it has to do only with Ephraim. It's amazing."
[5] Ephraim will long for and cry out to Judah for a mutual and equitable return.
[6] In context, Ephraim as the Nazarenes or "watchmen" are to cry out in all nations that Moshiach has come for atonement and return from the exile.
[7] All believers must publish these tov tidings.
[8] Spiritually.

[9] The Hebrew here is **kahal gadol** or "a large congregation." The congregation of Renewed Covenant Yisrael, consisting of the large remnant of the 12 tribes that once stood at Mt. Sinai.
[10] The catching away is the regathering of both houses back to the land.
[11] YHWH leads us back to the land, not man.
[12] Torah.
[13] Here YHWH states that it is Ephraim (later to become the ten-tribes of Yisrael) that is always and eternally His firstborn. As YHWH's eternal firstborn, he comes to a time of repentance through the Renewed Covenant. It is at that time that YHWH will be Master over all the tribes or clans of Yisrael, according to Jeremiah 31:1. The one returning as part of the great congregation from the nations is Ephraim YHWH's firstborn. Hebrews 12:23 confirms the centrality and spiritual primacy of firstborn Yisrael, the redeemed gathering and "congregation of the firstborn, having been enrolled in heaven...." YHWH says that all believers make up the membership of the "congregation of firstborn Yisrael," whose names are recorded in the Lamb's Book Of Life.
[14] Yahshua.
[15] All Yisrael will return by the same One who was responsible for the scattering.
[16] YHWH will redeem Yisrael from the hands of the stronger gentile nations.
[17] Both houses will flow back together. Note that Ephraim won't have to pander to orthodox separatists in unsaved Judah; who are now back in the land since 1948. Rather, the redeemed of both houses return together, as today neither redeemed Ephraim nor redeemed Judah are welcome as citizens. Only the unsaved in Yisrael seem to be welcome.
[18] The Moshiach who is the Tov Shepherd, the tov Torah, and the tov land.
[19] In the restored kingdom.
[20] The spotless virgin bride of Yahshua.

kohanim with fatness, and My people shall be satisfied with My tov, says יהוה . 15 This says יהוה; A voice was heard in Ramah, lamentation, and bitter weeping; Rachel weeping for her children; refusing to be comforted for her children, because they were not found.[1][2] 16 This says יהוה; Refrain your voice from weeping, and your eyes from tears: for your work shall be rewarded, says יהוה; and they shall shuv from the land of the enemy.[3] 17 And there is tikvah in your end, says יהוה, that your children shall shuv to their own country. 18 I have surely heard Ephraim lamenting himself;[4] You have chastised me, and I was chastised, as an untrained calf:[5] turn me back to you,[6] and I shall be turned; for You are יהוה My Elohim.[7] 19 Surely after that I was turned, I repented;[8] and after that I received Torah,[9] I smote upon my thigh:[10] I was ashamed,[11] yes, even ashamed, because I did bear the reproach of my youth.[12] 20 Is Ephraim My dear son?[13] Is he a pleasant child? For since I spoke against him, I do earnestly remember him still: therefore My inward parts are troubled for him;[14] I will surely have rachamim upon him, says יהוה. 21 Set up signposts,[15] make high heaps[16]: set your lev toward the highway, even the derech which you took: turn back,[17] O virgin of Yisrael,[18] turn back[19] to these your cities. 22 How long will you go about the olam,[20] O backsliding daughter?[21] For יהוה has created a new thing from nothing in the earth,[22] A woman shall surround a man.[23] 23 This says יהוה of hosts, the Elohim of Yisrael; They shall again use this speech in the land of Yahudah and in its cities, when I shall turn back their exile; יהוה bless you, O home of tzedakah, and mountain of set-apartness. 24 And there shall dwell in Yahudah itself, and in all the cities of it together, farmers, and those that go forth with flocks. 25 For I have filled the weary being, and I have replenished every sorrowful being.[24] 26 Upon this I woke up, and see; and my sleep was sweet to me[25] 27 See, the days will come, says יהוה, that I will sow Beit Yisrael and Beit Yahudah with the zera of man,[26] and with the zera of beast[27] 28 And it shall come to pass, that as I have watched over them, to pluck up, and to break down, and to throw down, and to destroy, and to afflict them; so will I watch

---

[1] In the literal pashat Rachel the wife of Jacob symbolically weeping over the Diaspora or the exile of scattered Yisrael in the galut. She is weeping for all of Yisrael's children, and her own children, Joseph and Benjamin, who are out of their homeland of Yisrael. Matthew chapter 2 quotes this in a remez/hint level. Bethlehem's children were killed due to Yisrael's disobedience of Torah, the very same reason Yisrael's 12 tribes were scattered to the ends of the earth to their spiritual and physical death. Disobedience is the thematic cord Matthew uses to tie this verse in the remez into its literal pashat.
[2] Despite her weeping and mourning, YHWH comforts her, as both houses will be returning. Ephraim represents Joseph's return, and Benjamin represents Judah's return, since Benjamin became part of Judah.
[3] The promised end of the exile comforts Rachel.
[4] YHWH comforts Rachel with proof of the end of the exile by telling her that He Himself has shema-ed Ephraim or non-Jewish Yisrael repenting.
[5] Ephraim laments his lack of instruction or Torah understanding. Egele or a bull is the tribal banner of Ephraim, later turned into idolatry by Ephraim.
[6] Ephraim cries for help in his teshuvah.
[7] Ephraim knows the ahava and patience of Pappa.
[8] True teshuvah for breaking the Torah.
[9] Instruction.
[10] Ephraim becomes amazed at his own blindness towards the eternal precepts of Torah, not just Judah's blindness towards Moshiach.
[11] A natural reaction when true repentance takes place.
[12] Ephraim sees his punishment as bearing the stupidity of his youthful ways, which included lust and paganism.
[13] A rhetorical question; If Ephraim is YHWH's dear Son, and furthermore is His firstborn, how can Ephraim not return together with Judah, despite not being recognized by the world or often even by themselves?

[14] YHWH is troubled until Ephraim is fully restored.
[15] Literal landmarks set up by Jeremiah and spiritual guideposts as well. This is addressed in detail at http://store.yourarmstoisrael.org/Qstore/Qstore.cgi?CMD=011&PROD=000007.
[16] Dolmans of stone; YHWH asks Yisrael to mark the route so they can return.
[17] Spiritually.
[18] All 12 tribes of verse 1.
[19] Physically.
[20] In prolonged exile.
[21] All Yisrael.
[22] This novum, or new thing, is directly linked to the healing of the backslidden daughter of Yisrael.
[23] In much Jewish literature, this was often viewed as a reference to the virgin birth of Moshiach. How does this all fit? The new thing is a human being born of the "seed of the woman" in fulfillment of Genesis 3:15, and is the means that actually brings about Ephraim and Judah's return; and it is the reason YHWH wants mother Rachel to stop crying.
[24] Caused by prolonged exile.
[25] Any dreams or visions of YHWH's restoration of Yisrael will indeed be a sweet time for the one understanding the meassge behind the dream.
[26] Limited intermingling between houses.
[27] A metaphor for gentiles or heathens. Both houses have the seed of Jacob mixed all over.

over them, to rebuild, and to plant them says יהוה.[1] 29 *In those days[2] they shall say no more, The ahvot have eaten a sour grape, and the children's teeth are blunted.[3] 30 But every one shall die for his own iniquity: every man that eats the sour grape, his teeth shall be set on edge. 31 See, the days are coming, says* יהוה, *that I will make a Brit Chadasha-Renewed Covenant with Beit Yisrael, and with Beit Yahudah:[4][5] 32 Not according to the covenant that I made with their ahvot in the day that I took them by the hand to bring them out of the land of Mitzrayim; which covenant they broke, although I was a husband to them, says* יהוה : [6] 33 *But this shall be the covenant that I will make with Beit Yisrael[7] after those days,[8] says* יהוה, *I will put My Torah in their inward parts, and write it on their levim; and will be their Elohim, and they shall be My People-Ami. 34 And they shall teach no more every man his neighbor, and every man his brother, saying, Know* יהוה: *for they shall all know Me,[9] from the least of them to the greatest* of them, says יהוה; *for I will forgive their iniquity, and I will remember their sin no more.[10] 35 This says* יהוה, *who gives the sun for a light by day, and the ordinances of the moon and of the chochavim for a light by night, who divides the sea when the waves of it roar;* יהוה *of hosts is His Name: 36 If those ordinances vanish from before Me, says* יהוה, *then the zera of Yisrael[11] also shall cease from being a nation before Me le-olam-va-ed.[12] 37 This says* יהוה; *If the shamayim above can be measured, and the foundations of the earth searched out beneath, I will also cast off all the zera of Yisrael for all that they have done, says* יהוה.[13] 38 *See, the days come, says* יהוה, *that the city[14] shall be rebuilt for* יהוה; *from the tower of Hanan-El to the Corner Gate. 39 And the measuring line shall yet go out straight ahead to the hill Garev, and shall turn to Goath. 40 And the whole valley of the dead bodies, and of the ashes, and all the fields to the Brook of Kidron, to the corner of the Horse Gate toward the east, shall be set-apart to* יהוה; *it shall not be plucked up, nor thrown down any more le-olam-va-ed.[15]*

---

[1] A clear-cut promise of full and total healing for both houses.
[2] At the time of restoration.
[3] An expression of those in exile.
[4] The Renewed Covenant was never cut with gentiles, or Christians but exclusively with both houses of Yisrael. This means all believers in the Renewed Covenant are Yisrael from either house or those who join with either house. If both of Yisrael's houses in fact became Judah, then why does YHWH specify another house by a different name 150 years after Ephraim had already gone into exile?
[5] It is this Renewed Covenant that ends the exile as renewal comes to both houses.
[6] Though YHWH was a husband to 4 million people that He personally took out of Egypt and then married at Sinai, only two stayed faithful to covenant. The Renewed Covenant is designed to make two houses faithful, not just two people.
[7] Both houses come into the Renewed Covenant but only Ephraim Yisrael needs a real introduction to Torah. Consequently after the days when the covenant is actually cut, there is an inner working in Ephraim out of a supernatural love to guard and perform Torah in their hearts. Judah on the other hand has the supernatural workings of the much-needed Ruach HaKodesh to bring their Torah walk to life. But these inward works are said to be ongoing and subsequent to the actual spilling of Moshiach's dom to cut the covenant.
[8] After the dom is spilled.
[9] "Knowing YHWH," is a first step that takes place through regeneration. YHWH, through Yahshua, does that regeneration. Therefore the commencement of the regeneration process is between YHWH and man, directly through His Son. Therefore the need is bypassed for any human instruments, to teach and instruct humanity, on how to know Him initially. All who truly desire to know can and will know Him, courtesy of Moshiach, without any human instrument. For the first time in Yisrael's history, man can

come to initially know YHWH's plan of salvation and His tov, without a human leader or rabbi, by simply beckoning Yahshua to reveal the Father-YHWH to him or herself through the revealed Word and its truth. Many have come to YHWH through His Son just by reading their Scriptures, without any human interference or input. After salvation, there is still the need for teachers and instructors. But that teaching role is to raise up the Yisraelite for maturity and fullness, in a higher revelation of the Word of YHWH. The ongoing need for teachers of the word, as it relates to the maturity of the individual by no means negates the promise of the Renewed Covenant. All the teaching is instilled after YHWH Himself, through His Son, sparks the flames of regeneration that brings one to that first step, on a long and exciting journey of knowing YHWH.
[10] In the Renewed Covenant both houses can be fully and unconditionally forgiven of all sins and transgressions.
[11] All 12 tribes.
[12] Yisrael's survival and the promised end of the exile and messianic redemption are guaranteed by the visibility of creation in the heavens. As long as these lights shine, the restoration and messianic redemption as well as the survival of both houses of Yisrael is personally guaranteed by Abba YHWH.
[13] YHWH also challenges us to remember that even as the heavens cannot be literally measured, neither can Yisrael be literally removed or replaced as the only single elect and chosen bride of YHWH, when found in their redeemed virgin state.
[14] Jerusalem.
[15] A description of Jerusalem rebuilt and restored ultimately in the millennium.

32 The word that came to Yirmeyahu from יהוה in the tenth year of Tzidkiyahu melech of Yahudah, which was the eighteenth year of Nebuchadnetzar. 2 For then the melech of Bavel's army besieged Yahrushalayim: and Yirmeyahu ha navi was imprisoned in the court of the guard, which was in the melech of Yahudah's bayit. 3 For Tzidkiyahu melech of Yahudah had imprisoned him, saying, Why do you prophesy, and say, This says יהוה, *See, I will give this city into the hand of the melech of Bavel, and he shall take it;* 4 *And Tzidkiyahu melech of Yahudah shall not escape out of the hand of the Chaldeans, but shall surely be delivered into the hand of the melech of Bavel, and shall speak with him mouth to mouth, and his eyes shall see his eyes;* 5 *And he shall lead Tzidkiyahu to Bavel, and there shall he shall be until I visit him,* says יהוה: *though you fight with the Chaldeans, you shall not prosper?* 6 And Yirmeyahu said, The word of יהוה came to me, saying, 7 *See, Haname-El the son of Shallum your uncle shall come to you, saying, Buy my field that is in Anathoth: for the right of redemption is yours to buy it.* 8 So Haname-El my uncle's son came to me in the court of the guard according to the word of יהוה, and said to me, Buy my field, I ask you, that is in Anathoth, which is in the country of Benyamin: for the right of inheritance is yours, and the redemption is yours; buy it for yourself. Then I knew that this was the word of יהוה. 9 And I bought the field of Haname-El my uncle's son that was in Anathoth, and weighed for him the silver, even seventeen shekels of silver. 10 And I signed the deed, and sealed it, and took witnesses, and weighed the silver in the scales. 11 So I took the deed of the purchase, both that which was sealed according to the Torah and custom, and that which was open: 12 And I gave the deed of the purchase to Baruch the son of Neriyah, the son of Maaseyah, in the sight of Haname-El my uncle's son, and in the

presence of the witnesses that signed the deed of the purchase, before all the Yahudim[1] that sat in the court of the guard. 13 And I commanded Baruch before them, saying, 14 This says יהוה of hosts, the Elohim of Yisrael; *Take these deeds, this deed of the purchase, both which is sealed, and this deed which is open; and put them in an earthen vessel, that they may remain for many days.* 15 For this says יהוה of hosts, the Elohim of Yisrael; *Houses and fields and vineyards shall be possessed again in this land.* 16 Now when I had delivered the deed of the purchase to Baruch the son of Neriyah, I made tefillah to יהוה, saying, 17 Ah Master יהוה! See, You have made the shamayim and the earth by Your great Power and ourstretched arm, and there is nothing too hard for You: 18 You show loving-kindness to thousands, and You repay the iniquity of the ahvot into the bosom of their children after them: the Great, the Mighty El, יהוה of hosts, is His Name, 19 Great in counsel, and mighty in work: for Your eyes are open upon all the halachot of the sons of men: to give every one according to his halacha, and according to the fruit of his doings: 20 For You have set signs and wonders in the land of Mitzrayim, even to this day, and in Yisrael, and among other men; and have made Your Name great, even to this day; 21 And have brought forth Your people Yisrael out of the land of Mitzrayim with signs, and with wonders, and with a strong hand, and with an outstretched arm, and with great awesome deeds; 22 And have given them this land, which You did swear to their ahvot to give them, a land flowing with milk and honey; 23 And they came in, and possessed it; but they obeyed not Your voice, neither had their halacha in Your Torah; they have done nothing of all that You commanded them to do: therefore You

---

[1] "Jews" is a term that had begun to refer to the south (all three tribes of Judah, Benjamin and Levi) at about this time and in other contemporary books like Esther and Nehemiah some 70 years later. This term, however, never refers to both houses anywhere in the Tanach, and very rarely in the Renewed Covenant.

have caused all this evil to come upon them: 24 See the siege mounds, they are come to the city to take it; and the city is given into the hand of the Chaldeans, that fight against it, because of the sword, and of the famine, and of the pestilence: and what You have spoken is coming to pass; and, see, you see it. 25 Yet You, O Master יהוה, have said to me, Buy the field for silver, and take witnesses, for the city is given into the hand of the Chaldeans. 26 Then came the word of יהוה to Yirmeyahu, saying, 27 *See, I am* יהוה*, the Elohim of all flesh: is there any thing too hard for Me?* 28 Therefore this says יהוה*; See, I will give this city into the hand of the Chaldeans, and into the hand of Nebuchadnetzar melech of Bavel, and he shall take it: 29 And the Chaldeans, that fight against this city, shall come and set fire to this city, and burn it with the houses, upon whose roofs they have offered incense to Baal, and poured out drink offerings to other elohim, to provoke Me to anger. 30 For the children of Yisrael and the children of Yahudah[1] have only done evil before Me from their youth: for the children of Yisrael[2] have only provoked Me to anger with the work of their hands, says* יהוה*. 31 For this city has been to Me as a provocation of My anger and of My wrath from the day that they built it even to this day; so that I should remove it from before My face, 32 Because of all the evil of the children of Yisrael and of the children of Yahudah,[3] which they have done to provoke Me to anger, they, their melechim, their leaders, their kohanim, and their neviim, and the men of Yahudah, and the inhabitants of Yahrushalayim. 33 And they have turned their back to Me, and not their face: though I taught them, rising up early and teaching them, yet they have not listened to receive instruction in Torah. 34 But they set their abominations in the Bayit, which is called by My Name, to defile it. 35 And they built the high places of* Baal[4]*, which are in the Valley of the Son of Hinnom, to cause their sons and their daughters to pass through the fire to Molech; which I commanded them not to do, neither came it into My mind, that they should do this abomination, to cause Yahudah to sin. 36 And now therefore this says* יהוה *, the Elohim of Yisrael, concerning this city, of which you say, It shall be delivered into the hand of the melech of Bavel by the sword, and by the famine, and by the pestilence; 37 See, I will gather them out of all countries, where I have driven them in My anger, and in My wrath, and in great wrath; and I will bring them again to this place, and I will cause them to dwell safely:[5] 38 And they shall be My people, and I will be their Elohim: 39 And I will give them one lev, and one halacha,[6] that they may fear Me le-olam-va-ed, for their tov, and the tov of their children after them: 40 And I will make an everlasting covenant with them,[7] that I will not turn away from them, to do them tov; but I will put My fear in their levim, that they shall not depart from Me. 41 Yes, I will gilah over them to do them tov, and I will plant them in this land in emet[8] with My whole lev and with My whole being. 42 For this says* יהוה*; Like I have allowed all this great evil upon this people, so will I bring upon them all the tov that I have promised them. 43 And fields shall be bought in this land, of which you say, It is desolate without man or beast; it is given into the hand of the Chaldeans. 44 Men shall buy fields for silver, and sign deeds, and seal them, and take witnesses in the land of Benyamin, and in the places around Yahrushalayim, and in the cities of Yahudah, and in the cities of the mountains, and in the cities of the valley, and in the*

---

[1] Both houses need cleansing by Moshiach Yahshua.
[2] Both houses.
[3] Both houses.
[4] Literally "The lord."
[5] Both houses driven into exile and both will return together.
[6] Both houses must be in agreement over Torah and the identity of King Moshiach. Until then, any attempt to reunite the two houses by changing immigration laws, is of the flesh and not of the Father.
[7] The one promised in Jeremiah 31:31.
[8] In compliance with Torah and Yahshua Who is The Truth.

cities of the south: for I will cause their exile to shuv, says **יהוה**.

33 Moreover the word of **יהוה** came to Yirmeyahu the second time, while he was yet imprisoned in the court of the guard, saying, 2 *This says* **יהוה** *the Maker of it,* **יהוה** *that formed it, to establish it;* **יהוה** *is His Name; 3 Call to Me, and I will answer you, and show you great and mighty things, which you know not.* 4 For this says **יהוה**, the Elohim of Yisrael, concerning the houses of this city, and concerning the houses of the melechim of Yahudah, which are thrown down by the siege mounds, and by the sword; 5 *They come to fight with the Chaldeans, and to fill their places with the dead bodies of men, whom I have slain in My anger and in My wrath, and for all whose wickedness I have hid My face from this city. 6 See, I will bring it health and relief, and I will cure them, and will reveal to them the abundance of real shalom and emet.*[1] 7 *And I will cause the exile of Yahudah and the exile of Yisrael to shuv,*[2] *and will build them, as at the first.*[3] 8 *And I will cleanse them from all their iniquity, by which they have sinned against Me; and I will pardon all their iniquities, by which they have sinned, and by which they have transgressed against Me.*[4] 9 *And it shall be to Me for a Name of simcha, a hallel and an honor before all the nations of the earth, who shall shema all the tov that I will do to them: and they shall fear and tremble for all the tov and for all the shalom that I give to them.*[5] 10 This says **יהוה**; *Again there shall be heard in this place, which you say shall be desolate without man and without beast, even in the* cities of Yahudah, and in the streets of Yahrushalayim, that are desolate, without man, and without inhabitant, and without beast, 11 *The voice of simcha, and the voice of gilah, the voice of the bridegroom, and the voice of the bride,*[6] *the voice of them that shall say, Baruch Hashem* **יהוה** *of hosts! For* **יהוה** *is tov; for His rachamim endures le-olam-va-ed, of those that shall bring the offering of hallel into the Bayit of* **יהוה**. *For I will turn back the exile of the land, as at the first, says* **יהוה**.[7] 12 *This says* **יהוה** *of hosts; Again in this place, which is desolate without man and without beast, and in all its cities, shall be a dwelling place of shepherds causing their flocks to lie down.*[8] 13 *In the cities of the mountains, in the cities of the low country, and in the cities of the south, and in the land of Benyamin, and in the places around Yahrushalayim, and in the cities of Yahudah, shall the flocks pass again under the hands of him that counts them, says* **יהוה**.[9] 14 *See, the days come, says* **יהוה**, *that I will perform that tov thing which I have promised to Beit Yisrael and to Beit Yahudah.*[10] 15 *In those days, and at that time,*[11] *will I cause the Branch-Tzamach of tzedakah to grow up to David; and He shall execute mishpat and tzedakah in the land.*[12] 16 *In those days shall Yahudah be saved,*[13] *and Yahrushalayim shall dwell safely: and this is the Name that shall be proclaimed to her,* **יהוה**-*Tzidkanu-our Tzedakah.*[14]

---

[1] Through the Renewed Covenant.
[2] Note how it is YHWH who will cause this, not man's negotiations and outright compromise with unredeemed Judah, as is prevalent in the land today.
[3] As in the days of the first settlement of the land; the days of Joshua son of Nun.
[4] At the end of the exile both houses will be pardoned and forgiven by virtue of the Renewed Covenant. If Judah has not entered into it, she is not ready for the messianic redemption.
[5] The end of the exile and revelation of the ten tribes brings YHWH great fame in the earth.
[6] Hebrew; **"kol katan vekol kalah."**
[7] As in the days of the first settlement, in the days of Joshua son of Nun.
[8] Both spiritually- and physically-speaking.
[9] Yahshua the Great Shepherd will count all Yisrael, to make sure none are missing that have been chosen to be redeemed and return from exile.
[10] Healing, forgiveness, and restoration to YHWH and the land.
[11] The **atid lavoh.**
[12] Moshiach Yahshua.
[13] Jewish Yisrael will be redeemed by dom atonement.
[14] Note: As in Jeremiah 23:5, the Branch of David, the King Moshiach, is called YHWH our Righteousness.

17 For this says **יהוה**; *David shall never lack an heir to sit upon the throne of Beit Yisrael;[1] 18 Neither shall the kohanim the Leviim lack a man before Me to offer burnt offerings, and to kindle grain offerings, and to do sacrifice continually.[2] 19 And the* word of **יהוה** came to Yirmeyahu, saying, 20 This says **יהוה**; *If you can break My covenant with the day, and My covenant with the night, and that there should not be day and night in their season; 21 Then may also My covenant be broken with David My eved, that he should not have a son to rule upon his throne; and with the Leviim the kohanim, My avadim.[3] 22 As the host of the shamayim cannot be numbered, neither the sand of the sea measured: so will I multiply the zera of David My eved,[4] and the Leviim that serve to Me.[5]* 23 Moreover the word of **יהוה** came to Yirmeyahu, saying, 24 *Have you considered what people are saying, The two families that* **יהוה** *has chosen,[6] He has cast off and rejected? So they have despised My people, that they should be no more a nation before them.[7]* 25 This says **יהוה**;[8] *If My covenant is not with day and night, and if I have not appointed the ordinances of the shamayim and earth; 26 Then will I cast away the zera of Yaakov, and David My eved, so that I will not take any of his zera to be rulers over the zera of Avraham,*

Yitzchak, and Yaakov: for I will cause their exiles to shuv, and have rachamim on them.

34 The word which came to Yirmeyahu from **יהוה**, when Nebuchadnetzar melech of Bavel, and all his army, and all the malchutim of the earth from his dominion, and all the people, fought against Yahrushalayim, and against all its cities, saying, 2 This says **יהוה**, the Elohim of Yisrael; *Go and speak to Tzidkiyahu melech of Yahudah, and tell him, This says* **יהוה***; See, I will give this city into the hand of the melech of Bavel, and he shall burn it with fire: 3 And you shall not escape out of his hand, but shall surely be taken, and delivered into his hand; and your eyes shall see the eyes of the melech of Bavel, and he shall speak with you mouth to mouth, and you shall go to Bavel. 4 Yet shema the word of* **יהוה***, O Tzidkiyahu melech of Yahudah; This says* **יהוה** *concerning you, You shall not die by the sword: 5 But you shall die in shalom: and with the burnings of spices for your ahvot, the former melechim who were before you, so shall they burn spices for you; and they will lament for you, saying, Ah master! For I have spoken the word,* says **יהוה**. 6 Then Yirmeyahu ha navi spoke all these words to Tzidkiyahu melech of Yahudah in Yahrushalayim, 7 When the melech of Bavel's army fought against Yahrushalayim, and against all the cities of Yahudah that were left, against Lachish, and against Azekah: for only these walled cities remained of the cities of Yahudah. 8 This is the word that came to Yirmeyahu from **יהוה**, after the melech Tzidkiyahu had made a covenant with all the people who were at Yahrushalayim, to proclaim the year of shmeta-release[9] to them; 9 That everyone should let his male eved, and his female eved, being an Ivri man or woman, go free; that none should keep them, meaning a Yahudite his brother. 10 Now when all the leaders, and all the people, who

---

[1] This does not mean that a Davidic king will always be visible. It means every generation will have the seed of King David perpetuated, until the real Moshiach comes to take His eternal throne. Moreover, this reference is to all 12 tribes, here called House of Yisrael, not a separate ruler over the House of Ephraim. For more details, see: http://yourarmstoisrael.org/Articles_new/restoration/?page=7&type=12.
[2] The Levitical priesthood will never perish or be replaced, though it will take on a new role. For more details, see: http://yourarmstoisrael.org/Articles_new/restoration/?page=16&type=12.
[3] The Davidic Covenant is eternal and unconditional.
[4] Yisrael.
[5] Not only will the Levites not cease in their calling, but also they will be increased in great numbers. See: http://yourarmstoisrael.org/Articles_new/restoration/?page=16&type=12
[6] Since 721 BCE YHWH has had "two chosen (physical) families" – Judah and Ephraim.
[7] YHWH rebukes the ill will harbored towards the two houses by the surrounding nations who thought that YHWH had cast them off forever, rather than for merely a season for a time of exile and discipline.
[8] To the heathen nations.

[9] Deuteronomy 15; the year of **shmeta** or release.

had entered into the covenant, heard that everyone should let his male eved, and everyone his female eved, go free, that none should be served by them anymore, then they obeyed, and let them go. 11 But afterwards they changed their minds, and caused the male avadim and the female avadim, whom they had let go free, to shuv, and brought them into subjection again as male avadim and female avadim. 12 Therefore the word of יהוה came to Yirmeyahu from יהוה, saying, 13 This says יהוה, the Elohim of Yisrael; *I made a covenant with your ahvot in the day that I brought them forth out of the land of Mitzrayim, out of the bayit of slavery, saying,* 14 *At the end of seven years everyone should let his Ivri brother go free, which has been sold to you; and when he has served you six years, you shall let him go free from you: but your ahvot listened not to Me, neither inclined their ear.* 15 *And you recently turned, and had done right in My sight, in proclaiming shmeta-release everyone to his neighbor; and you had made a covenant before Me in the Bayit which is called by My Name:* 16 *But you turned back and defiled My Name, and caused every man his male eved, and every man his female eved, whom you had set free for their pleasure, to shuv, and have brought them into subjection again, to be your male and female avadim.* 17 Therefore this says יהוה; *You have not listened to Me, in proclaiming shmeta-release, everyone to his brother, and every man to his neighbor: see, I proclaim a shmeta for you, says* יהוה, *to the sword, to the pestilence, and to the famine; and I will make you to be removed into all the malchutim of the earth.* 18 *And I will give the men that have transgressed My covenant, who have not performed the words of the covenant which they made before Me, when they cut the calf in two, and passed between the parts of it,* 19 *The leaders of Yahudah, and the leaders of Yahrushalayim, the eunuchs, and the kohanim, and all the people of the land, who passed between the parts of the calf;* 20 *I will even give them into the hand of their enemies, and into the hand of them that seek their chayim: and their dead bodies shall be for food for the fowls of the shamayim, and for the beasts of the earth.* 21 *And Tzidkiyahu melech of Yahudah and his leaders will I give into the hand of their enemies, and into the hand of those that seek their chayim, and into the hand of the melech of Bavel's army, which has withdrawn from you.* 22 *See, I will command, says* יהוה, *and cause them to shuv to this city; and they shall fight against it, and take it, and burn it with fire: and I will make the cities of Yahudah a ruin without an inhabitant.*

35 The word that came to Yirmeyahu from יהוה in the days of Yehoyaqim the son of Yoshiyahu melech of Yahudah, saying, 2 *Go to the bayit of the Rechavites, and speak to them, and bring them into the Bayit of* יהוה, *into one of the rooms, and give them wine to drink.* 3 Then I took Yazanyah the son of Yirmeyahu, the son of Havatzinyah, and his brothers, and all his sons, and all the bayit of the Rechavites; 4 And I brought them into the Bayit of יהוה, into the room of the sons of Hanan, the son of Yigdalyah, a man of Elohim, who was by the room of the leaders, which was above the room of Maaseyah the son of Shallum, the keeper of the door: 5 And I set before the sons of the bayit of the Rechavites pots full of wine, and cups, and I said to them, Drink the wine. 6 But they said, We will drink no wine: for Yonadav the son of Rechav our abba commanded us, saying, You shall drink no wine, neither you, nor your sons le-olam-va-ed: 7 Neither shall you build a bayit, nor sow zera, nor plant a vineyard, nor have any possessions: but all your days you shall dwell in tents; that you may live many days in the land where you are strangers. 8 So have we obeyed the voice of Yonadav the son of Rechav our abba in all

that he has commanded us, to drink no wine at all in our days, we, our wives, our sons, and our daughters; 9 Nor to build houses for us to dwell in: neither have we vineyards, or fields, or zera: 10 But we have dwelt in tents, and have obeyed, and done according to all that Yonadav our abba has commanded us. 11 But it came to pass, when Nebuchadnetzar melech of Bavel came up into the land, that we said, Come, and let us go to Yahrushalayim for fear of the army of the Chaldeans, and for fear of the army of the Arameans: so we dwell in Yahrushalayim. 12 Then came the word of יהוה to Yirmeyahu, saying, 13 This says יהוה of hosts, the Elohim of Yisrael; *Go and tell the men of Yahudah and the inhabitants of Yahrushalayim, Will you not receive instruction to shema to My words?* Says יהוה. 14 *The words of Yonadav the son of Rechav, that he commanded his sons not to drink wine, are performed; to this day they drink none, but obey their abba's commandment: notwithstanding I have spoken to you, rising early and speaking; but you have not listened to Me. 15 I have sent to you also all My avadim the neviim, rising up early and sending them, saying, Make teshuvah now every man from his evil halacha, and change your doings, and go not after other elohim to serve them, and you shall dwell in the land which I have given to you and to your ahvot: but you have not inclined your ear, nor listened to Me. 16 The sons of Yonadav the son of Rechav have performed the commandment of their abba, which he commanded them; but this people have not listened to Me:* 17 Therefore this says יהוה Elohim of hosts, the Elohim of Yisrael; *See, I will bring upon Yahudah and upon all the inhabitants of Yahrushalayim all the evil that I have pronounced against them: because I have spoken to them, but they have not heard; and I have called to them, but they have not answered.* 18 And Yirmeyahu said to the bayit of the Rechavites, This says יהוה of hosts, the

Elohim of Yisrael; *Because you have obeyed the commandment of Yonadav your abba, and kept all his precepts, and done according to all that he has commanded you:* 19 Therefore this says יהוה of hosts, the Elohim of Yisrael; *Yonadav the son of Rechav shall not lack a man to stand before Me le-olam-va-ed.*

36 And it came to pass in the fourth year of Yehoyaqim the son of Yoshiyahu melech of Yahudah, that this word came to Yirmeyahu from יהוה, saying, 2 *Take a scroll, and write in it all the words that I have spoken to you against Yisrael, and against Yahudah,[1] and against all the nations, from the day that I first spoke to you, from the days of Yoshiyahu, even to this day.[2]* 3 *It may be that Beit Yahudah will shema all the evil which I purpose to do to them; that they may shuv every man from his evil halacha; that I may forgive their iniquity and their sin.* 4 Then Yirmeyahu called Baruch the son of Neriyah: and Baruch wrote from the mouth of Yirmeyahu all the words of יהוה, which He had spoken to him, upon a scroll. 5 And Yirmeyahu commanded Baruch, saying, I am shut up; I cannot go into the Bayit of יהוה: 6 Therefore go, and read from the scroll, all that you have written from my mouth, the words of יהוה in the hearing of the people in יהוה's Bayit upon the fasting day:[3] and also you shall read them in the hearing of all of Yahudah that comes out of their cities. 7 It could be they will still present their petition before יהוה, and will shuv everyone from his evil halacha: for great is the anger and the wrath that יהוה has pronounced against this people. 8 And Baruch the son of Neriyah did according to all that Yirmeyahu ha navi commanded him, reading in the scroll the words of יהוה in יהוה's Bayit. 9 And it came to pass in the fifth year of Yehoyaqim the son of

---

[1] Both houses.
[2] The Scroll of Jeremiah.
[3] Yom Kippur.

Yoshiyahu melech of Yahudah, in the ninth month, that they proclaimed a fast before יהוה to all the people in Yahrushalayim, and to all the people that came from the cities of Yahudah to Yahrushalayim. 10 Then read Baruch in the scroll the words of Yirmeyahu in the Bayit of יהוה, in the room of Gemaryah the son of Shaphan the sopher, in the upper courtyard, at the entrance of the New Gate of יהוה's Bayit, in the hearing of all the people. 11 When Michayah the son of Gemaryah, the son of Shaphan, had heard out of the scroll all the words of יהוה, 12 He went down into the melech's bayit, into the sopher's room: and, see, all the leaders sat there, even Elishama the sopher, and Delayah the son of Shemiyah, and El-Nathan the son of Achvor, and Gemaryah the son of Shaphan, and Tzidkiyahu the son of Hananyah, and all the leaders. 13 Then Michayah declared to them all the words that he had heard, when Baruch read the scroll in the hearing of the people. 14 Therefore all the leaders sent Yehudi the son of Nethanyah, the son of Shelemyah, the son of Cushi, to Baruch, saying, Take in your hand the scroll from which you have read in the hearing of the people, and come. So Baruch the son of Neriyah took the scroll in his hand, and came to them. 15 And they said to him, Sit down now, and read it in our hearing. So Baruch read it in their hearing. 16 Now it came to pass, when they had heard all the words, they were all afraid, and said to Baruch, We will surely tell the melech all of these words. 17 And they asked Baruch, saying, Tell us now, How did you write all these words at his mouth? 18 Then Baruch answered them, He pronounced all these words to me with his mouth, and I wrote them with ink in the scroll. 19 Then said the leaders to Baruch, Go, hide with Yirmeyahu; and let no man know where you are going. 20 And they went in to the melech into the court, but they put the scroll in the room of Elishama the sopher, and told all the words in the hearing of the

melech. 21 So the melech sent Yehudi to get the scroll: and he took it out of Elishama the sopher's room. And Yehudi read it in the hearing of the melech, and in the hearing of all the leaders who stood next to the melech. 22 Now the melech sat in the winterhouse in the ninth month: and there was a fire on the fireplace burning before him. 23 And it came to pass, that when Yehudi had read three or four sections, he cut it with the penknife, and cast it into the fire that was on the fireplace, until the entire scroll was consumed in the fire that was on the fireplace. 24 Yet they were not afraid, nor tore their garments, neither the melech, nor any of his avadim that heard all these words. 25 Nevertheless El-Nathan and Delayah and Gemaryah had pleaded with the melech that he would not burn the scroll: but he would not shema to them. 26 But the melech commanded Yerahme-El the son of the melech, and Serayah the son of Azriel, and Shelemyah the son of Avde-El, to seize Baruch the sopher and Yirmeyahu ha navi: but יהוה hid them. 27 Then the word of יהוה came to Yirmeyahu, after the melech had burned the scroll, and the words that Baruch wrote at the mouth of Yirmeyahu, saying, 28 *Take again another scroll, and write in it all the former words that were in the first scroll, which Yehoyaqim the melech of Yahudah has burned. 29 And you shall say to Yehoyaqim the melech of Yahudah,* This says יהוה; *You have burned this scroll, saying, Why have you written in it, saying, The melech of Bavel shall certainly come and destroy this land, and shall cause to cease from there man and beast? 30 Therefore this says* יהוה *concerning Yehoyaqim melech of Yahudah; He shall have none to sit upon the throne of David: and his dead body shall be cast out in the day to the heat, and in the night to the frost. 31 And I will punish him and his zera and his avadim for their iniquity; and I will bring upon them, and upon the inhabitants of Yahrushalayim, and upon the men of*

Yahudah, all the evil that I have pronounced against them; but they listened not. 32 Then took Yirmeyahu another scroll, and gave it to Baruch the sopher, the son of Neriyah; who wrote in it from the mouth of Yirmeyahu all the words of the scroll which Yehoyaqim melech of Yahudah had burned in the fire: and there were added besides the original words many similar words.[1] [2]

37 And melech Tzidkiyahu the son of Yoshiyahu ruled instead of Coniyah the son of Yehoyaqim, whom Nebuchadnetzar melech of Bavel made melech in the land of Yahudah. 2 But neither he, nor his avadim, nor the people of the land, did shema to the words of יהוה, which He spoke by ha navi Yirmeyahu. 3 And Tzidkiyahu the melech sent Yehucal the son of Shelemyah and Tzephanyah the son of Maaseyah the kohen to ha navi Yirmeyahu, saying, Make tefillah now to יהוה our Elohim for us. 4 Now Yirmeyahu came in and went out among the people: for they had not yet put him into prison. 5 Then Pharoah's army came forth out of Mitzrayim: and when the Chaldeans that besieged Yahrushalayim heard tidings about them, they departed from Yahrushalayim. 6 Then came the word of יהוה to ha navi Yirmeyahu, saying, 7 *This says* יהוה, *the Elohim of Yisrael; This shall you say to the melech of Yahudah, that sent you to Me to inquire of Me; See, Pharoah's army, which is come forth to help you, shall shuv to Mitzrayim into their own land. 8 And the Chaldeans shall come again, and fight against this city, and take it, and burn it with fire.* 9 This says יהוה; *Deceive not yourselves, saying, The Chaldeans shall surely depart from us: for they shall not depart. 10 For though you had smitten the whole army of the Chaldeans that fight against you, and there remained only one wounded man among them, yet they will*

still rise up every man in his tent, and burn this city with fire. 11 And it came to pass, that when the army of the Chaldeans left the siege of Yahrushalayim for fear of Pharoah's army, 12 Then Yirmeyahu went out of Yahrushalayim to go into the land of Benyamin, to receive his portion there in the midst of the people. 13 And when he was in the Gate of Benyamin, a captain of the guard was there, whose name was Yiryah, the son of Shelemyah, the son of Hananyah; and he took Yirmeyahu ha navi, saying, You are deserting us to the Chaldeans. 14 Then said Yirmeyahu; It is false; I am not deserting to the Chaldeans. But he listened not to him: so Yiryah took Yirmeyahu, and brought him to the leaders. 15 Therefore the leaders were angry with Yirmeyahu, and smote him, and put him in prison in the bayit of Yonathan the sopher: for they had made that the prison. 16 When Yirmeyahu had entered into the dungeon, and into the cells, Yirmeyahu had remained there many days; 17 Then Tzidkiyahu the melech sent, and took him out: and the melech asked him secretly in his bayit, and said, Is there any word from יהוה? And Yirmeyahu said, There is! For, He said, you shall be delivered into the hand of the melech of Bavel. 18 Moreover Yirmeyahu said to melech Tzidkiyahu, What have I sinned against you, or against your avadim, or against this people, seeing that you have put me in prison? 19 Where are your neviim now who prophesied to you, saying, The melech of Bavel shall not come against you, nor against this land? 20 Therefore shema now, I ask you, O my master the melech: let my petition, I ask you, be accepted before you; that you do not make me shuv to the bayit of Yonathan the sopher, lest I die there. 21 Then Tzidkiyahu the melech commanded that they should commit Yirmeyahu into the court of the guard, and that they should give him daily a piece of lechem from the bakers' street, until all the lechem in the city was gone. So Yirmeyahu remained in the court of the guard.

---

[1] YHWH's words can never be destroyed.
[2] A type of the renewal of the broken or burned First Covenant.

38 Then Shephatyah the son of Mattan, and Gedalyah the son of Pashur, and Yuchal the son of Shelemyah, and Pashur the son of Malchiyah, heard the words that Yirmeyahu had spoken to all the people, saying, 2 This says יהוה, *He that remains in this city shall die by the sword, by the famine, and by the pestilence: but he that goes forth to the Chaldeans shall live; for he shall have his chayim as his reward, and shall live.* 3 This says יהוה, *This city shall surely be given into the hand of the melech of Bavel's army, who shall take it.* 4 Therefore the leaders said to the melech, We beg you, let this man be put to death: for this he weakens the hands of the men of war that remain in this city, and the hands of all the people, in speaking such words to them: for this man seeks not the welfare of this people, but their harm. 5 Then Tzidkiyahu the melech said, See, he is in your hand: for the melech is not he that can do anything against you. 6 Then they took Yirmeyahu, and cast him into the dungeon of Malchiyah the son of Hammelech, that was in the court of the guard: and they let down Yirmeyahu with cords. And in the dungeon there was no mayim, but mud: so Yirmeyahu sank in the mud. 7 Now when Eved-Melech the Ethiopian, one of the eunuchs who was in the melech's bayit, heard that they had put Yirmeyahu in the dungeon; the melech was sitting in the Gate of Benyamin; 8 Eved-Melech went forth out of the melech's bayit, and spoke to the melech, saying, 9 My master the melech, these men have done evil in all that they have done to Yirmeyahu ha navi, whom they have cast into the dungeon; and he is likely to die of hunger in the place where he is: for there is no more lechem in the city. 10 Then the melech commanded Eved-Melech the Ethiopian, saying, Take from here thirty men with you, and take up Yirmeyahu ha navi out of the dungeon, before he dies. 11 So Eved-Melech took the men with him, and went into the bayit of the melech under the treasury, and took there

old cast clouts and old rotten rags, and let them down by cords into the dungeon to Yirmeyahu. 12 And Eved-Melech the Ethiopian said to Yirmeyahu, Put now these old cast clouts and rotten rags under your armpits under the cords. And Yirmeyahu did so. 13 So they drew up Yirmeyahu with cords, and took him up out of the dungeon: and Yirmeyahu remained in the court of the guard. 14 Then Tzidkiyahu the melech sent, and took Yirmeyahu ha navi to him into the third entrance that is in the Bayit of יהוה: and the melech said to Yirmeyahu, I will ask you something; hide nothing from me. 15 Then Yirmeyahu said to Tzidkiyahu, If I declare it to you, will you not surely put me to death? And if I give you counsel, will you not shema to me? 16 So Tzidkiyahu the melech swore secretly to Yirmeyahu, saying, As יהוה lives, that made us in this chayim, I will not put you to death, neither will I give you into the hands of these men that seek your chayim. 17 Then said Yirmeyahu to Tzidkiyahu, This says יהוה, the Elohim of hosts, the Elohim of Yisrael; *If you will surely go out to the melech of Bavel's leaders, then your being shall live, and this city shall not be burned with fire; and you shall live, and your bayit: 18 But if you will not go forth to the melech of Bavel's leaders, then shall this city be given into the hand of the Chaldeans, and they shall burn it with fire, and you shall not escape out of their hand.* 19 And Tzidkiyahu the melech said to Yirmeyahu, I am afraid of the Yahudim that have gone over to the Chaldeans, lest they deliver me into their hand, and they mistreat me. 20 But Yirmeyahu said, They shall not hand you over. Obey, I beg you, the voice of יהוה, which I speak to you: so it shall be well with you, and your being shall live. 21 But if you refuse to go out, this is the word that יהוה has shown me: 22 And, see, all the women that are left in the melech of Yahudah's bayit shall be brought forth to the melech of Bavel's leaders, and those women shall say, Your close chaverim have deceived you, and have prevailed against you: your feet are sunk in the mud, and they are turned away back. 23 So they shall bring out all your wives and your children to the Chaldeans: and you shall not escape out of their hand, but shall be taken by the hand of the melech of Bavel: and you shall cause this city to be burned with fire. 24 Then said Tzidkiyahu to Yirmeyahu, Let no man know of these words, and you shall not die. 25 But if the leaders shema that I have talked with you, and they come to you, and say to you, Declare to us now what you have said to the melech, hide it not from us, and we will not put you to death; also what the melech said to you: 26 Then you shall say to them, I presented my petition before the melech, that he would not cause me to shuv to Yonathan's bayit, to die there. 27 Then came all the leaders to Yirmeyahu, and asked him: and he told them according to all these words that the melech had commanded. So they stopped speaking with him, for the matter was not perceived. 28 So Yirmeyahu stayed in the court of the guard to the day that Yahrushalayim was taken: and he was there when Yahrushalayim was taken.

39 In the ninth year of Tzidkiyahu melech of Yahudah, in the tenth month, came Nebuchadnetzar melech of Bavel and all his army against Yahrushalayim, and they besieged it. 2 And in the eleventh year of Tzidkiyahu, in the fourth month, the ninth day of the month, the city was broken up. 3 And all the leaders of the melech of Bavel came in, and sat in the Middle Gate, even Nergal-Sharezer, Samgar-Nevo, Sarsechim, Rav-Saris, Nergal-Sharezer, Ravmag, with all the rest of the leaders of the melech of Bavel. 4 And it came to pass, that when Tzidkiyahu the melech of Yahudah saw them, and all the men of war saw them, then they fled, and went forth out of the city by night, by the derech of the melech's garden, by the gate between the two walls: and he went out to the desert plain. 5 But the Chaldeans' army

pursued after them, and overtook Tzidkiyahu in the plains of Yericho: and when they had taken him, they brought him up to Nebuchadnetzar melech of Bavel to Rivlah in the land of Hamath, where he gave mishpat against him. 6 Then the melech of Bavel killed the sons of Tzidkiyahu in Rivlah before his eyes: also the melech of Bavel killed all the nobles of Yahudah. 7 Moreover he put out Tzidkiyahu's eyes, and bound him with chains, to carry him to Bavel. 8 And the Chaldeans burned the melech's bayit, and the houses of the people, with fire, and broke down the walls of Yahrushalayim. 9 Then Nebuzar-Adan the captain of the army carried away into exile to Bavel the remnant of the people that remained in the city, and those that defected to him, with the rest of the people that remained. 10 But Nebuzar-Adan the captain of the army left the poor of the people, who had nothing, in the land of Yahudah, and gave them vineyards and fields at the same time. 11 Now Nebuchadnetzar melech of Bavel gave an order concerning Yirmeyahu to Nebuzar-Adan the captain of the army, saying, 12 Take him, and look after him, and do not harm him; but do for him whatever he shall say to you. 13 So Nebuzar-Adan the captain of the guard sent, and Nebushazban, Rav-Saris, and Nergal-Sharezer, Ravmag, and all the melech of Bavel's leaders; 14 They all took Yirmeyahu out of the court of the guard, and committed him to Gedalyah the son of Ahiqam the son of Shaphan, that he should take him home: so he dwelt among the people. 15 Now the word of יהוה came to Yirmeyahu, while he was shut up in the court of the guard, saying, 16 Go and speak to Eved-Melech the Ethiopian, saying, This says יהוה of hosts, the Elohim of Yisrael; *See, I will bring My words upon this city for evil, and not for tov; and they shall be accomplished in front of you in that day. 17 But I will deliver you in that day,* says יהוה: *and you shall not be given into the*

hands of the men of whom you are afraid.
18 For I will surely deliver you, and you
shall not fall by the sword, but your chayim
shall be for a prize to you: because you
have put your trust in Me, says יהוה.[1]

40 The word that came to Yirmeyahu
from יהוה, after that Nebuzar-
Adan the captain of the guard had let him
go from Ramah, when he had taken him
bound in chains among all that were carried
away exile of Yahrushalayim and Yahudah,
who were carried away into exile to Bavel.
2 And the captain of the guard took
Yirmeyahu, and said to him, יהוה Your
Elohim has pronounced this evil upon this
place. 3 Now יהוה has brought it, and done
according to all He has said: because you
have sinned against יהוה, and have not
obeyed His voice, therefore this thing is
come upon you. 4 And now, see, I loose
you this day from the chains which were
upon your hand. If it seems tov to you to
come with me into Bavel, come; and I will
look well after you: but if it seems wrong
for you to come with me into Bavel, remain
here: see, all the land is before you: where it
seems tov and convenient for you to go, you
may go there. 5 Now while he had not yet
replied Nebuzar-Adan said, Or go back to
Gedalyah the son of Ahiqam the son of
Shaphan, whom the melech of Bavel has
made governor over the cities of Yahudah,
and dwell with him among the people: or go
wherever it seems convenient for you to go.
So the captain of the guard gave him food
and a gift, and let him go. 6 Then went
Yirmeyahu to Gedalyah the son of Ahiqam
to Mizpah; and dwelt with him among the
people that were left in the land. 7 Now
when all the captains of the army who were
in the fields, even they and their men, heard

that the melech of Bavel had made Gedalyah
the son of Ahiqam governor in the land, and
had committed to him men, and women, and
children, and of the poor of the land, of those
that were not carried away in exile to Bavel;
8 Then they came to Gedalyah to Mizpah,
even Ishmael the son of Nethanyah, and
Yohanan and Yonathan the sons of Kareyah,
and Serayah the son of Tanhumeth, and the
sons of Ophai the Netophathite, and
Yezanyah the son of a Maachathite, they and
their men. 9 And Gedalyah the son of
Ahiqam the son of Shaphan swore to them
and to their men, saying, Fear not to serve
the Chaldeans: dwell in the land, and serve
the melech of Bavel, and it shall be well with
you. 10 As for me, see, I will dwell at
Mizpah to serve the Chaldeans, which will
come to us: but you, gather your wine, and
summer fruits, and oil, and put them in your
vessels, and dwell in your cities that you
have taken. 11 Likewise when all the
Yahudim that were in Moav, and among the
Ammonites, and in Edom, and that were in
all the countries,[2] heard that the melech of
Bavel had left a remnant of Yahudah, and
that he had set over them Gedalyah the son
of Ahiqam the son of Shaphan; 12 Even all
the Yahudim returned out of all places where
they were driven, and came to the land of
Yahudah, to Gedalyah, to Mizpah, and
gathered much wine and summer fruits.[3]
13 Moreover Yohanan the son of Kareyah,
and all the captains of the army that were in
the fields, came to Gedalyah to Mizpah,
14 And said to him, Do you know that
Baalis the melech of the Ammonites has sent
Ishmael the son of Nethanyah to kill you?
But Gedalyah the son of Ahiqam did not
believe them. 15 Then Yohanan the son of
Kareyah spoke to Gedalyah in Mizpah
secretly, saying, Let me go, I ask you, and I
will kill Ishmael the son of Nethanyah, and
no man shall know it: why should he kill

---

[1] He was rewarded for rescuing Jeremiah from the dungeon
and for trusting that Jeremiah was YHWH's prophet. He was a
black man from Ethiopia, a true Yisraelite who trusted YHWH
and was considered more righteous than many. Black or
darker-skinned people have always been a central part of
Yisrael's history. Many of the latter-day returning Yisraelites
are blacks from all nations, and it appears that many are
spiritually in tune with the message of the promised end-time
two-house reunion.

[2] If Jews were in all these nations they still must have their
dom within them to this day. And if this is true of Judah, how
much more is it true of Ephraim, who is more numerous and
has been exiled far longer?
[3] A type of the return that is yet in the future.

you, so that all the Yahudim who are gathered to you should be scattered, and the remnant in Yahudah perish? 16 But Gedalyah the son of Ahiqam said to Yohanan the son of Kareyah, You shall not do this thing: for you speak falsely to me about Ishmael.

41

Now it came to pass in the seventh month, that Ishmael the son of Nethanyah the son of Elishama, of the royal zera, and the leaders of the melech, even ten men with him, came to Gedalyah the son of Ahiqam to Mizpah; and there they did eat lechem together in Mizpah. 2 Then arose Ishmael the son of Nethanyah, and the ten men that were with him, and smote Gedalyah the son of Ahiqam the son of Shaphan with the sword, and killed him, whom the melech of Bavel had made governor over the land. 3 Ishmael also killed all the Yahudim that were with him, even with Gedalyah, at Mizpah, and the Chaldeans that were found there, and the men of war. 4 And it came to pass the second day after he had slain Gedalyah, and no man knew it, 5 That there came certain from Shechem, from Shiloh, and from Shomron, even eighty men, having their beards shaven, and their clothes torn, and having cut themselves, with offerings and incense in their hand, to bring them to the Bayit of יהוה. 6 And Ishmael the son of Nethanyah went forth from Mizpah to meet them, weeping all along as he went: and it came to pass, as he met them, he said to them, Come to Gedalyah the son of Ahiqam. 7 And it was so, when they came into the midst of the city, that Ishmael the son of Nethanyah killed them, and cast them into the midst of the pit, he, and the men that were with him. 8 But ten men were found among them that said to Ishmael, Slay us not: for we have treasures in the field, of wheat, and of barley, and of oil, and of honey. So he held back, and killed them not among their brothers. 9 Now the pit in which Ishmael had cast all

the dead bodies of the men, whom he had slain because of Gedalyah, was the one Asa the melech had made for fear of Baasha melech of Yisrael: and Ishmael the son of Nethanyah filled it with them that were slain. 10 Then Ishmael carried away into exile all the residue of the people that were in Mizpah, even the melech's daughters, and all the people that remained in Mizpah, whom Nebuzar-Adan the captain of the guard had committed to Gedalyah the son of Ahiqam: and Ishmael the son of Nethanyah carried them away into exile, and departed to go over to the Ammonites. 11 But when Yohanan the son of Kareyah, and all the captains of the army that were with him, heard of all the evil that Ishmael the son of Nethanyah had done, 12 Then they took all the men, and went to fight with Ishmael the son of Nethanyah, and found him by the great mayim that are in Giveon. 13 Now it came to pass, that when all the people who were with Ishmael saw Yohanan the son of Kareyah, and all the captains of the army that were with him, then they were in simcha. 14 So all the people that Ishmael had carried away into exile from Mizpah turned around and returned, and went to Yohanan the son of Kareyah. 15 But Ishmael the son of Nethanyah escaped from Yohanan with eight men, and went to the Ammonites. 16 Then took Yohanan the son of Kareyah, and all the captains of the army that were with him, all the remnant of the people whom he had recovered from Ishmael the son of Nethanyah, from Mizpah, after he had slain Gedalyah the son of Ahiqam, even mighty men of war, and the women, and the children, and the eunuchs, whom he had brought again from Giveon: 17 And they departed, and dwelt in the dwelling of Chimham, which is near Beth-Lechem, to go into Mitzrayim, 18 Because of the Chaldeans: for they were afraid of them, because Ishmael the son of Nethanyah had slain Gedalyah the son of Ahiqam, whom the melech of Bavel made governor in the land.

42 Then all the captains of the army, and Yohanan the son of Kareyah, and Yezanyah the son of Hoshayah, and all the people from the least even to the greatest, came near, 2 And said to Yirmeyahu ha navi, Let, we ask you, our petition be accepted before you, and make tefillah for us to יהוה Your Elohim, even for all this remnant, for we are left but only a few from many, as your eyes see us. 3 That יהוה Your Elohim may show us the derech in which we may walk, and the thing that we may do. 4 Then Yirmeyahu ha navi said to them, I have heard you; see, I will make tefillah to יהוה Your Elohim according to your words; and it shall come to pass, that whatever thing יהוה shall answer you, I will declare it to you; I will keep nothing back from you. 5 Then they said to Yirmeyahu, Let יהוה be an emet and faithful witness between us, if we do not even according to all things that יהוה Your Elohim shall send to us through you. 6 Whether it be tov, or whether it be evil, we will obey the voice of יהוה our Elohim, to whom we send you; that it may be well with us, when we obey the voice of יהוה our Elohim. 7 And it came to pass after ten days, that the word of יהוה came to Yirmeyahu. 8 Then he called Yohanan the son of Kareyah, and all the captains of the army that were with him, and all the people from the least even to the greatest, 9 And said to them, This says יהוה, the Elohim of Yisrael, to whom you sent me to present your petition before Him; 10 *If you will still stay in this land, then will I build you, and not pull you down, and I will plant you, and not pluck you up: for I relent of the evil that I have done to you. 11 Be not afraid of the melech of Bavel, of whom you are afraid; be not afraid of him, says* יהוה: *for I am with you to save you, and to deliver you from his hand. 12 And I will show rachamim to you, that he may have*

rachamim upon you, and cause you to shuv to your own land. 13 But if you say, We will not dwell in this land; neither obey the voice of יהוה *Your Elohim, 14 Saying, No; but we will go into the land of Mitzrayim, where we shall see no war, nor shema the sound of the shofar, nor have hunger of lechem; and there will we dwell:* 15 Then shema the word of יהוה, you remnant of Yahudah; This says יהוה of hosts, the Elohim of Yisrael; *If you indeed set your faces to enter into Mitzrayim, and go to sojourn there;* 16 *Then it shall come to pass, that the sword, which you feared, shall overtake you there in the land of Mitzrayim, and the famine, of which you were afraid, shall follow close after you there in Mitzrayim; and there you shall die.* 17 *So shall it be with all the men that set their faces to go into Mitzrayim to sojourn there; they shall die by the sword, by the famine, and by the pestilence: and none of them shall remain or escape from the evil that I will bring upon them.* 18 For this says יהוה of hosts, the Elohim of Yisrael; *As My anger and My wrath has been poured forth upon the inhabitants of Yahrushalayim; so shall My wrath be poured forth upon you, when you shall enter into Mitzrayim: and you shall be an oath, and an astonishment, and a curse, and a reproach; and you shall see this place no more.* 19 יהוה has said concerning you, O you remnant of Yahudah; Go not into Mitzrayim: know certainly that I have admonished you this day. 20 For you deceived your own levim, when you sent me to יהוה Your Elohim, saying, Make tefillah for us to יהוה our Elohim; and according to all that יהוה our Elohim shall say, so declare to us, and we will do it. 21 And now I have this day declared it to you; but you have not obeyed the voice of יהוה Your Elohim, in all the things about which He has sent me to you. 22 Now therefore know certainly that you shall die by the sword, by the famine, and by the pestilence, in the place where you desire to go and to sojourn.

43 And it came to pass, that when Yirmeyahu had made an end of speaking to all the people all the words of יהוה their Elohim, for which יהוה their Elohim had sent him to them, even all these words, 2 Then spoke Azaryah the son of Hosiyah, and Yohanan the son of Kareyah, and all the proud men, saying to Yirmeyahu, You speak falsely: יהוה our Elohim has not sent you to say, Go not into Mitzrayim to sojourn there: 3 But Baruch the son of Neriyah sets you against us, to deliver us into the hand of the Chaldeans, that they might put us to death, and carry us away into exile into Bavel. 4 So Yohanan the son of Kareyah, and all the captains of the army, and all the people, obeyed not the voice of יהוה, to dwell in the land of Yahudah. 5 But Yohanan the son of Kareyah, and all the captains of the army, took all the remnant of Yahudah, that had returned from all nations, where they had been driven, to dwell in the land of Yahudah; 6 Even men, and women, and children, and the melech's daughters, and every person that Nebuzar-Adan the captain of the guard had left with Gedalyah the son of Ahiqam the son of Shaphan, and Yirmeyahu ha navi, and Baruch the son of Neriyah. 7 So they came into the land of Mitzrayim: for they obeyed not the voice of יהוה: they came to Tahpanhes. 8 Then came the word of יהוה to Yirmeyahu in Tahpanhes, saying, 9 *Take great stones in your hand, and hide them in the clay in the brick courtyard, which is at the entrance of Pharaoh's bayit in Tahpanhes, in the sight of the men of Yahudah;* 10 *And say to them, This says* יהוה *of hosts, the Elohim of Yisrael; See, I will send and take Nebuchadnetzar the melech of Bavel, My eved, and will set his throne upon these stones that I have hid; and he shall spread his royal canopy over them.* 11 *And when he comes, he shall smite the land of Mitzrayim, and deliver such as are for death to death; and such as are for exile to exile; and such as are for the sword to the*
sword. 12 *And I will kindle a fire in the houses of the elohim of Mitzrayim; and he shall burn them, and carry them away captive: and he shall clothe himself with the land of Mitzrayim, as a shepherd puts on his garment; and he shall go out from there in shalom.* 13 *He shall break also the pillars of Beth-Shemesh,[1] that is in the land of Mitzrayim; and the houses of the elohim of the Mitzrites shall he burn with fire.*

44 The word that came to Yirmeyahu concerning all the Yahudim which dwell in the land of Mitzrayim, which dwell at Migdol, and at Tahpanhes, and at Noph, and in the country of Pathros, saying, 2 This says יהוה of hosts, the Elohim of Yisrael; *You have seen all the evil that I have brought upon Yahrushalayim, and upon all the cities of Yahudah; and, see, this day they are a desolation, and no man dwells in it,* 3 *Because of their wickedness which they have committed to provoke Me to anger, in that they went to burn incense, and to serve other elohim, whom they knew not, neither they, you, nor your ahvot.* 4 *However I sent to you all My avadim the neviim, rising early and sending them, saying, Oy Vey, do not do this abominable thing that I hate.* 5 *But they listened not, nor inclined their ear to turn from their wickedness, to burn no incense to other elohim.* 6 *Therefore My wrath and My anger was poured forth, and was kindled in the cities of Yahudah and in the streets of Yahrushalayim; and they are wasted and desolate, as at this day.* 7 Therefore now this says יהוה, the Elohim of hosts, the Elohim of Yisrael; *Why are you doing this great evil against your beings, to cut off from you man and woman, child and infant, out of Yahudah, to leave you no one to remain;* 8 *In that you provoke Me to wrath with the works of your hands, burning incense to other elohim in the land of Mitzrayim, where you have gone to dwell, that you might cut yourselves off, and*

---

[1] Literally: "The House of Sun Worship."

that you might be a curse and a reproach among all the nations of the earth? 9 Have you forgotten the wickedness of your ahvot, and the wickedness of the melechim of Yahudah, and the wickedness of their wives, and your own wickedness, and the wickedness of your wives, which they have committed in the land of Yahudah, and in the streets of Yahrushalayim? 10 They are not humbled even to this day, neither have they feared, nor had their halacha in My Torah, nor in My chukim, that I set before you and before your ahvot. 11 Therefore this says יהוה of hosts, the Elohim of Yisrael; *See, I will set My face against you for evil, and to cut off all Yahudah. 12 And I will take the remnant of Yahudah, that have set their faces to go into the land of Mitzrayim to sojourn there, and they shall all be consumed, and fall in the land of Mitzrayim; they shall even be consumed by the sword and by the famine: they shall die, from the least even to the greatest, by the sword and by the famine: and they shall be an oath, and an astonishment, and a curse, and a reproach. 13 For I will punish them that dwell in the land of Mitzrayim, as I have punished Yahrushalayim, by the sword, by the famine, and by the pestilence: 14 So that none of the remnant of Yahudah, who are gone into the land of Mitzrayim to sojourn there, shall escape or remain, that they should shuv to the land of Yahudah, to the place which they have a desire to shuv to dwell there: for none shall shuv but such as shall escape.* 15 Then all the men who knew that their wives and had burned incense to other elohim, and all the women that stood by, a great multitude, even all the people that dwelt in the land of Mitzrayim, in Pathros, answered Yirmeyahu, saying, 16 As for the word that you have spoken to us in the Name of יהוה, we will not shema to you. 17 But we will certainly do whatever thing goes forth out of our own mouth, to burn incense to the malka of the shamayim, and to pour out drink offerings to her, as we have done, we, and our ahvot,

our melechim, and our leaders, in the cities of Yahudah, and in the streets of Yahrushalayim: for then had we plenty of food, and were well, and saw no evil.[1] 18 But since we stopped burning incense to the malka of the shamayim, and to pour out drink offerings to her, we have lacked all things, and have been consumed by the sword and by the famine. 19 And when we burned incense to the malka of the shamayim, and poured out drink offerings to her, did we make cakes to worship her, and pour out drink offerings to her, without our husbands? 20 Then Yirmeyahu said to all the people, to the men, and to the women, and to all the people that had given him that answer, saying, 21 The incense that you burned in the cities of Yahudah, and in the streets of Yahrushalayim, you, and your ahvot, your melechim, and your leaders, and the people of the land, did not יהוה remember them, and came it not into His mind? 22 So that יהוה could no longer bear it, because of the evil of your doings, and because of the abominations which you have committed; therefore is your land a desolation, and an astonishment, and a curse, without an inhabitant, as it is this day. 23 Because you have burned incense, and because you have sinned against יהוה, and have not obeyed the voice of יהוה, nor had your halacha in His Torah, nor in His chukim, nor in His testimonies; therefore this evil has happened to you, as at this day; 24 Moreover Yirmeyahu said to all the people, and to all the women, Shema the word of יהוה, all Yahudah that are in the land of Mitzrayim: 25 This says יהוה of hosts, the Elohim of Yisrael, saying; *You and your wives have both spoken with your mouths, and fulfilled with your hand, saying, We will surely perform our vows that we have vowed, to burn incense to the malka of the shamayim, and to pour out drink offerings to her: you will surely accomplish your vows, and surely perform your vows. 26 Therefore shema the word of*

---

[1] Great deception.

יהוה, all Yahudah that dwell in the land of Mitzrayim; See, I have sworn by My great Name, says יהוה, that My Name shall no more be named in the mouth of any man of Yahudah [1] in all the land of Mitzrayim, saying, The Master יהוה lives. 27 See, I will watch over them for evil, and not for tov: and all the men of Yahudah that are in the land of Mitzrayim shall be consumed by the sword and by the famine, until there is an end of them. 28 Yet a small number that escape the sword shall shuv out of the land of Mitzrayim into the land of Yahudah, and all the remnant of Yahudah, that have gone into the land of Mitzrayim to sojourn there, shall know whose words shall stand, mine, or theirs. 29 And this shall be a sign to you, says יהוה, that I will punish you in this place, that you may know that My words shall surely stand against you for evil: 30 This says יהוה ; See, I will give Pharaoh-Hophra melech of Mitzrayim into the hand of his enemies, and into the hand of them that seek his chayim; as I gave Tzidkiyahu melech of Yahudah into the hand of Nebuchadnetzar melech of Bavel, his enemy, that sought his chayim.

45 The word that Yirmeyahu ha navi spoke to Baruch the son of Neriyah, when he had written these words in a scroll at the mouth of Yirmeyahu, in the fourth year of Yehoyaqim the son of Yoshiyahu melech of Yahudah, saying, 2 This says יהוה, the Elohim of Yisrael, to you, O Baruch; 3 You did say, Woe is me now! For יהוה has added grief to my sorrow; I fainted in my sighing, and I find no rest. 4 This shall you say to him, יהוה says this; See, that which I have built will I break down, and that which I have planted I will pluck up, even this whole land. 5 And do you seek great things for yourself? Seek them not: for, see, I will bring evil upon all flesh, says יהוה: but your chayim will I give

to you as a prize in all places where you go. [2]

46 The word of יהוה which came to Yirmeyahu ha navi against the gentiles; 2 Against Mitzrayim, against the army of Pharaoh-Necho melech of Mitzrayim, which was by the river Euphrates in Carchemish, which Nebuchadnetzar melech of Bavel smote in the fourth year of Yehoyaqim the son of Yoshiyahu melech of Yahudah. 3 Order the large shield and the smaller shield, and draw near to battle. 4 Harness the horses; and get up, you horsemen, and stand forth with your helmets; polish the spears, and put on the armor. 5 Why have I seen them broken and turned away back? And their mighty ones are beaten down, and are fled quickly, and did not look back: for fear was all around, says יהוה. 6 Let not the swift flee away, nor the mighty man escape; they shall stumble, and fall toward the north by the river Euphrates. 7 Who is this that comes up as a flood, whose mayim surges as the rivers? 8 Mitzrayim rises up like a flood, and his mayim are moved like the rivers; and he says, I will go up, and will cover the earth; I will destroy the city and the inhabitants of it. 9 Come up, you horses; and rage, you mirkavot; and let the mighty men come forth; the Ethiopians and the Libyans, that handle the shield; and the Lydians, that handle and bend the bow. 10 For this is the day of the Master יהוה of hosts, a day of vengeance, that He may avenge Him of His adversaries: and the sword shall devour, and it shall be satisfied and made drunk with their dom: for the Master יהוה of hosts has a sacrifice in the north country by the river Euphrates. 11 Go up into Gilead, and take balm, O virgin, the daughter of Mitzrayim: in vain shall you use many medicines; for you shall not be cured. 12 The nations have heard of your shame, and your cry has filled the land: for the mighty man has stumbled against the

---

[1] It is quite possible that the rabbinical ban against the Name enacted about 300 years later, was a partial fulfillment of this prophecy; for YHWH wanted His Name removed from Judah's lips due to their blatant pride and trust in false elohim.

[2] For faithfulness to Jeremiah and his trust in YHWH.

mighty, and they are fallen both together. 13 The word that **יהוה** spoke to Yirmeyahu ha navi, how Nebuchadnetzar melech of Bavel should come and smite the land of Mitzrayim. 14 *Declare in Mitzrayim, and publish in Migdol, and publish in Noph and in Tahpanhes: saying, Stand fast, and prepare, for the sword shall devour all around you.* 15 *Why are your brave men swept away? They stood not, because* **יהוה** *did drive them out.* 16 *He made many to fall, yes, one fell upon another: and they said, Arise, and let us go again to our own people, and to the land of our nativity, from the oppressing sword.* 17 *They did cry there, Pharaoh melech of Mitzrayim is but a noise; he has passed his appointed time.* 18 *As I live, says the Melech, whose Name is* **יהוה** *of hosts, Surely as Tabor is among the mountains, and as Carmel by the sea, so shall he come.* 19 *O you daughter dwelling in Mitzrayim, furnish yourself to go into exile: for Noph shall be waste and desolate without an inhabitant.* 20 *Mitzrayim is like a very pretty heifer, but destruction comes; it comes out of the north.* 21 *Also her hired men are in the midst of her like fat bulls; for they also shall turn and shall flee away together: they did not stand, because the day of their calamity came upon them, and the time of their punishment.* 22 *The voice of it shall go like a serpent; for they shall march with an army, and come against her with axes, as cutters of wood.* 23 *They shall cut down her forest, says* **יהוה**, *though it cannot be searched; because they are more than the grasshoppers, and are innumerable.* 24 *The daughter of Mitzrayim shall be ashamed; she shall be delivered into the hand of the people of the north.* 25 **יהוה** *of hosts, the Elohim of Yisrael, says; See, I will punish the multitude of No, and Pharaoh, and Mitzrayim, with their elohim, and their melechim; even Pharaoh, and all them that trust in him:* 26 *And I will deliver them into the hand of those that seek their lives, and into the hand of Nebuchadnetzar melech of Bavel, and into*

the hand of his avadim: and afterward it shall be inhabited, as in the days of old, says **יהוה**. 27 *But fear not, O My eved Yaakov, and be not broken, O Yisrael: for, see, I will save you from far off, and your zera from the land of their exile; and Yaakov shall shuv, and be in rest and at ease, and none shall make him afraid.* [1] 28 *Fear you not, O Yaakov My eved, says* **יהוה**: *for I am with you; for I will make a full end of all the nations where I have driven you: but I will not make a full end of you, but correct you in tov measure; yet will I not leave you fully unpunished.* [2]

47 The word of **יהוה** that came to Yirmeyahu ha navi against the Philistines, before Pharaoh smote Gaza. 2 This says **יהוה**; *See, mayim rise up out of the north, and shall be an overflowing flood, and shall overflow the land, and all that is in it; the city, and them that dwell in it: then the men shall cry, and all the inhabitants of it shall wail.* 3 *At the noise of the stamping of the hoofs of his strong horses, at the rushing of his mirkavot, and at the rumbling of his wheels, the ahvot shall not look back to their children for feebleness of hands;* 4 *Because of the day that comes to plunder all the Philistines, and to cut off from Tsor and Tzidon every helper that remains: for* **יהוה** *will plunder the Philistines, the remnant of the country of Caphtor.* 5 *Baldness is come upon Gaza; Ashkelon is cut off with the remnant of their valley: how long will you cut yourself?* 6 *O you Sword of* **יהוה**, *how long will it be until you rest? Put up yourself into your sheath, rest, and be still.* 7 *How can it be quiet, seeing* **יהוה** *has given it a charge against Ashkelon, and against the seashore? There has He appointed it.* [3]

---

[1] The Jewish remnant that will return from Babylon, unlike those who ran to Egypt.
[2] The advantage of being Yisrael: a remnant is guaranteed survival as long as the world stands.
[3] To be judged by Egypt, who will in turn be judged by Babylon.

48 Against Moav this says יהוה of hosts, the Elohim of Yisrael; *Woe to Nevo! For it is plundered: Kiryathayim is ashamed and taken: Misgav is ashamed and broken.* 2 *There shall be no more the hallel of Moav: in Heshbon they have devised evil against it; come, and let us cut it off from being a nation. Also you shall be cut down, O Madmen; the sword shall pursue you.* 3 *A voice of crying shall be from Horonaim, plunder and great destruction.* 4 *Moav is destroyed; her little ones have caused a cry to be heard.* 5 *For in the going up of Luhith continual weeping shall go up; for in the going down of Horonayim the enemies have heard a cry of destruction.* 6 *Flee, save your lives, and be like the bush in the wilderness.* 7 *For because you have trusted in your works and in your treasures, you shall also be taken: and Chemosh shall go forth into exile with his kohanim and his leaders together.* 8 *And the plunderer shall come upon every city, and no city shall escape: the valley also shall perish, and the plain shall be destroyed, as* יה *has spoken.* 9 *Give wings to Moav, that it may flee and get away: for the cities of it shall be desolate, without any to dwell in it.* 10 *Cursed be he that does the work of* יהוה *deceitfully, and cursed be he that keeps back his sword from dom.* 11 *Moav has been at ease from his youth, and he has settled on his lees, and has not been emptied from vessel to vessel, neither has he gone into exile: therefore his taste remained in him, and his scent is not changed.* 12 *Therefore, see, the days come, says* יהוה, *that I will send to him wanderers, that shall cause him to wander, and shall empty his vessels, and break their bottles.* 13 *And Moav shall be ashamed of Chemosh, as Beit Yisrael* [1] *was ashamed of Beth-El their confidence.* 14 *How do you say, We are mighty and strong men for the war?* 15 *Moav is plundered, and gone up out of her cities, and his chosen young men are gone down to the slaughter, says the* Melech, *whose Name is* יהוה *of hosts.* 16 *The calamity of Moav is near to come, and his affliction is soon.* 17 *All you that are around him, lament him; and all you that know his name, say, How is the strong staff broken, and the beautiful rod!* 18 *You daughter that inhabits Divon, come down from your tiferet, and sit in thirst; for the plunderer of Moav shall come upon you, and he shall destroy your strong holds.* 19 *O inhabitant of Aroer, stand by the derech and watch, ask him that flees, and her that escapes, and say, What has been done?* 20 *Moav is ashamed; for it is broken down: wail and cry; and tell it in Arnon, that Moav is plundered,* 21 *And mishpat is come upon the plain country; upon Holon, and upon Yahazah, and upon Mephaath,* 22 *And upon Divon, and upon Nevo, and upon Beth-Diblathayim,* 23 *And upon Kiryat-Chaim, and upon Beth-Gamul, and upon Beth-Meon,* 24 *And upon Keryoth, and upon Bozrah, and upon all the cities of the land of Moav, far and near.* 25 *The horn of Moav is cut off, and his arm is broken, says* יהוה. 26 *Make him drunk: for he magnified himself against* יהוה: *Moav also shall roll in his vomit, and he also shall be in derision.* 27 *For was not Yisrael a derision to you? Was he found among thieves? For when you speak of him, you shake your head.* 28 *O you that dwell in Moav, leave the cities, and dwell in the rock, and be like the dove that makes her nest in the sides of the cave's mouth.* 29 *We have heard the pride of Moav, (he is exceeding proud) his loftiness, and his arrogance, and his pride, and the haughtiness of his lev.* 30 *I know his wrath, says* יהוה; *but it shall not be so; his boastings are untrue and his deeds are false.* 31 *Therefore will I wail for Moav, and I will cry out for all Moav; My lev shall mourn for the men of Kir-Cheres.* 32 *O vine of Sivmah, I will weep for you with the weeping of Yazer: your plants are gone over the sea, they reach even to the sea of Yazer: the plunderer is fallen upon your summer fruits and upon your vintage.*

---

[1] All 12 tribes.

33 And simcha and gilah is taken from the plentiful field, and from the land of Moav; and I have caused wine to fail from the winepresses: none shall tread with shouting; their shouting shall be no shouting. 34 From the cry of Heshbon even to Elealeh, and even to Yahatz, have they uttered their voice, from Tzoar even to Horonayim, as a heifer of three years old: for the mayim also of Nimrim shall be dried up. 35 Moreover I will cause to cease in Moav, says יהוה, him that offers in the high places, and him that burns incense to his elohim. 36 Therefore My lev shall sound for Moav like flutes, and My lev shall sound like flutes for the men of Kir-Cheres: because the riches that they have gotten shall perish. 37 For every head shall be bald, and every beard clipped: upon all the hands shall be cuttings, and upon the waist sackcloth. 38 There shall be lamentation generally upon all the housetops of Moav, and in the streets also: for I have broken Moav like a vessel in which is no pleasure, says יהוה. 39 They shall wail, saying, How is it broken down! How has Moav turned their back with shame! So shall Moav be a derision and a shock to all around it. 40 For this says יהוה; See, he shall fly as an eagle, and shall spread his wings over Moav. 41 Keryoth is taken, and the strongholds are surprised, and the mighty men's levim in Moav in that day shall be as the lev of a woman in her labor. 42 And Moav shall be destroyed from being a people, because he has magnified himself against יהוה. 43 Fear, and the pit, and the trap, shall be upon you, O inhabitant of Moav, says יהוה. 44 He that flees from fear shall fall into the pit; and he that gets up out of the pit shall be taken in the trap: for I will bring upon it, even upon Moav, the year of their visitation of punishment, says יהוה. 45 They that fled stood under the shadow of Heshbon because of the force: but a fire shall come forth out of Heshbon, and a flame from the midst of Sihon, and shall devour the corner of Moav, and the keter of the head of the tumultuous ones. 46 Woe be to you, O

Moav! The people of Chemosh perish: for your sons and your daughters are taken captive. 47 Yet will I turn back the exile of Moav in the latter-days, says יהוה.[1] This far is the mishpat of Moav.[2]

49 Concerning the Ammonites, this says יהוה; Has Yisrael no sons? Has he no heir? Why then has their elohim Malcham inherited Gad, and his people dwell in its cities? 2 Therefore, see, the days come, says יהוה, that I will cause an alarm of war to be heard in Rabbah of the Ammonites; and it shall be a desolate heap, and her daughters shall be burned with fire: then shall Yisrael be heir to them that were his heirs, says יהוה. 3 Howl, O Heshbon, for Ai is plundered: cry, you daughters of Rabbah, dress with sackcloth; lament, and run to and fro by the walls; for their melech shall go into exile, and his kohanim and his leaders together. 4 Why do you boast in the valleys, your flowing valley, O backsliding daughter? That trusted in her treasures, saying, Who shall come against Me? 5 See, I will bring a fear upon you, says the Master יהוה of hosts, from all those that are around you; and you shall be driven out each one straight ahead; and none shall bring home the wanderer. 6 And afterward I will turn back the exile of the children of Ammon, says יהוה. 7 Concerning Edom, this says יהוה of hosts; Is chochma no more in Teman? Is counsel perished from the prudent? Has their chochma vanished? 8 Flee, turn back, dwell deep, O inhabitants of Dedan; for I will bring the calamity of Esav upon him, the time that I will punish him. 9 If grape gatherers come to you, would they not leave some gleaning grapes? If thieves by night, they will destroy only until they have enough. 10 But I have made Esav bare, I have uncovered his hiding places,

---

[1] Not as a nation, rather through Moshiach Yahshua's invitation.
[2] Since YHWH pronounced the utter destruction of Moav as a nation, the only means by which their captivity can be reversed in the latter days is if and when they individually enter the Renewed Covenant and become part of the Commonwealth of Yisrael.

and he shall not be able to hide himself: his zera is plundered, and his brothers, and his neighbors, and he is no more. 11 *Leave your fatherless children; I will preserve them alive; and let your widows trust in Me.* 12 For this says **יהוה** ; *See, they whose mishpat was not to drink of the cup have surely drunken; and are you he that shall altogether go unpunished? You shall not go unpunished, but you shall surely drink of it.* 13 *For I have sworn by Myself, says* **יהוה**, *that Bozrah shall become a desolation, a reproach, a waste, and a curse; and all the cities of it shall be everlasting wastelands.* 14 *I have heard a rumor from* **יהוה**, *and an ambassador is sent to the heathen, saying, Gather together, and come against her, and rise up to the battle.* 15 *For, see, I will make you small among the heathen, and despised among men.* 16 *Your evil has deceived you, and the pride of your lev, O you that dwell in the clefts of the rock, that hold the height of the hill: though you should make your nest as high as the eagle, I will bring you down from there says* **יהוה**. 17 *Also Edom shall be a desolation: everyone that goes by it shall be appalled, and shall hiss at all its plagues.* 18 *As in the overthrow of Sedom and Amorah and the neighboring cities,* says **יהוה**, *no man shall stay there, neither shall a ben adam dwell in it.* 19 *See, he shall come up like a lion from the swelling of Yarden against the dwelling of the strong: but I will suddenly make him run away from her: and who is a chosen man, that I may appoint over her? For who is like Me? And who will appoint Me a time? And who is that shepherd that will stand before Me?* 20 *Therefore shema the counsel of* **יהוה**, *that He has taken against Edom; and His purposes, that He has purposed against the inhabitants of Teman: Surely the least of the flock shall draw them out: surely He shall make their dwellings desolate before them.* 21 *The earth is moved at the noise of their fall, at the cry the noise of it was heard in the Red Sea.* 22 *See, he shall come up and fly as the eagle, and spread his wings over Bozrah: and at that day shall the lev of the mighty men of Edom be as the lev of a woman in her labor.* 23 *Concerning Dameshek. Hamath is ashamed, and Arpad: for they have heard evil tidings: they are fainthearted; there is sorrow on the sea; it cannot be quiet.* 24 *Dameshek has grown weak, and turns herself to flee, and fear has seized on her: anguish and sorrows have taken her, as a woman in labor.* 25 *How is the city of hallel not left, the city of My simcha!* 26 *Therefore her young men shall fall in her streets, and all the men of war shall be cut off in that day,* says **יהוה** of hosts. 27 *And I will kindle a fire in the wall of Dameshek, and it shall consume the palaces of Ben-Hadad.* 28 *Concerning Kedar, and concerning the malchutim of Hazor, which Nebuchadnetzar melech of Bavel shall smite,* this says **יהוה**; *Arise go up to Kedar, and plunder the men of the east.* 29 *Their tents and their flocks shall they take away: they shall take to themselves their curtains, and all their vessels, and their camels; and they shall cry to them, Fear is on every side.* 30 *Flee, get far off, dwell deep, O you inhabitants of Hazor,* says **יהוה** ; *for Nebuchadnetzar melech of Bavel has taken counsel against you, and has conceived a purpose against you.* 31 *Arise, get up to the wealthy nation, that dwells without care,* says **יהוה**, *which has neither gates nor bars, which dwells alone.* 32 *And their camels shall be a spoil, and the multitude of their cattle a plunder: and I will scatter into all winds them that are in the furthest corners; and I will bring their calamity from all sides of it,* says **יהוה**. 33 *And Hazor shall be a dwelling for jackals, and a ruin le-olam-va-ed: there shall no man stay there, nor any son of man dwell in it.* 34 The word of **יהוה** that came to Yirmeyahu ha navi against Eylam in the beginning of the malchut of Tzidkiyahu melech of Yahudah, saying, 35 This says **יהוה** of hosts; *See, I will break the bow of Eylam, the chief of their might.* 36 *And upon*

Eylam will I bring the four winds from the four quarters of the shamayim, and will scatter them toward all those winds; and there shall be no nation where the outcasts of Eylam shall not come. 37 For I will cause Eylam to be broken before their enemies, and before them that seek their chayim: and I will bring evil upon them even My fierce anger, says יהוה; and I will send the sword after them, until I have consumed them: 38 And I will set My throne in Eylam, and will destroy from there the melech and the leaders, says יהוה. 39 But it shall come to pass in the latter-days that I will bring again the exile of Eylam, says יהוה.[1]

50 The word that יהוה spoke against Bavel and against the land of the Chaldeans by Yirmeyahu ha navi. 2 Declare among the nations, and publish, and set up a banner; publish, and do not conceal: say, Bavel is taken, Bel is ashamed, Merodach is broken in pieces; her idols are ashamed, her images are broken in pieces. 3 For out of the north there comes up a nation against her,[2] which shall make her land desolate, and none shall dwell in it: they shall remove, they shall depart, both man and beast.[3] 4 In those days, and in that time, says יהוה, the children of Yisrael shall come, they and the children of Yahudah together,[4] going and weeping: they shall go, and seek יהוה their

Elohim.[5] 5 They shall ask the road to Tzion with their faces towards it, saying, Come, and let us[6] join ourselves to יהוה in an everlasting covenant[7] that shall not be forgotten.[8] 6 My people have been lost sheep:[9] their shepherds have caused them to go astray,[10] they have turned them away on the mountains:[11] [12] they have gone from mountain to hill,[13] they have forgotten their resting place.[14] 7 All that found them have devoured them:[15] and their adversaries said, We offend not, because they have sinned against יהוה, the dwelling of justice, even יהוה, the tikvah of their ahvot.[16]

---

[1] It appears that all these diverse judgments against all the incestuous offspring of Lot, or the fleshly offspring of Edom, are permanent unless reversed individually in the latter days by these individuals joining with the King and His Kingdom as part of the greater Commonwealth of Yisrael.
[2] The Medo-Persian Empire that consumed the Babylonian Empire
[3] Also a dual application with an end-time application as well.
[4] This is an indication that when Ephraim returns at the end of the age, they will go together with redeemed Judah from the nations under the banner of King Moshiach Yahshua, meeting all the conditions set forth for the true and permanent reunion as found in Ezekiel 37, which includes the fact that both houses will have the same King and the same Shepherd. This also indicates that the unsaved Jews in the land since 1948 are a prophetic fulfillment in their own right, but are not those spoken of here and in other similar passages. Both houses come together and return together, without one catching up with another group already back in the land, as unbelievers in the King Moshiach Yahshua.

[5] Both houses are finally seen returning to the Zion road together, as they flee the pagan practices of Babylon (verse 8). This joyful reunion is characterized by weeping tears of joy. This Jeremiah 50 passage is universally recognized as being set in an eschatological and prophetic time frame, due in part to the prophetic Hebraic idiom "in those days at that time," used in verse four. "In those days at that time" is said to be a Hebraic idiom signaling the end of this age.
[6] Both houses will be in one accord, with one King, and one constitution of Torah.
[7] Jeremiah 31:31 by Yahshua's dom of atonement.
[8] That will never be forgotten or added to since the one Yahshua cut with both houses is the last one between YHWH and man; it is designed to take all His children into eternity fully forgiven, safe and sound.
[9] Which is why Yahshua said He only came for "the lost sheep of the Bayit of Yisrael" (Matthew 15:24), meaning all of Jacob's children in the Matthew context, and those who desired to join them in the eternal covenant that shall not be forgotten.
[10] YHWH holds the shepherds accountable, not the people; which is why many people in false religious systems still can be saved and love YHWH and His Son.
[11] In the last days while the great restoration is being prepared, there will still be some false Yisraelite shepherds, suffering from what is known as the "Jerusalem Complex," who see themselves as the self-appointed modern Moses to bring the nation home by negotiating with the government and the orthodox, who control immigration. That is why this verse refers to this deception - taking place at the end of the age back on the very mountains of Yisrael themselves.
[12] These false shepherds have turned these believers away at the very brink of their return to safety, resulting quite often with a denial of their King Yahshua, who alone will bring the regathering to pass.
[13] False hopes of return/aliyah.
[14] The King who has promised to take them home without fleshly "wheeling and dealing" is Yahshua our true Resting Place.
[15] False shepherds who promise false hopes of return and an end of the exile.
[16] Some feel that they have the right to deceive Yisraelites because YHWH has forsaken them; and others who feel (wrongly) that loving Yahshua is idolatry.

8 *Flee from the midst of Bavel, and go forth out of the land of the Chaldeans, and be as the male goats[1] before the flocks.[2]* 9 *For, see, I will raise and cause to come up against Bavel a company of great nations from the north country:[3] and they shall set themselves in battle against her; from there she shall be taken: their arrows shall be as of a mighty expert man; one shall shuv in vanity.* 10 *And Chaldea shall be for plunder: all that plunder her shall be satisfied, says* **יהוה**. 11 *Because you were in simcha, because you had gilah, O you destroyers of My heritage, because you are grown fat as the heifer threshing grain, and you danced like the rams of the flock;* 12 *Your ima shall be very ashamed; she that bare you shall be ashamed: see, the last of the nations shall be a wilderness, a dry land, and a desert.* 13 *Because of the wrath of* **יהוה** *it shall not be inhabited, but it shall be wholly desolate: every one that goes by Bavel shall be appalled, and hiss at all her plagues.* 14 *Put yourselves in battle against Bavel all around: all you that bend the bow, shoot at her, spare no arrows: for she has sinned against* **יהוה**. 15 *Shout against her all around: she has given her hand: her foundations are fallen, her walls are thrown down: for it is the vengeance of* **יהוה***: take vengeance upon her; as she has done, now do to her.* 16 *Cut off the sower from Bavel, and him that handles the sickle in the time of harvest: for fear of the oppressing sword they shall turn everyone to his people, and they shall flee everyone to his own land.* 17 *Yisrael is a scattered sheep; the lions have driven him away: first the melech of Ashshur has devoured him;[4] and last this Nebuchadnetzar melech of Bavel has broken his bones.[5]* 18 *Therefore this says* **יהוה** *of hosts, the Elohim of Yisrael; See, I will punish the melech of Bavel and his land, as I have punished the melech of Ashshur.* 19 *And I will bring Yisrael back again to his dwelling, and he shall feed on Carmel and Bashan, and his being shall be satisfied upon Mount Ephraim and Gilead.[6]* 20 *In those days, and in that time,[7] says* **יהוה***, the iniquity of Yisrael shall be sought for, and there shall be none; and the sins of Yahudah, and they shall not be found: for I will pardon those whom I leave as a remnant.[8]* 21 *Go up against the land of Merathayim, and against the inhabitants of Pekud: waste and utterly destroy after them, says* **יהוה***, and do according to all that I have commanded you.* 22 *A sound of battle is in the land, and of great destruction.* 23 *How has the hammer of the whole earth been cut asunder and broken! How has Bavel become a desolation among the nations![9]* 24 *I have laid a trap for you, and you are also taken, O Bavel, and you were not aware: you are found, and also caught, because you have striven against* **יהוה**. 25 **יהוה** *has opened his armory, and has brought forth the weapons of his displeasure: for this is the work of the Master* **יהוה** *of hosts in the land of the Chaldeans.* 26 *Come against her from the furthest borders, open her storehouses: pile her up as heaps, and destroy her utterly: let nothing of hers be left.* 27 *Slay all her bullocks; let them go down to the slaughter: woe to them! For their day has come, the time of their visitation.* 28 *The voice of them that flee and escape out of the land of Bavel, to declare in Tzion the vengeance of* **יהוה** *our Elohim, the vengeance of His Beit HaMikdash.* 29 *Call together the archers against Bavel: all you that bend the bow, camp against it all around; let none of them escape: repay her according to her work;*

---

[1] Symbolic of courageous visionary leaders who lead others in fleeing the pagan practices of the nations.
[2] Rev. 18:4 where YHWH calls the people out of Babylonian pagan ways to prepare them for the restored kingdom on earth.
[3] Medo-Persia.
[4] Ephraim.
[5] Judah.

[6] Ephraim shall return.
[7] Last days.
[8] The saved, forgiven, and pardoned remnant of both houses shall all return.
[9] Dual application. The historic, as well as the eschatological Babylon, both of whom are characterized by Yisrael's two houses being set free from their bondage.

according to all that she has done, do to her: for she has been proud against יהוה, against the Set-Apart One of Yisrael. 30 Therefore shall her young men fall in the streets, and all her men of war shall be cut off in that day, says יהוה. 31 See, I am against you, O you most proud, says the Master יהוה of hosts: for your day has come, the time that I will visit you with punishment. 32 And the most proud shall stumble and fall, and none shall raise him up: and I will kindle a fire in his cities, and it shall devour all round him. 33 This says יהוה of hosts; The children of Yisrael and the children of Yahudah were oppressed together:[1] and all that took them captive held them fast; they refused to let them go. 34 Their Redeemer is strong; יהוה of hosts is His Name: He shall completely plead their cause, that he may give rest to the land of Yisrael, and bring unrest to the inhabitants of Bavel. 35 A sword is upon the Chaldeans, says יהוה, and upon the inhabitants of Bavel, and upon her leaders, and upon her wise men. 36 A sword is upon the liars; and they shall be fools: a sword is upon her mighty men; and they shall be broken. 37 A sword is upon their horses, and upon their mirkavot, and upon all the mingled people that are in the midst of her; and they shall become as women: a sword is upon her treasures; and they shall be robbed. 38 A drought is upon her mayim; and they shall be dried up: for it is the land of carved images, and they boast about their idols. 39 Therefore the wild beasts of the desert with the wild beasts of the islands shall dwell there, and the owls shall dwell in it: and it shall be no more inhabited le-olam-va-ed; neither shall it be dwelt in from generation to generation. 40 As Elohim overthrew Sedom and Amorah and the neighboring cities, says יהוה; so shall no man stay there, neither shall any ben adam dwell in it. 41 See, a people shall come from the north, and a great nation, and many

melechim shall be stirred up from the ends of the earth. 42 They shall hold the bow and the spear: they are cruel, and will not show rachamim: their voice shall roar like the sea, and they shall ride upon horses, every one put in battle, like a man to the battle, against you, O daughter of Bavel. 43 The melech of Bavel has heard the report of them, and his hands have grown weak: anguish took hold of him, and pains as of a woman in labor. 44 See, he shall come up like a lion from the swelling of Yarden to the dwelling of the strong: but I will make them suddenly run away from her: and who is a chosen man that I may appoint over her? For who is like Me? And who will appoint Me the time? And who is that shepherd that will stand before Me? 45 Therefore shema the counsel of יהוה, that He has taken against Bavel; and His purposes, that He has purposed against the land of the Chaldeans: Surely the least of the flock shall draw them away: surely He shall make their pasture a waste before them. 46 At the noise of the capture of Bavel the earth is moved, and the outcry is heard among the nations.

51 This says יהוה; See, I will raise up against Bavel, and against them that dwell in Lev-Kami[2] that rise up against Me, a destroying wind;[3] 2 And will send to Bavel destroyers that shall destroy her, and shall empty her land: for in the day of trouble they shall be against her all around. 3 Against him that bends let the archer bend his bow, and against him that stands ready in his armor: spare not her young men; destroy utterly all her army; 4 Therefore the slain shall fall in the land of the Chaldeans, and they that are thrust through in her streets. 5 For Yisrael has not been forsaken, nor Yahudah by His Elohim, יהוה of

---

[1] As we have been oppressed together, so we shall return together.

[2] Literally "those who live in the heart of those who rise against me."

[3] All the following Scriptures have a dual application, both the historic destruction by Medo-Persia, and the end-time application of the destruction of the Babylonian beast system.

hosts;[1] though their land was filled with sin against the Set-Apart One of Yisrael. 6 Flee out of the midst of Bavel, and deliver every man his own being:[2] be not cut off in her iniquity; for this is the time of יהוה 's vengeance; He will render to her a repayment. 7 Bavel has been a golden cup in יהוה 's hand that made all the earth drunk: the nations have drunk of her wine; therefore the nations went mad. 8 Bavel is suddenly fallen and destroyed: wail for her; take balm for her pain, if so she may be healed. 9 We would have healed Bavel, but she is not healed: forsake her, and let us go every one into his own country: for her impending mishpat reaches to the shamayim, and is lifted up even to the clouds. 10 יהוה has brought forth our tzedakah: come, and let us declare in Tzion the work of יהוה Our Elohim.[3] 11 Make bright the arrows; gather the shields: יהוה has raised up the ruach of the melechim of the Medes: for His plan is against Bavel, to destroy it; because it is the vengeance of יהוה , the vengeance of His Beit HaMikdash. 12 Set up the banner upon the walls of Bavel, make the watchmen strong, set up the watchmen, prepare the ambushes: for יהוה has both devised and done that which He spoke against the inhabitants of Bavel. 13 O you that dwell upon many mayim, abundant in treasures, your end has come, and the measure of your greed. 14 יהוה of hosts has sworn by Himself, saying, Surely I will fill you with men, as with caterpillars; and they shall lift up a shout against you. 15 He has made the earth by His power, He has established the olam by His chochma, and has stretched out the shamayim by His binah. 16 When He utters His voice, there is a multitude of mayim in the shamayim; and He causes the vapors to ascend from the ends of the earth:

He makes lightnings for the rain, and brings forth the wind out of His treasures. 17 Every man is brutish by his own da'at. Every refiner is ashamed by the carved image; for his molded image is a falsehood, and there is no breath in them. 18 They are vanity, the work of errors: in the time of their visitation of punishment they shall perish. 19 The portion of Yaakov is not like them; for He is the Maker of all things: and Yisrael is the rod of His inheritance:[4] יהוה of hosts is His Name. 20 You are My battle-axe and weapons of war: for with you will I break in pieces the nations, and with you will I destroy malchutim; 21 And with you will I break in pieces the horse and his rider; and with you will I break in pieces the mirkavah and his rider; 22 With you also will I break in pieces men and woman; and with you will I break in pieces old and young; and with you will I break in pieces the young man and the maidens; 23 I will also break in pieces with you the shepherd and his flock; and with you will I break in pieces the farmer and his yoke of oxen; and with you will I break in pieces captains and rulers. 24 And I will render to Bavel and to all the inhabitants of Chaldea all their evil that they have done to Tzion before your sight, says יהוה. 25 See, I am against you, O destroying mountain, says יהוה, which destroys all the earth: and I will stretch out My hand upon you, and roll you down from the rocks, and will make you a burnt mountain. 26 And they shall not take of you a stone for a corner, nor a stone for foundations; but you shall be desolate le-olam-va-ed, says יהוה. 27 Set you up a banner in the land, blow the shofar among the nations, prepare the nations against her, call together against her the malchutim of Ararat, Minni, and Ashchenaz; appoint a captain against her; cause the horses to come up as hairy locusts. 28 Prepare against her the nations with the melechim of the Medes, their captains, and all their

---

[1] Though painfully corrected and disciplined, neither house will ever be forsaken by YHWH. Yahshua and the Renewed Covenant is proof of that.
[2] This is a call that all returning Yisraelites must answer or be in trouble in the spirit.
[3] The works of enabling us through His truth to fully leave Babylon; and return to the eternal ways of Tzion.

[4] YHWH created the world to find and redeem His people. Yisrael is His inheritance and YHWH is ours.

rulers, and all the land of their dominion. 29 And the land shall tremble and sorrow: for every purpose of יהוה shall be performed against Bavel, to make the land of Bavel a desolation without an inhabitant. 30 The mighty men of Bavel have refused to fight, they have remained in their strongholds: their might has failed; they became as weak as women: they have burned her dwelling places; her bars are broken. 31 One courier shall run to meet another, and one messenger to meet another, to show the melech of Bavel that his city is taken on all sides, 32 And that the passages are blocked, and the bastions they have burned with fire, and his men of war are frightened. 33 For this says יהוה of hosts, the Elohim of Yisrael; The daughter of Bavel is like a threshing floor, it is time to thresh her: yet a little while, and the time of her harvest shall come. 34 Nebuchadnetzar the melech of Bavel has devoured me, he has crushed me, he has made me an empty vessel, he has swallowed me up like a dragon, he has filled his belly with My delicacies, he has cast me out. 35 The violence done to me and to my flesh be upon Bavel, shall the inhabitant of Tzion say; my dom be upon the inhabitants of Chaldea, Yahrushalayim shall say. 36 Therefore this says יהוה; See, I will plead your cause, and take vengeance for you; and I will dry up her sea, and make her springs dry. 37 And Bavel shall become heaps, a dwelling place for jackals, an astonishment and an hissing, without an inhabitant. 38 They shall roar together like lions: they shall yell as lion's cubs. 39 In their heat I will make their feasts, and I will make them drunk, that they may gilah, and sleep an everlasting sleep, and never wake up, says יהוה.[1] 40 I will bring them down like lambs to the slaughter, like rams with male goats. 41 Oh how is Sheshach been captured! And how is the hallel of the whole earth surprised! How is Bavel become an astonishment among the nations! 42 The sea

is come up upon Bavel: she is covered with the multitude of the waves of it. 43 Her cities are a desolation, a dry land, and a wilderness, a land in which no man dwells, neither does any ben adam pass by it. 44 And I will punish Bel in Bavel,[2] and I will bring forth out of his mouth that which he has swallowed up: and the nations shall not flow together any more to him: yes, the wall of Bavel shall fall. 45 My people, come out of the midst of her,[3] and deliver every man his own being from the fierce anger of יהוה. 46 And lest your lev faint, and you fear for the rumor that shall be heard in the land; a rumor shall both come one year, and after that in another year shall come a rumor, and violence in the land, ruler against ruler. 47 Therefore, see, the days come, that I will bring mishpat upon the carved images of Bavel: and her whole land shall be ashamed, and all her slain shall fall in the midst of her. 48 Then the shamayim and the earth, and all that is in it, shall shir for Bavel: for the plunderers shall come to her from the north, says יהוה. 49 As Bavel has caused the slain of Yisrael to fall, so at Bavel shall fall the slain of all the earth. 50 You that have escaped the sword, go away, do not stand still: remember יהוה far off,[4] and let Yahrushalayim come into your mind.[5] 51 We are ashamed, because we have heard reproach: shame has covered our faces: for strangers have come into the set-apart rooms of יהוה's Bayit. 52 Therefore, see, the days come, says יהוה, that I will do mishpat upon her carved images: and through all her land the wounded shall groan. 53 Though Bavel should mount up to the shamayim, and though she should fortify the heights of her strength, yet from Me shall plunderers come to her, says יהוה. 54 A sound of a cry comes from Bavel, and great destruction

---

[1] Eternal death.
[2] Bel was the chief deity of Babylon.
[3] Come out of her my people.
[4] An idiomatic expression for Ephraim Yisrael.
[5] Let both houses note that Babylon will be destroyed so that our restoration can occur. In all the far places where the exiles have gone, the return to Jerusalem will come to mind in a mighty way in the last days.

from the land of the Chaldeans: 55 Because **יהוה** *has plundered Bavel, and destroyed out of her the great voice;[1] when her waves do roar like great mayim, a noise of their voice is uttered: 56 Because the plunderer has come upon her, even upon Bavel, and her mighty men are taken, every one of their bows is broken: for* **יהוה** *the El of repayments shall surely repay her. 57 And I will make her leaders drunk, and her wise men, her captains, and her rulers, and her mighty men: and they shall sleep an everlasting sleep, and not wake,[2] says the Melech, whose Name is* **יהוה** *of hosts. 58 This says* **יהוה** *of hosts; The broad walls of Bavel shall be utterly broken, and her high gates shall be burned with fire; and the people shall labor in vain, and the nations shall be weary with her fire.* 59 The word which Yirmeyahu ha navi commanded Serayah the son of Neriyah, the son of Maaseyah, when he went with Tzidkiyahu the melech of Yahudah into Bavel in the fourth year of his malchut. And this Serayah was an army commander. 60 So Yirmeyahu wrote in a scroll all the evil that should come upon Bavel, even all these words that are written against Bavel. 61 And Yirmeyahu said to Serayah, When you come to Bavel, and shall see, and shall read all these words; 62 Then shall you say, O **יהוה**, you have spoken against this place, to cut it off, that none shall remain in it, neither man nor beast, but that it shall be desolate le-olam-va-ed. 63 And it shall be, when you have made an end of reading this scroll, that you shall bind a stone to it, and cast it into the midst of the River Euphrates: 64 And you shall say, Like this shall Bavel shall sink, and shall not rise from the evil that I will bring upon her: and they shall be weary. Up to here are the words of Yirmeyahu.

52 [3] Tzidkiyahu was twenty-one years old when he began to rule, and he reigned eleven years in Yahrushalayim. And his ima's name was Hamutal the daughter of Yirmeyahu of Livnah. 2 And he did that which was evil in the eyes of **יהוה**, according to all that Yehoyaqim had done. 3 For through the anger of **יהוה** it came to pass in Yahrushalayim and Yahudah, until He had cast them out from His presence, that Tzidkiyahu rebelled against the melech of Bavel. 4 And it came to pass in the ninth year of his malchut, in the tenth month, in the tenth day of the month, that Nebuchadnetzar melech of Bavel came, he and all his army, against Yahrushalayim, and pitched against it, and built siege walls against it all around. 5 So the city was besieged to the eleventh year of melech Tzidkiyahu. 6 And in the fourth month, on the ninth day of the month, the famine was heavy in the city, so that there was no lechem for the people of the land. 7 Then the city wall was broken, and all the men of war fled, and went forth out of the city by night by the derech of the gate between the two walls, which was by the melech's garden - now the Chaldeans were by the city all around - and they went by the derech of the desert plain. 8 But the army of the Chaldeans pursued after the melech, and overtook Tzidkiyahu in the plains of Yericho; and all his army was scattered from him. 9 Then they took the melech, and carried him up to the melech of Bavel to Rivlah in the land of Hamath; where he pronounced mishpat upon him.[4] 10 And the melech of Bavel killed the sons of Tzidkiyahu before his eyes: he killed also all the leaders of Yahudah in Rivlah. 11 Then he poked out the eyes of Tzidkiyahu; and the melech of Bavel bound him in chains, and carried him to Bavel, and put him in prison until the day of his death. 12 Now in the fifth month, on the tenth day

---

[1] Of deception.
[2] Eternal death of the false religious, and political, end-time Babylonian system.

[3] This chapter appears to have not been written by Jeremiah, based on the previous verse. Baruch his secretary possibly wrote it, though no one is sure.
[4] For breaking his pledge of loyalty.

of the month,[1] which was the nineteenth year of Nebuchadnetzar melech of Bavel, came Nebuzar-Adan, captain of the guard, who served the melech of Bavel, into Yahrushalayim, 13 And he burned the Bayit of יהוה, and the melech's bayit; and all the houses of Yahrushalayim, and all the houses of the great men, he burned with fire: 14 And all the army of the Chaldeans, that were with the captain of the guard, broke down all the walls of Yahrushalayim all around. 15 Then Nebuzar-Adan the captain of the guard carried away into exile certain of the poor people, and the remnant of the people that remained in the city, and those that defected to the melech of Bavel, and the rest of the multitude. 16 But Nebuzar-Adan the captain of the guard left certain of the poor of the land as vinedressers and farmers. 17 Also the columns of bronze that were in the Bayit of יהוה, and the bases, and the bronze sea that was in the Bayit of יהוה, the Chaldeans broke, and carried all the bronze items to Bavel. 18 The pots also, and the shovels, and the snuffers, and the bowls, and the spoons, and all the vessels of bronze with which they served, they took away. 19 And the basons, and the firepans, and the bowls, and the pots, and the menorahs, and the spoons, and the cups; all that were made of gold, and all that was made of silver, the captain of the guard took away. 20 The two columns, one sea, and twelve bronze bulls that were under the bases, which melech Shlomo had made in the Bayit of יהוה: the weight of the bronze vessels was impossible to figure. 21 And concerning the columns, the height of one pillar was eighteen cubits; and its circumference was twelve cubits; and the thickness of it was four fingers, hollow. 22 And a capital of bronze was on it; and the height of one capital was five cubits, with a network and pomegranates on the capitals all around, all bronze. The second pillar also and the pomegranates

were like the other pillar. 23 And there were ninety-six pomegranates on a side; and all the pomegranates upon the network were a hundred all around. 24 And the captain of the guard seized Serayah the Kohen Ha-Gadol, and Tzephanyah the second kohen, and the three doorkeepers: 25 He took also out of the city a eunuch, who had the charge of the men of war; and seven men of battle that were very close to the melech, who were found in the city; and the sopher of the army's leader, who mustered the people of the land; and seventy men of the people of the land, that were found in the midst of the city. 26 So Nebuzar-Adan the captain of the guard took them, and brought them to the melech of Bavel to Rivlah. 27 And the melech of Bavel smote them, and put them to death in Rivlah in the land of Hamath. In this manner Yahudah was carried away into exile out of their own land. 28 This is the people whom Nebuchadnetzar carried away into exile: in the seventh year three thousand twenty-three Yahudim:[2] 29 In the eighteenth year of Nebuchadnetzar he carried away into the exile from Yahrushalayim eight hundred thirty-two persons: 30 In the twenty-third year of Nebuchadnetzar, Nebuzar-Adan the captain of the guard carried away into exile seven hundred forty-five persons of the Yahudim: all the persons were four thousand six hundred. 31 And it came to pass in the thirty-seventh year of the exile of Jehoiachin melech of Yahudah, in the twelfth month, on the twenty-fifth day of the month, that Evil-Merodach melech of Bavel in the first year of his rule brought Jehoiachin melech of Yahudah, out of prison, 32 And spoke kindly to him, and set his throne above the throne of the melechim that were with him in Bavel,

---

[1] The Beit HaMikdash was set on fire on the afternoon of the 9th of the fifth month, but the fire did most of its damage on the 10th, and thus the 10th is so recorded.

[2] When Jehoiachin was exiled.

33 And changed his prison garments: and he did continually eat lechem before him all the days of his chayim. 34 And for his diet, there was a continual allowance given to him by the melech of Bavel, every day a portion to the day of his death, all the days of his chayim.

יחזקאל

Yehchezkel - Ezekiel
To Our Forefathers Yisrael

[1]Now it came to pass in the thirtieth year, on the fourth month, in the fifth day of the month, as I was among the captives by the river of Chevar, that the shamayim were opened, and I saw visions of Elohim. 2 In the fifth day of the month, which was the fifth year of melech Yehoyachin's exile, 3 The word of יהוה came expressly to Ezekiel the kohen, the son of Buzi, in the land of the Chaldeans by the river Chevar; and the hand of יהוה was upon him there. 4 And I looked, and, see, a whirlwind came out of the north, a great cloud, and a fire flashing itself, and a splendor was around it, and out of the midst of it like the color of glowing metal, out of the midst of the fire. 5 Also out of the midst of it came the likeness of four living creatures. And this was their appearance; they had the likeness of a man. 6 And every one had four faces, and every one had four wings. 7 And their feet were straight feet; and the soles of their feet were like the soles of a calf's foot: and they sparkled like the color of polished bronze. 8 And they had the hands of a man under their wings on their four sides; and each of the four had faces and wings. 9 Their wings were joined one to another; they turned not when they went; but each one went straightforward. 10 As for the likeness of their faces, the four had the face of a man, and the face of a lion on the right side: and the four had the face of an ox on the left side; the four also had the face of an eagle. 11 Such were their faces: with their wings stretched upward; two wings of each one touched one another, and two covered their bodies. 12 And they went each one straightforward: going where the Ruach was to go, they went; and they did not turn when they went. 13 As for the likeness of the living creatures, their appearance was like burning coals of fire, and like the appearance of torches: it went up and down among the living creatures; and the fire was bright, and out of the fire went out lightning. 14 And the living creatures ran back and out as the appearance of a flash of lightning. 15 Now as I beheld the living creatures, see one wheel was upon the earth by the living creatures, with its four faces. 16 The appearance of the wheels and their works was like the color of beryl: and the four had one likeness: and their appearance and their work was as it were a wheel in the middle of a wheel. 17 When they went, they went in just four directions: and they turned not when they went. 18 As for their rims, they were so high that they were awesome; and their rims were full of eyes all around the four of them. 19 And when the living creatures went, the wheels went beside them: and when the living creatures were lifted up from the earth, the wheels were lifted up. 20 Wherever the Ruach was to go, they went, because there the Ruach went; and the wheels were lifted together with them: for the Ruach of the living creatures was in the wheels. 21 When those went, these went; and when those stood, these stood; and when those were lifted up from the earth, the wheels were lifted up with them: for the Ruach of the living creature was in the wheels. 22 And the likeness over the heads of the living creatures was as the color of the awesome crystal, stretched out over their heads above. 23 And under the expanse their wings were straight, one toward another: every one had two, which covered one side, and every one had two, which covered the other side, of their bodies. 24 And when they went, I heard the

---

[1] Called the "illegal chapter" by the traditional Jewish rabbis, since it so vividly speaks of the Moshiach Yahshua as YHWH. Many rabbis teach that those who study this chapter risk insanity. **Ma'aseh Mirkavah** is the official name of this chapter.

noise of their wings, like the noise of great waters, as the voice of the Almighty, a tumult, as the noise of an army: and when they stood, they let down their wings. 25 And there was a voice from the expanse that was over their heads, when they stood, and had let down their wings. 26 And above the expanse that was over their heads was the likeness of a throne, as the appearance of a sapphire stone:[1] and upon the likeness of the throne was a likeness as the appearance of a Man[2] above upon it.[3] 27 And I saw as the color of glowing metal, as the appearance of fire around and inside it, from the appearance of His waist upward, and from the appearance of His waist downward, I saw as it were the appearance of fire, and splendor all around.[4] [5] 28 As the appearance of the bow that is in the cloud in the day of rain, so was the appearance of the splendor all around the throne. This was the appearance of the likeness of the tiferet of יהוה.[6] And when I saw it, I fell upon my face, and I heard a voice of one that spoke.[7] [8]

2 And He said to me, *Ben-adam, stand upon your feet, and I will speak to you.* 2 And the Ruach entered into me when He spoke to me, and set me upon my feet, that I heard Him that spoke to me. 3 And He said to me, *Ben-adam, I send you to the children of Yisrael,[9] to a rebellious nation that has rebelled against Me: they and their ahvot*

have transgressed against Me, even to this very day. 4 They are children hard of lev and stiff faced: yet I do send you to them; and you shall say to them, This says the Master יהוה: *5 And they, whether they will shema, or whether they will refuse-for they are a rebellious bayit-yet they shall know that there has been a navi among them. 6 And you, Ben-adam, do not be afraid of them, neither be afraid of their words, though thistles[10] and thorns[11] are with you, and you dwell among scorpions: be not afraid of their words, nor be discouraged by their stares, for they are a rebellious bayit. 7 And you shall speak My words to them, whether they will shema, or whether they will refuse: for they are most rebellious. 8 But you, Ben-adam, shema what I say to you; Be not rebellious like that rebellious bayit: open your mouth, and eat what I give you.* 9 And when I looked, see, a hand was sent to me; and, a scroll of a book was in it; 10 And He spread it before me; and there was writing inside and on the outside: and there was written in it lamentations, and mournings, and woes.

3 Moreover He said to me, *Ben-adam, eat what you find; eat this scroll, and go speak to Beit Yisrael.[12]* 2 So I opened my mouth, and He caused me to eat that scroll. 3 And He said to me, *Ben-adam, feed your stomach, and fill your stomach with this scroll that I give you.* Then did I eat it; and it was in my mouth as honey for sweetness. 4 And He said to me, *Ben-adam, go to Beit Yisrael, and speak with My words to them. 5 For you are not sent to a people of a foreign speech and of a difficult language, but to Beit Yisrael; 6 Not to many people of a foreign speech and of a difficult language, whose words you cannot understand. Surely, had I sent you to them; they would have listened to you. 7 But Beit Yisrael[13] will not shema to you; for they will not*

---

[1] Sephira.
[2] YHWH emanating as the Son of Man, the Moshiach.
[3] The pre-existing Son of YHWH, who was **echad** with the Abba. All mirkavah rides lead to the driver - the Moshiach fueled by the Ruach HaKodesh.
[4] What Yahshua looks like in an esteemed eternal state. No man has or can see the Abba; so it is most clear that even in this mirkavah ride, Ezekiel sees a **sephira**/manifestation of YHWH, the man Moshiach Yahshua.
[5] Matches much of the description of Yahshua in His esteemed state as seen in Revelation chapter 1.
[6] Hebrews 1:3.
[7] Ezekiel worships a man on a throne in heaven, or the express image of YHWH - the Son of Yahweh - which is why this chapter had been declared illegal for Jews according to the traditional rabbis.
[8] For a full treatment on the subject of **mirkavah** or the mirkavah of the spirit, see:
http://store.yourarmstoisrael.org/Qstore/Qstore.cgi?CMD=011&PROD=000261.
[9] All 12 tribes.

[10] Judah.
[11] Ephraim.
[12] All 12 tribes.
[13] All 12 tribes.

shema to Me: for all of Beit Yisrael are hard headed and hard hearted. 8 *See, I have made your face strong against their faces, and your forehead strong against their foreheads. 9 As adamant stone, harder than flint, have I made your forehead: fear them not, neither be discouraged at their stares, for they are a rebellious bayit.* 10 Moreover He said to me, *Ben-adam, all My words that I shall speak to you receive in your lev, and shema to them with your ears. 11 And go, to them of the exile, to the children of your people, and speak to them, and tell them, This says the Master* יהוה*; whether they will shema, or whether they will refuse.* 12 Then the Ruach took me up, and I heard behind me a voice of a great rushing, saying, Blessed be the tiferet of יהוה from His place. 13 I heard also the noise of the wings of the living creatures that touched one another, and the noise of the wheels beside them, and a noise of a great rushing. 14 So the Ruach lifted me up, and took me away, and I went in bitterness, in the heat of my ruach; but the hand of יהוה was strong upon me. 15 Then I came to them of the exile at Tel-Aviv, that dwelt by the river of Chevar, and I sat where they sat, and remained there stunned among them seven days. 16 And it came to pass at the end of seven days, that the word of יהוה came to me, saying, 17 *Ben-adam, I have made you a watchman to Beit Yisrael: therefore shema to the words from My mouth, and give them warning from Me. 18 When I say to the wicked, You shall surely die; and you give him no warning, nor speak to warn the wicked of his wicked halacha, to save his chayim; the same wicked man shall die in his iniquity; but his dom will I require at your hand. 19 Yet if you warn the wicked, and he turn not from his wickedness, nor from his wicked halacha, he shall die in his iniquity; but you have delivered your being. 20 Again, When a tzadik man turns from his tzedakah, and commits iniquity, and I lay a stumbling block before him, he shall die: because you*

have not given him warning, he shall die in his sin, and his tzedakah which he has done shall not be remembered; but his dom will I require at your hand. *21 Nevertheless if you warn the tzadik man, that the tzadik sin not, and he does not sin, he shall surely live, because he is warned; also you have delivered your being.* 22 And the hand of יהוה was there upon me; and He said to me, *Arise, go out into the plain, and I will talk with you there.* 23 Then I arose, and went out into the plain: and, see, the tiferet of יהוה stood there,[1] the same tiferet that I saw by the river of Chevar: and I fell on my face. 24 Then the Ruach entered into me,[2] and set me upon my feet, and spoke with me, and said to me, *Go, shut yourself inside your bayit. 25 But you, O Ben-adam, see, they shall put chains upon you, and shall bind you with them, and you shall not go out among them: 26 And I will make your tongue cleave to the roof of your mouth, so that you shall be dumb, and shall not be a reprover to them: for they are a rebellious bayit. 27 But when I speak with you, I will open your mouth, and you shall say to them, This says the Master* יהוה*; He that hears, let him shema; and he that refuses, let him refuse: for they are a rebellious bayit.*

4 *You also, Ben-adam, take a clay tablet, and lay it before you, and you shall inscribe upon it the city of Yahrushalayim: 2 And lay siege against it, and build a siege wall against it, and heap up a mound against it; set the camp against it, and set battering rams against it all around.[3] 3 Moreover take for yourself an iron pan, and set it as a wall of iron between you and the city: and set your face against it, and it shall be besieged, and you shall lay siege against it. This shall be a sign to Beit Yisrael.[4] 4 Lie also upon your left side, and lay the iniquity of Beit Yisrael upon it: according to the number of the*

---

[1] Yahshua.
[2] Many Yisraelites had the Ruach before Acts chapter 2.
[3] Judah.
[4] Ephraim.

days that you shall lie upon it you shall bear their iniquity. 5 For I have laid upon you the years of their iniquity, according to the number of the days, three hundred and ninety days: so shall you bear the iniquity of Beit Yisrael. [1] *6 And when you have accomplished them, lie again on your right side, and you shall bear the iniquity of Beit Yahudah forty days: I have appointed you each day for a year.* [2] [3] *7 Therefore you shall set your face toward the siege of Yahrushalayim, and your arm shall be uncovered, and you shall prophesy against it. 8 And, see, I will lay chains upon you, and you shall not turn from one side to another, until you have ended the days of your siege. 9 Take also wheat, and barley, and beans, and lentils, and millet, and spelt, and put them in one vessel, and make lechem from it, according to the number of the days that you shall lie upon your side, three hundred and ninety days shall you eat of it.* [4] *10 And your food that you shall eat shall be by weight, twenty shekels a day: from time to time shall you eat it. 11 You shall drink also mayim by measure, the sixth part of a hin: from time to time shall you drink. 12 And you shall eat it as barley cakes, and you shall bake it with human dung, in their sight.* 13 And **יהוה** said, *Even so shall the children of Yisrael eat their defiled food among the gentiles, where I will drive them.* [5] 14 Then said I, Oy Vey, Master **יהוה**! *See, my being has not been defiled: for from my youth up even until now have I not eaten of that which dies by itself, or is torn in pieces; neither came there any abominable meat into my mouth.* 15 Then He said to me, *See, I have given you cow's dung instead of man's dung, and you shall prepare your lechem with it.* 16 Moreover He said to me, *Ben-adam, see, I will break the supply of lechem in Yahrushalayim: and they shall eat lechem by weight, and with care; and they shall drink mayim by measure, with astonishment: 17 That they may lack lechem and mayim, and be appalled with one another, and consume away for their iniquity.*

5 *And you, Ben-adam, take a sharp sword, use it like a barber's razor, and cause it to pass upon your head and upon your beard: then take scales to weigh it, and divide the hair. 2 You shall burn with fire a third part in the midst of the city, when the days of the siege are fulfilled: and you shall take a third part, and smite around it with a knife: and a third part you shall scatter in the wind; and I will draw out a sword after them. 3 You shall also take a few hairs, and bind them on the edge of your garment. 4 Then take some hairs again, and cast them into the midst of the fire, and burn them in the fire; for from it shall come a fire that spreads to all Beit Yisrael.* [6] *5 This says the Master* **יהוה**; *This is Yahrushalayim: I have set it in the midst of the nations and countries that are around her. 6 And she has changed My mishpatim into wickedness more than the other nations, and My mishpatim more than the other countries that are around her: for they have refused My mishpatim and My mishpatim, they have not had their halacha in them. 7 Therefore this says the Master* **יהוה**; *Because you multiplied more than the nations that are around you,* [7] *and have not kept your halacha in My halachot, neither have you kept My mishpatim,*

---

[1] Ephraim's punishment was for 2,730 years, or 390 years times the multiple of 7 in Leviticus 26:27-28, or from 734BCE until 1996 CE. For more details, see http://yourarmstoisrael.org/misc/charts/?page=ephraim_and_j udahs_punishment.
[2] 390 days + 40 days is 430 years, from 596BCE to 166BCE and the removal of the punishment around the time of the victory of the Maccabees. For more details, see: http://yourarmstoisrael.org/misc/charts/?page=ephraim_and_j udahs_punishment.
[3] Based on both punishments being fully lifted by 1996 CE, we have seen a massive acceleration of Ephraimites rediscovering their ten-tribe heritage, and Jews returning to YHWH through Moshiach.
[4] Symbolic of Ephraim's food of affliction, eaten by Ezekiel, to identify with both houses.
[5] Both houses were driven among – and became – gentiles, or were influenced strongly by gentiles. Ephraim was never driven into Judah, as some falsely teach.

neither have you done according to the mishpatim of the nations that are all around about you; 8 Therefore this says the Master יהוה; *See, I, even I, am against you, and will execute mishpatim in your midst in the sight of the nations. 9 And I will do in you that which I have not done, and of which I will not do any more again, because of all your abominations. 10 Therefore the ahvot shall eat the sons in the midst of you, and the sons shall eat their ahvot; and I will execute mishpatim in you, and the whole remnant of you will I scatter into all the winds.[1] 11 Therefore, as I live,* says the Master יהוה; *Surely, because you have defiled My Set-Apart Place with all your detestable things, and with all your abominations, therefore will I also diminish you; neither shall My eye spare; neither will I have any pity. 12 A third part of you shall die with the pestilence, and with famine shall they be consumed in the midst of you: and a third part shall fall by the sword around you and I will scatter a third part into all the winds, and I will draw out a word after them. 13 In this manner shall My anger be accomplished, and I will cause My anger to rest upon them, and I will be comforted: and they shall know that I* יהוה *have spoken it in My zeal, when I have accomplished My anger upon them. 14 Moreover I will make you waste, and a reproach among the nations that are around you, in the sight of all that pass by. 15 So it shall be a reproach and an object of taunting, an instruction and astonishment to the nations that are around you, when I shall execute mishpatim in you in displeasure and in anger and in furious chastisements. I* יהוה *have spoken it. 16 When I shall send upon them the evil arrows of famine, which shall be for their destruction, and which I will send to destroy you: and I will increase the famine upon you, and will break your supply of lechem: 17 So will I send upon you famine and evil beasts, and they shall bereave you; and*

pestilence and dom shall pass through you; and I will bring the sword upon you. I* יהוה *have spoken it.*

6 And the word of יהוה came to me, saying, 2 *Ben-adam, set your face toward the mountains of Yisrael, and prophesy against them, 3 And say, You mountains of Yisrael, shema the word of the Master* יהוה; *This says the Master* יהוה *to the mountains, and to the hills, to the rivers, and to the valleys; See, I, even I, will bring a sword upon you, and I will destroy your high places. 4 And your altars shall be desolate, and your images shall be broken: and I will cast down your slain men before your idols. 5 And I will lay the dead corpses of the children of Yisrael before their idols; and I will scatter your bones around your altars. 6 In all your dwelling places the cities shall be laid waste, and the high places shall be desolate; that your altars may be laid waste and made desolate, and your idols may be broken and made to cease, and your sun-pillars may be cut down, and your works may be abolished. 7 And the slain shall fall in your midst, and you shall know that I am* יהוה. *8 Yet will I leave a remnant that you may have some that shall escape the sword among the nations, when you shall be scattered throughout the countries.[2] 9 And they that escape from you shall remember Me among the nations where they shall be carried as captives, because I am broken with their whorish lev, which has departed from Me, and with their eyes, which go whoring after their idols: and they shall despise themselves for the evils which they have committed in all their abominations. 10 And they shall know that I am* יהוה, *and that I have not said in vain that I would do this evil to them. 11 This says the Master* יהוה; *Strike with your hand, and stamp with your foot, and say, Oy for all the evil abominations of Beit Yisrael![3] For they*

---

[1] Both houses fully exiled.

[2] Yisrael has filled all the nations.
[3] All Yisrael.

shall fall by the sword, by the famine, and by the pestilence. 12 He that is far off[1] shall die of the pestilence; and he that is near[2] shall fall by the sword; and he that remains and is besieged shall die by the famine: this will accomplish My anger upon them. 13 Then shall you know that I am יהוה, when their slain men shall be among their idols around their altars, upon every high hill, in all the tops of the mountains, and under every green eytz, and under every thick oak eytz, the place where they did offer sweet fragrances to all their idols. 14 So will I stretch out My hand upon them, and make the land desolate, yes, more desolate than the wilderness toward Divlath, in all their dwellings: and they shall know that I am יהוה.

7 Moreover the word of יהוה came to me, saying, 2 Also, you Ben-adam, this says the Master יהוה to the land of Yisrael; An end, the end is come upon the four corners of the land. 3 Now is the end come upon you, and I will send My anger upon you, and will shophet you according to your halachot, and will repay you for all your abominations. 4 And My eye shall not spare you, neither will I have pity: but I will repay your halachot upon you, and your abominations shall be in your midst: and you shall know that I am יהוה. 5 This says the Master יהוה; An evil, only evil, see, it has come. 6 An end has come, the end has come: it watches for you; see, it has come. 7 The morning is come to you, O you that dwell in the land: the time has come; the day of trouble is near, and not of gilah in the mountains. 8 Now will I shortly pour out My anger upon you, and accomplish My anger upon you: and I will shophet you according to your halachot, and will repay you for all your abominations. 9 And My eye shall not spare, neither will I have pity: I will repay you according to your halachot and your abominations that are in the midst

of you; and you shall know that I am יהוה who smites you. 10 See the day, see, it is come: the morning has come; the rod has blossomed, pride has budded. 11 Violence is risen up into a rod of wickedness: none of them shall remain, nor any of their multitude, nor any of their riches: neither shall there be wailing for them. 12 The time has come, the day draws near:[3] let not the buyer rejoice, nor the seller mourn: for anger is upon all the multitude of them. 13 For the seller shall not return to that which is sold, although they were yet alive: for the vision is touching the whole multitude of them, who shall not return; neither shall any strengthen himself in their chayim of iniquity. 14 They have blown the shofar, even to make all ready; but none goes to the battle: for My anger is upon all the multitude of them. 15 The sword is outside, and the pestilence and the famine inside: he that is in the field shall die with the sword; and he that is in the city, famine and pestilence shall devour him. 16 But, they that escape shall escape, and shall be on the mountains like doves of the valleys, all of them mourning, everyone over his iniquity. 17 All their hands shall go limp, and all knees shall be weak as mayim. 18 They shall also gird themselves with sackcloth, and horror shall cover them; and shame shall be upon all their faces, and baldness upon all their heads. 19 They shall cast their silver in the streets, and their gold shall be removed: their silver and their gold shall not be able to deliver them in the day of the anger of יהוה: they shall not satisfy their beings, neither fill their stomachs: because it is the stumbling block of their iniquity. 20 As for the beauty of his ornament, He set it in excellency: but they made the images of their abominations and of their detestable things from it: therefore have I set it far from them. 21 And I will give it into the hands of the foreigners for a prey, and to the wicked of the earth for a spoil; and they shall defile it. 22 My face

[1] Ephraim.
[2] Yahudah.
[3] Of Yahudah's full capture.

will I turn also from them, and they shall defile My secret place: for the robbers shall enter into it, and defile it. 23 Make a chain: for the land is full of bloody crimes, and the city is full of violence. 24 And I will bring the worst of the gentiles, and they shall possess their houses: I will also make the pride of the strong to cease; and their set-apart places shall be defiled. 25 Destruction comes; and they shall seek shalom, and there shall be none. 26 Mischief shall come upon mischief, and report shall be upon report; then shall they seek a vision of ha navi; but the Torah shall perish from the kohen, and counsel from the zachanim. 27 The melech shall mourn, and the leaders shall be clothed with desolation, and the hands of the people of the land shall be troubled: I will do to them according to their own halacha, and according to their own rulings will I shophet them; and they shall know that I am יהוה.

8 And it came to pass in the sixth year, in the sixth month, in the fifth day of the month, as I sat in my bayit, and the zachanim of Yahudah sat before me, that the hand of the Master יהוה fell upon me. 2 Then I beheld, and see a likeness as the appearance of fire: from the appearance of His waist downward, fire; and from His waist upward, as the appearance of splendor, as the color of glowing metal. 3 And He stretched out the design of a hand, and took me by a lock of my head; and the Ruach lifted me up between the earth and the shamayim, and brought me in the visions of Elohim to Yahrushalayim, to the door of the inner gate that looks toward the north where was the seat of the image of lust, that provokes lust. 4 And, see, the tiferet of the Elohim of Yisrael was there, according to the vision that I saw in the plain. 5 Then He said to me, Ben-adam, lift up your eyes now toward the north. So I lifted up my eyes toward the north, and see northward of the altar gate this image of lust was in the entrance. 6 He said furthermore

to me, Ben-adam, do you see what they are doing? Even the great abominations that Beit Yisrael[1] commits here, that I should go far away from My Set-Apart Place? But turn again, and you shall see even greater abominations. 7 And He brought me to the door of the courtyard; and when I looked, see a hole in the wall. 8 Then He said to me, Ben-adam, dig now in the wall: and when I had dug into the wall, I saw a door. 9 And He said to me, Go in, and see the wicked abominations that they do there. 10 So I went in and saw; and see every design of creeping things, and abominable beasts, and all the idols of Beit Yisrael, portrayed upon the wall all around. 11 And there stood before them the seventy men of the zachanim of Beit Yisrael, and in the midst of them stood Ya-azanyah the son of Shaphan, with every man his censer in his hand; and a thick cloud of incense went up. 12 Then said He to me, Ben-adam, have you seen what the zachanim of Beit Yisrael do in the dark, every man in the rooms of his idols? For they say, יהוה does not see us; יהוה has forsaken the land. 13 He said also to me, Turn again, and you shall see even greater abominations that they do. 14 Then He brought me to the door of the gate of יהוה's Bayit which was toward the north; and, see, there sat women weeping for Tammuz. 15 Then said He to me, Have you seen this, O Ben-adam? Turn again, and you shall see greater abominations than these. 16 And He brought me into the inner courtyard of יהוה's Bayit, and, see, at the door of the hekel of יהוה, between the porch and the altar, were about twenty-five men,[2] with their backs toward the hekel of יהוה, and their faces toward the east; and they worshipped the sun toward the east. 17 Then He said to me, Have you seen this, O Ben-adam? Is it a small thing for Beit Yahudah that they commit the abominations that they commit here? For they have filled the land with violence, and have returned to

---

[1] Judah.
[2] The 24 orders of the priests, plus the Kohen HaGadol.

provoke Me to anger: and, see, they put the branch to My nose. 18 Therefore will I also deal in anger: My eye shall not spare, neither will I have pity: and though they cry in My ears with a loud voice, yet will I not shema to them.

9 He cried also in my ears with a loud voice, saying, *Let the avengers of the city draw near, every man with his destroying weapon in his hand.* 2 And, see, six men came from the path of the Upper Gate, which lies toward the north, and every man a killing weapon in his hand; and one man among them was clothed with linen, whose loins were girded with sephirot:[1] and they went in, and stood beside the bronze altar. 3 And the tiferet of the Elohim of Yisrael had gone up from the cheruv, where it had been, to the threshold of the Bayit. And He called to the Man clothed with linen, whose loins were girded with sephirot;[2] 4 And יהוה said to him, *Go through the midst of the city, through the midst of Yahrushalayim, and set a mark upon the foreheads of the men that sigh and that cry for all the abominations that are done in the midst of it.* 5 And to the others He said in my hearing, *Follow him through the city, and smite: let not your eye spare, neither have any pity:* 6 *Slay utterly old and young, both maidens, and little children, and women: but come not near to any man who has the mark; and begin at My Set-Apart Place.* Then they began with the zachanim who were in front of the Bayit. 7 And He said to them, *Defile the Bayit, and fill the courts with the slain: go out. And they went out, and killed those in the city.* 8 And it came to pass, while they were slaying them, and I was left, that I fell upon my face, and cried, and said, Oy, Master יהוה! Will You destroy all the remnant of Yisrael in Your pouring out of Your anger upon Yahrushalayim? 9 Then He said to me, *The iniquity of Beit Yisrael and Yahudah is exceeding great,[3] and the land is full of dom, and the city full of perverseness: for they say, יהוה has forsaken the land, and יהוה sees not.* 10 *And as for Me also, My eye shall not spare, neither will I have pity, but I will repay their halacha upon their head.* 11 And, see, the Man clothed with linen, whose loins were girded with sephirot, reported the matter, saying, *I have done as you have commanded me.[4]*

10 Then I looked, and, saw, in the expanse that was above the head of the cheruvim there appeared over them as it were a sapphire stone, as the appearance of the likeness of a throne.[5] 2 And He spoke to the Man clothed with linen, and said, *Go in between the wheels, even under the cheruv, and fill your hand with coals of fire from between the cheruvim, and scatter them over the city.* And He went in before my eyes. 3 Now the cheruvim stood on the right side of the Bayit, when the Man went in; and the cloud filled the inner courtyard. 4 Then the tiferet of יהוה went up from the cheruv, and stood over the threshold of the Bayit; and the Bayit was filled with the cloud, and the courtyard was full of the splendor of יהוה's tiferet. 5 And the sound of the cheruvim's wings was heard even to the outer courtyard, as the voice of El-Shaddai when He speaks. 6 And it came to pass, that when He had commanded the Man clothed with linen, saying, Take fire from between the wheels, from between the cheruvim; then He went in, and stood beside the wheels. 7 And one cheruv stretched out his hand from between the cheruvim to the fire that was between the cheruvim, and took of it, and put it into the hands of him that was clothed with linen: who took it, and went out. 8 And there appeared in the cheruvim the design of a Man's hand[6] under their wings. 9 And when

---

[1] The manifestations of YHWH: Aramaic Peshitta.
[2] Probably Yahshua.
[3] Two-house reference.
[4] The Son always obeys the Abba who always sends Him.
[5] Yahshua's throne.
[6] Yahshua.

I looked, see the four wheels by the cheruvim, one wheel by one cheruv, and another wheel by another cheruv: and the appearance of the wheels was as the color of a beryl stone. [1] 10 And as for their appearances, the four looked alike, as if a wheel had been in the middle of a wheel. 11 When they went, they went upon their four sides; they turned not as they went, but to the place where the head looked they followed it; they turned not as they went. 12 And their whole body, and their backs, and their hands, and their wings, and the wheels, were full of eyes all round about, even the wheels that the four had. 13 As for the wheels, they were called for in my hearing, O wheel. 14 And every one had four faces: the first face was the face of a cheruv, and the second face was the face of a Man, and the third the face of a lion, and the fourth the face of an eagle. 15 And the cheruvim were lifted up. This is the living creature that I saw by the river of Chevar. 16 And when the cheruvim went, the wheels went by them: and when the cheruvim lifted up their wings to mount up from the earth, the same wheels also moved not from beside them. 17 When they stood, these stood; and when they were lifted up, these lifted up also: for the Ruach of the living creature was in them. 18 Then the tiferet of יהוה departed from off the threshold of the Bayit, and stood over the cheruvim. 19 And the cheruvim lifted up their wings, and mounted up from the earth in my sight: when they went out, the wheels also were beside them, and everyone stood at the door of the east gate of יהוה's Bayit; and the tiferet of the Elohim of Yisrael was over them above. 20 This is the living creature that I saw under the Elohim of Yisrael by the river of Chevar; and I knew that they were the cheruvim. 21 Every one had four faces apiece, and every one four wings; and the likeness of the hands of a man was under their wings. 22 And the likeness of their faces was the same faces that I saw by the river of Chevar, their appearances and themselves: each one went straightforward.

11 Moreover the Ruach lifted me up, and brought me to the East Gate of יהוה's Bayit, which looks eastward: and see at the door of the gate twenty-five men; [2] among whom I saw Ya-azanyah the son of Atzur, and Pelatyah the son of Benayah, the leaders of the people. 2 Then said He to me, *Ben-adam, these are the men that devise mischief, and give wicked counsel in this city*: 3 *Who say, It is not near; let us build houses: this city is the cooking pot, and we are the meat. 4 Therefore prophesy against them, prophesy, O Ben-adam.* 5 And the Ruach of יהוה fell upon me, and said to me, *Speak; This says* יהוה*; This have you said, O Beit Yisrael: for I know the things that come into your mind, every one of them. 6 You have multiplied your slain in this city, and you have filled the streets of it with the slain.* 7 Therefore this says the Master יהוה; *Your slain who you have laid in the midst of it, they are the flesh, and this city is the cooking pot: but I will bring you out of the midst of it. 8 You have feared the sword; and I will bring a sword upon you*, says the Master יהוה. 9 *And I will bring you out of the midst of it, and deliver you into the hands of foreigners, and will execute mishpatim among you. 10 You shall fall by the sword; I will shophet you in the borders of Yisrael; and you shall know that I am* יהוה. 11 *This city shall not be your cooking pot, neither shall you be the meat in the midst of it; but I will shophet you in the borders of Yisrael: 12 And you shall know that I am* יהוה*: for you have not had your halacha in My mishpatim, neither did you execute My mishpatim, but have done after the manners of the gentiles that are around you.* 13 And it came to pass, when I prophesied, that Pelatyah the son of Benayah died. Then I fell down upon my face, and cried with a loud voice, and said, Oy, Master יהוה! Will You make a full end

---

[1] Another mirkavah/chariot in the Spirit.

[2] See footnote on Ezekiel 8:16.

of the remnant of Yisrael? 14 Again the word of יהוה[1] came to me, saying, 15 *Ben-adam, your brothers,[2] even your brothers,[3] the men of your relatives, and all Beit Yisrael, are those to whom the inhabitants of Yahrushalayim have said, Stay away from יהוה: to us is this land given in possession. 16 Therefore say, This says the Master יהוה; Although I have cast them far off[4] among the gentiles, and although I have scattered them among the countries, yet will I be to them as a little set-apart place in the countries where they shall come.[5] 17 Therefore say, This says the Master יהוה; I will even gather you from the peoples, and assemble you out of the countries where you have been scattered, and I will give you the land of Yisrael.[6] 18 And they shall come to the land, and they shall take away all the detestable things of the land and all the abominations from there.[7] 19 And I will give them lev echad,[8] and I will put a new Ruach inside you; and I will take the stony lev out of their flesh, and will give them a lev of flesh:[9] 20 That they may have a halacha in My Torot, and keep My mishpatim, and do them: and they shall be My people-Ami, and I will be their Elohim.[10] 21 But as for them whose lev does after the lev of their own detestable things and abominations, I will repay their halacha upon their own heads,* says the Master יהוה. 22 Then did the cheruvim lift up their wings, and the wheels beside them; and the tiferet of the Elohim of Yisrael was over above them. 23 And the tiferet of יהוה went up from the midst of the city, and stood upon the mountain, which is on the east side of the city.[11] 24 Afterwards the Ruach took me up, and brought me in a vision by the Ruach of Elohim into Chaldea, to those in the exile. So the vision that I had seen departed from me. 25 Then I spoke to those of the exile all the things that יהוה had shown me.

12 The word of יהוה also came to me, saying, 2 *Ben-adam, you dwell in the midst of a rebellious bayit, who have eyes to see, and see not; they have ears to shema, and shema not: for they are a rebellious bayit.[12] 3 Therefore, Ben-adam, prepare baggage for exile, and go into exile during the day in their sight; and you shall be exiled from your place to another place in their sight: it may be they will reconsider things, though they be a rebellious bayit. 4 Then shall you bring out your baggage by day in their sight, as baggage for exile: and you shall go out at evening in their sight also, like those that go out into exile. 5 Dig through the wall in their sight, and bring them out through it. 6 In their sight shall you bear it upon your shoulders, and carry it out in the twilight: you shall cover your face, that you do not see the land: for I have made you as a sign to Beit Yisrael.* 7 And I did as I was commanded: I brought out my baggage by day, as baggage for exile, and in the evening I dug through the wall with my hand; I brought it out in the twilight, and I carried it upon my shoulder in their sight. 8 And in the morning came the word of יהוה to me, saying, 9 *Ben-adam, has not Beit Yisrael, the rebellious bayit, said to you, What are you doing? 10 Say to them, This says the Master יהוה; This burden concerns the leaders in Yahrushalayim, and all Beit Yisrael that are among them.[13] 11 Say, I am your sign: like I have done, so*

---

[1] The word of YHWH is always Yahshua as seen in John 1:1 and elsewhere. The Word, Yahshua, gave the entire Tanach to the neviim.
[2] Ephraim.
[3] Judah.
[4] Ephraim.
[5] YHWH will provide a little protection to assure their survival as His people while in exile.
[6] Promise of restoration.
[7] In the restoration and regathering of both houses of Yisrael.
[8] Reunite us as one.
[9] By the new birth or circumcision of the lev.
[10] A reversal of the "Lo-Ami" curse of Hosea chapter 1.

[11] Mt. of Olives; the place where the shechinah always goes - to the east whenever YHWH removes it from the west.
[12] Both houses.
[13] A reference to some crossover of the ten tribes into Judah. Not a proof text that all the northern kingdom had returned; "that are among them" is a qualifier – not a determinative statement. For not all of Yisrael's northern kingdom were indeed "among them."

shall it be done to you: you shall be removed and go into exile. 12 And the leader that is among them shall bear his baggage upon his shoulders in the twilight, and shall go out: he shall dig through the wall to carry them out through it: he shall cover his face, that he see not the land with his eyes. 13 My net also will I spread upon him, and he shall be taken in My trap: and I will bring him to Bavel to the land of the Chaldeans; yet shall he not see it, though he shall die there. 14 And I will scatter toward every wind all that are around him who try to assist him, and all his chains; and I will draw out the sword after them. 15 And they shall know that I am יהוה, when I shall scatter them among the nations, [1] and disperse them in the countries. 16 But I will let a few men of theirs escape from the sword, from the famine, and from the pestilence; that they may confess all their abominations among the gentiles where they will go; and they shall know that I am יהוה. 17 Moreover the word of יהוה came to me, saying, 18 Ben-adam, eat your lechem with quaking, and drink your mayim with trembling and with anxiety; 19 And say to the people of the land, This says the Master יהוה to the inhabitants of Yahrushalayim, and of the land of Yisrael; They shall eat their lechem with anxiety, and drink their mayim with astonishment, that her land may be desolate from all that is in it, because of the violence of all those that dwell in it. 20 And the cities that are inhabited shall be laid waste, and the land shall be desolate; and you shall know that I am יהוה. 21 And the word of יהוה came to me, saying, 22 Ben-adam, what is that proverb that you have in the land of Yisrael, saying, The days are delayed, and every vision fails? 23 Tell them therefore, This says the Master יהוה; I will make this proverb to cease, and they shall no more use it as a proverb in Yisrael; but say to them, The days are at hand, and the matter

of every vision. 24 For there shall be no more any vain vision nor flattering divination inside Beit Yisrael.[2] 25 For I am יהוה: I will speak, and the word that I shall speak shall come to pass; it shall be no more delayed: for in your days, O rebellious bayit, will I say the word, and will perform it, says the Master יהוה. 26 Again the word of יהוה came to me, saying, 27 Ben-adam, see, they of Beit Yisrael say, The vision that he sees is for many days from now, and he prophesies of times that are far off. 28 Therefore say to them, This says the Master יהוה; None of My words will be delayed any more, but the word that I have spoken shall be done, says the Master יהוה.

13 And the word of יהוה came to me, saying, 2 Ben-adam, prophesy against the neviim of Yisrael that prophesy, and say to them that prophesy out of their own levim, Shema the word of יהוה; 3 This says the Master יהוה; Woe to the foolish neviim, that follow their own ruach, and have seen nothing![3] 4 O Yisrael, your neviim are like the foxes in the deserts. 5 You have not gone up into the gaps; neither built a wall of protection for Beit Yisrael to stand in the battle in the day of יהוה. 6 They have seen vanity and lying divination, saying, יהוה says: and יהוה has not sent them: and they have made others to tikvah that the false word would be confirmed. 7 Have you not seen a vain vision, and have you not spoken a lying divination, whereas you say, יהוה says it; yet I have not spoken? 8 Therefore this says the Master יהוה; Because you have spoken vanity, and seen lies, therefore, see, I am against you, says the Master יהוה. 9 And My hand shall be upon the neviim that see vanity, and that divine lies: they shall not be in the congregation of My people, neither shall they be written in the writing of Beit Yisrael, neither shall they enter into the

---

[1] Even Jewish Yisrael is among all nations. How much more Ephraim, greater in number, and in exile for a longer period of time.

[2] Both houses.
[3] Like the deniers of Yahshua; who attempt to reunite the two houses in their own strength.

land of Yisrael; and you shall know that I am the Master יהוה. 10 Because, they have seduced My people, saying, Shalom; and there was no shalom; and one built up a wall, while others coat it with whitewash: 11 Say to them who coat it with whitewash that it shall fall: there shall be an overflowing shower; and you, O great hailstones, shall fall; and a stormy wind shall tear it down. 12 See, when the wall is fallen, shall it not be said to you, Where is the coating with which you have coated? 13 Therefore this says the Master יהוה; I will even tear it with a stormy wind in My anger; and there shall be an overflowing shower in My anger, and great hailstones in My anger to consume it. 14 So will I break down the wall that you have coated with untempered mortar, and bring it down to the ground, so that the foundation of it shall be uncovered, and it shall fall, and you shall be consumed in the midst of it: and you shall know that I am יהוה. 15 By this will I accomplish My anger upon the wall, and upon them that have coated it with whitewash, and I will say to you, The wall is no more, neither they that coated it; 16 Such are the neviim of Yisrael who prophesy concerning Yahrushalayim, and who see visions of shalom for her, and there is no shalom, says the Master יהוה. [1] 17 Likewise, Ben-adam, set your face against the daughters of your people, who prophesy out of their own lev; and prophesy against them, 18 And say, This says the Master יהוה; Woe to the women that sew cushions to all joints, and make veils upon the heads of every size to hunt beings! Will you hunt the beings of My people, and will you save the beings alive that come to you? 19 And will you profane Me among My own people for handfuls of barley and for pieces of lechem, to slay the beings that should not die, and to save the beings alive that should not be alive, by your lying to My people that

shema to your lies? 20 Therefore this says the Master יהוה; See, I am against your cushions, with which you hunt the beings like birds, and I will tear them from your arms, and will let the beings go, even the beings that you hunt like birds. 21 Your veils also will I tear, and deliver My people out of your hand, and they shall be no more in your hand to be hunted; and you shall know that I am יהוה. 22 Because with lies you have made the lev of the tzadik sad, whom I have not made sad; and strengthened the hands of the wicked, that he should not return from his wicked halacha, by promising him chayim: 23 Therefore you shall see no more vanity, nor practice divinations: for I will deliver My people out of your hand: and you shall know that I am יהוה.

14 Then came certain of the zachanim of Yisrael to me, and sat before me. 2 And the word of יהוה came to me, saying, 3 Ben-Adam, these men have set up their idols in their lev, and put the stumbling block of their iniquity before their faces: should I let them seek Me? 4 Therefore speak to them, and say to them, This says the Master יהוה; Every man of Beit Yisrael that sets up his idols in his lev, and puts the stumbling block of his iniquity before his face, and comes to ha navi; I יהוה will answer him that comes according to the multitude of his idols; 5 That I may take hold of Beit Yisrael by their own lev, because they are all estranged from Me through their idols. 6 Therefore say to Beit Yisrael, This says the Master יהוה; Make teshuvah, and turn yourselves away from your idols; and turn away your faces from all your abominations. 7 For every one of Beit Yisrael, or of the stranger that sojourns in Yisrael, who separates himself from Me, and sets up his idols in his lev, and puts the stumbling block of his iniquity before his face, and comes to a navi to inquire of him concerning Me; I יהוה will answer him by Myself: 8 And I will set My face against that

---

[1] As it was then, there are many today, many who think they can bring two house unity in Yisrael without Moshiach as King over both houses; they are deceived and are whitewashed walls about to be exposed.

man, and will make him a sign and a proverb, and I will cut him off from the midst of My people; and you shall know that I am יהוה. 9 And if ha navi is deceived when he has spoken a thing, I יהוה have deceived that navi, and I will stretch out My hand upon him, and will destroy him from the midst of My people Yisrael. 10 And they shall bear the punishment of their iniquity: the punishment of ha navi shall be even as the punishment of him that goes to him; 11 That Beit Yisrael may not go astray from Me anymore, neither be defiled any more with all their transgressions; but that they may be My people-Ami, and I may be their Elohim, says the Master יהוה. 12 The word of יהוה came again to me, saying, 13 Ben-adam, when the land sins against Me by trespassing grievously, then will I stretch out My hand upon it, and will cut off the supply of the lechem, and will send famine upon it, and will cut off man and beast from it: 14 Though these three men, Noach, Daniyel, and Iyov, were in it, they should deliver only their own beings by their tzedakah, says the Master יהוה. 15 If I cause evil beasts to pass through the land, and they spoil it, so that it be desolate, that no man may pass through because of the beasts: 16 Though these three men were in it, as I live, says the Master יהוה, they shall deliver neither their sons nor their daughters;[1] they only shall be delivered, but the land shall be desolate. 17 Or if I bring a sword upon that land, and say, Sword, go through the land; so that I cut off man and beast from it: 18 Though these three men were in it, as I live, says the Master יהוה, they shall deliver neither their sons nor daughters, but they only shall be delivered themselves. 19 Or if I send a pestilence into that land, and pour out My anger upon it for dom, to cut off from it man and beast: 20 Though Noach, Daniyel, and Iyov, were in it, as I live, says the Master יהוה, they shall deliver neither their son nor daughter; they shall only deliver their own beings by

their tzedakah. 21 For this says the Master יהוה; How much more when I send My four sore mishpatim upon Yahrushalayim, the sword, and the famine, and the evil beast, and the pestilence, to cut off from it man and beast? 22 Yet, see, in it shall be left a remnant that shall be brought out, both sons and daughters: see, they shall come out to you, and you shall see their halacha and their doings: and you shall be comforted concerning the evil that I have brought upon Yahrushalayim, even concerning all that I have brought upon it. 23 And they shall comfort you, when you see their halachot and their doings: and you shall know that I have not done without a cause all that I have done in it, says the Master יהוה.

15 And the word of יהוה. came to me, saying, 2 Ben-adam, Why is the vine eytz better than any other eytz, or than a branch which is among the eytzim of the forest? 3 Shall wood be taken from it to make it into woodwork? Or will men take a peg of it to hang any vessel on it? 4 See, it is cast into the fire for fuel; the fire devours both its ends, and the middle of it is burned. Is it fit for any woodwork? 5 See, when it was whole, it was fit for no woodwork: how much less shall it be fit for any woodwork, when the fire has devoured it, and it is burned? 6 Therefore this says the Master יהוה; As the vine eytz is among the eytzim of the forest, which I have given to the fire for fuel, so will I give the inhabitants of Yahrushalayim. 7 And I will set My face against them; they shall go out from one fire, and another fire shall devour them; and you shall know that I am יהוה, when I set My face against them. 8 And I will make the land desolate, because they have committed a trespass, says the Master יהוה.

16 Again the word of יהוה came to me, saying, 2 Ben-adam, cause Yahrushalayim to know her abominations, 3 And say, This says the Master יהוה to

---

[1] YHWH has no grandchildren.

Yahrushalayim; Your birth and your origin is of the land of Canaan; your abba was an Amorite, and your ima a Hittite.[1] 4 And as for your birth, in the day you were born your navel cord was not cut, neither were you washed in mayim to clean you; you were not rubbed with salt at all, nor swaddled in cloth at all. 5 No eye pitied you, to do any of these to you, to have compassion upon you; but you were cast out in the open field, to the loathing of your chayim, in the day that you were born. 6 And when I passed by you, and saw you defiled in your own dom, I said to you when you were in your dom, Live; yes, I said to you when you were in your dom, Live. 7 I have caused you to multiply as the bud of the field, and you have increased and grown great, [2] and you are come in the finest ornaments: your breasts are fashioned, and your hair is grown, but before you were naked and bare. 8 Now when I passed by you, and looked upon you, see, your time was the time of ahava; and I spread My skirt over you, and covered your nakedness: yes, I swore to you, and entered into a covenant with you, says the Master יהוה, and you became Mine.[3] 9 Then I washed you with mayim; yes, I thoroughly washed away your dom from you, and I anointed you with oil. 10 I clothed you also with embroidered work, and sandals of leather, and I wrapped you in fine linen, and I covered you with silk. 11 I adorned you also with ornaments, and I put bracelets upon your hands, and a chain on your neck. 12 And I put a jewel on your forehead, and earrings in your ears, and a beautiful crown upon your head. 13 You were adorned with gold and silver; and your clothing was of fine linen, and silk, and embroidered work; you did eat fine flour, and honey, and oil: and you were exceedingly beautiful, and you did prosper into a malchut. 14 And your fame went out among the gentiles for your beauty: for it was perfect through My splendor, which I had put upon you, says the Master יהוה. 15 But you trusted in your own beauty, and played the harlot because of your fame, and poured out your fornications on everyone that passed by; who desired it. 16 And of your garments you did take, and adorned your high places with different colors, and played the harlot there: which should not have come about, neither shall it be so. 17 You have also taken your fair jewels of My gold and of My silver, which I had given you, and made for yourself images of males, and did commit whorings with them, 18 And took your embroidered garments, and covered them: and you have set My oil and My incense before them. 19 My food also which I gave you, fine flour, and oil, and honey, with which I fed you, you have even set it before them for sweet fragrances: and so it was, says the Master יהוה. 20 Moreover you have taken your sons and your daughters, whom you have bore to Me, and these have you sacrificed to them to be devoured. Were your whorings a small matter? 21 In that you have slain My children, and delivered them to cause them to pass through the fire before them. 22 And in all your abominations and your whorings you have not remembered the days of your youth, when you were naked and bare, and were defiled in your dom. 23 And it came to pass after all your wickedness-woe, woe to you! Says the Master יהוה. 24 That you have also built an arched place, and have made an high place in every street for yourself. 25 You have built your high place at every head of the path, and have made your beauty to be abhorred, and have opened your legs to everyone that passed by, and multiplied your whorings. 26 You have also committed fornication with the Mitzrites your neighbors, great of flesh; and have increased your whorings, to provoke Me to anger. 27 See, therefore I have stretched out My hand over you, and have diminished your normal food, and delivered you to the

---

[1] A reminder to all who boast in being Jewish, as their sole means of attaining YHWH's favor.
[2] As promised through physical multiplicity.
[3] Yisrael became His bride.

will of them that hate you, the daughters of the Philistines, who are ashamed of your lewd halacha. 28 You have played the whore also with the Ashurim, because you were unsatiable; you have played the harlot with them, and still were not satisfied. 29 You have moreover multiplied your fornications in the land of Canaan all the way to Chaldea; and yet even then you were not satisfied. 30 How weak is your lev, says the Master יהוה, seeing you do all these things, the deeds of a shameless whorish woman; 31 In that you build your arched place in the head of every path, and make your high place in every street; and have not been wise like a harlot, in that you have refused payment; 32 But as a wife that commits adultery, who takes foreigners instead of her husband! 33 They give gifts to all whores: but you give your gifts to all your lovers, and hire them, that they may come to you from everywhere for your whorings. 34 You are different from other women in your whorings, whereas none follows you to commit whorings: in that you give payment, and no payment is given to you, therefore you are different. 35 Therefore, O harlot, shema the word of יהוה : 36 This says the Master יהוה ; Because your filthiness was poured out, and your nakedness uncovered through your whorings with your lovers, and with all the idols of your abominations, and by the dom of your children, which you did give to them; 37 See, therefore I will gather all your lovers, with whom you have taken pleasure, and all them that you have loved, with all them that you have hated; I will even gather them around you, and will reveal your nakedness to them, that they may see all your nakedness. 38 And I will bring mishpat upon you, as women that break wedlock and shed dom are judged; and I will give you dom in anger and jealousy. 39 And I will also give you into their hand, and they shall throw down your arched place, and shall break down your high places: they shall strip you also of

your clothes, and shall take your beautiful jewels, and leave you naked and bare. 40 They shall also bring up a company against you, and they shall stone you with stones, and thrust you through with their swords. 41 And they shall burn your houses with fire, and execute mishpatim upon you in the sight of many women: and I will cause you to cease from playing the harlot, and you also shall no longer give gifts. 42 So will I make My anger toward you to cease, and My jealousy shall depart from you, and I will be calm, and will be angry no more. 43 Because you have not remembered the days of your youth, but have troubled Me in all these things; see, therefore I also will repay your halacha upon your head, says the Master יהוה : because of your abominations and fornications. 44 See, everyone that uses proverbs shall use this proverb against you, saying, Like ima, like daughter. 45 You are your ima's daughter, that despises her husband and her children; and you are the sister of your sisters, which despised their husbands and their children: your ima was a Hittite, and your abba an Amorite. [1] 46 And your elder sister is Shomron, she and her daughters that dwell at your left hand: and your younger sister that dwells at your right hand is Sodom and her daughters. 47 Yet you have adopted their halacha after their halachot, and done all their abominations: but, in all your halacha, you were corrupted more than they were in all their halachot. 48 As I live, says the Master יהוה , Sodom your sister has not done like you have, neither she nor her daughters, have done as you and your daughters have. 49 See, this was the iniquity of your sister Sodom, pride, fullness of lechem, and abundance of idleness was in her and in her daughters, neither did she strengthen the hand of the poor and needy. 50 And they were haughty, and committed abominations before Me: therefore I took them away as I saw tov. 51 Neither has Shomron committed half of your sins; but

---

[1] Judah.

you have multiplied your abominations more than them and have justified your sisters in all your abominations that you have done. [1] 52 You also, which have pleaded for your sisters, [2] bear your own shame for your sins that you have committed more abominable than them: they are more tzadik than you: yes, be ashamed also, and bear your shame, in that you have made your sisters seem tzadik. 53 When I shall bring again their exile, the exile of Sodom and her daughters, and the exile of Shomron and her daughters, then will I bring again the exile of your captives in the midst of them:[3] 54 That you may bear your own shame, and may be ashamed in all that you have done, in that you are a comfort to them. 55 When your sisters, Sodom and her daughters, shall return to their former estate, and Shomron and her daughters shall return to their former estate, then you and your daughters shall return to your former estate.[4] 56 For your sister Sodom was not mentioned by your mouth in the day of your pride, 57 Before your wickedness was uncovered, as at the time of your reproach of the daughters of Aram, and all that are around her, and the daughters of the Philistines, who despise you all around. 58 You shall bear your lewdness and your abominations, says יהוה. 59 For this says the Master יהוה; I will even deal with you as you have done, who have despised the oath in breaking the covenant. 60 Nevertheless I will remember My covenant with you in the days of your youth, and I will establish for you an everlasting covenant.[5] 61 Then you shall remember your halachot, and be ashamed, when you shall receive your sisters, your elder and your younger: and I will give them to you for daughters, but not by your own covenant.[6] 62 And I will establish My covenant with you; and you shall know that I am יהוה: 63 That you may remember, and be ashamed, and never open your mouth any more because of your shame, when I am pacified toward you for all that you have done, says the Master יהוה.

17 And the word of יהוה came to me, saying, 2 Ben-adam, put out a riddle, and speak a parable to Beit Yisrael; 3 And say, This says the Master יהוה; A great eagle with great wings, longwinged, full of feathers, which had different colors, came to Lebanon, and took the highest branch of the cedar:[7] 4 He cropped off the top of his young twigs,[8] and carried it into a land of traders; he set it in a city of merchants.[9] [10] 5 He took also of the zera of the land, and planted it in a fruitful field; he placed it by many waters, and set it as a willow eytz. 6 And it grew, and became a spreading vine of little size, whose branches turned toward him, and the roots of it were under him: so it became a vine, and brought out branches, and shot out shoots. 7 There was also another great eagle[11] with great wings and many feathers: and, see, this vine did bend her roots toward him, and shot out her branches toward him, that he might mayim it by the furrows of her plantation. 8 It was planted in a tov soil by many waters, that it might bring out branches, and that it might bear fruit, that it might be a tov vine. 9 Say, This says the Master יהוה; Shall it prosper? Shall he not pull up the roots of it, and cut off the fruit of it, so that it withers? It shall wither in all the leaves of her spring, even without great power or many people to pluck it up by the roots of it. 10 See, it is planted, shall it prosper? Shall it not utterly wither, when the east wind

---

[1] A warning not to run to Judah or Judaism for righteousness, but to Yahshua alone.
[2] Ephraim and Sodom.
[3] Both houses will return together. Unredeemed Judah in the land today is not the Jewish redeemed remnant; that remnant is still mostly in the galut-exile, and will return when Ephraim returns, not when the orthodox Jews of modern-day Jerusalem "allow it."
[4] A simultaneous return. This is clear.
[5] The Renewed Covenant through Yahshua.

[6] The two houses will be reached by YHWH's efforts and His covenant, not the other way around.
[7] Cedars of Lebanon or Jerusalem's temple.
[8] Jehoiachin.
[9] Nebuchadnezzar is the great eagle.
[10] City of merchants is Babylon.
[11] Pharaoh.

touches it? It shall wither in the furrows where it grew.[1] 11 Moreover the word of יהוה came to me, saying, 12 *Say now to the rebellious bayit, Know you not what these things mean? Tell them, See, the melech of Bavel has come to Yahrushalayim, and has taken the melech, and the leaders of it, and led them with him to Bavel; 13 And has taken one of the melech's zera, and made a covenant with him, and has taken an oath from him: he has also taken the mighty of the land: 14 That the malchut might be base, that it might not lift itself up, but that by guarding his covenant it might stand. 15 But he rebelled against him in sending his ambassadors into Mitzrayim, that they might give him horses and many people. Shall he prosper? Shall he escape that does such things? Or shall he break the covenant, and be delivered?[2]* 16 *As I live,* says the Master יהוה, *surely in the place where the melech dwells that made him melech, whose oath he despised, and whose covenant he broke, even with him in the midst of Bavel he shall die. 17 Neither shall Pharaoh with his mighty army and great company go in to help him in battle, by casting heap mounds, and building walls, to cut off many persons: 18 Seeing he despised the oath by breaking the covenant,[3] when, see, he had given his hand, and has done all these things, he shall not escape. 19 Therefore this says the Master יהוה; As I live, surely My oath that he has despised, and My covenant that he has broken, even it will I repay upon his own head.[4] 20 And I will spread My net upon him, and he shall be taken in My trap, and I will bring him to Bavel, and will plead with him there for his trespass that he has trespassed against Me.[5] 21 And all his fugitives with all his chains shall fall by the sword, and they that remain shall be scattered toward all the winds: and*

you shall know that I יהוה have spoken it. 22 *This says the Master* יהוה; *I will also take of the highest branch of the high cedar, and will set it; I will crop off from the top of his young twigs a tender one, and will plant it upon a high and eminent mountain:[6] [7] 23 In the mountain on the height of Yisrael will I plant it: and it shall bring out branches, and bear fruit, and be a tov cedar: and under it shall dwell all fowls of every wing; in the shadow of its branches they shall dwell.[8] 24 And all the eytzim of the field[9] shall know that I יהוה have brought down the high eytz,[10] have exalted the low eytz,[11] have dried up the green eytz,[12] and have made the dry eytz to flourish:[13] I יהוה have spoken and shall do it.*

18 The word of יהוה came to me again, saying, 2 *What do you mean, when you use this proverb concerning the land of Yisrael, saying, The ahvot have eaten sour grapes, and the children's teeth are blunted? 3 As I live,* says the Master יהוה, *you shall not have an occasion any more to use this proverb in Yisrael. 4 See, all beings belong to Me; the being of the abba, so also the being of the son is Mine: the being that sins, it shall die.[14] 5 But if a man be tzadik, and do that which is according to Torah and right, 6 And has not eaten upon the mountains, neither has lifted up his eyes to the idols of Beit Yisrael, neither has defiled his neighbor's wife, neither has come near to a woman in nidah, 7 And has not oppressed anyone, but has restored to the debtor his pledge, has plundered no one by violence, and has given his lechem to the hungry, and has*

---

[1] The east wind of judgment of Babylon will destroy the vine of Yisrael.
[2] Zedekiah's rebellion against Nebuchadnezzar for which he was blinded.
[3] Zedekiah broke the oath with Nebuchadnezzar.
[4] Zedekiah also broke YHWH's covenant.
[5] Zedekiah.

[6] Mt. Zion.
[7] Moshiach.
[8] Matthew 13.
[9] Nations.
[10] Judah.
[11] Ephraim.
[12] Large segments of both houses.
[13] Nations.
[14] This speaks of spiritual death in the Lake of Fire since all humanity dies physically both sinner and saint. The spirit of the lost does not live le-olam-va-ed in hell, but is burned and dies.

covered the naked with a garment; 8 He that has not charged interest, neither has taken any increase, that has turned back his hand from iniquity, and has executed true mishpat between man and man, 9 Has had their halacha in My mishpatim, and has kept My mishpatim, to deal truly; he is just, and he shall surely live, says the Master יהוה. 10 If he begets a son that is a robber, a shedder of dom, or one that does any of these same kind of things, 11 But he himself did not do any of these things, but has eaten upon the mountains, or defiled his neighbor's wife, 12 Has oppressed the poor and needy, has plundered by violence, has not restored the pledge, and has lifted up his eyes to the idols, has committed abomination, 13 Has lent on interest, and has taken increase: shall he then live? He shall not live: he has done all these abominations; he shall surely die; his dom shall be upon him. 14 Now, see, if he begets a son, that sees all his abba's sins that he has done, and considers it, and does not do anything like it, 15 Who has not eaten upon the mountains, neither has lifted up his eyes to the idols of Beit Yisrael, and has not defiled his neighbor's wife, 16 Neither has oppressed anyone, has not withheld the pledge, neither has plundered by violence, but has given his lechem to the hungry, and has covered the naked with a garment, 17 That has removed his hand from harming the poor, and has not received interest nor increase, has executed My mishpatim, has had their halacha in My mishpatim; he shall not die for the iniquity of his abba, he shall surely live. 18 As for his abba, because he oppressed, plundered his brother by violence, and did that which is not tov among his people, see, even he shall die in his iniquity. 19 Yet say you, Why? Does not the son bear the iniquity of the abba? When the son has done that which is according to Torah and right, and has kept all My mishpatim, and has done them, he shall surely live. 20 The being that sins, it shall die. The son shall not bear the

iniquity of the abba, neither shall the abba bear the iniquity of the son: the tzedakah of the tzadik shall be upon him, and the wickedness of the wicked shall be upon him. 21 But if the wicked will turn from all his sins that he has committed, and keep all My mishpatim, and do that which is according to Torah and right, he shall surely live, he shall not die. 22 All his transgressions that he has committed, they shall not be remembered against him: in his tzedakah that he has done he shall live. 23 Have I any pleasure at all that the wicked should die? Says the Master יהוה: and not that he should return from his own halachot, and live? 24 But when the tzadik turns away from his tzedakah, and commits iniquity, and does according to all the abominations that the wicked man does, shall he live? All his tzedakah that he has done shall not be mentioned: in his trespass that he has trespassed, and in his sin that he has sinned, in them shall he die. 25 Yet you say, The halacha of יהוה is not equal. Shema, Beit Yisrael; Is not My halacha equal? Are not your halachot unequal?[1] 26 When a tzadik man turns away from his tzedakah, and commits iniquities, and dies in them; for his iniquities that he has done shall he die. 27 Again, when the wicked man turns away from his wickedness that he has committed, and does that which is according to Torah and mishpat, he shall save his being alive. 28 Because he sees, and turns away from all his transgressions that he has committed, he shall surely live, he shall not die. 29 Yet says Beit Yisrael, The halacha of יהוה is not equal. O Beit Yisrael, are not My halachot equal? Are not your halachot unequal? 30 Therefore I will shophet you, O Beit Yisrael, every one according to his own halachot, says the Master יהוה . Make teshuvah, and turn yourselves from all your transgressions; so iniquity shall not be your ruin. 31 Cast away from you all your transgressions, by which you have transgressed; and make for

---

[1] Certainly we need His ways; to treat both houses equally.

yourselves a new lev and a new Ruach: for why will you die, O Beit Yisrael?[1] 32 For I have no pleasure in the death of him that dies, says the Master יהוה: therefore make teshuvah for yourselves, and live.

19 Moreover take up a lamentation for the leaders of Yisrael, 2 And say, What a lioness was your ima: she lay down among lions, she nourished her cubs among young lions. 3 And she brought up one of her cubs: it became a young lion, and it learned to catch the prey; it devoured men. 4 The nations also heard of him; he was taken in their pit, and they brought him with chains to the land of Mitzrayim. 5 Now when she saw that she had waited, and her tikvah was lost, then she took another of her cubs, and made him a young lion. 6 And he went up and down among the lions, he became a young lion, and learned to catch the prey, and devoured men.[2] 7 And he knew their desolate palaces, and he laid waste their cities; and the land was desolate, and the fullness of it, by the noise of his roaring. 8 Then the nations set themselves against him on every side from the provinces, and spread their net over him: he was taken in their pit. 9 And they put him in a cage in chains, and brought him to the melech of Bavel: they brought him in nets, that his voice should no more be heard upon the mountains of Yisrael.[3] 10 Your ima is like a vine in your dom, planted by the waters: she was fruitful and full of branches by reaBen-adamy waters. 11 And she had strong rods for the scepters of them that had rule, and her size was exalted among the thick branches, and she appeared in her height with the multitude of her branches. 12 But she was plucked up in anger, she was cast down to the ground, and the east wind dried up her fruit: her strong rods were broken and withered; the fire consumed them. 13 And now she is

planted in the wilderness,[4] in a dry and thirsty ground. 14 And fire is gone out of a rod of her branches, which has devoured her fruit, so that she has no strong rod to be a scepter to rule. This is a lament, and shall be for a lamentation.

20 And it came to pass in the seventh year, in the fifth month, the tenth day of the month, that certain of the zachanim of Yisrael came to inquire of יהוה, and sat before me. 2 Then came the word of יהוה to me, saying, 3 Ben-adam, speak to the zachanim of Yisrael, and say to them, This says the Master יהוה; Are you come to seek Me? As I live, says the Master יהוה, I will not be sought by you. 4 Will you shophet them, Ben-adam, will you shophet them? Make them to know the abominations of their ahvot: 5 And say to them, This says the Master יהוה; In the day when I chose Yisrael, and lifted up My hand to the zera of Beit Yaakov, and made Myself known to them in the land of Mitzrayim, when I lifted up My hand to them, saying, I am יהוה Your Elohim; 6 In the day that I lifted up My hand to them, to bring them out of the land of Mitzrayim into a land that I had searched out for them, flowing with milk and honey, which is the tiferet of all lands: 7 Then said I to them, Cast away every man the abominations of his eyes, and defile not yourselves with the idols of Mitzrayim: I am יהוה your Elohim. 8 But they rebelled against Me, and would not shema to Me: they did not cast away the abominations of their eyes, neither did they forsake the idols of Mitzrayim: then I said, I will pour out My anger upon them to accomplish My anger against them in the midst of the land of Mitzrayim. 9 But I acted not for My Name's sake, that it should not be defiled before the gentiles, among whom they were, in whose sight I made Myself known to them, in bringing them out of the land of Mitzrayim. 10 Therefore I caused them to go out of the land of Mitzrayim, and

---

[1] The calling of the new birth and renewal of Yisrael.
[2] King Jehoiakim.
[3] Zedekiah blinded and taken captive to Babylon.

[4] Exile of both houses.

brought them into the wilderness. 11 And I gave them My mishpatim, and showed them My mishpatim, which if a man does; he shall even live in them.[1] 12 Moreover also I gave them My Shabbats, to be a sign between Me and them, that they might know that I am יהוה that sets them apart. 13 But Beit Yisrael rebelled against Me in the wilderness:[2] they had their halacha not in My mishpatim, and they despised My mishpatim, which if a man do, he shall even live in them; and My Shabbats they greatly defiled: then I said, I would pour out My anger upon them in the wilderness, to consume them. 14 But I did not act for My Name's sake, that it should not be defiled before the gentiles, in whose sight I brought them out. 15 Yet also I lifted up My hand to them in the wilderness, that I would not bring them into the land which I had given them, flowing with milk and honey, which is the tiferet of all lands; 16 Because they despised My mishpatim, and they did not have their halacha in My mishpatim, but defiled My Shabbats: for their lev went after their idols. 17 Nevertheless My eye spared them from destroying them, neither did I make an end of them in the wilderness. 18 But I said to their children in the wilderness, Do not have your halacha in the mishpatim of your ahvot, neither observe their rulings, nor defile yourselves with their idols: 19 I am יהוה your Elohim; have your halacha in My mishpatim, and keep My mishpatim, and do them; 20 And set-apart My Shabbats; and they shall be a sign between Me and you, that you may know that I am יהוה Your Elohim. 21 Notwithstanding the children rebelled against Me: they had their own halacha not in My mishpatim, neither kept My mishpatim to do them, which if a man does, he shall even live in them; they defiled My Shabbats: then I said, I would pour out My anger upon them, to accomplish My anger against them in the wilderness.

22 Nevertheless I withdrew My hand, and acted not for My Name's sake, that it should not be defiled in the sight of the gentiles, in whose sight I brought them out. 23 I lifted up My hand to them also in the wilderness, that I would scatter them among the gentiles, and disperse them throughout the countries; 24 Because they had not executed My mishpatim, but had despised My mishpatim, and had defiled My Shabbats, and their eyes were seeking after their ahvot's idols. 25 Therefore I gave them also mishpatim that were not tov, and mishpatim by which they should not live;[3] 26 And I defiled them in their own gifts, in that they caused to pass through the fire all the firstborn, that I might stun them, so that they might know that I am יהוה 27 Therefore, Ben-adam, speak to Beit Yisrael, and say to them, This says the Master יהוה; Yet in this your ahvot have blasphemed Me, in that they have committed a trespass against Me. 28 For when I had brought them into the land, for the which I lifted up My hand to give it to them, then they saw every high hill, and all the thick eytzim, and they offered there their sacrifices, and there they presented the provocation of their offering: there also they made their sweet fragrances, and poured out there their drink offerings. 29 Then I said to them, What is the high place where you are going? And so the name of it is called Shrine of Idols up to this day. 30 Therefore say to Beit Yisrael, This says the Master יהוה; Are you defiling yourselves after the manner of your ahvot? And are you whoring after their abominations? 31 For when you offer your gifts, when you make your sons to pass through the fire, you defile yourselves with all your idols, even to this day: and shall I be sought for by you, O Beit Yisrael? As I live, says the Master יהוה, I will not be sought for by you. 32 And that which comes into your mind shall not be at all, when you say, We will be as the gentiles, as the

---

[1] We are not called to study Hebrew roots as some wrongly teach, but we are to live in them as a lifestyle.
[2] All 12 tribes.

[3] Degradation into things such as Easter, Christmas, and Lent.

families of the countries, to serve wood and stone. 33 *As I live*, says the Master יהוה, *surely with a mighty hand, and with a stretched out arm, and with anger poured out, will I rule over you: 34 And I will bring you out from the people, and will gather you out of the countries where you are scattered,[1] with a mighty hand, and with a stretched out arm, and with anger poured out. 35 And I will bring you into the wilderness of the people, and there will I plead with you face to face.[2] 36 Like I pleaded with your ahvot in the wilderness of the land of Mitzrayim, so will I plead with you, says the Master* יהוה. *37 And I will cause you to pass under the rod, and I will bring you into the bond of the covenant:[3] 38 And I will purge out from among you the rebels, and them that transgress against Me: I will bring them out of the countries where they sojourn, and they shall not enter into the land of Yisrael: and you shall know that I am* יהוה.[4] *39 As for you, O Beit Yisrael*, this says the Master יהוה; *if you will not shema to Me then go and serve everyone his idols, in the future also: but do not defile My set-apart Name any more with your gifts, and with your idols.[5] 40 For on My set-apart mountain, in the mountain on the height of Yisrael,* says the Master יהוה, *there all Beit Yisrael, all of them in the land, shall serve Me: there will I accept them, and there will I require your offerings, and the bikkurim of your offerings, with all your set-apart gifts. 41 I will accept you with your sweet fragrances, when I bring you out from the people, and gather you out of the countries in which you have been scattered; and I will be set-apart in you before the gentiles. 42 And you shall know that I am* יהוה, *when I shall bring you into the land of Yisrael, into the country for which I lifted up My hand to give it to your ahvot. 43 And there shall you remember your halachot, and all your doings, in which you have been defiled; and you shall despise yourselves in your own sight for all your evils that you have committed. 44 And you shall know that I am* יהוה, *when I have worked with you for My Name's sake, not according to your wicked halachot, nor according to your corrupt doings, O Beit Yisrael*, says the Master יהוה. 45 Moreover the word of יהוה came to me, saying, 46 *Ben-adam, set your face toward the south, and drop your word toward the south, and prophesy against the forest of the south field; 47 And say to the forest of the south, Shema the word of* יהוה; *This says the Master* יהוה; *See, I will kindle a fire in you, and it shall devour every green eytz in you, and every dry eytz: the flaming flame shall not be quenched, and all faces from the south to the north shall be burned in it.[6] 48 And all flesh shall see that I* יהוה *have kindled it: it shall not be quenched.* 49 Then said I, Oy, Master יהוה! They say of me, Does he not speak in parables?

21 And the word of יהוה came to me, saying, 2 *Ben-adam, set your face toward Yahrushalayim, and drop your word toward the set-apart places, and prophesy against the land of Yisrael, 3 And say to the land of Yisrael, This says* יהוה; *See, I am against you, and will draw out My sword out of its sheath, and will cut off from you the tzadik and the wicked. 4 Seeing then that I will cut off from you the tzadik and the wicked, therefore shall My sword go out of its sheath against all flesh from the south to the north:[7] 5 That all flesh may know that I* יהוה *have drawn out My sword out of its sheath: it shall not return any more. 6 Sigh therefore, you Ben-adam, with the breaking of your insides; and with bitterness sigh*

---

[1] The promise of restoration.
[2] YHWH pleads His offer of imparted righteousness to Yisrael while they still are in the nations, before their return to the land.
[3] Scattered Yisrael enters the eternal Renewed Covenant in the exile, as we pass under the rod of correction.
[4] Not all will be brought back. Only those who are chosen. None of the elect will be left behind in the nations.
[5] Those who name the Name of YHWH must remove themselves from all ties to paganism.

[6] Judah.
[7] Both houses.

before their eyes. 7 And it shall be, when they say to you, Why do you sigh? Then you shall answer, For the news I have received; because it comes: and every lev shall melt, and all hands shall be feeble, and every ruach shall faint, and all knees shall be weak as mayim: see, it comes, and shall be brought to pass, says the Master יהוה. 8 Again the word of יהוה came to me, saying, 9 Ben-adam, prophesy, and say, This says יהוה; Say, A sword, a sword is sharpened, and also polished: 10 It is sharpened to make a slaughter; it is polished that it may glitter: should we then have simcha; it is sharpened to cut off the family of My son and every other branch. 11 And He has given it to be polished, that it may be handled: this sword is sharpened, and it is polished, to give it into the hand of the slayer. 12 Cry and wail, Ben-adam: for it shall be upon My people, it shall be upon all the leaders of Yisrael: by reason of the sword terror shall be upon My people: therefore strike your thigh. 13 Clap your hands because this calamity is justified; if the royal family is rejected, it shall be no more says the Master יהוה. 14 You therefore, Ben-adam, prophesy, and clap, and let the sword be doubled the third time, the sword of the slain: it is the sword of the great slaughter, which surrounds them. 15 I have set the point of the sword against all their gates, so that their lev may faint, and their ruins be multiplied: Oy! It is made bright; it is wrapped up for the slaughter. 16 Sharpen yourself on the right hand, or on the left, wherever your face is turned. 17 I will also clap My hands together, and I will cause My anger to rest: I יהוה have said it. 18 The word of יהוה came to me again, saying, 19 Also, you Ben-adam, appoint two paths, that the sword of the melech of Bavel may come: both paths shall come out of one land: and place a signpost, choose it at the head of the path to the city. 20 Appoint a path, that the sword may come to Rabbath of the Ammonites, and to Yahudah into the walled Yahrushalayim.

21 For the melech of Bavel shall stand at the parting of the paths, at the fork of the two paths, to use divination: to make his arrows bright, he shall consult with images, he shall see his triumph. 22 At his right hand was the divination for Yahrushalayim, to appoint captains, to open the mouth of the slaughter, to lift up the voice with shouting, to appoint battering rams against the gates, to cast a siege, and to build a wall. 23 And it shall be to them as a false divination in their sight, to them that have sworn oaths: but he will call to remembrance the iniquity that they may be taken. 24 Therefore this says the Master יהוה; Because you have made your iniquity to be remembered, in that your transgressions are uncovered, so that in all your doings your sins do appear; because, you have been remembered, you shall be taken by the hand. 25 And you, profane wicked leaders of Yisrael, whose day has come, when iniquity shall have an end, 26 This says the Master יהוה; Remove the diadem, and take off the crown: this shall not be the same: exalt him that is low, and abase him that is high.[1] 27 I will overturn, overturn, overturn, it: and it shall be no more, until he comes whose right it is; and I will give it him.[2] 28 And you, Ben-adam, prophesy and say, This says the Master יהוה concerning the Ammonites, and concerning their reproach; even say, The sword, the sword is drawn: for the slaughter it is polished, to consume because of its glittering: 29 While they see false visions for you, while they divine a lie to you, to bring you upon the same necks of those that are slain, of the wicked, whose day is come, when their iniquity shall have an end. 30 Shall I cause it to return into its sheath? I will shophet you in the place where you were created, in the land of your

---

[1] A pattern set to emerge on Judah's throne.
[2] The crown of Judah would go from Jehoiachin to Zedekiah and then to Gedalyah the caretaker governor. The crown would remain vacant and "be no more" until the first coming of Yahshua, or the One to whom it really belongs. This has nothing to do with British Israelite fantasy involving Scotland, Ireland and England.

birth. [1] 31 *And I will pour out My indignation upon you there, I will blow against you in the fire of My anger, and deliver you into the hand of brutish men, skilful to destroy.* [2] 32 *You shall be for fuel to the fire; your dom shall be in the midst of the land; you shall be no more remembered: for I* יהוה *have spoken it.*

22 Moreover the word of יהוה came to me, saying, 2 *Now, you Ben-adam, will you shophet, will you shophet the bloody city? Yes, you shall show her all her abominations.* [3] 3 *Then say, This says the Master* יהוה, *The city sheds dom in the midst of it, that her time may come, and makes idols inside herself to defile herself.* 4 *You are become guilty in your dom that you have shed; and have defiled yourself in your idols which you have made; and you have caused your days to draw near, and are come even to the end of your years: therefore have I made you a reproach to the gentiles, and a mocking to all countries.* 5 *Those that be near, and those that be far from you, shall mock you, which are infamous and there is great confusion about you.* 6 *See, the leaders of Yisrael, everyone has used their power to shed dom in the city.* 7 *In you have they despised their abba and ima: in you have they dealt by oppression with the stranger:* [4] *in you have they troubled the fatherless and the widow.* 8 *You have despised My set-apart things, and have profaned My Shabbats.* 9 *In you are men that carry slander to shed dom: and in you they eat upon the mountains: in the midst of you they commit lewdness.* 10 *In you have they uncovered their ahvot's nakedness: in you have they slept with women in nidah.* 11 *And one has committed abomination with his neighbor's wife; and*

another has lewdly defiled his daughter-in-law; and another in you has humbled his sister, his abba's daughter.* [5] 12 *In you have they taken bribes to shed dom; in you they have taken forbidden interest and increase, and you have greedily gained from your neighbors by extortion, and have forgotten Me,* says the Master יהוה. 13 *See, therefore I have smitten My hand at your dishonest gain that you have made, and at your dom which has been shed in the midst of you.* 14 *Can your lev endure, or can your hands be strong, in the days that I shall deal with you? I* יהוה *have spoken it, and will do it.* 15 *And I will scatter you among the gentiles[6], and disperse you in the countries, and will consume your filthiness out of you.* 16 *And you shall defile yourself in the sight of the gentiles, and you shall know that I am* יהוה. 17 *And the word of* יהוה *came to me, saying,* 18 *Ben-adam, Beit Yisrael is to Me become dross: all they are bronze, and tin, and iron, and lead, in the midst of a furnace; they have become the dross of silver.* 19 *Therefore this says the Master* יהוה; *Because you are all become dross, see, therefore I will gather you into the midst of Yahrushalayim.* 20 *As they gather silver, and bronze, and iron, and lead, and tin, into the midst of the furnace, to blow the fire upon it, to melt it; so will I gather you in My displeasure, and in My anger, I will leave you there to melt you.* 21 *Yes, I will gather you, and blow upon you in the fire of My anger, and you shall be melted in the midst of it.* 22 *As silver is melted in the midst of the furnace, so shall you be melted in the midst of it; and you shall know that I* יהוה *have poured out My anger upon you.* 23 And the word of יהוה came to me, saying, 24 *Ben-adam, say to her, You are the land that is not cleansed, nor rained upon in the day of indignation.* 25 *There is a conspiracy of her neviim in the midst of her, like a roaring lion seeking the prey; they have devoured beings; they have taken*

---

[1] The Ammonites taunted the Jews when Nebuchadnezzar decided to invade Jerusalem rather than their land. YHWH assures them that their turn will come - in their own land - by the same sword.
[2] Babylonians.
[3] Those given a prophetic anointing by YHWH can shophet by the Word and the Spirit.
[4] Sadly this has not changed.

[5] Incest.
[6] That's where you'll find Ephraim. "Among the gentiles."

the treasures and precious things; they have made many widows in the midst of her. 26 Her kohanim have violated My Torah, and have profaned My set-apart things: they have put no difference between the set-apart and profane, neither have they shown difference between the unclean and the clean, and have hid their eyes from My Shabbats, and I am profaned among them. 27 Her leaders in the midst of it are like wolves seeking the prey, to shed dom, and to destroy beings, to get dishonest gain. 28 And her neviim have coated their evil with whitewash, seeing vanity, and divining lies to them, saying, This says the Master יהוה, when יהוה has not spoken. 29 The people of the land have used oppression, and robbery, and have troubled the poor and the needy: they have oppressed the stranger without mishpat. 30 And I sought for a man among them, that should make up the breach, and stand in the gap before Me for the land, that I should not destroy it: but I found none.[1] 31 Therefore have I poured out My indignation upon them; I have consumed them with the fire of My anger: their own halacha have I repayed upon their heads, says the Master יהוה.

23 The word of יהוה came again to me, saying, 2 Ben-adam, there were two women, the daughters of one ima:[2] 3 And they committed whorings in Mitzrayim; they committed whorings in their youth: there were their breasts pressed, and there their virgin nipples were squeezed. 4 And their names were Ochala the elder, and Ochaliva her sister: and they were Mine, and they bore sons and daughters. These were their names; Shomron is Ochala, and Yahrushalayim

Ochaliva. 5 And Ochala played the harlot when she was Mine; and she lusted for her lovers, the neighboring Ashurim, 6 Who were clothed with blue, captains and rulers, all of them desirable young men, horsemen riding upon horses. 7 So she committed her whorings with them, with all of them that were the chosen men of Ashshur, and with all for whom she lusted: with all their idols she defiled herself.[3] 8 Neither did she leave her whorings that she brought up from Mitzrayim: for in her youth they had lain with her, and they squeezed the breasts of her virginity, and poured out their whorings upon her. 9 Therefore I have delivered her into the hands of her lovers,[4] into the hands of the Ashurim, for whom she lusted. 10 They uncovered her nakedness: they took her sons and her daughters, and killed her with the sword: and she became famous among women; for they had executed their desired judgments upon her. 11 And when her sister Ochaliva[5] saw this, she was more corrupt in her perverted ahava than she, and in her whorings more than her sister in her whorings.[6] 12 She also lusted upon the Ashurim her neighbors; captains and rulers clothed most gorgeously, horsemen riding upon horses, all of them desirable young men. 13 Then I saw that she was defiled, that they both followed one evil halacha, 14 And that she increased her whorings: for when she saw men portrayed upon the wall, the images of the Chaldeans portrayed in red,[7] 15 Girded with belts upon their waist, flowing turbans on their heads, all of them looking like leaders, after the manner of the Babylonians of Chaldea, the land of their birth: 16 And as soon as she saw them with her eyes, she lusted upon them, and sent

---

[1] No human mediator did qualify. It was also extremely early to send the true mediator, the Moshiach Yahshua, as per First Timothy 2:5.
[2] The two sisters are the two houses. The one ima is Jerusalem, the capital of a united monarchy before the division of the kingdom. This chapter is compared to Second John, which is a complimentary book to this entire chapter. For a deep study, go to: http://store.yourarmstoisrael.org/Qstore/Qstore.cgi?CMD=011&PROD=1065766494.

[3] Ephraim never cared what kind of paganism it was, as long as it was some form of it.
[4] 721 BCE.
[5] Judah.
[6] Judah was worse than Ephraim. Thus why would an Ephraimite run to unbelieving Judah for Torah or any other instruction? Instead, that task has been assigned to the remnant of believing Judah.
[7] Babylonian idolatry.

messengers to seek them into Chaldea. [1]
17 And the Babylonians came to her into the bed of ahava, and they defiled her with their whorings, and she was defiled with them, and her being was alienated from them in disgust. 18 So she uncovered her whorings, and uncovered her nakedness: then My being was alienated from her, like My being was alienated from her sister. 19 Yet she multiplied her whorings, in calling to remembrance the days of her youth, in which she had played the harlot in the land of Mitzrayim. [2] 20 For she lusted upon their lovers, whose flesh is as the flesh of donkeys, and whose emission is like the emission of horses. 21 This you remembered and called for the lewdness of your youth, in squeezing your nipples by the Mitzrites when they squeezed the breasts of your youth. 22 Therefore, O Ochaliva, this says the Master יהוה; See, I will raise up your lovers against you, from whom your being is now alienated, and I will bring them against you on every side; [3] 23 The Babylonians, and all the Chaldeans, Pechod, and Shoa, and Qoa, and all the Ashurim with them: all of them desirable young men, captains and rulers, great masters famous ones, all of them riding upon horses. 24 And they shall come against you with mirkavot, wagons, and wheels, and with a congregation of peoples, which shall set against you armor and shield and helmet all around: and I will hand over your mishpat to them, and they shall shophet you according to their own mishpatim. 25 And I will set My jealousy against you, [4] and they shall deal furiously with you: they shall take away your nose and your ears; and your remnant shall fall by the sword: they shall take your sons and your daughters; and the fire shall devour your remnant. 26 They shall also strip you out of your clothes, and take away your beautiful jewels. 27 In this manner will I make your lewdness to cease from you, and your whorings brought from the land of Mitzrayim to stop: so that you shall not lift up your eyes to them, nor choose to remember Mitzrayim any more. 28 For this says the Master יהוה; See, I will deliver you into the hand of them who you hate, into the hand of them from whom your being is alienated: 29 And they shall deal with you hatefully, and shall take away all you have worked for, and shall leave you naked and bare: and the nakedness of your whorings shall be uncovered, both your lewdness and your whorings. 30 I will do these things to you, because you have gone whoring after the gentiles, and because you are defiled with their idols. [5] 31 You have had your halacha in the halacha of your sister; therefore will I give her cup into your hand. [6] 32 This says the Master יהוה; You shall drink of your sister's cup deep and large: you shall be laughed to scorn and had in derision; it contains much mishpat. 33 You shall be filled with drunkenness and sorrow, with the cup of astonishment and desolation, with the cup of your sister Shomron. 34 You shall even drink it and drain it out, and you shall break the sherds of it, and beat your own breasts: for I have spoken it, says the Master יהוה. 35 Therefore this says the Master יהוה; Because you have forgotten Me, and cast Me behind your back, therefore you will also bear your lewdness and your whorings without Me. 36 יהוה said moreover to me; Ben-adam, will you shophet Ochala and Ochaliva? Yes, declare to them their abominations; 37 That they have committed adultery, and dom is in their hands, and with their idols have they committed adultery, and have also caused their sons, whom they bore for Me, to pass through the fire, to devour them. 38 Moreover this they have done to Me:

---

[1] Judah sought idolatrous lovers from both Assyria and Babylon.
[2] Both sisters added yet more lovers.
[3] Against Jerusalem.
[4] YHWH is the jealous husband over Yisrael.

[5] YHWH allowed both houses to literally become what they lusted for: Heathen!
[6] Judah will inherit the same cup of judgment and exile as Ephraim.

they have defiled My Set-Apart Place on the same day, and have profaned My Shabbats. 39 *For when they had slain their children to their idols, then they came the very same day into My Set-Apart Place to profane it; and, see, this have they done in the midst of My Bayit. 40 And furthermore, both of you have sent for men to come from far, for whom a messenger was sent; and, see, they came to you: the ones for whom you did wash yourself, and painted your eyes, and adorned yourself with ornaments, 41 And sat upon a splendid couch, with a table prepared in front of it, on which you have set My incense and My oil. 42 And the sound of a crowd being at ease was with her:[1] and with the men of the common sort were brought drunkards from the wilderness, who put bracelets upon their hands, and beautiful crowns upon their heads. 43 Then I said to her that was worn out by adulteries, Will they now commit whorings with her, and she with them? 44 Yet they still went in to her, as they go in to a woman that plays the harlot: so went they in to Ochala and to Ochaliva, the lewd women. 45 And the tzadik men, they shall shophet them after the manner of adulteresses, and after the manner of women that shed dom; because they are adulteresses, and dom is in their hands.* 46 For this says the Master יהוה; *I will bring up a company upon them, and will give them to be taken away and plundered. 47 And the company shall stone them with stones, and dispatch them with their swords; they shall slay their sons and their daughters, and burn up their houses with fire. 48 In this manner will I cause lewdness to cease out of the land, that all remaining women in Yisrael may be taught not to do after your lewdness. 49 And they shall repay your lewdness upon you, and you shall bear the sins of your idols: and you shall know that I am the Master* יהוה.

24 Again in the ninth year, in the tenth month, in the tenth day of the month, the word of יהוה came to me, saying, 2 *Ben-adam, write the name of the day, even this same day: that the melech of Bavel set himself against Yahrushalayim this same day. 3 And uttter a parable to the rebellious bayit, and say to them, This says the Master* יהוה; *Set a pot, out it on, and also pour mayim into it: 4 Gather the pieces of meat into it, even every tov piece, the thigh, and the shoulder; fill it with the best bones. 5 Take the best of the flock, and pile the bones under it, and make it boil fully, and let the bones cook in it.* 6 Therefore this says the Master יהוה; *Woe to the bloody city, to the pot whose scum is in it, and whose scum is not gone out of it! Bring it out piece by piece; let no lot fall up on it.*

7 For her dom is in the midst of her; she set it upon the top of a rock; she poured it not upon the earth, to cover the dom with dust; 8 That it might cause anger to come up to take vengeance; I have set her dom upon the top of a rock, that it should not be covered. 9 Therefore this says the Master יהוה; *Woe to the bloody city! I will even make the pile for great for her fire. 10 Heap on the wood, kindle the fire, consume the flesh, and spice it well, and let the bones be burned. 11 Then set it upon the coals empty, that the bronze of it may be hot, and may burn, and that the filthiness of it may be melted in it, that the scum of it may be consumed. 12 She has wearied herself with lies, and her great scum did not go out of her: her scum shall be wasted in the fire. 13 In your filthiness is your lewdness: because I have cleansed you, but you were still not clean, you shall not be purged from your filthiness any more, until I have caused My anger to rest upon you. 14 I* יהוה *have spoken it: it shall come to pass, and I will do it; I will not hold back, neither will I spare, neither will I relent; according to your own halachot, and according to your doings, shall they shophet you,* says the Master יהוה.

---

[1] Orgies.

15 Also the word of יהוה came to me, saying, 16 Ben-adam, see, I take away from you the desire of your eyes1 with a stroke: yet neither shall you mourn nor weep, neither shall your tears run down. 17 Hold back from crying, make no mourning for the dead, bind the turban of your head upon you, 2 and put on your sandals upon your feet, and cover not your lips, and do not eat the lechem of men. 18 So I spoke to the people in the morning: and at evening my wife died; and I did the next morning as I was commanded. 19 And the people said to me, Will you not tell us what these things mean to us, that you do? 20 Then I answered them, as the word of יהוה came to me, saying, 21 Speak to Beit Yisrael, This says the Master יהוה; See, I will profane My Set-Apart Place, the excellency of your strength, the desire of your eyes, and that which your being pities; and your sons and your daughters whom you have left shall fall by the sword. 22 And you shall do as I have done: you shall not cover your lips, nor eat the lechem of men. 23 And your turbans shall be upon your heads, and your sandals upon your feet: you shall not mourn nor weep; but you shall waste away for your iniquities, and mourn with one another. 24 And Yehchezkel is a sign to you: according to all that he has done shall you do: and when this comes, you shall know that I am the Master יהוה. 25 Also, you Ben-adam, shall it not be in the day when I take away from them their strength, the simcha of their tiferet, the desire of their eyes, and that on which they set their minds, their sons and their daughters, 26 That he that escapes in that day shall come to you, to cause you to shema to it with your ears? 27 In that day shall your mouth be opened to him who has escaped, and you shall speak, and be no more dumb: and you shall be a sign to them; and they shall know that I am יהוה.

25 The word of יהוה came again to me, saying, 2 Ben-adam, set your face against the Ammonites, and prophesy against them; 3 And say to the Ammonites, Shema the word of the Master יהוה; This says the Master יהוה; Because you said, Aha, against My Set-Apart Place, when it was profaned; and against the land of Yisrael, when it was desolate; and against Beit Yahudah, when they went into exile;[3] 4 See, therefore I will deliver you to the men of the east4 for a possession, and they shall set their palaces in you, and make their dwellings in you: they shall eat your fruit, and they shall drink your milk. 5 And I will make Ravah a stable for camels, and the Ammonites a resting place for flocks: and you shall know that I am יהוה. 6 For this says the Master יהוה; Because you have clapped your hands, and stomped with your feet, and had gilah in lev with all your scorn against the land of Yisrael; 7 See, therefore I will stretch out My hand upon you, and will deliver you for a spoil to the gentiles; and I will cut you off from the nations, and I will cause you to perish out of the nations: I will destroy you; and you shall know that I am יהוה. 8 This says the Master יהוה; Because Moav and Seir do say, See, Beit Yahudah is like all the rest of the gentiles; 9 Therefore, see, I will open the side of Moav from the cities, from his cities that are on his frontiers, the tiferet of the country, Beth-Yeshimoth, Baal-Meon, and Kiriathayim, 10 I will give it to the men of the east along with the Ammonites, and will give them as a possession, that the Ammonites may not be remembered among the nations. 11 And I will execute mishpatim upon Moav; and they shall know that I am יהוה. 12 This says the Master יהוה; Because Edom has also dealt against the Beit Yahudah by taking vengeance, and has greatly offended Me, and revenged himself upon them; 13 Therefore this says the Master יהוה; I will also stretch out My hand upon Edom, and

---

1 Jerusalem.
2 Yisraelite men wear head coverings.

3 YHWH alone is allowed to discipline Yisrael. If man attempts to harm either house they will be destroyed.
4 Babylonians.

will cut off man and beast from it; and I will make it desolate from Teman; and those of Dedan shall fall by the sword. 14 And I will lay My vengeance upon Edom by the hand of My people Yisrael: and they shall do in Edom according to My anger; and they shall know My vengeance, says the Master יהוה . 15 This says the Master יהוה ; Because the Philistines also have dealt by revenge, and have taken vengeance with a spiteful lev, to destroy Yisrael for the old hatred; 16 Therefore this says the Master יהוה; See, I will stretch out My hand upon the Philistines, and I will cut off the Cherethim, and destroy the remnant of the seacoast. 17 And I will execute great vengeance upon them with furious rebukes; and they shall know that I am יהוה, when I shall lay My vengeance upon them.

26 And it came to pass in the eleventh year, in the first day of the month, that the word of יהוה came to me, saying, 2 Ben-adam, because that Tsor [1] has said against Yahrushalayim, Aha, she is broken that was the gateway of the nations: she is turned over to Me: I shall be filled, now she is laid waste: 3 Therefore this says the Master יהוה ; See, I am against you, O Tsor, and will cause many nations to come up against you, as the sea causes its waves to come up. 4 And they shall destroy the walls of Tsor, and break down her towers: I will also scrape her up from the dust, and make her like the top of a rock. 5 It shall be a place for the spreading of nets in the midst of the sea: for I have spoken it, says the Master יהוה : and it shall become a spoil to all the nations. 6 And her daughters that are in the field shall be slain by the sword; and they shall know that I am יהוה. 7 For this says the Master יהוה; See, I will bring upon Tsor, Nebuchadnetzar melech of Bavel, a melech of melechim, from the north, with horses, and with mirkavot, and with horsemen, and bands, and much people. 8 He shall slay with the sword your

daughters in the field: and he shall make a wall against you, and cast a siege mound against you, and lift up the shield against you. 9 And he shall set engines of war against your walls, and with his axes he shall break down your towers. 10 By reason of the abundance of his horses their dust shall cover you: your walls shall shake at the noise of the horsemen, and of the wheels, and of the mirkavot, when he shall enter into your gates, as men enter into a city in which there is a breach. 11 With the hoofs of his horses shall he tread down all your streets: he shall slay your people by the sword, and your strongholds shall go down to the ground. 12 And they shall make a spoil of your riches, and make a prey of your merchandise: and they shall break down your walls, and destroy your nice houses: and they shall lay your stones and your timber and your dust in the midst of the sea mayim. 13 And I will cause the noise of your songs to cease; and the sound of your harps shall be heard no more. 14 And I will make you like the top of a rock: you shall become a place to spread nets upon; you shall be built no more: for I יהוה have spoken it, says the Master יהוה. 15 This says the Master יהוה to Tsor; Shall not the coastlands shake at the sound of your fall, when the wounded cry, when the slaughter is made in the midst of you? 16 Then all the leaders of the sea shall come down from their thrones, and lay away their robes, and put off their embroidered garments: they shall clothe themselves with trembling; they shall sit upon the ground, and shall tremble at every moment, and be astonished at your fall. 17 And they shall take up a lamentation for you, and say to you, How are you destroyed, that were inhabited by seafaring men, the famous city, which was strong by the sea, she and her inhabitants, who caused their fear to be on all that lived there! 18 Now shall the coastlands tremble in the day of your fall; yes, the coastlands that are in the sea shall be troubled by your departure. 19 For this says the Master יהוה;

---

[1] Tyre.

When I shall make you a desolate city, like the cities that are not inhabited; when I shall bring up the deep of the sea upon you, and great waters shall cover you; 20 When I shall bring you down with them that descend into the pit, with the people of old time, and shall set you in the lower parts of the earth, in the desolate places of old, with them that go down to the pit, that you be not inhabited;[1] and I shall establish My tiferet in the land of the living;[2] 21 I will make you a horror, and you shall be no more: though you be sought for, yet shall you never be found again, says the Master יהוה.

27 The word of יהוה came again to me, saying, 2 Now, you Ben-adam, take up a lamentation for Tsor; 3 And say to Tsor, O you that are situated at the entrance of the sea, who are a merchant of the peoples for many coastlands, This says the Master יהוה; O Tsor, you have said, I am perfect in my beauty. 4 Your borders are in the midst of the seas; your builders have perfected your beauty. 5 They have made all your shipboards of fir eytzim from Senir: they have taken cedars from Lebanon to make masts for you. 6 Of the oaks of Bashan have they made your oars; they have made your benches of ivory, brought out of the coastlands of Chittim. 7 Fine linen with embroidered work from Mitzrayim, was that which you spread out to be your sail; blue and purple from the coastlands of Elishah was that which covered you. 8 The inhabitants of Tzidon and Arvad were your mariners: your wise men, O Tsor, that were in you, were your sailors. 9 The zachanim of Geval and their wise men were repairing your seams: all the ships of the sea with their mariners were in your ports to trade with your merchandise. 10 Those of Persia and of Lud and of Phut were in your army, your men of war: they hung the shield and helmet in you; they gave splendor to you. 11 The men

of Arvad were in your army and were upon your walls all around, and the Gammadites were in your towers: they hung their shields upon your walls all around; they made your beauty perfect. 12 Tarshish was your merchant by reason of the multitude of all kinds of riches; with silver, iron, tin, and lead, they traded in your merchandise. 13 Javan,[3] Tuval, and Meshech,[4] they were your merchants: they traded slaves and vessels of bronze in your markets. 14 They of Beit Togarmah traded in your merchandise with horses and horsemen and mules. 15 The men of Dedan were your merchants; many coastlands were your markets: they brought presents from horns of ivory and ebony. 16 Aram was your merchant by reason of the multitude of the items that you made: they gave you emeralds, purple, and embroidered work, and fine linen, and coral, and rubies. 17 Yahudah, and the land of Yisrael, they were your merchants: they traded in your market wheat of Minnith, and early figs, and honey, and oil, and balm. 18 Dameshek was your merchant in the multitude of the items that you made, from the multitude of your riches; the wine of Helbon, and white wool. 19 Dan[5] also and Javan dealing in your merchandise from Uzal: bright iron, cassia, and cane, were in your market. 20 Dedan was your merchant in precious clothes for mirkavot. 21 Arabia, and all the leaders of Qedar, they traded with you in lambs, and rams, and goats: in these were they your merchants. 22 The merchants of Sheva and Raamah, they were your merchants: they traded in your merchandise with the finest of all spices, and with all precious stones, and gold. 23 Haran, and Canneh, and Eden, the merchants of Sheva, Ashshur, and Chilmad, were your merchants. 24 These were your merchants in all sorts of things, in blue clothes, and embroidered work, and in chests of rich apparel, bound with cords, and made of

---

[1] Possible location of the Lake of Fire.
[2] The Renewed Jerusalem.
[3] Japan?
[4] Parts of modern Russia?
[5] Tribe of Dan and modern Japan?

cedar, among your items. 25 The ships of Tarshish did seek you in your market: and you were filled, and made very famous in the midst of the seas. 26 Your mariners have brought you into many waters: but the east wind[1] has broken you in the midst of the seas. 27 Your riches, and your merchandise, your mariners, and your sailors, your seam repairers, and the traders of your merchandise, and all your men of war, that are with you, and in your company, shall fall into the midst of the seas in the day of your ruin. 28 The borders shall shake at the sound of the cry of your sailors. 29 And all that handle the oar, the mariners, and all the sailors of the sea, shall come down from their ships, they shall stand upon the land; 30 And shall cause their voice to be heard against you, and shall cry bitterly, and shall cast up dust upon their heads, and roll themselves in ashes: 31 And they shall make themselves completely bald because of you, and clothe themselves with sackcloth, and they shall weep for you with bitterness of lev and bitter wailing. 32 And in their wailing they shall take up a lamentation for you, and lament over you, saying, What city is like Tsor, like the one destroyed in the midst of the sea? 33 When your items went out of the seas, you filled many peoples; you did enrich the melechim of the earth with the multitude of your riches and of your merchandise. 34 In the time when you shall be broken by the seas in the depths of the waters your merchandise and all your company in the midst of you shall fall. 35 All the inhabitants of the coastlands shall be astonished at you, and their melechim shall be very afraid, they shall be troubled in their faces 36 The merchants among the people shall whistle at you; you shall be a horror, and shall be no more le-olam-va-ed.

28 The word of יהוה came again to me, saying, 2 *Ben-adam, say to the*

leaders of Tsor, This says the Master יהוה; Because your lev is lifted up, and you have said, I am an El, I sit in the seat of Elohim, in the midst of the seas; yet you are just men, and not El, though you set your lev as the lev of Elohim: 3 See, are you wiser than Daniyel; has no secret been hidden from you? 4 With your wisdom and with your understanding you have gotten riches, and have gotten gold and silver into your treasures: 5 By your great wisdom and by your trade you have increased your riches, and your lev is lifted up because of your riches: 6 Therefore this says the Master יהוה; Because you have set your lev as the lev of Elohim; 7 See, therefore I will bring foreigners upon you, the fear of the nations: and they shall draw their swords against the beauty of your wisdom, and they shall defile your splendor. 8 They shall bring you down to the pit, and you shall die the deaths of those that are slain in the midst of the seas. 9 Will you then say to him that kills you, that you are Elohim? But you shall be a man, and not an El, in the hand of him that kills you. 10 You shall die the deaths of the uncircumcised by the hand of foreigners:[2] for I have spoken it, says the Master יהוה . 11 Moreover the word of יהוה came to me, saying, 12 Ben-adam, take up a lamentation for the melech of Tsor, and say to him, This says the Master יהוה ; You sealed up a pattern, full of wisdom, and perfect in beauty. 13 You[3] have been in Eden the garden of Elohim;[4] every precious stone was your covering, the ruby, topaz, and the diamond, the beryl, the onyx, and the jasper, the sapphire, the emerald, and the turquoise, and gold: the workmanship of your settings and your

---

[1] Wind of judgment.

[2] This is a clear hint or **remez** indicating that as a result of colonization by Solomon, Tyre was considered a Yisraelite colony, and as Yisraelites, they would be judged at the hands of gentiles.
[3] s.a.tan; the real spirit behind Tyre's greed.
[4] In the **pashat** this is a continuation of the prophecy of judgment against Tyre. But suddenly in verse 13 the text shifts to the Garden of Eden, and becomes a revelation (or a sod) about the true motivating spirit behind the greed of Tyre. It is none other than s.a.tan. Scripture often speaks in the literal, with a sudden shift to a yet deeper level of Hebraic understanding.

mountings was prepared for you in the day that you were created. 14 *You are the moshiach-like cheruv that covers;[1] and I had placed you upon the set-apart mountain of Elohim;[2] you have walked up and down in the midst of the stones of fire.[3] 15 You were perfect in your halachot from the day that you were created, until iniquity was found in you.[4] 16 By the multitude of your merchandise they have filled your midst with violence, and you have sinned: therefore I will cast you as a profane-one out of the mountain of Elohim:[5] and I will destroy you, O covering cheruv, from the midst of the stones of fire.[6] 17 Your lev was lifted up because of your beauty, you have corrupted your wisdom by reason of your splendor: I will cast you to the ground, I will lay you before melechim, that they may see you. 18 You have defiled your sanctuaries by the multitude of your iniquities, by the iniquity of your trade; therefore will I bring out a fire in your midst, it shall devour you,[7] and I will bring you to ashes upon the earth in the sight of all them that see you.[8] 19 All they that knew you among the nations shall be astonished at you: you shall be a waste before them, and never shall you be again.[9]* 20 Again the word of יהוה came to me, saying, 21 *Ben-adam, set your face against Tzidon, and prophesy against it,* 22 And say, This says the Master יהוה; *See, I am against you, O Tzidon; and I will be exalted in your midst: and they shall know that I am יהוה, when I shall have executed mishpatim in her, and shall be set-apart in her. 23 For I will send into her pestilence, and dom into her streets; and the wounded shall be judged in the midst of her by the sword upon her on every side; and they shall know that I am יהוה. 24 And there shall be no more a pricking brier to Beit Yisrael, nor a painful thorn to all that are around them, that despised them; and they shall know that I am the Master יהוה.* 25 This says the Master יהוה; *When I shall have gathered Beit Yisrael[10] from the people among whom they are scattered, and shall be set-apart in them in the sight of the gentiles, then shall they dwell in their land that I have given to My eved Yaakov. 26 And they shall dwell safely in it, and shall build houses, and plant vineyards; they shall dwell with confidence, when I have executed mishpatim upon all those that despise them all around them; and they shall know that I am יהוה their Elohim.*

29 In the tenth year, in the tenth month, on the twelfth day of the month, the word of יהוה came to me, saying, 2 *Ben-adam, set your face against Pharaoh melech of Mitzrayim, and prophesy against him, and against all of Mitzrayim: 3 Speak, and say, This says the Master יהוה ; See, I am against you, Pharaoh melech of Mitzrayim, the great dragon that lies in the midst of his rivers, which has said, My river is my own, and I have made it for myself. 4 But I will put hooks in your jaws, and I will cause the fish of your rivers to stick to your scales, and I will bring you up out of the midst of your rivers, and all the fish of your rivers shall cling to your scales. 5 And I will leave you thrown into the wilderness, you and all the fish of your rivers: you shall fall upon the open fields; you shall not be brought together, nor gathered: I have given you for food to the beasts of the field and to the fowls of the shamayim. 6 And all the inhabitants of Mitzrayim shall know that I am יהוה, because they have been a staff of reed to Beit Yisrael. 7 When they took hold of you by your hand, you did break them,*

---

[1] s.a.tan as the anointed one of heaven, covering the other messengers with YHWH's radiated glory, even as the true Moshiach did and still does.
[2] In heaven, in eternity past.
[3] Other heavenly beings.
[4] Until s.a.tan rebelled.
[5] Out of the heavens.
[6] He was the reflection of YHWH to other angels and covered them with light. He was their head covering.
[7] Lake of Fire for s.a.tan.
[8] YHWH's people will see s.a.tan's destruction after the millennium.
[9] Revelation 20:10.

[10] Both houses.

and tore all their shoulders: and when they leaned upon you, you broke them, and made all their parts to shake. 8 Therefore this says the Master **יהוה**; *See, I will bring a sword upon you, and cut off man and beast from you.* 9 *And the land of Mitzrayim shall be desolate and ruined; and they shall know that I am* **יהוה**: *because he has said, The river is mine, and I have made it.* 10 *See, therefore I am against you, and against your rivers, and I will make the land of Mitzrayim utterly wasted and desolate, from the tower of Seweneh even to the border of Ethiopia.* 11 *No foot of man shall pass through it, no foot of beast shall pass through it, and neither shall it be inhabited forty years.* 12 *And I will make the land of Mitzrayim desolate in the midst of the countries that are desolate, and her cities among the cities that are laid waste shall be desolate forty years: and I will scatter the Mitzrites among the nations, and will disperse them through the countries.* [1] 13 This says the Master **יהוה**; *At the end of forty years will I gather the Mitzrites from the nations where they were scattered:* 14 *And I will bring again the exile of Mitzrayim, and will cause them to return into the land of Pathros, into the land of their dwelling; and they shall be there a humble malchut.* 15 *It it shall be the humblest of malchutim; neither shall it exalt itself anymore above the nations: for I will diminish them so that they shall no more rule over the nations.* [2] 16 *And it shall be no more the confidence of Beit Yisrael,[3] which brings their iniquity to My remembrance, when they look to them for help: but they shall know that I am the Master* **יהוה**. 17 And it came to pass in the twenty-seventh year, in the first month, in the first day of the month, the word of **יהוה** came to me, saying, 18 *Ben-adam, Nebuchadnetzar melech of Bavel caused his army to serve a great service against Tsor: every head was*

made bald, and every shoulder was exposed: yet had he no wages, and his army, had no reward from Tsor, for the service that he had served against it: [4] 19 Therefore this says the Master **יהוה**; *See, I will give the land of Mitzrayim to Nebuchadnetzar melech of Bavel; and he shall take her multitudes, and take her spoils, and take her prey; and that shall then be the wages for his army.* 20 *I have given him the land of Mitzrayim for his labor with which he served against it, because they were working for Me*, says the Master **יהוה**. 21 *In that day will I cause the horn of Beit Yisrael to spring out, and I will give you an open mouth to speak for Me in the midst of them; and they shall know that I am* **יהוה**.[5]

30 The word of **יהוה** came again to me, saying, 2 Ben-adam, prophesy and say, This says the Master **יהוה**; *Howl you, Woe to that day.* 3 *For the day is near, even the day of* **יהוה** *is near,[6] a cloudy day; it shall be the time of the nations.[7]* 4 *And the sword shall come upon Mitzrayim, and great pain shall be in Ethiopia, when the slain shall fall in Mitzrayim, and they shall take away her multitudes, and her foundations shall be broken down.* 5 *Ethiopia, and Libya, and Kuv, and all the mingled people, all the sons of the land of the covenant, shall fall with them by the sword.* 6 This says **יהוה**; *They also that uphold Mitzrayim shall fall; and the pride of her power shall come down: from the tower of Seweneh shall they fall in it by the sword*, says the Master **יהוה**. 7 *And they shall be desolate in the midst of the countries that are desolate, and her cities shall be in the midst of the cities that are*

---

[1] YHWH always uses exiles, to humble the proud and lofty nations.
[2] Egypt never regained world dominance again.
[3] All 12 tribes.

[4] For YHWH's will to be done.
[5] Around the time Egypt is captured, Yisrael will shema the voice of deliverance.
[6] The end-times last seven years of this age, also known as the 70th week of Yisrael.
[7] In the literal or **pashat** it spoke of a historical judgment by YHWH upon the nations using Babylon as a tool of correction upon those who abused either house of Yisrael. In an end-time or eschatological setting, it speaks of Yisrael's re-gathering, during the 70th week of Yisrael.

wasted. 8 *And they shall know that I am* **יהוה***, when I have set a fire in Mitzrayim, and when all her helpers shall be destroyed.* 9 *In that day shall messengers go out from Me in ships to make the complacent Ethiopians afraid, and great pain shall come upon them, as in the day of Mitzrayim: for, see, it is coming.* 10 *This says the Master* **יהוה***; I will also make the multitudes of Mitzrayim to cease by the hands of Nebuchadnetzar melech of Bavel.* 11 *He and his people with him, the ruthless ones of the nations, shall be brought to destroy the land: and they shall draw their swords against Mitzrayim, and fill the land with the slain.* 12 *And I will make the rivers dry, and sell the land into the hand of the wicked: and I will make the land wasted, and all that is in it, by the hand of foreigners: I* **יהוה** *have spoken it.* 13 *This says the Master* **יהוה***; I will also destroy the idols, and I will cause their images to cease out of Noph; and there shall be no more be a leader in the land of Mitzrayim: and I will put a fear in the land of Mitzrayim.* 14 *And I will make Pathros desolate, and will set fire in Zoan, and will execute mishpatim in No.* 15 *And I will pour My anger upon Sin, the strength of Mitzrayim; and I will cut off the multitudes of No.* 16 *And I will set fire in Mitzrayim: Sin shall have great pain, and No shall be torn asunder, and Noph shall have daily distresses.* 17 *The young men of Aven and of Pi-beseth shall fall by the sword: and these cities shall go into exile.* 18 *At Tehaphnehes also the day shall be darkened, when I shall break in that place the yokes of Mitzrayim: and the pride of her strength shall cease in her: as for her, a cloud shall cover her, and her daughters shall go into exile.* 19 *And I will execute mishpatim in Mitzrayim: so they shall know that I am* **יהוה***.* 20 And it came to pass in the eleventh year, in the first month, in the seventh day of the month, that the word of **יהוה** came to me, saying, 21 *Ben-adam, I have broken the arm of Pharaoh melech of*

Mitzrayim; and, see, it shall not be bound up to be healed, to put a bandage to bind it, to make it strong to hold the sword. 22 Therefore this says the Master **יהוה**; *See, I am against Pharaoh melech of Mitzrayim, and will break his strong arms, and that which was broken; and I will cause the sword to fall out of his hand.* 23 *And I will scatter the Mitzrites among the nations, and will disperse them throughout the countries.* 24 *And I will strengthen the arms of the melech of Bavel, and put My sword in his hand: but I will break Pharaoh's arms, and he shall groan before him with the groanings of a wounded man near death.* 25 *But I will strengthen the arms of the melech of Bavel, and the arms of Pharaoh shall fall down; and they shall know that I am* **יהוה***, when I shall put My sword into the hand of the melech of Bavel, and he shall stretch it out upon the land of Mitzrayim.* 26 *And I will scatter the Mitzrites among the nations, and disperse them among the countries; and they shall know that I am* **יהוה***.*

31 And it came to pass in the eleventh year, in the third month, in the first day of the month, that the word of **יהוה** came to me, saying, 2 *Ben-adam, speak to Pharaoh melech of Mitzrayim, and to his multitudes; Who are you like in your greatness?* 3 *See, the Ashshurim were a cedar in Lebanon with fair branches, and with forest shade, and of a high size; and its top was among the thick foliage.* 4 *The waters made him great, the deep set him up on high with her rivers running round around his plants, and sent out her little rivers to all the eytzim of the field.* 5 *Therefore his height was exalted above all the eytzim of the field, and his branches were multiplied, and his branches became long because of the multitude of waters, when he shot out.* 6 *All the fowls of shamayim made their nests in his branches, and under his branches did all the beasts of the field bring out their young, and under*

his shadow dwelt all great nations. 7 *This it was fair in its greatness, in the length of his branches: for his root was by great waters.* 8 *The cedars in the garden of Elohim could not even hide him: the fir eytzim were not like his branches, and the chestnut eytzim were not like his branches; nor any eytz in the garden of Elohim was like him in his beauty.* 9 *I have made it pretty by the multitude of its branches: so that all the eytzim of Eden, that were in the garden of Elohim, envied him.* 10 Therefore this says the Master יהוה; *Because you have lifted up yourself in height, and have its top among the thick foliage, and its lev is lifted up in its height;* 11 *I have therefore delivered him into the hand of the elohim of the gentiles; they shall surely deal with him: I have driven them out for their wickedness.* 12 *And foreigners, the ruthless of the nations, have cut him off, and have left him: upon the mountains and in all the valleys his branches are fallen, and his branches are broken by all the rivers of the land; and all the nations of the earth have gone down from his shadow, and have left him.* 13 *Upon his ruin shall all the fowls of the shamayim remain, and all the beasts of the field shall be upon his branches:* 14 *To the end that none of all the eytzim by the waters exalt themselves for their height, neither shoot up their top among the thick foliage, neither their eytzim stand up in their height, all that drink mayim: for they are all delivered to death, to the depths of the earth, in the midst of the children of men, with them that go down to the pit.*[1] 15 This says the Master יהוה; *In the day when he went down to the grave I caused a mourning: I covered the deep for him, and I restrained the floods, and the great waters were stopped: and I caused Lebanon to mourn for him, and all the eytzim of the field fainted for him.* 16 *I made the nations to shake at the sound of his fall, when I cast him down to the grave with them that*

---

[1] It seems that the Lake of Fire is somewhere deep in the pit of the earth.

descend into the pit: and all the eytzim of Eden, the best of Lebanon, all that drink mayim, shall be comforted in the depths of the earth. 17 *They also went down into the grave with him to them that are slain with the sword; and they that were his arm, which dwelt under his shadow in the midst of the gentiles.* 18 *To whom are you to be compared to in tiferet and in greatness among the eytzim of Eden? Yet shall you be brought down with the eytzim of Eden to the depths of the earth: you shall lie in the midst of the uncircumcised with them that are slain by the sword. This is Pharaoh and his entire multitude, says the Master* יהוה.

32 And it came to pass in the twelfth year, in the twelfth month, in the first day of the month, that the word of יהוה came to me, saying, 2 *Ben-adam, take up a lamentation for Pharaoh melech of Mitzrayim, and say to him, You are like a young lion of the nations, and you are as a whale in the seas: and you came out with your rivers, and troubled the waters with your feet, and dirtied their rivers.* 3 *This says the Master* יהוה ; *I will therefore spread out My net over you with a company of many nations; and they shall bring you up in My net.* 4 *Then will I leave you upon the land, I will cast you out into the open field, and will cause all the fowls of the shamayim to remain upon you, and I will fill the beasts of the whole earth with your flesh.* 5 *And I will lay your flesh upon the mountains, and fill the valleys with your height.* 6 *I will also mayim the land in which you swim with your own dom, even to the mountains; and the rivers shall be full of it.* 7 *And when I shall put you out, I will cover the shamayim, and make the chochavim of it dark; I will cover the sun with a cloud, and the moon shall not give her light.* 8 *All the bright lights of the shamayim will I make dark over you, and set darkness upon your land, says the Master* יהוה. 9 *I will also trouble the levim of many peoples, when I shall bring your*

destruction among the nations, into countries that you have not known. 10 Yes, I will make many people shocked at you, and their melechim shall be greatly afraid of you, when I shall brandish My sword before them; and they shall tremble at every moment, every man for his own chayim, in the day of your fall. 11 For this says the Master יהוה; The sword of the melech of Bavel shall come upon you. 12 By the swords of the mighty will I cause your multitudes to fall, the ruthless of the nations, all of them: and they shall spoil the pride of Mitzrayim, and all the multitudes of it shall be destroyed. 13 I will destroy also all the beasts of it from near the great waters; neither shall the foot of man trouble them any more, nor the hoofs of beasts trouble them. 14 Then will I make their waters deep, and cause their rivers to run like oil, says the Master יהוה. 15 When I shall make the land of Mitzrayim desolate, and the country shall be destitute of what it had when it was full, when I shall smite all of them that dwell in it, then shall they know that I am יהוה. 16 This is the lamentation with which they shall lament her: the daughters of the nations shall lament her: they shall lament for her, even for Mitzrayim, and for all her multitudes, says the Master יהוה. 17 It came to pass also in the twelfth year, in the fifteenth day of the month, that the word of יהוה came to me, saying, 18 Ben-adam, wail for the multitudes of Mitzrayim, and cast them down, even her, and the daughters of the famous nations, to the depths of the earth, with them that go down into the pit. 19 Whom do you surpass in beauty? Go down, and be placed with the uncircumcised. 20 They shall fall in the midst of them that are slain by the sword: she is delivered to the sword: draw her and all her multitudes. 21 The strong among the mighty shall speak to them out of the midst of the grave with them that help him: they are gone down; they lie with the uncircumcised, slain by the sword.

22 Ashshur is there and all her company: her graves are around her: all of them slain, fallen by the sword: 23 Whose graves are set in the sides of the pit, and their company is around her grave: all of them slain, fallen by the sword, which caused fear in the land of the living. 24 There is Eylam and all her multitudes around their grave, all of them slain, fallen by the sword, which are gone down uncircumcised into the depths of the earth, which caused their terror in the land of the living; yet have they borne their shame with them that go down to the pit. 25 They have set for her a bed in the midst of the slain with all their multitudes: her graves are around it: all of them uncircumcised, slain by the sword: for the fear they caused in the land of the living, yet have they borne their shame with them that go down to the pit: they are put in the midst of them that be slain. 26 Then there is Meshech, Tuval, and all their multitudes: their graves are around it: all of them uncircumcised, slain by the sword, though they caused fear in the land of the living. 27 And they shall not lie with the mighty that are fallen of the uncircumcised, which are gone down to the grave with their weapons of war: and they have laid their swords under their heads, but their iniquities shall be upon their bones, though they were the fear of the mighty in the land of the living. 28 Yes, you shall be broken in the midst of the uncircumcised, and shall lie with them that are slain with the sword. 29 Then there is Edom, and her melechim, and all her leaders, which with their might are laid by them that were slain by the sword: they shall lie with the uncircumcised, and with them that go down to the pit. 30 Then there are the leaders of the north, all of them, and all the Tzidonians, who are gone down with the slain; with their fear that they instilled; they are ashamed of their might; and they lie uncircumcised with them that be slain by the sword, and bear their shame with them that go down to the pit. 31 Pharaoh shall

see them, and shall be comforted over all his multitudes, even Pharaoh and all his army slain by the sword, says the Master יהוה. 32 For I have caused My fear in the land of the living: and he shall be laid in the midst of the uncircumcised with them that are slain with the sword, even Pharaoh and all his multitudes, says the Master יהוה.

33 Again the word of יהוה came to me, saying, 2 Ben-adam, speak to the children of your people, and say to them, When I bring the sword upon a land, if the people of the land take a man from their borders, and make him their watchman: 3 If when he sees the sword come upon the land, he blows the shofar, and warns the people; 4 Then whoever hears the sound of the shofar, and takes not warning; if the sword come, and takes him away, his dom shall be upon his own head.[1] 5 He that heard the sound of the shofar, and took not the warning; his dom shall be upon himself. But he that takes warning shall deliver his being. 6 But if the watchman sees the sword come, and blows not the shofar, and the people are not warned; if the sword come, and take away[2] any person from among them, he is taken away in his iniquity; but his dom will I require at the watchman's hand.[3] 7 So you, O Ben-adam, I have set you as a watchman to Beit Yisrael;[4] therefore you shall shema to the word at My mouth, and warn them from Me. 8 When I say to the wicked, O wicked man, you shall surely die; if you do not speak to warn the wicked away from his own halacha, that wicked man shall die in his iniquity; but his dom will I require at your hand. 9 Nevertheless, if you warn the wicked of his own halacha to turn from it; if he does not turn from his own halacha, he shall die in his iniquity; but you have delivered your being. 10 Therefore, O you

Ben-adam, speak to Beit Yisrael; This, say, If our transgressions and our sins be upon us, and we waste away in them, how should we then live? 11 Say to them, As I live, says the Master יהוה, I have no pleasure in the death of the wicked; but that the wicked turn from his own halacha and live: make teshuvah, make teshuvah from your evil halachot; for why will you die, O Beit Yisrael? 12 Therefore, you Ben-adam, say to the children of your people, The tzedakah of the tzadik shall not deliver him in the day of his transgression: as for the wickedness of the wicked, he shall not fall by it in the day that he makes teshuvah from his wickedness; neither shall the tzadik be able to live because of his tzedakah in the day that he sins. 13 When I shall say to the tzadik, that he shall surely live; if he trusts in his own tzedakah, and commits iniquity, all his tzedakah shall not be remembered; but for the iniquity that he has committed, he shall die for it. 14 Again, when I say to the wicked, You shall surely die; if he makes teshuvah from his sin, and does that which is just and right; 15 if the wicked restores the pledge, and returns what he has robbed, and has a halacha in the mishpatim of chayim, without committing further iniquity; he shall surely live, he shall not die. 16 None of his sins that he has committed shall be remembered: he has done that which is according to Torah and mishpat; he shall surely live. 17 Yet the children of your people say, The halacha of יהוה is not equal: but as for them, their halacha is not equal. 18 When the tzadik turns from his tzedakah, and commits iniquity, he shall even die because of it. 19 But if the wicked turn from his wickedness, and do that which is according to Torah and mishpat, he shall live because of it. 20 Yet you say, The halacha of יהוה is not equal. O Beit Yisrael, I will shophet you every one after his own halachot. 21 And it came to pass in the twelfth year of our exile, in the tenth month, in the fifth day of the month that one that had escaped out of

---

[1] Watchmen of two-house restoration are expected to do their job.
[2] As can be seen the term "taken away" in both covenants is not a tov thing, or an escape, but a removal for judgment.
[3] Both are guilty.
[4] All 12 tribes.

Yahrushalayim came to me, saying, The city has been hit! 22 Now the hand of יהוה was upon me the evening, before the man that escaped came; and had had opened my mouth, before he came to see me in the morning; and my mouth was opened, and I was no longer silent. 23 Then the word of יהוה came to me, saying, 24 *Ben-adam, they that inhabit the ruins of the land of Yisrael are saying, Abraham was one, and he inherited the land: but we are many; the land is given to us for our inheritance. 25 Therefore say to them, This says the Master* יהוה; *You eat food with the dom, and lift up your eyes toward your idols, and shed dom: shall you still possess the land? 26 You stand upon your sword, you work abomination, and you defile everyone his neighbor's wife: so shall you possess the land? 27 Say this to them, This says the Master* יהוה; *As I live, surely they that are in the ruins shall fall by the sword, and him that is in the open field will I give to the beasts to be devoured, and they that are in the strongholds and the caves shall die of the pestilence. 28 For I will lay the land totally desolate, and the pride of her strength shall cease; and the mountains of Yisrael shall be desolate, that none shall pass through her. 29 Then shall they know that I am* יהוה, *when I have laid the land totally desolate because of all their abominations which they have committed. 30 Also, you Ben-adam, the children of your people still are talking against you by the walls and in the doors of the houses, they speak to each other saying, Please come and shema what the word is that comes out from* יהוה. *31 And they come to you, as people do, and they sit before you as My people, and they shema your words, but they will not do them: for with their mouth they show you much ahava, but their lev goes after their own greed. 32 And, see, you are to them as a very lovely song of one that has a pleasant voice, and can play well on an instrument: for they shema your words,*

but they do them not.[1] *33 And when this comes to pass – see, it will come – then shall they know that a navi has been among them.*

34 And the word of יהוה came to me, saying, 2 *Ben-adam, prophesy against the shepherds of Yisrael, prophesy, and say to them, This says the Master* יהוה *to the shepherds; Woe to the shepherds of Yisrael that do feed themselves! Should not the shepherds feed the flocks?*[2] *3 You eat the fat, and you clothe yourself with wool, you kill them that are fed: but you feed not the flock.*[3] *4 The diseased have you not strengthened, neither have you healed those who were sick, neither have you bound up those who were broken, neither have you brought back those who were driven away,*[4] *neither have you sought those which were lost;*[5] *but with force and with cruelty have you ruled over them. 5 And they were scattered, because there is no shepherd: and they became food to all the beasts of the field,*[6] *where they were scattered. 6 My sheep wandered through all the mountains, and upon every high hill: yes, My flock was scattered upon all the face of the earth, and none did search or seek after them.*[7]

7 Therefore, you shepherds, shema the word of יהוה; 8 As I live, says the Master יהוה, *surely because My flock became a prey, and My flock became food to every beast of the field, because there was no shepherd, neither did My shepherds search for My*

---

[1] The ongoing plague of both houses.
[2] Our national disaster was and is still caused by the shepherds who are afraid of truth, and of proclaiming truth, or who teach Yisrael how to return under man's approval rather, than YHWH's. A shepherd is to be financially provided for in all areas, to enable him to minister. But he is not to be in the ministry with solely a profit motive.
[3] Yisrael's shepherds must be able to teach Torah and Moshiach from both covenants.
[4] By exile. A true shepherd of Yisrael will be actively seeking all the lost and wandering sheep from both houses of Yisrael.
[5] Ephraim.
[6] Heathen.
[7] Which is one of many reasons why both houses were exiled. There were very few shepherds after YHWH's own lev.

flock,[1] but the shepherds fed themselves, and fed not My flock; 9 *Therefore, O you shepherds, shema the word of* יהוה ; 10 *This says the Master* יהוה; *See, I am against the shepherds; and I will require My flock at their hand, and cause them to cease from feeding the flock; neither shall the shepherds feed themselves any more; for I will deliver My flock from their mouth, that they may not be food for them.[2]* 11 *For this says the Master* יהוה; *See, I, even I, will both search My sheep, and seek them out.[3]* 12 *As a shepherd seeks out his flock in the day that he is among his sheep[4] that are scattered; so will I seek out My sheep, and will deliver them[5] out of all places where they have been scattered[6] in the cloudy and dark day.[7]* 13 *And I will bring them out from the nations, and gather them[8] from the countries, and will bring them to their own land, and feed them upon the mountains of Yisrael by the rivers, and in all the inhabited places of the country.[9]* 14 *I will feed them in a tov pasture, and upon the high mountains of Yisrael shall their fold be: there shall they lie down in a tov fold, and in a fat pasture shall they feed upon the mountains of Yisrael.[10]* 15 *I will feed My flock, and I will cause them to lie down, says the Master* יהוה.[11] 16 *I will seek that which was lost,[12] and bring again that which was driven away, and will bind up that which was broken, and will strengthen that which was sick: but I will destroy the fat and the strong; I will feed them with mishpat.[13]* 17 *And as for you, O My flock, this says the Master* יהוה; *See, I shophet between sheep and sheep, between the rams and the male goats.[14]* 18 *Is it a small thing for you to have eaten up the tov pasture, but must you tread down with your feet the remnant of your pastures? And to have drunk of the deep waters, but you must foul the remnant with your feet?[15]* 19 *And as for My flock, they eat that which you have trampled with your feet; and they drink that which you have dirtied with your feet.[16]* 20 *Therefore this says the Master* יהוה *to them; See, I, even I, will shophet between the fat and lean sheep.* 21 *Because you have thrust with side and with shoulder, and pushed all the diseased with your horns, until you have scattered them abroad;[17]* 22 *Therefore will I save My flock,[18] and they shall no more be a prey; and I will shophet between sheep[19] and sheep.[20]* 23 *And I will set up One Shepherd over them,[21] and He shall feed them,[22] even My*

---

[1] Too busy building their own perversion of the kingdom, such as the separate entity gentile church, or Judaism without Yahshua, or the one-house heresy that refuses to search for the ten tribes in the exile.
[2] As demonstrated historically, YHWH will remove all those who refuse to seek out His plan for His lost and wandering sheep within both exiled houses; both in the spirit and in the physical.
[3] "Search and seek" is why Yahshua came in direct fulfillment of this prophesy. He affirms such in John 10:16-17. He came to seek, find, regather, and restore both houses of Yisrael.
[4] This is a prophecy of the absolute necessity of the incarnation when YHWH/Yahshua would have to become as His sheep; and dwell on the earth among His sheep, in order to draw, find, and recover them.
[5] Personal salvation is part of the deliverance from exile.
[6] Every nation.
[7] A reference to the Great Tribulation that YHWH will use to regather His people home to the land of Yisrael.
[8] The gathering is not "a rapture" but a return, as seen in Mathew 24.
[9] All Yisrael will be regathered.
[10] The mountains refer to all the land, including the mountains of Ephraim.
[11] Because He alone is the Tov Shepherd, and He alone knows where to find His sheep.

[12] Quoted by Yahshua in Luke 19:10. He did not come to build a "gentile church," but to find the lost sheep of Yisrael who had become gentiles, and return them to the fold.
[13] In the process of reuniting the two houses and feeding the starving sheep, He will feed the false shepherds with judgment.
[14] Yahshua is coming to judge and settle all differences between the sheep of Judah and the sheep of Ephraim, as well as between the sheep and goats as spoken of in Matthew 25.
[15] Even the true remnant of Yisrael is constantly seduced by various deviant religions and false names for YHWH, taught by the shepherds who are responsible for their destruction in the first place.
[16] Leftover rot, with such teachings as "saved gentiles" and "messianic gentiles."
[17] Weak ones have been re-scattered, as believing leaders sent Ephraimites back into confusion by withholding Yisraelite recognition. Rather than gather the lost sheep, these shepherds continue to gore the sheep. Until they are healed and nurtured and taught their identity as Yisrael in Moshiach, they are considered diseased. Moshiach came to put an end to that.
[18] He is compelled by love to bring unity and restoration by His mission to earth, since no others are able and willing, nor do they know where to look for the so called "lost tribes."
[19] Ephraim.
[20] Judah.
[21] Over both folds of the sheep.
[22] His Torah.

Eved David;[1] He shall feed them, and He shall be their Shepherd.[2] 24 And I יהוה will be their Elohim, and My Eved David[3] a Sar among them; I יהוה have spoken it.[4] 25 And I will make with them a covenant of shalom,[5] and will cause the evil beasts to cease out of the land:[6] and they shall dwell safely in the wilderness, and sleep in the woods. 26 And I will make them and the places all around My hill a blessing;[7] and I will cause the showers to come down in season; there shall be showers of blessing.[8] 27 And the eytzim of the field shall yield their fruit, and the earth shall yield her increase, and they shall be safe in their land,[9] and shall know that I am יהוה, when I have broken the chains of their yoke,[10] and delivered them out of the hand of those that made them slaves.[11] 28 And they shall no more be a prey to the gentiles, neither shall the beast of the land devour them; but they shall dwell safely, and none shall make them afraid. 29 And I will raise up for them a planting place of fame, and they shall be no more consumed with hunger in the land, neither bare the shame of the gentiles any more.[12] 30 This shall they know that I יהוה their Elohim am with them, and that they, Beit Yisrael,[13] are My people-Ami, says the Master יהוה. 31 And you My flock, the flock of My pasture, are men,[14] and I am your Elohim, says the Master יהוה.

35 Moreover the word of יהוה came to me, saying, 2 *Ben-adam, set your face against Mount Seir, and prophesy against it, 3 And say to it, This says the Master יהוה; See, O Mount Seir, I am against you, and I will stretch out My hand against you, and I will make you desolate. 4 I will lay your cities waste, and you shall be desolate, and you shall know that I am יהוה. 5 Because you have had a perpetual hatred, and have shed the dom of the children of Yisrael by the force of the sword in the time of their calamity,[15] in the time that their iniquity had an end:[16] 6 Therefore, as I live, says the Master יהוה, I will prepare you for dom letting, and dom shall pursue you: since you have not hated dom, dom shall pursue you.[17] 7 And I will make Mount Seir most desolate, and cut off from it the one that leaves and the one that returns. 8 And I will fill its mountains with his slain men: in your hills, and in your valleys, and in all your rivers, they shall fall that are slain with the sword. 9 I will make you a perpetual waste place, and your cities shall not return: and you shall know that I am יהוה. 10 Because you have said, These two nations[18] and these two countries[19][20] shall be mine, and we will possess it; even though יהוה was there: 11 Therefore, as I live, says the Master יהוה, I will even do to you according to your own anger, and according to your envy that you have used out of your hatred against them; and I will make Myself known among them, when I have judged you. 12 And you shall know that I am יהוה, and that I have heard all your blasphemies that you have spoken*

---

[1] The greater or the "eschatological David" always refers to Moshiach, and not a resurrected literal David as Moshiach; David will of course rise also to reign under Yahshua; but not in place of Yahshua.
[2] One Shepherd over all 12 tribes.
[3] Moshiach Yahshua.
[4] The true solution to the exile.
[5] The Shepherd Yahweh coming to earth to seek His own sheep will make the Renewed and everlasting Covenant with all Yisrael, to place all under the authority of the greater, or end-time David.
[6] All gentile domination will cease.
[7] Jerusalem and its environment will be a blessing, not a place of gentile domination.
[8] The latter or kingdom rain.
[9] The olive and fig eytz will fully blossom again as all Yisrael dwells in safety.
[10] Exile.
[11] Foreign domination.
[12] The exile and foreign domination will be over in the coming kingdom on earth.
[13] All 12 tribes.
[14] The term "men" as connected to the men of YHWH's pasture, always refers to Yisrael as seen often in both

covenants. This term also often comes into play in the Renewed Covenant, in a sod, or mystery level of teaching hidden things.
[15] Great Tribulation and other end-time battles, as they had done throughout history.
[16] At the time of their redemption.
[17] When the Day of YHWH fully comes, Edom will be removed completely from the land of Yisrael; by a bloodletting from YHWH, and receive impending judgment, for their perpetual hatred of Yisrael over the birthright sold by Esau.
[18] Judah and Ephraim.
[19] Jerusalem and Shomron.
[20] Note that 150 years after Ephraim's exile into the nations YHWH still refers to Yisrael as two nations that never reunited; even at the time of the return from Babylon.

against the mountains of Yisrael, saying, They are laid desolate, they are given to us to consume. 13 And with your mouth you have boasted against Me, and have multiplied your words against Me: I have heard them all.¹ 14 This says the Master יהוה; When the whole earth has gilah, I will make you desolate.² 15 As you did rejoice because the inheritance of Beit Yisrael,³ became desolate, so will I do to you: you shall be desolate, O Mount Seir, and all of Edom, even all of it: and they shall know that I am יהוה.

36 Also, you Ben-adam, prophesy to the mountains of Yisrael, and say, You mountains of Yisrael, shema the word of יהוה : 2 This says the Master יהוה ; Because the enemy has said against you, Aha, even the heights of old are now our possession: 3 Therefore prophesy and say, This says the Master יהוה; Because they have made you desolate, and swallowed you up on every side, that you might be a possession to the remnant of the gentiles, and you are taken up in the lips of talkers, and are slandered by the nations: 4 Therefore, you mountains of Yisrael, shema the word of the Master יהוה; This says the Master יהוה to the mountains, and to the hills, to the rivers, and to the valleys, to the desolate ruins, and to the cities that are forsaken, who became a prey and a cause for derision to the remnant of the gentiles that are all around; 5 Therefore this says the Master יהוה; Surely in the fire of My jealousy have I spoken against the remnant of the gentiles, and against all of Edom, who have appointed My land into their possession with the simcha of all their lev, with scorn in their being, to cast it out for a prey. 6 Prophesy therefore concerning the land of Yisrael, and say to the mountains, and to the hills, to the rivers,

and to the valleys, This says the Master יהוה; See, I have spoken in My jealousy and in My anger, because you have borne the shame of the gentiles: 7 Therefore this says the Master יהוה; I have lifted up My hand in an oath, Surely the gentiles that are around you, they shall bear their own shame. 8 But you, O mountains of Yisrael, you shall shoot out your Netzarim⁴, and yield your fruit⁵ to My people Yisrael; for they are about to come back. 9 For, see, I am for you, and I will return to you, and you shall be tilled and sown: 10 And I will multiply men⁶ upon you, all of Beit Yisrael,⁷ even all of it: and the cities shall be inhabited, and the ruins shall be rebuilt: 11 And I will multiply upon you man and beast; and they shall increase and bring fruit: and I will place you in your old dwellings, and will do better to you than at your beginning: and you shall know that I am יהוה. 12 And I will cause men, even My people Yisrael, to have their path upon you, and they shall possess you, and you shall be their inheritance, and you shall no more be bereaved of men. 13 This says the Master יהוה; Because they say to you, Your land devours men, and has bereaved your nation; 14 Therefore you shall devour men no more, neither bereave your nation any more, says the Master יהוה. 15 Neither will I cause men to shema in you the shame of the gentiles any more,⁸ neither shall you bear the reproach of the gentiles any more, neither shall you cause your nations⁹ to fall any more, says the Master יהוה . 16 Moreover the word of יהוה came to me, saying, 17 Ben-adam, when Beit Yisrael dwelt in their own land, they defiled it by their own halacha and by their doings: their halacha was before Me as the uncleanness

---

¹ YHWH will answer all of Edom's talk of owning the land and their boast that Allah is the true mighty one: by removing them from the land of Yisrael, and from Mt. Seir their original homeland.
² During the **atid lavoh**, or messianic millennial kingdom.
³ Both houses.
⁴ Netsarim or branches. Early Torah-keepers who followed Yahshua were known as His **Netsarim** or branches. They are the ones returning from the nations and bringing fruit to and amongst Yisrael for YHWH.
⁵ Fruit of the Spirit.
⁶ Yisraelites.
⁷ All Yisrael will once again multiply on the land.
⁸ All pagan influences and customs will be removed at the end of the exile.
⁹ Judah and Ephraim.

of a woman in nidah. 18 *Therefore I poured My anger upon them for the dom that they had shed upon the land, and for their idols with which they had defiled it:* 19 *And I scattered them among the gentiles, and they were dispersed among the countries: according to their own halacha and according to their doings I judged them.* 20 *And when they entered in among the gentiles, where they went, they profaned My set-apart Name, when they said to them, These are the people of* יהוה*, and yet they have been removed from their land.* [1] 21 *But I had compassion and concern for My set-apart Name, which Beit Yisrael had profaned among the gentiles, wherever they went.* [2] 22 *Therefore say to Beit Yisrael, This says the Master* יהוה*; I do not this for your sakes, O Beit Yisrael, but for My set-apart Name's sake, which you have profaned among the gentiles, wherever you went.* [3] 23 *And I will set-apart My great Name, which was profaned among the gentiles, which you have profaned in the midst of them; and the gentiles shall know that I am* יהוה*, says the Master* יהוה*, when I shall be set-apart by you before their eyes.* [4] 24 *For I will take you out from among the gentiles, and gather you out of all countries,* [5] *and will bring you into your own land.* 25 *Then will I sprinkle clean mayim upon you,* [6] *and you shall be clean: from all your filthiness, and from all your idols, will I cleanse you.* [7] 26 *A new lev* [8] *also will I give you, and a new Ruach* [9] *will I put inside you: and I will take away the stony lev out of your flesh, and I will give you a lev of flesh.* [10] 27 *And I will put My Ruach HaKodesh inside you, and cause you to have a halacha in My mishpatim, and you shall guard My mishpatim, and do them.* [11] 28 *And you shall dwell in the land that I gave to your ahvot; and you shall be My people-Ami, and I will be your Elohim.* [12] 29 *I will also save you from all your uncleanness:* [13] *and I will call for the corn, and will increase it, and lay no famine upon you.* [14] 30 *And I will multiply the fruit of the eytz, and the increase of the field, that you shall receive no more the reproach of famine among the gentiles.* 31 *Then* [15] *shall you remember your own evil halachot, and your doings that were not tov, and shall despise yourselves in your own sight for your iniquities and for your abominations.* 32 *Not for your sakes do I do this, says the Master* יהוה*, let that be known to you: be ashamed and blush for your own halachot, O Beit Yisrael.* 33 *This says the Master* יהוה*; In the day that I shall have cleansed you from all your iniquities I will also cause you to dwell in the cities, and the ruins shall be rebuilt.* 34 *And the desolate land shall be tilled, whereas it had been in ruin in the sight of all that passed by.* 35 *And they shall say, This land that was desolate has become like the Garden of Eden; and the waste, desolate and ruined cities have become fenced and inhabited.* 36 *Then the gentiles that are left around you shall know that I* יהוה *rebuild the ruined places, and planted what had been desolate: I* יהוה *have spoken it, and I will do it.* 37 *This says the Master* יהוה*; I will yet once again allow Beit Yisrael to call upon Me, to do this for them; I will increase their men like a flock.* 38 *As the set-apart flock, as the flock of Yahrushalayim in her set-apart moadim; so shall the ruined cities be filled with flocks of*

---

[1] Exile is a defilement of the true Name. This verse is quoted in Romans 2:24, further validating the Yisraelite makeup of the congregation at Rome.

[2] YHWH is jealous over his true Name and will guard it.

[3] YHWH will end the exile of both houses by sending Moshiach, so that his Name YHWH is no longer hidden and abused among the nations.

[4] When Yisrael knows and uses the true Name, along with full obedience to His Torah.

[5] All 12 tribes are in all countries, not just Anglo-Saxon ones as some falsely teach.

[6] Renewed Covenant water mikvah.

[7] YHWH gives Yisrael the unmerited favor of the new birth at the end of the exile, at the dawn of the Messianic Age.

[8] Circumcised, or born-again in heart.

[9] The Set-Apart Spirit.

[10] YHWH will renew His covenant with Yisrael.

[11] Renewed Covenant Yisrael will both guard and do His Torah through the enabling of the indwelling Spirit after the new birth.

[12] Reversal of the Hosea 1, Lo-Ami curse.

[13] Saved from the judgment of breaking His Torah.

[14] No more famine of food or His word.

[15] At the end of the exile.

men:[1] and they shall know that I am יהוה.

37 The hand of יהוה was upon me, and carried me out in the Ruach HaKodesh of יהוה, and set me down in the midst of the valley which was full of bones, 2 And caused me to pass among them all around: and, see, there were very many in the open valley; and, see, they were very dry. 3 And He said to me, *Ben-adam, can these bones live?* And I answered, O Master יהוה, You know. 4 Again He said to me, *Prophesy to these bones, and say to them, O dry bones, shema to the word of* יהוה. 5 This says the Master יהוה to these bones; *See, I will cause breath to enter into you, and you shall live:[2] 6 And I will lay sinews upon you, and will bring up flesh upon you, and cover you with skin, and put breath in you, and you shall live; and you shall know that I am* יהוה.[3] 7 So I prophesied as I was commanded: and as I prophesied, there was a noise, and see a shaking, and the bones came together, bone to bone.[4] 8 And when I beheld, see, the sinews and the flesh came up upon them, and the skin covered them above: but there was no breath in them. 9 Then He said to me, *Prophesy to the wind, prophesy, Ben-adam, and say to the wind, This says the Master* יהוה*; Come from the four winds, O breath, and breathe upon these slain,[5] that they may live.[6]* 10 So I prophesied as He commanded me, and the breath came into them, and they lived, and stood up upon their feet, an exceeding great army.[7] 11 Then He said to me, *Ben-adam, these bones are the whole of Beit Yisrael:[8] see, they say, Our bones are dried, and our tikvah is lost: we are cut off.* 12 *Therefore prophesy and say to them, This says the Master* יהוה*; See, O My people, I will open your graves, and cause you to come up out* of your graves, and bring you into the land of Yisrael.[9] 13 And you shall know that I am יהוה, when I have opened your graves, O My people, and brought you up out of your graves, 14 And shall put My Ruach HaKodesh in you, and you shall live, and I shall place you in your own land: then shall you know that I יהוה have spoken it, and performed it*, says יהוה. 15 The word of יהוה [10] came again to me, saying, 16 *Moreover, you Ben-adam, take one piece of wood, and write upon it, For Yahudah, and for the children of Yisrael his friends: then take another piece of wood, and write upon it, For Yoseph, the piece of wood of Ephraim, and for all Beit Yisrael his friends:[11] 17 And join them one to another into one piece of wood; and they shall become echad in your hand.[12] 18 And when the children of your people[13] shall speak to you, saying, Will you not show us what you mean by these?[14] 19 Say to them, This says the Master* יהוה*; See, I will take the piece of wood of Yoseph, which is in the hand of Ephraim,[15] and the tribes of Yisrael his companions,[16] and will put them with the piece of wood of Yahudah, and make them one piece of wood, and they*

---

[1] Yisraelites.
[2] The bones of all Yisrael will be revived to live again.
[3] The nation will be fully revived and restored.
[4] "Bone to bone" is a two-house reference.
[5] Spiritually and physically.
[6] The breath of life returns to Yisrael from the same four corners to which they went, as it finds them there.
[7] Yisrael revived and fully restored.
[8] All 12 tribes.

[9] The end of the exile and our return to the land of Yisrael. This speaks of three resurrections: physical, spiritual, and national.
[10] Yahshua returns a second time to bring to pass the two-stick restoration of Yisrael.
[11] Both pieces of wood, or both houses, have friends who have joined them, but may not be biological Yisraelites. But in the restoration and regathering of both houses, they are included, because the Father considers them Yisrael.
[12] Both houses are destined to become one olive eytz in the hands of the end-time Son of Man, Yahshua our King.
[13] Most who ask about, or express an interest in the two sticks, are Yisraelites; or else they would be like most who read these verses and do not stop to ask and meditate upon them.
[14] This question still needs to be asked and the answer sought for. Most believers have no clue as to what the two wooden sticks represent, or of their significance in their own personal lives. The two sticks of the two-house reunion still raise many questions.
[15] Because Ephraim received the birthright from Joseph after he bypassed Menasheh, and because Ephraim became by far the largest and most predominant tribe of the north; also because their first king Jeroboam was an Ephraimite.
[16] The other 9 tribes.

shall be one in My hand.[1] [2] 20 And the two pieces of wood on which you write shall be in your hand before their eyes.[3] 21 And say to them, This says the Master **יהוה**; See, I will take the children of Yisrael from among the gentiles, where they have gone,[4] and will gather them on every side,[5] and bring them into their own land: 22 And I will make them[6] one nation[7] in the land upon the mountains of Yisrael;[8] and one Melech[9] shall be Melech over them all:[10] and they shall be no more two nations, neither shall they be divided into two kingdoms any more: [11] 23 Neither shall they defile themselves any more with their idols, nor with their detestable things, nor with any of their transgressions:[12] but I will save them out of all their dwelling places, in which they have sinned, and will cleanse them: so shall they be My people-Ami, and I will be their Elohim.[13] 24 And David My Eved shall be Melech over them; and they all shall have One Shepherd:[14] they shall also have their halacha in My mishpatim, and observe My mishpatim, and do them.[15] 25 And they shall dwell in the land that I have given to Yaakov My eved, in which your ahvot have dwelt; and they shall dwell in it, they, and their children, and their children's children le-olam-va-ed:[16] and My Eved David shall be their Leader le-olam-va-ed. [17] 26 Moreover I will make a covenant of shalom with them; [18] it shall be an everlasting covenant with them:[19] and I will place them,[20] and multiply them,[21] and will set My Set-Apart Place in their midst le-olam-va-ed. [22] 27 My dwelling place also shall be with them: And, I will be their Elohim, and they shall be My people-Ami.[23] 28 And the gentiles shall know that I **יהוה** will set Yisrael apart, when My Set-Apart

---

[1] The wonderful and earth-changing final event of this age. The House of Ephraim being rejoined to the House of Judah, after 2,700 years of division, strife, and civil war.
[2] The two houses can come together only in Moshiach's hand. Any attempts to seek church or Jewish leaders in summits of the flesh are ordained to result in failure. He and He alone can find us, revive us, and rejoin us – bone-to-bone, and stick-to-stick.
[3] Meaning "in your hand continually," implying that the two-house message is not a side issue, but is one that true neviim must continually present before the eyes of all Yisraelites, lest we forget the true meaning of "thy kingdom come" and our King's coming.
[4] That's where the ten tribes are. They are not in Jewish Yisrael, nor modern Jewry, other than by a small crossover representation. The"fullness of the gentiles" are just were YHWH said they'd be - in and among the gentiles, filling the gentile nations, often camouflaged as gentiles. For more details on the overall plan of YHWH to bring in the true kingdom, see the series of teachings at: http://yourarmstoisrael.org/Articles_new/restoration/?page=home&type=2.
[5] All sides and lands.
[6] Not man, or man's planning, or man's wisdom, or man's aliyah, or man's laws of immigration.
[7] Future tense. An unfulfilled prophecy.
[8] All Yisrael's territory shall be returned, including the Palestinian and Jordanian occupied West Bank, and all the mountains of Ephraim.
[9] Yahshua - YHWH's Son.
[10] Judah by and large sadly continues to reject Yisrael's One and only chosen King for both nations of Yisrael. The very fact that Jewish Yisrael does not claim the same King as Ephraim Yisrael, is further solid evidence that the two houses have never been fully reunited as some false teachings continue to foolishly claim. We have not missed the reunion, as it remains a future end-time event.
[11] When and only when the King comes.
[12] Clearly both houses remain defiled, both houses have sinned, and both houses have not been cleansed. The reunion could not have been a past event for had it been so, then no sin, disgusting practice, nor idolatry would now be found in either house.

[13] Both houses have not entered the final cleansing, so this remains a future prophecy.
[14] The restoration must have one King and Moshiach. It cannot be done apart from, and without the arrival of, the King Moshiach, as some have so foolishly tried to do. Some have mapped out plans, to make the two houses one, with just the Abba and Torah. But Scripture here indicates that the unifying supernatural power will be found in a King like David, also called David, who is to reappear in the end times. He and He alone will make both flocks fully obedient and subjected, as outlined in John 10:16-17.
[15] The true Moshiach will cause a renewed desire to perform Torah in both houses.
[16] When the kingdom is fully restored, all Yisrael that is redeemed and Torah-compliant will return physically to the land given to Yaakov, which includes Jordan, Lebanon, Syria, and other parts of the Middle East as well. Then the Greater David will usher in the greater Yisrael.
[17] Only the Moshiach lives forever, and as such the two-house reunion can take place only through Him; and not the Father alone or man's plans alone.
[18] Moshiach will bring peace between YHWH and the men of His flock, as well as between the two sheepfolds i.e., between the two houses. He has come to remove the long-held enmity between Judah and Ephraim.
[19] The Renewed Covenant with Yisrael is eternal in the sense that it will never be changed and is unconditional. As outlined in Hebrews 8 and Jeremiah 31:31, it was cut with both houses of Yisrael, not with true gentiles, who yet can join in the covenant, as long as Yahshua is their Moshiach and they follow His ways of Torah.
[20] In the land of Yisrael.
[21] According to the covenant promise of physical multiplicity.
[22] In the **pashat**/literal this speaks of the rebuilding of the millennial temple. In the **remez/hint**, it is Moshiach Himself as YHWH's tabernacle living among us.
[23] Another reference to the reversal of the curse of Lo-Ami, in Hosea chapter 1.

Place shall be in their midst le-olam-va-ed.[1]

38 And the word of **יהוה** came to me, saying, 2 Ben-adam, set your face against Gog, the land of Magog,[2] the chief leader of Meshech and Tuval,[3] and prophesy against him,[4] 3 And say, This says the Master **יהוה**; See I am against you, O Gog, the chief leader of Meshech and Tuval: 4 And I will turn you around, and put hooks into your jaws, and I will bring you out,[5] and all your army, horses and horsemen, all of them clothed with all sorts of armor, even a great company with armor and shields, all of them handling swords: 5 Persia,[6] Ethiopia, and Libya with them; all of them with shield and helmet: 6 Gomer,[7] and all his units; Beit Togarmah from the north quarters, and all his units: and many nations with you.[8] 7 Be prepared, prepare yourself, you, and all your groups that are assembled to you, and be a guard over them. 8 After many days you shall be visited: in the latter years[9] you shall come into the land that is brought back from the sword, and is gathered out of many peoples, against the mountains of Yisrael, which had been a continual waste: but it is brought out of the gentiles, and they all shall dwell safely. 9 You shall ascend and come like a storm, you shall be like a cloud to cover the land, you, and all your units, and many nations with you. 10 This says the Master **יהוה**; It shall also come to pass, that at the same time shall things come into your mind, and you shall devise an evil plan: 11 And you shall say, I will go up to the land of unwalled villages; I will go to them that are at rest from war, that dwell safely, all of them dwelling without walls, and having neither bars nor gates,[10] 12 To take a spoil, and to take a prey; to turn your hand upon the former ruined places that are now inhabited, and upon the people that are gathered out of the nations, which have gotten cattle and goods, that dwell in the midst of the land. 13 Sheba, and Dedan, and the merchants of Tarshish,[11] with all the young lions of it, shall say to you, Did you come there to take a spoil? Have you gathered your army to take a prey? To carry away silver and gold, to take away cattle and goods, to take a great spoil? 14 Therefore, Ben-adam, prophesy and say to Gog, This says the Master **יהוה**; In that day when My people of Yisrael dwell safely,[12] shall you not know it? 15 And you shall come from your place out of the northern parts, you, and many nations with you, all of them riding upon horses, a great congregation, and a mighty army: 16 And you shall come up against My people of Yisrael, as a cloud to cover the land; it shall be in the latter days,[13] and I will bring you against My land, that the gentiles may know Me, when I shall be set-apart in you, O Gog, before their eyes. 17 This says the Master **יהוה**; Are you the one I have spoken about in times past by My avadim the neviim of Yisrael, who prophesied in those days for many years that I would bring you against them? 18 And it shall come to pass at the same time when Gog shall come against the land of Yisrael, says the Master **יהוה** that My anger shall come up in My face. 19 For in My jealousy and in the fire of My anger have I spoken, Surely in that

---

[1] Another dual application; in the **pashat/**literal this speaks of the rebuilding of the millennial temple. In the **remez/hint,** it is Moshiach Himself as YHWH's tabernacle living among us.
[2] This understanding of the battle of Gog and Magog is covered in depth. See: "A Global Concept" at :
http://store.yourarmstoisrael.org/Qstore/Qstore.cgi?CMD=011&PROD=000121.
[3] An area due north of Yisrael. Many claim this is Russia and all the Moslem states of the former Soviet Union.
[4] After the kingdom has been fully restored, and the millennium is over, s.a.tan leads one final global revolt against the reunited and restored throne of David. We see this as a post-millennial event, as outlined chronologically in both Ezekiel chapters 37-39 and Revelation 20:8-9. There, as in these verses, YHWH destroys them on the mountains of Yisrael, after they have surrounded Jerusalem and the city of the set-apart ones.
[5] YHWH brings them in according to His plan, against their own reluctance.
[6] Iran.
[7] Some European nations.
[8] An all-out assault.
[9] End of the **atid lavoh.**

[10] As will be the case only in the millennium, not before, when the land is on high alert, and all of the exiles are not home.
[11] A coalition led by the USA, Spain and some others?
[12] Millennial reign.
[13] After the **atid lavoh.**

day there shall be a great shaking in the land of Yisrael; 20 So that the fishes of the sea, and the fowls of the shamayim, and the beasts of the field, and all creeping things that creep upon the earth, and all the men that are upon the face of the earth, shall shake at My presence, and the mountains shall be thrown down, and the steep places shall fall, and every wall shall fall to the ground.[1] 21 And I will call for a sword against him throughout all My mountains, says the Master יהוה: every man's sword shall be against his brother. 22 And I will plead against him with pestilence and with dom; and I will rain upon him, and upon his units, and upon the many nations that are with him, an overflowing rain, with great hailstones, fire, and brimstone.[2] 23 And I will magnify Myself, and set Myself apart; and I will be known in the eyes of many nations, and then they shall know that I am יהוה.

39 Therefore, Ben-adam, prophesy against Gog,[3] [4] and say, This says the Master יהוה; See, I am against you, O Gog, the chief leader of Meshech and Tuval: 2 And I will turn you around, and lead you forward, and will cause you to come up from the northern parts, and will bring you upon the mountains of Yisrael: 3 And I will smite your bow out of your left hand, and will cause your arrows to fall out of your right hand. 4 You shall fall upon the mountains of Yisrael, you, and all your units, and the nations that are with you: I will give you to every kind of ravenous bird, and to the beasts of the field to be devoured. 5 You shall fall in the open field: for I have spoken it, says the Master יהוה. 6 And I will send a fire on Magog,[5] and among them that dwell carelessly in the

coastlands:[6] and they shall know that I am יהוה. 7 So will I make My set-apart Name known in the midst of My people Yisrael; and I will not let them defile My set-apart Name any more: and the gentiles shall know that I am יהוה, the Set-Apart One in Yisrael.[7] 8 See, it shall come, and it shall be done, says the Master יהוה; this is the day of which I have spoken.[8] 9 And they that dwell in the cities of Yisrael shall go out, and shall set on fire and burn the weapons, both the shields and the armor, the bows and the arrows, and the clubs, and the spears, and they shall burn them with fire seven years:[9] 10 So that they shall take no wood out of the field, neither cut down any out of the forests; for they shall burn the weapons with fire: and they shall spoil those that plundered them, and rob those that robbed them, says the Master יהוה. 11 And it shall come to pass in that day, that I will give to Gog a graveyard in Yisrael, the valley of those passing by east of the sea: and they shall close off the valley and there shall they bury Gog and all his multitudes: and they shall call it The Valley of Hamon-Gog.[10] 12 And seven months shall Beit Yisrael be burying them, that they may cleanse the land.[11] 13 Yes, all the people of the land shall bury them; and it shall be to them for their fame in the day that I shall be lifted up, says the Master יהוה. 14 And they shall separate men, who shall pass through the land continually to bury those that remain upon the face of the land, to cleanse it: At the end of seven months shall they do a search. 15 And the travelers that pass through the land, and see a man's bones, shall set up a sign by it, until the undertakers have buried it in the

---

[1] As stated in the Scroll of Revelation, YHWH's response by supernatural power will be swift and immediate.
[2] A sudden destruction.
[3] Gog could be the leader known as anti-Moshiach, since he is not thrown into the Lake of Fire until after the millennium and the Gog-Magog war/rebellion.
[4] Aramaic Peshitta replaces Gog with China, making this a confederacy of Moslems, Russia, and China.
[5] Mongolia in Aramaic Peshitta.

[6] Japan according to Peshitta.
[7] The ultimate purpose of the battle of Gog and Magog is to preserve Yisrael in kingdom glory, reestablish YHWH's true name among his people Yisrael, and introduce it to the nations, to some even for the very first time.
[8] The start of the 8th day, or eternity when all things become new; or are considered fully renewed.
[9] Could be a remez and not seven literal years.
[10] Valley of Gog's Annihilation.
[11] Another use of the number seven, which may be a **gematria** or a hint of "full death," as opposed to seven literal months.

Valley of Hamon-Gog. 16 And also the name of the city shall be Hamonah. In this manner shall they cleanse the land. 17 And, you Ben-adam, this says the Master יהוה; Speak to every feathered fowl, and to every beast of the field saying, Assemble yourselves, and come; gather yourselves on every side to My sacrifice that I do sacrifice for you, even a great sacrifice upon the mountains of Yisrael, that you may eat flesh, and drink dom. 18 You shall eat the flesh of the mighty, and drink the dom of the leaders of the earth, of rams, of lambs, and of goats, of bulls, all of the fatlings of Bashan. 19 And you shall eat fat until you are full, and drink dom until you are drunk, at My sacrifice which I have sacrificed for you. 20 In this manner you shall be filled at My table with horses and mirkavot, with mighty men, and with all the men of war, says the Master יהוה. 21 And I will set My tiferet among the gentiles, and all the gentiles shall see My mishpat that I have executed, and My hand that I have laid upon them. 22 So Beit Yisrael[1] shall know that I am יהוה their Elohim from that day and forward. 23 And the gentiles shall know that Beit Yisrael went into exile for their iniquity: because they trespassed against Me, therefore I hid My face from them, and gave them into the hand of their enemies: so they all fell by the sword. 24 According to their uncleanness and according to their transgressions have I done to them, and have hid My face from them. 25 Therefore this says the Master יהוה; Now will I bring back again the exiles of Yaakov, and have rachamim upon the whole of Beit Yisrael,[2] and will be jealous for My set-apart Name; 26 After they have borne their shame, and all their trespasses by which they have trespassed against Me, when they dwelt safely in their land, with no one to make them afraid. 27 When I have brought them back again from the nations, and gathered them out of their enemies' lands, and am

set-apart through them in the sight of many nations; 28 Then shall they know that I am יהוה their Elohim, who caused them to be led into exile among the gentiles: but I have gathered them to their own land, and have left none of them there any more. [3] 29 Neither will I hide My face from them any more: for I have poured out My Ruach HaKodesh upon Beit Yisrael, [4] says the Master יהוה.

40 In the twenty-fifth year of our exile, in the beginning of the year, in the tenth day of the month, in the fourteenth year after that the city was smitten, the same day the hand of יהוה was upon me, and brought me back there. 2 In the visions of Elohim he brought me into the land of Yisrael, and set me upon a very high mountain towards the south, which was as the structure of a city. 3 And He brought me there, and, see, there was a Man, whose appearance was like the appearance of bronze, with a line of flax in his hand, and a measuring rod; and he stood in the gate. [5] 4 And the Man said to me, Ben-adam, see with your eyes, and shema with your ears, and set your lev upon all that I shall show you; for the purpose that I might show them to you are you brought here: declare all that you see to Beit Yisrael. [6] 5 And see a wall on the outside of the Bayit all around, and in the man's hand a measuring rod of six cubits long by the cubit and an hand wide: so he measured the width of the wall structure, one rod; and the height, one rod. 6 Then he came to the gate which looks toward the east, and went up the stairs of it, and measured the threshold of the gate, which was one rod wide; and the other threshold of the gate, which was one rod wide. 7 And every little room was one rod long, and one rod wide; and

---

[1] All 12 tribes.
[2] All 12 tribes.
[3] By definition, based on the full revelation of Scripture, "none of them" would mean none who are part of the elect remnant; since we know that many who hate YHWH and His Son, will not be returning spiritually or physically.
[4] All 12 tribes.
[5] Yahshua.
[6] A glimpse into the future of the New Jerusalem.

between the little rooms were five cubits; and the threshold of the gate by the porch of the gate inside was one rod. 8 He measured also the porch of the gate inside, one rod. 9 Then he measured the porch of the gate, eight cubits; and the posts of it, two cubits; and the porch of the gate was on the inside. 10 And the little rooms of the gate eastward were three on this side, and three on that side; they three were of one measure: and the posts had one measure on this side and on that side. 11 And he measured the width of the entry of the gate, ten cubits; and the length of the gate, thirteen cubits. 12 The space also before the little rooms was one cubit on this side, and the space was one cubit on that side: and the little rooms were six cubits on this side, and six cubits on that side. 13 He measured then the gate from the roof of one little room to the roof of another: the width was twenty-five cubits, door to door. 14 He made also posts of sixty cubits, even to the post of the courtyard around the gate. 15 And from the front of the gate of the entrance to the front of the porch of the inner gate were fifty cubits. 16 And there were narrow windows to the little rooms, and to their posts inside the gate all around, and likewise to the arches: and windows were all around inside: and upon each post were palm eytzim. 17 Then brought he me into the outside courtyard, and, see, there were rooms, and a pavement made for the courtyard all around: thirty rooms were upon the pavement. 18 And the pavement by the side of the gates over against the length of the gates was the lower pavement. 19 Then he measured the width from the front of the lower gate to the front of the inner courtyard outside, an hundred cubits eastward and northward. 20 And the gate of the outward courtyard that looked toward the north, he measured the length of it, and the width of it. 21 And the little rooms of it were three on this side and three on that side; and the posts of it and the arches of it were after the measure of the first gate: the length of it was fifty cubits,

and the width twenty-five cubits. 22 And their windows, and their arches, and their palm eytzim, were after the measure of the gate that looks toward the east; and they went up to it by seven steps; and the arches of it were in front of them. 23 And the gate of the inner courtyard was over against the gate toward the north, and toward the east; and he measured from gate to gate an hundred cubits. 24 After that he brought me toward the south, and see a gate toward the south: and he measured the posts of it and the arches of it according to these measures. 25 And there were windows in it and in the arches of it round about, like those windows: the length was fifty cubits, and the width twenty-five cubits. 26 And there were seven steps to go up to it, and the arches of it were in front of them: and it had palm eytzim, one on this side, and another on that side, upon the posts of it. 27 And there was a gate in the inner courtyard toward the south: and he measured from gate to gate toward the south an hundred cubits. 28 And he brought me to the inner courtyard by the south gate: and he measured the south gate according to these measures; 29 And the little rooms of it, and the posts of it, and the arches of it, according to these measures: and there were windows in it and in the arches of it round about: it was fifty cubits long, and twenty-five cubits wide. 30 And the arches round about were twenty-five cubits long, and five cubits wide. 31 And the arches of it were toward the outer courtyard; and palm eytzim were upon the posts of it: and the going up to it had eight steps. 32 And he brought me into the inner courtyard toward the east: and he measured the gate according to these measures. 33 And the little rooms of it, and the posts of it, and the arches of it, were according to these measures: and there were windows in it and in the arches of it round about: it was fifty cubits long, and twenty-five cubits wide. 34 And the arches of it were toward the outward courtyard; and palm eytzim were upon the posts of it, on this side, and on that side: and the going up to it had eight steps. 35 And he brought me to the north gate, and measured it according to these measures; 36 The little rooms of it, the posts of it, and the arches of it, and the windows to it round about: the length was fifty cubits, and the width twenty-five cubits. 37 And the posts of it were toward the outer courtyard; and palm eytzim were upon the posts of it, on this side, and on that side: and the going up to it had eight steps. 38 And the rooms and the entries of it were by the posts of the gates, where they washed the burnt offering. 39 And in the porch of the gate were two tables on this side, and two tables[1] on that side, to slay on it the burnt offering and the sin offering and the trespass offering. 40 And at the side outside, as one goes up to the entry of the north gate, were two tables; and on the other side, which was at the porch of the gate, were two tables.[2] 41 Four tables were on this side, and four tables on that side, by the side of the gate; eight tables, on which they killed their sacrifices. 42 And the four tables were of cut stone for the burnt offering, of a cubit and a half long, and a cubit and a half wide, and one cubit high: on which also they laid the instruments with which they killed the burnt offering and the sacrifice. 43 And inside were hooks, a hand wide, fastened round about: and upon the tables was the flesh of the offering. 44 And outside the inner gate were the rooms of the singers in the inner courtyard, which was at the side of the north gate; and they faced toward the south: one at the side of the east gate facing toward the north. 45 And he said to me, This room that faces toward the south is for the kohanim, the keepers of the duties of the Bayit. 46 And the room that faced toward the north is for the kohanim, the keepers of the charge of the altar: these are the sons of Tzadok among the sons of Levi, who come near to יהוה to serve Him. 47 So he measured the courtyard, a hundred cubits long, and a hundred cubits wide, foursquare; and the altar that was before the Bayit. 48 And he brought me to the porch of the Bayit, and measured each post of the porch, five cubits on this side, and five cubits on that side: and the width of the gate was three cubits on this side, and three cubits on that side. 49 The length of the porch was twenty cubits, and the width eleven cubits; and he brought me by the steps by which they went up to it: and there were pillars by the posts, one on this side, and another on that side.

41 Afterward He brought me to the Beit HaMikdash, and measured the posts, six cubits wide on the one side, and six cubits wide on the other side. 2 And the width of the door was ten cubits; and the sides of the door were five cubits on the one side, and five cubits on the other side: and He measured the length of it, forty cubits: and the width, twenty cubits. 3 Then He went inward, and measured the post of the door, two cubits; and the door, six cubits; and the width of the door, seven cubits. 4 So He measured the length of it, twenty cubits; and the width, twenty cubits, before the Beit HaMikdash: and he said to me, *This is the most Set-Apart Place.* 5 After He measured the wall of the Bayit, six cubits; and the width of every side room, four cubits, around the Bayit on every side. 6 And the side rooms were three, one over another, and thirty in order; and they entered into the wall which was of the Bayit for the side rooms all around, that they might be supported, but they were fastened to the wall of the Bayit. 7 And there was a widening, and a winding upwards to the side rooms: for the winding around the Bayit went still upward all around the Bayit: therefore the width of the Bayit was still upward, and so it increased from the lowest room to the highest by the midst. 8 I saw also the height of the Bayit all around: the foundations of the side

---

[1] For both houses in the millennium.
[2] For both now-restored houses.

rooms, were a full rod of six large cubits. 9 The thickness of the wall, which was for the side room outside, was five cubits: and that which was left was the place of the side rooms that were inside. 10 And between the rooms was the wideness of twenty cubits all around the Bayit on every side. 11 And the doors of the side rooms were toward the place that was left, one door toward the north, and another door toward the south: and the width of the place that was left was five cubits all around. 12 Now the building that was before the separate place at the end toward the west was seventy cubits wide; and the wall of the building was five cubits thick all around, and the length of it ninety cubits. 13 So He measured the Bayit, an hundred cubits long; and the separate place, and the building, with the walls of it, an hundred cubits long; 14 Also the width of the face of the Bayit, and of the separate place toward the east, an hundred cubits. 15 And He measured the length of the building over against the separate place that was behind it, and the galleries of it on the one side and on the other side, an hundred cubits, with the inner Beit HaMikdash, and the porches of the courtyard; 16 The door posts, and the narrow windows, and the galleries all around on their three stories, over against the door, paneled with wood all around, and from the ground up to the windows, and the windows were covered; 17 From the space above the door, even to the inner Bayit, and outside, and by all the walls all around, inside and outside, by measure. 18 And it was made with cheruvim and palm eytzim, so that a palm eytz was between a cheruv and a cheruv; and every cheruv had two faces; 19 So that the face of a man was toward the palm eytz on the one side, and the face of a young lion toward the palm eytz on the other side: it was made through the entire Bayit all around 20 From the ground to above the door were cheruvim and palm eytzim made, and on the wall of the Beit HaMikdash. 21 The posts of the Beit HaMikdash were

squared, and the front of the Set-Apart Place; the appearance of one as the appearance of the other. 22 The altar of wood was three cubits high, and the length of it two cubits; and the corners of it, and the length of it, and the walls of it, were of wood: and He said to me, *This is the table that is before* יהוה. 23 And the Beit HaMikdash and the Set-Apart Place had two doors. 24 And the doors had two panels apiece, two turning panels; two panels for the one door, and two panels for the other door. 25 And there were made on them, on the doors of the Beit HaMikdash, cheruvim and palm eytzim, like as were made upon the walls; and there were thick wood upon the front of the porch outside. 26 And there were narrow windows and palm eytzim on the one side and on the other side, on the sides of the porch, and upon the side rooms of the Bayit, and thick wood.

42 Then He brought me out into the outer courtyard, the path toward the north: and he brought me into the room that was over against the separate place, and which was before the building toward the north. 2 Along the length of an hundred cubits was the north door, and the width was fifty cubits. 3 Opposite the twenty cubits that were for the inner courtyard, and opposite the pavement that was for the outer courtyard, was gallery against gallery in three stories. 4 And before the rooms was a path of ten cubits width inward, a path of one cubit; and their doors toward the north. 5 Now the upper rooms were shorter: for the galleries were higher than these, higher than the lower, and than the middle ones of the building. 6 For they were in three stories, but had no pillars as the pillars of the courts: therefore the building was set back more than the lowest and the middle levels from the ground. 7 And the wall that was outside opposite the rooms, toward the outer courtyard facing the rooms, the length of it was fifty cubits. 8 For the length of the rooms that were in the outer courtyard was

fifty cubits: and, see, facing the Beit HaMikdash was a hundred cubits. 9 And from under these rooms was the entrance on the east side, as one goes into them from the outer courtyard. 10 The rooms were in the thickness of the wall of the courtyard toward the east, opposite the separate place, and opposite the building. 11 And the path in front of them was like the appearance of the rooms which were toward the north, as long as them, and as wide as them: and all their goings out were both according to their fashions, and according to their doors. 12 And according to the doors of the rooms that were toward the south was a door at the head of the path, even the path directly before the wall toward the east, as one enters them. 13 Then said He to me, *The north rooms and the south rooms, which are before the separate place, they are set-apart rooms, where the kohanim that approach to* יהוה *shall eat the most set-apart things: there shall they place the most set-apart things and the grain offering, and the sin offering, and the trespass offering; for the place is set-apart. 14 When the kohanim enter in it, then shall they not go out of the Set-Apart Place into the outer courtyard, but there they shall lay their garments aside in which they serve; for they are set-apart; and shall put on other garments, and shall approach those things which are for the people.* 15 Now when He had made an end of measuring the inner Bayit, he brought me out toward the gate facing toward the east, and measured it all around. 16 He measured the east side with the measuring rod, five hundred rods, with the measuring rod all around. 17 He measured the north side, five hundred rods, with the measuring rod all around. 18 He measured the south side, five hundred rods, with the measuring rod. 19 He turned around to the west side, and measured five hundred rods with the measuring rod. 20 He measured it by the four sides: it had a wall all around, five hundred rods long, and five hundred wide,

to make a separation between the Set-Apart Place from the common place.

43 Afterward he brought me to the gate, even the gate that looks toward the east: 2 And, see, the tiferet of the Elohim of Yisrael came from the path of the east: and His voice was like a noise of many waters: and the earth shone with His tiferet. 3 And it was according to the appearance of the vision which I saw, even according to the vision that I saw when I came to destroy the city: and the visions were like the visions that I saw by the river Chevar; and I fell upon my face.[1] 4 And the tiferet of יהוה came into the Bayit by the path of the gate facing toward the east. 5 So the Ruach took me up, and brought me into the inner courtyard; and, see, the tiferet of יהוה filled the Bayit. 6 And I heard Him speaking to me from the Bayit; and the Man[2] stood by me. 7 And He said to me, *Ben-adam, the place of My throne, and the place of the soles of My feet, where I will dwell in the midst of the children of Yisrael le-olam-va-ed, and My set-apart Name, shall Beit Yisrael no more defile, neither they, nor their melechim, by their whorings, nor by the corpses of their melechim on their high places.[3] 8 In their setting of their threshold by My thresholds, and their post by My posts, and the wall between Me and them, they have even defiled My set-apart Name by their abominations that they have committed: wherefore I have consumed them in My anger. 9 Now let them put away their whorings, and the corpses of their melechim, far from Me, and I will dwell in the midst of them le-olam-va-ed. 10 You Ben-adam, show this Bayit to Beit Yisrael,[4] that they may be ashamed of their iniquities: and let them measure the pattern. 11 And if they be ashamed of all that they have done, show them the design of the*

---

[1] Meaning Yahshua continues to appear to Ezekiel, in much the same manner as He had earlier.
[2] Yahshua.
[3] During the **atid lavoh**.
[4] All 12 tribes.

Bayit, and the structure of it, and the exits, and the entrances, and all the designs of it, and all the mishpatim of it, and all its Torot: and write it in their sight, that they may keep the whole design of it, and all the mishpatim of it, and do them. 12 This is the Torah of the Bayit; Upon the top of the mountain the whole limit of it all around shall be most set-apart. See, this is the Torah of the Bayit. 13 And these are the measures of the altar after the cubits: The cubit is a cubit and an hand width; even the bottom shall be a cubit, and the width a cubit, and the border of it by the edge of it all around shall be one span: and this shall be the upper part of the altar. 14 And from the base upon the ground even to the lower edge shall be two cubits, and the width one cubit; and from the lesser edge even to the greater edge shall be four cubits, and the width one cubit. 15 So the altar shall be four cubits; and from the altar and upward shall be four horns. 16 And the altar shall be twelve cubits long, twelve wide, square in the four squares of it. 17 And the edge shall be fourteen cubits long and fourteen wide in the four squares of it; and the border about it shall be half a cubit; and the bottom of it shall be a cubit about; and its stairs shall face east. 18 And He said to me, Ben-adam, this says the Master **יהוה**; These are the mishpatim of the altar in the day when they shall make it, to offer burnt offerings on it, and to sprinkle dom on it. 19 And you shall give to the kohanim the Leviim that be of the zera of Tzadok, which approach Me, to serve to Me, says the Master **יהוה**, a young bull for a sin offering. 20 And you shall take of the dom of it, and put it on the four horns of it, and on the four corners of the edge, and upon the border all around: in this manner shall you cleanse and purge it. 21 You shall take the bull also of the sin offering, and he shall burn it in the appointed place of the Bayit, outside the Set-Apart Place. 22 And on the second day you shall offer a male goat without blemish for a sin offering; and they

shall cleanse the altar, as they did cleanse it with the bull. 23 When you have made an end of cleansing it, you shall offer a young bull without blemish, and a ram out of the flock without blemish. 24 And you shall offer them before **יהוה**, and the kohanim shall cast salt upon them, and they shall offer them up for a burnt offering to **יהוה**. 25 Seven days shall you prepare every day a goat for a sin offering: they shall also prepare a young bull, and a ram out of the flock, without blemish. 26 Seven days shall they purge the altar and purify it; and they shall consecrate themselves. 27 And when these days are over, it shall be, that upon the eighth day, and thereafter, the kohanim shall make your burnt offerings upon the altar, and your shalom offerings; and I will accept you, says the Master **יהוה**.

44 Then He brought me back the entrance of the gate of the outside the Set-Apart Place that looks toward the east; and it was shut. 2 Then said **יהוה** to me; This gate shall be shut, it shall not be opened, and no man shall enter in by it; because **יהוה**, the Elohim of Yisrael, has entered[1] in by it, therefore it shall be shut.[2] 3 It is for the Sar;[3] the Sar, He shall sit in it to eat lechem before **יהוה**; He shall enter by the path of the porch of that gate, and shall go out by the path of the same. [4] 4 Then He brought me along the derech of the north gate before the Bayit: and I looked, and, see, the tiferet of **יהוה** filled the Bayit of **יהוה**: and I fell upon my face. 5 And **יהוה** said to me, Ben-adam, mark well, and see with your eyes, and shema

---

[1] Past tense prior to it actually being shut.
[2] This was fulfilled when Yahshua entered the Eastern Gate as recorded in the Tov News. Today the gate remains shut, in fulfillment of this prophecy. The Moslems think they have successfully stopped the coming of the "Jewish" Moshiach," by cementing the gate in the middle ages and putting graves in front of the Eastern Gate; since no Torah-keeping Jew – not to mention a priest - would step on graves. In fact, they were merely being used to fulfill this prophecy, proving that the Moshiach had actually already come.
[3] **Ha Sar**-The Prince - The Moshiach. Only He can walk through walls to get into that gate to perform millennial temple duties.
[4] That happened at His first advent and will happen again during millennial temple services.

with your ears all that I say to you concerning all the mishpatim of the Bayit of יהוה, and all the Torot of it; and mark well the entering in of the Bayit, with every going out of the Set-Apart Place. 6 And you shall say to the rebellious, even to Beit Yisrael, This says the Master יהוה; O Beit Yisrael, enough of all your abominations, 7 In that you have brought into My Set-Apart Place foreigners, uncircumcised in lev, and uncircumcised in flesh,[1] to be in My Set-Apart Place, to defile it, even My Bayit, when you offer My lechem, the fat and the dom, and they have broken My covenant because of all your abominations. 8 And you have not kept the charge of My set-apart things: but you have set others to guard My charge in My Set-Apart Place in your stead. 9 This says the Master יהוה; No stranger,[2] uncircumcised in lev, nor uncircumcised in flesh,[3] shall enter into My Set-Apart Place, even any son of a foreigner that is among the children of Yisrael. 10 And the Leviim that have gone far away from Me, when Yisrael went astray, who also went astray away from Me after their idols; even they shall bear their iniquity. 11 Yet they were avadim in My Set-Apart Place, having charge at the gates of the Bayit, and serving the Bayit: they did slay the burnt offering and the sacrifice of the people, and they did stand before them to serve to them. 12 But because they ministered to them in front of their idols, and caused Beit Yisrael to fall into iniquity; therefore have I lifted up My hand against them, says the Master יהוה, and they shall bear their iniquity. 13 And they shall not come near to Me, to perform the office of a kohen to Me, nor to come near to any of My set-apart things, in the Most Set-Apart Place: but they shall bear their shame, and their abominations which they have

committed. 14 But I will make those keepers of the charge of the Bayit, for all the service of it, and for all that shall be done in it.[4] 15 But the kohanim the Leviim, the sons of Tzadok, that kept the charge of My Set-Apart Place when the children of Yisrael went astray from Me, they shall come near to Me to serve Me, and they shall stand before Me to offer to Me the fat and the dom, says the Master יהוה:[5] 16 They shall enter into My Set-Apart Place, and they shall come near to My table, to serve Me, and they shall keep My charge. 17 And it shall come to pass, that when they enter in at the gates of the inner courtyard, they shall be clothed with linen garments; and no wool shall come upon them, while they serve in the gates of the inner courtyard, and inside the Bayit. 18 They shall have linen head coverings upon their heads, and shall have linen breeches upon their waist; they shall not dress themselves with any thing that causes sweat. 19 And when they go out into the outer courtyard, even into the outer courtyard to the people, they shall put off their garments in which they ministered, and lay them in the set-apart rooms, and they shall put on other garments; and they shall not mingle among the people with their garments. 20 Neither shall they shave their heads, nor allow their hair to grow long; they shall only trim their hair. 21 Neither shall any kohen drink wine, when they enter into the inner courtyard. 22 Neither shall they take for their wives a widow, or her that is divorced: but they shall take virgins of the zera of Beit Yisrael,[6] or a widow that had a kohen before.[7] 23 And they shall teach My people the difference between the set-apart and

---

[1] The binding act of circumcision is eternal, as seen here in the **atid lavoh**. If it will be a requirement to worship YHWH in His reign on earth, why would anyone claim that it has been abolished even if for only a short time.
[2] Clearly all the redeemed in the millennium are Yisraelites, because YHWH states that no gentiles or strangers will be worshipping Him.
[3] True Yisraelite worshippers must have both circumcisions; let no man fool you into losing your crown.

[4] Because the splendor of the millennial temple and millennial people will require greater set-apartness, He will raise up others to minister in place of the rejected, who will be somehow relegated to hard labor in the service.
[5] The sons of Tzadok are lifted as the other sons of Levi are demoted.
[6] Must be equally yoked. For instance, a Shabbat-keeper should never marry a Sunday-keeper.
[7] Because she knows the pressures and the trials of the ministry, and can be helpful to a kohen/priest seeking a wife.

profane, and cause them to discern between the unclean and the clean.[1] 24 And in a dispute they shall stand in mishpat; and they shall shophet according to My mishpatim: and they shall keep My torot and My mishpatim in all My moadim; and they shall set-apart My Shabbats. 25 And they shall not come near any dead person to defile themselves: except for abba, or for ima, or for son, or for daughter, for brother, or for sister that has had no husband, for these in the family they may defile themselves. 26 And after he is cleansed, they shall count for him seven days. 27 And in the day that he goes into the Set-Apart Place, to the inner courtyard, to serve in the Set-Apart Place, he shall offer his sin offering, says the Master יהוה. 28 And it shall be to them for an inheritance: I am their inheritance: and you shall give them no possession in Yisrael: I am their possession. 29 They shall eat the grain offering, and the sin offering, and the trespass offering; and every dedicated thing in Yisrael shall be theirs. 30 And the first of all the bikkurim of all things, and every contribution of all, of every sort of your offerings, shall be the kohen's: you shall also give to the kohen the first of your dough, that he may cause the bracha to rest in your Bayit. 31 The kohanim shall not eat anything that is dead by itself, or torn, whether it be fowl or beast.

45 Moreover, when you shall divide by lot the land for inheritance,[2] you shall offer a contribution to יהוה, a set-apart portion of the land: the length shall be the length of twenty-five thousand rods, and the width shall be ten thousand. This shall be set-apart in all the borders of it all around. 2 Of this there shall be for the Set-Apart Place five hundred in length, with five hundred in width, square all around; and fifty cubits all around as open space. 3 And of this measure shall you measure the length of twenty-five thousand, and the width of ten thousand: and in it shall be the Set-Apart Place and the most Set-Apart Place. 4 The set-apart portion of the land shall be for the kohanim the avadim of the Set-Apart Place, which shall come near to serve יהוה: and it shall be a place for their houses, and set-apart ground for the Set-Apart Place. 5 And the twenty-five thousand cubits of length, and the ten thousand of width, shall also the Leviim, the avadim of the Bayit, have for themselves, twenty rooms as a possession. 6 And you shall appoint the possession of the city five thousand cubits wide, twenty-five thousand long, besides the contribution of the set-apart portion: it shall be for the whole of Beit Yisrael.[3] 7 And a portion shall be for the Sar on the one side and on the other side of the contribution of the set-apart portion, and of the possession of the city, before the contribution of the set-apart portion, and before the possession of the city, from the west side westward, and from the east side eastward: and the length shall be alongside one of the portions, from the west border to the east border. 8 In the land shall be his possession in Yisrael: and My leaders shall no more oppress My people; and the rest of the land they shall give to Beit Yisrael according to their tribes. 9 This says the Master יהוה; Let it suffice you, O leaders of Yisrael: remove violence and plundering, and execute mishpat and justice, take away your oppressions from My people, says the Master יהוה. 10 You shall have just balances, and a just ephah, and a just bath. 11 The ephah and the bath shall be of one measure, that the bath may contain the tenth part of an homer, and the ephah the tenth part of an homer: the measure of it shall be after the homer. 12 And the shekel shall be twenty gerahs: twenty shekels, twenty-five shekels, fifteen shekels, shall be your minah. 13 This is the contribution that you shall offer; one-sixth part of an ephah of a homer of wheat, and

---

[1] If you love Yahshua, and are willing to learn that, you will surely walk as Yisrael.
[2] In the kingdom.

[3] All 12 tribes.

you shall give one-sixth part of an ephah of a homer of barley: 14 Concerning the ordinance of oil, the bath of oil, you shall offer one-tenth part of a bath out of the kor, which is a homer of ten baths; for ten baths are a homer: 15 And one lamb out of the flock, out of two hundred, out of the fat pastures of Yisrael; for a grain offering, and for a burnt offering, and for shalom offerings, to make reconciliation for them, says the Master **יהוה**. 16 All the people of the land shall give this contribution for the leader in Yisrael. 17 And it shall be the Sar's part to give burnt offerings, and grain offerings, and drink offerings, in the moadim, and in the Rosh Chodashim, and in the Shabbats, in all appointed times of Beit Yisrael: He shall prepare the sin offering, and the grain offering, and the burnt offering, and the shalom offerings, to make reconciliation for Beit Yisrael. [1] [2] 18 This says the Master **יהוה**; In the first month, in the first day of the month, you shall take a young bull without blemish, and cleanse the Set-Apart Place: 19 And the kohen shall take of the dom of the sin offering, and put it upon the posts of the Bayit, and upon the four corners of the edge of the altar, and upon the posts of the gate of the inner courtyard. 20 And you shall do the same on the seventh day of the month for everyone that goes astray, and for him that is foolish: so shall you reconcile the Bayit. 21 In the first month, in the fourteenth day of the month, you shall have the Pesach, a feast of seven days; matzah shall be eaten. 22 And upon that day shall the Sar[3] shall prepare for Himself and for all the people of the land a bull for a sin offering. 23 And for seven days of the moed He shall prepare a burnt offering to **יהוה**, seven bulls and seven rams without blemish daily for the seven days; and a male goat

daily for a sin offering. 24 And he shall prepare a grain offering of an ephah for a bull, and an ephah for a ram, and a hin of oil for an ephah. 25 In the seventh month, on the fifteenth day of the month, shall He do likewise on the moed for the seven days, according to the sin offering, according to the burnt offering, and according to the grain offering, and according to the oil.

46 This says the Master **יהוה**; The gate of the inner courtyard that looks toward the east shall be shut the six working days; but on the Shabbat it shall be opened, and in the day of the Rosh Chodesh it shall be opened.[4] 2 And the Sar shall enter by the path of the porch of that gate from the outside, and shall stand by the post of the gate, and the kohanim shall prepare His burnt offering and His shalom offerings, and He shall worship at the threshold of the gate: then He shall go out; but the gate shall not be shut until the evening.[5] 3 Likewise the people of the land shall worship at the door of this gate before **יהוה** in the Shabbats and in the Rosh Chodashim. 4 And the burnt offering that the Sar shall offer to **יהוה** on the Shabbat day shall be six lambs without blemish, and a ram without blemish. 5 And the grain offering shall be an ephah for a ram, and the grain offering for the lambs, as He shall be able to give, and a hin of oil for an ephah. 6 And in the day of the Rosh Chodesh it shall be a young bull without blemish, and six lambs, and a ram: they shall be without blemish. 7 And He shall prepare a grain offering, an ephah for a bull, and an ephah for a ram, and for the lambs according as His hand shall attain to, and a hin of oil for an ephah. 8 And when the Sar shall enter, He shall go in by the path of the porch of that gate, and He shall go out by the path of it. 9 But when the

---

[1] In the **atid lavo** Moshaich Himself will lead the sons of Tzadok and the sons of Yisrael in worshipping His Abba. If we are Yisrael we ought to do the same even now.
[2] Note also how all the feasts of YHWH are eternal, and have never been set aside.
[3] Moshiach walks the Torah walk, and proves He is the real Moshiach.

[4] It will be open to remind Yisrael of just how set-apart are Shabbat and Rosh Chodesh.
[5] In the **atid lavoh** sacrifices, Yahshua will teach all Yisrael that all worship must be directed to Abba YHWH. We will watch Him in action. He will work hand-in-glove with the sons of Tzadok.

people of the land shall come before **יהוה** *in the solemn moadim, He that enters in by the path of the north gate to worship shall go out by the path of the south gate; and he that enters by the path of the south gate shall go out by the path of the north gate: he shall not return by the path of the gate by which he came in, but shall go out opposite it.[1] 10 And the Sar in the midst of them, when they go in, He shall go in; and when they go out, He shall go out.[2] 11 And in the feasts and in the moadim the grain offering shall be an ephah to a bull, and ephah to a ram, and to the lambs as He is able to give, and a hin of oil for an ephah. 12 Now when the Sar shall prepare a voluntary burnt offering or shalom offerings voluntarily to* **יהוה***, one shall then open for Him the gate that looks toward the east, and He shall prepare His burnt offering and His shalom offerings, as He did on the Shabbat day: then He shall go out; and after His going out one shall shut the gate. 13 You shall prepare a burnt offering to* **יהוה** *daily of a lamb of the first year without blemish: you shall prepare it every morning. 14 And you shall prepare a grain offering for it every morning, one sixth of an ephah, and one third part of a hin of oil, to moisten the fine flour; a grain offering continually by a perpetual ordinance to* **יהוה***. 15 In this manner shall they prepare the lamb, and the grain offering, and the oil, every shachrit for a continual burnt offering. 16 This says the Master* **יהוה***; If the Sar gives a gift to any of His sons, the inheritance of it shall be His sons';[3] it shall be their possession by inheritance. 17 But if He gives a gift of His inheritance to one of His avadim,[4] then it shall be his to the year of yovel; after it shall it return to the Sar: but His inheritance shall be His sons' for them. 18 Moreover the Sar shall not take of the people's inheritance by oppression, to thrust them out of their possession;* but *He shall give His sons inheritance out of His own possession: that My people be not scattered every man from his possession.[5] 19* After He brought me through the entrance, which was at the side of the gate, into the set-apart rooms of the kohanim, which faced north: and, see, there was a place on the two sides westward. 20 Then He said to me, *This is the place where the kohanim shall boil the trespass offering and the sin offering, where they shall bake the grain offering; that they bear them not out into the outer courtyard, to set-apart the people.* 21 Then He brought me out into the outer courtyard, and caused me to pass by the four corners of the courtyard; and, see, in every corner of the courtyard there was a courtyard. 22 In the four corners of the courtyard there were courts joined of forty cubits long and thirty wide: these four corners were of one measure. 23 And there was a row of building stones all around them, all around them were four, and it was made for boiling places under the rows all around. 24 Then said He to me, *These are the places of those that boil, where the avadim of the Bayit shall boil the sacrifices of the people.*

47 Afterward He brought me again to the door of the Bayit; and, see, waters issued out from under the threshold of the Bayit eastward: for the front of the Bayit stood toward the east, and the waters came down from under from the right side of the Bayit, at the south side of the altar. 2 Then brought he me out by the path of the gate northward, and led me about the path outside to the outer gate by the path that looks eastward; and, see, there waters ran on the right side. 3 And when the Man that had the line in His hand went out eastward, he measured a thousand cubits, and he brought me through the waters; the waters were to the ankles. 4 Again He measured a thousand cubits, and brought me through

---

[1] Symbolic of moving forward and never backward in our walk with YHWH.
[2] Following Yahshua as our older brother on a daily basis.
[3] Sons of Yisrael.
[4] Kohanim.

[5] Because He rules and reigns in right-ruling. This is a prophecy stating that He will not abuse the people, unlike both houses in the days of their abusive kings.

the waters; the waters were to the knees. Again he measured a thousand cubits, and brought me through; the waters were to the waist. 5 Afterward He measured a thousand cubits; and it was a river that I could not pass over: for the waters were risen, waters to swim in, a river that could not be passed over. 6 And He said to me, *Ben-adam, have you seen this?* Then He brought me, and caused me to return to the bank of the stream. 7 Now when I had returned, see, at the bank of the stream were very many *eytzim* on the one side and on the other. 8 Then He said to me, *These waters flow out toward the east country, and go down into the desert, and enter the sea: which being made to flow into the sea, the waters shall be healed.*[1] 9 *And it shall come to pass, that everything that lives, which moves, wherever the streams shall go, shall live: and there shall be a very great multitude of fish,*[2] *because these waters shall come there: and they shall be healed; and everything shall live where the stream comes.* 10 *And it shall come to pass, that the fishers shall stand upon it from En-Gedi even to En-Eglaim; there shall be a place to spread out nets; their fish shall be the same kind, as the fish of the great sea, also very many.* 11 *But its swamps and the marshes shall not be healed; they shall be given over to salt.* 12 *And by the stream upon the banks of it, on this side and on that side, shall grow all eytzim for food, whose leaf shall not fade, neither shall the fruit of it be consumed: it shall bring out new fruit according to its months, because their waters they brought came out of the Set-Apart Place: and its fruit shall be for food, and its leaves for medicine.*[3] 13 This says the Master **יהוה**; *This shall be the border, by which you shall inherit the land according to the twelve tribes of Yisrael: Yoseph shall have two portions.* 14 *And you*

shall inherit it, one as well as another: concerning which I lifted up My hand to give it to your ahvot: and this land shall fall to you as your inheritance.* 15 *And this shall be the border of the land toward the north side, from the great sea, the halacha of Hethlon, as men go to Tzedad;* 16 *Hamath, Berothah, Sivrayim, which is between the border of Dameshek and the border of Hamath; Hatzar-Hattichon, which is by the coast of Hauran.* 17 *And the border from the sea shall be Hazar-Enan, the border of Dameshek, and the north northward, and the border of Hamath. This is the north side.* 18 *And the east side you shall measure from Hauran, and from Dameshek, and from Gilead, and from the land of Yisrael by Jordan, from the border to the eastern side of the sea. And this is the east side.* 19 *And the south side southward, from Tamar even to the waters of Merivah in Kadesh, along the river to the great sea. And this is the south side southward.* 20 *The west side also shall be the great sea from the border, until a man come opposite Hamath. This is the west side.* 21 *So shall you divide this land to you according to the tribes of Yisrael.* 22 *And it shall come to pass, that you shall divide it by lot for an inheritance to you, and to the foreigners that sojourn among you, which shall beget children among you: and they shall be to you as one born in the country among the children of Yisrael; they shall have inheritance with you among the tribes of Yisrael.*[4] [5] 23 *And it shall come to pass, that in whatever tribe that the stranger sojourns, there shall you give him his inheritance,* says the Master **יהוה**.[6]

48 *Now these are the names of the tribes. From the north end to the coast of the path of Hethlon, as one goes to Hamath, Hazar-Enan, the border of*

---

[1] Probably Dead Sea.
[2] An idiom meaning Yisraelites as seen elsewhere; YHWH will heal them through the healing waters of the age to come.
[3] Eternity described, as seen vividly is Revelation 22:1-3. The two banks represent two houses, both receiving life, food, and healing in an eternity with YHWH.
[4] All tribes must be open to all who wish to live with them.
[5] This will occur in the millennium.
[6] When all tribes are revealed more clearly in the kingdom, strangers can choose. But right now, we can only choose Yahshua to get in, since we do not always know tribal affiliation.

Dameshek northward, to the coast of Hamath; for these are his sides east and west; a portion for Dan. 2 And by the border of Dan, from the east side to the west side, a portion for Asher. 3 And by the border of Asher, from the east side even to the west side, a portion for Naphtali. 4 And by the border of Naphtali, from the east side to the west side, a portion for Menashseh. 5 And by the border of Menashseh, from the east side to the west side, a portion for Ephraim. 6 And by the border of Ephraim, from the east side even to the west side, a portion for Reuven. 7 And by the border of Reuven, from the east side to the west side, a portion for Yahudah. 8 And by the border of Yahudah, from the east side to the west side, shall be the offering which you shall offer of twenty-five thousand rods in width, and in length as one of the other parts, from the east side to the west side: and the Set-Apart Place shall be in the midst of it. 9 The land contribution that you shall offer to יהוה shall be twenty-five thousand cubits in length, and ten thousand in width. 10 And for them, even for the kohanim, shall be this set-apart land contribution; toward the north twenty-five thousand cubits in length, and toward the west ten thousand cubits in width, and toward the east ten thousand cubits in width, and toward the south twenty-five thousand cubits in length: and the Set-Apart Place of יהוה shall be in the midst of it. 11 It shall be for the kohanim that are set-apart from the sons of Tzadok; who have kept My charge, which did not go astray when the children of Yisrael went astray, as the Leviim went astray. 12 And this contribution of the land that is offered shall be to them a thing most set-apart by the border of the Leviim. 13 And opposite the border of the kohanim the Leviim shall have twenty-five thousand cubits in length, and ten thousand cubits in width: all the length shall be twenty-five thousand cubits, and the width ten thousand cubits. 14 And they shall not sell it, neither exchange it, nor transfer the bikkurim of the land: for it

is set-apart to יהוה . 15 And the five thousand cubits, that are left in the width opposite the twenty-five thousand cubits, shall be for common use of the city, for dwelling, and for open land: and the city shall be in the midst of it. 16 And these shall be the measures of it; the north side four thousand five hundred cubits, and the south side four thousand five hundred cubits, and on the east side four thousand five hundred cubits, and the west side four thousand five hundred cubits. 17 And the open spaces of the city shall be toward the north two hundred and fifty cubits, and toward the south two hundred and fifty cubits, and toward the east two hundred and fifty cubits, and toward the west two hundred and fifty cubits. 18 And the rest of the length opposite the contribution of the set-apart portion shall be ten thousand cubits eastward, and ten thousand cubits westward: and it shall be opposite the contribution of the set-apart portion; and the increase of it shall be for food to them that serve the city. 19 And they that work the city shall serve it out of all the tribes of Yisrael. 20 All the land contribution shall be twenty-five thousand cubits by twenty-five thousand cubits: you shall offer the set-apart land contribution foursquare, with the possession of the city. 21 And the remnant shall be for the Sar, on one side and on the other side of the set-apart land contribution, and of the possession of the city, over against the twenty-five thousand cubits of the contribution toward the east border, and westward over against the twenty-five thousand cubits toward the west border, opposite the portions for the Sar: and it shall be the set-apart land contribution; and the Set-Apart Place of the Bayit shall be in the midst of it. 22 Moreover from the possession of the Leviim, and from the possession of the city, being in the midst of that which is the Princes', between the border of Yahudah and the border of Benyamin, it shall be for the Sar.[1] 23 As for the rest of the tribes, from the east side to the west side, Benyamin shall have a portion. 24 And by the border of Benyamin, from the east side to the west side, Shimeon shall have a portion. 25 And by the border of Shimeon, from the east side to the west side, Yissacher has a portion. 26 And by the border of Yissacher, from the east side to the west side, Zevulon has a portion. 27 And by the border of Zevulon, from the east side to the west side, Gad has a portion. 28 And by the border of Gad, at the south side southward, the border shall be even from Tamar to the waters of Merivah in Kadesh, and to the river toward the Great Sea. 29 This is the land, which you shall divide by lot to the tribes of Yisrael for inheritance, and these are their portions, says the Master יהוה. 30 And these are the exits of the city on the north side, four thousand five hundred cubits.

31 And the gates of the city shall be called after the names of the tribes of Yisrael:[2] [3] three gates northward; one gate of Reuven, one gate of Yahudah, one gate of Levi. 32 And at the east side four thousand and five hundred cubits: and three gates; and one gate of Yoseph,[4] one gate of Benyamin, one gate of Dan. 33 And at the south side four thousand and five hundred cubits: and three gates; one gate of Shimeon, one gate of Yissacher, one gate of Zevulon. 34 At the west side four thousand and five hundred cubits, with their three gates; one gate of Gad, one gate of Asher, one gate of Naphtali. 35 It was all around eighteen thousand cubits: and the name of the city from that day forward even le-olam-va-ed shall be, יהוה-Shamma. יהוה-Is-There.[5]

---

[1] Even Moshiach has an initial land inheritance in Yisrael. Yet according to First Corinthians, He will turn over all things in the kingdom to the Father so that at the end of the age, He has no land inheritance, for He is YHWH in the flesh and does not need land.

[2] No gate for Christians or gentiles, meaning all believers must be part of the Commonwealth of Yisrael to enter the New Jerusalem.
[3] In a very interesting switch, the tribes have gates named in a different direction than the original order of camping around the wilderness tabernacle as found in Numbers. This is all part of YHWH keeping His word to make all things new, including tribal positioning in the age to come.
[4] Represents Ephraim and Menasheh.
[5] When YHWH is in our midst in that day, correct tribal positioning and human desire will no longer matter.

דניאל

Daniyel - Daniel
To Our Forefathers Yisrael

1 In the third year of the malchut of Yehoyaqim melech of Yahudah came Nebuchadnetzar melech of Bavel to Yahrushalayim, and besieged it. 2 And יהוה gave Yehoyaqim melech of Yahudah into his hand, with part of the vessels of the Bayit of Eloah: which he carried into the land of Shinar to the bayit of his eloah; and he brought the vessels into the treasure bayit of his eloah. 3 And the melech spoke to Ashpenaz the master of his eunuchs, that he should bring certain of the children of Yisrael, and of the melech's seed, and of the nobles; 4 Children in whom was no blemish, but well favored, and skilful in all chochmah, and skilled in da'at, and the binah of science, and such as had the ability to stand in the melech's palace, in order that they might teach them the learning and the tongue of the Chaldeans. 5 And the melech appointed for them a daily provision of the melech's food, and of the wine which he drank: nourishing them for three years, so that at the end of that time they might stand before the melech. 6 Now among these were of the children of Yahudah, Daniyel, Hananyah, Misha-el, and Azaryah:[1] 7 To whom the prince of the eunuchs gave names: for he gave to Daniyel the name of Belteshazzar; and to Hananyah, he gave the name of Shadrach; and to Misha-el, he gave the name of Meshach; and to Azaryah, he gave the name of Aved-Nego.[2] 8 But Daniyel purposed in his lev that he would not defile himself with the portion of the melech's food,[3] nor with the wine which he

drank: therefore he requested to the prince of the eunuchs permission to abstain that he might not defile himself. 9 Now Eloah had brought Daniyel into favor and tender love with the prince of the eunuchs. 10 And the prince of the eunuchs said to Daniyel, I fear my master the melech, who has appointed your food and your drink: for why should he see your faces looking worse than the other children your age? Then you would make me risk my life before the melech. 11 Then said Daniyel to Menezar, who the prince of the eunuchs had set over Daniyel, Hananyah, Misha-el, and Azaryah, 12 Test your avadim for ten days I ask you; and let them give us vegetables to eat,[4] and mayim to drink. 13 Then let our faces be looked upon before you, and the faces of the rest of children of Yisrael that eat of the portion of the melech's food: and then as you see fit, deal with your avadim. 14 So he consented to them in this matter, and tested them ten days.[5] 15 And at the end of ten days their faces appeared more beautiful and fuller than all the children who did eat the portion of the melech's food. 16 Thus Menezar took away the portion of their food, and the wine that they should drink; and gave them daily vegetables. 17 As for these four children, Eloah gave them da'at and skill in all learning and chochmah: and Daniyel had binah in all visions and dreams. 18 Now at the end of those days at the time that the melech had said he would bring them in, then the prince of the eunuchs brought them in before Nebuchadnetzar. 19 And the melech communed with them; and among them all was found none like Daniyel, Hananyah, Misha-el, and Azaryah: therefore they stood and served before the melech. 20 And in all matters of chochmah

---

[1] Jewish children of the Yahudite exile.
[2] Hanan-Yah: Yah is gracious changed to Shadrach or "inspiration of the sun"; Misha-El or El is without equal, changed to Meshach or "belonging to Aku"; and Azar-Yah meaning "Yah is my helper" changed to Aved-Nego or "servant of Nego". As always, the spirit of Babylon sun worship, seeks to create a false identity among Yahweh's exiled people, in order to hide and cover their true heritage in Yisrael through Yahshua.
[3] Kept kosher while in captivity and exile.

[4] So they can keep kosher in exile.
[5] Perhaps representing the ten tribes of "hungering" unclean Yisrael.

and binah, that the melech asked them, he found them ten times better[1] than all the magicians and astrologers that were in all his malchut. 21 And Daniyel continued to serve in that capacity even to the first year of melech Koresh.

2 And in the second year of the malchut of Nebuchadnetzar, he dreamed dreams, by which his ruach was troubled, and his sleep left him. 2 Then the melech commanded a call to be made to all the magicians, and the astrologers, and the sorcerers, and the Chaldeans, to explain to the melech his dreams. So they came and stood before the melech. 3 And the melech said to them, I have dreamed a dream, and my ruach was anxious to know the dream. 4 Then spoke the Chaldeans to the melech in Aramaic, O melech, live le-olam-va-ed: tell your avadim the dream, and we will explain the interpretation.[2] 5 The melech answered and said to the Chaldeans, I have forgotten the dream: if you will not make known to me the dream, along with the interpretation, you shall be cut in pieces, and your houses shall be made into dunghills. 6 But if you explain the dream, and the interpretation, you shall receive from me gifts and rewards and great honor: therefore explain to me the dream, and its interpretation. 7 They answered again and said, Let the melech tell his avadim the dream, and we will explain the interpretation. 8 The melech answered and said, I know of certainty that you are buying time, because you see the dream has gone from my memory. 9 But if you will not make known to me the dream, there is but one decree for you: for you have prepared lying and corrupt words to speak before me, until the time has changed: therefore tell me the dream, and I shall know that you can also explain the interpretation of it. 10 The Chaldeans answered before the melech, and

said, There is not a man upon the olam that can explain the melech's matter: therefore there is no melech, master, or ruler, that has asked such things at any time from any magician, or astrologer, or Chaldean. 11 And it is a rare thing that the melech requires, and there is no other person that can explain it before the melech, except the emet Eloah, whose dwelling is not with flesh. 12 For this cause the melech was angry and very furious, and commanded to destroy all the wise men of Bavel. 13 And the decree went forth that the wise men should be slain; and they sought Daniyel and his companions to be slain. 14 Then Daniyel answered with counsel and chochmah to Ariyoch the captain of the melech's guard, who had gone forth to kill the wise men of Bavel: 15 He answered and said to Ariyoch the melech's captain, Why is the decree given in such haste from the melech? Then Ariyoch made the thing known to Daniyel. 16 Then Daniyel went in, and desired of the melech that he would give him time, and that he would explain to the melech the interpretation. 17 Then Daniyel went to his bayit, and made the thing known to Hananyah, Misha-el, and Azaryah, his companions: 18 That they would desire rachamim of the Eloah of the shamayim concerning this secret; that Daniyel and his companions should not perish with the rest of the wise men of Bavel. 19 Then was the secret revealed to Daniyel in a night vision. Then Daniyel blessed the Eloah of the shamayim. 20 Daniyel answered and said, Blessed be the Name of Eloah le-olam-va-ed: for chochmah and might are His: 21 And He changes the times and the seasons: He removes melechim, and sets up melechim: He gives chochmah to the wise, and da'at to them that have binah: 22 He reveals the deep and secret things: He knows what is in the darkness, and the light dwells with Him. 23 I thank You, and hallel You, O Eloah of my ahvot, who has given me chochmah and might, and has made known to me now

---

[1] Another hidden reference to Ephraim's gifts among the heathen?
[2] From this point until the end of chapter 7, the text switches to Aramaic.

what we have desired of You: for You have now made known to us the melech's matter. 24 Therefore Daniyel went in to Ariyoch, whom the melech had ordained to destroy the wise men of Bavel: he went and said to him; Destroy not the wise men of Bavel: bring me in before the melech, and I will explain to the melech the interpretation. 25 Then Ariyoch brought in Daniyel before the melech in haste and said to him, I have found a man of the captives of Yahudah, [1] that will make known to the melech the interpretation. 26 The melech answered and said to Daniyel, whose name was Belteshatzar, Are you able to make known to me the dream that I have seen, and its interpretation? 27 Daniyel answered in the presence of the melech, and said, The secret, which the melech has demanded, cannot be declared by the wise men, the astrologers, the magicians, or the soothsayers. 28 But there is an Eloah in the shamayim that reveals secrets, and makes known to the melech Nebuchadnetzar what shall be in the latter-days. Your dreams, and the visions of your head upon your bed, were these; 29 As for you, O melech, your thoughts came into your mind upon your bed, what should come to pass in the future: and He that reveals secrets makes known to you what shall come to pass. 30 But as for me, this secret is not revealed to me for any chochmah that I may have more than any others, but for their sakes that shall make known the interpretation to the melech, and that you might know the thoughts of your lev. 31 You, O melech, saw, and saw a great image. This great image, whose brightness was excellent, stood before you; and the form of it was awesome. 32 This image's head was of fine gold, its breast and its strong ones of silver, its belly and its thighs of brass, 33 Its legs of iron, its feet part iron and part clay. 34 You saw it until a Stone was cut out without hands, which smote the image upon its feet that were of

iron and clay, and broke them to pieces. 35 Then was the iron, the clay, the brass, the silver, and the gold, broken to pieces together, and became like the chaff of the summer threshing floors; and the wind carried them away, that no place was found for them: and the Stone that smote the image became a great mountain, and filled the whole olam. 36 This is the dream; and now we[2] will tell the interpretation of it to the melech. 37 You, O melech, are a melech of melechim: for the Eloah of the shamayim has given you a malchut, power, and strength, and tiferet. 38 And wherever the children of men dwell, the beasts of the field and the fowls of the shamayim He has given all this into your hands, and has made you ruler over them all. You are this head of gold.[3] 39 And after you shall arise another malchut inferior to yours,[4] and another third malchut of brass, which shall bear rule over all the olam.[5] 40 And the fourth malchut shall be strong as iron: forasmuch as iron breaks in pieces and subdues all things: and as iron that breaks all these, shall it break in pieces and bruise.[6] 41 And whereas you saw the feet and toes, part of potters' clay, and part of iron, the malchut shall be divided;[7] but there shall be in it some of the strength of the iron, forasmuch as you saw the iron mixed with muddy clay. 42 And as the toes of the feet were part of iron, and part of clay, so the malchut shall be partly strong, and partly broken.[8] 43 And whereas you saw iron mixed with muddy clay, they shall mingle themselves with the seed of men: but they shall not cleave one to another, even as iron is not mixed with clay.[9] 44 And in the days of these melechim shall the

---

[1] Note that Ephraim is nowhere to be found, as their exile was almost 200 years earlier, in a totally different direction, with a different captor.

[2] In Yisrael, all serve YHWH and all have a strong sense of community.
[3] Babylonian Empire.
[4] Medo-Persian Empire.
[5] Greek Empire.
[6] Roman Empire.
[7] Rome into east and west.
[8] Revised not revived end-time Edomite Roman Empire, with a strong remnant of Roman influence, combined with other weaker parts and interests of mankind, represented by sinful muddy clay.
[9] Roman Edomite interest will overcome the others in the revised Roman Empire.

Eloah of the shamayim set up a malchut, which shall never be destroyed:[1] and the malchut shall not be left to other people,[2] but it shall break in pieces and consume all these malchuts, and it shall stand le-olam-va-ed.[3] 45 For as much as you saw that the Stone was cut out of the mountain without hands,[4] and that it broke in pieces the iron, the brass, the clay, the silver, and the gold; the great Eloah has made known to the melech what shall come to pass in the future: and the dream is certain, and the interpretation of it sure. 46 Then the melech Nebuchadnetzar fell upon his face, and worshipped Daniyel, and commanded that they should offer an offering and sweet incense to him. 47 The melech answered to Daniyel, and said, Of an emet it is, that your Eloah is the Eloah of Elohim, and a Master of Melechim, and a revealer of secrets, seeing you could reveal this secret. 48 Then the melech made Daniyel a great man, and gave him many great gifts, and made him ruler over the whole province of Bavel, and chief of the nobles over all the wise men of Bavel. 49 Then Daniyel requested of the melech, and he set Shadrach, Meshach, and Abed-Nego, over the affairs of the province of Bavel: but Daniyel sat in the very gate of the melech.

3 Nebuchadnetzar the melech made an image of gold, whose height was threescore cubits, and the breadth of it six cubits: he set it up in the plain of Dura, in the province of Bavel. 2 Then Nebuchadnetzar the melech sent to gather together the nobles, the governors, and the captains, the judges, the treasurers, the counselors, the sheriffs, and all the rulers of the provinces, to come to the dedication of the image which Nebuchadnetzar the melech had set up. 3 Then the nobles, the

governors, and captains, the judges, the treasurers, the counselors, the sheriffs, and all the rulers of the provinces, were gathered together to the dedication of the image that Nebuchadnetzar the melech had set up; and they stood before the image that Nebuchadnetzar had set up. 4 Then a herald cried aloud, To you it is commanded, O peoples, nations, and languages, 5 That at the time you hear the sound of the trumpet, flute, harp, sackbut, psaltery, and all kinds of music, you shall fall down and worship the golden image that Nebuchadnetzar the melech has set up: 6 And whoever does not fall down and worship; shall at that same hour be cast into the middle of a burning fiery furnace. 7 Therefore at that time, when all the people heard the sound of the trumpet, flute, harp, sackbut, psaltery, and all kinds of music, all the peoples, nations, and languages, fell down and worshipped the golden image that Nebuchadnetzar the melech had set up. 8 Then at that time certain Chaldeans came near, and accused the Yahudim. 9 They spoke and said to the melech Nebuchadnetzar, O melech, live le-olam-va-ed. 10 You, O melech, have made a decree, that every man that shall hear the sound of the trumpet, flute, harp, and psaltery, and all kinds of music, shall fall down and worship the golden image: 11 And whoever does not fall down and worship, that he should be cast into the middle of a burning fiery furnace. 12 There are certain Yahudim whom you have set over the affairs of the province of Bavel, Shadrach, Meshach, and Abed-Nego; these men, O melech, have not regarded you: they do not serve your eloah, nor worship the golden image which you have set up. 13 Then Nebuchadnetzar in his rage and fury commanded to bring Shadrach, Meshach, and Abed-Nego to him. Then they brought these men before the melech. 14 Nebuchadnetzar spoke and said to them, Is it emet, O Shadrach, Meshach, and Abed-Nego that you do not serve my eloah, nor worship the golden image that I have set

---

[1] The reign of Moshiach Yahshua.
[2] It will not be a "gentile kingdom" like the others, but will be for restored, redeemed and regathered Yisrael, by and through Moshiach Yahshua.
[3] The final restored kingdom to Yisrael with Yahshua on David's throne.
[4] Without any human origin.

up? 15 Now if you are ready the next time you hear the sound of the trumpet, flute, harp, psaltery, and all kinds of music, if you fall down and worship the image which I have made; all will be well: but if you worship not, you shall be cast in that same hour into the middle of a burning fiery furnace; and who is that eloah that shall deliver you out of my hands? 16 Shadrach, Meshach, and Abed-Nego, answered and said to the melech, O Nebuchadnetzar, there is no need to answer you in this matter. 17 If it be so, our Eloah whom we serve is able to deliver us from the burning fiery furnace, and He will deliver us out of your hand, O melech. 18 But if not, be it known to you, O melech, that we will not serve your eloah, nor worship the golden image that you have set up. 19 Then was Nebuchadnetzar full of fury, and the expression on his face was changed against Shadrach, Meshach, and Abed-Nego: therefore he spoke, and commanded that they should heat the furnace seven times more than it was normally heated. 20 And he commanded the mightiest men that were in his army to bind Shadrach, Meshach, and Abed-Nego, and to cast them into the burning fiery furnace. 21 Then these men were bound in their coats, their trousers, and their head coverings,[1] and their other garments, and were cast into the middle of the burning fiery furnace. 22 Therefore because the melech's commandment was urgent, and the furnace exceedingly hot, the flame of the fire killed those men that took up Shadrach, Meshach, and Abed-Nego. 23 And these three men, Shadrach, Meshach, and Abed-Nego, fell down bound into the middle of the burning fiery furnace. 24 Then Nebuchadnetzar the melech was astonished, and rose up in haste, and spoke, and said to his counselors, Did not we cast three men bound into the middle of the fire? They answered and said to the melech, True, O melech. 25 He answered and said, Look, I see four men loose, walking in the middle of the fire, and they are not hurt; and the form of the fourth is like the Bar-Elohim.[2] 26 Then Nebuchadnetzar came near to the mouth of the burning fiery furnace, and spoke, and said, Shadrach, Meshach, and Abed-Nego, you avadim of the Most High Eloah, come forth, and come here. Then Shadrach, Meshach, and Abed-Nego, came forth from the middle of the fire. 27 And the nobles, governors, and captains, and the melech's counselors, being gathered together, saw these men, upon whose bodies the fire had no power, nor was a hair of their head singed, nor were their garments changed, nor had the smell of fire come on them. 28 Then Nebuchadnetzar spoke, and said, Blessed be the Eloah of Shadrach, Meshach, and Abed-Nego, who has sent His Heavenly Messenger, and delivered His avadim that trusted in Him, and have changed the melech's word, and yielded their bodies, that they might not serve nor worship any eloah, except their own Eloah. 29 Therefore I make a new decree,[3] That every people, nation, and language, that speaks anything wrong against the Eloah of Shadrach, Meshach, and Abed-Nego, shall be cut in pieces, and their houses shall be made a dunghill: because there is no other Eloah that can deliver in this manner. 30 Then the melech promoted Shadrach, Meshach, and Abed-Nego, in the province of Bavel.

4 Nebuchadnetzar the melech, to all peoples, nations, and languages, that dwell in all the olam; Shalom be multiplied to you. 2 I thought it tov to explain the signs and wonders that the Most High Eloah has worked for me. 3 How great are His signs! And how mighty are His wonders! His malchut is an everlasting malchut, and His dominion is from generation to generation.

---

[1] Yisraelite men and women wore head coverings.

[2] A reference to Yahshua, the visible form of YHWH who has no form, and the fourth man in the fire described as the Bar Elohim (Aramaic) or Son of Elohim.
[3] After Yahweh's Son appears in the fire, a New, or Renewed Covenant decree is made. The same happened when Yahshua came to earth and was baptized by fire, in His Mission to the lost sheep of all Yisrael.

4 I Nebuchadnetzar was at rest in my bayit, and flourishing in my palace: 5 I saw a dream that made me afraid, and the thoughts upon my bed and the visions in my head troubled me. 6 Therefore I made a decree to bring in all the wise men of Bavel before me that they might make known to me the interpretation of the dream. 7 Then came in the magicians, the astrologers, the Chaldeans, and the soothsayers: and I told the dream to all of them; but they did not make known to me the interpretation of it. 8 But lastly Daniyel came in before me, whose name was Belteshazzar, according to the name of my eloah, and in whom is the Ruach of the Set-Apart Eloah: and in his presence I told him the dream, saying, 9 O Belteshazzar, master of the magicians, because I know that the Ruach of the Set-Apart Eloah is in you, and no secret is too difficult for you, tell me the visions of my dream that I have seen, and its interpretation. 10 This then was the vision of my head on my bed; I saw, and see a tree in the middle of the olam, and the height of it was great. 11 The tree grew, and was strong, and the height of it reached to the shamayim, and the sight of it to the ends of all the olam: 12 The leaves of it were beautiful, and the fruit of it abundant, and in it was food for all: the beasts of the field had shadow under it, and the fowls of the shamayim dwelt in its branches, and all flesh was fed by it. 13 I saw in the visions of my head upon my bed, and, see, a Watcher and a Set-Apart One came down from the shamayim; 14 He cried aloud, and said this, Cut down the tree, and cut off its branches, shake off its leaves, and scatter its fruit: let the beasts get away from under it, and the fowls from its branches: 15 Nevertheless leave the stump of its roots in the olam, even with a band of iron and brass, in the tender grass of the field; and let it be wet with the dew of the shamayim, and let its portion be with the beasts in the grass of the olam: 16 Let his lev be changed from a man's lev, and let a beast's lev be given to

him; and let seven times pass over him. 17 This matter is by the decree of the watchers, and the demand by the word of the set-apart ones: to the intent that the living may know that the most High rules in the malchut of men, and gives it to whomever He desires, and sets up over it the lowest of men. 18 This dream I melech Nebuchadnetzar have seen. Now you, O Belteshazzar, declare the interpretation of it, because all the wise men of my malchut are not able to make known to me the interpretation: but you are able; for the Ruach of the Set-Apart Eloah is in you. 19 Then Daniyel, whose name was Belteshazzar, was astonished for one hour, and his thoughts troubled him. The melech spoke, and said, Belteshazzar, let not the dream, or the interpretation of it, alarm you. Belteshazzar answered and said, My master, the dream is for them that hate you, and the interpretation of it is for your enemies. 20 The tree that you saw, which grew, and was strong, whose height reached to the shamayim, and the sight of it to all the olam; 21 Whose leaves were beautiful, and the fruit of it abundant, and in it was food for all; under which the beasts of the field dwelt, and upon whose branches the fowls of the shamayim had their dwelling: 22 It is you, O melech, that are grown and become strong: for your greatness is grown, and reaches to the shamayim, and your dominion to the ends of the olam. 23 And whereas the melech saw a watcher and a set-apart one coming down from the shamayim, and saying, Cut the tree down, and destroy it; yet leave the stump of the roots of it in the olam, even with a band of iron and brass, in the tender grass of the field; and let it be wet with the dew of the shamayim, and let his portion be with the beasts of the field, until seven times pass over him; 24 This is the interpretation, O melech, and this is the decree of the Most High, which is come upon my master the melech: 25 That they shall drive you from men, and your dwelling shall be with the beasts of the field, and they shall make you to eat grass as oxen, and they shall wet you with the dew of the shamayim, and seven times shall pass over you, until you know that the Most High rules in the malchut of men, and He gives it to whomever He desires. 26 And whereas they commanded to leave the stump of the tree roots; your malchut will remain yours, after you come to know that the shamayim do rule. 27 Wherefore, O melech, let my counsel be acceptable to you, and break off your sins by tzedakah, and your iniquities by showing rachamim to the poor; if it may lead to a lengthening of your shalom and prosperity. 28 All this came upon the melech Nebuchadnetzar. 29 At the end of twelve months he walked in the palace of the malchut of Bavel. 30 The melech spoke, and said, Is not this great Bavel, that I have built for the bayit of the malchut by the might of my power, and for the honor of my greatness? 31 While the word was in the melech's mouth, there fell a voice from shamayim, saying, O melech Nebuchadnetzar, to you it is spoken; The malchut has departed from you. 32 And they shall drive you from men, and your dwelling shall be with the beasts of the field: they shall make you to eat grass as oxen, and seven times shall pass over you, until you know that the Most High rules in the malchut of men, and He gives it to whomever He desires. 33 The same hour was the thing fulfilled upon Nebuchadnetzar: and he was driven from men, and did eat grass as oxen, and his body was wet with the dew of the shamayim, until his hairs were grown like eagles' feathers, and his nails like birds' claws. 34 And at the end of those days I Nebuchadnetzar lifted up my eyes to the shamayim, and my binah returned to me, and I blessed the Most High, and I praised and honored Him that lives le-olam-va-ed, whose dominion is an everlasting dominion, and His malchut is from generation to generation: 35 And all the inhabitants of the

olam are counted as nothing: and He does according to His will in the armies of the shamayim, and among the inhabitants of the olam: and no one can stop His hand, or say to Him, What are You doing? 36 At the same time my reasoning returned to me; and for the tiferet of my malchut, my honor and brightness returned to me; and my counselors and my masters sought me again; and I was established in my malchut, and excellent greatness was even added to me. 37 Now I Nebuchadnetzar hallel and extol and honor the Melech of the shamayim, because all His works are all emet, and all His halachot are tzadik: and those that walk in pride He is able to humble.

5 Belshatstar the melech made a great feast to a thousand of his masters, and drank wine before the thousands. [1] 2 Belshatstar, while he tasted the wine, commanded to bring in the golden and silver vessels that his abba Nebuchadnetzar[2] had taken out of the temple that was in Yahrushalayim; so that the melech, and his nobles, his wives, and his concubines, might drink from them. 3 Then they brought the golden vessels that were taken out of the Beit HaMikdash of the Bayit of Eloah which was at Yahrushalayim; and the melech, and his nobles, his wives, and his concubines, drank from them. 4 They drank wine, and praised the eloah of gold, and of silver, of brass, of iron, of wood, and of stone. 5 In the same hour came forth fingers of a Man's hand, and wrote over against the menorah upon the plaster of the wall of the melech's palace: and the melech saw the part of the hand that wrote. 6 Then the melech's face was changed, and his thoughts troubled him, so that the joints of his hips were loosed, and his knees knocked one against another. 7 The melech cried aloud to bring in the astrologers, the

---

[1] It is important to understand that the Scroll of Daniel is not written in a correct historical chronological order of events.
[2] Not a physical father, but one who occupied the same throne.

Chaldeans, and the soothsayers. And the melech spoke, and said to the wise men of Bavel, Whoever shall read this writing, and explain to me the interpretation of it, shall be clothed with scarlet, and have a chain of gold[1] around his neck, and shall be the third ruler in the malchut. 8 Then came in all the melech's wise men: but they could not read the writing, nor make known to the melech its interpretation. 9 Then was melech Belshatstar greatly troubled, and his face was changed, and his nobles were astonished. 10 Now the queen, by reason of the words of the melech and his masters, came into the banquet bayit: and the queen spoke and said, O melech, live le-olam-va-ed: let not your thoughts trouble you, nor let your face be changed: 11 There is a man in your malchut, in whom is the ruach of the set-apart Eloah; and in the days of your abba[2] light and binah and chochmah, like the chochmah of the Eloah, was found in him; whom the melech Nebuchadnetzar your abba made master over all the magicians, astrologers, Chaldeans, and soothsayers; 12 Since an excellent Ruach, and da'at, and binah, interpreting of dreams, and solving difficult problems, and explaining things, were found in the same Daniyel, whom the melech named Belteshazzar: now let Daniyel be called, and he will explain the interpretation. 13 Then was Daniyel brought in before the melech. And the melech spoke and said to Daniyel, Are you that same Daniyel, who is from the children of the captivity of Yahudah, whom the melech my abba brought out of Yahudah? 14 I have even heard about you, that the Ruach of the Eloah is in you, and that light and binah and excellent chochmah is found in you. 15 And now the wise men, the astrologers, have been brought in before me, that they should read this writing, and make known to me

the interpretation of it: but they could not explain the interpretation of the thing: 16 And I have heard about you, that you can make interpretations, and dissolve doubts: now if you can read the writing, and make known to me the interpretation of it, you shall be clothed with scarlet, and have a chain of gold around your neck, and shall be the third ruler in the malchut.[3] 17 Then Daniyel answered and said before the melech, Let your gifts be for yourself, and give your rewards to another; yet I will read the writing to the melech, and make known to him the interpretation. 18 O you melech, the Most High Eloah gave Nebuchadnetzar your abba a malchut, and greatness, and tiferet, and honor: 19 And for the greatness that He gave him, all peoples, nations, and languages, trembled and feared before him: whom he would he killed; and whom he would he kept alive; and whom he would he set up; and whom he would he put down. 20 But when his lev was lifted up, and his mind hardened in pride, he was deposed from the melech's throne, and they4 took his tiferet from him: 21 And he was driven from the sons of men; and his lev was made like the beasts, and his dwelling was with the wild donkeys: they fed him with grass like oxen, and his body was wet with the dew of the shamayim; until he knew that the Most High Eloah ruled in the malchut of men, and that He appoints over it whomever He desires. 22 And you his son, O Belshatstar, have not humbled your lev, though you knew all this; 23 But have lifted up yourself against יהוה the Master of the shamayim; and they have brought the vessels of His Bayit before you, and you, and your masters, your wives, and your concubines, have drunk wine in them; and you have praised the mighty ones of silver, and gold, of brass, iron, wood, and stone, which see not, nor hear, and know nothing: and to the Eloah in whose hand your breath is, and who owns all your halachot, have

---

[1] Chain of gold; gold is a symbol of divinity, symbolizing that Babylon sought to bind Yisrael to their national idols and customs, by promoting Daniel, one of their own, to divinity. This practice continues today in the custom of venerating saints and such.
[2] Not biological, but father in the throne room.

[3] Tried to bribe Daniel.
[4] Reference to the Father and Son.

you not given tiferet: 24 So then the part of the hand sent from Him; with this writing: 25 And this is the writing that was written, MENE, MENE, TEKEL, UPHARSIN. 26 This is the interpretation of these words: MENE; Eloah has numbered your malchut, and finished it. 27 TEKEL; You are weighed in the balances, and are found wanting. 28 PERES; Your malchut is divided, and given to the Medes and Persians. 29 Then commanded Belshatstar, to clothe Daniyel with scarlet, and put a chain of gold around his neck, and made a proclamation concerning him, that he should be the third ruler in the malchut. 30 In that night was Belshatstar the melech of the Chaldeans killed. 31 And Dareyawesh the Mede took the malchut, being about sixty-two years old.

6 It pleased Dareyawesh to set over the malchut an hundred and twenty nobles, who would be over the whole malchut; 2 And over these three governors; of whom Daniyel was one: so that the nobles might give account to them, and the melech should suffer no loss. 3 So Daniyel excelled above the governors and nobles, because an excellent Ruach was in him; and the melech thought about setting him over the whole malchut. 4 Then the governors and nobles sought to find an occasion against Daniyel concerning the malchut; but they could find no occasion nor fault; because he was faithful, neither was there any error or fault found in him. 5 Then said these men, We shall not find any wrongdoing in Daniyel, except we find it against him concerning the Torah of his Eloah. 6 Then these governors and nobles assembled together to the melech, and said this to him, Melech Dareyawesh, live le-olam-va-ed. 7 All the governors of the malchut, the governors, and the nobles, the counselors, and the captains, have consulted together to establish a royal decree, and to make a firm decree, that whoever shall ask a petition from any eloah or man for thirty days,

except you, O melech, he shall be cast into a den of lions. 8 Now, O melech, establish the decree, and sign the edict, that it be not changed, according to the law of the Medes and Persians, which changes not. 9 So melech Dareyawesh signed the writing and the decree. 10 Now when Daniyel knew that the writing was signed, he went into his bayit; and his windows being open in his room toward Yahrushalayim, he kneeled upon his knees three times a day,[1] and made tefillah, and gave hodu before his Eloah, as he did before. 11 Then these men assembled, and found Daniyel praying and making supplication before his Eloah. 12 Then they came near, and spoke before the melech concerning the melech's decree; Did you not sign a decree, that every man that shall ask a petition of any eloah or man within thirty days, except you, O melech, shall be cast into the den of lions? The melech answered and said, The thing is emet, according to the law of the Medes and Persians, which changes not. 13 Then they answered and said before the melech, That Daniyel, which is of the children of the captivity of Yahudah,[2] does not regard you, O melech, nor the decree that you have signed, but makes his petition three times a day. 14 Then the melech, when he heard these words, was very displeased within himself, and set his lev against Daniyel to deliver him: and he labored until the going down of the sun to deliver him. 15 Then these men assembled to the melech, and said to the melech, Know, O melech, that the law of the Medes and Persians is, That no decree which the melech establishes can be changed. 16 Then the melech gave the command, and they brought Daniyel, and cast him into a den of lions. Now the melech spoke and said to Daniyel, Your Eloah whom you serve continually, He will deliver you. 17 And a stone was brought and laid upon the mouth of the den; and the

---

[1] **Shachrit, Mincha** and **Ma'ariv** facing Jerusalem.
[2] No references to Ephraim being in Babylon and thus they could not return from Babylon with the Jews, since they were never there.

melech sealed it with his own signet, and with the signet of his nobles; that the situation concerning Daniyel may not be changed. 18 Then the melech went to his palace, and passed the night fasting: neither were instruments of music brought before him: and his sleep left him. 19 Then the melech arose very early in the shachrit, and went in a hurry to the den of lions. 20 And when he came to the den, he cried with a pained voice to Daniyel: and the melech spoke and said to Daniyel, O Daniyel, servant of the living Eloah, is your Eloah, whom you serve continually, able to deliver you from the lions? 21 Then said Daniyel to the melech, O melech, live le-olam-va-ed. 22 My Eloah has sent His Heavenly Messenger, and has shut the lions' mouths, that they have not hurt me: forasmuch as before Him my innocence was found; and also before you, O melech, have I done no harm. 23 Then was the melech exceedingly in simcha for him, and commanded that they should take Daniyel up out of the den. So Daniyel was taken up out of the den, and no manner of hurt was found upon him, because he believed in his Eloah. 24 And the melech commanded, and they brought those men who had accused Daniyel, and they cast them into the den of lions, with their children, and their wives; and the lions overpowered them, and broke all their bones in pieces before they reached the bottom of the den. 25 Then melech Dareyawesh wrote to all peoples, nations, and languages, that dwell in all the olam; Shalom be multiplied to you. 26 I make a decree, That in every dominion of my malchut men tremble and fear before the Eloah of Daniyel: for He is the living Eloah, steadfast le-olam-va-ed, and His malchut shall not be destroyed, and His dominion shall be even to the end of time. 27 He delivers and rescues, and He works signs and wonders in the shamayim and in olam, and He has delivered Daniyel from the power of the lions. 28 So Daniyel prospered in the malchut of Dareyawesh, and in the malchut of Koresh the Persian.

7 In the first year of Belshatstar melech of Bavel Daniyel had a dream and visions of his head upon his bed: then he wrote the dream, giving a summary of the matters. 2 Daniyel spoke and said, I saw in my vision by night, and, see, the four winds of the shamayim strove upon the great sea. 3 And four great beasts came up from the sea, different one from another. 4 The first was like a lion, and had eagle's wings: I saw until the wings of it were plucked, and it was lifted up from the olam, and made stand upon the feet as a man, and a man's lev was given to it.[1] 5 And see another beast, a second, like a bear, and it raised up itself on one side, and it had three ribs in the mouth of it between the teeth of it: and they said this to it, Arise, devour much flesh.[2] 6 After this I saw, and see another, like a leopard, which had upon the back of it four wings of a fowl; the beast had also four heads; and dominion was given to it. [3] 7 After this I saw in the night visions, and see a fourth beast, dreadful and terrible, and exceedingly strong; and it had great iron teeth: it devoured and broke in pieces, and trampled down the residue with its feet: and it was diverse from all the beasts that were before it; and it had ten horns. [4] 8 I considered the horns, and, see, there came up among them another little horn,[5] before whom three of the first horns were plucked up by the roots: and, see, in this horn were eyes like the eyes of man, and a mouth speaking proud things. 9 I saw until the thrones[6] were cast down, and the Ancient of Days did sit, whose garment was white as snow, and the hair of His head like the pure wool: His throne was like the fiery flame,

[1] Babylonian Empire.
[2] Medo-Persia divided among three co-regents.
[3] Greece later divided among Alexander's four generals.
[4] Rome, and the later end-time European union, or the revised Roman Empire.
[5] The end-time literal anti-Moshiach, a forgery of the real Yahshua.
[6] YHWH is being described as seated on two thrones (**karsavan** in Aramaic).

and His wheels as burning fire.[1] 10 A fiery stream issued and came forth from before Him: a thousand thousands served Him, and ten thousand times ten thousand stood before Him: the Shophet was seated, and the scrolls were opened. 11 Then because of the voice of the proud words that the horn spoke: I saw even until the beast was slain, and his body destroyed, and given to the burning flame. 12 As concerning the rest of the beasts, they had their dominion taken away: yet their lives were prolonged for a season and time. 13 I saw in the night visions, and, see, one like Bar Enosh[2] [3] came with the clouds of the shamayim, and came to the Ancient of Days,[4] and they brought Him near before Him. 14 And there was given to Him dominion, and tiferet, and a malchut that all peoples, nations, and languages, should serve Him: His dominion is an everlasting dominion, which shall not pass away, and His malchut that shall not be destroyed.[5] 15 I Daniyel was grieved in my ruach in the middle of my body, and the visions of my head troubled me. 16 I came near to one of them that stood by,[6] and asked him the emet of all this. So he told me, and made me understand the interpretation of these things. 17 These great beasts, which are four, are four melechim, which shall arise out of the olam. 18 But the kidushim of the Most High shall take the malchut, and possess the malchut, le-olam-va-ed. 19 Then I desired to know the emet of the fourth beast, which was different from all the others, exceedingly dreadful, whose teeth were of iron, and his nails of brass; who devoured, broke in pieces, and trampled the others with his feet; 20 And of the ten horns that were in his head, and of the others that came up, and before whom the three fell; even that horn that had eyes, and a mouth that spoke

very great things, whose look was more proud than his companions. 21 I saw, and the same horn makes war with the kidushim, and prevailed against them; 22 Until the Ancient of Days came, and mishpat was given to the kidushim of the Most High; and the time came that the kidushim possessed the malchut.[7] 23 This he said, The fourth beast shall be the fourth malchut upon the olam, which shall be diverse from all kingdoms, and shall devour the whole olam, and shall tread it down, and break it in pieces. 24 And the ten horns out of this malchut are ten melechim that shall arise: and another shall rise after them; and he shall be different from the first, and he shall subdue three melechim. 25 And he shall speak proud words against the Most High, and shall wear out the kidushim of the Most High, and intends to change the appointed times[8] and Torot:[9] and they shall be given into his hand until a time and times and half a time.[10] [11] 26 But his mishpat shall be established, and they shall take away his dominion, to consume and to destroy it to the end of the age. 27 And the malchut and dominion, and the greatness of the malchut under the whole shamayim, shall be given to the people of the kidushim of the Most High,[12] whose malchut is an everlasting malchut, and all dominions shall serve and obey Him. 28 This is the end of the matter. As for me, Daniyel, my thoughts much troubled me, and my face changed: but I kept the matter in my lev.

8 In the third year of the malchut of melech Belshatstar a vision appeared to me, Daniyel, like what appeared to me the

---

[1] Abba YHWH.
[2] Aramaic term for Son of Man.
[3] Yahshua.
[4] Abba YHWH.
[5] The Messianic reign of Yahshua in the millennial kingdom and beyond into eternity.
[6] Heavenly messengers.

[7] Yisrael will possess the kingdom fully restored only when Yahshua returns. Not before, by any manmade programs of two-house restoration.
[8] Feasts.
[9] Torah or Torot.
[10] Three and a half years.
[11] The end-time anti-Moshiach is a man who will resemble the world's counterfeit "Jesus," who teaches that the feasts and Torah are not eternally binding. The end-time anti-Moshiach will look and sound much like the religious makeover called "Jesus," coming in the same anti-nomian spirit, and many will readily and easily accept him, since it is the only version of the "Christ" they have ever known.
[12] Given to reborn Yisrael.

first time. 2 And I saw in a vision; and it came to pass, when I saw, that I was at Shushan in the palace, which is in the province of Eylam; and I saw in a vision, and I was by the river of Ulai. 3 Then I lifted up my eyes, and saw, and, see, there stood before the river a ram which had two horns: and the two horns were high; but one was higher than the other, and the higher came up last. 4 I saw the ram pushing westward, and northward, and southward; so that no beasts could stand before him, neither was there any that could deliver out of his hand; but he did according to his will, and became great. 5 And as I was considering, see, a male goat came from the west on the face of the whole olam, and touched not the ground: and the goat had a very noticeable horn between his eyes. 6 And he came to the ram that had two horns, which I had there seen standing before the river, and ran in to him with the fury of his power. 7 And I saw him come close to the ram, and he was moved by bitterness against him, and smote the ram, and broke his two horns: and there was no power in the ram to stand before him, but he cast him down to the ground, and trampled upon him: and there was none that could deliver the ram out of his hand. 8 Therefore the male goat grew very great: and when he was strong, the great horn was broken; and in its place came up four very noticeable ones toward the four winds of the shamayim.[1] 9 And out of one of them came forth a little horn, which grew exceedingly great, toward the south, and toward the east, and toward the pleasant land.[2] 10 And it grew great, even to the hosts of the shamayim; and it cast down some of the hosts and of the chochavim to fall to the olam, and trampled upon them.[3] 11 Yes, he magnified himself even to the Prince of the host,[4] and he took the daily sacrifice away, and His Set-Apart Place was cast down.[5] 12 And an army was given to him against the daily sacrifice by reason of transgression, and it cast down the eternal emet to the ground; and it acted, and prospered.[6] 13 Then I heard one kadosh speaking, and another kadosh said to the one who spoke, When shall this vision come to be concerning the daily sacrifice, and the abomination of desolation, to give both the Set-Apart Place and the army to be trampled under foot? 14 And he said to me, Until two thousand three hundred days; then shall the Set-Apart Place be cleansed. 15 And it came to pass, when I, Daniyel, had seen the vision, and sought for the meaning, then, see; there stood before me the appearance of a Man. 16 And I heard a Man's voice[7] between the banks of Ulai, which called, and said, Gavriel, make this man to understand the vision. 17 So he came near where I stood: and when he came, I was afraid, and fell upon my face: but he said to me, Understand, O son of man: for at the time of the end shall the vision be done. 18 Now as he was speaking with me, I was in a deep sleep on my face toward the ground: but he touched me, and set me upright. 19 And he said, Behold, I will make you know what shall be in the end times of wrath: for at the time appointed the end shall be. 20 The ram which you saw having two horns are the melechim of Media and Persia. 21 And the rough goat is the melech of Greece: and the great horn that is between his eyes is the first melech. 22 Now that being broken, where the four stood up in its place, four kingdoms shall stand up out of the nation, but not in its power. 23 And in the latter time of their malchut, when the transgressors have filled their measure with

---

[1] The ram with two horns is Medo-Persia, the male goat is Greece, the notable horn is Alexander, and the four noticeable horns were the four generals who took over Alexander the Great's empire.
[2] Anti-Moshiach.
[3] s.a.tan is the father of the anti-Moshiach, and is the same one who caused the rebellion in the heavens in ages past.
[4] Yahshua.
[5] In the literal, this refers to Antiochus Epiphanies; in the end times, it refers to Daniel's little horn, or the very anti-Moshiach himself.
[6] Behavior of anti-Moshiach after the "abomination of desolation" in the middle of the Great Tribulation.
[7] The voice of Yahshua.

sin, a melech of fierce purpose, skilled in the hidden things, shall stand up. 24 And his power shall be mighty, but not by his own power: and he shall destroy with intensity, and shall prosper, and act, and shall seek to destroy the mighty and the set-apart people.[1] 25 And through his skilled policies he shall cause deception to prosper in his hand; and he shall magnify himself in his lev, and by shalom shall destroy many:[2] he shall also stand up against the Sar of all Princes; [3] but he shall be broken and defeated easily. 26 And the vision of the ma'ariv and the shachrit that was told is emet: Therefore seal the vision; for it shall come to pass after many days. 27 And I Daniyel fainted, and was sick certain days; afterwards I rose up, and did the melech's business; and I was still amazed at the vision, but no one else understood it.[4]

9 In the first year of Dareyawesh the son of Achashverosh, of the seed of the Medes, who was made melech over the realm of the Chaldeans; 2 In the first year of his malchut I Daniyel understood by the Scripture scrolls, the number of the years, stated in the word of יהוה that came to Yirmeyahu the ha navi, to accomplish the seventy years regarding the desolation of Yahrushalayim. 3 And I set my face to יהוה Eloah, to seek by tefillah and supplication, with fasting, and sackcloth, and ashes: 4 And I made tefillah to יהוה My Eloah, and made my confession, and said, O יהוה, the great and dreadful El, keeping the covenant and rachamim to them that love Him, and to them that keep His mitzvot; 5 We have sinned, and have committed iniquity, and have done wickedly, and have rebelled, even by departing from Your precepts and from

Your tzadik mishpatim: 6 Neither have we hearkened to Your avadim the neviim, who spoke in Your Name to our melechim, our nobles, and our ahvot, and to all the people of the land. 7 O יהוה, tzedakah belongs to You, but to us shame of face, as at this day; to the men of Yahudah, and to the inhabitants of Yahrushalayim,[5] and to all Yisrael,[6] that are near,[7] and that are far off,[8] through all the countries where You have driven them,[9] because of their trespass that they have trespassed against You.[10] 8 O יהוה, to us belongs shame of face, to our melechim, to our nobles, and to our ahvot, because we have sinned against You.[11] 9 To יהוה our Eloah belong rachamim and forgiveness, though we have rebelled against Him; 10 Neither have we obeyed the voice of יהוה our Eloah, to have our halacha in His Torot, which He set before us by His avadim the neviim. 11 Yes, all Yisrael has transgressed Your Torah,[12] even by departing, that they might not obey Your voice; therefore the curse is poured upon us,[13] and the oath that is written in the Torah of Moshe the eved of Eloah, because we have sinned against Him. 12 And He has confirmed His words, which He spoke against us, and against our leaders that judged us, by bringing upon us a great evil: for under the whole shamayim has not been done such destruction as has been done upon Yahrushalayim. 13 As it is written in the Torah of Moshe, all this evil is come upon us: yet we did not make our tefillot

---

[1] Anti-Moshiach will attack both houses of Yisrael, YHWH's people, and the redeemed remnant of both houses, which is why this time is referred to as Yaakov's Trouble.
[2] Many false peace treaties, including one with Jewish Yisrael.
[3] The true Moshiach Yahshua.
[4] When one receives a true vision of the end times, with the regathering and restoration of all Yisrael, others will often not have a clue as to YHWH's true declared purpose in the earth.

[5] Judah.
[6] Ephraim.
[7] Judah in Babylon with Daniel.
[8] Ephraim in all nations "far off" from Daniel; this term "far off" is a Hebraic idiomatic expression used in Ephesians 2, when Rav Shaul speaks of making both houses into one new man called "Yisrael."
[9] Ephraim Yisrael.
[10] May all believers become like Daniel, who prayed and fasted for the repentance and return of both houses of Yisrael. Those are the kinds of tefillot that move YHWH to answer us with new kingdom revelation, and with the appearing and understanding of Moshiach.
[11] Daniel prays for the fathers of both houses, realizing there is enough sin to go around.
[12] Both houses. Therefore our correction and learning must come from redeemed Judah, not unregenerate Orthodox Judah.
[13] The curse of Torah or disobedience, as well-outlined in Galatians.

before יהוה our Eloah, that we might make teshuvah from our iniquities, and understand Your emet. 14 Therefore has יהוה watched over the evil, and brought it upon us: for יהוה our Eloah is tzadik in all His works which He does: for we did not obey His voice. 15 And now, O יהוה our Eloah, that has brought Your people forth out of the land of Mitzrayim with a mighty hand, and has gotten great fame for Your Name, as at this day; we have sinned, we have done wickedly. 16 O יהוה, according to all Your tzedakah, I ask You, let Your anger and Your fury be turned away from Your city Yahrushalayim, Your set-apart mountain: because for our sins, and for the iniquities of our ahvot, Yahrushalayim and Your people have become a reproach to all that are around us. 17 Now therefore, O our Eloah, hear the tefillah of Your servant, and his supplications, and cause Your face to shine upon Your Set-Apart Place that is desolate, for יהוה's sake. 18 O My Eloah, incline Your ear, and hear; open Your eyes, and see our desolations, and the city which is called by Your Name: for we do not present our supplications before You because of our tzedakah, but because of Your great rachamim. 19 O יהוה, hear; O יהוה, forgive; O יהוה, shema and do not wait, for Your own sake, O My Eloah: for Your city and Your people are called by Your Name. [1] 20 And while I was still speaking, and praying, and confessing my sin and the sin of my people Yisrael, [2] and presenting my supplication before יהוה my Eloah for the set-apart mountain of My Eloah; 21 Yes, while I was still speaking in tefillah, even the man Gavriel, whom I had seen in the vision at the beginning, came close to me and touched me, around the time of the maariv offering. 22 And he informed me, and talked with me, and said, O Daniyel, I am now come forth to give you skill and binah. 23 At the beginning of your supplications the commandment came forth,

and I am come to explain things to you; for you are greatly beloved: therefore understand the matter, and consider the vision. 24 Seventy weeks are determined upon your people[3] and upon your set-apart city, [4] to finish the transgression, and to make an end of sins, [5] and to make reconciliation for iniquity,[6] and to bring in everlasting tzedakah, [7] and to seal up the vision and prophecy, [8] and to anoint the Most Set-Apart. [9] 25 Know therefore and understand, [10] that from the going forth of the commandment [11] to restore and to rebuild Yahrushalayim until The [12] Moshiach the Sar [13] shall be sixty-nine weeks: [14] [15] the street shall be built again, and the wall, even in troubled times. [16]

---

[3] The 70 weeks of Yisrael not Daniel.
[4] Jerusalem.
[5] Bring in final and full atonement and end Yisrael's rebellion.
[6] Between Yisrael and YHWH and between Ephraim and Judah.
[7] Eternal life clothed in His purity.
[8] Seal up and fulfill all the prophecies of Moshiach ben Yosef or the dying suffering Moshiach that brings Daniel's people final atonement and an end to their iniquity.
[9] Until the kingdom comes; and Yahshua is anointed on David's throne.
[10] The ha navi Daniel gave us the time frame so that we could narrow down who Moshiach would be.
[11] The year 445 B.C.E. was the 20th year of Artaxerxes, when Nehemiah said the king let him go to rebuild Jerusalem, on the new moon of Aviv (Neh. 2).
[12] Note: Definite article "the." Not one of many Moshiachs, as Orthodox Judaism teaches today.
[13] Moshiach had to come before the Temple was again destroyed. That places Him before 70 C.E. The term "weeks" here means "sets of seven (years)" therefore 69 weeks (7+62 years) or sets of seven totals 483 years. The Moshiach had to come 483 years after this decree was issued.
[14] 69 weeks of years or 69 times 7 or 483 years.
[15] 483 years from then would appear to come out at 38 C.E. but there is another factor. Prior to 701 B.C.E., a year was exactly 360 days long, which is why a circle has 360 degrees. That year, calendars around the world all had to be recalculated due to a planetary pass-by that changed an earth-year to 365 days. In the 19th century, Sir Robert Anderson recognized that any prophetic year has 360 days. All together we are dealing with 173,880 days, or, as we count them today, or 476 years and 25 days. Taking into account lunar cycles and intercalculary years as measured prior to 360 C.E., Anderson calculated that this 483-year period ended in 32 C.E. on Aviv 10 – the day Yisrael is commanded to select a lamb, four days before Passover; the very day on which Yahshua, upon seeing Jerusalem, said, "If only you had known this, your day what could lead to your peace, but you did not recognize the time of your visitation." (Luke19: 42-44). This was the day anyone reading Daniel should have known the Moshiach was to appear.
[16] As told in Nehemiah and Ezra.

---

[1] Yah-rushalayim and Yah-huda both contain the Name Yah.
[2] Both houses.

26 And after sixty-two weeks Ye-karet Moshiach;[1] shall Moshiach be cut off,[2] [3] but not for Himself:[4] and the people of the prince that shall come[5] shall destroy the city and the Set-Apart Place;[6] and the end of it shall be with a flood,[7] and to the end of the war desolations are determined.[8] 27 And he[9] shall confirm the covenant with many for one week: and in the middle of the week he shall cause the sacrifice and the oblation to cease, and for the overspreading of abominations he shall make it desolate,[10] even until the complete end of the olam hazeh, and that which has been determined shall be poured upon the one who lays waste.[11]

10 In the third year of Koresh melech of Persia a thing was revealed to Daniyel, whose name was called Belteshazzar; and the thing was emet, but the time appointed was a long time in the future: and he understood the thing, and had binah of the vision. 2 In those days I Daniyel was mourning three full weeks. 3 I ate no desirable bread, neither came meat or wine in my mouth, neither did I anoint myself at all, until three whole weeks were fulfilled. 4 And in the twenty-fourth day of the first month, as I was by the side of the great river, which is Tigris; 5 Then I lifted up my eyes, and looked, and see a certain Man clothed in linen, whose loins were girded with fine gold of Uphaz:[12] 6 His body also was like the beryl, and His face as the appearance of lightning, and his eyes as lamps of fire, and His strong ones and His feet like polished brass, and the voice of His words like the voice of a multitude.[13] 7 And I Daniyel alone saw the vision: for the men that were with me saw not the vision; but a great fear fell upon them, so that they ran away to hide themselves. 8 Therefore I was left alone, and saw this great vision, and there remained no strength in me: for my comeliness was destroyed in me, and I retained no strength. 9 Yet I heard the voice of His words: and when I heard the voice of His words, then I was stunned lying with my face towards the ground. 10 And, see, a hand touched me, which set me upon my knees and upon the palms of my hands. 11 And He said to me, O Daniyel, a man greatly beloved, understand the words that I speak to you, and stand up: for to you I am now sent. And when He had spoken this word to me, I stood up trembling. 12 Then He said to me, Fear not, Daniyel: for from the first day that you did set your lev to understand, and to humble yourself before your Eloah, your words were heard, and I have come in response to your words. 13 But the prince of Persia withstood me twenty-one days:[14] but, see, Micha-el, one of the chief heavenly messengers, came to help me; since I had been all alone with the prince of Persia. 14 Now I have come to make you understand what shall befall your people[15] in the latter days: for the vision is yet for many days. 15 And when he had spoken such words to me, I set my face toward the ground, and I became silent. 16 And, see, one who looked like the sons of men touched my lips: then I opened my

---

[1] The Actual Hebrew.
[2] **Ye-karet Moshiach** or Moshiach will be killed or slaughtered.
[3] Of the 483 years from the command to rebuild until the Moshiach, 49 of those years were given over to full completion of the rebuilding. From that time, it was 434 years to the crucifixion or cutting off of Moshiach.
[4] For both houses of Yisrael in answer to Daniel's petition in Chapter 9 verse 7.
[5] Rome in the person of Titus in 70 CE, and the end-time revised Roman Empire in the person of anti-Moshiach. This is a dual prophecy, with both a historical and an end-time application.
[6] Temple on Mt. Moriah.
[7] The flood of exile.
[8] To the end of the Jewish revolt against Rome, only ruin will occur.
[9] Anti-Moshiach.
[10] A yet-future event; like in the time of Antiochus Epiphanies in 150 BCE, who perpetrated the same abomination. Another dual prophecy, with both a historical and an end-time application.
[11] Three applications here. First the historical Antiochus Epiphanies, second the literal end-time anti-Moshiach, and lastly the non-historical Jesus, who has been disguised as a gentile, who eats bacon and worships on Sunday, standing in the Renewed Covenant congregation, as YHWH, but is in fact a false moshiach, unlike the true Yahshua who loved, lived, and taught His Abba's Torah.
[12] Yahshua again.
[13] The same Yahshua described in Revelation chapter 1.
[14] A governing demonic principality.
[15] Yisrael.

mouth, and spoke, and said to him that stood before me, O my master, because of the vision my pains are within me, and I have retained no strength. 17 For how can the servant of this my master talk with you my master? As for me, there remains no strength left in me; neither is there breath left in me. 18 Then there came again the One with the appearance of a Man; who touched me and strengthened me, 19 And said, O man greatly beloved, fear not: shalom aleichem, be strong, yes, be strong. And when He had spoken to me, I was strengthened, and said, Let My Master speak; for you have strengthened me. 20 Then said He, Do you now know why I have come to you? And now will I return to fight with the prince of Persia: and when I am gone, see, the prince of Greece shall come.[1] 21 But I will explain to you that which is noted in the Katav of Emet: and there is none that stands with me in these things, but Micha-el your prince.[2]

11 And in the first year of Dareyawesh the Mede, I, stood to confirm and to strengthen him. 2 And now will I explain to you the emet. Behold, there shall arise three melechim in Persia; and the fourth shall be far richer than all: and by his strength through his riches he shall stir up all against the rule of Greece. 3 And a mighty melech shall stand up, that shall rule with great dominion, and do according to his will. 4 And after he shall arise, his malchut shall be broken, and shall be divided toward the four winds of the shamayim; and not to his posterity, nor according to his dominion which he ruled: for his malchut shall be plucked up, even for others beside these. 5 And the melech of the south shall be strong, and one of his nobles; and he shall gain power over him, and have dominion; his dominion shall be a great dominion. 6 And at the end of some

years they shall join themselves together; for the melech's daughter of the south shall come to the melech of the north to make an agreement: but she shall not retain the power of the arm; neither shall he stand, nor his arm: but she shall be given up, and they that brought her, and he that begat her, and he that strengthened her in these times. 7 But out of a branch of her roots shall one arise in his place, which shall come with an army, and shall enter into the stronghold of the melech of the north, and shall deal against them, and shall prevail:[3] 8 And shall also carry captive into Mitzrayim their eloah, with their nobles, and with their precious vessels of silver and of gold; and he shall continue more years than the melech of the north. 9 So the melech of the south shall come into his malchut, and shall return into his own land. 10 But his sons shall be stirred up, and shall assemble a multitude of great forces: and one shall certainly come, and overflow, and pass through: then shall he return, and be stirred up, even to his stronghold. 11 And the melech of the south shall be moved with bitterness, and shall come forth and fight with him, even with the melech of the north: and he shall set forth a great multitude; but the multitude shall be given into his hand. 12 And when he has taken away the multitude, his lev shall be lifted up; and he shall cast down many ten thousands: but he shall not be strengthened by it. 13 For the melech of the north shall return, and shall set forth a multitude greater than the former, and shall certainly come after certain years with a great army and with much riches. 14 And in those times there shall many stand up against the melech of the south: also the robbers of your people shall exalt themselves to establish the vision; but they shall fall. 15 So the melech of the north shall come, and build a seige, and take the most protected cities: and the strong ones of the

---

[1] YHWH's battles have always been with Greek paganism and the systems that resist His will.
[2] Gabriel communicates top priority messages to Yisrael, while Michael is the warring messenger fighting Yisrael's battles.

[3] These skirmishes describe the dealings and wars between the four generals who took over Alexander the Great's Empire. They have all been fulfilled up until verse 28.

south shall not withstand, neither his chosen people, neither shall there be any strength to withstand. 16 But he that comes against him shall do according to his own will, and none shall stand before him: and he shall stand in the Splendid Land, which by his hand shall be consumed. 17 He shall also set his face to enter with the strength of his whole malchut, and upright ones with him; this shall he do: and he shall give him the daughter of women, corrupting her: but she shall not stand on his side, neither be for him. 18 After this shall he turn his face to the coastlands, and shall take many: but a prince shall bring the reproach against him to an end; with the reproach removed he shall turn back upon him. 19 Then he shall turn his face toward the strongholds of his own land: but he shall stumble and fall, and not be found. 20 Then shall stand up in his place a raiser of taxes in the tiferet of the malchut: but within a few days he shall be destroyed, neither in anger, nor in battle. 21 And in his place shall stand up a vile person, to whom they shall not give the honor of the malchut: but he shall come in shalom, and obtain the malchut by flatteries. 22 And with the strong ones of a flood shall they be swept away from before him, and shall be broken; yes, also the prince of the covenant. 23 And after the covenant made with him he shall work deceitfully: for he shall come up, and shall become strong with a small people. 24 He shall enter in shalom even upon the fattest places of the province; and he shall do that which his ahvot have not done, nor his ahvot's ahvot; he shall scatter among them the prey, and spoil, and riches: yes, and he shall devise his plots against the strongholds, but only for a time. 25 And he shall stir up his power and his courage against the melech of the south with a great army; and the melech of the south shall be stirred up to battle with a very great and mighty army; but he shall not stand: for they shall devise plots against him. 26 Yes, those that ate of his food shall destroy him, and his army shall be swept

away: and many shall fall down slain. 27 And both these melechim's levim shall desire to do mischief, and they shall speak lies at the same table; but it shall not prosper: for yet the end shall be at the time appointed. 28 Then shall he return into his land with great riches; and his lev shall be against the set-apart covenant; and he shall act, and return to his own land. 29 At the appointed time he shall return, and come toward the south; but it shall not be as the former, or as the latter times. 30 For the ships of Chittim shall come against him: therefore he shall be grieved, and return, and have indignation against the set-apart covenant: and shall act; he shall even return, and consider them that forsake the set-apart covenant. 31 And strong ones shall stand on his part, and they shall pollute the Set-Apart Place of strength, and shall take away the daily sacrifice, and they shall set up the abomination that makes desolate.[1] 32 And such as do wickedly against the covenant shall he corrupt by flatteries:[2] but the people that do know their Eloah shall be strong, and do mighty acts.[3] 33 And they that understand among the people shall instruct many: yet they shall fall by the sword, and by flame, by captivity, and by spoil, many days. 34 Now when they shall fall, they shall be assisted with a little help: but many shall join them with flatteries. 35 And some of them of binah shall fall, to test them, and to purge them, and to make them white, even to the time of the end: because it is yet for a time appointed. 36 And the melech shall do according to his will; and he shall exalt himself, and magnify himself above every el, and shall speak awful things against the El of all Eloahs, and shall prosper until the indignation be accomplished:[4] for what is determined shall be done.[5] 37 Neither shall he regard the

---

[1] Dual prophecy as seen elsewhere.
[2] Anti-Moshiach.
[3] Redeemed Yisrael will arise against him.
[4] Anti-Moshiach will attempt to make and proclaim himself YHWH, until Yahweh shortens those days.
[5] Until the end of Yisrael's 70th week and the coming of Yahshua.

Eloah of his ahvot, [1] nor the desire of women,[2] nor regard any eloah: for he shall magnify himself above all. 38 But in his place, shall he honor the eloah of force:[3] and an eloah whom his ahvot knew not shall he honor with gold, and silver, and with precious stones, and pleasant things. 39 This shall he do in the best strongholds with a strange eloah, whom he shall acknowledge and increase with tiferet: and he shall cause them to rule over many, and shall divide the land for gain.[4] 40 And at the time of the end shall the melech of the south push at him: and the melech of the north shall come against him like a whirlwind, with mirkavot, and with horsemen, and with many ships; and he shall enter into the countries, and shall overflow and pass over. 41 He shall enter also into the Splendid Land, and many countries shall be overthrown: but these shall escape out of his hand, even Edom, and Moab, and the chief of the children of Ammon.[5] 42 He shall stretch forth his hand also upon the countries: and the land of Mitzrayim shall not escape. 43 But he shall have power over the treasures of gold and of silver, and over all the precious things of Mitzrayim: and the Libyans and the Ethiopians shall be found at his feet.[6] 44 But tidings out of the east and out of the north shall trouble him: therefore he shall go forth with great fury to destroy, and utterly to do away with many. 45 And he shall pitch the tents of his palace between the seas in the splendid set-apart mountain; yet he shall come to his end, and none shall be able to help him.[7]

12 And at that time shall Micha-el stand still, [8] the great prince of battle who stands over[9] the children of your people: [10] and there shall be a time of trouble,[11] such as never was since there was a nation even to that time: and at that time your people shall be delivered,[12] everyone that shall be found written in the scroll.[13] 2 And many of them that sleep in the dust of the olam shall awake, some to everlasting life, and some to shame and everlasting contempt.[14] 3 And they that be wise shall shine as the brightness of the firmament; and they that turn many to tzedakah[15] as the chochavim le-olam-va-ed. 4 But you, O Daniyel, hide the words, and seal the scroll, even to the time of the end: many shall run to and fro, and da'at shall be increased.[16] 5 Then I Daniyel looked, and, see, there stood two others, the one on this side of the bank of the river, and the other on that side of the bank of the river. 6 And one said to the Man clothed in linen, who was upon the mayim of the river,[17] How long shall it be to the end of these wonders? 7 And I heard the Man clothed in linen, who was upon the mayim of the river, when He held up His right hand and His left hand to the shamayim, and swore by Him that lives le-olam-va-ed [18] that it shall be for a time, times, and a half a time; [19] and when He shall have accomplished the scattering and the restored power of the set-apart people,

---

[1] A Yisraelite from the tribe of Dan (Genesis 49:17-18), who denies the Torah and the faith.
[2] Possibly a homosexual Yisraelite from the tribe of Dan.
[3] s.a.tan.
[4] Confederacy of ten kings.
[5] Due to their allegiance to anti-Moshiach and hatred for both houses.
[6] All the Muslim countries are in league with anti-Moshiach, having the same designs on the land of Yisrael.
[7] He will plant his world headquarters on Mt. Moriah in Jerusalem; but will be destroyed with his allies.

[8] **Ya Amod** means to "stand still" or "freeze," as in a "do nothing" position, which allows the Great Tribulation to commence and occur, and it is Michael that is removed and taken out of the way in Second Thessalonians 2:6-7, the great restrainer of evil against Yisrael.
[9] Or looks out for.
[10] Yisrael.
[11] Great Tribulation.
[12] From Yaakov's Trouble, upon both houses of Yisrael.
[13] The Scroll of the Redeemed, or Lamb's Book Of Life.
[14] Resurrection of the righteous was and is the only hope of the believer, not rapture.
[15] A true Yisraelite is not ashamed of the evangelism of the true Good News, and is actively involved in this wise activity to Jew and non-Jew, despite the pressures of misguided men.
[16] All knowledge, both worldly and prophetic.
[17] The man is Yahshua, and the two banks symbolize Yahshua standing in His ministry to both houses of Yisrael, and using those like Daniel gifted as latter-day neviim with the end-time knowledge of the kingdom restored to Yisrael.
[18] Further evidence that this was Yahshua is found in Revelation chapter 10, which describes a very similar scene.
[19] Three and a half years.

all these things shall be finished.[1] 8 And I heard, but I understood not: then I said, O My Master, what shall be the end of these matters? 9 And he said, Go your way, Daniyel: for the words are closed up and sealed until the time of the end.[2] 10 Many shall be purified, and made white, through Tribulation; but the wicked shall do wickedly: and none of the wicked shall understand;[3] but the wise shall understand. 11 And from the time that the daily sacrifice shall be taken away, and the abomination that makes desolate set up, there shall be a thousand two hundred ninety days.[4] 12 Blessed is he that waits,[5] and comes to the one thousand three hundred thirty-fifth day.[6] 13 But go you your way until the end of the age: for you shall rest, and stand up[7] in your portion at the end of the age.

---

[1] Yisrael's 70th week concludes Yisrael's history for this present age.
[2] Until Moshiach declares them.
[3] Evil's price is often paid in stupidity, not just judgment.

[4] Three and a half years.
[5] An extra 45 days.
[6] 45 extra days after the end of the 1,290 days, is to provide Yisrael with thirty days to mourn their blindness towards Yahshua and His mission (Zechariah 12:10-14), as was the 30 days for Moshe's death in Deut. 34, and 15 extra days to cleanse the temple of the defilement of the abomination of desolation and prepare it for the **atid lavoh** millennial temple.
[7] Rise again to your feet in the resurrection.

הושיע

Hoshea - Hosea
To Our Forefathers Yisrael

1 The word of **יהוה** that came to Hoshea,[1] the son of Be-Eri, in the days of Uzziyah, Yotham, Ahaz, and Hizqiyahu, melechim of Yahudah, and in the days of Yerovoam the son of Yoash, melech of Yisrael. 2 The beginning of the words of **יהוה** through Hoshea. And **יהוה** said to Hoshea, *Go, take a wife of whoring and children of whoring: for the land has committed great whorings, departing from* **יהוה**. 3 So he went and took Gomer the daughter of Divlayim;[2] who conceived, and bore him a son. 4 And **יהוה** said to him, *Call his name Yizre-El;*[3][4] *for yet a little while, and I will avenge the dom of Yizre-El upon the Beit Yehu, and will cause the malchut to cease from Beit Yisrael.*[5] 5 *And it shall come to pass at that day, that I will break the bow of Yisrael, in the valley of Yizre-El.*[6] 6 *And she conceived again, and bore a daughter. And Elohim said to him, Call her name Lo-Ruchamah:*[7] *for I will no more have rachamim upon Beit Yisrael; but I will utterly take them away.*[8] 7 *But I will have rachamim upon Beit Yahudah,*[9] *and will save them by* **יהוה** *their Elohim, and will not save them by bow, nor by sword, nor by battle, by horses, nor by horsemen.* 8 Now when she had weaned Lo-Ruchamah, she conceived, and bore a son. 9 *Then said Elohim, Call his name Lo-Ami: for you are not My people, and I will not be*

Your Elohim.[10] 10 *Yet the full number of the children of Yisrael*[11] *shall be as the sand of the sea,*[12] *that cannot be measured nor numbered; and it shall come to pass, that in the place*[13] *where it was said to them, You are not My people-Lo Ami, there it shall be said to them,*[14] *You are the sons*[15] *of the living El - B'nai-Elohim.*[16][17][18] 11 *Then*[19] *shall the children of Yahudah*[20] *and the children of Yisrael*[21] *be gathered together,*[22][23] *and appoint for themselves One Head,*[24]

---

[10] Strong's Hebrew # 3818 meaning "not My people."
[11] Both houses. The sand of the sea hyperbole in Hosea 1:10 does not refer exclusively to Jewish-Yisrael. It does not and cannot ever refer solely to Jewish-Yisrael, who is mathematically disqualified, if counted alone. It is this remnant from both houses (as seen in verse 11) that are the re-establishing of the historical, social people of Yisrael. The multitudes of these renewed Yisraelites will be those returning from the Lo-Ami and Lo-Ruchamah status or Ephraim. This truth is confirmed again in Hosea 2:23 and 1 Peter 2:10.
[12] A metaphor first given to the patriarchs that promises literally billions of biological offspring.
[13] Ultimately the land of Yisrael, where the restored will abide.
[14] The same people who were not a people and with no mercy will become children of YHWH in numbers that humans cannot count or fathom. Notice the term "them," meaning that the latter-day children of YHWH are not a new people, but the same revived people.
[15] And daughters.
[16] Sonship is restored through YHWH's Son Yahshua as seen in verse 11.
[17] Peter, the great apostle, states that the royal Renewed Covenant believer-priesthood of First Peter 2:9-10 are the same children of Elohim spoken about by Hosea 1:10. He even goes so far as calling this recreated priesthood "a set-apart" nation.
[18] Those who identify themselves as born-again children of Elohim in the latter days, are declaring themselves to be the actual literal offspring of the former Lo-Ami and Lo-Ruchamah.
[19] In the days when YHWH reveals His children, through regeneration by the Ruach, or the born-again experience that leads to the birth of His children.
[20] Yahudah.
[21] Ephraim.
[22] Hosea 1:11 is truly a great glorious time as both scattered and assimilated houses are seen returning from all the nations, or the gentiles. The Children of Elohim come out of the earth of rejection from both houses, back to YHWH and the land of Yisrael. The re-gathering is simultaneous, and cannot have one house being restored, while the other remains in exile. They were exiled separately, but will return together at the same time.
[23] See Ezekiel 37:16-28.
[24] The re-gathering is a result of favor to those who choose One Head. We know that this One Head is the same for both houses, as Ezekiel 37:24 states that both houses will be reunited under the power and authority of the One King and Shepherd. (Note that one house does not appoint Torah alone, while the other appoints Moshiach. Both houses must

---

[1] A prophet to the northern kingdom, with a few words of restoration and hope for the south as well.
[2] Gomer is symbolic of Yisrael as the adulterous bride to YHWH.
[3] Meaning the gathering and collection of the previously scattered seed. Literally "El will scatter, El will sow."
[4] Strong's Hebrew #3157; TWOT # 582.
[5] All innocent dom will be avenged when YHWH brings an end to the nation of the north, as a viable independent nation, but not the scattered individuals from that nation.
[6] Ephraim will be broken and destroyed by being placed in a metaphoric valley of scattering.
[7] Strong's Hebrew # 3819 meaning "No Mercy."
[8] A people known as "no mercy" taken away in exile.
[9] Yahudah spared during Hosea's chayim and in small part throughout the generations.

and they shall come up out of the land:[1] for great shall be the Day of Yizre-El.[2]

2 *Say to your brothers, Oy My People-Ami! And to your sisters, Oy compassioned one-ruchamah![3] 2 Plead with your mother, plead: for she is not My wife, neither am I her husband: let her therefore put away her whoring out of her sight, and her adulteries from between her breasts; 3 Lest I strip her naked, and make her as in the day that she was born, and make her as a wilderness, and set her like a dry land, and kill her with thirst. 4 And I will not have rachamim upon her children; for they are the children of whoring. 5 For their mother has played the whore: she that conceived them has done shamefully: for she said, I will run after my lovers, that give me my bread and my mayim, my wool and my linen, my oil and my drink. 6 Therefore, behold, I will hedge up your way with thorns, and make a wall,[4] that she shall not find her paths. 7 And she shall follow after her lovers, but she shall not overtake them; and she shall seek them, but shall not find them: then shall she say, I will go and make teshuvah to my first husband; for then was it better with me than now.[5] 8 For she did*

not know that I gave her corn, and wine, and oil, and multiplied her silver and gold, which she prepared for Baal.[6] *9 Therefore will I turn from her, and take away My corn in its season, and My wine in the season, and will recover My wool and My linen given to cover her for her nakedness. [7] 10 And now will I uncover her shame in the sight of her lovers, and none shall deliver her out of My hand. 11 I will also cause all her gilah to cease, her chagim, her Rosh Chodashim, and her Shabbats, and all her moadim.[8] 12 And I will destroy her vines and her fig trees, of which she has said, These are my rewards that my lovers have given me: and I will make them a forest, and the beasts of the field shall eat them. 13 And I will visit upon her the days of the Baalim, in which she burned incense to them, and she decked herself with her earrings and her jewels, and she went after her lovers, and forgot Me, says* יהוה. *14 Therefore, behold, I will lead her, and bring her into the wilderness, and speak comfortably[9] to her.[10] 15 And I will give her vineyards from there, and the valley of Achor[11] for a door of tikvah: and she shall sing there, as in the days of her youth, and as in the day when she came up out of the land of Mitzrayim.[12] 16 And it shall be at that day, says* יהוה, *that you shall call Me Ishi-My Husband; and shall no more call*

appoint the same Head, and the same Torah, for the sake of reunification and unity.) So the Moshiach, the King and Great Shepherd, is the only means by which both houses can be eternally secure in the final re-gathering. Any attempt to reunite the two exiled houses through political, immigration, military or culturally mandated programs by man, is doomed to failure. Man does not cause the restoration and neither can he stop it. All who do so outside of YHWH's Moshiach alone are fools in a fishbowl of vanity. Individuals from both houses appoint the King/Shepherd or the Greater David/Moshiach, and then both become one in His hand as the Day of Jezreel is brought to pass.
[1] The earth of exile and unemunah.
[2] The day of the ingathering of the scattered and sown seed of both houses of Yisrael.
[3] After the two houses come together by appointing One Head, Judah will see Ephraim not merely as my brother in the Nazarene Yisraelite faith, but as part of Yisrael as he cries out to Ephraim "Ami." Also to Judah's believing sisters in Ephraim, Judah will cry out O Ruchamah, or "You who have now received mercy." As the two houses come together through Yahshua, we must change our view and thinking about our spiritual brothers, seeing them as fellow parts of the physical people of Yisrael, as we see them as part of "Ami," My people, and Your people.
[4] The wall of separation between YHWH and Ephraim, and between Ephraim and Judah.
[5] Ephraim will one day realize how tov things were with YHWH, since these dumb idols only bring death and rejection.

[6] Or the "lord."
[7] Why should YHWH give Ephraim all these blessings and have him turn them over to s.a.tan?
[8] The removal of the true appointed times of YHWH from Ephraim were part of their punishment. Conversely the reinstitution of the feasts to Ephraim is a sign of their return. Today, by and large Ephraim continues in pagan feasts and holidays, until they acknowledge Yahshua and His Torah and make a full teshuvah.
[9] The tov speaking, or comfortable speaking, is the proclamation of the besorat of the kingdom restored.
[10] Like the first exodus, Ephraim will be lured back to YHWH while in the wilderness of the nations.
[11] Achor is trouble or the "valley of trouble." In the Valley of Achor, Ephraim will have the door of hope open to return. In the Great Tribulation, Ephraim will fully respond to YHWH's call of comfort.
[12] She will rejoice in the Great Tribulation, as YHWH opens the door for Ephraim's repentance and return. Ephraim will sing the song of Moshe for Torah once again, as they did when they left Egypt under the Redeemer's hand.

Me Baali-my lord.¹ 17 For I will take away the names of Baalim out of her mouth, and they shall no more be remembered by their names.² 18 And in that day will I make a covenant for them with the beasts of the field and with the fowls of the shamayim, and with the creeping things of the ground: and I will break the bow and the sword and the battle out of the earth, and will make them to lie down safely.³ 19 And I will take you to Me le-olam-va-ed; I will take you back to Me in right standing, and in mishpat, and in loving rachamim, and in chesed.⁴ 20 I will take you to Me as a bride in faithfulness: and you shall know יהוה. 21 And it shall come to pass in that day, I will shema, says יהוה, I will shema in the shamayim, and they shall shema in the earth; 22 And the earth shall answer with the corn, and the wine, and the oil; and they shall answer Yizre-El.⁵ 23 And I will sow her to Me in the earth;⁶ and I will have Ruchama upon her that had not obtained Ruchama; and I will say to them who were not My people, Lo-Ami, You are My people-Ami; and they shall say, You are My Elohim.⁷ ⁸

3 *Then said יהוה to me, Go again, love a woman beloved of her friend, yet an adulteress, according to the ahava of יהוה toward the children of Yisrael, who look to other elohim, and love their raisin cakes.⁹ 2 So I bought her to me for fifteen pieces of* silver, for one and a half homers of barley: *3 And I said to her, You shall abide with me many days; you shall not play the whore, and you shall not be given to another man: so will I also be towards you. 4 For the children of Yisrael shall abide many days without a melech,¹⁰ and without a prince, and without a sacrifice,¹¹ and without an altar,¹² and without a shoulder garment,¹³ and burning of incense:¹⁴ 5 Afterwards shall the children of Yisrael make teshuvah,¹⁵ and seek יהוה their Elohim, and David their Melech;¹⁶ and shall come with fear to יהוה and His abundant tov in the latter-days.¹⁷*

4 *Shema the word of יהוה, you children of Yisrael: for יהוה has a controversy with the inhabitants of the land, because there is no emet, no rachamim, nor knowledge of Elohim in the land. 2 By swearing, and lying, and killing, and stealing, and committing adultery, they break out, and domshed follows domshed. 3 Therefore shall the land mourn, and every one that dwells in it shall languish, with the beasts of the field, and with the fowls of the shamayim; yes, the fishes of the sea also shall be taken away. 4 Yet let no man strive, nor reprove another: for your people are engaged in controversy like those striving with a kohen. 5 Therefore shall you fall in the day, and the navi also shall fall with you in the night, and I will destroy your mother. 6 My people are destroyed for lack of knowledge: because you have rejected knowledge, I will also reject you, that you shall not be a kohen to*

---

¹ When Ephraim returns, they will give up the generic term "lord" that they used to refer to all their other lovers and use "YHWH My Husband," to distinguish Him and to display His greatness, in their return.
² YHWH will remove all the false names and substitutes for YHWH from Ephraim, through sound teaching.
³ A Renewed Covenant will be made with Ephraim allowing them to be in safety in their return. See Jeremiah 23:6.
⁴ YHWH's promise to Ephraim to take them back will be unconditional and eternal, imparting unmerited favor and a Renewed Covenant.
⁵ The wonderful and awesome Day of Jezre-El will be known and understood by all the earth and all who dwell in it, as YHWH returns the captivity of the exiles of Tzion. The earth responds in affirmation with abundant production.
⁶ Sown in order to be re-gathered.
⁷ The curses reversed by YHWH through Yahshua.
⁸ This confession is happening even in our day.
⁹ Through Hosea's personal experiences, YHWH shows how Ephraim Yisrael has acted with Him, and how He feels as a broken hearted husband.

¹⁰ A reference to both houses without Moshiach.
¹¹ A reference to the destruction of the temple.
¹² A reference to no means of atonement.
¹³ A reference to the Kohen HaGadol losing his function in the earthly tabernacle.
¹⁴ A reference to lack of temple worship.
¹⁵ After many days of abiding without a King, and the means of dom atonement, due to unemunah.
¹⁶ In the ends times, a remnant of all Yisrael will return to YHWH by seeking both Him and David their resurrected King. This of course is a reference to the "Greater David," or the Son of David, the Moshiach Yahshua.
¹⁷ This return from unfaithfulness will occur in the latter days after seeking YHWH through the King Yahshua. Just as Hosea's wife was taken back, so YHWH has taken back His bride.

Me: seeing you have forgotten the Torah of Your Elohim, [1] I will also forget your children. [2] 7 As they were increased, [3] so they sinned against Me: therefore will I change their tiferet into shame. 8 They feed upon the sin of My people, and they set their lev on their iniquity. 9 And it shall be, like people, like kohen: and I will punish them both for their halachot, and reward all their doings. 10 For they shall eat, and not have enough: they shall commit whorings, and shall not increase: because they have stopped obeying יהוה. 11 Whoring and new wine take away their lev. 12 My people ask counsel of their own imaginations, and their blind man's staff leads them: for the ruach of whoring has caused them to go astray, and they have gone whoring away from their Elohim. 13 They sacrifice upon the tops of the mountains, and burn incense upon the hills, under oaks and poplars and elms, because their shadow is tov: therefore your daughters shall commit whorings, and your spouses shall commit adultery. 14 I will not punish your daughters when they commit whorings or your spouses when they commit adultery: for the men themselves are separated with whores, and they sacrifice with cult prostitutes: a people that does not understand shall fall. 15 Though you, Yisrael, [4] played the whore, yet let not Yahudah become guilty also; and go not to Gilgal, neither go up to Beth-Aven, nor swear by an oath saying, as יהוה lives. 16 For Yisrael is stubborn like a backslidden heifer: now would יהוה feed them like a lamb in a large place. 17 Ephraim is joined to idols: leave him alone. [5] 18 Their drink is sour: they have committed whorings continually: her rulers widely love shame. 19 The wind has bound her up in her wings, [6] and they shall yet be ashamed because of their sacrifices.

5 Shema to this, O kohanim; and pay attention, Beit Yisrael; and give ear, O house of the melech; for mishpat is coming to you, because you have been a trap to Mitzpah, and a net spread over Tavor. 2 And the rebel hunters have deepened their slaughter, so I will chastise them all. 3 I know Ephraim, and Yisrael is not hidden from Me: [7] but now, O Ephraim, you commit whorings, and Yisrael is defiled. [8] 4 They will not change their doings to make teshuvah to their Elohim: for the ruach of whoring is in the midst of them, and they have not known יהוה. [9] 5 And the pride of Yisrael does testify to Elohim's face: therefore shall Yisrael and Ephraim fall in their iniquity: Yahudah also shall fall with them. [10] 6 They shall go with their flocks and with their herds to seek יהוה; but they shall not find Him; He has withdrawn Himself from them. [11] 7 They have acted treacherously against יהוה: for they have begotten strange children: [12] now shall a Rosh Chodesh [13] devour them with their portions. 8 Blow the shofar in Giveah, and the shofar in Ramah: cry aloud at Beth-Aven, behind you, O Benyamin. 9 Ephraim shall be desolate in the day of rebuke: among the tribes of Yisrael have I made known that which shall surely be. [14] 10 The leaders of Yahudah were like those that

---

[1] Ephraim Yisrael was destroyed for rejecting Torah knowledge, as were the Levites. Religions like to quote this verse out of context by using it without the Torah reference.
[2] Ephraim's children forgot their heritage and ancestry, because their fathers forgot YHWH and His Torah.
[3] Physical multiplicity.
[4] Ephraim.
[5] Ephraim cannot be rejoined to YHWH, as long as he is joined to idols.

[6] YHWH will carry Ephraim to all four corners of the earth, as a judgment for his sacrifices and idolatrous worship.
[7] The ten tribes may be lost to the world, but YHWH knows their location, and He alone is finding them and gathering them. YHWH reiterates this truth.
[8] Ephraim Yisrael is not hidden, but sure is defiled.
[9] Even today many Ephraimites claim to know YHWH and believe in Moshiach, but little do they know that a whoring spirit is still among them, as many refuse to return to Torah living.
[10] Both houses will fall to the sword of exile.
[11] Until the coming of Moshiach.
[12] "Strange" is a synonym for gentiles. Yisrael has brought forth strange gentile children before YHWH.
[13] Fifth month or Av. The historical month of destruction for both houses.
[14] Ephraim or the ten tribes would cease as recognizable Yisraelites, as they would assimilate with the gentiles, and thus be indistinguishable from them. YHWH announced this to all Yisrael ahead of the actual events.

remove a border:[1] therefore I will pour out My wrath upon them like mayim. [2] 11 Ephraim is oppressed and broken in My mishpat, because he willingly walked after Tsaw.[3] [4] 12 Therefore will I be to Ephraim as a moth,[5] and to Beit Yahudah as rottenness. 13 When Ephraim saw his sickness, and Yahudah saw his wound, then Ephraim went to the Ashurite, and sent to Melech Yarev: yet he could not heal you, nor cure you of your wound.[6] 14 For I will be to Ephraim as a lion, and as a young lion to Beit Yahudah:[7] I, even I,[8] will tear and go away; I will take away,[9] and none shall rescue them. 15 I will go and return to My place,[10] until they acknowledge their offence, and seek My face: in their affliction[11] they will seek Me early.[12] [13]

6 Come, and let us[14] make teshuvah to יהוה: for He has torn, and He will heal us; He has smitten, and He will bind us up.[15] 2 After two days[16] will He revive us:[17] on the third day He will raise us up,[18] and we shall live in His sight.[19] 3 Then shall we know, how to follow forward to know יהוה:[20] His going forth is prepared as the morning;[21] and He shall come to us as the rain, as the malchut rain and the teaching rain upon the earth.[22] *4 O Ephraim, what shall I do to you? O Yahudah, what shall I do to you? For your attempts to be tov before Me is as a morning cloud, and as the early dew it goes away. 5 Therefore have I cut at them by the niviim; I have slain them by the words of My mouth: and My mishpatim are as the light that goes forth.[23] 6 For I desired rachamim, and not sacrifice; and the knowledge of Elohim more than burnt offerings.[24] [25] 7 But like Adam they have transgressed the covenant:[26] there have they dealt treacherously against Me. 8 Gilead is a city of theirs that works iniquity, and is polluted with dom. 9 And as groups of robbers wait for a man, so the company of kohanim murder on the way to Shechem:[27] for they commit wickedness. 10 I have seen a horrible thing in Beit Yisrael; there are the*

---

[1] They also perverted the Torah, the landmark they were to guard and establish before both houses.
[2] Water again is symbolic of exile.
[3] A popular idol.
[4] Ephraim's idolatry often has been blatant.
[5] Difficult to be apprehended.
[6] Ephraim often ran to neighbors around Yisrael for help, as opposed to YHWH.
[7] Both houses will be ripped apart from the land and from YHWH.
[8] Duality of Powers in the heavens. In Hebrew **Ani; Ani.**
[9] To the judgment of global exile.
[10] Yahshua will return to His place in the heavens, after His resurrection.
[11] Yaakov's Trouble or the Great Tribulation.
[12] They will seek relief and protection early on at the outset of the Great Tribulation.
[13] Since they did not want Yahshua to rescue them, He returned to His place in the heavens, waiting to reappear for them at the time designated by the Abba, after they acknowledge their sin in His rejection and crucifixion.
[14] Both houses.
[15] YHWH has corrected, but YHWH will heal when both houses make teshuvah.
[16] Two thousand years according to 2nd Peter 3:8 and Psalm 90:4, which establishes the principle of a day equaling one thousand years in YHWH's sight. We see that again in the creation account. After two days or 2,000 years, both houses will be quickened or revived to righteousness and restoration and healing in our nation. We see this coming to pass with the two-house healing and revival that began to accelerate in 1996, exactly 2,000 years after Yahshua's birth in 4 BCE. For more information, see
http://store.yourarmstoisrael.org/Qstore/Qstore.cgi?CMD=011&PROD=000067 and
http://store.yourarmstoisrael.org/Qstore/Qstore.cgi?CMD=011&PROD=000078.
[17] The "us" is both houses of Yisrael.
[18] The third day is the start of the 3rd set of 1,000 years after the offering of the kingdom by Moshiach Yahshua. Beginning around 1996 CE; the third day has begun. Both houses are in a season of revival that leads to the resurrected life of the millennial kingdom. Two-house revival is the means to the end, with the end being the life of the kingdom restored in the millennial reign of Yahshua, which commences 7,000 years after Adam and Eve, or 3,000 years - 3 days - after Yahshua's first coming.
[19] When both houses have been given eternal life through Yahshua, we will live in His sight and in His presence, or literally "before YHWH," as opposed to being broken and wounded, living out in the nations, away from His face and His presence.
[20] The whole purpose of the Renewed Covenant is to have both houses renewed by sins forgiven, so we can move on to "know YHWH" from the least of us, to the greatest among us according to Jeremiah 31:31-34.
[21] His coming or going forth to meet with us, is from the dawn or "morning of creation," prepared for us from the foundation of the world.
[22] In Hebrew **malchosh** and **yoreh** are the root forms of "king" and "teach." King-rain or latter-rain is ruling power and teaching rain, and "early rain" is the learning experienced under the Set-Apart Spirit, prior to the kingdom on earth.
[23] YHWH has done everything He can to bring both houses to their senses.
[24] His desire is for both houses to know Him personally not merely be religious.
[25] Yahshua quotes this in Matthew 9:13, further substantiating that He is speaking to Yisraelites who are familiar with the Hosea 6:6 passage.
[26] Torah.
[27] Home to many priests.

whorings of Ephraim, Yisrael is defiled.[1] 11 Also, O Yahudah, He has appointed a harvest for you,[2] when I return the captivity of My people.[3][4]

7 When I would have healed Yisrael, then the iniquity of Ephraim was revealed, and the wickedness of Shomron: for they commit falsehood; and the thief comes in, and the band of robbers raids outside. 2 And they consider not in their levim that I remember all their wickedness: now their own doings have surrounded them; they are before My face. 3 They make the melech have gilah with their wickedness, and the rulers with their lies. 4 They are all adulterers, as an oven heated by the baker, who ceases stirring the fire after he has kneaded the dough, until it be leavened. 5 In the day of our melech the rulers have made him sick with bottles of wine; he stretched out his hand to the scorners. 6 For they have made ready their lev like an oven, while they lie in wait: their baker sleeps all night; in the morning it burns as a flaming fire. 7 They are all hot as an oven,[5] and have devoured their judges; all their melechim are fallen:[6] there is none among them that calls to Me. 8 Ephraim, has mixed himself among the peoples;[7] Ephraim is a half-baked cake not turned.[8] 9 Strangers have devoured his strength,[9] and he knows it not:[10] yes, gray hairs are upon him, yet he knows it not.[11] 10 And the Excellence of Yisrael testifies to His face: but they do not make teshuvah to יהוה their Elohim, nor do they seek Him for all this. 11 Ephraim also is like a silly dove[12] without lev:[13] they call to Mitzrayim, they go to Ashshur.[14] 12 When they go, I will spread My net upon them; I will bring them down as the fowls of the shamayim; I will chastise them, as their assembly[15] has heard. 13 Woe to them! For they have strayed far from Me: destruction to them! Because they have transgressed against Me: though I have redeemed them, yet they have spoken lies against and about Me.[16] 14 And they have not cried to Me with their lev, when they wailed upon their beds: they assemble themselves for corn and wine, and they rebel against Me.[17] 15 Though I have disciplined and strengthened their arms, yet do they imagine mischief against Me. 16 They make teshuvah, but not to El-Elyon: they are like a deceitful bow: their rulers

---

[1] Ephraim is defiled by unclean spiritual and sexual practices.
[2] Personal salvation through rebirth.
[3] Judah will also experience a revival when Ephraim does, pointing out that the restoration and revival of all Yisrael is a simultaneous event, with no one left out. Judah will experience a harvest of souls, when Ephraim experiences a return to the Torah covenant and the land of Yisrael.
[4] We see the duality of echad in this verse.
[5] Hot with desire for sin.
[6] In the history of Ephraim in the north, not one single king is ever recorded as being pleasing to YHWH, as opposed to Judah, that at least had a few whom YHWH commended.
[7] Ephraim's desire was to mix and hang out with the nations and their elohim, so YHWH gave them their desire, by scattering them among the gentiles, so as to become one with the pagans.
[8] A cake or loaf that has not turned back to YHWH, and is not ready to be nourishment for anyone, since Ephraim is like a loaf or cake that looks tov, but on closer examination is not ready, or fully prepared to give and provide life in YHWH. The expression can also mean that Ephraim tends to be a bit "looney" at times.

[9] "Strangers," is an idiomatic expression for pagans, who have sapped his strength and his love to serve YHWH.
[10] Simply because he doesn't know who he is. How can he know what has occurred to him in his walk with YHWH?
[11] He is from Yisrael of old, but does not realize it. And he will have been around a long time (gray hair) before he finally sees that his problem was his penchant for paganism.
[12] Ironically but not surprisingly, the dove is the symbol for returning Ephraim, or most in Christianity. That dove is a sign from YHWH to most Christians, as to who they really are, since Ephraim is likened unto a gullible and gentle dove, that believes anything, and worships anything.
[13] Without a heart to stand firm for truth in their own national heritage as Yisrael. That is why poor "dove-like" silly Ephraim runs to traditional synagogues, where they often find acceptance as "perceived" equal heirs in Yisrael. That is why Ephraimites with an inferiority problem often caused by vexation from Judah, run to undergo long and difficult conversion procedures to become "Jewish" and thus fit into Yisrael. Often they are so weak in heart, that they willingly deny Yahshua to be accepted back into Judah, or to make aliyah-immigration back to the land of Yisrael. All of those chasing the acceptance of men through a conversion process overseen by a Bet Din (traditional Jewish rabbinical court) are in fact worshipping at the throne of Judaism, acting silly and displaying an unstable feeble heart.
[14] Ephraim has never met a false idol or doctrine from which he did not seek help, or by which he was not allured.
[15] Here Ephraim, though a nation of people, is called a kehela or ekklesia or a "congregation," as Ephraim is also called throughout the Renewed Covenant, as part of restored Yisrael.
[16] Today, though redeemed by Moshiach's dom, Ephraim sadly still misrepresents the true Torah-keeping Yahshua, and His true mission to restore Yisrael.
[17] They assemble as one for the provision; but not for the Provider.

shall fall by the sword for the rage of their tongue:1 this shall be their derision in the land of Mitzrayim.

8 Set the shofar to your mouth. The enemy shall come as an eagle against the Bayit of יהוה, [2] because they have transgressed My covenant,[3] and trespassed against My Torah. 2 Yisrael shall cry to Me, My Elohim, we know You. 3 Yisrael has cast off what is tov:[4] the enemy shall pursue him. 4 They have set up melechim, but not by Me: they have made rulers, and I knew it not: from their silver and their gold have they made for themselves idols, that they may be cut off. [5] 5 Your golden calf, O Shomron, has been cast off; My anger is kindled against them: how long will it be before they can be declared innocent? [6] 6 For from Yisrael was it made: the workman made it; therefore it cannot be Elohim: but the calf of Shomron shall be broken in pieces. 7 For they have sown the wind, and they shall reap the whirlwind:[7] the stalk has no bud, it shall yield no grain:[8] if it does yield, the strangers shall swallow it up.[9] 8 Yisrael is swallowed up: now shall they be among all the nations as a vessel in which is no pleasure. [10] 9 For they have gone up to Ashshur, a wild donkey alone by himself: [11] Ephraim has hired lovers. [12] 10 Yes, though they have sold themselves to idols among the nations, now will I gather them, [13] [14] after they have suffered a little from the burden of a melech[15] and rulers.[16] 11 Because Ephraim has made many altars for sin, the altars shall be counted to him for sin. 12 I have written to him the great and numerous things from My Torah,[17] but they were counted as a strange thing. [18] 13 They sacrifice flesh for the sacrifices of My offerings, and eat it; but יהוה accepts them not; now He will remember their iniquity, and visit their sins: they shall return to Mitzrayim.[19] 14 For Yisrael has forgotten his Maker, and built palaces; and Yahudah has multiplied fenced cities: but I will send a fire upon its cities, and it shall devour its palaces.[20]

9 Do not gilah, O Yisrael, with simcha, as other peoples: for you have gone whoring from Your Elohim, you have loved a reward upon every threshing floor.[21] 2 The floor and the winepress shall not feed them, and the new wine shall fail in her. 3 They shall not dwell in יהוה's land; but Ephraim shall return to Mitzrayim, and they shall eat unclean things22 in Ashshur. 4 They shall not offer wine offerings to יהוה, neither shall they be pleasing to Him: their sacrifices shall be to them as the bread of mourners; all that eat it shall be polluted: for their bread for their being shall not come into the Bayit of יהוה. 5 What will you do in the solemn day, and in the day of the moadim of

---

[1] For falsely accusing YHWH.
[2] Assyria and Egypt.
[3] Broke and forsook Torah.
[4] Torah.
[5] Cut off from the nation due to paganism.
[6] Not until Moshiach Yahshua comes.
[7] The whirlwinds will carry them to the earth's nations, where they will remain pagan and barren.
[8] Ephraim is dead in sin and cannot produce life.
[9] Strangers, or non-Yisraelites, will swallow up the ten tribes by assimilation end exile.
[10] The House of Yisrael or Ephraim was swallowed up, having settled among the gentiles, as the Hebrew word "swallowed" is **bala**, which literally means "to do away with something or someone by swallowing." It can also mean, "to devour," or "to swallow down." This is the same word used for human consumption of food. Typically, a piece of meat when swallowed disappears and becomes part of the flesh after digestion. So it was with the House of Yisrael-Ephraim. They became Lo-Ami (not My people) among the nations, and their identity was lost. How then can that identity be found in Judah, when it was YHWH's intention for them to lose their identity among the gentiles, the very status that they had whored after? Amos 9:9 makes it clear that The House of Yisrael-Ephraim will be sifted among the nations or gentiles, as grain is shaken in a sieve, yet they would not be lost to YHWH.

[11] Ephraim is wild and independent from YHWH and from the rest of the nation of Yisrael.
[12] Ephraim traded in YHWH for pleasure and whoring.
[13] The promise of restoration and regathering.
[14] After 2 days or 2,000 years after Yahshua.
[15] King of Assyria.
[16] Pagan leaders in pagan lands.
[17] In both the giving of Torah and the specific instructions of Torah.
[18] To this day Ephraim and most of Christianity see Torah as a strange and outdated "Jewish document," rather than their own constitution and marriage certificate to YHWH.
[19] Through Assyria, as many who were taken to Assyria were resettled in Egypt, an Assyrian colony at that time.
[20] YHWH will bring proper and measured judgments against both houses.
[21] Ephraim's penchant for paganism.
[22] Non-kosher.

יהוה ? 6 *For, see, they shall soon go because of destruction: Mitzrayim shall gather them up, Memphis shall bury them: the pleasant places for their silver, nettles shall possess them: thorns shall be in their tents. 7 The days of punishment have come, the days of repayment have come; Yisrael shall know it: the navi is a fool, the spiritual man is mad, for the multitude of your iniquity, the hatred is great.* [1] *8 The watchman of Ephraim was with My Elohim:* [2] *but the navi is a trap and a stumbling block in all his halachot, hatred is in the Beit his Elohim.* [3] *9 They have deeply corrupted themselves, as in the days of Giveah: therefore He will remember their iniquity; He will punish them for their sins. 10 I found Yisrael like grapes in the wilderness; I saw your ahvot as the bikkurim in the fig tree in the beginning: but they went to Baal-peor, and separated themselves for his shame; and their abominations were a result of their misplaced ahava.* [4] *11 As for Ephraim, their tiferet shall fly away like a bird,* [5] *they are cut off from the birth,* [6] *and from the womb, and from the conception.* [7] *12 Though they bring up their children, yet will I make them childless,* [8] *that there shall not be a man left: woe to them when I depart from them!* [9] *13 Ephraim, as I saw like Tzor, planted in a pleasant place:* [10] *but Ephraim shall bring forth his children to the murderer.* [11] *14 Give them, O* **יהוה** *: what will You give? Give them a miscarrying womb and dry breasts.* [12] *15 All their wickedness is in Gilgal: for there I hated them: for the wickedness of their doings I will drive them out of My Bayit, I will love them no more: all their rulers are rebels. 16 Ephraim is smitten, their root is dried up, they shall bear no fruit: yes, though they bring forth, yet will I kill even the beloved fruit of their womb. 17 My Elohim will cast them away, because they did not shema to Him: and they shall be wanderers among the nations.* [13]

10 *Yisrael is a degenerate* [14] *empty vine, he brings forth fruit to himself:* [15] *according to the multitude of his fruit* [16] *he has increased the altars; the better his land the better the pagan pillars they built. 2 Their lev is divided;* [17] *now shall they be found guilty: He shall break down their altars; He shall destroy their pillars. 3 For now they shall say, We have no melech, because we feared not* **יהוה** *; what then should a melech do for us? 4 They have spoken words, swearing falsely in making a covenant:* [18] *therefore mishpat will spring up as poisoned weeds in the furrows of the field. 5 The inhabitants of Shomron shall fear because of the calf of Beth-Aven: for the people there shall mourn over it, and also the kohanim* [19] *there who rejoiced over it, for its former tiferet, because it has departed from it. 6 It shall be also carried to Ashshur for a present to Melech Yarev: Ephraim shall receive shame, and Yisrael shall be ashamed of his own counsel. 7 As*

---

[1] Ephraim's confusion is in great part spiritual. They seek the ruach but the wrong kinds of spiritual experiences. Their hatred for Torah is often inexplicable.
[2] Only the watchmen who look out for the welfare of Ephraim really are doing YHWH's will. All the false prophets who do not love Ephraim's welfare and return to the Commonwealth of Yisrael and its ways, are dangerous traps for Ephraim.
[3] Because of the seducing spirits and the false neviim.
[4] Ephraim became as abominable as the idols they worshipped.
[5] Again the bird or dove has become the symbol for Ephraim in exile, though many think of it as a religious symbol.
[6] No Yisraelite identity.
[7] A full and final end to the kingdom of the north as it was. They would fly way into exile where no Yisraelites would be conceived, born or raised up for YHWH. They would become gentile parents of strange non-Yisraelite children.
[8] They will bring up their own children but not for YHWH, and He will not allow them to raise up seed for Him.
[9] When they became Lo-Ami in 721 BCE.
[10] Some of the places of exile were quite beautiful and pleasant in the natural.
[11] They will be presented to s.a.tan the murderer and father of all idolatry and rebellion against YHWH.
[12] Barrenness and inability to raise up seed in Yisrael for YHWH.
[13] They will become the "fullness of the nations" by virtue of their wanderings.
[14] Literally meaning "foreign vine."
[15] Not for Yisrael, but for paganism.
[16] Rotten fruit.
[17] Mixed worship. Some truth mixed with error, which is the most dangerous kind.
[18] Ephraim often made covenants with their neighbors, seeking help.
[19] Of Ephraim.

for Shomron, her melech is cut off as the foam upon the mayim. 8 The high places of Aven, the sin of Yisrael, shall be destroyed: the thorn and the thistle shall come up on their altars; and they shall say to the mountains, Cover us; and to the hills, Fall on us. 9 O Yisrael, you have sinned from the days of Giveah: there they stood: the battle in Giveah against the children of iniquity shall not overtake them. 10 It is in My desire that I should correct them; and peoples shall be gathered against them,[1] when I bind them for their double guilt.[2] 11 And Ephraim is as a heifer that is being taught, and loves to tread out the corn; but I passed over upon her fair neck:[3] I will make Ephraim to ride;[4] Yahudah shall plow,[5] and Yaakov shall break his clods.[6][7] 12 Sow to yourselves in tzedakah, reap in rachamim; break up your fallow ground: for it is time to seek יהוה, until He comes and rains tzedakah upon you.[8] 13 You have plowed wickedness, you have reaped iniquity; you have eaten the fruit of lies: because you did trust in your own halacha, in the multitudes of your mighty men.[9] 14 Therefore shall a tumult arise among your people, and all your fortresses shall be spoiled, as Shalman spoiled Beth-Arvel in the day of battle: the mother was dashed in pieces falling upon her children. 15 So shall Beth-El do to you because of your great wickedness: in a morning shall the melech of Yisrael utterly be cut off.

11 When Yisrael was a child, then I loved Him, and called My Son out of Mitzrayim.[10] 2 They called them, so they went out from them: they sacrificed to Baalim, and burned incense to carved images. 3 I taught Ephraim to walk,[11] taking them by their arms; but they knew not that I healed them.[12] 4 I drew them with cords of a man, with cords of ahava:[13] and I was to them as they that take off the yoke on their jaws,[14] and I bent down to feed them.[15] 5 Let him then return into the land of Mitzrayim, and the Ashurite shall be his melech, because they refused to make teshuvah to Me. 6 And the sword shall abide on his cities, and shall consume his branches[16], and devour them, because of their own counsels. 7 And My people are committed to backslide from Me: though they have called to El-Elyon, none would exalt Him.[17] 8 How shall I give you up, Ephraim? How can I just hand you over, Yisrael?[18] How shall I make you as Admah? How shall I set you as Zevoim? My lev churns within Me, My rachamim are being lit for you. 9 I will not execute the fierceness of My full anger, I will not return to destroy Ephraim:[19] for I am El, and not man; the Set-Apart One in the midst of you: and I will not come to you in full enmity. 10 They shall have their halacha in יהוה: He shall roar like a Lion:[20] when He shall roar,[21] then the children of Yisrael[22] shall tremble

---

[1] To remove them from Shomron and the north.
[2] In rejecting Torah and the true Moshiach Yahshua when they accepted a false gentile substitute.
[3] Ephraim likes to teach and work for YHWH, but often without instruction, experience, Torah and understanding, and thus YHWH passes them by.
[4] For training.
[5] The more mature one will plow.
[6] A combination of the teamwork of both houses can free Yisrael into breaking the clusters of dirt that surround their reality to YHWH.
[7] When Ephraim bears the yoke and Judah plows as one, Yaakov is produced from the twain.
[8] Both houses need to sow righteousness and work as one seeking YHWH, until the Master comes with the kingdom or latter rain.
[9] Ephraim trusted in his large numbers, instead of imparted righteousness.

---

[10] In the literal, this is a reference to all 12 tribes; and in the **remez** or hint application, this is a reference to Moshiach's coming out of Egypt.
[11] When YHWH joined him to Jacob and the other tribes.
[12] YHWH healed them of Egyptian idolatry. Yet they returned to it often, not realizing they were supposed to be healed.
[13] YHWH never stopped drawing Ephraim with love.
[14] YHWH's desire has been and remains to remove the yoke of bondage and exile from Ephraim.
[15] Fully seen in His Son coming as the Manna of the heavens.
[16] Eparim Yisrael is called the wild olive branches in Romans 11.
[17] There is a big difference between calling to Him and exalting Him.
[18] Listen to the Abba's lev for Ephraim, and pledge to never give Him up, even in the face of impending judgment.
[19] Here is YHWH's pledge to punish, but never to destroy Ephraim. This pledge guarantees that the ten tribes are not lost, since the Almighty would consider that destruction.
[20] In the person of Moshiach Yahshua, the Lion of Judah.
[21] Be manifest.
[22] Of Ephraim Yisrael.

from the west.[1] 11 *They shall tremble as a bird out of Mitzrayim, and as a dove[2] out of the land of Ashshur: and I will place them back in their own houses,*[3] *says* יהוה. 12 *Ephraim surrounds Me with lies, and Beit Yisrael with deceit:[4] but Yahudah still rules with El, and is faithful to the Set-Apart-One.*[5]

12 Ephraim feeds on wind, and follows after the east wind:[6] he daily increases lies and desolation; and they make a covenant with the Ashurim, and their oil is sent to Mitzrayim. 2 יהוה has also a controversy with Yahudah,[7] and will punish Yaakov[8] according to their halachot; according to their doings will he repay them. 3 He took his brother by the heel in the womb, and by his strength he had power with Elohim: 4 Yes, he had power over the Heavenly Malach, and prevailed: he wept, and made tefillot to Him: he found Him in Beth-El, and there He spoke with us; 5 Even יהוה Elohim of hosts; יהוה is His memorial.[9] 6 Therefore make teshuvah to Your Elohim: keep rachamim and mishpat and wait on Your Elohim continually. 7 Yet Yaakov is a merchant, the balances of deceit are in his hand: he loves to oppress. 8 And Ephraim said, Yes, I have become rich, I have found substance: in all my labors they shall find no iniquity in me that is sin. 9 And I who am יהוה Your Elohim from the land of Mitzrayim will yet make you to dwell in sukkot, as in the days of the solemn moed of Sukkot.[10] 10 I have also spoken to you by the niviim, and I have multiplied visions, and used parables, by the service of the niviim. 11 Is there iniquity in Gilead? Surely, yet they are vanity: they sacrifice bullocks in Gilgal; yes, their altars are as many as the heaps in the furrows of the fields. 12 And Yaakov fled into the country of Aram, and Yisrael served for a wife, and for a wife he kept sheep. 13 And by a navi יהוה brought Yisrael out of Mitzrayim, and by a navi was he guarded.[11] 14 Ephraim provoked Him to anger most bitterly: therefore shall He leave his dom-guilt upon him, and his reproach shall His Master repay to him.[12]

13 When Ephraim spoke there was trembling, he was exalted in Yisrael; but when he offended in Baal worship, he lost his power. 2 And now they sin more and more, and have made molten images of their silver, and idols according to their own understanding, all of it the work of the craftsmen: they say to them, Let the men that sacrifice kiss the calves. 3 Therefore they shall be as the morning cloud and as the early dew that passes away, as the chaff that is driven with the whirlwind out of the threshing floor, and as the smoke out of the chimney. 4 Yet I am יהוה Your Elohim from the land of Mitzrayim, and you shall know no other elohim but Me: for there is no Savior besides Me. 5 I knew you in the wilderness, in the land of great drought. 6 When they were they filled; and satisfied, and their lev was exalted; they forgot Me. 7 Therefore I will be to them as a lion: as a leopard by the path will I observe them:[13] 8 I will meet them as a bear that is missing her young,

---

[1] Though scattered throughout the globe, many are in the west and will return spiritually and physically from the west when Moshiach roars.
[2] Modern symbol of Ephraim.
[3] Latter-day **aliyah** to the land of Yisrael.
[4] Ephraim became totally depraved.
[5] Judah never was fully cut off; and had a remnant of authority in their dealings with Elohim.
[6] This has a dual application. First, it shows that much of Ephraim has headed west of Jerusalem, even though they initially headed east and northeast. Second; the Hebraic idiomatic expression "east wind" indicates judgment or the "wind of judgment."
[7] A controversy; but not a full divorce.
[8] Both houses.
[9] YHWH's Name is Yaakov's memorial. Most of Yaakov dishonors YHWH by not honoring that memorial Name.
[10] YHWH will humble Ephraim by having them live in shanty booths year-round, as they were supposed to do voluntarily at the appointed time during Sukkoth, but did not.
[11] Only someone with a true prophetic lev and ruach can guard over Ephraim's silliness and Yahudah's hatred without a cause towards Moshiach.
[12] Until the coming of the Moshiach, when all dom and other guilt would be removed forever to those individuals responding to the Tov News.
[13] By hiding His face.

and will rip open the casing of their lev, and there will I devour them like a lion: the wild beast shall tear them. 9 O Yisrael,[1] you have destroyed yourself; but in Me is your help. 10 Where is your melech now to save you in all your cities? And your rulers of whom you said, Give me a melech and rulers?[2] 11 I gave you a melech in My anger, and took him away in My wrath.[3] 12 The iniquity of Ephraim is bound up; his sin is hidden. 13 The pains of a travailing woman shall come upon him: he is an unwise son;[4] for he will not stay long in the place of childbirths.[5] 14 I will ransom them[6] from the power of the grave; I will redeem them from death: O death, where is your victory; O grave, where is your sting? Your consolation is hidden from My eyes.[7][8] 15 Though he be fruitful among his brothers,[9] an east wind shall come,[10] the wind of יהוה shall come up from the wilderness, and his spring shall become dry, and his fountain shall be dried up: it shall spoil the treasure of all his pleasant vessels. 16 Shomron shall become desolate; for she has rebelled against her Elohim: they shall fall by the sword: their infants shall be dashed in pieces, and their women with child shall be ripped up.

14 O Yisrael, make teshuvah to יהוה Your Elohim; for you have fallen by your iniquity. 2 Take with you words of Torah, and make teshuvah to יהוה: and say to him, Take away all our iniquity, and receive us graciously: so will we render the bulls, the fruit of our lips. 3 Ashur shall not save us; we will not ride upon horses: neither will we say any more to the work of our own hands, You are our elohim: for in You the fatherless finds rachamim.[11] 4 I will heal their backsliding, I will love them instantly: for My anger will be turned away from him. 5 I will be as the dew to Yisrael:[12] he shall grow as the lily, and cast forth his roots as Lebanon. 6 His branches shall spread,[13] and his beauty shall be as the olive tree,[14] and his smell as Levanon. 7 They that dwell under his shadow shall return;[15] they shall revive[16] as the corn, and grow as the vine: their fragrance shall be as the wine of Levanon. 8 Ephraim shall say, What have I to do any more with idols? I have heard Him, and observed Him: I am like a green fig tree.[17] From Me is your fruit found.[18] 9 Who is wise, and he shall understand these things? Discerning, and he shall know them?[19] For the halachot of יהוה are right, and the just shall have their halacha in these things:[20] but the transgressors shall fall in it.[21]

---

[1] Ephraim.
[2] In order to be like all the pagan nations.
[3] King Shaul.
[4] One of the two sons of Luke 15.
[5] In the land and culture of Yisrael that births Yisraelites.
[6] Ephraim Yisrael.
[7] This verse is quoted to the Corinthian Yisraelites in First Corinthians 15:54; proving once again that the congregation at Corinth was Yisraelite in nature and Ephraimite in character.
[8] The grave cannot and will not be consoled in its loss of power over mankind.
[9] Through physical multiplicity.
[10] Wind of judgment that carried Ephraim west.

[11] Recommended words of full repentance.
[12] Ephraim.
[13] In the **atid lavoh** or millennial kingdom.
[14] Restored and fully healed as seen in Romans 11. This olive tree reference is further proof that Ephraim and Judah, and their companions, make up the olive tree – not Jew and gentile being grafted into a "Jewish tree," as is so commonly taught.
[15] Under the shadow of the olive tree.
[16] Revival of all Yisrael.
[17] Like a Yisraelite again. The fig tree is one of the original symbols of Yisrael.
[18] May YHWH hasten that day.
[19] The spiritually mature and discerning understand that this is what YHWH is doing in our time and generation. He is making Ephraim a green fig tree again, and reviving the olive tree and its emanating shade.
[20] Restoration truths.
[21] The spiritually proud and untaught will fall over Ephraim's latter-day confession, repentance, and return, seeing it as a perceived threat to their exclusivity as Yisrael, rather than as an end-time promise.

יואל

Yoel - Joel
To Our Forefathers Yisrael

1 The word of **יהוה** that came to Yoel the son of Pethu-El. 2 *Hear this, you old men, and give ear, all you inhabitants of eretz Yisrael. Has this been in your days, or even in the days of your ahvot?[1] 3 Tell your children of it, and let your children tell their children, and their children another generation.* 4 *That which the gnawing locust has left the swarming locust has eaten; and that which the swarming locust has left the crawling locust has eaten; and that which the crawling locust has left the consuming locust has eaten.[2] 5 Awake, you drunkards, and weep; and wail, all you drinkers of wine, because of the new wine; for it is cut off from your mouth.* 6 *For a nation is come up upon My land, strong, and without number, whose teeth are the teeth of a lion, and he has the fangs of a great lion.[3]* 7 *He has laid My vine waste, and barked My fig tree: he has made it clean bare, and cast it away; the branches of it are made white.* 8 *Wail like a virgin girded with sackcloth for the husband of her youth.* 9 *The grain offering and the drink offering is cut off from the Bayit of* **יהוה***; the kohanim,* **יהוה** *'s avadim, mourn.* 10 *The field is ravaged, the land mourns; for the corn is ruined: the new wine is dried up, the oil fails.* 11 *Be you ashamed, O you farmers; wail, O you vinedressers, for the wheat and for the barley; because the harvest of the field is perished.* 12 *The vine is dried up, and the fig tree droops; the pomegranate tree, the palm tree also, and the apple tree, even all the trees of the field, are withered: because simcha is withered*

away from the sons of men. 13 *Gird yourselves, and lament, you kohanim: wail, you avadim of the altar: come, lie all night in sackcloth, you avadim of My Elohim: for the grain offering and the drink offering is withheld from the Bayit of Your Elohim.* 14 *Set-Apart a fast, call a miqra kodesh, gather the zachanim and all the inhabitants of eretz Yisrael into the Bayit of* **יהוה** *Your Elohim, and cry out to* **יהוה***,* 15 *Oy! For the day! For the Yom* **יהוה** *is at hand, and as destruction from the Almighty shall it come.* 16 *Is not the grain cut off before our eyes, yes, simcha and gilah from the Bayit of our Elohim?* 17 *The seed is rotten under their clods, the storehouses are laid desolate, and the barns are broken down; for the corn is withered.* 18 *How do the beasts groan! The herds of cattle are perplexed, because they have no pasture; yes, the flocks of sheep also perish.* 19 *O* **יהוה***, to You will I cry: for the fire has devoured the pastures of the wilderness, and the flame has burned all the trees of the field.* 20 *The beasts of the field cry also to You: for the rivers of mayim have dried up, and the fire has devoured the pastures of the wilderness.[4]*

2 *Blow the shofar in Tzion, and sound an alarm in My set-apart mountain: let all the inhabitants of eretz Yisrael tremble: for the Yom* **יהוה** *comes, for it is near at hand;* 2 *A day of darkness and of gloominess, a day of clouds and of thick darkness, as the morning dew upon the mountains: a great people and a strong; there has not been anything ever the like, neither shall there be any more after it, even to the years of many generations.[5]* 3 *A*

---

[1] The time for both houses to be purified through the time of Yakkov's Trouble or the Great Tribulation, a time unlike any other in world or Yisraelite history.
[2] Nothing shall escape YHWH's judgment one way or another. However, the saved will be protected either through martyrdom, or YHWH's providence for both houses, during this time of Great Distress.
[3] Babylon in a historical context, and the final Babylon led by anti-Moshiach in a latter-day context.

[4] As Kepha tells us the world that now stands is reserved for fiery judgment.
[5] Revised latter-day Roman Babylonian empire led by anti-Moshiach.

- 643 -

fire devours in front of them; and behind them a flame burns: eretz Yisrael is as the Gan Eden before them, and behind them a desolate wilderness; yes, and nothing shall escape from them. 4 The appearance of them is as the appearance of horses; and as horsemen, so shall they run. 5 Like the noise of mirkavot on the tops of mountains shall they leap, like the noise of a flame of fire that devours stubble, as a strong people set in battle array. 6 Before their face the people shall be pained: all faces shall gather blackness. 7 They shall run like mighty men; they shall climb the wall like men of war; and they shall march every one in his ways, and they shall not break their ranks: 8 Neither shall one press another; they shall walk every one in his path: and when they fall from the weight of their armor, they shall not be trampled. 9 They shall rush on the city; they shall run on the wall, they shall climb up on the houses; they shall enter in at the windows like a thief. 10 The earth shall quake before them; the shamayim shall tremble: the sun and the moon shall be darkened, and the chochavim shall withdraw their shining: 11 And יהוה shall utter His voice before His army: for His camp is very great: for He is strong that executes His word: for the Yom יהוה is great and very terrible; and who can survive it? 12 Therefore also now, says יהוה teshuvah to Me with all your lev, and with fasting, and with weeping, and with mourning: 13 And tear your lev, and not your garments, and turn to יהוה Your Elohim: for He is full of unmerited favor and rachamim, slow to anger, and of great chesed, and relents from evil.[1] 14 Who knows if mankind will turn and relent, and leave a bracha behind him; even a grain offering and a drink offering to יהוה Your Elohim? 15 Blow the shofar in Tzion, set-apart a fast, and call a miqra kodesh: 16 Gather the people, set-apart the congregation, assemble the zachanim,

gather the children, and those that nurse: let the bridegroom go forth from his chamber, and the bride out of her closet. 17 Let the kohanim, the avadim of יהוה, weep between the porch and the altar, and let them say, Spare Your people, O יהוה, and give not Your heritage to reproach, that the heathen should rule over them: why should they say among the peoples, Where is their Elohim? 18 Then will יהוה be jealous for eretz Yisrael, and pity His people. 19 Yes, יהוה will answer and say to His people, Behold, I will send you corn, and wine, and oil, and you shall be satisfied by them: and I will no more make you a reproach among the heathen: 20 But I will remove far off from you the northern army, and will drive him into a land barren and desolate, with his face toward the east sea, and his rear toward the western sea, and his stink shall come up, and his smell shall come up because he has boasted to do great things. 21 Fear not, O eretz Yisrael; be in gilah and simcha: for יהוה will do great things. 22 Be not afraid, you beasts of the field: for the pastures of the wilderness do spring forth, for the tree bears her fruit, the fig tree and the vine do yield their strength. 23 Gilah then, you children of Tzion, and simcha in יהוה Your Elohim: for He has given you the former rain moderately, and He will cause the rain to come down for you, the former rain, and the latter rain as before.[2] 24 And the floors shall be full of wheat, and the pots shall overflow with wine and oil. 25 And I will restore to you[3] the years that the swarming locust has eaten, the crawling locust, and the consuming locust, and the gnawing locust, My great army that I sent among you. 26 And you shall eat in plenty, and be satisfied, and praise the Name of יהוה Your Elohim that has dealt wondrously with you: and My people shall never be put to shame. 27 And you shall know that I am in the midst of

---

[1] Even during the Great Tribulation, along with the historical exile to Babylon, when repentance takes place, YHWH reveals His kindness.

[2] Two-house renewal during the Great Tribulation.

[3] The ultimate aim and goal of the Great Tribulation is to punish the heathen and restore a remnant of both houses of Yisrael, who have been so terribly plundered.

Yisrael, and that I am יהוה Your Elohim, and there is no one else: and My people shall never be put to shame. 28 And it shall come to pass afterward, that I will pour out My Ruach upon all flesh; and your sons and your daughters shall prophesy, your old men shall dream dreams, your young men shall see visions:[1] 29 And also upon the avadim and upon the female avadim in those days will I pour out My Ruach.[2] 30 And I will show wonders in the shamayim and on the earth, dom, and fire, and pillars of smoke. 31 The sun shall be turned into darkness, and the moon into dom, before the great and the terrible Yom[3] יהוה comes.[4] 32 And it shall come to pass, that whoever shall call on the Name of יהוה shall be delivered:[5] for in Har Tzion and in Yahrushalayim shall be deliverance and escape,[6] as יהוה has said, and among the remnant survivors whom יהוה shall call.[7]

3 For, behold, in those days, and in that time, when I shall turn back the captivity of Yahudah and Yahrushalayim,[8] 2 I will also gather all nations, and will bring them down into the Valley of Yehoshaphat, and will plead and enter mishpat with them there for My people and for My heritage Yisrael, whom they have scattered among the nations, and parted My land.[9] 3 And they have cast lots for My people; and have given a boy for a harlot, and sold a girl for wine, that they might drink.[10] 4 Yes, and what have you to do with Me, O Tsor, and Tzidon, and all the coasts of Philistia? Will you render Me a pay back? And if you pay Me back, swiftly and speedily will I not return your pay back upon your own head;[11] 5 Because you have taken My silver and My gold, and have carried them into your temples: 6 The children also of Yahudah and the children of Yahrushalayim have you sold to the Greeks, that you might remove them far from their border.[12] 7 Behold, I will raise them out of the place where you have sold them,[13] and will return upon your own head what you have done: 8 And I will sell your sons and your daughters into the hand of the children of Yahudah, and they shall sell them to the Sabeans, to a people far off: for יהוה has spoken it. 9 Proclaim this among the nations; Prepare war, wake up the mighty men, let all the men of war draw near; let them come up: 10 Beat your ploughshares into swords, and your pruning-hooks into spears: let the weak say, I am strong. 11 Assemble yourselves, and come, all you heathen, and gather yourselves together all around יהוה, who will break your might there. Cause your mighty ones to come down with you. 12 Let the heathen be awakened, and come up to the Valley of Yehoshaphat: for there will I sit to shophet all the heathen on every side. 13 Put in the sickle, for the harvest is ripe:[14] come, get down; for the winepress is full, the pots overflow; for their wickedness is

---

[1] By definition, Joel's children's are Yisraelites, which means in the temple in Acts 2, those gathered were Yisraelites, and Yisrael was renewed according to promise, rather than a separate non-Yisraelite entity being birthed. See notes on Acts 2:16.

[2] This was fulfilled in Acts 2 as step one to the renewal of both houses. Step 2 is at the end of the Great Tribulation, when Yisrael is fully restored, and fully endowed and empowered by the Ruach, with all Yisrael following Yahshua and His Torah.

[3] The same day is great for Yisrael and dreadful for the perishing heathen.

[4] Cosmic disturbance immediately precedes Yahshua's coming, followed by His return and a final outpouring of His Ruach.

[5] In order to be delivered in and from the Great Tribulation, it will be an absolute necessity to know and call on YHWH's true Name, even as the Name of YHWH protects the 144,000 themselves during the Great Tribulation.

[6] The escape is to Mt Zion and Yahrushalayim, not to heaven. Those chosen and surviving the Great Tribulation along with all the resurrected believers will find survival and escape in the land of Yisrael, not in a made-up escape in a rapture bus.

[7] Called, chosen remnant Yisrael from both houses.

[8] Restoration.

[9] After Yisrael is regathered, all nations will be judged for how they treated exiled Yisrael, and for pursuing a non-Scriptural partitioning of the land of Yisrael. This yet-to-be-formed valley, will be created when Yahshua touches down on the Mt of Olives, as the mountain separates, creating the Valley of Yehoshaphat.

[10] YHWH will punish the sell-off of Yisrael and her land.

[11] Will the Edomites be able to stop YHWH from regathering Yisrael back to the land? Any attempts to stop it will be paid back to them.

[12] Further evidence, that among the Greeks today are both Yahudites and Ephraimites.

[13] Which is why YHWH sent Rav Shaul to heavily Greek areas such as Athens and Corinth.

[14] The harvest of Yisrael.

great. 14 *Multitudes, multitudes in the Valley of Decision: for Yom* יהוה *is near in the Valley of Decision.[1]* 15 *The sun and the moon shall be darkened, and the chochavim shall withdraw their shining.* 16 יהוה *also shall roar out of Tzion, and utter His voice from Yahrushalayim; and the shamayim and the earth shall shake: but* יהוה *will be the tikvah of His people, and the strength of b'nai Yisrael.[2]* 17 *So shall you know that I am* יהוה *Your Elohim dwelling in Tzion, My set-apart mountain: then shall Yahrushalayim be set-apart, and there shall no gerim pass through her any more.[3]* 18 *And it shall come to pass in that day, that the mountains shall drop down new wine; and the hills shall flow with milk; and all the rivers of Yahudah shall flow with mayim; and a fountain shall come forth from the Bayit of* יהוה *and shall bring mayim to the Valley of Shittim.[4]* 19 *Mitzrayim shall be a desolation, and Edom shall be a desolate wilderness, for the violence against the children of Yahudah, because they have shed innocent dom in their land.[5]* 20 *But Yahudah shall dwell le-olam-va-ed, and Yahrushalayim from generation to generation.[6]* 21 *For I will avenge their dom that I have not avenged and will not absolve the offenders: for* יהוה *dwells in Tzion.[7]*

---

[1] All nations will be judged for their treatment of Yisrael.
[2] The return is great for Yisrael and dreadful for the earth's multitudes, in the Valley of Decision. It is possible that this is the earthly perspective of the "Great White Throne Judgment" of Revelation 20 and that this is what John saw in a vision.
[3] Only born-again Yisraelites will rule and reign with Moshiach in the **atid lavoh** or millennium.

[4] **Atid lavoh** or millennium.
[5] Kingdom justice.
[6] A word of joy, and warning, to all Edomites and others who seek Yahudah's destruction.
[7] When YHWH dwells in Tzion all the dom of exiled and tortured Yisrael, will at long last be avenged.

עמוס

Amoz - Amos
To Our Forefathers Yisrael

1 The words of Amoz, who was among the shepherds of Tekoa, which he saw concerning Yisrael in the days of Uzziyah melech of Yahudah, and in the days of Yerovoam the son of Yoash melech of Yisrael, two years before the earthquake. 2 And he said, יהוה will roar from Tzion, and utter His voice from Yahrushalayim; and the pastures of the shepherds shall mourn, and the top of Carmel shall wither. 3 This says יהוה; *For three transgressions of Dameshek, and for four, I will not turn away the punishment of it; because they have threshed Gilead with threshing instruments of iron: 4 But I will send a fire into the bayit of Haza-El, which shall devour the palaces of Ben-Hadad. 5 I will break also the bar of Dameshek, and cut off the inhabitant from the plain of Aven, and him that holds the scepter from the Beit Eden: and the people of Aram shall go into exile to Kir, says יהוה. 6 This says יהוה; For three transgressions of Gaza, and for four, I will not turn away the punishment of it; because they carried away captive the whole exile, to deliver them up to Edom: 7 But I will send a fire on the wall of Gaza, which shall devour the palaces of it: 8 And I will cut off the inhabitant from Ashdod, and him that holds the scepter from Ashkelon, and I will turn My hand against Ekron: and the remnant of the Philistines shall perish, says the Master יהוה. 9 This says יהוה; For three transgressions of Tzor, and for four, I will not turn away the punishment of it; because they delivered up the whole exile to Edom, and remembered not the brotherly covenant:[1] 10 But I will send a fire on the wall of Tzor that shall devour the palaces of it. 11 This says יהוה ; For three transgressions of Edom, and for four, I will not turn away the punishment of it; because*

he did pursue his brother with the sword, and did cast off all pity, and his anger did tear perpetually, and he kept his wrath le-olam-va-ed: 12 But I will send a fire upon Teman, which shall devour the palaces of Bozrah. 13 This says יהוה ; *For three transgressions of the children of Ammon, and for four, I will not turn away the punishment of it; because they have ripped up the women with child in Gilead, that they might enlarge their border: 14 But I will kindle a fire in the wall of Ravah, and it shall devour the palaces of it, with shouting in the day of battle, with a storm in the day of the whirlwind: 15 And their melech shall go into exile, he and his princes together, says* יהוה.

2 *This says* יהוה ; *For three transgressions of Moav, and for four, I will not turn away the punishment of it; because he burned the bones of the melech of Edom into lime: 2 But I will send a fire upon Moav, and it shall devour the palaces of Keriyoth: and Moav shall die with a tumult, with shouting, and with the sound of the shofar: 3 And I will cut off the shophet from the midst of it, and will slay all the princes of it with him, says* יהוה. *4 This says* יהוה ; *For three transgressions of Yahudah, and for four, I will not turn away the punishment of it; because they have despised the Torah of* יהוה, *and have not kept His commandments, and their lies have caused them to go astray, after the halacha that their ahvot have walked: 5 But I will send a fire upon Yahudah, and it shall devour the palaces of Yahrushalayim. 6 This says* יהוה; *For three transgressions of Yisrael,[2] and for four, I will not turn away the punishment of it; because they sold the tzadik for silver, and the poor for a*

---

[1] Between Solomon and Hiram in the Yisraelite empire.

[2] Ephraim or non-Jewish Yisrael.

pair of sandals; 7 They crush the head of the poor in the dust of the earth, and they turn aside the derech of the meek: and a man and his abba go into the same young girl, to profane My set-apart Name: 8 And they lay themselves down upon clothes taken in pledge by every altar, and they drink the wine of the condemned in the bayit of their elohim. 9 Yet I destroyed the Amorite before them, whose height was like the height of the cedars, and they were as strong as the oaks; yet I destroyed their fruit from above, and their roots from beneath. 10 Also I brought you up from the land of Mitzrayim, and led you forty years through the wilderness, to possess the land of the Amorite. 11 And I raised up your sons to be neviim, and your young men to be Nazarites. Is it not so, O children of Yisrael? says יהוה. 12 But you gave the Nazarites wine to drink; and commanded ha neviim, saying, Prophesy not! 13 Behold, I am weighed down by your sin, as a cart is weighed down that is full of sheaves. 14 Therefore the safe place shall perish from the swift, and the strong shall not strengthen his power, neither shall the mighty deliver himself: 15 Neither shall he stand that handles the bow; and he that is swift of foot shall not deliver himself: neither shall he that rides the horse deliver himself. 16 And he that is courageous among the mighty shall flee away naked in that day, says יהוה.

3 Shema to this word that יהוה has spoken against you, O children of Yisrael, against the whole family that I brought up from the land of Mitzrayim, saying, 2 You only have I known of all the families of the earth: therefore I will punish you for all your iniquities. 3 Can two walk together, except they are in agreement?[1] 4 Will a lion roar in the forest, when he has

no prey? Will a young lion cry out of his den, if he has taken nothing? 5 Can a bird fall in a trap upon the earth, where no trap exists? Does a trap spring up from the earth, if it has not taken prey? 6 Shall a shofar be blown in the city, and the people not tremble? Shall there be evil in a city, if יהוה has not allowed it? 7 Surely the Master יהוה will do nothing, but He reveals His secrets to His avadim ha neviim.[2] 8 The lion has roared,[3] who will not fear? The Master יהוה has spoken, who would refrain from prophesying? 9 Publish in the palaces at Ashdod, and in the palaces in the land of Mitzrayim, and say, Assemble yourselves upon the mountains of Shomron, and behold the great tumults in its midst, and the oppressed in its midst. 10 For they know not to do right, says יהוה, they store up violence and robbery in their palaces. 11 Therefore this says Master יהוה; An adversary[4] there shall be around the land; and he shall bring down your strength from you, and your palaces shall be spoiled. 12 This says יהוה; As the shepherd takes out of the mouth of the lion two legs, or a piece of an ear; so shall the children of Yisrael be rescued that dwell in Shomron, as in the corner of a bed, or the edge of a couch.[5] 13 Shema, and testify in Bet Yaakov, says the Master יהוה, the Elohim of hosts, 14 That in the day that I shall visit the transgressions of Yisrael upon him I will also visit the altars of Beth-El: and the horns of the altar shall be cut off, and fall to the ground. 15 And I will smite the winter bayit as well as the summer bayit; and the houses of ivory shall perish, and the great houses shall have an end, says יהוה.

---

[1] Both houses need to come into agreement over the King, the Torah, the validity of the Renewed Covenant, and the equality of all believers. As long as we promote the false and hateful doctrine of Jew and Gentile "one in Moshiach," as opposed to the "One Yisrael" message, we cannot walk back to Tzion as He has ordained.

[2] The prophets of Yisrael in these last days are hearing one main message. "Restoration." YHWH is revealing His workings through the prophets willing to take a stand and not run from opposition. Yisrael's redemption and regathering will come from prophetic voices preparing the people of the exile for Yahshua's return to bring the kingdom fully restored to Yisrael. This secret is being revealed in our generation.
[3] Yahshua is roaring kingdom restoration through His neviim.
[4] Assyria.
[5] A remnant of Ephraim will remain in the land, while most are taken away by Assyria.

4 Shema this word, you bulls of Bashan,[1] that are in the mountain of Shomron, who oppress the poor, who crush the needy, who say to their masters, Bring, and let us drink. 2 The Master יהוה has sworn by His set-apartness, that, the days shall come upon you, that He will take you away with hooks, and your offspring with fishhooks. 3 And you shall go out at the breaches, every woman to the breach before her; and you shall be cast out toward Harmon, says יהוה. 4 Come to Beth-El, and transgress; at Gilgal multiply transgression; and bring your sacrifices every shachrit, and your ma'aseh after three years: 5 And offer a sacrifice of hodu with chametz, and proclaim and publish the terumah offerings: for you have loved this, O children of Yisrael, says the Master יהוה. 6 And I also have given you a shortage of food in all your cities, and want of lechem in all your places: yet have you not made teshuvah to Me, says יהוה. 7 And also I have withheld the rain from you, when there were still three months to the harvest: and I caused it to rain upon one city, and caused it not to rain upon another city: one piece was rained upon, and the piece where it did not rain withered. 8 So two or three cities wandered to one city, to drink mayim; but they were not satisfied: yet have you not made teshuvah to Me, says יהוה. 9 I have smitten you with blight and mildew: when your gardens and your vineyards and your fig trees and your olive trees increased, the creeping locust devoured them: yet have you not made teshuvah to Me, says יהוה. 10 I have sent among you the plague after the manner of Mitzrayim: your young men have I slain with the sword, and have taken away your horses; and I have made the stink of your camps to come up to your nostrils: yet have you not made teshuvah to Me, says יהוה. 11 I have overthrown some of you, as Elohim overthrew Sedom and Amorah, and you were as a burning stick plucked out of the burning: yet have you not

made teshuvah to Me, says יהוה. 12 Therefore this will I do to you, O Yisrael: and because I will do this to you, prepare to meet Your Elohim, O Yisrael. 13 For, see, He that formed the mountains, and created the wind, and declared to man His thoughts, that made the morning darkness, and treads upon the high places of the earth, יהוה, The Elohim of hosts, is His Name.

5 Shema this word, which I take up against you, even a lamentation, O Bet Yisrael.[2] 2 The virgin of Yisrael is fallen; she shall no more rise:[3] she is forsaken upon her land; there is none to raise her up. 3 For this says the Master יהוה; The city that went out by a thousand shall leave but a hundred, and that which went forth by a hundred shall leave but ten,[4] to the Bet Yisrael.[5] 4 For this says יהוה to Bet Yisrael,[6] Seek Me, and you shall live: 5 But seek not Beth-El, nor enter into Gilgal, and pass not to Beer-Sheva: for Gilgal shall surely also go into exile, and Beth-El shall come to nothing also. 6 Seek יהוה, and you shall live;[7] lest He break out like fire upon Bet Yoseph, and devour it, and there be none to quench it in Beth-El. 7 You who turn mishpat to wormwood, and cease doing tzedakah in the earth, 8 Seek him that made Pleiades and Orion, and turns the shadow of death into the morning, and made the day dark with night: that called for the mayim of the sea, and poured them out upon the face of the earth: יהוה is His Name: 9 Who brings destruction against the strong, so that destruction comes against the fortress. 10 They hate him that rebukes in the gate, and they hate him that speaks the emet. 11 Therefore because you trample

---

[1] Gentiles.
[2] This judgment in prophecy is spoken against Ephraim Yisrael.
[3] The north will cease to be a vibrant identifiable nation for all times until the coming of Moshiach, when individuals will be joined to Judah; not the entire former nation itself which will not rise again.
[4] In the **remez**, a reference to the ten tribes.
[5] Only a remnant of redeemed individuals from Ephraim will return to YHWH and to the land.
[6] Ephraim.
[7] The invitation to live eternally and repent has always been open to individuals from Ephraim.

upon the poor, and take grain taxes from him: you have built houses of hewn stone, but you shall not dwell in them; you have planted pleasant vineyards, but you shall not drink wine from them. 12 *For I know your manifold transgressions and your mighty sins: they afflict the tzadik, they take a bribe, and they turn aside the poor in the gate from their rights.* 13 *Therefore the wise man shall keep silent in that time; for it is an evil time.* 14 *Seek tov, and not evil, that you may live: and so* יהוה, *the Elohim of hosts shall be with you, as you have spoken.* 15 Hate the evil, and love the tov, and establish mishpat in the gate: it may be that יהוה Elohim of hosts will be gracious to the remnant of Yoseph.[1] 16 Therefore יהוה, the Elohim of hosts, יהוה, says this; *Wailing shall be in all the streets; and they shall say in all the highways, Oy! Oy! And they shall call the farmer to mourning, and professional mourners to wailing.* 17 *And in all the vineyards there shall be wailing: for I will pass through you, says* יהוה. 18 *Woe to you that desire the Yom* יהוה*![2] To what end is it for you? The Yom* יהוה *is darkness, and not light.[3]* 19 *As if a man did flee from a lion, and a bear met him; or went into the bayit, and leaned his hand on the wall, and a serpent bit him.* 20 *Shall not the Yom* יהוה *be darkness, and not light? Even very dark, and no brightness in it?[4]* 21 *I hate, I despise your moadim, and I am not pleased with your miqra Qedoshim.[5]* 22 *Though you offer Me burnt offerings and your grain offerings, I will not accept them: neither will I regard the shalom offerings of your fattened beasts.* 23 *Take away from Me the noise of your shirim; for I will not*

shema *the melody of your stringed instruments.[6]* 24 *But let mishpatim run down as mayim, and tzedakah as a mighty stream.* 25 *Have you offered to Me sacrifices and offerings in the wilderness forty years, O Bet Yisrael?* 26 *But you have borne the tabernacle of your Moloch and Chiyun your idols, the cochav of your elohim, which you made as an idol for yourselves.* 27 *Therefore will I cause you to go into exile beyond Dameshek, says* יהוה, *whose Name is The Elohim of hosts.*

6 *Woe to those that are at ease in Tzion,[7] and trust in the mountain of Shomron,[8] which is named chief of the nations, to whom the Bet Yisrael came!* 2 *Pass to Calneh, and see; and from there go you to Hamath the great: then go down to Gath of the Philistines: are you better than these malchutim? Or their border greater than your border?* 3 *You that put far away the soon-coming evil day, and cause the seat of violence to come near;* 4 *That lies upon beds of ivory, and stretches themselves upon their couches, and eats the lambs out of the flock, and the calves out of the midst of their stall;* 5 *That chants to the sound of the stringed instruments, and invents for themselves instruments of music, like David;* 6 *That drinks wine in bowls, and anoints themselves with the finest ointments: but they are not grieved or pained for the affliction of Yoseph.[9]* 7 *Therefore now shall they go into exile with the first that go into exile,[10] and the banquet of those that stretched themselves out in comfort shall be removed.* 8 *The Master*

---

[1] He was in the person of Moshiach.
[2] This is a stern warning to all who desire the fictitious rapture, as they see it as the day of YHWH's return. It is not something to be anticipated at all.
[3] The text is a dual prophecy of Ephraim's impending Assyrian exile, as well as Ephraim's end-time role in Yaakov's Trouble.
[4] The rapture is seen as a good, positive, and "light"-related event in false religions; yet YHWH warns those who want to be "taken up" that there is nothing pleasant about that day.
[5] Ephraim had changed the appointed times and made their own holidays, and YHWH states they are not His. That tendency is found today in the celebration of X Mass and Easter.

[6] Is this how YHWH views Sunday melodies from Ephraim?
[7] How many who are biological Zion, do not know their heritage in Yisrael, because of a religious sleep, that tells them that falsehood is truth, and that all is well, when all is not well for Yisrael in exile.
[8] The people of Ephraim, and the false worship offered at Mt. Gerazim and Dan.
[9] How many are the multitudes of believers and unbelievers who care nothing of the captivity and lost condition of Joseph or Ephraim Yisrael? Apathy towards Joseph's plight will soon reveal the wrath of YHWH.
[10] Those not moved to care and action to return Joseph to the House of David, will themselves be put into, or remain in, captivity in the nations, with little hope of return, until they submit to the Master's revealed will for both houses of Yisrael.

יהוה has sworn by Himself, says יהוה the Elohim of hosts, *I hate the pride of Yaakov, and hate his palaces: therefore will I deliver up the city[1] with all that is in it.* 9 *And it shall come to pass, if there remain ten men in one bayit,[2] that they shall die.* 10 *And a man's uncle shall take him up, or an undertaker, to bring out his bones from the bayit,[3] and shall say to him that is by the sides of the bayit, Is there yet any with you? And he shall say, No. Then shall he say, Hold your tongue for we may not make mention of the Name of* יהוה.[4] 11 *For, behold,* יהוה *commands, and He will smite the great bayit[5] with breaches, and the little bayit[6] with clefts.[7]* 12 *Shall horses run upon the rock? Will one plow there with oxen? For you have turned mishpat into poison, and the fruit of tzedakah into wormwood:[8]* 13 *You who gilah in things of nothing, who say, Have we not taken for us horns by our own strength?* 14 *But, behold, I will raise up against you a nation, O Bet Yisrael,* says יהוה *the Elohim of hosts; and they shall afflict you from the entrance of Hamath to the river of the wilderness.*

7 This has the Master יהוה shown me; He formed locust swarms at the beginning of the late crop; and, see, it was the late crop after the melech's tribute. 2 And it came to pass, that when they had made an end of eating the grass of the land, then I said, O Master יהוה, forgive, I beg You: how shall Yaakov survive? For he is small. 3 יהוה relented for this: *It shall not be,* says יהוה. 4 This has the Master יהוה shown to me: behold, the Master יהוה called the people to shophet them by fire, and it devoured the great deep, and did eat up a part of it. 5 Then said I, O Master יהוה,

cease, I beg You: how shall Yaakov survive? For he is small. 6 יהוה relented for this: *This also shall not be,* says the Master יהוה. 7 This He showed me: and, behold, יהוה stood upon a wall made by a plumb-line, with a plumb-line in His hand. 8 And יהוה said to me, *Amoz, what do you see?* And I said, A plumb-line. Then said יהוה, *Behold, I will set a plumb-line in the midst of My people Yisrael: I will not again pass by them any more:* 9 *And the idol temples of Yitzchak shall be desolate, and the pagan shrines of Yisrael shall be laid waste; and I will rise up against Bet Yerovoam [9] with the sword.* 10 Then Amatzyah the kohen of Beth-El sent to Yerovoam melech of Yisrael, saying, Amoz has conspired against you in the midst of Bet Yisrael: the land is not able to bear all his words. 11 For this Amoz says, Yerovoam shall die by the sword, and Yisrael shall surely be led away captive out of their own land. 12 Also Amatzyah said to Amoz, O you seer, go, flee into the land of Yahudah, and there eat lechem, and prophesy there:[10] 13 But prophesy not again any more at Beth-El: for it is the melech's worship place, and it is the melech's court. 14 Then answered Amoz, and said to Amatzyah, I was no navi, neither was I a navi's son; but I was a shepherd, and a gatherer of wild figs: 15 And יהוה took me as I followed the flock, and יהוה said to me, *Go, prophesy to My people Yisrael.[11]* 16 Now therefore shema the word of יהוה: *You have said, Prophesy not against Yisrael, and drop not your word against the Bet Yitzchak.* 17 Therefore this says יהוה; *Your wife shall be a harlot in the city, and your sons and your daughters shall fall by the sword, and your land shall be divided by line;[12] and you shall die in a polluted*

---

[1] Shomron the capital of the north.
[2] "Ten men" in "one house" is a reference to the ten dying unrepentant tribes of Ephraim Yisrael.
[3] House of Ephraim.
[4] So that YHWH's Name may not be profaned among heathen Ephraim, until he is revived in the latter days of this age.
[5] Ephraim.
[6] Yahudah is numerically small.
[7] Both houses will undergo periodic and ongoing judgment.
[8] False doctrines.

[9] Ephraim.
[10] Ephraim trying to send the prophet to Yahudah.
[11] Ephraim.
[12] Into two houses.

land: and Yisrael shall surely go into exile out of its land.

8 This has the Master יהוה shown me: and behold a basket of summer fruit. 2 And He said, *Amoz, what do you see?* And I said, A basket of summer fruit. Then said יהוה to me, *The end is come upon My people of Yisrael;[1] I will not again pass by them anymore.* 3 And the shirim of the Set-Apart Place shall produce wailings in that day, says the Master יהוה: there shall be many dead bodies in every place; they shall cast them forth with silence. 4 Shema this, you that swallow up the needy, even to do away with the poor of the land, 5 Saying, When will the Rosh Chodesh be gone, that we may sell our corn? And the Shabbat, that we may set forth wheat, making the ephah small, and the shekel large, and falsifying the balances by deceit? 6 That we may buy the poor as avadim for silver, and the needy for a pair of sandals; yes, and sell the refuse of the wheat? 7 יהוה the Excellency of Yaakov has sworn, Surely I will never forget any of their works. 8 Shall not the land tremble for this, and everyone mourn that dwells in it? And it shall rise up wholly as a flood; and it shall be cast out and drowned, as by the flood of Mitzrayim.[2] 9 And it shall come to pass in that day, says the Master יהוה, that I will cause the sun to go down at noon, and I will darken the earth in the clear day:[3] 10 And I will turn your moadim[4] into mourning, and all your shirim into lamentation; and I will bring up sackcloth upon all loins, and baldness upon every head; and I will make it as the mourning of an only son,[5] and the end of it as a bitter day. 11 Behold, the days come, says the Master יהוה, that I will send a famine in the land, not a famine of lechem, nor a thirst for mayim, but of hearing the words of יהוה:[6] 12 And they shall wander from sea to sea, and from the north even to the east, they shall run to and fro to seek the word of יהוה, and shall not find it.[7] 13 In that day shall the beautiful virgins and young men faint for thirst. 14 They that swear by the sin of Shomron, and say, Your elohim, O Dan, lives; and by the false halacha coming from Beer-Sheva; even they shall fall, and never rise up again.[8]

9 I saw יהוה standing upon the altar: and He said, *Smite the lintel of the door, that the posts may shake: and cut them in the head, all of them; and I will slay the last of them with the sword: he that tries to flee shall not flee away, and he that tries to escape shall not be delivered.* 2 Though they dig into the grave, there shall My hand take them; though they climb up to the shamayim, there will I bring them down: 3 And though they hide themselves in the top of Carmel, I will search and take them out from there; and though they are hidden from My sight in the bottom of the sea, there will I command the serpent, and he shall bite them: 4 And though they go into exile before their enemies, there will I command the sword, and it shall slay them: and I will set My eyes upon them for evil, and not for tov. 5 And the Master יהוה of hosts is He that touches the land, and it shall melt, and all that dwell in it shall mourn: and it shall rise up like a massive flood; and it shall be drowned, as by the flood of Mitzrayim. 6 It is He that builds His dwelling places in the shamayim, and has founded His possessions on the earth; He that calls for the mayim of the sea, and pours them out upon the face of the land:[9] יהוה is His Name.[10] 7 Are you

---

[1] Ephraim.
[2] Exile foretold.
[3] A reference to the gross darkness at the death of Yahshua, whose rejection by the leaders of Jewish Yisrael, ultimately led to the floodwaters of global exile.
[4] Ephraim's false replacement holidays.
[5] A hint or **remez** that Yahshua the only Son will be killed in a day when it is pitch dark at noon, and a day that will clearly add Yahudah to join Ephraim in the floodwaters of global dispersion.

[6] That famine continues to this day.
[7] Because the children of the land and their Torah, are off of the land, due to exile.
[8] The death of the nation of Ephraim Yisrael. Only individuals from Ephraim will re-enter the covenant by Moshiach at His coming.
[9] The waters of global exile.
[10] Not "Lord."

not as children of the Ethiopians to Me, O children of Yisrael? Says יהוה. Have not I brought up Yisrael out of the land of Mitzrayim? And the Philistines from Caphtor, and the Arameans from Kir? 8 Behold, the eyes of the Master יהוה are upon the sinful malchut,[1] and I will destroy it from off the face of the earth; except that I will not utterly destroy Bet Yaakov, says יהוה. 9 For, see, I will command, and I will sift Bet Yisrael among all nations,[2] like corn is sifted in a sieve,[3] yet the least kernel of grain shall not fall upon the earth.[4] 10 All the sinners of My people shall die by the sword, who say, The evil shall not overtake nor find us. 11 In that day I will raise up the Sukkah of David[5] that has fallen, and close up the breaches of it;[6] and I will raise up its ruins,[7] and I will rebuild it as in the days of old:[8] 12 That they[9] may possess the remnant of Adam,[10] and of all the nations, who are called by My Name, says יהוה that does

this.[11] 13 Behold, the days come, says יהוה, that the plowman shall overtake the reaper, and the treader of grapes him that sows seed; and the mountains shall drip with sweet wine, and all the hills shall melt.[12] 14 And I will bring again the exile of My people of Yisrael, and they shall build the waste cities, and inhabit them; and they shall plant vineyards, and drink the wine from them; they shall also make gardens, and eat the fruit from them. 15 And I will plant them upon their land, and they shall no more be pulled up out of their land which I have given them, says יהוה Your Elohim.

---

[1] Ephraim.

[2] Ephraim is among all nations, not just a few in Europe.

[3] Amos 9:9 makes it clear that The House Of Israel/Ephraim will be sifted among the nations or Goyim, as grain is shaken in a sieve. The House Of Israel was not sifted just south of Shomron into Judah as some still teach.

[4] Amos 9:9 states "but not a kernel of grain will fall to the ground." Ephraim would lose their identity as a nation but not their existence. Ephraim's existence would be preserved for later re-gathering in the Day of Jezreel. Ephraim as a nation was scattered among the gentiles, but preserved individually, so that not one would fall into the ground of oblivion.

[5] All twelve tribes.

[6] By definition, the Tabernacle of David is made up of the identical components of the people that David ruled. Those people, as Scripture clearly displays, were twelve tribes plus strangers. The Tabernacle of David was being rebuilt in the apostolic age with the same components that made up the Tabernacle of David before it fell into ruin by division end exile.

[7] The word in Acts 15:19, referring to redeemed individuals coming out of the nations, is "returning." The word in the inspired Greek is **epistrepho** (reverting), rather than several other Greek words that could be used for fresh converts turning for the first time. The same word **epistrepho**, is found in First Thessalonians 1:9, referencing those leaving idolatry and returning to YHWH. Returning from what to what? From the first Davidic Tabernacle to the rebuilt one. Returnees by definition also belonged to the original.

[8] Non-Jewish Yisraelites or Ephraim are part of YHWH's massive rebuilding efforts as seen in Acts 15:16. Only Yisraelites made up the Tabernacle of David. Non-Jewish believers, Ephraimites and non-biological Yisraelites rejoin Israel, and by virtue of this rejoining, restoration, and rebuilding of David's fallen Tabernacle (Acts 15:14-16), believing Yisrael is alive and well, thriving and flourishing under Yahshua, Yisrael's King.

[9] Restored Yisrael.

[10] Mankind or Edom as it appears in some translations.

[11] The rebuilt Tabernacle of David will be made up of a remnant of individuals from all nations, who become Yisrael, as they know and trust in YHWH's true Name. The knowledge and usage of the true Name, is a sign that one is actually a real returning Yisraelite.

[12] The rebuilt Tabernacle of David will overflow with an abundance of harvest, seed, and new wine. That means restored souls, the restored word, and the restored ruach.

עובדיה

Ovadyah - Obadiah
To Our Forefathers Yisrael

The vision of Ovadyah.[1] This says יהוה Elohim concerning Edom; *We have heard a report from יהוה, and an ambassador is sent among the nations, Arise, and let us rise up against him in battle. 2 Behold, I have made you small among the nations: you are greatly despised. 3 The pride of your lev has deceived you, you that dwell in the clefts of the rock, whose dwelling is high; that says in his lev, Who shall bring me down to the ground? 4 Though you exalt yourself as the eagle, and though you set your nest among the stars, even from there will I bring you down*, says יהוה. *5 If thieves came to you, if robbers by night, how cut off you'd be! Would they not have stolen until they had enough? If the grape gatherers came to you, would they not leave some grapes? 6 How are the things of Esav searched out! How are his hidden things sought for! 7 All the men of your confederacy have brought you even to the border: the men that were at shalom with you have deceived you, and prevailed against you; they that eat your bread have laid an ambush under you: there is no understanding in him. 8 Shall I not in that day*, says יהוה, *even destroy the wise men out of Edom, and understanding out of the mount of Esav? 9 And your mighty men, O Teman, shall be dismayed, to the end that everyone of the mount of Esav may be cut off by slaughter. 10 Because of your chamas[2] against your brother Yaakov, shame shall cover you, and you shall be cut off le-olam-va-ed.[3] 11 In the day that you stood on the other side, in the day that the strangers carried away captive his forces,*

and foreigners entered into his gates, and cast lots upon Yahrushalayim, even you were as one of them. 12 But you should not have looked for the day of your brother's disaster, in the day that he became a stranger; neither should you have rejoiced over the children of Yahudah in the day of their destruction; neither should you have spoken proudly in the day of distress.[4]

13 You should not have entered into the gate of My people in the day of their calamity; yes, you should not have looked idly by upon their affliction in the day of their calamity, nor have laid hands on their wealth in the day of their calamity; 14 Neither should you have stood in the crossway, to cut off those of his that did escape; neither should you have delivered up those of his that did remain in the day of distress. 15 For the day of יהוה is near upon all the nations: as you have done, it shall be done to you: your reward shall return upon your own head.[5] 16 For as you have drunk upon My Set-Apart mountain, so shall all the nations drink continually, yes, they shall drink, and they shall swallow down, and they shall be as though they had not been. 17 But upon Har Tzion shall be deliverance, and there shall be set-apartness; and Bet Yaakov shall possess their possessions.[6] 18 And Bet Yaakov shall be a fire, and Bet Yoseph the flame, and Bet Esav for stubble, and they[7] shall kindle them, and devour them; and there shall not be any remaining of Bet Esav; for יהוה has

---

[1] A proselyte from Edom to Yisrael, as recorded in First Kings 18, who withstood Ahab and Jezebel. More evidence that Yisrael has always been made up of anyone who desired to be Yisrael; including willing Edomites.
[2] Violence in Hebrew is **chamas**, as in the Edomite terrorist murderers.
[3] Fully in the kingdom.

[4] Esau's hateful attitude towards Jewish Yisrael.
[5] Though YHWH speaks to Esau, the principle is the same, Yahudah and Ephraim should not take joy in their brother's calamity or blindness, but seek to assist and be involved in bringing healing between the two houses. The two houses have often treated each other as Esau has towards Yahudah.
[6] In the **olam habah** or age to come, Esau and the pagans will be under the feet of King Yahshua and His people Yisrael. The deliverance of both houses during the Great Tribulation will result in an escape to Mt. Zion, not to a rapture.
[7] Both houses together.

spoken it. [1] 19 *And they of the south shall possess the Har of Esav; and they of the plain the Philistines: and they shall possess the fields of Ephraim, and the fields of Shomron: and Benyamin shall possess Gilead.* [2] 20 *And the captivity of this host of the children of Yisrael* [3] *shall possess that of* the Canaanites, even to Tzarephath; and the captivity of Yahrushalayim, which is in Sepharad, shall possess the cities of the south. [4] 21 *And saviors shall come up on Har Tzion to shophet the Har of Esav;* [5] *and the malchut shall be* יהוה*'s.*

---

[1] A beautiful prophesy of the end-time return to Zion of the House of Joseph or Ephraim Yisrael, that will be the light or flame that tips the scales in the Arab- or Edomite-Jewish wars. When Joseph finds his place in redeemed Yisrael in combination with brother Yahudah, Yisrael will burn the entire remnant of Edom as fire burns stubble.

[2] When the two houses defeat Edom, then all things even within the land will be restored, with Benjamin returning to the east bank of Gilead and not Judah. It is the time of the restoration of all things.

[3] The reunited two houses of Joseph and Judah will posses all the land given to Jacob, and the exiles will be returning from places such as Zarapheth and Sepharad or France and Spain. Perhaps the most breath-taking pronouncement regarding Obadiah 1:20, is found in the writings of Don Isaac Abarbanel. He said "Zarapheth is France and so too the exiles of **Sepherad** (verse 20b) is Spain. Do not err just because Zarapheth (France) is spoken of and Angleterre (England) is not recalled (in this verse). For there too (i.e., to England), did the exiles go, for lo and behold that island is considered a part of **Zarapheth** (France) and in the beginning belonged to it, and in their ancient books they call it the isles of Zarapheth (the isles of France), even though it later separated itself from Zarapheth (France) and became a kingdom (England) in its own right. Those children of Israel, who completely left (Hebraic) religion due to the weight of troubles and persecutions, remain in Spain in their thousands and tens of thousands, in huge communities [before 1492]. They shall return and request the Lord [their Elohim]."

[4] See note on verse 18.

[5] In context, those saviors are redeemed Yisraelites, with the correct kingdom restoration message coming out of the nations of their exile to bring salvation to all Yisrael with their faithful two-house restoration message. In that day, Edom will be fully destroyed and subjected, as the end of the exile means the beginning of the kingdom of our father David.

יונה

Yonah - Jonah
To Our Forefathers Yisrael

1 Now the word of **יהוה** came to Yonah the son of Amittai, saying, 2 *Arise, go to Nineveh, that great city, and proclaim against it; for their wickedness is come up before Me.*[1] 3 But Yonah rose up to flee to Tarshish[2] from the presence of **יהוה**, and went down to Yapho; and he found a ship going to Tarshish: so he paid the fare, and went down into it, to go with them to Tarshish from the presence of **יהוה**. 4 But **יהוה** sent out a great wind into the sea, and there was a mighty storm in the sea, so that the ship was likely to be broken. 5 Then the mariners were afraid, and cried every man to his elohim, and cast out the cargo that was in the ship into the sea, to lighten the load. But Yonah had gone down into the lowest parts of the ship; and he lay down, and was fast asleep. 6 So the captain came to him, and said to him, what does all this mean you, sleeper? Arise, call upon Your Elohim, if so be that Your Elohim will think upon us, so that we do not perish. 7 And they said every one to his fellow, Come, and let us cast lots, that we may know what man has brought this evil upon us. So they cast lots, and the lot fell upon Yonah. 8 Then they said to him, Tell us, we beg you, for whose cause has this evil come upon us; What is your occupation? And where do you come from? What is your country? And from what people are you? 9 And he said to them, I am an Ivri; and I fear **יהוה**, the Elohim of the shamayim, who has made the sea and the dry land. 10 Then were the men exceedingly afraid, and said to him, Why have you done this? For the men knew that he fled from the presence of **יהוה**, because he had told them. 11 Then they said to him, What shall we do to you, that the sea may be calm for

us? For the sea raged, and was growing more stormy. 12 And he said to them, Take me up, and cast me into the sea; then shall the sea be calm for you: for I know that for my sake this great storm is upon you. 13 Nevertheless the men rowed hard to bring it to the land; but they could not: for the sea raged, and was tempestuous against them. 14 Therefore they cried to **יהוה**, and said, We ask You, O **יהוה**, we ask You, let us not perish for this man's chayim, and lay not upon us innocent dom: for You, O **יהוה**, have done as it pleased You. 15 So they took up Yonah, and cast him overboard into the sea: and the sea ceased from raging. 16 Then the men feared **יהוה** exceedingly, and offered a sacrifice to **יהוה**, and made vows. 17 Now **יהוה** had prepared a great fish to swallow up Yonah. And Yonah was in the belly of the fish three days and three nights.[3]

2 Then Yonah made tefillah to **יהוה** His Elohim out of the fish's belly, 2 And said, I cried by reason of my affliction to **יהוה**, and He heard me; out of the belly of Sheol I cried, and You heard my voice. 3 For You had cast me into the deep, in the midst of the seas; and the floods surrounded me about: all Your breakers and Your waves passed over me. 4 Then I said, I am cast out of Your sight; yet I will look again toward Your Set-Apart Bet HaMikdash. 5 The waters surrounded me, even to the being: the deep closed around me, the weeds were wrapped around my head. 6 I went down to the bottoms of the mountains; the earth with its bars behind me le-olam-va-ed: yet have You brought up my chayim from corruption, O **יהוה** My Elohim. 7 When my being fainted within me I remembered **יהוה**: and my tefillah came in

---

[1] An appeal to non-Yisraelite Assyrians.
[2] Probably modern Spain.

[3] Yahshua refers to this as the main sign and type of His resurrection.

to You, into Your Set-Apart Bet HaMikdash. 8 They that observe lying vanities forsake their own rachamim. 9 But I will sacrifice to You with the voice of hodu; I will pay that which I have vowed. Yahshua is from **יהוה**. 10 And **יהוה** spoke to the fish, and it vomited out Yonah upon the dry land.

3 And the word of **יהוה** came to Yonah the second time, saying, 2 *Arise, go to Nineveh, that great city, and proclaim the message that I tell you.* 3 So Yonah arose, and went to Nineveh, according to the word of **יהוה**. Now Nineveh was an exceedingly great city of three days' journey. 4 And Yonah began to enter into the city a day's journey, and he proclaimed, and said; yet forty days, and Nineveh shall be overthrown. 5 So the people of Nineveh believed Elohim, and proclaimed a fast, and put on sackcloth, from the greatest of them even to the least of them.[1] 6 For word came to the melech of Nineveh, and he arose from his throne, and he laid his robe before him, and covered himself with sackcloth, and ashes. 7 And he caused it to be proclaimed and published through Nineveh by the decree of the melech and his nobles, saying, Let neither man nor beast, herd nor flock, taste anything: let them not eat, nor drink mayim: 8 But let man and beast be covered with sackcloth, and cry mightily to Elohim: yes, let everyone make teshuvah from his evil way, and from the violence that is in their hands. 9 Who can tell if Elohim will turn and relent, and turn away from His fierce anger that we perish not? 10 And Elohim saw their works that they turned from their evil way; and Elohim repented of the evil, that He had said that He would do to them; and He did it not.

4 But it displeased Yonah exceedingly, and he was very angry.[2] 2 And he made tefillah to **יהוה**, and said, O **יהוה**, was not this what I said, when I was yet in my country? Therefore I fled before to Tarshish: for I knew that You are an El full of favor, and full of rachamim, slow to anger, and great in rachamim, and relenting from doing evil. 3 Therefore now, O **יהוה**, I beg You, take my chayim from me; for it is better for me to die than to live. 4 Then said **יהוה**, *Do you have a right to be angry?* 5 So Yonah went out of the city, and sat on the east side of the city, and there made himself a sukkah, and sat under it in the shadow, until he might see what would become of the city. 6 And **יהוה** Elohim prepared a plant, and made it to come up over Yonah, that it might be a shadow over his head, to deliver him from his grief. So Yonah was exceedingly in gilah because of the plant. 7 But Elohim prepared a worm when the morning rose the next day, and it attacked the plant that it withered. 8 And it came to pass, when the sun did rise, that Elohim prepared a strong east wind; and the sun beat upon the head of Yonah, that he fainted, and wished to die, and said, It is better for me to die than to live. 9 And Elohim said to Yonah, *Do you have a right to be angry because of the plant?* And he said, I do have a right to be angry, even to my death. 10 Then said **יהוה**, *You have had pity on the plant, for which you have not labored, neither made it grow; which came up in a night, and perished in a night:* 11 *And should not I spare Nineveh, that great city, where there are more than one hundred twenty thousand persons that cannot discern between their right hand and their left hand; and also many cattle?*[3]

---

[1] Non-native Yisraelites believe in YHWH as they periodically always have. The idea that those from the nations only started to believe in Acts 2 is a dispensational falsehood.

[2] A familiar attitude by Yisraelites when those of the nations join Yisrael.
[3] A Yisraelite with wrong priorities. His comfort and security was more important than seeing a pagan nation in full repentance. Sadly, this attitude prevails among professing believers even until this day. They won't teach non-Jews Torah, because they don't want to see others become equal, and function as equal heirs of the blessings of obedience to Torah.

מיכה

Mikah - Micah

To Our Forefathers Yisrael

1 The word of **יהוה** that came to Mikah the Moresheth in the days of Yotham, Ahaz, and Hizkiyahu, melechim of Yahudah, that he saw concerning Shomron and Yahrushalayim. 2 *Shema, all you people; shema, O olam, and all that are in them: and let* **יהוה** *Elohim be witness against you,* **יהוה** *from His Set-Apart Beit HaMikdash. 3 For, behold,* **יהוה** *comes forth out of His place, and will come down, and tread upon the high places of the earth. 4 And the mountains shall melt under Him, and the valleys shall be torn, as wax in front of a fire, and as the mayim that are poured down a steep place. 5 For the transgression of Yaakov is all this happening, and for the sins of the Bet Yisrael.* [1] *What is the transgression of Yaakov? Is it not Shomron?* [2] *And what are the idol temples of Yahudah? Are they not in Yahrushalayim? 6 Therefore I will make Shomron as a heap of the field, and as plantings of a vineyard: and I will pour down the stones of it into the valley, and I will reveal the foundations of it. 7 And all the graven images of it shall be beaten to pieces, and all the gifts of it shall be burned with the fire, and all the idols of it will I lay desolate: for she gathered it from the hire of a harlot, and they shall return to the hire of a harlot. 8 Therefore I will wail and howl, I will go stripped and naked: I will make a lamentation like the jackals, and mourning like owls. 9 For her wound is incurable; for it is come to Yahudah; he is come to the gate of My people, even to Yahrushalayim. 10 Rejoice not at Gath, weep not at all: in the house of Aphrah roll yourselves in the dust. 11 Pass away, beautiful inhabitant, having your shame naked: O inhabitant of Tza-Anan your wound will be like that of Beth-Etzel;*

12 *For the inhabitant of Maroth waited carefully for tov: but evil came down from* **יהוה** *to the gate of Yahrushalayim. 13 O you inhabitant of Lachish, bind the mirkavah to the swift horse: she is the beginning of sin to the daughter of Tzion: for the transgressions of Yisrael were found in you. 14 Therefore shall you abandon the possessions of Moresheth-Gath: the shrines of falsehood shall be a lie to the melechim of Yisrael. 15 Yet will I bring an heir to you, O inhabitant of Mareshah: he shall exalt the tifereth of Yisrael le-olam-va-ed. 16 Make yourselves bald, and pull out your hair for your delicate children; enlarge your baldness as the eagle; for they are gone into captivity from you.* [3]

2 Woe to them that devise iniquity, and work evil on their beds! When the morning is light, they practice it, because it is in the power of their hand. 2 And they covet fields, and take them by violence; and houses, and take them away: so they oppress a man and his house, even a man and his inheritance. 3 Therefore this says **יהוה** ; *Behold, against this family do I devise an evil, from which you shall not remove your necks; neither shall you walk away proudly: for this time is evil. 4 In that day shall one take up a parable against you, and lament with a bitter lamentation, and say, We are utterly plundered: He has changed the inheritance of my people: how has He removed it from me! Turning away from us He has divided our fields. 5 Therefore you shall have no one in the congregation of* **יהוה** *to divide the land by lot. 6 Don't you preach, say the false neviim, you shall not preach to them, so that shame shall not overtake them. 7 O you that are named Bet Yaakov, is the Ruach of*

---

[1] Ephraim.
[2] Ephraim's capital.

[3] Both houses are destined to go into exile.

יהוה limited? Are these His doings? Do not My words do tov to him that walks as a tzadik? 8 Even of late My people have risen up as an enemy: you pull off the robe with the garment from the poor that they lose their tikvah, as men who invite war. 9 The women of My people have you cast out from their pleasant houses; from their children have you taken away My tifereth le-olam-va-ed. 10 Arise, and depart; for this is no place for your rest: because it is polluted, it shall destroy you, even with a heavy destruction. 11 If a man walking in the ruach of falsehood does lie, saying, I will prophesy to you being overwhelmed by wine and strong drink; even he shall be ha navi of this people. 12 I will surely assemble, O Yaakov, all of you; I will surely gather the remnant of Yisrael;[1] I will put them together as the sheep of Bozrah,[2] as the flock in the midst of their fold: they shall make great noise by reason of the multitude of men.[3] 13 The path-breaker shall come up before them: they shall break out, and will pass through the gate, and go out by it: and their Melech shall pass before them, and **יהוה** at their head.[4]

3 And I said, Shema, I ask you, O heads of Yaakov, and you rulers of Bet Yisrael; should you not know mishpat? 2 Who hate the tov, and love the evil; who tear away the skin from My people, and their flesh from off their bones; 3 Who also eat the flesh of My people, and strip their skin from off them; and they break their bones, and chop them in pieces, as for a pot, and as meat within the cooking pot. 4 Then shall they cry to **יהוה**, but He will not shema them: He will even hide His face from them at that time, as they have behaved themselves evil in their deeds. 5 This says **יהוה** concerning the neviim that

lead My people into error, that bite with their teeth, and cry, Shalom; they even preach war against him who does not provide lechem for them. 6 Therefore night shall be to you, that you shall not have a vision; and it shall be dark to you, that you shall not divine; and the sun shall go down over the neviim, and the day shall be dark over them. 7 Then shall the seers be ashamed, and the diviners embarrassed: yes, they shall all cover their lips; for there is no answer from Elohim. 8 But truly I am full of the power by the Ruach of **יהוה**, and of mishpat, and of might, to declare to Yaakov his transgression, and to Yisrael his sin. 9 Shema to this, I ask you, you heads of Bet Yaakov, and rulers of Bet Yisrael, that abhor mishpat, and pervert all that is right. 10 They build up Tzion with dom, and Yahrushalayim with iniquity. 11 The heads of Yisrael shophet for reward and bribes, and the kohanim teach for pay, and the neviim divine for money: yet they lean on **יהוה**, and say, Is not **יהוה** among us? No evil can come upon us. 12 Therefore because of you Tzion shall be plowed as a field, and Yahrushalayim shall become heaps, and the Har HaBayit[5] like a forest.[6]

4 But in the latter-days it shall come to pass, that the Har HaBayit of **יהוה** shall be established on the top of the mountains, and it shall be exalted above the hills; and the nations shall flow to it.[7] 2 And many nations[8] shall come, and say, Come, and let us go up to the mountain of **יהוה**, and to the Bayit of the Elohim of Yaakov; and He will teach us His halachot, and we will have our halacha in His paths: for the

---

[1] Despite all the judgment, YHWH will one day gather all of His remnant flock.
[2] Take all the exiles of the two houses and bring them together by making them one.
[3] A multitude of remnant Yisraelites will be gathered.
[4] Millennial rule as Yisrael follows their King Yahshua in and out of the gates of Jerusalem.

[5] Same house of Acts 2. The temple.
[6] Micah prophesies exile and judgment on both houses of Yisrael. Unlike some others, he is not sent to merely one house.
[7] All nations will follow YHWH and His Torah through Moshiach.
[8] Not just limited to Jewish Yisrael. What will be fulfilled in that day has begun in our day, which is the preparation of a remnant from all nations, preparing to return to Zion and to Torah, as opposed to the earlier days of false and evil prophets.

Torah shall go forth from Tzion, and the word of יהוה from Yahrushalayim.[1] 3 And He shall shophet among many peoples, and rebuke strong nations far off;[2] and they shall beat their swords into plowshares, and their spears into pruning hooks: nation shall not lift up a sword against nation, neither shall they learn war any more.[3] 4 But they shall sit every man under his vine and under his fig tree;[4] and none shall make them afraid: for the mouth of יהוה of hosts has spoken it. 5 For all peoples will walk every one in the name of his elohim, and we will walk in the Name of יהוה our Elohim le-olam-va-ed.[5] 6 *In that day,*[6] *says* יהוה, *will I assemble her that was outcast,*[7] *and I will gather her that is driven out, and her that I have afflicted;*[8] *7 And I will make her that was lame a remnant,*[9] *and her that was cast far off*[10] *a strong nation*[11] *and* יהוה *shall reign over them in Har Tzion from that time forward, even le-olam-va-ed. 8 And you, gloomy ruler, the stronghold of the daughter of Tzion, your time has come, even the first dominion the former Ruler of the malchut shall come*[12] *to the daughter of Yahrushalayim.*[13] *9 Now why do you cry out aloud? Is there no melech in you? Is your counselor perished? For pains have taken you as a woman in travail. 10 Be in pain, and labor to bring forth, O daughter of Tzion, like a woman in travail: for now shall you go forth out of the city, and you shall dwell in the field, and you shall go even to Bavel; there shall you be delivered;*

there יהוה *shall redeem you from the hand of your enemies. 11 Now also many nations are gathered against you, that say, Let her be defiled, and let our eye look upon Tzion. 12 But they know not the thoughts of* יהוה, *neither do they understand His counsel: for He shall gather them as the sheaves into the threshing floor. 13 Arise and thresh them, O daughter of Tzion: for I will make your horn iron, and I will make your hoofs brass: and you shall beat in pieces many nations: and I will dedicate their gain to* יהוה, *and their wealth to* יהוה *of the whole earth.*

5 Now gather yourself in troops, O daughter of troops: He has laid siege against us: they shall smite the Shophet of Yisrael with a rod upon the cheek.[14] 2 But you, Beth-Lechem Ephratah, though you are little among the thousands of towns of Yahudah, yet out of you shall He come forth to Me that is to be Ruler in Yisrael; whose goings forth have been from of old, from everlasting.[15] 3 Therefore will He give them up, until the time that she who travails has brought forth:[16] then the remnant of His brothers shall return to the children of Yisrael. 4 And He shall stand and feed Yisrael in the strength of יהוה, in the majesty of the Name of יהוה His Elohim;[17] and they shall dwell:[18] for now shall He be great to the ends of the earth. 5 And this Man shall be The-Shalom,[19] when the Ashurite shall come into our land: and when he shall tread in our palaces, then shall we raise against him seven shepherds, and eight

---

[1] All nations will keep Torah in the millennial kingdom.
[2] "Far off"; is a term used of scattered Ephraim Yisrael and the far-off Ephraimite nations.
[3] Millennial bliss.
[4] YHWH sees all of the redeemed living in the atid lavoh, as Yisraelites living in peace under the fig tree, a symbol of national Yisrael. This is the same metaphor that Yahshua used when he saw Nathaniel under the fig tree, and proclaimed him to be a Yisraelite in whom their was no guile.
[5] Walking in YHWH's eternal Name is a mark of Yisrael and will be so forever.
[6] Hebraic idiom for the latter-days.
[7] Ephraim-Yisrael.
[8] Yahudah was afflicted and exiled but never outcast.
[9] Yahudah.
[10] Ephraim.
[11] Both houses will be restored into a strong nation.
[12] YHWH Himself in the person of Yahshua.
[13] The kingdom will be restored to Yisrael with Jerusalem as the capital. That is the message of the tov news.

[14] Yahshua.
[15] Yahshua was born in Bethlehem, but came there from eternity past, because He existed in eternity past.
[16] Born in Yahudah, Moshiach will give Yahudah up, until Ephraim has brought forth children to Yahshua on a massive scale, and then a remnant of Yahudah will return to YHWH and their brothers the righteous children of the House of Yisrael. This event has begun, but will take place fully at Yahshua's return.
[17] Yahshua's strength and authority came from the Greater YHWH, His Father, as well as His usage of the Name of YHWH.
[18] Both houses will dwell safely in Yahshua's arms.
[19] The Prince of Peace who brings shalom between both houses and between Yisrael and YHWH.

principal men.[1] [2] 6 And they[3] shall waste the land of Ashshur with the sword,[4] and the land of Nimrod[5] in the entrances of it: and He shall deliver us from Ashshur, when they come into our land, and when he treads within our borders. 7 And the remnant of Yaakov shall be in the midst of many nations[6] as dew from יהוה, as the showers upon the grass that tarries not for man, nor waits for the sons of men.[7] 8 And the remnant of Yaakov shall be among the goyim[8] in the midst of many nations as a lion among the beasts of the forest, as a young lion among the flocks of sheep: who, if he goes through, both treads down, and tears in pieces, and none can deliver.[9]

9 Your hand shall be lifted up upon your adversaries, and all your enemies shall be cut off.[10] 10 *And it shall come to pass in that day,* says יהוה, *that I will cut off your horses out of the midst of you, and I will destroy your mirkavot: 11 And I will cut off the cities of your land, and throw down all your strong holds: 12 And I will cut off witchcrafts out of your hand; and you shall have no more magicians: 13 Your graven images also will I cut off, and your pillars out of the midst of you; and you shall no more worship the work of your hands. 14 And I will pluck up your Asherim out of the midst of you: so will I destroy your cities. 15 And I will execute vengeance in anger and fury upon the heathen, such as they have not heard of before.*[11]

---

[1] Restored and redeemed Yisrael will overcome all her former enemies.
[2] Seven Shepherds: meaning prefect care for the flock; and eight men: meaning new beginnings for all Yisrael in Moshiach.
[3] Moshiach and Yisrael's ruling leaders.
[4] Moshiach will reverse Ephraim's captivity.
[5] Moshiach will also reverse Yahudah's captivity.
[6] **Bekerev amim rabim;** Yisrael is in the midst of all the world's nations as morning dew soon to disappear from sitting in those nations, to return to the land of Yisrael.
[7] First of two similar pronouncements, this one for Ephraim.
[8] No need to wonder where the 10 tribes are. They are gentiles living among the gentiles.
[9] Second of two similar pronouncements, this one for Yahudah, with references to lions.
[10] In the millennium when restoration is complete.
[11] After both houses are rescued from the nations, YHWH will judge all the nations where Yisrael went, as seen in verses 10-15. This may be part of the rod of iron rulership exercised by Yahshua in the **atid lavoh.**

---

6 Shema now what יהוה says; *Arise, contend before the mountains, and let the hills shema Your voice. 2 Shema, O mountains,* יהוה *'s controversy, and you strong foundations of the earth: for* יהוה *has a controversy with His people, and He will reprove Yisrael. 3 O My people, what chave I done to you? And how have I wearied you? Answer Me! 4 For I brought you up out of the land of Mitzrayim, and redeemed you out of the house of bondage; and I sent before you Moshe, Aharon, and Miryam. 5 O My people, remember now how Balak melech of Moav consulted, and what Balaam the son of Beor answered him from Shittim to Gilgal; that you may know the tzedakah of* יהוה. 6 With what shall I come before יהוה, and bow myself before El-Elyon Elohim? Shall I come before Him with burnt offerings, with calves of a year old? 7 Will יהוה be pleased with thousands of rams, or with ten thousands of rivers of oil? Shall I give my firstborn for my transgression, the fruit of my body for the sin of my being? 8 He has shown you, O man, what is tov. What does יהוה require of you? But to do tzedakah, and to love rachamim, and to have a humble halacha with Your Elohim. 9 יהוה's voice cries to the city, and the man of chochma shall see Your Name:[12] shema the rod, and to the One who has appointed it. 10 *Are there yet the treasures of wickedness in the house of the wicked, and the short measure that is abominable? 11 Shall I count them as innocent who have the unjust scales, and bags of false weights? 12 For the rich men who do so are full of violence, and the inhabitants who do so have spoken lies, and their tongue is deceitful in their mouth. 13 Therefore also will I make you sick in smiting you, in making you desolate because of your sins. 14 You shall eat, but not be satisfied; and your insides shall be empty. You shall store up, but not save; and*

---

[12] Wise men still seek only the true Name.

that which you save will I give up to the sword. 15 You shall sow, but you shall not reap; you shall tread the olives, but not anoint yourselves with oil; and make sweet wine, but shall not drink wine. 16 For the statutes of Omri are kept, and all the works of Beit Ahav, and you have your halacha in their counsels; that I should make you a desolation, and your inhabitants a hissing: therefore you shall bear the reproach of My people.

7 Woe is me! For I am as when they have gathered the summer fruits, as the grape gleanings of the harvest: there is no cluster to eat: my being desired the first ripe fruit. 2 The tov man is perished out of the earth: and there is none upright among men: they all lie in wait for dom; they hunt every man his brother with a net. 3 That they may do evil with both hands earnestly, the ruler asks, and the shophet asks for a bribe; and the ruler, he utters only the desire of his being: 4 The best of them is as a brier: the most upright is sharper than a thorn hedge: the day of your watchmen and your visitation comes; now shall be their perplexity. 5 Trust not in a chaver, put no confidence in a neighbor or guide: guard the doors of your mouth from your wife. 6 For the son dishonors the father, the daughter rises up against her mother, the daughter-in-law against her mother-in-law; a man's enemies are the men of his own house.[1]
7 Therefore I will look to יהוה; I will wait for the Elohim of My Yahshua: My Elohim will shema to me. 8 Do not gilah against me, O my enemy: when I fall, I shall yet rise; when I sit in darkness, יהוה shall be a Light to me. 9 I will bear the affliction of יהוה because I have sinned against Him, until He pleads my cause, and executes mishpat for me: He will bring me forth to the Light, and I shall behold His tzedakah.

10 Then she that is my enemy shall see it, and shame shall cover her who said to me, Where is יהוה your Elohim? My eyes shall behold her: now shall she be trodden down as the mud in the streets. 11 In the day that your walls are to be built, it is a day to be lifted up. 12 In that day also he shall come even to you from Ashshur, and from the fortified cities of Mitzrayim, to the river and from sea to sea, and from mountain to mountain. 13 Nevertheless the land shall be desolate because of them that dwell there, for the fruit of their doings. 14 Shepherd Your people with Your rod, the flock of Your heritage, who dwell alone in a forest, in the midst of Carmel: let them feed in Bashan and Gilead, as in the days of old. 15 *According to the days of your coming out of the land of Mitzrayim will I show to him marvelous things. 16 The nations shall see and be ashamed at all their might: they shall lay their hand upon their mouth; their ears shall be deaf.* 17 They shall lick the dust like a serpent, they shall move out of their holes like worms of the earth: they shall be afraid of יהוה our Elohim, and shall fear because of You. 18 Who is an El like You; that pardons iniquity, and passes over the transgression of the remnant of His heritage? He retains not His anger le-olam-va-ed, because He delights in rachamim. 19 He will return again, He will have rachamim on us; He will trample our iniquities; and You will cast all their sins into the depths of the sea. 20 You will perform the emet to Yaakov, and the rachamim to Avraham, which You have sworn to our ahvot from the days of old.

---

[1] Yisrael's state at the time of Micah, and Yisrael's state at the time when Yahshua arrived, with the same divisive message of the coming kingdom restored to Yisrael.

נחום

Nachum - Nahum
To Our Forefathers Yisrael

1 The burden of Nineveh. The scroll of the vision of Nachum the Elkoshite. 2 El is jealous, and יהוה revenges; יהוה revenges, and is furious; יהוה will take vengeance on His adversaries, and He reserves wrath for His enemies. 3 יהוה is slow to anger, and great in power, and will not acquit the wicked: יהוה has His derech in the whirlwind and in the storm, and the clouds are the dust of His feet. 4 He rebukes the sea, and makes it dry, and dries up all the rivers: Bashan withers, and Carmel too, and the flower of Levanon withers. 5 The mountains quake at Him, and the hills melt, and the earth is burned at His presence, yes, the world, and all that dwell therein. 6 Who can stand before His indignation? And who can survive the fierceness of His anger? His fury is poured out like fire, and the rocks are thrown down by Him. 7 יהוה is tov, a stronghold in the day of trouble; and He knows those that trust in Him. 8 But with an overrunning flood He will make an utter end of the place of Nineveh, and darkness shall pursue His enemies. 9 What do you imagine against יהוה? He will make an utter end of it: affliction shall not rise up the second time. 10 For while they are entangled as thorns, and while they are drunk as drunkards, they shall be devoured as fully dry stubble. 11 There is one come out of you, that imagines evil against יהוה, a wicked counselor. 12 This says יהוה: *Though they be quiet, and likewise many, yet they shall be cut down, when he shall pass away. Though I have afflicted you, I will afflict you no more. 13 For now will I break his yoke from off you, and will burst your chains asunder.*[1] 14 And יהוה has given a commandment concerning you, that no more of your name be sown: out of the bayit of your elohim will I cut off the graven image and the molten image: I will appoint your grave; for you are vile. 15 *Behold upon the mountains the feet of Him that brings tov tidings, that publishes shalom! O Yahudah, observe your moadim, perform your vows: for Beliya'al shall no more pass through you; he is utterly cut off.*[2]

2 *He that dashes in pieces is come up before your face: guard the roads, watch the derech, make your loins strong, and fortify your power mightily. 2 For* יהוה *will restore the excellency of Yaakov, as the excellency of Yisrael: for the oppressors have trampled on them, and destroyed their vine branches.*[3] *3 The shield of his mighty men is made red, the valiant men are in scarlet: the mirkavot shall be with flaming torches in the day of his preparation, and the horsemen shall be terribly shaken. 4 The mirkavot shall rage in the streets, they shall rush one another in the broad ways: they shall seem like flaming torches, they shall run like lightning. 5 He shall remember his nobles: they shall stumble in their walk; they shall hurry to the wall, and the defense shall be prepared. 6 The gates of the rivers shall be opened, and the palace shall be dissolved. 7 And Huzzav the Malcha shall be led away captive northward, she shall be brought up, and her female servants, beating on their breasts, mourn in their hearts like doves. 8 But Nineveh of old was like a pool of mayim: but now flee away. Stop, stop, shall they cry; but none shall look back. 9 Plunder the spoil of silver, take the spoil of gold: for there is no limit to the treasure, the wealth of all the precious objects. 10 She is empty, and void, and wasted: and the heart melts, and the knees shake together, and much pain is in all*

---

[1] Speaking of Assyria.
[2] Assyria would no longer hassle Yahudah after they captured Ephraim. They would soon be captured by Babylon.
[3] Unlike Assyria, Yisrael will in fact be restored.

loins, and the faces of them all gather blackness in shame. 11 Where is the dwelling of the lions, and the feeding place of the young lions, where the lion, even the old lion, walked, and the lion's cub, and none made them afraid? 12 The lion did tear in pieces enough for his cubs, and strangled for his lionesses, and filled his holes with prey, and his dens with flesh. 13 Behold, I am against you, says יהוה of hosts, and I will burn her mirkavot in the smoke, and the sword shall devour your young lions: and I will cut off your prey from the earth, and the voice of your messengers and your deeds shall no more be heard.

3 Woe to the bloody city! It is all full of lies and robbery; the plunder in it cannot be estimated; 2 The noise of a whip, and the noise of the rattling of the wheels, and of the snorting horses, and of the jumping mirkavot. 3 The horseman lifts up both the bright sword and the glittering spear: and there is a multitude of slain, and a great number of bodies; and there is no end of their bodies; they stumble upon their bodies: 4 Because of the multitude of her whorings of the well-favored harlot, the mistress of witchcrafts, that brings and trains up all nations through her whorings, and families through her witchcrafts. 5 Behold, I am against you, says יהוה of hosts; and I will lift up your skirts upon your face, and I will show the nations your nakedness, and the malchutim your shame. 6 And I will cast abominable filth upon you, and make you as a fool, and will set you as a spectacle. 7 And it shall come to pass, that all they that look upon you shall flee from you, and say, Nineveh is laid waste: who will wail for her? Where shall I seek comforters for you? 8 Are you better than Yawan of Ammon? Which was situated among the rivers, that had the mayim all around it, whose rampart was the sea, and her wall was mayim? 9 Ethiopia and Mitzrayim were her strength, and it was

unlimited; Put and Luvim were your helpers. 10 Yet was she carried away, she went into captivity: her young children also were dashed in pieces at the top of all the streets: and they cast lots for her honorable men, and all her great men were bound in chains. 11 You also shall be drunk: you shall be in hiding; you also shall seek strength because of the enemy. 12 All your strong holds shall be like fig trees with the ripened figs: if they are shaken, they shall even fall into the mouth of the eater. 13 Behold, your people in the midst of you are women: the gates of your land shall be set wide open unto your enemies: the fire shall devour your bars. 14 Draw mayim for the siege, fortify your strong holds: mix the clay, and tread the morter, make strong the foundations. 15 There shall the fire devour you; the sword shall cut you off, it shall eat you up like the locust: because you have become many like the crawling locust, and multiplied like the swarming locusts. [1] 16 You have multiplied your merchants above the stars of heaven: the locust spoils you, and flies away. 17 Your officials[2] are like the locusts, and your captains as the great grasshoppers, which settle in the hedges in the cold day, but when the sun arises they flee away, and the place where they are going is not known. [3] 18 Your shepherds slumber, O melech of Ashshur: your nobles shall dwell in the dust: your people are scattered upon the mountains, and no man gathers them. 19 There is no healing of your injury; your wound is grievous: all that hear the news shall clap their hands over you: for your wickedness has gone forth against every man continually. [4]

---

[1] Ephraim taken captive in Assyria began to multiply rapidly and were referred to as "swarming locusts."
[2] Aramaic Peshitta has "Nazarites" – which, if accurate, makes a clear case for Ephraimites who maintained Nazarite vows even in captivity in Assyria.
[3] No one knows for sure where most Assyrians went.
[4] Unlike Yisrael, Assyria will never be gathered together, or restored to world domination as a nation or empire.

צפניה

Tzephanyah - Zephaniah
To Our Forefathers Yisrael

1 The word of **יהוה** which came unto Tzephanyah the son of Cushi,[1] the son of Gedalyah, the son of Amaryah, the son of Hizkiyah, in the days of Yoshiyahu the son of Amon, melech of Yahudah. 2 *I will utterly consume all things from eretz Yisrael, says* **יהוה**. 3 *I will consume man and beast; I will consume the fowls of the shamayim, and the fishes of the sea, and the stumbling-blocks with the wicked; and I will cut off man from off eretz Yisrael, says* **יהוה**. 4 *I will also stretch out My hand upon Yahudah, and upon all the inhabitants of Yahrushalayim; and I will cut off the remnant of Baal from this place, and the name of the leading kohanim of idolatry with the kohanim; 5 And them that worship the host of the shamayim upon the housetops; and them that worship and that swear by* **יהוה**, *and that swear by Malcham at the same time;*[2] *6 And them that are turned back from* **יהוה**; *and those that have not sought* **יהוה**, *nor inquired of Him. 7 Keep silent at the presence of the Master* **יהוה**: *for Yom* **יהוה**[3] *is at hand: for* **יהוה** *has prepared a sacrifice, He has invited His guests. 8 And it shall come to pass in the day of* **יהוה**'*s sacrifice, that I will punish the rulers, and the melech's children, and all such as are clothed with strange apparel.*[4] *9 In the same day also will I punish all those that do violence and plunder, who fill their masters' bayits with violence and deceit. 10 And it shall come to pass in that day, says* **יהוה**, *that there shall*

be the noise of a cry from the Fish Gate, and an howling from the second quarter, and a great crashing from the hills. 11 Howl, ye inhabitants of Maktesh, for all the merchant people are cut down; all they that bear silver are cut off. 12 And it shall come to pass at that time, that I will search Yahrushalayim with candles, and punish the men that despise their watchmen: that say in their lev, **יהוה** *will not do tov, neither will He do evil. 13 Therefore their goods shall become a spoil, and their bayits a desolation: they shall also build bayits, but not inhabit them; and they shall plant vineyards, but not drink the wine of it. 14 The great Yom* **יהוה** *is near, it is near, and approaching greatly, even the voice of the Yom* **יהוה**: *then the mighty man shall cry out bitterly. 15 That day is a day of wrath, a day of trouble and tribulation, a day of waste and desolation, a day of darkness and gloominess, a day of clouds and thick darkness,*[5] *16 A day of the shofar*[6] *and alarm against the fenced cities, and against the high towers. 17 And I will bring tribulation upon men, that they shall walk like blind men, because they have sinned against* **יהוה** : *and their dom shall be poured out as dust, and their flesh as dung. 18 Neither their silver nor their gold shall be able to deliver them in the Yom of* **יהוה**'*s wrath; but the fire of His jealousy shall devour the whole earth: for He shall make even a speedy end of all them that dwell in the earth.*

2 *Gather yourselves together, yes, gather together, O nation without discipline;*[7]

---

[1] A black Yisraelite; as a son of Cush.
[2] Those who take YHWH's Name to their lips cannot mix that truth with other false names, or judgment is guaranteed.
[3] What began as a historical judgment against Yahudah and spoke specifically about the coming Babylonian captivity, quickly expands to include the final seven years of this age known as the "Day of YHWH" or "Yom YHWH," which is a global judgment. Prophecy often must be understood in dual or even multiple applications.
[4] Anyone not wearing the garments of Renewed Covenant Yisrael will be considered a stranger or a gentile, offering strange worship fire.

[5] The Great Tribulation leads into the wrath of the Yom YHWH. Yisraelite believers will go through, both fully guarded or martyred.
[6] Or the day of Yom Teruah.
[7] A clarion end-time call to gather all Yisrael from both houses, to prepare us not only for the coming Tribulation, but also for the great day of Yahshua's return. The cry of that period

2 *Before the decree comes forth, before the day pass as the chaff, before the fierce anger of* יהוה *comes upon you, before the Yom of* יהוה *'s anger come upon you.* [1] 3 *Seek* יהוה, *all you meek of the earth, who have done His mishpat of Torah; seek tzedakah, seek meekness: it may be that you shall be hidden in the Yom of* יהוה *'s anger.* [2] 4 *For Gaza shall be forsaken, and Ashkelon a desolation: they shall drive out Ashdod at the noonday, and Ekron shall be rooted up.* 5 *Woe unto the inhabitants of the sea coast, the nation of Crete! The word of* יהוה *is against you also; O Kanaan, the land of the Philistines, I will even destroy you, that there shall be no inhabitant.* 6 *And the seacoast shall be dwellings and cottages for shepherds, and folds for flocks.* 7 *And the coast shall be for the remnant of Bet Yahudah; they shall feed there: in the bayits of Ashkelon shall they lie down in the evening: for* יהוה *their Elohim shall visit them, and turn back their captivity.* [3] 8 *I have heard the reproach of Moav, and the revilings of the children of Ammon, by which they have reproached My people, and magnified themselves against their border.* 9 *Therefore as I live, says* יהוה *of hosts, the Elohim of Yisrael, Surely Moav shall be as Sodom, and the children of Ammon as Gomorrah, even the breeding of weeds, and salt pits, and a waste forever: the remnant of My people shall plunder them,* [4] *and the remnant of My people shall possess them.* 10 *This shall they have in return for their pride, because they have reproached and magnified themselves against the people of* יהוה *of hosts.* 11 יהוה *will be a fright to them: for He will destroy all the melechim of the earth; and men* [5] *shall worship Him,*

every one from his place, even all the isles of the seas. [6] 12 *Yes Ethiopians also, you too shall be slain by My sword.* 13 *And He will stretch out His hand against the north, and destroy Ashshur; and will make Nineveh a desolation, and dry like a wilderness.* 14 *And flocks shall lie down in the midst of her, all the beasts of the nations: both the pelican and the owls shall lodge in the upper tops of her columns; their voice shall sing in the windows; desolation shall be in her gates: for He shall uncover the cedar foundations and lay them bare.* 15 *This is the rejoicing city that dwelt carelessly, that said in her lev, I am, and there is none beside me: how is she become a desolation, a place for beasts to lie down in! Everyone that passes by her shall whistle and shake his hand.*

3 Woe to her that is filthy and polluted, to the oppressing city! 2 She obeyed not the voice; she received not correction; she trusted not in יהוה; she drew not near to her Elohim. 3 Her rulers within her are roaring lions; her judges are evening wolves; they leave no bones until tomorrow. 4 Her neviim are light and treacherous persons: her kohanim have polluted the Set-Apart Place, they have done violence to the Torah. 5 יהוה is Tzadik in the midst of her; He will not do iniquity: every morning He brings His mishpatim to light, He fails not; but the unjust knows no shame. 6 *I have cut off the nations: their towers are desolate; I made their streets waste, that none passes by: their cities are destroyed, so that there is no man, that there is none inhabitant.* 7 *I said, Surely you will fear Me, you will receive Torah; so their dwelling should not be cut off, howsoever I punished them: but they rose early, and corrupted all their doings.* 8 *Therefore wait upon Me, says* יהוה, *until the day that I rise up to the plunder: for My determination is to gather the nations, that I may assemble all malchutim, to pour upon*

---

immediately preceding His return is: "Gather, gather, and gather."
[1] Now is the time to prepare the restoration of our people through proclaiming the Good News and Torah obedience.
[2] The trust of the believer is in YHWH hiding and guarding us, not chartering a flight for us.
[3] These may be key and significant hiding places during the Great Tribulation.
[4] A redeemed remnant from both houses will conquer, reign, and rule over all the sons of Edom, Moab, and Ammon.
[5] "Men" is an idiomatic expression for Yisrael.

[6] Or places of Yisraelite dispersion.

them My indignation, even all My fierce anger: for all the earth shall be devoured with the fire of My jealousy.[1] 9 For then will I return to the people [2] a pure clean language,[3] that they may all call upon the Name of **יהוה** ,[4] to serve Him with one consent. 10 From beyond the rivers of Ethiopia My worshippers, even the daughter of My dispersed, shall bring My offering.[5] 11 In that day shall you not be ashamed of all your doings, in what you have transgressed against Me: for then I will take away out of the midst of you those that gilah in your pride, and you shall no more be haughty because of My Set-Apart har.[6] 12 I will also leave in the midst of you an afflicted and poor people, and they shall trust in the Name of **יהוה**.[7] 13 The remnant of Yisrael shall not do iniquity, nor speak lies; neither shall a deceitful tongue be found in their mouth: for they shall feed and lie down, and none shall make them afraid.[8] 14 Roni Bat Tzion; shout aloud, O Yisrael; be in simcha and gilah with all the lev, O Bat Yahrushalayim.

15 **יהוה** has taken away your judgments He has cast out your enemy: the Melech of Yisrael, even **יהוה**, is in the midst of you: you shall not see nor fear evil any more.[9] 16 In that day it shall be said to Yahrushalayim, Fear not: and to Tzion, Let not your hands be weak. 17 **יהוה** your Elohim in the midst of you is mighty; He will save,[10] He will gilah over you with simcha; He will rest in His ahava for you, He will simcha over you with shirim. 18 I will gather all those[11] that grieve for the set-apart congregation,[12] who are among you, to whom the reproach of exile was a burden. 19 Behold, at that time I will deal with all that afflict you: and I will save her that is lame, and gather her that was driven out;[13] and I will get for them tehilla and fame in every land where they have been put to shame.[14] 20 At that time will I bring you again, even in the time that I gather you: for I will make your name a tehilla among all peoples of the earth, when I turn back your captivity before your eyes, says **יהוה**.[15]

---

[1] During the Yom YHWH.
[2] Yisrael.
[3] Hebrew restored to all His people.
[4] The restoration to redeemed Yisrael of the Hebrew language is to bring unity, purity, and the restoration of YHWH's true and only eternal Name.
[5] Many Yisraelites are found on the African continent in many countries such as Zimbabwe and South Africa. Ethiopia remains mostly Yahudite, and beyond her rivers many Ephraimites are found. From there, they shall again worship YHWH and also return.
[6] In context, the African Yisraelites in dispersion will no longer be ashamed of their pagan customs and Torah violations, as they return from exile back to YHWH's mountain in Jerusalem.
[7] The African exiles will come to trust in YHWH, though initially in great poverty, as seen in Africa today.
[8] The rewards for the remnant from both houses.

[9] Moshiach in Jerusalem at long last.
[10] Yahshua the Savior of YHWH.
[11] Both houses. He doesn't gather one and leave one lost in exile.
[12] Of Yisrael.
[13] He will gather the woman Yisrael, who had become lame in her standing with YHWH.
[14] All nations will literally see the end of our exile and the actual restoration of the people. This will not be done secretly or in a corner.
[15] The entire hope and promise of restoration summed up in a single verse of promise. The name of Yisrael will be a praise for all nations.

חבקוק

Chabakook - Habakkuk
To Our Forefathers Yisrael

1 The burden which Chabakook ha navi did see. 2 O **יהוה**, how long shall I cry, and You will not hear! even cry out to You because of violence, and You will not save! 3 Why do You show me iniquity, and cause me to behold perversity? For ruin and violence are before me: and there are strife and contention that arise. 4 Therefore the Torah is slack, and mishpat does not go forth: for the wicked do enclose around the tzadik; therefore wrong rulings go forth. 5 See among the heathen nations, and regard, and wonder marvelously: for I will work a work in your days, which you will not believe, though it is told you.[1] 6 For, see, I raise up the Chaldeans, that bitter and hasty nation, who shall march through the breadth of eretz Yisrael, to possess the dwelling places that are not theirs. 7 They are frightening and dreadful: their rulings and their dignity shall proceed from themselves. 8 Their horses also are swifter than the leopards, and are fiercer than the evening wolves: and their horsemen shall spread themselves, and their horsemen shall come from far; they shall fly as the eagle that runs to eat. 9 They shall come all for violence: their faces are like the east wind, and they shall gather the captives as the sand. 10 And they shall scoff at the melechim, and the rulers shall be a scorn to them: they shall deride every stronghold; for they shall seize territory, and take it. 11 Then shall his mind change, and he shall pass on as a wind, and his army shall be found guilty before his mighty one. 12 Are You not from everlasting, O **יהוה** my Elohim, my Kadosh One? We shall not die. O **יהוה**, You have ordained them for mishpat; and, O mighty Elohim, You have established them for correction. 13 You are of purer eyes than to behold evil, and cannot look on iniquity: why do You look upon them that act treacherously, and hold Your tongue when the wicked devours the man that is more tzadik than he? 14 And make men as the fishes of the sea, as the creeping things, that have no ruler over them?[2] 15 They take up all of them with the angle, they catch them in their net, and gather them in their dragnet: therefore they have simcha and gilah. 16 Therefore they offer sacrifice to their net, and burn incense to their dragnet; because by them their portion is fat, and their food made plenty. 17 Why do they empty their net continually, and do not spare to slay the nations without rachamim?

2 I will stand upon my watch, and station myself upon the tower, and will watch to see what He will say to me, and what I shall answer when I am reproved. 2 And **יהוה** answered me, and said, *Write the vision, and make it plain upon tablets, that he may run that reads it. 3 For the vision is yet for an appointed time, it shall speak in the end, and not lie: though it lingers, wait for it; because it will surely come, it will not delay. 4 See, the being who is lifted up is not upright in him: but the just shall live by His emunah.[3] 5 Yes also, because he transgresses by wine, he is a proud man, neither stays at home, who enlarges his desires as the grave, and is like death, and cannot be satisfied, but gathers to himself all nations, and heaps to himself all peoples: 6 Shall not all these take up a parable against him, and a taunting proverb against him, and say, Woe to him that increases that which is not his! how long? And to him that loads himself with earthly goods! 7 Shall they not rise up*

---

[1] Quoted by Rav Shaul in regard to his own work among Ephraim Yisrael.

[2] A **remez** of Shepherd-less Yisrael.
[3] Yisraelites need faith in Yahshua, but also the faith of Yahshua to walk as He did.

suddenly that shall bite you, and awake that shall trouble you, and you shall be for plunder to them? 8 Because you have spoiled many nations, all the remnant of the people shall spoil you; because of men's dom, and for the violence against eretz Yisrael, and against the city, and of all that dwell there. 9 Woe to him that covets an evil gain for his house, that he may set his nest on high, that he may be delivered from the power of evil! 10 You have consulted shame to your house by cutting off many peoples, and have sinned against your being. 11 For the stone shall cry out of the wall, and the beam out of the timber shall answer it. 12 Woe to him that builds a town with dom, and establishes a city by iniquity! 13 See, is it not of יהוה of hosts that the nations shall labor only for fire, and the nations shall weary themselves for nothing? 14 For the earth shall be filled with the da'at of the tiferet of יהוה, as the waters cover the sea.[1] 15 Woe to him that gives his neighbor drink, that pours from your wineskin to him, and makes him drunk also, that you may look on their nakedness! 16 You are filled with shame for tiferet: drink also, and be exposed as uncircumcised: the cup of יהוה 's right hand[2] shall be turned to you, and shame shall be on your tiferet. 17 For the violence of Levanon shall cover you, and the plunder of beasts, which made them afraid, because of men's dom, and for your violence against eretz Yisrael, and the city, and of all that dwell in it. 18 What profit is the carved image to the maker who has carved it; a molten image, and a teacher of lies that the maker of its work trusts in what he has made, to make dumb idols? 19 Woe to him that says to the wood, Awake; to the dumb stone, Arise, it shall teach! See, it is laid over with gold and silver, and there is no breath at all inside it. 20 But יהוה is in His Beit HaMikdash: let all the earth keep silent before Him.

---

[1] The promise of the removal of all Chaldean pagan influences in the millennial kingdom.
[2] Yahshua.

3 A tefillah of Chabakook ha navi for erroneous utterances. 2 O יהוה, I have heard Your speech, and was afraid: O יהוה, revive Your work in the midst of the years, in the midst of the years make known; in anger remember rachamim. 3 Eloah came from Teman, and the Kadosh-One from Har Paran. Selah. His tiferet covered the heavens, and the earth was full of His tehilla. 4 And His brightness was as the light; He had horns coming out of His hand: and there was the hiding of His power. 5 Before Him went the pestilence, and burning coals went forth at His feet. 6 He stood, and measured the earth: He beheld, and drove asunder the nations; and the ancient mountains were scattered, the ancient hills did bow: His ways are everlasting. 7 I saw the tents of Cushan in affliction: and the curtains of the land of Midian did tremble. 8 Was יהוה displeased against the rivers? Was Your anger against the rivers? Was Your anger against the sea that You did ride upon Your horses and Your mirkavot of salvation? 9 You uncover Your bow; Your arrows were abundant according to Your word. Selah. You did cut through the earth with rivers. 10 The mountains saw You, and they trembled: the storms of the water pass over: the deep uttered its voice, and lifted up its hands on high. 11 The sun and moon stood still in their dwelling: at the light of Your arrows they went, and at the shining of your glittering spear. 12 You did march through the land in indignation, You did thresh the heathen in anger. 13 You went forth for the salvation of Your people, even for salvation with Your anointed; You wounded the head out of the house of the wicked, by laying bare from the foundation to the neck. Selah. 14 You did strike through with his own arrows the head of his leaders: they came out as a whirlwind to scatter me: their rejoicing was as to devour the poor secretly. 15 You did walk through the sea with Your horses, through the heap of great waters. 16 When I heard, my belly trembled; my lips quivered at the voice: rottenness entered into my bones, and I trembled in myself, that I might rest in the day of trouble: when he comes up to the people, he will invade them with his troops. 17 Although the fig tree shall not blossom, neither shall fruit be in the vines; the yield of the olive tree shall fail,[1] and the fields shall yield no food; the flock shall be cut off from the fold, and there shall be no herd in the stalls: 18 Yet I will gilah in יהוה, I will simcha in the Elohim of my Yahshua.[2] 19 יהוה the Master is My strength, and He will make my feet like those of deer, and He will make me to have my halacha upon my high places, that I may sing His tehilla.[3]

To the chief singer on my stringed instruments.

---

[1] The olive tree – or both houses of Yisrael – will fail to stop their ongoing captivity.

[2] Despite the nation of Yahudah's imminent fall, and despite the fact that their history that was glorious is turning to exile, on a personal level he will maintain his personal faith and trust in YHWH, despite the national and worldly events around him.
[3] He realizes that even when YHWH judges a nation, He does continue to make individuals stand tall and in truth.

חגי

Chaggai - Haggai

To Our Forefathers Yisrael

1 In the second year of Daryawesh the melech, in the sixth month, on the first day of the month, came the word of יהוה by Chaggai ha navi to Zeruvavel the son of Shealti-el, governor of Yahudah, and to Yahoshua the son of Yehotsadak, the Kohen HaGadol, saying, 2 This says יהוה of hosts, *This people say, The time is not come, the time that יהוה's Bayit should be rebuilt.* 3 Then came the word of יהוה through Chaggai ha navi, saying, 4 *Is it time for you, to dwell in your paneled houses, and this Bayit lie in waste?[1]* 5 Now therefore this says יהוה of hosts; *Consider your ways.[2] [3]* 6 *You have sown much, and bring in little; you eat, but you have not enough; you drink, but you are not filled with drink; you clothe yourself, but there is none warm; and he that earns wages earns wages to put it into a bag with holes.[4]* 7 This says יהוה of hosts; *Consider your halachot.[5]* 8 *Go up to the mountain, and bring wood, and build the Bayit; and I will take pleasure in it, and I will be esteemed,* says יהוה.[6] 9 *You looked for much, and, see, it came to little; and when you brought it home, I did blow upon it. Why? says* יהוה *of hosts. Because of My Bayit that is ruined, and you run every man to his own bayit.[7]* 10 *Therefore the shamayim over you have withheld the dew, and the earth has withheld her fruit.* 11 *And I called for a* drought upon the land, and upon the mountains, and upon the corn, and upon the new wine, and upon the oil, and upon that which the ground brings forth, and upon men, and upon cattle, and upon all the labor of their hands. 12 Then Zeruvavel the son of Shealtiel, and Yahoshua the son of Yehotsadak, the Kohen HaGadol, with all the remnant of the people,[8] obeyed the voice of יהוה their Elohim, and the words of Chaggai ha navi, as יהוה their Elohim had sent him, and the people did fear before יהוה . 13 Then spoke Chaggai יהוה's messenger, יהוה's message to all the people, saying, *I am with you, says* יהוה. 14 And יהוה stirred up the ruach of Zeruvavel the son of Shealtiel, governor of Yahudah, and the ruach of Yahoshua the son of Yehotsadak, the Kohen HaGadol, and the ruach of all the remnant of the people; and they came and did work on the Bayit of יהוה of hosts, their Elohim, 15 In the twenty-fourth day of the sixth month, in the second year of Daryawesh the melech.

2 In the seventh month, in the twenty-first day of the month, came the word of יהוה through ha navi Chaggai, saying, 2 *Speak now to Zeruvavel the son of Shealtiel, governor of Yahudah, and to Yahoshua the son of Yehotsadak, the Kohen HaGadol and to the residue of the people, saying,* 3 *Who is left among you that saw this Bayit in its former tiferet? And how do you see it now? Is it not in your eyes by comparison as nothing?* 4 *Yet now be strong, O Zeruvavel, says* יהוה*; and be strong, O Yahoshua, son of Yehotsadak, the Kohen HaGadol; and be strong, all you people of eretz Yisrael, says* יהוה*, and work: for I am with you, says* יהוה *of hosts:* 5 *According to the word that I covenanted*

---

[1] Is it ok to follow all kinds of wealth and prosperity doctrines, while the Tabernacle or Sukkah of David remains fallen and not rebuilt? Has not the time come to rebuild YHWH's tabernacle of David, His way according to His pattern?
[2] What version of the kingdom are you proclaiming? Consider your ways.
[3] A call to Yahudah.
[4] The result of not following the pattern of Acts 1:6 and the restoration message of the last hour. Tithing to a work that is not following the pattern of rebuilding YHWH's House of David, also can result in reaping nothing in return for your giving.
[5] A second call to Ephraim.
[6] YHWH's perfect will is rebuilding His fallen House of David.
[7] Most religions look to rebuild their own house, kingdom, or version of the evangel with little concern for the House of Jabob that remains in ruins.

[8] Of Yahudah.

with you when you came out of Mitzrayim, so My Ruach remains among you: fear not. 6 For this says **יהוה** of hosts; *Yet once, it is a little while, and I will shake the shamayim, and the earth, and the sea, and the dry land;* 7 *And I will shake all nations, and the desire of all nations shall come: and I will fill this Bayit with tiferet,* says **יהוה** of hosts. 8 *The silver is Mine, and the gold is Mine,* says **יהוה** of hosts. 9 *The tiferet of this latter Bayit shall be greater than of the former,* says **יהוה** of hosts: *and in this place will I give shalom,*[1] says **יהוה** of hosts.[2] 10 On the twenty-fourth day of the ninth month, in the second year of Daryawesh, came the word of **יהוה** by Chaggai ha navi, saying, 11 This says **יהוה** of hosts; *Now ask the kohanim concerning the Torah saying,* 12 *If one bears set-apart meat in the fold of his garment, and with the edge he touches bread, or pottage, or wine, or oil, or any food, shall it be set-apart? And the kohanim answered and said, No.* 13 Then said Chaggai, If one that is defiled by a dead body touches any of these, shall it be defiled? And the kohanim answered and said, It shall be defiled. 14 Then answered Chaggai, and said, *So is this people, and so is this nation before Me,* says **יהוה**; *and so is every work of their hands; and that which they offer there is defiled.* 15 *And now, I ask you, consider from this day forward, from before a stone was laid upon a stone in the Beit HaMikdash of* **יהוה**:

16 *Since those days were, when one came to a heap of twenty measures, there were but ten: when one came to the winepress to draw out fifty vessels out of the press, there were but twenty.* 17 *I smote you with blight and with mildew and with hail in all the labors of your hands; yet you made no teshuvah to Me,* says **יהוה**. 18 *Consider now from this day and forward, from the twenty forth day of the ninth month, even from the day that the foundation of* **יהוה**'s *Beit HaMikdash was laid; consider it.* 19 *Is the seed yet in the storehouse? Yes, but the vine, and the fig tree, and the pomegranate, and the olive tree, have not brought forth fruit yet: from this day will I bless you.* 20 And again the word of **יהוה** came to Chaggai in the twenty-fourth day of the month, saying, 21 *Speak to Zeruvavel, Governor of Yahudah, saying, I will shake the shamayim and the earth;* 22 *And I will overthrow the throne of malchutim, and I will destroy the strength of the malchutim of the heathen; and I will overthrow the chariots, and those that ride in them; and the horses and their riders shall come down, every one by the sword of his brother.* 23 *In that day,* says **יהוה** of hosts, *will I take you, O Zeruvavel, My eved, the son of Shealti-El,* says **יהוה**, *and will make you as a signet: for I have chosen you,* says **יהוה** of hosts.[3]

---

[1] From this rebuilt House, the call for individual and national shalom would go forth to all Yisrael.
[2] The latter House had an empty Holy of Holies. So how can this be? The latter esteem was present within the person of Yahshua of Nazareth, and the esteem He brought, exceeded that of the former House, as He entered this rebuilt House, being the fullness of that esteem.

[3] YHWH overturns the curse of Jeremiah 22:30 placed on all the offspring of Coniah, allowing Moshiach Yahshua to be born through Solomon.

זכריה

Zecharyah - Zachariah
To Our Forefathers Yisrael

1 In the eighth month, in the second year of Dareyawesh, came the word of יהוה to Zecharyah, the son of Berechyah, the son of Iddo ha navi, saying, 2 יהוה *has been very displeased with your ahvot.* 3 *Therefore say to them, This says* יהוה *of hosts; Teshuvah to Me, says* יהוה *of hosts, and I will turn to you, says* יהוה *of hosts.* 4 *Be not as your ahvot, to whom the former neviim have cried, saying, This says* יהוה *of hosts; Make teshuvah now from your evil ways, and from your evil doings: but they did not shema, nor heed to Me, says* יהוה. 5 *Your ahvot, where are they? And ha neviim, do they live forever?* 6 *But My words and My chukim, which I commanded My avadim ha neviim, did they not take hold of the levim of your ahvot? And they made teshuvah and said, As* יהוה *of hosts thought to do to us, according to our ways, and our doings, so has He dealt with us.* 7 Upon the twenty-fourth day of the eleventh month, which is the month Sevat, in the second year of Dareyawesh, came the word of יהוה to Zecharyah, the son of Berechyah, the son of Iddo ha navi, saying, 8 *I saw by night, and see a man riding upon a red horse, and he stood among the myrtle trees that were in the bottom; and behind him there were red horses, speckled, and white.* 9 Then said I, my master, what are these? And the heavenly messenger that talked with me said to me, I will show you what these are. 10 And the man that stood among the myrtle trees answered and said, These are they whom יהוה has sent to have your halacha back and forth throughout the earth. 11 And they answered the heavenly messenger of יהוה that stood among the myrtle trees, and said, We have walked back and forth throughout the earth, and, see, all the earth sits in shalom, and is at rest. 12 Then the heavenly messenger of יהוה answered and said, O יהוה of hosts,

how long will You not have rachamim on Yahrushalayim and on the cities of Yahudah, against which you were enraged these seventy years? 13 And יהוה answered the heavenly messenger that talked with me with tov words and comforting words. 14 So the heavenly messenger that communed with me said to me, Proclaim, saying, This says יהוה of hosts; *I am jealous for Yahrushalayim and for Tzion with a great jealousy.* 15 *And I am very, very displeased with the nations that are at ease: for I was but a little angry at My people, but they furthered the affliction.* 16 Therefore this says יהוה; *I shall return to Yahrushalayim with rachamim: My Bayit shall be rebuilt in it,* says יהוה of hosts, *and a surveyor's line shall be stretched out upon Yahrushalayim.*[1] 17 Proclaim saying, This says יהוה of hosts; *My cities through prosperity shall yet be spread abroad; and* יהוה *shall yet comfort Tzion, and shall yet choose Yahrushalayim.*[2] 18 Then lifted I up my eyes, and saw, and see four horns. 19 And I said to the heavenly messenger that talked with me, What are these? And he answered me; These are the horns of the gentiles that have scattered Yahudah, Yisrael, and Yahrushalayim.[3] 20 And יהוה showed me four carpenters. 21 Then said I, What have these come to do? And he spoke, saying, *These are the horns which have scattered Yahudah, so that no man did lift up his head to help: but these are come to frighten and uproot them, to cast down the*

---

[1] Speaking of historical return from Babylon, as well as an end-time application.
[2] Restoration of the capital and the land, both in 500 BCE and in the end-times.
[3] The four winds or horns that have scattered both houses. These gentile nations are Babylon, Medo-Persia, Greece, and Rome.

horns of the nations, which lifted up their horn over the land of Yahudah to scatter it.[1]

2 I lifted up my eyes again, and looked, and see a man with a measuring line in his hand. 2 Then said I, Where are you going? And He said to me, To measure Yahrushalayim, to see what is the width and what is the length. 3 And, see, the heavenly messenger that talked with me went forth, and another heavenly messenger went out to meet him, 4 And said to him, Run, speak to this young man, saying, Yahrushalayim shall be inhabited as towns without walls for the multitude of men and cattle in it:[2] 5 For I Myself am to her, says יהוה, a wall of fire all round, and will be the tiferet in the midst of her.[3] 6 Oh, Oh, come forth, and flee from the land of the north,[4] says יהוה: for I have spread you abroad as the four winds of the shamayim, says יהוה. 7 Deliver yourself, O Tzion, who dwells with the daughter of Bavel.[5] 8 For this says יהוה of hosts; Due to His tiferet has He sent Me to the nations who plundered you: for he that touches you touches the apple of My eye.[6] 9 For, see, I will stretch out My hand against them, and they shall be a spoil for their avadim: and you shall know that יהוה of hosts has sent Me.[7] 10 Shir and gilah, O Bat Tzion: for, look, I will come, and I will dwell in the midst of you, says יהוה.[8] 11 And many nations shall be joined to יהוה in that day, and shall be My people:[9] and I will dwell in the midst of you, and you shall know that יהוה of hosts has sent Me to you. 12 And יהוה shall inherit Yahudah as His portion in the set-apart land, and shall choose Yahrushalayim again.[10] 13 Be silent, all flesh, before יהוה: for He is risen out of His set-apart dwelling.

3 And he showed me Yahoshua the Kohen HaGadol[11] standing before the heavenly messenger of יהוה, and s.a.tan standing at his right hand to resist him. 2 And יהוה said to s.a.tan, יהוה rebuke you, O s.a.tan; even יהוה who has chosen Yahrushalayim rebuke you: is not this a brand plucked out of the fire?[12] 3 Now Yahoshua was clothed with filthy garments, and stood before the heavenly messenger. 4 And He answered and spoke to those that stood before Him, saying, Take away the filthy garments from him. And to him He said, See, I have caused your iniquity to pass from you, and I will clothe you with a change of raiment.[13] 5 And I said; Let them set a clean turban upon his head. So they set a clean turban upon his head, and clothed him with garments. And the heavenly messenger of יהוה stood by. 6 And the heavenly messenger of יהוה protested to Yahoshua, saying, 7 This says יהוה of hosts; If you will have your halacha in My ways, and if you will keep My charge, then you shall also shophet My Bayit, and shall also keep My courts, and I will give you places to have your halacha among these that stand by.[14] 8 Hear now, O Yahoshua the Kohen HaGadol, you, and your chaverim that sit before you:[15] for they are men of symbol: for, see, I will bring forth

---

[1] The four carpenters are symbolic of the Ruach sent to offset the abuse of the four winds of exile and the four gentile nations that have abused Yisraelites in their exile.
[2] In the final restoration under Moshiach.
[3] When Yahshua as YHWH reigns from David's throne.
[4] Ephraim will return from the way in which he went.
[5] Yahudah also will return.
[6] Yisrael is and always will be the apple of His eye. The nations who were used by YHWH to hold Yisrael in captivity in their exile, will all be judged by Yahshua the King, for exceeding the correction appointed by YHWH.
[7] Yahshua is returning to establish the kingdom, but also to punish the nations of their exile.
[8] Here we have YHWH living in Jerusalem, being sent by YHWH. The duality of YHWH is seen here.
[9] We have Yisrael being joined with the nations or Ephraim, as one people, in the days when Yahshua comes to reign. Note that many nations will be joined to YHWH, as YHWH joins all nations into one people called "Yisrael."

[10] Restoration of the capital, and Jewish Yisrael.
[11] A historical figure foreshadowing the real Kohen HaGadol over Yisrael, Yahshua the Moshiach.
[12] Duality of YHWH; one rebukes s.a.tan, and the other chooses Jerusalem.
[13] Foreshadowing the conversion of the priesthood from dirty sinners to the tzedakah of YHWH, by the work of Moshiach, as well as symbolizing the purity of the High Priest Yahshua, who does the cleansing for all the other sons of Levi.
[14] A promise to all the kohanim, if they become cleansed by Moshiach.
[15] Other shamashim or priests.

My Eved the Tsemach-Branch.[1] 9 *For see the Stone that I have laid before Yahoshua; upon one stone shall be seven eyes:*[2] *see, I will engrave the graving of it,* says **יהוה** *of hosts, and I will remove the iniquity of that land*[3] *in one day.*[4] 10 *In that day, says* **יהוה** *of hosts, shall you call every man his neighbor under the vine and under the fig tree.*[5]

4 And the heavenly messenger that talked with me came again, and woke me up, as a man that is awakened out of his sleep, 2 And said to me, What do you see? And I said, I have looked, and see a menorah all of gold, with a bowl upon the top of it, and on its stand seven lamps, and seven spouts to the seven lamps, which are at the top of it: 3 And two olive trees by it, one upon the right side of the bowl, and the other upon the left side of it.[6] [7] 4 So I answered and spoke to the heavenly messenger that talked with me, saying, What are these, my master?[8] 5 Then the heavenly messenger that talked with me answered and said to me, Don't you know what these are? And I said, No, my master.[9] 6 Then he answered and spoke to me, saying, This is the word of **יהוה** to Zeruvavel, saying, *Not by might, not by power, but by My Ruach, says* **יהוה** *of*

hosts. 7 *Who are you, O great har? Before Zeruvavel you shall become a plain: and he shall bring forth the headstone of it with shouts of, Favor, favor to it.* 8 Moreover the word of **יהוה** came to me, saying, 9 *The hands of Zeruvavel have laid the foundation of this Bayit; his hands shall also finish it; and you shall know that* **יהוה** *of hosts has sent Me to you.*[10] 10 *For who has despised the day of small beginnings? For they shall have gilah, and shall see the plum-line in the hand of Zeruvavel with those seven; they are the eyes of* **יהוה**, *which diligently search through the whole earth.*[11] 11 Then I responded, and said to Him, What are these two olive trees, one upon the right side of the menorah and one upon the left side? 12 And I responded again, and said to him, What are these two olive branches that through the two golden pipes empty the golden oil out of themselves? 13 And He answered me and said; *Don't you know what these are?* And I said, No, My Master.[12] 14 Then said He, *These are the two anointed ones, who stand by the Master of the whole earth.*[13] [14] [15]

5 Then I turned, and lifted up my eyes, and looked, and see a flying Torah scroll. 2 And He said to me, *What do you see?* And I answered, I see a flying Torah scroll; the length is twenty cubits, and the width ten cubits. 3 Then He said to me, *This*

---

[1] YHWH, speaking directly to Yahshua, points the shamashim to Him, and identifies Him as the Branch or the **Tsemach**. A clear reference to the Moshiach and High Priest being Yahshua by Name.
[2] The stone is Moshiach, and the seven eyes are symbolic of perfection and perfect spiritual vision.
[3] Yisrael.
[4] Now the High priest called "Yahshua," called "the Stone with perfect vision and character," is further identified as the One who will forgive the nation's sin in a single day. We saw that occur in one day, the day He died on Golgotha and proclaimed, "it is finished."
[5] In the day that Yisrael and her leaders are cleansed, all the people trusting in YHWH by Yahoshua the High Priest, will be considered neighbors or equals, and all will be dwelling or sitting under the fig tree, a symbol of national Yisrael.
[6] He saw two olive trees, both being congregations of Yisrael, both representing the Abba; both sending forth an anointed witness, both producing an individual witness to prophecy and together both representing the whole people of Yisrael.
[7] Additionally Revelation 11:4 makes mention of the same two olive trees seen by Zechariah here in chapter 4.
[8] Most believers still can't answer this question.
[9] YHWH is astounded by most people's inability to pick up on the two-house concept. This same blindness was seen in Zacharyah, even though he prophesied much about it.

[10] "The word" speaks a prophecy that was fulfilled when Zeruvavel finished the building of the temple.
[11] Zecharia understands the rebuilding prophecy, but not the two olive trees as part of that rebuilding.
[12] Still puzzled.
[13] These two olive trees are the Two Houses (Isaiah 8:14, Jeremiah 31:31, Jeremiah 11:16-17), Two Nations (Ezekiel 35:10), Two Chosen Families (Ezekiel 33:24), Two Backslidden Sisters (Ezekiel 23:2-4), Two Olive Branches (Zechariah 4:11-14, Jeremiah 11:16-17), Two Sticks (Ezekiel 37:15-28), Two Witnesses (Revelation 11:3-4), Two Lamp Stands (Revelation 11:3), Two Silver Trumpets for the whole Assembly (Numbers 10:2-3), Two Advents (Hebrews 9:28), Two Cherubim (Exodus 25:18-20), Two Spies from Ephraim and Judah (Numbers 13: 6, 8), Two Congregations (Rev. 1:20), based on the principle that one lampstand; equals one assembly.
[14] For a fully detailed study, see:
http://yourarmstoisrael.org/Articles_new/restoration/?page=5&type=12
[15] In Yahshua's ministry, the mystery of Zechariah 4 is finally and fully revealed.

is the curse that goes forth over the face of the whole earth:[1] for everyone that steals shall be judged according to its contents; and everyone who swears falsely, shall be judged according to it. 4 I will bring it forth, says יהוה *of hosts, and it shall enter into the bayit of the thief, and into the bayit of him that swears falsely by My Name: and it shall remain in the midst of his bayit, and shall consume it along with the timber and the stones.* 5 Then the heavenly messenger that talked with me went forth, and said to me, Lift up your eyes, and see what is this that goes forth. 6 And I said, What is it? And he said, This is an ephah-measure that goes forth. He said moreover, In it are the transgressions of all the earth. 7 And, see, a talent-measure of lead was lifted up: and a woman was sitting in the midst of the ephah-measure. 8 And he said, This is wickedness. And he cast her into the midst of the ephah; and he cast the talent of lead upon its mouth. 9 Then lifted I up my eyes, and looked, and, see, there came out two women,[2] and the wind was in their wings;[3] for they had wings like the wings of a stork: and they lifted up the ephah-measure between the earth and the shamayim. [4] 10 Then said I to the heavenly messenger who talked with me, Where do these who bear the ephah-measure go?[5] 11 And he said to me, To build it a bayit in the land of Shinar: and it shall be established, and set there upon her own base.[6]

6 And I turned, and lifted up my eyes, and looked, and, see, there came four chariots out from between two mountains; and the mountains were mountains of bronze. 2 In the first chariot were red horses; and in the second chariot black horses; 3 And in the third chariot white horses; and in the fourth chariot strong speckled horses. 4 Then I answered and said to the heavenly messenger that talked with me, What are these, my master? 5 And the heavenly messenger answered and said to me, These are the four spirits of the shamayim, which go forth from standing before יהוה of all the earth. 6 The chariot with black horses goes forth into the north country; and the chariot with white horses follows after them; and the chariot with speckled horses goes forth toward the south country. 7 And the red horses went forth, and sought to go that they might have your halacha to and fro in all the earth: and He said, Go now, have your halacha to and fro in all the earth. So they walked to and fro through the earth. 8 Then He called out to me, and spoke to me, saying, See, these that go toward the north country have quieted My ruach in the north country.[7] 9 And the word of יהוה came to me, saying, 10 *Receive gifts from the returning exiles, even from Heldai, from Tobiyah, and from Yedayah, who have come back from Bavel, and the same day, enter into the bayit of Yoshiyah the son of Tzephanyah;* 11 *Then take the silver and gold, and make a keter, and set it on the head of Yahoshua the son of Yehotsadaq, the Kohen HaGadol;* 12 *And speak to him, saying, This says* יהוה *of hosts, saying, See the Man whose Name is the Tsemach-Branch; and He shall grow up out of His place, and He shall rebuild the Beit HaMikdash of* יהוה:[8] 13 *Even He shall rebuild the Beit HaMikdash of* יהוה; *and*

---

[1] The strength of sin is the Torah, and those who break it are under a curse.
[2] Symbolic of Yahudah and Ephraim.
[3] Taken to the four corners of the earth in their iniquity.
[4] Being judged by the heavens and earth.
[5] Or where are the two houses headed because of their sins?
[6] To wickedly build the house of Jacob based on Babylonian customs, traditions, and vanities. Shinar is Babylon. Both houses found to be full of sin, were scattered to the winds only to settle in Babylon and its abominable customs.

[7] These very well could be the four horsemen and chariots of the apocalypse in Revelation 6, which are designed to really get things going in Jacob's Trouble. It may well be that since in the prior vision Yisrael was scattered to Babylon or Shinar, that these horsemen are YHWH's judgment on the unsaved and unrepentant living in Babylon's ways; but just like Jeremiah 30:7, this verse states Jacob's redeemed remnant will be saved out of Jacob's Trouble by protection.
[8] Another amazing prophecy of the Kohen HaGadol named Yahshua, anointed by YHWH to rebuild the temple of YHWH. In Ephesians 2, we find this fulfilled as Yahoshua the Moshiach builds His temple, with stones from both houses, fitly framed together. Even the words "see the man" is right from the evangels and were pronounced by Pilate. Certainly Yahshua's Name appears as the King and Priest over Renewed Covenant Yisrael, several times in the First Covenant.

He shall bear the tiferet, and shall sit and rule upon His throne;[1] and He shall be a Kohen upon His throne:[2] and the counsel of shalom shall be between them both.[3] 14 And the ketarim shall be to Helem, and to Tobiyah, and to Yedayah, and to Chen the son of Tzephaniah, for a memorial in the Beit HaMikdash of יהוה.[4] 15 And they that are far off[5] shall come and build the Beit HaMikdash of יהוה, and you shall know that יהוה of hosts has sent Me to you.[6] And this shall come to pass, if you will diligently obey the voice of יהוה Your Elohim.

7 And it came to pass in the fourth year of melech Dareyawesh, that the word of יהוה came to Zecharyah in the fourth day of the ninth month, even in Chislev; 2 When they had sent Sheretzer and Regem-Melech to Beth-El, with their men, to pray before יהוה, 3 And to speak to the kohanim who were in the Bayit of יהוה of hosts, and to ha neviim, saying, Should I weep in the fifth month, separating myself, as I have done these so many years?[7] 4 Then came the word of יהוה of hosts to me, saying, 5 Speak to all the people of the land, and to the kohanim, saying, When you fasted and mourned in the fifth and seventh month, even those seventy years, did you really fast to Me, or for Me? 6 And when you did eat, and when you did drink, did

you not eat for yourselves, and drink for yourselves? 7 Should you not shema the words that יהוה has proclaimed through the former neviim, when Yahrushalayim was inhabited and in prosperity, with all the cities around her, when men inhabited the south and the plain? 8 And the word of יהוה came to Zecharyah, saying, 9 This says יהוה of hosts, saying, Execute true right-ruling, and show rachamim and compassion every man to his brother: 10 And oppress not the widow, nor the fatherless, the stranger, nor the poor; and let none of you imagine evil against his brother in your lev. 11 But they refused to shema, and pulled away the shoulder, and covered their ears, that they should not shema.[8] 12 Yes, they made their levim as flint, lest they should shema the Torah, and the words which יהוה of hosts has sent by His Ruach through the former neviim: therefore came a great wrath from יהוה of hosts. 13 Therefore it is come to pass, that as He called, and they would not shema; so they called, and I would not shema, says יהוה of hosts: 14 But I scattered them with a whirlwind among all the nations[9] whom they knew not. And eretz Yisrael was desolate after them, so that no man passed through nor returned: for they made the pleasant land a waste.

8 Again the word of יהוה of hosts came to me, saying, 2 This says יהוה of hosts; I was jealous for Tzion with great jealousy, and I was jealous for her with great wrath.[10] 3 This says יהוה; I shall return to Tzion, and will dwell in the midst of Yahrushalayim: and Yahrushalayim shall be called The City of Emet; and the har of יהוה of hosts the Set-Apart har.[11] 4 This says יהוה of hosts; There shall yet old men and old women dwell in the streets of

---

1 This anointed High Priest is also Yisrael's King, who rebuilds the temple. According to Torah, no mortal man can be both High Priest and King, other than YHWH Himself in the person of Moshiach. The same Yahshua, in the millennial atid lavoh, will physically restore the temple, first rebuilt in the Spirit realm of His universal body.
2 See notes on verses 12 and 13.
3 In addition, this Moshiach Yahoshua will bring peace between the two roles of King and High Priest, as well as Judah and Ephraim. The reference to "both" is a direct link to the shalom that will occur between both houses during His reign.
4 The Scepter over both houses remained in Judah until Moshiach arrived.
5 The often-recurring Hebraic idiomatic expression always referring to the ten tribes of non-Jewish Yisrael. We see this term in such places as Daniel 9:7 and Ephesians 2:13. This is a clear indication that Ephraimites will work along with Moshiach to rebuild the spiritual and physical nation and temple on Mt. Moriyah.
6 Moshiach talking in first person.
7 The exiles of Yahudah wanted to know if they should continue fasting on the 9th of the fifth month in commemoration of the destruction of the temple now that the Babylonian exile had ended.

8 Both houses.
9 Yisrael is in all the nations.
10 YHWH states that He will be jealous for all of Zion, whom He misses and will bring all Yisrael back to Zion. Both the House of Judah and the House of Yisrael will return as seen in Zechariah 8:13.
11 Final fulfillment in the millennium.

Yahrushalayim, and every man with his staff in his hand for old age.¹ 5 And the streets of the city shall be full of boys and girls playing in its streets. 6 This says יהוה of hosts; If it be marvelous in the eyes of the remnant of this people in these days, should it also be marvelous in My eyes? Says יהוה of hosts.² 7 This says יהוה of hosts; See, I will save My people from the east country, and from the west country;³ 8 And I will bring them, and they shall dwell in the midst of Yahrushalayim: and they shall be My people - Ami,⁴ and I will be their Elohim, in emet and in tzedakah. 9 This says יהוה of hosts; Let your hands be strong, you that shema in these days these words by the mouth of ha neviim, who were there in the days that the foundation of the Bayit of יהוה of hosts was laid, that the Beit HaMikdash might be rebuilt. 10 For before these days there was no work for man, nor any work for beast; neither was there any shalom to him that came and went, because of the affliction: for I set all men every one against his neighbor. 11 But now I will not be to the residue of this people as in the former days, says יהוה of hosts. 12 For the zera shall be prosperous; the vine shall give her fruit, and the ground shall give her increase, and the shamayim shall give their dew; and I will cause the remnant of this people to possess all these things.⁵ 13 And it shall come to pass, that as you were a curse among the heathen, O Bet Yahudah, and Bet Yisrael;⁶ so will I save you, and you shall be a blessing: fear not, but let your hands be strong. 14 For this says יהוה of hosts; As I thought to punish you, when your ahvot provoked Me to anger, says יהוה of hosts, and I relented not: 15 So again have I thought in these

days to do well to Yahrushalayim and to Bet Yahudah: fear not. 16 These are the things that you shall do; Speak every man the emet to his neighbor; execute the mishpatim of emet and shalom in your gates: 17 And let none of you imagine evil in your levim against his neighbor; and love no false oath: for all these are things that I hate, says יהוה. 18 And the word of יהוה of hosts came to me, saying, 19 This says יהוה of hosts; The fast of the fourth month, and the fast of the fifth, and the fast of the seventh, and the fast of the tenth, shall be to Bet Yahudah for simcha and gilah, and joyous pleasant moadim;⁷ therefore love the emet and shalom.⁸ 20 This says יהוה of hosts; It shall yet come to pass, that there shall come nations, and the inhabitants of many cities:⁹ 21 And the inhabitants of one city shall go to another, saying, Let us go speedily to pray before יהוה, and to seek יהוה of hosts: I will go also. 22 Yes, many people and strong nations shall come to seek יהוה of hosts in Yahrushalayim, and to pray before יהוה. 23 This says יהוה of hosts; In those days¹⁰ it shall come to pass, that ten men¹¹ shall take hold¹² out of all languages of the nations,¹³ even shall take hold of the tzitzit¹⁴ of him that is a Yahudite, saying, We will go with you:¹⁵ for we have heard that Elohim is with you. ¹⁶

---

¹ Human longevity will be restored in the millennium.
² If Yisrael's restoration is great on earth, how much more in heaven?
³ From the horror of both dispersions.
⁴ A reversal of the Lo Ami curse of Hosea 1:9.
⁵ The latter-day Yisraelites will have all curses removed, as opposed to those of the years of former exile. The remnant of both houses will inherit all things through Moshiach.
⁶ A confirmation that Yisrael's remnant, will come into the blessing from both houses of Yisrael.

⁷ This is the answer to the question of those who came earlier from Medo-Persia wanting to know if they should continue in the various fasts of Yahudah, which were man-made. Here YHWH says that in the great restoration of all things, He will take these various days of fasting like that of the 9ᵗʰ of the 5ᵗʰ month and the fast of Gedlayah in the 7ᵗʰ month and literally turn them into appointed times somewhat equal and similar to the current feasts of Vayiqra 23.
⁸ Ephraim will be invited and expected to rejoice with Judah, based on the principle of Yisraelite brotherhood to "rejoice with those who rejoice" as found in the Brit Chadasha.
⁹ The end of the exile in the atid lavoh.
¹⁰ Latter-days.
¹¹ Ten tribes of Yisrael.
¹² Literally "seek out."
¹³ The ten tribes will come out of all nations speaking all languages – not Hebrew.
¹⁴ Fringes on a four-cornered garment.
¹⁵ In unity as echad.
¹⁶ Ephraim goes with a remnant of Yahudah, who has come to know YHWH as promised in Jeremiah 31:31. The idea that Ephraim is supposed to "take hold" of unredeemed Judah is not Scripturally-based. This verse, taken in context with Jeremiah 31:31, states that Ephraim must join a born-again Ruach-filled Jew of the Renewed Covenant, in his or her return.

9 The burden of the word of **יהוה** against the land of Hadrach, and Dameshek that shall be a gift to him: when the eyes of man, and all the tribes of Yisrael, are on **יהוה**. 2 And Hamath also which borders Dameshek; and Tsor, and Tzidon, though they have become very wise. 3 And Tsor did build herself a stronghold, and heaped up silver as the dust, and fine gold as the mud of the streets. 4 See, **יהוה** will cast her out, and He will destroy her power in the sea; and she shall be devoured with fire. 5 Ashkelon shall see it, and fear; Gaza also shall see it, and be very sorrowful, and Ekron; for her expectation has dried up; and the melech shall perish from Gaza, and Ashkelon shall not be inhabited. 6 *And strangers shall dwell in Ashdod, and I will cut off the pride of the Philistines. 7 And I will take away his dom out of his mouth, and his abominations from between his teeth: but he that remains, even he, shall be for our Elohim, and he shall be as a governor in Yahudah, and Ekron as a Yevusite. 8 And I will cause to dwell over My Bayit a governor, because of him that passes by, and because of him that returns: and no oppressor shall come against them anymore: for now have I seen with My eyes. 9 Rejoice greatly, O Bat Tzion; shout, O Bat Yahrushalayim: see, your Melech comes to you: He is Tzadik, and having salvation; humble, and riding upon a donkey, and upon a colt the foal of a donkey.*[1] *10 And I will cut off the chariot from Ephraim, and the horse from Yahrushalayim, and the battle bow shall be cut off:*[2] *and He shall speak shalom to the nations: and His dominion shall be from sea even to sea, and from the river even to the ends of the earth. 11 As for You also, by the dom of Your covenant I have sent forth*

Your prisoners out of the pit[3] *where there is no mayim.*[4] *12 Turn to the stronghold, you prisoners of hope in the congregation:*[5] *even today do I declare that I will render double to you;*[6] *13 When I have bent Yahudah for Me, and filled the bow with Ephraim, and raised up your sons, O Tzion, against your sons, O Greece, and made you as the sword of a mighty man.*[7] *14 And* **יהוה** *shall be seen over them,*[8] *and His arrow shall go forth as the lightning: and the Master* **יהוה** *shall blow the shofar, and shall go with whirlwinds from the south.*[9] *15* **יהוה** *of hosts shall shield and defend them; and they shall devour, and subdue with sling stones; and they shall drink, and make a noise as if with wine; and they shall be filled like bowls, like the corners of the altar.*[10] *16 And* **יהוה** *their Elohim shall save them in that Day as the flock of His people:*[11] *for they shall be as the stones of a keter,*[12] *sparkling in His land.*[13] *17 For how great is His tov, and how great is His beauty! Grain shall make the young men cheerful, and new wine the maids.*[14]

10 Ask **יהוה** for rain in the time of the latter-ruling-rain; so **יהוה** shall make bright clouds, and give them showers of rain, the plants in the field to everyone.

---

[3] Lake of Fire
[4] The dom of Moshiach, and the covenant He brings, will set all of Yisrael's captives and exiles free by ending spiritual thirst.
[5] Both houses are called "prisoners of hope."
[6] Double power to set both houses free.
[7] The final end-time spiritual battle will be between Hebraic culture in Torah and Greco-Roman culture that has imprisoned Yisrael's children for 2,700 years. The plan of YHWH to defeat this spiritual and religious bondage over the exiles of Yisrael, is to reunite both houses into a physical and spiritual force, where truth and Torah replaces error and religion. Today and in the days ahead, YHWH will continue to reunite us by filling the bow of Judah with the arrows of Ephraim, in the great end-time struggle for truth versus error.
[8] He will "be seen" or empower the sons of Tzion, in their struggle to reclaim their Hebraic heritage and land.
[9] Yahshua will come alongside them, cover them in protection, and return as lightning with the sound of the shofar, and will arrive from the south or from the House of Judah.
[10] YHWH will fight in this battle between cultures and fill Yisrael with the new wine of spiritual and military power, over all heathen influences found in the nation.
[11] Both houses made into the one flock of His own choosing.
[12] Twelve stones for the twelve tribes.
[13] Part of the battle will be both houses fighting to retake all of the Biblical land promised to our fathers.
[14] How fulfilling is the tov fruit and taste of restoration.

---

[1] Fulfilled when Yahshua entered Jerusalem to offer Jewish Yisrael the kingdom.
[2] Moshiach will enter Jerusalem to bring peace between Ephraim and Judah as He cuts off the weapons and levim bent towards war against each other. This two-house healing will then be extended from sea to sea over all nations on earth in His everlasting reign.

2 *For the idols have spoken vanity, and the diviners have seen falsehood, and have told false dreams; they comfort in vain: therefore they wandered about as a flock, they were troubled, because there was no shepherd. 3 My anger was kindled against the shepherds, and I punished the goats: for* יהוה *of hosts has visited His flock Bet Yahudah, and has made them as His splendid horse in the battle. 4 From them shall came forth the Rosh Pina; out of them the nail; out of them the battle bow; and out of them rulers together.[1] 5 And they shall be as mighty men, which tread down their enemies in the mud of the streets in the battle: and they shall fight,[2] because* יהוה *is with them, and the riders on horses shall be confounded. 6 And I will strengthen Bet Yahudah, and I will save the Bet Yoseph, and I will bring them back again; for I have rachamim upon them: and they shall be as though I had not cast them off: for I am* יהוה *their Elohim, and will shema them.[3] 7 And they of Ephraim shall be like a mighty man, and their lev shall rejoice as through wine: yes, their children shall see it, and have gilah; their lev shall rejoice in* יהוה.[4] *8 I will whistle[5] for them, and gather them;[6] for I have redeemed them: and they shall increase as they have increased.[7] 9 And I will scatter them among the nations: and they shall remember Me in far countries;[8] and they shall live together with their children, and return again.[9] 10 I will bring them again also out of the land of Mitzrayim, and gather them out of Ashshur; and I will bring them into the land of Gilead and Levanon; and yet these lands shall not be enough for them.[10] 11 And He shall pass through the sea with affliction, and shall smite the waves in the sea, and all the depths of the river shall dry up: and the pride of Ashshur shall be brought down, and the scepter of Mitzrayim shall depart away.[11] 12 And I will strengthen them in* יהוה; *and they shall have your halacha up and down in His Name,[12] and proclaim the besarot of His Name[13] says* יהוה.

11 Open your doors, O Levanon, that the fire may devour your cedars. 2 Howl, O cypress; for the cedar is fallen; because the mighty are spoiled: howl, O you oaks of Bashan; for the dense forest has come down.[14] 3 There is a voice of the howling of the shepherds; for their tiferet is ruined: a voice of the roaring of young lions; for the forest and pride of Yarden is spoiled. 4 *This says* יהוה *my Elohim; Feed the flock of the slaughter; 5 Whose owners slay them, and hold themselves guiltless: and they that sell them say, Barchu-et-* יהוה *; for I am rich: and their own shepherds do not pity them. 6 For I will no more pity the inhabitants of the land, says* יהוה*: but, I will deliver the men every one into his neighbor's hand, and into the hand of his melech: and they shall smite the land, and out of their hand I will not deliver them.[15] 7 So I will feed the flock destined for slaughter, even you, O poor of the flock.*

---

[1] The Scepter remained in Judah until Moshiach arrived.
[2] In the end-time Greco-Roman versus Zion spiritual battle.
[3] YHWH will regather both houses simultaneously in the end-times by His mercy. When we call, He will answer, as all is restored.
[4] In the restoration, Ephraim will be raised up and no longer discarded as an outcast. They will be filled with the new wine of the Spirit and with newfound bravery, as they join with Judah in the battle against the sons of Greece and their culture.
[5] YHWH's whistle is a shofar.
[6] YHWH's will is to regather Ephraim.
[7] YHWH even now is whistling for Ephraim's return. They are being called out of the nations, in order to be redeemed and manifested to the world. They continue to increase spiritually in their return, even as when they increased in times past by physically filling the nations.
[8] Hebraic idiom for Ephraimite dispersions.
[9] YHWH promises a return of Ephraim from among the *goyim*. Ephraim will be returning from among the nations or *goyim* in far-away places. They are not found totally in modern Judah as some teach, but in all the nations. YHWH's will is to revive Ephraim and their children in all nations and far-away places.
[10] So massive will be Ephraim's end-time revival and return to the land of Yisrael, that no room will be found for their housing in Judah, so they will have to settle in all the land promised to the patriarchs, such as in Lebanon, and the eastern side of Jordan in modern-day Jordan and Iraq.
[11] All the lands of their exile will no longer be able to hold Ephraim captive, as YHWH overcomes their strongholds.
[12] Ephraim's strength in their latter-day return will be resting and strengthening themselves in the true Name of YHWH. Notice that their return is linked to the knowledge of the Name of the Abba.
[13] Aramaic Peshitta.
[14] The prophesied destruction of the Temple on Mt. Moriah in 70 CE.
[15] Babylonian exile.

And I took to Myself two staffs; the one I called Beauty, and the other I called Unity; and I fed the flock.[1] 8 Three shepherds also I cut off in one month; and My very being despised them, and their being also abhorred Me.[2] 9 Then said I, I will not feed you: that which dies, let it die; and what is to be cut off, let it be cut off; and let the rest eat every one the flesh of another.[3] 10 And I took My staff, even Beauty, and cut it in half, that I might break My covenant that I had made with all the non-Yisraelite peoples. 11 And it was broken in that day: and so the poor of the flock that waited upon me knew that it was the word of יהוה. 12 And I said to them, If you think tov, give me My price; and if not, refrain. So they weighed for My price thirty pieces of silver.[4] 13 And יהוה said to me, Cast it to the potter: it is the splendid price that I was valued by them. And I took the thirty pieces of silver, and cast them to the potter in the Bayit of יהוה.[5] 14 Then I cut asunder My other staff, even Unity, that I might break the brotherhood between Yahudah and Yisrael.[6] 15 And יהוה said to me, Take again the instruments of a foolish shepherd. 16 For, look, I will raise up a shepherd in eretz Yisrael, which shall not visit those that are cut off,[7] neither shall he seek the young ones,[8] nor heal that which is broken,[9] nor feed those that stand still:[10] but he shall eat

the flesh of the fat, and tear their claws in pieces.[11] 17 Woe to the idol shepherd that leaves the flock! the sword shall be upon his arm, and upon his right eye: his arm shall wither, and his right eye shall be blinded.[12]

12 The burden of the word of יהוה concerning Yisrael, says יהוה, who stretches forth the shamayim, and lays the foundation of the earth, and forms the ruach of man within him. 2 See, I will make Yahrushalayim a cup of trembling to all the people around her, when they shall be in the siege both against Yahudah and against Yahrushalayim.[13] 3 And in that day will I make Yahrushalayim a burdensome stone for all nations: all that burden themselves with it shall be cut in pieces,[14] though all the nations of the earth be gathered together against it.[15] 4 In that day, says יהוה, I will smite every horse with stupor, and his rider with confusion: and I will open My eyes upon Bet Yahudah, and will smite every horse of the nations with blindness. 5 And the leaders of Yahudah shall say in their lev, The inhabitants of Yahrushalayim are stronger than we are in יהוה of hosts their Elohim. 6 In that day will I make the leaders of Yahudah like a fire pot among the wood, and like a torch of fire in a sheaf; and they shall devour all the peoples all around, on the right hand and on the left: and Yahrushalayim shall be inhabited again in her own place, even in Yahrushalayim.[16] 7 יהוה also shall save the tents of Yahudah first,[17] that the tiferet of Bet David[18] and the tiferet of the inhabitants of Yahrushalayim[19] do not magnify

---

[1] YHWH will rescue both houses from destruction and will feed them truth.
[2] Three sons of King Ahaziah.
[3] YHWH's attitude towards the kings of both houses, who were in the most part wicked.
[4] Yahshua betrayed for thirty pieces of silver.
[5] The rejection of Yahshua, the "beauty of the covenant" for thirty pieces of silver, was pre-figured in the breaking of the staff called Beauty.
[6] The breaking of the second staff was to show that the Unity between Judah and Ephraim was still broken even after the return of Judah from Babylon. Zechariah sealed the display of that broken brotherhood by breaking His staff called "Unity" or "Binders," symbolizing the dissolution of all prior remaining unity. If the Jewish people today are all Yisrael as many falsely teach, then the staff should not have been broken – because according to this false notion, brotherhood was restored at the time of Ezra and Nehemiah. But YHWH shows us different, since Zechariah ministered after the exile was over.
[7] Ephraim.
[8] Judah.
[9] Yisrael's unity.
[10] Who are still in the land of Yisrael.

[11] The end-time anti-Moshiach.
[12] Another reference to the end-time anti-Moshiach, the personification of all of Yisrael's false shepherds through the centuries.
[13] Final end-time battle for Jerusalem.
[14] The nations would be better off keeping their nose out of YHWH's business of restoration, but if they don't, they will be destroyed.
[15] All the world's nations come against Jerusalem to wrestle it away from the people of Yisrael by any means possible.
[16] YHWH will make the Yahudim military unbeatable.
[17] In other words; they will be the first to return to the land of Yisrael before Ephraim, as began in 1948 and continues.
[18] The other non-Jewish tribes in the house of David.
[19] Others such as non-Yisraelite inhabitants.

themselves against Yahudah.[1] 8 In that day shall **יהוה** defend the inhabitants of Yahrushalayim; and he that is feeble among them in that day shall be like David; Bet David shall be like Elohim,[2] as the Malach **יהוה** before them.[3] 9 And it shall come to pass in that day that I will seek to destroy all the nations that come against Yahrushalayim. 10 And I will pour upon Bet David, [4] and upon the inhabitants of Yahrushalayim, the Ruach of unmerited favor and of rachamim: and they shall look upon Me whom they have pierced,[5] [6]and they shall mourn for Him, as one mourns for His only son, and they will be in bitterness for Him, as one that is in bitterness for the loss of his firstborn.[7] 11 In that day shall there be a great mourning in Yahrushalayim, as the mourning of Hadad-Rimmon in the valley of Megiddo. 12 And the land shall mourn, every family apart; the family of Bet David apart, and their wives apart; the family of the bayit of Nathan apart, and their wives apart; [8] 13 The family of the bayit of Levi apart, and their wives apart; the family of Shimei apart, and their wives apart; 14 All the families that remain, every family apart, and their wives apart.

13 In that day [9] there shall be a fountain opened to Bet David and to the inhabitants of Yahrushalayim for sin and for uncleanness.[10] 2 And it shall come to pass in that day, says **יהוה** of hosts, that I will cut off the names of the idols out of the land, [11] and they shall no more be remembered: and also I will cause ha neviim and the unclean ruach to pass out of the land.[12] 3 And it shall come to pass, that when any shall yet prophesy, then his abba and his ima that begat him shall say to him, You shall not live; for you speak lies in the Name of **יהוה**: and his abba and his ima that begat him shall cut him in pieces when he prophesies. 4 And it shall come to pass in that day that ha neviim shall be ashamed everyone of his vision, when he has prophesied; neither shall they wear hairy skin to deceive: 5 But he shall say, I am no navi, I am a farmer; for man taught me to keep cattle from my youth. 6 And one shall say to Him, What are these wounds in Your hands? Then He shall answer, Those with which I was wounded in the bayit of My chaverim. 7 Awake, O sword, against My Shepherd, and against the Man that is My Fellow Companion, [13] says **יהוה** of hosts: smite the Shepherd, and the sheep shall be scattered: and I will turn My hand over the little ones. [14] 8 And it shall come to pass, that in all eretz Yisrael, says **יהוה**, two parts in it shall be cut off and die; but the third part shall be left in it.[15] 9 And I will bring the third part through the fire, and will refine them as silver is refined, and will try them as gold is tried: they shall call on My Name,[16] and I will shema them: I will say, It is My people - Ami: and they shall say, **יהוה** is the Name of My Elohim![17]

14 See, Yom **יהוה** comes, and your spoil shall be divided in the midst of you. 2 For I will gather all nations against Yahrushalayim to battle; and the

---

[1] YHWH will bring all the House of David back to the land, but not before Yahudah, so that the Ephraimites cannot magnify themselves over Yahudah – thereby reinforcing the error of Replacement Theology, that non-Jewish believers who break Torah are somehow the "New Yisrael."
[2] Unbeatable in power and might, against all nations seeking to remove Jerusalem from Yisrael's care.
[3] Yisrael will be as strong as Yahshua Himself.
[4] All 12 tribes.
[5] YHWH was pierced in the first person.
[6] Both houses will see Yahshua.
[7] Yisrael will mourn over YHWH's first brought-forth Son.
[8] The term "apart" indicates orthodox Jewish people, who do religious activity where men and women are separate.
[9] Last days.
[10] The fountain of redemption dom from Emanuel's veins.

[11] Moshiach is returning to remove all false names for YHWH out of the land of Yisrael by force, since man did not act when given the freedom to do so unilaterally.
[12] Renewal of the people and their land.
[13] Yahshua.
[14] Yahshua smitten and the sheep scattered in the **remez**-hint level of Hebraic understanding.
[15] In the final battle for the land, only Jerusalem will be as strong as Elohim, and will be the safest part of the land to be in.
[16] The inhabitants of Jerusalem and the true remnant of Yisrael, will all know and call on His Name, and no longer suppress it.
[17] Not any another false title or name.

city shall be taken, and the houses rifled, and the women ravished; and half of the city shall go forth into captivity, and the residue of the people shall not be cut off from the city.[1] 3 Then shall יהוה go forth, and fight against those nations, as when He fought in the day of battle. 4 And His feet shall stand in that day upon the Mount of Olives, which is before Yahrushalayim on the east,[2] and the Mount of Olives shall split in the middle toward the east and toward the west, and there shall be a very great valley; and half of the har shall move toward the north, and half of it toward the south.[3] 5 And you shall flee to the valley of the mountains; for the valley of the mountains shall reach to Atzal: yes, you shall flee, like you fled from before the earthquake in the days of Uzziyah melech of Yahudah: and יהוה Elohim shall come, and all the kidushim with Him.[4] 6 And in that day, there is no light; it will be dark:[5] 7 But it shall be one day which shall be known to יהוה alone, not day, or night: but it shall come to pass, that at evening time it shall be light. 8 And it shall be in that day, that living waters shall go out from Yahrushalayim; half of them toward the eastern sea, and half of them toward the western sea: in summer and in winter it shall it be. 9 And יהוה shall be Melech over all the earth: in that day shall there be יהוה echad, and His Name echad.[6] 10 All the land shall be changed into a plain from Geba to Rimmon south of Yahrushalayim: and it shall be lifted up, and inhabited in its place, from Benyamin's Gate to the place of

the First Gate, to the Corner Gate, and from the tower of Hanane-El to the melech's winepresses. 11 And men shall dwell in it, and there shall be no more utter destruction; but Yahrushalayim shall be safely inhabited. 12 And this shall be the plague with which יהוה will plague all the nations that have fought against Yahrushalayim; Their flesh shall consume away while they stand upon their feet, and their eyes shall consume away in their sockets, and their tongues will decay in their mouths.[7] 13 And it shall come to pass in that day, that a great confusion from יהוה shall be among them; and they shall lay hold every one on the hand of his neighbor, and his hand shall rise up against the hand of his neighbor. 14 And Yahudah also shall fight at Yahrushalayim; and the wealth of all the nations all around shall be gathered together, gold, and silver, and garments, in great abundance.[8] 15 And so shall be the plague of the horse, of the mule, of the camel, and of the donkey, and of all the beasts that shall be in these tents, as this plague. 16 And it shall come to pass, that every one that is left of all the nations which came against Yahrushalayim shall even go up from year to year to worship the Melech, יהוה of hosts, and to observe and guard the Sukkot - Feast of Tabernacles.[9] 17 And it shall be, that anyone who will not come up of all the families of the earth to Yahrushalayim to worship the Melech, יהוה of hosts, even upon them shall be no rain.[10] 18 And if the family of Mitzrayim does not go up, and enter in, they have no rain; this shall be the plague, by which יהוה will smite the nations that do not come up to keep the Sukkot - Feast of Tabernacles. 19 This shall be the

---

[1] The city will be temporarily overcome until Yahshua goes forth. This does not contradict other prophecies speaking of Jerusalem's might and strength in the final battle of this age. This is seen as just a temporary low tide of battle.
[2] Yahshua returns as said in Acts 1:11.
[3] In order to form the Valley of Jehosaphat, and to clear the way for mankind to head west back into paradise. For more details, see: **An Altar Of Authority** at:
http://store.yourarmstoisrael.org/Qstore/Qstore.cgi?CMD=011 &PROD=1065766783
[4] These are the resurrected believers from both the First and Renewed Covenants.
[5] His coming will light up the earth around the globe so that every eye will see Him, but He comes against the background of pitch darkness.
[6] His Name and His people who bear His Name will alone be left standing in the age to come.

[7] YHWH will visit the attackers with nuclear fallout.
[8] As promised in Torah, Yisrael would be the eternal head and not the tail in the age to come.
[9] Every subdued and defeated nation will worship YHWH in the person of Yahshua and observe Torah, including the feasts.
[10] Draught is the punishment for breaking Torah and not observing the feasts. All nations will observe the feasts in the millennium, so they cannot be "Jewish feasts" or the exclusive possession of Jewish Yisrael.

punishment of Mitzrayim, and the punishment of all the nations that do not come up to observe and guard the Sukkot - Feast of Tabernacles. 20 *In that day shall there be upon the bells of the horses, Kadosh-Le-* יהוה*; and the pots in* יהוה*'s Bayit shall be like the bowls before the altar.*

21 *Yes, every pot in Yahrushalayim and in Yahudah shall be set-apart to* יהוה *of hosts: and all they that sacrifice shall come and take them, and cook in them: and in that day there shall be no more Kanaanite merchants in the Bayit of* יהוה *of hosts.*

מלאכי

Malachi - Malachi

To Our Forefathers Yisrael

1 The burden of the word of **יהוה** to Yisrael by Malachi. 2 *I have loved you,* says **יהוה***. Yet you say, In what way have You loved us? Was not Esav Yaakov's brother?* Says **יהוה***: yet I loved Yaakov,* 3 *And I hated Esav, and laid his mountains and his heritage waste for the jackals of the wilderness.* 4 *Yet Edom says, We are beaten down, but we will return and rebuild the desolate places;* this says **יהוה** of hosts, *They shall build, but I will throw down; and they shall call them, The borders of wickedness, and, The people against whom* **יהוה** *has indignation forever.* 5 *And your eyes shall see, and you shall say,* **יהוה** *will be magnified from beyond the borders of Yisrael.* 6 *A son honors his abba, and an eved his master: if then I am an Abba, where is My honor? And if I am a Master, where is reverence for Me?* Says **יהוה** of hosts to you, *O kohanim, that despise My Name. And you say, In what way have we despised Your Name?* 7 *You offer unclean foods upon My altar; and you say, In what way have we polluted You? By saying, The table of* **יהוה** *is despicable.* 8 *And if you offer the blind for sacrifice, is it not evil? And if you offer the lame and sick, is it not evil? Offer it now to your governor; will he be pleased with you, or will he accept you favorably?* Says **יהוה** of hosts. 9 *And now, seek the face of El that He will show unmerited favor to us: this disaster has been brought on by your own doing; so I will not show you favor,* says **יהוה** of hosts. 10 *Who is there among you that would guard My doors or kindle a fire on My altar for nothing? I have no pleasure in you,* says **יהוה** of hosts, *neither will I accept an offering at your hand.* 11 *For from the rising of the sun even to the going down of the same My Name shall be great among the nations; and in every place incense* shall be offered to My Name, and a pure offering: for My Name shall be great among the nations* says **יהוה** of hosts.[1] 12 *But you have profaned it, in that you say, The table of* **יהוה** *is polluted; and its fruit, even its food, is despicable.* 13 *You said also, Behold, what a burden is it! And you have sneered at it,* says **יהוה** of hosts*; and you brought that which was torn, and the lame, and the sick; this you brought as My offering: should I accept this from your hand?* says **יהוה***. 14 But cursed be the deceiver, who has in his flock a perfect male, and vows, and yet sacrifices to* **יהוה** *a corrupt thing: for I am a great Melech,* says **יהוה** of hosts*, and My Name is feared among the nations.*[2]

2 *And now, O kohanim, this commandment is for you.* 2 *If you will not shema, and if you will not lay it to lev, to give tiferet to My Name,*[3] says **יהוה** of hosts, *I will even send a curse upon you, and I will curse your blessings: yes, I have cursed them already, because you do not lay it to lev.* 3 *Behold, I will corrupt your zera, and spread dung upon your faces, even the dung of your moadim; and one shall take you away with it.*[4][5] 4 *And you shall know that I have sent this commandment to you, that My covenant might be with Levi,* says **יהוה** of hosts. 5 *My covenant was with him for chayim and shalom; and I gave them to him for the fear*

---

[1] Through the Tov News, Yahweh's Name is being restored and declared among the nations once again, after being banned by religion for 2,500 years or so. The nations (or Ephraim) are doing the proclaiming in obedience to, and in accord with, the Tov News.
[2] See note on verse 11.
[3] Yisrael and her leaders have no choice. Withholding the true Name (regardless of the excuse) will result in a curse from YHWH. This is plain and simple for all to understand.
[4] Keeping the feasts without giving honor to YHWH's Name and obeying His Torah results in corruption.
[5] One of the reasons (among many) that Jewish Yisrael was exiled was the denial and desecration of the Name.

by which he feared Me, and was in awe of My Name.[1] 6 The Torah of truth was in his mouth, and iniquity was not found in his lips: he had his halacha with Me in shalom and equity, and did turn many away from their iniquity. 7 For the kohen's lips should keep knowledge, and they should seek the Torah at his mouth: for he is the messenger of יהוה of hosts. 8 But you have departed from the halacha; you have caused many to stumble at the Torah; you have corrupted the covenant of Levi, says יהוה of hosts. 9 Therefore have I also made you despicable and low before all the people, according as you have not kept My halachot, but have shown partiality in applying the Torah. 10 Have we not all one Abba?[2] Has not one El created us? Why do we deal treacherously every man against his brother, by profaning the covenant of our ahvot? 11 Yahudah has dealt treacherously, and an abomination is committed in Yisrael [3] and in Yahrushalayim; for Yahudah has profaned the set-apartness of יהוה which He loved, and has married the daughter of a strange elohim. 12 יהוה will cut off the man that does this, also his son and his son's son, out of the tabernacles of Yaakov,[4] and him that offers an offering to יהוה of hosts. 13 And this have you done again, covering the altar of יהוה with tears, with weeping, and with crying, so that He regards not the offering any more, or receives it with tov will from your hand. 14 Yet you say, Why? Because יהוה has been a witness between you and the wife of your youth, against whom you have dealt treacherously: yet she is your companion, and the wife of your covenant.[5] 15 And did not He make them echad? Yet he had the remnant of the Ruach. And why echad?

That he might seek a seed of Elohim. [6] Therefore take heed to your ruach, and let none deal treacherously against the wife of his youth. 16 For יהוה, the Elohim of Yisrael, says that He hates divorce: like the one who covers his sin with his garment, says יהוה of hosts: therefore guard your ruach, that you deal not treacherously with her. 17 You have wearied יהוה with your words. Yet you say, In what way have we wearied Him? When you say, Everyone that does evil is tov in the sight of יהוה, and He delights in them; or, Where is the Elohim of mishpat?[7]

3 Behold, I will send My messenger, and He shall prepare the Way[8] before Me:[9] [10] and יהוה, whom you seek,[11] shall suddenly[12] come to His Beit HaMikdash, [13] even the messenger of the covenant,[14] whom you delight in: see, He shall come, says יהוה of hosts. 2 But who may endure the day of His coming? And who shall stand when He appears? For He is like a refiner's fire, and like launderers' soap:[15] [16] 3 And He shall sit as a refiner and purifier of silver: and He shall purify b'nai Levi, and purge them as gold and silver, that they may offer to יהוה an offering in tzedakah.[17] 4 Then shall the offering of Yahudah and Yahrushalayim be pleasant to יהוה, as in the days of old, and as in former years. 5 And I will come near to you for mishpat; and I will be a swift witness against the sorcerers, and against the adulterers, and against false swearers, and against those

---

[1] Levi and the kohanim used to be in ahava with His Name, to proclaim and seek shelter in it – until the rabbinical ban pronounced around 350 BCE.
[2] Judah and Ephraim need to get this settled.
[3] Both houses stand guilty before YHWH.
[4] That is exactly what happened to both houses as they were removed from the Tabernacle of David that had fallen.
[5] Rampant divorce in both houses of Yisrael was another reason for our exile.

[6] That Yisrael would collectively be His son.
[7] False accusations cause YHWH to quickly lose patience.
[8] First-century Torah-believers were first known as members of "the Way."
[9] Yochanan HaMatbeel.
[10] Notice YHWH who is coming to Jerusalem, speaks here in the first person.
[11] YHWH in the manifestation of Yahshua.
[12] With great surprise to Yisrael.
[13] A response to verse 17: "Where is the Elohim of right ruling?" He is coming in person physically to His Temple.
[14] Yahshua the messenger of the Renewed Covenant, with both houses according to Jeremiah 31:31.
[15] Yahshua's mission is to fully refine and clean up all Yisrael.
[16] This is YHWH speaking about YHWH.
[17] He will cleanse and restore the kohanim of Yisrael as well. For more details, see:
http://yourarmstoisrael.org/Articles_new/restoration/?page=16&type=12.

that oppress the wage earner in his wages, the widow, and the fatherless, and that turn away the stranger from his rights in Yisrael,[1] and fear Me not, says יהוה of hosts. 6 For I am יהוה, I change not; therefore you sons of Yaakov are not consumed.[2] 7 Even from the days of your ahvot you have gone away from My Torot, and have not guarded them. Make teshuvah to Me, and I will return to you, says יהוה of hosts. But you said, In what way shall we make teshuvah? 8 Will a man rob Elohim? Yet you have robbed Me. But you say, In what way have we robbed You? In the ma'aser and the terumah. 9 You are cursed with a curse: for you have robbed Me, even this whole nation. 10 Bring all the ma'aser into the storehouse, that there may be food in My House, and prove Me now in this thing, says יהוה of hosts, if I will not open to you the windows of the heavens, and pour you out a bracha, so that there shall not be room enough to receive it. 11 And I will rebuke the devourer[3] for your sakes, and he shall not destroy the fruits of your ground; neither shall your vine cast her fruit before its time in the field, says יהוה of hosts. 12 And all nations shall call you blessed: for you shall be a land of delight, says יהוה of hosts. 13 Your words have been harsh against Me, says יהוה. Yet you say, What have we spoken against You? 14 You have said, It is worthless to serve Elohim: and what profit is it that we have kept His Torot, and that we have had our halacha in meekness before יהוה of hosts? 15 So now we will call the proud happy; yes, they that work wickedness are lifted up; yes, they that test Elohim, even they are delivered. 16 Then they that feared יהוה spoke often one to another:[4] and יהוה listened, and heard it, and a Scroll of

Remembrance[5] [6] was written before Him for them that fear יהוה, and that thought upon His Name. 17 And they shall be Mine, says יהוה of hosts, in that day when I make up My jewels;[7] and I will spare them, as a man spares his own son that serves him.[8] 18 Then shall you make teshuvah,[9] and discern between the tzadik and the wicked, between him that serves Elohim and him that serves Him not.[10]

4 *For, see, the day comes, that shall burn as an oven; and all the proud, yes, and all that do wickedly, shall be stubble: and the day that comes shall burn them up, says יהוה of hosts, that it shall leave them neither root nor branch.[11] 2 But to you that fear My Name[12] shall the Sun of tzedakah arise with healing in His four-cornered tzitzit; and you shall go forth, and grow up as calves of the stall.[13] 3 And you shall tread down the wicked; for they shall be ashes[14] under the soles of your feet in the day that I shall do this, says יהוה of hosts. 4 Remember the Torah of Moshe My eved, which I commanded to him in Horeb for all Yisrael, with the chukim and mishpatim.[15] 5 Behold, I will send you Eliyahu Ha Navi*

---

[1] Yahshua came to fix the pride of those who do not let non-Jewish Yisraelites back into full commonwealth rights and citizenship.
[2] What an eternally comforting truth. Since YHWH changes not, Yisrael is His only eternal bride.
[3] s.a.tan.
[4] Regular or casual conversation.

[5] A special book.
[6] This is neither the Lamb's Book of Eternal Life nor the Book of Life. This is a special book for those believers who walk in Torah, and who use, pronounce, worship, sing, and have casual conversations between themselves and others, using YHWH's true and wonderful Name. The context here is that YHWH listens even to casual conversation amongst believers using His real and true Name. This verse speaks against those who claim we are not to use YHWH's Name in casual conversation. For more details, see:
http://yourarmstoisrael.org/Editorials/?page=BACKSLIDDEN_SACRED_TRUE_NAMERS&type=3.
[7] Referring to true Name believers, who are called jewels in the nation.
[8] Spared from YHWH's wrath.
[9] In the end-time restoration and regathering of all Yisrael.
[10] In context here, those who use the correct Name serve Him, and those who do not, or stubbornly refuse to use the correct Name due to religious tradition, do not serve Him, These are YHWH's words, not man's opinion.
[11] The end of the lost is to be burned and cease to exist.
[12] Fearing His Name is again associated with right-standing before YHWH and eternal life.
[13] Yahshua's fringes will grow and mature us into a full healing in our return to Yisrael.
[14] End of the lost is annihilation, not eternal life in hell.
[15] Remembering His Torah is a mark of returning Yisrael. In the restoration of Yisrael, all Yisrael will keep His Torah, since YHWH states that it was given for all Israel, not just for Jewish-Yisrael.

before the coming of the great and dreadful Yom יהוה*:[1] 6 And he shall turn the lev of the ahvot to the children, and the lev of the children to their ahvot,[2] lest I come and smite the earth with a curse through utter destruction.[3]*

---

[1] Elijah will announce the coming of the kingdom as the day that is great for redeemed Yisrael, but dreadful for those who are not regenerated Yisrael.

[2] The fathers are the patriarchs, and we are the children. Elijah's job is to fully prepare the two-house restoration, by turning Yisrael away from the pagan nations and their practices, and back to Torah and the ways of the patriarchs, in order to prepare us for the return of King Moshiach.

[3] The restoration and regathering of Yisrael back to Torah and the land, is what withholds the earth from an eternal curse. Our presence here and our return to Yisrael spiritually and physically, allows YHWH to lift any curse on the earth.

תהלים

Tehillim - Psalms

To Our Forefathers Yisrael

Alef

1 [1] Blessed is the man that walks not in the counsel of the wicked, nor stands in the halacha of sinners, nor sits in the seat of the scoffers.

2 But his delight is in the Torah of **יהוה**; and in His Torah does he meditate day and night.

3 And he shall be like a tree planted by the rivers of mayim that brings forth its fruit in its season; his leaf also shall not wither; and whatever he does shall prosper.

4 The wicked are not so: but are like the chaff that the wind drives away.

5 Therefore the wicked shall not stand in the mishpat, nor sinners in the congregation of the tzadikim.[2]

6 For **יהוה** knows the halacha of the tzadikim: but the halacha of the wicked shall perish.

Bet

2 [3] Why do the nations rage, and the people imagine a vain thing?

2 The melechim of the earth set themselves and the rulers take counsel together, against **יהוה**, and against His Moshiach,[4] saying,

3 Let us break their bands asunder, and cast away their cords from us.

4 He that sits in the shamayim shall laugh: **יהוה** shall have them in derision.

5 Then shall He speak to them in His anger, and trouble them in His heavy displeasure.

6 Yet have I set My melech upon My set-apart Har Tzion.[5]

7 I will declare the decree: **יהוה** has said to Me, You are My Son;[6] this day have I brought You forth.[7]

8 Ask of Me, and I shall give You the nations for Your inheritance, and the furthest parts of the earth for Your possession.[8]

9 You shall break them with a rod of iron; you shall dash them in pieces like a potter's vessel.

10 Be wise now therefore, O melechim: be instructed, shophtim of the earth.

11 Serve **יהוה** with fear, and gilah with trembling.

12 Kiss the Son,[9] lest He be angry, and you perish from the halacha,[10] when His anger is kindled even slightly. Blessed are all they that put their trust in Him.[11]

Gimel

3 [12] **יהוה**, how are they increased that trouble me! Many are they that rise up against me.

2 Many there are who say of my being, There is no help for him in Elohim. Selah.

3 But You, O **יהוה**, are a shield for me; my tiferet and the lifter of my head.

4 I cried to **יהוה** with my voice, and He heard me out of His set-apart har. Selah.

5 I laid me down and slept; and I awoke for **יהוה** sustained me.

6 I will not be afraid of ten thousands of people, that have set themselves against me all around.7 Arise, O **יהוה**; save me, O my Elohim: for You have smitten all my enemies upon the cheek; You have broken the teeth of the wicked.

8 Salvation belongs to **יהוה**: Your bracha is upon Your people. Selah.

---

[1] The life of a Torah-honoring Nazarene Yisraelite that is pleasing to YHWH.
[2] Yisrael.
[3] A messianic psalm with many details of Moshiach Yahshua.
[4] Hebrew: **Meshecho.**
[5] Moshiach Yahshua.
[6] Yahshua.

[7] Hebrew: **B'nee atah ani hayom yeladtecha.**
[8] The Son of YHWH will inherit all nations as decreed by YHWH.
[9] Nashku Bar.
[10] The name of the first-century faith in Yahshua; "The Way" or the Nazarenes.
[11] Hebrew: **Ashrai kol chosai bo.**
[12] The believer and his trust at all times.

Daled

4 [1] Shema to me when I call, O Elohim of my tzedakah: You have given me relief when I was in distress; have rachamim upon me, and shema my tefillah.

2 O you sons of men, how long will you turn my tiferet into shame? How long will you love vanity, and seek after falsehood? Selah.

3 But know that **יהוה** has set-apart him that is tzadik for Himself: **יהוה** will shema when I call to Him.

4 Stand in awe, and sin not: commune with your own lev upon your bed, and be still. Selah.

5 Offer the sacrifices of tzedakah, and put your trust in **יהוה**.

6 There be many that say; Who will show us any tov? **יהוה**, lift up the light of Your face upon us.

7 You have put simcha in my lev, more than in the time that their grain and their wine increased.

8 I will both lay me down in shalom, and sleep: for You alone O, **יהוה**, make me dwell in safety.

Hey

5 [2] Shema to my words, O **יהוה**, consider my meditation.

2 Shema to the voice of my cry, My Melech, and My Elohim: for to you will I make tefillah.

3 My voice shall You shema in the morning, O **יהוה**; in the morning will I direct my tefillah to You, and will look up.

4 For You are not an El that has pleasure in wickedness: neither shall evil dwell with You.

5 The foolish proud do not stand in Your sight: You hate all the workers of iniquity.

6 You shall destroy them that speak falsehood: **יהוה** abhors the bloody and deceitful man.

7 But as for me, I will come into Your Bayit in the multitude of Your rachamim: and in

Your fear will I worship toward Your Set-Apart Beit HaMikdash.

8 Lead me, O **יהוה**, in Your tzedakah because of my enemies; make Your halacha straight before my face.

9 For there is no faithfulness in their mouth; their inward part is very wicked; their throat is an open grave; they flatter with their tongue.

10 Destroy them, O Elohim; let them fall by their own counsels; cast them out in the multitude of their transgressions; for they have rebelled against You.

11 But let all those that put their trust in You gilah: let them le-olam-va-ed shout for simcha, because You defend them: let them also that love Your Name[3] be joyful in You.

12 For You, **יהוה**, will bless the tzadik; with favor will You surround him as with a shield.

Vav

6 [4] O **יהוה**, rebuke me not in Your anger, neither discipline me in Your displeasure.

2 Have rachamim upon me, O **יהוה**; for I am weak: O **יהוה**, heal me; for my bones are fading away.

3 My being is also very troubled: but You, O **יהוה** - how long?

4 Return, O **יהוה**, deliver my being: save me for Your rachamim's sake.

5 For in death there is no remembrance of You: in the grave who shall give You hodu?

6 I am weary with my groaning; all night I flood my bed; in mayim I drench my couch with my tears.

7 My eye is consumed because of grief; it grows old because of all my enemies.

8 Depart from me, all you workers of iniquity; for **יהוה** has heard the voice of my weeping.

9 **יהוה** has heard my pleading; **יהוה** will receive my tefillah.

10 Let all my enemies be ashamed and very troubled: let them return suddenly and be ashamed.

---

[1] The shalom of a believing Yisraelite.
[2] YHWH will favor the righteous over the wicked.
[3] A special joy to those loving the true Name.
[4] Looking to YHWH in tears and trouble.

Zayin

7 [1] O יהוה my Elohim, in You do I put my trust: save me from all them that persecute me, and deliver me:

2 Lest he tear my being like a lion, rending it in pieces, while there is none to deliver.

3 O יהוה My Elohim, if I have done this; if there be iniquity in my hands;

4 If I have rewarded evil to him that was at shalom with me; or if I have delivered him without cause who is my enemy.

5 Then let the enemy persecute my being, and take it; yes, let him trample down my chayim upon the earth, and lay my honor in the dust. Selah.

6 Arise, O יהוה, in Your anger, lift Yourself up because of the rage of my enemies: and awake for me to the mishpat that You have commanded.

7 So shall the congregation of the nations surround You:[2] for their sakes therefore return on high.

8 יהוה shall shophet the nations: shophet me, O יהוה, according to my tzedakah, and according to my integrity that is in me.

9 Oh let the wickedness of the wicked come to an end; but establish the just: for the Tzadik Elohim tries the levim and kidneys.

10 My defense is on Elohim, who saves the tzadik in lev.

11 Elohim shophets the tzadikim, and El is angry at the wicked every day.

12 If he does not make teshuvah, He will sharpen His sword; He has bent His bow, and made it ready.

13 He has also prepared for Himself instruments of death; He ordains His arrows against the persecutors.

14 See, he who is bound with iniquity and has conceived evil, and brought forth falsehood.

15 He made a pit, and dug it, and has fallen into the ditch, which he made.

16 His evil shall return upon his own head, and his violent dealings shall come down upon the top of his head.

17 I will hallel יהוה according to His tzedakah: and will shir hallel to the Name of יהוה most high.[3]

Chet

8 [4] O יהוה our Master, how excellent is Your Name in all the earth! You who have set Your tiferet above the shamayim.

2 Out of the mouth of babes and sucklings have You ordained strength because of Your enemies, that You might silence the enemy and the avenger.

3 When I consider Your shamayim, the work of Your fingers, the moon and the chochavim, which You ordained;

4 What is man, that You are mindful of him? And the ben Adam, that You visit him?

5 For You have made him a little lower than the heavenly messengers, and have crowned him with tiferet and honor.

6 You made him to have rule over the works of Your hands; You have put all things under his feet:

7 All sheep and oxen, and also the beasts of the field;

8 The fowl of the air, and the fish of the sea, and whatever passes through the paths of the seas.

9 O יהוה our Master, how excellent is Your Name in all the earth![5]

Tet

9 [6] I will tehilla You, O יהוה, with my whole lev; I will show forth all Your marvelous works.

2 I will be in simcha and gilah in You: I will shir tehillot to Your Name,[7] O Most High.

3 When my enemies turn back, they shall fall and perish at Your shechinah.

---

[1] The view of the wicked.
[2] Renewed Covenant Yisrael; the assembly of the nations.
[3] Our songs must have His true Name or they are not considered fitting worship songs.
[4] Man's position in creation.
[5] Among reborn Yisrael.
[6] Rejoicing in YHWH's protection, deliverance, and victory over nations.
[7] Not to Your titles or translated name.

4 For You have maintained my right and my cause; You sat in the throne judging right.

5 You have rebuked the nations, You have destroyed the wicked, You have put out their name le-olam-va-ed.

6 O my enemy, your ruin is le-olam-va-ed: and You have destroyed cities; even their remembrance has perished with them.

7 But יהוה shall endure le-olam-va-ed: He has prepared His throne for mishpat.

8 And He shall shophet the olam in tzedakah; He shall serve mishpat to the nations in tzedakah.

9 יהוה also will be a refuge for the oppressed, a refuge in times of trouble.

10 And they that know Your Name will put their trust in You:[1] for You, יהוה, have not forsaken those that seek You.

11 Sing tehillot to יהוה, who dwells in Tzion: declare among the nations His deeds.

12 He remembers those who seek domshed, He remembers them: He forgets not the cry of the humble.

13 Have rachamim upon me, O יהוה; consider my trouble that I allow from them that hate me, You that lift me up from the shaarai mavet:

14 That I may show forth all Your tehilla in the gates of the daughter of Tzion: I will gilah in Your salvation.

15 The nations are sunk down in the pit that they made: into the net where they hid is their own foot taken.

16 יהוה is known by the mishpat that He executes: the wicked is trapped in the work of his own hands. Higayon. Selah.

17 The wicked shall be turned into Sheol, along with all the nations that forget Elohim.

18 For the needy shall not always be forgotten: the tikvah of the poor shall not perish le-olam-va-ed.

19 Arise, O יהוה; let not man prevail: let the nations be judged in Your sight.

20 Put them in fear, O יהוה: so that the nations may know that they themselves are just men. Selah.

Yud

10 [2] Why do you stand far off, O יהוה? Why do You hide Yourself in times of trouble?

2 The wicked in his pride does persecute the poor: let them be taken in the same plans that they have imagined.

3 For the wicked boasts of his lev's desire, and blesses the greedy, whom יהוה despises.

4 The wicked, through the pride of his face, will not seek after Elohim: Elohim is not in his thoughts at all.

5 His halachot are always prosperous; Your mishpat are far above his sight: as for all His enemies, He snorts at them.

6 He has said in his lev, I shall not be moved: for I shall never be in adversity.

7 His mouth is full of cursing and deceit and fraud: under his tongue is evil and vanity.

8 He sits in the hiding places of the villages: in the secret places does he murder the innocent: his eyes are on the lookout against the helpless.

9 He lies in wait secretly as a lion in his den: he lies in wait to catch the helpless: he does catch the helpless, when he draws him into his net.

10 He crouches, and lies low, that the helpless may fall by his strength.

11 He says in his lev, El has forgotten: He hides His face; He will never see it.

12 Arise, O יהוה; O El, lift up Your hand: forget not the lowly.

13 Why does the wicked scorn Elohim? He has said in his lev, You will not require it.

14 You have seen it; for You see evil and grief, to repay with Your hand: the poor commits himself to You; You are the helper of the fatherless.

---

[1] One cannot trust fully without knowing His Name.

[2] Where is YHWH in the face of evil?

15 Break the arm of the wicked and the evil man: seek out his wickedness until you find no more.

16 יהוה is Melech le-olam-va-ed: the nations shall perish out of His land.[1]

17 יהוה, You have heard the desire of the humble: You will prepare their lev, You will cause Your ear to shema them:

18 To shophet the fatherless and the oppressed, that the man of the earth may no more oppress.

Yud Aleph

11 [2] In יהוה put I my trust: Why do you say to my being, Flee as a bird to your har?

2 For, look, the wicked bend their bow; they make ready their arrow upon the string that they may secretly shoot at the tzadik in lev.

3 If the foundations are destroyed, what can the tzadikim do?

4 יהוה is in His Set-Apart Beit HaMikdash, יהוה's throne is in the shamayim: His eyes observe, His eyelids test, the children of men.

5 יהוה tries the tzadikim: but the wicked and those that love violence His being hates.

6 Upon the wicked He shall rain snares, fire and brimstone, and a horrible storm: this shall be the portion of their cup.

7 For יהוה is Tzadik, He loves tzedakah; His face does observe the tzadik.

Yud Bet

12 [3] Help, יהוה; for the tzadik man ceases; for trust has ceased from among the children of men.

2 They speak vanity each one with his neighbor: with flattering lips and with a double lev do they speak.

3 יהוה shall cut off all flattering lips, and the tongue that speaks proud things:

4 Who has said, With our tongue will we prevail; our lips are our own: who is master over us?

5 Because of the oppression of the poor, because of the sighing of the needy, now will I arise, says יהוה; I will set him in safety from him that snorts at him.

6 The words of יהוה are pure words: as silver tried in a furnace of the earth, purified seven times.[4]

7 You shall keep them, O יהוה, You shall preserve them from this generation le-olam-va-ed.

8 The wicked walk on every side, when vanity is exalted among the sons of men.

Yud Gimel

13 [5] How long will You forget me, O יהוה? Le-olam-va-ed? How long will You hide Your face from me?

2 How long shall I take counsel in my being, having sorrow in my lev daily? How long shall my enemy be exalted over me?

3 Consider and shema to me, O יהוה My Elohim: enlighten my eyes, lest I sleep the sleep of death;

4 Lest my enemy say, I have prevailed against him; and those that trouble me gilah when I am moved.

5 But I have trusted in Your rachamim; my lev shall gilah in Your salvation.

6 I will shir to יהוה, because He has dealt abundantly tov with me.

Yud Daled

14 The fool has said in his lev, There is no Elohim. They are corrupt, they have done abominable works; there is none that does tov.

2 יהוה looked down from the shamayim upon the children of men, to see if there were any that did understand, and seek Elohim.

---

[1] All heathen nations will be removed from the land of Yisrael in the **atid lavoh.**
[2] YHWH does right.
[3] YHWH does right by His Word.

[4] Each original Word was tested seven times; before it was allowed to be recorded.
[5] YHWH will hear and do right.

3 They are all turned aside, they are all together become filthy: there is none that does tov, no, not one.

4 Have all the workers of iniquity no da'at? Who eat up my people as they eat lechem, and call not upon יהוה.

5 There they are in great fear: for Elohim is in the generation of the tzadikim.

6 You have shamed the counsel of the poor, because יהוה is his refuge.

7 Oh that the Yahshua of Yisrael did come from Tzion! When יהוה brings back the exiles of His people, Yaakov shall gilah, and Yisrael shall be in simcha.[1]

Tet Vav

15 [2] יהוה, who shall abide in Your sukkah? Who shall dwell in Your Set-Apart har?

2 He that has their halacha in tzadik mitzvot, and works tzedakah, and speaks the emet in his lev.

3 He that does not backbite with his tongue, nor does evil to his neighbor, nor takes up a reproach against his neighbor.

4 In whose eyes a vile person is despised; but he honors them that fear יהוה. He that swears to his own hurt, and yet keeps the vow.

5 He that puts not his money to interest, nor takes a bribe against the innocent. He that does these things shall never be moved.

Tet Zayin

16 [3] Preserve me, O El: for in You do I put my trust.

2 O my being, you have said to יהוה, You are יהוה: I have no tov qualities without You;

3 But to the kidushim that are in the earth, and to the excellent ones, in whom is all my delight.

4 Their sorrows shall be multiplied that run after other elohim: their drink offerings of

dom will I not offer, nor take up their names into my lips.[4]

5 יהוה is the portion of my inheritance and of my cup: You preserve my lot.

6 The property lines are given to me in pleasant places; yes, I have a tov inheritance.

7 I will bless יהוה, who has given me counsel: my kidneys also instruct me in the night seasons.

8 I have set יהוה always before me: because He is at my right hand, I shall not be moved.

9 Therefore my lev is in simcha, and my tiferet has gilah: my flesh also shall rest in tikvah.

10 *For You will not leave My Being in Sheol; neither will You allow Your Set-Apart One to see corruption.[5][6]*

11 *You will show me the derech of chayim:[7] in Your shechinah is fullness of simcha; at Your Right Hand [8] there are pleasures and victories[9] le-olam-va-ed.[10]*

Yud Zayin

17 [11] Shema tzedakah, O יהוה, attend to my cry, shema to my tefillah, that goes not out of tainted lips.

---

[1] When both houses return to the land and receive Yahshua.

[2] A description of the righteous Yisraelite.

[3] The resurrection of Moshiach and all of Nazarene Yisrael.

[4] A Yisraelite must refuse to compromise with pagan substitute names and titles for YHWH.

[5] Yahshua the Set-Apart-One of Yisrael was not allowed to stay in the grave for more than three days and nights; thereby-bypassing corruption. In Psalms 16:10 we see the Set-Apart-One of Yisrael, as the One and Only One who did not have His corpse corrupt in the grave (**sheol**) but would see the light of resurrection life by receiving the path of life according to verse 11. This new resurrected life is said to be found at the right hand of YHWH, as confirmed in Psalm 110:1 and 5. This verse is one of the most quoted in all of the inspired Renewed Covenant Scriptures.

[6] The Hebrew word for "Your Holy One" is **kedoshecha**, but the Masoretes and their anti-missionary friends have changed the word to **chasdecha** meaning "Your Kind or Merciful One," which of course can be applied to anyone, as opposed to The Set-Apart One of Yisrael. **Kedoshecha**, therefore can only refer to Yahshua or Abba YHWH. Since Abba never took on flesh we are left with a clear reference to Yahshua and His bodily resurrection. David also did not qualify based on his own confessions in Psalm 51 and elsewhere, as he was far from a "holy one."

[7] Abba will show His Son the path of resurrection life.

[8] Where Yahshua sits.

[9] Hebrew: **Netzach.**

[10] For all Nazarene Yisraelite followers of truth.

[11] The righteous differs from the wicked.

2 Let my mishpat come forth from Your shechinah; let Your eyes observe the things that are equal.
3 You have proved my lev; You have visited me in the night; You have tried me, and shall find nothing evil; I am purposed that my mouth shall not transgress.
4 Concerning the works of men, by the word of Your lips I have kept myself from the paths of the destroyer.
5 Hold up my goings in Your halacha, that my footsteps slip not.
6 I have called upon You, for You will shema to me, O El: incline Your ear to me, and shema to my speech.
7 Show Your marvelous loving chesed, O You that saves by Your Right Hand[1] to those who put their trust in You from those that rise up against them.
8 Keep me as the apple of Your eye; hide me under the shadow of Your wings,
9 From the wicked that oppress me, from my deadly enemies, who surround me.
10 They are enclosed in their own fat: with their mouth they speak proudly.
11 They have now surrounded us in our steps: they have set their eyes to cast us to the earth;
12 Like a lion that is greedy of his prey, and as it were a young lion hiding in secret places.
13 Arise, O יהוה, disappoint him, cast him down: deliver my being from the wicked, by Your sword:
14 From men by Your hand, O יהוה from men of the olam, whose portion is in this chayim only, and whose wombs You fill with Your treasure: they are full of children, and leave the rest of their substance to their babies.
15 As for me, I will observe Your face in tzedakah: I shall be satisfied, when I awake, with Your likeness.[2]

Yud Chet

18 [3] I will love you, O יהוה My strength.

2 יהוה is My Rock, and My fortress, and my deliverer; My El, My strength, in whom I will trust; My shield, and the horn of My salvation, My high tower.
3 I will call upon יהוה who is worthy to be given tehilla: so shall I be saved from my enemies.
4 The cords of death surrounded me, and the floods of Beliya'al made me afraid.
5 The cords of Sheol surrounded me: the snares of death were before me.
6 In my distress I called upon יהוה and cried to My Elohim: He heard my voice out of His Beit HaMikdash, and my cry came before Him, even into His ears.
7 Then the earth shook and trembled; the foundations also of the hills moved and were shaken, because He was angry.
8 There went up smoke out of His nostrils, and fire out of His mouth; coals were kindled by it.
9 He bowed the shamayim also, and came down: and darkness was under His feet.
10 And He rode upon a cheruv, and did fly: yes, He did fly upon the wings of the wind.
11 He made darkness His covering; His citadel around Him was dark mayim and thick clouds of the skies.
12 At the brightness that was before Him His thick clouds passed, hail stones and coals of fire.
13 יהוה also thundered in the shamayim, and the Highest gave His voice; hail and coals of fire.
14 Yes, He sent out His arrows, and scattered them; and He shot out lightnings, and confused them.
15 Then the channels of mayim were seen, and the foundations of the olam were uncovered at Your rebuke, O יהוה, at the blast of the breath of Your nostrils.
16 He sent from above, He took me, He drew me out of many mayim.

---

[1] Yahshua.
[2] All Nazarene Yisraelite believers will be resurrected to Yahshua's likeness, which is our great reward.

---

[3] The great works of YHWH.

17 He delivered me from my strong enemy, and from those who hated me: for they were too strong for me.

18 They confronted me in the day of my calamity: but **יהוה** was My support.

19 He brought me forth also into a large place; He delivered me, because He delighted in me.

20 **יהוה** rewarded me according to my tzedakah; according to the cleanness of my hands has He repaid me.

21 For I have kept the halachot of **יהוה**, and have not departed wickedly from My Elohim.

22 For all His mishpatim were before me, and I did not put away His chukim from before me.

23 I was also tzadik before Him, and I kept myself from my iniquity.

24 Therefore has **יהוה** repaid me according to my tzedakah, according to the cleanness of my hands in His eyesight.

25 With the tender You will show Yourself tender; with a tzadik man You will show Yourself Tzadik;

26 With the pure You will show Yourself pure; and with the crooked You will show Yourself hard to figure out.

27 For You will save the afflicted people;[1] but will bring down high looks.

28 For You will light my candle: **יהוה** My Elohim will enlighten my darkness.

29 For by You I have run through a troop; and by My Elohim have I leaped over a wall.

30 As for El, His halacha is perfect: the word of **יהוה** is tried: He is a shield to all those that trust in Him.

31 For who is Eloah besides **יהוה**? Or who is a Rock except our Elohim?

32 It is El that clothes me with strength, and makes my halacha perfect.

33 He makes my feet like deer's feet, and sets me upon my high places.

34 He teaches my hands to war, so that a bow of steel is broken by my arms.

35 You have also given me the shield of Your salvation: and Your right hand[2] supports me, and Your gentleness has made me great.

36 You have enlarged my steps under me; that my feet did not slip.

37 I have pursued my enemies, and overtaken them: neither did I turn back until they were consumed.

38 I have wounded them so that they were not able to rise: they are fallen under my feet.

39 For You have clothed me with strength to the battle: You have subdued under me those that rose up against me.

40 You have also given me the necks of my enemies; that I might destroy them that hate me.

41 They cried, but there was none to save them: even to **יהוה**, but He did not answer them.

42 Then did I beat them as small as the dust before the wind: I did cast them out as the dirt in the streets.

43 You have delivered me from the strivings of the people; and You have made me the head of the nations: a people whom I have not known shall serve me.[3]

44 As soon as they shema about me, they shall obey me: the foreigners shall submit themselves to me.

45 The foreigners shall fade away, and be afraid from their strongholds.

46 **יהוה** lives; and blessed be My Rock; and let the Elohim of My Yahshua be exalted.

47 It is El that avenges me, and subdues the nations under me.

48 He delivers me from my enemies: yes, You lift me up above those that rise up against me: You have delivered me from the violent man.

49 Therefore will I give hodu to You, O **יהוה**, among the nations, and shir tehillot to Your Name.[4]

---

[1] Yisrael in all ages.

[2] A metaphor for Yahshua.
[3] David as well as Yahshua; the Greater end-time David.
[4] All thanks and praise must be done unto YHWH's true Name, and sealed in Yahshua's Name.

50 Great deliverance He gives to His melech; and shows rachamim to His anointed, to David, and to His zera le-olam-va-ed.

Yud Tet

19 [1] The shamayim declare the tiferet of El; and the expanse shows His handiwork.

2 Day-to-day utters speech, and night-to-night reveals da'at.

3 There is no speech nor language, where their voice is not heard.

4 Their line is gone out through all the earth, and their words to the end of the olam. In them has He set a sukkah for the sun,

5 Which is like a bridegroom coming out of his chamber, and has gilah as a strong man to run a race.

6 Its going forth is from the end of the shamayim, and its circuit to the other end: and there is nothing hidden from its heat.

7 The Torah of יהוה is perfect, returning the being: the testimony of יהוה is sure, making wise the simple.[2]

8 The chukim of יהוה are right, bringing simcha to the lev: the commandment of יהוה is pure, enlightening the eyes.

9 The fear of יהוה is clean, enduring le-olam-va-ed: the mishpat of יהוה are true and tzadik altogether.

10 More to be desired are they than gold, yes, than much fine gold: sweeter also than honey and the honeycomb.

11 Moreover by them is Your eved warned: and in keeping of them there is great reward.

12 Who can understand his own errors? Cleanse me from secret sin.

13 Keep back Your eved also from presumptuous sins; let them not have rule over me: then shall I be a tzadik, and then I shall be innocent from the great transgression.[3]

14 Let the words of my mouth, and the meditation of my lev, be acceptable in Your sight, O יהוה, My strength, and My Redeemer.

Chaph

20 [4] יהוה shema in the day of trouble; the Name of the Elohim of Yaakov does defend you;[5]

2 Send help from the Set-Apart Place, and strengthen you out of Tzion;

3 Remember all Your offerings, and accept Your burnt sacrifice; Selah.

4 Grant things according to Your own lev, and fulfill all Your counsel.

5 We will gilah in Your salvation, and in the Name of our Elohim we will set up our banners: יהוה fulfill all Your petitions.

6 Now I know that יהוה saves His anointed;[6] He will shema to him from His set-apart shamayim with the saving strength of His right hand.[7]

7 Some trust in mirkavot, and some in horses: but we will remember the Name of יהוה our Elohim.[8]

8 They are brought down and fallen: but we are risen and stand tzadik.

9 Save, יהוה: let the Melech shema to us when we call.

Chaph Aleph

21 [9] The melech shall simcha in Your strength, O יהוה; and in Your salvation how greatly shall he gilah!

2 You have given him his lev's desire, and have not withheld the request of his lips. Selah.

3 For You put before him the brachot of tov things: You set a keter of pure gold on his head.

---

[1] The ways of YHWH to His servant.
[2] Torah and testimony in Yahshua is the complete package for a Nazarene Yisraelite.
[3] Denial of Yahshua as Savior and King.

[4] The great Name of YHWH.
[5] Just like Yahshua defends us in YHWH's Name.
[6] Yisraelite servants.
[7] Yahshua.
[8] Remember His Name for deliverance in the physical and the spiritual.
[9] Destruction of YHWH's enemies.

4 He asked chayim from You, and You gave it him, even length of days le-olam-va-ed.[1]

5 His tiferet is great in Your salvation: honor and majesty have You laid upon him.

6 For You have made him most blessed le-olam-va-ed: You have made him gilah in the simcha of Your shechinah.

7 For the melech trusts in יהוה, and through the rachamim of the Most High he shall not be moved.

8 Your hand reaches all Your enemies: Your right hand[2] shall find out those that hate You.

9 You shall make them as a fiery oven in the time of Your anger: יהוה shall swallow them up in His anger, and the fire shall devour them.

10 Their fruit shall You destroy from the earth, and their zera from among the children of men.

11 For they intended evil against You: they imagined a mischievous plan, which they are not able to perform.

12 Therefore shall You make them turn their back, when You shall make ready Your arrows upon Your bowstrings against their faces.

13 Be exalted, יהוה, in Your own strength: so will we shir and hallel Your might.

Chaph Bet

22 [3] [4]Eli-Yahuweh Eli-Yahuweh? Lama azavtani,[5] and are far from saving Me and from the words of My roaring?

2 O My Elohim, I cry in the daytime, but You do not answer Me; and in the night season, and I find no rest.

3 But You are Set-Apart, O You that lives in the tehillot of Yisrael.

4 Our ahvot trusted in You: they trusted, and You did deliver them.

5 They cried to You, and were delivered: they trusted in You, and were not ashamed.

6 *But I am a worm, and no man; a reproach of men, and despised by the people.*[6]

7 *All they that see Me laugh Me to scorn: they shoot out the lip, they shake the head saying,*

8 *He trusted on* יהוה *that He would deliver Him: let Him deliver Him, seeing He delighted in Him.*

9 *But You are He that took Me out of the womb:*[7] *You did make Me tikvah when I was upon My ima's breasts.*

10 *I was cast upon You from the womb: You are My El from My ima's belly.*

11 *Be not far from Me; for trouble is near; for there is none to help.*

12 *Many bulls have surrounded Me: strong bulls of Bashan have encircled.*[8]

13 *They open their mouths against Me, as a ravening and a roaring lion.*

14 *I am poured out like mayim, and all My bones are out of joint: My lev is like wax; it is melted in the midst of My inward parts.*

15 *My strength is dried up like a potsherd; and My tongue cleaves to My jaws; and You have brought Me into the dust of death.*

16 *For dogs*[9] *have surrounded Me: the congregation of the wicked have encircled Me: they pierced*[10] *My hands and My feet.*

---

[1] Eternal life.

[2] Yahshua.

[3] The death of the Moshiach.

[4] The number *22* can also be listed as Bet; Bet or 2; 2 showing that in the sod or fourth level of Hebraic understanding, that the death and impalement of Moshiach Yahshua was for both houses or "Bet" Yahudah and "Bet" Ephraim."

[5] My El-Yahuweh My El-Yahuweh, why have You left me? The folks near the execution stake thought He called for Elijah (Matthew 27:46-49). Elijah in Hebrew is Eli-Yahu so we can know that He was calling for someone whose name sounded almost indistinguishable from Eliyahu, thus the rendering of Eli-Yahuweh.

[6] Despised by the leaders of the people.

[7] Virgin Birth.

[8] We see that around Yahshua's execution stake were many enemies and the terms "bulls" as a metaphor for demons, and "mighty ones of Bashan" are a metaphor for foreigners, strangers or non-Yisraelite pagans.

[9] Heathen or non-believers.

[10] **Karu** in Hebrew. The LXX does in fact use the term "pierced," and Yahshua and His talmidim also used the LXX, thereby substantiating its validity. Furthermore, in the Aramaic Peshitta text, as well as the Dead Sea Scrolls, the term "kaaru" is used, which means "pierced." The only way the Masorete text can support its translation of "like a lion" is by using the Word **ka-ari** instead of kaar-u by changing the vav at the end to a yud. Yet it is only the Masorete (i.e., handed-down / traditional) Jewish text that even attempts to make this change; a change that contradicts all other known and accepted Hebrew, Aramaic, or Greek aforementioned versions – most notably the Dead Sea Scrolls, and the Aramaic Peshitta. Additionally "like a lion" does not fit the context of a vivid crucifixion scene.

17 *I count all My bones:[1] they look and stare upon Me.*
18 *They part My garments among them, and cast lots for My raiment.[2]*
19 *But be not far from Me, O יהוה: O My strength, make haste to help Me.*20 *Deliver My being from the sword; My only chayim from the power of the dog.*
21 *Save Me from the lion's mouth:[3] from the horns of the wild beasts;[4] You have listened to Me.*
22 *I will declare Your Name to My brothers;[5] in the midst of the congregation[6] will I hallel You.*
23 *You that fear יהוה, hallel Him; all you the zera of Yakkov, give Him tiferet; and fear Him, all you zera of Yisrael.*
24 For He has not despised nor abhorred the affliction of the afflicted; neither has He hidden His face from Him; but when He cried to Him, He heard.
25 My tehillot shall be for You in the great congregation:[7] I will pay My vows before them that fear Him.
26 The meek shall eat and be satisfied: Those that seek Him shall hallel יהוה. Their lev shall live le-olam-va-ed.[8]
27 All the ends of the olam shall remember[9] and make teshuvah to יהוה: and all the families of the nations shall worship before You.
28 For the malchut is יהוה 's: and He is the Ruler among the nations.
29 All they that be fat upon earth shall eat and worship: all they that go down to the dust shall bow before Him: and none can keep alive his own being.[10]
30 A zera shall serve Him;[11] it shall be declared by יהוה for a coming generation.[12]

31 They shall come,[13] and shall declare His tzedakah[14] to a people[15] that shall be born, that He has done this.[16]

Caph Gimel

23 [17] יהוה is my Shepherd; I shall not want.
2 He makes me to lie down in green pastures: He leads me beside the still mayim.
3 He restores my being: He leads me in the paths of tzedakah for His Name's sake.[18]
4 Yes, though I walk through the valley of the shadow of death, I will fear no evil: for You are with me; Your rod and Your staff they comfort me.
5 You prepare a table before me in the presence of my enemies: You anoint my head with oil; my cup runs over.
6 Surely tov and rachamim shall follow me all the days of my chayim: and I will dwell in the Bayit of יהוה le-olam-va-ed.

Caph Daled

24 [19] The earth is יהוה 's, and the fullness[20] of it; the olam, and they that dwell in it.
2 For He has founded it upon the seas, and established it upon the floods.
3 Who shall ascend into the har of יהוה? Or who shall stand in His Set-Apart Place?
4 He that has clean hands, and a pure lev; who has not brought his being to vanity, nor sworn deceitfully.
5 He shall receive the bracha from יהוה, and tzedakah from the Elohim of his salvation.
6 This is the generation of them that seek Him, that seek Your face, O Elohim of Yaakov. Selah.

---

[1] As the Paschal Lamb, none were broken.
[2] Fulfilled at Yahshua's death in Matthew 27:35-36.
[3] Judah.
[4] Ephraim.
[5] Both houses of Yisrael.
[6] Of Renewed Covenant Yisrael.
[7] The great and enlarged congregation of Yisrael restored.
[8] Eternal life to those who receive this news and praise Him for it.
[9] The impalement and Tov News.
[10] They all need the Impaled One to have life past the grave.
[11] A redeemed remnant seed from both houses.
[12] The Besarot is for each coming generation.

[13] The messengers of that remnant seed of Yaakov.
[14] Yahshua's righteousness.
[15] Faithful Yisrael.
[16] Finished the work of atonement and redemption.
[17] The Tov Shepherd.
[18] He restored us because of love and His great Name.
[19] The King of Esteem.
[20] Hebrew: **Meloah**, same word from the root **maleh** or "full." Ephraim would fill the nations **melo hagoyim** (Gen. 48:19) just as all YHWH's creation fills the earth. Same word. Same principle.

7 Lift up your head, O you gates; and be lifted up, you everlasting doors; and the Melech of Tiferet shall come in.
8 Who is this Melech of Tiferet? יהוה strong and mighty, יהוה mighty in battle.
9 Lift up your heads, O you gates; even lift them up, you everlasting doors; and the Melech of Tiferet shall come in.
10 Who is this Melech of Tiferet? יהוה of hosts, He is the Melech of Tiferet. Selah.[1]

Caph Hey

25 [2] To You, O יהוה, do I lift up my being.
2 O my Elohim, I trust in You: let me not be ashamed, let not my enemies' triumph over me.
3 Yes, let none that wait on You be ashamed: let them be ashamed who transgress without cause.
4 Show me Your halachot, O יהוה; teach me Your halachot.
5 Lead me in Your emet, and teach me: for You are the Elohim of My Yahshua; on You do I wait all day.
6 Remember, O יהוה, Your tender rachamim and Your loving cheseds; for they have been le-olam-va-ed.
7 Remember not the sins of my youth, nor my transgressions: according to Your rachamim remember me for Your tov's sake, O יהוה.
8 Tov and Tzadik is יהוה: therefore will He teach sinners the halacha.
9 The meek will He guide in mishpat: and to the meek will He teach His halacha.
10 All the paths of יהוה are rachamim and emet to such as keep His covenant and His testimonies.[3]
11 For Your Name's sake, O יהוה, pardon my iniquity; for it is great.[4]
12 What man is he that fears יהוה? He teaches him in the halacha that he shall choose.

13 His being shall dwell at ease; and his zera shall inherit the earth.
14 The secret of יהוה is with them that fear Him; and He will show them His covenant.[5]
15 My eyes are always toward יהוה; for He shall pluck my feet out of the net.
16 Turn to me, and have rachamim upon me; for I am desolate and afflicted.
17 The troubles of my lev are enlarged: O bring me out of my distresses.
18 Look upon my affliction and my pain; and forgive all my sins.
19 Consider my enemies; for they are many; and they hate me with cruel hatred.
20 O guard my being, and deliver me: let me not be ashamed; for I put my trust in You.
21 Let integrity and tzedakah preserve me; for I wait on You.
22 Redeem Yisrael,[6] O Elohim, out of all his troubles.

Caph Vav

26 [7] Shophet me, O יהוה; for I have walked in my integrity: I have trusted also in יהוה; therefore I shall not slide.
2 Examine me, O יהוה, and prove me; test my kidneys and my lev.
3 For Your loving chesed is before my eyes: and I have had my halacha in Your emet.
4 I have not sat with vain persons; neither will I go in with pretenders.
5 I have hated the congregation of evildoers; and will not sit with the wicked.
6 I will wash my hands in innocence: so will I walk around Your altar, O יהוה:
7 That I may publish with the voice of hodu, and tell of all Your wonderful works.
8 יהוה, I have loved the dwelling place of Your Bayit, and the place where Your honor dwells.
9 Gather not my being with sinners, nor my chayim with bloody men,

---

[1] Repeated twice; once for each house as an invitation to enter.
[2] Walking upright.
[3] Torah and the testimony of Yahshua's resurrection.
[4] YHWH forgives sin to uphold the greatness of His Name.

[5] Yisrael.
[6] Both houses.
[7] A set-apart walk.

10 In whose hands are evil, and their right hand is full of bribes.

11 But as for me, I will have my halacha in my integrity: redeem me, and be full of rachamim to me.

12 My foot stands in an even place: in the congregations will I bless יהוה.[1]

Caph Zayin

27 [2] יהוה is my Light and My Yahshua; whom shall I fear? יהוה is the strength of my chayim; of whom shall I be afraid?

2 When the wicked, even my enemies and my foes, came upon me to eat up my flesh, they stumbled and fell.

3 Though an army should encamp against me, my lev shall not fear: though war should rise against me, in this will I be confident.

4 One thing have I desired of יהוה, and that will I seek after; that I may dwell in the Bayit of יהוה all the days of my chayim, to observe the beauty of יהוה, and to inquire in His Beit HaMikdash.

5 For in the time of trouble He shall hide me in His citadel: in the secret of His sukkah shall He hide me; He shall set me up upon a Rock.

6 And now shall my head be lifted up above my enemies all around me: therefore will I offer in His sukkah sacrifices of simcha; I will shir, yes, I will shir tehillot to יהוה.

7 Shema, O יהוה, when I cry with my voice: have rachamim also upon me, and answer me.

8 When You said, *Seek My face*; my lev said to You, Your face, יהוה, will I seek.

9 Hide not Your face far from me; put not Your eved away in anger: You have been my help; leave me not, neither forsake me, O Elohim of my salvation.

10 When my abba and my ima forsake me, then יהוה will take me up.

11 Teach me Your halacha, O יהוה, and lead me in a smooth derech, because of my enemies.

12 Deliver me not over to the will of my enemies: for false witnesses have risen up against me, and such as breathe out cruelty.

13 I would have fainted, unless I had believed to see the tov of יהוה in the land of the living.

14 Wait on יהוה: be of tov courage, and He shall strengthen your lev: wait, I say, on יהוה.

Caph Chet

28 [3] To You will I cry, O יהוה my Rock; be not silent before me: lest, if You be silent to me, I will become like them that go down into the pit.

2 Shema the voice of my supplications, when I cry to You, when I lift up my hands toward Your Set-Apart Place.

3 Draw me not away with the wicked, and with the workers of iniquity, who speak shalom to their neighbors, but evil is in their levim.

4 Give them according to their deeds, and according to the wickedness of their endeavors: give them according to the work of their hands; render to them what they deserve.

5 Because they regard not the works of יהוה, nor the works of His hands, He shall destroy them, and not build them up.

6 Barchu-et-יהוה, because He has heard the voice of my supplications.

7 יהוה is My strength and My shield; my lev trusted in Him, and I am helped: therefore my lev has great gilah; and with my shir will I hallel Him.

8 יהוה is their strength, and He is the saving strength of His anointed.

9 Save Your people, and bless Your inheritance: feed them also, and lift them up le-olam-va-ed.[4]

---

[1] A Yisraelite believer is most safe in the congregation of redeemed Yisrael.
[2] Loving YHWH without fear.

[3] Relationship with YHWH.
[4] YHWH's plan for Yisrael; save, bless and feed.

Caph Tet

29 [1] Give to יהוה, O you sons of the mighty, give to יהוה tiferet and strength.

2 Give to יהוה the tiferet due to His Name;[2] worship יהוה in the beauty of set-apartness.

3 The voice of יהוה is upon the mayim: the El of tiferet thunders: יהוה is upon many mayim.

4 The voice of יהוה is powerful; the voice of יהוה is full of majesty.

5 The voice of יהוה breaks the cedars; yes, יהוה breaks the cedars of Levanon.

6 He makes them also to skip like a calf; Levanon and Siryon like a young wild ox.

7 The voice of יהוה divides the flames of fire.

8 The voice of יהוה shakes the wilderness; יהוה shakes the wilderness of Kadesh.

9 The voice of יהוה makes the deers to give birth, and strips the forests: and in His Beit HaMikdash everyone speaks of His tiferet.

10 יהוה sits upon the flood; yes, יהוה sits as Melech le-olam-va-ed.

11 יהוה will give strength to His people; יהוה will bless His people with shalom.

Lamed

30 [3] I will extol You, O יהוה; for You have lifted me up, and have not made my foes to gilah over me.

2 O יהוה My Elohim, I cried to You, and You have healed me.

3 O יהוה, You have brought up my being from the grave: You have kept me alive, that I should not go down to the pit.

4 Sing to יהוה, O you kidushim of His, and give hodu at the remembrance of His set-apartness.

5 For His anger endures but for a moment; in His favor is chayim: weeping may endure for a night, but simcha comes in the morning.

6 And in my ease I said, I shall never be moved.

7 יהוה, by Your favor You have made my har to stand strong: You did hide Your face, and I was troubled.

8 I cried to You, O יהוה; and to יהוה I made my plea.

9 What profit is there in my dom, when I go down to the pit? Shall the dust hallel You? Shall it declare Your emet?

10 Shema, O יהוה, and have rachamim upon me: יהוה, be my helper.

11 You have turned my mourning into dancing: You have put off my sackcloth, and clothed me with simcha;

12 So I will shir halleluyah to You, and not be silent. O יהוה My Elohim, I will give hodu to You le-olam-va-ed.

Lamed Aleph

31 [4] In You, O יהוה, do I put my trust; let me never be ashamed: deliver me in Your tzedakah.

2 Bow down Your ear to me; deliver me speedily: be My strong Rock, for a Bayit of defense to save me.

3 For You are my Rock and My fortress; therefore for Your Name's sake lead me,[5] and guide me.

4 Pull me out of the net that they have laid secretly for me: for You are my strength.

5 *Into Your hand I commit My ruach:*[6] You have redeemed me, O יהוה El of emet.

6 I have hated them that regard lying vanities: but I trust in יהוה.

7 I will be in simcha and gilah in Your rachamim: for You have considered my trouble; You have known my being in adversities;

8 And have not shut me up into the hand of the enemy: You have set my feet in a large place.

9 Have rachamim upon me, O יהוה, for I am in trouble: my eye is consumed with grief, yes, my being and my belly.

---

[1] The Voice of YHWH.
[2] How beautiful is His Name to Yisrael.
[3] YHWH our Helper.

[4] YHWH our Rock.
[5] He leads us for His Name's sake.
[6] Quoted by Moshiach Yahshua.

10 For my chayim is consumed with grief, and my years with sighing: my strength fails because of my iniquity, and my bones are consumed.

11 I was a reproach among all my enemies, but especially among my neighbors, and a fear to my chaverim: they that did see me outside ran from me.

12 I am forgotten as a dead man out of mind: I am like a broken vessel.

13 For I have shema-ed the slander of many: fear was on every side: while they took counsel together against me, they planned to take away my chayim.

14 But I trusted in You, O יהוה: I said, You are My Elohim.

15 My times are in Your hand: deliver me from the hand of my enemies, and from them that persecute me.

16 Make Your face to shine upon Your eved: save me for Your rachamim's sake.

17 Let me not be ashamed, O יהוה; for I have called upon You: let the wicked be ashamed, and let them be silent in the grave.

18 Let the lying lips be put to silence; that speak grievous things proudly and contemptuously against the tzadikim.

19 Oh how great is Your tov, which You have laid up for them that fear You; which You have worked for them that trust in You before the sons of men!

20 You shall hide them in the secret of Your presence from the pride of man: You shall keep them secretly in a citadel from the strife of tongues.

21 Barchu-et יהוה: for He has showed me His marvelous chesed in a strong city.

22 For I said in my haste, I am cut off from before Your eyes: nevertheless You heard the voice of my supplications when I cried to You.

23 O love-et יהוה, all you His kidushim: for יהוה preserves the faithful, and fully rewards the proud doer.

24 Be of tov courage, and He shall strengthen your lev, all you that tikvah in יהוה.

Lamed Bet

32 [1] Blessed is he whose transgression is forgiven, whose sin is covered.

2 Blessed is the man to whom יהוה does not impute iniquity, and in whose ruach there is no deceit.

3 When I kept silence, my bones became old through my groaning all the day long.

4 For day and night Your hand was heavy upon me: my moisture is turned into the drought of summer. Selah.

5 I acknowledged my sin to You, and my iniquity I did not hide. I said, I will confess my transgressions to יהוה; and You forgave the iniquity of my sin. Selah.

6 For this shall every one that is tzadik make tefillah to You in a time when You may be found: surely in the floods of great mayim they shall not come near to him.

7 You are my hiding place; You shall preserve me from trouble; You shall surround me with shirim of deliverance. Selah.

8 I will instruct you and teach you in the halacha in which you shall go: I will guide you with My eye.

9 Be not as the horse, or as the mule, which have no binah: whose mouths must be held in with bit and muzzle, lest they come near to you.

10 Many sorrows shall be to the wicked: but he that trusts in יהוה, rachamim shall surround him.

11 Be in simcha in יהוה, and gilah, you tzadikim: and shout for simcha, all you that are tzadik in lev.

Lamed Gimel

33 [2] Rejoice in יהוה, O you tzadikim: for hallel is fitting for the tzadikim.

2 Hallel יהוה with the harp: shir to Him with the guitar and an instrument of ten strings.

3 Sing to Him a new shir; play skillfully with a loud noise. [3]

---

[1] YHWH our hiding place.
[2] YHWH's word for Yisrael.
[3] Yisrael must make noise when worshipping their King.

4 For the word of יהוה is right; and all His works are done in emet.
5 He loves tzedakah and mishpat: the earth is full of the tov of יהוה.
6 By the word of יהוה were the shamayim made;[1] and all the host of them by the breath of His mouth.
7 He gathers the mayim of the sea together as a heap: He lays up the deep in storehouses.
8 Let all the earth fear יהוה: let all the inhabitants of the olam stand in awe of Him.
9 For He spoke, and it was done; He commanded, and it stood fast.
10 יהוה brings the counsel of the nations to nothing: He makes the plans of the people of no effect.
11 The counsel of יהוה stands le-olam-va-ed, the thoughts of His lev to all generations.
12 Blessed is the nation whose Elohim is יהוה: and the people whom He has chosen for His own inheritance.[2]
13 יהוה looks from the shamayim; He beholds all the sons of men.
14 From the place of His dwelling place He looks upon all the inhabitants of the earth.
15 He makes their levim alike; He considers all their works.
16 There is no melech saved by the multitude of an army: a mighty man is not delivered by much strength.
17 A horse is a worthless thing for safety: neither shall he deliver anyone by his great strength.
18 See, the eyes of יהוה are upon them that fear Him, upon them that tikvah in His rachamim;
19 To deliver their being from death, and to keep them alive in famine.
20 Our being waits for יהוה; He is our help and our shield.
21 For our lev shall gilah in Him, because we have trusted in His set-apart Name.[3]

22 Let Your rachamim, O יהוה, be upon us, according to the tikvah we have in You.

Lamed Daled

34 [4] I will bless יהוה at all times: His hallel shall continually be in my mouth.
2 My being shall make its boast in יהוה: the humble shall shema of it, and are in simcha.
3 O magnify יהוה with me, and let us exalt His Name together.[5]
4 I sought יהוה and He heard me, and delivered me from all my fears.
5 They looked to Him, and were lightened: and their faces were not ashamed.
6 This poor man cried, and יהוה heard Him, and saved him out of all his troubles.
7 The heavenly messenger of יהוה encamps all around them that fear Him, and delivers them.
8 O taste and see that יהוה is tov: blessed is the man that trusts in Him.
9 O fear יהוה, you His kidushim: for there is no lack to them that fear Him.
10 The young lions do lack, and suffer hunger: but they that seek יהוה shall not lack any tov thing.
11 Come, you children, shema to me: I will teach you the fear of יהוה.
12 What man is he that desires chayim, and loves many days, that he may see tov?
13 Keep your tongue from evil, and your lips from speaking deceit.14 Depart from evil, and do tov; seek shalom, and pursue it.
15 The eyes of יהוה are upon the tzadikim, and His ears are open to their cry.
16 The face of יהוה is against them that do evil, to cut off the remembrance of them from the earth.
17 The tzadikim cry, and יהוה hears, and delivers them out of all their troubles.
18 יהוה is near to them that are of a broken lev; and saves such as be of a contrite ruach.

[1] By Moshiach Yahshua.
[2] Yisrael.
[3] Trusting in YHWH's true Name brings only joy and revelation.
[4] YHWH's eye on the righteous of Yisrael.
[5] Judah and Ephraim are called to magnify YHWH's Name as one.

19 Many are the afflictions of the tzadikim: but יהוה delivers them out of them all.
20 He keeps all His bones: not one of them is broken.[1]
21 Evil shall slay the wicked: and they that hate the tzadikim shall be ruined.
22 יהוה redeems the being of His avadim: and none of them that trust in Him shall be condemned.

Lamed Hey

35 [2] Plead my cause, O יהוה, with them that strive with me: fight against them that fight against me.
2 Take hold of shield and armor, and stand up for my help.
3 Draw out also the spear, and stop the way of those that persecute me: say to my being, I am Your Yahshua.
4 Let them be ashamed and put to shame that seek after my being: let them be turned back and brought to confusion that plan my hurt.
5 Let them be as chaff before the wind: and let the heavenly messenger of יהוה chase them.
6 Let their halacha be dark and slippery: and let the heavenly messenger of יהוה persecute them.
7 For without cause have they hid their net for me in a pit, which without cause they have dug for my being.
8 Let destruction come upon him unawares; and let his net that he has hid catch himself: into that very destruction let him fall.
9 And my being shall have simcha in יהוה: it shall gilah in His salvation.
10 All my bones shall say, יהוה, who is like You, who delivers the poor from him that is too strong for him, yes, the poor and the needy from him that spoils him?
11 False witnesses did rise up; they lay to my charge things that I knew not.
12 They rewarded me evil for tov to the bereaving of my being.

13 But as for me, when they were sick, my clothing was sackcloth: I humbled my being with fasting; and my tefillah returned into my own bosom.
14 I behaved myself as though he had been my chaver or brother: I bowed down heavily, as one that mourns for his ima.
15 But in my adversity they had simcha, and gathered themselves together: yes, the smiters gathered themselves together against me, and I knew it not; they did tear me, and ceased not:
16 With hypocritical mockers in the moadim, they gnashed upon me with their teeth.
17 יהוה, how long will You look on? Rescue my being from their destructions, my chayim from the lions.
18 I will give You hodu in the great congregation:[3] I will hallel You among a mighty nation.
19 Let not them that are my enemies wrongfully gilah over me: neither let them wink with the eyes who hate me without a cause.
20 For they speak not shalom: but they plan deceitful matters against them that are quiet in the land.
21 Yes, they opened their mouth wide against me, and said, Aha, aha, our eye has seen it.
22 This you have seen, O יהוה: keep not silent: O יהוה, be not far from me.
23 Stir up Yourself, and awake to my mishpat, even to my cause, My Elohim and My Master.
24 Shophet me, O יהוה My Elohim, according to Your tzedakah; and let them not gilah over me.
25 Let them not say in their levim, Aha, our desire is done: let them not say, We have swallowed him up.
26 Let them be ashamed and brought to confusion together that gilah at my hurt: let them be clothed with shame and dishonor that magnify themselves against me.

---

[1] Moshiach's bones could not be broken according to Exodus 12.
[2] YHWH fights our enemies.

[3] Of Redeemed Yisrael.

27 Let them shout for simcha, and be in simcha, that favor my tzadik cause: yes, let them say continually, Let יהוה be magnified, who has pleasure in the shalom of His eved.

28 And my tongue shall speak of Your tzedakah and of Your tehilla all the day long.

Lamed Vav

36 [1] The transgression of the wicked testifies to the evil within his lev, no fear of Elohim is before his eyes.

2 For he flatters himself in his own eyes, until his iniquity be found to be hateful.

3 The words of his mouth are iniquity and deceit: he has ceased to be wise, and to do tov.

4 He plans evil upon his bed; he sets himself in a halacha that is not tov; he despises not evil.

5 Your rachamim, O יהוה, is in the shamayim; and Your faithfulness reaches to the clouds.

6 Your tzedakah is like the great mountains; Your mishpat are a great deep: O יהוה You preserve man and beast.

7 How excellent is Your loving chesed, O Elohim! Therefore the children of men put their trust under the shadow of Your wings.

8 They shall be abundantly satisfied with the abundance of Your Bayit; and You shall make them drink of the river of Your pleasures.

9 For with You is the fountain of chayim: in Your light shall we see light.

10 O continue Your loving chesed to them that know You; and Your tzedakah to the tzadik in lev.

11 Let not the foot of pride come against me, and let not the hand of the wicked remove me.

12 There are the workers of iniquity fallen: they are cast down, and shall not be able to rise.

Lamed Zayin

37 [2] Do not be moved because of evildoers, neither be envious against the workers of iniquity.

2 For they shall soon be cut down like the grass, and wither as the green herb.

3 Trust in יהוה, and do tov; so shall you dwell in the land, and truly you shall be fed.

4 Delight yourself in יהוה; and He shall give you the desires of your lev.

5 Commit your halacha to יהוה; trust in Him; and He shall bring it to pass.

6 And He shall bring forth your tzedakah as the light, and your mishpat as the noonday.

7 Rest in יהוה, and wait patiently for Him: do not be moved because of him who prospers in his halacha, because of the man who brings wicked plans to pass.

8 Cease from anger, and forsake anger: do not be moved by any means to do evil.

9 For evildoers shall be cut off: but those that wait upon יהוה, they shall inherit the earth.[3]

10 For yet a little while, and the wicked shall be no more: yes, you shall diligently consider his place, and it shall not be.[4]

11 But the meek shall inherit the earth; and shall delight themselves in the abundance of shalom.

12 The wicked plots against the tzadik, and gnashes at him with his teeth.

13 יהוה shall laugh at him: for He sees that his Yom HaDin is coming.

14 The wicked have drawn out the sword, and have bent their bow, to cast down the poor and needy, and to slay those of tzadik behavior.

15 Their sword shall enter into their own lev, and their bows shall be broken.

16 A little that a tzadik man has is better than the riches of many wicked.

17 For the arms of the wicked shall be broken: but יהוה upholds the tzadikim.

---

[1] YHWH our Protector.

[2] YHWH will destroy the evildoers.
[3] The promises for believing Yisrael; The **Yom HaDin** or Judgment Day will make all things right.
[4] The soul that sins without redemption shall die in the Lake of Fire (Ezekiel 18:4).

18 יהוה knows the days of the tzadik: and their inheritance shall be le-olam-va-ed.
19 They shall not be ashamed in the evil time: and in the days of famine they shall be full.
20 But the wicked shall perish, and the enemies of יהוה shall be as the fat of lambs: they shall be consumed; into smoke shall they consume away.[1]
21 The wicked borrows, and pays not again: but the tzadik shows rachamim, and gives.
22 For such as are blessed of Him shall inherit the earth; and they that be cursed of Him shall be cut off.
23 The steps of a tov man are ordered by יהוה: and He delights in his halacha.
24 Though he falls, he shall not be utterly cast down: for יהוה upholds him with His hand.
25 I have been young, and now am old; yet have I not seen the tzadikim forsaken, or his zera begging lechem.
26 He is always full of rachamim, and lends; and his zera is blessed.
27 Depart from evil, and do tov; and dwell le-olam-va-ed.
28 For יהוה loves mishpat, and forsakes not His kidushim; they are preserved le-olam-va-ed: but the zera of the wicked shall be cut off.
29 The tzadikim shall inherit the earth, and dwell in it le-olam-va-ed.
30 The mouth of the tzadik speaks chochma, and his tongue talks of mishpat.
31 The Torah of His Elohim is in his lev; none of his steps shall slide.
32 The wicked watches the tzadik, and seeks to slay him.
33 יהוה will not leave him in his hand, nor condemn him when he is judged.
34 Wait on יהוה, and keep His halacha, and He shall exalt you to inherit the earth: when the wicked are cut off, you shall see it.
35 I have seen the wicked in great power, and spreading himself like a native green tree.

36 Yet he passed away, and, look, he was not: yes, I sought him, but he could not be found.
37 Mark the perfect man, and observe the tzadik: for the end of that man is shalom.
38 But the transgressors shall be destroyed together: the end of the wicked shall be cut off.[2]
39 But the salvation of the tzadikim is of יהוה: He is their strength in the time of trouble.
40 And יהוה shall help them and deliver them: He shall deliver them from the wicked, and save them, because they trust in Him.

Lamed Chet

38 [3] O יהוה, rebuke me not in Your anger: neither discipline me in Your hot displeasure.
2 For Your arrows have pierced me, and Your hand pressures me.
3 There is no soundness in my flesh because of Your anger; neither is there any rest in my bones because of my sin.
4 For my iniquities are gone over my head: as a heavy burden they are too heavy for me.[4]
5 My wounds stink and fester because of my foolishness.
6 I am troubled; I am bowed down greatly; I go depressed in mourning all day long.
7 For my loins are filled with burning: and there is no soundness in my flesh.
8 I am feeble and broken: I have roared by reason of the stress of my lev.
9 יהוה, all my desire is before You; and my groaning is not hidden from You.
10 My lev throbs, my strength fails me: as for the light of my eyes, it also is gone from me.
11 My lovers and my chaverim stand aloof from me; and my family stands far away.
12 They also that seek after my chayim lay snares for me: and they that seek my hurt

---

[1] Souls of the lost or unredeemed die.
[2] Death in the Lake of Fire; where their existence will cease.
[3] Walking with YHWH can be difficult.
[4] Only Yahshua can carry them.

speak mischievous things, and imagine deceit all day long.

13 But I, as a deaf man, heard not; and I was like a dumb man that opens not his mouth.

14 So I was as a man that hears not, and in whose mouth are no rebukes.

15 For in You, O יהוה, do I have tikvah: You will shema, O יהוה My Elohim.

16 For I said, Shema to me, lest otherwise they should gilah over me: when my foot slips, they would then magnify themselves over me.

17 For I am ready to fall away from You, and my sorrow is continually before me.

18 For I will declare my iniquity; I will be sorry for my sin.

19 But my enemies are lively, and they are strong: and they that hate me wrongfully are multiplied.

20 They also that render evil for tov are my adversaries; because I follow the thing that is tov.

21 Forsake me not, O יהוה: O My Elohim, be not far from me.

22 Hurry to help me, O יהוה My Yahshua.[1]

Lamed Tet

39 [2] I said, I will take heed to my halachot, that I sin not with my tongue: I will keep my mouth with a muzzle, while the wicked is before me.

2 I was dumb with silence, I held my silence, even from tov; and my sorrow was stirred.

3 My lev was hot within me, while I was meditating the fire burned: then spoke I with my tongue,

4 יהוה, make me to know my end, and the measure of my days, what it is; that I may know how brief I really am.

5 See, You have made my days like handbreadths; and my age is as nothing before You: truly every man in his best condition is altogether vanity. Selah.

6 Surely every man walks as a shadow: surely their turmoil is in vain: he heaps up riches, and knows not who shall gather them.

7 And now, יהוה, what do I wait for? My tikvah is in You.

8 Deliver me from all my transgressions: make me not the reproach of the foolish.

9 I was dumb; I opened not my mouth; because You did it.

10 Remove Your stroke away from me: I am consumed by the blow of Your hand.

11 When You correct man for iniquity with rebukes, You make his beauty to consume away like a moth: surely every man is vanity. Selah.

12 Shema my tefillah, O יהוה, and give ear to my cry; hold not Your silence at my tears: for I am a stranger with You, and a sojourner, as all my ahvot were.[3]

13 O spare me so that I may recover strength, before I go away, and am no more.

Mem

40 [4] I waited patiently for יהוה; and He inclined to me, and listened to my cry.

2 He brought me up also out of a horrible pit, out of the muddy clay, and set my feet upon a Rock, and established my goings.

3 And He has put a new shir in my mouth, even hallel to our Elohim: many shall see it, and fear, and shall trust in יהוה.

4 Blessed is that man that makes יהוה his trust, and has not turned to the proud, nor such as turn aside to lies.

5 Many, O יהוה My Elohim, are Your wonderful works that You have done, and Your thoughts towards us: there is none to compare to You: if I would declare and speak of them, they are more than can be numbered.

6 *Sacrifice and offering You did not desire;*

---

[1] Hebrew: **teshuati.**
[2] YHWH listens in all our trials.

---
[3] Yisrael's fathers were all strangers at one time, and we should be very sensitive to Ephraim and others who are returning to the Commonwealth of Yisrael.
[4] Moshiach is coming.

but a body You[1] have prepared for Me;[2 3] burnt offering and sin offering You did not require.[4]

7 *Then said I, observe, I will come: in the volume of the scroll it is written all about Me,[5 6 7]*

8 *I delight to do Your will, O My Elohim: yes, Your Torah is within My lev.[8]*

9 *I have preached tzedakah in the great congregation:[9] I will not refrain My lips O* יהוה, *You know My tzedakah.[10]*

10 *I have not hidden Your tzedakah within My lev; but I have declared Your faithfulness and Your salvation: I have not concealed Your loving chesed and Your emet from the great congregation of Yisrael.*

11 Withhold not Your tender rachamim from me, O יהוה: let Your loving chesed and Your emet continually preserve me.

12 For innumerable evils have surrounded me: my iniquities have taken hold of me, so that I am not able to look up; they are more than the hairs of my head: therefore my lev fails me.

13 Be pleased, O יהוה, to deliver me: O יהוה, hurry to help me.

14 Let them be ashamed and abased together that seek after my being to destroy it; let them be driven backward and put to shame that wish me evil.

15 Let them be ruined as a reward of their shame that say to me, Aha, aha.

16 Let all those that seek You gilah and have simcha in You: let those who love Your salvation say continually, יהוה be magnified.

17 But I am poor and needy; yet יהוה thinks about me: You are my help and My Deliverer; do not delay, O My Elohim.

Mem Aleph

41 [11] Blessed is he that considers the poor: יהוה will deliver him in time of trouble.

2 יהוה will preserve him, and keep him alive; and he shall be blessed upon the earth: and You will not deliver him to the will of his enemies.

3 יהוה will strengthen him upon his sick bed: You will bring recovery for his sickness on his bed.

4 I said, יהוה, be full of rachamim to me: heal my being; for I have sinned against You.

5 My enemies speak evil of me, When shall he die, and his name perish?

6 And if he comes to visit, he speaks vanity: his lev gathers iniquity to itself; when he goes out, he tells it.

7 *All that hate Me whisper together against Me: against Me do they plan My hurt.[12]*

8 *An unclean Beliya'al, they say, cleaves to Him: and now that He lies He shall rise up again no more.*

9 *Yes, My own familiar chaver, in whom I trusted, which did eat of My lechem, has lifted up his heel against Me.*

10 *But You, O* יהוה, *be full of rachamim to Me, and raise Me up, that I may repay them.*

---

[1] Abba YHWH.
[2] The most wonderful work.
[3] In Psalm 40:6 the Masorete text (Psalm 40:7 in the Stone Edition) has purposely changed the phrase "a body you have prepared for me," as properly quoted again in Hebrews 10:5, and verified by the Dead Sea Scrolls. This verse speaks of a man who has a special body prepared for Him by YHWH, to come to earth because the scrolls of Torah testify of Him. Now if you were a counter-Yahshua missionary evangelist, you'd want this verse tampered with also. That is exactly what they did. They changed Psalm 40:6 to "you opened my ears."
[4] From the LXX, Dead Sea Scrolls, and Brit Chadasha.
[5] Moshiach with a prepared body.
[6] Ivrim/Hebrews 10:5-7.
[7] The Masorete text reads in the Hebrew as follows, **be megilath sefer katuv alie**. The Hebrew is correct in the Masorete. The prefix **be** means "in"; the length of the scrolls it is written about Me. The prefix "**be**" means "in," not "with." If the text did say "with" as some claim, the Hebrew prefix or qualifier **eem** would be used – but it is not.
[8] Moshiach Yahshua speaking in first person.
[9] The besarot is for all who desire to be in and part of the great and enlarged congregation of Yisrael.
[10] Moshiach is called YHWH our Righteousness or YHWH Tzidkaynu in Jeremiah 23:6.

[11] Yahshua's betrayal predicted.
[12] In verses 7-12 Yahshua speaks through David in the first person, speaking of his accusers, betrayal, resurrection and ultimate ascension to Abba YHWH. Isn't it interesting how Yahshua and the Brit Chadasha writers knew this, and were extra careful not to apply any other verses in this Psalm to Yahshua, except indeed those with a dual fulfillment (verses 7-12) i.e., with both an immediate and a Messianic application. Verse 9 is a perfect example of this, where someone at the family table did the betrayal, whom we know to be Absalom, David's son, and later Judas, Yahshua's son in the truth.

11 *By this I will know that You chose Me, because My enemy does not triumph over Me.*
12 *And as for Me, You uphold Me in My integrity, and set Me before Your face le-olam-va-ed.*
13 Blessed is יהוה Elohim of Yisrael from everlasting, and to everlasting. Amein, and Amein.

Mem Bet

42 ¹ As the deer throbs after the mayim brooks, so throbs my being after You, O Elohim.
2 My being thirsts for Elohim, for the living El: when shall I come and appear before Elohim?
3 My tears have been my food day and night, while they continually say to me, Where is Your Elohim?
4 When I remember these things, I pour out my being within me: for I had gone with the multitude, I went with them to the Bayit of Elohim, with the voice of simcha and tehilla, with a multitude that kept the moadim.
5 Why are you cast down, O my being? And why are you in turmoil within me? Tikvah in Elohim: for I shall yet hallel Him for the help of His face.
6 O My Elohim, my being is cast down within me: therefore will I remember you from the land of Yarden, and from the heights of Hermon, and from Har Mitzar.
7 Deep calls to deep at the noise of Your waterfalls: all Your waves and Your billows are gone over me.
8 Yet יהוה will command His loving chesed in the daytime, and in the night His shir shall be with me, and my tefillah to the El of my chayim.
9 I will say to El My Rock, Why have You forgotten me? Why do I go mourning because of the oppression of the enemy?
10 Like a sword in my bones, my enemies reproach me; while they say daily to me, Where is your Elohim?

11 Why are you cast down, O my being? And why are you in turmoil within me? Tikvah in Elohim: for I shall yet hallel Him, who is the health of my face, and My Elohim.

Mem Gimel

43 ² Shophet me, O Elohim, and plead my cause against a wicked nation: O deliver me from the deceitful and unjust man.
2 For You are the Elohim of my strength: why do You cast me off? Why do I go mourning because of the oppression of the enemy?
3 O send out Your light and Your emet: let them lead me; let them bring me to Your set-apart har, and to Your sukkot.
4 Then will I go to the altar of Elohim, to El my exceeding simcha: yes, upon the harp will I hallel You, O Elohim My Elohim.
5 Why are you cast down, O my being? And why are you in turmoil within me? Tikvah in Elohim: for I shall yet hallel Him, who is the health of my face, and My Elohim.

Mem Daled

44 ³ We have heard with our ears, O Elohim, our ahvot have told us, what work You did in their days, in the times of old.
2 How You did drive out the nations with Your hand, and planted them; how You did afflict the people, and cast them out.
3 For they did not get the land in their possession by their own sword, neither did their own arm save them: but Your right hand, and Your arm,⁴ and the light of Your face, because You had showed favor to them.
4 You are my Melech, O Elohim: command deliverances for Yaakov.⁵

---
¹ YHWH is master over all depression and despondency.
² YHWH who pleads our cause.
³ YHWH and His history with His people.
⁴ Yahshua.
⁵ Nazarene Yisraelites experience many various deliverances from YHWH, not merely one or two.

5 Through You will we push down our enemies: through Your Name will we trample them under that rise up against us.
6 For I will not trust in my bow, neither shall my sword save me.
7 But You have saved us from our enemies, and have put them to shame that hated us.
8 In Elohim we will boast all day long, and hallel Your Name le-olam-va-ed. Selah.
9 But You have cast us off, and put us to shame; and do not go forth with our armies.
10 You make us turn back from the enemy: and those who hate us plunder us for themselves.
11 You have given us like sheep appointed for food; and have scattered us among the nations.[1]
12 You sold Your people for nothing, and have set no price on them.
13 You make us a reproach to our neighbors, a scorn and a mockery to them that are around us.
14 You make us a swear word among the nations, a shaking of the head among the peoples.
15 My confusion is continually before me, and the shame of my face has covered me,
16 For the voice of him that slanders and blasphemes; because of the enemy and the avenger.
17 All this has come upon us; yet have we not forgotten You, neither have we been false in Your covenant.
18 Our lev is not turned back; neither have our steps departed from Your halacha;
19 Yet You have broken us in the place of jackals, and covered us with the shadow of death.
20 If we have forgotten the Name of our Elohim,[2] or stretched out our hands to a strange el;
21 Would not Elohim search this out? For He knows the secrets of the lev.
22 Yes, for Your sake are we killed all day long; we are counted as sheep for the slaughter.[3]

23 Awake, why do You sleep, O יהוה?
Arise, cast us not off le-olam-va-ed.
24 Why do you hide Your face, and forget our affliction and our oppression?
25 For our being is bowed down to the dust: our belly cleaves to the earth.
26 Arise and be our help, and redeem us for Your rachamim's sake.

Mem Hey

45 [4] My lev is overflowing with a tov matter: I address my works to the melech: my tongue is the pen of a speedy writer.
2 You are fairer than the children of men: favor is poured into Your lips: therefore Elohim has blessed You le-olam-va-ed.
3 Gird Your sword upon Your thigh, O most mighty one, with Your tiferet and Your majesty.
4 And in Your majesty ride prosperously because of emet and meekness and tzedakah; let Your right hand lead to awesome things.
5 Your arrows are sharp in the lev of the melech's enemies; by which the nations fall under You.[5]
6 *Your throne, O Elohim, is le-olam-va-ed: the sceptre of Your malchut is a scepter of tzedakah.[6][7]*
7 *You loved tzedakah, and hated wickedness: therefore Elohim, Your*

---

[3] In Romans 8:36 this verse is attributed to Roman (not Catholic) believers, further validating their Yisraelite heritage.
[4] Moshiach has a throne.
[5] Starting with verse 2 thru 17, these verses speak of Moshiach Yahshua.
[6] The Elohim seated on a throne is Yahshua according to Ivrim/Hebrews 1:8-9. The Hebrew is: **kesecha elohim.**
[7] This is the Father speaking to the Son, proclaiming the Son's throne as righteous and everlasting, and as one that is received directly from Abba YHWH.

---

[1] To fulfill the promise of physical multiplicity.
[2] Yes; Yisrael certainly has chosen to forget YHWH's Name.

Elohim,[1] [2] has anointed You[3] with the oil of simcha above Your fellows.[4]

8 *All Your garments smell of myrrh, and aloes, and cassia, out of the ivory citadels, by which they have made You gilah.[5]*

9 Melechim's daughters were among Your honorable women: upon Your right hand did stand the queen in gold from Ophir.

10 Shema, O daughter, and consider, and incline your ear; forget also your own people, and your abba's bayit;

11 So shall the Melech greatly desire your beauty: He is your Master; worship him.

12 And the daughter of Tyre shall be there with a gift; even the rich among the people shall seek your favor.

13 The Melech's daughter is beautiful within: her clothing is embroidered with gold.[6]

14 She shall be brought to the Melech in raiment of needlework: the virgins[7] her companions[8] that follow her shall be brought to You.

15 With simcha and gilah shall they be brought: they shall enter into the Melech's palace.

16 Instead of Your ahvot shall be Your children, whom You appoint leaders in all the earth.[9]

17 I will make Your Name to be remembered in all generations:[10] therefore shall the people hallel You le-olam-va-ed.[11]

---

[1] The Elohim over Yisrael on the throne with the scepter also has an Elohim over Him. The Father Elohim is Elohim over Yahshua Elohim. The Hebrew here is: **elohim elohecha,** or "Elohim Your Elohim."

[2] Throughout the Brit Chadasha, Yahshua calls Abba "His Elohim" and we see that right in this verse.

[3] Abba YHWH has anointed the lesser Elohim as King over Yisrael, by calling Him the Moshiach King, or in the Hebrew **meshichecha,** or literally "Your Moshiach", meaning Abba YHWH's designated "Anointed One," or Moshiach for Yisrael, who has been given a throne.

[4] Above other fellow Yisraelites; no one has Yahshua's power or position with the Father.

[5] Metaphors describing the beauty and sweetness of King Yahshua.

[6] The nation as a whole.

[7] Dom-washed Yisrael.

[8] Those who join Yisrael by choice in and through Yahshua.

[9] Yisrael will rule the nations in the **atid lavoh.**

[10] The King, who received His throne from Abba, will make sure that Yahweh's Name is remembered for and to all generations, through its proclamation by the people of Renewed Covenant Yisrael. We see this fulfilled in John chapter 17:6.

Mem Vav

46 [12] Elohim is our refuge and strength, a very present help in trouble.

2 Therefore we will not fear, though the earth is removed, and though the mountains are carried into the midst of the sea;

3 Though the mayim rage and foam, though the mountains shake with its swelling. Selah.

4 There is a river, whose streams make joyful the city of Elohim, the Set-Apart Place of the sukkot of the Most High.

5 Elohim is in the midst of her; she shall not be moved: Elohim shall help her, early in the morning.

6 The nations raged, the malchutim were moved: He uttered His voice, the earth melted.

7 יהוה of hosts is with us; the Elohim of Yaakov is our refuge. Selah.

8 Come, observe the works of יהוה, what ruins He has made in the earth.

9 He makes wars to cease to the ends of the earth; He breaks the bow, and cuts the spear; He burns the mirkavah in the fire.

10 *Be still, and know that I am Elohim: I will be exalted among the nations; I will be exalted in the earth.*

11 יהוה of hosts is with us; the Elohim of Yaakov is our refuge. Selah.

Mem Zayin

47 [13] O clap your hands, all you peoples; shout to Elohim with the voice of triumph.

2 For יהוה most high is terrible; He is a great Melech over all the earth.

3 He shall subdue the nations under us, and the nations under our feet.[14]

4 He chooses our inheritance for us, the excellence of Yaakov[15] whom He loved. Selah.

---

[11] The job of Yisraelites is to make YHWH's Name known for all generations.

[12] YHWH is our refuge.

[13] The praises of YHWH.

[14] In the **atid lavoh.**

[15] All believers who follow Torah have inherited eternal life, and the inheritance of the ways of Yisrael. Selah

5 Elohim is gone up with a shout, **יהוה** with the sound of a shofar.
6 Sing tehillot to Elohim, shir tehillot: shir tehillot to our Melech; shir tehillot.
7 For Elohim is the Melech of all the earth: shir tehillot with binah.
8 Elohim reigns over the nations: Elohim sits upon the throne of His set-apartness.
9 The leaders of the earth are gathered together, even the people of the Elohim of Avraham: for the guardians of the earth belong to Elohim: He is greatly exalted.[1]

Mem Chet

48 [2] Great is **יהי**, and greatly to be praised in the city of our Elohim, in the har of His set-apartness.
2 Beautiful on high, the simcha of the whole earth, is Har Tzion, on the sides of the north, the city of the great Melech.
3 Elohim is known in her citadels as her refuge.
4 For, look, the melechim were assembled, they passed by together.
5 They saw it, and so they marveled; they were troubled, and rushed away.
6 Fear took hold upon them there, and pain, as of a woman in travail.
7 You broke the ships of Tarshish with an east wind.
8 As we have heard, so have we seen in the city of **יהוה** of hosts, in the city of our Elohim: Elohim will establish it le-olam-va-ed. Selah.
9 We have thought of Your loving chesed, O Elohim, in the midst of Your Beit HaMikdash.
10 According to Your Name, O Elohim, so is Your tehillah to the ends of the earth: Your Right Hand[3] is full of Tzedakah.
11 Let Har Tzion gilah, let the daughters of Yahudah be in simcha, because of Your mishpatim.
12 Walk around Tzion, and go around her: count her towers.
13 Mark well her ramparts; consider her citadels; that you may tell it to the following generation.
14 For this Elohim is our Elohim le-olam-va-ed: He will be our guide even to our death.

Mem Tet

49 [4] Shema, all you nations; shema, all you inhabitants of the olam:
2 Both low and high, rich and poor, together.
3 My mouth shall speak of chochma; and the meditation of my lev shall bring binah.
4 I will incline my ear to a parable: I will open my riddles upon the harp.
5 Why should I fear in the days of evil, when the iniquity of my supplanters shall surround me?
6 They that trust in their wealth, and boast themselves in the multitude of their riches;
7 None of them can by any means redeem his brother, nor give to Elohim a ransom for him:[5]
8 For the redemption of their being is precious,[6] and it ceases le-olam-va-ed:[7] 9 That he should still live le-olam-va-ed, and not see corruption.[8]
10 For he sees that wise men die, likewise the fools and the senseless persons perish, and leave their wealth to others.
11 Their inward thought is, that their houses shall continue le-olam-va-ed, and their dwelling places to all generations; they call their lands after their own names.[9]
12 Nevertheless man does not remain in honor: he is like the beasts that perish.
13 This halacha of theirs is folly: yet their disciples approve of their sayings. Selah.

---

[1] All gathered by Yahshua into Yisrael.
[2] YHWH reigns for Tzion.
[3] Yahshua.
[4] The ransomed of YHWH.
[5] No human can redeem another, which by definition means Yahshua was not merely man, but YHWH the Creator. Also Yahshua was the kinsman redeemer who died for His Yisraelite brothers who had become orphans, and all who would join them.
[6] Beyond natural human capability or ritual.
[7] Meaning it can be done only as a one-time event; and then it ceases, unlike manmade attempts at salvation, which are ongoing and never seem to end.
[8] Those who are redeemed.
[9] A pagan practice.

14 Like sheep they are laid into the grave; death shall feed on them; and the tzadik shall have rule over them in the morning;[1] and their beauty shall consume in the grave far from their dwelling.

15 But Elohim will redeem my being from the power of the grave:[2] for He shall receive me. Selah.

16 Be not afraid when one is made rich, when the tiferet of his bayit is increased;

17 For when he dies he shall carry nothing away: his tiferet shall not descend after him.

18 Though while he lived he blessed his being: and men will hallel you, when you do well for yourself.

19 He shall go to the generation of his ahvot; they shall never see light.

20 Man that has honor, but does not understand why, is like the beasts that perish.

Nun

50 [3] The mighty El, even יהוה, has spoken, and shall call the earth from the rising of the sun to its going down.

2 Out of Tzion, the perfection of beauty, Elohim has shined.

3 Our Elohim shall come,[4] and shall not keep silent: a fire shall devour those before Him, and it shall be very stormy around Him.

4 He shall call to the shamayim from above, and to the earth, that He may shophet His people.

5 Gather My kidushim together to Me; those that have made a covenant with Me by sacrifice.[5]

6 And the shamayim shall declare His tzedakah: for Elohim is the Shophet Himself. Selah.

7 Shema, O My people, and I will speak; O Yisrael, and I will testify against you: I am Elohim, even Your Elohim.

8 I will not reprove you for your sacrifices or your burnt offerings, to have been continually before Me.

9 I will take no bullock out of your bayit, nor male goats out of your folds.

10 For every beast of the forest is Mine, and the cattle upon a thousand hills.

11 I know all the fowls of the mountains: and the wild beasts of the field are Mine.

12 If I were hungry, I would not tell you: for the olam is Mine, and the fullness of it.

13 Will I eat the flesh of bulls, or drink the dom of goats?

14 Offer to Elohim hodu; and pay your vows to the most High:

15 And call upon Me in the day of trouble: I will deliver you, and you shall give Me tiferet.

16 But to the wicked Elohim says, What have you to do with declaring My chukim, or that you should take My covenant in your mouth?

17 Seeing you hate Torah, and cast My words behind you.

18 When you saw a thief, then you were pleased with him, and have been partakers with adulterers.

19 You gave your mouth to evil, and your tongue creates deceit.

20 You sit and speak against your brother; you slander your own ima's son.

21 These things have you done, and I kept silent; you thought that I was altogether such a one as yourself: but I rebuke you, and set it in order before your eyes.

22 Now consider this, you that forget Eloah, lest I tear you in pieces, and there be none to deliver.

23 Anyone offering hallel glorifies Me: and to him that orders his behavior in tzedakah, to him will I show the Yahshua of Elohim.

Nun Aleph

51 [6] Have rachamim upon me, O Elohim, according to Your loving chesed: according to the multitude of Your tender rachamim blot out my transgressions.

---

[1] Of resurrection.
[2] The Redeemer Yahshua must be Elohim, not a mere man.
[3] Yahshua returns to Tzion.
[4] Yahshua will return to Tzion.
[5] At His return, all Yisrael from both houses will be gathered to Yahshua.

[6] YHWH who pardons original sin.

2 Wash me thoroughly from my iniquity, and cleanse me from my sin.

3 For I acknowledge my transgressions: and my sin is ever before me.

4 Against You, and You alone, have I sinned, and done this evil in Your sight: that You might be justified when You speak, and be clear when You shophet.

5 See, I was shapen in iniquity; and in sin did my ima conceive me.[1]

6 See, You desire emet in the inward parts: and in the inward parts You shall make me to know chochma.

7 Purge me with hyssop, and I shall be clean: wash me, and I shall be whiter than snow.

8 Make me to shema, simcha and gilah; let the bones which You have broken gilah.

9 Hide Your face from my sins, and blot out all my iniquities.

10 Create in me a clean lev, O Elohim; and renew a right ruach within me.

11 Cast me not away from Your shechinah; and take not Your Set-Apart Ruach from me.

12 Restore to me the simcha of Your Yahshua; and uphold me with Your free Ruach.

13 Then will I teach transgressors Your halachot; and sinners shall be turned to You.

14 Deliver me from bloodguilt, O Elohim, Elohim of My salvation: and my tongue shall shir aloud of Your tzedakah.

15 O יהוה, open my lips; and my mouth shall show forth Your hallel.

16 For You do not desire sacrifice; or else would I give it: You delight not in burnt offering.

17 The sacrifices of Elohim are a broken ruach: a broken and a contrite lev, O Elohim, You will not despise.

18 Do tov in Your tov pleasure to Tzion: rebuild the walls of Yahrushalayim.

19 Then shall You be pleased with the sacrifices of tzedakah, with burnt offerings and whole burnt offerings: then shall they offer young bulls upon Your altar.

Nun Bet

52 Why do you boast in evil, O mighty man? The tov of El endures continually.

2 Your tongue plans evils; like a sharp razor, working deceitfully.

3 You love evil more than tov, and lying rather than to speak tzedakah. Selah.

4 You love all kinds of devouring words, O deceitful tongue.

5 El shall likewise destroy you le-olam-va-ed, He shall take you away, and pluck you out of your dwelling place, and root you out of the land of the living. Selah.

6 The tzadikim also shall see, and fear, and shall laugh at him:

7 See; this is the man that did not make Elohim his strength; but trusted in the abundance of his riches, and strengthened himself in his wickedness.

8 But I am like a green olive tree in the Bayit of Elohim:[2] I trust in the rachamim of Elohim le-olam-va-ed.

9 I will hallel You le-olam-va-ed, because You have done it: and I will wait on Your Name; for it is tov before Your kidushim.[3]

Nun Gimel

53 [4] The fool has said in his lev, There is no Elohim. Corrupt are they, and have done abominable iniquity: there is none that does tov.

2 Elohim looked down from the shamayim upon the children of men, to see if there were any that did understand, that did seek Elohim.

3 Every one of them has gone astray: they are altogether become filthy; there is none that does tov, no, not one.

---

[1] Original sin.

[2] All Renewed Covenant believers in the House of Yisrael are part of the Olive Tree.
[3] Those in the Olive Tree knowing YHWH's Name, wait for His return in Yahshua.
[4] YHWH's many enemies.

4 Have the workers of iniquity no da'at? Who eat up my nation as they eat lechem: they have not called upon Elohim.

5 There they are in great fear, where no fear was: for Elohim has scattered the bones of them that encamp against you: you have put them to shame, because Elohim has despised them.

6 Oh that the Yahshua of Yisrael would come out of Tzion! When Elohim brings back the exiles of His people, Yaakov shall gilah, and Yisrael shall be in simcha.[1]

Nun Daled

54 [2] Save me, O Elohim, by Your Name,[3] and shophet me by Your strength.

2 Shema to my tefillah, O Elohim; give ear to the words of my mouth.

3 For foreigners have risen up against me, and oppressors seek after my being: they have not set Elohim before them. Selah.

4 See, Elohim is My helper: **יהוה** is with them that uphold my being.

5 He shall reward evil to my enemies: cut them off in your emet.

6 I will freely sacrifice to You: I will hallel Your Name, O **יהוה**; for it is tov.

7 For He has delivered me out of all trouble: and my eye has seen His desire upon my enemies.

Nun Hey

55 [4] Give Your ear to my tefillah, O Elohim; and hide not Yourself from my pleading.

2 Attend to me, and shema me: I mourn in my complaint, and make noise;

3 Because of the voice of the enemy, because of the oppression of the wicked: for they cast iniquity upon me, and in their anger they hate me.

4 My lev is very pained within me: and the fears of death have fallen upon me.

5 Fearfulness and trembling are come upon me, and horror has overwhelmed me.

6 And I said, Oh that I had wings like a yonah! For then would I fly away, and be at rest.

7 See, then would I wander far off, and remain in the wilderness. Selah.

8 I would run and escape from the wind and storm.

9 Destroy, O **יהוה**, confuse and divide their tongues: for I have seen violence and strife in the city.

10 Day and night they go about it upon its walls: evil also and sorrow are in the midst of it.

11 Wickedness is in the midst of it: oppression and deceit depart not from her streets.

12 *For it was not an enemy that reproached Me; then I could have dealt with it: neither was it he that hated Me that did magnify himself against Me; then I would have hidden Myself from him:*[5]

13 *But it was you, a man My equal, My guide, and My acquaintance.*

14 *We took sweet counsel together, and walked to the Bayit of Elohim in the crowd.*

15 Let death seize upon them, and let them go down quickly into Sheol: for wickedness is in their dwellings, and among them.

16 As for me, I will call upon Elohim; and **יהוה** shall save me.

17 At shacrit, and mincha, and at maariv, will I make tefillah, and cry aloud: and He shall shema to my voice.

18 He has delivered my being in shalom from the battle that was against me: for there were many with me.

19 El shall shema, and afflict them, even He that abides from old. Selah. Because they have no changes,[6] therefore they fear not Elohim.

20 He has put forth his hands against such as be at shalom with him: he has broken his promise.

---

[1] The promise of the kingdom restored, when the exiles of both houses are returned.
[2] YHWH the Deliverer.
[3] Salvation is in YHWH's Name through Yahshua.
[4] Our YHWH who listens.

---

[5] Yahshua speaks in the first person.
[6] Hope of changes or change.

21 The words of his mouth were smoother than butter, but war was in his lev: his words were softer than oil, yet were they drawn swords.

22 Cast your burden upon יהוה, and He shall sustain you: He shall never allow the tzadikim to be moved.

23 But You, O Elohim, shall bring them down into the pit of destruction: bloody and deceitful men shall not live out half their days; but I will trust in You.

Nun Vav

56 [1] Be full of rachamim to me, O Elohim: for man would swallow me up; the daily fighting oppresses me.

2 My enemies would swallow me up daily: for there are many that fight against me, O most High.

3 When I am afraid, I will trust in You.

4 In Elohim I will hallel His word, in Elohim I have put my trust; I will not fear what flesh can do to me.

5 Every day they twist my words: all their thoughts are against me for evil.

6 They gather themselves together, they hide themselves, and they mark my steps, when they wait for my being.

7 Shall they escape by iniquity? In Your anger cast down the nations, O Elohim.

8 You count my wanderings: You put my tears into Your wineskin: are they not in Your book?

9 When I cry to You, then shall my enemies turn back: this I know; for Elohim is for me.

10 In Elohim will I hallel His word: in יהוה will I hallel His word.[2]

11 In Elohim have I put my trust: I will not be afraid what man can do to me.

12 Your vows are upon me, O Elohim: I will render tehillot to You.

13 For You have delivered my being from death: will not You deliver my feet from falling, that I may have my halacha before Elohim in the light of the living?

Nun Zayin

57 [3] Be full of rachamim to me, O Elohim, be full of rachamim to me: for my being trusts in You: yes, in the shadow of Your wings will I make my refuge, until these calamities have past.

2 I will cry to Elohim most high; to El that performs all things for me.

3 He shall send from the shamayim, and save from the reproach of him that would swallow me up. Selah. Elohim shall send forth His rachamim and His emet.

4 My being is among lions: and I lie even among them that are set on fire, even the sons of men, whose teeth are spears and arrows, and their tongue a sharp sword.

5 Be exalted, O Elohim, above the shamayim; let Your tiferet be above all the earth.

6 They have prepared a net for my steps; my being is bowed down: they have dug a pit before me, into the midst of which they are fallen themselves. Selah.

7 My lev is fixed, O Elohim, my lev is fixed: I will shir and give halleluyahs.

8 Awake, my tiferet; awake, guitar and harp: I myself will awake early.

9 I will hallel You, O יהוה, among the peoples: I will shir to You among the nations.

10 For Your rachamim is great to the shamayim, and Your emet to the clouds.

11 Be exalted, O Elohim, above the shamayim: let Your tiferet be above all the earth.

Nun Chet

58 [4] Do you indeed speak tzedakah, O congregation?[5] Do you shophet uprightly, you sons of men?

2 Yes, in lev you work wickedness; you weigh the violence of your hands in the earth.

---

[1] YHWH can be trusted.
[2] The Word is Yahshua.

[3] YHWH our refuge.
[4] YHWH judges rightly.
[5] Of Yisrael.

3 The wicked are estranged even from the womb: they go astray as soon as they are born, speaking lies.

4 Their poison is like the poison of a serpent: they are like the deaf cobra that stops its ear;

5 Which will not shema to the voice of charmers, whisperers or the wise.

6 Break their teeth, O Elohim, in their mouth: break out the great teeth of the young lions, O יהוה.

7 Let them melt away as mayim that runs continually: when He bends His bow to shoot His arrows, let them be as cut in pieces.

8 As a snail that melts, let every one of them pass away: like the untimely birth of a woman, that they may not see the sun.

9 Before your pots can feel the thorns, may He blow them away; green and blazing alike.

10 The tzadikim shall gilah when he sees the vengeance: He shall wash his feet in the dom of the wicked.

11 So that a man shall say, Truly there is a reward for the tzadikim: truly He is an Elohim that shophets the earth.

Nun Tet

59 ¹Deliver me from my enemies, O my Elohim: defend me from them that rise up against me.

2 Deliver me from the workers of iniquity, and save me from bloody men.

3 For, look, they lie in wait for my being: the mighty are gathered against me; not for my transgression, nor for my sin, O יהוה.

4 They run and prepare themselves without my fault: awake to help me, and observe.

5 You therefore, O יהוה Elohim of hosts, the Elohim of Yisrael, awake to visit all the nations: be not full of rachamim to any wicked transgressors. Selah.

6 They return at evening: they make a noise like a dog, and go around the city.

7 See, they belch out with their mouth: swords are in their lips: for who, say they, does shema?

8 But You, O יהוה, shall laugh at them; You shall have all the nations in derision.

9 Because of his strength will I wait upon You: for Elohim is my defense.

10 The Elohim of my rachamim shall go before me: Elohim shall let me see my desire upon my enemies.

11 Slay them not, lest my people forget: scatter them by Your power; and bring them down, O יהוה our shield.

12 For the sin of their mouth and the words of their lips let them even be taken in their pride: and for cursing and lying which they speak.

13 Consume them in anger, consume them that they may not be: and let them know that Elohim rules in Yaakov to the ends of the earth. Selah.

14 And at evening let them return; and let them make a noise like a dog, and go around the city.

15 Let them wander up and down for food, and complain if they are not satisfied.

16 But I will shir of Your power; yes, I will shir aloud of Your rachamim in the morning: for You have been my defense and refuge in the day of my trouble.

17 To You, O my Strength, will I shir: for Elohim is my defense, the Elohim of my rachamim.

Samech

60 ² O Elohim, You have cast us off, You have scattered us, You have been displeased; O turn Yourself to us again.

2 You have made the land to tremble; You have broken it: heal the breaches of it; for it shakes.

3 You have showed Your people hard things: You have made us to drink the wine of fear.

---

¹ YHWH will take vengeance.

² YHWH and Yisrael.

4 You have given a banner to them that fear You, that it may be displayed because of the emet. Selah.

5 That Your beloved may be delivered;[1] save with Your right hand,[2] and shema to me.

6 Elohim has spoken in His set-apartness; *I will gilah, I will divide Shechem, and measure out the valley of Succoth.*

7 *Gilead is Mine, and Menashsheh is Mine; Ephraim also is the strength of My head,[3] Yahudah is My Lawgiver;[4]*

8 *Moav is My washpot; over Edom will I cast out My shoe: Philistia, scream out because of Me.*

9 Who will bring me into the strong city? Who will lead me into Edom?

10 Will not You, O Elohim, who had cast us off? And you; O Elohim, who did not go out with our armies?

11 Give us help from trouble: for vain is the help of man.

12 Through Elohim we shall do valiantly: for He it is that shall trample down our enemies.

Samech Alef

6 1 [5] Shema my cry, O Elohim; attend to my tefillah.

2 From the ends of the earth will I cry to You, when my lev is overwhelmed: lead me to the Rock that is higher than I.

3 For You have been a shelter for me, and a strong tower from the enemy.

4 I will abide in Your sukkah le-olam-va-ed: I will trust in the shelter of Your wings. Selah.

5 For You, O Elohim, have listened to my vows: You have given me the heritage of those that fear Your Name.[6]

6 You will prolong the melech's chayim: and his years as many generations.

7 He shall abide before Elohim le-olam-va-ed: O prepare rachamim and emet, which may preserve him.

8 So will I shir hallel to Your Name le-olam-va-ed, that I may daily perform my vows.

Samech Bet

6 2 [7] Truly my being waits upon Elohim: from Him comes My Yahshua.

2 He only is my Rock and My Yahshua; He is my defense; I shall not be greatly moved.

3 How long will you imagine evil against a man? You shall be slain all of you: as a leaning wall shall you be, and as a tottering fence.

4 They only consult to cast him down from His excellency: they delight in lies: they bless with their mouth, but they curse inwardly. Selah.

5 My being, finds rest in Elohim alone; for my tikvah is from Him.

6 He only is my Rock and My Yahshua: He is my defense; I shall not be moved.

7 In Elohim is My Yahshua and my tiferet: the Rock of my strength, and my refuge, is in Elohim.

8 Trust in Him at all times; you people, pour out your lev before Him: Elohim is a refuge for us. Selah.

9 Surely men of low degree are vanity, and men of high degree are a lie: if weighed in the scales, they are altogether lighter than vanity.

10 Trust not in oppression, and do not put false tikvah in robbery: if riches increase, set not your lev upon them.

11 Elohim has spoken once; twice have I heard this; that power belongs to Elohim.

12 Also to You, O יהוה, belongs rachamim: for You give to every man according to his mitzvot.

---

[1] Both houses.
[2] Yahshua.
[3] Ephraim is the power that will proclaim salvation, or the Head of Yisrael, who is Head over all; even our King Yahshua.
[4] Yahudah is the Torah-proclaimer, and the Torah-guardian.
[5] YHWH our shelter and Rock.
[6] Reverencing YHWH's true Name is considered a heritage to be passed down in all Yisraelite generations.

[7] Waiting upon YHWH.

Samech Gimel

63 [1] O Elohim, you are my El; early will I seek You: my being thirsts for You, my flesh longs for You in a dry and thirsty land, where no mayim is;
2 To see Your power and Your tiferet, so as I have seen You in the Set-Apart Place.
3 Because Your loving chesed is better than chayim, my lips shall hallel You.
4 So will I bless You while I live: I will lift up my hands in Your Name.[2]
5 My being shall be satisfied as with marrow and abundance; and my mouth shall hallel You with joyful lips:
6 When I remember You upon my bed, and meditate on You in the night watches.
7 Because You have been my help, therefore in the shadow of Your wings will I gilah.
8 My being follows hard after You: Your right hand upholds me.[3]
9 But those that seek my being, to destroy it, shall go into the lower parts of the earth.
10 They shall fall by the sword: they shall be the portion for foxes.
11 But the melech shall gilah in Elohim; everyone that swears by Him shall have tiferet: but the mouth of them that speak lies shall be stopped.

Samech Daled

64 [4] Shema to my voice, O Elohim, in my tefillah: preserve my chayim from fear of the enemy.
2 Hide me from the secret counsel of the wicked; from the insurrection of the workers of iniquity:
3 Who sharpen their tongue like a sword, and bend their bows to shoot their arrows, even bitter words:
4 That they may shoot in secret at the blameless: suddenly do they shoot at him, and fear not.

5 They encourage themselves in an evil matter: they commune by laying snares secretly; they say, Who shall see them?
6 They search out iniquities; they accomplish a diligent search: both the inward thought of every one of them, and the lev, is deep.
7 But Elohim shall shoot at them with an arrow; suddenly shall they be wounded.
8 So they shall make their own tongue to fall upon themselves: all that see them shall flee away.
9 And all men shall fear, and shall declare the work of Elohim; for they shall wisely consider His doing.
10 The tzadikim shall be in simcha in יהוה, and shall trust in Him; and all the tzadik in lev shall be immortal.

Samech Hey

65 [5] Tehilla waits for You, O Elohim, in Tzion: and to You shall the vow be performed.
2 O You that hears all tefillah, to You shall all flesh come.
3 Iniquities prevail against me: as for our transgressions, You shall purge them away.
4 Blessed is the man whom You choose, and whom You cause to approach You, that he may dwell in Your courts: we shall be satisfied with the tov of Your Bayit, even of Your Set-Apart Beit HaMikdash.
5 By awesome deeds in tzedakah will You answer us, O Elohim of our salvation; You are the confidence of all the ends of the earth, and of them that are far off[6] upon the sea:
6 Who by His strength established the mountains; being clothed with power:
7 Who stills the noise of the seas, the noise of their waves, and the tumult of the nations.
8 They also that dwell in the furthest parts are afraid at Your signs: You make the outgoings of the morning and evening to gilah.

---

[1] Blessing YHWH.
[2] Yisrael lifts up hands in YHWH's Name.
[3] Yahshua.
[4] YHWH protects.

[5] YHWH controls nature and its gifts.
[6] Ephraim Yisrael.

9 You visit the earth, and give mayim to it: You greatly enrich it with the river of Elohim, which is full of mayim: You prepare grain for them, when You have so provided for it.

10 You give mayim to the ridges of it abundantly: You deepen its furrows: You make it soft with showers: You bless its growth.

11 You top the year with Your tov; and Your paths drip with abundance.

12 They drip upon the pastures of the wilderness: and the little hills gilah on every side.

13 The pastures are clothed with flocks; the valleys also are covered with grain; they shout for simcha, they also shir.

Samech Vav

66 [1] Make a joyful noise to Elohim, all you lands:

2 Sing forth the honor of His Name:[2] make His hallel beautiful.

3 Say to Elohim, How awesome are You in Your works! Through the greatness of Your power shall Your enemies submit themselves to You.

4 All the earth shall worship You, and shall shir to You; they shall shir to Your Name. Selah.

5 Come and see the works of Elohim: He is awesome in His doings toward the children of men.

6 He turned the sea into dry land: they went through the flood on foot: there did we gilah in Him.

7 He rules by His power le-olam-va-ed; His eyes observe the nations: let not the rebellious exalt themselves. Selah.

8 O bless our Elohim, you nations, and make the voice of His hallel to be heard:

9 Who holds our being in chayim, and allows not our feet to be moved.

10 For You, O Elohim, have proved us: You have tried us, as silver is tried.

11 You brought us into the net; you laid affliction on our loins.

12 You have caused men to ride over our heads; we went through fire and through mayim: but You brought us out into a wealthy place.

13 I will go into Your Bayit with burnt offerings: I will pay my vows to You,

14 Which my lips have uttered, and my mouth has spoken, when I was in trouble.

15 I will offer to You burnt sacrifices of fatlings, with the incense of rams; I will offer young bulls with goats. Selah.

16 Come and shema; all you that fear Elohim, and I will declare what He has done for my being.

17 I cried to Him with my mouth, and He was extolled with my tongue.18 If I regard iniquity in my lev, יהוה will not shema me:

19 But truly Elohim has heard me; He has attended to the voice of my tefillah.

20 Blessed be Elohim, who has not turned away my tefillah, nor His rachamim from me.

Samech Zayin

67 [3] Elohim be full of rachamim to us, and bless us; and cause His face to shine upon us; Selah.

2 That Your halacha may be known upon the earth, Your saving health among all nations.

3 Let the nations hallel You, O Elohim; let all the nations hallel You.

4 O let the nations be in simcha and shir for simcha: for You shall shophet the nations in tzedakah, and govern the nations upon earth. Selah.

5 Let the nations hallel You, O Elohim; let all the nations hallel You.

6 Then shall the earth yield her increase; and Elohim, even our own Elohim, shall bless us.

7 Elohim shall bless us; and all the ends of the earth shall fear Him.

[1] YHWH's works are awesome.
[2] Worship must be geared to YHWH's Name – not any substitutes.
[3] YHWH shall be praised by all nations in the kingdom.

Samech Chet

68 [1] Let Elohim arise, let His enemies be scattered: let them also that hate Him flee before Him.

2 As smoke is driven away, so He drives them away: as wax melts before the fire, so let the wicked perish at the shechinah of Elohim.

3 But let the tzadikim be in simcha; let them gilah before Elohim: yes, let them be exceedingly in gilah.

4 Sing to Elohim, shir tehillot to His Name: extol Him that rides upon the shamayim by His Name Yah, and gilah before Him.

5 An Abba of the fatherless, and a Shophet of the widows, is Elohim in His set-apart dwelling place.

6 Elohim make a home for the lonely: He brings out those who are bound with chains: but the rebellious dwell in a dry land.

7 O Elohim, when You went forth before Your people, when You did march through the wilderness; Selah:

8 The earth shook, the shamayim also dripped at the shechinah of Elohim: even Sinai itself was moved at the shechinah of Elohim, the Elohim of Yisrael.

9 You, O Elohim, did send a plentiful rain, by which You did confirm Your inheritance, when it was weary.

10 Your flock has lived in it: You, O Elohim, have prepared of Your tov for the poor.

11 יהוה gave the word: great was the company of those that published it.

12 Melechim of armies did flee in a hurry: and she that stopped at home divided the plunder.

13 Though you have lain down among the thorns, yet shall you be as the wings of a yonah covered with silver, and her feathers with yellow gold.

14 When the Almighty scattered melechim in it, it was white as snow in Tsalmon.

15 The har of Elohim is as the har of Bashan; a high har as the har of Bashan.

16 Why do you leap, you high hills? This is the har which Elohim desires to dwell in; yes, יהוה will dwell in it le-olam-va-ed.

17 The mirkavot of Elohim are twenty thousand, even thousands of heavenly messengers: יהוה came from Sinai, into the Set-Apart Place.

18 You have ascended on high, You have led exiles captive:[2] You have received gifts for men;[3] Yes, for the rebellious also, that Yah-Elohim might dwell among them.

19 Blessed be יהוה, who daily loads us with benefits, even the El of our Yahshua. Selah.

20 He that is our El is the El of salvation; and to יהוה, My Master, belongs the escapes from death.

21 But Elohim shall wound the head of His enemies, and the hairy scalp of such a one as goes on still in His trespasses.

22 יהוה said, I will bring again from Bashan,[4] I will bring My people again from the depths of the sea:[5]

23 That your foot may be dipped in the dom of your enemies, and the tongue of your dogs in the same.

24 They have seen Your goings, O Elohim; even the goings of My El, My Melech, in the Set-Apart Place.

25 The singers went before, the players on instruments followed after; among them were the young women playing with tambourines.

26 Bless you Elohim in the congregations, even יהוה,[6] from the fountain of Yisrael.

27 There is little Benyamin with their ruler, the leaders of Yahudah and their council, the leaders of Zevulon, and the leaders of Naphtali.

28 Your Elohim has commanded your strength: strengthen, O Elohim, that which You have worked for us.

---

[1] Our history.

[2] Yahshua/YHWH has come to free the exiles of Yisrael both spiritually as seen in Ephesians 4:8 and physically as seen in Ezekiel 37.

[3] From Abba for Yisrael.

[4] From the heathen.

[5] He will end the exile and restore both houses.

[6] Does your Yisraelite congregation bless YHWH or another deity?

29 Because of Your Beit HaMikdash at Yahrushalayim shall melechim bring presents to You.

30 Rebuke the oppressors, the multitude of the wild bulls: the idols of the heathen, which are covered in silver until each one submits himself: scatter the nations that delight in war.

31 Rulers shall come out of Mitzrayim; Ethiopia shall soon stretch out her hands to Elohim.

32 Sing to Elohim, you malchutim of the earth; O shir tehillot to the יהוה; Selah:

33 To Him that rides upon the shamayim of the shamayim, which were ancient; look, He does send out His voice, a mighty voice.

34 Give strength to Elohim: His excellency is over Yisrael, and His strength is in the clouds.

35 O Elohim, You are awesome out of Your set-apart places: the El of Yisrael is He that gives strength and power to His people. Barchu-et-Elohim.

Samech Tet

69 [1] Save me, O Elohim; for the mayim are come in to my being.

2 I sink in deep mud, where there is no standing: I am come into deep mayim, where the floods overflow me.

3 *I am weary of my crying: my throat is dried: my eyes pine away while I wait for My Elohim.*

4 *They that hate Me without a cause are more than the hairs of My head: they that would destroy Me, being My enemies wrongfully, are mighty: then I restored that which I took not away.* [2] [3]

5 O Elohim, You know my foolishness; and my sins are not hidden from You.

6 Let not them that wait on You, O Master יהוה of hosts, be ashamed for my sake: let not those that seek You be ashamed for my sake, O Elohim of Yisrael.

7 Because for Your sake I have borne reproach; shame has covered My face.

8 *I am become a stranger to My brothers, and an alien to My ima's children.* [4]

9 *For the zeal for Your Bayit has eaten Me up; and the reproaches of them that reproached You have fallen upon Me.* [5]

10 When I wept, and chastened my being with fasting, that was to my reproach.

11 I made sackcloth also my garment; and I became a proverb to them.

12 They that sit in the gate speak against me; and I was the shir of the drunkards.

13 But as for me, my tefillah is to You, O יהוה, in an acceptable time: O Elohim, in the multitude of Your rachamim You listened to me, in the emet of Your salvation.

14 Deliver me out of the mud, and let me not sink: let me be delivered from them that hate me, and out of the deep mayim.

15 Let not the water's flood overflow me, neither let the deep swallow me up, and let not the pit shut her mouth upon me.

---

[1] Yahshua's suffering.

[2] Yahshua is speaking in the first person. The thing He did not steal was authority from Abba and the covenant from Yisrael, as some claim through Replacement Theology. Rather, He reconciled and restored Abba to Yisrael, and Yisrael to Torah and to each other.

[3] In the **pashat** or literal it does apply to a guilty man and not Yahshua; but the Renewed Covenant is a highly esoteric book, employing metaphors, allegories, mysteries, euphemisms, and the like. If we but merely skip down one level of understanding to the **remez**, then the hint of Psalm 69:4a points directly to Yahshua. Also in John 15:25, Yahshua knowing that Psalm 69:5 did not apply to Him; purposely and masterfully did not quote it. We see this many times in the Renewed Covenant, where Yahshua or one of the apostles

will quote a verse seemingly (and sometimes shockingly) out of its primary context, and then apply it to the Moshiach, without quoting the entire chapter. This is all part of the Hebraic method of understanding and brings about no contradictions whatsoever.

[4] Yahshua had zeal to rebuild Yisrael, and was rejected by many in Judah and also among His own physical relatives.

[5] Yahshua had zeal to rebuild Yisrael, as well as build the spiritual Temple through which YHWH could function and dwell. In order to display His zeal for the cleansing, and purification of the true Temple that He was appointed to build in the Spirit, He displayed that zeal in the natural by using the dishonest charlatan moneychangers as an example or type of what He was sent to do as YHWH's Moshiach in the Spirit realm. We find that truth in Matthew 16:18, as well as in Ephesians 2:21-22, where Moshiach's plans to build the Temple of His Father YHWH in the Spirit realm is neatly displayed and outlined. The cleansing of the sons of Levi by removing the leaven from their courts is a type of what He has done for all Yisrael in the realm of the Spirit. Proper Hebraic understanding of all issues is that everything seen in the natural has a corresponding copy in the spiritual and everything seen in the spiritual realm by Spirit beings, has a physical equivalent in the natural realm. Thus the Spirit and physical realms are merged into echad or one entire package.

16 Shema to me, O יהוה; for Your loving chesed is tov: turn to me according to the multitude of Your tender rachamim.

17 And hide not Your face from Your eved; for I am in trouble: shema to me speedily.

18 Draw near to my being, and redeem it: deliver me because of my enemies.

19 You have known my reproach, and my shame, and my dishonor: my adversaries are all before You.

20 Reproach has broken my lev; and I am full of heaviness: and I looked for some to take pity, but there was none; and for comforters, but I found none.

21 *They gave Me also gall for My food; and in My thirst they gave Me vinegar to drink.[1]*

22 *Let their table become a trap before them: and that which should have been for their welfare,[2] let it become a trap.[3]*

23 *Let their eyes be darkened, that they see not; and make their loins continually to shake.[4]*

24 *Pour out Your indignation upon them, and let Your wrathful anger take hold of them.*

25 *Let their dwelling place be desolate; and let none dwell in their tents.[5][6]*

26 *For they persecute Him whom You have smitten; and they talk to the grief of those whom You have wounded.*

27 *Add iniquity to their iniquity: and let them not come into Your tzedakah.*

28 *Let them be blotted out of Sefer HaChayim, and not be written with the tzadikim.*

29 But I am poor and sorrowful: let Your salvation, O Elohim, set me up on high.

30 I will hallel the Name of Elohim with a shir, and will magnify Him with hodu.

31 This also shall please יהוה better than an ox or bullock that has horns and hoofs.

32 The humble shall see this, and be in simcha: and your lev shall live that seek Elohim.

33 For יהוה hears the poor, and despises not His exiles.[7]

34 Let the shamayim and earth hallel Him, the seas, and everything that moves in it.

35 For Elohim will save Tzion, and will rebuild the cities of Yahudah: that they may dwell there, and have it in their possession.

36 The zera also of His avadim shall inherit it: and they that love His Name shall dwell in it.[8]

Ayin

70 [9] Make haste, O Elohim, to deliver me; make haste to help me, O יהוה.

2 Let them be ashamed and abased that seek after my being: let them be turned backward, and put to confusion, that desire my hurt.

3 Let them be turned back for a reward of their own shame that say, Aha, aha.

4 Let all those that seek You gilah and be in simcha in You: and let such as love Your Yahshua[10] say continually, Let Elohim be magnified.

---

[1] Psalm 69:21 was referred to by both Moshiach and John in his besorah. But the meaning is far deeper than that. Those at the execution stake misunderstood Him, even as do the anti-missionaries to this day. He was not merely fulfilling a verse of Scripture in verse 21. The significance is far greater. According to Numbers 5, His final thoughts at the time of His death were about His bride. He was dying for Yisrael. As such the cry "I thirst," was more than a fulfillment of a single verse. It was a heartfelt cry of agony, in that He desired to buy back - to redeem, and to be with, His bride. According to Numbers 5, He needed to drink the water of bitterness or vinegar in order to drink the bitter water demanded for a bride to drink in the Torah (instruction) regarding "A Jealous Husband." In the death of Moshiach, He, the Righteous Bridegroom became the unrighteous bride, and therefore in order for His belly to swell, as did the unfaithful woman's in Numbers 5, He had to drink the bitter water or waters of bitterness. Not only does Yahshua importantly fulfill Psalm 69:21, He more importantly fulfills the "Law Of a Jealous Husband," when the husband knows or suspects that his wife has been unfaithful. When crying out "it is finished" (**tetelestai** in the Greek of John 19:28-30) in Hebrew He actually cried **kalah** meaning in the **pashat**/literal "accomplished" but in secondary application or **remez**/hint meaning "bride." The Hebrew word for "finished" is **kalah**; the same word as "bride."
[2] The execution stake.
[3] Speaking of Jewish Yisrael.
[4] Speaking of Jewish Yisrael.
[5] Verse 25 speaks of David in the **pashat** and Judas in the **remez**. Yahshua has the full authority He needs to take any verse in any part of Scripture, both in and out of context, in order to make a point. In this reference to Judas's betrayal, He does just that.
[6] A secondary application would be to Judah's leaders with whom Judas conspired.
[7] Both houses.
[8] Every citizen of the **atid lavoh**/millennium will love His true Name – Yahweh.
[9] YHWH can hurry if need be.
[10] Hebrew: **yeshuatecha**; "your Yahshua."

5 But I am poor and needy: make haste to me, O Elohim: You are My help and My Deliverer; O יהוה, make no delay.

Ayin Aleph

71 [1] In You, O יהוה, do I put my trust: let me never be put to confusion.
2 Deliver me in Your tzedakah, and cause me to escape: incline Your ear to me, and save me.
3 Be my strong dwelling place, to where I may continually resort: You have given commandment to save me; for You are My Rock and My fortress.
4 Deliver me, O my Elohim, out of the hand of the wicked, out of the hand of the unrighteous and cruel man.
5 For You are my tikvah, O Master יהוה: You are my trust from my youth.
6 On You have I leaned from the womb: You are He that took me out of my ima's inward parts: my hallel shall be continually of You.
7 I am as a wonder to many; but You are my strong refuge.
8 Let my mouth be filled with Your hallel and with Your honor all the day.
9 Cast me not off in the time of old age; forsake me not when my strength fails.
10 For my enemies speak against me; and they that lay in wait for my being take counsel together,
11 Saying, Elohim has forsaken him: persecute and take him; for there is none to deliver him.
12 O Elohim, be not far from me: O My Elohim, rush to my help.
13 Let them be ashamed and consumed that are adversaries to my being; let them be covered with reproach and dishonor that seek my hurt.
14 But I will tikvah continually, and will yet hallel You more and more.

15 My mouth shall show forth Your tzedakah and Your salvation all the day; for I know not the numbers of it.
16 I will go in the strength of the Master יהוה: I will make mention of Your tzedakah, even of You only.
17 O Elohim, You have taught me from my youth: and to this day have I declared Your wonderful works.
18 Now also when I am old and grayheaded, O Elohim, forsake me not; until I have shown Your strength to this generation, and Your power to every one that is to come.
19 Your tzedakah also, O Elohim, is very high, who has done these great things: O Elohim, who is like You!
20 You, who have shown me great and evil troubles, shall quicken me again, and shall bring me up again from the depths of the earth.[2]
21 You shall increase my greatness, and comfort me on every side.
22 I will also hallel You with the guitar, even Your emet, O My Elohim: to You will I shir with the harp, O You Set-Apart-One of Yisrael.
23 My lips shall greatly gilah when I shir to You; and my being, which You have redeemed.
24 My tongue also shall talk of Your tzedakah all the day long: for they are ashamed, for they are brought to shame, that seek my hurt.

Ayin Bet

72 [3] Give the melech Your mishpatim, O Elohim, and Your tzedakah to the melech's son.
2 He shall shophet Your people with tzedakah, and Your poor with mishpat.
3 The mountains shall bring shalom to the people, and the little hills, by tzedakah.
4 He shall shophet the poor of the people; He shall save the children of the needy, and shall break in pieces the oppressor.

---

[1] YHWH our refuge.

[2] Resurrection is the tikvah of Yisrael.
[3] YHWH's millennium.

5 They shall fear You as long as the sun and moon endure, throughout all generations.
6 He shall come down like rain upon the mowed grass: as showers that give mayim the earth.
7 In His days shall the tzadikim flourish; and the abundance of shalom as long as the moon endures.
8 He shall have rule also from sea to sea, and from the river to the ends of the earth.[1]
9 They that dwell in the wilderness shall bow before Him; and His enemies shall lick the dust.
10 The melechim of Tarshish and of the coastlands shall bring presents: the melechim of Sheva and Seva shall offer gifts.
11 Yes, all melechim shall fall down before Him: all nations shall serve Him.[2]
12 For He shall deliver the needy when He cries; the poor also, and him that has no helper.
13 He shall spare the poor and needy, and shall save the beings of the needy.
14 He shall redeem their being from deceit and violence: and precious shall their dom be in His sight.
15 And He shall live, and to Him shall be given of the gold of Sheva: tefillah also shall be made for Him continually; and daily shall He be given tehilla.
16 There shall be a handful of grain in the earth upon the top of the mountains; the fruit of it shall shake like Levanon: and they of the city shall flourish like grass of the earth.
17 His Name shall endure le-olam-va-ed: His Name shall be continued as long as the sun: and men shall be blessed in Him: all nations shall call Him blessed.[3]
18 Blessed be יהוה Elohim, the Elohim of Yisrael, who only does wonderful things.

19 And blessed is His esteemed Name le-olam-va-ed: and let the whole earth be filled with His tiferet; Amein, and Amein.
20 The tefillot of David the son of Yishai are ended.

Ayin Gimel

73 [4] Truly Elohim is tov to Yisrael, even to such as are of a clean lev.
2 But as for me, my feet were almost gone; my steps had well near slipped.
3 For I was envious of the foolish, when I saw the prosperity of the wicked.
4 For there are no pains in their death: but their strength is firm.
5 They are not in trouble as other men; neither are they plagued like other men.
6 Therefore pride circles them about as a chain; violence covers them as a garment.
7 Their eyes stand out with abundance: they have more than the lev could wish.
8 They are corrupt, and speak wickedly concerning oppression: they speak with arrogance.
9 They set their mouth against the shamayim, and their tongue weaves through the earth.
10 Therefore His people return here: and they drain mayim of a full cup.
11 And they say, How does El know? And is there da'at in the most High?
12 See, these are the wicked, who prosper in the olam hazeh; they increase in riches.
13 Truly I have cleansed my lev in vain, and washed my hands in innocence.
14 For all the day long have I been plagued, and chastened every morning.
15 If I say, I will speak this; see, I would have deceived the generation of your children.
16 When I thought to know this, it was too painful for me;
17 Until I went into the Set-Apart Place of El; then I understood their end.

---

[1] Yahshua.
[2] King Yahshua.
[3] YHWH is not His "old" or First Covenant or "Jewsih" Name, but rather His only eternal Name, and will endure as long as the sun, and beyond into eternity.

[4] Appealing to YHWH.

18 Surely You did set them in slippery places: You cast them down into destruction.

19 How are they brought into ruin, as in a moment! They are utterly consumed with terrors.

20 As a dream when one awakes; so, O יהוה, when You awake, You shall despise their image.

21 So my lev was grieved, and I was pierced in my kidneys.

22 So foolish was I, and ignorant: I was as a beast before You.

23 Nevertheless I am continually with You: You have supported me by my right hand.

24 You shall guide me with Your counsel, and afterward receive me to tiferet.

25 Whom have I in the shamayim but You? And there is none upon the earth that I desire beside You.

26 My flesh and my lev fails: but Elohim is the strength of my lev, and my portion le-olam-va-ed.

27 For, look, they that are far from You shall perish: You have destroyed all them that go whoring away from You.

28 But it is tov for me to draw near to Elohim: I have put my trust in the Master יהוה, that I may declare all Your works.

Ayin Daled

74 ¹ O Elohim, why have You cast us off le-olam-va-ed? Why does Your anger smoke against the sheep of Your pasture?

2 Remember Your congregation,² which You have purchased of old;³ the rod of Your inheritance, which You have redeemed; this Har Tzion, where You have lived.

3 Lift up Your feet to the perpetual ruins; even all that the enemy has done wickedly in the Set-Apart Place.

4 Your enemies roar in the midst of Your meeting places; they set up their own signs as true signs.

5 A man was famous according to how he had lifted up axes upon the thick trees.

6 But all the carved work of it they break down with axes and hammers.

7 They have cast fire into Your Set-Apart Place, they have defiled You by casting down the dwelling place of Your Name to the ground.

8 They said in their levim, Let us destroy them together: they have burned up all the meeting places of El in the land.

9 We see not our signs: there is no longer a navi: neither is there among us anyone that knows how long.

10 O Elohim, how long shall the adversary reproach? Shall the enemy blaspheme Your Name le-olam-va-ed?

11 Why do you withdraw Your hand, even Your right hand?⁴ Pluck it out of Your bosom.

12 For Elohim is My Melech of old, working salvation in the midst of the earth.

13 You did divide the sea by Your strength: You broke the head of Liviathan in the mayim.

14 You broke the heads of Leviathan in pieces, and gave him to be food to the people inhabiting the wilderness.

15 You did cleave open the fountain and the flood: You dried up mighty rivers.

16 The day is Yours, the night also is Yours: You have prepared the light and the sun.

17 You have set all the borders of the earth: You have made summer and winter.

18 Remember this, that the enemy has reproached, O יהוה, and the foolish people have blasphemed Your Name.⁵

19 O deliver not the being of Your turtledove to the multitude of the wicked: forget not the congregation of Your poor le-olam-va-ed.

---

¹ YHWH's discipline of Yisrael.
² Congregation of Yisrael.
³ By the dom of the Torah covenant, when Moshe sprinkled the scroll.

⁴ Yahshua came from the bosom of the Father.
⁵ The leaders of Jewish Yisrael.

20 Have respect to the covenant: for the dark places of the earth are full of the dwellings of cruelty.

21 O let not the oppressed return ashamed: let the poor and needy hallel Your Name.

22 Arise, O Elohim, plead Your own cause: remember how the foolish man slanders You daily.

23 Forget not the voice of Your enemies: the tumult of those that rise up against You increases continually.

Ayin Hey

75 [1] To You, O Elohim, do we give hodu, to You do we give hodu: and Your Name is near; Your wonderful works shall be declared.

2 When I shall seize the moed I will shophet uprightly.

3 The earth and all the inhabitants of it are dissolved: I set up the pillars of it. Selah.

4 I said to the fools, Deal not foolishly: and to the wicked, Lift not your pride:

5 Lift not your pride on high: and speak not with a stiff neck.

6 For promotion comes neither from the east, nor from the west, nor from the south.[2]

7 But Elohim is the Shophet: He puts down one, and sets up another.

8 For in the hand of יהוה there is a cup, and the wine is red; it is full of mixture; and He pours it out: draining even its dregs, all the wicked of the earth shall drink it.

9 But I will declare le-olam-va-ed; I will shir tehillot to the Elohim of Yaakov.

10 All the pride of the wicked also will I cut off; but the horns of the tzadikim shall be exalted.

Ayin Zayin

76 [3] In Yahudah is Elohim known: His Name is great in Yisrael.[4]

2 In Yahrushalayim also is His sukkah, and His dwelling place in Tzion.

3 There He broke the arrows of the bow, the shield, and the sword, and the battle. Selah.

4 You are more beautiful and excellent than the mountains of prey.

5 The stout-hearted are stripped, they have slept their sleep: and none of the men of might have found their hands.

6 At Your rebuke, O Elohim of Yaakov, both the mirkavah and horse are cast into a dead sleep.

7 You, You, are to be feared: and who may stand in Your sight when You are angry?

8 You did cause mishpat to be heard from the shamayim; the earth feared, and was still,

9 When Elohim arose to mishpat, to save all the meek of the earth. Selah.

10 Surely the anger of man shall hallel You: with the remainder of their anger shall You cloth Yourself.

11 Vow, and pay to יהוה Your Elohim: let all that be around Him bring presents to Him that ought to be feared.

12 He shall cut off the ruach of leaders: He is terrible to the melechim of the earth.

Ayin Zayin

77 [5] I cried to Elohim with my voice, even to Elohim with my voice; and He listened to me.

2 In the day of my trouble I sought יהוה: my hand was stretched out in the night, and ceased not: my being refused to be comforted.

3 I remembered Elohim, and was troubled: I complained, and my ruach was overwhelmed. Selah.

4 You ceased the vision of my eyes: I am so troubled that I cannot speak.

5 I have considered the days of old, the years long past.

6 I call to remembrance my shir in the night: I commune with my own lev: and my ruach made diligent search.

7 Will יהוה cast off le-olam-va-ed? And will He be favorable no more?

---

[1] YHWH's cup.
[2] In Yisrael it comes from the North, the dwelling place of YHWH.
[3] YHWH will rule rightly.
[4] It is our responsibility as re-born Yisrael, to make His Name known.

[5] YHWH is patient with our complaints.

8 Is His rachamim gone le-olam-va-ed? Does His promise pine away le-olam-va-ed?

9 Has El forgotten to show favor? Has He in His anger shut up His tender rachamim? Selah.

10 And I said, This is my infirmity: it is another type of visitation of the right hand of the most high.

11 I will remember the deeds of Yah: surely I will remember Your wonders of old.

12 I will meditate also on all Your work, and talk of Your doings.

13 Your halacha, O Elohim, is in the Set-Apart Place: who is so great an El as our Elohim?

14 You are the El that does wonders: You have declared Your strength among the people.

15 You have with Your Arm redeemed Your people, the sons of Yaakov and Yoseph.[1] Selah.

16 The mayim saw You, O Elohim, the mayim saw You; they were afraid: the depths also were troubled.

17 The clouds poured out mayim: the skies sent out a sound: Your arrows also went out.

18 The voice of Your thunder was in the shamayim: the lightnings lightened the olam: the earth trembled and shook.

19 Your derech is in the sea, and Your derech in the great mayim, and Your footsteps are not known.

20 You led Your people like a flock by the hand of Moshe and Aharon.

Ayin Chet

78 [2] Give ear, O My people, to My Torah:[3] incline your ears to the words of My mouth.

2 I will open My mouth in a parable: I will utter dark sayings of old:[4]

3 That we have heard and known, and our ahvot have told us.

4 We will not hide them from their children, showing to the generation to come the tehillot of יהוה, and His strength, and His wonderful works that He has done.

5 For He established a testimony in Yaakov,[5] and appointed a Torah in Yisrael, which He commanded our ahvot, that they should make them known to their children:

6 That the generation to come might know them, even the children who would be born; who would arise and declare them to their children:

7 That they might set their tikvah upon Elohim, and not forget the works of El, but keep His mitzvot:

8 And might not be as their ahvot, a stubborn and rebellious generation; a generation that set not their lev right, and whose ruach was not steadfast with El.

9 The children of Ephraim, being armed, and carrying bows, turned back in the day of battle.[6]

10 They kept not the covenant of Elohim, and refused to have their halacha in His Torah;[7]

11 And forgot His works, and His wonders that He had showed them.[8]

12 Marvelous things did He in the sight of their ahvot, in the land of Mitzrayim, in the field of Tzoan.

13 He divided the sea, and caused them to pass through; and He made the mayim to stand as a heap.

---

reveal His truths only to the repentant and not to mockers, as did His Father. According to the Word of YHWH, being chosen or elected by YHWH for salvation is a requisite to receive any kind of healing or understanding of deep eternal truths. Places in Tanach such as Jeremiah 1:5 and Exodus 3:4-6 make it clear that YHWH chooses His vessels first by divine election and appointment, and then and only then, does He reveal truth and understanding from Torah through riddles or parables (**drash**) to the elect. According to Psalm 78:2, Yahshua would bring things of old from Yisrael's history or First Covenant, and also new things that were previously hidden.
[5] The testimony of the resurrection of His Son Yahshua.
[6] Turned back to Egypt in their hearts.
[7] Ephraim, or non-Jewish Yisraelites in Yahshua, remain blind to their heritage as the ten tribes and blind to the eternality of YHWH's loving eternal instructions.
[8] Ephraim has amnesia concerning their heritage and history, seeing themselves as gentiles. This continues until they turn to Torah, and then they snap out of their blindness.

---

[1] Yahshua has redeemed both houses including Beit Yoseph.
[2] The works of YHWH in Yisrael.
[3] Both houses.
[4] Matthew 13:34-35 says Yahshua spoke only in parables to the crowds, so that they couldn't understand. Psalm 78:2, states that parables were used in Yisrael to clear things up not to confuse people. How is this reconciled? Yahshua would

14 In the daytime also He led them with a cloud, and all the night with a pillar of fire.
15 He split the rocks in the wilderness, and gave them to drink as out of the great depths.
16 He brought streams also out of the Rock, and caused mayim to run down like rivers.
17 And they sinned again against Him by provoking the Most High in the wilderness.
18 And they tested El in their lev by asking food for their lust.
19 Yes, they spoke against Elohim; they said, Can El furnish us a table in the wilderness?
20 See, He smote the Rock, that the mayim gushed out, and the streams overflowed; can He give lechem also? Can He provide meat for His people?
21 Therefore יהוה heard this and was angry, so a fire was kindled against Yaakov,[1] and anger also came up against Yisrael;[2]
22 Because they believed not in Elohim, and trusted not in His Yahshua:[3]
23 Though He had commanded the clouds from above, and opened the doors of the shamayim,
24 And had rained down manna upon them to eat, and had given them of the grain of the shamayim.
25 Man did eat heavenly messengers' food: He sent them food to their satisfaction.
26 He caused an east wind to blow in the shamayim: and by His power He brought in the south wind.
27 He rained flesh also upon them as dust, and feathered fowls as the sand of the sea:
28 And He let it fall in the midst of their camp, around their dwellings.
29 So they did eat, and were well filled: for He gave them their own desire;
30 They were not removed from their lust. Their food was still in their mouths,
31 The anger of Elohim came upon them, and slew their most satisfied, and smote down the chosen men of Yisrael.

32 For all this they sinned still, and believed not His wonderful works.
33 Therefore their days He did consume in vanity, and their years in trouble.
34 When He slew them, then they sought Him: and they made teshuvah and inquired early after El.
35 And they remembered that Elohim was their Rock, and El-Elyon their Redeemer.
36 Nevertheless they did flatter Him with their mouth, and they lied to Him with their tongues.
37 For their lev was not right with Him, neither were they true to His covenant.
38 But He, being full of rachamim, forgave their iniquity, and destroyed them not: many times He turned His anger away, and did not stir up all His anger.
39 For He remembered that they were but flesh; a wind that passes away, and comes not again.
40 How often did they provoke Him in the wilderness, and grieve Him in the desert!
41 Yes, they turned back and tested El, and limited the Set-Apart One of Yisrael.[4]
42 They remembered not His hand,[5] nor the day when He delivered them from the enemy.
43 How He had worked His signs in Mitzrayim, and His wonders in the field of Tzoan:
44 And had turned their rivers into dom; and their streams, that they could not drink.
45 He sent divers sorts of flies among them, which devoured them; and frogs, which destroyed them.
46 He gave also their increase to the caterpiller, and their labor to the locust.
47 He destroyed their vines with hail, and their sycamore trees with frost.
48 He gave up their cattle also to the hail, and their flocks to bolts of fire.
49 He cast upon them the fierceness of His anger, and indignation, and trouble, by sending evil messengers among them.

---

[1] All 12 tribes.
[2] Ephraim Yisrael.
[3] Hebrew: **Beshuato.**

[4] Limiting His power and love to restore to just one house is sinful.
[5] Yahshua.

50 He made a derech for His anger; He spared not their being from death, but gave their chayim over to the pestilence;
51 And smote all the firstborn in Mitzrayim; the first-fruits of their strength in the tents of Ham:
52 But made His own people to go forth like sheep, and guided them in the wilderness like a flock.
53 And He led them on safely, so that they feared not: but the sea overwhelmed their enemies.
54 And He brought them to the border of His set-apart land, even to this har,[1] which His right hand[2] had purchased.
55 He cast out the nations also before them, and divided them an inheritance by measure, and made the tribes of Yisrael to dwell in their tents.
56 Yet they tested and provoked El-Elyon, and kept not His testimonies:
57 But turned back, and dealt unfaithfully like their ahvot: they were turned away like a deceitful bow.
58 For they provoked Him to anger with their high places, and moved Him to jealousy with their carved images.
59 When Elohim heard all this, He was angry, and greatly abhorred Yisrael:
60 So that He forsook the tent at Shiloh, the tent which He placed among men;
61 And delivered His strength into exiles,[3] and His tiferet into the enemy's hand.
62 He gave His people over also to the sword; and was angry at His inheritance.
63 The fire consumed their young men; and their virgins were not given to marriage.
64 Their kohanim fell by the sword; and their widows did not weep.
65 Then יהוה awoke as one out of sleep, and like a mighty man that shouts because of wine.
66 And He smote His enemies backwards: He put them to a perpetual reproach.

67 Moreover He rejected the tent of Yoseph, and chose not the tribe of Ephraim:[4]
68 But chose the tribe of Yahudah, Har Tzion which He loved.[5]
69 And He built His Set-Apart Place like high citadels, like the earth which He has established le-olam-va-ed.
70 He chose David His eved, and took him from the sheepfolds:
71 From tending the ewes, He brought him to feed Yaakov His people, and Yisrael His inheritance.
72 So He fed them according to the integrity of His lev; and guided them by the skillfulness of His hands.

Ayin Tet

79 [6] O Elohim, the nations are come into Your inheritance; Your Set-Apart Beit HaMikdash have they defiled; they have laid Yahrushalayim in ruins.
2 The dead bodies of Your avadim have they given to be food to the fowls of the shamayim, the flesh of Your kidushim to the beasts of the earth.
3 Their dom have they shed like mayim around Yahrushalayim; and there was none to bury them.
4 We are become a reproach to our neighbors, a scorn and derision to them that are around us.
5 How long, יהוה? Will You be angry le-olam-va-ed? Shall Your jealousy burn like fire?
6 Pour out Your anger upon the nations that have not known You, and upon the malchutim that have not called upon Your Name.
7 For they have devoured Yaakov, and laid waste his dwelling place.
8 O remember not against us former iniquities: let Your tender rachamim speedily meet us: for we are brought very low.

---

[1] Mt. Tzion.
[2] Yahshua.
[3] Both houses.

[4] By proclaiming them Lo-Ami and Lo-Ruchama.
[5] To preserve the Torah, and birth the Moshiach.
[6] YHWH will avenge Yisrael.

9 Help us, O Elohim of our Yahshua, for the tiferet of Your Name: and deliver us, and purge away our sins, for Your Name's sake.[1]

10 Why should the nations say, Where is their Elohim? Let Him be known among the nations in our sight by the revenging of the dom of Your avadim that is shed.

11 Let the sighing of the prisoner come before You; according to the greatness of Your power preserve those that are appointed to die;

12 And render to our neighbors sevenfold into their bosom their reproach, with which they have reproached You, O יהוה.

13 So we, Your people and sheep of Your pasture will give You hodu le-olam-va-ed: we will show forth Your hallel to all generations.

Peh

80 [2] Shema, O Shepherd of Yisrael, You that lead Yoseph like a flock;[3] You that live between the cheruvim, shine forth.

2 Before Ephraim and Benyamin and Menashsheh stir up Your strength, and come and save us.[4]

3 Help us make teshuvah to You, O Elohim,[5] and cause Your face to shine;[6] and we shall be saved.[7]

4 O יהוה Elohim of hosts, how long will You be angry against the tefillot of Your people?

5 You feed them with the lechem of tears; and give them tears to drink in great measure.

6 You make us a strife to our neighbors: and our enemies laugh among themselves.

7 Help us make teshuvah, O Elohim of hosts, and cause Your face to shine; and we shall be saved.

8 You have brought a vine out of Mitzrayim: You have cast out the nations, and planted it.

9 You prepared room before it, and did cause it to take deep root, and it filled the land.

10 The hills were covered with its shadow, and its twigs were like the tov cedars.

11 She sent out her branches to the sea, and to the river.

12 Why have You then broken down her hedges, so that all they who pass by the roads do pluck her fruit?

13 The boar out of the woods wastes it, and the wild beast[8] of the field does devour it.

14 Return,[9] we beseech You, O Elohim of hosts: look down from the shamayim, and observe, and visit this vine;[10]

15 And the vineyard that Your right hand has planted, and the branch that You made strong for Yourself.

16 It is burned with fire, it is cut down: they perish at the rebuke of Your face.

17 Let Your hand be upon the Man of Your right hand,[11] upon the Ben-Adam whom You made strong for Yourself.

18 So will we not backslide from You: quicken us, and we will call upon Your Name.[12]

19 Help us make teshuvah, O יהוה Elohim of hosts, cause Your face to shine; and we shall be saved.

Peh Alef

81 [13] Sing aloud to Elohim our strength: make a joyful noise to the Elohim of Yaakov.

2 Take a psalm, and bring here the tambourine, the pleasant harp with the guitar.

---

[1] His beautiful Name forgives sins.
[2] YHWH will save us.
[3] YHWH loves the ten exiled tribes who became gentiles, and has sent his Son Moshiach Ben Yosef to lead them back home in the spirit and in the natural.
[4] YHWH answered this prayer very nicely by sending salvation, or Yah saves – Yahshua – to bring Ephraim Yisrael home.
[5] The cry of Ephraim Yisrael to YHWH.
[6] The face or full manifestation of YHWH is the face of Yahshua.
[7] Spiritually, and as a nation.

[8] Heathen.
[9] In His second coming.
[10] He answered this prayer by sending Yahshua His Son.
[11] Yahshua also called the "son of man".
[12] Yisrael needs to be quickened in order to call on YHWH's Name.
[13] YHWH's love for Joseph.

3 Blow the shofar on the Rosh Chodesh, at the concealed moon,[1] on our solemn feast day.
4 For this was a statute-chuk for Yisrael, and a Torah-mishpat of the Elohim of Yaakov.[2]
5 This He ordained in Yahoseph[3] for a testimony,[4] [5]when He went out through the land of Mitzrayim: where I heard a language that I understood not.[6]
6 I removed his shoulder from the burden: his hands were delivered from the pots.
7 You called in trouble, and I delivered you; I answered you in the covering of thunder: I proved you at the mayim of Meribah. Selah.
8 Shema, O My people, and I will testify to you: O Yisrael, if you will shema to Me;
9 There shall no strange elohim be in you; neither shall you worship any strange el.
10 I am יהוה Your Elohim, who brought you out of the land of Mitzrayim: open your mouth wide, and I will fill it.
11 But My people would not shema to My voice; and Yisrael would have none of Me.
12 So I gave them up to their own levim's lust: and they walked in their own counsels.
13 Oh that My people had listened to Me, and Yisrael had walked in My halachot!

14 I would have subdued their enemies quickly, and turned My hand against their adversaries.
15 The haters of יהוה should have submitted themselves to Him: and their time of punishment will endure le-olam-va-ed.
16 He should have fed them also with the finest of the wheat: and with honey out of the Rock should I have satisfied you.

Peh Bet

82 [7] Elohim stands in the congregation of El; He shophets among the elohim.
2 He says; How long will you shophet unjustly, and accept the persons of the wicked? Selah.
3 Defend the poor and fatherless: do justice to the afflicted and needy.
4 Deliver the poor and needy: rescue them out of the hand of the wicked.
5 They know not, neither will they understand; they walk on in darkness: all the foundations of the earth are shaken.
6 *I have said, You are elohim; and all of you are children of the Most High.*
7 *But you shall die like men, and fall like one of the leaders.*[8]
8 Arise, O Elohim, shophet the earth: for You shall inherit all nations.[9]

Peh Gimel

83 [10] Keep not silent, O El: hold not Your silence, and be not still, O Elohim.2 For, look, Your enemies make a tumult: and they that hate You have lifted up their head.
3 They have taken crafty counsel against Your people, and consulted against Your treasured ones.

---

[1] The concealed moon or **keseh** associated with the shofar is Yom Teruah or the Feast of Trumpets, held on the first day of the seventh month. Yom Teruah is the day on which Moshiach will come to gather the scattered seed of Joseph and reunite them with Judah.
[2] The restoration and regathering of both houses of Yisrael on Yom Teruah; is both a **chuk** or ordinance with hidden meanings, as well as a **mishpat** or eternal right-ruling that makes perfect sense. Therefore it is eternally binding on Yisrael and Joseph in two (logical-illogical) different ways.
[3] Joseph. Normally Yoseph is spelled as **yud, vav, samech, peh sofit**. However in this verse Joseph is spelled **yud, hey, vav, samech, peh sofit**, with the added letter **hey** or the breath of YHWH. This highly unusual spelling indicates the very breath of YHWH coming into the House of Joseph or the 10 tribes of the northern kingdom, in order to revive them after 2,000 years, so they can enter the kingdom. The added **hey** is representative of both eternal life and the kingdom as the inheritance for Joseph.
[4] According to Hebrew tradition, Joseph was officially raised up and appointed viceroy of Egypt on Yom Teruah or the first day of the seventh month.
[5] The restoration and regathering of Joseph on Yom Teruah is a witness or testimony for and to Joseph, that he will not remain in the nations separate from Judah forever.
[6] Just like today, Joseph-Ephraim speaks many non-Hebraic languages, sometimes hard to understand.

---

[7] YHWH's mighty sons of Yisrael.
[8] All Yahshua's talmidim are like elohim (John 10:35-36) or mighty in power as Yahshua referred to. But verse 7 here reminds even His "elohim-disciples," that when it comes time to meet the grave, we will die like mere men.
[9] In a latter-day context this is Ephraim.
[10] YHWH identifies Yisrael's historical and end-time enemies.

4 They have said, Come, and let us cut them off from being a nation; that the name of Yisrael may be remembered no more.

5 For they have consulted and conspired together with one lev: they are a confederate against You:

6 The tents of Edom, and the Ishmaelites; of Moav, and the Hagarites;

7 Geval, and Ammon, and Amalek; the Philistines with the inhabitants of Tsor;

8 Ashshur also is joined with them: they have helped the children of Lot. Selah.

9 Do to them as to the Midyan; as to Sisera, as to Yavin, at the brook of Kison:

10 Who perished at Endor: they became as dung for the earth.

11 Make their nobles like Orev, and like Zeev: yes, all their leaders as Zevah, and as Tzalmunna:

12 Who said, Let us take to ourselves the houses of Elohim in our possession.

13 O My Elohim, make them like a wheel; as the stubble before the wind.

14 As the fire burns a forest, and as a flame sets the mountains on fire;

15 So persecute them with Your whirlwind, and make them afraid with Your storm.

16 Fill their faces with shame; that they may seek Your Name, O יהוה.

17 Let them be ashamed and troubled le-olam-va-ed; yes, let them be put to shame, and perish:

18 That men may know that You, whose Name alone is יהוה, are the most high over all the earth.[1]

Peh Daled

84 [2] How lovely are Your sukkot, O יהוה of hosts!

2 My being longs, yes, even faints for the courts of יהוה: my lev and my flesh cries out for the living El.

3 Yes, the sparrow has found a bayit, and the swallow a nest for herself, where she may lay her young, even Your altars, O יהוה of hosts, My Melech, and My Elohim.

4 Blessed are they that dwell in Your Bayit: they will still be giving You tehilla. Selah.

5 Blessed is the man whose strength is in You; in whose lev are Your halachot.

6 Who passing through the valley of Baca makes it a well; the rain also fills the pools.

7 They go from strength to strength, every one of them in Tzion appears before Elohim.[3]

8 O יהוה Elohim of hosts, shema to my tefillah: give ear, O Elohim of Yaakov. Selah.

9 See, O Elohim our shield, and look upon the face of Your anointed.

10 For one day in Your courts is better than a thousand days elsewhere. I would rather be a doorkeeper in the Bayit of My Elohim, than to dwell in the tents of wickedness.

11 For יהוה Elohim is a sun and shield: יהוה will give favor and tiferet: no tov thing will He withhold from them that have their halacha in tzedakah. 12 O יהוה of hosts, blessed is the man that trusts in You.

Peh Hey

85 [4] יהוה, You have been favorable to Your land: You have brought back the exiles of Yaakov.[5]

2 You have forgiven the iniquity of Your people; You have covered all their sin.[6] Selah.

3 You have taken away all Your anger: You have turned Yourself from the fierceness of Your anger.

4 Turn us, O Elohim of our Yahshua, and cause Your anger toward us to cease.

5 Will You be angry with us le-olam-va-ed? Will You draw out Your anger to all generations?

6 Will You not revive us again: that Your people may gilah in You?[7]

---

7 Show us Your rachamim, O יהוה, and grant us Your Yahshua.[1]

8 I will shema what El-יהוה will speak: for He will speak shalom to His people, and to His kidushim: but let them not turn again to folly.

9 Surely His Yahshua[2] is near to them that fear Him; that tiferet may dwell in our land.

10 Chesed and emet shall meet; tzedakah and shalom shall kiss each other.[3]

11 Emet shall spring out of the earth; and tzedakah shall look down from the shamayim.

12 Yes, יהוה shall give that which is tov; and our land shall yield her increase.

13 Tzedakah shall go before Him; and shall set us in the halacha of His steps.

Peh Vav

86

[4] Incline Your ear, O יהוה, answer me: for I am poor and needy.

2 Preserve my being; for I am dedicated: O My Elohim, save Your eved that trusts in You.

3 Give me rachamim, O יהוה: for I cry to You daily.

4 Bring simcha to the being of Your eved: for to You, O יהוה, do I lift up my being.

5 For You יהוה, are tov, and ready to forgive; and abundant in rachamim to all those that call upon You.

6 Shema, O יהוה, to my tefillah; and attend to the voice of my supplications.

7 In the day of my trouble I will call upon You: for You will answer me.

8 Among the elohim there is none like You, O יהוה; neither are there any works like Your works.

9 All nations whom You have made shall come and worship before You, O יהוה; and shall give tiferet to Your Name.[5]

10 For You are great, and do wonderful things: You are Elohim alone.

11 Teach me Your halacha, O יהוה; I will walk in Your emet: unite my lev to fear Your Name.[6]

12 I will hallel You, O יהוה My Elohim, with all my lev: and I will esteem Your Name le-olam-va-ed.

13 For great is Your rachamim towards me: and You have delivered my being from the lowest Sheol.

14 O Elohim, the proud have risen against me, and the mobs of violent men have sought after my being; and have not set You before them.

15 But You, O יהוה, are an El full of rachamim, and favor, longsuffering, and abundant in rachamim and emet.

16 O turn to me, and have rachamim upon me; give Your strength to Your eved, and save the son of Your female eved.

17 Show me a sign for tov; that they who hate me may see it, and be ashamed: because You, יהוה, have helped me, and comforted me.

Peh Zayin

87

[7] His foundation is in the set-apart mountains.

2 יהוה loves the gates of Tzion; more than all the dwellings of Yaakov.

3 Wonderful things are spoken about you, O city of Elohim. Selah.

4 I will make mention of Rahav and Bavel to them that know me: see Philistia, and Tsor, with Ethiopia; this man was born there.[8]

5 And of Tzion it shall be said, This one and that man was born in her: and the Highest Himself shall establish her.

6 יהוה shall write, when He writes up the registers of the nations, that this man was born there. Selah.[9]

---

[1] Hebrew: **Ve-yeshuecha.**
[2] Hebrew: **Yisho.**
[3] Only in and through the person and ministry of Moshiach Yahshua.
[4] YHWH who listens and delivers.
[5] This is decreed for the **atid lavoh.**

[6] A unified lev will fear and treasure YHWH's Name.
[7] YHWH's love for Tzion.
[8] Zionists or Yisraelites will be born in many lands including these.
[9] Through the new birth, many of the nations or Ephraimites will be counted and listed in the registers of Tzion as if they had never been exiled.

7 And the singers and the players on instruments shall be there: all my fountains are in you.[1]

Peh Chet

88 [2] O **יהוה** Elohim of My salvation; I have cried day and night before You:

2 Let my tefillah come before You: shema to my cry;

3 For my being is full of troubles: and my chayim draws near to the grave.

4 I am counted with them that go down into the pit: I am as a man that has no strength:

5 Free among the dead, like the slain that lie in the grave, whom You remember no more: and they are cut off from Your hand.

6 You have laid me in the lowest pit, in darkness, in the depth.

7 Your anger lies heavy upon me, and You have afflicted me with all Your waves. Selah.

8 You have put away my chaverim far from me; you have made me an abomination to them: I am shut up, and I cannot come forth.

9 My eye mourns by reason of affliction: **יהוה**, I have called daily upon You, I have stretched out my hands to You.

10 Will You show wonders to the dead? Shall the dead arise and hallel You? Selah.

11 Shall Your loving chesed be declared in the grave? Or Your faithfulness in the place of destruction?

12 Shall Your wonders be known in the dark? And Your tzedakah in the land of forgetfulness?

13 But to You have I cried, O **יהוה**; and during shacrit shall my tefillot come before You.

14 **יהוה**, why do You cast off my being? Why do You hide Your face from me?

15 I am afflicted and have been ready to die from my youth up: I have borne frightening things from You.

16 Your fierce anger covers me; Your terrors have silenced me.

17 They came around me daily like mayim; they surround me in unison.

18 Lover and chaver have You put far from me, and my chaver is the darkness.

Peh Tet

89 [3] I will shir of the rachamim of **יהוה** le-olam-va-ed: with my mouth will I make known Your faithfulness to all generations.

2 For I have said, Chesed shall be built up le-olam-va-ed: Your faithfulness shall You establish in the shamayim.

3 I have made a covenant with My chosen, I have sworn to David My eved,

4 Your zera will I establish le-olam-va-ed, and build up Your throne to all generations. Selah.

5 And the shamayim shall hallel Your wonders, O **יהוה**: Your faithfulness also in the congregation of the kidushim.

6 For who in the shamayim can be compared to **יהוה**? Who among the sons of the mighty is like **יהוה**?

7 El is greatly to be feared in the kahal of the kidushim, and to be had in reverence by them that are around Him.

8 O **יהוה** Elohim of hosts, who is a strong Yah like You? And Your faithfulness is all around You.

9 You rule the raging of the sea: when the waves of it arise, You quiet them.

10 You have broken the proud in pieces, as one that is slain; You have scattered Your enemies with Your strong arm.

11 The shamayim are Yours, the earth also is Yours: as for the olam and the fullness of it, You have founded them.

12 The north and the south You have created them: Tavor and Hermon shall gilah in Your Name.

13 You have a Mighty Arm: strong is Your hand, and high is Your Right Hand.[4]

---

[1] In Tzion for His children.
[2] YHWH tries His faithful.

[3] YHWH's covenant with David's Throne.
[4] Yahshua.

14 Justice and mishpat are the dwelling place of Your throne: rachamim and emet shall go before Your face.

15 Blessed is the people that know the joyful sound: they shall walk, O יהוה, in the light of Your face.

16 In Your Name shall they gilah all the day: and in Your tzedakah shall they be exalted.

17 For You are the tiferet of their strength: and in Your favor our horn shall be exalted.

18 For יהוה is our defense; and the Set-Apart One of Yisrael is our Melech.

19 Then You spoke in a vision to Your set-apart one, and said, I have given help to one that is mighty; I have exalted one chosen out of the people.

20 I have found David My eved; with My set-apart oil have I anointed Him:

21 With whom My hand shall be established: My Arm[1] also shall strengthen Him.

22 The enemy shall not put taxes upon him; nor the sons of wickedness afflict him.

23 And I will beat down his foes before his face, and plague them that hate him.

24 But My faithfulness and My rachamim shall be with him: and in My Name shall his horn be exalted.[2]

25 I will set his hand also in the sea, and his right hand in the rivers.

26 He shall cry to Me, You are My Abba, My El, and the Rock of My salvation.

27 Also I will make Him My firstborn, higher than the melechim of the earth.[3]

28 My rachamim will I keep for him le-olam-va-ed, and My covenant shall stand fast with him.

29 His zera also will I make to endure le-olam-va-ed, and his throne as the days of the shamayim.[4]

30 If his children forsake My Torah, and walk not in My mishpatim;

31 If they break My chukim, and keep not My mitzvot;

32 Then will I visit their transgression with the rod, and their iniquity with stripes.

33 Nevertheless My loving chesed will I not utterly remove from him, nor allow My faithfulness to pine away.

34 My covenant will I not break, nor alter the thing that has gone out of My lips.

35 Once have I sworn by My set-apartness that I will not lie to David.

36 His zera shall endure le-olam-va-ed, and his throne as the sun before Me.

37 It shall be established le-olam-va-ed as the moon, and as a faithful witness in the shamayim. Selah.[5]

38 But You have shunned and spurned, You have been angry at Your anointed.

39 You have made void the covenant of Your eved: You have profaned his keter by casting it to the ground.[6]

40 You have broken down all his hedges; You have brought his strongholds to ruin.

41 All that pass by the derech plunder him: he is a reproach to his neighbors.

42 You have set up the right hand of his adversaries; You have made all his enemies to gilah.

43 You have also turned the edge of his sword, and have not made him to stand in the battle.

44 You have made his tiferet to cease, and cast his throne down to the ground.

45 The days of his youth have You shortened: You have covered him with shame. Selah.

46 How long, יהוה? Will You hide Yourself; le-olam-va-ed? Shall Your anger burn like fire?

47 Remember how short my time is: why have You made all men in vain?

48 What man is he that lives, and shall not see death? Shall he deliver his own being from the hand of the grave? Selah.

---

[1] Yahshua.
[2] YHWH's Name is what exalted David.
[3] Many different meanings; David, Ephraim-Yisrael, all 12 tribes, and Yahshua Himself, can all be inferred from this verse.
[4] David's Throne is forever.

[5] The Throne of David as seen here is in the heavens, and is where Yahshua sits; not in London, Ireland or elsewhere. For more details, see: **One Hundred and Eighty Degrees Apart** http://yourarmstoisrael.org/Articles_new/restoration/?page=7&type=12
[6] Not true. The Ruach truly recorded David's frustration.

49 יהוה, where are Your former rachamim, that You swore to David in Your emet?
50 Remember, יהוה, the reproach of Your avadim; how I do bear in my bosom the reproach of all the mighty people;
51 With which Your enemies have reproached, O יהוה; with which they have reproached the footsteps of Your anointed.
52 Blessed be יהוה le-olam-va-ed. Amein, and Amein.

Tzadey

90 ¹ יהוה, You have been our dwelling place in all generations.
2 Before the mountains were brought forth, or before You had formed the earth and the olam hazeh, even from everlasting to everlasting, You are El.
3 You turn man to destruction; and say, Return, You children of men.
4 For a thousand years in Your sight are but as yesterday when it is past, and as a watch in the night.
5 You carry them away as with a flood; they are as a sleep: in the morning they are like grass which springs up.
6 In the morning it flourishes, and grows up; in the evening it is cut down, and withers.
7 For we are consumed by Your anger, and by Your anger are we troubled.
8 You have set our iniquities before You, our secret sins in the light of Your face.
9 For all our days have passed away in Your anger: we spend our years as a whisper.
10 The days of our years are seventy years; and if by reason of strength they be eighty years, yet still, the best of them is but strength, labor and sorrow; for it is soon cut off, and we fly away.
11 Who knows the power of Your anger and the fear of Your wrath?
12 So teach us to number our days, that we may apply our levim to chochma.

13 Return, O יהוה, how long? And be sorry for Your avadim.
14 O satisfy us early with Your rachamim; that we may gilah and be in simcha all our days.
15 Give us simcha according to the days that You have afflicted us, and the years that we have seen evil.
16 Let Your work appear to Your avadim, and Your tiferet to their children.
17 And let the beauty of יהוה our Elohim be upon us: and establish the work of our hands upon us; O confirm the work of our hands.

Tzady Aleph

91 ² He that dwells in the secret place of the Most High shall abide under the shadow of the Almighty.
2 I will say of יהוה, He is My refuge and My fortress: My Elohim; in Him will I trust.
3 Surely He shall deliver you from the trap of the hunter, and from the destructive pestilence.
4 He shall cover you with His feathers, and under His wings shall you trust: His emet shall be your shield and armor.
5 You shall not be afraid for the terror by night; nor of the arrow that flies by day,
6 Nor for the pestilence that walks in darkness; nor for the destruction that ravages at noonday.
7 A thousand shall fall at your side, and ten thousand at your right hand; but it shall not come near you.³
8 Only with your eyes shall you observe and see the reward of the wicked.
9 Because you have made יהוה, who is my refuge, even the most High, your dwelling place;
10 There shall no evil befall you, neither shall any plague come near your dwelling.
11 For He shall give His heavenly messengers charge over you, to keep you in all your halachot.

---

¹ Psalms 90-100 were written by Moshe and compiled by David according to most scholars.
² With YHWH, Yisrael cannot be defeated.
³ Overcoming the enemies of YHWH as Yisrael.

12 They shall bear you up in their hands, lest you dash your foot against a stone.
13 You shall trample upon the lion and cobra: the young lion and the serpent shall you trample under feet.
14 *Because he has set his ahava upon Me, therefore will I deliver him: I will set him on high, because he has known My Name.*
15 *He shall call upon Me, and I will answer him: I will be with him in trouble; I will deliver him, and honor him.*
16 *With long chayim will I satisfy him, and show him My Yahshua.*[1] [2]

Tzady Bet

92 [3] It is a tov thing to give hodu to יהוה, and to shir tehillot to Your Name, O most High:[4]
2 To show forth Your loving chesed in the morning, and Your faithfulness every night,
3 Upon an instrument of ten strings, and upon the guitar; upon the harp with a solemn sound.
4 For You, יהוה, have made me simcha through Your works: I will shout for the works of Your hands.
5 O יהוה, how great are Your works! And Your thoughts are very deep.
6 A senseless man knows this not; neither does a fool understand this.
7 When the wicked spring up as the grass, and when all the workers of iniquity do flourish; it is so that they shall be destroyed le-olam-va-ed:
8 But You, יהוה, are most high le-olam-va-ed.
9 For, look, Your enemies, O יהוה look, Your enemies shall perish; all the workers of iniquity shall be scattered.
10 But my horn shall You exalt like the horn of a wild ox: I shall be anointed with fresh oil.
11 My eye also shall see my desire on my enemies, and my ears shall shema my desire of the wicked that rise up against me.

12 The tzadikim shall flourish like the palm tree: he shall grow like a cedar in Levanon.
13 Those that are planted in the Bayit of יהוה shall flourish in the courts of our Elohim.
14 They shall still bring forth fruit in old age; they shall be fat and flourishing;
15 To show that יהוה is Tzadik: He is My Rock, and there is no unrighteousness in Him.

Tzady Gimel

93 [5] יהוה reigns, He is clothed with majesty; יהוה is clothed with strength, with which He has clothed Himself: the olam also is established, so that it cannot be moved.
2 Your throne is established from old: You are from everlasting.
3 The floods have lifted up, O יהוה, the floods have lifted up their voice; the floods lift up their waves.
4 יהוה on high is mightier than the noise of many mayim, yes, than the mighty waves of the sea.
5 Your witnesses are very trustworthy: set-apartness is befitting to Your Bayit, O יהוה, le-olam-va-ed.

Tzady Dalet

94 [6] O יהוה El, to whom vengeance belongs; O El, to whom vengeance belongs, shine forth.
2 Lift Yourself up, Shophet of the earth: render punishment to the proud.
3 יהוה, how long shall the wicked, how long shall the wicked triumph?
4 How long shall they utter and speak in arrogance? And all the workers of iniquity boast in themselves?
5 They break in pieces Your people, O יהוה, and afflict Your heritage.
6 They slay the widow and the stranger, and murder the fatherless.

---

[1] Hebrew: **Beshuati.**
[2] By knowing YHWH's true Name, you will be set on high, have longer life, and have Yahshua shown to you.
[3] YHWH will give the righteous all the victories.
[4] Praises must be sung to YHWH's true Name.

[5] YHWH reigns.
[6] YHWH will judge right.

7 Yet they say, Yah shall not see, neither shall the Elohim of Yaakov regard it.

8 Understand, you senseless among the people: and you fools, when will you be wise?

9 He that planted the ear, shall He not shema? He that formed the eye, shall He not see?

10 He that chastises the nations, shall He not correct? He that teaches man da'at, shall He not know?

11 יהוה knows the thoughts of man, that they are worthless.

12 Blessed is the man whom You chasten, O Yah, and whom You teach out of Your Torah;

13 That You may give him rest from the days of adversity, until the pit be dug for the wicked.

14 For יהוה will not cast off His people, neither will He forsake His inheritance.[1]

15 But mishpat shall return to tzedakah: and all the tzadik in lev shall follow it.

16 Who will rise up for me against the evildoers? Or who will stand up for me against the workers of iniquity?

17 Unless יהוה had been my helper, my being had almost lived without answers.

18 When I said, My foot slips; Your rachamim, O יהוה, held me up.

19 When anxious thoughts were within me Your comforts delighted my being.

20 Shall the seat of iniquity have chavurah with You, they who framed evil by a decree?

21 They gather themselves together against the being of the tzadikim, and condemn the innocent dom.

22 But יהוה is my defense; and My Elohim is the Rock of My refuge.

23 And He shall bring upon them their own iniquity, and shall cut them off in their own wickedness; yes, יהוה our Elohim shall cut them off.

Tzady Hey

95 [2] O come, let us shir to יהוה: let us make a joyful noise to the Rock of our salvation.

2 Let us come before His shechinah with hodu, and make a noise full of simcha to Him with tehillim.

3 For יהוה is a great El, and a great Melech above all elohim.

4 In His hand are the deep places of the earth: the strength of the hills are His also.

5 The sea is His, and He made it: and His hands formed the dry land.

6 O come, let us worship and bow down: let us kneel before יהוה our Maker.

7 For He is our Elohim; and we are the nation of His pasture, and the sheep of His hand. Today if you will shema to His voice,

8 Harden not your lev, as in the provocation, and as in the day of temptation in the wilderness:[3]

9 When your ahvot tested me, to try and prove Me, even though they saw My work.

10 Forty years long was I grieved with this generation, and said, It is a people that do go astray in their lev, and they have not known My halachot:

11 To whom I swore in My anger that they should not enter into My rest.

Tzady Vav

96 [4] O shir to יהוה a new shir: shir to יהוה, all the earth.

2 Sing to יהוה, bless His Name; show forth His Yahshua from day to day.

3 Declare His tiferet among the nations, His wonders among all people.

4 For יהוה is great, and greatly to be praised: He is to be feared above all elohim.

5 For all the elohim of the nations are idols: but יהוה made the shamayim.

6 Honor and majesty are before Him: strength and beauty are in His Set-Apart Place.

---

[1] Both houses.

[2] YHWH our Maker.
[3] Quoted in Hebrews 3:8 and Hebrews 3:15, substantiating that the Ivrim were members of both houses. Most of the Renewed Covenant is written to the exiles of both houses.
[4] YHWH rules from the wood of Golgotha.

7 Give to יהוה, O you kindreds of the people, give to יהוה tiferet and strength.
8 Give to יהוה the tiferet due to His Name: bring an offering, and come into His courts.[1]
9 O worship יהוה in the beauty of set-apartness: fear Him, all the earth.
10 Proclaim among the nations that יהוה reigns from the wood:[2] the olam also shall be established that it shall not be moved: He shall shophet the people in tzedakah.
11 Let the shamayim gilah, and let the earth be in simcha; let the sea roar, and the fullness of it.
12 Let the field be full of simcha, and all that is in it: then shall all the trees of the wood gilah,
13 Before יהוה: for He comes,[3] for He comes to shophet the earth: He shall shophet the olam with tzedakah, and the people with His emet.

Tzady Zayin

97 [4] יהוה reigns; let the earth gilah; let the multitude of the coastlands be in simcha over it.
2 Clouds and darkness are all around Him: tzedakah and mishpat are the dwelling place of His throne.
3 A fire goes before Him, and burns up His enemies all around.
4 His lightnings shall light the olam: the earth saw, and trembled.
5 The hills melted like wax at the shechinah of יהוה, at the shechinah of יהוה of the whole earth.
6 The shamayim declare His tzedakah, and all the nations see His tiferet.
7 Put to shame are all they that serve carved images, who boast themselves in idols: worship Him, all you elohim.

8 Tzion heard, and was in simcha; and the daughters of Yahudah had simcha because of Your mishpatim, O יהוה.
9 For You, יהוה, are high above all the earth: You are exalted far above all elohim.
10 You that love יהוה, hate evil: He preserves the beings of His kidushim; He delivers them out of the hand of the wicked.
11 Light is sown for the tzadikim, and simcha for the tzadik in lev.
12 Gilah in יהוה, you tzadikim; and give hodu at the remembrance of His set-apartness.

Tzady Chet

98 [5] O shir to יהוה a new shir; for He has done marvelous things: His right hand, and His Set-Apart Arm,[6] has gotten Him the victory.
2 יהוה has made known His Yahshua:[7] His tzedakah has He openly shown in the sight of the nations.[8]
3 He has remembered His rachamim and His emet toward Beit Yisrael:[9] all the ends of the earth have seen the Yahshua[10] of our Elohim.
4 Make a joyful noise to יהוה, all the earth: make a loud noise, and gilah, and shir hallel.
5 Sing to יהוה with the harp; with the harp, and the voice of a psalm.
6 With trumpets and the sound of a shofar make a joyful noise before יהוה, the Melech.
7 Let the sea roar, and the fullness of it; the olam, and they that dwell in it.
8 Let the rivers clap their hands: let the hills be in simcha together,
9 Before יהוה; for He comes to shophet the earth:[11] with tzedakah shall He shophet the olam, and the people with equity.

---

[1] Yisrael cannot enter His courts with titles like HaShem and Adonai, without identifying who that Adonai is.
[2] Moshiach from the tree of sacrifice; this text appeared in first-century manuscripts according to eyewitnesses and some "church" historians. The Dead Sea Scrolls and the LXX confirm this reading. For more details, see: **Psalm 96** http://www.godrules.net/library/clarke/clarkepsa96.htm commentary on verse 10.
[3] Through Yahshua.
[4] YHWH author of Light and nature.

[5] YHWH will remember and show Yahshua to Ephraim.
[6] Yahshua.
[7] Hebrew: **Yeshuato.**
[8] Ephraim Yisrael.
[9] Ephraim Yisrael – the ten tribes of the north.
[10] Hebrew: **Yeshuat.**
[11] YHWH is coming to earth as promised.

Tzady Tet

99 [1] **יהוה** reigns; let the people tremble: He sits between the cheruvim; let the earth be moved.

2 **יהוה** is great in Tzion; and He is high above all the nations.

3 Let them hallel Your great and terrible Name; for it is set-apart.[2]

4 The melech's strength also loves mishpat; You do establish equity, You execute mishpat and tzedakah in Yaakov.

5 Exalt **יהוה** our Elohim, and worship at His footstool; for He is Set-Apart.

6 Moshe and Aharon among His kohanim, and Schmuel were among them that called upon His Name; they called upon **יהוה**, and He answered them.[3]

7 He spoke to them in the cloudy column: they guarded His witness, and the ordinances that He gave them.

8 You answered them, O **יהוה** our Elohim: You were an El that forgave them, though You took vengeance on their evil inventions.

9 Exalt **יהוה** our Elohim, and worship at His set-apart har; for **יהוה** our Elohim is Set-Apart.

Kuf

100 [4] Make a noise of simcha to **יהוה**, all you lands.

2 Serve **יהוה** with simcha: come before His shechinah with singing.

3 Know that **יהוה** He is Elohim: it is He that has made us, and not we ourselves; we are His people, and the sheep of His pasture.

4 Enter into His gates with hodu, and into His courts with hallel: be full of hodu for Him, and bless His Name.

5 For **יהוה** is tov; His rachamim is everlasting; and His emet endures to all generations.

Kuf Aleph

101 [5] I will shir of rachamim and mishpat: to You, O **יהוה**, will I shir.

2 I will behave myself wisely in a perfect halacha. O when will You come to me? I will walk within my bayit with a pure lev.

3 I will set no wicked thing before my eyes: I hate the work of them that turn away; it shall not cleave to me.

4 A crooked lev shall depart from me: I will not know a wicked person.[6]

5 Whoever secretly slanders his neighbor, him will I cut off: him that has a high look and a proud lev will not I allow.

6 My eyes shall be upon the faithful of the land, that they may dwell with me: he that has his halacha in my pure halacha, he shall serve me.

7 He that works deceit shall not dwell within my bayit:[7] he that tells lies shall not stay in my sight.8 Each morning I will destroy all the wicked of the land; that I may cut off all wicked doers from the city of **יהוה**.

Kuf Bet

102 [8] Shema to my tefillah, O **יהוה**, and let my cry come to You.

2 Hide not Your face from me in the day when I am in trouble; incline Your ear to me: in the day when I call answer me speedily.

3 For my days are consumed like smoke, and my bones are burned as a furnace.

4 My lev is smitten, and withered like grass; so that I forget to eat my lechem.

5 By reason of the voice of my groaning my bones cleave to my skin.

6 I am like a pelican of the wilderness: I am like an owl of the desert.

7 I watch, and am as a sparrow alone upon the roof.

---

[1] YHWH is fully Set-Apart.
[2] The only Name that is set-apart.
[3] If Moses, Aaron, and Samuel did, then all Yisrael has no choice other than rebellion or religious pride.
[4] YHWH desires to be approached with joy and singing.

[5] YHWH will cut off the evildoers.
[6] Yisraelites must distance themselves from the unsaved and unrighteous.
[7] Redeemed Yisrael.
[8] YHWH will subdue all nations by His Name.

8 My enemies reproach me all the day; and they that are mad against me are sworn against me.

9 For I have eaten ashes like lechem, and mingled my drink with weeping,

10 Because of Your indignation and Your anger: for You have lifted me up, and cast me down.

11 My days are like a shadow that declines; and I am withered like grass.

12 But You, O יהוה, shall endure le-olam-va-ed; and Your remembrance to all generations.

13 You shall arise, and have rachamim upon Tzion: for the time to favor her, yes, the set time, has come.[1]

14 For Your avadim take pleasure in her stones, and favors the dust of it.

15 So the nations shall fear the Name of יהוה,[2] and all the melechim of the earth Your tiferet.

16 When יהוה shall build up Tzion, He shall appear in His tiferet.[3]

17 He will regard the tefillah of the destitute, and not despise their tefillah.

18 This shall be written for the generation to come: and the people who shall be created shall hallel-Yah.[4]

19 For He has looked down from the height of His Set-Apart Place; from the shamayim did יהוה observe the earth;

20 To shema the groaning of the prisoner;[5] to loose those that are appointed to death;

21 To declare the Name of יהוה in Tzion, and His hallel in Yahrushalayim;[6]

22 When the nations[7] are gathered together, and the malchutim, to serve יהוה.

23 He humbled my strength in the halacha; He shortened my days.

24 I said, O My El, take me not away in the midst of my days: Your years are throughout all generations.

25 Of old have You laid the foundation of the earth: and the shamayim are the work of Your hands.

26 They shall perish, but You shall endure: yes, all of them shall grow old like a garment; as a vesture shall You change them, and they shall be changed:[8]

27 But You are the same, and Your years shall have no end.

28 The children of Your avadim shall continue, and their zera shall be established before You.[9]

Kuf Gimel

103

[10] Bless יהוה, O my being: and all that is within me; bless His Set-Apart Name.

2 Bless יהוה, O my being, and forget not all His benefits:

3 Who forgives all your iniquities; who heals all your diseases;

4 Who redeems your chayim from destruction; who crowns you with loving chesed and tender rachamim;

5 Who satisfies your mouth with tov things; so that your youth is renewed like the eagle's.

6 יהוה who is doing tzedakah and mishpat for all that are oppressed.

7 He made known His halacha to Moshe, His acts to b'nai Yisrael.

8 יהוה is full of rachamim and favor, slow to anger, and abundant in chesed.

9 He will not always chide: neither will He keep His anger le-olam-va-ed.

10 He has not dealt with us after our sins; nor rewarded us according to our iniquities.

11 For as the shamayim are high above the earth, so great is His rachamim toward them that fear Him.

---

[1] When the two houses begin to come together, the set time to have rachamim is very near.
[2] One way or another, by choice or by stripes, all men will use the Name of YHWH in the age to come.
[3] When you begin to see the two houses identified and built up, Yahshua/YHWH will appear.
[4] The one new man from the two houses will proclaim the set time of Tzion's favor, to a generation to enter the atid lavoh.
[5] The exiles of Yisrael.
[6] YHWH will bring Yisrael restoration in order to fully declare His true Name in Tzion.
[7] Ephraim.

---

[8] All creation will be changed in the renewal of all things at the end of the age.
[9] Regenerated Yisrael will live forever after their change to immortality.
[10] YHWH our Healer and King.

12 As far as the east is from the west, so far has He removed our transgressions from us.[1]

13 Like an abba pities his children, so יהוה pities them that fear Him.

14 For He knows our frame; He remembers that we are just dust.

15 As for man, his days are as grass: as a flower of the field, so he flourishes.

16 For the wind passes over it and it is gone; and its place shall know it no more.

17 But the rachamim of יהוה is from everlasting to everlasting upon them that fear Him, and His tzedakah to the children's children;

18 To such as keep His covenant, and to those that remember His mitzvot to do them.

19 יהוה has prepared His throne in the shamayim; and His malchut rules over all.

20 Bless יהוה, you His heavenly messengers, that excel in strength, that do His mitzvot, that shema to the voice of His word.

21 Bless יהוה, all His hosts, you avadim of His, who do His pleasure.

22 Bless יהוה, all His works in all places of His rule: bless יהוה, O my being!

Kuf Daled

104 [2] Bless יהוה, O my being. O יהוה My Elohim, You are very great; You are clothed with honor and majesty.

2 Who covers Yourself with light as with a garment:[3] who stretches out the shamayim like a curtain:

3 Who lays the beams of His rooms in the mayim: who makes the clouds His mirkavah: who walks on the wings of the wind:

4 Who makes His heavenly messengers ruachim; His avadim a flaming fire:

5 Who laid the foundations of the earth, that it should not be removed le-olam-va-ed.

6 You covered it with the deep as with a garment: the mayim stood above the mountains.

7 At Your rebuke they ran; at the voice of Your thunder they rush away.

8 They go up by the mountains; they go down by the valleys to the place that You have founded for them.

9 You have set a border that they may not pass over; that they return not again to cover the earth.

10 He sends the springs into the valleys, which run among the hills.

11 They give drink to every beast of the field: the wild donkeys quench their thirst.

12 By them shall the fowls of the shamayim have their dwelling place, which shir among the branches.

13 He gives mayim to the hills from His upper rooms: the earth is satisfied with the fruit of Your works.

14 He causes the grass to grow for the cattle, and herb for the service of man: that He may bring forth food out of the earth;

15 And wine that makes simcha the lev of man, and oil to make his face to shine, and lechem that strengthens man's lev.

16 The trees of יהוה are full of sap; the cedars of Levanon, which He has planted;

17 Where the birds make their nests: as for the stork, the cypress trees are her bayit.

18 The high hills are a refuge for the wild goats; and the rocks for the gophers.

19 He created the moon for moadim: the sun knows its going down.

20 You make darkness, and it is night: in it all the beasts of the forest do creep.

21 The young lions roar after their prey, and seek their food from El.

22 The sun rises, they gather themselves together, and lay down in their dens.

23 Man goes forth to his work and to his labor until the evening.

24 O יהוה, how manifold are Your works! In chochma have You made them all: the earth is full of Your riches.

---

[1] Through His Son Yahshua.
[2] YHWH; the Provider and Sustainer.
[3] Tallit; YHWH is covered; why aren't you?

25 There is the great and wide sea, in it are innumerable things creeping, both small and great beasts.

26 There go the ships: also that Leviathan, whom You have made to play in it.

27 These all wait upon You; that You may give them their food in due season.

28 What You give them they gather: You open your hand, they are filled with tov.

29 You hide Your face, they are troubled: You take away their breath, they die, and return to their dust.

30 You send forth Your Ruach, they are created: and You renew the face of the earth.

31 The tiferet of יהוה shall endure le-olam-va-ed: יהוה shall gilah in His works.

32 He looks on the earth, and it trembles: He touches the hills, and they smoke.

33 I will shir to יהוה as long as I live: I will shir hallel to My Elohim while I have my being.

34 My meditation on Him shall be sweet: I will be in simcha in יהוה.

35 Let the sinners be consumed out of the earth, and let the wicked be no more. Bless יהוה, O my being! Hallel יהוה. Halleluyah!

Kuf Hey

105 [1] O give hodu to יהוה; call upon His Name: make known His deeds among the nations.

2 Sing to Him, shir tehillim to Him: talk of all His wonderful works.

3 Make your boast in His set-apart Name: let the lev of them gilah that seek יהוה.

4 Seek יהוה, and His strength: seek His face evermore.

5 Remember His marvelous works that He has done; His wonders, and the mishpatim of His mouth;

6 O you zera of Avraham His eved, you children of Yaakov His chosen.

7 He is יהוה our Elohim: His mishpatim are in all the earth.

8 He has remembered His covenant le-olam-va-ed, the word that He commanded to a thousand generations.

9 Which covenant He made with Avraham, and His oath to Yitzchak:

10 And confirmed the same to Yaakov for a chuk, and to Yisrael for an everlasting covenant:[2]

11 Saying, To you will I give the land of Kanaan, the lot of your inheritance:[3]

12 When they were but a few men in number; very few indeed, and foreigners in it.

13 When they went from one nation to another, from one malchut to another people;

14 He allowed no man to do them wrong: yes, He reproved melechim for their sakes;

15 Saying, *Touch not My anointed, and do My neviim no harm.*[4]

16 Moreover He called for a famine upon the land: He broke the whole supply of lechem.

17 He sent a man before them, even Yoseph, who was sold as an eved:

18 Whose feet they hurt with shackles: his neck was laid in iron:

19 Until the time that His word came: the Word of יהוה[5] tried him.

20 The melech sent and loosed him; even the ruler of the people, and let him go free.

21 He made him master of his bayit, and ruler of all his substance:

22 To bind his leaders at his pleasure; and teach his zechanim chochma.

23 Yisrael also came into Mitzrayim; and Yaakov sojourned in the land of Ham.

24 And He increased His people greatly;[6] and made them stronger than their enemies.

25 He turned their lev to hate His people, to deal deceitfully with His avadim.

---

[1] YHWH's people and their history.

[2] The land covenant to all Yisrael is called a Torah forever just like the feasts.

[3] Yisrael's covenant right to the land will last for 1,000 generations, or about 1 million years, way into eternity.

[4] This verse often misquoted, when taken in proper context means Yisrael the nation is YHWH's anointed, not some Pentecostal preacher on TV.

[5] Yahshua.

[6] As per the covenant of physical multiplicity.

26 He sent Moshe His eved, and Aharon whom He had chosen.

27 They showed His signs among them, and wonders in the land of Ham.

28 He sent darkness, and made it dark; and they rebelled not against His word.

29 He turned their mayim into dom, and killed their fish.

30 Their land brought forth frogs in abundance, in the rooms of their melechim.

31 He spoke, and there came divers sorts of flies, and lice in all their coasts.

32 He gave them hail for rain, and flaming fire in their land.

33 He smote their vines also and their fig trees; and broke the trees of their coasts.

34 He spoke, and the locusts came, and caterpillars, without number,

35 And did eat up all the herbs in their land, and devoured the fruit of their ground.

36 He smote also all the firstborn in their land, the first of all their strength.

37 He brought them forth also with silver and gold: and there was not one feeble person among their tribes.[1]

38 Mitzrayim was in simcha when they departed: for the fear of them fell upon them.

39 He spread a cloud for a covering; and fire to give light in the night.

40 The people asked, and He brought quails, and satisfied them with the lechem of the shamayim.

41 He opened the Rock, and the mayim gushed out; it ran in the dry places like a river.

42 For He remembered His set-apart promise, to Avraham His eved.

43 And He brought forth His people with simcha, and His chosen ones with singing:

44 And gave them the lands of the nations: and they inherited the labor of the nations;

45 That they might observe His chukim, and observe His Torot. Hallel יהו.

Kuf Vav

106

[2] Hallel יהוה. O give hodu to יהוה; for He is tov: for His rachamim endures le-olam-va-ed.

2 Who can utter the mighty acts of יהוה? Who can show forth all His hallel?

3 Blessed are they that keep mishpat, and he that does tzedakah at all times.

4 Remember me, O יהוה, with the favor that You give to Your people: O visit me with Your Yahshua[3];

5 That I may see the tov of Your chosen, that I may gilah in the simcha of Your nation, that I may tiferet with Your inheritance.

6 We have sinned with our ahvot, we have committed iniquity; we have done wickedly.

7 Our ahvot understood not Your wonders in Mitzrayim; they remembered not the multitude of Your rachamim; but provoked Him at the sea, even at the Sea of Reeds.

8 Nevertheless He saved them for His Name's sake; that He might make His mighty power to be known.

9 He rebuked the Sea of Reeds also, and it was dried up: so He led them through the depths, as through the wilderness.

10 And He saved them from the hand of him that hated them, and redeemed them from the hand of the enemy.

11 And the mayim covered their enemies: there was not one of them left. 12 Then they believed His words; they sang His hallel.

13 They soon forgot His works; they waited not for His counsel:

14 But lusted exceedingly in the wilderness, and tested El in the desert.

15 And He gave them their request; but sent leanness into their inner being.

16 They envied Moshe also in the camp, and Aharon the kadosh of יהוה.

17 The earth opened and swallowed up Dathan, and covered the company of Aviram.

---

[1] YHWH's will for Yisrael.

[2] More History from YHWH's perspective.
[3] Hebrew: **BeYeshuatecha.**

18 And a fire was kindled in their company; the flame burned up the wicked.

19 They made a calf in Horeb, and worshipped the molten image.

20 So they changed My tiferet into the similitude of an ox that eats grass.

21 They forgot El their Savior, who had done great things in Mitzrayim;

22 Wondrous works in the land of Ham, and awesome things by the Sea of Reeds.

23 Therefore He said that He would destroy them, had not Moshe His chosen stood before Him in the breach, to turn away His anger, lest He should destroy them.

24 Yes, they then despised the pleasant land, they believed not His word:

25 But murmured in their tents, and listened not to the voice of **יהוה**.

26 Therefore He lifted up His hand against them, to overthrow them in the wilderness:

27 To throw their zera also among the nations, and to scatter them in the lands.[1]

28 They joined themselves also to Baal-Peor, and ate the sacrifices of the dead.

29 So they provoked Him to anger with their inventions: and the plague broke in upon them.

30 Then stood up Phinehas, and executed mishpat: and so the plague was stopped.

31 And that act was counted to Him for tzedakah to all generations le-olam-va-ed.

32 They angered Him also at the mayim of Merivah, so that Moshe suffered because of them:

33 Because they provoked his ruach, so that he spoke rashly with his lips.

34 They did not destroy the nations, concerning whom **יהוה** commanded them:

35 But were mingled among the nations, and learned their works.

36 And they served their idols: which were a trap to them.

37 Yes, they sacrificed their sons and their daughters to demons,[2]

38 And shed innocent dom, even the dom of their sons and of their daughters, whom they sacrificed to the idols of Kanaan: and the land was polluted with dom.

39 So they were defiled with their own works, and went whoring with their own inventions.

40 Therefore was the anger of **יהוה** kindled against His people; He loathed His own inheritance.

41 And He gave them into the hands of the nations; and they that hated them ruled over them.

42 Their enemies also oppressed them, and they were brought into subjection under their hand.

43 Many times did He deliver them; but they provoked Him with their counsel, and were brought low for their iniquity.

44 Nevertheless He regarded their affliction, when He heard their cry:

45 And He remembered His covenant with them, and relented according to the multitude of His rachamim.

46 He made them also to be pitied by all those that carried them into exile.

47 Save us, O **יהוה** our Elohim, and gather us from among the nations, to give hodu to Your set-apart Name, and to triumph in Your hallel.[3]

48 Blessed is **יהוה** Elohim of Yisrael from everlasting to everlasting: and let all the people say, Amein. Hallel **יהוה**.

Kuf Zayin

107 [4]O give hodu to **יהוה**, for He is tov: for His rachamim endures le-olam-va-ed.

2 Let the redeemed of **יהוה** say so, whom He has redeemed from the hand of the enemy;[5]

---

[1] Known in Hebrew as the **Galut**.
[2] Hebrew: **Shaddim**. Unclean spirits. YHWH is called **El-Shaddai** for He is the highest power over all spirits or shaddim and thus **El-Shaddai**.

[3] The final ingathering will be to bring restoration so that ultimately His Name will be known and worshipped in all the earth.
[4] YHWH desires praise from the children of men.
[5] Proclaim the besarot loudly, without condition, and freely.

3 And gathered them out of the lands, from the east, and from the west, from the north, and from the south.[1]

4 They wandered in the wilderness in a solitary derech; they found no city to dwell in.

5 Hungry and thirsty, their being fainted in them.

6 Then they cried to יהוה in their trouble, and He delivered them out of their distresses.

7 And He led them forth by the right derech; that they might go to a city to settle.

8 Oh that men would hallel יהוה for His tov, and for His wonderful works to the children of men!

9 For He satisfies the longing being, and fills the hungry being with tov.

10 Such as sit in darkness and in the shadow of death, being shackled in affliction and iron;[2]

11 Because they rebelled against the words of El, and despised the counsel of the Most High:

12 Therefore He brought down their lev with labor; they fell down, and there was none to help.

13 Then they cried to יהוה in their trouble, and He saved them out of their distresses.

14 He brought them out of darkness and the shadow of death, and broke their chains in pieces.

15 Oh that men would hallel יהוה for His tov, and for His wonderful works to the children of men!

16 For He has broken the gates of brass, and cut the bars of iron in pieces.

17 Fools because of their transgression, and because of their iniquities, are afflicted.

18 Their being despises all manner of food; and they draw near to the gates of death.

19 Then they cry to יהוה in their trouble; and He saves them out of their distresses.

20 He sent His Word, and healed them, and delivered them from their destructions.[3]

21 Oh that men would hallel יהוה for His tov, and for His wonderful works to the children of men!

22 And let them sacrifice the sacrifices of hodu, and declare His works with gilah.

23 They that go down to the sea in ships, that do business in the great mayim;

24 These see the works of יהוה, and His wonders in the deep.

25 For He commands, and raises the stormy wind, which lifts up the waves of it.

26 They go up to the shamayim, they go down again to the depths: their being is melted because of trouble.

27 They reel back and forth, and stagger like a drunk man, and all there chochma is gone.

28 Then they cry to יהוה in their trouble, and He brings them out of their distresses.

29 He makes the storm calm, so that its waves are still.

30 Then they are in simcha because the sea is silenced; so He brings them to their desired haven.

31 Oh that men would hallel יהוה for His tov, and for His wonderful works to the children of men!

32 Let them exalt Him also in the congregation of the people, and hallel Him in the congregation of the zechanim.

33 He turns rivers into a wilderness, and the mayim springs into dry ground;

34 A fruitful land into barrenness, for the wickedness of them that dwell in it.

35 He turns the wilderness into a pool of mayim, and dry ground into mayim springs.

36 And there He makes the hungry to dwell, that they may prepare a city for a dwelling place;

37 And sow the fields, and plant vineyards, which may yield fruits of increase.

38 He blesses them also, so that they are multiplied greatly; and allows not their cattle to decrease.

39 But when they are diminished and brought low through oppression, affliction, and sorrow,

---

[1] Yisrael's end-time redeemed will come forth from all four winds.
[2] Ephraim Yisrael based on Isaiah chapter 9:1-3.
[3] Yahshua.

40 He pours contempt upon their leaders, and causes them to wander in the wilderness, where there is no derech.
41 Yet He raises the poor up from affliction, and makes their families His flock.
42 The tzadikim shall see it, and gilah: and all iniquity will shut its mouth.
43 Whoever is wise, will observe these things, even they shall understand the loving chesed of **יהוה**.

Kuf Chet

108 [1] O Elohim, my lev is fixed; I will shir and give hallel, even with my tiferet.
2 Awake, guitar and harp: I myself will awake early.
3 I will hallel You, O **יהוה**, among the people: and I will shir tehillot to You among the nations.
4 For Your rachamim is great above the shamayim: and Your emet reaches to the clouds.
5 Be exalted, O Elohim, above the shamayim: and Your tiferet above all the earth;
6 That Your beloved may be delivered: save with Your right hand,[2] and answer me.
7 Elohim has spoken in His set-apartness; I will gilah, I will divide Shechem, and measure out the Valley of Sukkot.
8 Gilead is Mine; Menashsheh is Mine; Ephraim also is the strength of My head;[3] Yahudah is My Lawgiver;[4]
9 Moav is My washpot; over Edom will I cast out My shoe; over Philistia will I triumph.
10 Who will bring me into the strong city? Who will lead me into Edom?
11 Will not You, O Elohim, who have cast us off? And will You not, O Elohim, go forth with our armies?
12 Give us help from trouble: for worthless is the help of man.

13 Through Elohim we shall do valiantly, for He it is that shall trample down our enemies.

Kuf Tet

109 [5] Hold not Your silence, O Elohim of My hallel;
2 For the mouth of the wicked and the mouth of the deceitful are open against me: they have spoken against me with a lying tongue.
3 They surrounded me about also with words of hatred; and fought against me without a cause.
4 For my ahava they are my adversaries: but I give myself to tefillah.
5 And they have rewarded me evil for tov, and hatred for my ahava.
6 Set a wicked man over him: and let s.a.tan stand at his right hand.
7 When he shall be judged, let him be condemned: and let his tefillah become sin.
8 Let his days be few; and let another take his office.
9 Let his children be fatherless, and his wife a widow.[6]
10 Let his children always wander, and beg: let them seek their lechem also out of their ruins.
11 Let the creditor set a trap for all that he has; and let the foreigners plunder his labor.
12 Let there be none to extend rachamim to him: neither let there be any to favor his fatherless children.
13 Let his descendants be cut off; and in the generation following let their name be blotted out.
14 Let the iniquity of his ahvot be remembered with **יהוה**; and let not the sin of his ima be blotted out.
15 Let them be before **יהוה** continually, that He may cut off the memory of them from the earth.

---

[1] YHWH marches with Yisrael's army.
[2] Yahshua.
[3] See note on Psalm 60:7.
[4] See note on Psalm 60:7.

[5] YHWH sees the betrayal of Yahshua and David.
[6] In the literal **pashat**, it speaks of the betrayal of Moshiach Yahshua (in verses 1-14); of course it also speaks of David's enemies. Verses 8-10 specifically speak of Judas-Yahudah as confirmed in the Renewed Covenant. It speaks of David in the **pashat** and Judas in the **remez**.

16 Because that he remembered not to show rachamim, but persecuted the poor and needy man, that he might even slay the broken in lev.

17 As he loved cursing, so let it come to him: as he delighted not in bracha, so let it be far from him.

18 As he clothed himself with cursing as with his garment, so let it come into his inward parts like mayim, and like oil into his bones.

19 Let it be to him as the garment that covers him, and for a girdle with which he is clothed continually.

20 Let this be the reward of my adversaries before יהוה, and of them that speak evil against my being.

21 But do this for me, O Elohim יהוה, for Your Name's sake: because Your rachamim is tov, deliver me.

22 For I am poor and needy, and my lev is wounded within me.

23 I am gone like the shadow when it lengthens: I am tossed up and down as the locust.

24 My knees are weak through fasting; and my flesh grows lean from lack of abundance.

25 I became also a reproach to them: when they looked upon me they shook their heads.

26 Help me, O יהוה My Elohim: O save me according to Your rachamim:

27 That they may know that this is Your hand; that You, יהוה, have done it.

28 Let them curse, but You bless me: when they arise, let them be ashamed; but let Your eved gilah.

29 Let my adversaries be clothed with shame, and let them cover themselves with their own confusion, as with a mantle.

30 I will greatly hallel יהוה with my mouth; yes, I will hallel Him among the multitude.

31 For He shall stand at the right hand of the poor, to save them from those that condemn them.

Kuf Yud

110 [1] יהוה said to My Adon,[2] Sit at My right hand, until I make Your enemies Your footstool.

2 יהוה shall send the rod of Your strength out of Tzion: rule in the midst of Your enemies.

3 Your people shall be willing in the day of Your power, in the splendors of set-apartness from the womb of the morning: You have the dew of your youth.[3]

4 יהוה has sworn, and will not repent, You are a Kohen le-olam-va-ed[4] after the order of Melech-Tzedek.[5]

---

[1] Yahshua/YHWH sits at the Father's right hand.
[2] David's Master was and is Yahshua.
[3] Moshiach's power was from the womb.
[4] Yahshua will be an eternal priest; for as YHWH's Son, He will not remain dead like the sons of Aaron.
[5] YHWH has installed Moshiach at His right hand as the King of Righteousness over believing Yisrael. This subject is detailed in Hebrews/Ivrim chapters 6-7.

5 יהוה at Your Right Hand[1] [2] [3] shall strike through melechim in the Day of His anger.[4] 6 He shall shophet among the nations, He shall fill the places with the dead bodies; He

shall wound the leaders over many countries. 7 He shall drink of the brook in its derech: therefore shall He lift up the head.[5]

Kuf Yud Aleph

111 [6] Hallel יהוה; I will hallel יהוה with my whole lev, in the congregation of the tzadik, and in the congregation.

2 The works of יהוה are great, sought out by all them that have pleasure in it.

3 His work is honorable and full of tiferet: and His tzedakah endures le-olam-va-ed.

4 He has made His wonderful works to be remembered: יהוה shows favor and is full of rachamim.

5 He has given food to them that fear Him: He will be le-olam-va-ed mindful of His covenant.

6 He has shown His people the power of His works, that He may give them the heritage of the nations.[7]

7 The works of His hands are emet and mishpat; all His mitzvot are sure.

8 They stand fast le-olam-va-ed, and are done in emet and tzedakah.

9 He sent redemption to His people: He has commanded His covenant le-olam-va-ed: set-apart and awesome is His Name.

10 The fear of יהוה is the beginning of chochma: a tov binah have all those that do His mitzvot: His hallel endures le-olam-va-ed.

Kuf Yud Bet

112 [8] Hallel You יהוה. Blessed is the man that fears יהוה, who delights greatly in His mitzvot.

2 His zera shall be mighty upon the earth: the generation of the tzadik shall be blessed.

3 Wealth and riches shall be in His bayit: and His tzedakah endures le-olam-va-ed.

---

[1] David's **Adon** or Master of verse one at YHWH's right hand is further identified as YHWH in verse 5. Psalm 110:5 reads in the original Hebrews as "YHWH at thy right hand" or **"YHWH al yemenecah."** The original meaning of verse 5 qualifies the **Adon** of verse 1 as the Master YHWH and not David, since it has one YHWH talking to another YHWH, called Master/**Adon** in verse 1; but qualified as YHWH in verse 5. Being aware of this, the crafty Masoretes, just as they did 134 other times in the Masoretic Tanach, substituted "Adonai" or "my master" for the Tetragrammaton -YHWH as they did here in Psalm 110:5. Now we have to understand that the Brit Chadasha writers knew and possessed the original Hebrew of Psalm 110, where the "Adonai" or "Master" of verse 1, was qualified by verse 5 as "YHWH at thy right hand," and quoted it as such throughout the Brit Chadasha. They used the Hebrew translations, which at the time had not yet been tampered with by the Masoretes. With this understanding, when going to the Greek we see the usage of two Greek equivalents for LORD "Kurios said to my **Kurios**" to indicate that one **Kurios** was talking to the other **Kurios,** in order to represent the Hebrew qualifier of verse 5 as YHWH, seated at YHWH's right hand of honor. We can therefore ascertain that the Greek double-use of **Kurios** is actually a translation of the actual Hebrew prior to Masorete editing. The Aramaic Peshitta nails this down by stating in verse one that Eloah said to My Mar-Yah or Master-Yah, identifying David's Adonai or Mar-Yah, as the Master Yah. Moreover, Yahshua quotes this with the original verse 5 in answer to a question regarding His identity in Matthew 26:64, identifying Himself as YHWH. Immediately the High Priest in Matthew 26:65 cries charges of blasphemy, which according to Jewish law (not Torah law) is the pronunciation of the ineffable and outlawed Name of Yahweh. No other sin or violation of Jewish Law (not Torah law) is considered blasphemy. Even claiming to be "The Messiah" does not meet halachic criteria as blasphemy. The Jewish custom described in Matthew 26:65 of "ripping the garment," and saying the **Shema** is associated only with the verbal utterance of YHWH's Name by the lips of a man. Even Matthew had succumbed to the ban in order to reach Jews with his scroll. That explains the usage of the euphemism Power instead of YHWH, in the same verse in found in the Greek text of Matthew 26:64.

[2] Dake's Annotated Bible page 601, note b; "One manuscript reads, 'YHWH said to My YHWH' and this should be the case as in the original Hebrew of v.5 it reads, 'YHWH at thy (YHWH's) right hand.' But out of the extreme reverence for the name of YHWH, the ancient custodians of the sacred text substituted Adonai for YHWH in 134 passages."

[3] Yahshua properly quoted Psalm 110:5 as it appeared before the change. We know this from the definition of blasphemy found in the Talmud as it lines up with Matthew's evangel. This is the view of R. Meir: "But the Sages maintain: [blasphemy] with use of the ineffable Name, is punishable by death: with the employment of substitutes, it is the object of an injunction [But not punishable by death]." Talmud San.56a. "Jacob states that since 'Jose' is used as a substitute, it proves that even if the longer Names are not employed, but merely the Tetragrammaton, the guilt of blasphemy is incurred; i.e., of forty-two letters." Talmud San. 60a. Our Rabbis taught: "He who hears [the Name blasphemed] and he who hears it from the person who first heard it [i.e., from the witness who testifies],"are both bound to rend their garments. But the witnesses are not obliged to rend their clothes [when they hear themselves repeating the blasphemy in the course of their testimony], because they had already done so on first hearing it." San.60a.

[4] A reference to the Second Advent.

---

[5] He will lift up and bring esteem to His Father YHWH.
[6] YHWH's works are to be honored.
[7] Renewed Yisrael will reign with Yahshua.
[8] YHWH guards those who ahava Him and obey Him.

4 To the tzadik there rises light in the darkness: he is favorable and full of rachamim to the tzadikim.
5 A tov man shows favor, and lends: he will guide his affairs with discretion.
6 Surely he shall not be moved le-olam-va-ed: the tzadikim shall be in everlasting remembrance.
7 He shall not be afraid of evil tidings: his lev is fixed, trusting in יהוה.
8 His lev is established, he shall not be afraid, until he see his desire upon his enemies.
9 He has dispersed, he has given to the poor; His tzedakah endures le-olam-va-ed; his horn shall be exalted with honor.
10 The wicked shall see it, and be grieved; he shall gnash with his teeth, and melt away: the desire of the wicked shall perish.

Kuf Yud Gimel

113 [1] Hallel יהוה. Hallel Him; O you avadim of יהוה, hallel the Name of יהוה.
2 Blessed be the Name of יהוה from this time forth and le-olam-va-ed.[2]
3 From the rising of the sun to the going down of the same יהוה's Name is to be praised.[3]
4 יהוה is high above all nations, and His tiferet above the shamayim.
5 Who is like יהוה our Elohim, who dwells on high,
6 Who looks down to observe the things that are in the shamayim, and in the earth!
7 He raises up the poor out of the dust, and lifts the needy out of the dunghill;
8 That he may set him with leaders, even with the leaders of His people.
9 He makes the barren woman to keep her bayit, and to be a simcha-filled ima of children. Hallel-יהוה.

Kuf Yud Daled

114 [4] When Yisrael went out of Mitzrayim, the Beit Yaakov from a people with a strange language;
2 Yahudah became His set-apart place, and Yisrael His rule.[5]
3 The sea saw it, and ran: Yarden was driven back.
4 The mountains skipped like rams, and the little hills like lambs.
5 What bothered you, O Sea of Reeds; that you fled? And you Yarden, that you were driven back?
6 You mountains, that you skipped like rams; and you little hills, like lambs?
7 Tremble, O earth, at the shechinah of יהוה, at the shechinah of the Eloah of Yaakov;
8 Who turned the Rock into a pool of mayim, the flint into a fountain of mayim.

Kuf Tet Vav

115 [6] Not to us,[7] O יהוה, not to us,[8] but to Your Name give tiferet, for Your rachamim, and for Your emet's sake.[9]
2 Why should the nations say, Where is now their Elohim?
3 But our Elohim is in the shamayim: He has done whatever He has pleased.
4 Their idols are silver and gold, the work of men's hands.
5 They have mouths, but they speak not: eyes they have, but they see not:
6 They have ears, but they shema not: noses they have, but they smell not:
7 They have hands, but they touch not: feet they have, but they walk not: neither do they speak through their throat.
8 They that make them are like them; so is every one that trusts in them.
9 O Yisrael, trust in יהוה: He is their help and their shield.

---

[1] YHWH's Name is to be praised all day long.
[2] YHWH the eternal and only covenant Name.
[3] All day.

[4] The YHWH of the Exodus.
[5] Both houses play a role.
[6] YHWH rules over all dumb idols.
[7] Judah.
[8] Ephraim.
[9] Yisraelites are to seek honor only for His Name, not for ourselves, or any Name under heaven.

10 O beit Aharon, trust in יהוה: He is their help and their shield.

11 You that fear יהוה, trust in יהוה: He is their help and their shield.

12 יהוה has been mindful of us: He will bless us; He will bless the bayit of Yisrael;[1] He will bless the bayit of Aharon.

13 He will bless them that fear יהוה, both small and great.

14 יהוה shall increase you more and more, you and your children.[2]

15 You are blessed of יהוה who made the shamayim and earth.

16 The shamayim, are the shamayim of יהוה: but the earth has He given to the children of men.

17 The dead do not hallel יהוה, neither those that go down into silence.

18 But we will bless יהוה from this time forth and le-olam-va-ed. Hallel יהוה.

Kuf Tet Zayin

116

[3] I love יהוה, because He has heard my voice and my supplications.

2 Because He has inclined His ear to me, therefore will I call upon Him as long as I live.

3 The sorrows of death surrounded me, and the pains of Sheol came upon me: I found trouble and sorrow.

4 Then called I upon the Name of יהוה; O יהוה, I beg You, deliver my being.

5 Full of unmerited favor is יהוה, and He is tzadik; yes, our Elohim is full of rachamim.

6 יהוה preserves the simple: I was brought low, and He helped me.

7 Return to your rest, O my being; for יהוה has treated you well.

8 For You have delivered my being from death, my eyes from tears, and my feet from falling.

9 I will have my halacha before יהוה in the land of the living.

10 I believed, therefore have I spoken: I was greatly afflicted:

11 I said in my haste; All men are liars.

12 What shall I render to יהוה for all His benefits toward me?

13 I will lift up the cup of Yahshua, and call upon the Name of יהוה.

14 I will pay my vows to יהוה now in the presence of all His people.

15 Precious in the sight of יהוה is the death of His kidushim.[4]

16 O יהוה, truly I am Your eved; I am Your eved, and the son of Your female eved: You have loosed my chains.

17 I will offer to You the sacrifice of hodu, and will call upon the Name of יהוה.

18 I will pay my vows to יהוה now in the presence of all His people,

19 In the courts of יהוה's Bayit, in the midst of you, O Yahrushalayim. Hallel יהוה.

Kuf Yud Zayin

117

[5] O hallel יהוה, all you nations: hallel Him, all you people.

2 For His rachamim and chesed is great toward us: and the emet of יהוה endures le-olam-va-ed. Hallel יהוה.

Kuf Yud Tet

118

[6] O give hodu to יהוה; for He is tov: because His rachamim endures le-olam-va-ed.

2 Let Yisrael now say, that His rachamim endures le-olam-va-ed.

3 Let Beit Aharon now say, that His rachamim endures le-olam-va-ed.

4 Let them now that fear יהוה say; that His rachamim endures le-olam-va-ed.

5 I called upon Yah in distress: Yah answered me, and set me in a large place.

6 יהוה is on my side; I will not fear: what can man do to me.

7 יהוה takes my part with them that help me: therefore shall I see my desire upon them that hate me.

---

[1] All 12 tribes.
[2] The eternal and ongoing promise of physical multiplicity.
[3] YHWH is the cup of our salvation.
[4] To the believer death is a precious event, ending in glorification, and immortality.
[5] YHWH's great kindness.
[6] YHWH/Yahshua is the Stone that the builders rejected.

8 It is better to trust in יהוה than to put confidence in man.

9 It is better to trust in יהוה than to put confidence in leaders.

10 All nations surrounded me all around: but in the Name of יהוה will I destroy them.[1]

11 They surrounded me, yes, they surrounded me all around: but in the Name of יהוה I will destroy them.

12 They surrounded me around like bees; they are quenched as burning thorns: for in the Name of יהוה I will destroy them.

13 You have pushed hard at me that I might fall: but יהוהhelped me.

14 Yah is my strength and shir, and has become My Yahshua.[2]

15 The voice of gilah and Yahshua is in the sukkot of the tzadikim: the Right Hand of יהוה[3] does valiantly.

16 The Right Hand of יהוה is exalted: the Right Hand of יהוה does valiantly.[4]

17 I shall not die, but live,[5] and declare the works of Yah.

18 Yah has chastened me hard: but He has not given me over to death.

19 Open to me the gates of tzedakah: I will go into them, and I will give hallel to יהוה:

20 This is the gate of יהוה, into which the tzadikim shall enter.

21 I will hallel You: for You have heard me, and have become My Yahshua.[6]

22 The Stone[7] that the builders[8] rejected has become the Rosh Pina[9] of the corner.

23 This is יהוה's doing;[10] it is marvelous in our eyes.

24 This is the day which יהוה has made; we will gilah and be in simcha in it.[11]

25 Save now, I beseech You, O יהוה: O יהוה, I beseech You, send now prosperity.

26 Baruch haba beshem יהוה: we have blessed You from the Bayit of יהוה.

27 El is יהוה, who has showed us light: bind the sacrifice for the moed with cords, to the horns of the altar.

28 You are My El, and I will hallel You: You are My Elohim, I will exalt You.

29 O give hodu to יהוה; for He is tov: for His chesed endures le-olam-va-ed.

Kuf Yud Tet

119

[12] Blessed are the undefiled in the halacha, who walk in the Torah of יהוה.

2 Blessed are they that keep His testimonies, and that seek Him with their whole lev.

3 They also do no iniquity: they walk in His halachot.

4 You have commanded us to keep Your precepts diligently.

5 O that my halachot were directed to keep Your chukim!

6 Then shall I not be ashamed, when I look into all Your mitzvot.

7 I will hallel You with tzedakah of lev, when I shall have learned Your tzadik mishpatim.

8 I will keep Your chukim: Do not forsake me utterly.

9 How shall a young man cleanse his halacha? By guarding it according to Your word.

10 With my whole lev have I sought You: O let me not wander far from Your mitzvot.

11 Your word have I hid in my lev, that I might not sin against You.[13]

12 Blessed are You, O יהוה: teach me Your chukim.

13 With my lips have I declared all the mishpatim of Your mouth.

---

[1] YHWH's true Name destroys His enemies.
[2] Hebrew: **LeYeshua;** The Father became our Yahshua by sending the fullness of "the brought forth One" Himself.
[3] Yahshua causes the rejoicing and the deliverance.
[4] YHWH has exalted His Son.
[5] Because of YHWH's right hand, Yahshua.
[6] Hebrew: **LeYeshua.** The Father sent all of His essence into a prepared body and brought forth Yahshua His Son; not an object of worship, but one of deliverance and full freedom from sin.
[7] Yahshua.
[8] The leaders of Jewish Yisrael.
[9] Cornerstone.
[10] The Father caused it to happen.

[11] The day of salvation, or the day when Yahshua died by rejection.
[12] YHWH's Torah is perfect.
[13] Yisraelites must memorize the Word.

14 I have had simcha in the halacha of Your testimonies, as much as in all riches.

15 I will meditate in Your precepts, and have respect for Your halachot.

16 I will delight myself in Your chukim: I will not forget Your word.

17 Deal abundantly tov with Your eved, that I may live, and keep Your word.

18 Open my eyes, that I may observe wonderful things out of Your Torah.

19 I am a sojourner in the earth: hide not Your mitzvot from me.

20 My being is in anguish for the longing that it has to perform Your mishpatim at all times.

21 You have rebuked the proud that are cursed, who do go astray from Your mitzvot.

22 Remove from me reproach and contempt; for I have kept Your testimonies.

23 Rulers also did sit and speak against me: but Your eved did meditate in Your chukim.

24 Your testimonies also are my delight and my counselors.

25 My being cleaves to the dust: quicken me according to Your word.

26 I have declared my halachot, and You heard me: teach me Your chukim.

27 Make me to understand the halacha of Your precepts: so shall I talk of Your wonderful works.

28 My being melts for heaviness: strengthen me according to Your word.

29 Remove from me the derech of lying: and grant me Your Torah with favor.

30 I have chosen the halacha of emet: Your mishpatim have I laid before me.

31 I have stuck to Your testimonies: O יהוה, put me not to shame.

32 I will run to the derech of Your mitzvot, when You shall enlarge my lev.

33 Teach me, O יהוה, the halacha of Your chukim; and I shall keep it to the end.

34 Give me binah, and I shall keep Your Torah; yes, I shall observe it with my whole lev.

35 Make me to go in the derech of Your mitzvot; for in it do I delight.

36 Incline my lev to Your testimonies, and not to covetousness.

37 Turn away my eyes from beholding vanity; and quicken me in Your halacha.

38 Establish Your word to Your eved, who is devoted to Your fear.

39 Turn away my reproach that I fear: for Your mishpatim are tov.

40 See, I have longed after Your precepts: quicken me in Your tzedakah.

41 Let Your rachamim come also to me, O יהוה, even Your Yahshua,[1] according to Your word.

42 So shall I have something to answer him that slanders me: for I trust in Your word.

43 And take not the word of emet fully out of my mouth; for I have hoped in Your mishpatim.

44 So shall I keep Your Torah continually le-olam-va-ed.

45 And I will walk in liberty:[2] for I seek Your precepts.

46 I will speak of Your testimonies also before melechim, and will not be ashamed.

47 And I will delight myself in Your mitzvot, which I have loved.

48 My hands also will I lift up to Your mitzvot, which I have loved; and I will meditate in Your chukim.

49 Remember the word to Your eved, upon which You have caused me to tikvah.

50 This is my comfort in my affliction: for Your word has quickened me.

51 The proud have had me in great derision: yet have I not departed from Your Torah.

52 I remembered Your mishpatim of old, O יהוה; and have comforted myself.

53 Horror has taken hold upon me because of the wicked that forsake Your Torah.

54 Your chukim have been my shirim in the bayit of my pilgrimage.

55 I have remembered Your Name, O יהוה, in the night, and have kept Your Torah.[3]

56 This I had, because I kept Your precepts.

---

[1] Hebrew: **Te-yshuatcha.**
[2] The true freedom of and in the Spirit comes from following Torah.
[3] One cannot truly keep Torah without guarding YHWH's Name.

57 You are my portion, O יהוה: I have said that I would keep Your words.
58 I sought Your favor with my whole lev: be full of rachamim to me according to Your word.
59 I thought on my halachot, and then I turned my feet to Your testimonies.
60 I hurried, and did not delay to keep Your mitzvot.
61 The mobs of the wicked have robbed me: but I have not forgotten Your Torah.
62 At midnight I will rise to give hodu to You because of Your tzadik mishpatim.
63 I am a companion of all those that fear You, and of them that keep Your precepts.
64 The earth, O יהוה, is full of Your rachamim: teach me Your chukim.
65 You have dealt well with Your eved, O יהוה, according to Your word.
66 Teach me tov mishpatim and da'at: for I have believed Your mitzvot.
67 Before I was afflicted I went astray: but now have I kept Your word.
68 You are tov, and do tov; teach me Your chukim.
69 The proud have forged a lie against me: but I will keep Your precepts with my whole lev.
70 Their lev is as fat as grease; but I delight in Your Torah.
71 It is tov for me that I have been afflicted; that I might learn Your chukim.
72 The Torah of Your mouth is better to me than thousands of gold and silver pieces.
73 Your hands have made me and fashioned me: give me binah, that I may learn Your mitzvot.
74 They that fear You will be in simcha when they see me; because I have hoped in Your word.
75 I know, O יהוה, that Your mishpatim are right, and that You in faithfulness have afflicted me.
76 Let, I beg You, Your great chesed be for my comfort, according to Your word to Your eved.

77 Let Your tender rachamim come to me, that I may live: for Your Torah is my delight.
78 Let the proud be ashamed; for they dealt perversely with me without a cause: but I will meditate in Your precepts.
79 Let those that fear You turn to me, and those that have known Your testimonies.
80 Let my lev be sound in Your chukim; that I be not ashamed.
81 My being faints for Your Yahshua:[1] but I tikvah in Your word.
82 My eyes pine away for Your word, saying, When will it comfort me?
83 For I am become like a wineskin in the smoke; yet do I not forget Your chukim.
84 How many are the days of Your eved? When will You execute mishpat on them that persecute me?
85 The proud have dug pits for me, they do not follow after Your Torah.
86 All Your mitzvot are faithful: they persecute me wrongfully; help me.
87 They had almost consumed me upon earth; but I forsook not Your precepts.
88 Quicken me after Your loving chesed; so shall I keep the testimony of Your mouth.
89 Forever, O יהוה, Your word is settled in the shamayim.[2]
90 Your faithfulness is to all generations: You have established the earth, and it abides.
91 They continue this day according to Your ordinances: for all are Your avadim.
92 Unless Your Torah had been my delight, I would have perished in my affliction.
93 I will never forget Your precepts: for with them You have quickened me.
94 I am Yours, save me; for I have sought Your precepts.
95 The wicked have waited for me to destroy me: but I will consider Your testimonies.
96 I have seen an end of all perfection: but Your commandment is exceedingly broad.

---

[1] Hebrew: **teshuatecha.**
[2] Yahshua is eternal.

97 O how I love Your Torah! It is my meditation all the day.
98 You through Your mitzvot have made me wiser than my enemies: for they are always with me.
99 I have more binah than all my teachers: for Your testimonies are my meditation.
100 I understand more than the aged, because I keep Your precepts.
101 I have refrained my feet from every evil halacha, that I might keep Your word.
102 I have not departed from Your mishpatim: for You have taught me.
103 How sweet are Your words to my taste! Yes, sweeter than honey to my mouth!
104 Through Your precepts I get binah: therefore I hate every false halacha.
105 Your word is a lamp to my feet, and a light to my derech.
106 I have sworn, and I will perform it, that I will keep Your tzadik mishpatim.
107 I am afflicted very much: quicken me, O יהוה, according to Your word.
108 Accept, I beg You, the terumah offerings of my mouth, O יהוה, and teach me Your mishpatim.
109 My being is continually in my hand: yet I do not forget Your Torah.
110 The wicked have laid a trap for me: yet I did not go astray from Your precepts.
111 Your testimonies have I taken as a heritage le-olam-va-ed: for they are the rejoicing of my lev.
112 I have inclined my lev to perform Your chukim le-olam-va-ed, even to the end.
113 I hate worthless thoughts: but Your Torah do I love.
114 You are my hiding place and my shield: I tikvah in Your word.
115 Depart from me, you evildoers: for I will keep the mitzvot of My Elohim.
116 Uphold me according to Your word, that I may live: and let me not be ashamed of my tikvah.
117 Hold me up, and I shall be safe: and I will have respect to Your chukim continually.

118 You have trampled down all those that go astray from Your chukim: for their deceit is falsehood.
119 You put away all the wicked of the earth like dross: therefore I love Your testimonies.
120 My flesh trembles for fear of You; and I am in awe of Your mishpatim.
121 I have done mishpat and justice: leave me not to my oppressors.
122 Guarantee Your eved's well being: let not the proud oppress me.
123 My eyes pine away for Your Yahshua,[1] and for the word of Your tzedakah.
124 Deal with Your eved according to Your rachamim, and teach me Your chukim.
125 I am Your eved; give me binah, that I may know Your testimonies.
126 It is time for You, יהוה, to work: for they have made void Your Torah.
127 Therefore I love Your mitzvot above gold; yes, above fine gold.
128 Therefore I esteem all Your precepts concerning all things to be right; and I hate every false halacha.
129 Your testimonies are wonderful: therefore does my being keep them.
130 The entrance of Your words gives light; it gives binah to the simple.
131 I opened my mouth, and panted: for I longed for Your mitzvot.
132 Look upon me, and be full of rachamim to me, as You used to do to those that loved Your Name.
133 Order my steps in Your word: and let not any iniquity have rule over me.
134 Deliver me from the oppression of man: so will I keep Your precepts.
135 Make Your face to shine upon Your eved; and teach me Your chukim.
136 Rivers of mayim run down my eyes, because they keep not Your Torah.[2]
137 Righteous are You, O יהוה, and tzadik are Your mishpatim.
138 Your testimonies that You have commanded are tzadik and very faithful.

---

[1] Hebrew: **Leyeshuatecha.**
[2] Judah's lev for Ephraim's blindness.

139 My zeal has consumed me, because my enemies have forgotten Your words.

140 Your word is very pure: therefore Your eved loves it.

141 I am small and despised: yet I do not forget Your precepts.

142 Your tzedakah is an everlasting tzedakah, and Your Torah is the emet.

143 Trouble and anguish have taken hold on me: yet Your mitzvot are my delights.

144 The tzedakah of Your testimonies is everlasting: give me binah, and I shall live.

145 I cried with my whole lev; shema to me, O יהוה: I will keep Your chukim.

146 I cried to You; save me, and I shall keep Your testimonies.

147 I rise before dawn and cry for help: I hope in Your word.

148 My eyes go before the night watches, that I might meditate in Your word.

149 Shema to my voice according to Your loving chesed: O יהוה, quicken me according to Your mishpat.

150 They draw near that follow after evil: they are far from Your Torah.

151 You are near, O יהוה; and all Your mitzvot are emet.

152 Concerning Your testimonies, I have known from the past that You have founded them le-olam-va-ed.

153 Consider my affliction, and deliver me: for I do not forget Your Torah.

154 Plead my cause, and deliver me: quicken me according to Your word.

155 Yahshua[1] is far from the wicked: for they seek not Your chukim.

156 Great are Your tender rachamim, O יהוה: quicken me according to Your mishpatim.

157 Many are my persecutors and my enemies; yet I do not decline from Your testimonies.

158 I beheld the transgressors, and was grieved; because they kept not Your word.

159 Consider how I love Your precepts: quicken me, O יהוה, according to Your loving chesed.

160 Your word is true from Bereshet: and every one of Your tzadik mishpatim endures le-olam-va-ed.

161 Rulers have persecuted me without a cause: but my lev stands in awe of Your word.

162 I gilah at Your word, as one that finds great plunder.

163 I hate and abhor lying: but Your Torah do I love.

164 Seven times a day do I give You hallel; because of Your tzadik mishpatim.

165 Great shalom have those who love Your Torah: and nothing shall offend them.

166 יהוה, I have hoped for Your Yahshua,[2] and done Your mitzvot.

167 My being has kept Your testimonies; and I love them exceedingly.

168 I have kept Your precepts and Your testimonies: for all my halachot are before You.

169 Let my cry and come near before You, O יהוה: give me binah according to Your word.

170 Let my pleading come before You: deliver me according to Your word.

171 My lips shall utter hallel, when You have taught me Your chukim.

172 My tongue shall speak of Your word: for all Your mitzvot are tzedakah.

173 Let Your hand[3] help me; for I have chosen Your precepts.

174 I have longed for Your Yahshua,[4] O יהוה; and Your Torah is my delight.[5]

175 Let my being live, and it shall hallel You; and let Your mishpatim help me.

176 I have gone astray like a lost sheep;[6] seek Your eved; for I do not forget Your mitzvot.

Kuph Chaf

120 [7] In my distress I cried to יהוה, and He heard me.

[1] Hebrew: **Yeshua.**
[2] Hebrew: **LeYeshuatecha.**
[3] Yahshua.
[4] Hebrew: **LeYeshuatecha.**
[5] The true halacha for both houses; Yahshua and Torah, with neither being neglected.
[6] The cry and confession of returning Yisrael.
[7] YHWH the Master of the tongue, war and peace.

2 Deliver my being, O יהוה, from lying lips, and from a deceitful tongue.

3 What shall be given to you? Or what shall be done to you, you false tongue?

4 Sharp arrows of the mighty; with coals of oak.

5 Woe is me, that I sojourn in Mesech; that I dwell in the tents of Kedar!

6 My being has long lived with him that hates shalom.

7 I am for shalom: but when I speak, they are for war.

Kuf Chaf Aleph

121 [1] I will lift up my eyes to the hills, from where does my help come?

2 My help comes from יהוה, Maker of the shamayim and earth.

3 He will not allow your foot to be moved: He that keeps you will not slumber.

4 See, He that keeps Yisrael shall neither slumber nor sleep.

5 יהוה is your keeper: יהוה is your shade at your right hand.[2]

6 The sun shall not smite you by day, nor the moon by night.

7 יהוה shall preserve you from all evil: He shall preserve your being.

8 יהוה shall preserve your going out and your coming in from this time forth, and even le-olam-va-ed.

Kuf Chaf Bet

122 [3] I had great simcha when they said to me, Let us go into the Bayit of יהוה.

2 Our feet shall stand within your gates, O Yahrushalayim.

3 Yahrushalayim is built as a city that is compact together:

4 Where the tribes go up, the tribes of Yah, to the testimony of Yisrael, to give hodu to the Name of יהוה.[4]

5 For there are the set thrones of mishpat, the thrones of Beit David.[5]

6 Shaalu shalom Yahrushalayim: they shall prosper that love You.

7 Peace be within your walls, and prosperity within your citadels.

8 For my brothers[6] and companions[7] sakes, I will now say, Shalom be within you.

9 Because of the Bayit of יהוה our Elohim I will seek Your tov.

Kuf Chaf Gimel

123 [8] To You lift I up my eyes, O you that lives in the shamayim.

2 See, as the eyes of the avadim look to the hand of their masters, and as the eyes of a female eved to the hand of her mistress; so our eyes will wait upon יהוה our Elohim, until that He has rachamim upon us.

3 Have rachamim upon us, O יהוה, have rachamim upon us: for we are exceedingly filled with contempt.

4 Our being is exceedingly filled with the scorning of those that are at ease, and with the contempt of the proud.

Kuf Chaf Daled

124 [9] If it had not been יהוה who was on our side, now may Yisrael say;

2 If it had not been יהוה who was on our side, when men rose up against us:

3 Then they would have swallowed us up quickly, when their anger was kindled against us:

4 Then the mayim would have overwhelmed us, the stream would have gone over our being:

5 Then the proud mayim would have gone over our being.

6 Blessed be יהוה, who has not given us as a prey to their teeth.

---

[1] YHWH Master of all, who never sleeps.
[2] Yahshua is YHWH the shade and right hand of Abba.
[3] Master over Jerusalem and all 12 tribes.
[4] YHWH's desire is for all who claim to be from the 12 tribes to approach Him in His true Name of YHWH.

[5] All believers will have thrones in the Renewed Yahrushalayim in the malchut.
[6] 12 tribes.
[7] Those non-Yisraelites who join Yisrael in the two-house reunion.
[8] YHWH who overcomes contempt.
[9] YHWH is our great escape.

7 Our being has escaped as a bird out of the trap of the bird hunters: the trap is broken, and we have escaped.

8 Our help is in the Name of **יהוה**, who made the shamayim and earth.[1]

Kuf Chaf Hey

125 [2] They that trust in **יהוה** shall be as Har Tzion, which cannot be removed, but abides le-olam-va-ed.

2 As the mountains are all around Yahrushalayim, so **יהוה** is all around His people, from this time forward and even le-olam-va-ed.

3 For the rod of the wicked shall not rest upon the lot of the tzadikim; lest the tzadikim put forth their hands to iniquity.

4 Do tov, O **יהוה**, to those that are tov, and to them that are tzadik in their levim.

5 As for such that turn aside to their crooked halachot, **יהוה** shall lead them forth with the workers of iniquity: but shalom shall be upon Yisrael.

Kuf Chaf Vav

126 [3] When **יהוה** turned back the exiles of Tzion, we were like them that dream.

2 Then was our mouth filled with laughter, and our tongue with singing: then said they among the nations, **יהוה** has done great things for them.

3 **יהוה** has done great things for us; of which we are in simcha.

4 Turn back our exiles, O **יהוה**, as the streams in the south.

5 They that sow in tears shall reap in simcha.[4]

6 He that goes forth and weeps, bearing precious zera, shall doubtless come again with gilah, bringing his sheaves with him.[5]

Kuf Chaf Zayin

127 [6] Except **יהוה** build the bayit, they labor in vain that build it:[7] except **יהוה** guard the city, the watchman wakes in vain.

2 It is vain for you to rise up early, to sit up late, to eat the lechem of sorrow: so He gives His beloved sleep.

3 See, children are a heritage from **יהוה**: and the fruit of the womb is His reward.

4 As arrows are in the hand of a mighty man; so are children of one's youth.

5 Blessed is the man that has his quiver full of them: they shall not be ashamed, but they shall speak with their enemies in the gate.

Kuf Chaf Chet

128 [8] Blessed is every one that fears **יהוה**; that has their halacha in His halachot.

2 For you shall eat the labor of your hands: great blessing shall you have, and it shall be well with you.

3 Your wife shall be as a fruitful vine by the sides of your bayit: your children like olive plants all around your table.[9] [10]

4 See, that is how the man shall be blessed who fears **יהוה**.[11]

5 **יהוה** shall bless you out of Tzion: and you shall see the tov of Yahrushalayim all the days of your chayim.

6 Yes, you shall see your children's children, and shalom upon Yisrael.[12]

---

[1] We can escape the enemy through YHWH's true Name.
[2] YHWH the hedge around Yisrael.
[3] YHWH who brings back the captivity of Tzion.
[4] All 12 tribes.
[5] Referring to Yahshua scattering his Word in all Yisraelite nations, and then returning to harvest that seed, for great is the Day of Jezreel. A secondary application would be the seed representing both houses returning, when He returns.

[6] YHWH the Master Builder.
[7] Let this word sink in deep for those who deny Yahshua as YHWH's King, yet attempt to rebuild the nation, or the two houses, with the orthodox, but without the greater end-time David.
[8] YHWH's table with olive plants.
[9] A man who walks in YHWH's Torah will wind up raising little faithful Yisraelites symbolized by the olive plants at his table.
[10] This is also a picture of the way Abba-YHWH sees us looking down at His nation.
[11] Can you see it? Both houses at the same table as olive plants.
[12] If you desire to live as and with His nation.

Kuf Chaf Tet

129 [1] Often they have afflicted me from my youth, may Yisrael now say:

2 Often they have afflicted me from my youth: yet they have not prevailed against me.

3 The plowers plowed upon my back: they made their furrows long.4 **יהוה** is Tzadik: He has cut asunder the cords of the wicked.

5 Let them all be ashamed and turned back that hate Tzion.

6 Let them be as the grass upon the housetops, which withers before it grows up:

7 With which the reapers do not fill their hands; nor he that binds sheaves his bosom.

8 Neither do they who pass by say, The bracha of **יהוה** be upon you: we bless you in the Name of **יהוה**.

Kuf Lamed

130 [2] Out of the depths have I cried to You, O **יהוה**.

2 **יהוה**, shema to my voice: let Your ears be attentive to the voice of my supplications.

3 If You, Yah, should mark iniquities, O **יהוה**, who shall stand?

4 But there is forgiveness with You, that You may be feared.

5 I wait for **יהוה**; my being does wait, and in His Word do I tikvah.

6 My being waits for **יהוה** more than they that watch for the morning: I say, more than they that watch for the morning.

7 Let Yisrael tikvah in **יהוה**: for with **יהוה** there is rachamim, and with Him is abundant redemption.

8 And He shall redeem Yisrael from all their iniquities.

Kuf Lamed Aleph

131 [3] **יהוה**, my lev is not haughty, nor my eyes proud: neither do I concern myself in great matters, or in things too wonderful for me.

2 Surely I have behaved and quieted myself, as a child that is weaned by its ima: my being is even as a weaned child.

3 Let Yisrael tikvah in **יהוה**: from this time forward and le-olam-va-ed.

Kuf Lamed Bet

132 [4] O **יהוה**, remember David, and all his afflictions:

2 How he swore to **יהוה**, and vowed to the mighty Elohim of Yaakov;

3 Surely I will not come into the sukkah of my bayit, nor go up into my bed;

4 I will not give sleep to my eyes, or slumber to my eyelids,

5 Until I find a place for **יהוה**, a Dwelling Place for the mighty Elohim of Yaakov.

6 See, we heard of it at Ephrata: we found it in the fields of the forest.

7 We will go into His sukkot: we will worship at His footstool.

8 Arise, O **יהוה**, into Your rest; You, and the ark of Your strength.

9 Let Your kohanim be clothed with tzedakah; and let Your kidushim shout for simcha.

10 For Your eved David's sake do not turn away the face of Your anointed.

11 **יהוה** has sworn in emet to David; He will not turn from it; Of the fruit of your body will I set upon your throne.

12 If your children will keep My covenant and My testimony that I shall teach them, their children shall also sit upon your throne le-olam-va-ed.

13 For **יהוה** has chosen Tzion; He has desired it for His dwelling place.

14 This is My rest le-olam-va-ed: here will I dwell; for I have desired it.

15 I will abundantly bless her provision: I will satisfy her poor with lechem.

16 I will also clothe her kohanim with Yahshua:[5] and her kidushim shall shout aloud for simcha.

---

[1] YHWH will cut down those who hate Zion and her two-house restoration.
[2] Abundant redemption is in YHWH.
[3] Yisrael's hope.

[4] YHWH who establishes David's Throne forever.
[5] Hebrew:**Yesha.**

TEHILLIM – PSALMS 132

17 There will I make the horn of David to bud: I have ordained a lamp for My anointed.
18 His enemies will I clothe with shame: but upon himself shall His keter flourish.

Kuf Lamed Gimel

133 [1] Hinai ma-tov uma-nayim shevet achim gam yachad! [2]
2 It is like the precious ointment upon the head; that ran down upon the beard, even Aharon's beard: that went down to the collar of his robe;
3 As the dew of Hermon, and as the dew that descends upon the mountains of Tzion: for there יהוה commands the bracha, even chayim le-olam-va-ed. [3]

Kuf Lamed Daled

134 [4]See; bless יהוה, all you avadim of יהוה, which by night stand in the Bayit of יהוה.
2 Lift up your hands in the Set-Apart Place, and bless יהוה.
3 יהוה that made the shamayim and earth bless you out of Tzion.

Kuf Lamed Hey

135 [5]Hallel יהוה. Hallel the Name of יהוה; hallel Him O you avadim of יהוה.
2 You that stand in the Bayit of יהוה, in the courts of the Bayit of our Elohim,
3 Hallel יהוה; for יהוה is tov: shir tehillot to His Name; for it is pleasant.
4 For Yah has chosen Yaakov to Himself, and Yisrael for His peculiar treasure.
5 For I know that יהוה is great, and that our יהוה is above all elohim.
6 Whatever יהוה pleased, that did He in the shamayim, and in the earth, in the seas, and all deep places.

7 He causes the vapors to ascend from the ends of the earth; He made lightning for the rain; He brings the wind out of His treasuries.
8 Who smote the firstborn of Mitzrayim, both of man and beast.
9 Who sent signs and wonders into the midst of you, O Mitzrayim, upon Pharaoh, and upon all his avadim.
10 Who smote great nations, and slew mighty melechim;
11 Sihon melech of the Amorites, and Og melech of Bashan, and all the malchutim of Kanaan:
12 And gave their land for a heritage, a heritage to Yisrael His people.
13 Your Name, O יהוה, endures le-olam-va-ed; and Your memorial, O יהוה, throughout all generations.
14 For יהוה will shophet His people, and have rachamim on His avadim. 15 The idols of the nations are silver and gold, the work of men's hands.
16 They have mouths, but they speak not; eyes, but they see not;
17 They have ears, but they shema not; neither is there any breath in their mouths.
18 They that make them are like them: so is every one that trusts in them.
19 Bless יהוה, O Beit Yisrael: bless יהוה, O Beit Aharon:
20 Bless יהוה, O Beit Levi: you that fear יהוה, bless יהוה.
21 Blessed be יהוה out of Tzion, who dwells at Yahrushalayim. Hallel יהוה.

Kuf Lamed Vav

136 [6] O give hodu to יהוה; for He is tov: for His rachamim endures le-olam-va-ed.
2 O give hodu to the Elohim of elohim: for His rachamim endures le-olam-va-ed.
3 O give hodu to the Master of sovereigns: for His rachamim endures le-olam-va-ed.
4 To Him who alone does great wonders: for His rachamim endures le-olam-va-ed.

---

[1] YHWH promises brotherhood between Judah and Ephraim.
[2] See; how tov and how pleasant it is for brothers to dwell together in unity.
[3] YHWH desires two-house unity among those chosen for eternal life by Moshiach.
[4] YHWH does His blessings from Tzion.
[5] YHWH chooses.

[6] YHWH's mercy endures forever.

5 To Him that by chochma made the shamayim: for His rachamim endures le-olam-va-ed.
6 To Him that stretches out the earth above the mayim: for His rachamim endures le-olam-va-ed.
7 To Him that made great lights: for His rachamim endures le-olam-va-ed:
8 The sun to rule by day: for His rachamim endures le-olam-va-ed:
9 The moon and chochavim to rule by night: for His rachamim endures le-olam-va-ed.
10 To Him that smote Mitzrayim and their firstborn: for His rachamim endures le-olam-va-ed:
11 And brought Yisrael out from among them: for His rachamim endures le-olam-va-ed:
12 With a strong hand, and with a stretched out arm: for His rachamim endures le-olam-va-ed.
13 To Him who divided the Sea of Reeds into parts: for His rachamim endures le-olam-va-ed:
14 And made Yisrael to pass through the midst of it: for His rachamim endures le-olam-va-ed:
15 But overthrew Pharaoh and his army in the Sea of Reeds: for His rachamim endures le-olam-va-ed.
16 To Him who led His people through the wilderness: for His rachamim endures le-olam-va-ed.
17 To Him who smote great melechim: for His rachamim endures le-olam-va-ed:
18 And slew famous melechim: for His rachamim endures le-olam-va-ed:
19 Sihon melech of the Amorites: for His rachamim endures le-olam-va-ed:
20 And Og the melech of Bashan: for His rachamim endures le-olam-va-ed:
21 And gave their land for a heritage: for His rachamim endures le-olam-va-ed:
22 Even a heritage to Yisrael His eved: for His rachamim endures le-olam-va-ed.
23 Who remembered us in our low estate: for His rachamim endures le-olam-va-ed:

24 And has redeemed us from our enemies: for His rachamim endures le-olam-va-ed.
25 Who gives food to all flesh: for His rachamim endures le-olam-va-ed.
26 O give hodu to the El of the shamayim: for His rachamim endures le-olam-va-ed.

Kuf Lamed Zayin

137 [1] By the rivers of Bavel, there we sat down, yes, we wept, when we remembered Tzion.
2 We hung our harps upon the willows in the midst of it.
3 For there they that carried us away in exile demanded of us a shir; and they that ruined us required that we gilah, saying, Sing to us one of the shirim of Tzion.
4 How shall we shir יהוה's shir in a strange land?
5 If I forget you, O Yahrushalayim, let my right hand forget me.
6 If I do not remember you, let my tongue cleave to the roof of my mouth; if I prefer not Yahrushalayim above my highest simcha.
7 Remember, O יהוה, the children of Edom in the day of Yahrushalayim; who said, Ruin it, ruin it, even to its foundation.
8 O daughter of Bavel,[2] who are to be destroyed; in simcha shall he be, that rewards you as you have treated us.
9 In simcha shall he be, that takes and dashes your little ones against the stones.

Kuf Lamed Chet

138 [3] I will hallel You with my whole lev: before the mighty will I shir tehillot to You.
2 I will worship toward Your Set-Apart Beit HaMikdash, and hallel Your Name for Your loving chesed and for Your emet: for You have magnified Your Word and Your Name above all.[4]

---

[1] YHWH the end of our exile.
[2] Medo-Persia.
[3] YHWH's Word and Name.
[4] Yahshua and YHWH's Name are above all.

3 In the day when I cried You answered me, and strengthened me with strength in my being.
4 All the melechim of the earth shall hallel You, O יהוה, when they shema the words of Your mouth.
5 Yes, they shall shir in the halachot of יהוה: for great is the tiferet of יהוה.
6 Though יהוה be high, yet has He respect to the lowly: but the proud He knows far off.
7 Though I walk in the midst of trouble, You will revive me: You shall stretch forth Your hand against the anger of my enemies, and Your right hand[1] shall save me.
8 יהוה will perfect that which concerns me: Your rachamim, O יהוה, endures le-olam-va-ed: forsake not the works of Your own hands.

Kuf Lamed Tet

139 [2] O יהוה, You have searched me, and know me.
2 You know my sitting down and my rising up; You understand my thoughts from far off.
3 You sift my derech and my lying down, and are acquainted with all my halachot.
4 For there is not a word in my tongue, but see, O יהוה, You know it all.
5 You have closed me in behind and before, and laid Your hand upon me.
6 Such da'at is too wonderful for me. it is too high, I cannot attain to it.
7 Where shall I go from Your Ruach? Or where shall I flee from Your Shechinah?
8 If I ascend up into the shamayim, You are there: if I make my bed in Sheol, see, You are there.
9 If I take the wings of the morning, and dwell in the farthest parts of the sea;
10 Even there shall Your hand lead me, and Your right hand[3] shall hold me.
11 If I say, Surely the darkness shall cover me; even the night shall be light around me.

12 Yes, the darkness hides not from You; but the night shines as the day: the darkness and the light are both alike to You.
13 For You have possessed my kidneys: You have covered me in my ima's womb.
14 I will hallel You; for I am fearfully and wonderfully made: marvelous are Your works; and that does my being know full well.
15 My bones were not hidden from You, when I was shaped in the hidden place, and knit together in the lowest parts of the earth.
16 Your eyes did see my unformed body, yet in Your book all my members were already written, which were formed, when as yet there was none of them.[4]
17 How precious also are Your thoughts to me, O El! How great is their sum!
18 If I should count them, they are more in number than the sand: when I awake, I am still with You.
19 Surely You will slay the wicked, O Eloah: depart from me therefore, you men of domshed!
20 For they speak against You wickedly, and Your enemies take Your Name in vain.[5]
21 Do not I hate them, O יהוה, that hate You? And am not I grieved with those that rise up against You?
22 I hate them with a full hatred: I count them as my enemies.
23 Search me, O El, and know my lev: test me, and know my thoughts:
24 And see if there be any wicked halacha in me, and lead me in the halacha that is everlasting.

---

[1] Yahshua.
[2] YHWH is everywhere.
[3] Yahshua.

[4] YHWH knows us before formation, and sees us as if we were already conceived.
[5] Bring it to nothing, as do most religious leaders today.

Kuf Mem

140 [1] Deliver me, O **יהוה**, from the evil man: preserve me from the violent man;

2 Who imagine evil in their levim; continually are they gathered together for war.

3 They have sharpened their tongues like a serpent; cobras' poison is under their lips. Selah.

4 Keep me, O **יהוה**, from the hands of the wicked; preserve me from the violent man; who has purposed to overthrow my goings.

5 The proud have hidden a trap for me, and with cords; they have spread a net by the roadside; they have set traps for me. Selah.

6 I said to **יהוה**, You are My El: shema the voice of my supplications, O **יהוה**.

7 O Elohim **יהוה**, the strength of My Yahshua,[2] You have covered my head in the day of battle.

8 Grant not, O **יהוה**, the desires of the wicked: further not his wicked plan; lest they exalt themselves. Selah.

9 As for the heads of those that surround me, let the evil of their own lips cover them.

10 Let burning coals fall upon them: let them be cast into the fire; into deep pits that they rise not up again.

11 Let not a slanderer be established in the earth: evil shall hunt the violent man to overthrow him.

12 I know that **יהוה** will maintain the cause of the afflicted, and the rights of the poor.

13 Surely the tzadikim shall give hodu to Your Name: the tzadik shall dwell in Your shechinah.

Kuf Mem Aleph

141 [3] **יהוה**, I cry to You: hurry back to me; shema to my voice, when I cry to You.

2 Let my tefillah be set forth before You as incense; and the lifting up of my hands as maariv.

3 Set a watch, O **יהוה**, before my mouth; guard the door of my lips.

4 Let not my lev be inclined to any evil thing, to practice wicked works with men that work iniquity: and let me not eat of their delicacies.

5 Let the tzadikim smite me; it shall be a pleasure: and let him rebuke me; only let not the oil of the wicked anoint me, for my tefillah has been against their evil.

6 When their shophtim are overthrown in stony places, they shall shema to my words; for they are sweet.

7 Our bones are scattered at the grave's mouth, as when one cuts and cleaves wood upon the earth.

8 But my eyes are to You, O Elohim **יהוה**: in You is my trust; leave not my being destitute.

9 Keep me from the snares that they have laid for me, and the traps of the workers of iniquity.

10 Let the wicked fall into their own nets, while I escape.

Kuf Mem Bet

142 [4] I cried to **יהוה** with my voice; with my voice to **יהוה** did I make my pleading.

2 I poured out my complaints before Him; I showed Him my troubles.

3 When my ruach was overwhelmed within me, then You knew my derech. In the halacha that I walk, they have secretly laid a trap for me.

4 I looked on my right hand, and beheld, but there was no man that would know me: refuge failed me; no man cared for my being.

5 I cried to You, O **יהוה**: I said, You are my refuge and my portion in the land of the living.

6 Attend to my cry; for I am brought very low: deliver me from my persecutors; for they are stronger than I.

---

[1] YHWH will rescue us.
[2] Hebrew: **Yeshuati.**
[3] YHWH traps the wicked in their own nets.

[4] YHWH who lovingly and patiently allows us to complain to Him.

7 Bring my being out of prison, that I may hallel Your Name: the tzadikim shall surround me; for You shall deal abundantly with me.

Kuf Mem Gimel

143 [1] Shema to my tefillah, O **יהוה**, give ear to my supplications: in Your faithfulness answer me, and in Your tzedakah.

2 And enter not into mishpat with Your eved: for in Your sight shall no man living be justified.

3 For the enemy has persecuted my being; he has smitten my chayim down to the ground; he has made me to dwell in darkness, as those that have been long dead.

4 Therefore is my ruach overwhelmed within me; my lev within me is desolate.

5 I remember the days of old; I meditate on all Your works; I ponder the work of Your hands.

6 I stretch forth my hands to You: my being thirsts after You, as a thirsty land. Selah.

7 Shema me speedily, O **יהוה**: my ruach fails: hide not Your face from me, lest I be like them that go down into the pit.

8 Cause me to shema Your loving chesed in the morning; for in You do I trust: cause me to know the halacha in which I should walk; for I lift up my being to You.

9 Deliver me, O **יהוה**, from my enemies: I flee to You to hide me.

10 Teach me to do Your will; for You are My Elohim: Your Ruach is tov; lead me into the land of tzedakah.

11 Quicken me, O **יהוה**, for Your Name's sake: for Your tzedakah's sake bring my being out of trouble.

12 And by Your rachamim cut off my enemies, and destroy all them that afflict my being: for I am Your eved.

Kuf Mem Dalet

144 [2] Blessed be **יהוה** my strength, who teaches my hands to war,

and my fingers to fight:

2 My tov, and My fortress; My high tower, and My deliverer; My shield, in whom I trust; who subdues nations under me.

3 **יהוה**, what is man, that You are mindful of him! And the ben Adam, that You take account of him!

4 Man is like vanity: his days are as a shadow that passes away.

5 Bow Your shamayim, O **יהוה**, and come down: touch the mountains, and they shall smoke.

6 Cast forth lightning, and scatter them: shoot out Your arrows, and destroy them.

7 Send Your hand from above; rescue me, and deliver me out of great mayim, from the hand of foreign children;

8 Whose mouths speaks vanity, and their right hand is a right hand of falsehood.

9 I will shir a new shir to You, O Elohim: upon a guitar and an instrument of ten strings will I shir tehillot to You.

10 It is He that gives Yahshua[3] to melechim: who delivers David His eved from the hurtful sword.

11 Rescue me, and deliver me from the hand of foreign children, whose mouth speaks vanity, and their right hand is a right hand of falsehood:

12 That our sons may be as plants grown up in their youth; that our daughters may be as corner stones, polished after the likeness of a palace:

13 That our storehouses may be full, supplying all kinds of supply: that our sheep may bring forth thousands and ten thousands in our streets:

14 That our oxen may be strong to labor; that there be no breaking in, nor going out; that there be no complaining in our streets.[4]

15 Blessed are the people, that have this situation: yes, blessed are that people, whose Elohim is **יהוה**.

---

[3] Hebrew: **teshua.**
[4] Avoiding foreign customs and living a Yisraelite lifestyle just like Yahshua and the apostles, will allow us to avoid the foreign children and their customs that are an obstacle to both our personal and national material prosperity.

---

[1] YHWH will show us favor in all trials.
[2] YHWH who gives Yahshua to the kings of the earth.

Kuf Mem Hey

145

[1] I will extol You, my Elohim, O Melech; and I will bless Your Name le-olam-va-ed.

2 Every day will I bless You; and I will hallel Your Name le-olam-va-ed.

3 Great is **יהוה**, and greatly to be praised; and His greatness is unsearchable.

4 One generation shall hallel Your works to another, and shall declare Your mighty acts.

5 I will speak of the beautiful honor of Your majesty, and of Your wonderful works.

6 And men shall speak of the might of Your awesome acts: and I will declare Your greatness.

7 They shall abundantly utter the memory of Your great tov, and shall shir about Your tzedakah.

8 **יהוה** is full of favor, and full of rachamim; slow to anger, and of great rachamim.

9 **יהוה** is tov to all: and His tender rachamim are over all His works.

10 All Your works shall hallel You, O **יהוה**; and Your kidushim shall bless You.

11 They shall speak of the tiferet of Your malchut, and talk of Your power;

12 To make known to the sons of men His mighty acts, and the beautiful majesty of His malchut.

13 Your malchut is an everlasting malchut, and Your rule endures throughout all generations. **יהוה** is faithful in His words, and set-apart in all His works.[2]

14 **יהוה** upholds all that fall, and raises up all those that are bowed down.

15 The eyes of all wait upon You; and You give them their food in due season.

16 You open Your hand, and satisfy the desire of every living thing.

17 **יהוה** is tzadik in all His halachot, and set-apart in all His works.

18 **יהוה** is near to all them that call upon Him, to all that call upon Him in emet.

19 He will fulfill the desire of those that fear Him: He also will shema to their cry, and will save them.

20 **יהוה** preserves all those that love Him: but all the wicked will He destroy.

21 My mouth shall speak the hallel of **יהוה**: and let all flesh barchu His set-apart Name le-olam-va-ed.[3]

Kuf Mem Vav

146

[4] Hallel You **יהוה**. Hallel **יהוה**, O my being.

2 While I live I will hallel **יהוה**: I will shir tehillot to My Elohim while I have chayim.

3 Put not your trust in leaders, nor in a ben Adam, in whom there is no help.

4 His breath goes forth, he returns to his earth; in that very day his thoughts perish.

5 Blessed is he that has the El of Yaakov for his help, whose tikvah is in **יהוה** His Elohim:

6 Who made the shamayim, and earth, the sea, and all that is in it: who keeps emet le-olam-va-ed:

7 Who is doing mishpat for the oppressed: who gives food to the hungry. **יהוה** looses the prisoners:

8 **יהוה** opens the eyes of the blind: **יהוה** raises them that are bowed down: **יהוה** loves the tzadikim:

9 **יהוה** preserves the foreigners[5]; He relieves the fatherless and widow: but the halacha of the wicked He turns upside down.

10 **יהוה** shall reign le-olam-va-ed, even Your Elohim, O Tzion, to all generations. Hallel **יהוה**.

Kuf Mem Zayin

147

[6] Hallel **יהוה**. For it is tov to shir tehillot to our Elohim; for it is pleasant; and hallel is comely.

---

[1] YHWH's everlasting malchut.
[2] LXX, DSS.

[3] His Name YHWH is for all believing flesh, not just Jews.
[4] YHWH; the only trustworthy One.
[5] By making them part of Yisrael's Commonwealth.
[6] His works for Yisrael.

2 יהוה builds up Yahrushalayim:[1] He gathers together the outcasts of Yisrael.[2][3]
3 He heals the broken in lev, and binds up their wounds.[4]
4 He counts the number of the chochavim; He calls them all by their names.
5 Great is our יהוה, and of great power: His binah is infinite.
6 יהוה lifts up the meek: He casts the wicked down to the ground.
7 Sing to יהוה with hodu; shir tehillot upon the harp to our Elohim:
8 Who covers the shamayim with clouds, who prepares rain for the earth, who makes grass grow upon the mountains.
9 He gives to the beast its food, and to the young ravens who cry to Him.
10 He delights not in the strength of the horse: He takes no pleasure in the legs of a man.
11 יהוה takes pleasure in those that fear Him, in those that have tikvah in His rachamim.
12 Hallel יהוה, O Yahrushalayim: Hallel Your Elohim, O Tzion.
13 For He has strengthened the bars of your gates; He has blessed your children within you.
14 He makes shalom in your borders, and fills you with the finest of the wheat.
15 He sends forth His commandment upon the earth: His word runs very swiftly.
16 He gives snow like wool: He scatters the frost like ashes.
17 He casts forth His hail like morsels: who can stand before His cold?
18 He sends out His word, and melts them: He causes His wind to blow, and the mayim flows.
19 He shows His word to Yaakov, His chukim and His mishpatim to Yisrael.
20 He has not dealt like that with any other nation: and as for His mishpatim, they have not known them. Hallel יהוה.

Kuf Mem Chet

148 [5] Hallel יהוה; hallel יהוה from the shamayim, hallel Him in the heights.
2 Hallel Him, all His heavenly messengers: hallel Him, all His hosts.
3 Hallel Him, sun and moon: hallel Him, all you chochavim of light.
4 Hallel Him, you shamayim of shamayim, and you mayim that are above the shamayim.
5 Let them hallel the Name of יהוה: for He commanded, and they were created.
6 He has also established them le-olam-va-ed: He has made a decree that shall not pass.
7 Hallel יהוה from the earth, you sea creatures, and all the depths:
8 Fire, and hail; snow, and vapor; stormy winds fulfilling His word:
9 Mountains, and all hills; fruitful trees, and all cedars:
10 Beasts, and all cattle; creeping things, and flying fowls:
11 Melechim of the earth, and all nations; leaders, and all shophtim of the earth:
12 Both young men, and virgins; old men, and children:
13 Let them hallel the Name of יהוה: for His Name alone is excellent; His tiferet is above the earth and the shamayim.
14 He also exalts the horn of His people, the hallel of all His kidushim; even of the children of Yisrael, a people near to Him. Hallel יהוה.

Kuf Mem Tet

149 [6] Hallel יהוה. Sing to יהוה a new shir, and His tehillot in the congregation of the kidushim.[7]
2 Let Yisrael gilah in Him that made Him: let the children of Tzion be in simcha over their Melech.

[1] Judah.
[2] Ephraim Yisrael.
[3] In our generation this work is spreading and he is revealing this more and more. He builds up Jerusalem and simultaneously gathers the outcasts all over the world.
[4] Both houses are in need of this healing.

[5] Let everything praise YHWH.
[6] YHWH will rule all nations.
[7] In Yisrael.

3 Let them hallel His Name in the dance: let them shir tehillot to Him with the tambourine and harp.
4 For **יהוה** takes pleasure in His people: He will beautify the meek in Yahshua.[1]
5 Let the kidushim be joyful in tiferet: let them shir aloud upon their beds.
6 Let the high tehillot of El be in their mouths, and a two-edged sword in their hand;
7 To execute vengeance upon the nations, and punishments upon the peoples;
8 To bind their melechim with chains, and their nobles with shackles of iron;
9 To execute upon them the written mishpat: this honor have all His kidushim. Hallel **יהוה**.

Kuf Nun

150 [2] Hallel **יהוה**. Hallel El in His Set-Apart Place: hallel Him in the expanse of His power.
2 Hallel Him for His mighty acts: hallel Him according to His excellent greatness.
3 Hallel Him with the sound of the shofar: hallel Him with the guitar and harp.
4 Hallel Him with the tambourine and dance: hallel Him with stringed instruments and flutes.
5 Hallel Him with the loud cymbals: hallel Him upon the high sounding cymbals.
6 Let everything that has breath hallel-Yah. Hallel- **יהוה**.

Kuf Nun Aleph (LXX)[3]

151 [4] I was small among my brothers and youngest in my abba's bayit: I tended my abba's sheep.
2 My hands formed a musical instrument, and my fingers tuned a guitar
3 And who shall tell my **יהוה**? The Master Himself, He Himself will shema.
4 He sent forth His heavenly messenger, and took me from my abba's sheep, and He anointed me with the oil of His anointing.
5 My brothers were handsome and tall; but **יהוה** did not take pleasure in them.
6 I went forth to meet the Philistine; and he cursed me by his idols.
7 But I drew his own sword, and beheaded him, and removed reproach from the children of Yisrael.

---

[1] Hebrew: **BeYeshua.**
[2] Let all who have breath praise Yah.
[3] Found in the LXX-Septuagint.
[4] YHWH raised up David and his future throne.

משלי

Mishle - Proverbs
To Our Forefathers Yisrael

1 The Mishle of Shlomo ben David, melech of Yisrael;
2 To know chochmah and discipline; to perceive the words of binah;
3 To receive the discipline of chochmah, tzedakah, and mishpat, and equity;
4 To give insight to the simple, to the young man da'at and discretion.
5 A wise man will shema, and will increase learning; and a man of binah gets wise counsel:
6 To understand a Mishle, and the interpretation; the words of the wise, and their riddles.
7 The fear of **יהוה** is the beginning of da'at: but fools despise chochmah and discipline.
8 My son, shema the discipline of your abba, and forsake not the Torah of your ima:
9 For they shall be an ornament of favor for your neck, as necklaces around your neck.
10 My son, if sinners entice you, do not consent to them.
11 If they say, Come with us, let us lie in wait for dom, let us ambush the innocent without any cause:
12 Let us swallow them up alive as the grave; and whole, as those that go down into the pit:
13 So then we shall find all precious goods, we shall fill our houses with spoil:
14 Cast in your lot among us; let us all have one purse:
15 My son, walk not with them in their halacha; hold back your foot from their halacha:
16 For their feet run to do evil, and hurry to shed dom.
17 Surely in vain the net is spread in the sight of any bird.
18 And they lie in wait for their own dom; they ambush their own lives.

19 So are the halachot of everyone that is greedy for gain; that takes away the chayim of its owners.
20 Wisdom calls outside; she[1] utters her voice in the streets:
21 She utters in the main place of concourse, in the openings of the gates: in the city she utters her words, saying,
22 How long, you simple ones, will you love simplicity? And the scorners delight in their scorning, and fools hate da'at?
23 Make teshuvah at My correction: behold, I will pour out My Ruach to you, I will make known My words to you.
24 Because I have called, and you refused; I have stretched out My hand, and no man regarded it;
25 But you have ignored all My counsel, and would receive none of My correction:
26 I also will laugh at your calamity; I will mock when your fear comes;
27 When your fear comes as desolation, and your destruction comes as a whirlwind; when distress and anguish come upon you.
28 Then shall they call upon Me, but I will not answer; they shall seek Me early, but they shall not find Me:
29 Because they hated da'at, and did not choose the fear of **יהוה**:
30 They would receive none of My counsel: they despised all My correction.
31 Therefore shall they eat of the fruit of their own halacha, and be filled with their own counsel.
32 For the teshuvah of the simple shall slay them, and the prosperity of fools shall destroy them.
33 But anyone who listens to Me shall dwell safely, and shall be at ease from fear of evil.

---

[1] Wisdom in Hebraic binah is associated with the female character aspects of the manifestations of YHWH, and has most often been associated with the motherly care of YHWH known as the Ruach HaKodesh, or Set-Apart Spirit, the gentle "mothering care" of Father YHWH.

2 My son, if you will receive My words, and hide My commandments with you;
2 So that you incline your ear to chochmah, and apply your lev to binah;
3 Yes, if you shout out for da'at, and lift up your voice for binah;
4 If you seek her as silver, and search for her as for hidden treasures;
5 Then shall you understand the fear of יהוה, and find the da'at of Elohim.
6 For יהוה gives chochmah: out of His mouth comes da'at and binah.
7 He lays up sound chochmah for the tzadik: He is a shield to them that have an upright halacha.
8 He guards the halachot of mishpat, and preserves the halacha of His kidushim.
9 Then shall you understand tzedakah, and mishpat, and equity; yes, every tov halacha.
10 When chochmah enters into your lev, and da'at is pleasant to your being;
11 Discretion shall preserve you; binah shall guard you:
12 To deliver you from the halacha of the evil man, from the man that speaks perverted things;
13 Who leaves the halachot of uprightness, to have a halacha in the halachot of darkness;
14 Who rejoices to do evil, and delights in the perversities of the wicked;
15 Whose halachot are crooked, and are perverted in their halachot:
16 To deliver you from the strange woman, even from the stranger who flatters with her words
17 Who forsakes the Guide of her youth, and forgets the covenant of her Elohim.
18 For her bayit has sunken to death, and her halachot to the dead.
19 None that go into her return again, neither do they retake hold of the halachot of chayim.[1]
20 So walk in the halacha of tov men, and guard the halachot of the tzadik.

21 For the upright shall dwell on the earth, and the perfect shall remain in it.[2]
22 But the wicked shall be cut off from the earth, and the transgressors shall be rooted out of it

3 My son, forget not My Torah; but let your lev guard My commandments:
2 For length of days, and long chayim, and shalom, shall they add to you.
3 Let not rachamim and emet forsake you: bind them around your neck; write them upon the table of your lev:
4 So shall you find favor and tov binah in the sight of Elohim and man.
5 Trust in יהוה with all your lev; and lean not to your own binah.
6 In all your halachot acknowledge Him, and He shall direct your halach.
7 Be not wise in your own eyes: fear יהוה, and depart from evil.
8 It shall be health to your navel, and marrow to your bones.
9 Honor יהוה with your substance, and with the firstfruits of all your increase:[3]
10 So shall your barns be filled with plenty, and your presses shall burst out with new wine.
11 My son, despise not the chastening of יהוה; neither be weary of His correction:
12 For whom יהוה loves He corrects; even as an Abba with the son in whom He delights.
13 Happy is the man that finds chochmah, and the man that gains binah.[4]
14 For its gain is better than the merchandise of silver and fine gold.
15 She is more precious than rubies: and all the things you desire are not to be compared to her.
16 Length of days is in her right hand; and in her left hand riches and honor.
17 Her halachot are halachot of pleasantness, and all her halachot are shalom.

---

[1] Sexual perversity is a path of no return and those in its trap find it almost impossible to return to the peace of YHWH.

[2] Home of the **atid lavoh;** or millennial kingdom.
[3] The tithe of all.
[4] Two aspects of YHWH's manifestations, both the masculine and feminine as revealed by the Son of YHWH.

18 She is the eytz chaim to them that take hold of her: and happy is everyone that takes hold of her.

19 **יהוה** by chochmah founded the earth; by binah has He established the shamayim.

20 By His da'at the depths are broken up, and the clouds drop down the dew.

21 My son, let not them depart from your eyes: guard sound chochmah and discretion:

22 So shall they be chayim to your being, and adornment to your neck.

23 Then shall you walk in your halacha safely, and your foot shall not stumble.

24 When you lie down, you shall not be afraid: yes, you shall lie down, and your sleep shall be sweet.

25 Be not afraid of sudden fear, neither of the desolation of the wicked, when it comes.

26 For **יהוה** shall be your confidence, and shall guard your foot from being taken.

27 Withhold not any tov from them to whom it is due, when it is in the power of your hand to do it.

28 Say not to your neighbor, Go, and come again, and tomorrow I will give; when you have his needs with you.

29 Plan no evil against your neighbor, seeing He dwells securely beside you.

30 Strive not with a man without reason, if He has done you no harm.

31 Envy not the oppressor, and choose none of his halachot.

32 For the perverted are an abomination to **יהוה**: but His secret counsel is with the tzadikim.

33 The curse of **יהוה** is in the bayit of the wicked: but He gives brachot the dwelling of the tzadik.

34 Surely He scorns the scorners: but He gives favor to the humble.

35 The wise shall inherit tiferet: but shame shall be the disgrace of fools.

4 Shema, you children of Yisrael, to the discipline of an Abba, and shema to know binah.

2 For I give you tov teaching, forsake not My Torah.

3 For I was My abba's son, tender and the only beloved in the sight of my ima.[1]

4 He taught me also, and said to me, Let your lev retain My words: guard My commandments, and live.

5 Get chochmah, get binah: forget it not; neither decline from the words of My mouth.[2]

6 Forsake her not, and she shall preserve you: love her, and she shall guard you.

7 Wisdom is the main thing; therefore get chochmah: and with all your getting of things get binah.

8 Exalt her, and she shall promote you: she shall bring you to honor, when you do embrace her.

9 She shall give to your head an ornament of favor: a keter of tiferet shall she deliver to you.

10 Shema, O My son, and receive My sayings; and the years of your chayim shall be many.

11 I have taught you in the halacha of chochmah; I have led you in right halachot.

12 When you go, your steps shall not be hindered; and when you run, you shall not stumble.

13 Take firm hold of discipline; do not let her go: guard her; for she is your chayim.

14 Enter not into the halacha of the wicked, and go not in the halacha of evil men.

15 Avoid it, do not pass by it, turn from it, and pass on by it.

16 For they do not sleep, except they have first done mischief; and their sleep is taken away, unless they first cause someone to fall.

17 For they eat the lechem of wickedness, and drink the wine of violence.

18 But the halacha of the tzadik is as the shining light, that shines more and more until the perfect day of the olam habah.

19 The halacha of the wicked is as darkness: they know not at what they stumble.

---

[1] Yisrael.
[2] Living Torah.

20 My son, pay attention to My words;
incline your ear to My sayings.
21 Let them not depart from your eyes;
guard them in the midst of your lev.
22 For they are chayim to those that find
them, and health to all their flesh.[1]
23 Guard your lev with all diligence; for out
of it are the issues of chayim.
24 Put away from you a perverted mouth,
and perverted lips put far from you.
25 Let your eyes look right on, and let your
eyelids look straight before you.
26 Ponder the halacha of your feet, and let
all your halachot be established.
27 Turn not to the right hand nor to the left:
remove your foot from evil.

5 My son, shema to My chochmah, and
bow your ear to My binah:
2 That you may regard discretion, and that
your lips may guard da'at.
3 For the lips of a strange woman drop as a
honeycomb, and her mouth is smoother
than oil:
4 But her end is bitter as wormwood, sharp
as a two-edged sword.
5 Her feet go down to death; her steps take
hold on the grave.
6 She does not ponder the halacha of
chayim, her halachot are unstable, that you
cannot know them.
7 Shema to Me now therefore, O you
children of Yisrael and depart not from the
words of My mouth.
8 Remove your halacha far from her, and
come not near the door of her bayit:
9 Lest you give up your honor to others, and
your years to the cruel:
10 Lest strangers be filled with your
strength; and your labors be in the bayit of a
stranger;
11 And you shall have remorse in your old
age, when your flesh and your body are
consumed,
12 And say, How have I hated discipline,
and my lev despised correction;

13 And have not obeyed the voice of my
teachers, nor inclined my ears to those that
instructed me!
14 I was almost in every kind of evil in the
midst of the congregation.[2]
15 Drink waters out of your own cistern,
and running waters out of your own well.
16 Let your fountains be dispersed abroad,
and rivers of waters in the streets.
17 Let them be only your own, and not
strangers' with you.
18 Let your fountain be blessed: and gilah
with the wife of your youth.
19 Let her be as the loving deer and
pleasant mountain roe; let her breasts satisfy
you at all times; and be captivated always
by her love.
20 And why will you, My son, be misled
with a strange woman, and embrace the
bosom of a stranger?
21 For the halachot of men are before the
eyes of יהוה, and He ponders their entire
goings.
22 His own iniquities shall take away the
wicked himself, and He shall be held with
the cords of his own sins.
23 He shall die without discipline; and in
the greatness of his folly He shall go astray.

6 My son, if you are a guarantor for
your friend, if you have shaken your
hand with a stranger,
2 You are trapped with the words of your
mouth, you are taken with the words of
your mouth.
3 Do this now, My son, deliver yourself,
when you are come into the hand of your
friend; go, humble yourself, and urge your
friend.
4 Give no sleep to your eyes, nor slumber to
your eyelids.
5 Deliver yourself as a gazelle from the
hand of the hunter, and as a bird from the
hand of the trapper.
6 Go to the ant, you lazy one; consider her
halachot, and be wise:

---

[1] The Torah as taught by the Ruach, is medicine and healing
for YHWH's true people.

[2] Going to a congregation does not necessarily mean you love
YHWH.

7 They have no guide, overseer, or ruler, yet she;

8 Provides her food in the summer, and gathers her food in the harvest.

9 How long will you sleep, O lazy one? When will you arise out of your sleep?

10 Yet a little sleep, a little slumber, a little folding of the hands to sleep:

11 And then poverty will come upon you, and distress will overtake you.

12 A man of Beliya'al, a wicked man, walks with a perverted mouth.

13 He winks with his eyes, he speaks with his feet, he points with his fingers;[1]

14 Perversity is in his lev, he devises mischief continually; he sows discord.

15 Therefore shall his calamity come suddenly; suddenly shall he be broken without remedy.

16 These six things does יהוה hate: yes, seven are an abomination to Him:

17 A proud look, a lying tongue, and hands that shed innocent dom,

18 A lev that plans wicked imaginations, feet that are swift in running to mischief,

19 A false witness that speaks lies, and he that sows discord among brothers.[2]

20 My son, guard your abba's commandment, and forsake not the Torah of your ima:

21 Bind them continually upon your lev, and tie them around your neck.

22 When you move about, it shall lead you; when you sleep, it shall guard you; and when you awake, it shall talk with you.

23 For the commandment is a lamp; and the Torah is light; and reproofs of discipline are the halacha of chayim:

24 To guard you from the evil woman, from the flattery of the tongue of a strange woman.

25 Lust not after her beauty in your lev; neither let her take you with her eyelids.

26 For by means of a whorish woman a man is brought to a piece of lechem: and the adulteress will hunt for the precious chayim.

27 Can a man take fire in his bosom, and his clothes not get burned?

28 Can one walk upon hot coals, and his feet not be burned?

29 So he that goes in to his neighbor's wife; whosoever touches her shall not be innocent.

30 Men do not despise a thief, if he steals to satisfy his being when he is hungry;

31 But if he is caught, he shall restore sevenfold; he shall give all the substance of his bayit.

32 But whoever commits adultery with a woman lacks binah: he that does it destroys his own being.

33 A wound and dishonor shall he get; and his reproach shall not be wiped away.

34 For jealousy enrages a man: therefore he will not spare in the day of vengeance.

35 He will not regard any ransom; neither will he rest content, though you give him many bribes.

7 My son, guard My words, and treasure My commandments with you.

2 Keep My commandments, and live; and My Torah as the apple of your eye.

3 Bind them upon your fingers; write them upon the table of your lev.

4 Say to chochmah, You are My sister; and call binah your counselor:

5 That they may guard you from the strange woman, from the stranger who flatters with her words.

6 For at the window of my bayit I looked through my lattice,

7 And beheld among the simple ones, I discerned among the youths, a young man void of binah,

8 Passing through the street near her corner; and he went on the path to her bayit,

9 In the twilight, in the evening, in the black and dark night:

10 And, behold, there met him a woman with the attire of a harlot, and a subtil lev.

11 She is loud and stubborn; her feet do not stay in her bayit:

---

[1] Walks in secret and confusing ambiguity, along with a foul mouth.
[2] Seven sins all Yisraelites must avoid.

12 Now is she outside, in the streets, and lies in wait at every corner.

13 So she caught him, and kissed him, and with a hardened face said to him,

14 I have shalom offerings with me; this day have I paid my vows.

15 Therefore I came forth to meet you, diligently to seek your face, and I have found you.

16 I have decked my bed with coverings of tapestry, with carved works, with fine linen of Mitzrayim.

17 I have perfumed my bed with myrrh, aloes, and cinnamon.

18 Come, let us take our fill of love until the morning: let us delight ourselves with love.

19 For my husband is not at home, he is gone a long journey:

20 He has taken a bag of money with him, and will come home on the day of Rosh Chodesh.

21 With her many words she caused him to yield, with the flattering of her lips she seduces him.

22 He goes after her immediately, as an ox goes to the slaughter, or as a fool to the correction of the prison;

23 Until a dart strikes through his liver; as a bird rushing to the trap that did not know it would take his chayim.

24 Shema to Me now, O you children of Yisrael, and pay attention to the words of My mouth.

25 Let not your lev sink down to her halachot, go not astray in her halachot.

26 For she has cast down many wounded: yes, many strong men have been slain by her.

27 Her bayit is the halacha of the grave, going down to the rooms of death.

8 Does not chochmah call?[1] And binah lifts her voice?

2 She stands in the top of the heights; between the paths she has taken her stand.

3 She utters at the gates, at the entry of the city, at the coming in at the doors.

4 *To you, O men, I call; and My voice is to the sons of man.*

5 *O you simple, understand chochmah: and, you fools, be of a binah lev.*

6 *Shema; for I will speak of excellent things; and the opening of My lips shall be right things.*

7 *For My mouth shall speak emet; and wickedness is an abomination to My lips.*

8 *All the words of My mouth are in tzedakah; there is nothing perverted or perverse in them.*

9 *They are all plain to him that understands, and right to them that find da'at.*

10 *Receive My discipline, and not silver; and da'at rather than choice gold.*

11 *For chochmah is better than rubies; and all the things that may be desired are not to be compared to it.*

12 *I, chochmah, dwell with insight, and find out da'at and foresight.*

13 *The fear of יהוה is to hate evil: pride, and arrogance, and the evil halacha, and the perverted mouth, that do I hate.*

14 *Counsel is mine, and sound chochmah: I am binah; I have strength.*

15 *By me melechim reign, and rulers decree tzedakah.*

16 *By me rulers rule, and nobles, even all the judges of the earth.*

17 *I love them that love me; and those that seek me early shall find me.*

18 *Riches and honor are with me; yes, durable riches and tzedakah.*

19 *My fruit is better than gold, yes, than fine gold; and My revenue than choice silver.*

20 *I lead in the halacha of tzedakah, in the midst of the halachot of mishpat:*

21 *That I may cause those that love me to inherit substance; and I will fill their treasures.*

22 *יהוה possessed me in the beginning of His halacha, before His works of old.*

23 *I was set up from everlasting, from the beginning, before the earth was.*

---

[1] In this chapter **chochma**/wisdom is personified throughout as Yahshua, confirming First Corinthians 1:30 and Luke 11:49 that Moshiach is YHWH's chochma personified.

24 When there were no depths, I was brought forth; when there were no fountains abounding with mayim.
25 Before the mountains were settled, before the hills was I brought forth:
26 While as yet He had not made the earth, or the fields, or the highest part of the dust of the world.
27 When He prepared the shamayim, I was there: when He set a compass upon the face of the depth:
28 When He established the clouds above: when He strengthened the fountains of the deep:
29 When He gave to the sea His decree, that the waters should not pass His commandment: when He appointed the foundations of the earth:
30 Then I was by Him, as one brought up with Him: and I was daily His delight, having gilah always before Him;
31 Having gilah in the habitable part of His earth; and My delights were with the sons of men.
32 Now therefore shema to Me, O you children of Yisrael: for blessed are they that guard My halachot.[1]
33 Shema discipline, and be wise, and refuse it not.
34 Blessed is the man that listens to me, watching daily at My gates, waiting at the posts of My doors.
35 For whoever finds me finds chayim, and shall obtain favor from יהוה.
36 But he that sins against me wrongs his own being: all they that hate me love death.

9 Wisdom has built her bayit; she has cut out its seven pillars:
2 She has killed her beasts; she has mingled her wine; she has also furnished her table.
3 She has sent forth her young women: she utters upon the highest places of the city,
4 Who is simple, let him turn in here: as for him that wants binah, she says to him,
5 Come, eat of my lechem, and drink of the wine that I have mingled.

6 Forsake the foolish, and live; and go in the halacha of binah.
7 He that reproves a scorner gets to himself shame: and he that rebukes a wicked man gets himself a blot.
8 Reprove not a scorner, lest he hate you: rebuke a wise man, and he will love you.
9 Give discipline to a wise man, and he will be yet wiser: teach a tzadik man, and he will increase in learning.
10 The fear of יהוה is the beginning of chochmah: and the da'at of the Set-Apart-One is binah.
11 For by me your days shall be multiplied, and the years of your chayim shall be increased.
12 If you are wise, you shall be wise for yourself: but if you scorn, you alone shall bear it.
13 A foolish woman is loud: she is simple, and knows nothing.
14 For she sits at the door of her bayit, on a seat in the high places of the city,
15 To call passengers who go right on their paths:
16 Whoever is simple, let him turn in here: and as for him that lacks binah, she says to him,
17 Stolen waters are sweet, and lechem eaten in secret is pleasant.
18 But he knows not that the dead are there; and that her guests are in the depths of the grave.

10 The Mishle of Shlomo. A wise son makes an abba have gilah: but a foolish son is the heaviness of his ima.
2 Treasures of wickedness profit nothing: but tzedakah delivers from death.
3 יהוה will not allow the being of the tzadik to hunger: but He casts away the substance of the wicked.
4 The poor deals with a lazy hand: but the hand of the diligent makes rich.
5 He that gathers in summer is a wise son: but he that sleeps in harvest is a son that causes shame.

---

[1] Torah.

6 Blessings are upon the head of the tzadik: but violence covers the mouth of the wicked.

7 The memory of the tzadik is blessed: but the name of the wicked shall rot.

8 The wise in lev will receive commandments: but the one with foolish lips shall fall.

9 He that has an upright halacha walks safely: but he that perverts his halachot shall be known.

10 He that winks with the eye causes sorrow: but the one with foolish lips shall fall.

11 The mouth of a tzadik man is a well of chayim: but violence covers the mouth of the wicked.

12 Hatred stirs up strifes: but love cover all sins.

13 In the lips of him that has binah chochmah is found: but a rod is for the back of him that is void of binah.

14 Wise men lay up da'at: but the mouth of the foolish is near destruction.

15 The rich man's wealth is his strong city: the destruction of the poor is their poverty.

16 The labor of the tzadik is for chayim: the fruit of the wicked to sin.

17 He is already in the halacha of chayim that heeds discipline: but he that refuses correction goes astray.

18 He that hides hatred with lying lips, and he that utters slander, is a fool.

19 In the multitude of words sin is never absent: but he that refrains his lips is wise.

20 The tongue of the tzadik is as choice silver: the lev of the wicked is worth little.

21 The lips of the tzadik feed many: but fools die for want of chochmah.

22 The blessing of יהוה makes rich, and He adds no sorrow with it.

23 It is as sport to a fool to do mischief: but a man of binah has chochmah.

24 The fear of the wicked, it shall come upon him: but the desire of the tzadik shall be granted.

25 As the whirlwind passes, so is the wicked no more: but the tzadik is an everlasting foundation.

26 As vinegar to the teeth, and as smoke to the eyes, so is the lazy one to them that send him.

27 The fear of יהוה prolongs days: but the years of the wicked shall be shortened.

28 The tikvah of the tzadik shall be simcha: but the expectation of the wicked shall perish.

29 The halacha of יהוה is strength to the upright: but destruction shall be to the workers of iniquity.

30 The tzadik shall never be shaken: but the wicked shall not inhabit the earth.

31 The mouth of the tzadik brings forth chochmah: but the perverted tongue shall be cut out.

32 The lips of the tzadik know what is acceptable: but the mouth of the wicked speaks perversities.

11 A false balance is abomination to יהוה: but a tzadik weight is His delight.[1]

2 When pride comes, then comes shame: but with the humble is chochmah.

3 The integrity of the upright shall guide them: but the perverseness of transgressors shall destroy them.

4 Riches profit not in the day of anger: but tzedakah delivers from death.

5 The tzedakah of the perfect shall direct his halacha: but the wicked shall fall by his own wickedness.

6 The tzedakah of the upright shall deliver them: but transgressors shall be taken away by their greed.

7 When a wicked man dies, his expectation shall perish: and the tikvah of unjust men perishes.

8 The tzadik is delivered out of trouble, and the wicked comes to his place.

---

[1] When both houses are treated equally with equal weights and measures, YHWH is delighted.

9 A hypocrite with his mouth destroys his neighbor: but through da'at shall the tzadik be delivered.

10 When it goes well with the tzadik, the city rejoices: and when the wicked perish, there is shouting.

11 By the blessing of the upright the city is exalted: but the mouth of the wicked overthrows it.

12 He that is void of chochmah despises his neighbor: but a man of binah holds his silence.

13 A slanderer reveals secrets: but he that is of a faithful ruach conceals the matter.

14 Where no counsel is, the people fall: but in the multitude of counsels there is safety.

15 He that is guarantor for a stranger shall suffer for it: and he that hates shaking hand in pledge is safe.

16 A gracious woman retains honor: and strong men retain riches.

17 The merciful man does tov to his own being: but he that is cruel troubles his own flesh.

18 The wicked works a deceitful work: but to him that sows tzedakah shall be a sure reward.

19 As tzedakah leads to chayim: so he that pursues evil pursues it to his own death.

20 They that are of a perverted lev are an abomination to יהוה: but such as are upright in their halacha are His delight.

21 Though hand join in hand, the wicked shall not be unpunished: but the seed of the tzadik shall be delivered.

22 As a jewel of gold in a pig's snout, so is a beautiful woman who is without discretion.

23 The desire of the tzadik is only tov: but the expectation of the wicked is anger.

24 There is one that scatters, and yet increases; and there is one that withholds more than is right, but it leads to poverty.

25 The generous being shall be enriched: and he that waters shall be watered also himself.

26 He that withholds corn, the people shall curse him: but blessing shall be upon the head of him that sells it.

27 He that diligently seeks tov obtains unmerited favor: but he that seeks mischief, it shall come to him.

28 He that trusts in his riches shall fall: but the tzadik shall flourish as a branch.

29 He that troubles his own bayit shall inherit the wind: and the fool shall be eved to the wise of lev.

30 The fruit of the tzadik is an eytz chaim; and he that wins beings is wise.[1]

31 Behold, the tzadik shall be repaid in the earth: how much more the wicked and the sinner!

12 Whoever loves discipline loves da'at: but he that hates correction is stupid.

2 A tov man obtains the favor of יהוה: but a man of wicked devices will He condemn.

3 A man shall not be established by wickedness: but the root of the tzadik shall not be moved.

4 A virtuous woman is a keter to her husband: but she that makes him ashamed is as rottenness in his bones.

5 The thoughts of the tzadik are right: but the counsels of the wicked are deceit.

6 The words of the wicked are to lie in wait for dom: but the mouth of the upright shall deliver them.

7 The wicked are overthrown, and are no more: but the bayit of the tzadik shall stand.

8 A man shall be commended according to his chochmah: but he that is of a perverse lev shall be despised.

9 He that is despised, and has an eved, is better than he that honors himself, and lacks lechem.

10 A tzadik man regards the chayim of his beast: but the compassion of the wicked is cruel.

11 He that tills his land shall be satisfied with lechem: but he that follows vain pursuits is void of binah.

---

[1] Soul-winning is a Hebraic mandate, not a Christian invention. True Hebraic understanding is evangelistic-minded.

12 The wicked desires the net of evil men: but the root of the tzadik yields fruit.

13 The wicked is trapped by the transgression of his lips: but the tzadik shall come out of trouble.

14 A man shall be satisfied with tov by the fruit of his mouth: and the reward of a man's hands shall be given back to him.

15 The halacha of a fool is right in his own eyes: but he that listens to counsel is wise.

16 A fool's anger is presently known: but a clever man covers shame.

17 He that speaks emet shows forth tzedakah: but a false witness deceit.

18 Rash speaking is like the piercing of a sword: but the tongue of the wise is health.

19 The lip of emet shall be established le-olam-va-ed: but a lying tongue is but for a moment.

20 Deceit is in the lev of them that imagine evil: but the counselors of shalom, have simcha.

21 There shall no evil happen to the tzadik: but the wicked shall be filled with mischief.

22 Lying lips are an abomination to יהוה: but they that deal truly are His delight.

23 A clever man conceals da'at: but the lev of fools proclaims foolishness.

24 The hand of the diligent shall bear rule: but the lazy shall be under compulsory labor.

25 Heaviness in the lev of man makes him depressed: but a tov word makes it have simcha.

26 The tzadik is more excellent than his neighbor: but the halacha of the wicked seduces them.

27 The lazy man roasts not that which he took in hunting: but the possessions of a diligent man are precious.

28 In the halacha of tzedakah is chayim; and in that pathway there is no death.

13 A wise son hears his abba's discipline: but a scorner hears not rebuke.

2 A man shall eat tov by the fruit of his mouth: but the being of the transgressors shall eat violence.

3 He that guards his mouth guards his chayim: but he that opens wide his lips shall have destruction.

4 The being of the lazy one desires, and has nothing: but the being of the diligent shall be made rich.

5 A tzadik man hates lying: but a wicked man is loathsome, and comes to shame.

6 Righteousness guards him that is upright in the halacha: but wickedness overthrows the sinner.

7 There is one that makes himself rich, yet has nothing: there is one that makes himself poor, yet has great riches.

8 The ransom of a man's chayim are his riches: but the poor hears not rebuke.

9 The light of the tzadik has gilah: but the lamp of the wicked shall be put out.

10 By pride comes only contention: but chochmah is with those who take advice.

11 Wealth gotten by vanity shall be diminished: but he that gathers by labor shall increase.

12 Hope deferred makes the lev sick: but when the desire comes, it is an eytz chaim.

13 He who despises the word shall be destroyed: but he that fears the commandment shall be rewarded.

14 The Torah of the wise is a fountain of chayim, to depart from the traps of death.

15 Tov binah gives favor: but the halacha of transgressors is hard.

16 Every clever man deals with da'at: but a fool lays open his folly.

17 A wicked messenger falls into mischief: but a faithful ambassador is a healing.

18 Poverty and shame shall be to him that refuses discipline: but he that regards correction shall be honored.

19 The desire accomplished is sweet to the being: but it is abomination to fools to depart from evil.

20 He that has his halacha with wise men shall be wise: but a companion of fools shall be destroyed.

21 Evil pursues sinners: but to the tzadik tov shall be repaid.

22 A tov man leaves an inheritance to his children's children: and

the wealth of the sinner is laid up for the tzadik.

23 Much food is in the tillable ground of the poor: but lack of mishpat sweeps it away.

24 He that spares his rod hates his son: but he that loves him chastens him diligently.

25 The tzadik eats to the satisfying of his being: but the belly of the wicked shall have lack.

14 Every wise woman builds her bayit: but the foolish breaks it down with her hands.

2 He that has halacha in his uprightness fears הוהי: but he that is perverse in his halachot despises Him.

3 In the mouth of the foolish is a rod of pride: but the lips of the wise shall preserve them.

4 Where no oxen are, the crib is clean: but much increase comes from the strength of the ox.

5 A faithful witness will not lie: but a false witness will utter lies.

6 A scorner seeks chochmah, and finds it not: but da'at is easy to him that understands.

7 Go from the presence of a foolish man, when you perceive not in him the lips of da'at.

8 The chochmah of the clever is to understand His halacha: but the folly of fools is deceit.

9 Fools make a mockery of sin: but among the tzadik there is favor.

10 The lev knows its own bitterness; and a stranger does not share its simcha.

11 The bayit of the wicked shall be overthrown: but the sukkah of the upright shall flourish.[1]

12 There is a halacha that seems right to a man, but the ends of it are the halachot of death.[2]

13 Even in laughter the lev is in pain; and the end of that simcha is heaviness.

14 The backslider in lev shall be filled with his own halachot: but a tov man shall be satisfied from within.

15 The simple believes every word: but the clever man looks carefully at all his steps.

16 A wise man fears, and departs from evil: but the fool rages, and is confident.

17 He that is quick to be angry deals foolishly: and a man of wicked devices is hated.

18 The simple inherit folly: but the clever are crowned with da'at.

19 The evil man bows before the tov; and the wicked man at the gates of the tzadik.

20 The poor is hated even by his own neighbor: but the rich has many friends.

21 He that despises his neighbor sins: but he that has rachamim on the poor is blessed.

22 Do they not go astray that devise evil? But rachamim and emet shall be for them that devise tov.

23 In all labor there is profit: but the talk of the lips leads only to poverty.

24 The keter of the wise is their riches: but the foolishness of fools is folly.

25 A true witness delivers beings: but a deceitful witness speaks lies.

26 In the fear of הוהי is strong confidence: and His children in Yisrael shall have a place of refuge.

27 The fear of הוהי is a fountain of chayim, to depart from the traps of death.

28 In the multitude of people is the melech's honor:[3] but in the lack of people is the destruction of the prince.

29 He that is slow to anger is of great binah: but he that is hasty of ruach exalts folly.

30 A sound lev is the chayim of the flesh: but jealousy the rottenness of the bones.

31 He that oppresses the poor reproaches His Maker: but he that honors Him has rachamim on the poor.

32 The wicked is taken away in his wickedness: but the tzadik has tikvah in his death.

---

[1] A reference to redeemed Yisrael.
[2] Religion versus relationship with YHWH through Yahshua and His Torah.

[3] The multitudes of Yisrael are an honor and testimony to the covenant-keeping power of the King Yahshua.

33 Wisdom rests in the lev of him that has binah: but that which is in the midst of fools is made known.

34 Righteousness exalts a nation: but sin is a reproach to any people.

35 The melech's favor is toward a wise eved: but his anger is against him that causes shame.[1]

15 A soft answer turns away anger: but harsh words stir up anger.

2 The tongue of the wise uses da'at right: but the mouth of fools pours out foolishness.

3 The eyes of יהוה are in every place, beholding the evil and the tov.

4 A wholesome tongue is an eytz chaim: but perverseness of tongue crushes the ruach.

5 A fool despises his abba's discipline: but he that regards correction is clever.

6 In the bayit of the tzadik is much treasure: but the income of the wicked is trouble.

7 The lips of the wise disperse da'at: but the lev of the foolish does not do so.

8 The sacrifice of the wicked is an abomination to יהוה: but the tefillah of the upright is His delight.

9 The halacha of the wicked is an abomination to יהוה: but He loves him that follows after tzedakah.

10 Correction will be harsh to him that forsakes the halacha: and he that hates correction shall die.

11 The grave and destruction are before יהוה: how much more the levim of the children of Yisrael and of men?

12 A scorner loves not one that reproves him: neither will he go to the wise.

13 A lev of simcha makes a cheerful face: but by sorrow of the lev the ruach is crushed.

14 The lev of him that has binah seeks da'at: but the mouth of fools feeds on foolishness.

15 All the days of the afflicted are evil: but he that has a lev of simcha has a continual moed.

16 Better is little with the fear of יהוה than great treasure with trouble.

17 Better is a dinner of herbs where love is, than a fatted calf where hatred is.

18 An angry man stirs up strife: but he that is slow to anger appeases strife.

19 The halacha of the lazy man is as a hedge of thorns: but the halacha of the tzadik is a highway.

20 A wise son makes an abba have gilah: but a foolish man despises his ima.

21 Folly is simcha to him that is destitute of chochmah: but a man of binah has halacha uprightly.

22 Without counsel purposes are disappointed: but in the multitude of counselors they are established.

23 A man has simcha by the answer of his mouth: and a word spoken in due season, how tov is it!

24 The halacha of chayim leads upward to the wise that he may depart from the grave beneath.

25 יהוה will destroy the bayit of the proud: but He will establish the border of the widow.

26 The thoughts of the wicked are an abomination to יהוה: but the words of the pure are pleasant words.

27 He that is greedy of unjust gain troubles his own bayit; but he that hates bribes shall live.

28 The lev of the tzadik studies how to answer: but the mouth of the wicked pours out evil things.

29 יהוה is far from the wicked: but He hears the tefillah of the tzadik.

30 The light of the eyes brings gilah in the lev: and a tov report gives marrow to the bones.

31 The ear that hears the correction of chayim stays among the wise.

32 He that refuses discipline despises his own being: but he that hears correction gets binah.

---

[1] Yisraeltes should be careful never to bring shame to King Yahshua by their behavior and lifestyle.

33 The fear of יהוה is the discipline of chochmah; and before honor is humility.

16 The preparations of the lev in man, and the answer of the tongue, is from יהוה.

2 All the halachot of a man are clean in his own eyes; but יהוה weighs the spirits.

3 Commit your mitzvot to יהוה, and your thoughts shall be established.

4 יהוה has made all things for Himself: yes, even the wicked for the day of evil.

5 Everyone that is proud in lev is an abomination to יהוה: though evil joins in hand with others, it shall not be unpunished.

6 By rachamim and emet iniquity is purged: and by the fear of יהוה men depart from evil.

7 When a man's halachot please יהוה, He makes even his enemies to be at shalom with him.

8 Better is a little with tzedakah than great income without right.

9 A man's lev plans his own halacha: but יהוה directs his steps.

10 An oath is on the lips of the melech: his mouth transgresses not in mishpat.

11 A tzadik weight and balance are יהוה's: all the weights of the bag are His work.[1]

12 It is an abomination for melechim to commit wickedness: for the throne is established by tzedakah.

13 Righteous lips are the delight of melechim; and they love him that speaks what is right.

14 The anger of a melech is as a messenger of death: but a wise man will pacify it.

15 In the light of the melech's face is chayim; and his favor is as a cloud of the latter malchut rain.

16 How much better is it to get chochmah than gold! And to get binah rather than to chose silver!

17 The highway of the upright is to depart from evil: he that guards His halacha preserves his being.

18 Pride goes before destruction, and a haughty ruach before a fall.

19 Better it is to be of a humble ruach with the humble, than to divide the spoil with the proud.

20 He that handles a matter wisely shall find tov: and whoever trusts in יהוה, happy is he.

21 The wise in lev shall be called clever: and the sweetness of the lips increases learning.

22 Understanding is a wellspring of chayim to him that has it: but the discipline of fools is folly.

23 The lev of the wise teaches his mouth, and adds learning to his lips.

24 Pleasant words are as a honeycomb, sweet to the being, and health to the bones.

25 There is a halacha that seems right to a man, but the ends of it are the halachot of death.

26 He that labors; labors for himself; for his mouth drives him on.

27 A worthless man digs up evil: and in his lips there is as a burning fire.

28 A perverted man sows strife: and a whisperer separates best friends.

29 A violent man entices his neighbor, and leads him into the halacha that is not tov.

30 He shuts his eyes to devise perverted things: moving his lips he brings evil to pass.

31 The gray hair is a keter of tiferet, if it be found in the halacha of tzedakah.

32 He that is slow to anger is better than the mighty; and he that rules over his ruach than he that takes a city.

33 The lot is cast into the lap; but every decision by it is of יהוה.

17 Better is a dry morsel of lechem, with rest, than a bayit full of offerings with strife.

2 A wise eved shall have rule over a son that causes shame, and shall have part of the inheritance among the brothers.

3 The refining pot is for silver, and the furnace for gold: but יהוה tries the levim.

---

[1] All Yisraelites are His work and we are equal in His sight.

4 An evil-doer gives heed to false lips; and a liar gives ear to a nasty tongue.

5 Whoever mocks the poor reproaches His Maker: and he that has gilah at calamities shall not be unpunished.

6 Grandchildren are the keter of old men; and the tiferet of the children in Yisrael are their ahvot.

7 Excellent speech does not fit a fool: much less do lying lips befit a prince.

8 A bribe is as a precious stone in the eyes of its owner: wherever it turns, it prospers for him.

9 He that covers a transgression seeks love; but he that repeats a matter separates friends.

10 A correction enters more into a wise man than an hundred stripes into a fool.

11 An evil man seeks only rebellion: therefore a cruel messenger shall be sent against him.

12 Let a bereaved bear meet a man, rather than a fool in his folly.

13 Whoever rewards evil for tov, evil shall not depart from his bayit.

14 The beginning of strife is like the releasing of mayim: therefore stop a fight before it breaks forth.

15 He that justifies the wicked, and he that condemns the tzadik, both are abominations to יהוה.

16 What tov is wealth in the hands of a fool who has no desire to get chochmah?

17 A friend loves at all times, and a brother is born for adversity.[1]

18 A man void of binah shakes hands in a pledge, and becomes a guarantor in the presence of his friend.

19 He loves transgression that loves strife: and he that exalts his gate seeks destruction.

20 He that has a perverted lev finds no tov: and he that has a perverse tongue falls into mischief.

21 He that brings forth a fool does it to his sorrow: and the abba of a fool has no simcha.

22 A lev of simcha does tov like medicine: but a broken ruach dries the bones.

23 A wicked man takes a bribe behind the back to pervert the halachot of mishpat.

24 Wisdom is before him that has binah; but the eyes of a fool are in the ends of the earth.

25 A foolish son is a grief to his abba, and bitterness to her that bore him.

26 Also to punish the tzadik is not tov, nor to smite leaders for speaking emet.

27 He that has da'at spares his words: and a man of binah is of an excellent ruach.

28 Even a fool, when he holds his shalom, is counted as wise: and he that shuts his lips is regarded as a man of binah.

18 The inactive separatist seeks his own desire; he breaks out against all sound chochmah.[2]

2 A fool has no delight in binah, but only in revealing his lev.

3 When the wicked man comes, then comes also shame, disfavor and iniquity.

4 The words of a man's mouth are as deep waters, and the wellspring of chochmah as a flowing brook.

5 It is not tov to accept the person of the wicked, to overthrow the tzadik in mishpat.

6 A fool's lips enter into contention, and his mouth calls for blows.

7 A fool's mouth is his destruction, and his lips are the trap of his being.

8 The words of a slanderer are as wounds, and they go down into the innermost parts of the belly.

9 He also that is lazy in his work is brother to him that is a great waster.

10 The Name of יהוה is a strong tower: the tzadik runs into it, and is safe.[3]

11 The rich man's wealth is his strong city, like a high wall in his own conceit.

12 Before destruction the lev of man is haughty, and before honor is humility.

---

[1] A believing Yisraelite brother.

[2] The separate entity called the "church" has forsaken the Commonwealth of Yisrael and her Torah, and thus has left all true wisdom behind. They have sought their own desire, not YHWH's.

[3] By clear directive, those who don't know and don't use it are not safe.

13 He that answers a matter before he hears it, it is folly and shame to him.

14 The ruach of a man will sustain his infirmity; but a crushed ruach who can bear?

15 The lev of the clever gets da'at; and the ear of the wise seeks da'at.

16 A man's gift makes room for him, and brings him before great men.

17 He that is first in his own cause seems tzadik; until another comes and examines him.

18 The lot causes contentions to cease, and separates between the mighty.

19 A brother offended is harder to be won than a strong city:[1] and contentions are like the bars of a castle.

20 A man's belly shall be satisfied with the fruit of his mouth; and with the increase of his lips shall he be filled.

21 Death and chayim are in the power of the tongue: and they that love it shall eat the fruit of it.

22 Whoever finds a wife finds a tov thing, and obtains favor from יהוה.

23 The poor beseeches; but the rich answers roughly.

24 A man that has friends must show himself friendly: and there is a friend that sticks closer than a brother.[2]

19

Better is the poor that has a halacha of integrity, than he that is perverse in his lips, and is a fool.

2 Also, desire without da'at, it is not tov; and he that rushes in with his feet sins.

3 The foolishness of man perverts his halacha: and his lev is angry against יהוה.

4 Wealth makes many friends; but the poor is separated from his neighbor.

5 A false witness shall not be unpunished, and he that speaks lies shall not escape.

6 Many will entreat the favor of the prince: and every man is a friend to him that gives bribes.

7 All the brothers of the poor do hate him: how much more do his friends go far from him? He pursues them with words, yet they are gone.

8 He that gets chochmah loves his own being: he that guards binah shall find tov.

9 A false witness shall not be unpunished, and he that speaks lies shall perish.

10 Luxury is not fitting for a fool; much less for an eved to have rule over rulers.

11 The discretion of a man makes him patient; and it is to his tiferet to overlook a transgression.

12 The melech's anger is as the roaring of a lion; but his favor is as dew upon the grass.

13 A foolish son is the calamity of his abba:[3] and the contentions of a wife are like continual drippings through the roof.

14 House and riches are the inheritance of ahvot and a clever wife is from יהוה.

15 Laziness casts one into a deep sleep; and an idle being shall suffer hunger.

16 He that guards the commandment[4] guards his own being; but he that despises His halachot shall die.

17 He that has pity upon the poor lends to יהוה; and that which he has given will be repaid to him again.

18 Discipline your son while there is tikvah, and let not your being spare him tzadik because of his crying.

19 A man of great anger shall suffer punishment: for if you deliver him, you will have to do so again.

20 Shema to counsel, and receive discipline, that you may be wise in your latter end.

21 There are many plans in a man's lev; nevertheless the counsel of יהוה shall stand.

22 What is desirable in a man is his chesed: and a poor man is better than a liar.

23 The fear of יהוה leads to chayim: and he that has it shall stay satisfied; he shall not be visited with evil.

24 A lazy man hides his hand in his bosom, and will not so much as bring it to his

---

[1] Yisraelite brothers must work had to be reconciled to those they are at odds with. Without miracles, reconciliation is often impossible.
[2] Yahshua our Savior.

[3] Yisrael as YHWH's son has often brought Abba calamity.
[4] Torah.

mouth again.

25 Beat a scorner, and the simple will beware: and reprove one that has binah, and he will understand da'at.

26 He that plunders his abba, and chases away his ima, is a son that causes shame, and brings reproach.

27 Cease, My son Yisrael, to shema the discipline that causes you to go astray from the words of da'at.

28 A worthless witness despises mishpat: and the mouth of the wicked devours iniquity.

29 Judgments are in store for scorners, and stripes for the back of fools.

20 Wine is a mocker, strong drink is a brawler: and whosoever is deceived by it is not wise.

2 The fear of a melech is as the roaring of a lion: whoever provokes Him to anger sins against his own being.

3 It is an honor for a man to cease from strife: but every fool will be meddling.

4 The lazy one will not plow by reason of the cold; therefore shall he beg in harvest, and have nothing.

5 Counsel in the lev of man is like deep mayim; but a man of binah will draw it out.

6 Most men will proclaim every one his own virtues: but a faithful man who can find?

7 The tzadik man has a halacha in his own integrity: his children in Yisrael are blessed after him.

8 A melech that sits on the throne of mishpat scatters away all evil with his eyes.

9 Who can say, I have made my lev clean, I am pure from my sin?

10 Different weights, and different measures, both of them are an abomination to יהוה.[1]

11 Even a child is known by his doings, whether his work is pure, or whether it is right.

12 The hearing ear, and the seeing eye, יהוה has made both of them.

13 Love not sleep, lest you come to poverty; open your eyes, and you shall be satisfied with lechem.

14 It is nothing, it is nothing, says the buyer: but when he is gone, then he boasts.

15 There is gold, and a multitude of rubies: but the lips of da'at are a precious jewel.

16 Take his garment that is guarantor for a stranger: and take it as a pledge when it is for foreigners.

17 Bread gained by deceit is sweet to a man; but afterwards his mouth shall be filled with gravel.

18 Every purpose is established by counsel: and with tov advice war can be waged.

19 He that goes about as a slanderer reveals secrets: therefore do not associate with him that flatters with his lips.

20 Whoever curses his abba or his ima, his lamp shall be put out in obscure darkness.

21 An inheritance may be gotten with quick greed at the beginning; but the end of it shall not be blessed.

22 Do not say, I will repay the evil; but wait on יהוה, and He shall save you.

23 Divers weights are an abomination to יהוה; and a false balance is not tov.

24 Man's steps are from יהוה; what then does a man understand about his own halacha?

25 It is a trap to the man who devours that which is set-apart, and afterwards vows to make inquiry.

26 A wise melech scatters the wicked, and turns the wheel over them.

27 The ruach of man is the lamp of יהוה, searching all the inward parts of the belly.

28 Chesed and emet preserve the melech: and his throne is upheld by rachamim.

29 The tiferet of young men is their strength: and the tiferet of old men is their gray head.

30 The wounds of a blow clean away evil: so do stripes to the inward parts of the lev.

---

[1] Both houses of Yisrael are to use the same weights and measures when measuring such things as paganism and human traditions needing to be exposed. We cannot demand that one house be submitted or subservient to another in the restoration. Both houses have much to let go of, and much to learn from one another, as we walk together back to Tzion.

21

The melech's lev is in the hand of יהוה, as with the rivers of mayim: He turns it wherever He desires.

2 Every halacha of a man is right in his own eyes: but יהוה ponders the levim.

3 To do tzedakah and mishpat is more acceptable to יהוה than sacrifice.

4 A high look, and a proud lev, and the work of the wicked, is sin.

5 The thoughts of the diligent lead only to plenty; but the rash haste only to lack.

6 The getting of treasures by a lying tongue is a vanity tossed to and fro by those that seek death.

7 The spoil of the wicked shall destroy them; because they refuse to do mishpat.

8 The halacha of a guilty man is perverted and strange: but as for the pure, his work is right.

9 It is better to dwell in a corner of the housetop, than with a brawling woman in a wide bayit.

10 The being of the wicked desires evil: his neighbor finds no favor in his eyes.

11 When the scorner is punished, the simple is made wise: and when the wise is instructed, he receives da'at.

12 The tzadik man wisely considers the bayit of the wicked: but Elohim overthrows the wicked for their wickedness.

13 Whoever shuts his ears at the call of the poor, he also shall call himself, but shall not be heard.

14 A bribe in secret pacifies anger: and a bribe in the bosom strong anger.

15 It is simcha to the tzadik to do mishpat: but destruction shall be to the workers of iniquity.

16 The man that wanders out of the halacha of binah[1] shall remain in the congregation of the dead.[2]

17 He that loves pleasure shall be a poor man: he that loves wine and oil shall not be rich.

18 The wicked shall be a ransom for the tzadik, and the transgressor for the upright.

19 It is better to dwell in the wilderness, than with a contentious and angry woman.

20 There is treasure to be desired and oil in the dwelling of the wise; but a foolish man swallows it up.

21 He that follows after tzedakah and rachamim finds chayim, tzedakah, and honor.

22 A wise man climbs the city of the mighty, and casts down the strength of its confidence.

23 Whoever guards his mouth and his tongue guards his being from troubles.

24 The proud and haughty, Scorner is his name, who deals in proud anger.

25 The desire of the lazy kills him; for his hands refuse to labor.

26 He covets with greed all the day long: but the tzadik gives and spares not.

27 The sacrifice of the wicked is an abomination: how much more, when he brings it with a wicked mind?

28 A false witness shall perish: but the man that hears and obeys speaks emet.

29 A wicked man hardens his face: but as for the upright, he is established in his halacha.

30 There is no chochmah or binah or counsel that can stand against יהוה.

31 The horse is prepared for the day of battle: but true safety is of יהוה.

22

A tov name is rather to be chosen than great riches, and loving favor rather than silver and gold.

2 The rich and poor meet together:[3] יהוה is the Maker of them all.

3 A clever man foresees the evil, and hides himself: but the simple pass on, and are punished.

4 By humility and the fear of יהוה are riches, and honor, and chayim.

5 Thorns and traps are in the halacha of the perverted: he that guards his being shall be far from them.

---

[1] Or back to familiar yet incorrect systems and places of worship.

[2] Religious assemblies that have vain doctrines substituted for Torah, or those that have Torah, but not the King and Giver of Torah, the Moshiach Yahshua. YHWH calls them the assemblies of the dead.

[3] In Yisraelite brotherhood.

6 Train up a child in the halacha he should go: and when he is old, he will not depart from it.[1]

7 The rich rules over the poor, and the borrower is eved to the lender.

8 He that sows iniquity shall reap vanity: and the rod of his anger perishes.

9 He that has a tov generous eye shall be blessed; for he gives of his lechem to the poor.

10 Cast out the scorner, and contention shall go out; yes, strife and reproach shall cease.[2]

11 He that loves pureness of lev, whose speech is clean, the melech shall be his friend.

12 The eyes of יהוה preserve da'at, and He overthrows the words of the transgressor.

13 The lazy man says, There is a lion outside, I shall be slain in the streets.

14 The mouth of strange women is a deep pit: he that is denounced by יהוה shall fall in it.

15 Foolishness resides in the lev of a child; but the rod of correction shall drive it far from him.

16 He that oppresses the poor to increase his own riches, and he that gives to the rich, shall surely come to poverty.

17 Bow down your ear, and shema the words of the wise, and apply your lev to My da'at.

18 For it is a pleasant thing if you guard them inside you; they shall all be ready on your lips.

19 That your trust may be in יהוה, I have caused you to know these things today, even to you.

20 Have not I written to you excellent things in counsel and da'at,

21 That I might make you know the certainty of the words of emet; that you might answer with words of emet to them that are sent to you?

22 Rob not the poor, because he is poor: neither oppress the afflicted in the gate:

23 For יהוה will plead their cause, and plunder the being of those that plundered them.

24 Make no friendship with an angry man; and with a furious man you shall not go:

25 Lest you learn his halachot, and get yourself trapped.

26 Be not one of them that shakes hands, or of those that are guarantors for debts.

27 If you have nothing to pay, why should they take away your bed from under you?

28 Remove not the ancient landmark, which your ahvot have set.[3]

29 Do you see a man diligent in his business? He shall stand before melechim; he shall not stand before the obscure.

23 When you sit to eat with a ruler, consider diligently what is before you:

2 And put a knife to your throat, if you are a man given to appetite.

3 Do not desire his delicacies: for they are deceitful food.

4 Labor not to be rich: cease from your own chochmah.

5 Will you set your eyes upon that which is nothing? For riches certainly make themselves wings; they fly away as an eagle towards the shamayim.

6 Eat not the lechem of him that has an evil eye,[4] neither desire his food delicacies:

7 For as he thinks in his lev, so is he: Eat and drink, he says to you; but his lev is not with you.

8 The piece which you have eaten shall you vomit up, and lose your sweet words.

9 Speak not in the ears of a fool: for he will despise the chochmah of your words.

10 Remove not the old landmark; and enter not into the fields of the fatherless:

11 For their Redeemer is mighty; He shall plead their cause with you.

---

[1] All Yisraelite parents must teach the halacha of Yahshua and His Torah to their offspring, in order to counted as faithful parents by YHWH, and to train Yisrael's next believing generation.
[2] Disobedient, mocking, and sinful Yisraelites, must be put outside the camp for division and strife to cease.

[3] Yisrael must return to the ancient paths, not seek new gentile ones by removing the ancient truths.
[4] Is cheap.

12 Apply your lev to discipline, and your ears to the words of da'at.

13 Withhold not correction from the child: for if you correct him with the rod, he shall not die.

14 You shall correct him with the rod, and shall deliver his being from the grave.

15 My son, if your lev is wise, My lev shall gilah, even I.

16 Yes, My kidneys shall gilah, when your lips speak right things.

17 Let not your lev be jealousy of sinners: but be in the fear of יהוה all day long.

18 For surely there is an end to all things; and your expectation shall not be cut off.

19 Shema, My son, and be wise, and guide your lev in the halacha.

20 Be not among heavy drinkers; among gluttonous eaters of meat:

21 For the drunkard and the glutton shall come to poverty: and slumber shall clothe a man with rags.

22 Shema to your abba that brought you forth and do not despise your ima when she is old.

23 Buy the emet, and sell it not; also chochmah, and discipline, and binah.

24 The abba of the tzadik shall greatly gilah: and he that brings forth a wise child shall have simcha from him.

25 Your abba and your ima shall be in simcha, and she that bore you shall gilah.

26 My son, give me your lev, and let your eyes observe My halachot.

27 For a whore is like a deep ditch; and a strange woman is a narrow pit.

28 She also lies in wait as for a prey, and increases the transgressors among the men of Yisrael.

29 Who has woe? Who has sorrow? Who has contentions? Who has complaints? Who has wounds without cause? Who has redness of eyes?

30 They that stay long drinking wine; they that go to seek mixed wine.

31 Look not upon the wine when it is red, when it gives its color in the cup, when it flows smoothly.

32 In the end it bites like a serpent, and stings like an adder.

33 When your eyes shall behold strange women, your lev shall utter perverse things.

34 Yes, you shall be as he that lies down in the midst of the sea, or as he that lies upon the top of a mast.

35 They have smote me, and I was not sick; they have beaten me, and I felt it not: when I shall awake, I will seek it yet again.

24 Be not envious of evil men, neither desire to be with them.

2 For their lev studies destruction, and their lips talk of mischief.

3 Through chochmah is the bayit built; and by binah it is established:[1]

4 And by da'at shall the rooms be filled with all precious and pleasant riches.

5 A wise man is strong; yes, a man of da'at increases strength.

6 For by wise counsel you shall make war: and in a multitude of counselors there is safety.

7 Wisdom is too high for a fool: he opens not his mouth in the gate.

8 He that plans to do evil shall be called a mischievous person.

9 The purpose of foolishness is sin: and the scorner is an abomination to men.

10 If you faint in the day of adversity, your strength is small.

11 Deliver them that are drawn to death, and redeem those that are ready to be slain;[2]

12 If you say, Behold, we did not know; does not He that ponders the lev consider it? And He that guards your being, does He not know it? And shall not He repay to every man according to his works?

13 My son, eat honey, because it is tov; and the honeycomb, which is sweet to your taste:

14 So shall the da'at of chochmah be to your being: when you have found it, then there shall be a reward, and your expectation shall not be cut off.

---

[1] All three pillars of Elohim will rebuild Yisrael: **Chochma, binah** and the Son of Yah **Tiferet.**

[2] Yisrael is to evangelize without regret, remorse, or guilt.

15 Lay not in wait, O wicked man, against the dwelling of the tzadik; spoil not his resting place:

16 For a tzadik man falls seven times, and rises up again: but the wicked shall fall into mischief.

17 Rejoice not when your enemy falls, and let not your lev be in simcha when he stumbles:

18 Lest יהוה see it, and it displeases Him, and He turn away His anger from him.

19 Do not concern yourself because of evil men, neither be envious of the wicked;

20 For there shall be no reward to the evil man; the lamp of the wicked shall be put out.

21 My son, fear יהוה and the melech: and meddle not with them that are given to change:

22 For their calamity shall rise suddenly; and who knows the ruin of them both?

23 These things also belong to the wise. It is not tov to show partiality in mishpat.

24 He that says to the wicked, You are tzadik; the people shall curse, nations shall abhor him:

25 But to them that rebuke him shall be delight, and a tov blessing shall come upon them.

26 Every man shall kiss his lips[1] when a mishpat is given in answer.

27 Prepare your work outside, and make it fit for yourself in the field; and afterwards build your bayit.

28 Be not a witness against your neighbor without a cause; and deceive not with your lips.

29 Do not say, I will do to him as he has done to me: I will render to the man according to his work.

30 I went by the field of the lazy, and by the vineyard of the man without binah;

31 And, see, it was all grown over with thorns, and nettles had covered the face of it, and its stone wall was broken down.

32 Then I saw, and considered it well: I looked at it, and received discipline.

33 Yet a little sleep, a little slumber, a little folding of the hands to sleep:

34 So shall your poverty come suddenly; and your lack as a runner.

25 These are also Mishle of Shlomo, which the men of Hizqiyahu melech of Yahudah copied.

2 It is the tiferet of Elohim to conceal a matter: but the honor of melechim is to search out a matter.

3 The shamayim for height, and the earth for depth, and the lev of melechim is unsearchable.

4 Take away the dross from the silver, and there shall come forth a vessel from the refiner.

5 Take away the wicked from before the melech, and his throne shall be established in tzedakah.

6 Do not exalt yourself in the presence of the melech, and stand not in the place of great men:

7 For better if it is said concerning you, Come up here; than that you should be removed from the presence of the prince whom your eyes have seen.

8 Do not rush to strive, lest you know not what to do in the end, when your neighbor has put you to shame.

9 Debate your cause with your neighbor himself; and do not disclose a secret to another:

10 Lest he that hears it puts you to shame, and your bad reputation never leaves.

11 A word spoken at the right time is like apples of gold in settings of silver.

12 As an earring of gold, and an ornament of fine gold, so is a wise one's reproof to an obedient ear.

13 As the cold of snow in the time of harvest, so is a faithful messenger to those that send him: for he refreshes the being of his masters.

14 Whoever boasts about his gifts falsely, is like clouds and wind without rain.

15 By patience is a prince persuaded, and a soft tongue breaks the bone.

---

[1] Esteem.

16 Have you found honey? Eat only as much as you need, lest you be satisfied and vomit it.

17 Do not visit your neighbor's bayit often; lest he become weary of you, and then hate you.

18 A man that bears false witness against his neighbor is like a club, and a sword, and a sharp arrow.

19 Confidence in an unfaithful man in time of trouble is like a broken tooth, and a foot out of joint.

20 As he that takes away a garment in cold weather, and as vinegar on soda, so is he that sings songs to a heavy lev.

21 If your enemy is hungry, give him lechem to eat; and if he is thirsty, give him mayim to drink:

22 For you shall heap coals of fire upon his head, and יהוה shall reward you.

23 The north wind drives away rain: and a backbiting tongue angry looks.

24 It is better to dwell in the corner of the housetop, than with a brawling woman in a wide bayit.

25 Like cold mayim to a thirsty being, so is tov news from a far country.

26 A tzadik man giving into the path of the wicked is as a troubled fountain, and a corrupt spring.

27 It is not tov to eat much honey: or for men to search for tiferet after tiferet.

28 He that has no rule over his own ruach is like a city that is broken down without walls.

26 As snow in summer, and as rain in harvest, so honor is not fitting for a fool.

2 As the bird by wandering, as the swallow by flying, so a curse without cause shall not come.

3 A whip for the horse, a bridle for the donkey, and a rod for the fool's back.

4 Answer not a fool according to his folly, lest you also be like him.

5 Answer a fool according to your chochma, lest he think himself wise in his own conceit.

6 He that sends a message by the hand of a fool cuts off feet, and drinks damage.

7 The legs of the lame are not equal: so is a parable in the mouth of fools.[1]

8 As he that binds a stone in a sling, so is he that gives honor to a fool.

9 As a thorn goes up into the hand of a drunkard, so is a parable in the mouth of fools.[2]

10 The great Elohim that formed all things both rewards the fool, and rewards transgressors.

11 As a dog returns to his vomit, so a fool returns to his folly.[3]

12 Do you see a man wise in his own conceit? There is more tikvah for a fool than for him.

13 The lazy man says, There is a lion in the path; a lion is in the streets.

14 As the door turns upon its hinges, so does the lazy upon his bed.

15 The lazy hides his hand in his bosom; it pains him to bring it again to his mouth.

16 The lazy one is wiser in his own conceit than seven men that can render a reason.

17 He that passes by, and meddles in someone else's strife, is like one that takes a dog by the ears.

18 As a madman, who casts firebrands, arrows, and death,

19 So is the man that deceives his neighbor, and says, I was only joking.

20 Where no wood is, there the fire goes out: so where there is no slanderer, the strife ceases.

21 As coals are to burning coals, and wood to fire; so is a contentious man to kindle strife.

22 The words of a slanderer are as wounds that go down into the innermost parts of the belly.

---

[1] Yahshua's parables are foolish gibberish to the anti-Yahshua missionaries.

[2] See note for verse 7.

[3] This speaks of Yisraelites who know Yahshua and yet succumb to the anti-missionaries, as referenced in Second Kepha 2:22.

23 Burning lips and a wicked lev are like a clay pot covered with silver dross.
24 He that hates pretends with his lips, and lays up deceit within him;
25 When he speaks nice, believe him not: for there are seven abominations in his lev.
26 Hatred is covered by deceit; its wickedness shall be shown before the whole congregation of Yisrael.
27 Whoever digs a pit shall fall in it: and he that rolls a stone, it will return on him.
28 A lying tongue hates its victims; and a flattering mouth works ruin.

27 Boast not about tomorrow; for you know not what a day may bring forth.
2 Let another man praise you, and not your own mouth; a stranger, and not your own lips.
3 A stone is heavy, and the sand weighty; but a fool's anger is heavier than them both.
4 Wrath is cruel, and displeasure is outrageous; but who is able to stand before jealousy?
5 Open rebuke is better than secret love.
6 Faithful are the wounds of a friend; but the kisses of an enemy are deceitful.
7 The satisfied one loathes the honeycomb; but to the hungry being every bitter thing is sweet.
8 As a bird that wanders from her nest, so is a man that wanders from his place.
9 Ointment and perfume gilah the lev: so does the sweetness of a man's counsel given from the lev.
10 Your own friend, and your abba's friend, forsake not; neither go into your brother's bayit in the day of your calamity: for better is a neighbor that is near than a brother far off.
11 My son, be wise, and make My lev in simcha, that I may answer him who reproaches me.
12 A clever man foresees the evil, and hides himself; but the simple pass on, and are punished.

13 He that becomes a guarantor for a stranger, his garment will be taken from him and held as a pledge for another stranger.
14 He that greets his friend with a loud voice early in the morning, it shall be counted as a curse to him.
15 A continual dripping on a very rainy day and a contentious woman are alike.
16 Whoever hides her can hide the wind, and keep the perfume on his right hand from being known.
17 Iron sharpens iron; so a man sharpens the face of his friend.
18 Whoever guards the fig tree[1] shall eat the fruit of it:[2] so he that waits on His Master shall be honored.[3]
19 As in mayim face answers to face, so the lev of man to man.
20 Sheol and destruction are never full; so the eyes of man are never satisfied.
21 As the fining pot for silver, and the furnace for gold; so is a man to his praise.
22 Though you pound a fool in a mortar among wheat with a pestle, yet will not his foolishness depart from him.
23 Be diligent to know the state of your flocks, and look well to your herds.
24 For riches are not le-olam-va-ed: and does the keter endure to every generation?
25 The hay appears, and the tender grass shows itself, and herbs of the mountains are gathered.
26 The lambs are for your clothing, and the goats are the price of the field.
27 And you shall have goats' milk enough for your food, for the food of your household, and for the maintenance of your young women.

---

[1] Symbolic of national Yisrael.
[2] We are called to guard the restoration and regathering of both houses; and if we do, we will eat the full fruit and reward of our labor.
[3] Waits for His return to finish the task of restoring the fig tree.

28

The wicked flee when no man pursues: but the tzadik are bold as a lion.

2 For the transgressions of a land, many are the rulers over it: but by a man of binah and da'at the state of it shall be prolonged.

3 A poor man that oppresses the poor is like a sweeping rain that leaves no food.

4 They that forsake the Torah praise the wicked: but such as guard the Torah contend with them.

5 Evil men understand not mishpat: but they that seek יהוה understand all things.

6 Better is the poor that has halacha in his uprightness, than he that is perverted in his halachot, though he is rich.

7 Whoever guards the Torah is a wise son: but he that is a companion of gluttons shames his abba.

8 He that by interest and unjust gain increases his substance, he shall gather it for others that will pity the poor.

9 He that turns away his ear from hearing the Torah, even his tefillah shall be an abomination.[1]

10 Whoever causes the tzadik to go astray in an evil halacha, he shall fall himself into his own pit: but the upright shall have tov things in possession.

11 The rich man is wise in his own conceit; but the poor that has binah searches him out.

12 When tzadik men are strong, there is great tiferet: but when the wicked rise, the tiferet diminishes.

13 He that covers his sins shall not prosper: but whoever confesses and forsakes them shall have rachamim.

14 Happy is the man that fears Elohim always: but he that hardens his lev shall fall into mischief.

15 As a roaring lion, and a charging bear; so is a wicked ruler over the poor people.

16 The prince that lacks binah is also a great oppressor: but he that hates greed shall prolong his days.

17 A man that does violence to the dom of any person shall flee to the pit; let no man help him.

18 Whoever has upright halacha shall be saved: but he that is perverse in his halachot shall fall at once.

19 He that works his land shall have plenty of lechem: but he that follows after worthless persons shall have great poverty.

20 A faithful man shall abound with blessings: but he that hurries to be rich shall not be innocent.

21 To show partiality with people is not tov: for a piece of lechem a man will transgress.

22 He that runs to be rich has an evil eye, and considers not that poverty shall come upon him.

23 He that rebukes a man shall find more favor than he that flatters with the tongue.

24 Whoever robs his abba or his ima, and says, It is not a transgression; the same is the companion of a destroyer.

25 He that is of a proud lev stirs up strife: but he that puts his trust in יהוה shall be made to prosper.

26 He that trusts in his own lev is a fool: but whoever has wise halacha, he shall be delivered.

27 He that gives to the poor shall not lack: but he that hides his eyes from them shall have many curses.

28 When the wicked rise, men hide themselves: but when they perish, the tzadik increase.

29

He, that being often reproved hardens his neck, shall suddenly be destroyed, without cure.

2 When the tzadik are in authority, the people gilah: but when the wicked bears rule, the people mourn.

3 Whoever loves chochmah brings gilah to his abba: but a companion of harlots destroys wealth.

4 The melech by mishpat establishes the land: but he that receives bribes overthrows it.

---

[1] What does that say for the prayers of those who claim to love Moshiach but don't keep His eternal commands found in Torah?

5 A man that flatters his neighbor spreads a net for his feet.
6 In the transgression of an evil man there is a trap: but the tzadik does sing and gilah.
7 The tzadik considers the cause of the poor: but the wicked desires not to know it.
8 Scornful men bring a city into flames: but wise men turn away anger.
9 If a wise man contends with a foolish man, whether he rages or laughs, there is no shalom.
10 The domthirsty hate the upright: but the tzadik seek his being.
11 A fool utters his entire mind: but a wise man guards it until later.
12 If a ruler listens to lies, all his avadim become wicked.
13 The poor and the oppressor have this in common: יהוה gives light to both their eyes.
14 The melech that faithfully judges the poor, his throne shall be established le-olam-va-ed.
15 The rod and correction give chochmah: but a child left to himself brings his ima to shame.
16 When the wicked are multiplied, transgression increases: but the tzadik shall see their fall.
17 Correct your son, and he shall give you rest and give delight to your being.
18 Where there is no vision, the people perish: but he that guards the Torah, happy is he.[1]
19 An eved will not be corrected by words: for though he understands he will not answer.
20 Do you see a man that is hasty in his words? There is more tikvah for a fool than for him.
21 He that delicately brings up his eved from childhood shall have him become his son in the end.
22 An angry man stirs up strife, and a furious man abounds in transgression.

23 A man's pride shall bring him low: but honor shall uphold the humble in ruach.
24 Whoever is partner with a thief hates his own being: he hears himself put under oath but answers nothing.
25 The fear of man brings a trap: but whoever puts his trust in יהוה shall be safe.
26 Many seek the ruler's favor; but every man's mishpat comes from יהוה.
27 An unjust man is an abomination to the tzadik: and he that is upright in halacha is an abomination to the wicked.

30 The words of Agur the son of Yacheh, even the prophecy: the man spake to Ithi-El, and Uchal,
2 Surely I am more stupid than any man, and have not the binah of a man.
3 I neither learned chochmah, nor have the da'at of the Set-Apart-One.
4 Who has ascended up into the shamayim, or descended? Who has gathered the wind in His fists? Who has bound the waters in a garment? Who has established all the ends of the earth? What is His Name,[2] and what is His Son's Name,[3] if you can tell?[4]
5 Every word of Eloah is pure: He is a shield to them that put their trust in Him.
6 Add not to His words, lest He reprove you, and you be found a liar.[5]
7 Two things have I asked of You; deny me not before I die:
8 Remove far from me vanity and lies: give me neither poverty nor riches; feed me my portion of lechem:
9 Lest I be full, and deny You, and say, Who is יהוה? Or lest I be poor, and steal,

[1] Yisrael in these last days must carry a vision of restoration from YHWH's will and His Word, based on all of the Torah.

[2] YHWH.
[3] Yahshua Ben YHWH.
[4] This is a riddle of the Designer-Creator and His Son the Creator, and most of the world's population does not know either one. Most believe them to be g-d and je-us; when the true Names of YHWH and Yahshua remain unknown to the minds and hearts of mankind. What was a riddle in Solomon's time; is just as much of a riddle in our time. Yet knowing this is the key to being a child of the coming resurrection.
[5] This does not speak of translations where men are bound to attempt to explain or elaborate in all translations and all languages. YHWH speaks to those who would dare to alter the original autograph manuscripts.

and take the Name of **יהוה** My Elohim in vain.[1]

10 Accuse not an eved to his master, lest he curse you, and you be found guilty.

11 There is a generation that curses their abba, and does not bless their ima.

12 There is a generation that is pure in their own eyes, and yet is not washed from their filthiness.

13 There is a generation, O how haughty are their eyes! And their eyelids are lifted up.

14 There is a generation, whose teeth are as swords, and their jaw-teeth as knives, to devour the poor from off the earth, and the needy from among men.

15 The leech has two daughters, crying, Give me, give me.[2] There are three things that are never satisfied, yes, four things that never say, It is enough:

16 The grave; and the barren womb; the soil that is not filled with mayim; and the fire which never says, It is enough.

17 The eye that mocks his abba, and despises to obey his ima, the ravens of the valley shall pick it out, and the young eagles shall eat it.[3]

18 There be three things which are too wonderful for me, yes, four which I know not:

19 The way of an eagle in the air; the way of a serpent upon a rock; the way of a ship in the midst of the sea; and the way of a man with a girl.

20 Such is the halacha of an adulterous woman; she eats, and wipes her mouth, and says, I have done no wickedness.

21 For three things the earth trembles, and for four which it cannot bear:

22 For an eved when he reigns; and a fool when he is filled with food;

23 For an odious woman when she is married; and a female eved that replaces her mistress.

24 There are four things that are little upon the earth, but they are exceedingly wise:

25 The ants are a people not strong, yet they prepare their food in the summer;

26 The conies are a weak species, yet make they their houses in the rocks;

27 The locusts have no melech, yet they travel in formation;

28 The spider is caught with two hands, yet is in the melech's palaces.

29 There are three things which go well, yes; four are beautiful in their going:

30 A lion that is strongest among beasts, and turns not away from any;

31 A greyhound; and a male goat also; and a melech, whose army is with him.

32 If you have done foolishly in lifting yourself up, or if you have thought evil, lay your hand upon your mouth.

33 Surely the pressing of milk brings forth butter, and the pressing of the nose brings forth dom: so the pressing of anger brings forth strife.

31 The words of melech Lemu-El, a message that his ima taught him.

2 What, My son? And what, the son of My womb? And what, the son of My vows?

3 Give not your strength to women, nor your halachot to that which destroys melechim.

4 It is not for melechim, O Lemu-El, it is not for melechim to drink wine; nor for rulers to drink strong drink:

5 Lest they drink, and forget the Torah, and pervert the mishpat of any of the afflicted.

6 Give strong drink to him that is ready to perish, and wine to those that are of heavy levim.

7 Let him drink, and forget his poverty, and remember his misery no more.

8 Open your mouth for those who cannot speak for themselves and are appointed to destruction.

---

[1] Meaning becoming so sinful in stealing, that YHWH's Name and His Set-Apartness are lost and brought to nothing.
[2] Both houses of Israel have to learn to give and not take, as they are transformed from leeches to sons and daughters of YHWH. They are learning that it is more blessed to give than to receive.
[3] When the unsaved are taken away in judgment, as believers will be left behind to be protected.

9 Open your mouth, judge righteously, and plead the cause of the poor and needy.

10 Who can find a virtuous woman?[1] For her price is far above rubies.

11 The lev of her husband does safely trust in her, so that he shall have no need of spoil.

12 She will do him tov and not evil all the days of her chayim.

13 She seeks wool, and linen, and works willingly with her hands.

14 She is like the merchants' ships; she brings her food from far.

15 She rises also while it is still night, and provides food to her household, and a portion to her young women.

16 She considers a field, and buys it: with the fruit of her hands she plants a vineyard.

17 She girds her loins with strength, and strengthens her arms.

18 She perceives that her merchandise is tov: her lamp goes not out at night.

19 She lays her hands to the spindle, and her hands hold the linen.

20 She stretches out her hand to the poor; yes, she reaches out her hands to the needy.

21 She is not afraid of the snow for her household: for all of her household is clothed in scarlet.

22 She makes herself quilts; her clothing is silk and purple.

23 Her husband is known in the gates, when he sits among the zachanim of the land.

24 She makes fine linen, and sells it; and delivers girdles to the merchants.

25 Strength and honor are her clothing; and she shall gilah in time to come.

26 She opens her mouth with chochmah; and on her tongue is the Torah of chesed.

27 She looks well to the halachot of her household, and eats not the lechem of idleness.

28 Her children in Yisrael rise up, and call her blessed; her husband also, and he praises her:

29 Many daughters have done virtuously, but you have risen over them all.

30 Favor is deceitful, and beauty is vain: but a woman that fears יהוה, she shall be be given tehilla.

31 Give her of the fruit of her hands; and let her own mitzvot praise her in the gates.

---

[1] In this verse starts the **eshet chayil** or "virtuous woman" chapter.

איוב

Iyov - Job
To Our Forefathers Yisrael

*The Jewish Talmud cites nine opinions of when Job lived, ranging from
Jacob to the time of Ezra. There is even a strong view that the entire book
is a parable and not an actual series of events.*

1 There was a man in the land of Uz, whose name was Iyov; and that man was perfect and tzadik, one that feared Eloah, and turned aside from evil. 2 And there were born to him seven sons and three daughters. 3 His possessions also was seven thousand sheep, and three thousand camels, and five hundred yoke of oxen, and five hundred female donkeys, and a very great bayit with avadim; so that this man was the greatest of all the men of the east.[1] 4 And his sons went and feasted in their bayits, every one on his own day;[2] and sent and called for their three sisters to eat and to drink with them. 5 And it was so, when the days of their feasting were over, that Iyov sent for them and set them apart, and rose up early in the morning, and offered burnt offerings according to their number: for Iyov said, It may be that my sons have sinned and cursed Eloah in their levim.[3] This did Iyov continually. 6 Now there was a day when the sons of Eloah[4] came to present themselves before יהוה, and s.a.tan came also among them. 7 And יהוה said to s.a.tan, *From where are you coming?* Then s.a.tan answered יהוה, and said, From going to and fro on the earth,[5] and from walking up and down in it. 8 And יהוה said to s.a.tan, *Have you considered My eved Iyov, that there is none like him in the earth, a perfect and a tzadik man, one that fears Eloah, and turns away from evil?* 9 Then s.a.tan answered יהוה, and said, Does Iyov

fear Eloah for nothing? 10 Have not You made a hedge about him, and about his bayit, and about all that he has on every side? You have blessed the work of his hands, and his possessions are increased in the land. 11 But put forth Your hand now, and touch all that he has, and he will curse You to Your face.[6] 12 And יהוה said to s.a.tan, *See, all that he has is in your hand; only against his chayim do not put forth your hand.* So s.a.tan went forth from the shechinah of יהוה. 13 And there was a day when his sons and his daughters were eating and drinking wine in their eldest brother's bayit: 14 And there came a messenger to Iyov, and said, The oxen were plowing, and the donkeys feeding beside them: 15 And the robbers fell on them, and took them away; yes, they have slain the avadim with the edge of the sword; and only I have escaped to tell you. 16 While he was yet speaking, there came also another, and said, The fire from Eloah has fallen from the shamayim, and has burned up the sheep, and the avadim, and consumed them; and I alone escaped to tell you. 17 While he was yet speaking, there came also another, and said, The Chaldeans came out with three bands, and fell on the camels, and have carried them away, yes, and slain the avadim with the edge of the sword; and I alone have escaped to tell you. 18 While he was yet speaking, there came also another, and said, Your sons and your daughters were eating and drinking wine in their eldest brother's bayit: 19 And, behold, there came a great wind from the wilderness, and smote the four corners of the bayit, and it

---

[1] A Hebrew.
[2] On their birthday, rather than YHWH's feasts. Birthdays are highly frowned upon in Yisraelite culture, and are always associated with paganism, curses and death. Hebrews remember the day of one's passing, not the day of one's birth.
[3] During the drunken birthday celebration.
[4] Fallen heavenly messengers.
[5] s.a.tan's home.

---

[6] A lie since no man can see YHWH's face other than through His Son.

fell on the young men, and they are dead; and I alone have escaped to tell you. 20 Then Iyov arose, and tore his mantle, and shaved his head, and fell down on the ground, and worshipped, 21 And said, Naked came I out of my ima's womb, and naked shall I return there: יהוה gave, and יהוה has taken away: Barchu-et-Shem-יהוה. 22 In all this Iyov did not sin, nor charge Eloah foolishly.

2 Again there was a day when the sons of Eloah[1] came to present themselves before יהוה, and s.a.tan came also among them to present himself before יהוה. 2 And יהוה said to s.a.tan, *From where have you come from?* And s.a.tan answered יהוה, and said, From going to and fro on the earth, and from walking up and down in it. 3 And יהוה said to s.a.tan, *Have you considered My eved Iyov, that there is none like him on the earth, a perfect and a tzadik man, one that fears Eloah, and turns away from evil? And still he holds fast his integrity, even though you moved Me against him, to destroy him without a cause.* 4 And s.a.tan answered יהוה, and said, Skin for skin, all that a man has will he give for his chayim. 5 But put forth Your hand now, and touch his bone and his flesh, and he will curse You to Your face. 6 And יהוה said to s.a.tan, *See, he is in your hand; but spare his chayim.* 7 So s.a.tan went forth from the shechinah of יהוה, and smote Iyov with sore boils from the sole of his foot to his head. 8 And he took him pottery pieces to scrape himself with; and he sat down among the ashes. 9 Then said his wife to him; Do you still retain your integrity? Curse Eloah, and die! 10 But he said to her, You speak as one of the foolish women speaks. What? Shall we receive tov from Eloah, and not receive evil? In all this Iyov did not sin with his lips. 11 Now when Iyov's three chaverim heard of all this evil that had come on him, they came everyone from his own place; Eliphaz the Temanite,

and Bildad the Shuhite, and Tzophar the Na'amathite: for they had made an appointment together to come to mourn with him and to comfort him. 12 And when they lifted up their eyes far off, and did not recognize him, they lifted up their voice, and wept; and they tore every one his mantle, and sprinkled dust on their heads toward the shamayim. 13 So they sat down with him on the ground seven days and seven nights,[2] and none spoke a word to him: for they saw that his grief was very great.

3 After this opened Iyov his mouth, and cursed his birthday. 2 And Iyov spoke, and said, 3 Let the day perish in which I was born, and the night in which it was said, There is a male child conceived. 4 Let that day be darkness; let not Eloah regard it from above, neither let light shine on it. 5 Let darkness and the shadow of death stain it; let a cloud dwell over it; let the blackness of the day frighten it. 6 As for that night, let darkness seize it; let it not be joined to the days of the rest of the year, let it not be counted in the number of the months. 7 Look, let that night be silent, let no voice of simcha come into it. 8 Let them curse it that curse the day, who are ready to raise up Leviathan. 9 Let the chochavim of its twilight be dark; let it look for light, but have none; neither let it see the dawning of the next day: 10 Because it did not shut the doors of my ima's womb, nor hid sorrow from my eyes. 11 Why did I not die in the womb? Why did I not give up the ruach when I came out of the belly? 12 Why did the knees receive me? Or the breasts for me to suck? 13 For by now I would have been lying in shalom, I should have died: then would I be at rest, 14 With the melechim and counselors of the earth, who built ruin for themselves; 15 Or with princes that had gold, who filled their bayits with silver: 16 Or as a hidden untimely birth; as infants who never saw light. 17 There the wicked

---

[1] Fallen heavenly messengers.

[2] Sitting **Shiva**.

cease from causing trouble; and there the weary are at rest. 18 There the prisoners rest together; they shema not the voice of the oppressor. 19 The small and great are there; and the eved is free from his master. 20 Why is light given to him that is in misery, and chayim to the bitter of being; 21 Who longs for death, but it comes not; and digs for it more than for hidden treasures; 22 Who rejoice exceedingly, and are in simcha, when they can find Sheol? 23 Why is light given to a man whose halacha is hidden, and whom Eloah has hedged in? 24 For my sighing comes before I eat, and my groanings pour out like mayim. 25 For the thing that I greatly feared has come on me, and that which I was afraid of has come to me. 26 I was not in safety, neither had I rest, neither was I quiet; yet trouble came.

4 Then Eliphaz the Temanite answered and said, 2 If we start to speak with you, will you be grieved? But who can withhold himself from speaking? 3 See, you have instructed many, and you have strengthened the weak hands. 4 Your words have held him that was falling, and you have strengthened the weak knees. 5 But now it is come on you, and you fainted; it touches you, and you are troubled. 6 Is not this your fear, your confidence, your tikvah, and the uprightness of your halacha? 7 Remember, please, who being innocent ever perished? Or when were the tzadikim ever cut off? 8 Even as I have seen, they that plow iniquity, and sow wickedness, reap the same. 9 By the blast of Eloah they perish, and by the Ruach of His nostrils are they consumed. 10 The roaring of the lion, and the voice of the fierce lion, and the teeth of the young lions, are broken. 11 The old lion perishes for lack of prey, and the cubs of the lioness are scattered abroad. 12 Now a word was secretly brought to me, and my ear received a little of it. 13 In thoughts from the visions of the night, when deep sleep falls on men, 14 Fear came on

me, and trembling, which made all my bones to shake. 15 Then a ruach passed before my face; the hair of my body stood up: 16 It stood still, but I could not discern the form of it: an image was before my eyes; there was silence, and I heard a voice, saying, 17 Shall mortal man be more tzadik than Eloah? Shall a man be cleaner than His Maker? 18 See, He puts no trust in His avadim; and His heavenly messengers He charged with straying: 19 How much more those that dwell in bayits of clay, whose foundation is in the dust, who are crushed before the moth? 20 They are destroyed from morning to evening: they perish le-olam-va-ed without anyone regarding it. 21 See their pride departs and they die, even without chochma.

5 Call now, if there is anyone that will answer you; and to which of the kidushim will you turn? 2 For anger kills the foolish man, and envy slays the simple. 3 I have seen the foolish taking root: but suddenly his home was cursed. 4 His children are far from safety, and they are crushed in the gate, neither is there anyone to deliver them. 5 Whose harvest the hungry eats up, and takes it out of the thorns, and the robber swallows up their possessions. 6 Although affliction does not come out of the dust, neither does trouble spring out of the ground; 7 Yet man is born for trouble, as the sparks fly upward. 8 I would seek El, and to Eloah would I commit my cause: 9 Who does great and unsearchable things; marvelous things without number: 10 Who gives rain on the earth, and sends mayim on the fields: 11 To set up on high those that are low; that those who mourn may be exalted to safety. 12 He disappoints the schemes of the crafty, so that their hands cannot perform their work. 13 He takes the wise in their own craftiness: and the counsel of the schemers is carried away. 14 They meet with darkness in the daytime, and grope in the noonday as in the night. 15 But

He saves the poor from the sword, from their mouth, and from the hand of the mighty. 16 So the poor have tikvah, and iniquity stops her mouth. 17 See, happy is the man whom Eloah corrects: therefore despise not the chastening of the Almighty: 18 For He bruises, and binds up: He wounds, and His hands make whole. 19 He shall deliver you in six troubles: yes, in seven there shall no evil touch you. 20 In famine He shall redeem you from death: and in war from the power of the sword. 21 You shall be hidden from the scourge of the tongue: neither shall you be afraid of the destruction when it comes. 22 At destruction and famine you shall laugh: neither shall you be afraid of the beasts of the earth. 23 For you shall be in covenant with the stones of the field: and the beasts of the field shall be at shalom with you. 24 And you shall know that your tent shall be in shalom; and you shall visit your tent, and shall not sin. 25 You shall know also that your zera shall be great, and your offspring as the grass of the earth.[1] 26 You shall come to Sheol in a ripe old age, like a stack of grain comes in its season. 27 Look this is what we have searched for, so shema to it, and know it for your own tov.

6 But Iyov answered and said, 2 Oh that my grief was thoroughly weighed, and my calamity laid on scales! 3 For now it would be heavier than the sand of the sea: therefore my words are rash. 4 For the arrows of the Almighty are within me, their poison saps up my ruach: the arrows of Eloah do set themselves in array against me. 5 Does the wild donkey bray when he has grass? Or does the ox neigh over its fodder? 6 Can that which is unsavory be eaten without salt? Or is there any taste in the white of an egg? 7 My being refuses to touch them. They are as food when I am sick. 8 Oh that I might have my request; and that Eloah would grant me the thing that I

long for! 9 Even that it would please Eloah to destroy me; that He would let loose His hand, and cut me off! 10 Then should I yet have comfort; I would rejoice in pain: let Him not spare; for I have not concealed the words of the Set-Apart One. 11 What is my strength, that I should have tikvah? And what is my end, that I should prolong my chayim? 12 Is my strength the strength of stones? Or is my flesh of bronze? 13 Is not my help in me? And is ability driven far from me? 14 To him that is afflicted pity should be shown from his friend; but he forsakes the fear of the Almighty. 15 My brothers have dealt deceitfully as a brook, and as the stream of brooks they pass away; 16 Which are dark because of the ice, and in which the snow is hidden: 17 When it is warm, they vanish: when it is hot, they are consumed out of their place. 18 The paths of their halacha are turned aside; they go to nothing, and perish. 19 The passengers of Tema looked, the travelers of Sheba waited for them. 20 They were ashamed because they had hoped; they came there, and were ashamed. 21 For now you are nothing; you see my casting down, and are afraid. 22 Did I say, Bring to me? Or, Give me a reward from your possessions? 23 Or, Deliver me from the enemy's hand? Or, redeem me from the hand of the mighty? 24 Teach me, and I will hold my tongue: and cause me to understand in which halacha I have gone astray. 25 How harsh are right words! But what does your arguing reprove? 26 Do you imagine to reprove the words, and the speeches of one that is in despair, which are as wind? 27 Yes, you overwhelm the fatherless, and you dig a grave for your friend. 28 Now therefore be content, look on me; for it is evident to you if I lie. 29 Relent, please, let it not be iniquity; yes, Relent, my tzedakah is in it. 30 Is there iniquity in my tongue? Or does my mouth speak emet?

7 Is there not an appointed time to man on earth? Are not his days also like the

---

[1] The promise of the Hebrews becoming great in their physical multiplicity.

days of a hired eved? 2 As an eved earnestly desires the shade, and as a hired man looks for the reward of his work: 3 So am I made to possess months of vanity, and wearisome nights are appointed to me. 4 When I lie down, I say, When shall I arise, and the night be gone? And I am full of tossing back and forth until the dawning of the day. 5 My flesh is clothed with worms and clods of dust; my skin is broken, and festers. 6 My days are swifter than a weaver's shuttle, and are spent without tikvah. 7 O remember that my chayim is wind: my eyes shall no more see tov. 8 The eye of him that has seen me shall see me no more: your eyes are on me, and I am not. 9 As the cloud is consumed and vanishes away: so is he that goes down to Sheol; he shall come up no more. 10 He shall return no more to his bayit; neither shall his place know him any more. 11 Therefore I will not refrain my mouth; I will speak in the anguish of my ruach; I will complain in the bitterness of my being. 12 Am I a sea, or a whale, that You have set a watch over me? 13 When I say, my bed shall comfort me; my couch shall ease my complaint; 14 Then You scare me with dreams, and terrified me through visions: 15 So that my being chooses strangling, and death rather than my chayim. 16 I loathe it; I would not live always: leave me alone; for my days are vanity. 17 What is man, that You should magnify him? And that You should set Your lev on him? 18 And that You should visit him every morning, and try him every moment? 19 How long will You stay and not depart from me, nor leave me alone until I swallow down my saliva? 20 I have sinned; what have I done to You, O You watcher of men? Why have You set me as a target against You, so that I am a burden to myself? 21 And why do You not pardon my transgression, and take away my iniquity? For now shall I sleep in the dust; and You shall seek me in the morning, but I shall not be.

8 Then answered Bildad the Shuhite, and said, 2 How long will you speak these things? And how long shall the words of your mouth be like a strong wind? 3 Does El pervert mishpat? Or does the Almighty pervert justice? 4 If your children have sinned against Him, and He has cast them away for their transgression; 5 If you would continually seek Eloah, and make your supplication to the Almighty; 6 If you were pure and tzadik; surely now He would arise for you, and make the dwelling of your tzedakah prosperous. 7 Though your beginning was small, yet your latter end should greatly increase. 8 For ask of the former generation, and prepare yourself for the research of their ahvot: 9 For we are but of yesterday, and know nothing, because our days on earth are as a shadow: 10 Shall not they teach you, and tell you, and utter words out of their lev? 11 Can the papyrus grow up without mud? Can the reed grow without mayim? 12 While it is yet green, and not cut down, it withers before any other herb. 13 So are the paths of all that forget El; and the hypocrite's tikvah shall perish: 14 Whose tikvah shall be cut off, and whose trust shall be a spider's web. 15 He shall lean on his bayit, but it shall not stand: he shall hold onto it fast, but it shall not endure. 16 He is green before the sun, and his branch shoots forth in his garden. 17 His roots are wrapped around a heap, and sees the place of stones. 18 If he destroys him from his place, then it shall deny him, saying, I have not seen you. 19 See, this is the simcha of his derech, and out of the earth shall others grow. 20 See, El will not cast away a perfect man; neither will He help the evil-doers: 21 Until He fills your mouth with laughing, and your lips with gilah. 22 They that hate you shall be clothed with shame; and the dwelling place of the wicked shall come to nothing.

9 Then Iyov answered and said, 2 Truly I know it is so: but how should a man be tzadik with Eloah? 3 If he will contend

with Him, he cannot answer Him one time out of a thousand. 4 He is wise in lev, and mighty in strength: who has hardened himself against Him, and still prospered? 5 Who removes the mountains, and they know it not: who overturns them in His anger. 6 Who shakes the earth out of its place, and the pillars of it tremble. 7 Who commands the sun, and it rises not; and seals up the chochavim. 8 Who alone spreads out the shamayim, and treads on the waves of the sea. 9 Who makes Aldebaran, Orion, and Pleiades, and the rooms of the south. 10 Who does great things past finding out; yes, and wonders without number. 11 See, He goes by me, and I see Him not: He passes on also, but I perceive Him not. 12 See, He takes away, who can hinder Him? Who will say to Him, What are You doing? 13 Eloah will not withdraw His anger; the proud helpers do stoop under Him. 14 How much less shall I answer Him, and choose out my words to reason with Him? 15 Who, though I were a tzadik, yet would I not answer, but I would make tefillah to my Shophet. 16 If I had called, and He had answered me; yet would I not believe that He had listened to my voice. 17 For He breaks me with a storm, and multiplies my wounds without cause. 18 He will not allow me to take my ruach, but fills me with bitterness. 19 If I speak of strength, look, He is strong: and if of mishpat, who shall set me a time to plead? 20 If I justify myself, my own mouth shall condemn me: if I say, I am perfect; it shall also prove me a liar. 21 Am I perfect? Yet would I not know my being: I would still despise my chayim. 22 It is all the same, therefore I said it, He destroys the perfect and the wicked. 23 If the scourge slays suddenly, He will laugh at the trial of the innocent. 24 The earth is given into the hand of the wicked: He covers the faces of the shophtim of it; if it is not He, then who does it? 25 Now my days are swifter than a messenger: they flee away, they see no tov. 26 They are passed away as the swift ships:

as the eagle that hurries to its prey. 27 If I say, I will forget my complaint; I will leave off my heaviness, and comfort myself: 28 I am afraid of all my sorrows; I know that you will not hold me innocent. 29 If I am wicked, why then do I labor in vain? 30 If I wash myself with snow mayim, and my hands with soap; 31 Yet shall You plunge me in the ditch, and my own clothes shall abhor me. 32 For He is not a man, as I am, that I should answer Him that we should come together in mishpat. 33 Neither is there any mediator between us; that might lay his hand on us both.[1] 34 Let Him take His rod away from me, and let not His fear frighten me: 35 Then would I speak, and not fear Him; but it is not so within me.

10 My being is weary of my chayim; I will leave my complaint to myself; I will speak in the bitterness of my being. 2 I will say to Eloah, Do not condemn me; show me why You strive against me. 3 Is it tov to You that You should oppress, that You should despise the work of Your hands, and shine on the counsel of the wicked? 4 Have You eyes of flesh? Or do You see as man sees? 5 Are Your days as the days of man? Are Your years as man's days? 6 That You inquire after my iniquity, and search out my sin? 7 You know that I am not wicked; and there is none that can deliver out of Your hand. 8 Your hands have made me and fashioned me together all around; yet You destroy me. 9 Remember, I beg You, that You have made me as the clay; and will You bring me into dust again? 10 Have You not poured me out as milk, and curdled me like cheese? 11 You have clothed me with skin and flesh, and have fenced me with bones and sinews. 12 You have granted me chayim and favor, and Your visitation has preserved my ruach. 13 And these things have You hid in Your lev: I know that this is with

---

[1] Before Yahshua was revealed, no mediator was there. This leads one to suspect that this took place before the Torah was given, since even under Torah a mediation system took place supervised by the sons of Aaron.

You. 14 If I sin, then target me, and do not acquit me from my iniquity. 15 If I were wicked, woe to me; and if I were a tzadik, yet will I not lift up my head. I am full of confusion; therefore see my affliction; 16 For it increases. You hunted me as a fierce lion: and again You show Yourself marvelous against me. 17 You renew Your witnesses against me, and increase Your indignation on me; changes and an army are against me. 18 Why then have You brought me forth out of the womb? Oh that I had given up the ruach, and no eye had seen me! 19 I should have been as though I had not been; I should have been carried from the womb directly to Sheol. 20 Are not my days few? Cease then, and leave me alone, that I may take comfort a little, 21 Before I go to where I shall not return, even to the land of darkness and the shadow of death; 22 A land of darkness, as dark as darkness itself; and of the shadow of death, without any order, where the light is as darkness.

11 Then answered Tzophar the Na'amathite, and said, 2 Should not the multitude of your words be answered? And should a man full of talk be justified? 3 Should your lies make men hold their silence? And when you mock him, shall no man make you ashamed? 4 For you have said, my teaching and chayim is pure, and I am clean in Your eyes. 5 But oh that Eloah would speak, and open His lips against you; 6 And that He would show you the secrets of chochma; that they are double to that which is! Know therefore that Eloah requires from you less than your iniquity deserves. 7 Can you by searching find out Eloah? Can you find out the Almighty to complete da'at? 8 It is as high as the shamayim; what can you do? Deeper than Sheol; what can you know? 9 The measure of it is longer than the earth, and wider than the sea. 10 If He cuts off, and shuts up, or gathers together, then who can stop Him?[1]

11 For He knows false men: He sees wickedness also; will He not then consider it? 12 For a vain man would be wise, though man is born like a wild donkey's colt. 13 If you prepare your lev, and stretch out your hands toward Him; 14 If iniquity is in your hand, put it far away, and let not wickedness dwell in your tents. 15 For then shall you lift up your face without spot; yes, then you shall be steadfast, and shall not fear: 16 Because then you shall forget your misery, and remember it as mayim that pass away: 17 And your chayim shall be clearer than the noonday; you shall shine forth, you shall be as the morning. 18 And you shall be secure, because there is tikvah; yes, you shall search yourself, and then you shall take your rest in safety. 19 Also you shall lie down, and none shall make you afraid; yes, many shall seek your favor. 20 But the eyes of the wicked shall fail, and they shall not escape, and their tikvah shall be the giving up of their ruach.

12 And Iyov answered and said, 2 No doubt but you are the people, and chochma shall die with you. 3 But I have binah as well as you; I am not inferior to you: yes, who knows not such things as these? 4 I am as one mocked by his neighbor, who calls on Eloah, and He answers him: the tzadik man is laughed to scorn. 5 He that is ready to slip with his feet is as a lamp despised in the thought of him that is at ease. 6 The tents of robbers prosper, and they that provoke El are secure; into whose hand Eloah brings abundantly. 7 But ask now the beasts, and they shall teach you; and the fowls of the air, and they shall tell you: 8 Or speak to the earth, and it shall teach you: and the fishes of the sea shall declare to you. 9 Who among all these does not know that the hand of יהוה has done this? 10 In Whose hand is the being of every living thing, and the ruach of all mankind. 11 Does not the ear

---

[1] Mankind can never stop the end-time regathering of both houses of Yisrael, despite unemunah in the message, or fleshly attempts to bring it about by man's human efforts alone.

discern words? And the mouth taste His food? 12 With the aged is chochma; and in length of days binah. 13 With Him is chochma and strength, He has counsel and binah. 14 See, He breaks down, and it cannot be built again: He imprisons a man, and there can be no release. 15 See, He withholds the mayim, and they dry up: also He sends them out, and they overwhelm the earth. 16 With Him is strength and chochma: the deceived and the deceiver are His. 17 He leads counselors away spoiled, and makes shophtim into fools. 18 He looses the bond of melechim, and girds their loins with a girdle. 19 He leads princes away spoiled, and overthrows the mighty. 20 He removes the speech of the trusted, and takes away the binah of the aged. 21 He pours contempt on princes, and weakens the strength of the mighty. 22 He discovers deep things out of darkness, and brings to light the shadow of death. 23 He increases the nations, and destroys them: He enlarges the nations, and straitens them again. 24 He takes away the lev of the leaders of the peoples of the earth, and causes them to wander in a wilderness where there is no derech. 25 They grope in the dark without light, and He makes them stagger like a drunken man.

13 Look, my eye has seen all this, my ear has heard and understood it. 2 What you know, the same do I know also: I am not inferior to you. 3 Surely I would speak to the Almighty, and I desire to reason with El. 4 But you are forgers of lies; you are all physicians of no value. 5 O that you would altogether hold your silence! And then it would be your chochma. 6 Shema now my reasoning, and shema to the pleadings of my lips. 7 Will you speak wickedly for El? And talk deceitfully for Him? 8 Will you accept His person? Will you contend for El? 9 Would it be tov with you if He should search you out? Or as one man mocks another, do you mock Him? 10 He will surely reprove you, if you do

secretly display partiality. 11 Shall not His excellence make you afraid? And His fear fall on you? 12 Your memories are like ashes, your bodies as bodies of clay. 13 Hold your silence, leave me alone, that I may speak, and let come on me whatever will be. 14 Why do I take my flesh in my teeth, and put my chayim in my hand? 15 Though He slay me, yet will I trust in Him: but I will maintain my own halacha before Him. 16 He also shall be my salvation: for a hypocrite shall not come before Him. 17 Shema diligently to my speech, and my declaration with your ears. 18 See now, I have prepared my case; I know that I shall be justified. 19 Who is he that will strive with me? For then I would keep silent, and die. 20 Only do not two things to me: then will I not be hidden from Your face. 21 Withdraw Your hand far from me: and let not Your fear make me afraid. 22 Then call, and I will answer: or let me speak, and You can answer me. 23 How many are my iniquities and sins? Make me to know my transgression and my sin. 24 Why do You hide Your face, and count me as Your enemy? 25 Will You break a leaf driven to and fro? And would You pursue dry stubble? 26 For You write bitter things against me, and make me to possess the iniquities of my youth. 27 You put my feet also in the stocks, and look closely at all my paths; You set a limit for the soles of my feet. 28 And he, as a rotten thing, wastes away, as a garment that is moth eaten.

14 Man that is born of a woman is of few days, and full of trouble. 2 He comes forth like a flower, and is cut down: he flees also as a shadow, and continues not. 3 And do You open Your eyes on such a one, to bring me into mishpat with You? 4 Who can bring a clean thing out of an unclean? Not one. 5 Seeing his days are determined, the numbers of his months are with You, You have appointed his bounds that he cannot pass; 6 Turn from him, that he may rest, until as a hired man, he enjoys

his day. 7 For there is tikvah for a tree, if it were cut down, that it would sprout again, and that its tender branch will not cease.[1] 8 Though its root grows old in the earth, and the stump dies in the ground; 9 Yet through the scent of mayim it will bud, and bring forth foliage like a plant. 10 But man dies, and wastes away: yes, man gives up the ruach, and where is he? 11 As the mayim disappear from the sea, and the river dries up: 12 So man lies down, and rises not: until the shamayim are no more, they shall not awake, nor be raised out of their sleep. 13 O that You would hide me in Sheol, that You would keep me concealed, until Your anger is past, that You would appoint me a set time, and remember me![2] 14 If a man dies, shall he live again? All the days of my appointed time will I wait, until my change comes.[3] 15 You shall call, and I will answer You: You will yearn for the work of Your hands.[4] 16 For now You number my steps; do You not also watch over my sin? 17 My transgression is sealed up in a bag, and You cover my iniquity. 18 And surely the mountain falling comes to nothing, and the rock is removed out of its place. 19 The mayim wears away the stones: You wash away the things that grow out of the dust of the earth; and You destroy the tikvah of man. 20 You prevail le-olam-va-ed against him, and he passes: You change his countenance, and send him away. 21 His sons come to honor, and he will not know it; and they are brought low, but he will not perceive it. 22 But his flesh on him shall have pain, and his being within him shall mourn.

15 Then answered Eliphaz the Temanite, and said, 2 Should a wise man answer with vain da'at, and fill his belly with the east wind? 3 Should he reason with unprofitable talk? Or with speeches by which he can do no tov? 4 Yes, you have done away with reverence, and withheld tefillah before El. 5 For your mouth utters your iniquity, and you choose the tongue of the deceitful. 6 Your own mouth condemns you, and not I: yes, your own lips testify against you. 7 Are you the first man that was born? Or were you made before the hills? 8 Have you heard the secret of Eloah? And do you limit chochma to yourself only? 9 What do you know, that we do not know? What do you understand, that is not in us? 10 With us are both the gray-headed and very aged men, much older than your abba. 11 Are the comforts of El only with you? Is there any secret thing with you? 12 Why does your lev mislead you away? And why do your eyes flash? 13 That you turn your ruach against El, and let such words come out of your mouth? 14 Who is man, that he should be clean? And he who is born of a woman, that he should be tzadik? 15 See, He puts no trust in His kidushim; yes, the shamayim are not clean in His sight. 16 How much more abominable and filthy is man, who drinks iniquity like mayim? 17 I will show you, shema me; and that which I have seen I will declare; 18 Which wise men have told from their ahvot, and have not hidden it: 19 Unto whom alone the earth was given, and no stranger passed among them. 20 The wicked man travails with pain all his days, and very few years is given to the ruthless. 21 A dreadful sound is in his ears: in his shalom the destroyer shall come on him. 22 He believes not that he shall return out of darkness, and he is destined for the sword. 23 He wanders abroad for lechem, saying, Where is it? Yet he knows that the day of darkness is already at hand. 24 Trouble and anguish shall make him afraid; they shall prevail against him, as a melech ready for the battle. 25 For he stretches out his hand against El, and strengthens himself against the Almighty.

---

[1] As is the hope of Yisrael to see Yisrael's olive tree restored.
[2] After the wrath has passed in the resurrection of the dead, or the promised catching up of our mortal bodies.
[3] Job hoped for a change from mortal to immortal, not in a rapture. Yisrael holds to that same hope according to First Corinthians 15.
[4] In the day of resurrection.

26 He runs on Him, even on his neck, with the multitude of his shields: 27 Because he covers his face with his fatness, and puts layers of fat on his flanks. 28 And he dwells in desolate cities, and in bayits which no man inhabits, which are ready to become heaps. 29 He shall not be rich, neither shall his possessions continue, neither shall he prolong the possessions of it on the earth. 30 He shall not depart out of darkness; the flame shall dry up his branches, and by the ruach of his mouth shall he go away. 31 Let him that is deceived not trust in vanity: for vanity shall be his reward. 32 It shall be accomplished before its time, and his branch shall not be green. 33 He shall shake off his unripe grape as the vine, and shall cast off his flower as the olive. 34 For the congregation of hypocrites shall be desolate, and fire shall consume the tents of bribery. 35 They conceive mischief, and bring forth vanity, and their belly prepares deceit.

16 Then Iyov answered and said, 2 I have heard many such things: miserable comforters are you all. 3 Shall your empty words have an end? Or what emboldens you that you even answer? 4 I also could speak as you do: if your being were in my place, I could heap up words against you, and shake my head at you. 5 But I would rather strengthen you with my mouth, and the moving of my lips would bring relief to your grief. 6 Though I speak, my grief is not relieved: and though I refrain, does it leave me? 7 But now He has made me weary: but you have stunned all my company. 8 And you have filled me with wrinkles; which is a witness against me: and my lean body coming on me bears witness with my face. 9 He tears me in his anger, he who hates me: he gnashes on me with his teeth; my enemy sharpens his eyes on me.[1] 10 They have opened wide their mouth; they have smitten me on the cheek with reproach; they have gathered themselves together against me. 11 El has delivered me to the perverse, and turned me over into the hands of the wicked. 12 I was at ease,[2] but He has broken me asunder: He has also taken me by my neck, and shaken me to pieces, and set me up for His target. 13 His archers encircle me all around, He cleaves my kidneys in two, and does not spare; He pours out my bile on the ground. 14 He breaks me with breach upon breach, He runs on me like a giant. 15 I have sewed sackcloth on my skin, and laid my horn in the dust. 16 My face is red from weeping, and on my eyelids are the shadows of death; 17 Not for any injustice in my hands: also my tefillah is pure. 18 O earth, do not cover my dom, and let my cry have no place. 19 Also now, behold, my witness is in the shamayim, and My Defender is on high. 20 My chaverim scorn me: but my eye pours out tears to Eloah. 21 O that one might plead for a man with Eloah, as a man pleads with his neighbors! 22 When a few years are past, then I shall go the derech from which I shall not return.

17 My ruach is broken, my days are extinct, Sheol is ready for me. 2 Are there not mockers with me? And does not my eye continue to see their provocation? 3 Please lay down a pledge with me; who is he that will strike hands with me? 4 For You have hid their lev from binah: therefore You shall not exalt them. 5 He that speaks flattery to his chaverim, even the eyes of his children shall fail. 6 He has made me also a byword of the people; but beforehand I was as a drum. 7 My eye also is dim by reason of my sorrow, and all my members are like shadows. 8 Upright men shall be astonished at this, and the innocent shall stir up himself against the hypocrite. 9 The tzadik also shall hold on to his halacha, and he that has clean hands shall be stronger and stronger. 10 But as for all of you, do you return, and come now: for

---

[1] Eliphaz; the comforter.

[2] The true sin of Job; being at ease and not laboring for the Master.

I cannot find one wise man among you. 11 My days are past; my purposes are broken off, even the thoughts of my lev. 12 They change the night into day: the light is short because of darkness. 13 If I wait, then Sheol is my bayit: I have made my bed in the darkness. 14 I have said to corruption, You are my abba: to the worm, You are my ima, and my sister. 15 And where is now my tikvah? As for my tikvah, who shall see it? 16 They shall go down to the bars of Sheol, they shall descend together into the dust.

18 Then answered Bildad the Shuhite, and said, 2 How long will it be until you make an end of your words? Tell us and afterwards we will speak. 3 Why are we counted as beasts, and reputed as unworthy in your sight? 4 He tears himself in his anger: shall the earth be forsaken for your sake? And shall the rock be removed out of its place? 5 Yes, the light of the wicked shall be put out, and the spark of his fire shall not shine. 6 The light shall be dark in his tent, and his candle shall be put out with him. 7 The steps of his strength shall be impeded, and his own counsel shall overthrow him. 8 For he is cast into a net by his own feet, and he walks into a pit. 9 The net shall take him by the heel, and the robber shall prevail against him. 10 The snare is laid for him in the ground, and a trap for him in the way. 11 Terrors shall make him afraid on every side, and shall chase him to his feet. 12 His strength shall be removed, and destruction shall be ready at his side. 13 It shall devour parts of his skin: even the firstborn of death shall devour his strength. 14 His confidence shall be rooted out of his tent, and it shall bring him to the melech of terrors. 15 It shall dwell in his tent, because it is none of his: brimstone shall be scattered on his bayit. 16 His roots shall be dried up beneath, and above shall his branch be cut off. 17 His memory shall perish from the earth, and he shall have no name in the street. 18 He shall be driven from light into darkness, and chased out of the olam hazeh. 19 He shall neither have son or nephew among his people, nor any remaining in his dwellings. 20 They that come after him shall be astonished at his day, as those who were before them were frightened. 21 Surely such are the dwellings of the wicked, and this is the place of him that knows not El.

19 Then Iyov answered and said, 2 How long will you trouble my being, and break me in pieces with words? 3 These ten times have you insulted me: you are not ashamed that you make yourselves strange to me. 4 And indeed I have gone astray, my error remains with myself. 5 If indeed you will magnify yourselves against me, and plead against me with insults: 6 Know now that Eloah has overthrown me, and has encircled me with His net. 7 See, I cry out of wrong, but I am not heard: I cry aloud, but there is no mishpat. 8 He has fenced up my path that I cannot move, and He has set darkness in my paths. 9 He has stripped me of my tiferet, and taken the keter from my head. 10 He has destroyed me on every side, and I am gone: and my tikvah has He removed like a tree. 11 He has also kindled His anger against me, and He counts me to Him as one of His enemies. 12 His troops come together, and raise up their false halacha against me, and encamp round about my tent. 13 He has put my brothers far from me, and my acquaintances are fully estranged from me. 14 My relatives have failed me, and my closest chaverim have forgotten me. 15 They that dwell in my bayit, and my maids, treat me as a ger: I am an alien in their sight. 16 I call my eved, and he gives me no answer; I have to beg him with my mouth. 17 My breath is strange to my wife, though I implored for the children of my own body. 18 Yes, young children despise me; I arise, and they speak against me. 19 All my intimate chaverim loathe me: and those whom I have

loved have turned against me. 20 My bone cleaves to my skin and to my flesh, and I am escaped with the skin of my teeth. 21 Have pity on me; have pity on me, O you my chaverim; for the hand of Eloah has struck me. 22 Why do you persecute me as does El, and are not satisfied with my flesh's suffering? 23 Oh that my words were now written! Oh that they were printed in a scroll! 24 That they were graven with an iron pen and lead in the rock le-olam-va-ed! 25 For I know that my Redeemer lives, and that He shall stand at the latter-day on the earth:[1] 26 And after my skin has been taken off and worms destroy this body, yet in my flesh shall I see Eloah:[2] 27 Whom I shall see for myself, and my eyes shall behold, and not another;[3] though my kidneys will be consumed within me. 28 But what you should be saying is, Why do we persecute him, seeing that a tov report will follow me and vindicate me?[4] 29 Be afraid of the sword: for anger brings the punishment of the sword; that you may know there is mishpat.

20 Then answered Tzophar the Na'amathite, and said, 2 Therefore do my thoughts cause me to answer, and I will make haste. 3 I have heard the reproach that insults me, and the ruach of my binah causes me to answer. 4 Don't you know this of old, since man was placed on the earth, 5 That the triumphing of the wicked is short, and the simcha of the hypocrite is but for a moment? 6 Though his pride mounts up to the shamayim, and his head reaches to the clouds; 7 Yet he shall perish le-olam-va-ed like his own dung: they who have seen him shall say, Where is he? 8 He shall fly away as a dream,[5] and shall not be found: yes, he shall be chased away as a vision of the night. 9 The eye also which saw him shall see him no more; neither shall his place any more behold him. 10 His children shall seek to please the poor, and his hands shall restore their goods. 11 His bones are full of the sins of his youth, which shall lie down with him in the dust. 12 Though wickedness is sweet in his mouth, though he hide it under his tongue; 13 Though he fondles it, and forsakes it not; but keeps it still within his mouth: 14 Yet his food in his stomach is turned, it is the bitterness of cobras within him. 15 He has swallowed down riches, and he shall vomit them up again: El shall cast them out of his belly. 16 He shall suck the poison of cobras: the viper's tongue shall slay him. 17 He shall not see the rivers, the floods, or the brooks of honey and butter. 18 That which he labors for shall he restore, and shall not swallow it down: according to his possessions shall the restitution be, and he shall not rejoice in them. 19 Because he has oppressed and has forsaken the poor; because he has violently taken away a bayit which he did not build; 20 Surely he shall not feel ease in his belly, he shall not keep that which he desired. 21 There shall none of his posterity be left; therefore his tov will not be remembered. 22 In the fullness of his sufficiency he shall be in distress: every hand of the wicked shall come on him. 23 When he is about to fill his belly, Eloah shall cast the fury of His anger on him, and shall rain it on him while he is yet eating. 24 He shall flee from the iron weapon, but the bow of steel shall strike him through. 25 It is drawn, and comes out of the body; yes, the glittering sword comes out of his gall: terrors are on him. 26 All darkness shall be hid in his secret places: a fire not blown shall consume him; it shall be ill with him that is left in his tent. 27 Then the

---

[1] Job knew his only hope was in the living Redeemer and the coming of Moshiach, who Himself would stand on the earth at the end of days.
[2] Job's hope was that the Redeemer would come to earth and give him a new changed immortal body, by which he would then be able to see YHWH, which is exactly what Yahshua did and has come to do.
[3] He expected the living YHWH to be His personal Savior by taking on flesh, so as to allow Job with his own eyes, and not merely through the ruach, to see the Redeemer on the earth in Job's new immortal and resurrected body.
[4] From the Aramaic Peshitta; Job rebukes them for not following the tov report of His promised redemption and resurrection for the righteous ones.

[5] Throughout Scripture, it is the wicked that are taken away, never the redeemed.

shamayim shall reveal his iniquity; and the earth shall rise up against him. 28 The increase of his bayit shall depart, and his goods shall flow away in the day of His anger. 29 This is the portion of a wicked man from Eloah, and the heritage appointed to him by El.

21 But Iyov answered and said, 2 Shema diligently my speech, and let this be your comfort. 3 Allow me that I may speak; and after I have spoken, you can mock more. 4 As for me, is my complaint to man? And if it were so, why should not my ruach be troubled? 5 Look at me, and be astonished, and lay your hand on your mouth. 6 Even when I remember I am afraid, and trembling takes hold on my flesh. 7 Why do the wicked live, become old, yes, are mighty in power? 8 Their zera is established in their sight with them, and their offspring before their eyes. 9 Their bayits are safe from fear, neither is the rod of Eloah on them. 10 Their bull breeds, and fails not; their cow gives birth, without miscarriage. 11 They send forth their little ones like a flock, and their children dance. 12 They take the tambourine and harp, and rejoice at the sound of the flute. 13 They spend their days in wealth, and in a moment go down to Sheol. 14 Therefore they say to El, Depart from us; for we desire not the da'at of Your halacha. 15 Who is the Almighty that we should serve Him? And what profit should we have, if we make tefillah to Him? 16 See, their tov is not in their hand: the counsel of the wicked is far from me. 17 How often is the candle of the wicked put out! And how often comes their destruction on them! Eloah distributes sorrows in His anger. 18 They are as stubble before the wind, and as chaff that the storm carries away. 19 You claim that Eloah lays up His iniquity for His children: He rewards him, and he shall know it. 20 His eyes shall see his destruction, and he shall drink of the anger of the Almighty. 21 For what pleasure has he in his bayit after him, when the number of his months is cut off in the midst? 22 Shall any teach El da'at? Seeing He even shophets those that are exalted. 23 One dies in his full strength, being wholly at ease and shalom. 24 His breasts are full of milk, and his bones are moistened with marrow. 25 And another dies in the bitterness of his being, and never eats with pleasure. 26 They shall lie down alike in the dust, and the worms shall cover them both. 27 See, I know your thoughts, and the schemes that you wrongfully imagine against me. 28 For you say, Where is the bayit of the prince? And where are the dwelling places of the wicked? 29 Have you not asked them that go by their own halacha? And do you not know those signs, 30 That the wicked is reserved to the Day of destruction?[1] They shall be brought forth to the Day of anger. 31 Who shall declare his halacha to his face? And who shall repay him for what he has done? 32 Yet shall he be brought to Sheol, and shall remain in the tomb. 33 The clusters of mud of the valley shall be sweet to him, and every man shall follow after him, as there are innumerable ones who went before him. 34 Why then do you comfort me in vain, seeing in your answers there remains falsehood?

22 Then Eliphaz the Temanite answered and said, 2 Can a man be profitable to El, as he that is wise may be profitable to himself? 3 Is it any pleasure to the Almighty, that you are tzadik? Or is it to His advantage that you make your halacha perfect? 4 Would He reprove you if you feared Him? Will He enter with you into mishpat? 5 Is not your wickedness great? And your iniquities infinite? 6 For you have taken a pledge from your brother for nothing, and stripped the naked of their clothing. 7 You have not given mayim to the weary to drink, and you have withheld lechem from the hungry. 8 But as for the mighty man, he has the earth; and the honorable man dwells in it. 9 You have sent

---

[1] In the age to come.

widows away empty, and the arms of the fatherless you have broken. 10 Therefore snares are around you, and sudden fear troubles you; 11 Or darkness, that you cannot see; and an abundance of mayim cover you. 12 Is not Eloah in the heights of the shamayim? And behold the heights of the chochavim, how high they are! 13 And you say, How does El know? How can He shophet through the dark cloud? 14 Thick clouds are a covering to Him, that He sees not; and He walks in the circuit of the shamayim. 15 Have you marked the old halacha in which wicked men have trodden? 16 Who were cut down before their time, whose foundation was swept away with a flood: 17 Who said to El, Depart from us: and what can the Almighty do for us? 18 Yet He filled their bayits with tov things: but the counsel of the wicked is far from me. 19 The tzadikim see it, and are glad: and the innocent laugh them to scorn. 20 If they are not prostrated because of their stubbornness, then their remnant the fire will consume. 21 Agree with Him and serve Him, and be at shalom: thereby tov shall come to you. 22 Receive, I beg you, the Torah from His mouth, and lay up His words in your lev. 23 If you teshuvah to the Almighty, you shall be built up, you shall put away iniquity far from your tents. 24 Then shall you lay up gold as dust, and the gold of Ophir as the stones of the brooks. 25 Yes, the Almighty shall be your defense, and you shall have plenty of silver. 26 For then shall you have your delight in the Almighty, and shall lift up your face to Eloah. 27 You shall make your tefillah to Him, and He shall shema you, and you shall pay your vows to Him. 28 You shall also decree a thing, and it shall be established to you: and the light shall shine on your halacha. 29 When men are cast down, then you shall say, There is lifting up; and He shall save the humble person. 30 Shall He deliver one who is not innocent? Deliverance is by the pureness of your hands.

23 Then Iyov answered and said, 2 Even today is my complaint bitter: His hand is now heavier and increases my groaning. 3 Oh that I knew where I might find Him! That I might come even to His seat! 4 I would present my cause before Him, and fill my mouth with arguments. 5 I would know the words with which He would answer me, and understand what He would say to me. 6 Will He plead against me with His great power? No; but He would put strength in me. 7 There the tzadikim might reason with Him; so I should be delivered le-olam-va-ed from My Shophet. 8 See, I go forward, but He is not there; and backward, but I cannot perceive Him: 9 On the left hand, where He does work, but I cannot behold Him: He hides Himself on the right hand, that I cannot see Him:[1] 10 But He knows the halacha that I take: when He has tried me, I shall come forth as gold. 11 My foot has held to His steps, His halacha have I kept, and not declined. 12 Neither have I backslidden from the commandment of His lips; I have esteemed the words of His mouth more than my necessary food. 13 But He is in echad, and who can turn Him? And what His being desires, even that He does. 14 For He performs the thing that He has appointed for me: and many such things are with Him. 15 Therefore am I troubled at His shechinah: when I consider it, I am afraid of Him. 16 For El makes my lev soft, and the Almighty troubles me: 17 Because I was not cut off before the darkness, neither has He covered the darkness from my face.

24 Times are not hidden from the Almighty, and why do those who know Him not see more days? 2 Some remove the landmarks; they violently take away flocks, and feed on it. 3 They drive away the donkey of the fatherless; they take the widow's ox for a pledge. 4 They turn the needy out of the way: the poor of the earth hide themselves together. 5 See, as wild

---

[1] An esoteric reference to Yahshua as YHWH's right arm.

donkeys in the desert, they go forth to their work; rising for a prey: the wilderness yields food for them and for their children. 6 They reap each one his corn in the field: and they gather the vintage of the wicked. 7 They cause the naked to lodge without clothing, that they have no covering in the cold. 8 They are wet with the showers of the mountains, and embrace the rock for want of a shelter. 9 They pluck the fatherless from the breast, and take a pledge from the poor. 10 They cause him to go naked without clothing, and they take away the sheaf from the hungry; 11 Who make oil within their walls, and tread their own winepresses, and allow thirst. 12 Men groan from out of the city, and the being of the wounded cry out: yet Eloah lays not folly to them. 13 They are of those that rebel against the light; they know not the halacha of it, nor abide in the paths of it. 14 The murderer rising with the light kills the poor and needy, and in the night is as a thief. 15 The eye also of the adulterer waits for the twilight, saying, No eye shall see me: and disguises his face. 16 In the dark they dig through bayits, which they have marked for themselves in the daytime: they know not the light. 17 For the morning is to them even as the shadow of death: if one knows them, they are in the terrors of the shadow of death. 18 He is swift as the mayim; their portion is cursed in the earth: he beholds not the way of the vineyards. 19 Drought and heat consume the snow mayim: so does Sheol consume those who have sinned. 20 The womb shall forget him; the worm shall feed sweetly on him; he shall be no more remembered; and wickedness shall be broken as a tree. 21 He treats the barren that bears not with evil: and does no tov to the widow. 22 He draws also the mighty with His power: He rises up, so that man is sure of chayim. 23 Though he is given safety, wherein he rests; yet his eyes are on his own evil ways. 24 They are exalted for a little while, but are gone and brought low; they are taken out of the way as all the others, and cut off as the tops of the ears of corn. 25 And if it is not so, who will make me a liar, and make my speech worthless?

25 Then answered Bildad the Shuhite, and said, 2 Dominion and fear are with Him, He makes shalom in His high places. 3 Is there any number to His armies? And on whom does not His light arise? 4 How then can a man be justified with El? Or how can he be clean that is born of a woman? 5 See even the moon, shines not; yes, the chochavim are not pure in His sight. 6 How much less man, that is a worm? And the ben-Adam; who is a worm?

26 But Iyov answered and said, 2 How have you helped him that is without power? How did you save the arm that has no strength? 3 How have you counseled him that has no chochma? And how have you plentifully declared the thing as it is? 4 To whom have you uttered words? And whose ruach came from you? 5 Dead things are formed from under the mayim, and the inhabitants of it. 6 Sheol is naked before Him, and destruction has no covering. 7 He stretches out the north over the empty place, and hangs the earth on nothing. 8 He binds up the mayim in His thick clouds; and the cloud is not torn under them. 9 He holds back the Face of His throne, and spreads His cloud on it. 10 He has circled the mayim with boundaries, until day and night come to an end. 11 The pillars of the shamayim tremble and are astonished at His reproof. 12 He divides the sea with His power, and by His binah He smites through the proud. 13 By His Ruach He has adorned the shamayim; His hand has formed the crooked serpent. 14 Look, these all are parts of His halacha: but how little of that portion is heard from Him? But even the thunder of His power; who can understand?

27 Moreover Iyov continued his parable, and said, 2 As El lives, who has turned aside my mishpat; and the Almighty, who has troubled my being; 3 All the while my ruach is in me, and the ruach of Eloah is in my nostrils; 4 My lips shall not speak wickedness, nor my tongue utter deceit. 5 Eloah forbid that I should tell you that you are right: until I die I will not remove my integrity from me. 6 My tzedakah I will hold on to, and will not let it go: my lev shall not reproach me so long as I live. 7 Let my enemy be as the wicked, and he that rises up against me as the unrighteous. 8 For what is the tikvah of the hypocrite, though he has gained all, when Eloah takes away his being? 9 Will El shema to his cry when trouble comes on him? 10 Will he delight himself in the Almighty? Will he always call on Eloah? 11 I will teach you by the hand of El: that which is with the Almighty will I not conceal. 12 See, all you have seen it; why then are you altogether vain? 13 This is the portion of a wicked man with El, and the heritage of oppressors, which they shall receive of the Almighty. 14 If his children are multiplied, it is for the sword: and his offspring shall not be satisfied with lechem. 15 Those that remain from him shall be buried in death: and his widows shall not weep. 16 Though he heap up silver as the dust, and prepare clothing as the clay; 17 He may prepare it, but the tzadik shall put it on, and the innocent shall divide the silver. 18 He builds his bayit as a moth, and as a booth that a watchman makes. 19 The rich man shall lie down, but he shall not be gathered:[1] he opens his eyes, and he is not. 20 Terrors take hold on him as mayim of a flood; a storm steals him away in the night. 21 The east wind carries him away, and he departs: and as a storm hurls him out of his place. 22 For Eloah shall cast him out without pity, and not spare: he cannot escape out of his hand. 23 Men shall clap their hands before him, and shall hiss him out of his place.

28 Surely there is a mine for the silver, and a place for gold where they refine it. 2 Iron is taken out of the earth, and bronze is melted out of the stone. 3 He sets an end to darkness, and searches out all perfection: the stones of darkness, and the shadow of death. 4 The flood breaks out from the inhabitant; even the mayim forgotten by the foot: they are dried up; they are gone away from men. 5 As for the earth, out of it comes lechem: and under it is turned up as if it were fire.[2] 6 The stones of it are the place of sapphires:[3] and it has dust of gold. 7 There is a path which no fowl knows, and which the vulture's eye has not seen: 8 Wild beasts have not trodden it, nor the fierce lion passed by it. 9 He puts forth his hand on the rock; He overturns the mountains by the roots. 10 He cuts out rivers among the rocks; and His eye sees every precious thing. 11 He binds the floods from overflowing; and the thing that is hidden He brings to light. 12 But where shall chochma be found? And where is the place of binah? 13 Man knows not the price of it; neither is it found in the land of the living. 14 The depth says, It is not in me: and the sea says, It is not with me. 15 It cannot be gotten for gold; neither shall silver be weighed for the price of it. 16 It cannot be valued with the gold of Ophir, with the precious onyx, or the sapphire. 17 The gold and the crystal cannot equal it: and the exchange of it shall not be for jewels of fine gold. 18 No mention shall be made of coral, or of pearls: for the price of chochma is above rubies. 19 The topaz of Ethiopia shall not equal it; neither shall it be valued with pure gold. 20 From where then comes chochma? And where is the place of binah? 21 Seeing it is hidden from the eyes of all living, and kept closed from the fowls of the air. 22 Destruction and death say; We have heard the fame of it with our ears. 23 Eloah understands the halacha it brings,

---

[1] At the ingathering of the Nations at Yahshua's return.

[2] Possible location of the Lake of Fire spoken of in Revelation 20.
[3] In the earth, men can only see YHWH's **sefirot** or manifestations.

and He knows the place of it. 24 For He looks to the ends of the earth, and sees under the whole shamayim; 25 To make the weight for the winds; and He weighs the mayim by measure. 26 When He makes a decree for the rain, and a path for the lightning and the thunder: 27 Then He did see it, and declare it; He prepared it, yes, and searched it out. 28 And to man He said, *See, the fear of יהוה, that is chochma; and to depart from evil is binah.*

29 Moreover Iyov continued his parable, and said, 2 Oh that I were as in months past, as in the days when Eloah preserved me; 3 When His candle shined on my head, and when by His light I walked through the darkness; 4 As I was in the days of my youth, when the secret of Eloah was in my tent; 5 When the Almighty was yet with me, when my children were around me; 6 When I washed my steps with butter, and the rock poured me out rivers of oil; 7 When I went out to the gate through the city, when I prepared my seat in the street! 8 The young men saw me, and hid themselves: and the aged arose, and stood up. 9 The princes refrained from talking, and laid their hand on their mouth. 10 The nobles held their silence, and their tongues cleaved to the roofs of their mouths. 11 When the ear heard me, then it blessed me; and when the eye saw me, it gave witness to me: 12 Because I delivered the poor that cried, and the fatherless, and him that had no one to help him. 13 The blessing of him that was ready to perish came on me: and I caused the widow's lev to sing for simcha. 14 I put on tzedakah, and it clothed me: my mishpat was as a robe and a keter. 15 I was eyes to the blind, and feet to the lame. 16 I was an abba to the poor: and the case, which I did not know, I searched out. 17 And I broke the jaws of the wicked, and plucked the plunder out of his teeth. 18 Then I said, I shall die in my nest, and I shall multiply my days as the sand. 19 My root was spread out by the mayim, and the

dew lay all night on my branch. 20 My tiferet was fresh in me, and my bow was renewed in my hand. 21 Unto me men listened, and waited, and kept silence at my counsel. 22 After my words they spoke not again; and my speech dropped on them. 23 And they waited for me as for the rain; and they opened their mouth wide as for the latter rain. 24 I laughed on those, who believed not; and the light of my countenance they cast not down. 25 I chose out the halacha for them, and sat as a ruler, and dwelt as a melech in the army, as one that comforts the mourners.

30 But now they that are younger than I have me in derision, whose ahvot I would have disdained to have put with the dogs of my flock. 2 Yes, the strength of their hands; of what use would it have been to me? 3 For want and famine they were dried up; fleeing into the wilderness in former times a desolate and a waste. 4 Who cut up salty herbs by the bushes, and juniper tree roots for their food. 5 They were driven forth from among men, they shouted at them as at a thief; 6 To dwell in the clefts of the valleys, in the caves of the earth, and in the rocks. 7 Among the bushes they cried; under the nettles they were gathered together. 8 They were children of fools, yes, children of wicked men: they were lower than the earth. 9 And now am I their song, yes, I am their byword. 10 They abhor me; they flee far from me, and refrain not to spit in my face. 11 Because He has loosed my cord, and afflicted me, they have also thrown off restraint before me. 12 Upon my right hand rise the youth; they push away my feet, and they raise up against me the derech of their destruction. 13 They have broken my path, they set forward my calamity, and they have no one to restrain them. 14 They came on me as a wide breaking in of mayim: in the desolation they rolled themselves on me. 15 Destruction has turned on me: they pursue my being as the wind: and my welfare passes away as a

cloud. 16 And now my being is poured out on me; the days of affliction have taken hold on me. 17 My bones are pierced in me in the night season: and my sinews take no rest. 18 By the great force of my disease is my garment changed: it binds me around as the collar of my coat. 19 He has cast me into the mud, and I am become like dust and ashes. 20 I cry to You, and You do not shema me: I stand up, and You regard me not. 21 You have become cruel to me: with Your strong hand You oppose me. 22 You lift me up to the wind; You cause me to ride on it, and dissolve my possessions. 23 For I know that You will bring me to death, and to the bayit appointed for all living. 24 But He will not stretch out His hand against me to kill me, though I cry in destruction. 25 Did not I weep for him that was in trouble? Was not my being grieved for the poor? 26 When I looked for tov, then evil came to me: and when I waited for light, there came darkness. 27 My inward parts boiled, and rested not: the days of affliction were before me. 28 I went mourning without the sun: I stood up, and I cried in the congregation. 29 I am a brother to dragons, and a companion to owls. 30 My skin is black on me, and my bones are burned with heat. 31 My harp also is turned to mourning, and my flute into the voice of them that weep.

31 I made a covenant with my eyes; why then should I think on a maid? 2 For what portion of Eloah is there from above? And what inheritance of the Almighty from on high? 3 Is not destruction to the wicked? And strange punishment to the workers of iniquity? 4 Does He not see my halacha, and count all my steps? 5 If I have walked with vanity, or if my foot has been led to deceit; 6 Let me be weighed in an even balance, that Eloah may know my integrity. 7 If my step has turned away from His halacha, and my lev walked after my eyes, and if any spot has cleaved to my hands; 8 Then let me sow, and let another

eat; yes, let my offspring be rooted out. 9 If my lev has been deceived by a woman, or if I have laid wait at my neighbor's door; 10 Then let my wife grind for another, and let others bow down on her. 11 For this is a heinous crime; yes, it is an iniquity to be punished by the shophtim. 12 For it is a fire that consumes to destruction, and would root out all my increase. 13 If I did despise the cause of my male eved or of my female eved, when they complained against me; 14 Then what shall I do when El rises up? And when He visits, what shall I answer Him? 15 Did not He that made me in the womb make him also? And did not the Echad Himself fashion us in the womb? 16 If I have withheld from the poor their desire, or have caused the eyes of the widow to lose tikvah; 17 Or have eaten my morsel myself alone, and the fatherless have not eaten of it; 18 For from my youth he was brought up with me, as with an abba, and I have guided her from my ima's womb; 19 If I have seen any perish for want of clothing, or any poor without a covering; 20 If his loins have not blessed me, and if he did not warm himself with the fleece of my sheep; 21 If I have lifted up my hand against the fatherless, when I saw I had help in the gate: 22 Then let my arm fall from my shoulder blade, and my arm be broken from the bone. 23 For destruction from El was a terror to me, and by reason of His excellence I could not endure. 24 If I have made gold my tikvah, or have said to the fine gold, You are my confidence; 25 If I had gilah because my wealth was great, and because my hand had gotten much; 26 If I beheld the sun when it shined, or the moon walking in brightness; 27 And my lev has been secretly enticed, or my mouth has kissed my hand: 28 This also would be an iniquity to be punished by the Shophet: for then I would have denied the El that is above. 29 If I rejoiced at the destruction of him that hated me, or lifted up myself when evil found him: 30 Neither have I allowed my mouth to sin by wishing a curse to his being. 31 If the men of my tent did not say, Who is there that has not been satisfied with some food? 32 The ger did not lodge in the street: but I opened my doors to the traveler. 33 If I covered my transgressions like Adam, by hiding my iniquity in my bosom: 34 Did I fear a great multitude, or did the contempt of families frighten me, that I kept silent, and went not out of the door? 35 Oh that one would shema me! See, my desire is, that the Almighty would answer me, and that my accuser had written an accusation bill. 36 Surely I would take it on my shoulder, and bind it as a keter to me. 37 I would declare to Him the number of my steps; as a prince, would I go near to Him. 38 If my land cries against me, or that the furrows likewise of it complain; 39 If I have eaten the fruits of it without payment, or if I have caused the owners of it to die. 40 Let thistles grow instead of wheat, and weeds instead of barley. The words of Iyov are now finished.

32 So these three men ceased to answer Iyov, because he was tzadik in his own eyes. 2 Then was kindled the anger of Elihu the son of Barach-El the Buzite, of the kindred of Ram: against Iyov was his anger kindled, because he justified himself rather than Eloah. 3 Also against his three chaverim was his anger kindled, because they had found no real answer, and yet had condemned Iyov. 4 Now Elihu had waited until Iyov and the others had spoken, because they were older than him. 5 When Elihu saw that there was no answer in the mouth of these three men, then his anger was kindled. 6 And Elihu the son of Barach-El the Buzite answered and said, I am young, and you are aged; so I was afraid, and did not show you my opinion. 7 I said, Days should speak, and many years should teach chochma. 8 But there is a ruach in man: and the inspiration of the Almighty gives them binah. 9 Great men are not always wise: neither do the aged

always understand mishpat. 10 Therefore I said, Shema to me; I also will show my opinion. 11 See, I waited for your words; I listened to your reasoning, while you searched out what to say. 12 Yes, I attended to you, and, behold, there was none of you that convinced Iyov, or that answered his words: 13 Lest you should say, We have found out chochma: El thrusts him down, not man. 14 Now he has not directed his words against me: neither will I answer him with your speeches. 15 They were amazed, they answered no more: they left off speaking. 16 When I had waited - for they spoke not, but stood still, and answered no more - 17 I said, I will answer also my part; I also will show my opinion. 18 For I am full of words, the ruach within me constrains me. 19 See, my belly is as wine that has no opening; it is ready to burst like new wineskins. 20 I will speak, that I may be relieved: I will open my lips and answer. 21 Let me not show partiality, neither let me give flattering words to any man. 22 For I know better than to give flattery; for in so doing my Maker would soon take me away.[1]

33 Yet, Iyov, I ask you please, shema to my speeches, and shema to all my words. 2 See, now I have opened my mouth, my tongue has spoken in my mouth. 3 My words shall be of the tzedakah of my lev: and my lips shall utter da'at clearly. 4 The Ruach of El has made me, and the Ruach of the Almighty has given me chayim. 5 If you can answer me, set your words in order before me, stand up. 6 See, you and I are the same before El: I also am formed out of the clay. 7 See, nothing about me shall make you afraid; neither shall my pressure be heavy on you. 8 Surely you have spoken in my hearing, and I have heard the voice of your words, saying, 9 I am clean without transgression, I am innocent; neither is there iniquity in me.

---

[1] As seen throughout Scripture, the term "taken away" is not a tov thing (as in a fictitious "rapture"), but a terrible thing with judgment impending.

10 See, He finds occasions against me; He counts me as His enemy, 11 He puts my feet in the stocks; He marks all my paths. 12 See, in this you are not tzadik: I will answer you, that Eloah is greater than man. 13 Why do you complain against Him? For He doesn't give answers about all His matters. 14 For El speaks once, or twice, yet a man perceives it not. 15 In a dream, in a vision of the night, when deep sleep falls on men, in slumbering on the bed; 16 Then He opens the ears of men, and seals their instructions, 17 That He may withdraw man from His own purpose, and hide pride from man. 18 He keeps back his being from Sheol, and his chayim from perishing by the sword. 19 He is chastened also with pain on his bed, and the multitude of his bones with strong pain: 20 So that his chayim abhors lechem, and his being desirable food. 21 His flesh wastes away, that it cannot be seen; and his bones that were not seen stick out. 22 Yes, his being draws near to Sheol, and his chayim to the destroyers. 23 If there be a messenger with him, a mediator, one among a thousand, to show to man His tzedakah: 24 Then He shows unmerited favor to him, and says, Deliver him from going down to Sheol: I have found a ransom. 25 His flesh shall be fresher than a child's: he shall return to the days of his youth:[1] 26 He shall make tefillah to Eloah, and He will show unmerited favor to him: and He shall see his face with simcha: for He will restore to man his own tzedakah.[2] 27 He looks on men, and if any say, I have sinned, and perverted that which was right, and it did not profit; 28 He will deliver his being from going into Sheol, and his chayim shall see the light. 29 See, all these things works El often with man, 30 To bring back his being from Sheol, to be enlightened with the light of the living.[3] 31 Take note, O Iyov, shema to me tov: hold your silence, and I will speak. 32 If you have anything to say, answer me: speak, for I desire to justify you. 33 If not, shema to me: hold your silence, and I shall teach you chochma.

34 Furthermore Elihu answered and said, 2 Shema to my words, O you wise men; and give ear to me, you that have da'at. 3 For the ear tries words, as the mouth tastes food. 4 Let us choose for us mishpat: let us know among ourselves what is tov. 5 For Iyov has said, I am tzadik: and El has taken away my mishpat. 6 Should I lie against my right? My wound is incurable without any transgression on my part. 7 What man is like Iyov, who drinks up the mocking of others like mayim? 8 Who goes in the company with the workers of iniquity, and walks with wicked men. 9 For he has said, It profits a man nothing that he should delight himself with Eloah. 10 Therefore shema to me, you men of binah: far be it from Eloah, that He should do wickedness; and from the Almighty, that He should commit iniquity. 11 For the work of a man shall He render to him, and cause every man to find his own reward according to his own halacha. 12 Yes, surely El will not do wickedly, neither will the Almighty pervert mishpat. 13 Who has given Him authority over the earth? Or who has laid out the whole olam hazeh? 14 If He set His lev on man, if He gather to Himself man's ruach and his breath;[4] 15 All flesh shall perish together, and man shall turn again to dust. 16 If now you have binah, shema to this: shema to the voice of my words. 17 Shall he that hates mishpat govern? And will you condemn him that is the most tzadik? 18 Is it fit to say to a melech, You are worthless? And to princes, You are evil? 19 How much less to him that shows no partiality towards princes, or regards the rich over the poor? For they all are the work of His hands. 20 In a moment shall they die, and the people shall be troubled at midnight, and pass away: and the mighty

---

[1] In the resurrection.
[2] YHWH did that through His Son.
[3] Resurrection from the grave.

[4] Redeemed spirits go to YHWH; waiting for a rejoining with a new resurrected body.

shall be taken away[1] without hand. 21 For His eyes are on the halacha of man, and He sees his entire goings. 22 There is no darkness, nor shadow of death, where the workers of iniquity may hide themselves. 23 For He will not lay on man more than is right; that he is able to enter into mishpat with El. 24 He shall break in pieces mighty men without number, and set others in their place. 25 Therefore He knows their works, and He overturns them in the night, so that they are destroyed. 26 He strikes them as wicked men in the open sight of others; 27 Because they turned back from Him, and would not consider any of His halachot: 28 So that they cause the cry of the poor to come to Him, and He shemas the cry of the afflicted. 29 When He gives shalom, who then can make trouble? And when He hides His face, who then can behold Him? Whether it be done against a nation, or against a man: 30 That the hypocrite should not rule, lest the people be trapped. 31 Surely it is right to say to El, I have borne my chastisement, I will not offend any more: 32 That which I see not teach me: If I have done iniquity, I will do no more. 33 Must Eloah have your consent to punish, that you can reject it? Will you choose while others don't? Therefore tell me what you know. 34 Let men of binah tell me, and let a wise man shema to me. 35 Iyov has spoken without da'at, and his words were without chochma. 36 My desire is that Iyov may be tried to the very end because his answers are the same as wicked men. 37 For he adds rebellion to his sin, he claps his hands among us, and multiplies his words against El.

35

Elihu spoke moreover, and said, 2 Do you think you are right, when you said; My tzedakah is more than El's? 3 For you said; What advantage will it be to you? And, What profit shall I have, if I am cleansed from my sin? 4 I will answer you, and your companions with you. 5 Look to the shamayim, and see; and behold the clouds which are higher than you. 6 If you sin, what would you do against Him? Or if your transgressions are multiplied, what would you do to Him? 7 If you are tzadik, what would you give Him? Or what does He receive from your hand? 8 Your wickedness may hurt a man as you are; and your tzedakah may profit the son of man. 9 By reason of the multitude of oppressions they make the oppressed to cry: they cry out by reason of the arm of the mighty. 10 But none says, Where is Eloah My Maker, who gives shirim in the night; 11 Who teaches us more than the beasts of the earth, and makes us wiser than the fowls of the shamayim? 12 There they cry, but none gives an answer, because of the pride of evil men. 13 Surely El will not shema vanity, neither will the Almighty regard it. 14 Although you say you do not see Him, yet mishpat is before Him; therefore trust in Him. 15 But now, because it is not so, He has not visited in His anger; He does not harm extreme arrogance of being. 16 Therefore does Iyov open his mouth in vain; he multiplies words without da'at.

36

Elihu also proceeded, and said, 2 Allow me a little more time, and I will show you that I have yet to speak on Eloah's behalf. 3 I will fetch my da'at from afar, and will ascribe tzedakah to My Maker. 4 For truly my words shall not be false: He that is perfect in da'at is with you. 5 See, El is mighty, and despises no one: He is mighty in strength and chochma. 6 He preserves not the chayim of the wicked: but does mishpat to the poor. 7 He withdraws not His eyes from the tzadikim: but with melechim are they on the throne; yes, He does establish them le-olam-va-ed, and they are exalted. 8 And if they be bound in fetters, and be held in cords of affliction; 9 Then He shows them their work, and their transgressions that they have exceeded. 10 He opens also their ear to discipline, and commands that they make teshuvah from

---

[1] The lost are taken or caught away, never the righteous.

iniquity. 11 If they obey and serve Him, they shall spend their days in prosperity, and their years in pleasures. 12 But if they obey not, they shall perish by the sword, and they shall die without da'at. 13 But the hypocrites in lev heaps up anger: let them cry not when He binds them. 14 They die in their youth, and their chayim is among the unclean. 15 He delivers the poor in his affliction, and opens their ears in oppression. 16 Even so would He have removed you out of trouble into a broad place, where there is no trouble; so that which should be set on your table should be full of rich food. 17 But you are now filled with the mishpat upon the wicked; mishpat and tzedakah have taken hold of you. 18 Because there is anger, beware lest He take you away with His stroke: then even a great ransom cannot deliver you. 19 Will He value your riches? No, not gold, nor all the forces of your strength. 20 Desire not the night, when people are cut off in their place. 21 Take heed, regard not iniquity: for this have you chosen rather than affliction. 22 See, El is exalted by His power: who is a Teacher like Him? 23 Who has assigned Him His halacha? Or who can say, You have done iniquity? 24 Remember to magnify His work, which men behold. 25 Every man may see it; man may behold it even far off. 26 See, El is great, and we know Him not, neither can the number of His years be searched out. 27 For He makes small the drops of mayim: they pour down rain according to the mist of it: 28 Which the clouds do drop and distil on man abundantly. 29 Also can any understand the spreading of the clouds, or the noise of His sukkah? 30 See, He spreads His light on it, and covers the bottom of the sea. 31 For by them He shophets the people; He gives food in abundance. 32 With clouds He covers the light; and commands it not to shine by the cloud that comes between. 33 Its noise reveals it; the cattle also reveal what is coming.

37 At this also my lev trembles, and is moved out of its place. 2 Shema attentively the noise of His voice, and the sound that goes out of His mouth. 3 He directs it under the whole the shamayim, and His lightning to the ends of the earth. 4 After it a voice roars: He thunders with the voice of His excellency; and He will not hold them back when His voice is heard. 5 El thunders marvelously with His voice; great things He does, which we cannot comprehend. 6 For He says to the snow, *Be on the earth*; likewise to the small rain, and to the great rain of His strength. 7 He seals up the hand of every man; that all men may know His work. 8 Then the beasts go into dens, and remain in their places. 9 Out of the south comes the whirlwind: and cold out of the north. 10 By the Ruach of El frost is given: and the width of the mayim becomes ice. 11 Also by moisture He loads the thick clouds: He scatters His bright cloud: 12 And they swirl around by His counsels: that they may do whatever He commands them on the face of the earth. 13 He causes it to come, whether for correction, or for His land, or for rachamim. 14 Shema to this, O Iyov: stand still, and consider the wondrous works of El. 15 Do you know when Eloah disposed them, and caused the light of His cloud to shine? 16 Do you know the balancing of the clouds, the wondrous works of Him who is perfect in da'at? 17 How your garments are warm, when He quiets the earth by the south wind? 18 Have you joined Him to spread out the sky, which is strong, and as a hard mirror? 19 Teach us what we shall say to Him; for we cannot order our speech by reason of darkness. 20 Shall it be told to Him that I speak? If a man speaks to Him, surely He shall be swallowed up. 21 And now men do not see the bright light that is in the clouds: but the wind passes, and cleanses them. 22 Fair-weather comes out of the north: Eloah is awesome in majesty. 23 Touching the Almighty, we cannot find Him out: He is excellent in power, and in mishpat, and in plenty of tzedakah: He will not afflict. 24 Men do therefore fear Him: He respects no one wise in their own lev.

38

Then יהוה answered Iyov out of the whirlwind, and said,[1] 2 *Who is this that darkens counsel by words without da'at? 3 Gird up your loins like a man; for now I will demand from you, and answer Me if you can. 4 Where were you when I laid the foundations of the earth? Declare, it if you have binah. 5 Who has laid the measures of it, if you know? Or who has stretched the line on it?[2] 6 On what are the foundations of it fastened? Or who laid the cornerstone of it; 7 When the morning chochavim sang as echad, and all the sons of Eloah[3] shouted for simcha? 8 Or who shut up the sea with doors, when it broke forth, as if it had issued out of the womb? 9 When I made the cloud its garment, and thick darkness its swaddling band, 10 And broke up for it My decreed place, and set bars and doors to it, 11 And said, Up to here shall you come, but no further: and here shall your proud waves be stopped? 12 Have you ever commanded the morning; and caused the dawn to know its place; 13 That it might take hold of the ends of the earth, that the wicked might be shaken out of it? 14 So that their bodies will be changed to clay under a seal; and be thrown into a heap. 15 And from the wicked light is withheld, and their lifted arm shall be broken. 16 Have you entered into the sources of the sea? Or have you walked in search of the depth? 17 Have the gates of death been opened to you? Or have you seen the doors of the shadow of death? 18 Have you perceived the width of the earth? Declare the width if you know it all. 19 Where is the path to where light dwells? And as for darkness, where is its place, 20 That you should find its boundary, and that you should know the paths to its source, 21 Do you know it, because you were born back then? Or because the number of your days goes back to that time? 22 Have you entered into the treasures of the snow? Or have you seen the treasures of the hail, 23 Which I have reserved for the time of trouble,[4] prepared for the day of battle and war? 24 By what manner is the light divided, or the east wind scattered all over the earth? 25 Who has divided a watercourse for the overflowing of mayim, or a derech for the clap of thunder; 26 To cause it to rain on the earth, where no man is; in the wilderness, in which there is no man; 27 To satisfy the desolate and waste places; and to cause the bud of the tender herb to spring forth? 28 Does the rain have an abba? Or who has brought forth the drops of dew? 29 Out of whose womb came the ice? And the frost of the shamayim, who has birthed it? 30 The mayim harden like a stone, and the face of the deep is frozen. 31 Can you stop the movement of Pleiades, or loose the path of Orion? 32 Can you bring forth the constellations in its season? Or can you lead the Bear with his sons? 33 Do you know the laws of the shamayim? Can you set the dominion of the shamayim in the earth? 34 Can you lift up your voice to the clouds, that abundance of mayim may cover you? 35 Can you send lightning, so that they go, and say to you, Here we are! 36 Who has put chochma in the inward parts? Or who has given binah to the lev? 37 Who can number the clouds in chochma? Or who can tip over the wineskins of the shamayim, 38 When the dust grows into hardness, and the clods cleave fast together? 39 Will you hunt the prey for the lion? Or fill the appetite of the young lions, 40 When they couch in their dens, and sit in secret to lie in wait? 41 Who provides for the raven his food? When his young ones cry to El, and wander for lack of food..*

---

[1] When YHWH breaks forth in personal or redemptive revelation as with Iyov, He uses YHWH and not Eloah or Elohim.
[2] Job did not know it was Yahshua, since that was progressively revealed later on.
[3] Heavenly sons; or messengers.

[4] Great Tribulation.

39 *Do you know the time when the wild mountain goat bears young ones? Or can you observe when the deer give birth? 2 Can you number the months that they are complete? Or do you know the time when they bring forth? 3 They bow down, they bring forth their young ones, their labor pains are ended. 4 Their young ones are thriving, they grow up in the field; they go forth, and do not return to them. 5 Who has set the wild donkey free? Or who has loosed the yoke of the wild donkey, 6 Whose home I have made the wilderness, and the barren land his dwellings? 7 He scorns the multitude of the city; neither regards the shouts of the driver. 8 The range of the mountains is his pasture, and he searches after every green thing. 9 Will the wild ox be willing to serve you, or abide by your feeding trough? 10 Can you bind the yoke on the neck of the wild ox? Or will he plough the valleys behind you? 11 Will you trust him, because his strength is great? Or will you leave your labor to him? 12 Will you believe him that he will bring home your grain, and gather it into your barn? 13 Did you give the fine wings to the peacocks? Or wings and feathers to the ostrich? 14 She leaves her eggs in the earth, and warms them in the dust, 15 And forgets that a foot may crush them, or that a wild beast may break them. 16 She treats her young harshly, as though they were not hers: her toil is in vain without fear; 17 Because Eloah has deprived her of chochma, neither has He imparted binah to her. 18 When she lifts herself on high, she laughs at the horse and his rider. 19 Have you given the horse strength? Have you clothed his neck with thunder? 20 Can you make him leap like a grasshopper? The splendor of his nostrils is terrible. 21 He paws in the valley, and has gilah in his strength: He goes on to meet the armed men. 22 He mocks at fear, and is not afraid; neither turns back from the sword. 23 The quiver rattles against him, the glittering spear and the shield. 24 He swallows the ground with fierceness and rage: and does not stand still when the shofar is sounded. 25 He says at the blast of the shofar, Aha; and He smells the battle from far, the thunder of the commanders, and the shouting. 26 Does the hawk fly by your chochma, and stretch her wings toward the south? 27 Does the eagle mount up at your command, and make its nest on high? 28 It dwells and abides on the rock, on the cliff of the rock, and the stronghold. 29 From there it seeks the prey, and its eyes behold far off. 30 Her young ones also suck up dom: and where the slain are, there it is.*

40 *Moreover* יהוה *answered Iyov, and said, 2 Shall he that contends with the Almighty instruct Him? He that reproves Eloah, let him answer. 3 Then Iyov answered* יהוה*, and said, 4 See, I am unworthy; what shall I answer You? I will lay my hand on my mouth. 5 Once have I spoken; but I will not answer: yes, twice; but I will proceed no further. 6 Then answered* יהוה *to Iyov out of the whirlwind, and said, 7 Gird up your loins now like a man: I will ask things of you, and you declare the answers to Me. 8 Will you also disannul My mishpat? Will you condemn Me, that you may be a tzadik? 9 Have you an arm like El?1 Or can you thunder with a voice like Him? 10 Deck yourself now with majesty and excellency; and dress yourself with tiferet and splendor. 11 Cast abroad the rage of your anger: and behold everyone that is proud, and bring him low. 12 Look on everyone that is proud, and bring him low; and tread down the wicked in their place. 13 Hide them in the dust together; and bind their faces in obscurity. 14 Then will I also confess to you that your own right hand can save you. 15 See now Behemoth-hippopotamus, which I made with you; he eats grass as an ox. 16 See, his strength is in his loins, and his force is in his stomach muscles. 17 He moves his tail like a cedar: the sinews of his*

---
[1] Moshiach.

thighs are wrapped together. 18 His bones are as tubes of bronze; his bones are like bars of iron. 19 He is the start of the derech of El: His Maker made him powerful to fight. 20 Surely the mountains bring him food, where all the beasts of the field play. 21 He lies under the shady trees, under the cover of the reed, and fens. 22 The shady trees cover him with their shadow; the willows of the stream surround him. 23 See, if the river rages he has no fear: he trusts that he can draw up the Yarden River into his mouth. 24 Can one catch him with a hook or a net: or pierce his nose through a trap?

41 Can you draw out Leviathan[1] with a hook? Or his tongue with a cord which you let down? 2 Can you put a hook into his nose? Or pierce his jaw through with a hook? 3 Will he plead with you? Will he speak soft words to you? 4 Will he make a covenant with you? Will you take him as an eved le-olam-va-ed? 5 Will you play with him as with a bird? Or will you leash him for your young girls? 6 Shall trading partners bargain over him? Shall they part him among the merchants? 7 Can you fill his skin with harpoons? Or his head with fishing spears? 8 Try to capture him, such a battle you will never forget. 9 See any expectation regarding him is worthless: shall not one be cast down just at the sight of him? 10 None is so fierce that dares to stir him up: who then is able to stand before Me? 11 Who has given anything to Me, that I should repay him? Whatever is under the whole the shamayim is Mine. 12 I will not conceal his parts, nor his power, nor his fair frame. 13 Who can remove the surface of his skin? Or who can come to him with a double bridle? 14 Who can open the doors of his face? His teeth are terrible all around. 15 His scales are his pride, closed together as with a binding seal. 16 One is so near to another, so that no air can come between them. 17 They are joined one to another, they stick together, that they cannot be separated. 18 By his sneezing a light does shine, and his eyes are like the eyelids of the morning. 19 Out of his mouth goes smoke, and sparks of fire leap out. 20 Out of his nostrils goes smoke, as out of a boiling pot or kettle. 21 His ruach kindles coals, and a flame goes out of his mouth. 22 In his neck remains strength, and fear proceeds from him. 23 The folds of his flesh are joined together: they are firm in themselves; they cannot be moved. 24 His lev is as firm as a stone; yes, as hard as a piece of lower millstone. 25 When he raises himself to stand, the mighty are afraid: by reason of his crashing they are amazed. 26 The sword that reaches him cannot hold him: the spear, the dart, nor the lance. 27 He reckons iron as straw, and bronze as rotten wood. 28 The arrow cannot make him flee: sling stones are like stubble to him. 29 Darts are counted as stubble: he laughs at the shaking of a spear. 30 Sharp stones make up his underbelly: he sprawls on the mud like a sledge. 31 He makes the deep to boil and bubble like a pot: He makes the sea like a pot of ointment. 32 He makes a path to shine after him; one would think the deep to be gray. 33 Upon earth there is none like him, who is made without fear. 34 He beholds all high things: He is a melech over all the children of pride.

42 Then Iyov answered יהוה , and said, 2 I know that You can do everything, and that no thought can be withheld from You. 3 Who is he that hides counsel without da'at? Therefore have I uttered what I understood not; things too wonderful for me, which I knew not. 4 Shema, I beg You, and I will speak: I did ask You, and You did answer me. 5 I have heard of You before by the hearing of the ear: but now my eye sees You.[2] 6 Now I despise myself, and repent in dust and ashes. 7 And it was so, that after יהוה had

---

[1] In the literal, this is a ferocious perhaps extinct sea monster, or sea dinosaur. In the **remez** or hint level of understanding, this is an allegory or metaphor for s.a.tan himself.

[2] The trials brought Job from head knowledge to personal heart knowledge.

spoken these words to Iyov, יהוה said to Eliphaz the Temanite, *My anger is kindled against you, and against your two chaverim: for you have not spoken of Me the thing that is right, like My eved Iyov has. 8 Therefore take now seven bullocks and seven rams, and go to My eved Iyov, and offer up for yourselves a burnt offering; and My eved Iyov shall make tefillah for you: for him will I accept: lest I deal with you after your folly, in that you have not spoken of Me the thing which is right, like My eved Iyov.* 9 So Eliphaz the Temanite and Bildad the Shuhite and Tzophar the Na'amathite went, and did according to what יהוה commanded them: יהוה also accepted Iyov. 10 And יהוה turned the captivity of Iyov, when he made tefillah for his chaverim: also יהוה gave Iyov twice as much as he had before. 11 Then came to him all his brothers, and all his sisters, and all those that had been of his relatives before, and did eat lechem with him in his bayit: and they sympathized with him, and comforted him over all the evil that יהוה had allowed upon him: every man also gave him a piece of silver, and every one a ring of gold. 12 So יהוה blessed the latter end of Iyov more than his beginning: for he had fourteen thousand sheep, and six thousand camels, and a thousand yoke of oxen, and a thousand female donkeys. 13 He had also seven sons and three daughters. 14 And he called the name of the first, Yemima; and the name of the second, Ketziyah; and the name of the third, Keren-Happuch. 15 And in all the land were no women found as beautiful as the daughters of Iyov: and their abba gave them a full inheritance among their brothers. 16 After this Iyov lived one hundred forty years, and saw his sons, and his grandchildren, even to the fourth generation. 17 So Iyov died, being old and satisfied with a fullness of days.

Shir HaShirim - Song of Songs

To Our Forefathers Yisrael

1 The shir ha-shirim, which is Shlomo's.[1]

2 Let Him kiss me with the kisses of His mouth: for your love is better than wine.

3 Because of the fragrance of Your good perfumes Your Name is as ointment poured forth,[2] therefore do the virgins love You.

4 Draw me, we will run after You: the melech has brought me into His inner rooms: we will be in simcha and gilah in You, we will remember your love more than wine: the tzadikim love You.

5 I am black,[3] but lovely, O daughters of Yahrushalayim, as the tents of Kedar, as the curtains of Shlomo.

6 Look not upon me, because I am black, because the sun has looked upon me: my ima's children were angry with me; they made me the keeper of the vineyards; but my own vineyard have I not kept.

7 Tell me, O You whom my being loves, where You feed, where You make your flock to rest at noon: for why should I be as one that is veiled by the flocks of your companions?

8 If you know not, O you fairest among women, go your way in the footsteps of the flock, and feed your little goats beside the shepherds' tents.

9 I have compared You, O My love, to a company of horses in Pharaoh's mirkavot.

10 Your cheeks are lovely with rows of jewels, your neck with chains of gold.

11 We will make You borders of gold with studs of silver.

12 While the melech sits at His table, my spikenard sends forth its smell.

13 A bundle of myrrh is My Beloved to me; he shall lie all night between my breasts.

14 My Beloved is to me as a cluster of henna flowers in the vineyards of En-Gedi.

15 See, You are fair, my love; see, You are fair; You have doves' eyes.

16 See, You are handsome, My Beloved, yes, pleasant: also our bed is green.

17 The beams of our house are cedar, and our rafters of cypress.

2 I am the Rose of Sharon, and the Lily of the Valleys.[4]

2 As the lily among the thorns, so is my love among the daughters.[5]

3 As the apple tree among the trees of the wood, so is My Beloved among the sons. I sat down under His shadow with great delight, and His fruit was sweet to my taste.

4 He brought me to the banqueting house, and His banner over me was love.[6]

5 Strengthens me with raisin cakes, comforts me with apples: for I am sick for love.

6 His left hand is under my head, and His right hand does embrace me.

7 I charge you, O you daughters of Yahrushalayim, by the gazelles, and by the deer of the field, that you stir not, nor awake my love, until He so pleases.

8 The voice of My Beloved! He is coming leaping upon the mountains, skipping upon the hills.[7]

---

[1] In the **remez** or hint level of Hebraic understanding, the entire scroll is a love letter between Yisrael the bride and YHWH her Maker and Husband. The so-called church; has claimed this love song as a love song between them and YHWH. This doctrine stakes a not so subtle claim to being the new Yisrael thus replacing Jewish Yisrael. Their interpretation of this song in such manner is just one more attempt by the institutionalized church to replace the scripture's true intent. The so-called church has applied this entire scroll, to a new and improved gentile church bride, as opposed to Yisrael, who in fact remains YHWH's eternal bride. The very terminology that sees the so-called church, as Yahshua's bride, is pure doctrinal anti-Semitism.

[2] YHWH's Name.

[3] Very possibly a reference in the literal-**pashat;** to Solomon's dark skin.

[4] Yisrael's bridegroom is Yahshua/YHWH; as viewed by Yisrael's daughters.

[5] Of Tzion.

[6] Yisrael has been brought to His feasts and His loving banner.

[7] The promise and anticipation of Yahshua's return.

9 My Beloved is like a gazelle or a young stag: see, He stands behind our wall, He looks out the windows, showing Himself through the lattice.

10 My Beloved spoke, and said to me, Rise up, my love, my fair one, and come away.

11 For, look, the winter is past, the rain is over and gone;[1]

12 The flowers appear on the earth; the time of the singing of birds has come, and the voice of the turtledove is heard in our land;[2]

13 The fig tree puts forth her green figs,[3] and the vines with the tender grapes give a good smell. Arise, my love, my fair one, and come away.

14 O My dove, that are in the clefts of the rock, in the secret places of the stairs, let me see your countenance, let me hear your voice; for sweet is your voice, and your countenance is lovely.

15 Catch the foxes, the little foxes that spoil the vines: for our vines have tender grapes.[4]

16 My Beloved is mine, and I am His:[5] He feeds among the lilies.

17 Until the day break, and the shadows flee away, turn, My Beloved, and be like a gazelle or a young stag upon the mountains of Bether.

3 By night on my bed I sought Him whom my being loves: I sought Him, but I found Him not.

2 I will rise now, and go about the city in the streets, and in the broad ways I will seek Him whom my being loves: I sought Him, but I found Him not.

3 The watchmen that go around the city found me: to whom I said, Did You see Him whom my being loves?

4 Scarcely I passed from them, but I found Him whom my being loves: I held Him, and would not let Him go, until I had brought Him into my ima's house, and into the inner rooms of her that conceived me.

5 I charge you, O you daughters of Yahrushalayim, by the gazelles, and by the deer of the field, that you stir not, nor awake my love, until He so pleases.

6 Who is this that comes out of the wilderness like pillars of smoke, perfumed with myrrh and frankincense, with all powders of the merchants?

7 See his bed, which is Shlomo's; sixty valiant men are around it, of the valiant of Yisrael.

8 They all hold swords, being experts in war: every man has his sword upon his thigh because of fear in the night.

9 King Shlomo made himself a mirkavah from the woods of Levanon.

10 He made its pillars of silver, the bottom of gold, the covering of it in purple, and the middle being paved with love, by the daughters of Yahrushalayim.

11 Go forth, O you daughters of Tzion, and see melech Shlomo with the keter with which his ima crowned him in the day of his wedding, and in the day of the simcha of his lev.

4 See, You are fair, my love; see, You are fair; You have doves' eyes within your locks: your hair is as a flock of goats, coming down from Mount Gilead.

2 Your teeth are like a flock of sheep that are shorn, which came up from the washing; all of them bear twins, and none is barren among them.

3 Your lips are like a thread of scarlet, and your speech is lovely: your cheeks are like a piece of a pomegranate.

4 Your neck is like the tower of David built for an armory, on which there hangs a thousand shields, all the shields of mighty men.

5 Your two breasts are like two young gazelles that are twins, who feed among the lilies.

---

[1] The return of Moshiach after the winter of the Great Tribulation.
[2] The millennium or **atid lavoh.**
[3] Yisrael will once again blossom over the entire earth as in Solomon's days.
[4] Foxes are a type of demons who try and destroy Yisrael's fruitfulness in Moshaich.
[5] **Ani dodi ve dodi lee.** The eternal covenant between Yahshua and Yisrael, is beautifully expressed in these profound words.

6 Until the day breaks, and the shadows flee away, I will go my way to the mountain of myrrh, and to the hill of frankincense.

7 You are all fair, My love; there is no spot in You.[1]

8 Come with Me from Levanon, My bride, with me from Levanon: look from the top of Amana, from the top of Shenir and Hermon, from the lions' dens, from the mountains of the leopards.

9 You have encouraged My lev, My sister, My bride; you have encouraged My lev with one of your eyes, with one bead of your necklace.

10 How fair is your love, my sister, and My bride! How much better is your love than wine! And the fragrance of your perfumes than all spices!

11 Your lips, O my bride, drop as the honeycomb: honey and milk are under your tongue; and the smell of your garments is like the smell of Levanon.

12 A garden locked is My sister, My bride; a spring shut, a fountain locked.

13 Your plants are an orchard of pomegranates; with pleasant fruits; with henna flower, with spikenard,

14 Spikenard and saffron; calamus and cinnamon, with all trees of frankincense; myrrh and aloes, with all the chief spices:

15 A fountain of gardens, a well of living mayim, and streams from Levanon.

16 Awake, O north wind; and come, O south; blow upon my garden that the spices may flow out. Let my Beloved come into His garden, and eat His pleasant fruits.[2]

5 I am come into my garden, My sister, My bride: I have gathered My myrrh with My spice; I have eaten My honeycomb with My honey; I have drunk My wine with My milk: eat, O friends; drink, yes, drink abundantly, O beloved.

2 I sleep, but my lev awakes: it is the voice of My Beloved that knocks, saying, Open to Me, My sister, My love, My dove, My undefiled: for My head is filled with dew, and My locks with the drops of the night.

3 I have put off My coat; how shall I put it on? I have washed My feet; how shall I defile them?

4 My Beloved put in His hand by the latch of the door, and my inside feelings were moved for Him.

5 I rose up to open to My Beloved; and my hands dripped with myrrh, and my fingers with sweet smelling myrrh, upon the handles of the lock.

6 I opened to My Beloved; but My Beloved had withdrawn Himself, and was gone: my being failed when He spoke: I sought Him, but I could not find Him; I called to Him, but He gave me no answer.

7 The watchmen that went around the city found me, they smote me, they wounded me; the keepers of the walls took away my veil from me.

8 I charge you, O daughters of Yahrushalayim, if you find My Beloved, that you tell Him, that I am sick for love.

9 Why is your Beloved greater than another Beloved, O you fairest among women? Why is your Beloved greater than another beloved, that you have placed us under an oath?

10 My Beloved is dazzling and ruddy, the head among ten thousand.

11 His head is as the finest gold; His locks are wavy, and black as a raven.[3]

12 His eyes are as the eyes of doves by the rivers of mayim, washed with milk, and fitly set.

13 His cheeks are as a bed of spices, as sweet flowers: His lips like lilies, dripping sweet smelling myrrh.

14 His hands are as gold rings set with the beryl: His belly is as bright ivory overlaid with sapphires.

---

[1] Redeemed Yisrael has no spot or blemish because of the bridegroom.

[2] Yisrael has much fruit to offer her Beloved while she abides in the vine.

[3] Description of a man of color.

15 His legs are as pillars of marble, set upon sockets of fine gold: His countenance is as Levanon, excellent as the cedars.
16 His mouth is most sweet: yes, He is altogether lovely. This is My Beloved, and this is My friend, O daughters of Yahrushalayim.

6 Where is Your Beloved gone, O fairest among women? Where has your Beloved turned aside, that we may seek Him with you?
2 My Beloved is gone down into His garden, to the beds of spices, to feed in the gardens, and to gather lilies.
3 I am My Beloved's, and My Beloved is mine: He feeds among the lilies.
4 You are beautiful, O my love, as fair as Tirzah, lovely as Yahrushalayim, terrible as an army with banners.
5 Turn away your eyes from me, for they have overcome me: your hair is as a flock of goats that appeared from Gilead.
6 Your teeth are as a flock of sheep which go up from the washing, where everyone bears twins, and there is not one barren among them.
7 As two pieces of a pomegranate are your cheeks behind your veil.
8 There are sixty queens, and eighty concubines, and virgins without number.
9 My dove, my undefiled is but one; she is the only one of her ima; she is the choicest one of her that bare her. The daughters saw her, and blessed her; yes, the malchas and the concubines, they give tehilla to her.
10 Who is she that shines forth as the morning, fair as the moon, clear as the sun, and awesome as an army with banners?
11 I went down into the garden of nuts to see the fruits of the valley, and to see whether the vine flourished, and the pomegranates budded.
12 I did not know, My desire made me like the mirkavot of nobility.
13 Teshuvah, and shuv, O Shulamite; shuv, shuv, that we may look upon you. What will

you see in the Shulamite? As it were the dance companies of two armies.[1]

7 How beautiful are your feet in sandals, O prince's daughter! The curves of your thighs are like jewels, the work of the hands of a skilled workman.
2 Your navel is like a round bowl, let it not lack wine: your body is like a heap of wheat set about with lilies.
3 Your two breasts are like two young gazelles that are twins.
4 Your neck is as a tower of ivory; your eyes like the pools in Heshbon, by the gate of Bath-Ravvim: your nose is as the tower of Levanon that looks toward Damascus.
5 Your head upon you is like Carmel, and the hair of your head like purple; the melech is held by the ringlets.
6 How fair and how pleasant are you, O love, for delights!
7 Your stature is like a palm tree, and your breasts to clusters of grapes.
8 I said, I will go up to the palm tree, I will take hold of its tips: now also your breasts shall be as clusters of the vine, and the smell of your nose like apples;
9 And the roof of your mouth like the best wine for my Beloved, that makes me move my lips and my teeth.
10 I am My Beloved's, and His desire is toward me.
11 Come, my Beloved, let us go forth into the field; let us stay in the villages.
12 Let us get up early to the vineyards; let us see if the vine has budded, whether the tender grapes appears, and the pomegranates bud forth: there will I give You my love.
13 The love-apples give a smell, and at our gates are all manner of pleasant fruits, new and old,[2] which I have laid up for You, O My Beloved.

---

[1] Yisrael is likened unto a woman who returns to her bridegroom to be seen as the two rejoicing houses of Yahudah and Ephraim At their return to YHWH through Yahshua, both dance for joy in their renewal and restoration before their Beloved.
[2] The fruits found in both covenants manifest in a close bond between Yahshua and Renewed Covenant Yisrael.

8 O that You were as my brother that sucked the breasts of my ima! When I should find You outside, I would kiss You; yes, I should not be despised.

2 I would lead You, and bring You into my ima's house, who would instruct Me: I would cause You to drink of spiced wine of the juice of My pomegranate.

3 His left hand should be under my head, and His right hand should embrace me.

4 I have put you under oath, O daughters of Yahrushalayim; that you stir not, nor awake my love, until He so pleases.

5 Who is this that comes up from the wilderness, leaning upon her Beloved? I raised you up under the apple tree: there your ima brought you forth: there she brought you forth that bare you.

6 Set me as a seal upon Your lev, as a seal upon Your arm: for love is strong as death; jealousy is cruel as the grave: the coals of it are coals of fire, which has a most vehement flame.

7 Many mayim cannot quench love, neither can the floods drown it: if a man would give all the substance of his house for love, it would utterly be scorned.

8 We have a little sister, and she has no breasts: what shall we do for our sister in the day when she shall be spoken for?

9 If she is a wall, we will build upon her a palace of silver: and if she is a door, we will enclose her with boards of cedar.

10 I am a wall, and my breasts like towers: then was I in His eyes as one that found favor.

11 Shlomo had a vineyard at Baal-Hamon; he leased the vineyard to keepers; everyone for its fruit was to bring a thousand pieces of silver.

12 My vineyard, which is mine, is before me: O Shlomo, You must have a thousand, and those that keep the fruit two hundred.

13 You that dwell in the gardens, the companions listen to Your voice: let me hear it.[1]

14 Hurry, My Beloved, and be like to a gazelle or a young stag upon the mountains of spices.

---

[1] Redeemed Yisrael listens carefully for the voice of the Master Yahshua both in and out of the vineyard.

רות

Root - Ruth
To Our Forefathers Yisrael

1 Now it came to pass in the days when the shophtim ruled, that there was a famine in the land. And a certain man of Beth-Lechem Yahudah went to sojourn in the country of Moav, he, and his wife, and his two sons. 2 And the name of the man was Eli-Melech, and the name of his wife Naomi, and the name of his two sons Machlon and Chilyon, Ephrathites[1] of Beth-Lechem Yahudah. And they came into the country of Moav, and continued there. 3 And Eli-Melech Naomi's husband died; and she was left, with her two sons. 4 And they took wives from the women of Moav; the name of the one was Orpah, and the name of the other Root:[2] and they dwelled there about ten years. 5 And Machlon and Chilyon both died; and the woman was left without her two sons and her husband. 6 Then she arose with her daughters-in-law; that she might return from the country of Moav: for she had heard in the country of Moav how that יהוה had visited His people in giving them lechem. 7 And she went forth out of the place where she was, with her two daughters-in-law with her; and they went on the way to return to the land of Yahudah. 8 And Naomi said to her two daughters-in-law, Go, return each of you to your ima's bayit: יהוה deal kindly with you, as you have dealt with the dead, and with me. 9 יהוה grant you that you may find rest, each of you in the bayit of a husband. Then she kissed them; and they lifted up their voice, and wept. 10 And they said to her, Surely we will return with you to your people.[3] 11 And Naomi said, Turn back again, my daughters: why will you go

with me? Are there more sons in my womb, that they may be your husbands? 12 Turn again, my daughters, go your way; for I am too old to have a husband. If I should say, I have tikvah, that I should have a husband also tonight, should I bear sons? 13 Would you wait for them until they were grown? Would you keep yourselves back from having husbands? No, my daughters; for it grieves me much for your sakes that the hand of יהוה has gone out against me. 14 And they lifted up their voice, and wept again: and Orpah kissed her ima-in-law; but Root clung to her. 15 And she said, See, your sister-in-law is gone back to her people, and to her elohim: return and follow your sister-in-law also. 16 And Root said, Do not urge me to leave you, or to return from following after you: for where you go, I will go; and where you lodge, I will lodge: your people shall be my people, and Your Elohim My Elohim:[4] 17 Where you die, will I die, and there will I be buried: יהוה do so to me, and more also, if anything but death separates you and me.[5] 18 When she saw that she was steadfast in mind to go with her, then she stopped discouraging her.[6] 19 So the two of them went until they

---

[1] Noble Ephraimites.
[2] For a full study on the significance of this Scroll of Ruth, see: http://store.yourarmstoisrael.org/Qstore/Qstore.cgi?CMD=011&PROD=000111.
[3] A desire to become Yisrael.

[4] She desired to become Yisrael, and so she was Yisrael. No conversions were necessary. Men do not have the right to dictate to anyone the terms of engrafting or being part of Yisrael. YHWH has made the way open and simple to all through Moshiach's dom and a personal desire. It's a tov thing Ruth was never dragged before any religious body before being recognized as a Yisraelite. Her citizenship was based solely on her confession of emunah. Most modern Jewish legal courts (including vast segments of Messianic Judaism and the one-house movement), established and based on extra-Biblical Talmudic oral law, would not have found her qualified to be a Yisraelite.

[5] Biological non-Yisraelites are a part of believing Yisrael as was Ruth. They cannot be wished away. Why would we want to discourage those who desire to make a 100% commitment to Torah and to the Giver of Torah; leaving them instead to be classified as "gentiles," unless we had an apartheid agenda for restoring Yisrael?

[6] That's how a non-biological Yisraelite becomes Yisrael. Grab tight and don't let go, when you are chased away.

came to Beth-Lechem. And it came to pass, when they were come to Beth-Lechem, that all the city was moved about them, and they said, Is this Naomi? 20 And she said to them, Call me not Naomi, call me Mara: for the Almighty has dealt very bitterly with me. 21 I went out full, and יהוה has brought me home again empty: why then do you call me Naomi, seeing that יהוה has testified against me, and the Almighty has afflicted me? 22 So Naomi returned, and Root the Moavitess, her daughter-in-law, with her, who returned out of the country of Moav: and they came to Beth-Lechem in the beginning of barley harvest around Yom HaBikkurim.

2 And Naomi had a kinsman of her husband's, a mighty man of wealth, of the family of Eli-Melech; and his name was Boaz. 2 And Root the Moavitess said to Naomi, Let me now go to the field, and glean ears of corn after him in whose sight I shall find favor. And she said to her, Go, my daughter. 3 And she went, and came, and gleaned in the field after the reapers: as it turned out she came to the part of the field belonging to Boaz, who was of the family of Eli-Melech. 4 And see, Boaz came from Beth-Lechem, and said to the reapers, יהוה be with you. And they answered him, יהוה bless you.[1] 5 Then said Boaz to his eved that was set over the reapers, Whose young woman is this? 6 And the eved that was set over the reapers answered and said, It is the Moavite young woman that came back with Naomi out of the country of Moav: 7 And she said, I ask you, let me glean and gather after the reapers among the sheaves: so she came, and has continued even from the morning until now, then she stayed a little in the bayit. 8 Then said Boaz to Root, have you heard, my daughter? Go not to glean in another field, neither go from here, but stay

here close to my young women: 9 Let your eyes be on the field that they reap, and go after them: have I not charged the young men that they shall not touch you? And when you are thirsty, go to the vessels, and drink of that which the young men have drawn from. 10 Then she fell on her face, and bowed herself to the ground, and said to him, Why have I found favor in your eyes, that you should take notice of me, seeing I am a strange foreigner? 11 And Boaz answered and said to her, It has fully been shown me, all that you have done for your ima-in-law since the death of your husband: and how you have left your abba and your ima, and the land of your nativity, and are come to a people[2] which you knew not before. 12 יהוה repay your work, and may a full reward be given to you by יהוה Elohim of Yisrael; under whose wings you have come to trust.[3] 13 Then she said, Let me find favor in your sight, my master; for that you have comforted me, and for that you have spoken friendly to your female eved, though I be not like to one of your female avadim. 14 And Boaz said to her, At mealtime come here, and eat of the lechem, and dip your lechem in the vinegar. And she sat beside the reapers: and he passed parched corn to her, and she did eat, and was satisfied, and left. 15 And when she was risen up to glean, Boaz commanded his young men, saying, Let her glean even among the sheaves, and do not restrain her: 16 And let some corn fall by the handfuls for her, and leave them, that she may glean them, and rebuke her not. 17 So she gleaned in the field until evening, and beat out that she had gleaned: and it was about an ephah of barley. 18 And she took it up, and went into the city: and her ima-in-law saw what she had gleaned: and she brought forth, and gave to her what she had reserved after she was satisfied. 19 And her ima-in-law said to her; Where have you gleaned today? And where did you work? Blessed be He that did

---

[1] Here is a perfect example of YHWH's Name being used in casual greeting. This shows that the usage of YHWH's Name is not limited to liturgy or congregational prayer. This also shows that using YHWH's Name in casual greeting and conversation was never considered to be using His Name in vain.

[2] Come to Yisrael, to become Yisrael, and YHWH will reward you.
[3] The reward is in salvation and being Yisrael.

take knowledge of you. And she showed her ima-in-law with whom she had worked, and said, The man's name with whom I worked today is Boaz. 20 And Naomi said to her daughter-in-law, Blessed be he of יהוה, who has not forsaken His kindness to the living and to the dead. And Naomi said to her, The man is a near kinsman of ours, one of our kinsman redeemers. 21 And Root the Moavitess said, He said to me also, You shall stay close to my young men, until they have ended all my harvest. 22 And Naomi said to Root her daughter-in-law, It is good, my daughter, that you go out with his young women too, that they meet you not in any other field. 23 So she kept close to the young women of Boaz to glean to the end of barley harvest and of the wheat harvest of Shavout; and dwelt with her ima-in-law.

3 Then Naomi her ima-in-law said to her, My daughter, shall I not seek rest for you, that it may be well with you? 2 And now is not Boaz of our family, with whose young women you were? See, he is winnowing barley tonight in the threshing floor. 3 Wash yourself therefore, and anoint yourself, and put your garment upon you, and get down to the floor: but do not make yourself known to the man, until he has finished eating and drinking. 4 And it shall be, when he lies down, that you shall mark the place where he shall lie, and you shall go in, and uncover his feet, and lay down; and he will tell you what you shall do. 5 And she said to her, All that you say to me I will do. 6 And she went down to the floor, and did according to all that her ima-in-law told her. 7 And when Boaz had eaten and drunk, and his lev was full of simcha, he went to lie down at the end of the heap of corn: and she came softly, and uncovered his feet, and laid down. 8 And it came to pass at midnight, that the man was afraid, and he turned: and, see, he found a woman lying at his feet. 9 And he said, Who are you? And she answered, I am Root your female eved: spread your covering over your female eved; for you are a near kinsman redeemer. 10 And he said, Blessed are you of יהוה,[1] my daughter: for you have shown more kindness in the latter end than at the beginning, because you followed not young men, whether they are poor or rich. 11 And now, my daughter, fear not; I will do to you all that you require: for all the city of my people does know that you are a virtuous woman. 12 And now it is true that I am your near kinsman: however there is a kinsman nearer than I. 13 Stay this night, and it shall be in the morning, that if he will redeem you tov, let him redeem you: but if he will not redeem you, then I will redeem you, as יהוה lives: lie down until the morning. 14 And she lay at his feet until the morning: and she rose up before anyone could see anyone else. And he said; Let it not be known that a woman came into the floor. 15 Also he said, Bring the mantle that you have upon you, and hold it. And when she held it, he measured six measures of barley, and laid it on her: and she went into the city. 16 And when she came to her ima-in-law, she said; Is that you, my daughter? And she told her all that the man had done to her. 17 And she said, These six measures of barley he gave me; for he said to me, Do not go empty to your ima-in-law. 18 Then said she, Sit still, my daughter, until you know how the matter will fall: for the man will not rest, until he has finished the matter this day.

4 Then went Boaz up to the gate, and sat down there: and, see, the kinsman of whom Boaz spoke came by; to whom he said, Hey! Turn aside, and sit down here. And he turned aside, and sat down. 2 And he took ten men of the zachanim of the city, and said, Sit down here. And they sat down. 3 And he said to the kinsman, Naomi that is come again out of the country of Moav sells a parcel of land, which was our brother Eli-Melech's: 4 And I thought to disclose it to you, saying, Buy it before the inhabitants,

_____

[1] All greetings were done in YHWH's true Name.

and before the zachanim of my people. If you will redeem it, redeem it: but if you will not redeem it, then tell me, that I may know: for there is none to redeem it beside you; and I am after you. And he said, I will redeem it. 5 Then said Boaz, On the day you buy the field from the hand of Naomi; you must acquire also Root the Moavitess, the wife of the dead, to raise up the name of the dead for and upon his inheritance. 6 And the kinsman redeemer said, I cannot redeem it for myself, lest I ruin my own inheritance: redeem my right for yourself; for I cannot redeem it. 7 Now this was the manner in former time in Yisrael concerning redeeming and concerning changing, for to confirm all things; a man plucked off his sandal, and gave it to his neighbor: and this was a testimony in Yisrael. 8 Therefore the kinsman said to Boaz, Buy it for you. So he drew off his sandal. 9 And Boaz said to the zachanim, and to all the people, You are witnesses this day, that I have bought all that was Eli-Melech's, and all that was Chilyon's and Machlon's, from the hand of Naomi. 10 Moreover Root the Moavitess, the wife of Machlon, have I purchased to be my wife, to raise up the name of the dead upon his inheritance, that the name of the dead be not cut off from among his brothers, and from the gate of his place: you are witnesses this day. 11 And all the people that were in the gate, and the zachanim, said, We are witnesses. **יהוה** make the woman that is come into your House like Rachel and like Leah, which two did build Beit Yisrael[1] [2];

and prove your worth in Ephratah, and proclaim the Name in Beth-Lechem: [3] 12 And let your bayit be like the bayit of Peretz, whom Tamar bare to Yahudah, of the zera which **יהוה** shall give you by this young woman. 13 So Boaz took Root, and she was his wife: and when he went in to her. **יהוה** gave her conception, and she bore a son. 14 And the women said to Naomi, Blessed be **יהוה**, who has not left you this day without a redeemer, that His Name may be famous in Yisrael.[4] 15 And he shall be to you a restorer of your life,[5] and a sustainer of your old age: for your daughter-in-law, who loves you, and who is better to you than seven sons, has born him. 16 And Naomi took the child, and laid it in her bosom, and became a nurse to it. 17 And the women who were her neighbors gave him a name, saying, There is a son born to Naomi; and they called his name Oved: he is the abba of Yishai, the abba of David.[6] 18 Now these are the generations of Perets: Perets begat Hetzron, 19 And Hetzron begat Ram, and Ram begat Amminadav, 20 And Amminadav begat Nachshon, and Nachshon begat Salmon, 21 And Salmon begat Boaz, and Boaz begat Oved, 22 And Oved begat Yishai, and Yishai begat David.[7]

---

[1] Ruth became a Yisraelite but more than that. She became a matriarch just like Leah and Rachel. That was despite of her Moabite background. This is the one and only pattern to follow for those washed in Yahshua's dom. Regardless of how they get into the Commonwealth of Yisrael, they are to be considered equal to Rachel and Leach; and the men to Abraham Isaac, and Jacob. Non-Israelites become Yisrael, even as Ruth did and are accepted, not just allowed to worship. Acceptance and allowance are often worlds apart.

[2] All non-Jews can and should build the House of Yisrael as a reunited people following in the work and ministry of Yahshua, to build or restore the nation. All females who restore and rebuild Yisrael are considered to be matriarchs like Ruth, who had no Yisraelite domlines before marrying Boaz. Therefore in Yisrael there are no longer Jews and non-Jews, but all believers in their Kinsmen Redeemer are Yisrael, and are expected to rebuild the nation of Yisrael. Through her

offspring (King David) she was certainly used to build the Tabernacle of David, which we are now being called to rebuild.

[3] As a builder of Yisrael, Ruth was told to proclaim YHWH's Name in Bethlehem. Anyone who refuses to do so is disqualified from building in Yisrael according to His correct and revealed pattern.

[4] The Redeemer has come to bless us in YHWH's Name, so that we in turn can proclaim His Name and make it famous to returning Yisrael.

[5] Our Kinsmen Redeemer has come to restore life and inheritance among us His people Yisrael.

[6] The second generation of converts like Obed, and all future generations are considered natural Yisraelites along with the initial converts. In Judaism, all the heirs of converts who maintain a continual sense of Jewish community are considered Jews. If this applies to Jews, most certainly it applies for any and all Yisraelites. Was Obed, the son of Ruth and Boaz, considered a Moabite or a Yisraelite? After one generation, offspring are considered Yisrael. If it works in Judaism, it must also work in Biblical Yisrael. The full proof that Obed was considered a Yisraelite, is found in the fact that YHWH placed him in the lineage of the Moshiach as seen in verses 17-22.

[7] And thus Ruth became the great grandmother of King David, clearly part of the future Tabernacle of David.

איכה

Echah - Lamentations
To Our Forefathers Yisrael

1 How does the city sit alone, that was full of people! How she is become as a widow she that was great among the nations, and princess among the provinces, how she has become an eved! 2 She weeps heavy in the night, and her tears are on her cheeks: among all her lovers she has none to comfort her: all her friends have dealt treacherously with her, they are become her enemies. 3 Yahudah is gone into exile because of affliction, and because of great labor: she dwells among the nations,[1] she finds no rest: all her persecutors overtook her between the narrow places. 4 The ways of Tzion do mourn, because none come to the moadim: all her gates are desolate: her kohanim sigh, her virgins are afflicted, and she is in bitterness. 5 Her adversaries have become the rulers, her enemies prosper; for יהוה has afflicted her for the multitude of her transgressions: her children are gone into exile before the enemy. 6 And from the daughter of Tzion all her beauty is departed: her rulers are become like harts that find no pasture, and they go without strength before their pursuer. 7 Yahrushalayim remembered in the days of her affliction and of her miseries all her pleasant things that she had in the days of old, when her people fell into the hand of the enemy, and none did help her: the adversaries saw her, and did mock her Shabbats. 8 Yahrushalayim has grievously sinned; therefore she has been removed: all that honored her despise her, because they have seen her nakedness: yes, she sighed, and turned away. 9 Her filthiness is in her skirts; she remembers not her last end; therefore she came down wonderfully: she had no comforter.[2] O יהוה, behold my affliction: for the enemy has magnified himself. 10 The adversary has spread out his hand upon all her pleasant things: for she has seen that the heathens entered into her Set-Apart Place, whom You did command that they should not enter into Your congregation. 11 All her people sigh, they seek lechem; they have given their pleasant things for food to relieve their being: see, O יהוה, and consider; for I am become despised. 12 Is it nothing to you, all you that pass by? See, and see if there is any sorrow like my sorrow, which is done to me, by which יהוה has afflicted me in the day of His fierce anger. 13 From above He sent fire into my bones, and it prevailed against them: He has spread a net for my feet, He has turned me back: He has made me desolate and faint all the day. 14 The yoke of my transgressions is bound by His hand: they are wreathed, and come up upon my neck: He has made my strength to fall, יהוה has delivered me into their hands, from whom I am not able to rise up.[3] 15 יהוה has trodden under foot all my mighty men in the midst of me: He has called a company against me to crush my young men: יהוה has trodden the virgin, the daughter of Yahudah, as in a winepress. 16 For these things I weep; my eye runs down with water, because the comforter that should relieve my being is far from me: my children are desolate, because the enemy has prevailed. 17 Tzion spreads forth her hands, and there is none to comfort her: יהוה has commanded concerning Yaakov, that his adversaries should be around him: Yahrushalayim is as an unclean woman in niddah among them. 18 יהוה is Tzadik; for I have rebelled against His Torah: shema all my people, and behold my sorrow: my virgins and my

---

[1] If Yahudah is in the nations, how much more Ephraim who has been there far longer and is numerically greater than Yahudah.
[2] Lacked the Ruach HaKodesh as it remains so to this day.

[3] Babylonian exile and captivity.

young men are gone into exile. 19 I called for my lovers, but they deceived me: my kohanim and my zachanim died in the city, while they sought food to relieve their souls. 20 See, O יהוה; for I am in distress: my inward parts are troubled; my lev is turned within me; for I have grievously rebelled: from abroad the sword has bereaved us, at home there is death. 21 They have heard me sigh: there is none to comfort me: all my enemies have heard of my trouble; they are glad that You have done it: You will bring on the day that You have announced to them also, and they shall be like me. 22 Let all their wickedness come before You; and do to them, as You have done to me for all my transgressions: for my sighs are many, and my lev is faint.

2 How has יהוה covered the daughter of Tzion with a cloud in His anger, and cast down from the shamayim to the earth the beauty of Yisrael, and remembered not His footstool in the day of His anger! 2 יהוה has swallowed up all the pastures of Yaakov, and has not pitied: He has thrown down in His wrath the strong holds of the daughter of Yahudah; He has brought them down to the ground: He has polluted the malchut and its rulers. 3 He has cut off in His fierce anger all the horns of Yisrael: He has drawn back His right hand from before the enemy, and He burned against Yaakov like a flaming fire, that devours all things all around. 4 He has bent His bow like an enemy: He stood with His right hand as an adversary, and killed all that were pleasant to the eye in the Tabernacle of the daughter of Tzion: He poured out His fury like fire. 5 יהוה was as an enemy: He has swallowed up Yisrael, He has swallowed up all her palaces: He has destroyed her strongholds, and has increased in the daughter of Yahudah mourning and lamentation. 6 And He has violently taken away His Tabernacle,1 as if it were of a garden: He has destroyed the places of the

congregation: יהוה has caused the moadim and Shabbats to be forgotten in Tzion, and has despised in the indignation of His anger both the melech and the kohen. 7 יהוה has cast off His altar, He has rejected His Set-Apart Place, He has given up into the hands of the enemy the walls of her palaces; they have made a noise in the Bayit of יהוה, as in the day of a solemn moed. 8 יהוה has purposed to destroy the wall of the daughter of Tzion: He has stretched out a line, He has not withdrawn His hand from destroying it: therefore He made her forces and the wall to lament; they languished together. 9 Her gates are sunk into the ground; He has destroyed and broken her bars: her melech and her rulers are among the nations: the Torah is no more; her neviim also find no further vision from יהוה. 10 The zachanim of the daughter of Tzion sit upon the ground, and keep silent: they have cast dust upon their heads; they have girded themselves with sackcloth: the virgins of Yahrushalayim hang down their heads to the ground. 11 My eyes do fail with tears, my inward parts are troubled, my liver is poured upon the earth, for the destruction of the daughter of my people; because the children and the infants languish in the streets of the city. 12 They say to their mothers, Where is the corn and wine? When they languished as the wounded in the streets of the city, when their being was poured out into their mothers' bosom. 13 What thing shall I take to witness for you? What thing shall I liken to you, O daughter of Yahrushalayim? What shall I equal to you, that I may comfort you, O virgin daughter of Tzion? For your breach is great like the sea: who can heal you? 14 Your neviim have seen vain and foolish things for you: and they have not discovered your iniquity, to turn away your exile; but have seen visions for you that are false and misleading messages. 15 All that pass by clap their hands at you; they hiss and shake their head at the daughter of Yahrushalayim, saying, Is this the city that

---

1 All 12 tribes or both houses in David's tabernacle.

men call The Perfection of Beauty, The joy of the whole earth? 16 All your enemies have opened their mouth against you: they hiss and gnash their teeth: and they say, We have swallowed her up: certainly this is the day that we looked for; we have found, we have seen it. 17 יהוה has done that which He had devised; He has fulfilled His word that He had commanded in the days of old: He has thrown down, and has not pitied: and He has caused your enemy to gilah over you, He has set up the horn of your adversaries. 18 Their lev cried to יהוה, O wall of the daughter of Tzion, let tears run down like a river day and night: give yourself no rest; let not the apple of Your eye cease. 19 Arise, cry out in the night: in the beginning of the watches pour out your lev like water before the face of יהוה: lift up your hands toward Him for the life of your young children, that faint for hunger at the top of every street. 20 See, O יהוה, and consider to whom You have done this. Shall the women eat the fruit of their womb, children the size of a hand? Shall the kohen and the navi be slain in the Set-Apart-Place of יהוה? 21 The young and the old lie on the ground in the streets: my virgins and my young men are fallen by the sword; You have slain them in the day of Your anger; You have killed, and not pitied. 22 You have called as in a moed my terrors all around, so that in the day of יהוה's anger none escaped nor remained: those that I have nursed and brought up has my enemy consumed.

3 I am the man that has seen affliction by the rod of His wrath. 2 He has led me, and brought me into darkness, but not into light. 3 Surely against me is He turned; He turned His hand against me all the day. 4 My flesh and my skin has He made old; He has broken my bones. 5 He has built against me, and surrounded me with bitterness and hardship. 6 He has set me in dark places, as they that are dead of old. 7 He has hedged me around, so that I cannot get out: He has made my chains heavy. 8 Also when I cry and shout, He shuts out my tefillah. 9 He has enclosed my ways with cut stone; He has made my paths crooked. 10 He was to me as a bear lying in wait, and as a lion in secret places. 11 He has turned aside my ways, and pulled me in pieces: He has made me desolate. 12 He has bent His bow, and set me as a mark for the arrow. 13 He has caused the arrows of His quiver to enter into my kidneys. 14 I was a derision to all my people; and their song all the day. 15 He has filled me with bitterness; He has made me drunk with wormwood.[1] 16 He has also broken my teeth with gravel stones; He has covered me with ashes. 17 And You have removed my being far off from shalom: I have forgotten prosperity. 18 And I said, my strength and my tikvah has perished from before יהוה: 19 As I remember my affliction and my misery, the wormwood and the bitterness. 20 My being has them still in remembrance, and is humbled in me. 21 This I recall to my mind, therefore have I tikvah. 22 It is because of יהוה's rachamim that we are not consumed, because His rachamim fail not. 23 They are new every morning: great is Your faithfulness. 24 יהוה is my portion, says my being; therefore will I tikvah in Him. 25 יהוה is tov to them that wait for Him, to the being that seeks Him. 26 It is tov that a man should both have tikvah and quietly wait for the Yahshua of יהוה. 27 It is tov for a man that he bears a yoke in his youth. 28 He sits alone and keeps silent, because He has borne it upon Him. 29 He puts His mouth in the dust; if so there may be tikvah. 30 He gives His cheek to him that smites Him: he is filled full with reproach. 31 For יהוה will not cast off le-olam-va-ed: 32 But though He causes grief, yet will He have rachamim according to the multitude of His rachamim. 33 For He does not afflict in simcha nor grieve the children of men. 34 To crush under His feet all the prisoners of the earth, 35 To turn aside the

---

[1] False emunahs and doctrines.

right of a man before the face of El-Elyon, 36 To subvert a man in his cause, יהוה does not approve. 37 Who is He that spoke, and it came to pass, has יהוה not commanded it? 38 Out of the mouth of El-Elyon proceeds the evil and the tov? 39 Why does a living man complain, for the punishment of his sins? 40 Let us search and try our ways, and teshuvah to יהוה. 41 Let us lift up our lev with our hands to El in the shamayim. 42 We have transgressed and have rebelled: You have not pardoned. 43 You have covered with anger, and persecuted us: You have slain, You have not pitied. 44 You have covered Yourself with a cloud that our tefillah should not pass through. 45 You have made us as scum and refuse in the midst of the nations. 46 All our enemies have opened their mouths against us. 47 Fear and a snare has come upon us, desolation and destruction. 48 My eye runs down with rivers of water for the destruction of the daughter of my people. 49 My eye trickles down, and ceases not, without any stop, 50 Until יהוה looks down, and beholds from the shamayim. 51 My eye affects my lev because of all the daughters of my city. 52 My enemies hunted me down, like a bird, without cause. 53 They have cut off my life in the dungeon, and cast a stone on top of me. 54 Waters flowed over my head; then I said, I am cut off. 55 I called upon Your Name, O יהוה, out of the lowest dungeon. 56 You have heard my voice: hide not Your ear at my breathing, at my cry. 57 You drew near in the day that I called upon You: You said, *Fear not.* 58 O יהוה, You have pleaded the causes of my being; You have redeemed my life. 59 O יהוה, You have seen my oppression: shophet my cause. 60 You have seen all their vengeance and all their plans against me. 61 You have heard their reproach, O יהוה, and all their plans against me; 62 The lips of those that rose up against me, and their plans against me all the day. 63 See their sitting down, and their rising

up; I am their music. 64 Repay them, O יהוה, according to the works of their hands. 65 Give them sorrow of lev, Your curse be upon them. 66 Persecute and destroy them in anger from under the shamayim of יהוה.

4 How is the gold become dim! How is the most fine gold changed! The stones of the Set-Apart Place are poured out at the top of every street. 2 The precious sons of Tzion, who were comparable to fine gold, how they are now reckoned as earthen pitchers, the work of the hands of the potter! 3 Even the sea monsters draw out the breast, they nurse their young ones: the daughter of my people has become cruel, like the ostriches in the wilderness. 4 The tongue of the nursing child clings to the roof of his mouth for thirst: the young children ask lechem, and no man breaks it for them. 5 They that did feed delicately are desolate in the streets: they that were brought up in scarlet embrace dunghills. 6 For the punishment of the iniquity of the daughter of my people is greater than the punishment of the sin of Sodom, that was overthrown as in a moment, and no hands wearied in destroying her. 7 Her Nazarites were purer than snow, they were whiter than milk, they were more ruddy in body than rubies, and their polish was like sapphire: 8 Their appearance is blacker than a coal; they are not known in the streets: their skin cleaves to their bones; it is withered, it is become dry like wood. 9 Those that be slain with the sword are better than they that be slain with hunger: for these pine away, stricken for want of the fruits of the field. 10 The hands of the compassionate women have boiled their own children: they were their food in the destruction of the daughter of my people. 11 יהוה has accomplished His fury; He has poured out His fierce anger, and has kindled a fire in Tzion, and it has devoured its foundations. 12 The melechim of the earth, and all the inhabitants of the world, would not have believed that the adversary and the

enemy would have entered into the gates of Yahrushalayim. 13 For the sins of her neviim, and the iniquities of her kohanim, that have shed the dom of the just in the midst of her, 14 They have wandered as blind men in the streets; they have polluted themselves with innocent dom, so that men could not touch their garments. 15 They cried to them, Depart it is unclean; depart, depart, do not touch them: when they fled away and wandered among the nations they said, They shall no more go to sojourn there. 16 The anger of **יהוה** has exiled them; He will no more regard them: they did not respect the kohanim; they showed no favor to the zachanim. 17 As for us, our eyes failed in our vain watch for help: in our watchtower we have watched for a nation that could not save us. 18 They hunt our steps that we cannot go in our streets: our end is near, our days are fulfilled; for our end is come. 19 Our persecutors are swifter than the eagles of the shamayim: they pursued us upon the mountains, they laid wait for us in the wilderness. 20 The breath of our nostrils, the anointed of **יהוה**, was taken in their pits, of whom we said, Under His shadow we shall live among the nations. 21 Gilah and be in simcha, O daughter of Edom, that dwells in the land of Uz; this cup also shall pass through to you: you shall be drunk, and shall make yourself naked. 22 The punishment of your iniquity is accomplished, O daughter of Tzion; He will no more carry you away into exile: He will visit your iniquity, O daughter of Edom; He will discover your sins.[1]

5 Remember, O **יהוה**, what is come upon us: consider, and behold our reproach. 2 Our inheritance is turned to strangers, our houses to aliens. 3 We are orphans and fatherless, our mothers are as widows. 4 We have drunken our water for money; our wood is sold to us. 5 Our necks are under persecution: we labor, and have no rest. 6 We have given our hand to the Mitzrites, and to the Ashurim, to be satisfied with lechem. 7 Our ahvot have sinned, and are no more; and we have borne their iniquities. 8 Servants have ruled over us: there is none that does deliver us out of their hand. 9 We have gotten our lechem with the peril of our lives because of the sword of the wilderness. 10 Our skin was black like an oven because of the terrible famine. 11 They ravished the women in Tzion, and the young women in the cities of Yahudah. 12 Princes are hung up by their hand: the faces of the elderly were not honored. 13 They took the young men to grind, and the children fell under the wood. 14 The zachanim have ceased from the gate, the young men from their music. 15 The simcha of our lev is ceased; our dance is turned into mourning. 16 The keter is fallen from our head: woe to us; for we have sinned! 17 For this our lev is faint; for these things our eyes are dim. 18 Because of the Mt. Tzion, which is desolate, the foxes walk upon it. 19 You, O **יהוה**, remain le-olam-va-ed; Your throne from generation to generation. 20 Why do You forget us le-olam-va-ed, and forsake us for so long a time? 21 Turn us to You, O **יהוה**, and we shall be turned; renew our days as of old.[2] 22 But You have utterly rejected us; You are very angry with us, exceedingly!

---

[1] Though Jewish Yisrael's exile was temporal (lasting 70 years), Edom's would be permanent in the end times. But through Yahshua they can still join the Commonwealth of Yisrael as individuals. For more details on Edom's future as part of greater Yisrael, see: http://yourarmstoisrael.org/Articles_new/restoration/?page=24&type=12

[2] The liturgy for the **eytz chaim** Torah cantorial.

קהלת

Koheleth - Ecclesiastes
To Our Forefathers Yisrael

1 The words of the Qoheleth, ben David, melech in Yahrushalayim. 2 Vanity of vanities, says the Qoheleth, vanity of vanities; all is vanity. 3 What profit has a man of all his labor that he toils under the sun? 4 One generation passes away, and another generation comes: but the earth abides forever. 5 The sun also rises, and the sun goes down, and hurries to its place where it arose. 6 The wind goes toward the south, and turns around to the north; it whirls around continually, and the wind returns again according to its circuits. 7 All the rivers run into the sea; yet the sea is not full; to the place from where the rivers come, there they return again. 8 All things are wearisome; man is not satisfied with utterance: the eye is not satisfied with seeing, nor the ear filled with hearing. 9 The thing that has been, it is that which shall be; and that which is done is that which shall be done: and there is no new thing under the sun. 10 Is there anything of which it may be said, See, this is new? It has been already of old time, which was before us.[1] 11 There is no remembrance of former things; neither shall there be any remembrance of things that are to come with those that shall come after. 12 I the Qoheleth was melech over Yisrael in Yahrushalayim. 13 And I gave my lev to seek and search out by chochma concerning all things that are done under the shamayim: this evil task has Elohim given to the sons of men to be humbled by it. 14 I have seen all the works that are done under the sun; and, behold, all is vanity and vexation of ruach. 15 That which is crooked cannot be made straight: and that which is lacking cannot be numbered. 16 I communed with my own lev, saying, See, I am come to great estate, and have gotten more chochma than all they that have been before me in Yahrushalayim: yes, my lev has seen much chochma and da'at. 17 And I set my lev to know chochma, and to know transgression and folly: I perceived that this too is vexation of ruach. 18 For in much chochma is much grief: and he that increases da'at[2] increases sorrow.

2 I said in my lev, Come now, I will prove you with rejoicing, therefore enjoy pleasure: and, behold, this also is vanity. 2 I said of laughter, It is mad: and of rejoicing, What does it do? 3 I sought in my lev to give myself to wine, while guiding my lev with chochma; and how to lay hold on folly, until I might see what was that tov for the sons of men, to do under the shamayim all the days of their life. 4 I made great works; I built my houses; I planted my vineyards: 5 I made me gardens and orchards, and I planted trees in them of all kind of fruits: 6 I made my pools of water, to water the wood that brings forth trees: 7 I got servants and maidens, and had servants born in my bayit; also I had great possessions of great and small cattle above all that were in Yahrushalayim before me: 8 I gathered also silver and gold, and the peculiar treasures of melechim and of the provinces: I got for myself men singers and women singers, and the delights of the sons of men, and I appointed for myself butlers and waitresses. 9 So I was great, and increased more than all that were before me in Yahrushalayim: also my chochma remained with me. 10 And whatever my eyes desired I kept not from them, I withheld not my lev from any simcha; for my lev rejoiced in all my labor: and this was my portion of all my labor. 11 Then I looked on all the works that my hands had

---

[1] That is why the Renewed Covenant is not new.

[2] Worldly knowledge.

made, and on the labor that I had labored to do: and, behold, all was vanity and vexation of ruach, and there was no gain under the sun. 12 And I turned myself to behold chochma, and transgression, and folly: for what can the man do that comes after the melech? Even that which has been already done. 13 Then I saw that chochma is better than folly, as far as light is better than darkness. 14 The wise man's eyes are in his head; but the fool has his halacha in darkness: and I myself perceived also that one event happens to them all. 15 Then said I in my lev, As it happens to the fool, so it happens even to me; and why was I then more wise? Then I said in my lev, that this also is vanity. 16 For there is no remembrance of the wise more than of the fool forever; seeing that which now is in the days to come shall all be forgotten. And how dies the wise man? As the fool. 17 Therefore I hated life; because the work that is done under the sun is grievous to me: for all is vanity and vexation of ruach. 18 Yes, I hated all my labor that I had taken under the sun: because I should leave it to the man that shall be after me. 19 And who knows whether he shall be a wise man or a fool? Yet shall he have rule over all my labor that I have labored, and in which I have shown myself wise under the sun. This is also vanity. 20 Therefore I went about to cause my lev to despair of all the labor which I toiled under the sun. 21 For there is a man whose labor is in chochma, and in da'at, and in equity; yet to a man that has not labored for it shall he leave it for his portion. This also is vanity and a great evil. 22 For what has man from all his labor, and of the vexation of his lev, in which he has labored under the sun? 23 For all his days are sorrows, and his work grievous; yes, his lev takes not rest even in the night. This is also vanity. 24 There is nothing better for a man, than that he should eat and drink, and that he should make his being enjoy tov in his labor. This also I saw, that it was from the hand of Elohim. 25 For who can eat, or

who else can drink except He? 26 For Elohim gives to a man what is tov in His sight, chochma, and da'at, and simcha: but to the sinner He gives toil, to gather and to heap up, that He may give to Him that is tov before Elohim. This also is vanity and vexation of ruach.

3 To every thing there is a season, and a time to every purpose under the shamayim: 2 A time to be born, and a time to die; a time to plant, and a time to pluck up that which is planted; 3 A time to kill, and a time to heal; a time to break down, and a time to build up; 4 A time to weep, and a time to laugh; a time to mourn, and a time to dance; 5 A time to cast away stones, and a time to gather stones together; a time to embrace, and a time to refrain from embracing; 6 A time to get, and a time to lose; a time to keep, and a time to cast away; 7 A time to rend, and a time to sew; a time to keep silent, and a time to speak; 8 A time to love, and a time to hate; a time of war, and a time of shalom. 9 What profit has he that works from his toil? 10 I have seen the toil, which Elohim has given to the sons of men to be humbled in it. 11 He has made every thing beautiful in His time: also He has set the ages in their lev, so that no man can find out the work that Elohim made from the beginning to the end. 12 I know that there is no tov in them, but for a man to gilah, and to do tov in his life. 13 And also that every man should eat and drink, and enjoy the tov of all his labor, it is the gift of Elohim. 14 I know that, whatever Elohim does, it shall be forever:[1] nothing can be added to it, nor anything taken from it: and Elohim does it, that men should fear before Him. 15 That which has been is now; and that which is to be has already been; and Elohim requires that which is past. 16 And moreover I saw under the sun instead of mishpat, that evil was there; and instead of tzedakah, that iniquity was there. 17 I said in my lev,

---

[1] Yisrael therefore is His forever eternal and only bride.

Elohim shall shophet the tzadik and the wicked: for there is a time there for every purpose and for every work. 18 I said in my lev concerning the situation of the sons of men, that Elohim might manifest them, and that they might see that they themselves are beasts. 19 For that which befalls the sons of men befalls beasts; even one thing befalls them: as the one dies, so dies the other; yes, they have all one breath; so that a man has no preeminence above a beast: for all is vanity. 20 All go to one place; all are of the dust, and all turn to dust again.[1] 21 Who knows the ruach of man that goes upward, and the ruach of the beast that goes downward to the earth?[2] 22 Wherefore I perceive that there is nothing better, than that a man should gilah in his own works; for that is his portion: for who shall bring him to see what shall be after him?

4 So I returned, and considered all the oppression that is done under the sun: and behold the tears of such as were oppressed, and they had no comforter; and on the side of their oppressors there was power; but they had no comforter. 2 Therefore I praised the dead who are already dead more than the living who are yet alive. 3 Yes, better is he than both of them, who has not yet been born, who has not seen the evil work that is done under the sun. 4 Again, I considered all toil, and skill of work, that brings envy between man and his neighbor. This is also vanity and vexation of ruach. 5 The fool folds his hands together, and eats his own flesh. 6 Better is a handful with quietness, than both the hands full with toil and vexation of ruach. 7 Then I looked again, and I saw vanity under the sun. 8 There is one who is alone, and there is not a second; yes, he has neither child nor brother: yet there is no end of all his labors; neither is his eye satisfied with riches; neither does he say, For whom do I labor, and bereave my being of tov? This is also vanity, yes, it is an evil toil. 9 Two are better than one; because they have a tov reward for their labor.[3] 10 For if they fall, the one will lift up his fellow: but woe to him that is alone when he falls; for he has not another to help him up. [4] 11 Again, if two lie together, then they have heat:[5] but how can one be warm alone? 12 And if one prevails against him, two shall withstand him; and a threefold cord is not quickly broken.[6] 13 Better is a poor and a wise child than an old and foolish melech, who will no more be admonished. 14 For out of prison he comes to reign; whereas also he that is born in his malchut has been born miserable. 15 I considered all the living who walk under the sun, with the young men that shall rise up in their place. 16 There is no end of all the people, even of all that have been before them: they also that come after shall not gilah in him. Surely this also is vanity and vexation of ruach.

5 Keep your foot when you go to the Bayit of Elohim, and be more ready to shema, than to give the sacrifice of fools: for they consider not that they do evil. 2 Be not hasty with your mouth, and let not your lev be hasty to utter anything before Elohim: for Elohim is in the shamayim, and you upon the earth: therefore let your words be few. 3 For a dream comes through the greatness of a task;[7] and a fool's voice is known by his many words. 4 When you vow a vow to Elohim, do not delay to pay it; for He has no pleasure in fools: pay that

---

[1] This speaks of the body, not the spirit; as seen in many Scriptures.
[2] The difference is clear here. Upon death the believer's spirit goes up to YHWH, and the body to the earth to sleep with the bodies of the beasts. For more details see: http://yourarmstoisrael.org/Articles_new/articles/?page=what_happens_when_a_messianic_be&type=6.
[3] Being involved in YHWH's two-house restoration is far better than focusing on man's plan, or reviving only one house back to Torah. A two-house laborer has a great reward from YHWH.
[4] Both houses in Moshiach's body need each other.
[5] The heat that can be produced by two-house brotherhood.
[6] With Yahshua as the third cord, both houses can come together. Those who try to reunite the two houses in their own strength working with orthodox rabbis and such without Yahshua as King are not doing YHWH's work, His way.
[7] The greatness of restoring Yisrael causes all of us who long for that day to dream.

which you have vowed. 5 Better is it that you should not vow, than that you should vow and not pay. 6 Allow not your mouth to cause your flesh to sin; neither say before the heavenly messenger, that it was an error: why should Elohim be angry at your voice, and destroy the work of your hands? 7 For in the multitude of dreams and many words there are also divers vanities: rather fear Elohim. 8 If you see the oppression of the poor, and the violent perverting of mishpat and justice in a province, marvel not at the matter: for he that is higher than the highest regards this; and there are higher ones over them. 9 Moreover the increase of the earth is for all: the melech himself is served by the field. 10 He that loves silver shall not be satisfied with silver; nor he that loves abundance with increase: this is also vanity. 11 When goods increase, those who eat them are increased: and what tov is there to the owners, except the beholding of them with their eyes? 12 The sleep of a working man is sweet, whether he eats little or much: but the abundance of the rich will not allow him to sleep. 13 There is a sore evil that I have seen under the sun, namely, riches kept for its owners to do evil. 14 But those riches perish by evil use: and he begets a son, and there is nothing in his hand. 15 As he came forth from his mother's womb, naked shall he return to go as he came, and shall take nothing of his labor, which he may carry away in his hand. 16 And this also is a sore evil, that in all points as he came into the olam hazeh, so shall he go: and what profit has he that has labored for the wind? 17 All his days also he eats in darkness, and he has much sorrow and wrath with his sickness. 18 Behold that which I have seen: it is tov and pleasant for one to eat and to drink, and to enjoy the tov of all his labor that he toils under the sun all the days of his life, which Elohim gives him: for it is his portion. 19 Every man also to whom Elohim has given riches and wealth, and has given him power to eat of it, and to take his portion, and to gilah in his

labor; this is the gift of Elohim. 20 For he shall not much remember the days of his life; because Elohim answers him in the simcha of his lev.

6 There is an evil that I have seen under the sun, and it is common among men: 2 A man to whom Elohim has given riches, wealth, and honor, so that he wants nothing for his being of all that he desires, yet if Elohim gives him not power to eat it, but a stranger eats it: this is vanity, and it is an evil disease. 3 If a man beget an hundred children, and lives many years, so that the days of his years are many, and if his being be not filled with tov, and also if he has no burial; I say, that an untimely birth is better than him. 4 For he comes in with vanity, and departs in darkness, and his name shall be covered with darkness. 5 Moreover he has not seen the sun, nor known anything: this one has more rest than the other 6 Yes, though he live a thousand years twice told, yet he has seen no tov: do not all go to one place? 7 All the labor of man is for his mouth, and yet the appetite is not filled. 8 For what has the wise more than the fool? What advantage has the poor, who knows to walk before the living? 9 Better is the sight of the eyes than the wandering of the desire: this is also vanity and vexation of ruach. 10 That which has been is named already, and it is known that it is man: neither may he contend with Him that is mightier than he. 11 Seeing there be many things that increase vanity, what advantage has the man? 12 For who knows what is tov for man in this life, all the days of his vain life that he spends as a shadow? For who can declare to a man what shall be after him under the sun?

7 A tov name is better than precious oil; and the day of death than the day of one's birth. 2 It is better to go to the bayit of mourning, than to go to the bayit of feasting: for that is the end of all men; and the living will lay it to his lev. 3 Sorrow is

better than laughter: for by the sadness of the countenance the lev is made better. 4 The lev of the wise is in the bayit of mourning; but the lev of fools is in the bayit of gilah. 5 It is better to shema the rebuke of the wise, than for a man to shema the song of fools. 6 For as the crackling of thorns under a pot, so is the laughter of the fool: this also is vanity. 7 Surely oppression makes a wise man mad; and a bribe destroys the lev. 8 Better is the end of a thing than the beginning of it: and the patient in ruach is better than the proud in ruach. 9 Be not hasty in your ruach to be angry: for anger rests in the bosom of fools. 10 Don't you say, What is the cause that the former days were better than these? For you do not inquire wisely concerning this. 11 Wisdom is tov with an inheritance: and by it there is profit to them that see the sun. 12 For chochma is a defense, and money is a defense: but the excellency of da'at is, that chochma gives life to them that have it. 13 Consider the work of Elohim: for who can make straight, what He has made crooked? 14 In the day of prosperity be full of simcha, but in the day of adversity consider: Elohim also has appointed one as well as the other, to the end that man should find nothing after him. 15 All things have I seen in the days of my vanity: there is a just man that perishes in his tzedakah, and there is a wicked man that prolongs his life in his evil. 16 Be not over tzadik; neither make yourself over wise: why should you destroy yourself?[1] 17 Be not wicked overmuch, neither be foolish: why should you die before your time? 18 It is tov that you should take hold of this; yes, also from this withdraw not your hand: for he that fears Elohim shall follow all these things. 19 Wisdom strengthens the wise more than ten mighty men who are in the city. 20 For there is not a just man upon earth that does tov, and sins not.[2] 21 Also take no heed to all words that are spoken; lest you shema

your servant curse you: 22 For many times as also your own lev knows you likewise have cursed others. 23 All this have I proved by chochma: I said, I am wise; but it was far from me. 24 That which is far off, and exceeding deep, who can find it out?[3] 25 I applied my lev to know, and to search, and to seek out chochma, and the reason of things, and to know the evil of folly, even of foolishness and transgression: 26 And I find more bitter than death the woman, whose lev is snares and nets, and her hands as shackles: the one who pleases Elohim shall escape from her; but the sinner shall be taken by her. 27 Behold, this have I found, says the Qoheleth, counting one by one, to find out the conclusion: 28 What yet my being seeks, but I found not: one man among a thousand have I found; but a woman among all those have I not found. 29 Behold, this only have I found, that Elohim has made man upright; but they have sought out many devices.

8 Who is as the wise man? And who knows the interpretation of a thing? A man's chochma makes his face to shine, and the boldness of his face shall be changed. 2 I counsel you to keep the melech's commandment, because of the oath of Elohim. 3 Be not hasty to go out of His sight: stand not in an evil thing; for He does whatever pleases Him. 4 Where the word of a melech is, there is power: and who may say to him, What are you doing? 5 Whoever keeps the commandment shall know no evil thing: and a wise man's lev discerns both time[4] and mishpat. 6 Because to every purpose there is time and mishpat, therefore the misery of man is great upon him. 7 For he knows not what shall be: for who can tell him when it shall be? 8 There is no man that has power over the ruach to retain the ruach; neither has he power in the

---

[1] A balanced life is the key.
[2] Hebrews always believed in original sin and the passing of that sin to all men.

[3] "Far off" is a reference often used of Ephraim Yisrael's exiles and no one can find this out without revelation from YHWH Himself.
[4] A wise heart can discern the time and season of Yisrael's restoration.

day of death: and there is no discharge in a war; neither shall evil deliver those that are given to it. 9 All this have I seen, and applied my lev to every work that is done under the sun: there is a time in which one man rules over another to his own hurt. 10 And so I saw the wicked buried, who had come and gone from the place of the set-apart, and they were forgotten in the city where they had so done: this is also vanity. 11 Because sentence against an evil work is not executed speedily, therefore the lev of the sons of men is fully set in them to do evil. 12 Though a sinner do evil an hundred times, and his days be prolonged, yet surely I know that it shall be well with them that fear Elohim, who fear before Him: 13 But it shall not be well with the wicked; neither shall he prolong his days, which are as a shadow; because he does not fear before Elohim. 14 There is a vanity which is done upon the earth; that there be just men, to whom it happens according to the work of the wicked; again, there be wicked men, to whom it happens according to the work of the tzadik: I said that this also is vanity. 15 Then I commended gilah, because a man has no better thing under the sun, than to eat, and to drink, and to be in happiness: for that shall abide with him from his labor all the days of his life, which Elohim gives him under the sun. 16 When I applied my lev to know chochma, and to see the task that is done upon the earth, even though one sees no sleep day or night. 17 Then I beheld all the work of Elohim, that a man cannot find out the work that is done under the sun: because though a man labor to seek it out, yet he shall not find it; yes further; though a wise man claim to know it, yet shall he not be able to find it.

9 For all this I considered in my lev even to declare all this that the tzadik, and the wise, and their works, are in the hand of Elohim: no man knows whether love or hatred awaits him. 2 All things come alike to all: there is one event to the tzadik, and to the wicked; to the tov and to the clean, and to the unclean; to him that brings sacrifices, and to him that does not bring sacrifices: as is the tov, so is the sinner; and he that swears, as he that fears an oath. 3 This is an evil among all things that are done under the sun, that there is one event to all: yes, also the lev of the sons of men is full of evil, and transgression is in their lev while they live, and then they go to the dead. 4 For to him that is joined to all the living there is tikvah: for a living dog is better than a dead lion. 5 For the living know that they shall die: but the dead know not any thing, neither have they any more a reward; for the memory of them is forgotten.[1] 6 Also their love, and their hatred, and their envy, is now perished; neither have they any more a portion forever in any thing that is done under the sun. 7 Go your way, eat your bread with simcha, and drink your wine with a happy lev; for Elohim now accepts your works. 8 Let your garments be always white; and let your head lack no oil. 9 Live joyfully with the wife whom you love all the days of the life of your vanity, which He has given you under the sun, all the days of your vanity: for that is your portion in this life, and in your labor which you toil under the sun. 10 Whatever your hand finds to do, do it with your might; for there is no work, nor device, nor da'at, nor chochma, in the grave, where you go. 11 I returned, and saw under the sun, that the race is not to the swift, nor the battle to the strong, neither the bread to the wise, nor the riches to men of binah, nor the favor to men of skill; but time and chance happens to them all. 12 For man also knows not his time: as fish that are taken in an evil net, and as the birds that are caught in a snare; so are the sons of men snared in an evil time, when it falls suddenly upon them. 13 This chochma have I seen also under the sun, and it seemed great to me: 14 There was a little city, and few men within it; and there came

---

[1] Their body and soul die – not their redeemed ruach.

a great melech against it, and besieged it, and built great bulwarks against it: 15 Now there was found in it a poor wise man, and he by his chochma he delivered the city; yet no man remembered that same poor man. 16 Then said I, Wisdom is better than strength: nevertheless the poor man's chochma is despised, and his words are not heard.

17 The words of wise men are heard in quiet more than the cry of him that rules among fools. 18 Wisdom is better than weapons of war: but one sinner destroys much tov.

10 Dead flies cause the oil of the perfumer to send forth a stinking smell: so does a little folly to him that is in reputation for chochma and honor. 2 A wise man's lev is at his right hand; but a fool's lev at his left. 3 Yes also, when he that is a fool walks by the way, his chochma fails him, and he says to every one that he is a fool. 4 If the ruach of the ruler rises up against you, leave not your place; for yielding pacifies great offences. 5 There is an evil that I have seen under the sun, as an error that proceeds from the ruler: 6 Folly is set in great dignity, and the rich sit in low place. 7 I have seen servants upon horses, and rulers walking as servants upon the earth. 8 He that digs a pit shall fall into it; and whoever breaks a hedge, a serpent shall bite him. 9 Whoever removes stones shall be hurt with them; and he that splits wood shall be endangered by it. 10 If the iron is blunt, and one does not sharpen the edge, then he needs more strength: but chochma is profitable to make right. 11 Surely the serpent will bite without being charmed; then in vain is the charmer. 12 The words of a wise man's mouth are gracious; but the lips of a fool will swallow himself up. 13 The beginning of the words of his mouth is foolishness: and the end of his talk is wicked transgression. 14 A fool also is full of words: a man cannot tell what shall be; and what shall be after him, who can tell

him? 15 The labor of the foolish wearies every one of them, because he knows not how to go to the city. 16 Woe to you, O land, when your melech is a child, and your rulers eat in the morning! 17 Blessed art you, O land, when your melech is the son of nobles, and your rulers eat in due season, for strength, and not for drunkenness! 18 By much laziness the building decays; and through idleness of the hands the bayit drops through. 19 A feast is made for laughter, and wine makes happy: but money answers all things. 20 Curse not the melech, no not in your thought; and curse not the rich in your bedroom: for a bird of the air shall carry the voice, and that which has wings shall tell the matter.

11 Cast your bread upon the waters: for you shall find it after many days. 2 Give a portion to seven, and also to eight; for you know not what evil shall be upon the earth. 3 If the clouds are full of rain, they empty themselves upon the earth: and if the tree falls toward the south, or toward the north, in the place where the tree falls, there it shall be. 4 He that observes the wind shall not sow; and he that regards the clouds shall not reap. 5 As you know not what is the way of the ruach, nor how the bones do grow in the womb of her that is with child: even so you know not the works of Elohim who makes all. 6 In the morning sow your seed, and in the evening withhold not your hand: for you know not which shall prosper, either this or that, or whether they both shall be alike and tov. 7 Truly the light is sweet, and a pleasant thing it is for the eyes to behold the sun: 8 But if a man lives many years, and gilahs in them all; yet let him remember the days of darkness; for they shall be many. All that comes is vanity. 9 Gilah, O young man, in your youth; and let your lev encourage you in the days of your youth, and walk in the ways of your lev, and in the sight of your eyes: but know, that for all these things Elohim will bring you into judgment.

10 Therefore remove sorrow from your lev, and put away evil from your flesh: for childhood and youth are vanity.

12 Remember now your Creators[1] in the days of your youth, while the evil days come not, nor the years draw near, when you shall say, I have no pleasure in them; 2 While the sun, or the light, or the moon, or the stars, be not darkened, nor the clouds return after the rain: 3 In the day when the keepers of the bayit shall tremble, and the strong men shall bow themselves, and the grinders cease because they are few, and those that look out of the windows will become dim, 4 And the doors shall be shut in the streets, when the sound of the grinding is low, and he shall rise up at the voice of the bird, and all the daughters of music shall be brought low; 5 Also when they shall be afraid of that which is high, and fears shall be in the way, and the almond tree shall flourish, and the grasshopper shall be a burden, and desire shall fail: because man goes to his everlasting home, and the mourners go about the streets: 6 Or ever the silver cord

be loosed, or the golden bowl be broken, or the pitcher be broken at the fountain, or the wheel broken at the cistern. 7 Then shall the dust return to the earth as it was: and the ruach shall return to Elohim who gave it.[2] 8 Vanity of vanities, says the Qoheleth; all is vanity. 9 And moreover, because the Qoheleth was wise, he still taught the people da'at; yes, he listened and sought out, and set in order many proverbs. 10 The Qoheleth sought to find out acceptable words: and that which was written was upright, even words of truth. 11 The words of the wise are as goads, and as nails arranged by workmen, which are given from One Shepherd.[3] 12 And further, by these, my son, be admonished: of making many books there is no end; and much study is a weariness of the flesh. 13 Let us shema the conclusion of the whole matter: Fear Elohim, and keep His mitzvot: for this is the entire duty of all mankind. 14 For Elohim shall bring every work into mishpat, with every secret thing, whether it is tov, or whether it is evil.

---

[1] **Et borecha**. Literally: "your creators". A reference to the plurality of divinity; also the **aleph taf** or **et** (in the actual Hebrew) before "Creators" is a direct object pointer, indicting that the Creators are aleph taf.

[2] This is the truth plainly outlined by those open to receive it.
[3] In Yisrael's rebuilding, the Tov Shepherd distributes our tasks and the tools such as nails.

אסתר

Hadasah - Esther

To Our Forefathers Yisrael

1 Now it came to pass in the days of Achashverosh (this is Achashverosh that reigned, from India even to Ethiopia, over one hundred twenty-seven provinces)[1] 2 That in those days, when the Melech Achashverosh sat on the throne of his malchut, which was in Shushan the palace,[2] 3 In the third year of his reign, he made a feast to all his princes and his avadim; the powers of Persia and Media, the nobles and princes of the provinces, being before him: 4 He showed the riches of his beautiful malchut and the honor of his excellent majesty many days, even one hundred eighty days. 5 And when those days were expired, the melech made a feast to all the peoples that were present in Shushan the palace, both to great and small, seven days, in the court of the garden of the melech's palace; 6 Where there were white, green, and blue, hangings, fastened with cords of fine linen and purple to silver rings and pillars of marble: the beds were of gold and silver, upon a pavement of red, and blue, and white, and black, marble. 7 And they served drinks in vessels of gold - the vessels being diverse one from another - and royal wine in abundance, according to the generosity of the melech. 8 And the drinking was according to the law; no one was compelled: for so the melech had appointed to all the officers of his bayit, that they should serve according to every man's pleasure. 9 Also Vashti the malcha made a feast for the women in the royal bayit that belonged to Melech Achashverosh. 10 On the seventh day, when the lev of the melech was filled with wine, he commanded Mehuman, Biztha, Harvona, Bigtha, and Avagtha, Zethar, and Carcas, the seven eunuchs that served in the presence of Achashverosh the melech, 11 To bring Vashti the malcha before the melech with her royal crown, to show the people and the princes her beauty: for she was lovely to look at. 12 But the Malcha Vashti refused to come at the melech's commandment given by his eunuchs: therefore the melech was very angry, and his anger burned inside of him. 13 Then the melech said to the wise men, who knew the times - for this was the melech's custom; he discussed matters in the presence of those who understood law and judgment- 14 And the next to him was Carshena, Shethar, Admatha, Tarshish, Meres, Marsena, and Memucan, the seven princes of Persia and Media, who saw the melech's face, and who sat in the highest and foremost positions in the malchut. 15 What shall we do to the Malcha Vashti according to law, because she has not performed the commandment of Melech Achashverosh by the eunuchs? 16 And Memucan answered before the melech and the princes, Vashti the malcha has not done wrong to the melech only, but also to all the princes, and to all the peoples that are in all the provinces of the Melech Achashverosh. 17 For this rebellion of the malcha shall be known to all women, so that they shall despise their husbands, when it shall be reported. Then Melech Achashverosh commanded Vashti the malcha to be brought in before him, but she did not come. 18 Likewise shall the ladies of Persia and Media say to all the melech's princes, that they have heard of the deed of the malcha. Then shall there arise much contempt and anger. 19 If it please the melech, let there be issued a royal

---

[1] Many scholars feel this was none other than the well-known Artaxeres, who was a friend of the Jews based on many events, including those detailed in the scroll of Esther.
[2] The Jews in Babylon, who chose not to return with Ezra and Nehemiah, were later swallowed up in the captivity of Babylon, by the combined might of Medo-Persia. These captured exiles from Babylon circa 490 BCE are the Jews of the Book of Esther. They were called Jews by then, because all the Jews descended primarily from the three southern tribes, as were both Mordechai and Esther.

commandment from him, and let it be written among the laws of the Persians and the Medes, that it be not altered, That Vashti come no more before Melech Achashverosh; and let the melech give her royal position to another that is better than she. 20 And when the melech's decree that he shall make shall be published throughout all his empire - for it is great - all the wives shall give to their husbands honor, both great and small. 21 And the guidance pleased the melech and the princes; and the melech did according to the words of Memucan: 22 For he sent letters into all the melech's provinces, into every province according to the written decree, and to every people after their language, that every man should bear the rule in his own bayit, and that it should be published according to the language of every people.

2 After these things, when the anger of Melech Achashverosh was appeased, he remembered Vashti, and what she had done, and what was decreed against her. 2 Then said the melech's avadim that attended to him, Let there be lovely young virgins sought for the melech: 3 And let the melech appoint officers in all the provinces of his malchut, that they may gather together all the lovely young virgins to Shushan the palace, to the bayit of the women to the custody of Hegai the melech's eunuch, guardian of the women; and let their things for purification be given them to them: 4 And let the virgin that pleases the melech become malcha instead of Vashti. And the guidance pleased the melech; and he did so. 5 Now in Shushan the palace there was a certain Yahudite,[1] whose name

was Mordechai, the son of Yair, the son of Shimei, the son of Kish, a Benyamite; 6 Who had been carried away from Yahrushalayim with the captivity that had been carried away with Yechonyah melech of Yahudah, whom Nebuchadnetzar the melech of Bavel had carried away. 7 And he brought up Hadasah, that is, Esther, his uncle's daughter: for she had neither abba nor ima, and the virgin was lovely and beautiful; whom Mordechai took for his own daughter, when her abba and ima were dead. 8 So it came to pass, when the melech's commandment and his decree was heard, and when many virgins were gathered together to Shushan the palace, to the custody of Hegai, that Esther was brought also to the melech's bayit, to the custody of Hegai, guardian of the women. 9 And the virgin pleased him, and she obtained kindness from him; and he quickly gave her things for purification, with such things as belonged to her, and seven avadim, which were to be given to her, out of the melech's bayit: and he preferred her and her female avadim to the best place of the bayit of the women. 10 Ester had not revealed her national identity nor her relatives: for Mordechai had ordered her that she should not declare it. 11 And Mordechai walked every day before the court of the women's bayit, to know how Esther was doing, and what would become of her. 12 Now when every virgin's turn had come to go in to Melech Achashverosh, after she had been purified twelve months, according to the manner of the women; for in this manner were the days of their purifications accomplished; six months with the oil of myrrh, and six months with sweet odors. 13 Then came every virgin to the melech; whatever she desired was given to her to go with her out from the bayit of the women to the melech's bayit. 14 In the evening she went, and the next day she

---

[1] The thought of anyone having to become Jewish is nonsensical prior to 921 BCE when the Tabernacle of David split. The term "Jew," or "Jews," is not mentioned in Scripture prior to 490 BCE. The term "Jew" does not even appear in the Scriptures in social-historical Yisrael until the nation split into two houses and is first referenced here in the Scroll of Esther, which took place after the first return of Yahudah from the Babylonian captivity. Yahudim did not exist as Jews separately from Yisrael until the kingdom split in 921 BCE. Any ties to social and historical Yisrael prior to that date would lead one to Yisraelite, and certainly not Jewish, status.

Mordechai was considered a Jew, because he came from Benyamin, a southern tribe.

returned into the second bayit of the women, to the custody of Shaashgaz, the melech's eunuch, who kept the concubines: she came in to the melech no more, unless the melech delighted in her, so that she was called by name a second time. 15 Now when the turn of Esther, the daughter of Avihail the uncle of Mordechai, who had taken her for his daughter, had come to go in to the melech, she required nothing but what Hegai the melech's eunuch, the guardian of the women, had advised. And Esther obtained favor in the sight of all those that looked upon her. 16 So Esther was taken to Melech Achashverosh into his royal bayit in the tenth month, which is the month Teveth, in the seventh year of his reign. 17 And the melech loved Esther above all the women, and she obtained favor and kindness in his sight more than all the virgins; so that he set the royal crown upon her head, and made her malcha instead of Vashti. 18 Then the melech made a great feast to all his princes and his avadim, even Esther's Feast; and he made a release to the provinces, and gave gifts, according to the means of a melech. 19 And when the virgins were gathered together the second time, then Mordechai sat in the melech's gate. 20 Esther had not yet showed her relatives or her national identity; as Mordechai had ordered her: for Esther followed the commandment of Mordechai, just like when she was brought up with him. 21 In those days, while Mordechai sat in the melech's gate, two of the melech's eunuchs, Bigthan and Teresh, of those who guarded the palace door, were angry, and sought to lay hands on the Melech Achashverosh. 22 And the matter became known to Mordechai, who told it to Esther the malcha; and Esther informed the melech in Mordechai's name. 23 And when an investigation was made of the matter, it was confirmed; therefore they were both hanged on a tree: and it was written in the scroll of the chronicles before the melech.

3 After these things did Melech Achashverosh promote Haman the son of Hammedatha the Agagite, and advanced him, and set his seat above all the princes that were with him. 2 And all the melech's avadim, that were in the melech's gate, bowed, and reverenced Haman: for the melech had so commanded concerning him. But Mordechai bowed not, nor did him reverence. 3 Then the melech's avadim, who were in the melech's gate, said to Mordechai, Why do you transgress the melech's commandment? 4 Now it came to pass, when they spoke daily to him, and he listened not to them, that they told Haman, to see whether Mordechai's words would stand: for he had told them that he was a Yahudite. 5 And when Haman saw that Mordechai bowed not, nor did him reverence, then was Haman full of anger. 6 And he thought it despicable to lay hands on Mordechai alone; for they had showed him the identity of the people of Mordechai: therefore Haman sought to destroy all the Yahudim that were throughout the whole malchut of Achashverosh, even the people of Mordechai. 7 In the first month, that is, the month Nisan, in the twelfth year of Melech Achashverosh, they cast Pur, that is, the lots, before Haman from day to day, and from month to month, to the twelfth month, which is, the month Adar. 8 And Haman said to Melech Achashverosh, There is a certain people scattered abroad and dispersed among the nation [1] in all the provinces of your malchut; and their laws are diverse from all peoples; neither do they keep the melech's laws: therefore it is not for the melech's benefit to let them remain alive. 9 If it please the melech, let it be written that they may be destroyed: and I will pay ten thousand talents of silver to the hands of those that have the duties of the business, to bring it into the melech's treasuries. 10 And the melech took his ring from his hand, and gave it to Haman the son of Hammedatha the Agagite, the Yahudim's

---

[1] Jewish Yisrael.

enemy. 11 And the melech said to Haman, The silver is given to you, the people also, to do with them as it seems tov to you. 12 Then were the melech's Sophrim called on the thirteenth day of the first month, and there was written according to all that Haman had commanded to the melech's lieutenants, and to the governors that were over every province, and to the rulers of every people of every province according to the written decree, and to every people in their own language; in the name of Melech Achashverosh it was written, and sealed with the melech's seal. 13 And the letters were sent by messenger posts into all the melech's provinces, to destroy, to kill, and to cause to perish, all the Yahudim, both young and old, little children and women, in one day, even upon the thirteenth day of the twelfth month, which is the month Adar, and to take their plunder as a plunder. 14 The copy of the decree was issued as a commandment to be given in every province and was published to all the people, that they should be ready for that day. 15 The posts went out, being quickened by the melech's commandment, and the decree was given in Shushan the palace. And the melech and Haman sat down to drink; but the city of Shushan was in confusion.

4 When Mordechai perceived all that was done, Mordechai tore his clothes, and put on sackcloth with ashes, and went out into the middle of the city, and cried with a loud and a bitter cry; 2 And came before the melech's gate: for none might enter into the melech's gate clothed with sackcloth. 3 And in every province, wherever the melech's commandment and his decree came, there was great mourning among the Yahudim, and fasting, and weeping, and wailing; and many lay in sackcloth and ashes. 4 So Esther's maids and her eunuchs came and told it to her. Then was the malcha exceedingly in pain; and she sent clothing to clothe Mordechai,

and to take away his sackcloth from him: but he refused. 5 Then called Esther for Hatach, one of the melech's eunuchs, who was appointed to serve her, and gave him a commandment to Mordechai, to know what it was, and why it was. 6 So Hatach went forth to Mordechai to the street of the city, which was before the melech's gate. 7 And Mordechai told him of all that had happened to him, and of the sum of the money that Haman had promised to pay in to the melech's treasuries for the Yahudim, to destroy them. 8 Also he gave him the copy of the writing of the decree that was given at Shushan to destroy them, to show it to Esther, and to declare it to her, and to order her that she should go in to the melech, to make petition to him, and to make a request before him for her people. 9 And Hatach came and told Esther the words of Mordechai. 10 Again Esther spoke to Hatach, and gave him commandment to Mordechai; 11 All the melech's avadim, and the people of the melech's provinces, do know, that anyone, whether man or woman, who shall come to the melech into the inner court, who is not called, will be put to death by his law, except the one to whom the melech shall hold out the golden scepter, that he may live: but I have not been called to come in to the melech these thirty days. 12 And they told Mordechai Esther's words. 13 Then Mordechai commanded this answer to Esther, Think not to yourself that you shall escape in the melech's bayit, more than all the other Yahudim. 14 For if you keep silent at this time, then shall their relief and deliverance arise for the Yahudim from another place; but you and your abba's bayit shall be destroyed: and who knows whether you have come to the malchut for such a time as this?[1] 15 Then Esther ordered them to return to Mordechai with this

---

[1] Yisraelites cannot keep silent when either house of Yisrael is being mistreated or persecuted. We must speak up for both houses, using love and equal weights and measures. If we keep silent we lose YHWH's blessing. We have been brought into the kingdom in these last days to proclaim deliverance and relief to all Yisralels captives.

answer, 16 Go, gather together all the Yahudim that are present in Shushan, and fast for me, and neither eat nor drink three days and nights: I also and my virgins will fast as well; and then I will go in to the melech, which is not according to the law: and if I perish, I perish.[1] 17 So Mordechai went his way, and did according to all that Esther had commanded him.

5 Now it came to pass on the third day, that Esther put on her royal apparel, and stood in the inner court of the melech's bayit, opposite the melech's bayit: and the melech sat upon his royal throne in the royal bayit, over against the gate of the bayit. 2 And it was so, when the melech saw Esther the malcha standing in the court, that she obtained favor in his sight: and the melech held out to Esther the golden scepter that was in his hand. So Esther drew near, and touched the top of the scepter. 3 Then said the melech to her, What do you desire, Malcha Esther? And what is your request? It shall be given to you even to the half of the malchut. 4 And Esther answered, If it seem tov to the melech, let the melech and Haman come this day to the banquet that I have prepared for him. 5 Then the melech said, Hurry and get Haman, that he may do as Esther has said. So the melech and Haman came to the banquet that Esther had prepared. 6 And the melech said to Esther at the banquet of wine, What is your petition? And it shall be granted you: and what is your request? Even to the half of the malchut it shall be given. 7 Then answered Esther, and said, My petition and my request is this; 8 If I have found favor in the sight of the melech, and if it please the melech to grant my petition, and to perform my request, let the melech and Haman come to the banquet that I shall prepare for them, and I will do tomorrow as the melech has said. 9 Then went Haman forth that day with gilah and with a lev of simcha: but

when Haman saw Mordechai in the melech's gate, that he did not stand up, nor move for him, he was full of indignation against Mordechai. 10 Nevertheless Haman refrained himself: and when he came home, he sent and called for his friends, and Zeresh his wife. 11 And Haman told them of the beauty of his riches, and the multitude of his children, and all the things in which the melech had promoted him, and how he had advanced him above the princes and avadim of the melech. 12 Haman said moreover, Esther the malcha did not let any man come in with the melech to the banquet that she had prepared except myself; and tomorrow I am invited with her and also with the melech. 13 Yet all this means nothing to me, as long as I see Mordechai the Yahudite sitting at the melech's gate. 14 Then said Zeresh his wife and all his friends to him, Let gallows be made of fifty cubits high, and tomorrow speak to the melech that Mordechai may be hanged on it: then go in joyfully with the melech to the banquet. And the thing pleased Haman; and he ordered the gallows to be made.

6 On that night the melech could not sleep, and he commanded someone to bring the scroll of records of the chronicles; and they were read before the melech. 2 And it was found written, that Mordechai had informed him of Bigthana and Teresh, two of the melech's eunuchs, the guards of the palace door, who sought to lay hands on the Melech Achashverosh. 3 And the melech said, What honor and dignity has been done to Mordechai for this? Then said the melech's avadim that attended to him, There is nothing done for him. 4 And the melech said, Who is in the court? Now Haman had come into the outward court of the melech's bayit, to speak to the melech to hang Mordechai on the gallows that he had prepared for him. 5 And the melech's avadim said to him, Behold, Haman stands in the court. And the melech said, Let him come in. 6 So Haman came in. And the

---

[1] We must be willing to lose all for the kingdom message of Yisrael's restoration.

melech said to him, What shall be done to the man whom the melech delights to honor? Now Haman thought in his lev, To whom would the melech delight to do honor more than to myself? 7 And Haman answered the melech, For the man whom the melech delights to honor, 8 Let the royal apparel be brought which the melech wears, and the horse that the melech rides upon, and the royal crown that is set upon his head: 9 And let this apparel and horse be delivered to the hand of one of the melech's most noble princes, that they may array the man completely whom the melech delights to honor, and bring him on horseback through the streets of the city, and proclaim before him, So shall it be done to the man whom the melech delights to honor. 10 Then the melech said to Haman, Hurry, and take the apparel and the horse, as you have said, and do so to Mordechai the Yahudite, that sits at the melech's gate: let nothing fail of all that you have spoken. 11 Then took Haman the apparel and the horse, and arrayed Mordechai, and brought him on horseback through the streets of the city, and proclaimed before him, So shall it be done to the man whom the melech delights to honor. 12 And Mordechai came again to the melech's gate. But Haman hurried back to his bayit mourning, and having his head covered. 13 And Haman told Zeresh his wife and all his friends everything that had happened to him. Then said his wise men and Zeresh his wife to him, If Mordechai is of the zera of the Yahudim, you shall not prevail against him, but shall surely fall before him.[1] 14 And while they were yet talking with him, the melech's eunuchs came, and quickly brought Haman to the banquet that Esther had prepared.

7 So the melech and Haman came to banquet with Esther the malcha. 2 And the melech said again to Esther on the second day at the banquet of wine, What is

your petition, Malcha Esther? And it shall be granted you: and what is your request? And it shall be performed, even to the half of the malchut. 3 Then Esther the malcha answered and said, If I have found favor in your sight, O melech, and if it please the melech, let my life be given me at my petition, and my people at my request: 4 For we have been sold, I and my people, to be destroyed, to be slain, and to perish. But if we had been sold even as slaves, I would have remained silent, although the enemy could not make up the damage to the melech. 5 Then the Melech Achashverosh answered and said to Esther the malcha, Who is he, and where is he, that does presume in his lev to do so? 6 And Esther said, The adversary and enemy is this wicked Haman. Then Haman was afraid before the melech and the malcha. 7 And the melech arising from the banquet of wine in anger went into the palace garden: and Haman stood up to make a request for his life to Esther the malcha; for he saw that there was evil determined against him by the melech. 8 Then the melech returned out of the palace garden into the place of the banquet of wine; and Haman fell upon the bed on which Esther was. Then said the melech, Will he force the malcha sexually also before me in the bayit? As the word went out of the melech's mouth, they covered Haman's face. 9 And Havonah, one of the eunuchs, said before the melech, Behold also, the gallows fifty cubits high, which Haman had made for Mordechai, who had spoken tov for the melech, stands at the bayit of Haman. Then the melech said, Hang him on it. 10 So they hanged Haman on the gallows that he had prepared for Mordechai. Then was the melech's anger abated.

8 On that day did the Melech Achashverosh give the bayit of Haman the Yahudim's enemy to Esther the malcha. And Mordechai came before the melech; for Esther had told him how he was related to

---

[1] Would to YHWH all the gentiles would grab hold of this principle.

her. 2 And the melech took off his ring, which he had taken from Haman, and gave it to Mordechai. And Esther set Mordechai over the bayit of Haman. 3 And Esther spoke yet again before the melech, and fell down at his feet, and besought him with tears to put away the mischief of Haman the Agagite, and his evil device that he had devised against the Yahudim. 4 Then the melech held out the golden scepter toward Esther. So Esther arose, and stood before the melech, 5 And said, If it please the melech, and if I have found favor in his sight, and the thing seems right before the melech, and I be pleasing in his eyes, let it be written to reverse the letters devised by Haman the son of Hammedatha the Agagite, which he wrote to destroy the Yahudim who are in all the melech's provinces: 6 For how can I endure to see the evil that shall come to my people? Or how can I endure to see the destruction of my relatives? 7 Then the Melech Achashverosh said to Esther the malcha and to Mordechai the Yahudite, Behold, I have given Esther the bayit of Haman, and him they have hanged upon the gallows, because he laid his hand upon the Yahudim. 8 Write also for the Yahudim, whatever you like, in the melech's name, and seal it with the melech's ring: for the writing which is written in the melech's name, and sealed with the melech's ring, no man can reverse. 9 Then were the melech's Sophrim called at that time in the third month, that is, the month Sivan, on the twenty-third day; and it was written according to all that Mordechai commanded to the Yahudim, and to the lieutenants, and the deputies and rulers of the provinces which are from India to Ethiopia, [1] a hundred twenty-seven provinces, to every province according to their writing, and to every people after their language, and to the Yahudim according to their writing, and according to their language. 10 And he wrote in the Melech Achashverosh's name,

and sealed it with the melech's ring, and sent letters by messenger posts on horseback, and riders on mules, camels, and young mares: 11 In which the melech granted the Yahudim who were in every city to gather themselves together, [2] and to stand for their life, to destroy, to slay, and to cause to perish, all the power of the peoples and provinces that would assault them, both little ones and women, and to take the plunder from them for a plunder, 12 Upon one day in all the provinces of Melech Achashverosh, namely, upon the thirteenth day of the twelfth month, which is the month of Adar. 13 The copy of the writing for a commandment to be given in every province was published to all peoples, that the Yahudim should be ready that day to avenge themselves on their enemies. 14 So the messenger posts that rode upon mules and camels went out, being rushed by the melech's commandment. And the decree was given at Shushan the palace. 15 And Mordechai went out from the presence of the melech in royal apparel of blue and white, and with a great crown of gold, and with a garment of fine linen and purple: and the city of Shushan rejoiced and was in simcha. 16 The Yahudim had light, and gilah, and simcha, and kavod. 17 And in every province, and in every city, wherever the melech's commandment and his decree was declared, the Yahudim had simcha and gilah, a feast and a Yom-Tov. And many of the people of the land became Yahudim; [3] for the fear of the Yahudim fell upon them.

9 Now in the twelfth month, that is, the month Adar, on the thirteenth day of the same, when the melech's commandment

---

[1] We see Yisraelites throughout Asia and Asia Minor. If that is true of Yahudah, how much more of the numerically larger non-Jewish Yisraelites?

[2] Yahudah was scattered into every Persian city, just like Ephraim was scattered into every city on the earth as the "fullness of the nations."
[3] Many in Asia and the Middle East became Yahudim. Since the Chaldeans were included, many Chaldeans also became Yisrael. So the dom of both houses remains fully intermingled in fulfillment of the **nivrechu** promise given to Abraham in Genesis 12:3. See notes on Gen. 12:3 for more details.

and his decree drew near to be done to the Yahudim, in the same day that the enemies of the Yahudim hoped to have power over them, it was turned around, so that the Yahudim had rule over those who hated them. 2 The Yahudim gathered themselves together in their cities throughout all the provinces of the Melech Achashverosh, to lay hands on those who had sought their hurt: and no man could withstand them; for the fear of them fell upon all people. 3 And all the rulers of the provinces, and the lieutenants, and the deputies, and officers of the melech, helped the Yahudim; because the fear of Mordechai fell upon them. 4 For Mordechai was great in the melech's bayit, and his fame went out throughout all the provinces: for this man Mordechai grew greater and greater. 5 So the Yahudim smote all their enemies with the stroke of the sword, and slaughter, and destruction, and did what they desired to those that hated them. 6 And in Shushan the palace the Yahudim killed and destroyed five hundred men. 7 And Parshandatha, and Dalphon, and Aspatha, 8 And Poratha, and Adalya, and Aridatha, 9 And Parmashta, and Arisai, and Aridai, and Vayetzatha, 10 The ten sons of Haman the son of Hammedatha, the enemy of the Yahudim, they killed; but on the plunder they laid not their hands. 11 On that day the number of those that were slain in Shushan the palace was brought before the melech. 12 And the melech said to Esther the malcha, The Yahudim have slain and destroyed five hundred men in Shushan the palace, and the ten sons of Haman; what have they done in the rest of the melech's provinces? Now what is your petition? And it shall be granted you: or what is your further request? and it shall be done. 13 Then said Esther, If it please the melech, let it be granted to the Yahudim who are in Shushan to do tomorrow also according to today's decree, and let Haman's ten sons be hanged upon the gallows. 14 And the melech commanded it to be done: and the decree was given at Shushan; and they hanged Haman's ten sons. 15 For the Yahudim that were in Shushan gathered themselves together on the fourteenth day also of the month Adar, and killed three hundred men at Shushan; but the plunder was not touched. 16 But the other Yahudim that were in the melech's provinces gathered themselves together, and stood up for their lives, and had rest from their enemies, and killed of their foes seventy and five thousand, but they laid not their hands on the plunder, 17 On the thirteenth day of the month Adar; and on the fourteenth day of the same month they rested, and made it a day of feasting and simcha. 18 But the Yahudim that were at Shushan assembled together on the thirteenth day; and on the fourteenth; and on the fifteenth day of the same they rested, and made it days of feasting and gilah. 19 Therefore the Yahudim of the villages, that dwelt in the unwalled towns, made the fourteenth day of the month Adar a day of gilah and feasting, and a tov day, and of sending portions one to another. 20 And Mordechai wrote these things, and sent letters to all the Yahudim that were in all the provinces of the Melech Achashverosh, both near and far, 21 To establish this among them, that they should observe the fourteenth day of the month Adar, and the fifteenth day of the same, yearly, 22 As the days in which the Yahudim rested from their enemies, and the month which was turned from sorrow to simcha, and from mourning into a Yom-Tov: that they should make them days of feasting and simcha, and of sending portions one to another, and gifts to the poor. 23 And the Yahudim undertook to do as they had begun, and as Mordechai had written to them; 24 Because Haman the son of Hammedatha, the Agagite, the enemy of all the Yahudim, had devised against the Yahudim to destroy them, and had cast Pur, that is, the lot, to consume them, and to destroy them; 25 But when Esther came before the melech, he commanded by letters that his wicked device, which he devised against the Yahudim, should return upon his own head, and that he and his sons should be hanged on the gallows. 26 Therefore they called these days Purim after the name of Pur. Therefore for all the words of this letter, and of that which they had seen concerning this matter, and which had come to them, 27 The Yahudim ordained, and took upon them, and upon their zera, and upon all such as joined themselves to them,[1] so as it should not fail, that they would keep these two days according to their decree, and according to their appointed time every year; 28 And that these days should be remembered and kept throughout every generation, every family, every province, and every city; and that these days of Purim should not fail from among the Yahudim, nor the memorial of them perish from their zera. 29 Then Esther the malcha, the daughter of Avihail, and Mordechai the Yahudite, wrote with all authority, to confirm this second letter of Purim. 30 And he sent the letters to all the Yahudim, to the hundred twenty-seven provinces of the malchut of Achashverosh, with words of shalom and emet,

31 To confirm these days of Purim in their appointed times, according to what Mordechai the Yahudite and Esther the malcha had established for them, and as they had decreed for themselves and for their zera, the matters of their fastings and their lamenting. 32 And the decree of Esther confirmed these matters of Purim; and it was written in the scroll.

10 And the Melech Achashverosh laid a compulsory labor upon the land, and upon the islands of the sea.[2] 2 And all the acts of his power and of his might, and the declaration of the greatness of Mordechai, with which the melech made him great, are they not written in the scroll of the chronicles of the melechim of Media and Persia? 3 For Mordechai the Yahudite was second to Melech Achashverosh, and great among the Yahudim, and accepted by the multitude of his brothers, seeking the wealth of his people, and speaking shalom to all his zera.

---

[1] Many joined with Jewish Yisrael and had offspring who obviously became Yisrael and are dispersed in the world to this day.

[2] Home to many of Ephraim Yisrael.

Ezrah - Ezra

To Our Forefathers Yisrael

1 Now in the first year of Koresh melech of Persia, so that the word of **יהוה** by the mouth of Yirmeyahu might be fulfilled, **יהוה** stirred up the ruach of Koresh melech of Persia, so that he made a proclamation throughout all his malchut, and put it also in writing, saying, 2 This says Koresh melech of Persia, **יהוה** Elohim of the shamayim has given me all the malchuts of the earth; and He has commanded me to rebuild a Bayit for Him at Yahrushalayim, which is in Yahudah. 3 Who is there among you of all of His people? His Elohim be with him, and let him go up to Yahrushalayim, which is in Yahudah, and rebuild the Bayit of **יהוה** Elohim of Yisrael - He is the Elohim - that is in Yahrushalayim. 4 And whoever remains in any place where he sojourns, let the men of his place help him with silver, and with gold, and with goods, and with beasts, besides the terumah offerings for theBayit of Elohim that is in Yahrushalayim. 5 Then the heads of the ahvot of Yahudah and Benyamin rose up,[1] and the kohanim, and the Leviim, with all those whose ruach Elohim had raised, to go up to rebuild the Bayit of **יהוה** which is at Yahrushalayim. 6 And all those around them strengthened their hands with vessels of silver, with gold, with goods, and with beasts, and with precious things, besides all that was willingly offered. 7 Also Koresh the melech brought forth the vessels of the Bayit of **יהוה**, which Nebuchadnetzar had brought out of Yahrushalayim, and had put them in the Bayit of his elohim; 8 Even those did Koresh melech of Persia bring forth by the hand of Mithredath the treasurer, and numbered them to Sheshbatzar, the leader of Yahudah. 9 And this is the number of them: thirty dishes of gold, a thousand dishes of silver, twenty-nine knives, 10 Thirty basons of gold, silver basons four hundred and ten, and a thousand other vessels. 11 All the vessels of gold and of silver were five thousand four hundred. All these did Sheshbatzar bring up with those of the exile that were brought up from Bavel to Yahrushalayim.

2 Now these are the children of the province that returned from the exile, of those that had been carried away, whom Nebuchadnetzar the melech of Bavel had carried away to Bavel, these came again to Yahrushalayim and Yahudah, every one to his own city; 2 Who came with Zeruvvavel: Yeshua, Nehemyah, Seraiyah, Reelayah, Mordechai-Bilashon, [2] Mispar, Bigvai, Rehum, Baanah. The number of the men of the people of Yisrael: 3 The children of Parosh, two thousand one hundred seventy-two. 4 The children of Shephatyah, three hundred seventy-two. 5 The children of Arah, seven hundred seventy-five. 6 The children of Pahath-Moav, of the children of Yeshua and Yoav, two thousand eight hundred twelve. 7 The children of Eylam, one thousand two hundred fifty-four. 8 The children of Zattu, nine hundred forty-five. 9 The children of Zaccai, seven hundred sixty. 10 The children of Bani, six hundred forty-two. 11 The children of Bevai, six hundred twenty-three. 12 The children of Azgad, a thousand two hundred twenty-two. 13 The children of Adonikam, six hundred sixty-six. 14 The children of Bigvai, two thousand fifty-six. 15 The children of Adin, four hundred fifty-four. 16 The children of Ater of Hizkiyahu, ninety-eight. 17 The

---

[1] Not Ephraim or the other ten tribes, since Ephraim never was part of the Babylonian exile having gone into Assyria some 200 years earlier.

[2] This is the Mordechai from the Book of Esther recorded here as **Mordechai-Bilashon**, because he was proficient in many languages. He returned from exile with Ezra and Nehemiah.

children of Bezai, three hundred twenty-three. 18 The children of Yorah, one hundred twelve. 19 The children of Hashum, two hundred twenty-three. 20 The children of Givar, ninety-five. 21 The children of Beth-Lechem, one hundred twenty-three. 22 The men of Netophah, fifty-six. 23 The men of Anathoth, a hundred twenty-eight. 24 The children of Azmaveth, forty-two. 25 The children of Kiryath-Arim, Chephirah, and Beeroth, seven hundred forty-three. 26 The children of Ramah and Geva, six hundred twenty-one. 27 The men of Michmas, a hundred twenty-two. 28 The men of Beth-El and Ai, two hundred twenty-three. 29 The children of Nebo, fifty-two. 30 The children of Magvish, one hundred fifty-six. 31 The children of the other Eylam, one thousand two hundred fifty-four. 32 The children of Harim, three hundred twenty. 33 The children of Lod, Hadid, and Ono, seven hundred twenty-five. 34 The children of Yericho, three hundred forty-five. 35 The children of Senaah, three thousand six hundred and thirty. 36 The kohanim: the children of Yedaiyah, of the bayit of Yeshua, nine hundred seventy-three. 37 The children of Immer, one thousand fifty-two. 38 The children of Pashur, one thousand two hundred forty-seven. 39 The children of Harim, one thousand seventeen. 40 The Leviim: the children of Yeshua and Kadmi-El, of the children of Hodavyah, seventy-four. 41 The singers: the children of Asaph, one hundred twenty-eight. 42 The children of the gatekeepers: the children of Shallum, the children of Ater, the children of Talmon, the children of Achuv, the children of Hatita, the children of Shovai, in all one hundred thirty-nine. 43 The Nethinim: the children of Tziha, the children of Hasupha, the children of Tavaoth, 44 The children of Keros, the children of Siaha, the children of Padon, 45 The children of Levanah, the children of Hagavah, the children of Achuv, 46 The children of Hagav, the children of Shalmai, the children of Hanan, 47 The children of Gidd-El, the children of Gahar, the children of Reayah, 48 The children of Rezin, the children of Nekoda, the children of Gazzam, 49 The children of Uzza, the children of Paseah, the children of Besai, 50 The children of Asnah, the children of Mehunim, the children of Nephusim, 51 The children of Bakbuk, the children of Hachupha, the children of Harhur, 52 The children of Batzluth, the children of Mehida, the children of Harsha, 53 The children of Barkos, the children of Sisera, the children of Thamah, 54 The children of Netziyah, the children of Hatipha. 55 The children of Shlomo's avadim: the children of Sotai, the children of Sophereth, the children of Peruda, 56 The children of Yaalah, the children of Darkon, the children of Gidd-El, 57 The children of Shephatyah, the children of Hattil, the children of Pochereth of Tzevaim, the children of Ami. 58 All the Nethinim, and the children of Shlomo's avadim, were three hundred ninety-two. 59 And these were those who went up from Tel-melah, Tel-harsa, Cheruv, Addan, and Immer: but they could not show their abba's lineage, and their zera, whether they were of Yisrael: 60 The children of Delayah, the children of Toviyah, the children of Nekoda, six hundred fifty-two. 61 And of the children of the kohanim: the children of Havayah, the children of Koz, the children of Barzillai; which took a wife of the daughters of Barzillai the Gileadite, and was called after their name: 62 These sought to register among those that were numbered by genealogy, but they were not found: therefore they were counted as polluted, and removed from the priesthood. 63 And the governor said to them, that they should not eat of the most set-apart things, until there stood up a kohen with Urim and with Thummim. 64 The whole congregation together was forty-two thousand three hundred sixty,[1] 65 Beside their avadim and

---

[1] As seen elsewhere, most Yahudites didn't return from Babylon, let alone Ephraim from out in the nations. A remnant returned, but not all Yisrael. They have never yet been fully reconstituted.

their maids, of whom there were seven thousand three hundred thirty-seven: and there were among them two hundred singing men and singing women. 66 Their horses were seven hundred thirty-six; their mules, two hundred forty-five; 67 Their camels, four hundred thirty-five; their donkeys, six thousand seven hundred twenty. 68 And some of the heads of the ahvot, when they came to the Bayit of יהוה which is at Yahrushalayim, offered freely for the Bayit of Elohim to set it up in its place: 69 They gave after their ability to the treasury for the work sixty-one thousand drams of gold, and five thousand pounds of silver, and one hundred sets of the kohanim's garments. 70 So the kohanim, and the Leviim, and some of the people, and the singers, and the gatekeepers, and the Nethinim, dwelt in their cities, and all Yisrael[1] in their cities.

3 And when the seventh month had come, and the children of Yisrael were in their cities, the people gathered themselves together as echad to Yahrushalayim. 2 Then stood up Yeshua the son of Yotzadak, and his brothers the kohanim, and Zeruvvavel the son of Shealti-El, and his brothers, and rebuilt the altar of the Elohim of Yisrael, to offer burnt offerings on it, as it is written in the Torah of Moshe the man of Elohim. 3 And they set the altar upon its bases; for fear was upon them because of the people of those countries: and they offered burnt offerings on it to יהוה, even burnt offerings for shacrit and maariv. 4 They kept also the Chag Sukkot, as it is written, and offered the daily burnt offerings by number, according to the mishpat, as the duty of each day required; 5 And afterward they offered the continual burnt offering, both for the Rosh Chodashim, and for all the

moadim of יהוה that were set-apart, and of everyone that willingly offered a terumah offering to יהוה. 6 From the first day of the seventh month they began to offer burnt offerings to יהוה. But the foundation of the Beit HaMikdash of יהוה was not yet laid. 7 They gave money also to the stonemasons, and to the carpenters; and food, and drink, and oil, to those of Tzidon, and to those of Tyre, to bring cedar logs from Levanon to the Sea of Yapho, according to the grant and permission that they had from Koresh melech of Persia. 8 Now in the second year of their coming to the Bayit of Elohim at Yahrushalayim, in the second month, began Zeruvvavel the son of Shealti-El, and Yeshua the son of Yotzadak, and the remnant of their brothers the kohanim and the Leviim, and all those that were come out of the exile to Yahrushalayim; and appointed the Leviim, from twenty years old and upward, to oversee the work of the Bayit of יהוה. 9 Then stood Yeshua with his sons and his brothers, Kadmi-El and his sons, the sons of Yahudah, together, to oversee the workmen in the Bayit of Elohim: the sons of Henadad, with their sons and their brothers the Leviim. 10 And when the builders laid the foundation of the Beit HaMikdash of יהוה, they set the kohanim in their robes with shofars, and the Leviim the sons of Asaph with cymbals, to tehilla יהוה, after the order established by David melech of Yisrael. 11 And they sang together by division in giving tehilla and giving hodu to יהוה; because He is tov, for His chesed endures le-olam-va-ed toward Yisrael. And all the people shouted with a great shout, and gave tehilla to יהוה, because the foundation of the Bayit of יהוה was laid. 12 But many of the kohanim and Leviim and heads of the ahvot, who were older men, that had seen the first Bayit, when the foundation of this Bayit was laid before their eyes, wept with a loud voice; yet many others shouted aloud for simcha: 13 So that the people could not discern the noise of the

---

[1] Obviously "all Yisrael" here is limited to those who returned with Jewish Yisrael, and not the false notion that the fullness of all 12 tribes returned. The qualifier for the "all Yisrael" is found earlier in this very same verse with the term "some of the people."

shout of simcha from the noise of the weeping of the people: for the people shouted with a loud shout, and the noise was heard far off.

4 Now when the adversaries of Yahudah and Benyamin heard that the children of the exile had rebuilt the Beit HaMikdash to יהוה Elohim of Yisrael; 2 Then they came to Zeruvvavel, and to the heads of the ahvot, and said to them, Let us rebuild with you: for we seek your Elohim, as you do; and we do sacrifice to Him since the days of Esar-Haddon melech of Ashshur, who brought us here.[1] 3 But Zeruvvavel, and Yeshua, and the rest of the heads of the ahvot of Yisrael, said to them, You have nothing to do with us to rebuild a Bayit to our Elohim; but we ourselves together will rebuild to יהוה Elohim of Yisrael, as melech Koresh the melech of Persia has commanded us. 4 Then the people of the land weakened the hands of the people of Yahudah, and troubled them in building,[2] 5 And hired counselors against them, to frustrate their purpose, all the days of Koresh melech of Persia, even until the reign of Dareyawesh melech of Persia. 6 And in the reign of Achashverosh, in the beginning of his reign, they wrote to him an accusation against the inhabitants of Yahudah and Yahrushalayim. 7 And in the days of Artahshashta, Bishlam, Mithredath, Taveel, and the rest of their companions, wrote to Artahshashta melech of Persia; and the writing of the letter was written in the Aramaic tongue, and translated from the Aramaic tongue. 8 Rehum the governor and Shimshai the sopher all wrote a letter against Yahrushalayim to Artahshashta the melech like this: 9 Rehum the governor, and Shimshai the sopher, and the rest of their companions; the shophtim, the emissaries,

the counsels, the officials, the people of Erek, of Bavel, of Shushan, of Dehavites, of the Eylamites, 10 And the rest of the nations who the great and noble Osnappar brought over, and placed in the cities of Shomron, and the rest that are on this side of the river, at this time. 11 This is the copy of the letter that they sent to him, even to Artahshashta the melech; Your avadim the men on this side of the river, at such a time. 12 Be it known to the melech, that the Yahudim[3] who came up from you to us have come to Yahrushalayim, building the rebellious and the evil city, and have set up the walls, and repaired its foundations. 13 Be it known now to the melech, that, if this city is rebuilt, and the walls set up again, then will they not pay excise, or tax, and will cause the revenue of the melech to suffer loss. 14 Now because we have eaten salt from the melech's palace, and it was not right for us to see the melech being shamed like this, therefore have we sent and certified this letter to the melech; 15 That a search may be made in the scroll of the records of your ahvot: so shall you find in the scroll of the records, and know that this city is a rebellious city, and hurtful to melechim and provinces, and that they have been responsible for revolts within it in the past which is the reason this city was destroyed. 16 We inform the melech that, if this city is rebuilt again, and the walls of it set up again, by this action you shall have no portion of land on this side of the river. 17 Then sent the melech an answer to Rehum the governor, and to Shimshai the sopher, and to the rest of their companions that dwell in Shomron, and to the rest beyond the river, Shalom, at this time. 18 The letter that you sent to us has been plainly read before me. 19 And I commanded, and a search has been made, and it is found that this city in times past has made insurrection against melechim, and that rebellion and sedition have been

[1] Assyrian colonists who settled in the north after Ephraim's expulsion, and mixed with the remaining Ephraimites, who came to be known as Samaritans and were actually Ephraimites who were dom-related to the Jewish exiles that returned.
[2] This was basically another Ephraimite attempt to stop Jerusalem-based worship.
[3] Only called Yahudim after their exile and return from Babylon.

made in it. 20 There have been mighty melechim also over Yahrushalayim, who have ruled over all countries beyond the river; and tax, excise, and toll, was paid to them. 21 Now make a decree to these men to cease, so that this city not be rebuilt, until a commandment from me shall be given to do so. 22 Beware that you do not fail to do this: why should damage increase to the hurt of the melechim? 23 Now when the copy of melech Artahshashta's letter was read before Rehum, and Shimshai the sopher, and their companions, they went up in a hurry to Yahrushalayim to the Yahudim, and made them cease by force and power. 24 Then ceased the work of the Bayit of Elohim that is at Yahrushalayim. So it ceased until the second year of the reign of Dareyawesh melech of Persia.

5 Then ha neviim, Chaggai, and Zacharyah the son of Iddo, prophesied to the Yahudim that were in Yahudah and Yahrushalayim in the Name of the Elohim of Yisrael.[1] 2 Then rose up Zeruvvavel the son of Shealti-El, and Yeshua the son of Yotzadak, and began to rebuild the Bayit of Elohim which is at Yahrushalayim: and with them were ha neviim of Elohim helping them.[2] 3 At the same time came to them Tatnai, the governor on this side of the river, and Shethar-Boznai, and their companions, and said this to them, Who has commanded you to rebuild this Bayit, and to raise up this wall? 4 And then we told them, all the names of the men that were doing the building. 5 But the eye of their Elohim was upon the zachanim of the Yahudim, so that they could not force them to cease, until the matter came to Dareyawesh: and then they returned an answer by letter concerning this matter. 6 The copy of the letter that Tatnai, governor on this side of the river, and

Shethar-boznai, and his companions the officials, who were on this side the river, sent to Dareyawesh the melech: 7 They sent a letter to him, in which was written this; Unto Dareyawesh the melech, all shalom. 8 Be it known to the melech, that we went into the province of Yahudah, to the Bayit of the great Elohim, which is rebuilt with great stones, and timber is laid in the walls, and this work goes forward, and prospers in their hands. 9 Then we asked those zachanim, and said to them this, Who commanded you to rebuild this Bayit, and to raise up these walls? 10 We asked their names also, to inform you, that we might write the names of the men that were their leaders. 11 And this they returned us answer, saying, We are the avadim of the Elohim of the shamayim and earth, and we now rebuild the Bayit that was built many years ago, which a great melech of Yisrael built and set up. 12 But after our ahvot had provoked the Elohim of the shamayim to wrath, He gave them into the hand of Nebuchadnetzar the melech of Bavel, the Chaldean, who destroyed this Bayit, and carried the people away into Bavel. 13 But in the first year of Koresh the melech of Bavel the same melech Koresh made a decree to rebuild this Bayit of Elohim. 14 And the vessels also of gold and silver of the Bayit of Elohim, which Nebuchadnetzar took out of the Beit HaMikdash that was in Yahrushalayim, and brought them into the Beit HaMikdash of Bavel, those did Koresh the melech take out of the Beit HaMikdash of Bavel, and they were delivered to one, whose name was Sheshbatstsar, whom he had made governor; 15 And said to him, Take these vessels, go, carry them into the Beit HaMikdash that is in Yahrushalayim, and let the Bayit of Elohim be rebuilt in its place. 16 Then came the same Sheshbatstsar, and laid the foundation of the Bayit of Elohim that is in Yahrushalayim: and since that time, even until now it is being rebuilt, and yet it is not finished. 17 Now therefore, if it seems tov to the

---

[1] The prophets with vision and a message of correction always spearhead true revival moves, such as the end-time restoration of both houses of Yisrael.
[2] Both ha neviim and laborers must work together in Yisrael's restoration.

melech, let there be a search made in the melech's treasure bayit, which is there at Bavel, whether it is true, that a decree was made by Koresh the melech to rebuild this Bayit of Elohim at Yahrushalayim, and let the melech send his decision to us concerning this matter.

6 Then Dareyawesh the melech made a decree, and a search was made in the bayit of the records, where the treasures of Bavel were kept. 2 And there was found at Achmetha, in the palace that is in the province of the Medes, a roll, and in it was a record with this written: 3 In the first year of Koresh the melech the same Koresh the melech made a decree concerning the Bayit of Elohim at Yahrushalayim, Let the Bayit be rebuilt, the place where they offered sacrifices, and let the foundations of it be strongly laid; the height of it sixty cubits, and the width of it sixty cubits; 4 With three rows of great stones, and a row of new timber: and let the expenses be given out of the melech's bayit: 5 And also let the golden and silver vessels of the Bayit of Elohim, which Nebuchadnetzar took out of the Beit HaMikdash which is at Yahrushalayim, and brought to Bavel, be restored, and brought again to the Beit HaMikdash which is at Yahrushalayim, every piece to its place, and place them in the Bayit of Elohim. 6 Now therefore, Tatnai, governor beyond the river, Shethar-Boznai, and your companions the officials, who are beyond the river, stay away from the city and the Beit HaMikdash: 7 Leave the work of this Bayit of Elohim alone; let the governor of the Yahudim and the zachanim of the Yahudim rebuild this Bayit of Elohim in its place. 8 Moreover I make a decree what you shall do for the zachanim of these Yahudim for the building of this Bayit of Elohim: that from the melech's goods, even from the expenses beyond the river, that immediately all expenses be paid to these men, that they be not hindered. 9 And that which they have need of, both young bullocks, and rams, and

lambs, for the burnt offerings of the Elohim of the shamayim, wheat, salt, wine, and oil, according to the orders of the kohanim which are at Yahrushalayim, let it be given to them daily without fail: 10 That they may offer sacrifices of sweet savors to the Elohim of the shamayim, and make tefillah for the life of the melech, and of his sons. 11 Also I have made a decree, that whoever shall alter this word, let timber be pulled down from his bayit, then reset, and let him be hanged on it; and let his bayit be made into a dunghill for this. 12 And the Elohim that has caused His Name to dwell there will destroy all of the melechim and peoples that shall put their hand to alter and to destroy this Bayit of Elohim which is at Yahrushalayim. I Dareyawesh have made a decree; let it be done quickly. 13 Then Tatnai, governor on this side of the river, Shethar-Boznai, and their companions, according to all that Dareyawesh the melech had sent, so they did and obeyed immediately. 14 And the zachanim of the Yahudim rebuilt, and they prospered through the prophesying of Chaggai ha navi and Zacharyah the son of Iddo. And they rebuilt, and finished it, according to the commandment of the Elohim of Yisrael, and according to the commandment of Koresh, and Dareyawesh, and Artahshashta melech of Persia.[1] 15 And this Bayit was finished on the third day of the month Adar, which was in the sixth year of the reign of Dareyawesh the melech. 16 And the children of Yisrael, the kohanim, and the Leviim, and the rest of the children of the exile, kept the dedication of the Bayit of Elohim with simcha, 17 And offered at the dedication of the Bayit of Elohim an hundred bullocks, two hundred rams, four hundred lambs; and for a sin offering for all Yisrael, twelve male goats, according to the number of the tribes of Yisrael.[2] 18 And

---

[1] The same command was renewed and confirmed three times.
[2] A sacrifice made representing all 12 tribes. This in no way indicates or even implies that the fullness of all 12 tribes were present, as only 42,000 Jews had returned, proving that Judah had not fully returned – much less Ephraim.

they set the kohanim in their divisions, and the Leviim in their divisions, for the service of Elohim, which is at Yahrushalayim; as it is written in the scroll of Moshe. 19 And the children of the exile kept the Pesach upon the fourteenth day of the first month. 20 For the kohanim and the Leviim were cleansed together, all of them were clean, and killed the Pesach for all the children of the exile, and for their brothers the kohanim, and for themselves. 21 And the children of Yisrael, who were come again out of exile,[1] and all such as had separated themselves to join them from the filthiness of the heathen of the land, to seek יהוה Elohim of Yisrael, did eat, 22 And kept the moed of Chag Matzot seven days with simcha: for יהוה had made them full of simcha, and turned the lev of the melech of Ashshur to them, to strengthen their hands in the work of the Bayit of Elohim, the Elohim of Yisrael.

7 Now after these things, in the reign of Artahshashta melech of Persia, Ezra the son of Seraiyah, the son of Azaryah, the son of Hilkiyah, 2 The son of Shallum, the son of Tzadok, the son of Ahituv, 3 The son of Amaryah, the son of Azaryah, the son of Meraioth, 4 The son of Zerahyah, the son of Uzzi, the son of Buchi, 5 The son of Avishua, the son of Phinehas, the son of El-Azar, the son of Aharon the Kohen HaGadol: 6 This Ezra went up from Bavel; and he was a skilled sopher in the Torah of Moshe, which יהוה Elohim of Yisrael had given: and the melech granted him all his requests, according to the hand of יהוה His Elohim upon him. 7 And there went up some of the children of Yisrael,[2] and of the kohanim, and the Leviim, and the singers, and the gatekeepers, and the Nethinim, to Yahrushalayim, in the seventh year of Artahshashta the melech. 8 And he came to Yahrushalayim in the fifth month, which was in the seventh year of the melech. 9 For upon the first day of the first month he

began to go up from Bavel, and on the first day of the fifth month he came to Yahrushalayim, according to the tov hand of His Elohim upon him. 10 For Ezra had prepared his lev to seek the Torah of יהוה, and to do it, and to teach in Yisrael chukim and mishpatim.[3] 11 Now this is the copy of the letter that the melech Artahshashta gave to Ezra the kohen, the sopher, even a sopher of the words of the commandments of יהוה, and of His chukim to Yisrael. 12 Artahshashta, melech of melechim, to Ezra the kohen, a sopher of the Torah of the Elohim of the shamayim, perfect shalom, at such a time. 13 I make a decree that all they of the people of Yisrael, and of His kohanim and Leviim, in my realm, who are minded by their own terumah to go up to Yahrushalayim, may go with you. 14 Forasmuch as you are sent by the melech, and by his seven counselors, to inquire concerning Yahudah and Yahrushalayim, according to the Torah of your Elohim that is in your hand; 15 And to carry the silver and gold, which the melech and his counselors have freely offered to the Elohim of Yisrael, whose dwelling is in Yahrushalayim, 16 And all the silver and gold that you can find in all the province of Bavel, with the terumah offering of the people, and of the kohanim, offering willingly for the Bayit of their Elohim which is in Yahrushalayim: 17 That you may quickly buy with this money your bullocks, rams, lambs, with their grain offerings and their drink offerings, and offer them upon the altar of the Bayit of Your Elohim that is in Yahrushalayim. 18 And whatever shall seem tov to you, and to your brothers, to do with the rest of the silver and the gold, that do after the will of your Elohim. 19 The vessels also that are given to you for the service of the Bayit of Your Elohim, those deliver to the Elohim of Yahrushalayim. 20 And whatever more shall be needed for the Bayit of your

---

[1] Specifically the Babylonian exile, since Ephraim is not even the topic here.
[2] Many of Yahudah stayed behind.

[3] According to Jewish legend, if Moshe had not proven worthy to receive Torah, Ezra was next in line.

Elohim, which you shall have occasion to give, give it out of the melech's treasure bayit. 21 And I, Artahshashta the melech, do make a decree to all the treasurers who are beyond the river, that whatever Ezra the kohen, the sopher of the Torah of the Elohim of the shamayim, shall require from you, let it be done immediatly, 22 Up to a hundred talents of silver, and to a hundred measures of wheat, and to a hundred baths of wine, and to a hundred baths of oil, and salt without measure. 23 Whatever is commanded by the Elohim of the shamayim, let it be diligently done for the Bayit of the Elohim of the shamayim: for why should there be wrath against the malchut of the melech and his sons? 24 Also we inform you, that as for the kohanim and Leviim, singers, gatekeepers, Nethinim, or avadim of the Bayit of Elohim, it shall not be lawful to impose tax, excise, or any tolls, upon them. 25 And you, Ezra, after the wisdom of your Elohim, that is in your hand, set magistrates and shophtim, who may judge all the people that are beyond the river, all such as know the Torot of your Elohim; and teach them that know them not. 26 And whoever will not do the Torah of your Elohim, and this decree of the melech, let judgment be executed immediately upon him, whether it be to death, or to banishment, or to confiscation of personal goods, or to imprisonment. 27 Blessed be יהוה Elohim of our ahvot, who has put such a thing as this in the melech's lev, to beautify the Bayit of יהוה which is in Yahrushalayim: 28 And has extended rachamim to me before the melech, and his counselors, and before all the melech's mighty leaders. And I was strengthened as the hand of יהוה My Elohim was upon me, and I gathered together out of Yisrael leading men to go up with me.

8 These are now the heads of their ahvot, and this is the genealogy of those that went up with me from Bavel, in the reign of Artahshashta the melech. 2 Of the sons of Phinehas; Gershom: of the sons of Ithamar; Dani-El: of the sons of David; Hattush. 3 Of the sons of Shechanyah, of the sons of Pharosh; Zacharyah: and with him were numbered by genealogy of the males a hundred fifty. 4 Of the sons of Pahath-Moav; Elyeho-Eynai the son of Zerahyah, and with him two hundred males. 5 Of the sons of Shechanyah; the son of Yahazi-El, and with him three hundred males. 6 Of the sons also of Adin; Eved the son of Yonathan, and with him fifty males. 7 And of the sons of Eylam; Yeshayah the son of Athalyah, and with him seventy males. 8 And of the sons of Shephatyah; Tzevadyah the son of Micha-El, and with him eighty males. 9 Of the sons of Yoav; Ovadyah the son of Yehi-El, and with him two hundred and eighteen males. 10 And of the sons of Shelomith; the son of Yosiphyah, and with him a hundred sixty males. 11 And of the sons of Bebai; Zacharyah the son of Bevai, and with him twenty-eight males. 12 And of the sons of Azgad; Yohanan the son of Hakkatan, and with him a hundred ten males. 13 And of the last sons of Adonikam, whose names are these, Eliphelet, Yei-El, and Shemayah, and with them sixty males. 14 Of the sons also of Bigvai; Uthai, and Zavud, and with them seventy males. 15 And I gathered them together to the river that runs to Ahava; and there we stayed in tents three days: and I viewed the people, and the kohanim, and found there none of the sons of Levi. 16 Then sent I for Eli-Ezer, for Ari-El, for Shemayah, and for Elnathan, and for Yariv, and for Elnathan, and for Nathan, and for Zacharyah, and for Meshullam, leaders; also for Yoyariv, and for Elnathan, men of understanding. 17 And I sent them with a commandment for Iddo the leader at the place Casiphya, and I told them what they should say to Iddo, and to his brothers the Nethinim, at the place Casiphya, that they should bring to us avadim for the Bayit of our Elohim. 18 And by the tov hand of our Elohim upon us they brought us a man of

understanding, of the sons of Mahli, the son of Levi, the son of Yisrael; and Sherevyah, with his sons and his brothers, eighteen; 19 And Hashavyah, and with him Yeshayah of the sons of Merari, his brothers and their sons, twenty; 20 Also of the Nethinim, whom David and the leaders had appointed for the service of the Leviim, two hundred twenty Nethinim: all of them were designated by name. 21 Then I proclaimed a fast there, at the river of Ahava, that we might afflict ourselves before our Elohim, to seek from Him a right halacha for us, and for our little ones, and for all our substance. 22 For I was ashamed to require of the melech a band of soldiers and horsemen to help us against the enemy in the way: because we had spoken to the melech, saying, The hand of our Elohim is upon all them for tov that seek Him; but His power and His wrath is against all them that forsake Him. 23 So we fasted and besought our Elohim for this: and He was moved by us. 24 Then I separated twelve of the heads of the kohanim, Sherevyah, Hashavyah, and ten of their brothers with them, 25 And weighed to them the silver, and the gold, and the vessels, even the offering of the Bayit of our Elohim, which the melech, and his counselors, and his masters, and all Yisrael there present, [1] had offered: 26 I even weighed to their hand six hundred fifty talents of silver, and silver vessels a hundred talents, and of gold a hundred talents; 27 Also twenty basons of gold, of a thousand drams; and two vessels of fine copper, precious as gold. 28 And I said to them, You are set-apart to יהוה; the vessels are set-apart also; and the silver and the gold are terumah offerings to יהוה Elohim of your ahvot. 29 Watch, and keep them, until you weigh them before the heads of the kohanim and the Leviim, and heads of the ahvot of Yisrael, at Yahrushalayim, in the rooms of the Bayit of יהוה. 30 So the kohanim and the Leviim took the weight of the silver, and the gold, and the vessels, to bring them to Yahrushalayim to the Bayit of our Elohim. 31 Then we departed from the river of Ahava on the twelfth day of the first month, to go to Yahrushalayim: and the hand of our Elohim was upon us, and He delivered us from the hand of the enemy, and from such as laid in wait by the way. 32 And we came to Yahrushalayim, and stayed there three days. 33 Now on the fourth day was the silver and the gold and the vessels weighed in the Bayit of our Elohim by the hand of Meremoth the son of Uriyah the kohen; and with him was El-Azar the son of Phinehas; and with them was Yotzavad the son of Yeshua, and Noadyah the son of Binnui, the Leviim; 34 By number and by weight of everyone: and all the weight was written at that time. 35 Also the children of those that had been carried away, who were come out of the exile, offered burnt offerings to the Elohim of Yisrael, twelve bullocks for all Yisrael,[2] ninety-six rams, seventy-seven lambs, twelve male goats for a sin offering: all this was a burnt offering to יהוה. 36 And they delivered the melech's decrees to the melech's viceroys, and to the governors beyond the river: and they lifted up the people, and the Bayit of Elohim.

9 Now when these things were done, the leaders came to me, saying, The people of Yisrael, and the kohanim, and the Leviim, have not separated themselves from the people of the lands, and are doing according to their abominations, even of the Canaanites, the Hittites, the Perizzites, the Yevusites, the Ammonites, the Moavites, the Mitzrites, and the Amorites. 2 For they have taken their daughters for themselves, and for their sons: so that the set-apart zera has been mingled with the peoples of those lands: yes, even the hand of the leaders and rulers have been foremost in this trespass. 3 And when I heard this thing, I tore my

---

[1] This offering is by "all Yisrael there present," or 42,360 Jews. It does not say all Yisrael was present.

[2] They offered on behalf of all Yisrael, not that all Yisrael was present.

garment and my mantle, and plucked off the hair of my head and my beard, and sat down astonished. 4 Then were assembled to me every one that trembled at the words of the Elohim of Yisrael, because of the transgression of the exiles; and I sat astonished until the maariv sacrifice. 5 And at the maariv sacrifice I arose up from my heaviness; and having torn my garment and my mantle, I fell upon my knees, and spread out my hands to יהוה my Elohim. 6 And said, O my Elohim, I am ashamed and blush to lift up my face to You, my Elohim: for our iniquities are increased way over our head, and our trespass is risen up to the shamayim. 7 Since the days of our ahvot have we been in a great trespass even until this day; and for our iniquities have we, our melechim, and our kohanim, been delivered into the hand of the melechim of the lands, to the sword, to exile, and to be a plunder, and to confusion of face, as it is this until this day. 8 And now for a little time rachamim has been shown from יהוה our Elohim, to leave us a remnant to escape, and to give us a nail in His Set-Apart Place, that our Elohim may lighten our eyes, and give us a little revival in our bondage. [1] 9 For we were slaves; yet our Elohim has not forsaken us in our bondage, but has extended rachamim to us in the sight of the melechim of Persia, to give us a revival, to set up the Bayit of our Elohim, and to repair its desolations, and to give us a wall in Yahudah and in Yahrushalayim. 10 And now, O our Elohim, what shall we say after this? For we have forsaken Your commandments, 11 Which You have commanded by Your avadim ha neviim, saying, The land, which you go to possess it, is an unclean land with the filthiness of the people of the lands, with their abominations, who have filled it from one end to another with their uncleanness. 12 Now therefore give not your daughters to their sons, neither take their daughters to your sons, nor seek their shalom or their wealth le-olam-va-ed: that you may be strong, and eat the tov of the land, and leave it as an inheritance to your children le-olam-va-ed. 13 And after all that has come upon us for our evil deeds, and for our great trespass, seeing that You our Elohim have punished us even less than our iniquities deserve, and have given us such deliverance as this; 14 Should we again break Your commandments, and join in union with the people of these abominations? Would You not be angry with us until You have consumed us, so that there should be no remnant or survivor? 15 O יהוה Elohim of Yisrael, You are tzadik: for we still remain as a remnant, as it is this day: behold, we are before You in our trespasses: for there is no one to stand before You about this.

10 Now when Ezra had prayed, and when he had confessed, weeping and casting himself down before the Bayit of Elohim, there assembled to him out of Yisrael a very great congregation of men and women and children: for the people wept very bitterly. 2 And Shechanyah the son of Yehi-El, one of the sons of Eylam, answered and said to Ezra, We have trespassed against our Elohim, and have taken strange wives from the peoples of the land: yet now there is hope in Yisrael concerning this thing. 3 Now therefore let us make a covenant with our Elohim to put away all the wives, and such as are born from them, according to the counsel of my master, and of those that tremble at the commandment of our Elohim; and let it be done according to the Torah. 4 Arise; for this matter belongs to you: we also will be with you: be of tov courage, and do it. 5 Then Ezra arose, and made the heads of the kohanim, the Leviim, and all Yisrael, to swear that they should do according to this word. And they swore. 6 Then Ezra rose up from before the Bayit of Elohim, and went into the room of Yohanan the son of Eliashiv: and when he came there, he did

---

[1] This is exactly what both houses need in this final hour of the age. A "little revival" in our national bondage.

eat no lechem, nor drink water: for he mourned because of the transgression of those that had been carried away. 7 And they made proclamation throughout Yahudah and Yahrushalayim to all the children of the exile, that they should gather themselves together to Yahrushalayim; 8 And that whoever would not come within three days, according to the counsel of the leaders and the zachanim, all his substance should be forfeited, and himself separated from the congregation of the exiles. 9 Then all the men of Yahudah and Benyamin gathered themselves together to Yahrushalayim within three days. It was the ninth month, on the twentieth day of the month; and all the people sat in the street of the Bayit of Elohim, trembling because of this matter, and because of the huge downpour. 10 And Ezra the kohen stood up, and said to them, You have transgressed, and have taken strange wives, to increase the trespass of Yisrael. 11 Now therefore make confession to יהוה Elohim of your ahvot, and do His pleasure: and separate yourselves from the peoples of the land, and from the strange wives. 12 Then all the congregation answered and said with a loud voice, As you have said, so must we do. 13 But the people are many, and it is a time of much rain, and we are not able to stand outside, neither is this a work of one or two days: for we are many that have transgressed in this thing. 14 Let now our rulers of all the congregation stand, and let all them who have taken strange wives in our cities come at scheduled times, and with them the zachanim of every city, and its shophtim, until the fierce wrath of our Elohim for this matter has turned away from us. 15 Only Yonathan the son of Asah-El and Yahatzyah the son of Tikvah gave them support about this matter: and Meshullam and Shavethai the Levite helped them. 16 And the children of the exile did so. And Ezra the kohen, with certain heads of the ahvot, after the bayit of their ahvot, and all of them by their names, were separated, and sat down on the first day of the tenth month to examine the matter. 17 And they had finished the list with all the men who had taken strange non-Yisraelite wives by the first day of the first month. 18 And among the sons of the kohanim there were found that had taken strange wives: namely, of the sons of Yeshua the son of Yotzadak, and his brothers; Maaseyah, and Eli-Ezer, and Yariv, and Gedalyah. 19 And they gave their hands in a pledge that they would put away their strange wives; and being guilty, they offered a ram of the flock for their trespass. 20 And of the sons of Immer; Hanani, and Zevadyah. 21 And of the sons of Harim; Maaseyah, and Eliyah, and Shemayah, and Yehi-El, and Uzziyah. 22 And of the sons of Pashur; Elyo-Eynai, Maaseyah, Yishmael, Nethan-El, Yotzavad, and El-Asah. 23 Also of the Leviim; Yotzabad, and Shimei, and Kelayah - the same is Kelita - Pethahyah, Yahudah, and Eli-Ezer. 24 Of the singers also; Eliashv: and of the gatekeepers; Shallum, and Telem, and Uri. 25 Moreover of Yisrael: of the sons of Parosh; Ramiyah, and Yeziyah, and Malchiyah, and Miamin, and Eleazar, and Malchijah, and Benayah. 26 And of the sons of Eylam; Mattanyah, Zacharyah, and Yehi-El, and Avdi, and Yeremoth, and Eliyah. 27 And of the sons of Zattu; Elyo-Eynai, Eliashiv, Mattanyah, and Yeremoth, and Zavad, and Aziza. 28 Of the sons also of Bevai; Yehohanan, Hananyah, Zavai, and Athlai. 29 And of the sons of Bani; Meshullam, Malluch, and Adayah, Yashuv, and Sheal, and Ramoth. 30 And of the sons of Pahath-Moav; Adna, and Chelal, Benayah, Maaseyah, Mattanyah, Bezal-El, and Binnui, and Menashsheh. 31 And of the sons of Harim; Eli-Ezer, Yishiyah, Malchiyah, Shemayah, Shimeon, 32 Benyamin, Malluch, and Shemaryah. 33 Of the sons of Hashum; Mattenai, Mattattah, Zavad, Eliphelet, Yeremai, Menashsheh, and Shimei. 34 Of the sons of Bani; Maadai, Amram, and Uel,

35 Benayah, Bedeyah, Chelluh, 36 Vanyah, Meremoth, Eliashiv, 37 Mattanyah, Mattenai, and Yaasau, 38 And Bani, and Binnui, Shimei, 39 And Shelemyah, and Nathan, and Adayah, 40 Machnadevai, Shashai, Sharai, 41 Azare-El, and Shelemyah, Shemaryah,

42 Shallum, Amaryah, and Yosef 43Of the sons of Nebo; Yei-El, Mattithyah, Zavad, Zevina, Yadau, and Yoel, Benayah. 44 All these had taken foreign wives: and some of them had wives by whom they had children.[1]

---

[1] Even through this disobedience, Yisrael's seed was mixed in many nations, fulfilling YHWH's purpose.

נחמיה

Nechemyah - Nehemiah
To Our Forefathers Yisrael

1 The words of Nechemyah the son of Hachalyah. And it came to pass in the month Chislev, in the twentieth year, as I was in Shushan[1] the palace, 2 That Hanani, one of my brothers, came, along with certain men of Yahudah; and I asked them concerning the Yahudim that had escaped the captivity, and concerning Yahrushalayim. 3 And they said to me, The remnant[2] that is left of the captivity there in the province are in great affliction and reproach: the wall of Yahrushalayim also is broken down, and its gates are burned with fire. 4 And it came to pass, when I heard these words, that I sat down and wept, and mourned for certain days, and fasted, and made tefillah before the Elohim of the shamayim, 5 And said, I beg You, O יהוה Elohim of the shamayim, the great and awesome El, that keeps covenant and rachamim for them that love Him and shomer His commandments: 6 Let Your ear now be attentive, and Your eyes open, that You may shema the tefillah of Your eved, which I pray before You, day and night, for the children of Yisrael Your avadim, and confess the sins of the children of Yisrael,[3] which we have sinned against You: both I and my abba's house have sinned. 7 We have dealt very corruptly against You, and have not kept the commandments, nor the chukim, nor the mishpatim, which You commanded Your eved Moshe. 8 Remember, I beg You, the word that You commanded Your eved Moshe, saying, If you transgress, I will scatter you abroad among the nations:[4] 9 But if you teshuvah to Me, and keep My commandments, and do them; though you were cast out to the uttermost parts of the shamayim, yet will I

gather them from there, and will bring them to the place that I have chosen to set My Name there. [5] 10 Now these are Your avadim and Your people, whom You have redeemed by Your great power, and by Your strong hand. 11 O יהוה, I beg You, let now Your ear be attentive to the tefillah of Your eved, and to the tefillot of Your avadim, who desire to fear Your Name:[6] and I make tefillah that You prosper Your eved this day, grant him rachamim in the sight of this man. For I was the melech's cupbearer.

2 And it came to pass in the month Nisan, [7] in the twentieth year of Artahshashta the melech, that wine was set before him: and I took up the wine, and gave it to the melech. Now I had not ever before been sad in his presence. 2 And the melech said to me, Why is your face sad, seeing you are not sick? This is nothing else but sorrow of lev. Then I was very much afraid, 3 And said to the melech, Let the melech live le-olam-va-ed: why should not my face be sad, when the city, the place of my abbas' tombs, lies in waste, and its gates are consumed with fire? 4 Then the melech said to me, For what do you make request? So I made tefillah to the Elohim of the shamayim. 5 And then I said to the melech, If it please the melech, and if your eved has found favor in your sight, that you would send me to Yahudah, to the city of my ahvot's tombs, that I may rebuild it. 6 And the melech said to me - the queen also sitting by him - For how long shall your

---

[1] Medio-Persia.
[2] Yahudah.
[3] Prayer for all 12 tribes.
[4] Known as the **galut.**

[5] All Yisrael's prophets knew the importance of the Name.
[6] All Yisrael needs this desire.
[7] Notice the usage of the Babylonian names of months that do not appear in Scripture until the 70 years that Yahudah spent in Babylon. The Scripture accurately records this transition into pagan names of months; but nowhere gives approval to it. Yisraelites should do their very best to refrain from using them, and should stick to the numbering system designated for months in the Torah.

journey be? And when will you return? So it pleased the melech to send me; and I set for him a time. 7 Moreover I said to the melech, If it pleases the melech, let letters be given to me to the governors beyond the river, that they may let me pass through until I come into Yahudah; 8 And a letter to Asaph the keeper of the melech's forest, that he may give me timber to make beams for the gates of the palace that belong to the Bayit, and for the wall of the city, and for the house that I shall enter into. And the melech gave them to me, according to the tov hand of My Elohim upon me. 9 Then I came to the governors beyond the river, and gave them the melech's letters. Now the melech had sent captains of the army and horsemen with me. 10 When Sanballat the Horonite, and Toviyah the Ammonite official, heard of it, it exceedingly grieved them that there had come a man to seek the welfare of the children of Yisrael.[1] 11 So I came to Yahrushalayim, and was there three days. 12 And I arose in the night, I and some few men with me; neither did I tell any man what My Elohim had put in my lev to do at Yahrushalayim: neither was there any beast with me, except the beast that I rode on. 13 And I went out by night by the gate of the valley, even before the Jackals Fountain, and to the Dung Gate, and viewed the walls of Yahrushalayim, which were broken down, and the gates that were consumed with fire. 14 Then I went on to the Fountain Gate, and to the melech's pool: but there was no place for the beast that was under me to pass. 15 Then I went up in the night by the brook, and viewed the wall, and turned back, and entered by the gate of the valley, and so I returned. 16 And the heads knew not where I went, or what I did; neither had I as yet told it to the Yahudim, nor to the kohanim, nor to the nobles, nor to the heads, nor to the rest that did the work. 17 Then I said to them, You see the distress that we are in, how Yahrushalayim lies

waste, and the gates of it are burned with fire: come, and let us build up the wall of Yahrushalayim, that we be no more a reproach. 18 Then I told them of the hand of My Elohim which was tov upon me; and also the melech's words that he had spoken to me. And they said, Let us rise up and build. So they strengthened their hands for this tov work. 19 But when Sanballat the Horonite, and Toviyah the eved, the Ammonite, and Geshem the Arabian, heard it, they laughed us to scorn, and despised us, and said, What is this thing that you do? Will you rebel against the melech? [2] 20 Then I answered them, and said to them, The Elohim of the shamayim, He will prosper us; therefore we His avadim will arise and build: but you have no portion, or rights, or memorial, in Yahrushalayim.

3 Then Eli-ashiv the Kohen HaGadol rose up with his brothers the kohanim, and they built the Sheep Gate; they set it apart, and set up the doors; they set that apart as well as far as the tower of Hanane-El. 2 And next to him built the men of Yericho. And next to them built Zaccur the son of Yimri. 3 But the Fish Gate did the sons of Hassena'ah build, who also laid its beams, and set up its doors, its locks, and its bars. 4 And next to them repaired Meremoth the son of Uriyah, the son of Koz. And next to them repaired Meshullam the son of Berechyah, the son of Meshezave-El. And next to them repaired Tzadok the son of Ba-Ana. 5 And next to them the Tekoites repaired; but their nobles did not put their necks to the work of their Master. 6 Moreover the Old Gate repaired Yehoyada the son of Paseyah, and Meshullam the son of Besodeyah; they laid its beams, and set up its doors, and its locks, and its bars. 7 And next to them repaired Melatyah the Giveonite, and Yadon the Meronothite, the men of Giveon, and of Mizpah, to the throne of the governor on

---

[1] When one carries a true burden for all Yisrael, he will not be received well, and the opponents will be many.

[2] Those who try and rebuild Yisrael with the King Yahshua's blessings can always count on being mocked and scorned.

this side of the river. 8 Next to him repaired Uzzi-El the son of Harhayah, of the goldsmiths. Next to him also repaired Hananyah the son of one of the perfumers, and they fortified Yahrushalayim to the Broad Wall. 9 And next to them repaired Rephayah the son of Hur, the head of the half part of Yahrushalayim. 10 And next to them repaired Yedayah the son of Harumaph, even opposite his own house. And next to him repaired Hattush the son of Hashavniyah. 11 Malchiyah the son of Harim, and Hashuv the son of Pahath-Moav, repaired the other section, and the Tower of the Furnaces. 12 And next to him repaired Shallum the son of Halohesh, the head of the half part of Yahrushalayim, he and his daughters. 13 The Valley Gate repaired Hanun, and the inhabitants of Tzanoah; they built it, and set up its doors, its locks, and its bars, and a thousand cubits on the wall to the Dung Gate. 14 But the Dung Gate was repaired by Malchiyah the son of Rechav, the head of part of Beth-HaKerem; he built it, and set up its doors, its locks, and its bars. 15 But the Gate of the Fountain repaired Shallun the son of Chol-Hozeh, the head of part of Mitzpah; he built it, and covered it, and set up its doors, its locks, and its bars, and the wall of the Pool of Shiloach by the melech's garden, and the stairs that go down from the city of David. 16 After him repaired Nechemyah the son of Azvuk, the head of half the part of Beth-Tzur, to the place opposite the tombs of David, and to the pool that was made, and to the house of the mighty men. 17 After him repaired the Leviim, Rehum the son of Bani. Next to him repaired Hashavyah, the head of half of Keilah, in his district. 18 After him repaired their brothers, Bavai the son of Henadad, the head of half of the district of Keilah. 19 And next to him repaired Ezer the son of Yeshua, the head of Mitzpah, another section opposite the going up to the armory at the turning of the wall. 20 After him Baruch the son of Zavvai earnestly repaired the other section, from

the turning of the wall to the door of the house of Eli-ashiv the Kohen HaGadol. 21 After him repaired Meremoth the son of Uriyah the son of Koz another section, from the door of the house of Eli-Ashiv even to the end of the house of Eli-ashiv. 22 And after him repaired the kohanim, the men of the plain. 23 After him repaired Benyamin and Hashuv opposite their house. After him repaired Azaryah the son of Maaseyah the son of Ananyah by his house. 24 After him repaired Binnui the son of Henadad another section, from the house of Azaryah to the turning of the wall, even to the corner. 25 Palal the son of Uzai, over against the turning of the wall, and the tower which lies out from the melech's high house, that was by the court of the prison. After him Pedayah the son of Parosh. 26 Moreover the Nethinim dwelt in Ophel, to the place opposite the Water Gate toward the east, and the tower that projects outward. 27 After them the Tekoites repaired another section, opposite the great tower that projects out, even to the wall of Ophel. 28 From above the Horse Gate repaired the kohanim, every one opposite his own house. 29 After them repaired Tzadok the son of Yimmer opposite his house. After him repaired also Shemayah the son of Shechanyah, the keeper of the east gate. 30 After him repaired Hananyah the son of Shelemyah, and Hanun the sixth son of Tzalaph, another section. After him repaired Meshullam the son of Berechyah opposite his room. 31 After him repaired Malchyah the goldsmith's son to the place of the Nethinim, and of the merchants, opposite the Miphchad Gate, and to the going up of the corner. 32 And between the going up of the corner to the Sheep Gate repaired the goldsmiths and the merchants.

4 But it came to pass, that when Sanballat heard that we built the wall, he was angry, and took great indignation, and mocked the Yahudim. 2 And he spoke before his brothers and the army of

Shomron,[1] and said, What are these feeble Yahudim doing? Will they fortify themselves? Will they sacrifice? Will they complete it in a day? Will they revive the stones out of the heaps of the rubbish that are burned? 3 Now Toviyah the Ammonite was by him, and he said, Whatever they build, if a fox goes up, even he shall break down their stone wall. 4 Shema, O our Elohim; for we are despised: and turn their reproach upon their own head, and make them as a prey in a land of captivity: 5 And cover not their iniquity, and let not their sin be blotted out from before You: for they have provoked You to anger before the builders. 6 So we built the wall; and the entire wall was joined together up to the half of it: for the people had a mind and lev to work. 7 But it came to pass, that when Sanballat, and Toviyah, and the Arabians, and the Ammonites, and the Ashdodites, heard that the walls of Yahrushalayim were being repaired, and that the broken places began to be fixed, then they were very angry,[2] [3] 8 And conspired all of them together to come and to fight against Yahrushalayim, and to harm it. 9 Nevertheless we made our tefillah to our Elohim, and set a watch against them day and night, because of them. 10 And Yahudah said, The strength of the bearers of burdens is weakening, and there is much rubbish; so that we are not able to build the wall. 11 And our adversaries said, They shall not know, neither see, until we come in the midst among them, and slay them, and cause the work to cease. 12 And it came to pass, that when the Yahudim who dwelt by them came, they said to us ten times, From all places wherever you turn they are against us. 13 So I set in the lower places behind the wall, and on the higher places, I set the people according to their families

with their swords, their spears, and their bows. 14 And I looked, and rose up, and said to the nobles, and to the heads, and to the rest of the people, Be not afraid of them: remember **יהוה**, who is great and terrible, and fights for your brothers, your sons, and your daughters, your wives, and your houses. 15 And it came to pass, when our enemies heard that it was known to us, and Elohim had brought their counsel to nothing, that we returned all of us to the wall, everyone to his work. 16 And it came to pass from that time foward that the half of my avadim worked in the work and the other half of them held the spears, the shields, and the bows, and the breastplates; and the heads were behind all the Bayit of Yahudah. 17 They, who built on the wall, and they that bore burdens, with those that loaded, everyone with one of his hands worked in the work, and with the other hand held a weapon.[4] 18 For the builders, everyone had his sword girded by his side, and so built. And he that sounded the shofar was by me. 19 And I said to the nobles, and to the heads, and to the rest of the people, The work is great and large, and we are separated upon the wall, one far from another. 20 In whatever place therefore you shema the sound of the shofar, join us there: our Elohim shall fight for us. 21 So we labored in the work: and half of them held the spears from the rising of the morning until the chochavim appeared. 22 Likewise at the same time I said to the people, Let every one with his eved sleep within Yahrushalayim, that in the night they may be a guard for us, and labor on the day. 23 So neither I, nor my brothers, nor my avadim, nor the men of the guard who followed me, none of us took off our clothes, except that every one put them off for washing.

5 And there was a great cry of the people and of their wives against their

---

[1] Those Samaritans that were colonized by the Assyrians. Here they mock Judah in another classic two-house battle of hate and bitterness.
[2] Just like all those who don't want to see David's Tabernacle being rebuilt, because they are building their own version of Yisrael.
[3] The message of restoration will often bring out fierce anger.

[4] A true description of the two-house fight to rebuild; a sword along with hard labor.

brothers the Yahudim. 2 For some said, We, our sons, and our daughters, are many: therefore we take up corn for them, that we may eat, and live. 3 Some also were there that said, We have mortgaged our lands, vineyards, and houses, that we might buy corn, because of the famine. 4 There were also those that said, We have borrowed money for the melech's tax that is upon our lands and vineyards. 5 Yet now our flesh is as the flesh of our brothers, our children as their children: and, see, we bring into bondage our sons and our daughters to be avadim, and some of our daughters are brought to subjection already: neither is it in power of our hands; for other men have our lands and vineyards. 6 And I was very angry when I heard their cry and these words. 7 Then my lev ruled me, and I rebuked the nobles, and the heads, and said to them, You charge interest, everyone from his brother. And I called out a great congregation against them. 8 And I said to them, We according to our ability have redeemed our brothers the Yahudim, who were sold to the nations;[1] and will you now sell your brothers? Or shall they be sold to us? Then they were silent, and found nothing to answer. 9 Also I said, It is not tov what you do: should you not rather have your halacha in the fear of our Elohim because of the reproach of our heathen enemies? 10 I and my brothers, and my avadim, are lending them money and corn: I ask you, let us stop with this interest. 11 Please restore, to them, even this day, their lands, their vineyards, their olive-yards, and their houses, also the hundredth part of the money, and the corn, the wine, the oil that you took from them. 12 Then they said, We will restore it to them, and will require nothing from them; so will we do as you have said. Then I called the kohanim, and took an oath from them, that they should do according to this promise. 13 Also I shook my garment, and said, So Elohim shake out every man from his house, and from his property, that performs not this promise, even so he shall be shaken out, and emptied. And the entire congregation said, Amein, and gave tehilla יהוה. And the people did according to this promise. 14 Moreover from the time that I was appointed to be their governor in the land of Yahudah, from the twentieth year even to the thirty-second year of Artahshashta the melech, that is, twelve years, I and my brothers have not eaten the lechem of their governors. 15 But the former governors that were before me laid burdens on the people, and had taken from them lechem and wine, beside forty shekels of silver; yes, even their avadim bore rule over the people: but I did not do that, because of my fear of Elohim. 16 Yes, also I continued in the work of this wall, neither bought we any land: and all my avadim were gathered there to the work. 17 Also there were at my table a hundred fifty of the Yahudim and heads, beside those that came to us from among the heathen that are around us. [2] 18 Now that which was prepared for me daily was one ox and six choice sheep; also fowls were prepared for me, and once in ten days of all sorts of wine: yet for all this I required not the food for the governor, because the bondage was heavy upon this people. 19 Think upon me, my Elohim, for tov, according to all that I have done for this people.

6 Now it came to pass, when Sanballat and Toviyah, and Geshem the Arabian, and the rest of our enemies, heard that I had built the wall, and that there was no breach

---

[1] Nehemiah 5:8 has nothing at all to do with proving that all twelve tribes returned as some claim. If anything, it proves that only Jews returned. The issue here is Nehemiah's wrath at fellow Jews violating Torah by subjecting other Jews to the bondage of slavery, when YHVH had set all of Jewish-Israel apart from the Goyim or the Babylonian pagans. Ephraim never returned from Babylonian exile because they were never in Babylon as a nation, only as individuals mixed in with Judah.

[2] Many heathen joined Nehemiah and became Judah or Jewish Yisraelites. How about those who join Ephraim? Using equal weights and measures, one would have to surmise that they also become Yisrael, since there is no respecter of persons with YHWH.

left in it, though at that time I had not set up the doors upon the gates; 2 That Sanballat and Geshem sent to me, saying, Come, let us meet together in one of the villages in the plain of Ono. But they thought to do me evil. 3 And I sent messengers to them, saying, I am doing a great work, so that I cannot come down: why should the work cease, while I leave it, and come down to you? 4 Yet they sent to me four times in this manner; and I answered them the same way. 5 Then Sanballat sent his eved to me in like manner the fifth time with an open letter in his hand; 6 In which was written, It is reported among the nations, and Gashmu says it, that you and the Yahudim think to rebel: for which cause you build the wall that you may be their melech, according to these words. 7 And you have also appointed neviim to proclaim about you at Yahrushalayim, saying, There is a melech in Yahudah: and now shall it be reported to the melech according to these words. Come now therefore, and let us take counsel together. 8 Then I sent to him, saying, There are no such things done as you have said, but you are creating them out of your own lev. 9 For they all made us afraid, saying, Their hands shall be weakened from the work, that it be not finished. Now therefore, O Elohim, strengthen my hands. 10 Afterward I came to the house of Shemayah the son of Delayah the son of Mehetav-El, who was restrained; and he said, Let us meet together in the Bayit of Elohim, within the Beit HaMikdash, and let us shut the doors of the Beit HaMikdash: for they will come to slay you; yes, in the night will they come to slay you. 11 And I said, Should such a man as I flee? And who is there, that, being as I am, would go into the Beit HaMikdash to save his life? I will not go in. 12 And, see, I discerned that Elohim had not sent him; but that he pronounced this prophecy against me: for Toviyah and Sanballat had hired him. 13 Therefore he was hired, that I should be afraid, and do so, and sin, and that they

might have a matter for an evil report, that they might reproach me. 14 My Elohim, think upon Toviyah and Sanballat according to these their works, and on the niviyah Noadyah, and the rest of the neviim, that would have put me in fear. 15 So the wall was finished on the twenty-fifth day of the month Elul, in fifty-two days. 16 And it came to pass, that when all our enemies heard about it, and all the heathen that were around us saw these things, they were much cast down in their own eyes: for they perceived that this work was the work of our Elohim. 17 And in those days the nobles of Yahudah sent many letters to Toviyah, and the letters of Toviyah came to them. 18 For there were many in Yahudah loyal to him, because he was the son-in-law of Shechanyah the son of Arah; and his son Yehohanan had married the daughter of Meshullam the son of Berechyah. 19 Also they reported his tov deeds before me, and uttered my words to him. And Toviyah sent letters to put me in fear.

7 Now it came to pass, when the wall was built, and I had set up the doors, and the gatekeepers and the singers and the Leviim were appointed, 2 That I gave my brothers Hanani, and Hananyah the head of the palace, authority over Yahrushalayim: for he was a faithful man, and feared Elohim above most. 3 And I said to them, Let not the gates of Yahrushalayim be opened until the sun is hot; and while they stand by, let them shut the doors, and bolt them: and appoint guards of the inhabitants of Yahrushalayim, every one in his watch, and every one in front of his house. 4 Now the city was large and great: but the people inside were few, and the houses were not built. 5 And My Elohim put into my lev to gather together the nobles, and the heads, and the people, that they might be counted by genealogy. And I found a register of the genealogy of those who came up first, and found all that was written in them, 6 These are the children of the province, that went

up out of the captivity, of those that had been carried away, whom Nebuchadnetzar the melech of Bavel had carried away, and had returned to Yahrushalayim and to Yahudah, every one to his city; 7 Who came with Zeruvvabel, Yeshua, Nechemyah, Azaryah, Raamayah, Nachamani, Mordechai, Bilshan, Mitspereth, Bigvai, Nechum, Baanah. The numbers, of the men of the people of Yisrael[1] was this; 8 The children of Parosh, two thousand one hundred seventy-two. 9 The children of Shephatyah, three hundred seventy-two. 10 The children of Arah, six hundred fifty-two. 11 The children of Pahath-moav, of the children of Yeshua and Yoav, two thousand eight hundred eighteen. 12 The children of Eylam, a thousand two hundred fifty-four. 13 The children of Zattu, eight hundred forty-five. 14 The children of Zacchai, seven hundred sixty. 15 The children of Binnui, six hundred forty-eight. 16 The children of Bevai, six hundred twenty-eight. 17 The children of Azgad, two thousand three hundred twenty-two. 18 The children of Adonikam, six hundred sixty-seven. 19 The children of Bigvai, two thousand sixty-seven. 20 The children of Adin, six hundred fifty-five. 21 The children of Ater of Hizqiyahu, ninety-eight. 22 The children of Hashum, three hundred twenty-eight. 23 The children of Bezai, three hundred twenty-four. 24 The children of Hariph, one hundred twelve. 25 The children of Giveon, ninety-five. 26 The men of Beth-Lechem and Netophah, one hundred eighty-eight. 27 The men of Anathoth, one hundred twenty-eight. 28 The men of Beth-Azmaveth, forty-two. 29 The men of Kiryath-Yearim, Chephirah, and Beeroth, seven hundred forty-three. 30 The men of Ramah and Geva, six hundred twenty-one. 31 The men of Michmas, one hundred and twenty-two. 32 The men of Beth-El and Ai, one hundred twenty-three. 33 The men of the other Nebo, fifty-two. 34 The children

of the other Eylam, one thousand two hundred fifty-four. 35 The children of Harim, three hundred twenty. 36 The children of Yericho, three hundred forty-five. 37 The children of Lod, Hadid, and Ono, seven hundred twenty-one. 38 The children of Senaah, three thousand nine hundred thirty. 39 The kohanim: the children of Yedayah, of the house of Yeshua, nine hundred seventy-three. 40 The children of Immer, a thousand fifty-two. 41 The children of Pashur, a thousand two hundred forty-seven. 42 The children of Harim, a thousand and seventeen. 43 The Leviim: the children of Yeshua, of Kadmi-El, and of the children of Hodevah, seventy-four. 44 The singers: the children of Asaph, an hundred forty-eight. 45 The gatekeepers: the children of Shallum, the children of Ater, the children of Talmon, the children of Akkuv, the children of Hatita, the children of Shovai, one hundred thirty-eight. 46 The Nethinim: the children of Ziha, the children of Hashupha, the children of Tavaoth, 47 The children of Keros, the children of Sia, the children of Padon, 48 The children of Levana, the children of Hagava, the children of Shalmai, 49 The children of Hanan, the children of Gidd-El, the children of Gahar, 50 The children of Reayah, the children of Rezin, the children of Nekoda, 51 The children of Gazzam, the children of Uzza, the children of Phaseah, 52 The children of Besai, the children of Meunim, the children of Nephishesim, 53 The children of Bakbuk, the children of Hakupha, the children of Harhur, 54 The children of Batzlith, the children of Mehida, the children of Harsha, 55 The children of Barkos, the children of Sisera, the children of Tamah, 56 The children of Netziah, the children of Hatipha. 57 The children of Shlomo's avadim: the children of Sotai, the children of Sophereth, the children of Perida, 58 The children of Yaala, the children of Darkon, the children of Gidd-El, 59 The children of Shephatyah, the children of Hattil, the children of Pochereth of

---

[1] Jewish Yisrael.

Tzevaim, the children of Amon. 60 All the Nethinim, and the children of Shlomo's avadim, were three hundred ninety-two. 61 And these were they who went up also from Telmelah, Telharesha, Cheruv, Addon, and Immer: but they could not show their abba's house, nor their offspring, whether they were of Yisrael.[1] 62 The children of Delayah, the children of Toviyah, the children of Nekoda, six hundred forty-two. 63 And of the kohanim: the children of Havayah, the children of Koz, the children of Barzillai, which took one of the daughters of Barzillai the Gileadite to wife, and was called after their name. 64 These sought their place among those that were counted by genealogy, but it was not found: therefore they were seen as polluted, and barred from the priesthood.[2] 65 And the governor said to them, that they should not eat of the most set-apart things, until there stood up a kohen with the Urim and Thummim. 66 The whole congregation together was forty-two thousand three hundred sixty, 67 Besides their male and female avadim, of whom there were seven thousand three hundred thirty-seven: and they had two hundred forty-five singing men and singing women. 68 Their horses, seven hundred thirty-six: their mules, two hundred forty-five: 69 Their camels, four hundred thirty-five: six thousand seven hundred twenty donkeys. 70 And some of the heads of the ahvot gave to the work. The governor gave to the treasury a thousand drams of gold, fifty basons, five hundred thirty kohanim garments. 71 And some of the heads of the ahvot gave to the treasury of the work twenty thousand drams of gold, and two thousand two hundred pounds of silver. 72 And that which the rest of the people gave was twenty thousand drams of gold, and two thousand pounds of silver, and sixty-seven kohanim garments. 73 So the kohanim, and the Leviim, and the gatekeepers, and the singers, and some of the people, and the Nethinim, and all Yisrael,[3] dwelt in their cities; and when the seventh month came, the children of Yisrael were in their cities.

8 And all the people gathered themselves together as echad into the street that was before the Water Gate; and they spoke to Ezra the sopher to bring the scroll of the Torah of Moshe, that יהוה had commanded to Yisrael. 2 And Ezra the kohen brought the Torah before the congregation both of men and women, and all that could shema with understanding, upon the first day of the seventh month, which is Yom Teruah. 3 And he read from it in the open space that was before the Water Gate from the morning until midday, before the men and the women, and those that could understand; and the ears of all the people were attentive to the scroll of the Torah. 4 And Ezra the sopher stood upon a pulpit of wood, which they had made for that purpose; and beside him stood Mattithyahu, and Shema, and Anayah, and Uriyah, and Hilkiyah, and Maaseyah, on his right hand; and on his left hand, Pedayah, and Misha-El, and Malchiyah, and Hashum, and Hashvadana, Zacharyah, and Meshullam. 5 And Ezra opened the scroll in the sight of all the people - for he was high above all the people - and when he opened it, all the people stood up: 6 And Ezra blessed יהוה, the great Elohim. And all the people answered, Amein, Amein, with lifting up their hands: and they bowed their heads, and worshipped יהוה with their faces to the ground. 7 Also Yeshua, and Bani, and Sherevyah, Yamin, Akkuv,

---

[1] These people could not prove their Yisraelite heritage, yet were still counted by Nehemiah as Yisraelites. The same applies today. If someone dwells with and makes teshuvah with Yisrael, they must be reckoned as Yisrael, without any kind of formal rabbinical conversion.
[2] The offspring of Barzillai were barred from the priesthood, not barred from the nation of Yisrael. Proving genealogy may be critical in determining eligibility to be a kohen, but cannot and should not bar one from being part of both the physical and spiritual nation of Yisrael.
[3] As seen elsewhere in Second Chronicles and such, the term "all Yisrael" was often qualified by the term "all Yisrael who were present." The same would apply here. The total of around 50,000 returning exiles cannot be considered all of Judah (most of whom remained in Babylon), let alone the full return of Ephraim.

Shavvethai, Hodiyah, Maaseyah, Kelita, Azaryah, Yozavad, Hanan, Pelayah, and the Leviim, helped the people to understand the Torah: and the people stood in their place. 8 So they read in the scroll in the Torah of Elohim distinctly, and gave the sense of it, and caused them to understand the reading. 9 And Nechemyah, who is the governor, and Ezra the kohen and sopher, and the Leviim that taught the people, said to all the people, This day is set-apart to יהוה Your Elohim; mourn not, nor weep. For all the people wept when they heard the words of the Torah. 10 Then he said to them, Go your way, eat the fat of his tov, and drink the sweetness of it, and send portions to those for whom nothing is prepared: for this day is set-apart to our יהוה : neither be sorry; for the simcha of יהוה is your strength. 11 So the Leviim silenced all the people, saying, Keep silent, for the day is set-apart; so don't be grieved. 12 And all the people went their way to eat, and to drink, and to send portions, and to make great gilah, because they had understood the words that were declared to them.[1] 13 And on the second day were gathered together the heads of the ahvot of all the people, the kohanim, and the Leviim, to Ezra the sopher, to further understand the words of the Torah. 14 And they found written in the Torah that יהוה had commanded by Moshe, that the children of Yisrael should dwell in sukkot in the moed of the seventh month: 15 And that they should publish and proclaim in all their cities, and in Yahrushalayim, saying, Go forth to the mountain, and fetch olive branches, and pine branches, and myrtle branches, and palm branches, and branches of thick trees, to make sukkot, as it is written. 16 So the people went out, and brought them, and made themselves sukkot, everyone upon the roof of his house, and in their courts, and in the courts of the Bayit of Elohim, and in the street of the Water Gate, and in the street of the Gate of Ephraim. 17 And all the congregation of those that were come again out of the captivity made sukkot, and sat under the sukkot: for since the days of Yahoshua ben Nun to that day the children of Yisrael had not done so. And there was very great simcha. 18 Also day by day, from the first day to the last day, he read in the scroll of the Torah of Elohim. And they kept the moed seven days; and on the eighth day there was a miqra qodesh, according to the manner.

9 Now on the twenty-fourth day of this month the children of Yisrael were assembled with fasting, and with sackclothes, and earth upon them. 2 And the zera of Yisrael separated themselves from all the gerim, [2] and stood and confessed their sins, and the iniquities of their ahvot. 3 And they stood up in their place, and read in the scroll of the Torah of יהוה their Elohim one-fourth part of the day; and another fourth part they confessed, and worshipped יהוה their Elohim. 4 Then stood up upon the stairs, of the Leviim, Yeshua, and Bani, Kadmi-El, Shebanyah, Bunni, Sherebiyah, Bani, and Chenani, and cried with a loud voice to יהוה their Elohim. 5 Then the Leviim, Yeshua, and Kadmi-El, Bani, Hashavniyah, Shereviah, Hodiyah, Shevanyah, and Pethachyah, said, Stand up and bless יהוה your Elohim le-olam-va-ed: and blessed be Your beautiful Name, which is exalted above all brachot and tehillot.[3] 6 You, You alone, are יהוה; You have made the shamayim, the shamayim of shamayim, with their entire host, the earth, and all things that are in them, the seas, and all that is in them, and You preserve them all; and the host of the shamayim worships You. 7 You are יהוה the Elohim, who did choose Avram, and brought him forth out of Ur of the Chaldees, and gave him the name of Avraham; 8 And found his lev faithful before You, and You

---

[1] When restored Yisrael understands Torah, great joy breaks out.

[2] Being true Yisrael requires separation.
[3] His Name is higher and more important than all of man's praise and worship.

made a covenant with him to give the land of the Canaanites, the Hittites, the Amorites, and the Perizzites, and the Yevusites, and the Girgashites, to give it to his zera, and have performed Your words; for You are Tzadik: 9 And did see the affliction of our ahvot in Mitzrayim, and heard their cry by the Sea of Reeds; 10 And showed signs and wonders upon Pharoah, and on all his avadim, and on all the people of his land: for You knew that they dealt proudly against them. So You made Your Name great, as it is this day. 11 And You did divide the sea before them, so that they went through the midst of the sea on the dry land; and their persecutors You threw into the deeps, as a stone into the mighty waters. 12 Moreover You led them in the day by a cloudy pillar; and in the night by a pillar of fire, to give them light in the halacha in which they should go. 13 You came down also upon Mount Sinai, and spoke with them from the shamayim, and gave them mishpatim, and true torot, tov chukim and commandments: 14 And made known to them Your set-apart Shabbat, and commanded for them precepts, chukim, and laws, by the hand of Moshe Your eved: 15 And gave them lechem from the shamayim for their hunger, and brought forth water for them out of the Rock for their thirst, and promised them that they should go in to possess the land which You had sworn to give them. 16 But they and our ahvot dealt proudly, and hardened their necks, and listened not to Your commandments, 17 And refused to obey, neither were mindful of Your wonders that You did among them; but hardened their necks, and in their rebellion appointed a leader to return to their bondage: but You are Eloah, ready to pardon, gracious and full of rachamim, slow to anger, and of great kindness, and forsook them not. 18 Yes, when they had made a molten calf, and said, These are your Elohim that brought you up out of Mitzrayim, and had worked great provocations and blasphemies; 19 Yet You in Your manifold rachamim forsook them not in the wilderness: the pillar of the cloud departed not from them by day, to lead them in the way; neither the pillar of fire by night, to show them light, and the way in which they should go. 20 You gave also Your tov Ruach to instruct them, and withheld not Your manna from their mouth, and gave them water for their thirst. 21 Yes, forty years did You sustain them in the wilderness, so that they lacked nothing; their clothes did not grow old, and their feet did not swell. 22 Moreover You gave them malchutim and nations, and did divide them by their lots: so they possessed the land of Sihon, and the land of the melech of Cheshbon, and the land of Og melech of Bashan. 23 Their children also You multiplied as the chochavim of the shamayim, and brought them into the land, concerning which You had promised to their ahvot, that they should go in to possess it. [1] 24 So the children went in and possessed the land, and You subdued before them the inhabitants of the land, the Canaanites, and gave them into their hands, with their melechim, and the people of the land, that they might do with them, as they desired. 25 And they took strong cities, and a fat land, and possessed houses full of all items, wells dug, vineyards, and olive-yards, and fruit trees in abundance: so they did eat, and were filled, and became fat, and delighted themselves in Your great tov. 26 Nevertheless they were disobedient, and rebelled against You, and cast Your Torah behind their backs, and killed Your neviim that testified against them to turn them to You, and they worked great provocations. 27 Therefore You delivered them into the hand of their enemies, who distressed them: and in the time of their trouble, when they cried to You, You heard them from the shamayim; and according to Your manifold rachamim You gave them saviors, who

---

[1] Yisrael in the ancient world was the largest nation of all. Today, they remain so as well, though camouflaged in the nations.

saved them out of the hand of their enemies. 28 But after they had rest, they did evil again before You: therefore You left them in the hand of their enemies, so that they had the dominion over them: yet when they returned, and cried to You, You heard them from the shamayim; and many times You did deliver them according to Your rachamim; 29 And testified against them, that You might bring them again to Your Torah: yet they dealt proudly, and listened not to Your commandments, but sinned against Your mishpatim - which if a man does, he shall live in them - and withdrew the shoulder, and hardened their neck, and would not shema. 30 Yet for many years You had patience with them, and testified against them by Your Ruach through Your neviim: yet they would not pay attention: therefore You gave them into the hands of the people of the lands. 31 Nevertheless for Your great rachamim's sake You did not utterly consume them, nor forsake them; for You are an El of rachamim and unmerited favor. 32 Now therefore, our Elohim, the great, the Mighty, and the awesome El, who keeps covenant and rachamim, let not all the trouble seem little before You, that has come upon us, on our melechim, on our heads, and on our kohanim, and on our neviim, and on our ahvot, and on all Your people, since the time of the melechim of Ashshur to this day. 33 Yet You are just in all that has been brought upon us; for You have done right, but we have done wickedly: 34 Neither have our melechim, our heads, our kohanim, or our ahvot, kept Your Torah, nor listened to Your commandments and Your testimonies, with which You did testify against them. 35 For they have not served You in their malchut, and in Your great tov that You gave them, and in the large and rich land which You gave them, neither did they turn from their wicked works. 36 Behold, we are avadim this day, and for the land that You gave to our ahvot to eat its fruit and its tov, behold, we are avadim in it: 37 And it yields much

increase to the melechim whom You have set over us because of our sins: also they have dominion over our bodies, and over our cattle, at their pleasure, and we are in great distress. 38 And because of all this we make a sure pledge, and write it; and our heads, the Leviim, and kohanim, set their seal on it.

10 Now those that sealed were, Nechemyah, the governor, the son of Hachaliyah, and Tzidkiyah, 2 Serayah, Azaryah, Yirmeyahu, 3 Pashur, Amaryah, Malchiyah, 4 Hattush, Shevanyah, Malluch, 5 Harim, Meremoth, Ovadyah, 6 Dani-El, Ginnethon, Baruch, 7 Meshullam, Aviyah, Miyamin, 8 Maatzyah, Bilgai, Shemayah: these were the kohanim. 9 And the Leviim: both Yeshua the son of Azanyah, Binnui of the sons of Henadad, Kadmi -El; 10 And their brothers, Shevanyah, Hodiyah, Kelita, Pelayah, Hanan, 11 Micha, v Hashviyah, 12 Zaccur, Sherevyah, Shevanyah, 13 Hodiyah, Bani, Beninu. 14 The heads of the people; Parosh, Pahath-Moav, Eylam, Zatthu, Bani, 15 Bunni, Azgad, Bevai, 16 Adoniyah, Bigvai, Adin, 17 Ater, Hizkiyah, Azzur, 18 Hodiyah, Hashum, Betzai, 19 Hariph, Anathoth, Nevai, 20 Magpiash, Meshullam, Hezir, 21 Meshezave-El, Tzadok, Yahdua, 22 Pelatyah, Hanan, Anayah, 23 Hoshea, Hananyah, Hashuv, 24 Hallohesh, Pileha, Shovek, 25 Rehum, Hashavnah, Maaseyah, 26 And Ahiyah, Hanan, Anan, 27 Malluch, Harim, Baanah. 28 And the rest of the people, the kohanim, the Leviim, the gatekeepers, the singers, the Nethinim, and all they that had separated themselves from the people of the lands to the Torah of Elohim, their wives, their sons, and their daughters, everyone having knowledge, and having understanding; 29 They joined with their brothers, their nobles, and entered into a curse, and into an oath, to have their halacha in Elohim's Torah, which was given by Moshe the eved of Elohim, and to shomer and do all the commandments of

יהוה our Master, and His mishpatim and His chukim; 30 And that we would not give our daughters as wives to the peoples of the land, nor take their daughters as wives for our sons:[1] 31 And if the people of the land bring items or any food on the Shabbat day to sell, that we would not buy it from them on the Shabbat, or on a set-apart day: and that we would rest in the schmitta-seventh year, and remove every debt due us. 32 Also we made commands for ourselves, to give yearly one-third part of a shekel for the service of the Bayit of our Elohim; 33 For the Lechem of the Faces, and for the continual grain offering, and for the continual burnt offering, of the Shabbats, of the Rosh Chodashim, for the set-apart moadim, and for the set-apart things, and for the sin offerings to make an atonement for Yisrael, and for all the work of the Bayit of our Elohim. 34 And we cast the lots among the kohanim, the Leviim, and the people, for the wood offering, to bring it into the Bayit of our Elohim, after the houses of our ahvot, at the yearly moadim, to burn upon the altar of יהוה our Elohim, as it is written in the Torah: 35 And to bring the bikkurim of our ground, and the bikkurim of all fruit of all trees, yearly, to the Bayit of יהוה: 36 Also the firstborn of our sons, and of our cattle, as it is written in the Torah, and the firstlings of our herds and of our flocks, to bring to the Bayit of our Elohim, to the kohanim that serve in the Bayit of our Elohim: 37 And that we should bring the bikkurim of our dough, and our offerings, and the fruit of all manner of trees, of wine and of oil, to the kohanim, to the rooms of the Bayit of our Elohim; and the ma'aser of our ground to the Leviim, that those same Leviim might have the ma'aser in all the cities of our labor. 38 And the kohen the son of Aharon shall be with the Leviim, when the Leviim take ma'aser: and the Leviim shall bring up the ma'aser

from the ma'aser to the Bayit of our Elohim, to the rooms, into the treasury house. 39 For the children of Yisrael and the children of Levi shall bring the offering of the corn, of the new wine, and the oil, to the rooms, where the vessels of the sanctuary are, and the kohanim that serve, and the gatekeepers, and the singers: and we will not forsake the Bayit of our Elohim.

11 And the heads of the people dwelt at Yahrushalayim: the rest of the people also cast lots, to bring one of ten to dwell in Yahrushalayim the set-apart city, and nine parts to dwell in other cities. 2 And the people blessed all the men that willingly offered themselves to dwell at Yahrushalayim. 3 Now these are the heads of the province that dwelt in Yahrushalayim: but in the cities of Yahudah dwelt everyone in his own possession in their cities - Yisrael,[2] the kohanim, and the Leviim, and the Nethinim, and the children of Shlomo's avadim. 4 And at Yahrushalayim dwelt certain of the children of Yahudah, and of the children of Benyamin. Of the children of Yahudah; Athayah the son of Uzziyah, the son of Zacharyah, the son of Amaryah, the son of Shephatyah, the son of Mahalal-El, of the children of Peretz; 5 And Maaseyah the son of Baruch, the son of Col-Hozeh, the son of Hazayah, the son of Adayah, the son of Yoyariv, the son of Zacharyah, the son of Shiloni. 6 All the sons of Peretz that dwelt at Yahrushalayim were four hundred sixty-eight brave men. 7 And these are the sons of Benyamin; Sallu the son of Meshullam, the son of Yoed, the son of Pedayah, the son of Kolaiyah, the son of Maaseyah, the son of Ithi-El, the son of Yeshiyah. 8 And after him Gabbai, Sallai, nine hundred twenty-eight. 9 And Yoel the son of Zichri was their overseer: and Yahudah the son of Senuah was second over the city. 10 Of the kohanim: Yedayah the son of Yoyariv,

---

[1] Yisrael in order to survive must not intermarry outside the nation. In modern understanding that would mean we cannot marry anyone not fully in love with Moshiach and born-again and fully Torah-compliant.

[2] In this context it is used as a generic term for the non-priestly "common people."

Yachin. 11 Serayah the son of Hilkiyah, the son of Meshullam, the son of Tzadok, the son of Meraioth, the son of Ahituv, was the head of the Bayit of Elohim. 12 And their brothers that did the work of the Bayit were eight hundred twenty-two: and Adayah the son of Yeroham, the son of Pelalyah, the son of Amzi, the son of Zacharyah, the son of Pashur, the son of Malchiyah, 13 And his brothers, heads of the ahvot, two hundred forty-two: and Amashai the son of Azare-El, the son of Ahasai, the son of Meshillemoth, the son of Immer, 14 And their brothers, mighty men of bravery, one hundred twenty-eight: and their overseer was Zavdi-El, the son of one of the great men. 15 Also of the Leviim: Shemayah the son of Hashuv, the son of Azrikam, the son of Hashbiyah, the son of Bunni; 16 And Shavethai and Yozavad, of the heads of the Leviim, had the oversight of the outward work of the Bayit of Elohim. 17 And Mattanyah the son of Micha, the son of Zavdi, the son of Asaph, was the leader to begin the giving of hodu in tefillah: and Bakbuchiyah the second among his brothers, and Avda the son of Shammua, the son of Galal, the son of Yeduthun. 18 All the Leviim in the set-apart city were two hundred eighty-four. 19 Moreover the gatekeepers, Akkuv, Talmon, and their brothers that kept guard at the gates, were one hundred seventy-two. 20 And the residue of Yisrael, of the kohanim, and the Leviim, were in all the cities of Yahudah, every one in his inheritance. 21 But the Nethinim dwelt in Ophel: and Ziha and Gispa were over the Nethinim. 22 The overseer also of the Leviim at Yahrushalayim was Uzzi the son of Bani, the son of Hashbiyah, the son of Mattanyah, the son of Micha. Of the sons of Asaph, the singers were over the work of the Bayit of Elohim. 23 For it was the melech's commandment concerning them, that a certain portion should be to the singers, due everyday. 24 And Pethayah the son of Meshezab-El, of the children of Zerah the son of Yahudah, was the melech's deputy in all matters concerning the people. 25 And for the villages, with their fields, some of the children of Yahudah dwelt at Kiryath-Arba, and in its villages, and at Divon, and in its villages, and at Yekavtzel, and its villages, 26 And at Yeshua, and at Moladah, and at Beth-Phelet, 27 And at Hazar-Shual, and at Beer-Sheva, and in its villages, 28 And at Ziklag, and at Mechonah, and in its villages, 29 And at En-Rimmon, and at Tzareah, and at Yarmuth, 30 Zanoah, Adullam, and in their villages, at Lachish, and its fields, at Azekah, and in its villages. And they dwelt from Beer-Sheva to the valley of Hinnom. 31 The children also of Benyamin from Geva dwelt at Michmash, and Aiya, and Beth-El, and in their villages, 32 And at Anathoth, Nob, Ananyah, 33 Hazor, Ramah, Gittayim, 34 Hadid, Tzevoim, Nevallat, 35 Lod, and Ono, the Valley of Craftsmen. 36 And of the Leviim were divisions in Yahudah, and in Benyamin.

12 Now these are the kohanim and the Leviim that went up with Zeruvvavel the son of Shealti-El, and Yeshua: Serayah, Yirmeyahu, Ezra, 2 Amaryah, Malluch, Hattush, 3 Shechanyah, Rehum, Meremoth, 4 Iddo, Ginnetho, Aviyah, 5 Miamin, Maadiyah, Bilgah, 6 Shemayah, and Yoyariv, Yediyah, 7 Sallu, Amok, Hilkiyah, Yedayah. These were the heads of the kohanim and of their brothers in the days of Yeshua. 8 Moreover the Leviim: Yeshua, Binnui, Kadmi-El, Shereviyah, Yahudah, and Mattanyah, who were over the hodu, he and his brothers. 9 Also Bakvukyah and Unni, their brothers, were opposite them in the guard duties. 10 And Yeshua begat Yoiakim, Yoiakim also begat Eli-Ashiv, and Eli-Ashiv begat Yoyada, 11 And Yoyada begat Yonathan, and Yonathan begat Yahdua. 12 And in the days of Yoiakim were kohanim, the heads of the ahvot: of Serayah, Merayah; of

Yirmeyahu, Hananyah; 13 Of Ezra, Meshullam; of Amaryah, Yehohanan; 14 Of Melicu, Yonathan; of Shevanyah, Yoseph; 15 Of Harim, Adna; of Merayoth, Helkai; 16 Of Iddo, Zacharyah; of Ginnethon, Meshullam; 17 Of Aviyah, Zichri; of Miniamin, of Moadiyah, Piltai; 18 Of Bilgah, Shammua; of Shemayah, Yehonathan; 19 And of Yoyariv, Mattenai; of Yedayah, Uzzi; 20 Of Sallai, Kallai; of Amok, Ever; 21 Of Hilkiyah, Hashbiyah; of Yedayah, Nethan-El. 22 The Leviim in the days of Eli-Ashiv, Yoyada, and Yohanan, and Yahdua, were recorded heads of the ahvot: also the kohanim, to the reign of Dareyawesh the Persian. 23 The sons of Levi, the heads of the ahvot, were written in the scroll of the chronicles, even until the days of Yohanan the son of Eli-Ashiv. 24 And the heads of the Leviim: Hashbiyah, Sherevyah, and Yeshua the son of Kadmi-El, with their brothers opposite them, to give tehilla and to give hodu, according to the commandment of David the man of Elohim, watch opposite watch. 25 Mattanyah, and Bakbuchiyah, Ovadyah, Meshullam, Talmon, Akkuv, were gatekeepers keeping the guard at the storerooms of the gates. 26 These were in the days of Yoiakim the son of Yeshua, the son of Yotzadak, and in the days of Nechemyah the governor, and of Ezra the kohen, the sopher. 27 And at the dedication of the wall of Yahrushalayim they sought the Leviim out of all their places, to bring them to Yahrushalayim, to keep the dedication with simcha, both with hodu, and with singing, with cymbals, psalteries, and with harps. 28 And the sons of the singers gathered themselves together, both out of the countryside around Yahrushalayim, and from the villages of Netophathi; 29 Also from the house of Gilgal, and out of the fields of Geva and Azmaveth: for the singers had built their villages around Yahrushalayim. 30 And the kohanim and the Leviim purified themselves, and purified the people, and the gates, and the

wall. 31 Then I brought up the heads of Yahudah upon the wall, and appointed two great companies of them that gave hodu, of which one went on the right hand upon the wall toward the Dung Gate: 32 And after them went Hoshayah, and half of the heads of Yahudah, 33 And Azaryah, Ezra, and Meshullam, 34 Yahudah, and Benyamin, and Shemayah, and Yirmeyahu, 35 And certain of the kohanim's sons with trumpets; namely, Zacharyah the son of Yonathan, the son of Shemayah, the son of Mattanyah, the son of Michayah, the son of Zaccur, the son of Asaph: 36 And his brothers, Shemayah, and Azara-El, Milalai, Gilalai, Maai, Nethan-El, and Yahudah, Hanani, with the musical instruments of David the man of Elohim, and Ezra the sopher before them. 37 And at the Fountain Gate, which was opposite them, they went up by the stairs of the city of David, at the going up of the wall, above the house of David, even to the Water Gate eastward. 38 And the other company of them that gave hodu went opposite them, and I after them, and the half of the people upon the wall, from beyond the Tower of the Furnaces even to the broad wall; 39 And from above the Gate of Ephraim, and above the Old Gate, and above the Fish Gate, and the tower of Hanan-El, and the Tower of Meah, even to the Sheep Gate: and they stood still in the Prison Gate. 40 So stood the two companies of them that gave hodu in the Bayit of Elohim, and I, and the half of the heads with me: 41 And the kohanim; Elyakim, Maaseyah, Minyamin, Michayah, Elyoeynai, Zacharyah, and Hananyah, with trumpets; 42 And Maaseyah, and Shemayah, and Eleazar, and Uzzi, and Yehohanan, and Malchiyah, and Eylam, and Ezer. And the singers sang loud, with Yezrayah their overseer. 43 Also that day they offered great sacrifices, and had gilah: for Elohim had made them gilah with great simcha: the wives also and the children had gilah: so that the simcha of Yahrushalayim was heard even far off. 44 And at that time were some appointed over the rooms for the treasures, for the offerings, for the bikkurim, and for the ma'aser, to gather into them from the fields of the cities the portions of the Torah for the kohanim and Leviim: for Yahudah had gilah for the kohanim and for the Leviim that stood up. 45 And both the singers and the gatekeepers kept the guard of their Elohim, and the guard of the purification, according to the commandment of David, and of Shlomo his son. 46 For in the days of David and Asaph of old there were heads of the singers, and songs to give tehilla and hodu to Elohim. 47 And all Yisrael [1] in the days of Zeruvvavel, and in the days of Nechemyah, gave the portions of the singers and the gatekeepers, every day their portion: and they separated the set-apart things to the Leviim; and the Leviim set them apart to the children of Aharon.

13 On that day they read in the scroll of Moshe in the audience of the people; and in it was found written, that the Ammonite and the Moavite should not come into the congregation of Elohim le-olam-va-ed; 2 Because they met not the children of Yisrael with lechem and with water, but hired Bilam against them, that he should curse them: but our Elohim turned the curse into a bracha. 3 Now it came to pass, when they had heard the Torah that they separated from Yisrael all the mixed multitude. 4 And before this, Eli-Ashiv the kohen, having the oversight of the room of the Bayit of our Elohim, was allied to Toviyah: 5 And he had prepared for him a great room, where in times past they laid the grain offerings, the frankincense, and

the vessels, and the ma'aser of the corn, the new wine, and the oil, which was commanded to be given to the Leviim, and the singers, and the gatekeepers; and the offerings of the kohanim. 6 But in all this time I was not at Yahrushalayim: for in the thirty-second year of Artahshashta melech of Bavel I came to the melech, and after certain days I obtained leave from the melech to return: 7 And I came to Yahrushalayim, and understood of the evil that Eli-ashiv did for Toviyah, in preparing him a room in the courts of the Bayit of Elohim. 8 And it grieved me much: therefore I cast out all the household items of Toviyah out of the room. 9 Then I commanded, and they cleansed the rooms: and there brought I again the vessels of the Bayit of Elohim, with the grain offering and the frankincense. 10 And I perceived that the portions of the Leviim had not been given to them: for the Leviim and the singers, that did the work, had fled every one to his field. 11 Then contended I with the heads, and said, Why is the Bayit of Elohim forsaken? And I gathered them together, and set them in their place. 12 Then brought from all Yahudah the ma'aser of the corn and the new wine and the oil to the storehouse. 13 And I appointed treasurers over the storehouses, Shelemiyah the kohen, and Tzadok the sopher, and of the Leviim, Pedayah: and next to them was Hanan the son of Zaccur, the son of Mattanyah: for they were counted faithful, and their duty was to distribute to their brothers. 14 Remember me, O my Elohim, concerning this, and wipe not out my tov mitzvot that I have done for the Bayit of My Elohim, and for its duties. 15 In those days saw I in Yahudah some treading wine presses on the Shabbat, and bringing in sheaves, and loading donkeys; as also wine, grapes, and figs, and all manner of burdens, which they brought into Yahrushalayim on the Shabbat day: and I testified against them in the day in which they sold food. 16 There dwelt men of Tsor

---

[1] The Nehemiah 12:47 reference is a reference to "all Israel," with Zerubbavel in Judah (one house). This joint rebuilding of the temple and the set-apart city in an eschatological context has yet to take place! The **Shechinah** Presence will return when all twelve tribes are involved in rebuilding. Because only Jewish-Yisrael rebuilt the Temple and city with Ezra and Nehemiah, there is no record of the **Shechinah** Presence falling as it had under Solomon and will again in the millennium. The withholding of the **Shechinah** or Divine Presence was a clear sign from YHVH that all Yisrael did not return with the Babylonian exiles in 500 BCE.

also there, who brought fish, and all manner of items, and sold on the Shabbat to the children of Yahudah, and in Yahrushalayim. 17 Then I contended with the nobles of Yahudah, and said to them, What evil thing is this that you do, to profane the Shabbat? 18 Did not your ahvot do this, and did not our Elohim bring all this evil upon us, and upon this city? Yet now you bring more wrath upon Yisrael by profaning the Shabbat. 19 And it came to pass, that when the gates of Yahrushalayim began to be dark before the Shabbat, [1] I commanded that the gates should be shut, and charged that they should not be opened until after the Shabbat: and some of my avadim I assigned at the gates, that no burden should be brought in on the Shabbat day. 20 So the merchants and sellers of all kind of items lodged outside Yahrushalayim once or twice. 21 Then I testified against them, and said to them, Why do you lodge around the wall? If you do this again, I will lay hands on you. From that time forth they came no more on the Shabbat. 22 And I commanded the Leviim that they should cleanse themselves, and that they should come and guard the gates, to set-apart the Shabbat day. Remember me, O My Elohim, concerning this also, and pardon me according to the greatness of Your rachamim. 23 In those days also I saw Yahudim that had married wives of Ashdod, of Ammon, and of Moav:

24 And their children spoke half in the speech of Ashdod, and could not speak in the Yahudim's language, but according to the language of each people. 25 And I contended with them, and cursed them, and smote certain of them, and plucked off their hair, and made them swear by Elohim, saying, You shall not give your daughters to their sons, nor take their daughters to your sons, nor for yourselves. 26 Did not Shlomo melech of Yisrael sin by these same things? Yet among many nations was there no melech like him, who was beloved by his Elohim, and Elohim made him melech over all Yisrael: nevertheless outlandish women caused even him to sin. 27 Shall we then hearken to you to do all this great evil, to transgress against our Elohim in marrying strange wives? 28 And one of the sons of Yoyada, the son of Eli-Ashiv the Kohen HaGadol, was son-in-law to Sanballat the Horonite: therefore I chased him from me. 29 Remember them, O my Elohim, because they have defiled the order of the kohanim, and the covenant of the office of the kohanim, and of the Leviim. 30 And so I cleansed them from all gerim, and appointed the duties of the kohanim and the Leviim, everyone in his own work; 31 And for the wood offering, at moadim, and for the bikkurim. Remember me, O My Elohim, for tov!

---

[1] Shabbat begins at sundown, not at sunrise.

Divre HaYamim Alef - First Chronicles

To Our Forefathers Yisrael

1 Adam, Sheth, Enosh, 2 Kenan, Mahalal-El, Yered, 3 Henoch, Methuselah, Lamech, 4 Noach, Shem, Ham, and Yapheth. 5 The sons of Yapheth; Gomer, and Magog, and Madai, and Yavan, and Tuval, and Meshech, and Tiras. 6 And the sons of Gomer; Ashchenaz, and Diphath, and Togarmah. 7 And the sons of Yavan; Elishah, and Tarshishah, Kittim, and Rodanim. 8 The sons of Ham; Cush, and Mitzraim, Put, and Canaan. 9 And the sons of Cush; Seva, and Havilah, and Savta, and Raamah, and Savtecha. And the sons of Raamah; Sheva, and Dedan. 10 And Cush begat Nimrod: he began to be mighty upon the earth. 11 And Mitzraim begat Ludim, and Anamim, and Lehavim, and Naphtuhim, 12 And Pathrusim, and Casluhim, from who came the Philistines, and the Caphthorim. 13 And Canaan begat Tzidon his firstborn, and Heth, 14 The Yevusite also, and the Amorite, and the Girgashite, 15 And the Hivite, and the Arkite, and the Sinite, 16 And the Arvadite, and the Tzemarite, and the Hamathite. 17 The sons of Shem; Eylam, and Ashshur, and Arphaxad, and Lud, and Aram, and Uz, and Hul, and Gether, and Meshech. 18 And Arphaxad begat Shelah, and Shelah begat Ever. 19 And to Ever were born two sons: the name of the one was Peleg; because in his days the earth was divided: and his brother's name was Yoktan. 20 And Yoktan begat Almodad, and Sheleph, and Hatzarmaveth, and Yerah, 21 Hadoram also, and Uzal, and Diklah, 22 And Eyval, and Avima-El, and Sheva, 23 And Ophir, and Havilah, and Yovav. All these were the sons of Yoktan. 24 Shem, Arphaxad, Shelah, 25 Ever, Peleg, Reu, 26 Serug, Nahor, Terah, 27 Avram; the same is Avraham. 28 The sons of Avraham; Yitschaq, and Ishma-El. 29 These are their generations: The firstborn of Ishma-El, Nevayoth; then Kedar, and Adveel, and Mivsam, 30 Mishma and Dumah, Massa, Hadad, and Tema, 31 Yetur, Naphish, and Kedemah. These are the sons of Ishma-El. 32 Now the sons of Keturah, Avraham's concubine: she bore Zimran, and Yokshan, and Medan, and Midiyan, and Yishbak, and Shuah. And the sons of Yokshan; Sheva, and Dedan. 33 And the sons of Midiyan; Ephah, and Epher, and Hanok, and Avida, and Eldaah. All these are the sons of Keturah. 34 And Avraham begat Yitschaq. The sons of Yitschaq; Esau and Yisrael. 35 The sons of Esau; Eliphaz, Reuel, and Yeush, and Yaalam, and Korah. 36 The sons of Eliphaz; Teman, and Omar, Tzephi, and Gatam, Kenaz, and Timna, and Amalek. 37 The sons of Reuel; Nahath, Zerah, Shammah, and Mizzah. 38 And the sons of Seir; Lotan, and Shoval, and Tzibeon, and Anah, and Dishon, and Ezer, and Dishan. 39 And the sons of Lothan; Hori, and Homam: and Timna was Lotan's sister. 40 The sons of Shobal; Alyan, and Manahath, and Eybal, Shephi, and Onam. And the sons of Tzibeon; Ayah, and Anah. 41 The sons of Anah; Dishon. And the sons of Dishon; Amram, and Eshban, and Yithran, and Cheran. 42 The sons of Ezer; Bilhan, and Zavan, and Yakan. The sons of Dishan; Uz, and Aran. 43 Now these are the melechim that reigned in the land of Edom before any melech reigned over the children of Yisrael; Bela the son of Beor: and the name of his city was Dinhavah. 44 And when Bela was dead, Yovab the son of Zerah of Bozrah reigned in his place. 45 And when Yovab was dead, Husham of the land of the Temanites reigned in his place. 46 And when Husham was dead, Hadad the son of Bedad, who killed Midiyan in the field of Moav, reigned in his place: and the name of his city was Avith. 47 And when Hadad was dead, Samlah of Masrekah reigned in his place. 48 And when Samlah was dead, Shaul of Rehovoth by the river reigned in his place. 49 And when Shaul was dead, Baal-hanan the son of Achbor reigned in his place. 50 And when Baal-hanan was dead, Hadad reigned in his place: and the name of his city was Pai; and his wife's name was Mehetab-El, the daughter of Matred, the daughter of Mezahav. 51 Hadad died also. And the rulers of Edom were; chief Timnah, chief Alyah, chief Yetheth, 52 Chief Oholibamah, chief Elah, chief Pinon, 53 Chief Kenaz, chief Teman, chief Mibzar, 54 Chief Magdi-El, chief Iram. These are the rulers of Edom.

2 These are the sons of Yisrael; Reuven, Shimeon, Levi, and Yahudah, Yissachar, and Zevulun, 2 Dan, Yoseph, and Benyamin, Naphtali, Gad, and Asher. 3 The sons of Yahudah; Er, and Onan, and Shelah: the three were born to him of the daughter of Shua the Canaanitess. And Er, the firstborn of Yahudah, was evil in the sight of יהוה; and He killed him. 4 And Tamar his daughter in law bore him Perets and Zerah. All the sons of Yahudah were five. 5 The sons of Perets; Hezron, and Hamul. 6 And the sons of Zerah; Zimri, and Eythan, and Heman, and Calcol, and Dara: five of them in all. 7 And the sons of Carmi; Achan, the troubler of Yisrael, who transgressed in the cursed thing. 8 And the sons of Eythan; Azaryah. 9 The sons also of Hezron, that were born to him; Yerahme-El, and Ram, and Cheluvai. 10 And Ram begat Amminadav; and Amminadav begat Nahshon, leader of the children of Yahudah; 11 And Nahshon begat Salma, and Salma begat Boaz, 12 And Boaz begat Oved, and Oved begat Yishai, 13 And Yishai begat his firstborn Eliyav, and Abinadav the second, and Shimma the third, 14 Nethan-El the fourth, Raddai the fifth, 15 Otzem the sixth, David the seventh:

16 Whose sisters were Tzeruyah, and Avigayil. And the sons of Tzeruyah; Avishai, and Yoav, and Asah-El, three. 17 And Avigail bore Amasa: and the abba of Amasa was Yether the Ishmaelite. 18 And Calev the son of Hetzron begat children of Azuvah his wife, and of Yerioth: her sons are these; Yesher, and Shovav, and Ardon. 19 And when Azuvah was dead, Calev took Ephrath as his wife, who bore him Hur. 20 And Hur begat Uri, and Uri begat Betzal-El. 21 And afterward Hetzron went in to the daughter of Machir the abba of Gilead, who he married when he was seventy years old; and she bore him Seguv. 22 And Segub begat Yair, who had twenty-three cities in the land of Gilead. 23 And he took Geshur, and Aram, with the towns of Yair, from them, with Kenath, and its towns, even sixty towns. All these belonged to the sons of Machir the abba of Gilead. 24 And after Hetzron was dead in Calev-Ephratah, then Aviah Hetzron's wife bore him Ashur the abba of Tekoa. 25 And the sons of Yerahme-El the firstborn of Hetzron were, Ram the firstborn, and Bunah, and Oren, and Otzem, and Ahiyah. 26 Yerahme-El had also another wife, whose name was Atarah; she was the ima of Onam. 27 And the sons of Ram the firstborn of Yerahme-El were, Maaz, and Yamin, and Eker. 28 And the sons of Onam were, Shammai, and Yada. And the sons of Shammai; Nadav, and Avishur. 29 And the name of the wife of Avishur was Avihayil, and she bore him Ahban, and Molid. 30 And the sons of Nadav; Seled, and Appayim: but Seled died without children. 31 And the son of Appayim was Yishi. And the sons of Yishi; Sheshan. And the children of Sheshan; Ahlai. 32 And the sons of Yada the brother of Shammai; Yether and Yonathan: and Yether died without children. 33 And the sons of Yonathan; Peleth, and Zaza. These were the sons of Yerahme-El. 34 And Sheshan had no sons, but daughters. And Sheshan had an eved, a Mitzrite, whose name was Yarha. 35 And

Sheshan gave his daughter to Yarha his eved as a wife; and she bore him Attai. 36 And Attai begat Nathan, and Nathan begat Zavad, 37 And Zavad begat Ephlal, and Ephlal begat Oved, 38 And Oved begat Yehu, and Yehu begat Azaryah, 39 And Azaryah begat Heletz, and Heletz begat El-asah, 40 And El-asah begat Sisamai, and Sisamai begat Shallum, 41 And Shallum begat Yechamyah, and Yechamyah begat Elishama. 42 Now the sons of Calev the brother of Yerahme-El were, Meysha his firstborn, who was the abba of Ziph; and the sons of Mareshah the abba of Hevron. 43 And the sons of Hevron; Korah, and Tappuah, and Rekem, and Shema. 44 And Shema begat Raham, the abba of Yorkeam: and Rekem begat Shammai. 45 And the son of Shammai was Maon: and Maon was the abba of Beth-tzur. 46 And Ephah, Calev's concubine, bore Haran, and Moza, and Gazez: and Haran begat Gazez. 47 And the sons of Yahdai; Regem, and Yotham, and Geyshan, and Pelet, and Ephah, and Shaaph. 48 Maachah, Calev's concubine, bore Shever, and Tirhanah. 49 She bore also Shaaph the abba of Madmannah, Sheva the abba of Machbenah, and the abba of Givea: and the daughter of Calev was Achsah. 50 These were the sons of Calev the son of Hur, the firstborn of Ephratah; Shoval the abba of Kiryath-Yearim, 51 Salma the abba of Beth-Lechem, Hareph the abba of Beth-Gader. 52 And Shoval the abba of Kiryath-Yearim had sons; Haroeh, and half of the Menuhothites. 53 And the families of Kiryath-Yearim; the Yithrites, and the Puhites, and the Shumathites, and the Mishraites; from them came the Tzorathites, and the Eshtaolites. 54 The sons of Salma; Beth-Lechem, and the Netophathites, Atroth, the bayit of Yoab, and half of the Menahthites, the Tzorites. 55 And the families of the Sophrim who dwelt at Yabetz; the Tirathites, the Shimathites, and Sucathites. These are the Kenites that came from Hemath, the abba of the bayit of Rechav.

3 Now these were the sons of David, who were born to him in Hevron; the firstborn Amnon, of Ahinoam the Yizreelitess; the second Dani-El, of Avigail the Carmelitess: 2 The third, Assalom the son of Maachah the daughter of Talmai melech of Geshur: the fourth, Adoniyah the son of Haggith: 3 The fifth, Shephatyah of Avital: the sixth, Yithream by Eglah his wife. 4 These six were born to him in Hevron; and there he reigned seven years and six months: and in Yahrushalayim he reigned thirty-three years. 5 And these were born to him in Yahrushalayim; Shimea, and Shovav, and Nathan, and Shlomo, four, of Bath-shua the daughter of Ammi-El: 6 Yivhar also, and Elishama, and Eliphelet, 7 And Nogah, and Nepheg, and Yaphiya, 8 And Elishama, and Elyada, and Eliphelet, nine. 9 These were all the sons of David, beside the sons of the concubines, and Tamar their sister. 10 And Shlomo's son was Rehovoam, Avia his son, Asa his son, Yehoshaphat his son, 11 Yoram his son, Ahazyahu his son, Yoash his son, 12 Amazyahu his son, Azaryah his son, Yotham his son, 13 Ahaz his son, Hizqiyahu his son, Menashsheh his son, 14 Amon his son, Yoshiyahu his son. 15 And the sons of Yoshiyahu were, the firstborn Yochanan, the second Yehoyaqim, the third Tzidqiyahu, the fourth Shallum. 16 And the sons of Yehoyaqim: Yekonyah his son, Tzidqiyahu his son. 17 And the sons of Yekonyah; Shealtiel his son, 18 Malchiram also, and Pedayah, and Shenatzar, Yechamyah, Hoshama, and Nedavyah. 19 And the sons of Pedayah were, Zeruvvavel, and Shimei: and the sons of Zeruvvavel; Meshullam, and Hananyah, and Shelomith their sister: 20 And Hashuvah, and Ohel, and Berechyah, and Hasadyah, Yushav-hesed, five. 21 And the sons of Hananyah; Pelatyah, and Yeshayah: the sons of Rephayah, the sons of Arnan, the sons of Ovadiah, the sons of Shechanyah. 22 And the sons of Shechanuah; Shemayah; and the sons of

Shemayah; Hattush, and Yigal, and Bariyah, and Nearyah, and Shaphat, six. 23 And the sons of Nearyah; Elyoeynai, and Hizqiyah, and Azrikam, three. 24 And the sons of Elyoeynai were, Hodayah, and Elyashiv, and Pelayah, and Akkuv, and Yohanan, and Dalayah, and Anani, seven.

4 The sons of Yahudah; Perets, Hetzron, and Carmi, and Hur, and Shoval. 2 And Reayah the son of Shoval begat Yahath; and Yahath begat Ahumai and Lahad. These are the families of the Tzorathites. 3 And these were of the abba of Eytam; Yezreel, and Yishma, and Yidvash: and the name of their sister was Hatzelelponi: 4 And Penu-El the abba of Gedor and Ezer the abba of Hushah. These are the sons of Hur, the firstborn of Ephratah, the abba of Beth-Lechem. 5 And Ashur the abba of Tekoa had two wives, Helah and Naarah. 6 And Naarah bore him Ahuzzam, and Hepher, and Temeni, and Haahashtari. These were the sons of Naarah. 7 And the sons of Helah were, Tzereth, and Tsohar, and Ethnan. 8 And Cotz begat Anuv, and Tobevah, and the families of Aharh-El the son of Harum. 9 And Yavetz was more honorable than his brothers: and his ima called his name Yavetz, saying, Because I bore him with sorrow. 10 And Yabetz called on the Elohim of Yisrael, saying, Oh that You would bless me indeed, and enlarge my border, and that Your hand might be with me, and that You would keep me from evil, that it may not grieve me! And Elohim granted him that which he requested. 11 And Cheluv the brother of Shuah begat Mehir, who was the abba of Eshton. 12 And Eshton begat Beth-Rapha, and Paseah, and Tehinnah the abba of Ir-nahash. These are the men of Rechah. 13 And the sons of Kenaz; Othniel, and Serayah: and the sons of Othniel; Hathath. 14 And Meonothai begat Ophrah: and Serayah begat Yoav, the abba of Ge-Charashim; for they were craftsmen. 15 And the sons of Calev the son

of Yephunneh; Iru, Elah, and Naam: and the sons of Elah, even Kenaz. 16 And the sons of Yehalele-El; Ziph, and Ziphah, Tireya, and Asare-El. 17 And the sons of Ezra were, Yether, and Mered, and Epher, and Yalon: and she bore Miryam, and Shammai, and Ishbah the abba of Eshtemoa. 18 And his wife Yehudiyah bore Yered the abba of Gedor, and Hever the abba of Socho, and Yekuthiel the abba of Zanowah. And these are the sons of Bithyah the daughter of Pharoah, who Mered took. 19 And the sons of his wife Hodiyah the sister of Naham, the abba of Keilah the Garmite, and Eshtemoa the Maachathite. 20 And the sons of Shimon were, Amnon, and Rinnah, Ben-Hanan, and Tulon. And the sons of Yishi were, Zoheth, and Ben-Zoheth. 21 The sons of Shelah the son of Yahudah were, Er the abba of Lecah, and La-dah the abba of Mareshah, and the families of the bayit of them that wrought fine linen, of the bayit of Ashvea, 22 And Yokim, and the men of Chozeba, and Yoash, and Saraph, who had the dominion in Moav, and Yashuvi-Lehem. But the records were ancient. 23 These were the potters, and those that dwelt at Netaim and Gederah: there they dwelt with the melech for his work. 24 The sons of Shimeon were, Nemu-El, and Yamin, Jariv, Zerah, and Shaul: 25 Shallum his son, Mivsam his son, Mishma his son. 26 And the sons of Mishma; Hamu-El his son, Zachur his son, Shimei his son. 27 And Shimei had sixteen sons and six daughters; but his brothers had not many children, neither did any of their family multiply, like the children of Yahudah. 28 And they dwelt at Beer-sheva, and Moladah, and Hazar-Shual, 29 And at Bilhah, and at Etzem, and at Tolad, 30 And at Bethu-El, and at Hormah, and at Tziklag, 31 And at Beth-Marcavoth, and Hatzar-Susim, and at Beth-Birei, and at Shaarayim. These were their cities until the reign of David. 32 And their villages were, Eytam, and Ayin, Rimmon, and Tochen, and Ashan, five cities: 33 And all their villages that were around the same cities, as far as Baal. These were their dwellings, and their genealogy. 34 And Meshovab, and Yamlech, and Yoshah the son of Amatzyahu, 35 And Yoel, and Yehu the son of Yoshivyah, the son of Serayah, the son of Asi-El, 36 And Elyoeynai, and Yaakovah, and Yeshohayah, and Asayah, and Adiel, and Yesimiel, and Benayah, 37 And Ziza the son of Shiphi, the son of Allon, the son of Yedayah, the son of Shimri, the son of Shemayah; 38 These mentioned by their names were leaders in their families: and the bayit of their ahvot increased greatly. 39 And they went to the entrance of Gedor, even to the east side of the valley, to seek pasture for their flocks. 40 And they found rich pasture and tov, and the land was wide, and quiet, and peaceful; for some Hamites had dwelt there formerly. 41 And these written by name came in the days of Hizqiyahu melech of Yahudah, and destroyed their tents, and the homes that were found there, and destroyed them utterly to this day, and dwelt in their place: because there was pasture there for their flocks. 42 And some of them, even of the sons of Shimeon, five hundred men, went to Mount Seir, having as their commanders Pelatyah, and Ne-aryah, and Rephayah, and Uzzi-El, the sons of Yishi. 43 And they killed the rest of the Amalekites that escaped, and dwelt there to this day.

5 Now the sons of Reuven the firstborn of Yisrael, for he was the firstborn; but because he defiled his abba's bed, his birthright was given to the sons of Yoseph the son of Yisrael:[1] and the genealogy is not listed after the birthright. 2 For Yahudah prevailed above his brothers, and from him came the Ruler;[2] but the birthright was Yoseph's.[3] 3 The sons, of Reuven the firstborn of Yisrael were, Hannoch, and Pallu, Hezron, and Carmi. 4 The sons of Yoel; Shemayah his son, Gog his son, Shimi his son, 5 Micah his son, Reaya his son, Baal his son, 6 Beerah his son, whom Tilgath-Pileser melech of Ashshur carried away captive: he was leader of the Reuvenites.[4] 7 And his brothers by their families, when the genealogy of their generations was listed, were the chief, Yeiel, and Zecharyah, 8 And Bela the son of Azaz, the son of Shema, the son of Yoel, who dwelt in Aroer, even to Nebo and Baal-Meon: 9 And he inhabited eastward to the entering in of the wilderness from the river Euphrates: because their cattle were multiplied in the land of Gilead. 10 And in the days of Shaul they made war with the Hagarites, who fell by their hand: and they dwelt in their tents throughout all the east land of Gilead. 11 And the children of Gad dwelt opposite them, in the land of Bashan to Salchah: 12 Yoel the chief, and Shapham the next, and Yaanai, and Shaphat in Bashan. 13 And their brothers of the bayit of their ahvot were, Micha-El, and Meshullam, and Sheva, and Yorai, and Yachan, and Ziya, and Hever, seven. 14 These are the children of Avihail the son of Huri, the son of Yaroah, the son of Gilead, the son of Micha-El, the son of Yeshishai, the son of Yahdo, the son of Buz; 15 Ahi the son of Avdiel, the son of Guni, chief of the bayit of their ahvot. 16 And they dwelt in Gilead in Bashan, and in her towns, and in all the suburbs of Sharon, within their borders. 17 All these were listed by genealogies in the days of Yotham melech of Yahudah, and in the days of Yerovoam melech of Yisrael. 18 The sons of Reuven, and the Gadites, and half the tribe of Menashsheh, of brave men, men able to bear shield and sword,

---

[1] As the firstborn, Reuben son of Leah was the true birthright recipient. But he had sex with Bilah Jacob's concubine, and therefore the **mishpat bachor** was given to Yoseph/Joseph. But then Jacob bypasses Joseph and gives it to Ephraim in Genesis 48:18-19. This is confirmed in Jeremiah 31:9 where Ephraim is reckoned as Yisrael's firstborn. In the Renewed Covenant all believers are called the "Congregation of Ephraim or the firstborn," showing clear evidence that the writer of Hebrews considered non-Jewish believers as the descendants of Ephraim Yisrael (Hebrews 12:23). So Ephraim from Joseph is recorded in Yisrael's history as the firstborn, even though Reuben was the true biological firstborn.

[2] Moshiach.
[3] Actually given by Jacob to Ephraim, Joseph's son.
[4] In phase one of Ephraim's exile that took place in several stages over about 15 years.

and to shoot with bow, and skilled in war, were forty-four thousand seven hundred sixty, that went out to the war. 19 And they made war with the Hagarites, with Yetur, and Nephish, and Nodav. 20 And they were helped against them, and the Hagarites were delivered into their hand, and all that were with them: for they cried to Elohim in the battle, and He answered them; because they put their trust in Him. 21 And they took away their cattle; of their camels fifty thousand, and of sheep two hundred and fifty thousand, and of donkeys two thousand, and of men a hundred thousand. 22 For there fell down many dead, because the war was of Elohim. And they dwelt in their place until the exile. 23 And the children of the half tribe of Menashsheh dwelt in the land: they increased from Bashan to Baal-Hermon and Senir, and to Mount Hermon. 24 And these were the heads of the bayit of their ahvot, even Epher, and Yishi, and Eliel, and Azriel, and Yeremeyah, and Hodavyah, and Yahdiel, mighty men of bravery, famous men, and heads of the bayit of their ahvot. 25 And they transgressed against the Elohim of their ahvot, and went whoring after the elohim of the people of the land, who Elohim destroyed before them. 26 And the Elohim of Yisrael stirred up the ruach of Pul melech of Ashshur, and the ruach of Tilgath-Pileser melech of Ashshur, and he carried them away, even the Reuvenites, and the Gadites, and the half tribe of Menashsheh,[1] and brought them to Halah, and Habor, and Hara, and to the river Gozan, to this day.[2][3]

6 The sons of Levi; Gershom, Kohath, and Merari. 2 And the sons of Kohath; Amram, Yitzhar, and Hevron, and Uzzi-El. 3 And the children of Amram; Aharon, and Moshe, and Miryam. The sons also of Aharon; Nadav, and Avihu, Elazar, and Yithamar. 4 El-Azar begat Phinehas, Phinehas begat Avishua, 5 And Avishua begat Bukki, and Bukki begat Uzzi, 6 And Uzzi begat Zerahyah, and Zerahyah begat Merayoth, 7 Merayoth begat Amaryah, and Amaryah begat Ahituv, 8 And Ahituv begat Tzadok, and Tzadok begat Ahimaatz, 9 And Ahimaatz begat Azaryah, and Azaryah begat Yohanan, 10 And Yohanan begat Azaryah, he is the one that executed the kohen's office in the Bet HaMikdash that Shlomo built in Yahrushalayim: 11 And Azaryah begat Amaryah, and Amaryah begat Ahituv, 12 And Ahituv begat Tzadok, and Tzadok begat Shallum, 13 And Shallum begat Hilkiyah, and Hilkiyah begat Azaryah, 14 And Azaryah begat Serayah, and Serayah begat Yehotzadak, 15 And Yehotzadak went into captivity, when יהוה carried away Yahudah and Yahrushalayim by the hand of Nebuchadnetzar. 16 The sons of Levi; Gershom, Kohath, and Merari. 17 And these are the names of the sons of Gershom; Livni, and Shimei. 18 And the sons of Kohath were, Amram, and Yizhar, and Hevron, and Uzzi-El. 19 The sons of Merari; Mahli, and Mushi. And these are the families of the Leviim according to their ahvot. 20 Of Gershom; Livni his son, Yahath his son, Zimmah his son, 21 Yoah his son, Iddo his son, Zerah his son, Yeatherai his son. 22 The sons of Kohath; Amminadav his son, Korah his son, Assir his son, 23 Elkanah his son, and Evyasaph his son, and Assir his son, 24 Tahath his son, Uri-El his son, Uzziyah his son, and Shaul his son. 25 And the sons of Elkanah; Amasai, and Ahimoth. 26 As for Elkanah:

---

[1] The first to settle in Moshe's day now became the first to leave in a limited phase to an exile that would be complete in 721 BCE with the fall of Shomron.
[2] Around 440 BCE, Ezra (the writer of Chronicles) said that Ephraim (ten tribes) was scattered in "Halah, Habor, Hara, and to the River Gozan to this day." The prophet Ezra penned these words more than 250 years after (Ephraim) the House of Israel was scattered, and more than 50 years after Judah's return from Babylon to rebuild the Temple. So Ezra, the leader of the Jewish post-Babylonian return, did not consider Yisrael reunited at the time of the Second Temple's restoration. Steven M. Collins, in his book The Ten Lost Tribes of Israel Found, states "Halah, Habor and Gozan were in the Mesopotamian region of the Assyrian empire, but the cities of the Medes were located southeast of the Caspian Sea in

modern Iran. It is likely that the Assyrians settled the Yisraelites in many different areas of their empire (not just Nineveh), in order to prevent them from consolidating their strength.
[3] They went to Assyria, and the towns of the Medes in the east; NIV Study Bible 1995 p.550.

the sons of Elkanah; Zophai his son, and Nahath his son, 27 Eliav his son, Yeroham his son, Elkanah his son. 28 And the sons of Schmuel; the firstborn Yoel, and Aviyah. 29 The sons of Merari; Mahli, Livni his son, Shimei his son, Uzza his son, 30 Shimea his son, Haggiyah his son, Asayah his son. 31 And these are the men who David set over the service of song in the Bayit of יהוה, after the Ark came to rest. 32 And they served before the dwelling place of the Tabernacle of the congregation with singing, until Shlomo had built the Bayit of יהוה in Yahrushalayim: and then they performed their duties according to their order. 33 And these are they that performed their duties with their children. Of the sons of the Kohathites: Heman a singer, the son of Yoel, the son of Schmuel, 34 The son of Elkanah, the son of Yeroham, the son of Eliel, the son of Towah, 35 The son of Zuph, the son of Elkanah, the son of Mahath, the son of Amasai, 36 The son of Elkanah, the son of Yoel, the son of Azaryah, the son of Tzephanyah, 37 The son of Tahath, the son of Assir, the son of Evyasaph, the son of Korah, 38 The son of Yizhar, the son of Kohath, the son of Levi, the son of Yisrael. 39 And his brother Asaph, who stood on his right hand, even Asaph the son of Beracyahu, the son of Shimea, 40 The son of Micha-El, the son of Baaseyah, the son of Malchiyah, 41 The son of Ethni, the son of Zerah, the son of Adayah, 42 The son of Eythan, the son of Zimmah, the son of Shimei, 43 The son of Yahath, the son of Gershom, the son of Levi. 44 And their brothers the sons of Merari stood on the left hand: Eythan the son of Kishi, the son of Avdi, the son of Malluch, 45 The son of Hashabyah, the son of Amatzyah, the son of Hilkiyah, 46 The son of Amtzi, the son of Bani, the son of Shemer, 47 The son of Mahli, the son of Mushi, the son of Merari, the son of Levi. 48 Their brothers also the Leviim were appointed to all manner of service of the Tabernacle of the bayit of Elohim. 49 But

Aharon and his sons offered upon the altar of the burnt offering, and on the altar of incense, and were appointed for all the work of the Most Set-Apart Place, and to make an atonement for Yisrael, according to all that Moshe the eved of Elohim had commanded. 50 And these are the sons of Aharon; El-Azar his son, Phinehas his son, Avishua his son, 51 Bukki his son, Uzzi his son, Zerahyah his son, 52 Merayoth his son, Amaryah his son, Ahituv his son, 53 Tzadok his son, Ahimaatz his son. 54 Now these are their dwelling places throughout their settlements in their borders, of the sons of Aharon, of the families of the Kohathites: for theirs was the lot. 55 And they gave them Hevron in the land of Yahudah, and the suburbs all around about it. 56 But the fields of the city, and the villages of it, they gave to Calev the son of Yephunneh. 57 And to the sons of Aharon they gave the cities of Yahudah, namely, Hevron, the city of refuge, and Livnah with its suburbs, and Yattir, and Eshtemoa, with their suburbs, 58 And Hilen with its suburbs, Debir with its suburbs, 59 And Ashan with its suburbs, and Beth-Shemesh with its suburbs: 60 And out of the tribe of Benyamin; Geba with its suburbs, and Alemeth with its suburbs, and Anathoth with its suburbs. All their cities throughout their families were thirteen cities. 61 And to the sons of Kohath, which were left of the family of that tribe, were cities given out of the half tribe, namely, out of the half tribe of Menashsheh, by lot, ten cities. 62 And to the sons of Gershom throughout their families out of the tribe of Yissachar, and out of the tribe of Asher, and out of the tribe of Naphtali, and out of the tribe of Menashsheh in Bashan, thirteen cities. 63 Unto the sons of Merari were given by lot, throughout their families, out of the tribe of Reuven, and out of the tribe of Gad, and out of the tribe of Zevulun, twelve cities. 64 And the children of Yisrael gave to the Leviim these cities with their suburbs. 65 And they gave by lot out of the tribe of the children of Yahudah, and out of the tribe of the children of Shimeon, and out of the tribe of the children of Benyamin, these cities, which are called by their names. 66 And the residue of the families of the sons of Kohath had cities of their borders out of the tribe of Ephraim. 67 And they gave to them, of the cities of refuge, Shechem in Mount Ephraim with its suburbs; they gave also Gezer with its suburbs, 68 And Yokmeam with its suburbs, and Beth-Horon with its suburbs, 69 And Ayalon with its suburbs, and Gath-Rimmon with its suburbs: 70 And out of the half tribe of Menashsheh; Aner with its suburbs, and Bileam with its suburbs, for the family of the remnant of the sons of Kohath. 71 Unto the sons of Gershom were given out of the family of the half tribe of Menashsheh, Golan in Bashan with its suburbs, and Ashtaroth with its suburbs: 72 And out of the tribe of Yissachar; Kedesh with its suburbs, Daverath with its suburbs, 73 And Ramoth with its suburbs, and Anem with its suburbs: 74 And out of the tribe of Asher; Mashal with its suburbs, and Abdon with its suburbs, 75 And Hukok with its suburbs, and Rehob with its suburbs: 76 And out of the tribe of Naphtali; Kedesh in Galil with its suburbs, and Hammon with its suburbs, and Kiryathaim with its suburbs. 77 Unto the rest of the children of Merari were given out of the tribe of Zevulun. Rimmon with its suburbs, Tabor with its suburbs: 78 And on the other side Yarden by Yericho, on the east side of Yarden, were given them out of the tribe of Reuven, Bezer in the wilderness with its suburbs, and Yahzah with its suburbs, 79 Kedemoth also with its suburbs, and Mephaath with its suburbs: 80 And out of the tribe of Gad; Ramoth in Gilead with it suburbs, and Mahanayim with its suburbs, 81 And Heshbon with its suburbs, and Yazer with its suburbs.

7 Now the sons of Yissachar were, Tola, and Puah, Yashuv, and Shimron, four.

2 And the sons of Tola; Uzzi, and Rephayah, and Yeriel, and Yahmai, and Yivsam, and Schmuel, heads of their abba's bayit. Of Tola: they were brave men of might in their generations; whose number was in the days of David twenty-two thousand six hundred. 3 And the sons of Uzzi; Yizrahyah: and the sons of Yizrahyah; Micha-El, and Ovadyah, and Yoel, Yishiyah, all five of them were ruling men. 4 And with them, by their generations, after the bayit of their ahvot, were bands of soldiers for war, thirty-six thousand men: for they had many wives and sons. 5 And their brothers among all the families of Yissachar were brave men of might, listed in all by their genealogies sixty seven thousand. 6 The sons of Benyamin; Bela, and Becher, and Yediya-El, three. 7 And the sons of Bela; Etzbon, and Uzzi, and Uzziel, and Yerimoth, and Iri, five; heads of the bayit of their ahvot, mighty men of bravery; and were listed by their genealogies twenty-two thousand and thirty-four. 8 And the sons of Becher; Zemirah, and Yoash, and Eliezer, and Elyoeynai, and Omri, and Yerimoth, and Aviyah, and Anathoth, and Alameth. All these are the sons of Becher. 9 And the number of them, after their genealogy by their generations, heads of the bayit of the ahvot, mighty men of bravery, were twenty thousand two hundred. 10 The sons also of Yediyael; Bilhan: and the sons of Bilhan; Yeush, and Benyamin, and Ehud, and Chenaanah, and Zethan, and Tharshish, and Ahishahar. 11 All these the sons of Yediyael, by the heads of their ahvot, mighty men of bravery, were seventeen thousand two hundred soldiers, fit to go out for war and battle. 12 Shuppim also, and Huppim, the children of Ir, and Hushim, the sons of Aher. 13 The sons of Naphtali; Yahtziel, and Guni, and Yetzer, and Shallum, the sons of Bilhah. 14 The sons of Menashsheh; Ashriel, who she bore: but his concubine the Aramean bore Machir the abba of Gilead: 15 And Machir took as his wife the sister of Huppim and Shuppim,

whose sister's name was Maachah; and the name of the second was Tzelophehad: and Tzelophehad had daughters. 16 And Maachah the wife of Machir bore a son, and she called his name Peresh; and the name of his brother was Sheresh; and his sons were Ulam and Rakem. 17 And the sons of Ulam; Bedan. These were the sons of Gilead, the son of Machir, the son of Menashsheh. 18 And his sister Hammoleketh bore Ishod, and Aviezer, and Mahalah. 19 And the sons of Shemida were, Ahyan, and Shechem, and Likhi, and Aniyam. 20 And the sons of Ephraim; Shuthelah, and Bered his son, and Tahath his son, and Eladah his son, and Tahath his son, 21 And Zavad his son, and Shuthelah his son, and Ezer, and Elead, who the men of Gath that were born in that land killed, because they came down to take away their cattle. 22 And Ephraim their abba mourned many days, and his brothers came to comfort him.[1] 23 And when he went in to his wife, she conceived, and bore a son, and he called his name Beriah, because it went evil with his bayit.[2] 24 And his daughter was Sherah, who built Beth-Horon the lower and the upper, and also Uzzen-Sherah. 25 And Rephah was his son, also Resheph, and Telah his son, and Tahan his son, 26 Laadan his son, Ammihud his son, Elishama his son, 27 Nun his son, Yahoshua his son. 28 And their possessions and dwellings were Beth-El and its towns, and eastward Naaran, and westward Gezer, with their towns; Shechem also and its towns, to Gaza and its towns: 29 And by the borders of the children of Menashsheh, Beth-shean and its towns, Taanach and its towns, Megiddo and its towns, Dor and its towns. In these dwelt the children of Yoseph the son of Yisrael. 30 The sons of Asher; Imnah, and Isuah, and Yishuai, and Beriah, and Serah their sister. 31 And the sons of Beriah; Heber, and Malchi-El, who

is the abba of Birzoth. 32 And Heber begat Yaphlet, and Shomer, and Hotham, and Shua their sister. 33 And the sons of Yaphlet; Pasach, and Bimhal, and Ashvath. These are the children of Yaphlet. 34 And the sons of Shamer; Ahi, and Rohgah, Yehuvvah, and Aram. 35 And the sons of his brother Helem; Tzophah, and Yimna, and Shelesh, and Amal. 36 The sons of Tzophah; Suah, and Harnepher, and Shual, and Beri, and Yimrah, 37 Betzer, and Hod, and Shamma and Shilshah, and Yithran, and Beera. 38 And the sons of Yether; Yephunneh, and Pispah, and Ara. 39 And the sons of Ulla; Arah, and Haniel, and Retziya. 40 All these were the children of Asher, heads of their abba's bayit, chosen ones, mighty men of bravery, chief leaders. And the number throughout the genealogy of them that were fit for war and to battle was twenty - six thousand men.

8 Now Benyamin begat Bela his firstborn, Ashvel the second, and Aharah the third, 2 Nohah the fourth, and Rapha the fifth. 3 And the sons of Bela were, Addar, and Gera, and Avihud, 4 And Avishua, and Naaman, and Ahoah, 5 And Gera, and Shephuphan, and Huram. 6 And these are the sons of Ehud: these are the heads of the ahvot of the inhabitants of Geba, and they removed them to Manahath: 7 And Naaman, and Ahiah, and Gera, he removed them, and begat Uzza, and Ahihud. 8 And Shaharaim begat children in the country of Mov, after he had sent them away; Hushim and Baara were his wives. 9 And he begat of Hodesh his wife, Yovab, and Tzivia, and Meysha, and Malcham, 10 And Yeuz, and Shachia, and Mirma. These were his sons, heads of the ahvot. 11 And of Hushim he begat Avituv, and Elpaal. 12 The sons of Elpaal; Eber, and Misham, and Shamer, who built Ono, and Lod, with its towns. 13 Beriah also, and Shema, who were heads of the ahvot of the inhabitants of Ayalon, who drove away the inhabitants of Gath: 14 And Ahyo, Shashak,

---

[1] A type or foreshadow of Judah, that would come to comfort their brothers Ephraim in the latter-day two-house restoration.
[2] A prophecy revealing that Ephraim's House – though chosen – would experience much trouble and anguish in their future.

and Yeremoth, 15 And Tzebadyah, and Arad, and Eder, 16 And Michel, and Yispah, and Yoha, the sons of Beriyah; 17 And Tzevadyah, and Meshullam, and Hezqui, and Hever, 18 Yishmerai also, and Yezliah, and Jovab, the sons of Elpaal; 19 And Yakim, and Zichri, and Zavdi, 20 And Elieynai, and Tzillethai, and Eli-El, 21 And Adayah, and Berayah, and Shimrath, the sons of Shimhi; 22 And Yishpan, and Hever, and Eli-El, 23 And Avdon, and Zichri, and Hanan, 24 And Hananyah, and Eylam, and Antothiyah, 25 And Yiphedeyah, and Penu-El, the sons of Shashak; 26 And Shamsherai, and Sheharyah, and Athalyah, 27 And Yareshyah, and Eliyah, and Zichri, the sons of Yeroham. 28 These were heads of the ahvot, by their generations, rulers of men. These dwelt in Yahrushalayim. 29 And at Giveon dwelt the abba of Giveon; whose wife's name was Maachah: 30 And his firstborn son Avdon, and Tzur, and Kish, and Baal, and Nadav, 31 And Gedor, and Ahyo, and Zecher. 32 And Mikloth begat Shim-ah. And these also dwelt with their brothers in Yahrushalayim, alongside them. 33 And Ner begat Kish, and Kish begat Shaul, and Shaul begat Yonathan, and Malchi-shua, and Avinadab, and Esh-baal. 34 And the son of Ynathan was Merib-baal; and Merib-baal begat Micah. 35 And the sons of Micah were, Pithon, and Melech, and Taarea, and Ahaz. 36 And Ahaz begat Yehoadah; and Yehoadah begat Alemeth, and Azmaveth, and Zimri; and Zimri begat Motza, 37 And Motza begat Binea: Rapha was his son, El-asah his son, Azel his son: 38 And Azel had six sons, whose names are these, Azrikam, Bocheru, and Yishmael, and Shearyah, and Ovadyah, and Hanan. All these were the sons of Atzel. 39 And the sons of Eshek his brother were, Ulam his firstborn, Yehush the second, and Eliphelet the third. 40 And the sons of Ulam were mighty men of bravery, archers, and had many sons, and grandsons, a hundred and fifty. All these are of the sons of Benyamin.

9 So all Yisrael was listed by genealogies; and, behold, they were written in the scroll of the melechim of Yisrael and Yahudah, who were carried away to Bavel for their transgression. 2 Now the first inhabitants that dwelt in their possessions in their cities were, the Yisraelites, the kohanim, Leviim, and the Nethinims. 3 And in Yahrushalayim dwelt some of the children of Yahudah, and some of the children of Benyamin, and some of the children of Ephraim, and Menashsheh;[1] 4 Uthai the son of Ammihud, the son of Omri, the son of Yimri, the son of Bani, of the children of Perets the son of Yahudah. 5 And of the Shilonites; Asayah the firstborn, and his sons. 6 And of the sons of Zerah; Yeuel, and their brothers, six hundred and ninety. 7 And of the sons of Benyamin; Sallu the son of Meshullam, the son of Hodavyah, the son of Hasenuah, 8 And Yibneyah the son of Yeroham, and Elah the son of Uzzi, the son of Michri, and Meshullam the son of Shephatyah, the son of Reuel, the son of Yibniyah; 9 And their brothers, according to their generations, nine hundred and fifty-six. All these men were rulers of a abba's bayit in their abba's houses. 10 And of the kohanim; Yedayah, and Yehoyariv, and Yachin, 11 And Azaryah the son of Hilkiyah, the son of Meshullam, the son of Tzadok, the son of Merayoth, the son of Ahituv, the chief of the Bayit of Elohim; 12 And Adayah the son of Yeroham, the son of Pashur, the son of Malchiyah, and Maasai the son of Adiel, the son of Yahzerah, the son of Meshullam, the son of Meshillemith, the son of Yimmer; 13 And their brothers, heads of the bayit of their ahvot, a thousand seven hundred sixty; very able men for the work of the service of the Bayit of Elohim. 14 And of the Leviim; Shemayah the son of Hasshub, the son of Azrikam, the son of

---

[1] Even before King David's reign, some of the tribes of the north settled amongst Judah. That is clear. Also some from the south migrated north. So that is also clear. What is clearer still is that both houses have a small representation of all 12 tribes, but certainly not the full number of those tribes.

Hashabyah, of the sons of Merari; 15 And Bakbakkar, Heresh, and Galal, and Mattanyah the son of Micah, the son of Zichri, the son of Asaph; 16 And Ovadiah the son of Shemayah, the son of Galal, the son of Yeduthun, and Berechyah the son of Asa, the son of Elkanah, that dwelt in the villages of the Netophathites. 17 And the gatekeepers were, Shallum, and Akkub, and Talmon, and Ahiman, and their brothers: Shallum was the chief; 18 Who up until then waited in the melech's gate eastward: they were gatekeepers for the camps of the children of Levi. 19 And Shallum the son of Kore, the son of Eviasaph, the son of Korah, and his brothers, of the bayit of his abba, the Korahites, were over the work of the service, guards of the gates of the Tabernacle: and their ahvot, being guards over the host of יהוה, were keepers of the entrance. 20 And Phinehas the son of El-Azar was the chief over them in times past, and יהוה was with him. 21 And Zecharyah the son of Meshelemyah was gatekeeper of the door of the Tabernacle of the congregation. 22 All these which were chosen to be gatekeepers in the gates were two hundred and twelve. These were listed by their genealogy in their villages, whom David and Schmuel the seer did ordain in their set appointed office. 23 So they and their children had the oversight of the gates of the Bayit of יהוה, namely, the Bayit of the Tabernacle, by watches. 24 In four quarters were the gatekeepers, toward the east, west, north, and south. 25 And their brothers, that were in their villages, were to come after seven days from time to time with them. 26 For these Leviim, the four chief gatekeepers, were in their office of trust, and were over the rooms and treasuries of the Bayit of Elohim. 27 And they were all night around the Bayit of Elohim, because the duty was upon them, concerning the opening of them every morning. 28 And certain of them had the duty of the service vessels, that they should bring them in and out by count. 29 Some of them also were appointed to oversee the vessels, and all the instruments of the Set-Apart Place, and the fine flour, and the wine, and the oil, and the frankincense, and the spices. 30 And some of the sons of the kohanim made the ointment of the spices. 31 And Mattityiah, one of the Leviim, who was the firstborn of Shallum the Korahite, was entrusted with the things that were made in the pans. 32 And others of their brothers, of the sons of the Kohathites, were in charge of the Lechem of His Presence, to prepare it every Shabbat. 33 And these are the singers, rulers of the ahvot of the Leviim, in the rooms, and were exempted from other duties: for they were employed in that work day and night.[1] 34 These rulers of the ahvot of the Leviim were rulers throughout their generations; these dwelt at Yahrushalayim. 35 And in Giveon dwelt the abba of Giveon, Yehiel, whose wife's name was Maachah: 36 And his firstborn son Avdon, then Tzur, and Kish, and Baal, and Ner, and Nadav, 37 And Gedor, and Ahyo, and Zecharyah, and Mikloth. 38 And Mikloth begat Shimeam. And they also dwelt with their brothers at Yahrushalayim. 39 And Ner begat Kish; and Kish begat Shaul; and Shaul begat Yonathan, and Malchi-shua, and Avinadab, and Esh-baal. 40 And the son of Yehonathan was Meriv-baal: and Meriv-baal begat Micah. 41 And the sons of Micah were, Pithon, and Melech, and Tahrea, and Ahaz. 42 And Ahaz begat Yarah; and Yarah begat Alemeth, and Azmaveth, and Zimri; and Zimri begat Motza; 43 And Motza begat Binea; and Rephayah his son, El-asah his son, Atzel his son. 44 And Atzel had six sons, whose names are these, Azrikam, Bocheru, and Yishmael, and Shearyah, and Ovadyah, and Hanan: these were the sons of Atzel.

10 Now the Philistines fought against Yisrael; and the men of Yisrael fled from before the Philistines, and fell down

---

[1] Musicians were full-time employees.

dead in Mount Gilboa. 2 And the Philistines followed hard after Shaul, and after his sons; and the Philistines killed Yonathan, and Avinadav, and Malchi-Shua, the sons of Shaul. 3 And the battle went strongly against Shaul, and the archers hit him, and he was wounded by the archers. 4 Then said Shaul to his armor-bearer, Draw your sword, and thrust me through with it; lest these uncircumcised come and abuse me. But his armor-bearer would not; for he was very afraid. So Shaul took a sword, and fell upon it. 5 And when his armor-bearer saw that Shaul was dead, he fell likewise on the sword, and died. 6 So Shaul died, and his three sons, and all his bayit died together. 7 And when all the men of Yisrael that were in the valley saw that they fled, and that Shaul and his sons were dead, then they forsook their cities, and fled: and the Philistines came and dwelt in them. 8 And it came to pass the next day, when the Philistines came to strip the slain, that they found Shaul and his sons fallen in Mount Gilboa. 9 And when they had stripped him, they took his head, and his armor, and sent into the land of the Philistines all around, to carry the news to their idols, and to the people. 10 And they put his armor in the bayit of their elohim, and fastened his head in the temple of Dagon. 11 And when all Yavesh-Gilead heard all that the Philistines had done to Shaul, 12 They arose, all the brave men, and took away the body of Shaul, and the bodies of his sons, and brought them to Yavesh, and buried their bones under the oak in Yavesh, and fasted seven days. [1] 13 So Shaul died for his transgression that he committed against יהוה , even against the word of יהוה , which he did not keep, and also for asking counsel from one that had a familiar ruach; 14 And he did not ask of יהוה: therefore He killed him, and turned over the malchut to David the son of Yishai.

11 Then all Yisrael gathered themselves to David to Hevron, saying, Behold, we are your bone and your flesh. 2 And moreover in times past, even when Shaul was melech, you were the one that led out and brought in Yisrael: and יהוה your Elohim said to you, You shall feed My people Yisrael, and you shall be chief over My people Yisrael. 3 Then came all the zachanim of Yisrael to the melech to Hevron; and David made a covenant with them in Hevron before יהוה ; and they anointed David melech over Yisrael, according to the word of יהוה by Schmuel. 4 And David and all Yisrael went to Yahrushalayim, which is Yevus; where the Yevusites were the inhabitants of the land. 5 And the inhabitants of Yevus said to David, You shall not come here. Nevertheless David took the castle of Tzion, which is the city of David. 6 And David said, Whoever smites the Yevusites first shall be chief and commander. So Yoav the son of Tzeruyah went up first, and was chief. 7 And David dwelt in the castle; therefore they called it the city of David. 8 And he built the city all around, even from Millo all around: and Yoav repaired the rest of the city. 9 So David grew greater and greater: for יהוה Tzevaot was with him. 10 These also are the heads of the mighty men whom David had, who strengthened themselves with him in his malchut, and with all Yisrael, to make him melech, according to the word of יהוה concerning Yisrael. [2] 11 And this is the number of the mighty men whom David had; Yashoveam, son of a Hachmonite, the chief of the thirty: he lifted up his spear against three hundred slain by him at one time. 12 And after him was El-Azar the son of Dodo, the Ahohite, who was one of the three mighty men. 13 He was with David at Pas-Dammim, and there the Philistines were gathered together to battle, where was a field of ground full of barley; and the people fled from before the Philistines.

---

[1] The tradition of seven days of sitting **shiva**.

[2] United monarchy as both houses submit to David.

14 And they set themselves in the midst of that field, and delivered it, and killed the Philistines; and יהרה saved them by a great deliverance. 15 Now three of the thirty commanders went down to the rock to David, into the cave of Adullam; and the army of the Philistines camped in the valley of Rephaim. 16 And David was then in the stronghold, and the Philistines' watchpost was then at Beth-Lechem. 17 And David longed, and said, Oh that one would give me drink of the mayim of the well of Beth-Lechem, that is at the gate! 18 And the three broke through the host of the Philistines, and drew mayim out of the well of Beth-Lechem, that was by the gate, and took it, and brought it to David: but David would not drink of it, but poured it out to יהרה, 19 And said, My Elohim forbids me, that I should do this thing: shall I drink the dom of these men that have put their lives in jeopardy? For with the jeopardy of their lives they brought it. Therefore he would not drink it. These things did these three mighty men. 20 And Avishai the brother of Yoav, he was chief of the three: for lifting up his spear against three hundred, he killed them, and made a name among the three. 21 Of the three, he was more honorable than the two; for he was their commander: however he attained not to the position of the first three. 22 Benayah the son of Yehoiada, the son of a brave man of Kavzeel, who had done many acts; he killed two lion-like men of Moav: also he went down and killed a lion in a pit on a snowy day. 23 And he killed an Mitzrite, a man of great size, five cubits high; and in the Mitzrite's hand was a spear like a weaver's beam; and he went down to him with a staff, and plucked the spear out of the Mitzrite's hand, and killed him with his own spear. 24 These things did Benayah the son of Yehoiada, and had the name among the three mightiest. 25 Behold, he was honorable among the thirty, but attained not to the first three: and David set him over his court. 26 Also the brave men of the armies

were, Asahel the brother of Yoav, El-Hanan the son of Dodo of Beth-Lechem, 27 Shammoth the Harorite, Heletz the Pelonite, 28 Ira the son of Ikkesh the Tekoite, Abi-ezer the Anatothite, 29 Sibbechai the Hushathite, Ilai the Ahohite, 30 Maharai the Netophathite, Heled the son of Baanah the Netophathite, 31 Ithai the son of Rivai of Gibeah, that pertains to the children of Benyamin, Benayah the Pirathonite, 32 Hurai of the brooks of Gaash, Aviel the Arvathite, 33 Atzmaveth the Baharumite, Eliahva the Shaalbonite, 34 The sons of Hashem the Gizonite, Yonathan the son of Shage the Hararite, 35 Ahyam the son of Sacar the Hararite, Eliphal the son of Ur, 36 Hepher the Mecherathite, Ahiyah the Pelonite, 37 Hetzro the Carmelite, Naarai the son of Ezbai, 38 Yoel the brother of Nathan, Mivhar the son of Haggeri, 39 Tzelek the Ammonite, Naharai the Berothite, the armor-bearer of Yoav the son of Tzeruyah, 40 Ira the Yithrite, Gareb the Yithrite, 41 Uriah the Hittite, Tzabad the son of Ahlai, 42 Adina the son of Shiza the Reuvenite, a commander of the Reuvenites, and thirty with him, 43 Hanan the son of Maachah, and Yoshaphat the Mithnite, 44 Uzzia the Ashterathite, Shama and Yehiel the sons of Hothan the Aroerite, 45 Yediya-El the son of Shimri, and Joha his brother, the Titzite, 46 Eli-El the Mahavite, and Yeribai, and Yoshavyah, the sons of Elnaam, and Yithmah the Moavite, 47 Eli-El and Oved, and Yasi-El the Metsovite.

12 Now these are they that came to David to Ziklag, while he yet kept himself hidden because of Shaul the son of Kish: and they were among the mighty men, helpers of the war. 2 They were armed with bows, and could use both the right hand and the left in hurling stones and shooting arrows out of a bow, even of Shaul's brothers of Benyamin. 3 The chief was Ahiezer, then Yoash, the sons of

Shemaah the Giveathite; and Yeziel, and Pelet, the sons of Atzmaveth; and Berachyah, and Yehu the Anatothite, 4 And Ysmayah the Giveonite, a mighty man among the thirty, and over the thirty; and Yirmeyahu, and Yahazie-El, and Yohanan, and Yosavad the Gederathite, 5 Eluzai, and Yerimoth, and Bealyah, and Shemaryah, and Shephatyahu the Haruphite, 6 Elkanah, and Yesiah, and Azare-El, and Yoezer, and Yashoveam, the Korhites, 7 And Yoelah, and Tzevadyah, the sons of Yeroham of Gedor. 8 And of the Gadites there separated themselves to David at the stronghold in the wilderness men of might, men of war fit for the battle, that could handle shield and spear, whose faces were like the faces of lions, and were as swift as the gazelles upon the mountains; 9 Ezer the first, Ovadyah the second, Eliav the third, 10 Mishmannah the fourth, Yirmeyahu the fifth, 11 Attai the sixth, Eli-El the seventh, 12 Yohanan the eighth, Elzavad the ninth, 13 Yirmeyahu the tenth, Machvanai the eleventh. 14 These were of the sons of Gad, commanders of the army: the least was over an hundred, and the greatest over a thousand. 15 These are they that went over the Yarden River in the first month, when it had overflown all its banks; and they put to flight all of them of the valleys, both toward the east, and toward the west. 16 And there came of the children of Benyamin and Yahudah to the stronghold to David. 17 And David went out to meet them, and answered and said to them, If you are come in shalom to help me, my lev shall be knit to you: but if you are come to betray me to my enemies, seeing there is no violence in my hands, the Elohim of our ahvot look see it, and rebuke it. 18 Then the Ruach came upon Amatsai, who was chief of the commanders, and he said, Yours we are, David, and we are on your side, you son of Yishai: shalom, shalom be to you, and shalom be to your helpers; for your Elohim helps you. Then David received them, and made them commanders of the band. 19 And some of Menashsheh went over to David, when he came with the Philistines against Shaul to battle: but they did not help Shaul: for the leaders of the Philistines upon advisement sent him away, saying, He might go to his master Shaul with our heads. 20 As he went to Ziklag, those of Menashsheh who went over to him, Adnah, and Yozavad, and Yediya-El, and Micha-El, and Yozavad, and Elihu, and Tzilthai, commanders of the thousands that were of Menashsheh. 21 And they helped David against the band of the raiders: for they were all mighty men of bravery, and were commanders in the host. 22 For at that time day by day men came to David to help him, until it was a great army, like the host of Elohim. 23 And these are the numbers of the tribes that were ready armed to the war, and came to David to Hevron, to turn the malchut of Shaul to him, according to the word of יהוה. 24 The children of Yahudah that bore shield and spear were six thousand and eight hundred, ready and armed for war. 25 Of the children of Shimeon, mighty men of bravery for war, seven thousand and one hundred. 26 Of the children of Levi four thousand and six hundred. 27 And Yehoiada was the leader of the Aharonites, and with him were three thousand and seven hundred; 28 And Tzadok, a young man mighty in bravery, and of his abba's bayit twenty-wo commanders. 29 And of the children of Benyamin, the relatives of Shaul, three thousand: for until then the greatest part of them had guarded the duties of the bayit of Shaul. 30 And of the children of Ephraim twenty thousand and eight hundred, mighty men of bravery, famous throughout the bayit of their ahvot. 31 And of the half tribe of Menashsheh eighteen thousand, who were designated by name, to come and make David melech. 32 And of the children of Yissachar, who were men that had binah of the times, to know what Yisrael should do; the heads of them were two hundred; and all their brothers were at their commandment. [1] 33 Of Zevulun, such as went forth to battle, expert in war, with all the instruments of war, fifty thousand, who could keep rank: they were not of a double lev. [2] 34 And of Naphtali a thousand commanders, and with them with shield and spear thirty seven thousand. 35 And of the Danites expert in war twenty eight thousand six hundred. 36 And of Asher, such as went forth to battle, expert in war, forty thousand. 37 And on the other side of Yarden, of the Reuvenites, and the Gadites, and of the half tribe of Menashsheh, with all manner of instruments of war for the battle, a hundred twenty thousand. 38 All these men of war, that could keep rank, came with a perfect lev to Hevron, to make David melech over all Yisrael: and all the rest also of Yisrael were of one lev to make David melech. [3] 39 And there they were with David three days, eating and drinking: for their brothers had prepared for them. 40 Moreover they that were near them, even from as far away as Yissachar and Zevulun and Naphtali, brought lechem on donkeys, and on camels, and on mules, and on oxen, and meat, meal, cakes of figs, and bunches of raisins, and wine, and oil, and oxen, and sheep abundantly: for there was simcha in Yisrael. [4]

13 And David consulted with the commanders of thousands and hundreds, and with every leader. 2 And David said to all the congregation of Yisrael, If it seems tov to you, and that it be of יהוה our Elohim, let us send abroad to our brothers everywhere, that are left in all the land of Yisrael, and with them also to the kohanim and Leviim who are in their cities and suburbs, that they may gather themselves to us: [5] 3 And let us bring again the Ark of our Elohim to us: for we sought Him not with it in the days of Shaul. 4 And all the congregation said that they would do so: for the thing was right in the eyes of all the people. 5 So David gathered all Yisrael together, from Shihor of Mitzrayim even to the entering of Hamath, to bring the Ark of Elohim from Kiryath-Yearim. 6 And David went up, and all Yisrael, to Baalah, that is, to Kiryath-Yearim, which belonged to Yahudah, to bring up from there the Ark of Elohim יהוה, that dwells between the cheruvim, whose Name is called on it. 7 And they carried the Ark of Elohim in a new cart out of the bayit of Avinadav: and Uzza and Ahyo led the wagon. 8 And David and all Yisrael played before Elohim with all their might, and with singing, and with harps, and with lyres, and with timbrels, and with cymbals, and with shofars. 9 And when they came to the threshing floor of Chidon, Uzza put forth his hand to hold the Ark; for the oxen stumbled. 10 And the anger of יהוה was kindled against Uzza, and He killed him, because he put his hand to the Ark: and there he died before Elohim. 11 And David was displeased, because יהוה had broken out upon Uzza: therefore that place is called Perez-Uzza to this day. 12 And David was afraid of Elohim that day, saying, How shall I bring the Ark of Elohim home to me? 13 So David brought not the Ark home to himself to the city of David, but carried it aside into the bayit of Oved-Edom the Gittite. 14 And the Ark of Elohim remained with the family of Oved-Edom in his bayit three months. And יהוה blessed the bayit of Oved-Edom, and all that he had.

---

[1] Many leading the end-time two-house revival are most likely from Issachar. Though small in number, as seen here with only 200 sent to David, they knew what Yisrael had to do in uniting the House of David with the House of Saul, later to become the House of Yisrael, and they had a keen understanding of the times that they were in, knowing that unity was at hand. Today many of Yissachar are leading the two-house restoration, as they know both the times we are in, as well as what Yisrael has to do.
[2] Many in the two-house restoration movement who are faithful warriors and know how to keep rank are from Zevulon. These Yisraelites are tireless workers for the restoration, yet do not seek leadership positions, and avoid double-mindedness in their calling.
[3] The days of Yisrael's splendor, unity and might, as all 12 tribes were in harmony and unity.
[4] Two-house advocates strive to recapture that joy as we prepare the way for Moshiach's return.

---

[5] The call to all Yisrael to become echad.

14 Now Hiram melech of Tzor sent messengers to David, and timber of cedars, with masons and carpenters, to build him a bayit. 2 And David perceived that יהוה had confirmed him as melech over Yisrael, for his malchut was lifted up on high, because of His people Yisrael. 3 And David took more wives at Yahrushalayim: and David begat more sons and daughters. 4 Now these are the names of his children which he had in Yahrushalayim; Shammua, and Shovav, Nathan, and Shlomo, 5 And Yivhar, and Elishua, and Elpalet, 6 And Nogah, and Nepheg, and Yaphiya, 7 And Elishama, and Beelyada, and Eliphalet. 8 And when the Philistines heard that David was anointed melech over all Yisrael, all the Philistines went up to seek David. And David heard of it, and went out against them. 9 And the Philistines came and made a raid in the valley of Rephaim. 10 And David inquired of Elohim, saying, Shall I go up against the Philistines? And will You deliver them into my hand? And יהוה said to him, Go up; for I will deliver them into your hand. 11 So they came up to Baal-Perazim; and David killed them there. Then David said, Elohim has broken in upon my enemies by my hand like the breaking forth of the waters: therefore they called the name of that place Baal-Perazim. 12 And when they had left their elohim there, David gave a commandment, and they were burned with fire. 13 And the Philistines yet again made a raid in the valley. 14 Therefore David inquired again of Elohim; and Elohim said to him, Go not up after them; turn away from them, and come upon them over against the mulberry trees. 15 And it shall be, when you shall shema a sound of howling in the tops of the mulberry trees, that then you shall go out to battle: for Elohim has gone forth before you to smite the army of the Philistines. 16 David therefore did as Elohim commanded him: and they killed the army of the Philistines from Giveon even to Gazer. 17 And the fame of David went out into all lands; and יהוה brought the fear of him upon all nations.[1]

15 And David made for himself houses in the city of David, and prepared a place for the Ark of Elohim, and pitched for it a tent. 2 Then David said, None should carry the Ark of Elohim but the Leviim: for יהוה has chosen them to carry the Ark of Elohim, and to attend to Him le-olam-va-ed. 3 And David gathered all Yisrael together to Yahrushalayim, to bring up the Ark of יהוה to the place, which he had prepared for it. 4 And David assembled the children of Aharon, and the Leviim: 5 Of the sons of Kohath; Uri-El the chief, and his brothers a hundred and twenty: 6 Of the sons of Merari; Asayah the chief, and his brothers two hundred and twenty: 7 Of the sons of Gershom; Yoel the chief, and his brothers an hundred and thirty: 8 Of the sons of Elizaphan; Shemayah the chief, and his brothers two hundred: 9 Of the sons of Hevron; Eli-El the chief, and his brothers eighty: 10 Of the sons of Uzzi-El; Amminadav the chief, and his brothers an hundred and twelve. 11 And David called for Tzadok and Aviathar the kohanim, and for the Leviim, for Uri-El, Asayah, and Yoel, Shemayah, and Eli-El, and Amminadav, 12 And said to them, You are the heads of the ahvot of the Leviim: set yourselves apart, both you and your brothers, that you may bring up the Ark of יהוה Elohim of Yisrael to the place that I have prepared for it. 13 For because you did it not the first time, יהוה our Elohim broke out against us, for that we sought not the right ruling. 14 So the kohanim and the Leviim set themselves apart to bring up the Ark of יהוה Elohim of Yisrael. 15 And the children of the Leviim bore the Ark of Elohim upon their shoulders with the poles on it, as Moshe commanded according to the word of יהוה. 16 And David spoke to the heads of the Leviim to appoint their brothers to be the singers with instruments

---

[1] Yisrael became a global colonizing power under King David, with the seed of Yisrael sprinkled in all nations.

of music, lyres and harps and cymbals, sounding, by lifting up their voices with simcha. 17 So the Leviim appointed Heman the son of Yoel; and of his brothers, Asaph the son of Berechyahu; and of the sons of Merari their brothers, Ethan the son of Kushayah; 18 And with them their brothers of the second rank, Zechariyh, Ben, and Yaazi-El, and Shemiramoth, and Yehi-El, and Unni, Eliav, and Benayah, and Maaseyah, and Mattityahu, and Eli-pheleh, and Mikneyah, and Oved-Edom, and Yei-El, the gatekeepers. 19 So the singers, Heman, Asaph, and Ethan, were appointed to sound with cymbals of bronze; 20 And Zecharyah, and Azi-El, and Shemiramoth, and Yehi-El, and Unni, and Eliav, and Maaseyah, and Benayah, with harps according to Alamoth; 21 And Mattityahu, and Eli-Pheleh, and Mikneyah, and Oved-Edom, and Yei-El, and Azazyah, with harps on the Sheminith to excel. 22 And Chenanyah, chief of the Leviim, in songs: he instructed about the songs, because he was skilful. 23 And Berechyahu and Elkanah were doorkeepers for the Ark. 24 And Shebanyah, and Yehoshaphat, and Nethane-El, and Amasai, and Zecharyah, and Benayah, and Eliezer, the kohanim, did blow with the shofars before the Ark of Elohim: and Oved-Edom and Yehiyah were doorkeepers for the Ark. 25 So David, and the zachanim of Yisrael, and the commanders over thousands, went to bring up the Ark of the covenant of יהוה out of the bayit of Oved-Edom with simcha. 26 And it came to pass, when Elohim helped the Leviim that bore the Ark of the Covenant of יהוה, that they offered seven bullocks and seven rams. 27 And David was clothed with a robe of fine linen, and all the Leviim that bore the Ark, and the singers, and Chenanyah the master of the song with the singers: David also had upon himself a shoulder garment of linen. 28 So all Yisrael brought up the Ark of the Covenant of יהוה with shouting, and with sound of the horn, and with shofars, and with cymbals, making

a noise with harps and lyres. 29 And it came to pass, as the Ark of the Covenant of יהוה came to the city of David, that Michal the daughter of Shaul looking out from a window saw melech David dancing and playing: and she despised him in her lev.

16

So they brought the Ark of Elohim, and set it in the midst of the tent that David had pitched for it: and they offered burnt sacrifices and shalom offerings before Elohim. 2 And when David had made an end of offering the burnt offerings and the shalom offerings, he blessed the people in the Name of יהוה.[1] 3 And he dealt to every one of Yisrael, both man and woman, to every one a loaf of lechem, and a tov piece of meat, and a container of wine. 4 And he appointed certain of the Leviim to attend before the Ark of יהוה, and to bring to remembrance, and to hodu and give tehilla to יהוה Elohim of Yisrael: 5 Asaph the chief, and next to him Zecharyah, Yei-El, and Shemiramoth, and Yehi-El, and Mattityahu, and Eliav, and Benayah, and Oved-Edom: and Yei-El with harps and with lyres; but Asaph made a sound with cymbals; 6 Benayah also and Yahazi-El the kohanim with shofars continually before the Ark of the Covenant of Elohim. 7 Then on that day David first delivered this psalm of hodu to יהוה into the hand of Asaph and his brothers. 8 Give hodus to יהוה, call upon His Name[2] make known His deeds among the nations. 9 Sing to Him, sing tehillim to Him, talk of all His wondrous works. 10 Tiferet in His Set-Apart Name: let the levim of those rejoice that seek יהוה. 11 Seek יהוה and His strength, seek His face continually. 12 Remember His marvelous works that He has done, His wonders, and the mishpatim of His mouth; 13 O you zera of Yisrael His eved: you children of Yaakov, His chosen ones.[3] 14 He is יהוה our Elohim; His

---

[1] There remains no other way to seal Yisrael but by the true Name.
[2] Yisrael must call upon his Name, not His title.
[3] His eternal bride; He has no other elect.

mishpatim are in all the earth. 15 Be you mindful always of His covenant; the word that He commanded to a thousand generations; 16 Even of the covenant that He made with Avraham, and of His oath to Yitschaq; 17 And has confirmed the same to Yaakov for a Torah, and to Yisrael for an everlasting covenant,[1] 18 Saying, To you will I give the land of Canaan, the lot of your inheritance; 19 When you were but few, even a few, and strangers in it. 20 And when they went from nation to nation, and from one malchut to another; 21 He allowed no man to do them wrong: yes, He reproved melechim for their sakes, 22 Saying, Touch not My anointed, and do My neviim no harm. 23 Sing to יהוה, all the earth; show forth from day to day His salvation. 24 Declare His tiferet among the nations; His marvelous works among all nations. 25 For great is יהוה, and greatly to be praised: He also is to be feared above all elohim. 26 For all the elohim of the nations are idols: but יהוה made the shamayim. 27 Tiferet and honor are in His presence; strength and simcha are in His place. 28 Ascribe to יהוה, you kindreds of the nations, give to יהוה tiferet and strength. 29 Ascribe to יהוה the tiferet due to His Name:[2] bring an offering, and come before Him: worship יהוה in the tiferet of set-apartness. 30 Fear before Him, all the earth: the world also shall be established, that it is not moved. 31 Let the shamayim be in simcha, and let the earth rejoice: and let men say among the nations, יהוה reigns.[3] 32 Let the sea roar, and the fullness of it: let the fields gilah, and all that is in it. 33 Then shall the trees of the forest sing out at the presence of יהוה, because He comes to shophet the earth. 34 O hodu le יהוה; ke tov; for His chesed endures le-olam-va-ed. 35 And say, Save us, O Elohim of our salvation, and gather us together,[4] and

deliver us from the nations, that we may give hodu to Your set-apart Name,[5] and boast in Your tehilla. 36 Blessed be יהוה Elohim of Yisrael le-olam-va-ed. And all the people said, Amein, and praised יהוה. 37 So he left there Asaph and his brothers; before the Ark of the Covenant of יהוה, to attend before the Ark continually, as each day work required: 38 And Oved-Edom with their brothers, sixty-eight; Oved-Edom also the son of Yeduthun and Hosah to be gatekeepers: 39 And Tzadok the kohen, and his brothers the kohanim, before the Tabernacle of יהוה in the high place that was at Giveon, 40 To offer burnt offerings to יהוה upon the altar of the burnt offering continually shacrit and ma'ariv, and to do according to all that is written in the Torah of יהוה, which He commanded Yisrael; 41 And with them Heman and Yeduthun, and the rest that were chosen, who were designated by name, to give hodu to יהוה, because His rachamim endures le-olam-va-ed; 42 And with them Heman and Yeduthun with shofars and cymbals for those that should sound aloud, and with musical instruments for the songs of Elohim. And the sons of Yeduthun were gatekeepers. 43 And all the people departed every man to his bayit: and David returned to bless his bayit.

17 Now it came to pass, as David sat in his bayit, that David said to Nathan ha navi, See, I dwell in a bayit of cedars, but the Ark of the Covenant of יהוה remains under curtains. 2 Then Nathan said to David, Do all that is in your lev; for Elohim is with you. 3 And it came to pass the same night, that the word of Elohim came to Nathan, saying, 4 *Go and tell David My eved, This says יהוה, You shall not build Me a bayit to dwell in: 5 For I have not dwelt in a bayit since the day that I brought up Yisrael even until this day; but have gone from tent to tent, and from one Tabernacle to another. 6 Wherever I have*

---

[1] The land of Yisrael belongs to Yisrael forever.
[2] Enjoy the beauty of His true Name.
[3] We are to proclaim YHWH's Name and kingdom in all nations, not suppress it in any nation.
[4] Those who are regathered from the nations back to the things of Yisrael will give praise and honor to His true Name.

---

[5] Our thanksgiving is to be directed to His Name.

walked with all Yisrael, did I ever speak a word to any of the shophtim of Yisrael, whom I commanded to feed My people, saying, Why have you not built Me a bayit of cedars? 7 Now therefore this shall you say to My eved David, This says יהוה *Tzevaot, I took you from the sheepfold, even from following the sheep, that you should be ruler over My people Yisrael: 8 And I have been with you wherever you have walked, and have cut off all your enemies from before you, and have made you a name like the name of the great men that are in the earth. 9 Also I will ordain a place for My people Yisrael, and will plant them, and they shall dwell in their place, and shall be moved no more; neither shall the children of wickedness ruin them any more, as at the beginning,* [1] [2] *10 And since the time that I commanded shophtim to be over My people Yisrael. Moreover I will subdue all your enemies. Furthermore I tell you that* יהוה *will build you a bayit. 11 And it shall come to pass, when your days are expired that you must go to be with your ahvot, that I will raise up your zera after you, which shall be from your sons; and I will establish his malchut. 12 He shall build Me a bayit, and I will establish his throne le-olam-va-ed. 13 I will be his abba, and he shall be My son:* [3] *and I will not take My rachamim away from him, as I took it from him that was before you: 14 But I will settle him in My bayit and in My malchut le-olam-va-ed: and his throne shall be established le-olam-va-ed.* 15 According to all these words, and according to all this vision, so did Nathan speak to David. 16 And David the melech came and sat before יהוה, and said, Who am I, O יהוה Elohim, and what is my bayit, that You have brought me this far? 17 And yet this was a small thing in Your eyes, O Elohim; for You have also spoken of Your eved's bayit for a great while to come, and have regarded me according to the position of a man of exalted position, O יהוה Elohim. 18 What can David speak more to You for the honor of Your eved? For You know Your eved. 19 O יהוה, for Your eved's sake, and according to Your own lev, have You done all this greatness, in making known all these great things. 20 O יהוה, there is none like You, neither is there any Elohim beside You, according to all that we have heard with our ears. 21 And what one nation in the earth is like Your people Yisrael, whom Elohim went to redeem to be His own people, to make Yourself a Name of greatness and awesomeness, by driving out the nations from before Your people, whom You have redeemed out of Mitzrayim?[4] 22 For Your people Yisrael did You make Your own people le-olam-va-ed; and You, יהוה, became their Elohim. [5] 23 Therefore now, יהוה, let the thing that You have spoken concerning Your eved and concerning his bayit be established le-olam-va-ed, and do as You have said. 24 Let it even be established, that Your Name may be magnified le-olam-va-ed,[6] saying, יהוה Tzevaot is the Elohim of Yisrael, even an Elohim to Yisrael: and let the bayit of David Your eved be established before You. 25 For You, O my Elohim, have told Your eved that You will build him a bayit: therefore Your eved has found it in his lev to make tefillah before You. 26 And now, יהוה, You are Elohim, and have promised this tov to Your eved: 27 Now therefore let it please You to bless the bayit of Your eved, that it may be before You le-olam-va-ed: for You blessed it, O יהוה, and it shall be blessed le-olam-va-ed.

---

[1] See notes on Second Samuel 7:10.
[2] Deuteronomy 29:28, **eretz acheret** or "another land" or "new world land." See note at Deuteronomy 29:28. For more details, see:
http://yourarmstoisrael.org/icles_new/guest/?page=eretz_ache rit.
[3] Moshiach.

[4] YHWH chose Yisrael to make His true Name great.
[5] Only Yisrael is ever referred to as YHWH's elect in both covenants. Any other manmade reference to an elect separate from historic Yisrael is a doctrine of deception and anti-Semitism.
[6] Nothing can be clearer. His Name did not change when Moshiach arrived. It is found more than 200 times preserved in the Aramaic Peshitta as Mar-Yah.

18

Now after this it came to pass, that David killed the Philistines, and subdued them, and took Gath and its towns out of the hand of the Philistines. 2 And he killed Moav; and the Moavites became David's avadim, and brought gifts. 3 And David killed Hadadezer melech of Tzovah to Hamath, as he went to establish his dominion by the river Euphrates. 4 And David took from him a thousand mirkavot, and seven thousand horsemen, and twenty thousand footmen: David also hamstrung all the mirkavah horses, but left from them a hundred mirkavot. 5 And when the Arameans of Dameshek came to help Hadadezer melech of Tzovah, David killed of the Arameans twenty-two thousand men. 6 Then David put watch-posts in Aram of Dameshek; and the Arameans became David's avadim, and brought gifts. So יהוה preserved David wherever he went. 7 And David took the shields of gold that were on the avadim of Hadadezer, and brought them to Yahrushalayim. 8 Likewise from Tivhath, and from Chun, cities of Hadadezer, David brought very much bronze, with which Shlomo made the bronze sea, and the pillars, and the vessels of bronze. 9 Now when Tou melech of Hamath heard how David had killed all the army of Hadadezer melech of Tzovah; 10 He sent Hadoram his son to melech David, to inquire of his welfare, and to congratulate him, because he had fought against Hadadezer, and killed him - for Hadadezer had war with Tou - and with him all manner of vessels of gold and silver and bronze. 11 Them also melech David set-apart to יהוה, with the silver and the gold that he brought from all these nations; from Edom, and from Moav, and from the children of Ammon, and from the Philistines, and from Amalek. 12 Moreover Avishai the son of Tzeruyah killed of the Edomites in the Valley of Salt eighteen thousand. 13 And he put watch-posts in Edom; and all the Edomites became David's avadim. So יהוה preserved David wherever

he went. 14 So David reigned over all Yisrael,[1] and executed judgment and justice among all his people. 15 And Yoav the son Tzeruyah was over the army; and Yehoshaphat the son of Ahilud, recorder. 16 And Tzadok the son of Ahituv, and Avimelech the son of Aviathar, were the kohanim; and Shavsha was sopher; 17 And Benayah the son of Yehoyada was over the Cherethites and the Pelethites; and the sons of David were heads all around the melech.

19

Now it came to pass after this, that Nahash the melech of the children of Ammon died, and his son reigned in his place. 2 And David said, I will show chesed to Hanun the son of Nahash, because his abba showed chesed to me. And David sent messengers to comfort him concerning his abba. And the avadim of David came to Hanun in the land of the children of Ammon to comfort him. 3 And the heads of the children of Ammon said to Hunan; Is David honoring your abba in your eyes because he has sent comforters to you? Have not his avadim come here to spy out the land? 4 So Hanun took David's avadim, and shaved them, and cut off their garments in the midst at their buttocks, and sent them away. 5 Then there went certain men, who told David how the men were served. And he sent to meet them: for the men were greatly ashamed. And the melech said, Stay at Yericho until your beards are grown, and then return.[2] 6 And when the children of Ammon saw that they had made themselves a bad stench to David, Hanun and the children of Ammon sent a thousand talents of silver to hire them mirkavot and horsemen out of Mesopotamia, and out of Aram-Maachah, and out of Tzovah. 7 So they hired thirty-two thousand mirkavot, and the melech of Maachah and his people; who came and pitched before Medeva. And the children of Ammon gathered themselves together from their cities, and came to

---

[1] United nation.
[2] Yisraelite men must wear beards and not be clean-shaven.

battle. 8 And when David heard of it, he sent Yoav, and all the army of the mighty men. 9 And the children of Ammon came out, and put on the battle array before the gate of the city: and the melechim that had come were by themselves in the field. 10 Now when Yoav saw that the battle was set against him before and behind, he chose out of all the choice men of Yisrael, and put them in battle array against the Arameans. 11 And the rest of the people he delivered to the hand of Avishai his brother, and they set themselves in battle array against the children of Ammon. 12 And he said, If the Arameans are too strong for me, then you shall help me: but if the children of Ammon are too strong for you, then I will help you. 13 Be of tov courage, and let us behave ourselves valiantly for our people, and for the cities of our Elohim: and let יהוה do that what is tov in His sight. 14 So Yoav and the people that were with him drew near before the Arameans to the battle; and they fled before him. 15 And when the children of Ammon saw that the Arameans were fled, they likewise fled before Avishai his brother, and entered into the city. Then Yoav came to Yahrushalayim. 16 And when the Arameans saw that they were being killed before Yisrael, they sent messengers, and brought the Arameans that were beyond the river: and Shophach the commander of the army of Hadadezer went before them. 17 And it was told David; and he gathered all Yisrael, and passed over Yarden, and came upon them, and set up in battle array against them. So when David had put the battle in array against the Arameans, they fought with him. 18 But the Arameans fled before Yisrael; and David killed of the Arameans seven thousand men who fought in mirkavot, and forty thousand footmen, and killed Shophach the commander of the army. 19 And when the avadim of Hadadezer saw that they were killed by Yisrael, they made shalom with David, and became his avadim: neither would the Arameans help the children of Ammon any more.

20 And it came to pass, at the turn of the year, at the time that melechim go out to battle, Yoav led the power of the army, and wasted the country of the children of Ammon, and came and besieged Rabbah. But David tarried at Yahrushalayim. And Yoav killed Rabbah, and destroyed it. 2 And David took the crown of their melech from off his chief, and found it to weigh a talent of gold, and there were precious stones in it; and it was set upon David's chief: and he brought also exceeding much plunder out of the city. 3 And he brought out the people that were in it, and put them to work with saws, and with harrows of iron, and with axes. This is how David dealt with all the cities of the children of Ammon. And David and all the people returned to Yahrushalayim. 4 And it came to pass after this, that there arose war at Gezer with the Philistines; at which time Sibbechai the Hushathite killed Sippai, that was one of the children of the giant: and they were subdued. 5 And there was war again with the Philistines; and Elhanan the son of Yair killed Lahmi the brother of Golyath the Gittite, whose spear staff was like a weaver's beam. 6 And yet again there was war at Gath, where was a man of great size, whose fingers and toes were twenty-four, six on each hand, and six on each foot: and he also was the son of the giant. 7 But when he defied Yisrael, Yonathan the son of Shimea David's brother killed him. 8 These were born to the giant in Gath; and they fell by the hand of David, and by the hand of his avadim.

21 And s.a.tan stood up against Yisrael, and provoked David to number Yisrael.[1] 2 And David said to Yoav and to the rulers of the people, Go, number Yisrael from Beer-Sheva even to Dan; and bring the number of them to me, that I may

---

[1] See note on Second Samuel 24:1.

know it. 3 And Yoav answered, **יהוה** make His people an hundred times so many more as they be: but, my master the melech, are they not all my master's avadim? Why then does my master require this thing? Why will he be a cause of trespass to Yisrael? 4 Nevertheless the melech's words prevailed against Yoav. Therefore Yoav left, and went throughout all Yisrael, and came to Yahrushalayim. 5 And Yoav gave the sum of the number of the people to David. And all those of Yisrael were one million one hundred thousand men that drew sword: and Yahudah was four hundred seventy thousand men that drew sword. 6 But Levi and Benyamin he did not count: for the melech's word was abominable to Yoav. 7 And Elohim was displeased with this thing; therefore He killed Yisrael. 8 And David said to Elohim, I have sinned greatly, because I have done this thing: but now, I beg You, do away the iniquity of Your eved; for I have done very foolishly. 9 And **יהוה** spoke to Gad, David's seer, saying, *10 Go and tell David, saying, This says* **יהוה***, I offer you three things: choose one of them, that I may do it to you.[1]* 11 So Gad came to David, and said to him, This says **יהוה***, Choose for yourself 12 Either three years' famine; or three months to be destroyed before your foes, while the sword of your enemies overtakes you; or else three days the sword of* **יהוה***, even pestilence, in the land, with the heavenly messenger of* **יהוה** *destroying throughout all the borders of Yisrael*. Now therefore consider yourself what word I shall bring again to Him that sent me. 13 And David said to Gad, I am in a great trouble: let me fall now into the hand of **יהוה** ; for very great are His rachamim: but let me not fall into the hand of man. 14 So **יהוה** sent pestilence upon Yisrael: and there fell of Yisrael seventy thousand men. 15 And Elohim sent a heavenly messenger to Yahrushalayim to destroy it: and as he was destroying, **יהוה** beheld, and He relented of the evil, and said

to the heavenly messenger that was destroying, *It is enough, hold back now your hand*. And the heavenly messenger of **יהוה** stood by the threshing floor of Ornan the Yevusi. 16 And David lifted up his eyes, and saw the heavenly messenger of **יהוה** stand between the earth and the shamayim, having a drawn sword in his hand stretched out over Yahrushalayim. Then David and the zachanim of Yisrael, who were clothed in sackcloth, fell upon their faces. 17 And David said to Elohim, Is it not I that commanded the people to be numbered? I have sinned and done evil indeed; but as for these sheep, what have they done? Let Your hand, I make tefillah to You, O **יהוה** My Elohim, be on me, and on my abba's bayit; but not on Your people, that they should be plagued. 18 Then the heavenly messenger of **יהוה** commanded Gad to say to David, that David should go up, and set up an altar to **יהוה** in the threshing floor of Ornan the Yevusi. 19 And David went up at the saying of Gad, which he spoke in the Name of **יהוה**.[2] 20 And Ornan turned back, and saw the heavenly messenger; and his four sons with him hid themselves. Now Ornan was threshing wheat. 21 And as David came to Ornan, Ornan looked and saw David, and went out of the threshing floor, and bowed himself to David with his face to the ground. 22 Then David said to Ornan, Grant me the place of this threshing floor, that I may build an altar here to **יהוה**: you shall grant it me for the full price: that the plague may be stayed from the people. 23 And Ornan said to David, Take it for you, and let my master the melech do that which is tov in his eyes: look, I give you the oxen also for burnt offerings, and the threshing instruments for wood, and the wheat for the grain offering; I give it all. 24 And melech David said to Ornan, No; but I will truly buy it for the full price: for I will not take that which is yours for **יהוה**, nor offer burnt offerings without cost. 25 So David gave to Ornan for the place six hundred shekels of

---

[1] Chesed.

[2] A true prophet does not prophesy in any other name.

gold by weight. 26 And David built there an altar to **יהוה**, and offered burnt offerings and shalom offerings, and called upon **יהוה**; and He answered him from shamayim by fire upon the altar of burnt offering. [1] 27 And **יהוה** commanded the heavenly messenger; and he put up his sword again into its sheath. 28 At that time when David saw that **יהוה** had answered him in the threshing floor of Ornan the Yevusi, then he sacrificed there. 29 For the Tabernacle of **יהוה**, which Moshe made in the wilderness, and the altar of the burnt offering, were at that time in the high place at Giveon. 30 But David could not go before it to seek Elohim: for he was afraid because of the sword of the heavenly messenger of **יהוה**.

22 Then David said, This is the Bayit of **יהוה** Elohim, and this is the altar of the burnt offering for Yisrael. 2 And David commanded to gather together the strangers that were in the land of Yisrael; and he set stonemasons to cut stones to build the Bayit of Elohim. 3 And David prepared iron in abundance for the nails for the doors of the gates, and for the clamps; and bronze in abundance without weight; 4 Also cedar trees in abundance: for the Tzidonians and those of Tzor brought much cedar wood to David. 5 And David said, Shlomo my son is young and tender, and the bayit that is to be built for **יהוה** must be exceedingly great, for a tiferet Name throughout all the countries: I will therefore now make preparation for it. So David prepared abundantly before his death. 6 Then he called for Shlomo his son, and commanded him to build a bayit for **יהוה** Elohim of Yisrael. 7 And David said to Shlomo, My son, as for me, it was in my mind to build a bayit to the Name of **יהוה** My Elohim: 8 But the word of **יהוה** came to me, saying, *You have shed dom*

abundantly, and have made great wars: you shall not build a bayit to My Name, because you have shed much dom upon the earth in My sight. 9 Behold, a son shall be born to you, who shall be a man of rest; and I will give him rest from all his enemies all around: for his name shall be Shlomo, and I will give shalom and rest to Yisrael in his days. 10 He shall build a Bayit for My Name; and he shall be My son, and I will be his Abba; and I will establish the throne of his malchut over Yisrael le-olam-va-ed. 11 Now, my son, **יהוה** be with you; and prosper you, and build the Bayit of **יהוה** Your Elohim, as He has said to you. 12 Only **יהוה** give you chochma and binah, and give you charge concerning Yisrael, that you may guard the Torah of **יהוה** your Elohim. 13 Then shall you prosper, if you take heed to fulfil the statutes and mishpatim that **יהוה** commanded Moshe concerning Yisrael: be strong, and of tov courage; fear not, nor be dismayed. 14 Now, behold, in my trouble I have prepared for the Bayit of **יהוה** an hundred thousand talents of gold, and a million talents of silver; and of bronze and iron without weight; for it is in abundance: timber also and stone have I prepared; and you may add to it. 15 Moreover there are workmen with you in abundance, hewers and workers of stone and timber, and all manner of skilled men for every manner of work. 16 Of the gold, the silver, and the bronze, and the iron, there is no number. Arise therefore, and build, and **יהוה** be with you. 17 David also commanded all the leaders of Yisrael to help Shlomo his son, saying, 18 Is not **יהוה** your Elohim with you? And has He not given you rest on every side? For He has given the inhabitants of the land into my hand; and the land is subdued before **יהוה**, and before His people. 19 Now set your lev and your being to seek **יהוה** your Elohim; arise therefore, and build the Set-Apart Place of **יהוה** Elohim, to bring the Ark of the Covenant of **יהוה**, and the set-apart vessels of Elohim,

---

[1] David bought two altars: one on Mt. Moriah, the other on the Mt. Of Olives.
See **An Altar Of Authority** at:
http://store.yourarmstoisrael.org/Qstore/Qstore.cgi?CMD=011&PROD=1065730379.

into the Bayit that is to be built for the Name of **יהוה**.

23 So when David was old and full of days, he made Shlomo his son melech over Yisrael. 2 And he gathered together all the leaders of Yisrael, with the kohanim and the Leviim. 3 Now the Leviim were numbered from the age of thirty years and upward: and their number chief by chief, man by man, was thirty-eight thousand. 4 Of which, twenty-four thousand were to set forward the work of the Bayit of **יהוה**; and six thousand were officers and shophtim: 5 Moreover four thousand were gatekeepers; and four thousand praised **יהוה** with the instruments which I made, said David, to tehilla with it. 6 And David divided them into courses among the sons of Levi, namely, Gershon, Kohath, and Merari. 7 Of the Gershonites were, Laadan, and Shimei. 8 The sons of Laadan; the chief was Yehi-El, and Zetham, and Yo-El, three. 9 The sons of Shimei; Shelomith, and Hazi-El, and Haran, three. These were the heads of the ahvot of Laadan. 10 And the sons of Shimei were, Yahath, Zina, and Yeush, and Beriyah. These four were the sons of Shimei. 11 And Yahath was the chief, and Zizah the second: but Yeush and Beriyah had not many sons; therefore they were reckoned, according as one abba's bayit. 12 The sons of Kohath; Amram, Yishar, Hevron, and Uzzi-El, four. 13 The sons of Amram; Aharon and Moshe: and Aharon was separated, that he should sanctify the most set-apart things, he and his sons le-olam-va-ed, to burn incense before **יהוה**, to attend to Him, and to bless in His Name le-olam-va-ed.[1] 14 Now concerning Moshe the man of Elohim, his sons were named of the tribe of Levi. 15 The sons of Moshe were, Gershom, and Eliezer. 16 Of the sons of Gershom, Shevuel was the chief. 17 And the sons of Eliezer were, Rehavyah the chief. And Eliezer had no other sons; but

the sons of Rehaviah were very many. 18 Of the sons of Yitzhar; Shelomith the chief. 19 Of the sons of Hevron; Yeriyah the first, Amaryah the second, Yahazie-El the third, and Yekameam the fourth. 20 Of the sons of Uzzi-El; Michah the first, and Yesiyah the second. 21 The sons of Merari; Mahli, and Mushi. The sons of Mahli; El-Azar, and Kish. 22 And El-Azar died, and had no sons, but daughters: and their brothers the sons of Kish took them. 23 The sons of Mushi; Mahli, and Eder, and Yeremoth, three. 24 These were the sons of Levi after the bayit of their ahvot; even the heads of the ahvot, as they were counted by number of names chief by chief, that did the work for the service of the Bayit of **יהוה**, from the age of twenty years and upward. 25 For David said, **יהוה** Elohim of Yisrael has given rest to His people that they may dwell in Yahrushalayim le-olam-va-ed: 26 And also to the Leviim; they shall no more carry the Tabernacle, nor any vessels of it for the service of it. 27 For by the last words of David the Leviim were numbered from twenty years old and above: 28 Because their duty was to wait on the sons of Aharon for the service of the Bayit of **יהוה**, in the courts, and in the rooms, and in the purifying of all the set-apart things, and the work of the service of the Bayit of Elohim; 29 Both for the Lechem of The Faces, and for the fine flour for the grain offering, and for the unleavened cakes, and for that which is baked in the pan, and for that which is fried, and for all manner of measures and sizes; 30 And to stand every shacrit to give hodu and tehilla to **יהוה**, and likewise at maariv; 31 And to offer all burnt sacrifices to **יהוה** on the Shabbats, on the Rosh Chodashim, and on the Moadim, by number, according to the order commanded to them, continually before **יהוה**: 32 And that they should keep the duty of the Tabernacle of the congregation, and the duty of the Set-Apart Place, and the duty of the sons of Aharon

---

[1] Blessings that are Biblical and eternal are done only in YHWH's Name.

their brothers, in the service of the Bayit of יהוה.

24 Now these are the divisions of the sons of Aharon. The sons of Aharon; Nadav, and Avihu, El-Azar, and Ithamar. 2 But Nadav and Avihu died before their abba, and had no children: therefore El-Azar and Ithamar executed the kohen's office. 3 And David divided them, both Tzadok of the sons of El-Azar, and Ahimelech of the sons of Ithamar, according to their offices in their service. 4 And there were more leaders found of the sons of El-Azar than of the sons of Ithamar; and so were they divided. Among the sons of El-Azar there were sixteen chief men of the bayit of their ahvot, and eight among the sons of Ithamar according to the bayit of their ahvot. 5 So they were divided by lot, one group with another; for the officials of the Set-Apart Place, and officials of the Bayit of Elohim, were of the sons of El-Azar, and of the sons of Ithamar. 6 And Shemayah the sopher the son of Nethane-El, one of the Leviim, wrote them before the melech, and the leaders, and Tzadok the kohen, and Ahimelech the son of Aviathar, and before the heads of the ahvot of the kohanim and Leviim: one principal household being taken for El-Azar, and one taken for Ithamar. 7 Now the first lot came forth to Yehoyariv, the second to Yedayah, 8 The third to Harim, the fourth to Seorim, 9 The fifth to Malchiyah, the sixth to Miyamin, 10 The seventh to Hakkoz, the eighth to Abiyah, 11 The ninth to Yeshua, the tenth to Shecanyah, 12 The eleventh to Eliashiv, the twelfth to Yakim, 13 The thirteenth to Huppah, the fourteenth to Yesheveab, 14 The fifteenth to Bilgah, the sixteenth to Immer, 15 The seventeenth to Hezir, the eighteenth to Aphses, 16 The nineteenth to Pethahyah, the twentieth to Yehezkel, 17 The twenty-first to Yachin, the twenty-second to Gamul, 18 The twenty-third to Delayah, the twenty-fourth to Maazyah. 19 These were the offices in

their service to come into the Bayit of יהוה, according to their mishpat, under Aharon their abba, as יהוה Elohim of Yisrael had commanded him. 20 And the rest of the sons of Levi were these: Of the sons of Amram; Shuvael: of the sons of Shuva-El; Yehdeiyah. 21 Concerning Rehavyah: of the sons of Rehavyah, the first was Yishiyah. 22 Of the Yitzharites; Shelomoth: of the sons of Shelomoth; Yahath. 23 And the sons of Hevron; Yeriyah the first, Amaryah the second, Yahazie-El the third, Yekameam the fourth. 24 Of the sons of Uzzi-El; Michah: of the sons of Michah; Shamir. 25 The brother of Michah was Yishiyah: of the sons of Yishiyah; Zecharyah. 26 The sons of Merari were Mahli and Mushi: the sons of Yaaziyah; Beno. 27 The sons of Merari by Yaaziyah; Beno, and Shoham, and Zaccur, and Ivri. 28 Of Mahli came El-Azar, who had no sons. 29 Concerning Kish: the son of Kish was Yerahme-El. 30 The sons also of Mushi; Mahli, and Eder, and Yerimoth. These were the sons of the Leviim after the bayit of their ahvot. 31 These also cast lots as did their brothers the sons of Aharon in the presence of David the melech, and Tzadok, and Ahimelech, and the heads of the ahvot of the kohanim and Leviim, even the heads of the ahvot as well as his younger brothers.

25 Moreover David and the commanders of the army separated for the service some of the sons of Asaph, and of Heman, and of Yeduthun, who should prophesy with harps, with lyres, and with cymbals: and the number of the workmen according to their service was: 2 Of the sons of Asaph; Zaccur, and Yoseph, and Nethanyah, and Asharelah, the sons of Asaph under the hands of Asaph, who prophesied according to the order of the melech. 3 Of Yeduthun: the sons of Yeduthun; Gedalyah, and Zeri, and Yeshayah, Hashavyah, and Mattityahu, six, under the hands of their abba Yeduthun,

who prophesied with a harp, to give hodu and to tehilla יהוה. 4 Of Heman: the sons of Heman; Bukkiyah, Mattanyah, Uzzi-El, Shevu-El, and Yerimoth, Hananyah, Hanani, Elyathah, Giddalti, and Romamti-ezer, Yoshbekashah, Mallothi, Hothir, and Mahaziyoth: 5 All these were the sons of Heman the melech's seer in the words of Elohim, to lift up the horn. And Elohim gave to Heman fourteen sons and three daughters. 6 All these were under the hands of their abba for singing in the Bayit of יהוה, with cymbals, harps, and lyres, for the service of the Bayit of Elohim, according to the melech's order to Asaph, Yeduthun, and Heman. 7 So the number of them, with their brothers that were instructed in the songs of יהוה, even all that were skilled, was two hundred eighty-eight. 8 And they cast lots, for their duty, the small as well as the great, the teacher as well as the student. 9 Now the first lot came forth for Asaph to Yoseph: the second to Gedalyah, who with his brothers and sons were twelve: 10 The third to Zaccur, he, his sons, and his brothers, were twelve: 11 The fourth to Yitsri, he, his sons, and his brothers, were twelve: 12 The fifth to Nethanyah, he, his sons, and his brothers, were twelve: 13 The sixth to Bukkiyah, he, his sons, and his brothers, were twelve: 14 The seventh to Yesharelah, he, his sons, and his brothers, were twelve: 15 The eighth to Yeshayah, he, his sons, and his brothers, were twelve: 16 The ninth to Mattanyah, he, his sons, and his brothers, were twelve: 17 The tenth to Shimei, he, his sons, and his brothers, were twelve: 18 The eleventh to Azar-El, he, his sons, and his brothers, were twelve: 19 The twelfth to Hashabyah, he, his sons, and his brothers, were twelve: 20 The thirteenth to Shuva-El, he, his sons, and his brothers, were twelve: 21 The fourteenth to Mattityahu, he, his sons, and his brothers, were twelve: 22 The fifteenth to Yeremoth, he, his sons, and his brothers, were twelve: 23 The sixteenth to Hananyah, he, his sons, and his brothers,

were twelve: 24 The seventeenth to Yoshbekashah, he, his sons, and his brothers, were twelve: 25 The eighteenth to Hanani, he, his sons, and his brothers, were twelve: 26 The nineteenth to Mallothi, he, his sons, and his brothers, were twelve: 27 The twentieth to Elyathah, he, his sons, and his brothers, were twelve: 28 The one and twentieth to Hothir, he, his sons, and his brothers, were twelve: 29 The two and twentieth to Giddalti, he, his sons, and his brothers, were twelve: 30 The three and twentieth to Mahaziyoth, he, his sons, and his brothers, were twelve: 31 The four and twentieth to Romamti-ezer, he, his sons, and his brothers, were twelve.

26 Concerning the divisions of the gatekeepers: Of the Korhites was Meshelemyah the son of Kore, of the sons of Asaph. 2 And the sons of Meshelemyah were, Zecharyah the firstborn, Yediya-El the second, Zevavyah the third, Yathniel the fourth, 3 Eylam the fifth, Yehohanan the sixth, Elioeynai the seventh. 4 Moreover the sons of Oved-Edom were, Shemayah the firstborn, Yehozabad the second, Yoah the third, and Sacar the fourth, and Nethane-El the fifth, 5 Ammi-El the sixth, Yissachar the seventh, Peulthai the eighth: for Elohim blessed him. 6 Also to Shemayah his son were sons born, that ruled throughout the bayit of their abba: for they were mighty men of bravery. 7 The sons of Shemayah; Othni, and Repha-El, and Oved, Elzavad, whose brothers were strong men, Elihu, and Semachyah. 8 All these of the sons of Oved-Edom: they and their sons and their brothers, able men for strength for the service, were sixty-two of Oved-Edom. 9 And Meshelemiyah had sons and brothers, strong men, eighteen. 10 Also Hosah, of the children of Merari, had sons; Simri the chief, for though he was not the firstborn, yet his abba made him the chief; 11 Hilkiyah the second, Tevayiah the third, Zecharyah the fourth: all the sons and brothers of Hosah were thirteen. 12 Among

these were the divisions of the gatekeepers, even among the chief men, having duties like their brothers, to attend in the Bayit of יהוה. 13 And they cast lots, as well the small as the great, according to the bayit of their ahvot, for every gate. 14 And the lot eastward fell to Shelemyah. Then for Zecharyah his son, a wise counselor, they cast lots; and his lot came out northward. 15 To Oved-Edom southward; and to his sons the porches. 16 To Shuppim and Hosah the lot came forth westward, with the Shallecheth-Gate, by the ascending highway, guard corresponding with guard. 17 Eastward were six Leviim, northward four a day, southward four a day, and toward the porches two and two. 18 At Parbar westward, four at the highway, and two at Parbar. 19 These are the divisions of the gatekeepers among the sons of Kore, and among the sons of Merari. 20 And of the Leviim, Ahiyah was over the treasures of the Bayit of Elohim, and over the treasures of the set-apart things. 21 As concerning the sons of Laadan; the sons of the Gershonite Laadan, heads of their ahvot, even of Laadan the Gershonite, were Yehi-eli. 22 The sons of Yehi-eli; Zetham, and Yo-El his brother, which were over the treasures of the Bayit of יהוה. 23 Of the Amramites, and the Yizharites, the Hevronites, and the Uzzielites: 24 And Shevuel the son of Gershom, the son of Moshe, was chief of the treasures. 25 And his brothers by Eli-ezer; Rehaviah his son, and Yeshayah his son, and Yoram his son, and Zichri his son, and Shelomith his son. 26 Shelomith and his brothers were over all the treasures of the set-apart things, that David the melech, and the heads of the ahvot, the commanders over thousands and hundreds, and the commanders of the army, had set-apart. 27 Out of the plunders won in battles did they set-apart to maintain the Bayit of יהוה. 28 And all that Schmuel the seer, and Shaul the son of Kish, and Avner the son of Ner, and Yoav the son of Tzeruyah, had set-apart; and whoever had

set-apart anything, it was under the hand of Shelomith, and of his brothers. 29 Of the Yitzharites, Chenanyah and his sons were for the outward duties over Yisrael, for officers and shophtim. 30 And of the Hevronites, Hashaviyah and his brothers, men of bravery, a thousand seven hundred, were officers among them of Yisrael on the west side of the Yarden in all the duties of יהוה, and in the service of the melech. 31 Among the Hevronites was YeriYah the chief, among the Hevronites, according to the generations of his ahvot. In the fortieth year of the reign of David they were sought for, and there were found among them mighty men of bravery at Yazer of Gilead. 32 And his brothers, men of bravery, were two thousand seven hundred heads of the ahvot, who melech David made rulers over the Reuvenites, the Gadites, and the half tribe of Menashsheh, for every matter pertaining to Elohim, and in the affairs of the melech.

27 Now the children of Yisrael after their number, the heads of the ahvot and commanders of thousands and hundreds, and their officers that served the melech in any matter of the divisions, that came in and went out month by month throughout all the months of the year, of every division were twenty four thousand. 2 Over the first course for the first month was Yashoveam the son of Zavdiel: and in his course were twenty four thousand. 3 Of the children of Perez was the chief of all the commanders of the host for the first month. 4 And over the course of the second month was Dodai an Ahohite, and of his course was Mikloth also the chief: in his course likewise were twenty four thousand. 5 The third commander of the army for the third month was Benayah the son of Yehoyada, a chief kohen: and in his course were twenty-four thousand. 6 This is that Benayah, who was mighty among the thirty, and above the thirty: and in his course was Ammizavad his son. 7 The fourth commander for the

fourth month was Asah-El the brother of Yoav, and Zevadyah his son after him: and in his course were twenty-four thousand. 8 The fifth commander for the fifth month was Shamhuth the Yizrahite: and in his division were twenty-four thousand. 9 The sixth commander for the sixth month was Ira the son of Ikkesh the Tekoite: and in his division were twenty-four thousand. 10 The seventh commander for the seventh month was Helez the Pelonite, of the children of Ephraim: and in his division were twenty-four thousand. 11 The eighth commander for the eighth month was Sibbecai the Hushathite, of the Zarhites: and in his division were twenty-four thousand. 12 The ninth commander for the ninth month was Aviezer the Anetothite, of the Benyamites: and in his division were twenty-four thousand. 13 The tenth commander for the tenth month was Maharai the Netophathite, of the Zarhites: and in his division were twenty-four thousand. 14 The eleventh commander for the eleventh month was Benayah the Pirathonite, of the children of Ephraim: and in his division were twenty-four thousand. 15 The twelfth commander for the twelfth month was Heldai the Netophathite, of Othni-El: and in his division were twenty-four thousand. 16 Furthermore over the tribes of Yisrael: the chief of the Reuvenites was Eliezer the son of Zichri: of the Shimeonites, Shephatyah the son of Maachah: 17 Of the Leviim, Hashavyah the son of Kemu-El: of the Aaronites, Tzadok: 18 Of Yahudah, Elihu, one of the brothers of David: of Yissachar, Omri the son of Micha-El: 19 Of Zevulun, Yishmayah the son of Ovadyah: of Naphtali, Yerimoth the son of Azri-El: 20 Of the children of Ephraim, Hoshea the son of Azazyah: of the half tribe of Menashsheh, Yoel the son of Pedayah: 21 Of the half tribe of Menashsheh in Gilead, Iddo the son of Zecharyah: of Benyamin, Yaasi-El the son of Avner: 22 Of Dan, Azar-El the son of Yeroham. These were the leaders of the tribes of Yisrael. 23 But David took not the number of them from twenty years old and under: because יהוה had said He would increase Yisrael like to the stars of the shamayim.[1] 24 Yoav the son of Tzeruyah began a census, but he did not finish, because wrath fell against Yisrael; neither was the number put in the account of the chronicles of melech David. 25 And over the melech's treasures was Azmaveth the son of Adi-El: and over the storehouses in the fields, in the cities, and in the villages, and in the castles, was Yehonathan the son of Uzziyah: 26 And over them that did the work of the field for tilling the ground was Ezri the son of Chelub: 27 And over the vineyards was Shimei the Ramathite: over the increase of the vineyards for the wine cellars was Zavdi the Shiphmite: 28 And over the olive trees and the sycomore trees that were in the low plains was Baal-hanan the Gederite: and over the stores of oil was Yoash: 29 And over the herds that fed in Sharon was Shitrai the Sharonite: and over the herds that were in the valleys was Shaphat the son of Adlai: 30 Over the camels also was Ovil the Yishmaelite: and over the donkeys was Yehdeyah the Meronothite: 31 And over the flocks was Yaziz the Hagerite. All these were the rulers of the property that was melech David's. 32 Also Yonathan David's uncle was a counselor, a wise man, and a sopher: and Yehi-El the son of Hachmoni was with the melech's sons: 33 And Ahithophel was the melech's counselor: and Hushai the Archite was the melech's companion: 34 And after Ahithophel was Yehoyada the son of Benayah, and Aviathar: and the general of the melech's army was Yoav.

28 And David assembled all the leaders of Yisrael, the leaders of the tribes, and the commanders of the companies that ministered to the melech by division, and the commanders over the thousands, and commanders over the

---

[1] David believed in the promise of physical multiplicity.

hundreds, and the stewards over all the substance and possessions of the melech, and his sons, with the officers, and with the mighty men, and with all the brave men, to Yahrushalayim. 2 Then David the melech stood up upon his feet, and said, Hear me, my brothers, and my people: As for me, I had in my lev to build a Bayit of rest for the Ark of the Covenant of יהוה, and for the footstool of our Elohim, and had made ready for the building: 3 But Elohim said to me, *You shall not build a Bayit for My Name, because you have been a man of war, and have shed dom.* 4 But יהוה Elohim of Yisrael chose me before all the bayit of my abba to be melech over Yisrael le-olam-va-ed: for He has chosen Yahudah to be the chief; and of the bayit of Yahudah, the bayit of my abba; and among the sons of my abba He was pleased with me to make me melech over all Yisrael: 5 And from all my sons, for יהוה has given me many sons, He has chosen Shlomo my son to sit upon the throne of the malchut of יהוה over Yisrael. 6 And He said to me, *Shlomo your son, he shall build My Bayit and My courts: for I have chosen him to be My son, and I will be His Abba. 7 Moreover I will establish his malchut le-olam-va-ed, if he is steadfast to do My commandments and My mishpatim, as at this day.* 8 Now therefore in the sight of all Yisrael, the congregation of יהוה, and in the audience of our Elohim, keep and seek for all the commandments of יהוה your Elohim: that you may possess this tov land, and leave it as an inheritance for your children after you le-olam-va-ed. 9 And you, Shlomo my son, know the Elohim of your abba, and serve Him with a perfect lev and with a willing mind: for יהוה searches all levim, and understands all the intents of the thoughts: if you seek Him, He will be found by you; but if you forsake Him, He will cast you off le-olam-va-ed. 10 Take heed now; for יהוה has chosen you to build a Bayit for the Set-Apart Place: be strong, and do it. 11 Then David gave to Shlomo his son the pattern of the porch, and

of the houses of it, and of the treasuries of it, and of the upper rooms of it, and of the inner parlors of it, and of the place of the rachamim seat, 12 And the pattern of all that he had by the Ruach, of the courts of the Bayit of יהוה, and of all the rooms all around, of the treasuries of the Bayit of Elohim, and of the treasuries of the set-apart things: 13 Also for the divisions of the kohanim and the Leviim, and for all the work of the service of the Bayit of יהוה, and for all the vessels of service in the Bayit of יהוה. 14 He gave of gold by weight for things of gold, for all instruments of all manner of service; silver also for all instruments of silver by weight, for all instruments of every kind of service: 15 Even the weight for the menorahs of gold, and for their lamps of gold, by weight for every menorah, and for the lamps of it: and for the menorahs of silver by weight, both for the menorah, and also for the lamps of it, according to the use of every menorah. 16 And by weight he gave gold for the table of the Lechem of His Faces, for every table; and likewise silver for the tables of silver: 17 Also pure gold for the forks, and the bowls, and the cups: and for the golden basons he gave gold by weight for every bason; and likewise silver by weight for every bason of silver: 18 And for the altar of incense refined-gold by weight, and gold for the pattern of the mirkavah of the cheruvim,[1] that spread out their wings, and covered the Ark of the Covenant of יהוה. 19 All this, said David, יהוה made me understand in writing by His hand upon me, even all the works of this pattern. 20 And David said to Shlomo his son, Be strong and of tov courage, and do it: fear not, nor be dismayed: for יהוה Elohim, even my Elohim, will be with you; He will not fail you, nor forsake you, until you have finished all the work for the service of the Bayit of יהוה. 21 And, behold, the divisions of the kohanim and the Leviim,

---

[1] The chariot ride into the eternal dom atonement of our Yahshua.

even they shall be with you for all the service of the Bayit of Elohim: and there shall be with you for all manner of work every willing skillful man, for any manner of service: also the leaders and all the people will be fully at your commandment.

29 Furthermore David the melech said to all the congregation, Shlomo my son, whom alone Elohim has chosen, is yet young and tender, and the work is great: for the palace is not for man, but for יהוה Elohim. 2 Now I have prepared with all my might for the Bayit of my Elohim the gold for things to be made of gold, and the silver for things of silver, and the bronze for things of bronze, the iron for things of iron, and wood for things of wood; onyx stones, and stones to be set, glistering stones, and divers colors, and all manner of precious stones, and marble stones in abundance. 3 Moreover, because I have set my affection to the Bayit of My Elohim, I have provided from my own posessions, gold and silver, that I have given to the Bayit of my Elohim, over and above all that I have prepared for the Set-Apart Bayit, 4 Even three thousand talents of gold, of the gold of Ophir, and seven thousand talents of refined silver, to overlay the walls of the Bayit: 5 The gold for things of gold, and the silver for things of silver, and for all manner of work to be made by the hands of craftsmen. And who then is willing to consecrate his service this day to יהוה? 6 Then the heads of the ahvot and leaders of the tribes of Yisrael, and the commanders of thousands and of hundreds, with the rulers of the melech's work, offered willingly, 7 And gave for the service of the Bayit of Elohim of gold five thousand talents and ten thousand darics, and of silver ten thousand talents, and of bronze eighteen thousand talents, and one hundred thousand talents of iron. 8 And those who had precious stones gave them to the treasury of the Bayit of יהוה, by the hand of Yehi-El the Gershonite. 9 Then the people had gilah, for they offered willingly, because with

perfect lev they offered willingly to יהוה: and David the melech also rejoiced with great simcha. 10 And David blessed יהוה before the entire congregation: and David said, Barchu-et, יהוה Elohim of Yisrael our Abba, le-olam-va-ed. 11 Yours, O יהוה, is the greatness, and the power, and the tiferet, and the victory, and the majesty: for all that is in the shamayim and on the earth is Yours; Yours is the malchut, O יהוה, and You are exalted as head above all. 12 Both riches and honor come from You, and You reign over all; and in Your hand is power and might; and in Your hand it is to make great, and to give strength to all. 13 Now therefore, our Elohim, we hodu You, and tehilla the tiferet of Your Name. 14 But who am I, and what are my people that we should be able to offer so willingly like this? For all things come from You, and of Your own have we given You. 15 For we are strangers before You, and sojourners, as were all our ahvot: our days on the earth are as a shadow, and without permanence. 16 O יהוה our Elohim, all this in store that we have prepared to build You a Bayit for Your Set-Apart Name comes from Your hand, and is all Your own. 17 I know also, My Elohim, that You try the levim, and have pleasure in uprightness. As for me, in the uprightness of my lev I have willingly offered all these things: and now have I seen with simcha Your people, who are present here, to offer willingly to You. 18 O יהוה Elohim of Avraham, Yitschaq, and of Yisrael, our ahvot, keep this le-olam-va-ed in the intent of the thoughts of the lev of Your people, and prepare their levim toward You: 19 And give to Shlomo my son a perfect lev, to keep Your commandments, Your testimonies, and Your statutes, and to do all these things, and to build the palace, for which I have made provision. 20 And David said to all the congregation, Now bless יהוה Your Elohim. And the entire congregation blessed יהוה Elohim of their ahvot, and bowed down their heads, and worshipped יהוה, and honored the melech.

21 And they sacrificed sacrifices to יהוה, and offered burnt offerings to יהוה, the next day, even a thousand bullocks, a thousand rams, and a thousand lambs, with their drink offerings, and sacrifices in abundance for all Yisrael: 22 And did eat and drink before יהוה on that day with great simcha. And they made Shlomo the son of David melech the second time, and anointed him to יהוה to be the chief leader, and Tzadok to be the kohen. 23 Then Shlomo sat on the throne of יהוה as melech instead of David his abba, and prospered; and all Yisrael obeyed him. 24 And all the leaders, and the mighty men, and all the sons of melech David, submitted themselves to Shlomo the melech. 25 And יהוה magnified Shlomo exceedingly in the sight of all Yisrael, and bestowed upon him such royal majesty as had not been on any melech before him in Yisrael. 26 So David the son of Yishai reigned over all Yisrael.[1] 27 And the time that he reigned over Yisrael was forty years; seven years he reigned in Hevron, and thirty-three years he reigned in Yahrushalayim. 28 And he died in a tov old age, full of days, riches, and honor: and Shlomo his son reigned in his place. 29 Now the acts of David the melech, from the first to the last last, behold, they are written in the scroll of Schmuel the seer, and in the Scroll of Nathan ha navi, and in the Scroll of Gad the seer,[2] 30 With all his reign and his might, and the times that passed over him, and over Yisrael, and over all the kingdoms of the countries.[3]

---

[1] The very words we long for in the work of Yahshua.
[2] These two scrolls are missing.
[3] David's malchut included more than just the land of Yisrael; it included many of the earth's known nations. Surely Yisraelite seed has been deposited in all those nations through assimilation, and forbidden intermarriage and sexual relations.

דברי הימים ב

Divre HaYamim Bet - Second Chronicles
To Our Forefathers Yisrael

1 And Shlomo the son of David was strengthened in his malchut, and יהוה his Elohim was with him, and made him exceedingly great. 2 Then Shlomo spoke to all Yisrael, to the captains of thousands and of hundreds, and to the shoftim, and to every leader in all Yisrael, the heads of the ahvot. 3 So Shlomo, and the entire congregation with him, went to the high place that was at Giveon; for there was the Tabernacle of the congregation of Elohim, which Moshe the eved of יהוה had made in the wilderness. 4 But the Ark of Elohim had David brought up from Kirjath-Yearim to the place that David had prepared for it: for he had pitched a tent for it at Yahrushalayim. 5 Moreover the bronze altar, that Betzal-el the son of Uri, the son of Hur, had made, he put before the Tabernacle of יהוה: and Shlomo and the congregation sought it. 6 And Shlomo went up there to the bronze altar before יהוה, which was at the Tabernacle of the congregation, and offered a thousand burnt offerings upon it. 7 In that night did Elohim appear to Shlomo, and said to him, Ask what I shall give you. 8 And Shlomo said to Elohim, You have showed great rachamim to David my abba, and have made me to reign in his place. 9 Now, O יהוה Elohim let Your promise to David my abba be established: for You have made me melech over a people like the dust of the earth in multitude.[1] 10 Give me now chochma and da'at, so that I may go out and come in before this people: for who can shophet this Your people, that is so great? 11 And Elohim said to Shlomo, *Because this was in your lev, and you have not asked riches, wealth, or honor, nor the chayim of your enemies, neither yet have you asked for long*

chayim for yourself; but have asked chochma and da'at for yourself, that you may shophet My people, over whom I have made you melech: 12 *Wisdom and da'at is granted to you; and I will give you riches, and wealth and honor, such as none of the melechim have had that have been before you; neither shall any have after you.* 13 Then Shlomo came from his journey to the high place that was at Giveon to Yahrushalayim, from before the Tabernacle of the congregation, and reigned over Yisrael. 14 And Shlomo gathered mirkavot and horsemen: and he had a thousand and four hundred mirkavot, and twelve thousand horsemen, which he placed in the mirkavah cities, and with the melech at Yahrushalayim. 15 And the melech made silver and gold at Yahrushalayim as plenty as stones, and cedar trees and sycomore trees that are in the plains for abundance. 16 And Shlomo had horses brought out of Mitzrayim, and linen yarn: the melech's merchants received the linen yarn at a price. 17 And they brought forth from Mitzrayim a mirkavah for six hundred shekels of silver, and an horse for an hundred fifty: and so they brought out horses for all the melechim of the Hittites, and for the melechim of Aram, by their own means.

2 And Shlomo determined to build a Bayit for the Name of יהוה, and a bayit for his malchut. 2 And Shlomo enrolled seventy thousand men to bear burdens, and eighty thousand to cut stone in the mountains, and three thousand six hundred to oversee them. 3 And Shlomo sent to Huram the melech of Tsor, saying, As you did deal with David my abba, and did send him cedars to build him a bayit to dwell in, even so deal with me. 4 See, I build a Bayit to the Name of יהוה My

---

[1] Shlomo refers to the promise of Genesis 13:16 knowing full well the promise of physical multiplicity.

Elohim, to dedicate it to Him, and to burn before Him sweet incense, and for the continual Lechem of the Faces, and for the burnt offerings for shachrit and maariv, and on the Shabbats, and on the Rosh Chodashim, and on the solemn moadim of יהוה our Elohim. This is an ordinance le-olam-va-ed to Yisrael. 5 And the Bayit that I build is great: for great is our Elohim above all elohim. 6 But who is able to build Him a Bayit, seeing the shamayim and the shamayim of shamayim cannot contain Him? Who am I then, that I should build Him a Bayit, except only to burn sacrifice before Him? 7 Send me now a man skilled to work in gold, and in silver, and in bronze, and in iron, and in purple, and crimson, and blue, and that can engrave with the skilled men that are with me in Yahudah and in Yahrushalayim, whom David my abba did provide. 8 Send me also cedar trees, cypress trees, and algum trees, out of Levanon: for I know that your avadim know how to cut timber in Levanon; and, see, my avadim shall be with your avadim, 9 Even to prepare for me timber in abundance: for the Bayit that I am about to build shall be wonderful and great. 10 And, see, I will give to your avadim, the cutters that cut timber, twenty thousand measures of ground wheat, and twenty thousand measures of barley, and twenty thousand baths of wine, and twenty thousand baths of oil. 11 Then Huram the melech of Tsor answered in writing, which he sent to Shlomo saying, Because יהוה has loved His people, He has made you melech over them. 12 Huram said moreover, Barch-et יהוה Elohim of Yisrael, that made the shamayim and earth, Who has given to David the melech a wise son, endued with chochma and binah, that might build a Bayit for יהוה, and a bayit for his malchut. 13 And now I have sent a skilled man, having binah, of Huram-Avi, 14 The son of a woman of the daughters of Dan, and his abba was a man of Tsor, [1] skillful in working with gold, with silver, with bronze, with iron, with stone, with timber, with purple, with blue, and with fine linen, and with crimson; also to engrave any kind of engraving, and to accomplish any plan given to him, with your skilled men, and with the skilled men of my master David your abba. 15 Now therefore the wheat, and the barley, the oil, and the wine, which my master has spoken of, let him send to his avadim: 16 And we will cut wood out of Levanon, as much as you shall need: and we will bring it to you in rafts by Sea to Yapho; and you shall carry it up to Yahrushalayim. 17 And Shlomo numbered all the gerim [2] that were in the land of Yisrael, according to the same numbering that David his abba had numbered them; and they were totaled up to be a hundred fifty three thousand six hundred gerim. 18 And he set seventy thousand of them to be bearers of burdens, and eighty thousand to be cutters in the mountain, and three thousand six hundred overseers to make the people work.

3 Then Shlomo began to build the Bayit of יהוה at Yahrushalayim on Mount Moriah, where יהוה appeared to David his abba, in the place that David had prepared in the threshing floor of Ornan the Yevusite. 2 And he began to build in the second day of the second month, in the fourth year of his reign. 3 Now these are the foundations that Shlomo laid for the building of the Bayit of Elohim. The length by cubits after the first measure was seventy cubits, and the width twenty cubits. 4 And the porch that was in the front of the Bayit, the length of it was according to the width of the bayit, twenty cubits, and the height was an hundred and twenty: and he covered the inside with pure gold. 5 And the greater

---

[1] A Yisraelite living in modern day Lebanon or ancient Tyre; Yisraelites already lived all over the world due to colonialism, as highlighted in the days of David and especially Solomon.
[2] The alien and stranger were always subject to second-class citizenship, in direct contradiction to Torah. Many Ephraimites were also later numbered to join these **gerim** as laborers for the House of David under Solomon, sowing even more cords of division within the nation.

bayit he paneled with cypress trees, which he covered with fine gold, and carved palm trees and flowers on it. 6 And he covered the bayit with precious stones for beauty: and the gold was gold of Parvayim. 7 He covered the bayit, the beams, the posts, and the walls, and the doors, with gold; and carved cheruvim on the walls. 8 And he made the Most Set-Apart Bayit, the length was the same as the width of the bayit, twenty cubits, and the width twenty cubits: and he covered it with fine gold, amounting to six hundred talents. 9 And the weight of the nails was fifty shekels of gold. And he covered the upper rooms with gold. 10 And in the Most Set-Apart Bayit he made two cheruvim of sculptured work, and covered them with gold.[1] 11 And the wings of the cheruvim were twenty cubits long: one wing of the one cheruv was five cubits, reaching to the wall of the bayit: and the other wing was likewise five cubits, reaching to the wing of the other cheruv.[2] 12 And one wing of the other cheruv was five cubits, reaching to the wall of the bayit: and the other wing was five cubits also, joining to the wing of the other cheruv.[3] 13 The wings of these cheruvim spread themselves forth twenty cubits: and they stood on their feet, and their faces were inward. 14 And he made the vail of blue, and purple, and crimson, and fine linen, and worked cheruvim on it. 15 Also he made before the Bayit two pillars thirty-five cubits high, and the capital that was on the top of each of them was five cubits. 16 And he made wreaths of chains, as in the speaking place, and put them on the heads of the pillars; and made a hundred pomegranates, and put them on the chains. 17 And he reared up the pillars before the Beit HaMikdash, one on the right hand, and the other on the left; and called the name of

the one on the right hand Yachin, and the name of the one on the left Boaz.[4]

4 Moreover he made an altar of bronze, twenty cubits was the length, and twenty cubits was the width, and ten cubits the height. 2 Also he made a molten Sea of ten cubits from brim to brim, round all about, and five cubits in height; and a line of thirty cubits measured all around. 3 And under it were figures like oxen, all around: ten in a cubit, all the way around the Sea. Two rows of oxen were cast, when it was cast. 4 It stood on twelve oxen, three looking toward the north, and three looking toward the west, and three looking toward the south, and three looking toward the east: and the Sea was set above upon them, and all their back parts were inward. 5 And the thickness of it was a handbreadth, and the brim of it like the work of the brim of a cup, with flowers of lilies; and it received and held three thousand baths. 6 He made also ten basins, and put five on the right hand, and five on the left, to wash in them:[5] such things as they offered for the burnt offering they washed in them; but the Sea was for the kohanim to wash in. 7 And he made ten menorahs of gold according to their form, and set them in the Beit HaMikdash, five on the right hand, and five on the left.[6] 8 He made also ten tables, and placed them in the Beit HaMikdash, five on the right side, and five on the left.[7] And he made an hundred bowls of gold. 9 Furthermore he made the court of the kohanim, and the great court, and doors for the court, and covered the doors with bronze. 10 And he set the Sea on the right side eastward, over against the south. 11 And Huram made the pots, and

---

[1] A type of the desired purity and holiness YHWH desires for both houses of Yisrael in His presence.
[2] Both houses are equally loved and treated with equal weights and measures by the Father.
[3] When both houses learn to touch each other in love and equity, then the presence of YHWH appears in our midst.

[4] Two pillars both symbolic of YHWH's congregation or the temple of His presence, being made up of two solid houses of Yisrael.
[5] Symbolic of the ten tribes being a divided people from the rest of Yisrael; needing washing by Yahshua to become one again.
[6] Symbolizing the division of the ten tribes of Yisrael, yet eventually reflecting the Light of Moshiach.
[7] Symbolizing the division of the ten tribes of Yisrael; yet eventually called to uphold the bread of life; the Moshiach.

the shovels, and the bowls. And Huram finished the work that he was to make for melech Shlomo for the Bayit of Elohim; 12 The two pillars, and the bowl-shaped capitals which were on the top of the two pillars, and the two wreaths to cover the two bowl-shaped capitals which were on the top of the pillars; 13 And four hundred pomegranates on the two wreaths; two rows of pomegranates on each wreath, to cover the two bowl-shaped capitals that were upon the pillars. 14 He made also stands, and made basins upon the stands; 15 One Sea, and twelve oxen under it. 16 The pots also, and the shovels, and the forks, and all their instruments, did Huram his master craftsman make to melech Shlomo for the Bayit of יהוה of bright bronze. 17 In the plain of the Yarden did the melech cast them, in the clay ground between Succoth and Tzeredathah. 18 So Shlomo made all these vessels in great abundance: for the weight of the bronze could not be discovered. 19 And Shlomo made all the vessels that were for the Bayit of Elohim, the golden altar also, and the tables on which the Lechem of The Faces was set; 20 Moreover the menorahs with their lamps of pure gold, that they should burn after the correct manner before the Speaking Place, 21 And the flowers, and the lamps, and the snuffers, he made of gold, of perfect gold; 22 And the snuffers, and the bowls, and the spoons, and the censers, of pure gold: and the entry of the Bayit, the inner doors for the Most Set-Apart place, and the doors of the Bayit of the Beit HaMikdash, were of gold.

5 Then all the work that Shlomo made for the Bayit of יהוה was finished: and Shlomo brought in all the things that David his abba had dedicated; and the silver, and the gold, and all the instruments, he put among the treasures of the Bayit of Elohim. 2 Then Shlomo assembled the zachanim of Yisrael, and all the heads of the tribes, the leaders of the ahvot of the children of Yisrael, to Yahrushalayim, to bring up the Ark of the Covenant of יהוה out of the city of David, which is Tzion. 3 Therefore all the men of Yisrael assembled themselves to the melech in the moed that was in the seventh month. 4 And all the zachanim of Yisrael came; and the Leviim took up the Ark. 5 And they brought up the Ark, and the Tabernacle of the congregation, and all the set-apart vessels that were in the Tabernacle, these did the kohanim and the Leviim bring up. 6 Also melech Shlomo, and all the congregation of Yisrael that were assembled to him before the Ark, sacrificed sheep and oxen, which could not be counted or numbered for multitude. 7 And the kohanim brought in the Ark of the Covenant of יהוה to His place, to the Speaking Place of the Bayit, into the Most Set-Apart Place, even under the wings of the cheruvim: 8 For the cheruvim spread forth their wings over the place of the Ark, and the cheruvim covered the Ark and the poles. 9 And they drew out the poles of the Ark, that the ends of the poles were seen from the Ark before the Speaking Place; but they were not seen from outside the veil. And there it is to this day. 10 There was nothing in the Ark except the two tablets that Moshe put in at Horeb, when יהוה made a Covenant with the children of Yisrael, when they came out of Mitzrayim. 11 And it came to pass, when the kohanim were come out of the Set-Apart Place - for all the kohanim that were present were set-apart, and did not yet serve by their assigned division - 12 Also the Leviim who were the singers, all of them of Asaph, of Heman, of Yeduthun, with their sons and their brothers, being dressed in white linen, having cymbals and lyres and harps, stood at the east end of the altar, and with them a hundred and twenty kohanim sounding with shofars: 13 It came even to pass, as the shofar blowers and singers were as echad, to make one sound to be heard in tehilla and hodu to יהוה; when they lifted up their voice with the shofars and cymbals and

instruments of music, and gave tehilla to to **יהוה** , saying, For He is tov; for His chesed endures le-olam-va-ed: that then the Bayit was filled with a cloud, even the Bayit of **יהוה**; 14 So that the kohanim were not able to stand to serve because of the cloud: for the tiferet of **יהוה** filled the Bayit of Elohim.

6 Then said Shlomo, **יהוה** has said that He would dwell in the thick darkness. 2 But I have built a Bayit of dwelling for You, and a place for Your dwelling le-olam-va-ed. 3 And the melech turned his face, and blessed the whole congregation of Yisrael: and all the congregation of Yisrael stood. 4 And he said, Blessed be **יהוה** Elohim of Yisrael, who has with His hands fulfilled that which He spoke with His mouth to my abba David, saying, 5 *Since the day that I brought forth My people out of the land of Mitzrayim I chose no city among all the tribes of Yisrael to build a Bayit in, that My Name might be there; neither chose I any man to be a ruler over My people Yisrael: 6 But I have chosen Yahrushalayim, that My Name might be there;[1] and have chosen David to be over My people Yisrael.* 7 Now it was in the lev of David my abba to build a Bayit for the Name of **יהוה**[2] Elohim of Yisrael. 8 But **יהוה** said to David my abba, *Since it was in your lev to build a Bayit for My Name, you did well in that it was in your lev:* 9 *But you shall not build the Bayit; but your son who shall come forth out of your loins, he shall build the Bayit for My Name.* 10 Now **יהוה** therefore has performed His word that He has spoken: for I have risen up in the place of David my abba, and am set on the throne of Yisrael, as **יהוה** promised, and have built the Bayit for the Name of **יהוה** Elohim of Yisrael. 11 And in it I have put the Ark, in which is the Covenant of **יהוה**, that He made with the children of Yisrael.

12 And he stood before the altar of **יהוה** in the presence of all the congregation of Yisrael, and spread forth his hands:[3] 13 For Shlomo had made a bronze scaffold, of five cubits long, and five cubits wide, and three cubits high, and had set it in the middle of the court: and upon it he stood, and kneeled down upon his knees before all the congregation of Yisrael, and spread forth his hands toward the shamayim, 14 And said, O **יהוה** Elohim of Yisrael, there is no Elohim like You in the shamayim, nor on the earth; who keeps Covenant, and shows rachamim to Your avadim, that have their halacha before You with all their levim: 15 You who have kept with Your eved David my abba that which You have promised him; and spoke with Your mouth, and have fulfilled it with Your hand, as it is this day. 16 Now therefore, O **יהוה** Elohim of Yisrael, keep with Your eved David my abba that which You have promised him, saying, There shall not cease a man from your lineage in My sight to sit upon the throne of Yisrael; yet only if your children take heed to their way to have their halacha in My Torah, as you have had your halacha before Me. 17 Now then, O **יהוה** Elohim of Yisrael, let Your word be verified, which You have spoken to Your eved David. 18 But will Elohim indeed dwell with men on the earth? See, the shamayim and the shamayim of shamayim cannot contain You; how much less this Bayit which I have built! 19 Have respect therefore to the tefillah of Your eved, and to his supplication, O **יהוה** My Elohim, to shema to the cry and the tefillah that Your eved brings before You: 20 That Your eyes may be open upon this Bayit day and night, upon the place of which You have said that You would put Your Name there; to shema to the tefillah which Your eved prays toward this place. 21 Shema therefore to the supplications of Your eved, and of Your people Yisrael, which they shall make

---

[1] YHWH attaches great significance to His Name finding rest among His true people.
[2] Is your congregation building or home a house dedicated for and to His true Name YHWH?

[3] In Hebraic understanding, he is transferring all the power and manifestations of YHWH to the people.

toward this place: and shema from Your dwelling place, even from the shamayim; and when You shema, forgive. 22 If a man sin against his neighbor, and an oath be laid upon him to make him swear, and the oath come before Your altar in this Bayit; 23 Then shema from the shamayim, and do, and shophet Your avadim, by repaying the wicked, by recompensing his way upon his own head; and by justifying the tzadik, by giving him according to his tzedakah. 24 And if Your people Yisrael be smitten before their enemy, because they have sinned against You; and shall make teshuvah and confess Your Name, [1] and make tefillah and supplication before You in this Bayit; 25 Then shema from the shamayim, and forgive the sin of Your people Yisrael, and bring them again to the land which You gave to them and to their ahvot. 26 When the shamayim are shut up, and there is no rain, because they have sinned against You; yet if they make tefillah toward this place, and confess Your Name,[2] and teshuvah from their sin, when You do afflict them; 27 Then shema from the shamayim, and forgive the sin of Your avadim, and of Your people Yisrael, when You have taught them the tov halacha, in which they should have their halacha; and send rain upon Your land, which You have given to Your people for an inheritance. 28 If there be famine in the land, if there be pestilence, if there be blight, or mildew, locusts, or grasshoppers; if their enemies besiege them in the cities of their land; or if there be any plague or sickness: 29 Then whatever tefillah or whatever supplication shall be made by any man, or of all Your people Yisrael, when each one shall know his own plague and his own grief, and shall spread forth his hands to this Bayit: 30 Then shema from the shamayim Your dwelling place, and forgive, and render to every man according to all his halachot, whose lev You alone know; for You alone know the levim

of the children of men: 31 That they may fear You, to have their halacha in Your ways, so long as they live in the land which You gave to our ahvot. 32 Moreover concerning the stranger, which is not of Your people Yisrael, but is come from a far country for Your great Name's sake,[3] and Your mighty hand, and Your stretched-out Arm; if they come and make tefillah in this Bayit; 33 Then shema from the shamayim, even from Your dwelling place, and do according to all that the stranger calls to You for; that all people of the earth may know Your Name,[4] and fear You, as does Your people Yisrael, and may know that this Bayit which I have built is called by Your Name. 34 If Your people go out to war against their enemies by the way that You shall send them, and they make tefillah to You toward this city that You have chosen, and the Bayit which I have built for Your Name; 35 Then shema from the shamayim their tefillah and their supplication, and maintain their cause. 36 If they sin against You, for there is no man which sins not, and You are angry with them, and deliver them over to their enemies, and they carry them away captives[5] to a land far off or near;[6] 37 Yet if they think of their errors in the land where they are carried captive, and make teshuvah and make tefillah to You in the land of their captivity, saying, We have sinned, we have done wrong, and have dealt wickedly; 38 If they return to You with all their lev and with all their being in the land of their captivity, where they have been carried captives, and make tefillah toward their land, which You gave to their ahvot, and toward the city which You have chosen, and toward the Bayit which I have built for Your Name: 39 Then shema from the

---

[1] Notice that true confession cannot happen apart from YHWH's true Name.
[2] Confession must occur in YHWH's true Name.
[3] Notice that those far-away strangers truly seeking YHWH, are actually drawn – and never repulsed – by the truth of the true Name.
[4] Foreigners are sent out to declare the Name in their nations.
[5] Exile is considered the ultimate discipline by YHWH towards Yisrael.
[6] Two-house reference; as "far off" refers to Ephraim and "near" to Judah.

shamayim, even from Your dwelling place, their tefillah and their supplications, and maintain their cause, and forgive Your people who have sinned against You. [1] 40 Now, my Elohim, let, I beg You, Your eyes be open, and let Your ears be attentive to the tefillah that is made in this place. 41 Now therefore arise, O יהוה Elohim, into Your resting place, You, and the Ark of Your strength: let Your kohanim, O יהוה Elohim, be clothed with salvation, and let Your kidushim gilah in Your tov. 42 O יהוה Elohim, turn not away the face of Your anointed: remember the rachamim of David Your eved.

7 Now when Shlomo had made an end of making tefillah, the fire came down from the shamayim, and consumed the burnt offering and the sacrifices; and the tiferet of יהוה filled the Bayit. 2 And the kohanim could not enter into the Bayit of יהוה, because the tiferet of יהוה had filled יהוה's Bayit. 3 And when all the children of Yisrael saw how the fire came down, and the tiferet of יהוה upon the Bayit, they bowed themselves with their faces to the ground upon the pavement, and worshipped, and gave tehilla to יהוה, saying, For He is tov; for His chesed endures le-olam-va-ed. 4 Then the melech and all the people offered sacrifices before יהוה. 5 And melech Shlomo offered a sacrifice of twenty-two thousand oxen, and a hundred twenty thousand sheep: so the melech and all the people dedicated the Bayit of Elohim. 6 And the kohanim waited on their offices: the Leviim also with the instruments of music for יהוה, which David the melech had made to give tehilla to יהוה, because His chesed endures le-olam-va-ed, when David gave tehilla also by their hands; and the kohanim sounded shofars before them, and all Yisrael stood. 7 Moreover Shlomo set apart the middle of the court that was before the Bayit of יהוה:

for there he offered burnt offerings, and the fat of the shalom offerings, because the bronze altar which Shlomo had made was not able to receive the burnt offerings, and the meat offerings, and the fat. 8 Also at the same time Shlomo kept the moed seven days, and all Yisrael with him, a very great congregation, from the entering in of Hamath to the river of Mitzrayim.[2] 9 And in the eighth day they made a miqra kodesh: for they kept the dedication of the altar seven days, and the moed seven days. 10 And on the twenty-third day of the seventh month he sent the people away into their tents, with simcha and happy levim; for the tov that יהוה had showed to David, and to Shlomo, and to Yisrael His people. 11 So Shlomo finished the Bayit of יהוה, and the melech's bayit: and all that entered into Shlomo's lev to make in the Bayit of יהוה, and in his own bayit, he prosperously accomplished. 12 And יהוה appeared to Shlomo by night, and said to him, *I have heard your tefillah, and have chosen this place to Myself for a Bayit of sacrifice. 13 If I shut up the shamayim that there is no rain, or if I command the locusts to devour the land, or if I send pestilence among My people; 14 If My people, who are called by My Name,[3] shall humble themselves, and make tefillah, and seek My face, and teshuvah from their wicked ways; then will I shema from the shamayim, and will forgive their sin, and will heal their land. 15 Now My eyes shall be open, and My ears attentive to the tefillah that is made in this place. 16 For now have I chosen and set-apart this Bayit, that My Name may be there le-olam-va-ed: and My eyes and My*

---

[1] A promise to the exiles of Yisrael, that their tefillot will always be heard if they face home.

[2] Many Yisraelites came, including those from other nations such as Egypt. Yisrael has always been a mixed seed in all nations, even before there was such a term or person known as a Jew, or the official two-house division.

[3] Most anti-Torah and anti-True Name believers love to quote this verse as some sort of a "fix all" to their needs or problems. The only problem here is that YHWH says He will only hear His people called by His Name. Since this was given in a First Covenant context before the revelation of the Name of Yahshua, that Name must be YHWH. Moreover, Yahshua came in the Father's Name to make it binding on us, the people of Renewed Covenant Yisrael, in our own walk with Him.

lev shall be there perpetually. 17 And as for you, if you will have your halacha before Me, as David your abba had his halacha before Me, and do according to all that I have commanded you, and shall observe My chukim and My mishpatim; 18 Then will I establish the throne of your malchut, as I have covenanted with David your abba, saying, There shall not cease from your lineage a man to be ruler in Yisrael. 19 But if you turn away, and forsake My chukim and My mishpatim, which I have set before you, and shall go and serve other elohim, and worship them; 20 Then will I pluck them up by the roots out of My land which I have given them; and this Bayit, which I have set apart for My Name, will I cast out of My sight, and will make it to be a proverb and a mockery among all nations. 21 And this Bayit, which is high, shall be an astonishment to everyone that passes by it; so that they shall say, Why has יהוה *done this to this land, and to this Bayit? 22 And it shall be answered, Because they forsook* יהוה *Elohim of their ahvot, who brought them forth out of the land of Mitzrayim, and laid hold on other elohim, and worshipped them, and served them: therefore has He brought all this evil upon them*

8 And it came to pass at the end of twenty years, that Shlomo had built the Bayit of יהוה, and his own bayit, 2 That the cities that Huram had restored to Shlomo, Shlomo built them, and caused the children of Yisrael to dwell there.[1] 3 And Shlomo went to Hamath-Tzovah, and prevailed against it. 4 And he built Tadmor in the wilderness, and all the storage cities, which he built in Hamath. 5 Also he built Beth-Horon the upper, and Beth-Horon the lower, fenced cities, with walls, gates, and bars; 6 And Baalath, and all the storage cities that Shlomo had, and all the mirkavah cities, and the cities of the horsemen, and all that Shlomo desired to build in Yahrushalayim, and in Levanon,[2] and throughout all the lands of his rule.[3] 7 As for all the people that were left of the Hittites, and the Amorites, and the Perizzites, and the Hivites, and the Yevusites, who were not of Yisrael, 8 But of their children, who were left after them in the land, whom the children of Yisrael did not destroy, Shlomo made them compulsory labor until this day. 9 But of the children of Yisrael did Shlomo make no avadim for his work; but they were men of war, and heads of his captains, and captains of his mirkavot and horsemen. 10 And these were the rulers of melech Shlomo's officers, even two hundred fifty, that ruled over the people. 11 And Shlomo brought up the daughter of Pharaoh out of the city of David to the bayit that he had built for her: for he said, My wife shall not dwell in the bayit of David melech of Yisrael, because the place is set-apart, where the Ark of יהוה has come to rest. 12 Then Shlomo offered burnt offerings to יהוה on the altar of יהוה, that he had built before the porch, 13 Even according to the daily requirement, offering according to the mishpatim of Moshe, on the Shabbats, and on the Rosh Chodashim, and on the shalosh regalim, three times in the year, even in the moed of Pesach, and in the moed of Shavout, and in the moed of Sukkot. 14 And he appointed, according to the order of David his abba, the courses of the kohanim to their service, and the Leviim to their charges, to give tehilla and serve before the kohanim, as the duty of each day required: the gatekeepers also by their courses at every gate: for so had David the man of Elohim commanded. 15 And they departed not from the commandment of the melech to the kohanim and Leviim concerning any matter, or concerning the

---

[1] Solomon settles Yisraelites in the areas that would later become part of Phoenicia. That nation would grow into a huge nation with many documented Yisraelite ties. Phoenicia had colonies across the globe and formed an alliance with Solomon, allowing for international colonies and trade. Read more in: The Lost Ten Tribes Of Israel Chapter 2 By Steven M Collins.

[2] The early colony that later incorporated many Yisraelites.
[3] Yisraelites settled in many lands and no doubt assimilated with local populations, furthering the seeding of all nations with Yisrael's seed.

treasures. 16 Now all the work of Shlomo was prepared from the day of the foundation of the Bayit of יהוה, until it was finished. So the Bayit of יהוה was perfected. 17 Then went Shlomo to Ezion-GeVer, and to Eloth, at the seaside in the land of Edom.[1] 18 And Huram sent him by the hands of his avadim ships, and avadim that had knowledge of the sea; and they went with the avadim of Shlomo to Ophir,[2] and took from there four hundred fifty talents of gold, and brought them to melech Shlomo.

9 And when the malcha of Sheba heard of the fame of Shlomo, she came to prove Shlomo with hard questions at Yahrushalayim, with a very great company,[3] and camels that carried spices, and gold in abundance, and precious stones: and when she was come to Shlomo, she communed with him all that was in her lev. 2 And Shlomo answered all her questions: and there was nothing hidden from Shlomo which he told her not. 3 And when the malcha of Sheba had seen the chochma of Shlomo, and the Bayit that he had built, 4 And the food of his table, and the sitting of his avadim, and the service of his waiters and, and their attire; his cupbearers also, and their attire; and the ascent by which he went up into the Bayit of יהוה; there was no more ruach in her. 5 And she said to the melech, It was a true report which I heard in my own land of your acts, and of your chochma: 6 But I believed not their words, until I came, and my eyes have seen it: and, see, not even half of the greatness of your

chochma was told to me: for you far exceed the fame that I heard. 7 Blessed are your men, and blessed are these: Your avadim that stand continually before you, and shema your chochma. 8 Blessed be יהוה Your Elohim, who delighted in you to set you on His throne, to be melech for יהוה Your Elohim: because Your Elohim loved Yisrael, to establish them le-olam-va-ed, therefore He made you melech over them, to do mishpat and justice. 9 And she gave the melech a hundred twenty talents of gold, and of spices great abundance, and precious stones: neither was there any other similar spices as the kind the malcha of Sheba gave melech Shlomo. 10 And the avadim also of Huram, and the avadim of Shlomo, who brought gold from Ophir, brought algum trees and precious stones. 11 And the melech made from the algum trees stairs to the Bayit of יהוה, and to the melech's palace, and harps and lyres for singers: and there were none such as these seen before in the land of Yahudah. 12 And melech Shlomo gave to the malcha of Sheba all her desires, whatever she asked, beside that which she had brought to the melech. So she returned, and went away to her own land, she and her avadim. 13 Now the weight of gold that came to Shlomo in one year was six hundred sixty-six talents of gold; 14 Beside that which traders and merchants brought. And all the melechim of Arabia[4] and rulers of the countries brought gold and silver to Shlomo. 15 And melech Shlomo made two hundred shields of beaten gold: six hundred shekels of beaten gold went into one shield. 16 And three hundred shields he made of beaten gold: three hundred shekels of gold went into one shield. And the melech put them in the bayit of the forest of Levanon. 17 Moreover the melech made a great throne of ivory, and covered it with pure gold. 18 And there

---

[1] Non-Yisraelite areas conquered by David who turned them into settlements of Yisraelites; These Yisraelites mixed with local Edomites, Arameans, Ammonites, Tzidonians and many other nations. Much of the promise of physical multiplicity began to take place during Solomon's global reign, by colonization prior to exile.

[2] Much speculation about the location of Ophir; some say America, but certainly a far-off land across the seas where Yisraelites settled.

[3] That would become mixed with Yisraelite seed as per the historical accounts of the Queen and her people. And. According to Ethiopian tradition, Sheba (called Makeda) married Solomon, and their son, Menelik the First, founded the royal dynasty of Ethiopia. For more details, see note on First Kings 10:13.

[4] Yisraelites settled throughout Arabia and the Persian Gulf as well. It is easy to see how YHWH began to fill all nations with Yisrael's seed. Over the course of thousands of years, this seed exploded in each and every place they settled; as they did in Egypt, causing the first historic Egyptian exodus.

were six steps to the throne, with a footstool of gold, which were fastened to the throne, and stays on each side of the sitting place, and two lions standing by the armrests: [1] 19 And twelve lions stood there on the one side and on the other upon the six steps. There was not the like made in any malchut. 20 And all the drinking vessels of melech Shlomo were of gold, and all the vessels of the bayit of the forest of Levanon were of pure gold: none were of silver; for silver had little value in the days of Shlomo. 21 For the melech's ships went to Tarshish with the avadim of Huram: [2] once every three years came the ships of Tarshish bringing gold, and silver, ivory, and apes, and peacocks. 22 And melech Shlomo passed all the melechim of the earth in riches and chochma. 23 And all the melechim of the earth sought the presence of Shlomo, [3] to shema the chochma that Elohim had put in his lev. 24 And they brought every man his present, vessels of silver, and vessels of gold, and clothing, armor, and spices, horses, and mules, year by year. [4] 25 And Shlomo had four thousand stalls for horses and mirkavot, and twelve thousand horsemen; whom he stationed in the mirkavah cities, and with the melech at Yahrushalayim. 26 And he reigned over all the melechim [5] from the river even to the land of the Philistines, and to the border of Mitzrayim. [6] 27 And the melech made silver in Yahrushalayim as stones, and cedar trees he made as plenty as the sycamore trees that are in the low plains. 28 And they brought to Shlomo horses out of Mitzrayim, and out of all lands. [7] [8] 29 Now the rest of the acts of Shlomo, first and last, are they not written in the scroll of Nathan the navi, [9] and in the prophecy of Ahiyah the Shilonite, and in the visions of Iddo the seer against Yerovoam the son of Nebat? 30 And Shlomo reigned in Yahrushalayim over all Yisrael for forty years. 31 And Shlomo slept with his ahvot, and he was buried in the city of David his abba: and Rehovoam his son reigned in his place.

10 And Rehovoam went to Shechem: for to Shechem all Yisrael had come to make him melech. [10] 2 And it came to pass, when Yerovoam the son of Nebat, who was in Mitzrayim, where he had fled from the presence of Shlomo the melech, heard it, that Yerovoam returned out of Mitzrayim. 3 And they sent and called him. So Yerovoam and all Yisrael came and spoke to Rehovoam, saying, 4 Your abba made our yoke hard: now therefore lighten the hard service of your abba, and his heavy yoke that he put upon us, and we will serve you. 5 And he said to them, Return to me after three days. And the people departed. 6 And melech Rehovoam took counsel with the elderly men that had stood before Shlomo his abba while he yet lived, saying, What counsel do you give me to return an answer to this people? 7 And they spoke to him, saying, If you are kind to this people, and please them, and speak tov words to

---

[1] See note on First Kings 10:19-20.
[2] Europe and Spain in particular. Many Yisraelites oversaw the colonies set up across the Mediterranean Ocean, settling there as well. Europe housed many Yisraelite traders, who came and went; thus beginning a large Yisraelite representation in Europe. From history we know, that many of these same Yisraelite settlers and traders found their way from Europe to the New World, including America and North America.
[3] All means all. We see Yisrael's influence being global, with all kings serving Solomon as vassal states or colonies of Yisraelite settlement. These gifts could have been a combination of tribute and free-will gifts.
[4] This appears to be some sort of annual tribute and gift. The fact that all kings and nations brought annual gifts is a clear indication of the scope and size of this vast empire. Historians through s.a.tan's deception, have continually underplayed and misrepresented Solomon's empire, limiting it to an empire based solely in the Middle East, as opposed to all continents. This was done for many reasons, some anti-Semitic; nevertheless, the result has been to obscure and blur the truth of the promise to turn all the world's nations into the offspring of Jacocb.
[5] Yisrael reigned over all the world's kings and all of the Middle East from the Euphrates to the Mediterranean to Egypt and Lebanon in the north.

[6] Not only was Yisrael's seed mixed in Egypt from the time of the exodus, but also Solomon married Pharoh's daughter. So Egypt can be added as another nation, though Hamite in origin that became filled with Yisraelite offspring.
[7] All kings from all the earth's lands brought horses indicating that Yisraelite influence as a colonial power extended to all these lands.
[8] For more details, see The Lost Ten Tribes Found by Steven M. Collins 1992 CPA Books Boring Oregon.
[9] Missing scroll.
[10] Both houses attempted to continue to be one.

them, they will be your avadim le-olam-va-ed. 8 But he forsook the counsel that the elderly men gave him, and took counsel with the young men that were brought up with him, that stood before him. 9 And he said to them, What advice do you give me so I can return an answer to this people, who have spoken to me, saying, Lighten the yoke that your abba did put upon us? 10 And the young men that were brought up with him spoke to him, saying, This shall you answer the people that spoke to you, saying, Your abba made our yoke heavy, but you make it light for us; Say my little finger shall be thicker than my abba's loins. 11 Now my abba put a heavy yoke upon you, I will surely add to your yoke: my abba chastised you with whips, but I will chastise you with scorpions. 12 So Yerovoam and all the people came to Rehovoam on the third day, as the melech commanded, saying, Come again to me on the third day. 13 And the melech answered them harshly; and melech Rehovoam forsook the counsel of the elderly men, 14 And answered them after the advice of the young men, saying, My abba made your yoke heavy, but I will add to it: my abba chastised you with whips, but I will chastise you with scorpions. 15 So the melech listened not to the people: for the cause and turn of events was from Elohim, so that יהוה might perform His word, which He spoke by the hand of Ahiyah the Shilonite to Yerovoam the son of Nebat.[1][2] 16 And when all Yisrael

saw that the melech would not shema to them, the people answered the melech, saying, What portion have we in David?[3] And we have no inheritance in the son of Yishai: every man to your tents,[4] O Yisrael: and now, David, see to your own bayit.[5] So all Yisrael went to their tents.[6] 17 But as for the children of Yisrael that dwelt in the cities of Yahudah, Rehovoam reigned over them.[7] 18 Then melech Rehovoam sent Hadoram that was over the compulsory labor; and the children of Yisrael stoned him with stones, that he died.[8] But melech Rehovoam rushed to get up to his mirkavah, to flee to Yahrushalayim. 19 And Yisrael[9] rebelled against the bayit of David to this day.[10]

11 And when Rehovoam had come to Yahrushalayim, he gathered of the bayit of Yahudah and Benyamin a hundred eighty thousand chosen men, who were warriors, to fight against Yisrael, that he might bring back the malchut again to Rehovoam. 2 But the word of יהוה came to

being hidden or camouflaged in and among the gentiles as gentiles.
[2] First Kings 12:12 serves as a second Torah witness of YHWH's will and hand in the division.
[3] Ephraim's jealousy towards Judah, that the king is a descendent of Judah. This jealousy will never go away until Moshiach removes it from Ephraim's believing offspring, as outlined in Isaiah 11:13-14.
[4] Feelings of inferiority, among Ephraim.
[5] Ephraim tells Judah to get lost, just like the Jewish king Rehovoam told them to get chained in added compulsory labor.
[6] And eventually YHWH moved these tents into the nations.
[7] Second Chronicles 10:17 states that some Ephraimites lived in Judah. That is accepted. The only Yisraelites who did not return to their tents (in Yisrael), were those already settled in Judah. These folks returned home to their tents in Judah, where Rehoboam reigned. To put it another way, all northern Yisraelites went back north, except for those previously submitted to Rehoboam in the cities of Judah. Only some, who already lived in Judah, returned to Judah. This verse does not prove – or even hint at – a past full reunion of the two houses of Yisrael.
[8] The ultimate manifestation of jealousy is murder. This pattern is often repeated in our nation's history. Judah enslaves Ephraim or makes them feel like second-class citizens under tribute, and then Ephraim lashes out in jealousy and kills Jews. Only in our day and later on through Yahshua's return, will we see this pattern of conduct finally ended.
[9] Ephraim-Yisrael.
[10] This is an ongoing prophecy as Ephraim rebels in many ways, not the least of which is changing the Torah and separating themselves from the rest of Yisrael, into such abominations as Sunday worship and many other unclean practices.

[1] YHWH caused the split and division of the monarchy into two separate Yisraelite houses. It was His will for these events to take place for many small reasons, with the overriding one being that this was His designated and chosen method by which to fulfill covenant to the patriarchs, that the nations of the world would become Yisraelite nations, filled with Jacob's offspring. While there were many methods or circumstances that YHWH could have used, and in smaller ways did use, the overriding method by which He chose to accomplish that plan for this age was through the preordained division and scattering of both houses of Yisrael into global exile. Here we see the confirmation of the plan. The end result of the plan was that the world's nations or gentiles, would look, act, and behave, just like the Yisraelite settlers among them, and that Yisrael would be camouflaged among the nations, with most Yisraelites looking and acting like their gentile counterparts. This was both a prophetic measure, as well as a protective measure; guaranteeing that Yisrael's seed could never be eliminated by massive persecutions or killings, due to their

Shemayah the man of Elohim, saying, 3 *Speak to Rehovoam the son of Shlomo, melech of Yahudah, and to all Yisrael in Yahudah and Benyamin, saying,* [1] 4 *This says* יהוה*, You shall not go up, nor fight against your brothers: return every man to his bayit: for this matter of the division is from Me.* [2] And they obeyed the words of יהוה , and returned from going against Yerovoam. 5 And Rehovoam dwelt in Yahrushalayim, and built cities for defence in Yahudah. 6 He built even Beth-Lechem, and Etam, and Tekoa, 7 And Beth-Zur, and Shoco, and Adullam, 8 And Gath, and Mareshah, and Ziph, 9 And Adoraim, and Lachish, and Azekah, 10 And Tzorah, and Aiyalon, and Hevron, which are fenced cities in Yahudah and in Benyamin. 11 And he fortified the strongholds, and put captains in them, and stores of food, and oil and wine. 12 And in every city he put shields and spears, and made them exceedingly strong, having Yahudah and Benyamin on his side. 13 And the kohanim and the Leviim that were in all Yisrael resorted to him out of all their coasts. 14 For the Leviim left their suburbs and their possession, and came to Yahudah and Yahrushalayim: [3] for Yerovoam and his sons had ordered them to cease from executing the kohen's office to יהוה :

15 And he ordained for himself priests for the high places, and for the goats, and for the calves that he had made. 16 And after them out of all the tribes of Yisrael such as set their levim to seek יהוה Elohim of Yisrael came to Yahrushalayim, to sacrifice to יהוה Elohim of their ahvot. [4] 17 So they strengthened the malchut of Yahudah, and made Rehovoam the son of Shlomo strong for three years: for three years they had his halacha in the way of David and Shlomo. 18 And Rehovoam took him Mahalath the daughter of Yerimoth the son of David to be his wife, and Abihayil the daughter of Eliav the son of Yishai; 19 Who bore him children; Yeush, and Shamariyah, and Zaham. 20 And after her he took Maachah the daughter of Avshalom; who bore him Aviyah, and Attai, and Ziza, and Shelomith. 21 And Rehovoam loved Maachah the daughter of Avshalom above all his wives and his concubines: for he took eighteen wives, and sixty concubines; and begat twenty-eight sons, and sixty daughters. 22 And Rehovoam made Aviyah the son of Maachah the head, to be ruler among his brothers: for he thought about making him melech. 23 And he dealt wisely, and dispersed from among all his children throughout all the countries of Yahudah and Benyamin, to every fenced city: and he gave them food in abundance. And he sought many wives for them. [5]

12 And it came to pass, when Rehovoam had established the malchut, and had strengthened himself, he forsook the Torah of יהוה, and all Yisrael

---

[1] See Note on Second Chronicles 10:17.
[2] The Father created this clear historical boundary in 921 BCE and only He can penetrate the boundaries of division and ultimately bring healing. 1 Kings 11:11-12, 26, 31-35, 1 Kings 12:24, 1 Kings 12:15, 24 and 2 Chronicles 11:4, all cry out loud to any truth-seeker, that the impenetrable boundaries between both houses were created by YHWH according to His will. As Sovereign, He also chose not to fully heal that animosity and division, until after the coming of His beloved Son Yahshua, the greater and latter-day David. Ephesians 2:11-22 cannot be any clearer. It is YHWH's desire that the two sets of Commonwealth Israelites, "those near" (Judah), still in the land when Ephesians was written, and "those far" (House of Israel-Ephraim globally scattered), are made one, after enmity prevailed for about 1,000 years before Yahshua. Ephesians chapter two brings full light to Yisrael's full end-time restoration as does John 10:16.
[3] More cross-migration is seen. The priests and levites headed south to join Rehoboam in Yahudah, joining Benjamin and others from the north. As seen many times, significant cross-migration was prevalent enough, so that today both houses, while maintaining their basic character, also include a random sampling or sprinkling of all twelve tribes. But neither house contains the fullness of the 12 tribes. That fullness remains found in the nations not in Judah.

[4] This verse is one of several cited to show that Ephraimites are allegedly all found among the Jewish people. What this verse says is that from among all the tribes of Yisrael, those who had hearts set on serving YHWH came to Jerusalem to make offerings. The verse does not say that all of the north or most of the north had these hearts, or that any of them settled in Jerusalem. Actually the text insinuates that they came to Jerusalem to sacrifice and worship – not to settle down permanently.
[5] According to YHWH's will to propagate Yisrael's seed. While modern society frowns on polygamy and the possession of concubines, YHWH allowed it in Yisrael; all towards the purpose of bringing to pass His promises to make Yisrael more numerous than all nations.

with him.[1] 2 And it came to pass, that in the fifth year of melech Rehovoam Shishak melech of Mitzrayim came up against Yahrushalayim, because they had transgressed against יהוה, 3 With twelve hundred mirkavot, and sixty thousand horsemen: and the people were without number that came with him out of Mitzrayim; the Lubims, the Sukkiims, and the Ethiopians. 4 And he captured the fenced cities that pertained to Yahudah, and came to Yahrushalayim. 5 Then came Shemayah the navi to Rehovoam, and to the rulers of Yahudah, that were gathered together to Yahrushalayim because of Shishak, and said to them, This says יהוה, *You have forsaken Me, and therefore have I also left you in the hand of Shishak.* 6 Then the rulers of Yisrael and the melech humbled themselves; and they said, יהוה is Tzadik. 7 And when יהוה saw that they humbled themselves, the word of יהוה came to Shemayah, saying, *They have humbled themselves; therefore I will not destroy them, but I will grant them some deliverance; and My wrath shall not be poured out upon Yahrushalayim by the hand of Shishak. 8 Nevertheless they shall be his avadim; that they may know My service, and the service of the malchutim of the countries.* 9 So Shishak melech of Mitzrayim came up against Yahrushalayim, and took away the treasures of the Bayit of יהוה, and the treasures of the melech's bayit; he took all: and carried away also the shields of gold which Shlomo had made. And then melech Rehovoam made shields of bronze to replace them, and committed them to the hands of the head of the guard, that guarded the entrance of the melech's bayit. 11 And when the melech entered into the Bayit of יהוה, the guard came and fetched them, and brought them again into the guard chamber. 12 And when he humbled himself, the wrath of יהוה turned from him that he would not destroy him altogether: and also in Yahudah things went

well. 13 So melech Rehovoam strengthened himself in Yahrushalayim, and reigned: for Rehovoam was forty-one years old when he began to reign, and he reigned seventeen years in Yahrushalayim, the city which יהוה had chosen out of all the tribes of Yisrael, to put His Name there. And his mother's name was Naamah an Ammonitess.[2] 14 And he did evil, because he prepared not his lev to seek יהוה. 15 Now the acts of Rehovoam, the first and last, are they not written in the Scroll of Shemayah the navi, and of Iddo the seer concerning genealogies?[3] And there were wars between Rehovoam and Yerovoam continually.[4] 16 And Rehovoam slept with his ahvot, and was buried in the city of David: and Aviyah his son reigned in his place.

13 Now in the eighteenth year of melech Yerovoam began Aviyah to reign over Yahudah. 2 He reigned three years in Yahrushalayim. His mother's name also was Michayah the daughter of Uriel of Giveah. And there was war between Aviyah and Yerovoam.[5] 3 And Aviyah joined the battle with an army of brave men of war, even four hundred thousand chosen men: Yerovoam also set the battle against him with eight hundred thousand chosen men, being mighty men of bravery. 4 And Aviyah stood up upon Mount Zemarayim, which is in the mountains of Ephraim, and said, Shema to me, Yerovoam, and all Yisrael; 5 Don't you know that יהוה Elohim of Yisrael gave the malchut over Yisrael to David le-olam-va-ed, even to him and to his sons by a covenant of salt? 6 Yet Yerovoam the son of Nebat, the eved of

---

[1] Both houses had become unfaithful to YHWH.

[2] She was a non-naturalized Yisraelite; therefore in Judah, there is plenty of Ammonite dom. So it is wrong for Judah to make Ephraim prove Yisraelite domlines, when their own is mixed and without proof. Therefore in determining who is a Yisraelite, the only criteria that can be used is who belongs to Moshiach and guards His commandments; and who doesn't.
[3] Missing scrolls.
[4] Sadly the two-house wars continue unabated usually in theological issues, sometimes through the centuries in actual warfare.
[5] Two-house battles.

Shlomo the son of David, has risen up, and has rebelled against his master. 7 And there are gathered to him vain men, the children of Beliya-al, and have strengthened themselves against Rehovoam the son of Shlomo, when Rehovoam was young and tenderhearted, and could not withstand them. 8 And now you think to withstand the malchut of יהוה in the hand of the sons of David; because you are a great multitude, and there are with you golden calves, which Yerovoam made for you as your elohim. 9 Have you not cast out the kohanim of יהוה, the sons of Aharon, and the Leviim, and have made for yourselves priests after the manner of the nations of other lands? So that whoever comes to consecrate himself with a young bullock and seven rams, the same may be a kohen for them that are not elohim. 10 But as for us, יהוה is our Elohim, and we have not forsaken Him; and the kohanim, who serve יהוה, are the sons of Aharon, and the Leviim wait upon their business: 11 And they burn to יהוה every shachrit and every maariv burnt sacrifices and sweet incense: the Lechem of The Faces also they set in order upon the pure table; and the menorah of gold with its lamps, to burn every maariv: for we keep the charge of יהוה our Elohim; but you have forsaken Him. 12 And, see, Elohim Himself is with us as our Captain, and His kohanim with sounding shofars to sound the alarm against you. O children of Yisrael, fight not against יהוה Elohim of your ahvot; for you shall not prosper. 13 But Yerovoam caused an ambush to come about behind them: so they were before Yahudah, and the ambush was behind them. 14 And when Yahudah looked back, see, the battle was before and behind: and they cried to יהוה, and the kohanim sounded with the shofars. 15 Then the men of Yahudah gave a shout: and as the men of Yahudah shouted, it came to pass, that Elohim killed Yerovoam and all Yisrael before Aviyah and Yahudah. 16 And the children of Yisrael fled before Yahudah: and Elohim

delivered them into their hand. 17 And Aviyah and his people killed them with a great slaughter: so there fell down slain of Yisrael five hundred thousand chosen men. 18 So the children of Yisrael were humbled at that time, and the children of Yahudah prevailed, because they relied upon יהוה Elohim of their ahvot. [1] 19 And Aviyah pursued after Yerovoam, and took cities from him, Beth-El with its towns, and Yeshnah with its towns, and Ephron with its towns. 20 Neither did Yerovoam recover his strength again in the days of Aviyah: and יהוה struck him, and he died. 21 But Aviyah grew mighty, and married fourteen wives, and begat twenty-two sons, and sixteen daughters. 22 And the rest of the acts of Aviyah, and his ways, and his sayings, are written in the Scroll of the navi Iddo.

14 So Aviyah slept with his ahvot, and they buried him in the city of David: and Asa his son reigned in his place. In his days the land was quiet ten years. 2 And Asa did that which was tov and right in the eyes of יהוה His Elohim: 3 For he took away the altars of the strange elohim, and the idol temples, and broke down the images, and cut down the Asherim: 4 And commanded Yahudah to seek יהוה Elohim of their ahvot, and to do the Torah and the mishpatim. 5 Also he took away out of all the cities of Yahudah the idol temples and the images: and the malchut was quiet before him. 6 And he built fenced cities in Yahudah: for the land had rest, and he had no war in those years; because יהוה had given him rest. 7 Therefore he said to Yahudah, Let us build these cities, and make around them walls, and towers, gates, and bars, while the land is yet before us; because we have sought יהוה our Elohim, we have sought Him, and He has given us rest on every side. So they built and prospered. 8 And Asa had an army of men

---

[1] Oh that this was always the case with both houses of Yisrael.

that bore shields and spears, out of Yahudah three hundred thousand; and out of Benyamin, that bore shields and drew bows, two hundred eighty thousand: all these were mighty men of bravery. 9 And there came out against them Zerah the Ethiopian with an army of a million men, and three hundred mirkavot; and came to Mareshah. 10 Then Asa went out against him, and they set the battle in the valley of Tzephathah at Mareshah. 11 And Asa cried to יהוה His Elohim, and said, יהוה, it is nothing for You to help, whether with many, or with them that have no power: help us, O יהוה our Elohim; for we rest on You, and in Your Name[1] we go against this multitude. O יהוה, You are our Elohim; let not man prevail against You. 12 So יהוה killed the Ethiopians before Asa and before Yahudah; and the Ethiopians fled. 13 And Asa and the people that were with him pursued them to Gerar: and the Ethiopians were overthrown, that they could not recover themselves; for they were destroyed before יהוה, and before His army; and they carried away very much spoil. 14 And they smote all the cities all around Gerar; for the fear of יהוה came upon them: and they plundered all the cities; for there was very much spoil in them. 15 They smote also the tents of cattle, and carried away sheep and camels in abundance, and returned to Yahrushalayim.

15 And the Ruach of Elohim came upon Azaryah the son of Oved: 2 And he went out to meet Asa, and said to him, Shema to me, Asa, and all Yahudah and Benyamin; יהוה is with you, while you be with Him; and if you seek Him, He will be found of you; but if you forsake Him, He will forsake you. 3 Now for a long season Yisrael has been without the true Elohim, and without a teaching kohen, and without Torah.[2] 4 But when they in their trouble did teshuvah to יהוה Elohim of Yisrael, and sought Him, He was found of them.[3] 5 And

in those times there was no shalom to him that went out, nor to him that came in, but great vexations were upon all the inhabitants of the countries. 6 They were beaten down nation-by-nation, and city-by-city: for Elohim did vex them with all adversity. 7 Be strong therefore, and let not your hands be weak: for your work shall be rewarded.[4] 8 And when Asa heard these words, and the prophecy of Oved the navi, he took courage, and put away the abominable idols out of all the land of Yahudah and Benyamin, and out of the cities which he had taken from Mount Ephraim, and renewed the altar of יהוה, that was before the porch of יהוה. 9 And he gathered all Yahudah and Benyamin, and the gerim[5] with them out of Ephraim and Menashsheh,[6] and out of Shimeon: for they came over to him out of Yisrael in abundance, when they saw that יהוה his Elohim was with him.[7] 10 So they gathered themselves together at Yahrushalayim in the third month, in the fifteenth year of the reign of Asa. 11 And they offered to יהוה the same time, from the spoil that they had brought, seven hundred oxen and seven thousand sheep. 12 And they entered into a covenant to seek יהוה Elohim of their ahvot with all their lev and with all their being; 13 That whoever would not seek יהוה Elohim of Yisrael should be put to death, whether small or great, whether man or woman. 14 And they swore to יהוה with a loud voice, and with shouting, and with shofars, and with cornets. 15 And all Yahudah had gilah at the oath: for they had sworn with all their lev, and sought Him with their whole desire; and He was found by them: and יהוה gave them rest all round.

---

[1] We fight all Yisraelite battles in the Name of YHWH.
[2] Speaking of Ephraim Yisrael.
[3] In past times.

[4] Encouraging Yahudah to walk upright; not like Ephraim.
[5] Note that Ephraimites immediately after the split, though still biological Yisraelites, are still referred to as strangers dwelling amongst Yahudah. Since they were considered gentile strangers then, how much more today?
[6] Again we see limited but apparent crossover. Here for the first time Shimeon is mentioned as being found in Judah.
[7] Ephraimites will be drawn to Yahudah when Yahudah walks upright. What happened in Asa's day will happen again in our day, according to Zachariah 8:23, and again in the **atid lavoh** by Moshiach Himself in Ezekiel 37:16-28.

16 And also concerning Maachah the mother of Asa the melech, he removed her from being malcha, because she had made an idol in an Asherah: and Asa cut down her idol, and stamped it, and burnt it at the brook Kidron. 17 But the idol temples were not taken away out of Yisrael: nevertheless the lev of Asa was perfect all his days. 18 And he brought into the Bayit of Elohim the things that his abba had dedicated, and that he himself had dedicated, silver, and gold, and vessels. 19 And there was no more war to the thirty-fifth year of the reign of Asa.

16 In the thirty-sixth year of the reign of Asa, Baasha Melech of Yisrael came up against Yahudah, and rebuilt Ramah, with the intent that he might let no one go out or come in to Asa melech of Yahudah. 2 Then Asa brought out silver and gold out of the treasures of the Bayit of יהוה and of the melech's bayit, and sent to Ben-Hadad melech of Aram, that dwelt at Dameshek, saying, 3 There is a covenant between me and you, as there was between my abba and your abba: see, I have sent you silver and gold; go, break your covenant with Baasha melech of Yisrael, that he may depart from me. 4 And Ben-Hadad listened to melech Asa, and sent the captains of his armies against the cities of Yisrael; and they smote Iyon, and Dan, and Abel-Mayim, and all the storage cities of Naphtali. 5 And it came to pass, when Baasha heard it, that he stopped the rebuilding of Ramah, and let his work cease. 6 Then Asa the melech took all Yahudah; and they carried away the stones of Ramah, and its timber, with which Baasha was building; and he built with it Geva and Mitzpah. 7 And at that time Hanani the seer came to Asa melech of Yahudah, and said to him, Because you have relied on the melech of Aram, and not relied on יהוה Your Elohim, therefore the army of the melech of Aram has escaped out of your hand. 8 Were not the Ethiopians and the Luvims a huge army, with very many mirkavot and horsemen? Yet, because you did rely on יהוה, He delivered them into your hand. 9 For the eyes of יהוה run to and fro throughout the whole earth, to show Himself strong on the behalf of those whose lev is perfect toward Him. In this matter you have done foolishly: therefore from now on you shall have wars. 10 Then Asa was angry with the seer, and put him in a prison; for he was in a rage with him because of this thing. And Asa oppressed some of the people at the same time. 11 And, see, the acts of Asa, first and last, see, they are written in the scroll of the melechim of Yahudah and Yisrael. 12 And Asa in the thirty-ninth year of his reign was diseased in his feet, until his disease was exceedingly great: yet in his disease he looked not to יהוה, but to the physicians.[1] 13 And Asa slept with his ahvot, and died in the forty-first year of his reign. 14 And they buried him in his own tomb, which he had made for himself in the city of David, and laid him in the bed which was filled with sweet odours and divers kinds of spices prepared by the perfumers skill: and they made a very great burnt offering for him.

17 And Yehoshaphat his son reigned in his place, and strengthened himself against Yisrael. 2 And he placed forces in all the fenced cities of Yahudah, and set watch-posts in the land of Yahudah, and in the cities of Ephraim, which Asa his abba had taken.[2] 3 And יהוה was with Yehoshaphat, because he had his halacha in the first ways of his abba David, and sought not any Baalim; 4 But looked to יהוה Elohim of his abba, and had his halacha in His mishpatim, and not after the doings of Yisrael. 5 Therefore יהוה established the malchut in his hand; and all Yahudah brought to Yehoshaphat presents; and he had riches and honor in great abundance.

---

[1] This is not a rebuke for the fact that he sought medical treatment. Rather the rebuke is over the fact that he totally neglected YHWH in favor of medical treatment. YHWH creates both means of healing, natural and supernatural, and wants us to keep Him as the focus of all healings.
[2] Some Ephraimite cities remained under Yahudite control.

6 And his lev was encouraged in the ways of יהוה: moreover he took away the idol temples and Asherim out of Yahudah. 7 Also in the third year of his reign he sent to his rulers, Ben-Hail, and Ovadyah, and Zacharyah, and Nethan-el, and Michayah, to teach in the cities of Yahudah. 8 And with them he sent Leviim, even Shemayah, and Nethanyah, and Zevadyah, and Asah-el, and Shemiramoth, and Yehonathan, and Adoniyah, and Toviyah, and Tov-adoniyah, Leviim; and with them Elishama and Yehoram, kohanim. 9 And they taught in Yahudah, and had the scroll of the Torah of יהוה with them, and went around throughout all the cities of Yahudah, and taught the people.[1] 10 And the fear of יהוה fell upon all the malchutim of the lands that were all around Yahudah, so that they made no war against Yehoshaphat. 11 Also some of the Philistines brought Yehoshaphat presents, and compulsory labor and silver; and the Arabians brought him flocks, seven thousand seven hundred rams, and seven thousand seven hundred male goats. 12 And Yehoshaphat grew great exceedingly; and he built in Yahudah castles, and cities of storage. 13 And he had much business in the cities of Yahudah: and the men of war, mighty men of bravery, were in Yahrushalayim. 14 And these are their numbers according to the bayit of their ahvot: Of Yahudah, the captains of thousands; Adnah the head, and with him mighty men of bravery three hundred thousand. 15 And next to him was Yehohanan the captain, and with him two hundred eighty thousand. 16 And next to him was Amatsyah the son of Zichri, who willingly offered himself to יהוה; and with him two hundred thousand mighty men of bravery. 17 And of Benyamin; Elyada a mighty man of bravery, and with him armed men with bow and shield two hundred thousand. 18 And next to him was Yehozavad, and with him a hundred eighty thousand ready prepared for the war.

19 These served the melech, beside those whom the melech put in the fenced cities throughout all Yahudah.

18 Now Yehoshaphat had riches and honor in abundance, and was aligned with Ahav by marriage. 2 And after certain years he went down to Ahav to Shomron. And Ahav killed sheep and oxen for him in abundance, and for the people that he had with him, and persuaded him to go up with him to Ramoth-Gilead. 3 And Ahav melech of Yisrael said to Yehoshaphat melech of Yahudah, Will you go with me to Ramoth-Gilead? And he answered him, I am as you are, and my people as your people; and we will be with you in the war.[2] 4 And Yehoshaphat said to the melech of Yisrael, Inquire, I ask you, for the word of יהוה today. 5 Therefore the melech of Yisrael gathered together four hundred men of the neviim, and said to them, Shall we go to Ramoth-Gilead to battle, or shall I refrain? And they said, Go up; for Elohim will deliver it into the melech's hand. 6 But Yehoshaphat said, Is there not here a navi of יהוה besides these that we might inquire of him? 7 And the melech of Yisrael said to Yehoshaphat, There is yet one man, by whom we may inquire of יהוה: but I hate him; for he never prophesied tov to me, but always evil: he is Michayah the son of Yimla. And Yehoshaphat said, Let not the melech say such things. 8 And the melech of Yisrael called for one of his officers, and said, Fetch quickly Michayah the son of Imla. 9 And the melech of Yisrael and Yehoshaphat melech of Yahudah sat both on their thrones, clothed in their robes, and they sat in an open place at the entrance of the gate of Shomron; and all the neviim prophesied before them. 10 And Tzidekiyahu the son of Chenanyah had made for himself horns of iron, and said, This says יהוה, *With these you shall push Aram until they be consumed.* 11 And all

---

[1] Real Jewish revival.

the neviim prophesied likewise, saying, Go up to Ramoth-Gilead, and prosper: for יהוה shall deliver it into the hand of the melech. 12 And the messenger that went to call Michayah spoke to him, saying, See, the words of the neviim declare tov to the melech with one accord; let your word therefore, I beg you, be like one of theirs, and speak tov. 13 And Michayah said, As יהוה lives, even what My Elohim says, that will I speak. 14 And when he was come to the melech, the melech said to him, Michayah, shall we go to Ramoth-Gilead to battle, or shall I refrain? And he said, Go up, and prosper: and they shall be delivered into your hand. 15 And the melech said to him, How many times shall I admonish you that you say nothing but the emet to me in the Name of יהוה? 16 Then he said, I did see all Yisrael scattered upon the mountains, as sheep that have no shepherd: and יהוה said, *These have no master; let them return therefore each man to his bayit in shalom.* 17 And the melech of Yisrael said to Yehoshaphat, Did I not tell you that he would not prophesy tov to me, but evil? 18 Again he said, Therefore shema the word of יהוה ; I saw יהוה sitting upon His throne, and all the armies of the shamayim standing on His right hand and on His left.[1] 19 And יהוה said, *Who shall entice Ahav melech of Yisrael, so that he may go up and fall at Ramoth-Gilead?* And one spoke saying after this manner; and another saying after another manner. 20 Then there came out a ruach, and stood before יהוה, and said, I will entice him. And יהוה said to him, In what way? 21 And he said, I will go out, and be a lying ruach in the mouth of all his neviim. And יהוה said, *You shall entice him, and you shall also prevail: go out, and do so.* 22 Now therefore, see, יהוה has put a lying ruach in the mouth of these your neviim, and יהוה has spoken evil against you. 23 Then Tzidqiyahu the son of Chenanyah came near, and smote Michayah upon the cheek, and said, Which way went

the Ruach of יהוה from me to speak to you? 24 And Michayah said, See, you shall see on that day when you shall go into an inner chamber to hide yourself. 25 Then the melech of Yisrael said, Take Michayah, and carry him back to Amon the leader of the city, and to Yoash the melech's son; 26 And say, This says the melech, Put this fellow in the prison, and feed him with the lechem of affliction and with mayim of affliction, until I return in shalom. 27 And Michayah said, If you certainly return in shalom, then יהוה has not spoken by me. And he said, Shema, all you people. 28 So the melech of Yisrael and Yehoshaphat the melech of Yahudah went up to Ramoth-Gilead. 29 And the melech of Yisrael said to Yehoshaphat, I will disguise myself, and will go to the battle; but put on your robes. So the melech of Yisrael disguised himself; and they went to the battle. 30 Now the melech of Aram had commanded the captains of the mirkavot that were with him, saying, Fight not against small or great, except only against the melech of Yisrael. 31 And it came to pass, when the captains of the mirkavot saw Yehoshaphat, that they said, It is the melech of Yisrael. Therefore they circled around him to fight: but Yehoshaphat cried out, and יהוה helped him; and Elohim moved them to depart from him. 32 For it came to pass, that, when the captains of the mirkavot perceived that it was not the melech of Yisrael, they turned back again from pursuing him. 33 And a certain man drew a bow unwittingly, and killed the melech of Yisrael between the joints of the harness: the king said to his mirkavah man, Turn around, that you may take me out of the battle; for I am wounded. 34 And the battle increased that day: but the melech of Yisrael stayed in his mirkavah against the Arameans until the evening: and about the time of the sundown he died.

19 And Yehoshaphat the melech of Yahudah returned to his bayit in shalom to Yahrushalayim. 2 And Yehu the

---

[1] Michayah saw a heavenly vision.

son of Hanani the seer went out to meet him, and said to melech Yehoshaphat, Should you help the wicked, and love them that hate **יהוה**? Therefore wrath is upon you from **יהוה**. 3 Nevertheless there are tov things found in you, in that you have taken away the Asherim out of the land, and have prepared your lev to seek Elohim. 4 And Yehoshaphat dwelt at Yahrushalayim: and he went out again throughout the people from Beer-Sheva to Mount Ephraim, and brought them back to **יהוה** Elohim of their ahvot. 5 And he set shoftim in the land throughout all the fenced cities of Yahudah, city by city, 6 And said to the shoftim, Take heed what you do: for you shophet not for man, but for **יהוה**, who is with you in the mishpat. 7 And now let the fear of **יהוה** be upon you; take heed and do it: for there is no iniquity with **יהוה** our Elohim, or partiality of persons, or taking any gifts. 8 Moreover in Yahrushalayim did Yehoshaphat set up the Leviim, and the kohanim, and the heads of the ahvot of Yisrael, to administer the mishpatim of **יהוה**, and to settle disputes, when they returned to Yahrushalayim. 9 And he charged them, saying, This shall you do in the fear of **יהוה**, faithfully, and with a perfect lev. 10 And what cause soever shall come to you if your brothers that dwell in their cities, between dom and dom, between Torah and commandment, chukim and mishpatim, you shall even warn them that they trespass not against **יהוה**, and so wrath come upon you, and upon your brothers: this do, and you shall not trespass. 11 And, see, Amariyah the head kohen is over you in all matters of **יהוה**; and Tzevadyah the son of Ishmael, the ruler of the bayit of Yahudah, for all the melech's matters: also the Leviim shall be officers before you. Deal courageously, and **יהוה** shall be with the tov.

20 It came to pass after this also, that the children of Moav, and the children of Ammon, and with them others beside the Ammonites, came against Yehoshaphat to battle. 2 Then there came some that told Yehoshaphat, saying, There comes a great multitude against you from beyond the sea on this side of Aram; and, see, they are in Hatzatzon-Tamar, which is En-Gedi. 3 And Yehoshaphat feared, and set himself to seek **יהוה**, and proclaimed a fast throughout all Yahudah. 4 And Yahudah gathered themselves together, to ask help from **יהוה**: even out of all the cities of Yahudah they came to seek **יהוה**. 5 And Yehoshaphat stood in the congregation of Yahudah and Yahrushalayim, in the Bayit of **יהוה**, before the new court, 6 And said, O **יהוה** Elohim of our ahvot, are not You Elohim in the shamayim? And don't You rule over all the malchutim of the nations? And in Your hand is there not power and might, so that none is able to withstand You? 7 Are not You our Elohim, who did drive out the inhabitants of this land before Your people Yisrael, and gave it to the zera of Avraham Your friend le-olam-va-ed? 8 And they dwelt in it, and have built You a Set-Apart Place in it for Your Name, saying, 9 If, when evil comes upon us, as the sword, mishpat, or pestilence, or famine, if we stand before You in this Bayit, and in Your presence, for Your Name is in this Bayit,[1] and cry to You in our affliction, then You will shema and help. 10 And now, see, the children of Ammon and Moav and Mount Seir, whom You would not let Yisrael invade, when they came out of the land of Mitzrayim, but they turned from them, and destroyed them not; 11 See, look, how they reward us, to come and to cast us out of Your possession, which You have given us to inherit. 12 O our Elohim, will You not shophet them? For we have no might against this great company that comes against us; neither know we what to do: but our eyes are upon You. 13 And all Yahudah stood before **יהוה**, with their little ones, their wives, and their children. 14 Then

---

[1] His Name is with Yisrael always.

upon Yahazi-el the son of Zacharyah, the son of Benayah, the son of Yei-el, the son of Mattanyah, a Levite of the sons of Asaph, came the Ruach of יהוה in the middle of the congregation; 15 And he said, Shema, all Yahudah, and you inhabitants of Yahrushalayim, and you melech Yehoshaphat, This says יהוה to you, *Be not afraid nor dismayed by reason of this great multitude; for the battle is not yours, but Elohim's.* 16 *Tomorrow go down against them: see, they come up by the cliff of Tziz; and you shall find them at the end of the brook, before the wilderness of Yeru-el.* 17 *You shall not need to fight in this battle: position yourselves, and stand still, and see the salvation of* יהוה *with you, O Yahudah and Yahrushalayim: fear not, nor be dismayed; tomorrow go out against them: for* יהוה *will be with you.* 18 And Yehoshaphat bowed his head with his face to the ground: and all Yahudah and the inhabitants of Yahrushalayim fell before יהוה , worshipping יהוה . 19 And the Leviim, of the children of the Kohathites, and of the children of the Korhites, stood up to give tehilla to יהוה Elohim of Yisrael with a loud voice on high. 20 And they rose early in the morning, and went forth into the wilderness of Tekoa: and as they went forth, Yehoshaphat stood and said, Shema to me, O Yahudah, and you inhabitants of Yahrushalayim; Believe in יהוה your Elohim, so shall you be established; believe His neviim, so shall you prosper.[1] 21 And when he had consulted with the people, he appointed singers to יהוה, who should give tehilla to the beauty of set-apartness; as they went out before the army, and to say, Give tehilla to יהוה ke le-olam-chasdo.[2] 22 And when they began to sing and to give tehilla, יהוה set ambushes against the children of Ammon, Moav, and Mount Seir, who were coming against Yahudah; and they were killed. 23 For the children of Ammon and

Moav stood up against the inhabitants of Mount Seir, utterly to kill and destroy them: and when they had made an end of the inhabitants of Seir, each one helped to destroy one another. 24 And when Yahudah came toward the watchtower in the wilderness, they looked to the multitude, and, see, there were dead bodies fallen to the earth, and none escaped. 25 And when Yehoshaphat and his people came to take away the spoil from them, they found among them an abundance of riches with the dead bodies, and precious jewels, which they stripped off for themselves, more than they could carry away: and they spent three days gathering the spoil, it was so much. 26 And on the fourth day they assembled themselves in the valley of Berach-Yah; for there they blessed יהוה: therefore the name of the same place is called, The Valley of Berach-Yah, to this day. 27 Then they returned, every man of Yahudah and Yahrushalayim, and Yehoshaphat in front of them, to go again to Yahrushalayim with simcha; for יהוה had made them to gilah over their enemies. 28 And they came to Yahrushalayim with lyres and harps and shofars to the Bayit of יהוה. 29 And the fear of Elohim was on all the malchutim of those countries, when they had heard that יהוה fought against the enemies of Yisrael. 30 So the realm of Yehoshaphat was quiet: for His Elohim gave him rest all around. 31 And Yehoshaphat reigned over Yahudah: he was thirty-five years old when he began to reign, and he reigned twenty-five years in Yahrushalayim. And his mother's name was Azuvah the daughter of Shilhi. 32 And he had his halacha in the way of Asa his abba, and departed not from it, doing that which was right in the sight of יהוה . 33 But the idol temples were not taken away: for as yet the people had not prepared their levim towards the Elohim of their ahvot. 34 Now the rest of the acts of Yehoshaphat, the first and last, see, they are written in the Scroll of Yehu the son of

---

[1] Only those with a prophetic calling can deliver Yisrael from the exile. There are simply too many other obstacles otherwise.
[2] For his kindness is forever.

Hanani,[1] who is mentioned in the scroll of the melechim of Yisrael. 35 And after this did Yehoshaphat melech of Yahudah join with Ahazyah melech of Yisrael, and did wickedly in doing so:[2] 36 And he joined himself with him to make ships to go to Tarshish:[3] and they made the ships in Ezion-Gever. 20:37 Then Eli-ezer the son of Dodavah of Mareshah prophesied against Yehoshaphat, saying, Because you have joined yourself with Ahaziyah, יהוה has broken your works. And the ships were broken, that they were not able to go to Tarshish.[4]

21 Now Yehoshaphat slept with his ahvot, and was buried with his ahvot in the city of David. And Yehoram his son reigned in his place. 2 And he had brothers the sons of Yehoshaphat, Azaryah, and Yehi-el, and Zacharyah, and Azaryah, and Micha-el, and Shephatyah: all these were the sons of Yehoshaphat melech of Yisrael. 3 And their abba gave them great gifts of silver, and of gold, and of precious things, with fenced cities in Yahudah: but the malchut he gave to Yehoram; because he was the firstborn. 4 Now when Yehoram had risen up over the malchut of his abba, he strengthened himself, and killed all his brothers with the sword, and others also of the rulers of Yisrael. 5 Yehoram was thirty-two years old when he began to reign, and he reigned eight years in Yahrushalayim. 6 And he had his halacha in the way of the melechim of Yisrael,[5] like as did the bayit of Ahav: for he had the daughter of Ahav as his wife: and he worked that which was evil in the eyes of יהוה. 7 Yet יהוה would not destroy the bayit of David, because of the covenant that He had made with David, and

as He promised to give a light to him and to his sons le-olam-va-ed. 8 In his days the Edomites revolted from under the rule of Yahudah, and made themselves a melech. 9 Then Yehoram went forth with his rulers, and all his mirkavot with him: and he rose up by night, and killed the Edomites who surrounded him, and the captains of the mirkavot. 10 So the Edomites revolted from under the hand of Yahudah to this day. The same time also did Livnah revolt from under his hand; because he had forsaken יהוה Elohim of His ahvot. 11 Moreover he made idol temples in the mountains of Yahudah, and caused the inhabitants of Yahrushalayim to commit fornication, and led Yahudah astray. 12 And there came a written parchment to him from Eliyahu the navi,[6] saying, This says יהוה Elohim of David your abba, *Because you have not had your halacha in the ways of Yehoshaphat your abba, nor in the ways of Asa melech of Yahudah, 13 But have had your halacha in the way of the melechim of Yisrael,[7] and have made Yahudah and the inhabitants of Yahrushalayim to go whoring, like the whoredoms of the bayit of Ahav, and also have slain your brothers from your abba's bayit, who were better than you: 14 See, with a great plague יהוה will smite your people, and your children, and your wives, and all your goods: 15 And you shall have great sickness by disease of your intestines, until your intestines fall out by reason of the sickness day by day.* 16 Moreover יהוה stirred up against Yehoram the ruach of the Philistines, and of the Arabians, that were near the Ethiopians: 17 And they came up into Yahudah, and broke into it, and carried away all the substance that was found in the

---

[1] Missing scroll.
[2] He sought unity around compromise and idolatry, in the same way many today try and unite the so-called church with Judah, instead of calling people totally out of the church, so that end-time Yisrael can be birthed.
[3] Europe and Spain.
[4] So that he could not reach some of the colonies planted by Solomon, with a warped and perverted version of kingdom unity.
[5] Ephraim.

[6] Many have wondered how a letter can come from Elijah well after had had been taken away. We are left with two options. The first was that he was taken to the skies and then removed to another spot in Yisrael away from harm, and not to heaven itself. Or that he had written this letter prior to his being snatched to heaven, having obeyed YHWH to write a letter about events before it happened, so as to puinish Yehoram with dire fear and mental disturbance; in that he was actually getting letters from dead people speaking for YHWH, with YHWH's true words.
[7] Ephraim.

melech's bayit, and his sons also, and his wives; so that there was not one son left to him, except Yehoahaz, the youngest of his sons. 18 And after all this יהוה smote him in his intestines with an incurable disease. 19 And it came to pass, that in process of time, after the end of two years, his intestines fell out by reason of his sickness: so he died of a serious disease. And his people made no burning funeral for him like the burning funeral for his ahvot. 20 Thirty-two years old was he when he began to reign, and he reigned in Yahrushalayim eight years, and departed without being desired by anyone. But they buried him in the city of David, but not in the tombs of the melechim.

22 And the inhabitants of Yahrushalayim made Ahaziyah his youngest son melech in his place: for the raiding band of men that came with the Arabians to the camp had slain all the older sons. So Ahaziyah the son of Yehoram melech of Yahudah reigned. 2 Forty-two years old was Ahaziyah when he began to reign, and he reigned one year in Yahrushalayim. His mother's name also was Athalyah the daughter of Omri. 3 He also had his halacha in the ways of the bayit of Ahav: for his mother was his counselor to do wickedly. 4 And he did evil in the sight of יהוה like the bayit of Ahav: for they were his counselors to his destruction after the death of his abba. 5 He had his halacha also after their counsel, and went with Yehoram the son of Ahav melech of Yisrael to war against Haza-el melech of Aram at Ramoth-Gilead: and the Arameans killed Yoram. 6 And he returned to be healed in Yezreel because of the wounds that were given him at Ramah, when he fought with Haza-el melech of Aram. And Azaryah the son of Yehoram melech of Yahudah went down to see Yehoram the son of Ahav at Yezre-el, because he was sick. 7 And the destruction of Ahaziyah was of Elohim by coming to Yoram: for when he was come,

he went out with Yehoram against Yehu the son of Nimshi, whom יהוה had anointed to cut off the bayit of Ahav. 8 And it came to pass, that, when Yehu was executing mishpat upon the bayit of Ahav, and found the rulers of Yahudah, and the sons of the brothers of Ahaziyah, that served Ahaziyah, he killed them. 9 And he sought for Ahaziyah: and they caught him, for he was hidden in Shomron, and brought him to Yehu: and when they had slain him, they buried him properly: Because, they said, he is the son of Yehoshaphat, who sought יהוה with all his lev. So the bayit of Ahaziyah had no power to still keep the malchut. 10 But when Athalyah the mother of Ahaziyah saw that her son was dead, she arose and destroyed all the royal zera of the bayit of Yahudah. 11 But Yehoshavath, the daughter of the melech, took Yoash the son of Ahaziyah, and stole him from among the melech's sons that were slain, and put him and his nurse in a bedroom. So Yehoshavath, the daughter of melech Yehoram, the wife of Yehoyada the kohen, for she was the sister of Ahaziyah, hid him from Athalyah, so that she killed him not. 12 And he was with them hidden in the Bayit of Elohim six years: and Athalyah reigned over the land.[1]

23 And in the seventh year Yehoyada strengthened himself, and took the captains of hundreds, Azaryah the son of Yeroham, and Ishmael the son of Yehohanan, and Azaryah the son of Oved, and Maaseyah the son of Adayah, and Elishaphat the son of Zichri into covenant with him. 2 And they went about in Yahudah, and gathered the Leviim out of all the cities of Yahudah, and the heads of the ahvot of Yisrael, and they came to Yahrushalayim. 3 And the entire congregation made a covenant with the melech in the Bayit of Elohim. And he said to them, See, the melech's son shall reign,

---

[1] Yoash is a type of Yahshua, who has been hidden from Yahudah for 6,000 years, yet is to be revealed in the millennial kingdom.

as יהוה has said of the sons of David. 4 This is the thing that you shall do; A third part of you entering on the Shabbat, from the kohanim and of the Leviim, shall be gatekeepers for the doors; 5 And a third part shall be at the melech's bayit; and a third part at the Foundation Gate: and all the people shall be in the courts of the Bayit of יהוה. 6 But let none come into the Bayit of יהוה, except the kohanim, and those that serve from the Leviim; they shall go in, for they are set-apart: but all the people shall guard the charge of יהוה. 7 And the Leviim shall surround the melech all round, every man with his weapons in his hand; and whoever else comes into the bayit, he shall be put to death: but you be with the melech when he comes in, and when he goes out. 8 So the Leviim and all Yahudah did according to all things that Yehoyada the kohen had commanded, and took every man his men that were to come in on the Shabbat, with them that were to go out on the Shabbat: for Yehoyada the kohen did not dismiss the priestly divisions. 9 Moreover Yehoyada the kohen delivered to the captains of hundreds spears, and large shields, and smaller shields, that had been melech David's, which were in the Bayit of Elohim. 10 And he set all the people, every man having his weapon in his hand, from the right side of the Beit HaMikdash to the left side of the Beit HaMikdash, along by the altar and the Beit HaMikdash, by the melech all around. 11 Then they brought out the melech's son, and put upon him the crown, and gave him the testimony, and made him melech. And Yehoyada and his sons anointed him, and said, Let the melech live! 12 Now when Athalyah heard the noise of the people running and praising the melech, she came to the people into the Bayit of יהוה: 13 And she looked, and, see, the melech stood at his pillar at the entering in, and the rulers and the shofars by the melech: and all the people of the land had gilah, and sounded with shofars, also the singers with instruments of music, and such

as taught to sing and offer tehilla. Then Athalyah tore her clothes, and said, Treason, Treason. 14 Then Yehoyada the kohen brought out the captains of hundreds that were set over the army, and said to them, Take her forth from the ranks: and whoever follows her, let him be slain with the sword. For the kohen said, Slay her not in the Bayit of יהוה. 15 So they laid hands on her; and when she came to the entering of the Horse Gate by the melech's bayit, they killed her there. 16 And Yehoyada made a covenant between him, and between all the people, and between the melech that they should be יהוה's people. 17 Then all the people went to the bayit of Baal, and broke it down, and broke his altars and his images in pieces, and killed Mattan the priest of Baal before the altars. 18 Also Yehoyada appointed the offices of the Bayit of יהוה by the hand of the kohanim the Leviim, whom David had distributed in the Bayit of יהוה, to offer the burnt offerings of יהוה, as it is written in the Torah of Moshe, with gilah and with shirim, as David ordained it. 19 And he set the gatekeepers at the gates of the Bayit of יהוה, that none who were unclean in any way should enter in. 20 And he took the captains of hundreds, and the nobles, and the rulers of the people, and all the people of the land, and brought down the melech from the Bayit of יהוה : and they came through the high gate into the melech's bayit, and set the melech upon the throne of the malchut. 21 And all the people of the land had gilah: and the city was quiet, after they had slain Athalyah with the sword.

24 Yoash was seven years old when he began to reign, and he reigned forty years in Yahrushalayim. His mother's name also was Tziviah of Beer-Sheva. 2 And Yoash did that which was right in the sight of יהוה all the days of Yehoyada the kohen. 3 And Yehoyada took for him two wives; and he begat sons and daughters. 4 And it came to pass after this, that Yoash

decided to repair the Bayit of יהוה. 5 And he gathered together the kohanim and the Leviim, and said to them, Go out to the cities of Yahudah, and gather from all Yisrael money to repair the Bayit of Your Elohim from year to year, and see that you go quickly to the matter. But the Leviim did not hurry to do it. 6 And the melech called for Yehoyada the kohen, and said to him, Why have you not required of the Leviim to bring out of Yahudah and out of Yahrushalayim the collection, according to the commandment of Moshe the eved of יהוה, and of the congregation of Yisrael, for the Tabernacle of witness? 7 For the sons of Athalyah, that wicked woman, had broken up the Bayit of Elohim; and also all the dedicated things of the Bayit of יהוה did they offer to Baalim. 8 And at the melech's commandment they made a chest, and set it outside at the gate of the Bayit of יהוה. 9 And they made a proclamation throughout Yahudah and Yahrushalayim, to bring in to יהוה the collection that Moshe the eved of Elohim laid upon Yisrael in the wilderness. 10 And all the rulers and all the people had gilah, and brought in, and cast into the chest, until they had made an end of giving. 11 Now it came to pass, at that time that the chest was brought to the melech's office by the hand of the Leviim, and when they saw that there was much money, the melech's sopher and the high kohen's officer came and emptied the chest, and took it and carried it back to its place again. This they did every day, and gathered money in abundance. 12 And the melech and Yehoyada gave it to such as did the work of the service of the Bayit of יהוה, and they hired masons and carpenters to repair the Bayit of יהוה, and also such as worked with iron and bronze to fix the Bayit of יהוה. 13 So the workmen labored and the work was finished by them, and they set the Bayit of Elohim in its proper form, and strengthened it. 14 And when they had finished it, they brought the rest of the money before the melech and Yehoyada,

from which were made vessels for the Bayit of יהוה, even vessels to serve, and to offer with, and spoons, and vessels of gold and silver. And they offered burnt offerings in the Bayit of יהוה continually all the days of Yehoyada. 15 But Yehoyada grew older, and was full of days when he died; a hundred thirty years old he was when he died. 16 And they buried him in the city of David among the melechim, because he had done tov in Yisrael, both toward Elohim, and toward His Bayit. 17 Now after the death of Yehoyada came the rulers of Yahudah, and bowed before the melech. Then the melech listened to them. 18 And they left the Bayit of יהוה Elohim of their ahvot, and served Asherim and idols: and wrath came upon Yahudah and Yahrushalayim for their trespass. 19 Yet He sent neviim to them, to bring them back again to יהוה; and they testified against them: but they would not shema. 20 And the Ruach of Elohim came upon Zacharyah the son of Yehoyada the kohen, who stood above the people, and said to them, This says Elohim, *Why do you transgress the mishpatim of* יהוה *, that you cannot prosper? Because you have forsaken* יהוה*, He has also forsaken you.* 21 And they conspired against him, and stoned him with stones at the commandment of the melech in the court of the Bayit of יהוה. 22 So Yoash the melech remembered not the kindness which Yehoyada Zacharyah's abba had done to him, but killed his son. And when he died, he said, יהוה look upon it, and repay it! 23 And it came to pass at the end of the year, that the army of Aram came up against him: and they came to Yahudah and Yahrushalayim, and destroyed all the rulers of the people from among the people, and sent all their spoil to the melech of Dameshek. 24 For the army of the Arameans came with a small company of men, and יהוה delivered a very great army into their hand, because they had forsaken יהוה Elohim of their ahvot. So they executed mishpat against Yoash. 25 And when they were departed from him, for they left him very sick, his own avadim conspired against him for the dom of the sons of Yehoyada the kohen, and killed him on his bed, and he died: and they buried him in the city of David but they buried him not in the tombs of the melechim. 26 And these are they that conspired against him; Zavad the son of Shimeath an Ammonitess, and Yehozavad the son of Shimrith a Moavitess. 27 Now concerning his sons, and the others that conspired against him, and the repairing of the Bayit of Elohim, see, they are written in the scroll of the melechim. And Amatzyahu his son reigned in his place.

25 Amatzyahu was twenty-five years old when he began to reign, and he reigned twenty-nine years in Yahrushalayim. And his mother's name was Yehoaddan of Yahrushalayim. 2 And he did that which was right in the sight of **יהוה**, but not with a perfect lev. 3 Now it came to pass, when the malchut was established to him, that he killed the avadim that had killed the melech his abba. 4 But he did not kill their children, but did as it is written in the Torah in the scroll of Moshe, where **יהוה** commanded, saying, *The ahvot shall not die for the children, neither shall the children die for the ahvot, but every man shall die for his own sin.* 5 Moreover Amatzyahu gathered Yahudah together, and made them captains over thousands, and captains over hundreds, according to the houses of their ahvot, throughout all Yahudah and Benyamin: and he numbered them from twenty years older and above, and found them to be three hundred thousand choice men, able to go forth to war, that could handle the spear and shield. 6 He hired also a hundred thousand mighty men of bravery out of Yisrael for a hundred talents of silver.[1] 7 But there came a man of Elohim to him, saying, O melech, let not the army of Yisrael go with you; for **יהוה** is

not with Yisrael, with all the children of Ephraim.[2] 8 But if you will go, do it, be strong for the battle: Elohim shall make you fall before the enemy: for Elohim has power to help, and to cast down. 9 And Amatzyahu said to the man of Elohim, But what shall we do about the hundred talents that I have given to the army of Yisrael? And the man of Elohim answered, **יהוה** is able to give you much more than this. 10 Then Amatzyahu separated the army that had come to him out of Ephraim, to go home again: therefore their anger was greatly kindled against Yahudah, and they returned home in great anger.[3] 11 And Amatzyahu strengthened himself, and led forth his people, and went to the Valley of Salt, and killed of the children of Seir ten thousand. 12 And another ten thousand left alive did the children of Yahudah carry away captive, and brought them to the top of the rock, and cast them down from the top of the rock, that they all were broken in pieces. 13 But the soldiers of the army which Amatzyahu sent back, that they should not go with him to battle, fell upon the cities of Yahudah, from Shomron even to Beth-Horon, and killed three thousand of them, and took much spoil. 14 Now it came to pass, after that Amatzyahu returned from the slaughter of the Edomites, that he brought the elohim of the children of Seir, and set them up to be his elohim, and bowed down himself before them, and burned incense to them. 15 Therefore the anger of **יהוה** was kindled against Amatzyahu, and He sent to him a navi, who said to him, Why have you sought after the elohim of the very people, who could not deliver their own people out of your hand? 16 And it came to pass, as he talked with him, that the melech said to him, Are you appointed to give the melech counsel? Stop! Why should you be killed? Then ha navi

---

[1] That naturally led to more limited crossover.

[2] We are given a clear warning to all who seek to reunite both houses in the flesh, and not through Yahshua as King in the Ruach, along with full Torah compliance by both houses.
[3] More hatred; more hard feelings; more jealousy; without the return of Yahshua, it can never end. The scars and the history run too deep.

stopped, and said, I know that Elohim has determined to destroy you, because you have done this, and have not listened to my counsel. 17 Then Amatzyahu melech of Yahudah took advice, and sent to Yoash, the son of Yehoahaz, the son of Yehu, melech of Yisrael, saying, Come, let us see one another face to face. 18 And Yoash melech of Yisrael sent to Amatzyahu melech of Yahudah, saying, The thistle that was in Levanon sent to the cedar that was in Levanon, saying, Give your daughter to my son as a wife: and there passed by a wild beast that was in Levanon, and trampled the thistle. 19 You have said, See, I have killed the Edomites; and your lev lifted you up to boast: stay now at home; why should you meddle with me to your own hurt, that you should fall, even you, and all of Yahudah with you? 20 But Amatzyahu would not shema; for it came from Elohim, that He might deliver them into the hand of their enemies, because they sought after the elohim of Edom. 21 So Yoash the melech of Yisrael went up; and they saw one another face to face, both he and Amatzyahu melech of Yahudah, at Beth-Shemesh, which belongs to Yahudah. [1] 22 And Yahudah was killed before Yisrael, and they fled every man to his tent. 23 And Yoash the melech of Yisrael took Amatzyahu melech of Yahudah, the son of Yoash, the son of Yehoahaz, at Beth-Shemesh, and brought him to Yahrushalayim, and broke down the wall of Yahrushalayim from the Gate of Ephraim to the corner gate, four hundred cubits 24 And he took all the gold and the silver, and all the vessels that were found in the Bayit of Elohim with Oved-Edom, and the treasures of the melech's bayit, the hostages also, and returned to Shomron. 25 And Amatzyahu the son of Yoash melech of Yahudah lived after the death of Yoash son of Yehoahaz melech of Yisrael fifteen years. 26 Now the rest of the acts of Amatzyahu, the first and

last, see, are they not written in the scroll of the melechim of Yahudah and Yisrael? 27 Now from the time that Amatzyahu turned away from following יהוה they made a conspiracy against him in Yahrushalayim; and he fled to Lachish: but they sent to Lachish after him, and killed him there. 28 And they brought him upon horses, and buried him with his ahvot in the city of Yahudah.

26 Then all the people of Yahudah took Uzziyah, who was sixteen years old, and made him melech in the place of his abba Amatzyahu. 2 He built Eloth, and restored it to Yahudah, after the melech slept with his ahvot. 3 Sixteen years old was Uzziyah when he began to reign, and he reigned fifty-two years in Yahrushalayim. His mother's name also was Yecholyah of Yahrushalayim. 4 And he did that which was right in the sight of יהוה, according to all that his abba Amatzyahu did. 5 And he sought Elohim in the days of Zacharyah, who had binah in the visions of Elohim: and as long as he sought יהוה, Elohim made him to prosper. 6 And he went forth and warred against the Philistines, and broke down the wall of Gath, and the wall of Yavneh, and the wall of Ashdod, and built cities around Ashdod, and among the Philistines. 7 And Elohim helped him against the Philistines, and against the Arabians that dwelt in Gur-Baal, and the Mehunims. 8 And the Ammonites gave gifts to Uzziyah: and his name spread abroad even to the entrance of Mitzrayim; for he strengthened himself exceedingly. 9 Moreover Uzziyah built towers in Yahrushalayim at the Corner Gate, and at the Valley Gate, and at the turning of the wall, and fortified them. 10 Also he built towers in the desert, and dug many wells: for he had much cattle, both in the low country, and in the plains: farmers also, and vine dressers in the mountains, and in Carmel: for he loved the soil. 11 Moreover Uzziyah had an army of fighting men, that

---

[1] Very appropriate for two wicked kings to meet in the place called the "House of the Sun," or sun worship.

went out to war by divisions, according to the number of their account by the hand of Yei-el the sopher and Maaseyah the ruler, under the hand of Chananyah, one of the melech's captains. 12 The whole number of the head of the ahvot of the mighty men of bravery was two thousand six hundred. 13 And under their hand there was an army, three hundred seven thousand five hundred, that made war with mighty power, to help the melech against the enemy. 14 And Uzziyah prepared for them throughout all the army shields, and spears, and helmets, and body armor, and bows, and slings to cast stones. 15 And he made in Yahrushalayim machines, invented by skilled men, to be on the towers and upon the corners, to shoot arrows and great stones with. And his name spread far abroad; for he was marvellously helped, until he became strong. 16 But when he was strong, his lev was lifted up to his own destruction: for he transgressed against יהוה his Elohim, and went into the Beit HaMikdash of יהוה to burn incense upon the altar of incense.[1] 17 And Azaryah the kohen went in after him, and with him eighty kohanim of יהוה, that were brave men: 18 And they withstood Uzziyah the melech, and said to him, This has nothing to do with you Uzziyah, to burn incense to יהוה, but only for the kohanim the sons of Aharon, that are set-apart to burn incense: go out of the Set-Apart place; for you have trespassed; neither shall it be for your honor before יהוה Elohim. 19 Then Uzziyah was angry, and had a censer in his hand to burn incense: and while he was angry with the kohanim, the leprosy even rose up in his forehead before the kohanim in the Bayit of יהוה, from beside the incense altar. 20 And Azaryah the head kohen, and all the kohanim, looked upon him, and, see, he was leprous in his forehead, and they threw him out from there; he himself hurried to get out, because יהוה had struck him. 21 And Uzziyah the melech was a leper to the day of his death, and dwelt in a separate bayit, being a leper; for he was cut off from the Bayit of יהוה: and Yotham his son was over the melech's bayit, giving mishpat to the people of the land. 22 Now the rest of the acts of Uzziyah, the first and last, was recorded by Yeshayahu ha navi, the son of Amotz. 23 So Uzziyah slept with his ahvot, and they buried him with his ahvot in the field of the burial that belonged to the melechim; for they said, He is a leper: and Yotham his son reigned in his place.

27 Yotham was twenty-five years old when he began to reign, and he reigned sixteen years in Yahrushalayim. His mother's name also was Yerushah, the daughter of Tzadok. 2 And he did that which was right in the sight of יהוה, according to all that his abba Uzziyah did: however, he entered not into the Beit HaMikdash of יהוה. And the people did still act corruptly. 3 He built the High Gate of the Bayit of יהוה, and on the wall of Ophel he built much. 4 Moreover he built cities in the mountains of Yahudah, and in the forests he built castles and towers. 5 He fought also with the melech of the Ammonites, and prevailed against them. And the children of Ammon gave him in that same year a hundred talents of silver, and ten thousand measures of wheat, and ten thousand of barley. So much did the children of Ammon pay to him, both the second year, and the third. 6 So Yotham became mighty, because he prepared his halachot before יהוה His Elohim. 7 Now the rest of the acts of Yotham, and all his wars, and his halacha, see, they are written in the scroll of the melechim of Yisrael and Yahudah. 8 He was twenty-five years old when he began to reign, and reigned sixteen years in Yahrushalayim. 9 And Yotham slept with his ahvot, and they buried him in the city of David: and Ahaz his son reigned in his place.

---

[1] A job reserved only for the priests.

28 Ahaz was twenty years old when he began to reign, and he reigned sixteen years in Yahrushalayim: but he did not do that which was right in the sight of יהוה, like David his abba: 2 For he had his halacha in the ways of the melechim of Yisrael,1 and made also molten images for the Baalim. 3 Moreover he burnt incense in the Valley of the son of Hinnom,[2] and burnt his children in the fire, after the abominations of the nations whom יהוה had cast out before the children of Yisrael. 4 He sacrificed also and burnt incense in the idol temples, and on the hills, and under every green tree. 5 Therefore יהוה His Elohim delivered him into the hand of the melech of Aram; and they killed him, and carried away a great multitude of them captive, and brought them to Dameshek. And he was also delivered into the hand of the melech of Yisrael, who killed him with a great slaughter. 6 For Pekah the son of Remaliah killed in Yahudah a hundred twenty thousand in one day, who were all brave men; because they had forsaken יהוה Elohim of their ahvot. 7 And Zichri, a mighty man of Ephraim, killed Maaseyah the melech's son, and Azricham the leader of the bayit, and Elchanah that was next to the melech. 8 And the children of Yisrael carried away captive their brothers two hundred thousand, women, sons, and daughters, and took also away much spoil from them, and brought the spoil to Shomron.[3] 9 But a navi of יהוה was there, whose name was Oved: and he went out before the army that came to Shomron, and said to them, See, because יהוה Elohim of Your ahvot was angry with Yahudah, He has delivered them into your hand, and you have slain them in a rage that reaches up to the shamayim. 10 And now you desire to keep under the children of Yahudah and Yahrushalayim for bondmen and bondwomen to you: but are there not with

you, your sins against יהוה Your Elohim? 11 Now shema to me therefore, and return the captives again, which you have taken captive of your brothers: for the fierce wrath of יהוה is upon you. 12 Then certain of the heads of the children of Ephraim, Azaryah the son of Yohanan, Berechiyah the son of Meshillemoth, and Yehizkiyah the son of Shallum, and Amatsa the son of Hadlai, stood up against them that came from the war, 13 And said to them, You shall not bring in the captives here: for whereas we have offended against יהוה already, you intend to add more to our sins and to our trespass: for our trespass is great, and there is fierce wrath against Yisrael.[4] 14 So the armed men left the captives and the spoil before the rulers and the entire congregation. 15 And the men which were designated by name rose up, and took the captives, and the spoil and clothed all that were naked among them, and dressed them, and gave them sandals, and gave them to eat and to drink, and anointed them, and carried all their feeble upon donkeys, and brought them to Yericho, the city of palm trees, to their brothers: then they returned to Shomron.[5] 16 At that time did melech Ahaz send to the melechim of Ashshur to help him. 17 For again the Edomites had come and smote Yahudah, and carried away captives. 18 The Philistines also had invaded the cities of the low country, and of the south of Yahudah, and had taken Beth-Shemesh, and Ayalon, and Gederoth, and Shocho with its villages, and Timnah with its villages, Gimzo also with its villages: and they dwelt there. 19 For יהוה brought Yahudah low because of Ahaz melech of Yisrael; for he made Yahudah, [6] and

---

1 Ephraim.
2 Gei-Hinnom.
3 Another battle; and another case of crossover from Yahudah to Ephraim through battle.

4 Ephraim.
5 A very interesting example of YHWH forbidding major crossover, since this battle and capture involved 200,000 of Yahudah. The only time YHWH allowed crossover was in a very limited basis. Here he sends his navi Oved to stop what surely would have been the end of Judah due to massive assimilation and a heightened presence of idolatry. These and many other Scriptures prove conclusively that the two houses never reunited and remain divided until this hour.
6 Spiritually and physically.

transgressing heavily against **יהוה**. 20 And Tilgath-Pileser melech of Ashshur came to him, and distressed him, but did not help him. 21 For Ahaz took away a portion out of the Bayit of **יהוה**, and out of the bayit of the melech, and from the rulers, and gave it to the melech of Ashshur: but it did not help him. 22 And in the time of his distress did he trespass even more against **יהוה**: this is that melech Ahaz. 23 For he sacrificed to the elohim of Dameshek, who killed him: and he said, Because the elohim of the melechim of Aram helps them, therefore will I sacrifice to them, that they may help me. But they were his ruin, and of all Yisrael. 1 24 And Ahaz gathered together the vessels of the Bayit of Elohim, and cut in pieces the vessels of the Bayit of Elohim, and closed the doors of the Bayit of **יהוה**, and he made pagan altars in every corner of Yahrushalayim. 25 And in every city of Yahudah he made idol temples to burn incense to other elohim, and provoked **יהוה** Elohim of his ahvot to anger. 26 Now the rest of his acts and of all his ways, the first and last, see, they are written in the scroll of the melechim of Yahudah and Yisrael. 27 And Ahaz slept with his ahvot, and they buried him in the city, even in Yahrushalayim: but they brought him not into the tombs of the melechim of Yisrael: and Hizqiyahu his son reigned in his place.

29 Hizqiyahu began to reign when he was twenty-five years old, and he reigned twenty-nine years in Yahrushalayim. And his mother's name was Aviyah, the daughter of Zacharyah. 2 And he did that which was right in the sight of **יהוה**, according to all that David his abba had done. 3 He in the first year of his reign, in the first month, opened the doors of the Bayit of **יהוה**, and repaired them. 4 And he brought in the kohanim and the Leviim, and gathered them together into the East Street, 5 And said to them, Shema to me, you Leviim, set yourselves apart, and set-apart

the Bayit of **יהוה** Elohim of your ahvot, and carry out the filth still in the Set-Apart Place. 6 For our ahvot have trespassed, and done that which was evil in the eyes of **יהוה** our Elohim, and have forsaken Him, and have turned away their faces from the dwelling of **יהוה**, and turned their backs. 7 Also they have shut up the doors of the porch, and put out the lamps, and have not burned incense nor offered burnt offerings in the Set-Apart Place to the Elohim of Yisrael. 8 Therefore the wrath of **יהוה** was upon Yahudah and Yahrushalayim, and He has delivered them to trouble, to astonishment, and to hissing, as you see with your eyes. 9 For, see, our ahvot have fallen by the sword, and our sons and our daughters and our wives are in captivity for this. 10 Now it is in my lev to make a covenant with **יהוה** Elohim of Yisrael, that His fierce wrath may turn away from us. 11 My sons; be not now negligent: for **יהוה** has chosen you to stand before Him, to serve Him, and that you should serve Him, and burn incense. 12 Then the Leviim arose, Mahath the son of Amatsai, and Yoel the son of Azaryah, of the sons of the Kohathites: and of the sons of Merari, Kish the son of Avdi, and Azaryah the son of Yehalel-el: and of the Gershonites; Yoah the son of Tzimmah, and Eden the son of Yoah: 13 And of the sons of Elizaphan; Shimri, and Yei-el: and of the sons of Asaph; Zacharyah, and Mattanyah: 14 And of the sons of Heman; Yehi-el, and Shimei: and of the sons of Yeduthun; Shemayah, and Uzzi-el. 15 And they gathered their brothers, and set themselves apart, and came, according to the commandment of the melech, by the words of **יהוה**, to cleanse the Bayit of **יהוה**. 16 And the kohanim went into the inner part of the Bayit of **יהוה**, to cleanse it, and brought out all the uncleanness that they found in the Beit HaMikdash of **יהוה** into the court of the Bayit of **יהוה**. And the Leviim took it, to carry it out abroad into the brook Kidron. 17 Now they began on the first day of the

---

1 Ruin of both houses.

first month to set it apart, and on the eighth day of the month they came to the porch of יהוה: so they set apart the Bayit of יהוה in eight days; and on the sixteenth day of the first month they made an end. 18 Then they went in to Hizqiyahu the melech, and said, We have cleansed all the Bayit of יהוה, and the altar of burnt offering, with all its vessels, and the lechem of the Table of The Faces, with all its vessels. 19 Moreover all the vessels, which melech Ahaz in his reign did cast away in his transgression, have we prepared and set-apart, and, see, they are before the altar of יהוה. 20 Then Hizqiyahu the melech rose early, and gathered the rulers of the city, and went up to the Bayit of יהוה . 21 And they brought seven bullocks, and seven rams, and seven lambs, and seven male goats, for a sin offering for the malchut, and for the Set-Apart Place, and for Yahudah. And he commanded the kohanim the sons of Aharon to offer them on the altar of יהוה. 22 So they killed the bullocks, and the kohanim received the dom, and sprinkled it on the altar: likewise, when they had killed the rams, they sprinkled the dom upon the altar: they killed also the lambs, and they sprinkled the dom upon the altar. 23 And they brought forth the male goats for the sin offering before the melech and the congregation; and they laid their hands upon them: 24 And the kohanim killed them, and they made reconciliation with their dom upon the altar, to make atonement for all Yisrael:[1] for the melech commanded that the burnt offering and the sin offering should be made for all Yisrael.[2] 25 And he appointed the Leviim in the Bayit of יהוה with cymbals, with lyres, and with harps, according to the commandment of David, and of Gad the melech's seer, and Nathan ha navi: for so

was the commandment of יהוה by His neviim. 26 And the Leviim stood with the instruments of David, and the kohanim with the shofars. 27 And Hizqiyahu commanded to offer the burnt offering upon the altar. And when the burnt offering began, the songs of יהוה began also with the shofars, and with the instruments ordained by David melech of Yisrael. 28 And all the congregation worshipped, and the singers sang, and the trumpeters sounded: and all this continued until the burnt offering was finished. 29 And when they had made an end of offering, the melech and all that were present with him bowed themselves, and worshipped. 30 And Hizqiyahu the melech and the rulers commanded the Leviim to sing and give tehilla to יהוה with the words of David, and of Asaph the seer. And they sang tehillim with gilah, and they bowed their heads and worshipped. 31 Then Hizqiyahu answered and said, Now you have set-apart yourselves to יהוה, come near and bring sacrifices and hodu offerings into the Bayit of יהוה . And the congregation brought in sacrifices and hodu offerings; and burnt offerings by as many as were of a moved lev. 32 And the number of the burnt offerings, which the congregation brought, was seventy bullocks, a hundred rams, and two hundred lambs: all these were for a burnt offering to יהוה. 33 And the set-apart things were six hundred oxen and three thousand sheep. 34 But the kohanim were too few, so that they could not skin all the burnt offerings: therefore their brothers the Leviim did help them, until the work was ended, and until the other kohanim had set themselves apart: for the Leviim were more upright in lev to set themselves apart than the kohanim. 35 And also the burnt offerings were in abundance, with the fat of the shalom offerings, and the drink offerings for every burnt offering. So the service of the Bayit of יהוה was re-established. 36 And Hizqiyahu had gilah, with all the people, in that Elohim had

---

[1] Atonement has only been and always will be by dom alone.
[2] The sacrifices at the cleansing of the temple were to represent all Yisrael or all 12 tribes before YHWH. That in no way even implies that all 12 tribes were fully represented there in person, or fully returned back to Judah. To use a ceremony that called for reconciliation for all 12 tribes and claim that all 12 tribes in all their fullness had actually returned in the days of Hezekiah; is pure fantasy, not to mention historical revisionism.

prepared the people: for the task was done suddenly and promptly.

30 And Hizqiyahu sent to all Yisrael and Yahudah, and wrote letters also to Ephraim and Menashsheh, that they should come to the Bayit of יהוה at Yahrushalayim, to keep the Pesach to יהוה Elohim of Yisrael.[1] 2 For the melech had taken counsel, and his rulers, and the entire congregation in Yahrushalayim, to keep the Pesach in the second month. 3 For they could not keep it at that time, because the kohanim had not set themselves apart sufficiently, neither had the people gathered themselves together to Yahrushalayim. 4 And the thing pleased the melech and the entire congregation. 5 So they established a decree to make a proclamation throughout all Yisrael, from Beer-Sheva even to Dan, that they should come to keep the Pesach to יהוה Elohim of Yisrael at Yahrushalayim: for they had not done it for a long time as it had been commanded.[2] 6 So the postal runners went with the letters from the melech and his rulers throughout all Yisrael and Yahudah, and according to the commandment of the melech, saying, You children of Yisrael, teshuvah again to יהוה Elohim of Avraham, Yitzchak, and Yisrael,[3] and He will return to the remnant of you, that are escaped out of the hand of the melechim of Ashshur.[4][5][6] 7 And be not you like your ahvot, and like your brothers, who trespassed against יהוה Elohim of their ahvot, who then gave them up to desolation, as you see. 8 Now be you not stiff-necked, as your ahvot were, but yield yourselves to יהוה, and enter into His Set-Apart Place, which He has set-apart le-olam-va-ed: and serve יהוה Your Elohim, that the fierceness of His wrath may turn away from you. 9 For if you teshuvah again to יהוה, your brothers and your children shall find rachamim before them that lead them captive,[7] so that they shall come again into this land: for יהוה Your Elohim is full of unmerited favor and rachamim, and will not turn away His face from you, if you teshuvah to Him. 10 So the postal runners passed from city to city through the country of Ephraim and Menashsheh even to Zevulun: but they laughed them to scorn, and mocked them.[8] 11 Nevertheless some from Asher and Menashsheh and of Zevulun humbled themselves, and came to Yahrushalayim.[9] 12 Also in Yahudah the hand of Elohim was to give them one lev[10] to do the commandment of the melech and of the rulers, by the word of יהוה. 13 And there were assembled at Yahrushalayim many people to keep the moed of Chag Matzoth in the second month, a very great congregation. 14 And they arose and took away the altars that were in Yahrushalayim, and all the altars for incense they took away, and cast them into the brook Kidron. 15 Then they killed the Pesach on the fourteenth day of the second month: and the kohanim and the Leviim were ashamed, and set themselves apart, and brought in the burnt offerings into the Bayit of יהוה. 16 And they stood in their place according

---

[1] Hezekiah issues an invitation to both houses to make teshuvah.
[2] Verse 5 of Second Chronicles 30 makes it clear that the division was so sharp that this was a one-time historic event, never repeated before or since. No reunion took place here.
[3] Any true revival of Yisrael must occur by invitation to both houses, not to Jewish Yisrael alone.
[4] The Assyrian exile had already begun; but was not yet complete as it was carried out in stages.
[5] Verse 6 reiterates that only a small remnant was even in the land of Ephraim to attend, since most had gone to Assyria. Remnant means "remaining trace or leftover part" according to Webster's Dictionary.
[6] The messengers of verse 6 remind the remnant that there is not much left to the House of Yisrael and that unless they head south for repentance, a similar tragedy will befall them.

[7] According to verse 9, their brothers and children were already in captivity and had not returned. These are some of the ones who became the **melo ha Goyim**.
[8] How did Ephraim react? Did the whole nation accept the invitation to return to YHWH? No; they stayed away, did not come in masses and mocked the messengers and the message. The leftover portion mocked the call to repentance. That is not an appropriate definition of unity.
[9] Verse 11 states that only "some" of the small remnant humbled themselves to come to Jerusalem. Righteous Anna of Asher, in Luke's evangel, was surely descended from those few who did go down and sojourn in Judah. Does this mean that all of Asher joined all of Judah? The text does not imply that, instead expressly stating that "some" came, thus emphasizing the oddity – not the normalcy – of Ephraim-Yisrael's coming to Judah.
[10] Yahudah had one heart. No such heart fell upon the tribes of the north.

to the commandment, according to the Torah of Moshe the man of Elohim: the kohanim sprinkled the dom, which they received from the hand of the Leviim. 17 For there were many in the congregation that were not set-apart: therefore the Leviim had the charge of the killing of the Pesach for everyone that was not clean, to set them apart to יהוה. 18 For a multitude of the people, even many of Ephraim, [1] and Menashsheh, Yissachar, and Zevulun, had not cleansed themselves, yet did they eat the Pesach otherwise than it was written. But Hizqiyahu made tefillah for them, saying, יהוה is tov and He will pardon everyone,[2] 19 That prepares his lev to seek Elohim, יהוה Elohim of His ahvot, though he be not cleansed according to the purification of the Set-Apart Place. 20 And יהוה listened to Hizqiyahu, and healed the people. 21 And the children of Yisrael that were present[3] at Yahrushalayim kept the moed of Chag Matzoth seven days with great gilah: and the Leviim and the kohanim gave tehilla to יהוה day-by-day, singing with loud instruments to יהוה. 22 And Hizqiyahu spoke comfortably to all the Leviim that taught the tov da'at of יהוה: and they did eat throughout the moed seven days, offering shalom offerings, and making confession to יהוה Elohim of their ahvot. 23 And the whole congregation took counsel to keep another seven days: and they kept another seven days with gilah. 24 For Hizqiyahu melech of Yahudah did give to the congregation a thousand bullocks and seven thousand sheep; and the rulers gave to the congregation a thousand bullocks and ten thousand sheep: and a great number of kohanim set themselves

apart. 25 And all the congregation of Yahudah, with the kohanim and the Leviim, and the entire congregation that came out of Yisrael,[4] and the gerim that came out of the land of Yisrael, and that dwelt in Yahudah, had gilah. 26 So there was great simcha in Yahrushalayim: for since the time of Shlomo the son of David melech of Yisrael there was nothing like it in Yahrushalayim. 27 Then the kohanim the Leviim arose and blessed the people: and their voice was heard, and their tefillah came up to His Set-Apart Dwelling, even to the shamayim.

31 Now when all this was finished, all Yisrael that was present[5] went out to the cities of Yahudah, and broke the images in pieces, and cut down the Asherim, and threw down the idol temples and the altars out of all Yahudah and Benyamin, in Ephraim also and Menashsheh, until they had utterly destroyed them all. Then all the children of Yisrael returned, every man to his possession, into their own cities.[6] 2 And Hizqiyahu appointed the divisions of the kohanim and the Leviim after their divisions, every man according to his service, the kohanim and Leviim for burnt offerings and for shalom offerings, to serve, and to give hodu, and to give tehilla in the gates of the tents of יהוה. 3 He appointed also the melech's portion from his substance for the burnt offerings, for the shacrit and maariv burnt offerings, and the burnt offerings for the Shabbats, and for the Rosh Chodashim, and for the set moadim, as it is written in the Torah of יהוה. 4 Also he commanded the people that dwelt in Yahrushalayim to give the portion of the kohanim and Leviim to them, that they

---

[1] Many, but not a fullness by any means.
[2] Verse 18 indicates that the few, who did appear, did so with impure hearts and defiled hands. Can anyone with an open mind and heart, seeking truth at any expense and price, honestly declare that this limited Passover is the fulfillment of the glorious two-stick millennial reunion promised for the future, when no iniquity or mocking spirits will be found in either house of Israel? The answer is an obvious "No."
[3] The term "who were present" defines the limitations of the "many" in verse 18. The ones who did not mock, but responded are the ones who were present. The very language here indicates that many were not present.

[4] Limited to those who came.
[5] As final confirmation, that the reunion is yet future. Second Chronicles 31:1 qualifies the "all Yisrael" (northerners) present at the Passover, with the qualifier "all Yisrael who were present." Not all Yisrael joined Judah. Scripture does not record any follow-up feasts that year, or any other year for that matter, displaying with forceful clarity that this was a one-time event, with some attendance from a leftover apostate populace.
[6] Notice they returned without settling in Judah.

- 952 -

might be encouraged in the Torah of **יהוה**. 5 And as soon as the commandment came abroad, the children of Yisrael brought in abundance the firstfruits of corn, wine, and oil, and honey, and of all the increase of the fields; and the tithe of all things they brought in abundantly.¹ 6 And concerning the children of Yisrael and Yahudah, that dwelt in the cities of Yahudah, they also brought in the tithe of oxen and sheep, and the tithe of set-apart things which were set-apart to **יהוה** their Elohim, and laid them up by heaps.² 7 In the third month they began to lay the foundation of the heaps, and finished them in the seventh month. 8 And when Hizqiyahu and the rulers came and saw the heaps, they blessed **יהוה**, and His people Yisrael. 9 Then Hizqiyahu questioned the kohanim and the Leviim concerning the heaps. 10 And Azaryah the head kohen of the Bayit of Tzadok answered him, and said, Since the people began to bring the offerings into the Bayit of **יהוה**, we have had enough to eat, and have left plenty: for **יהוה** has blessed His people; and that which is left is in this great storage. 11 Then Hizqiyahu commanded to prepare rooms in the Bayit of **יהוה**; and they prepared them, 12 And brought in the offerings and the tithes and the dedicated things faithfully: over which Chonanyah the Levite was ruler, and Shimei his brother was the next. 13 And Yehi-el, and Azazyah, and Nahath, and Asah-el, and Yerimoth, and Yozavad, and Elel, and Ismachiyah, and Mahath, and Benayah, were overseers under the hand of Chonanyah and Shimei his brother, at the commandment of Hizqiyahu the melech, and Azaryah the ruler of the Bayit of Elohim. 14 And Kore the son of Imnah the Levite, the gatekeeper toward the east, was over the terumah of Elohim, to distribute the offerings of **יהוה**, and the most set-apart things. 15 And next were Eden, and Minyamin, and Yeshua, and Shemayah, Amaryah, and Shecanyah, in the cities of the kohanim, in their appointed office, to give to their brothers by divisions, as well to the great as to the small: 16 Beside the males, from three years older and upward, even to everyone that enters into the Bayit of **יהוה**, his daily portion for their service in their duties according to their divisions; 17 Both to the kohanim by the bayit of their ahvot, and the Leviim from twenty years old and upward, in their duties by their divisions; 18 And to the genealogy of all their little ones, their wives, and their sons, and their daughters, through the entire congregation: for in their appointed office they set themselves apart in set-apartness: 19 Also of the sons of Aharon the kohanim, who were in the fields of the suburbs of their cities, in every city, the men that were designated by name, to give portions to all the males among the kohanim, and to all that were counted by genealogies among the Leviim. 20 And this did Hizqiyahu throughout all Yahudah, and did that which was tov and right and full of emet before **יהוה** His Elohim. 21 And in every mitzvah that he began in the service of the Bayit of Elohim, and in the Torah, and in the mishpatim, to seek His Elohim, he did it with all his lev, and prospered.

32

After these things, and their establishment, Sennacherib melech of Ashshur came, and entered into Yahudah, and encamped against the fenced cities, and thought to win them for himself. 2 And when Hizqiyahu saw that Sennacherib had come, and that he was purposed to fight against Yahrushalayim, 3 He took counsel with his rulers and his mighty men to stop the mayim of the fountains that were outside the city: and they did help him. 4 So there was gathered much people together, who stopped all the fountains, and the brook that ran through the middle of the land, saying, Why should

---

¹ Those Ephraimites that had just kept the Passover.
² Another reference to limited crossover.

the melechim of Ashshur[1] come, and find much mayim? 5 Also he strengthened himself, and built up all of the wall that was broken, and raised up to the towers, and another wall outside, and repaired Millo in the city of David, and made spears and shields in abundance. 6 And he set captains of war over the people, and gathered them together to him in the street of the gate of the city, and spoke comfortably to them, saying, 7 Be strong and courageous, be not afraid nor dismayed for the melech of Ashshur, nor for all the multitude that is with him: for there be more with us than with him: 8 With him is an arm of flesh; but with us is יהוה our Elohim to help us, and to fight our battles. And the people found rest by the words of Hizqiyahu melech of Yahudah. 9 After this did Sennacherib melech of Ashshur send his avadim to Yahrushalayim - but he himself laid siege against Lachish and all his power with him - to Hizqiyahu melech of Yahudah, and to all Yahudah that were at Yahrushalayim, saying, 10 This says Sennacherib melech of Ashshur, On what do you trust, that you stay in the siege in Yahrushalayim? 11 Does not Hizqiyahu persuade you to die by famine and by thirst, saying, יהוה our Elohim shall deliver us out of the hand of the melech of Ashshur? 12 Has not the same Hizqiyahu taken away His idol temples and His altars, and commanded Yahudah and Yahrushalayim, saying, You shall worship before one altar, and burn incense upon it? 13 Know you not what I, and my ahvot have done to all the peoples of other lands? Were the elohim of the nations of those lands in any way able to deliver their lands out of my hand? 14 Who was there among all the elohim of those nations that my ahvot utterly destroyed, which could deliver their people out of my hand, that Your Elohim should be able to deliver you out of my hand? 15 Now therefore let not Hizqiyahu deceive you, nor

persuade you on this matter, neither believe him: for no elohim of any nation or malchut was able to deliver his people out of my hand, and out of the hand of my ahvot: how much less shall Your Elohim deliver you out of my hand? 16 And his avadim spoke even more things against יהוה Elohim, and against His eved Hizqiyahu. 17 He wrote also letters to rail on יהוה Elohim of Yisrael, and to speak against Him, saying, As the elohim of the nations of the other lands have not delivered their people out of my hand, so shall not the Elohim of Hizqiyahu deliver His people out of my hand. 18 Then they cried with a loud voice in the speech of Yahudah to the people of Yahrushalayim that were on the wall, to frighten them, and to trouble them; that they might take the city. 19 And they spoke against the Elohim of Yahrushalayim, as against the elohim of the peoples of the earth, which are the work of the hands of man. 20 And for this cause Hizqiyahu the melech, and the navi Yeshayahu the son of Amotz, made tefillot and cried to the shamayim. 21 And יהוה sent a heavenly messenger, who cut off all the mighty men of bravery, and the leaders and captains in the camp of the melech of Ashshur. So he returned with shame to his own land. And when he had come into the bayit of his elohim, they that were his own offspring killed him there with the sword. 22 So יהוה saved Hizqiyahu and the inhabitants of Yahrushalayim from the hand of Sennacherib the melech of Ashshur, and from the hand of all others, and guided them on every side. 23 And many brought gifts to יהוה to Yahrushalayim, and presents to Hizqiyahu melech of Yahudah: so that he was magnified in the sight of all nations from then on. 24 In those days Hizqiyahu was sick, near to death, and made tefillah to יהוה and He spoke to him, and He gave him a sign. 25 But Hizqiyahu rendered not again according to the tov done to him; for his lev was lifted up in pride: therefore there was wrath upon him,

---

[1] Assyria had many rulers over districts and the Ephraimite exile was spread all over these districts and lands.

and upon Yahudah and Yahrushalayim. 26 Notwithstanding Hizqiyahu humbled himself for the pride of his lev, both he and the inhabitants of Yahrushalayim, so that the wrath of יהוה came not upon them in the days of Hizqiyahu. 27 And Hizqiyahu had exceeding riches and honor: and he made himself treasuries for silver, and for gold, and for precious stones, and for spices, and for shields, and for all manner of pleasant jewels; 28 Storehouses also for the increase of corn, and wine, and oil; and stalls for all kinds of beasts, and folds for flocks. 29 Also he provided for himself cities, and possessions of flocks and herds in abundance: for Elohim had given him very much substance. 30 Hizqiyahu himself also stopped the upper watercourse of Gihon, and brought it straight down to the west side of the city of David. And Hizqiyahu prospered in all his works. 31 However in the business of the ambassadors sent from the rulers of Bavel, who sent to him to seek information about all the wonders that were done in the land, Elohim left him alone, to test him, that He might know all that was in his lev. 32 Now the rest of the acts of Hizqiyahu, and his tov mitzvot, see, they are written in the vision of Yeshayahu the navi, the son of Amotz, and in the scroll of the melechim of Yahudah and Yisrael. 33 And Hizqiyahu slept with his ahvot, and they buried him in the best of the tombs of the sons of David: and all Yahudah and the inhabitants of Yahrushalayim gave him great honor at his death. And Menashsheh his son reigned in his place.

33 Menashsheh was twelve years old when he began to reign, and he reigned fifty-five years in Yahrushalayim: 2 But did that which was evil in the sight of יהוה, like the abominations of the nations, who יהוה had cast out before the children of Yisrael. 3 For he rebuilt again the idol temples which Hizqiyahu his abba had broken down, and he raised up altars for the Baalim, and made Asherim, and worshipped all the hosts of the shamayim, and served them. 4 Also he built altars in the Bayit of יהוה; about which יהוה had said, In Yahrushalayim shall My Name be le-olam-va-ed. 5 And he built altars for all the hosts of shamayim in the two courts of the Bayit of יהוה. 6 And he caused his children to pass through the fire in the Valley of the son of Hinnom: also he observed pagan times, and used enchantments, and used witchcraft, and dealt with a familiar ruach, and with spiritists: he did much evil in the sight of יהוה, to provoke Him to anger. 7 And he set a carved image, an idol that he had made, in the Bayit of Elohim, of which Elohim had said to David and to Shlomo his son, *In this Bayit, and in Yahrushalayim, which I have chosen before all the tribes of Yisrael, will I put My Name le-olam-va-ed:*[1] 8 *Neither will I any more remove the foot of Yisrael from out of the land which I have appointed for your ahvot; only if they will take heed to do all that I have commanded them, according to the whole Torah and the chukim and the ordinances by the hand of Moshe.* 9 So Menashsheh made Yahudah and the inhabitants of Yahrushalayim to go astray, and to do worse than the nations, whom יהוה had destroyed before the children of Yisrael. 10 And יהוה spoke to Menashsheh, and to His people: but they would not shema. 11 Therefore יהוה brought upon them the captains of the army of the melech of Ashshur, which took Menashsheh among the thorns, and bound him with bronze shackles, and carried him to Bavel. 12 And when he was in affliction, he sought יהוה His Elohim, and humbled himself greatly before the Elohim of His ahvot,[2] 13 And made tefillah to Him: and He was intreated by him, and listened to his supplication, and brought him again to Yahrushalayim into his malchut. Then Menashsheh knew that יהוה He was

---

[1] His Name is upon Yisrael forever.
[2] True teshuvah.

Elohim. 14 Now after this he built a wall outside the city of David, on the west side of Gihon, in the valley, even to the enterance of the Fish Gate, and it went around Ophel, and he raised it up to a very great height, and put captains of war in all the fenced cities of Yahudah. 15 And he took away the strange elohim, and the idol out of the Bayit of יהוה, and all the altars that he had built on the Mount of the Bayit of יהוה, and in Yahrushalayim, and cast them out of the city. 16 And he repaired the altar of יהוה, and sacrificed on it shalom offerings and hodu offerings, and commanded Yahudah to serve יהוה Elohim of Yisrael. 17 Nevertheless the people did sacrifice still in the idol temples, yet to יהוה their Elohim only. 18 Now the rest of the acts of Menashsheh, and his tefillah to His Elohim, and the words of the seers that spoke to him in the Name of יהוה Elohim of Yisrael, see, they are written in the scroll of the melechim of Yisrael. 19 His tefillah also, and how Elohim was moved by him, and all his sin, and his trespass, and the places in which he built idol temples, and set up Asherim and graven images, before he was humbled: see, they are all written among the sayings of the seers. 20 So Menashsheh slept with his ahvot, and they buried him in his own bayit: and Amon his son reigned in his place. 21 Amon was twenty-two years old when he began to reign, and reigned two years in Yahrushalayim. 22 But he did that which was evil in the sight of יהוה, as did Menashsheh his abba: for Amon sacrificed to all the carved images which Menashsheh his abba had made, and served them; 23 And humbled not himself before יהוה, as Menashsheh his abba had humbled himself; but Amon trespassed more and more. 24 And his avadim conspired against him, and killed him in his own bayit. 25 But the people of the land killed all them that had conspired against melech Amon; and the people of the land made Yoshiyahu his son melech in his place.

34 Yoshiyahu was eight years old when he began to reign, and he reigned in Yahrushalayim thirty-one years. 2 And he did that which was right in the sight of יהוה, and had his halacha in the halachot of David his abba, and turned neither to the right hand, nor to the left. 3 For in the eighth year of his reign, while he was yet young, he began to seek after the Elohim of David his abba: and in the twelfth year he began to purge Yahudah and Yahrushalayim of the idol temples, and the Asherim, and the carved images, and the molten images. 4 And they broke down the altars of Baalim in his presence; and the images, that were high above them, he cut down; and the Asherim, and the carved images, and the molten images, he broke in pieces, and made dust of them, and strowed it upon the graves of them that had sacrificed to them. 5 And he burnt the bones of their priests upon their altars, and cleansed Yahudah and Yahrushalayim. 6 And so he did in the cities of Menashsheh, and Ephraim, and Shimeon, even to Naphtali, with their ruins all around. [1] 7 And when he had broken down the altars and the Asherim, and had beaten the graven images into powder, and cut down all the idols throughout all the land of Yisrael, he returned to Yahrushalayim. 8 Now in the eighteenth year of his reign, when he had purged the land, and the Bayit, he sent Shaphan the son of Azalyah, and Maaseyah the leader of the city, and Yoah the son of Joahaz the recorder, to repair the Bayit of יהוה His Elohim. 9 And when they came to Hilkiyah the Kohen HaGadol, they delivered the money that was brought into the Bayit of Elohim, which the Leviim that kept the doors had gathered from the hand of Menashsheh and Ephraim, and of the remnant of Yisrael, and of all Yahudah and Benyamin; and they returned to

---

[1] His cleansing reached into territories of Ephraim that were under Judah's control. This is not any kind of proof that the two houses already have had their reunion.

Yahrushalayim.[1] 10 And they put it in the hand of the workmen that had the oversight of the Bayit of יהוה, and they gave it to the workmen that worked in the Bayit of יהוה, to repair and strengthen the Bayit: 11 Even to the craftsmen and builders they gave it, to buy hewn stone, and timber for couplings, and to floor the houses that the melechim of Yahudah had destroyed. 12 And the men did the work faithfully: and the overseers were Yahath and Ovadyah, the Leviim, of the sons of Merari; and Zacharyah and Meshullam, of the sons of the Kohathites, to oversee; and others of the Leviim, all that were skilled with instruments of music. 13 Also they who oversaw the bearers of burdens, and were overseers of all those that did work in any manner of service: and of the Leviim there were scribes, and officers, and gatekeepers. 14 And when they brought out the money that was brought into the Bayit of יהוה, Hilkiyah the kohen found a scroll of the Torah of יהוה given by Moshe. 15 And Hilkiyah answered and said to Shaphan the sopher, I have found the scroll of the Torah in the Bayit of יהוה . And Hilkiyah delivered the scroll to Shaphan. 16 And Shaphan carried the scroll to the melech, and brought the melech word back again, saying, All that was committed to your avadim, they did it. 17 And they have gathered together the money that was found in the Bayit of יהוה, and have delivered it into the hand of the overseers, and to the hand of the workmen. 18 Then Shaphan the sopher told the melech, saying, Hilkiyah the kohen has given me a scroll. And Shaphan read it before the melech. 19 And it came to pass, when the melech had heard the words of the Torah, that he tore his clothes. 20 And the melech commanded Hilkiyah, and Ahikam the son of Shaphan, and Avdon the son of Micah, and Shaphan the sopher, and Asayah an eved of the melech's, saying, 21 Go, inquire of יהוה for me, and for them that are left in Yisrael and in Yahudah,

concerning the words of the scroll[2] that is found: for great is the wrath of יהוה that is poured out upon us, because our ahvot have not kept the word of יהוה, to do after all that is written in this scroll. 22 And Hilkiyah, and they that the melech had appointed, went to Huldah the neviyah, the wife of Shallum the son of Tikvath, the son of Hasrah, keeper of the wardrobe - now she dwelt in Yahrushalayim in the second quarter - and they spoke to her to that effect. 23 And she answered them, This says יהוה Elohim of Yisrael, *Tell the man that sent you to Me,* 24 *This says* יהוה, *See, I will bring evil upon this place, and upon the inhabitants of it, even all the curses that are written in the scroll that they have read before the melech of Yahudah:* 25 *Because they have forsaken Me, and have burned incense to other elohim, that they might provoke Me to anger with all the works of their hands; therefore My wrath shall be poured out upon this place, and shall not be quenched.* 26 *And as for the melech of Yahudah, who sent you to inquire of* יהוה, *so shall you say to him, This says* יהוה *Elohim of Yisrael concerning the words which you have heard;* 27 *Because your lev was tender, and you did humble yourself before Elohim, when you heard His words against this place, and against its inhabitants and humbled yourself before Me, and did tear your clothes, and weep before Me; I have even heard you also, says* יהוה. 28 *See, I will gather you to your ahvot, and you shall be gathered to your grave in shalom, neither shall your eyes see all the evil that I will bring upon this place, and upon the inhabitants of it.* So they brought the melech word again. 29 Then the melech sent and gathered together all the zachanim of Yahudah and Yahrushalayim. 30 And the melech went up into the Bayit of יהוה, and all the men of Yahudah, and the inhabitants of Yahrushalayim, and the kohanim, and the Leviim, and all the

---

[1] Both houses contributed to the well-being of the temple.

[2] An attempt to reach those of both houses, with yet another call to repentance.

people, great and small: and he read in their ears all the words of the scroll of the covenant that was found in the Bayit of יהוה. 31 And the melech stood in his place, and made a covenant before יהוה, to have their halacha after יהוה, and to keep His mishpatim, and His testimonies, and His chukim, with all His lev, and with all His being, to perform the words of the covenant that is written in this scroll. 32 And he caused all that were present in Yahrushalayim and Benyamin to stand by it. And the inhabitants of Yahrushalayim did according to the covenant of Elohim, the Elohim of their ahvot. 33 And Yoshiyahu took away all the abominations out of all the countries that pertained to the children of Yisrael, and made all that were present in Yisrael[1] to serve, even to serve יהוה their Elohim. And all his days they did not depart from following יהוה, the Elohim of their ahvot.

35 Moreover Yoshiyahu kept a Pesach to יהוה in Yahrushalayim: and they killed the Pesach on the fourteenth day of the first month. 2 And he set the kohanim in their duties, and encouraged them to the service of the Bayit of יהוה, 3 And said to the Leviim that taught all Yisrael, who were set-apart to יהוה, Put the Set-Apart Ark in the Bayit which Shlomo the son of David melech of Yisrael did build; it shall not be a burden upon your shoulders: serve יהוה Your Elohim, and His people Yisrael, 4 And prepare yourselves by the houses of your ahvot, after your divisions, according to the writing of David melech of Yisrael, and according to the writing of Shlomo his son. 5 And stand in the Set-Apart Place according to the divisions of the families of the ahvot of your brothers the people, and after the division of the families of the Leviim. 6 So kill the Pesach, and set yourselves apart, and prepare your brothers,

so that they may do according to the word of יהוה by the hand of Moshe. 7 And Yoshiyahu gave to the people, of the flock, lambs and kids, all for the Pesach offerings, for all that were present, to the number of thirty-three thousand bullocks: these were of the melech's substance. 8 And his rulers gave willingly to the people, to the kohanim, and to the Leviim: Hilkiyah and Zacharyah and Yehi-el, rulers of the Bayit of Elohim, they gave to the kohanim for the Pesach offerings two thousand six hundred small cattle, and three hundred oxen. 9 Chonanyah also, and Shemayah and Nethan-el, his brothers, and Hashavyah and Yei-el and Yozabad, head of the Leviim, gave to the Leviim for Pesach offerings five thousand small cattle, and five hundred oxen. 10 So the service was prepared, and the kohanim stood in their place, and the Leviim in their courses, according to the melech's commandment. 11 And they killed the Pesach, and the kohanim sprinkled the dom from their hands, and the Leviim skinned them. 12 And they removed the burnt offerings, so that they might give according to the divisions of the families of the people, to offer to יהוה, as it is written in the scroll of Moshe. And so they did with the oxen. 13 And they roasted the Pesach with fire according to the ordinance: but the other set-apart offerings they cooked in pots, and in caldrons, and in pans, and divided them speedily among all the people. 14 And afterward they made ready for themselves, and for the kohanim: because the kohanim the sons of Aharon were busy in offering the burnt offerings and the fat until night; therefore the Leviim prepared for themselves, and for the kohanim the sons of Aharon. 15 And the singers the sons of Asaph were in their places, according to the commandment of David, and Asaph, and Heman, and Yeduthun the melech's seer; and the gatekeepers waited at every gate; they might not depart from their service; for their brothers the Leviim prepared for them. 16 So all the service of

---

[1] Another reference to Ephraim as being present amongst Judah, but not as having been fully reunited with Judah.

יהוה was prepared the same day, to keep the Pesach, and to offer burnt offerings upon the altar of יהוה, according to the commandment of melech Yoshiyahu. 17 And the children of Yisrael that were present[1] kept the Pesach at that time, and the moed of Chag Matzoth seven days. 18 And there was no Pesach like to that kept in Yisrael from the days of Schmuel the navi; neither did all the melechim of Yisrael [2] ever shomer such a Pesach as Yoshiyahu kept, and the kohanim, and the Leviim, and all Yahudah and Yisrael that were present, [3] and the inhabitants of Yahrushalayim. 19 In the eighteenth year of the reign of Yoshiyahu was this Pesach kept. 20 After all this, when Yoshiyahu had prepared the Beit HaMikdash, Necho melech of Mitzrayim came up to fight against Carchemish by the Euphrates River: and Yoshiyahu went out against him. 21 But he sent ambassadors to him, saying, What have I to do with you, you melech of Yahudah? I come not against you this day, but against the bayit with which I have war: for Elohim commanded me to hurry: refrain from meddling with Elohim, who is with me, that He does not destroy you. 22 Nevertheless Yoshiyahu would not turn his face from him, but disguised himself, that he might fight with him, and listened not to the words of Necho from the mouth of Elohim, and came to fight in the Valley of Megiddo. 23 And the archers shot at melech Yoshiyahu; and the melech said to his avadim, Take me away; for I am severely wounded. 24 His avadim therefore took him out of that mirkavah, and put him in the second mirkavah that he had; and they brought him to Yahrushalayim, and he died, and was buried in one of the tombs of his ahvot. And all Yahudah and Yahrushalayim mourned for Yoshiyahu.

25 And Yirmeyahu lamented for Yoshiyahu: and all the singing men and the singing women spoke of Yoshiyahu in their lamentations until this day, and made them an ordinance in Yisrael: and, see, they are written in the lamentations. 26 Now the rest of the acts of Yoshiyahu, and his tov mitzvot, according to that which was written in the Torah of יהוה, 27 And his mitzvot, the first and last, see, they are written in the scroll of the melechim of Yisrael and Yahudah.

36 Then the people of the land took Yehoahaz the son of Yoshiyahu, and made him melech in his abba's place in Yahrushalayim. 2 Yehoahaz was twenty-three years old when he began to reign, and he reigned three months in Yahrushalayim. 3 And the melech of Mitzrayim turned aside and took Yahrushalayim, and imposed on the land a hundred talents of silver and a talent of gold. 4 And the melech of Mitzrayim made Eliakim his brother melech over Yahudah and Yahrushalayim, and changed his name to Yehoyakim. And Necho took Yehoahaz his brother, and carried him to Mitzrayim. 5 Yehoyakim was twenty-five years old when he began to reign, and he reigned eleven years in Yahrushalayim: and he did that which was evil in the sight of יהוה his Elohim. 6 Against him came up Nebuchadnezzar melech of Bavel, and bound him in bronze shackles, to carry him to Bavel. 7 Nebuchadnezzar also carried the vessels of the Bayit of יהוה to Bavel, and put them in his temple at Bavel. 8 Now the rest of the acts of Yehoyakim, and his abominations which he did, and that which was found in him, see, they are written in the scroll of the melechim of Yisrael and Yahudah: and Yehoyakin his son reigned in his place. 9 Yehoyakin was eight years old when he began to reign, and he reigned three months and ten days in Yahrushalayim: and he did that which was evil in the sight of יהוה.

---

[1] "The children of Yisrael that were present"...By inspiration the Ruach HaKodesh keeps adding this phrase indicating when used that Scripture does not speak of all of Ephraim, but only those few who chose to be present. We cannot ignore this simplistic yet true recurring phrase.
[2] Ephraim.
[3] See note for verse 17 above.

10 And at the turn of the year,[1] melech Nebuchadnezzar sent, and brought him to Bavel, with the valuable vessels of the Bayit of יהוה, and made Tzidqiyahu his brother melech over Yahudah and Yahrushalayim. 11 Tzidqiyahu was twenty-one years old when he began to reign, and reigned eleven years in Yahrushalayim. 12 And he did that which was evil in the sight of יהוה His Elohim, and humbled not himself before Yirmeyahu ha navi speaking from the mouth of יהוה. 13 And he also rebelled against melech Nebuchadnetzar, who had made him swear by Elohim: but he stiffened his neck, and hardened his lev from turning to יהוה Elohim of Yisrael. 14 Moreover all the heads of the kohanim, and the people, transgressed very much just like all the abominations of the nations; and polluted the Bayit of יהוה which He had set-apart in Yahrushalayim. 15 And יהוה Elohim of their ahvot sent for them by His messengers, rising up early, and sending them; because He had rachamim on His people, and on His dwelling place: 16 But they mocked the messengers of Elohim, and despised His words, and misused His neviim, until the wrath of יהוה arose against His people, until there was no remedy. 17 Therefore He brought upon them the melech of the Chaldeans, who killed their young men with the sword in the bayit of their Set-Apart Place, and had no rachamim upon young men or maidens, older men, or those that were frail: He gave them all into his hand.

18 And all the vessels of the Bayit of Elohim, great and small, and the treasures of the Bayit of יהוה, and the treasures of the melech, and of his rulers; all these he brought to Bavel. 19 And they burnt the Bayit of Elohim, and broke down the wall of Yahrushalayim, and burnt all the palaces of it with fire, and destroyed all the valuable vessels in it. 20 And those that had escaped from the sword he carried away to Bavel; where they were avadim to him and his sons until the reign of the malchut of Persia: 21 To fulfill the word of יהוה by the mouth of Yirmeyahu, until the land had enjoyed her Shabbats: for as long as she lay desolate she kept Shabbat, to fulfill seventy years.[2] 22 Now in the first year of Koresh melech of Persia, so that the word of יהוה spoken by the mouth of Yirmeyahu might be accomplished, יהוה stirred up the ruach of Koresh melech of Persia, so that he made a proclamation throughout all his malchut, and put it also in writing, saying, 23 This says Koresh melech of Persia, All the malchutim of the earth has יהוה Elohim of the shamayim given me; and He has charged me to build him a Bayit in Yahrushalayim, which is in Yahudah. Who is there among you from all His people? יהוה His Elohim be with him, and now let him go and make aliyah.

---

[1] Equinox.

[2] Ten seven-year periods.

The Renewed Covenant Of Our MarYah Yahshua

Promised To Both Our Houses of Yisrael.

When they therefore had come together, they asked Him, saying, Master, will You at this time restore again the malchut to Yisrael?

Ma'aseh Shlichim-Acts 1:6

³¹הִנֵּה יָמִים בָּאִים נְאֻם יהוה וְכָרַתִּי אֶת בֵּית יִשְׂרָאֵל וְאֶת בֵּית יְהוּדָה בְּרִית חֲדָשָׁה׃ ³²לֹא כַבְּרִית אֲשֶׁר כָּרַתִּי אֶת אֲבוֹתָם בְּיוֹם הֶחֱזִיקִי בְיָדָם לְהוֹצִיאָם מֵאֶרֶץ מִצְרָיִם אֲשֶׁר הֵמָּה הֵפֵרוּ אֶת בְּרִיתִי וְאָנֹכִי בָּעַלְתִּי בָם נְאֻם יהוה׃ ³³כִּי זֹאת הַבְּרִית אֲשֶׁר אֶכְרֹת אֶת בֵּית יִשְׂרָאֵל אַחֲרֵי הַיָּמִים הָהֵם נְאֻם יהוה נָתַתִּי אֶת תּוֹרָתִי בְּקִרְבָּם וְעַל לִבָּם אֶכְתֲּבֶנָּה וְהָיִיתִי לָהֶם לֵאלֹהִים וְהֵמָּה יִהְיוּ לִי לְעָם׃ ³⁴וְלֹא יְלַמְּדוּ עוֹד אִישׁ אֶת רֵעֵהוּ וְאִישׁ אֶת אָחִיו לֵאמֹר דְּעוּ אֶת יהוה כִּי כוּלָּם יֵדְעוּ אוֹתִי לְמִקְטַנָּם וְעַד גְדוֹלָם נְאֻם יהוה כִּי אֶסְלַח לַעֲוֹנָם וּלְחַטָּאתָם לֹא אֶזְכָּר עוֹד׃

Yirmiyahu/Jeremiah 31:31-34

מתיתיהו

The Besorah According To

Mattityahu – Matthew

To All Nations

1 The scroll of the generations of **יהושע**[1] the Moshiach, Ben David, the Son of Avraham. 2 Avraham begat Yitzchak; and Yitzchak begat Yaakov; and Yaakov begat Yahudah and his brothers; 3 And Yahudah begat Peretz and Tzerah of Tamar; and Peretz begat Hetsron; and Hetsron begat Ram; 4 And Ram begat Amminadav; and Amminadav begat Nahshon; and Nahshon begat Salmon; 5 And Salmon begat Boaz of Rachav;[2] and Boaz begat Oved of Ruth;[3] and Obed begat Yishai; 6 And Yishai begat David the melech; and David the melech begat Shlomo of her that had been the wife of Uriah;[4] 7 And Shlomo begat Rehovoam; and Rehovoam begat Aviyah; and Aviyah begat Asa; 8 And Asa begat Yahoshaphat; and Yahoshaphat begat Yoram; and Yoram begat Uzziyah;[5] 9 And Uzziyah begat Yoatham; and Yoatham begat Achaz; and Achaz begat Hizqiyahu; 10 And Hizqiyahu begat Menashsheh; and Menashsheh begat Amon; and Amon begat Yoshiyahu; 11 And Yoshiyahu begat Yehkonia[6] and his brothers, about the time they were carried away to Bavel: 12 And after the exile to Bavel, Yehkonia begat Shealtiel; and Shealtiel begat Zeruvavel; 13 And Zeruvavel begat Avihud; and Avihud begat Elyaqim; and Elyaqim begat Azor; 14 And Azor begat Tzadok; and Tzadok begat Achim; and Achim begat Elihud; 15 And Elihud begat El-Azar; and El-Azar begat Mattan; and Mattan begat Yaakov; 16 And Yaakov begat Yoseph. This Yoseph was the

---

[1] The True Name of YHWH's Only Begotten Son, recovered as it initially appeared prior to His days on earth, meaning YHWH who does the saving. The use of Yahoshua rather than Y'shua or Yeshua as the name of Moshiach, greatly depends on the historical context. For the *Restoration Scriptures True Name Edition*, we have opted for Yahoshua because in terms of our research, this was the form the Name had in terms of pre-Babylonian captivity, as well as its clear linkage in the prophetic Scriptures, such as in Zechariah 6:11-12. Add to that the fact that Yahshua came in His Father's name, which most obviously contains the letter **hey** as in **Yah**oshua. However, in terms of what Moshiach was actually called at the time of His first advent, both the Peshitta Aramaic and Old Syriac texts refer to him as **yud-shen-vav-ayin** rather than **yud hey vav shen ayin**. We have opted for the full name including the letter **hey** as revealed prior to corruption.
[2] A non-biological Yisraelite and a whore to boot is considered a Yisraelite because she willfully joined Yisrael and performed the mitzvah of hiding the spies. She is honored as a Yisraelite by being placed in Moshiach's lineage.
[3] Ruth became a mother in Yisrael as a Yisraelite in Moshiach's lineage, yet was never considered Jewish.
[4] Uriah was a Hittite and yet his wife is considered a Yisraelite; as was he, since he was even in David's army.
[5] Actually Matthew leaves out three descendants of Jehosophat here (Ahaziah, Joash, and Amaziah), because Jehosophat's son Jehoram married cursed King Ahab's (husband of Jezebel of the House of Yisrael) daughter (2nd Chronicles 18:1, 21:1, 4-7). So while YHWH did not curse the entire House of Judah, He did curse the House of Ahab; and by marrying into the House of Ahab Jehoram brought cursed domlines into the House of Judah, or Solomon's downline. As such, YHWH cursed three generations of Jehoram's offspring without cursing the entire lineage forever as seen in Exodus 20:4-5, where YHWH allows that kind of curse for only three generations before it is lifted. So while they are counted or listed physically elsewhere, they cannot be considered ancestors of Moshiach. Were Matthew to include the three missing kings as most anti-missionaries want him to (Ahaziah, Joash, and Amaziah), his genealogy would be invalid and most Jews would have laughed him to scorn. So the three so-called missing kings are not missing at all. YHWH through Matthew intentionally leaves them out.
[6] YHWH cursed Jechoniah in Jeremiah 22:24-30. That curse was lifted clearly in Zerubabel his grandson, as confirmed by YHWH through Haggai in chapter 2 verses 20-23. In those verses the royal signet seal of kingly favor taken from Jechoniah is returned to Zerubabel. Moreover, the curse was for Jechoniah to be childless; which we see was reversed as he certainly had children. This obstacle to Yahshua being Moshiach no longer exists and was removed some 500 years before His birth.

gowra-guardian[1] of Miryam, from whom was born יהושע, who is called the Moshiach. 17 So all the generations from Avraham to David are fourteen generations; and from David until the carrying away into Bavel are fourteen generations; and from the carrying away into Bavel to the Moshiach are fourteen generations. [2] 18 Now the birth of יהושע the Moshiach was in this manner: When His ima Miryam was espoused to Yoseph[3], before they came together, she was found to be with Child of the Ruach HaKodesh.[4] 19 Then Yoseph her baalah-husband[5], being a tzadik man, and not willing to make her a public example, desired to put her away and conceal her.

20 But while he thought on these things, see, the heavenly messenger of the Master יהוה[6] appeared to him in a dream, saying, Yoseph, ben David, fear not to take to you Miryam your wife: for that which is conceived in her is from the Ruach HaKodesh. 21 And she shall bring forth a Son, and you shall call His Name יהושע: for He shall save His people[7] from their sins. 22 Now all this was done, that it might be fulfilled what was spoken by the Master יהוה through ha navi, saying, 23 See, a virgin[8] shall be with Child, and shall bring forth a Son, and they[9] shall call His Name Emmanu-El,[10] which when interpreted[11] means, Elohim with us. 24 Then Yoseph being raised from sleep did as the heavenly messenger of the Master יהוה had told him, and took to himself his wife: 25 And had no sexual relations with her until she had brought forth her firstborn Son: and he called His Name יהושע.

2 Now when יהושע was born in Beth-Lechem of Yahudah in the days of Herod the melech, see, there came astrologers from the east to Yahrushalayim, 2 Saying, Where is He that is born Melech of the Yahudim? For we have seen His cochav in the east, and have come to worship Him. 3 When Herod the melech had heard these things, he was troubled, and all Yahrushalayim with him. 4 And when he

---

[1] The Aramaic term **gowra** is mistranslated as "husband" in all Greek manuscripts. **Gowra** in proper context is a guardian or legal guardian or legal caretaker, as seen in the Torah in Deuteronomy 25:5-6 where Yisraelites are given the command to establish a **gowra** or a legal guardian. Most likely this Joseph took Mary's deceased father's place and became her **gawra** as Boaz did in Ruth 2:20, where he is called the **gowra** for Ruth in the Aramaic Targum. (Boaz was Ruth's **gowra** before he ever became her husband.) This Joseph (in verse 16) was Mary's legal guardian. In verse 19, however, the Aramaic/Hebrew word is **baalah** that can only mean "husband." The Aramaic Peshitta clearly uses the two different words (**gowra** and **baalah**) to show that one Joseph (in verse 16) was Mary's guardian, whereas the other Joseph (in verse 19) was Mary's husband. With this clarification, we see that there are indeed 14 generations from Babylonian captivity to Yahshua's birth (in accordance with Matthew's bold insistence in verse 17 that there are three sets of 14 generations), versus only 13 if the two Josephs were to be accounted as one and the same. If we count Joseph the **gowra**/legal guardian as #12, Mary as #13 and Yahshua as #14, we have a perfect set of 14. Therefore this genealogy is clearly Miryam's genealogy and not Joseph's. In order to be the Moshiach, Yahshua had to inherit the throne from Solomon – not Nathan as Christianity teaches. Nathan never sat on the throne, and David's many prophecies indicate that the lineage of the Moshiach would be through Solomon alone and never through another one of his sons. Therefore Luke's account does not give Mary's genealogy, whereas Matthew's account does give Mary's genealogy, as he counts Mary as number 13 in the final set of 14, thereby allowing verse 17 make perfect sense. One can pick up on this only in the Aramaic Peshitta text, which not only is the primacy text from which all Greek translations have come, but also is the only one that differentiates between **gowra** and **baalah**.
[2] The **gematria**, or numerical value of David in Hebrew is 14. The three sets of 14 indicate that Yahshua is from the royal House of David. As seen in study note # 5, when using the Aramaic Peshitta, one can see that there were three perfect sets of 14, dropping the three cursed kings along with differentiating between the guardian Joseph and the later husband Joseph.
[3] Mathew is now finished with the genealogies of the past having made his point; and now switches to the future, further separating the two Josephs after making a net summation of the past in verse 17.
[4] At no time is this Yoseph the **baalah** or husband of Mary ever called Yahshua's father.
[5] See study note on verse 16 above.

[6] Mar-Yah or Master Yah in the actual Aramaic.
[7] Yisrael.
[8] **Almah** in Hebrew, and **parthenos** in Greek and **betulah** in Aramaic.
[9] The "they" Matthew speaks of are the Jews who expected the long-awaited Moshiach, as Rashi and other scholars have stated. The "they" Matthew speaks of is also a euphemism for the "prophets of Yisrael."
[10] A title not a name. The Jews were waiting for a divine visitation, and not someone with a name like "Immanu-el Glickstein." Matthew, operating in the **remez** level of **PaRDes**, takes the freedom to say that through this virgin birth, the long-held concept of Moshiach would finally be brought to pass – not that a baby actually named "Immanu-el" would show up. Moreover, the Hebrew title contains two smaller words ("**Emanu**" and "**El**"). The prophets of Yisrael all believed that Moshiach was eternal ("**El**") and that Moshiach would come to Yisrael ("**Emanu**" or "with us" in Yisrael) – further substantiating a concept and not a proper name for Moshiach.
[11] A proper personal noun or name cannot be interpreted, but must be transliterated. But the common title Emanu-El can be and is interpreted here.

had gathered all the main kohanim and Sophrim of the people together, he demanded of them where the Moshiach would be born. 5 And they said to him, In Beth-Lechem of Yahudah: for this is written by ha navi, 6 And you Beth-Lechem, in the land of Yahudah, are not the least among the princes of Yahudah: for out of you shall come a Governor that shall rule My people Yisrael. [1] 7 Then Herod, when he had privately called the magicians, inquired of them diligently what time the cochav appeared. 8 And he sent them to Beth-Lechem, and said, Go and search diligently for the young Child; and when you have found Him, bring me word again, that I may come and worship Him also. 9 When they had heard the melech, they departed; and, see, the cochav, which they saw in the east, went before them, until it came and stood over where the young Child was. 10 When they saw the cochav, they rejoiced with exceeding great simcha. 11 And when they had come into the bayit, they saw the young Child with Miryam His ima, and fell down, and worshipped Him: and when they had opened their treasures, they presented to Him gifts; gold, and frankincense, and myrrh. 12 And being warned of יהוה in a dream that they should not return to Herod, they departed into their own country another way. 13 And when they were departed, see, the heavenly messenger of the Master יהוה appeared to Yoseph in a dream, saying, Arise, and take the young Child and His ima, and flee into Mitzrayim, and stay there until I bring you word: for Herod will seek the young Child to destroy Him. 14 When he arose, he took the young Child and His ima by night, and departed into Mitzrayim: 15 And was there until the death of Herod: that it might be fulfilled what was spoken by the Master יהוה through ha navi, saying, Out of Mitzrayim have I called My Son. 16 Then Herod, when he saw that he was mocked by the wise

men, was exceedingly angry, and sent forth, and killed all the children that were in Beth-Lechem, and in all its coasts, from two years old and under, according to the time which he had diligently inquired of the wise men. 17 Then was fulfilled that which was spoken by Yirmeyahu ha navi, saying, 18 In Ramah was there a voice heard, lamentation, and weeping, and great mourning, Rachel weeping for her children, and she would not be comforted, because they are no more. [2] 19 But when Herod was dead, see, a heavenly messenger of the Master יהוה appeared in a dream to Yoseph in Mitzrayim, 20 Saying, Arise, and take the young Child and His ima, and go into the land of Yisrael: for they are dead who sought the young Child's chayim. 21 And he arose, and took the young Child and His ima, and came into the land of Yisrael. 22 But when he heard that Archelaus did reign in Yahudah in the place of his abba Herod, he was afraid to go there: notwithstanding, being warned by יהוה in a dream, he turned aside into the parts of Galil: 23 And He came and dwelt in a city called Natzareth: that it might be fulfilled what was spoken by the neviim, He shall be called a Notsri.

3 In those days came Yochanan HaMatbeel, proclaiming in the wilderness of Yahudah, 2 And saying, Make teshuvah: for the malchut ha shamayim[3] is offered. [4] 3 For this is he that was spoken of by ha navi Yeshayahu, saying, The voice of one crying in the wilderness, Prepare the way of the Master יהוה , make His paths straight. 4 And the same Yochanan had his clothing from camel's hair, and a leather girdle all around his loins; and his food was locusts and wild honey. 5 Then went out to him

---

[2] The destruction of Yahudah's children matched those of Ephraim's children who were killed or dispersed some 700 years prior. The tears of Rachel are for all Yisrael's return from death, as seen in Jeremiah 31:17.
[3] The long-awaited Heavenly King; and His solution to Yisrael's exile and two-bayit division.
[4] Hebrew **keruvah** meaning "offered."

Yahrushalayim, and all of Yahudah, and the entire region all around the Yarden River, 6 And were immersed by him in the Yarden River, confessing their sins. 7 But when he saw many of the Prushim and Tzadukim come to his mikvah, he said to them, O generation of vipers, who has warned you to flee from the wrath to come? 8 Bring forth therefore fruits of perfect[1] teshuvah: 9 And think not within yourselves, We have Avraham as our abba: for I say to you that יהוה is able of these stones to raise up children for Avraham. 10 And now also the axe is laid to the root of the eytzim: therefore every eytz, which brings not forth tov fruit, is cut down, and cast into the fire.[2] 11 I indeed mikvah you with the mayim of teshuvah: but He that comes after me is mightier than I, whose sandals I am not worthy to bear:[3] He shall mikvah you with the fire of the Ruach HaKodesh, 12 Whose fan is in His hand, and He will thoroughly purge His floor,[4] and gather His wheat into the storehouse; but He will burn up the chaff with unquenchable fire. 13 Then came יהושע from Galil to the Yarden River to Yochanan, to be immersed by him. 14 But Yochanan forbad Him, saying, I have need to be immersed by You, and You come to me? 15 And יהושע answering said to him, *Allow it to be so now: for this will allow us to fulfill all tzedakah.* Then he allowed Him. 16 And יהושע, when He was immersed, He went up immediately out of the mayim: and, see, ha shamayim were opened over Him, and Yochanan saw the Ruach of יהוה descending like a yonah, and resting upon Him: 17 And see a voice from ha shamayim, saying, *This is My beloved Son, in whom I am well pleased.*

4 Then was יהושע led up by the Ruach into the wilderness to be tempted by ha s.a.tan. 2 And when He had fasted forty days and forty nights, He was hungry afterward. 3 And when the tempter came to Him, he said, If You are the Son of Elohim, command that these stones be made lechem. 4 But He answered and said, *It is written, Man shall not live by lechem alone, but by every word that proceeds out of the mouth of* יהוה. 5 Then s.a.tan took Him up into the Set-Apart city, and set Him on a pinnacle of the Beit HaMikdash, 6 And said to Him, If You are the Son of Elohim, cast Yourself down: for it is written, He shall give His heavenly messengers charge concerning You: and in their hands they shall bear You up, lest at any time You dash Your foot against a stone. 7 יהושע said to him, *It is written again, You shall not test the Master* יהוה *Your Elohim.* 8 Again, s.a.tan took Him up into an exceedingly high mountain, and showed Him all the malchutim of the olam hazeh, and the tifereth of them; 9 And said to Him, All these things will I give You, if You will fall down and worship me and bare Your head to me.[5] 10 Then said יהושע to him, *Go, s.a.tan: for it is written, You shall worship* יהוה *Your Elohim, and Him only shall you serve.* 11 Then s.a.tan left Him, and, see, heavenly messengers came and attended to Him. 12 Now when יהושע had heard that Yochanan was cast into prison, He departed into Galil; 13 And leaving Natzareth, He came and dwelt in the city of Nachum, which is upon the sea coast, in the borders of Zevulon and Naphtali:[6] 14 That it might be fulfilled what was spoken by Yeshayahu ha navi, saying, 15 The land of Zevulon, and the land of Naphtali, by the way of the sea, beyond the Yarden River, Galil of the gentiles;[7] [8] 16 The people who sat in

---

[1] Hebrew Shem Tov reference.
[2] Moshiach would come to refine both houses into one, by removing all the bad fruit.
[3] Shem Tov reference.
[4] A clear reference to Yisrael.

[5] Hebrew Shem Tov reference; Proof that our Moshiach wore a head covering as a man.
[6] Land of Ephraim Yisrael.
[7] This is a key passage identifying Yahshua's true mission. He dwelt and ministered mostly in the north, the former home of Ephraim Yisrael, to bring them back. Notice these verses even mention the tribes from the north that were allegedly missing; yet Yahshua knew where to find them living as gentiles.
[8] Even in His day it was known that Ephraim Yisrael had become the fullness of the gentiles, hence the term "Galilee of the gentiles," who would see the light and return to the kingdom.

darkness saw great Light; and to those who sat in the region and shadow of death Light is sprung up.[1] 17 From that time יהושע began to proclaim, and to say, Teshuvah: for the malchut ha shamayim[2] is offered. 18 And יהושע, walking by the Sea of Galil, saw two brothers, Shimon called Kepha, and Andri his brother, casting a net into the sea: for they were fishermen. 19 And He said to them, Follow Me, and I will make you fishers of men.[3] 20 And they immediately left their nets, and followed Him. 21 And going on from from there, He saw two other brothers, Yaakov the son of Zavdi, and Yochanan his brother, in a ship with Zavdi their abba, mending their nets; and He called them. 22 And they immediately left the ship and their abba, and followed Him. 23 And יהושע went about all Galil, [4] teaching [5] in their synagogues, and proclaiming the besarot of the malchut, and healing all manner of sickness and all manner of disease among the people of Yisrael. 24 And His fame went throughout all Aram-Syria:[6] and they brought to Him all sick people that were taken with divers diseases and torments, and those who were possessed with shadim, and those which were lunatics, and those that had paralyses; and He healed them. 25 And there followed Him great multitudes[7] of people from Galil, and from Decapolis, and from Yahrushalayim, and from Yahudah, and from beyond the Yarden River.[8]

5 And seeing the multitudes,[9] He went up into a mountain: [10] and when He was seated, His talmidim came to Him: 2 And He opened His mouth, and taught them, saying, 3 *Blessed are the poor in ruach: for theirs is the malchut ha shamayim. 4 Blessed are they that mourn: for they shall be comforted. 5 Blessed are the meek: for they shall inherit the Land.[11] 6 Blessed are they that do hunger and thirst after tzedakah: for they shall be filled. 7 Blessed are the racham givers: for they shall obtain rachamim. 8 Blessed are the pure in lev: for they shall see* יהוה. 9 *Blessed are the shalom-makers: for they shall be called b'nai* יהוה. 10 *Blessed are those who are persecuted for tzedakah's sake: for theirs is the malchut ha shamayim. 11 Blessed are you, when men shall revile you, and persecute you, and shall say all manner of evil against you falsely, for My sake. 12 Gilah, and be in great simacha: for great is your reward in ha shamayim: for so persecuted they the neviim who were before you. 13 You are the salt of the earth: but if the salt has lost its taste, how shall it be salted? It is no longer tov for anything, but to be cast out, and to be trodden under the feet of men.[12] 14 You are the light of the olam hazeh.[13] A city that is set on a hill cannot be hidden. 15 Neither do men light a candle, and put it under a bushel, but on a menorah; and it gives light to all that are in the bayit. 16 Let your light so shine before men, that they may see your tov mitzvot, and esteem Your Abba who is in ha shamayim. 17 Think not that I am come to destroy the Torah, or the neviim: I have not come to destroy, but to completely reveal it in its*

---

[1] The very ones from the spiritually dark north.
[2] According to Acts 1:8 the kingdom of heaven was when Yisrael's exile was over and the King Moshiach would arrive to regather and restore both houses of Yisrael.
[3] A fulfillment of the promise that Yisrael would multiply like fishes in the midst of the earth in Beresheth 48:16. Fishermen trained by Yahshua certainly knew how to catch the multitudes of Yisrael through the Great Commission.
[4] In search of lost gentile Ephraim.
[5] Torah.
[6] Home to many exiles of Yisrael and the route north to the lands of Ephraim's Assyrian captivity.
[7] **Melo Hagoyim.**
[8] Starting to gather talmidim from Galilee of the gentiles and Yahudah.

[9] Multitudes speak of the offspring of Jacob that would fill all the earth.
[10] The mighty "Mount of Reversal" where all the curses upon the multitudes of Ephraim were reversed in this Sermon on the Mount. For full details on this sermon and the reversing of Ephraim's curses go to: **Mt. of Reversal** at: http://yourarmstoisrael.org/Articles_new/restoration/?page=25 &type=12.
[11] Yisrael.
[12] What mankind has done to YHWH's true Name, bringing it to naught.
[13] Renewed Covenant Yisrael.

intended fullness. 18 For truly I say to you, Until the current shamayim and earth pass away, not one yud or one nekudah shall by any means pass from the Torah, until all be fulfilled. 19 Whoever therefore shall break one of the least Torah commandments, and shall teach men so, he shall be called the least in the malchut ha shamayim: but whoever shall do and teach the commands, the same shall be called great in the malchut ha shamayim. 20 For I say to you, Except your tzedakah shall exceed the tzedakah of the Sophrim and Prushim, you shall in no case enter into the malchut ha shamayim. 21 You have heard that it was said by them of old time, You shall not kill; and whoever shall kill shall be in danger of the mishpat: 22 But I say to you, That whoever is angry with his brother without a cause shall be in danger of the mishpat: and whoever shall say to his brother, Raca, you nothing idiot, shall be in danger of the Sanhedrin: but whoever shall say, You fool, shall be in danger of Gei-Hinnom fire. 23 Therefore if you bring your gift to the altar, and there remember that your brother has anything against you; 24 Leave your gift before the altar, and go your way; first be reconciled to your brother, and then come and offer your gift. 25 Agree with your adversary quickly, while you are in the way with him; lest at any time the adversary deliver you to the shophet, and the shophet deliver you to the officer, and you be cast into prison. 26 Truly I say to you, You shall by no means come out from there, until you have paid the last penny. 27 You have heard that it was said by them of old time, You shall not commit adultery: 28 But I say to you, That whoever looks on a woman to lust after her has committed adultery with her already in his lev. 29 And if your right eye seduces[1] you, pluck it out, and cast it from you: for it is better for you that one of your members should perish, than for your whole body to be cast into Gei-Hinnom. 30 And if

your right hand seduces[2] you, cut if off, and cast it from you: for it is more profitable for you that one of your members should perish, rather than your whole body should be cast into Gei-Hinnom. 31 It has been said, Whoever shall put away his wife, let him give her a Get of divorce. 32 But I say to you, That whoever shall put away his wife, except for the cause of fornication, causes her to commit adultery: and whoever shall marry her that is divorced commits adultery.[3] 33 Again, you have heard that it has been said by them of old time, You shall not swear falsely, but shall perform to the Master יהוה your oaths: 34 But I say to you, Swear not at all; neither by ha shamayim; for it is יהוה's throne: 35 Nor by the earth; for it is His footstool: neither by Yahrushalayim; for it is the city of the Awesome Melech. 36 Neither shall you swear by your head, because you cannot not make one hair white or black. 37 But let your communication be, Ken, ken; Lo, lo: for whatever is more than this comes from the wicked one. 38 You have heard that it has been said, An eye for an eye, and a tooth for a tooth: 39 But I say to you, That you resist not man's evil: but whoever shall smite you on your right cheek, turn to him the other one also. 40 And if any man will sue you at the court, and takes away your coat, let him have your cloke also. 41 And whoever shall compel you to go a mile, go with him two. 42 Give to him that asks you, and from him that would borrow from you, turn not you away. 43 You have heard that it has been said; You shall love your neighbor, and hate your enemy. 44 But I say to you, Love your enemies, bless them that curse you, do tov to them that hate you, and make tefillah for those who despitefully use you, and persecute you; 45 That you may be the children of your Abba who is in ha shamayim: for He makes His sun to rise on the evil and on the tov, and sends rain on the tzadikim and on the those who are not

---

[1] Shem Tov Hebrew reference.

[2] Shem Tov Hebrew reference.
[3] Moshiach's teaching before His dom was spilled. Afterwards, all sins can be forgiven according to Matthew 12.

tzadikim. 46 *For if you only love them who love you, what reward have you? Do not even the tax collectors the same?* 47 *And if you greet your brothers only, what do you do more than others? Do not even the tax collectors do so?* 48 *Be therefore perfect, even as Your Abba who is in ha shamayim is perfect.*

6 *Take heed that you do not your mitzvot before men, to be seen by them: otherwise you have no reward from Your Abba who is in ha shamayim.* 2 *Therefore when you perform your mitzvot, do not sound a shofar before you, as the hypocrites do in the synagogues and in the streets, that they may have tifereth from men. Truly I say to you, They have their reward.* 3 *But when you perform mitzvot, let not your left hand know what your right hand does:* 4 *That your mitzvot may be in secret: and Your Abba who sees in secret Himself shall reward you openly.* 5 *And when you make tefillah, you shall not be as the hypocrites are: for they love to petition standing in the synagogues and in the corners of the streets, so that they may be seen of men. Truly I say to you, They have their reward.* 6 *But you, when you make tefillah, enter into your tallit or onto your couch*[1]*, and when you have shut your door, make tefillah to Your Abba who is in secret; and Your Abba who sees in secret shall reward you openly.* 7 *But when you make tefillah, use not vain repetitions, as the heathen do:*[2] *for they think that they shall be heard for their long tefillot.* 8 *Be not therefore like them: for do you not see that Your Abba knows what things you have need of, before You even ask Him?* 9 *After this manner therefore make tefillah: Our Abba who is in ha shamayim, kadosh shmecha.*[3] 10 *Your malchut come. Your ratzon be done in the earth, as it is in ha shamayim.* 11 *Give us*

today our daily lechem. 12 *And forgive us our debts, as we forgive our debtors.* 13 *And lead us not into temptation, but deliver us from evil: For Yours is the malchut, and the power, and the tifereth, le-olam-va-ed. Amein.* 14 *For if you forgive men their trespasses, your heavenly Abba will also forgive you:* 15 *But if you forgive not men their trespasses, neither will Your Abba forgive your trespasses.* 16 *Moreover when you fast, be not, as the hypocrites, who make a sad countenance: for they disfigure their faces that they may appear to men to fast. Truly I say to you, They have their reward.* 17 *But you, when you fast, anoint your head, and wash your face;* 18 *That you appear not to men to be fasting, but to Your Abba who is in secret: and Your Abba, who sees in secret, shall reward you openly.* 19 *Lay not up for yourselves treasures upon earth, where moth and rust does corrupt, and where thieves break through and steal:* 20 *But lay up for yourselves treasures in ha shamayim, where neither moth nor rust does corrupt, and where thieves do not break through nor steal:* 21 *For where your treasure is, there will your lev be also.* 22 *The light of the body is the eye: if therefore your eye is single, your whole body shall be full of light.* 23 *But if your eye is evil,*[4] *your whole body shall be full of darkness. If therefore the light that is in you be darkness, how great is that darkness!* 24 *No man can serve two masters: for either he will hate the one, and love the other; or else he will hold to the one, and despise the other. You cannot serve* יהוה *and Mammon.* 25 *Therefore I say to you, Take no thought for your chayim, what you shall eat, or what you shall drink; nor yet for your body, what you shall put on. Is not chayim more than food, and the body more than clothing?* 26 *See the birds of the air: for they sow not, neither do they reap, nor gather into barns; yet your Heavenly Abba feeds them. Are you*

---

[1] Shem Tov reference.
[2] Yahshua sees all believers as part of Yisrael, and not as the heathen.
[3] All set-apart and acceptable prayer must acknowledge and reverence His true Name. That's what Yahshua did.

[4] Stingy when it comes to sharing or distributing YHWH's riches of eternal truth and love.

not much better than they are? 27 Which of you by taking thought can add one cubit to his height? 28 And why do you fixate with your clothing? Consider the lilies of the field, how they grow; they toil not, neither do they spin: 29 And yet I say to you, That even Shlomo in all his tifereth was not dressed like one of these. 30 Therefore, if יהוה so clothes the grass of the field, which today is, and tomorrow is cast into the oven, shall He not much more clothe you, O you of little emunah? 31 Therefore take no thought, saying, What shall we eat? Or, What shall we drink? Or, with what shall we be clothed? 32 For after all these things do the gentiles seek:[1] for your Heavenly Abba knows that you have need of all these things. 33 But you seek first the malchut of יהוה, and His tzedakah;[2] and all these things shall be added to you.[3] 34 Take therefore no thought for tomorrow: for tomorrow shall take thought for the things of its own: Sufficient for one day is the evil of that day.

7 Shophet not, that you be not judged. 2 For with what mishpat you shophet, you shall be judged: and with what measure you apply, it shall be measured to you again. 3 And why do you see the splinter that is in your brother's eye, but consider not the log that is in your own eye? 4 Or how will you say to your brother, Let me pull out the splinter out of your eye; and, see, a log is in your own eye? 5 You hypocrite, first cast out the log out of your own eye; and then shall you see clearly to remove the splinter out of your brother's eye. 6 Give not that which is set-apart to the dogs,[4] neither cast you your pearls before pigs, lest they trample them under their feet, and turn again and tear at you. 7 Ask, and it

shall be given you;[5] seek, and you shall find; knock, and it shall be opened to you: 8 For everyone that asks receives; and he that seeks finds; and to him that knocks it shall be opened. 9 Or what man is there of you, who if his son asks for lechem, will he give him a stone? 10 Or if he asks for a fish, will he give him a serpent? 11 If you then, being evil, know how to give tov gifts to your children, how much more shall Your Abba who is in ha shamayim give tov things and His tov Ruach[6] to them that ask Him? 12 Therefore all things whatever you would that men should do to you, do you also to them: for this is the Torah and the neviim. 13 Enter in at the narrow gate: for wide is the gate, and broad is the way, that leads to destruction, and many there be who go in that gate: 14 Because narrow is the gate, and narrow is the way, that leads to chayim, and few there be that find it. 15 Beware of false niviim, who come to you in sheep's clothing, but inwardly they are ravening wolves. 16 You shall know them by their fruits. Do men gather grapes from thorns, or figs from thistles? 17 Even so every tov eytz brings forth tov fruit; but a corrupt eytz brings forth evil fruit. 18 A tov eytz cannot bring forth evil fruit; neither can a corrupt eytz bring forth tov fruit. 19 Every eytz that brings not forth tov fruit is cut down, and cast into the fire. 20 Therefore by their fruits you shall know them. 21 Not every one that says to Me, Master, Master, shall enter with Me into the malchut ha shamayim; but he that does the will of My Abba who is in ha shamayim.[7] 22 Many will say to Me in that day, Master, Master, have we not prophesied in Your Name? And in Your Name have cast out shadim? And in Your Name[8] done many wonderful mitzvot? 23 And then will I profess to them, I never knew you: depart from Me, you that work

---

[1] Yisraelites have more pressing eternal spiritual issues to be concerned with.
[2] A correct perspective and longing to serve YHWH for Yisrael's restoration, leaves little time for seeking other activities.
[3] If you have the right message you have His promise of abundance. If abundance is missing it is also possible that you have the right Elohim but the wrong message.
[4] The Besarot is for all who would desire to be part of Yisrael.

[5] In context the "you" here is Yisrael; as opposed to the gentile pagan dogs.
[6] Shem Tov reference.
[7] As outlined in Torah.
[8] Of course there's a problem since most who are doing works for Yahshua do it in names that are not His nor His Father's.

Torah-less-ness. [1] 24 Therefore whoever hears these sayings of Mine, and does them,[2] I will liken him to a wise man, who built his bayit upon a rock: 25 And the rain descended, and the floods came, and the winds blew, and beat upon that bayit; and it fell not: for it was founded upon a rock. 26 And every one that hears these sayings of Mine, and does them not, shall be like a foolish man, who built his bayit upon the sand:[3] 27 And the rain descended, and the floods came, and the winds blew, and beat upon that bayit;[4] and it fell: and great was the fall of it. 28 And it came to pass, when יהושע had ended these sayings, the people were astonished at His Torah and conduct:[5] 29 For He taught them as one having authority, and not as the Sophrim.

8 When He had come down from the mountain, great multitudes[6] followed Him. 2 And, see, there came a leper and worshipped Him, saying, Master, if You will, You can make me clean. Will You heal me?[7] 3 And יהושע put forth His hand, and touched Him, saying, I will; be clean. And immediately His leprosy was cleansed. 4 And יהושע said to Him, See that you tell no man; but go your way, show yourself to the kohen, and offer the gift that Moshe commanded, for a testimony to them. [8] 5 And when יהושע had entered into City of Nachum,[9] there came to Him a centurion, beseeching Him, 6 And saying, Master, my eved lies at home sick of paralysis, grievously tormented. 7 And יהושע said to him, I will come and heal him. 8 The centurion answered and said, Master, I am not worthy that You should come under my roof: but speak the word only, and my eved shall be healed. 9 For I am a sinful man under authority, having soldiers under me: and I say to this man, Go, and he goes; and to another, Come, and he comes; and to my eved, Do this, and he does it. 10 When יהושע heard it, He marveled, and said to them that followed, Truly I say to you, I have not found so great emunah, no, not in Yisrael. [10] 11 And I say to you, That many shall come from the east and west, and shall sit down with Avraham, and Yitzchak, and Yaakov, in the malchut ha shamayim. [11] 12 But the children of the malchut[12] shall be cast out into the outer darkness of Gei-Hinnom: and there shall be weeping and gnashing of teeth. 13 And יהושע said to the centurion, Go your way; and as you have believed, so be it done to you. And his eved was healed in the exact same hour. 14 And when יהושע had come into Kepha's bayit, He saw his wife's ima in bed, and sick with a fever. 15 And He touched her hand, and the fever left her: and she arose, and attended to them. 16 When the evening had come, they brought to Him many that were possessed with shadim: and He cast out the shadim with His word, and healed all that were sick: 17 That it might be fulfilled which was spoken by Yeshayahu ha navi, saying, He Himself took our infirmities, and carried our sicknesses. 18 Now when יהושע saw great multitudes [13] around Him; He gave a commandment to depart to the other side.[14] 19 And a certain sopher came, and said to Him, Master; I will follow You wherever You go. 20 And יהושע said to him, The foxes have holes, and the birds of the air have nests; but the Ben Adam, the virgin's Son,[15] has no where to lay His head. 21 And another of His talmidim said to Him, Rabbi, allow me first to go and bury my abba.

---

[1] Living a lifestyle void of obedience to Yahshua's eternal Torah.
[2] Torah.
[3] Gentiles, whose lifestyles don't follow His Torah.
[4] House can apply to the individual in the pashat or the entire 12 tribes of the House of Yisrael in the **remez**.
[5] Shem Tov reference.
[6] Multitudes of physical remnant Yisrael.
[7] Shem Tov reference.
[8] The real Yahshua ordered His followers to perform Torah.
[9] Capernaum.

[10] A clear reference to Jewish Yisrael, only in Judea.
[11] The prophesied return of the scattered Yisraelite nations; as seen in Matthew 15:24.
[12] The children of Yahudah in Judea.
[13] **Melo hagoyim** in the north.
[14] A reference to both the other shore in the pashat and the **sitrah hora** or "world of dark spirits" in the sod/mystery.
[15] Shem Tov reference.

22 But **יהושע** said to him, *Follow Me; and let the dead bury their own dead.* 23 And when He had entered into a ship, His talmidim followed Him. 24 And, see, there arose a great tempest in the sea, insomuch that the ship was covered with waves: but He was asleep. 25 And His talmidim came to Him, and awoke Him, saying, Master, save us: we perish! 26 And He said to them, *Why are you fearful, O you of so little emunah?* Then He arose, and rebuked the winds and the sea; and there was a great calm. 27 But the men marveled, saying, What manner of man is this, that even the winds and the sea obey Him! 28 And when He had come to the other side into the country of the Girgashites, there met Him two men possessed with shadim, coming out of the tombs, exceedingly fierce, so that no man might pass by that way. 29 And, see, they cried out, saying, What have we to do with You, **יהושע**, Son of Elohim? Are You come here to torment us before the time? 30 And there was off in the distance a herd of many pigs feeding. 31 So the shadim besought Him, saying, If You cast us out, allow us to go away into the herd of pigs. 32 And He said to them, *Go.* And when they had come out, they went into the herd of pigs: and, see, the whole herd of pigs ran violently down a steep place into the sea, and perished in the mayim. 33 And they that kept them fled, and went their way into the city, and told everything that had happened to the ones who were possessed by the shadim. 34 And, see, the whole city came out to meet **יהושע**: and when they saw Him, they besought Him that He would depart out of their coasts.[1]

9 And He entered into a ship, and passed over, and came into His own city. 2 And, see, they brought to Him a man sick from paralyses, lying on a bed: and **יהושע** seeing their emunah said to the sick from paralyses; *Son, be of tov ruach; your sins are forgiven you.* 3 And, see, certain of the Sophrim said within themselves, This Man blasphemes. 4 And **יהושע** knowing their thoughts said, *Why do you think evil in your levim?* 5 *For which is easier, to say, Your sins are forgiven you; or to say, Arise, and walk?*[2] 6 *But that you may know that the Ben Adam has power on earth to forgive sins,* (then He said to the sick of the paralysis,) *Arise, take up your mat, and go to your bayit.* 7 And he arose, and departed to his bayit. 8 But when the multitudes saw it, they marveled, and gave tehilla to **יהוה**, who had given such power to men. 9 And as **יהושע** passed forth from from there, He saw a man, named Mattityahu, sitting at the tax office: and He said to Him, *Follow Me.* And he arose, and followed Him. 10 And it came to pass, as **יהושע** sat to eat in the bayit, see; many tax collectors, violent men,[3] and sinners came and sat down with Him and His talmidim. 11 And when the Prushim saw it, they said to His talmidim, Why does your Rabbi eat with tax collectors and sinners? 12 But when **יהושע** heard that, He said to them, *They that are whole need not a physician, but they that are sick.* 13 *But go and learn what this means, I desire rachamim, and not sacrifice: for I am not come to call the tzadikim, but sinners to teshuvah.* 14 Then came to Him the talmidim of Yochanan HaMatbeel, saying, Why do we and the Prushim fast often, but Your talmidim fast not? 15 And **יהושע** said to them, *Can the children of the Bridegroom[4] mourn, as long as the Bridegroom is with them? But the days will come, when the Bridegroom shall be taken from them, and then shall they fast.* 16 *No man puts a piece of new cloth on an old garment, for that which is put in to fill it up takes from the garment, and the tear is made worse.* 17 *Neither do men put new wine into old wineskins: lest the wineskins break, and the wine runs out, and the wineskins perish: but they put new wine into*

---

[2] Neither. Only YHWH can do both.
[3] Shem Tov reference.
[4] Clear reference to Yisrael.

[1] Following Yahshua can be bad for the pig business.

new wineskins, and both are preserved.[1] 18 While He spoke these things to them, see, there came a certain ruler, and worshipped Him, saying, My daughter is even now dead: but come and lay Your hand upon her, and she shall live. 19 And יהושע arose, and followed him, and so did His talmidim. 20 And, see, a woman, who was diseased with an issue of dom for twelve years, came behind Him, and touched the tzitzit of His garment:[2] 21 For she said within herself, If I may just touch His tzitzit, I shall be whole.[3] 22 But יהושע turned around, and when He saw her, He said, *Daughter, be of tov comfort; your emunah has made you whole.* And the woman was made whole from that hour.[4] 23 And when יהושע came into the ruler's bayit, and saw the flute players and the people making noise, 24 He said to them, *Give place: for the girl is not dead, just sleeping.* And they laughed Him to scorn. 25 But when the people were put out, He went in, and took her by the hand, and the girl arose. 26 And the fame of it went abroad into all that land. 27 And when יהושע departed from there, two blind men[5] followed Him, crying, and saying, Ben David, have rachamim on us. 28 And when He had come into the bayit, the blind men came to Him: and יהושע said to them, *Do you believe that I am able to do this?* They said to Him, Yes, Master. 29 Then He touched their eyes, saying, *According to your emunah be it to you.* 30 And their eyes were opened; and יהושע strictly commanded them, saying, *See that no man knows it.* 31 But they, when they had departed, they published His fame in all that country. 32 As they went out, see, they brought to Him a dumb man possessed by s.a.tan. 33 And when the s.a.tan was cast out, the dumb spoke: and the multitudes marveled, saying, It was never so seen in Yisrael. 34 But the Prushim said, He casts out shadim through the prince of the shadim. 35 And יהושע went about all the cities and villages, teaching in their synagogues,[6] and proclaiming the besaroth of the malchut, and healing every sickness and every disease among the people. 36 But when He saw the multitudes, He was moved with rachamim on them, because they fainted, and were scattered abroad, as sheep having no shepherd. 37 Then He said to His talmidim, *The harvest truly is great, but the workers are few;* 38 *Make tefillah therefore to the Master of the harvest, that He will send forth workers into His harvest.*

10 And when He had called to Him His twelve talmidim, He gave them power against unclean shadim, to cast them out, and to heal all kinds of sickness and all kinds disease. 2 Now the names of the twelve shlichim [7] are these; The first, Shimon, who is called Kepha, and Andri his brother; Yaakov the son of Zavdi, and Yochanan his brother; 3 Philip, and Bartholomi; Toma, and Mattiyahu the tax collector; Yaakov the son of Alphai, and Lavai, whose last name was Thaddai; 4 Shimon the Zealot,[8] and Yahudah from Qerioth, who also betrayed Him. 5 These twelve יהושע sent forth, and commanded them, saying, *Go not the way of the gentiles by staying away from pagan practices,*[9] [10]

---

[1] The new wineskins are the Renewed Covenant Yisraelites and the new wine is the purified Torah that Yahshua came to deliver, void of man's additions and traditions.
[2] Twelve years symbolizes the 12 tribes who were considered to be a bleeding unfaithful unclean woman who had gone away from YHWH. One touch from the Master brought her to wholeness, as Yahshua has purposed to do for all Yisrael.
[3] Malachi 4:2.
[4] Yisrael healed.
[5] Both houses of Yisrael in the **remez** or hint level crying to Moshiach

[6] In unbelieving synagogues.
[7] For the 12 thrones over the 12 tribes in the **atid lavoh**/messianic age.
[8] Luke 6:15.
[9] Since Ephraim had become the "fullness of the gentiles" this verse is often seen as a contradiction. Not so. It is simply Moshiach telling His talmidim that as they search for Yisrael's lost sheep, they are not to go the way of or the pagan path of the gentiles. This order is a mere restatement of Yirmeyahu/Jeremiah 10:1-5. This is confirmed by the Aramaic Peshitta.
[10] Lamsa's Peshitta p. 961.

and into any city of the Shomronim[1] enter not: 6 But go rather to the lost sheep that have strayed [2] from Beit Yisrael. [3] 7 And as you go, proclaim, saying, The malchut ha shamayim[4] is offered. 8 Heal the sick, cleanse the lepers, raise the dead, and cast out shadim: freely you have received, freely give. 9 Take neither gold, nor silver, nor brass in your purses, 10 Nor a bag for your journey, neither two coats, neither sandals, nor your staffs: for the workman is worthy of his food. 11 And into whatever city or town you shall enter, inquire who in it is worthy; and there abide until you go from there. 12 And when you come into a bayit, greet those in it. 13 And if the bayit is worthy, let your shalom come upon it: but if it is not worthy, let your shalom return to you. 14 And whoever shall not receive you, nor shema your words, when you depart out of that bayit or city, shake off the dust of your feet. 15 Truly I say to you, It shall be more tolerable for the land of Sedom and Amorah in the Yom HaDin, than for that city. 16 See, I send you forth as sheep in the midst of wolves: be therefore wise as serpents, and harmless as doves. 17 But beware of men: for they will deliver you up to their congregational councils, and they will scourge you in their congregations; 18 And you shall be brought before governors and melechim for My sake, for a testimony against them and the gentiles.[5] 19 But when they seize you, take no thought how or what you shall speak: for it shall be given to you in that same hour what you shall speak. 20 For it is not you that speaks, but the Ruach of Your Abba who speaks in you. 21 And the brother shall deliver up the brother to death, and the abba the child: and the children shall rise up against their parents, and cause them to be put to death.[6] 22 And you shall be hated by all men for My Name's sake: but he that endures to the end shall be saved.[7] 23 But when they persecute you in this city, flee into another: for truly I say to you, you shall not have covered the cities of Yisrael,[8] until the Ben Adam has returned. [9] 24 The talmid is not above His Teacher, nor the eved above His Master. 25 It is enough for the talmid that he is as His teacher, and the eved as His Master. If they have called the Master of Beit Yisrael Beel-Zevuv, how much more shall they call them of His household? 26 Fear them not therefore: for there is nothing covered, that shall not be revealed; and hidden, that shall not be made known. 27 What I tell you in darkness, that speak in light: and what you shema in the ear, that proclaim upon the housetops. 28 And fear them not who kill the body, but are not able to kill the being: but rather fear Him who is able to destroy both being and body in Gei-Hinnom. 29 Are not two sparrows sold for a copper coin? And yet one of them shall not fall on the ground without Your Abba. 30 Are not the very hairs of your head all numbered?[10] 31 Fear not therefore, you are of more value than many sparrows. 32 Whoever therefore shall confess and give tehilla to Me before men, Him will I confess and give tehilla for[11] him also before My Abba who is in ha shamayim. 33 But whoever shall deny Me

[1] Due to the intense hatred between Jews and Shomronites, Yahshua wanted to display His love for those Ephraimites by opening the way Himself in Yochanan/John 4. This was a crucial task and He wanted to do it right. After displaying the proper manner to reach them by modeling His love for Ephraim in Shomron, He would later command and allow the disciples to do likewise in Acts 1:8. So this is not an injunction against going to the Ephraimites in Shomron. Rather it's a matter of timing and proper instructions from the Master.
[2] Shem Tov reference.
[3] In this broad context House of Yisrael refers to all twelve tribes; and not merely Ephraim, as many Dual Covenant theologians teach.
[4] Kingdom restored as seen in Acts 1:8.
[5] Can it be any clearer? The pagans and their antinomian groups will persecute believers who are all part of Yisrael for keeping Torah and a Yisraelite lifestyle.
[6] Yisrael will not be divided by two houses any more, but by love or hate for Moshiach Yahshua.
[7] Yisrael means overcomer or one who perseveres with El.
[8] The Aramaic is even more two-bayit-friendly using "the House of Yisrael," rather than "cities of Yisrael."
[9] A verse often cited to refute two-bayit truth. Actually it further supports it by stating that the talmidim will be still proclaiming the kingdom in Yisraelite cites at the time the Moshiach returns. These cities could not be limited to first-century Judea, since certainly all of Judea was covered with the tov news in a few months or years perhaps. Here we see that there are so many Yisraelite cities to cover across the globe in all nations, that the talmidim will still be going to these Yisraelite cities until the Son of Man returns.
[10] Shem Tov reference.
[11] Shem Tov reference.

before men, him will I also deny before My Abba who is in ha shamayim. 34 *Think not that I am come to send shalom on the earth: I came not to send shalom, but a sword.*[1] 35 *For I am come to set a man at odds against his abba, and the daughter against her ima, and the daughter-in-law against her ima-in-law. 36 And a man's foes shall be they of his own household. 37 He that loves abba or ima more than Me is not worthy of Me: and he that loves son or daughter more than Me is not worthy of Me. 38 And he that takes not his execution stake, and follows after Me, is not worthy of Me. 39 He that finds his chayim shall lose it: and he that loses his chayim for My sake shall find it. 40 He that receives you receives Me, and he that receives Me receives Him that sent Me. 41 He that receives a navi in the name of a navi shall receive a navi's reward; and he that receives a tzadik man in the name of a tzadik man shall receive a tzadik man's reward. 42 And whoever shall give a drink to one of these little ones, even just a cup of cold mayim in the name of a talmid, truly I say to you, he shall in no way lose his reward.*

11 And it came to pass, when יהושע had made an end of commanding His twelve talmidim, He departed from there to teach and to proclaim in their cities. 2 Now when Yochanan had heard in the prison the mitzvot of the Moshiach, he sent two of his talmidim,[2] 3 And said to Him, Are You the One that should come, or do we look for another? 4 יהושע answered and said to them, *Go and show Yochanan again those things that you do shema and see: 5 The blind receive their sight, and the lame walk, the lepers are cleansed, and the deaf shema, the dead are raised up, and the poor have the besarot proclaimed to them and are acquitted.*[3] 6 *And blessed is he,*

who shall not be offended by Me. 7 And as they departed, יהושע began to say to the multitudes concerning Yochanan, *What did you go out into the wilderness to see? A reed shaken with the wind? 8 But what did you go out to see? A man clothed in fine clothing? See, they that wear fine clothing are in melechim's houses. 9 But what did you go out to see? A navi? Yes, I say to you, and more than a navi. 10 For this is he, of whom it is written, See, I send My messenger before Your face, who shall prepare Your way before You. 11 Truly I say to you, Among them that are born of women there has not risen a greater than Yochanan HaMatbeel: nevertheless he that is least in the malchut ha shamayim is greater than him. 12 And from the days of Yochanan HaMatbeel until now the malchut ha shamayim has been administered by force and has been oppressed, and senseless*[4] *persons have been controlling it by violence.*[5] 13 *For all the neviim and the Torah prophesied concerning Yochanan.*[6] 14 *And if you will receive it, this is Eli-Yahu, who was supposed to come. 15 He that has ears to shema, let him shema. 16 But to what shall I liken this generation? It is like children sitting in the markets, and calling to their friends, 17 And saying, We have played for you, and you have not danced; we have mourned for you, and you have not lamented. 18 For Yochanan came neither eating nor drinking, and they said, He has a shad. 19 The Ben Adam came eating and drinking, and they say, See a gluttonous man, and wine drinker, a friend of tax collectors and sinners. So fools shophet the wise.*[7] 20 *Then He began to rebuke the cities where most of His mighty mitzvot were done, because they did not make teshuvah: 21 Woe to you, Chorazin! Woe to you, Beth Tsaida!*[8] *For if the mighty*

---

[1] To divide Yisrael based on loyalty to the King not by two-bayit division any more.
[2] Symbolic of inquiring Yahudah and Ephraim.
[3] Shem Tov reference.
[4] Unregenerated.
[5] Shem Tov and Peshitta, with this possible reference to the rule of the Pharisees under Rome.
[6] Notice according to Shem Tov they spoke "concerning" not "until" John the Immerser.
[7] Shem Tov reference.
[8] In first-century Judea.

mitzvot, which were done in you, had been done in Tsur and Tsidon,[1] they would have repented long ago in sackcloth and ashes. 22 But I say to you, It shall be more tolerable for Tsur and Tsidon at the Yom HaDin, than for you. 23 And you, City of Nachum, which is exalted to ha shamayim, shall be brought down to Gei-Hinnom: for if the mighty mitzvot, which have been done in you, had been done in Sedom, it would have remained until this day. 24 But I say to you, That it shall be more tolerable for the land of Sedom in the Yom HaDin, than for you. 25 At that time יהושע made tefillah and said, I thank you, O Abba, Master of ha shamayim and earth, because You have hidden these things from the wise and prudent, and have revealed them to babes. 26 Even so, Abba: for so it seemed tov in Your sight. 27 All things are delivered to Me by My Abba: and no man knows the Son, but the Abba; neither knows any man the Abba, but the Son, and he to whom the Son will reveal Him. 28 Come to Me, all you that labor and are heavy laden, and I will give you rest and help you to bear your yoke. [2] 29 Take My yoke upon you, and learn about Me; for I am meek and lowly in lev: and you shall find rest for your beings. 30 For My yoke is gentle, and My burden is light.

12 At that time יהושע went on the Shabbat through the cornfields; and His talmidim were hungry, and began to pluck the ears of corn, and to eat. 2 But when the Prushim saw it, they said to Him, See, Your talmidim do that which is not proper[3] to do upon the Shabbat. 3 But He said to them, Have you not read what David did, when he was hungry, and they that were with him; 4 How he entered into the Bayit of the Master יהוה, and did eat from the Lechem of the Faces, which was not permitted in Torah for him to eat, neither for them who were with him, but only for the kohanim? 5 Or have you not read in the Torah, how that on the Shabbat the kohanim in the Beit HaMikdash profane the Shabbat, and are blameless? 6 But I say to you, That in this place is One greater than the Beit HaMikdash. 7 But if you had known what this means, I will have rachamim, and not sacrifice, you would not have condemned the innocent. 8 For the Ben Adam is Master even of the Shabbat. 9 And when He was departed from there, He went into their synagogue: 10 And, see, there was a man who had his hand withered. And they asked Him, saying, Is it permitted in the Torah to heal on the Shabbat? -So that they might accuse Him. 11 And He said to them, What man shall there be among you, that shall have one sheep, and if it fall into a pit on the Shabbat, will he not lay hold on it, and lift it out? 12 How much then is a man better than a sheep? So then it is permitted in Torah to do mitzvot on the Shabbat. 13 Then He said to the man, Stretch forth your hand. And he stretched it forth; and it was restored whole, just like the other. 14 Then the Prushim went out, and took council against Him, how they might destroy Him. 15 But when יהושע knew it, He withdrew Himself from there: and great multitudes[4] followed Him, and He healed them all; 16 And commanded them that they should not make Him known: 17 That it might be fulfilled what was spoken by Yeshayahu ha navi, saying, 18 See My Eved, whom I have chosen; My Beloved, in whom My being is well pleased: I will put My Ruach upon Him, and He shall show Torah's mishpatim to the gentiles. [5] 19 He shall not strive, nor cry out; neither shall any man shema His voice in the streets. 20 A crushed reed shall He not break, and smoking flax shall He not quench, until He brings forth mishpatim to victory. 21 And in His Name shall the gentiles trust.[6] 22 Then was brought to Him one possessed with a shad, blind, and dumb:

---

[1] Lands of Ephraimite dispersion.
[2] Shem Tov reference.
[3] Shem Tov reference.

[4] Yisrael.
[5] Ephraim.
[6] His Son has revealed the Name of YHWH to all nations.

and He healed him, so completely that the blind and dumb both spoke and saw. 23 And all the people of Yisrael were amazed, and said, Is not this Ben David? 24 But when the Prushim heard it, they said, This fellow does not cast out shadim, except by Beel-Zevuv the prince of the shadim. 25 And יהושע knew their thoughts, and said to them, *Every malchut divided against itself is brought to desolation; and every city or bayit divided against itself shall not stand: 26 And if s.a.tan cast out s.a.tan, he would be divided against himself; how then would his malchut stand? 27 And if I by Beel-Zevuv cast out shadim, by whom do your children cast them out? Therefore they shall be your shophtim. 28 But if I cast out shadim by the Ruach of יהוה, then the malchut of יהוה has come to you. 29 Or else how can one enter into a strong man's bayit, and spoil his goods, except he first bind the strong man? And then he will spoil his bayit. 30 He that is not with Me is against Me; and he that gathers not with Me scatters abroad.* [1] *31 Therefore I say to you, All manner of sin and blasphemy shall be forgiven to men: but the blasphemy against the Ruach HaKodesh shall not be forgiven to men. 32 And whoever speaks a word against the Ben Adam, it shall be forgiven him: but whoever speaks against the Ruach HaKodesh, it shall not be forgiven him, neither in the olam hazeh, and neither in the olam habah.*[2] *33 Either make the eytz tov, and its fruit tov; or else make the eytz corrupt, and its fruit corrupt: for the eytz is known by its fruit. 34 O generation of vipers, how can you, being evil, speak tov things? For out of the abundance of the lev the mouth speaks. 35 A tov man out of the tov treasure of the lev brings forth tov things: and an evil man out of the evil treasure brings forth evil things. 36 But I say to you, That every idle word that men shall speak, they shall give account of it on the Yom HaDin. 37 For by your words you shall be declared tzadik, and by your words you shall be condemned.* 38 Then certain of the Sophrim and of the Prushim answered, saying, Rabbi, we would see a sign from You. 39 But He answered and said to them, *An evil and adulterous generation seeks after a sign; and there shall no sign be given to it, but the sign of the navi Yonah: 40 For as Yonah was three days and three nights in the fish's belly; so shall the Ben Adam be three days and three nights in the lev of the earth. 41 The men of Nineveh shall rise in the Yom HaDin with this generation, and shall condemn it: because they repented at the proclaiming of Yonah; and, see, a Greater than Yonah is here. 42 The Malcha of Sheba shall rise up in the Yom HaDin with this generation, and shall condemn it: for she came from the uttermost parts of the earth to shema the chochma of Shlomo; and, see, a Greater than Shlomo is here. 43 When the unclean ruach has gone out of a man, it walks through dry places, seeking rest, and finds none. 44 Then it says, I will return to my bayit from where I came out; and when it returns, it finds it empty, swept, and decorated. 45 Then it goes, and takes with it seven other shadim more wicked than itself, and they enter in and dwell there: and then the last state of that man is worse than the first. Even so shall it be also in this wicked generation.* 46 While He yet talked to the people, see, His ima and His brothers stood outside, desiring to speak with Him. 47 Then one said to Him, See, Your ima and Your brothers stand outside, desiring to speak with You. 48 But He answered and said to him that told Him, *Who is My ima? And who are My brothers?* 49 And He stretched forth His hand toward His talmidim, and said, *See My ima and My brothers! 50 For whoever shall do the will of My Abba who is in ha shamayim, the same is My brother, and sister, and ima.*

---

[1] Gather Yisrael.
[2] Attributing the works of Yahshua to s.a.tan's power. No believer would willfully do that as did the Prushim.

13 The same day יהושע went out of the bayit,[1] and sat by the seaside.[2] 2 And great multitudes were gathered together to Him, so that He went into a ship, and sat;[3] and the whole multitude stood on the shore. 3 And He spoke many things to them in parables, saying, *See, a sower went forth to sow;[4] 4 And when he sowed, some seeds fell by the way side, and the birds came and devoured them up: 5 Some fell upon stony places, where they had not much earth: and immediately they sprung up, because they had no deepness of earth: 6 And when the sun was up, they were scorched; and because they had no root, they withered away. 7 And some fell among thorns; and the thorns sprung up, and choked them: 8 But others fell into tov ground, and brought forth fruit, some a hundredfold, some sixtyfold, some thirtyfold. 9 Who has ears to shema, let him shema.* 10 And the talmidim came, and said to Him, Why do You speak to them in parables? 11 He answered and said to them, *Because it is given to you to know the mysteries of the malchut ha shamayim, but to them it is not given. 12 For whoever has, to him shall be given, and he shall have more abundance: but whoever has not, from him shall be taken away even what he has. 13 Therefore I speak to them in parables: because seeing they see not; and hearing they shema not, neither do they understand. 14 And in them is fulfilled the prophecy of Yeshayahu, which said, By hearing you shall shema, and shall not understand; and seeing you shall see, and shall not perceive: 15 For this people's lev has become thickened, and their ears are dull of hearing, and their eyes they have closed; lest at any time they should see with their eyes, and shema with their ears, and should understand with their lev, and should make teshuvah, and I should heal them. 16 But blessed are your eyes, for they see: and your ears, for they shema. 17 For truly I say to you, That many neviim and tzadikim have desired to see those things which you see, and have not seen them; and to shema those things which you shema, and have not heard them.* [5] 18 *Shema therefore the parable of the sower. 19 When any one hears the word of the malchut, and understands it not, then comes the wicked one, and catches away that which*[6] *was sown in his lev. This is he who received seed by the way side. 20 But he that received the seed into stony places, the same is he that hears the word, and immediately with simcha receives it; 21 Yet has he not root in himself, but endures for a while: for when tribulation or persecution arises because of the word, immediately he is offended.*[7] *22 He also that received seed among the thorns is he that hears the word; and the cares of the olam hazeh, and the deceitfulness of riches, choke the word, and he becomes unfruitful. 23 But he that received seed into the tov ground is he that hears the word, and understands it; who also bears fruit, and brings forth, some a hundredfold, some sixty, some thirty.* 24 Another parable He put forth to them, saying, *The malchut ha shamayim is like a man who sowed tov seed in his field: 25 But while men slept, his enemy came and sowed tares among the wheat, and went his way. 26 But when the blade was sprung up, and brought forth fruit, then appeared the tares also. 27 So the avadim of the master came and said to him, Sir, did you not sow tov seed in your field? From where then have the tares come from? 28 He said to them, An enemy has done this. The avadim said to him, Will you then that we go and gather them up? 29 But he said, No; lest while you gather up the tares, you root up also the*

---

[1] Left the bayit of Yahudah to also search for Ephraim.
[2] The seaside is a type of the nations where Ephraim was scattered.
[3] Yisraelite rabbis sit when they teach.
[4] The sower is Yahshua in the literal, and Judah in the hint understanding, as the seed he sows or Torah comes from the storehouses of Yahudah.

[5] True Yisraelites listen to Moshiach's Torah.
[6] False understandings of the correct message of the regathering and restoration of both houses into one kingdom.
[7] Has anyone ever become offended over the two-bayit message? Have you?

wheat with them. 30 *Let both grow together until the harvest: and in the time of the harvest I will say to the reapers, Gather together first the tares,[1] and bind them in bundles to burn them: but gather the wheat into My barn.* 31 Another parable He put forth to them, saying, *The malchut ha shamayim is like a grain of mustard seed, which a man took, and sowed in his field:* 32 *Which indeed is the least of all seeds: but when it is grown, it is the greatest among herbs, and becomes a eytz, so that the birds of the air come and lodge in its branches.* 33 Another parable He spoke to them; *The malchut ha shamayim is like chametz, which a woman took, and hid in three measures of meal, until the whole was leavened.*[2] 34 All these things spoke יהושע to the multitude in parables; and without a parable He spoke not to them: 35 That it might be fulfilled what was spoken by ha navi, saying, I will open My mouth in parables; I will utter things that have been kept secret[3] from the days of old.[4] 36 Then יהושע sent the multitude away, and went into the bayit: and His talmidim came to Him, saying, Declare to us the parable of the tares of the field. 37 He answered and said to them, *He that sows the tov seed is the Ben Adam;* 38 *The field is the olam hazeh; the tov seed are the children of the malchut;[5] but the tares are the children of the wicked one;* 39 *The enemy that sowed them is s.a.tan; the harvest is the end of the olam hazeh; and the reapers are the heavenly messengers.* 40 *As the tares are gathered and burned in the fire; so shall it be at the end of this olam hazeh.* 41 *The Ben Adam shall send forth His heavenly messengers, and they shall gather out of His* malchut all things that offend, and those who do Torah-less-ness;[6] 42 *And shall cast them into a furnace of fire: where there shall be wailing and gnashing of teeth.* 43 *Then shall the tzadikim shine forth as the sun in the malchut of their Abba. He who has ears to shema, let him shema.* 44 *Again, the malchut ha shamayim is like a treasure[7] hidden in a field; which when a man has found, he hides, and because of simcha goes and sells all that he has, and buys that single field.* 45 *Again, the malchut ha shamayim is like a merchant, seeking precious pearls:* 46 *Who, when he had found one pearl of great price,[8] went and sold all that he had, and bought it.* 47 *Again, the malchut ha shamayim is like a net that was cast into the sea, and gathered in every kind:* 48 *Which, when it was full, they drew to shore, and sat down, and gathered the tov into vessels, but took the bad away.* 49 *So shall it be at the end of the olam hazeh: the heavenly messengers shall come forth, and separate the wicked from among the tzadikim,[9]* 50 *And shall cast them into the furnace of fire: where there shall be wailing and gnashing of teeth.* 51 יהושע said to them, *Have you understood all these things?* They said to Him, Oh yes, Master. 52 Then He said to them, *Therefore every sopher which is instructed about the malchut ha shamayim is like an abba of children, [10] who brings forth out of his treasure things new and old.[11]* 53 And it came to pass, that when יהושע had finished these parables, He departed from there. 54 And when He had come into His own country, He taught them in their synagogues, so that they were astonished, and said, from where has this Man this chochma, and these mighty mitzvot? 55 Is not this the carpenter's Son? Is not His ima called Miryam? And His brothers, Yaakov,

---

[1] Notice: That unbelievers and the disobedient are gathered first and taken away first; not believers who are gathered after the great taking away of the lost. Pray to be left behind like Noach during the coming Great Tribulation.
[2] Speaking of the sinfulness of the teaching that YHWH is three separate persons, which in the end days Yahshua said would be prevalent.
[3] His entire ministry and the entire Brit Chadasha are delivered in a manner that unveils the hidden or sod.
[4] Yisrael's history.
[5] B'nai Yisrael.

[6] Torah mockers who claim to be saved.
[7] Yisrael mixed in all the earth.
[8] Yisrael.
[9] Wicked taken away. No rapture here.
[10] Shem Tov reference: A father of born again children of Yisrael, teaches restoration truth from both covenants.
[11] From both covenants.

and Yoseph, and Shimon, and Yahudah? 56 And His sisters, are they not all with us? From where then has this Man all these things? 57 And they were offended by Him. But יהושע said to them, *A Navi is not unappreciated, except in His own country, and in His own bayit.* 58 And He did not many mighty mitzvot there because of their unbelief.[1]

14 At that time Herod the district ruler heard about the fame of יהושע, 2 And said to his avadim, This is Yochanan HaMatbeel; he is risen from the dead; and therefore mighty mitzvot do manifest themselves in him. 3 For Herod had laid hold on Yochanan, and bound him, and put him in prison because of Herodias, his brother Philip's wife. 4 For Yochanan said to him, it is not permissible in Torah for you to have her. 5 And when he would have put him to death, he feared the multitude, because they counted him as a navi. 6 But when Herod's birthday was kept, the daughter of Herodias danced before them, and pleased Herod. 7 So he promised with an oath to give her whatever she would ask. 8 And she, being previously instructed by her ima, said, Give me here Yochanan HaMatbeel's head on a dish. 9 And the melech was sorry: nevertheless for the oath's sake, and those who sat with him as guests over food, he commanded the head to be given to her. 10 And he sent, and beheaded Yochanan in the prison. 11 And his head was brought on a dish, and given to the girl: and she brought it to her ima. 12 And his talmidim came, and took up the body, and buried it, and went and told יהושע. 13 When יהושע heard of it, He departed from there by ship into a desert place apart: and when the people had heard of it, they followed Him on foot out of the cities. 14 And יהושע went forth, and saw a great multitude, and was moved with rachamim towards them, and He healed their sick ones. 15 And when it was

evening, His talmidim came to Him, saying, This is a desert place, and the sunlight is now past; send the multitude away, that they may go into the villages, and buy themselves food. 16 But יהושע said to them, *They need not depart; you give them to eat.* 17 And they said to Him, We have here only five loaves, and two fishes. 18 He said, *Bring them here to Me.* 19 And He commanded the multitude to sit down on the grass, and took the five loaves,[2] and the two fishes,[3] and looking up to ha shamayim, He said the bracha, and broke it, and gave the loaves to His talmidim, and the talmidim to the multitude. 20 And they did all eat, and were filled: and they took up of the fragments that remained twelve baskets full.[4] 21 And they that had eaten were about five thousand men, beside women and children. 22 And immediately יהושע constrained His talmidim to get into a ship, and to go before Him to the other side, while He sent the multitudes away. 23 And when He had sent the multitudes away, He went up into a mountain alone to make tefillah: and when the evening had come, He was there alone. 24 But the ship was now in the midst of the sea, tossed with waves: for the wind was contrary to it. 25 And in the fourth watch of the night יהושע went to them, walking on the sea. 26 And when the talmidim saw Him walking on the sea, they were troubled, saying, It is a ruach; and they cried out for fear. 27 But immediately יהושע spoke to them, saying, *Be of tov courage; it is I; be not afraid.* 28 And Kepha answered Him and said, Master, if it is You, command me to come to You on the mayim. 29 And He said, *Come.* And when Kepha had come down out of the ship, he walked on the mayim, to go to יהושע. 30 But when he saw the wind boisterous, he was afraid; and beginning to sink, he cried out, saying,

---

[1] He could have; but chose not to.

[2] The five loaves represent the Torah that all 12 tribes receive upon their return.
[3] Torah instructions, for both houses of Yisrael.
[4] Notice the true manna and sustenance from the Master is placed for safekeeping in 12 baskets, one for each of the 12 tribes He came to restore.

Master, save me. 31 And immediately יהושע stretched forth His hand, and caught him, and said to him, *O man of little emunah, why did you doubt?* 32 And when they had come into the ship, the wind ceased. 33 Then they that were in the ship came and worshipped Him, saying, Of an emet You are the Son of יהוה. 34 And when they had gone over, they came into the land of Gennesar. 35 And when the men of that place had knowledge of His arrival, they sent out into all that country all around, and brought to Him all that were diseased; 36 And begged Him that they might only touch the tzitzit of His garment: and as many as touched were completely healed.

15 Then came to יהושע Sophrim and Prushim, who were from Yahrushalayim, saying, 2 Why do Your talmidim transgress the tradition of the zachanim? For they do not wash their hands when they eat food. 3 But He answered and said to them, *Why do you also transgress the commandment of* יהוה *by your tradition?* 4 For יהוה *commanded, you saying, Honor your abba and ima: and, He that curses abba or ima, let him die the death. 5 But you say, Whoever shall say to his abba or his ima, It is a gift,* [1] *by whatever you would have been profited by me; 6 And does not honor his abba or his ima,* [2] *he shall be free.* [3] *This is how you have made the commandment of* יהוה *of no effect by your tradition. 7 You hypocrites, well did Yeshayahu prophesy about you, saying, 8 This people draws near to Me with their mouth, and honors Me with their lips; but their lev is far from Me. 9 But in vain they do worship Me, teaching as doctrines the commandments of men.* 10 And He called the multitude, and said to them, *Shema, and understand: 11 Not that which goes into the mouth defiles a man; but that which comes out of the mouth, this defiles a man.* [4] 12 Then came His talmidim, and said to Him, Did You know that the Prushim were offended, after they heard this teaching? 13 But He answered and said, *Every plant, which My heavenly Abba has not planted, shall be rooted up. 14 Leave them alone: they are blind leaders of the blind. And if the blind lead the blind, both shall fall into the ditch.* 15 Then answered Kepha and said to Him, Declare to us this parable. 16 And יהושע said, *Are you also yet without understanding? 17 Do you not yet understand, that whatever enters in at the mouth goes into the belly, and is cast out into the sewer? 18 But those things that proceed out of the mouth come forth from the lev; and they defile the man. 19 For out of the lev proceed evil thoughts, murders, adulteries, fornications, thefts, false witness, and blasphemies: 20 These are the things that defile a man: but to eat with unwashed hands defiles not a man.* 21 Then יהושע went from there, and departed into the coasts of Tsur and Tsidon. 22 And, see, a woman of Kanaan[5] came out of the same coasts, and cried to Him, saying, Have rachamim on me, O Master, Ben David; my daughter is heavily vexed with a shad. 23 But He answered her not a word. And His talmidim came and sought Him, saying; Send her away; for she cries after us. 24 But He answered and said, *They did not send Me*[6] *but to the lost sheep of the Bayit of Yisrael.*[7] 25 Then she came and worshipped Him, saying, Master, help me. 26 But He answered and said, *It is not right to take the children's lechem, and to cast it to dogs.*[8] 27 And she said, Emet, sir: yet the dogs eat

---

[1] To YHWH.
[2] By taking their needed money as a donation to YHWH.
[3] From honoring them.

[4] Yahshua is not allowing unclean foods; He is stating that the human heart is the problem not YHWH's word. This is further confirmed in verse 13.
[5] An alternate rendering of the Hebrew word for Canaanite could be merchant.
[6] Shem Tov reference: A reference to the plurality of divinity. Shem Tov reference.
[7] This incident is interesting in that the talmidim wanted to send her away seeing that in the natural she was a Canaanite woman. Yet Yahshua apparently knew she had Yisraelite heritage due to His response that indicated that He would not abandon her, since He had come for the lost sheep of Yisrael, which apparently He knew her to be.
[8] A possible test for her. Not necessarily an indication that she was a true dog, or gentile

of the crumbs that fall from their masters' table. 28 Then יהושע answered and said to her, *O woman, great is your emunah: be it to you even as you will.* And her daughter was made whole from that very hour. 29 And יהושע departed from there, and came near to the Sea of Galil; and went up into a mountain, and sat down there. 30 And great multitudes came to Him, having with them those that were lame, blind, dumb, maimed, and many others, and cast them down at יהושע's feet; and He healed them: 31 So that the multitude wondered, when they saw the dumb speak, the maimed made whole, the lame to walk, and the blind to see: and they gave tehilla to the Elohim of Yisrael. 32 Then יהושע called His talmidim to Him, and said, *I have rachamim on the multitude, because they continue with me now for three days, and have nothing to eat: and I will not send them away without food, lest they faint in the way.* 33 And His talmidim said to Him, From where should we have so much lechem in the wilderness, so as to feed so great a multitude? 34 And יהושע said to them, *How many loaves have you?* And they said, Seven, and a few little fishes. 35 And He commanded the multitude to sit down on the ground. 36 And He took the seven loaves and the fishes, and gave hodu, and broke them, and gave to His talmidim, and the talmidim to the multitude. 37 And they did all eat, and were filled: and they collected from the broken pieces that were left seven baskets full. 38 And they that did eat were four thousand men, beside women and children. 39 And He sent away the multitude, and entered the boat, and came into the coasts of Magdala.

16

The Prushim also with the Tzadukim came, and testing Him desired that He would show them a single sign from ha shamayim. 2 He answered and said to them, *When it is evening, you say, It will be fair weather: for the sky is red.* 3 *And in the morning, It will be foul weather today: for the sky is red and overcast. O you hypocrites, you can discern the face of the sky; but can you not discern the signs of the times?*[1] 4 *The offspring of evildoers seeks*[2] *after a sign; and there shall no sign be given to it, but the sign of the navi Yonah. And He left them, and departed.* 5 And when His talmidim were come to the other side, they had forgotten to take lechem. 6 Then יהושע said to them, *Take heed and beware of the chametz of the Prushim and of the Tzadukim.* 7 And they reasoned among themselves, saying, It is because we have taken no lechem. 8 Which when יהושע perceived, He said to them, *O you of little emunah, why do you reason among yourselves, that you have brought no lechem? 9 Do you not yet understand, neither remember the five loaves and the five thousand, and how many baskets you took up? 10 Neither the seven loaves and the four thousand, and how many baskets you took up? 11 How is it that you did not understand that I spoke not to you concerning lechem, but that you should beware of the chametz of the Prushim and of the Tzadukim?* 12 Then they understood how that He commanded them not to beware of the chametz of lechem, but of the teachings[3] and behavior[4] of the Prushim and of the Tzadukim. 13 When יהושע came into the coasts of Caesarea Philippi, He asked his talmidim, saying, *Who do men say that I the Ben Adam am?* 14 And they said, Some say that You are Yochanan HaMatbeel: some, Eli-Yahu; and others, Yirmeyahu, or one of the neviim. 15 He said to them, *But who do you say that I am?* 16 And Shimon Kepha answered and said, You are the Moshiach, the Son of the living Elohim who has come into the olam hazeh.[5] 17 And יהושע answered and said to him, *Blessed are you, Shimon Bar Yonah: for flesh and dom has not revealed this to you,*

---

[1] Unable to perceive that Yisrael's exile was starting to come to an end.
[2] Shem Tov reference.
[3] Added teachings.
[4] Shem Tov reference.
[5] Shem Tov reference.

but My Abba who is in ha shamayim. 18 And I say also to you, That you are Kepha, and upon this Rock I will restore[1] My congregation[2] as a Bayit of tefillah;[3] and the gates of Gei-Hinnom shall not prevail against it. 19 And I will give to you the keys of the malchut ha shamayim: and whatever you shall bind on earth shall be; having been bound in ha shamayim: and whatever you shall loose on earth shall be; having been loosed in ha shamayim.[4] 20 Then He commanded His talmidim that they should tell no man that He was יהושע the Moshiach. 21 From that time forth יהושע began to show to His talmidim, how that He must go to Yahrushalayim, and suffer many things from the zachanim and main kohanim and Sophrim, and be killed, and be raised again the third day. 22 Then Kepha took Him, and began to rebuke Him, saying, Be it far from You, Master: this shall not be to You. 23 But He turned, and said to Kepha, Get behind Me, s.a.tan: you are an offence to Me: for you do not desire the things that be of יהוה, but those that be of men. 24 Then said יהושע to His talmidim, If any man will come after Me, let him deny himself, and take up his execution stake, and follow Me. 25 For whoever will save his chayim shall lose it: and whoever will lose his chayim for My sake shall find it. 26 For how is a man profited, even if he shall gain the entire olam hazeh, and lose his own being? Or what shall a man give in exchange for his being? 27 For the Ben Adam shall come in the tiféreth of His Abba with His heavenly messengers; and then He shall reward every man according to his

mitzvot.[5] 28 Truly I say to you, There are some standing here, who shall not taste of death, until they see the Ben Adam coming in His malchut.[6]

17 And after six days יהושע took Kepha, Yaakov, and Yochanan his brother, and brought them up into an high mountain alone to make tefillah,[7] 2 And while He was making tefillah[8] He was transformed before them: and His face did shine as the sun, and His clothing was white as the light. 3 And, see, there appeared to them Moshe and Eli-Yahu talking with Him about what would happen to Him in Yahrushalayim.[9] 4 Then answered Kepha, and said to יהושע, Master, it is tov for us to be here: if You will, let us make here three sukkot; one for You, and one for Moshe, and one for Eli-Yahu.[10] 5 While He yet spoke, see, a bright cloud overshadowed them and they were greatly alarmed:[11] and see a Bat-Kol out of the cloud, which said, This is My beloved Son, in whom I am well pleased; shema to Him. 6 And when the talmidim heard it, they fell on their face, and were very afraid. 7 And יהושע came and touched them, and said, Arise, and be not afraid. 8 And when they had lifted up their eyes, they saw no man, except יהושע only. 9 And as they came down from the mountain, יהושע commanded them, saying, Tell the vision to no man, until the Ben Adam be risen again from the dead. 10 And His talmidim asked Him, saying, Why then do the Sophrim say that Eli-Yahu must first come? 11 And יהושע answered and said to them, Eli-Yahu truly shall first come, and restore all things. 12 But I say to you, That Eli-Yahu has come already, and they knew him not, but have done to him whatever they desired. Likewise shall also the Ben Adam suffer from them. 13 Then the

---

[1] Greek word is **oikodomeo**. Strong's Greek # 3618, meaning rebuild, repair and restore.
[2] Ecclesia or congregation of Yisrael; Not a new and separate gentile entity called "the church." Shem Tov Matthew shows that Yahshua's congregation is the fulfillment of Isaiah 56:7, where all who keep Shabbat and all who guard His Name YHWH, will enter the rebuilt House of Prayer for all nations.
[3] Shem Tov reference.
[4] Meaning if heaven allows a ruling already, its is allowable by the talmidim. If heaven doesn't allow it, it is not to be allowed by the talmidim. Binding means disallow, loosing means allow. These are Hebraic idiomatic expressions that have nothing to do with binding and loosing demons. Although we as Renewed Covenant Yisrael certainly do have that imparted authority over demons.

[5] Done as a believer.
[6] That happens in a vision in the very next chapter.
[7] Shem Tov reference.
[8] Shem Tov reference.
[9] Shem Tov reference; and Luca/Luke 9:31.
[10] Based on Kepha's understanding of Zecharyah 14:16-21.
[11] Shem Tov reference.

talmidim understood that He spoke to them of Yochanan HaMatbeel. 14 And when they had come to the multitude, there came to Him a certain man, kneeling down to Him, and saying, 15 Master, have rachamim on my son: for he is tormented by an evil ruach, and very tormented: for often he falls into the fire, and often into the mayim. 16 And I brought him to Your talmidim, and they could not cure him. 17 Then **יהושע** answered and said, *O faithless and perverse generation who deny,*[1] *how long shall I be with you? How long shall I allow you? Bring him here to Me.* 18 And **יהושע** rebuked the shad; and he departed out of him: and the child was cured from that very hour. 19 Then came the talmidim to **יהושע** alone, and said, Why could not we cast it out? 20 And **יהושע** said to them, *Because of your unbelief: for truly I say to you, If you have emunah as a grain of mustard seed, you shall say to this mountain, Remove from here to there; and it shall remove; and nothing shall be impossible to you. 21 However this kind goes out only by tefillah and fasting.* 22 And while they stayed in Galil, **יהושע** said to them, *The Ben Adam shall be betrayed into the hands of men: 23 And they shall kill Him, and the third day He shall be raised again.* And they were exceedingly sorry. 24 And when they were come to City of Nachum, they that received tax money came to Kepha, and said, Does not your Rabbi pay tax? 25 He said, Yes. And when he was come into the bayit, **יהושע** anticipated this and said to him, saying, *What do you think, Shimon Kepha? Of whom do the melechim of the earth take toll or tax? From their own children, or from strangers?* 26 Kepha said to Him, From strangers. **יהושע** said to him, *Then are the children exempt. 27 Nevertheless, lest we should offend them, go to the sea, and cast a hook, and take up the fish that first comes up; and when you have opened its mouth, you shall find a piece of money: that take, and give them for Me and you.*

18 At the same time came the talmidim to **יהושע**, saying, Who is the greatest in the malchut ha shamayim?
2 And **יהושע** called a little child to Him, and set Him in the midst of them, 3 And said, *Truly I say to you, Except you turn to Me, and then become as little teachable children, you shall not enter into the malchut ha shamayim. 4 Whoever therefore shall humble himself as this little child, the same is the greatest in the malchut ha shamayim. 5 And whoever shall receive one such little child in My Name receives Me. 6 But whoever shall offend one of these little ones who believe in Me, it were better for him that a millstone were hung around his neck, and that he were drowned in the depth of the sea. 7 Woe to the olam hazeh because of offences and confusion! For it must be that offences come; but woe to that man by whom the offence and confusion*[2] *comes! 8 So if your hand or your foot offend you, cut them off, and cast them from you: it is better for you to enter into chayim lame or maimed, rather than having two hands or two feet to be cast into everlasting fire. 9 And if your eye offends you, pluck it out, and cast it from you: it is better for you to enter into chayim with one eye, rather than having two eyes to be cast into Gei-Hinnom fire. 10 Take heed that you despise not one of these little ones; for I say to you, That in ha shamayim their heavenly messengers do always see the face of My Abba who is in ha shamayim. 11 For the Ben Adam has come to save that which was lost.*[3] *12 So what do you think? If a man has an hundred sheep, and one of them goes astray, does he not leave the ninety-nine, and go into the mountains, and seek that one that has gone astray? 13 And if so be that he finds it, truly I say to you, he has simcha more over that sheep, than of the ninety-nine who went not astray. 14 Even so it is not the will of Your*

---

[1] Shem Tov reference.
[2] Shem Tov reference.
[3] That's the whole point of His coming; to seek and rescue Yisrael's scattered sheep.

Abba who is in ha shamayim that one of these little ones should perish.[1] 15 And if your brother shall trespass against you, go and tell him his fault between you and him alone: if he shall shema you, you have gained your brother. 16 But if he will not shema you, then take with you one or two more witnesses, that in the mouth of two or three witnesses every word may be established. 17 And if he shall neglect to shema them, tell it to the congregation of Yisrael: but if he neglects to shema the congregation of Yisrael, let him be to you like a heathen man and a tax collector. 18 Truly I say to you, Whatever you shall bind on earth shall be bound in ha shamayim: and whatever you shall loose on earth shall be loosed in ha shamayim. 19 Again I say to you, That if two of you shall agree on earth as touching any thing that they shall ask, it shall be done for them by My Abba who is in ha shamayim. 20 For where two or three will assemble together[2] in My Name, there am I in the midst of them.[3] 21 Then came Kepha to Him, and said, Master, how often shall my brother sin against me, and I forgive him? Up to seven times? 22 יהושע said to him, I did not say to you, up to seven times: but, up to seventy times seven.[4] 23 Therefore is the malchut ha shamayim like a certain melech, who would take account of his avadim. 24 And when he had begun to settle, one was brought to him, who owed him ten thousand talents. 25 But as he had nothing with which to pay, his master commanded him to be sold, and his wife, and children, and all that he had, and payment to be made. 26 The eved therefore fell down, and worshipped him, saying, master, have patience with me, and I will pay you all. 27 Then the master of that eved was moved with rachamim, and released

him, and forgave him the debt. 28 But the same eved went out, and found one of his fellow avadim, who owed him an hundred pieces of money: and he laid hands on him, and took him by the throat, saying, Pay me what you owe. 29 And his fellow eved fell down at his feet, and begged him, saying, Have patience with me, and I will pay you all. 30 And he would not: but went and cast him into prison, until he should pay the debt. 31 So when his fellow avadim saw what was done, they were very sad and angry, and came and told their master all that was done. 32 Then his master, after he had called him, said to him, O you wicked eved of Biliyaal, I forgave you all that debt, because you begged me: 33 Should not you have also have had rachamim on your fellow eved, even as I had rachamim on you? 34 And his master was angry, and delivered him to the torturers, until he should pay all that was due to him. 35 So likewise shall My heavenly Abba do also to you, if you from your levim do not forgive every one his brother their trespasses.[5]

19 And it came to pass, that when יהושע had finished these sayings, He departed from Galil, and came into the coasts of Yahudah beyond the Yarden River; 2 And great multitudes followed Him; and He healed them there. 3 The Prushim also came to Him, tempting Him, and saying to Him, Is it permitted in Torah for a man to put away his wife for any and every cause? 4 And He answered and said to them, Have you not read, that He who made them in Bereshet made them male and female, 5 And said, For this cause shall a man leave abba and ima, and shall cleave to his wife: and the two shall be one flesh?[6] 6 Wherefore they are no more two, but basar echad. What therefore יהוה has joined together, let not man put asunder. 7 They said to Him, Why did Moshe then

---

[1] The point being that Yahshua cares for every lost sheep of Yisrael, including those who still think they are just believing gentiles.
[2] Moadim and Shabbat.
[3] Yisraelite remnants, gathering in His true Name.
[4] Between Yahudah and Ephraim there must be unlimited amounts of forgiveness so that long held mistrusts can be healed.

[5] A tremendous halachic ruling of proper behavior and loving compassion, within Renewed Covenant Yisrael.
[6] YHWH's will for marriages and Yisrael's two-bayit restoration. See Ephesians 5:31-32.

command to give a Get, and to put her away? 8 He said to them, *Moshe because of the hardness of your levim allowed you to put away your wives: but from the beginning and from eternity*[1] *it was not so. 9 And I say to you, Whoever shall divorce his wife, except it be for fornication, and shall marry another, commits adultery: and whoever marries her who has been divorced does commit adultery.*[2] 10 His talmidim said to Him, If the case of the man be so with his wife, it is not tov to marry. 11 But He said to them, *All men cannot receive your saying, except those to whom it is given. 12 For there are some eunuchs, who were so born from their ima's womb: and there are some eunuchs, who were made eunuchs by men: and there are eunuchs, who have made themselves eunuchs for the malchut ha shamayim's sake. He that is able to receive it let him receive it.* 13 Then were brought to Him little children, that He should put His hands on them, and say a bracha: and the talmidim rebuked them. 14 But יהושע said, *Allow little children, and do not forbid them, to come to Me: for of such is the malchut ha shamayim.* 15 And He laid His hands on them, and departed from there. 16 And, see, one came and said to Him, Tov Master, what tov thing shall I do, that I may have eternal chayim in the olam haba?[3] 17 And He said to him, *Why do you call Me tov? There is none tov but one, that is,* יהוה :[4] *but if you will enter into chayim, keep the Torah commandments.*[5] 18 He said to Him, Which ones? יהושע said, *You shall do no murder, You shall not commit adultery, You shall not steal, You shall not bear false witness, 19 Honor your abba and your ima: and, You shall love your neighbor as yourself.*[6] 20 The young man said to Him, All these things have I kept from my youth up: what do I lack yet? 21 יהושע said to him, *If you will be perfect, go and sell what you have, and give to the poor, and you shall have treasure in ha shamayim: and come and follow Me.* 22 But when the young man heard that saying, he went away sorrowful and angry:[7] for he had great possessions. 23 Then said יהושע to His talmidim, *Truly I say to you, That it is very hard for a rich man to enter into the malchut ha shamayim. 24 And again I say to you, It is easier for a large rope*[8] *to go through the eye of a needle, than for a rich man to enter into the malchut of* יהוה. 25 When His talmidim heard it, they were exceedingly amazed, saying, Who then can be saved?[9] 26 But יהושע beheld them, and said to them, *With men this is impossible; but with* יהוה *all things are possible.* 27 Then answered Kepha and said to Him, See, we have forsaken all, and followed You; what shall we have therefore? 28 And יהושע said to them, *Truly I say to you, Those of you who have followed Me, in the regeneration*[10] *when the Ben Adam shall sit on the throne of His esteem, you also shall sit upon twelve thrones, administering mishpat over the twelve tribes of Yisrael.*[11] 29 *And every one that has forsaken houses, or brothers, or sisters, or abba, or ima, or wife, or children, or lands, for My Name's sake,*[12] *shall receive a hundredfold, and shall inherit everlasting chayim.*

---

[1] Shem Tov reference.
[2] Before Yahshua's dom was shed and forgave all manner of sin; That is the real untainted tov news. But once a believing couple marries they cannot ever be divorced.
[3] Shem Tov reference.
[4] Yahshua is not denying being YHWH in the flesh; He is merely saying to this Yisraelite that by using the term "good" does he realize what he's actually saying? Torah alone defines what is tov.
[5] Torah keeping alone does not save us. What Yahshua is saying in essence is, "are you really perfect or as perfect as you think you are?"
[6] Obviously the others are just as important. Rabbinic teaching includes citing only certain key passages as a starting point, and expecting the student or follower to know the rest of the verses by heart. This is what is taking place here.
[7] Shem Tov reference.
[8] See note on Mark 10:25.
[9] Because in Hebraic understanding wealth is a sign of YHWH's favor.
[10] Olam habah.
[11] Clearly Yahshua speaks of Yisrael reborn not a separate entity apart from Yisrael which man has built using false variations of His Name and His plan.
[12] For the only true Name.

30 *But many that are first shall be last; and the last shall be first.*

20 For the malchut ha shamayim is like a man that is a farm owner, who went out early in the morning to hire workers into his vineyard. 2 And when he had agreed with the workers for a penny a day, he sent them into his vineyard. 3 And he went out about the third hour, and saw others standing idle in the marketplace, 4 And said to them, You too go into the vineyard, and whatever is right I will give you. And they went their way. 5 Again he went out about the sixth and ninth hour, and did likewise. 6 And about the eleventh hour he went out, and found others standing idle, and said to them, Why do you stand here all the day idle? 7 They say to him, Because no man has hired us. He said to them, You too go also into the vineyard; and whatever is right, that shall you receive. 8 So when evening had come, the owner of the vineyard said to his manager, Call the workers, and give them their pay, beginning from the last to the first. 9 And when those came who were hired around the eleventh hour, they received every man a silver piece. 10 *But when the first came, they thought that they would receive more; and they likewise received every man a silver piece. 11 And when they had received it, they murmured against the owner of the vineyard, 12 Saying, These last group has worked just one hour, and you have made them equal to us, who have borne the burden and heat of the day. 13 But he answered one of them, and said, Friend, I do you no wrong: did you not agree with me for a silver piece? 14 Take what is yours, and go your way: I will give to this last man, as also I gave to you. 15 Is it not permitted in Torah for Me to do what I will with my own? Is your eye evil,[1] because I am tov? 16 So the last shall be first, and the first last: for many are called, but few chosen.* 17 And **יהושע** going up to

Yahrushalayim, took the twelve talmidim aside in the way, and said to them, 18 *See, we go up to Yahrushalayim; and the Ben Adam shall be betrayed to the main kohanim and to the Sophrim, and they shall condemn Him to death, 19 And shall deliver Him to the gentiles to mock, and to scourge, and to impale Him: and the third day He shall rise again.*[2] 20 Then came to Him the ima of Zavdi's children with her sons, worshipping Him, and desiring a certain request from Him. 21 And He said to her, *What do you want?* She said to Him, Grant that my two sons may sit, one on Your right hand, and the other on the left, in Your malchut. 22 But **יהושע** answered and said, *You know not what you ask. Are you able to drink of the cup that I shall drink of, and to be immersed with the mikvah that I am immersed with?* They said to Him, We are able. 23 And He said to them, *You shall drink indeed of My cup, and be immersed with the mikvah that I am immersed with: but to sit on My right hand, and on My left, is not Mine to give, but it shall be given to them for whom it is prepared by My Abba.* 24 And when the ten heard it, they were moved with indignation against the two brothers. 25 But **יהושע** called them to Him, and said, *You know that the princes of the goyim exercise dominion over them, and they that are great exercise authority upon them. 26 But it shall not be so among you: but whoever will be great among you, let him be your eved;*[3] 27 And whoever will be first among you, let him be your eved:[4] 28 Even as the Ben Adam came not to be attended to, but to serve, and to give His chayim a ransom for many.* 29 And as they departed from Yericho, a great multitude followed Him. 30 And, see, two blind men sitting by the way side, when they heard that **יהושע** passed by, cried out, saying, Have rachamim on us, O Master, Ben

---

[1] Stingy.

[2] Notice according to Yahshua Himself the Jews are not the killers of Moshiach.
[3] Notice the contrast between His talmidim, the Yisraelites; and the non-believers who are the true gentiles.
[4] Kingdom greatness is fine; but it's done by service to others.

David. 31 And the multitude rebuked them, because they desired them to keep silent: but they cried out even more, saying, Have rachamim on us, O Master, Ben David. 32 And יהושע stood still, and called them, and said, *What do you want Me to do for you?* 33 They said to Him, Master, that our eyes may be opened. 34 So יהושע had rachamim on them, and touched their eyes: and immediately their eyes received sight, and they followed Him.[1]

21 And when they drew near to Yahrushalayim, and had come to Beth Phagi, to the Mount of Olives, then יהושע sent two talmidim,[2] 2 Saying to them, *Go into the village opposite you, and immediately you shall find an donkey tied, and a colt with her: loose them, and bring them to Me.* 3 *And if any man says anything to you, you shall say, the Master has need of them; and immediately he will send them.* 4 All this was done, that it might be fulfilled what was spoken by ha navi, saying, 5 Tell you the daughter of Tzion, See, your Melech comes to you, meek, and sitting upon a donkey, even a colt the foal of a donkey. 6 And the talmidim went, and did as יהושע commanded them, 7 And brought the donkey, and the colt, and put on them their clothes, and they set Him on it. 8 And a very great multitude spread their garments in the road; others cut down branches from the eytzim, and spread them in the road. 9 And the multitudes that went before, and that followed, cried out, saying, Hoshia-na to the Savior[3] the Ben David: Blessed is He that comes in the Name of the Master יהוה; Hoshia-na in the highest. 10 And when He had come into Yahrushalayim, all the city was stirred up, saying, Who is this? 11 And the multitude said, This is יהושע HaNavi of Natzreth of Galil. 12 And יהושע went into the Beit HaMikdash of יהוה, and cast out all them that sold and bought in the Beit HaMikdash, and overthrew the tables of the moneychangers, and the seats of them that sold doves, 13 And said to them, *It is written, My Bayit shall be called the Bayit of tefillah; but you have made it a den of thieves and violent men.*[4] 14 And the blind and the lame came to Him in the Beit HaMikdash; and He healed them. 15 And when the main kohanim and Sophrim saw the wonderful things that He did, and the children crying in the Beit HaMikdash saying let the Son of Elohim be praised,[5] and saying, Hoshia-na to the Ben David; they were very displeased, 16 And said to Him, Do You shema what they say? And יהושע said to them, *Yes; have you never read, Out of the mouth of babies and those who are nursed, You have perfected tehilla?* 17 And He left them, and went out of the city into Beth Anya; and He spent the night there. 18 Now in the morning as He returned into the city, He was hungry. 19 And when He saw a fig eytz on the way, He came to it, and found nothing on it, but leaves only, and said to it, *Let no fruit grow on you ever again.* And at once the fig eytz withered away. 20 And when the talmidim saw it, they marveled, saying, How quickly the fig eytz did wither away! 21 יהושע answered and said to them, *Truly I say to you, If you have emunah, and doubt not, you shall not only do that which is done to the fig eytz, but also if you shall say to this mountain, Be removed, and be thrown into the sea; it shall be done.* 22 *And all things, whatever you shall ask in tefillah, believing, you shall receive.* 23 And when He was come into the Beit HaMikdash, the main kohanim and the zachanim of the people came to Him as He was teaching, and said, By what authority and power do You do these things? And who gave You this authority and power?[6] 24 And יהושע answered and said to them, *I will ask you one thing, which if you tell Me, I will tell*

---

[1] Both houses have their eyes opened by Moshiach, as represented in the two blind men.
[2] A type of both houses ready to rejoice at Pesach in brotherhood restored.
[3] Shem Tov reference.

[4] Shem Tov reference.
[5] Shem Tov reference.
[6] Shem Tov reference.

you by what authority I do these things. 25 Yochanan's mikveh and authority, where did it come from? From ha shamayim, or from men? And they reasoned among themselves, saying, If we shall say, From ha shamayim; He will say to us, Why did you not then believe him? 26 But if we shall say, Of men; we fear the people; for all believed that Yochanan was a navi. 27 And they answered יהושע, and said, We cannot tell. And He said to them, *Neither do I tell you by what authority I do these things. 28 But what do you think? A certain man had two sons; and He came to the first, and said, Son, go work today in My vineyard. 29 He answered and said, I will not: but afterward he repented, and went.*[1] *30 And He came to the second, and said likewise. And he answered and said, I go, sir: and went not.*[2] *31 Which of the two sons did the will of His Abba?* They said to Him, The first.[3] יהושע *said to them, Truly I say to you, that the tax collectors and the harlots go into the malchut of* יהוה *before you.* [4] *32 For Yochanan came to you in the way of tzedakah, and you believed him not: but the tax collectors and the harlots believed him: and you, when you had seen it, made no teshuvah afterwards, that you might believe him. 33 Shema another parable: There was a certain farm owner, who planted a vineyard,*[5] *and placed a hedge around it, and dug a winepress in it, and built a tower, and leased it out to farmers, and went into a far country:*[6] *34 And when the time of the fruit drew near, He sent His avadim to the farmers, that they might receive the fruits of it. 35 And the farmers took His avadim, and beat one, and killed another, and stoned another. 36 Again, He sent other avadim more than the first: and they did to them likewise. 37 But last of all He sent to them*

His Son, saying, They will reverence My Son. 38 But when the farmers saw the Son, they said among themselves, This is the heir; come, let us kill Him, and let us seize on His inheritance.[7] *39 And they caught Him, and cast Him out of the vineyard, and killed Him. 40 When the Master therefore of the vineyard comes, what will He do to those farmers?* 41 They said to Him, He will miserably destroy those wicked men, and will lease His vineyard to other farmers, who shall render Him the fruits in their seasons. 42 יהושע said to them, *Did you never read in the Ketuvim, The Stone that the builders rejected, the same has become the Head of the corner: this is the Master* יהוה *'s doing, and it is marvelous in our eyes? 43 Therefore I say to you, The malchut of* יהוה *shall be taken from you, and given to a people*[8] [9] *bringing forth the fruits of it. 44 And whoever shall fall on this Stone shall be broken: but on whomever it shall fall, it will grind him to powder and they will be broken apart.*[10] 45 And when the main kohanim and Prushim had heard His parables, they perceived that He spoke about them. 46 But when they sought to lay hands on Him, they feared the multitude, because the people trusted Him as a Navi.

22 And יהושע answered and spoke to them again by parables, and said, *2 The malchut ha shamayim is like a certain melech, who made a marriage for his Son,*[11] *3 And sent forth his avadim to call them that were invited to the wedding: and they would not come. 4 Again, he sent forth*

---

[1] Ephraim Yisrael.
[2] Yahudah Yisrael.
[3] Ephraim.
[4] Before Yahudah that is. It has been 2,000 years and Jewish Yisrael still hasn't fully come in. All the other groups named, have been the first to repent.
[5] Yisrael is the vineyard of the Beloved as seen in Yeshayahu chapter 5.
[6] Heaven.

[7] The inheritance is the right to rule over Yisrael.
[8] Not the church or a different nation. Given to "a nation" as Yahshua said. Strong's Greek #1484. The Greek word here means "tribe" or "a group from the same company or race." The kingdom was removed from Yahudah for a long season and given to Ephraim, as this was made official by the transfer of the scepter from the tribe of Yahudah to the tribe of Gad. We can understand this in light of the previous parables in the same chapter about two sons, with one returning to obedience while the other does not. See http://yourarmstoisrael.org/Articles_new/restoration/?page=21&type=12.
[9] Alternate meaning: "given to a future generation" of the same people.
[10] Shem Tov reference.
[11] Shemot 4:22-23; Yisrael is YHWH's national son.

other avadim, saying, *Tell them who are invited, See, I have prepared my dinner: my oxen and my fatted calf are killed, and all things are ready: come to the marriage.* 5 *But they made light of it, and went their ways, one to his farm, another to his merchandise: 6 And the remnant took his avadim, and treated them spitefully, and killed them. 7 But when the melech heard of this, He was angry: and he sent forth his armies, and destroyed those murderers, and burned up their city. 8 Then He said to his avadim, The wedding is ready, but those who were invited[1] were not worthy. 9 Go therefore into the highways, and as many as you shall find, invite to the marriage. 10 So those avadim went out into the highways, and gathered together as many as they found, both bad and tov: and the wedding was furnished with guests. 11 And when the melech came in to see the guests, he saw there a man who did not have on a wedding garment: 12 And he said to him, Friend, how did you come in here not having on a wedding garment? And he was speechless.[2] 13 Then said the melech to the avadim, Bind him hand and foot, and take him away, and cast him into outer darkness; there shall be weeping and gnashing of teeth. 14 For many are called, but few are chosen.*

15 Then went the Prushim, and took counsel how they might entangle Him in His talk. 16 And they sent out to Him their talmidim with the Herodians, saying, Rabbi, we know that You are true and faithful,[3] and teach the Way of Elohim in emet, neither do You care what any man thinks: for You regard not the person of men. 17 Tell us therefore, What do You think? Is it permitted in Torah to give tax to Caesar, or not? 18 But יהושע perceived their wickedness, and said, *Why do you try Me, you hypocrites? 19 Show Me the tax money.* And they brought to Him a silver piece.

20 And He said to them, *Whose likeness and inscription is this?* 21 They said to Him, Caesar's. Then He said to them, *Give obediently therefore to Caesar the things which are Caesar's; and to יהוה the things that are יהוה's.* 22 When they had heard these words, they marveled, and left Him, and went their way. 23 The same day came to Him the Tzadukim, who say that there is no resurrection, and asked Him, 24 Saying, Master, Moshe said, If a man dies, having no children, his brother shall marry his wife, and raise up seed for his brother. 25 Now there were among us seven brothers: and the first, when he had married a wife, he died and, having no children, left his wife to his brother: 26 Likewise the second also, and the third, all the way to the seventh. 27 And last of all, the woman died also. 28 Therefore in the resurrection whose wife shall she be from the seven? For they all had her as a wife. 29 יהושע answered and said to them, *You are led astray, not knowing the Ketuvim, nor the power of יהוה. 30 For in the resurrection they neither marry, nor are given in marriage, but are as the heavenly messengers of יהוה in ha shamayim. 31 But as touching the resurrection of the dead, have you not read that which was spoken to you by Elohim, saying, 32 I am the Elohim of Avraham, and the Elohim of Yitzchak, and the Elohim of Yaakov? Elohim is not the Elohim of the dead, but of the living.* 33 And when the multitude heard this, they were astonished at His Torah. 34 But when the Prushim had heard that He had put the Tzadukim to silence, they were gathered together. 35 Then one of them, who was a Torah master, asked Him a question, testing Him, and saying, 36 Rabbi, which one is the great commandment in the Torah? 37 יהושע said to him, *You shall love the Master יהוה Your Elohim with all your lev, and with all your being, and with your entire mind.[4] 38 This is the first and greatest*

---

[1] Some of Jewish Yisrael.
[2] Staying in the context with the two sons of the same father, the son who tries to sneak into the kingdom without dom atonement and imputed righteousness is Yahudah; Romans 10:1-4.
[3] Shem Tov reference: "Faithful" implies Torah observance.

[4] The Shema of Devarim 6:4-5.

commandment. 39 *And the second is like it; You shall love your neighbor as yourself.*
40 *On these two commandments hang all the Torah and the neviim.*[1] 41 While the Prushim were gathered together, **יהושע** asked them, 42 Saying, *What do you think of the Moshiach? Whose Son is He?* They said to Him, Ben David. 43 He said to them, *How then does David in the Ruach call Him the Master* **יהוה**,[2] *saying,* 44 *The Master* **יהוה** *said to my Master, Sit you on My right hand, until I make Your enemies Your footstool?*[3] 45 *If David then calls Him Master* **יהוה**, *how is He then David's son?* 46 And no man was able to answer Him a word, and from that day on no one asked Him any more questions.

23 Then spoke **יהושע** to the multitude, and to His talmidim, 2 *Saying, The Sophrim and the Prushim sit in Moshe's seat:* 3 *All therefore that Moshe said*[4] *that they invite you to observe, that observe and do; but do not do after their mitzvot: for they say, and do not.*[5][6] 4 *For they bind heavy burdens too grievous to bear, and lay them on men's shoulders; but they themselves will not move them with one of their fingers.* 5 *But all their mitzvot they do to be seen by men: they make large their tephillin, and lengthen their tzitziyot,* 6 *And love the best seats at moadim, and the main seats in the synagogues,* 7 *And greetings in the markets, and to be called, Rabbi, Rabbi, by men.* 8 *But as for you do not desire to be called Rabbi:*[7] *for one is your Rabbi, even the Moshiach; and all you are brothers.*
9 *And call no man abba upon the earth: for one is your Abba, who is in ha shamayim.* 10 *Neither be called teachers: for one is your Teacher, even the Moshiach.* 11 *But he that is greatest among you shall be your eved.* 12 *And whoever shall exalt himself shall be humbled; and he that shall humble himself shall be exalted.* 13 *But woe to you, Sophrim and Prushim, hypocrites! For you shut up the malchut ha shamayim from men: for you neither go in yourselves, neither do you allow them that are entering to go in.* 14 *Woe to you, Sophrim and Prushim, hypocrites! For you devour widows' houses, and for show and lengthy exposition*[8] *make long tefillot: therefore you shall receive the greater damnation.* 15 *Woe to you, Sophrim and Prushim, hypocrites! For you travel sea and land to make one Yireh-* **יהוה**,[9] *and when he is made, you make him twofold more a child of Gei-Hinnom than yourselves.* 16 *Woe to you, blind guides, who say, Whoever shall swear by the Beit HaMikdash, it is nothing; but whoever shall swear by the gold of the Beit HaMikdash, he is a debtor!* 17 *You blind fools: for what is greater, the gold, or the Beit HaMikdash that sets apart the gold?* 18 *And, Whosoever shall swear by the altar, it is nothing; but whoever swears by the gift that is upon it, he is guilty.* 19 *You blind fools: for which is greater, the gift, or the altar that sets apart the gift?* 20 *Whoever therefore shall swear by the altar, swears by it, and by all things on it.* 21 *And whoever shall swear by the Beit HaMikdash, swears by it, and by Him that dwells in it.* 22 *And he that shall swear by ha shamayim swears by the throne of* **יהוה**, *and by Him that sits on it.* 23 *Woe to you,*

---

[1] Torah can't be "done away with," indeed, Yahshua says the Torah and the prophets hang on these two big ones; that is, these two big ones expand into the details, which are contained in the Torah and the prophets. They don't replace the 613 laws; they are the foundation of those laws.
[2] **MarYah** in Aramaic a reference to Moshiach being YHWH.
[3] Tehillim/Psalms 110:1-5.
[4] Hebrew in the singular as in "he said," or **yomer** versus the plural "they say," or **yaamru**. The one giving the sayings is a single person or Moshe the Torah-giver.
[5] This verse fits in with the entire chapter when taken from the Hebrew Shem Tov Matthew. Moshiach contrasts the things they teach from what Moshe taught in Torah. For a full treatment on this understanding go to: http://yourarmstoisrael.org/Articles_new/restoration/?page=13&type=12.
[6] This does not mean as some teach that all things that Judaism teaches, even when wrong, believers must follow. That is not what Moshiach is teaching.

[7] The Hebrew Shem Tov uses the word **tirzu**, which is desire. That definition is quite telling. It states that a man should not desire title and yet if YHWH bestows a title including rabbi, that's fine. He is attacking a bad heart attitude, not one or two particular "Jewish" religious titles, while allowing others to be permissible.
[8] Shem Tov reference.
[9] Non-Jewish convert deemed righteous. Literally "YHWH fearer."

Sophrim and Prushim, hypocrites! For you pay tithe of mint and anise and cummin, and have omitted the weightier matters of the Torah, mishpat, rachamim, and emunah: these needed to have been done, and not to leave the others undone. 24 You blind guides, who strain at a gnat, and swallow a camel. 25 Woe to you, Sophrim and Prushim, hypocrites! For you make clean the outside of the cup and of the dish, but inside they are full of extortion and unrighteousness. 26 You blind Prush, cleanse first that which is inside the cup and dish, that the outside of them may be clean also. 27 Woe to you, Sophrim and Prushim, hypocrites! For you are like white washed tombs, which indeed appear beautiful outside, but inside are full of dead men's bones, and all uncleanness. 28 Even so you also outwardly appear tzadik to men, but inside you are full of hypocrisy and Torah-less-ness. 29 Woe to you, Sophrim and Prushim, hypocrites! Because you build the tombs of the neviim, and decorate the graves of the tzadik, 30 And say, If we had been alive in the days of our ahvot, we would not have taken part with them in the dom of the neviim. 31 Therefore you are witnesses against yourselves, that you are the children of those that killed the neviim. 32 Fill you up then the measure of your ahvot. 33 You serpents, you generation of vipers, how can you escape the damnation of Gei-Hinnom? 34 Therefore, see, I send to you neviim, and wise men, and Sophrim: and some of them you shall kill and destroy; and some of them you shall scourge in your synagogues, and persecute them from city to city: 35 That upon you may come all the tzadik dom shed upon the earth, from the dom of the tzadik Hevel to the dom of Zacharyah son of Yehoidai[1], whom you killed between the Beit HaMikdash and the altar. 36 Truly I say to you, All these things shall come upon this generation. 37 O Yahrushalayim, Yahrushalayim, you that kills the neviim, and stones those who are sent to you, how often would I have gathered your children together, even as a hen gathers her chicks under her wings, but you were not willing! 38 See, your Bayit is left to you desolate.[2] 39 For I say to you, You shall not see Me again, until you shall surely learn to say, Baruch Haba BeShem HaAdon יהוה.[3]

24 And יהושע went out, and departed from the Beit HaMikdash: and His talmidim came to Him to show Him the buildings of the Beit HaMikdash. 2 And יהושע said to them, Do you not see all these things? Truly I say to you, There shall not be left here one stone upon another that shall not be thrown down. 3 And as He sat upon the Mount of Olives, the talmidim came to Him privately, saying, Tell us, when shall these things be? And what shall be the sign of Your coming, and of the end of this age? 4 And יהושע answered and said to them, Take heed that no man deceive you. 5 For many shall come in My Name, saying, I am the Moshiach; and shall deceive many. 6 And you shall shema of wars and rumors of wars: see that you be not troubled or become foolish:[4] for all these things must come to pass, but the end is not yet. 7 For nation shall rise against nation, and malchut against malchut: and there shall be famines, and pestilences, and earthquakes, in divers places. 8 All these are the beginning of sorrows. 9 Then shall they deliver you up to be afflicted, and shall kill you: and you shall be hated by all nations for My Name's sake. 10 And then shall many be offended, and shall betray one another, and shall hate one another. 11 And many false neviim shall rise, and shall deceive many. 12 And because Torah-less-ness shall abound, the ahava of many shall grow cold. 13 But he that shall endure

---

[1] Second Chronicles 24:20-21. According to kirch father Jerome, the Hebrew copy he had read correctly as son of Yehoidai and not Barachai.

[2] The Temple on Moriyah; and the House of Yahudah as a whole.

[3] Learning YHWH's true Name in Yisrael is a prerequisite for Yahshua's return. He is waiting for that to occur, before He returns.

[4] Shem Tov reference.

to the end, the same shall be saved. 14 And this besarot of the malchut shall be proclaimed in all the olam hazeh for a witness to all nations;[1] and then shall the end come.[2] 15 When you therefore shall see the abomination of desolation, spoken of by Daniyel the navi, stand in the Beit HaMikdash, (whoever reads, let him understand:)[3] 16 Then let them who are in Yahudah flee into the mountains: 17 Let him who is on the housetop not come down to take anything out of his bayit: 18 Neither let him who is in the field return back to take his clothes. 19 And woe to them that are with child, and to them that are nursing children in those days! 20 But make tefillah that your flight is not in the winter, neither on the Shabbat day:[4] 21 For then shall be Great Tribulation, such as was not since the beginning of the olam hazeh to this time, no, nor ever shall be. 22 And except those days are shortened, there should no flesh survive: but for the elect[5] and for the sake of those chosen,[6] those days shall be shortened. 23 Then if any man say to you, See, here is the Moshiach, or there; believe it not. 24 For there shall arise false Moshiachs, and false neviim, and shall show great signs and wonders; insomuch that, if it became possible, they shall deceive the very elect and chosen.[7][8] 25 See, I have told you before it occurs. 26 Therefore if they shall say to you, See,

He is in the desert; do not go: see, He is in the secret rooms; believe it not. 27 For as the lightning comes out of the east, and shines even to the west; so shall also the coming of the Ben Adam be. 28 For wherever the dead body is, there will the eagles be gathered together. 29 Immediately after the Tribulation[9] of those days shall the sun be darkened, and the moon shall not give its light, and the cochavim shall fall from ha shamayim, and the powers of ha shamayim shall be shaken: 30 And then shall appear the sign of the Ben Adam in ha shamayim: and then shall all the tribes of the land[10] mourn, and they shall see the Ben Adam coming on the clouds of ha shamayim with power and great tiferet. 31 And He shall send His heavenly messengers with a great sound of a shofar, and they shall gather together His elect from the four winds,[11] from one end of ha shamayim to the other.[12] 32 Now learn a parable of the fig eytz; When its branch is yet tender, and puts forth leaves, you know that summer fruit is near: 33 So likewise, when you shall see all these things,[13] know that it is near, even at the doors. 34 Truly I say to you, This generation shall not pass, until all these things are fulfilled. 35 Ha Shamayim and earth shall pass away, but My words shall not pass away. 36 But of that day and hour knows no man, no, not even the heavenly messengers, but My Abba only. 37 But as the days of Noach were, so shall also the coming of the Ben Adam be. 38 For as in the days that were before the flood they were eating and drinking, marrying and giving in marriage, until the day that Noach entered into the ark, 39 And knew not until the flood came, and took them all away; so shall also the coming of

---

[1] All the latter-day Yisraelite nations.
[2] The message of the kingdom restored and eternally established is the only right message.
[3] How can the believers see the "abomination of desolation" if they are no longer on earth? The believers will be reading the Book of Daniel during the Great Tribulation. There is no rapture here; for if there was why would we need the book of Daniel or any other book, if there was a pre-tribulation rapture? For more details see:
http://yourarmstoisrael.org/Articles_new/restoration/?page=10&type=12.
[4] Believers were expected to always keep Shabbat and will be doing so at the time both before and after the Great Tribulation.
[5] In the Brit Chadasha the congregation of the redeemed is called the elect. Never are unsaved Jews, or other unsaved peoples called elect anywhere in the Brit Chadasha, or in the rest of scripture for that matter.
[6] The chosen and elect are one and the same people.
[7] Within the deceived "tribulation elect," there is a "very elect" that cannot be deceived.
[8] Shem Tov reference.

[9] It is very clear when Moshiach returns – after the Tribulation.
[10] All nations, and all of Yisrael's 12 tribes. Double meaning.
[11] "Four winds," is an idiomatic expression used only to refer to the locations of exile for both houses of Yisrael. It is found in Torah and the Renewed Covenant.
[12] Regathering of Yisrael's two houses according to Isaiah 11:12.
[13] Take careful note. Do not be deceived. Believers will see these things as the Master says here.

the Ben Adam be.[1] 40 Then shall two be in the field; one shall be taken, and the other left. 41 Two women shall be grinding at the mill; one shall be taken, and the other left. 42 Watch therefore: for you know not what hour your Master is coming.[2] 43 But know this; that if the owner of the bayit had known in what hour the thief would come, he would have watched, and would not have allowed his bayit to be broken into. 44 Therefore you also stay ready: for in such an hour as you think not the Ben Adam will come. 45 Who then is a faithful and wise eved, whom his Master has made ruler over His household, to give them food in due season? 46 Blessed is that eved, whom His Master when He comes shall find so doing. 47 Truly I say to you, That He shall make him ruler over all His goods and children.[3] 48 But if an evil eved shall say in his lev, My Master delays His coming; 49 And shall begin to smite his fellow avadim, and to eat and drink with the drunks; 50 The Master of that eved shall come in a day when he looks not for Him, and in an hour that he is not aware of, 51 And shall cut him in pieces, and appoint him a portion with the hypocrites: and there shall then be weeping and gnashing of teeth.

25 Then shall the malchut ha shamayim be like to ten virgins, who took their lamps, and went forth to meet the Bridegroom.[4] 2 And five of them were wise, and five were foolish.[5] 3 They that were foolish took their lamps, and took no oil with them: 4 But the wise took oil in their vessels with their lamps. 5 While the Bridegroom tarried, they all slumbered and slept. 6 And at midnight there was a cry made, See, the Bridegroom comes; go out to meet him. 7 Then all those virgins arose, and trimmed their lamps. 8 And the foolish said to the wise, Give us from your oil; for our lamps have gone out. 9 But the wise answered, saying, Not so; lest there not be enough for you and us: instead go to them that sell, and buy for yourselves. 10 And while they went to buy, the Bridegroom came; and they that were ready went in with him to the marriage: and the door was shut. 11 Afterward came also the other virgins, saying, Master, Master, open to us. 12 But he answered and said, Truly I say to you, I know you not. 13 Watch therefore, for you know neither the day nor the hour in which the Ben Adam comes. 14 For the malchut ha shamayim is like a man traveling into a far country, who called His own avadim, and delivered to them His goods. 15 And to one He gave five talents, to another two, and to another one; to every man according to his own ability; and immediately He took his journey. 16 Then he that had received the five talents went and traded with the same, and made five other talents. 17 And likewise he that had received two, he also gained another two. 18 But he that had received one talent went and dug in the earth, and hid His Master's money. 19 After a long time the Master of those avadim came, and settled accounts with them. 20 And so he that had received five talents came and brought another five talents, saying, Master, you delivered to me five talents: see, I have gained beside them five talents more. 21 His Master said to him, Well done, you tov and faithful eved: you have been faithful over a few things, I will set you over many things: enter into the simcha of Your Master. 22 He also that had received two talents came and said, Master, You delivered to me two talents: see, I have gained two more talents besides them. 23 His Master said to him, Well done, tov and faithful eved; you have been faithful over a few things, I will set you over many things: enter into the simcha of Your Master. 24 Then he who had received the one talent came and said, Master, I knew

---

[1] Those taken away didn't fly away in Noach's day, but were taken away by the waters of judgment. In like manner will the tribulation take the lost away, while the saved are left behind.
[2] Redeemed Yisrael will be protected and will overcome, as all others are taken away.
[3] Shem Tov reference.
[4] Ten: representing ten returning tribes of Ephraim, who hear and accept the latter-day revelation of the regathering.
[5] Not all returning from the nations stay in the truth of Yahshua and His Torah, as First Yochanan testifies.

You that You are a hard shrewd Man, reaping where You have not sown, and gathering where You have not scattered seed: 25 And I was afraid, and went and hid Your talent in the earth: see, there You have what is Yours.[1] 26 His Master answered and said to him, You wicked and lazy eved, you supposedly knew that I reap where I sowed not, and gather where I have not scattered seed: 27 You should have at least deposited My silver with the bankers, and then at My coming I would have received My own with interest. 28 Take therefore the talent from him, and give it to him who owns ten talents. 29 For to every one that has shall be given, and he shall have abundance: but from him that has not; shall be taken away even that which he has.[2] 30 And cast the unprofitable eved into outer darkness: there shall be weeping and gnashing of teeth. 31 When the Ben Adam shall come in His tifereth, and all the set-apart heavenly messengers with Him, then shall He sit upon the throne of His tifereth:[3] 32 And before Him shall be gathered all nations: and He shall separate them one from another, as a Shepherd divides His sheep from the goats:[4] 33 And He shall set the sheep on His right hand, but the goats on the left. 34 Then shall the Melech say to them on His right hand, Come, you blessed of My Abba, inherit the malchut prepared for you from the foundation of the olam hazeh: 35 For I was hungry, and you gave Me food: I was thirsty, and you gave Me drink: I was a stranger,[5] and you took Me in: 36 Naked, and you clothed Me: I was sick, and you visited Me: I was in prison,

and you came to Me. 37 Then shall the tzadikim answer Him, saying, Master, when did we see You hungry, and fed You? Or thirsty, and gave You to drink? 38 When did we see You as a stranger, and took You in? Or naked, and clothed You? 39 Or when did we see You sick, or in prison, and visited You? 40 And the Melech shall answer and say to them, Truly I say to you, whenever you have done it to one of the least of these My brothers; you have done it to Me.[6] 41 Then shall He say also to them on the left hand, Depart from Me, you cursed, into everlasting fire, prepared for s.a.tan and his shadim:[7] 42 For I was hungry, and you gave Me no food: I was thirsty, and you gave Me no drink: 43 I was a stranger, and you took Me not in: naked, and you clothed Me not: sick, and in prison, and you visited Me not. 44 Then shall they also answer Him, saying, Master, when did we see You hungry, or thirsty, or a stranger, or naked, or sick, or in prison, and did not attend to You? 45 Then shall He answer them, saying, Truly I say to you, In so far as you did it not to one of the least of these, you did it not to Me.[8] 46 And these shall go away into everlasting punishment: but the tzadikim into chayim eternal.

26 And it came to pass, when יהושע had finished all these sayings, He said to His talmidim, 2 You know that after two days is the moed of the Pesach, and the Ben Adam is betrayed to be impaled. 3 Then assembled together the main kohanim, and the Sophrim, and the zachanim of the people, to the palace of the Kohen HaGadol, who was called Qayapha, 4 And they consulted just how they might seize יהושע by subtilty, and kill Him.

---

[1] Sadly most believers including many who know the true message of the restoration of the kingdom remain silent watchman on Tzion's walls.
[2] An eternal Torah. YHWH gives more to the faithful and loyal than to the merely intelligent, shrewd, or cautious self-preservation-type personalities.
[3] David's throne in Yahrushalayim, as the kingdom is fully come.
[4] King Moshaich will take all nations and look within each for Yisraelites who have become His sheep through accepting the good news of forgiveness. A second application could be the way the non Jewish Yisraelite nations treated brother Yahudah.
[5] Referring to the returning Ephraimites who need special care and instruction.

[6] The Master's love and care for both Yahudah and Ephraim's recovered sheep in the nations.
[7] Demons and s.a.tan burn in the Lake of Fire forever, since they are immortal beings. Lost man dies a second death and perishes.
[8] This should send chills down the spine of those who do not seek love and care for all brethren in both two houses of redeemed Yisrael. It seems that this issue of love and healing between Yahudah and Ephraim can have eternal consequences to those who have been quickened by this understanding, and yet fail to walk it out in love.

5 But they said, Not on the moed day, lest there be an uproar among the people. 6 Now when **יהושע** was in Beth Anya, in the bayit of Shimon the jar merchant, [1] 7 There came to Him a woman having an alabaster box of very precious ointment, and poured it on His head, as He sat at the table to eat. 8 But when His talmidim saw it, they had indignation, saying, For what purpose is this wasted? 9 For this ointment might have been sold for much, and given to the poor. 10 When **יהושע** understood it, He said to them, *Why do you trouble the woman? For she has done a tov work upon Me. 11 For you have the poor always with you; but Me you do not have always. 12 For in that she has poured this ointment on My body, she did it for My burial preperation. 13 Truly I say to you, Wherever this besarot shall be proclaimed in the whole olam hazeh, there shall also be told what this woman has done for me, as a memorial to her.* 14 Then one of the twelve, called Yahudah from Qerioth, went to the Kohanim HaGadolim, 15 And said to them, What will you give me, and I will deliver Him to you? And they covenanted with him for thirty pieces of silver. 16 And from that time on, he sought an opportunity to betray Him. 17 Now before[2] [3] the moed of Chag Matzoth the talmidim came to **יהושע** , saying to Him, Where will You that we prepare for You to eat the Pesach?[4] 18 And he said, *Go into the city to a man who will be a volunteer for the task,* [5] *and say to him, The Master said, My time is at hand; I will keep the Pesach at your bayit with My talmidim.* 19 And the talmidim did as

יהושע had commanded them; and they made ready the Pesach. 20 Now when the evening had come, He sat down with the twelve.[6] [7] 21 And as they did eat, He said, *Truly I say to you, that one of you shall betray Me.* 22 And they were exceedingly sorrowful, and began each one of them to say to Him, Master, is it I? 23 And He answered and said; *He that dips his hand with Me in the dish, the same shall betray Me. 24 The Ben Adam goes as it is written of Him: but woe to that man by whom the Ben Adam is betrayed! It had been tov for that man if He had not even been born.* 25 Then Yahudah, who betrayed Him, answered and said, Rabbi, is it I? He said to him, *You have spoken it.* 26 And as they were eating, **יהושע** took lechem, and made the bracha, and broke it, and gave it to the talmidim, and said, *Take, eat; this is My body.* 27 And He took the cup, and gave hodu, and gave it to them, saying, *Drink all of it; 28 For this is My dom of the Renewed Covenant that is shed for many for the remission of sins. 29 But I say to you, I will not drink of this fruit of the vine again, until that day when I drink it new with you in My Abba's malchut.* 30 And when they had sung a song, they went out to the Mount of Olives. 31 Then said **יהושע** to them, *All of you shall be offended and grieved because of Me this night: for it is written, I will smite the Shepherd, and the sheep of the flock shall be scattered abroad.* [8] *32 But after I am risen again, I will go before you into Galil.* 33 Kepha answered and said to Him, Though all men shall be offended because of You, yet will I never be offended. 34 **יהושע** said to him, *Truly I say*

---

[1] See notes on Mark 14:3.
[2] Strong's Greek # 4413. The Greek word here is **protos**, which depending on the context, can mean "before" as in the first of a series of sequential events, or "first" as in a number. Obviously here it means "before" or the first in a series of sequential preparation events, because Yahshua died on the afternoon of preparation and as such was dead before Passover.
[3] Hebrew, Aramaic and Talmud Bavli. Sanhedrin 43, all testify that Yahshua was hung on Passover before Unleavened Bread.
[4] We see here again that it was not yet Passover, so it certainly couldn't be the first Day of Unleavened Bread, which is the day after Passover.
[5] Shem Tov reference.

[6] Every orthodox rabbi even to this day has a Passover before the Passover, as a training lesson. Today this practice is seen in the Lubavitch movement when they gather the night before Pesach for what they call the Moshiach's Supper, looking forward to the coming of Moshiach. Some consider it a Pesach even though it is officially just a preparation. Yahshua looked and acted as if it were the Passover, without it actually being the Passover. This seeming contradiction is fully understood from a Hebraic mindset.
[7] All 12 tribes represented.
[8] This speaks of the House of Yahudah's scattering in 70 CE after the Moshiach will be killed.

to you, *That this night, before the cock crows, you shall deny Me three times.* 35 Kepha said to Him, Though I should die with You, yet will I not deny You. Likewise also said all the talmidim. 36 Then came **יהושע** with them to a place called Gethsemane, and said to the talmidim, *Sit here, while I go and make tefillah over there.* 37 And He took with Him Kepha and the two sons of Zavdi, and began to be sorrowful and very heavy hearted. 38 Then said He to them, *My being is exceedingly sorrowful, even to death: stay here, and watch with Me.* 39 And He went a little further, and fell on His face, and made tefillah, saying, *O My Abba, if it is possible, let this cup pass from Me: nevertheless not as I will, but as You will.* 40 And He came to the talmidim, and found them asleep, and said to Kepha, *What, could you not watch with Me one hour?* 41 *Watch and make tefillah, so that you enter not into temptation: the human ruach indeed is willing, but the flesh is weak.* 42 He went away again the second time, and made tefillah, saying, *O My Abba, if this cup may not pass away from Me, except I drink it, let Your will be done.* 43 And He came and found them asleep again: for their eyes were heavy. 44 And He left them, and went away again, and made tefillah the third time, saying the same words. 45 Then He came to His talmidim, and said to them, *Sleep on now, and take your rest: see, the hour is at hand, and the Ben Adam is betrayed into the hands of sinners.* 46 *Rise, let us be going: see, he is at hand that does betray Me.* 47 And while He yet spoke, see, Yahudah, one of the twelve, came, and with him a great multitude with swords and clubs, from the main kohanim and the zachanim of the people. 48 Now he that betrayed Him gave them a sign, saying, Whomever I shall kiss, it is Him: seize Him. 49 And immediately he came to **יהושע**, and said, Shalom, Rabbi; and kissed Him. 50 And **יהושע** said to him, *Beloved friend, why have you come, what have you done?*[1] Then they came, and arrested **יהושע**, and took Him. 51 And, see, one of them who

was with **יהושע** stretched out his hand, and drew his sword, and struck an eved of the Kohen HaGadol's, and cut off his ear. 52 Then said **יהושע** to him, *Put up again your sword into the sheath: for all those that take the sword shall perish with the sword.* 53 *Do you not understand that I can meet My enemies*[2] *and that I can now make tefillah to My Abba, and He shall presently give Me more than twelve legions of heavenly messengers?* 54 *But how then shall the Ketuvim of the Tanach be fulfilled, that it has to be this way?* 55 In that same hour said **יהושע** to the multitudes, *Are you come out against a thief, as if we were thieves,*[3] *with swords and clubs to take Me? I sat daily with you teaching in the Beit HaMikdash, and you did not seize Me.* 56 *But all this was done, that the Ketuvim of the neviim might be fulfilled.* Then all the talmidim forsook Him, and fled. 57 And they that had laid hold on **יהושע** led Him away to Qayapha the Kohen HaGadol, where the Sophrim and the Zachanim were assembled. 58 But Kepha followed Him from far off to the Kohen HaGadol's palace, and went in, and sat with the avadim, to see the result. 59 Now the main kohanim, and zachanim, and all the Sanhedrin, sought false witness against **יהושע**, to put Him to death; 60 But found none: yes, though many false witnesses came, yet they found none. At the end came two false witnesses, 61 And said, This Fellow said, I am able to destroy the Beit HaMikdash of Elohim, and to build it in three days. 62 And the Kohen HaGadol stood, and said to Him, Don't You respond? What is all this that these witness against You? 63 But **יהושע** kept His silence. And the Kohen HaGadol answered and said to Him, I put You under oath before the living Elohim, that You tell us whether You are The Moshiach, the Son of the Almighty.

---

64 יהושע said to him, *You have said it: nevertheless I say to you, After this you shall see the Ben Adam sitting at the right hand of יהוה,*[1] *and coming in the clouds of ha shamayim.* 65 Then the Kohen HaGadol tore his clothes, saying, He has spoken blasphemy; what further need do we have for witnesses? See, now you have heard His blasphemy.[2] 66 What do you think? They answered and said, He is guilty of death. 67 Then they did spit in His face, and beat Him; and others slapped Him with the palms of their hands, 68 Saying, Prophesy to us, Oh You Moshiach, Who is he that smote You? 69 Now Kepha sat outside in the palace: and a girl came to him, saying, You also were with יהושע of Galil. 70 But he denied it before them all, saying, I know not what you are saying. 71 And when he was gone out into the porch, another girl saw him, and said to them that were there, This fellow was also with יהושע of Natzareth. 72 And again he lied with an oath saying, I do not know the man. 73 And after a while came to him those that stood by, and said to Kepha, Surely you also are one of them from this Navi's group;[3] for your speech gives you away. 74 Then he began to curse and to swear, saying, I don't know the Man. And immediately the cock crowed. 75 And Kepha remembered the word of יהושע, which said to him, *Before the cock crows, you shall deny Me three times.* And he went out, and wept bitterly.

27 When the morning had come, all the main kohanim and zachanim of the people took counsel against יהושע to put Him to death: 2 And when they had bound Him, they led Him away, and delivered Him to Pontius Pilate the governor. 3 Then Yahudah, who had betrayed Him, when he saw that he was condemned, repented, and brought again the thirty pieces of silver to the main kohanim and zachanim, 4 Saying, I have sinned in that I have betrayed the innocent dom. And they said, What is that to us? You take care of that. 5 And he cast down the pieces of silver in the Beit HaMikdash, and departed, and went and hanged himself. 6 And the main kohanim took the silver pieces, and said, It is not right according to Torah to put the coins into the treasury, because it is the price of dom. 7 And they took counsel, and bought with the coins the Potter's Field, to bury strangers[4] in. 8 Therefore that field is called, Akel-Dama, to this day. 9 Then was fulfilled that what was spoken by Zecharyah[5] ha navi, saying, And they took the thirty pieces of silver, the price of Him that was appraised, whom the children of Yisrael did appraise; 10 And gave the silver for the Potter's Field, as the Master יהוה appointed me. 11 And יהושע stood before the governor: and the governor asked Him, saying, are You Melech of the Yahudim? And יהושע said to him, *You have said it.* 12 And when He was accused by the main kohanim and zachanim, He answered nothing. 13 Then said Pilate to Him, Do You shema how many things they witness against You? 14 And He answered him not a word; insomuch that the governor marveled greatly. 15 Now at the time of the moed the governor used to release to the people a prisoner, whom they desired. 16 And they had then a notable prisoner who was almost meshugas,[6] called Bar-Abba taken in a case of murder who had been placed in a dungeon. 17 Therefore when they were gathered together, Pilate said to them, Whom do you wish that I release to you? Bar-Abba, or יהושע who is called the Moshiach? 18 For he knew that for envy and hatred without a cause[7] they had delivered Him. 19 When he sat down on the mishpat seat, his wife sent to him, saying, Have nothing to do with that

---

[1] Quoting Psalm 110:5; "YHWH at thy right hand."
[2] The rabbinic version, not the biblical one, which classifies blasphemy as cursing with the Name or eliminating the Name, as opposed to actually pronouncing it.
[3] Shem Tov reference.

[4] Non-Yisraelites.
[5] Shem Tov reference and Peshitta.
[6] Shem Tov reference.
[7] Shem Tov reference.

Tzadik-Man: for I have suffered many things today in a dream because of Him. 20 But the main kohanim and zachanim persuaded the multitude that they should ask for Bar-Rabba, and destroy יהושע. 21 The governor answered and said to them, Which of the two do you desire that I release to you? They said, Bar-Rabba. 22 Pilate said to them, What shall I do then with יהושע who is called the Moshiach? They all said to him, Let Him be hanged. 23 And the governor said, Why, what evil has He done? But they cried out even more, saying, Let Him be hanged on a eytz. 24 When Pilate saw that he could not prevail nothing, but that rather a tumult was made, he took mayim, and washed his hands before the multitude, saying, I am innocent of the dom of this Tzadik: You see to it. 25 Then answered all the people, and said, His dom be on us, and on our children.[1] 26 Then he released Bar-Abba to them: and when he had scourged יהושע, he delivered Him to be impaled. 27 Then the soldiers of the governor the horsemen of the court,[2] took יהושע into the common hall, and gathered to Him the whole band of soldiers. 28 And they stripped Him, and put on Him a scarlet robe. 29 And when they had platted a crown of thorns, they put it upon His head, and a reed in His right hand: and they bowed the knee before Him, and mocked Him, saying, Hail, Melech of the Yahudim! 30 And they spit at Him, and took the reed, and smote Him on the head. 31 And after they had mocked Him, they took the robe off from Him, and put His own clothing on Him, and led Him away to impale Him. 32 And as they came out, they found a man of Cyrene, Shimon by name: they compelled him to bear His execution stake. 33 And when they were come to a place called Golgotha, that is to say, a place of a skull,[3] 34 They gave Him vinegar to

drink mingled with gall: and when He had tasted it, He would not drink. 35 And they impaled Him, and parted His garments, casting lots: that it might be fulfilled what was spoken by ha navi, They parted My garments among them, and upon My vesture did they cast lots. 36 And sitting down they watched Him there; 37 And set up over His head His accusation written, THIS IS יהושע THE MELECH OF THE YAHUDIM. [4] 38 Then were there two thieves impaled with Him, one on the right hand, and another on the left.[5] 39 And they that passed by reviled Him, shaking their heads, 40 Saying, You that will destroy the Beit HaMikdash, and build it in three days, save Yourself. If You are the Son of Elohim, come down from the execution stake. 41 Likewise also the main kohanim mocking Him, with the Sophrim and zachanim, said, 42 He saved others; Himself He cannot save. If He is the Melech of Yisrael, let Him now come down from the execution stake, and we will believe Him. 43 He trusted in Elohim; let Him deliver Him now, if He will have Him: for He said, I am the Son of Elohim. 44 The thieves also, who were impaled with Him, reviled Him in the same way. 45 Now from 12 noon there was darkness over all the olam[6] until 3 in the afternoon. 46 And at about 3 o'clock יהושע cried with a loud voice, saying, *Eli-Yahuweh, Eli-Yahuweh, lama sabachthani?* That is to say, *My Elohim Yahuweh, My Elohim Yahuweh, why have You forsaken Me?* 47 Some of them that stood there, when they heard that, said, This Man calls for Eli-Yahu.[7] 48 And immediately one of them ran, and took a sponge, and filled it with vinegar, and put it on a reed, and gave Him to drink. 49 The rest said, Leave Him alone, let us see whether Eli-Yahu will come to save Him. 50 יהושע, when He had cried again with a loud voice, He dismissed the Ruach.

---

[1] From a non-anti Semitic and positive outlook, may YHWH answer this prayer that Moshaich's dom be on all Yahudah for His loving redemption.
[2] Shem Tov reference.
[3] Mt. Of Olives.

[4] YHWH – Yahshua Hanotzrei Vemelech HaYahudim.
[5] Certainly a picture of YHWH's two sons; Judah and Ephraim.
[6] Shem Tov reference.
[7] Because Eli-Yahu-weh sounds like Eli-Yahu.

51 And, see, the veil of the Beit HaMikdash was rent in two from the top to the bottom; [1] and the earth did quake, and the rocks rent; 52 And the graves were opened; and many bodies of the kidushim that slept arose, 53 And came out of the graves after His resurrection, and went into the set-apart city, and appeared to many. 54 Now when the centurion, and they that were with him, watching יהושע, saw the earthquake, and those things that were done, they feared greatly, saying, Truly this was the Son of the Almighty. 55 And many women were there looking from far off, who followed יהושע from Galil, attending to Him: 56 Among them were Miryam from Magdala, and Miryam the ima of Yaakov and Yoseph, and also the ima of Zavdi's children. 57 When the evening had come, there came a rich man of Ramathayim, named Yoseph, who also himself was יהושע's talmid: 58 He went to Pilate, and asked for the body of יהושע. Then Pilate commanded the body to be delivered. 59 And when Yoseph had taken the body, he wrapped it in a clean linen cloth, 60 And laid it in his own new tomb, which he had cut out in the rock: and he rolled a great stone to the door of the tomb, and departed. 61 And there was Miryam from Magdala, and the other Miryam, opposite the tomb. 62 Now the next day, that followed the day of the preparation, the main kohanim and Prushim came together to Pilate, 63 Saying, Sir, we remember that that deceiver said, while He was yet alive, After three days I will rise again. 64 Command therefore that the tomb be made secure until the third day, lest His talmidim come by night, and steal Him away, and say to the people, He is risen from the dead: so that the last perversion shall be worse than the first ones. 65 Pilate said to them, You have a guard: go your way; make it as secure as you can. 66 So they went, and made the tomb secure, sealing the stone, and setting a guard.

28 In the evening of the Shabbat,[2] as it began to dawn, towards the first of the week,[3] came Miryam of Magdala and the other Miryam to see the tomb. 2 And, see, there was a great earthquake: for the heavenly messenger of the Master יהוה descended from ha shamayim, and came and rolled back the stone from the door, and sat upon it. 3 His appearance was like lightning, and His clothing white as snow: 4 And for fear of him the guards did shake, and became as dead men. 5 And the heavenly messenger answered and said to the women, Fear not: for I know that you seek יהושע, who was impaled. 6 He is not here: for He is risen, as He said. Come; see the place where the Master יהושע lay. 7 And go quickly, and tell His talmidim that He is risen from the dead; and, see, He goes before you into Galil; there shall you see Him: see, I have told you. 8 And they departed quickly from the tomb with fear and great simcha; and did run to bring His talmidim word. 9 And as they went to tell His talmidim, see, יהושע met them, saying, *Greetings. May the Name[4] deliver you.*[5] And they came and held Him by the feet, and worshipped Him. 10 Then said יהושע to them, *Be not afraid: go tell My brothers that they go into Galil, and there shall they see Me.* 11 Now when they were going, see, some of the guards came into the city, and showed the main kohanim all the things that were done. 12 And when they were assembled with the zachanim, and had taken counsel, they gave large money to the

---

[2] Around **havdalah** or 6PM.
[3] Strongs Greek # 4521 can mean a full 7-day week. Thus **mia sabbaton** in this case means "one week" (meaning "full," not "partial") or one of the full weeks during the omer count. It can also mean one of the weekly Shabbats. Putting the two meanings together, we get the following timing for His resurrection: After Shabbat at around 6-7PM, being officially on the first of the week, at the end of the first weekly Shabbat of the seven weekly Shabbats, in between firstfruits and Pentecost. In other evangels, the term **mia sabbaton** only means one of the weekly Shabbats.
[4] Shem Tov reference. Of His Father YHWH.
[5] Fascinating insight to what was truly said.

---

[1] The veil to the set-apart place, not the most set-apart place.

horsemen soldiers,[1] 13 Saying, Say that, His talmidim came by night, and stole Him away while we slept. 14 And if this comes to the governor's attention, we will persuade him, and protect you. 15 So they took the money, and did as they were taught: and this saying is commonly reported in secret[2] among the Yahudim until this day. 16 Then the eleven talmidim went away into Galil, into a mountain where יהושע had appointed them. 17 And when they saw Him, they worshipped Him: but some still doubted. 18 And יהושע came and spoke to them, saying, *All Power is given to Me in ha shamayim and in the earth.* 19 *Go therefore, and make talmidim of all nations,*[3] *mikvahing them in My Name:*[4] 20 *Teaching them to shomer all things, which I have commanded you:*[5] *and, see, I am with you always, even to the end of the olam hazeh.* Amein.

---

[1] Shem Tov reference.
[2] Shem Tov reference.

---

[3] All latter-day Yisraelite nations.
[4] The original reading almost without question did not have the later Trinitarian addition. For firm understanding and further detail see: **A Close Look At Matthew 28:19** at: www.focus-search.com/shc/matt2819.
[5] Torah.

מרקוס

The Besorah According To

Yochanan-Moshe-Markus – Mark
To All Nations

1 The beginning of the Besorah of יהושע the Moshiach, the Son of יהוה; 2 As it is written in the neviim, See, I send My messenger before Your face, which shall prepare Your way before You. 3 The voice of one crying in the wilderness, Prepare you the way of the Master יהוה,[1] make His paths straight. 4 Yochanan did mikvah in the wilderness, and proclaim the mikvah of teshuvah for the remission of sins. 5 And there went out to him all the land of Yahudah, and those of Yahrushalayim, and were all immersed by him in the river of Yarden, confessing their sins. 6 And Yochanan was clothed with camel's hair, and with a girdle of a skin around his loins; and he did eat locusts and wild honey; 7 And proclaimed, saying, There comes One mightier than I after me, whose sandal strap I am not worthy to stoop down and loosen. 8 I indeed have immersed you with mayim: but He shall mikvah you with the Ruach HaKodesh. 9 And it came to pass in those days that יהושע came from Natzareth of Galilee, and was immersed of Yochanan in the Yarden. 10 And immediately coming up out of the mayim, He saw the shamayim opened, and the Ruach like a yonah descending upon Him: 11 And there came a voice from the shamayim, saying, *You are My beloved Son, in whom I am well pleased.* 12 And immediately the Ruach drove Him into the wilderness. 13 And He was there in the wilderness forty days, tempted by s.a.tan; and was with the wild beasts; and the heavenly messengers attended to Him. 14 Now after Yochanan was put in prison, יהושע came into Galilee, proclaiming the besarot of the malchut of יהוה, 15 And saying, *The time is fulfilled, and the*

malchut of יהוה *is at hand: make teshuvah, and believe the besarot.* [2] 16 Now as He walked by the Sea of Galil, He saw Shimon and Andri his brother casting a net into the sea: for they were fishermen. 17 And יהושע said to them, *Follow Me, and I will make you to become fishers of men.* [3] 18 And immediately they forsook their nets, and followed Him. 19 And when He had gone a little further, He saw Yaakov the son of Zavdi, and Yochanan his brother, who also were in the boat mending their nets. 20 And immediately He called them: and they left their abba Zavdi in the boat with the hired avadim, and went after Him. 21 And they went into the city of Nachum; and immediately on the Shabbat He entered into the synagogue, and taught. 22 And they were astonished at His teaching: for He taught them as one that had authority, and not as the Sophrim. 23 And there was in their synagogue a man with an unclean ruach; and he cried out, 24 Saying, Leave us alone; what have we to do with You, You יהושע of Natzareth? Are You come to destroy us? I know You who You are, the Kadosh One of יהוה. 25 And יהושע rebuked him, saying, *Be silent, and come out of him.* 26 And when the unclean ruach had torn him, and cried with a loud voice, he came out of him. 27 And they were all amazed, insomuch that they questioned among themselves, saying, What thing is this? What new teaching is this? For with authority He commands even the shadim, and they do obey Him. 28 And immediately His fame spread abroad throughout all the

---

[1] MarYah in Aramaic text.

[2] The King was here and Yisrael was about to be restored and enter the Kingdom.
[3] A fulfillment of the promise that Yisrael would multiply like fishes in the midst of the earth in Beresheth 48:16. Fishermen trained by Yahshua certainly knew how to catch the multitudes of Yisrael through the Great Commission.

regions all around about Galil. [1] 29 And immediately, when they were come out of the synagogue, they entered into the bayit of Shimon and Andri, with Yaakov and Yochanan. 30 But Shimon's wife's ima lay sick of a fever, and immediately they told Him about her. 31 And He came and took her by the hand, and lifted her up; and immediately the fever left her, and she attended to them. 32 And at evening, when the sun did set, they brought to Him all that were diseased, and them that were possessed with shadim. 33 And the entire city was gathered together at the door. 34 And He healed many that were sick of different diseases, and cast out many shadim; and allowed not the shadim to speak, because they knew Him. 35 And in the morning, rising up a great while before day, He went out, and departed into a solitary place, and there made tefillah. 36 And Shimon and they that were with Him followed after Him. 37 And when they had found Him, they said to Him, All the men of Yisrael seek for You. 38 And He said to them, *Let us go into the next towns that I may proclaim there also: for therefore came I forth.* [2] 39 And He proclaimed in their synagogues throughout all Galil, and cast out shadim. 40 And there came a leper to Him, beseeching Him, and kneeling down to Him, and saying to Him, If You will, You can make me clean. 41 And יהושע , moved with rachamim, put out His hand, and touched him, and said to him, *I will; be clean.* 42 And as soon as He had spoken, immediately the leprosy departed from him, and he was cleansed. 43 And He strictly ordered him, and immediately sent him away; 44 And said to him, *See you say nothing to any man: but go your way, show yourself to the kohen, and offer for your cleansing those things which Moshe commanded, for a testimony to them.* [3]

45 But he went out, and began to greatly publish it, and to spread abroad the matter, insomuch that יהושע could no more openly enter into the city, but was outside in desert places: and they came to Him from every quarter.

2 And again He entered into Kfar Nachum, after some days; and it became known that He was in the bayit. 2 And immediately many were gathered together, [4] insomuch that there was no room to receive them, no, not even around the door: and He proclaimed the word to them. 3 And they came to Him, bringing one sick of the palsy, who was carried by four men. [5] 4 And when they could not come near to Him for the press, they removed the roof where He was: and when they had broken it up, they let down the bed where the sick of the palsy lay. 5 When יהושע saw their emunah, He said to the sick of the palsy, *Son, your sins are forgiven you.* 6 But there were certain of the Sophrim sitting there, and reasoning in their levim, 7 Why does this man speak blasphemies like this? Who can forgive sins but Elohim only? [6] 8 And immediately when יהושע perceived in His Ruach that they so reasoned within themselves, He said to them, *Why do you reason these things in your levim? 9 Which is easier to say to the sick of the palsy, Your sins are forgiven you; or to say, Arise, and take up your bed, and walk?* [7] *10 But that you may know that the Ben Adam has power on earth to forgive sins,* He said to the sick of the palsy, *11 I say to you, Arise, and take up your bed, and go your way into your bayit.* 12 And immediately he arose, took up the bed, and went out before them all; so that they were all amazed, and esteemed יהוה, saying, We never saw anything like this. 13 And He went out again by the

---

[1] See comments for Matthew 4:15.
[2] That is the primary reason for His coming. To reach Yisraelites in all their towns both in Yahudah and all the nations.
[3] The real Yahshua encouraged His talmidim to follow Torah.

[4] The ingathering of Yisrael.
[5] The four men symbolic of the four corners or four winds of the earth, bringing sick and lost Yisraelites to the Master.
[6] Which is why Yahshua was YHWH the sent One from YHWH the Greater. YHWH can forgive sins on earth as it is done in the heavens.
[7] Neither, only YHWH can do both.

seaside; and all the multitudes[1] came to Him, and He taught them. 14 And as He passed by, He saw Levi the son of Alphaeus sitting at the tax office, and said to him, *Follow Me.* And he arose and followed Him. 15 And it came to pass, that, as **יהושע** sat at meat in his bayit, many tax collectors and sinners sat also together with **יהושע** and His talmidim: for there were many, and they followed Him. 16 And when the Sophrim and Prushim saw Him eat with tax collectors and sinners, they said to His talmidim, How is it that He eats and drinks with tax collectors and sinners? 17 When **יהושע** heard it, He said to them, *They that are whole have no need of the physician, but they that are sick: I came not to call the tzadikim, but sinners to teshuvah.*[2] 18 And the talmidim of Yochanan and of the Prushim used to fast: and they came and said to Him, Why do the talmidim of Yochanan and of the Prushim fast, but Your talmidim fast not? 19 And **יהושע** said to them, *Can the children of the Bridegroom fast, while the Bridegroom is with them? As long as they have the Bridegroom with them, they cannot fast. 20 But the days will come, when the bridegroom shall be taken away from them, and then shall they fast in those days. 21 No man also sews a piece of new cloth on an old garment: otherwise the new piece that filled it up takes away from the old, and the tear is made worse. 22 And no man puts new wine into old wineskins: or else the new wine bursts the wineskins, and the wine is spilled, and the wineskins will be ruined: but new wine must be put into new wineskins.*[3] 23 And it came to pass, that He went through the cornfields on the Shabbat; and His talmidim began, as they went, to pluck the ears of corn. 24 And the Prushim said to Him, See, why do they do on the Shabbat day that which is not allowed?

25 And He said to them, *Have you never read what David did, when he had need, and was hungry, he, and they that were with him? 26 How he went into the Bayit of the Master יהוה,[4] and did eat the Bread of the Presence, which is not lawful to eat except for the kohanim, and gave also to them that were with him?*[5] 27 And He said to them, *The Shabbat was made for man, and not man for the Shabbat: 28 Therefore the Ben Adam is Master also of the Shabbat.*

3 And He entered again into the synagogue; and there was a man there who had a withered hand. 2 And they watched Him, whether He would heal him on the Shabbat; that they might accuse Him. 3 And He said to the man that had the withered hand, *Stand up.* 4 And He said to them, *Is it lawful to do tov on the Shabbat, or to do evil? To save chayim, or to kill?* But they held their silence. 5 And when He had looked all around them with anger, being grieved for the hardness of their levim, He said to the man, *Stretch out your hand.* And he stretched it out: and his hand was restored whole as the other. 6 And the Prushim went out, and immediately took counsel with the Herodians against Him, how they might destroy Him. 7 But **יהושע** withdrew Himself with His talmidim to the sea: and a great multitude from Galil[6] followed Him, and from Yahudah,[7] 8 And from Yahrushalayim, and from Idumaea, and from beyond Yarden; and those around Tsor and Tsidon, a great multitude, when they had heard what great things He did,

---

[1] A reference to Yisrael's promised multitudes.
[2] In Scripture, the sick are equated with the wayward or backslidden First Covenant sheep of lost Yisrael.
[3] Meaning Moshiach's mission was to renew the wineskin, not the wine of Torah. Yisrael is the wineskin and Renewed Covenant Yisrael is the new wineskin.

[4] In the Greek the name "Aviathar" appears rather than his correct father Ahimelech who was the High Priest in David's time, and thus the Old Syriac Aramaic is quoted.
[5] **Kal VaChomer.** Weightier versus lighter matters. When two Torah principles that are both valid seem to contradict, the weightier or more important allows action that often violates or seems to violate the lesser matters. The overriding principle in the spirit of Torah is what is called **yeshuat nefesh** or the saving of life, which takes higher precedent than any other statute, and can include breaking all 613 mitzvoth to save a single human life. This is the principal at work here. David would have died without food. And that took precedence over the Shabbat, especially since the Shabbat was made for man, and if a man were dead, what tov would the Shabbat do for him?
[6] Ephraimites.
[7] Jews.

came to Him. 9 And He spoke to His talmidim, that a small boat should wait for Him because of the multitude, lest they should throng Him. 10 For He had healed many; so that that they pressed upon Him for to touch Him, as many as had plagues. 11 And unclean ruachim, when they saw Him, fell down before Him, and cried, saying, You are the Son of Elohim. 12 And He strictly ordered them that they should not make Him known. 13 And He went up into a mountain, and called to Him whom He would: and they came to Him. 14 And He ordained twelve, that they should be with Him, and that He might send them out to proclaim,[1] 15 And to have power to heal sicknesses, and to cast out shadim: 16 And Shimon He surnamed Kepha; 17 And Yaakov the son of Zavdi, and Yochanan the brother of Yaakov; and He surnamed them B'nai Regash, which is, The Sons of Thunder: 18 And Andri, and Philip, and Bartholomew, and Matthew, and Thomas, and Yaakov the son of Alphaeus, and Thaddaeus, and Shimon the Zealot, 19 And Yahudah from Qerioth, who also betrayed Him: and they went into a bayit. 20 And the multitude[2] came together again, so that they could not so much as eat lechem. 21 And when His relatives heard it, they went out to seize Him: for they said, He is out of His mind. 22 And the Sophrim that came down from Yahrushalayim said, He has Beel-Zevuv, and by the prince of the shadim He casts out shadim. 23 And He called them to Him, and said to them in parables, *How can s.a.tan cast out s.a.tan? 24 And if a malchut is divided against itself, that malchut cannot stand. 25 And if a bayit is divided against itself, that bayit cannot stand.*[3] 26 *And if s.a.tan rise up against himself, and be*

divided, he cannot stand, but has an end. 27 *No man can enter into a strong man's bayit, and spoil his goods, except he will first bind the strong man; and then he will spoil his bayit. 28 Truly I say to you, All sins shall be forgiven to the sons of men, and whatever blasphemies they shall blaspheme: 29 But he that shall blaspheme against the Ruach HaKodesh has no forgiveness, but is in danger of eternal damnation:* 30 Because they said, He has an unclean ruach.[4] 31 There came then His brothers and His ima, and, standing outside, sent to Him, calling Him. 32 And the multitude sat about Him, and they said to Him, See, Your ima and Your brothers outside seek for You. 33 And He answered them, saying, *Who is My ima, or My brothers?* 34 And He looked all around to those who sat around Him, and said; *See My ima and My brothers! 35 For whoever shall do the will of* **יהוה**, *the same is My brother, and My sister, and ima.*

4 And He began again to teach by the sea side: and there was gathered to Him a great multitude, so that He entered into a boat, and sat in the sea; and the whole multitude was by the sea on the land.[5] 2 And He taught them many things by parables, and said to them in His teaching, 3 *Shema; See, there went out a sower to sow: 4 And it came to pass, as he sowed, some fell by the way side, and the fowls of the air came and devoured it up. 5 And some fell on stony ground, where it had not much earth; and immediately it sprang up, because it had no depth of earth: 6 But when the sun was up, it was scorched; and because it had no root, it withered away. 7 And some fell among thorns, and the thorns grew up, and choked it, and it yielded no fruit. 8 And some fell on tov*

---

[1] For all twelve tribes.
[2] Promised multitudes.
[3] In the **pashat** or literal understanding, Yahshua explains how illogical their argument is since s.a.tan would be interested in casting out clean messengers but never himself. In the **remez**, He is stating the principle, that so long as Yisrael remains divided into two houses or malchutim, they will be open to various forms of division and diverse fallings and failings, that would not take place were the malchut already restored to Yisrael.

[4] Attributing the works of Yahshua to s.a.tan's power. No believer would willfully do that as did the Prushim.
[5] The sea in scripture is a type of the world and by sitting in the sea with His talmidim, He is portraying that through His word all those whom the 12 talmidim represent scattered in the nations will come to His truth and His message of restoration and healing.

ground, and did yield fruit that sprang up and increased; and brought out, some thirty, and some sixty, and some an hundred. 9 And He said to them, *He that has ears to shema, let him shema.* 10 And when He was alone, the twelve that were with Him, asked Him about the parable. 11 And He said to them, *To you it is given to know the mystery of the malchut of* יהוה*: but to them that are outside, all these things are done in parables:* [1] 12 *That seeing they may see, and not perceive; and shema-ing they may shema, and not understand; lest at any time they should do teshuvah, and their sins should be forgiven them.* 13 And He said to them, *Don't you know this parable? And how then will you know all other parables?* 14 *The sower sows the word.* 15 *And these are they by the way side, where the word is sown; but when they have heard, s.a.tan comes immediately, and takes away the word that was sown in their levim.* 16 *And these are they likewise which are sown on stony ground; who, when they have heard the word, immediately receive it with gilah;* 17 *And have no root in themselves, and so endure but for a time: afterward, when affliction or persecution arises for the word's sake, immediately they are offended.* 18 *And these are those that are sown among thorns; such as shema the word,* 19 *And the cares of this olam hazeh, and the deceitfulness of riches, and the desires for other things entering in, choke the word, and it becomes unfruitful.* 20 *And these are they which are sown on tov ground;* [2] *such as shema the word, and receive it, and bring out fruit, some thirtyfold, some sixty, and some a hundred.* 21 And He said to them, *Is a candle brought to be put under a bushel, or under a bed? And not to be set on a menorah?* [3] 22 *For there is nothing hid,* which shall not be manifested; neither was any thing kept secret, but that it should come abroad. 23 *If any man has ears to shema, let him shema.* 24 And He said to them, *Take heed what you shema: with what measure you use, it shall be measured to you: and to you that shema shall more be given.* 25 *For he that has, to him shall be given: and he that has not, from him shall be taken even that which he has.* [4] 26 And He said, *So is the malchut of* יהוה*, as if a man should cast seed into the ground;* 27 *And should sleep, and rise night and day, and the seed should spring and grow up, he knows not how.* [5] 28 *For the earth brings out fruit by itself; first the blade, then the ear, after that the full corn in the ear.* 29 *But when the fruit is brought out, immediately he puts in the sickle, because the harvest is come.* 30 And He said, *To what shall we compare the malchut of* יהוה*? Or with what comparison shall we compare it?* 31 *It is like a grain of mustard seed, which, when it is sown in the earth, is less than all the seeds that be in the earth:* 32 *But when it is sown, it grows up, and becomes greater than all herbs, and shoots out great Netzarim-Branches; so that the fowls of the air may lodge under the shadow of it.* [6] 33 And with many such parables He spoke the word to them, as they were able to shema to it. 34 But without a parable He spoke not to them: and when they were alone, He expounded all things to His talmidim. 35 And the same day, when the evening was come, He said to them, *Let us pass over to the other side.* 36 And when they had sent away the multitude, they took Him along as He was in the boat. And there were also with Him other little ships. 37 And there arose a great storm of wind,

---

[1] Believing Yisraelites get the message directly while those outside of believing Yisrael must come through parables. So parables were given to reveal history and future revelation to regathered Yisrael, while blinding the eyes of those outside, in order to force them to inquire on their own.
[2] Yisrael redeemed and forgiven is the tov solid soil that receives His word.
[3] Once Yisrael receives Moshiach's teaching, we are to let our truth and light shine in all the House of Yisrael.

[4] A spiritual law.
[5] Since we don't know where exactly every lost sheep is, we are to scatter the word of the malchut to all four corners of the globe so that it can reach our brothers; and then they can be touched and appear as fruits in the kingdom.
[6] A clear reference to Yisrael's beginnings with Avraham, and the growth to the present day, where there is so much leaven in both houses, one does not know where to begin to clear bayit. Thankfully Moshiach Yahshua does know and has been doing so.

and the waves beat into the boat, so that it was now full. 38 And He was in the stern, asleep on a cushion: and they woke Him, and said to Him, Rabbi, don't You care that we perish? 39 And He arose, and rebuked the wind, and said to the sea, *Shalom, be still.* And the wind ceased, and there was a great calm. 40 And He said to them, *Why are you so fearful? How is it that you have no emunah?* 41 And they feared exceedingly, and said one to another, What manner of Man is this, that even the wind and the sea obey Him?

5 And they came over to the other side of the sea, into the country of the Gadarenes. 2 And when He was come out of the boat, immediately there met Him out of the tombs a man with an unclean ruach, 3 Who had his dwelling among the tombs; and no man could bind him, not even with chains: 4 Because he had often been bound with shackles and chains, and had pulled the chains apart, and the shackles he had broken in pieces: neither could any man tame him. 5 And always, night and day, he was in the mountains, and in the tombs, crying, and cutting himself with stones. 6 But when he saw יהושע far off, he ran and worshipped Him, 7 And cried with a loud voice, and said, What have I to do with You, יהושע: You, Son of El-Elyon? I ask You by Elohim, that You torment me not. 8 For He said to him, *Come out of the man, you unclean ruach.* 9 And He asked him, *What is your name?* And he answered, saying, My name is Legion: for we are many. 10 And he begged Him much that He would not send them away out of the country. 11 Now there was there near to the mountains a great herd of pigs feeding. 12 And all the shadim begged Him, saying, Send us into the pigs, that we may enter into them. 13 And immediately יהושע gave them leave. And the unclean ruachim went out, and entered into the pigs: and the herd ran violently down a steep place into the

sea, they were about two thousand;[1] and were choked in the sea.[2] 14 And they that fed the pigs fled, and told it in the city, and in the country. And they went out to see what it was that was done. 15 And they come to יהושע, and saw him that was possessed with the s.a.tan, and had the legion, sitting, and clothed, and in his right mind: and they were afraid. 16 And they that saw it told them what happened to him that was possessed with the s.a.tan, and also concerning the pigs. 17 And they began to beg Him to depart out of their coasts. 18 And when He was come into the boat, he that had been possessed with the s.a.tan begged that he might go with Him. 19 But יהושע allowed it not, but said to him, *Go home to your chaverim, and tell them what great things the Master יהוה has done for you, and how He has had rachamim on you.* 20 And He departed, and began to publish in Dekapolis[3] how great things יהושע had done for him: and all men did marvel. 21 And when יהושע was passed over again by boat to the other side, many people gathered to Him: and He was near to the sea. 22 And, see, there came one of the shamashim of the synagogue, Yair by name; and when he saw Him, he fell at His feet, 23 And begged Him greatly, saying, My little daughter lies at the point of death: I beg you, come and lay Your hands on her, that she may be healed; and she shall live. 24 And יהושע went with him; and many people followed Him, and thronged him.[4] 25 And a certain woman, who had an issue of dom for twelve years, 26 And had suffered many things by many physicians, and had spent all that she had, and was not better, but rather grew worse, 27 When she

---

[1] In the hint or **remez** level this account teaches us that for 2,000 years (symbolized by the 2,000 pigs) – the time between Yahshua's comings – both houses of Yisrael would enter into the pigs or into pagan practice and worship, resulting in death in the sea symbolizing the exile and spiritual death into the nations.
[2] We were choked in the sea of nations.
[3] Meaning "ten cities" symbolic of the ten tribes of Ephraim-Yisrael receiving the besarot; and the healing emanating from that message.
[4] The multitudes of Yisrael.

had heard of **יהושע**, she came in the crowd behind, and touched His garment. 28 For she said, If I may touch even His tzitzit, I shall be whole. 29 And immediately the fountain of her dom was dried up; and she felt in her body that she was healed of that plague. [1] 30 And **יהושע** , immediately knowing in Himself that Power had gone out of Him, turned around to the crowd, and said, *Who touched My clothes?* 31 And His talmidim said to Him, You see the multitude thronging You, and You say, Who touched Me? 32 And He looked all around about to see her that had done this thing. 33 But the woman fearing and trembling, knowing what was done in her, came and fell down before Him, and told Him all the emet. 34 And He said to her, *Daughter of Yisrael, your emunah has made you whole; go in shalom, and be whole of your affliction.* [2] 35 While He yet spoke, there came from the shamesh of the synagogue's bayit, someone who said, Your daughter is dead: why trouble the Master any further? 36 As soon as **יהושע** heard the word that was spoken, He said to the shamesh of the synagogue, Be not afraid, only believe. 37 And He allowed no man to follow Him, except Kepha, and Yaakov, and Yochanan the brother of Yaakov. 38 And He came to the bayit of the shamesh of the synagogue, and saw the tumult, and those that wept and wailed greatly. 39 And when He had come in, He said to them, *Why do you make this commotion, and weep? The child is not dead, but only sleeping.* 40 And they laughed at Him. But when He had put them all out, He took the abba and the ima of the child, and those that were with Him, and entered in where the child was lying. 41 And He took the child by the hand, and said to her, *Talitha cumi;* which is, translated, Little girl, I say to you,

arise.[3] 42 And immediately the child arose, and walked; for she was of the age of twelve years. [4] And they were astonished with great astonishment. 43 And He ordered them many times that no one should know it; and commanded that something should be given to her to eat.

6 And He went out from there, and came into His own country; and His talmidim followed Him. 2 And when the Shabbat had come, He began to teach in the synagogue: and many hearing Him were astonished, saying, From where has this Man these things? And what chochmah is this, which is given to Him, that even such mighty mitzvot are done by His hands? 3 Is not this the carpenter, the Son of Miryam, the brother of Yaakov, and Yoseph, and of Yahudah, and Shimon? And are not His sisters here with us? And they were offended by Him. 4 But **יהושע** said to them, *A Navi is not without honor, except in His own country, and among His own kin, and in His own bayit.* 5 And He could do no mighty mitzvot there, except that He laid His hands upon a few sick folk, and healed them.[5] 6 And He marveled because of their unbelief. And He went around their villages, teaching. 7 And He called to Him the twelve, and began to send them out two by two; and He gave them power over unclean ruachim; 8 And commanded them that they should take nothing for their journey, except a staff only; no bag, no lechem, no copper in their money belts: 9 But to wear sandals; and not put on two coats. 10 And He said to them, *In whatever place you enter into a bayit, there abide until you depart from that place. 11 And whoever shall not receive you, nor shema*

---

[1] The woman is Yisrael, the twelve years are one for each tribe and the tzitzit are symbolic of remembering all YHWH's Torot and the power that goes from the Torah and Moshiach that flows back to Yisrael, who then is made whole.
[2] Biblical emunah in Yahshua and Torah will lead us to shalom and wholeness.

[3] An alternate rendering for **Talitha Cumi** would be "you who are under the tallit rise."
[4] When this child of Yisrael is healed, she represents all Yisraelites who receive the message of the malchut as a little child, and each of those twelve years of age, represents the resurrection of all 12 tribes to new life by Moshiach. Once alive they are given new manna or bread to eat as seen in verse 43.
[5] He chose not to do so, because there was no emunah there to move Him into action.

you, when you depart from there, shake off the dust under your feet for a testimony against them. Truly I say to you, It shall be more tolerable for Sedom and Amorah in the Yom HaDin, than for that city. 12 And they went out, and proclaimed that men[1] should make teshuvah. 13 And they cast out many shadim, and anointed with oil many that were sick, and healed them. 14 And melech Herod heard of Him; (for His Name had been spread abroad:) and he said, That Yochanan HaMatbeel had risen from the dead, and therefore mighty mitzvot do show themselves in him. 15 Others said, That it is Eli-Yahu. And others said, That it is a navi, or someone as one of the neviim. 16 But when Herod heard this, he said, It is Yochanan, whom I beheaded: he is risen from the dead. 17 For Herod himself had sent out and seized Yochanan, and bound him in the prison for Herodias' sake, his brother Philip's wife: for he had married her. 18 For Yochanan had said to Herod, It is not permitted in the Torah for you to have your brother's wife. 19 Therefore Herodias had a quarrel against him, and would have killed him; but she could not: 20 For Herod feared Yochanan, knowing that he was a just man and one who was set-apart, and observed him; and when he heard him, he was very convicted, and heard him with gilah. 21 And when a convenient day had come, Herod on his birthday made a supper to his great men, high captains, and head men of Galilee; 22 And when the daughter of Herodias came in, and danced, and pleased Herod and those who sat with him, the melech said to the girl, Ask from me whatever you will, and I will give it you. 23 And he swore to her, Whatever you shall ask of me, I will give it you, up to half of my malchut. 24 And she went out, and said to her ima, What shall I ask for? And she said, The head of Yochanan the Immerser. 25 And she came in immediately with haste to the melech, and asked, saying, I will that you give me immediately in a dish the head

of Yochanan the Immerser. 26 And the melech was exceedingly sorry; yet for his oath's sake, and for their sakes who sat with him, he would not refuse her. 27 And immediately the melech sent an executioner, and commanded his head to be brought: and he went and beheaded him in the prison, 28 And brought his head in a dish, and gave it to the girl: and the girl gave it to her ima. 29 And when his talmidim heard of it, they came and took up his corpse, and laid it in a tomb. 30 And His talmidim gathered themselves together to יהושע, and told Him all things, both what they had done, and what they had taught. 31 And He said to them, *Come aside by yourselves into a quiet place, and rest a while:* for there were many coming and going, and they had no time for themselves, so much as to eat. 32 And they departed into a quiet place by boat privately. 33 And the people saw them departing, and many knew Him, and ran there on foot from all cities, and came before them, and came together to Him. 34 And יהושע, when He came out, saw many people, and was moved with rachamim toward them, because they were as sheep not having a shepherd: and He began to teach them many things.[2] 35 And when the day was now far gone, His talmidim came to Him, and said, This is a deserted place, and now the hour is late: 36 Send them away, that they may go into the country all around, and into the villages, and buy themselves lechem: for they have nothing to eat. 37 He answered and said to them, *You give them something to eat.* And they said to Him, Shall we go and buy two hundred silver pieces of lechem, and give them to eat? 38 He said to them, *How many loaves do you have? Go and see.* And when they knew, they said, Five, and two fishes. 39 And He commanded them to make them all sit down in groups upon the green grass. 40 And they sat down in ranks, by hundreds, and by

---

[1] Yisraelites.

[2] He was moved by Yisrael's lost sheep who lacked any true guidance and provider.

fifties. 41 And when He had taken the five loaves[1] and the two fishes, He looked up to the shamayim, and said the bracha, and broke the loaves, and gave them to His talmidim to set before them; and the two fishes He divided[2] among them all. 42 And they did all eat, and were filled. 43 And they took up twelve baskets full of the fragments,[3] and also of fishes. 44 And those that did eat of the loaves were about five thousand men. 45 And immediately He made His talmidim get into the boat, and to go to the other side to Beth Saida, while He sent away the people. 46 And when He had sent them away, He departed into a mountain to make tefillah. 47 And when evening was come, the boat was in the midst of the sea, and He was alone on the land. 48 And He saw them toiling in rowing; for the wind was against them: and about the fourth watch of the night He came to them, walking upon the sea, and would have passed right by them. 49 But when they saw Him walking upon the sea, they thought it was a ruach, and cried out: 50 For they all saw Him, and were troubled. And immediately He talked with them, and said to them, Be of tov courage: it is I; be not afraid. 51 And He went up to them and into the boat; and the wind ceased: and they were exceedingly amazed within themselves beyond description, and wondered. 52 For they considered not the miracle of the loaves: for their lev was hardened. 53 And when they had passed over, they came into the land of Gennesar, and drew to the shore. 54 And when they were come out of the boat, immediately they knew Him, 55 And ran throughout that whole region all around, and began to carry in beds those that were sick, to where they heard He was. 56 And wherever He entered, into villages, or cities, or country, they laid the sick in the streets, and begged Him that they might touch only His tzitzit: and as many as touched Him were made whole.

7 Then came together to Him the Prushim, and certain of the Sophrim, which came from Yahrushalayim. 2 And when they saw some of His talmidim eat lechem with defiled, that is to say, with unwashed, hands, they found fault. 3 For the Prushim, and all the Yahudim, except they wash their hands often, eat not, holding to the tradition of the zachanim. 4 And when they come from the market, except they wash, they eat not. And many other things there are, which they have received and hold fast to such, as the washing of cups, and pots, copper vessels, and tables. 5 Then the Prushim and Sophrim asked Him, Why don't Your talmidim have their halachot according to the tradition of the zachanim, but eat lechem with unwashed hands? 6 He answered and said to them, *Well has Yeshayahu prophesied of you hypocrites, as it is written, This people honors Me with their lips, but their lev is far from Me. 7 But in vain do they worship Me, teaching as Torah the commandments of men. 7 Laying aside the commandment of* יהוה*, you guard the traditions of men, such as the washing of pots and cups: and many other such things you do. 9 And He said to them, Full well you do reject the commandments of* יהוה*, that you may keep your own tradition. 10 For Moshe said, Honor your abba and your ima; and, Whoever curses abba or ima, let him die in death: 11 But you say, If a man shall say to his abba or ima, It is Corban, that is to say, a gift to* יהוה*, from whatever you might have received from me; he shall be free. 12 And you no longer allow him to do any tov matter for his abba or his ima;* [4] *13 Making the word of* יהוה *of no effect through your tradition, which you have delivered: and many similar things you do.* 14 And when He had called all the people to Him, He said to them, *Shema to Me every*

---

[1] See note on Matthew 14:19.
[2] He came for those two groups of fishes that were divided.
[3] From the two fishes and the five loaves, He filled 12 baskets, meaning that He takes a divided people and regathers them neatly placed into 12 baskets full, symbolizing the fullness of the tribes in the regathering.

[4] See notes on Matthew 15:5-6.

one of you, and understand: 15 *There is nothing from outside a man, that entering into him can defile him: but the things which come out of him, those are they that defile the man.* 16 *If any man has ears to shema, let him shema.* 17 And when He had entered into the bayit away from the people, His talmidim asked Him concerning the parable. 18 And He said to them, *Are you also without understanding? Do you not perceive, that things from outside that enter into the man, it cannot defile him;* [1] 19 *Because it enters not into his lev, but into the belly, and out into the stomach, and is then eliminated purging all foods?* 20 And He said, *That which comes out of the man that defiles the man.* 21 *For from within, out of the lev of men, proceeds evil thoughts, adulteries, fornications, murders,* 22 *Thefts, covetousness, wickedness, deceit, lasciviousness, an evil eye, blasphemy, pride, foolishness:* 23 *All these evil things come from within, and defile the man.* 24 And from there He arose, and went into the borders of Tsor and Tsidon, and entered into a bayit, and would have no man know it: but He could not be hidden. 25 For a certain woman, whose young daughter had an unclean ruach, heard of Him, and came and fell at His feet: 26 The woman was a Greek, a Syro-Phoenician by nation; and she begged Him that He would cast out s.a.tan out of her daughter. 27 But יהושע said to her, *Let the children first be filled: for it is not right to take the children's lechem, and to cast it to the dogs.* 28 And she answered and said to Him, Yes, Master: yet the dogs under the table eat of the children's crumbs. 29 And He said to her, *For this saying go your way; the s.a.tan has gone out of your daughter.* [2] 30 And when she was come to her bayit, she found the

s.a.tan gone out, and her daughter laid upon the bed. 31 And again, departing from the coasts of Tsor and Tsidon, He came to the Sea of Galil, through the midst of the coasts of Decapolis. [3] 32 And they brought to Him one that was deaf, and had an impediment in his speech; and they begged Him to put His hand upon him. 33 And He took him aside from the multitude, and put His fingers into his ears, and He spit, and touched his tongue; 34 And looking up to the shamayim, He sighed, and said to him, *Ephphatha,* that is, Be opened. 35 And immediately his ears were opened, and the binding of his tongue was loosed, and he spoke plainly. 36 And He ordered them that they should tell no man: but the more He ordered them, so much the more they published it; 37 And were beyond measure astonished, saying, He has done all things well: He makes both the deaf to shema, and the dumb to speak.

8 In those days the multitudes [4] being very great, and having nothing to eat, יהושע called His talmidim to Him, and said to them, 2 *I have rachamim on the multitude, because they have now been with Me three days, and have nothing to eat:* [5] 3 *And if I send them away fasting to their own houses,* [6] *they will faint by the way: for some of them came from far.* [7] 4 And His talmidim answered Him, From where can a man satisfy these men with lechem here in the wilderness? 5 And He asked them, *How many loaves do you have?* And they said, seven. 6 And He commanded the people to sit down on the ground: and He took the seven loaves, and said the bracha, and broke them, and gave to His talmidim to set it before them; and they did set it before the people. 7 And they had a few small fishes: and He said the bracha, and commanded to

---

[1] Yahshua in no way is reversing any laws of **kashrut**, for if He even considered reversing one, He could not by definition be the Moshiach. No, instead the topic here regards the traditions of washing hands so as to be considered ritually pure. This was pure tradition finding no basis in Torah instructions. Yahshua gives Yisrael the understanding that washed or unwashed hands do not change a man or woman's heart. That is all that is taking place here.
[2] See comments Matthew 15:24 and 15:26.

[3] Ten towns full of Ephraimites from the north.
[4] Of Yisrael.
[5] Without Moshiach, Yisrael's multitudes remain hungry for truth.
[6] Division is not the answer to our hunger for truth. Our own houses are not what He came to build.
[7] Ephraimites.

set them also before them. 8 So they did eat, and were filled: and they took up of the broken pieces that were left seven baskets. 9 And they that had eaten were about four thousand: and He sent them away. 10 And immediately He entered into a boat with His talmidim, and came into the parts of Dalmanutha. 11 And the Prushim came out, and began to question Him, seeking from Him a sign from the shamayim, trying Him. 12 And He sighed deeply in His Ruach, and said, *Why does this generation seek after a sign? Truly I say to you, There shall no sign be given to this generation.* 13 And He left them, and entering into the boat again departed to the other side. 14 Now the talmidim had forgotten to take lechem, neither did they have in the boat with them more than one loaf. 15 And He ordered them, saying, *Watch out, beware of the chametz of the Prushim, and of the chametz of Herod.* 16 And they reasoned among themselves, saying, It is because we have no lechem. 17 And when **יהושע** knew it, He said to them, *Why do you reason, because you have no lechem? Don't you yet perceive and understand? Are your levim still hardened? 18 Having eyes, don't you see? And having ears, don't you shema? And do you not remember? 19 When I broke the five loaves among five thousand, how many baskets full of fragments took you up?* They say to Him, Twelve. 20 *And when the seven among four thousand, how many baskets full of fragments took you up?* And they said, Seven. 21 And He said to them, *How is it then that you do not understand?* 22 And He came to Beth-Saida; and they brought a blind man to Him, and begged Him to touch him. 23 And He took the blind man by the hand, and led him out of the town; and when He had spit on his eyes, and put His hands upon him, He asked him if he saw anything. 24 And he looked up, and said, I see men as trees, walking. 25 After that He put His hands again upon his eyes, and made him look up: and he was

restored, and saw every man clearly. [1] 26 And He sent him away to his bayit, saying, Neither go into the town, nor tell it to anyone in the town. [2] 27 And **יהושע** went out, and His talmidim, into the towns of Caesarea Philippi: and on the way He asked His talmidim, saying to them, *Who do men[3] say that I am?* 28 And they answered, Yochanan the Immerser: but some say, Eli-Yahu; and others, One of the neviim. 29 And He said to them, *But who do you say that I am?* And Kepha answered and said to Him, You are The Moshiach. 30 And He ordered them that they should tell no man about Him. 31 And He began to teach them, that the Ben Adam must suffer many things, and be rejected of the zachanim, and by the head kohanim, and Sophrim, and be killed, and after three days rise again. 32 And He spoke that saying openly. And Kepha took Him, and began to rebuke Him. 33 But when He had turned around and looked at His talmidim, He rebuked Kepha, saying, *Get behind Me, s.a.tan: for you are not thinking on the things that are from* **יהוה**, *but the things that are from men.* 34 And when He had called the people to Him with His talmidim also, He said to them, *Whoever will come after Me, let him deny himself, and take up his execution stake, and follow Me. 35 For whoever will save his chayim shall lose it; but whoever shall lose his chayim for My sake and that of the besarot, the same shall save it. 36 For what shall it profit a man, if he shall gain the whole olam hazeh, and lose his own being? 37 Or what shall a man give in exchange for his being? 38 Whoever*

---

[1] Before two-bayit restoration is revealed, a man is blind to his own heritage, and that of other men. Men all look fuzzy and all look the same, like gentiles, among gentiles. But when Yahshua touches us a second time or returns to this earth to restore perfect understanding and vision completing the restoration process, then instead of seeing men of Yisrael as mere uniform trees, the Master's touch will open our eyes to restoration; with our vision having fully been restored. Ezekiel 34:31 refers to Yisraelites as the **men** of YHWH's pasture; thus when restoration truth affects an individual, the trees come into focus and the trees of Yisrael are clearly seen for who they truly are.
[2] Because the restoration of Yisrael is by a personal revelation.
[3] Yisraelites according to the Biblical definition of men.

therefore shall be ashamed of Me and of My words in this adulterous and sinful generation; of him also shall the Ben Adam be ashamed, when He comes in the tifereth of His Abba with the set-apart heavenly messengers.

9 And He said to them, *Truly I say to you, That there be some of you that stand here, who shall not taste of death, until they have seen the malchut of* יהוה[1] *come with Power.* 2 And after six days יהושע took with Him Kepha, and Yaakov, and Yochanan, and led them up into an high mountain apart by themselves: and He was transformed before them. 3 And His raiment became shining, exceedingly white as snow; like no launderer on earth can whiten them. 4 And there appeared to them Eli-Yahu with Moshe: and they were talking with יהושע .[3] 5 And Kepha answered and said to יהושע, Rabbi, it is tov for us to be here: and let us make three sukkot; one for You, and one for Moshe, and one for Eli-Yahu.[4] 6 For he did not know what to say; for they were very afraid. 7 And there was a cloud [5] that overshadowed them: and a voice came out of the cloud, saying, *This is My beloved Son: shema to Him.*[6] 8 And suddenly, when they had looked around, they saw no man any more, except יהושע only with themselves. 9 And as they came down from the mountain, He ordered them that they should tell no man what things they had seen, until the Ben Adam had risen from the dead. 10 And they kept that saying within

themselves, questioning one another what this rising from the dead should mean. 11 And they asked Him, saying, Why say the Sophrim that Eli-Yahu must first come? 12 And He answered and told them, *Eli-Yahu truly comes first, and restores all things;*[7] *and how it is written of the Ben Adam, that He must suffer many things, and be despised.* 13 *But I say to you, That Eli-Yahu has indeed come,*[8] *and they have done to him whatever they desired, as it is written of him.* 14 And when He came to His talmidim, He saw a great multitude around them, and the Sophrim disputing with them. 15 And immediately all the people, when they beheld Him, were greatly amazed, and running to Him greeted Him. 16 And He asked the Sophrim, *What are you disputing about with them?* 17 And one of the multitude answered and said, Master, I have brought to you my son, who has a dumb ruach; 18 And whenever he seizes him, he tears him: and he foams, and gnashes with his teeth, and wastes away: and I spoke to Your talmidim that they should cast it out; and they could not. 19 He answered him, and said, *O unbelieving generation, how long shall I be with you? How long shall I put up with you? Bring him to Me.* 20 And they brought him to Him: and when he saw Him, immediately the ruach tore at him; and he fell on the ground, and rolled about foaming. 21 And He asked his abba, *How long has this been happening to him?* And he said, From childhood. 22 And often it casts him into the fire, and into the mayim, to destroy him: but if You can do anything, have rachamim on us, and help us. 23 יהושע said to him, *If you can believe, all things are possible to him that believes.* 24 And immediately the abba of the child cried out, and said with tears, Master, I believe; help my unbelief. 25 When יהושע saw that the people came running together, He rebuked the foul ruach, saying

---

[1] David's throne, back on earth and restored, ruling all 12 tribes.
[2] Speaks of a time just six days later, when the talmidim see the malchut come in a vision before they taste death. They see this on the 7th day after Yahshua's prophesy, a type of the millennium or the **atid lavoh**.
[3] According to Luke and Matthew about His soon-coming atonement in Yahrushalayim, that opens the way for malchut entry.
[4] They thought that the malchut had come, not realizing that it was just a vision of the malchut, and as such they were required to build sukkot and celebrate Tabernacles according to Zacharyah 14:16-21. So actually, Kepha makes a pretty sharp discernment of malchut responsibility.
[5] Kingdom **shechinah or** presence.
[6] Notice this is My Son, not the Father's New Covenant Name.

---

[7] At the return of Moshiach the literal Eliyahu will appear. Malachi 4: 5-6.
[8] Yochanan the Immerser came for the first advent of Yahshua, in Eliyahu's ruach and power.

to him, *You dumb and deaf ruach, I charge you, come out of him, and enter no more into him.* 26 And the ruach cried out, after causing convulsions, and came out of him: and he was as one who was dead; so that many said, he is dead. 27 But **יהושע** took him by the hand, and lifted him up; and he arose. 28 And when He had come into the bayit, His talmidim asked Him privately, Why could we not cast it out? 29 And He said to them, *This kind can come out by nothing, other than tefillah and fasting.* 30 And they departed from there, and passed through Galil; and He did not desire that any man should know it. 31 For He taught His talmidim, and said to them, *The Ben Adam is delivered into the hands of men, and they shall kill Him; and after He is killed, He shall rise the third day.* 32 But they understood not that saying, and were afraid to ask Him. 33 And He came to city of Nachum: and being in the bayit He asked them, *What was it that you disputed among yourselves on the way?* 34 But they held their silence: for on the way they had argued among themselves, who should be the greatest. 35 And He sat down, and called the twelve, and said to them, *If any man desires to be first, the same shall be last of all, and eved of all.* [1] 36 And He took a child, and set him in the midst of them: and when He had taken him in His arms, He said to them, 37 *Whoever shall receive one such child in My Name, receives Me: and whoever shall receive Me, receives not Me, but Him that sent Me.* 38 And Yochanan answered Him, saying, Rabbi, we saw one casting out shadim in Your Name, and he doesn't follows us: and we forbade him, because he doesn't follows us. 39 But **יהושע** said, *Forbid him not: for there is no man who shall do a miracle in My Name that can ever speak evil of Me. 40 For he that is not against us is for us. 41 For whoever shall give you a cup of mayim to drink in My Name, because you belong to*

The Moshiach, truly I say to you, he shall not lose his reward. 42 And whoever shall offend one of these little ones that believe in Me, it is better for him that a millstone were hung around his neck, and he were cast into the sea.* [2] *43 And if your hand offends you, cut it off: it is better for you to enter into chayim maimed, than having two hands to go into Gei-Hinnom, into the fire that never shall be quenched: 44 Where their worm dies not, and the fire is not quenched. 45 And if your foot offend you, cut it off: it is better for you to enter crippled into chayim, than having two feet to be cast into Gei-Hinnom, into the fire that never shall be quenched: 46 Where their worm dies not, and the fire is not quenched. 47 And if your eye offends you, pluck it out: it is better for you to enter into the malchut of* יהוה *with one eye, than having two eyes to be cast into Gei-Hinnom fire: 48 Where their worm dies not, and the fire is not quenched. 49 For every one shall be salted with fire, and every sacrifice shall be salted with salt. 50 Salt is tov: but if the salt has lost its saltiness, with what will you season it? Have salt in yourselves,* [3] *and have shalom one with another.* [4]

10 And He arose from there, and came into the coasts of Yahudah by the other side of the Yarden: and the people gathered to Him again; and, as He usually did, He taught them again. 2 And the Prushim came to Him, and asked Him, Is it permitted in the Torah for a man to put away his wife? Trying Him. 3 And He answered and said to them, *What did Moshe command you?* 4 And they said, Moshe allowed us to write a Get, and to put her away. 5 And **יהושע** answered and said to them, *For the hardness of your lev he wrote*

[1] A principle for Yisraelite living. Service is the road to greatness. Among gentiles rulership leads to domination.

[2] The little children are the children of Yisrael.
[3] All Torah sacrifices were seasoned with salt a preservative. "Have salt in yourselves" is a Hebraic idiomatic expression, saying in essence "you are the new living Yisraelite sacrifices, and as such must season all you do in the malchut with salt." For more details see:
http://yourarmstoisrael.org/Articles_new/restoration/?page=27&type=12
[4] "One with another" is a two-bayit reference.

you this precept. 6 But from the beginning of the creation **יהוה** *made them male and female. 7 For this cause shall a man leave his abba and ima, and cleave to his wife; 8 And the two shall be one flesh: so then they are no more two, but one flesh.* [1] *9 What therefore* **יהוה** *has joined together let not man separate.* 10 And in the bayit His talmidim asked Him again about the same matter. 11 And He said to them, *Whoever shall put away his wife, and marry another, commits adultery against her. 12 And if a woman shall put away her husband, and be married to another, she commits adultery.* 13 And they brought young children to Him, that He should touch them: and His talmidim rebuked those that brought them. 14 But when **יהושע** saw it, He was much displeased, and said to them, *Allow the little children to come to Me, and forbid them not: for of such people is the malchut of* **יהוה**. *15 Truly I say to you, Whoever shall not receive the malchut of* **יהוה** *as a little child, he shall not enter into it.* 16 And He took them up in His arms, put His hands upon them, and said a bracha upon them. 17 And when He had gone out into the way, there came one running, and bowed before Him, and asked Him, Tov Rabbi, what shall I do that I may inherit eternal chayim? 18 And **יהושע** said to him, *Why do you call Me tov? There is none tov but One, that is,* **יהוה**.[2] *19 You know the mitzvot, Do not commit adultery, Do not kill, Do not steal, Do not bear false witness, Defraud not, Honor your abba and ima.* [3] 20 And he answered and said to Him, Rabbi, all these have I observed from my youth. 21 Then **יהושע** beholding him

loved him, and said to him, *One thing you lack: go your way, sell whatever you have, and give to the poor, and you shall have treasure in the shamayim: and come, take up the execution stake, and follow Me.* 22 And he was sad at that saying, and went away grieved: for he had great possessions. 23 And **יהושע** looked around and said to His talmidim, *How hardly shall they that have riches enter into the malchut of* **יהוה**. 24 And the talmidim were astonished at His words. But **יהושע** answered again, and said to them, *Children, how hard is it for them that trust in riches to enter into the malchut of* **יהוה**. *25 It is easier for a large rope*[4] *to go through the eye of a needle, than for a rich man to enter into the malchut of* **יהוה**. 26 And they were totally astonished, saying among themselves, Who then can be saved? 27 And **יהושע** looking at them said, *With men it is impossible, but not with* **יהוה**: *for with* **יהוה** *all things are possible.* 28 Then Kepha began to say to Him, Look, we have left all, and have followed You. 29 And **יהושע** answered and said, *Truly I say to you, There is no man that has left bayit, or brothers, or sisters, or abba, or ima, or wife, or children, or lands, for My sake, and that of the besarot, 30 That he shall receive an hundredfold now in this time, houses, and brothers, and sisters, and mothers, and children, and lands with persecutions; and in the olam habah eternal chayim. 31 But many that are first shall be last; and the last first.* 32 And they were in the way going up to Yahrushalayim; and **יהושע** went before them: and they were amazed; and as they followed, they were afraid. And He took again the twelve, and began to tell them what things should happen to Him, 33 Saying, *See, we go up to Yahrushalayim; and the Ben Adam shall be delivered to the head kohanim, and to the Sophrim; and they shall condemn Him to death, and shall deliver Him to the goyim: 34 And they shall*

---

[1] Applies to Yahshua and Yisrael becoming one flesh, as well as the two houses being one again, as well as a man and his wife.
[2] In essence Yahshua is asking, "Do you realize what you're saying by calling Me tov?" That is freewill recognition of His deity by the young ruler, and a confirmation of Yahshua's own testimony about Himself, when in John 10 He refers to Himself as the Tov Shepherd. This verse has been twisted to mean that Yahshua is saying that only Abba is tov, but the truth here is just the opposite. Both He and Abba are tov, and as such He confronts the rich young ruler with this truth.
[3] Notice that Yahshua teaches Torah to those who are and would be His followers.

[4] Peshitta: **gemala** can mean rope or camel and here in context means rope.

mock Him, and shall scourge Him, and shall spit upon Him, and shall kill Him:[1] and the third day He shall rise again. 35 And Yaakov and Yochanan, the sons of Zavdi, came to Him, saying, Rabbi, we would that You should do for us what we desire. 36 And He said to them, *What would you desire that I should do for you?* 37 They said to Him, Grant to us that we may sit, one on Your right hand, and the other on Your left hand, in Your tifer:th. 38 But **יהושע** said to them, *You know not what you ask: can you drink of the cup that I drink of? And be immersed with the mikvah that I am immersed with?* 39 And they said to Him, We can. And **יהושע** said to them, *You shall indeed drink of the cup that I drink of; and with the mikvah that I am immersed with shall you be immersed:* 40 *But to sit on My right hand and on My left hand is not mine to give; but it shall be given to them for whom it is prepared.* 41 And when the ten heard it, they began to be much displeased with Yaakov and Yochanan.[2] 42 But **יהושע** called them to Him, and said to them, *You know that they who are chosen to rule over the goyim exercise dominion over them; and their great ones exercise authority upon them.*[3] 43 *But so shall it not be among you: but whoever will be great among you, shall be your eved:* 44 *And whoever of you desires to be the first, shall be eved of all.* 45 *For even the Ben Adam came not to be attended to, but to serve, and to give His chayim a ransom for many.* 46 And they came to Yericho: and as He went out of Yericho with His talmidim and a great number of people, blind Bartimai, the son of Timai, sat by the highway side begging. 47 And when he heard that it was **יהושע** of Natzareth, he began to cry out, and say, **יהושע**, Ben

David, have rachamim on me. 48 And many ordered him that he should hold his silence: but he cried out even more, Oy! Ben David, have rachamim on me. 49 And **יהושע** stood still, and commanded him to be called. And they called the blind man, saying to him, Be of tov comfort, rise; He calls for you. 50 And he, casting away his garment, rose, and came to **יהושע**. 51 And **יהושע** answered and said to him, *What do you desire that I should do for you?* The blind man said to Him, Master, that I might receive my sight. 52 And **יהושע** said to him, *Go your way; your emunah has made you whole.* And immediately he received his sight, and followed **יהושע** in the Way.[4]

11 And when they came near to Yahrushalayim, to Beth-Phage and Beth-Anya, at the Mount of Olives, He sent out two of His talmidim,[5] 2 And said to them, *Go your way into the village opposite you: and as soon as you enter into it, you shall find a colt tied, on which never man sat; loose him, and bring him.* 3 *And if any man says to you, Why are you doing this? You say that the Rabbi has need of it; and immediately he will send him here.* 4 And they went their way, and found the colt tied by the door outside in a place where two ways met;[6] and they loosed him. 5 And certain of them that stood there said to them, What are you doing, loosing the colt? 6 And they said to them even as **יהושע** had commanded: and they let them go. 7 And they brought the colt to **יהושע**, and cast their garments on him; and He sat upon him. 8 And many spread their garments in the way: and others cut down branches off the trees, and spread them in the way. 9 And they that went before, and they that followed, shouted, saying, Hoshia-na;

---

[1] According to Yahshua, the gentiles or Romans would do the actual killing. Not the Jews.
[2] The ten here symbolize Ephraim Yisrael, or the 10 tribes who are jealous of their brothers from Yahudah, for seeking special privilege and position in the family. The Bible calls this a vexation of Ephraim that causes Yahudah to be the recipient of Ephraim's jealousy.
[3] Further evidence that believers are never referred to as "gentiles" in Scripture.

[4] Early Nazarene Yisraelites were known as members of "The Way"; after Yahshua's proclamation in John 14:6.
[5] These two talmidim represent the two houses, who both are called to do their preparation job to prepare the way for His triumphal return to Yahrushalayim as King of Yisrael at His second coming.
[6] Both houses will begin the restoration with the official arrival of the King to Yahrushalayim, as the "two ways" of Yahudah and Ephraim become one.

Baruch Habah Beshem HaAdon יהוה :
10 Blessed is the malchut of our abba David that comes in the Name of יהוה: Hoshia-na in the highest. 11 And יהושע entered into Yahrushalayim, and into the Beit HaMikdash: and when He had looked around at all things, and the evening had come, He went out to Beth-Anya with the twelve. 12 And on the next day, when they had come from Beth-Anya, He was hungry: 13 And seeing a fig tree[1] far off having leaves, He came, to see if He might find anything on it: and when He came to it, He found nothing but leaves; for the time of figs had not yet come. 14 And יהושע answered and said to it, *No man eat fruit from you after this le-olam-va-ed.* And His talmidim heard it.[2] 15 And they came to Yahrushalayim: and יהושע went into the Beit HaMikdash, and began to cast out those that sold and bought in the Beit HaMikdash, and overthrew the tables of the moneychangers, and the seats of them that sold yonahs; 16 And would not allow that any man should carry any vessel through the Beit HaMikdash. 17 And He taught, saying to them, *Is it not written, My Bayit shall be called a Beit Tefillah for all nations?*[3] *But you have made it a den of thieves.* 18 And the Sophrim and head kohanim heard it, and sought how they might destroy Him: for they feared Him, because all the people were astonished at His teaching. 19 And when evening had come, He went out of the city. 20 And in the morning, as they passed by, they saw the fig tree dried up from the roots. 21 And Kepha calling it to remembrance said to Him, Rabbi, see, the fig tree that You cursed has withered away. 22 And יהושע answering said to them, *Have emunah in יהוה.* 23 *For truly I say to you, That whoever shall say to this mountain, Be*

removed, and be cast into the sea; and shall not doubt in his lev, but shall believe that those things, which He said, shall come to pass; he shall have whatever He said. 24 *Therefore I say to you, What things you desire, when you make tefillah, believe that you receive them, and you shall have them.* 25 *And when you stand making tefillah, forgive, if you have any matter against any: that your Abba also who is in the shamayim may forgive you your trespasses.* 26 *But if you do not forgive, neither will your Abba who is in the shamayim forgive your trespasses.* 27 And they come again to Yahrushalayim: and as He was walking in the Beit HaMikdash, there came to Him the head kohanim, and the Sophrim, and the zachanim, 28 And said to Him, By what authority are You doing these things? And who gave You this authority to do these things? 29 And יהושע answered and said to them, *I will also ask you one question, and answer Me, and I will tell you by what authority I do these things.* 30 *The mikvah from Yochanan, was it from the shamayim, or from men? Answer Me.* 31 And they reasoned within themselves, saying, If we shall say, From the shamayim; He will say, Why then did you not believe him? 32 But if we shall say, Of men; they feared the people: for all men reckoned Yochanan, that he was a navi indeed. 33 And they answered and said to יהושע, We cannot tell. And יהושע answering said to them, *Neither do I tell you by what authority I do these things.*

12 And He began to speak to them by parables. *A certain man planted a vineyard, and set a hedge around it, and dug a place for the winepress, and built a tower, and rented it out to farmers, and went into a far country. 2 And at the season he sent to the farmers an eved, that he might receive from the farmers of the fruit of the vineyard. 3 And they caught him, and beat him, and sent him away empty. 4 And again he sent to them another eved; and at him*

---

[1] Symbol of national Yisrael.
[2] This was not a curse on the nation as some teach, but a curse on "fruit eating," meaning the fruit from Yisrael would come from the new wine of Moshiach, not the old figs of the Prushim.
[3] The plan was always to gather Yisrael and make all nations echad in Yisrael.

they cast stones, and wounded him in the head, and sent him away shamefully handled. 5 And again he sent another; and him they killed, and many others; beating some, and killing some. 6 Having yet therefore one Son, His well beloved, He sent him lastly also to them, saying, They will reverence My Son. 7 But those farmers said among themselves, This is the heir; come, let us kill him, and the inheritance shall be ours. 8 And they took him, and killed him, and cast him out of the vineyard. 9 What shall therefore the master of the vineyard do? He will come and destroy the farmers, and will give the vineyard to others. 10 And have you not read this Katav; The Stone, which the builders rejected, has become the Head of the corner:[1] 11 This was the Master יהוה 's doing, and it is marvelous in our eyes? 12 And they sought to lay hold on Him, but feared the people: for they knew that He had spoken the parable against them: and they left Him, and went their way. 13 And they sent to Him certain of the Prushim and of the Herodians, to catch Him in His words. 14 And when they had come, they said to Him, Rabbi, we know that You are emet, and are not concerned with man's opinion: for You regard not the person of men, but teach the Way of Elohim in emet: Is it permitted according to Torah to give taxes to Caesar, or not? 15 Shall we give, or shall we not give? But He, knowing their hypocrisy, said to them, Why do you test Me? Bring Me a penny, that I may see it. 16 And they brought it. And He said to them, Whose image and inscription is this? And they said to Him, Caesar's. 17 And יהושע answering said to them, Render to Caesar the things that are Caesar's, and to יהוה the things that are יהוה 's. And they marveled at Him. 18 Then come to Him the Tzadukim, who say there is no resurrection; and they asked Him, saying, 19 Rabbi, Moshe Rabainu wrote to us, If a man's brother dies, and leaves his wife behind

him, and leaves no children, that his brother should take his wife, and raise up zera for his brother. 20 Now there were seven brothers: and the first took a wife, and dying left no zera. 21 And the second took her, and died, neither left her any zera: and the third likewise. 22 And the seven all had her, and left no zera: last of all the woman died also. 23 In the resurrection therefore, when they shall rise, whose wife shall she be? Since all seven had her as a wife. 24 And יהושע answering said to them, Do you not therefore make grave errors, because you know not the Ketuvim, or the power of יהוה? 25 For when they shall rise from the dead, they neither marry, nor are given in marriage; but are as the heavenly messengers who are in the shamayim. 26 And concerning the dead, that they will rise: have you not read in the Torah of Moshe, how in the bush יהוה spoke to him, saying, I am the Elohim of Avraham, and the Elohim of Yitzchak, and the Elohim of Yaakov? 27 He is not the Elohim of the dead, but the Elohim of the living: you therefore do greatly go astray. 28 And one of the Sophrim came, and having heard them reasoning together, and perceiving that He had answered them well, asked Him, Which is the first commandment of all? 29 And יהושע answered him, The first of all the commandments is, Shema, O Yisrael; the Master יהוה is our Elohim, the Master יהוה is Echad: 30 And you shall love the Master יהוה your Elohim with all your lev, and with all your being, and with all your mind, and with all your strength: this is the first commandment. 31 And the second is like it, namely this; You shall love your neighbor as yourself. There are no other commandments greater than these. 32 And the sopher said to Him, Well, Rabbi, You have said the emet: for there is one Elohim; and there is no other besides Him: 33 And to love Him with all the lev, and with all the understanding, and with all the being, and with all the strength, and to love your neighbor as yourself, is

---

[1] See notes on Matthew 21:33-44.

more than all the burnt offerings and sacrifices. 34 And when יהושע saw that He answered discreetly, He said to him, *You are not far from the malchut of יהוה.* And no man after that did ask Him any questions. 35 And יהושע responding said, while He taught in the Beit HaMikdash, *How do the Sophrim say that the Moshiach is the Ben David? 36 For David himself said by the Ruach HaKodesh, the Master יהוה said to My Master, Sit at My right hand, until I make Your enemies Your footstool. 37 David therefore himself called Him Master; in what way then is He His Son?* And the common people heard Him with gilah.[1] 38 And He said to them in His teaching, *Beware of the Sophrim, who ahava to go in long clothing, and ahava greetings in the marketplaces, 39 And the best seats in the synagogues, and the best places at moadim: 40 Who devour widows' houses, and for a public show make long tefillot: these shall receive greater damnation.* 41 And יהושע sat over against the treasury, and beheld how the people cast money into the treasury: and many that were rich cast in much. 42 And there came a certain poor widow, and she threw in two small copper coins, which make a cent. 43 And He called to Him His talmidim, and said to them, *Truly I say to you, That this poor widow has put more in, than all those who have put into the treasury: 44 For all they did put in of their abundance; but she of her poverty did put in all that she had, even all her livelihood.*

13 And as He went out of the Beit HaMikdash, one of His talmidim said to Him, Rabbi, see what manner of stones and what buildings are here! 2 And יהושע answering said to him, *Do you see these great buildings? There shall not be left one stone upon another that shall not be thrown down.* 3 And as He sat upon the Mount of Olives opposite the Beit

HaMikdash, Kepha and Yaakov and Yochanan and Andri asked Him privately, 4 Tell us, when shall these things be? And what shall be the sign when all these things shall be fulfilled? 5 And יהושע answering them began to say, *Take heed lest any man deceive you: 6 For many shall come in My Name, saying, I am the Moshiach; and shall deceive many. 7 And when you shall shema of wars and rumors of wars, be not troubled: for such things must indeed be; but the end shall not be yet. 8 For nation shall rise against nation, and malchut against malchut: and there shall be earthquakes in different places, and there shall be famines and troubles: these are the Shivlai HaMoshiach.[2] 9 But take heed to yourselves: for they shall deliver you up to councils; and in the synagogues you shall be beaten: and you shall be brought before rulers and melechim for My sake, for a testimony to them. 10 And the besarot must first be published among all nations.[3] 11 But when they shall lead you away, and deliver you up, take no thought beforehand what you shall speak, neither do you premeditate: but whatever shall be given you in that hour, what you shall speak: for it is not you that speaks, but the Ruach HaKodesh. 12 Now the brother shall betray the brother to death, and the abba the son; and children shall rise up against their parents, and shall cause them to be put to death. 13 And you shall be hated of all men for My Name's sake: but he that shall endure to the end,[4] the same shall be saved. 14 But when you shall see the abomination of desolation, spoken of by Daniel the navi,[5] set up where it should not be, (let him that reads understand,) then let them that be in Yahudah flee to the mountains: 15 And let him that is on the housetop not go down into the bayit, neither enter in, to take any*

---

[1] Moshiach is both the Son of David and the Master of David, a revelation that can become reality only by a revelation from YHWH Himself.

[2] Known as Yaakov's Trouble or **Shivlei HaMashiach** – the birth pains of Moshiach.
[3] All Yisraelite nations, who by Yahshua's time had already begun to be filled with Ephraimites.
[4] Of this age.
[5] In order to see it, believers must be on earth during the 70th week of Yisrael.

thing out of his bayit: 16 And let him that is in the field not turn back again to take up his garment. 17 But woe to them that are with child, and to them that nurse in those days! 18 And make tefillah you that your flight is not in the winter. 19 For in those days shall be Tribulation, such as was not from the beginning of the creation that יהוה created to this time, neither shall be ever again. 20 And except that the Master יהוה had shortened those days, no flesh should be saved: but for the elect's sake,[1] whom He has chosen, He has shortened the days. 21 And then if any man shall say to you, Look, here is the Moshiach; or, look, He is there; believe him not: 22 For false Moshiachs and false niviim shall rise, and shall show signs and wonders, to seduce, if it were possible, even the chosen people. 23 But take you heed: see, I have foretold you all things. 24 But in those days, after that Tribulation, the sun shall be darkened, and the moon shall not give her light, 25 And the chochavim of the shamayim shall fall, and the powers that are in the shamayim shall be shaken. 26 And then shall they see the Ben Adam coming on the clouds with great Power and tifereth.[2] 27 And then shall He send His heavenly messengers, and shall gather together His chosen people from the four winds,[3] from the uttermost parts of the earth to the uttermost parts of the shamayim. 28 Now learn a parable of the fig tree; When her branch is yet tender, and puts out leaves, you know that summer is near: 29 So in like manner, when you shall see these things come to pass, know that it is near, even at the doors. 30 Truly I say to you, that this generation shall not pass, until all these

things be done.[4] 31 Heaven and earth shall pass away: but My words shall not pass away.[5] 32 But of that day and that hour knows no man, no, not the heavenly messengers who are in the shamayim, neither the Son, but the Abba alone. 33 Take heed, watch and make tefillah: for you know not when the time is. 34 For the Ben Adam is like a man taking a far journey, who left His Bayit, and gave authority to His avadim, and to every man his work assignment, and commanded the doorkeeper to watch. 35 Watch therefore: for you know not when the Master of the Bayit comes, at evening, or at midnight, or at twilight, or in the morning: 36 Lest coming suddenly He finds you sleeping. 37 And what I say to you I say to kol Yisrael, Shomer!

14 After two days was the moed of the Pesach, and of Chag Matzoth: and the head kohanim and the Sophrim sought how they might seize Him by trickery, and put Him to death. 2 But they said, Not on the moed day,[6] lest there be an uproar of the people. 3 And being in Beth-Anya in the bayit of Shimon the jar merchant,[7] as He sat at dinner, there came a woman having an alabaster flask of ointment of pistachio very precious; and she broke the flask, and poured it on His head. 4 And there were some that were displeased among themselves, and said, Why was this waste of the ointment made? 5 For it might have been sold for more than three hundred pieces of silver, and given to the poor. And they murmured against her. 6 And יהושע said, Leave her alone; why do you trouble her? She has done a tov mitzvah for Me. 7 For you have the poor with you always, and

---

[1] YHWH's one elect is Yisrael, since YHWH does not have two sets of elect, rather two parts to the one elect. If everywhere in the Brit Chadasha "elect" refers to the body of believers, it must also apply here, meaning Renewed Covenant Yisrael will certainly go through the Great Tribulation.
[2] As seen in verse 24, Yahshua's return is after the Great Tribulation. Nothing can be plainer.
[3] The term four winds throughout Scripture is always speaking of Yisrael and the ingathering of the exiles as seen in Devarim 30:4, Ezekiel 37:9, and elsewhere. This ingathering has nothing to do with a "rapture" of any church.

[4] The rebirth of the state of Yisrael in 1948 and the recapture of Yahrushalayim in 1967. The generation that sees these events will be the final generation or generations.
[5] Meaning He taught Torah and His words were Torah, for only Torah (Genesis-Revelation) cannot pass away.
[6] His arrest was scheduled before Passover.
[7] The Hebrew for "leper" is ga-rabba and for "jar merchant" in Aramaic the word is garava. Torah would not allow Yahshua to be defiled by a leper and so the understanding of "jar merchant" is more probable.

whenever you desire, you may do them tov: but Me you have not always. 8 She has done what she could: she has come before the time to anoint My body for its burial. 9 Truly I say to you, Wherever this besorat shall be proclaimed throughout the whole olam hazeh, what she has done shall be spoken of for her remembrance. 10 And Yahudah from Qerioth, one of the twelve, went to the head kohanim, to betray Him to them. 11 And when they heard it, they were had gilah, and promised to give him money. And he sought how he might conveniently betray Him. 12 And before the first day of Chag Matzoth, when they killed the Pesach,[1] His talmidim said to Him, Where do You desire that we go and prepare so that You may eat the Pesach?[2] 13 And He sends out two of His talmidim, and said to them, *Go into the city, and there shall meet you a man bearing a pitcher of mayim: follow him. 14 And wherever he shall go in, say you to the owner of the bayit, The Rabbi said, Where is the guest room, where I shall eat the Pesach with My talmidim? 15 And he will show you a large upper room furnished and prepared: there make it ready for us.* 16 And His talmidim went out, and came into the city, and found it as He had said to them: and they made ready the Pesach. 17 And in the evening He came with the twelve. 18 And as they sat and did eat, **יהושע** said, *Truly I say to you, one of you who eats with Me shall betray Me.* 19 And they began to be sorrowful, and to say to Him one by one, Is it I? and another said, Is it I? 20 And He answered and said to them, *It is one of the twelve that dips with Me in the dish. 21 The Ben Adam indeed going, as it is written of Him: but woe to that man by whom the Ben Adam is betrayed! Tov were it for that man if he had never been born.* 22 And as they did eat,

יהושע took matzah, and said the bracha, and broke it, and gave it to them, and said, *Take, eat: this is My body.* 23 And He took the Cup of Geulah, and when He had given hodu, He gave it to them: and they all drank of it. 24 And He said to them, *This is My dom of the Renewed Covenant, which is shed for many. 25 Truly I say to you, I will drink no more of the fruit of the vine, until that day that I drink it new in the malchut of* **יהרה**.[3] 26 And when they had sung a hymn, they went out to the Mount of Olives. 27 And **יהושע** said to them, *All you shall be offended because of Me this night: for it is written, I will smite the Shepherd, and the sheep shall be scattered. 28 But after I am risen, I will go before you into Galil.* 29 But Kepha said to Him, Although all shall be offended; yet I will not. 30 And **יהושע** said to him, *Truly I say to you, That this day, even in this night, before the cock crows twice, you shall deny Me three different times.* 31 But he spoke the more vehemently, If I should die with You, I still will not deny You in any way. Likewise said all of them. 32 And they came to a place that was named Gat Sh'manim: and He said to His talmidim, *Sit here, while I shall make tefillah.* 33 And He took with Him Kepha and Yaakov and Yochanan, and He began to be very pressed down, and to be deeply distressed; 34 And said to them, *My being is exceedingly sorrowful to death: tarry here, and watch.* 35 And He went forward a little, and fell on the ground, and made tefillah that, if it were possible, the hour might pass from Him. 36 And He said, *Abba, Abba, all things are possible for You; take away this cup from Me: nevertheless not what I will, but what You will.* 37 And He comes, and finds them sleeping, and He said to Kepha, *Shimon, are you sleeping? Couldn't you watch just one hour? 38 Watch and make tefillah, lest you enter into temptation. The human ruach truly is ready, but the flesh is weak.* 39 And again He went away, and made tefillah, and spoke

---

[1] The Greek word **protos** means "before" in this context and certainly not "first." Most translators have translated **protos** as "first" instead of "before." But the Passover is killed and prepared before the first day of Unleavened Bread.
[2] They were preparing a Moshiach's Passover, a tradition held by many rabbis sometime before the actual Passover. See notes for Matthew 26:20.

[3] When He consummates the marriage with His bride Yisrael.

the same words. 40 And when He returned, He found them asleep again, for their eyes were heavy, neither did they know what to answer Him. 41 And He came the third time, and said to them, *Sleep on now, and take your rest: it is enough, the hour has come; see, the Ben Adam is betrayed into the hands of sinners.* 42 *Rise up, let us go; look, he that betrays Me is here.* 43 And immediately, while He yet spoke, came Yahudah, one of the twelve, and with him a great multitude with swords and clubs, from the head kohanim and the Sophrim and the zachanim. 44 And he that betrayed Him had given them a sign, saying, Whomever I shall kiss, that is Him; take Him, and lead Him away safely. 45 And as soon as he was come, he went immediately to Him, and said, Rabbi, Rabbi; and kissed Him. 46 And they laid their hands on Him, and took Him. 47 And one of them that stood by drew a sword, and smote an eved of the Kohen HaGadol, and cut off his ear. 48 And יהושע answered and said to them, *Are you come out, against a thief, with swords and with clubs to take Me?* 49 *I was daily with you in the Beit HaMikdash teaching, and you took Me not: but the Ketuvim must be fulfilled.* 50 And they all forsook Him, and fled. 51 And there followed Him a certain young man, having a linen cloth cast around his naked body; and the men laid hold on him: 52 And he left the linen cloth, and fled from them naked.[1] 53 And they led יהושע away to the Kohen HaGadol: and with Him were assembled all the head kohanim and the zachanim and the Sophrim. 54 And Kepha followed Him far off, even into the palace of the Kohen HaGadol: and he sat with the avadim, and warmed himself at the fire. 55 And the head kohanim and all the Sanhedrin sought for a witness against יהושע to put Him to death; and found none. 56 For many bore false witness against Him, but their witness did not agree. 57 And there arose some, and bore false witness against Him, saying, 58 We heard

Him say, I will destroy this Beit HaMikdash that is made with hands, and within three days I will build another made without hands. 59 But neither in this accusation did their witness agree. 60 And the Kohen HaGadol stood up in the midst, and asked יהושע, saying, do You answer nothing? What is this that they witness against You? 61 But He maintained His silence, and answered nothing. Again the Kohen HaGadol asked Him, and said to Him, Are You The Moshiach, the Son of the Blessed? 62 And יהושע said, *I Am: and you shall see the Ben Adam sitting on the Right Hand of Power,*[2] *and coming on the clouds of the shamayim.* 63 Then the Kohen HaGadol tore his clothes, and said, Why do we need any further witnesses? 64 You have heard the blasphemy: what do you think? And they all condemned Him to be guilty of death. 65 And some began to spit on Him, and to cover His face, and to buffet Him, and to say to Him, Prophesy: and the avadim did strike Him with the palms of their hands. 66 And as Kepha was beneath in the palace, there came one of the eved girls of the Kohen HaGadol: 67 And when she saw Kepha warming himself, she looked at Him, and said, And you also were with יהושע of Natzareth. 68 But he denied it, saying, I know Him not; neither do I understand what you say. And he went out into the porch; and the cock crew. 69 And an eved girl saw him again, and began to say to them that stood by, He is one of them. 70 And he denied it again. And a little after, they that stood by said again to Kepha, Surely you are one of them: for you are a Galilaean, and your speech is like theirs. 71 But he began to curse and to swear, saying, I know not this man of whom

---

[1] Probably was Moshe-Markus.

[2] A euphemism for YHWH as it appears in Psalm 110:5. Yahshua pronounced the true Name of Yahweh as He correctly quoted Psalm 110:5 to show that YHWH would sit on the right hand of YHWH. According to Jewish man-made fabrication, at that time this was the only crime labeled as blasphemy. We see that in verses 63-64, that they heard the blasphemy, and we know that Yahshua said nothing other than quote Psalm 110:5. He was killed for saying YHWH's Name. Scripture calls on us to proclaim and declare His Name, just like our Master, even in the face of possible death.

you speak. 72 And the second time the cock crowed. And Kepha recalled to mind the word that יהושע said to him, *Before the cock crows twice, you shall deny Me three times.* And when he thought about it, he wept.[1]

15

And immediately in the morning the head kohanim held a consultation with the zachanim and Sophrim and the whole Sanhedrin, and bound יהושע, and carried Him away, and delivered Him to Pilate. 2 And Pilate asked Him, Are You the Melech of the Yahudim? And He answering said to him, *You say it.* 3 And the head kohanim accused Him of many things: but He answered nothing. 4 And Pilate asked Him again, saying, You answer nothing? Look at how many things they witness against You. 5 But יהושע again answered nothing; so that Pilate marveled. 6 Now at that moed he released one prisoner to them, whomever they desired. 7 And there was one named Bar-Rabba, who was bound with them that had made insurrection with him, who had committed murder in the insurrection. 8 And the multitude crying aloud began to desire him to do as he had always done for them. 9 But Pilate answered them, saying, Do you wish that I release to you the Melech of the Yahudim? 10 For He knew that the head kohanim had delivered Him because of envy. 11 But the head kohanim moved the people, that he should release Bar-Rabba to them. 12 And Pilate answered and said again to them, What will you then that I shall do to Him whom you call the Melech of the Yahudim? 13 And they cried out again, Impale Him! 14 Then Pilate said to them, Why, what evil has He done? And they cried out the more exceedingly, Impale Him. 15 And so Pilate, willing to content the people, released Bar-Rabba to them, and delivered יהושע , when he had scourged

Him, to be impaled. 16 And the soldiers led Him away into the hall, called Praetorium; and they called together the whole company of soldiers. 17 And they clothed Him with purple, and platted a crown of thorns, and put it around His head, 18 And began to salute Him, Hail, Melech of the Yahudim! 19 And they smote Him on the head with a reed, and did spit upon Him, and bowing their knees they mockingly worshipped Him. 20 And when they had mocked Him, they took off the purple from Him, and put His own clothes on Him, and led Him out to impale Him. 21 And they compelled one Shimon a Cyrenian, who passed by, coming out of the country, the abba of Alexander and Rufus, to bear His execution stake. 22 And they brought Him to the place Golgotha, which is, being interpreted, The place of a skull.[2] 23 And they gave Him wine to drink mingled with myrrh: but He received it not. 24 And when they had impaled Him, they parted His garments, casting lots for them, what every man should take. 25 And it was 9 o'clock in the morning, and they impaled Him. 26 And the inscription of His accusation was written above, *Y-AHSHUA H-ANOTZREI W-EMELECH H-AYAHUDIM.*[3] 27 And with Him they impaled two thieves; the one on His right hand, and the other on His left.[4] 28 And the Katav was fulfilled, that said, And He was numbered with the transgressors.[5] 29 And they that passed by blasphemed Him, wagging their heads, and saying, Ah, You that destroys the Beit HaMikdash, and builds it in three days, 30 Save yourself, and come down from the execution stake. 31 Likewise also the head kohanim mocking said among themselves with the Sophrim, He saved others; Himself He cannot save. 32 Let the Moshiach the

---

[1] Such detail found about Kepha's behaviors leads scholars to suggest that Peter is really the author behind Moshe/Mark's besorah.

[2] Mount of Olives.
[3] YHWH-Yud Hey Vav Hey.
[4] A hint of the two houses; with the repentant thief being a type of Ephraim, and the unrepentant a type of Yahudah, with Yahshua holding His hands towards both sinning brothers, beckoning them to come together in Him.
[5] Of both houses of Yisrael.

Melech of Yisrael descend now from the execution stake that we may see and believe. And they that were impaled with Him reviled Him. 33 And when 12 noon had come, there was darkness over the whole land until the ninth hour. 34 And at 3 o'clock in the afternoon יהושע cried with a loud voice, saying, *Eli-Yahuweh, Eli-Yahuweh, lama sabachthani?* Which is, being interpreted, My Yahu-weh, My Yahu-weh, why have You forsaken Me? 35 And some of them that stood by, when they heard it, said, See, He calls for Eli-Yahu.[1] 36 And one ran and filled a sponge full of vinegar, and put it on a reed, and gave Him to drink, saying, Leave Him alone; let us see whether Eli-Yahu will come to take Him down. 37 And יהושע cried with a loud voice, and gave up the ruach. 38 And the veil of the Beit HaMikdash was torn in two[2] from the top to the bottom. 39 And when the centurion, who stood opposite Him, saw that He cried out, and gave up the ruach, he said, Truly this Man was the Son of the Almighty.[3] 40 There were also women looking on far off: among whom was Miryam of Magdala, and Miryam the ima of Yaakov the Less and of Yoseph, and Shlomo; 41 Who also, when He was in Galil, followed Him, and attended to Him; and many other women who came up with Him to Yahrushalayim. 42 And now when the evening had come, because it was the preparation, that is, the day before the Shabbat,[4] 43 Yoseph of Ramathayim, a prominent Sanhedrin member, who also believed in and waited for the malchut of יהרה, came, and went in boldly to Pilate, and asked for the body of יהושע. 44 And Pilate marveled that He was already dead:

and he called the centurion, and asked Him whether He had already been dead. 45 And when he knew it from the centurion, he gave the body to Yoseph. 46 And he bought fine linen, and took Him down, and wrapped Him in linen, and laid Him in a tomb that was cut out of a rock, and rolled a stone to the door of the tomb. 47 And Miryam from Magdala and Miryam the ima of Yoseph beheld the place where He was laid.

16 And when the Shabbat had past,[5] Miryam from Magdala, and Miryam the ima of Yaakov, and Shlomo, had bought sweet spices that they might come and anoint Him. 2 And very early in the morning mia-ton-sabbat-on,[6] they came to the tomb at the rising of the sun.[7] 3 And they said among themselves, Who shall roll away for us the stone from the door of the tomb? 4 And when they looked, they saw that the stone was already rolled away: for it was very great. 5 And entering into the tomb, they saw a young man sitting on the right side, clothed in a long white garment; and they were greatly frightened. 6 And He said to them, Be not afraid: You seek יהושע of Natzareth, who was impaled: He is risen; He is not here: see the place where they laid Him. 7 But go your way, tell His talmidim and Kepha that He went before you into Galil: there shall you see Him, as He said to you. 8 And they went out quickly, and fled from the tomb; for they trembled and were amazed: neither said they anything to any man; for they were afraid. 9 Now when יהושע had risen early

---

[1] The only way these learned Hebrew sophrim could possibly have thought He was seeking Eliyahu, or Elijah in English, was if the words He was crying out were almost exactly like the sound of **Eli-Yahu**. And it was. He was calling for Yah-u-weh His El or **Eli-yah-u-weh**.
[2] Torn into two equal pieces symbolizing equal access to YHWH for both houses of redeemed Yisrael.
[3] Based on seeing the veil of the Hekel rent from the Mount of Olives, for if He were behind the Beit HaMikdash to the west at "Gordon's Calvary," he wouldn't have seen anything.
[4] Approaching the night of Aviv 14, with Aviv 15 being an annual Shabbat.

[5] After Havdalah.
[6] Retained the Greek since that served all best. Greek is **mia ton sabbaton** or "one of the Shabbats" not "first day." since the word "first" does not appear in the Greek and the word "day" also is missing. Just after one of the Shabbats, very early, would have been say 6-7 PM, and after this time reckoning, they got to the tomb around the rising of the sun at dawn. Moreover, one of the Shabbats refers to one of the seven weekly Shabbats between the start of the omer count on the 16th of Aviv, ending seven weeks later. For more details on this see: **Understanding Omer** http://store.yourarmstoisrael.org/Qstore/Qstore.cgi?CMD=011 &PROD=1065766335.
[7] By the time they arrived at sunrise, the blessed Master had been long gone, having risen at the end of Shabbat.

mia-ton-sabbat-on, [1] He appeared first to Miryam from Magdala, out of whom He had cast seven shadim. 10 And she went and told them that had been with Him, as they mourned and wept. 11 And they, when they had heard that He was alive, and had been seen by her, they believed not. 12 After that He appeared in another form to two of them, as they walked, and went into the country. 13 And they went and told it to the rest: neither did the rest believe them. 14 Afterward He appeared to the eleven as they sat to eat, and upbraided them for their unbelief and hardness of lev, because they believed not those who had seen Him after He had risen. 15 And He said to them, *Go into all the olam hazeh, and proclaim the besarot to every creature. 16 He that believes and is immersed shall be saved; but he that believes not shall be damned.*

17 *And these signs shall follow them that believe; In My Name shall they cast out shadim; they shall speak with new tongues; 18 They shall take up serpents; and if they drink any deadly thing, it shall not hurt them; they shall lay hands on the sick, and they shall recover.* 19 So then after יהושע had spoken to them; He was received up into the third shamayim, and sat down on the right hand of יהוה.[2] 20 And they went out, and proclaimed everywhere, יהוה working with them, and confirming the word with signs following. Amein.

---

[1] Retained the Greek since that served all best.

[2] As per Psalm 110:5.

לוקא

The Besorah According To

Luka – Luke

To All Nations

1 Since many have taken in hand to set forth in order a declaration of those things that are most surely believed among us, 2 Even as they delivered them to us, which from the beginning were eyewitnesses, and avadim of the word; 3 It seemed tov to me also, having had perfect understanding of all things from the very beginning, to write to you in order, most excellent Theophilos, [1] 4 That you might know the certainty of those things, in which you have been instructed. 5 There was in the days of Herod, the melech of the province of Yahudah, a certain kohen named Zacharyah, of the division of Abiyah: and his wife was one of the daughters of Aharon, and her name was Elisheva. 6 And they were both tzadikim before the Master יהוה, having their halacha in all the chukim and mishpatim of the Master יהוה blameless. 7 And they had no child, because Elisheva was barren, and they both were now advanced in years. 8 And it came to pass, that while he served in the kohen's office before יהוה in the order of his division, 9 According to the custom of the kohen's office, he was chosen by lot to burn incense when he went into the Beit HaMikdash of the Master יהוה. 10 And the whole multitude of the people were making tefillot outside at the time of incense. 11 And there appeared to him a heavenly messenger of the Master יהוה standing on the right side of the altar of incense. 12 And when Zacharyah saw him, he was troubled, and fear fell upon him. 13 But the heavenly messenger said to him, Fear not, Zacharyah: for your tefillah is heard; and your wife Elisheva shall bear you a son, and you shall call his name Yochanan. 14 And you shall have simcha and gladness; and many shall rejoice at his birth. 15 For he shall be great in the sight of the Master יהוה, and shall drink neither wine nor strong drink; [2] and he shall be filled with the Ruach HaKodesh, even from his ima's womb. 16 And many of the children of Yisrael shall he return to the Master יהוה their Elohim. 17 And he shall go before Him in the Ruach and power of Eli-Yahu, to turn the levim of the ahvot to the children, [3] and the disobedient to the chochmah of the just; to make ready a people prepared for the Master יהוה. 18 And Zacharyah said to the heavenly messenger, How shall I know this? For I am an old man, and my wife advanced in years. 19 And the heavenly messenger answering said to him, I am Gavriel, that stands in the shechinah of יהוה; and am sent to speak to you, and to show you this tov news. 20 And, see, you shall be dumb, and not able to speak, until the day that these things shall be performed, because you believed not my words, which shall be fulfilled in their season. 21 And the people waited for Zacharyah, and marveled that he waited so long in the Beit HaMikdash. 22 And when he came out, he could not speak to them: and they perceived that he had seen a vision in the Beit HaMikdash: for he beckoned to them, and remained dumb. 23 And it came to pass, that, as soon as the days of his service were accomplished, he departed to his own bayit. 24 And after those days his wife Elisheva conceived, and hid herself five months, saying, 25 The Master יהוה

---

[1] The book of Luke was written originally to Theophilus, who served as High Priest from 37 to 42 C.E. Theophilus was both a priest and a Sadducee. It would appear that this evangel was intended to be used by others as well, and was likely targeted at Sadducee readers. Theophilus was the son of Annas and the brother-in-law of Caiaphas.

[2] A Nazarite.
[3] To turn the fathers of Yahudah to the forthcoming children of YHWH, or returning Ephraim; to prepare Yisrael as a people for Yahshua by replacing disobedience with Torah.

has dealt with me in the days in which He looked on me, to take away my reproach among men. 26 And in the sixth month the heavenly messenger Gavriel was sent from יהוה to a city of Galil, named Natzareth, 27 To a virgin engaged to a man whose name was Yoseph, from the bayit of David; and the virgin's name was Miryam. 28 And the heavenly messenger came in to her, and said, Greetings, you that are highly favored, יהוה is with you: favored are you among women. 29 And when she saw him, she was troubled at his saying, and wondered in her mind what manner of greeting this should be. 30 And the heavenly messenger said to her, Fear not, Miryam: for you have found favor with יהוה. 31 And, see, you shall conceive in your womb, and bring forth a Son, and shall call His Name יהושע. 32 He shall be great and shall be called the Son of the Highest: and the Master יהוה Elohim shall give to Him the throne of His abba David:[1] 33 And He shall reign over the Beit Yaakov le-olam-va-ed; and of His malchut there shall be no end.[2] 34 Then said Miryam to the heavenly messenger, How shall this be, seeing I know not a man? 35 And the heavenly messenger answered and said to her, The Ruach HaKodesh shall come upon you, and the power of the El-Elyon shall overshadow you: therefore also that Set-Apart-One which shall be born of you shall be called the Son of יהוה. 36 And, see, your cousin Elisheva, she has also conceived a son in her old age: and this is the sixth month with her, who was called barren. 37 For with יהוה nothing shall be impossible. 38 And Miryam said, See the female eved of the Master יהוה; be it to me according to Your word. And the heavenly messenger departed from her. 39 And Miryam arose in those days, and went into the hill country with speed, into a city of Yahudah; 40 And entered into the bayit of

Zacharyah, and greeted Elisheva. 41 And it came to pass, that, when Elisheva heard the greeting of Miryam, the baby leaped in her womb; and Elisheva was filled with the Ruach HaKodesh: 42 And she spoke out with a loud voice, and said, Blessed are you among women, and favored is the fruit of your womb. 43 And who am I that the ima of my Master should come to me? 44 For see, as soon as the voice of your greeting sounded in my ears, the baby leaped in my womb for simcha. 45 And favored is she that believed: for there shall be an accomplishing of those things that were told her from the Master יהוה. 46 And Miryam said, My being does magnify the Master יהוה, 47 And my ruach has rejoiced in Elohim My Savior.[3] 48 For He has regarded the low estate of His female eved: for, see, from now on all generations shall call me favored. 49 For He that is mighty has done to me great things; and set-apart is His Name. 50 And His rachamim is on them that fear Him from generation to generation. 51 He has showed strength with His Arm;[4] He has scattered the proud in the imagination of their levim. 52 He has put down the mighty from their seats, and exalted them of low degree. 53 He has filled the hungry with tov things; and the rich He has sent empty away. 54 He has helped His son Yisrael,[5] in remembrance of His rachamim; 55 As He spoke to our ahvot, to Avraham, and to his zera le-olam-va-ed. 56 And Miryam stayed with her about three months, and returned to her own bayit. 57 Now Elisheva's full time came that she should be delivered; and she brought forth a son. 58 And her neighbors and her cousins heard how יהוה had showed great rachamim upon her; and they rejoiced with her. 59 And it came to pass, that on the eighth day they came to brit milah the child; and they called him Zacharyah, after the name of his abba.[6] 60 And his ima

---

[1] Not the throne of Roman pontiffs.
[2] Yahshua rules over the House of Yisrael forever. This verse, among many others, shows that He came to renew Yisrael forever, and did not come to establish a separate entity apart from historic and physical Yisrael.
[3] Miryam, a sinner needs salvation.
[4] Metaphor for Yisrael's Moshiach.
[5] The nation of Yisrael is also the son of YHWH.
[6] In Yisrael male children are named at **brit milah** not at birth.

answered and said, Not so; but he shall be called Yochanan. 61 And they said to her, There is no one from your family that is called by this name. 62 And they made signs to his abba, how he would have him called. 63 And he asked for a writing tablet, and wrote, saying, His name is Yochanan. And they all marveled. 64 And his mouth was opened immediately, and his tongue loosed, and he spoke, and praised יהוה. 65 And fear came on all that dwelt round around them: and all these sayings were noised abroad throughout all the hill country of province of Yahudah. 66 And all they that heard them laid them up in their levim, saying, What manner of child shall this be! And the hand of the Master יהוה was with him. 67 And his abba Zacharyah was filled with the Ruach HaKodesh, and prophesied, saying, 68 Blessed be the Master יהוה Elohim of Yisrael; for He has visited and redeemed His people, 69 And has raised up a horn of salvation for us in the bayit of His eved David; 70 As He spoke by the mouth of His set-apart neviim, who have been since the olam hazeh began: 71 That we should be saved from our enemies, and from the hand of all that hate us; 72 To perform the rachamim promised to our ahvot, and to remember His set-apart covenant;[1] 73 The oath that He swore to our abba Avraham,[2] 74 That He would grant to us, that we being delivered out of the hand of our enemies might serve Him without fear, 75 In set-apartness and tzedakah before Him, all the days of our chayim. 76 And you, child, shall be called ha navi of El-Elyon: for you shall go before the face of the Master יהוה [3] to prepare His ways; 77 To give the knowledge of salvation to His people by the remission of their sins, 78 Through the tender rachamim of our

Elohim; by which the dayspring from on high has visited us, 79 To give Light to them that sit in darkness and in the shadow of death,[4] to guide our feet into the halacha of shalom. 80 And the child grew, and grew strong in ruach, and was in the deserts until the day of his open showing to Yisrael.

2 And it came to pass in those days, that there went out a decree from Caesar Augustus, that all the land [5] should be registered. 2 And this registration was first made when Quirinius was governor of Syria-Aram. 3 And all went to be registered, every one to his own city. 4 And Yoseph also went up from Galil, out of the city of Natzareth, into the province of Yahudah, to the city of David, which is called Beth-Lehem; because he was of the bayit and lineage of David: 5 To be registered with Miryam his engaged wife, being great with child. 6 And so it was, that, while they were there, the days were filled that she should give birth. 7 And she brought forth her firstborn Son, and wrapped Him in swaddling clothes,[6] and laid Him in a sukkah-feeding trough; because there was no room for them in the inn. 8 And there were in the same country shepherds abiding in the field, keeping watch over their flock by night. 9 And, see, the heavenly messenger of the Master יהוה came upon them, and the tifereth of יהוה shone around them: and they were greatly afraid. 10 And the heavenly messenger said to them, Fear not: for, see, I bring you tov news of great simcha, which shall be to all the people of Yisrael. 11 For to you is born this day in the city of David a Savior, which is the Moshiach the Master יהוה.[7] 12 And this shall be your sign; You shall find the baby wrapped in swaddling clothes, lying in a sukkah feeding trough. 13 And suddenly there was with the heavenly messenger a

---

[1] The Immerser and the Moshiach were coming to prepare Yisrael for the malchut, not to look for pagans to bring into Yisrael without any repentance.
[2] The blessings of Moshiach and physical multiplicity, which always are considered a single promise, that goes hand in hand.
[3] The Ruach HaKodesh speaking through Zachariah considered Yahshua to be the full manifestation of YHWH Himself.

[4] A clear reference to Moshiach's work among the northern tribes, as seen in Isaiah 9:1-3.
[5] Land of Yisrael.
[6] Menorah clothe strips used to light the menorah.
[7] As it literally appears in the Aramaic. Moshiach the Master YHWH or Mar-Yah.

multitude of the heavenly messengers praising יהוה, and saying, 14 Tifereth to יהוה in the highest, and on earth shalom, and tov among men, with whom He is pleased. 15 And it came to pass, as the heavenly messengers were gone away from them into the shamayim, the shepherds said one to another, Let us now go to Beth-Lechem, and see this thing which has come to pass, which the Master יהוה has made known to us. 16 And they came with speed, and found Miryam, and Yoseph, and the baby lying in a sukkah-feeding trough. 17 And when they had seen it, they made known abroad the saying which was told them concerning this child. 18 And all they that heard it marveled at those things which were told them by the shepherds. 19 But Miryam kept all these things, and pondered them in her lev. 20 And the shepherds returned, esteeming and praising יהוה for all the things that they had heard and seen, as it was told to them. 21 And when eight days were accomplished for the brit milah of the Child, His Name was called יהושע, which was so named by the heavenly messenger before He was conceived in the womb. 22 And when the days of her cleansing according to the Torah of Moshe were accomplished, they brought Him to Yahrushalayim, to present Him before the Master יהוה; 23 As it is written in the Torah of the Master יהוה, Every male that opens the womb shall be called set-apart to the Master יהוה; 24 And to offer a sacrifice according to that which is said in the Torah of the Master יהוה, A pair of turtledoves, or two young pigeons. 25 And, see, there was a man in Yahrushalayim, whose name was Shimeon; and the same man was just and devout, waiting for the comforting restoration of Yisrael: [1] and the Ruach HaKodesh was upon him. 26 And it was revealed to him by the Ruach HaKodesh, that he should not see death, before he had seen the Master יהוה's Moshiach. 27 And

he came by the Ruach into the Beit HaMikdash: and when the parents brought in the Child יהושע, to do for Him after the command of the Torah, 28 Then took he Him up in his arms, and blessed יהוה, and said, 29 יהוה, now allow Your eved depart in shalom, according to Your word: 30 For my eyes have seen Your salvation, 31 That You have prepared before the face of all peoples[2]; 32 A Light to unveil[3] the gentiles, and the tifereth of Your people Yisrael. [4] 33 And Yoseph and His ima marveled at those things that were spoken about Him. 34 And Shimeon blessed them, and said to Miryam His ima, See, this Child is set for the fall and rising[5] again of many in Yisrael; and for a sign which shall be spoken against; 35 And a sword shall pierce through your own being also, that the thoughts of many levim may be revealed. 36 And there was one Anna, a neviyah, the daughter of Phenu-El, of the tribe of Asher:[6] she was advanced in years, and had lived with a husband seven years from her virginity; 37 And she was a widow of about eighty-four years, who departed not from the Beit HaMikdash, but served יהוה with fastings and tefillot night and day. 38 And she coming in that instant gave hodu likewise to the Master יהוה, and spoke of Him to all them that looked for redemption in Yahrushalayim.[7] 39 And when they had performed all things according to the Torah of the Master יהוה, they returned into Galil, to their own city Natzareth. 40 And the Child grew, and became strong in Ruach, filled with chochmah: and the rachamim of יהוה was upon Him. 41 Now His parents went to Yahrushalayim every year at the moed of the Pesach. 42 And

---

[1] Further evidence that non-Jewish Yisrael or the 10 tribes had not been reunited with Yahudah after the Babylonian captivity.

[2] Ephraim Yisraelite nations or peoples.
[3] Unveil their blindness to Torah and their own lineage to Yaakov.
[4] In context Jewish Yisrael.
[5] Fall of Yahudah and rising of Ephraim, a clear cut prophesy of Moshiach's mission between both houses of Yisrael.
[6] Proof that some mixing or overlap occurred between the two houses.
[7] Interesting how her message of Yisrael's redemption, i.e. the end of the exile and return of all the tribes, was the same burden expressed by the same Ruach that moved Shimeon.

when He was twelve years old, they went up to Yahrushalayim for the moed. 43 And when they had fulfilled the days of Chag Matzoth, as they returned, the Child יהושע stayed behind in Yahrushalayim; and Yoseph and His ima did not know it. 44 But thinking He was in the company, they went a day's journey; and they sought Him among their relatives and acquaintances. 45 And when they found Him not, they turned back again to Yahrushalayim, seeking Him. 46 And it came to pass, that after three days they found Him in the Beit HaMikdash, sitting in the midst of the Torah teachers, both hearing them, and asking them questions. 47 And all that heard Him were astonished at His understanding and answers. 48 And when they saw Him, they were amazed: and His ima said to Him, Son, why have You dealt with us like this? See, Your abba and I have sought You anxiously. 49 And He said to them, *How is it that you sought Me? Did you not know that I must be about My Abba's business?* 50 And they understood not the saying that He spoke to them. 51 And He went down with them, and came to Natzareth, and was subject to them: but His ima kept all these sayings in her lev. 52 And יהושע increased in chochmah and stature, and in favor with יהוה and man.

3 Now in the fifteenth year of the reign of Tiberius Caesar, Pontius Pilate being governor of the province of Yahudah, and Herod being district ruler of Galil, and his brother Philip district ruler of Yetur and of the region of Trachonitis, and Lusanias the district ruler of Abilene, 2 Annas and Caiaphas being the High Kohanim, the word of יהוה came to Yochanan the son of Zacharyah in the wilderness. 3 And he came into all the country around Yarden, proclaiming the mikvah of teshuvah for the remission of sins; 4 As it is written in the scroll of the words of Yeshayahu ha navi, saying, The voice of one crying in the wilderness, Prepare the way of the Master יהוה, make His paths straight. 5 Every valley shall be filled, and every mountain and hill shall be brought low; and the crooked shall be made straight, and the rough ways shall be made smooth; 6 And all flesh shall see the salvation of יהוה. 7 Then said he to the multitude that came forth to be immersed by him, O generation of vipers, who has warned you to flee from the wrath to come? 8 Bring forth therefore fruits worthy of teshuvah, and begin not to say within yourselves, We have Avraham as our abba: for I say to you, That יהוה is able of these stones to raise up children to Avraham.[1] 9 And now also the axe is laid to the root of the trees: every tree therefore which brings not forth tov fruit is cut down, and thrown into the fire. 10 And the people asked him, saying, What shall we do then? 11 He answered and said to them, He that has two coats, let him impart to him that has none; and he that has food, let him do likewise. 12 Then came also tax collectors to be immersed, and said to him, Teacher, what shall we do? 13 And he said to them, take no more than that which is appointed to you. 14 And the soldiers likewise demanded of him, saying, And what shall we do? And he said to them, Do violence to no man, neither accuse any falsely; and be content with your wages. 15 And as the people were in expectation, and all men wondered in their levim about Yochanan, whether he were the Moshiach, or not; 16 Yochanan answered, saying to them all, I indeed mikvah you with mayim; but one mightier than I is coming, the straps of whose sandals I am not worthy to unloose: He shall mikvah you with the Ruach HaKodesh and with fire: 17 Whose winnowing fork is in His hand, and He will thoroughly purge His floor,[2] and will gather the wheat into His storehouse; but the chaff He will burn with fire unquenchable fire. 18 And many other things in his exhortation he

---

[1] This does not negate the two-bayit emet at all. Rather what is being proclaimed is that ethnic origin does not lead to a free pass to salvation. One must be born again.
[2] Yisrael.

proclaimed to the people. 19 But Herod the district ruler, being rebuked by him for Herodias his brother Philip's wife, and for all the evils which Herod had done, 20 Added this also to them, that he locked up Yochanan in prison. 21 Now when all the people were immersed, it came to pass, that יהושע also being immersed, and making tefillot, the shamayim were opened, 22 And the Ruach HaKodesh descended in a bodily shape like a yonah upon Him, and a voice came from the shamayim, which said, *You are My beloved Son; in You I am well pleased.* 23 And יהושע Himself began to be about thirty years of age, being (as was supposed) the Son of Yoseph, who was the son of Eli,[1] 24 Who was the son of Mattityahu, who was the son of Levi, who was the son of Meleki, who was the son of Yanna, who was the son of Yoseph, 25 Who was the son of Mattityahu, who was the son of Amos, who was the son of Nachum, who was the son of Hesli, who was the son of Nogah, 26 Who was the son of Maath, who was the son of Mattityahu, who was the son of Shimi, who was the son of Yoseph, who was the son of Yahudah, 27 Who was the son of Yochanan, who was the son of Rephayah, who was the son of Zeruvavel, who was the son of Shealtiel, who was the son of Neri, 28 Who was the son of Meleki, who was the son of Addi, who was the son of Qosam, who was the son of Elmodam, who was the son of Er, 29 Who was the son of Yehoshua, who was the son of Eliezer, who was the son of Yorim, who was the son of Mattityahu, who was the son of Levi, 30 Who was the son of Shimeon, who was the son of Yahudah, who was the son of Yoseph, who was the son of Yonan, who was the son of Elyakim, 31 Who was the son of Melea, who was the son of Menna, who was the son of Mattatha, who was the son of Nathan, who was the son of David,[2]

32 Who was the son of Yishai, who was the son of Oved, who was the son of Boaz, who was the son of Salmon, who was the son of Nachshon, 33 Who was the son of Aminadav, who was the son of Aram, who was the son of Hetsron, who was the son of Perets, who was the son of Yahudah, 34 Who was the son of Yaakov, who was the son of Yitzchak, who was the son of Avraham, who was the son of Terah, who was the son of Nachor, 35 Who was the son of Saruch, who was the son of Re-u, who was the son of Pheleg, who was the son of Ever, who was the son of Shela, 36 Who was the son of Qeynan, who was the son of Arpakshad, who was the son of Shem, who was the son of Noach, who was the son of Lamech, 37 Who was the son of Methushelach, who was the son of Hanoch, who was the son of Yared, who was the son of Mahala-el, who was the son of Qayin, 38 Who was the son of Enosh, who was the son of Sheth, who was the son of Adam, who was of Elohim.[3]

4 And יהושע being full of the Ruach HaKodesh returned from the Yarden, and was led by the Ruach into the wilderness, 2 Being forty days tested of the s.a.tan. And in those days He did eat nothing: and when they were ended, He afterward was hungry. 3 And the s.a.tan said to Him, If You are the Son of Elohim, command this stone that it be made lechem. 4 And יהושע answered him, saying, *It is written, That man shall not live by lechem alone, but by every word of* יהוה. 5 And the s.a.tan, taking Him up into a high mountain, showed Him all the malchutim of the olam hazeh in a moment of time. 6 And the s.a.tan said to Him, All this power will I give You, and the tifereth of them: for that is delivered to me; and to whomever I will, I give it. 7 If You therefore will worship me, all shall be Yours. 8 And יהושע

---

[1] Yoseph's genealogy; not Mary's as is commonly taught. For important insights study footnotes on Matthew chapter 1.
[2] All the lineage references before this verse proceeded from Nathan, David's son, through Eli, Joseph's father. This Joseph son of Eli, is a different Joseph than Joseph son of Jacob in Matthew 1:16. For important insights study footnotes on Matthew chapter 1.
[3] Peshitta.

answered and said to him, *Get behind Me, s.a.tan: for it is written, You shall worship* יהוה *Your Elohim, and Him only shall you serve.* 9 And he brought Him to Yahrushalayim, and set Him on a pinnacle of the Beit HaMikdash, and said to Him, If You are the Son of Elohim, cast yourself down from here: 10 For it is written, He shall give His heavenly messengers charge over You, to keep You: 11 And in their hands they shall bear You up, lest at any time You dash Your foot against a stone. *12* And יהושע answering said to him, *It is said, You shall not try the Master* יהוה *your Elohim.* 13 And when the s.a.tan had ended all the trial, he departed from Him for a while. 14 And יהושע returned in the power of the Ruach into Galil: and there was published His fame through all the regions all around.[1] 15 And He taught in their synagogues, being esteemed by all. 16 And He came to Natzareth, where He had been brought up: and, according to His practice, He went into the synagogue on Shabbat, and stood up to read. 17 And there was delivered to Him the scroll of ha navi Yeshayahu. And when He had opened the scroll, He found the place where it was written, 18 *The Ruach of the Master* יהוה *is upon Me, because He has anointed Me to proclaim the besarot to the poor; He has sent Me to heal the brokenhearted, to proclaim deliverance to the captives, and recovering of sight to the blind, to set at liberty those that are bruised,* [2] 19 *To proclaim the acceptable year of the Master* יהוה. 20 And He rolled up the scroll, and He gave it again to the shamash, and sat down. And the eyes of all of those that were in the synagogue were glued on Him. 21 And He began to say to them, *This day is this Katav fulfilled in your ears.*[3] 22 And all

bare Him witness, and wondered at the favorable words that proceeded out of His mouth. And they said, Is not this Moshiach Ben Yoseph?[4] 23 And He said to them, *You will surely say to Me this mishle, Physician, heal Yourself: whatever we have heard done in the city of Nachum, do also here in Your country.* 24 And He said, *Truly I say to you, No navi is accepted in his own country.* 25 *But I tell you the emet; many widows were in Beit Yisrael in the days of Eli-Yahu, when the shamayim were shut up three years and six months, when great famine was throughout all the land;*[5] 26 *But to none of them was Eli-Yahu sent, except to Tsarephath, a city of Tsidon, to a woman that was a widow.* 27 *And many lepers were in Beit Yisrael in the time of Elisha ha navi; and none of them was cleansed, except Naaman the Aramean.* 28 And all those in the synagogue, when they heard these things, were filled with wrath, 29 And rose up, and threw Him out of the city, and led Him to the brow of the hill on which their city was built, that they might cast Him down headlong.[6] 30 But He passing through the midst of them went His way,[7] 31 And came down to the city of Nachum, a city of Galil, and He taught them on the Shabbat. 32 And they were astonished at His teaching: for His word was with authority.

---

[4] In first-century understanding, the Moshiach would come in two persons – one to suffer and regather the ten lost tribes, and the other to reign on David's throne. The plain declaration here is that Yahshua is Joseph's stepson, but on the **remez** or hint understanding the question being raised in light of Yahshua's pronouncement of Isaiah 61 coming to fulfillment was: Is this man whom we knew as a boy really the Moshiach ben (or "son of") Yoseph, or the suffering Moshiach to die in a war (over evil) in order to return Yisrael's exiles?
[5] The House of Yisrael as seen in Old Syriac manuscript is telling. Rather than simply "Yisrael," Yahshua's pronouncement was that just as YHWH visited the widow woman from the House of Yisrael or ten tribes, and just as YHWH visited Naaman from the Aramens, among whom Ephraim mixed, He would come and rescue those same ten tribes and deliver them, using these two figures as examples of His mission as Moshiach ben Yosef. The response of brother Yahudah can be seen in verses 28-29.
[6] Sadly not much has changed. When Yahudah/Jewish Yisrael is confronted with the reality of his brother's return through Moshiach's favor, they choose either to ignore it, or get angry with those who are merely the messengers for the malchut.
[7] Regardless of the opponents of two-bayit restoration, they will not deter Yahshua who merely goes about His way shown Him by the Father.

---

[1] In the area of the northern tribes of Ephraim.
[2] The exiles of Yisrael who need spiritual sight, freedom from exile and sin, and a remarriage to their King. The concept here is one of liberty or yovel/jubilee for the exiles of the nation.
[3] The official announcement that Yisrael's nightmare of national exile was over and that the regathering process had begun; that very day in that very synagogue.

33 And in the synagogue there was a man, who had an unclean ruach of a shad, and cried out with a loud voice, 34 Saying, Leave us alone; what have we to do with You, יהושע of Natzareth? Have You come to destroy us? I know You who You are; the Set-Apart One of יהוה. 35 And יהושע rebuked him, saying, *Be silent, and come out of him.* And when the s.a.tan had thrown him in their midst, he came out of him, and hurt him not. 36 And they were all amazed, and spoke among themselves, saying, What a word is this! For with authority and power He commands the shadim, and they come out. 37 And His fame Him went out into every place of the country all around. [1] 38 And He arose out of the synagogue, and entered into Shimon's bayit. And Shimon's ima-in-law was taken with a great fever; and they asked Him concerning her. 39 And He stood over her, and rebuked the fever; and it left her: and immediately she stood and waited on them. 40 Now when the sun was setting, all they that had any sick with divers diseases brought them to Him; and He laid His hands on each one of them, and healed them. 41 And shadim also came out of many, crying out, and saying, You are the Moshiach the Son of Elohim. And He rebuking them allowed them not to speak: for they knew that He was The Moshiach. 42 And when it was day, He departed and went into a desert place: and the people sought Him, and came to Him, and tried to keep Him from leaving them. 43 And He said to them, *I must proclaim the malchut of* יהוה *to other cities*[2] *also: for that reason I am I sent.* 44 And He proclaimed in the synagogues of Galil.[3]

5 And it came to pass, that, as the people pressed upon Him to shema the word of יהוה, He stood by the lake of Gennesaret, 2 And saw two boats standing by the lake: but the fishermen were gone out of them, and were washing their nets.

3 And He entered into one of the boats, which was Shimon's, and asked that he would pull out a little from the land. And He sat down, and taught the people out of the ship.[4] 4 Now when He had ceased speaking, He said to Shimon, *Pull out into the deep, and let down your nets for a catch.* 5 And Shimon answering said to Him, Master, we have toiled all night, and have taken nothing: nevertheless at Your word I will let down the net. 6 And when they had this done, they caught a great multitude of fishes: and their net broke. 7 And they beckoned to their partners, who were in the other ship, that they should come to help them. And they came, and filled both the boats, so that they began to sink.[5] 8 When Shimon Kepha saw it, he fell down at יהושע's knees saying, Depart from me; for I am a sinful man, O Master. 9 For he was astonished, and all that were with Him, at the catch of the fishes which they had taken:[6] 10 And so was also Yaakov, and Yochanan, the sons of Zavdi, who were partners with Shimon. And יהושע said to Shimon, *Fear not; from now on you shall catch men.*[7] 11 And when they had brought their boats to land, they forsook all, and followed Him. 12 And it came to pass, when He was in a certain city, see a man full of leprosy: who seeing יהושע fell on his face, and asked Him, saying, Master, if You will, You can make me clean. 13 And He put forth His hand, and touched him, saying, *I will: be clean.* And immediately the leprosy departed from him. 14 And He ordered him to tell no man, *But go, and show yourself to the kohen, and offer for your cleansing, according as Moshe commanded, as a testimony to them.* 15 But

---

[1] The North.
[2] Of Yisrael.
[3] Territory of the ten tribes.

[4] Two ships are symbolic of Yahshua's calling to both houses with the tov news of the kingdom. Sitting in one boat symbolizes that His teaching will come to both houses from the bayit of Yahudah.
[5] Both houses sinking need rescue from Moshiach, since the olam hazeh is full of Yisraelite fish. The only thing lacking are more fishers of these men.
[6] When people discover the truth of Yisrael's multitudes, 4-5 billion strong, they are astonished, and can only worship the Melech.
[7] Men are Yisrael, as per Ezekiel 34:31.

all the more His fame went all around: and great multitudes[1] came together[2] to shema, and to be healed by Him of their infirmities. 16 And He withdrew Himself into the wilderness, and made tefillah. 17 And it came to pass on a certain day, as He was teaching, that there were Prushim and teachers of the Torah sitting by, who were come out of every town of Galil, and the province of Yahudah, and Yahrushalayim: and the power of the Master יהוה was present to heal them. 18 And, see, men brought in a bed a man who was taken with a paralysis: and they sought a means to bring him in, and to lay him before Him. 19 And when they could not find how they might bring him in because of the multitude, they went up to the roof, and let him down through the tiling with his pallet into the midst before יהושע. 20 And when He saw their emunah, He said to him, *Man, your sins are forgiven you.* 21 And the Sophrim and the Prushim began to reason, saying, Who is this who speaks blasphemies? Who can forgive sins, but Elohim alone? 22 But when יהושע perceived their thoughts, He answering said to them, *What are you reasoning in your levim? 23 Which is easier, to say, Your sins are forgiven you; or to say, Rise up and walk? 24 But that you may know that the Ben Adam has power upon earth to forgive sins,* (He said to the sick of the paralysis,) *I say to you, Arise, and take up your pallet, and go into your bayit.* 25 And immediately he rose up before them, and took up that on which he lay, and departed to his own bayit, esteeming יהוה . 26 And they were all amazed, and they esteemed יהוה, and were filled with fear, saying, We have seen strange things today. 27 And after these things He went forth, and saw a tax collector, named Levi, sitting at the tax office: and He said to him, *Follow Me.* 28 And he left all, rose up, and followed Him. 29 And Levi made Him a great

reception in his own bayit: and there was a great company of tax collectors and of others that sat down with them. 30 But the Sophrim and Prushim grumbled against His talmidim, saying, Why do You eat and drink with tax collectors and sinners? 31 And יהושע answering said to them, *They that are whole need not a physician; but they that are sick. 32 I came not to call the tzadikim, but sinners to teshuvah.* [3] 33 And they said to Him, Why do the talmidim of Yochanan fast often, and make tefillot, and likewise the talmidim of the Prushim; but yours eat and drink? 34 And He said to them, *Can you make the children of the Bridegroom fast, while the bridegroom is with them? 35 But the days will come, when the bridegroom shall be taken away from them, and then shall they fast in those days.* 36 And He spoke also a parable to them; *No man puts a piece of a new garment upon an old; otherwise the new one makes a tear, and also the piece that was taken out of the new one does not match the old. 37 And no man puts new wine into old wineskins; else the new wine will burst the wineskins, and be spilled, and the wineskins shall perish. 38 But new wine must be put into new wineskins; and both are preserved.* [4] *39 No man also having drunk old wine immediately desires new: for He said, The old is better.* [5]

6 And it came to pass on the second Shabbat after the first, that He went through the corn fields; and His talmidim plucked the ears of corn, and did eat, rubbing them in their hands. 2 And certain of the Prushim said to them, Why do You do that which is prohibited in Torah on the Shabbat? 3 And יהושע answering them said, *Have you not read so much as this, what David did, when he was hungry, and they who were with Him; 4 How he went*

---

[1] Multitudes of Ephraim.
[2] Were gathered.

[3] Sick wandering exiles.
[4] New wine of Yahshua's Torah teachings must be put into Renewed Covenant Yisrael, not merely physical Yisrael.
[5] New wine must be drunk along with old wine, not old wine alone. A reminder to those who want Moshiach's wine, without Moshiach.

into the Bayit of the Master יהוה, and did take and eat the Lechem of His Faces,[1] and gave also to those that were with Him; which it is not lawful to eat except for the kohanim alone?[2] 5 And He said to them, *Therefore the Ben Adam is Master also of the Shabbat.*[3] 6 And it came to pass also on another Shabbat, that He entered into the synagogue and taught: and there was a man whose right hand was withered. 7 And the Sophrim and Prushim watched Him, whether He would heal on the Shabbat; that they might find an accusation against Him. 8 But He knew their thoughts, and said to the man who had the withered hand, *Rise up, and stand forth in the midst.* And he arose and stood forth. 9 Then said יהושע to them, *I will ask you one thing; Is it lawful on the Shabbat to do tov, or to do evil? To save chayim, or to destroy it?*[4] 10 And looking all around upon them all, He said to the man, *Stretch forth your hand.* And he did so: and his hand was restored whole as the other. 11 And they were filled with bitterness; and discussed with each other what they might do to יהושע. 12 And it came to pass in those days, that He went out into a mountain to make tefillah, and continued all night in tefillah to יהוה. 13 And when it was day, He called to Himself His talmidim: and from them He chose twelve, whom also He named shlichim [5] 14 Shimon (whom He also named Kepha) and Andri his brother, Yaakov and Yochanan, Philip and Bartholomi, 15 Mattityahu and Toma, Yaakov the son of Alphai, and Shimon called Zealot, 16 And Yahudah the brother of Yaakov, and Yahudah from Qerioth, who also was the traitor. 17 And He came down with them, and stood in the plain, and the crowd of His talmidim, and a great multitude of people out of all the provinces of Yahudah and Yahrushalayim, and from the sea coast of Tsor and Tsidon, who came to shema Him, and to be healed of their diseases; 18 And they that were vexed with shadim: and they were healed. 19 And the whole multitude sought to touch Him: for there went power out of Him, and healed them all. 20 And He lifted up His eyes on His talmidim, and said, *Blessed are you poor: for yours is the malchut of* יהוה. *21 Blessed are you that hunger now: for you shall be filled. Blessed are you that weep now: for you shall laugh. 22 Blessed are you, when men shall hate you, and when they shall separate you from their company, and shall reproach you, and publish your names as evil, for the Ben Adam's sake. 23 Rejoice in that day, and leap for simcha: for, see, your reward is great in the shamayim: for in the like manner did their ahvot to the neviim. 24 But woe to you that are rich! For you have received your consolation. 25 Woe to you that are full! For you shall hunger. Woe to you that laugh now! For you shall mourn and weep. 26 Woe to you, when all men shall speak well of you! For so did their ahvot to the false neviim. 27 But I say to you who shema, Love your enemies, do tov to them who hate you, 28 Bless them that curse you, and make tefillah for them who despitefully use you. 29 And to him that smites you on one cheek offer also the other; and he that takes away your robe forbid him not to take your shirt also. 30 Give to every man that asks from you; and of him that takes away your goods do not ask them to return it. 31 And as you would desire that men should do to you, do also to them likewise. 32 For if you only love them who love you, what blessing have you? For sinners also ahava those that love them. 33 And if you only do tov to them who do tov to you, what blessing have you? For even sinners also do the same. 34 And if you lend to them from whom you hope to receive again, what*

---

[1] Showbread.
[2] See notes on Mark 2:26.
[3] Meaning He alone knows what constitutes a violation of Shabbat and would never engage in it.
[4] Yahshua has to reinforce the principle of **yeshuat nefesh,** or the saving of life, that overrides all laws and regulations. This is the heart of the Torah, and is what Yahshua is reintroducing to all Yisrael.
[5] One for each tribe of Yisrael, showing that the restoration of Yisrael is the tov news of the malchut.

blessing have you? For sinners also lend to sinners, to receive as much again. 35 But love you your enemies, and do tov, and lend, hoping for nothing in return; and your reward shall be great, and you shall be the children of El-Elyon: for He is kind to the thankless and to the evil. 36 Be therefore full of rachamim, as your Abba also is full of rachamim. 37 Judge not, and you shall not be judged: condemn not, and you shall not be condemned: forgive, and you shall be forgiven: 38 Give, and it shall be given to you; tov measure, pressed down, and shaken together, and running over, shall men give into your bosom. For with the same measure with which you measure it shall be measured back to you again. 39 And He spoke a parable to them, Can the blind lead the blind? Shall they not both fall into the ditch? 40 The talmid is not above His Master: but every one that is perfect shall be as His Master. 41 And why do you see the mote that is in your brother's eye, but perceive not the beam that is in your own eye? 42 Or how can you say to your brother, Brother, let me pull out the mote that is in your eye, when you yourself see not the beam that is in your own eye? You hypocrite, cast out first the beam out of your own eye, and then shall you see clearly to pull out the mote that is in your brother's eye. [1] 43 For a tov tree brings not forth corrupt fruit; neither does a corrupt tree bring forth tov fruit. 44 For every tree is known by its own fruit. For from thorns men do not gather figs, nor from a bramble bush do they gather grapes. 45 A tov man out of the tov treasure of his lev brings forth that which is tov; and an evil man out of the evil treasure of his lev brings forth that which is evil: for out of the abundance of the lev his mouth speaks. 46 And why do you call Me, Master, Master, and do not the things that I say? [2] 47 Whoever comes to Me, and hears My sayings, and does them, I will show you to whom he is like: [3] 48 He is like a man who built a bayit, and dug deep, and laid the foundation on a rock: and when the flood arose, the stream beat vehemently upon that bayit, and could not shake it: for it was founded upon a rock. [4] 49 But he that hears, and does not what I say, is like a man that built a bayit upon the earth without a foundation; against which the stream did beat vehemently, and immediately it fell; and the ruin of that bayit was great. [5]

7 Now when He had ended all His sayings in the audience of the people, He entered into the city of Nachum. 2 And a certain centurion's eved, who was dear to Him, was sick, and ready to die. 3 And when he heard of יהושע, he sent zachanim of the Yahudim, asking Him that He would come and heal his eved. 4 And when they came to יהושע, they asked Him immediately, saying, That he was worthy for whom He should do this: 5 For he loves our nation, and he has built us a synagogue. 6 Then יהושע went with them. And when He was now not far from the bayit, the centurion sent chaverim to Him, saying to Him, Master, trouble not yourself: for I am not worthy that You should enter under my roof: 7 Therefore neither thought I myself worthy to come to You: but just say Your word, and my eved shall be healed. 8 For I also am a man set under authority,[6] having under me soldiers, and I say to one, Go, and he goes; and to another, Come, and he comes; and to my eved, Do this, and he does it. 9 When יהושע heard these things, He marveled at him, and turned around, and said to the people that followed Him, I say to you, I have not found

---

[1] In the great return both houses need to walk in mercy, not holding one bayit better than the other or lifting one above the other, and not criticizing and finding fault with one bayit's errors and shortcomings without first seeing the sin and error in our own eyes or our own bayit. Both houses are in a time where splinters and beams are being removed through teaching, understanding, and mutual acceptance.

[2] Torah.
[3] Torah keepers.
[4] Redeemed Torah-observant Yisrael; the one united bayit set on Yahshua as King.
[5] Those who claim to be redeemed but do not perform the eternal commands of Torah.
[6] The centurion perceived well, that even Yahshua was under the Abba's authority, who remains the Greater YHWH.

so great emunah, no, not in Yisrael. [1]
10 And they that were sent, returning to the
bayit, found the eved whole that had been
sick. 11 And it came to pass the day after,
that He went into a city called Naim; and
many of His talmidim went with Him, and
many people. 12 Now when He came near
to the gate of the city, see, there was a dead
man carried out, the only son of his ima,
and she was a widow: and many people of
the city were with her. 13 And when
יהושע saw her, He had compassion on her,
and said to her, *Weep not.* 14 And He came
and touched the casket: and they that
carried him stood still. And He said, *Young
man, I say to you, Arise.* 15 And he that was
dead sat up, and began to speak. And He
delivered him to his ima. 16 And there
came a fear on all: and they esteemed יהוה,
saying, That a great Navi has risen up
among us; and, That Elohim has visited His
people. 17 And this news about Him went
forth throughout all the province of
Yahudah, and throughout the entire region
all around. 18 And the talmidim of
Yochanan showed him of all these things.
19 And Yochanan calling to him two of His
talmidim[2] sent them to יהושע, saying, Are
You He that should come? Or do we look
for another? 20 When the men were come
to Him, they said, Yochanan HaMatbeel has
sent us to You, saying, Are You He that
should come? Or should we look for
another?[3] 21 And in that same hour He
cured many of their infirmities and plagues,
and shadim; and to many that were blind He
gave them sight. [4] 22 Then יהושע
answering said to them, *Go your way, and
tell Yochanan what things you have seen
and heard; how that the blind see, the lame
walk, the lepers are cleansed, the deaf
shema, the dead are raised, and to the poor*

the besarot is proclaimed. 23 And favored is
he, whoever shall not be offended by Me. [5]
24 And when the messengers of Yochanan
had departed, He began to speak to the
people concerning Yochanan, *What went
you out into the wilderness to see? A reed
shaken with the wind? 25 But what went
you out for to see? A man clothed in soft
garments? See, those who are splendidly
dressed, and live delicately, are in
melechim's courts. 26 But what went you
out to see? A navi? Yes, I say to you, and
much more than a navi. 27 This is He, of
whom it is written, See, I send My
messenger before Your face, who shall
prepare Your way before You. 28 For I say
to you, Among those that are born of
women there is not a greater navi than
Yochanan the HaMatbeel: but he that is
least in the malchut of* יהוה *is greater than
he.* 29 And all the people that heard Him,
even the tax collectors, declared Elohim to
be Tzadik, being immersed by the mikvah
of Yochanan. 30 But the Prushim and
Torah-teachers rejected the counsel of יהוה
for themselves, not being immersed by him.
31 And יהושע said, *To what shall I liken
the men of this generation? And what are
they like? 32 They are like children sitting
in the marketplace, and calling one to
another, and saying, We have played the
flute for you, and you have not danced; we
have lamented for you, and you have not
wept. 33 For Yochanan the HaMatbeel
came neither eating lechem nor drinking
wine; and you say, He has a s.a.tan. 34 The
Ben Adam has come eating and drinking;
and you say, See a gluttonous man, and a
winedrinker, a chaver of tax collectors and
sinners! 35 But chochmah is justified by all
its works*[6]. 36 And one of the Prushim
desired that He would eat with him. And He
went into the Prush's bayit, and sat down to
eat. 37 And, see, a woman in the city, who

---

[1] Either the centurion was a true non-Yisraelite, or Yahshua
limited His remarks to the lack of emunah He found in Jewish
Yisrael.
[2] Representing both houses of Yisrael.
[3] Are you Moshiach ben/Son of Yosef or ben/Son of David?
The question was not: Are you the Moshiach? Rather, the
question was: Which one are you? The ruling One, or the
dying One?
[4] Answered by demonstration.

[5] My role to die and regather Yisrael.
[6] Aramaic Peshitta fits the text. Despite all the heavenly music
and repenting going on around them, the leaders of Jewish
Yisrael refused to hear, and as such their works showed their
true heart towards Moshiach.

was a sinner, when she knew that **יהושע** sat to eat in the Prush's bayit, brought an alabaster vase of oil, 38 And stood at His feet behind Him weeping, and began to wash His feet with tears, and did wipe them with the hairs of her head, and kissed His feet, and anointed them with the oil. 39 Now when the Prush who had invited Him saw it, he spoke to himself, saying, This Man, if He were a navi, would have known who and what manner of woman this is that touches Him: for she is a sinner. 40 And **יהושע** answering said to him, *Shimon, I have something to say to you.* And he said, Master, say it. 41 *There was a certain creditor who had two debtors: the one owed five hundred pence, and the other fifty. 42 And when they had nothing to pay, he forgave them both. Tell Me therefore, which of them will love him most?* [1] 43 Shimon answered and said, I suppose that he, to whom he forgave most. And He said to him, *You have rightly judged.* 44 And He turned to the woman, and said to Shimon, *See this woman? I entered into your bayit, you gave Me no mayim for My feet: but she has washed My feet with tears, and wiped them with the hairs of her head. 45 You gave Me no kiss: but this woman since the time I came in has not ceased to kiss My feet. 46 My head with oil you did not anoint: but this woman has anointed My feet with perfume. 47 Therefore I say to you, Her sins, which are many, are forgiven; for she loved much: but to whom little is forgiven, the same loves little.* 48 And He said to her, *Your sins are forgiven.* [2] 49 And they that sat at the table with Him began to say within themselves, Who is this that forgives sins also? 50 And He said to the woman, *Your emunah has saved you; go in shalom.*

8 And it came to pass afterward, that He went throughout every city and village, proclaiming and showing the besarot of the malchut of **יהוה**: and the twelve were with Him, 2 And certain women, who had been healed of shadim and infirmities, Miryam called Magdala, out of whom went seven shadim, 3 And Yochana the wife of Chuza Herod's manager, and Shoshanna, and many others, who attended to Him from their substance. 4 And when many people were gathered together, and had come to Him out of every city, He spoke by a parable: 5 *A sower went out to sow his zera: and as he sowed, some fell by the way side; and it was trodden down, and the fowls of the air devoured it. 6 And some fell upon a rock; and as soon as it sprung up, it withered away, because it lacked moisture. 7 And some fell among thorns; and the thorns sprang up with it, and choked it. 8 And some fell on tov ground, and sprang up, and produced fruit a hundredfold. And when He had said these things, He cried, He that has ears to shema let him shema.* 9 And His talmidim asked Him, What is this parable about? 10 And He said, *To you it is given to know the mysteries of the malchut of **יהוה**: but to others in parables; that seeing they might not see, and hearing they might not understand. 11 Now the parable is this: The seed is the word of **יהוה**. 12 Those by the way side are those that shema; then comes the s.a.tan, and takes away the word out of their levim, lest they should believe and be saved. 13 Those on the rock are those, who, when they shema, receive the word with simcha; and these have no root, which for a while believe, and in time of trial fall away. 14 And that which fell among thorns are they, who, when they have heard, go forth, and are choked with the cares and riches and pleasures of this chayim, and bring no fruit to perfection. 15 But that zera on the tov ground are those, who in an honest and tov lev, having heard the word, keep it, and bring forth fruit with patience. 16 No man, when he has lit a candle, covers it with a vessel, or puts it under a bed; but sets it on a menorah that those who enter in may see*

---

[1] A reference to both houses. Who will love Him the most in their return? The bayit that was the guiltiest. That applies to individuals as well.
[2] The woman is a type of forgiven Yisrael.

the light. 17 For nothing is secret that shall not be made manifest; neither any thing hid, that shall not be known and come abroad. [1] 18 *Be careful therefore how you shema: for whoever has, to him shall be given; and whoever has not, from him shall be taken even that which he seems to have.* 19 Then came to Him His ima and His brothers, and could not come to Him because of the crowd. 20 And it was told to Him by certain men who said, Your ima and Your brothers stand outside, desiring to see You. 21 And He answered and said to them*, My ima and My brothers are those who shema the word of* **יהוה***, and are doing it.*[2] 22 Now it came to pass on a certain day, that He went into a ship with His talmidim: and He said to them, *Let us go over to the other side of the lake.* And they set out. 23 But as they sailed He fell asleep: and there came down a storm of wind on the lake; and they were filled with mayim, and were in jeopardy. 24 And they came to Him, and awoke Him, saying, Master, Master, we perish. Then He arose, and rebuked the wind and the raging of the mayim: and they ceased, and there was a calm. 25 And He said to them*, Where is your emunah?* And they being afraid wondered, saying one to another, What manner of man is this; for He commands even the winds and mayim, and they obey Him? 26 And they arrived at the country of the Gadarenes, which is opposite Galil. 27 And when He went forth to land, there met Him out of the province a certain man, who had a shad a long time, and wore no clothes, neither stayed in any bayit, but in the tombs. 28 When he saw **יהושע**, he cried out, and fell down before Him, and with a loud voice said, What do we have in common, **יהושע**, Son of El-Elyon? I beg You, torment me not. 29 For He had commanded the shad to come out of the man. For often it had caught him: and he was kept bound with chains and in shackles;

and he broke the bands, and was driven by the shad into the wilderness. 30 And **יהושע** asked him, saying, *What is your name?* And he said, Legion: because many shadim were entered into him. 31 And they asked Him that He would not command them to go out into the bottomless pit. 32 And there was there a herd of many swine feeding on the mountain: and they asked Him that He would allow them to enter into them. And He allowed them. 33 Then went the shadim out of the man, and entered into the swine: and the herd ran violently down a steep place into the lake, and were choked. 34 When they that fed them saw what was done, they fled, and went and told it in the city and in the country. 35 Then they went out to see what was done; and came to **יהושע**, and found the man, out of whom the shadim had departed, sitting at the feet of **יהושע**, clothed, and in his right mind: and they were afraid. 36 They also which saw it told them by what means he that was possessed of the shadim was healed. 37 Then the whole multitude of the country of the Gadarenes all around asked Him to depart from them; for they were taken with great fear: and He went up into the ship, and returned back again. 38 Now the man out of whom the shadim were departed asked Him if he might stay with Him: but **יהושע** sent him away, saying, 39 *Return to your own bayit, and show how great things* **יהוה** *has done to you.* And he went his way, and published throughout the whole city how great things **יהושע** had done to him. [3] 40 And it came to pass, that, when **יהושע** returned, the people gladly received Him: for they were all waiting for Him. 41 And, see, there came a man named Yair, and he was a shamash of the synagogue: and he fell down at **יהושע**'s feet, and asked Him to come into his bayit: 42 For he had one only daughter, about twelve years of age, and she lay dying. But as He went the people

---

[1] The unveiling of the mystery of the ingathering of the exiles into the restored kingdom will be proclaimed abroad as a light to all nations.
[2] All Yisrael that hears and does the mitzvot.

[3] Notice YHWH and Yahshua are **echad**.

thronged Him.[1] 43 And a woman having an issue of dom twelve years, who had spent all her living upon physicians, neither could be healed by any,[2] 44 Came behind Him, and touched the tzitzit of His garment:[3] and immediately her issue of dom stopped. 45 And **יהושע** said, *Who touched Me?* When all denied it, Kepha and they that were with Him said, Master, the multitudes throng You and press You, and yet You ask, Who touched Me? 46 And **יהושע** said, *Somebody has touched Me: for I perceive that power has gone out of Me.* 47 And when the woman saw that she was not hidden,[4] she came trembling, and falling down before Him, she declared to Him before all the people the reason she had touched Him and how she was healed immediately. 48 And He said to her, *Daughter, be of tov comfort: your emunah has made you whole; go in shalom.*[5] 49 While He yet spoke, there came one from the shamash of the synagogue's bayit, saying to Him, Your daughter is dead; trouble not the Master.[6] 50 But when **יהושע** heard it, He answered him, saying, *Fear not: believe only, and she shall be made whole.*[7] 51 And when He came into the bayit, He allowed no man to go in, except Kepha, and Yaakov, and Yochanan, and the abba and the ima of the girl. 52 And all wept, and mourned her: but He said, *Weep not; she is not dead, but only sleeping.*[8] 53 And they laughed Him to scorn, knowing that she was dead. 54 And

He put them all out, and took her by the hand, and called, saying, *Young girl, arise.* 55 And her ruach returned, and she arose immediately: and He commanded them to give her something to eat. 56 And her parents were astonished: but He ordered them that they should tell no man what was done.

9 Then He called His twelve talmidim[9] together, and gave them power and authority over all shadim, and to cure diseases. 2 And He sent them to proclaim the malchut of **יהוה**, and to heal the sick. 3 And He said to them, *Take nothing for your journey, neither staffs, nor bags, neither lechem, neither money; neither have two coats apiece. 4 And whatever bayit you enter into, there abide, and then depart. 5 And whoever will not receive you, when you go out of that city, shake off the very dust from your feet for a witness against them.* 6 And they departed, and went through the towns, proclaiming the besarot, and healing everywhere. 7 Now Herod the district ruler heard about all that was done by Him: and he was perplexed, because that it was said by some, that Yochanan was risen from the dead; 8 And by some, that Eli-Yahu had appeared; and by others, that one of the old neviim had risen again. 9 And Herod said, Yochanan have I beheaded: but who is this, of whom I shema such things? And he desired to see Him. 10 And the shlichim, when they had returned, told Him all that they had done. And He took them, and went aside privately into a desert place belonging to the city called Beth-Saida. 11 And the people, when they knew it, followed Him: and He received them, and spoke to them of the malchut of **יהוה**, and healed them that had need of healing. 12 And when the day began to wane, then came the twelve, and said to Him, Send the multitude away, that they may go into the towns and country all around, and lodge, and get food: for we are

---

[1] Twelve years old. The number "12" showing that this girl is a type of Yisrael, with all her 12 tribes, dying unless the Moshiach intervenes.
[2] See note on Matthew 9:20. A woman bleeding was considered unfit and unclean in Torah.
[3] Malachi 4:2.
[4] The unveiling of the sick woman with an issue of dom, to be healed by Moshiach's power to restore and heal all 12 tribes. This is the tov news of the malchut.
[5] Yisrael's national healing is found in bowing the knee to Moshiach.
[6] The two women are a type of the two houses of Yisrael. While one is healed, the other lies dead. The living but ill one is Yahudah; and the dead one is Ephraim. But when Yahshua finishes His work of atonement, the dead resurrected husband (Yahshua) will bring life and healing to both of Yisrael's daughters.
[7] See note for Luke 8:42.
[8] Yisrael's problem was and remains not merely death, but spiritual slumber regarding the times of her redemption.

[9] For the 12 tribes.

here in a desert place. 13 But He said to them, *You give them to eat.* And they said, We have only five loaves and two fishes;[1] unless we go and buy food for all this people. 14 For there were about five thousand men. And He said to His talmidim, *Make them sit down by fifties in a company.*[2] 15 And they did so, and made them all sit down. 16 Then He took the five loaves and the two fishes, and looking up to the shamayim, He said the bracha, and broke them, and gave to the talmidim to set before the multitude.[3] 17 And they did eat, and were all filled: and there was taken up from the fragments that remained to them twelve baskets.[4] 18 And it came to pass, as He was alone making tefillot, His talmidim were with Him: and He asked them, saying, *Who do the people say that I am?* 19 They answering said, Yochanan HaMatbeel; but some say, Eli-Yahu; and others say, that one of the old neviim has risen again. 20 He said to them, *But who do you say that I am?* Kepha answering said, The Moshiach of יהוה. 21 And He strictly ordered them, and commanded them to tell this to no man. 22 Saying, *The Ben Adam must suffer many things, and be rejected by the zachanim and chief kohanim and Sophrim, and be killed, and be raised the third day.* 23 And He said to them all, *If any man will come after Me, let him deny himself, and take up his execution stake daily, and follow Me. 24 For whoever will save his chayim shall lose it: but whoever will lose his chayim for My sake, the same shall save it. 25 For what is a man advantaged, if he gains the whole olam hazeh, and loses himself, or be thrown away? 26 For whoever shall be ashamed of Me and of My words, of him shall the Ben Adam be ashamed, when He shall come with the tifereth of His Abba,* accompanied by the set-apart heavenly messengers. *27 But I tell you the emet, there be some standing here, who shall not taste of death, until they see the malchut of* יהוה. 28 And it came to pass about eight days after these sayings, He took Kepha and Yochanan and Yaakov, and went up into a mountain to make tefillah. 29 And as He made tefillah, the appearance of His countenance was altered, and His garment was white and dazzling. 30 And, see, there talked with Him two men, who were Moshe and Eli-Yahu: 31 Who appeared in ti!ereth, and spoke of His death that He would accomplish at Yahrushalayim. 32 But Kepha and they that were with Him were heavy with sleep: and when they awoke, they saw His tifereth, and the two men that stood with Him. 33 And it came to pass, as they departed from Him, Kepha said to יהושע, Master, it is tov for us to be here: and let us make three sukkot; one for You, and one for Moshe, and one for Eli-Yahu: not knowing what he said. 34 While He spoke, there came a cloud, and overshadowed them: and they feared as they entered into the cloud. 35 And there came a voice out of the cloud, saying, *This is My beloved Son: shema Him.*[5] 36 And when the voice was past, יהושע was found alone. And they kept it quiet, and told no man in those days any of those things that they had seen. 37 And it came to pass, that on the next day, when they were come down from the mountain, many people met Him.

38 And, see, a man of the company cried out, saying, Master, I beg You, look upon my son: for he is my only child. 39 And, see, a ruach seizes him, and he suddenly cries out; and it convulses him with foaming, and it hardly departs from him bruising him. 40 And I asked Your talmidim to cast it out; and they could not. 41 And יהושע answering said, *O unbelieving and perverse generation, how long shall I be with you, and put up with you? Bring your son here.* 42 And as He

---

[1] That's enough manna. Five loaves represent all five books of Torah, and the two fishes represent both houses of the multitudes of Yisrael, who will be fed Torah by the Moshiach.
[2] In order for both houses to receive **yovel**, or jubilee, from slavery to exile and sin.
[3] YHWH uses people to bring restoration and work His purposes in the earth.
[4] See note on Matthew 14:20.

[5] See notes on Mark 9:5, Matthew 17:1.4.5.

was coming, the shad threw him down, and tore at him. And יהושע rebuked the shad, and healed the child, and delivered him again to his abba. 43 And they were all amazed at the mighty power of יהוה. But while they all marveled every one at all the things that יהושע did, He said to His talmidim, 44 *Let these sayings sink down into your ears: for the Ben Adam shall be delivered into the hands of men.* 45 But they understood not this saying, and it was hidden from them, that they perceived it not: and they feared to ask Him about that saying. 46 Then there arose a dispute among them, which of them should be greatest. 47 And יהושע , perceiving the thoughts of their levim, took a child, and set him by His side, 48 And said to them, *Whoever shall receive this child in My Name receives Me: and whoever shall receive Me receives Him that sent Me: for he that is least among you all, the same shall be great.* 49 And Yochanan answered and said, Master, we saw one casting out shadim in Your Name; and we rebuked him, because he is not with us as Your follower. 50 And יהושע said to him, *Forbid him not: for he that is not against us is for us.* 51 And it came to pass, when the time had come that He should be offered up, He prepared His face to go to Yahrushalayim, 52 And sent messengers before His face: and they went, and entered into a village of the Shomronites, to make ready for Him.[1] 53 And they did not receive Him, because His face was directed though He would go to Yahrushalayim. [2] 54 And when His talmidim Yaakov and Yochanan saw this, they said, Master, will You that we command fire to come down from the shamayim, and consume them, even as Eli-Yahu did? 55 But He turned, and rebuked them, and said, *You know not what manner of ruach you are of.* 56 *For the Ben Adam*

has not come to destroy men's lives, but to save them. And they went to another village. 57 And it came to pass, that, as they went in the way, a certain man said to Him, Master, I will follow You wherever You go. 58 And יהושע said to him, *Foxes have holes, and birds of the air have nests; but the Ben Adam has nowhere to lay His head.* 59 And He said to another, *Follow Me.* But he said, Master, allow me first to go and bury my abba. 60 יהושע said to him, *Let the dead bury their dead: but you go and proclaim the malchut of יהוה.* 61 And another also said, Master, I will follow You; but let me first entrust my home to someone and then come.[3] 62 And יהושע said to him, *No man, having put his hand to the plough, and looking back, is fit for the malchut of יהוה.*

10 After these things He appointed seventy others,[4] and sent them two by two before His face into every city and place, where He Himself would come. 2 Therefore said He to them, *The harvest truly is great, but the laborers are few: make tefillah therefore the Master of the harvest, that He would send forth laborers into His harvest. 3 Go your ways: see, I send you forth as lambs among wolves.[5] 4 Carry neither purse, nor bag, nor sandals: and greet no man along the way. 5 And into whatever bayit you enter, first say, Shalom to this bayit. 6 And if the son of shalom is there, your shalom shall rest upon it: if not, it shall return to you again. 7 And in the same bayit remain, eating and drinking such things as they give you: for the laborer is worthy of his wages. Go not from bayit to bayit.[6] 8 And into whatever city you enter, and they receive you, eat such things as are set before you: 9 And heal the sick that are there, and say to them, The malchut of יהוה has come near to you.*

---

[1] Samaritans were Ephraimites as seen in John 4 and in historical records. See: **Tov or Bad Samaritan** at: http://store.yourarmstoisrael.org/Qstore/Qstore.cgi?CMD=011&PROD=000158.
[2] Samaritans didn't like Jews either, and we see the hatred between the two houses on display.

[3] Aramaic Peshitta.
[4] Perhaps a Sanhedrin for those in the exile.
[5] Lambs are Yisrael; wolves are pagans.
[6] Stay in and among the visible people of Yisrael for now, before going to the nations.

10 *But into whatever city you enter, and they receive you not, go out into the streets, and say,* 11 *Even the very dust of your city, which cleaves on us, we do wipe off against you: notwithstanding be you sure of this, that the malchut of* יהוה *is offered to you.*[1] 12 *But I say to you, that it shall be more tolerable in that day for Sedom, than for that city.* 13 *Woe to you, Chorazin! woe to you, Beth-Saida! For if the mighty works had been done in Tsor and Tsidon, which have been done in you, they would have a great while ago made teshuvah, sitting in sackcloth and ashes.* 14 *But it shall be more tolerable for Tsor and Tsidon at the Yom HaDin, than for you.*[2] 15 *And you, the city of Nachum that is exalted to the shamayim shall be thrown down to Sheol.* 16 *He that hears you hears Me; and he that despises you despises Me; and he that despises Me despises Him that sent Me.* 17 And the seventy returned again with simcha, saying, Master, even the shadim were subject to us through Your Name. 18 And He said to them, *I beheld s.a.tan as lightning fall from the shamayim.* 19 *See, I give to you power to tread on serpents and scorpions, and over all the power of the enemy: and nothing shall by any means hurt you.* 20 *But rejoice not, that the shadim are subject to you; but rather rejoice, because your names are written in the shamayim.*[3] 21 In that hour יהושע rejoiced in His ruach, and said, *I thank You, O Abba, Sovereign of the shamayim and earth, that You have hid these things from the wise and prudent, and have revealed them to babes: even so, Abba; for so it seemed tov in Your sight* 22 *All things are delivered to Me by My Abba: and no man knows who the Son is, but the Abba; and who the Abba is, but the Son, and he to whom the Son wishes to reveal Him.* 23 And He turned to His talmidim, and said privately, *Blessed are*

the eyes which see the things that you see: 24 *For I tell you, that many neviim and melechim have desired to see those things which you see, and have not seen them; and to shema those things which you shema, and have not heard them.*[4] 25 And, see, a certain Torah teacher stood up, and tested Him, saying, Master, what shall I do to inherit eternal chayim? 26 He said to Him, *What is written in the Torah? How do you read it?* 27 And he answering said, You shall love the Master יהוה Your Elohim with all your lev, and with all your being, and with all your strength, and with all your mind; and your neighbor as yourself. 28 And He said to him, *You have answered right: these do, and you shall live.* 29 But he, willing to justify himself, said to יהושע, And who is my neighbor? 30 And יהושע answering said, *A certain man went down from Yahrushalayim to Yericho, and fell among thieves, who stripped him of his garment, and wounded him, and departed, leaving him half dead.* 31 *And by chance there came down a certain kohen that way: and when he saw him, he passed by on the other side.* 32 *And likewise a Levite, when he was at the place, came and looked at him, and passed by on the other side.* 33 *But a certain Shomronite, as he journeyed, came to where he was: and when he saw him, he had compassion on him,* 34 *And went to him, and bound up his wounds, pouring in oil and wine, and set him on his own beast, and brought him to an inn, and took care of him.* 35 *And in the morning when he departed, he took out two pieces of silver, and gave them to the innkeeper, and said to him, Take care of him; and whatever more you spend, when I come again, I will repay you.* 36 *Which of these three, do you think, was a neighbor to him that fell victim among the thieves?* 37 And he said, He that showed rachamim to him. Then said יהושע to him, *Go, and do likewise.*

---

[1] Aramaic **krubat**, an offered near event or thing.
[2] Former Phoenician coastline where many Ephraimites migrated. Yahshua compares Ephraim's state of teshuvah with Yahudah's ongoing pride.
[3] Lamb's Book of Life.
[4] A clear reference to the prophets of Yisrael and their ancient desire for all Yisrael to be redeemed; also for the exile and captivity of both houses to be brought to an end in the full restoration of David's Tabernacle.

38 Now it came to pass, as they went, that He entered into a certain village: and a certain woman named Martha received Him into her bayit. 39 And she had a sister called Miryam, who also sat at יהושע's feet, and heard His word. 40 But Martha was occupied with much serving, and came to Him, and said, Master, don't You care that my sister has left me to serve alone? Speak to her therefore that she help me. 41 And יהושע answered and said to her, *Martha, Martha, you are worried and troubled about many things:* 42 *But one thing is required: and Miryam has chosen that tov part, which shall not be taken away from her.*

11 And it came to pass, that, as He was making tefillot in a certain place, when He ceased, one of His talmidim said to Him, Master, teach us to make tefillah, as Yochanan also taught His talmidim. 2 And He said to them, *When you make tefillah, say, Our Abba who are in the shamayim, Set-Apart be Your Name. Your malchut come. Your ratzon be done, as in the shamayim, also in the earth.*[1] 3 *Give us day by day our daily lechem.* 4 *And forgive us our sins; for we also forgive every one that is indebted to us. And lead us not into trial; but deliver us from the wicked one.* 5 And He said to them, *Which of you shall have a chaver, and shall go to him at midnight, and say to him, Chaver, lend me three loaves;* 6 *For a chaver of mine in his journey has come to me, and I have nothing to set before him?* 7 *And he from within shall answer and say, Trouble me not: the door is now shut, and my children are with me in bed; I cannot rise and give you.* 8 *I say to you, if he will not rise and give him because he is his chaver, yet because of his persistence he will rise and give him as much as he needs.* 9 *And I say to you, Ask, and it shall be given you; seek, and you shall find; knock, and it shall be opened to*

you. 10 *For every one that asks receives; and he that seeks finds; and to him that knocks it shall be opened.* 11 *If a son shall ask lechem from any of you that is an abba, will he give him a stone? Or if he asks for a fish, will he for a fish give him a serpent?* 12 *Or if he shall ask for an egg, will he offer him a scorpion?* 13 *If you then, being evil, know how to give tov gifts to your children: how much more shall your Heavenly Abba give the Ruach HaKodesh to them that ask Him?* 14 And He was casting out a shad, and it was dumb. And it came to pass, when the shad was gone out, the dumb spoke; and the people wondered. 15 But some of them said, He casts out shadim through Baal-Zevuv the chief of the shadim. 16 And others, testing Him, sought from Him a sign from the shamayim. 17 But He, knowing their thoughts, said to them, *Every malchut divided against itself is brought to desolation; and a bayit divided against a bayit falls*[2]. 18 *If s.a.tan also were divided against himself, how shall his malchut stand? Because you say that I cast out shadim through Baal-Zevuv.* 19 *And if I by Baal-Zevuv cast out shadim, by whom do your sons cast them out? Therefore shall they be your shophtim.* 20 *But if I with the finger of* יהוה *cast out shadim no doubt the malchut of* יהוה *is offered to you.* 21 *When a strong-armed man keeps his palace, his goods are safe:* 22 *But when a stronger one than he shall come upon him, and overcome him, he takes from him all his armor in which he trusted, and divides his spoils.* 23 *He that is not with Me is against Me: and he that gathers not with Me scatters.*[3] 24 *When the unclean ruach is gone out of a man, he walks through dry places, seeking rest; and finding none, he said, I will return to my bayit where I came from.* 25 And when he is

---

[1] The **kadesh**. A prayer for the coming restored malchut to all Yisrael, as the earthly Yahrushalayim becomes free like the Yahrushalayaim above.

[2] See note on: Mark 3:25. Also note the exact wording "bayit against a bayit". Two-bayit reference.
[3] People will either gather Yisrael or scatter her anew. Both houses must work together on His agenda, not their own kingdom.

coming, he finds it swept and garnished.
26 Then he goes, and takes with him seven
other shadim more wicked than himself;
and they enter in, and dwell there: and the
last state of that man is worse than the first.
27 And it came to pass, as He spoke these
things, a certain woman of the company
lifted up her voice, and said to Him, Blessed
is the womb that bore You, and the breasts
which You have sucked. 28 But He said,
Yes rather, favored are they that shema the
word of יהוה, *and guard it.* 29 And when
the people were gathered thick together, He
began to say, *This is an evil generation:*
they seek a sign; and there shall no sign be
given it, but the sign of Yonah ha navi.
30 For as Yonah was a sign to the
Ninevites, so also shall the Ben Adam be to
this generation. 31 The queen of the south
shall rise up in the Yom HaDin with the
men of this generation, and condemn them:
for she came from the ends of the earth to
shema the chochmah of Shlomo; and, see, a
greater than Shlomo is here. 32 The men of
Nineveh shall rise up in the Yom HaDin
with this generation, and shall condemn it:
for they repented at the proclaiming of
Yonah; and, see, a greater than Yonah is
here. 33 No man, when he has lit a candle,
puts it in a secret place, neither under a
bushel, but on a menorah, that those who
come in may see the light. 34 The light of
the body is the eye: therefore when your eye
is single, your whole body also is full of
light; but when your eye is sick, your body
also is full of darkness. [1] *35 Take heed*
therefore that the light that is in you be not
darkness. 36 If your whole body therefore
be full of light, having no part dark, the
whole shall be full of light, as when the
bright shining of a candle does give you
light. [2] 37 And as He spoke, a certain Prush
asked Him to dine with him: and He went
in, and sat down to eat. 38 And when the

Prush saw it, he marveled that He had not
first washed before dinner. 39 And יהושע
said to him, *Now do you Prushim make*
clean the outside of the cup and the platter;
but your inward part is full of greed and
wickedness. 40 You fools, did not He that
made that which is on the outside make that
which is within also? 41 But rather give
kindness of such things as you have within;
and, see, all things are clean to you. 42 But
woe to you, Prushim! For you tithe mint
and rue and all manner of herbs, and pass
over mishpatim and the ahava of יהוה:
these you should have done, and not to
leave the others undone. 43 Woe to you,
Prushim! For you love the uppermost seats
in the synagogues, and greetings in the
markets. 44 Woe to you, Sophrim and
Prushim, hypocrites! For you are as graves
that are not seen, and the men that walk
over them are not aware of them. 45 Then
answered one of the Torah teachers, and
said to Him, Master, with this saying You
insulted us also.[3] 46 And He said, *Woe to*
you also, you Torah teachers! For you load
men[4] with burdens hard to bear, and you
yourselves touch not the burdens with one
of your fingers. 47 Woe to you! For you
build the tombs of the neviim, and your
ahvot killed them. 48 Truly you bear witness
that you allow the deeds of your ahvot: for
they indeed killed them, and you built their
tombs. 49 Therefore also said the chochmah
of Elohim, I will send them neviim and
shlichim, and some of them they shall slay
and persecute: 50 That the dom of all the
neviim that was shed from the foundation of
the olam hazeh may be required of this
generation; 51 From the dom of Abel to the
dom of Zacharyah, who perished between
the altar and the Beit HaMikdash: truly I
say to you, It shall be required of this
generation. 52 Woe to you, Torah teachers!
For you have taken away the key of

---

[1] Stingy people don't have the necessary receptivity to
malchut things. Financial greed is a tov indicator of a state of
mind, which is not fully open to the things of the malchut.
[2] YHWH expects His children to be generous with others,
especially so in extending rachamim and compassion, which
is the lev of the Torah.

[3] A man called to Yisrael's restoration cannot worry about
people's responses or reactions.
[4] Men in Scripture are almost always a veiled reference to
Yisrael, the men of His pasture. These leaders were
preventing the restoration of the malchut, by rejecting the offer
of the malchut as well as its King.

knowledge:[1] you entered not in yourselves, and them that were entering in you hindered. 53 And as He said these things to them, the Sophrim and the Prushim began to oppose Him vehemently, and to provoke Him to speak on many subjects: 54 Laying in wait for Him, and seeking to catch something out of His mouth, that they might accuse Him.

12 In the meantime, when there were gathered together an innumerable multitude of people, so that they trampled one another, He began to say to His talmidim first, *Beware of the chametz of the Prushim, which is hypocrisy. 2 For there is nothing covered that shall not be revealed; neither hidden, that shall not be known. 3 Therefore whatever you have spoken in darkness shall be heard in the light; and that which you have spoken in the ear in inner rooms shall be proclaimed upon the housetops. 4 And I say to you My chaverim, Be not afraid of them that kill the body, and after that have no more that they can do. 5 But I will show you whom you shall fear: Fear Him, which after He has killed has power to thrown into Gei-Hinnom; yes, I say to you, Fear Him. 6 Are not five sparrows sold for two copper coins, and not one of them is forgotten before* יהוה? *7 But even the very hairs of your head are all numbered. Fear not therefore: you are of more value than many sparrows. 8 Also I say to you, Whoever shall confess Me before men, Him shall the Ben Adam also confess before the heavenly messengers of* יהי: *9 But he that denies Me before men shall be denied before the heavenly messengers of* יהי. *10 And whoever shall speak a word against the Ben Adam, it shall be forgiven him: but to him that blasphemes against the Ruach HaKodesh it shall not be forgiven. 11 And when they bring you to the synagogues, and to rulers, and authorities, take no thought how or what thing you shall answer, or what*

you shall say: 12 For the Ruach HaKodesh shall teach you in the same hour what you ought to say. 13 And one of the company said to Him, Master, speak to my brother, that he divide the inheritance with me. 14 And He said to him, Man, who made Me a shophet or a divider over you?[2] 15 And He said to them, Take heed, and beware of greed: for a man's chayim consists not in the abundance of the things that he possesses. 16 And He spoke a parable to them, saying, The ground of a certain rich man brought forth plentifully: 17 And he thought within himself, saying, What shall I do, because I have no room where to store my fruits? 18 And he said, This will I do: I will pull down my barns, and build larger ones; and there will I store all my fruits and my goods. 19 And I will say to my being, Being, you have much goods laid up for many years; take it easy, eat, drink, and be celebrate. 20 But יהוה *said to him, You fool, this night your being shall be required from you: then whose shall those things be, which you have prepared? 21 So is he that lays up treasure for himself, and is not rich toward* יהי.[3] *22 And He said to His talmidim, Therefore I say to you, Take no thought for your chayim, what you shall eat; neither for the body, what you shall put on. 23 Your chayim is more than food, and your body is more than a garment. 24 Consider the ravens: for they neither sow nor reap; which neither have storehouses nor barns; and* יהוה *feeds them: how much more are you better than the fowls? 25 And which of you by worrying can add to his height one cubit? 26 If you then are not able to do the thing that is least, why worry about the rest? 27 Consider the lilies how they grow: they toil not, they spin not; and yet I say to you, that Shlomo in all his tifereth was not dressed like one of these. 28 If then* יהוה *so clothe the grass, which today is in the field, and tomorrow is thrown into the oven; how*

---

[1] The key is the Name of salvation Yahshua or YHWH saves. Without the Name of YHWH the door does not open (Acts 4:12).

[2] Like Yahshua, we who are serious about restoration ought to avoid worldly entanglements that are not absolutely essential.
[3] Yisraelites must be building the kingdom of Yisrael, not bigger barns, symbolic of bigger plans for, of, and by self.

much more will He clothe you, O you of little trust? 29 And seek not what you shall eat, or what you shall drink, neither keep worrying. 30 For all these things do the gentiles of the olam hazeh seek after: and your Abba knows that you have need of these things.[1] 31 But rather seek the malchut of **יהוה**; and all these things shall be added to you. 32 Fear not, little flock;[2] for it is your Abba's tov pleasure to give you the malchut. 33 Sell what you have, and give in kindness; provide yourselves bags which grow not old, a treasure in the shamayim that fails not, where no thief approaches, neither moth corrupts. 34 For where your treasure is, there will your lev be also. 35 Let your loins be bound, and your lights burning; 36 And you yourselves like men[3] that wait for their Master, when He will return from the wedding; that when He is coming and knocks, they may open to Him immediately. 37 Blessed are those avadim, whom the Master when He is coming shall find watching: truly I say to you, that He shall gird himself, and make them to sit down to eat, and will go around and serve them. 38 And if He shall come in the second watch, or come in the third watch, and find them watching, favored are those avadim. 39 And this know, that if the owner of the bayit had known what hour the thief would come, he would have watched, and not have allowed his bayit to be broken into. 40 Be you therefore ready also: for the Ben Adam is coming at an hour when you think not. 41 Then Kepha said to Him, Master, are You speaking this parable to us, or even to everyone? 42 And **יהושע** said, Who then is that faithful and wise steward, whom His Master shall make ruler over His household, to give them their portion of food in due season? 43 Blessed is that eved, whom His Master when He comes shall find so doing. 44 Of an emet I say to you, that He will make

him ruler over all that He has. 45 But if that eved says in his lev, My Master delays His coming; and shall begin to beat the male avadim and female avadim, and to eat and drink, and to be drunk; 46 The Master of that eved will come in a day when he looks not for Him, and at an hour when he is not aware, and will cut him in two, and will appoint him his portion with the unbelievers. 47 And that eved, who knew His master's will, and did not prepare himself, neither did according to His will, shall be beaten with many stripes. 48 But he that knew not, and did commit things worthy of stripes, shall be beaten with few stripes. For to whom much is given, of him shall be much required: and to whom men have committed much, of him they will ask the most. 49 I am come to send fire on the earth; and how I wish that it be already kindled?[4] 50 But I have a mikvah to be immersed with; and how am I greatly afflicted until it be accomplished! 51 Do you think that I am come to give shalom on earth? I tell you, No; but rather division: 52 For from now on there shall be five in one bayit divided, three against two, and two against three. 53 The abba shall be divided against the son, and the son against the abba; the ima against the daughter, and the daughter against the ima; the ima-in-law against her daughter-in-law, and the daughter-in-law against her ima-in-law. [5] 54 And He said also to the people, When you see a cloud rise out of the west, immediately you say, There is coming a shower; and so it is. 55 And when you see the south wind blow, you say, There will be heat; and it comes to pass. 56 You hypocrites, you can discern the face of the sky and of the earth; but how is it that you do not discern this time? 57 Yes, and why even yourselves you shophet not what is right? 58 When you go with your adversary to the ruler, as you are in the way, give

---

[1] Yisraelite believers are not gentiles. There is no such thing as saved gentiles.
[2] The redeemed remnant from both houses is referred to here as a small "called out" flock. Remnant Yisrael, as opposed to all of physical Yisrael will be a very small remnant.
[3] Like a Yisraelite.

[4] He was sent to purify and cleanse the earth.
[5] His claim to be YHWH's Son will cause great division in the bayit. What bayit? The people of Yisrael will be greatly divided, as well as each family unit within Yisrael.

diligence that you may be delivered from him; lest he drag you to the shophet, and the shophet deliver you to the officer, and the officer cast you into prison. 59 *I tell you, you shall not depart from there, until you have paid the very last coin.*

13 There were present at that season some that told Him of the Galilaeans, whose dom Pilate had mingled with their sacrifices. 2 And **יהושע** answering said to them, *Do you think that these Galilaeans were sinners above all the Galilaeans, because they suffered such things? 3 I tell you, No: but, except you make teshuvah, you shall all likewise perish.*[1] *4 Or those eighteen, upon whom the tower in Siloam fell, and killed them, do you think that they were sinners above all men that dwelt in Yahrushalayim? 5 I tell you, No: but, except you make teshuvah, you shall all likewise perish. 6 He spoke also this parable; A certain man had a fig tree*[2] *planted in his vineyard; and he came and sought fruit on it, and found none. 7 Then he said to the dresser of his vineyard, See, these three years I came seeking fruit on this fig tree, and found none: cut it down; why should the ground be wasted? 8 And he answering said to him, Master, leave it alone this year again, until I shall dig around it, and cast manure on it: 9 And if it bears fruit, well: and if not, then after that You shall cut it down.*[3] 10 And He was teaching in one of the synagogues on the Shabbat. 11 And, see, there was a woman who had a ruach of infirmity eighteen years, and was bent over, and could in no way lift herself up. 12 And when **יהושע** saw her, He called her to Him, and said to her, *Woman, you are loosed from yours infirmity.* 13 And He laid His hands on her: and immediately she was made straight, and esteemed **יהוה**. 14 And the Rabbi of the synagogue answered with indignation, because **יהושע** had healed

on the Shabbat, and said to the people, There are six days in which men ought to work: in them therefore come and be healed, and not on the Shabbat. 15 **יהושע** then answered him, and said, *You hypocrite, does not each one of you on the Shabbat loose his ox or his donkey from the stall, and lead him away to watering? 16 And should not this woman, being a daughter of Avraham, whom s.a.tan has bound, see, these eighteen years, be set free from this bond on the Shabbat?*[4] 17 And when He had said these things, all His adversaries were ashamed: and the entire nation had gilah for all the wonderful things that were done by Him. 18 Then He said, *To what is the malchut of* **יהוה** *like? And to what shall I compare it? 19 It is like a grain of mustard seed, which a man took, and threw into his garden; and it grew, and grew into a great tree; and the fowls of the air lodged in the branches of it.*[5] 20 And again He said, *To what shall I liken the malchut of* **יהוה**? *21 It is like leaven, which a woman took and hid in three measures of meal, until the whole was leavened.*[6] 22 And He went through the cities and villages, teaching, and journeying toward Yahrushalayim. 23 Then someone said one to Him, Master, are there few that will be saved? And He said to them, *24 Strive to enter in at the narrow gate: for many,*[7] *I say to you, will seek to enter in, and shall not be able. 25 Once the Master of the bayit is risen up, and has shut the door, and you begin to stand outside, and to knock on the door, saying, Master, Master, open to us; and He shall answer and say to you, I know you not where you are from: 26 Then shall you begin to say, We ate and drank in your presence, and You have*

---

[1] Yahudites as well as Ephraimites must repent from sin, to prevent a second death of perishing in the Lake of Fire.
[2] The secondary symbol of the nation of Yisrael, following the Olive Tree, both making up YHWH's vineyard.
[3] YHWH's patience with all Yisrael.

[4] The woman is a type of Yisrael, with 18 being the number of life or **chayim**; meaning when Yisrael meets Yahshua, all things are made straight as said in Isaiah chapter 40.
[5] A parable of Renewed Covenant Yisrael's growth in accordance with physical multiplicity, so that it contains both spirit-born and spiritually dead members. Fowls represent shadim and falsehoods.
[6] See note on Matthew 13:33.
[7] Many from the multitudes of Yisrael.

taught in our streets. 27 *But He shall say, I tell you, I know you not where you are from; depart from Me, all you workers of Torah-less-ness.*[1] 28 *There shall be weeping and gnashing of teeth, when you shall see Avraham, and Yitzchak, and Yaakov, and all the neviim, in the malchut of* יהוה, *and you yourselves thrown out.*[2] 29 *And they shall come from the east, and from the west, and from the north, and from the south, and shall sit down in the malchut of* יהוה.[3] 30 *And, see, there are last which shall be first, and there are first which shall be last.*[4] 31 The same day there came certain of the Prushim, saying to Him, Get going, and depart from here: for Herod will kill You. 32 And he said to them, *You go, and tell that fox, See, I cast out shadim, and I do cures today and tomorrow, and the third day I shall be finished. 33 Nevertheless I must walk today, and tomorrow, and the day following: for it cannot be that a navi perishes outside of Yahrushalayim. 34 O Yahrushalayim, Yahrushalayim, which kills the neviim, and stones them that are sent to you; how often would I have gathered your children together, as a hen does gather*[5] *her chicks under her wings, and you O Yisrael did not want it! 35 See, your Beit Yisrael is left to you desolate: and truly I say to you, You shall not see Me, until the time come when you shall say, baruch habah beshem HaAdon* יהוה.[6]

14 And it came to pass, as He went into the bayit of one of the chief Prushim to eat lechem on the Shabbat, that they watched Him. 2 And, see, there was a certain man before Him who had the dropsy. 3 And יהושע answering spoke to the Torah teachers and Prushim, saying, *Is it permitted in Torah to heal on the Shabbat?* 4 And they held their silence. And He took him, and healed him, and let him go; 5 And answered them, saying, *Which of you shall have a donkey or an ox fall into a pit, and will not immediately pull him out on the Shabbat day?* 6 And they could not answer Him about these things. 7 And He put forth a parable to those who were invited, when He noted how they chose out the best places at moadim; saying to them, 8 *When you are invited by any man to a wedding, do not sit down in the best place; lest he invite a more honorable man than you; 9 And he that invited both of you comes and says to you, Give this man the best place; and you begin with shame to take the last place. 10 But when you are invited, go and sit down in the last place; that when he that invited you comes, he may say to you, Chaver, go up higher: then shall you have honor in the presence of those that sit at the moed with you. 11 For whoever exalts himself shall be humbled; and he that humbles himself shall be exalted.* 12 Then he said he also to the one that invited Him, *When you make a dinner or a supper, call not your chaverim, nor your brothers, neither your relatives, nor your rich neighbors; lest they also invite you again, and a repayment be made to you. 13 But when you observe a moed, call the poor, the maimed, the lame, and the blind:*[7] 14 *And you shall be favored; for they cannot repay you: for you shall be repaid at the resurrection of the just.* 15 And when one of them that was reclining with Him, heard these things, he said to Him, Blessed is he that shall eat lechem in the malchut of יהוה 16 Then He said to him, *A certain man*

---

[1] Without Torah obedience, Yahshua will not recognize one's service, or the spirit under which that person operates.
[2] Notice that all of the Hebrew patriarchs and by implication matriarchs, will be there so this is not a rejection of Yisrael. Rather it is a rejection of one generation of leaders, who willfully rejected Him.
[3] In contrast to the Jewish leaders of that generation, the reference here is to the return of the exiles of Yisrael from the four corners of the earth to which they were scattered. Four-corner references, such as Isaiah 11:12 and Jeremiah 31:8, always refer to Yisrael alone and her return in the last days through Moshiach. These verses then are not a removal of the malchut from Yisrael, but rather an expansion of the malchut to all Yisrael, even those at the earth's four corners, that is Ephraim Yisrael.
[4] Role reversal of the two houses. Ephraim enters before Yahudah, who fully enters at the Second Advent.
[5] Gathering Yisrael. The true and primary mission of Moshiach.
[6] Rather than gather Yisrael at that time, the bayit would remain divided and therefore desolate of unity and immediate healing.

[7] When a Biblical feast is celebrated.

made a great supper, and invited many:
17 And sent his eved at supper time to say
to them that were invited, Come; for all
things are now ready. 18 And they all began
making excuses. The first said to him, I have
bought a piece of property, and I must go
and see it: I ask you have me excused.
19 And another said, I have bought five
yoke of oxen, and I go to try them out: I ask
you have me excused. 20 And another said,
I have married a wife, and therefore I
cannot come.[1] 21 So that eved came, and
showed His Master these things. Then the
Master of the bayit being angry said to his
eved, Go out quickly into the streets and
lanes of the city, and bring in here the poor,
and the crippled, the lame, and the blind.[2]
22 And the eved said, Master, it is done as
you have commanded, and yet there is still
room. 23 And the Master said to the eved,
Go out into the highways and hedges, and
compel them to come in, that My bayit may
be filled.[3] 24 For I say to you, That none of
those men who were invited shall taste of
My supper. [4] 25 And there went great
multitudes with Him: and He turned, and
said to them, 26 If any man come to Me,
and hate not his abba, and ima, and wife,
and children, and brothers, and sisters, yes,
and his own chayim also, he cannot be My
talmid. [5] 27 And whoever does not bear his
execution stake, and come after Me, cannot
be My talmid. 28 For which of you,
intending to build a tower, sits not down
first, and counts the cost, whether he has
sufficient supplies to finish it?
29 Otherwise, after he has laid the
foundation, and is not able to finish it, all
that see it begin to mock him, 30 Saying,
This man began to build, and was not able

to finish.[6] 31 Or what melech, going to
make war against another melech, sits not
down first, and consults whether he is able
with ten thousand to meet him that is
coming against him with twenty thousand?
32 If not, while the other is yet a great way
off, he sends a delegation, and desires
conditions of shalom. 33 So likewise, any of
you that forsakes not all that he has, he
cannot be My talmid. 34 Salt is tov: but if
the salt becomes tasteless, with what shall it
be seasoned?[7] 35 It is neither fit for the
land[8], nor yet for the dunghill; but men[9]
cast it out. He that has ears to shema let
him shema.

15

Then drew near to Him all the tax
collectors and sinners to shema
Him. 2 And the Prushim and Sophrim
grumbled, saying, This Man receives
sinners, and eats with them. 3 And He
spoke this parable to them, saying, 4 What
man among you, having a hundred sheep, if
he loses one of them, does not leave the
ninety and nine in the wilderness, and go
after that which is lost, until he finds it?[10]
5 And when he has found it, he lays it on
his shoulders, rejoicing.[11] 6 And when he is
coming home, he calls together his
chaverim and neighbors, saying to them,
Rejoice with me; for I have found My sheep
that was lost. 7 I say to you, that likewise
simcha shall be in the shamayim over one
sinner that repents, more than over ninety-
nine tzadikim, who need no teshuvah. 8 Or
what women having ten pieces of silver, if
she loses one piece, does not light a candle,
and sweep the bayit,[12] and seek diligently
until she finds it?[13] 9 And when she has
found it, she calls her chaverim and her

---

[1] Yahudah's many excuses regarding why Yahshua, cannot
be the promised King.
[2] The global call to Ephraim.
[3] Non-biological Yisraelites, who become redeemed Yisrael by
invitation.
[4] First-century Jewish leaders.
[5] **Kal VaChomer**. If you love your family, how much more
should you love Me? This is not a signal to hate physical
family.

[6] Those who fall away after an initial expression of trust, like
those who have fallen prey to the anti-Yahshua missionaries
and who now are mocked as those who are dazed and
confused, and as those without endurance.
[7] See note on Mark 9:50.
[8] Of Yisrael.
[9] Other Yisraelites.
[10] The one is a type of Ephraim.
[11] The heart of Moshiach in returning the exiles to the fold.
[12] Of Yisrael.
[13] A reference to the ten tribes and their rediscovery.

neighbors together, saying, Rejoice with me; for I have found the piece that I had lost. [1] 10 Likewise, I say to you, there is simcha in the presence of the heavenly messengers of יהוה over one sinner that repents. 11 And He said, A certain man had two sons:[2] 12 And the younger of them said to his abba, Abba, give me the portion of goods that belongs to me. And he divided to them his living. 13 And not many days after the younger son gathered all things together, and took his journey into a far country,[3] and there wasted his substance with riotous living. 14 And when he had spent all, there arose a mighty famine in that land; and he began to be in want. 15 And he went and joined himself to a citizen of that country; and he sent him into his fields to feed swine. 16 And he was longing to fill his belly with the pods that the swine did eat: and no man gave to him. 17 And when he came to himself, he said, How many hired avadim of my abba's have lechem enough and to spare, and I perish with hunger! 18 I will arise and go to my abba, and will say to him, Abba, I have sinned against the shamayim, and before you, 19 And am no more worthy to be called your son: make me as one of your hired avadim. [4] 20 And he arose, and came to his abba. But when he was yet a great way off, his abba saw him, and had compassion, and ran, and fell on his neck, and kissed him.[5] 21 And the son said to him, Abba, I have sinned against the shamayim, and in your sight, and am no more worthy to be called your son. 22 But the abba said to his avadim, Bring forth the best robe, and put it on him; and put a ring on his hand, and shoes on his feet: 23 And bring here the

fatted calf, and kill it; and let us eat, and celebrate: 24 For this my son was dead, and is alive again; he was lost, and is found. And they began to be celebrate. [6] 25 Now his elder son[7] was in the field: and as he came and drew near to the bayit, he heard music and dancing. 26 And he called one of the avadim, and asked what these things meant.[8] 27 And he said to him, Your brother is come; and your abba has killed the fatted calf, because he has received him safe and sound. 28 And he was angry, and would not go in: therefore his abba came out, and pleaded with him. [9] 29 And he answering said to his abba, See, these many years do I serve you, neither transgressed I at any time your commandment:[10] and yet you never gave me a goat, that I might celebrate with my chaverim: 30 But as soon as this your son[11] was come, who has devoured your living with harlots, you have killed for him the fatted calf. 31 And he said to him, Son, you are always with Me, and all that I have is yours. 32 It was right that we should celebrate, and be in simcha: for this your brother was dead, and is alive again; and was lost, and is found. [12]

16 And He said also to His talmidim, There was a certain rich man, who had a steward; and the same steward was accused of wasting his wealth. 2 And he called him, and said to him, How is it that I shema this about you? Give an account of your stewardship; for you may no longer be steward. 3 Then the steward said to himself, What shall I do? For my master takes away from me the stewardship: I cannot dig; to beg I am ashamed. 4 I know what to do, so that, when I am put out of the stewardship,

---

[1] The proper attitude of the woman; a type of a righteous Yisraelite, towards the return of anyone from the ten tribes.
[2] This parable is all about the two biological sons of the Abba YHWH, Yahudah and Ephraim, and displays how Yahudah should not react to Ephraim's return, as opposed to the correct reaction outlined earlier in verses 1-10.
[3] In scripture Ephraim Yisrael are those referred to as far off, or far away from Jerusalem, in such places as Ephesians 2:13,17 and Daniel 9:7.
[4] Ephraim's true repentance and confession.
[5] Abba YHWH's reaction to Ephraim's return.

[6] Rejoicing at Ephraim's return in the Abba's House.
[7] Yahudah.
[8] Many in Judah have always had a problem with understanding what Ephraim's return really meant.
[9] Yahudah's typical initial reaction to Ephraim's return from the nations. This reaction is still prevalent today.
[10] Upheld Torah.
[11] Notice the reaction of Yahudah; "your son," not "my brother." He refuses to recognize Ephraim as a brother, seeing him rather as a pagan who betrayed YHWH, and remains a pig farmer.
[12] The Father's commentary on family reunion.

they may receive me into their houses. 5 So he called every one of his master's debtors to him, and said to the first, How much do you owe my master? 6 And he said, A hundred measures of oil. And he said to him, Take your bill, and sit down quickly, and write fifty. 7 Then said he to another, And how much do you owe you? And he said, A hundred measures of wheat. And he said to him, Take your bill, and write eighty. 8 And the master commended the unjust steward, because he had done wisely: for the children of this olam hazeh are in their generation wiser than the children of light.[1] 9 And I say to you, Make for yourselves chaverim of the mammon of unrighteousness; that, when you fail, they may receive you into everlasting dwellings. [2] 10 He that is faithful in that which is least is faithful also in much: and he that is unjust in the least is unjust also in much. 11 If therefore you have not been faithful in the unrighteous mammon, who will commit to your trust the emet riches?[3] 12 And if you have not been faithful in that which is another man's, who shall give you that which is your own? 13 No eved can serve two masters: for either he will hate the one, and love the other; or else he will hold to the one, and despise the other. You cannot serve יהוה and wealth. 14 And the Prushim also, who were covetous, heard all these things: and they ridiculed Him. 15 And He said to them, You are they which justify yourselves before men; but יהוה knows your levim: for that which is highly esteemed among men is abomination in the sight of יהוה.[4] 16 The Torah and the neviim

were concerning Yochanan:[5] since that time the malchut of יהוה is proclaimed, and every man presses into it. 17 And it is easier for the shamayim and earth to pass, than one letter of the Torah to fail. 18 Whoever puts away his wife, and marries another, commits adultery: and whoever marries her that is put away from her husband commits adultery. 19 There was a certain rich man, which was clothed in purple and fine linen, and fared very well every day:[6] 20 And there was a certain beggar named El-Azar, who was laid at his gate, full of sores, 21 Desiring to be fed with the crumbs that fell from the rich man's table: moreover the dogs came and licked his sores. 22 And it came to pass, that the beggar died, and was carried by the heavenly messengers into Avraham's Bosom: the rich man also died, and was buried; 23 And in Sheol he lifts up his eyes, being in torment, and saw Avraham far off, and El-Azar in his bosom. 24 And he cried and said, Abba Avraham, have rachamim on me, and send El-Azar, that he may dip the tip of his finger in mayim, and cool my tongue; for I am tormented in this flame. 25 But Avraham said, Son, remember that you in your lifetime received your tov things, and likewise El-Azar evil things: but now he is comforted, and you are tormented. 26 And beside all this, between us and you there is a great gulf fixed: so that those who would pass from here to you cannot; neither can they pass to us that would come from there.[7] 27 Then he said, I ask you therefore, abba Avraham that you would send him to my abba's bayit: 28 For I have five brothers; that he may testify to them,

[1] A stern rebuke that shows how worldly children of s.a.tan are more shrewd in money matters than Yisraelites, who ought to be the best stewards around, since they are full of the Ruach's wisdom and discernment. Yet due to this lack of financial shrewdness, the majority of Yisraelites wrongly believe that asking for money for the malchut is begging or carnal. In this fault, Yahshua shines His light by teaching us that we have much to learn from the children of darkness, when it comes to funding YHWH's will in the earth.
[2] A sarcastic addendum that though we can learn from the world, we cannot go to the carnal for everlasting life and blissful eternal dwelling. That can only be given by Yahshua.
[3] A key position in the kingdom of Moshiach.
[4] Putting greed before YHWH.
[5] See note on Matthew 11:13.
[6] This is not a parable, but a real afterlife account. In a parable, names are not used. Here they are; so we should see this as a true account of the afterlife.
[7] Abraham's bosom was the abode of the righteous before Moshiach. When Moshiach came, He emptied Abraham's Bosom and took the spirits (not bodies) of the trusting to heaven. Today the believer's spirit is righteous and according to Hebrews 11, joins the patriarchs and matriarchs in heaven waiting for the resurrection of the last day. For details see: **What Happens When A Messianic Believer Dies?** http://yourarmstoisrael.org/Articles_new/articles/?page=what_happens_when_a_messianic_be&type=6.

lest they also come into this place of torment. 29 Avraham said to him, They have Moshe Rabainu and the neviim; let them shema them. 30 And he said, No, Abba Avraham: but if one went to them from the dead, they will make teshuvah. 31 And he said to him, If they shema not to Moshe Rabainu and the neviim, neither will they be persuaded, though one rose from the dead. [1]

17 Then said He to the talmidim, *It is impossible that offences will not come: but woe to him, through whom they come!* 2 *It were better for him that a millstone were hung around his neck, and he was thrown into the sea rather, than that he should offend one of these little ones.* 3 *Take heed to yourselves: If your brother trespasses against you, rebuke him; and if he makes teshuvah, forgive him.* 4 *And if he trespasses against you seven times in a day, and seven times in a day turn again to you, saying, I make teshuvah; you shall forgive him.* [2] 5 And the shlichim said to יהושע, Increase our emunah. 6 And יהושע said, *If you had emunah as a grain of mustard seed, you might say to this mulberry tree, Be plucked up by the root, and be planted in the sea; and it should obey you.* [3] [4] 7 *But which of you, having an eved plowing or feeding cattle, will say to him immediately, when he is come from the field, Go and sit down to eat?* 8 *But would you not rather say to him, Make ready for my supper, and dress yourself, and serve me, until I have eaten and drank? and afterward you shall eat and drink?* 9 *Does he thank that eved because he did the things that were commanded him? I think not.* 10 *So likewise you, when you shall have done all those things that are commanded you, say, We*

are unworthy avadim: we have done only that which was our duty to do. 11 And it came to pass, as He went to Yahrushalayim that He passed through the midst of Shomron and Galil. [5] 12 And as He entered into a certain village, there He met ten men [6] that were lepers, who stood far off: [7] 13 And they lifted up their voices, and said, יהושע, Master, have rachamim on us. [8] 14 And when He saw them, He said to them, *Go show yourselves to the kohanim.* And it came to pass, that, as they went, they were cleansed. [9] 15 And one of them, when he saw that he was healed, turned back, and with a loud voice esteemed יהוה, 16 And fell down on his face at His feet, giving Him hodu: and he was a Shomronite. 17 And יהושע answering said, *Were there not ten cleansed? But where are the nine?* 18 *There are not found any that returned to give tifereth to יהוה, except this stranger.* [10] 19 And He said to him, *Arise, go your way: your emunah has made you whole.* [11] 20 And the Prushim demanded to know, when the malchut of יהוה should come, He answered them and said, *The malchut of יהוה is not coming with observation:* 21 *Neither shall they say, See here! or, see there! For, see, the malchut of יהוה is within you.* [12] 22 And He said to the talmidim, *The days will come, when you shall desire to see one of the days of the Ben Adam, and you shall not see it.* 23 *And they shall say to you, See here; or, see there: go not after them, nor follow them.* 24 *For as*

---

[1] The Torah speaks of Moshiach; and if they won't believe the witness of the author Moshe, they won't believe even though Yahshua rises.
[2] Behavior in Yisrael.
[3] The issue is not how great our emunah is, but how big our YHWH is, since even a tiny seed of emunah moves him.
[4] The **remez** or hint is that our emunah in the message of the kingdom is likened unto the trees of tzedakah or Yisrael, planted in the sea of nations; and with our emunah we find them and plant them in Torah, even while they wander in the nations.

[5] The north or land of Ephraim where Shomron was the capital.
[6] Ten men are the ten tribes of non-Jewish Yisrael. They are lepers, as leprosy is likened unto an ongoing state of ritual uncleanness, since Ephraim became unclean in the nations as gentiles.
[7] Far off. A catch term or scriptural euphemism for the ten tribes who were far off from Yisrael and Torah.
[8] The voice of Ephraim in their return to Yisrael.
[9] Yahshua, instructs the ten tribes, in their return to perform Torah, which is what they were doing when they became cleansed.
[10] While YHWH is calling all ten tribes to return in **teshuvah**, only a remnant from Ephraim Yisrael will answer that call, while others receive the blessings of Moshiach, but won't return in full obedience and thanksgiving.
[11] Only a full return through Yahshua leads to complete wholeness.
[12] It starts with an inward desire. Inward desire leads to entry. This does not mean that the malchut won't manifest on earth.

the lightning, that flashes out from one part under the shamayim, and shines to the other part under the shamayim; so shall also the Ben Adam be in His day. 25 But first He must suffer many things, and be rejected by this generation. 26 And as it was in the days of Noach, so shall it be also in the days of the Ben Adam. 27 They did eat, they drank, they married wives, they were given in marriage, until the day that Noach entered into the ark, and the flood came, and destroyed them all. 28 Likewise also as it was in the days of Lot; they did eat, they drank, they bought, they sold, they planted, they built; 29 But the same day that Lot went out of Sedom it rained fire and brimstone from the Master **יהוה** from the shamayim, and destroyed them all. ¹ 30 Even so shall it be in the day when the Ben Adam is revealed. 31 In that day, he who shall be upon the housetop, with his belongings in the bayit, let him not come down to take it away: and he that is in the field, let him likewise not return back. 32 Remember Lot's wife. 33 Whoever shall seek to save his chayim shall lose it; and whoever shall lose his chayim shall preserve it. 34 I tell you, in that night there shall be two men in one bed; the one shall be taken, and the other shall be left. 35 Two women shall be grinding together; the one shall be taken, and the other left. 36 Two men shall be in the field; the one shall be taken, and the other left. 37 And they answered and said to Him, Where, Master? And He said to them, Wherever the body is, there will the eagles be gathered together.²

18 And He spoke a parable to them to this end, that men ought always to make tefillah, and not to faint; 2 Saying, There was in a city a shophet, who feared not **יהוה**, neither regarded man:³ 3 And there was a widow in that city; and she came to him, saying, Do right to me regarding my adversary. 4 And he would not for a while: but afterward he said to himself, Though I fear not Elohim, nor regard man; 5 Yet because this widow troubles me, I will avenge her, lest by her continual coming she wears me out. 6 And **יהושע** said, Shema what the unjust shophet said. 7 And shall not **יהוה** do tov to His own elect, who cry day and night to Him, though He bear long with them? 8 I tell you that He will do tov them speedily. Nevertheless when the Ben Adam comes, shall He find emunah in the earth?⁴ 9 And He spoke this parable to certain people who trusted in themselves that they were tzadik, and despised others: 10 Two men went up into the Beit HaMikdash to make tefillah; the one a Prush, and the other a tax collector. 11 The Prush stood and made tefillah within himself, Elohim, I thank You, that I am not as other men are, extortionists, unjust, adulterers, or even as this tax collector. 12 I fast twice in the week, I give tithes of all that I possess. 13 And the tax collector, standing far off, would not lift up so much as his eyes to the shamayim, but smote his breast, saying, Elohim be merciful to me a sinner. 14 I tell you, this man went down to his bayit justified rather than the other: for every one that exalts himself shall be humbled; and he that humbles himself shall be exalted. ⁵ 15 And they brought to Him also infants, that He would touch them: but when His talmidim saw it, they rebuked them. 16 But

---

¹ Judgment came the same day that the righteous were sealed and protected, and in like manner shall be the return of Moshiach. There will not be any interval between the sealing and protection of the righteous, and the coming of judgment, as pre-tribulation rapture theology teaches.
² It is clear from this verse and the comparison to Noach's days, that the ones "taken away" are not the saved but the lost. If there was any doubt, this verse seals it, as the talmidim asked where will those "taken away" go, and what will be their end. Yahshua, answers them by telling them that those "taken away" will go to the vultures for food and judgment. As Yisrael, you ought to pray to be left behind.

³ Yisraelite Torah justice.
⁴ True Torah-based trust in Moshiach.
⁵ The Prush represents Yahudah, and the "far off" tax collector represents the heathen Ephraimites. If Ephraim humbles himself, he can and will return in full acceptance by the Father. Yahudah, on the other hand, must also show this attitude of repentance and change or they will be like the one who has the right liturgy in prayer, but does not return to the Commonwealth of Yisrael justified by Moshiach.

יהושע called them to Him, and said, *Allow the little children to come to Me, and forbid them not: for of such is the malchut of* יהוה. 17 *Truly I say to you, Whoever shall not receive the malchut of* יהוה *as a little child shall in no way enter there.* 18 And a certain ruler asked Him, saying, Tov Master, what shall I do to inherit eternal chayim? 19 And יהושע said to him, *Why do you call Me tov? No one is tov, except One, that is,* יהוה.[1] 20 *You know the commandments, Do not commit adultery, Do not kill, Do not steal, Do not bear false witness, Honor your abba and your ima.* 21 And he said, All these have I kept from my youth up. 22 Now when יהושע heard these things, He said to him, *Yet you lack one thing: sell all that you have, and distribute to the poor, and you shall have treasure in the shamayim: and come, follow Me.* 23 And when he heard this, he was very sorrowful: for he was very rich. 24 And when יהושע saw that he was very sorrowful, He said, *How hardly shall they that have riches enter into the malchut of* יהוה. 25 *For it is easier for a large rope*[2] *to go through a needle's eye, than for a rich man to enter into the malchut of* יהוה. 26 And they that heard it said, Who then can be saved? 27 And He said, *The things, which are impossible with men, are possible with* יהוה. 28 Then Kepha said, Look, we have left all, and followed You. 29 And He said to them, *Truly I say to you, There is no man that has left bayit, or parents, or brothers, or wife, or children, for the malchut of* יהוה*'s sake,* 30 *Who shall not receive manifold more in this present time, and in the olam haba chayim everlasting.* 31 Then He took aside the twelve, and said to them, *See, we go up to Yahrushalayim, and all things that are written by the neviim concerning the Ben Adam shall be accomplished.* 32 *For He shall be delivered to the gentiles, and shall be mocked, and insulted, and spit on:* 33 *And they shall scourge Him, and put Him to death: and the third day He shall rise again.*[3] 34 And they understood none of these things: and this saying was hidden from them, neither knew they the things that were spoken. 35 And it came to pass, that as He was coming near to Yericho, a certain blind man sat by the way side begging: 36 And hearing the multitude pass by, he asked what it meant. 37 And they told him, that יהושע of Natzareth passes by. 38 And he cried, saying, יהושע, Ben David, have rachamim on me. 39 And those who went before rebuked him, that he should hold his shalom: but he cried much more, You Ben David, have rachamim on me. 40 And יהושע stood, and commanded him to be brought to Him: and when he had come near, He asked him, 41 Saying, *What will you that I shall do for you?* And he said, Master, that I may receive my sight. 42 And יהושע said to him, *Receive your sight: your emunah has saved you.* 43 And immediately he received his sight, and followed Him, esteeming יהוה: and all the people, when they saw it, gave hallel to Elohim.

19 And יהושע entered and passed through Yericho. 2 And, see, there was a man named Zakkai, which was the chief among the tax collectors, and he was rich. 3 And he sought to see יהושע who He was; and could not due to the pressing crowds, because he was little in height. 4 And he ran ahead, and climbed up into a sycamore tree to see Him: for He was to pass that way. 5 And when יהושע came to the place, He looked up, and saw him, and said to him, *Zakkai, hurry, and come down; for today I must abide at your bayit.* 6 And he hurried, and came down, and received Him with simcha. 7 And when they saw it, they all grumbled, saying, That He was gone to be guest with a man that is a sinner. 8 And Zakkai stood, and said to יהושע; See, Master, the half of my goods I give to

---

[1] See note on Matthew 19:17.
[2] See note on Mark 10:25.

[3] As confirmed in Mark 10 the gentiles or non-Jews did the actual killing according to Yahshua Himself.

the poor; and if I have taken any thing from any man by false accusation, I restore all things to him fourfold.[1] 9 And **יהושע** said to him, *This day is salvation come to this bayit because he also is a b'nai Avraham. 10 For the Ben Adam has come to seek and to save that which was lost.* [2] 11 And as they heard these things, He added another parable, because He was near to Yahrushalayim, and because they thought that the malchut of **יהוה** should immediately appear. 12 He said therefore, *A certain nobleman went into a far country to receive for himself a malchut, and to return. 13 And he called his ten avadim,* [3] *and delivered to them ten pounds, and said to them, Occupy until I come. 14 But his citizens hated him, and sent a message after him, saying, We will not have this man to reign over us. 15 And it came to pass, that when he returned, having received the malchut, then he commanded these avadim to be called to him, to whom he had given the money that he might know how much every man had gained by trading. 16 Then came the first, saying, Master, your pound has gained ten pounds. 17 And he said to him, Well done, you tov eved: because you have been faithful in very little, take authority over ten cities. 18 And the second came, saying, Master, your pound has gained five pounds. 19 And He said likewise to him, Take authority also over five cities. 20 And another came, saying, Master, see, here is your pound, which I have kept laid up in a napkin: 21 For I feared you, because you are a harsh man: you take up that which you laid not down, and reap that which you did not sow. 22 And he said to him, Out of your own mouth will I shophet you, you wicked eved. You supposedly knew that I was a harsh man, taking up what I* laid not down, and reaping what I did not sow: 23 *Then why didn't you put my money into the bank, that at my coming I might have collected my own with interest? 24 And he said to them that stood by, Take from him the pound, and give it to him that has ten pounds. 25 And they said to Him, Master, he has ten pounds. 26 For I say to you, That to every one who has shall be given; and from him that has not, even that which he has shall be taken away from him. 27 But these enemies, who did not desire that I should reign over them, bring here, and slay them before me.* 28 And when He had spoken this, He went ahead, ascending up to Yahrushalayim. 29 And it came to pass, when He was come near to Beth-Phagi and Beth Anya, at the mount called the Mount of Olives, He sent two of His talmidim, [4] 30 Saying, *Go into the village opposite you; in which as you enter you shall find a colt tied, on which no man has sat: loose him, and bring him here. 31 And if any man asks you, Why do you loose him? This shall you say to him, Because the Master has need of him.* 32 And they that were sent went their way, and found it even as He had said to them. 33 And as they were loosing the colt, the owners of it said to them, Why do you loose the colt? 34 And they said, the Master has need of him. 35 And they brought him to **יהושע**: and they threw their garments upon the colt, and they set **יהושע** on it. 36 And as He went, they spread their clothes in the way. 37 And when He had come near, even now at the descent of the Mount of Olives, the whole multitude of the talmidim began to have gilah and give tehilla to **יהוה** with a loud voice for all the mighty mizvot that they had seen; 38 Saying, Blessed be the Melech that is coming in the Name of the Master **יהוה**: shalom in the shamayim, and tifereth in the highest. 39 And some of the Prushim from among the multitude said to Him, Master, rebuke Your talmidim. 40 And He answered and said to them, *I tell*

---

[1] Torah repentance always includes restitution – not just diverse sorrows.
[2] Nothing can be clearer. Yahshua visited Zakkai because he was a lost sheep of Yisrael; Yahshua stated that was the main and primary purpose for His coming.
[3] Another reference to the ten tribes of Yisrael coming home and waiting, sometimes faithfully, sometimes unfaithfully, for His return to establish the kingdom on earth.

[4] See note on Matthew 21:1.

you that, if these should hold their shalom, the stones would immediately cry out. 41 And when He came near, He beheld the city, and wept over it, 42 Saying, *If you only knew, even in this your day, the things which belong to your shalom! but now they are hidden from your eyes. 43 For the days shall come upon you, that your enemies shall cast a trench around you, and surround you, and press you in on every side, 44 And shall lay you even with the ground, and your children within you; and they shall not leave in you one stone upon another; because you knew not the time of your visitation.*[1] 45 And He went into the Beit HaMikdash, and began to cast out them that sold there, and them that bought; 46 Saying to them, *It is written, My Bayit is the Bayit of Tefillah: but you have made it a den of thieves.* 47 And He taught daily in the Beit HaMikdash. But the chief kohanim and the Sophrim and the chief of the people sought to destroy Him, 48 And could not find what they might do: for all the people were very attentive to shema Him.

20 And it came to pass, that on one of those days, as He taught the people in the Beit HaMikdash, and proclaimed the besarot; the chief kohanim and the Sophrim came to Him with the zachanim, 2 And spoke to Him, saying, Tell us, by what authority do You do these things? Or who is He that gave You this authority? 3 And He answered and said to them, *I will also ask you one thing; and answer Me: 4 The mikvah of Yochanan, was it from the shamayim, or from men?* 5 And they reasoned among themselves, saying, If we shall say, From the shamayim; He will say, Why then didn't you believe him? 6 But if we say, Of men; all the people will stone us: for they are persuaded that Yochanan was a navi. 7 And they answered, that they could not tell where it was from. 8 And יהושע said to them, *Neither do I tell you by what authority I do these things.* 9 Then He

began to speak to the people this parable; *A certain man planted a vineyard,*[2] *and leased it forth to farmers, and went into a far country for a long time. 10 And at the season he sent an eved to the farmers, that they should give him of the fruit of the vineyard: but the farmers beat him, and sent him away empty. 11 And again he sent another eved: and they beat him also, and treated him shamefully, and sent him away empty. 12 And again he sent a third: and they wounded him also, and threw him out. 13 Then said the master of the vineyard, What shall I do? I will send my beloved son: it may be they will reverence him when they see him. 14 But when the farmers saw him, they reasoned among themselves, saying, This is the heir: come; let us kill him, that the inheritance may be ours. 15 So they cast him out of the vineyard, and killed him. What therefore shall the master of the vineyard do to them? 16 He shall come and destroy these farmers, and shall give the vineyard to others. And when they heard it, they said, Let it not be. 17 And He beheld them, and said, What is this then that is written, The stone that the builders rejected, the same has become the Rosh Pina? 18 Everyone who falls upon that stone shall be broken; but on whoever it shall fall, it will grind him to powder.* 19 And the chief kohanim and the Sophrim the same hour sought to lay hands on Him; but they feared the people: for they perceived that He had spoken this parable against them. 20 And they watched Him, and sent forth spies, who pretended to be just men, that they might trap Him in His words, that so they might deliver Him to the power and authority of the governor. 21 And they asked Him, saying, Master, we know that You say and teach rightly, neither are You partial to any man, but teach the halacha of Elohim truly: 22 Is it right for us to give taxes to Caesar, or not? 23 But He perceived their craftiness, and said to them, *Why do you try Me? 24 Show Me a silver*

---

[1] Speaking of Jewish Yisrael.

[2] Isaiah 5.

piece. *Whose image and inscription does it have?* They answered and said, Caesar's. 25 And He said to them, *Render therefore to Caesar the things that are Caesar's, and to* יהוה *the things that are* יהוה*'s.* 26 And they could not catch Him in His words before the people: and they marveled at His answer, and held their silence. 27 Then came to Him certain of the Tzadukim, who deny that there is any resurrection; and they asked Him, 28 Saying, Master, Moshe Rabainu wrote to us, If any man's brother die, having a wife, and he die without children, that his brother should take his wife, and raise up zera for his brother. 29 There were therefore seven brothers: and the first took a wife, and died without children. 30 And the second took her as a wife, and he died childless. 31 And the third took her; and in like manner all seven also: and they all left no children, and died. 32 Last of all the woman died also. 33 Therefore in the resurrection whose wife is she? For all seven had her as a wife. 34 And יהושע *answering said to them, The children of the olam hazeh marry, and are given in marriage:* 35 *But those who shall be accounted worthy to obtain the olam haba, and the resurrection from the dead, neither marry, nor are given in marriage:* 36 *Neither can they die any more: for they are like the heavenly messengers; and are the children of Elohim, being the children of the resurrection.* 37 *Now that the dead are raised, even Moshe showed at the bush, when he called the Master* יהוה *the Elohim of Avraham, and the Elohim of Yitzchak, and the Elohim of Yaakov.* 38 *For He is not the Elohim of the dead, but of the living: for all live to Him.* 39 Then certain of the Sophrim answering said, Master, You have well said. 40 And after that they did not ask Him any question at all. 41 And He said to them, *How do they say that the Moshiach is David's Son?* 42 *And yet David himself said in the Scroll of Tehillim, the Master* יהוה *said to My Master, Sit on My right hand,* 43 *Until I make Your enemies Your*

footstool. 44 *David therefore called Him Master, how is he then His Son?* 45 Then in the presence of all the people He said to His talmidim, 46 *Beware of the Sophrim, who desire to walk in long robes, and love greetings in the markets, and the highest seats in the synagogues, and the best places at moadim;* 47 *Who devour widows' houses, and for a show make long tefillot: these shall receive greater damnation.*

21 And He looked up, and saw the rich men casting their gifts into the treasury. 2 And He saw also a certain poor widow casting in there her two small coins. 3 And He said, *Of an emet I say to you, that this poor widow has thrown in more than all of them:* 4 *For all these have of their abundance thrown into the offerings to Elohim: but she of her poverty has thrown in all that she had to live on.* 5 And as some spoke of the Beit HaMikdash, how it was adorned with beautiful stones and gifts, He said, 6 *As for these things which you see, the days will come, in which there shall not be left one stone upon another, that shall not be thrown down.* 7 And they asked Him, saying, Master, but when shall these things be? And what sign will there be when these things shall come to pass? 8 And He said, *Take heed that you be not deceived: for many shall come in My Name, saying, I am the Moshiach; and the time draws near: go not therefore after them.* 9 *But when you shall shema of wars and unrest, be not terrified: for these things must first come to pass; but the end is not immediately.* [1] 10 Then He said to them, *Nation shall rise against nation, and malchut against malchut:* 11 *And great earthquakes shall be in divers places, and famines, and pestilences; and fearful sights and great signs shall there be from the shamayim.* 12 *But before all these, they shall lay their hands on you, and persecute you, delivering*

---

[1] Notice how believers are going to be present in the Great Tribulation, and as such, are to heed Yahshua's warnings. If they were to be raptured, no warning would be necessary. The elect in both covenants speak only of Yisrael.

you up to the synagogues, and into prisons, being brought before melechim and rulers for My Name's sake. 13 And it shall turn into a testimony for you. 14 Settle it therefore in your levim, not to meditate before what you shall answer: 15 For I will give you a mouth and chochmah, that all your adversaries shall not be able to refute nor resist. 16 And you shall be betrayed both by parents, and brothers, and family, and chaverim; and some of you shall they cause to be put to death. 17 And you shall be hated of all men for My Name's sake. 18 But there shall not a hair of your head perish. 19 Possess your lives by your endurance to the end. 20 And when you shall see Yahrushalayim surrounded with armies, then know that the destruction of it is near.[1] 21 Then let those who are in province of Yahudah flee to the mountains; and let them which are in the midst of it depart out; and let not them that are in the countries enter into it.[2] 22 For these are the days of vengeance, that all things which are written may be fulfilled. 23 But woe to them that are with child, and to them that nurse, in those days! For there shall be great distress in the land, and wrath upon this people. 24 And they shall fall by the edge of the sword, and shall be led away captive into all nations:[3] and Yahrushalayim shall be trodden down by the gentiles, until the times of the gentiles be fulfilled.[4] 25 And there shall be signs in the sun, and in the moon, and in the stars; and upon the earth distress of nations, with perplexity; the sea and the waves roaring;[5] 26 Men's levim failing them for fear, and for looking after those things that are coming on the earth: for the powers of the shamayim shall be shaken. 27 And then shall they see the Ben Adam coming on clouds with a large army[6] and great tifereth. 28 And when these things begin to come to pass, then look up, and lift up your heads; for your redemption draws near. 29 And He spoke to them a parable; See the fig tree, and all the trees;[7] 30 When they already budded, you see and know for yourselves that summer is now near at hand. 31 So likewise, when you see these things come to pass, know that the malchut of יהוה is near at hand. 32 Truly I say to you, This generation shall not pass away, until all be fulfilled. 33 Heaven and earth shall pass away: but My words shall not pass away. 34 And take heed to yourselves, lest at any time your levim be weighed down with gluttony, and drunkenness, and worries of this chayim, and so that day come upon you suddenly. 35 For as a trap shall it come on all them that dwell on the face of the whole earth. 36 Watch therefore, and make tefillah always, that you may be accounted worthy to escape[8] all these things that shall come to pass, and to stand before the Ben Adam. 37 And in the daytime He was teaching in the Beit HaMikdash; and at night He went out, and stayed on the mount that is called the Mount of Olives. 38 And all the people came early in the morning to Him in the Beit HaMikdash, to shema to Him.

22 Now the moed of Chag Matzoth drew near, which is called the

---

[1] 70 CE under Titus the Roman general, along with an end-time application as well.
[2] By heeding this warning, Nazarene Yisraelites were not killed or annihilated in the Jewish revolt against Rome. As a consequence of fleeing Yahrushalayim and not fighting alongside traditional Jews against Rome, the early Nazarene Yisraelites were physically removed and thrown out from the synagogue, fulfilling yet another prophecy by Moshiach.
[3] What happened to Ephraim Yisrael back in 721 BCE was about to happen to Yahudah in 70 CE. Both houses would find themselves dispersed throughout the nations, only to be gathered back together in the latter days, as is now occurring. This process finds its culmination in the millennial **atid lavoh**.
[4] Not to be confused with the "fullness of the gentiles" which speaks of Ephraim's seed (10 tribes) filling the earth. The "time of the gentiles" refers to the pagans' control over Jerusalem coming to an end. That event, as prophesied here, already took place in 1967 CE when the state of Yisrael recaptured Jerusalem from Jordan ending a 2,000-year domination of Jerusalem by non-Yisraelite foreign powers and religious orders.

[5] These events could not happen before 1967. Now they are right up the road.
[6] Peshitta.
[7] The fig tree (Jewish Yisrael) and all the trees (the nations) all bud at the same time (post-1996 CE) as Yisrael is awakened simultaneously in all the nations. The fig tree (Yahudah) and the other trees (Ephraim) both wake up and perceive one another, as a budding part of the people of Yisrael.
[8] Escape death and famine – not the Tribulation itself.

Pesach.[1] 2 And the chief kohanim and Sophrim sought how they might kill Him; but they feared the people. 3 Then entered s.a.tan into Yahudah surnamed Qerioth, being from the number of the twelve. 4 And he went his way, and communed with the chief kohanim and captains, how he might betray Him to them. 5 And they were glad, and covenanted to give him money. 6 And he promised, and sought opportunity to betray Him to them in the absence of the multitude. 7 Then approached Chag Matzoth, when the Pesach must be killed.[2] 8 And He sent Kepha and Yochanan, saying, *Go and prepare for us the Pesach that we may eat.* 9 And they said to Him, Where do You want us to prepare? 10 And He said to them, *See, when you enter into the city, there shall a man meet you, bearing a pitcher of mayim; follow him into the bayit where he enters in.* 11 *And you shall say to the owner of the bayit, The Master says to you, Where is the guest room, where I may eat the Pesach with My talmidim?* 12 *And he shall show you a large upper room furnished: there make ready.* 13 And they went, and found as He had said to them: and they made ready the Pesach. 14 And when the hour was come, He sat down, and the twelve shlichim with Him.[3] 15 And He said to them, *With desire I have desired to eat this Pesach with you before I suffer:* 16 *For I say to you, I will not any more eat of it, until it be fulfilled in the malchut of* יהוה.[4] 17 And He took the cup, and gave hodu, and said, *Take this, and divide it among yourselves:* 18 *For I say to you, I will not drink of the fruit of the vine, until the malchut of* יהוה *shall come.* 19 And He took matzah, and said the bracha, and broke it, and gave it to them, saying, *This is My body which is given for*

you: this do in remembrance of Me. 20 Likewise also the cup after supper, saying, *This cup is the Renewed Covenant in My dom, which is shed for you.* 21 *But, see, the hand of him that betrays Me is with Me on the table.* 22 *And truly the Ben Adam goes, as it was determined: but woe to that man by whom He is betrayed!* 23 And they began to inquire among themselves, which of them it was that should do this thing. 24 And there was also a strife among them, which of them should be the greatest. 25 And He said to them, *The melechim of the gentiles exercise rule over them; and they that exercise authority upon them are called doers of tov.* 26 *But you shall not be so:[5] but he that is greatest among you, let him be as the least; and he that is a leader, be as he that does serve.* 27 *For who is greater, he that sits down, or he that serves the one sitting? Is it not he that sits to eat? But I am among you as one that serves.* 28 *You are those who have continued with Me in My trials.[6]* 29 *And I appoint to you a malchut, as My Abba has appointed to Me;* 30 *That you may eat and drink at My table in My malchut, and sit on thrones being shophets over the twelve tribes of Yisrael.[7]* 31 And He said, *Shimon, Shimon, see, s.a.tan has desired to have you, that he may sift you as wheat:* 32 *But I have made tefillah for you, that your emunah fails not: and when you have repented, strengthen your brothers.* 33 And He said to Him, Master, I am ready to go with You, both into prison, and to death. 34 And He said, *I tell you, Kepha, the cock shall not crow this day, before you shall three times deny that you know Me.* 35 And He said to them, *When I sent you without purse, and bag, and sandals, did you lack anything?* And they said, Nothing. 36 Then said He to them, *But now, he that has a purse, let him*

---

[1] Technically it starts at sundown just after the Passover meal.
[2] See notes on Mark 14:12.
[3] A type of the kingdom; and all 12 tribes of Yisrael in full and total restoration harmony.
[4] Notice that He wants to, and all is prepared, but He says very clearly that He will not. This assures us that he had a "rabbinical Pesach," traditionally held the night before, as did most rabbis (since he was a rabbi after all), without actually eating it that year.

[5] Proof that all believers are part of physical and spiritual Yisrael.
[6] Yahshua commends those who endure and overcome, not those who confess and don't follow.
[7] If Yahshua came to build a "gentile church" with a few token Jews thrown in, rather than rebuilding Yisrael from the nations, He certainly would never have made this statement.

take it, and likewise his bag: and he that has no sword, let him sell his garment, and buy one. 37 *For I say to you, that this that was written must yet be accomplished in Me, I was reckoned among the transgressors: for the things concerning Me must be fulfilled.* 38 And they said, Master, see, here are two swords. And He said to them, *It is enough.*[1] 39 And He came out, and went, as He was accustomed, to the Mount of Olives; and His talmidim also followed Him. 40 And when He was at the place, He said to them, *Make tefillah that you enter not into trial.* 41 And He was withdrawn from them about a stone's throw, and kneeled down, and made tefillah, 42 Saying, *Abba, if You be willing, remove this cup from Me: nevertheless not My will, but Yours, be done.* 43 And there appeared a heavenly messenger to Him from the shamayim, strengthening Him. 44 And being in an agony He made tefillah more earnestly: and His sweat became like great drops of dom as He fell down to the ground. 45 And when He rose up from tefillah, and came to His talmidim, He found them sleeping due to sorrow, 46 And said to them, *Why do you sleep? Rise and make tefillah, lest you enter into trial.* 47 And while He yet spoke, see a multitude, and he that was called Yahudah, one of the twelve, went before them, and drew near to יהושע to kiss Him. 48 But יהושע said to him, *Yahudah, do you betray the Ben Adam with a kiss?* 49 When those who were around Him saw what would follow, they said to Him, Master, shall we smite with the sword? 50 And one of them smote the eved of the Kohen HaGadol, and cut off his right ear. 51 And יהושע answered and said, *Enough already.* And He touched the ear of the one who was struck, and healed him.[2] 52 Then יהושע said to the chief kohanim, and captains of the Beit HaMikdash, and the zachanim, who had come to Him, *Have you*

come out, like against a thief, with swords and staves? 53 *When I was daily with you in the Beit HaMikdash, and you did not even point your hands against Me: but this is your time, and the power of darkness.* 54 Then they took Him, and led Him, and brought Him into the Kohen HaGadol's bayit. And Kepha followed far off. 55 And when they had kindled a fire in the midst of the hall, and were sat down together, Kepha sat down among them. 56 But a certain eved girl beheld him as he sat by the fire, and earnestly looked at him, and said, This man was also with Him. 57 And he denied Him, saying, Woman, I know Him not. 58 And after a little while another saw him, and said, You are also one of them. And Kepha said, Man, I am not. 59 And about the space of one hour later another confidently affirmed, saying, Of an emet this fellow also was with Him: for he is a Galilaean. 60 And Kepha said, Man, I know nothing of what you are saying. And immediately, while he was yet speaking, the cock crew. 61 And יהושע turned, and looked at Kepha. And Kepha remembered the word of יהושע, how He had said to him, *Before the cock crows, You shall deny Me three times.* 62 And Kepha went out, and wept bitterly. 63 And the men that held יהושע mocked Him, and smote Him. 64 And when they had blindfolded Him, they struck Him on the face, and asked Him, saying, Prophesy, who is it that smote You? 65 And many other things blasphemously they spoke against Him. 66 And as soon as it was day, the zachanim of the people and the chief kohanim and the Sophrim came together, and led Him into their council chamber, saying, 67 Are You Moshiach? Tell us. And He said to them, *If I tell you, you will not believe: 68 And if I also ask you, you will not answer Me, nor let Me go. 69 Hereafter shall the Ben Adam sit on the right hand of the Power of* יהוה. 70 Then said they all, Are You then the Son of El-Elyon? And He said to them, *You say that I am.* 71 And they said, What need we

---

[1] A **remez** or hint of the two swords being YHWH's two-edged word, being enough to reunite both houses after all things concerning our Suffering King were to be fulfilled.
[2] Peshitta.

any further witness? For we ourselves have heard from His own mouth.[1]

23

And the whole multitude of them arose, and led Him to Pilate. 2 And they began to accuse Him, saying, We found this fellow perverting the nation, and forbidding giving taxes to Caesar, saying that He Himself is the Moshiach, a Melech. 3 And Pilate asked Him, saying, Are You the Melech of the Yahudim? And He answered him and said, *You said it.* 4 Then said Pilate to the chief kohanim and to the people, I find no fault in this Man. 5 And they were angrier, saying, He stirs up the people, teaching throughout all the province of Yahudah, beginning from Galil to this place. 6 When Pilate heard of Galil, he asked whether the Man were a Galilaean. 7 And as soon as he knew that He belonged to Herod's jurisdiction, he sent Him to Herod, who himself also was at Yahrushalayim at that time. 8 And when Herod saw יהושע, he was exceedingly in simcha: for he had desired to see Him for a long time, because he had heard many things about Him; and he hoped to have seen some miracle done by Him. 9 Then he questioned with Him in many words; but He answered him nothing. 10 And the chief kohanim and Sophrim stood and vehemently accused Him. 11 And Herod with his men of war insulted Him, and mocked Him, and dressed Him in a scarlet robe, and sent Him again to Pilate. 12 And the same day Pilate and Herod were made chaverim: for before they were at enmity between themselves. 13 And Pilate, when he had called together the chief kohanim and the rulers of the people, 14 Said to them, You have brought this Man to me, as one that perverts the people: and, see, I, having examined Him before you, have found no fault in this Man concerning those things of which you accuse Him: 15 No, not even Herod: for I sent you to him; and, see, nothing worthy of death is done to Him.

16 I will therefore chastise Him, and release Him. 17 For because of a necessity he must release one to them at the moed. 18 And they cried out all at once, saying, Away with this Man, and release to us Bar-Abba: 19 Who for a certain uprising made in the city, and for murder, was thrown into prison 20 Pilate therefore, willing to release יהושע, spoke again to them. 21 But they cried, saying, Impale Him, impale Him. 22 And he said to them the third time, Why, what evil has He done? I have found no cause of death in Him: I will therefore chastise Him, and let Him go. 23 And they insisted with loud voices, requiring that He might be impaled. And the voices of them and of the chief kohanim prevailed. 24 And Pilate gave sentence that it should be as they required. 25 And he released to them, the one that for sedition and murder was thrown into prison, whom they had desired; but he delivered יהושע to their will. 26 And as they led Him away, they laid hold upon one Shimon, a Cyrenian, coming out of the country, and on him they laid the execution stake, that he might bear it after יהושע. 27 And there followed Him a great group of people, and of women, who also mourned and lamented Him. 28 But יהושע turning to them said, *Daughters of Yahrushalayim, weep not for Me, but weep for yourselves, and for your children. 29 For, see, the days are coming, in the which they shall say, Blessed are the barren, and the wombs that never bore, and the breasts which never nursed. 30 Then shall they begin to say to the mountains, Fall on us; and to the hills, Cover us. 31 For if they do these things in a green tree, what shall be done in the dry?*[2] [3] 32 And there were also two other, wicked ones, led with Him to be put to death. 33 And when they were come to the place, which is called The Skull, there they impaled Him, with the wicked ones, one on

---

[1] See notes on Mark 14:62.

[2] Yahshua prophecies the soon destruction of Jerusalem and the Beit HaMikdash.
[3] The green tree is Yahudah in the land. The dry tree is Yahudah's full exile in the nations.

the right hand, and the other on the left.[1] 34 Then said **יהושע**, *Abba, forgive them; for they know not what they do.* And they parted His garment, and cast lots. 35 And the people stood staring. And the rulers also with them sneering, saying, He saved others; let Him save Himself, if He is the Moshiach, the chosen of Elohim. 36 And the soldiers also mocked Him, coming to Him, and offering Him vinegar, 37 And saying, If You are the Melech of the Yahudim, save Yourself. 38 And an inscription also was written over Him in letters of Greek, and Latin, and Ivrit, THIS IS THE MELECH OF THE YAHUDIM. 39 And one of the wicked ones who were hanged blasphemed against Him, saying, If You are the Moshiach, save Yourself and us. 40 But the other answering rebuked him, saying, Don't you fear Elohim, seeing you are under the same condemnation? 41 And we indeed justly; for we receive the due reward of our deeds: but this Man has done nothing wrong. 42 And he said to **יהושע**, Master, remember Me when You come into Your malchut. 43 And **יהושע** said to him, *Truly I say to you, Today shall you be with Me in Gan-Aden.*[2] 44 And it was about the sixth hour, and there was a darkness over all the earth until the ninth hour. 45 And the sun was darkened, and the veil of the Beit HaMikdash was torn in the midst.[3] 46 And when **יהושע** had cried with a loud voice, He said, *Abba, into Your hands I commit My ruach:* and having said this, He gave up the Ruach. 47 Now when the centurion saw what was done, he esteemed Elohim, saying, Certainly this was a Tzadik Man. 48 And all the people that came together to that sight, beholding the things that were done, smote their breasts, and returned. 49 And all His acquaintances, and the

women that followed Him from Galil, stood far off, beholding these things. 50 And, see, there was a man named Yoseph a Sanhedrin member; and he was a tov man, and a tzadik - 51 He had not agreed with the counsel and their deed - he was from Ramathayim, a city of Yahudah: who also himself waited for the malchut of **יהוה**. 52 This man went to Pilate, and asked for the body of **יהושע**. 53 And he took it down, and wrapped it in linen, and laid it in a tomb that was cut in stone, in which never a man before was laid. 54 And that day was the preparation, and the Shabbat drew near.[4] 55 And the women also, who came with Him from Galil, followed after, and beheld the tomb, and how His body was laid. 56 And they returned, and prepared spices and ointments; and rested on the Shabbat day according to the commandment.

24 Now upon one of the weekly Shabbats,[5] very early towards the morning,[6] they came to the tomb, bringing the spices that they had prepared, and certain others with them. 2 And they found the stone rolled away from the tomb. 3 And they entered in, and found not the body of **יהושע**. 4 And it came to pass, as they were much perplexed about it, see, two men[7] stood by them in shining garments: 5 And as they were afraid, and bowed down their faces to the earth, they said to them, Why seek you the living among the dead? 6 He is not here, but is risen: remember how He spoke to you when He was yet in Galil, 7 Saying, *The Ben Adam must be delivered into the hands of sinful men, and be impaled, and the third day rise again.* 8 And they remembered His words, 9 And returned from the tomb, and told all these things to the eleven, and to all the rest. 10 It was Miryam from Magdala, and Yochanan, and Miryam the ima of Yaakov, and other

---

[1] See note on Mark 15:27.
[2] The thief on the tree was the last person in Abraham's bosom or Paradise before it was liberated at Moshiach's ascension in accordance with Luke 16.
[3] To the Set-Apart Place, not the Most Set-Apart Place. **See: Within The Veil.**
http://store.yourarmstoisrael.org/Qstore/Qstore.cgi?CMD=011&PROD=1065766819

[4] Annual Shabbat of Aviv 15.
[5] **mia ton sabbaton** in Greek. The words "first" and "day" do not appear in the Greek.
[6] Say about 6-8 PM during **havdallah** or **motzei** Shabbat.
[7] Possibly as a dual witness to Yahudah and Ephraim.

women that were with them, who told these things to the shlichim. 11 And their words seemed to them as idle tales, and they believed them not.[1] 12 Then arose Kepha, and ran to the tomb; and stooping down, he beheld the linen clothes laid by themselves, and departed, wondering within himself about all that which had come to pass. 13 And, see, two of them went that same day to a village called Amma-Us, which was from Yahrushalayim about six miles.[2] 14 And they talked together about all those things that had happened. 15 And it came to pass, that, while they communed together and reasoned, **יהושע** Himself drew near, and went with them.[3] 16 But their eyes were restrained so that they could not recognize Him. 17 And He said to them, *What manner of communications are these that you have with each other, as you walk, and are sad?* 18 And one of them, whose name was Qleophas, answering said to Him, Are You only a ger[4] in Yahrushalayim, and have not known the things that have come to pass in it in these days? 19 And He said to them, *What things?* And they said to Him, Concerning **יהושע** of Natzareth, who was a Navi mighty in mitzvot and word before Elohim and all the people: 20 And how the chief kohanim and our rulers delivered Him to be condemned to death, and have impaled Him. 21 But we trusted that it was Him who should have redeemed Yisrael:[5] and besides all this, today is the third day since these things were done. 22 Yes, and certain women also of our group made us astonished, who were earlier at the tomb; 23 And when they found not His body, they came, saying, that they had also seen a vision of heavenly messengers, who said

that He was alive. 24 And certain of those who were with us went to the tomb, and found it even as the women had said: but Him they did not see. 25 Then He said to them, *O fools, and slow of lev to believe all that the neviim have spoken:* 26 *Did not the Moshiach have to suffer all these things, in order to enter into His tifereth?* 27 And beginning at Moshe Rabainu and all the neviim, He expounded to them in all the Ketuvim the things concerning Himself.[6] 28 And they drew near to the village, where they went: and He made them think He was going to a far place. [7] 29 But they constrained Him, saying, Remain with us: for it is toward evening, and the day is nearly dark. And He went in to stay with them. 30 And it came to pass, as He sat to eat with them, He took lechem, and said the bracha, and broke it, and gave some to them. 31 And their eyes were opened, and they knew Him; and He vanished out of their sight. 32 And they said one to another, Were not our minds dull within us, while He talked with us on the road, and interpreted the Ketuvim to us?[8] 33 And they rose up the same hour, and returned to Yahrushalayim, and found the eleven gathered together, and them that were with them, 34 Saying, our Master is risen indeed, and has appeared to Shimon. 35 And they told what things were done on the road, and how He was known by them in the breaking of lechem. 36 And as they spoke, **יהושע** Himself stood in the midst of them, and said to them, *Shalom Aleichem.* 37 But they were confused and frightened, and thought that they had seen a ruach. 38 And He said to them, *Why are you troubled? And why do thoughts arise in your levim?* 39 *See My hands and My feet, that it is I Myself: handle Me and understand, and see; for a ruach has no flesh and bones, as you see*

---

[1] Probably because they were women in a male-dominated society.
[2] A type of both houses, wandering in exile outside of Yahrushalayim, blind to their Moshiach and His Torah.
[3] Two-bayit brotherhood waiting for a revelation from Yahshua.
[4] For returning Ephraimites who have been called strangers or non-Yisraelites, don't feel bad. You're in very elite company, as here Yahshua's own disciples called Him a "stranger."
[5] The plain truth: that the true Moshiach must redeem and reunite both houses.

[6] The ultimate study.
[7] Peshitta: Note the language in the Aramaic ("to a far place") as opposed to the Greek. Possibly to Europe, Africa, Asia Minor, and elsewhere to gather in the exiles through post-resurrection appearances.
[8] Peshitta.

Me have. [1] 40 And when He had spoken this, He showed them His hands and His feet. 41 And while they yet believed not for simcha, and wondered, He said to them, *Have you here any food?* 42 And they gave Him a piece of broiled fish, and a honeycomb. 43 And He took it, and did eat before them. 44 And He said to them, *These are the words that I spoke to you, while I was yet with you, that all things must be fulfilled, which were written in the Torah of Moshe, and in the neviim, and in the Tehillim, concerning Me.* 45 Then opened He their understanding, that they might understand the Ketuvim, 46 And said to them, *So it is written, and so it was necessary that the Moshiach suffer, and rise from the dead on the third day: 47 And that teshuvah and remission of sins should be proclaimed in His Name among all nations,* [2] *beginning at Yahrushalayim. 48 And you are witnesses of these things. 49 And, see, I send the Promise of My Abba upon you: but remain in the city of Yahrushalayim, until you be clothed with power from on high.* 50 And He led them out as far as to Beth-Anya, and He lifted up His hands, and blessed them. [3] 51 And it came to pass, while He blessed them, He departed from them, and went up into the shamayim. 52 And they worshipped Him, and returned to Yahrushalayim with great simcha: 53 And were continually in the Beit HaMikdash, giving tehilot and brachot to יהוה. Amein. [4]

---

[1] This text declares that Yahshua did not rise as a spirit or an invisible spirit. Rather, He arose as a human without the dom since that was shed for our atonement and forgiveness. While it was a different form of body, or a spiritual body, it was still with a form, having both flesh and bones, which allowed the talmidim to touch and feel Him.
[2] The fullness of all nations or Ephraim Yisrael.

[3] Possibly the Aaronic Benediction.
[4] That's why in Acts chapter 2, they were in the Abba's House, or the Beit HaMikdash, when the Ruach HaKodesh fell, since they were carefully commanded not to depart from the tarrying place, until the promise of the Ruach HaKodesh had arrived. This will become critical in understanding Renewed Covenant Yisrael, in the follow-up of Luke's account as found in the Scroll of Acts.

יוחנן

The Besorah According To

Yochanan – John
To All Nations

1 Bereshet was the Torah, and the Torah was with יהוה, and the Torah was יהוה. 2 The same was in the beginning with יהוה. 3 All things were made by Him; and without Him was not anything made that was made. 4 In Him was chayyim; and the chayyim was the Light of men. 5 And the Light shines in darkness; and the darkness comprehended it not. 6 There was a man sent from יהוה, whose name was Yochanan. 7 The same came for a witness, to bear witness of the Light, that all men through Him might believe. 8 He was not that Light, but was sent to bear witness of that Light. 9 That was the emet Light, which lights every man that comes into the olam hazeh. 10 He was in the olam hazeh, and the olam hazeh was made by Him, and the olam hazeh knew Him not. 11 He came to His own, and His own received Him not.[1] 12 But as many as received Him, to them gave He power to become the sons of יהוה, even to them that believe on His Name: 13 Which were born, not of dom, nor of the will of the flesh, nor of the will of man, but of יהוה. 14 And the Torah was made flesh, and dwelt among us, and we saw His tifereth, the tifereth as of the only brought forth of the Abba, full of unmerited favor and emet. 15 Yochanan bore witness of Him, and cried, saying, This was He of who I spoke, He that comes after me is preferred before me: for He was before me. 16 And of His fullness all we have received, unmerited favor upon unmerited favor. 17 For the Torah was given by Moshe; its unmerited favor and emet came by יהושע the Moshiach. 18 No man has seen the Abba at any time; the only brought forth Son, who was in the bosom of the Abba, He has declared Him. 19 And this is the witness of Yochanan, when the Yahudim sent kohanim and Leviim from Yahrushalayim to ask him, Who are you? 20 And he confessed, and denied not; but confessed, I am not the Moshiach. 21 And they asked him, What then? Are you Eliyahu? And he said, I am not. Are you Ha Navi? And he answered, No. 22 Then said they to him, Who are you? That we may give an answer to them that sent us. What are you saying about yourself? 23 He said, I am the voice of one crying in the wilderness, Make straight the derech of the Master יהוה, as said ha navi Yeshayahu. 24 And they that were sent were of the Prushim. 25 And they asked him, and said to him, Why are you doing mikvahs, if you are not the Moshiach, nor Eliyahu, neither Ha Navi? 26 Yochanan answered them, saying, I mikvah with mayim: but there stands One among you, whom you know not; 27 He it is, who coming after me is preferred before me, whose sandals I am not worthy to unloose. 28 These things were done in Beth-Avara beyond Yarden, where Yochanan was doing mikvah. 29 The next day Yochanan sees יהושע coming to him, and said, Behold the Lamb of יהוה, who takes away the sin of the olam hazeh. 30 This is He of whom I said, After me comes a Man who is preferred before me: for He was before me. 31 And I knew Him not: but that He should be made manifest to Yisrael,[2] therefore am I come mikvahing with mayim. 32 And Yochanan bore witness, saying, I saw the Ruach descending from the shamayim like a yonah, and it stayed upon Him. 33 And I knew Him not: but He that sent me to mikvah with mayim, the same said to me, Upon whom you shall see the Ruach

---

[1] The leadership of Jewish Yisrael, not the people who heard Him gladly.

[2] The true and primary purpose of His coming.

descending, and remaining on Him, the same is He who mikvahs with the Set-Apart Ruach. 34 And I saw, and bore witness that this is the Son of יהוה.[1] 35 Again the next day after Yochanan stood up with two of his talmidim; 36 And looking right at יהושע as He walked, he said, Behold the Lamb of יהוה! 37 And the two-talmidim heard Him speak, and they followed יהושע. 38 Then יהושע turned, and saw them following, and said to them, *What are you seeking?* They said to Him, Rabbi (Teacher), where do You live? 39 He said to them, *Come and see.* They came and saw where He dwelt, and stayed with Him that day: for it was about the tenth hour. 40 One of the two who heard Yochanan speak, and followed Him, was Andri, Shimon Kepha's brother. 41 He first found his own brother Shimon, and said to him, We have found the Moshiach. 42 And he brought him to יהושע. And when יהושע saw him, He said, You are Shimon bar Yonah: you shall be called Kepha, A stone. 43 The day following יהושע wished to go into Galil, and found Philip, and said to him, *Follow Me.* 44 Now Philip was of Beth-Tsaida, the city of Andri and Kepha. 45 Philip finds Nathan-El, and said to him, We have found Him, of whom Moshe in the Torah, and the neviim, did write, יהושע of Natzareth, the Son of Yoseph.[2] 46 And Natahan-El said to him, Can there any tov thing come out of Natzareth? Philip said to him, Come and see. 47 יהושע saw Natahan-El coming to Him, and said of him, *Behold an Yisraelite indeed, in whom is no guile!* 48 Natahan-El said to Him, From where do You know me? יהושע answered and said to him, *Before Philip called you, when you were under the fig tree, I saw you.*[3] 49 Natahan-El answered and said to Him, Rabbi, You are

the Son of יהוה; You are Melech Yisrael. 50 יהושע answered and said to him, *Because I said to you, I saw you under the fig tree, you believe? You shall see greater things than these.* 51 And He said to him, *Truly, truly, I say to you, From now on you shall see the shamayim opened, and the heavenly messengers of* יהוה *ascending and descending upon the Ben Adam.*[4]

2 And on Yom Shleshi there was a marriage in Qanah of Galil; and the ima of יהושע was there: 2 And both יהושע was invited, and His talmidim, to the marriage. 3 And when they needed more wine, the ima of יהושע said to Him, They have no wine. 4 יהושע said to her, *Woman, what have I to do with you? My hour has not yet come.*[5] 5 His ima said to the avadim, Whatever He says to you, do it.[6] 6 And there were set there six stone jars, after the manner of the purifying of the Yahudim, containing two or three gallons apiece. 7 יהושע said to them, *Fill the stone jars with mayim.* And they filled them up to the brim. 8 And He said to them, *Draw out with them now, and bring them to the master of ceremonies of the wedding.* And they took them. 9 When the master of ceremonies of the wedding had tasted the mayim that was made wine, and knew not where it came from - but the avadim who drew the mayim knew - the master of ceremonies of the wedding called the bridegroom, 10 And said to him, Every man at the beginning does serve tov wine; and when men have drunk, afterwards that which is poorer: but you have kept the tov wine until now. 11 This is the beginning of the nisim that יהושע did in Qanah of Galil, and manifested forth His tifereth; and His

---

[1] Not a son but "the" Son. Not the Father in a costume.
[2] In the literal, this is the stepson of Yoseph, but in the hint application, Philip confesses that Moshiach ben Yosef or the Suffering Moshiach, has arrived to die and regather the lost sheep of Yisrael.
[3] Yahshua sees all true believers as standing under the fig tree, symbolic of national Yisrael. He does not recognize any believer that does not abide in the Commonwealth of Yisrael, under the fig tree.

[4] A reference to the time when Yaakov/Yisrael saw YHWH on the top of the ladder in Genesis 28:12; and the reference here is to the fact that Yisrael as a nation will again see YHWH fully manifested in Yahshua of Nazareth. That initial event occurred in Beth El, and Yahshua mentions it here to let Yisrael know that He is coming to properly rebuild the House of El through His appearing.
[5] The hour to break His Nazarite vow.
[6] Note how Miryam was fully subject to YHWH in Him, and didn't pull fleshly rank.

talmidim believed on Him.[1] 12 After this He went down to the City of Nachum, with His ima, and His brothers, and His talmidim: and they continued there a few days. 13 And the Yahudim's Pesach was at hand, and יהושע went up to Yahrushalayim, 14 And found in the Beit HaMikdash those that sold oxen and sheep and doves, and the changers of money sitting: 15 And when He had made a whip of small cords, He drove them all out of the Beit HaMikdash, and the sheep, and the oxen; and poured out the changers' money, and overthrew the tables; 16 And said to them that sold doves, *Take these things away; make not My Abba's Bayit into a Bayit of merchandise.* [2] 17 And His talmidim remembered that it is written, The zeal for Your Bayit has given Me courage[3] and eaten Me up. 18 Then answered the Yahudim and said to Him, What sign will You show us, seeing that You are doing these things? 19 יהושע answered and said to them, *Destroy this Beit HaMikdash, and in three days I will raise it up.* 20 Then said the Yahudim, Forty-six years this Beit HaMikdash was being built, and will You raise it up in three days? 21 But He spoke of the Beit HaMikdash of His body.[4] 22 When therefore He was risen from the dead, His talmidim remembered that He had said this to them; and they believed the kituvim,[5] and the word which יהושע had said. 23 Now when He was in Yahrushalayim at the Pesach, during the moed, many believed in His Name,[6] when they saw the nisim that He did. 24 But יהושע did not commit Himself to them, because He knew all men,[7] 25 And needed not that any should testify of man: for He knew what was in the sons of men.

3 There was a man of the Prushim, named Nakdimon, a ruler of the Yahudim: 2 The same came to יהושע by night, and said to Him, Rabbi, we know that You are a moreh come from Elohim: for no man can do these nisim that You are doing, except Elohim be with Him. 3 יהושע answered and said to him, *Truly, truly, I say to you, Except a man be born again/brit halev,* [8] *he cannot see the malchut of* יהוה. [9] 4 Nakdimon said to Him, How can a man be born when he is old? Can he enter the second time into his ima's womb, and be born? 5 יהושע answered, *Truly, truly, I say to you, Except a man is born of mayim and of the Ruach, he cannot enter into the malchut of* יהוה. [10] 6 *That which is born of the flesh is flesh; and that which is born of the Ruach is Ruach.* [11] 7 *Marvel not that I said to you, You must be born from above.* 8 *The wind blows where it desires, and you shema the sound of it, but cannot tell where it comes from, and where it goes: so is every one that is born of the Ruach.* 9 Nakdimon answered and said to Him, How can these things be? 10 יהושע answered and said to him, *Are you a moreh of Yisrael, and you do not know not these things?* [12] [13] 11 *Truly, truly, I say to you, We*[14] *speak what we do know, and testify what we have seen; and you receive not our*

---

[1] As Moshiach ben Yosef, the gatherer of Yisrael's exiles, it was necessary that His work begin in the northern territories of the exiles of the House of Yisrael as seen here.
[2] The moneychangers were allowed to be there according to Torah in Deuteronomy 14:24-26. What they were not allowed to do was operate in dishonesty, and on days when work was forbidden as per Torah.
[3] Aramaic Peshitta.
[4] His physical body, as well as the Commonwealth of Yisrael, who would be revived or raised up on the third day, or the beginning of the third millennium after Yahshua's first coming according to Hosea 6:2.
[5] Hosea 6:2, Psalm 16:10.
[6] Emunah in the true Name is essential according to the Word.

[7] He knew the hearts of all Yisrael both tov and bad.
[8] A Hebraic requirement to follow and obey Torah as recorded in Deuteronomy 10:16, where YHWH requires Yaakov/Yisrael to have circumcised hearts.
[9] Yisrael restored under Moshiach, through the new birth.
[10] A reference to Ezekiel 36:25-27, where Renewed Covenant Yisrael was promised to have a new lev to obey, along with a change of thinking, as well as having mayim poured on them to purify them. That water is both the water that poured from Yahshua's side on the stake, as well as the sealing into the emunah by full water immersion in Yahshua's Name. The Ezekiel reference is a clear statement that Yahshua came to pour water m on unclean Yisrael, not to birth a separate gentile entity apart from historic Yisrael.
[11] The principle of "like kind."
[12] True teachers of Yisrael teach people how to be born again and follow Torah, and Nakdimon was not doing that.
[13] Teachers who don't know Yahshua or who are still "seeking" truth should be students in Yisrael, not teachers.
[14] He and the Father in Him.

witness. 12 *If I have told you earthly things, and you believe not, how shall you believe, if I tell you of heavenly things?* 13 *And no man has ascended up to the shamayim, but He that came down from the shamayim, even the Ben Adam who is in the shamayim.*[1] 14 *And as Moshe lifted up the serpent in the wilderness, even so must the Ben Adam be lifted up:*[2] 15 *That whoever believes in Him should not perish, but have eternal chayim.* 16 *For* יהוה *so loved the olam hazeh, that He gave His only brought forth Son, that whoever believes in Him should not perish, but have everlasting chayim.* 17 *For* יהוה *sent not His Son into the olam hazeh to condemn the olam hazeh; but that the olam hazeh through Him might be saved.* 18 *He that believes on Him is not condemned: but he that believes not is condemned already, because he has not believed in the Name*[3] *of the only brought forth Son of* יהוה. 19 *And this is the condemnation, that Light has come into the olam hazeh, and men loved darkness rather than Light, because their deeds were evil.* 20 *For everyone that does evil hates the Light, neither comes to the Light, lest his deeds should be exposed.* 21 *But he that does emet comes to the Light, that his deeds may be made manifest, that they are done through Elohim.* 22 After these things came יהושע and His talmidim into the province of Yahudah; and there He tarried with them, and was doing mikvahs. 23 And Yochanan also was mikvahing in Ayin near to Salim, because there was much mayim there: and they came, and were immersed. 24 For Yochanan was not yet cast into prison. 25 Then there arose a question between some of Yochanan's talmidim and the Yahudim about cleansing ceremonies. 26 And they came to Yochanan, and said to him, Rabbi, he that was with You beyond Yarden, to whom You bore witness, see, the same does mikvahs, and all men come to Him. 27 Yochanan answered and said, A man can receive nothing, except it be given Him from the shamayim. 28 You yourselves bear me witness that I said; I am not the Moshiach, but that I am sent before Him. 29 He that has the bride is the Bridegroom: but the chaver of the bridegroom, who stands and hears Him, rejoices greatly because of the Bridegroom's voice: in His voice, my simcha therefore is complete. 30 He must increase, but I must decrease. 31 He that comes from above is above all: he that is of the earth is earthly and speaks of the earth: He that comes from the shamayim is above all.[4] 32 And what He has seen and heard, that He testifies; and no man receives His testimony.[5] 33 He that has received His testimony has received the seal that Elohim is emet. 34 For He whom יהוה has sent speaks the words of יהוה: for יהוה gives not the Ruach to Him by limited increments. 35 The Abba love the Son, and has given all things into His hand. 36 He that believes on the Son has everlasting chayim: and he that believes not on the Son shall not see chayim; but the wrath of יהוה remains upon Him.

4 When therefore the Master knew how the Prushim had heard that יהושע made and immersed more talmidim than Yochanan, 2 Though יהושע Himself did not do mikvahs, but His talmidim. 3 He left Yahudah, and departed again into Galil. 4 And He needed go through Shomron.[6] 5 He came to a city of Shomron, which is called Shechem, near to the parcel of ground that Yaakov gave to his son Yoseph.[7] 6 Now Yaakov's Well was there.

---

[1] This does not mean that believers' ruachs do not go to heaven as some claim. Rather, it means what it says. That no one before Yahshua's death, burial and resurrection went to heaven, as seen in Luke 16, where they were preserved in Abraham's Bosom or Paradise, later to be released at Moshiach's ascension.
[2] Numbers 21:6-9. Look at Golgotha and live.
[3] What is His Name? Without knowing it and all that it entails, a man stands condemned.
[4] The Son pre-existed as YHWH's Word. Proverbs 30:4.
[5] Yahshua alone while in heaven, has seen and heard things from the Father and desires to reveal them to us if we know who Yahshua truly is.
[6] The need was the actual calling by His Father to open up the door to the former capital of Ephraim.
[7] This entire fascinating event takes place in a land given to Yoseph and his children Ephraim and Menashsheh. Later Shomron would be the actual capital of the northern kingdom.

יהושע therefore, being wearied with His journey, sat on the well: and it was about the sixth hour. 7 There came a woman of Shomron to draw mayim: יהושע said to her, *Give Me to drink.* 8 His talmidim had gone away to the city to buy food. 9 Then said the woman of Shomron to Him, How is it that You, being a Yahudite, ask a drink from me, which am a woman of Shomron? For the Yahudim have no dealings with the Shomronites.[1] [2] 10 יהושע answered and said to her, *If you knew the gift of Elohim, and whom it is that said to you, Give Me a drink; you would have asked Him, and He would have given you living mayim.* 11 The woman said to Him, Master, You have no bucket, and the well is deep: from where then do You have this living mayim? 12 Are You greater than our abba Yaakov, who gave us the well, and drank from it himself, and his children, and his cattle?[3] 13 יהושע answered and said to her, *Whoever drinks of this mayim shall thirst again:* 14 *But whoever drinks of the mayim that I shall give him shall never thirst; but the mayim that I shall give him shall be in him a well of mayim springing up into everlasting chayim.* 15 The woman said to Him, Master, give me this mayim, that I thirst not, neither come here to draw. 16 יהושע said to her, *Go, call your husband, and come here.* 17 The woman answered and said, I have no husband. יהושע said to her, *You have well said, I have no husband:* 18 *For you have had five husbands; and He whom you now have is not your husband:*[4]

what you have said is emet. 19 The woman said to Him, Master, I perceive that You are a Navi.[5] 20 Our ahvot worshipped in this mountain; and yet You say, that in Yahrushalayim is the place where men[6] should worship. 21 יהושע said to her, *Woman, believe Me, the hour comes, when you shall neither in this mountain,[7] nor at Yahrushalayim, worship the Abba.* 22 *You worship you know not what: we know what we worship: for salvation is from the Yahudim.*[8] 23 *But the hour comes, and now is, when the emet worshippers shall worship the Abba in Ruach and in emet: for the Abba seeks such to worship Him.* 24 *Elohim is Ruach: and they that worship Him must worship Him in Ruach and in Emet.*[9] 25 The woman said to Him, I know that the Moshiach comes, when He has come, He will tell us all things. 26 יהושע said to her, *I that speak to you am He.* 27 And at this time came His talmidim, and marveled that He talked with the woman: yet no man said, What do You want with her? Or, Why do You talk with her?[10] 28 The woman then left her mayim jug, and went on her derech into the city, and said to the men, 29 Come, see a Man, who told me all things that I ever did: is not this the Moshiach? 30 Then they went out of the city, and came to Him. 31 In the meantime His talmidim urged Him, saying, Master, eat something. 32 But He said to them, *I have food to eat that you know*

---

[1] That was an understatement. The animosity between them was thick and traced back to the split in the House of David back in 921 BCE. The Samaritans were half-breeds (a mixture of Assyrian settlers and those from Ephraim who remained behind) who, while claiming to be Yisraelites, practiced many expressions of paganism, mixed into their lifestyle.
[2] For more details, see these audio selections:
Tov Samaritan Bad Samaritan
http://store.yourarmstoisrael.org/Qstore/Qstore.cgi?CMD=011&PROD=000158 ; also
The Yisraelite Woman Of Shechem
http://store.yourarmstoisrael.org/Qstore/Qstore.cgi?CMD=011&PROD=000051.
[3] She makes a direct claim to being a Yisraelite from Yaakov's loins in the land of Yoseph. It was common knowledge at the time that despite Jewish objections, Samaritans were in fact children of historic Yisrael.
[4] Meaning Yahshua Himself, making sure she has no ideas.

[5] Note that Yahshua rebuked her immoral lifestyle, but never responded to her claim to be a Yisraelite connected to Yaakov, since that was common knowledge. Also from history we know that many early first-century believers came from Shomron. We have to assume they had offspring in later generations of believers, meaning many of their children today are still in the believing community.
[6] Yisraelites.
[7] Mt. Gerazim.
[8] A strong statement regarding Ephraim's spiritual ignorance and depravity, without Moshiach and Torah. In their return they must grab hold of Yahshua and those from Yahudah who follow Yahshua, in order to return in a manner pleasing to the Father. We see that in Zechariah 8:23, where all ten tribes grab the tzitzit of regenerated Yahudah.
[9] Those who do so are called in scripture the "Yisrael of YHWH."
[10] It was unheard of for a rabbi to be alone with a woman, let alone a Samaritan woman who was considered to be less than a pagan.

nothing about. 33 Therefore said the talmidim one to another, Has any man brought Him anything to eat? 34 יהושע said to them, *My food is to do the will of Him that sent Me, and to finish His mitzvah. 35 Do you not say, There are yet four months, and then comes the harvest? See, I say to you, Lift up your eyes, and look at the fields; for they are white already to harvest.* [1] 36 *And he that reaps receives wages, and gathers fruit to chayim eternal: that both he that sows and he that reaps may gilah as echad.*[2] 37 *And in this case is that saying emet, One sows, and another reaps.* 38 *I sent you to reap that on which you bestowed no labor: other men labored, and you have entered into their labors.* 39 And many of the Shomronites of that city believed on Him for the saying of the woman, which she testified, He told me all that ever I did. 40 So when the Shomronites were come to Him, they asked Him to stay with them: and He stayed there two days.[3] 41 And many more believed because of His own word; 42 And said to the woman, Now we believe, not because of your saying: for we have heard Him ourselves, and know that this is indeed the Moshiach, the Savior of the olam hazeh. 43 Now after two days He departed from there, and went into Galil.[4] 44 For יהושע Himself testified, that a Navi has no honor in His own country. 45 Then when He had come into Galil, the Galileans received Him, having seen all the nisim that He did at Yahrushalayim at the moed: for they also went to the moed.[5] 46 So יהושע came again into Qanah of Galil, where He made the mayim wine. And there was a certain nobleman, whose son was sick at the City of Nachum. 47 When he heard that יהושע had come out of Yahudah into Galil, he went to Him, and asked Him if He would come down, and heal his son: for he was at the point of death. 48 Then said יהושע to him, *Except you see signs and wonders, you will not believe.* 49 The nobleman said to Him, Master, come down before my child dies. 50 יהושע said to him*, Go on your way; your son lives.* And the man believed the word that יהושע had spoken to him, and he went on his derech. 51 And as he was now going down, his avadim met him, and told him, saying, Your son lives. 52 Then he asked the time when his son began to improve. And they said to him, Yesterday at the seventh hour the fever left him. 53 So the abba knew that it was at the same hour, in which יהושע said to him, Your son lives: and he himself believed, and his bayit as well. 54 This is the second ness that יהושע did, when He came out of Yahudah into Galil.

5 After this there was a moed of the Yahudim; and יהושע went up to Yahrushalayim. 2 Now there is at Yahrushalayim by the sheep market a mikvah, which is called in the Ivrit tongue Beth Chesed,[6] having five porches.[7] 3 In these lay a great multitude of impotent folks, blind, crippled, and paralyzed, waiting for the moving of the mayim. 4 For a heavenly messenger went down at a certain season into the mikvah, and stirred the mayim: whoever was first in after the stirring of the mayim was made well of whatever disease he had. 5 And a certain

---

[1] This was said around Shavuot, the early or spring harvest, referencing the four months until the fall harvest of the latter ingathering at Sukkoth or Tabernacles. The very terminology of the feast that references Yisrael's final ingathering from the nations, is a statement about the nature of His mission in coming. He also reminds the talmidim, that because he has reached out to Ephraim here for the very first time in such a bold manner, the door to Ephraim has been opened, and the harvest was white and ready for immediate restoration in the northern kingdom. This is why he prohibited the 70 from going to Shomron earlier, until He had shown them His love for Ephraim by modeling what they were to do. Then in the Great Commission, He allows them to go to Shomron, since in this interaction; He has officially opened the doors to Ephraim's return.

[2] Yisraelites are the reapers, and the Son of Man is the sower of the word of reconciliation.

[3] He stayed for two days or 2,000 years, and has been staying primarily (not exclusively) in the House of Ephraim for that time.

[4] From one former territory of the north to another.

[5] Ephraimites at the feasts.

[6] House of Mercy.

[7] For the five books of Torah, symbolizing the great mercy outlined in the Torah.

man was there, who had an illness thirty-eight years. 6 When יהושע saw him lying down, He knew that he had been in that condition for a long time, said to him, *Do you wish to be made well?* 7 The impotent man answered Him, Master, I have no one, when the mayim is stirred, to put me into the mikvah: but while I am coming, another steps down before me. 8 יהושע said to him, *Rise, take up your quilt, and walk.* 9 And immediately the man was made well, and took up his quilt, and walked: and that day was the Shabbat. 10 The Yahudim therefore said to him that was cured, It is Shabbat: it is not allowed by Torah for you to carry your quilt. 11 He answered them, He that made me well, the same One said to me, Take up your quilt, and walk. 12 Then they asked him, What man is that who said to you, Take up your quilt, and walk? 13 And he that was healed did not who it was: for יהושע had moved Himself away, into a large multitude in that place. 14 Afterward יהושע found him in the Beit HaMikdash, and said to him, *Behold, you are made well: sin no more, lest a worse thing come to you.* 15 The man departed, and told the Yahudim that it was יהושע, who had made him well. 16 And therefore did the Yahudim persecute יהושע, and sought to kill Him, because He had done these things on the Shabbat. 17 But יהושע answered them, *My Abba works until now, and I work.* [1] 18 Therefore the Yahudim sought even more to kill Him, because He not only had broken the Shabbat,[2] but said also that Elohim was His Abba, making Himself equal with Elohim. [3] 19 Then answered יהושע and said to them, *Truly, truly, I say to you, The Son can do nothing by Himself, but only what He sees the Abba doing: for the things He does, these also does the Son likewise.*[4] 20 *For the Abba loves the Son, and shows Him all things that He Himself does: and He will show Him greater works than these that you may marvel. 21 For as the Abba raises the dead, and makes alive; even so the Son makes alive whom He will. 22 For the Abba shophets no man, but has entrusted all mishpat to the Son: 23 That all men should honor the Son, even as they honor the Abba. He that honors not the Son honors not the Abba who has sent Him.*[5] 24 *Truly, truly, I say to you, He that hears My word, and believes on Him that sent Me, has everlasting chayim, and shall not come into condemnation; but has passed from death to chayim. 25 Truly, truly, I say to you, The hour is coming, and now is, when the dead shall shema the voice of the Son of* יהוה: *and they that shema shall live. 26 For as the Abba has chayim in Himself; so has He given to the Son to have chayim in Himself; 27 And has given Him authority to execute mishpat also, because He is the Ben Adam. 28 Marvel not at this: for the hour is coming, that all that are in the graves shall shema His voice, 29 And shall come forth; they that have done tov, to the resurrection of chayim; and they that have done evil, to the resurrection of damnation. 30 I can by My own self do nothing: as I shema, I shophet: and My mishpat is righteous; because I seek not My own will, but the will of the Abba who has sent Me. 31 If I bear witness of Myself, My witness is not emet. 32 There is another*[6] *that bears witness of Me; and I know that the witness which He witnesses of Me is emet. 33 You sent to Yochanan, and He bore witness to the Emet. 34 But I receive not testimony from man: but these things I say, that you might be saved. 35 He was a burning and a shining*

---

[1] This does not mean that Yisrael can now work on Shabbat. It means when it comes to the Father's work of rebuilding Yisrael, and healing injured sheep, we are to do the Father's work without cessation, seven days a week. Worldly and personal labors, especially renumeration labors as an employee of another, remains forbidden.
[2] A false accusation.
[3] Another false accusation. Throughout the scroll of John, He says that while being YHWH, He is the lesser YHWH, subject and in full dependence on Abba YHWH. At no time does He connote the Sent One as equal to the Sender.

---

[4] Here Yahshua clarifies that He is fully reliant on the Father, thus negating their false accusation.
[5] This is a clear warning, to those running to embrace any emunah system that leaves out Yahshua as YHWH's Son.
[6] Note the Father is a second witness and thus must be the other power in the plurality of **echad**.

light: and you were willing for a season to gilah in His light. 36 But I have a greater witness than that of Yochanan: for the works which the Abba has given Me to finish, the same works that I do, bear witness of Me, that the Abba has sent Me. 37 And the Abba Himself, who has sent Me, has borne witness of Me. You have neither heard His voice at any time, nor seen His appearance. 38 And you have not His word living and abiding in you: for whom He has sent, Him you believe not. 39 Search the Ketuvim;[1] for in them you think you have eternal chayim: and these are those, which testify of Me. 40 And you will not come to Me, that you might have chayim.[2] 41 I receive not honor from men. 42 But I know you, that you have not the ahava of Elohim in you. 43 I am come in My Abba's Name, and you receive Me not: if another shall come in His own name, him you will receive.[3] 44 How can you believe, you who receive honor from each other, and seek not the honor that comes from יהוה only? 45 Do not think that I will accuse you to the Abba: there is one that accuses you, even Moshe, in whom you trust.[4] 46 For had you believed Moshe, you would have believed Me: for he wrote of Me. 47 But if you believe not his Ketuvim, how shall you believe My words?[5]

6 After these things יהושע went over the Sea of Galil, which is the Sea of Kinnereth. 2 And a great multitude followed Him, because they saw His nisim that He did on those that were diseased. 3 And יהושע went up into a mountain, and there He sat with His talmidim. 4 And the Pesach, a moed of the Yahudim, was near. 5 When יהושע then lifted up His eyes, and saw a great company come to Him, He said to Philip, *Where shall we buy lechem that these may eat?* 6 And this He said to test him: for He Himself knew what he would do. 7 Philip answered Him, Two hundred pieces of silver worth of lechem is not enough for them, so that each one of them may take a little. 8 One of His talmidim, Andri, Shimon Kepha's brother, said to Him, 9 There is a lad here, who has five barley loaves, and two small fishes: but what are they among so many?[6] 10 And יהושע said, *Make the men[7] sit down.* Now there was much grass in the place. So the men sat down, in number about five thousand. 11 And יהושע took the loaves; and when He had said the bracha, He distributed to the talmidim, and the talmidim to them that were sitting down; and likewise from the fishes as much as they could. 12 When they were filled, He said to His talmidim, *Gather up the fragments that remain, that nothing be lost.* 13 Therefore they gathered them together, and filled twelve baskets with the fragments of the five barley loaves, which remained over and above that which they had eaten.[8] 14 Then those men, when they had seen the ness that יהושע did, said, This is truly Ha Navi[9] that should come into the olam hazeh. 15 When יהושע therefore perceived that they would come and take Him by force, to make Him Melech Yisrael, He departed again into a mountain Himself alone. 16 And when evening came, His talmidim went down to the sea, 17 And entered into a ship, and went over the sea toward the Kfar Nachum. And it was now dark, and יהושע had not come to them. 18 And the sea arose because of a great wind that blew. 19 So when they had rowed about twenty-five or

---

[1] Tanach.
[2] Some of the saddest words in scripture.
[3] YHWH saves and became Yahshua, and thus the Son's Name contains both the Name and the action taken by the Father on our behalf. Since Moshiach is a literal person on earth, so is the end-time anti-Moshiach, who will come in his own Name and authority and not that of Yahweh's. s.a.tan's promotion of a generic mighty one, fits in well with the concept of coming in his own name and authority.
[4] This does not mean the Yisraelites should not trust Moshe's words; rather, He is using a **Kal va Chomer** argument stating that if you trust Moshe, a servant in the House, how much more should you trust the Builder of the entire House of Yisrael.
[5] Since they are the same with the same authority.

[6] See notes on Matthew 14:19, Mark 6:41.
[7] Men in scripture are usually "Yisrael." Gentiles are usually referred to as pigs or dogs.
[8] See important note on Matthew 14:20.
[9] Deut.18: 18.

thirty furlongs, they saw יהושע walking by the sea,[1] and drawing near to the ship: and they were afraid. 20 But He said to them, *It is I; be not afraid.* 21 Then they willingly received Him into the ship: and immediately the ship was at the province where they were going. 22 The day following, the people who stood on the other side of the sea saw that there was no other boat there, except for the one into which His talmidim had entered, and that יהושע had not entered with His talmidim. 23 But other boats from Tiberias came from near the place where they had eaten lechem, after יהושע had said the bracha: 24 When the people therefore saw that יהושע was not there, neither His talmidim, they also took boats, and came to the City of Nachum, seeking for יהושע. 25 And when they had found Him at the seaport, they said to Him, Rabbi, when did You come here? 26 יהושע answered them and said, *Truly, truly, I say to you, You seek Me, not because you saw the nisim, but because you did eat of the loaves, and were filled. 27 Labor not for the food that perishes, but for that food that endures to everlasting chayim, which the Ben Adam shall give you: for Him has the Abba sealed.* 28 Then they said to Him, What should we do, that we might do the works of Elohim? 29 יהושע answered and said to them, *This is the mitzvah of Elohim, that you believe on Him whom He has sent.* 30 They said therefore to Him, What sign will You show us, that we may see, and believe You? What mitzvah do You perform? 31 Our ahvot did eat manna in the desert; as it is written, He gave them manna from the shamayim to eat. 32 Then יהושע said to them, *Truly, truly, I say to you, Moshe gave you not that manna from the shamayim; but My Abba gives you the emet lechem from the shamayim. 33 For the lechem of Elohim is He who comes down from the shamayim, and gives chayim to the olam hazeh.* 34 Then they said to

Him, Master, Always and le-olam-va-ed give us this lechem. 35 And יהושע said to them, *I AM the lechem of chayim: he that comes to Me shall never hunger; and he that believes on Me shall never thirst. 36 But I said to you, That you also have seen Me, and believe not. 37 All that the Abba gives to Me shall come to Me; and he that comes to Me I will in no way cast out. 38 For I came down from the shamayim, not to do My own will, but the will of Him that sent Me. 39 And this is the Abba's will who has sent Me, that of all those He has given Me I should lose nothing, but should raise it up again at the last day.[2] 40 And this is the will of Him that sent Me, that everyone who sees the Son, and believes on Him, may have everlasting chayim: and I will raise him up at the last day.* 41 The Yahudim then murmured at Him, because He said, I AM the lechem who came down from the shamayim.[3] 42 And they said, Is not this יהושע, the ben of Yoseph,[4] whose abba and ima we know? How is it then that He said, I came down from the shamayim? 43 יהושע therefore answered and said to them, *Murmur not among yourselves. 44 No man can come to Me, except the Abba who has sent Me draws him: and I will raise him up at the last day. 45 It is written by the navi, And they shall be all taught of יהוה.[5] Every man therefore that has heard, and has learned from the Abba, comes to Me. 46 Not that any man has seen the Abba, except the One who is from[6] יהוה, he has seen the Abba. 47 Truly, truly, I say to you, He that believes on Me has everlasting chayim. 48 I am that lechem of chayim. 49 Your ahvot did eat manna in the wilderness, and are dead. 50 This is the lechem that comes down from the shamayim*

---

[1] He was by the sea not crossing it, since He was traveling from Tiberius to Capernaum, both on the same side of the lake.

[2] The Father's will is resurrection not rapture.
[3] Just like in the wilderness with the first descent of manna. Here, some 1500 years later, they still complain about heavenly bread.
[4] Moshiach ben Yosef, the Moshiach who would suffer so that Ephraim Yisrael could return to Yahudah.
[5] Isaiah 54:13. Here Yahshua refers to himself as YHWH, who has arrived to teach all Yisrael.
[6] Greek:"**para**" meaning, "out from" or "taken out from". See John 1:18.

that a man may eat of it, and not die. 51 I am the living lechem who came down from the shamayim: if any man eats of this lechem, he shall live le-olam-va-ed: and the lechem that I will give is My flesh, which I will give for the chayim of the olam hazeh. 52 The Yahudim therefore argued among themselves, saying, How can this man give us His flesh to eat?[1] 53 Then יהושע said to them, *Truly, truly, I say to you, Except you eat the flesh of the Ben Adam, and drink His dom; you have no chayim in you. 54 Whoever eats My flesh, and drinks My dom, has eternal chayim; and I will raise him up on the last day. 55 For My flesh is meat indeed, and My dom is drink indeed. 56 He that eats My flesh, and drinks My dom, dwells in Me, and I in him. 57 As the living Abba has sent Me, and I live by the Abba: so he that eats of Me, even he shall live by Me.[2] 58 This is that lechem[3] that came down from the shamayim: not as your ahvot did eat manna, and are dead: he that eats of this lechem shall live le-olam-va-ed.* 59 These things said He in the synagogue, as He taught in the City of Nachum. 60 Many therefore of His talmidim, when they had heard this, said, Oy! This is a difficult teaching; who can shema and obey it? 61 When יהושע knew within Himself that His talmidim murmured, He said to them, *Does this offend you[4] 62 What if you shall see the Ben Adam ascend up to where He was before? 63 It is the Ruach that makes alive; the flesh profits nothing: the words that I speak to you, they are Ruach, and they are chayim.[5] 64 But there are some of you that believe not.* For יהושע

knew from Bereshet[6] whom they were that believed not, and who should betray Him. 65 And he said, *Therefore said I to you that no man can come to Me, except it is given to him by My Abba.* 66 From that time on many of His talmidim backslid, and had their halacha no longer with Him. 67 Then said יהושע to the twelve, *Will you also go away?* 68 Then Shimon Kepha answered Him, Rabbi, to whom shall we go? You have the words of eternal chayim. 69 And we believe and are sure that You are the Moshiach, the Son of the living יהוה. 70 יהושע answered them, *Have not I chosen you twelve, and yet one of you is a shad?* 71 He spoke of Yahudah from Qerioth the son of Shimon: for he it was that was chosen to betray Him, being one of the twelve.

7 After these things יהושע walked only in Galil: for He would not walk in the province of Yahudah because the Yahudim sought to kill Him.[7] 2 Now the Yahudim's moed of Sukkoth was at hand.[8] 3 His brothers therefore said to Him, Depart from here,[9] and go into Yahudah, that Your talmidim also might see the works that You are doing. 4 For there is no one who does anything in secret, who himself seeks to be known openly. If You do these nisim, show Yourself to the olam hazeh. 5 For neither did His brothers believe in Him.[10] 6 Then יהושע said to them, *My time is not yet[11] come: but your time to go up is always ready. 7 The olam hazeh cannot hate you; but Me it hates, because I testify against it, that its deeds are evil. 8 Go up to this moed: I do not go up to this moed; for My time is*

---

[1] Cannibalism is forbidden in Torah.
[2] Yahshua is in no way promoting cannibalism. Rather He is speaking in the **sod** or esoteric, stating that spiritual abiding is the key and that symbols of that spiritual trust and abiding can be soon found in his flesh and dom, which will serve as symbols and reminders of his date with the execution stake. His flesh will soon represent the true bread of life that had been under prior discussion.
[3] His sacrificed flesh.
[4] Truth will always offend overly-sensitive people, and in Yisrael a battle-tested army cannot afford to be too sensitive, or they'll turn their backs on truth, and on the men who are bold enough to proclaim truth, who do not look at men's faces for reactions.
[5] "Chayim" literally means "lives" as in temporal + eternal lives.

[6] Bereshet/Genesis chapter one.
[7] Not all Jews. Just the Jewish leaders in Judea.
[8] These references don't change YHWH's feasts into Jewish feasts, but simply point out that Ephraim is still in the nations, or else they too would be celebrating them like they were supposed to. All these references to the Jewish feasts merely prove that Ephraim had not returned at that time, and this is the Ruach's way of hinting that Ephraim was missing.
[9] Northern territory.
[10] Physical brothers; for if they were spiritual brothers, they would be "unbelieving spiritual brothers" – surely an oxymoron.
[11] Apparently He had taken a new Nazarite vow, and appears to have done this throughout His life on earth.

not yet come. 9 When He had said these words to them, He stayed still in Galil. 10 But when His brothers had gone up, then He went also up to the moed, but not openly, but as it were in secret. 11 Then the Yahudim sought Him at the moed, and said, Where is He? 12 And there was much murmuring among the people concerning Him: for some said, He is a tov man: others said, No; but He just deceives the people. 13 But no man spoke openly about Him for fear of the Yahudim. 14 Now about the midst of the moed **יהושע** went up into the Beit HaMikdash, and taught. 15 And the Yahudim marveled, saying, How does this man know how to read the scrolls, having never learned in a yeshiva?[1] 16 **יהושע** answered them, and said, *My teaching is not Mine, but His who sent Me.* 17 *If any man desires His will, he shall know of the teaching, whether it be from* **יהוה**, *or if I speak from my own thoughts.* 18 *He that speaks of himself seeks his own tifereth: but He that seeks the tifereth of the One who sent Him, the same is emet, and there is no unrighteousness in Him.* 19 *Did not Moshe give you the Torah, and yet none of you keeps the Torah? Why do you try to kill Me?* 20 The people answered and said, You have a shad: who is trying to kill You? 21 **יהושע** answered and said to them, *I have done one mitzvah, and you all marvel.* 22 *Moshe therefore gave you brit milah; - not because it is from Moshe, but from the ahvot - and you on the Shabbat brit milah a man.* 23 *If a man on the Shabbat receives brit milah, that the Torah of Moshe is not broken; are you angry with Me, because I have made a man fully healed on the Shabbat?* 24 *Shophet not according to appearance, but shophet a tzadik mishpat.* 25 Then said some of them from Yahrushalayim, Is not this the One whom they seek to kill? 26 But look, He speaks boldly, and they say nothing to Him.

Perhaps our rulers have found out that this is the actual Moshiach? 27 But on the other hand we know this man and where He comes from: but when the Moshiach comes, no man will know where He is from. 28 Then cried **יהושע** in the Beit HaMikdash as He taught, saying, *You both know Me, and you know where I am from: and I am not come by Myself, but He that sent Me is Emet, who you know not.* 29 *But I know Him: for I am from Him, and He has sent Me.* 30 Then they sought to take Him: but no man laid hands on Him, because His hour had not yet come. 31 And many of the people believed on Him, and said, When the Moshiach comes; will He do more nisim than those that this Man has done? 32 The Prushim heard the people muttering such things about Him; and the Prushim and the chief kohanim sent officers to seize Him. 33 Then said **יהושע** to them, *Yet a little while am I with you, and then I go to Him that sent Me.* 34 *You shall seek Me, and shall not find Me: and where I am, there you cannot come.* 35 Then said the Yahudim among themselves, Where will He go, that we shall not find Him? Will He go to the dispersed among the Greeks, and teach the Greeks?[2] 36 What kind of saying is this that He said, You shall seek Me, and shall not find Me: and where I am, there you cannot come? 37 On Shimini Atzereth, the last great day of the moed, **יהושע** stood and cried, saying, *If any man thirsts, let him come to Me, and drink.*[3] 38 *He that believes on Me, as the Kituvim*[4] *have said, out of His*

---

[1] Deuteronomy 31:10-13 commands the entire Torah to be read at Sukkoth in a year of **schmeetah** or sabbatical year, and that's exactly what Yahshua was doing. This ability is what shocked the rabbis.

[2] The word here is Greeks, and taken along with the term "dispersed," it refers to Yisrael's non-Jewish exiles among the Greek nations. That would include Corinth, Athens, and all the other Greek-dominated countries and cities at that time, such as Antioch. From many sources such as First Maccabees 12:19-23, we know that the Jews knew that the Greeks and Spartans were physical brothers from the same race. This passage is one of the clearest references to Ephraim Yisrael in the nations at the time of Yahshua, and not back in the land. The mocking tone of this question also displays the ongoing animosity between Yisrael's two houses. For many more details see **The Greeks Of the Brit Chadasha** available in video and audio at:
http://store.yourarmstoisrael.org/Qstore/Qstore.cgi?CMD=011 &PROD=000209.
[3] This invitation is given twice in John. Once to Ephraim, and once to Yahudah, for both houses to **shema** and return.
[4] Isaiah 12:3, Jeremiah 17:13.

belly shall flow rivers of mayim chayim. 39 And this He spoke of the Ruach, which they that believe on Him would receive: for the Set-Apart Ruach was not yet given; because **יהושע** was not yet esteemed. 40 Many of the people therefore, when they heard this saying, said, Truly this is HaNavi of Devarim. 41 Others said, This is the Moshiach. But some said, Shall the Moshiach come out of Galil? 42 Have not the Kituvim said, that the Moshiach comes from the zera of David, and out of the town of Beth-Lechem, where David was from? 43 So there was a division among the people because of Him. 44 And some of them would have taken Him; but no man laid hands on Him. 45 Then came the officers to the chief kohanim and Prushim; and they said to them, Why have you not brought Him to us? 46 The officers answered, Never has any man spoken like this man. 47 Then answered the Prushim, Are you also deceived? 48 Have any of the rulers or any of the Prushim believed on Him? 49 But these people[1] who know not the Torah are cursed. 50 Nakdimon said to them - he that came to **יהושע** by night, being one of them - 51 Does our Torah shophet any man[2], before it hears him, and knows what he does? 52 They answered and said to him, Are you also from Galil? Search, and look: for out of Galil neviim do not come forth.[3] 53 And every man went to his own bayit.

8 **יהושע** went to the Mount of Olives. 2 And early in the morning He came again into the Beit HaMikdash, and all the people came to Him; and He sat down, and taught them. 3 And the scribes and Prushim brought to Him a woman taken in adultery; and when they had placed her in the midst, 4 They said to Him, Master, this woman was taken in adultery, in the very act. 5 Now Moshe in the Torah commanded us,

that such should be stoned: but what are you saying? 6 This they said, tempting Him, that they might be able to accuse Him. But **יהושע** stooped down, and with His finger wrote on the ground, as though He heard them not. 7 So when they continued asking Him, He lifted Himself up, and said to them, *He that is without sin among you, let him be the first to cast a stone at her.* 8 And again He stooped down, and wrote on the ground.[4] 9 And they which heard it, being convicted by their own conscience, went out one by one, beginning with the eldest, even to the youngest: and **יהושע** was left alone, with the woman standing in the midst. 10 When **יהושע** had Himself lifted up, and saw no one but the woman, He said to her, *Woman, where are your accusers? Has no man condemned you?* 11 She said, No man, Master. And **יהושע** said to her, *Neither do I condemn you: go, and sin no more.* 12 Then spoke **יהושע** again to them, saying, *I am the Light of the olam hazeh: he that follows Me shall not walk in darkness, but shall have the Light of chayim.* 13 The Prushim therefore said to Him, You bare witness of Yourself; Your witness is not emet. 14 **יהושע** answered and said to them, *Though I bear witness of Myself, yet My witness is emet: for I know where I came from, and where I am going; but you cannot tell where I came from, or where I go. 15 You shophet after the flesh; I shophet no man. 16 And yet if I do shophet, My mishpat is emet: for I am not alone, but I and the Abba that sent Me. 17 It is also written in your Torah, that the testimony of two men is emet. 18 I am one that bears witness of Myself, and the Abba that sent Me bears witness of Me.*[5] 19 Then they said to Him, Where is Your Abba? **יהושע** answered *You neither know Me, nor My Abba: if you knew*

---

[1] **Am HaAretz** or the common unlearned people.
[2] Yisraelite.
[3] In their anger they must have forgotten about Nachum and Yonah.

[4] He upheld the Torah and the mercy of the Torah, all the while fulfilling prophecy by writing the names of those who were forsaking the living water, into the dust of the earth, as prophesied in Jeremiah 17:13.
[5] This passage gives insight into the two powers of Father and Son that serve as dual witnesses. Yahshua Himself declares the Father and Son as **echad,** yet two witnesses according to Torah, not one witness in different costumes.

Me, *you would have known My Abba also.* 20 These words spoke **יהושע** in the treasury, as He taught in the Beit HaMikdash: and no man laid hands on Him; for His hour had not yet come. 21 Then said **יהושע** again to them, *I go on My derech, and you shall seek Me, and shall die in your sins: where I go, you cannot come.* 22 Then said the Yahudim, Will He kill Himself? Because He said, Where I go, you cannot come. 23 And He said to them, *You are from beneath; I am from above: you are of the olam hazeh; I am not of the olam hazeh. 24 I said therefore to you, that you shall die in your sins: for if you believe not that I AM, you shall die in your sins.*[1] 25 Then said they to Him, Who are you? And **יהושע** said to them, *Even though I have just begun to speak to you; 26 I have many things to say and to shophet you for: but He that sent Me is emet; and I speak to the olam hazeh those things which I have heard from Him.* 27 They did not understood that He spoke to them of the Abba. 28 Then said **יהושע** to them, *When you have lifted up the Ben Adam, then shall you know that I AM, and that I do nothing by Myself; but as My Abba has taught Me, I speak these things. 29 And He that sent Me is with Me: the Abba has not left Me alone; for I do always those things that please Him.*[2] 30 As He spoke these words, many believed on Him. 31 Then said **יהושע** to those Yahudim who believed on Him, *If you continue in My word, then are you My talmidim indeed;*[3] *32 And you shall know the emet, and the emet shall make you free.* 33 They answered Him, We are Avraham's zera, and were never in bondage to any man: how are You saying, you shall be

made free?[4] 34 **יהושע** answered them, *Truly, truly, I say to you, Whoever commits sin is the eved of sin. 35 And the eved stays not in the Bayit le-olam-va-ed: but a son stays le-olam-va-ed. 36 If the Son therefore shall make you free, you shall be free indeed. 37 I know that you are Avraham's zera; but you seek to kill Me, because My word has no place in you. 38 I speak that which I have seen with My Abba: and you do that which you have seen with your abba.* 39 They answered and said to Him, Avraham is our abba. **יהושע** said to them, *If you were Avraham's children, you would do the works of Avraham. 40 But now you seek to kill Me, a man that has told you the emet, which I have heard from* **יהוה***: this Avraham did not do. 41 You do the deeds of your abba.* Then they said to Him, We are not born of fornication; we have one Abba, even Elohim.[5] 42 **יהושע** said to them, *If* **יהוה** *Elohim were your Abba, you would love Me: for I proceeded forth and came from* **יהוה** *Elohim; neither came I by My own accord, but He sent Me. 43 Why do you not understand My speech? Even because you cannot shema My word. 44 You are of your abba s.a.tan,*[6] *and the lusts of your abba you will do. He was a murderer from Bereshet, and stayed not in the emet, because there is no emet in him. When he speaks a lie, he speaks his own lie: for he is a liar, and the abba of it. 45 And because I tell you the emet, you do not believe Me. 46 Which of you can rebuke Me because of sin? And if I say the emet, why do you not believe Me? 47 He that is of* **יהוה** *hears* **יהוה** *'s words: you therefore shema them not, because you are not of* **יהוה***.* 48 Then answered the Yahudim, and said to Him, Don't we say the emet, that You are a

---

[1] It is required that every man or woman believe in Yahshua as the **I AM** of Exodus 3:14-15, or the consequences will be a second and eternal death. This includes all from the House of Judah.
[2] Full obedience to Torah that He learned from much suffering. He learned from the Father, and therefore is not the Father, who learns from no man.
[3] The test of discipleship is endurance to the end of one's life on earth.
[4] A true case of brain fade; Egypt, Babylon and Assyria were three such times when Yisrael was enslaved.
[5] Even then the accusations of Yahshua being illegitimate were circulating.
[6] This is not to say all Jews are shadim, since most of the multitudes and the writers of the Renewed Covenant were Jews. Rather any unbeliever that hates Yahshua is a child of s.a.tan. This is a general application text, not a condemnation of Jews.

Shomronite, and have a shad?[1] 49 **יהושע** answered, *I have not a shad; but I honor My Abba, but you do dishonor Me.*[2] 50 *And I seek not My own tifereth: there is One that seeks and shophets. 51 Truly, truly, I say to you, If a man shomers My words, he shall never see death.* 52 Then said the Yahudim to Him, Now we know that You have a shad. Avraham is dead, and the neviim; and You are saying, If a man shomers My words, he shall never taste death. 53 Are You greater than our abba Avraham, who is dead? And the neviim who are dead: who do You make Yourself to be? 54 **יהושע** answered, *If I honor Myself, My honor is nothing: it is My Abba that honors Me; the One who you say, is your Elohim: 55 Yet you have not known Him; but I know Him: and if I should say, I don't know Him, I shall be a liar like yourselves: but I know Him, and guard His Word. 56 Your abba Avraham rejoiced to see My day: and he saw it, and had gilah.*[3] 57 Then said the Yahudim to Him, You are not yet fifty years old, and You have seen Avraham? 58 **יהושע** said to them, *Truly, truly, I say to you, Before Avraham was, I AM.*[4] 59 Then took they up stones to cast at Him: but **יהושע** hid Himself, and went out of the Beit HaMikdash, going through the midst of them, and so went away.[5]

9 And as **יהושע** passed by, He saw a man who was blind from his birth. 2 And His talmidim asked Him, saying, Master, who did sin, this man, or his parents, that he was born blind? 3 **יהושע** answered, *Neither has this man sinned, nor His parents: but that the works of Elohim should be made manifest through Him. 4 I must do the works of Him that sent Me, while it is day: the night comes, when no man can do works. 5 As long as I am in the olam hazeh, I am the Light of the olam hazeh.* 6 When He had spoken this, He spat on the ground, and made clay with the saliva, and He anointed the eyes of the blind man with the clay, 7 And said to Him, *Go, wash in the Mikvah of Shiloach* - which is by interpretation, Sent - He went on his derech therefore, and washed, and came seeing. 8 The neighbors therefore, and those who before had seen him blind, said, Is not this he that sat and begged? 9 Some said, This is that man: others said, No he only resembles him: but he said, I am the one. 10 Therefore said they to him, How were your eyes opened? 11 He answered and said, A Man they call **יהושע** made clay, and anointed My eyes, and said to me, Go to the Mikvah of Shiloach, and wash: and I went and washed, and I received My sight. 12 Then they said to him, Where is He? He said, I don't know. 13 They brought to the Prushim him that was blind before. 14 And it was Shabbat when **יהושע** made the clay, and opened his eyes. 15 Then again the Prushim asked him how he had received his sight. He said to them, He put clay upon my eyes, and I washed, and do see. 16 Therefore said some of the Prushim, This Man is not from Elohim, because He shomers not the Shabbat. Others said, How can a man that is a sinner do such nisim? And there was a division among them. 17 They said to the blind man again, What do you say you about Him, who has opened your eyes? He said to them, I say He is a Navi. 18 But the Yahudim did not believe him, who had been blind, and received his sight, until they called in the parents of him that had received his sight. 19 And they asked them, saying, Is this your son, who you say was born blind? How then does he now see? 20 His parents answered them and said, We know that this is our son, and that he was born blind: 21 But by what means he now sees, we don't know; or who has

---

[1] A dual accusation. That He is shad-driven, and is an Ephraimite, again displaying the contempt and hate between Yisrael's two houses.
[2] Notice how he so identified with Ephraim Yisrael as Moshiach ben Yosef, in that he refuses to answer the Samaritan accusation, seeing himself as a Yisraelite in suffering, like they themselves were.
[3] Genesis 22.
[4] A claim to be YHWH.
[5] They understood His claim to be YHWH even if some today don't.

opened his eyes we don't know: he is bar mitzvah;[1] ask him: he can speak for himself. 22 These words spoke his parents, because they feared the Yahudim: for the Yahudim had agreed already, that if any man did confess that He was the Moshiach, he would then be put out of the synagogue.[2] 23 Because of this his parents said, He is bar mitzvah; ask him. 24 Then they again called the man that was blind, and said to him, Give Elohim the tehilla: we know that this man is a sinner. 25 He answered and said, Whether He is a sinner or not, I don't know: one thing I know, that, before I was blind, but now I see. 26 Then said they to him again, What did He to you? How did he open your eyes? 27 He answered them, I have told you already, and you do not shema: why do you want to shema it again? Do you also desire be His talmidim? 28 Then they abused him, and said, You are His talmid; but we are Moshe's talmidim. 29 We know that Elohim spoke to Moshe: as for this fellow, we don't even know where He comes from. 30 The man answered and said to them, Why here is an interesting thing, that you don't know from where He comes from, and yet He has opened my eyes. 31 Now we know that Elohim hears not to sinners: but if any man be a worshipper of Elohim, and does His will, He hears to him. 32 Since the olam hazeh began it was never heard that any man opened the eyes of one that was born blind. 33 If this man were not from Elohim, He could do nothing. 34 They answered and said to him, You were altogether born in sins, and yet you teach us? And they cast him out. 35 יהושע heard that they had cast him out; and when He had found him, He said to him, *Do you believe on the Son of* יהוה*?* 36 He answered and said, Who is He, Master, that I may believe on Him? 37 And יהושע said to him, *You have seen Him, and it is He that is speaking with you right now.* 38 And he said, Master, I

believe. And he worshipped Him. 39 And יהושע said, *For mishpat I am come into this olam hazeh, that they who see not might see; and that they who see might be made blind.* 40 And some of the Prushim who were with Him heard these words, and said to Him, Are we blind also? 41 יהושע said to them, *If you were blind, you would have no sin: but now you say, We see; therefore your sin remains.*

10 *Truly, truly, I say to you, He that enters not by the door into the sheepfold, but climbs up some other derech, the same is a thief and a robber. 2 But he that enters in by the door is the Shepherd of the sheep. 3 To Him the doorkeeper opens; and the sheep shema His voice: and He calls His own sheep by name, and leads them out. 4 And when He puts forth His own sheep, He goes before them, and the sheep follow Him: for they know His voice. 5 And a stranger will they not follow, but will flee from him: for they know not the voice of strangers.* 6 This figure of speech יהושע used with them: but they understood not these things that He spoke to them. 7 Then said יהושע to them again, *Truly, truly, I say to you, I am the door of the sheep. 8 All that ever came before Me are thieves and robbers: but the sheep did not shema them. 9 I am the door: by Me if any man enters in, he shall be saved, and shall go in and out, and find pasture. 10 The thief comes not, but to steal, and to kill, and to destroy: I am come that they might have chayim, and that they might have it more abundantly. 11 I am the Tov Shepherd: the Tov Shepherd gives His chayim for the sheep. 12 But he that is a hired person, and not the Shepherd, whose own the sheep are not, sees the wolf coming, and leaves the sheep, and runs away: and the wolf catches them, and scatters the sheep. 13 The hired person runs away, because he is a hired person, and cares not for the sheep. 14 I am the Tov Shepherd, and know My sheep, and am*

---

[1] A child of the covenant, and thus 13 and older.
[2] The leaders agreed, not the people who heard him gladly.

known by My sheep.[1] 15 *As the Abba knows Me, even so know I the Abba: and I lay down My chayim for the sheep.* 16 *And other sheep I have, which are not of this fold: them also I must bring in, and they shall shema My voice; and there shall be one fold, and one Shepherd.*[2] 17 *Therefore does My Abba love Me, because I lay down My chayim, that I might take it again.*[3]

18 *No man takes it from Me, but I lay it down by Myself. I have power to lay it down, and I have power to take it again. This commandment have I received from My Abba.*[4] 19 There was a division therefore again among the Yahudim for these sayings.[5] 20 And many of them said, He has a shad and is meshugas; why do you shema to Him?[6] 21 Others said, These are not the words of Him that has a shad. Can a shad open the eyes of the blind?[7] 22 And it was at Yahrushalayim at Chanukah, and it was winter. 23 And **יהושע** walked in the Beit HaMikdash in Shlomo's Porch. 24 Then came the Yahudim around Him,

and said to Him, How long do You make us doubt? If You are the Moshiach, tell us plainly. 25 **יהושע** answered them, *I told you, and you believed not: the works that I do in My Abba's Name, they bear witness of Me. 26 But you believe not, because you are not My sheep, as I said to you. 27 My sheep shema My voice, and I know them, and they follow Me: 28 And I give to them eternal chayim; and they shall never perish, neither shall any man snatch them out of My hand. 29 My Abba, who gave them to Me, is greater than all; and no man is able to snatch them out of My Abba's hand. 30 I and My Abba are Echad.*[8] 31 Then the Yahudim took up stones again to stone Him. 32 **יהושע** answered them, *Many tov works have I shown you from My Abba; for which of those works do you stone Me?*

33 The Yahudim answered Him, saying, For a tov mitzvah we don't stone You not; but for blasphemy; because You, being only a man, make Yourself Elohim.[9] 34 **יהושע** answered them, *Is it not written in your Torah, I said, You are elohim? 35 If He called them elohim, to whom the word of* **יהוה** *came, then the Kituvim cannot be broken;*[10] 36 *Why do you say of Him, whom Abba has set-apart, and sent into the olam hazeh, You blaspheme; because I said, I am the Son of Elohim?*[11] [12] 37 *If I do not the works of My Abba, believe Me not. 38 But if I do, though you believe Me not, believe the works: that you may know, and believe, that the Abba is in Me, and I in Him.*

---

[1] Ezekiel 34:11-31 is where YHWH Himself promises to come to earth to look for and find His lost sheep. The speech here is used to alert anyone familiar with scripture that Yahshua Himself is the One who has come to look for and return Yisrael's wandering exiles back to the fold.

[2] A plain reference to the other fold or flock of Yisrael, Ephraim Yisrael, that Yahshua says He must bring in by command of the Father. Note that even before He died and rose, He had two existing Yisraelite flocks, not one. Through His mission as the Tov Shepherd, both folds will become **echad**.

[3] The Father loves Yahshua, because He is faithful to His primary mission of taking two Yisraelite folds, and making them one Yisrael, knowing YHWH.

[4] The mission to die for both houses is called a commandment by Yahshua.

[5] The truth about the true purpose of Yahshua's death, which is to restore and regather both houses of Yisrael, brings sharp division among the Jewish community. It seems like whenever Yahudah hears of YHWH's love for both houses as in Luke 15, it brings out the worst in them. The message of the true kingdom always brings division, and those who teach the truth will always be labeled as divisive. Yet it is that message alone that heals and ends vexation and jealousy.

[6] Yahshua was called insane and demon-influenced due to His teachings regarding His Shepherd's role in the regathering of both houses of Yisrael. Today, those Jews who oppose YHWH's plan to reunite non-Jewish Yisrael with Jewish Yisrael are also accused of being insane and promoting a teaching of demons, as seen here in this text. Nevertheless, YHWH is working in the earth, as more and more believers are seeing the two-bayit restoration.

[7] Both houses are being restored as blindness is removed. Yahudah's blindness to Yahshua, and Ephraim's blindness to Torah and their Hebraic identity, constitutes blindness removed from each bayit. This is healing and is not a demonic activity as Yahshua Himself taught us.

[8] Aramaic: "are of one accord". Father and Son are both in **echad**, and in full power and authority sharing in full accord, yet all flows from the Father into Yahshua.

[9] Not true. He only stated the fact that He is **echad** with YHWH, and is the same substance as YHWH. He didn't make that up.

[10] Psalm 82:6.

[11] The point made here is that all recipients of the Word of YHWH are made mighty in inner strength, and are thus called "Elohim" or "strong mighty ones." Based on that word assignment, Yahshua asks the obvious question. Why is it not blasphemy for you and suddenly it is for Me? If you are elohim, how much more is the Creator Elohim, again proving that those arguing with Him, were religious but ignorant of scripture.

[12] The one difference between YHWH's Son and all the other elohim in Yisrael, is found in the same Psalm, Psalm 82 verse 7: "but as men" you shall die. Yahshua in His eternal existence is distinguished from other human elohim.

39 Therefore they sought again to take Him: but He escaped out of their hand, 40 And He went away again beyond Yarden into the place where Yochanan at first immersed; and there He stayed. 41 And many came to Him, and said, Yochanan did not even do one ness: but all the things that Yochanan spoke about this Man are emet. 42 And many believed on Him there.

11 Now a certain man was sick, named El-Azar, of Beth Anya, the town of Miryam and her sister Martha. 2 It was that Miryam who anointed יהושע with ointment, and wiped His feet with her hair, whose brother El-Azar was sick. 3 Therefore his sisters sent to Him, saying, Master, see, he whom You love is sick. 4 When יהושע heard that, He said, *This sickness is not to death, but for the tiferleth of* יהוה, *that the Son of* יהוה *might be esteemed by this.* 5 Now יהושע loved Martha, and her sister, and El-Azar. 6 When He had heard that he was sick, He stayed two days still in the same place where He was. 7 Then after that He said to His talmidim, *Let us go into Yahudah again.* 8 His talmidim said to Him, Master, the Yahudim recently sought to stone You; and You go there again? 9 יהושע answered, *Are there not twelve hours in the day? If any man walks in the day, he stumbles not, because he sees the Light of the olam hazeh.* 10 *But if a man walks in the night, he stumbles, because there is no Light in him.* 11 These things He said: and after that He said to them, *Our chaver El-Azar sleeps; but I go, that I may awake him out of sleep.* 12 Then said His talmidim, Master, if he sleeps, he shall do well. 13 But יהושע spoke of His death: but they thought that He had spoken of taking a rest in sleep. 14 Then said יהושע to them plainly, *El-Azar is dead.* 15 *And I am glad for your sake that I was not there, to the intent you may believe; nevertheless let us go to him.* 16 Then said Toma, who is called the Twin, to his fellow talmidim, Let us also go, that

we may die with Him. 17 Then when יהושע came, He found that he had been in the tomb for four days already. 18 Now Beth-Anya was near to Yahrushalayim, about two miles away: 19 And many of the Yahudim came to Martha and Miryam, to comfort them concerning their brother. 20 Then Martha, as soon as she heard that יהושע was coming, went and met Him: but Miryam sat still in the bayit. 21 Then said Martha to יהושע, Master, if You had been here, my brother would not have died. 22 But I know, that even now, whatever You will ask of יהוה, יהוה will give it You. 23 יהושע said to her, *Your brother shall rise again.* 24 Martha said to Him, I know that he shall rise again in the resurrection on the last day. 25 יהושע said to her, *I Am the resurrection, and the chayim: he that believes in Me, though he were dead, yet shall he live:* 26 *And whoever lives and believes in Me shall never die. Do you believe this?* 27 She said to Him, Yes, Master: I believe that You are the Moshiach, the Son of יהוה, who should come into the olam hazeh. 28 And when she had said so, she went on her derech, and called Miryam her sister secretly, saying, The Master has come, and calls for you. 29 As soon as she heard that, she arose quickly, and came to Him. 30 Now יהושע had not yet come into the town, but was in that place where Martha met Him. 31 The Yahudim then who were with her in the bayit, comforting her, when they saw Miryam, that she rose up quickly and went out, followed her, saying, She goes to the tomb to weep there. 32 Then when Miryam had come to where יהושע was, and saw Him, she fell down at His feet, saying to Him, Master, if You had been here, my brother would not have died. 33 When יהושע therefore saw her weeping, and the Yahudim also weeping who came with her, He groaned in the Ruach, and was troubled, 34 And said, *Where have you laid Him?* They said to Him, Master, come and see. 35 יהושע wept. 36 Then said the Yahudim,

Behold how He loved him! 37 And some of them said, Could not this Man, who opened the eyes of the blind, have caused that even this man should not have died? 38 יהושע therefore again being troubled within came to the tomb. It was a cave, and a stone was placed at the entrance. 39 יהושע said, *Take away the stone.* Martha, the sister of him that was dead, said to Him, Master, by this time he stinks: for he has been dead four days. 40 יהושע said to her, *Did I not say to you, that, if you would believe, you would see the tifereth of* יהוה*?* 41 Then they took away the stone from the place where the dead man was laid. And יהושע lifted up His eyes, and said, *Abba, todah that You have heard Me. 42 And I know that You shema Me always: but because of the people who stand by I said it, that they may believe that You have sent Me.* 43 And when He had spoken, He cried out with a loud voice, *El-Azar, uhrah vetzeah; come forth.* 44 And he that was dead came forth, bound hand and foot with burial clothes: and his face bound with a burial napkin. יהושע said to them, *Loose him, and let him go.* 45 Then many of the Yahudim who came to Miryam, and had seen the things that יהושע did, believed on Him. 46 But some of them went to the Prushim, and told them what things יהושע had done. 47 Then gathered the chief kohanim and the Prushim a Sanhedrin, and said, What do we do? For this Man does many nisim. 48 If we just leave Him alone, all men will believe on Him: and the Romans shall come and take away our position, Beit HaMikdash and nation. 49 And one of them, named Qayapha, being the Kohen HaGadol that same year, said to them, You know nothing at all, 50 Nor do you consider that it is better for us that one man should die for the people, than for the entire nation to perish.[1] 51 And this he spoke not by himself: but being Kohen HaGadol that year, he prophesied that

יהושע should die for that nation;[2] 52 And not for that nation only, but that also He should gather together into echad the b'nai Elohim that were scattered abroad.[3] 53 Then from that day forward they took counsel together to put Him to death. 54 יהושע therefore walked no more openly among the Yahudim; but went there to a country near to the wilderness, into a city called Ephraim, and there continued with His talmidim.[4] 55 And the Yahudim's Pesach was at hand: and many went out of the country up to Yahrushalayim before the Pesach, to purify themselves. 56 Then they sought for יהושע , and spoke among themselves, as they stood in the Beit HaMikdash, What do you think, will He not come to the moed? 57 Now both the chief kohanim and the Prushim had given a commandment, that, if any man knew where He was, he should reveal it, that they might seize Him.

12 Then יהושע six days before the Pesach came to Beth Anya, where El-Azar was who יהושע had raised from the dead. 2 There they made Him a supper; and Martha served: but El-Azar was one of

---

[2] The House of Yahudah.
[3] "The children of Yisrael or Elohim that were already scattered abroad" can only be referring to non-Jewish or Ephraim Yisrael, from the ten northern tribes. No other group of people possibly fits this description. Note that they were not pagans, but already covenant people in exile. Note also that they are called "children of Elohim," an end-time term referring to the 10 tribes of the north according to Hosea 1:10. Since Yahudah was mostly in the land of Yisrael at the time of this prophecy, it certainly points to Ephraim Yisrael. Ciaphas pronounces this, and the Ruach elaborates by saying that it is far better for Yahshua to die than for both houses to perish. Both those in the land, and those scattered abroad, return by His death according to Ciaphas and John, so that both folds can become one again.
[4] Once the Ruach had declared the reason for Yahshua's death, we see an immediate **remez**, or hint application, of the gathering of the exiles of Ephraim back home. Rather than walk in Judea, where He would be prematurely arrested, Yahshua went into the wilderness to a city called Ephraim. Since Ephraim is in the wilderness of the nations, and since Yahudah's leaders no longer welcomed Him, he continued in Ephraim and remained there with His talmidim. This is again a prophetic declaration by the Ruach in the **remez**, that Yahshua will be rejected by Yahudah's elders, only to find refuge among scattered Ephraim in the wilderness of the nations. In so doing, He would remain there with His disciples for the better part of the next 2,000 years. The Ruach places these Scriptures in spiritual sequence and the message is clear. Yahshua has found His talmidim primarily among returning Ephraim, and will continue to do so until His return.

---

[1] Jewish Yisrael.

them that sat at the table with Him.[1] 3 Then Miryam took an alabaster of tov pistachio,[2] very expensive, and anointed the feet of **יהושע**, and wiped His feet with her hair: and the bayit was filled with the fragrance of the oil.[3] 4 Then said one of His talmidim, Yahudah from Qerioth, Shimon's son, who would betray Him, 5 Why was this ointment not sold for three hundred silver pieces, and given to the poor? 6 This he said, not because he cared for the poor; but because he was a thief, and had the moneybag, and stole what was put in it. 7 Then said **יהושע**, *Leave her alone: she has kept it for the day of My burial. 8 For the poor you always have with you; but Me you do not have always.* 9 Many people of the Yahudim therefore knew that He was there: and they came not for **יהושע**'s sake only, but that they might also see El-Azar, who He had raised from the dead. 10 But the chief kohanim conspired that they might put El-Azar also to death; 11 Because on account of him many of the Yahudim went away, and believed on **יהושע**. 12 On the next day many of the people that had come early for the moed, when they heard that **יהושע** was coming to Yahrushalayim, 13 Took branches of palm trees, and went forth to meet Him, and cried, Hoshia-na: Blessed is the Melech of Yisrael; Baruch haba beshem HaAdon **יהוה**. 14 And **יהושע**, when He had found a young donkey, sat on it; as it is written, 15 Fear not, daughter of Tsiyon: see, your Melech comes, sitting on a donkey's colt. 16 These things His talmidim understood not at that time: but when **יהושע** was esteemed, then they recalled that these things were written about Him, and that they had done these things to Him. 17 The people therefore that were with Him when He called El-Azar out of His tomb, and raised him from the dead, bore witness.

18 For this cause the people also met Him, for that they heard that He had done this ness. 19 The Prushim therefore said among themselves, Do you perceive how you prevail nothing? Behold, the entire olam has gone after Him. 20 And there were certain Greeks among them that came up to worship at the moed:[4] 21 The same came near to Philip, who was from Beth-Tsaida of Galil, and sought him, saying, sir, we would like to see **יהושע**. 22 Philip comes and tells Andri: and Andri and Philip tell **יהושע**. 23 And **יהושע** answered them, saying, *The hour has come, that the Ben Adam should be esteemed.[5] 24 Truly, truly, I say to you, Except a grain of wheat falls into the ground and dies, it stays alone: but if it dies, it brings forth much fruit.[6] 25 He that loves his chayim shall lose it; and he that hates his chayim in the olam hazeh shall keep it to chayim eternal. 26 If any man serve Me, let him follow Me; and where I am, there shall also My eved be: if any man serve Me, him will My Abba honor. 27 Now My being is troubled; and what shall I say? Abba, save Me from this hour: but it was for this cause that I came to this hour. 28 Abba, bring tifereth Your Name. Then there came a voice from the shamayim, saying, I have both esteemed it, and will tifereth it again.[7] 29 The people therefore, that stood by, and who heard to it, said that it thundered: others said, A heavenly messenger spoke to Him. 30* **יהושע** answered and said, *This voice came not because of Me, but for Your sakes.[8] 31 Now is the mishpat of the olam*

---

[1] This could have been one of those pre-Pesach rehearsal meals, done by most rabbis in the first century that Yahshua later did with the 12 talmidim.
[2] Hebraic Roots Version, p.232.
[3] A true thanksgiving offering by Miryam for what Yahshua did by raising her brother. This is the true worship, that doesn't seek a gift, but returns in pure adoration.
[4] See note on John 7:35.
[5] What prompted Yahshua to say this at this juncture was the return of these select Ephraimites, who were attending the feasts, and wanted more perfect instruction and so came to seek Moshiach. When Yahshua perceived of the return of the children of exiled Yisrael scattered abroad, He knew that His time had come to bring back not just these few, but the "fullness of the gentiles" as seen in Genesis 48:19.
[6] In context, Ephraim's massive return depends upon the grain of wheat (Yahshua) falling into the ground at death, in order to bring forth much fruit among the exiles of non Jewish Yisrael.
[7] In the ministry of Moshiach, and in the future ministry of his people among his people by the Ruach. The esteeming of YHWH's Name is an ongoing restoration work as well.
[8] That we would know of a certainty that the Father expects us to esteem and proclaim His true Name.

hazeh: now shall the prince of the olam hazeh be cast out. 32 And I, if I be lifted up from the earth, will draw all men[1] to Me. 33 This He said, signifying what death He should die. 34 The people answered Him, We have heard out of the Torah that the Moshiach remains on earth le-olam-va-ed: and how are you saying, The Ben Adam must be lifted up? Who is this Ben Adam? 35 Then יהושע said to them, *Yet a little while is the Light with you. Walk while you have the Light, lest darkness come upon you: for he that walks in darkness knows not where he goes. 36 While you have Light, believe in the Light, that you may be the children of Light.* These things spoke יהושע, and departed, and was hidden from them. 37 But though He had done so many nisim before them, yet they believed not on Him: 38 That the saying of Yeshayahu ha navi might be fulfilled, which he spoke saying יהוה, who has believed our report? And to whom has the Arm of the Master יהוה been revealed? 39 Therefore they could not believe, because Yeshayahu said again, 40 He has blinded their eyes, and hardened their hearts; that they should not see with their eyes, nor understand with their hearts, and be turned, and I would heal them. 41 These things said Yeshayahu, when he saw His tifereth, and spoke of Him. 42 Nevertheless among the chief rulers also many believed on Him; but because of the Prushim they did not confess Him, lest they should be put out of the synagogue: 43 For they love the tehilla of men more than the tehilla of יהוה .[2] 44 יהושע cried and said, *He that believes on Me, believes not on Me, but on Him that sent Me. 45 And he that sees Me sees Him that sent Me. 46 I have come a Light into the olam hazeh that whoever believes on Me should not live in darkness. 47 And if any man shema My words, and believe not, I shophet him not: for I came not to shophet the olam, but to save the olam hazeh. 48 He that rejects Me, and receives not My words, has One that shophets him: the word that I have spoken, the same shall shophet him on the last day. 49 For I have not spoken by Myself; but the Abba who sent Me, He gave Me a commandment, what I should say, and what I should speak. 50 And I know that His commandment is chayay olam: whatever I speak therefore, even as the Abba said to Me, so I speak.*

13 Now before the moed of the Pesach, when יהושע knew that His hour had come and that He should depart out of the olam hazeh back to the Abba, having loved His own who were in the olam hazeh, He loved them to the end. 2 During supper, s.a.tan put into the heart of Yahudah from Qerioth, Shimon's son, the desire to betray Him; 3 יהושע knowing that the Abba had given all things into His hands, and that He had come from יהוה, and was going to יהוה ; 4 Rose from supper, and laid aside His garments; and took a towel, and girded Himself. 5 After that He poured mayim into a bason, and began to observe Rachatz and wash the talmidim's feet, and to wipe them with the towel with which He was girded. 6 Then He came to Shimon Kepha: and Kepha said to Him, Master, do You wash my feet? 7 יהושע answered and said to him, *What I do you do not know now; but you shall know after this.* 8 Kepha said to Him, You shall never wash my feet. יהושע answered him, *If I wash you not, you have no part with Me.* 9 Shimon Kepha said to Him, Master, not my feet only, but also my hands and my head.[3] 10 יהושע said to him, *He that is bathed need not wash except his feet, but is clean already: and you are clean, but not all.* 11 For He knew who should betray Him; therefore He said, You are not all clean. 12 So after He had washed their feet, and had taken off His garments, and was sitting down again, He said to them, *Now do*

---

[1] The drawing back of Yisrael.
[2] One of the saddest verses in Scripture.
[3] Kepha realized that this was not a mere ritualistic bathing or washing, but a symbolic act, and therefore realized his need for full and total cleansing by Moshiach.

you know what I have done to you? 13 You call Me Master and Rabbi: and you say well; for I AM. 14 If I then, your Rabbi and Master, have washed your feet; you also should wash one another's feet. 15 For I have given you an example that you should do as I have done to you. 16 Truly, truly, I say to you, The eved is not greater than His Master; neither He that is sent greater than He that sent Him. 17 If you know these things, happy are you if you do them. [1] 18 I speak not of you all: I know whom I have chosen: but that the Ketuvim may be fulfilled, He that eats lechem with Me has lifted up his heel against Me. [2] 19 Now I tell you before it comes to pass, so that, when it is come to pass, you may believe that I AM. 20 Truly, truly, I say to you, He that receives whomever I send receives Me; and he that receives Me receives Him that sent Me. 21 When יהושע had said this, He was troubled in Ruach, and testified, and said, Truly, truly, I say to you, that one of you shall betray Me. 22 Then the talmidim looked at each other, not knowing of whom He spoke. 23 Now there was leaning on יהושע's bosom one of His talmidim, whom יהושע loved. [3] 24 Shimon Kepha therefore beckoned to him that He should ask who it was that He spoke about. 25 He then lying on יהושע's breast said to Him, Master, who is it? 26 יהושע answered, It is he, to whom I shall give a matzoh piece, when I have dipped it. And when He had dipped the matzoh piece, He gave it to Yahudah from Qerioth, the son of Shimon. 27 And after the matzoh piece s.a.tan entered into him. Then said יהושע to him, What you are doing, do quickly. [4] 28 Now no man at the table knew why He said this to him. 29 For some of them thought, because Yahudah

had the moneybag, that יהושע had said to him, Buy those things that we need for the moed; or, that he should give something to the poor. 30 He then having received the matzoh piece went out immediately: and it was night. 31 Therefore, when he had gone out, יהושע said, Now is the Ben Adam esteemed, and יהוה is esteemed in Him. 32 If יהוה be esteemed in Him, יהוה shall also esteem Him in Himself, and shall esteem Him immediately. 33 Little children, yet a little while I am with you. You shall seek Me: and as I said to the Yahudim, Where I go, you cannot come; so now I say to you. 34 A renewed commandment I give to you, That you have ahava towards one another; as I have loved you, that you also ahava one another. 35 By this shall all men know that you are My talmidim, if you have ahava one to another. 36 Shimon Kepha said to Him, Master, where are you going? יהושע answered him, Where I go, you cannot follow Me now; but you shall follow Me afterwards. 37 Kepha said to Him, Master, why can't I follow You now? I will lay down my chayim for your sake. 38 יהושע answered him; Will you lay down your chayim for My sake? Truly, truly, I say to you, The cock shall not crow, until you have denied Me three times.

14 Let not your heart be troubled: you believe in יהוה, believe also in Me. 2 In My Abba's Bayit are many abiding chambers: if it were not so, I would have told you. I go to prepare a place for you. [5] 3 And if I go and prepare a place for you, I will come again, and receive you to Myself; that where I am, there you may be also. 4 And where I go you know, and the derech you know. 5 Toma said to Him, Master, we know not where You are going; so how can we know the derech? 6 יהושע said to him, I am the derech, the emet, and the chayim: no man comes to the Abba, except through Me. 7 If you had known Me, you would have

---

[1] True and contented believers know Yahshua as YHWH manifested fully in flesh, but also know that the Father is greater. For more details see: http://www.yourarmstoisrael.org/Articles_new/articles/?page=greater_and_lesser&type=8.
[2] Psalm 41:9.
[3] Yochanan the author.
[4] A double infilling of s.a.tan after the initial influence of verse 2.

[5] Dual application. Heavenly dwellings, and earthly dwellings, in the Renewed Yahrushalayim on earth.

known My Abba also: and from now on you know Him, and have seen Him. 8 Philip said to Him, Master, show us the Abba, and it will be enough for us. 9 **יהושע** said to him, *Have I been so long a time with you, and yet have you not known Me, Philip? He that has seen Me has seen the Abba; how then are you saying, show us the Abba? 10 Do you not believe that I am in the Abba, and the Abba is in Me? The words that I speak to you I speak not from Myself: but the Abba that dwells in Me, He does the works. 11 Believe Me that I am in the Abba, and the Abba in Me: or else believe Me because of the works. 12 Truly, truly, I say to you, He that believes on Me, the works that I do shall he do also; and greater works than these shall he do; because I go to My Abba.*[1] *13 And whatever you shall ask in My Name, that will I do, that the Abba may be esteemed in the Son.*[2] *14 If you shall ask anything in My Name, I will do it.*[3] *15 If you love Me, keep My mitzvot.*[4] *16 And I will ask the Abba, and He shall give you another Comforter, that He may stay with you le-olam-va-ed; 17 Even the Ruach of Emet; whom the olam hazeh cannot receive, because it sees Him not, neither knows Him: but you know Him; for He dwells with you, and shall be in you. 18 I will not leave you orphans: I will come to you after a little while. 19 Yet a little while, and the olam hazeh will see Me no more; but you will see Me: because I live, you shall live also. 20 At that day you shall know that I am in My Abba, and you in Me, and I in you. 21 He that has My mitzvot, and keeps them,*[5] *he it is that loves Me: and he who loves Me, shall be loved by My Abba, and I will love him, and will reveal Myself to him.*

22 Yahudah, not from Qerioth, said to Him, Master, how is it that You will reveal Yourself to us, and not to the olam hazeh? 23 **יהושע** answered and said to him, *If a man loves Me, he will guard My words: and My Abba will love him, and We will come to him, and make Our stay with him. 24 He that loves Me not keeps not My sayings: and the word which you shema is not mine, but the Abba's who sent Me. 25 These things have I spoken to you, being yet present with you. 26 But the Comforter, which is the Set-Apart Ruach, whom the Abba will send in My Name, He shall teach you all things, and bring all things to your remembrance, whatever I have said to you. 27 Shalom I leave with you, My own shalom I give to you: but not as the olam hazeh gives, it. Let not your heart be troubled, neither let it be afraid. 28 You have heard what I said to you, I go away, and come again to you. If you loved Me, you would gilah, because I said, I go to the Abba: for My Abba is greater than I.*[6] *29 And now I have told you before it comes to pass, so that, when it is come to pass, you might believe. 30 I will no longer talk much with you: for the prince of the olam hazeh is coming, and has nothing against Me. 31 But that the olam hazeh may know that I love My Abba; and as the Abba gave Me mitzvot, even so I do them. Rise up; let us go away from here.*

15 *I am the Emet Vine, and My Abba is the Gardener.*[7] *2 Every branch in Me that bears not fruit He takes away: and every branch that bears fruit, He purges it, that it may bring forth more fruit. 3 Now you are clean through the word that I have spoken to you. 4 Stay in Me, and I in you. As the branch cannot bear fruit by itself, except it stay in the Vine; neither can you, except you stay in Me. 5 I am the Vine, you*

---

[1] Greater numerically and quantitatively, not in terms of actually raising dead people on a weekly basis. This means that Yahshua's followers not having the full measure of the Spirit cannot possibly do what only He could do.
[2] Prayers in Nazarene Yisrael must be sealed in Yahshua's Name.
[3] In His Name and according to His will (First John 5:14).
[4] A short but sweet warning to all who love Yahshua. The proof is full Torah compliance.
[5] Torah-keeping is a precondition in order for Yahshua to reveal Himself to individual Yisraelites.

[6] Please see:
http://www.yourarmstoisrael.org/Articles_new/articles/?page=g reater_and_lesser&type=8 for more details.
[7] This discourse is given in light of Isaiah 5, where the vineyard is Yisrael and the Beloved who owned the vineyard is Abba-YHWH.

are the branches: He that stays in Me, and I in him, the same brings forth much fruit: for without Me you can do nothing. 6 If a man stays not in Me, he is cast forth as a branch, and is withered; and men gather them, and cast them into the fire, and they are burned.[1] 7 If you stay in Me, and My words stay in you, you shall ask what you desire, and it shall be done for you. 8 By this is My Abba esteemed, that you bear much fruit; so shall you be My talmidim. 9 As the Abba has loved Me, so have I loved you: continue in My ahava. 10 If you keep My mitzvot, you shall stay in My ahava; even as I have kept My Abba's mitzvot, and stay in His ahava. [2] 11 These things have I spoken to you, that My simcha might remain in you, and that your simcha might be full. 12 This is My commandment, That you love one another, as I have loved you. 13 Greater ahava has no man than this that a man lay down His chayim for His chaverim. 14 You are My chaverim, if you do what I command you. 15 No longer do I call you avadim; for the eved knows not what his Master does: but I have called you chaverim; for all things that I have heard from My Abba I have made known to you. 16 You have not chosen Me, but I have chosen you, and ordained you, that you should go and bring forth fruit, and that your fruit should remain: whatever you shall ask of the Abba in My Name, He will give it to you. [3] 17 These things I command you, that you love one another. 18 If the olam hazeh hates you, you know that it hated Me before it hated you. 19 If you were of the olam hazeh, the olam hazeh would love its own: but because you are not of the olam hazeh, but I have chosen you out of the olam hazeh, therefore the olam hazeh hates you.

20 Remember the word that I said to you, The eved is not greater than His Master. If they have persecuted Me, they will also persecute you; if they have guarded My words, they will guard yours also. 21 But all these things will they do to you for My Name's sake, because they know not Him that sent Me. 22 If I had not come and spoken to them, they would have no sin: but now they have no excuse for their sin. 23 He that hates Me hates My Abba also. [4] 24 If I had not done among them the works that no other man did, they would have no sin: but now have they both seen and hated both My Abba and Me. 25 But this comes to pass, that the word might be fulfilled that is written in their Torah, They hated Me without a cause. 26 But when the Comforter will come, whom I will send to you from the Abba, the Ruach of Emet, which proceeds from the Abba, He shall testify of Me: 27 And you also shall bear witness, because you have been with Me from the beginning.

16 These things have I spoken to you, that you should not stumble. 2 They shall put you out of the synagogues:[5] yes, the time comes, that whoever kills you will think that he does יהוה's service. 3 And these things will they do to you, because they have not known Me or the Abba. 4 But these things have I told you, so that when the time shall come, you may remember that I told you about them. And these things I did not tell you before, because I was with you. 5 But now I go on My derech to Him that sent Me; and none of you asks Me, Where are you going? 6 But because I have said these things to you, sorrow has filled your heart. 7 Nevertheless I tell you the emet; It is better for you that I go away: for if I go not away, the Comforter will not come to you; but if I depart, I will send Him to you. 8 And when He is come, He will reprove the olam hazeh of sin, and of tzedakah, and of

---

[1] Those who deny Him, after having at one time believed in Him.
[2] Both Yahshua and Yisrael must guard YHWH's Torah as a sign of affection, submission and obedience. To claim a love for Yahshua apart from Torah obedience will result in being cut off from the Vine, along with suffering the consequences of that removal.
[3] Yisrael is chosen and as such is the restored nation of His choosing.

[4] Let the House of Yahudah take careful note.
[5] The early Nazarenes were officially thrown out at the council of Yavneh in 70CE, with the addition of the curse on the Nazarenes in the **Shmone Esreh** –18 Benedictions - called the **Birchat HaMinim**. At that point this prophecy officially came true.

mishpat: 9 *Of sin, because they believe not on Me;* 10 *Of tzedakah, because I go to My Abba, and you see Me no more;* 11 *Of mishpat, because the ruler of the olam hazeh is being judged.* 12 *I have yet many other things to say to you, but you cannot grasp them now.* [1] 13 *But when He, the Ruach of Emet, has come, He will guide you into all emet: for He shall not speak of Himself; but whatever He shall shema, that shall He speak: and He will show you things to come in the future.* 14 *He shall esteem Me: for He shall receive from Me what is Mine, and shall show it to you.* 15 *All things that the Abba has are Mine: that is why I said, that He shall take of Mine, and shall show it to you.* 16 *A little while, and you shall not see Me: and again, a little while later, and you shall see Me, because I go to the Abba.* 17 Then said some of His talmidim among themselves, What is this that He said to us, A little while, and you shall not see Me: and again, a little while, and you shall see Me: and, Because I go to the Abba? 18 They said therefore, What is this that He said, A little while? We do not understand what He said. 19 Now יהושע knew that they desired to ask Him, and said to them, *Do you inquire among yourselves what I said, A little while, and you shall not see Me: and again, a little while, and you shall see Me?* 20 *Truly, truly, I say to you, That you shall weep and lament, but the olam hazeh shall gilah: and you shall be sorrowful, but your sorrow shall be turned into simcha.* 21 *A woman when she is in labor has grief, because her hour has come: but as soon as she is delivered of the child, she remembers no more the pain, for the simcha that a son is born into the olam hazeh.* [2] 22 *And you now therefore have sorrow: but I will see you again, and your heart shall gilah, and your simcha no man takes from you.* 23 *And in that day you shall ask Me nothing. Truly, truly, I say to you, Whatever you shall ask the Abba in My Name, He will give it you.* 24 *Until now have you asked nothing in My Name: now ask, and you shall receive, that your simcha may be full.* 25 *These things have I spoken to you in figures of speech: but the time comes, when I shall no more speak to you in figures of speech, but I shall show you in the pashat things concerning the Abba.* 26 *At that day you shall ask in My Name: and I say not to you, that I will ask the Abba for you:* 27 *For the Abba Himself loves you, because you have loved Me, and have believed that I came out from within* יהוה. 28 *I came out from the Abba, and have come into the olam hazeh: again, I leave the olam hazeh, and go back to the Abba.* 29 His talmidim said to Him, See, now You speak in pashat, and speak without drash. 30 Now we are sure that You know all things, and need not that any man should ask You: by this we believe that You came forth from within* יהוה. 31 יהושע said to them, *Do you now believe?* 32 *Behold, the hour comes, yes, is now come, that you shall be scattered, every man to his own, and shall leave Me alone: and yet I am not alone, because the Abba is with Me.* 33 *These things I have spoken to you, that in Me you might have shalom. In the olam hazeh you shall have tribulation: but be of tov courage; I have overcome the olam hazeh.* [3]

17 These words spoke יהושע, and lifted up His eyes to the shamayim, and said, *Abba, the hour has come esteem Your Son, that Your Son also may esteem You:* 2 *As You have given Him power over all flesh that He should give eternal chayim to as many as You have given Him.* 3 *And this is eternal chayim, that they might know You, the only emet* יהוה, *and* יהושע *the*

---

[1] Yahshua teaches His people in stages called "progressive revelation."
[2] In Hebraic culture when a son is born, the mother is immediately informed. When a daughter is born, the news is withheld from the mother for a while. Here Yahshua speaks of the immediate joy the believers will have upon the news of His resurrection, and return to the Father.

[3] Yahshua teaches Yisrael how to overcome, and thus fulfill the role He has for Yisrael. Yisrael means an overcomer, and Yahshua overcame this world, so all Yisrael can follow His lead.

Moshiach, whom You have sent. 4 *I have esteemed You on the earth: I have finished the work that You gave Me to do.* 5 *And now, O Abba, esteem Me by Your own self with the esteem that I had with You before the olam hazeh was created.*[1] 6 *I have manifested Your Name to the men whom You gave Me out of the olam hazeh[2]: yours they were, and You gave them to Me; and they have kept Your word.* 7 *Now they have known that all things whatever You have given Me are from You.* 8 *For I have given to them the words which You gave Me; and they have received them, and have known surely that I came out from You, and they have believed that You did send Me.* 9 *I request for them: I request not for the olam hazeh, but for those whom You have given Me; for they are yours.* 10 *And all Mine are Yours, and Yours are Mine; and I am esteemed in them.* 11 *And now I am no more in the olam hazeh, but these are in the olam hazeh, and I come to You Set-Apart Abba, shomer through Your own Name those whom You have given Me, that they may be echad, as we are echad.*[3] 12 *While I was with them in the olam hazeh, I guarded them in Your Name: those that You gave Me I have kept, and none of them is lost, except the son of perdition; that the Ketuvim might be fulfilled.*[4] 13 *And now I return to You; but these things I speak in the olam hazeh, that they might have My simcha completed within themselves.* 14 *I have given them Your word; and the olam hazeh has hated*

them, *because they are not of the olam hazeh, even as I am not of the olam hazeh.* 15 *I request not that You should take them out of the olam hazeh, but that You should keep them from the evil.*[5] 16 *They are not of the olam hazeh, even as I am not of the olam hazeh.* 17 *Set them apart through Your emet: Your word is emet.*[6] 18 *As You have sent Me into the olam hazeh, even so have I also sent them into the olam hazeh.* 19 *And for their sakes I set Myself apart, that they also might be set-apart through the emet.* 20 *Neither do I make tefillah I for these alone, but for them also who shall believe on Me through their word;*[7] 21 *That they all may be echad; as You, Abba, are with Me, and I with You, that they also may be echad with Us: that the olam hazeh may believe that You have sent Me.* 22 *And the tifereth, which You gave Me, I have given them; that they may be echad, even as we are echad:* 23 *I with them, and You with Me, that they may be perfected into echad; and that the olam hazeh may know that You have sent Me, and have loved them, as You have loved Me.* 24 *Abba, I will that they also, whom You have given Me, be with Me where I am; that they may see My tifereth, which You have given Me: for You loved Me before the foundation of the olam hazeh.* 25 *O Tzadik-Abba, the olam hazeh has not known You: but I have known You, and these have known that You have sent Me.*

---

[1] Eternality of the brought-forth Son. See Proverbs chapter 8.

[2] Because Jewish Yisrael was under a manmade rabbinical ban against saying the Name of YHWH, over time it fell from usage, and men forgot how to pronounce and declare it properly. Among Yahshua's many ministries, one of His main ones was to reveal and restore YHWH's Name to the men of Renewed Covenant Yisrael. By using the Name revealed to us by Yahshua, we show ourselves to have the seal of being proclaimed His talmidim, the true Yisrael of YHWH. For more details see:
http://yourarmstoisrael.org/Articles_new/?page=home&type=1
and
http://store.yourarmstoisrael.org/Qstore/Qstore.cgi?CMD=011&PROD=000252.

[3] Take note that the true Name of YHWH does and will yet guard His people in their testings and trials. It is Yahshua's means, through which He protects and guards His talmidim. The vital importance of the true Name even determines protection or lack of protection for His people.

[4] See John 13:18.

[5] There is no rapture theology here. Yahshua's prayer was for us to be guarded in the truth and in the Name of YHWH, not for us to fly out on a rapture shuttle.

[6] Torah and Tanach was the only word recorded at this time. The Renewed Covenant had not yet been written.

[7] All of redeemed Yisrael.

26 *And I have declared to them Your Name, and will yet declare it: that the ahava with which You have loved Me may be in them, and I in them* [1]

18 After **יהושע** had spoken these words, He went forth with His talmidim over the brook Qidron, where there was a garden, into which He entered, with His talmidim. 2 And Yahudah also, who betrayed Him, knew the place: for **יהושע** often would stay there with His talmidim. 3 Yahudah then, having received a band of men and officers from the chief kohanim and Prushim, came there with lanterns and torches and weapons. 4 **יהושע** therefore, knowing all things that should come upon Him, went forward, and said to them, *Whom do you seek?* 5 They answered Him, **יהושע** of Natzareth. **יהושע** said to them, *I AM.* And Yahudah also, which betrayed Him, stood with them. 6 As soon as He had said to them, *I AM,* they went backwards, and fell to the ground. 7 Then He asked them again, *Whom do you seek?* And they said, **יהושע** of Natzareth. 8 **יהושע** answered, *I have told you that I AM: if therefore you seek Me, let these go their way:* 9 That the saying might be fulfilled, that He spoke, *Of those whom You gave Me have I lost none.* 10 Then Shimon Kepha having a sword drew it, and smote the Kohen HaGadol's eved, and cut off his right ear. The eved's name was Melech. 11 Then said **יהושע** to Kepha, *Put up your sword into the sheath: the cup, which My Abba has given Me, shall I not drink it?* 12 Then the company of soldiers and the captain and officers of the Yahudim took

יהושע, and bound Him, 13 And led Him away to Hanan first; for he was abba-in-law of Qayapha, who was the Kohen HaGadol that same year. 14 Now Qayapha was he, who gave counsel to the Yahudim, that it was better that one man should die for the people. [2] 15 And Shimon Kepha followed **יהושע**, and so did another talmid: that talmid was known to the Kohen HaGadol, and went in with **יהושע** into the palace of the Kohen HaGadol. 16 But Kepha stood at the door outside. Then went out that other talmid, [3] who was known to the Kohen HaGadol, and spoke to her that guarded the door, and brought in Kepha. 17 Then said the eved girl that guarded the door to Kepha, Are not you also one of this Man's talmidim? He said, I am not. 18 And the avadim and officers stood there, who had made a fire of coals; for it was cold: and they warmed themselves: and Kepha stood with them, and warmed himself. 19 The Kohen HaGadol then asked **יהושע** about His talmidim, and about His doctrine. 20 **יהושע** answered him, *I spoke openly to the olam hazeh; I always taught in the synagogue, and in the Beit HaMikdash, where the Yahudim always assemble; and in secret have I said nothing. 21 Why do you ask Me? Ask those who heard Me, what I have said to them: see, they know what I said.* 22 And when He had spoken this, one of the officers who stood by struck **יהושע** with the palm of his hand, saying, is that the way You answer the Kohen HaGadol? 23 **יהושע** answered him, *If I have spoken evil, bear witness of the evil: but if well, why did you strike Me?* 24 Now Hanan had sent Him bound to Qayapha the Kohen HaGadol. 25 And Shimon Kepha stood and warmed himself. They said therefore to him, Are not you also one of His talmidim? He denied it, and said, I am not. 26 One of the avadim of the Kohen HaGadol, being a relative of the one whose ear Kepha cut off, said, Did I not see you in the garden with

---

[1] The final item in this Kohen HaGadol's prayer is the understanding that not only does the Name of YHWH protect and guard Yisrael, but also it is the means by which Yahshua loves His people. He states here that He will continue to declare YHWH's true Name until the end of time so that His disciples can receive His love, even as Yahshua receives the Father's love, also through and by the Name of YHWH. The Name of YHWH then is the "love channel," through which we receive that unconditional acceptance and sonship. Moreover all High Priests had to carry YHWH's Name as found in the tetragrammaton on their foreheads in the First Covenant. Yahshua being the High Priest of the Renewed Covenant also must carry and have YHWH's Name upon Him as He ministers to His Father on our behalf.

[2] As seen earlier, for the people found in both houses.
[3] Yochanan the Beloved himself, speaking in the second person.

Him? 27 Kepha then denied again: and immediately the cock crew. 28 Then they led יהושע from Qayapha to the hall of mishpat: and it was early; but they themselves went not into the Mishpat Hall, lest they should be defiled; so that they might eat the Pesach. 29 Pilate then went out to them, and said, What accusation do you bring against this Man? 30 They answered and said to him, If he were not an evildoer, we would not have brought Him up to you. 31 Then said Pilate to them; You take Him, and shophet Him according to your Torah. The Yahudim therefore said to him, It is not lawful for us to put any man to death:[1] 32 That the word of יהושע might be fulfilled, that He spoke, signifying what kind of death He should die. 33 Then Pilate entered into the Mishpat Hall again, and called יהושע, and said to Him, Are You the Melech of the Yahudim? 34 יהושע answered him, *Are you asking this on your own, or did others tell you this about Me?* 35 Pilate answered, Am I a Yahudite? Your own nation and the chief kohanim have brought You to me: what have You done? 36 יהושע answered, *My malchut is not of this olam hazeh: if My malchut were of this olam hazeh, then would My avadim fight, that I should not be delivered to the Yahudim: but now is My malchut not from here.* 37 Pilate therefore said to Him, Are You a melech then? יהושע answered, *You are right in saying that I AM a Melech. For this very reason was I born, and for this cause I came into the olam hazeh, that I should bear witness to the Emet. Everyone that is of the Emet hears to My voice.* 38 Pilate said to Him, What is emet? And when he had said this, he went out again to the Yahudim, and said to them, I find in Him no fault at all. 39 But you have a custom that I should release to you one prisoner on the Pesach: will you therefore that I release to you the Melech of the Yahudim? 40 Then they all cried again,

saying: Not this man, but Bar-Rabba. Now Bar-Rabba was a robber.

19 Then Pilate therefore took יהושע, and scourged Him. 2 And the soldiers wove a crown of thorns, and put it on His head, and they put on Him a purple robe,[2] 3 And said, Hail, Melech of the Yahudim! And they smote Him with their hands. 4 Pilate therefore went forth again, and said to them, Behold, I bring Him forth to you, that you may know that I find no fault in Him. 5 Then came יהושע forth, wearing the crown of thorns, and the purple robe. And Pilate said to them, Behold the Man! 6 When the chief kohanim therefore and officers saw Him, they cried out, saying, Impale Him, impale Him! Pilate said to them, You take Him, and impale Him: for I find no fault in Him. 7 The Yahudim answered him; We have a Torah, and by our Torah He has to die, because He made Himself the Son of Elohim.[3] 8 When Pilate therefore heard that saying, he was even more afraid; 9 And went again into the Mishpat Hall, and said to יהושע, Where are You from? But יהושע gave him no answer. 10 Then said Pilate to Him, You speak not to me? Don't you know that I have power to impale You, and have power to release You? 11 יהושע answered, You would have no power at all against Me, unless it was given to you from above: therefore he that delivered Me to you has the greater sin. 12 And from that time on Pilate sought to release Him: but the Yahudim cried out, saying, If you let this Man go, you are not Caesar's chaver: whoever makes Himself a Melech speaks against Caesar. 13 When Pilate therefore heard that saying, he brought יהושע forth, and sat down in the mishpat seat in a place that is called Pavement, but in Ivrit, Gavatha. 14 And it was during the preparation for the Pesach, at about noon he said to the Yahudim, Behold Your Melech!

---

[1] Under Roman occupation.

[2] Carrying the curse of the earth symbolized by the thorns.
[3] They were fully and willfully ignorant of such verses as Psalm 2:7, Psalm 2:12, Proverbs 30:4, Psalm 82:6 and others.

15 But they cried out, Away with Him, away with Him, impale Him. Pilate said to them, Shall I impale Your Melech? The Kohan HaGadol answered; We have no melech but Caesar. 16 Then Pilate delivered Him to them to be impaled. And they took יהושע, and led Him away. 17 And He bearing His stake went forth into a place called the Place of The Skull, which is called in Ivrit; Golgotha: 18 Where they impaled Him, and two others with Him, on either side one, and יהושע in the midst.[1] 19 And Pilate wrote on a stone sign, and put it on the stake. And the writing was, יהושע HaNotsri WeMelech HaYahudim– YHWH. 20 This sign then read many of the Yahudim: for the place where יהושע was impaled was near to the city: and it was written in Ivrit, and Greek, and Latin. 21 Then said the chief kohanim of the Yahudim to Pilate, Write not, The Melech of the Yahudim; but that He said, I am Melech of the Yahudim. 22 Pilate answered, What I have written, I have written. 23 Then the soldiers, when they had impaled יהושע, took His garments, and made four parts,[2] to every soldier a part; and also His coat: now the coat was without seam, woven from the top throughout. 24 They said therefore among themselves, Let us not tear it, but cast lots for it, to see whose it should be: that the Katav might be fulfilled, which said, They parted My clothes among them, and for My robe they did cast lots. These things therefore the soldiers did. 25 Now there stood by the stake of יהושע His ima, and His ima's sister, Miryam the wife of Qlophah, and Miryam from Magdala. 26 When יהושע therefore saw His ima, and the talmid standing by, whom He loved, He said to His ima, *Woman, see your Son!* 27 Then He said to the talmid, *See your ima!* And from that hour that talmid took her to his own home. 28 After this, יהושע knowing that all things were now

accomplished, that the Kituvim might be fulfilled, said, *I thirst.* 29 Now there was set a vessel full of vinegar: and they filled a sponge with vinegar, and put it upon hyssop, and lifted it to His mouth. 30 When יהושע therefore had received the vinegar, He said, *KALA:*[3] and He bowed His head, and dismissed His Ruach. 31 The Yahudim therefore, because it was the Preparation Day, that the bodies should not remain upon the stake on the Shabbat, - for that Shabbat day was a high day[4] - besought Pilate that their legs might be broken, and that they might be taken away.[5] 32 Then came the soldiers, and broke the legs of the first, and of the other who were impaled with Him. 33 But when they came to יהושע, and saw that He was dead already, they broke not His legs: 34 But one of the soldiers with a spear pierced His side, and instantly came out dom and mayim. 35 And he that saw it bore witness, and his witness is emet: and he knows that what He said is emet, that you might believe. 36 For these things were done, that the Kituv should be fulfilled, A bone of His shall not be broken. 37 And again another Kituv said, They shall look on Him whom they pierced. 38 And after this Yoseph of Ramathayim, being a talmid of יהושע, but secretly for fear of the Yahudim, asked Pilate if he could take away the body of יהושע: and Pilate gave him permission. He came therefore, and

---

[1] See note in Matthew 27:38.
[2] Thus signifying His death was the atonement for all Yisrael from both houses scattered to the four corners of the earth.

[3] In the Greek he is saying "it is finished." But in the Hebrew there is another significant utterance that many have missed. In the Hebrew the word for "finish" or "is finished" is kala also meaning bride. The last words uttered by Yahshua prior to His death was a cry for His kala to return and be cleansed and forgiven, showing that even while dying He had Yisrael on his mind and in his heart. In essence by crying for the kahal or the congregation/bride of Yisrael, He is displaying the true reason He hanged Himself on the tree. An alternative word for finished is neshalem, whose root word is shalom. Combining these two variations in Hebrew, we get Shalom My bride! YHWH has only one bride and the Son was sent to fetch that wandering bride, even as Eliezer was sent to fetch a bride for Yitzchak. That one word kala is the message of the kingdom in a nutshell.
[4] Meaning around 3 PM, when the 14th of Aviv officially began, one day before the annual Shabbat of the 15th. Clearly he was not impaled on a Friday, but the day before the annual Shabbat of Aviv 15.
[5] For more details see:
http://yourarmstoisrael.org/Articles_new/articles/index.php?page=why_i_believe_the_passover_slaug&type=1.

took the body of **יהושע**. 39 And there came also Nakdimon, who in the beginning came to **יהושע** by night, and brought a mixture of myrrh and aloes, about a hundred-pint weight. 40 Then they took the body of **יהושע**, and wound it in linen clothes with the spices, as the manner of the Yahudim is to bury. 41 Now in the place where He was impaled there was a garden; and in the garden a new tomb, where no man was ever laid. 42 There they laid **יהושע** because of the Yahudim's Preparation Day; for the tomb was nearby.

20 And on one of the weekly Shabbats[1] came Miryam from Magdala early, when it was still dark, to the tomb, and saw the stone taken away from the tomb. 2 Then she ran, and came to Shimon Kepha, and to the other talmid, whom **יהושע** loved, and said to them, They have taken away **יהושע** out of the tomb, and we know not where they have laid Him. 3 Kepha therefore went forth, and that other talmid, and came to the tomb. 4 So they ran both together: and the other talmid did outrun Kepha, and came first to the tomb. 5 And stooping down, and looking in, he saw the linen clothes lying; yet he did not go in.[2] 6 Then came Shimon Kepha following him, and went into the tomb, and saw the linen clothes lie, 7 And the cloth, that was around His head, not lying with the linen clothes, but wrapped together in a place by itself. 8 Then went in also that other talmid, who came first to the tomb, and he saw, and believed.[3] 9 For as yet they knew not the kituv, that He must rise again from the dead.[4] 10 Then the talmidim went away again to their own home. 11 But Miryam stood outside at the tomb weeping: and as she wept, she stooped down, and looked into the tomb, 12 And saw two heavenly messengers in white sitting, one at the head, and the other at the feet, where the body of **יהושע** had lain. 13 And they say to her, Woman, why do you weep? She said to them, Because they have taken away My Master and I know not where they have laid Him.[5] 14 And when she had said that, she turned herself back, and saw **יהושע** standing, and knew not that it was **יהושע**. 15 **יהושע** said to her, *Woman, why do you weep? Whom do you seek?* She, supposing Him to be the gardener, said to Him, Master, if you have taken Him away, tell me where you have laid Him, and I will take Him away.[6] 16 **יהושע** said to her, *Miryam.* She turned herself, and said to Him, Rabboni; which is to say, My Master. 17 **יהושע** said to her, *Touch Me not; for I am not yet ascended to My Abba:[7] but go to My brothers, and say to them, I ascend to My Abba, and Your Abba; and to My Elohim, and Your Elohim.[8]* 18 Miryam from Magdala came and told the talmidim that she had seen **יהושע**, and that He had spoken these things to her. 19 Then the same day at evening, being Yom Rishon, when the doors were shut where the talmidim were assembled for fear of the Yahudim, came **יהושע** and stood in their midst, and said to them, *Shalom alaichem.* 20 And when He had said this, He showed them His hands and His side. Then were the talmidim in gilah, when they saw **יהושע**. 21 Then said **יהושע** to them again, *Shalom alaichem: as My Abba has sent Me, even so I send you. 22 And when He had said this, He breathed on them, and said to them, Receive the Set-Apart Ruach: 23 If you forgive the sins of any, they are forgiven; If you withhold forgiveness of a man's sins*

---

[1] **Mia ton sabbaton** in the Greek. The words "first" and "day" do not appear in the Greek. On one of the weekly Shabbats at about sundown, during the season of counting the omer.
[2] Because he was a kohen and could not defile himself with the dead. That's also the reason Yochanan the Beloved was well-known by the Kohen HaGadol of Yisrael.
[3] Only after Peter became defiled, and so John was not defiled, since contact with the dead had already been made.
[4] Isaiah 53:10-11 and Psalm 16:10.

[5] See details at p 108-109 at http://yourarmstoisrael.org/misc/?page=handbook&type=1.
[6] See **Home and Garden** at: http://store.yourarmstoisrael.org/Qstore/Qstore.cgi?CMD=011&PROD=000180.
[7] He had not yet ascended to offer his dom in the Most Set-Apart Place in the heavens, and as such could not be ceremonially defiled by sinful flesh.
[8] Note that Yahshua Himself has an Elohim, and even after his ascension to heaven, He had Abba as his Elohim as seen throughout the Book of Revelation. Regardless of the approach one takes, one is always left with the eternal truth of YHWH the greater, and YHWH the lesser, being **echad** for all eternity.

they are kept.[1] 24 But Toma, one of the twelve, called the Twin, was not with them when יהושע came. 25 The other talmidim therefore said to Him, We have seen יהושע. But He said to them, Except I shall see in His hands the print of the nails, and put my finger into the print of the nails, and thrust my hand into His side, I will not believe. 26 And after eight days again His talmidim were inside and Toma with them: then came יהושע, the doors being shut, and stood in the midst, and said, *Shalom alaichem.* 27 Then He said to Toma, *Reach here your finger, and see My hands; and reach here your hand, and thrust it into My side: and be not faithless, but believing.* 28 And Toma answered and said to Him, My Master and My Elohim. 29 יהושע said to him, *Toma, because you have seen Me, you have believed: blessed are they that have not seen, and yet have believed.*[2] 30 And many other signs truly did יהושע in the presence of His talmidim, which are not written in this scroll: 31 But these are written; that you might believe that יהושע is the Moshiach, the Son of יהוה; and that by believing you might have chayim through His Name.

21 After these things יהושע showed Himself again to the talmidim at the Sea of Kinnereth; and in this manner did He show Himself. 2 There were together Shimon Kepha, and Toma called the Twin, and Natahan-El of Qanah in Galil, and the sons of Zavdi, and two others of His talmidim. 3 Shimon Kepha said to them,

I'm going fishing. They said to him, We'll also go with you. They went forth, and climbed into a boat immediately; and that night they caught nothing. 4 But when the morning was now come, יהושע stood on the shore: but the talmidim knew not that it was יהושע. 5 Then יהושע said to them, *Children, have you any food?* They answered Him, No. 6 And He said to them, *Cast the net on the right side of the ship,*[3] *and you shall find.* They cast therefore, and now they were not able to draw it in for the multitude of fishes. 7 Therefore that talmid whom יהושע loved said to Kepha, It is יהושע. Now when Shimon Kepha heard that it was יהושע, He put on his outer fisher's coat - for he was stripped - and did cast himself into the sea. 8 And the other talmidim came in a little boat - for they were not far from land, but as it were about a hundred yards - dragging the net with the fishes. 9 As soon then as they were come to land, they saw a fire of coals there, and fish laid on it, and lechem. 10 יהושע said to them, *Bring of the fish that you have now caught.* 11 Shimon Kepha went up, and drew the net to land[4] full of great fishes,[5] one hundred fifty three: for even though there were so many, yet was not the net broken.[6] 12 יהושע said to them, *Come and break your fast.* And none of the talmidim did ask Him, Who are You? Knowing that it was the Master Yah.[7] 13 יהושע then came, and took lechem, and gave it to them, and

---

[1] One must be very careful here to understand this in the light of all of Katav, including Yahshua's admonition to Yisrael to forgive all men 70 times 7. This declaration can be understood only in terms of evangelism and sharing the Tov News (glad tidings) of eternal life in Moshiach. When we proclaim as we are sent by YHWH, and men respond to the Tov News of Moshiach, that person has been forgiven by us personally, in the sense that we were the ones delivering the message, and likewise when we do not deliver the message of the only one by whom man can be saved, we do not allow for forgiveness to flow through us. Thus in essence, we don't forgive others their sins. This declaration is all about delivering the message, and not about the establishment of a religious hierarchy that has power to send people to a second death.

[2] Future generations.

[3] The right side is symbolic of **rachamim**/mercy in the understanding of a Hebrew, and the phrase "right side" or **tsad hayamin**, has a numeric Hebrew value of 204, the same as the word **tzadik** or "righteous one." Here at the command of the "Righteous One" in a sea of rachamim, fish will be caught. The fish of course are Yisrael (see Gen. 48:16) and the sea of course is the nations.

[4] Bringing the scattered fish of lost Yisrael back to the land of Yisrael.

[5] Genesis 48:16 where Yisrael is prophesied to be like multitudes of great fish in the earth's midst.

[6] 153 is the numerical value of the name **Betzalel,** the maker of the wilderness tabernacle after the pattern received from YHWH. This means the children of Yisrael would be made into YHWH's image and pattern, into a renewed congregation, after the disciples drew them out of the sea of nations. For more details see: http://store.yourarmstoisrael.org/Qstore/Qstore.cgi?CMD=011&PROD=000240.

[7] Mar-Yah in Aramaic, improperly translated in Greek simply as "Lord," instead of "Master-Yah."

also fish. 14 This is now the third time that יהושע showed Himself to His talmidim, after He was risen from the dead. 15 So when they had eaten, יהושע said to Shimon Kepha, *Shimon, bar Yonah, Do you love Me more than these?* He said to Him, Yes, Master Yah; You know that I love you. He said to him, *Feed My lambs.* 16 He said to him again the second time, *Shimon, bar Yonah, do you love Me?* He said to Him, Yes, Master Yah; You know that I love You. He said to him, *Feed My sheep.* 17 He said to him the third time, *Shimon, bar Yonah, do you love Me?* Kepha was grieved because He said to him the third time, Do you love Me? And he said to Him, Master Yah, You know all things; You know that I love You. יהושע said to him, *Feed My lambs. 18 Truly, truly, I say to you, When you were young, you dressed yourself, and walked wherever you desired: but when you shall be old, you shall stretch forth your hands, and another shall dress you, and carry you where you do not want to go.*

19 This He spoke, signifying by what death Kepha should esteem יהוה.[1] And when He had spoken this, He said to him, *Follow Me.* 20 Then Kepha, turning around, saw the talmid whom יהושע loved following; who also was the one that leaned on His breast at supper, who said, Master Yah, who is he that betrays You? 21 Kepha seeing Him said to יהושע, Master Yah, and what about him? 22 יהושע said to him, *If I desire that he lives until I come, what is that to you? You just follow Me.* 23 Then this saying went abroad among the brothers, that this talmid would not die: yet יהושע said not to him, you shall not die; but, *If I choose that he remains alive until I come, what is that to you?* 24 This is the talmid who testifies of these things, and wrote these things: and we know that his testimony is emet. 25 And there are also many other things that יהושע did, which, if they should all be written one by one,[2] I suppose that even the olam hazeh itself, could not contain those written scrolls. Amein.

---

[1] By hanging bound hand and foot upside down. Then this prophecy was fulfilled.
[2] The four evangels are summations of the major events of Moshiach's life. Were all His teachings and nisim actually recorded, that would entail the finite and the mortal, capturing in words the infinite and immortal Son of YHWH, which is beyond human limitation and possibility. But enough has been recorded, so that mankind is without excuse, real or imagined.

מעשה שליכים

Ma'aseh Shlichim - Acts
To All Nations

When attending "Bible College" or seminary or other such religious-based classes, often the teacher or instructor will make a startling statement that seems logical, but is the cause for great misunderstandings of the true faith of the disciples. Usually the remark will sound something like this: "The Book of Acts is a historical book used to record the transition between the Jewish dispensation and the 'New Yisrael' church. Therefore this book should not and cannot be used for doctrine, or to establish church theological positions as the rest of scripture, which can, and should be used for doctrine." Now years later, understanding the Two-House truth, we can understand why this was taught to many. These statements were designed to keep believers away from Torah and a first-century Yisraelite lifestyle. As you will shortly see, the Book of Acts is a most Hebraic resource, showing vividly the practice of Torah in the life of all believers in Moshiach. In this book, we see the apostles wrestling with how to incorporate the returning non-Jews into a Torah-based lifestyle. As such, these issues are all doctrinal issues ranging from ecclesiology (the study of just who is the one true elect bride of YHWH), to soteriology (the study of salvation itself). Therefore the Book of Acts must be viewed and studied not merely as a historical or transitional document as some claim, but as a worthy book from which we can derive practical instruction, as well as settle ongoing doctrinal issues, as we receive clarity from its pages. Second Timothy 3:16 reminds us of this truth, by stating that all scripture is profitable for any and every use, including doctrine. Let those that have been discouraged from doing so in the past, begin to look to this book again, not merely as a record of early Nazarene history, but as a guidebook in our cultural readaptation back into the Commonwealth of Yisrael.

1 The first scroll have I made, O Theophilos,[1] of all that יהושע began both to do and to teach, 2 Until the day in which He was taken up, after He through the Ruach HaKodesh had given His Torah to the shlichim whom He had chosen: 3 To whom also He showed Himself alive after His passion by many infallible proofs, being seen by them forty days, and speaking of the things pertaining to the malchut of יהוה. 4 And, being assembled together with them, He commanded them that they should not depart from Yahrushalayim, but wait for the Promise of Abba, which, He said, you have heard from Me. 5 For Yochanan HaMatbeel truly immersed with mayim; but you shall be immersed with the Ruach HaKodesh not many days from now. 6 When they therefore had come together, they asked Him, saying, Master, will You at this time restore again the malchut to Yisrael?[2] 7 And

He said to them, *It is not for you to know the times or the moadim, which Abba has put under His own authority.*[3] 8 *But you shall receive Power, after the Ruach HaKodesh has come upon you: and you shall be witnesses to Me both in Yahrushalayim, and in all Yahudah, and in Shomron, and to the four corners of the olam.*[4] 9 And when He had spoken these

---

[1] See note on Luke 1:3.
[2] When there is togetherness in believing Yisrael, the main concern will be the restoration and regathering of the two houses. These folks hardly agreed on anything, but with one accord were concerned that Yahshua was returning to the Father without Ephraim and Yahudah first being joined again as one in YHWH's hand. This question set in a future tense, is valid and ample evidence that the restoration was paramount in Yahshua's ministry, and moreover has never fully taken place previously, at the time of the Jews' return from Babylonian exile, nor in Hezekiah or Josiah's days, as some erroneously claim.
[3] Yahshua answered them in the future tense in verses 7-8, illustrating that His Father had not yet revealed the exact future timing of the full restoration to anyone. The question posed by the disciples and Moshiach's answer, forever dismisses any attempt to contrive or fabricate some supposedly well-known, past reunion of the two houses, five hundred years before Yahshua came in the flesh.
[4] Note the plan for regathering Yisrael clearly outlined. In context, this commission is given in response to the disciples' question on how to restore Yisrael. He told them that they could not know when it would be fully accomplished, but He told them the method by which it would come to pass. He sent them out to all Yisrael, both in Judea, in Samaria and the entire world. There is only one Great Commission, not three. In all three areas, lost sheep of Yisrael are to be found.

things, while they looked, He was taken up; and a cloud received Him out of their sight. 10 And while they looked steadfastly toward the shamayim as He went up, see, two men stood by them in white apparel;[1] 11 Who also said, You men of Galil, why do you stand gazing up into the shamayim? This same יהושע, who is taken up from you into the shamayim, shall so come in like manner as you have seen Him go into the shamayim.[2] 12 Then they returned to Yahrushalayim from the har called Olivet, which is from Yahrushalayim a Shabbat day's journey.[3] 13 And when they came back, they went up into an upper room, where there were staying Kepha, and Yaakov, and Yochanan, and Andri, Philip, and Toma, Bartholomi, and Matityahu, Yaakov the son of Alphai, and Shimon the Zealot, and Yahudah the brother of Yaakov. 14 These all continued with one accord in the tefillot and supplication,[4] with the women, and Miryam the ima of יהושע, and with His brothers. 15 And in those days Kepha stood up in the midst of the talmidim - the number of names together were about a hundred twenty - and said, 16 Men and brothers, this Katav had to have been fulfilled, which the Ruach HaKodesh by the mouth of David spoke before concerning Yahudah, who was a guide to them that took יהושע. 17 For he was numbered with us, and had obtained part of this service. 18 Now this man purchased a field with the reward of iniquity; and falling head first, he burst open in the middle, and all his intestines gushed out. 19 And it was known to all the dwellers at Yahrushalayim; so that field is called in their own language, Hacal-Dama, that is to say, The Field of

Dom. 20 For it is written in the Scroll of Tehillim, Let his dwelling be desolate, and let no man dwell in it: and let his office of service be given to another. 21 It is therefore necessary that one of these men who have been with us all the time that the Savior יהושע went in and out among us, 22 Beginning from the mikvah of Yochanan HaMatbeel, to the same day that He was taken up from us, one must be ordained to be a witness with us of His resurrection. 23 And they appointed two, Yoseph called Bar-Abba, who was surnamed Justus, and Matityahu. 24 And they made tefillah, and said, You, Master יהוה, who knows the levim of all men, show which of these two You have chosen,[5] 25 That he may take part of this service and calling, from which Yahudah by transgression fell, that he might go to his own place.[6] 26 And they gave out their lots; and the lot fell upon Mattityahu; and he was numbered with the eleven shlichim.

2 And when the moed of Shavuot was fully counted by the omer, they were all with one accord in one place. 2 And suddenly there came a sound from the shamayim as of a rushing mighty wind, and

---

[1] In context, one messenger representing both houses that would be coming together by the proclaiming of the tov news.
[2] Physically, bodily and back to the Mt. of Olives.
[3] As determined by the Sanhedrin of that day. This concept became part of the Jewish oral law.
[4] The upper room was the place where the tefillah meeting of the leaders of Renewed Covenant Yisrael took place, but was not the place where the Ruach HaKodesh fell. The error of superimposing this tefillah venue onto and into the events of chapter 2 has resulted in untold horror, tragedy and error, as seen in the alleged birth of a so-called gentile church.

[5] They prayed and asked simply because there were twelve disciples from each of the twelve tribes ordained for kingdom rulership, and the one that needed to be chosen was one who was first and foremost faithful and also would be from the same tribe that Judas was from. Only YHWH knew that for certain.
[6] As opposed to a faithful Yisraelite, who is said to be gathered to his people.

it filled all the Bayit [1] where they were sitting. 3 And there appeared to them divided tongues like as of fire, and it sat upon each of them. [2] 4 And they were all filled with the Ruach HaKodesh, and began to speak with other tongues, as the Ruach HaKodesh gave them the utterance. [3] 5 And there were dwelling at Yahrushalayim Yahudim, [4] devout men, out of every nation [5] under the shamayim. 6 Now when this was noised abroad, the multitude came together, [6] and were confused, because that every man heard them speak in his own language. [7] 7 And they were all amazed and marveled, saying one to another, See, are not all these who speak Galilaeans? 8 How then do we shema them speaking in our own native language? 9 Parthians, and Medes, and Eylamites, and those Yisraelites dwelling in Aram, among whom were Yahudim, and those from Kappadokia, those from Pontos, and also Asia Minor, [8] [9] 10 Phrygia, and Pamphulia, in Mitzrayim, and in the parts of Libya near Cyrene, and Yahudim and Gerim from Rome, along with Yireh יהרה , [10] [11] 11 Cretes and Arabians, [12] we do shema them speak in our tongues the wonderful works of Elohim. 12 And they were all amazed and stunned, and were in doubt, saying one to another, What does this mean? [13] 13 Others mocking said, These men are full of new wine. 14 But Kepha, standing up with the eleven, lifted up his voice, and said to them, You men of Yahudah, and all you that are staying at Yahrushalayim, [14] be this known to you, and shema to my words: 15 For these men are not drunk, as you suppose, seeing it is but nine o'clock in the morning.

---

[1] The House is not a room. And is not an upper room. It is merely a Hebraic way of identifying the place as the House of YHWH on Moriyah. Even in the land of Yisrael today, the Temple Mount is known as Har HaBayit or the Mountain of the House. The Ruach fell in the temple or the "House" of YHWH, since that was the only place Yisraelites would be gathered by commandment according to Deut. 16 and Lev. 23. Had these Yisraelites been in an upper room, the Set-Apart-Ruach could not have been given, since they would be in disobedience to the Torah, as would YHWH if He gave it to those who were not in His House but rather in a tefillah room of their own choosing. The so-called church as a separate entity from Yisrael, was never born on that day, since the events were promised and prophesied and fulfilled to Yisraelites in the Temple in YHWH's House. For a full treatment of Yisrael's promised renewal on this day, see:
A Celebration Of Renewed Life:
http://yourarmstoisrael.org/Articles_new/restoration/?page=18 &type=twelve or **Help I Can't Find the Church In My Bible** at:
http://store.yourarmstoisrael.org/Qstore/Qstore.cgi?CMD=011 &PROD=000050.
[2] Another indication that Yisrael was being renewed, as opposed to a gentile church being birthed, as the Torah was also given in voices of thunderings, or (as the sages teach) in the 70 known tongues of the nations. The Torah was now being placed in their hearts, and this sign of divided tongues indicated that very implanting within the disciples.
[3] See: **The Father's Promise To Ephraim And Tongues** http://store.yourarmstoisrael.org/Qstore/Qstore.cgi?CMD=011 &PROD=000104
[4] Note that these people were not pagans but returning Yisraelites in varying stages of return. No pagans would go and worship YHWH on Shavuot. Later in verses 8-11 we see that these men were Yisaelites but not Jews, even though the term Jew is used here to include other Yisraelites both natural and by conversion.
[5] The term "every nation" is indicative of non-Jewish Yisraelites, since this was before the exile of 70CE and the Jews at that time had not yet been exiled to every nation under heaven like they are today, which had in fact occurred to Ephraim at that time.
[6] The "multitudes of the nations." We see both the devout Jews and the multitudes from the nations coming together around the feasts as the restoration work begins.
[7] Native tongue of the many Yisraelite nations that were visiting.

[8] The Parthians and Medes in Acts 2:9, are identified as an area where Ephraim (ten tribes) were scattered, according to I Chronicles 5:26. The Gozan River was in the area of Medo-Persia. They later formed a large part of the Scythian peoples, who later would settle Northwest Europe as the invading Anglo-Saxon and barbarian nations. The Eylamites in Acts 2:9, were most likely descendents of Ullam, son of Sheresh, son of Maachah, son of Manasseh, son of Joseph. "Eylamites descended from Ullan, son of Maachah, son of Menashsheh, son of Joseph..." *Kol Shofar Monthly Newsletter*, Vol.2 No.6 p.2.
[9] The exiles from Pontos, Galatia, Kappadokia and Asia, were all to be considered the dispersed exiled chosen people according to Peter in 1 Peter 1.1.
[10] Known in Hebrew as Yireh-YHWH or YHWH fearers who were not natives.
[11] Clearly many non-Yisraelites by birth were also in YHWH's House joining Yisrael and thus being Yisrael as seen by the term **gerim** and **Yire-YHWH** converts. Notice that Libyans and Egyptians also become Yisrael and received the seal of the Ruach.
[12] Arabs can and have always been welcome to become Yisrael based on Torah terms.
[13] Most believers still don't clearly see the significance of this event, seeing it as the birth of a new religion or non-Yisraelite entity, rather than as the fulfillment of Jeremiah 31:31.
[14] A clear two-house reference. The Yahudim, and those non-Yahudim staying for the feast.

16 But this is that which was spoken by ha navi Yo-El;[1] 17 *And it shall come to pass in the yamim acharonim, said* יהוה, *I will pour out from My Ruach upon all flesh: and your sons and your daughters shall prophesy, and your young men shall see visions, and your old men shall dream dreams: 18 And on My avadim and on My female avadim I will pour out in those days of My Ruach; and they shall prophesy: 19 And I will show wonders in the shamayim above, and signs in the olam beneath; dom, and fire, and vapor of smoke: 20 The sun shall be turned into darkness, and the moon into dom, before that great and terrible Yom* יהוה *comes:*[2] *21 And it shall come to pass, that whoever shall call on the Name of the Master* יהוה *shall be saved.*[3] 22 You men of Yisrael,[4] shema to these words; יהושע of Natzareth, a man approved of יהוה among you by nisim and wonders and signs, which יהוה did through Him in the midst of you, as you yourselves also know: 23 Him, being delivered by the determined counsel and foreknowledge of יהוה, you have taken, and by the hands of Torah-less men, you have impaled and killed:[5] 24 Whom יהוה has raised up, having demolished the pains of death: because it was not possible for Sheol[6] to hold Him. 25 For David spoke concerning Him, I saw My יהוה always before My face, for He is on My right hand, that I should not be moved: 26 Therefore did My lev have gilah, and My tongue had simcha; moreover also My body shall rest in tikvah: 27 Because You will not leave My being in Sheol, neither will You allow the Set-Apart One of Yisrael to see corruption. 28 You have made known to Me the ways of chayim; You shall make Me full of simcha with Your presence. 29 Men and brothers, let me freely speak to you of the patriarch David, that he is both dead and buried, and his tomb is with us to this day. 30 Being a navi, and knowing that יהוה had sworn with an oath to him, that of the fruit of his loins, according to the flesh, he would raise up the Moshiach to sit on his throne; 31 He seeing this before spoke of the resurrection of the Moshiach, that His being was not left in the grave, neither did His flesh see corruption. 32 This יהושע has יהוה raised up, of which we all are witnesses. 33 Therefore being by the right hand of יהוה exalted, and having received from Abba the promise of the Ruach HaKodesh, He has sent out all this, which you now see and shema. 34 For David is not ascended into the shamayim:[7] but He said Himself, *the Master* יהוה *said to My Master, Sit at My right hand*, 35 Until I make Your enemies Your footstool. 36 Therefore let kol Beit Yisrael know [8] assuredly, that the Master יהוה has made that same יהושע, whom you have impaled, both Melech and Moshiach. 37 Now when they heard this, they were pierced in their lev, and said to Kepha and to the rest of the shlichim, Men and brothers, what shall we do?

---

[1] Yoel's prophesy in Joel 2:28-32 was given exclusively to Yisraelites and not to pagans or gentiles. Peter states that this Yisraelite prophecy is fulfilled in the men and women standing there that day. This prophecy states that the "all flesh" under consideration in the context of Joel 2:27, is the flesh of Yisrael and Yisrael alone. In Joel 2:27, YHWH states that this promise is to Yisrael, since it is He who dwells in the midst of Yisrael. YHWH further elaborates about this last days outpouring of the Ruach upon all Yisraelite flesh in Joel chapter 2:28, 29. The promised outpouring of the Ruach HaKodesh would take place upon your sons, your daughters, your old men, your young men, your men servants, and your female servants. Obviously the key word here is "your" or Joel's people. If we are honest with scripture and we let scripture interpret scripture, the "all flesh" that received the Ruach had to be Yisrael's sons, daughters, young men, old men and all sojourners among them. Yisrael was being renewed without any new church being born.

[2] At the second coming.

[3] **MarYah** in the Peshitta; literally meaning that to call on YHWH through Yahshua is salvation itself.

[4] Again the multitudes from all the nations despite not being Jewish or speaking Hebrew are called "Yisrael" by Peter.

[5] Yahshua's death was arranged by the will of the Father, in order to redeem man individually and Yisrael collectively, as seen in John 10:16-17. This was and remains the Father's plan to cleanse all His children from both houses. The Jews did not kill Moshiach. The Father's predetermined plan did.

[6] The grave.

[7] David's spirit ascended only after the resurrection of Moshiach, and his body remains in the grave for the return of Moshiach. For more details see **Restoring Heaven's Gates** at:
http://store.yourarmstoisrael.org/Qstore/Qstore.cgi?CMD=011&PROD=1065734337

[8] In the setting, an obvious reference to kol or all Yisrael, or those returning from both houses.

38 Then Kepha said to them, Teshuvah, and be immersed every one of you in the Name of the Master-Yah[1] יהושע the Moshiach for the forgiveness of sins, and you shall receive the gift of the Ruach HaKodesh. 39 For the promise is to you, and to your children, and to all that are far off,[2] even as many as יהוה our Elohim shall call. [3] 40 And with many other words did He testify and exhort them, saying, Save yourselves from this sinful generation. 41 Then they that gladly received his word were immersed: and the same day there were added to them about three thousand beings.[4] 42 And they continued steadfastly in the shlichim's Torah and chavurah, and in breaking of lechem, and in the tefillot.[5] 43 And fear came upon every being: and many wonders and signs were done by the shlichim. 44 And all that believed were ecahd, and had all things be-yachad; 45 And sold their possessions and goods, and divided them to all men, as every man had need. 46 And they, continuing daily as echad in the Beit HaMikdash,[6] breaking lechem from bayit to bayit,[7] [8]did eat their food with simcha and a pure lev, 47 Offering tehilla to יהוה, and having favor with all the people. And יהוה added to the congregation of Yisrael daily all those being saved.

3 Now Kepha and Yochanan went up together into the Beit HaMikdash at the hour of tefillah, being the ninth hour. 2 And a certain man lame from his ima's womb was carried, whom they laid daily at the gate of the Beit HaMikdash which is called Yahpha Gate, to ask assistance from those that entered into the Beit HaMikdash; 3 Who seeing Kepha and Yochanan about to go into the Beit HaMikdash asked for assistance. 4 And Kepha, staring at him with Yochanan, said, Look at us. 5 And he listened to them, expecting to receive something from them. 6 Then Kepha said, Silver and gold I have none; but what I have I give you: In the Name of יהושע the Moshiach of Natzareth rise up and walk. 7 And he took him by the right hand, and lifted him up: and immediately his feet and ankle bones received strength. 8 And he leaped up and stood, and he walked, and entered the Beit HaMikdash with them, walking, and leaping, and giving tehilla to Elohim. 9 And all the people saw him walking and giving tehilla to Elohim: 10 And they knew that it was the one who sat for assistance at the Yahpha gate of the Beit HaMikdash: and they were filled with wonder and amazement at that which had happened to him. 11 And as the lame man who was healed held Kepha and Yochanan, all the people ran together to them in the porch that is called Shlomo's, greatly wondering. 12 And when Kepha saw it, he answered to the people, You men of Yisrael,[9] why do you marvel at this? Or why do you look you so intently at us, as though by our own power or set-apartness we have made this man to walk? 13 The Elohim of Avraham, and of Yitzchak, and of Yaakov, the Elohim of our ahvot, has esteemed His Son יהושע; whom you delivered up, and denied Him in the presence of Pilate, when he was determined to let Him go. 14 But you denied the Kadosh-One and the Tzadik of Yisrael, and desired that a murderer to be released to you; 15 And killed the Prince of Chayim, whom יהוה has raised from the dead; of

---

[1] Aramaic Mar-Yah Yahshua, a clear reference to His deity.
[2] A Hebraic idiom as outlined in Ephesians 2:13 and Daniel 9:7 and elsewhere, that speak of the 10 tribes of Ephraim Yisrael.
[3] The perpetual promise to all of Joel's regenerated children, even as many as are generations away.
[4] Further proof that this event could not have taken place in the so called "upper room" since that tiny upper room of the last supper can't hold 3,000 people, or even 120, and certainly did not have a mikvah pool.
[5] Three times daily.
[6] The final proof that these events did not birth an upper room church, as by definition they could not continue in the temple, unless they were there in the first place.
[7] This is a **remez** (scriptural hint) on the unity of Yisrael being restored from house to house, between Yahudah and Ephraim.
[8] See **House To House** teaching available at: http://store.yourarmstoisrael.org/Qstore/Qstore.cgi?CMD=011&PROD=1065734072

[9] All Yisrael.

which we are witnesses. 16 And His Name through emunah in His Name has made this man strong, whom you see and know: yes, the emunah, which is by Him, has given Him this perfect soundness in the presence of all of you. 17 And now, brothers, I know that through ignorance you did it, as did also your rulers. 18 But those things, which Elohim before had shown by the mouth of all His neviim, that the Moshiach should suffer, He has now fulfilled. 19 Make teshuvah therefore, and be converted in lev, that your sins may be blotted out, when the times of refreshing shall come from the presence of the Master יהוה; 20 And He shall send יהושע the Moshiach, who before was proclaimed to you: 21 Whom the shamayim must receive until the times of the restoration of all things, which יהוה has spoken by the mouth of all His set-apart neviim since the olam began. [1] 22 For Moshe truly said to the ahvot, A Navi shall the Master יהוה Your Elohim raise up to you from your brothers, like me; you shall shema to Him in all things and whatever He shall say to you. 23 And it shall come to pass, that every being, which will not shema that Navi, shall be destroyed from among the people of Yisrael. 24 Yes, and all the neviim from Schmuel and those that followed after, as many as have spoken, have likewise foretold of these days. 25 You are the children of the neviim, and of the covenant that יהוה made with our ahvot, saying to Avraham, And in your zera shall all the nations of the olam be blessed/mixed. [2] 26 To you first יהוה, having raised up His Son יהושע, sent Him to give you brachot, in turning away all of you from your iniquities.

4 And as they spoke to the people, the kohanim, and the leaders of the Beit HaMikdash, and the Tzadukim, came upon them, 2 Being disturbed that they taught the people of Yisrael, and proclaimed through יהושע the resurrection from the dead. 3 And they laid hands on them, and put them in prison until the next day: for it was now evening. 4 But many of them who heard the word believed; and the number of the men were about five thousand. 5 And it came to pass on the next day, that their rulers, and zachanim, and Torah Sophrim, 6 And Hanan the Kohen HaGadol, and Cayapha, and Yochanan, and Alexander, and as many as were from the mishpocha of the Kohen HaGadol, were gathered together at Yahrushalayim. 7 And when they had set the talmidim in their midst, they asked, By what power, or by what Name, have you done this? 8 Then Kepha, filled with the Ruach HaKodesh, said to them, You rulers of the people, and zachanim of Yisrael, 9 If we are examined today because of the tov mitzvah done to the impotent man, by what means he is made healthy; 10 Be it known to you all, and to kol Yisrael,[3] that by the Name of יהושע the Moshiach of Natzareth, whom you impaled, whom יהוה raised from the dead, even by Him does this man stand here before you healthy. 11 This is the Stone that was rejected by you builders, that has become the Rosh Pina. 12 Neither is there salvation in any other: for there is no other Name under the shamayim given among men, whereby we must be saved. 13 Now when they saw the boldness of Kepha and Yochanan, and perceived that they were unlearned and ignorant men, they marveled; and they took special note, that they had been with יהושע.[4] 14 And beholding the man who was healed standing with them, they could say nothing against it. 15 But when they had commanded them to go outside out of the Sanhedrin, they conferred among themselves, 16 Saying, What shall we do to these men? For that

---

[1] This does not mean that Yahshua will not return until all things are fully restored as some teach. Rather He will not return until He has begun an irreversible process in all things that need restoration, such as His Father's Name, Torah and the two houses of Yisrael. What he starts will be completed in the **atid lavoh** (millennium).
[2] See note on Genesis 12:3.

[3] **Kol Yisrael**; both houses.
[4] Yahshua can take all kind of Yisraelites, and turn them into Torah scholars.

indeed a notable nes has been done by them is manifest to all them that dwell in Yahrushalayim; and we cannot deny it. 17 But that it spreads no further among the people, let us strictly threaten them that they speak to no man in this Name from now on. 18 And they called them, and commanded them not to speak at all nor teach in the Name of יהושע. 19 But Kepha and Yochanan answered and said to them, Whether it is right in the sight of Elohim to shema to you more than to יהוה, you can shophet. 20 We just cannot stop speaking about the things, which we have seen, and heard. 21 So when they had further threatened them, they let them go, finding nothing on how they might punish them, because of the people: for all men gave tehilla to יהוה for that which was done. 22 For the man was above forty years old, on whom this nes of healing was done. 23 And being let go, they went to their own people, and reported all that the chief kohanim and zachanim had said to them. 24 And when they heard that, they lifted up their voice to יהוה with one accord, and said, Master יהוה, You are Elohim, who has made the shamayim, and the olam, and the sea, and all that is in them: 25 Who by the mouth of Your servant David has said, Why did the heathen rage, and the people imagine worthless things? 26 The melechim of the olam stood up, and the rulers were gathered together against the Master יהוה, and against His Moshiach. 27 For of an emet against Your Set-Apart Son יהושע, whom You have anointed, both Herod, and Pontius Pilate, with the gentile pagans, and the people of Yisrael, were gathered together, 28 To do whatever Your hand and Your counsel determined before to be done. 29 And now, Master יהוה, see their threats: and grant to Your avadim, that with all boldness they may speak Your word, 30 By stretching out Your hand to heal; and that signs and wonders may be done by the Name of Your Set-Apart Son יהושע. 31 And when they had made tefillah, the

place was shaken where they were assembled together; and they were all filled with the Ruach HaKodesh, and they spoke the word of יהוה with boldness. 32 And the multitude of them that believed were echad: no one claimed that any of the things, which he possessed, was his own; but they had all things in be-yachad. 33 And with great power gave the shlichim witness of the resurrection of the Savior יהושע: and great favor was upon them all. 34 Neither was there any among them that lacked: for as many as were possessors of lands or houses sold them, and brought the prices of those things that were sold, 35 And laid them down at the shlichim's feet: and then distributions were made to every man according as he had need. 36 And Yoseph, who by the shlichim was surnamed Bar-Navah,[1] which is, being interpreted, The Son of Encouragement a Levite, and of the country of Cyprus, 37 Had a field, and sold it, and brought the money, and placed it at the disposal of the shlichim.

5 But a certain man named Chananyah, with Shappirah his wife, sold a field, 2 And kept back part of the proceeds, his wife also knowing about it, and brought a certain part, and laid it at the shlichim's feet. 3 But Kepha said, Chananyah, why has s.a.tan filled your lev to lie to the Ruach HaKodesh, to keep back part of the price of the field? 4 While it remained in your care, was it not your own? And after it was sold, was it not under your own authority? Why have you conceived this thing in your lev? You have not lied to men, but to יהוה.[2] 5 And Chananyah hearing these words fell down, and gave up the Ruach: and great fear came on all them that heard these things. 6 And the young men arose, wrapped him up, and carried him out, and buried him. 7 And it was about three hours later, when his wife, not knowing what was

---

[1] Aramaic.
[2] The Set-Apart Spirit here is clearly called YHWH, since YHWH and His Power are one.

done, came in. 8 And Kepha asked to her, Tell me whether you sold the field for this much? And she said, Yes, for this much. 9 Then Kepha said to her, How is it that you have agreed together to tempt the Ruach of the Master יהוה? See, the feet of those who have buried your husband are at the door, and shall carry you out. 10 Then fell she down at his feet immediately, and yielded up the Ruach: and the young men came in, and found her dead, and, carried her out, and buried her next to her husband. 11 And great fear came upon all the congregation of Yisrael, and upon as many as heard these things. 12 And by the hands of the shlichim were many signs and wonders done among the people; and they were all with one accord in Shlomo's Porch. 13 And of the rest of those in the Beit HaMikdash, they dared not join themselves to them: but the people magnified them. 14 And believers were added to יהוה, more and more even multitudes both of men and women. 15 So that they brought out the sick into the streets, and laid them on mats and couches, that at the least the shadow of Kepha passing by might overshadow some of them. 16 There came also a multitude out of the cities round around Yahrushalayim, bringing sick folks, and those who were troubled with shaddim [1] : and they were healed every one. 17 Then the Kohen HaGadol rose up, and all they that were with him, which is the sect of the Tzadukim, and were filled with indignation, 18 And laid their hands on the shlichim, and put them in the common prison. 19 But a heavenly messenger of the Master יהוה opened the prison doors at night, and brought them out, and said, 20 Go, stand and speak in the Beit HaMikdash to the people of Yisrael all the words of this Way of chayim. 21 And when they heard that, they entered into the Beit HaMikdash early in the morning, and taught. But the Kohen HaGadol came, and they that were with him, and called the Sanhedrin together, and

all the Sanhedrin of the children of Yisrael and sent word to the prison to have them brought out. 22 But when the officers came, and found them not in the prison, they returned, and told, 23 Saying, The prison truly we found shut with all safety, and the guards standing outside the doors: but when we had opened the doors, we found no man inside. 24 Now when the Kohen HaGadol and the captain of the Beit HaMikdash and the chief kohanim heard these things, they were puzzled and wondered how this could happen. 25 Then came one and told them, saying, See, the men whom you put in prison are standing in the Beit HaMikdash, and teaching the people of Yisrael. 26 Then the captain with the officers brought the talmidim in without violence: for they feared the people, lest they should be stoned. 27 And when they had brought them, they sat them before the Sanhedrin: and the Kohen HaGadol asked them, 28 Saying, Did not we strictly command you that you should not teach in this Name? [2] And, see, you have filled Yahrushalayim with your teaching, and now you intend to bring this man's dom upon us. 29 Then Kepha and the other shlichim answered and said, We must first obey Elohim rather than men. 30 The Elohim of our ahvot raised up יהושע , whom you killed and hanged on a tree of execution. 31 This very one has יהוה exalted with His right hand to be the Prince and Savior, to grant teshuvah to Yisrael, and the forgiveness of sins. 32 And we are His witnesses of these things; and so is also the Ruach HaKodesh, whom Elohim has given to them that obey Him. [3] 33 When they heard these words, they were enraged, and took counsel to murder them. 34 Then stood up one in the Sanhedrin, a Prush, named Gamliel, an honored Torah teacher, held in the highest esteem among all the

---

[1] Hebrew word for demons.

[2] Not much has changed. When you teach His word in YHWH's and Yahshua's true Name, you'll often be told to be quiet.
[3] Only those who obey his commandments truly receive the Ruach.

people of Yisrael, who commanded that the shlichim be taken out of the chamber for a while; 35 And said to them, You men of Yisrael,[1] take heed to yourselves what you intend to do to these men. 36 For before these days rose up Todah, boasting himself to be somebody great; to whom a number of men, about four hundred, joined themselves: he was killed; and all, that obeyed him, were scattered, and brought to nothing. 37 After this man rose up Yahudah of Galil in the days of the taxing, and drew away many people after him: he also perished; and all those who obeyed him were dispersed. 38 And now I say to you, Refrain from hurting these men, and leave them alone: for if these ideas or this work be from men, it will come to nothing: 39 But if it be of Elohim, you cannot overthrow it; lest you be found in a fight against Elohim. 40 And they agreed with him: and when they had called the shlichim, and had beaten them, they commanded that they should not speak in the Name of יהושע , and let them go. 41 And they departed from the presence of the Sanhedrin, rejoicing that they were counted worthy to suffer shame for His Name. 42 And daily in the Beit HaMikdash, and in every bayit, they ceased not to teach and proclaim יהושע the Moshiach.

6 And in those days, when the number of the talmidim was multiplied, there arose a murmuring of the Hellenists against the Ivrim, because their widows were neglected in the daily distribution.[2] 2 Then the twelve called the multitude of the talmidim to them, and said, It is not right that we should leave the word of יהוה, and serve food. 3 Therefore, brothers, look for seven men of honest report, full of the Ruach of the Master יהוה and chochma,

whom we may appoint over this business. 4 But we will give ourselves continually to tefillah, and to the service of the word. 5 And the saying pleased the entire multitude: and they chose Stephanos, a man full of emunah and the Ruach HaKodesh, and Philip, and Prochoros, and Nikanor, and Timon, and Parmenas, and Nikolaos a Yisraelite of Antioch:[3] 6 Who were set before the shlichim: and when they had made tefillah, they laid their hands on them. 7 And the word of יהוה increased; and the number of the talmidim multiplied in Yahrushalayim greatly; and a large group of the kohanim and others from the Yahudite emunah were obedient to the Netsarim emunah. 8 And Tsephanyah, full of emunah and power, did great wonders and nisim among the people. 9 Then there arose certain of the synagogue, which is called the Synagogue of the Libertines, and Cyrenians, and Alexandrians, and of them of Cilicia and of Asia Minor, disputing with Tsephanyah.[4] 10 And they were not able to resist the chochma and the Ruach by which he spoke. 11 Then they instigated other men, who said, We have heard him speak blasphemous words against Moshe, and against Elohim. 12 And they stirred up the people, and the zachanim, and the Sophrim, and all these came upon him, and caught him, and brought him to the Sanhedrin, 13 And set up false witnesses, who said, This man ceases not to speak blasphemous words against the Set-Apart Place, and the Torah: 14 For we have heard him say, that this יהושע of Natzareth shall destroy this place, and shall change the ways that Moshe delivered to us. 15 And all that sat in the Sanhedrin, looking steadfastly at him, saw

---

[1] Both houses.
[2] This conflict prevails in the congregation to this day. There are those who are content with the lies of their fathers and desire to perpetuate a Hellenistic approach to Yahshua, including diverse forms of paganism. The Hebrew, on the other hand, desires a full and rewarding return to the emunah that was initially and eternally given to the people of Nazarene inheritance.

[3] Greeks converts, especially in Asia Minor, were clearly lost sheep as outlined elsewhere.
[4] More early fighting between Yahudite believers and Greek converts, who assembled in various places, including this place known as the Synagogue of Freedom or Freemen. There is little doubt that these were in fact the early seeds of the later-developed Roman-Greek church system, that paraded and boasted in their status as freemen, or those freed from obedience and compliance to Torah.

his face as if it had been the face of a heavenly messenger.

7 Then said the Kohen HaGadol said, Are these things the emet? 2 And he said, Men, brothers, and ahvot, shema to me; The Elohim of tiferet appeared to our abba Avraham, when He was in Mesopotamia, before he dwelt in Charran, 3 And said to him, Get out of your country, and from your mishpocha, and come into the land that I shall show you. 4 Then he came out of the land of the Chaldaeans, and dwelt in Charran: and from there, when his abba was dead, he moved into this land, in which you now dwell. 5 And He gave him no inheritance in it, no, not so much as to set his foot on: yet He promised that He would give it to him for a possession, and to his zera after him, when as yet he had no children. 6 And Elohim spoke saying, That his zera should sojourn in a strange land; and that they should bring them into bondage, and mistreat them with evil four hundred years. 7 And the nation to whom they shall be in bondage will I shophet, said יהוה: and after that shall they come out, and serve Me in this place. 8 And He gave him the covenant of Brit Milah: and so Avraham brought out Yitzchak, and brit-milahed him the eighth day; and Yitzchak brought out Yaakov; and Yaakov brought out the twelve ahvot. 9 And the ahvot, moved with envy, sold Yoseph into Mitzrayim: but Elohim was with him, 10 And delivered him out of all his afflictions, and gave him favor and chochma in the sight of Pharaoh melech of Mitzrayim; and He made him governor over Mitzrayim and all his bayit. 11 Now there came a famine over all the land of Mitzrayim and Kanaan, and great affliction: and our ahvot found no food. 12 But when Yaakov heard that there was corn in Mitzrayim, He sent out our ahvot first. 13 And at the second time Yoseph was made known to his brothers;[1] and Yoseph's mishpocha was made known to Pharaoh. 14 Then Yoseph sent, and called his abba Yaakov to him, and all his mishpocha, seventy-five beings.[2] 15 So Yaakov went down into Mitzrayim, and died, he, and our ahvot, 16 And were carried over into Shechem, and laid in the tomb that Avraham bought for a sum of money from the sons of Chamor the abba of Shechem. 17 But when the time of the promise drew near, which Elohim had sworn to Avraham, the people grew and multiplied in Mitzrayim, 18 Until another melech arose, who knew not Yoseph. 19 The same dealt deceitfully with our people, and mistreated our ahvot; so that they made them cast out their young children, so that they might not live. 20 In which time Moshe was born, and was favored and pleasing to Elohim, and was raised in his abba's bayit three months: 21 And when he was exposed, Pharaoh's daughter took him in, and nourished him even as her own son. 22 And Moshe was learned in all the chochma of the Mitzrites, and was mighty in words and in deeds. 23 And when he was forty years old, it came into his lev to visit his brothers the children of Yisrael.[3] 24 And seeing one of them mistreated, he defended him, and avenged him that was oppressed, and smote the Mitzrite: 25 For he supposed his brothers would have understood how Elohim by his hand would deliver them: but they understood not. 26 And the next day he shown himself to them as they fought, and would have made them echad again, saying, Men, you are brothers; why do you do wrong one to another? 27 But he that did his neighbor wrong pushed him away, saying, Who made you a ruler and a shophet over us? 28 Will you kill me, as you did the Mitzrite yesterday?

---

[1] Speaking in **remez**/hint of the revelation of Yoseph or the 10 tribes of Ephraim to Yahudah, the second time Moshiach comes.
[2] Quoting LXX.
[3] It's never too late to leave Egypt and return to your people Yisrael.

29 Then Moshe ran at this saying, and was a stranger in the land of Midyan, where he brought out two sons. 30 And when forty years were expired, there appeared to him in the wilderness of Har Sinai the Malach יהוה[1] from the Master יהוה in a flame of fire in a bush. 31 When Moshe saw it, he wondered at the sight: and as he drew near to see it, the voice of the Master יהוה came to him, 32 Saying, I am the Elohim of your ahvot, the Elohim of Avraham, and the Elohim of Yitzchak, and the Elohim of Yaakov. Then Moshe trembled, and dared not look. 33 Then said the Master יהוה to him, Take off your sandals from your feet: for the place where you stand is set-apart ground. 34 I have seen, yes I have seen the affliction of My people who are in Mitzrayim, and I have heard their groaning, and am come down to deliver them. And now come, I will send you into Mitzrayim. 35 This Moshe whom they refused, saying, Who made you a ruler and a shophet? The same one did יהוה send to be a ruler and a deliverer by the hand of the Malach-יהוה who appeared to him in the bush. 36 He brought them out, after that He had shown wonders and signs in the field of Mitzrayim, and in the Sea of Reeds, and in the wilderness for forty years. 37 This is that Moshe, who said to the children of Yisrael, A Navi shall the Master יהוה your Elohim raise up to you from your brothers, like me; to Him shall you shema. 38 This is he, that was in the ekklesia-congregation of Yisrael in the wilderness[2][3] with the Malach-יהוה

who spoke to him on Har Sinai, and with our ahvot: who received the living words[4] to give to us: 39 To whom our ahvot would not obey, but threw him from them, and in their levim turned back again into Mitzrayim, 40 Saying to Aharon, Make us mighty ones to go before us: for as for this Moshe, who brought us out of the land of Mitzrayim, we do not know what is become of him. 41 And they made a calf in those days, and offered sacrifices to the idol, and rejoiced in the works of their own hands. 42 Then Elohim turned, and gave them up to worship the chochavim of the shamayim; as it is written in the scroll of the neviim, O you people of Yisrael, why have you offered to Me slain beasts and sacrifices during forty years in the wilderness? 43 Yes, you took up the tent of Moloch, and the chochav of your mighty one Remphan-Derphan, and made images to worship: and so I will carry you away beyond Bavel.[5] 44 Our ahvot had the tent of witness in the wilderness, as He had appointed, speaking to Moshe, that he should make it according to the pattern that he had seen. 45 Which also our ahvot that came after brought in with Yahoshua son of Nun, into this land of the gentiles, whom Elohim drove out before the face of our ahvot, up until the days of David; 46 Who found favor before יהוה, and desired to find a tent for the Elohim of Yaakov. 47 But Shlomo built Him a Bayit. 48 But El-Elyon dwells not in temples made with hands; as said ha navi, 49 *Heaven is My throne, and the olam is My footstool: what bayit will you build Me?* Says the Master יהוה: *or what is the place of My rest?* 50 *Has not My hand made all these*

---

[1] Yahshua.
[2] Acts 7:38 speaks of the **ekklesia** or congregation (translated as "church" in most English Bibles) that was in the wilderness, which clearly indicates that those of first-century Yisrael thought that the people being called forth in Moshiach, were "one and the same" with those of ancient Yisrael. YHWH's Ruach, not man, wrote this Acts 7 quotation. He placed this verse here, to make sure that the disciples understood, just as Stephen the Jewish martyr understood things. Namely, that the Renewed Covenant Yisraelite community was the historic and prophetic continuation of the people of Yisrael, made up of twelve tribes plus strangers. It is not the birth of a new and separate entity of elect called "the church." It is the historic continuation through Moshiach's renewal of Yisrael. But, ultimately, this congregation has a name, and it is not "Messianic Judaism" or "Christian church," but "Yisrael." Hence the term "ekklesia" or "congregation" of Yisrael.

[3] In The LXX (Greek Septuagint) the Hebrew word for "congregation" or "**kahal**" Yisrael was translated by 70 Jewish rabbis in 150 CE into the Greek word **ekklesia** – the same word used here and for all Renewed Covenant congregations throughout the Renewed Covenant; meaning that the authors considered the congregations that believed in Yahshua as the same Yisrael that was at Mt. Sinai.
[4] Apparently Stephen also believed that the Torah was still in effect after Yahshua came, since he calls the Torah's teachings "ongoing" or "living words."
[5] Speaking of Yisrael's exile to all four corners of the earth.

things? 51 You stiff-necked and uncircumcised [1] in lev and ears, you do always resist the Ruach HaKodesh: as your ahvot did, so do you. 52 Which of the true neviim have not your ahvot persecuted? And they have also killed those who spoke before of the coming of the Tzadik-One; whom you now have betrayed by murder: 53 Who have received the Torah like the very commands given to heavenly messengers, but have not kept it. 54 When they heard these things, they were enraged, and they gnashed on him with their teeth. 55 But he, being full of the Ruach HaKodesh, looked up staring into the shamayim, and saw the tiferet of **יהוה**, and **יהושע** standing on the right hand of El-Elyon, 56 And said, See, I see the shamayim opened, and the Ben-Adam standing on the right hand of **יהוה** . [2] 57 Then they cried out with a loud voice, and covered their ears, and ran upon him with one accord, 58 And cast him out of the city, and stoned him: and the witnesses laid down their clothes at a young man's feet, whose name was Shaul. 59 And they stoned Tsephanyah, while he was calling upon Elohim, and saying, Master **יהושע**, receive My Ruach. 60 And he kneeled down, and cried with a loud voice, Master **יהושע**; lay not this sin against them. And when he had said this, he died.

8 And Shaul was approving of Tsephanyah's death. And at that time there was a great persecution against the congregation of Yisrael at Yahrushalayim; and they were all scattered abroad throughout the regions of Yahudah and Shomron, except the shlichim. [3] 2 And devout men carried Tsephanyah to his burial, and mourned over him in great human sorrow. 3 As for Shaul, he made havoc of the congregation of Yisrael, entering into every bayit, and haling men and women throwing them into prison. 4 Therefore they that were scattered abroad went everywhere proclaiming the word. 5 Then Philip went down to the city of Shomron, [4] and proclaimed the Moshiach to them. 6 And the people with one accord gave heed to those things that Philip spoke, hearing and seeing the nisim that he did. 7 For shaddim, crying with loud voices, came out of many that were possessed with them: and many who were paralyzed, and that were lame, were healed. 8 And there was great simcha in that city. [5] 9 But there was a certain man, called Shimon, who in the past in the same city used sorcery, and bewitched the people of Shomron, claiming to be someone great: 10 To whom they all gave heed, from the least to the greatest, saying, This man is the great power of Elohim. 11 And to him they paid careful attention, because for a long time he had amazed them with sorceries. 12 But when they believed Philip proclaiming the things concerning the malchut of **יהוה**, and the Name of **יהושע** the Moshiach, they were immersed, both men and women. 13 Then Shimon himself believed also: and when he was immersed, he continued with Philip, and was impressed, beholding the nisim and signs that were done. 14 Now when the shlichim who were at Yahrushalayim heard that Shomron had received the word of **יהוה** , they sent to them Kepha and Yochanan: 15 Who, when they had come down, made tefillah for them, that they might receive the Ruach HaKodesh: 16 For until then He had not fallen upon them: they

---

[1] In the twenty times the word "uncircumcised" appears in most English translations, only once, here in Acts 7:51, does it appear in the Greek as **aperitome** (a negation of **peritome**). Surprisingly this one exception refers not to gentiles but to Jews. The other nineteen times it is an altogether different word, **akrobustia** and as shared elsewhere in the footnotes on Galatians, it refers to Ephraim returning as those whose foreskins were cut according to covenant, but nevertheless tossed away by a willful forsaking of the covenant.
[2] Why standing? Because Yahshua honored him as the first Renewed Covenant martyr, and stood in his honor.

[3] This among many other persecutions was used by YHWH, to spread both the message, and the people of the message, so that they would go gathering the lost sheep.
[4] A city of Ephraim.
[5] See: **Tov or Bad Samaritan** at:
http://store.yourarmstoisrael.org/Qstore/Qstore.cgi?CMD=011&PROD=000158.

only were immersed in the Name of the Savior יהושע . 17 Then they laid their hands on them, and they received the Ruach HaKodesh. 18 And when Shimon saw that through laying on of the shlichim's hands that the Ruach HaKodesh was given, he offered them money,[1] 19 Saying, Give me also this power, that on whoever I lay hands; he may receive the Ruach HaKodesh. 20 But Kepha said to him, Your money perishes with you, because you have thought that the gift of יהוה may be purchased with money. 21 You have nothing to do with this our emunah: for your lev is not right in the sight of יהוה. 22 Repent therefore of your wickedness, and make tefillah to Elohim, if perhaps the thoughts of your lev may be forgiven you. 23 For I perceive that you are poisoned with bitterness, bound by Torah violations. 24 Then answered Shimon, and said, Make tefillah to the Savior for me, that none of these things that you have spoken come upon me. 25 And, when they had testified and proclaimed the word of יהוה, returned to Yahrushalayim, and proclaimed the besarot in many villages of the Shomronim. 26 And a heavenly messenger of the Master יהוה spoke to Philip, saying, Arise, and go toward the south to the derech that goes down from Yahrushalayim to Aaza, which is desert. 27 And he arose and went: and, see, a man of Kush, a faithful believer,[2] a treasurer of great authority under Candace malqa of the Kushim, who was in charge of all her treasure, and had come to Yahrushalayim for to worship,[3] 28 Was returning, and sitting in his mirkavah

reading Yeshayahu ha navi. 29 Then the Ruach said to Philip, Go near, and join this mirkavah. 30 And Philip ran to him, and heard him reading Yeshayahu ha navi, and said; Do you understand what you read? 31 And he said, How can I, except some man should teach me? And he desired that Philip would come up and sit with him. 32 The place of the Katav from where he read was this, He was led as a sheep to the slaughter; and like a Lamb is dumb before His shearer, so He opened not His mouth: 33 In His humiliation His mishpat was taken away: and who shall declare His generation? For His chayim is taken from the olam. 34 And the faithful believer asked Philip, and said, I ask you, of whom does ha navi speak this? Of himself, or of some other man? 35 Then Philip opened his mouth, and began at the same Katav, and proclaimed to him יהושע. 36 And as they went on their derech, they came to a certain mayim: and the faithful believer said, See, here is mayim; what does stop me from being immersed? 37 And Philip said, If you believe with all your lev, you may. And he answered and said, I believe that יהושע the Moshiach is the Son of יהוה. 38 And he commanded the mirkavah to stop: and they both went down into the mayim, both Philip and the faithful believer; and he immersed him. 39 And when they were come up out of the mayim, the Ruach of the Master יהוה caught Philip away to another place, so that the faithful believer saw him no more: and he went on his derech with gilah.[4] 40 But Philip was found at Ashdod: and passing through he proclaimed in all the cities, until he came to Caesarea.

9 And Shaul, yet breathing out threatenings and slaughter against the

---

[1] See: **Shimon Magus The First Pope** at http://store.yourarmstoisrael.org/Qstore/Qstore.cgi?CMD=011&PROD=000101.
[2] This man was not a eunuch as most translations render these verses. He was a faithful convert and was in Jerusalem for one of the three feasts of Deuteronomy 16:16. The Torah forbids a eunuch from worshipping in the temple or from being a convert in Yisrael according to Deuteronomy 23:1. All eunuchs are excluded from the people of Yisrael. The solution is found in the Aramaic word for both eunuch and faith-filled man; which is **Mahimna**, which in this case clearly means a faithful believer, to whom Phillip proclaimed Yahshua.
[3] A black man, who had joined himself to Yisrael, either as a stranger in the gates, or a seeking Ephraimite.

[4] When this man returned to Kush or Ethiopia, he went around proclaiming the tov news, and much of Ethiopia and later India received the tov news. If this man had children and he was as an Ephraimite or even a Yahudite, then today millions of Ethiopians are believing Yisraelites. As we see, Yisrael is not limited to the white Caucasians. Rather Yisrael is Yoseph's coat of many colors.

talmidim of the Savior, went to the Kohen HaGadol, 2 And desired letters from him to Dameshek to the synagogues,[1] that if he found any of this Way, whether they were men or women, he might bring them bound to Yahrushalayim. 3 And as he journeyed, he came near Dameshek: and suddenly there shone all around him a light from the shamayim: 4 And he fell to the ground, and heard a voice saying to him, *Shaul, Shaul, why are you persecuting Me?*[2] 5 And he said, Who are You, Master? And He said, *I am* **יהושע** *whom you are persecuting: it is hard for you to offer against Me this worthless resistance.* 6 And he trembling and astonished said, Master, what will you have me to do? And **יהושע** said to him, *Arise, and go into the city, and it shall be told to you what you must do.* 7 And the men who journeyed with him stood speechless, hearing a voice, but seeing no man. 8 And Shaul arose from the ground; and when his eyes were opened, he saw no man: but they led him by the hand, and brought him into Dameshek. 9 And he was three days without sight, and neither did eat nor drink. 10 And there was a certain talmid at Dameshek, named Chananyah; and **יהושע** said to him in a vision, *Chananyah.* And he said, See, Hinani, my Master **יהוה**. 11 And **יהושע** said to him, *Arise, and go into the street which is called Yashar, and ask in the bayit of Yahudah for one called Shaul, of Tarsus: for, see, he makes tefillah,*[3] 12 *And has seen in a vision a man named Chananyah coming in, and putting his hand on him, that he might receive his sight.* 13 Then Chananyah answered, Master, I have heard from many about this man, how much evil he has done to Your kidushim at Yahrushalayim: 14 And here he

has authority from the chief kohanim to imprison all that call on Your Name. 15 But the Master **יהוה** said to him, *Arise and go: for he is a chosen vessel to Me, to bear My Name before the nations, and melechim, and the children of Yisrael:*[4] 16 *For I will show him how many great things he must suffer for My Name's sake.*[5] 17 And Chananyah went his derech, and entered into the bayit; and putting his hands on him said, Brother Shaul, the Savior, even **יהושע**, that appeared to you in the derech as you came, has sent me, that you might receive your sight, and be filled with the Ruach HaKodesh. 18 And immediately there fell from his eyes something like scales: and he received sight immediately, and arose, and was immersed. 19 And when he had received food, he was strengthened. Then Shaul stayed for a while with the talmidim that were at Dameshek. 20 And right away he proclaimed **יהושע** in the synagogues,[6] that Yahshua is the Son of **יהוה**. 21 But all that heard him were amazed, saying; Is not this the one that destroyed those who called on this Name in Yahrushalayim, and came here for that purpose, that he might bring them bound to the chief kohanim? 22 But Shaul increased even more in strength, and confused the Yahudim who dwelt at Dameshek, proving that this is the Moshiach. 23 And after many days, the Yahudim took counsel to kill him: 24 But Shaul knew their laying in wait. And they watched the gates day and night to kill him. 25 Then the talmidim took him by night, and let him down from the wall in a basket. 26 And when Shaul was come to Yahrushalayim, he desired to join himself to the talmidim: but they were

---

[1] True believers prior to the Hellinization of the faith met in Torah-honoring synagogues and congregations.
[2] Note that Yahshua chose to speak Hebrew not Greek, as Shaul is his Hebrew name. He also calls him Shaul not Paul.
[3] The **remez** here is beautiful as Rav Shaul is in a place known as the straight and narrow way, and from the House of Yahudah ready to be called to the nations to find his Ephraimite brothers, yet is still blind to that call in the House of Yahudah where he is residing.

[4] Many today still don't truly understand the call of Rav Shaul to the children of Yisrael in Judea and in the nations, seeing him as some sort of apostle to pagan gentiles alone. Also note that the call of Rav Shaul (as it is with all of us) is the proclamation of the kingdom, sealed in and by the Name of YHWH. Most versions of the tov news are devoid of the true Name and therefore not sealed by the Father.
[5] Those who use the true Names of the Father and the Son will be under extraordinary pressure to compromise.
[6] A pattern we see throughout his ministry, and the pattern given to him by the Father YHWH.

all afraid of him, and believed not that he was a talmid. 27 But Bar-Nava took him, and brought him to the shlichim, and declared to them how he had seen the Master יהוה in the derech,[1] and that he had spoken to him, and how he had proclaimed boldly at Dameshek in the Name of יהושע. 28 And he was with them coming in and going out at Yahrushalayim. 29 And he spoke boldly in the Name of the Savior יהושע, and disputed against the Hellenists: and they went about to murder him.[2] 30 Which when the brothers knew, they brought him down to Caesarea, and sent him out to Tarsus. 31 Then had the congregations of Yisrael shalom throughout all Yahudah and Galil and Shomron, and were built up; having their halacha in the fear of יהוה, and in the comfort of the Ruach HaKodesh, and were multiplied. 32 And it came to pass, as Kepha passed through various cities, he came down also to the kidushim who dwelt at Lod. 33 And there he found a certain man named Anyah, who had been bound to his mat eight years, and was sick from paralysis. 34 And Kepha said to him, Anyah, יהושע the Moshiach makes you healthy: arise, and take your mat. And he arose immediately. 35 And all that dwelt at Lod and Sharon saw him, and turned to יהוה. 36 Now there was at Yapho a certain talmida named Tavitha, which by interpretation is called Dorcas: this woman was full of tov mitzvot and kind acts that she did. 37 And it came to pass in those days, that she was sick, and died: who when they had washed her, they laid her in an upper room. 38 And since Lod was near to Yapho, and the talmidim had heard that Kepha was there, they sent to him two men, desiring him that he would not delay to come to them. 39 Then Kepha arose and went with them. When he was come, they brought him into the upper chamber: and all the widows stood by him weeping, and showing the coats and garments that Dorcas made, while she was with them. 40 But Kepha put them all out, and kneeled down, and made tefillah; and turning to the body said, Tavitha, arise. And she opened her eyes: and when she saw Kepha, she sat up. 41 And he gave her his hand, and lifted her up, and when he had called the kidushim and widows, he presented her alive. 42 And it was known throughout all Yapho; and many believed in יהושע because of it. 43 And it came to pass, that he stayed many days in Yapho with Shimon a leather-tanner.

10 There was a certain man in Caesarea called Cornelius, a captain of the Italian regiment, 2 A devout man, a Yireh-יהוה along with all his bayit, who gave much assistance to the people, and made tefillah to Elohim always. 3 He saw in a vision evidently about three o'clock a heavenly messenger of יהוה coming in to him, and saying to him, Cornelius. 4 And when he looked at him, he was afraid, and said, What is it, Master? And he said to him, your tefillot and your mitzvot have come up as a memorial before Elohim. 5 And now send men to Yapho, and call for Shimon, who is called Kepha: 6 He lodges with one Shimon a tanner, whose bayit is by the sea: 7 And when the heavenly messenger who spoke to Cornelius was departed, he called two of his household avadim, and a devout soldier from those that waited on him continually; 8 And when he had declared all these things to them, he sent them to Yapho. 9 On the next day, as they went on their journey, and drew near to the city, Kepha went up to the housetop to make tefillah about noon: 10 And he became very hungry, and desired to eat: but while they prepared food for him, he fell into a trance, 11 And he saw the shamayim opened, and a certain vessel descending to him, as it had been a great

---

[1] Mar-Yah in Aramaic used in reference to Moshiach, showing Moshiach to be YHWH fully manifested.
[2] The same battle rages today. Hebrews who desire the faith of Yahshua versus those with a mere mental assent in the Greco-Roman version called Jes-s. How could Paul be a Hellenist, when he argued with them over their false anti-Torah views?

sheet knit at the four corners,[1] and let down to the olam: 12 In it were all manner of four-footed beasts of the olam, and wild beasts, and creeping things, and fowls of the air.[2] 13 And there came a voice to him, *Rise, Kepha; kill, and eat.* 14 But Kepha said, Not so, Master; for I have never eaten anything that is not set-apart or that is unkosher. 15 And the voice spoke to him again the second time, *What* יהוה *has cleansed, that you should not call unkosher.*[3] 16 This was done three times: and the vessel was received up again into the shamayim. 17 Now while Kepha doubted in himself what this vision which he had seen should mean,[4] see, the men who were sent from Cornelius had arrived and asked for Shimon's bayit, and stood outside the gate, 18 They called out, and asked whether Shimon, who was surnamed Kepha, were lodged there. 19 While Kepha thought on the vision, the Ruach said to him, *See, three men seek you.*[5] 20 *Arise therefore, and go down, and go with them, doubting nothing: for I have sent them.* 21 Then Kepha went down to the men who were sent to him from Cornelius; and said, See, I am the one whom you seek: what is the cause for which you came? 22 And they said, Cornelius the captain, a tzadik man, and one that is a Yireh-יהוה, and has a tov report among all the nation of the Yahudim, was instructed by Elohim through a set-

apart heavenly messenger to send for you to his bayit, and to shema words from you. 23 Kepha invited them in, and lodged them. And the next day Kepha went away with them, and certain brothers from Yapho accompanied him. 24 And the next day after they entered into Caesarea, Cornelius was waiting for them, and had called together his relatives and close friends. 25 And as Kepha was coming in, Cornelius met him, and fell down at his feet, and worshipped him. 26 But Kepha took him up, saying, Stand up; I myself also am only a man. 27 And as he talked with him, he went in, and found many that had come together. 28 And he said to them, You know how that it is rabbincally forbidden for a man that is a Yahudi to keep company, or come to one of another nation;[6] but יהוה has shown me that I should not call any man common, unkosher or unclean.[7] 29 Therefore I came to you without hesitation, as soon as I was sent for: I ask therefore for what purpose you have sent for me? 30 And Cornelius said, Four days ago I was fasting until this hour; and at 3 o'clock in the afternoon I made tefillah in my bayit, and, see, a man stood before me in bright clothing, 31 And said, Cornelius, your tefillot are heard, and your mitzvot are had in remembrance in the sight of Elohim. 32 Send therefore to Yapho, and call here Shimon, whose surname is Kepha; he is lodged in the bayit of Shimon a tanner by the sea: who, when he comes, shall speak to you. 33 Immediately therefore I sent for you; and you have done well that you have come. Now therefore we are all here present before Elohim, to shema all things that are

---

[1] Four-cornered sheet represents the four corners of Yisrael's exiles. Yisrael's exiles were scattered into the four corners of the globe.
[2] Unclean foods are not even considered to be food according to YHWH's commands.
[3] In context as seen later, YHWH was not reversing the eternal laws of keeping kosher, but was showing Kepha that Yisrael's exiles were about to return in an unclean state or condition. As such, his unkosher attitude towards them had to change, or they would not be received back into the commonwealth. The vision is well-timed, as Cornelius the non-Jew, is about to seek his rightful place among the people of Yisrael. The "kill and eat" part, would soon be understood as YHWH showing Kepha that all men who were willing, would soon be considered clean, regardless of whether or not they were Jewish.
[4] If YHWH was reversing the kosher food laws, then why did Peter not know it, and why was he confused and not sure, since certain groups claim that this was exactly what was being done here.
[5] The voice of YHWH came three times, one for each of the three arriving men.

[6] A completely rabbinical command not found in Torah, that went right along with the same mentality that added the wall of separation into the outer court in Solomon's temple. This idea of not sharing Torah with other nations is unscriptural. What Yisrael was forbidden from doing was mixing or dwelling with other nations, but was never prohibited to teach and be a light to and for them.
[7] Here then is the full understanding of the vision. It was not as many false religions teach to reverse the eternal laws of YHWH. Rather, it was to show the Jews that those previously unclean men and women in the globe's four corners, would be cleansed by Yahshua's mercy, and as such should be received into the community of Yisrael.

commanded you by Elohim. 34 Then Kepha opened his mouth, and said, Of a emet I perceive that יהוה is not respecter of persons: 35 But in every nation those that fear Him, and work tzedakah, [1] are accepted by Him. 36 The word that the Master יהוה sent to the children of Yisrael, proclaiming shalom by יהושע the Moshiach: He is Master of all: 37 That word, I say, you know, which was published throughout all Yahudah, and began at Galil, after the mikvah that Yochanan HaMatbeel proclaimed; 38 How יהוה anointed יהושע of Natzareth with the Ruach HaKodesh and with power: who went about doing all tov, and healing all that were oppressed of s.a.tan; for יהוה was with Him. 39 And we are witnesses of all things which He did both in the land of the Yahudim, and in Yahrushalayim; whom they killed and hanged on a tree: 40 Him יהוה raised up on the third day, and shown Him openly; 41 Not to all the people, but to witnesses chosen before by יהוה, even to us, who did eat and drink with Him after He rose from the dead. 42 And He commanded us to proclaim to the people, and to testify that it is He who was ordained by יהוה to be the Shophet of the living and dead. 43 To Him give all the neviim witness that through His Name whoever believes in Him shall receive remission of sins. 44 While Kepha yet spoke these words, the Ruach HaKodesh fell on all them who heard the word. 45 And the Yahudim who believed were astonished, all those who came with Kepha, because that on the nations also was poured out the same gift of the Ruach HaKodesh. 46 For they heard them speak with other languages, and magnify יהוה. Then answered Kepha, 47 Can any man forbid mayim for their mikvah, that these should not be immersed, who have received the Ruach HaKodesh as well as we have? 48 And he commanded them to be immersed in the Name of יהושע. [2] Then they asked him to stay certain days.

11 And the shlichim and brothers that were in Yahudah heard that the nations had also received the word of יהוה. 2 And when Kepha was come up to Yahrushalayim, they that were of the Brit Milah contended with him, 3 Saying, You went in with uncircumcised men, and did eat with them. 4 But Kepha rehearsed the matter from the beginning, and explained it in order to them, saying, 5 I was in the city of Yapho making tefillah: and in a trance I saw a vision, A certain vessel descended, as it had been a great sheet, let down from the shamayim by four corners; and it came even to me: 6 When I had intently looked inside, I considered, and saw four-footed beasts of the olam, and wild beasts, and creeping things, and fowls of the air. 7 And I heard a voice saying to me, *Arise, Kepha; kill and eat.* 8 But I said, Not so, Master: for nothing common or unkosher has at any time entered into my mouth. 9 But the voice answered me again from the shamayim, *What יהוה has cleansed, that call not common.* 10 And this was done three times: and all were drawn up again into the shamayim. 11 And, see, immediately there were three men already who had come to the bayit where I was, sent from Caesarea to me. 12 And the Ruach told me go with them, doubting nothing. Moreover these six brothers accompanied me, and we entered into the man's bayit: 13 And he showed us how he had seen a heavenly messenger in his bayit, who stood and said to him, Send men to Yapho, and call for Shimon, whose surname is Kepha; 14 Who shall tell you words, whereby you and all your bayit shall be saved. 15 And as I began to speak, the Ruach HaKodesh fell on them, as on us at the beginning. 16 Then I remembered the word of יהושע, how that He said, *Yochanan HaMatbeel indeed immersed with*

---

[1] Faith and mitzvoth.

[2] Proper method of mikvah is in Yahshua's Name and His authority.

mayim; but you shall be immersed with the Ruach HaKodesh. 17 Forasmuch then as יהוה gave them the same gift as He did to us, who believed on יהושע the Moshiach; who was I, that I could withstand יהוה? 18 When they heard these things, they became silent, and gave tehilla to יהוה, saying, Then has יהוה also to the nations granted teshuvah to chayim. 19 Now they who were scattered abroad upon the persecution that arose over Tsephanyah traveled as far as Phoenicia, and Cyprus, and Antioch, proclaiming the word to none but to the Yahudim only.[1] 20 And some of them were men of Cyprus and Cyrene, who, when they were come to Antioch, spoke to the Hellenists, proclaiming יהושע the Moshiach. 21 And the hand of the Master יהוה was with them: and a great number believed, and returned to יהוה. 22 Then tidings of these things came to the ears of the congregation of Yisrael, which was in Yahrushalayim: and they sent out Bar-Nava, that he should go as far as Antioch. 23 Who, when he came, and had seen the favor of יהוה, had gilah, and exhorted them all, that with a full purpose of lev they must cleave to יהוה. 24 For he was a tov man, and full of the Ruach HaKodesh and of emunah: and many people were added to יהוה. 25 Then Bar-Nava departed to Tarsus, to seek Shaul:[2] 26 And when he had found him, he brought him to Antioch. And it came to pass, that for a full year they assembled themselves with the congregation of Yisrael, and taught many people. And the talmidim were called Notsrim first in Antioch.[3] 27 And in those

[1] If Yahudah, was scattered in these areas, how much more and further was Ephraim scattered? Phoenicia was a well-known colony of Yisrael in the days of Solomon, as outlined in scripture and by author Steven Collins in *The Ten Lost Tribes Of Israel Found.*
[2] To find someone who actually spoke Greek.
[3] This term is "Christian" as it appears in both the Greek and Aramaic versions. This was a derogatory term, as those at Antioch made fun of the "little moshiachs". The fact that the Aramaic preserves this term through transliteration from the Greek and not translation, is further evidence that this was a title assigned "by men to men," and never by YHWH; For when YHWH speaks, such as in Galatians 6:16, or through the use of **ekklessia**, all believers in Yahshua are called and known as Yisrael. If one is called "Christian", it is man's

days came neviim from Yahrushalayim to Antioch. 28 And there stood up one of them named Hagavus, and signified by the Ruach that there should be great famine throughout all the olam: which came to pass in the days of Claudius Caesar. 29 Then the talmidim, every man according to his ability, determined to send relief to the brothers who dwelt in Yahudah: 30 Which also they did, and sent it to the zachanim by the hands of Bar-Nava and Shaul.

12 Now about that time Herod the melech stretched out his hands to do evil to certain of the congregation of Yisrael. 2 And he killed Yaakov the brother of Yochanan with the sword. 3 And because he saw it pleased the unbelieving Yahudim, he proceeded further to take Kepha also. These were the days of Chag Matzoth. 4 And when he had apprehended him, he put him in prison, and delivered him to four squads of soldiers to guard him; intending after Pesach to bring him out to the people. 5 Kepha therefore was kept in prison: but made tefillah was made without ceasing by the congregation of Yisrael to יהוה for him. 6 And when Herod would have brought him out, the same night Kepha was sleeping between two soldiers, bound with two chains: and the guards in front of the door guarded the prison. 7 And, see, the heavenly messenger of the Master יהוה came upon him, and a light shone in the prison: and he touched Kepha on the side, and raised him up, saying, Arise up quickly. And his chains fell off from his hands. 8 And the heavenly messenger said to him, Gird yourself, and tie your sandals. And so he did. And he said to him, Cast your garment around you, and follow me. 9 And he went out, and followed him; and did not know that it was real which was done by the heavenly messenger; but thought he saw a vision. 10 When they were past the first and the second guard posts, they came to

terminology. If one is called Yisrael, he has adopted YHWH's terminology and viewpoint.

the iron gate that leads to the city; which opened to them on its own accord: and they went out, and passed on through one street; and at once the heavenly messenger departed from him. 11 And when Kepha had come to himself, he said, Now I know for sure, that the Master יהוה has sent His heavenly messenger, and has delivered me out of the hand of Herod, and from all the expectation of the people among the unbelieving Yahudim. 12 And when he had realized this, he came to the bayit of Miryam the ima of Yochanan, whose surname was Moshe-Markus; where many were gathered together making tefillah. 13 And as Kepha knocked at the door of the gate, a young girl came to shema, named Rhoda. 14 And when she knew Kepha's voice, she did not open the gate due to uncontrollable simcha, but ran in, and told how Kepha stood outside the gate. 15 And they said to her, You are meshugas. But she constantly affirmed that it was even so. Then they said, It is his heavenly messenger. 16 But Kepha continued knocking: and when they had opened the door, and saw him, they were astonished. 17 But he, beckoning to them with the hand to be quiet, declared to them how the Master יהוה had brought him out of the prison. And he said, Go show these things to Yaakov, and to the brothers. And he departed, and went into another place. 18 Now as soon as it was day, there was no small stir among the soldiers, about what had become of Kepha. 19 And when Herod had sought for him, and found him not, he questioned the guards, and commanded that they should be put to death. And he went down from Yahudah to Caesarea, and stayed there. 20 And Herod was highly displeased with them of Tsor and Tzidon: but they came with one accord to him, and, having made Blastus the melech's eunuch their friend, desired shalom; because their country was nourished by the melech's country. 21 And upon a set day Herod, arrayed in royal apparel, sat upon his

throne, and made a verbal address to them. 22 And the people gave a shout, saying, It is the voice of a mighty one, and not of a man. 23 And immediately the heavenly messenger of the Master יהוה killed him, because he gave not יהוה the tiferet: and he was eaten by worms, and gave up the Ruach. 24 But the word of יהוה grew and multiplied. 25 And Bar-Nava and Shaul returned from Yahrushalayim, when they had fulfilled their service, and took with them Yochanan, whose surname was Moshe-Markus.

13 Now there were in the congregation of Yisrael that was at Antioch certain neviim and teachers; as Bar-Nava, and Shimeon that was called Niger, [1] and Lucius of Cyrene, and Manachem, who had been brought up with Herod the tetrarch, and Shaul. 2 As they made tefillah and fasted to יהוה, the Ruach HaKodesh said, *Separate for Me Bar-Nava and Rav Shaul for the work for which I have called them.* 4 So they, being sent out by the Ruach HaKodesh, departed to Seleukia; and from there they sailed to Cyprus. 5 And when they were at Salamis, they proclaimed the word of יהוה in the synagogues of the Yahudim: and they had also Yochanan-Moshe-Markus with them. 6 And when they had gone through the island to Paphos, they found a certain sorcerer, a false navi, a Yahudite, whose name was Bar-Yeshua: [2] 7 Who was with the deputy of the country, Sergeus Paulus, a wise man; who called for Bar-Nava and Shaul, and desired to shema the word of Elohim. 8 But Elymas the sorcerer (for so is his name by interpretation) withstood them, seeking to turn away the deputy from

---

[1] A man of color in exile most likely Ephraim Yisrael.
[2] A very interesting **remez**-hint here with this Jew named Jess a real devil in disguise, seeking to stop Yisrael from hearing the Tov News. Historically we have seen this play out, as the devil has again disguised himself as a person named "Jesus the son," or "bar-Jesus," who breaks Torah, eats bacon, and hates Jews. This is mere sorcery designed to enslave and confuse the masses from recognizing and accepting the real Yahshua, who lived and does yet live.

the emunah. 9 Then Shaul, who also is called Paul, filled with the Ruach HaKodesh, set his eyes on him, 10 And said, O full of all deceit and all mischief, you child of the devil, you enemy of all tzedakah, will you not cease to pervert the right halachot of the Master יהוה? 11 And now, see, the hand of the Master יהוה is upon you, and you shall be blind, not seeing your sun for a season.[1] And immediately there fell on him a mist and darkness; and he went about seeking someone to lead him by the hand. 12 Then the deputy, when he saw what was done, believed, being astonished at the Torah of the Master יהוה. 13 Now when Shaul and his company left from Paphos, they came to Perga in Pamphylia: and Yochanan Moshe-Mark departed from them and returned to Yahrushalayim. 14 But when they departed from Perga, they came to Antioch in Pisidia, and went into the synagogue on the Shabbat, and sat down.[2] 15 And after the reading of the Torah parsha and the haftarah the rulers of the synagogue sent to them, saying, Men and brothers, if you have any word of exhortation for the people, go ahead and say it. 16 Then Shaul stood up, and beckoning with his hand said, Men of Yisrael, and you that fear Elohim,[3] pay attention! 17 The Elohim of this people of Yisrael chose our ahvot, and exalted the people when they dwelt as strangers in the land of Mitzrayim, and with a Mighty Arm He brought them out. 18 And for forty years He preserved them in the wilderness. 19 And when He had destroyed seven nations in the land of Kanaan, He divided their land by inheritance. 20 And after that He gave to them shophtim for around four hundred fifty years, until Schmuel ha navi. 21 And afterward they desired a melech:

and יהוה gave to them Shaul the son of Kish, a man from the tribe of Benyamin, for about forty years. 22 And when He had removed him, He raised up David to be their melech; and regarding him He gave testimony, and said, I have found David the son of Yishai, a man after My own lev, who shall do all My will. 23 Of this man's zera has יהוה according to His promise raised up for Yisrael a Savior, יהושע: 24 Whom Yochanan HaMatbeel had first proclaimed even before His coming by the mikvah of teshuvah, to all the people of Yisrael. 25 And as Yochanan HaMatbeel fulfilled his course, he said, Who do you think that I am? I am not He. But, see, there comes One after me, whose sandals I am not worthy to loose. 26 Men and brothers, children of the race of Avraham, and whoever among you are Yireh-יהוה,[4] to you is the word of this salvation sent. 27 For they that dwell at Yahrushalayim, and their rulers, because they knew Him not, nor the voices of the neviim that are read every Shabbat, they have fulfilled those words by condemning Him. 28 And though they found no cause of death in Him, yet they desired Pilate that He should be killed. 29 And when they had fulfilled all that was written of Him, they took Him down from the tree, and laid Him in a tomb. 30 But יהוה raised Him from the dead: 31 And He was seen many days by those who came up with Him from Galil to Yahrushalayim, who are His witnesses to the people. 32 And we declare to you the besarot, how that the promise which was made to the ahvot, 33 יהוה has fulfilled the same promise to us their children,[5] in that He has raised up יהושע again; as it is also written in the Tehillim Bet, *You are My Son, this day have I begotten You.* 34 And since He raised Him up from the dead, no more to return to corruption, He said this, *I will give You the sure rachamim of David.* 35 For this reason He said also in another

---

[1] A valid punishment, considering Jesus is affiliated with sun infatuation such as Sun Day, Easter Sun-Day, and Whit Sun-Day and Sun-Day Pentecost worship and more.
[2] Following the pattern and looking for the lost sheep in both houses, while still keeping Shabbat. In all the nations this remained Shaul's pattern.
[3] Men of Yisrael are Yahuduah and the Yireh-YHWH or YHWH-fearers were mostly returning Ephraim.

[4] Two-house reference.
[5] Note: That even strangers and Yire-YHWH were called Yisrael's children by Rav Shaul.

mizmor, You shall not allow Your Kadosh One to see corruption. 36 For David, after he had served his own generation by the will of יהוה, died, and was laid with his ahvot, and saw corruption: 37 But He, whom יהוה raised again, saw no corruption. 38 Be it known to you therefore, men and brothers, that through this Man is proclaimed to you the forgiveness of sins: 39 And by Him all that believe are justified from all things, from which you could not be justified by the Torah of Moshe. 40 Beware therefore, lest that come upon you, which is spoken of in the neviim; 41 *See, you despisers, and wonder, and perish: for I work a work in your days, a work which you shall in no way believe, though a man declare it to you.* 42 And when the Yahudim were gone out of the synagogue, the non-Yahudim begged that these words might be proclaimed to them the next Shabbat. 43 Now when the congregation was dismissed, many of the Yahudim and religious proselytes followed Shaul and Bar-Nava: who were speaking to them, and persuaded them to continue in the favor of יהוה. 44 And the next Shabbat almost the entire city came together to shema the word of יהוה. 45 But when the Yahudim saw the multitudes, they were filled with envy, and spoke against those things, which were spoken by Shaul, contradicting and blaspheming him. 46 Then Shaul and Bar-Nava grew bold, and said, It was necessary that the word of יהוה should first have been spoken to you: but seeing you put it away from you, and shophet yourselves unworthy of everlasting chayim, look, we turn to the nations. 47 For this is what יהוה commanded us, saying, *I have set you to be a light of the nations that you should be for salvation to the ends of the olam.* 48 And when the non-Yahudim heard this, they were full of simcha, and gave tehilla to the word of יהוה: and as many as were ordained to eternal chayim believed. 49 And the word of the Master יהוה was published throughout that entire region. 50 But the Yahudim stirred up the devout and honorable women, and the ruling men of the city, and raised persecution against Shaul and Bar-Nava, and expelled them out of their borders. 51 But they shook off the dust of their feet against them, and came to Ikoniom. 52 And the talmidim were filled with simcha, and with the Ruach HaKodesh.

14 And it came to pass in Ikonium, that they went both together into the synagogue of the Yahudim, and so spoke, that a great multitude both of the Yahudim and also of the Greeks believed.[1]
2 But the unbelieving Yahudim stirred up the non-Yahudim, and affected their minds with evil against the brothers. 3 So they remained there a long time speaking boldly in the Master יהוה, who gave testimony to the word of His favor, and granted signs and wonders to be done by their hands. 4 But the multitude of the city was divided: a part sided with the Yahudim, and a part sided with the shlichim. 5 And when there was an assault made both of the non-Yahudim, and also of the Yahudim with their rulers, to use them despitefully, and to stone them, 6 They were made aware of it, and fled to Lustra and Derbe, cities of Lukaonia, and to the region all around: 7 And there they proclaimed the besarot. 8 And there sat a certain man at Lustra, impotent in his feet, being a cripple from his ima's womb, who never had walked: 9 The same heard Shaul speak: who firmly looked at him, and perceived that he had emunah to be healed, 10 Said with a loud voice, Stand up straight on your feet. And he leaped and walked. 11 And when the people saw what Shaul had done, they lifted up their voices, saying in the speech of the Lukaonians, The mighty ones have come down to us in the likeness of men. 12 And they called Bar-Nava, Zeus; and Shaul, Hermes, because he was the chief speaker. 13 Then the priest of Zeus, who was before

---

[1] Two houses in the synagogue.

their city, brought oxen and wreaths to the gates, and wanted to sacrifice to them along with the people. 14 Which when the shlichim, Bar-Nava and Shaul, heard of it, they tore their clothes, and ran in among the people, crying out, 15 And saying, Sirs, why do you do these things? We also are men of like passions with you, and proclaim to you that you should teshuvah from these vanities to the living Elohim, who made the shamayim, and olam, and the sea, and all things that are in them: 16 Who in times past allowed all nations to have their halacha in their own ways. 17 Nevertheless he left not Himself without witness, in that He did tov, and gave us rain from the shamayim, and fruitful moadim, filling our levim with food and simcha. 18 And with these sayings they barely restrained the people, so that they did not sacrifice to them. 19 And there came there certain Yahudim from Antioch and Ikonium, who persuaded the people to turn against the shlichim, and, having stoned Shaul, drew him out of the city, thinking he was dead. 20 But, as the talmidim stood all around him, he rose up, and came into the city: and the next day he departed with Bar-Nava to Derbe. 21 And when they had proclaimed the besarot to that city, and had taught many, they returned again to Lustra, and to Ikonium, and Antioch, 22 Exhorting the talmidim, and reminding them to continue in the emunah, and that we must through great tribulation[1] enter into the malchut of יהוה. 23 And when they had ordained zachanim in every congregation of Yisrael, and had made tefillah and fasted, they commended them to יהושע, on whom they believed. 24 And after they had passed throughout Pisidia, they came to Pamphulia. 25 And when they had proclaimed the word of the Master יהוה in Perge, they went down into Attalia: 26 And from there they sailed to Antioch, from where they had been recommended to the favor of the Master

יהוה for the work that they fulfilled. 27 And when they had come, and had gathered the congregation of Yisrael together, they rehearsed all that יהוה had done with them, and how he had opened the door of emunah to the nations. 28 And there they stayed a long time with the talmidim.

15 And certain men which came down from Yahudah taught the brothers, and said, Except you become brit-milahed after the manner of Moshe, you cannot be saved.[2] 2 When therefore Shaul and Bar-Nava had no small dissension and disputation with them, they determined that Shaul and Bar-Nava, and certain others of them, should go up to Yahrushalayim to the shlichim and zachanim about this question. 3 And being sent on their derech by the congregation of Yisrael, they passed through Phoenicia and Shomron, declaring the return of the nations: and they caused great simcha to all the brothers. 4 And when they had come to Yahrushalayim, they were received by the congregation of Yisrael, and by the shlichim and zachanim, and they declared all things that יהוה had done trough them. 5 But there rose up certain of the sect of the Prushim who believed, saying, That it was needful to give them brit milah, and to command them to keep the Torah of Moshe.[3] 6 And the shlichim and zachanim came together to

---

[2] This is what was known as the "works of the law" or man's dogmas that started returning Ephraimites off on the wrong foot by circumcising them before they held true faith, conviction, and understanding. These promoters of their own "works of the law" of their community, violated the pattern of Abraham and the patriarchs along with Moses and others who were circumcised after they knew what they believed, and were ready to fulfill more Torah mitzvoth. For more details see: **The Mother of Us All** at:
http://store.yourarmstoisrael.org/Qstore/Qstore.cgi?CMD=011&PROD=1065767021
[3] The question becomes when to circumcise them and learn all of Torah, not if they should move on to full compliance. The argument centers around when. The Pharisees said that circumcision and Torah obedience are not progressive, but rather prerequisites to kingdom entry and salvation. The Pauline view is that these things will come in due time, but by not allowing YHWH to work progressively and selectively, these men will be confused, hardened, discouraged and not ready for unity and reconciliation with their Yahudite brothers.

---

[1] A reference to the Great end-time Tribulation, or Yisrael's trouble.

consider this matter. 7 And when there had been much disputing, Kepha rose up, and said to them, Men and brothers, you know how that a long time ago יהוה made choices among us, that the nations by my mouth should shema the word of the besorat, and believe. 8 And יהוה, who knows the levim, bore them witness, giving them the Ruach HaKodesh even as He did to us; 9 And put no difference between us and them; purifying their levim by emunah.[1] 10 Now therefore why do you tempt יהוה, to put a yoke upon the neck of the talmidim, which neither our ahvot nor we were able to bear?[2] 11 But we believe that through the favor of יהושע the Moshiach we shall be saved, even as they will. 12 Then the entire multitude kept silent, and gave audience to Bar-Nava and Shaul, declaring what nisim and wonders יהוה had done among the nations by them. 13 And after they had kept silent, Yaakov answered, saying, Men and brothers, shema to me: 14 Shimeon has declared how יהוה at first did visit the nations, to take out from them a people for His Name.[3] 15 And to this agree the words of the neviim; as it is written,[4] 16 After this I will return, and will rebuild[5] again the Sukkah of David, which has fallen down; and I will rebuild again its ruins, and I will set it up once more:[6]

17 That the remnant of men might seek after the Master יהוה, and all the nations, upon whom My Name is called,[7] said the Master יהוה, who does all these things. 18 Known to יהוה are all His works from the beginning of the olam. 19 Because of this, my mishpat is that we trouble not them, who are from among the nations and who are returning[8] to יהוה: 20 But that we write to them, that they abstain from pollutions of idols, and from fornication, and from things strangled, and from dom.[9] 21 For Moshe from old times has in every city those that proclaim his teachings, with His Torah being read in the synagogues every Shabbat.[10][11] 22 Then it pleased the shlichim and zachanim, with the entire congregation of Yisrael, to send chosen men of their own company to Antioch with Shaul and Bar-Nava; namely, Yahudah surnamed Bar-Savas, and Sila, key men among the brothers: 23 And they gave them written letters to be delivered saying;

Obviously, the components are the twelve tribes living in harmony and unity under the new and Greater David, the Moshiach Yahshua Himself. Verse 17 of Acts 15 tells you that this rebuilding will be done by finding and rescuing the nations, or the gentiles "upon whom My Name is (already) called."

[7] Yisraelite nations.

[8] The Greek word here in verse 19, often wrongly translated as merely "turning" (to Elohim), which is Strong's Greek # 1994 **epistrepho**. **Epistrepho** literally means "returning, reverting or coming again." These "gentiles" are returning. One cannot return unless they at some prior point were Yisrael, making up part of David's Sukkaah, or dwelling place!

[9] To start their progressive journey back, with circumcision towards the end of that journey, they are to now rejoin Yahudah, in the rebuilt tabernacle. The place to do so was at the feasts in table fellowship. So by forsaking idolatry and fornication, they would remove two major abominations that Jews would find repulsive. Things not strangled and not having dom are food principles of **shochet**, where the animal must not be strangled, but will have its throat cut along with having all its dom drained out. This will allow common kosher food at the table of brotherhood. These four items are not the full requirement for returnees from the nations, but merely a start, so as not to place the full Torah obligations on them too fast.

[10] The returning tribes were to continue their Torah education in the Shabbat portions read every week, in every city, from which they came. Then, eventually all the details would be received and incorporated into their lifestyles. Sadly most religions stop reading in the previous verse, and try to make a case for non-Jews not having to obey all of Torah. A careful study of these verses proves that YHWH requires all Yisrael to be equal with identical requirements, and the identical benefits and blessings, associated with Torah compliance.

[11] Note also that all believers are required to keep and guard the Shabbat, and not to pick their own favorite day of worship, out of the proverbial hat.

---

[1] Note that all believers are Yisrael and there is to be no difference between believers, meaning divisions into Jew and non-Jew or Torah-keeping versus those who are told they do not have to keep Torah; all such classification is an abomination to YHWH. All Yisrael must follow Torah and love Yahshua.

[2] Added "works of law" of men being taught as if they were Torah, and clouding the difference between man's law and YHWH's Torah. This burden Peter speaks of is man's "works of law" that is being presented as if it were the real and full Torah. Neither Yisraelites of that day nor the talmidim could keep all those added burdens.

[3] Ephraimites and others coming from out of the pagan nations will be called to carry and proclaim His Name. Yisrael will be a people that knows and proclaims YHWH's Name.

[4] Amos 9:11-12.

[5] Strong's Greek # 456 **anoikodomeo**. "To rebuild" in a future tense. Greek equivalent of Hebrew **banah**; Strong's Hebrew #1129, as used ("to rebuild") in Jeremiah 31:4. This means that the rebuilding of both houses into the Tabernacle of David of all twelve tribes was still a future event in the first century, not an alleged past one in 520 BCE as some try to claim.

[6] The focus of the Renewed Covenant in Acts 15:15-16 is the rebuilding, the return, the re-establishment of the Tabernacle of David, which had fallen. Thus for the Tabernacle of David to be rebuilt, the original components would have to be used.

The shlichim and zachanim and brothers send greetings to the brothers, which are of the nations in Antioch and Syria and Cilicia: 24 Forasmuch as we have heard, that certain which went out from us have troubled you with words, subverting your beings, saying, You must be brit-milahed first, and keep the Torah immediately: to whom we gave no such commandment: 25 It seemed tov to us, being assembled as echad, to send chosen men to you with our beloved Bar-Nava and Shaul, 26 Men that have hazarded their chayim for the Name of our Master יהושע ha Moshiach. 27 We have sent therefore Yahudah and Sila, who shall also tell you the same things by mouth. 28 For it seemed tov to the Ruach HaKodesh, and to us, to lay upon you no greater burden than these necessary initial things; 29 That you abstain from meats offered to idols, and from dom, and from things strangled, and from fornication: if you guard yourselves regarding these, you shall do well. Be strong! 30 So when they were dismissed, they came to Antioch: and when they had gathered the multitude together, they delivered the letter: 31 Which when they had read, they rejoiced for the encouragement. 32 And Yahudah and Sila, being neviim also themselves, exhorted the brothers with many words, and confirmed them. 33 And after they had stayed a while, they were let go in shalom from the brothers back to the shlichim. 34 But it pleased Sila to stay there still. 35 Shaul also and Bar-Nava continued in Antioch, teaching and proclaiming the word of יהוה, with many others also. 36 And some days later Shaul said to Bar-Nava, Let us go again and visit our Yisraelite brothers in every city where we have proclaimed the word of יהוה, and see how they are doing. 37 And Bar-Nava determined to take with them Yochanan, whose surname was Moshe-Markus. 38 But Shaul thought it not tov to take him with them, because he departed from them from Pamphylia, and continued not with them in the work.

39 And the contention was so sharp between them that they departed after separating from each other: and so Bar-Nava took Moshe-Markus, and sailed to Cyprus; 40 And Shaul chose Sila, and departed, being recommended by the brothers to the favor of יהוה. 41 And he went through Syria and Cilikia, confirming the congregations of Yisrael.

16 Then he came to Derbe and Lustra: and, see, a certain talmid was there, named Timtheous, the son of a certain woman, who was a Yahudite, and believed; but his abba was a Greek: 2 Which was well reported of by the brothers that were at Lustra and Ikonium. 3 Shaul desired to have him travel with him; and took him and conducted brit-milah for him because of the Yahudim who were in those quarters:[1] for they all knew that his abba was a Greek. 4 And as they went through the cities, they delivered to them the decrees to keep that were ordained by the shlichim and zachanim who were at Yahrushalayim. 5 And so were the congregations of Yisrael established in the emunah, and increased in number daily. 16 Now when they had gone throughout Phrygia and the region of Galutyah, they were forbidden by the Ruach HaKodesh to proclaim the word in Asia Minor,[2] 7 After they were come to Mysia, they desired to go into Bitunyah: but the Ruach did not allow them. 8 And they passing by Mysia came down to Troas. 9 And a vision appeared to Shaul in the night; There stood a man of Makedonia, and begged him, saying, Come over into

---

[1] Proof that circumcision was approved of in Renewed Covenant Yisrael, as long as done in proper order. Obviously this man was mature enough to be ready to travel with Rav Shaul, as opposed to John Mark and thus ready for a full Torah commitment.
[2] Apparently based on his first journey, there was a proliferation and abundance of the tov news in Asia, and YHWH wanted Rav Shaul to head west to reach Greek-speaking wandering sheep in Eastern Europe.

Makedonia, and help us.[1] 10 And after he had seen the vision, immediately we sought to go into Makedonia, knowing for sure that יהוה had called us to proclaim the besarot to them. 11 We left Troas; we came with a straight course to Samothrake, and the next day to Neapolis; 12 And from there to Philippi, which is the main city of that part of Makedonia, and a colony:[2] and we were in that city abiding certain days. 13 And on the Shabbat we went out of the city by a riverside, where tefillah was always made; and we sat down, and spoke to the women who assembled there.[3] 14 And a certain woman named Lydyah, a seller of purple, from the city of Thyatira, who worshipped יהוה,[4] listened to us: whose lev יהוה opened, that she received those things that were spoken of by Shaul. 15 And when she was immersed, and her household, she asked us, saying, If you have judged me to be faithful to יהוה, come into my bayit, and stay there. And she urged us. 16 And it came to pass, as we went to Shabbat tefillot, a certain young girl possessed with a Ruach of divination met us, who brought her masters much profit by fortune telling: 17 The same followed Shaul and us, and cried, saying, These men are the avadim of El-Elyon, who show to us the derech of salvation. 18 And this she did many days. But Shaul, being disturbed, turned and said to the Ruach, I command you in the Name of יהושע the Moshiach to come out of her. And he came out the same hour. 19 And when her masters saw that the ongoing possibility of further gain was gone, they caught Shaul and Sila, and dragged them into the marketplace to the rulers, 20 And brought them to the authorities, saying,

These men, being Yahudim, do exceedingly trouble our city, 21 And teach customs,[5] which are not lawful for us to receive, neither to observe, being Romans.[6] 22 And the multitude rose up together against them: and the authorities tore off their clothes, and commanded to beat them. 23 And when they had laid many stripes upon them, they cast them into prison, commanding that the prison guard keep them safely: 24 Who, having received such a charge, threw them into the inner prison, and made their feet secure in the stocks. 25 And at midnight Shaul and Sila made tefillah, and sang tehillim to יהוה: and the prisoners heard them. 26 And suddenly there was a great earthquake, so that the foundations of the prison were shaken: and immediately all the doors were opened, and everyone's chains were loosed. 27 And the keeper of the prison woke out of his sleep, and seeing the prison doors open, he drew out his sword, and would have killed himself, supposing that the prisoners had escaped. 28 But Shaul shouted with a loud voice, saying, Do yourself no harm: for we are all here. 29 Then the keeper of the prison called for a light, and ran in, and came trembling, and fell down before Shaul and Sila, 30 And having led them out, he said, Sirs, what must I do to be saved? 31 And they said, Believe on the Master יהושע the Moshiach, and you shall be saved, and also your bayit. 32 And they spoke to him the word of the Master יהוה, and to all that were in his bayit. 33 And he took them in that same hour of the night, and washed their stripes; and was immersed, he and all his mishpocha, right away. 34 And when he had brought them into his bayit, he prepared food before them, and rejoiced, believing in יהוה with all his bayit. 35 And when it was day, the authorities sent the prison officers, saying, Let those men go. 36 And the keeper of the prison told this to Shaul, The authorities have

---

[1] A vision from YHWH that allowed the tov news to reach the lost sheep of Yisrael in a key area. This vision is directly related to the regathering of the two houses, since it is YHWH directing Rav Shaul's steps, so as to find those wandering sheep in Europe.
[2] Former or current Yisraelite colony?
[3] An Ephraimite or Jewish congregation in exile meeting on Shabbat consisting of only women, which is fine in Yisrael.
[4] Not a pagan even though not a believer, and certainly proof that Rav Shaul did not go looking for true pagans, but lost Yisraelites. The pattern is firm and secure as we see in all his travels.

[5] Torah.
[6] Not much has changed in religious circles.

sent to let you go: now therefore depart, and go in shalom. 37 But Shaul said to them, They have beaten us openly uncondemned, being Roman citizens, and have cast us into prison; and now do they throw us out privately? No! Indeed; let them come here themselves and bring us out. 38 And the prison officers told these words to the authorities: and they feared, when they heard that they were Romans. 39 And they came and pleaded with them, and brought them outside the gates, and desired them to depart out of the city. 40 And they went out of the prison, and entered into the bayit of Lydyah and when they had seen the brothers, they comforted them, and left.

17 Now when they had passed through Apollonia, they came to Tesloniqyah, where was a synagogue of the Yahudim: 2 And Shaul, as his manner was,[1] went in, and for three Shabbats reasoned with them out of the Ketuvim, 3 Opening and alleging, that the Moshiach needed to have suffered, and risen again from the dead; and that this **יהושע**, whom I proclaim to you, is the Moshiach. 4 And some of them believed,[2] and joined with Shaul and Sila; and of the devout Greeks a great multitude,[3] and many of the leading women. 5 But the Yahudim who believed not, moved with envy, took some wicked men from the city streets, and gathered a large mob, and caused disturbances in the city, and assaulted the bayit of Jason, and sought to bring them out to the people. 6 And when they found them not, they drew Jason and certain brothers to the rulers of the city, crying, These that have turned the olam upside down have come here also; 7 Whom Jason has received: and these all do contrary to the decrees of Caesar, saying that there is another melech, named **יהושע**. 8 And they troubled the people and the rulers of the city, when they heard these

things. 9 And when they had taken bail from Jason, and from the others, they let them go. 10 And the brothers immediately sent away Shaul and Sila by night to Berea: who coming there went into the synagogue of the Yahudim. 11 These were more noble than those in Tesloniqyah, in that they received the word with all readiness of mind, and searched the Ketuvim daily, whether those things were so. 12 Therefore many of them believed; also many honorable women and men who were Greeks. 13 But when the Yahudim of Tesloniqyah had knowledge that the word of **יהוה** was proclaimed by Shaul at Berea, they came there also, and stirred up the people. 14 And then immediately the brothers sent away Shaul to go as it were to the sea: but Sila and Timtheous stayed there still. 15 And they that conducted his trip brought Shaul to Athens: and receiving a commandment to Sila and Timtheous to come to him fast, they departed. 16 Now while Shaul waited for them at Athens, his Ruach was stirred in him, when he saw the city totally given to idolatry. 17 Therefore he disputed in the synagogue with the Yahudim, and with the devout persons,[4] and in the market daily with them that met with him. 18 Then certain philosophers of the Epioureans, and of the Stoicks, encountered him. And some said: What will this babbler say? Others said, He seems to be a proclaimer of strange mighty ones: because he proclaimed to them **יהושע** , and the resurrection. 19 And they arrested him, and brought him to Areopagus, saying, May we know what is this new teaching, that you bring? 20 For you bring certain strange things to our ears: we would like to know therefore what these things mean. 21 For all the Athenians and strangers who were there, spent their time in nothing else, but either to tell, or to shema some new thing. 22 Then Shaul stood in the midst of Areopagus, and said, You men of Athens, I perceive that in all things you are very

---

[1] As seen, he was not looking for pagans.
[2] Yahudites.
[3] Ephraimites.

[4] Ephraimites.

religious. 23 For as I passed by, and looked at your devotions, I found an altar with this inscription, TO THE UNKNOWN MIGHTY ONE. Whom you therefore ignorantly worship, him I do declare to you. 24 יהוה that made the olam and all things in it, seeing that He is Ruler of the shamayim and the olam, dwells not in temples made with hands; 25 Neither is worshipped with men's hands, as though He needed anything, seeing He gives to all chayim, and breath, and all things; 26 And has made all from one dom, all nations of men[1] to dwell on all the face of the olam, and has determined the times before appointed, [2] and the bounds of their dwelling; 27 That they should seek Him, if possibly they might reach out for him, and find him, though He be not far from any one of us: 28 For in Him we live, and move, and have our being; as certain also of your own poets have said, For we are also his offspring. 29 Now then since we are the offspring of יהוה, we should not think that El-Elyon is anything like gold, or silver, or stone, graven by man's mind or devices. 30 For the past times of ignorance יהוה overlooked; but now commands all men every where to make teshuvah: 31 Because He has appointed a Yom Din, in which He will shophet the olam in tzedakah by that Man whom He has ordained; by which He has given proof to all men, in that He has raised Him from the dead. 32 And when they heard of the resurrection of the dead, some mocked: and others said, We will shema to you again on this matter. 33 So Shaul departed from among them. 34 But certain men joined him, and believed: among whom was Dionusios the Areopagite, and a woman named Damaris, and others with them.

18 After these things Shaul departed from Athens, and came to Corinth;

2 And found a certain Yahudi named Aquila, born in Pontus, who had recently come from Italy, with his wife Priscilla; because Claudius had commanded all Yahudim to depart from Rome and they came to them. 3 And because he was of the same trade, he stayed with them, and they worked together: for by their occupation they were tallit makers.[3] 4 And he reasoned in the synagogue every Shabbat, and persuaded the Yahudim and the Greeks.[4] 5 And when Sila and Timtheous were come from Makedonia, Shaul was pressed in the Ruach, because the Yahudim opposed and blasphemed as he testified that יהושע was the Moshiach. 6 And when they opposed themselves, and blasphemed, he shook off his garment, and said to them, Your dom be upon your own heads; I am clean: from now on I will go to the nations. 7 And he departed there, and entered into a certain man's bayit, named Justus, one that worshipped יהוה, whose bayit was next to the synagogue. 8 And Crispus, the rabbi of the synagogue, believed on יהושע with all his bayit; and many of the Corinthians hearing believed, and were immersed. 9 Then spoke the Master יהוה to Shaul in the night by a vision, *Be not afraid, but speak, and do not keep silent: 10 For I am with you, and no man shall attack you to hurt you: for I have many people in this city.* 11 And he stayed there a year and six months, teaching the word of יהוה among them. 12 And when Gallion was the proconsul of Achaia, the unbelieving Yahudim made insurrection with one accord against Shaul, and brought him to the mishpat bema, 13 Saying, This fellow persuades men to worship Elohim contrary to the Torah. 14 And when Shaul was now about to open his mouth, Gallion said to the Yahudim, If it were a matter of criminal wrong or wicked lewdness, O you Yahudim, there would be a reason that I should shema you: 15 But if it were a

---

[1] All of mankind comes from Adam and Eve and even later from Noach. Therefore the promise to fill all nations with the seed of one man, Jacob, should not be surprising or shocking.
[2] Moadim, or feasts, or appointed times.

[3] Makers of tallits or tefillot-prayer shawls.
[4] Both houses in the synagogue.

question of words and names,[1] and of your Torah, you can settle it; for I do not wish to be a shophet of such matters. 16 And he removed all of them from the mishpat bema. 17 Then all the pagans [2] took Sosthenes, the rabbi of the synagogue, and beat him before the mishpat seat. And Gallion cared for none of those things. 18 And Shaul after this stayed there yet a tov while, and then took his leave from the brothers, and sailed from there into Aram, and with him Priscilla and Aquila; having shaved his head in Cenchrea: for he was under a Nazarite vow. 19 And he came to Ephesos, and left them there: but he himself entered into the synagogue, and reasoned with the Yahudim. 20 When they desired him to stay longer with them, he declined; 21 But bade them farewell, saying, I must by all means keep this moed[3] that comes in Yahrushalayim: but I will return again to you, if יהוה wills. And he sailed from Ephesos. 22 And when he had landed at Caesarea, and went up, and greeted the congregation of Yisrael, then he went down to Antioch. 23 And after he had spent some time there, he departed, and went over all the country of Galutyah and Phrygia, strengthening all the talmidim. 24 And a certain Yahudi named Apollos, born at Alexandria, an eloquent man, and mighty in the Ketuvim, came to Ephesos. 25 This man was instructed in the Torah and halacha of the Master יהוה; and being fervent in the Ruach, he spoke and taught diligently the things of יהוה, knowing only the mikvah of Yochanan HaMatbeel. 26 And he began to speak boldly in the synagogue: and when Aquila and Priscilla had heard him, they took him to them, and expounded to him the Way of יהוה more fully. 27 And when he was disposed to pass into Achaia, the brothers wrote, exhorting the talmidim to receive him, and when he arrived, helped them much who had believed through favor: 28 For he mightily refuted the Yahudim, publicly, showing by the Ketuvim that יהושע was in fact the Moshiach.

19 And it came to pass, that, while Apollos was at Corinth, Shaul having passed through the upper borders came to Ephesos: and finding certain talmidim, 2 He said to them, Have you received the Ruach HaKodesh when you believed? And they said to him, We have not even heard whether there is any Ruach HaKodesh. 3 And he said to them, Into what then were you immersed? And they said, Into Yochanan HaMatbeel's mikvah. 4 Then said Shaul, Yochanan HaMatbeel truly immersed with the mikvah of teshuvah, saying to the people, that they should believe on Him who should come after Him, that is, on Moshiach יהושע. 5 When they heard this, they were immersed in the Name of the Master יהושע. 6 And when Shaul had laid his hands upon them, the Ruach HaKodesh came on them; and they spoke with tongues, and prophesied. 7 And all the men were about twelve. 8 And he went into the synagogue, and spoke boldly for around three months, disputing and persuading the things concerning the malchut of יהוה. 9 But when some were hardened, and believed not, but spoke evil of the Way before the multitude, he departed from them, and separated the talmidim, and they midrashed daily in the yeshiva of Tyrannus. 10 And this continued for around two years; so that all those who dwelt in Asia Minor Minor heard the word of the Master יהושע, Yahudim, Greeks and Arameans. 11 And יהוה worked special nisim by the hands of Shaul: 12 So that even from the clothes on his body were brought to the sick handkerchiefs or aprons, and the diseases departed from them, the shadim went out from them, and the insane were restored.

---

[1] Rav Shaul clearly was teaching the true Name of YHWH, and the Jews of Corinth freaked out as many Jewish brothers often do still today. They dragged him to the government officials, because of his use of the true Name and the tov news as well.
[2] Peshitta.
[3] Rav Shaul kept, and taught others how to guard, the feasts.

13 Then certain roving Yahudite, exorcists, took it upon themselves to call out over those who had shadim in the Name of the Master יהושע, saying, We adjure you by יהושע who Shaul proclaims. 14 And there were seven sons of Skeua, a Yahudite, and the head of the roving exorcising priests, which did the same thing. 15 And the evil shad answered and said, יהושע I know, and Shaul I know; but who are you? 16 And the man in whom the evil Ruach was leaped on them, and overcame them, and prevailed against them, so that they fled out of that bayit naked, beaten and wounded. 17 And this was known to all the Yahudim and Greeks [1] also dwelling at Ephesos; and fear fell on them all, and the Name of the Savior יהושע was magnified. 18 And many that believed came, and confessed, and showed their satanic deeds. 19 Many of them also who used magic brought their books together, and burned them before all men: and they counted the price of the books, and found it fifty thousand pieces of silver. 20 So mightily grew the word of יהוה and prevailed. 21 After these things were ended, Shaul purposed in the Ruach, when he had passed through Makedonia and Achaia, to go to Yahrushalayim, saying, After I have been there, I must also see Rome. 22 So he sent into Makedonia two of them that attended to him, Timtheous and Erastos; but he himself stayed in Asia Minor Minor for a while. 23 And the same time there arose a big stir about the Way. 24 For a certain man named Demetrius, a silversmith, who made silver shrines for Artemis the pagan mighty one, brought no small gain to the craftsmen; 25 When he called together the shrine makers, and said, Sirs, you know that by this craft we have our wealth. 26 Moreover you see and shema, that not alone at Ephesos, but almost throughout all of Asia Minor, this Shaul has persuaded and turned away many people, saying that they are not mighty ones which we make with

our hands: 27 So that not only our livelihood is in danger to come to nothing; but also that the Beit HaMikdash of the great female mighty one Artemis should be despised, and her magnificence should be destroyed, whom all in Asia Minor and the olam worships. 28 And when they heard these sayings, they were full of wrath, and cried out, saying, Great is Artemis of the Ephesians. 29 And the entire city was filled with confusion: and having caught Gaius and Aristarchus, men of Makedonia, Shaul's companions in travel, they rushed with one accord into the theatre. 30 And when Shaul would have entered into the mob, the talmidim did not allow him. 31 And certain of the officials of Asia Minor, who were his friends, sent to him, desiring him that he would not risk his chayim in the theatre. 32 Some therefore cried one thing, and some another: for the mob was confused; and most did not know why they had come together. 33 And they drew Alexander out of the multitude, the Yahudim putting him forward. And Alexander motioned for silence with his hand, and would have made his defence to the people. 34 But when they knew that he was a Yahudi, all with one voice for about two hours cried out, Great is Artemis of the Ephesians. 35 And when the mayor had quieted the people, he said, You men of Ephesos, what man is there that knows not how that the city of the Ephesians is a worshipper of the great female mighty one Artemis, and her image which fell down from Zeus in heaven? 36 Seeing then that these things cannot be spoken against, you should be quiet, do nothing in haste. 37 For you have brought here these men, who are neither robbers of temples, nor blasphemers of your female mighty one. 38 Therefore if Demetrius, and the craftsmen who are with him, have a matter against any man, the courts are open, and there are proconsuls: let them accuse one another. 39 But if you inquire any thing concerning any other matters, it shall be determined in a lawful court.

---

[1] Two houses.

40 For we are in danger to be called to an account for this day's riot, there being no reason we can give to account of this mob scene. 41 And when he had spoken, he dismissed the crowd.

20 And after the uproar had ceased, Shaul called to him the talmidim, and embraced them, and departed to go into Makedonia. 2 And when he had gone over those parts, and had given them much exhortation, he came into Greece, 3 And there he stayed three months. And when the unbelieving Yahudim laid in wait for him, as he was about to sail into Syria, he purposed to return through Makedonia. 4 And there accompanied him into Asia Minor Sopater of Berea; and of the Tesloniqyah, Aristarchos and Secundos; and Gaios of Derbe, and Timtheous; and of Asia Minor, Tuchicos and Trophimos. 5 These going on ahead waited for us at Troas. 6 And we sailed away from Philippi after the days of Chag Matzoth,[1] and came to them to Troas in five days; where we stayed seven days. 7 And after havdalah, when the talmidim stayed together to break lechem, Shaul proclaimed to them, ready to depart the next day; and continued his speech until midnight. 8 And there were many lights in the upper chamber, where they were gathered together. 9 And there sat in a window a certain young man named Eutuchos, who fell into a deep sleep: and as Shaul was proclaiming a long teaching, he sunk down with sleep, and fell down from the third loft, and was picked up dead. 10 And Shaul went down, and fell on him, and embraced him and said, Don't worry; for his chayim is now in Him. 11 When he therefore was come up again, and had broken lechem, and eaten, and talked a long while, even until daybreak he then departed. 12 And they brought the young man alive, and rejoiced exceedingly. 13 And we went ahead by ship, and sailed to Assos, there

intending to take in Shaul: for so had he appointed, having gone there by land. 14 And when he met with us at Assos, we took him in, and came to Mitulene. 15 And we sailed there, and came the next day opposite Chios; and the next day we arrived at Samos, and stayed at Trogullium; and the next day we came to Miletus. 16 For Shaul had determined to sail by Ephesos, because he would not spend the time in Asia Minor: for he rushed, if it were still possible for him, to be at Yahrushalayim for the Yom Shavuot.[2] 17 And from Miletus he sent to Ephesos, and called the zachanim of the congregation of Yisrael. 18 And when they had come to him, he said to them, You know, from the first day that I came into Asia Minor, what kind of lifestyle I had with you at all times, 19 Serving יהוה with all humility of mind, and with many tears, and temptations, what befell me by the lying in wait of the unbelievingYahudim: 20 And how I kept back nothing that was profitable for you, but have shown you, and have taught you publicly, and from bayit to bayit,[3] 21 Testifying both to the Yahudim, and also to the Greeks,[4] teshuvah toward יהוה, and emunah toward our Master יהושע the Moshiach. 22 And now, see, I go bound in the Ruach to Yahrushalayim, not knowing the things that shall befall me there: 23 Except that the Ruach HaKodesh witnesses in every city, saying that prison and afflictions await me. 24 But none of these things move me, neither count I my chayim dear to myself, so that I might finish my course with simcha, and the service, which I have received from the Master יהושע, to testify the besarot of the favor of יהוה. 25 And now, see, I know that you all, among whom I have gone proclaiming the malchut of יהוה, shall see my face no more. 26 Therefore I take you to record this day that I am pure from the dom of all men.

---

[1] All these men kept the feast of Unleavened Bread with Ephraimites in Philippi.

[2] He kept the feasts and counted the omer as well.
[3] "House to house" in **remez**/hint level of Hebraic understanding, is to Jews and to Greeks and Armenians, so that his work was to all Yisrael in the nations.
[4] Two-house reference.

27 For I have not held back to declare to you all the counsel of יהוה. 28 Take heed therefore to yourselves, and to all the flock, over which the Ruach HaKodesh has made you overseers, to feed the congregation of Yisrael of יהוה, which He has purchased with His own dom.[1] 29 For I know this, that after my departing shall grievous wolves enter in among you, not sparing the flock.[2] 30 Also of your own selves shall men arise, speaking perverse things, to draw away talmidim after themselves. 31 Therefore watch, and remember, that for about three years I ceased not to warn every one night and day with tears. 32 And now, brothers, I commend you to יהוה, and to the word of His favor, which is able to build you up, and to give you an inheritance among all them who are set-apart. 33 I have coveted no man's silver, or gold, or apparel. 34 Yes, you yourselves know, that these hands have supplied my necessities, for me and for those that were with me. 35 I have shown you all things, how that by working hard you also must support the weak, and to remember the words of the Master יהושע, how He said, *It is more blessed to give than to receive.* 36 And when he had spoken this, he kneeled down, and made tefillah with them all. 37 And they all wept hard, and fell on Shaul's neck, and kissed him, 38 Sorrowing most of all for the words that he spoke, that they should see his face no more. And they accompanied him to the ship.

21 And it came to pass, that after we had separated from them, and had launched, we came with a straight course to Coos, and the day following to Rhodes, and from there to Patara: 2 And finding a ship sailing over to Phoenicia, we went aboard, and set out. 3 Now when we had seen Cyprus, we left it on the left hand, and sailed into Syria, and landed at Tsor: for there the ship was to unload her cargo. 4 And finding talmidim, we stayed there seven days: who said to Shaul through the Ruach that he should not go up to Yahrushalayim. 5 And when we had accomplished those days, we departed and went our derech; and they all brought us on our derech, with their wives and children, until we were out of the city: and we kneeled down on the shore, and made tefillah. 6 And when we had taken our leave one of another, we sailed; and they returned home again. 7 And when we had finished our course from Tsor, we came to Ptolemais, and greeted the brothers, and stayed with them one day. 8 And the next day we that were of Shaul's group departed, and came to Caesarea: and we entered into the bayit of Philip the Proclaimer, who was one of the seven; and stayed with him. 9 And the same man had four daughters, virgins, who did prophesy. 10 And as we stayed there many days, there came down from Yahudah a certain navi, named Hagav. 11 And when he was come to us, he took Shaul's girdle, and bound his own hands and feet, and said, This said the Ruach HaKodesh, *So shall the Yahudim at Yahrushalayim bind the man that owns this girdle, and shall deliver him into the hands of the pagans.* 12 And when we heard these things, both we, and those of that place, begged him not to go up to Yahrushalayim. 13 Then Shaul answered, What do you mean by weeping and breaking my lev? For I am ready not only to be bound, but also to die at Yahrushalayim for the Name of the Master יהושע.[3] 14 And when he would not be persuaded, we ceased, saying, The will of יהוה be done. 15 And after those days we prepared, and went up to Yahrushalayim. 16 There went with us also certain of the talmidim of Caesarea, and brought with them Menason of Cyprus, an old talmid, with whom we should lodge. 17 And when we were come to

---

[1] The dom of YHWH Elohim is a reference to His deity.
[2] All kinds, but in context and specifically, anti-Yahshua missionaries.
[3] Are you ready to die for the **kiddushat hashem,** or the set-apartness of the name Yahweh?

Yahrushalayim, the brothers received us with simcha. 18 And the day following Shaul went in with us to Yaakov; and all the zachanim were present. 19 And when he had greeted them, he declared particularly what things יהוה had done among the nations by his service. 20 And when they heard it, they gave tehilla to יהוה, and said to him, You see, brother, how many tens of thousands there are who believe among the Yahudim;[1] and they are all zealous for the Torah: 21 And they are wrongly informed about you, that you teach all the Yahudim who are among the nations to forsake Moshe's Torah, saying that they should not brit milah their children, neither to walk after the halacha of Torah.[2] 22 What is this therefore? The multitudes will shema that you have come. 23 So do what we tell you: We have four men who have a Nazarite vow on them; 24 Take them, and cleanse yourself with them, and pay their expenses, that they may shave their heads: and then all will know that those things, of which they were informed about you, are false and nothing; but that you yourself also have your halacha orderly, guarding all of the Torah. [3] 25 As touching the returning nations which believe, we have written and concluded that they observe no such thing, except only that they keep themselves from things offered to idols, and from dom, and

from strangled things, and from fornication.[4] 26 Then Shaul took the men, and the next day cleansed himself with them and entered into the Beit HaMikdash, to signify the completion of the days of their separation, until the offering should be given for every one of them. 27 And when the seven days were almost ended, the Yahudim who were of Asia Minor, when they saw him in the Beit HaMikdash, stirred up all the people, and laid hands on him, 28 Crying out, Men of Yisrael, help: This is the man, that teaches all men everywhere against the people of Yisrael, and the Torah, and this set-apart place: and furthermore he brought Greeks[5] into the Beit HaMikdash, and has polluted this set-apart place. 29 For they had seen before with him in the city Trophimos the Ephesian, whom they supposed that Shaul had brought into the Beit HaMikdash. 30 And all the city was moved, and the people ran together: and they took Shaul, and dragged him out of the Beit HaMikdash: and immediately shut the doors. 31 And as they went about to kill him, news came to the chief captain of the company, that all Yahrushalayim was in an uproar. 32 He immediately took soldiers and centurions, and ran down to them: and when they saw the chief captain and the soldiers, they stopped beating Shaul. 33 Then the chief captain came near, and took him, and commanded him to be bound with two chains; and demanded to know who he was, and what he had done. 34 And some cried one thing, some another, among the multitude: and when he could not know the real reason for the tumult, he commanded him to be carried into the headquarters. 35 And when he came to the stairs, so it was, that had to be carried by the soldiers because of the violence of the people. 36 For the multitude of the unbelieving people followed after him, shouting, Away with him. 37 And as Shaul was about to be led into the headquarters,

---

[1] This is a reference to Devarim/Deuteronomy 33:17, where Yisrael was prophesied to become the tens of thousands of Ephraim Yisrael and the thousands of Menashsheh. Many of these settled amongst Judah, and along with Jewish Yisrael, loved Yahshua and His Torah.
[2] Rav Shaul taught and performed circumcision as seen in Acts 16:1. What he did not allow was immediate circumcision to those coming to faith, as the first step in that return, but postponed it to be one of the last steps.
[3] This is a test by the shamashim designed to do three things. First, to see if Rav Shaul objects. If so, they'll know that the accusations are true. Secondly, this Torah mitzvah is designed to be a witness to other Jews, that the accusation is a lie. Thirdly, it is a mitzvah to the poor brothers, and they can receive assistance in ending their vow. If there ever was a time, or place, or an opportunity for Rav Shaul to refuse to perform this Torah mitzvah, or to tell the shamashim that they were wrong, or any other such thing, this was his big chance. He had the attention of the entire believing Jewish leadership, as well as the leaders of unbelieving Yahudah. But as seen a couple of verses later, he did obey, and did show the world for all times, that he did and taught the Torah, but just didn't do it in the way the Pharisees demanded that he do it.

[4] See notes on Acts 15:19-21.
[5] Returning Ephraimites who were despised in their return.

he said to the chief captain, May I speak to you? Who said, Can you speak Greek? 38 Are not you that Mitzrite, who a while back made a revolt, and led out into the wilderness four thousand men that were assassins? 39 But Shaul said, No. I am a man, a Yahudi of Tarsus, a city in Cilicia, a citizen of a well known city: and, I beg you, allow me to speak to the people. 40 And when he had given him permission, Shaul stood on the stairs, and motioned with the hand to the people. And when there was a great silence, he spoke to them in the Ivrit tongue, saying,

22 Men, brothers, and ahvot of Yisrael, [1] shema to my defence, which I make to you now. 2 And when they heard that he spoke in the Ivrit tongue, they kept even quieter and he said, 3 I am indeed a man who am a Yahudi, born in Tarsus, a city in Cilicia, yet brought up in this city at the yeshiva of Gamliel, and taught according to the perfect manner of the Torah of the ahvot, and was zealous toward Elohim, as you all are this day. 4 And I persecuted the Way to the death, binding and delivering into prisons both men and women. 5 As also the Kohen HaGadol does bear me witness, and all the zachanim of the Sanhedrin: from whom also I received letters to the brothers, and went to Dameshek, to bring them who were there bound to Yahrushalayim, to be punished. 6 And it came to pass, that, as I made my journey, and had come near to Dameshek around noon, suddenly there shone from the shamayim a great light all around me. 7 And I fell to the ground, and heard a voice saying to me, *Shaul, Shaul, why do you persecute Me?* 8 And I answered, Who are You, Master? And He said to me, *I am* **יהושע** *of Natzareth, whom you persecute.* 9 And they that were with me saw the light, and were afraid; but they did not shema the voice of Him that spoke to me. 10 And I said, What shall I do, Master? And **יהושע**

said to me, *Arise, and go into Dameshek; and there it shall be told you all things which are appointed for you to do.* 11 And when I could not see for the tiferet of that light, being led by the hand of those that were with me, I came into Dameshek. 12 And one Chananyah, a devout man following the Torah, having a tov report of all the Yahudim who dwelt there, 13 Came to me, and stood, and said to me, Brother Shaul, receive your sight. And the same hour I looked up at him. 14 And he said, The Elohim of our ahvot has chosen you, that you should know His will, and see that Tzadik-One, and should shema the voice from His mouth. 15 For you shall be His witness to all men[2] of what you have seen and heard. 16 And now why do you delay? Arise, and be immersed, and wash away your sins, calling on the Name of **יהוה**. 17 And it came to pass, that, when I was come again to Yahrushalayim, even while I made tefillah in the Beit HaMikdash, I came into a trance; 18 And saw Him saying to me, *Hurry, and get quickly out of Yahrushalayim: for they will not receive your testimony concerning Me.* 19 And I said, Master, they know that I imprisoned and beat in every synagogue those that believed on You:[3] 20 And when the dom of Your martyr Tsephanyah was shed, I also was standing by, and approving of his death, and held the garments of those that killed him. 21 And He said to me, *Depart: for I will send you far from here to the nations.*[4] 22 And they gave him their attention up to this word, and then lifted up their voices, and said, Away with such a fellow from the olam: for it is not fit that he should live.[5] 23 And as they shouted, they cast off their clothes, and threw dust into

---

[1] Jewish Yisrael.

[2] Not just to pagans, but all men filling the nations.
[3] First-century Yisraelites did not go to Sunday church and neither should we.
[4] To all Yisraelite nations or Ephraim.
[5] The crowd wanted him dead, for he had the nerve to go out and bring Ephraim home to be equal heirs in Yisrael. When they heard of YHWH's love for the nations, they lost control. The same attitude sadly holds true today in both believing and non-believing Judah.

the air, 24 The chief captain commanded him to be brought into the headquarters, and ordered that he should be examined after a scourging and beating; that he might know the reason they shouted against him. 25 And as they bound him with straps, Shaul said to the captain that stood by, Is it lawful for you to scourge a man that is a Roman citizen, and yet uncondemned? 26 When the captain heard that, he went and told the chief captain, saying, Be careful what you do: for this man is a Roman citizen. 27 Then the chief captain came, and said to him, Tell me, are you a Roman citizen? He said, Yes. 28 And the chief captain answered, I paid a great price for my citizenship. And Shaul said, But I was freely born as a Roman citizen. 29 Then right away those who should have examined him left him alone: and the chief captain also was worried, after he knew that he was a Roman citizen, because he had bound him unlawfully. 30 On the next day, because he desired to know the true reason why he was accused by the unbelieving Yahudim, he unbound and released him, and commanded the chief kohanim and all their Sanhedrin to appear, and brought Shaul down, and set him before them.

23 And Shaul, intently beholding the Sanhedrin, said, Men and brothers, I have lived in all tov conscience before יהוה until this day. 2 And the Kohen HaGadol Chananyah commanded them that stood by him to hit him on the mouth. 3 Then said Shaul to him, יהוה shall hit you, you whited wall: for you sit to shophet me by the Torah, and then command me to be hit contrary to the Torah. 4 And they that stood by said, Do you even revile Elohim's Kohen HaGadol? 5 Then said Shaul, I did not know brothers, that he was the Kohen HaGadol: for it is written, You shall not speak evil of the ruler of your people. [1] 6 But when Shaul perceived that the one part were Tzadukim, and the other Prushim,

he cried out in the Sanhedrin, Men and brothers, I am a Prush, the son of a Prush: because of my tikvah in the resurrection of the dead - the meechayai hamaytiim - I am being questioned. 7 And when he had so said, there arose a dissension between the Prushim and the Tzadukim: and the multitude was divided. 8 For the Tzadukim say that there is no resurrection, or heavenly messengers, and shaddim: but the Prushim confess both. 9 And there arose a great tumult: and the Sophrim who were of the Prushim's viewpoint arose, saying, We find no evil in this man: but if a Ruach or a heavenly messenger has spoken to him, let us not fight against Elohim. 10 And when there arose a great dissension, the chief captain, fearing lest Shaul might have been pulled to pieces by them, commanded the soldiers to go down, and to take him by force from among them, and to bring him into the headquarters. 11 And the night following יהושע stood by him, and said, *Be of tov ruach, Shaul: for as you have testified of Me in Yahrushalayim, so must you bear witness in Rome.*[2] 12 And when it was daylight, certain of the Yahudim banded together, and bound themselves under a curse, saying that they would neither eat nor drink until they had killed Shaul. 13 And there were more than forty who had made this conspiracy. 14 And they came to the chief kohanim and zachanim, and said, We have bound ourselves under a great curse, that we will eat nothing until we have killed Shaul. 15 Now therefore you with the Sanhedrin tell the chief captain that he bring him down to you tomorrow, and pretend as if you are seeking more information from him: and we, whenever he comes near, are ready to kill him. 16 And when Shaul's nephew heard of their lying in wait, he went and entered into the headquarters, and told Shaul. 17 Then Shaul called one of the centurions to him, and said, Bring this young man to the chief captain: for he has

---

[1] An obvious reference to his bad eyesight.

[2] Two-house reference.

something to tell him. 18 So he took him, and brought him to the chief captain, and said, Shaul the prisoner called me to him, and asked me to bring this young man to you, who has something to tell you. 19 Then the chief captain took him by the hand, and went with him aside privately, and asked him, What is that you have to tell me? 20 And he said, The unbelieving Yahudim have agreed to ask you that you would bring down Shaul tomorrow into the Sanhedrin, as though they would inquire something of him more fully. 21 But do not yield to them: for they lie in wait for him more than forty men who, have bound themselves with an oath, that they will neither eat nor drink until they have killed him: and now they are ready, looking for the promise from you. 22 So the chief captain then let the young man depart, and said, See that you tell no man that you have shown these things to me. 23 And he called to him two centurions, saying, Make ready two hundred soldiers to go to Caesarea, and seventy horsemen, and two hundred spearmen, at three o'clock in the morning; 24 And provide them beasts that they may set Shaul on them, and bring him safely to Felix the governor. 25 And he wrote a letter after this manner: 26 Claudius Lysias sends greetings to the most excellent Governor Felix. 27 This man was taken by the Yahudim, and would have been killed by them: then came I with an army, and rescued him, having understood that he was a Roman citizen. 28 And when I wanted to know the reason why they accused him, I brought him out into their Sanhedrin: 29 Whom I perceived to be accused of questions about their Torah, but to have nothing laid to his charge worthy of death or even of prison. 30 And when it was told to me how that the Yahudim laid in wait for the man, I sent right away to you, and gave commandment to his accusers also to speak before you exactly what they had against him. Farewell. 31 Then the soldiers, as it was commanded them, took Shaul, and

brought him by night to Antipatris. 32 On the next day they left the horsemen to go with him, and returned to the headquarters: 33 Who, when they came to Caesarea, and delivered the letter to the governor, presented Shaul also before him. 34 And when the governor had read the letter, he asked what province he was from. And then he understood that he was of Cilicia; 35 I will shema to you, when your accusers are also come, he said. And he commanded him to be kept in Herod's Praetorium.

24 And after five days Chananyah the Kohen HaGadol descended with the zachanim, and with a certain orator named Tertullus, who informed the governor against Shaul. 2 And when he was called out, Tertullus began to accuse him, saying, Seeing that by you we enjoy great shalom, and that very worthy deeds are done to this nation by your care, 3 We accept it always, and in all places, most noble Felix, with all hodu. 4 But, that I not weary you with long explanations, I ask you that you would shema to us in your kindness just a few of our words. 5 For we have found this man a pestilent fellow, and a mover of sedition among all the Yahudim throughout the olam, and a ringleader of the sect of the Notsrim[1]: 6 Who also has gone about to profane the Beit HaMikdash: whom we took, and would have judged according to our Torah. 7 But the chief captain Lysias came upon us, and with great violence took him away out of our hands, 8 Commanding his accusers to come to you: so that by examining him yourself you will have the knowledge of all these things, of which we accuse him. 9 And the Yahudim also agreed, saying that these things were so.

---

[1] Yisraelite believers were first called **Notsrim**, a fulfillment of the prophecies that YHWH would save a preserved handful of remnant Yisraelites. The terms "preserved" and "watchmen," depending on the context in the First Covenant, both mean **Notsrim**. Since today Notsrim in Hebrew means Christian; and since neither the true first-century disciples nor the modern Nazarenes care to be lumped in with that term as it is used today, it may be preferable to use **Netsarim**. **Netsarim** means branches; seeing that we are the true branches of the Vine, who scripture tells us is Yahshua our King.

10 Then Shaul, after that the governor had motioned to him to speak, answered, Knowing that you have been for many years a shophet to this nation, I gladly defend myself: 11 So that you may understand, about twelve days ago I went up to Yahrushalayim to worship. 12 And they neither found me in the Beit HaMikdash disputing with any man, nor stirring up the people, neither in the synagogues, nor in the city: 13 Neither can they prove the things of which they now accuse me. 14 But this I confess to you, that after the Way which they call heresy, so I worship the Elohim of my ahvot, believing all things which are written in the Torah and in the Neviim:[1] 15 Having tikvah toward Elohim, which they themselves also believe, that there shall be a resurrection of the dead, both of the tzadikim and unjust. 16 It is for this reason that I labor, to always have a conscience void of offence toward Elohim, and toward men. 17 Now after many years I came to bring assistance to my nation, and terumah offerings. 18 At which time certain Yahudim from Asia Minor found me cleansed in the Beit HaMikdash, neither with multitude, nor with tumult. 19 Who should be here before you, and object, if they had something against me. 20 Or else let those here say, if they have found any evil doing in me, while I stood before the Sanhedrin, 21 Except it be for this one declaration, that I shouted standing among them, It is regarding the resurrection of the dead that I am called into questioning by you this day. 22 And when Felix heard these things, having more exact knowledge of the Way, he deferred and said, When Lysias the chief captain shall come down, I will decide your matter. 23 And he commanded a captain to keep Shaul, and to let him have liberty, and that he should not forbid any of his acquaintances to attend to or visit him. 24 And after certain days,

when Felix came with his wife Drusilla, who was a female Yahudite, he sent for Shaul, and heard him concerning the emunah in the Moshiach. 25 And as he reasoned of tzedakah, self-control, and the mishpat to come, Felix trembled, and answered, Go your derech for now; when I have some time, I will call for you. 26 He hoped also that money should have been given to him by Shaul, that he might free him: therefore he sent for him often, and communed with him. 27 But after two years Porcius Festus succeeded Felix: and Felix, willing to do the unbelieving Yahudim a favor, left Shaul in prison.

25 Now when Festus had come into the province, after three days he ascended from Caesarea to Yahrushalayim. 2 Then the Kohen HaGadol and the leaders of the Yahudim informed him against Shaul, and begged him, 3 Asking a favor from him, that he would send him to Yahrushalayim, laying wait in the derech to kill him. 4 But Festus answered, that Shaul should be kept at Caesarea, and that he himself would depart there shortly. 5 Let them therefore, said he, which among you are able, go down with me, and accuse this man, if there be any wickedness in him. 6 And when he had stayed among them more than ten days, he went down to Caesarea; and the next day sitting on the mishpat seat commanded Shaul to be brought out. 7 And when he had come, the unbelieving Yahudim who came down from Yahrushalayim stood around, and laid many and grievous complaints against Shaul, which they could not prove. 8 When he answered for himself he said, Neither against the Torah of the Yahudim, neither against the Beit HaMikdash, nor yet against Caesar, have I offended in any thing at all. 9 But Festus, willing to do the unbelieving Yahudim a favor, answered Shaul, and said, Will you go up to Yahrushalayim, and there be judged of these things before me? 10 Then said Shaul, I stand at Caesar's

---

[1] Both traditional Judaism and Christianity will always consider Nazarene Yisraelites heretics. Even pagans will see fit to pass some kind of judgment.

mishpat seat, where I ought to be judged: to the Yahudim have I done no wrong, as you very well know. 11 For if I be an offender, or have committed anything worthy of death, I refuse not to die: but if there be none of these things of which these accuse me, no man may deliver me to them. I appeal to Caesar. 12 Then Festus, when he had conferred with the Sanhedrin, answered, Have you appealed to Caesar? To Caesar shall you go. 13 And after certain days Melech Agrippa and Bernice came to Caesarea to greet Festus. 14 And when they had been there many days, Festus declared Shaul's cause to the melech, saying, There is a certain man left in prison by Felix: 15 About whom, when I was at Yahrushalayim, the chief kohanim and the zachanim of the Yahudim informed me, desiring to have mishpat against him. 16 To whom I answered, It is not the manner of the Romans to deliver any man to die, before the one accused has an opportunity to answer the accusers face to face, and have a chance to answer for himself concerning the crime laid against him. 17 Therefore, when they were come here, without any delay on the next day I sat on the mishpat seat, and commanded the man to be brought out. 18 Against whom when the accusers stood up, they brought none of the accusations about such things as I thought: 19 But had certain questions against him of their own worship, and about someone named יהושע , who was dead, whom Shaul affirmed to be alive. 20 And because I was uncertain about these matters, I asked him whether he would go to Yahrushalayim, and there be judged on these matters. 21 But when Shaul had appealed to be kept for a hearing before Augustus, I commanded him to be kept until I might send him to Caesar. 22 Then Agrippa said to Festus, I would also like to shema the man myself. Tomorrow, he said, you shall shema him. 23 And the next day, when Agrippa had come, and Bernice, with

great show, and had entered into the place of hearing, with the commanders, and important men of the city, at Festus's commandment Shaul was brought out. 24 And Festus said, Melech Agrippa, and all men who are here present with us, you see this man, about whom all the multitude of the Yahudim have dealt with me, both at Yahrushalayim, and also here, screaming that he should not live any longer. 25 But when I found that he had committed nothing worthy of death, and that he himself had appealed to Augustus, I have determined to send him. 26 Of whom I have no certain charges to write to my master. Therefore I have brought him out before you, and especially before you, O melech Agrippa, so that, after your examination, I might have something to charge him with. 27 For it seems to me unreasonable to send a prisoner, and not signify the crimes brought against him.

26 Then Agrippa said to Shaul, You are permitted to speak for yourself. Then Shaul stretched out the hand, and answered for himself: 2 I think of myself as favored, Melech Agrippa, because I shall answer for myself this day before you touching all the things of which I am accused of the Yahudim: 3 Especially because I know you to be expert in all customs and questions which are among the Yahudim: therefore I ask you to shema to me patiently. 4 My manner of chayim from my youth, which was in the beginning among my own nation at Yahrushalayim, know all the Yahudim; 5 Who knew me from the beginning, if they would testify, that after the strictest sect of our observance I lived as a Prush with their excellent teaching. 6 And now I stand and am judged for the tikvah of the promise made by יהוה to our ahvot: 7 To which promise our twelve tribes, instantly serving Elohim day and night, have tikvah to come. For which tikvah's sake, Melech Agrippa, I am

accused by the Yahudim.[1] 8 Why should it be thought a thing incredible with you, that יהוה should raise the dead? 9 I truly thought to myself, that I should to do many things contrary to the Name of יהושע of Natzareth. 10 Which thing I also did in Yahrushalayim: and many of the kidushim did I lock in prison, having received authority from the chief kohanim; and when they were put to death, I gave my voice against them. 11 And I punished them often in every synagogue, and compelled them to blaspheme; and being exceedingly mad at them, I persecuted them even to foreign cities. 12 While doing this, as I went to Dameshek with authority and commission from the chief kohanim, 13 At midday, O Melech, I saw on the road a light from the shamayim, greater than the brightness of the sun, shining all around me and on those who journeyed with me. 14 And when we were all fallen to the ground, I heard a voice speaking to me, and saying in the Ivrit tongue, *Shaul, Shaul, why do you persecute Me? It is hard for you to offer against Me this worthless resistance.* 15 And I said, Who are You, Master? And He said, *I am* יהושע *whom you persecute.* 16 *But rise, and stand upon your feet: for I have appeared to you for this purpose, to make you a servant and a witness both of these things which you have seen, and of those things which I will reveal to you;* 17 *Delivering you from the people,[2] and from the nations,[3] to whom I now send you,* 18 *To open their eyes, and to turn them from darkness to light, and from the power of s.a.tan to* יהוה, *that they may receive forgiveness of sins, and an inheritance among them who are set-apart by emunah that is in Me.* 19 Therefore, O Melech Agrippa, I was not disobedient to the heavenly vision: 20 But showed it first to

them of Dameshek, and at Yahrushalayim, and throughout all the borders of Yahudah, and then to the nations,[4] that they should make teshuvah and turn to יהוה, and do mitzvot meet for teshuvah. 21 For these reasons the Yahudim caught me in the Beit HaMikdash, and went about to kill me. 22 Having therefore obtained help from יהוה, I continue to this day, witnessing both to small and great, saying no other things than those, which the neviim and Moshe Rabainu said, would come: 23 That the Moshiach should suffer, and that He should be the first that should rise from the dead, and should show Light to the people, and to the nations.[5] 24 And as he was speaking for himself, Festus said with a loud voice, Shaul, you are beside yourself; much learning has made you meshugas. 25 But he said, I am not meshugas, most noble Festus; but speak out the words of emet and common sense. 26 For the melech knows of these things, before whom also I speak freely: for I am persuaded that none of these things are hidden from you; for this thing was not done in a corner. 27 Melech Agrippa, do you believe the neviim? I know that you believe. 28 Then Agrippa said to Shaul, You almost persuaded me to be a Moshiach-ite. 29 And Shaul said, I would to Elohim, that not only you, but also all that shema me today, might become fully as I am, except for these chains. 30 And when he had spoken all this, the melech rose up, and the governor, and Bernice, and they that sat with them: 31 And when they had left, they talked between themselves, saying, This man does nothing worthy of death or of prison. 32 Then said Agrippa to Festus; This man could have been set free, if he had not appealed to Caesar.

27 And when it was determined that we should sail into Italy, they delivered Shaul and certain other prisoners to one named Julius, a captain of the

---

[1] The promises were made to all twelve tribes, and Rav Shaul states plainly that he has this hope of the resurrection of the dead for all twelve tribes defining his emunah and his mission. The twelve tribes are found today in both houses of Yisrael.
[2] Yahudah.
[3] Ephraim.

[4] Two-house reference.
[5] Two-house reference.

Augustan regimen. 2 And entering into a ship from Adramyttium, we launched, meaning to sail by the borders of Asia Minor; with Aristarchos, a Makedonian of Tesloniqyah, being with us. 3 And the next day we touched at Tzidon. And Julius courteously treated Shaul, and gave him liberty to go to his friends to refresh himself. 4 And when we had launched from there, we sailed under Cyprus, because the winds were contrary. 5 And when we had sailed over the sea of Cilicia and Pamphylia, we came to Mura, a city of Lucia. 6 And there the captain found a ship from Alexandria sailing into Italy; and he put us on board. 7 And when we had sailed slowly many days, and barely were come opposite Cnidus, the wind did not allow us to proceed, we sailed close to Crete, off Salmone; 8 And, hardly passing it, came to a place which is called The Fair Havens; near the city of Lasea. 9 Now we remained there a long time, even until the Yom Kippur Yahudite fast was past,[1] and since it had become dangerous for anyone to sail, Shaul admonished them, 10 And said to them, Sirs, I perceive that this voyage will be with hurt and much damage, not only of the cargo and ship, but also of our chayim. 11 Nevertheless the captain believed the navigator and the owner of the ship, more than those things that were spoken by Shaul. 12 And because the harbor was not suited to winter in, most advised to depart from there also, if by any means they might get to Phoenicia, and spend the winter there; which is a harbor of Crete, facing southwest and northwest. 13 And when the south wind blew softly, supposing that they had obtained their purpose, leaving there, they sailed close by Crete. 14 But not long after there arose against us a hurricane, called Euroclydon. 15 And when the ship was caught, and could not hold up against the wind, we yielded control of it. 16 And passing under a certain island that is called Clauda, we could hardly retain the ship's

lifeboat: 17 Which when they had taken it up, we girded up and prepared the ship and, feared lest we should fall into the downward rapids, we pulled down the sail, and drifted. 18 And we being exceedingly tossed with the hurricane, the next day they began to throw our belongings into the sea; 19 And the third day we cast out with our own hands the rigging of the ship. 20 And when neither sun nor chochavim in many days appeared, and the hurricane beat on us, all tikvah that we should be saved was then lost. 21 But after a long abstinence from food Shaul stood out in the midst of them, and said, Sirs, you should have listened to me, and not have sailed from Crete, only to have experienced this harm and loss. 22 And now I exhort you to be of tov courage: for there shall be no loss of any man's chayim among you, but only of the ship. 23 For there stood by me this night a heavenly messenger of יהוה, whose I am, and whom I serve, 24 Saying, Fear not, Shaul; you must be brought before Caesar: and, look, יהוה has given you all them that sail with you. 25 Therefore, sirs, be of tov courage: for I believe יהוה, that it shall be even as it was told to me. 26 But first we must run aground upon a certain island. 27 But when the fourteenth night was come, as we were driven up and down in the Adriatic Sea, about midnight the sailors determined that they had drawn near to some country; 28 And taking sounding measurements, they found it twenty fathoms: and when they had gone a little further, they sounded again, and found it fifteen fathoms. 29 Then fearing lest we should run aground, they dropped four anchors out of the stern, and made tefillah for the day to come. 30 And as the sailors were about to flee out of the ship, when they had let down the lifeboat into the sea, under pretense as though they would have cast out anchors to fasten the ship, 31 Shaul said to the captain and to the soldiers, If these people do not stay in the ship, they cannot survive. 32 Then the soldiers cut off

---

[1] Peshitta.

the ropes of the lifeboat, and let it fall off. 33 And while the day was dawning, Shaul besought them all to take food, saying, This day is the fourteenth day that you have stayed and continued fasting, having taken nothing. 34 Therefore I beg you to take some food: for this is for your health: for there shall not a hair fall from the head of any of you. 35 And when he had spoken, he took lechem, and gave hodu to **יהוה** in presence of them all: and when he had broken it, he began to eat. 36 Then were they all of tov courage, and they also took some food. 37 And we were in all in the ship two hundred seventy six beings. 38 And when they had eaten enough, they lightened the ship, and cast out the wheat into the sea. 39 And when it was day, they did not recognize the land: but they discovered a certain bay with a shore, into which they planned, if it were possible, to run the ship. 40 And when they had cut off the anchors, they threw them into to the sea, and loosed the rudder ropes, and hoisted up the main sail to the wind, and made it to shore. 41 And falling into a place where two seas met, they ran the ship aground; and the front stuck fast, and remained unmovable, but the back of it was broken with the violence of the waves. 42 And the soldiers' counsel was to kill the prisoners, lest any of them should swim away, and escape. 43 But the captain, willing to save Shaul, kept them from their purpose; and commanded that those who could swim should cast themselves first into the sea, and go to land: 44 And the rest, some on boards, and some on broken pieces of the ship. And so it came to pass, that they all escaped safely to land.

28 And having come to safety, then they learned that the island was called Melita. 2 And the barbarians who lived there shown us much kindness: for they kindled a fire, and received each one of us, because of the falling rain, and because of the cold. 3 And when Shaul had gathered a bundle of sticks, and laid them on the fire, there came a viper out of the heat, and bit his hand. 4 And when the barbarians saw the creature hanging on his hand, they said among themselves, No doubt this man is a murderer, who, though he has escaped the sea, yet justice does not allow him to have his chayim. 5 And he shook off the viper into the fire, and felt no harm. 6 But they looked to see when he would swell up, or die suddenly: but after they had looked a great while, and saw no harm come to him, they changed their minds, and said that he was a mighty elohim. 7 In the same area were lands belonging to the chief of the island, whose name was Publius; who received us, and lodged us at his home for three days most courteously. 8 And it came to pass, that the abba of Publius lay sick of a fever and of a bowel pain: to whom Shaul entered in, and made tefillah, and laid his hands on him, and healed him. 9 So when this was done, others also, who had diseases in the island, came, and were healed: 10 Who also honored us with many honors; and when we departed, they gave us such basic things as were necessary. 11 And after three months we departed in a ship from Alexandria, which had wintered on the island, whose carved figurehead was Castor and Pollux. 12 And landing at Syracuse, we stayed there three days. 13 And from there we got hold of a compass, and came to Rhegium: and after one day the south wind blew, and we came the next day to Puteoli: 14 Where we found brothers, and were invited to stay with them for seven days: and so we went toward Rome. 15 And from there, when the brothers heard of us, they came to meet us as far as Appiiforum, and the Three Taverns: who when Shaul saw, he gave hodu to **יהוה**, and took courage. 16 And when we came to Rome, the captain delivered the prisoners to the captain of the guard: but Shaul was allowed to dwell by himself with a soldier that kept him. 17 And it came to pass, that after three days

Shaul called the rulers of the Yahudim together: and when they were come together, he said to them, Men and brothers, though I have committed nothing against the Yahudite people, or the Torah of our ahvot, yet was I delivered prisoner from Yahrushalayim into the hands of the Romans. 18 Who, when they had examined me, would have let me go, because there was no reason for death to me. 19 But when the unbelieving Yahudim spoke against it, I was obliged to appeal to Caesar; not that I had anything to accuse my nation of. 20 For this cause therefore have I called for you, to see you, and to speak with you: because it is for the tikvah of Yisrael[1] [2] that I am bound with these chains. 21 And they said to him, We neither received letters out of the province of Yahudah concerning you, neither did any of the brothers that came here show or speak any lashon hara against you. 22 But we desire to shema from you what you think: for as concerning this sect, we know that everywhere it is spoken against.[3] 23 And when they had appointed him a day, there came many to him into his lodging; to whom he expounded and testified the malchut of יהוה, persuading them concerning יהושע, both out of the Torah of Moshe, and out of the neviim,

from morning until evening.[4] 24 And some believed the things that were spoken, and some believed not. 25 And when they agreed not among themselves, they departed, after Shaul had spoken one final word, Well did the the Ruach HaKodesh speak by Yeshayahu ha navi to our ahvot, 26 Saying, *Go to this people, and say, Hearing you shall shema, and shall not understand; and seeing you shall see, and not perceive: 27 For the lev of this people is grown hardened, and their ears are dull of hearing, and their eyes have they closed; lest they should see with their eyes, and shema with their ears, and understand with their lev, and should be returned back, and I should heal them.* 28 Be it known therefore to you, that the יהושע of יהוה is being sent to the nations,[5] and that they will shema to it. 29 And when he had said these words, the Yahudim departed, and had great reasoning and arguing among themselves. 30 And Shaul dwelt two full years in his own rented bayit at his own expense, and received all that came in to him, 31 Proclaiming the malchut of יהוה, and teaching those things about יהושע the Moshiach: with all confidence, no man forbidding him.[6]

---

[1] Rav Shaul's ministry to the nations was for the hope of the restoration, regathering, and homecoming of all Yisraelites and never to establish a separate non-Yisraelite entity.
[2] Both houses.
[3] Being a Torah-keeping Nazarene Yisraelite will cause your enemies to multiply.

[4] Notice that the message remains the same; it is the message of the kingdom, spoken of by Yahshua as being restored through Him, and all the Scriptures speak of this kingdom.
[5] Two-house reference
[6] Of course this was to change later as he was slain as a martyr.

Publisher's Note-This "missing chapter" is educational and informative, particularly historically speaking. Moreover in the light of the purposes of this unique edition, which seeks to show the overwhelming evidence for two-house restoration, we have included the "missing chapter" of Acts. We feel, however, based on lack of valid second and third witnesses, that while this may be a very useful missing chapter, it must nonetheless be considered an item of topical interest and therefore must remain solely apocryphal. What you are about to read below cannot be considered Scripture and is not presented as such.

29 [1] And Shaul, full of the blessings of Moshiach, and abounding in the Ruach, departed out of Romulus, [2] determining to go into Sepharad[3], for he had a long time proposed to journey there, and was minded also to go from there to Britain. 2 For he had heard in Phoenicia that certain of the children of Yisrael, about the time of the Ashurian captivity, had escaped by sea to Barat-Anat[4] as spoken be the Navi[5] [Esdra], and called by the Romulusans – Barat-Anat.[6] 3 And יהוה commanded the besorot to be preached far off to the nations, and to the lost sheep of the House of Yisrael.[7] 4 And no man hindered Shaul; for he testified boldly of יהושע before the tribunes and among the people; and he took with him certain of the brothers who abode with him at Romulus, [8] and they took shipping at Ostrium and having the winds favorable, were brought safely into a haven of Sepharad - Spain. 5 And many people were gathered together from the towns and villages, and the hill country; for they had heard of the conversion to the Shlichim, and the many nisim, which he had wrought. 6 And Shaul preached mightily in Spain, and great multitudes believed and were converted, for they perceived he was a sholiach sent from יהוה . 7 And they departed out of Sepharad, and Shaul and his company finding a ship in Armorica sailing to Barat-Anat[9], they were, passing along the south Coast, they reached a port called Raphinus. [10] 8 Now when it was voiced abroad that the sholiach[11] had landed on

---

[1] Apocryphal. From the *Sonnini Manuscript (SM)*, a.k.a. *The Long Lost Chapter of the Acts of the Apostles*. SM was translated from the Greek by C.S. Sonnini during the reign of Louis XVI who held the French throne from 1774 to 1793; from an original manuscript found in the archives of Constantinople, and was presented to him by the Sultan Abdoul Achmet. Found interleaved in a copy of *Sonnini's Travels in Turkey and Greece* and purports to be the concluding portion of the book of Acts. Details the approximately six-year history of Shaul/Paul's 4th and 5th missionary journeys, which here includes Sepharad - Spain (See Acts 15:28; Romans 15:24, 28) and Barat-Anat (though some scholars dispute this) after his forced residence and subsequent trial and acquittal in Romulus. He later is arrested again and returns to Romulus to be martyred while supporting and defending the thousands of other Nazarene believers during the reign of the Roman Emperor Nero. Modern Christian congregations often view their ministries as living-out "Acts 29" (the as yet un-written chapter) - yet few grasp the true calling and purpose that Rav Shaul exhibits in this chapter – namely, the search for and regathering of scattered Ephraimites back to their true calling as Yisraelites. While admittedly speculative, it is interesting and yet possible that this apocryphal manuscript has remained so under the purposeful hand of YHWH during the mandatory galut (diaspora/scattering) and punishment of Ephraim into the nations. For had it been considered canonical during any of the preceding 2,700 years of history, Ephraim's identity would likely have been revealed prematurely thereby violating the Torah-mandated exile. Because the punishment came from YHWH through His Torah, it thus was impossible for man to "see" its prophetic and historical significance at any time prior to the end of Ephraim's punishment.

Apocryphal Source:
"Travels in Turkey and Greece undertaken by order of Louis XVI, and with the authority of the Ottoman Court, by C.S. Sonnini, member of several scientific or literary societies of the Society of Agriculture of Paris, and of the Observers of Men. Mores multorum videt et ubes. Hor., London: Printed for T.N. Longman and O. Rees, Paternoster Row, 1801."

[2] Rome – traditionally thought to have been named after one of two legendary/mythic figures: Romulus (of Romulus and Remus). Others believe it to comes from the false elohim Roma. We use "Romulus" herein.
[3] Spain. Also "Iveria" (Iberia) from "Ivrim" meaning Hebrews; further from the Hebrew root "ever" – meaning one who has "crossed over."

[4] Also "Berit-Anat," considered by 17th-century scholars Sammes and Bochart to be the ancient Phoenician name for Britain. In English sometimes referred to as: "The Tin Islands" or "Islands of Tin," as this metal was highly traded in the ancient maritime sailing routes in this area. Related to "Berit-Am," meaning "people of the covenant" or "covenant of the people." Britain was the then-farthest most-inhabited large group of islands north and west of Yisrael – the British Isles, including Scotland. Romulus had by then conquered the greater part of Barat-Anat.
[5] Prophet.
[6] See the footnote regarding Barat-Anat at Acts 29:2.
[7] Acts 9:15; 22:21. The northern tribes – Ephraimites.
[8] See the footnote regarding Romulus at Acts 29:1.
[9] See the footnote regarding Barat-Anat at Acts 29:2.
[10] This is the Roman name for London. In Saxon times there was still standing in Sandwich an old house called the "House of the Apostles"; tradition has it that Shaul was one of these Apostles.
[11] Apostle.

their coast, great multitudes of the inhabitants met him, and they treated Shaul courteously and he entered in at the east gate[1] of their city, and lodged in the bayit of an Ivri and one of his own nation. 9 And on the morrow he came and stood upon Mount Lud[2] and the people thronged at the gate, and assembled in the Broadway, and he preached Moshiach to them, and they believed the Word and the testimony of יהושע. 10 And in the evening the Ruach HaKodesh fell upon Shaul, and he prophesied, saying, See in the last days the Elohim of Shalom shall dwell in the cities, and the inhabitants of it shall be numbered:[3] and in the seventh numbering of the people,[4] their eyes shall be opened,[5] and the kavod[6] of their inheritance will shine out before them.[7] The nations shall come up to worship on the Mount that testifies of the patience and long suffering of a servant of יהוה.[8] 11 And in the yamim acharonim new tidings of the besorot[9] shall issue out of Yahrushalayim,[10] and the levim of the people shall rejoice, and see, fountains shall be opened,[11] and there shall be no more plague. 12 In those days there shall be wars and rumors of war; and a melech shall rise up,[12] and His sword,[13] shall be for the

healing of the nations,[14] and His peacemaking shall abide, and the kavod of His kingdom a wonder among princes. 13 And it came to pass that certain of the Druids came to Shaul privately, and shown by their rites and ceremonies they were descended from the Yahudim[15] who escaped from bondage in the land of Mitzrayim,[16] and the sholiach believed these things, and he gave them the kiss of shalom. 14 And Shaul abode in his lodgings three months confirming in the emunah and preaching Moshiach continually. 15 And after these things Shaul and his brothers departed from Raphinus[17] and sailed to Atium in Galut-Yah.[18] 16 And Shaul preached in the Romulusan garrison and among the people, exhorting all men to repent and confess their sins. 17 And there came to him certain of the Belgae[19] to enquire of him of the new teaching, and of the Man יהושע; And Shaul opened his lev to them and told them all things that had befallen him, and how Moshiach יהושע came into the world to save sinners; and they departed pondering among themselves the things which they had heard. 18 And after much preaching and toil, Shaul and his fellow laborers passed into Helvetia, and came to Mount Pontius Pilate, where he who condemned the Master יהושע dashed

---

[1] Interestingly he enters via the east gate of that city – for he brings news of Moshiach Yahshua, the One Who will enter through the Eastern Gate of Yahrushalayim.
[2] Ludgate Hill and Broadway, where "St. Paul's Cathedral" stands in London, England.
[3] An allusion to how YHWH has bound the geographical boundaries of the nations by the number of Yisraelites they would hold. Devarim/Deuteronomy 32:8.
[4] An allusion to the seven-fold multiplied punishment of Ephraim after they did not make teshuvah (repented). This Torah requirement is found at Wayiqra/Leviticus 26:28.
[5] After the seven-fold count of punishment ends, their eyes are opened to their identity as Yisraelites.
[6] Glory.
[7] Yahoshua/Joshua 16:4-5,8-9; 24:30 Shoftim/Judges 2:9. They have the same inheritance as one of the two tov spies who claimed the land of promise - namely, Yahoshua – Himself an Ephraimite, and thus a type of namesake for the scattered tribes whose eyes have now been opened.
[8] Mt. Tzion. Micah 4:2.
[9] Glad tidings; tov news.
[10] Yeshayahu/Isaiah 2:3; Micah 4:2.
[11] Bamidbar/Numbers 33:9 when all twelve tribes of the children of Yisrael pitched their tents at the dessert of Eylim where they found twelve fountains of water – one for each tribe.
[12] Moshiach Yahshua.
[13] Torah.

[14] All nations who come to worship in Ruach and in truth; but particularly returning Ephraim Yisraelites who have been away from Torah the longest.
[15] Not that the Druids – mostly truly pagan people – are themselves Yahudim, but that some Yahudim appear to also have been dispersed as far as these "Isles far off" and the Druids absorbed and utilized certain Yehudite practices among their rituals. It also could be that these Druids were actually Ephraimites who still held on to certain rituals of the true worship from Yahrushalayim and, in the confusion of the exile, considered these to be of the "Yahudim" rather than more correctly "of Yisrael."
[16] Egypt.
[17] See the footnote regarding Raphinus at Acts 29:7.
[18] Gallia in Latin, a.k.a. The Celts. Consisting mostly of scattered Ephraimites.
[19] One of three peoples inhabiting the Roman "Gaul – Belgae, Aquitani and the Celts. From whom the Dutch likely descend i.e., Holland, Belgium. Sadly – even in modern times there exists in Belgium (among all of Europe) much anti-semitic tension and even notorious outright antagonism towards Jewish people. Perhaps this is a leftover manifestation of the Ephraimite hatred of the ways of their brother Yahudah.

himself down headlong,[1] and so miserably perished. 19 Immediately a torrent gushed out of the mountain and washed his body, broken in pieces, into a lake. 20 And Shaul stretched out his hands upon the mayim, and made tefillah to יהוה; saying O יהוה Elohim, give a sign to all nations that here Pontius Pilate who condemned Your only-begotten Son, plunged down headlong into the pit. 21 And while Shaul was yet speaking, see, there came a great earthquake, and the face of the mayim was changed, and the form of the lake became like the Ben Adam hanging in an agony upon the Stake.[2] 22 And a voice came out of the shamayim[3] saying; Even Pilate has escaped the wrath to come for he washed his hands before the multitude at the dom shedding of the Master יהושע. 23 When, therefore, Shaul and those that were with

him saw the earthquake, and heard the voice of the malach,[4] they esteemed יהוה, and they were mightily strengthened in the Ruach. 24 And they journeyed and came to Mount Julius where stood two pillars,[5] one on the right hand and one on the left hand, erected by Caesar Augustus. 25 And Shaul, filled with the Ruach HaKodesh, stood up between the two pillars, saying, Men and brothers these stones that you see this day shall testify of my journey here; and I say, they shall remain until the outpouring of the Ruach upon all nations, neither shall the derech be hindered throughout all generations. 26 And they went out and came to Illtricum, intending to go by Makedonia into Asia, and grace was found in all the congregations, and they prospered and had shalom. Amein.

---

[1] Thought to be the mountain where Pontius Pilate committed suicide and thus bears his name.
[2] Cross, pole used by the Romans for impaling victims. Greek: **stauroo**.
[3] A **bat kol**.

[4] Angel, messenger.
[5] Possibly refers to two bronze pillars Caesar Augustus requested be placed at the entrance to his Mausoleum in Rome with engraved descriptions in Greek and Latin of all his achievements as Emperor. Known in Latin as **Res Gestae Divi Augustae** or simply abbreviated RG. A similar inscription was placed at Ankyra in GalutYah – the then new Roman territory where; Shaul would make his declaration at these columns or pillars (whether this verse speaks of Rome or GalutYah is unclear) and uses them as evidence of his travels and presence there to preach the besarot and regather Ephraim, as well as prophesying that the pillars would remain there until the outpouring of the ruach upon all nations. The RG remains a historical artifact to this day.

יעקב

Yaakov – James

To Believing Remnant Yisrael

1 Yaakov, an eved of יהוה and the Master יהושע the Moshiach to the twelve tribes who are scattered abroad in the galut: Shalom. [1] 2 My Yisraelite brothers, [2] count it all simcha when you fall into divers trials; 3 Knowing this, that the trying of your emunah produces patience. 4 But let patience be a perfect work, that you may be perfect and complete, wanting nothing. [3] 5 If any of you lack chochma, let him ask of יהוה who gives to all men liberally, without reproach; and it shall be given to him. 6 But let him ask in emunah, nothing wavering. For he that wavers is like a wave of the sea driven with the wind and tossed. 7 For let not that man think that he shall receive anything from the Master יהוה. 8 A double minded[4] man[5] is unstable in all his ways. 9 Let the brother of low degree gilah in that he is exalted:[6] 10 But the rich, in that he is made low: because as the flower of the grass he shall pass away. 11 For the sun is no sooner risen with a burning heat, so that it withers the grass, and the flower falls, and the pretty appearance of it perishes: so also shall the rich man fade away in the course of his chayim. 12 Blessed is the man that endures trials: for when he is tried, he shall receive the keter of chayim that יהוה has promised to those that love Him.[7] 13 Let no man say when he is tempted, I am tempted by יהוה

for יהוה cannot be tempted with evil, neither does He tempts any man:[8] 14 But every man[9] is tempted, when he is drawn away by his own desires, and is taken away.[10] 15 Then when desire has conceived, it births sin: and sin, when it is spread, brings forth death. 16 Do not go astray, my beloved Yisraelite brothers. 17 Every tov gift and every perfect gift is from above, and comes down from the Abba of Lights, in whom there is no changing, nor shadows that turn. 18 Of His own will He brought us forth with the Torah of emet, that we should be the bikkurim of His recreation.[11] 19 So then, my beloved Yisraelite brothers, let every man be swift to hear, slow to speak, and slow to anger: 20 For the wrath of man does not bring about the tzedakah of יהוה. 21 Therefore lay aside all filthiness and the multitude of evils, and receive with meekness the engrafted Torah, [12] which is able to save your beings. 22 But be doers of the Torah,[13] and not hearers only deceiving yourselves.[14] 23 For if any be a hearer of the Torah, and not a doer, he is like a man beholding his natural face in a mirror: 24 For he sees himself, and goes away, and immediately forgets what type of man he was. [15] 25 But whoever looks into the

---

[8] "Man" is a synonym for "Yisrael," and Yisraelites know that YHWH tries and tests us, but never tempts us. That job is done by s.a.tan.
[9] See the footnote regarding "man" in James 1:8.
[10] Just like the lost during the Great Tribulation, as the saved are left behind, and the lost are "taken away."
[11] Yaakov expects his Hebrew readers to understand Shavuot and Bikkurim, both referred to as first-fruit feasts. We will be the first-fruits to rise from the dead at Yahshua's return.
[12] The promise to both houses found in Jeremiah 31:31.
[13] The only word that believers knew was Torah, since most of the Renewed Covenant had not yet been written.
[14] Torah-keeping guards us from possible self-deceptions.
[15] When the exiles hear the Torah and do not perform it, they continue in the path of all who are Yisrael; and at one time knew who they were, but became the lost tribes due to a departure from doing Torah. Since they did not continue in observing it, they need to be constantly reminded that they are the lost sheep of the House of Yisrael. They need to look into the mirror of Torah, in order to have their memory jarred as to their identity. Looking carefully at Torah then will reestablish their identity and end their amnesia.

---

[1] This scroll is written to all twelve tribes of Yisrael, who are all said to be in the galut or dispersion. If the House of Yahudah had returned in 520 BCE in the days of Ezra, then Yaakov would not be addressing all twelve tribes still in dispersion, but only the Jews.
[2] The born-again believers are called brothers from the 12 tribes. Yakkov, Yahshua's half-brother, had no problem understanding just who the believers in Moshiach truly are.
[3] Even in exile, Yisrael can be fully provided for through one's own patience, as they wait on YHWH.
[4] The imagery here is that double-mindedness is likened unto spiritual exile, a situation the 12 tribes can well identify with.
[5] "Men" in Scripture almost always refers to Yisarel in a believing context.
[6] Speaking of the former **Lo-Ami** or Ephraim Yisrael.
[7] Being Yisrael means that by trusting YHWH, a man can overcome trials and be rich in faith.

perfect Torah of freedom, and continues in it, he will not be a forgetful hearer, but a doer of the mitzvot; this man shall be blessed in his mitzvot. [1] 26 If any man among you seems to be a servant of the Master, and controls not his tongue, deceives his own lev, and this man's service is in vain.[2] 27 Pure and undefiled service to Abba יהוה is this: to visit the fatherless and widows in their affliction, and to keep himself unspotted from the world.[3]

2 My Yisraelite brothers, have not the emunah in our Master יהושע the Moshiach, the Master of tifereth, with partiality.[4] 2 For if there comes into your synagogue a man with a gold ring, in costly apparel, and there comes in also a poor man in soiled clothing; 3 And you show favor to him that wears the beautiful clothing, and say to him, Sit here in a tov place; and say to the poor, Stand over there, or sit here under my footstool: 4 Are you not then being partial among yourselves, and have become shophtim with evil thoughts? 5 Listen carefully, my beloved Yisraelite brothers, Has not יהוה chosen the poor of this world rich in emunah, and heirs of the malchut which He has promised to them that love Him? 6 But you have despised the poor.[5] Is it not rich men that oppress you, and drag you before their mishpat bema? 7 Do they not blaspheme that worthy Name by which you are called? 8 If you fulfill the royal Torah according to the Katav, You shall love your neighbor as yourself; you will do well: 9 But if you show partiality among men, you commit sin, and are convicted by the Torah as transgressors.[6]

10 For whosoever shall keep the entire Torah, and yet offend in one point, he is guilty of all.[7] 11 For He that said, Do not commit adultery, said also, Do not kill. Now even if you commit no adultery, yet if you kill, you are become a transgressor of the Torah.[8] 12 So act, and do, as those that shall be judged by the Torah of liberty. 13 For He shall have mishpat without rachamim that has shown no rachamim; for you exalt yourselves by desiring rachamim instead of mishpat.[9][10] 14 What does it profit, my Yisraelite brothers, if a man says he has emunah, and has not mitzvot? Can emunah save him? 15 If a brother or sister is naked, and destitute of daily food, 16 And one of you says to them, Depart in shalom, may you be warm and filled; but you give them not those things that are needful to the body; what use is it? 17 Even so emunah, if it has not mitzvot, is dead, being alone. 18 Yes, a man may say, You have emunah, and I have mitzvot: show me your emunah without your mitzvot, and I will show you my emunah by my mitzvot.[11] 19 You believe that there is Elohim echad; you do well: the shadim also believe, and tremble.[12] 20 But will you know, O vain man[13], that emunah without mitzvot is dead? 21 Was not Avraham our abba[14] made tzadik by mitzvot, when he had

---

[1] See footnote for James 1:24. A doer of Torah will soon remember his ancient heritage, causing the amnesia of his heritage to dissipate.
[2] **Lashon hara** or "evil speech," that can defile a Yisraelite's walk and calling.
[3] In Hebraic mindset, it is not merely believing that displays a man's character, but his performance of what he believes, as opposed to a mere mental assent to facts.
[4] A warning to all returning Yisraelites.
[5] And thereby violated Torah.
[6] If Yahudah shows partiality towards Yahudah alone and doesn't receive Ephraim back, they are considered transgressors, just as if they had abused the poor.
[7] What one point is under discussion? Showing partiality. If a Jewish believer keeps the whole Torah, and yet mistreats or refuses to recognize Ephraim, it is as if he has violated the entire Torah. There is much more on this in Galatians or Galut-Yah.
[8] See the footnote for James 2:10.
[9] Aramaic Peshitta.
[10] These verses (8-13) are a call to returning Yisrael to walk in mercy and patience towards the other house, so that our national civil war can be over and our unity can be a shalom offering before YHWH.
[11] Yaakov is not negating either. Rather he is showing the exiles the difference between a balanced Hebraic approach to faith in Yahshua, as opposed to the Greco-Roman heretical approach, that had begun to seep in.
[12] The point here is the emunah in a superpower or an almighty is nice, but it is necessary to trust in YHWH alone, and then act like it, unlike demons that neither use YHWH's Name, nor do they act like Him.
[13] Reference to Yisrael.
[14] Believers are both the physical and spiritual offspring of Abraham.

offered Yitzchak his son upon the altar? 22 Do you see how emunah worked with his mitzvot, and by mitzvot was his emunah made perfect? 23 And the Katav was fulfilled which said, Avraham believed יהוה , and it was counted to him for tzedakah: and he was called the chaver of יהוה. 24 You see then how that by mitzvot a man is made tzadik, and not by emunah only.[1] [2] 25 Likewise also was not Rahav the harlot made tzadik by mitzvot, when she had received the spies, and had sent them out another way? 26 For as the body without the ruach is dead, so emunah without mitzvot is dead also.

3 My Yisraelite brothers, not many should be rabbis, [3] knowing that we shall receive a stronger mishpat.[4] 2 For in many things we offend all people. If any man offend not in Torah, the same is a perfect man, and able also to bridle the whole body. 3 Behold, we put bits in the horses' mouths, so that they may obey us; and we turn their whole body. 4 Behold also the ships, which though they be so great, and are driven by fierce winds, yet they are turned around with a very small rudder, in any way that the captain desires. 5 Even so the tongue is a little member, and yet boasts great things. Behold, how great a matter a little fire ignites! 6 And the tongue is a fire, and the sinful world a forest: so is the tongue among our members, it can defile the whole body, and sets on fire the course of our Yisraelite race that rolls on like a wheel; and it burns on with the fire of Gei-

Hinnom.[5] 7 For every kind of beasts, and of birds, and of serpents, and of things in the sea, is tamed, and has been tamed by mankind: 8 But the tongue can no man tame; it is unruly evil, and full of deadly poison.[6] 9 With it we bless Elohim, even our Abba; and with it we curse men, who are made after the image of the Master יהוה. 10 Out of the same mouth proceeds brachot and cursing. My Yisraelite brothers, these things should not be so.[7] 11 Does a fountain send forth at the same place sweet mayim and bitter? 12 Can the fig tree, my Yisraelite brothers, bear olive berries? Or a vine, figs? So likewise saltwater cannot be made sweet. 13 Who is a wise man and endued with training among you? Let him show a tov lifestyle with his mitzvot in meekness of chochma. 14 But if you have bitter envy and self-seeking in your levim, boast not, and lie not against the emet. 15 This chochma descends not from above, but is earthly, sensual, and from s.a.tan. 16 For where envy and strife is, there is confusion and every evil work. 17 But the chochma that is from above is first pure, then full of shalom, gentle, and ready to obey, full of rachamim and tov fruits, without partiality, and without hypocrisy.[8] 18 And those that make shalom sow the fruit of tzedakah in shalom.[9]

4 From where come wars and fighting among you? Do they not come from your desires that war in your members? 2 You desire, and have not: you kill, and desire to have, and cannot obtain: you strive and fight; yet you have not, because you ask not. 3 You ask, and receive not, because

---

[1] Unlike Luther, Abraham and other Torah-keepers understand this very well. The Torah is an outlet through which we shower Abba with obedience, and our fellow man with set-apart living. It is the natural expression of our faith.
[2] If Abraham was justified by the work he did in Genesis 22, it seems that that work was truly completed in order for him to be commended.
[3] Usage of the word rabbi is due to the obvious reference to believers attending a synagogue in chapter 2, verse 2, as well as this scroll being sent to all twelve tribes, who called their teachers "rabbi."
[4] Sentencing by YHWH takes into account the greater responsibilities given to teachers, and more will be required of teachers, as opposed to this being any sort of personal condemnation, which, based on Romans 8:1, is not for any believer.

[5] The Aramaic describes the tongue as a destructive tool to the Yisraelite race that is like a wheel symbolizing the ongoing iniquity of the people of Yisrael.
[6] Sadly in Yisrael's history, our tongues have gotten us in much trouble with YHWH, and with our fellow brother.
[7] Remember that not even Yisraelites can curse other Yisraelites, since Torah tells us that no man can curse what YHWH has blessed.
[8] Heavenly wisdom is ready to obey and do all of Torah, without jealousy and arguing, and also without partiality towards either returning house of Yisrael.
[9] When all twelve tribes come together in harmony and love, it is a shalom offering before YHWH, and received as a fruit or grain offering as in the Tanach.

you ask wickedly, that you may satisfy your lusts. 4 You adulterers and adulteresses, know you not that chavurah with worldly things is enmity with יהוה ? Whoever therefore wants to be a chaver of worldly things is the enemy of יהוה. 5 Do you think that the Katav said in vain, The ruach that dwells in us is being provoked to envy? 6 But He gives more favor. Therefore He said, יהוה *resists the proud, but gives favor to the humble.* 7 Submit yourselves therefore to יהוה. Resist s.a.tan, and he will flee from you. 8 Draw near to יהוה, and He will draw near to you. Cleanse your hands, you sinners; and purify your levim, you double minded. 9 Lament, and mourn, and weep: let your laughter be turned to mourning, and your simcha to heaviness. 10 Humble yourselves in the sight of the Master יהוה , and He shall lift you up. 11 Speak not evil one of another, Yisraelite brothers. He that speaks evil of his brother, and shophets his brother, speaks evil of the Torah, and shophets the Torah: But if you shophet the Torah, you are not a doer of the Torah, but a shophet of it.[1] 12 There is one Lawgiver and Shophet, who is able to save and to destroy: who are you to shophet your neighbor? 13 Come now, you that say, Today or tomorrow we will go into such a city, and continue there a year, and buy and sell, and prosper: 14 You do not know what shall be tomorrow. For what is your chayim? It is even a vapor that appears for a little time, and then vanishes away. 15 For what you should say is, The Master יהוה willing, we shall have chayim, and do this, or that.[2] 16 But now you gilah in your boastings: all such pride is evil.

17 Therefore to him that knows to do tov, and does it not, to him it is sin.[3]

5 Come now, you rich men, weep and howl for your miseries that shall come upon you. 2 Your riches are corrupted, and your garments are moth-eaten. 3 Your gold and silver is tarnished; and their rust shall be a witness against you, and shall eat your flesh, as it was fire. You have stored up treasure together for the yamim acharonim. 4 Behold, the wages of the laborers who have reaped your fields, which you hold back by fraud, cries: and the cries of those who have reaped have entered into the ears of the Master יהוה Tsevaoth. 5 You have lived in pleasure on the earth, and been in luxury; you have nourished your levim, as in a day of slaughter. 6 You have condemned and killed the tzadik; and he does not resist you. 7 Be patient therefore, Yisraelite brothers, to the coming of the Master יהוה. Behold, the farmer waits for the precious fruit of the earth, and has great patience for it, until it receives the early and latter-rain. 8 Be you also patient; establish your levim: for the coming of the Master draws near.[4] 9 Grumble not one against another, Yisraelite brothers, lest you be condemned: behold, the Shophet stands before the door.[5] 10 Take, my Yisraelite brothers, the neviim, who have spoken in the Name of the Master יהוה , as our example of suffering, affliction, and of patience. 11 Behold, we count them blessed who endure. You have heard of the patience of Iyov, and have seen the purpose of the Master יהוה; that the Master יהוה is full of pity, and full of tender rachamim. 12 But above all things, my Yisraelite brothers,

---

[1] Yahudah and Ephraim must both be doing Torah, not judging each other's styles and quirks in applying the Torah; for if we do so we become Torah judges, rather that doers of Torah on an equal footing with others in Yisrael. If we are always judging others, we have no time to get reacquainted with His love for all Yisrael.
[2] Yisraelites take one day at a time, even as our Master taught us to do.

[3] Knowing the Word is not the answer. Knowing it and not obeying it is sin. Obedience is knowing the Word and obeying it.
[4] Even the rich will have to give account for their riches at Yahshua's coming. Are you investing what you have in the kingdom, or in yourself alone, on an ongoing basis?
[5] All Yisrael must unlearn the vanity of our fathers, as they were a people of constant murming and complaining. We on the other hand, who are called to be renewed Yisraelites, must learn how not to complain, but rather to give praise while we walk in restoration love.

swear not, neither by the shamayim, neither by the olam, neither by any other oath: but let your yes be yes; and your no, no; lest you fall into condemnation. [1] 13 Is any among you afflicted? Let him make tefillah. Is any in tov mood? Let him sing from the Tehillim. 14 Is any sick among you? Let him call for the shamashim of the congregation; and let them make tefillah over him, anointing him with oil in the Name of יהוה : [2] 15 And the tefillah of emunah shall save the sick, and יהוה shall raise him up; and if he has committed sins, they shall be forgiven him. 16 Confess your faults one to another, and make tefillah one for another, that you may be healed. The effectual fervent tefillot of a tzadik man is powerful accomplishing much. 17 Eliyahu was a man subject to many emotions as we are, and he made tefillah earnestly that it would not rain: and it rained not on the earth for three years and six months. 18 And he made tefillah again, and the shamayim gave rain, and the earth brought forth her fruit. 19 Yisraelite brothers, if any of you does stray from the emet, and one of you turns him back; 20 Let him know, that he who turns the sinner from the error of his derech, shall save a being from death, and shall even wipe out a multitude of sins. [3]

---

[1] This is not a reversal of Torah-based vow taking, rather a simplification of it to fewer words, so that s.a.tan cannot get a foothold within the saying of longer vows, where the tongue is given more room to set more forests on fire.
[2] True healing that lasts and is not simply dramatics is done in petition to YHWH; not any other name or substitute title.

[3] An apparent reference to those Yisraelites thinking of leaving true faith in Yahshua by denying Him. Notice these stray sheep can be rescued while straying, but not after they have denied and forsaken Yahshua. By displaying a strong stance against the evil forces that steal wayward sheep into denying Yahshua as YHWH's Son, there is a promised reward of extra mercy to those fighting those anti-missionary battles in front line positions. Their deeds cover other shortcomings they may have before YHWH, since He counts this battle as most crucial.

עברים

Ivrim - Hebrews

To Believing Remnant Yisrael

1 Elohim, who at various times and in different ways spoke in times past to the ahvot of Yisrael by the niviim, 2 has in these yamim acharonim spoken to us by His Son, whom He has appointed heir of all things, through whom also He made the olamim;[1] 3 Who being the brightness of His tiereth, and the express image of His Person, and upholding all things by the word of His power, when He had by Himself purged our sins, sat down on the right hand of the Majesty on high; 4 Being made so much better than the heavenly malachim, as He has inherited a more excellent Name than them.[2] 5 For to which of the heavenly malachim said He at any time, *You are My Son, this day have I brought You forth?* And again, *I will be to Him an Abba, and He shall be to Me a Son?*[3] 6 And again, when He brings in the first brought-forth into the olam, He says, *And let all the heavenly malachim of Elohim worship Him.* 7 And of the heavenly malachim He says, *Who makes His heavenly malachim ruachim, and His avadim a flame of fire.* 8 But to the Son He says, *Your throne, O Elohim, is le-olam-va-ed: a scepter of tzedakah is the scepter of Your malchut. 9 You have loved tzedakah, and hated iniquity; therefore Elohim, even Your Elohim,[4] [5] has anointed You with the oil of gladness above Your fellows. 10 And, You, יהוה, in the beginning have laid the foundation of the earth; and the shamayim are the works of Your hands: 11 They shall perish; but You remain; and they all shall grow old as does a garment; 12 And like a mantle You shall fold them up, and they shall be changed: but You are the same, and*

Your years shall not fail. 13 But to which of the heavenly malachim said He at any time, *Sit on My right hand, until I make Your enemies Your footstool?* 14 Are they not all serving ruachim, sent forth to serve those who shall be heirs of salvation?

2 Therefore we have to give the more earnest attention to the things which we have heard, lest at any time we should let them slip.[6] 2 For if the word spoken by heavenly malachim[7] was firm, and every transgression and act of disobedience received a correct reward; 3 How shall we escape, if we neglect so great a salvation; which at first began to be spoken by the Master Himself, and was confirmed to us by them that heard Him; 4 יהוה also bearing them witness, both with signs and wonders, and with different nisim, and gifts of the Ruach HaKodesh, according to His own will? 5 For it is not to the heavenly malachim that He has subjected the olam habah, of which we speak. 6 But someone[8] in a certain place has testified, saying, What is man, that You are mindful of him? Or the Ben Adam, that You visited Him? 7 You made him a little lower than the heavenly malachim; You crowned him with tiereth and honor, and did set him over the works of Your hands: 8 You have put all things in subjection under His feet. For in that He put all in subjection under Him, He left nothing that is not put under Him.[9] But now we see not yet all things put under Him. 9 But we see יהושע, who was made a little lower than the heavenly malachim for the suffering of death, crowned with tiereth

---

[1] The true Creator.
[2] The Name of YHWH.
[3] Plurality in echad.
[4] Moshiach has an Elohim and is not another Name for the Father, but is His brought-forth Son.
[5] Yahshua has an Elohim, even though He is Elohim.
[6] These warnings to believing Yisrael are sprinkled throughout the Brit Chadasha and should be very sobering to the faithful.
[7] Torah was given with the assistance of heavenly malachim.
[8] The writer of Ivrim certainly knows who and where the Scripture is, but is writing to both houses, and as Yisraelites he expects them to know where all theses Tanach quotes can be found.
[9] Except Abba Himself of course.

and honor; that He by the favor of **יהוה**, should taste death for every man. 10 For it was fitting for Him, for whom are all things, and by whom are all things, in bringing many sons[1] to tifereth, to make the Sar of their salvation perfect through sufferings. 11 For both He that sets-apart and those who are being set-apart are all echad: for which reason He is not ashamed to call them Yisraelite brothers,[2] 12 Saying, *I will declare Your Name to My Yisraelite brothers,[3] in the midst of the congregation will I sing tehilla to You.* 13 And again, *I will put My trust in Him.* And again, *Behold I and the children[4] that* **יהוה** *has given Me.* 14 Since the children[5] share in flesh and dom, He also Himself likewise took part of the same; that through death He might destroy him that had the power of death, that is, s.a.tan; 15 And deliver them who through fear of death were all their lifetime subject to slavery. 16 For truly He took not on Himself the nature of heavenly malachim; but He took on Himself the offspring of Avraham. 17 So in every way it behooved Him to be made like His Yisraelite brothers, so that He might be full of rachamim as a faithful Kohen Gadol in things pertaining to **יהוה** , to make atonement for the sins of the people. [6] 18 For in that He Himself has suffered being tried, He is able to help them that are tried.

3 Therefore, set-apart brothers, partakers of the heavenly calling, consider the Sholiach and Kohen Gadol of our confession, ha Moshiach **יהושע**; 2 Who was faithful to Him that appointed Him, as also Moshe was faithful in all his bayit.[7] 3 For this Man was counted worthy of more tifereth than Moshe, seeing that He who has

built the bayit has more honor than the bayit.[8] 4 For every bayit is built by some man; but He that built all things is Elohim. 5 And Moshe truly was faithful in all his bayit,[9] as an eved, for a testimony of those things that were to be spoken later; 6 But ha Moshiach as a Son over His own Bayit; whose bayit we are, if we hold fast the confidence and the gilah of our tikvah firm to the end. 7 Therefore as the Ruach HaKodesh says, *Today if you will hear His voice, 8 Harden not your levim, as in the rebellion, in the day of trials in the wilderness: 9 When your ahvot tried Me, proved Me, and saw My works forty years.[10] 10 Therefore I was grieved with that generation, and said, They do always go wayward in their levim; and they have not known My halachot. 11 So I swore in My wrath, They shall not enter into My rest.* 12 Shema, Yisraelite brothers, lest there be in any of you an evil lev of unbelief, in departing from the living Elohim. 13 But exhort one another daily, while it is called today; lest any of you become hardened through the deceitfulness of sin. 14 For we are made partakers of ha Moshiach, if we hold onto the beginning of our confidence firm to the end; 15 While it is said, today if you will shema His voice, harden not your levim, as in the rebellion. 16 For some, when they had heard, did rebel: was it not those that came out of Mitzrayim with Moshe? Although not all of them. 17 But with whom was He grieved for forty years? Was it not with them that had sinned, whose bodies fell in the wilderness? 18 And to whom did He swear that they should not

---

[1] Of Yisrael.
[2] In YHWH and in Yisrael.
[3] Any faith or religion that does not do what Yahshua did, which is teach Abba's only true Name to the brethren in the congregation, is not Yahshua's ministry, though it may be one of their own making.
[4] Of Yisrael and of YHWH.
[5] Of Yisrael.
[6] Of Yisrael.
[7] Beit Yisrael where Mose Rabianu served.

[8] Moshiach Yahshua is the builder of Renewed Covenant Yisrael, whereas Moshe served in that house. The builder is always greater than the worker in the house. This contrasts the greatness of Yahshua and Moshe to these Hebrews, a continuing problem to modern-day Nazarenes who desire to see Moshe or Torah on some sort of equal footing with Yahshua, a problem prevalent in the first century as well. There simply is no equal comparison between the Creator and the created.
[9] First-Covenant Yisrael was a foreshadow of the renewal that was to come through the Builder Himself.
[10] The Ruach that speaks today is begging Renewed Covenant Yisrael to do differently and have different results than the death of our fathers. He wants us to obey and have eternal life.

enter into His rest, but to them that believed not? 19 So we see that they could not enter in because of unbelief.

4 Let us therefore fear, while the promise of entering into His rest remains, lest any of you should seem to come short of it. 2 For to us was the besarot proclaimed, as well as to them: [1] but the word proclaimed did not profit them, since it was not mixed with emunah in them that heard it. 3 For we who have believed do enter into the rest, as He said, *As I have sworn in My wrath, if they shall enter into My rest:* for behold the works were finished from the foundation of the olam. 4 For He spoke in a certain place of the seventh day in this manner, *And Elohim did rest the seventh day from all His works.* 5 And in this place again, *If they shall enter into My rest.* 6 Seeing therefore it stands that some will surely enter into it, and they to whom it was first proclaimed entered not because of unbelief: 7 Again, after so long a time; He appointed another day as it is written above, for David said, Today if you will shema His voice, harden not your levim. [2] 8 For if Yehoshua son of Nun had given them rest, then would He not afterward have spoken of another day. 9 There remains therefore a Shabbat-keeping to the people of Elohim. [3] 10 For He that is entered into His rest, He also has ceased from his own works, as יהוה did from His. 11 Let us labor therefore to enter into that future Shabbat, lest any man fall after the same example of unbelief. 12 For the word of יהוה is quick, and powerful, and sharper than any two-edged sword, piercing even to the dividing between the being and the ruach, and between the joints and marrow and bone, and is a discerner of the thoughts and intents of the lev. 13 Neither is there any creature that is not manifest in His sight: but all things are naked and open

before the eyes of Him to whom we have to answer. 14 Seeing then that we have a great Kohen Gadol, that is passed into the shamayim, יהושע the Son of יהוה, let us hold fast our confession. [4] 15 For we have not a Kohen HaGadol who cannot be touched with the feeling of our weaknesses; but He was in all points tried like we are, yet He was without sin. 16 Let us therefore come boldly to the kesay of favor, that we may obtain rachamim, and find favor to help in our time of need.

5 For every Kohen HaGadol taken from among men is appointed for men in things pertaining to יהוה, that he may offer both gifts and sacrifices for sins: 2 Who can have ruchama on the ignorant who go astray; for that he himself also is surrounded with weakness. [5] 3 And because of these he is obliged, to sacrifice for the people, and also for himself, on account of his own sins. 4 And no man takes this honor to himself, but he that is called of יהוה, as was Aharon. 5 So also ha Moshiach esteemed not Himself to be made a Kohen Gadol; but He that said to Him, *You are My Son, today have I brought You forth.* 6 As He says also in another place, *You are a Kohen le-olam-va-ed after the order of Melech-Tzadik.* 7 Who in the days of His flesh, when He had offered up tefillot and supplications with strong crying and tears to Him that was able to save Him from death, and was heard; 8 Though He was the Son, yet He learned obedience by the things that He suffered; 9 And He grew to be perfect, and He became the author of eternal salvation to all them that obey Him; [6] 10 Called of יהוה a Kohen HaGadol after the

---

[1] Other non-believing or drawing-back Yisraelites.
[2] A second chance to a hardened people.
[3] YHWH's people honor that second chance through obedience to all manner of rest that He has prepared for us as witnessed by our weekly Shabbat observance.

[4] Making confession in Moshiach as YHWH's Son is the easy part. Holding onto that confession without succumbing to deception and seducing teachings, is the challenge for all Yisrael. Finishing the race is what determines if you enter the eternal Shabbat.
[5] The High Priest can have ruchama on those going astray, but cannot bring them back. Only the eternal High Priest Moshiach, who loves the deceived despite their ignorance and deception, can do that.
[6] The emphasis is on obeying.

order of Melech-Tzadik. 11 About whom we have many things to say, but some are hard to explain, seeing you are dull of hearing.[1] 12 For when by this time you ought to be morehs, you have the need that someone teach you again the first principles of the primary writings of יהוה;[2] and have become those that need milk, and not strong meat. 13 For everyone that uses milk is unskilled in the word of tzedakah: for he is a baby. 14 But strong meat belongs to them that are mature, even those who by reason of using the word, have their senses exercised to discern both tov and evil.

6 Therefore leaving the elementary principles of the teaching of ha Moshiach, let us go on to perfection; not laying again the foundation of teshuvah from past evil works, and of emunah toward יהוה, 2 Of the teaching of mikvot, and of laying on of hands, and of our resurrection from the dead, and of eternal mishpat.[3] 3 And this will we do, if the Master יהוה permits. 4 For it is impossible for those who were once enlightened, and have tasted of the heavenly gift, and were made partakers of the Ruach HaKodesh, 5 And have tasted the tov word of יהוה, and the powers of the olam habah, 6 And they fall away, to renew them again to teshuvah; seeing they impale by themselves the Son of יהוה again, and put Him to an open shame.[4] 7 For the earth

which drinks in the rain that comes upon it, and brings forth plants fit for them by whom it is tilled, receives brachot from Elohim: 8 But that which bears thorns and thistles is rejected, and is near to cursing; whose end is to be burned.[5] 9 But, beloved, we expect better things from you, and things that accompany salvation; that's why we speak like this. 10 For יהוה is not unrighteous to forget your work and labor of ahava, which you have shown toward His Name, in that you have served the kidushim, and still do serve.[6] 11 And we desire that every one of you show the same eagerness to the full assurance of your tikvah to the end:[7] 12 That you be not lazy in the malchut, but followers of them who through emunah and patience will inherit the promises. 13 For when יהוה made a promise to Avraham, because He could swear by no one greater, He swore by Himself, 14 Saying, *Surely in brachot I will bless you, and multiplying I will multiply you.*[8] 15 And so, after he had patiently endured, he obtained the promise.[9] 16 For men truly swear by the greater than themselves: and in every dispute among them the true settlement is by oath. 17 In like manner יהוה, willing more abundantly to show to the heirs of promise that His

---

[1] YHWH wanted to reveal many mysteries of Malkitzedek through the centuries to believers, but because of their falling away from Yahshua into forms of first-century Judaism and false Jewish concepts, He simply cannot speak about these advanced topics. Nothing has changed. Today we spend much time chasing many who have exchanged Yahshua for Moses, and monotheism in plurality for extreme monotheism that denies the Son and the Father as echad. Therefore many mysteries of the faith remain veiled and unexplored.
[2] Torah.
[3] The things religion calls crucial, the Word calls elementary. The problem with today's believers is called "Believer's Boredom," where they cannot enter the deep things of YHWH because, every week they are told by false teachers to stay away from Torah, and delve deeper into the elementary school program of Moshiach. The problem then results in Yisraelites staying home, completely bored, dazed, and confused. Only the truth of Torah, Yahshua and the eternal matters of the Commonwealth of Yisrael can keep us busy, on fire, and maturing in the emunah.
[4] Let this word be a loving warning to all those on the verge of denying the Renewed Covenant and Moshiach's gift of eternal life in favor of Jewish fables. A man or woman who falls away

fully in their heart, cannot return, regardless of one's effort to reach them or their seeming openness to listen. Scripture soberly tells us that if they have tasted the life of the new wine and fall away, it becomes impossible to renew them to life. What they have done is they have impaled Moshiach again and shamed Him openly before the world by falling away; a supposed weakness before this world that seems to indicate that Yahshua can't even guard His own.
[5] Burned with cessation of being. That is the Scriptural destination of those who start out as believers, but wind up in some perversion of the truth about Abba and His Son.
[6] All of His work done His way will have His rewards. One manifestation of His work is the proclaiming of the besarot in the true Name as seen here.
[7] Endurance, endurance, endurance; are the three keys in YHWH's word.
[8] Notice that this one promise to Avraham of physical multiplicity dominates Scripture in both covenants, for from it comes a nation whose seed filled the globe, a Moshiach who saves that globe, and YHWH's manifold wisdom and kingdom declared in that same congregation. Believing this promise saved Abraham. As Abraham's children, do we believe what Abraham believed about the fullness of the nations?
[9] Not in its end-time fulfillment, but being the first recipient of it.

promise was unchangeable,[1] sealed it by an oath: 18 That by two immutable things, the promise and the tikvah, in which it was impossible for יהוה to lie, we might have a strong encouragement, we who have fled for refuge to lay hold upon the tikvah set before us: 19 Which tikvah we have as an anchor of our being, both sure and firm, and that tikvah enters within the veil;[2] 20 There יהושע has previously entered in for our sakes, even יהושע , made a Kohen HaGadol le-olam-va-ed after the order of Melech-Tzadik.[3]

7 For this Melech-Tzadik, melech of Salem, kohen of El-Elyon, who met Avraham returning from the slaughter of the melechim, and blessed him; 2 To whom also Avraham gave a ma-aser; first being by interpretation Melech of Tzedakah, and after that also Melech of Salem, which is, Melech of Shalom; 3 Neither His ima nor abba are recorded in the genealogies, without beginning of days, nor end of chayim; but made like the Son of יהוה; abides as a Kohen continually. 4 Now consider how great this Man was, to whom even the patriarch Avraham gave the ma-aser of the best. 5 And truly they that are of the sons of Levi, who receive the office of the kohanim, have a mitzvah to take the ma-aser from the people according to the Torah, that is, from their Yisraelite brothers, even though they come out of the loins of Avraham: 6 But He whose descent is not recorded in their genealogies received the ma-aser from Avraham, and blessed Him that had the promises. 7 And without any contradiction the lesser is blessed by the greater. 8 And here mortal men receive the ma-aser; but there He received them, of whom Ketuvim says that He lives continually. 9 And one might say, that through Avraham even Levi, who received

the ma-aser, gave ma-aser.[4] 10 For he was yet in the loins of his abba Avraham, when Melech-Tzadik met him. 11 If therefore perfection were by the Levitical priesthood - for under it the people received the Torah - what further need was there that another kohen should arise after the order of Melech-Tzadik, and not be called after the order of Aharon? 12 For the priesthood being transferred, there is made of necessity an adjustment also in the Torah.[5] 13 For He of whom these things are spoken of pertains to another tribe, of which no man ever served at the altar. 14 For it is evident that our Master sprang out of Yahudah; of which tribe Moshe said nothing concerning the priesthood. 15 And it is yet clearer: that after the likeness of Melech-Tzadik there arises another Kohen, 16 Who is not appointed by the Torah of a carnal mitzvah, but by the power of an endless chayim. 17 For He testifies, *You are a Kohen le-olam-va-ed after the order of Melech-Tzadik.* 18 For there is truly a setting-aside of the former command, because of its weakness and unprofitableness.[6] 19 For the Torah made nothing perfect, [7] but the bringing in of a better tikvah did; through which we draw nigh to יהוה. 20 And He confirmed it to us by an oath:[8] 21 For those kohanim were made without an oath; but this One with an oath by Him that said to Him, the Master יהוה swore and will not relent, You are a Kohen le-olam-va-ed; after the order of-Melech-Tzadik: 22 By that יהושע was made a Guarantor of a better covenant.

---

[1] To Yisrael.
[2] Our hope and promise is within the veil and penetrates within the veil, but we ourselves do not enter there. Only Yahshua can do that.
[3] He entered as High Priest, not we who are merely priests.

[4] As part of Yisrael.
[5] The Torah was not done away with, but adjusted or slightly altered, to accommodate a better, more complete priesthood and sacrifice. Strong's Greek # 3346 **metatithaymee** means "moved from one place to another, not eliminated." So the priesthood was shifted, not eliminated. Shifted from Aaron to Malkitzedek and from Vayiqra to Bereshet, still within the Torah itself.
[6] Not a setting-aside of the entire Torah, but only the transfer of the priesthood from one tribe to another, and of the forsaking of the old priestly order to establish the new. This is not a replacement of Torah by the Renewed Convent; rather, one priesthood is established instead of the other by transfer within the nation of Yisrael itself.
[7] Pertaining to atonement and priesthood. The ongoing subject is the sacrifices and the priesthood, not the Torah itself.
[8] Lamsa's Peshitta p.1200.

23 And they truly were many kohanim, because they were not allowed to continue by reason of their death: 24 But this Man, because He is Immortal, [1] has an unchangeable priesthood. 25 Therefore He is able also to save them to the uttermost that come to יהוה through Him, seeing He lives le-olam-va-ed to make intercession for them. 26 For such a Kohen HaGadol became fully fit for us, who is set-apart, harmless, undefiled, separate from sinners, and made higher than the shamayim; 27 Who need not daily, as those Kohanim HaGadolim, to offer up sacrifice, first for his own sins, and then for the people's: for this He did once, when He offered up Himself. 28 For the Torah makes men Kohanim HaGadolim, who have human weakness; but the word of the oath, which was after the Torah, appointed the Son, who has been perfected le-olam-vaed.

8 Now of the things that we have spoken this is the summary: We have such a Kohen HaGadol, who is set on the right hand of the throne of the Majesty in the shamayim; 2 An attendant of the Set-Apart Place, and of the emet Tent of Meeting, which יהוה pitched, and not man. 3 For every Kohen HaGadol is appointed to offer gifts and sacrifices: So it was also necessary that this Man have something to offer. 4 For if He were on earth, He would not be a kohen, seeing that there are kohanim that offer gifts according to the Torah: 5 Who serve as the example and shadow of heavenly things, as Moshe was admonished by Elohim when he was about to make the Tent of Meeting: for, *See,* He said, *that you make all things according to the pattern shown to you on the Mount.* 6 But now יהושע ha Moshiach has obtained a greater service, by which He also is the Mediator of a more advantageous [2] covenant, which

was given as Torah [3] based upon more advantageous promises. 7 For if that first covenant had been faultless, then should no place have been sought for the second. 8 For finding fault with them, [4] He says, *Behold, the days come,* says the Master יהוה, *when I will make a Renewed Covenant with Beit Yisrael and with Beit Yahudah:* [56] 9 *Not according to the covenant that I made with their ahvot in the day when I took them by the hand to lead them out of the land of Mitzrayim; because they continued not in My covenant, and I regarded them not,* [7] says the Master יהוה. 10 *For this is the covenant that I will make with Beit Yisrael* [8] *after those days,* says the Master יהוה; *I will put My Torah into their mind, and write it on their levim: and I will be their Elohim, and they shall be My*

---

[3] Strong's Greek # 3549; **nomotheteo** translated as *established* in most translations, is better translated as "to enact law," or "sanction by law," meaning the Renewed Covenant is established by virtue of the fact that it is given as The Torah renewed in us.
[4] The Torah and First Covenant were not the problem; the problem as clearly stated here was with them. The next verse qualifies "the them."
[5] Both houses had faults, causing the need for a new priesthood, a new sacrifice, and a Renewed Covenant. According to this promise quoted from Jeremiah 31:31, there are no gentiles in the Renewed Covenant, as it was cut exclusively with Yisrael's two houses. Those two houses are Jews and Ephraimites, not Jews and gentiles. Of course non-biological Yisraelites also join as the friends of Yisrael (Ezekiel 37.16-17).
[6] Note also that Paul or Barnabas (the author of Hebrews) in his era also considered Yisrael divided and Ephraim as being still assimilated in the nations. This reference here alone fully and totally refutes any fictitious claims that the two houses reunited 525 years before Rav Shaul or Barnabas wrote Hebrews, during the return of Yahudah from Babylon.
[7] An anti-missionary favorite. The text was changed from "though I was a husband to them," to "I disregarded them." The reason for the change is that this paraphrase is not meant to be an exact quote. Rather it is a paraphrase to show that only one generation of Yisrael was discarded, not the whole nation. That is, the one-generation that died in the wilderness was discarded, without the entire nation being discarded. The point is that those who don't enter the Renewed Convent will be discarded like those in the wilderness; and not that all Yisraelites will be replaced by a gentile church. Therefore this is not a text that teaches that the church is the "New Yisrael," or that the Jews have been discarded.
[8] The Renewed Covenant is not only designed to bring eternal life and forgiveness to all Yisrael, but also to take the eternal Torah and place it within the hearts of the returning Ephraimites, who will then have the desire to freely obey it. This promise of a subsequent work in Ephraim Yisrael after salvation in the Renewed Covenant is what we see today. Yahudah is not mentioned here because they come into the Renewed Covenant with a decent grasp of Torah (though not always living it), and therefore YHWH focuses in on Ephraim's return to Torah.

---

[1] Only Moshiach is immortal. Believers do not become immortal, until the return of Moshiach.
[2] Strong's Greek # 2909; **kreitton** meaning "more advantageous," or "more useful," as opposed to strictly "better."

people: 11 *And they shall not teach every man his neighbor, and every man his brother, saying, Know the Master* יהוה *for all shall know Me, from the least to the greatest of them.* 12 *For I will forgive their unrighteousness, and their sins and their Torah-less-ness will I remember no more.* 13 In that He says, a Renewed Covenant, He has made the first old. Now that which decays and becomes old is near disappearing.[1]

9 Then truly the first covenant also had regulations of worship, and an earthly Set-Apart Place. 2 For there was a Tent of Meeting made; the first area, where the menorah, and the table, and the lechem of the shechinah was; which is called the set-apart place. 3 And after the second veil, the area of the Tent of Meeting which is called the Kadosh HaKadoshim; 4 Which had the golden censer, and the Ark of the Covenant covered on all sides with gold, in which was the golden pot that had manna, and Aharon's rod that budded, and the tablets of the covenant; 5 And over it the cheruvim of tifereth shadowing the mercy seat; of which we won't now speak in detail. 6 Now when these things were prepared, the kohanim went always into the Makom Kadosh of the Tent of Meeting, performing the services. 7 But into the Kadosh HaKadoshim went the Kohen HaGadol alone once every year, with dom, which he offered for himself, and for the sins of the people: 8 The Ruach HaKodesh therefore signifying, that the way into the Makom Kadosh was not yet made manifest, while the first Tent of Meeting was still standing:[2] 9 Which was a parable[3]

for the time then present, in which were offered both gifts and sacrifices, that could not make the one that did the service perfect, regarding his conscience; 10 Which stood only in food offerings and drink offerings, and different washings, and flesh-related regulations, imposed on the kohanim until the time of reformation.[4] 11 But ha Moshiach has now become a Kohen HaGadol of tov things to come, by a greater and more perfect Tent of Meeting, not made with hands, that is to say, not of this creation; 12 Neither by the dom of goats and calves, but by His own dom He entered in once into the Kadosh HaKdoshim, having obtained eternal redemption for us. 13 For if the dom of bulls and of goats, and the ashes of a red heifer sprinkling the defiled, sets-apart the flesh: 14 How much more shall the dom of ha Moshiach, who through the eternal Ruach offered Himself without blemish to Elohim, purify your conscience from dead works to serve the living Elohim? 15 And for this cause He is the Mediator of the Renewed Covenant, by means of His death, for the redemption of the sins that were done in the first covenant, so that those who are called, might receive the promise of eternal inheritance. 16 For where a will is presented it shows the death of its maker. 17 For a covenant is in force only after men are dead: otherwise it is useless while its maker lives. 18 For this reason not even the first covenant was dedicated without dom. 19 For when Moshe had spoken every precept to all the people according to the Torah, he took the dom of calves and of goats, with mayim, and scarlet wool, and hyssop, and sprinkled both the scroll, and all the people, 20 Saying, This is the dom

---

[1] The first thing to grasp is that the topic through these chapters is the priesthood. So what is about to grow old and pass away is the priesthood that then ministered in the temple. Not the Torah itself. Even the language bears this up, as the term "near disappearing" means that the temple had not yet been destroyed, and therefore the Levitical priesthood was still functional despite Yahshua's role as Malkitzedek. In essence then, this is a prophesy of the temple's imminent destruction, along with all its altars, priesthood and functions that will soon be changed or altered forever.

[2] Meaning Yahshua's way into the Holy of Holies was not accomplished as long as the earthly priests did their service. Our way into the Set-Apart Place also was not made manifest. It does not mean that believers enter the Holy of Holies. None

do. The veil that ripped was that of the Hekel curtain, gaining us access into the Holy Place, as our Kohen HaGadol does His work alone in the Holy of Holies, a place to where no believers have ever gone, for we are priests not the High Priest of the nation. For details: obtain **Within the Veil** at: http://store.yourarmstoisrael.org/Qstore/Qstore.cgi?CMD=011&PROD=1065766819

[3] Temple and Tabernacle Services.

[4] Reformation of the priesthood, and not the annulling of the Torah.

of the covenant which **יהוה** has commanded for you. 21 In like manner he sprinkled with dom both the Tent of Meeting, and all the vessels of the service. 22 And almost all things are by the Torah purged with dom; and without the shedding of dom is no forgiveness. 23 It was therefore necessary that the copies of the heavenly things should be purified with these; but the heavenly things themselves with better sacrifices than these. 24 For ha Moshiach is not entered into the Set-Apart Place made with hands, which is a copy of the true one; but into the shamayim itself, now to appear in the presence of **יהוה** for us: [1] 25 For He does not need to offer Himself often, as the Kohen HaGadol who enters into the Kadosh HaKadoshim every year with dom that is not His own; 26 For then He would have to suffer often from the foundation of the olam: but now once at the end of the olam hazeh, He has appeared to abolish sin by the sacrifice of Himself. 27 And as it is appointed to men once to die, but after this the mishpat: [2] 28 So Ha Moshiach was once offered to bear the sins of many; and to those that look for Him shall He appear the second time for our deliverance, this time not carrying our sins.

10 For the Torah having a shadow of tov things to come, and not the very image of the things, can never with those sacrifices which they offered year by year continually, make those who draw near perfect. 2 Otherwise would they not have ceased to be offered? Because then the worshippers once cleansed should have had no more awareness of their sins. 3 But in those sacrifices there is a yearly reminder of sins. 4 For it is impossible that the dom of bulls and goats can take away sins. 5 Therefore when He comes into the olam hazeh, He says, *Sacrifice and offering You did not desire, but a body You have*

prepared for Me: [3] 6 *In burnt offerings and sacrifices for sin You have had no pleasure.* 7 *Then said I, Behold, I come: in the volume of the scroll it is written of Me, to do Your will, O* **יהוה**. 8 In the above quote when He said, *Sacrifice and offering and burnt offerings and offering for sin You did not desire, neither do You have pleasure in them; which are offered according to the Torah*; 9 Then He said, *Behold, I come to do Your will, O* **יהוה**. He takes away the first, that He may establish the second. [4] 10 By that desire we are now set-apart through the offering of the body of **יהושע** ha Moshiach once for all. 11 And every kohen stands daily serving and offering the same sacrifices, which can never take away sins: 12 But this Man, after He had offered one sacrifice for sins le-olam-va-ed, sat down on the on the right hand of **יהוה**; 13 Waiting from then on until all His enemies are made His footstool. 14 For by one offering He has perfected le-olam-va-ed them that are being set-apart. 15 And the Ruach HaKodesh also is a witness for us: for after that He had said before, 16 *This is the covenant that I will make with them after those days,* says the Master **יהוה**, *I will put My laws into their levim, and in their minds will I write them;* 17 *And their sins and Torah-less-ness will I remember no more.* 18 Now where forgiveness of these is, there is no more offering for sin. 19 Having therefore, Yisraelite brothers, boldness to enter into the Makom Kadosh by the dom of **יהושע**, [5] 20 By a new and living way, which He has set-apart for us, through the veil, that is to say, His flesh; 21 And having a Kohen HaGadol over the Beit HaMikdash of **יהוה**; [6] 22 Let us draw near with a true lev in full assurance of emunah, having our levim sprinkled from an evil conscience, and our bodies washed with pure mayim. 23 Let us hold fast the

---

[1] If all believers were Kohen Gadols in the Holy of Holies as religion teaches, we wouldn't need Yahshua to be there for us.
[2] No such thing as reincarnation.

[3] Accurately quoting the LXX.
[4] Takes away the first sacrificial system and priesthood to establish the second. Not referring to Torah itself.
[5] We can enter the Holy Place but not the Holy of Holies.
[6] Yisrael.

confession of our emunah without wavering; (for He is faithful that promised;) 24 And let us care for one another to stir up ahava and tov mitzvot: 25 Not forsaking the assembling of ourselves together, as the manner of some is; but exhorting one another: and so much the more, as you see the Yom approaching.[1] 26 For if we sin willfully after that we have received the da'at of the emet, there remains no more sacrifice for sins, 27 But a certain fearful anticipation of mishpat and fire, which shall devour His enemies. 28 He that despised Moshe's Torah died without rachamim under two or three witnesses: 29 Of how much worse punishment, do you think, he shall deserve, who has trampled under foot the Son of יהוה, and has counted the dom of the covenant, by which He was made kadosh as a common thing, and has insulted the Ruach of favor?[2] 30 For we know Him that has said, *Vengeance belongs to Me, I will repay*, says the Master יהוה. And again, יהוה *shall shophet His people.*[3] 31 It is a fearful thing to fall into the hands of the living Elohim. 32 But remember the former days, in which, after you were enlightened, you endured great fights and sufferings;[4] 33 On one hand you were exposed to reproaches and pressures; and on the other hand you became sharers with those who were so treated. 34 And you had pity on those who were prisoners and you allowed the seizure of your property cheerfully, for you yourselves know that you have a better and more enduring possession in the shamayim.[5] 35 Do not lose your confidence, which has great reward. 36 For you have need of patience, that, after you have done the will of יהוה, you will receive the promise.[6] 37 In yet a little while, He that shall come will come, and will not tarry. 38 *But the just shall live by My emunah: but if anyone draws back, My being shall have no pleasure in him.*[7] 39 But we are not of those who draw back to perdition; but of them that believe to the saving of the being.[8]

11 Now emunah is the substance of things hoped for, the evidence of things not seen. 2 For by it zichnai-Yisrael obtained a tov report.[9] 3 Through emunah we understand that the olamim were framed by the word of Elohim, so that things that are seen were made by the invisible. 4 By emunah Hevel offered to יהוה a more excellent sacrifice than Qayin, by which he obtained witness that he was tzadik, יהוה testifying of His gifts: and by it he being dead yet speaks. 5 By emunah Chanok was translated that he should not see death; and was not found, because יהוה had translated him: for before His translation he had this testimony; that he pleased יהוה. 6 But without emunah it is impossible to please Him: for he that comes to יהוה must believe that He is, and that He is a rewarder of those that diligently seek Him. 7 By emunah Noach, being warned by יהוה of things not seen as yet, moved with fear, made an ark to save his bayit; by it he condemned the olam, and became heir of the tzedakah that is by emunah. 8 By emunah Avraham, when he was called to go out into

---

[1] Some do not guard YHWH's feasts and are considered unaware of the times and seasons of His return.

[2] This is another warning to those who leave the faith, and not to unbelievers. It is worse to have the truth and then abandon it, than to never have known and experienced the truth. The Hebraic idiomatic expression "trample under foot" means to erase Yahshua and His dom from the Torah equation, and try to attain right-standing with YHWH based on other criteria. Those who deny Yahshua in the end have brought great insult to YHWH's love and Ruach.

[3] YHWH judges Yisrael.

[4] A call to teshuvah for Hebrews who wind up denying Yahshua.

[5] Our future inheritance is in the heavens where the tabernacle and the High Priest are. Heaven as the home for the Yisraelite is not a Greco-Roman pagan doctrine, as can be seen here and elsewhere; though one day heaven and earth will meet and become one.

[6] Patience for reward can overcome temptation to fall away and return to rabbinic Judaism or any other religion.

[7] Yisrael is called to have faith in Yahshua and the faith of Yahshua and walk as He walked.

[8] If anyone turns back and denies Yahshua after believing, YHWH will have no pleasure in that action, or in the eternal second death of the one drawing back. Yisraelites are expected to move forward, not turn back. We are called to be Yisrael, not Mrs. Lot.

[9] What is so beautiful about this hall of fame honor roll is that it proves that since the beginning of humanity, YHWH has always had one (not two) group of elect. Not Yisrael and the church, or Jew and Gentile, but rather one community of emunah. This is heaven's perspective.

a place that he would later receive as an inheritance, obeyed; and he went out, not knowing where he was going. 9 By emunah he sojourned in the land of promise, as in a strange country, dwelling in tents with Yitzchak and Yaakov, the heirs with him of the same promise:[1] 10 For he looked for a city that has foundations, whose Builder and Maker is יהוה. 11 Through emunah also Sarah herself received strength to conceive offspring, and was delivered of a child when she was past age, because she deemed Him faithful who had promised. 12 Therefore sprang forth one, from him almost dead, even later as many as the cochavim of the sky in multitude, and as the sand which is by the sea shore innumerable.[2] 13 These all died in emunah, not having received the heavenly promised land,[3] but having seen it far off, and were persuaded of it, and embraced it, and confessed that they were gerim and pilgrims on the earth. 14 For they that say such things declare plainly that they seek a country. 15 And truly, if they had been mindful of that country from where they came out, they might have had the opportunity to return. 16 But now they desire a better country, that is, a heavenly one:[4] therefore יהוה is not ashamed to be called their Elohim: for He has prepared for them a city.[5] 17 By emunah Avraham, when he was tried, offered up Yitzchak: and he that had received the promises offered up his only brought-forth son, 18 Of whom it was said, That in Yitzchak shall your zera be called: 19 Accounting that יהוה was able to raise him up, even from the dead; from where also he received Him in a figure.[6] 20 By emunah Yitzchak blessed Yaakov and Esav concerning things to come. 21 By emunah Yaakov, when he was dying, blessed both the sons of Yoseph; and worshipped, leaning upon the top of his staff. 22 By emunah Yoseph, when he died, made mention of the exodus of the B'nai Yisrael; and gave them a commandment concerning his bones. 23 By emunah Moshe, when he was born, was hidden three months by his parents, because they saw he was a beautiful child; and they were not afraid of the melech's commandment. 24 By emunah Moshe, when he was grown, refused to be called the son of Pharaoh's daughter; 25 Choosing rather to suffer affliction with the people of יהוה, than to enjoy the pleasures of sin for a short while; 26 Esteeming the reproach of ha Moshiach as greater riches than the treasures in Mitzrayim: for he looked forward to receive the reward.[7] 27 By emunah he forsook Mitzrayim, not fearing the wrath of the melech: for he endured, as seeing Him who is invisible. 28 Through emunah he kept the Pesach, and the sprinkling of dom, lest He that destroyed the firstborn should touch them. 29 By emunah they passed through the Sea of Reeds as by dry land: which the Mitzrites attempting to do were drowned. 30 By emunah the walls of Yericho fell down, after they were circled around for seven days. 31 By emunah the harlot Rachav did not perish with them that believed not, when she had received the spies with shalom. 32 And what more shall I say? For the time would fail me to tell of Gidyon, and of Baraq, and of Shimshon, and of Yiphtah; of David also, and Schmuel, and of the niviim: 33 Who through emunah subdued malchutim, worked tzedakah, obtained promises, stopped the mouths of lions, 34 Quenched the violence of fire, escaped the edge of the sword, out of weakness were made strong, became valiant in fight, routed the armies of the foreigners. 35 Women received their dead raised to chayim again: and others were tortured, not accepting deliverance; that they might obtain a better resurrection: 36 And others had trials of cruel mockings and scourgings, yes, and also chains and

---

[1] The promise of physical multiplicity.
[2] See footnote on Hebrews 11:9.
[3] Peshitta. Heaven contextually inferred by verse 16.
[4] Not a pagan hope. It is a core Hebraic doctrine.
[5] The Renewed Yahrushalayim.
[6] As a figure or type of the coming Moshiach who would also die.

[7] Moshe Rabainu had a basic understanding of Moshiach.

imprisonment: 37 They were stoned, they were sawn asunder, were tempted, were slain with the sword: they wandered about in sheepskins and goatskins; being destitute, afflicted, tormented; 38 (Of whom this olam was not worthy:) they wandered in deserts, and in mountains, and in dens and caves of the earth. 39 And these all, having obtained a tov report through emunah, received not the promise: 40 יהוה having provided for us too; so that they without us should not be made perfect. [1]

12 Therefore seeing that we also are surrounded with so great a cloud of Yisraelite witnesses,[2] let us lay aside every weight, and the sin that does so easily beset us, and let us run with patience the race that is set before us, 2 Looking to יהושע the Author and Finisher of our emunah; who for the simcha that was set before Him endured the execution tree, despising the shame, and has sat down at the right hand of the throne of יהוה. 3 For consider Him that endured such opposition from sinners against Himself, lest you be weary and faint in your own lives. 4 Ye have not yet resisted to dom, striving against sin.[3] 5 And you have forgotten the exhortation that speaks to you as to children, *My son, despise not the chastening of the Master* יהוה, *nor grow weak when you are rebuked by Him*: 6 *For whom the Master* יהוה *loves He chastens, and scourges every son whom He receives.* 7 If you endure discipline, יהוה deals with you as with sons; for what son does the abba not discipline? 8 But if you are without discipline, by which we all are trained, then are you gerim, and not sons.[4] 9 Furthermore we have had ahvot of our flesh who corrected us, and we gave them respect: shall we not much rather be subject to the Abba of Ruachim, and live? 10 For they

truly for a few days disciplined us after their own understanding; but He for our profit, that we might be partakers of His Set-Apart nature.[5] 11 Now no discipline for the present seems to be fun, but sorrowful: nevertheless afterwards it yields fruits of shalom to those who are trained by that discipline. 12 Therefore lift up the hands that hang down, and the feeble knees; 13 And make straight paths for your feet, lest that which is lame be turned out of the way; but let it rather be healed. 14 Follow shalom with all men, and set-apartness, without which no man shall see יהוה: 15 Taking heed lest any man fall short of the favor of יהוה; lest any root of bitterness spring up to harm you, and by which many be defiled; 16 Lest there be any fornicator, or profane person, as Esav, who for one morsel of meat sold his birthright.[6] 17 For you know how that afterward, when he would have inherited the bracha, [7] he was rejected: for he had no chance of recovery, though he sought it carefully with tears. 18 For you have not come to the Mount that might be touched, and that burned with fire, nor to blackness, and darkness, and tempest, 19 And the sound of a shofar, and the voice of words; which voice they that heard begged that the word should not be spoken to them any more: 20 For they could not endure what was commanded, And if so much as a beast touched the mountain, it was to be stoned, or thrust through with a spear: 21 And so terrible was the sight that Moshe said, I exceedingly fear and quake: 22 But you have come to Har Tzion, and to the city of the living Elohim, the heavenly Yerushalayim, and to an innumerable multitude of heavenly malachim,

---

[1] Meaning all believers of all times are Yisrael, and all will inherit the kingdom as echad and not separately in some sort of dispensational reckoning.
[2] Kol Yisrael.
[3] His battle against sin caused His dom to be spilled. Our fight to rule over sin though tough, has yet to result in that same high cost.
[4] Personal discipline by YHWH in our lives is a sure sign that we are Yisrael and not gerim or goyim.

[5] To make Yisrael back into the original nation of kohanim.
[6] Ephraimites stuck in Christianity, who don't take the two-house message and their identity seriously, act the same way. Since you have the birthright, you should not take it lightly, nor trade it in for other psuedo-truths. For more details, see: **The Second Worst Sale In History**
http://yourarmstoisrael.org/Articles_new/restoration/?page=15 &type=12 .
[7] Of the firstborn. Ephraim remains YHWH's eternal firstborn. Don't let go of that right!

23 To the gathering [1] and congregation of the firstborn, [2] that is enrolled in the shamayim, and to יהוה the Shophet of all, and to the ruachim of tzadikim made perfect, [3] 24 And to יהושע the Mediator of the Renewed Covenant, and to the dom of sprinkling, that speaks better things than that of Hevel. 25 See that you refuse Him not that speaks. For if they escaped not who refused Him that spoke on earth, how much more shall we not escape, if we turn away from Him that speaks from the shamayim: 26 Whose voice then shook the earth: but now He has promised, saying, *Yet once more I shake not the earth only, but also the shamayim.* 27 And this word, Yet once more, signifies the removing of those things that are shaken, the things that have been made, that those things that cannot be shaken may remain. [4] 28 Therefore receiving a malchut that cannot be moved let us have favor, by which we may serve יהוה acceptably with reverence and fear: 29 For our Elohim is a consuming fire.

13 Let Yisraelite brotherly ahava continue. [5] 2 Be not forgetful to entertain gerim: [6] for in that manner some have entertained heavenly malachim unaware. 3 Remember them that are in prison, as in prison with them; and them who suffer adversity, for you also are human. 4 Marriage is honorable in all situations, and the bed undefiled: but whoremongers and adulterers יהוה will shophet. 5 Let your behavior be without greed; and be content with such things as you have: for the Master יהוה Himself has said, *I will never leave you, nor forsake you.*

6 So that we may boldly say, יהוה is my Helper, and I will not fear what man shall do to me. 7 Remember those who lead you, who have spoken to you the word of יהוה: whose outcome follow, imitate their mitzvot and emunah. 8 יהושע ha Moshiach the same yesterday, and today, and le-olam-va-ed. [7] 9 Be not carried about with different and strange doctrines. [8] For it is a tov thing that the lev is established with favor; not with foods, which has not profited those that have been occupied with that. [9] 10 We have an altar, [10] from which they have no right to eat, who serve the earthly Tent of Meeting. 11 For the bodies of those beasts, whose dom is brought into the Set-Apart Place by the Kohen HaGadol for sin, are burned outside the camp. 12 Therefore יהושע also, that He might set-apart the people of Yisrael with His own dom, suffered outside the gate. 13 Let us go forth therefore to Him outside the camp, bearing His reproach. 14 For we have no lasting city here, but we seek the one to come. 15 By Him therefore let us offer the sacrifice of tehilla to יהוה continually, that is, the fruit of our lips giving hodu to His Name. [11] 16 But to do tov and to share don't forget: for with such sacrifices יהוה is well pleased. 17 Listen to your spiritual leaders, and obey them: for they watch for your beings, as those that must give account to יהוה, that they may do it with simcha, and not with grief: for that is unprofitable for you. 18 Make tefillot for us: for we trust we have a tov conscience, in all things willing to live honestly. 19 But I ask you exceedingly to do this, that I may be

---

[1] Restoration and regathering of all the exiles into one set-apart congregation.
[2] According to Shemoth/Exodus 4:22-23, that firstborn congregation is eternally Yisrael. Let your part in Yisrael sink in deep.
[3] Departed justified spirits go to heaven, and the body and soul, or the being, goes into the dust waiting the day of resurrection.
[4] Only eternal matters and eternal things not created for corruption will survive the final shaking known as "the time of Yaakov's trouble."
[5] Written to Hebrews, so He must mean between both houses that have entered the Renewed Covenant.
[6] Non-Yisraelites (non-believers) or even heavenly malachim.

[7] That means He taught and kept Torah then. And had Yisrael as a bride then. Since He is the same forever, it is His followers who have changed for the worse into anti-Torah lifestyles and cultures, all the while professing Him as King.
[8] Strange, as in strangers, as in non-Torah teachings and customs.
[9] We are to be more preoccupied with spiritual matters than with foods, diets, herbs, and weight loss.
[10] Outside the camp in the east, facing west, where Golgotha was. For details see **Altar of Authority** at: http://store.yourarmstoisrael.org/Qstore/Qstore.cgi?CMD=011 &PROD=1065766783
[11] Without His true Name, the thanksgiving is not considered kosher.

restored to you sooner. 20 Now the Elohim of shalom, that brought again from the dead our Master יהושע, that Great Roei of the sheep, through the dom of the everlasting covenant, 21 Make you perfect in every tov mitzvah to do His will, working in you that which is well pleasing in His sight, through יהושע ha Moshiach; to whom be tifereth le-olam-va-ed. Amein.

22 And I beg you, brothers, allow for this word of exhortation: for I have written a letter to you in just a few words. 23 Know that our brother Timtheous has been set free; if he comes shortly, I will see you with him. 24 Salute all your spiritual leaders, and all the kidushim. The Yisraelites of Italy salute you. 25 Favor be with you all. Amein.

Kepha Aleph - First Peter
To The Believing Remnant Of Yisrael

1 Shimon Kepha, a sholiach of יהושע the Moshiach, to the pilgrims of the galut in Pontos, Galut-Yah, Kappadokia, Asia, and Bithunia,[1] 2 Chosen[2] according to the foreknowledge of Abba יהוה, and set-apart by the Ruach, for obedience[3] and sprinkling of the dom of יהושע the Moshiach: favor to you and shalom be multiplied. 3 Blessed be the Elohim and Abba of our Master יהושע the Moshiach, who according to His abundant rachamim has begotten us again to a living tikvah through the resurrection of יהושע the Moshiach from the dead, 4 To an inheritance incorruptible and undefiled and that does not fade away, reserved in the shamayim for you,[4] 5 Who are kept by the power of יהוה through emunah for salvation and deliverance ready to be revealed in the yamim acharonim. 6 In this you greatly gilah, though now for a little while, if need be, you have been burdened by various trials, 7 That the testing of your emunah, being much more precious than gold that perishes, though it is tested by fire, may be found to tehilla, honor, and tifereth at the revelation of יהושע the Moshiach, 8 Whom having not seen, you love. Though now you do not see Him, yet believing, you gilah with simcha unspeakable and full of tifereth, 9 Receiving the end of your emunah - the salvation of your beings. 10 Of this salvation the neviim have inquired and searched carefully, who prophesied of the favor that would come to you, 11 By searching to know what, or in what time frame, the Ruach of the Moshiach that was in them was indicating concerning Moshiach, when it testified beforehand of the sufferings of the Moshiach, and the esteem that would follow. 12 To them it was revealed that they weren't really serving themselves, but were ministering to us the things which now have been reported to you through those who have proclaimed the besarot to you by the Ruach HaKodesh sent from the shamayim; things which heavenly messengers desire to look into. 13 Therefore prepare the loins of your mind, be sober, and rest your tikvah fully upon the favor that is to be brought to you at the revelation of יהושע the Moshiach; 14 As obedient children,[5] not conforming yourselves to the former lusts, as in your ignorance; 15 But as He who called you is Set-Apart, you also be set-apart in all your conduct, 16 Because it is written, *Be set-apart, for I am Set-Apart.*[6] 17 And if you call on Abba, who without partiality shophets according to each one's mitzvot,[7] conduct yourselves throughout the time of your sojourning in fear; 18 Knowing that you were not redeemed with corruptible things, like silver or gold, from your futile spiritual conduct received by tradition from your ahvot, 19 But with the precious dom of the Moshiach, as of a Lamb without blemish and without spot. 20 He indeed was foreordained before the foundation of the olam, but was manifest in these last times for you 21 Who through Him believe in יהוה, who raised Him from the dead and gave Him tifereth, so that your emunah and tikvah are in יהוה. 22 Since you have cleansed your beings in obeying the emet[8]

---

[1] All areas of Yisraelite exile. The seven congregations of revelation in Asia Minor as well.
[2] Writing to the chosen people.
[3] Guarding Torah.
[4] A key reference to our spirit's reward in the heavens. Emunah in life in heaven with YHWH is originally a Hebraic concept, not a Greco-Roman one.
[5] Torah-keepers.
[6] Kepha applies a Scripture about Yisrael's priesthood in the First Covenant to Renewed Covenant Yisrael, since only Yisrael is ever called YHWH's priests.
[7] YHWH does take into account Torah faithfulness in believers' lives.
[8] Torah.

through the Ruach in sincere ahava of the brothers, love one another fervently with a clean lev,[1] 23 Having been born again, not of corruptible zera but incorruptible, through the word of יהוה which lives and abides le-olam-va-ed, 24 Because all flesh is as grass, and all the tifereth of man as the flower of the grass. The grass withers, and its flower falls away, 25 But the word of יהוה endures le-olam-va-ed. Now this is the word that by the besarot was proclaimed to you.

2 Having laid aside all evil, and all deceit, and hypocrisies, and envies, and all lashon hara,[2] 2 As newborn babes, desire the sincere milk of the word that you may grow by it: 3 If so be that you have tasted that the Master יהוה is tov. 4 To whom coming, as to a living Stone, disallowed indeed by men, but chosen of יהוה, and precious, 5 You also, as lively stones, are built up as a spiritual bayit,[3] a set-apart priesthood, to offer up spiritual sacrifices, acceptable to יהוה by יהושע the Moshiach.[4] 6 Therefore also it is contained in the Katav, *Behold, I lay in Tzion a chief corner stone, elect, precious: and he that believes on Him shall not be put to shame.*
7 To you therefore who believe He is precious: but to those who are disobedient, the Stone that the builders disallowed, the same is made the Rosh Pina, 8 And a Stone of stumbling, and a Rock of offence, even to them who stumble at the word, being disobedient: to which they also were appointed. 9 But you are a chosen generation, a royal priesthood, a set-apart nation,[5] and a peculiar people; that you should show forth the tehillot of Him who has called you out of darkness into His marvelous Light:[6] 10 Who in times past

were Lo-Ami-Not a People[7] but are now the people of יהוה: who were Lo-Ruchama – No-Mercy, but now have obtained rachamim.[8] 11 Dearly beloved, I beg you as strangers and sojourners in the olam hazeh, abstain from fleshly lusts, which war against the being; 12 Having your behavior honest among the gentiles:[9] that, when they speak against you as evildoers, they may by your mitzvot, which they shall behold, esteem יהוה in a future day of personal visitation. 13 Submit yourselves to every ordinance of man for יהוה's sake: whether it is to the melech, as supreme; 14 Or to governors, as to those that are sent by Him for the punishment of evildoers, and for the tehilla of those that do well. 15 For so is the will of יהוה, that with well doing[10] you may put to silence the ignorance of foolish men: 16 As free, and not using your liberty for a cloak of evil, but as the avadim of יהוה. 17 Honor all men. Love the brotherhood. Fear יהוה. Honor the melech.[11] 18 Avadim, be subject to your human masters with all fear; not only to the tov and gentle, but also to the crooked ones. 19 For this is true favor, if because of a tov conscience to יהוה, anyone endures with grief, or suffering wrongfully. 20 For what tifereth is it, if, when you are beaten for

---

[1] The bond of perfection that will hold all of believing Yisrael together.
[2] Against brethren.
[3] The House or Tabernacle of David restored.
[4] The calling of every Yisraelite.
[5] Yisrael is not just a mystical body but also a literal nation.
[6] Believers are not just individuals, but a nation. The nation of Yisrael regathered from exile.

[7] In times past, Ephraim Yisrael alone was called **Lo-Ami** by YHWH. Today the non-Jews in the exile who now believe in Yisrael's Moshiach, are called the former **Lo-Ami** or "Not My People" pronounced in Hosea 1:9 and Hosea 2:23. Kepha quotes Hosea directly and attributes these prophecies about the ten tribes as finding full fulfillment in the non-Jewish Yisraelite believers in the exile, who are coming to the emunah, in order to form a royal priesthood. This answers the question of whether Kepha knew about the two houses being restored.
[8] Kepha quotes Hosea 1:8 the **Lo-Ruchama** pronouncement over Ephraim or non-Jewish Yisrael. And he directly attributes it to the exiles of Pontos, Galut-Yah, and Asia etc., whom he calls the chosen people. Through Moshiach, the **Lo-Ruchama** exiles, become recipients of both mercy and compassion, as foretold in Hosea 2:23. It is most vital to see the direct connection between the actual prophecy and its fulfillment among the latter-day believing non-Jews. A fuller treatment is available at
http://yourarmstoisrael.org/Articles_new/restoration/?page=home&type=2
[9] Believers are called the chosen people or Yisrael, and the non-believers who walk in lust are referred to as gentiles, confirming that the term "saved gentile" or "believing gentile" is an oxymoron.
[10] Torah-keeping.
[11] The King Moshiach is honored for starting the end of our exile, when we truly love each other as equal heirs in Yisrael.

your own faults, you shall take it patiently? But if, when you do well, and still suffer for it, and you take it patiently, this is acceptable with יהוה. 21 For even to this were you called: because Moshiach also suffered for us, leaving us an example, that you should follow His steps: 22 Who did no sin, neither was deceit found in His mouth: 23 Who, when He was reviled, reviled not again; when He suffered, He threatened not; but committed Himself to Him that shophets righteously: 24 Who His own self carried our sins in His own body on the tree that we, being dead to sins, should live to tzedakah: by whose stripes you were healed.[1] 25 Because you were as sheep going astray; but now have made teshuvah[2] to the Shepherd and Guardian[3] of your beings.

3 Likewise, wives, be in subjection to your own husbands; that, if any obey not the word, they also may without the word be won by the behavior of the wives; 2 While they behold your pure behavior coupled with your fear of יהוה. 3 Whose adorning let it not be that outward adorning of plaiting the hair, and of wearing of gold, or of putting on of apparel; 4 But let it be the hidden man of the lev, that which is not corruptible, even the ornament of a meek and quiet ruach, which is in the sight of יהוה of great price.[4] 5 For after this manner in the former times the set-apart women also, who trusted in יהוה , adorned themselves, being in proper relationship to their own husbands: 6 Even as Sarah obeyed Avraham, calling him master: whose daughters you are, as long as you do

well, and are not frightened by them with any fear. 7 In like manner, you husbands, dwell with them according to da'at, giving honor to the wife, as to the weaker vessel, and as being heirs together of the favor of chayim; that your tefillot be not hindered. 8 Finally, be you all of an echad mind, having rachamim on each another, love as brothers, be tender of lev, be courteous: 9 Not rendering evil for evil, or railing for railing: on the contrary, brachot; knowing that you are called to this, that you should inherit the great bracha. 10 For he that will love chayim, and see tov days, let him refrain his tongue from lashon hara, and his lips that they speak no deceit: 11 Let him make teshuvah from evil, and do tov; let him seek shalom, and pursue it.[5] 12 For the eyes of the Master יהוה are over the tzadik, and His ears are open to their tefillot: but the face of the Master יהוה is against them that do evil. 13 And who is he that will harm you, if you are followers of that which is tov? 14 But and if you suffer for tzedakah's sake, favored are you: and be not afraid of their terror threats, neither be troubled;[6] 15 But set-apart the Master יהוה Elohim in your levim: and be ready always to give an answer to every man that asks you for a reason of the tikvah[7] that is in you with meekness and fear: 16 Having a tov conscience; that, when they speak lashon hara about you, like evildoers, they may be ashamed that falsely accuse your tov behavior in Moshiach. 17 For it is better, if the will of יהוה be so, that you suffer for well doing, rather than for evil doing. 18 For Moshiach also has once suffered for sins, the Tzadik for the unjust, that He might bring us to יהוה, being put to death in the flesh, but quickened by the Ruach: 19 Through which He also went and

---

[1] A promise given to Yisrael in Yeshayahu 53 and applied again to believers, because as Yisrael they are the heirs of that promise.
[2] "Returned" or **epistrepho** in Strong's Greek # 1994. These non-Jews were returning to faith, not coming for the first time, because they were the lost sheep.
[3] **Metatron** (Aramaic), the Guardian of Yisrael in the wilderness.
[4] Yisraelite women must not dress like the world. They ought to be fully covered, so other righteous men can focus in on YHWH alone. Dressing modestly is a very serious issue with YHWH, which no true woman of YHWH should take lightly. Scripture teaches us that the outward dress of a woman is indicative of the modesty in her heart towards YHWH.

[5] Many Yisraelites seek peace once or twice, but don't go on to pursue peace.
[6] A tov word for all Yisrael after 9/11/01.
[7] According to Paul, the reason he was in prison and the reason we suffer is for the hope of Yisrael, which is the end of the exile and the regathering of both houses of Yisrael back into His kingdom (Acts 28:20).

proclaimed to the ruachim in prison; [1] 20 Who before that time were disobedient, when the patience of **יהוה** waited in the days of Noach, while the ark was being prepared, when few, that is, eight beings were saved by mayim. 21 Whose true likeness and reality also saves us, even mikvah, [2] not the putting away of the filth of the flesh, but the answer of a tov conscience towards **יהוה** , by the resurrection of **יהושע** the Moshiach: 22 Who is gone into the shamayim, and is on the right hand of **יהוה**; heavenly messengers and authorities and powers being made subject to Him. [3]

4 Since then the Moshiach has suffered for us in the flesh, arm yourselves likewise with the same mind: for he that has suffered in the flesh has ceased from sin; 2 That he no longer should live the rest of his time in the flesh for the lusts of men, but for the will of **יהוה**. 3 For in past times in our chayim it sufficed us to have done the will of the gentiles, [4] when we walked in indecencies, lusts, drunkenness, orgies, wild parties, and detestable idolatries: [5] 4 They think it strange that you do not associate with them in that same excess of loose living, even speaking lashon hara about you: 5 Who shall give an account to Him that is ready to shophet the living and the dead. 6 For this reason was the besarot proclaimed also to them that are dead, that they might be judged as men in the flesh, but live according to **יהוה** in the Ruach. 7 But the end of all things is at hand: be therefore sober, and be attentive in tefillah. 8 And above all things have fervent ahava among yourselves: for ahava shall cover a

multitude of sins. 9 Be like mishpocha one to another without grumbling. 10 As every man has received a gift, [6] even so serve the same gift to another, as tov stewards of the manifold favor of **יהוה**. 11 If any man speaks, let him speak the oracles of **יהוה**; if any man serve, let him do it with the ability which **יהוה** gives: that in all things **יהוה** may be esteemed through **יהושע** the Moshiach, to whom be tehilla and the rule in Yisrael le-olam-va-ed. Amein. 12 Beloved, think it not strange concerning the fiery trials which are to test you, as though some strange thing has happened to you:13 But gilah, in the fact that you share Moshiach's sufferings; that, when His tiferet shall be revealed, you may be gilah also with exceeding simcha. 14 If you are reproached for the Name of Moshiach, [7] happy are you; for the Ruach of tiferet and of **יהוה** rests upon you: on their part He is evil spoken of, but on your part He is praised. 15 But let none of you suffer as a murderer, or as a thief, or as an evildoer, or as a busybody in other men's matters. 16 Yet if any man suffer as a Notzri in Yisrael, let him not be ashamed; but let him esteem **יהוה** in this matter. 17 For the time has come that Yom HaDin must begin in the Beth **יהוה**: and if it first begins with us, what shall be the end of them that obey not besarot of **יהוה**? [8] 18 And if the tzadikim barely are saved, where shall the wicked and the sinner appear? 19 So then let those that suffer according to the will of **יהוה** commit the keeping of their beings to Him in well doing, as to a faithful Creator.

5 Therefore the zachanim who are among you I exhort, who am also a zachan, and a witness of the sufferings of Moshiach, and also a partaker of the tifereth

---

[1] **Tartaros:** is a special place of the imprisoned spirits at the time of the flood (Genesis 6).
[2] Apparently mikvah is an important part of Yisrael's teshuvah. For some, the waters of Noach were a killing of filthy flesh, but for those chosen few, it was salvation. The same holds true today. If one is clean within, the mikvah still saves. If one is not clean within, it is just a cleansing flood on one's temporal flesh.
[3] Two shared powers, two shared thrones (Revelation 22:1 Daniel 7:9) in one YHWH-Echad.
[4] Kepha doesn't consider you a gentile and neither should you.
[5] Gentiles still do these things. Yisraelites have overcome them.

[6] A gift; not all gifts are tongues.
[7] Yah-shua.
[8] Great question. If many of the former faithful deny His divinity and His Messiahship, and we are then judged, what about the world? YHWH always cleanses Yisrael first (to obtain clean vessels for His use), before He tells them to go out and cleanse the world through the message of the **besarot**.

that shall be revealed: 2 Feed the flock of יהוה which is among you, taking the oversight of it, not by compulsion, but willingly; not for greed or dirty gain, but of a willing mind; 3 Neither as being masters over those trusted to you, but by being examples to the flock. 4 And when the Roei-HaGadol shall appear, you shall receive a keter of tifereth that fades not away.5 Likewise, you younger Yisraelites, submit to the shamashim. Yes, all of you are to be subject one to another, and be clothed with humility: for יהוה resists the proud, and gives favor to the humble. 6 Humble yourselves therefore under the mighty hand of יהוה, that He may exalt you in due time: 7 Casting all your anxiety upon Him; for He cares for you. 8 Be sober, be vigilant; because your enemy s.a.tan, as a roaring lion, walks around on earth, seeking whom he can devour:

9 Whom resist steadfast in the emunah, knowing that the same afflictions are experienced in your brothers that are all over the olam.[1] 10 But the Elohim of all favor, who has called us to His eternal tifereth by Moshiach יהושע, after that you have suffered a while, make you perfect, establish, strengthen, and settle you. 11 To Him be tifereth and rule over kol Yisrael le-olam-va-ed. Amein. 12 By Sila, a faithful brother to you, as I count him to be, I have written briefly, exhorting, and testifying that this is the true favor of יהוה by which you stand. 13 The congregation that is at Bavel,[2] elected together with you, salutes you; and so does Moshe-Marcus my son. 14 Greet one another with a kiss of ahava. Shalom be with you all that are in Moshiach יהושע. Amein.

---

[1] Scattered Yisrael and her exiles are being tested in the entire world.

[2] The Jewish emissary in a congregation among the dispersed Jews in Babylon (many left from the 580 BCE exile choosing not to return) is finishing his letter to the exiles of Ephraim Yisrael, also elected. We see one select house writing to the other select house, even as we see in the allegorical style of Second Yochanan.

כאפא ב

Kepha Bet - Second Peter
To the Believing Remnant of Yisrael

1 Shimon Kepha, an eved and a sholiach of יהושע ha Moshiach, to them that have obtained like precious emunah with us through the tzedakah of יהוה and our Savior יהושע ha Moshiach: 2 Favor and shalom be multiplied to you through the da'at of יהוה, and of יהושע our Master, 3 According as His divine power has given to us all things that pertain to chayim and Shabbat-guarding piety,[1] through the da'at of Him that has called us to tifereth and power: 4 By these are given to us exceeding great and precious promises: that by these you might be partakers of the divine nature, having escaped the corruption that is in the olam hazeh through lust. 5 And beside this, giving all diligence, add to your emunah power; and to power da'at; 6 And to da'at temperance; and to temperance patience; and to patience Shabbat-guarding piety; 7 And to Shabbat-guarding piety, brotherly kindness; and to brotherly kindness ahava. 8 For if these things be in you, and abound, they shall cause that you shall neither be inactive nor unfruitful in the da'at of our Master יהושע ha Moshiach. 9 But he that lacks these things is blind, and cannot see far off,[2] and has forgotten that he was purged from his old sins. 10 For this reason, brothers, give diligence to make your calling and election sure: for if you do these things, you shall never fall: 11 For in this manner an entrance shall be provided for you abundantly into the everlasting malchut[3] of our Master and Savior יהושע ha Moshiach. 12 And so I will not be negligent to put you always in remembrance of these things, though you know them, and are established in the present emet. 13 Yes, I think it is right, as long as I am in this earthly tent, to stir you up by a reminder; 14 Knowing that shortly I must put off my earthly tent, even as our Master יהושע ha Moshiach has shown me. 15 Moreover I will endeavor that you may be able after my death to have these things always as a reminder. 16 For we have not followed cunningly devised fables, when we made known to you the power and coming of our Master יהושע ha Moshiach, but were eyewitnesses of His majesty.[4] 17 For He received from Abba יהוה honor and tifereth, when there came a voice to Him from the excellent tifereth, *This is My beloved Son, in whom I am well pleased.* 18 And this voice that came from the shamayim we heard, when we were with Him in the Har-Kadosh. 19 We have also a more sure word of prophecy; to which you do well that you take heed, as to a Light that shines in a dark place, until the day dawns, and the Day Star rises in your levim: 20 Knowing this first that no prophesy of the Ketuvim is of any private interpretation.[5] 21 For the prophecy came not in ancient time by the will of man: but set-apart men of יהוה spoke as they were moved by the Ruach HaKodesh.

2 But there were false niviim also among the people, even as there shall be false morim among you, who privately shall bring in damnable heresies, even

---

[1] Strong's Greek # 2150 **eusebeia**, literally meaning "tov well-done Shabbat-keeping," is a key word used throughout the epistles of the Renewed Covenant. The root word is # 2152 Greek root **eusebia**. There is no Greek word for Shabbat for obvious reasons and in the Hebraic mind (i.e., that of the authors of the Scriptures), a Shabbat-keeper was one whose lifestyle was pious, or **eu sebio**, or into faithful Shabbat-keeping, and all that it entails. One could not be considered pious without being a Shabbat-keeper, and it was considered a basic test of piety then, as it is now. Therefore the translators did not transliterate this word, but translated it, and put the word "godly" or "godliness" in the text instead of the true meaning of a pious life bent toward Shabbat piety. The Restoration Scriptures has restored this key word in its correct context throughout the letters to Renewed Covenant Yisrael.
[2] One who does not walk in full Torah truth and a life of visible fruit in the Ruach, cannot see the Ephraimites who are "far off" in their ongoing return to our nation.
[3] The restored kingdom.
[4] According to the Torah requirement of two or three.
[5] It belongs to all Yisrael.

denying the Master that bought them,[1] and bring upon themselves swift destruction. 2 And many shall follow their paths of destruction; because of them the Halacha of Emet shall be evil spoken of. 3 And through greed shall they with fabricated words make merchandise of you: whose mishpat now is from a long time and lingers not, and their damnation does not slumber. 4 For if יהוה spared not the heavenly malachim that sinned, but cast them down to the Tartaros,[2] and delivered them into chains of darkness, to be reserved for mishpat; 5 And spared not the ancient olam-hazeh, but saved Noach the eighth person, a proclaimer of tzedakah, bringing in the flood upon the olam-hazeh of the wicked; 6 And turning the cities of Sedom and Amora into ashes condemned them with an overthrow, making them an example to those that after should live wickedly; 7 And delivered just Lot, oppressed with the filthy behavior of the wicked: 8 (For that tzadik dwelling among them, in seeing and hearing, tortured his tzadik being from day to day with their anti-Torah deeds;) 9 The Master יהוה knows how to deliver the Shabbat-guarding pious ones out of trials, and to reserve the unjust until Yom HaDin to be punished: 10 But mostly those that walk after the flesh in the lust of uncleanness, and despise government. Presumptuous are they, self-willed, they are not afraid to speak evil of the honored. 11 Whereas heavenly malachim, which are greater in power and might, bring not a slanderous accusation against them before יהוה. 12 But these, as natural brute beasts,[3] made to be taken and destroyed, speak evil of the things that they understand not;[4] and shall utterly perish in their own corruption; 13 And shall receive

the reward of unrighteousness, as they that count it pleasure to indulge in the daytime. Spots they are and blemishes, revelling themselves with their own deceptions while they celebrate their moeds with you; [5] 14 Having eyes full of adultery, that cannot cease from sin; enticing unstable beings, having a lev of greed they have exercised covetous practices; children under a curse: 15 Who have forsaken the tzadik derech, and have gone astray, following the way of Bilam the son of Be'or, who loved the wages of unrighteousness; 16 But was rebuked for his Torah-less-ness: the dumb donkey speaking with a man's voice forbad the madness of ha navi. 17 These are wells without mayim, clouds that are carried with a tempest; to whom the mist of darkness is reserved le-olam-va-ed. 18 For when they speak arrogant nonsense, they entice through the lusts of the flesh, through many indecencies, those that had indeed escaped from them who live in error. 19 While they promise them liberty, they themselves are the avadim of corruption: for of whom a man is overcome, of the same is he brought in bondage. 20 For if after they have escaped the pollutions of the olam hazeh through the da'at of the Master and Savior יהושע ha Moshiach, then they are again entangled therein, and overcome, the latter-end is worse with them than the beginning.[6] 21 For it had been better for them not to have known the halacha of tzedakah, than, after they have known it, to turn from the set-apart mitzvoth [7] delivered to them. 22 But it is happened to them according to the mishle emet, The dog has returned to its

---

[1] Prevalent in the ever-growing apostasy found in the messianic movement from where the final apostasy comes from. For more information see: **Is It Us?**
http://store.yourarmstoisrael.org/Qstore/Qstore.cgi?CMD=011&PROD=1065766902
[2] A special holding prison for unclean spirits before the flood.
[3] A metaphor for gentiles or heathen.
[4] Spiritual matters.

[5] More evidence that all believers kept YHWH's feasts.
[6] Yisrael is said to overcome, not be overcome. This confirms Ivrim 6:4 and the great dangers of falling away.
[7] Torah and Moshiach.

own vomit again; and the pig that was washed to her rolling in the mud.[1]

3 This second letter, beloved, I now write to you; in both letters I have stirred up your sincere minds by way of a reminder: 2 That you may be mindful of the words which were spoken before by the set-apart neviim, and by the directions from us the shlichim of the Master and Savior: 3 Knowing this first, that there shall come in the acharit hayamim scoffers, walking after their own lusts, 4 And saying, Where is the promise of His coming? For since the ahvot[2] fell asleep, all things continue as they were from the Bereshet of the creation. 5 For this they willingly are ignorant of this fact, that by the word of יהוה the shamayim were of old, and the earth standing out of the mayim and in the mayim: 6 Through which the olam that then was, being overflowed with mayim, perished: 7 But the shamayim and the earth, which are now, by the same word [3] are kept in store, reserved for the fire at the Yom HaDin and destruction of wicked men. 8 But, beloved, be not ignorant of this one thing, that one day is with Master יהוה as a thousand years, and a thousand years as one day. 9 The Master יהוה is not slack concerning His promise, as some men count slackness; but is longsuffering towards us, not willing that any should perish,[4] but that all should come to teshuvah. 10 But the day of the Master יהוה will come as a thief in the night; in which the shamayim shall pass away with a great noise, and the elements shall melt with fervent heat, the earth also and the works that are in it shall be burned up. 11 Seeing then that all these things shall be dissolved, what manner of persons should you be in all set-apart conduct and Shabbat-guarding piety, 12 Looking for and earnestly desiring the coming of the Yom יהוה, in which the shamayim being on fire shall be dissolved, and the elements shall melt with fervent heat! 13 Nevertheless we, according to His promise, look for renewed shamayim and a renewed olam, where tzedakah dwells. 14 So then, beloved, seeing that you look for such things, be diligent that you may be found by Him in shalom, without spot, and blameless. 15 And consider the long patience of our Master as salvation; even as our beloved brother Shaul also according to the chochmah given to him has written to you; 16 As also in all his letters, speaking in them of these things; in which some things are hard to understand, which they that are unlearned and unstable twist, as they do also the other Ketuvim, to their own destruction.[5] 17 You then, beloved ones, seeing you know these things[6] beforehand, beware lest you also, being led away with the delusion[7] of Torah-less-ness, fall from your own steadfastness.[8] 18 But grow in favor, and in the da'at of our Master and Savior יהושע ha Moshiach. To Him be tifereth both now and le-olam-va-ed. Amein.

---

[1] A warning to Ephraim that they are not to return to their old Shabbat-breaking lifestyle, since they are no longer pigs but Yisraelites.
[2] Of our people Yisrael.
[3] The same tested word that guaranteed creation and destruction earlier.
[4] In the coming fire.
[5] The way YHWH has designed Rav Shaul's letters, is that they are a bit difficult to grasp through a Greco-Roman mindset. As such, YHWH tests us to see if we will adopt a Hebrew mindset instead. Also by twisting the true pro-Torah meanings of Rav Shaul's letters, we see for ourselves how highly unstable and immature we still are. So rather than complain about them and ignore them, or remove them (thinking incorrectly that they somehow violate Torah), let us use them as a test of our spiritual progress, which is what they were designed for. Even many rabbis fall into this immature and dangerous category. YHWH Himself calls us through Kepha, to use Paul's letters as an ongoing test of our personal maturity and stability, in the things of Yahshua and His restored kingdom.
[6] About developing a mature attitude and understanding concerning Rav Shaul's letters.
[7] The delusion that Rav Shaul is anti-Torah puts one in a delusion of lawlessness, when that is not the message being delivered by YHWH through him. Many in those days were denying Yahshua as YHWH's Son, because of delusions and misconceptions about Paul. Peter steps forward to warn Torah-guarding Yisraelites, not to do likewise, and not to fall prey to such delusion.
[8] This is a lifelong pursuit.

Yochanan Alef - First John
To The Believing Remnant of Yisrael

1 That which was from the Bereshet, which we[1] have heard, which we have seen with our eyes, which we have looked upon, and our hands have handled, concerning the word of chayim. 2 And the chayim was manifested, and we have seen, and bear witness to, and declare to you that eternal chayim, that was with Abba and was manifested to us. 3 We announce to you that which we have seen and heard; that we declare to you, that you also may have chavurah with us; and truly our chavurah is with Abba and with His Son יהושע ha Moshiach. 4 And these things we write to you that your simcha may be full. 5 This is the message which we have heard from Him and declare to you, that יהוה is Light and in Him is no darkness at all. 6 If we say that we have chavurah with Him, and walk in darkness, we lie and do not practice the emet. 7 But if we walk in the Light as He is in the Light, we have chavurah with one another, [2] and the dom of יהושע ha Moshiach His Son cleanses us from all sin. 8 If we say that we have no sin, we deceive ourselves, and the emet is not in us. 9 If we confess our sins, He is faithful and just to forgive us our sins and to cleanse us from all unrighteousness. 10 If we say that we have not sinned, we make Him a liar, and His word is not in us.

2 My little children of Yisrael, these things I write to you, so that you may not sin. But if anyone sins, we have an Intercessor with Abba, יהושע ha Moshiach Ha-Tzadik. 2 And He Himself is the atonement offering for our sins, and not for ours only but also for the whole olam hazeh. [3] 3 Now by this we know that we know Him, if we guard His mitzvot. [4] 4 He who says, I know Him, and does not guard His mitzvot, is a liar, and the emet is not in him. [5] 5 But whoever keeps His word; truly the ahava of יהוה is perfected in him. By this we know that we are in Him. [6] 6 He who says he stays in Him, should himself also have his halacha just as He had His halacha. [7] 7 Brothers, I write no new mitzvah to you, but an old mitzvah, which you have had, from Bereshet. The old mitzvah is the word that you have heard from Bereshet.[8] 8 Again, a new mitzvah I write to you, which thing is emet in Him and in you, because the darkness is passing away, and the emet of Light is already shining. 9 He who says he is in the Light, and hates his brother, is in darkness until now.[9] 10 He who loves his brother stays in the Light, and there is no cause for stumbling in him. 11 But he who hates his brother is in darkness and has his halacha in darkness, and does not know where he is going, because the darkness has blinded his eyes. [10] 12 I write to you, little children, because your sins are forgiven for His Name's sake. 13 I write to you, ahvot, [11]

---

[3] This is not teaching globalism or salvation for every human, but rather displays the scope of His atonement as embracing all peoples and all Yisraelites in all nations.
[4] Keeping Torah is a true yet simple test of anyone claiming discipleship status and or Yisraelite citizenship.
[5] How true.
[6] Torah perfects Yisrael's ahava for Abba and Yahshua, and gives us assurance of salvation.
[7] An evangelical talk without Yahshua's Torah walk is a lie.
[8] Genesis.
[9] In light of the two houses of Yisrael being restored, the hatred among brothers refers to Yahudah and Ephraim. The Tov News is that in Yahshua's Light, there can be no more of that historical hatred.
[10] A key rebuke to all who deny Ephraim's existence as the latter-day gentiles, returning through Moshiach to join Yahudah in the Light.
[11] Proof that mature believers in Yisrael are called spiritual fathers. Not a violation of Matthew 23 since there, Yahshua rebukes man's bestowing of titles as opposed to YHWH doing the bestowing Himself.

---

[1] "We"; i.e., all 12 tribes symbolized by the 12 shlichim.
[2] Two-House reference.

because you have known Him who is from Bereshet. I write to you, young men, because you have overcome the wicked one. I write to you, little children, because you have come to know Abba. 14 I have written to you, ahvot, because you have known Him who is from the Bereshet. I have written to you, young men, because you are strong, and the word of יהוה stays in you, and you have overcome the wicked one. 15 Do not love the olam hazeh or the things in the olam hazeh. If anyone loves the olam hazeh, the ahava of Abba is not in him. 16 For all that is in the olam hazeh; the lust of the flesh, the lust of the eyes, and the pride of chayim; is not of Abba but is of the olam hazeh. 17 And the olam hazeh is passing away, and the lust of it; but he who does the will of יהוה lives le-olam-vaed. 18 Little children, it is the last hour; and as you have heard that the anti-Moshiach is coming, even now many anti-Moshiachs have come, by which we know that it is the final hour. 19 They went out from us, but they were not of us; for if they had been of us, they would have continued with us; but they went out that they might be made manifest, that none of them were of us.[1] 20 But you have an anointing from the Set-Apart One, and you know all things. 21 I have not written to you because you do not know the emet, but because you know it, and that no lie is of the emet.[2] 22 Who is a liar but he who denies that יהושע is ha Moshiach? He is anti-Moshiach who denies Abba and the Son.[3] 23 Whoever denies the Son does not have Abba either; but he who

acknowledges the Son has Abba also.[4] 24 As for you, let that stay in you which you have heard from Bereshet. If what you heard from Bereshet stays in you, you also will stay in the Son and in Abba.[5] 25 And this is the promise that He has promised us; eternal chayim.[6] 26 These things I have written to you concerning those who try to deceive you.[7] 27 But the anointing which you have received from Him stays in you, and you do not need that anyone teach you differently;[8] but as the same anointing teaches you concerning all emet things, and is emet, and is not a lie, and just as it has taught you, then you will stay in Him.[9] 28 And now, little children, stay in Him, so that when He appears, we may have confidence and not be ashamed before Him at His coming. 29 If you know that He is Tzadik, you know that everyone who practices tzedakah is born of Him.

3 Behold what manner of ahava Abba has bestowed on us, that we should be called b'nai יהוה ! Therefore the olam hazeh does not know us, because it did not know Him.[10] 2 Beloved, now we are b'nai יהוה; and it has not yet been revealed what we shall be, but we know that when He is revealed, we shall be like Him, for we shall see Him as He is. 3 And everyone who has this tikvah in Him purifies himself, just as He is pure. 4 Anyone who commits sin violates Torah, for sin is the transgression of the Torah.[11] 5 And you know that He was manifested to take away our sins,[12] and in Him there is no sin. 6 Whoever stays in

---

[1] Those who deny Yahshua, the Renewed Covenant, and the plurality of divinity. Specifically those who left the faith, not a particular local assembly; that is not considered leaving the faith.

[2] Yisraelite believers can guard themselves from apostasy in the here and now. Once a Yisraelite becomes a heretic by denying either the Father or His Son, Ivrim/Hebrews 6:4 states that it is no longer possible to return them to truth. See also Hebrews 10:29 and Second Peter 2:20-22.

[3] Those who teach unscriptural ideas of the Abba and Son being the same as opposed to two powers (not persons) of the One-Echad are called liars. This would also apply to those who bypass Yahshua entirely, claiming only the need for the Father as their Savior. That also is a devilish spirit.

[4] From this alone we see the "grave" errors of rabbinic Judaism.

[5] In other words, if you really understand Torah from Bereshet forward, you will always stay in the Son. Denying the Son displays one's ignorance of Torah and Torah justification.

[6] The promise of life eternal is conditional based on our ability to recognize that the Father is not the Son and the Son is not the Father, and by a trust in both.

[7] Such as anti-Yahshua missionaries.

[8] We all need solid Biblical teaching.

[9] If one listens to His teaching and not liars.

[10] Children of YHWH are reborn children of Yisrael.

[11] Therefore most believers who consider themselves "saints" are still sinning sinners. It may be a great time for a personal reality check, based on Scripture's definition of sin and sinful behavior.

[12] Take away our sins, not our Torah.

Him does not sin.[1] Whoever sins has neither seen Him nor known Him. 7 Little children, let no one deceive you. He who does tzedakah[2] is tzadik, just as He is Tzadik. 8 He who sins is of s.a.tan, for s.a.tan has sinned from Bereshet. For this purpose the Son of יהוה was manifested, that He might destroy the works of s.a.tan. 9 Whoever has been born of יהוה does not sin, for His Zera remains in him; and he cannot sin, because he has been born of יהוה.[3] 10 In this the b'nai יהוה and the children of s.a.tan are manifest: Whoever does not do tzedakah is not of יהוה, nor is he who does not love his brother.[4] 11 For this is the message that you heard from Bereshet, that we should love one another,[5] 12 Not as Qayin, who was of the wicked one, and murdered his brother. And why did he murder him? Because his works were evil and his brother's were tzadik. 13 Do not marvel, my brothers, if the olam hazeh hates you. 14 We know that we have passed from death to chayim, because we have ahava for the brothers. He who does not love his brother stays in death. 15 Whoever hates his brother is a murderer, and you know that no murderer has eternal chayim abiding in him. 16 By this we know ahava, because He laid down His chayim for us. And we also ought to lay down our chayim for our brothers.[6] 17 But whoever has this olam's necessities, and sees his brother in need, and shuts his lev from him, how does the ahava of יהוה live in him? 18 My little children let us not love in word or in tongue, but in mitzvot and in emet. 19 And by this we know that we are of the emet, and shall establish our levim before Him. 20 For if our lev condemns us, יהוה is greater than our lev, and knows all things. 21 Beloved, if our lev does not condemn us, we have confidence toward יהוה . 22 And whatever we ask we receive from Him, because we guard His mitzvoth, and do those things that are pleasing in His sight.[7] 23 And this is His great mitzvah: that we should believe on the Name[8] of His Son יהושע Ha Moshiach and love one another, as He gave us that mitzvah. 24 Now he who keeps His mitzvot stays in Him, and He in him. And by this we know that He stays in us, by the Ruach that He has given us.

4 Beloved, do not believe every ruach, but test all the ruachim, whether they are of יהוה ; because many false niviim have gone out into the olam hazeh. 2 By this you know the Ruach of יהוה: Every ruach that confesses that יהושע ha Moshiach has come in the flesh is of יהוה, 3 And every ruach that does not confess that יהושע ha Moshiach has come in the flesh is not of יהוה.[9] And this is the ruach of the anti-Moshiach, which you have heard was coming, and is now already in the olam hazeh. 4 You are of יהוה, little children, and have overcome them,[10] because He who is in you is greater than he who is in the olam hazeh. 5 They are of the olam-hazeh.[11] Therefore they speak as of the olam-hazeh, and the olam-hazeh hears them. 6 We are of יהוה . He who knows יהוה hears us; he who is not of יהוה does not hear us. By this we know the Ruach of emet and the ruach of error. 7 Beloved, let us love one another, for ahava is of יהוה; and everyone who has ahava is born of יהוה and knows יהוה. 8 He who does not have ahava does not know יהוה, for יהוה is Ahava. 9 In this the ahava of יהוה was manifested toward us; that יהוה has sent His only begotten Son into the olam hazeh, that we might live through Him. 10 In this is found that ahava, not that we loved יהוה, but that He loved

---

[1] As a lifestyle. All can fall into sin.
[2] Torah.
[3] See footnote for 1 John 3:4.
[4] Doing Torah and loving all Yisrael.
[5] Because His banner over both returning houses is ahava.
[6] Not by dying for them but by living for them.

[7] That and Moshiach is what identifies us as reborn Yisrael.
[8] Meaning that false names are not kosher for the believer.
[9] Very simple. Many false Moshiachs came in the flesh. What Yochanan speaks of here is a coming in the flesh from eternity past to this olam hazeh as stated in Micah 5:2. A warning to those who deny His pre-existence, and subsequent virgin birth. These denials were already problems back in the first century CE.
[10] False doctrines, anti-missionaries and lying spirits.
[11] Anti-Yahshua missionaries in all their variations.

us and sent His Son to be the atonement for our sins. 11 Beloved, if **יהוה** so loved us; we also should love one another.[1] 12 No one has seen **יהוה** at any time. If we love one another, **יהוה** stays in us, and His ahava has been perfected in us. 13 By this we know that we stay in Him, and He in us, because He has given us from His Ruach. 14 And we have seen and testify that the Abba has sent the Son as Savior of the olam-hazeh.[2] 15 Whoever confesses that **יהושע** is the Son of **יהוה**, **יהוה** stays in him, and he in **יהוה**.[3] 16 And we have known and believed the ahava that **יהוה** has for us. **יהוה** is Ahava, and he who stays in ahava, stays in **יהוה**, and **יהוה** in him. 17 Ahava has been perfected among us in this: that we may have boldness in the Yom HaDin; because as He is, so are we in this olam-hazeh.[4] 18 There is no fear in ahava; but perfect ahava casts out fear, because fear involves punishment. But he who fears punishment has not been made perfect in ahava. 19 We love Him because He first loved us.[5] 20 If someone says, I love **יהוה**, and hates his brother, he is a liar; for he who does not love his brother whom he has seen, how can he love **יהוה** whom he has not seen? 21 And this mitzvah we have from Him: that he who loves **יהוה** must love his brother also.

5 Everyone who believes that **יהושע** is Ha Moshiach is begotten of **יהוה**: and every one that loves Him that begat, loves Him also that is begotten of Him. 2 By this we know that we love the b'nai **יהוה**, when we love **יהוה**, and guard His mitzvot.[6] 3 For this is the ahava of **יהוה**, that we guard His mitzvot: and His mitzvot are not heavy and hard.[7] 4 For whoever is born of **יהוה** overcomes the olam-hazeh:

and this is the victory that overcomes[8] the olam-hazeh, even our emunah. 5 Who is he who overcomes the olam-hazeh, but he that believes that **יהושע** is the Son of **יהוה**? 6 This is He that came by mayim and dom, even **יהושע** Ha Moshiach; not by mayim only, but by mayim and dom.[9] And it is the Ruach that bears witness of this, because the Ruach is emet. 7 For there are three that bear witness: 8 The Ruach, and the mayim, and the dom: and these three agree as Echad. 9 If we receive the witness of men, the witness of **יהוה** is greater: for this is the witness of **יהוה** that He has testified concerning His Son. 10 He that believes on the Son of **יהוה** has the witness in himself: he that believes not **יהוה** has made Him a liar; because he believes not the witness that **יהוה** gave of His Son. 11 And this is the witness, that **יהוה** has given to us eternal chayim, and this chayim is in His Son. 12 He that has the Son has chayim; and he that has not the Son of **יהוה** has not chayim. 13 These things have I written unto you that believe on the Name of the Son of **יהוה**; that you may know that you have eternal chayim, and that you may believe on the Name of the Son of **יהוה**. 14 And this is the confidence that we have in Him, that, if we ask anything according to His will, He shema's us:[10] 15 And if we know that He shema's us, whatever we ask, we know that we have the petitions that we desired of Him. 16 If any man sees his brother sin a sin, which is not unto death, he shall ask, and He shall give him chayim for them that sin not unto death. There is a sin unto death: I do not say that he shall make tefillah for

---

[1] Two-House admonition.
[2] So much for those who believe that only the Abba is called Savior. Technically, He saves through the Son making Him the Savior-Designer, not the Savior-Executor.
[3] Staying in Him is harder than believing in Him.
[4] Torah guardians.
[5] Quite an understatement.
[6] Torah trains us in ahava.
[7] Despite what religion claims.

[8] Notice the frequency of the word yisra-els. "Yisrael" means "overcomer with El," and therefore those trusting in Moshiach are overcomers, or Yisrael in Hebrew.
[9] He shed dom and gushed water from His side.
[10] All answered prayer is based on His will, not on commands given to YHWH by the proud and arrogant through formulas.

it.[1] 17 All unrighteousness is sin: and there is a sin that is not unto death. 18 We know that whoever is born of יהוה sins not;[2] but he that is begotten of יהוה shomers himself, and the wicked one touches him not. 19 And we know that we are of יהוה, and that the whole olam-hazeh lies in the wicked one. 20 And we know that the Son of יהוה has come, and has given us binah, that we may know Him that is Emet, and we are in Him that is Emet, even in His Son יהושע ha Moshiach. He is the Elohim-Emet, and is eternal chayim. 21 B'nai Yisrael, guard yourselves [3] from idols. [4] Amein.

---

[1] Once someone truly falls away, they cannot be brought back, which is why we guard our emunah before it happens and why we don't pray for those who have turned their back on Moshiach Yahshua forever, as stated by the Ruach here. This may not be what we like to hear, but this is what Scripture teaches us here and in Ivrim/Hebrews 6:4. The purpose of this Scripture is to make sure all Yisraelites work overtime to guard their faith while they still have it, and while they still can. Of course, all things are still possible with YHWH on an exception basis, based on His mercy.
[2] As a lifestyle.

[3] Each individual.
[4] Yisrael warned again about their historic desire for idolatry.

Yochanan Bet - Second John
To Believing Remnant Yisrael

1 The zachen[1] to the chosen elect lady Kuira[2] and her children,[3] whom I love in the emet; and not I only, but also all they that have known the emet;[4] 2 For the emet's sake, which dwells in us, and shall be with us le-olam-va-ed.[5] 3 Favor be with you, rachamim, and shalom, from Abba, and from the Master יהושע the Moshiach, the Son of Abba, in emet and ahava. 4 I rejoiced greatly because I found your children having their halacha in emet,[6] as we have received the same commandment from the Abba.[7] 5 And now I beseech you, lady, [8] not as though I wrote a new commandment to you, but that which we had from Bereshet, [9] that we love one another.[10] 6 And this is ahava, that we have our halacha after His commandments. This is the commandment, as you have heard from Bereshet, that you should have your halacha in it.[11] 7 For many deceivers have entered into the olam hazeh, who confess not that יהושע the Moshiach has come in the flesh. This is a deceiver and an anti-Moshiach.[12]

8 Shomer yourselves, that we lose not those things for which we have worked and attained, but that we receive a full reward.[13] 9 Everyone committing Torah violation, by not staying in the teaching of the Moshiach, has not Elohim. He that stays in the teaching of the Moshiach has both the Abba and the Son.[14] 10 If anyone comes to you, and brings not this teaching,[15] receive him not into your house, neither offer him shalom:[16] 11 For he that greets him even with a shalom, is a partaker of his wicked works.[17] 12 Having many things to write to you, I would not write with paper and ink: but I trust to come to you, and speak panayim-el-panayim, that our simcha may be full.[18] 13 The children of your elect sister greet you. Amein.[19]

---

[1] John - representing the House of Yahudah.
[2] Kuria - representing the House of Ephraim.
[3] Ephraim's multitudes.
[4] The common bond that unites both houses in truth and love. Both Kuria and her children and all those with John.
[5] The truth of the kingdom restored which is an everlasting truth.
[6] Through Moshiach, Yahudah learns to rejoice greatly with Ephraim's return and position in the truth of restoration.
[7] Torah.
[8] Ephraim.
[9] Torah.
[10] That's what Moshiach came to do; to end the war between the two houses.
[11] YHWH wants us to walk in this truth of Yisrael's redemption and healing that dates back to the Book of Genesis.
[12] Brother Yahudah warning Ephraim not to become so caught up in being like Yahudah, that she gives up and forfeits her elect status as Moshiach's redeemed. Even in those days, just as today in larger numbers, many who are Ephraim have such a zeal for anything perceived to be Jewish, that they even go so far as denying Yahshua as YHWH manifested as the Son of YHWH. Note the tender care and affection of the elder sister.

[13] It is up to the individual Yisraelite to guard the truth of YHWH coming in the flesh as Yahshua. It's not only the job of the rabbi or spiritual leader. It's your job. Today, just as back then, Ephraimites and Yahudites are tossing in their elected lady status for a bowl of lentils and some orthodox tzitzit. For assistance in guarding what Moshiach has given His elect, see:
http://yourarmstoisrael.org/misc/?page=handbook&type=1.
[14] Let this verse be the clearest and most clarion of all warnings to both chosen sisters. Any doctrine that denies Yahshua as YHWH manifested in the flesh commits sin, and is a violator of the Torah they claim to trust. The actual denial of Yahshua by either house, especially returning Ephraim, results in that poor soul not having the Father either. John deals with many falling away, even as we do today. They were falling away from the true Nazarene faith, since there was no false church system to fall away from in those days.
[15] Plurality of divinity (Biblical monotheism), and the divinity of Moshiach.
[16] If someone is known as a denier of Yahshua and the truth that He is YHWH's Only begotten Son (and not just another Name for the Father, or any similar perversion), as a believer, we are forbidden to allow him entry or even to say a hearty "shalom." In this manner, both elected ladies will protect themselves. Of course Yahudah in the person of John, is seen as being the caring and older guardian of newly returning Ephraim.
[17] Very personal, plain and chilling.
[18] Just the way it should be; Yahudah and Ephraim face to face.
[19] One elect sister writing to another; a continuation of the two twisted sisters of Ezekiel 23, becoming straightened out in righteousness by the truth of Moshiach and His kingdom.

Yochanan Gimel - Third John

To Believing Remnant Yisrael

1 The zachen to the beloved Gaios, whom I love in the emet. 2 Beloved, I wish above all things that you may prosper and be in health, even as your chayim prospers. 3 For I rejoiced greatly, when the brothers came and testified of the emet that is in you even as you have your halacha in the emet. 4 I have no greater simcha than to shema that my children have their halacha in emet. 5 Beloved, do faithfully whatever you do for the brothers,[1] and for gerim;[2] 6 Who have borne witness of your ahava before the congregation: who if you send them forward worthy of Elohim, you shall do tov: 7 Because that for His Name's sake they went forth, taking nothing from the gentiles.[3] 8 Therefore we should receive such men, that we might be their fellow helpers for the emet. 9 I wrote to the congregation: but Diotrephes, who loves to be in the first position among them, receives us not.

10 So, if I come, I will remember his deeds which he does, gossiping against us with malicious words: and not content with that, neither does he himself receive the brothers, and forbids them that would, and casts them out of the congregation.[4] 11 Beloved, follow not that which is evil, but that which is tov. He that does tov is of יהוה: but he that does evil has not seen יהוה. 12 Demetrios has a tov report among all men, and about the emet itself: yes, and we also bear record of him; and you know that our witness is emet. 13 I have many things to write, but I will not with ink and pen write to you: 14 But I trust I shall shortly see you, and we shall speak panayim-el-panayim. Shalom be to you. Our chaverim greet you. Greet the chaverim by name.

---

[1] Biological Yisraelites.
[2] Believers not born as physical Yisraelites who have become Yisrael through Yahshua.
[3] A clear reference that believers are Yisraelites, not gentiles; and those who live like Yisrael are to do the work of YHWH to bring honor to His true Name staying set-apart from the pagans.

[4] Sheep stealing.

Yahudah - Jude
To Believing Remnant Yisrael

1 Yahudah, the eved of **יהושע** ha Moshiach, and brother of Yaakov, to them that are set-apart by Abba **יהוה**, and preserved in **יהושע** ha Moshiach, and called: 2 Rachamim to you, and shalom, and ahava, be multiplied. 3 Beloved, when I gave all diligence to write to you of the common salvation, it was needful for me to write to you, and exhort you that you should earnestly contend for the emunah which was once for all time delivered to the kidushim. 4 For there are certain men who slipped in secretly, who were before of old ordained to this condemnation, wicked men, turning the favor of our Elohim into indecency, and denying the only Master Elohim, and our Master **יהושע** ha Moshiach.[1] 5 I will therefore put you in remembrance, though you once knew this, how that the Master **יהוה**, having saved the people out of the land of Mitzrayim, afterward destroyed them that believed not. 6 And the heavenly malachim who kept not their first dwelling, but left their own dwelling, He has reserved in everlasting chains under darkness for the mishpat of the great Yom HaDin. 7 Even as Sedom and Amora, and the cities around them in like manner, giving themselves over to fornication, and going after strange flesh, are set forth as an example, suffering the mishpat of eternal fire. 8 Likewise also these filthy dreamers defile the flesh, reject authority, and speak evil of His tifereth. 9 Yet Mika-el the chief malach, when contending with the s.a.tan about the body of Moshe, did not bring against him a railing accusation, but said, the Master **יהוה** rebuke you. 10 But these speak evil of those things that they do not know: but what they know naturally, as unreasoning beasts,[2] in those things they corrupt themselves. 11 Woe to them! For they have gone in the way of Qayin, and ran with greed after the delusion of Bil'am for a reward, and perished in the rebellion of Qorach. 12 These are rocky reefs in your moadim of ahava to **יהוה**, when they feast[3] with you, feeding themselves without fear: clouds they are without mayim, carried about by the winds; trees whose fruit decays, twice dead,[4] plucked up by the roots; 13 Raging waves of the sea, foaming out their own shame; wandering cochavim, for whom is reserved the blackness of darkness le-olam-va-ed. 14 And Hanok also, the seventh from Adam, prophesied of these, saying, Behold, the Master **יהוה** comes with ten thousands of His kidushim,[5] 15 To execute mishpat upon all, and to convince all that are wicked among them of all their wicked deeds, which they have wickedly committed, and of all their harsh words which wicked sinners have spoken against Him. 16 These are murmurers, complainers, walking after their own lusts; and their mouth speaks proud words, being respecters of persons in order to seek gain. 17 But, beloved, remember the words which were spoken before by the shlichim of our Master-Yah **יהושע** ha Moshiach; 18 How that they told you there should be mockers in the yamim acharonim, who should walk after their own wicked lusts. 19 These are those who cause divisions, sensual, having not the Ruach. 20 But you, beloved, build yourselves up in your most set-apart emunah, making tefillot in the Ruach HaKodesh,[6] 21 Shomer yourselves in the ahava of Elohim, looking for the rachamim

---

[1] Denial of duality of powers.
[2] A metaphor for pagan gentiles.
[3] Moadim.
[4] Appointed to the second death.
[5] Book of Enoch.
[6] In His will, not only in tongues.

of our Master-Yah יהושע ha Moshiach to eternal chayim. 22 And have ruchama on some who doubt, making a difference: 23 And others save with fear, pulling them out of the fire; hating even a garment defiled by the things of the flesh. 24 Now to Him that is able to keep you from falling, and to present you blameless before the presence of His shechina with exceeding simcha, 25 To the only Elohim our Savior, through יהושע ha Moshiach our Master-Yah be tifereth and majesty, authority and power, both now and le-olam-va-ed. Amein.

רומיא

Romiyah - Romans
To The Believing Remnant Of Yisrael

1 Shaul, an eved of יהושע ha Moshiach, called to be a sholiach, set-apart to the besorah of יהוה, 2 Which He had promised before by His niviim in the set-apart Kituvim, 3 Regarding His Son יהושע ha Moshiach our Savior, who was born of the zera of David in the flesh; 4 And declared to be the Son of יהוה with power, according to the Ruach of set-apartness, by His resurrection from the dead: 5 By whom we have received unmerited favor and the calling of a sholiach, for obedience to the emunah that bears His Name among all nations.[1] 6 Among whom are you also the called of יהושע ha Moshiach: 7 To all that be in Romiyah,[2] beloved of יהוה, called to be kidushim: unmerited favor to you and shalom from יהוה our Abba, and the Savior יהושע ha Moshiach. 8 First, I thank my Elohim through יהושע ha Moshiach for you all, that your emunah is spoken of throughout the whole olam hazeh. 9 For יהוה is my witness, whom I serve with my ruach in the besorah of His Son, that without ceasing I make mention of you always in my tefillot; 10 Making requests, if at all possible that I might have a prosperous journey by the will of יהוה to come to you. 11 For I long to see you, that I may impart to you some spiritual gift, so that you may be established; 12 That is, that I may be comforted together with you by the mutual emunah both yours and mine. 13 Now I would not have you ignorant, brothers, that oftentimes I purposed to come to you, but was previously hindered, that I might have some fruit among you also, even as among other nations. 14 I am a debtor both to the Greeks, and to the foreigners;[3] both to the wise, and to the unwise. 15 So, as much as in me is, I am ready to proclaim the besorah to you that are at Romiyah also. 16 For I am not ashamed of the besorah of ha Moshiach: for it is the power of יהוה for salvation to every one that believes; to the Yahudi first, and also to the Greek and Aramean.[4] 17 For by the besorah is the tzedakah of יהוה revealed from emunah to emunah:[5] as it is written, The tzadik shall live by emunah.[6] 18 For the wrath of יהוה is revealed from the shamayim against all wickedness and all unrighteousness of men, who suppress the emet in unrighteousness; 19 Because that which could be known about יהוה is manifest in them; for יהוה has shown it to them.[7] 20 For the invisible things coming from Him from the creation of the olam hazeh are clearly seen, being understood by the things of creation, even His eternal power and divine nature; so that they are without excuse:[8] 21 Because that, when they knew יהוה, they esteemed Him not as Elohim, neither did they show hodu; but became vain in their imaginations, and

---

[1] The faith is to all nations in whom the seed of Yaakov is found. The word **ethnos** does not necessarily mean gentiles pagans and cannot be limited to such. Rav Shaul was an apostle to the nations, not the pagans in the nations.
[2] Correct Aramaic word.

[3] Notice the contrast between Greeks and foreigners. The Greeks of that day were known to be Yisraelites, as stated in First Maccabees 12. For more details see **The Greeks Of The Brit Chadasha** at:
http://store.yourarmstoisrael.org/Qstore/Qstore.cgi?CMD=011&PROD=000209
[4] **Arami** Strong's Hebrew # 761, using both the Greek and Aramaic versions. In either case, the Greeks were known to be Yisraelites, and the Arameans were the actual ancestors of the patriarchs of Yisrael as recorded in Torah. The seven congregations in Asia Minor in Revelation in the area of modern Turkey were also known areas of northward Ephraimite migration. Using both the Greek and Aramean here, the message to the Yisraelite nations along with Yahudah becomes even more evident.
[5] Emunah for the Jew and the Greek/Aramean, thus the two-fold, two-house pronouncement.
[6] Actually more accurately "the just shall live by His faith," or have the faith of Yahshua, not merely faith in Yahshua.
[7] Creation or the witness of creation.
[8] Creation testifies of YHWH in the absence of human messengers, so mankind has no excuse.

and their foolish lev was darkened. [1]
22 Claiming themselves to be wise, they became fools,[2] 23 And changed the tifereth of the incorruptible Elohim into an image made like corruptible man, such as birds, and four footed beasts, and other creeping things. 24 Therefore יהוה also gave them up to uncleanness through the lusts of their own levim, to dishonor their own bodies between themselves: 25 Who changed the emet of יהוה into a lie,[3] and worshipped and served the creation more than the Creator, baruch shemoh. 26 For this cause יהוה gave them up to vile affections: for even their women did change the natural sexual relations into that which is against nature: 27 And likewise also the men, leaving the natural sexual relationship of the woman, burned in their lust one toward another; men with men committing shameful acts, and receiving back in their own selves repayment for their error. 28 And even as they did not like to retain יהוה in their da'at, יהוה gave them over to a wasted mind, to do those things that are improper; 29 Being filled with all unrighteousness, fornication, wickedness, covetousness, maliciousness; full of envy, murder, fighting, deceit, evil thinking; whisperers, 30 Backbiters, haters of יהוה, despiteful, proud, boasters, inventors of evil things, disobedient to parents, 31 Without binah or discernment, covenant breakers, cold and without ahava, unforgiving, ruthless: 32 Who knowing the mishpat of יהוה, that those who commit such things are worthy of death, not only do the same, but also take pleasure in others that do them.

2 Therefore you are inexcusable, O man, whomever you are that judges: for in your mishpat of another, you condemn yourself; because you who judges do the same things. 2 But we are sure that the mishpat of יהוה is according to emet against those who commit such things. 3 And do you really think, O man, that shophet them who do such things, and do the same, that you shall escape the mishpat of יהוה? 4 Or do you stand against the riches of His rachamim and tolerance and patience; by not knowing that the rachamim of יהוה can lead you to teshuvah? 5 But after your hardness and unrepentant lev you are storing up for yourself great wrath against the Yom of His wrath and the revelation of the tzadik mishpat of יהוה; 6 Who will render to every man according to his mitzvot: [4] 7 To them who by continuing patiently in well doing seek for tifereth and honor and immortality, eternal chayim:[5] 8 But to those that are contentious against the emet, and do not obey the emet, but actually obey unrighteousness, will come indignation and wrath, 9 Tribulation and anguish, upon every being that does evil, upon the Yahudi first, and also upon the Greek and Aramean;[6] 10 But tifereth, honor, and shalom, to every man that does tov mitzvot, to the Yahudi first, and also to the Greek and Aramean:[7] 11 For there is no partiality with יהוה. 12 For as many as have sinned without Torah da'at shall also perish without Torah da'at: and as many as have sinned with Torah da'at shall be judged by that Torah da'at; 13 For not the hearers of Torah da'at are just before יהוה, but the doers of the Torah shall be tzadikim.[8] 14 For when the nations, which have not Torah da'at, do by nature the things contained in the Torah, these, having not the Torah da'at, have an inbred Torah for themselves: 15 Which shows the work of the Torah written on their levim, their conscience also bearing witness, and their

---

[1] Notice this cannot be speaking of pagans, since those being addressed once knew Him as YHWH and Savior, and became foolish and darkened. This again is another indication that Rav Shaul knew exactly who these people once were.
[2] At one time they were not foolish.
[3] The truth given to them in the past.

[4] Even believers will be held responsible for their actions after salvation.
[5] Man can attain immortality by Moshiach, but does not have it apart from Moshiach.
[6] This is a clear indication that both houses enter the Great Tribulation, as opposed to the nations flying to heaven in an unscriptural rapture.
[7] See note on Romans 1:16.
[8] Rav Shaul obviously taught Torah.

thoughts will either accuse or else excuse one another. 16 In the Yom when יהוה shall shophet the secrets of men[1] by יהושע ha Moshiach according to my besorah. 17 See, you are called a Yahudi, who trusts in the Torah, and make your boast in your Elohim, 18 And knows His will, and approve of the excellent things, that are being instructed in the Torah; 19 And are confident that you yourself are a guide to the spiritually blind, a light to those who are in darkness, 20 An instructor of the foolish, a rabbi of babies, who see themselves as the pattern of da'at and the emet that is in the Torah. 21 You therefore who teaches another, don't you also teach yourself? You that proclaim that a man should not steal, do you steal? 22 You that say a man should not commit adultery, do you commit adultery? You that hate idolatry, do you rob temples? 23 You that make your boast in the Torah, through breaking the Torah do you dishonor יהוה ? 24 For the Name of יהוה is blasphemed among the nations through you, as it is written.[2] 25 For brit-milah truly profits, if you keep the Torah: but if you are a breaker of the Torah, your brit-milah has been made akrobustia.[3][4] 26 Therefore if the

akrobustia[5] keep the tzedakah of the Torah, shall not his akrobustia be again counted for brit-milah?[6] 27 And shall not the akrobustia by nature, if they completely perform[7] the Torah, judge you, even though you follow the letter and the brit-milah, but still transgress the Torah? 28 For he is not a Yahudi, which is one outwardly; neither is that brit-milah, which is outward in the flesh: 29 But he is a Yahudi, who is one inwardly; and brit-milah is that of the lev, in the Ruach, and not in the letter; whose tehilla is not of men, but from יהוה.[8]

3 What advantage then has the Yahudi? Or what profit is there in brit-milah? 2 Much in every way: primarily, because they were the first to be entrusted with the oracles of יהוה and the first to believe in His word.[9] 3 For what if some did not believe? Shall their unbelief nullify emunah in יהוה? 4 By no means: yes, let יהוה be emet, but every man a liar; as it is written, That You might be proven tzadik by Your words, and triumph when You shophet. 5 But if our unrighteousness establishes the tzedakah of יהוה,[10] what shall we say? Is יהוה unrighteous when He inflicts wrath? I speak as a man. 6 By no means: for then how shall He shophet the olam hazeh? 7 For if the emet of יהוה has increased through my lying nature for His tiphereth; why am I still judged as a sinner? 8 And not rather - as we be slanderously reported, and as some affirm that we say - Let us do evil,

---

[1] A hint or **remez** to the men of Yisrael according to Ezekiel 34:31.
[2] This reference was given to the House of Yisrael or Ephraim, stating that because of their conduct, YHWH's Name was desecrated among all the nations. Clearly Rav Shaul is identifying the believers in Rome as the very same ones who desecrated the Name, as originally admonished in Ezekiel 36:20-23.
[3] Circumcision is tov after faith comes and after a slow progressive incorporation back into Torah life. To start a believer that has been wandering the nations for 2,700 years with circumcision, is the heresy proclaimed by the Jerusalem Council and rebuked by Rav Shaul in Galatians.
[4] The word for uncircumcision is **akrobustia,** meaning "tossed-away foreskins," or those once Yisrael, previously confirmed by circumcision. Those who have now tossed it all away, including their obedience to Torah, and their precious heritage to become mixed with and become one flesh with the nations. This term appears throughout the Brit Chadasha when speaking of returning Ephraim Yisrael. If these were true pagans in Rome, the Greek word to be used would be the word **aperitome** or the negation of the word **peritome** (Strong's Greek # 4061) for circumcision. This unique term gives us great insight that these were the lost sheep of Yisrael, the **akrobustia** and not the **apaeritome** or true pagans, that had never been circumcised. This word was put into the inspiration of scripture, to differentiate between the "tossed away foreskinned ones," as opposed to the never-circumcised pagans. Even Greek scholars are stumped by this unique and unusual term, and cannot explain how and

why it appears throughout scripture. But with a proper two-house understanding, it makes perfect sense.
[5] **Akrobustia** is always a reference to Ephraim Yisrael, who tossed away their rights and their benefits of belonging to the circumcision, or to the people of historic Yisrael.
[6] If returning Ephraim guards Torah, won't YHWH accept them back?
[7] Execute and perform; Strong's Greek #5055 **teleo.**
[8] This does not mean that the real Jews are now the Christians. It means that a real Jew will have both the heart circumcision and the flesh circumcision, and the **akrobustia** or returning Ephraimte will also have both. In this way all are equal in Yisrael having both the physical and spiritual circumcision in place. If either one is missing, then that person cannot be part of the true Yisrael of YHWH despite their boasting.
[9] Aramaic Peshitta.
[10] By Moshiach.

that tov may come?[1] Their condemnation for this is le-olam-va-ed.[2] 9 What then? Are we better them they? No, in no way: for we have before proven that the Yahudim and Greeks and Arameans, that they are all under sin; 10 As it is written, There is not one tzadik, no, not one: 11 There is none that understands, there is none that seeks after Elohim. 12 They are all gone out of the halacha; they have all together become worthless; there is none that does tov, no, not one. 13 Their throat is an open tomb; with their languages they have spoken deceit; the poison of asps is under their lips: 14 Whose mouths are full of cursing and bitterness: 15 Their feet are swift to shed dom: 16 Destruction and misery are in their halachot: 17 And the halacha of shalom have they not known: 18 There is no fear of Elohim before their eyes. 19 Now we know that what things the Torah says, it says to those who are living by Torah: that every mouth may be stopped, and all the olam hazeh may become guilty before **יהוה** .[3] 20 Therefore by the mitzvot of the Torah alone without heartfelt emunah there shall no flesh be justified in His sight: for by the Torah comes the da'at of sin. 21 But now the tzedakah of **יהוה** apart from the Torah is manifested, being witnessed by the Torah and the neviim;[4] 22 Even the tzedakah of **יהוה** which is by emunah on **יהושע** ha Moshiach to all and upon all them that believe: for there is no difference:[5] 23 For all have sinned, and come short of the tifereth of **יהוה**; 24 Being justified freely by His unmerited favor through the redemption that is in Moshiach **יהושע** : 25 Who **יהוה** has set forth to be a keporah

through emunah in His dom, to declare His tzedakah for the remission of sins that are past. 26 To declare, I say, at this time His tzedakah: that He might be tzadik, and the justifier of anyone who believes on **יהושע**. 27 Where is man's boasting then? It is worthless. By what Torah is man made tzadik? By mitzvot alone? No: but by the Torah of emunah. 28 Therefore we conclude that a man is made a tzadik by emunah apart from the mitzvot of the Torah. 29 Is He the Elohim of the Yahudim only? Is He not also Elohim of the nations? Yes, of course, of the nations also: 30 Since it is Elohim-Echad, who shall justify the brit-milah by emunah, and the akrobustia through emunah. 31 Do we then make void the Torah through personal emunah? By no means: actually we establish the Torah.[6]

4 What shall we say then about Avraham our abba,[7] who lived in the flesh, before Elohim called him? 2 For if Avraham were justified by mitzvot alone, he has something to boast about; but not before **יהוה**. 3 For what says the Ketuvim? Avraham believed **יהוה**, and it was counted to him for tzedakah.[8] 4 Now to him that performs mitzvoth alone is the reward not given as unmerited favor, but as a debt. 5 But to him that works not, but believes on Him that makes tzadik the unrighteous, his emunah is counted as tzedakah. 6 Even as David also described the blessed status of the man, to whom **יהוה** imputes tzedakah without mitzvot, 7 Saying, Blessed are they whose Torah-less-ness is forgiven, and whose sins are covered. 8 Blessed is the man to whom **יהוה** will not impute sin. 9 Does this blessed status come upon the brit-milah only, or also upon the akrobustia also? For we say that emunah was imputed to

---

[1] Rav Shaul never taught or allowed Torah-less living among his students; and those who accused him of such things were liars, as there remain many of those same liars today.
[2] A sober warning to all who insist that the Pauline epistles negate Torah for all believers.
[3] Both Torah-keepers and those who don't obey Torah are all guilty before YHWH.
[4] Faith in Moshiach spoken of in Torah, yet eternal life needs to be received apart from Torah by an open heart to His corporal reality.
[5] No difference between both houses and pagans. All need Yahshua and Torah, and all receive Yahshua apart from Torah, by an expression or exercise of personal trust.

[6] Will religion ever get this right? Faith in Yahshua brings us back home and establishes Torah.
[7] Father of all Yisraelite nations.
[8] He was saved by emunah in the promise of physical multiplicity. If he is our father of faith, we must believe exactly what he believed. That Yisrael would become more than the sand of the sea and more than the dust of the earth and spread out to many nations.

Avraham as tzedakah. 10 How was it then imputed? When he was in brit-milah, or in akrobustia? Not in brit-milah, but in akrobustia.[1] 11 And he received the sign of brit-milah, as a seal of the tzedakah of his emunah while he was yet akrobustia: that he might be the abba of all them that believe, though they may not be circumcised; that tzedakah might be imputed to them also: 12 And the abba of brit-milah to them who are not of the brit-milah only, but who also have their halacha in the steps of the emunah of our abba Avraham, which he had being yet akrobustia.[2] 13 For the promise, that he should be the heir of the olam hazeh, was not to Avraham, or to his zera, through the Torah, but through the tzedakah of his emunah. 14 For if those who are of the Torah alone are the heirs, emunah is made void, and the promise made of none effect: 15 Because the Torah works wrath: for where no Torah is, there is no transgression. 16 Therefore it is of emunah, that it might be by unmerited favor; to the end that the promise might be made certain to all the zera; not to that only which is of the Torah,[3]

but to those also who are of the emunah of Avraham; who is the abba of us all,[4] 17 As it is written, *I have made you an abba of many nations*, before Him whom he believed, even יהוה, who makes alive the dead, and calls those things which are not as though they were. 18 Who against tikvah believed in tikvah, that he might become the abba of many nations; according to that which was spoken, *so shall your zera be.*[5] 19 And being not weak in emunah, he considered not his own body almost dead, when he was about one hundred years old, neither the deadness of Sarah's womb: 20 He did not doubt the promise of יהוה through any unbelief; but was strong in emunah, giving tifereth to יהוה; 21 And being fully persuaded that, what He had promised, He was able also to perform.[6] 22 And therefore it was imputed to him for tzedakah. 23 Now it was not written for his sake alone, that it was imputed to him alone; 24 But for us also, to whom it shall be imputed, if we believe on Him that raised up יהושע our Savior from the dead; 25 Who was delivered for our willful transgressions, and was raised again for our justification.

5 Therefore being justified by emunah, we have shalom with יהוה through our Savior יהושע ha Moshiach: 2 By whom also we have access by this emunah into this unmerited favor in which we stand, and rejoice in the tikvah of the tifereth of יהוה. 3 And not only so, but we tifereth in tribulations also: knowing that tribulation works patience; 4 And patience, experience; and experience, tikvah: 5 And tikvah makes us bold; because the ahava of יהוה is shed abroad in our levim by the Ruach HaKodesh that is given to us. 6 For when we were yet without strength, in due time ha Moshiach died for the unrighteous.

---

[1] Some two-house critics use this single verse as some sort of alleged proof text, attempting to negate all other clear **akrobustia** references to Ephraim, by stating that Abraham was not an Ephraimite. They claim that because YHWH still called him **akrobustia**, then **akrobustia** cannot mean "tossed-away foreskins," but simply means "never uncircumcised." The problem with that is that through their ignorance, they forgot that as a descendant of Noah who knew right from wrong (i.e., Torah principles), paganism had set into the family – even into Abraham's father Terah and all in his house. Therefore from YHWH's point of view, Abraham's house had tossed away all the truth and set-apartness of Noach and his son Shem, and thereby the act or covenant of circumcision was tossed away by Abraham's house, only to again be renewed with Abraham. YHWH knowing that Abraham's ancestors had become **akrobustia**, applies this term to Abraham before the renewal of the rite, as opposed to using the word **aperitome**, which would have meant that all of Abraham's ancestors were pagans and had no Torah knowledge.
[2] He was the father through Isaac and Jacob of both houses. Of the Jews, by being the father of the circumcised and of the **akrobustia** Ephraimites who are returning, by being himself a returnee - a crossover - or one who **evers** as a returning Hebrew. In Hebrew, one who crosses over is called an **iberi**; **iberi** comes from the root word **eber** meaning "to cross over to truth from paganism." So both before and after his circumcision, he still fathered one of the two houses of Yisrael, despite one being circumcised and the other **akrobustia**, since he at one time was both. YHWH accepted him in both states, even as he accepts both houses in their wanderings and their unfaithfulness, in their return through Moshiach.
[3] Yahudah in first-century terms.

[4] Ephraim Yisrael who shares the patriarchs with Jewish Yisrael. This applies physically as well as spiritually.
[5] All of these chosen nations were to come through Jacob. Ishmael and Esav were never promised to birth nations but only a single great nation.
[6] Fill the world with his seed through Jacob.

7 Hardly for a tzadik will one die: yet maybe for a tov man some would even dare to die. 8 But יהוה manifested His ahava toward us, in that, while we were yet sinners, ha Moshiach died for us.[1] 9 Much more then, being made tzadik by His dom, we shall be saved from wrath through Him. 10 For if, when we were enemies, we were restored to יהוה[2] by the death of His Son, much more, being restored, shall we be saved by His chayim.[3] 11 And not only this, but we also simcha in יהוה through our Savior יהושע ha Moshiach, by whom we have now received the keporah. 12 Therefore, as by one man sin entered into the olam hazeh, and death by sin; and so death passed upon all men, for all have sinned: 13 For until the Torah sin was in the olam hazeh: but sin is not imputed when there is no Torah. 14 Nevertheless death reigned from Adam to Moshe, even over all those that had not sinned after the sin of Adam's transgression, who is the type of Him that was to come. 15 But the gift is not like the fall of man. For if through the fall of one man many died, how much more through the unmerited favor of יהוה, and His gift of unmerited favor, which also came by one Man, יהושע ha Moshiach, is increased for many more. 16 And the fall of man is not as great as is the gift: for the mishpat of one led to the condemnation of many, but the free gift of forgiveness from many offences, resulted in the justification of many more. 17 For if by one man's offence death reigned by one; much more they who receive overflowing unmerited favor and the gift of tzedakah shall reign in chayim by One, יהושע ha Moshiach. 18 Therefore as by the offence of one mishpat came upon all men to condemnation; even so by the tzedakah of One the free gift came upon all men for justification and victory to chayim. 19 For

as by one man's disobedience many were made sinners, so by the obedience of One shall many be made tzadik. 20 Moreover the Torah entered, that trespasses would officially increase. But where sin increased, unmerited favor did much more abundantly increase: 21 So that as sin has reigned to death, even so might unmerited favor reign through tzedakah to eternal chayim by יהושע ha Moshiach our Savior.

6 What shall we say then? Shall we continue in sin, so that unmerited favor may increase more than sin? 2 Let it not be! How shall we, that are dead to sin, live any longer in it? 3 Know you not, that as many of us as were immersed into יהושע ha Moshiach were immersed into His death? 4 Therefore we are buried with Him by mikvah into death: that like our Moshiach who was raised up from the dead by the tifereth of Abba, even so we also should have our halacha in a new chayim. 5 For if we have been planted together in the likeness of His death, we shall be also raised in the likeness of His resurrection: 6 Knowing this, that our old man[4] has been impaled with Him, that the body of sin might be destroyed, that from now on we should not serve sin. 7 For he that is dead is freed from serving sin. 8 Now if we are dead with ha Moshiach, we believe that we shall also live with Him: 9 Knowing that ha Moshiach being raised from the dead dies no more; death has no more dominion over Him. 10 For in that He died, He died to sin once: but in that He lives, He lives to יהוה. 11 In like manner consider yourself also to be dead indeed to sin, but alive to יהוה through יהושע ha Moshiach our Savior. 12 Let not sin therefore have rule in your mortal body, that you should obey it in its hurtful desires. 13 Neither yield your members as instruments of unrighteousness to sin: but yield yourselves to יהוה, as those that are alive from the dead, and your

---

[1] Note: Before we were circumcised as an act of obedience.
[2] Both houses were restored even while in sin and of course we as individuals as well.
[3] We are justified and redeemed by His dom, but we are saved by His life.

[4] Old nature and inclination toward evil called the **yetzer harah.**

members as instruments of tzedakah to יהוה. 14 For sin shall not have dominion over you: for you are not under the law of sin,[1] but under unmerited favor. 15 What then? Shall we sin again, because we are free from the law of sin, but under unmerited favor? Let it not be. 16 Know you not, that to whom you yield yourselves avadim to obey, His avadim you become; whether of sin to death, or of Torah obedience to tzedakah? 17 But יהוה be given hodu that you were the avadim of sin, but you have obeyed from the lev that form of instruction that was delivered to you. 18 Being then made free from sin, you became the avadim of tzedakah. 19 I speak like a man does because of the limitations of your comprehension in the flesh: for as you have yielded your body's members as avadim to uncleanness and to Torah-lessness; even so now yield your body's members as avadim to tzedakah and set-apartness. 20 For when you were the avadim of sin, you were free from tzedakah. 21 What fruit did you have then in those things that you are now ashamed of? For the end of those things is death. 22 But now being made free from sin, having become avadim to יהוה, you have your fruit to set-apartness, with the end result being everlasting chayim. 23 For the wages of sin is death, but the gift of יהוה is eternal chayim through יהושע ha Moshiach our Master.

7 Know you not, brothers, for I speak to them that know the Torah, how that the Torah has dominion over a man as long as he lives? 2 For the woman who has a husband is bound by the Torah to her husband so long as he lives; but if the husband is dead, she is loosed from the torah of her husband.[2] 3 So then if, while her husband lives, she is married to another man, she shall be called an adulteress: but if her husband is dead, she is free from the torah of her husband; so that she is not an adulteress, though she gets married to another man. 4 So you see, my brothers, you also have become dead to the torah of your husband by the body of ha Moshiach; that you should be married to another, even to Him who is raised from the dead, that we should bring forth fruit to יהוה.[3] 5 For when we were in the flesh, the passions of sins, through the Torah, did work in our members to bring forth fruit to death.[4] 6 But now we are delivered from the torah of our husband, that being dead to what we were held by; that we should serve in newness of Ruach, and not in the oldness of the letter. 7 What shall we say then? Is the Torah a sinful or sin-causing instrument? Let it not be! No, I had not known about sin, except by the Torah: for I had not known lust, except the Torah had said, *You shall not covet.* 8 But sin, by means of the commandment, provoked in me all manner of desire. For without the Torah sin was dead. 9 For I was alive without the Torah once:[5] but when the commandment came, sin revived, and I died. [6] 10 And the commandments, which were ordained to bring chayim, I found to bring death. 11 For sin, taking opportunity by the commandments, deceived me, and by it killed me. 12 Therefore the Torah is set-apart, and the mitzvoth are set-apart, and just, and tov. 13 Then was that which is tov made into death for me? Let it not be! But sin, that it might appear to be sin, working death in me by that which is tov; that sin by the mitzvoth might become exceedingly

---

[1] Not the Torah itself, but the "law of sin", which enslaved us, spoken of further in chapter 7:23, 25 and elsewhere.
[2] Not the entire Torah but only that aspect of the Torah.
[3] The death is not to the Torah, but to the particular ordinance of a man and his wife. Since Yisrael was the adulterous bride, YHWH couldn't take her back unless the husband died, and unless she was forgiven, which is what happened when Yahshua died. Yisrael was free from the marriage covenant, and YHWH in His love took her back after death, fulfilling both the law of an adulterous woman and the law of jealousy. For more details see:
http://store.yourarmstoisrael.org/Qstore/Qstore.cgi?CMD=011&PROD=000262
[4] The flesh sought loopholes to avoid Torah, and thus led to sin. The flesh and the Torah are a deadly combination, whereas the Torah and the Moshaich, bring life.
[5] Adam and Eve.
[6] All humanity.

sinful.[1] 14 For we know that the Torah is full of the Ruach: but I am of the flesh, sold under sin. 15 For I do not know what is going on: for what I purpose to do in obeying Torah, that I do not do; but what I hate in the olam hazeh, that I wind up doing. 16 If then I do that which I do not want to do, I consent to the Torah that it is tov.[2] 17 Now then it is no more I that do sinful deeds, but sin that dwells in my flesh. 18 For I know that in me that is, in my flesh, dwells no tov thing: for the choice and desire to do the right thing is present with me; but how to perform that which is tov evades me. 19 For the tov that I should do I do not: but the evil that I desire not, that I wind up doing. 20 Now if I do what I should not do, it is no more I that do it, but sin that dwells in me. 21 I find then an interesting Torah, that, when I would do tov by the Torah, evil is still present with me. 22 For I delight in the Torah of יהוה after the inward man: 23 But I see another torah in my members, warring against the Torah of my mind,[3] and bringing me into captivity to the torah of sin, which is in my members. 24 O wretched man that I am! Who shall deliver me from the body of this death?[4] 25 Hodu be to יהוה through יהושע ha Moshiach our Savior. So then with the mind I myself serve the Torah of יהוה, but with the flesh the torah of sin.

8 There is therefore now no condemnation to those who are in ha Moshiach יהושע, who have their halacha not after the flesh, but after the Ruach.

2 For the Torah of the Ruach of chayim in Moshiach יהושע has made me free from the torah of sin and death.[5] 3 For what the Torah could not do, because it was powerless regarding man's weak flesh, יהוה sending His own Son in the likeness of that same sinful flesh, and for sin, condemned all sin in man's flesh: 4 That the tzedakah of the Torah might be fulfilled in us, who have their halacha not after the flesh, but after the Ruach.[6] 5 For they that are after the flesh do mind the things of the flesh; but they that are after the Ruach the things of the Ruach. 6 For to be carnally minded is death; but to be spiritually minded is chayim and shalom. 7 Because the carnal mind is enmity against יהוה: for it is not subject to the Torah of יהוה, neither indeed can be.[7] 8 So then they that are in the flesh cannot please יהוה.[8] 9 But you are not in the flesh, but in the Ruach, if in fact the Ruach of יהוה dwells in you. Now if any man does not have the Ruach of ha Moshiach, he is none of His.[9] 10 And if ha Moshiach be in you, the body is dead because of sin; but the Ruach is chayim because of tzedakah. 11 But if the Ruach of Him that raised up יהושע from the dead lives in you, He that raised up ha Moshiach from the dead shall also bring chayim to your mortal bodies by His Ruach that dwells in you. 12 Therefore, brothers, we are debtors, not to the flesh, to live after the flesh and its torah. 13 For if you live after the flesh, you shall die: but if you allow the Ruach to mortify the deeds and desires of your body, you shall live. 14 For as many as are led by the Ruach of יהוה, they are the sons of יהוה. 15 For you have not received the Ruach of bondage again to fear, but you have received the Ruach of adoption,

---

[1] It comes down to this. The Torah and the flesh are a deadly combination, for the flesh seeks violation and loopholes. The Spirit and Moshiach in us seeks obedience not loopholes, and as such the Torah appeals to the flesh until that flesh is destroyed by Moshiach, and thus Torah can become helpful and a blessing again. So YHWH's challenge was removing us from our fallen condition – not removing the Torah from fallen man.
[2] Therefore the sin nature needs to be impaled – not the set-apart Torah itself.
[3] The battle is between the Torah in his heart and mind, versus the law of sin and death in his flesh. The battle is between these two factors, not between law and unmerited favor, since walking in Torah is a life full of unmerited favor, and walking in unmerited favor is a life full of laws.
[4] He cries out for deliverance from the wretched body, not the "wretched Torah" as some have tried to teach.

[5] Contrast between true versus evil torah of sin.
[6] Walking in the Ruach will cause all believers to obey Torah.
[7] The carnal mind is the mind of the flesh.
[8] Because people in the flesh cannot be in obedience to Torah, unlike those in the Ruach.
[9] He is none of His and cannot follow Torah.

whereby we cry, Abba, Abba. [1] 16 The Ruach itself bears witness with our Ruach, that we are b'nai יהוה: 17 And if children, then heirs; heirs of יהוה, and joint-heirs with ha Moshiach; so that since we suffer with Him, we will also be esteemed together. 18 For I'm sure that the sufferings of this present time are not worthy to be compared with the tifereth that shall be revealed in us. 19 For the intense expectation of all creation waits for the manifestation of the sons of יהוה. 20 For creation was made subject to vanity, not willingly or originally, but by reason of Him who has subjected creation to wait in tikvah, 21 Because the creation itself also shall be delivered from the bondage of corruption into the beautiful liberty of the b'nai יהוה. 22 For we know that all of creation groans and travails in pain together until now. 23 And not only creation, but we ourselves, who have the bikkurim of the Ruach, even we ourselves groan within ourselves, waiting for the adoption, specifically, the redemption of our body. 24 For we are saved by tikvah: but tikvah that is seen is not tikvah: for what a man actually sees, he does not need to have tikvah for! 25 But if we have tikvah for what we do not yet see, then with patience we willingly wait for it. 26 Likewise the Ruach also helps our weaknesses: for we know not what we should make tefillah for as we should: but the Ruach makes tefillah for us with groanings that cannot be described. 27 And He that searches the levim knows what is the mind of the Ruach, because the Ruach makes tefillah for the kidushim according to the will of יהוה. 28 And we know that all things work together for tov to them that ahava יהוה, to them who are the called[2] according to His purpose. 29 For whom He did foreknow, He

also did predestinate to be conformed to the image of His Son, that He might be the Bachor among many Yisraelite brothers. [3] 30 Moreover whom He did predestine, those He also called: and whom He called, those He also justified: and whom He justified, those He also esteemed. 31 What shall we then say to these things? If יהוה is for us, who can be against us? 32 He that spared not His own Son, but delivered Him up for us all, how shall He not with Him also freely give us all things? 33 Can anyone bring any charge against יהוה's chosen people? It is יהוה that makes us tzedakah. 34 Who is the only One that could condemn His chosen people? It is ha Moshiach who died, yes. But instead of condemning us, He has risen, to the right hand of יהוה, and He now makes intercession for us.[4] 35 Who then shall separate us from the ahava of ha Moshiach? Shall tribulation, or distress, or persecution, or famine, or nakedness, or peril, or sword? 36 As it is written, For your sake we are killed all day long; we are counted as sheep for the slaughter. [5] 37 No, in all these things we are more than conquerors through Him that loved us. 38 For I am persuaded, that neither death, nor chayim, nor heavenly malachim, nor principalities, nor powers, nor things present, nor things to come, 39 Nor height, nor depth, nor any other creation, shall be able to separate us from the ahava of יהוה, which is in Moshiach יהושע our Savior.

9 I say the truth in ha Moshiach, I lie not, my conscience also bearing me witness in the Ruach, HaKodesh 2 That I have great heaviness and continual sorrow in my lev. 3 For if it were possible I myself would wish to be banished from ha Moshiach for my brothers, my kinsmen

---

[1] Every human needs adoption into YHWH's family including Yahudah, and as such we become the Yisrael of YHWH, crying to Abba through Yahshua, and even our speech and lifestyle resemble that of the Hebrew speaker. Notice what doesn't come out from our mouth is false titles and substitutes.
[2] The chosen people in every sense of the phrase.

[3] YHWH's plan for all Yisrael is to be one people, all being brothers, unlike the gentiles whose tier systems are sad and infamous.
[4] Meaning how can He condemn us, when He's busy helping and praying for us.
[5] A quote from Eliyahu about Yisrael's leaders being killed. This is further evidence that those being persecuted for Moshiach in Rav Shaul's day were from the same nation as the ones being slaughtered in Eliyahu's day.

according to the flesh: [1] 4 Who are Yisraelites; to whom pertains the adoption, and the tifereth, and the covenants, and the giving of the Torah, and the worship, and the promises; 5 Who are the ahvot, from whom ha Moshiach came in the flesh, who is the Elohim over all, **יהוה** the blessed One le-olam va-ed. 6 Not as though the word of **יהוה** has failed in Yisrael. For they are not all still Yisrael, who are from Yisrael: [2] 7 Neither, because they are the zera of Avraham, are they all b'nai Yisrael: but, *In Yitzchak shall your zera be called.*[3] [4] 8 That is, those who are children of the flesh, these are not the b'nai **יהוה**: but the b'nai-brit are counted as the zera.[5] 9 For this is the word of promise, *At this time will I come, and Rivkah shall have a son.* 10 And not only this; but when Rivkah also had conceived by one, even by our abba Yitzchak; 11 For the children being not yet born, neither having done any tov or evil, that the purpose of **יהוה** according to choice might stand, not of works, but of Him that does the calling; 12 It was said to her, *The older boy shall serve the younger.*[6] 13 As it is written, *Yaakov have I loved, but Esav have I hated.* 14 What shall we say

then? Is there unrighteousness with **יהוה**? Let it not be! 15 For He says to Moshe, *I will have rachamim on whom I will have rachamim, and I will have ruchama on whom I will have ruchama.* 16 So then it is not within reach of him that wishes, nor of him that strives in the flesh to be Yisrael, but of **יהוה** that shows rachamim. 17 For the Katav says to Pharaoh, *Even for this same purpose have I raised you up, that I might show My power in you, and that My Name might be declared throughout all the earth.*[7] 18 Therefore He has rachamim on whom He will have rachamim, and He hardens the levim of those He does not choose. 19 You might say then to me, Why does He find fault with some that He does not choose? For who has resisted His will? 20 No but, O man, who are you that replies and talks back to **יהוה**? Shall the thing formed say to Him that formed it, Why have you made me this way? 21 Does not the potter have power over the clay, from the same lump to make one vessel to honor, and another to dishonor?[8] 22 What if **יהוה**, willing to show His wrath, and to make His power known, endured with much patience the vessels of wrath prepared for destruction:[9] 23 And that He might make known the riches of His tifereth on the vessels of rachamim, that He had prepared beforehand for tifereth,[10] 24 Even us, whom He has called, not of the Yahudim only, but also of the nations?[11] 25 As He says also in Hoshea, *I will call them My People-Ami, who were not My People-Lo-Ami; and will call her Ruchamah, who were Lo-*

---

[1] Jewish Yisrael or Bet Yahudah.
[2] One of the most misquoted and misunderstood verses used even by haters of Jewish Yisrael. It simply means that some Yahudim did not receive the living Word, but there are other parts of Yisrael that have, where the word has taken hold such as in non-Jewish or Ephraim Yisrael. Moreover, being born biological Yisrael, is just step one in a two-step process that must be followed up by the new birth. So the expression "not all Yisrael are Yisrael," applies to anyone who may be biological Yisrael but has not been regenerated by the Ruach HaKodesh.
[3] First Jewish Yisrael in order to be Yisrael must become like Isaac. Isaac was a regenerated individual in covenant relationship with YHWH the chosen offspring of Abraham. We see this confirmed in Galatians 4:28. So then Yisrael as a nation cannot be divided along the lines of spiritual or physical Yisrael, since unless one can claim both physical birth and spiritual rebirth, one may be a biological Yisraelite like those in Yahudah, and yet not be regenerated like Isaac was.
[4] Take note: Being a descendant of Abraham does not mean someone is a physical Yisraelite. Rather physical Yisraelite descent must be found to be through Isaac and Jacob. Moreover, the Ishmaelites cannot be biological Yisrael, though the door is open for them to join and dwell with Yisrael, at which point after being born again they are to be considered Yisrael both physically and spiritually.
[5] As stated, the Yisrael of YHWH is both physical and spiritual Yisrael, and if one is merely physical Yisrael, they cannot be like Isaac, a child of promise. This applies equally to both houses.
[6] Yisrael called to be the head and not the tail.

[7] When YHWH calls His Yisrael, it is a display of choice not human will; and moreover it is for the purpose of representing all that He is, including His Name YHWH.
[8] Note that the lump is the same, from which both Jews and non-Jews come. That is the lump of the seed of Yaakov filling all nations.
[9] The vessels of wrath were Ephraim Yisrael, with whom YHWH has shown extraordinary patience.
[10] Both Yahudah and Ephraim.
[11] Both houses have a redeemed remnant prepared to be vessels of honor.

Ruchama.[1] 26 And it shall come to pass, that in the place where it was said to them, Ye are not My People-Lo Ami; there shall they be called children of the living Elohim.[2] 27 Yeshayahu also cries on behalf of Yisrael, Though the number of b'nai Yisrael be as the sand of the sea; only a remnant shall be saved:[3] 28 For He will finish the work, and cut it short in tzedakah: because a short work will the Master יהוה make upon the earth.[4] 29 And as Yeshayahu said before, *Except the Master יהוה Tzevaoth had left us a zera, we had been as Sedom, and been made like Amora.* 30 What shall we say then? That the nations, who followed not after the Torah of tzedakah, have attained to tzedakah, even the tzedakah that comes by emunah. 31 But Yisrael,[5] which followed after the Torah of tzedakah, has not attained to the goal of the Torah of tzedakah. 32 Why not? Because they sought it not by emunah, but as it were by the mitzvot of the Torah alone. For they stumbled at that Stumbling Stone; 33 As it is written, *See, I lay in Tzion a Stumbling*

Stone and Rock of Offence: and whoever believes on Him shall not be ashamed.[6]

10 Yisraelite brothers, my lev's desire and tefillah to יהוה for Yisrael is, that they might be saved.[7] 2 For I bear them record that they have a zeal for יהוה, but not according to da'at. 3 For they being ignorant of יהוה's tzedakah, go about to establish their own tzedakah,[8] have not submitted themselves to the tzedakah of יהוה. 4 For ha Moshiach is the actual goal of the Torah for an eternal tzadik standing to everyone that believes. 5 For Moshe describes the tzedakah that comes from the Torah: That the man who does those things shall live by them.[9] 6 But the tzedakah that is of emunah speaks in this manner; Say not in your lev, Who shall ascend into the shamayim? That is, to bring ha Moshiach down from above: 7 Or, Who shall descend into the deep? That is, to bring up ha Moshiach again from the dead. 8 But what does Torah actually say? The word is near you, even in your mouth, and in your lev: that is, the word of emunah, which we proclaim;[10] 9 That if you shall confess with your mouth the Master יהושע, and shall believe in your lev that יהוה has raised Him from the dead, you shall be saved.[11] 10 For with the lev man believes to tzedakah; and with the mouth confession is made to Yahshua. 11 For the Katav says, *Whoever believes on Him shall not be ashamed.*

---

[1] Rav Shaul makes a direct reference to the non-Jewish believers coming to Moshiach being the very northern exiles spoken about by Hosea in chapter one. Hosea was never sent to gentiles. As such, Rav Shaul continues to unravel the mystery of the identity of those responding from the nations. Note also the contextual connection between the nations being favored in verse 24, and the fact that Hosea spoke of these exact same people in verse 25, thus establishing a direct connection between the latter-day -nations, and the Ephraimites of Hosea chapter 1 verses 8-9, and chapter 2 verse 23.

[2] From Hosea 1:10, this is still speaking of the nations, those who were the former Lo-Ami not My people, the exact same people who will supernaturally appear in the end times as the "children of the living Elohim". Again the key connection is the word "them." "Them" refers to the 10 tribes of the north, and the word "they" (the same people) refers to their end-time restoration as YHWH's acceptable children from non Jewish-Yisrael.

[3] Isaiah 1:9: From all the billions of Yisraelites, Isaiah sees that only a remnant from each house will be saved, and come to eternal life as Yahshua takes those two remnant peoples and makes them one in His hand. In this understanding, Isaiah is greatly distressed, as are many quickened Yisraelites today, who can't understand why their families won't receive Moshiach and live an Yisraelite lifestyle.

[4] The restoration and awakening of both houses will be a complete finished work by Moshiach's redemption. Yet more than that, it will only be in operation for a limited time from 1996 CE until Yahshua's return and the final ingathering of the nation. See:

http://yourarmstoisrael.org/misc/charts/?page=ephraim_and_j udahs_punishment

[5] In context, a clear reference to Jewish Yisrael.

[6] Many in Jewish and non-Jewish Yisrael stumbled over Moshiach as found in Isaiah 8:14.

[7] For all Yisrael, but the upcoming verses deal with Jewish Yisrael in context.

[8] "Works of the law."

[9] One of the weightier matters is faith in Moshiach. If, Jewish Yisrael is going to live by Torah, they also should accept the aspect of the Torah that will lead them to a right standing with YHWH.

[10] Deuteronomy 30:12-14: Rav Shaul is actually saying that the word that we preach is what the Torah aimed at, which is to take the same word given for all times to Yisrael, and by faith in Moshiach, place it in the hearts and mouths of regathered Yisrael. This is a direct statement showing that Rav Shaul is merely preaching the internalization of Torah rather than its abrogation.

[11] Saved from judgment, death, Lake of Fire, the grave, sin, bondage, and slavery, and being in discipleship to s.a.tan. Yisrael must never ridicule the concept of personal salvation as many have done, wrongly thinking it to be a non-Hebraic concept.

12 For there is no difference between the Yahudi and the Greek or the Aramean: for the same Master **יהוה** is over all and is rich in rachamim to all that call upon Him. 13 *For whoever shall call upon the Name of the Master* **יהוה** *shall be saved.*[1] 14 How then shall they call on Him in whom they have not believed? And how shall they believe in Him of whom they have not heard? And how shall they shema without a proclaimer? 15 And how shall they proclaim, except they be sent? As it is written, How beautiful are the feet of them that proclaim the besorah of shalom, and bring besorah of tov things! 16 But they have not all obeyed the besorah. For Yeshayahu says, **יהוה**, who has believed our report? 17 So then emunah comes by hearing, and hearing by the word of **יהוה**. 18 But I say, Have they not heard? Yes truly, their sound went into all the earth, and their words to the ends of the olam hazeh. 19 But I say, Did not Yisrael know? First Moshe says, I will provoke you to jealousy by them that are not a people at all, a Lo-Ami, and by this foolish nation I will anger you.[2] 20 But Yeshayahu is very bold, and says, *I was found by them that sought Me not; I was made manifest to them that asked not after Me.*[3] 21 But to Yisrael[4] He says, *All day long I have stretched forth My hands to a disobedient and quarrelsome people.*

11 I say then, did **יהוה** cast away His people? By no means. For I also am a Yisraelite, of the zera of Avraham, of the tribe of Benyamin.[5] 2 **יהוה** has not cast away His people whom He knew and chose beforehand. Don't you know what the

Katav says of Eliyahu? How He even pleads with **יהוה** against Yisrael, saying, 3 **יהוה**, they have killed Your niviim, and overthrown Your altars; and I am left alone, and they seek my chayim. 4 But what says the word of **יהוה** to him? *I have reserved for Myself seven thousand men, who have not bowed the knee to the image of Baal.* 5 Even so then at this present time also there is a remnant according to His election by unmerited favor.[6] 6 And if by unmerited favor, then is it no more of mitzvot: otherwise unmerited favor is not unmerited favor. But if it is of mitzvot, then is it no more unmerited favor: unless work is not work. 7 What then? Yisrael has not obtained that which they seek for; but the chosen remnant has obtained it, and the rest were blinded.[7] 8 According as it is written, **יהוה** has given them the ruach of slumber, eyes that they should not see, and ears that they should not shema; to this day. 9 And David says, Let their table be made a snare, and a trap, and a stumbling-block, and a reward to them: 10 Let their eyes become darkened, that they may not see, and be hunchbacked always.[8] 11 I say then, have they stumbled that they should fall le-olam-va-ed? Let it not be: but rather through their fall salvation has gone out to the nations, for to provoke them to jealousy.[9] 12 Now if their temporal fall brought riches to the olam hazeh, and the diminishing of their believing numbers brought riches to the nations; how much more the fullness of their return from blindness? 13 For I speak to you nations, because I am the sholiach to the nations, I magnify my work by explaining this: 14 If by any means I may provoke to emulation those who are of my

---

[1] Make your past calling and election sure and secure, by calling on YHWH, and not on any other abominable titles.
[2] Moshe in Deuteronomy 32:21 spoke of a part of Yisrael that would become a foolish Lo-Ami, and that would wind up provoking the rest of the nation to jealousy. Of course that speaks of Ephraim provoking Yahudah.
[3] Isaiah 65:11: a reference to Ephraim of the nations, seeking YHWH as opposed to Jewish Yisrael that in part believes that loving the true Moshiach, is not a critical part of Torah zeal.
[4] Jewish Yisrael.
[5] Speaking of Jewish Yisrael, not being forsaken despite problems with unemunah.

[6] Both houses have a faithful remnant. Out of the billions of Yisraelites that He used to fulfill covenant, YHWH deals with His remnant today, even as He did in the days of Ephraim's apostasy.
[7] Deals with Jewish Yisrael who did not attain right standing, as opposed to Ephraim Yisrael who did, though not even seeking it at all.
[8] Jewish Yisrael.
[9] Ephraim gets it while Yahudah is blinded. But in the end times both houses start seeing clearly.

flesh, and might save some of them.[1] 15 For if their temporal setting aside be the reconciling of the olam hazeh, what shall the receiving of them back be, but chayim from the dead?[2] 16 For if the bikkurim is set-apart, the lump is also set-apart: and if the root is set-apart, so are the branches-netsarim.[3] 17 And if some of the branches were broken off, and you, being a wild olive tree,[4] were grafted in among them, and with them you partake of the Root and fatness of the olive tree; 18 Boast not against the cultivated branches. But if you boast, you better remember that you do not bear the Root, but the Root bears you.[5] 19 You will say then, The cultivated branches were broken off,[6] that I might be grafted in.[7] 20 True; because of unbelief they were broken off, and you stand by emunah. Be not arrogant, but fear: 21 For if יהוה spared not the cultivated branches, shomer, He may not spare you either. 22 See therefore the chesed and severity of יהי: on those who fell, severity; but towards you, chesed,

if you continue in His chesed: otherwise you also shall be cut off. 23 And they also, if they abide not still in their unbelief, shall be grafted in: for יהוה is able to graft them in again.[8] 24 For if you were cut out of the olive tree which is uncultivated, and were grafted contrary to nature into a tov olive tree: how much more shall these, who are the cultivated branches, be grafted into their own olive tree as well? 25 For I would not, brothers, that you should be ignorant of this mysterious secret, lest you should be wise in your own pride and conceit; that partial blindness has happened to Yisrael,[9] until the fullness of the nations - the melo hagoyim - comes in.[10] [11] 26 And so all Yisrael shall be saved:[12] as it is written, *There shall come out of Tzion the Deliverer, and shall turn away wickedness from Yaakov:* 27 *For this is My covenant with them, when I shall take away their sins.* 28 As concerning the besorah, they are enemies for your sakes: but as far as being chosen, they are beloved for the sake of the

---

[1] From Yahudah.
[2] If Yahudah's blindness brought life to Ephraim, how much more will Yahudah's regeneration bring greater life in the kingdom?
[3] The olive tree parable speaks of Yisrael and Yahudah not Yahudah alone. Here the first-fruits are the patriarchs Abraham, Isaac, and Jacob. The lump represents the immediate descendents of those patriarchs, the Root is Yahshua and the branches are both houses. This understanding is detailed in extra great length at: http://yourarmstoisrael.org/Articles_new/restoration/?page=5&type=12 and is an absolutely recommended study. According to Jeremiah 11:13-14, the branches are Yahudah and Ephraim, with the cultivated ones being Yahudah, and the wild ones being Ephraim, but both being Yisrael. When the cultivated branch does not believe, he is cut off. When the wild one does not believe, he is cut off. The issue then is not who is the olive tree, since it is clearly both houses of Yisrael mentioned by name in Jeremiah 11:13-14 and Zechariah chapter 4: The issue is which of the branches have faith in the Root or the Moshiach. That will determine whether that branch abides or is removed. Another excellent study, proving beyond a shadow of doubt that this olive tree is not Jewish with non-Jews grafted in, but rather is all Yisraelite branches that get grafted back into their own tree by faith is found at: http://yourarmstoisrael.org/Articles_new/guest/?page=the_tora h_of_kilayim_and_the_olive_tree&type=13 Understanding the composition of the olive tree parable is a key to Yisrael's return, and your understanding of the two houses.
[4] Ephraim Yisrael.
[5] Yahshua bears all Yisraelites, and decides who is in and who is out.
[6] Jewish Yisrael.
[7] Replacement Theology is still around today, believing that in order for non-Jews to return or come in to the Olive tree, Jews have to have their place taken from them as Yisrael.

[8] All are Yisrael. Whether you abide with and as Yisrael depends on your faith in Moshiach, and your lifestyle to walk as He walked, and not as pagans walk.
[9] If we let Scripture interpret Scripture, then Isaiah 8:14 speaks of both houses as being blind. Yahudah is blind as to who is their Moshiach. Ephraim is blind as to who they are as the other house of Yisrael, and to the relevancy of Torah in their lives, seeing it through a dark glass as a strange Jewish thing, rather than as their own marriage certificate and heritage. Traditionally these verses have been taught to mean that some Jews see and believe, and some just don't. That meaning is seen as fallacious, when one understands that the olive tree is not strictly Jewish, and that both houses are said to be blind, which is why the terminology "partial blindness" is used to indicate that all twelve tribes are blind in differing areas.
[10] The only other time this term is used in scripture is in Genesis 48:19. Yakkov laid his hands on Ephraim his grandson and said that his seed would literally become the fullness of the nations or the melo-hagoyim. The mystery of the olive tree is not that some day gentiles will be part of Yisrael. That was never a mystery as all of the First Covenant spoke of the gentiles seeing the light of YHWH and Torah. The mystery of the olive tree is the identity of those who are not Jewish coming out of the nations into Moshiach. So this partial blindness on both houses according to Rav Shaul will come to an end only when the "fullness of the gentiles" comes in. The Hebraic idiom is a reference to the seed of the ten tribes collectively known as Ephraim-Yisrael. When the remnant of all ten tribes comes in, then Yisrael's blinders will be lifted and the kingdom will begin. For more details, we strongly recommend you study: http://yourarmstoisrael.org/Articles_new/restoration/?page=5& type=12.
[11] For more details, also see notes on Genesis 48:19.
[12] When the melo-hagoyim comes in.

ahvot.[1] 29 For the gifts and calling of **יהוה** are without teshuvah.[2] 30 For as you in times past have not believed **יהוה**, yet have now obtained rachamim through their unbelief: 31 Even so have these also now not believed, that through your rachamim they also may re-obtain rachamim. 32 For **יהוה** has put all Yisrael in various forms of unbelief, that He might have rachamim upon all Yisrael. 33 O the depth of the riches both of the chochmah and da'at of **יהוה** ! How unsearchable are His mishpatim, and His halachot past finding out! 34 For who has really known the mind of the Master **יהוה**? Or who has been His advisor? 35 Or who has first given anything to Him, in order to receive something back from Him? 36 For from Him, and through Him, and to Him, are all things: to whom be tifereth le-olam-va-ed. Amein.

12 I beg you therefore, Yisraelite brothers, by the rachamim of **יהוה**, that you present your bodies a living sacrifice, set-apart, acceptable to **יהוה** , which is your act of reasonable worship. 2 And be not conformed to this olam hazeh: but be transformed by the ongoing renewing of your mind, that you may discern what is that tov, acceptable, and even the perfect, will of **יהוה** . 3 For I say, through the unmerited favor given to me, to every man that is among you, not to think of himself more highly than he should;[3] but to think soberly, as **יהוה** has dealt to every man the measure of emunah. 4 For as we have many members in the one body of Yisrael, and all members have not the same role: 5 So we, being many, are one body of Yisrael in ha Moshiach, and each one members one of another. 6 Having then gifts differing according to the unmerited favor that is given to us, whether prophecy, let us prophesy according to the measure of

emunah; 7 Or some service, let us serve: or he that teaches, let him teach; 8 Or he that exhorts, on exhortation: he that gives, let him do it with simplicity; he that oversees, with diligence; he that shows rachamim, with simcha. 9 Let ahava be without deceit in full sincerity. Despise that which is evil; cleave to that which is tov. 10 Be kind and tender to one another with brotherly ahava; in honor preferring another over yourself; 11 Not idle in your duty; fervent in ruach; serving your **יהוה** ; 12 Having gilah in tikvah; be patient in tribulation; continue steadfast in tefillah; 13 Distributing to the necessity of kidushim; be given to hospitality. 14 Bless them who persecute you: bless, and do not curse. 15 Gilah with them that do gilah, and weep with those that weep. 16 Be of the same mind one toward another. Mind not prideful things and position, but associate with the humble. Be not wise in your own estimation. 17 Repay to no man evil for evil. Do things honestly and right in the sight of all men. 18 If it is possible, on your part, live in shalom with all men. 19 Dearly beloved, revenge not yourselves, but rather give place to wrath: for it is written, *Vengeance is mine; and repayment*, says **יהוה**. 20 Therefore if your enemy is hungry, feed him. If he is thirsty, give him drink: for in so doing you shall heap coals of fire on His head.[4] 21 Be not overcome by evil, but overcome evil with tov.

13 Let every Yisraelite be subject to civil governing powers. For there is no power but from **יהוה**: the civil powers that exist are ordained of **יהוה**. 2 Whoever therefore resists the civil power, resists the ordained institution of **יהוה**: and they that resist, shall receive mishpat on themselves. 3 For civil shophtim are not a menace to tov mitzvot, but to cause men to fear doing evil. Will you then not be afraid of the authorities? Do that which is tov, and you

---

[1] Speaking of YHWH's special love for Jewish Yisrael, for the sake of the covenants by YHWH with the patriarchs.
[2] To both houses.
[3] Judah and Ephraim must see each other as equal heirs of salvation, with neither house thinking that one is more important, or more special before YHWH.

---

[4] A Hebraic idiomatic expression meaning: "you'll blow his mind with love."

shall have tehilla from the same authorities: 4 For he is the eved of יהוה to you for tov. But if you do that which is evil, then be afraid; for he bears not the sword in vain: for he is the eved of יהוה, an instrument to execute wrath upon the one that does evil. 5 Therefore we must be subject, not only for fear of wrath, but also because of our conscience. 6 For this cause pay taxes also: for they are יהוה's instruments, attending continually upon this very thing. 7 Render therefore to all their dues: tax to whom tax is due; custom to whom custom; reverence to whom reverence is due; honor to whom honor is due. 8 Owe no man any thing, but to love one another: for he that loves another has fulfilled the Torah.[1] 9 For this, *you shall not commit adultery, you shall not kill, you shall not steal, you shall not bear false witness, you shall not covet*; and if there is any other mitzvah, it is briefly comprehended in this saying, namely; *ahavta re'echa camocha - you shall love your neighbor as yourself.*[2] 10 Ahava seeks no evil to its neighbor: therefore ahava is the completion of the Torah chayim. 11 And that, knowing the time, that now it is high time to awake out of sleep: for now is our salvation nearer than when we first came to believe. 12 The night is far spent, the Yom is at hand: let us therefore cast off the deeds of darkness, and let us put on the tallit of Light. 13 Let us have an honest halacha, as in the day; not in wild parties and drunkenness, not in living together before marriage and indecencies, not in fighting or envying. 14 But put on יהושע ha Moshiach, and make not any provision for the flesh, to fulfill the lusts thereof.[3]

14 Him that is weak in the emunah receive, but not criticizing his thoughts. 2 For one believes that he may eat all things: another, who is weak, eats only vegetables. 3 Let not him that eats meat despise him that eats no meat; and let not him who does not eat meat shophet him that eats meat: for יהוה has received kol Yisrael. 4 Who are you that judges another man's eved? To his own Master יהוה he stands or falls. Yes, he shall be held up too: for יהוה is able to make him stand. 5 One man esteems one day above another: another esteems every day alike. Let every man be fully persuaded in his own mind.[4] 6 He that regards the day of eating, regards it to יהוה; and he that regards not the day, to יהוה he does not regard it. He that eats, eats to יהוה, for he gives יהוה hodu; and he that eats not, before יהוה he eats not, and neither gives יהוה hodu. 7 For no Yisraelite man lives for himself, and no man dies to himself. 8 For whether we live, we live for יהוה; and whether we die, we die for יהוה: whether we live, or whether we die, we belong to and for יהוה. 9 For to this end ha Moshiach both died, and rose, and was revived, so that He might be the Master יהוה both of the dead and the living. 10 But why do you shophet your brother? Or why do you despise your brother over these secondary issues? For we shall all stand before the bema seat of our Moshiach. 11 For it is written, *As I live,* says the Master יהוה, *every knee shall bow to Me, and every tongue shall confess to the Master* יהוה. 12 So then each one of us shall give account of himself to יהוה. 13 Let us not therefore shophet one another any more: but rather be mindful of this that

---

[1] Not that we don't have to do the commands, but rather that a Torah-keeper's attitude should manifest as love, submission and forgiveness.
[2] It is briefly understood as love, but it is a descriptive summation, not a release from obeying all of Torah.
[3] The actual armor of YHWH, as described in Ephesians 6. See notes in and on Ephesians 6.

[4] The word "eat" is used six times in these verses. The issue obviously is food. Some eat meat, some don't and the same goes for vegetables. Some eat meat on Thursday some eat meat only on Monday. Some fast every morning, some fast only one morning a week. We are not to make issues out of things that YHWH says are gray areas, such as what days we fast or eat certain clean foods. In a case of a gray area, do not criticize a new brother, or a weak brother, in the ways of Yisrael. This applies only to gray areas that remain unaddressed by detail in Scripture. Therefore verse 5 does not talk about Shabbat at all, or "pick your own Shabbat," or your own favorite day for your own worship days, simply because first the topic is eating habits, and secondly because Shabbat is not a gray area. The Spirit would never tell mankind to pick his own day in direct violation of His Word.

no man put any unnecessary stumbling-block or an occasion to fall into his brother's path. 14 I know, and am persuaded by the Savior **יהושע**, that there is nothing unclean of itself: but to him that esteems anything to be unclean, to him it is unclean.[1] 15 But if your brother is grieved with your food choice, now you are no longer walking in ahava. Do not destroy him with your food choices, for whom ha Moshiach died.[2] 16 Let not then your tov be evil spoken of: 17 For the malchut of **יהוה** is not food and drink; but tzedakah, and shalom, and simcha in the Ruach HaKodesh.[3] 18 For he that in these choices serves ha Moshiach is acceptable to **יהוה**, and approved of men. 19 Let us therefore follow after the things that make for shalom, and things with which we may edify one another. 20 For food choices will not destroy the work of **יהוה**. All things indeed are pure;[4] but it is evil for that man who eats so as to cause stumbling. 21 It is tov neither to eat meat, nor to drink wine, or anything whereby your brother stumbles, or is offended, or is made weak. 22 Have you a certain food emunah? Keep it to yourself before **יהוה**. Favored is he that condemns not himself in that thing which he allows.[5] 23 And he that doubts and eats violates his own emunah, because he eats not with emunah: for whatever is not of emunah is sin.[6]

15 We then that are strong ought to bear the weaknesses of the weak, and not to please ourselves. 2 Let every one of us please his neighbor for his tov and edification. 3 For even ha Moshiach pleased not Himself; but, as it is written, *The reproaches of them that reproached You fell on Me.* 4 For all things that were written in Tanach were written for our learning, that we through patience and comfort of the Ketuvim might have tikvah. 5 Now the Elohim of patience and comfort, grant you the ability to regard one another with equal worth according to Moshiach **יהושע** : 6 That you may with one mind and one mouth esteem **יהוה**, even the Abba of our Savior **יהושע** ha Moshiach. 7 Therefore receive one another, as ha Moshiach also received us to the tifereth of **יהוה**. 8 Now I say that **יהושע** ha Moshiach was an eved to Yisrael for the emet of **יהוה**, to confirm the promises made to our ahvot: 9 And that the nations might all esteem **יהוה** for His rachamim; as it is written, For this cause I will confess You among the nations, and shir to Your Name. 10 And again He says, *Gilah, you nations, with His people.*[7] 11 And again, Hallel the Master **יהוה**, all you nations; and laud Him, all you people.[8] 12 And again, Yeshayahu says, There shall be a Root of Yishai, and He that shall rise to reign over the nations; in Him shall the nations trust. 13 Now the Elohim of tikvah fill you with all simcha and shalom in believing, that you may abound in your tikvah, through the power of the Ruach HaKodesh. 14 And I myself also am persuaded of you, my brothers, that you also are full of much tov, filled with all da'at, able also to admonish one another. 15 Nevertheless, brothers, I have written more boldly partially to remind you, because of the unmerited favor that is given to me of **יהוה**, 16 That I should be the eved of **יהושע** ha Moshiach to the nations, serving in the besorah of **יהוה**, that the offering up of the nations might be acceptable, being set-apart by the Ruach

---

[1] Again gray area issues that are not black or white cannot be judged to be clean or unclean like Shabbat-breaking and eating pig certainly can be.
[2] As can be seen, the entire chapter does not depart from this theme and again has nothing on earth to do with Shabbat, or making up your own holidays.
[3] Man's choices don't matter; it is what the Ruach says about our food and drink choices, which we receive with joy.
[4] Both meat and vegetables as outlined by Torah.
[5] Meaning when alone, in your food choices and such, don't do anything against the Torah, lest you wind up condemning yourself with your own unclean behavior.
[6] Meaning we better get our Yisraelite values from full emunah in Torah and the faith of Moshiach, and not man or man's emotions or dogmas.

[7] Here YHWH's will is outlined. All nations are to join and rejoice with His people Yisrael, not try and have Yisraelites mix and assimilate with the nations or gentile expressions of faith.
[8] All nations are to serve YHWH and not their own elohim.

HaKodesh. 17 I have therefore a cause for boasting through יהושע ha Moshiach in those things that pertain to יהוה. 18 For I will not dare to speak of any of those things that ha Moshiach has not done through me, to make the nations obedient, by word and demands, 19 Through mighty signs and wonders, by the power of the Ruach of יהוה; so that from Yahrushalayim, and all around Illurikon, I have fully proclaimed the besorah of ha Moshiach. 20 Yes, so have I strived to proclaim the besorah, not where ha Moshiach was already named, lest I should build upon another man's foundation: 21 But as it is written, To whom He was not spoken of, they shall see: and they that have not heard shall understand. 22 For which cause also I have been much hindered from coming to you. 23 But now having no more a place in these parts, and having a great desire these many years to come to you; 24 Whenever I take my journey into Sepharad, I will come to you: for I trust to see you in my journey, and that you will escort me there, after I have more or less fully enjoyed my visit with you. [1] 25 But now I go to Yahrushalayim to serve the kidushim. 26 For it has pleased them of Makedonia and Achaia to make a certain contribution for the poor kidushim who are at Yahrushalayim. 27 It has pleased them truly; and their debtors they are. For if the nations have been made partakers of their spiritual things, their duty is also to attend to them in material things. [2] 28 When therefore I have performed this, and have sealed for them this fruit, I will return through you into Sepharad. 29 And I am sure that, when I come to you, I shall come in the fullness of the brachas of the besorah of ha Moshiach. 30 Now I beg you, brothers, for the Savior יהושע ha Moshiach's sake, and for the ahava of the

Ruach, that you strive together with me in your tefillot to יהוה for me; 31 That I may be delivered from them that do not believe in Yahudah; and that my offering which I have for Yahrushalayim may be accepted by the kidushim; 32 That I may come to you with simcha by the will of יהוה, and may be refreshed with you. 33 Now the Elohim of shalom be with you all. Amein.

16 I commend to you Phoebe our sister, who is an eved of the congregation that is at Cenchrea: 2 That you receive her in יהוה, as becomes kidushim, and that you assist her in whatever business she has need of: for she has been a great help to many, and to myself also. 3 Greet Priscilla and Aqulas my helpers in Moshiach יהושע : 4 Who have for my chayim laid down their own necks: to whom not only I give hodu, but also all the congregations of the Yisraelite nations. 5 Likewise greet the congregation that is in their bayit. Greet my well beloved Epainetos, who is the bikkurim of Achaia to ha Moshiach. 6 Greet Miryam, who worked very hard for us. 7 Greet Andronikos and Junia, my relatives, and my fellow prisoners, who are of note among the shlichim, who also were in ha Moshiach before me.[3] 8 Greet Amplias my beloved in יהוה. 9 Greet Urbanos, our helper in ha Moshiach, and Stachus my beloved. 10 Greet Apelles approved in ha Moshiach. Greet those who are of Aristobulos' bayit. 11 Greet Herodion my relative. Greet them that are of the bayit of Narkissus, who are in יהוה. 12 Greet Truphania and Truphosa, who labor in יהוה . Greet the beloved Persis, who labored much in יהוה. 13 Greet Rufus chosen in יהוה , and his ima and mine. 14 Greet Asugritos, Phlegon, Hermas, Patrobas, Hermes, and the brothers, which are with them. 15 Greet Philologos, and Julia, Nereus, and his sister, and Olumpas, and all the kidushim that are with them.

---

[1] Spain and Rome were both areas of known prophetic Yisraelite migration as found in Obadiah 1:20. Rav Shaul always was out in the nations, looking for the lost sheep of the house of Yisrael.
[2] Both houses should take tov care of each other.

[3] Junia was a female apostle in Yisrael.

16 Greet one another with a set-apart kiss. The Yisraelite congregations of ha Moshiach greet you. 17 Now I beg you, brothers, mark those who cause divisions and stumbling contrary to the Torah that you have learned; and avoid them. 18 For they that are such serve not our Savior יהושע ha Moshiach, but their own belly; and by tov words and fair speeches deceive the levim of the simple. 19 For your obedience is reported to all men. I am glad therefore on your behalf: but yet I would have you wise to that which is tov, but simple concerning evil. 20 And the Elohim of shalom shall bruise s.a.tan under your feet shortly. The unmerited favor of our Savior יהושע ha Moshiach be with you. 21 Timtheous my fellow worker and Lucius, and Jason, and Sosipater, my relatives, greet you. 22 I Tertius, who wrote this letter, greet you in יהוה.

23 Gaios my host, and the whole congregation, greets you. Erastos the treasurer of the city greets you, and Quartus a brother. 24 The unmerited favor of our Savior יהושע ha Moshiach be with you all. 25 Now to Him that is able to establish you according to my besorah, and the proclaiming of יהושע ha Moshiach, according to the revelation of the mystery, which was kept hidden since the olam hazeh began, 26 But now is made manifest, by the Ketuvim of the niviim, according to the commandment of the everlasting Elohim, made known to all nations for the obedience of the emunah: 27 To יהוה the only wise One, be tifereth through יהושע ha Moshiach le-olam-ve-ed. Amein.

Qorintyah Alef - First Corinthians

To The Believing Remnant Of Yisrael

1 Shaul, called to be an sholiach of יהושע ha Moshiach through the will of יהוה , and Sosthenes our Yisraelite brother, 2 To the Yisraelite congregation of יהוה which is at Qorintyah, to them that are set-apart in ha Moshiach יהושע, called to be kidushim, with all that in every place call upon the Name of יהושע ha Moshiach our Master, both theirs and ours: 3 Unmerited favor to you, and shalom, from יהוה our Father, and from the Master יהושע ha Moshiach. 4 I thank my Elohim always on your behalf, for the unmerited favor of יהוה which is given to you by יהושע ha Moshiach; 5 That in every thing you are enriched by Him, in all words, and in all da'at; 6 Even as the witness of ha Moshiach was confirmed in you: 7 So that you were not lacking any gift; while waiting for the coming of our Master יהושע ha Moshiach: 8 Who shall also strengthen you to the end, that you may be blameless in the day of our Master יהושע ha Moshiach. 9 יהוה is faithful, by who you were called to the chavurah of His Son יהושע ha Moshiach our Master. 10 Now I appeal to you, Yisraelite brothers, by the Name of our Master יהושע ha Moshiach that you all speak as echad, and that there be no divisions among you; but that you be perfectly joined together in the same mind and in the same opinion. 11 For it has been declared to me of you, my Yisraelite brothers, by those who are of bayit Chloe, that there are contentions and disputes among you. 12 Now this I say, because some among you say, I am of Shaul; and I am of Apollos; and I am of Kepha; and I am of ha Moshiach. 13 Is ha Moshiach divided? Was Shaul impaled for you? Or were you immersed in the name of Shaul? 14 I thank יהוה that I immersed none of you, but Crispos and Gaios; 15 So that no one should

say that I had immersed in my own name. 16 And I immersed also the bayit of Tsephanyah: besides them, I do not know whether I immersed anyone else. 17 For ha Moshiach sent me not to mikvah, but to proclaim the besarot: not with chochmah of words, lest the offering of ha Moshiach should be made of no effect. 18 For the proclaiming of the execution stake is to them that are perishing foolishness; but to us who are being saved it is the power of יהוה. 19 For it is written, *I will destroy the chochmah of the wise, and will bring to nothing the understanding of the prudent.* 20 Where is the wise? Where is the sopher? Where is the debator of the olam hazeh? Has not יהוה made foolish the chochmah of the olam hazeh? 21 For after that in the chochmah of יהוה the olam hazeh by worldly chochmah knew not יהוה , it pleased יהוה by the foolishness of proclaiming to save them that believe. 22 For the Yahudim require a sign, and the Greeks seek after chochmah:[1] 23 But we proclaim ha Moshiach impaled, to the Yahudim a stumbling-block, and to the Greeks foolishness;[2] 24 But to those who are called, both Yahudim and Greeks, ha Moshiach is the power of יהוה, and the chochmah of יהוה.[3] 25 For the foolishness of יהוה is wiser than men; and the weakness of יהוה is stronger than men. 26 For you see your calling, my Yisraelite brothers, how that not many wise men after the flesh, not many mighty, not many noble, are called: 27 But יהוה has chosen the foolish things of the olam hazeh to embarrass the wise; and יהוה has chosen the weak things of the olam hazeh to

---

[1] Two-House reference.
[2] Two-House reference.
[3] The power and **chochmah** to save individuals, and regather both houses through Moshiach.

embarrass the things that are mighty; 28 And Elohim has chosen those from humble families of the olam hazeh, those who are despised, those יהוה has chosen, yes, and the ones who are not, to bring to nothing those that are something: 29 That no flesh should boast in His presence. 30 But of Him are you in ha Moshiach יהושע, who is from יהוה and has been made to us chochmah, and tzedakah, and set-apartness, and redemption: 31 That, as it is written, He that boasts, let him boast in יהוה.

2 And I, Yisraelite brothers, when I came to you, came not with excellence of speech or of chochmah, declaring to you the witness of יהוה. 2 For I determined not to know any thing among you, except יהושע ha Moshiach, and Him impaled. 3 And I was with you in weakness, and in fear, and in much trembling. 4 And my speech and my proclaiming was not with enticing words of man's chochmah, but in a demonstration of the Ruach and of power: 5 That your emunah should not stand in the chochmah of men, but in the power of יהוה. 6 Yet we speak chochmah among those that are mature: yet not the chochmah of the olam hazeh, or of the rulers of the olam hazeh, that comes to nothing: 7 But we speak the chochmah of יהוה in a sod mystery, even the hidden chochmah, that יהוה has ordained before the olam hazeh to our tifereth: 8 Which none of the rulers of the olam hazeh knew: for had they known it, they would not have impaled the Master of Tifereth. 9 But as it is written, Eye has not seen, nor ear heard, neither has it entered into the lev of man, the things which Elohim has prepared for them that love Him. 10 But יהוה has revealed them to us by His Ruach: for the Ruach searches all things, yes, the deep things of יהוה. 11 For who knows the things of a man, except the ruach of man, which is in him? Even so the things of Elohim no man knows, but the Ruach of Elohim. 12 Now we have received, not the

ruach of the olam hazeh, but the Ruach, which is from Elohim; that we might know all the things that are freely given to us by יהוה. 13 Which things also we speak, not in the words which man's chochmah teaches, but which the Ruach HaKodesh teaches; comparing spiritual matters with spiritual matters. 14 But the natural material man receives not the things of the Ruach of יהוה: for they are foolishness to him: neither can he know them, because they need spiritual discernment. 15 But he that is spiritual judges all things, yet he himself is judged by no man. 16 For who has known the mind of the Master יהוה, that He may give Him Torah lessons? But we have the mind of ha Moshiach.

3 And I, Yisraelite brothers, could not speak to you as spiritual ones, but as to worldly ones, even as to babies in ha Moshiach. 2 I have fed you with milk, and not with meat: for before now you were not able to bear it, neither now are you able. 3 For you are still worldly: since there is among you ongoing envying, and strife, and divisions, are you not worldly, and walking as natural men? 4 For while one says, I am of Shaul; and another, I am of Apollos; are you not still worldly? 5 Who then is Shaul, and who is Apollos, but avadim through whom you believed, even as the Master יהוה gave to every man? 6 I have planted, Apollos gave mayim; but יהוה gave the increased growth. 7 So then neither is he that plants anything, neither he that gives mayim anything; but יהוה who gives the increase. 8 Now he that plants and he that gives mayim are echad: and every man shall receive his own reward according to his own labor. 9 For we are Yisraelite laborers together with יהוה: you are יהוה's field, you are יהוה's building.[1] 10 According to the unmerited favor of יהוה which is given to me, as a wise master builder, I have laid the foundation, and another builds on it. But

---

[1] The congregation is the rebuilt Tabernacle of David the true building of YHWH; and the very field He purchased in Matthew 13.

let every man take heed how he builds on it.[1] 11 For another foundation can no man lay than that which has been laid, which is **יהושע** ha Moshiach.[2] 12 Now if any man builds upon this foundation gold, silver, precious stones, wood, hay, and straw; 13 Every man's mitzvot shall be made manifest: for the Light of Yom HaDin shall declare it, because it shall be revealed by fire; and the fire[3] shall try every man's mitzvot of what sort it is. 14 If any man's mitzvot remain which he has built on, he shall receive a reward. 15 If any man's mitzvot shall be burned, he shall suffer loss: but he himself shall be saved; as one who has been saved by a fire. 16 Know you not that you are the Beit HaMikdash of **יהוה**, and that the Ruach of **יהוה** dwells in you? 17 If any man defiles the Beit HaMikdash of **יהוה**, him shall **יהוה** destroy; for the Beit HaMikdash of **יהוה** is set-apart, which you are.[4] 18 Let no man deceive himself. If any man among Yisrael seems to be wise in this olam hazeh, let him become a natural fool, that he may be spiritually wise. 19 For the chochmah of the olam hazeh is foolishness with **יהוה**. For it is written, *He catches the wise in their own craftiness.* 20 And again, the Master **יהוה** knows the thoughts of the naturally wise, that they are worthless. 21 Therefore let no man boast in other men. For all things are yours; 22 Whether Shaul, or Apollos, or Kepha, or the olam hazeh, or chayim, or death, or the olam habah; all things are yours; 23 And you are ha Moshiach's; and ha Moshiach is **יהוה**'s.

4 Let a man regard all of us, as simple avadim of ha Moshiach, and caretakers of the sod mysteries of **יהוה**. 2 Moreover it is required in caretakers that a man is found faithful. 3 But with me it is a very small thing that I should be judged by you, or of man's mishpat: yes, I do not even shophet myself. 4 For I do not know of any matter against myself; yet am I not declared tzadik by that: but He that judges me is the Master **יהוה**. 5 Therefore shophet nothing before the time, until **יהושע** comes, who both will bring to light the hidden things of darkness, and will make manifest the thoughts of the levim: and then shall every man have tehilla from the Master **יהוה**. 6 And these things, my Yisraelite brothers, I have in an explainable picture applied to myself and to Apollos for your sakes; that you might learn by us not to think of any man above that which is written, that not one of you be puffed up in favor of one against another. 7 For who makes you to differ from each other? And what do you have that you did not first receive? Now if you did receive it, why do you boast, as if you had not received it? 8 Now you are full, now you are rich, you have reigned as melechim apart from us: and I wished indeed that you did reign, that we also might reign with you. 9 For I think that **יהוה** has set forth the shlichim to be last in all things, as if we were condemned to death: for we have become a spectacle to the olam hazeh, and to the heavenly malachim, and to all men. 10 We are fools for ha Moshiach's sake, but you are wise in ha Moshiach; we are weak, but you are strong; you are honorable, but we are despised. 11 Even to this present hour we both hunger, and thirst, and are scantily clad, and beaten, and have no permanent home; 12 And labor, working with our own hands: being cursed, we return brachot; being persecuted, we suffer: 13 Being defamed, we help: we are made as the filth of the olam hazeh, and are the revilement of all men to this day. 14 I write not these things to shame you, but as my be loved children I warn you. 15 For though you have ten thousand Torah

---

[1] Yisrael must be rebuilt according to First Covenant pattern, with Moshiach being the Head Corner Stone.
[2] The rebuilding of Yisrael and restoration of the exiles cannot be built by any man or religion that omits the foundation and Chief Corner Stone the Moshiach Yahshua. Unlike some who teach otherwise, scripture indicates that both houses cannot truly come together without a heartfelt emunah in Yahshua as the promised King Moshiach. Any other building plan results in leaning or crumbling towers without a strong foundation.
[3] Judgment.
[4] Individually and collectively we are the temple of His dwelling.

teachers in ha Moshiach, yet you do not have many spiritual ahvot: for in ha Moshiach יהושע I have begotten you through the besarot. 16 Therefore I appeal to you be imitators[1] of me. 17 For this cause have I sent to you Timtheous, who is my be love d ben emunah, and faithful in יהוה, who shall bring you into remembrance of my halacha which is in ha Moshiach, as I teach everywhere in every Yisraelite congregation. 18 Now some are puffed up, as though I were not coming to you. 19 But I will come to you shortly, if the Master יהוה wills, and will know, not the words of those who are puffed up, but the power. 20 For the malchut of יהוה is not in speech only, but in power. 21 What do you desire? Shall I come to you with a rod of correction, or in ahava, and in the ruach of meekness?

5 It is commonly reported that there is fornication among you, and the kind of fornication not even mentioned among the pagan gentiles,[2] that one should have his abba's wife. 2 And you are boasting in this behavior, instead of mourning, that he that has done this sin might be removed outside the camp. 3 For I truly, I remain absent in body, but present in the Ruach, I have judged already, as though I were present, concerning him that has so done this sin, 4 In the Name of our Master יהושע ha Moshiach, when you are gathered together, and my ruach, with the power of our Master יהושע ha Moshiach, 5 To deliver such a one to s.a.tan for the destruction of the flesh,[3] that his ruach may be saved in theYom of the Master יהושע . 6 Your boasting is not good. Don't you know that a little chametz leavens the whole lump? 7 Clean out therefore the old chametz, that you may be a new lump, as you are unleavened. For even ha Moshiach our

Pesach was sacrificed for us: 8 So then let us keep the moed,[4] not with old chametz, neither with the chametz of malice and wickedness; but with the unleavened matzah of sincerity and emet. 9 I wrote to you in a prior letter not to associate with fornicators and immoral persons: 10 I did not mean with the fornicators out in the olam hazeh, or with the covetous, or swindlers, or with idolaters; since you would literally have to leave the olam hazeh. 11 But now I have written to you not to keep company or associate, with any man that is called a Yisraelite brother who is a fornicator, or covetous, or an idolater, or a reviler, or a drunkard, or a swindler; with such a one do not even eat. 12 For what business do I have with judging those that are in the olam hazeh? But you may shophet them that are in the Yisraelite congregation.[5] 13 But those that are in the olam hazeh יהוה judges. Therefore put that wicked person outside the camp yourselves.

6 How dare any of you, having a matter against another Yisraelite, go to court before the unsaved, and not before the Bet Din of the kidushim? 2 Do you not know that the kidushim shall shophet the olam hazeh? And if you shall judge the entire olam hazeh, are you unworthy and unable to shophet even the smallest matters? 3 Don't you know that we shall shophet the heavenly malachim? How much more things that pertain to this chayim? 4 If then you have mishpatim to render in things pertaining to this chayim, why then do you appoint as shophtim in the Bet Din those who are least esteemed in the Yisraelite congregation. 5 I speak to your shame. Is it so, that there is not a wise man among you to sit on the Bet Din? No, not even one that shall be able to shophet between Yisraelite

---

[1] Imitators not followers.
[2] Note the difference between believers in Yisrael's commonwealth, as opposed to the true gentiles or the pagans. The unfortunate term "saved gentile" is and always will be an oxymoron.
[3] A term for excommunication, which is an eternal Torah principle of dealing with improper or unclean conduct.

[4] Note that this Ephraimite, non-Jewish, congregation guarded the feast as an eternal order from YHWH. All believers in all ages are expected and commanded to keep YHWH's feasts. This is not a reference to the cheap substitute of manmade communion. This is the real thing.
[5] Only and solely by the word of YHWH, not based on hearsay, allegation, or emotional likes and dislikes.

brothers? 6 But Yisraelite brother goes to court against Yisraelite brother, and that before the unbelievers! 7 Now therefore you are all already at fault, because you go to court one against another. Why do you not rather receive being wronged? Why do you not rather allow yourselves to be cheated? 8 No, you do wrong, and cheat, even your Yisraelite brothers. 9 Know you not that the unrighteous shall not inherit the malchut of יהוה? Be not deceived: neither fornicators, nor idolaters, nor adulterers, nor effeminate, nor homosexuals, 10 Nor thieves, nor covetous, nor drunkards, nor revilers, nor swindlers, shall inherit the malchut of יהוה.[1] 11 And such were some of you: but you are washed, but you are set-apart, but you are declared to be tzadik in the Name of the Master יהושע, and by the Ruach of our Elohim. 12 All things are permitted to me, but not all things profit: all things are permitted for me, but I will not be brought under the power of any.[2] 13 Foods for the stomach, and the stomach for foods: but יהוה shall destroy both it and them. Now the body is not for fornication, but for יהוה; and יהוה for the body. 14 And יהוה who has raised up יהושע, will also raise us by His own power. 15 Don't you know that your bodies are the members of ha Moshiach? Shall I then take the members of ha Moshiach, and make them the members of a harlot? Let it never be! 16 What? Know you not that he who is joined to a harlot is one body? For the two, says He, shall become basar echad. 17 But he that is joined to יהוה becomes one with Him in Ruach. 18 Flee fornication. Every sin that a man does is outside the body; but he that commits fornication sins against his own body. 19 Do you not know that your body is the Beit HaMikdash of the Ruach HaKodesh which is in you, which you have from יהוה, and you are not your own?

20 For you are bought with a price: therefore bring tifereth to יהוה in your body, and in your ruach, which are from Him.

7 Now concerning the matters of which you wrote to me: It is tov for a man not to touch a woman. 2 Nevertheless, to avoid fornication, let every man have his own wife, and let every woman have her own husband. 3 Let the husband render to the wife the ahava he owes her: and likewise also the wife to her husband. 4 The wife does not have full authority over her own body, without the husband: and likewise also the husband does not have full authority over his own body, without the wife. 5 Do not deprive one another, except it be with consent for a short time, that you may give yourselves to fasting and tefillot; and afterwards come together again, so that s.a.tan does not tempt you in the area of self-control. 6 But I speak this as a concession, but it is not part of the Torah. 7 For I would prefer that all men were like myself in purity. But every man has his own proper gift from יהוה, one after this manner, and another after that. 8 I say therefore to the unmarried and the widows, It is tov for them if they remain single even as I am now. 9 But if they do not have the self-control, let them marry: for it is better to marry than to burn with passion. 10 And to the married I command, yet not I, but יהוה, Let not the wife depart from her husband: 11 But and if she departs let her remain unmarried, or be reconciled to her husband: and let not the husband divorce his wife. 12 But to the rest speak I, not יהוה: If any Yisraelite brother has a wife that believes not, and she is pleased to stay with him, let him not divorce her. 13 And the woman who has a husband that believes not, and if he is pleased to stay with her, let her not leave him. 14 For the unbelieving husband is set-apart by the wife, and the unbelieving wife is set-apart by the husband: otherwise your children would be

---

[1] These prohibitions and warnings are straight out of Torah, and are being restated to these troubled and confused Yisraelites.
[2] Speaking of gray areas not forbidden in Torah, but that does not serve his inner man or his spiritual growth.

unclean; but now are they set-apart.[1] 15 But if the unbelieving insists on departing, let him depart. A Yisraelite brother or a sister is not under bondage in such cases: but יהוה has called us to have shalom. 16 For who knows, O wife, whether you shall bring salvation to your husband? Or how knows, O man, whether you shall bring salvation to your wife? 17 But as the Master יהוה has distributed a purpose to every man, as יהושע has called each one; so let him have his halacha. And this is what I ordain in all congregations of Yisrael. 18 Is any man called being circumcised? Let him not become uncircumcised. Is any called in uncircumcision? Let him not be circumcised. [2]19 Brit Milah is nothing, and uncircumcision[3] is nothing, but the keeping of the Torah of יהוה is everything.[4] 20 Let every man remain in the same calling in which he was before he was called to salvation. 21 Were you called being an eved? It matters not: but even though you can be made free, choose rather to serve. 22 For he that was called in יהושע, being an eved, is יהושע's freeman: likewise also he that was called, being free, is ha Moshiach's eved. 23 Ye were bought with a price; do not be the avadim of men. 24 Yisraelite brothers, let every man, in whatever station of chayim he was called, remain in it serving יהוה . 25 Now concerning virgins I have no Torah commandment of יהוה : yet I give my mishpat, as one that has obtained the rachamim of יהוה to be faithful. 26 I suppose therefore that this is tov due to the present distress and persecutions, I say, that it is tov for a man or a woman to remain as a virgin. 27 Are you married to a wife? Seek not to be divorced. Are you divorced from a wife? Do not seek a wife. 28 But and if you marry, you have not sinned; and if a virgin marry, she has not sinned. Nevertheless such shall have pressure in the flesh: but I will spare you more details. 29 But this I say, Yisraelite brothers, the time is short: from now on, even those who have wives should act as though they had none; 30 And they that weep, as though they wept not; and they that have gilah, as though they have none; and they that buy, as though they did not possess anything. 31 And they that use this olam hazeh, as not misusing it, for the design of the olam hazeh passes away. 32 But I would have you without worldly cares. He that is unmarried cares for the things that belong to יהוה, how he may please יהוה: 33 But he that is married cares for the things that are of the olam hazeh, how he may please his wife. 34 There is a difference also between a wife and a virgin or a single. The unmarried woman cares for the things of יהוה, that she may be set-apart both in body and in ruach: but she that is married cares for the things of the olam hazeh, how she may please her husband. 35 And this I speak for your own tov; not to

---

[1] These are spiritual unseen laws at work in the Heavenlies. If the house has one believing spouse, the likelihood for the other spouse to be saved, as well as the children, are increased greatly. Set-apart means they are under a spiritual covering, with a great advantage and head start in coming to eternal life. That motive alone should cause many unequally yoked relationships to consider staying the course.

[2] It is essential to go to the Greek here for exact clarification. The word for circumcision meaning Yisraelites is peritemno (Strong's Greek # 4059), a form of peritome meaning "circumcised." Let that Yisraelite already circumcised, walk in Yahshua and not seek uncircumcision or epispaomai. This is a very rare word for uncircumcised which usually appears as akrobustia or aperitome. This word comes from the days of Antiochus Epiphanes, when Jewish Yisraelite men hid or concealed their circumcision in order to be considered Greek. So in essence, Rav Shaul states that all Corinthian Yisraelites must not be ashamed or try and hide their Yisraelite roots and heritage in Moshiach. And finally, the last word used here for "uncircumcised," as in a person who is uncircumcised is the word akrobustia. Akrobustia means "tossed-away-foreskinned ones," thereby alluding to Ephraim (the northern kingdom) who had been circumcised only to toss it all away to paganism. These returning Ephraimites should not seek another circumcision now since they were circumcised before breaking the Torah. These are the plain and literal understandings. The overriding theme in this verse as with the verses on marriage, being single, and divorce, is that whatever state one is in as a believing Nazarene Yisraelite, one should remain in that calling, without seeking another's status or another's calling.

[3] Peritome and akrobustia - a clear two-house reference in the Greek.

[4] The keeping of Torah is the main thing for all believers. This declaration is not in opposition to circumcision. Rather it is simple Kal VaChomer – meaning if one thing like circumcision is an important issue, then how much more the keeping of all the commands of Torah, which includes circumcision. So circumcision is a waste of time if your life is not in obedience to Torah. For example, this is like someone who seeks circumcision, only to continue to celebrate pagan days like Christmas. Only within a Torah framework does circumcision matter at all. That is exactly what is being expressed here.

place a restraint on you, but for that which is proper, so that you may serve **יהוה** without distraction. 36 But if any man thinks that he behaves himself improperly toward his maiden, if she is past the marriage age, and his need requires marriage, let him do what he desires, he sins not: let them marry. 37 But he that stands steadfast in his lev, having no necessity for marriage, but has power over his own desire, and has determined in his lev that he will keep his maiden single, also does well. 38 So then as for ahvot, he that gives her in marriage does well; but he that gives her not in marriage does even better. 39 The wife is married by the Torah as long as her husband lives; but if her husband is dead, she is at liberty to be married to whom she desires; of course only to those of like emunah.[1] 40 But she is happier if she remains unmarried, in my opinion: and I think also that I have the Ruach of **יהוה**.

8 Now as regarding food offered to idols, we know that we all have da'at. Da'at puffs up, but ahava edifies. 2 And if any man think that he knows anything, he knows nothing yet as he should know. 3 But if any man love **יהוה**, this person is known by Him. 4 As concerning therefore the eating of food that is offered in sacrifice to idols, we know that an idol is nothing in the olam hazeh, and that there is no other Elohim but the Echad of Yisrael. 5 For though there be many so-called elohim and masters, whether in the shamayim or on earth, as there are many mighty ones, and many masters, 6 But to us there is but One Elohim, Abba, from whom are all things, and we in Him; and One Master **יהוה** ha Moshiach, through whom are all things, and through whom we live. 7 However every man does not have that correct da'at: for some with a clear conscience being aware of

the idolatrous sacrifice, still eat things offered to idols and their conscience being weak becomes defiled. 8 But food commends us not to **יהוה**: for neither, if we eat this kind of food, are we better in His sight; neither, if we do not eat this kind of food, are we worse in His sight. 9 But beware lest by any means this liberty of yours becomes a stumbling-block to those that are weak. 10 For if any believing man sees you who has a true da'at of **יהוה** sitting to eat in the idol's temple, shall not the conscience of him who is weak be encouraged to eat those things which are offered to idols? 11 And through your indifference shall the weak Yisraelite brother perish, for whom ha Moshiach died? 12 But when you sin in this manner against the Yisraelite brothers, and wound their weak conscience, don't you sin against ha Moshiach Himself. 13 So, if meat causes my Yisraelite brother to stumble, I will eat no meat while the olam hazeh stands, lest I cause my Yisraelite brother to stumble.

9 Am I not a sholiach? Am I not a free man? Have I not seen **יהושע** ha Moshiach our Master? Are not you my work in **יהוה**? 2 If I am not a sholiach to others, yet doubtless I am to you: for you are the seal of my sholiach's work in **יהוה**. 3 My answer to them that do examine my credentials is this, 4 Have we not authority to eat and to drink? 5 Have we not authority to travel with a sister, a wife, or relative, just like the other shlichim, and other brothers of the Master **יהושע**, and Kepha? 6 Or is it only Bar-Nabah and I alone, that have no authority to stop secular work? 7 What officer or soldier goes into a war at any time at his own expenses? Who plants a vineyard, and eats not of its fruit? Or who feeds a flock, and eats not from the milk of the flock? 8 Do I say these things, as a man would talk? Or does not the Torah say the same thing also? 9 For it is written in the Torah of Moshe, *You shall not muzzle the mouth of the ox that treads out the corn. Is*

---

[1] This is exactly how Yahshua was able to remarry Yisreal by becoming the dead Husband, freeing her to remarry her Husband and Master. For more details see: **Coming Clean** at http://store.yourarmstoisrael.org/Qstore/Qstore.cgi?CMD=011&PROD=000262

יהוה concerned only about the oxen? 10 Or does He say it for all our sakes? Yes. For our sakes, no doubt, this is written: that he that plows should plow in tikvah; and that he that threshes should thresh in tikvah so that both can be partakers of His tikvah of harvest. 11 If we have sown to you the spiritual things, is it too much if we should reap your material things? 12 If others are partakers of this authority over you, what about us? But we have not used this authority; but we put up with all things, lest we should hinder the besarot of ha Moshiach. 13 Do you not know that those who serve the Set-Apart Place receive their provision from the things of the Set Apart Place? And those who serve at the altar have their share of the offerings from the altar? 14 Even so has יהוה ordained that those who proclaim the besarot should live from the besarot.[1] 15 But I have used none of these things: neither have I written that these compensations should be done to me: for it were better for me to die, than that any man should make my boasting worthless. 16 For though I proclaim the besarot, I have nothing to boast about: for necessity is laid upon me; yes, woe to me, if I proclaim not the besarot! 17 For if I do this thing voluntarily, then I have a reward: but if not voluntarily I am entrusted with mere management duties. 18 What is my reward then? Truly that, when I proclaim the besarot, I may make the besarot of ha Moshiach without cost, that I do not abuse my authority in the besarot. 19 For though I am free from all men, yet have I made myself an eved to all, so that I might gain more beings. 20 And to the Yahudim I became as a Yahudite, that I might gain the Yahudim; to them that are under the Torah, as under the Torah,[2] that I might gain them that are under the Torah;[3] 21 To them that are without Torah, as without Torah, being

not without Torah before יהוה, but guarded by the Torah for ha Moshiach, that I might gain them that are without Torah.[4] 22 To the weak I became as one who is weak, that I might gain the weak: I am made all things to all men, that I might by any means lead some to salvation. 23 And this I do for the sake of the besarot that I might be a fellow partaker of it with you. 24 Don't you know that they who run in a race all run, but only one receives the prize? So when you run, run in such a way that you may obtain it. 25 And every man that competes for the prize controls himself in all things. Now they do it to obtain a corruptible crown; but we an incorruptible one. 26 So I run, not with uncertainty; so I fight, not as one that aimlessly beats the air: 27 But I conquer and subdue my body, so that when I have proclaimed to others, I myself should not become a castaway.

10 Moreover, Yisraelite brothers, I would not that you should be ignorant,[5] how that all our ahvot[6] were under the cloud, and all passed through the sea; 2 And were all immersed into Moshe in the cloud and in the sea; 3 And did all eat the same spiritual food; 4 And did all drink the same spiritual drink: for they all drank of that spiritual Rock that followed them:[7] and that Rock was and is ha Moshiach. 5 But with many of them יהוה was not well pleased: for they were overthrown in the wilderness. 6 Now these things were our examples, to the intent we should not lust

---

[1] Yisraelite congregations are expected to provide for their hard working leaders.
[2] "Under the Torah" means guarded or protected by its loving boundaries. Yisrael and specifically Jewish Yisrael were all protected under the Torah's covering from pagan dominance.
[3] House of Judah.

[4] Ephraim Yisrael, or House of Yisrael.
[5] How many born again people sadly remain ignorant of the fact that their physical fathers were the ones coming out of Egypt? This chapter is written so that your ignorance in this area can pass.
[6] Rav Shaul, a Jewish Rabbi and Pharisee, stated that the physical fathers of the Corinthian congregation, or ekklesia, were the very ones who along with his physical fathers (notice the term "our"), left Egypt, and disobeyed YHWH in the wilderness. Also note the term "all our fathers" which means all the patriarchs we share, and also can mean the fathers of us all! All Jewish believers along with the Ephraimites at Corinth, had the same biological fathers who experienced the same historical events.
[7] Notice that the Rock (Yahshua-YHWH) was spiritual; not the physical ancestors of the Corinthian Ephraimite brothers.

after evil things, as they also lusted. [1]
7 Neither let us be idolaters, as were some of them; as it is written, The people sat down to eat and drink, and rose up to play. 8 Neither let us commit fornication, as some of them committed, and there fell in one day twenty three thousand. 9 Neither let us test ha Moshiach, as some of them also tested, and were destroyed by serpents. 10 Neither let us murmur, as some of them also murmured, and were destroyed by the destroyer. 11 Now all these things happened to them for examples: and they are written as our warning,[2] upon whom the ends of the olam hazeh have come. 12 Therefore let him that thinks he stands take careful watch, lest he fall. 13 There has no trial come upon you but such as is common to all men: but יהוה is faithful, who will not allow you to be tempted above that which you are able to bear; but will with the trial also make a way of escape, that you may be able to bear it. 14 Therefore, my dearly be loved, flee from idolatry.[3] 15 I speak as to wise men; you are the shophet of what I say. 16 The kiddish cup of bracha which we bless, is it not the sharing of the dom of ha Moshiach? The matzah which we break, is it not the sharing of the body of ha Moshiach? 17 For we being many are one lechem, and one body: for we are all partakers of that lechem echad.[4] 18 Behold Yisrael whose observance is after the flesh:[5] are not those who eat of the sacrifices partakers of the altar? 19 What then do I say? That the idol is anything, or that which is offered in

sacrifice to idols is anything? 20 But I say, that the things that the gentiles sacrifice,[6] they sacrifice to shadim, and not to Elohim: and I would not that you should have chavurah with shadim. [7] [8] 21 Ye cannot drink the kiddish cup of יהוה, and the cup of shadim: you cannot be partakers of יהוה's table, and the table of shadim. 22 Do we provoke יהוה to jealousy? Are we stronger than He is? 23 All things are permitted for me, but all things are not profitable: all things are permitted for me, but all things do not build up my emunah. 24 Let no man seek his own interests only, but every man another's well-being and welfare. 25 Whatever is sold in the meat market, that eat, asking no questions for conscience sake:[9] 26 For the earth is the Master יהוה's, and the fullness of it. 27 If any of them that believe not invite you to a feast, and you desire to go; whatever is set before you, eat, asking no question for conscience sake. [10] 28 But if any man say to you, This is offered in sacrifice to idols, do not eat it for his sake that showed it, and for conscience sake: for the earth is the Master יהוה's, and the fullness thereof: 29 The conscience, of which I speak is not yours, but others: for why is my liberty judged by another man's conscience? 30 For if I by unmerited favor be a partaker, why should evil be spoken against me for that thing for which I give hodu? 31 Therefore whether you eat, or

---

[1] These things that happened to our forefathers "to serve as our examples" that we should not repeat the very same mistakes of our Yisraelite forefathers."

[2] The warning is simple. It happened to Yisrael before and it can happen to the last few generations of Yisrael as well.
[3] If Ephraim is going to truly be repatriated back into Yisrael with Yahudah, he has to fully and completely renounce all forms of idolatry on an ongoing basis.
[4] From this verse alone, all emunah in separate entity theology is shown to be from the devil. Any division of YHWH's people into Jew and Gentile, or any other form of division outside Yisrae'ls Commonwealth, is seen as the establishment of a separate entity or expression. Once we understand that YHWH has only one Elect, and we understand that it is not for Yisraelites to run to gentile practice, but for redeemed non-Jews to run to Yisraelite practice, all our understanding of the rest of scripture will fall neatly into line.
[5] An obvious reference to unsaved parts of Jewish Yisrael.

[6] The mixed worship of Corinthian Yisraelites is compared and contrasted to the worship of gentiles who by definition are pagans. One cannot be a saved gentile any more than one can be a clean pig. Gentiles worship demons. Yisraelites worship YHWH through His Son. Born again believers were from the first century onward seen as Yisraelites.
[7] They may seem harsh but Scripture is clear here. A Torah-guarding born-again Yisraelite cannot have close fellowship with anyone who sees himself as a gentile; for by Biblical definition, gentiles worship demons!
[8] Yisraelites become one with others when they worship. We should neither have close fellowship with Yisrael after the flesh (unregenerate Yahudah) as stated in verse 18 nor with gentiles in false systems of worship, or with pagans. Our shared community is to be with other Nazarene Yisraelites.
[9] This does not mean we can eat unkosher (unclean) foods. Rather that if an animal is clean as defined in Torah, the people of Yisrael should just eat since they are not held responsible for the origins of the meat. In pagan areas, it was not always possible to determine beyond any doubt whether or not the meat had been used in a pagan temple rite.
[10] Meaning as long as it is clean/kosher and the origin cannot be determined, a Yisraelite may eat with a clear conscious.

drink, or whatever you do, do all to the tifereth of יהוה. 32 Give no offence, neither to the Yahudim,[1] nor to the nations,[2] nor to the Yisraelite congregation [3] of יהוה : 33 Even as I please all men in all things, not seeking my own advantage, but the advantage of many, that they may be saved.

11

Be imitators of me, even as I also am of ha Moshiach. 2 Now I praise you, Yisraelite brothers, that you remember me in all things, and keep the chukim and mishpatim,[4] as I delivered them to you. 3 But I would have you to know, that the head of every man is ha Moshiach; and the head of the woman is the man; and the head of ha Moshiach is יהוה.[5] 4 Every man making tefillot or prophesying, having his head veiled and hanging down, dishonors his head.[6] 5 But every woman that makes tefillot or prophesies with her head uncovered dishonors her head: for that is the same as if she were shaven.[7] 6 For if the woman does not have a head covering, let her also be shorn: but if it is a shame for a woman to be shorn or shaven, let her be covered. 7 For a man indeed ought not to

veil his head,[8] because he is the image and tifereth of יהוה : but the woman is the tifereth of the man. 8 For the man is not from the woman; but the woman from the man. 9 Neither was the man created for the woman; but the woman for the man. 10 For this cause ought the woman to have a symbol of authority on her head because of the unclean fallen shadim.[9] 11 Nevertheless neither is the man independent of the woman, neither the woman independent of the man, in יהוה. 12 For as the woman is from the man, even so is the man also through the woman; but all things are from יהוה. 13 Shophet for yourselves: is it proper that a woman prays to יהוה uncovered? 14 Does not nature itself teach you, that, if a man has long hair,[10] it is a shame to him? 15 But if a woman has long hair, it is a tifereth for her: for her hair is given to her as a covering.[11] 16 But if any man seems to be contentious, we have no such custom of contention, neither the congregations of יהוה.[12] 17 Now in declaring this to you I do not commend you, since when you come together you have not made progress but have become worse.[13] 18 For first of all, when you come together in the Yisraelite congregation, I shema that there are divisions among you; and I partly believe it. 19 For there must be

---

[1] Unbelieving Yahudim.
[2] Unbelieving Ephraimites or pagans.
[3] The redeemed of both houses and those who join them.
[4] Statutes and judgments.
[5] The Father is the head of Yahshua, not His co-equal, for The Father was, is, and always will be greater; that is scripture. But we cannot inherit eternal life without the Son.
[6] Head veiled (Strong's Greek # 2596 **kata**, meaning hanging down). This is not any kind of prohibition against yarmulkes or skull caps, since all the priests of Yisrael as well as the kings wore them. As His kings and priests, Revelation 1:6, we also as Yisraelite men are required to wear head coverings especially in public worship and in times of ministry. The prohibition here is against veils hanging down like a woman, since that was a sign of cross-dressing which is forbidden in Torah as found in Deuteronomy 22:5. Also the veil even if in the form of long hair worn over the forehead as a woman, is also a type of cross-dressing, or gender confusion, or such the principle being taught here is the Torah warning against all cross-dressing, whether it be veiling the face as the temple prostitutes did in Athens and Corinth, or using long hair for similar purposes. For more details on this subject see: **Reclaiming A Lost Priestly Tool** available at:
http://store.yourarmstoisrael.org/Qstore/Qstore.cgi?CMD=011 &PROD=1065766858
[7] Denominations can and indeed have fought over ladies' head coverings. For Yisraelite ladies however, this is not an option but like their male counterparts their head must be covered in public worship settings, and by choice in private settings. If a woman does not wear a head covering she is acting like a pagan, since pagan female temple prostitutes shaved their heads as seen here.

[8] With a hang-me-down veil, or long hanging frontal hair.
[9] This is a clear reference back to Genesis 6 where women who were not under a spiritual authority or covering like Noach's were molested and had demons co-habitate with them. Due to the reality of unclean demons desiring to physically violate and emotionally scar women through vaginal entry, women are strongly urged to do what is proper and not make this a contentious issue like some who feel this is not important.
[10] Worn like a woman, but OK for Nazarite vows and such other pursuits of YHWH.
[11] The point being that nature is the ultimate instructor. If women have longer hair, it is because YHWH is saying that women are to be covered. Nature and Scripture each teach likewise.
[12] The congregations of Yisrael have no custom that makes this a side issue or worse yet a contentious one. It is a main issue showing rebellion or submission to kingdom life and must not be treated as a side issue and must not be made into a contentious matter. It is given to the congregations as divine guidance. Rav Shaul states here clearly that this Corinthian custom of contention is not found in other congregations in Renewed Covenant Yisrael.
[13] In many issues including the one he has addressed for 16 verses.

controversies and also heresies among you, that those who are approved may be made manifest among you.[1] 20 When you come together therefore into one place as Yisrael, this is not to eat יהושע's supper. 21 For in eating every one takes his own supper first: and one is hungry, and another is drunk. 22 What's going on? Don't you have houses to eat and to drink meals in? Or do you despise the Yisraelite congregation of יהוה, and shame those that have nothing? What shall I say to you? Shall I tehilla you for this? I will not give you tehilla. 23 For I have received from יהוה that which also I delivered to you, that the Master יהושע the same night in which He was betrayed took lechem: 24 And when He had said the bracha, He broke it, and said, *Take, eat: this is My body, which is broken for you: this do in remembrance of Me.* 25 After the same manner also He took the kiddush cup, after He had eaten, saying, *This cup of redemption is the Brit Chadasha in My dom: this do, as often as you drink it, in remembrance of Me.* 26 For as often as you eat this lechem, and drink this cup, you do show יהושע's death until He returns.[2] 27 Therefore whosoever shall eat this lechem, and drink this cup of the Master יהוה, unworthily,[3] shall be guilty of the body and dom of the Master יהוה. 28 But let a man examine himself, and so let him eat of that lechem, and drink of that cup. 29 For he that eats and drinks unworthily, eats and drinks damnation to himself, not discerning the body of the Master יהוה.[4]

30 For this reason many are weak and sickly among you, and many are dead.[5] 31 For if we would shophet ourselves, we should not be judged. 32 But when we are judged, we are disciplined by יהוה, that we should not be condemned with the olam hazeh. 33 Therefore, my Yisraelite brothers, when you come together to eat, wait one for the other. 34 And if any man hunger, let him eat at home; so that when you come together it is not for condemnation. And the rest of the Pesach procedures I will set in order when I come.

12 Now concerning spiritual gifts, my Yisraelite brothers, I would not have you ignorant. 2 Ye know that you were gentiles,[6] carried away to and by those dumb idols, even as you were led. 3 Therefore I want you to understand, that no man speaking by the Ruach of יהוה calls יהושע a curse: and that no man can say that יהושע is the Master יהוה,[7] but by the Ruach HaKodesh. 4 Now there are diversities of gifts, but the same Ruach. 5 And there are differences in callings, but the same Master יהוה. 6 And there are diversities of powers and manifestations,[8] but it is the same Elohim who works all and through all. 7 But the manifestation of the Ruach is given to every man to profit himself and all others. 8 For to one is given by the Ruach the word of chochmah; to another the word of da'at by the same Ruach; 9 To another emunah by the same Ruach; to another the gifts of healing by the same Ruach; 10 To another the working of nisim; to another prophecy; to another discerning of ruachim; to another divers kinds of languages; to another the interpretation of diverse languages: 11 But all these are done by that one and the same

---

[1] Therefore believers are responsible for making sure that heresy is not being taught and thereby will be recognized as those approved by the word.
[2] "As often as you do this" means that when the proper time rolls around annually on the 14th of Aviv between the evenings, that is to say 3-6 PM, then do it in remembrance of Me. This does not mean that a believing congregation is to do this as often as they feel like it. Rather they are to do it by submitting to the times and frequencies that Yahshua did, since after all, we are remembering what He did, not what the church council or the elder board command us to do. Communion is taken once a year during Passover, not as an event divorced from Passover.
[3] Is later defined in verse 29 as not discerning His broken body for our sins, and the great eternal consequences associated with that, as well as not discerning the unity and love required in the body of Yisrael before this meal can ever be shared.
[4] See note #53 on verse 27.

[5] There cannot be unforgiveness and divisions in the camp during this solemn time. Many had already found that out the hard way.
[6] Note the tense here. These are non-Jewish Yisraelites and it's time for believers to walk like Yahshua walked.
[7] Mar-Yah in Aramaic; showing Yahshua to be the Master-Yah Himself.
[8] YHWH works differently in every Yisraelite's life.

Ruach, dividing to every man individually as He will. 12 For as the body of Yisrael is one, and has many members, and all the members of that one body, being many, are still one body: so also is ha Moshiach. 13 For by one Ruach are we all immersed into one body, whether we be Yahudim or Greeks or Arameans, whether we be eved or free; and have been all made to drink of Ruach echad. 14 For the body is not one member, but many. 15 If the foot shall say, Because I am not the hand, I am not of the body; is it therefore not of the body? 16 And if the ear shall say, Because I am not the eye, I am not of the body; is it therefore not of the body? 17 If the whole body was an eye, where would the hearing be? If the whole body were for hearing, what part would the smelling come from? 18 But now has Elohim set the members every one of them in the body, as it has pleased Him. 19 And if they were all the same member, where would the body be? 20 But now there are indeed many members, yet just one body. 21 And the eye cannot say to the hand, I have no need of you: nor can the head say to the feet, I have no need of you. 22 No, rather those members of the body, which seem to be weakest, are the most necessary: 23 And those members of the body, which we think to be less respected, upon these we present greater respect; and our uncomely parts we dress up with greater care. 24 For our nicer looking parts have no need for special attention: but Elohim has blended the body together, having given more abundant respect to the parts that lack respect or are inferior: 25 That there should be no discord or division in the body; but that the members should have the same ahava one for another. 26 And whether one member suffers, all the members suffer with it; or if one member be honored, all the members gilah with it. 27 Now you are the body of ha Moshiach, and members individually. 28 And יהוה has set some in the Yisraelite congregation, first shlichim, secondarily niviim, thirdly moriim, after

that nisim, then gifts of healings, helpers, leaders, and diverse languages. 29 Are all shlichim? Are all niviim? Are all moriim? Are all workers of nisim? 30 Do all have the gifts of healings? Do all speak with diverse languages? Do all interpret? 31 But seek earnestly the best gifts: and yet I will show you a more excellent halacha.

13 Though I speak with the diverse languages of men and of heavenly malachim, and have not ahava, I am become as sounding brass, or a clanging cymbal. 2 And though I have the gift of prophecy, and understand all sod mysteries, and all da'at; and though I have all emunah, so that I could remove mountains, and have not ahava, I am nothing. 3 And though I distribute all my material things to feed the poor, and though I give my body to be burned, and have not ahava, it profits me nothing. 4 Ahava suffers long, and is kind; ahava envies not; ahava does not boast, is not puffed up, 5 Does not behave itself indecently, seeks not its own, is not easily provoked, thinks no evil; 6 Has no gilah in Torah-less-ness, but simchas in the emet; 7 Bears all things, believes all things, tikvahs for all tov things, endures all things. 8 Ahava never fails: but whether there are prophecies, they shall fail; whether there be diverse languages, they shall cease; whether there be da'at, it shall vanish away.[1] 9 For we know in part, and we prophesy in part. 10 But when that which is Perfect has come, then that which is in part shall be done away.[2]

---

[1] All these gifts of the Spirit will one day vanish away and cease, the question then is when?
[2] The perfect one is Yahshua. When Yahshua returns, we will see Him and therefore all temporary manifestations will no longer be needed. "The perfect" cannot be speaking of the completion of the Bible, as some believe, since all translations are not perfect and moreover as seen in verse 12 the perfect object that comes has a face, not a book cover. Therefore all the gifts remain in full operation until His return. Of course, this means so do the abuses of those same gifts. Returing Ephraimites and Jews coming out of the Sunday system often are scared of these manifestations and merely dismiss them because they are too discomforting; however, that is sadly setting aside the written Word in exchange for imagined emotional tranquility. Truth is truth, regardless of some people's excess and abuse.

11 When I was a child, I spoke as a child, I understood as a child, I thought as a child: but when I became a man, I put away childish things. 12 For now we see in a mirror, dimly; but then panayim-el-panayim:[1] now I know in part; but then shall I know Him, even as also He has known me. 13 And now abides these three - emunah, tikvah, ahava; but the greatest of these is ahava.[2]

14 Follow after ahava, and desire spiritual gifts, but specifically that you may prophesy. 2 For he that speaks in an unknown language[3] speaks not to men, but to Elohim: for no man understands him; but in the Ruach he speaks sod mysteries. 3 But he that prophesies speaks to men to edification, and encouragement, and comfort. 4 He that speaks in an unknown language edifies himself; but he that prophesies [4] edifies the Yisraelite congregation. 5 I would that you all spoke with diverse languages, but rather that you prophesied: for greater is he that prophesies than he that speaks with diverse languages, unless the same one interpret, that the Yisraelite congregation may receive edifying. 6 Now, Yisraelite brothers, if I come to you speaking with diverse languages, what shall I profit you, except I shall speak to you either by revelation, or by da'at, or by prophesying, or by teaching? 7 And even lifeless instruments that give musical sounds, whether flute or harp, except they give a distinct sound, how shall it be known what is played on the flute or harp? 8 For if the shofar gives out an uncertain sound, who shall prepare himself for the battle? 9 So likewise, unless you utter by the tongue words that are easy to be understood, how shall it be known what is spoken? For you shall be speaking into the air. 10 There are, undoubtedly, so many kinds of voices and sounds in the olam hazeh, and none of them is without significance. 11 Therefore if I know not the meaning of the voice, I shall be to him that speaks a foreigner, and he that speaks shall be a foreigner[5] to me. 12 So since, you are zealous for spiritual gifts, seek gifts that will allow you to excel in the edifying of the entire Yisraelite congregation. 13 Therefore let him that speaks in an unknown language makes tefillah that he may also be given the interpretation. 14 For if I make tefillah in an unknown langauge, my Ruach makes tefillah, but my understanding is unfruitful. 15 What then shall I do? I will make tefillah with the Ruach, and I will make tefillah with the binah also: I will sing with the Ruach, and I will sing with the binah also. 16 Or else when you shall bless with the Ruach, how shall he that is in a place of not being learned say, Amein; when you give hodu, seeing he does not understand what you are saying? 17 For you truly do well to give hodu in the Ruach, but the others are not edified. 18 I thank my Elohim; I speak with diverse languages more than all of you combined: 19 Yet in the Yisraelite congregation I had rather speak five words with my understanding, that by my voice I might teach others also, than ten thousand words in an unknown language. 20 Yisraelite brothers, be not children in binah: but in evil and Torah breaking that's where you can be children, but in binah be men.

---

[1] The Perfect One with a face is Yahshua and when He returns we will be with Him face to face and all gifts of the Spirit naturally will cease.
[2] After all the gifts of the Ruach cease, these three things will remain: emunah, hope, and love. Love lasts forever both in this world and the age to come.
[3] These tongues are not gibberish or lip gyrations, but true and fully recognized languages spoken in the world today.
[4] Prophecy is a forth-telling of the written Word more than a declaration of the future, which usually falls under the category of words of knowledge about specific things that YHWH reveals.

[5] As opposed to a Yisraelite speaking in prophecy, or tongues plus interpretation. If there are tongues without interpretation, then instead of the Yisraelites being built up and edified, Scripture compares that chaos to two pagans speaking to each other in different languages.

21 In the Torah it is written, *With men of other diverse languages and other lips will I speak to this people; and yet for all that will they not hear Me*, says the Master יהוה.[1] 22 So diverse languages are for a sign, not to them that believe, but to them that believe not: but prophesying serves not for unbelievers, but for those who believe. 23 If therefore the whole Yisraelite congregation comes together into one place, and all speak with diverse languages, and there comes in a visitor or those that are unlearned in the gifts, or even unbelievers, will they not say that you are meshugoyim? 24 But if all prophesy, and there comes in a visitor, one that believes not, or one who is unlearned, he will be convinced by all the words, and he will be set right by all the words: 25 And the secrets of his lev will be openly revealed; and so falling down on his face he will worship Elohim, and report that Elohim is truly among you. 26 How is it then, Yisraelite brothers? When you come together, each one of you has a mizmor, has a different doctrine, has a language, has a revelation, and has an interpretation. Let all things be done to build up the people of Yisrael. 27 If any man speaks in an unknown language, let two, or at most three take their turns, and let someone interpret. 28 But if there is no interpreter, let him keep silent in the Yisraelite congregation; and let him speak to himself, and to His Elohim. 29 Let the neviim speak two or three in their turns, and let the others discern their words. 30 If anything is simultaneously revealed to another that sits by, let the first hold his silence and not interrupt. 31 For you may all prophesy one by one in your turn, that all may learn, and all may be comforted. 32 And the ruachim of the neviim are subject to the neviim.[2] 33 For Elohim is not the author of confusion, but of shalom, as He is in all congregations of the kidushim. 34 Let your women keep silent in the congregations: for it is not permitted for them to speak; but they are commanded to be under obedience, as also says the Torah. 35 And if they will learn any thing, let them ask their husbands at home: for it is a shame for women to speak out in the Yisraelite congregation.[3] 36 What? Came the word of יהוה out from you only? Or came it to you only? 37 If any man thinks himself to be a navi, or a spiritual being, let him acknowledge that the things that I write to you are in fact from the Torah of יהוה. 38 But if any man is ignorant, let him be ignorant.[4] 39 Wherefore, Yisraelite brothers, seek to prophesy, and also forbid not to speak with diverse languages. 40 Of course let all things be done decently and in order.

15 Moreover, Yisraelite brothers, I declare to you the besarot which I proclaimed to you, which also you have received, and in which you stand; 2 By which also you are saved, if you keep in memory what I proclaimed to you, unless you have believed in vain. 3 For I delivered to you first of all that which I also received, how that ha Moshiach died for our sins according to the Ketuvim; 4 And that He was buried, and that He rose again the third day according to the Ketuvim:[5] 5 And that He was seen of Kepha, then of the twelve: 6 After that, more than five hundred Yisraelite brothers saw Him at once; of

---

[1] Tongues were given to assist others in identifying the ten tribes of returning Yisrael. For an extensive teaching identifying Ephraim as those gifted in tongues with interpretation in the Renewed Covenant see: **The Promise To Ephraim**:
http://www.yourarmstoisrael.net/audio/promise_to_ephraim.ram
[2] Meaning that no one with a word from YHWH has to do anything like interrupt, disrupt worship or liturgy, or the like. If he has the true and pure gift, he can hold that word even for months, until he has an unction or an opening in the service, to give it without causing confusion.
[3] This does not mean women cannot talk or minister. It simply means that they cannot shout out questions to their husbands during meetings. They need to wait until they arrive home. This condition was caused because the first-century Nazarene Yisraelite synagogues met in places where the men and women sat separate, and had to yell across the room to get one another's attention. The cause of this command to keep silent is not the women themselves, but rather the orthodox Jewish seating arrangement of the early Nazarene Yisraelites who met in synagogues until about 130 CE.
[4] Yisraelites should teach only those who want to be taught, not those who think they have nothing more to learn or unlearn! Move on from these to others.
[5] Hosea 6:2 Yisrael and Yahshua both YHWH's Son, were raised after 3 days to life.

whom a great many remain alive, but some are dead. 7 After that, He was seen by Yaakov; then of all the shlichim. 8 And last of all He was seen by me also, ignorant and imperfectly trained as I was. 9 For I am the least of the shlichim, that am not even fit to be called a sholiach, because I persecuted the Yisraelite congregation of Elohim. 10 But by the unmerited favor of יהוה today I am what I am: and His unmerited favor that was showered upon me was not in vain; but I labored even more abundantly than them: yet not I, but the unmerited favor of יהוה which was in me. 11 Therefore whether it was I, or them; so we proclaimed, and so you believed. 12 Now if ha Moshiach is proclaimed that He rose from the dead, how say some among you that there is no resurrection of the dead? 13 But if there is no resurrection of the dead, then is ha Moshiach not risen: 14 And if ha Moshiach has not risen, then is our proclaiming in vain, and your emunah is also in vain. 15 Yes, and worse than that we are found to be false witnesses of יהוה; because we have testified about יהוה that He raised up ha Moshiach: whom He did not raise up, if it be that the dead rise not. 16 For if the dead rise not, then ha Moshiach is not raised: 17 And if ha Moshiach is not raised, your emunah is in vain; you are still in your sins. 18 Then those also who died with emunah in ha Moshiach have perished. 19 If for this chayim only we have tikvah in ha Moshiach, we are of all men most miserable. 20 But now is ha Moshiach risen from the dead, and become the bikkurim of them that died. 21 For since by man came death, by Man came also the resurrection of the dead. 22 For as in Adam all die, even so in ha Moshiach shall all be made alive. 23 But every man in his own order: ha Moshiach the bikkurim; afterwards they that are ha Moshiach's at His coming. 24 Then comes the end of this olam hazeh, when He shall have delivered up the malchut to יהוה, even Abba; when He shall have put down

all rule and all authority and power. 25 For He must reign, until He has put all enemies under His feet. 26 The last enemy that shall be destroyed is death. 27 For He has put all things under His feet. But when He says, all things are put under Him, it is clear that the one who did put all things under Him, Abba Himself is excluded. [1] 28 And when all things shall be subdued under Him, then shall the Son also Himself be subject to Abba that put all things under Him, so that יהוה may be all in all. [2] 29 Otherwise what shall they do who are immersed for the dead, if the dead rise not at all? Why are they then immersed for the dead? [3] 30 And why do we stand in jeopardy every hour? 31 I affirm by my boasting over you that I have in ha Moshiach יהושע our Master, I die daily. 32 If after the manner of men I have fought with beasts at Ephesos, [4] what advantage is it to me, if the dead rise not? Let us eat and drink; for tomorrow we die. 33 Be not deceived: evil company corrupts tov manners and habits. 34 Awake to tzedakah, and sin not; for some have not the da'at of Elohim: I speak this to your shame. 35 But someone will say, How are the dead raised up? And with what body do they come? 36 You fool, that which you sow is not made alive, except it die: 37 And that which you sow, you sow not the body that shall be, but the bare grain, that it may by chance result in wheat, barely or even some other grain: 38 But Elohim gives it a body as it has pleased Him, and to every seed its own body. 39 All flesh is not the same flesh: but there is one kind of flesh of men, another flesh of beasts, another of fishes, and another of birds. 40 There are also

---

[1] When are wayward Yisraelites going to get this straight? The Father is never under Yahshua's authority nor does He take orders from Yahshua as an equal; but He was, is, and always will be in this age and the age to come, over Yahshua and not under Him.

[2] Let freedom's truth ring in this verse. When the age-to-come dawns and Yahshua rules on David's throne, He still takes all commands and orders from the greater part of YHWH.

[3] This is not approving of mikvah by proxy as practiced by the Mormons. Rather it was a memorial service or act to remember the memory of the blessed dead, similar to the modern rabbinical Jewish memorial service known as **Yizkor**, in the hope of resurrection.

[4] Local anti-Yahshua missionaries.

heavenly bodies, and earthly bodies: but the tifereth of the heavenly is one kind, and the tifereth of the earthly is another kind. 41 There is one tifereth of the sun, and another tifereth of the moon, and another tifereth of the cochavim: for one cochav differs from another cochav in tifereth. 42 So also is the resurrection of the dead. It is sown in corruption; it is raised in incorruption: 43 It is sown in dishonor; it is raised in tifereth: it is sown in weakness; it is raised in power: 44 It is sown a natural body; it is raised a spiritual body. There is a natural body, and there is a spiritual body. 45 And so it is written, The first man Adam was made a living being; the last Adam was made a chayim giving Ruach. 46 But the spiritual Adam was not first, but the natural Adam; and afterwards the spiritual one. 47 The first man is of the earth, earthy: the second man is the Master יהוה from the shamayim. 48 As is the earthy, so also are those that are earthy: and as is the heavenly, so also are those that are heavenly. 49 And as we have borne the image of the earthy, we shall also bear the image of the heavenly. 50 Now this I say, Yisraelite brothers, that flesh and dom cannot inherit the malchut of יהוה ; [1] neither does corruption inherit incorruption. 51 Behold, I show you a sod mystery; We shall not all die, but we shall all be changed,[2] 52 In a moment, in the twinkling of an eye, at the last shofar: for the shofar shall sound, and the dead shall be raised incorruptible, and we shall be changed. [3] 53 For this corruptible must put on incorruption, and this mortal must put on immortality. 54 So when this corruptible shall have put on incorruption, and this mortal shall have put on immortality, then shall be brought to pass the saying that is written, Death is swallowed up in victory. 55 O death, where is your sting? O grave, where is your victory? 56 The sting of death is sin; and the strength of sin is the Torah violations. 57 But thanks be to יהוה, who gives us the victory through our Master יהושע ha Moshiach. 58 Therefore, my beloved Yisraelite brothers, be steadfast, unmovable, always abounding in the mitzvot and assignments of the Master יהוה, for you must know that your labor is not in vain in Him.

16 Now concerning the collection for the kidushim, as I have given orders to the Yisraelite congregations of Galutyah, the same applies to you. 2 After one of the Shabbats[4] let every one of you lay aside and store up, what יהוה has prospered Him with, so that there be no collections when I come.[5] 3 And when I come, whoever you shall approve by your letters, them will I send to bring your liberal gift to Yahrushalayim. 4 And if it is right that I go also, they shall go with me. 5 Now I will come to you, when I shall pass through Makedonia: for I do pass through Makedonia. 6 And it may be that I will remain, and spend the winter with you, that you may bring me on my journey wherever I go. 7 For I will not see you now on the way; but I trust to stay a while with you, if יהוה permits. 8 But I will stay at Ephesos until Shavuot.[6] 9 For a great and effective door has opened to me, but there are many adversaries. 10 Now if Timtheous comes, see that he may be with you without worry: for he works the mitzvot of the Master יהוה, as I also do. 11 Let no man therefore despise him: but send him forth in shalom, that he may come to me: for I am waiting for him with my other Yisraelite brothers. 12 As touching our Yisraelite brother Apollos, I greatly desired him to come to

---

[1] In other words our body must - and will - be changed.
[2] One last final generation that will escape death and be changed without dying.
[3] Changed - not raptured. For more details regarding resurrection truth versus rapture fantasy. see: **A Stumbling Block To Restoration** at:
http://yourarmstoisrael.org/Articles_new/restoration/?page=10&type=12

[4] In the Greek **kata mia sabbaton** literally "after one of the Shabbats."
[5] Giving should be prepared before and with thought, as a serious and conscientious worshipper of YHWH. He desired collections (not tithes) to be made before or after Shabbat.
[6] Rav Shaul, like us, must guard YHWH's eternal feasts.

you with the Yisraelite brothers: but his desire was not to come at this time; but he will come when he shall have a convenient time. 13 Watch, stand fast in the emunah, be like men, and be strong. 14 Let all your mitzvot be done with ahava. 15 I appeal to you, Yisraelite brothers, you know the bayit of Tsephanyah, how they are the bikkurim from Achaia, and that they have fully dedicated themselves to the service of the kidushim, 16 Submit yourselves to them, and to everyone that helps us, and labors with us. 17 I am in simcha about the coming of Tsephanyah and Fortunatos and Achaicos: for that which was lacking on your part they have supplied.

18 For they have refreshed my ruach and yours: therefore recognize them that are like that. 19 The congregations of Asia Minor greet you. Aqulas and Priscilla greet you warmly in the Master, with the Yisraelite congregation that is in their bayit. 20 All the Yisraelite brothers greet you. Greet one another with a set-apart kiss. 21 The salutation of Shaul with my own hand. 22 If any man love not the Master יהושע ha Moshiach, let him be a curse. Maranatha.[1] Oh Master come! 23 The unmerited favor of our Master יהושע ha Moshiach be with you. 24 My ahava be with you all in ha Moshiach יהושע. Amein.

---

[1] An Aramaic term meaning "Master come." In the Hebrew however, **Mah aaron atah** can mean "will you be at the coming" or "will you be gathered at the coming." Either or both Semitic understandings remain Scriptural. Some claim that this phrase in the Hebrew served as a code word between believers, so as to differentiate their friends from their foes. By Rav Shaul placing the term here, he identifies his deep love and friendship even for the worldly Yisraelite believers at Corinth in code.

קורנתי ב

Qorintyah Bet - Second Corinthians
To The Believing Remnant Of Yisrael

1 Shaul, a sholiach of **יהושע** ha Moshiach by the will of **יהוה**, and Timtheous our brother, to the Yisraelite congregation of **יהוה** which is at Qorintyah, with all the kidushim that are in all Achaia: 2 Unmerited favor be to you and shalom from **יהוה** our Abba, and from the Master **יהושע** ha Moshiach. 3 Blessed be **יהוה**, even the Abba of our Master **יהושע** ha Moshiach, the Abba of all rachamim, and the Elohim of all comfort; 4 Who comforts us in all our tribulation that we may be able to comfort those who are in any trouble, by the comfort with which we ourselves are comforted by Elohim. 5 For as the sufferings of ha Moshiach abound in us, so our comforts also abound by ha Moshiach. 6 And whether we be afflicted, it is for your comfort and salvation, being worked out in enduring the same sufferings, which we also suffer: or if we are comforted, it is for your comfort and salvation. 7 And our tikvah for you is steadfast, knowing, that as you are partakers of the sufferings, so shall you be also of the comforts. 8 For we would not, brothers, have you ignorant of our trouble that came to us in Asia Minor, that we were weighed down, beyond our strength, so that we despaired even of our chayim: 9 But we were even ready to die, that we should not trust in ourselves, but in **יהוה** who raises the dead: 10 Who delivered us from so great a death, and does deliver: in whom we trust that He will yet deliver us; 11 You also helping together by making tefillah for us that for the gift bestowed upon us by the means of many persons, hodu may be given to many on our behalf. 12 For our gilah is this, the testimony of our conscience, in simplicity, sincerity and cleanliness, not with fleshly wisdom, but by the unmerited favor of **יהוה**, we have had our behavior in the olam hazeh, and even more so to you.

13 For we write no other things to you, than what you read or acknowledge; and I trust you shall acknowledge even to the end; 14 As also you have understood us in part, that we are also your gilah, even as you also are our gilah in the Yom of the Master **יהושע**. 15 And in this confidence I desired and intended to come to you before, that you might have a double benefit; 16 And to pass by you into Makedonia, and to come again out of Makedonia to you, and by you to be brought on my way toward the province of Yahudah. 17 When I was therefore considering this, did I do so lightly? Or the things that I plan, do I plan according to the flesh; that with me there should be the confusion of yes, yes, and no, no? 18 But as **יהוה** is emet, our word toward you was not even yes and no. 19 For the Son of **יהוה**, **יהושע** ha Moshiach, who was proclaimed among you by us, even by me and Sila and Timtheous, was not yes and no, but in Him was yes. 20 For all the promises of **יהוה** in Him are yes, and in Him amein, to the tifereth of **יהוה** through us. 21 Now He who establishes us with you as echad in ha Moshiach, and has anointed us all, is **יהוה**; 22 Who has also sealed us, and given the pledge of the Ruach in our levim. 23 Moreover I call **יהוה** for a record upon my being, that to spare you I decided not to come yet to Qorintyah. 24 Not that we have rule over your emunah, but are helpers of your simcha: for by emunah you stand.

2 But I determined this within myself that I would not come again to you in sadness. 2 For if I make you sorry, who is he then that makes me have simcha, but the same ones who are made sorry by me? 3 And I wrote this same to you, lest, when I came, I should have sorrow from the ones I ought to gilah with; having confidence in

you all, that my simcha is your simcha as well. 4 For out of much affliction and anguish of lev I wrote to you with many tears; not that you should be made sad, but that you might know the abundant ahava which I have for you. 5 But if anyone has caused grief, he has not made me sad only, but to a certain degree all of you: therefore the news will not be a shock to you. 6 The rebuke of many persons is sufficient for such a man. 7 So that from now on you should forgive him, and comfort him, lest perhaps such a one should be swallowed up with excessive sorrow. 8 Therefore I appeal you that you would confirm your ahava toward him. 9 For that is why I wrote to you, that I might know by your words to me, whether you are obedient in all things.[1] 10 To whom you forgive anything, I forgive also: for anything I have forgiven, to whomever I forgave it, it is for your sakes that I forgave it in the presence of ha Moshiach; 11 Lest s.a.tan should get an advantage over us: for we are not ignorant of his devices. 12 Furthermore, when I came to Troas to proclaim the besarot of ha Moshiach, and a door was opened to me by יהוה, 13 I had no rest in my ruach, because I did not find Teitus my brother: therefore I left them, I went from there into Makedonia. 14 Now thanks be to יהוה, who always causes us to triumph in ha Moshiach, and makes manifest the fragrance of His chochmah through us in every place. 15 For we are to יהוה a sweet fragrance of ha Moshiach, in them that are being saved, and in them that are perishing: 16 To the one we are the fragrance of death to death; and to the other the fragrance of chayim to chayim. And who is worthy for these things? 17 For we are not as many, who corrupt the word of יהוה: but as men of sincerity, according to the emet, in the sight of יהוה, we speak through Moshiach.

3 Do we begin again to commend ourselves? Or do we need, as some

others, letters of recommendation to you, or letters of recommendation from you? 2 You are our letter written on our levim, known and read by all men: 3 For you are known to be the letter of ha Moshiach served by us, written not with ink, but with the Ruach of the living Elohim; not in tables of stone, but on fleshy tables of the living lev.[2] 4 And this is the trust we have through ha Moshiach towards יהוה: 5 Not that we are sufficient in ourselves to think anything of ourselves; but our sufficiency is from יהוה; 6 Who also has made us worthy avadim of the Renewed Covenant; not of the letter, but of the Ruach: for the letter kills, but the Ruach gives chayim. [3] 7 But if the administration of death, written and engraved in stones, was full of so much tiereth, that the b'nai Yisrael could not behold the face of Moshe for the tiereth of his countenance; which tiereth was not lasting: [4] 8 Why then should not the administration of the Ruach be with even more tiereth?[5] 9 For if the administration of condemnation was with tiereth, much

---

[1] Yisraelite community living such as care, love, and discipline.

[2] A promise to Yisrael found in Ezekiel 36:25-27.
[3] Not a comparison between law and grace, but between Ruach-led Torah obedience versus mandated legalism. Legalism is man-imposed regulations upon another man, as found in Galatians.
[4] The subject in verse 7 is the beauty on Moshe's face that did not last. This does not say that the Torah does not last or that the Torah was passing away, as many have falsely claimed. The issue is the fading tiereth/cloud of beauty, on Moshe's face. The comparison here then is between the tiereth of the First Covenant, compared to the greater tiereth of the Renewed Covenant, since one is found on faces and tablets, whereas the other is found in the renewed heart.
[5] The comparison is between the greater tiereth of the Renewed Covenant versus the fading tiereth of the First Covenant. What was fading was the tiereth, not the entire Torah.

more does the administration of tzedakah exceed in tifereth.[1] [2] 10 For even that which was made in tifereth had no tifereth in this respect, by reason of the tifereth that exceeds it.[3] 11 For if that which was not lasting was with tifereth, how much more that which remains is full of tifereth.[4] [5] 12 Seeing then that we have such tikvah, we speak and conduct ourselves bravely: 13 And not as Moshe, who put a veil over his face that the b'nai Yisrael should not look on the tifereth that was not lasting:[6] 14 But their minds were blinded: for until this day there remains the same veil not taken away in the reading of the Tanach; which veil is removed by ha Moshiach.[7] 15 But even to this day, when Torah is read,

the veil is upon their lev.[8] 16 Nevertheless whenever a man makes teshuvah to the Master יהוה, the veil shall be taken away by the Ruach HaKodesh. 17 Now the Master יהוה is that very Ruach: and where the Ruach of the Master יהוה is, there is freedom. 18 But we all, with an open face seeing ourselves in a mirror see the tifereth of the Master יהוה, and are changed into the same likeness from tifereth to tifereth, even by the Ruach of the Master יהוה.[9]

4 Therefore we are not weary of this service, just as we are not weary of the rachamim we have received, and so we don't lose lev; 2 But have renounced the hidden things of shame, not practicing cunning, nor handling the word of יהוה deceitfully; but by the manifestation of the emet commending ourselves to every man's conscience in the sight of Elohim. 3 But if our besarot is hid, it is hid to them that are lost and perishing: 4 In whom the elohim of this olam has blinded the minds of those who believe not, lest the light of the tifereth filled besarot of ha Moshiach, who is the image and likeness of יהוה, should shine on them. 5 For we proclaim not ourselves, but ha Moshiach יהושע the Master; and ourselves your avadim for יהושע's sake. 6 For יהוה, who commanded the Light to shine out of darkness, has shone in our levim, to give the Light of the chochmah of the tifereth of יהוה in the face of יהושע ha Moshiach. 7 But we have this treasure in earthen vessels, that the excellency of the power may be of יהוה, and not of us. 8 We are distressed on every side, yet not overwhelmed; we are perplexed, but not conquered; 9 Persecuted, but not forsaken; cast down, but not destroyed; 10 Always bearing about in our bodies the death of the Master יהושע, that the chayim also of יהושע might be made manifest in our

---

[1] The tifereth of the administration of condemnation does not mean that Torah-keeping and Torah itself is futile leading to death. It means that the knowledge of sin that leads to death comes from Torah. Torah, not the Renewed Covenant, defines sin. In that sense it was and continues to be the instrument of death in that it defines sin and the wages of sin, which is death. The comparison here is that if the Torah which pointed out our sins was full of His tifereth, how much more the work of the Ruach HaKodesh in writing the same Torah in our hearts and Yahshua granting forgiveness of our sins. What has more tifereth? The covenant that points out our sins, or the covenant that takes our sins away forever? The covenant that puts Torah on stone tablets, or puts Torah in our hearts? That's the issue here. The Torah is not the issue. The tifereth of the covenant that forgives us by definition more full of tifereth, yet recognizing that Torah also has its own measure of tifereth.

[2] The ongoing comparison is between administrations and not the Torah itself. What has more tifereth? The administration that placed the Torah on stone tablets before Yisrael through a man, or the placing of the same Torah in men's hearts by the Ruach without the administration of a man? Therefore the issue is between administrations of Torah and not the Torah itself.

[3] The issue again is tiferth versus greater tifereth, not grace versus law.

[4] The greater tifereth and greater administration of that tifereth has exceeded that of the stone delivery and the human lawgiver, since now the Lawgiver is YHWH and the tablets are regenerated hearts.

[5] **Kal VaChomer**. If this is true… how much truer is that? If this be done….aren't we then to do that other thing even more? A basic principle of Torah understanding and interpretation from the first century school of Hillel.

[6] The veil covered the tifereth that was passing away, since it was on a human being and not on the inner tablets of the heart, where it is now being guarded and can never fade or pass away.

[7] The veil of focusing in on the lesser and temporal tifereth blinds Jewish Yisrael to the greater tifereth, seen only when the veil is removed by Moshiach. In other words, the veil of the tifereth of the Torah still covers the tifereth emanating from Torah, but only Moshiach can lift that veil for Jewish Yisrael to see the even greater tifereth of the Renewed Covenant and its greater administration.

[8] So they can't see the greater tifereth of the covenant that removes sins, found by violation of Torah.

[9] Our own tiferet seen by gazing into a mirror is greater than that on Moshe's face. Why? Because the Administrator is the Ruach of YHWH, or YHWH, as opposed to Moshe the man.

body. 11 For we who live are always delivered to death for יהושע's sake, that the chayim also of יהושע might be made manifest in our mortal bodies. 12 So then death is close to us, but chayim is in you. 13 We having the same Ruach of emunah, as it is written, I believed, and therefore have I spoken; we also believe, and therefore we also speak; 14 Knowing that He who raised up the Master יהושע shall raise us up also by יהושע, and shall present us with you. 15 For all things are for your sakes that the abundant unmerited favor might through the hodus of many overflow to the tifereth of יהוה. 16 For this reason we faint not; but though our outward man perish, yet the inward man is renewed day by day. 17 For our light and tiny afflictions, which is just for a moment, prepares for us a far greater and limitless tifereth, le-olam-va-ed; 18 We look not and gilah not at the things, that are seen, but at the things that are not seen: for the things that are seen are temporal; but the things that are not seen are le-olam-va-ed.

5 For we know that if our earthly bayit of this tent were destroyed, we still have a building of Elohim, a bayit not made with hands, eternal in the shamayim.[1] 2 For in this we groan, earnestly desiring to be clothed with our bayit, which is from the shamayim: 3 So that then, unlike now, we will not be found naked. 4 For we that are in this tent do groan, because of its weight: not because we are willing to leave it, but rather to add to it and put on the other body, so that mortality might be swallowed by chayim. 5 Now He that has prepared us for the same purpose is Elohim, who also has given to us the pledge of His Ruach. 6 Therefore we are always confident, knowing that, while we are at home in the

body, we are absent from יהוה: 7 For we have our halacha by emunah, not by sight: 8 This is why we are confident, I say, willing rather to be absent from the body, and to be present with our יהוה. 9 Therefore we labor, that, whether present or absent from home, we may be pleasing to Him. 10 For we must all appear before the bema seat of ha Moshiach; that every one may receive the things done with his body, according to what He has done, whether it be tov or bad. 11 Knowing therefore the fear of יהוה, we persuade and win men; so that we are understood by יהוה; and I trust also by you in your consciences. 12 For we commend not ourselves again to you, but we give you an occasion to boast about us, that you may have something to answer them who take pride in appearance, and not in lev. 13 For if we are wrong, we answer to Elohim: or if we are tzadik, it is for your cause. 14 For the ahava of ha Moshiach compels us; because we have judged this to be emet, that if One died for all, then all were dead: 15 And that He died for all, that those who live should not from now on live for themselves, but for Him who died for them, and rose again. 16 And from now on we know no man after the body: yes, though we have known ha Moshiach after the body, yet now we don't know Him any longer in this way. 17 Therefore if any man is in ha Moshiach, he is a renewed creation: old things have passed away; behold, all things have become renewed. 18 And all things are of יהוה, who has restored us to Himself by יהושע ha Moshiach, and has given to us the service of restoration; [2] 19 Definitely then יהוה was in ha Moshiach, restoring the olam to Himself, not counting their trespasses against them; and has committed to us the word of

---

[1] The promise to Renewed Covenant believers. This is one main reason why the tifereth of the Renewed Covenant exceeds the tifereth of the First Covenant. First Covenant believers went to Abraham's Bosom, but now that Moshiach has led captivity captive, our spirits have an abiding place in the heavens, and our bodies await the resurrection of the last day.

[2] The commission to all Yisrael. He has restored us to Him individually, as well as restored us as a nation. Now, having experienced this dual restoration, we have been ordained as Yisraelites to serve Him in the cause of reconciling other lost sheep back to Himself, and restoring all Yisraelites to each other as YHWH rebuilds and restores the Tabernacle of David, which had fallen.

restoration. [1] 20 Now then we are ambassadors for ha Moshiach, as though Elohim is asking you through us: we beg you on Moshiach's behalf, be restored to יהוה. 21 For He has made Him to be sin for us, who knew no sin; that we might be made the tzedakah of יהוה in Him.

6 We then, as workers together with Him, appeal to you also that you receive not the unmerited favor of יהוה in vain. 2 For He said, *I have heard you in a time accepted, and in the day of salvation have I helped you: behold, now is the accepted time; behold, now is the day of salvation.* 3 Giving no offence in anything that the service of restoration is not blamed: 4 But in all things showing ourselves to be the avadim of Elohim, in much patience, in afflictions, in hardships, in distresses, 5 In scourgings, in imprisonments, in tumults, in labors, in vigils, in fastings; 6 In clean Torah living, in da'at, in longsuffering, in chesed, in the Ruach HaKodesh, in sincere ahava, 7 In the word of emet, in the power of Elohim, in the armor of tzedakah on the right hand and on the left, 8 In honor and dishonor, in evil report and tov report: as deceivers, and yet emet; 9 In unknown, and yet well known; in dying, and, behold, we live; in chastening, and yet not killed; 10 As sad, yet always in gilah; in poverty, yet making many rich; as having nothing, and yet possessing all things. 11 O Qorintyahim, we have told you everything, our lev is exposed. 12 You are not constrained by us, but you are restrained by your own levim. 13 Now repay me the same way, I speak to my children, be you also increased in your ahava for me. 14 Do not unite together in marriage with unbelievers: for what fellowship has tzedakah with Torah-less-ness? And what mingling has Light with darkness? 15 And what accord or covenant has ha Moshiach with s.a.tan? Or what portion has he that believes with an unbeliever? 16 And what union has the Beit HaMikdash of יהוה with idols? For you are the Beit HaMikdash of the living Elohim; as יהוה has said, *I will dwell in them, and walk in them; and I will be their Elohim, and they shall be My ami/people.* [2] 17 *Therefore come out from among them, and be set-apart*, says the Master יהוה, *and touch not the unclean things; and I will receive you,* [3] 18 *And will be an Abba to you, and you shall be My sons and daughters*, says the Master יהוה the Almighty.

7 Having therefore these promises, dearly beloved, let us cleanse ourselves[4] from all filthiness of the flesh and ruach, perfecting our set-apartness in the fear of יהוה. 2 Receive us; we have wronged no man, we have corrupted no man, we have defrauded no man. 3 I speak this not to condemn you: for I have said before, that you are in our levim to die and live with you. 4 Great is my boldness of speech towards you, great is my boasting about you: I am filled with comfort, I am exceedingly in simcha in all our tribulation. 5 For, when we were come into Makedonia, our flesh had no rest, but we were troubled on every side; around us fightings and disputes, within were fears and pressure. 6 Nevertheless Elohim, that comforts those that are cast down, comforted us by the coming of Teitus; 7 And not by His coming only, but by the comfort with which he was comforted by you, when he told us of your longing desire, your mourning, your zeal towards me; so that I had even more simcha. 8 For though I made you sorry with a letter, I do not regret it, though I did regret it before: for I perceive that the same letter

---

[1] The message of restoration is both vertical and horizontal, and has been given to all believing Yisraelites.

[2] A reference to Ephraim Yisrael, as Rav Shaul paraphrases Hosea 2:23.

[3] If we as Yisrael come out from among the nations of exile, and the pagan religions of exile, YHWH will surely restore and receive us back, both individually and as a nation. How does Yisrael achieve that separation? By not touching or partaking of all the unclean things prohibited in Torah, as well as by walking out from the many cathedrals of error and anti-nomianism, which Scripture calls "Babylon."

[4] Yisrael must respond in obedience to the clear purity laws of Torah in order to truly inherit the promises of YHWH regarding sonship and inheritance in the kingdom.

has made you sad, though it was only for a little while.[1] 9 Now I have gilah, not that you were made sorry, but that you sorrowed leading you to full teshuvah: for you were made sorry according to the things of יהוה, that you might not be damaged by us in any way. 10 For sorrow according to the things of יהוה leads to teshuvah and to salvation that never needs to be repented of: but the sorrow of the olam hazeh works death. 11 For look; the very thing that was distressing you, that you sorrowed over according to the things of יהוה, that has resulted from your great effort, yes in your apology, yes in your anger over your sin, yes in your fear of Elohim, yes in your ahava, desire, zeal, and righting of all wrongs! In all things you have proven yourselves to be clear in this matter. 12 So, although I wrote to you, I did not write for the cause of him who had done the wrong, nor for the cause of the one that suffered the wrong, but that our care for you in the sight of Elohim might appear to be evident to you. 13 Therefore we were comforted in your comfort: yes, and exceedingly with even more simcha because of the simcha of Teitus, because his ruach was refreshed by all of you. 14 For if I boasted anything to him about you, I am not ashamed; but as we spoke all things to you in emet, even so our boasting, which I made before Teitus, was truthful. 15 And his deep ahava is more abundant toward you, while he remembers your obedience, how with respect and awe you received him. 16 I gilah therefore that I have confidence in you in all things.

8 Moreover, brothers, we want you to know the unmerited favor of יהוה bestowed on the Yisraelite congregations of Makedonia; 2 How that even in great trial of affliction, the plenty of their simcha despite their deep poverty overflowed into their rich liberality. 3 For to their credit and power, yes I bear witness, that even beyond their ability they were willing to give of themselves; 4 Begging us with much urgency that we would receive the gift, so they could take part in the service of this mitzvah to the kidushim. 5 And this they did, not only as we expected, but first they gave themselves to יהוה, and then to us by the will of יהוה. 6 So that we desired Teitus, that as he had begun, so he would also finish with you the same unmerited favor as well. 7 Therefore, as you excel in all things, in emunah, and clean speech, and in Torah da'at, and in all diligence, and in your ahava for us, see that you excel in the unmerited favor of giving also. 8 I speak not by Torah commandment, but about the sincerity of others, to prove the sincerity of your ahava. 9 For you know the unmerited favor of our Master יהושע ha Moshiach, that, though He was rich, yet for your sake He became poor, that through His poverty you might be made spiritually rich. 10 And with this background I give my advice: for this is for your advantage, who have begun before in your own desire about a year ago, to now do. 11 Now therefore perform the actual mitzvah; that as there was a readiness to perform the mitzvah, so there may be a performance of it also from that which you have. 12 For if there is a willing mind, then every man can give according to what a man has, and not according to what he has not, and then his gift is acceptable. 13 This advice is not intended to relieve other men, for you to be burdened: 14 But that there may be equality, that now at this time your plenty may be a supply for their needs, so that their plenty also may be a supply for your needs: that there may be equality:[2] 15 As it is written, He that had gathered

---

[1] The letter of stern and ongoing rebuke, found in First Corinthians, covering many areas of misbehavior and error in the Yisraelite congregation.

[2] When Yisrael is being restored, equality must be prevalent in all undertakings including giving to each other. This midrash or explanation is not talking about tithing or paying tithes which is an eternal Torah command starting at a minimum of ten percent of one's gross income. Tithing is not something an individual does arbitrarily. Instead, what is being addressed here is free-will **terumah** offerings, or the care and maintenance of the people of scattered Yisrael, where one does have the freedom to dispense according to personal decisions, based upon one's own abundance, however great or small that may be.

much had nothing extra; and he that had gathered little had no lack.[1] 16 But hodu be to יהוה, who put the same care for you into the lev of Teitus. 17 For indeed he accepted our appeal; but being more eager to receive it, on his own accord he went to see you. 18 And we have sent with him the brother, whose tehilla is in the besarot throughout all the Yisraelite congregations; 19 And not only that, but he was also chosen by the Yisraelite congregations to travel with us with this financial relief, which is administered by us to the tifereth of the same Master, and to also encourage you to do likewise: 20 We are therefore careful in the collection and distribution, that no man should blame us in this plenty that is administered by us: 21 For we are careful to do the honest things, not only in the sight of יהוה, but also in the sight of men. 22 And we have sent with them our brother, whom we have often proved diligent in many things, but now much more diligent, because of the great trust which he has in you. 23 If anyone asks about Teitus, he is my partner and fellow helper concerning you: or if anyone asks about our brothers, they are the shlichim of the Yisraelite congregations, and the very tifereth of ha Moshiach. 24 Therefore show them, and all the Yisraelite congregations, the proof of your ahava, and of our boasting on your behalf by the performance of your intentions.

9 For as touching the service to the kidushim, it is not necessary for me to write to you: 2 For I know the eagerness of your mind, for which I boast of you to them of Makedonia, that Achaia was ready to give a year ago; and your zeal has provoked very many. 3 Yet have I sent the brothers to you, lest our boasting of you should be worthless in this matter; that, as I said, you should be ready: 4 Perhaps if some from Makedonia come with me, and find you unprepared-we speak, not you-you would then be ashamed about our confident boasting. 5 Therefore I thought it necessary to ask the brothers, that they would go before me to you, and make up beforehand your gift, about which you gave notice before, that the gift might be ready, as a bracha for you, and not as an act of extortion. 6 But this I say, He who sows sparingly shall also reap sparingly; and he who sows bountifully shall reap also bountifully. 7 Every man according as he purposed in his lev, so let him give; not grudgingly, or of necessity: for Elohim loves a cheerful giver.[2] 8 And Elohim is able to make all unmerited favor abound towards you; that you, always having all sufficiency in all things, and may abound to every tov mitzvah: 9 As it is written, He has dispersed liberally; He has given to the poor: His tzedakah remains le-olam-va-ed. 10 Now He that gives seed to the sower including lechem for food, shall supply and multiply your seed sown, and increase the fruits of your tzedakah; 11 Being enriched in every way in all liberality, which causes us to give and perfect our hodu to Elohim. 12 For the administration of this service not only supplies the needs of the kidushim, but it causes an overflowing of hodus by many Yisraelites to Elohim; 13 Through the actual evidence of this service they give tifereth to יהוה for your confession and subjection to the besarot of ha Moshiach, and for your liberal distribution to them, and to all men; 14 And by their tefillot for you, who long after you for the great unmerited favor of יהוה in you. 15 Hodu also be to יהוה for His incomparable gift.[3]

10 Now I Shaul myself appeal to you by the meekness and gentleness of ha Moshiach, who in presence am lowly

---

[1] Speaking of YHWH's equitable system of manna distribution. Note the Yisraelite connection, as Rav Shaul applies a scripture about equity in Yisrael to the Corinthians, which is further evidence of their spiritual and physical roots as Yisrael.

[2] Again this speaks of free-will care giving for other Yisraelites, where the percentages are arbitrary. The tithe is not arbitrary, and is not an option, as Rav Shaul admits here by stating that he is talking and not the Torah.
[3] Moshiach Yahshua.

when among you, but being absent still have confidence towards you: 2 But I appeal to you, not to be troubled when I arrive, since I think I will have to be bold and brave against some, who think that we walk according to the flesh. 3 For though we are walking in the flesh, we do not war according to the flesh: 4 For the weapons of our warfare are not carnal, but mighty through our Elohim to the pulling down of strongholds; 5 Casting down imaginations, and every high human matter that exalts itself against the da'at of יהוה , taking captive every thought to be obedient to Moshiach; 6 And we are ready to revenge all disobedience among some, when your obedience is complete.[1] 7 Do you look on things after the outward appearance? If any man trusts that he belongs to Moshiach, let him rethink and understand, that, as he belongs to ha Moshiach, even so we belong to ha Moshiach. 8 For even if I should boast more of our authority, that יהוה has given us, not for your destruction but for your edification, I should not be ashamed: 9 I am hesitant so that I may not terrify you by my letter. 10 For his letters, they say, are weighty and powerful; but his bodily presence is weak, and his speech is weak. 11 Let the ones who think this understand, that, such as we are in word by letter when we are absent, so will we be also in action when we are present. 12 For we dare not count or compare ourselves with those who are proud of, or who commend, themselves, for they measure themselves by themselves, and comparing themselves among themselves, are not wise.[2] 13 But we will not boast of things outside our limits, but according to the limits of the authority that יהוה has distributed to us, the limit needed to reach out even to you. 14 For we stretch not ourselves beyond our limits of authority, as if we did not ever reach you: for we have come all the way to you also by proclaiming the besorat of ha Moshiach:

15 Not boasting of things beyond our limited measure, that is, of other men's labors; but having tikvah, that as your emunah is increased, we also shall be increased by you, according to our limits among you, 16 And so we shall proclaim the besorat in the regions beyond you, so as not to boast in another man's limited authority or what others have accomplished. 17 But he that boasts, let him boast about יהוה. 18 For not he that praises himself is approved, but whom the Master יהוה praises.

11 I would that you could bear with me a little in my folly: and indeed you are bearing with me. 2 For I am jealous over you with the jealousy of יהוה: for I have given you in marriage to one Husband, that I may present you as an innocent virgin to ha Moshiach. 3 But I fear, lest by any means, as the serpent beguiled Chava through his tricks, so your minds should also be corrupted away from the simplicity that is in ha Moshiach. 4 For when some- one comes and proclaims another יהושע, whom we have not proclaimed, or if you receive another ruach, which you have not before received, or another besorat, which you have not before accepted, sometimes you still put up with it! 5 For I suppose I am not inferior to the most distinguished shlichim. 6 But though I may be unskilled in speech,[3] yet not in da'at; for we have been fully transparent and open among you in all things. 7 Have I committed an offence in humbling myself that you might be exalted, because I have proclaimed to you the besorat of יהוה without pay? 8 I robbed other Yisraelite congregations, taking assistance from them, to do you tov service. 9 And when I was present with you, and was in lack, I was a burden to no man: for that which was lacking for me the brothers who came from Makedonia supplied: and in all things I have kept myself from being burdensome to you, and so will I continue

---

[1] Obedience to community and Torah is always key.
[2] Yisraelites must compare their lives to Yahshua, not to one another.

[3] Which is why Peter warns those evil persons who take Paul's hard-to-understand words, and then twist them into justifications for breaking Torah (Second Kepha 3:16-17).

to keep myself. 10 As the emet of ha Moshiach is in me, no man shall stop me from this boasting in the regions of Achaia. 11 Why? Because I don't love you? יהוה knows I do. 12 But what I do, that I will do, that I may cut off any opportunity from those who desire opportunity; that in whatever they boast, they may not be found equal to us. 13 For such are false shlichim, deceitful workers, transforming themselves into the shlichim of ha Moshiach. 14 And no marvel; for s.a.tan himself is transformed into a malach of light. 15 Therefore it is no great thing if s.a.tan's avadim also become transformed as the avadim of tzedakah; whose end shall be according to their deeds. 16 I say again, Let no man think me to be a fool; if otherwise, yet still as a fool then receive me, that I may boast myself a little. 17 That which I speak here, I speak it not according to יהוה, but as it were foolishly, in this confidence of boasting. 18 Seeing that many boast after the flesh, I will boast also. 19 For you listen to and put up with fools, despite you yourselves being wise. 20 For you allow them to dominate you, even if a man brings you into bondage, or if a man devours you, or if a man takes from you, or if a man exalts himself, or if a man hits you in the face. 21 I speak this as concerning reproach, as though we have been weak. But in things that others are bold - I speak foolishly - I am bold also. 22 Are they Ivrim? So am I. Are they Yisraelites? So am I. Are they the zera of Avraham? So am I! 23 Are they avadim of ha Moshiach? - I speak as a fool - I am even more; in labors more abundant, in beatings above my limit, in prison more frequently, in near-death experiences more often. 24 From the unbelieving Yahudim five times I received thirty-nine stripes. 25 Three times was I beaten with rods, once was I stoned, three times I was shipwrecked, a night and a day I have been in the deep; 26 In many journeys, often, in perils of waters, in perils of robbers, in perils by my own countrymen, in perils by

the heathen, in perils in the city, in perils in the wilderness, in perils in the sea, in perils among false brothers; 27 In toils and hardships, in making tefillot often, in hunger and thirst, in much fasting, in cold and in nakedness. 28 Beside those things that are outside attacks and pressures, that which comes upon me daily, the care and well being of all the Yisraelite congregations. 29 Who is sick, that I do not feel their pain? Who stumbles in their halacha, and does not have my inward sympathy? 30 If I must boast, I will boast of the things that concern my own sufferings and weaknesses. 31 The Elohim and Abba of our Master יהושע ha Moshiach, who is blessed le-olam-va-ed, knows that I do not lie. 32 In Dameshek the governor under Aretas the melech guarded the city of Dameshek with a guard, who desired to apprehend me: 33 And through a window in a basket was I let down by the wall, and escaped from his hands.

12 To boast is indeed useless for me. I prefer to relate visions and revelations of יהוה. 2 I knew a man in ha Moshiach about fourteen years ago - whether in the body, I cannot tell; or whether out of the body, I cannot tell:[1] יהוה knows - such a one was caught up to the third shamayim.[2] 3 And I knew such a man - whether in the body, or out of the body, I cannot tell: יהוה knows - 4 How he was caught up into Paradise, and heard unspeakable words, which it is not lawful for a man to utter.[3] 5 In such a one will I boast: yet about myself I will not boast anymore, except in my weaknesses. 6 For though I would desire to boast more, I shall not be a fool; for I speak the emet: but now I will stop, lest any man should think of me above that which he sees me to be, or that he hears me to be. 7 And lest I should be exalted above measure through the

---

[1] The man is Rav Shaul talking in the first person.
[2] Three heavens of creation.
[3] Words or conversations taking place between The Father and His Son and/or their set-apart messengers.

abundance of the revelations I have received, there was given to me a thorn in the flesh, a messenger of s.a.tan to buffet me, lest I should exalt myself. 8 For this thing I sought יהוה three times, that it might depart from me. 9 And He said to me, *My unmerited favor is sufficient for you: for My strength is made perfect in your weakness.* With great gilah therefore will I rather boast in my weaknesses, so that the power of ha Moshiach may rest upon me. 10 Therefore I take pleasure in my weaknesses, in reproaches, in necessities, in persecutions, in distresses for ha Moshiach's sake: for when I am physically weak, then am I spiritually strong. 11 I have become a fool in boasting; you have compelled me: for I should have been commended by you: for in nothing am I behind the most distinguished of the shlichim, though I be nothing. 12 Truly the signs of a sholiach were done among you in all patience, in signs, and wonders, and mighty mitzvot. 13 For in what manner were you inferior to other Yisraelite congregations, except that I myself was not burdensome to you? Forgive me this wrong! 14 Behold, the third time I am ready to come to you; and I will not be burdensome to you: for I seek nothing from you but just yourselves: for children should not provide for the parents, but the parents for the children. 15 And I will very willingly pay my expenses and give all of myself for your beings; yet the more I love you, the less I am loved. 16 But so be it, I did not burden you: nevertheless, as a shrewd man, I caught you with your guile. 17 Did I make any financial gain from you, by any of them whom I sent to you? 18 I urged Teitus to go to you, and with him I sent a brother. Did Teitus make a gain of you? Did not we have the same Ruach-led halacha? Was not our halacha in the same steps? 19 Again, do you think that we still need to keep defending and apologizing to you? We speak before יהוה in ha Moshiach: but we do all things, dearly beloved, for you to be built up. 20 For I

fear, lest, when I come, I shall not find you the way I would like, and that I shall act among you as you would not like: lest there be strife, jealousy, anger, contention, slander, gossip, boasting, and tumults: 21 And perhaps, when I come again, my Elohim will humble me, as I shall bewail many who have sinned already, and have not made teshuvah of the uncleanness and fornication and indecency that they have committed.

13 This is the third time I am coming to you. In the mouth of two or three witnesses shall every word be established. 2 I told you before, and say again before I come, as if I were present, as on my second visit; I write to those who keep sinning until now and have not made teshuvah, and to all others, that, if I come again, I will not spare, though I am absent now: 3 Since you seek a proof of ha Moshiach speaking through me, who has never been powerless among you but powerful among you: 4 For though He was impaled through weakness, yet He lives by the power of יהוה. For we also are weak in Him, but we shall live with Him by the power of יהוה towards you. 5 Examine yourselves, whether you be in the emunah; test yourselves. Know you not yourselves, how that יהושע ha Moshiach is in you, unless you are rejects? 6 But I trust that you shall know that we are not rejected. 7 Now I make tefillah to יהוה that you do no evil; not so that we should appear approved, but that you should do that which is honest, though we may appear to be rejects before you. 8 For we can do nothing against the emet, but for the emet. 9 For we are in simcha, when we are weak, and you are strong: and this also we wish, even your perfection. 10 Therefore I write these things being absent, lest being present I should use harshness, according to the power, that יהוה has given to me for your edification, and not destruction. 11 Finally, brothers, farewell. Be perfect, be of tov comfort, be echad, live in shalom; and the Elohim of

ahava and shalom shall be with you. 12 Greet one another with a set-apart kiss. 13 All the kidushim greet you. 14 The unmerited favor of the Master יהושע ha Moshiach, and the ahava of יהוה, and the chavurah of the Ruach HaKodesh, be with you all. Amein.

גלטיא

Galutyah - Galatians

To The Believing Remnant Of Yisrael

1 Shaul, a sholiach, not of men, neither by man, but by **יהושע** ha Moshiach, and Abba **יהוה**, who raised Him from the dead; 2 And all the Yisraelite brothers, who are with me, to the Yisraelite congregations of Galutyah:[1][2][3] 3 Unmerited favor to you and shalom from Abba **יהוה**, and from our Master **יהושע** ha Moshiach, 4 Who gave Himself for our sins, that He might deliver us from the evil olam hazeh, according to the will of **יהוה** our Abba: 5 To whom be tifereth le-olam-va-ed. Amein. 6 I am shocked that you are so soon removed from Him that called you to the unmerited favor of ha Moshiach to another version of the besarot: 7 Which is not another; but there are some that trouble you, and do pervert the besarot of ha Moshiach. 8 But though we, or a messenger from the shamayim, proclaim any other besarot to you than that which we have proclaimed to you, let him be accursed.[4] 9 As we said before, so I repeat, if any man proclaims any other besarot[5] to you than the one you have received, let him be accursed.[6][7] 10 For do I now persuade men, or **יהוה**? Or do I seek to please men? For if I still sought to please men, I should not be the eved of ha Moshiach. 11 But I certify to you, my Yisraelite brothers, that the besarot, which was proclaimed by me, is not received from man. 12 For I neither received it from man, neither was I taught it from men, but through the revelation of **יהושע** ha Moshiach. 13 For you have heard of my former halacha in the past in the Yahudite religion, how that I intensely and continually persecuted the Yisraelite congregation of **יהוה**, and tried to destroy it: 14 And I progressed in the Yahudite religion above many of my equals in my own nation; above all I was especially zealous of the teachings of my ahvot. 15 But when it pleased **יהוה**, who chose me from my birth, and called me by His unmerited favor, 16 To reveal His Son in me, that I might proclaim Him among the heathen; immediately I conferred not with flesh and dom: 17 Neither did I go to Yahrushalayim to them who were shlichim before me; but I went into Arabia, and returned again to Dameshek. 18 Then after three years I went up to Yahrushalayim to see Kepha, and stayed with him fifteen days. 19 But the other shlichim I did not see, other than Yaakov the Master's brother. 20 Now the things that I write to you, behold, before **יהוה** , I do not lie. 21 Afterwards I came into the regions of Aram and Cilicia; 22 And was not known personally by sight by any of the Yisraelite congregations in the province of Yahudah who were in ha Moshiach: 23 But they had heard only, that he who had persecuted us in times past now proclaims the emunah that he once destroyed. 24 And they esteemed **יהוה** because of me.

2 Then fourteen years after I went up again to Yahrushalayim with Bar-Nabah, and took Teitus with me also. 2 And I went up by sod-revelation, and

---

[1] Literally meaning "the exiles of Yah." The Hebrew root for Diaspora is galut; hence the term Galut-Yah. According to Peter these were chosen people of the dispersion scattered through modern day Turkey and the former area of Aramea.
[2] The English term "gentile" probably comes from the word galut (exile) by reversing the L and the T and adding an N at the end and thus the word "gentile," which even etymologically has ties to the exiles of Yisrael. Ezra 4:1, First Chronicles 5:6, Ezekiel 25:3 all use galut or a form of that word to describe exiles of both houses of Yisrael. The area of Galatia had major remnants of both houses in the first century.
[3] Since the congregations of Yisrael were Torah-based, he is writing to exiles from the ten tribes who desire a full Torah-obedient lifestyle.
[4] A warning to Yahudah.
[5] Literally means "the tov news" of Yisrael's freedom from slavery or exile.
[6] A warning to Ephraim.
[7] Since the tov news is the actual freeing of the exiles of Yisrael that were in slavery, the perversion of that message is considered another evangel. This perversion forces the freed Galatians to become slaves again to a different set of masters.

communicated to them concerning the besarot that I proclaim among the nations,[1] but privately to them who were of tov reputation, lest by any means I should labor, or had labored, in vain. 3 But neither Teitus, who was with me, being an Aramean, was compelled to be circumcised immediately:[2] 4 And because of false Yisraelite brothers who sneaked in, and who came in to secretly spy out our liberty that we have in ha Moshiach יהושע, that they might bring us into slavery:[3] 5 To whom we gave no place by yielding in submission to them, no, not for an hour; that the emet of the besarot[4] might remain among you. 6 But of those who were considered to be somewhat important-whatever they were, it makes no difference to me: יהוה accepts no man's person – for those who seemed to be somewhat important added nothing additional or new to me: 7 But on the contrary, when they saw that the besarot of the akrobustia[5] was

committed to me, as was the besarot of the brit milah to Kepha; 8 For He that worked vigorously in Kepha for his calling as a sholiach to the brit milah, the same One was mighty in me toward the nations: 9 And when Yaakov, Kepha, and Yochanan, who seemed to be pillars, perceived the unmerited favor that was given to me, they gave to me and Bar-Nabah the right hand of chavurah; that we should go to the heathen, and they to the brit milah. 10 Only they desired that we should remember the poor; the same mitzvah which I also was eager to do. 11 But when Kepha had come to Antioch,[6] I withstood him to his face, because he was at fault. 12 For before certain men came from Yaakov, he did eat with the peoples:[7] but when they had come, he withdrew and separated[8] himself, fearing them that were of the Yahudim.[9] [10] 13 And the other Yahudim joined with him in his hypocrisy; so that even Bar-Nabah was led astray with their hypocrisy.[11] 14 But when I saw that they walked not uprightly

---

[1] Ending the exile of the House of Ephraim-Yisrael.

[2] At least not compelled before entering maturity and a full understanding of what His return meant. As seen later, part of the Galatian heresy was circumcising people who didn't even believe, or who had not grown in any understanding. The proper order of things would be first to trust in Yahshua, and then seal that growth and faith with circumcision. Rather, man used circumcision as an entry point into the community, as did the Jerusalem group or the Qumran community at the Dead Sea.

[3] The tov news was the proclamation of freedom from slavery and from religion to the exiles of Galut-Yah. These certain brothers from Jerusalem were coming in quietly under the radar and reversing the truth of Scripture by using circumcision in a wrong chronological manner and by manmade standards as requirements for community entry and favor in the community. This was known as "works of the law" or "works of man's laws."

[4] Divine plan for ending the House of Yisrael's exile.

[5] The Greek word used in Galatians 2:7 for Shaul's ministry to the uncircumcised is the word akrobustia (Strong's Greek # 203), which literally means "tossed-away foreskins." He was contrasting his ministry to the uncircumcised or the "akrobustia" with James and Peter's ministry to the circumcised or the "peritome" (Strong's Greek # 4061). The same word peritome is used in describing the mission of James, Peter and John. This peritome means those living and abiding in circumcision identity, or in other words, the "House of Yahudah." The choice of "akrobustia" is fitting, as it describes just what Shaul was doing in the nations, or among the Galut-Yah. He was first and foremost looking for the lost sheep of the House of Yisrael (Ephraim), as per Yahshua's instructions. Akrobustia, does not mean "pagan gentiles" per se, but a select group within the gentiles or nations. The term akrobustia, as opposed to peritome, means those who were circumcised, but through disobedience and outright rebellion had their foreskins tossed away, thus becoming like one who is born and raised as an

uncircumcised (aperitome) pagan gentile. The opposite of a ministry to the peritome (which James and Peter had) would have been one to the aperitome or "never-circumcised." Yet Shaul did not claim a ministry to the aperitome or never-circumcised. His ministry, according to his own description, was to the akrobustia, or those who had undergone circumcision but had tossed it all away!

[6] Due north 300 miles from Jerusalem, as detailed in Scripture, which was once part of Assyria, the initial area of Ephraimite dispersion.

[7] Am-amaya in Aramaic meaning "the nations" or "the people with similar spiritual or kinship connections held in spiritual darkness." According to the Aramaic Targum or elaboration on Isaiah 9:2, the people (Hebrew "am") walking in darkness, were the House of Yisrael (ten tribes). They were the am-amaya.

[8] Hebrew word for separated is prush. So Peter separated or became a Prush or a Pharisee in his separatist behavior.

[9] What message were they coming with? A different message that placed prior conditions upon returning Ephraimites in order for them to even be saved. That is and was a message of slavery. We see these same folks in Acts 15:1-3.

[10] They came with added conditions established by the Jerusalem rabbinate, placing immediate preconditions such as circumcision upon these returning exiles.

[11] Instead of unity between Yisrael's two warring houses, this message from the Jerusalem legalists was renewing old wounds and stifling the reconciliation between the two houses that Moshiach came to bring, and was hence another evangel.

according to the emet of the besarot,[1] I said to Kepha in front of them all, If you, being a Yahudite in the Light, [2] live like the Arameans in the darkness,[3] [4] and not as do the Yahudim, why do you compel the peoples in darkness to live as do the Yahudim in Light?[5] 15 For we who are from the Yahudite nature,[6] are not from the peoples; the sinners,[7] [8] [9] 16 Knowing that a man is not ever declared right by the works of law,[10] [11] [12] but by the emunah on יהושע

ha Moshiach, even we who have believed in יהושע ha Moshiach, that we might be declared tzadik by the emunah on ha Moshiach, and not by the works of law: for by works of law shall no flesh ever be declared tzadik.[13] 17 But if, while we seek to be declared tzadik by ha Moshiach, we ourselves also are found to be sinners, is therefore Moshiach now a Servant of the sin in our lives? Let it never be! 18 For if I build again the things that I destroyed,[14] I make myself a transgressor.[15] 19 For I through the law I am dead to the law[16] that I might live to יהוה.[17] 20 I am impaled with ha Moshiach: nevertheless I live; yet not I, but ha Moshiach lives in me: and the chayim which I now live in the flesh I live by the emunah of the Son of יהוה,[18] who loved me, and gave Himself for me. 21 I do

---

[1] The truth of the tov news according to the final ruling of Acts 15 is that returning Yisraelites had to neither perform nor obey any immediate and enforceable act to receive entry into the Commonwealth of Yisrael. However, the ruling strongly implied that like Abraham circumcision would follow at a later date (24 years later), when personal maturity comes.

[2] Living in the light as per Esther 8:16.

[3] Who were the Arameans? Whose fathers were they? In Aramaic, the Targum Onkelos (the Aramaic translation of Deuteronomy 26:5 used in all the ancient first-century synagogues during the time of Yahshua) reads: "An Aramean tried to destroy my father. The Aramean was Laban, Jacob's uncle and Jacob is our father whom Laban tried to destroy. The ten tribes later were known as Greeks, Arameans and even Romans according to rabbinical literature. In rabbinical literature Edom is often spelled **Erom** or **Aram** as in Aramean.

[4] Arameans, or "the peoples," were considered to be in darkness as in Isaiah 9:2.

[5] The overriding thought being expressed here is that of light versus darkness, not Jew versus gentile. If Peter who is a son of light lives in darkness through separation from his returning Ephraimite brothers, then he is in no position to ask them or appeal to them to live in the light.

[6] Light.

[7] Darkness.

[8] Rav Shaul reminds Peter that the Jews have the Light to show to those Arameans who desired table fellowship. Rather than being loving and shining the Light, Peter did the same thing to the Aramean Yisraelites that Laban the Aramean did to Jacob. Peter tried to destroy them in their quest for full and equal repatriation back into the commonwealth. As soon as the "circumcision-first club" arrived, he betrayed the Aramean Yisraelites and the message of restoration to both houses. This betrayal displayed contempt and hypocrisy, which was sinful, as well as against the illuminated nature of a regenerated Yahudite.

[9] The ultimate result of his actions was the denial of full and equal rights as redeemed Yisrael to the Arameans, without any preconditions for salvation. He needed to be rebuked, as he suddenly changed from a restorer of Yisrael, into a Pharisee/**Prush** meaning "a Separatist."

[10] Not a term referring to Torah since it is never found in Torah or the Renewed Covenant. Here is the source for this very term. *Dead Sea Scrolls 4Q-255-264a, 5Q11 column 5, Lines 20-24*: "They are to be enrolled by rank, one man higher than his fellow—as the case may be—by virtue of his understanding and works. Thus each will obey his fellow, the inferior his superior.

[11] A catch phrase or "code" vividly describing what the "circumcision-first club" was doing. They were mimicking the Qumran community, by having a self-designated "teacher of tzedakah" and his elders decide what salvation and acceptance before YHWH entails. This list includes mostly manmade regulations, along with some Scriptural commands that are either taken out of proper understanding, or misapplied. For example, teaching that no one can be saved until they first avoid pig (i.e. observe the dietary instructions),

---

and performed circumcision, would be taking Scriptural commands out of their proper understanding and misapplying them. The truth is that most of us entered these truths later on down our journey of salvation and not before. This phrase "works of law" will appear throughout Galatians, and does not refer to Torah-keeping. This phrase "works of law" is not found in any of Shaul's other letters, or anywhere else in Scripture; as such it has no second or third witness. Therefore it cannot be referring to Torah. For when YHWH confirms a truth in the earth, it is found in several places in His word. The very fact that this term is so isolated and limited in scope to the "circumcision-first club" in one particular community, should lead any open-minded individual to the understanding that the phrase "works of law" does not speak of YHWH's Torah, but rather of man's perverted permutations.

[12] "Works of law" or "works of nomos" can mean any type of law. Examples of the use of **nomos** can be for farming laws, sanitation laws, army laws, driving laws, transportation laws, federal aviation laws, building code laws, etc. All these laws are described in Greek with the word **nomos** and unless the context allows for it, the word **nomos** does not necessarily mean YHWH's **nomos** or Torah.

[13] If YHWH's Torah cannot declare a man to be in right standing with YHWH, what makes anyone think that man's own set of rules and half-truths or "works of law" can make any man justified? Thus it is clear that neither by Torah, nor by man's "works of law," can a person be justified.

[14] Manmade religion in his life that was destroyed when Rav Shaul came to Moshiach and Torah.

[15] He would violate the real Torah, because he would knowingly be sinning again by partaking in various forms of error and religious elitism, and thus destroy the two-house restoration.

[16] Dead to all of man's attempts at "works of law" such as Peter had encountered in the incident where he broke table fellowship under their pressure. He died to that form of elitism forever and wants no part of it either for himself or others in Galut-Yah.

[17] Life in YHWH and His Torah of equality for all is far better than death in man's ranking systems of spiritual apartheid.

[18] Note: Not just the faith in Yahshua, but now he lives the actual Torah faith of Yahshua. There is a big difference between "faith in" and "faith of." Both are needed for the returning Yisraelite.

not frustrate the unmerited favor of **יהוה**: for if becoming a tzadik came by the law,[1] then ha Moshiach has died in vain.

3 O foolish Galutyah, who has put you under a spell, that you should not obey the emet, since **יהושע** ha Moshiach has been clearly set forth, before your eyes as impaled among you? 2 This only would I learn from you: Did you receive the Ruach HaKodesh by the works of law, or by your obedience [2] to emunah? 3 Are you so foolish? Having begun your halacha in the Ruach HaKodesh, are you now made perfect by the flesh?[3] 4 Have you suffered so many things for nothing? If it is yet for nothing. 5 He that supplies you with the Ruach HaKodesh, and works great nisim among you, does He it by the works of law, or by your hearing and emunah?[4] 6 Even as Avraham believed **יהוה**, and it was counted to him for tzedakah.[5] 7 Know therefore that those who are of the emunah, the same are b'nai Avraham. [6] 8 And the Scripture, foreseeing that **יהוה** would justify the heathen through emunah, proclaimed before the besarot to Avraham, saying, *In you shall all nations be blessed.*[7] 9 So then they that are of emunah are blessed with faithful believing Avraham. 10 For as many as are followers of the works of law are under the curse:[8] for it is written, Cursed is every one

that continues not in all things that are written in the scroll of the Torah to do them.[9] 11 But that no man is declared a tzadik by the law[10] in the sight of **יהוה**, it is evident: for, The tzadik shall live by emunah. 12 And the law is not made by emunah:[11] [12] but, The man that does what is written in it shall live in them.[13] 13 Ha Moshiach has redeemed us from the curse of the Torah,[14] being made a curse for us: for it is written, Cursed is every one that hangs on a tree:[15] 14 That the bracha upon Avraham might come upon the nations through **יהושע** ha Moshiach; that we might receive the promise of the Ruach HaKodesh through emunah. 15 Yisraelite brothers, I speak after the manner of men; Even if a covenant is a man's covenant, yet still if it is confirmed,

---

[1] This applies to both YHWH's Torah and man's ranking systems of spirituality.
[2] True obedience to true Torah.
[3] Following man's ranking for spiritual positioning will guarantee a life led by the flesh. We cannot begin in Sinai's eternal Torah and His Ruach, and then complete that journey by submitting to man's rules that are either not Biblical, or are reversed or somehow rearranged.
[4] This is a rhetorical question and a style used often by Rav Shaul. YHWH works among us based on our faith – not based on man's ranking systems of and by the flesh.
[5] Justification and tzedakah can only come by emunah alone.
[6] Physical Yisraelites from either house do not become complete until they express saving faith in Moshiach. Even though Avraham had the physical part right, he still had to receive personal redeeming faith.
[7] See notes on Genesis 12:3; this prophecy had a dual application and was fulfilled in the sense that all nations would receive the hope of salvation in Moshiach, the seed of promise. An alternative reading is "in you all nations will have your seed mixed in" or engrafted.
[8] Those who substitute man's requirements like the community regulations by the "teacher of tzedakah" in Qumran or at Jerusalem, are under a curse for two reasons.

The first reason is they have changed and thereby violated YHWH's own eternal Word. And the second reason is stated in part B of this same verse as; "Cursed is every one that continues not in all things which are written in the scroll of the Torah to do them."
[9] Being meticulous about keeping the requirements of the true Torah given by Moshe and yet still refusing to fully accept the returning House of Yisrael/Ephraim is rejecting the stranger, a violation of many explicit warnings not to do so in the Torah (such as Leviticus 19:34). Ephraimites making teshuvah must not be regarded as less than a Jew by requiring immediate actions on things set as conditions. Those who follow "works of law" may think they are doing all of Torah but are not. In direct violation of Torah they are showing no love to the returning strangers from the nations.
[10] Any law including Torah.
[11] Aramaic Peshitta reads: "not made by faith."
[12] Made by YHWH, not man's emunah.
[13] If these spiritual separatists were doing real Torah they wouldn't shut out the non-Jew or returning stranger, by assigning him Jewish superiors in the kingdom, but would rather treat him as an equal.
[14] The curse of the Torah was the death incurred by violating any or all of its precepts, and in context, by rejecting returning Ephraim by placing many pre-conditions on them. These Yahudim had put themselves under the curse of violating Torah. According to James 2:10-12, this one violation was enough to put them under a curse. The Torah itself is not a curse as some teach, but its violation by these separatists was.
[15] "Moshiach died to remove these curses and set us free, not to remove the Torah itself. If He removed the Torah's curses, why would we want to be in slavery again by following a new "works of law" program by those who practiced spiritual apartheid?"

no man sets it aside, or adds to it.[1][2] 16 Now to Avraham and his zera were the promises made. He said not, And to zerot, as of many; but as of one, And to your zera, which is ha Moshiach.[3] 17 And this I say, that the Avrahamic covenant, that was confirmed by יהוה through ha Moshiach, in the Torah,[4] and came four hundred and thirty years later, cannot disannul the Avrahamic covenant, so that it should make the promise of none effect.[5] 18 For if the inheritance is from the Torah, it is no more by the word of promise: but יהוה gave it to Avraham by promise. 19 What purpose then does the Torah serve? It was added because of transgressions,[6] until the Zera should come to whom the promise was made; and heavenly messengers through the hands of a Mediator ordained it[7]. 20 Now a Mediator does not represent one party,[8] but יהוה is one. 21 Is the Torah then against the promises of יהוה? Let it never be! For if there had been a Torah given that could have given us chayim, then truly tzedakah would have been by the Torah.[9] 22 But the

Scripture has concluded all under sin, that the promise by emunah of יהושע ha Moshiach might be given to them that believe.[10] 23 But before the Netsarim emunah came; the Torah was guiding and guarding us while we were confined from the emunah about to be revealed.[11][12][13] 24 Therefore the Torah was the pathfinder for us going forward to the derech of Moshiach, that by trusting emunah in Him we may be declared tzadik.[14][15] 25 But after that emunah has come we are no longer under schoolmasters.[16][17][18]

---

[1] No man can annul or replace any of YHWH's covenants from Abraham until now. All new covenants are merely stacked upon prior covenants, with some having greater importance than the older ones, but all are eternal and all are applicable for all generations. Instead of dispensationalism, Scripture teaches the principal of the "stacking" of covenants.

[2] On this one principle alone, Torah cannot have been replaced or annulled. That's the whole point. How can we disallow Ephraim equal citizenship, while claiming to uphold Torah, when even the Abrahamic Covenant promises that all non-Jewish nations would receive the full blessings of Abraham?

[3] The Seed, or the Moshiach, blesses all the nations (the mixed seed of Abraham), and since Jews and Ephraimites are in all the nations, you have two marvelous concurrent truths flowing from Golgotha. You have the Seed (Moshiach) going into all the nations, and with His Word (Mark 4:14), to gather into one, Abraham, Isaac and Yisrael's scattered physical seed.

[4] The Moshiach or YHWH's brought-forth Word is the actual giver of the Torah and not The Father YHWH who was the source.

[5] The same principle must be applied to all covenants. A newer one never annuls a prior one. That would have to mean that just as Torah never negated the Abrahamic Covenant, neither does the Renewed Covenant annul the Torah.

[6] Because of man's apostasy, so that man could clearly see what he has done wrong and why. It was added to make the need for a personal redeemer clearer.

[7] The Mediator was and remains Yahshua, for First Timothy 2:5 teaches us that there is only one eternal Mediator between man and YHWH.

[8] Yahshua represents both YHWH The Father and Yisrael.

[9] He states the obvious. That since the Torah itself couldn't impart eternal life, how can a cheap and sinful substitute called "works of law" accomplish that impartation?

[10] All Yisraelites and would-be Yisraelites must come through personal faith in Moshiach. All laws, both man's and YHWH's, just are not designed or empowered to do either.

[11] Aramaic Peshitta.

[12] While out in the nations, the blessed Torah protected and preserved Yisrael, while we waited patiently for the coming of Moshiach. The same applies today as we await His return.

[13] Isaiah 56:1.

[14] Aramaic Peshitta.

[15] As Romans 10:4 states, Moshiach is the **teleo** or the goal at which the Torah's path aims.

[16] "Plural in the Aramaic. "Tutors" or "schoolmasters." The Torah is a singular item and as such cannot be referred to here in the Aramaic. The tutor and tutors are two different categories. The tutor or schoolmaster is the Torah. The false tutors thought that they were the guardians of tradition and local assembly life. These tutors or schoolmasters believed that in order to protect the Torah, there had to be additional fences around it and thus they added regulations, making sure no Torah could ever be broken, since there were too many fences around it. Those fences were called "works of law." These tutors were the same ones using these fences to keep returning Ephraim out in the nations, by subjecting Ephraim to the slavery of second class citizenship, instead of enjoying the true Torah freedom that Moshiach came to accomplish by setting all of Yisrael's exiles free. This is perfectly applied by Yahshua in Matthew 21:33-43 and by using drash or allegory in Luke 15:11-32.

[17] The false or many tutors of Yisrael had always sought to replace the only true Tutor or the real Torah as seen in Ezekiel 20:18-25 where YHWH says, "do not walk in the statutes of their fathers," and repeats this in Matthew 23:1-4 and Matthew 23:13-15. These tutors that we are no longer under shut out the entry to the kingdom of heaven from men. "Men" as stated elsewhere, are lost Yisraelites as per Ezekiel 34:30-31. These fences by these tutors are also addressed in Acts 15:10-11, and called the "burdens upon men." The "men" are Yisrael, and the burdens are various forms of self-righteousness, summed up in the term "works of law."

[18] The Aramaic word for "tutors" is **taraa** and for "door" is **tarea** The **taraa-tutors** were locking the door-**tarea** for the **galut-yah** to return to the Commonwealth of Yisrael and their Torah covenant, while Yahshua, is the **Tarea** or The Door back to Yisrael. As the Moshiach Yahshua stated in John 10:9, He came to do the opposite. He came to open the door to the kingdom. So once faith in the Door came, we are no longer under these **tarra** or tutors, who try to keep returning Yisraelites out of the door. Faith in Yahshua as the Door, unlocks the kingdom's door for both houses of Yisrael.

26 For you are all b'nai **יהוה** by emunah in ha Moshiach **יהושע**.[1] 27 For as many of you as have been immersed into ha Moshiach have put on ha Moshiach. 28 There is neither Yahudite nor Aramean nor Greek,[2] there is neither eved nor free, and there is neither male nor female: for you are all Yisrael echad in ha Moshiach **יהושע**.[3] 29 And if you are Moshiach's, then are you Avraham's zera,[4] and heirs according to the promise.[5]

4 Now I say, That the heir, as long as he is a child, differs nothing from an eved, even though he is master over all of them; 2 But is under guardians and stewards of the bayit[6] until the time that has been set by his abba.[7] [8] 3 Even so, when we were children, we were in slavery under the elements of the olam hazeh:[9] 4 But when the fullness of the time had come,[10] [11] [12] **יהוה** sent forth His Son,[13] made of a woman,[14] made under the law,[15] [16] 5 To redeem those who were under the law,[17] [18]that we might receive the adoption as sons.[19] [20] 6 And because you are sons, **יהוה** has sent forth the Ruach HaKodesh of His own Son into your levim, crying, Abba, Abba.[21] 7 So then you are no longer an eved, but a son; and if a son, then an heir of **יהוה** through ha Moshiach.[22]

---

[1] Thanks to Yahshua, both houses are now equal, no longer under tutors, but under the guidance of the living Torah Yahshua, and His own written guidelines.

[2] All believers are now Yisrael, and as such your former designation becomes totally irrelevant. Regardless of how you entered Yisrael, you are now Yisrael, and your life should reveal and reflect this truth to all you meet.

[3] Who is who is determined by what is what. If the body of Moshiach is Yisrael renewed, then by definition all its parts or members are Yisrael.

[4] Abraham's sperm! Sperm is derived from the Greek word **sperma** (Strong's Greek # 4690). **Sperma** means "Something sown, seed, including the male sperm, offspring, a remnant, issue, seed." The noun is purely physical, pertaining to literal male semen and their offspring, giving forth a remnant issue (people). So if you belong to Moshiach, then you are descendants of Abraham, and his "heirs according to the promise." The Bible does not add the word "spiritual" before sperm and neither should anyone else. The Theological Wordbook of the Old Testament says: "**Zera** (Hebrew equivalent for the Greek **sperma**) refers to semen." The word is regularly used as a collective noun in the singular (never plural). This is an important aspect of the promise doctrine, for Hebrew never uses the plural of this root to refer to posterity or offspring. Thus the word is deliberately flexible enough to denote either one person (Moshiach) who epitomizes the whole group, or the many persons in that entire lineage of natural-spiritual descendants.

[5] Salvation is a revelation of who you are and were, despite the fact that you didn't know it. The fact that you belong to Yahshua then becomes the proof and the doorway into the revelation that you are Avraham's seed both physically and spiritually.

[6] House of Yisrael.

[7] All Yisrael remains in bondage to their masters the guardians, despite the fact that Yisrael was chosen to be the head and not the tail of the nations, and despite Yisrael's full divine inheritance in YHWH. The guardians were and yet are enslaving all Yisrael.

[8] The House of Yisrael/Ephraim Joseph was sold into bondage as slaves to serve under the watchful eye of his host culture's guardians and stewards as a disciplinary measure until such a time when their Father would bring them mercy and would set them free from their bondage and from their captivity.

[9] The children of Yisrael were slaves to the world, its elementary base matters, and its civil and religious guardians while roaming the nations.

[10] See note on Genesis 48:19. The fullness of the nations is the seed of Ephraim Yisrael.

[11] See note on Romans 11:25-16. All Yisrael will be saved when the fullness of the gentiles or Ephraim Yisrael comes in.

[12] Luke 4:18;the task of ransoming the captives and setting them free belongs to Moshiach.

[13] Yahshua.

[14] Made or brought forth as a human by and through the nation of Yisrael. In Scripture the woman is always a metaphor for the nation of Yisrael, as seen in Revelation 12, Ezekiel 23, Jeremiah 3:20, Jeremiah 31:32, and elsewhere.

[15] Greek word is **nomos**; Aramaic word is **namosa** and means any law, principle, norm, rule, or custom (secular or religious). It does not mean the Torah of Sinai unless specifically ascertaining it from a given context.

[16] In context Yisrael gave birth to Moshiach when the fullness of the nations were due to be awakened, and when the Moshiach would be born in Yisrael yet under the domination, rulership, oppression, and slavery of Rome politically and under various systems of "works of law" spiritually. He was born under national slave laws for sure.

[17] In order that He might redeem those who were under the laws of the dominating power of their master's rules, authority and manmade slave structures like Roman or Herodian rule.

[18] "Moshe the author of Torah was born from the woman Yisrael, under the law, rule and authority of Egypt. Likewise Yahshua was born of the woman Yisrael, and born under the law, rule, and authority, of Rome.

[19] According to Lamentations 5:1-3 and Hosea 4:6 and other references, Yisrael though an heir of all had through rebellion and spiritual adultery become the tail and the slaves. Galatians 4:1 begins with the cold hard fact that Yisrael was no different than a slave, due to guardians and others enslaving her by their **nomos** or manmade regulations. They had become orphans from YHWH.

[20] Nevertheless, despite having become orphans, in the latter days when the "fullness of time" determined by The Father came, Yisrael was once again resorted to sonship and readopted into YHWH's eternal family.

[21] Note that when we have the true Ruach of YHWH, we cry and speak in Hebrew, and we avoid false titles for Abba YHWH.

[22] Our current standing after Moshiach's liberation work. It is this liberty we must guard lest more **nomos** and manmade spiritual rankings, rules, and rulers return to bring us back into slavery.

8 Back then, when you knew not יהוה, you did service to those who by nature are not יהוה Elohim.[1] 9 But now, after that you have known יהוה, or rather are known by יהוה, how do you return again back to the weak and poor elementary matters,[2] to which you desire again to be in slavery?[3] 10 You shomer days, and months, and times, and years.[4] 11 I am concerned about you, lest I have labored among you for nothing. 12 Yisraelite brothers, put yourself in my place, just as once I put myself in your place. You have not offended me at all. 13 You know how through weakness of the flesh I proclaimed the besarot to you before. 14 And in my trial that was in my flesh you did not despise or reject me; but received me as a messenger of Elohim, even as ha Moshiach יהושע .[15] Where then were the brachot and rachamim you had toward me? For I bear you record, that, if it had been possible, you would have plucked out your own eyes, and have given them to me.[5] 16 Have I therefore become your enemy, because I tell you the emet?[6] 17 They do not desire tov for you, but they desire to dominate you and exclude you from Yisrael that your desire may be to serve them. 18 But it is tov to always desire after pleasant things, and not only when I am present with you.[7] 19 My little children, of whom I am again in birth pains until ha Moshiach be formed in you again,[8] 20 I desire to be present with you now, and to change my tone; but now I stand in doubt of you. 21 Tell me, you that desire to be under the law;[9] do you not shema to the Torah?[10] [11] 22 For it is written, that Avraham had two sons, the one by a female eved, the other by a free woman. 23 But he who was from the female eved was born after the flesh;[12] but he from the free woman was by promise.[13] 24 Which things are allegories:[14] for these are the two covenants; the one from the Mount Sinai, that brings forth slavery, which is Hagar. 25 For this Hagar is Mount Sinai in Arabia, and corresponds to Yahrushalayim that now exists, and is in slavery with her children.[15] 26 But the Yahrushalayim that is above is free,[16] which

---

[1] Before Moshiach came to liberate Yisrael, they were in bondage to political rulers and their false spiritual leaders, as well as their false mighty ones like Jupiter, Zeus, Hermes etc. Now that Nazarene Yisrael knows YHWH, they must avoid all slave masters, even those coming from Jerusalem and from Yahudah, if coming with a different tov news.

[2] This cannot be speaking of Torah, since Torah is YHWH's Word, and is eternal and thus can never be described as weak, poor or elementary by a Jewish rabbi. What these exiles were returning to was not Torah, but man's nomos in all its variations and permutations, with much of it coming from Jerusalem, leading to a return to slavery to men.

[3] The only way not to give in to that desire is to obey Yahshua alone and follow His walk as to how to incorporate Torah "decently and in order," on a progressive basis.

[4] Calendars and holidays given by those who bring "works of law." This included a pagan calendar of important days and seasons given to them by their masters. Yisrael once set free, must stick to Torah and not the times of their earthly masters.

[5] Clear evidence that Rav Shaul's trial in the flesh was bad eyes or bad eyesight. His relationships with the Galut-Yah were so strong that they accepted him with his weakness, and would have done all they could to restore his eyes. Now he is trying to restore them back to the truth and correct spiritual vision.

[6] In his attempt to stop them from returning to man's "works of law" he had made many enemies. In our pursuit and guarding of the truth, enemies will be made from former close friends.

[7] Desiring freedom in Moshiach and His Torah is a tov thing. Desiring their religious rankings and perverted programs for self-righteousness pursuits, will lead right back to the domination of Ephraim by Yahudah, and thus a complete negation of Yahshua's restoration work.

[8] A season of error always needs apostolic oversight until truth can overcome bondage to error. As the one who birthed this congregation, He has gone into spiritual labor until Yisrael returns to truth.

[9] **Nomos** of man's laws or the "works of law."

[10] The Torah is what you should be hearing to keep you and guard you from man's **nomos** and all his tutors.

[11] The upcoming allegory has nothing to do with Torah. The issue is over the correct interpretation of Torah. In this case, the ones calling for immediate circumcision for the returning Ephraimites did not have a proper understanding of when and why it should be done. These false teachers were the masters, and the Galatians the slaves, who submitted to their manmade laws and requirements. It was the Torah that had the promise of their return and redemption, not these masters in Jerusalem.

[12] Ishmael and Esau.

[13] Yitzchak.

[14] This allegory is a story portraying an underlying truth. It is the Hebraic method of interpretation known as **drash**.

[15] This does not teach that the Torah is bondage. In this allegory or story, Mt. Sinai corresponds to, or is like, Jerusalem that produces slaves. Spiritually, the residents at Jerusalem were by and large unsaved and were the ones who were working at "works of law" for their own religious community, so as to make one believer subservient to another. Moreover, Edom or Rome was in full and total military and political occupation of all the residents of Jerusalem. It was that way in Yahshua's day, and remains so today. Jerusalem operating in, by, and under, the ruach of Ishmael or Edom, continues to enslave Yisraelites still looking for freedom in all the wrong places. Note again, that the Torah does not produce slaves, but rather it is the people and leaders at Jerusalem operating through the ruach of the slave woman Hagar, who are coming down to Galatia attempting to do the same to Ephraim, as they have done to many in Judah.

[16] Free from slavery and doctrinal perversion of any kind.

is the ima of us all.[1] 27 For it is written, Gilah, you barren that did not bear; break forth[2] and shout for simcha,[3] you that did not have labor: for the barren and deserted one has many more children[4] than she who has had a husband.[5] 28 Now[6] we, Yisraelite brothers, are like Yitzchak was;[7] we are the children of promise.[8] 29 But as it was then, he that was born after the flesh persecuted him that was born after the Ruach HaKodesh, even so, it is now.[9] 30 Nevertheless what do the Ketuvim tell us to do? *Cast out the female eved and her son: for the son of the female eved shall not be heir with the son of the free woman.*[10]

---

[1] The Jerusalem above, operating through the Spirit of YHWH and Isaac, sets Yisrael free to be like Yahshua and His Torah, and produces men and women like Yahshua, not like the earthly Jerusalem. All born-again Yisraelites must pledge allegiance to the Jerusalem above; which has begotten us through the Ruach, and not the spirit of Edom that has placed Yisrael's children into functional and terminal slavery. The comparison is not law or Torah versus grace, as some falsely teach, but two different women, operating by two different spirits from two different Jerusalem's, producing two different kinds of children. One prepared for the devil, one set-apart for YHWH. Despite the clear admonition of Scripture, many still insist in taking this allegory and turning it into an alleged literal diatribe against the Torah.
[2] Across the globe.
[3] Publish the tov news.
[4] Ephraim's offspring (4 billion, see notes on Devarim 1:10-11) is far more than the 16 or so million of Yahudah.
[5] The former barren one is Ephraim Yisrael, who had no husband due to her divorce. Subsequently and consequentially, she had no children. Now in and through the tov news, she who was divorced and barren is remarried and renewed, and is conceiving multitudes of Yistraelite children for YHWH, since she now operates in full obedience and compliance to Moshiach and His Torah. The former divorced woman (Ephraim or non-Jewish Yisrael), is still more fruitful than Yahudah, bound in large part by the ruach of Ishmael working in the earthly city of Jerusalem among its residents.
[6] At this moment in time after Moshiach's first coming.
[7] Isaac was both physical and spiritual Yisrael, and so are all believers in Moshiach, since this verse is clear that we are like Isaac and not limited to just spiritual or physical Yisraelite status, but now we can claim both roles and positions. This applies for saved Yahudim and Ephraimites.
[8] Promised seed through Avraham, Yitzchak, and Yaakov.
[9] The earthy Jerusalem is full of the seed of Esau/Edom/Rome and its religious influences, along with many secular Yahudim, who believe in nothing but themselves, which is a form of idolatry. These elements seek to persecute the tiny Nazarene Yisraelite remnant still walking and living for Yahshua and Torah both in the galut/diaspora and back in the land. As it was then, so it remains today. Today some in Jerusalem seek Ephraim's return to the land, but relegate them to second-tier status if they believe in Yahshua, in their vain attempts to put themselves in the very place of YHWH.
[10] This is more than another exhortation. It is a Biblical command that we are to do as did our father Abraham; namely, throw out from among the people those who are arriving to change obedience to the true Torah, and turn it instead into obedience to their own "teacher of righteousness" and his "works of **nomos**." Based on this precedent in Yisrael,

31 So then, Yisraelite brothers, we are not children of the female eved, but of the free woman.[11]

5 Stand fast therefore in the liberty in which ha Moshiach has made us free, and be not harnessed again under the yoke of slavery. 2 Behold, I Shaul say to you, that if you become circumcised,[12] ha Moshiach shall profit you nothing.[13] 3 For I testify again[14] to every man that is circumcised, that he is a debtor to do the whole Torah.[15] 4 Ha Moshiach is become of no effect to you, whoever of you are declared to be a tzadik by the Torah; you are fallen from unmerited favor.[16][17] 5 For we through the Ruach HaKodesh wait for the tikvah of tzedakah[18] by emunah.

Rav Shaul appeals to the Galut-Yah to take immediate action and send these legalists back on their way to Yahrushalayim.
[11] Free to serve Moshiach and follow the true Torah that holds the promise of repatriation to all who desire to become Yisrael, or find their way home to Yisrael.
[12] Circumcised as a manmade precondition for salvation, as opposed to an act of obedience after salvation like Abraham and Moses.
[13] First warning is to Yahudah.
[14] Second warning is for Ephraim.
[15] Which is why circumcision must be done decently and in order, because once the token or seal is received, that Yisraelite is pledged to full and immediate compliance, which can become so frustrating, that a new convert can give up and fall away from YHWH.
[16] No law – including YHWH's Torah – can forgive sin. Only YHWH the Savior does that. So man's law is bondage, and YHWH's law is a guide for the redeemed, but not an instrument of redemption.
[17] Someone who trusts in Torah for their salvation, has fallen from favor, simply because they have not understood the favor or the tov news. The tov news is that Yahshua is the Door for eternal life apart from works of law, or Torah-keeping, which was and always will be a path to Moshiach and then a guide to His already-redeemed people.
[18] The resurrection from the dead and the coming **olam habah**.

6 For in **יהושע** ha Moshiach neither brit milah is anything, nor akrobustia; but emunah which works by ahava.[1] 7 You did run well before; who did hinder you that you should not obey the emet?[2] 8 This persuasion comes not of Him that has called you.[3] 9 A little chametz leavens the whole lump.[4] 10 I have confidence in you through **יהוה**, that you will not think any differently: but he that troubles you shall bear his mishpat, whoever he is.[5] 11 And I, Yisraelite brothers, if I yet proclaim brit milah, why do I suffer persecution? Then is the stumbling-block of the execution stake ceased.[6] 12 I desire that they who trouble you were even cut off.[7] 13 For, Yisraelite brothers, you have been called to liberty;[8] only use not liberty as an occasion for the flesh, but by ahava serve one another.[9] 14 For all the Torah is fulfilled in one word, even in this; *You shall love your neighbor as yourself.*[10] 15 But if you bite and devour one another, take heed that you are not consumed by each other.[11] 16 This I say then, have your halacha in the Ruach HaKodesh, and you shall not fulfill the desires of the flesh. 17 For the flesh craves what is harmful to the Ruach HaKodesh, and the Ruach HaKodesh opposes the desires of the flesh: and these two are contrary to one another: so that you cannot do whatever you please. 18 But if the Ruach HaKodesh leads you, you are not under the law.[12] 19 Now the works of the flesh are well known, among which are these; Adultery, fornication, uncleanness,[13] indecency 20 Idolatry, witchcraft, hatred, quarrels, jealousies, rage, strife, selfish ambition, stubbornness, heresies, 21 Envy, murder, drunkenness, wild indecent parties, and all such things: about which I warn you again as I have also done in times past, that those who practice such things as a halacha shall not inherit the malchut of **יהוה**. 22 But the fruit of the Ruach HaKodesh is ahava, simcha, shalom, patience, chesed, rachamim, trust worthiness, 23 Gentleness, self-control: there is no true Torah that is against this kind of fruit. 24 And they that are ha Moshiach's have controlled the flesh with its affections and desires. 25 If we live in the Ruach HaKodesh, let us also have our halacha in the Ruach HaKodesh.[14] 26 Let us not desire worthless tifereth, provoking or ridiculing one another, or envying one another.

---

[1] This holds true eternally. First, that circumcision is an act of love to seal one's faith, not to establish it; and neither the Yahudite, the circumcised, nor the **akrobustia** the "tossed-away foreskinned ones" have any ranking or special standing over the other. Neither house of Yisrael should see circumcision or lack thereof as a means of a spiritual rank over and above the other, but as something that the individual in YHWH's decent order must do on his own. Circumcision avails nothing in the sense that if abused it establishes one part of Yisrael as master and the other as slaves. So it avails nothing in terms of restoring equality in Yisrael, yet is a mandate to the individual in his or her walk with YHWH. Moshiach came to free both houses, and establish equality, not a new system of "works of law," or ranking, based on an immediate response to mandated corporate physical circumcision rather than personal physical circumcision.

[2] Rhetorical question here. Obviously it was the club from Jerusalem.

[3] They were tricked and persuaded by men and the ruach of Hagar, Ishmael and Rome. They were not being led by YHWH, who had called them to a different understanding.

[4] Which is why Rav Shaul comes down hard and teaches us to cast out the bondwoman.

[5] Judgment will come to those perverting the door to Ephraim's return, and YHWH appeals through Rav Shaul that we all agree with the truth, and not be found later being judged with those who have taken circumcision which is just part of the tov news, and pervert it into making it the tov news itself.

[6] If the message is circumcision like that done by those who placed it before growth and maturity, or before even the message of salvation itself, then why is Rav Shaul persecuted, since that would put him in accord with those who pervert the message? He is being persecuted for putting the dom of Yahshua before circumcision.

[7] A little play on words. He wants them circumcised or "cut off" from the presence of the congregations of the Galut-Yah.

[8] The end of the exile or galut.

[9] This new freedom is to bring unity and harmony between Yisrael's two houses, as we serve each other in equality and truth, not as a new license to engage in the individual temporal pleasures of the flesh.

[10] This is a summation of the Ruach behind the true Torah, and not some sort of license to neglect the rest of Torah, as Yahshua personally warned us about in Matthew 5:17-19.

[11] When spiritual standing is sought by "works of law" or by any precondition, what ultimately takes places is biting competition, and/or the subjecting of believers into masters and slaves; the end of these "works of law," is not restoration, but division, and the consuming of others in an attempt to promote one's own flesh before man.

[12] A clear reference to the **nomos** of the "circumcision club" and/or other legal systems of spiritual ranking. The true Spirit of Truth (Torah) will lead you to obey the Torah from the Jerusalem above, and not from the Jerusalem below, which is a law written and operated under the Ruach of Ishmael and Esau.

[13] A desire to break Torah's standards of unclean or prohibited things.

[14] Not in man.

6 Yisraelite brothers, if a man is overtaken in a trespass, you who are the spiritual ones restore him in the ruach of gentleness; while guarding yourself, lest you also be tempted. 2 Bear one another's burdens, and so complete in practice the Torah of ha Moshiach.[1] 3 For if a man thinks himself to be something, when he is nothing, he deceives himself. 4 But let every man examine his own mitzvot, and then shall he have gilah in himself alone, and not in another. 5 For every man shall bear his own burden. 6 Let him that is taught in the word share with him that teaches in all tov things.[2] 7 Be not deceived; Elohim is not mocked: for whatever a man sows, that shall he also reap. 8 For he that sows to his flesh shall from the flesh reap corruption; but he that sows into the Ruach HaKodesh shall from the Ruach HaKodesh reap everlasting chayim. 9 And let us not be weary in doing well: for in due season we shall reap, if we do not grow weary. 10 So then, as we have the opportunity, let us do tov to all men, especially to those who are of the household of believing Yisrael. 11 You see how large a letter I have written to you with my own hand. 12 Those who desire to make a nice show of your flesh, they compel you to be circumcised; in order to avoid suffering persecution for the execution stake of ha Moshiach.[3][4] 13 For those who are circumcised do not keep the Torah;[5] but desire to have you circumcised, that they may boast over your flesh.[6] 14 But יהוה forbid that I should boast, except in the execution stake of our Master יהושע ha Moshiach, through whom the olam hazeh is impaled to me, and I am impaled to the olam hazeh.[7] 15 For in ha Moshiach יהושע neither brit milah, nor akrobustia, has strength but a renewed creation.[8] 16 And as many as have their halacha according to this mishpat, shalom be upon them, and rachamim, be upon the Yisrael of יהוה.[9] 17 From now on let no man trouble me: for I bear in my body the marks of the Master יהושע. 18 Yisraelite brothers, the unmerited favor of our Master יהושע ha Moshiach be with your ruach. Amein.

---

[1] If Yahshua nailed the Torah to the cross, as alleged by some, then what Torah is this speaking of? No doubt it is the same one that His Abba has.
[2] The Yisraelite man or woman is obliged to care and provide for their teachers, so that the teachings won't be hindered by lack of material necessities.
[3] Preaching circumcision without Moshiach, or as a precondition for Moshiach's acceptance of the individual is all about parading foreskins in a numbers game or show, even as modern-day denominations fill out commitment cards of those who professed J-s-s, to make a nice show of big numbers, and among whom many have sadly had no regeneration experience. Ephraim uses "decision cards"; Yahudah uses "circumcision clubs." Same wrong motive and same wrong reasoning. Circumcision is required only after true salvation and maturity.
[4] Circumcision is widely accepted in Yahudah and the atonement of Yahshua is not. It is sinful to place circumcision above the offence of the message of the tree of execution, in order to avoid ridicule and persecution. The same practice is found in many modern "messianic" congregations, where there is such an emphasis on "Hebraic or Jewish things," that the execution stake and the Son of YHWH almost become afterthoughts.

[5] Because they violate the equality of believers as outlined in Torah which commands Yisraelites to love, care, and nurture the strangers or non-Jews in the gates as equal heirs in Yisrael and moreover as those who abide by the same Torah.
[6] That identifies you as someone belonging to his or her sect or religious order that places preconditions and rankings on believers.
[7] The stake is where our hope lies. The dom of atonement has purchased us, and as such, we are dead to any allegiance to the world or any of its claims on our lives.
[8] The strength to become regenerated as a new creation comes only from YHWH's Ruach, and not by any act of circumcision or any other commandment of YHWH or men.
[9] As many from both houses living by the priority rule of becoming born of the Ruach and then learning how to follow Torah, upon those with this understanding and proper spiritual priority is placed the title of "Yisrael." The true "Yisrael of YHWH" is composed of returning and redeemed exiles from both houses, and those who desire to join with their King and His Torah.

Ephsiyah - Ephesians
To The Believing Remnant Of Yisrael

1 Shaul, a sholiach of **יהושע** ha Moshiach by the will of **יהוה**, to the kidushim which are at Ephesos, and to the faithful Yisraelites in ha Moshiach **יהושע**: 2 Unmerited favor be to you, and shalom, from **יהוה** our Abba, and from the Master **יהושע** ha Moshiach. 3 Blessed be the Elohim and Abba of our Master **יהושע** ha Moshiach, who has blessed us with all spiritual brachot in ha shamayim in ha Moshiach: 4 Even as He has chosen us in Him before the foundation of the olam, that we should be set-apart and without spot before Him in ahava: 5 Having predestinated us for the adoption of children by **יהושע** ha Moshiach to Himself, according to the tov pleasure of His will,[1] 6 To the tehilla of the tifereth of His unmerited favor, by which He has made us accepted in the Beloved. 7 In whom we have redemption through His dom, the forgiveness of sins, according to the riches of His unmerited favor; 8 Which He has abounded toward us in all chochmah and binah; 9 Having made known to us the mystery of His will, according to His tov pleasure which He has purposed in Himself: 10 That in the administration of the fullness of times He might gather together in one all things in ha Moshiach, both which are in the shamayim, and which are on the earth; even in Him:[2] 11 In whom also we have

obtained an inheritance, being predestinated according to the purpose of Him who works all things after the counsel of His own will: 12 That we should be the tehillah of His tifereth, who were the first to trust in ha Moshiach. 13 In whom you also trusted, after you heard the word of emet, the besarot of your salvation: in whom also, after you believed, were then sealed with the Ruach HaKodesh of promise, 14 Who is the pledge from **יהוה** of our future inheritance until the redemption of the purchased possession, our bodies, to the tehillah of His tifereth. 15 Therefore, after I heard of your emunah in the Master **יהושע**, and your ahava to all the kidushim, 16 Do not stop to give hodu for you, making mention of you in my tefillot; 17 That the Elohim of our Master **יהושע** ha Moshiach, the Abba of tifereth, may give to you the Ruach of chochmah and revelation in the da'at of Him: 18 So that the eyes of your understanding being enlightened; to know what is the tikvah of His calling, and what are the riches of the tifereth of His inheritance in the kidushim, 19 And what is the exceeding greatness of His power to us, who believe, according to the working of His mighty power, 20 Which He worked in ha Moshiach, when He raised Him from the dead, and seated Him at His own right hand in the shamayim, 21 Far above all principality, and power, and might, and dominion, and every name that is named, not only in the olam hazeh, but also in the olam haba:[3] 22 And has put all things under His feet, and gave Him to be the head over all things in the Yisraelite congregation, 23 Which is His body, the complete extension of Him who fills all in all.

---

[1] All believers are adopted into YHWH's family. There is no such thing as the Yahudim being the real chosen children and non-Jews being merely adopted. All human beings are sinners and all need adoption into YHWH's family, including Jewish Yisrael.

[2] This text alone destroys any form of separate entity theology where Yahudim have synagogues for Shabbat and Christians have churches for Sunday worship and where YHWH's word is divided into two covenants. Both Yahudim, and Torah-honoring non-Yahudim, are called to be in one body, as Yahshua gathers all His children into one body. That includes all His children in heaven, all the heavenly messengers, and all of creation that He came to gather into one. All things scattered are being gathered, which by definition must include Yisrael's exiles, from both houses.

[3] Hebraic understanding of time is non-dispensational; One's salvation is received in this world, in order to enter the next. Just two periods of time, without man-made dispensations.

2 And you has He made alive, who were dead in trespasses and sins; 2 In which in times past you walked according to the course of this olam, according to the prince of the power of the air,[1] the ruach that now operates in Torah-breaking children: 3 Among whom also we all used to have our conduct in times past in the lusts of our flesh, fulfilling the desires of our flesh and of the mind; and were by nature the children of wrath, even as were others. 4 But יהוה, who is rich in rachamim, for His great love through which He loved us, 5 Even when we were dead in our sins, has made us alive together with ha Moshiach - by unmerited favor you are saved - 6 And has raised us up together, and made us sit together in the heavenly places in ha Moshiach יהושע:[2]

7 That in the olam haba He might show the exceeding riches of His unmerited favor in chesed toward us through ha Moshiach יהושע. 8 For by unmerited favor are you saved through emunah; and that not of yourselves: it is the gift of יהוה: 9 Not by our mitzvot, lest any man should boast.[3]

10 For we are His masterpiece, recreated in ha Moshiach יהושע to tov mitzvot, which יהוה has ordained beforehand that we should perform as our halacha. [4]

11 Therefore remember, that you being in times past gentiles in the flesh,[5] who are called Uncircumcision[6] by those called the Brit-Milah in the flesh made by hands;

12 That at that time you were without ha Moshiach, being excluded, aliens from the Commonwealth of Yisrael, as gerim from the covenants of promise, having no tikvah, and without Elohim in the olam hazeh:[7] 13 But now in ha Moshiach יהושע you who sometimes were far off[8] are made near by the dom of ha Moshiach. 14 For He is our shalom, who has made both echad,[9] and has broken down the middle wall of partition between us;[10] 15 Having abolished in His flesh the enmity,[11] even the law of commandments contained in human dogma;[12] for to make in Himself from the

---

[1] s.a.tan is called the ruler of the air because he controls that atmosphere, but also because unlike redeemed Yisrael, he will inherit nothing but air.

[2] All Yisrael is seated together positionally in the Heavens. Therefore, we must seat ourselves on earth as one nation, where all believers are considered the commonwealth of Yisrael; no longer divided amongst ourselves under designations such as "Jew" and "gentile."

[3] Salvation is by dom atonement and YHWH's acceptance of the dom for our atonement. It has never been by keeping Torah.

[4] Here is the contrast. Works don't save us, but YHWH's ordained works known as Torah are the ones ordained for they are written, as The Way YHWH desires for us to walk. Scripture speaks much about the difference between man's works and ordained works that allow us to be His masterpieces.

[5] Note that these Ephraimite believers in Ephesus, were no longer pagans or gentiles.

[6] Not much has changed. Most saved Yahudim refuse to call Ephraimites Yisrael, but keep referring to them as "saved gentiles."

[7] Before Moshiach, non-Yahudim were considered unclean dogs outside of the nation of Yisrael.

[8] "Far off" is a Hebraic idiomatic expression used throughout Scriptures, including in Daniel 9:7 when he prayed for both houses. The one in Babylon and the one far off. The fact that Rav Shaul applies this term to the non-Jewish believers here is solid evidence that he identified these folks as returning Ephraim Yisrael.

[9] In order to make two entities into one commonwealth, those near and those far, there must exist two Yisraelite entities in need of shalom-peace between themselves. Yahshua came to bring an end to the civil war between the two houses of Yisrael that make up the commonwealth, as this Scripture so vividly declares.

[10] The middle wall is not the Torah, but the manmade partition that the Yahudim illegally added to the temple repaired in the days of Zerubbabel, separating the outer court into subdivisions, including the manmade court of the gentiles. This court did not exist in the wilderness tabernacle, or in Solomon's temple, and most importantly it does not exist in the actual temple in Heaven. This is the earthly partition Yahshua came to remove so that all true worshippers entering the temple of YHWH would be considered Yisrael.

[11] Moshiach came to end the enmity or hatred and enemy status between Yisrael's two houses. Nevertheless, some still want to continue in that enmity despite Yahshua's revealed will for all believers to be considered Yisrael.

[12] Yahshua came to abolish the human dogmas or doctrines that fueled the enmity between the two houses, such as the partition barrier that established the unlawful court of the gentiles.

two ¹ one renewed man, ² so making shalom;³ 16 And that He might reconcile both⁴ to **יהוה** in one body⁵ by the execution stake, having slain the enmity through it:⁶ 17 And came and proclaimed shalom to you who were far off,⁷ and to them that were near.⁸ 18 For through Him we both⁹ have access by one Ruach to Abba. 19 Now therefore you are no more gerim and foreigners, but fellow citizens with the kidushim, forming the household of **יהוה**; Beit Yisrael.¹⁰ 20 Beit Yisrael is built upon the foundation of the shlichim and neviim, **יהושע** ha Moshiach Himself being the Rosh Pina;¹¹ 21 In whom all the bayit being joined together¹² grows into a set-apart Bet HaMikdash in **יהוה**: 22 In whom you also are being built together as the Beit HaMikdash of Elohim through the Ruach.¹³

3 For this cause I Shaul, am the prisoner of **יהושע** ha Moshiach for you

nations, ¹⁴ 2 If you have heard of the administration of the unmerited favor of **יהוה** which is given to me for you:¹⁵ 3 How that by revelation He made known to me the mystery; as I wrote before in few words, 4 So that, when you read this, you may understand my da'at into the mystery of ha Moshiach;¹⁶ 5 Which in other olamim was not made known to the sons of men, as it is now revealed to His set-apart shlichim and neviim by the Ruach;¹⁷ 6 That the nations should be fellow heirs, united in shalom in the same body, and partakers of His promise in ha Moshiach by the besarot:¹⁸ 7 Of which I was made a servant, according to the gift of the unmerited favor of **יהוה** given to me by the working of His power.¹⁹ 8 To me, who am the least of all kidushim, is this unmerited favor given, that I should proclaim among the nations the unsearchable riches of ha Moshiach; 9 And that all men would see what is the purpose of the administration of this mystery, ²⁰ which from the beginning of the olam has been hidden in **יהוה**, who created all things

---

¹ From the multitudes of the two houses, He took those chosen, from the remnant of Yahudah and the remnant of Ephraim and has made them into one new man. Notice that the one new man is composed of those from these two prior entities. Like all men, the new man too has a name: Yisrael.
² See previous footnote for this verse.
³ In fulfillment of many promises such as: Isaiah 11:13-14, and Ezekiel 37:15-28, and Hosea chapter one.
⁴ Both houses.
⁵ Renewed Covenant Yisrael.
⁶ To bring life and restoration between the two houses, Yahshua first had to destroy the hatred and enmity, before instituting shalom through the one new man, with the name of Yisrael.
⁷ Ephraim or non-Jewish Yisrael, as per Daniel 9:7, Ezekiel 11:16 and other places.
⁸ Yahudah, near to home or near to Yahrushalayim, the center of YHWH's world.
⁹ Not only are both houses Yisrael, but both houses share the same Moshiach, Ruach HaKodesh, and homeland in the land of Yisrael.
¹⁰ Non-Jewish believers must see themselves as Scripture declares them to be. Not as strangers, not as foreigners, not as aliens, but as citizens of physical and spiritual Yisrael; and as the set-apart ones, making up the renewed congregation of YHWH. Until Ephraimites see their heritage clearly, and receive it by faith in Scripture, the nation will remain divided and in exile.
¹¹ All true Yisraelite congregations will feature the Moshiach, as well as a foundation in the writings of the Tanach (First Covenant), and the foundational writings of the apostles of the Brit Chadasha.
¹² Note that Yahshua's first coming started an ongoing process of joining with each other, to be completed at His return, and not before by man's efforts.
¹³ This temple is called the Tabernacle of David, which is being rebuilt, into a home for all Yisraelites, and also for YHWH through His Ruach HaKodesh. Through the ministry of our Moshiach, the Booth of David with all twelve tribes fully present and represented is being raised up.

---

¹⁴ For what cause? The ones outlined in chapter two. To bring the non-Jews in; and return them to Yisrael. Rav Shaul is going to the far corners of the globe, in all the "far away" places, to bring them into the Commonwealth of Yisrael. For more details see:
http://store.yourarmstoisrael.org/Qstore/Qstore.cgi?CMD=011&PROD=000012
¹⁵ He was administering YHWH's unmerited favor for salvation and their return to the nation of Yisrael.
¹⁶ The mystery of Moshiach regards the nature of His mission, which is the restoration and regathering of both houses of Yisrael. Rav Shaul states, that this insight into the true meaning of the tov news is given, administered, and received by revelation alone.
¹⁷ See the footnote for Ephesians 3:4.
¹⁸ That's the crux of the message: The rebuilding and re-gathering of Yisreal, not the building of a gentile church. But this understanding will come only by the word of YHWH, and the illumination of revelation.
¹⁹ A servant to the nations, to regather the wandering sheep of Yisrael.
²⁰ Rav Shaul prayed that all men would come to understand the real reason he went to the nations, which was not to meet pagans, but to bring Yisrael back into covenant.

by **יהושע** ha Moshiach:[1] [2] 10 For the intent that now through the one reunited Yisraelite congregation, principalities and authorities in the shamayim might learn the manifold chochmah of **יהוה**,[3] 11 According to the eternal purpose that He purposed in ha Moshiach **יהושע** our Master:[4] 12 In whom we have boldness and access with confidence by the emunah in Him. 13 So I desire that you faint not at my tribulations for you, which is your tifereth. 14 For this cause I bow my knees to the Abba of our Master **יהושע** ha Moshiach, 15 Of whom the whole mishpochah in the shamayim and on the earth is named,[5] 16 That He would grant you, according to the riches of His tifereth, to be strengthened with might by His Ruach in your inner man; 17 That ha Moshiach may dwell in your levim by emunah; that you, being rooted and grounded in ahava, 18 May be able to comprehend with all kidushim what is the width and length and depth and height; 19 To know the ahava of ha Moshiach, which passes human da'at; that you might be filled with all the fullness of **יהוה**. 20 Now to Him that is able to do exceeding abundantly above all that we ask or think, according to the power that is at work in us, 21 To Him be tifereth in the Yisraelite congregation through ha Moshiach **יהושע** throughout all olamim, le-olam-va-ed. Amein.

4 I therefore, the prisoner of **יהושע**, beg of you that your halacha is worthy of the rank to which you are called, 2 With all humility and meekness, with patience, bearing with one another in ahava; 3 Being eager to guard the unity of the Ruach in the bond of shalom.[6] 4 There is one body and one Ruach, even as you are called in one tikvah of your calling;[7] 5 One Master **יהוה**, one emunah, one mikvah, 6 One Elohim and Abba of us all, who is above us all, and through us all, and in you all.[8] 7 But to every one of us is given unmerited favor according to the measure of the gift of the Moshiach. 8 That is why it says, When He ascended up on high, He led captivity captive,[9] and gave spiritual gifts to men. 9 (Now that He ascended, what is it but that He also descended first into the lower parts of the earth? 10 He that descended is the same One also that ascended up far above all the shamayim, that He might fill all things.) 11 And He gave some, shlichim; and some, neviim; and some, proclaimers; and some, roehim and morim; 12 For the perfecting of the kidushim, for the mitzvot of service, for the rebuilding of the body of ha Moshiach: 13 Until we all come into the unity of national emunah, and the full chochmah of the Son of **יהוה**, into a mature and perfect man, according to the same measure and the same stature of the fullness that Moshiach Himself has: 14 That we no longer be children, tossed around, and carried away with every wind of teaching, by the tricks of men, and human cleverness, used by those who lie in wait to deceive you; 15 But speaking the emet in ahava, that we may progress and grow through Him, who is the Head of kol Yisrael, even ha Moshiach: 16 From whom the whole body

---

[1] The tov news is the unveiling of the means and the reasons for Moshiach's coming, to rebuild the Tabernacle of David for YHWH to inhabit forever. The Creator is Yahshua; and He came to rebuild His nation and all who desire to be part of it under His leadership.

[2] Yahshua is the Creator.

[3] In scattering and then re-gathering His people, thereby using Yisrael as an object lesson to show His future and end-time faithfulness to all created spirits as well.

[4] The purpose He just outlined in the preceding verses.

[5] Yahshua is the personification of Yisrael and is called Yisrael in Hosea 11:1 and Isaiah 49:3. So if Yahshua's Name is prophetically known as Yisrael, then we His people are the children of Yisrael, and all who belong to Yahshua in heaven and on earth, are surely part of the Yisraelite family. Moreover, if Yahshua carries the Name of His Father, as well as all of His titles, since they are echad, then the Father is also "Father Yisrael," or the Father of Yisrael and the children of Yisrael.

[6] Be eager to guard the truth of the peaceful reunification of our people at all times.

[7] Both houses have been promised the same hope.

[8] As far as YHWH is concerned, there is only one faith and one people. That's is the body of Renewed Covenant Yisrael, where there are no Jews or Arameans or Greeks but all are Yisrael.

[9] The righteous in Abraham's Bosom. See notes on Luke 16.

joined and knit together by what every joint supplies, according to the working of every member doing its share, causing growth for the body, building itself up in ahava. 17 This I say therefore, and testify in יהוה, that from now on you conduct your halacha not as other gentiles walk, in the vanity of their mind, [1] 18 Having their binah darkened, being alienated from the chayim of Elohim through the ignorance that is in them, because of the blindness of their lev:[2] 19 Who being past feeling have given themselves over to indecency, to perform all uncleanness with greediness. 20 But you have not learned your chayim in Moshiach that way; 21 If you have heard about Him, and have been taught by Him, as the emet is in יהושע. 22 That you put off concerning the former way of chayim the old man, which is degenerated with deceitful lusts; 23 And be renewed in the ruach of your mind; 24 And that you put on the renewed man, which after Elohim is recreated in tzedakah and real set-apartness. 25 Therefore put away lying, and speak every man the emet with his neighbor: for we are members one of another.[3] 26 Be angry, but sin not: let not the sun go down upon your wrath:[4] 27 Do not give s.a.tan a chance or opening. 28 Let him that stole steal no more: but rather let him labor, working with his hands the thing that is tov, that he may have something to give to him that needs.[5] 29 Let no lashon harah proceed out of your mouth, but that, which is tov, and useful for edification, that it may impart brachot to the hearers. 30 And grieve not the Ruach HaKodesh of יהוה, with which you are sealed for the yom of redemption.

31 Let all bitterness, and wrath, and anger, and loud yelling, and lashon hara, be put away from you, along with all malice: 32 And be you kind towards one another, tenderhearted, forgiving one another, even as יהוה for ha Moshiach's sake has already forgiven you.

5 Be therefore followers of יהוה, as dear children; 2 And have a halacha of ahava, as ha Moshiach also has loved us, and has given Himself for us an offering and a sacrifice to יהוה for a sweet smelling fragrance. 3 But fornication, and all uncleanness, or greed for gain, let it not be even once named among you, as is fitting for kidushim in Yisrael; 4 Neither cursing, nor foolish talking, nor insults, not even flattery, since none of these are necessary: but rather the giving of hodu. 5 For this you know, that no one who whores around, no unclean person, no covetous man, no one who is an idolater, has any inheritance in the malchut of ha Moshiach and of יהוה. 6 Let no man deceive you with meaningless words: for because of these things comes the wrath of יהוה upon the children of disobedience. 7 Be not partakers with them. 8 For you were once darkness, but now are you in the Light of יהוה: have your halacha as children of Light: 9 For the fruits of Light are found in chesed and tzedakah and emet; 10 Learn to discern what is acceptable to יהוה. 11 And have no chavurah with the unfruitful deeds of darkness, but rather condemn them.[6] 12 For it is a shame to even speak of those things that are done by them in secret. 13 But all things that are under condemnation are made manifest by the Light: for whatever is manifested is manifested by Light. 14 Therefore He said, *Awake you that sleep, and arise from the dead, and ha Moshiach shall give you Light.* 15 See then that your

---

[1] Yisraelites cannot imitate and follow the ways of the gentiles, since Yisraelites are not gentiles, as we see here in the comparisons between believers and gentiles. Believers must not walk or talk like gentiles, which includes referring to themselves as a so-called "gentile believer."
[2] This does not - and cannot - be a description of a believer, who walks in light and revelation. Gentiles are blind and walk in spiritual darkness.
[3] Unlike religion, where people become members of a denomination, in Yisrael we become members of each other.
[4] Anger is a human emotion. But prolonged anger or inbred anger will destroy from within; thus, Yisraelites are encouraged to "let it go" before the new day dawns.
[5] A true Yisraelite can be detected by fruits of repentance.

[6] The behavior not the individual.

halacha is detailed and alert, not as fools, but as wise, 16 Taking advantage of the time and opportunity you are given, because the days are evil. 17 Therefore be not unwise, but understand what the will of יהוה is.[1] 18 And be not drunk with wine, in which there is excess; but be filled with the Ruach; 19 Speaking to yourselves with the Tehillim and songs of tehilla and spiritual songs, singing and making melody in your lev to the Master יהוה; 20 Giving hodu always for all things to Abba יהוה in the Name of our Master יהושע ha Moshiach;[2] 21 Submit yourselves one to another in the fear of יהוה.[3] 22 Wives, submit yourselves to your own husbands, as you would to יהושע. 23 For the husband is the head of the wife, even as ha Moshiach is the Head of the Yisraelite congregation: and He is the Savior of the body. 24 Therefore as the Yisraelite congregation is subject to ha Moshiach, so let the wives be to their own husbands in everything. 25 Husbands, love your wives, even as ha Moshiach also loved the Yisraelite congregation, and gave Himself for it; 26 That He might set it apart and cleanse it with the washing of mayim by the word, 27 That He might present it to Himself a beautiful Yisraelite congregation, not having spots, or wrinkles, or any such thing; but that it should be set-apart and without blame. 28 Like this men should love their wives even as their own bodies. He that loves his wife loves himself. 29 For no man ever yet hated his own flesh; but nourishes and cherishes it, even as יהושע the Yisraelite congregation: 30 For we are members of His body, of His flesh, and of His bones. 31 For this cause shall a man leave his abba and ima, and shall be joined to his wife, and the two shall be basar-echad.[4] 32 This is a great sod: but I speak concerning ha Moshiach and the Yisraelite congregation.[5] 33 However let every one of you as an individual so love his wife even as himself; and the wife see that she respect her husband.

6 Children, obey your parents in the Master: for this is right before יהוה. 2 *Honor your abba and ima*-which is the first commandment with promise,[6]3 *That it may be well with you, and you may live long on the land.* 4 Parents, provoke not your children to anger: but bring them up in the Torah and admonitions of the Master. 5 Avadim, be obedient to them that are your masters according to the flesh, with fear and trembling, in sincerity of lev, as to Moshiach; 6 Not with eye-service, as hypocrites; but as the avadim of ha Moshiach, doing the will of יהוה from the lev; 7 With a tov will doing service for men, as if to יהוה , and not to men: 8 Knowing that whatever tov thing any man does, the same shall he receive from יהוה, whether he be an eved or free. 9 And, you masters, do the same things to them, refrain from threatening them: knowing that Your own Master יהוה also is in the shamayim; neither is there any partiality with Him. 10 Finally, my brothers, be strong in יהוה, and in the power of His might. 11 Put on the whole armor of Elohim, that you may be able to stand against the strategies of s.a.tan. 12 Because we wrestle not against flesh and dom, but against principalities, against authorities, against the rulers of the darkness of this olam, against spiritual wickedness in high places. 13 Therefore take up the whole armor of Elohim, that you

---

[1] Regarding who you are, and how you are to behave as returning Yisrael.
[2] Returning Yisraelites are commanded to pray to the Father in Yahshua's Name, never to Yahshua directly.
[3] In Yisrael, community holds people accountable.
[4] There's the pashat or literal understanding. Two people becoming one.

[5] Mystery? Yes. The pashat/literal understanding is the two persons becoming one. The secret behind the literal is that in Yahshua the two individual houses become one. That is the mystery behind the uniting of man and woman. Yahshua and Yisrael become one in the **remez** or hint level of understanding. But in the **sod** or secret level as Yahshua marries Yisrael, both houses remarry each other, thereby establishing shalom. That is also known as "the mystery" of the kingdom.
[6] Quoting one of the ten words/commandments as further evidence that the Ephesian believers will one day inherit the actual land of Yisrael, along with Jewish Yisrael.

may be able to withstand in the evil day, and having done all, to stand, stand even more. 14 Stand therefore, having your waist wrapped around with emet, and having on the breastplate of tzedakah; 15 And your feet fitted with the preparation of the besarot of shalom; 16 Above all, taking the shield of emunah, with which you shall be able to quench all the fiery arrows of the wicked one. 17 And take the helmet of salvation, and the sword of the Ruach, which is the word of **יהוה**:[1] 18 Making tefillot always with all intercession and supplication in the Ruach, and watching in the Ruach with all endurance and petitions for all the kidushim; 19 And for me, that words may be given to me, that I may open my mouth boldly, to make known the mystery of the besarot,[2] 20 For which I am an envoy in prison: that in prison I may speak boldly, as I should speak. 21 But that you also may know my affairs, and how I am doing, Tuchikos, a beloved brother and faithful eved in the Master, shall make known to you all things: 22 Whom I have sent to you for the same purpose, that you might know our affairs, and that He might comfort your levim. 23 Shalom be to the brothers, and ahava with emunah, from Abba **יהוה** and the Master **יהושע** ha Moshiach. 24 Unmerited favor be with all them that love our Master **יהושע** ha Moshiach in sincerity. Amein.

---

[1] He is not describing a Roman soldier for the simple reason that Isaiah, whom Rav Shaul is quoting, never saw a Roman soldier. He is quoting Isaiah 59:17. In context with Isaiah 59:16, Yahshua is the one being described as YHWH's armor. So in essence, these verses are telling Yisrael to put on Yahshua and His fullness.

[2] We all need prayer for boldness, to proclaim the two houses in the face of the darkness of organized religion.

Phylypsiyah - Philippians
To The Believing Remnant Of Yisrael

1 Shaul and Timtheous, the avadim of **יהושע** ha Moshiach, to all the kidushim in ha Moshiach **יהושע** who are at Phylypseyah, with the teaching overseers and shamashim: 2 Unmerited favor be to you, and shalom, from **יהוה** our Abba, and from the Master **יהושע** ha Moshiach. 3 I give hodu to my Elohim upon every remembrance of you, 4 Always in every one of my tefillot for you I make my request with simcha, 5 For your chavurah in the besarot from the first day until now; 6 Being confident of this very thing, that He who has begun a tov work in you will complete it until the Yom of **יהושע** ha Moshiach: 7 Even as it is right for me to think this of all of you, because I have you in my lev; because both in my imprisonment, and in the defense and confirmation of the besarot, you all are partakers of my unmerited favor. 8 For **יהוה** is my witness, how greatly I long after you all with the affections of **יהושע** ha Moshiach. 9 And this is my tefillah, that your ahava may abound more and more in chochmah and in all discernment; 10 That you may choose and discern the things that are excellent; that you may be sincere and without offence until the Yom of ha Moshiach; 11 Being filled with the fruits of tzedakah, which are by **יהושע** ha Moshiach, to the tifereth and praise of **יהוה**. 12 But I desire that you should understand, brothers, that the things that happened to me have turned out for the advancement of the besarot; 13 So that the reasons for my imprisonment in ha Moshiach are manifest to all the palace, and to Caesar's court and also in all other places; 14 And many of the brothers in the Master are growing more confident by my imprisonment and are much more bold to speak the word without fear. 15 Some indeed proclaim ha Moshiach because of envy and strife; and some also in tov will and ahava: 16 The former proclaim ha Moshiach for selfish ambition, not sincerely, thinking they are adding pressure and stress to my imprisonment: 17 But the latter out of ahava, knowing that I am set for the defense of the besarot. 18 What then? In every way, whether in pretence, or in emet, ha Moshiach is proclaimed; and in that I have gilah, yes, and will have more gilah. 19 For I know that this shall turn into my deliverance through your tefillot, and the gift of the Ruach of **יהושע** ha Moshiach, 20 According to my intense longing and my tikvah, that in nothing I shall be ashamed, but that with all boldness, as always, so now also ha Moshiach shall be magnified in my body, whether it be by chayim, or by my death. 21 For to me to live is ha Moshiach, and to die is gain.[1] 22 But if I live in the body, this is the ongoing fruit of my labor: yet what I shall choose I do not know. 23 For I am torn between two desires, having a desire to depart, and to be with ha Moshiach; which is far better:[2] 24 Nevertheless to remain in the body is more needful for you.[3] 25 And having this confidence, I know that I shall stay here for now, and continue with you for your progress and simcha in believing; 26 That your gilah may be more abundant in **יהושע** ha Moshiach for me by my coming to you again. 27 Only let your behavior be worthy of the besarot of ha Moshiach: that whether I come and see you, or whether I am absent, I may hear of your

---

[1] In order for death to be considered a gain, there must be something to be gained immediately upon death.
[2] A departure from the body is a release to be with Moshiach upon death. Once we discover where Moshiach is now, we'll discover where we'll be, while we await the resurrection of the last day.
[3] To complete His calling.

affairs, that you stand fast in one ruach, with one mind striving as echad for the emunah of the besarot; 28 And in nothing be terrified by your adversaries: whose personal conduct is the sign of their future destruction, but your conduct speaks of salvation, from **יהוה**. 29 For to you it is given on Moshiach's behalf, not only to believe on Him, but also to suffer for His sake; 30 Having the same trials that you saw in me, and now shema to be in me.

2 If therefore you have received any encouragement in ha Moshiach, or any comfort, or ahava, or any chavurah of the Ruach, or any affection, or rachamim, 2 Complete my simcha, that you are likeminded, having the same ahava, being in echad accord, in echad mind. 3 Let nothing be done through strife or pride or conceit; but in lowliness of mind let each esteem the other better than themselves. 4 A Yisraelite should look not only on his own things, but every man also on the things of others. 5 Let this mind be in you, which was and is also in ha Moshiach **יהושע** : 6 Who, being in the form of Elohim, thought it not a thing to be grasped at, to be equal with **יהוה** :[1] 7 But made Himself of no reputation, and took upon Himself the form of a eved, and was made in the likeness of men:[2] 8 And being found fashioned as a man, He humbled Himself, and became obedient to death, even the death of the execution stake. 9 Therefore **יהוה** also has highly exalted Him, and given Him the Name which is above every name:[3] 10 That at the Name of **יהושע** every knee should bow, of things in the shamayim, and things on earth, and things under the earth;[4] 11 And that every tongue should confess that **יהושע** ha Moshiach is

Master, to the tifereth of the Master Abba **יהוה**. 12 Therefore, my beloved, as you have always obeyed, not only in my presence, but now much more in my absence, work out your own salvation with fear and trembling.[5] 13 For it is **יהוה** who works in you both to will and to do of His tov pleasure. 14 Do all things without murmurings and disputes: 15 So that you may be the blameless and harmless, sons of **יהוה** , without spot, in the midst of a crooked and perverse generation, among whom you shine as lights in the olam hazeh; 16 For you are to them the light of chayim,[6] that I may gilah in the Yom of ha Moshiach, that I have not run randomly, neither labored in vain. 17 Yes, and if my dom be offered in the sacrifice and service for your emunah, I have simcha, and gilah with you all. 18 For the same reason also do you simcha, and gilah with me. 19 But I trust in the Master **יהושע** to send Timtheous shortly to you, that I also may be of tov comfort, when I know your condition. 20 For I have no man likeminded, who will genuinely care for your condition. 21 For all seek their own agendas, and not the things that are **יהושע** ha Moshiach's. 22 But you know his record, that, as a son with an abba, he has served with me in the besarot. 23 Therefore I plan to send him shortly, as soon as I see how it goes with me. 24 But I trust in **יהוה** that I also myself shall come shortly. 25 Yet I thought it necessary to send to you Epaphroditos, my brother, and chaver in labor, and fellow soldier, your sholiach, who also attended to my needs. 26 For he longed for you, and was full of heaviness, because you had heard that he had been sick. 27 For indeed he was sick even close to death: but **יהוה** had rachamim on him; and not on him only, but on me also, so that I should not have sorrow upon sorrow. 28 I sent him to you even more eagerly, so that when you see him again, you may gilah, that I might be

---

[1] Yahshua was and remains YHWH's visible form, yet did not think it was something to be boastful or conceited about.
[2] Rather than parade about to seize Abba's position, He humbled Himself to man's lowly position.
[3] The Name. The Father's own Name as prophesied in Isaiah 45:23. He would be recognized and known as YHWH in the flesh, which no other man in history could be known as.
[4] Isaiah 45:23-24.

[5] Meaning walk it out with reverence and Torah guidance, realizing before whom you walk.
[6] Peshitta.

less sorrowful. 29 Receive him therefore in the Master with all simcha; and hold him in high regard: 30 Because for the work of ha Moshiach he was near death, not regarding his chayim, to supply to me what you could not.

3 Finally, my brothers, gilah in our Master. To write the same things to you over and over again, to me is not a bother, but it is safe for you. 2 Beware of dogs,[1] beware of evil workers,[2] beware of the mutilation.[3] 3 For we are the brit milah,[4] who worship יהוה in the Ruach, and gilah in ha Moshiach יהושע, and have no confidence in the flesh.[5] 4 Though I too could have confidence in the flesh. If any other man thinks of trusting in the flesh, I could even more so: 5 I was circumcised the eighth day, of the race of Am-Yisrael, of the tribe of Benyamin, an Ivri son of an Ivri; regarding Torah, a Prushi; 6 Concerning zeal, persecuting the Renewed Yisraelite congregation; regarding the right conduct that is in the Torah, blameless. 7 But what things were once gains for me; I counted lost for ha Moshiach. 8 Yes doubtless, and I count all things to be lost for the better excellence of the chochmah of ha Moshiach יהושע My Master: for whom I have suffered the loss of all things, and do count them as garbage, that I may gain more of ha Moshiach, 9 And be found in Him, not having mine own tzedakah, which is from the Torah, but that which is through the emunah of ha Moshiach, the tzedakah that is from יהוה by emunah:[6] 10 That I may know Him, and the power of His resurrection, and the chavurah of His sufferings, being made conformable even to a death like His; 11 That by any means necessary I might attain to the resurrection of the dead. 12 Not as though I had already attained it, or was already perfected: but I follow after, so that I may apprehend the reasons why I was also apprehended by ha Moshiach יהושע. 13 Brothers, I count not myself to have apprehended: but this one thing I do, forgetting those things that are behind me, I reach and strive for those things that are yet before me, 14 I press on toward the goal for the prize of victory of the high calling of יהוה in ha Moshiach יהושע. 15 Let us therefore, as many as are mature, have this mind: and if in anything you think differently, יהוה shall reveal even this to you. 16 Nevertheless, in the main issues we have all already attained maturity, so let us have our halacha by the same rule, let us mind the same thing. 17 Brothers, be imitators together of me, and mark them who have that same halacha just as you have us as an example. 18 For many have wrong halacha, of whom I have told you often, and now tell you even with weeping, that they are the enemies of the execution stake of ha Moshiach:[7] 19 Whose end is destruction, whose elohim is their belly, and whose tifereth is in their shameful conduct, who mind earthly things. 20 For our labor and behavior is from the shamayim; from where we also look and eagerly wait for the return of the Savior, the Master יהושע ha Moshiach: 21 Who shall change our poor lowly body, that it may be refashioned just like His new esteemed body, according to His own working by which He is able to subdue all things under His control.

4 Therefore, my brothers dearly beloved and longed for, my simcha and keter, stand fast in the Master, my dearly beloved. 2 I beseech Euodia, and beseech Suntuche, that they be of the same

---

[1] Pagans or gentiles and their conduct.
[2] Adversaries of the tov news.
[3] Circumcision, or those who desire to turn believers into traditional Jews.
[4] Yisrael.
[5] Paul does not negate circumcision at all, but merely states that a believer is not to trust in anything but Yahshua for right-standing before YHWH.
[6] Torah was never given to impart salvation or an eternal right-standing with YHWH. It was used to lead us to Moshiach, and now guides us by Moshiach, who alone imparts righteousness. Moshiach Yahshua uses Torah to guard us from being led astray.

[7] Such folks as anti-Yahshua missionaries, and replacement theologians.

mind in the Master. 3 And I ask you also, emet chaverim, help those women who labored with me in the besarot, with Qlemes also, and with others of my fellow laborers, whose names are in the Scroll of Chayim.[1] 4 Gilah in יהוה always: and again I say, Gilah. 5 Let your moderation and humility be known to all men. The Master is at hand. 6 Be anxious for nothing; but in every thing by tefillah and supplication with hodu let your requests be made known to יהוה. 7 And the shalom of יהוה, which passes all binah, shall keep your levim and minds through ha Moshiach יהושע. 8 Finally, brothers, whatever things are emet, whatever things are honest, whatever things are just, whatever things are pure, whatever things are lovely, whatever things are of tov report; if there be any virtue, and if there be any tehilla, think on these things. 9 Those things, which you have both learned, and received, and heard, and seen in me, do: and the Elohim of shalom shall be with you.[2] 10 But I had gilah in יהוה greatly, that now again recently your care and concern for me has revived again; though you were concerned in the past, but you lacked the means. 11 Not that I speak in respect of want: for I have learned, in whatever state I am in to be content. 12 I know what it is to be poor, and I know what it is to be rich: I have gone through and experienced many things, both to be full and to be hungry, to have plenty and be in want.[3]

13 I have the strength to do all things through ha Moshiach who strengthens me. 14 Yet you have done well, that you did share during my affliction. 15 Now you in Phylypseyah should know, that in the beginning of the besarot in the nations, when I departed from Makedonia, no Yisraelite congregation communicated with me regarding giving and receiving assistance, but you alone. 16 For even in Tesloniqyah you sent again and again to meet my needs. 17 Not because I desire a gift: but I desire spiritual fruit that may multiply in your account. 18 But I have all, and abound: I am full, having received from Epaphroditos the things that were sent from you, as an odor of a sweet-smelling sacrifice, acceptable and well pleasing to יהוה. 19 But My Elohim shall supply all your needs according to His riches by the tifereth of ha Moshiach יהושע. 20 Now to יהוה our Abba be tifereth le olam-va-ed. Amein. 21 Greet every set-apart one in ha Moshiach יהושע. The brothers who are with me greet you. 22 All the kidushim greet you, most of all those that believe in Caesar's household. 23 The unmerited favor of our Master יהושע ha Moshiach be with you all. Amein.

---

[1] Lamb's Book of Life.
[2] This is not boasting, but a reminder that YHWH requires mature believers and leaders to lead by example.
[3] Peshitta.

Qolesayah - Colossians
To The Believing Remnant Of Yisrael

1 Shaul, a sholiach of **יהושע** ha Moshiach by the will of **יהוה**, and Timtheous our brother, 2 To the kidushim and faithful brothers in ha Moshiach who are at Qolesayah: Unmerited favor be to you, and shalom, from **יהוה** our Abba and the Master **יהושע** ha Moshiach. 3 We give hodu to **יהוה** the Abba of our Master **יהושע** ha Moshiach, making tefillot always for you, 4 Since we heard of your emunah in ha Moshiach **יהושע**, and of the ahava which you have to all the kidushim, 5 For the tikvah that is laid up for you in the shamayim, of which you heard before in the word of the emet of the besarot; 6 Which is come to you, as it has in all the olam; and brings forth fruit, as it does also in you, since the day that you heard of it, and knew the unmerited favor of **יהוה** in emet: 7 As you also learned of Epaphras our dear fellow eved, who is for you also a faithful eved of ha Moshiach; 8 Who also declared to us your ahava in the Ruach. 9 For this cause we also, since the day we heard of it, do not cease to make tefillot for you, and to desire that you might be filled with the da'at of His will in all chochmah and spiritual binah; 10 That you might have a halacha worthy of the Master fully pleasing, being fruitful in every tov mitzvah, and increasing in the da'at of Elohim; 11 Strengthened with all koach, according to His beautiful power, to all patience and endurance with simcha; 12 Giving hodu to Abba, who has made us fit to be partakers of the inheritance of the kidushim in light: 13 Who has delivered us from the power of darkness, and has translated us into the malchut of His dear Son: 14 In whom we have redemption through His dom, even the forgiveness of sins: 15 Who is the image of the invisible Elohim, the firstborn of all creation: 16 For by Him were all things created, that are in the shamayim, and that are on earth, visible and invisible, whether they are thrones, or dominions, or principalities, or powers: all things were created by Him, and for Him:[1] 17 And He is before all things, and by Him all things consist. 18 And He is the head of the body, the congregation of Yisrael: who is the beginning, the firstborn from the dead; that in all things He might be the first. 19 For it pleased Abba that in Him should all fullness dwell; 20 And, having made shalom through the dom of His execution stake, through Him to restore all things to Himself;[2] whether they be things on earth, or things in the shamayim. 21 And you, that were sometimes alienated and enemies in your mind by wicked works, yet now has He restored.[3] 22 In the body of His flesh through death, to present you set-apart and blameless and without reproach in His sight: 23 If you continue in the emunah grounded and settled, and be not moved away from the tikvah of the besarot, about which you have heard, and which was proclaimed to every creature that is under the shamayim; by which I Shaul have been made an eved; 24 Who now have simcha in my sufferings for you, that now fills up that which is lacking in the afflictions of ha Moshiach in my own flesh for His body's sake, which is the congregation of Yisrael: 25 Of which I am made an eved, according to the administration of Elohim's gift, which is given to me for you, to fulfill the word of **יהוה**; 26 Even the mystery that has been hidden from olamim and from

---

[1] Yahshua the Son of Ha Abba, is the Creator who followed The Father's blueprint.
[2] Since Yahshua's dom came to restore all things, that restoration by definition must also include the people of Yisrael scattered into two houses.
[3] The alienated ones were Ephraim Yisrael, who have now been restored to YHWH and to their brothers in Yahudah.

generations, but now is revealed to His kidushim: 27 To whom יהוה would make known what is the riches of the tifereth of this mystery among all the nations;[1] which is ha Moshiach in you, the tikvah of tifereth: 28 Whom we proclaim, warning every man, and teaching every man in all chochmah; that we may present every man mature in ha Moshiach יהושע : 29 For which I also labor, striving according to His working, which works in me with His power.[2]

2 For I want you to know what a great struggle I have for you, and for them at Laodikeia, and for as many as have not seen my face in the flesh; 2 That their levim might be in full shalom, being knit together in ahava, to all the riches of the full assurance of binah, to the acknowledgement of the mystery of Abba יהוה and of ha Moshiach;[3] 3 In whom are hidden all the treasures of chochmah and da'at. 4 And this I say, lest any man should beguile you with enticing words. 5 For though I am absent in the flesh, yet am I with you in the Ruach, having simcha and beholding your orderliness, and the firmness of your emunah in ha Moshiach. 6 As you have therefore received ha Moshiach יהושע the Master, so have your halacha in Him:[4] 7 Rooted and built up in Him, established in the emunah, as you have been taught, abounding in the emunah with hodu. 8 Beware lest any man devour you through philosophy and vain deceit, after the traditions of men, after the elementary matters of the olam hazeh, and not after ha Moshiach. 9 For in Him dwells all the fullness of El-Elyon in bodily form. 10 And you are complete in Him, who is the head of all principality and power:[5] 11 In

whom also you are circumcised with the brit milah made without hands, in putting off the body of the sins of the flesh by the brit milah of ha Moshiach:[6] 12 Buried with Him in mikvah, by which also you are risen with Him through the emunah in the operation of יהוה, who has raised Him from the dead.[7] 13 And you, being dead in your sins and the uncircumcision of your flesh, has He made alive together with Him, having forgiven you all your trespasses; 14 Blotting out the handwriting of ordinances that was against us, which was contrary to us,[8] and took it out of the way, nailing it to His execution stake; 15 And having spoiled principalities and powers, He made a show of them openly, triumphing over them in it. 16 Let no individual man therefore judge you in meat, or in drink, or in respect of a moed, or of the Rosh Chodesh, or of the Shabbat days: 17 Which are shadows of things to come; except the Yisraelite body of ha Moshiach.[9] 18 Let no man beguile you of your reward in a false humility and in the worshipping of heavenly messengers,

---

[1] The fullness of all the end-time nations (Genesis 49:1), or the seed of Ephraim (Genesis 48:19) in those nations. Moshiach is now in us.
[2] To bring in the nations, with and by YHWH's power in Him.
[3] One of the mysteries of Renewed Covenant Yisrael is that Abba and Son form the **echad**.
[4] We received Him in joy and confidence, not letting any man entice us away from Him.
[5] Our completeness is in Yahshua not any branch of religion.
[6] All Renewed Covenant Yisraelites have had their hearts circumcised by Yahshua as we had the old nature and body cut off for a new nature and body to be given at His return. Now that this is done, the physical circumcision follows at a later time, not the other way around as practiced in traditional Judaism and in the Galatian heresy.
[7] Raised in newness of life or a new nature.
[8] This is not the Torah but rather the curses of the adulterous woman, or Yisrael, being nailed to the execution stake as the full and final fulfillment of Numbers 5:23, where the curses were kept in a list in a book. All the ordinances of Torah that we as Yisrael broke, were nailed to the stake. Furthermore YHWH's Torah, or any other part of His word, cannot be against man but for man, for in the Torah itself it states that the Torah was given for man's good. Furthermore, if the Torah was nailed to the stake, that means by definition sin no longer exists, since where there is no Torah, sin cannot be charged. Thankfully, only the lists of broken Yisraelite ordinances were nailed to the Master's stake.
[9] Since Yisrael is expected to follow all of YHWH's eternal ways, when we do the eternal ordinances, no one outside the body of Renewed Covenant Yisrael can, or has the right to, judge the manner in which we celebrate. The premise here is not if we celebrate, but proper guidance when we celebrate. No one but the congregation of Yisrael, can guide us in the manner that we celebrate. Moreover, verse 17 states that when we do these eternal moadim, we show forth the future kingdom to come, not things in the past. So if the celebration itself is a prophetic foreshadow of coming things, how is it that the celebrating of them takes anyone back to, or back "under the law," when Rav Shaul states just the opposite.

spiritually standing on things that he has not seen, empty-headed things, created by his fleshly mind,[1] 19 And not holding to the Head, from which all the body knit together by joints and ligaments receives nourishment, and grows with the increase of Elohim. 20 Therefore if you are dead with ha Moshiach from the elements of the olam hazeh, why, as though living in the olam hazeh, are you subject to ordinances,[2] 21 Touch not; taste not; handle not; 22 Which all are to perish with man's using; after the commandments and teachings of men?[3] 23 Whose rules have a show of wisdom in positive attitude, human-will worship, or self-humiliation of the body type worship, and neglecting of the body type worship; but these have no eternal value except for the satisfying and parading of the flesh.

3 If you then be risen with ha Moshiach, seek those things which are above, where ha Moshiach sits on the right hand of יהוה.[4] 2 Set your affection on things above, not on things on the earth. 3 For you are dead, and your life is hidden with ha Moshiach in יהוה. 4 When ha Moshiach, who is our chayim, shall appear, then shall you also appear with Him in tifereth. 5 Put to death therefore your bodily members which are upon the earth; fornication, uncleanness, perverted affections, evil desire, and covetousness, which is idolatry: 6 For which things' sake the wrath of יהוה comes on the children of disobedience: 7 In which you also had your halacha in the past, when you lived in them. 8 But now you also put off all these; anger, wrath, malice, blasphemy, and filthy speech out of your mouth. 9 Lie not one to another, seeing that you have put off the old man with his wicked deeds; 10 And have put on the renewed man, which is renewed in da'at after the image of Him that created him: 11 Where there is neither Greek, or Yahudite, brit milah, or uncircumcision, foreigner or, Scythian,[5] [6] bond, or free: but ha Moshiach is all, and in all Yisrael.[7] 12 Put on therefore, as the chosen people of יהוה , set-apart and beloved, rachamim, chesed, humbleness of mind, meekness, and endurance; 13 Bearing one another, and forgiving one another, if any man has a quarrel against anyone else: even as ha Moshiach forgave you, so also do you. 14 And above all these things put on ahava, which is the bond of perfection. 15 And let the shalom of Elohim rule in your levim, to which also you are called in one body;[8] and be full of hodu. 16 Let the word of ha Moshiach dwell in you richly in all chochmah; teaching and admonishing one another in the Tehillim and with Ruach-filled shirim, singing with unmerited favor in your levim to the Master. 17 And whatever you do in word, or mitzvah, do all in the Name of the Master יהושע , giving hodu to Abba יהוה through Him. 18 Wives, submit yourselves to your own husbands, as it is fit in the Master. 19 Husbands, love your wives, and be not bitter against them. 20 Children, obey your parents in all things: for this is well pleasing to יהוה. 21 Ahvot, provoke not your

---

[1] No one but Moshiach and His chosen people can guide us in approaching the moadim, since other pagan religions do strange things such as worshipping the creation, or self-flagellation.
[2] The carnal ones mentioned in verse 18. Yisrael had traded truth in Torah for Colossian legends and "works of the law," i.e., man's law, such as angel worship and false humility, as a means of atonement.
[3] The manmade "works of law" that the Colossians followed, were manmade as it states here. Is anyone prepared to argue that Torah is not divine, but merely manmade? Rav Shaul was attempting to get these Yisraelites back to YHWH's Torah, under community guidance and away from the vain temporal perishing ordinances of man, that had set in Colossia and also in Galatia.
[4] His Torah and His gift of eternal life, instead of manmade ordinances like taste not, and touch not, which will pass away, even while man is using them.

[5] The Scythians were Ephraimites according to Talmud Kiddushin 71A, stating that Scythians will return to Yisrael, when the prophet Elijah comes. Also the Greeks were not pure heathen, but lost Yisraelites, as explained in the video **The Greeks of the Brit Chadasha** available at:
http://store.yourarmstoisrael.org/Qstore/Qstore.cgi?CMD=011&PROD=000209
[6] The Greek word Strong's Greek # 915 for "Barbarian" is actually "foreigner"; and here Rav Shaul compares a foreigner to a non-foreigner or a Scythian, showing that many Scythians were biological Yisraelites in the believing congregation.
[7] In other words, all believers are part of Yisrael, regardless of how or what part of the nation you came from. Who is who in biblical understanding, is determined by what is what.
[8] Yisrael.

children to anger, lest they be discouraged. 22 Avadim, obey in all things your masters according to the flesh; not with eye-service, as men pleasers; but in sincerity of lev, fearing the Master יהוה: 23 And whatever you do, do it heartily, as to יהוה, and not to men; 24 Knowing that from the Master יהוה you shall receive the reward of the inheritance: for you serve יהושע ha Moshiach. 25 But he that does wrong shall receive for the wrong that he has done: and there is no partiality of persons.

4 Masters, give to your avadim that which is just and fair; knowing that you also have the Master יהוה in the shamayim. 2 Continue in the tefillot, and watch in the same with hodu; 3 Offer tefillah also for us, that Elohim would open to us a door for the word, to speak the mystery of ha Moshiach, for which I am also in prison: 4 That I may make things clear, as I should speak. 5 Have your halacha in chochmah towards those that are outside the emunah, redeeming the time. 6 Let your speech be always with unmerited favor, seasoned with salt, that you may know how you should answer every man. 7 All my affairs shall Tuchikos tell you, who is a beloved brother and a faithful eved in the Master: 8 Whom I have sent to you for the same purpose, that he might know your affairs, and bring shalom to your

levim; 9 With Onesimos, a faithful and beloved brother, who is one of you. They shall make known to you all things that are done here. 10 Aristarchus my fellow prisoner salutes you, and Moshe-Marcus, the nephew of Bar-Navah, about whom you received my instructions: if he comes to you, receive him; 11 And Yeshua, who is called Justus, who is a Yahudite. These only are my fellow workers for the malchut of יהוה, who have been a comfort to me. 12 Epaphras, who is one of you, an eved of ha Moshiach, salutes you, always laboring fervently for you in tefillot, that you may stand perfect and complete in all the will of יהוה. 13 For I bear him record, that he has a great zeal for you, and for those that are in Laodikeia, and for those in Hierapolis. 14 Luka, the beloved physician, and Demas, greet you. 15 Salute the brothers who are in Laodekeia, and Numpha, and the remnant congregation that meets in his bayit.

16 And when this letter is read among you, make sure that it is read also in the congregation of the Laodikeians; and that you also read the letter from Laodikeia.

17 And say to Archippos, Take heed to the calling, which you have received in the Master, that you complete it. 18 This greeting is with my own hand - Shaul. Remember my imprisonment. Unmerited favor be with you. Amein.

תסלוניקיא א

Tesloniqyah Alef - First Thessalonians

To The Believing Remnant Of Yisrael

1 Shaul, and Sila, and Timtheous, to the congregation of the Tesloniqyah [1] which is in Abba **יהוה** and in the Master **יהושע** ha Moshiach: unmerited favor be to you, and shalom, from **יהוה** our Abba, and the Master **יהושע** ha Moshiach. 2 We give hodu to **יהוה** always for you all, making mention of you in our tefillot; 3 Remembering without ceasing your mitzvot in the emunah, and labor of ahava, and patience of tikvah in our Master **יהושע** ha Moshiach, in the sight of **יהוה** our Abba; 4 Knowing, beloved brothers, your choosing by **יהוה**. 5 For our besarot came not to you in word only, but also in power, and in the Ruach HaKodesh,[2] and in much assurance; as you know what manner of men we were among you for your sake. 6 And you became followers of us, and of the Master, having received the word in much tribulation, with the simcha of the Ruach HaKodesh: 7 So that you were examples to all that believe in Makedonia and Achaia.[3] 8 For from you sounded forth the word of the Master not only in Makedonia and Achaia, but also in every place, so that your emunah towards **יהוה** is spread abroad; so that we do not need to speak anything more about you. 9 For they themselves relate to us what manner of entry we first had with you, and how you made teshuvah towards **יהוה** from idols to serve the living and emet Elohim; 10 And to wait for His Son from the shamayim, who He raised from the dead, even **יהושע**, who delivers us from the wrath to come.[4]

2 For yourselves, brothers, know our entrance in and among you, that it was not a waste of time: 2 But even after we had suffered and were shamefully treated before, as you know, at Philippi, we were bold in our Elohim to speak to you the besarot of **יהוה** in much struggle. 3 For our appeal was not by deceit, nor by uncleanness, nor by guile: 4 But as we were allowed by **יהוה** to be put in trust with the besarot, even so we speak; not as pleasing men, but **יהוה**, who tries our levim. 5 For neither at any time did we use flattering words to make you believe, as you know, nor under a secret desire based upon greed; **יהוה** is witness: 6 We sought not support, neither from you, nor from others, when we could have been burdensome to you, as the shlichim of ha Moshiach. 7 But we were gentle among you, even as a nursing ima nurses her children: 8 So having this affectionate desire towards you, we were willing to have imparted to you, not the besarot of **יהוה** only, but also our own beings, because you were dear to us. 9 For you remember, brothers, our labor and toil: for laboring night and day when with you, because we would not be burdensome to any of you, we proclaimed to you the besarot of Elohim. 10 You are witnesses, along with **יהוה** also, how set-apart and justly and without blame we behaved ourselves among you that believe: 11 As you know how we exhorted and comforted and oversaw each one of you, as an abba does with his children, 12 That you would have your halacha worthy of **יהוה**, who has called you to His malchut and tifereth. 13 For this cause also we give hodu to **יהוה** without ceasing, because, when you received the word of **יהוה** which you heard from us, you received it not as the word of men, but as it is in emet, the word of **יהוה**, that also works in you that believe. 14 For you, brothers, became followers of the

---

[1] Aramaic pronunciation.
[2] Everywhere the Tov News is shared, miracles of changed lives and changed thinking occur.
[3] See notes on First Timothy 1:3.
[4] The Lake of Fire and divine protection during the soon-coming Great Tribulation.

congregations of יהוה which in Yahudah are in ha Moshiach יהושע: for you also have suffered similar things from your own countrymen, even as they have of the Yahudim of Judea:[1] 15 Who both killed the Master יהושע,[2] and their own neviim, and have persecuted us; and they please not יהוה, and are contrary to all men: 16 Forbidding us to speak to the nations so that they might be saved, to fill up their sins all the way: for His wrath is come upon them to the uttermost.[3] 17 But we, brothers, being taken from you for a short time in presence, not in lev, tried even more earnestly to see your face with great desire. 18 Therefore we would have come to you, even I Shaul, again; but s.a.tan hindered us. 19 For what is our tikvah, or simcha, or keter of gilah? All of you are; now and even then in the presence of our Master יהושע ha Moshiach at His coming? 20 For you are our tifereth and simcha.

3 So when we could no longer stand it, we thought it tov to be left at Athens alone; 2 And sent Timtheous, our brother, and servant of יהוה, and our fellow-laborer in the besarot of ha Moshiach, to establish you, and to encourage you concerning your emunah: 3 That no man should be moved by these afflictions: for you yourselves know that we are appointed to this.[4] 4 For truly, when we were with you, we told you before that we should suffer tribulation; even as it came to pass, as you know. 5 For this cause, when I could no longer stand it, I sent to know about your emunah, lest by

some means the tempter had tempted you, and our labor among you be in vain. 6 But now when Timtheous came from you back to us, and brought us the besarot of your emunah and ahava, and that you have tov memories of us all the time, desiring greatly to see us again, as we also to see you again: 7 Therefore, brothers, we were comforted over you in all our tribulation and distress by your emunah: 8 For now we live, if you stand fast in the Master. 9 For what hodu can we render to יהוה again for you, for all the simcha in which we rejoiced for your sakes before our Elohim; 10 In maariv and shacrit with many tefillot, so that we might see your face, and might complete that which is lacking in your emunah? 11 Now יהוה Himself our Abba, and our Master יהושע ha Moshiach, direct our way back to you. 12 And יהוה make you to increase and abound in ahava one toward another, and toward kol Yisrael, even as we do to you: 13 To establish your levim blameless in set-apartness before יהוה, our Abba, at the coming of our Master יהושע ha Moshiach with all His kidushim.

4 Furthermore we beg you, brothers, and exhort you by the Master יהושע, that as you have received from us how you ought to have your halacah in pleasing יהוה, so you would excel more and more. 2 For you know what commands we gave you by the Master יהושע. 3 For this is the will of יהוה, even your set-apartness that you should abstain from fornication: 4 That every one of you should know how to possess his own body as a vessel in set-apartness and honor; 5 Not in the lust of passions, even as the gentiles who know not יהוה:[5] 6 That no man take advantage or defraud his brother in Yisrael in any matter: because יהוה is the revenger of all such behavior, as we also have warned you and testified. 7 For יהוה has not called us to unclean behavior, but to set-apartness.

---

[1] Non-believing Yahudim were persecuting believing Yahudim in the province of Yahudah, as were Thessalonian believers who were being persecuted by Thessalonian unbelievers. Both houses were being persecuted for being the believing remnant of Yisrael, by non-believing Yisraelites.

[2] Not literally killed, but Rav Shaul speaks specifically of those leaders who were involved in the conspiracy according to Psalm 2 and Acts 2:23. The charge here is directed at the Jewish leaders, not the nation, since many Jews followed Him, and without them there would not be a Brit Chadasha.

[3] In addition to conspiring against Moshiach, some Yahudim (not those like Shaul himself) that did not believe (not all Yahudim) also tried to stop Ephraim from returning home as seen in Galatians. They caused confusion and corruption to enter into both houses of Yisrael, fighting against her promised restoration by Yahshua.

[4] The Great Tribulation.

[5] Nothing can be clearer; gentiles are pagans and don't know YHWH. Non-Jewish believers are Yisraelites who do know YHWH.

8 Therefore he that despises another Yisraelite, despises not man, but יהוה Himself, who has also given us His Ruach HaKodesh. 9 But as touching brotherly ahava you need not that I write to you again: for you yourselves are taught by יהוה to love one another. 10 And indeed you do love all the brothers who are in all of Makedonia: but we beg you, brothers that you increase in this even more; 11 And that you study to be quiet, and to do your own business, and to work with your own hands, as we commanded you; 12 That you may have your halacha honestly toward them that are outside the emunah, and that you may lack nothing. 13 But I would not have you to be ignorant, brothers, concerning those who are dead, that you sorrow not, even as unbelievers who have no tikvah. 14 For if we believe that יהושע died and rose again, even them also who have died believing in יהושע will Elohim bring with Him.[1] 15 For this we say to you by the word of יהוה, that we who are alive and remain until the coming of the Master shall not be resurrected before those who are already dead in the emunah. 16 For יהושע Himself shall descend from the shamayim with a shout, with the voice of the chief heavenly messenger,[2] and with the shofar and the tekiyah-ge-dolah of יהוה: and the dead in Moshiach shall rise first: 17 Then we who are alive and remain at His return shall be caught up together with them onto the clouds, to meet the Master in the air:[3] and so shall we ever be with the Master.[4] 18 So then comfort one another with these words.

5 But of the times and the seasons, brothers, you have no need that I write to you. 2 For you know perfectly that the Yom of יהוה comes as a thief in the night.[5] 3 For when they shall say, Shalom-ve betachon;[6] then sudden destruction comes upon them, as labor pains upon a woman in labor;[7] and they shall not escape. 4 But you, brothers, are not in darkness, that that day should overtake you as a thief.[8] 5 You are all the children of Light, and the children of the Day: we are not of the night, or of the darkness. 6 Therefore let us not sleep, as do others; but let us watch and be sober. 7 For they that sleep, sleep in the night; and they that get drunk, get drunk in the night. 8 But let us, who are of the Day, be sober, putting on the breastplate of emunah and ahava; and as a helmet, the tikvah of salvation. 9 For יהוה has not appointed us to wrath, but to obtain deliverance by our Master יהושע ha Moshiach,[9] 10 Who died for us, that, whether we are awake or dead, we should live together with Him. 11 Therefore comfort yourselves together, and edify one another, even as also you already do. 12 And we ask you, brothers, to know them who labor among you, and are over you in יהוה, and who admonish you; 13 And to honor them very highly in ahava for their work's sake. And be at shalom among yourselves. 14 Now we exhort you, brothers, correct them that are unruly, comfort those who lack courage, support the weak, be patient toward all men. 15 See that none repay evil for evil to any man; but always follow that which is tov, both among yourselves, and to all men. 16 Gilah always. 17 Make tefillah without ceasing. 18 In all things give hodu: for this is the will of יהוה

---

[1] At the ingathering of Yisrael.
[2] Gabriel.
[3] Strong's Greek #109 meaning "air" or lower denser air around the earth, not heaven itself. The clouds belong to the earth's atmosphere, not the heavens. This is the first and blessed resurrection, held in two brief stages as Moshiach returns just prior to the 1,000-year reign. This concept is simple, when we allow YHWH to renew our minds. Yahshua makes things as plain as He can in John 17:15, where He prays that believers be not removed from the earth, thus eliminating any chance of an alleged rapture.
[4] He meets us to change us in the air, since the earth is under a curse. Then after rising to be changed, we return with Him to reign.

[5] For unbelievers.
[6] "Peace and security," as in today's Middle East peace processes.
[7] In Hebraic thought, this is called the birth pains of the Moshiach, or **shivlai Ha Moshiach** that precede His anticipated arrival. The woman in labor is Yisrael, as seen in this letter to an Ephraimite congregation.
[8] No such thing as an imminent return, but rather an anticipated one.
[9] Deliverance from the hour of testing, not removal from the hour of testing. We will experience His trials, not His wrath, which is poured out fully at His return. See John 17:15.

in ha Moshiach יהושע for you. 19 Quench not the Ruach HaKodesh. 20 Do not reject prophecies. 21 Test them all; hold fast to what is tov. 22 Abstain from all forms of evil. 23 And the very Elohim of shalom separate you completely; so that your whole ruach, nephesh and gooff be preserved without blemish, until the coming of our Master יהושע ha Moshiach.[1] 24 Faithful is He that called you, who also will shomer all of His word.

25 Brothers, offer many tefillot for us. 26 Greet all the brothers with a set-apart kiss. 27 I charge you by the Master that this letter is read to all the set-apart brothers. 28 The unmerited favor of our Master יהושע ha Moshiach be with you. Amein.

---

[1] All three parts are considered echad.

תסלוניקיא ב

Tesloniqyah Bet - Second Thessalonians
To The Believing Remnant Of Yisrael

1 Shaul, and Sila, and Timtheous, to the congregation of Tesloniqyah in יהוה our Abba and the Master יהושע ha Moshiach: 2 Favor to you, and shalom, from יהוה our Abba and the Master יהושע ha Moshiach. 3 We are bound to give hodu to יהוה always for you, brothers, as it is proper, because your emunah grows exceedingly, and the ahava of all Yisrael toward each other abounds more and more; 4 So that we ourselves boast in you in the congregations of יהוה for your patience and emunah even in all your persecutions and tribulations that you endure: 5 Which is clear evidence of the tzadik mishpat of יהוה yet to come to the olam hazeh, that you may be counted worthy of the malchut of יהוה, for which you also now suffer: 6 Seeing it is a righteous thing with יהוה to repay tribulation to them that trouble you;[1] 7 And to you who are undergoing tribulation rest with us, when the Master יהושע shall be revealed from the shamayim with His mighty heavenly messengers, 8 In flaming fire taking vengeance on them that know not יהוה, and that obey not the besarot of our Master יהושע ha Moshiach: 9 Who shall be punished with everlasting destruction away from the presence of יהוה, and from the tifereth of His power; 10 When He shall come to be esteemed in His kidushim, and to be admired by all those who believe in that Day, because our testimony among you was believed. 11 Therefore also we make tefillah always for you, that our Elohim would count you worthy of this calling, to fulfill all the tov pleasure of His rachamim, and the work of emunah with power: 12 That the Name of our Master יהושע ha

Moshiach may be lifted up in you, and you in Him, according to the unmerited favor of our Elohim and the Master יהושע ha Moshiach.

2 Now we urge you, brothers, by the coming of our Master יהושע ha Moshiach, and by our gathering together to Him,[2] 2 That you be not soon shaken in mind, or troubled, neither by any ruach, nor by man's word, nor by letter as from us, that the Yom of ha Moshiach's coming is at hand. 3 Let no man deceive you by any means: for that Yom shall not come, except there come a falling away first,[3] and that man of sin will be revealed, the son of perdition; [4] 4 Who opposes and exalts himself above all that is called elohim, or that is worshipped; so that he as elohim sits in the Beit HaMikdash of elohim, declaring himself to be elohim.[5] 5 Remember, that, when I was still with you, I told you these things? 6 And now you know what withholds, this so that he might be revealed in his time. 7 For the mystery of Torah-less-ness does already work: only he who now lets it will let it, until he be taken out of the way.[6] 8 And then shall that Torah-less one

---

[1] The enemies of the Tov News will get their reward during the Great Tribulation.

[2] Gathering into the kingdom, not a flight to rapture. In Hebraic understanding this is the **kevutz galyut**, or the return and gathering of Yisrael's exiles from the four winds. This is the subject here.
[3] **Apostasia**. See: http://store.yourarmstoisrael.org/Qstore/ for the teaching **Is It Us?**
[4] The revealing of anti-Moshiach from the tribe of Dan.
[5] The physical temple will be rebuilt on Mt. Moriah in the literal understanding. In the spiritual understanding, it is the false portrayal of the gentile Moshiach called J-sus, as opposed to the historical Yahshua who has been seated in YHWH's temple, the body of Moshiach; and has caused massive falling away. Both applications in a latter-day context are appropriate. For more details, see: http://store.yourarmstoisrael.org/Qstore/Qstore.cgi?CMD=011 &PROD=000130.
[6] A reference to Mikael or Michael the arch messenger, who is said to be Yisrael's warring messenger. He will be taken out of the way by YHWH as prophesied in Daniel 12:1-2, when he is told to cease or freeze in standing up for Yisrael so that Jacob's Trouble, or the Great Tribulation, can commence. This

be revealed, whom יהושע shall consume with the Ruach of His mouth, and shall destroy with the brightness of His coming: 9 Even him, whose coming is after the working of s.a.tan with all unclean power and signs and lying wonders, 10 With all deceit and unrighteousness in those that are perishing; because they received not the ahava of the emet that they might be saved. 11 And for this reason יהוה shall send them strong delusion, that they should believe The Lie:[1] 12 That they all might be damned who believed not the emet, but had pleasure in unrighteousness. 13 But we are bound to give hodu always to יהוה for you, brothers beloved of the Master, because יהוה has from Bereshet chosen you to be saved through the set-apartness of the Ruach and emunah of the emet: 14 To which He called you by our besarot, to the obtaining of the tifereth of our Master יהושע ha Moshiach. 15 Therefore, brothers, stand fast, and hold the traditions[2] that you have been taught, whether by word, or our letter. 16 Now our Master יהושע ha Moshiach Himself, and יהוה, even our Abba, who has loved us, and has given us everlasting comfort and tov tikvah through unmerited favor, 17 Comfort your levim, and establish you in every tov word of the Ketuvim and in mitzvot.

3 Finally, brothers, make tefillah for us, that the word of יהוה may spread rapidly, and be praised, even as it has with you: 2 And that we may be delivered from unreasonable and wicked men: for all men have not emunah. 3 But the Master יהוה is faithful, who shall establish you, and shomer you from evil. 4 And we have

confidence in יהוה about you, that you both do and will do the things that we command you. 5 And the Master direct your levim into the ahava of יהוה, and into the patient waiting for ha Moshiach. 6 Now we command you, brothers, in the Name of our Master יהושע ha Moshiach that you withdraw yourselves from every brother that has his halacha disorderly, and not after the tradition that he received from us.[3] 7 For you know how you should follow us: for we ourselves behaved not disorderly among you; 8 Neither did we eat any man's bread without paying for it; but worked with labor and toil night and day, that we might not burden any of you: 9 Not because we have no power to do so, but to make ourselves an example for you to follow us. 10 For even when we were with you, this we commanded you, that if any would not work, neither should he eat. 11 For we hear that there are some who walk among you disorderly, not working at all, but are busybodies. 12 Now those that are like that we command and exhort by our Master יהושע ha Moshiach, that with shalom they should work, and eat their own bread. 13 But you, brothers, be not weary in well doing. 14 And if any man does not obey our word by this letter, note that man, and have no company with him, that he may be ashamed.[4] 15 Yet count him not as an enemy, but admonish him as a brother. 16 Now the Elohim of shalom Himself give you shalom always by all means. יהוה be with you all. 17 The greeting of Shaul with my own hand, which is my mark in every letter: so I write. 18 The unmerited favor of our Master יהושע ha Moshiach be with you all. Amein.

---

does not refer to the Set-Apart Spirit, for clearly the Set-Apart Spirit is in the earth during that time, as seen by those who get saved and come to emunah during that time.

[1] Allowing the false Moshiach, the anti-Moshiach, or the image of the false one, to replace the real Torah-keeping Yahshua. This has occurred and will yet occur more widely, because YHWH has allowed it.

[2] This is not a reference to the Oral Torah of the traditional rabbis, but to traditions of the first-century Nazarene Yisraelite community, such as service and worship procedures during feasts and Shabbat.

---

[3] The tradition of the ingathering of the exiles, not the tradition of the pre-tribulation rapture; for those who walk that way are called disorderly, as outlined throughout chapter two.

[4] A stern warning to those who can work but won't and who through laziness wait for a pre-tribulation rapture in the hills, shunning all responsibility to family and the community of Yisrael.

פילמן

Phileymon - Philemon

To Believing Remnant Yisrael

1 Shaul, a prisoner of **יהושע** ha Moshiach, and Timtheous our brother, to Phileymon our dearly beloved, and fellow laborer, 2 And to our beloved Apphia, and Archippus our fellow soldier, and to the congregation in your bayit: [1] 3 Favor to you, and shalom, from **יהוה** our Abba and the Master **יהושע** ha Moshiach. 4 I give hodu to my Elohim, making mention of you always in my tefillot, 5 Hearing of your ahava and emunah, that you have toward the Master **יהושע**, and toward all the kidushim; 6 That the sharing of your emunah may work itself out by the acknowledging of every tov thing that is in you in ha Moshiach **יהושע**. 7 For we have great simcha and consolation in your ahava, because the affections of the kidushim are refreshed by you, brother. 8 Therefore, though I might have much boldness in ha Moshiach to command you to do what is fitting, 9 Yet for ahava's sake I rather appeal to you, being such a one as Shaul the aged, and now also a prisoner of **יהושע** ha Moshiach. 10 I beg you for my ben emunah Onesimus, whom I have brought to emunah in my imprisonment: 11 Who in times past was to you unprofitable, but now he is profitable to you and to me: 12 Whom I have sent again: therefore receive him, that is, my own desire: 13 Whom I would have retained with me, so that in your place he has served me in the chains of the besarot:

14 But without your feedback I did nothing; so that your mitzvah should not be as it were from necessity, but willingly. 15 For perhaps he therefore departed from you for a while, that you should receive him back le-olam-va-ed; 16 Not now as an eved, [2] but above an eved, a beloved brother, especially to me, but how much more to you, both in the flesh, and in the Master? [3] 17 If you count me as your partner, receive him as you would me. 18 If he has wronged you, or owes you anything, put that on my account; 19 I Shaul have written this with my own hand, I will repay it: not to mention how you owe me indeed even your own chayim. 20 Yes, brother, let me have simcha over you in **יהוה**: refresh my tender affections in **יהוה**. 21 Having confidence in your obedience I wrote to you, knowing that you will also do even more than I say. 22 At the same time prepare for me also a place to stay: for I trust that through your tefillot I shall be given back to you. 23 Epaphras, my fellow prisoner in ha Moshiach **יהושע** greets you; 24 And Moshe-Marcus, Aristarchos, Demas, Luka, my fellow laborers. 25 The favor of our Master **יהושע** ha Moshiach be with your ruach. Amein

---

[1] Renewed Covenant Yisraelites often met at home.

[2] The Torah principle that a Hebrew must not own a Hebrew servant.
[3] This runaway slave had gotten saved while Rav Shaul was in prison in Rome. He appeals to Philemon as an Yisraelite, asking him to allow Onesimos the slave to remain free in service to Moshiach, and not to return to physical slavery. Here one Yisraelite appeals to another to remove slavery, since Yisraelites were sensitive to the plight of slaves, having been slaves in Egypt.

טימתאוס א

Timtheous Alef - First Timothy
To A Shepherd of Yisrael

1 Shaul, a sholiach of יהושע the Moshiach by the commandment of יהוה our Savior, and Master יהושע ha Moshiach our Tikvah; 2 To Timtheous, my own ben emunah: Unmerited favor, rachamim, and shalom, from יהוה our Abba and יהושע ha Moshiach our Master. 3 As I asked you to stay at Ephesos, when I went into Makedonia, [1] that you might command some that they teach no other teaching, 4 Neither give heed to bubbe mysehs and endless genealogies, which cause disputes, rather than building up your emunah. [2] 5 Now the goal of the above commandment is ahava out of a clean lev, a tov conscience, and sincere emunah: 6 From which some having turned aside to foolish words; 7 Desiring to be teachers of the Torah; understanding neither what they say, nor what they affirm. [3] 8 But we know that the Torah is tov, if a man uses it lawfully; 9 Knowing this, that the Torah is not made for a tzadik, but for the Torah-less and disobedient, for the wicked and for sinners, for Shabbat-breakers, [4] for wrong-doers for profane, for murderers of ahvot and murderers of imot, for killers, 10 For those who whore, for sodomites and lesbians, for kidnappers, for liars, for perjurers, and if there be any other thing that is contrary to sound Torah-keeping; 11 According to the beautiful besarot of the blessed Elohim, that was committed to my trust. [5] 12 And I give hodu to ha Moshiach יהושע our Master, who has empowered me, in that He counted me faithful, putting me into the service; 13 Even though before I was a blasphemer, and a persecutor, and insulter of believers: I obtained rachamim, because I did it ignorantly in unbelief. 14 And the unmerited favor of our Master was exceedingly abundant to me with the emunah and ahava that is in ha Moshiach י־הושע. 15 This is a faithful saying, and worthy of all acceptance: That ha Moshiach יהושע came into the olam hazeh to save sinners; of whom I am the worst. 16 But for this cause I obtained rachamim, that in me first יהושע ha Moshiach might show forth all patience, for a pattern to those who will believe on Him to chayim everlasting after me. 17 Now to the Melech, Eternal, Immortal, Invisible, the only wise Elohim, be honor and tifereth le-olam va-ed. 18 This charge I commit to you, my son Timtheous, according to the prophecies which went before upon you, that you by them might wage a tov campaign; 19 Holding your emunah, in a tov conscience; because those who have rejected this charge have had their emunah become shipwrecked:

---

[1] A hotbed of Ephraimite settlement, as Rav Shaul answered that call in the Macedonian vision (Acts 16. 8-13). Greek-speaking exiles were many and were from the lost tribes. For more details, see:
http://store.yourarmstoisrael.org/Qstore/Qstore.cgi?CMD=011&PROD=000209
[2] The entire basis for two-house truth and the Yisraelite character of most end-time nations is not based on any kind of genealogy, or any sort of birth validation. It is based only on Scripture and the many promises found for the children of the promise, who would be more than the children of the bondwoman. If the physical sons of Ishmael number one billion, the sons of Yaakov cannot number less. These and many other such promises are basis for the trust that most nations are filled with the seed of Yisrael.
[3] A Torah-teacher must be mature and not a new babe in Moshiach. A mature Yisraelite will use Torah as the full illumination of Yahshua's teaching. He or she will not use it to obtain salvation without King Yahshua.
[4] See note on Second Peter 1:3.

[5] The Tov News is the cure for Torah-breaking, not the cure for Torah itself.

20 Among those are Humenaios and Alexander; whom I have delivered to s.a.tan that they may learn not to blaspheme.[1]

2 I urge that, first of all, supplications, tefillot, intercessions, and hodu, be made for all men; 2 For melechim, and for all that are in authority; that we may lead a quiet and shalom-filled chayim in all Shabbat-guarding piety and seriousness. 3 For this is tov and acceptable in the sight of יהוה our Savior; 4 Who will have all men to be saved, and come to the knowledge of the emet. 5 For there is Elohim echad, and One Mediator between Elohim and men, the Man יהושע ha Moshiach;[2] 6 Who gave Himself a ransom for all, to be proclaimed in due time. 7 Of which I am ordained as a proclaimer, and a sholiach - I speak the emet in ha Moshiach, and do not lie - a teacher of the nations[3] in emunah and truth. 8 I desire therefore that men make tefillah everywhere, lifting up set-apart hands, without wrath or doubting. 9 In like manner also, that women adorn themselves in modest apparel, with decency and sensitive chochmah; not with braided hair, or gold, or pearls, or costly outfits;[4] 10 But that which becomes a woman professing Shabbat-guarding piety with tov mitzvot. 11 Let the woman learn in silence with all subjection.[5] 12 But I do not allow a woman to teach, or to usurp authority over the man, but to be in silence.[6] 13 For Adam was first formed, then Chavah. 14 And Adam was not deceived, but the woman being deceived was in the transgression.[7] 15 But she shall give brachot and chayim by the children she bears, if of course they continue in emunah and ahava and set-apartness with sensible behavior.

3 This is a true saying, if a man desires the office of a teaching-overseer or shamash, he desires a tov work. 2 A teaching overseeing shamash then must be blameless, the husband of one wife, [8] vigilant, sober, of tov behavior, given to hospitality, able to teach; 3 Not given to excessive wine, not a short-tempered brawler, not a lover of unjust gains; but patient and gentle; 4 One that oversees his own bayit well, having his children in subjection living in all purity; 5 For if a man knows not how to oversee his own bayit, how shall he take care of the congregation of יהוה ? 6 Not a new believer, lest being lifted up with pride he fall into the condemnation of s.a.tan. 7 Moreover he must have a tov report of them who remain outside Yisrael; lest he fall into reproach and the snare of the s.a.tan. 8 Likewise must the shamashim also be pure, not double-tongued, not given to much wine, not greedy for unjust gain; 9 Holding the divine mystery of the emunah in a clean conscience. 10 And let these shamashim also first be tested and examined; then let them use the office of a shamash, after having been found blameless. 11 Even so must their wives be of tov character, not slanderers, sober,

---

[1] "Delivered to s.a.tan" is a different way of saying that they were put outside, or removed from the camp of believing Yisrael for discipline and protection of the sheep.
[2] There is no approach to YHWH other than by Yisrael's King Moshiach Yahshua. This includes Torah-keeping without Yahshua as personal Savior.
[3] Strong's Greek # 1484 word is **ethnos** or "nations," not "pagans" or "gentiles." Here in Rav Shaul's own words, he outlines his calling to the nations, and the seed of Yisrael now filling those nations.
[4] Yisraelite women must dress very modestly, with the idea of covering rather than revealing. They thus reserve their bodies for Moshiach and their husbands; not for men whether saved or unsaved. Yisraelite women, who do not dress modestly, show that they have not yet fully escaped Babylon, where Sunday dress is often better left unreported.
[5] Silent ruach; not under a religious gag order.
[6] A Yisraelite woman can minister anywhere at any time, as this verse indicates. The main point being that she always must be under a man's covering whether it is denominational, ecclesiastical or marriage. Single women called to active ministry simply need to find a man, or set-apart men to be their spiritual covering, to whom they are truly accountable in deed and not in concept only.
[7] Divine order is the issue, not the verbal gagging of over half the human race.
[8] A leader in Yisrael in today's times cannot be a polygamist.

faithful in all things. 12 Let the shamashim be the husbands of one wife, overseeing their children and their own houses well.[1] 13 For they that have used the office of a shamash well gain a tov standing, and great increase with the emunah which is in ha Moshiach יהושע. 14 These things I write to you, hoping to come to you shortly: 15 But if I delay, that you may know how you ought to behave yourself in the Bet יהוה, which is the congregation of the living Elohim, the pillar and foundation of the Torah of emet.[2] 16 And without controversy great is the mystery of our Shabbat-guarding piety: He was manifest in the flesh, declared right in the Ruach, seen by heavenly messengers, proclaimed among the nations,[3] believed on in the olam hazeh, then received up into tifereth.

4 Now the Ruach speaks expressly, that in the yamim achranomim some shall depart from the emunah, giving heed to seducing ruachs, and teachings of shadim; 2 Speaking lies in hypocrisy; having their conscience branded with a hot iron; 3 Forbidding to marry, and commanding to abstain from foods, which יהוה has created to be received with hodu by those who believe and know the emet.[4][5] 4 For every creature of יהוה is tov, and nothing to be refused, if it be received with hodu:[6] 5 If it is set-apart by the word of יהוה and tefillah.[7] 6 If then you teach these things to the brothers, you shall be a tov eved of יהושע ha Moshiach, nourished up in the words of emunah and of tov teaching, which you have followed closely. 7 But refuse profane bubbe mysehs,[8] and exercise yourself rather by Shabbat-guarding piety. 8 For bodily exercise profits some: but Shabbat-guarding piety is profitable for all things, having the promise of the chayim that now is, and of the olam habah that is to come.[9][10] 9 This is a faithful saying and worthy of all acceptance. 10 For therefore we both labor and suffer reproach, because we trust in the living Elohim, who is the Savior of all men, specifically of those that believe.[11] 11 These things command and teach. 12 Let no man despise your youth; but be an example to the believers in Yisrael, in word, in behavior, in ahava, in ruach, in emunah, in purity. 13 Until I come, give attendance to reading Torah,[12] to exhortation, to teaching. 14 Neglect not the gift that is in you, which was given to you by prophecy, with the laying on of the hands of the shamashim. 15 Practice these

---

[1] Polygamy in these times is forbidden for men in all leadership positions in Yisrael.
[2] Since "truth" is defined as "Torah" in Psalm 119:142, the Nazarene Yisraelite congregation is the pillar of all truth, both Torah and Moshiach.
[3] Ephraim Yisrael.
[4] Forbidding to marry, as a human originated doctrine is demonic, for it leads to suppression and unnatural manifestations of sexuality. Only those to whom it is given by Yahshua can lead such a life.
[5] All foods are to be considered edible if they are considered food in the first place. But all unclean foods in Torah are not considered food. And as such, Rav Shaul tells returning Yisrael that only real foods or what YHWH calls food fit for human consumption should be received. This is confirmed in verse 5. So the heresy is religious doctrines that forbid certain clean foods.
[6] Verse 5 defines what creatures YHWH considers tov.
[7] Nothing should be refused and rejected if it is already previously set-apart by the word of YHWH and tefillah. So that tefillah and thanksgiving should only be given over foods that are already set-apart in YHWH's word; and the only place we find a menu of set-apart foods is in Torah. So the doctrine of demons is a religious attempt by demons to try and get mankind to abstain from foods on the list of clean foods, already set-apart by the word. Just like marriage that is already set-apart by the word, the demons try and stop people from marrying and instead introduce substitute perversities.
[8] Old ladies or grandma's fairy tales.
[9] The eternality of a Shabbat-keeping lifestyle, as found in Isaiah 66, will serve us well in this age and in the age to come, as opposed to bodily exercise whose benefits are limited to this age.
[10] The Yisraelite mind sees time divided into just two ages. This age and that age. This is how YHWH sees time as well. The redeemed in this age enter the next. This understanding is crucial in letting go of dispensational time frames, which also are doctrines of s.a.tan, since man cannot possibly know when one age begins and the next ends. Man has added ages, not found in scripture due to severe deceptions about ecclesiology (who it is that actually constitutes the single elect people of YHWH).
[11] This is not teaching universalism but rather, that atonement while made available to all men, specifically benefits only those believers who accept it.
[12] The Renewed Covenant had not yet been written.

things; give yourself fully to them; that your progress may appear to all Yisrael. 16 Take heed to yourself, and to your teachings; continue in them: for in doing this you shall both save yourself, and those that hear you.[1]

5 Rebuke not a shamash, but treat him as an abba in the emunah; and the younger men as brothers; 2 The elderly women as imas; the younger as sisters, with all purity. 3 Honor widows that are widows indeed. 4 But if any widow have children or nephews, let them first learn to show Shabbat-guarding piety at home, and let the children care for them and so repay their parents: for that is tov and acceptable before יהוה. 5 And she that is a widow indeed, and is all-alone, trusts in יהוה , and continues in supplications and tefillot both during maariv and shachrit. 6 But she that lives in pleasure is dead while she lives. 7 And these things command, that they may be blameless. 8 But if any does not provide for his own, especially for those of his own bayit, he has denied the emunah, and is worse than an infidel.[2] 9 Let not a widow be enrolled for community support under sixty years old, having been the wife of just one man, 10 Well reported of for tov mitzvot; if she has brought up children, if she has housed non-Yisraelite gerim, if she has washed the feet of the kidushim, if she has relieved the afflicted, if she has diligently followed every tov mitzvah, then let her be added to the community support rolls. 11 But the younger widows refuse for community enrollment: for when they will begin to be headstrong against ha Moshiach, they will marry; 12 Having guilt, because they have cast off their first emunah. 13 Also they learn to be idle, wandering about from bayit to bayit; and not only idle, but also become gossiping busybodies, speaking things that they should not. 14 I resolve therefore that the younger women marry, bear children, and guide the house, giving no occasion to the adversary to speak disdainfully. 15 For some women have already turned aside after s.a.tan. 16 If any man or woman that believes has widows in their homes, let them assist them, and let not the congregation be charged; so that the congregation can relieve them that are truly widows. 17 Let the shamashim that oversee well be counted worthy of double honor, especially they who labor in the word and in Torah.[3] 18 For the scripture says, *You shall not muzzle the ox that treads out the corn.* And, *The laborer is worthy of his reward.* 19 Against a shamash receive not an accusation, without two or three witnesses.[4] 20 Them that sin rebuke before all, so that others also may fear. 21 I adjure you before יהוה, and the Master יהושע ha Moshiach, and the elect heavenly messengers, that you shomer these things without preferring one over another, doing nothing by partiality. 22 Lay hands suddenly on no man, neither be a partaker of other men's sins: keep yourself clean.[5] 23 Drink mayim no longer, but use a little wine for your stomach's sake and your ongoing infirmities. 24 Some men sins are obvious leading to mishpat; but those of others will be seen later. 25 Likewise also the tov mitzvot of some are manifest now; and those who do not perform mitzvot cannot be hidden.

6 Let those who are believing avadim under a yoke count their own masters worthy of all honor, that the Name of יהוה and His teaching be not blasphemed. 2 And those that have believing masters, let them not despise them, because they are brothers; but rather do them service, because they are

---

[1] Doctrine that is correct saves. Incorrect doctrine leads astray.
[2] This applies first and foremost to the personal home, as well as the House of Yisrael; the community of faith.
[3] The leader of a Yisraelite Nazarene community, is one who is not merely a shamash but a teaching shamash.
[4] Do not believe any accusation against a shamash. The charge does not equal guilt, since the charge is often levied by s.a.tan. If witnesses cannot be found, all further thoughts and actions must be dropped.
[5] A Yisraelite minister must first be tested for doctrine, commitment, stability, consistency and purity.

faithful and beloved, partakers of the benefit of the masters. These things teach and exhort. 3 If any man teach otherwise, and consent not to wholesome words, even the words of our Master יהושע ha Moshiach, and to the teaching which is according to Shabbat-guarding piety; 4 He is proud, knows nothing, but is sick, engaging in questions and verbal battles, from which comes envy, contention, strife, blasphemy, evil suspicions, 5 Worthless disputes of men of corrupt minds, and destitute of the emet, supposing that serving יהוה is a means to unjust wealth and is the same as Shabbat-guarding piety: from such withdraw yourself. 6 But Shabbat-guarding piety with contentment is the great gain. 7 For we brought nothing into the olam hazeh, and it is certain we can carry nothing out of it. 8 And having food and clothing let us be content with these. 9 But they that will be rich fall into temptation and a trap, and into many foolish and hurtful lusts, which plunge men into destruction and perdition. 10 For the ahava of money is the root of all-evil: which while some have longed after, they have fallen from the emunah, and pierced themselves through with many sorrows.[1] 11 But you, O man of יהוה, flee these things; and follow after tzedakah, Shabbat-guarding piety, emunah, ahava, patience, and meekness. 12 Fight the tov fight of emunah, grab hold on eternal chayim, for which you are also called, and have professed a tov profession before many witnesses. 13 I give you charge in the sight of יהוה, who quickens all things, and before ha Moshiach יהושע, who before Pontius Pilate witnessed a tov confession; 14 That you keep this mitzvah[2] without spot, blameless, until the appearing of our Master יהושע ha Moshiach: 15 Who in His own timing shall show, just who is the blessed and only Eternal Ruler, the Melech HaMelechim, and Adon Adonim; 16 Who alone has immortality,[3] [4] dwelling in the Light that no man can approach; whom no man has seen, or can see: to whom be honor and power le-olam-va-ed. Amein. 17 Charge them that are rich in the olam hazeh, that they be not proud, nor trust in uncertain riches, but in the living Elohim, who gives us richly all things to enjoy; 18 That they do tov, that they are rich in tov mitzvot, ready to give tzedakah, willing to share their wealth; 19 Laying up in store for themselves a tov foundation for the olam habah, that they may grab hold of eternal chayim. 20 O Timtheous, guard that which is committed to your trust, avoiding profane and empty babblings, and the contradictions of false so-called worldly da'at: 21 Who some professing have strayed from the emunah. Unmerited favor be with you. Amein.

---

[1] Chasing money as opposed to having YHWH provide as per covenant obligation, is step one to a denial of the faith, as so often happens when mammon knocks YHWH off the throne in a believer's heart.

[2] To flee unjust gain and a love of money.
[3] Please see **Do You Have An Immortal Soul?** at: http://store.yourarmstoisrael.org/Qstore/Qstore.cgi?CMD=011&PROD=000083
[4] Only YHWH and Yahshua are immortal.

טימתאוס ב

Timtheous Bet - Second Timothy
To A Shepherd of Yisrael

1 Shaul, a sholiach of **יהושע** ha Moshiach by the will of **יהוה**, according to the promise of chayim, which is in **יהושע** ha Moshiach, 2 To Timtheous, my dearly beloved son: Unmerited favor, rachamim, and shalom, from Abba **יהוה** and **יהושע** ha Moshiach our Master. 3 I give hodu to **יהוה**, whom I served from boyhood with a clear conscience, that without ceasing, I have remembered you in my tefillot during maariv and shacrit; 4 Greatly desiring to see you, being mindful of your tears, that I may be filled with simcha; 5 When I call to remembrance the sincere emunah that is in you, which dwelt first in your grandmother Lois, and your ima Eunike; and I am persuaded in you also. 6 For this reason I remind you to stir up the gift of **יהוה**, which is in you by the laying on of my hands. 7 For **יהוה** has not given us the Ruach of fear; but of power, and of ahava, and of a sound mind. 8 Be not ashamed of the testimony of our Master, nor of me His eved: but be a partaker of the afflictions of the besarot according to the power of **יהוה**; 9 Who has saved us, and called us with a set-apart calling, not according to our man-made works, but according to His own purpose and favor, which was given to us in **יהושע** the Moshiach even before the olam began, 10 But now has been made manifest by the appearing of our Savior **יהושע** the Moshiach, who has abolished death, and has revealed chayim and immortality through the besarot: 11 To which I am appointed a proclaimer, and a sholiach, and a moreh to the nations.[1] 12 For which cause I also suffer these things: nevertheless I am not ashamed: for I know in whom I have believed, and am persuaded that He is able

to take care of me until that day. 13 Hold fast to the form of sound words, which you have heard of me, in emunah and in the ahava that is in **יהושע** the Moshiach. 14 That tov thing which was committed to you shomer by the Ruach HaKodesh who dwells in us. 15 This you know, that all those who are in Asia have turned away from me; of whom are Phugellos and Hermogenes.[2] 16 **יהוה** give rachamim to the bayit of Onesiphoros; for he often refreshed me, and was not ashamed of my imprisonment: 17 But, when he was in Romiyah, he searched me out very diligently, and found me. 18 **יהוה** grant to him that he may find rachamim in that day: and in all the ways he attended to me at Ephesos, you know very well.

2 You therefore, my son, be strong in the unmerited favor that is in **יהושע** the Moshiach. 2 And the things that you have heard from me among many witnesses, the same commit to other faithful men, who shall be able to teach others also.[3] 3 You therefore endure hardships, with us as a tov soldier of **יהושע** the Moshiach. 4 No man that goes to battle entangles himself with the affairs of this chayim; so that he may please Him who has chosen him to be a soldier. 5 And if anyone competes in a contest, he cannot receive the keter, except he competes by the rules. 6 The farmer that labors must be the first one to eat of his fruits. 7 Consider what I say; and **יהוה** give you da'at in all things. 8 Remember that **יהושע** the Moshiach of the zera of David was raised from the dead according to my besarot: 9 For which I suffer trouble, as a criminal, even

---

[1] The latter-day nations made up mostly of Yisraelites.

[2] First-century apostasy was prevalent as it is today. This is not a new phenomenon.
[3] Torah instruction and the besarot.

imprisoned; but the word of יהוה is not imprisoned. 10 Therefore I endure all things for the chosen people, that they may also obtain the salvation that is in יהושע the Moshiach with eternal tifereth. 11 It is a faithful saying: For if we are dead with Him, we shall also live with Him: 12 If we suffer, we shall also reign with Him: if we deny Him, He also will deny us: 13 If we believe not, yet He abides faithful: He cannot deny Himself. 14 Of these things put them in remembrance, charging them before יהוה that they not engage in word battles - that is useless - since it subverts the hearers of the word. 15 Study to show yourself approved before יהוה, a workman that needs not to be ashamed, rightly dividing the word of emet.[1] 16 But avoid profane and empty chatter: for they will increase unto more wickedness. 17 And their word will eat through people like gangrene: Humenaios and Philetos are of this group;[2] 18 Who concerning the emet have gone astray, saying that the resurrection is past already; and have overthrown the emunah of some. [3] 19 Nevertheless the foundation of the Master יהוה stands firm, having this seal; the Master יהוה knows those who are His. And, Let everyone that names the Name of the Moshiach depart from Torah breaking. 20 But in a great bayit there are not only vessels of gold and of silver, but also of wood and of earth; and some to honor, and some to dishonor.[4] 21 If a man therefore cleanses himself from unclean matters, he shall be a vessel of honor, set-apart, and fit for the Master's use, and prepared for every tov mitzvah. 22 Flee also youthful lusts: but follow righteousness, emunah, ahava, shalom, with them that call on יהוה out of a pure lev. 23 But foolish and unlearned questions avoid, knowing that they do breed arguments.[5] 24 And the eved of יהוה must not quarrel; but be gentle to all men, able to teach, patient, 25 In meekness instructing those that oppose Him; so יהוה somehow will give them teshuvah to their acknowledging of the emet; 26 And that they may come to their senses and leave the snare of s.a.tan, who has taken them captive to do his will.

3 This know also, that in the acharit hayamim perilous times shall come. 2 For men shall be lovers of their own selves, covetous, boasters, proud, blasphemers, disobedient to parents, unthankful, unclean, 3 Without natural affection, trucebreakers, false accusers, addicts to lust, fierce, despisers of those that are tov, 4 Traitors, hasty, proud and arrogant, lovers of pleasures more than lovers of יהוה; 5 Having a form of a Shabbat-guarding pious lifestyle,[6] but denying the power of it: from such turn away. 6 For these are the people who creep into and infect entire houses away from emunah, and lead captive women weighed down with sins, who are being led away with various lusts, 7 Always learning, and never able to come to the da'at of the emet. 8 Now as Yohane and Mamre opposed Moshe, so do these also resist the emet: people of corrupt minds, far from the emunah. 9 But they shall go no further: for their folly shall be manifest to all men, as was that of those men. 10 But you have fully known my teaching, manner of chayim, purpose, emunah, endurance, ahava, patience, 11 The persecutions, and afflictions, which came to me at Antioch, at Ikonion, at Lustra; what persecutions I endured: but out of them all יהוה delivered me. 12 Yes, and all that will live a Shabbat-guarding pious lifestyle in יהושע the Moshiach shall suffer persecution.

---

[1] A challenge to all Yisrael to study all of the Word and divide it properly, as opposed to manmade divisions like the so-called Old and New Testaments, or such as the dispensation of law versus grace.
[2] Heretics must be named publicly, to warn and protect others from falling into error.
[3] Like some today who teach that some will miss the rapture, or that the Great Tribulation has already begun.
[4] Yisrael contains both, as in days gone by, and as Moshiach taught in Matthew 13.

[5] In context, arguments about doctrines that are known to be false. We are to rebuke them and avoid long-term entanglement with them.
[6] Eu-sebeia or Shabbat piety in the Greek (Strong's Greek #2150). See note on Second Peter 1:3.

13 But evil men and imposters shall get worse and worse, deceiving, and being deceived.[1] 14 But you on the other hand continue in the things that you have learned and have been assured of, knowing from whom you have learned them; 15 And that from a child you have known the set-apart Ketuvim, which are able to make you wise for your salvation through emunah which is in יהושע ha Moshiach. 16 All the Ketuvim are given by the inspiration of יהוה, and are profitable for teaching, for reproof, for correction, as Torah in righteousness: 17 That the man of יהוה may be perfect, fully equipped for all tov mitzvot.

4 I charge you therefore before יהוה, and the Master יהושע the Moshiach, who shall judge the living and the dead at His appearing and His malchut; 2 Proclaim the word; be ready to do so during moadim, and at regular times; reprove, rebuke, exhort with all patience and teaching. 3 For the time will come when they will not endure sound teaching; but after their own lusts shall they add for themselves extra teachers, tickling the ears.[2] 4 And they shall turn away their ears from the emet, and shall be turned to bubbe mysehs. 5 But shomer yourself in all things, endure afflictions, do the work of a proclaimer, fulfill your service. 6 For I am now ready to be offered, and the time of my departure is at hand. 7 I have fought a tov fight, I have finished my course, and I have kept the emunah:[3] 8 And now there is laid up for me a keter of tzedakah, which יהושע, the Tzadik-Shophet, shall give me at that day:

and not to me only, but to all them also that love His appearing. 9 Do your best to come shortly to me: 10 For Demas has forsaken me, having loved the olam hazeh, and is departed to Thessalonike; Crescens to Galutyah, Teitus to Dalmatyah. 11 Only Luke is with me. Take Moshe-Mark, and bring him with you: for he is profitable to me for the service. 12 And Tuchikos have I sent to Ephesos. 13 The cloke that I left at Troas with Karpus, when you come, bring with you, and also the scrolls, but especially the parchment scrolls. 14 Alexander the coppersmith did me much evil: יהוה reward him according to his works: 15 You too shomer also; for he has greatly withstood our words.[4] 16 At my first answer no man stood with me, but all men forsook me: I pray that it may not be laid to their charge. 17 Notwithstanding יהוה stood with me, and strengthened me; that by me the proclaiming might be fully known, and that all the nations[5] might hear: and I was delivered out of the mouth of the lion. 18 And יהוה shall deliver me from every evil work, and will preserve me for His heavenly malchut: to Him be tifereth le olam va-ed. 19 Salute Prisca and Aqulas, and the bayit of Onesiphoros. 20 Erastos stayed in Corinth: but Trophimos have I left at Miletos sick. 21 Do your best to come before winter. Eubulos greets you, and Pudes, and Linos, and Klaudia, and all the brothers. 22 The Master יהושע ha Moshiach be with your ruach. Unmerited favor be with you. Amein.

---

[1] Those who devour the emunah of others throughout the centuries, such as the anti-Yahshua missionaries.
[2] Extra, non-Torah-based doctrines.
[3] A very commendable action among today's false prophets.

[4] It is not **lashon hara** to warn brothers of true wolves if three Torah witnesses can establish their error.
[5] The scattered Yisraelite nations.

טוטס

Teitus - Titus
To A Shepherd of Yisrael

1 Shaul, an eved of יהוה, and a sholiach of יהושע ha Moshiach, according to the emunah of יהוה's chosen ones,[1] and the acknowledging of the emet that is after a lifestyle of Shabbat-guarding piety;[2] 2 In the expectation of eternal chayim, which Elohim, who does not lie, promised before the olam hazeh; 3 But has in a time that now is at hand, manifested His word through proclaiming, which has been committed to me according to the commandment of Elohim our Savior; 4 To Teitus, my own ben emunah according to our common emunah: Favor, rachamim, and shalom, from Abba יהוה and the Master יהושע the Moshiach our Savior. 5 For this cause left I you in Crete, that you should set in order the things that are not done, and ordain zachanim in every city,[3] as I had appointed you: 6 If anyone is blameless, the husband of one wife,[4] having believing children not accused of loose living or of being unruly. 7 For a Yisraelite overseer must be blameless, as a spiritual manager of יהוה ; not self-seeking, not quick tempered, not excessive in the use of wine, not a brawler, not greedy for filthy gain; 8 But kind to gerim, a lover of tov men, sober, a tzadik, set-apart, self-controlled; 9 Holding fast to the trustworthy word as he has been taught, that he may be able by sound teaching to exhort the believers and rebuke the proud. 10 For there are many unruly men, big talkers, and deceivers, especially those who are circumcised unbelievers:[5] 11 Whose mouths must be stopped, who pervert entire houses of believers, teaching things they should not, for the sake of filthy gain.[6] 12 One of their own, even a so called navi of their own, said, The Cretans are always liars, evil beasts, lazy gluttons.[7] 13 This witness is emet. Therefore rebuke them sharply, so that the believers may be sound in the emunah;[8] 14 Not giving heed to certain Yahudite fables and commandments of men, who hate the emet and turn others from the emet.[9] 15 Unto the clean all things are clean: but to them that are defiled and unbelieving is nothing clean; but even their mind and conscience is defiled. 16 They profess that they know יהוה; but in mitzvot they deny Him, being abominable and disobedient, condemning every tov mitzvah.[10]

2 But you must speak the things that are proper for sound instruction: 2 Teach the older men to be sober, tahor, temperate, sound in emunah, in ahava and in patience. 3 Teach the older women likewise, that they

---

[1] Always and exclusively only a reference to the Commonwealth of Yisrael.
[2] See note in Second Kepha 1:3.
[3] Every Yisraelite city of exile in that area.
[4] Polygamy is forbidden for leaders in Renewed Covenant Yisrael.
[5] Anti-Yahshua missionaries, as seen by their actions in the next verse.

[6] The anti-missionary scourge was common then as it is today, and Rav Shaul is warning Titus and giving the young leader guidance.
[7] Again we are confronted with an attitude problem towards non-Jews, and specifically returning Ephraimites who filled Crete. Crete was a Greek-influenced and populated area and was home to many of the exiles of Yisrael. So naturally these anti-missionaries would pervert the truth of Yahshua, as well as cloak their message with statements that were harsh towards the exiles in Crete, who desired a return to Yisrael through Moshiach, rather than through traditional Judaism.
[8] Rebuke the anti-missionaries so that believers may remain sound.
[9] An eternal warning to Torah-keeping Yisraelites who love Moshiach to stay clear of these sorts, who will come with fables and myths, designed to steal and subvert you and your family. Notice that the way Rav Shaul dealt with this is by addressing the shepherds, for it is the shepherds who are responsible for guarding the sheep before the poison is swallowed.
[10] This does not speak of lawless believers. It speaks of unbelievers who claim to know Abba, but hate the Son and are also committed to remove entire houses and families from the gift of eternal life, given by YHWH who does not lie. These persons are worse than mere unbelievers; they are abominations before YHWH, because besides their unemunah, they also work against others who do believe.

be in their behavior as becomes set-apartness, not false accusers, not an eved to much wine, teachers of tov things; 4 That they may teach the young women to be modest, to love their husbands and their children, 5 To be sensible, tahor, tov homemakers, obedient to their own husbands, that the word of יהוה is not reproached. 6 Likewise exhort children to be sensible and modest. 7 In all things showing yourself as a living pattern of tov mitzvot: in teaching, showing perfection, sincerity, and seriousness. 8 Choose sound words for teaching, so that they cannot be condemned; so that he who opposes us may be ashamed, having no evil thing to say about us.[1] 9 Let avadim be obedient to their own masters, and to please them well in all things; not talking back or contentious; [2] 10 Not stealing but showing trustworthiness; so that they may embrace the teaching of יהוה our Savior in all things. 11 For the favor of יהוה that brings salvation has appeared to all men, [3] 12 Teaching us to renounce wickedness and worldly lusts, and to live sensibly, as tzadikim with a lifestyle of Shabbat-guarding piety, [4] in this present age; 13 Looking for that blessed tikvah, and the beautiful appearing of the great Elohim and our Savior יהושע ha Moshiach;[5] 14 Who gave Himself for us, that He might save us from all Torah breaking, and cleanse for Himself a renewed people, zealous of tov works. 15 These things speak and exhort and rebuke with all authority. Let no man despise you.

3 Remind the people of Yisrael to be subject to earthly rulers and governors,

to be ready to do every tov mitzvah, 2 To speak no lashon hara[6] of anyone, to not be quarrelsome, but gentle, showing meekness to all men. 3 For we ourselves also were once foolish, disobedient, deceived, serving various lusts and pleasures, living in evil and envy, being hated, and hating one another. 4 But after the chesed and ahava of יהוה our Savior toward man appeared, 5 Not by works of righteousness which we have done, but according to His rachamim He saved us, by the washing of regeneration and renewing work of the Ruach Hakodesh; 6 Which He shed on us abundantly through יהושע ha Moshiach our Savior; 7 That being declared a tzadik by His favor, we should be made heirs of the hope of eternal chayim. 8 This is a faithful saying, and these things I will that you affirm constantly, that those who believe in יהוה might be careful to maintain tov mitzvoth continually. [7] These things are tov and profitable to men. [8] 9 But avoid foolish endless questions, and genealogies, and contentions, and quarrels about the Torah with the Sophrim;[9] for they are unprofitable and vain. [10] 10 A man that is divisive or heretical after the first and second warning, just shun him;[11] 11 Knowing that he that is like that is perverted, and sins, being self-condemned. 12 When I shall send Artemas to you, or Tuchikus, be diligent to come to me to Nikopolis: for I have decided to spend the winter there. 13 Make sure that Zenas the sopher and Apollos are given a tov farewell on their journey so that they lack nothing. 14 And let all Yisrael also learn to maintain tov mitzvot in urgent needs and times, that they be not unfruitful. 15 All that are with me greet you. Greet them that love us in the emunah. Favor be with you all. Amein.

---

[1] Yisraelites are to be living examples, patterns and letters, open and available to the world, to read and consider.
[2] Employees must follow this pattern in service to their employers.
[3] Not that all men are saved, but that all men can be saved. From the world, YHWH's chosen and saved, then become Yisrael restored.
[4] See note in Second Kepha 1:3.
[5] Isaiah 43:10-11.
[6] No evil speaking.
[7] Torah mitzvoth are eternal.
[8] Not the manmade variety, but Torah-prescribed mitzvoth.
[9] Peshitta.
[10] Rav Shaul says that we should be doing the Torah, and not quarreling about it with others.
[11] Torah principle of putting someone outside the camp, to allow for a season of repentance and restoration.

גלינא

Gilyahna - Revelation

To The Believing Remnant Of
Yisrael In Asia
And Yisrael's Final Generation

1 The Revelation of **יהושע** the Moshiach, which **יהוה** gave to Him, to show to His avadim things which must shortly come to pass; and He sent and signified it by His heavenly messenger to His eved Yochanan: 2 Who bore witness of the Word of **יהוה**, and of the testimony of **יהושע** the Moshiach, and of all things that He saw. 3 Blessed is he that reads, and they that shema to the words of this prophecy, and shomer those things that are written in it: for the time is at hand. 4 Yochanan to the seven Yisraelite congregations, which are in Asia:[1] Unmerited favor be to you, and shalom, from Him who is, and who was, and who is to come; and from the seven Ruachim which are before His throne; 5 And from **יהושע** the Moshiach, who is the Faithful Witness, and the Bachor from the dead, and the Sar of the melechim of the olam. Unto Him that loved us, and washed us from our sins in His own dom, 6 And has made us melechim and kohanim to His Elohim and Abba; to Him be tifereth and dominion le-olam va-ed. Amein. 7 See, He comes with clouds; and every eye shall see Him, and those also who pierced Him: and all tribes[2] of the olam shall wail because of Him. Even so, amein. 8 *I am the Aleph and Taf, the Beginning and the End*, says the Master **יהוה**, who is, and who was, and who is to come, the Almighty. [3] 9 I Yochanan, who also am your brother, and chaver in tribulation, and in the malchut and endurance of **יהושע** the Moshiach, was on the island that is called Patmos, for the word of **יהוה**, and for the testimony of **יהושע** the Moshiach. 10 I was in the Ruach on Yom **יהוה**,[4] and heard behind me a great voice, as of a shofar, 11 Saying, *I am Aleph and Taf, the First and the Last: and, What you see, write in a scroll, and send it to the seven Yisraelite congregations which are in Asia; to Ephesos, and to Smyrna, and to Pergamos, and to Thyatira, and to Sardis, and to Philadelphia, and to Laodikeia.* 12 And I turned to see the voice that spoke with me. And when I turned, I saw seven golden menorot;[5] 13 And in the midst of the seven menorot one like the Ben Adam, clothed with a garment down to the feet, and wrapped around the chest with a golden band. 14 His head and His hairs were white like wool, as white as snow; and His eyes were as a flame of fire; 15 And His feet like fine brass, as if they burned in a furnace; and His voice as the sound of many streams of mayim. 16 And He had in His right hand seven cochavim: and out of His mouth went a sharp two-edged sword: and His face was as the sun shining in strength.[6] 17 And when I saw Him, I fell at His feet as dead. And He laid His right hand upon me, saying to me, *Fear not; I am the*

---

[1] "Today known as Asia Minor due north of the Middle East between Europe and Far East Asia. The former lands controlled by the Assyrians who were the conquerors of the ten northern tribes in 721 BCE, and the cities in which most of the early believers lived in outside of Yahrushalayim. Rav Shaul knew this and spent much time seeking the lost sheep of Beit Yisrael there. These Ephraimites would break into other nations such as the Scythians, Sacae, and Cimmerians." Collins p. 127, *The Lost Ten Tribes of Yisrael Found. Josephus, Antiquities* 11, chap 5 verse 2.
[2] A dual reference to the 12 tribes of Yisrael and all the nations of the earth.

[3] Clearly a hard-to-contest reference to Yahshua YHWH our Moshiach.
[4] Not the Lord's Day, but the "Day of YHWH," a Hebraic idiomatic expression for the entire time period when YHWH judges the earth. John was fast-forwarded in the Ruach by revelation, to see this entire period. This reference has absolutely nothing to do with any kind of alleged Sunday worship, or John receiving the Book of Revelation on a Sunday.
[5] Plural for menorahs.
[6] Same man seen by Ezekiel in chapter 1.

first and the last: 18 *I am He that lives, and was dead; and, see, I am alive le-olam va-ed. Amein; and have the keys of the grave and of death. 19 Write the things that you have seen, and the things that are, and the things which shall be after this; 20 The mystery of the seven cochavim that you saw in My right hand, and the seven golden menorot. The seven cochavim are the seven teaching overseers of the seven Yisraelite congregations: and the seven menorot that you saw are the seven Yisraelite congregations.* [1]

2 *Unto the teaching overseer of the congregation of Ephesos write; These things says He that holds the seven cochavim in His right hand, who walks in the midst of the seven golden menorot; 2 I know your mitzvot, and your labor, and your endurance, and how you can't bear those who are evil: and you have tried them who say they are shlichim, and are not, and have found them liars:* [2] *3 And have borne, and have endurance, and for My Name's sake have labored, and have not fainted. 4 Nevertheless I have something against you, because you have left your first ahava. 5 Remember therefore from where you are fallen, and make teshuvah, and do the first mitzvot; or else I will come to you quickly, and will remove your menorah out of its place, unless you make teshuvah.* [3] *6 But this you have, that you hate the mitzvot of the Nikolites, which I also hate.* [4] *7 He that has an ear, let him shema what the Ruach says to the Yisraelite congregations; To him that overcomes* [5] *I will give to eat of the eytz chaim, which is in the midst of the Gan Aden of Elohim. 8 And to the teaching overseer of the congregation in Smyrna write; These things says the first and the last, who was dead, and is alive; 9 I know your mitzvot, and tribulation, and poverty, but you are rich - and I know the blasphemy of them who say they are Yahudim, and are not, but are the synagogue of s.a.tan.* [6] *10 Fear none of those things that you shall suffer: see, s.a.tan shall cast some of you into prison, that you may be tried; and you shall have tribulation ten days: be faithful to death, and I will give you the keter chayim. 11 He that has an ear, let him shema what the Ruach says to the Yisraelite congregations; He that overcomes shall not be hurt by the second death.* [7] *12 And to the teaching overseer of the congregation in Pergamos write; These things says He who has the sharp sword with two edges; 13 I know your mitzvot, and where you dwell, even where s.a.tan's seat is: and you hold fast My Name,* [8] *and have not denied the emunah in Me, even in those days when Antipas was My faithful martyr, who was slain among you, where s.a.tan dwells. 14 But I have a few things against you, because you have there them that hold the teaching of Bilam, who taught Balaq to cast a stumbling block before the children of Yisrael, to eat things sacrificed to idols, and to commit fornication.* [9] *15 So have you also*

---

[1] These seven congregations are historic Yisraelite congregations and were addressed individually in their first-century historical context. While some of the principles and details in these admonitions have eternal applications to us today, they are not - nor do they represent - periods or dispensations in ecclesiastical history, as some dispensationalists have tried to portray in their sensationalist wresting of Scripture.

[2] This is not any kind of a reference to Rav Shaul, as some heretics have taught. Rather, it refers to those who entered after his departure, proven by the fact that the term "apostles" or "shlichim" is in the plural.

[3] A clear warning that a congregation can lose the approval of Yahshua, even after starting out well.

[4] Denominational systems that don't serve people, but have people serve them. For more details see: video http://store.yourarmstoisrael.org/Qstore/Qstore.cgi?CMD=011&PROD=000093

[5] Overcomes. A term used eight times in the Book of Revelation and ten times in the Brit Chadasha. Eight is the number of new beginnings; ten is the number for the wandering tribes of the north. "El Overcomes" is the literal translation of the term "Yisraelite." So Yahshua's admonition is that those who overcome through Him are His Yisrael.

[6] This is not a reference to Yahudim in general. It is a rebuke of those Ephraimites in Smyrna who don't understand their identity as members of the Commonwealth of Yisrael, who are non-Yahudim or non-Jewish Yisraelites; yet insist in calling themselves the new Yahudim. Rather than this being an attack on Yahudim, it is a rebuke to those who are not, but claim to be. Many modern religions fall into that trap by claiming to be the true or the real Yahudim in various forms of replacement theology. They stand rebuked.

[7] That is what salvation does. It allows humanity to escape the second death.

[8] A congregation that honors the true Name.

[9] Further validation of the Yisraelite makeup of this congregation.

those that hold the teaching of the Nikolites, which teaching I hate. 16 Make teshuvah; or else I will come to you quickly, and will fight against them with the sword of My mouth. 17 He that has an ear, let him shema what the Ruach says to the Yisraelite congregations; To him that overcomes will I give to eat of the hidden manna, and will give him a white stone, and in the stone a renewed name written, which no man knows other than he that receives it. 18 And to the teaching overseer of the congregation in Thyatira write; These things says the Son of יהוה, who has His eyes like a flame of fire, and His feet are like fine brass; 19 I know your mitzvot, and ahava, and service, and emunah, and your endurance, and your mitzvot; and the last to be more than the first. 20 But I have a few things against you, because you allow that woman Isavel, who called herself a naviyah, to teach and to seduce My avadim to commit fornication, and to eat things sacrificed to idols. [1] 21 And I gave her time to make teshuvah from her fornication; and she repented not. 22 See, I will cast her into a bed, and them that commit adultery with her into Great Tribulation, unless they make teshuvah of their deeds.[2] 23 And I will kill her children with death; and all the Yisraelite congregations shall know that I am He who searches the kidneys and levim: and I will give to every one of you according to your mitzvot. 24 But to you I say, and to the rest in Thyatira, as many as have not this teaching of uncleanness, and who have not known the depths of s.a.tan, as they call them; I will put upon you no other burden. 25 But that which you have already hold fast until I come. 26 And he that overcomes, and keeps My mitzvot to the end, to him will I give power over the gentiles:[3] 27 And He shall rule them with a rod of iron; as the vessels of a potter shall they be broken to pieces: even as I received from My Abba. 28 And I will give him the Morning Cochav. 29 He that has an ear, let him shema what the Ruach says to the Yisraelite congregations.

3 And to the teaching overseer of the congregation in Sardis write; These things says He that has the seven Ruachim of יהוה, and the seven cochavim; I know your mitzvot, that you have a name that you live, and yet are dead. 2 Be watchful, and strengthen the things that remain, that are ready to die: for I have not found your mitzvot perfect before יהוה. 3 Remember therefore how you have received and heard, and hold fast, and make teshuvah. If therefore you shall not watch, I will come upon you as a thief, and you shall not know what hour I will come upon you. 4 You have a few names even in Sardis who have not defiled their garments; and they shall walk with Me in white: for they are worthy. 5 He that overcomes, the same shall be clothed in white raiment; and I will not blot out his name out of the Scroll of Chayim, but I will confess his name before My Abba, and before His heavenly messengers.[4] 6 He that has an ear, let him shema what the Ruach says to the Yisraelite congregations. 7 And to the heavenly messenger of the congregation in Philadelphia write; These things says He that is set-apart, He that is emet, He that has the key of David, He that opens, and no man shuts; and shuts, and no man opens; 8 I know your mitzvot: see, I have set before you an open door, and no man can shut it: for you have a little strength, but have kept My word, and have not denied My Name.[5] 9 See, I will make them of the Synagogue of s.a.tan,[6] who say

---

[1] A particular woman leading sheep astray. This is not speaking of a ruach of any kind. It is a rebuke of an anti-Torah deceiver, who happens to be a woman.
[2] An unclean and unrighteous lifestyle will lead to being overcome by the Great Tribulation, as opposed to overcoming through it.
[3] Yisrael is called to rule with Moshiach over the heathen-gentiles; and therefore by definition cannot be the gentiles.

[4] The Book of Life here is the scroll of the living, and not the Lamb's Book of Life containing the names of the redeemed.
[5] A truly set-apart congregation refusing to deny the true Name of YHWH.
[6] See note for Revelation 2:9.

they are Yahudim, and are not, but do lie; see, I will make them to come and worship before your feet, and to know that I have loved you. 10 Because you have kept the word of My endurance, I also will shomer you in the hour of testing, [1] which shall come upon all of the olam hazeh, to test them that dwell in the olam. 11 See, I come quickly: hold fast what you have, that no man takes your keter. 12 Him that overcomes will I make a pillar in the Sukkah of My Elohim, and he shall go no more out: and I will write upon him the Name of My Elohim, and the name of the city of My Elohim, which is the Renewed Yahrushalayim, which comes down out of the shamayim from My Elohim: and I will write upon him My renewed Name. [2] 13 He that has an ear, let him shema what the Ruach says to the Yisraelite congregations. 14 And to the teaching overseer of the congregation of the Laodikeia write; These things says The Amein, the faithful and emet witness, the first cause of all the creation of יהוה; 15 I know your mitzvot that you are neither cold nor hot: I would that you were cold or hot. 16 So then because you are lukewarm, and neither cold nor hot, I will vomit you out of My mouth. 17 Because you say, I am rich, and increased with goods, and have need of nothing; and know not that you are wretched, and miserable, and poor, and blind, and naked: 18 I counsel you to buy from Me gold tried in the fire, that you may be rich; and white raiment, that you may be clothed, so that the shame of your nakedness does not appear; and anoint your eyes with ointment, that you may see. 19 As many as I love, I rebuke and chasten: be zealous therefore, and make teshuvah. 20 See, I stand at the door, and knock: if any man hears to My voice, and opens the door, I will come in to him, and will dine with him, and he with Me.

21 To him that overcomes will I grant to sit with Me in My throne, even as I also overcame, and am set down with My Abba in His throne. [3] 22 He that has an ear, let him shema what the Ruach says to the Yisraelite congregations.

4 After this I looked, and, see, a door was opened in the shamayim: and the first voice which I heard was as it were of a shofar talking with me; which said, Come up here, and I will show you things that must be after this. [4] 2 And immediately I was in the Ruach: and, see, a throne was set in the shamayim, and One sat on the throne. 3 And He who sat there looked like jasper and a ruby stone: and there was a rainbow around the throne, in sight like an emerald. 4 And all around the throne were twenty-four seats: and upon the seats I saw twenty-four zachanim sitting, clothed in white raiment; and they had on their heads ketarim of gold. [5] 5 And out of the throne came lightning and thundering and voices: and there were seven lamps of fire burning before the throne, which are the seven Ruachim of יהוה. 6 And before the throne there was a sea of glass like crystal: and in the midst of the throne, and all around the throne, were four beasts full of eyes before and behind. 7 And the first beast was like a lion, and the second beast like a calf, and the third beast had a face as a man, and the fourth beast was like a flying eagle. 8 And the four beasts had each of them six wings [6] around him; and they were full of eyes within: and they rest not day and night, saying, Kadosh, Kadosh, Kadosh, יהוה El-

---

[1] Divine protection during the Great Tribulation, and the "Day of YHWH," and certainly not a reference to the so-called "rapture."
[2] Note that Yahshua has the same Elohim over Him as we do. That would be Abba-YHWH.

[3] Yahshua and Abba YHWH share the same throne. Duality of powers in echad.
[4] John is in a vision fast forwarded in time, and as such sees things as YHWH opens a door in heaven for him to be carried up in the Ruach to receive and then to convey insight. He is about to see the entire 70th week of Daniel through the Ruach. This single person's vision cannot be twisted into a corporate flight to heaven for pig-eating Shabbat-breakers.
[5] The 24 elders are the 12 tribes represented in both covenants, or the 12 tribes of Yisrael plus the 12 apostles of Renewed Covenant Yisrael; therefore portraying that this entire vision is about Yisrael during the time known as the "Day of YHWH" and showing that all men in heaven are those who are yisra-el or overcomers with El.
[6] Seraphim

Shaddai, who was, and is, and is to come. 9 And when those beasts give tifereth and honor and hodu to Him that sat on the throne, who lives le-olam-va-ed, 10 The twenty-four zachanim fell down before Him that sat on the throne, and worshiped Him that lives le-olam-va-ed, and cast their ketarim before the throne, saying, 11 You are worthy, O יהוה, to receive tifereth and honor and power: for You have created all things, and for Your pleasure they are and were created.

5 And I saw in the right hand of Him that sat on the throne a scroll written within and on the backside, sealed with seven seals. 2 And I saw a strong heavenly messenger proclaiming with a loud voice, Who is worthy to open the scroll, and to loose the seals of it? 3 And no man in the shamayim, or in the olam, neither under the olam, was able to open the scroll, neither to look at it. 4 And I wept much, because no man was found worthy to open and to read the scroll, neither to look at it. 5 And one of the zachanim said to me, Weep not: see, the Lion of the tribe of Yahudah, the Root of David, has prevailed to open the scroll, and to loose its seven seals. 6 And I looked, and in the midst of the throne and of the four beasts, and in the midst of the zachanim, stood a Lamb as it had been slain, having seven horns and seven eyes, which are the seven Ruachim of יהוה sent forth into all the olam. 7 And He came and took the scroll out of the right hand of Him that sat upon the throne. 8 And when He had taken the scroll, the four beasts and the twenty-four zachanim fell down before the Lamb, having every one of them harps, and golden vials full of spices, which are the tefillot of kidushim. 9 And they sang a renewed song, saying, You are worthy to take the scroll, and to open its seals: for You were slain, and have redeemed us to יהוה by Your dom out of every kindred and tongue and people and nation; 10 And have made us melechim and kohanim to our

Elohim: and we shall reign in the olam. 11 And I looked, and I heard the voice of many heavenly messengers around the throne and the beasts and the zachanim: and the number of them was ten thousand times ten thousand, and thousands of thousands, 12 Saying with a loud voice, Worthy is the Lamb that was slain to receive power, and riches, and chochmah and strength and honor, and tifereth and bracha. 13 And every creature which is in the shamayim, and on the olam, and under the olam, and such as are in the sea, and all that are in them, I heard saying, Blessing, and honor, and tifereth, and power, be to Him that sits upon the throne, and to the Lamb le-olam-va-ed! 14 And the four beasts said, Amein. And the twenty-four zachanim fell down and worshipped Him that lives le-olam-va-ed.

6 And I saw when the Lamb opened one of the seals, and I heard, as it were the noise of thunder and one of the four beasts saying, Come and see. 2 And I saw, and see a white horse: and he that sat on him had a bow; and a keter was given to him: and he went forth conquering, and to conquer. 3 And when He had opened the second seal, I heard the second beast say, Come and see. 4 And there went out another horse that was red: and power was given to him that sat on it to take shalom from the olam, and that they should kill one another: and there was given to him a great sword. 5 And when He had opened the third seal, I heard the third beast say, Come and see. And I looked, and a black horse; and he that sat on it had a pair of balances in his hand. 6 And I heard a voice in the midst of the four beasts say, A measure of wheat for a penny, and three measures of barley for a penny; and see that you hurt not the oil and the wine. 7 And when He had opened the fourth seal, I heard the voice of the fourth beast say, Come and see. 8 And I looked, and saw a pale horse: and his name that sat on it was Death, and the grave

followed with him. And power was given to them over the fourth part of the olam, to kill with sword and with hunger and with death and with the beasts of the olam. 9 And when He had opened the fifth seal, I saw under the altar the beings of those that were slain for the word of **יהוה**, and for the testimony, which they held:[1] 10 And they cried with a loud voice, saying, How long, O **יהוה**, set-apart and emet, do You not judge and avenge our dom on them that dwell on the olam? 11 And white robes were given to each one of them; and it was said to them, that they should rest yet for a little while, until their fellow servants and their brothers, should also be killed as they were, was completed.[2] 12 And I looked when He had opened the sixth seal, and there was a great earthquake; and the sun became black as sackcloth of hair, and the moon became as dom;[3] 13 And the cochavim of the shamayim fell to the olam, even as a fig tree casts its unripe figs, when shaken by a strong wind. 14 And the shamayim departed as a scroll when it is rolled together; and every mountain and island were moved out of their places. 15 And the melechim of the olam and the great men and the rich men and the chief captains and the mighty men and every slave and every free man hid themselves in the dens and in the rocks of the mountains; 16 And said to the mountains and rocks, Fall on us, and hide us from the face of Him that sits on the throne, and from the wrath of the Lamb: 17 For the great Yom of His wrath is yet to come;[4] and who shall be able to stand?

7 And after these things I saw four heavenly messengers standing on the four corners of the olam, holding the four winds of the olam, that the wind should not blow on the olam, nor on the sea, nor on any tree. 2 And I saw another heavenly messenger ascending from the east, having the seal of the living Elohim: and he cried with a loud voice to the four heavenly messengers, to whom it was given to hurt the olam and the sea, 3 Saying, Hurt not the olam, neither the sea, nor the trees, until we have sealed the avadim of our Elohim in their foreheads. 4 And I heard the number of those who were sealed: and there were sealed a hundred forty four thousand from all the tribes of the children of Yisrael.[5] 5 Of the tribe of Yahudah were sealed twelve thousand. Of the tribe of Reuven were sealed twelve thousand. Of the tribe of Gad were sealed twelve thousand. 6 Of the tribe of Asher were sealed twelve thousand. Of the tribe of Naphtali were sealed twelve thousand. Of the tribe of Menashsheh were sealed twelve thousand. 7 Of the tribe of Shimeon were sealed twelve thousand. Of the tribe of Levi were sealed twelve thousand. Of the tribe of Yissacher were sealed twelve thousand. 8 Of the tribe of Zevulon were sealed twelve thousand. Of the tribe of Yoseph[6] were sealed twelve thousand. Of the tribe of Benyamin were sealed twelve thousand.[7] 9 After this I looked, and, a great multitude, which no

---

[1] Torah and the witness of Yahshua.
[2] Some Torah-guarding believers are chosen to be martyred during the Time of Yaakov's Trouble. This may not be popular theology, but it is Scripture.
[3] Cosmic disturbance is the sign that He is soon to return at the end of the Great Tribulation, not immediately upon the initial manifestation of the disturbance itself, as taught by some. There is a time gap between Matthew 24:29 and 30. The cosmic disturbance starts here but remains until after the 70th week of Yisrael, when the Master will return.
[4] Strong's Greek #2064 **erchomai,** meaning "still or "yet to come." This sheds a different light on this text, showing that His wrath is yet future at end of the 70th week of Yisrael, when the olam hazeh is judged, not at some mid- or early point, or

at this point, where allegedly the Tribulation ends and the wrath starts.
[5] These are not 144,000 Yahudim, since all 12 tribes are represented. These 144,000 are also not "Jewish Billy Grahams," since unlike those folks, these Yisraelites all use the true Names and are sealed with it, as seen in Revelation 14:1.They are sealed to proclaim the Name and His plan during the Great Tribulation.
[6] Yoseph is substituted for Ephraim and Dan. For Ephraim because Scripture often uses Yoseph and Ephraim interchangeably, and Dan is replaced by Yoseph because from Dan comes the end-time anti-Moshiach (Genesis 49:17-18) and this is YHWH's judgment on Dan by refusing to seal his children during a time of judgment when Dan himself will judged and not sealed. However, in the age to come, or the millennium, Dan does reconstitute its tribal inheritance in the land of Yisrael, as well as in the new Yahrushalayim coming out of the shamayim to the earth. So the judgment appears for a brief point and time only.
[7] Obviously the ten tribes are not lost, and this is proof that YHWH knows who they are and where they are.

man could number, of all nations and tribes and peoples and tongues stood before the throne and before the Lamb, clothed with white robes, and palms in their hands;[1] 10 And cried with a loud voice, saying, Salvation to our Elohim who sits upon the throne, and to the Lamb. 11 And all the heavenly messengers stood around the throne, and the zachanim and the four beasts, and fell before the throne on their faces, and worshipped יהוה, 12 Saying, Amein! Blessing and tifereth and chochmah and hodu and honor and power and might, be to our Elohim le-olam-va-ed. Amein. 13 And one of the zachanim answered, saying to me, Who are these who are arrayed in white robes? And where did they come from?[2] 14 And I said to him, Sir, you know. And he said to me, These are those who came out of the Great Tribulation, and have washed their robes, and made them white in the dom of the Lamb. 15 Therefore are they before the throne of יהוה, and serve Him day and night in His Sukkah: and He that sits on the throne shall dwell among them. 16 They shall hunger no more, neither thirst any more; neither shall the sun light on them, nor any heat. 17 For the Lamb who is in the midst of the throne shall feed them, and shall lead them to living fountains of mayim: and יהוה shall wipe away all tears from their eyes.

8 And when He had opened the seventh seal, there was silence in the shamayim for about half an hour. 2 And I saw the seven heavenly messengers who stood before יהוה; and to them were given seven shofars. 3 And another heavenly messenger came and stood at the altar, having a golden censer; and there was given to him much incense, that he should offer it with the tefillot of all the kidushim upon the golden altar that was before the throne. 4 And the smoke of the incense, which came with the tefillot of the kidushim, ascended up before

יהוה out of the heavenly messenger's hand. 5 And the heavenly messenger took the censer, and filled it with fire of the altar, and cast it onto the olam: and there were voices and thunderings and lightnings and an earthquake. 6 And the seven heavenly messengers who had the seven shofars prepared themselves to sound. 7 The first heavenly messenger sounded, and there followed hail and fire mingled with dom, and they were cast upon the olam: and a third part of the trees were burned up, and all the green grass was burned up. 8 And the second heavenly messenger sounded, and as it were a great mountain burning with fire was cast into the sea: and the third part of the sea became dom; 9 And a third part of the creatures that were in the sea that had chayim, died; and a third part of the ships were destroyed. 10 And the third heavenly messenger sounded, and there fell a great cochav from the shamayim, burning as if it were a lamp, and it fell upon a third of the rivers, and upon the fountains of mayim; 11 And the name of the cochav is called Wormwood: and a third part of the mayim became wormwood; and many men died from the mayim, because they were made bitter. 12 And the fourth heavenly messenger sounded, and a third part of the sun was smitten, and a third part of the moon, and a third part of the cochavim; so that a third of them were darkened, and a third part of both day and night did not shine. 13 And I looked, and listened to a heavenly messenger flying through the midst of the shamayim, saying with a loud voice, Woe, woe, woe, to the inhabitants of the olam because of the other voices of the shofar of the three heavenly messengers, which are yet to sound!

9 And the fifth heavenly messenger sounded, and I saw a cochav fall from the shamayim to the olam: and to him was given the key of the bottomless pit. 2 And he opened the bottomless pit; and there arose a smoke out of the pit, as the smoke

---

[1] Believers that were martyred - not raptured - during the Great Tribulation.
[2] See the footnote for Revelation 7:9.

of a great furnace; and the sun and the air were darkened because of the smoke of the pit. 3 And there came out of the smoke locusts upon the olam: and to them was given power, as the scorpions of the olam have power. 4 And it was commanded to them that they should not hurt the grass of the olam, neither any green thing, neither any tree; but only those men who do not have the seal of יהוה in their foreheads.[1] 5 And to them it was given that they should not kill them, but that they should be tormented for five months: and their torment was as the torment of a scorpion, when he stings a man. 6 And in those days shall men seek death, and shall not find it; and shall desire to die, and death shall flee from them. 7 And the shapes of the locusts were like horses prepared to battle; and on their heads were as it were ketarim like gold, and their faces were like the faces of men. 8 And they had hair like the hair of women, and their teeth were like the teeth of lions. 9 And they had breastplates, like breastplates of iron; and the sound of their wings was like the sound of chariots of many horses running to battle. 10 And they had tails like scorpions, and there were stings in their tails: and their power was to hurt men for five months.[2] 11 And they had a melech over them, who is the heavenly messenger of the bottomless pit, whose name in Ivrit is Avaddon, but in the Greek tongue his name is Apolluon. 12 One woe is past; and, see, there comes two more woes after this. 13 And the sixth heavenly messenger sounded, and I heard a voice from the four horns of the golden altar that is before יהוה, 14 Saying to the sixth heavenly messenger who had the shofar, Loose the four heavenly messengers which

are bound in the great River Euphrates.[3] 15 And the four heavenly messengers were loosed, who were prepared for the hour and day and month and year, in which to slay a third of mankind. 16 And the number of the army of the horsemen were two hundred million, and I heard the number of them. 17 And this is how I saw the horses in the vision, and those that sat on them, having breastplates of fire, and of jacinth, and brimstone: and the heads of the horses were as the heads of lions; and out of their mouths issued fire and smoke and brimstone. 18 By these three were the third part of mankind killed, by the fire and by the smoke and by the brimstone, that issued out of their mouths. 19 For their power is in their mouth, and in their tails: for their tails were like serpents, having heads, and with them they do their harm. 20 And the rest of the men who were not killed by these plagues still did not make teshuvah from the works of their hands, that they should not worship shadim, and idols of gold, and silver, and brass, and stone, and of wood: which cannot see, shema, nor walk: 21 Neither did they make teshuvah from their murders, nor from their sorceries, nor from their fornication, nor from their thefts.

10 And I saw another mighty heavenly messenger come down from the shamayim, clothed with a cloud: and a rainbow was upon his head, and his face was as it were the sun, and his feet as pillars of fire: 2 And he had in his hand a little scroll open: and he set his right foot upon the sea, and his left foot on the olam, 3 And cried with a loud voice, as when a lion roars: and when he had cried, seven thunders uttered their voices. 4 And when the seven thunders had uttered their voices, I was about to write: and I heard a voice from the shamayim saying to me, Seal up those things that the seven thunders uttered, and do not write them. 5 And the heavenly

---

[1] His Name in and upon their minds and hearts.
[2] Fallen demons kept in **Tartoros** (Second Kepha 2:4) from the time of the flood for their forbidden activities in Genesis 6, until the last years of this age, only to be released for YHWH's Tribulation purposes; and then tossed into the Lake of Fire. The fallen star that unlocks **Tartaros** is none other than s.a.tan himself.

[3] Please see: **The Four Unclean Spirits Of Eden:** http://store.yourarmstoisrael.org/Qstore/Qstore.cgi?CMD=011&PROD=000166

messenger whom I saw stood upon the sea and upon the olam lifted up his hand to the shamayim, 6 And swore by Him that lives le-olam va-ed, who created the shamayim, and the things that are in it, and the olam, and the things that are in it, and the sea, and the things that are in it, that time should no longer exist: 7 But in the days of the voice of the seventh heavenly messenger, when he shall begin to sound, the mystery of יהוה shall also be finished,[1] as He has declared to His avadim the niviim. 8 And the voice which I heard from the shamayim spoke to me again, and said, Go and take the little scroll that is open in the hand of the heavenly messenger who stands upon the sea and upon the olam. 9 And I went to the heavenly messenger, and said to him, Give me the little scroll. And he said to me, Take it, and eat it up; and it shall make your belly bitter, but it shall be in your mouth sweet as honey. 10 And I took the little scroll out of the heavenly messenger's hand, and ate it up; and it was in my mouth sweet as honey: and as soon as I had eaten it, my belly was bitter. 11 And he said to me, You must prophesy again before many peoples and nations and tongues and melechim.

11 And there was given to me a reed like to a rod: and the heavenly messenger stood, saying, Rise, and measure the Sukkah of יהוה, and the altar, and those that worship in it. 2 But the court that is outside the Beit HaMikdash leave out, and do not measure it; for it is given to the gentiles[2]: and the set-apart city shall they tread under foot forty two months. 3 And I will give power to My two witnesses,[3] and they shall prophesy a thousand two hundred sixty days, clothed in sackcloth. 4 These are the two olive trees, and the two menorot standing before the Elohim of the olam.[4] 5 And if any man will hurt them, fire proceeds out of their mouth, and devours their enemies: and if any man will hurt them, he must in like manner be killed. 6 These have power to shut the shamayim,[5] that it rain not in the days of their prophecy: and have power over mayim to turn them to dom,[6] and to smite the olam with all kind of plagues, as often as they desire. 7 And when they shall have finished their testimony, the beast that ascends out of the bottomless pit shall make war against them, and shall overcome them, and kill them. 8 And their dead bodies shall lie in the street of the great city, which spiritually is called Sedom and Mitzrayim, where also our Master was impaled. 9 And those of the peoples and tribes and tongues and nations shall see their dead bodies[7] three and a half days, and shall not allow their dead bodies to be put in graves. 10 And they that dwell upon the olam shall gilah over them, and celebrate, and shall send gifts to each other; because these two neviim tormented those that dwelt on the olam. 11 And after three and a half days the Ruach chayim from יהוה entered into them, and they stood upon their feet; and great fear fell upon those who saw them. 12 And they heard a great voice from the shamayim saying to them, *Come up here.* And they ascended up to the shamayim in a cloud; and their

---

[1] The mystery of the kingdom being restored to Yisrael being finished in its hidden stage, about to be fully revealed at long last.
[2] The new and rebuilt Temple in Yahrushalayim will have no court for the gentiles, simply because all who worship YHWH are Yisraelites, confirming the whole purpose and core of the two-house message.
[3] Moshe and Eliyahu; see footnote to Revelation 11:4 below.
[4] The two witnesses are Yahudah and Ephraim, as both houses are ordained to rise up and teach truth during the Day of YHWH, during Yisrael's 70th week. We know that these two witnesses are the two houses, because they are called two menorot or two lampstands. The seven congregations in Asia are called seven menorot in Revelation 1:20. So each congregation of believers is one menorah. Therefore two menorot are two congregations or groups of believers. This confirms the entire revelation to Zecharyah in chapter 4 of the two anointed olive trees who stand before YHWH. From each of these two houses comes one witness, or two individuals who represent the two houses. Moshe from Yahudah, since Levi was part of Yahudah, and Eliyahu from Ephraim. They do their ministry for 3½ years before being killed and then rising in Yahrushalayim. YHWH will never allow any true Biblical witness in the earth without both Yahudah and Ephraim being the two chosen and faithful representatives of His truth. For more details, see: http://yourarmstoisrael.org/Articles_new/restoration/?page=5&type=12
[5] Eliyahu.
[6] Moshe Rabainu.
[7] TV and mass media.

enemies saw them. 13 And the same hour there was a great earthquake, and the tenth part of the city fell, and in the earthquake seven thousand men were killed: and the remnant became afraid, and gave tifereth to the Elohim of the shamayim. 14 The second woe is past; and see, the third woe comes quickly. 15 And the seventh heavenly messenger sounded; and there were great voices in the shamayim, saying, The malchutim of the olam hazeh have become the malchutim of our Elohim, and of His Moshiach; and He shall reign le-olam va-ed. 16 And the twenty-four zachanim, who sat before יהוה on their seats, fell upon their faces, and worshipped יהי, 17 Saying, We give You hodu, O Master יהוה El-Shaddai, who was and who is and who is coming; because You have taken Your great power, and have reigned. 18 And the nations were angry, and Your wrath has come and the time of the dead that they should be judged, and that You should give rewards to Your avadim the niviim, and to the kidushim, and to them that fear Your Name, small and great; and should destroy them who destroy the olam. 19 And the Sukkah of יהוה was opened in the shamayim, and there was seen in His Sukkah the Ark of the Covenant: and there were lightnings and voices and thunderings and an earthquake, and great hail.

12 And there appeared a great wonder in the shamayim; a woman clothed with the sun, and the moon under her feet, and upon her head a keter of twelve cochavim: [1] 2 And she being with child cried, labored in birth, and pained to deliver. 3 And there appeared another wonder in the shamayim; and see a great red dragon, having seven heads and ten horns, and seven ketarim upon his heads. 4 And his tail drew a third part of the cochavim of the shamayim, and did cast them to the olam: and the dragon stood before the woman who was ready to deliver,

in order to devour her Child as soon as it was born.[2] 5 And she brought forth a male-Child, who was to rule all nations with a rod of iron: and her Child was caught up to יהוה, and to His throne.[3] 6 And the woman fled into the wilderness, where she has a place prepared by יהוה, that they should feed her there a thousand two hundred sixty days. [4] [5] 7 And there was war in the shamayim: Micha-El and his heavenly messengers fought against the dragon; and the dragon fought with his heavenly messengers, 8 And the dragon prevailed not; neither was their place found any more in the shamayim. 9 And the great dragon was cast out, that old serpent, called the s.a.tan, who deceives the entire olam hazeh: he was cast out into the olam, and his heavenly messengers were cast out with him. 10 And I heard a loud voice saying in the shamayim, Now has come salvation and strength and the malchut of our Elohim, and the power of His Moshiach: for the accuser of our brothers is cast down, who accused them before our Elohim day and night. 11 And they overcame him by the dom of the Lamb, and by the word of their testimony; and they loved not their lives to the death. 12 Therefore gilah, you shamayim, and you that dwell in them. Woe to the inhabitants of the olam and of the sea! For s.a.tan has come down to you, having great wrath, because he knows that he has but a short time. 13 And when the dragon saw that he was cast to the olam, he persecuted the woman who brought forth the male-Child. 14 And to the woman was given two wings of a great eagle, that she might fly into the wilderness, into her place, where she is nourished for a time, and times, and half a time, from the face of the

---

[1] Yisrael.

[2] s.a.tan versus Yisrael.
[3] Yahshua.
[4] 3½ years in the wilderness being guarded by YHWH.
[5] Actually this has a double meaning of Yahshua being born in Yisrael in the past, and a future prophetic time during the Great Tribulation, where through the test of endurance, His true body or Commonwealth children will yet be birthed during the **shivlai haMahshiach** or birth pains of Moshiach.

serpent.[1] 15 And the serpent cast out of his mouth mayim as a flood after the woman, that he might cause her to be carried away by the flood.[2] 16 And the ground helped the woman, and the earth opened her mouth, and swallowed up the flood, which the dragon cast out of his mouth.[3] 17 And the dragon was angry with the woman, and went to make war with the remnant of her seed,[4] that shomer the mitzvot of יהוה, and have the testimony of יהושע the Moshiach.[5]

13 And I stood upon the sand of the sea, and saw a beast rise up out of the sea, having seven heads and ten horns, and upon his horns ten ketarim, and upon his heads the names of blasphemy.[6] 2 And the beast which I saw was like a leopard, and his feet were as the feet of a bear and his mouth as the mouth of a lion: and the dragon gave him his power, and his seat, and great authority. 3 And I saw one of his heads as it were wounded to death; and his deadly wound was healed: and all of the olam hazeh marveled after the beast. 4 And they worshipped the dragon who gave power to the beast: and they worshipped the beast, saying, Who is like to the beast? Who is able to make war with him? 5 And there was given to him a mouth speaking great things and blasphemies; and power was given to him to continue forty-two months. 6 And he opened his mouth in blasphemy

against יהוה, to blaspheme His Name, and his Sukkah, and them that dwell in the shamayim. 7 And it was given to him to make war with the kidushim, and to overcome them: and power was given him over all tribes and tongues and nations. 8 And all that dwell in the olam shall worship him, whose names are not written in the Scroll of Life of the Lamb slain from the foundation of the olam. 9 If any man has an ear, let him shema. 10 He that leads into captivity shall go into captivity: he that kills with the sword must be killed with the sword. [7] Here is the endurance and the emunah of the kidushim. 11 And I looked and another beast came up out of the earth; and he had two horns like a lamb, and he spoke as a dragon.[8] 12 And he exercises all the power of the first beast before him, and causes the olam and those who dwell in it to worship the first beast, whose deadly wound was healed. 13 And he does great wonders, so that he makes fire come down from the shamayim on the olam in the sight of men, 14 And deceives them that dwell on the olam by the means of those nisim which he had power to do in the sight of the beast; saying to those that dwell on the olam, that they should make an image to the beast, who had the wound by a sword, and did live.[9] 15 And he had power to give life to the image of the beast, so that the image of the beast should both speak, and cause as many as would not worship the image of the beast to be killed. 16 And he causes all, both small and great, rich and poor, free and bond, to receive a mark in their right hand, or in their foreheads: 17 And that no man

---

[1] YHWH may provide an airlift by plane to the wilderness as He guards His bride for 3.5 years.
[2] Flood denotes exile, or removal to the wilderness of the nations.
[3] The gentile nations would absorb Yisrael and in many cases save life, by camouflaging them as they became one with and indistinguishable from the heathen gentiles. A dual application in previous history and in the end time as well.
[4] Nazarene Yisraelites.
[5] Let this be clear. Only those who have resurrection testimony and Torah witness are His remnant Yisrael. The rest will be carried away or taken away. Pray to be left behind.
[6] The beast or anti-Moshiach will rise from the community of nations, and will be considered Moshiach but will not come nor proclaim YHWH's Name; instead he will proclaim the many so-called names of blasphemy, such as goad and "lord" and Jes-s and all the other forbidden substitutes that bring YHWH's name to naught. The anti-Moshiach will propagate chilul hashem. He will be a political wheeler-dealer, with the second later beast in verse 11 working on the religious front, while anti-Moshiach works in the political and secular realm.

[7] When anti-Moshiach comes, turning around (teshuvah/repentance) for YHWH will be near impossible, as Torah-less-ness reigns. Now is the time to turn around.
[8] Looked like the true Lamb but was corrupted in two horns. This false prophet religious order is spearheaded by Catholics and Protestants; thus the reference to two horns coming out of the earth, or the curse of promoting the first political beast or anti-Moshiach, with the second beast, being in control of worship and religious matters. Non-Torah-keepers may find these insights insulting, but as Yahshua asked The Twelve, "will you also leave Me?"
[9] Clearly this false one-world religious order desires the beast to be worshipped and punishes those who don't conform. The dragon or s.a.tan gives the false prophet power to do miracles and wonders, all pointing people to trust in the first beast.

might buy or sell, except he that had the mark, or the name of the beast, or the number of his name.[1] 18 Here is chochmah. Let him that has understanding count the number of the beast: for it is the number of a man; and his number is six hundred sixty six.[2]

14 And I looked, and saw, a Lamb stood on Har Tzion, and with Him a hundred forty four thousand Yisraelites, having His Abba's Name written in their foreheads.[3] 2 And I heard a voice from the shamayim, as the voice of many mayim, and as the voice of a great thunder: and I heard the voice of harpists playing with their harps: 3 And they sung as it were a renewed song before the throne, and before the four beasts, and the zachanim: and no man could learn that song but the hundred forty four thousand, who were redeemed from the olam.[4] 4 These are they, which were not defiled with women; for they are virgins.[5] These are they who follow the Lamb wherever He goes. These were redeemed from among men, being the bikkurim to **יהוה** and to the Lamb. 5 And in their mouth was found no guile: for they are without fault before the throne of **יהוה**. 6 And I saw another heavenly messenger fly in the midst of the shamayim, having the everlasting besarot to proclaim to them that dwell in the olam, and to every nation and kindred and tongue and people, 7 Saying with a loud voice, Fear **יהוה** , and give tifereth to Him; for the hour of His judgment has come: and worship Him that made the shamayim and the olam and the

sea and the fountains of mayim. 8 And there followed another heavenly messenger, saying, Bavel is fallen, is fallen, that great city,[6] because she made all nations drink of the wine of the wrath of her fornication. 9 And the third heavenly messenger followed them, saying with a loud voice, If any man worship the beast and his image, and receive his mark in his forehead, or in his hand, 10 The same shall drink of the wine of the wrath of **יהוה**, which is poured out without mixture into the cup of His indignation; and he shall be tormented with fire and brimstone in the presence of the set-apart heavenly messengers, and in the presence of the Lamb: 11 And the smoke of their torment ascends up le-olam-va-ed: and they have no rest day or night, who worship the beast and his image, and whoever receives the mark of his name.[7] 12 Here is the endurance of the kidushim: here are those that shomer the commandments of **יהוה**, and the emunah of **יהושע**.[8] 13 And I heard a voice from the shamayim saying to me, *Write, Blessed are the dead who die in* **יהוה** *from this time forward: Yes,* says the Ruach, *that they may rest from their labors; and their mitzvot do follow them.* 14 And I looked, and see a white cloud, and upon the cloud One sat like the Ben Adam, having on His head a golden keter, and in His hand a sharp sickle. 15 And another heavenly messenger came out of the Sukkah, crying with a loud voice to Him that sat on the cloud, Thrust in Your sickle, and reap: for the time is come for You to reap; for the harvest of the olam is ripe. 16 And He that sat on the cloud thrust in His sickle into the olam; and the olam was reaped. 17 And another heavenly messenger came out of the Sukkah that is in the shamayim, he also having a sharp

---

[1] The mark of the beast is for those who don't conform to the one-world religious order. That order has as its mark the changing of the everlasting covenant or the 7th Yom Shabbat. This is, as best that we can ascertain, the single most overriding and defining mark of the beast.
[2] The numerical value of the words on the Roman pontiff's headpiece.
[3] The seal of the 144,000. Without a love and commitment to use and proclaim the true Name of YHWH, you can forget about being chosen for that precious assignment.
[4] See **Resurrection Music** at:
http://store.yourarmstoisrael.org/Qstore/Qstore.cgi?CMD=011 &PROD=000256
[5] Undefiled by false religion that leaves out either Yahshua as King and YHWH's Son, or Torah as a guide.

[6] Note that Bavel is a city of that time and also the end-time. Romiyah for sure.
[7] The result of their torment from the second death is forever and cannot be reversed, but their torment ends upon the second death.
[8] This is the formula to escape the second death. Emunah in Yahshua and Torah. If Torah is the standard in the last of the last days, and also of yesterday, then it must be so today, since YHWH and Yahshua never change.

sickle. 18 And another heavenly messenger came out from the altar, who had power over fire; and cried with a loud cry to Him that had the sharp sickle, saying, Thrust in Your sharp sickle, and gather the clusters of the vine of the olam; for her grapes are fully ripe. 19 And the heavenly messenger thrust in His sickle into the olam, and gathered the vine of the olam, and cast it into the great winepress of the wrath of יהוה.[1] 20 And the winepress was trodden outside the city, and dom came out of the winepress, even to the horse bridles, by the space of a thousand six hundred furlongs.

15 And I saw another sign in the shamayim, great and marvelous, seven heavenly messengers having the seven last plagues; for in them is filled up the wrath of יהוה. 2 And I saw as it were a sea of glass mingled with fire: and them that had gotten the victory over the beast and over his image and over his mark and over the number of his name, standing on the sea of glass, having the harps of Elohim. 3 And they sing the shir of Moshe the eved of the Master יהוה, and the shir of the Lamb, saying, Great and marvelous are Your mitzvot, Master יהוה El-Shaddai; tzadik and emet are Your halachot, O Melech of the kidushim. 4 Who shall not fear You, O Master יהוה, and glorify Your Name? For You alone are set-apart: for all nations shall come and worship before You; for Your mishpatim are made manifest. 5 And after that I looked, and, see, the Sukkah of the testimony in the shamayim was opened: 6 And the seven heavenly messengers came out of the Sukkah, having the seven plagues, clothed in pure and white linen, and having their breasts wrapped with golden girdles. 7 And one of the four beasts gave to the seven heavenly messengers seven golden vials full of the wrath of יהוה, who lives le-olam-va-ed. 8 And the Sukkah was filled with smoke from the tifereth of

יהוה, and from His power; and no man was able to enter into the Sukkah, until the seven plagues of the seven heavenly messengers were fulfilled.

16 And I heard a great voice out of the Sukkah saying to the seven heavenly messengers, Go your ways, and pour out the vials of the wrath of יהוה upon the olam. 2 And the first went, and poured out his vial upon the olam; and there fell severe and malignant sores[2] upon the men who had the mark of the beast, and upon them who worshipped his image. 3 And the second heavenly messenger poured out his vial upon the sea; and it became as the dom of a dead man: and every living being died in the sea. 4 And the third heavenly messenger poured out his vial upon the rivers and fountains of mayim; and they became dom.[3] 5 And I heard the heavenly messenger of the mayim say, You are Tzadik, O יהוה, who is and was and who shall be, because You have judged well. 6 For they have shed the dom of the kidushim and niviim, and You have given them dom to drink; for they are worthy. 7 And I heard another out of the altar say, Even so, Master יהוה El-Shaddai, emet and tzadik are Your mishpatim. 8 And the fourth heavenly messenger poured out his vial upon the sun; and power was given to him to scorch men with fire. 9 And men were scorched with great heat, and blasphemed the Name of יהוה, who has power over these plagues: and they did not make teshuvah to give Him tifereth. 10 And the fifth heavenly messenger poured out his vial upon the throne of the beast;[4] and his malchut was full of darkness; and they gnawed their tongues for pain, 11 And blasphemed the Elohim of the shamayim because of their pains and their sores, and did not make teshuvah from their deeds. 12 And the sixth heavenly messenger poured out his vial upon the great River

---

[1] Those branches of the vine that either had dried fruit or were barren.

[2] Final mishpatim before Moshiach will return. Skin Cancer.
[3] Drought.
[4] City of Romiyah.

Euphrates; and the mayim of it was dried up, so that the way of the melechim of the east might be prepared. 13 And I saw three unclean shadim like frogs come out of the mouth of the dragon and out of the mouth of the beast and out of the mouth of the false prophet. 14 For they are the ruachim of shadim, working nisim, who go forth to the melechim of the olam and to the entire olam hazeh, to gather them to the battle of that great Yom יהוה the Almighty. 15 *See, I come as a thief. Blessed is he that watches, and keeps his garments, lest he walk naked, and they see his shame.* 16 And He gathered them together into a place called in Ivrit, Har Meggido. 17 And the seventh heavenly messenger poured out his vial into the air; and there came a great voice out of the Sukkah of the shamayim, from the throne, saying, It is done. 18 And there were voices and thunders and lightnings and there was a great earthquake, such as was not since men were upon the olam, so mighty an earthquake, and so great. 19 And the great city was divided into three parts, and the cities of the nations fell: and great Bavel came to remembrance before יהוה, to give to her the cup of the wine of the fierceness of His wrath. 20 And every island fled away, and the mountains were not found.[1] 21 And there fell upon men a great hail out of the shamayim, every stone about the weight of a talent: and men blasphemed יהוה because of the plague of the hail; for the plague of it was exceedingly great.

17 And there came one of the seven heavenly messengers who had the seven vials, and talked with me, saying to me, Come here; I will show to you the judgment of the great whore that sits upon many mayim: 2 With whom the melechim of the olam have committed fornication, and the inhabitants of the olam have been made drunk with the wine of her fornication. 3 So he carried me away in the

Ruach into the wilderness: and I saw a woman sit upon a scarlet colored beast, full of names of blasphemy,[2] having seven heads and ten horns. 4 And the woman was arrayed in purple and scarlet color and decked with gold and precious stones and pearls, having a golden cup in her hand full of abominations and filthiness of her fornication: 5 And upon her forehead was a name written, MYSTERY, BAVEL THE GREAT, THE MOTHER OF HARLOTS AND ABOMINATIONS OF THE EARTH.[3] 6 And I saw the woman drunk with the dom of the kidushim, and with the dom of the martyrs of יהושע: and when I saw her, I wondered greatly. 7 And the heavenly messenger said to me, Why did you marvel? I will tell you the mystery of the woman, and of the beast that carries her, which has the seven heads and ten horns. 8 The beast that you saw was and is not; and shall ascend out of the bottomless pit, and go into perdition: and they that dwell on the olam shall wonder, whose names were not written in the Scroll of Chayim from the foundation of the olam hazeh, when they see the beast that was and is not and yet is. 9 And here is the mind that has chochmah. The seven heads are the seven mountains, on which the woman sits.[4] 10 And there are seven melechim: five are fallen and one is and the other has not yet come; and when he comes, he must continue a short space. 11 And the beast that was and is not, even he is the eighth and is of the seven and goes into destruction. 12 And the ten horns that you saw are ten melechim, who have received no malchut as yet; but receive power as melechim in just one hour with the beast. 13 These have one mind, and shall give their power and strength to the beast. 14 These shall make war with the Lamb, and the Lamb shall overcome them: for He is Master of masters and Melech of

---

[1] Seventh Shofar; nuclear fallout.

[2] Multiple false titles for YHWH.
[3] In order for Roman popery to be the mother of all falsehood, she must have daughters who left home and yet are still spiritual harlots.
[4] Romiyah.

melechim: and they that are with Him are called, the chosen and faithful people. 15 And he said to me, The mayim that you saw, where the whore sits, are peoples and multitudes and nations and tongues. 16 And the ten horns that you saw upon the beast, these shall hate the whore and shall make her desolate and naked, and shall eat her flesh, and burn her with fire. 17 For יהוה has put in their levim to fulfill His will and to agree and give their malchut to the beast, until the words of יהוה shall be fulfilled. 18 And the woman that you saw is that great city, [1] that reigns over the melechim of the olam.

18

And after these things I saw another heavenly messenger come down from the shamayim, having great power; and the olam was lit with his tifereth. 2 And he cried mightily with a strong voice, saying, Bavel the great has fallen, has fallen and has become the dwelling of shadim, and the haunt of every foul ruach, and a cage of every unclean and hateful bird. 3 For all nations have drunk of the wine of the wrath of her fornication and the melechim of the olam have committed fornication with her and the merchants of the olam have grown rich through the abundance of her delicacies. 4 And I heard another voice from the shamayim, saying, *Come out of her, My people-Ami,*[2][3] *that you be not partakers of her sins, so that you receive not of her plagues. 5 For her sins have reached to the shamayim, and* יהוה *has remembered her iniquities. 6 Reward her even as she rewarded you and repay her double according to her works: in the cup that she has filled, fill it double to her. 7 How much she has esteemed herself, and lived deliciously, so much torment and sorrow give her: for she says in her lev, I sit*

a malka, and am no widow, and shall see no sorrow. 8 Therefore shall her plagues come in one day, death and mourning and famine; and she shall be utterly burned with fire: for strong is the Master יהוה *Elohim who judges her. 9 And the melechim of the olam, who have committed fornication and lived deliciously with her, shall bewail her, and lament for her, when they shall see the smoke of her burning, 10 Standing far off for the fear of her torment, saying, Oy, Vey, that great city Bavel, that mighty city! For in one hour is your judgment come. 11 And the merchants of the olam shall weep and mourn over her; for no man buys their merchandise*[4] *any more: 12 The merchandise of gold and silver and precious stones and of pearls and fine linen and purple and silk and scarlet and all your wood and all the vessels of ivory and all the vessels of most precious wood and of brass and iron and marble, 13 And cinnamon and incense and ointments and frankincense and wine and oil and fine flour and wheat and beasts and sheep and horses and chariots and slaves and beings of men. 14 And the fruits that your being lusted after are departed from you, and all things which were dainty and tov have departed from you, and you shall find them no more at all. 15 The merchants of these things, who were made rich by her, shall stand far off for the fear of her torment, weeping and wailing, 16 And saying, Oy, Vey, that great city, that was clothed in fine linen and purple and scarlet and decked with gold and precious stones and pearls! 17 For in one hour so great riches have come to nothing. And every ship captain and all the passengers and sailors and as many as trade by sea, stood far off,*[5] *18 And cried when they saw the smoke of her burning, saying, What city is like this great city! 19 And they cast dust on their heads, and cried, weeping and wailing, saying, Oy, Vey that great city, in which all that had ships in*

---

[1] Romiyah and her popery.
[2] True Yisrael can indeed be found in the church system, as well as the nations. But in order to manifest that they are redeemed, Yisrael must manifest that reality by coming out of Bavel instead of continuing in its deception. This cry is not a prayer request but a command.
[3] No doubt the voice of Yahshua Himself.

---

[4] Products and/or pagan worship system.
[5] A term meaning Ephraimites, or traders with Romiyah from the ten tribes.

the sea were made rich because of her *wealth! For in one hour she is made desolate. 20 Gilah over her, you shamayim and you set-apart shlichim and niviim; for* יהוה *has avenged you on her.* 21 And a mighty heavenly messenger took up a stone like a great millstone, and cast it into the sea, saying, Just like this with violence shall that great city Bavel be thrown down, and shall be found no more at all. 22 And the voice of harpists and musicians and of flutists and trumpeters, shall be heard no more at all in you; and no craftsman of any craft, shall be found any more in you; and the sound of a millstone shall be heard no more at all in you; 23 And the light of a candle shall shine no more at all in you; and the voice of the bridegroom and of the bride shall be heard no more at all in you: for your merchants were the great men of the olam hazeh; for by your sorceries were all nations deceived. 24 And in her was found the dom of niviim, and of kidushim, and of all that were slain upon the olam hazeh.[1]

19 And after these things I heard a great voice of many people in the shamayim, saying, Hallel-u-Yah; Salvation and tiphereth and honor and power to יהוה our Elohim: 2 For emet and tzadik are His mishpatim: for He has judged the great whore, who did corrupt the olam with her fornication, and has avenged the dom of His avadim at her hand. 3 And again they said, Hallel-u-Yah. And her smoke rose up le-olam-va-ed. 4 And the twenty-four zachanim and the four beasts fell down and worshipped יהוה that sat on the throne, saying, Amein; Hallel-u-Yah. 5 And a voice came out of the throne, saying, Tehilla to our Elohim, all of you His avadim and you that fear Him, both small and great. 6 And I heard as it were the voice of a great multitude and as the voice of much mayim and as the voice of mighty thunderings, saying, Hallel-u-Yah: for the Master יהוה El-Shaddai reigns. 7 Let us be glad and gilah and give honor to Him: for the marriage of the Lamb has come, and His wife has made herself ready. 8 And to her was granted that she should be arrayed in fine linen, clean and white: for the fine linen is the tzedakah of kidushim.[2] 9 And He said to me, *Write, Blessed are they who are called to the marriage supper of the Lamb.* And He said to me, *These are the emet sayings of* יהוה. 10 And I fell at His feet to worship Him. And He said to me, *See that you do it not: I am your fellow Eved and from your brothers who have the testimony of* יהושע: *worship* יהוה: *for the testimony of* יהושע *is the Ruach of prophecy.*[3] 11 And I saw the shamayim opened and see a white horse; and He that sat upon it was called Faithful and Emet and in tzedakah He does shophet and make war. 12 His eyes were as a flame of fire and on His head were many ketarim; and He had a Name written, that no man knew, but He Himself. 13 And He was clothed with a robe dipped in dom: and His Name is called The Devar יהוה. 14 And the armies that were in the shamayim followed Him upon white horses, clothed in fine linen, white and clean. 15 And out of His mouth goes a sharp sword, that with it He should smite the nations: and He shall rule them with a rod of iron: and He treads the winepress of the fierceness and wrath of El-Shaddai. 16 And He has on His tallit and on His thigh a Name written, Melech-HaMelechim, and Adon-Adonim. 17 And I saw a heavenly messenger standing in the sun; and he cried with a loud voice, saying to all the fowls that fly in the midst of the shamayim, Come and gather yourselves together to the supper of the great Elohim; 18 That you may eat the flesh of melechim and the flesh of captains and the flesh of mighty men and the flesh of horses and of them that sit on them and the flesh of all men, both free and bond, both small and

---

[1] Final condemnation of the Roman Catholic Church that controls all nations, and destroys truth, along with the servants of truth.

[2] Yisrael.

[3] All worship must be directed to Abba and sealed in Yahshua's Name.

great.[1] 19 And I saw the beast, and the melechim of the olam, and their armies, gathered together to make war against Him that sat on the horse, and against His army. 20 And the beast was taken, and with him the navi sheker that wrought nisim before him, with which he deceived those that had received the mark of the beast, and those that worshipped his image. These both were cast alive into a Lake of Fire burning with brimstone. 21 And the remnant was slain with the sword of Him that sat upon the horse, whose sword proceeded out of His mouth: and all the fowls were filled with their flesh.

20 And I saw a heavenly messenger come down from the shamayim, having the key of the bottomless pit and a great chain in his hand. 2 And he laid hold on the dragon, that old serpent, who is s.a.tan, and bound him a thousand years, 3 And cast him into the bottomless pit, and shut him up, and set a seal upon him, that he should deceive the nations no more, until the thousand years are fulfilled: and after that he must be loosed for a short season. 4 And I saw thrones, and they sat upon them, and judgment was given to them: and I saw the beings of them that were beheaded for the witness of יהושע, and for the word of יהוה, and who had not worshipped the beast, or his image, neither had received his mark upon their foreheads, or in their hands; and they lived and reigned with Moshiach a thousand years. 5 This is the first resurrection. (But the rest of the dead lived not again until the thousand years were finished.) 6 Blessed and set-apart is he that has part in the first resurrection: on such the second death has no power, but they shall be kohanim of יהוה and of Moshiach and shall reign with Him a thousand years. 7 And when the thousand years are expired, s.a.tan shall be loosed out of his prison, 8 And shall go out to deceive the nations who are in the four quarters of

the olam, Gog and Magog, to gather them together to battle: the number of whom is as the sand of the sea. 9 And they came over the entire width of the olam, and surrounded the camp of the kidushim, and the beloved city:[2] and fire came down from יהוה out of the shamayim, and devoured them. 10 And s.a.tan that deceived them was cast into the Lake of Fire and brimstone, where the beast and the navi sheker are, and shall be tormented day and night le-olam-va-ed.[3] 11 And I saw a great white throne, and Him that sat on it, from whose face the olam and the shamayim fled away; and there was found no place for them. 12 And I saw the dead, small and great, stand before יהוה; and the scrolls were opened: and another scroll was opened, which is the Scroll of Chayim: and the dead were judged out of those things which were written in the scrolls, according to their own mitzvot.[4] 13 And the sea gave up the dead that were in it; and death and the grave delivered up the dead that were in them: and they were judged every man according to their own mitzvot.[5] 14 And death and the grave were cast into the Lake of Fire. This is the second death. 15 And whoever was not found written in the Scroll of Chayim was cast into the Lake of Fire.

21 And I saw a renewed shamayim and a renewed olam: for the first shamayim and the first olam had passed away; and there was no more sea. 2 And I Yochanan saw the set-apart city, the renewed Yahrushalayim, coming down

---

[1] Of those who were taken away.

[2] Yahrushalayim. Notice that the set-apart ones are citizens in Yisrael and thus must be Yisrael.
[3] Unclean spirit beings suffer forever since they have immortality within them. Human beings who reject the besarot also go to the Lake of Fire to die a second death, since they have no immortality within them to withstand and survive the Lake of Fire.
[4] The White Throne Judgment is for the lost. It is not a second opportunity. Having understood that, the reason that the scrolls are still opened, is to show mankind why YHWH is doing what He is about to do, even though He answers to no man. However, His justice demands that He shows His reasoning. Nevertheless, those who have never truly heard the besarot of Yahshua, but rather a cheap lawless imitation, will in fact have their works looked at carefully and fairly before YHWH makes a final judgment.
[5] See footnote for Revelation 20:12.

from יהוה out of the shamayim, prepared as a bride adorned for her husband. 3 And I heard a great voice out of the shamayim saying, See, the Sukkah of יהוה is with men, and He will dwell with them, and they shall be His people and יהוה Himself shall be with them, and be their Elohim. 4 And יהוה shall wipe away all tears from their eyes; and there shall be no more death, neither sorrow, nor crying, neither shall there be any more pain: for the former things have passed away. 5 And He that sat upon the throne said, *See, I make all things renewed.* And He said to me, *Write: for these words are emet and faithful.* 6 And He said to me, *Kalah. I am Aleph and Taf, the Beginning and the End. I will give to him that is thirsty of the fountain of the mayim chayim freely.* 7 *He that yis-ra-els shall inherit all things; and I will be his Elohim, and He shall be My son.* 8 *But the fearful and unbelieving and the abominable and murderers and those who whore and sorcerers and idolaters and all liars shall have their part in the lake which burns with fire and brimstone: this is the second death.* 9 And there came to me one of the seven heavenly messengers who had the seven vials full of the seven last plagues and talked with me, saying, Come here, I will show you the bride, the Lamb's wife. 10 And he carried me away in the Ruach to a great high mountain, and showed me that great city, the set-apart Yahrushalayim, descending out of the shamayim from יהוה, 11 Having the tifereth of יהוה: and its light was like a stone most precious, even like a jasper stone, clear as crystal; 12 And had a great and high wall, and had twelve gates, and at the gates twelve heavenly messengers, and names written on the gates, which are the names of the twelve tribes of the children of Yisrael:[1] 13 On the east

three gates; on the north three gates; on the south three gates; and on the west three gates. 14 And the wall of the city had twelve foundations, and in them the names of the twelve shlichim of the Lamb. 15 And he that talked with me had a golden reed to measure the city, and its gates, and its walls. 16 And the city lies foursquare and the length is as large as the width: and he measured the city with the reed, twelve thousand furlongs. The length and the breadth and the height of it are equal. 17 And he measured its wall, a hundred forty four cubits, according to the measure of the man, that is, of the heavenly messenger. 18 And the building of the wall of it was of jasper: and the city was pure gold, like clear glass. 19 And the foundations of the wall of the city were garnished with all manner of precious stones. The first foundation was jasper; the second, sapphire; the third, agate; the fourth, emerald; 20 The fifth, sardonyx; the sixth, ruby; the seventh, chrysolite; the eighth, beryl; the ninth, topaz; the tenth, chrysoprase; the eleventh, jacinth; the twelfth, amethyst. 21 And the twelve gates were twelve pearls; every gate was one pearl:[2] and the street of the city was pure gold, as if it were transparent glass. 22 And I saw no Sukkah in it: for the Master יהוה El-Shaddai and the Lamb are the Sukkah of it. 23 And the city had no need of the sun, neither of the moon, to shine in it: for the tifereth of יהוה did brighten it, and the Lamb is the Light of it. 24 And the nations of those that are saved shall walk in the Light of it: and the melechim of the olam do bring their tifereth and honor into it. 25 And the gates of it shall not be shut at all by day: for there shall be no night there. 26 And they shall bring the tifereth and honor of the nations into it. 27 And there shall by no means enter into it anyone that is unclean, or whoever works abomination,

---

[1] The New Yahrushalyaim is the eternal home of all believers in Moshiach. But there are only twelve gates for all twelve tribes of Yisrael. There is no gate for gentiles, or Christians, or Yahudim, and neither is there any other entry. Only dom-washed Yisraelites get into their promised eternal home. If you are a born-again believer, you must be a Yisraelite, as you will be entering through one of those twelve gates.

[2] The pearl of great price that Yahshua spoke of in Matthew 13 is a parable of the 12 separate pearly gates to the Renewed Yahrushalayim. By purchasing all those gates He allowed all Yisrael to enter their eternal home.

and or makes up lies: but only those who are written in the Lamb's Scroll of Chayim.

22 And he showed me a pure river of mayim chayim, clear as crystal, proceeding out of the throne of יהוה and of the Lamb. 2 In the midst of its street, on either side of the river, there was an eytz-chaim, that bore twelve kinds of fruits, and yielded their fruit every month: and the leaves of the tree were for the healing of the nations.[1] [2] 3 And there shall be no more curse: but the throne of the Master יהוה and of the Lamb shall be in it; and His avadim shall serve Him: 4 And they shall see His face; and His Name shall be in their foreheads.[3] 5 And there shall be no night there; and they need no candle, neither light of the sun; for יהוה-Elohim gives them light: and they shall rein le-olam-va-ed. 6 And he said to me, These sayings are faithful and emet: and יהוה Elohim of the set-apart niviim sent His heavenly Malach-יהוה to show to His avadim the things that must shortly be done. 7 *See, I come quickly: blessed is he that guards the sayings of the prophecy of this scroll.* 8 And I, Yochanan, saw these things, and heard them. And when I had heard and seen them, I fell down to worship before the feet of the Malach-יהוה who showed me these things.[4] 9 Then He said to me, *See that you do it not: for I am your fellow Eved, and of your brothers the niviim, and from them who shomer the sayings of this scroll: worship* יהוה.[5]

10 And He said to me, *Seal not the sayings of the prophecy of this scroll: for the time is at hand.*[6] 11 *He that is unjust, let him be unjust still: and he which is filthy, let him be filthy still: and he that is a tzadik, let him be a tzadik still: and he that is set-apart, let him be set-apart still. 12 And, see, I come quickly; and My reward is with Me, to give every man according to his mitzvot.*[7] 13 *I am Aleph and Taf, the Beginning and the End, the First and the Last.* 14 Blessed are they that do His commandments that they may have right to the eytz chaim, and may enter in through the gates into the city.[8] 15 For outside are dogs[9] and sorcerers and whores and murderers and idolaters and whoever loves to make lying a way of life. 16 *I יהושע have sent My heavenly messenger to testify to you these things in the Yisraelite congregations. I am the Root and the Offspring of David, and the Bright and Morning Cochav.* 17 And the Ruach and the bride of Yisrael say, *Come.* And let him that hears say, *Come.* And let him that is thirsty come. And whoever so desires, let him take the mayim chayim freely. 18 For I testify to every man that hears the words of the prophecy of this scroll, If any man shall add to these things, יהוה shall add to him the plagues that are written in this scroll: 19 And if any man shall take away from the words of the scroll of this prophecy, יהוה shall take away his part out of the Scroll of Chayim, and out of the set-apart city,

---

[1] The twelve fruits during twelve months for the healing of nations, indicates that all nations were composed of twelve tribes of Yisraelites. Moreover, the two trees of life, one on each side, are for the two houses and their ultimate and complete spiritual healing.
[2] Fruit indicates ongoing sustenance; and leaves indicate healing from sin.
[3] When we are all home, everyone will need the true Name to enter and will have it on their foreheads as a reward and seal of who we are. The true Name, therefore, is a not an optional issue in the New Yahrushalayim as well.
[4] The Messenger of YHWH has to be Yahshua, since He is talking in the first person and is the same one who says, "I am coming soon" in verses 7,12 and 13. This no doubt is the same Malach-YHWH that led our people in the wilderness for 40 years. Yahshua is not an angel, but is known as The Messenger, or Malach of His Presence, or the visible "lesser YHWH."
[5] Yahshua here tells John not to worship Him, but to redirect it to His Abba-YHWH. He accepts initial worship, but then is

under oath to redirect it to His Father. This confirms what He taught us in Matthew 6:9 in the true kadesh of praise.
[6] He reverses the admonition of Daniel 12:4, where Daniel is told to seal the visions.
[7] Performed as believers and disciples.
[8] Keeping Torah is a requirement to kingdom entry.
[9] A reference to gentiles who are kept out of the city, while Yisraelites are in the city.

and from the things that are written in this scroll.[1] 20 He who testifies of these things says, *Surely I come quickly.* Amein. Even so, come, Master יהושע.

21 The unmerited favor of our Master יהושע the Moshiach be with all the kidushim. Amein.

Am Yisrael Chai Forever in The Renewed Yahrushalayim

---

[1] This is a warning to those in the first century, working from the original inspired scrolls in Hebrew, Aramaic, Chaldean or Greek, not to make changes. Those scrolls did exist in the first century and those scribes are the ones that had the temptation to change the original autograph manuscripts. This sin cannot be committed today, since the originals are no longer available. This warning is not referring to later translators, who may have used an English-based text to translate again, or may have had to add such things as definite articles, adjectives, or other such methods as word reversal, in order to allow the translation to flow freely.

The Restoration Scriptures
True
Name Edition

Glossary

Definitions and explanations are provided below for selected words that appear in the text in Hebrew (H), Aramaic (A), Greek (G), Chaldean (C), or (P) for Persian

Abba (H)	Father YHWH
Acharit Hayamim (H)	Latter-Days
Achashverosh (H)	Ahasuerus the Persian King
Achor (H)	Trouble
Aden (H)	Eden
Adon (H)	Master
Adon Adonim (H)	Master of all Masters
Adonai (H)	Master
Aharon (H)	Aaron
Ahava (H)	Love
Ahavta Re'echa Camocha (H)	Love your neighbor as yourself
Ahvot or Avot (H)	Fathers
Akrobustia (G)	The previously circumcised Ephraimites, or those who counted their covenant circumcision as something to be tossed away and not treasured. They became reckoned by the Jews as those who behaved like the uncircumcised, and thus the usage of this special term of designation.
Al Tereh (H)	Fear Not
Alef-Taf (H)	First and last letters of Hebrew alphabet. Used to describe the Father-YHWH and YHWH-Yahshua
Aleph (H)	First letter in the Hebrew alphabet

I

Aliyah (H)	Return to the land of Yisrael, or to go up in an upward direction
Almah (H)	Virgin
Am (H)	Nation or People
Am Ha-Aretz (H)	Common or unlearned people
Am Rav (H)	A great or huge nation
Amein (H)	"So let it be" or "truly it is"; Amen
Ami (H)	My people
Amorah (H)	Gomorrah
Anakim (H)	Giants
Aram (H)	The Arameans
Aretz (H)	Earth, or Land of Yisrael
Artahshashta (P)	Artaxerxes King of Persia
Asham (H)	Sacrificial guilt offering
Asher (H)	Asher
Asherim or Asherahot (H)	Pagan groves of worship
Ashshur or Ashur (H)	Assyria
Ashurim (H)	Assyrians
Atah (H)	You
Atid Lavoh (H)	Millennium or Messianic Age
Avadim (H)	Servants or slaves
Avot or Ahvot(H)	Fathers
Avram (H)	Abraham
Azazel (H)	The Yom Kippur scapegoat
B'nai (H)	Children or Sons
B'nai Brit (H)	Children of the Covenant
B'nai Elohim (H)	Children of Elohim
B'nai Yisrael (H)	Children of Yisrael
B'nai-Brit (H)	Children of the Covenant
Ba'ali (H)	My lord
Baal (H)	The lord, or any lord other than YHWH
Baalah (A) (H)	Husband
Bachor or Bechor (H)	Firstborn
Bachorati (H)	My Birthright
Bala (H)	Swallow or consume
Bar (A)	Son
Bar Elohim (A & H)	Son of Elohim
Bar Enosh (A)	Son of Man
Bar Mitzvah (A) (H)	13-year-old male child of the covenant. A passage to manhood.
Bara (H)	Created from nothing

Barchu (H)	Blessed Are You
Barchu-Et (H)	Bless The
Barchu-Et-Shem-יהוה (H)	Bless The Name of YHWH
Bar-Navah (A)	Barnabas
Baruch Haba Beshem (H)	Blessed is He that comes in The Name of
Baruch Shemo (H)	Bless His Name
Basar-Echad (H)	One Flesh
Bat (H)	Daughter
Bat Kol (H)	Heavenly Voice of YHWH
Bavel (H)	Babylon or confusion
Bayit (H)	House
Baytim or Batyim or Bayitim (H)	Houses or homes (plural)
Bechor (H)	See "Bachor."
Bechorot (H)	Firstlings
Beit (H)	House
Beit Ahav (H)	House of Ahab
Beit David (H)	House of David
Beit Ephraim (H)	House of Ephraim
Beit HaMikdash (H)	YHWH's Temple on Mt. Moriah
Beit Tefillah (H)	House of Prayer
Beit Yaakov (H)	House of Jacob
Beit Yahudah (H)	House of Judah
Beit Yisrael (H)	House of Israel
Beit Yoseph (H)	House of Joseph
Belial (H)	s.a.tan
Bema Seat (H)	Judgment Seat
Ben (H)	Son
Ben David (H)	Son of David
Ben Emunah (H)	Son in The Faith
Ben-adam or Ben Adam (H)	Son of man pronounced, "Ben ad-am" when referring to someone other than Yahshua. "Ben Adam" when referring to Yahshua the Moshiach
Benyamin or Binyamin (H)	Benjamin
Berchati (H)	My Blessing
Beresheeth or Bereshet (H)	In the Beginning; or Scroll of Genesis
Besarot (H)	Good News
Besorah (H)	Gospel or Good News
Bet (H)	House, or second letter of Hebrew alphabet

Bet Din (H)	Torah Court of Law, or House of Judgment
Bet Ephraim (H)	House of Ephraim
Betachon (H)	Security or Safety
Beth Chesed (H)	House of Mercy
Beth-Lechem (H)	Bethlehem, or House of Bread
Betulah (H & A)	Young Woman or Maiden
Beulah (H)	Married
Be-Yachad (H)	As One, or In Common
Bikkurim (H)	Firstfruit Offering
Bilashon (H)	In the language
Biliyaal (H)	See "Belial."
Biliyaal or Belial (H)	s.a.tan
Binah (H)	Understanding
Binyamin (H)	See "Benyamin."
Birchat HaMinim (H)	Curse on the Nazarenes by traditional Jews in the Prayer Book
Bracha (H)	Blessing
Brachot (H)	Blessings
Brit Am (H)	Covenant People, or Covenant of the people
Brit Chadasha (H)	New or Renewed Covenant, or New Testament
Brit Halev (H)	Circumcision of the Heart
Brit Milah (H)	Circumcision
Bubbe Mysehs (H)	Fairy Tales, or Old Wives Tales
Chag (Singular) or Chagim (plural) (H)	Feast of Rejoicing; Indicates one or more of the three Ascension Feasts: Unleavened Bread, Pentecost and Tabernacles
Chag HaSukkot or Chag Sukkot (H)	Feast of Tabernacles
Chag Matzot (H)	Feast of Unleavened Bread
Chag Shavout (H)	Pentecost
Chai (H)	Life or 18 years of age depending on context
Chamas (H)	Violence
Chametz (H)	Leaven
Chananyah (H)	Ananais
Channah (H)	Hannah
Chanoch (H)	Enoch
Chatsrot (H)	Twin Silver Trumpets
Chava (H)	Eve
Chaver (H)	Friend or Sharer
Chaverim (H)	Friends or Companions
Chavurah (H)	Fellowship or Fellowship Time

Chayay Olam or Chayim Olam (H)	Eternal Life
Chayim (H)	Life
Chesed (H)	Kindness or Goodness
Chilul Hashem (H)	Desecration of the Name of YHWH by voiding it or misusing it.
Chochav (H)	Star
Chochavim (H)	Stars
Chochmah (H)	Wisdom
Chodashim (H)	Months
Chol-Ha-Moed (H)	Days that are Moadim but not Annual Shabbats or set-apart convocations.
Choresh (H)	Forest
Chuk (H)	An ordinance of Torah not fully logical or understood, yet fully and eternally binding
Chukim (H)	Statutes or ordinances (plural form of "Chuk")
Cubit (H)	About 18 inches or 1.5 feet
Cup of Geulah (H)	Cup of Redemption; the third of four Passover cups. The Master's cup of memorial blood
Da'at (H)	Knowledge
Dameshek (H)	Damascus
Dan (H)	Dan
Dareyawesh (P)	King Darius the Mede
Derech (H)	Way, or road, or path
Devar YHWH (H)	Word of YHWH
Divre HaYamim (H)	Chronicles
Dom (H)	Blood; Pronounced Dah-hm
Drash (H)	Allegoric level of Hebraic understanding
DSS (H)	Dead Sea Scrolls
Ecclesia (G)	See "Ekklesia."
Echad (H)	One, or Oneness, or Unity, or Compound Unity
Ed (H)	Witness
Edah (H)	Congregation
Edot (H)	Congregations
Egle (H)	Bull. The tribal banner of Ephraim Yisrael
Ekklesia or Ecclesia (G)	Congregation or Synagogue
El (H)	Single form of "Elohim"
El-Azar (H)	See "Eliezer."
El-Elohe-Yisrael (H)	Elohim the El of Yisrael
El-Elyon (H)	Most High
Eliezer or El-Azar (H)	Eliezer (son of Aaron the High Priest)
Elisheva (H)	Elizabeth

Eliyhau (H)	Elijah
Eloah (A)	Elohim in Aramaic
Elohim (H)	Title for YHWH; often used either for YWHH or in conjunction with the personal proper Name YHWH
El-Olam (H)	Master of the universe or world
El-Roi (H)	El My Shepherd, or El who shepherds
El-Shaddai (H)	Most High El, or El of over all shads or demons
Ema (H)	See "Ima."
Emanu-el (H)	El with us
Emet (H)	True, or truth, or truthful
Emot (H)	Mothers
Emot (H)	See "Imot."
Emunah (H)	Emunah or Faith
Epaph (H)	Unit of dry measure equal to about one bushel or about 33 litres, or a dry measure of about 64 US pints.
Ephod (H)	Shoulder garment worn by the High Priest
Ephraim (H)	Ephraim
Eretz Acherit (H)	Another Land or New World
Erom (A)	Edom
Et (H)	The
Et Borecha (H)	Literally: "your Creators"
Eu Sebio or Saveo (G)	Shabbat-guarding piety
Eved (H)	Servant or Slave
Eytz Chaim (H)	Tree of Life
Eytzim (H)	Trees (plural)
Gad (H)	Gad
Gadar-Peretz (H)	Restorer of the breach
Galil (H)	Area of Galilee or Sea of Galilee
Galut (H)	Exile or Diaspora
Galutyah (H)	Exiles of Yah
Gan (H)	Garden
Gan-Aden (H)	Paradise or Garden of Eden
Gat Sh'manim (H)	Gethsemane
Gavriel (H)	Gabriel the heavenly messenger
Gei-Hinnom (H)	Hell, or a valley of garbage-dumping outside ancient Jerusalem
Gematria (H)	Numerical value of Hebrew letters used to discover secrets about YHWH.
Ger (H)	Sojourner, or stranger, or convert to a form of Judaism
Gerim (H)	Plural for strangers, sojourners, or converts to a form of Judaism.

Get (H)	Certificate of Divorce
Gilah (H)	Rejoice
Gilgal from Gilgul (H)	Roll away, or revolving
Goalecha (H)	Your Redeemer or Redeemers
Golyath (H)	Goliath the giant
Gooff (H)	Physical Body
Gowra (A)	Guardian or Legal Guardian
Goy; Goyim (H)	Nation (as applied to either Yisrael or the gentiles depending on context). Also: an individual not born in Yisrael.
Ha (H)	Definite article: "The"
Ha Levi (H)	The Levite
Ha Moshiach (H)	The Moshiach
Ha navi or ha navi (H)	The or a prophet; not speaking of Yahshua
HaAdon (H)	The Master
Hacal-Dama (H)	Field of Dom
Haftarah (H)	Weekly portion from the Prophets read in the Shabbat service
Halacha (H)	Way, or way to walk or conduct one's life
Halachot (H)	Plural form of "Halacha"
Hallel (H)	Praise
Hallelu or Hallelu-et (H)	Praise to; or praise the
Hamas (H)	Violence
HaMitikun (H)	The Restoration
HaNavi (H)	The Prophet; speaking only of Yahshua
Har (H)	Mountain, mount, or hill
Har HaBayit (H)	Mountain of the House (Temple)
Har HaZaytim (H)	Mount of Olives
Har Tzion (H)	Mt. Zion
Har-Kadosh (H)	Set-Apart Mountain
Havdallah (H)	Closing service for Shabbat night
Heilel (H)	s.a.tan
Hekel (H)	Temple or Set-Apart Place in front of the Holy of Holies
He-Nayni or Henanei (H)	See "Hinayni."
Hephzi-nah (H)	Delight in her
Higayon (H)	Meditation or "to meditate"
Hinai Ma-Tov Uma-Nayim Shevet Aachim Gam Yachad (H)	See, how tov and how pleasant it is for brothers to dwell together in unity.

Hinayni or Hinani or He-Nayni or Hcnanei (H)	"Here am I," or "Here I am"
Hodu (H)	Give Thanks
Hoshianna (H)	Hosanna or Save Now
Ichavod (H)	The presence and beauty of YHWH has departed
Ima or Ema (H)	Mother
Imot or Emot (H)	Mothers
Ish (H)	Man
Isha (H)	Woman
Ivrim (H)	Hebrews (plural)
Ivri (H)	A Hebrew person
Ivrit (H)	The Hebrew language
Iyov (H)	Job
Kadesh (A)	Liturgical Prayer of praise in Matthew 6 and of the traditional Synagogue funeral service
Kadosh HaKedoshim (H)	Most Set-Apart Place or Holy of Holies
Kadosh Le-YHWH (H)	Set-Apart to YHWH
Kadosh or Kodesh (H)	Set-Apart
Kadosh or Kodesh Le (H)	Set-Apart to
Kadosh Shemecha (H)	Set-Apart is Your Name; hallowed is Your Name
Kadosh-One (H)	Set-Apart-One referring to Yahshua-YHWH or Father-YHWH
Kahal (H)	Congregation or Assembly
Kahal Gadol (H)	Large or great congregation or assembly
Kal va Chomer (H)	Principle of Hebraic interpretation that seeks the greater or weightier issue, when two commandments seem to contradict
Kala or Kalah (H)	Bride or Finished; as in "It is done"
Kanaan (H)	Land of Canaan
Kanaanite (H)	Canaanite
Karsavan (A)	Thrones (in plural form)
Kashrut (H)	Kosher laws of YHWH and the corresponding lifestyle
Kata (G)	Hanging facial veil
Katav (H)	"The" or "a" Scripture, as in a "single verse"
Kavod (H)	Esteem
Ke Etsem Ha Shamayim (H)	The body or bone of Heaven
Ke Le-Olam-Chasdo (H)	His Kindness is Everlasting

Ke Tov (H)	For He is good
Kedoshecha (H)	Your Set-Apart One
Kelalot (H)	Curses
Ken (H)	Yes or for sure
Kepha (H)	Peter
Keporah (H)	Dom Atonement
Kesay (H)	Throne or Seat of Authority
Ketarim (H)	Crowns
Keter (H)	Crown
Ketuvim or Kituvim(H)	Writings (i.e., those portions of the Tanach other than the Torah and neviim); or the Scriptures as a whole (in plural form)
Kevutz Galyut (H)	Ingathering of the Exiles
Kiddish (H)	Cup of Blessing and Separation
Kiddushat HaShem H)	The sanctification of the Name
Kidushim (H)	Saints
Kilayaim (H)	Torah command prohibiting mixing of seeds
Kiporah or Keporah(H)	Atonement or sin covering
Koach (H)	Strength or power
Kochav (H)	Star
Kochavim (H)	Stars
Kodesh (H)	See "Kadosh"
Kohanim (H)	Priests
Kohanim Gedolim (H)	High Priests
Kohanim HaGadolim (H)	The High Priests (plural)
Kohen (H)	Priest
Kohen HaGadol (H)	High Priest
Kol (H)	Voice or All
Kol Bet Yisrael (H)	All the House Of Israel
Kol Echad (H)	One voice
Kol Ha-Am (H)	All the people
Kol Shofar (H)	Voice of the Shofar
Koresh (H)	Cyrus
Kruvat (H)	An offered near event or thing
Kush (H)	Ethiopia
Kushite (H)	Person of color or Ethiopian
Lashon Hara (H)	Evil speaking, gossip or slander
Lashuv (H)	To return again
Lechayim (H)	To life or "long life"
Lechem (H)	Bread

Lechem Ha Panayim or Lechem HaPanayim (H)	Bread of The Faces, or Showbread in the ancient temple.
Le-Marbe (H)	To increase
Le-Olam-Va-Ed (H)	Forever; for eternity
Lev (H)	Heart
Lev Echad (H)	One heart, or one purpose
Levanon (H)	Lebanon
Levi (H)	Levi or tribe of Levi
Leviim (H)	Levites (plural)
Levim (H)	Hearts (plural)
Lo (H)	No
Lo-Ami (H)	Not My People
Lo-Ruchama (H)	No Compassion
LXX (G)	Septuagint (the Greek translation of the Hebrew Tanach, done circa 150 BCE)
Ma'aleh (H)	Filled
Ma'aseh (H)	Acts or works of
Ma'aseh Mirkavah (H)	Workings of the Chariot; official name for Ezekiel chapter one.
Ma'aser (H)	Tithe or Tithes or 10 %
Maariv or Ma'ariv (H)	Early Evening Prayer
Makom Kadosh (H)	Set-Apart Place
Malach (H)	Heavenly messenger or The Messenger; when referring to Yahshua
Malach-YHWH (H)	Messenger of YHWH or Yahshua
Malcha or Malka (H)	Queen
Malchut (H)	Kingdom, or The Kingdom
Malchut HaShamayim (H)	Kingdom of Heaven or the Heavens
Malchutim (H)	Kingdoms (plural)
Malki-Tzedek (H)	Melchesidek
Malkosh (H)	Latter rain or kingdom rain
Manna (H)	Wafers of honey, or the wilderness food of Yisrael. Literally: "What is this?"
Marah (H)	Bitter
Mar-Yah (A)	Aramaic for Master or Master-Yah
Matbeel (H)	Baptist
Mattityahu (H)	Matthew
Matzah (H)	Unleavened Bread
Matzoth (H)	Chag Matzoth, or Unleavened Bread, or plural form for matzah

Mayim (H)	Water or waters
Me-Camocha (H)	Who is like you?
MeChayai HaMaytiim (H)	Resurrection of the dead as a reality, hope, or doctrine
Melachim (H)	Angels or Heavenly Messengers
Melech (H)	King
Melech HaMelechim (H)	Kings of all Kings
Melechim (H)	Kings (plural)
Melech-Tzadik (H)	Malchitzedek or King of Righteousness
Melo Hagoyim (H)	Fullness of the gentiles
Mem (H)	Hebrew Letter
Menashsheh (H)	Manasseh
Menorah (H)	Seven-branched candleholder as used in the ancient temple
Menorot (H)	Seven-branched candleholders (plural)
Meshecho (H)	His Moshiach
Meshugas (H)	Crazy
Meshugoyim (H)	Lunatics or crazies (plural)
Metatron (A)	Guardian; The Guardian of Yisrael or Yahshua
Mezuzah or Mezuzot (H)	Scripture portions in a case posted on the doorposts
Mia-Ton-Sabbaton (G)	One of the Shabbats
Midrashed (H)	Discussed Scripture or theology openly
Mikvah (H)	Baptism, water immersion-purification, to baptize, to immerse
Mincha (H)	Afternoon prayer
Miqra Kedoshim (H)	Set-Apart assemblies or gatherings (Plural)
Miqra Kodesh or Miqra Qodesh(H)	Set-Apart gathering of believers ordered by Torah
Mirkavot (H)	Chariots (plural)
Miryam (H)	Mary
Mishle (H)	Proverbs or Proverb
Mishle Emet (H)	True Proverb
Mishpachot (H)	Families or tribes
Mishpat (H)	Judgment or right ruling
Mishpat Bachor (H)	Firstborn rights
Mishpatim (H)	Judgments or Right-Rulings that make perfect sense
Mishpocha (H)	Family
Mitzrayim (H)	Egypt
Mitzrites (H)	Egyptians

Mitzvah (H)	Single Commandment or Obedient Act, or command (verb)
Mitzvot or Mitzvoth (H)	YHWH's Commandments or man's obedient deeds, or obedient works of Torah done in complete submission and willingness
Mizmor (H)	Individual Psalm from The Book of Psalms
Moadim (H)	Appointed times, eternal feasts of YHWH (plural)
Moed (H)	Feast, appointed time
Moreh (H)	Teacher
Morim (H)	Teachers (plural)
Moshe (H)	Moses
Moshe Rabainu (H)	Moses Our Teacher, Moses Our Rabbi
Moshiach (H)	The Messiah or The Anointed One
Motzei Shabbat (H)	Sundown on Shabbat
Nachas (H)	Intense joy
Nakdimon (H)	Nicodemous
Naphtali (H)	Naphtali
Natzareth (H)	Nazereth
Navi (H)	Prophet
Navi Sheker (H)	The False Prophet of Revelation
Naviyah (H)	See "Neviyah."
Neir Tamid (H)	Eternal flame in front of Holy of Holies
Nekudah (H)	Point mark, such as a period
Nephesh (H)	Soul
Nephilim (H)	Giants before the Flood
Neshalem (H)	Peace to the bride or a finished action
Ness (H)	Individual miracle
Nethinim (H)	Singers-musicians
Netzarim (H)	Believers in Yahshua who keep Torah. Literally means "branches."
Neviim or Nevim (H)	Prophets (plural)
Neviyah or Naviyah (H)	Prophetess
Niddah or Nadah (H)	Period of menstruation; used in symbolic terms, as well, to portray uncleanness
Nigzar (H)	Cut off
Nisim (H)	Miracles (plural)
Nissi (H)	Banner
Nivrechu (H)	Mixed or intermingled
Noach (H)	Noah
Nokri (H)	Foreign or strange, as in foreign vine
Nomos (G)	Law or statutes

Notsrei Yisrael (H)	Nazarene Yisrael, or Preserved Ones
Notsrim (H)	Believers in Yahshua who keep Torah; Nazarenes
Oikodomeo (G)	Rebuild
Olam (H)	World or Earth
Olam Haba (H)	World or age to come; the reward of the redeemed
Olam Hazeh (H)	This age or world
Olamim (H)	Ages
Omer (H)	The standard measurement for food in Torah; About 2.5 lbs. About 1/10 of an ephah which is about 6.4 pints.
Oy (H)	A loud sigh
Panayim-El-Panayim (H)	Face to Face
PaRDeS (H)	Four levels of understanding Scripture (from most basic to deepest): Pashat (simple), Remez (hint), Drash (parables, riddles and allegories), and Sod (esoteric, mysterious level).
Parsha or Parashot (H)	Torah Portion; the name of the portion is based on the first few words in Hebrew in the first sentence of the Torah-reading portion. There are 52 Parshas, one for each of 52 Shabbats in the year.
Parthenos (G)	Virgin
Pashat (H)	Literal Level of Hebraic understanding
Pehter (H) or Peter (G)	As a proper noun, a name; but also a verb, meaning "to open" (as in the opening of a womb)
Pe-ot (H)	Long Sideburns, or Side Locks worn by male Torah-keepers
Pesach (H)	Passover
Peshitta (A)	Aramaic plain and preserved text of the east; the probable original language of the Renewed Covenant documents
Peter (G)	See "Pehter."
Pinchus or Pinchas (H)	Phineus
Prush (H)	Pharisee
Prushim (H)	Pharisees
Qayin (H)	Cain
Qoheleth (H)	Preacher
Racham (H)	Mercy (in singular form)
Rachamim (H)	Mercy or mercies
Rachatz (H)	Hand-washing ceremony during Passover meal
Raphechah or Rophechah (H)	Your healer or healers
Ratzon (H)	Will (as in YHWH's will and purpose)
Rav (H)	Rabbi or teacher

Rav Shaul (H)	Apostle Paul
Regalim (H)	Three ascension or foot feasts to Jerusalem.
Remez (H)	Hint level of Hebraic understanding
Rephaim (H)	Healed resurrected Spirits
Reuven (H)	Reuben
Roei (H)	Shepherd
Roei-HaGadol (H)	Chief Shepherd
Rohim (H)	Shepherds
Romiyah (H)	Rome
Roni (H)	Rejoice
Roni Bat Tzion (H)	Shout for joy daughter of Zion
Rosh Chodashim (H)	New Moons or new months
Rosh Pina (H)	Cornerstone
Ruach (H)	Spirit of Man or Beast
Ruach HaKodesh (H)	Set-Apart Spirit
Ruachim (H)	Spirits
Ruchama (H)	Compassion
s.a.tan (H)	Satan
Sanhedrin (H)	Ruling council of 70 elders in Jerusalem
Sar (H)	Prince or Ruler (Moshiach) or lower level prince
Schlichim or Shlichim (H)	Apostles, messengers, sent ones from YHWH
Schmuel (H)	Samuel
Seah (H)	Grain measurement
Sedom (H)	City of Sodom
Sefer HaChayim (H)	Book or Scroll of Life
Sefirot (H)	Manifestations of YHWH
Selah (H)	Pause and think about It
Sepharad (H)	Spain
Seraphim (H)	Heavenly Messengers
Shaalu Shalom (H)	Pray or ask for the peace
Shaar Yahshuv (H)	Isaiah's son
Shaarai Mavet (H)	Gates of death
Shabbat (H)	Sabbath Day
Shabbat-Shabbaton (H)	A Day of Rest; and a term used for certain ordained days of rest, such as the Day of Atonement
Shachrit or Shacrit (H)	Morning Prayer
Shad (H)	Demon or unclean spirit
Shadim (H)	Demons or unclean spirits (plural)
Shalom (H)	Peace
Shalom Alaichem (H)	Peace be to you

Shalom VeBetachon (H)	Peace and safety
Shalosh Regallim (H)	Three ascension feasts or literally foot festivals
Shamashim (H)	Local elders in a congregation (plural)
Shamayim (H)	The Heavens (singular and plural)
Shamesh (H)	Elder
Shatnetz (H)	A forbidden mixture of wool and cotton
Shavuot (H)	Feast of Weeks; Pentecost
Shechinah (H)	The Divine Presence
Shem Tov (H)	A Middle Ages Hebrew version of the book of Matthew translated from the Greek
Shema (H)	Hear or Listen
Shemesh (H)	Sun
Shemot (H)	Names
Sheol (H)	Grave or Pit
Sheva Yamim (H)	Seven days
Shevet (H)	Scepter
Shimeon (H)	Simeon
Shir (H)	Sing or Song
Shir HaShirim (H)	Song of Songs
Shirim (H)	Songs (plural)
Shiva (H)	Tradition (among traditional Jews) of mourning for seven days
Shivlai HaMoshiach H)	Birth Pains of The Moshiach, or another description of the Great Tribulation
Shlomo (H)	Solomon
Shmecha (H)	Your Name
Shmetah or Shmetha (H)	Seventh-year land Shabbat of release
Shmonai Esreh (H)	The Liturgical Piece of 18 benedictions that included the curse on the Nazarenes; still used today without the curse in modern Judaism
Shnai Machanot (H)	Two camps or companies
Shochet (H)	Ritual slaughterer of Kosher meat; a certified slaughterer
Shofar (H)	Ram's Horn
Sholiach (H)	Emissary or Apostle
Sholiachship (H)	Office of Sholiach
Shomer (H)	Watch, keep, observe, or guard
Shomerim or Shomrim (H)	Watchmen
Shomron (H)	Samaria

Shophet (H)	Judge, or to Judge
Shophtim (H)	Judges
Shuv (H)	Return
Siddur (H)	Prayer Book
Simcha (H)	Joy or Happiness
Sitrah Hora (H)	Other side, or dark underworld of spirits
Sod (H)	Mystical esoteric or secret level of Hebraic understanding
Sopher (H)	Scribe
Sophrim (H)	Scribes
Sperma (G)	Human seed or seed of fruit
Succoth (H)	See "Sukkot."
Sukkah (H)	Tabernacle or booth
Sukkot or Succoth or Sukkoth (H)	Feast of Tabernacles or Booths
Taf (H)	Last letter in the Hebrew alphabet
Tahor (H)	Pure
Tallit (H)	Prayer shawl
Talmid (H)	Student or disciple
Talmida (H)	Female student or disciple
Talmidim (H)	Disciples, students, or followers
Tanach (H)	Acronym for the "First Covenant" formed by: **T**orah (Law), **N**eviim (Prophets), and **K**ituvim (Writings)
Taraa (A)	Tutors
Tarea (A)	Door
Tartaros (G)	A special place of imprisoned spirits at the time of the flood and for the fallen angels of the flood
Tavah (H)	Ark of Noah
Techelet (H)	Cord of blue on the fringes
Tefillah (H)	Prayer (singular)
Tefillin (H)	Head and arm phylacteries
Tefillot (H)	Prayers (plural)
Tehilla (H)	Praise
Tehillim (H)	Praises or Book of Psalms
Tehilot (H)	Praises (plural)
Tekiyah (H)	Shout of a trumpet, long shofar blast, or shout
Tekiyah-Ge-Dolah (H)	Loud and long shofar blast
Teleo (G)	Goal or finished
Telestai (G)	Accomplished or finished
Terumah (H)	Free-will offering
Teshuvah (H)	Repentance or turning back

Tetragrammaton (G)	The four letters forming the divine Name YHWH
The Shema (H)	Deuteronomy 6:4
Tifereth or Tiferet (H)	Beauty, Glory
Tikvah (H)	Hope, expectation, baptism (depending on context)
Todah (H)	Thank you, thanks
Torah (H)	Instruction found in the Five Books of Moses, or instructions of Moses; mistranslated as "Law"
Torot (H)	Plural of Torah
Tov (H)	Good
Tsad HaYamin (H)	Right side
Tsemach (H)	Branch
Tsephanyah (H)	Stephen
Tsor (H)	Tyre
Tzadik (H)	A righteous man, woman or person
Tzadik Mishpat (H)	Righteous judgment or sentence
Tzadik Shophet (H)	Righteous judge
Tzadikim (H)	Righteous ones or persons
Tzaduk (H)	Sadducee
Tzadukim (H)	Sadducees
Tzarephath (H)	France
Tzedakah (H)	Righteousness or charity
Tzevaot (H)	Hosts
Tzevaoth (H)	Hosts
Tzitzit (H)	Fringes
Tzitziyot (H)	Fringes (plural)
Tziyon (H)	Zion
Urah-Vetzeah (H)	Rise and come out
Uzuvah (H)	Forsaken
Vayhee Beensoah HaAron (H)	Synagogue liturgy piece during removal of Torah from the ark; taken from Torah
Yaakov (H)	Jacob or James
Yachad (H)	Together, as in unity or common
Yachid (H)	Absolute unity
Yah (H)	Poetic short form of Yahweh
Yahpha Gate (H)	Beautiful Gate of ancient Temple
Yahrushalayim (H)	Jerusalem
Yahshua (H)	YHWH's only begotten Son; Hebrew Name for Moshiach (meaning "Yah saves" or "Salvation of Yah")
Yahudah (H)	Judah
Yahudi (H)	A Jew
Yahudim (H)	The Jewish People

Yam Suf (H)	Sea of Reeds
Yamim Acharonim (H)	Last Days
Yamim HaAcharonim (H)	The Latter-Days
Yapha (H)	Beautiful
Yapho (H)	City of Joppa
Yarden (H)	Jordan River, or Jordan
Yashar (H)	Straight
Yericho (H)	Jericho
Yeshayahu (H)	Isaiah
Yeshiva (H)	Torah class, school for Torah study
Yeshuat Nefesh (H)	Saving of life; the overriding principle of Torah
Yetzer Harah (H)	Evil nature or inclination in all humanity
Yev-arech-echah (H)	YHWH bless you
YHWH (H)	True Name of the Father
YHWH Nissi (H)	YHWH My Banner
YHWH Tzidkaynu (H)	YHWH Our Righteousness
YHWH-Yireh (H)	YHWH will be seen or YHWH will provide
Yireh-YHWH (H)	Yahweh-fearers or non-Jewish converts in the first century
Yirmeayahu (H)	Jeremiah
Yisrael (H)	Israel (the nation or land or person known as Jacob, depending on context)
Yisraelite (H)	Israelite
Yissacher or Yissaker (H)	Issachar
Yizrael (H)	Jezreal, or the gathering of the scattered seed of Yisrael
Yochanan (H)	John
Yochanan HaMatbeel (H)	John the Baptist
Yom (H)	Day
Yom Chameeshe (H)	Fifth Day
Yom Din or Yom HaDin (H)	Day of Judgment
Yom HaKippurim	Days of Atonement (plural)
Yom Kippur or Yom Ha Kippur (H)	Day Of Atonement
Yom Revee (H)	Fourth Day
Yom Rishon (H)	First day of the week
Yom Shanee (H)	Second Day
Yom Sheshi (H)	Sixth Day

Yom Shleshi or Yom Shlishi (H)	Third day
Yom Teruah (H)	Feast of Trumpets
Yom Tov (H)	Normal holiday that is either Biblical or manmade
Yonah (H)	Dove, or a proper name
Yoseph (H)	YHWH has added or enlarged
Yoseph (H)	Joseph
Yovel (H)	Jubilee or Year of Jubilee
Yud (H)	Smallest Hebrew letter, tenth letter of the Hebrew alphabet
Zachanim or Zechanim (H)	Elders of a nation or a faith
Zacharyah (H)	Zechariah
Zechanim (H)	See "Zachanim."
Zechen or Zachan (H)	Elder of a nation or faith
Zera (H)	Seed, Sperm
Zevulon (H)	Zebulon
Zichnai Yisrael (H)	Elders of Yisrael or of the faith

Bibliography

Ben-Yehuda, Ehud and Weinstein, David, eds. *Ben-Yehuda's English-Hebrew Hebrew-English Dictionary,* New York: Pocket Books, 1964.

BibleWorks 4.0, The Premier Biblical Exegesis and Research Program [CD Rom]. Hermeneutika, 1999, www.bibleworks.com.

Brenton, Sir Lancelot, C. L., ed. *The Septuagint With Apocrypha: Greek And English*, USA: Hendrickson Publishers, 2001.

Collins, Steven M. *The Lost Ten Tribes of Israel...Found!* Oregon: CPA Books, 1992.

Howard, George. *Hebrew Gospel of Matthew*, Georgia: Mercer University Press, 1995.

Interlinear Greek-English New Testament, Grand Rapids: Baker Book House, 1897.

Koniuchowsky, Rabbi Moshe Yoseph. *The Truth About All Israel* [CD Rom], Miami Beach: Your Arms To Israel, 2000.

Koniuchowsky, Rabbi Moshe Yoseph. The Messianic Believer's First Response Handbook, Miami Beach: Your Arms To Israel Publishing, 2003.

Koniuchowsky, Rivkah and Tocre, Yochanan, eds. *Nazarene Yisraelite Annual Siddur*, Margate: Your Arms To Israel Publishing, 2004.

Lamsa, George M., translator. *Holy Bible From The Ancient Eastern Text*, San Francisco: HarperSanFrancisco, 1968.

Roth, Andrew G. *Ruach Qadim, Recovering The Aramaic Origins Of The New Testament And Lost Vision Of The Nazarenes* [Standard Electronic Edition], 2003, andrewgabriel77@hotmail.com.

Scherman, Rabbi Nosson and Zlotowitz, Rabbi Meir, eds. *The Stone Edition Tanach*, New York: Mesorah Publications, Ltd., 2002.

Stern, David H., translator. *Complete Jewish Bible*, Clarksville: Jewish New Testament Publications, Inc., 1998.

Strong, James. *The Exhaustive Concordance Of The Bible*, Nashville: Abingdon Press, 1980.

The Scriptures, South Africa: Institute for Scripture Research, Ltd., 2000.

The Soncino Talmud [CD Rom], Brooklyn: Judaica Press and Davka Corp., 1995.

Trimm, James S., translator. *Hebraic-Roots Version "New Testament"*, Hurst: Society for the Advancement of Nazarene Judaism, 2001.

Whiston, William, translator. *Josephus, Complete Works*, Grand Rapids: Kregel Publications, 1981.

Wootten, Batya Ruth. Who Is Israel? And Why You Need To Know, Saint Cloud: Key of David Publishing, 1998.

Youhan, Paul, translator. Aramaic/English Interlinear New Testament [On-line], www.peshitta.org.

My Restoration Notes

My Restoration Notes

My Restoration Notes

My Restoration Notes

My Restoration Notes

<u>My Restoration Notes</u>

My Restoration Notes

My Restoration Notes

My Restoration Notes

My Restoration Notes

My Restoration Notes

My Restoration Notes